China

written and researched by

David Leffman, Simon Lewis and Jeremy Atiyah

this edition updated by

Mike Meyer and Susie Lunt

www.roughguides.com

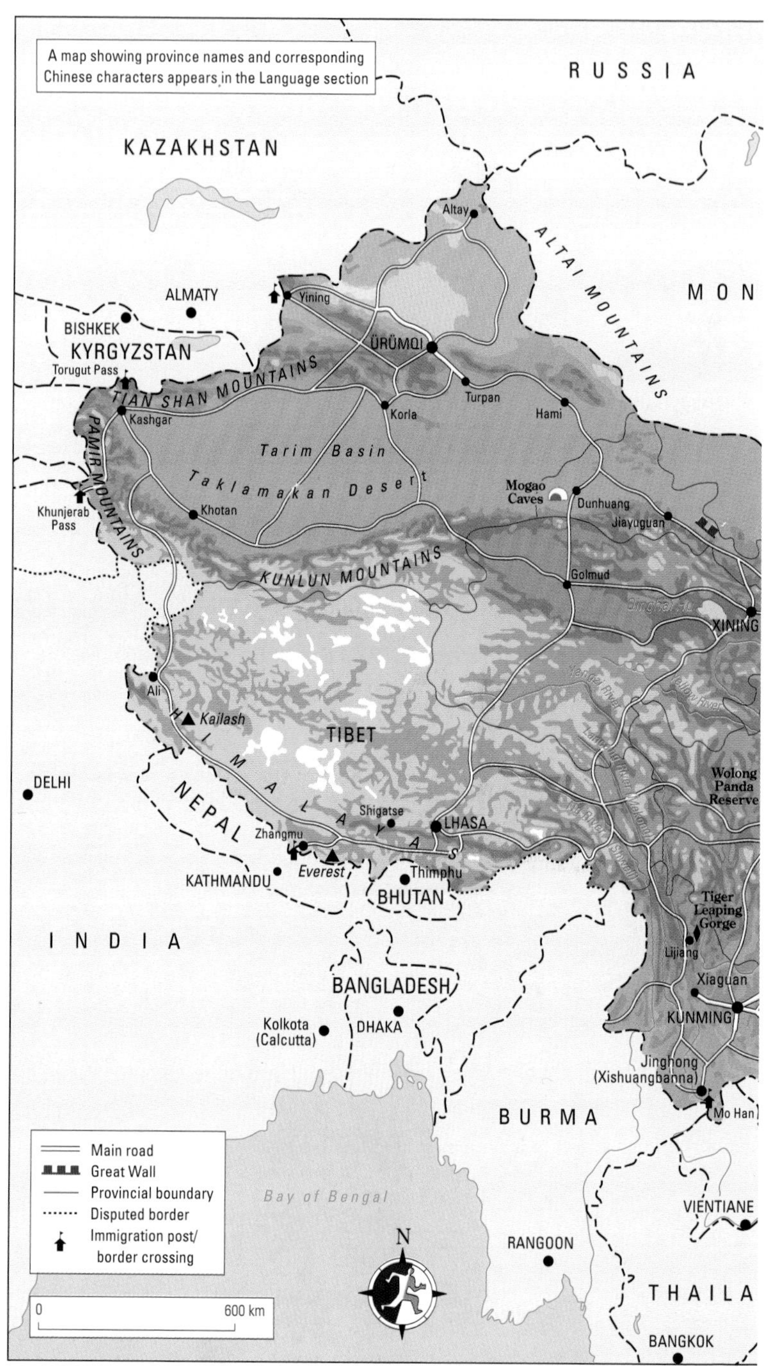

A map showing province names and corresponding Chinese characters appears in the Language section
RUSSIA
KAZAKHSTAN
Altay
ALTAI MOUNTAINS
ALMATY
Yining
MON
BISHKEK
KYRGYZSTAN
ÜRÜMQI
Torugut Pass
TIAN SHAN MOUNTAINS
Turpan
Hami
Kashgar
Korla
PAMIR MOUNTAINS
Tarim Basin
Taklamakan Desert
Mogao Caves
Dunhuang
Khunjerab Pass
Khotan
Jiayuguan
KUNLUN MOUNTAINS
Golmud
XINING
Ali
Kailash
TIBET
HIMALAYAS
Wolong Panda Reserve
DELHI
NEPAL
Shigatse
LHASA
Zhangmu
Everest
KATHMANDU
Thimphu
BHUTAN
Tiger Leaping Gorge
INDIA
Lijiang
Xiaguan
BANGLADESH
KUNMING
Kolkota (Calcutta)
DHAKA
Jinghong (Xishuangbanna)
Mo Han
BURMA
Main road
Great Wall
Provincial boundary
Disputed border
Immigration post/ border crossing
Bay of Bengal
VIENTIANE
N
RANGOON
THAILA
0
600 km
BANGKOK

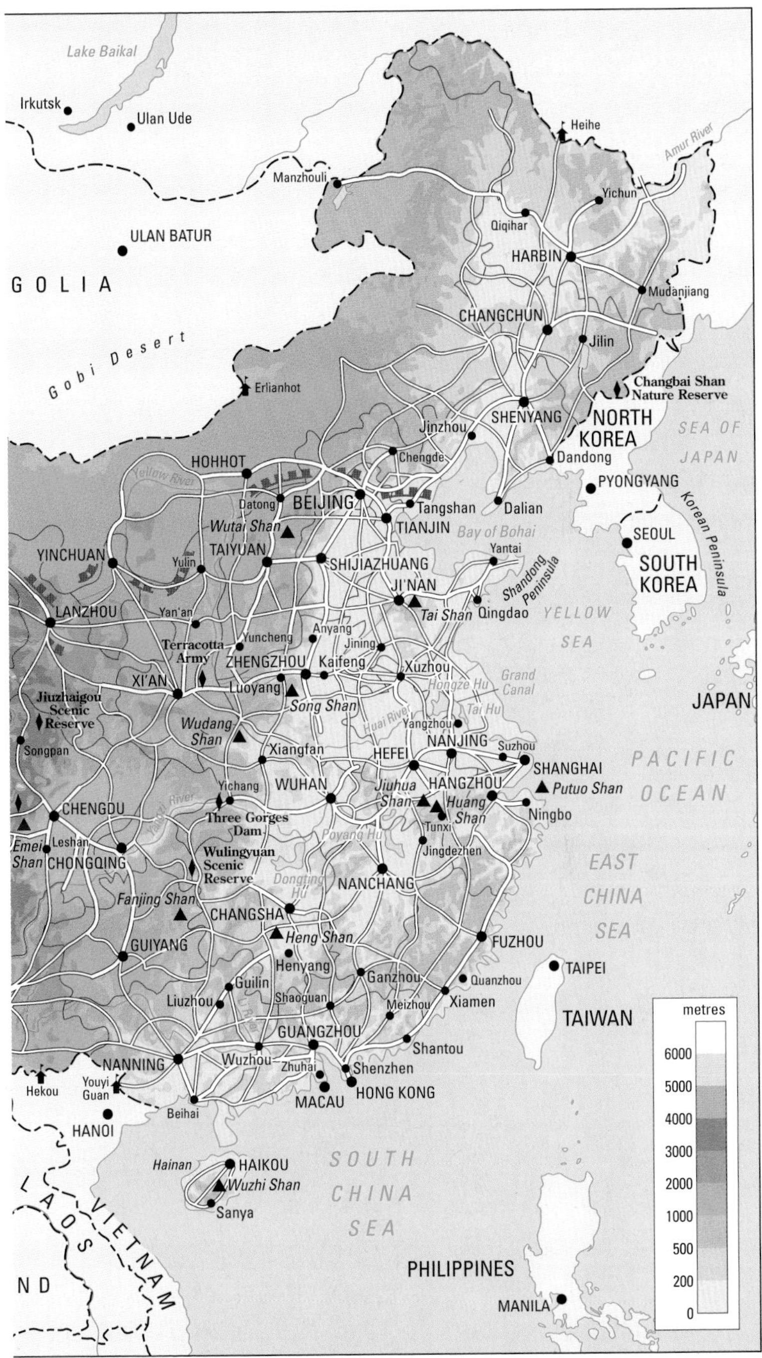
Lake Baikal
Irkutsk
Ulan Ude
ULAN BATUR
GOLIA
Gobi Desert
Manzhouli
Heihe
Amur River
Yichun
Qiqihar
HARBIN
Mudanjiang
CHANGCHUN
Jilin
Erlianhot
Changbai Shan Nature Reserve
SHENYANG
NORTH KOREA
SEA OF JAPAN
Jinzhou
Dandong
Chengde
PYONGYANG
HOHHOT
Yellow River
Datong
BEIJING
Tangshan
Dalian
Korean Peninsula
Wutai Shan
TIANJIN
Bay of Bohai
SEOUL
YINCHUAN
TAIYUAN
Yulin
SHIJIAZHUANG
Yantai
Shandong Peninsula
SOUTH KOREA
JI'NAN
LANZHOU
Yan'an
Tai Shan
Qingdao
YELLOW SEA
Anyang
Terracotta Army
Yuncheng
Jining
ZHENGZHOU
Kaifeng
Xuzhou
Grand Canal
XI'AN
Luoyang
Song Shan
Hongze Hu
Jiuzhaigou Scenic Reserve
Tai Hu
JAPAN
Huai River
Yangzhou
Wudang Shan
NANJING
Songpan
Xiangfan
Suzhou
HEFEI
SHANGHAI
PACIFIC OCEAN
Yichang
WUHAN
Jiuhua Shan
HANGZHOU
Putuo Shan
CHENGDU
Yangzi River
Huang Shan
Ningbo
Three Gorges Dam
Tunxi
Emei Shan
Leshan
Poyang Hu
CHONGQING
Jingdezhen
Wulingyuan Scenic Reserve
EAST CHINA SEA
Dongting Hu
NANCHANG
Fanjing Shan
CHANGSHA
Heng Shan
FUZHOU
GUIYANG
Henyang
TAIPEI
Ganzhou
Quanzhou
Guilin
Liuzhou
Li River
Shaoguan
Xiamen
Meizhou
TAIWAN
GUANGZHOU
Shantou
NANNING
Wuzhou
Zhuhai
Shenzhen
Hekou
Youyi Guan
HONG KONG
MACAU
Beihai
HANOI
Hainan
HAIKOU
SOUTH CHINA SEA
Wuzhi Shan
LAOS
VIETNAM
Sanya
PHILIPPINES
ND
MANILA
metres
6000
5000
4000
3000
2000
1000
500
200
0

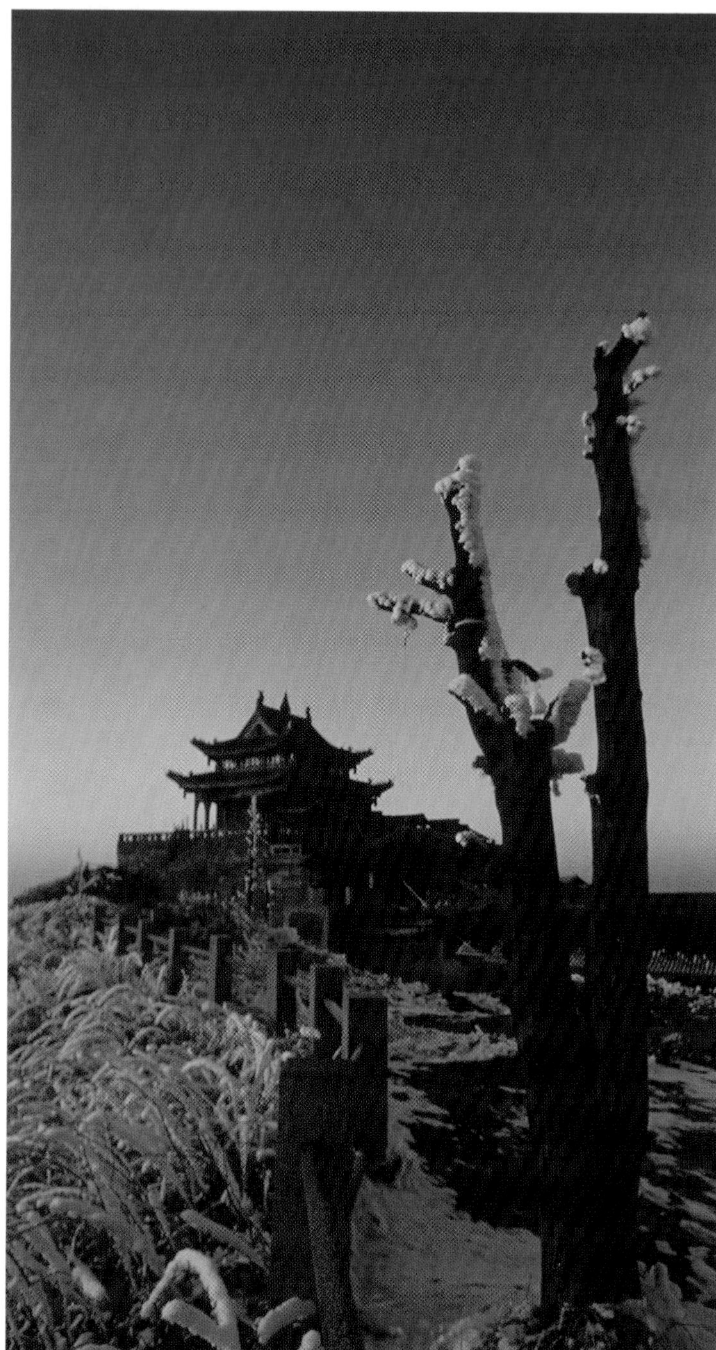

Introduction to China

China has grown up alone and aloof, cut off from the rest of Eurasia by the Himalayas to the south and the Siberian steppe to the north. For the last three millennia, while empires, languages and peoples in the rest of the world rose, blossomed and disappeared without trace, China has been busy largely recycling itself. The ferocious dragons and lions of Chinese statuary have been produced for 25 centuries or more, and the script still used today reached perfection at the time of the Han dynasty, two thousand years ago. Until the late nineteenth century, the only foreigners China saw – apart from occasional ruling elites of Mongol and Manchu origin, who quickly became assimilated – were visiting merchants from far-flung shores or uncivilized nomads from the wild steppe: peripheral, unimportant and unreal.

Today, while there is no sign of the Communist Party relinquishing power, the negative stories surrounding China – the runaway pollution, the oppression of dissidents, the harsh treatment of criminal suspects and the imperialist behaviour towards Tibet and other minority regions – are only part of the picture. As the Party moves ever further away from hard-line political doctrine and towards economic pragmatism, China is undergoing a huge commercial and creative upheaval. A

Fact file

• With an area of 9.6 million square kilometres, China is the fourth largest country in the world – practically the same size as the United States – and the most populous nation on earth, with around 1.3 billion people. Of these, 92% are of the Han nationality, with the remainder comprising about sixty ethnic minority groups such as Mongols, Uigurs and Tibetans. The main religions are Buddhism, Taoism and Confucianism, though the country is officially atheist. A third of China comprises fertile river plains, and another third arid deserts, plateaus or mountains. China's longest river is the Yangzi (6275km) and the highest peak is Qomolongma – Mount Everest (8850m), on the Nepalese border.

• China is a police state run by the Chinese Communist Party, the sole political organization, which is divided into Executive, Legislative and Judicial branches. The chief of state (President) and the head of government (Premier) are elected for five-year terms at the National People's Congress. After decades of state planning, the economy is now mixed, with state-owned enterprises on the decline and free-market principles ubiquitous. China's main exports are clothing, textiles, tea and fossil fuels, and its main trading partners are the US, Japan, South Korea and Europe.

country the size of ten Japans has entered the world market: Hong Kong-style city skylines are rearing up all across China, and tens of millions of people are finding jobs that earn them a spending power their parents could never have known. Whatever the reasons you are attracted to China, the sheer pace of change, visible in every part of Chinese life, will ensure that your trip is a unique one.

The first thing that strikes visitors to China is the extraordinary density of its **population**. In central and eastern China, villages, towns and cities seem to sprawl endlessly into one another

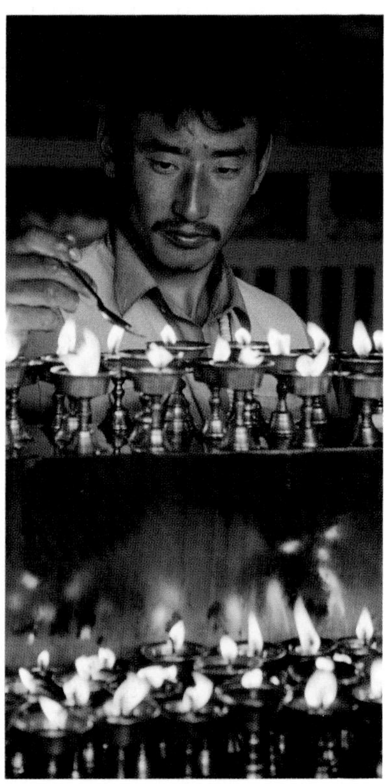

along the grey arteries of busy expressways. These are the Han Chinese heartlands, a world of chopsticks, tea, slippers, massed bicycles, shadow-boxing, exotic pop music, teeming crowds, chaotic train stations, smoky temples, red flags and the smells of soot and frying tofu. Move west or north away from the major cities, however, and the population thins out as it begins to vary: indeed, large areas of the People's Republic are inhabited not by the "Chinese", but by more than two hundred distinct ethnic minorities, ranging from animist hill tribes to urban Muslims. Here the landscape begins to dominate: green paddy fields and misty hilltops in the southwest, the scorched, epic vistas of the old Silk Road in the northwest, and the magisterial mountains of Tibet.

While travel around the country itself is seldom problematic, it would be wrong to pretend that it is an entirely easy matter to penetrate modern China. The tourist highlights – the Great Wall, the Forbidden City, the Terracotta Army and Yangzi gorges – are relatively few considering the size of the country. In particular, recent modernizations have, quite deliberately, destroyed much of the historic architecture which would have lent Chinese cities the character enjoyed by those in Europe or the Middle East. On top of this are the frustrations of travelling in a land where few people speak English, the writing system is alien and foreigners are regularly viewed as exotic objects of intense curiosity, or as fodder for overcharging – though overall you'll find that the Chinese, despite a reputation for curtness, are generally hospitable and friendly.

Urban pollution

A reliance on coal for power and heating, factories spewing untreated waste into the atmosphere, growing numbers of vehicles, and the sheer density of the urban population all conspire to make Chinese cities some of the most polluted on earth. Black sludge fills canals and streams; buildings are mired by soot; blue sky is only a memory; the population seems permanently stricken with bronchitis; and acid rain withers plants. In summer the worst spots are the Yangzi valley "furnaces" of Nanjing, Chongqing and Wuhan; winter in Xi'an, on the other hand, features black snow.

The Chinese government is finally begining to take pollution seriously, especially with the Beijing Olympics due in 2008: in the capital, at least, factories are being relocated and elderly, fume-belching minibuses have been scrapped or foisted on other cities.

Where to go

Inevitably, **Beijing** is on everyone's itinerary, and the Great Wall and the splendour of the Imperial City are certainly not to be missed. But with skyscrapers aplenty, Beijing can seem vast, soulless and functional. To get the best out of the place, you need to dig under the surface to find the more intimate, private city that exists in the dwindling number of *hutongs* – twisted, quaint alleyways. The capital also offers some of the best food and nightlife in the country, and is a good place to base yourself for a host of easy short trips. **Chengde**, just north of Beijing, has some stunning imperial buildings, constructed by emperors when this was their favoured retreat for the summer, while today's city residents escape to the quiet coastal towns of **Shanhaiguan** and **Beidaihe**, offering lush countryside, grand old fortresses and a welter of seaside kitsch.

North of the Great Wall, **Dongbei** (Manchuria) has long had a reputation for severely cold weather and hot-blooded warriors, but the expanses of countryside and milltowns stand out for their preserves of nature, history and minority culture. Dongbei's frontier with North Korea results in diverting border towns like **Dandong** and ports such as **Dalian**; the onion-domed cathedrals of **Harbin** and the local taste for vodka reveal Russia's proximity; while **Shenyang** tells the story of Dongbei's tumultuous history: the Manchus, Russians, Japanese, warlords, Nationalists and Communists each controlled it in the course of the last century.

Most visitors head for greater attractions south of the capital, along the **Yellow River Valley**, the cradle of Chinese civilization, where remnants of the dynastic age lie scattered in a unique landscape of loess terraces. The cave temples at **Datong** and **Luoyang** are magnificent, with huge Buddhist sculptures staring out impassively across their now industrialized settings. Of the historic capitals, **Xi'an** is the most obvious

Wildlife

Although China's varied geography and climate has created a wealth of wildlife habitats, the country's vast human population has put pressure on the environment, bringing some high-profile creatures to the edge of extinction. Most famous of these is the giant panda, which survives in pockets of high-altitude bamboo forest across the southwest. A few Siberian tigers haunt the northeastern highlands, while the critically endangered South China tiger can be found in reserves in Fujian and Guangxi. Less well-known rarities include the snub-nosed golden monkey and Chinese alligator, both of which it's possible – with a lot of luck – to see in the wild. Birdlife can be prolific, however, with freshwater lakes along the Yangzi and in western Guizhou, along with the vast saline Qinghai Lake, providing winter refuge for hosts of migratory wildfowl – including rare Siberian and black-necked cranes. For more on wildlife and the environment, see p.1213.

destination, where the celebrated Terracotta Army still stands guard over the tomb of Emperor Qin Shi Huang. Other less visited ancient towns, including sleepy **Kaifeng** in Henan and **Qufu**, the birthplace of Confucius in Shandong, hold architectural treasures as well as offering an intimate, human scale that's missing in the large cities. The area is also well supplied with holy mountains, providing a rare continuity with the past: grandmothers still shuffle their way up **Tai Shan**, perhaps the grandest and most imperial of the country's pilgrimage sites, to pay homage to deities as old as Chinese civilization itself; **Song Shan** in Henan sees followers of

Chinese cuisine

The Chinese can seem obsessed with eating, and each region boasts its own cuisine. Northern, Eastern, Cantonese and Sichuanese are the four major regional styles, but every area has its own specialities, including tear-jerkingly spicy tofu in Chengdu, salt-baked chicken in eastern Guangdong, boiled scorpions in Qufu, butter tea in Tibet, handmade noodles and mutton soup in the Northwest, elegant *dim sum* breakfasts in Guangzhou and Beijing duck in the capital. For snacking, noodle dishes, soups, and buns and dumplings stuffed with meats or vegetables are generally on sale at the nearest street corner. Eating is very much a social event: a selection of dishes is shared among family or friends, and most good restaurants are famously "hot and noisy". And despite the Western perception that all Chinese eat rice, in the north they favour noodles and plain buns. For more on Chinese food, see p.48.

the more contemporary kung-fu craze making the trek to the Shaolin Temple, where the art originated; and **Wutai Shan** in Shanxi features some of the best-preserved religious sites in the country, as well as a lush and pretty alpine setting.

Central China forms a basin around the middle reaches of Asia's longest river, the **Yangzi**, which feeds into the two massive freshwater **Poyang** and **Dongting** lakes en route to the sea. It was once a vital transport artery, and several thousand kilometres are still plied by regular passenger ferries through the provinces of Anhui, Hubei, Hunan and Jiangxi, providing one of the world's great river journeys past countless images of everyday Chinese life. A host of bustling riverside ports now thrive on industrial momentum, including **Wuhan**, a modern metropolis and former European concession. Relics of the past range from 2000-year-old tombs and third-century battlefields to the Hunanese village of **Shaoshan**, Mao Zedong's birthplace. Away from the river lurk some evocative landscapes: the classically Chinese cloud-and-pine-draped peaks of **Huang Shan** in Anhui; Hubei's **Wudang Shan**, covered in aged, esoteric Taoist temples; and the splintered cliffs and forested wilds of western Hunan's **Wulingyuan Scenic Reserve**.

Dominating China's east coast near the mouth of the Yangzi, **Shanghai** is the mainland's most Westernized city, a booming port where the Art Deco monuments of the old European-built Bund – the riverside business centre –

rub shoulders with a hyper-modern metropolis, crowned with two of the world's tallest skyscrapers. Around Shanghai are areas offering some of China's most characteristic scenery – low-lying and wet, crisscrossed with canals and dotted with historic towns. Jiangsu Province to the north is home to **Suzhou**, whose famous ornate gardens were built by Ming dynasty scholars and officials, while a short way to the west lies the city of **Nanjing**, crowded with relics from its tumultuous history as one-time capital of China. South of Shanghai, in Zhejiang Province at the terminus of the historic Grand Canal, **Hangzhou** is one of China's greenest and most scenic cities, located along Xi Hu, a historic lake whose shore and neighbouring hills abound with walking opportunities. Off the coast, an overnight journey by boat from Shanghai, the Buddhist island of **Putuo Shan** is superbly attractive, with beaches, rural walks and monasteries.

In China's southeast, comprising the coastal provinces of Fujian and Guangdong, as well as Hainan Island, you'll find all the paradoxes of any rapidly industrializing nation: incredible economic success back to back with chronic poverty, and a lust for modernity, refuted by staunch conservatism. Only a short hop from Hong Kong, the chaotic city of **Guangzhou** and the adjacent industrial sprawl of the **Pearl River Delta** have it all: skyscrapers and temples, beggars and businessmen, nightclubs and traditional opera, forgettable fast food and the finest in classical Chinese cuisine. In common with other cities across the region (the Fujian island

The Chinese script

Chinese characters are simplified images of what they represent, and their origins as pictograms can often still be seen, even though they have become highly abstract today. The earliest known examples of Chinese writing are predictions which were cut into "oracle bones" over three thousand years ago during the Shang dynasty, though the characters must have been in use long before as these inscriptions already amount to a highly complex writing system. As the characters represent concepts, not sounds, written Chinese cuts through the problem of communication in a country with many different dialects. However, learning the writing system is ponderous, taking children an estimated two years longer than with an alphabet. Foreigners learning Mandarin use the modern *pinyin* transliteration system of accented Roman letters – used throughout this book – to help memorize the sounds. For more on language, see p.1253.

port of **Xiamen** is the nicest of these), Guangzhou also has a fair scattering of European architecture, built by colonial victors after the nineteenth-century Opium Wars. Elsewhere, towns such as **Chaozhou** proudly retain their traditions, while the Guangdong–Fujian border is home to ethnic Hakka, who live as they have done for centuries in massive fortified apartments. **Hainan** at first glance seems to have no heritage at all, just a very nice beach, but there's a little more depth to the place if you dig hard enough – most rewarding is a visit to the Li villages in the island's central highlands.

Returned to Beijing in 1997, but retaining a degree of autonomy that's unprecedented in modern times, **Hong Kong** boasts one of the greatest cityscapes in the world. Its recent colonial heritage still lends it a refreshingly cosmopolitan atmosphere, and there's almost nothing Hong Kong cannot offer in the way of tourist facilities, from fine beaches to colonial remains to great eating, drinking and nightlife. **Macau**, too, is well worth a visit, if not for its casinos, then for its Baroque churches and fine Portuguese cuisine.

In the southwest of the country, Sichuan's **Chengdu** and Yunnan's **Kunming** remain two of China's most interesting and easy-going provincial

capitals, and the entire region is, by any standards, exceptionally diverse, with landscapes encompassing everything from snowbound summits and alpine lakes to steamy tropical jungles. The karst (limestone peak) scenery is particularly renowned, especially along the Li River between **Yangshuo** and **Guilin** in Guangxi. In Sichuan, pilgrims flock to see the colossal Big Buddha at **Leshan**, and to ascend the holy mountain of **Emei Shan**; to the east, the city of **Chongqing** marks the start of river trips down the Yangzi through the **Three Gorges**. As Yunnan and Guangxi share borders with Vietnam, Laos and Burma, while Sichuan rubs up against Tibet, it's not surprising to find that the region is home to near-extinct wildlife and dozens of ethnic autonomous regions; the attractions of the latter range from the traditional Naxi town of **Lijiang** and Dai villages of **Xishuangbanna** in Yunnan, to the exuberant festivals and textiles of Guizhou's Miao and the wooden architecture of Dong settlements in Guangxi's north.

The huge area of China referred to as the Northwest is where the people thin out and real wilderness begins. Inner Mongolia, just hours from Beijing, is already at the frontiers of Central Asia; here you can follow in the footsteps of Genghis Khan by going horse-riding on the endless grasslands of the steppe. To the south and west, the old **Silk Road** heads out of Xi'an right to and through China's western borders. Highlights en route start with the fabulous Buddhist sculptures at **Maiji Shan** and **Bingling Si** just outside **Lanzhou**, while south from Lanzhou lies the delightful rural retreat and Buddhist monastery town of **Xiahe**. Further to the west, in the northwestern part of Gansu, you'll find the terminus of the Great Wall of China, the famous last fort of **Jiayuguan**, and nearby, one of the major draws of all China, the lavish Buddhist cave art in the sandy deserts of **Dunhuang**.

West of here lie the mountains and deserts of vast Xinjiang, where China blends into old Turkestan and where simple journeys between towns are

epics of modern bus travel. The oasis cities of **Turpan** and remote **Kashgar**, with their donkey carts and bazaars, are the main attractions, though the blue waters of **Tian Chi**, offering alpine scenery in the midst of searing desert, are deservedly popular.

Tibet still sounds the most exotic of all travel possibilities – and so in some ways it is, especially if you come across the border from Nepal or brave the long road in from Golmud in Qinghai Province. Despite fifty years of (hardly enlightened) Chinese rule, coupled with a mass migration of Han Chinese into the region, the manifestations of Tibetan culture remain intact – the Potala Palace in **Lhasa**, red-robed monks, lines of pilgrims turning prayer wheels, butter sculptures and gory frescoes decorating monastery halls. And Tibet's mountain scenery, which includes **Mount Everest**, is possibly worth the trip in itself, even if opportunities for independent travel are more restricted than elsewhere in China.

When to go

China's **climate** is extremely diverse. The **south** is subtropical, with wet, humid summers (April to September) – when temperatures can approach 40°C – and a typhoon season on the southeast coast between July and September. Though it is often still hot enough to swim in the sea in December, the short winters, from January to March, can be surprisingly chilly.

Central China, around Shanghai and the Yangzi

Average daily maximum and minimum temperatures, and monthly rainfall

	Jan	Feb	Mar	Apr	May	June	July	Aug	Sept	Oct	Nov	Dec
Beijing												
max °C	1	4	11	21	27	31	31	30	26	20	9	3
min °C	-10	-8	-1	7	13	18	21	20	14	6	-2	-8
rainfall mm	4	5	8	17	35	78	243	141	58	16	11	3
Chongqing												
max °C	9	13	18	23	27	29	34	35	28	22	16	13
min °C	5	7	11	16	19	22	24	25	22	16	12	8
rainfall mm	15	20	38	99	142	180	142	122	150	112	48	20
Guilin												
max °C	16	17	20	25	29	31	32	32	31	27	23	19
min °C	8	10	14	19	23	25	26	26	24	19	15	12
rainfall mm	33	56	97	160	206	193	160	178	84	43	38	37
Hong Kong												
max °C	18	17	19	24	28	29	31	31	29	27	23	20
min °C	13	13	16	19	23	26	26	26	25	23	18	15
rainfall mm	33	46	74	137	292	394	381	367	257	114	43	31
Jilin												
max °C	-6	-2	6	16	23	29	31	29	24	16	5	-4
min °C	-18	-14	-6	3	10	16	21	19	11	3	-6	-15
rainfall mm	8	8	18	28	69	84	183	170	64	36	28	15
Kunming												
max °C	20	22	25	28	29	29	28	28	28	24	22	20
min °C	8	9	12	16	18	19	19	19	18	15	12	8
rainfall mm	8	18	28	41	127	132	196	198	97	51	56	15
Lhasa												
max °C	7	9	12	16	19	24	23	22	21	17	13	9
min °C	-10	-7	-2	1	5	9	9	9	7	1	-5	-9
rainfall mm	0	13	8	5	25	64	122	89	66	13	3	0
Shanghai												
max °C	8	8	13	19	25	28	32	32	28	23	17	12
min °C	1	1	4	10	15	19	23	23	19	14	7	2
rainfall mm	48	58	84	94	94	180	147	142	130	71	51	36
Ürümqi												
max °C	-11	-8	-1	16	22	26	28	27	21	10	-1	-8
min °C	-22	-19	-11	2	8	12	14	13	8	-1	-11	-13
rainfall mm	15	8	13	38	28	38	18	25	15	43	41	10
Wuhan												
max °C	8	9	14	21	26	31	34	34	29	23	17	11
min °C	1	2	6	13	18	23	26	26	21	16	9	3
rainfall mm	46	48	97	152	165	244	180	97	71	81	48	28

River, has brief, cold winters, with temperatures dipping below zero, and long, hot, humid summers. It's no surprise that three Yangzi cities – Chongqing, Wuhan and Nanjing – are proverbially referred to as China's three "furnaces". Rainfall here is high all year round. Farther north, the **Yellow River basin** marks a rough boundary beyond which central heating is fitted as standard in buildings, helping to make the region's harsh winters a little more tolerable. Winter temperatures in Beijing rarely rise above freezing from December to March, and freezing winds off the Mongolian plains add a vicious wind-chill factor. In summer, however, temperatures here can be well over 30°C. In the **Inner Mongolia** and **Manchuria**, winters are at least clear and dry, but temperatures remain way below zero, while summers can be uncomfortably warm. **Xinjiang** gets fiercely hot in summer, though without the humidity of the rest of the country, and winters are as bitter as anywhere else in northern China. **Tibet** is ideal in midsummer, when its mountain plateaux are pleasantly warm and dry; in winter, however, temperatures in the capital Lhasa frequently fall below freezing.

Overall, the best time to visit China is **spring** or **autumn**, when the weather is at its most temperate. In the spring, it's best to start in the south and work north or west as summer approaches; in the autumn, start in the north and work south.

35 things not to miss

It's not possible to see everything China has to offer in one trip – and we don't suggest you try. What follows is a selective and subjective taste of the country's highlights: gaudy temples, mouthwatering cuisine, exuberant festivals, pristine wildlife reserves and vibrant landscapes. They're all arranged in five colour-coded categories to help you find the very best things to see, do and experience. All entries have a page reference to take you straight into the guide, where you can find out more.

01 The Great Wall Page **138** • Once the division between civilizations, this monumental barrier still inspires awe.

02 Caohai, Guizhou Page **847** • Being punted around this shallow lake after rare birdlife is a wonderfully restful experience.

03 Ice Festival, Harbin, Heilongjiang Page **215** • "Lurid" and "outrageous" don't begin to describe the bizarre sculptures here – everything from life-size ice castles with rainbow lighting to fantastical snowy tableaux.

04 Dim sum Page **640** • The classic Cantonese breakfast; there's no better place to try it than Guangzhou.

05 Chengde, Hebei Page **169** • The emperors' former retreat from the heat of summer holds a string of pretty temples.

06 Xishuangbanna, Yunnan Page **904** • Make sure you glimpse the very different culture and lifestyle of one of China's many minorities.

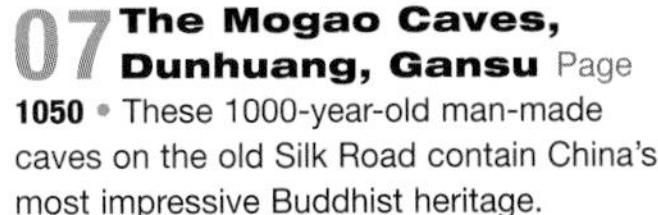

07 The Mogao Caves, Dunhuang, Gansu Page **1050** • These 1000-year-old man-made caves on the old Silk Road contain China's most impressive Buddhist heritage.

08 Lijiang, Yunnan Page **881** • What many people feel China ought to look like, a charming old town of narrow cobbled alleyways and courtyard houses.

09 Beijing duck Page **50** • A northern Chinese culinary speciality and absolutely delicious – crisp skin and juicy meat eaten in a pancake.

10 Forbidden City, Beijing Page **99** • Once centre of the Chinese imperial universe and off-limits to the hoi polloi, the emperor's impressive palace complex is now open to all.

11 The Hanging Temple and Yungang Caves Page **238** • Near Datong in Shanxi are two incredible sights: a temple clinging to a precipice and a series of grottoes containing a panoply of Buddhist statuary.

12 Labrang Monastery, Xiahe, Gansu Page **1034** • One of the most important Tibetan Buddhist monasteries, a riot of lavishly decorated halls, butter sculptures and ragged pilgrims.

13 The Li River, Guangxi Page **790** • Take a boat trip here to admire weird, contorted peaks of the sort you'll see on Chinese scroll paintings.

14 Leshan Buddha, Sichuan Page **949** • You'll feel a mere speck as you gaze up at the world's largest carved Buddha.

15 The Hong Kong cityscape Page **739** • Admire this electrifying skyline from Tsim Sha Tsui.

16
Longmen Caves Page **305** • A seemingly never-ending parade of Buddhist figurines and reliefs, near Luoyang in Henan.

17 The Jokhang, Lhasa Page **1134** • Stuffed with gorgeous statuary and perpetually wreathed in juniper smoke and incense, this temple is one of the holiest in Tibet.

18 Changbai Shan Page **211** • Just one of China's many invaluable nature reserves, well worth a visit – though you'd have to be exceptionally lucky to spot its rare Siberian tigers.

19 Mount Everest Page **1168** • The sight of the mountain towering above ensures you'll not regret the long drive up to Base Camp, which is as far (and, at an altitude of 5150m, as high) as most visitors to Tibet ever get.

20 The Bund, Shanghai Page **387** • An elegant parade of matronly colonial architecture, nestling incongruously at the heart of Shanghai's gaudy modernity.

21 Tai Shan, Shandong Page **339** • The taxing ascent of this holy peak is rewarded with some immaculate temples and pavilions.

22 Suzhou, Jiangsu Page **419** • A venerable mercantile city, dotted with elegant walled gardens.

23 Sisters' Meal Festival Page **839** • Join tens of thousands of locals in Taijiang, Guizhou, as they participate in this annual three-day showcase of ethnic Miao culture.

24 Skiing at Yabuli, Heilongjiang Page **224** • The very idea of a Chinese skiing holiday sounds off-the-wall – and thus all the more worth trying.

25 The Confucius Mansion Page **345** • The site of this lavish complex in Qufu, Shandong, was home to nearly eighty generations of the great sage's clan.

26 The Terracotta Army Page **287** • In Shaanxi near Xi'an, the former capital, these 2200-year-old, life-size soldiers guard the tomb of China's first emperor.

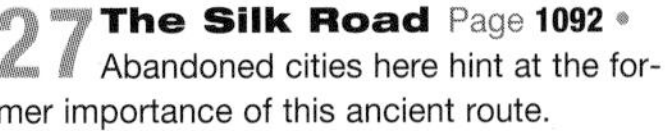

27 The Silk Road Page **1092** • Abandoned cities here hint at the former importance of this ancient route.

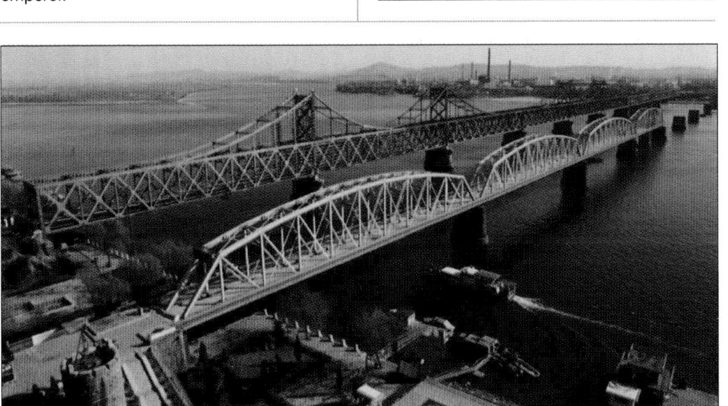

28 Old Yalu Bridge, Dandong, Liaoning Page **204** • This half-demolished bridge to North Korea is still a potent relic of the Korean war.

29 A cruise down the Yangzi River Page **962** • Enjoy some awesome scenery and a wealth of historic sights before they vanish below the waters of a new dam.

30 The Yellow River Page **263** • One of the world's great rivers, offering a tantalizing range of vistas, including the turbid Hukou Falls.

31 Sichuanese teahouses Page **930** • Relaxed places to gossip, read or socialize for the price of a cup of tea.

32 Yonghe Gong, Beijing Page **115** • This charismatic Tibetan temple is an explosion of ornament and colour.

33 Colonial architecture, Xiamen, Fujian Page **613** • Gulangyu Island here has some of the best architecture left by nineteenth-century Europeans.

34 Jiayuguan, Gansu Page **1045** • A famously lonely outpost looks out over the desert at the western tail of the Great Wall.

35 Kashgar's Sunday Market, Xinjiang Page **1103** • Crowds from all over Central Asia descend to trade livestock, carpets, knives and clothes at this weekly event.

Contents

using this Rough Guide

We've tried to make this Rough Guide a good read and easy to use. The book is divided into six main sections, and you should be able to find whatever you want in one of them.

Colour section

The front colour section offers a quick tour of China. The **introduction** aims to give you a feel for the place, with suggestions on where to go. We also tell you what the weather is like and include a basic country fact file. Next, our authors round up their favourite aspects of China in the **things not to miss** section – whether it's an amazing temple, a holy mountain or fantastic food. Right after this comes a full **contents** list.

Basics

The Basics section covers all the **pre-departure** nitty-gritty to help you plan your trip. This is where to find out which airlines fly to your destination, what paperwork you'll need, what to do about money and insurance, about Internet access, food, security, public transport – in fact just about every piece of **general practical information** you might need.

Guide

This is the heart of the Rough Guide, divided into user-friendly chapters, each of which covers a specific region. Every chapter starts with a list of **highlights** and an **introduction** that helps you to decide where to go, depending on your time and budget. Likewise, introductions to the various towns and smaller regions within each chapter should help you plan your itinerary. We start most town accounts with information on arrival and accommodation, followed by a tour of the sights, and finally reviews of places to eat and drink, and details of nightlife. Longer accounts also have a directory of practical listings. Each chapter concludes with **public transport** details for that region.

Contexts

Read Contexts to get a deeper understanding of what makes China tick. We include a history, articles about **martial arts, beliefs, art** and **music**, and a detailed further reading section that reviews dozens of **books** relating to the country.

Language

The **language** section gives useful guidance for speaking Mandarin Chinese and pulls together all the vocabulary you might need on your trip, including a comprehensive menu reader. Here you'll also find a glossary of words and terms peculiar to the country.

Index + small print

Apart from a **full index**, which includes maps as well as places, this section covers publishing information, credits and acknowledgements, and also has our contact details in case you want to send in updates and corrections to the book – or suggestions as to how we might improve it.

Map and chapter list

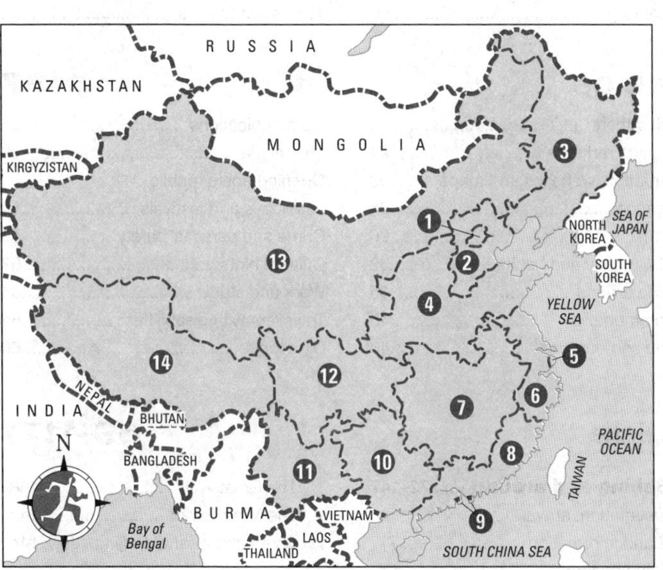

Contents

Colour section i–xxiv

Basics 9–67

Guide 69–1171

Contexts 1173–1252

Language 1253–1275

Index 1276–1290

map symbols

maps are listed in the full index using coloured text

Expressway
Major road
Minor road
Pedestrianized road
Steps
Path
Railway
Ferry route
Waterway
Canal
Wall
Airport
Point of interest
Temple/monastery
Buddhist temple
Pagoda
Mosque
Convent
Museum
Tower
Ruins
Viewpoint
Caves
Mountain peak
Mountain range
Waterfall
Cliffs
Tree
Bridge
Arch
Skiing area
Border crossing post
Metro station
Bus station/depot
Minibus stand/bus stop
Embassy/consulate
Statue
Hospital
Internet access
Telecom office
Information office
Post office
Hotel
Restaurant
Cable car
Gate
Building
Church/cathedral
Market
Park
Beach
Forest
Cemetery

Basics

Basics

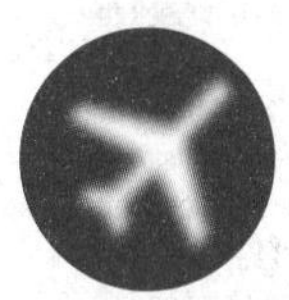

Getting there

China's most important long-haul international gateways are Beijing, Hong Kong and Shanghai, though many other Chinese cities are served by international flights, operated mainly by airlines based in East Asia. There are also well-established overland routes into China – including road and rail links from its Southeast Asian neighbours, as well as the alluring Trans-Siberian train from Moscow.

Fares to Hong Kong are at their highest during the fortnight before Christmas, the fortnight before Chinese New Year (see box on p.59) and from mid-June to early October. The cheapest time to fly there is the months of February (after Chinese New Year), May and November. For Beijing, peak season is generally summertime. Note also that flying on weekends is slightly more expensive; price ranges quoted below assume midweek travel.

You can often cut costs by going through a **specialist flight agent** – either a consolidator, who buys up blocks of tickets from the airlines and sells them at a discount, or a **discount agent**, who may also offer special student and youth fares plus travel insurance, rail passes, car rentals, tours and the like.

A further possibility is to see if you can arrange a **courier flight**, on which you shepherd a parcel through customs in return for a deeply discounted ticket. To take advantage, however, your schedule will have to be very flexible, and you may have to be satisfied with quite a short stay; courier flights are often best suited to lone travellers with very little luggage.

If China is only one stop on a much longer journey, you might want to consider buying a **Round-the-World** (**RTW**) ticket. Some travel agents can sell you an "off-the-shelf" RTW ticket that will have you touching down in about half a dozen cities (Hong Kong is on many itineraries); others will have to assemble one for you, which can be tailored to your needs but is apt to be more expensive. If you have a particular list of stopovers in mind, it's well worth calling the larger flight agents for a quote.

If your time is limited, you can't face the hassles of travelling on your own, or if you have a specialist interest such as cycling or bird-watching, then an **organized tour** of China, with flights, transport and accommodation included, might be worth considering. Though convenient, any tour including accommodation and internal travel is likely to work out more expensive per day than if you were travelling independently.

Booking flights online

Many airlines and discount travel websites offer you the opportunity to book your tickets **online**, cutting out the costs of agents and middlemen. Good deals can often be found through discount or auction sites, as well as through the airlines' own websites.

Online booking agents

Ⓦ **www.cheapflights.com** Bookings from the UK and Ireland only. Flight deals, travel agents, plus links to other travel sites.

Ⓦ **www.cheaptickets.com** Discount flight specialists.

Ⓦ **www.expedia.com** Discount airfares, all-airline search engine and daily deals.

Ⓦ **www.flyaow.com** Online air travel info and reservations site.

Ⓦ **www.flychina.com** Online broker specializing in flights between the US and China, as well as Chinese domestic flights. Use their Fare Finder to submit a request, then wait for their emailed confirmation or suggestion. Staff are helpful, and special offers are posted frequently.

Ⓦ **www.hotwire.com** Bookings from the US only. Last-minute savings of up to forty percent on regular fares. Travellers must be at least 18; no refunds, transfers or changes are allowed.

Ⓦ **www.lastminute.com** Offers good last-minute

holiday package and flight-only deals.

Ⓦ **www.priceline.com** Name-your-own-price website that has deals at around forty percent off standard fares. You can't specify flight times (although you do specify dates) and the tickets are non-refundable, non-transferable and non-changeable.

Ⓦ **www.skyauction.com** Bookings from the US only. Auctions tickets and travel packages using a "second bid" scheme. The best strategy is to bid the maximum you're willing to pay, since the winner is only charged just enough to beat the runner-up.

Ⓦ **www.travelocity.com** Provides access to SABRE, the most comprehensive central reservations system in the US.

Ⓦ **www.travelshop.com.au** Australian website offering discounted flights, packages, insurance and online bookings.

From the UK and Ireland

The only **nonstop flights** to China from the UK go from **London Heathrow** to either Hong Kong (12hr) or Beijing (10hr). It's not a problem to fly to China from other UK airports or from the Republic of Ireland, though you'll end up either catching a connecting flight to London or flying via your airline's hub city.

From the UK, the lowest available fares to Beijing from London start from around £400 in low season, rising to £600 in high season; to Hong Kong the corresponding range is about £450–700. Unfancied airlines such as Air China and Aeroflot themselves offer competitive fares; Aeroflot's £560 one-year open ticket on its Shanghai flight is the cheapest fares there from Europe. Even the more upmarket airlines such as British Airways can be worth approaching to see if they are running any special offers or promotions – if you catch them at the right time you can enjoy the luxury of a nonstop flight at a budget price.

As regards **RTW tickets**, a London–Bangkok–Manila–Hong Kong–London ticket costs less than £700, while an RTW ticket incorporating stopovers in Australia and the USA should come in well under £1000.

Airlines

Aeroflot UK Ⓣ020/7355 2233, Ⓦwww.aeroflot.co.uk. London–Moscow flights, with connections daily to Beijing and once a week to Shanghai and Hong Kong.

Air China UK Ⓣ020/7630 0919 or 7630 7678, Ⓦwww.air-china.co.uk. Five weekly nonstop flights from London Heathrow to Beijing, with keen fares.

Air France UK Ⓣ0845/084 5111, Ⓦwww.airfrance.co.uk; Republic of Ireland Ⓣ01/605 0383, Ⓦwww.airfrance.com/ie. Daily flights to Beijing, Shanghai and Hong Kong, via Paris.

British Airways UK Ⓣ0845/773 3377, Republic of Ireland Ⓣ1800/626747, Ⓦwww.ba.com. Flies from London Heathrow to Beijing four times a week, and to Hong Kong daily. Connections available from many UK airports.

Cathay Pacific UK Ⓣ08457/581581 or 020/8834 8888, Ⓦwww.cathaypacific.com/uk. At least one nonstop service to Hong Kong daily from London Heathrow, with connections from several UK airports and, through its sister airline Dragonair, links to more than a dozen cities on the Chinese mainland.

Emirates Airlines UK Ⓣ0870/243 2222, Ⓦwww.emirates.com. Daily flights from London Heathrow to Hong Kong via Dubai. Some good off-peak prices.

Finnair UK Ⓣ020/7408 1222, Republic of Ireland Ⓣ01/844 6565, Ⓦwww.finnair.com. From London Heathrow, Manchester and Glasgow to Helsinki, with three weekly flights from there to Beijing.

Gulf Air UK Ⓣ0870/777 1717, Ⓦwww.gulfairco.com. Daily from London Heathrow to Hong Kong via Dubai.

KLM UK Ⓣ0870/507 4074, Ⓦwww.klmuk.com. Flies from many UK regional airports to Amsterdam, from where it runs four flights weekly to Beijing and daily flights to Hong Kong.

Lufthansa UK Ⓣ08457/737747, Ⓦwww.luthansa.co.uk. Daily flights to Beijing, Shanghai and Hong Kong, via Frankfurt, with connections from UK and Irish airports.

Pakistan International Airlines UK Ⓣ020/7499 5500, Ⓦwww.fly-pia.com. London–Islamabad, with two weekly connections to Beijing; requires an overnight stop.

Singapore Airlines UK Ⓣ0870/608 8886, Republic of Ireland Ⓣ01/671 0722, Ⓦwww.singaporeair.com. A classy airline but a circuitous route, via Singapore from London Heathrow and Manchester. From their hub they have daily flights to Beijing, Hong Kong, Shanghai and Guangzhou.

Swiss International Airlines UK Ⓣ0845/601 0956, Ⓦwww.swiss.com. Daily flights to Beijing and Hong Kong, with connections to their Zürich hub from London, Birmingham, Manchester, Edinburgh and Dublin.

Thai Airways UK ⓣ0870/606 0911, ⓦwww.thaiair.com. Via Bangkok, they offer a whole range of gateways to China, including Beijing, Shanghai, Hong Kong, Guangzhou and Macau.
Virgin Atlantic Airways UK ⓣ01293/747 747, ⓦwww.virgin-atlantic.com. Four flights to Shanghai weekly and daily flights to Hong Kong. Slightly cheaper than British Airways or Cathay Pacific for the same high standard of service.

Flight agents and courier flight brokers

UK

Bridge the World UK ⓣ0870/444 7474, ⓦwww.bridgetheworld.com. Specializes in RTW tickets.
Co-op Travel Care Belfast ⓣ0870/902 0033, ⓦwww.travelcareonline.com. Flights and holidays.
Destination Group UK ⓣ020/7400 7045, ⓦwww.destination-group.com. Good discount airfares.
Flightbookers UK ⓣ0870/010 7000, ⓦwww.ebookers.com. Low fares on scheduled flights.
Flynow UK ⓣ0870/444 0045, ⓦwww.flynow.com. Large range of discounted tickets.
International Association of Air Travel Couriers UK ⓣ0800/074 6481 or 01305/216920, ⓦwww.aircourier.co.uk. Courier flights to Beijing and Hong Kong from London Gatwick or Heathrow.
North South Travel UK ⓣ & ⓕ01245/608291, ⓦwww.northsouthtravel.co.uk. Discounted fares worldwide; profits are used to support projects in the developing world, especially the promotion of sustainable tourism.
Quest Travel UK ⓣ0870/442 3542, ⓦwww.questtravel.com. Specialists in RTW discount fares.
STA Travel UK ⓣ0870/1600599, ⓦwww.statravel.co.uk. Worldwide specialists in low-cost flights and tours for students and under-26s, though other customers welcome.
Top Deck UK ⓣ020/7244 8000, ⓦwww.topdecktravel.co.uk. Long-established agent dealing in discount flights.
Trailfinders UK ⓣ020/7628 7628, ⓦwww.trailfinders.com. One of the best-informed and most efficient agents for independent travellers; produce a very useful quarterly magazine worth scrutinizing for round-the-world routes.
Travel Bag UK ⓣ0870/890 1456, ⓦwww.travelbag.co.uk. Discount flights.
Travel Cuts UK ⓣ020/7255 2082 or 7255 1944, ⓦwww.travelcuts.co.uk. Canadian company specializing in budget, student and youth travel and RTW tickets.

Republic of Ireland

Apex Travel ⓣ01/241 8000, ⓦwww.apextravel.ie. Discount flight specialists.
Aran Travel International ⓣ091/562595, ⓦhomepages.iol.ie/~arantvl/aranmain.htm. Good-value flights.
CIE Tours International ⓣ01/703 1888, ⓦwww.cietours.ie. General flight and tour agent.
Go Holidays ⓣ01/874 4126, ⓦwww.goholidays.ie. Package tour specialists.
Joe Walsh Tours ⓣ01/676 0991, ⓦwww.joewalshtours.ie. General budget-fares agent.
Lee Travel Cork ⓣ021/277111, ⓦwww.leetravel.ie. Flights and holidays.
McCarthy's Travel Cork ⓣ021/427 0127, ⓦwww.mccarthystravel.ie. General flight agent.
Trailfinders Dublin ⓣ01/677 7888, ⓦwww.trailfinders.ie. One of the best-informed and most efficient agents for independent travellers; produces a very useful quarterly magazine worth scrutinizing for RTW routes.
USIT ⓣ01/602 1600, ⓦwww.usitnow.ie. Student and youth flight specialists.

Organized tours

UK-based tour operators fall into two categories: those which offer a fully cosseted holiday and talk about the "romance" of China, and those which concern themselves with the "real" China – at the earthiest end of the market, these involve rugged overland trips in specially modified vehicles. The advantage of the latter tours is that they sometimes penetrate parts of China inaccessible by public transport.

Particularly good deals are the amazingly cheap off-season **flight-and-hotel** packages to Beijing which, at prices that often go below £500, provide six or seven nights in a four-star hotel effectively for free. Don't forget, though, that quoted prices in brochures usually refer to the low-season minimum, based on two people sharing – the cost for a single traveller in high season will always work out far more expensive.

Specialist tour operators

China Travel Service (CTS) UK ☎020/7836 9911, ⓦwww.ctshorizons.com. An extensive range of tours including very cheap off-season hotel-and-flight packages to Beijing. This China-based operator also has offices in many Chinese cities; see the guide for addresses.

Destinations Worldwide Holidays Republic of Ireland ☎01/855 6641, ⓦwww.destinations.ie. Undemanding two-week tours that include Hong Kong and Beijing.

Exodus UK ☎020/8675 5550, ⓦwww.exodus.co.uk. Offers some interesting and unusual overland itineraries in the wilds of Tibet, Inner Mongolia and the Northwest. Good-value three-week tours from £1700 including flights.

Explore Worldwide UK ☎01252/760000, ⓦwww.explore.co.uk. Big range of small-group tours and treks, including Tibet tours and trips along the Yangtse, as well as a Silk Road epic for under £2000. Some supplements for single travellers,

Hayes and Jarvis ☎0870/898 9890, ⓦwww.hayes-jarvis.com, ⓔres@hayesandjarvis.co.uk. Similar approach to Kuoni's, though note that their Beijing flight-and-hotel-only packages can be the cheapest around.

Haiwei Trails ⓦwww.haiweitrails.com. A British company with a Chinese base at Lijiang in Yunnan. They specialize in adventure travel, including bird-watching excursions, trekking and rafting, around the remoter parts of southwest China. A three-week hiking trip along the Tibet–Sichuan frontier, for example, starts at around £1400.

Imaginative Traveller UK ☎020/8742 8612, ⓦwww.adventurebound.co.uk. An emphasis on the unusual, with cycling tours, a panda trek in Sichuan and a Kathmandu–Lhasa–Kathmandu overland trip.

Kuoni Worldwide ☎01306/740500 ⓦwww.kuoni.co.uk. Packages China as a holiday experience; often in conjunction with side-trips to Bali or Bangkok. Seven nights Hong Kong–Shanghai–Beijing–Xi'an from £1200.

Magic of the Orient UK ☎01293/537700, ⓦwww.magic-of-the-orient.com. Tailor-made holidays sometimes off the beaten track, in Yunnan and along the Yangtze. An all-inclusive overland 12-day trip from Kunming to Hanoi costs just over £1000.

Naturetrek UK ☎01962/733051, ⓦwww.naturetrek.co.uk. Runs worldwide tours which specialize in spotting the local flora and fauna, including an annual 25-day overland trip from Chengdu to Lhasa costing around £4000.

Regent Holidays UK ☎0117/921 1711, ⓦwww.regent-holidays.co.uk. Offers interesting Trans-Siberian packages for individual travellers in either direction and with different possible stopover permutations. The basic Moscow–Beijing package, including a night in a Moscow hotel, costs around £400.

The Russia Experience UK ☎020 8566 8846, ⓦww.trans-siberian.co.uk. Besides detailing their Trans-Siberian packages, their website has a veritable mine of information about the railway.

World Expeditions UK ☎020/8870 2600, ⓦwww.worldexpeditions.co.uk. Offers a leisurely 18-day cycling tour (9 days of actual cycling) through Guangdong Province to Guilin – a good way to see real village life – for £1450 excluding flights. Also a 21-day Great Wall trek, starting in Beijing, that gets well off the beaten track for £1595 excluding flights.

From the US and Canada

There are more flights to **Hong Kong** from North America than elsewhere in China, though there's no shortage of flights to Beijing, and you can also choose to fly to a Chinese provincial city – Chinese, Japanese, Korean and Hong Kong airlines offer services to cities throughout China from their respective hubs. It takes around thirteen hours' **flying time** to reach Beijing from the West Coast; add seven hours or more to this if you start from the East Coast (including a stopover on the West Coast en route).

Round-trip fares to Hong Kong, Beijing and Shanghai are broadly comparable: in low season, expect to pay US$600–800 /CDN$950–1250 from the West Coast (Los Angeles, San Francisco, Vancouver), or US$800–1100/CDN$1250–1750 from the East coast (New York, Montreal, Toronto). To get a good fare during high season it's important to buy your ticket as early as possible, in which case you probably won't pay more than US$200/CDN$320 above what you would have paid in low season. For an **RTW** ticket taking in Beijing or Hong Kong, reckon on US$2200/CDN$3500.

Airlines

Air Canada ☎1-888/247-2262, ⓦwww.aircanada.ca. Daily direct flights to Beijing from Toronto, via Vancouver.

Air China US ⓣ1-800/982-8802 or 1-800/986-1985, Canada ⓣ416/581-8833, ⓦwww.airchina.com.cn. Daily nonstop flights to Beijing from New York, San Francisco, Los Angeles and Vancouver, with connections to all major cities in China. Also flies daily to Beijing from Montreal and Toronto via Vancouver. US connecting flights with Northwest Airlines.

All Nippon Airways ⓣ1-800/235-9262, ⓦsvc.ana.co.jp/eng/index.html. Japanese carrier with daily direct flights from New York, Washington, San Francisco, Los Angeles, Vancouver and Toronto to Tokyo. They operate onward flights to Beijing, Hong Kong, Shanghai, Dalian, Qingdao, Shenyang and Xiamen.

American Airlines ⓣ1-800/433-7300, ⓦwww.aa.com. Daily nonstop flights from New York, Dallas, Chicago and Los Angeles to Tokyo, with connections to Hong Kong and Beijing.

Asiana Airlines ⓣ1-800/227-4262, ⓦus.flyasiana.com. Korean airline flying nonstop to Seoul from Los Angeles (daily), San Francisco and Seattle (4 weekly) as well as flying direct from New York (4 weekly); connections to cities throughout China.

Cathay Pacific ⓣ1-800/233-2742, ⓦwww.cathay-usa.com. Daily service to Hong Kong from Los Angeles, New York, San Francisco, Toronto and Vancouver. Connections to more than a dozen Chinese cities with its subsidiary Dragonair.

China Eastern Airlines ⓣ1-800/200-5118, ⓦwww.ce-air.com. Daily flights from Los Angeles to Beijing, with connections to major Chinese cities.

EVA Airways ⓣ1-800/695-1188, ⓦwww.evaair.com. Taiwanese carrier; via Taipei, they operate daily flights to Hong Kong from New York (via Seattle), Los Angeles and San Francisco, plus three weekly flights from Vancouver to Hong Kong. Taipei–Macau connections also available.

Japan Air Lines ⓣ1-800/525-3663, ⓦwww.japanair.com. Daily nonstop service to Tokyo from New York, Los Angeles, San Francisco, Chicago and Vancouver, with connections to Beijing, Hong Kong, Shanghai, Dalian, Qingdao, Tianjin and Xiamen.

Korean Airlines ⓣ1-800/438-5000, ⓦwww.koreanair.com. Daily nonstop flights to Seoul from New York, Los Angeles, Chicago, Dallas, Washington, San Francisco and Atlanta; connections to Beijing, Hong Kong, Shanghai, Qingdao, Tianjin, Kunming and several other Chinese cities.

Northwest/KLM Airlines ⓣ1-800/447-4747, ⓦwww.nwa.com, ⓦwww.klm.com. Daily flights to Tokyo from Honolulu, Seattle, San Francisco, Los Angeles, Minneapolis, Detroit and New York, with connections to Beijing and Hong Kong.

United Airlines ⓣ1-800/538-2929, ⓦwww.ual.com. Daily nonstop flights from San Francisco to Shanghai and Chicago to Beijing, plus a daily nonstop service to Hong Kong from Chicago and San Francisco.

Travel agents and courier flight brokers

Air Brokers International ⓣ1-800/883-3273, ⓦwww.airbrokers.com. Consolidator and specialist in RTW tickets.

Airtreks.com ⓣ1-877-AIRTREKS or 415/912-5600, ⓦwww.airtreks.com. The website features an interactive database that lets you build and price your own RTW itinerary, with Beijing, Shanghai and Hong Kong all potential stopovers.

Air Courier Association ⓣ1-800/282-1202, ⓦwww.aircourier.org or www.cheaptrips.com. New York–Hong Kong courier flights for around $450. Membership costs around $40 a year.

Council Travel ⓣ1-800/2COUNCIL, ⓦwww.counciltravel.com. Nationwide organization that mostly specializes in student/budget travel. Flights from the US only.

International Association of Air Travel Couriers ⓣ308/632-3273, ⓦwww.courier.org. New York–Hong Kong courier flights. Annual membership $45.

STA Travel ⓣ1-800/781-4040, ⓦwww.sta-travel.com. Worldwide specialists in independent travel.

TFI Tours ⓣ1-800/745-8000 or 212/736-1140, ⓦwww.lowestairprice.com. Consolidator.

Travac ⓣ1-800/TRAV-800, ⓦwww.thetravelsite.com. Consolidator with offices in New York City and Orlando.

Travelers Advantage ⓣ1-877/259-2691, ⓦwww.travelersadvantage.com. Discount travel club; annual membership fee required.

Travel Avenue ⓣ1-800/333-3335, ⓦwww.travelavenue.com. Full-service travel agent that offers discounts in the form of rebates.

Travel Cuts Canada ⓣ1-800/667-2887, US ⓣ1-866/246-9762, ⓦwww.travelcuts.com. Canadian student-travel organization.

Worldtek Travel ⓣ1-800/243-1723, ⓦwww.worldtek.com. Discount travel agency for worldwide travel.

Tour operators

Prices below exclude flights to China unless otherwise stated.

Abercrombie & Kent ⓣ1-800/323-7308 or 630/954-2944, ⓦwww.abercrombiekent.com. Luxury tours; $4000 buys you a twelve-day "Highlights of China" trip covering Shanghai, Guilin, Xian and Beijing.

Absolute Asia ⓣ1-800/736-8187, ⓦwww.absoluteasia.com. Numerous tours of China lasting from between 6 and 23 days, in first-class accommodation, such as the 14-day "Art and History of China" tour which starts at $3700.

Adventure Center ⓣ1-800/228-8747 or 510/654-1879, ⓦwww.adventure-center.com. Their 21-day "Essence of China" package ($1500) starts out in Yanshuo and ends up in Beijing, with walking, hiking and biking opportunities along the way.

Adventures Abroad ⓣ1-800/665-3998 or 360/775-9926, ⓦwww.adventures-abroad.com. Small-group specialists offering a 13-day tour that weaves its way from Beijing to Shanghai ($2100).

Asian Pacific Adventures ⓣ1-800/825-1680 or 818/886-5190, ⓦwww.asianpacificadventures.com. Numerous tours of China, including the 17-day "Dragons, Drums and Art" excursion, starting at $3100 and covering Hong Kong, Guangzhou, Guiyang, Kaili, Rongjiang and Guilin.

Asia Transpacific Journeys ⓣ1-800/642-2742, ⓦwww.southeastasia.com. Their "China: Beyond the Wall" deluxe 18-day hiking tour starts at $4800.

Backroads ⓣ1-800/GO-ACTIVE or 510/527-1555, ⓦwww.backroads.com. Cycling and hiking throughout Beijing and south China's Guangdong Province; ten-day packages start at $4000.

Cross-Culture ⓣ1-800/491-1148 or 413/256-6303, ⓦwww.crossculturesinc.com. Offers several tours involving China, such as the nine-day "Yangtze River Cruise" from $3150, including airfare to China.

Geographic Expeditions ⓣ1-800/777-8183 or 415/922-0448, ⓦwww.geoex.com. Offers an eight-day "Classic China" tour taking in Beijing, Xi'an and Guilin, at $3000.

Himalayan Travel ⓣ1-800/225-2380 or 203/743-2349, ⓦwww.himalayantravelinc.com. Several tours throughout China including "China Unmasked", a twenty-day tour of Beijing, Hohhot, Shapatou, Chongqing, Yichang, Luoyang and Xi'an for $2000.

IST Cultural Tours ⓣ1-800/833-2111, ⓦwww.ist-tours.com. Theiir "China – New and Old" tour takes in Beijing and Shanghai ($700).

Journeys International ⓣ1-800/255-8735 or 734/665-4407, ⓦwww.journeys-intl.com. Tour operator specializing in ecotravel.

Maupintour ⓣ1-800/255-4266, ⓦwww.maupintour.com. Luxury tour operator. For $5000 you could go on their 17-day "China and its Ancient Waterways" package, which includes a three-night cruise on the Yangzi.

Mir Corp ⓣ206/624-7289, ⓦwww.mircorp.com. Specialists in Trans-Siberian rail travel, for small groups as well as individual travellers.

Mountain Travel Sobek ⓣ1-888/MTSOBEK or 510/527-8100, ⓦwww.mtsobek.com. Adventure tours such as "K2 and the Chinese Karakoram", thirty days of strenuous hiking and camping with a $5800 price tag to match.

Pacific Delight Tours ⓣ1-800/221-7179 or 212/818-1781, ⓦwww.pacificdelighttours.com. Numerous Yangzi River tours.

Pleasant Holidays ⓣ1-800/742-9244, ⓦwww.pleasantholidays.com. Air/hotel packages to Beijing; five nights start at a very reasonable $900.

REI Adventures ⓣ1-800/622-2236, ⓦwww.rei.com/travel. Cycling and hiking tours throughout China.

Worldwide Quest Adventures ⓣ1-800/387-1483 or 416/633-5666, ⓦwww.worldwidequest.com. On their 21-day "Hike the Great Wall" you get 11 days of trekking along the wall, all for $2600.

From Australia and New Zealand

The closest entry point into China from Australia and New Zealand is Hong Kong, though from Australia it's also possible to fly to Guangzhou, Shanghai and Beijing without changing planes. It's not a problem to fly elsewhere in China from either country if you catch a connecting flight along the way, though this can involve a long layover in the airline's hub city.

From Australia, some of the cheapest fares are with Royal Brunei Airlines, though they only serve Brisbane and Darwin. Their return fares, via a stopover in Brunei, are around A$1100 to Hong Kong from Brisbane or Darwin; A$1350 to Shanghai from Brisbane. Other good deals include Air China from Melbourne or Sydney direct to Guangzhou (A$1300), Shanghai (A$1500), and Beijing (A$1500); and Cathay Pacific direct to Hong Kong (A$1500 in low season; their fares are steep at other times). Qantas or British Airways are the only two operators to fly direct from Perth to Hong Kong (A$1800).

Flights **from New Zealand** are limited and therefore expensive: about the best deal is on Air New Zealand or Singapore from Auckland to Hong Kong (NZ$1750). Air New Zealand, Malaysian and other carriers also fly via other Southeast Asian hub cities to Hong Kong and elsewhere in China.

Airlines

Air China Australia ⓣ02/9232 7277, ⓦwww.airchina.com.cn/index_en.html. From Sydney or Melbourne, they fly twice weekly to Guangzhou, three times a week to Shanghai, and five times a week to Beijing. Connections to all major Chinese cities.

Air New Zealand New Zealand ⓣ0800/737000, ⓦwww.airnz.com. Auckland to Hong Kong five times a week, with connections to mainland Chinese cities.

British Airways Australia ⓣ02/8904 8800, New Zealand ⓣ0800/274847, ⓦwww.britishairways.com. Daily from Australian east-coast capitals to Hong Kong, with connections on Chinese airlines through to Shanghai, Beijing and other major cities.

Cathay Pacific Australia ⓣ131747, New Zealand ⓣ09/379 0861 or 0508/800454, ⓦwww.cathaypacific.com. Daily from Australian east-coast capitals to Hong Kong, with connections into a dozen or so cities across China with their sister airline Dragonair.

Malaysia Airlines Australia ⓣ132627, New Zealand ⓣ09/373 2741, ⓦwww.mas.com.my. Five flights a week from Australian east-coast capitals, plus Perth and Adelaide, to Hong Kong, Beijing, Shanghai or Guangzhou, to Kuala Lumpur, where after an overnight stay you connect onto their flights to Hong Kong, Beijing, Shanghai, Xiamen or Guangzhou.

Qantas Australia ⓣ131313, ⓦwww.qantas.com.au. At least daily from Australian east-coast capitals to Hong Kong, with connections on Chinese airlines through to Shanghai and Beijing.

Royal Brunei Airlines Australia ⓣ07/3017 5000, ⓦwww.bruneiair.com. From Brisbane to Hong Kong weekly, to Shanghai twice a week; also once a week from Darwin to Hong Kong. All flights via Brunei.

Singapore Airlines Australia ⓣ131011, New Zealand ⓣ09/303 2129, ⓦwww.singaporeair.com. Several flights weekly from Brisbane, Sydney, Melbourne and Auckland to Singapore, with connections to Beijing, Hong Kong, Shanghai, Guangzhou and Xiamen.

Thai Australia ⓣ1300/651960, ⓦwww.thaiair.com. Several flights weekly from Brisbane, Sydney and Melbourne, via Bangkok, to Hong Kong, Kunming, Guangzhou, Beijing, Shanghai, and Chengdu – and they allow you to fly into one city and return from another without a surcharge, as long as the return fare to each city is the same.

Vietnam Australia ⓣ02/9283 1355, ⓦwww.vietnamairlines.com.vn. Twice weekly from Sydney and Melbourne, via Hanoi, to Beijing, Kunming, and Guangzhou.

Travel agents

Budget Travel New Zealand ⓣ09/366 0061 or 0800/808040, ⓦwww.budgettravel.co.nz.

Destinations Unlimited New Zealand ⓣ09/373 4033.

Flight Centres Australia ⓣ133133 or 02/9235 3522, New Zealand ⓣ09/358 4310, ⓦwww.flightcentre.com.au.

Northern Gateway Australia ⓣ08/8941 1394, ⓦwww.northerngateway.com.au.

STA Travel Australia ⓣ1300/733035, ⓦwww.statravel.com.au, New Zealand ⓣ0508/782872, ⓦwww.statravel.co.nz.

Student Uni Travel Australia ⓣ02/9232 8444, ⓦwww.sut.com.au; New Zealand ⓣ0800/874823, ⓦwww.sut.co.nz.

Trailfinders Australia ⓣ02/9247 7666, ⓦwww.trailfinders.com.au.

Specialist tour operators

The Adventure Travel Company New Zealand ⓣ09/379 9755, ⓦwww.adventuretravel.co.nz. NZ agent for Peregrine (see p.18). Trekking and just sightseeing in China, Mongolia and Tibet; also organizes Trans-Siberian rail trips.

All About Asia Australia ⓣ1800/066526 or 07/3221 4417, ⓦwww.allaboutasia.com.au. Discount airfares, plus hotel and resort packages in Hong Kong and mainland China.

Asian Explorer Holidays Australia ⓣ03/9245 0777, ⓦwww.asianexplorer.com.au. Hong Kong getaway packages.

Birding Worldwide Australia ⓣ03/9899 9303, ⓦwww.birdingworldwide.com.au. Organizes group trips to China – including Tibet – for those wanting to glimpse typical, unique and rare bird species.

China Tours and Travel Australia ⓣ08/9321 3432 ⓕ03/9321 2190. Six-day to three-week packages to China by air, road, rail and river.

China Travel Service Australia ⓣ02/9211 2633, New Zealand ⓣ09/309 6458,

Ⓦwww.chinatravel.com.au. Covers package tours, transport and accommodation bookings for all the main sites in China, through sister organizations in the country.

Gateway Travel Australia Ⓣ02/9745 3333, Ⓦwww.russian-gateway.com.au. Eastern European and Russian specialists; useful for Trans-Siberian bookings.

Intrepid Adventure Travel Australia Ⓣ1300/360667 or 03/9473 2626, New Zealand Ⓣ0800/174043, Ⓦwww.intrepidtravel.com.au. Small-group tours, with the emphasis on cross-cultural contact and low-impact tourism. Covers the staples – Beijing, Shanghai, Xi'an, and the Yangzi – along with the Silk Road, Karakorum Highway, and minor sights.

Passport Travel Australia Ⓣ03/9867 3888, Ⓦwww.travelcentre.com.au. A few city-based packages to Beijing and Shanghai in particular, plus Trans-Siberian bookings.

Peregrine Adventures Australia Ⓣ03/9662 2700 or 02/9290 2770, Ⓦwww.peregrine.net.au; NZ bookings through the Adventure Travel Company (see p.17). Off-the-beaten-track excursions between Beijing and Xishuangbanna.

Sundowners Australia Ⓣ03/9672 5300 or 1800/337089, Ⓦwww.sundowners-travel.com. Tours of the Silk Road, plus Trans-Siberian rail bookings.

Travel Indochina Australia Ⓣ1300 365355, Ⓦwww.travelindochina.com.au. Covers the obvious China sights but goes a bit beyond them too; also arranges cross-border visas for Thailand, Laos, Vietnam and Cambodia.

Overland routes

China now has a number of **land borders** open to foreign travellers. When planning your route, think carefully about where you buy your Chinese visa – remember that Chinese visas must be used within three months of their date of issue, which may not be very useful if you are planning a long overland trip before arriving in China. Visas are obtainable in the capitals of virtually all European and Asian countries, though you may have to wait a few days for them to be issued (see p.22 for embassy addresses).

Via Moscow

One of the classic overland routes to China is through Russia on the so-called **Trans-Siberian Express**. As a one-off trip, the journey is highly recommended, and is a memorable way to begin or end one's stay in China. The awesome views of stately birch forests, velvety prairies, misty lakes and arid plateaus help time pass much faster than you'd think, and there are frequent stops during which you can wander the station platform for a few minutes, purchasing food and knick-knacks. The trains are comfortable and clean: second-class compartments contain four berths, while first-class have two and even boast a private shower.

There are actually two rail lines from Moscow to Beijing: the **Trans-Manchurian** line, which runs almost as far as the sea of Japan before turning south through Dongbei (Manchuria) to Beijing; and the **Trans-Mongolian** express, which cuts through Mongolia from Siberia. The Manchurian train takes about six days, the Mongolian train about five; the latter is more popular with foreigners, not just because it's a little quicker but also because of the allure of Mongolia. Trans-Mongolian Chinese Train #4 is the most popular service for foreign tourists, a scenic route that rumbles past Lake Baikal and Siberia, the grasslands of Mongolia, and the desert of northwest China, skirting the Great Wall. At the Mongolia–China border, you can watch as the undercarriage is switched to a different gauge. The one drawback of this route is that you might need an additional visa for Mongolia, though US citizens no longer require this.

Meals are included while the train is in China. In Mongolia, the dining car accepts payment in both Chinese and Mongolian currency; while in Russia, US dollars or Russian roubles can be used. It's worth having small denominations of US dollars as you can change these on the train throughout the journey, or use them to buy food from station vendors along the way – though experiencing the cuisine and people in the dining cars is part of the fun. You could attempt to order what's listed on the menu, but your requests for caviar, ox-tongue salad and fried chicken with pineapple will probably be scoffed at by the waiter, who will deliver vodka, bread, and Marlboros. Bring instant noodles and snacks as a backup, plenty of film, and that great long novel you've always wanted to read – such as the four-volume Chinese classic *Journey to the West*.

Tickets and packages

Booking tickets can be problematic, especially in summer, when you may need to book two or three months ahead to ensure a seat. Furthermore, sorting out your travel arrangements from abroad is a complex business – you'll need transit visas for Russia, as well as for Mongolia if you intend to pass through there, and if you plan on reaching or leaving Moscow by rail via Warsaw, you'll have to get a transit visa for Belarus too. It's therefore highly advisable to use an experienced **travel agent** who can organize all tickets, visas and stopovers if required, in advance. Visa processing is an especially helpful time saver which agents can offer, given the ridiculous queues and paperwork required for visas along the route. One firm offering these services as well as rail packages that you can book from abroad is Monkey Business (Ⓦwww.monkeyshrine.com), who have offices in Hong Kong and Beijing; for details of companies **at home** which can sort out Trans-Siberian travel; see the lists of specialist travel agents earlier in the Getting There section. If you want to book a ticket yourself, reckon on paying the equivalent of at least US$200 for second-class travel from Moscow to Bejing. For information on taking the train **from Beijing**, see p.81.

Via the Central Asian Republics

Until the collapse of the Soviet Union it was almost unthinkable to travel around places like **Kazakhstan** or **Kyrgystan** on your way to China. These days, although the old land routes between China and the West are certainly reawakening, they still present bureaucratic obstacles to travellers, which can sometimes be eased by the judicious distribution of a few low-denomination US dollar notes.

Almaty and Bishkek – respectively the former and current capitals of Kazakhstan and Kyrgystan – are both still linked by daily trains to Moscow (3 days), though getting Russian transit visas and booking berths on these trains is not easy from home; it's worth talking to the Trans-Siberian specialists listed earlier in Getting There, as some offer packages involving travel through Central Asia. It is now also possible to get into Central Asia without going through Russia at all. You can get to **Turkmenistan**, and thence to the rest of Central Asia, either from northeastern Iran or from Azerbaijan across the Caspian Sea, though again you'll need to look closely at the visa situation of the countries you plan to cross.

Crossing into China from Kazakhstan is perfectly straightforward – there are very comfortable twice-weekly trains from Almaty to Ürümqi, which take 35 hours and cost about US$75 for a berth in a four-berth compartment. There are also buses, which are less comfortable, but cheaper and faster (US$50; about 24hr). From Bishkek in Kyrgystan, Kashgar is only nine hours' drive away and the two cities are linked by buses in summer months. Foreigners, however, have had difficulties in trying to use these and have usually had to resort to expensive private transport run by local tour operators to help them across.

Via the Indian subcontinent

The land route from Europe to the Indian subcontinent goes through **Turkey** and **Iran** to **Pakistan**, a fairly straightforward trip on local buses and trains. Note that Iranian seven-day transit visas are routinely issued to Western travellers, with the exception of US citizens – though visa applications may take up to two months to be processed.

The routes from the subcontinent across the mountains to China are among the toughest in Asia. The first is from Pakistan into Xinjiang Province over the **Karakoram Highway**, along one of the branches of the ancient Silk Road. This requires no pre-planning, except for the fact that it is open only from May to October, and closes periodically due to landslips. The Karakoram Highway actually starts at Rawalpindi (the old city outside the capital Islamabad), and in theory you can get from here to Kashgar in four days on public buses. From Rawalpindi, first take one of the daily minibuses which run the arduous fifteen-hour trip up the Indus gorge to the village of Gilgit, where you'll have to spend a night. From Gilgit, the next destination is the border town of Sust, a five-hour journey. There are a couple of daily buses on this route. Once in Sust, immediately book your ticket to Tashkurgan in China (7hr) for the next morning – it costs 1200 rupees (about US$30). A few travellers have managed to talk their way into being issued a visa at the border, but you're strongly advised to have one already. The route is popular with cyclists, but there's no guarantee that you will be allowed to bike across the border; you'll probably have to load your bike on a bus for this part of the trip. For more on crossing the Chinese border here, see p.1109.

The other route tourists can use from the Indian subcontinent is **from Nepal into Tibet**. You can simply arrive in Kathmandu and arrange everything from there, with the exception of your Chinese visa, which is best arranged before you go – getting one in Nepal can not only be problematic, it's also likely to be valid for travel with a tour group in Tibet only. It's an expensive trip, as foreigners are forbidden from using the normal public buses and must book a jeep tour to Lhasa with a driver and a guide – expect to pay at least US$300. See p.1124 for more on crossing the Nepalese border into Tibet, and remember that regulations concerning this crossing are in a constant state of flux.

From India itself there are, for political reasons, no border crossings to China. For years the authorities have discussed opening a bus route from Sikkim to Tibet, north from Darjeeling, but it has yet to materialize.

From Vietnam

Vietnam has three border crossings with China – **Dong Dang**, 60km northeast of Hanoi; **Lao Cai**, 150km northwest; and the little-used **Mong Cai**, 200km south of Nanning. All three are open daily between 8.30am and 5pm. Vietnamese border guards are notoriously officious, though just about any problem can be resolved with small sums of US dollars.

A twice-weekly **direct train** service from Hanoi is advertised as running all the way to **Beijing** (60hr), passing through **Nanning** and **Guilin**. In practice, though, you'll have to leave the train at Dong Dang, walk across the border, and catch a minibus to the Chinese railhead, 15km away at Pingxiang, from where there's a connecting train for the 170-kilometre run northeast to Nanning, Guangxi's capital. Alternatively, there are good rail and road connections from Hanoi to Lang Son, from where a minibus can take you the last 5km to Dong Dang; thereafter you'll need to get across the border as described earlier, to catch the afternoon or evening Nanning train (¥40) from Pingxiang. Similarly, there are daily trains from Hanoi to Lao Cai, eleven hours away in Vietnam's mountainous and undeveloped northwest (near the pleasant resort of Sa Pa). From here, you can cross into Yunnan Province at Hekou (see p.872), from where a daily train service runs to the provincial capital, **Kunming**. From Mong Cai, there are regular buses to Nanning.

From Laos and Burma

Crossing into China **from Laos** also lands you in Yunnan, this time at Bian Mao Zhan in the Xishuangbanna region. Formalities are very relaxed and unlikely to cause any problems, though take some hard cash as you can't change traveller's cheques on the Chinese side. It's 220km on local buses north from here to the regional capital, Jinghong, with a likely overnight stop in the town of Mengla along the way (see p.914).

Entering China **from Burma** (Myanmar) is an interesting possibility too, with the old Burma Road cutting northeast from Rangoon (Yangon) to Lashio and the crossing at Wanding in Yunnan. At time of writing, it isn't officially open, however – though given the country's volatile tourist situation, it's worth asking about the latest state of affairs before applying for a Burmese visa.

Visas and red tape

All foreign nationals require a visa to enter the People's Republic of China. Visas are available worldwide from Chinese embassies and consulates and through specialist tour operators and visa agents.

Most nationalities need only a valid passport to enter **Hong Kong**, although the length of time you can stay varies. British citizens, Canadians, Australians, New Zealanders and Irish and most other European citizens can stay for three months; and Americans and South Africans for thirty days. If you are planning to enter China through Hong Kong, you'll find this is probably the most straightforward place of all to buy your Chinese visa.

Visas

Single-entry **tourist visas** must generally be used within three months of issue, are valid for from thirty to ninety days from your date of entry into China and cost around US$40 or the local equivalent. The authorities increase and decrease visa durations in order to control tourist traffic, and you're more likely to be given a visa for longer than thirty days outside the summer months. Note that **transit** through China requires a 'G' visa, valid for seven days, if you are in the country for longer than 24 hours.

To **apply** for a transit or a tourist "L" visa you have to submit an application form, one or two passport-size photographs, your passport (which must be valid for at least another six months from your planned date of entry into China) and the fee, which cannot be paid by personal cheque. If you apply in person, processing should take between three and five working days, but this varies from country to country – usually, if you are willing to pay a surcharge you can get your visa the next day.

The application form asks for some details of your trip, such as where in China you're going – you're not bound to stick to the itinerary you state. Don't put Tibet or Xinjiang down as these replies can lead to additional questioning of your motives for visiting. You'll also be asked your occupation – don't put writer, journalist or any media-related profession, as doing so may significiantly reduce your chances of securing a visa. "Computer operator" is a handy catchall alternative – don't worry about being economical with the truth as they never check up. Rarely, you may be asked for copies of any air-ticket reservations and hotel bookings you've made.

A **business** "F" visa is valid for three months and can be issued for multiple entries, though you'll need an official invitation from a government-recognized Chinese organization. Twelve-month **work** or "Z" visas again require an invitation, plus a health certificate. Students intending to **study** for less than six months need an invitation from a college; those staying for longer also need to fill in an extra form available from embassies, and need a health certificate.

Applying for a Chinese visa in Hong Kong

In Hong Kong, the standard one-month tourist visa for China can be obtained from any of the numerous travel agencies or direct from the visa office at the Lower Block, China Resources Building, 26 Harbour Rd (trilingual info on ⓣ3413 2300). For a sixty- or ninety-day multiple-entry visa, issued in two days, visit CTS at 78–83 Connaught Rd or 27–33 Nathan Rd (see p.714 for further details). Note that these visas are valid from the date of issue, not the date of entry. You can get a six-month multiple-entry business visa at Shoestring Travel, 27–33 Nathan Rd, for HK$600. No invitation letter is required, just a business card.

Chinese embassies and consulates

Australia 15 Coronation Drive, Yarralumla, ACT 2600 ☎02/6273 4780, Ⓦwww.chinaembassy.org.au. Also consulates at 77 Irving Rd, Toorak (visa & passport enquiries ☎03/9804 3683) and 539 Elizabeth St, Surry Hills (☎02/9698 7929).
Canada 515 St Patrick St, Ottawa, Ontario K1N 5H3 ☎613/234 2682 Ⓦwww.chinaembassycanada.org. Visas can also be obtained from the consulates in Calgary, Toronto and Vancouver.
Ireland 40 Ailesbury Road, Dublin 4 ☎01/269 1707.
Kazakhstan ul. Furmanova 137, Almaty ☎634966.
Kyrgystan ul. Toktogula 196, Bishkek ☎222423.
Laos Thanon Wat Nak Yai, Vientiane ☎315103.
Nepal Baluwatar, Toran Bhawan, Naxal, Kathmandu ☎412589. Visas available only through travel agents to those travelling with a tour group, see pp.1121–1125.
New Zealand 2–6 Glenmore Street, Wellington ☎04/474 9631, Ⓦwww.chinaembassy.org.nz; plus a consulate in Auckland ☎09/525 1589, Ⓦwww.chinaconsulate.org.nz.
Pakistan Ramna 4, Diplomatic Enclave, Islamabad. Issues only ten-day visas.
Russia ul. Druzhby 6, Moscow ☎095/145-1543 Ⓦwww.chinaembassy.ru.
Thailand 57 Rachadapisake Rd, Huay Kwang, Bangkok 10310 ☎02/245 7044; 111 Chang Lo Rd, Chiang Mai ☎053/272197.
UK 31 Portland Place, London W1B 1QD ☎020/7631 1430; Denison House, Denison Rd, Victoria Pk, Manchester M14 5RX ☎0161/224 7480; Ⓦwww.chinese-embassy.org.uk.
USA 2300 Connecticut Ave NW, Washington, DC 20008 ☎202/328-2517, Ⓦwww.chinese-embassy.org. Also consulates in Chicago, Houston, Los Angeles, New York and San Francisco.
Vietnam Tran Phu, Hanoi (round the corner from the main embassy building at 46 Hoang Dieu) ☎04/823 5517.

Visa extensions

Visa extensions are handled by the Foreign Affairs section of the **Public Security Bureau (PSB)**, so you can apply for one in any reasonably sized town. The amount of money you'll pay for this, and the amount of hassle you'll have, varies greatly depending on where you are, your nationality, and what season it is. The best time of day to apply for an extension is just after lunch, when corpulent cops are at their most content.

A first extension, valid for a month, is easy to obtain. Most Europeans pay ¥160, Americans a little less. However, you're basically at the mercy of the particular PSB office and they may decide to levy charges on top. In some small towns the charge may even be waived and the process take ten minutes; in cities it can take up to a week. The worst place to apply is Tibet – you'll be given a week at most. The next worst places to apply are Beijing and then Shanghai – they keep your passport for up to a week.

A second or third extension is harder to get – in major cities you will probably be turned away. PSB offices in small towns are a much better bet, and you'd be unlucky to come away without some kind of extension, though it may only be for ten or twenty days. You will be asked your reasons for wanting an extension – simply saying you want to spend more time in this wonderful country usually goes down well, or you could cite illness or transport delays. Don't admit to being low on funds. Fourth or even fifth extensions are possible, but you'll need to foster connections with a PSB office. Ask advice from a local independent travel agent – they often have the right sort of contacts. Alternatively, try going to a lawyer, though they'll charge a lot.

Don't overstay your visa even for a few hours – the fine is ¥500 a day, and if you're caught at the airport with an out-of-date visa the hassle that follows may mean you miss your flight.

Customs

You're allowed to **import** into China up to four hundred cigarettes, two litres of alcohol, twenty fluid ounces of perfume and up to fifty grams of gold or silver. You can't take in more than ¥6000, and amounts of foreign currency over US$5000 or equivalent must be declared. It's illegal to import printed matter, tapes or videos critical of the country, but don't worry too much about this, as confiscation is rare in practice, except in sensitive areas such as Tibet; here, some travellers have reported books specifically about Tibet being taken off them. Finally, note that **export restrictions** apply on items which are more than 100 years old, for which you require an export form available from Friendship Stores.

Information, websites and maps

The concept of a country promoting itself by giving out tourist information for free has not yet taken hold in China outside the biggest cities. There is a very thin scattering of tourist promotion offices in foreign capitals, though these government organizations are officious and generally unhelpful – their only function seems to be recommending possible tour operators and advising telephone callers to listen to long, useless and expensive recorded messages. A more promising source of immediate information is the Internet.

Similarly, inside the People's Republic, there is no such thing as a tourist office. **CITS** (Ⓦwww.cits.net), the state-accredited tour operator with a special responsibility for foreigners, was originally dressed up as such, but now it is just one of a large number of competing local operators who have no function other than selling tours and tickets, and renting cars. However, it may still be worthwhile dropping in on the local branch of CITS, or an affiliated organization (**CTS**, Ⓦwww.ctsho.com; or **CYTS**, Ⓦwww.chinatour.com/cyts), especially in out-of-the-way places, as it is sometimes here that you will find the only person in town who can speak English. You should assume that most leaflets, brochures and maps from these places will not be free. Other sources of information are your own hotel staff (in upmarket places), or any local English-speakers you happen to meet. Otherwise, in certain tourist centres, restaurant proprietors have taken it upon themselves to act as the local information office, giving advice in exchange for custom.

In Beijing, Shanghai and Guangzhou you'll find English-language magazines with bar, restaurant and other "what's on" **listings**, aimed mainly at the resident expatriate population. These are usually distributed free in bars and upmarket hotels. The local English-language newspaper, the *China Daily*, also has a few listings of forthcoming major cultural events in Beijing and one or two other large cities. In Hong Kong and Macau you are beset with information on all sides. For details of listings magazines in the two territories, see p.716 and p.768.

Chinese tourist offices abroad

For additional locations, see Ⓦwww.cnto.org/offices.htm.

Australia 19th floor, 44 Market St, Sydney, NSW 2000 Ⓣ02/9299 4057.

Canada 480 University Ave, Suite 806, Toronto, Ontario M5G 1V2 Ⓣ0416/599 6636.

UK 4 Glentworth St, London NW1 5PG Ⓣ020/7373 0888.

USA Suite 6413, 350 Fifth Ave, Empire State Building, New York, NY 10018 Ⓣ212/760-8218; Suite 201, 333 W Broadway, Glendale, CA 91024 Ⓣ818/545-7505.

Online resources

CCTV 9 Ⓦwww.cctv-9.com. The website of one of Chinese state television's English-language channels, featuring a live video stream plus other programmes available to watch on demand.

China Business World Ⓦwww.cbw.com. A corporate directory site with a useful travel section, detailing tours and allowing you to book flights and hotels.

China News Digest Ⓦwww.cnd.org. This US-based site provides in-depth coverage of current affairs in China, in both English and Chinese.

China Vista Ⓦwww.chinavista.com. China-based website with snippets about Chinese culture, history, attractions, and food.

Chuck@China Ⓦchake.topcities.com. A quirky, entertaining site maintained by an American English-language teacher in China, with revelations on all aspects of expat life.

International Campaign for Tibet Ⓦwww.savetibet.org. An authoritative source of current news from Tibet.

Sinomania Ⓦwww.sinomania.com. A California-based site with links to current Chinese news stories and a good popular music section, with MP3s available.

Yesasia ⓦ www.yesasia.com. Online shopping for Chinese movies, CDs, books, collectibles etc.
Zhongwen.com ⓦ www.zhongwen.com. Especially interesting if you're a student of Chinese, this site includes background on the Chinese script, several classic texts (with links to some English translations) and even a bunch of suggested renderings into Chinese of common Christian names.
ⓦ chinesefood.about.com. Everything you want to know about Chinese food, with an emphasis on cooking it for yourself.

Travel advisories

Australian Department of Foreign Affairs ⓦ www.dfat.gov.au. Advice and reports on unstable countries and regions.
British Foreign & Commonwealth Office ⓦ www.fco.gov.uk. Constantly updated advice for travellers on circumstances affecting safety in over 130 countries.
Canadian Department of Foreign Affairs ⓦ www.dfait-maeci.gc.ca/menu-e.asp. Country-by-country travel advisories.
US State Department Travel Advisories ⓦ travel.state.gov/travel_warnings.html. Website providing "consular information sheets" detailing the dangers of travelling in most countries of the world.

Maps

Street maps are available in China for almost every town and city. You can nearly always buy them in street kiosks, hotel shops and Xinhua bookshops, or from vendors in the vicinity of train and bus stations. Unfortunately the vast majority of maps are in Chinese only, which is a pity because the maps are a mine of information, showing bus routes, hotels, restaurants and tourist attractions. You'll nearly always find local bus, train and flight timetables printed on the back as well. The same vendors also sell pocket-sized provincial **road atlases**, again in Chinese only.

Cities most commonly visited by foreign tourists do produce English-language maps for foreigners. You'll find these on sale in upmarket hotels, at the principal tourist sights, such as big museums, or in CITS offices. In Beijing and Shanghai you'll find various editions of such maps, issued free in smart hotels and paid for by advertising. The situation is similar in Hong Kong and Macau, where the local tourist offices provide free maps which are adequate for most visitors' needs. For very detailed street maps of Hong Kong, have a look at the *Hong Kong Island Street Map* and the *Kowloon Street Map*, for sale in English-language bookshops.

Countrywide maps, which you should buy before you leave home, include the excellent 1:4,000,000 map from GeoCenter, which shows relief and useful sections of all neighbouring countries. Also worth considering is the recently published Collins map of the country, at 1:5,000,000. If you want very high-resolution maps showing details of terrain, especially useful for cyclists and trekkers in the wilderness parts of western China, the *Operational Navigation Charts* (Series ONC) – actually designed for pilots – are worth having a look at. One of the best maps of Tibet is *Stanfords Map of South-Central Tibet; Kathmandu–Lhasa Route Map*.

Map outlets

UK and Ireland

Blackwell's Map and Travel Shop 50 Broad St, Oxford OX1 3BQ ⓣ 01865/793550, ⓦ maps.blackwell.co.uk.
Easons Bookshop 40 O'Connell St, Dublin 1 ⓣ 01/858 3881, ⓦ www.eason.ie.
Heffers Map and Travel 20 Trinity St, Cambridge CB2 1TJ ⓣ 01865/333536, ⓦ www.heffers.co.uk.
Hodges Figgis Bookshop 56–58 Dawson St, Dublin 2 ⓣ 01/677 4754, ⓦ www.hodgesfiggis.com.
The Map Shop 30a Belvoir St, Leicester LE1 6QH ⓣ 0116/247 1400, ⓦ www.mapshopleicester.co.uk.
National Map Centre 22–24 Caxton St, London SW1H 0QU ⓣ 020/7222 2466, ⓦ www.mapsnmc.co.uk.
Newcastle Map Centre 55 Grey St, Newcastle-upon-Tyne NE1 6EF ⓣ 0191/261 5622.
Stanfords 12–14 Long Acre, London WC2E 9LP ⓣ 020/7836 1321, ⓦ www.stanfords.co.uk.
The Travel Bookshop 13–15 Blenheim Crescent, London W11 2EE ⓣ 020/7229 5260, ⓦ www.thetravelbookshop.co.uk.

US and Canada

Adventurous Traveler.com US ⓣ 1-800/282-3963, ⓦ adventuroustraveler.com.
Distant Lands 56 S Raymond Ave, Pasadena, CA 91105 ⓣ 1-800/310-3220, ⓦ www.distantlands.com.

Elliot Bay Book Company 101 S Main St, Seattle, WA 98104 ⓣ1-800/962-5311, ⓦwww.elliotbaybook.com.
Globe Corner Bookstore 28 Church St, Cambridge, MA 02138 ⓣ1-800/358-6013, ⓦwww.globercorner.com.
Map Link 30 S La Patera Lane, Unit 5, Santa Barbara, CA 93117 ⓣ1-800/962-1394, ⓦwww.maplink.com.
Rand McNally US ⓣ1-800/333-0136, ⓦwww.randmcnally.com.
The Travel Bug Bookstore 2667 W Broadway, Vancouver V6K 2G2 ⓣ604/737-1122, ⓦwww.swifty.com/tbug.
World of Maps 1235 Wellington St, Ottawa, Ontario K1Y 3A3 ⓣ1-800/214-8524, ⓦwww.worldofmaps.com.

Australia and New Zealand

The Map Shop 6–10 Peel St, Adelaide, SA 5000 ⓣ08/8231 2033, ⓦwww.mapshop.net.au.
Mapland 372 Little Bourke St, Melbourne, Victoria 3000 ⓣ03/9670 4383, ⓦwww.mapland.com.au.
MapWorld 173 Gloucester St, Christchurch ⓣ0800/627967 or 03/374 5399, ⓦwww.mapworld.co.nz.
Perth Map Centre 1/884 Hay St, Perth, WA 6000 ⓣ08/9322 5733, ⓦwww.perthmap.com.au.
Specialty Maps 46 Albert St, Auckland 1001 ⓣ09/307 2217, ⓦwww.ubdonline.co.nz/maps.

Insurance

You'd do well to take out an insurance policy before travelling to cover against theft, loss and illness or injury. Before paying for a new policy, however, it's worth checking whether you are already covered: some all-risks home insurance policies may cover your possessions when overseas, and many private medical schemes include cover when abroad. In Canada, provincial health plans usually provide partial cover for medical mishaps overseas, while holders of official student/teacher/youth cards in Canada and the US are entitled to meagre accident coverage and hospital in-patient benefits. Students will often find that their student health coverage extends during the vacations and for one term beyond the date of last enrolment.

After exhausting the possibilities above, you might want to contact a specialist travel insurance company. A typical travel insurance policy usually provides cover for the loss of baggage, tickets and – up to a certain limit – cash or cheques, as well as cancellation or curtailment of your journey. Most of them exclude so-called dangerous sports unless an extra premium is paid: in China this can mean scuba diving, white-water rafting, skiing, windsurfing and trekking, though probably not kayaking or jeep safaris. Many policies can be chopped and changed to exclude coverage you don't need – for example, sickness and accident benefits can often be excluded or included at will. If you do take medical coverage, ascertain whether benefits will be paid as treatment proceeds or only after return home, and whether there is a 24-hour medical emergency number. When securing baggage cover, make sure that the per-article limit – typically under £500/US$750 – will cover your most valuable possession. If you need to make a claim, you should keep receipts for medicines and medical treatment and, in the event you have anything stolen, you must obtain an official statement from the police.

Health

Low standards of public hygiene, stress and overcrowded conditions are to blame for most of the health problems that beset travellers in China. If you do get ill, medical facilities, at least in the big cities, are adequate, and the largest cities have high-standard international clinics. For minor complaints, every town has a pharmacy which can suggest remedies, and doctors who can treat you with traditional Chinese or Western techniques. You'll need to take a phrasebook or a Chinese speaker if you don't speak Chinese.

Before you go

No **vaccinations** are required for China, except for yellow fever if you're coming from an area where the disease is endemic, but a **hepatitis A** jab is recommended. A significant health hazard for travellers, Hepatitis A is a viral infection spread by contaminated food and water which causes an inflammation of the liver. Symptoms are yellowing of the eyes and skin, preceded by lethargy, fever and pains in the upper right abdomen. The traditional one-shot vaccine gives protection for three months.

The less common **hepatitis B** virus can be passed on through unprotected sexual contact, transfusions of unscreened blood and dirty needles. Though the disease occurs worldwide, it's especially prevalent in parts of Asia, so it's worth asking your doctor about the vaccine (three injections over six months), particularly if you intend to travel through Asia for six months or more. Additional injections to consider, depending on where you are going and when, are meningitis and **rabies** (a serious problem in Tibet and rural areas of China) – again, check with your doctor. Remember also that a **tetanus** booster is required every ten years.

Visit a doctor as **early** as possible before you travel to allow time to complete any courses of vaccinations you need. You should have all your shots **recorded** on an International Certificate of Vaccination. If you have any longstanding medical conditions, or are travelling with small children, consult your doctor and take any necessary medicine with you. It's also wise to get a dental check-up, and if you decide to take a course of anti-malarial tablets, start taking them before you go.

It's worth taking a **first-aid kit** with you, particularly if you will be travelling extensively outside the cities, where the language barrier can make getting hold of the appropriate medicines difficult. Include bandages, plasters, painkillers, oral rehydration solution, medication to counter diarrhoea, vitamin pills and antiseptic cream. A sterile set of hypodermics may be advisable if you will be in the country for a significant period, as re-use of hypodermics does occur in China.

General precautions

There's no point in being overconcerned with your health in China, but it's an easy place to become stressed and exhausted, leaving yourself vulnerable to infections. Travel at an easy pace, and treat yourself occasionally to upmarket accommodation and food. Take vitamin pills (you can buy them in many cities) if you think your diet is lacking in variety.

Personal hygiene is one area you can control and it pays to be meticulous. Wash your hands often and don't share drinks or cigarettes. When in the shower, always wear flip-flops or shower shoes, provided free at most hotels – look under the bed. The smallest cuts can become infected, so clean them thoroughly and apply an antiseptic cream, then keep them dry and covered.

With the majority of China's waterways highly contaminated, **water** is a potential cause of sickness. Don't drink unboiled tap water, or use it to clean your teeth; avoid ice in drinks, and the ice lollies sold by streetside entrepreneurs. The Chinese boil drinking water scrupulously, and every hotel room is equipped with a Thermos, which the floor attendant will fill for you. **Bottled water** is available from supermarkets, though it often tastes disgusting. If you stick to this and drink tea or carbonated drinks in restaurants, you should be fine. If you have to sterilize water yourself, boil it for at least ten minutes to kill micro-organisms; at altitude, however, water boils below 100°C, so you'll have to use other methods. **Iodine tablets** are effective, but leave the water tasting rank, and they are unsafe for pregnant women, babies and people with thyroid complaints. If you've got the space, a **water purifier**, which removes contaminants by filtration, is ideal – they're available from specialist outdoor equipment stores before you leave home.

As for **food**, eat at places which look busy and clean, stick to fresh, thoroughly cooked food, and you'll have few problems. Beware of food that has been precooked and kept warm for several hours. **Shellfish** are a potential hepatitis A risk in Asia, and best avoided if raw or not thoroughly cooked. Fresh fruit you've peeled yourself is safe; other uncooked foods may have been washed in unclean water. The other thing to watch for is **dirty chopsticks**, though many restaurants provide disposable sets; if you want to be really sure, bring your own pair.

Intestinal troubles

Diarrhoea is the most common illness to affect travellers, usually in a mild form while your stomach gets used to unfamiliar food. The sudden onset of diarrhoea with stomach cramps and vomiting indicates food poisoning. In both instances, get plenty of rest, drink lots of water, and in serious cases replace lost salts with oral rehydration solution (ORS); this is especially important with young children. Take a few sachets with you, or make your own by adding half a teaspoon of salt and three of sugar to a litre of cool, previously boiled water. While down with diarrhoea, avoid milk, greasy or spicy foods, coffee and most fruit, in favour of bland foodstuffs such as rice, dumplings, noodles and soup. If symptoms persist, or if you notice blood or mucus in your stools, consult a doctor.

Dysentery is inflammation of the intestine, indicated by diarrhoea with blood or mucus and abdominal pain. There are two strains. Bacillary dysentery has an acute onset with discomfort, fever and vomiting, plus severe abdominal pains with bloody, watery diarrhoea. In mild cases recovery occurs spontaneously within a week, but a serious attack will require antibiotics. Amoebic dysentery is more serious as bouts last for several weeks and often recur. The gradually appearing symptoms are marked by bloody faeces accompanied by abdominal cramps, but no vomiting or fever. A prompt course of antibiotics should restore you to health.

Giardiasis is distinguished by smelly burps or farts, discoloured faeces without blood or pus, and fluctuating diarrhoea; left untreated, these symptoms disappear but recur around once a month. Again the disease is treatable with an antibiotic, Flagyl, under medical supervision. If you're heading for Tibet, where the disease is a particular problem, you will not be able to get the appropriate antibiotics there, so take some with you (you may need to get a prescription from your doctor for this).

Typhoid and cholera are also spread by contaminated food or water, generally in localized epidemics. The varied symptoms of **typhoid** include headaches, high fever and constipation, followed by diarrhoea in the later stages. The disease is infectious and requires immediate medical treatment but it's also difficult to diagnose. The first indication of **cholera** is the sudden but painless onset of watery and unpredictable diarrhoea, later combined with vomiting, nausea and muscle cramps. The rapid dehydration caused by the diarrhoea rather than the intestinal infection itself is the main danger. However serious the vomiting and diarrhoea, you can treat cholera with plenty of oral rehydration solutions, but if you can't retain enough fluids, get medical help.

Finally, if you're suffering from diarrhoea, remember that oral drugs such as anti-malarial and contraceptive pills pass through your system too quickly to be absorbed effectively.

Mosquito-borne diseases

Mosquitoes are widespread throughout southern China, so travellers here need to be aware of the risk from mosquito-borne diseases, particularly if you're visiting tropical regions such as Hainan Island and southern Yunnan, or if you want to make a summer-time trip through southwestern China.

Carried by the *anopheles* mosquito, **malaria** is caused by a parasite which infects the blood and liver. Symptoms are flu-like fever with hammering headaches, shivering, and severe joint pain. If you're travelling in a high-risk area it is advisable to take **preventative tablets**, although medical opinion varies on the safety and effectiveness of the different drugs available. The current favourite is mefloquine, though some people experience unpleasant side effects with it, and the malarial parasite is showing resistance to it in some parts of China; consequently, it's best to talk the various options through with your doctor. Note that you need to start taking all anti-malarial medication some time before entering a malarial region, and then continue for a few weeks after leaving, as the parasite can lie dormant for a while; again, consult your doctor for advice. Women should always consult a doctor before taking any malarial prophylactics, as they can affect pregnancy. None of these precautions is infallible, however. A **blood test** will confirm the diagnosis and, if caught early, treatment can be quick and effective.

Aedes aegypti mosquitoes, identifiable by their black-and-white stripes, are responsible for transmitting **dengue fever**, a viral disease whose symptoms are similar to malaria, though there's sometimes also a rash spreading from the torso over the limbs and face. There's no cure, and though symptoms subside on their own after a week or so of rest, chronic fatigue can dog you for months afterwards. A more dangerous strain called **dengue haemorrhageic fever** primarily affects children. If you notice an unusual tendency to bleed or bruise, consult a doctor immediately.

The key measure with both diseases is to **avoid being bitten** in the first place. Mosquitoes are most active at dawn and dusk, so at these times wear long sleeves and trousers and avoid dark colours, and use **repellent** on exposed skin. Repellent containing about forty percent DEET (diethyl-toluamide) is effective, but the chemical is toxic and prolongued use can cause side-effects; keep it away from eyes and open wounds, and young children. Good alternatives based on natural ingredients are sold under the names Mosi-Guard Natural and Gurkha.

Most hotels and guesthouses in affected areas provide **mosquito nets**, but you may want to bring your own if you intend heading to any rural areas. A net which hangs from a single point is the most practical. Tuck the edges in well at night, sleep away from the sides and make sure the mesh is not torn. Many nets are already impregnated with mosquito repellant, but need retreating every six months; all the gear is available from travel clinics and good travel shops. Air conditioning and fans help keep mosquitoes away, as do **mosquito coils** – extremely effective indoors – and insecticide sprays, both available in China.

Respiratory infections

The most common hazard to your health in China is the host of **flu** infections that strike down a large proportion of the population, mostly in the winter months. The problem is compounded by the overcrowded conditions, chain-smoking, intense pollution and the widespread habit of spitting, which rapidly spreads infection. Initial symptoms are fever, sore throat, chills and a feeling of malaise, followed by prolongued bouts of bronchitis. Drink lots of fluids and get plenty of rest, though if symptoms persist you should seek medical advice.

More serious is **tuberculosis**, a respiratory disease transmitted by inhalation, and spread by coughing and spitting – so it's not hard to see why China has a high incidence. It strikes at the lungs and in a small number of cases can be fatal. There is no need for visitors to be overly worried about the disease – many people are immune thanks to previous, mild infections or through childhood vaccinations. Especially if your trip will involve spending a lot of time on crowded trains and buses, it's worth consulting your doctor about your TB-immune status.

Sexually transmitted diseases and AIDS

It is doubtful that China was ever, as the government suggests, a place where prostitution didn't exist and **sexually transmitted diseases** were a foreign problem – and this picture is certainly not true now. Thanks to the contemporary, more liberal, climate, a burgeoning sexual revolution and the refusal of many men to use condoms, STDs have flourished, **AIDS** among them. The government is becoming far more open about the problem, admitting recently to several million Chinese being infected with HIV. Paranoia about the disease, and its transmission by foreigners, is rife, and you may find that if you turn up at a Chinese hospital the first thing they will do is test you for it. The more common **gonorrhoea** and **syphilis**, identifiable by rashes around the genitals and painful discharge, are treatable with antibiotics, available from doctors.

As ever, it is extremely unwise to contemplate unprotected sex. Local Chinese **condoms** vary in quality, but imported brands are available in big cities. If it becomes essential for you to have an injection or blood transfusion in China, try to get to Hong Kong, where blood is reliably screened, and make sure that new, sterile needles are used – to be sure, bring your own. Similarly, don't undergo acupuncture unless you are sure that the equipment is sterile.

Environmental hazards

Parts of China are **tropical**, requiring a couple of weeks to acclimatize to the temperature and humidity, during which time you may feel listless and tire easily. Don't underestimate the strength of the sun in tropical areas such as Hainan Island, in desert regions such as Xinjiang or very high up, for example on the Tibetan plateau. **Sunburn** can be avoided by restricting your exposure to the sun and by liberal use of sunscreens, sometimes available in China. **Dark glasses** help to protect your eyes and a wide-brimmed hat is a good idea.

Drinking plenty of water will prevent **dehydration**, but if you do become dehydrated – signified by infrequent or irregular urination – drink a salt-and-sugar solution (see under "Intestinal Troubles", p.27). **Heat stroke** is more serious and may require hospital treatment. Symptoms are a high temperature, lack of sweating, a fast pulse and red skin. Reducing your body temperature with a lukewarm shower will provide initial relief.

High humidity can cause **heat rashes**, **prickly heat** and **fungal infections**. Prevention and cure are the same: wear loose clothes made of natural fibres, wash frequently and dry off thoroughly afterwards.

Talcum or anti-fungal powder and the use of mild antiseptic soap helps too.

At the other extreme, there are plenty of parts in China – Tibet and the north in particular – that get very **cold** indeed. Watch out here for **hypothermia**, where the core body temperature drops to a point that can be fatal. Symptoms are a weak pulse, disorientation, numbness, slurred speech and exhaustion. To prevent the condition, wear lots of layers and a hat (most body heat is lost through the head), eat plenty of carbohydrates, and try to stay dry and out of the wind. To treat hypothermia, get the victim into shelter, away from wind and rain, give them hot drinks – but not alcohol – and easily digestible food, and keep them warm. Serious cases require immediate hospitalization.

Altitude sickness

You should be aware of the dangers posed by the **high altitude** in several regions of China, including Tibet and areas of Xinjiang, Sichuan and Yunnan. At altitude, reduced air pressure means that the blood does not absorb oxygen efficiently and so – until your body adapts after a week or two, by producing more red blood cells – you may suffer from **AMS** (acute mountain sickness); most people feel some effects above 3000m. Symptoms vary, but include becoming easily exhausted, headaches, shortness of breath, sleeping disorders and nausea; they're intensified if you ascend to high altitude rapidly, for instance by flying direct from coastal cities to Lhasa. Relaxing for the first few days, drinking plenty of water, and taking painkillers will ease symptoms; some of Lhasa's hotels even have oxygen on hand. For most people the symptoms pass, although having acclimatized at one altitude you should still ascend slowly, or you can expect the symptoms to return. Medical opinion is divided about the usefulness of acetazolamide (Diamox) to ease the symptoms; discuss this with your doctor before you travel.

You should also be aware that if, for any reason, the body fails to acclimatize effectively to altitude, serious conditions can develop. To compensate for reduced oxygen in the body, the heart beats faster, trying to circulate available oxygen more rapidly. In consequence, fluid can be forced from the blood through thin membranes into the lungs or brain, causing potentially fatal **pulmonary oedema** (characterized by severe breathing trouble, a cough and frothy white or pink sputum), and **cerebral oedema** (causing severe headaches, loss of balance, other neurological symptoms and eventually coma). The only treatment for these is **rapid descent**: in Tibet, this means flying out to Kathmandu or Chengdu without delay. If symptoms have been serious, or persist afterwards, seek immediate medical treatment.

Getting medical help

Pharmacies, found in all towns, can help with minor injuries or ailments. Larger ones sometimes have a separate counter offering diagnosis and advice, though it's unlikely that staff will speak anything but Chinese, so take along a phrasebook or a Chinese speaker (see "Language", p.1264, for some useful phrases). The selection of reliable Asian and Western products available is improving (though always check expiry dates on brand-name products), and it's also possible to treat yourself for minor complaints with herbal medicines. Contraceptives are widely available, as are antibiotics. The staff will usually be able to help if you describe your symptoms.

Large hotels often have a **clinic** for guests offering diagnosis, advice and prescriptions – ask an English speaker from the reception desk to accompany you. Beijing, Shanghai, Guangzhou and Hong Kong and Macau have clinics specifically for foreigners where staff speak English. If you are seriously ill, head straight to a **hospital** – your accommodation or local CITS might be able to give you useful advice in an emergency. Addresses of clinics and hospitals can be found in the "Listings" sections of major towns and cities in the guide. You will be expected to pay for your treatment on the spot, but it should not be too expensive. Keep all medical bills and receipts so you can make an insurance claim when you get home.

If you're interested in being treated according to **traditional Chinese medicine** – of most use for minor and chronic complaints (see p.1204) – many hospitals and medical colleges have attached traditional institutes, while some hotels have their own massage or acupuncture services.

Travel health centres and online resources

Besides consulting the resources and clinics listed below, you can get practical information on staying healthy during your trip from the *Rough Guide to Travel Health.*

Websites

Ⓦhealth.yahoo.com Information on specific diseases and conditions, drugs and herbal remedies, as well as advice from health experts.
Ⓦwww.fitfortravel.scot.nhs.uk UK NHS website carrying information about travel-related diseases and how to avoid them.
Ⓦwww.istm.org The website of the International Society for Travel Medicine, with a full list of clinics specializing in international travel health.
Ⓦwww.tripprep.com Travel Health Online provides an online-only comprehensive database of necessary vaccinations for most countries, as well as destination and medical service provider information.

UK

British Airways Travel Clinics 156 Regent St, London W1 (Mon–Fri 9.30am–5.15pm, Sat 10am–4pm; no appointment necessary; Ⓣ020/7439 9584). Vaccinations, tailored advice from an online database plus a range of travel healthcare products.
Communicable Diseases Unit Brownlee Centre, Glasgow G12 0YN Ⓣ0141/211 1062. Travel vaccinations.
Hospital for Tropical Diseases Travel Clinic 2nd floor, Mortimer Market Centre, off Capper St, London WC1E 6AU (Mon–Fri 9am–5pm by appointment only; Ⓣ020/7388 9600; the £15 consultation fee is waived if you have your injections here). Their recorded Health Line (Ⓣ09061/337733; 50p/min) gives hints on hygiene and illness prevention as well as listing appropriate immunizations.
Liverpool School of Tropical Medicine Pembroke Place, Liverpool L3 5QA Ⓣ0151/708 9393 (walk-in clinic Mon–Fri 1–4pm). Appointment required for yellow fever, but not for other jabs.
MASTA (Medical Advisory Service for Travellers Abroad) Forty clinics around the UK (call Ⓣ0870/606 2782 or see Ⓦwww.masta.org for locations). Also operates a prerecorded 24hr Travellers' Health Line (Ⓣ0906/822 4100, 60p/min), giving written information tailored to your journey by return of post.
Trailfinders Immunization clinic at 194 Kensington High St, London (Mon–Fri 9am–5pm except Thurs to 6pm, Sat 9.30am–4pm; no appointment necessary; Ⓣ020/7938 3999).
Travel Medicine Services PO Box 254, 16 College St, Belfast 1 Ⓣ028/9031 5220. Offers medical advice before a trip and help afterwards in the event of a tropical disease.

Republic of Ireland

Dun Laoghaire Medical Centre 5 Northumberland Ave, Dun Laoghaire Co, Dublin Ⓣ01/280 4996, Ⓕ01/280 5603. Advice on medical matters abroad.
Travel Health Centre Department of International Health and Tropical Medicine, Royal College of Surgeons in Ireland, Mercers Medical Centre, Stephen's St Lower, Dublin Ⓣ01/402 2337. Expert pretrip advice and inoculations.
Tropical Medical Bureau Grafton Buildings, 34 Grafton St, Dublin 2, Ⓣ01/671 9200, Ⓦtmb.exodus.ie. Provides a comprehensive vaccination service.

US and Canada

Canadian Society for International Health 1 Nicholas St, Suite 1105, Ottawa, ON K1N 7B7 Ⓣ613/241-5785, Ⓦwww.csih.org. Distributes a free pamphlet, "Health Information for Canadian Travellers", containing an extensive list of travel health centres in Canada.
Centers for Disease Control 1600 Clifton Rd NE, Atlanta, GA 30333 Ⓣ1-800/311-3435 or 404/639-3534, Ⓦwww.cdc.gov. Publishes outbreak warnings, suggested inoculations, precautions and other background information for travellers. International Travelers Hotline on Ⓣ1-877/FYI-TRIP.
International SOS Assistance Eight Neshaminy Interplex Suite 207, Trevose, USA 19053-6956 Ⓣ1-800/523-8930, Ⓦwww.intsos.com. Members receive pre-trip medical referral info, as well as overseas emergency services designed to complement travel insurance coverage.
MEDJET Assistance Ⓣ1-800/863-3538, Ⓦwww.medjetassistance.com. Annual membership program for travellers (US$175 for individuals, $275 for families) that, in the event of illness or injury, will fly members home or to the hospital of their choice in a medically equipped and staffed jet.

Travel Medicine ⓣ1-800/872-8633, ⓕ1-413/584-6656, ⓦwww.travmed.com. Sells first-aid kits, mosquito netting, water filters, reference books and other health-related travel products.

Travelers Medical Center 31 Washington Square West, New York, NY 10011 ⓣ212/982-1600. Consultation service on immunizations and treatment of diseases for people travelling to developing countries.

Australia and New Zealand

Travellers' Medical and Vaccination Centres Australia: 27–29 Gilbert Place, Adelaide ⓣ08/8212 7522; 5/247 Adelaide St, Brisbane ⓣ07/3221 9066; 5/8–10 Hobart Place, Canberra ⓣ02/6257 7156; 2/393 Little Bourke St, Melbourne ⓣ03/9602 5788; Level 7, Dymocks Bldg, 428 George St, Sydney ⓣ02/9221 7133. New Zealand: 1/170 Queen St, Auckland ⓣ09/373 3531; 147 Armagh St, Christchurch ⓣ03/379 4000; Shop 15, Grand Arcade, 14–16 Willis St, Wellington ⓣ04/473 0991. For details of additional locations in both countries, plus online travel health information, see ⓦwww.tmvc.com.au.

Costs, money and banks

Compared with the rest of Asia, China is an expensive place to travel. Though it's always possible to eat and move around fairly cheaply, accommodation costs can be as high as in Europe or the US for comparable facilities, and daily expenses vary drastically, according to region. In descending order, the three main price "zones" are Hong Kong and Macau, the eastern seaboard, and the interior provinces, with some variation within these categories (for more, see "Accommodation", p.43). Basically, things get cheaper the farther west you go, though costs are always relatively more expensive in popular tourist spots.

The mainland **Chinese currency** is formally called **yuan** (¥), more colloquially known as **renminbi** (RMB, literally "the people's money") or **kuai**. One yuan breaks down into ten **jiao** or mao, with one jiao breaking down into ten **fen**. **Paper money** was invented in China and is still the main form of exchange, available in ¥100, ¥50, ¥20, ¥10, ¥5, and ¥1 notes, with a similar selection of mao. You occasionally come across tinny mao **coins**, and brass ¥5 pieces; people in rural areas may never have seen coins before and might not accept them. Be aware that China suffers regular outbreaks of **counterfeiting**, some of it very sophisticated – many businesses check notes for watermarks (something you should do too), or use ultraviolet lamps to reveal otherwise invisible fluorescent marks on the genuine article. At the time of writing, the exchange rate was approximately ¥13 to £1, ¥8 to US$1, ¥8 to €1, ¥5 to C$1, and ¥4.5 to A$1.

Hong Kong's currency is the Hong Kong **dollar** (HK$), divided into one hundred cents, while in **Macau** they use **pataca** (usually written M$ or ptca), in turn broken down into 100 avos. Both currencies are roughly equivalent to the yuan but, while Hong Kong dollars are accepted in Macau and southern China's Special Economic Zones and can be exchanged internationally, neither yuan or pataca are any use outside the mainland or Macau respectively. Tourist hotels in Beijing, Shanghai and Guangzhou also sometimes accept – even insist on – payment in Hong Kong or US dollars. Hong Kong dollars are available overseas, yuan and patacas are not, though both can be obtained in Hong Kong, and converted back at a bank before you leave the country.

Costs

Given the extreme regional variations, it's hard to make exact predictions of daily costs in China. But, wherever you are in **mainland China**, you should be able to keep your average daily budget for food and travel to a minimum £10/US$16 or so by eating in cheap and mid-range restaurants, and travelling on local buses or hard train classes. What really separates the east coast (including the whole of Dongbei) from the interior provinces, however, is the cost of **accommodation**. While budget travellers can find beds in western China for as little as £2/US$3 a night, on the east coast it's hard to find anything for less than £25/US$35. Fast or comfortable travel also comes at a premium – flights and train sleeper berths are at least five times as expensive as covering the same route by bus. In general, by doing everything cheaply and sticking mostly to the interior provinces you can survive on £20/US$32 a day; travel a bit more widely and in better comfort from time to time and you're looking at £35/US$55 a day; while travelling in style and visiting only key places along the east coast, you're looking at daily expenses of £60/US$95 and above.

Price tiering, where foreigners are charged more than Chinese for services, was formerly widespread but has now been officially banned. This means that you should pay the same as everyone else for accommodation, transport, or to enter museums or famous sights. In practice, some private transport or tour operators may still surcharge foreigners or you might be sold the most expensive option, without being informed of less costly alternatives; take comfort in the fact that Chinese tourists suffer the same treatment. **Student rates** are often available for entry fees, however, so it's worth getting hold of a **Chinese Student Card** – they are vaguely official-looking documents, adorned with your photograph and folded into a red plastic wallet. You can get one officially by studying, even briefly, in China; unofficially, budget tour agents geared up to foreign needs can often supply them for about ¥40. **ISIC cards** are also occasionally recognized, most likely in Beijing and Hong Kong.

To cut accommodation and shopping costs, try **bargaining** – it's usual for mid-range and upmarket hotels to knock thirty percent off their advertised rates without too much persuasion, and in low season skillful negotiators can net even higher discounts. At markets, you may initially be asked for up to ten times the going price for goods, so find out what others are paying first and be prepared to haggle.

Costs in **Hong Kong** and **Macau** are higher than for comparable services on the mainland, particularly for upmarket accommodation – though food and drink are again pretty reasonable and transport expenses negligible. The cheapest dorm beds will set you back £5/US$8, while it's hard to come by a decent double room for under £60/US$100. Staying at cheap lodgings and eating simply from noodle stalls will cost you about £20/US$32 a day, up to £25/US$40 with a mid-range restaurant meal thrown in. For more comfort and classier food, budget from £80/US$125 and up daily.

Carrying your money

Traveller's cheques, available through banks and travel agents, are the best way to carry your funds around; their exchange rate in China is fixed and actually better than for cash, and they can be replaced if lost or stolen – keep the **purchase agreement** and a list of the serial numbers separate from the cheques, and report any loss immediately to the issuing company. On the downside, in **mainland China** they can be cashed only at major branches of the Bank of China and tourist hotels (very few parts of the country have neither) and the process always involves lengthy paperwork. In **Hong Kong** and **Macau**, any bank or bureau de change will be happy to cash them.

When buying traveller's cheques, stick to brands such as Thomas Cook or American Express, as less familiar, bank-issued traveller's cheques won't be accepted in smaller places. The usual **fee** for buying them is one or two percent, though this may be waived if you buy the cheques through a bank where you have an account; you will also be charged a **commission** (often hidden in the exchange rate offered) for cashing them.

In case you find yourself in difficulties, it's worth taking along a small supply of **foreign currency** such as US, Canadian or Australian dollars, or British pounds, which are more widely exchangeable. There's a low-key and burgeoning **black market** in China for foreign currency, but the small differential in rates and the risks of getting ripped off or attracting police attention don't make it worthwhile.

Banks

Banks in major Chinese cities are sometimes open seven days a week, though foreign exchange is usually only available Monday to Friday, approximately between 9am and noon and again from 2pm to 5pm. All banks are closed for the first three days of the Chinese New Year, with reduced hours for the following eleven days, and at other holiday times. In Hong Kong, banks are generally open Monday to Friday from 9am to 4.30pm, until 12.30pm on Saturday, while in Macau they close thirty minutes earlier.

Credit and debit cards

Credit cards are a very handy backup source of funds; upmarket hotels in China accept them and – depending where you are – they can be used for cash withdrawals either in ATMs or over the counter. Visa and Mastercard are widely recognized in China, Amex less so, and other cards may not be. Remember that all cash advances are treated as loans, with interest accruing daily from the date of withdrawal; the Bank of China charges a **three percent fee** on top of this, though Hong Kong banks do not.

ATMs in China are common in cities and theoretically compatible with all manner of foreign cards, but periodically won't accept them; in Hong Kong, however, they function as advertised. When you can find a compliant ATM, you may also be able to make withdrawals using your **debit card** (or bank card marked with the Cirrus/Maestro symbol), which is not liable to interest payments, and subject only to a flat transaction fee which is quite small – your bank will able to advise on this. Make sure you have a personal identification number (PIN) that's designed to work overseas.

A compromise between traveller's cheques and plastic is **Visa TravelMoney**, a disposable pre-paid debit card with a PIN which works in all ATMs that take Visa cards. You load up your account with funds before leaving home, and when they run out you simply throw the card away. You can buy up to nine cards to access the same funds – useful for couples or families travelling together – and it's a good idea to buy at least one extra as a back-up in case of loss or theft. The card is available in most countries from branches of Thomas Cook and Citicorp. For **24-hour assistance** with the card, call the following toll-free numbers: in China, ⓣ10800/110 2911; in Hong Kong, ⓣ800/967025. For more information, check ⓦinternational.visa.com.

Wiring money

Wiring money from home basically involves someone paying money to you using an overseas branch of a money-transfer agent, allowing you to withdraw the same amount from their representative in China. The service isn't cheap or particularly convenient, however, so it should be considered a last resort. It's also possible to have money wired directly from a bank in your home country to a bank in China, although this is a more complex operation because it involves two separate institutions. If you go down this route, your home bank will need the address of the bank where you want to pick up the money and the address and telex number of the Beijing head office, which will act as the clearing house; money wired this way normally takes two working days to arrive, and costs around £25/$40 per transaction.

Money-wiring companies

Moneygram US ⓣ1-800/926-3947, Canada ⓣ1-800/933-3278, other countries international freephone ⓣ+800/6663 9472; ⓦwww.moneygram.com.
Western Union UK ⓣ0800/833833, Republic of Ireland ⓣ1800/395395, US & Canada ⓣ1-800/325-6000, Australia ⓣ1800/501500, New Zealand ⓣ09/270 0050; ⓦwww.westernunion.com.

Getting around

China is huge and, unless you concentrate on a small area, you're going to spend a good deal of your time – and budget – just getting around. Fortunately, public transport is comprehensive and reasonably priced considering the distances involved. You can fly to all regional capitals and many cities; the rail network extends to every province except Tibet (though that is soon to change); and a (decreasing) number of rivers are plied by passenger ferries, with a few vessels chugging between coastal ports and down to Hainan Island. If you're up to slow hours of rough riding, you can reach China's remotest corners on local transport – which covers everything from buses to tractors. Tibet is the one region where there are widespread restrictions on independent travel (see p.1121 for more details), though for reasons of military security or simply personal safety, a few other localities around the country are officially off-limits to foreigners.

While there are plenty of options, travel often requires planning, patience, and stamina. You need to weigh up the mental and physical rigours involved if you insist on travelling the cheapest way all the time – it's well worth covering long distances in as much comfort as possible. **Tours** are one way of taking the pressure off, and in some cases are the only practical way of getting out to certain sights; they're never cheap, but can be good value.

Public holidays – the Labour Day weekend in May (which actually lasts a week), Christmas and New Year, and especially a fortnight either side of the Spring Festival (Chinese New Year) – are rotten times to travel, as half China is on the move between family and workplace: ticket prices rise (legally, by no more than fifteen percent, though often by up to fifty), bus and train station crowds swell insanely, and even flights become scarce.

Trains

China's first rail lines were laid in the nineteenth century, and the country's current leaders have invested heavily in the network, seeing a healthy transport infrastructure as essential to economic growth. With US$42 billion earmarked for rail development between 2002 and 2005, services are constantly improving, with modern, high-speed engines on major lines slashing around twenty-five percent off journey times, and around 7000km of new track currently being laid – including, by 2006, a link **to Tibet**, whose geography has previously defied connection. All this means that China's rail network is vast and efficient, making train the safest, most reliable way to get around the country.

Timetables and tickets

The first step in train travel is getting hold of a **timetable**. Usually on display somewhere in the ticket office, or sold from stalls around the station, timetables can be hard to decipher; you need to be able to recognize the characters for both where you are and your destination, then memorize the train number and how many services there are, in case your first choice isn't available.

Tickets – always **one-way** – show the date of travel and destination, along with the train number, carriage and seat or berth number. They become available up to five days in advance, though demand frequently outstrips supply, so it's wise to plan ahead. It's easiest to book tickets through an **agent**, such as the CITS or a hotel travel service, though you'll pay a commission of ¥30 or more per person. Alternatively, many cities have downtown **advance purchase offices**, though some are so well hidden that even the Chinese don't seem to know about them; it makes sense to try these places first as train stations are often locat-

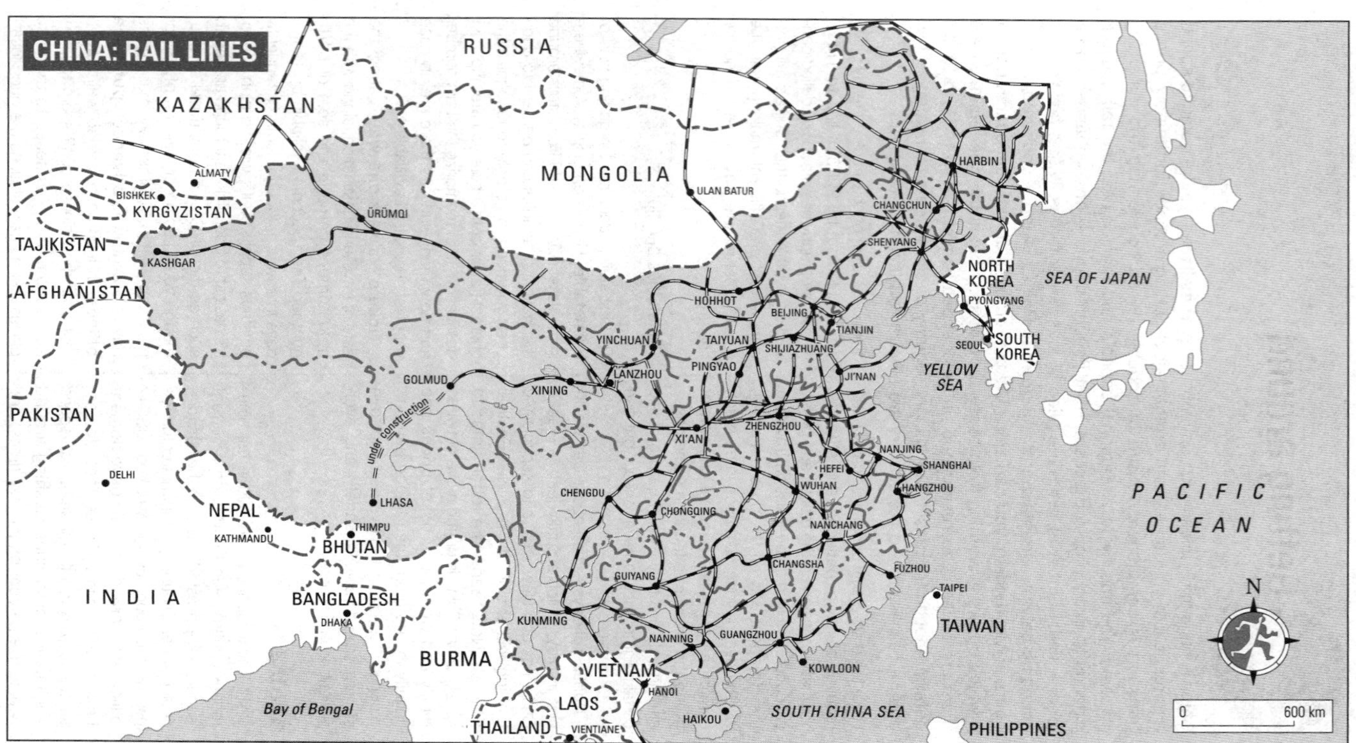
CHINA: RAIL LINES
RUSSIA
KAZAKHSTAN
MONGOLIA
ALMATY
BISHKEK
KYRGYZISTAN
TAJIKISTAN
AFGHANISTAN
PAKISTAN
KASHGAR
ÜRÜMQI
ULAN BATUR
HARBIN
CHANGCHUN
SHENYANG
NORTH KOREA
PYONGYANG
SEOUL
SOUTH KOREA
SEA OF JAPAN
HOHHOT
BEIJING
TIANJIN
YINCHUAN
TAIYUAN
SHIJIAZHUANG
PINGYAO
JI'NAN
YELLOW SEA
GOLMUD
XINING
LANZHOU
under construction
XI'AN
ZHENGZHOU
NANJING
SHANGHAI
HEFEI
HANGZHOU
WUHAN
DELHI
LHASA
CHENGDU
CHONGQING
NANCHANG
PACIFIC OCEAN
NEPAL
KATHMANDU
THIMPU
BHUTAN
CHANGSHA
FUZHOU
GUIYANG
TAIPEI
INDIA
BANGLADESH
DHAKA
KUNMING
NANNING
GUANGZHOU
TAIWAN
BURMA
VIETNAM
KOWLOON
HANOI
LAOS
Bay of Bengal
HAIKOU
SOUTH CHINA SEA
THAILAND
VIENTIANE
PHILIPPINES
N
0
600 km

ed far from city centres. If the office is run by the railway you won't pay a commission, whereas private operators charge a small mark-up. Otherwise, head to the **train station ticket office**; most premises are computerized nowadays and, while queues can still tie you up for an hour, you'll generally get what you're after in the end. At the counter, state your destination, the day you'd like to travel, and the class you want, or have it written down (station staff rarely speak English, though you may strike it lucky in big cities). If there's nothing else available, the you can ask the ticket office for an **unreserved ticket** (*wuzuo*, literally "no seat"), which doesn't give you an assigned seat but at least lets you on the train – though you might have to stand for the entire journey if you can't upgrade on board.

If you've bought a ticket but decide not to travel, you should be able to get most of the fare **refunded** by returning the ticket to a ticket office at least two hours before departure. If there's a window specifically for returned tickets (*tuipiao*), the people in the queue are actually a potential quick source of tickets – Chinese speakers are best placed to take advantage. If there is no other way of buying a ticket and you simply have to get on the train, try the **touts** who inevitably hang around busy stations, though be careful not to end up with a photocopied ticket instead of the real thing.

Boarding the train

Even if you've bought your ticket in advance, you should still turn up at the station with time to spare before your train leaves. All luggage has to be passed through **x-ray machines** at the station entrance to check for dangerous goods such as firecrackers – officials can get irate if you try to skip the procedure, but there's rarely anyone paying any attention to the monitors. Carry **film** through separately to avoid the possibility of getting it fogged. You then need to work out which platform your train leaves from – most stations have electronic departure boards in Chinese, or you can show your ticket to station staff who will point you in the right direction. Passengers are not allowed on to the platform until the train is in and ready to leave, which can result in some mighty stampedes when the gates open. To upgrade your ticket on board, make your way immediately to the controller's booth, in the hard-seat carriage next to the restaurant car (usually #8 – all carriages are numbered on the outside), where you can sign up for beds or seats as they become available.

Types of train

There are three types of train in China, each given their own code on timetables. **Express trains** are marked T- (for *tekuai*); **fast** are K- (*kuai*); **ordinary** (*putong che*) have a number only and are the slowest option. T- and K-trains reach 100–200kph and have modern fittings with text messages scrolled at the carriage's end announcing temperature, arrival time at next station, and speed. A few busy, short-haul express services, such as the Shenzhen–Guangzhou train, have double-decker carriages. **No-smoking** rules are often vigorously enforced. The numbered services, though older and stopping more frequently, can be well maintained, with smoking banned in sleeper carriages (leading to furtive huddles in the spaces in between). Some, however, are elderly plodders destined for the scrapheap whose interiors are crusty with cigarette smoke and sunflower seed husks on the linoleum floor. As always in China, the faster services are slightly more expensive.

Classes

There are four train **classes**. The best is **soft sleeper** (*ruanwo*), which costs slightly less than flying and is patronized by foreigners, party officials and successful entrepreneurs. It's a nice experience; there's a plush waiting room at most stations, and on the train itself you get a four-berth compartment with a soft mattress, fan, optional radio, and a choice of Western- or Chinese-style toilets. If you've a long way to travel and can afford it, soft sleeper is well worth the money, allowing you to arrive rested and ready to enjoy your destination.

Hard sleeper (*yingwo*), about two-thirds the price of *ruanwo*, is favoured by China's middle class and money-conscious foreigners, and hence is also the most difficult to

Sample train fares

The fares below are for one-way travel on express trains.

	Hard seat	Hard sleeper	Soft sleeper
From Beijing			
Guangzhou	¥225	¥615	¥840
Hong Kong	¥240	¥660	¥1025
Shanghai	¥150	¥415	¥570
Xi'an	¥155	¥430	¥590
From Xian			
Guangzhou	¥245	¥675	¥920
Turpan	¥235	¥650	¥895
Ürümqi	¥250	¥695	¥935

book in advance. It's not a bad way to travel, though dawn-to-dusk piped music and a relentless investigation of yourself and possessions by fellow passengers can wear thin. Carriages are divided into twenty sets of three-tiered **bunks**; the lowest bunk is the most expensive, but gets used as communal seating during the day and you may appreciate being able to withdraw to a higher level. The end tier of bunks is closest to night lights and the connecting space between carriages, where smokers congregate. Each set of six bunks has its own vacuum flask of boiled water (topped up from the urn at the end of each carriage), and you bring your own mugs and beverage. Every carriage also has a toilet and washbasin, which can become unsavoury; do what the locals do and carry a face towel to keep clean on long journeys. There are fairly spacious **luggage racks**, though make sure you chain your bags securely while you sleep.

Note that in either sleeper class, on boarding the carriage you will have your ticket exchanged for a metal tag by the attendant. The tag is swapped back for your ticket (so you'll be able to get through the barrier at the station) about half an hour before you arrive at your destination; you'll be woken up whatever hour of the day or night this happens to be.

Soft seat (*ruanzuo*) is increasingly available on services whose complete route takes less than a day. Seats are around the cost of an express-bus fare, have plenty of legroom, and are well padded. Much more common is **hard seat** (*yingzuo*), which is really only recommended for the impecunious – it costs around half the soft-seat fare – or on relatively short journeys. The basic hard-seat setup is a padded three-person bench with just enough room to sit, though more modern carriages are relatively comfortable. On older trains, the air is thick with cigarette smoke and every available inch of floorspace is crammed with travellers who were unable to book a seat – bear in mind that should you board a train with an unreserved ticket, you'll be standing with them. Again, you'll be the subject of intense and unabashed speculation, this time from peasants and labourers who can't afford to travel in better style. The best way to cope is to join in as best you can, whether you can speak Chinese or not; you'll probably end up playing cards, sharing food and drinking with them.

Food, though often expensive and pretty ordinary, is always available on trains, either as polystyrene boxes of rice and stir-fries wheeled around along with snacks, or in the restaurant car between soft sleeper section and the rest of the train. You can also buy snacks from vendors at train stations during the longer station stops.

Buses and minibuses

Despite the ever-widening net thrown by the rail lines, there are still many parts of China unreachable by train – in which case **buses** are often the only means of getting there. Cities may have one central **main bus sta-**

tion; or several separate suburban depots located on the side of town in which traffic is heading or arriving from (usually named after the relevent compass point); or both. **Private depots** – often with faster, more modern vehicles – are often located in the big squares outside train stations. Services are frequent, even to remote places, and some cities have so many competing depots it can be hard to find the right departure point.

Unlike train tickets, bus **tickets** are easy to buy: ticket offices at main stations are often computerized, queues are nowhere near as bad as at train stations, and – with the exception of backroads routes, which might only run every other day – you don't need to book in advance and are guaranteed a seat. At private depots, you often buy tickets from a nearby booth, or pay on board. You'll do this too if you hail a bus in passing; destinations are always displayed (in Chinese characters) on the front of the vehicle. Bus-station **timetables** are often inaccurate; ticket staff are pretty helpful, however.

As with trains, there are various types of bus, though there's not always a choice available for particular routes. If there is, the station staff will assume that foreigners will want the fastest, most comfortable service – which will also be the most expensive. **Ordinary buses** (*putong che*) are cheap and basic, with wooden or lightly padded seats; they're never heated or air-conditioned, so dress accordingly. Seats can be cramped and luggage racks tiny; you'll have to put anything bulkier than a satchel on the roof, your lap, or beside the driver. They tend to stop off frequently, so don't count on an average speed of more than 50km an hour. **Sleeper buses** (*wopu che*) cost a bit more than ordinary, have basic bunks instead of seats, and can be either comfortable or excruciatingly cramped; road travel at night is also more dangerous. Lower bunks (*xiapu*) are a bit more expensive than upper bunks (*shangpu*), but are better because you don't get thrown out of bed every time the bus takes a corner. Bags can sometimes be stored, if you get in early, otherwise there's a shoebox-sized luggage rack per bed and nothing else. One advantage to sleeper buses is that if they reach their destination before dawn, passengers are left to sleep on board until sunrise, saving the price of a hotel room. They are also relatively quick, stopping off less along the way. **Express buses** (*kuai che*) are the most expensive and have good legroom, comfy seats which may well recline, air conditioning and video – not always a welcome addition to the noise. Bulky luggage gets locked away in the belly of the bus, a fairly safe option as these buses operate on a speedy point-to-point basis, with no stops en route. The final option are **minibuses** (*xiao che*) seating up to twenty people, common on routes of less than 100km or so and typically costing a little more than the same journey by ordinary bus. They can be extremely cramped, however, and often circuit the departure point for hours until they have filled up.

There are a few **downsides** to bus travel. **Roads** are not always in good condition, though the number of fast expressways is continually rising. Drivers, mobile phones in one hand, wheel in the other, have the dangerous habit of saving fuel by coasting down hill or mountainsides in "angel gear" – neutral, with the engine off. **Airhorns** (banned in some places) can make the experience noisy, too, as drivers are obliged to announce their presence before overtaking anything, and so earplugs are seriously recommended. Take some **food** along, because though buses usually pull up at inexpensive roadhouses at mealtimes, they have been known to take two drivers and plough on for a full 24 hours without stopping. Only the most upmarket coaches have **toilets**; drivers generally pull up every few hours or if asked to do so by passengers (roadhouse toilets are some of the worst in the country, however). Owing to the frequent police checks on roads in China, buses are seldom illegally overcrowded. Finally, note that foreigners need to buy **PICC** insurance to use buses in some parts of rural China; see p.1020 for more.

Planes

China's airlines link all major cities. The main operators are Air China (Ⓦwww.airchina.com.cn), China Southern (Ⓦwww.cs-air.com) and China Eastern (Ⓦwww.ce-air.com), which – along with a few minor companies – are overseen by the Civil Aviation Administration of China, or **CAAC**. Flying is a luxury worth considering for long distances: prices compare with soft-sleeper train travel but journey times are far less; planes are generally modern and well maintained; and service is good – soft drinks, biscuits and souvenir trinkets are handed out along the way, and sometimes there's even a raffle.

Buying tickets from the local CAAC office, hotel desk or tour agent is seldom problematic, and there seem to be enough flights along popular routes to cope with demand. **Timetables** are displayed at airline offices, though country-wide schedules seem unobtainable outside major cities, where they are sold at CAAC offices. **Fares** are based on one-way travel (so a return ticket is the price of two one-way tickets) and officially fixed, though they can vary between airlines, and agents do sometimes offer illegal discounts. As an illustration, from Beijing, expect to pay at least ¥620 to Xi'an, ¥690 to Shanghai, ¥935 to Chengdu, ¥1055 to Guangzhou, ¥1190 to Kunming, ¥1440 to Ürümqi, and ¥1800 to Hong Kong.

Airlines frequently provide an **airport bus** running to and from the airport; as these can be 30km or more from city centres, it's worth finding out if a bus is available, if one isn't already listed in the relevant account in this guide. **Check-in time** for all flights is two hours before departure, and there's always a **departure tax** – currently ¥50 for internal flights.

Ferries

River and sea journeys are on the decline in China, with **passenger ferries** being made redundant by new and faster roads and rail lines. One of the world's great river journeys remains, however, namely the **Yangzi**, which is navigable for thousands of kilometres between the Sichuanese port of Chongqing and coastal Shanghai, a journey which takes you through the spectacular **Three Gorges** – itself under threat by the construction of a giant dam. Another favourite is the day-cruise down the **Li River** between Guilin and Yangshuo in southwestern Guangxi province, past a forest of pointy mountains looking just like a Chinese scroll painting. Other short ferry trips survive, mostly in rural areas – make use of them if you can, because doubtless they'll be gone in a few years. By sea, there are still passenger boats between Hong Kong and Xiamen in Fujian province, and down to Hainan Island.

Conditions on board are greatly variable, but on overnight trips there's always a choice of **classes** – sometimes as many as six – which can range from a bamboo mat on the floor, right through to the luxury of private cabins. Don't expect anything too impressive, however; many mainland services are cramped and overcrowded, and cabins, even in first class, are grimly functional. Toilets and food can be basic too, so plan things as best you can.

Driving and car rental

Driving a car across China is an appealing idea, but an experience as yet forbidden to foreign tourists – though bilingual road signs going up along new expressways suggest that the notion is being considered. It is possible, however, to **rent vehicles** for local use in Beijing and Shanghai, from rental companies at the airports. You need an international driving licence and a credit card to cover the deposit. Special licence plates make these rental vehicles easily identifiable to Chinese police, so don't try taking them beyond the designated boundaries. Rates are about ¥300 a day plus petrol.

The Chinese drive **on the right**, although in practice drivers seem to drive wherever they like – through red lights, even on the left. They use their horns instead of the brake, and lorries and buses plough ahead regardless while smaller vehicles get out of the way. It's straightforward to rent a vehicle in Hong Kong, where they drive on the left, but the place is so small – and public transport so good – that this is unlikely to be something you'll be desperate to try.

Elsewhere the only option is to rent a **taxi**, **minibus** or Chinese **jeep**, complete with driver. Prices are set by negotiating and average ¥400 a day, and you'll be expected to provide lunch for the driver. It's cheapest to approach drivers directly, though if you can't speak Chinese someone at your accommodation should be able to help, and some tour operators run vehicles too – and might include the services of an interpreter. In Tibet, renting a jeep with a driver is pretty much the only way to get to many destinations (see p.1125).

Bicycles

China has the highest number of **bicycles** of any country in the world, with about a quarter of the population owning one (despite many people ditching them in favour of motorbikes). Few cities have any hills and many have **bike lanes**, though **heavy traffic** can be a problem in big, congested metropolises such as Guangzhou and Beijing – drivers have a saying in China along the lines of "If they're on a bike, do what you like."

Rental shops or booths are common around the train stations, where you can rent a set of wheels for ¥5–10 a day. You will need to leave a deposit (¥200–400) and/or some form of ID, and you're fully responsible for anything that happens to the bike while it's in your care, so check brakes, tyre pressure and gearing before renting. Most rental bikes are bog-standard black rattletraps – the really de luxe models feature working bells and brakes. There are **repair shops** all over the place should you need a tyre patched or a chain fixed up (around ¥5). Note that there's little in the way of private insurance in China, so if the bike sustains any serious damage it's up to the parties involved to sort out responsibility and payment on the spot. To **avoid theft**, always use a bicycle chain or lock – they're available everywhere – and in cities, leave your vehicle in one of the ubiquitous designated **parking areas**, where it will be guarded by an attendant for a few mao.

An alternative to renting is to **buy a bike**, a sensible option if you're going to be based anywhere for a while – foreigners don't need licences, all department stores stock them (from about ¥500), and demand is so high that there should be little problem reselling the bike when you leave. The cheapest are solid, heavy, unsophisticated machines such as the famous Flying Pigeon brand, though multigeared mountain-bikes are becoming very popular – they're not always as sturdy as they look, however. You can also **take your own bike** into China with you; international airlines usually insist that the front wheel is removed, deflated, and strapped to the back, and that everything is thoroughly packaged. Inside China, airlines, trains and ferries all charge to carry bikes, and the ticketing and accompanying paperwork can be baffling. Where possible, it's easier to stick to long-distance buses and stow it for free on the roof, no questions asked. Another option is to see China on a **specialized bike tour** (see pp.14, 16 and 17 for operators); though by no means cheap, these can be an excellent way to start a longer stay in China.

Hitching

Hitching around China is basically possible, and in remoter areas might save some time in reaching sights. However, drivers will usually charge you the going bus fare, and have been known to renegotiate en route, threatening to leave you stranded if you won't pay extra. Given the added personal risks inherent in hitching, and the fact that public transport is becoming ever more available, it's not recommended as a means of getting around.

If you must hitch, don't do it alone. The best places to try are on town and city exit roads. Get the driver's attention by waving your hand, palm down, at them. Expect to bargain for the fare, and make sure that you have your destination written down in Chinese characters.

A few travellers hitch **into Tibet** on trucks as a way to get around government travel restrictions. Be aware that if you do this you are putting yourself at some risk, as conditions can be excruciatingly uncomfortable and sometimes extremely cold. If you are found, you might be arrested, have to pay a fine, and get kicked back the way you came, and your driver will be in serious trouble – some drivers have been severely beaten by police.

Organized tours

Chinese tour operators, such as the CITS, can almost always organize excursions, from local city sights to river cruises and multi-day cross-country trips. While you always pay for the privilege, sometimes these tours are not bad value: travel, accommodation and food – usually plentiful and excellent – are generally included, as might be the services of an interpreter and guide. And in some cases tours are the most practical (if not the only) way to see something really worthwhile, saving endless bother organizing local transport and accommodation.

As regards **adventure tours**, it's worth checking out **WildChina** (☎010/64039737, wwww.wildchina.com), an intriguing Beijing-based company. They run customized excursions around the nation's fringes for individuals and groups, with trekking and hiking a focus of many trips, though some tours have an architectural or cultural emphasis.

On the downside, there are disreputable operators who'll blatantly overcharge for mediocre services, foist guides on you who can't speak local dialects or are generally unhelpful and spend three days on what could better be done in an afternoon. In general, it helps to make exhaustive enquiries about the exact nature of the tour, such as exactly what the price includes and the departure and return times, before handing any money over. If you do have any trouble, many cities now have **tourist complaint hotlines**, whose phone numbers are displayed at sights or the local tourist office – though in practical terms, don't expect too much to result from a complaint.

Recommended tours

The following selection of tours will give you an idea of the cost and variety available; most are covered in more detail in the guide.

Bingling Caves Gansu Hope International Travel Agency, Lanzhou, Gansu (and other operators in Lanzhou). A one-day visit to the Bingling Si Buddhist cave complex outside Lanzhou. Car with driver, boat transport and entrance fee are included, giving approximately two hours at the site. ¥400–500 per person.

Birding/Wildlife Tours Heilongjiang Overseas Tourist Corporation, Harbin, Dongbei. April–June only. Fifteen days return to Harbin via bird reserves at Zhalong, Beier Hu and Manzhouli; all-inclusive. ¥5000 per person. Also organizes tours to other reserves such as Wolong (Sichuan).

Dong Villages Wind and Rain Bridge Travel Service, Sanjiang, Guangxi. Return to Sanjiang. Private car, driver, guide, interpreter fluent in English and local language, lunch in Dong house extra. Price negotiable as are destinations; full day from ¥500 per person.

Ice Festival CITS, Harbin, Dongbei. Ten-day circuit of ice festivals in Chanchun, Harbin and Jilin in the depths of winter (Jan–Feb). Fully inclusive, but well below freezing. ¥3000 per person.

Inner Mongolian grassland tour Inner Mongolia Luye International Travel Company, Hohhot (and many other operators in Hohhot). Two-day tour of the grasslands including all transport, meals, yurt accommodation, entertainment and a guide (non English-speaking). ¥250–300 per person.

Qinghai Hu Qinghai Jiaotong Luxingshe, Xining, Qinghai. Two-day trip to the great lake, Qinghai Hu, plus Bird Island and Chaka Slat Lake. All-inclusive. ¥600 per person.

Steam Train Tour CITS, Shengyang, Dongbei. Two-week tour of steam loco factories, workyards and museums in Beijing, Harbin and Jiamusi; also numerous rides. All-inclusive. ¥5000 per person.

Turpan Any tour operator in Turpan, Xinjiang. A one-day tour of the sights around Turpan – ancient cities, caves and underground irrigation channels. Transport only. ¥50 per person.

Xishuangbanna Villages Mengyuan Travel Service, Jinghong, Yunnan. Three- to four-day hiking through border regions. Transport connections, tents, food and English-speaking guide. ¥700 per person.

Yungang Caves CITS, Datong, Shanxi. Day tour of the caves, Hanging Temple and Yingxian Wooden Pagoda – China's oldest wooden structure. Lunch, bus and an unreliable guide. ¥50 per person.

Zuo River CITS, Nanning, Guangxi. Two days/one night return from Nanning; includes train connections, English-speaking guide, three-hour river trip, four big meals, hotel accommodation, one-hour Zhuang rock art tour. ¥500 per person.

City transport

Most Chinese cities are spread out over areas which defeat even the most determined walker, but all have some form of **public transit system**. Hong Kong, Beijing, Guangzhou, and Shanghai have efficient underground **metros**; elsewhere the **city bus** is the transport focus. These are cheap and run from around 6am to 9pm or later, but – Hong Kong's apart – are usually slow and hideously crowded. Pricier **private minibuses** often run the same routes in similar comfort but at greater speed – they're either numbered or have their destination written up at the front.

If you're in a hurry or can't face another bus journey, you'll find **taxis** cruising the streets in larger towns and cities, or hanging around the main transit points and hotels.

They're not bad value for a group, costing either a fixed rate within certain limits – ¥5 seems normal – or about ¥8 to hire and then ¥1–3 per kilometre. You'll also find (motorized- or cycle-) **rickshaws** and **motorbike taxis** outside just about every mainland bus and train station, whose highly erratic rates are set by bargaining beforehand.

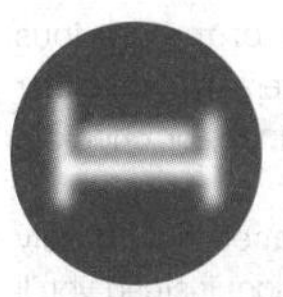

Accommodation

Accommodation in China is generally disappointing. Acres of marble and chrome aside, the Chinese rarely seem to realize that a hotel can be more than just a functional place to stay, but could be an interesting or enjoyable place in itself. What's lacking is variety – characterful old family-run institutions of the kind that can be found all over Asia and Europe simply don't exist in mainland China. Instead, most hotels are entirely anonymous and unmemorable, comprising purpose-built blocks with standardized interiors.

Despite the lack of variety, there is a vast **range of quality** in terms of comfort and service. A general rule is that newer hotels are almost always preferable, enjoying a honeymoon period of enthusiastic service and stain-free carpets before poor maintenance begins to take its toll. **Price**, however, is a poor guide to quality: Eastern China, for example, is far more expensive than western China, and large cities are more expensive than small ones. Hotels seldom seem to revise their prices either, so a once upmarket place might still charge high rates long after the facilities have deteriorated to the point of no return. In any case, **room rates** on display at reception often turn out to be merely the starting point in negotiations; staff are almost always amenable to **bargaining**. Getting thirty percent off the advertised price isn't unusual, and you might get even more of a discount in low season or where there's plenty of competition. Conversely, at popular tourist destinations during peak season hotels can charge considerably more. Polite enquiries might also persuade the receptionist to mention the existence of hitherto unsuspected cheaper rooms or a dormitory in another wing of the hotel.

One specific irritation for **foreigners** is the fact that plenty of hotels – normally the cheap ones – can't take them at all. Such hotels have not obtained permission to do so from local authorities and if they are caught housing foreigners illegally they face substantial fines. Nothing is ever certain in China, however. Sometimes the receptionists don't know that foreigners aren't allowed to stay and, if it is late at night, or if there is only one hotel in town, you will normally be allowed in anyway (being able to speak Chinese improves your chances, as does having a Chinese student card). And things may be changing: Yunnan recently passed a law allowing foreigners to stay at any available accommodation within the province.

Hotels in China are reasonably **secure** places, although you would be foolish to leave money or valuables lying about in your room. If you lock valuables such as cameras inside your bag before going out you are unlikely to have problems.

Finding a room

For international-class rooms, **booking ahead** is a routine procedure and you will undoubtedly find receptionists who speak English to take your call; besides hotel phone numbers, we've listed fax numbers or websites/email addresses throughout the guide. For any hotel below this category, however, the concept of booking ahead may be alien, and you won't make much headway without some spoken Chinese – though it's a good idea to call (or to ask someone to call for you) to see if vacancies exist before lugging your bag across town. One of the easier ways to book mid-range or better accommodation is to use a dedicated **website** – ⓦwww.sinohotelguide.com, for example, lists brief hotel descriptions and room rates in US dollars for several hundred hotels across the country.

To find a room **upon arrival**, time things so that you reach at your destination in broad daylight, then deposit your bag at a left-luggage office at the train or bus station and check out possible accommodation options. It's considered perfectly normal to ask to see the room before deciding to take it. If you can't find anywhere suitable, CITS can often tell you of convenient places to stay and can wrangle respectable discounts, though they only deal with two-star accommodation and up.

In some places, **touts** with hotel brochures and name cards will approach you outside stations. You won't lose much by following them as they are paid directly by the hotels concerned, not by surcharges on your room price. Sometimes, however, touts can inadvertently waste your time by taking you to hotels which turn out not to accept foreigners.

Checking in and out

The checking-in process involves filling in a detailed **form** (see opposite) giving details of your name, age, date of birth, sex and address, places where you are coming from and going to, how many days you intend staying and your visa and passport numbers. Filling in forms correctly is a serious business in bureaucratic China and if potential guests are unable to carry out this duty, the result is impasse. Upmarket hotels have English versions of these forms, and might fill them in for you, but hotels unaccustomed to foreigners usually have them in Chinese only, and might never have seen a foreign passport before – which explains the panic experienced by many hotel receptionists when they see a foreigner walk in the door. Opposite there's an example of this form in English and Chinese to help you complete it correctly.

You are always asked to **pay** in advance and, in addition, leave a **deposit** which may amount to as much as twice the price of the room. Assuming you haven't broken anything – check that everything works properly when you check in – deposits are reliably refunded; just don't lose the receipt. Note that as the official **hotel day** begins at 6am, arriving before this time means you have to pay a portion of the rate for the previous night. If you're staying several nights, either pay the whole lot in advance, or check in again every day.

Except in upmarket places, you hardly ever get a **key** from reception; instead you'll get a piece of paper which you take to the appropriate floor attendant who will give you a room card and open the door for you whenever you come in. Sometimes the floor attendant will offer you the key to keep, though if you want it you'll have to pay her another refundable deposit of ¥10–20. If your room has a **telephone**, men are advised to disconnect it if they don't want prostitutes calling up through the night – this can be a headache even in upmarket hotels.

Check-out time is noon, but if you have to leave early in the morning to catch a bus, for instance, you may be unable to find staff to refund your deposit, and might also encounter locked front doors or compound gates. This is most of a problem in rural areas, though often the receptionist sleeps behind the desk and can be woken up if you make enough noise.

Hotels

The different Chinese words for hotel are vague indicators of the status of the place. Sure signs of upmarket pretensions are the modern-sounding **dajiulou** or **dajiudian**, which translate as something like "big wine bar". The far more common term **binguan** is similarly used for smart new establishments, though it is also the name given to the older government-run hotels, many of which have now been renovated; foreigners can nearly always stay in these. **Fandian** (literally "restaurant") is used indiscriminately for top-class hotels as well as humble and obscure ones. Reliably downmarket – and rarely accepting foreigners – is **zhaodaisuo** ("guesthouse"), while the humblest of all is

临时住宿登记表

REGISTRATION FORM FOR TEMPORARY RESIDENCE

请用正楷填写 PLEASE WRITE IN BLOCK LETTERS

英文姓 Surname	英文名 First name	性别 Sex
中文姓名 Name in Chinese	国籍 Nationality	出生日期 Date of birth
证件种类 Type of certificate (eg passport)	证件号码 Certificate No.	签证种类 Type of visa
签证有效期 Valid date of visa	抵店日期 Date of arrival	离店日期 Date of departure
由何处来 From	交通工具 Carrier	往何处 To
永久地址 Permanent address		停留事由 Object of stay
职业 Occupation		
接待单位 Received by		房号 Room No.

lüguan ("inn"), where you might occasionally get to stay in some rural areas.

Whatever type of hotel you are staying in, there are two things you can rely on. One is a pair of plastic or paper slippers under the bed, that you use for walking to the bathroom, and the other is a vacuum flask of drinkable hot water that can be refilled any time by the floor attendant. **Breakfast** is sometimes included in the price; nearly all hotels, even fairly grotty ones, will have a restaurant where at least a basic breakfast of

Accommodation price codes

Accommodation in mainland China listed in this book has been given one of the following price codes, which represent the price of the cheapest **double room**. Where a spread of prices is indicated, this is because there are very few rooms for which the lower price code applies, or else the text will explain what extra facilities you get in the upper categories (usually an en-suite bathroom). In the cheaper hotels that have **dormitories** or that rent out individual beds in rooms, we give the price of a bed in yuan.

It should generally be noted that in the **off-season** – from October to June excluding holidays such as Chinese New Year – prices in tourist hotels are more flexible, and often lower, than during the peak summer months.

Note that the price codes do not take into account the **service charge** of fifteen percent added to bills in all mid-range and upmarket hotels.

❶ Up to ¥50	❹ ¥140–200	❼ ¥450–600
❷ ¥50–80	❺ ¥200–300	❽ ¥600–800
❸ ¥80–140	❻ ¥300–450	❾ Over ¥800

buns, pickles and rice porridge is served, usually between 7am and 8am.

Upmarket

In the larger cities – including virtually all provincial capitals – you'll find upmarket four- or five-star hotels, often managed by foreigners. Conditions in such hotels are comparable to those anywhere in the world, with all the usual **international facilities** on offer – such as swimming pools, gyms and business centres – though the finer nuances of service will sometimes be lacking. Prices for standard doubles in these places are upwards of ¥800 (❾ in our price-code scheme) and go as high as ¥1500, with a fifteen percent **service charge** added to the bill; the use of credit cards is routine. In **Hong Kong** and **Macau** the top end of the market is similar in character to the mainland, though prices are higher and service more efficient.

Even if you cannot afford to stay in the upmarket hotels, they can still be pleasant places to escape from the hubbub of life in China, and nobody in China blinks at the sight of a stray foreigner roaming around the foyer of a smart hotel. As well as air conditioning and clean toilets, you'll find cafés and bars (sometimes showing satellite TV), telephone and fax facilities and seven-days-a-week money changing (though this is not always open to non-guests).

Mid-range

Many urban Chinese hotels built nowadays are **mid-range,** and practically every town in China has at least one hotel of this sort. When new, they generally have clean, spacious, standard double rooms with attached bathroom, 24-hour hot water, TV and air conditioning – though after a couple of years the facilities can go into decline. Single rooms are rarely available in these places.

In remote places you should get a double in a mid-range establishment for ¥150–250, but expect to pay at least ¥350 in any sizeable city. Some mid-range hotels built during the dawn of tourism in 1980s, however, have been successfully upgraded, and might retain older, **cheaper wings** – though staff may initially deny their existence. These are often well maintained, if threadbare, and cost ¥100–200 for a double with bathroom, and as low as ¥25 for a dorm bed – but as staff seldom allow foreigners to share with Chinese, you may be asked to pay for a whole room.

Budget hotels

Cheap hotels, with doubles costing less than ¥100, vary in quality from the dilapidated to the perfectly comfortable. In many cities, they're commonly located near the train station, though in the major cities such as Beijing or Shanghai you may end up far from the centre.

Where you do manage to find a budget hotel that takes foreigners, you'll notice that the Chinese routinely **rent beds** rather than rooms – doubling up with one or more strangers – as a means of saving money. Foreigners are only very occasionally allowed to share rooms with Chinese people, but if there are three or four foreigners together it's often possible for them to share one big room. Otherwise, the saving grace for budget travellers is that tourist centres, including large cities such as Beijing, Shanghai and Guangzhou, tend to have one or two budget hotels with special **foreigners' dormitory** accommodation, costing around ¥20–50 per bed. The surest way to save money on accommodation in China, though, is to **go west**. Hotels in all of the Northwest, as well as Tibet, Sichuan and Yunnan, can be absurdly cheap, with double rooms available for as little as ¥50.

Hostels and guesthouses

There's a thin scattering of **IYHA hostels** on the mainland and in Hong Kong, where members get minor discounts. Hong Kong and Macau also have a large number of privately run **guesthouses** and hostels. They come in all shapes and sizes and the sheer variety comes as a serious relief after the dullness of mainland hotels. Prices for double rooms in these guesthouses are generally cheaper than in hotels in most of eastern China, and very cheap dormitories are also plentiful.

Youth hostel associations

UK and Ireland

Youth Hostel Association (YHA) ⓣ0870/770 8868, ⓦwww.yha.org.uk & www.iyhf.org. England and Wales.
Scottish Youth Hostel Association ⓣ0870/155 3255, ⓦwww.syha.org.uk.
Hostelling International Northern Ireland ⓣ028/9032 4733, ⓦwww.hini.org.uk.
Irish Youth Hostel Association Republic of Ireland ⓣ01/830 4555, ⓦwww.irelandyha.org.

US and Canada

Hostelling International-American Youth Hostels ⓣ202/783-6161, ⓦwww.hiayh.org.
Hostelling International Canada ⓣ1-800/663 5777 or 613/237 7884, ⓦwww.hostellingintl.ca.

Australia and New Zealand

Australia Youth Hostels Association ⓣ02/9261 1111, ⓦwww.yha.com.au.
Youth Hostelling Association New Zealand ⓣ0800/278299 or 03/379 9970, ⓦwww.yha.co.nz.

University accommodation

Another budget possibility always worth trying are rooms in **universities**, as more and more of them are willing to accommodate foreign tourists. These will have a building on campus termed something like the "Foreigners' Guesthouse" (*waibing zhaodaisuo*) or the "Foreign Experts' Building" (*waiguo zhuanjia lou*), designed primarily to accommodate foreign students or teachers. You would be unlucky not to find some obliging English-speaking student to help you find the right block once you're inside the campus. These buildings act like simple hotels and you have to fill in all the usual forms. Expect to pay around ¥50 a night, though some places are now charging tourists substantially more. Sometimes you find yourself put in to share with a resident foreign student who may be less than gracious about having you – but this happens only if the student concerned has paid for only one of the two beds in their room, so you needn't feel guilty about it. Although universities are friendly places to stay, the communal washing and toilet facilities can be grim, and campuses are often located far out in the suburbs.

Camping and pilgrims' inns

Camping is only really feasible in the wildernesses of western China where you are not going to wake up under the prying eyes of thousands of local villagers. In parts of Tibet, Qinghai, Xinjiang, Gansu and Inner Mongolia there are places within reach of hikers or cyclists where this is possible, though don't bother actually trying to get permission for it. This is the kind of activity which the Chinese authorities do not really have any clear idea about, so if asked they will certainly answer "no". The only kind of regular, authorized camping in China is by the nomadic Mongolian and Kazakh peoples of the steppe who have their own highly sophisticated felt tents (*mengu bao*), which tourists can ask to stay in (see p.988).

An alternative to camping are the **pilgrims' inns** at important monasteries and lamaseries. These are an extremely cheap, if rather primitive, form of accommodation, though vacancies disappear quickly. Foreigners are warmly welcomed in such places and, although the authorities are not particularly keen on you staying in them, you are most unlikely to be turned away if it is late in the day and you are really stuck.

Eating and drinking

The Chinese love to eat, and from market-stall buns and soup, right through to the intricate variations of regional cookery, China boasts one of the world's greatest cuisines. It's also far more complex than you might suspect from its manifestations overseas, and while food might not initially be a major reason for your trip, once here you may well find that eating becomes the highlight. However, the inability to order effectively sees many travellers missing out, and they leave desperate for a "proper meal", convinced that the bland stir-fries and dumplings served up in the cheapest canteens is all that's available. With a bit of effort you can eat well whatever your budget and ability with the language, though it can be monotonous eating solo for any length of time – meals are considered social events, and the process is accordingly geared to a group of diners sharing a variety of different dishes with their companions.

Though fresh ingredients are available from any market stall, there are very few opportunities to cook for yourself in China, and most of the time eating out is much more convenient and interesting. The **principles of Chinese cooking** are based on a desire for a healthy harmony between the qualities of different ingredients. For the Chinese, this extends right down to considering the *yin* and *yang* attributes of various dishes – for instance, whether food is "moist" or "dry", or "heating" or "cooling" in effect – but can also be appreciated in the use of ingredients with contrasting textures and colour, designed to please the eye as well as the palate. Recipes and ingredients themselves, however, are generally a response to more direct requirements. The chronic poverty of China's population is reflected in the traditionally scant quantity of meat used, while the need to preserve precious stocks of firewood led to the invention of quick cooking techniques, such as slicing ingredients into tiny shreds and stir-frying them. The reliance on eating whatever was immediately to hand also saw a readiness to experiment with anything edible; so, though you'd hardly come across them every day, items such as bear's paw, shark's fin, fish lips and even jellyfish all appear in Chinese cuisine.

For a comprehensive menu reader and useful phrases for ordering food and drink, see pp.1266–1271.

Ingredients and cooking methods

The after-effects of Maoist policies meant that as late as the 1980s the availability of good **ingredients** in China was pretty poor, leading to a miserably low standard of food served outside the highest-class hotels and restaurants. Now, in much of the country, market stalls are swamped under the weight of fresh produce, the restaurant industry is booming – though there is a growing national tendency to cover up poor cooking skills by using too much oil and flavour enhancer.

In the south, **rice** in various forms – long and short grain, noodles, or as dumpling wrappers – is the staple, replaced in the cooler north by **wheat**, formed into buns or noodles. Keep an eye out for **lamian** – literally "pulled noodles" – a Muslim treat made as you wait by pulling out ribbons of dough between outstretched arms, and serving them in a spicy soup (see p.1069).

Meat is held to be a generally invigorating substance and, ideally, forms the backbone of any meal – serving a pure meat dish is the height of hospitality. Pork is the most common meat used, except in areas with a strong Muslim tradition where it's replaced with mutton or beef. **Fowl** is considered especially good during old age or convalescence, and was quite a luxury in the past (chicken was once the most expensive meat in Beijing), though today most rural people in central and southern China seem to own a couple of hens, and the countryside is littered with duck farms. **Fish and seafood** are very highly regarded and can be extraordinarily expensive – partly because local pollution means that they often have to be imported – as are rarer game meats.

Eggs – duck, chicken or quail – are a popular nationwide snack, often flavoured by hard-boiling in a mixture of tea, soy sauce and star anise. There's also the so-called "thousand-year" variety, preserved for a few months in ash and straw – they look gruesome, with translucent brown albumen and green yolks, but actually have a delicate, brackish flavour. **Dairy products** serve limited purposes in China. Goat's cheese and yoghurt is eaten in parts of Yunnan and the Northwest, but milk is considered fit only for children and the elderly and is not used in cooking.

Vegetables accompany nearly every Chinese meal, used in most cases to balance tastes and textures of meat, but also appearing as dishes in their own right. Though the selection can be very thin in some parts of the country, there's usually a wide range on offer, from leafy greens to water chestnuts, mushrooms, bamboo shoots, seaweed and radish – even thin, transparent "glass" noodles, made out of pea starch, which the Chinese regard as vegetables too.

Soya beans are used very widely in Chinese cooking, being a good source of protein in a country where meat has often been a luxury. The beans themselves are small and green when fresh, and are sometimes eaten this way in the south. More frequently, however, they are salted and used to thicken sauces, fermented to produce **soy sauce**, or boiled and pressed to make white cakes of **tofu** (beancurd). Fresh tofu is flavourless and as soft as custard, though it can be or pressed further to create a firmer texture, or deep-fried until crisp. This is often smoked or cooked in stock, sliced thinly and used as a meat substitute in vegetarian cooking. Regional variations abound: in the west tofu is served heavily spiced; in Hunan

Vegetarian food

Vegetarianism has been practised for almost two thousand years in China for both religious and philosophical reasons, and its practitioners have included historical figures such as Cao Cao, the famous Three Kingdoms' warlord, and the pious sixth-century emperor Wu. Vegetarian cooking takes at least three recognized forms: plain **vegetable dishes**, commonly served at home or in ordinary restaurants; **imitation meat** dishes derived from Qing court cuisine, which use gluten, beancurd and potato to mimic the natural attributes of meat, fowl and fish; and **Buddhist cooking**, which often avoids onions, ginger, garlic and other spices considered stimulating.

Having said all this, strict vegetarians visiting China will find their options limited, despite a growing interest in veggie cuisine. Vegetables might be considered intrinsically healthy, but the Chinese also believe that they lack any physically fortifying properties, and **vegetarian diets** are unusual except for religious reasons. There's also a stigma of poverty attached to not eating meat, and no one can understand why foreigners wouldn't want it when they could clearly afford to gorge themselves on meat regularly. Although you can get vegetable dishes everywhere, be aware that cooking fat and stocks in the average dining room are of animal origins. If you really want to be sure that you are being served nothing of animal origin, tell your waiter that you are a Buddhist (see p.1266).

Things are easiest in big cities such as Beijing, Shanghai, and Guangzhou, which have real **vegetarian restaurants**; elsewhere, head for the nearest **temple**, many of which have dining rooms open to the public at lunchtime – some serve extraordinarily good food, worth sampling even if you're not vegetarian. When ordering in these places, note that imitation meat dishes are still called by their usual name, such as West Lake fish, honey pork or roast duck.

they grow mould on it (rather like cheese); in the south it's stuffed with meat; northerners make it spongy by freezing it; and everywhere it gets used in soup. The skin that forms on top of the liquid while tofu is being made is itself skimmed off, dried, and used as a wrapping for spring rolls and the like.

Seasonal availability is smoothed over by a huge variety of **dried**, **salted** and **pickled** vegetables, meats and seafood, which often characterize local cooking styles. There's also an enormous assortment of regional **fruit**, great to clean the palate or fill a space between meals.

When it finally comes to **preparing and cooking** these ingredients, be aware that there's far more on offer than simply chopping everything into small pieces and stir-frying them. A huge number of **spices** are used for their health-giving properties, to mask undesirable flavours or provide a background taste. **Marinating** removes blood (which is generally repugnant to the Chinese, though congealed pig's blood is a common rural dish in the south) – and tenderizes and freshens the flavour of meats. Chicken and fish are often cooked whole, though they may be dismembered before serving. Several cooking methods can be used within a single dish to maximize textures or flavours, including crisping by **deep frying** in flour or a batter; **steaming**, which can highlight an ingredient's subtler flavours; **boiling and blanching**, usually to firm meat as a precursor to other cooking methods; and **slow cooking** in a rich stock.

Regional cooking

Not surprisingly, given China's scale, there are a number of distinct **regional cooking styles**, divided into four major traditions. **Northern cookery** was epitomized by the imperial court and so also became known as Mandarin or Beijing cooking, though its influences are far wider than these names suggest. A solid diet of **wheat and millet buns**, noodles, pancakes and dumplings help to face severe winters, accompanied by the savoury tastes of dark soy sauce and bean paste, white cabbage, onions and garlic. The north's cooking has also been influenced by neighbours and invaders: Mongols brought their hotpots and grilled and roast meats, and Muslims a taste for mutton and chicken. Combined with exotic items imported by foreign merchants and vassal embassies visiting the court, imperial kitchens turned these rather rough ingredients and cooking styles into sophisticated marvels such as Beijing duck and bird's nest soup – though most northerners survive on soups of winter pickles, or fried summer greens eaten with a bun.

The central coast provinces produced the **Eastern style**, whose cooking delights in seasonal fresh seafood and river fish. Winters can still be cold and summers scorchingly hot, so dried and salted ingredients feature too, pepping up a background of rice noodles and dumplings. Based around Shanghai, eastern cuisine (as opposed to daily fare) enjoys little, delicate forms and light, fresh, sweet flavours, sometimes to the point of becoming precious – tiny meatballs are steamed in a rice coating and called "pearls", for example. **Red-cooking**, stewing meat in a sweetened wine and soy-sauce stock, is another characteristic of eastern dishes.

Western China is dominated by the boisterous cooking of **Sichuan** and **Hunan**, the antithesis of the eastern style. Here, there's a heavy use of chillies and pungent, constructed flavours – vegetables are concealed with "fish-flavoured" sauce, and even normally bland tofu is given enough spices to lift the top off your head. Yet there are still subtleties to enjoy in a cuisine which uses dried orange peel, aniseed, ginger and spring onions, and the cooking methods themselves – such as dry frying and smoking – are refreshingly unusual. Sichuan is also home of the now-ubiquitous **hotpot** (*huoguo*), for which you pay a set amount and are served with various raw meats and vegetables which you cook in boiling stock. For more on Sichuan cooking, see p.935.

Southern China is fertile and subtropical, a land of year-round plenty. When people say that southerners – specifically the **Cantonese** – will eat anything, they really mean it: fish maw, snake, dog and cane rat are some of the more unusual dishes here, strange even to other Chinese, though there's also a huge consumption of fruit and vegetables, fish and shellfish. Typically, the demand is for extremely fresh ingredients, quickly cooked and only lightly seasoned, though the south is also home to that famous mainstay of Chinese restaurants overseas, sweet-and-sour sauce. The tradition of **dim sum** – "little eats" – reached its pinnacle here, too, where a morning meal of tiny flavoured buns, dumplings and pancakes is washed down with copious tea, satisfying the Chinese liking for a varied assortment of small dishes. Nowadays *dim sum* (*dian xin* in Mandarin) is eaten all over China, but southern restaurants still have the best selection. For more on Cantonese and southern food, see p.642.

Hong Kong basically takes the best of Chinese cooking as its own, though heavily biased towards the southern style, while in **Macau** you'll get the chance to try the region's unique mix of Portuguese and Asian food, known as Macanese. Aside from the four major styles, almost every part of China has its own regional slant on food – the guide covers Yunnanes (p.862), Uigur (p.1069) and Tibetan (p.795) cooking.

Breakfast and snacks

Breakfast is not a big event by Chinese standards, more something to line the stomach for a few hours. Much of the country is content with a bowl of **zhou** (also known as congee, rice porridge) or sweetened soy milk, flavoured with pickles and accompanied by a heavy, plain bun or fried dough stick, the latter rather like a straight, savoury doughnut. Another favourite is a plain soup with rice noodles and perhaps a little meat. Most places also have countless small, early opening **snack stalls**, usually located around markets, train and bus stations. Here you'll get grilled chicken wings; kebabs; spiced noodles; baked yams and potatoes; boiled eggs; grilled corn and countless local treats. Look out also for steamed **buns**, which are either stuffed with meat or vegetables (*baozi*) or plain (*mantou*, literally "bald heads"). The buns originated in the north and are especially warming on a winter's day; a sweeter Cantonese variety is stuffed with barbecued pork. Another northern snack now found everywhere is the ravioli-like **jiaozi**, again with a meat or vegetable filling and either fried or steamed; **shuijiao** are boiled *jiaozi* served in soup. Some small restaurants specialize in *jiaozi*, containing a bewildering range of fillings and always sold by weight – see p.52 for details.

Western and international food

There's a fair amount of **Western and international food** available in China, though supply and quality varies from place to place. Hong Kong has the best range, with some excellent restaurants covering everything from French to Vietnamese cuisine, and there are a number of restaurants specializing in Western food in Guangzhou, Beijing, Yangshuo and Shanghai. Elsewhere, international-style hotels may have Western restaurants, often serving relatively expensive but huge **buffet breakfasts** of scrambled egg, bacon, toast, cereal, and coffee; and there's a growing number of **cafés** in many cities, offering fresh coffee and tea, along with **set meals** from ¥30–80 – steak hotplates are a current trend (the more expensive versions using imported beef), served with a drink, small soup and salad. *Shangdao Kafei* and *Coffee Language* are two widespread Taiwanese-owned chains, with branches in several cities. **Burger**, **fried-chicken** and **pizza** places are also ubiquitous, including domestic chains such as *Dicos* alongside genuine *McDonald's*, *KFC* and *Pizza Hut*.

Where to eat

In itself, getting fed is never difficult as everyone wants your custom. Walk past anywhere that sells cooked food and you'll be hailed by cries of *chi fan* – basically, "come and eat!"

Hotel dining rooms can be very flash affairs, with the most upmarket serving a range of foreign and regional Chinese food at ruinous cost, though more average establishments can often be extremely good value. Advantages include the possibility that staff may speak English, or that they might offer a **set menu** of small local dishes. Elsewhere, **restaurants** are often divided into two or three floors: the first will offer a canteen-like choice, upstairs will be pricier and have more formal dining arrangements, with waitress service and a written menu, while further floors (if they have them) are generally reserved for banquet parties or foreign tour groups and are unlikely to seat individuals. Note that the favoured atmosphere in a Chinese restaurant is *renao*, or "hot and noisy", rather than the often quiet norm in the West.

The cheapest **stalls and canteens** are necessarily basic, with simple food which is often much better than you'd expect from the furnishings. Though foreigners are generally given disposable chopsticks, it's probably worth buying your own set in case these aren't available – washing up frequently involves rinsing everything in a bucket of grey water on the floor and leaving it to dry on the pavement.

While small noodle shops and food stalls around train and bus stations have flexible hours, **restaurant opening times** tend to be early and short. Breakfast is usually under way by 6am, and will have wound up by 9am. Get up late and you'll have to join the first sitting for lunch at 11am or so, leaving you plenty of time to work up an appetite for the evening meal around 5pm. An hour later you'd be lucky to get a table in some places, and by 9pm the staff will be yawning and sweeping the debris off the tables around your ankles.

Ordering and dining

When **ordering**, unless eating a one-dish meal like Peking duck or a hotpot, try to select items with a range of tastes and textures – perhaps some seafood, meat and chicken, each cooked in a different manner; it's also usual to include a soup. In cheap places, servings of noodles or rice are huge, but as they are considered basic stomach fillers, quantities decline the more upmarket you go. Note that dishes such as *jiaozi* or some seafood, as well as fresh produce, are sold **by weight**: a *liang* is 50 grams, a *banjin* 250 grams, a *jin* 500 grams, and a *gongjin* one kilo.

Menus, where available, are often more of an indication of what's on offer than a definitive list, so don't be afraid to ask for a missing favourite. Note also that English menu translations tend to omit things that the Chinese consider might be unpalatable to foreigners. Our menu reader (see p.1266) will certainly help you order if you can't speak Chinese; otherwise, **pointing** is all that's required at street stalls and small restaurants, where the ingredients are displayed out the front in buckets, bundles and cages; canteens usually have the fare laid out or will have the selection scrawled illegibly on strips of paper or a board hung on the wall. You either tell the cook directly what you want or buy chits from a cashier, which you exchange at the kitchen hatch for your food and sit down at large communal tables or benches.

When you enter a **proper restaurant** you'll be escorted to a chair and promptly given a pot of tea, along with pickles and nuts in upmarket places. The only tableware provided is a spoon, bowl and a pair of chopsticks, and at this point the Chinese will ask for a flask of boiling water and a bowl to wash it all in – not usually necessary, but something of a ritual. A menu will be produced, if they have one, but otherwise you might be escorted through to the kitchen to make your choice. Alternatively, have a look at what other diners are eating – the Chinese are often delighted that a foreigner wants to eat Chinese food, and will indicate the best food on their table.

One thing to watch out for is getting the idea across when you want different items cooked together (say *yīkuàir*) – otherwise you might end up with separate plates of nuts, meat and vegetables when you thought you'd ordered a single dish of chicken with cashews and green peppers. Note also that unless you're specific about how you want your food prepared, it inevitably arrives stir-fried.

Dishes are all **served** at once, placed in the middle of the table for diners to share; eat fairly slowly, taking time to talk between helping yourself. To handle **chopsticks**, hold one halfway along its length like a pencil, then slide the other underneath and use them as an extension of your fingers to pick up the food – though note that rice is shovelled in using the chopsticks, with the bowl up against your lips, while soft or slippery foods such as tofu or mushrooms are managed with **spoons**. With some poultry dishes you can crunch up the smaller bones, but anything else is spat out on to the tablecloth or floor, more or less discreetly depending on the establishment – watch what others are doing. Soups tend to be bland and are consumed last (except in the south where they may be served first or as part of the main meal) to wash the meal down, the liquid slurped from a spoon or the bowl once the noodles, vegetables or meat in it have been picked out and eaten. **Desserts** aren't a regular feature in China, though in the south sweet soups and buns are eaten (the latter not confined to main meals), particularly at festive occasions.

Resting your chopsticks together across the top of your bowl means that you've **finished** eating. After a meal the Chinese don't hang around to talk over drinks as in the West, but get up straight away and leave. In canteens you'll **pay** up front, while at restaurants you ask for the bill and pay either the waiter or at the front till. **Tipping** is not expected in mainland China.

Drinking

Water is easily available in China, but never drink what comes out of the tap. **Boiled water** is always on hand in hotels and trains, either provided in large vacuum flasks or an urn, and you can buy **bottled spring water** at station stalls and supermarkets – read the labels and you'll see some unusual substances (such as radon) listed, which you'd probably want to avoid.

Tea

Tea was introduced into China from India around 1800 years ago, and was originally drunk for medicinal reasons. Although its health properties are still important, and some food halls sell nourishing or stimulating varieties by the bowlful, over the centuries a whole social culture has sprung up around this beverage, spawning teahouses which once held the same place in Chinese society that the local pub or bar does in the West. Plantations of neat rows of low tea bushes adorn hillsides across southern China, while the brew is enthusiastically consumed from the highlands of Tibet – where it's mixed with barley meal and butter – to every restaurant and household between Hong Kong and Beijing.

Often the first thing you'll be asked in a restaurant is *hè shénme chá* – "what sort of tea would you like?" Chinese tea comes in red, green and flower-scented **varieties**, depending on how it's processed; only Hainan produces Indian-style black tea. Some regional kinds, such as *pu'er* from Yunnan, Fujian's *tie guanyin*, Zhejiang's *longjing*, or Sichuan's *emei cha*, are highly sought after – if you like the local style, head for the nearest market and stock up. Though tea is never drunk with milk and only very rarely with sugar, the manner in which it's served also varies from place to place: sometimes it comes in huge mugs with a lid, elsewhere in dainty cups served from a miniature pot; there are also formalized **tea rituals** in parts of Fujian and Guangdong. When drinking in company, it's polite to top up others' cups before your own, whenever they become empty; if someone does this for you, lightly tap your first two fingers on the table to show your thanks. If you've had enough, leave your cup full, and in a restaurant take the lid off or turn it over if you want the pot refilled during the meal.

It's also worth trying some **Muslim tea**, which involves dried fruit, nuts, seeds, crystallized sugar and tea heaped into a cup with the remaining space filled with hot water, poured with panache from an immensely long-spouted copper kettle. Also known as *babao cha*, or Eight Treasures Tea, it's becoming widely available in upmarket restaurants everywhere, and is sometimes sold in packets from street stalls.

Alcohol

The popularity of **beer** – *pijiu* – in China rivals that of tea, and, for men, is the preferred mealtime beverage (drinking alcohol in public is considered improper for Chinese women, though not for foreigners). The first brewery was set up in the northeastern port of Qingdao by the Germans in the nineteenth century, and now, though the Tsingtao label is widely available, just about every province produces at least one brand of four percent Pilsner. Sold in litre bottles, it's always drinkable, often pretty good, and is actually cheaper than bottled water. Draught beer is becoming available across the country.

Watch out for the term "**wine**" on English menus, which doesn't usually carry the conventional meaning. China does actually have a couple of commercial vineyards producing the mediocre Great Wall and Dynasty labels, more of a status symbol than an attempt to rival Western growers. Far better are the local pressings in Xinjiang Province, where the population of Middle Eastern descent takes its grapes seriously. More often, however, "wine" denotes **spirits**, made from rice (*mijiu*), sorghum or millet (*baijiu*). Serving spirits to guests is a sign of hospitality, and they're always used for toasting at banquets. Again, local home-made varieties can be quite good, while mainstream brands – especially the expensive, nationally famous Maotai and Wuliangye – are pretty vile to the Western palate. **Imported beers and spirits** are sold in large department stores and in city bars, but are always expensive.

Western-style bars are found not only in Hong Kong and Macau, but also in the major mainland cities. These establishments serve both local and imported beers and spirits, and are popular with China's middle class as well as foreigners. Mostly, though, the Chinese drink alcohol with their meals – all restaurants serve at least local beer and *baijiu*.

Soft drinks

Canned products, usually sold unchilled, include various lemonades and colas, and the national sporting drink **Jianlibao**, an orange and honey confection which most foreigners find over-sweet. **Fruit juices** can be unusual and refreshing, however, flavoured with chunks of lychee, lotus and water chestnuts. **Coffee** is grown and drunk in Yunnan and Hainan, and imported brews are available in cafés; you can buy instant powder in any supermarket. **Milk** is sold in powder form as baby food, and increasingly in bottles for adult consumption as its benefits for invalids and the elderly become accepted wisdom. Sweetened **yogurt drinks**, available all over the country in little packs of six, are a popular treat for children, though their high sugar content won't do your teeth much good.

Communications

China's communications system has much improved in recent years and is still being rapidly updated. Internet access is cheap and increasingly available, international phone calls are reasonably priced, and on the whole it's easy to phone or fax abroad, even from obscure towns, while the international mail services are reliable to or from any of the cities. Domestic calls are nearly as reliable, and within the country mail is very rapid.

Mail

The Chinese mail service is, on the whole, fast and reliable, with letters taking less than a day to reach destinations in the same city, two or more days to other destinations in China, and up to several weeks to destinations abroad. Overseas postage rates are becoming expensive; a postcard costs ¥4.2, while a standard letter is ¥5.4 or more, depending on the weight. Ideally you should have mail franked in front of you to stop anyone stealing and reusing the stamps. An Express Mail Service (**EMS**) operates to most countries and to most destinations within China; besides cutting delivery times, the service ensures the letter or parcel is sent by registered delivery.

Main **post offices** are open seven days a week between 8am and 8pm; smaller offices may close earlier or for lunch, or be closed at weekends. As well as at post offices, you can post letters in green **postboxes**, though these are few and far between except in the biggest cities, or at tourist hotels, which usually have a postbox at the front desk. Envelopes can be frustratingly scarce; try the stationery sections of department stores.

To send **parcels**, turn up at the main post office with the goods you want to send and the staff will help you pack them, a service which costs only a few yuan; don't try to do it yourself, as your package will have to be unpacked to ensure it is packed correctly. You can buy boxes at the post office, or your goods will be sewn into a linen packet like a pillowcase. Once packed, but before the parcel is sealed, it must be checked at the customs window in the post office. In some parts of the country, especially the south, you'll find separate parcels offices near the post office. A one-kilogram parcel should cost from around ¥70 for surface mail, ¥120 by air to Europe. Though parcel post from China is reliable, you'll have to complete masses of paperwork, with forms in Chinese and French (the international language of postal services) only. If you are sending valuable goods bought in China, put the receipt or a photocopy of it in with the parcel, as it may be opened for customs inspection farther down the line.

Poste restante services are available in any city. A nominal fee has to be paid to pick up mail, which will be kept for several months, and you will sometimes need to present ID when picking it up. Mail is often eccentrically filed – to cut down on misfiling, your name should be printed clearly at the top of the letter and the surname underlined, but it's still worth checking all the other pigeonholes just in case. Have letters addressed to you c/o Poste Restante, GPO, town or city, province. You can also leave a message for someone in the poste restante box, but you'll have to buy a stamp.

Phones

Local calls are free from land lines, and long-distance China-wide calls are fairly cheap. Note that everywhere in China has an **area code** which must be used when phoning from outside that locality; area codes are given for all telephone numbers throughout the guide. International calls cost at least ¥16 a minute (much cheaper if you use an IP internet phone card – see below).

You can make international calls from offices of the state-run **China Telecom**, usually located next to or within the main post office and usually open 24 hours. You pay a deposit of ¥200 and are told to go to a particular booth. When you have finished, the charge for the call is worked out automatically and you pay at the desk. You may find that a minimum charge for three minutes applies. Calls to Britain cost ¥15 per minute, to the US and Australia ¥18, and to Hong Kong ¥5. You can also make IDD calls from streetside telephone shops (generally displaying "IDD" on a sign). These usually charge by the minute, but always check in advance.

Alternatively, tourist hotels offer direct dialling abroad from your room, but will add a surcharge, and a minimum charge equivalent to between one and three minutes will be levied even if the call goes unanswered. The **business centres** you'll find in most big hotels offer fax, telephone, Internet and telex services (as well as photocopying and typing), and you don't have to be a guest to use them – though prices for all these services are typically extortionate. Hotels also charge for receiving faxes, usually around ¥10 per page.

Card phones, widely available in major cities, are the cheapest way to make domestic long-distance calls (¥0.2 for 3min), and can also be used for international calls (generally over ¥10 for 3min). They take **IC Cards**, which come in units of ¥20, ¥50 and ¥100. There's a fifty percent discount after 6pm and on weekends. You will be cut off when your card value drops below the amount needed for the next minute.

Yet another option is the **IP** (Internet Phone) **card**, which can be used from any phone, and comes in ¥100 units. You dial a local number, then a PIN, then the number you're calling. Rates are as low as ¥2.4 per minute to the USA and Canada, ¥3.2 to Europe.

Cellular phones

Your home **cellular phone** may already be compatible with the Chinese network (visitors from North American should ensure their phones are GSM/Triband), though note that you will pay a premium to use it abroad, and that callers within China have to make an international call to reach your phone. For more information, check the manual that came with your phone, or with the manufacturer and/or your telephone service provider. Alternatively, once in China you can buy a GSM SIM card (around ¥100) from any outlet of China Mobile, which allows you to use your phone as though it's a local mobile; additionally, you'll need to buy prepaid cards to pay for the calls. In big cities you can even **rent mobile phones** – look for the ads in expat magazines. Making and receiving domestic calls this way costs ¥0.6 per minute.

Internet access

Domestic interest in the Internet is huge, and with personal computer ownership still low, there are cramped **Internet cafés** (*wangba*) throughout the country, crammed with young people surfing (and indulging in networked gaming). A good place to find Net cafés is in the vicinity of colleges and universities, around which there's usually a cluster. Alternatively, try the China Telecom office as a last resort, though note that many of their Net bars have closed down. In the unlikely event of your being turned away by a Net café, this is generally because many aren't licensed, and don't want the additional responsibility of hosting foreigners on the premises.

While getting online is cheap at ¥2–5 an hour, generally, you can't be sure of actually getting at the websites you want. In response to the perceived threat of free access to information, the government has constructed a **firewall** (wryly nicknamed the new Great Wall) to block access to politically sensitive sites. The way this is administered shifts regularly according to the mood among the powers that be – restrictions were loosened, for example, while Beijing was campaigning to be awarded the 2008 summer Olympics (the government was anxious to be seen not to be oppressing its subjects) – but in general you can be pretty sure you won't be able to access the BBC or CNN, or the White House, though newspaper websites tend to be left unhindered. Access to the search engine **Google** has actually been cut off from time to time; in 2002, for example, it was unavailable for a few days (because, officials claimed, if you typed "Jiang Zemin" into it a satirical game appeared among the top ten results).

The media

The Chinese news agency, Xinhua, is a national organization with an office in every province, a mouthpiece for the state which has a monopoly on domestic news. You can read their propaganda in the *China Daily*, the only English-language newspaper, which is scarce outside Beijing, though you can always get it online at ⓦwww.chinadaily.com.cn. The stories of economic success written in turgid prose may be numbing, but the paper also has a Beijing listings section and articles on uncontroversial aspects of Chinese culture. Other official English-language publications such as *Beijing Review* and *Business Beijing* are glossy titles, again very difficult to get hold of outside the capital, with articles on investment opportunities, the latest state successes, as well as interesting places to visit.

Much more interesting are the free **expat-geared magazines** available in Beijing, Shanghai and Guangzhou, which contain listings of local venues and events, plus classifieds and feature articles; they're closely monitored by the authorities, though this doesn't stop them sailing quite close to the wind at times. In large cities you'll also find copies of (generally uncensored) imported publications such as *Time, Newsweek* and the *Far Eastern Economic Review*. Try branches of the Friendship Store (the state-run department store) or big tourist hotels for these.

The main Chinese-language daily newspaper is the *People's Daily*, which has an online English edition at ⓦenglish.peopledaily.com.cn. Heavy **censorship** continues to affect the mainland Chinese-language press, though stories sometimes break that the Party would rather people didn't know about. In 2001, for example, the press exposed a scandal about blood-donation vans spreading AIDS through entire villages; and in 2002 the appalling conditions of mine workers and overtaxed peasants became a national issue thanks to crusading journalists. It's a brave editor who prints such stuff, however.

A good range of English-language newspapers and magazines are published in **Hong Kong**, including the *South China Morning Post*, the *Hong Kong Standard*, the *Eastern Express* and the *Far Eastern Economic Review.* Asian editions of a number of international magazines and newspapers are also produced here – *Time*, *Newsweek*, the *Asian Wall Street Journal* and *USA Today*, for example. Surprisingly, all these have so far remained free (and openly critical of Beijing on occasion), despite the former colony's changeover to Chinese control.

TV and radio

There is the occasional item of interest on mainland Chinese **television**, though you'd have to be very bored to resort to it for entertainment. Domestic travel and wildlife programmes are common, as are song-and-dance extravaganzas, the most entertaining of which feature dancers performing in fetishistic, tight-fitting military gear while party officials watch with rigor-mortis faces. Soap operas and historical dramas are popular, and often feature a few foreigners; also screened are 20-year-old American thrillers and war films. Chinese war films, in which the Japanese are shown getting mightily beaten, at least have the advantage that you don't need to speak the language to understand what's going on. The same goes for the flirty dating gameshows, where male contestants proudly state their qualifications and height. CCTV, the state broadcaster, has two English-language channels, 4 and 9, though they're of precious little interest. **Satellite TV** in English is available in the more expensive hotels.

On the **radio** you're likely to hear the latest soft ballads, often from Taiwan or Hong Kong, or versions of Western pop songs sung in Chinese. For news from home, you may want to bring a **shortwave radio** with you; see the websites of the BBC World Service (ⓦwww.bbc.co.uk/worldservice), Radio Canada (ⓦwww.rcinet.ca), the Voice of America (ⓦwww.voa.gov) and Radio Australia (ⓦwww.abc.net.au/ra) for schedules and frequencies.

Opening hours, public holidays and festivals

The general trend in offices – airlines, travel services and the like – is for relatively early opening and closing, with long lunch hours. Typical hours are 8–11.30am and 1.30–4.30pm, with a half day on Saturday. Generalization is difficult, though, as there is no real equivalent to the role that Sunday plays in the West as the day of rest. Post and telecommunications offices open daily, often until late at night. Shops, too, nearly all open daily, keeping long, late hours, especially in big cities. Although banks *usually* close on Sundays – or for the whole weekend – even this is not always the case.

Tourist **sights** such as parks, pagodas and temples open every day, usually between 8am and 5pm and without a lunch break. Most public parks open from about 6am, ready to receive the morning flood of shadow boxers. Museums, however, tend to have slightly more restricted hours, including lunch breaks and one closing day a week, often Monday or Tuesday. If you arrive at an out-of-the-way place that seems to be closed, however, don't despair – knocking or poking around will often turn up a drowsy doorkeeper. Conversely, you may find other places locked and deserted when they are supposed to be open.

Public holidays and festivals

A number of secular **public holidays** have been celebrated since 1949; offices close on these dates, though many shops will remain open. The most important of these holidays are January 1 (New Year's Day), May 1 (Labour Day) and October 1 (National Day) – the last two mark the beginning of week-long breaks for many people. There are a few other dates, March 8 (Women's Day), June 1 (Children's Day), July 1 (Chinese Communist Party Day) and August 1 (Army Day), which are celebrated by parades and festive activities by the groups concerned. Businesses and offices tend to operate normally on these dates.

The only traditional Chinese **festival** marked by an official holiday is also the biggest of all, the **Chinese New Year** or Spring Festival (see opposite). This sees nearly all shops and offices closing down for three days, and a large proportion of the population off work. Even after the third day, offices such as banks may operate on restricted hours until the official end of the holiday period, eleven days later. Other traditional Chinese festivals, such as the Qingming Festival and the Mid-autumn Festival, aren't marked by official holidays, though you may notice a growing tendency for businesses to operate restricted hours at these times.

Most festivals take place according to dates in the Chinese **lunar calendar**, in which the first day of the month is the time when the moon is at its thinnest, with the full moon marking the middle of the month. So, by the Gregorian calendar, such festivals fall on a different day every year. Most festivals celebrate the turning of the seasons or propitious dates, such as the eighth day of the eighth month (eight is a lucky number in China), and are times for gift giving, family reunion and feasting. In the countryside, lanterns are lit and **firecrackers** (banned in the cities) are set off. It's always worth visiting temples on festival days, when the air is thick with incense, and people queue up to kowtow to altars and play games that bring good fortune, such as trying to hit the temple bell with thrown coins.

Aside from the following national festivals, China's **ethnic groups** punctuate the year with their own ritual observances, and these are detailed in the appropriate chapters in the guide. In Hong Kong all the national Chinese festivals are celebrated.

Spring Festival

The **Spring Festival** is two weeks of festivities marking the beginning of a **new year** in the lunar calendar. In Chinese astrology (for more on which see "Contexts", p.1210), each year is associated with a particular animal from a cycle of twelve; 2003 is the Year of the Goat, for example, and the passing into a new phase is a momentous occasion. Each year it falls on a different date in the Gregorian calendar, but it's usually in late January or early February. There's a tangible sense of excitement in the run-up to the festival, when China is perhaps at its most colourful, with shops and houses decorated with good-luck messages and stalls and shops selling paper money, drums and costumes. However the festival is not an ideal time to be travelling the country – everything shuts down, and most of the population goes on the move, making travel impossible or extremely uncomfortable.

The first day of the festival is marked by a family feast at which *jiaozi* (dumplings) are eaten, sometimes with coins hidden inside. To bring luck, people dress in red clothes (red being regarded as a lucky colour) – a particularly important custom if the animal of their birth year is coming round again – and each family tries to eat a whole fish, since the word for fish sounds like the word for surplus. In the countryside, firecrackers are let off almost constantly to scare ghosts away and, on the fifth day, to honour **Cai Shen**, god of wealth. In the cities, where fireworks are banned, enterprising stallholders sell cassette tapes of explosions as a substitute. Another ghost-scaring tradition you may notice is the pasting up of images of door gods at the threshold. Outside the home, New Year is publicly celebrated at **temple fairs**, which feature acrobats, drummers, and clouds of smoke as the Chinese light incense sticks to placate the gods. After two weeks, the celebrations end with the **lantern festival**, when the streets are filled with multicoloured paper lanterns, a tradition dating from the Han dynasty. Many places also have flower festivals and street processions with paper dragons and other animals parading through the town. It's customary at this time to eat *tang yuanr*, a delicious sticky sweet made of rice and bean paste.

A holidays and festivals calendar

January/February Spring Festival. Celebrated during the first two weeks of the new lunar year.
February Tiancang Festival. On the twentieth day of the first lunar month Chinese peasants celebrate Tiancang, or Granary Filling Day, in the hope of ensuring a good harvest later in the year.
March Guanyin's Birthday. Guanyin, the Goddess of Mercy, and probably China's most popular deity, is celebrated, most colourfully in Taoist temples, on the nineteenth day of the second lunar month.
April 5 Qingming Festival. This festival, also referred to as Tomb Sweeping Day, is the time to visit the graves of ancestors and burn ghost money in honour of the departed.
April 13–15 Water Splashing Festival. Popular in Yunnan Province. Anyone on the streets is fair game for a soaking.
May 4 Youth Day. Commemorating the student demonstrators in Tian'anmen Square in 1919, which gave rise to the Nationalist "May Fourth Movement". It's marked in most cities with flower displays.
June 1 Children's Day. Most schools go on field trips, so if you're visiting a popular tourist site be prepared for mobs of kids in yellow baseball caps.
June/July Dragon-boat Festival. On the fifth day of the fifth lunar month dragon-boat races are held in memory of the poet Qu Yuan, who drowned himself in 280 BC. Some of the most famous venues for this festival in the country are Yueyang in Hunan Province, and Hong Kong. The traditional food to accompany the celebrations is *zongzi* (lotus-wrapped rice packets).
August/September Ghost Festival. The Chinese equivalent of Halloween, this is a time when ghosts from hell are supposed to walk the earth. It's not celebrated so much as observed; it's regarded as an inauspicious time to travel, move house or get married.
September/October Moon Festival. On the fifteenth day of the eighth month of the lunar calendar the Chinese celebrate the Moon Festival,

also known as the Mid-autumn Festival, a time of family reunion that is celebrated with fireworks and lanterns. Moon cakes, containing a rich filling of sugar, lotus-seed paste and walnut, are eaten, and plenty of Maotai is consumed. In Hong Kong, the cakes sometimes contain salted duck egg yolks.

September/October Double Ninth Festival. Nine is a number associated with *yang*, or male energy, and on the ninth day of the ninth lunar month such qualities as assertiveness and strength are celebrated. It's believed to be a good time for the distillation (and consumption) of spirits.

September 28 Confucius Festival. The birthday of Confucius is marked by celebrations at all Confucian temples. It's a good time to visit Qufu, in Shandong Province, when elaborate ceremonies are held in the temple there (see p.344).

October 1 National Day. Everyone has a day off to celebrate the founding of the People's Republic. TV is even more dire than usual as it's full of programmes celebrating Party achievements.

December 25 Christmas. This is marked as a religious event only by the faithful, but for everyone else it's an excuse for a feast and a party.

Crime and personal safety

Despite the new veneer of individual freedom, China remains a police state, with the state interfering with and controlling the lives of its subjects to a degree most Westerners would find it hard to tolerate – as indeed many of the Chinese do. This should not affect foreigners much, however, as the state on the whole takes a hands-off approach to visitors – they are anxious that you have a good time rather than come away with a bad impression of the country. Indeed, Chinese who commit crimes against foreigners are treated much more harshly than if their victims had been native.

Crime is a growth industry in China, with official corruption and juvenile offences the worst problems. Much crime is put down to spiritual pollution by foreign influences, the result of increasing liberalization. But serious social problems such as mass unemployment are more to blame, as is the let's-get-rich attitude that has become the prevailing ideology.

The police

The police, known as the Public Security Bureau or **PSB** (*gong'an ju* in Chinese), are recognizable by their green uniforms and caps, though there are a lot more around than you might at first think, as plenty are undercover. They have much wider powers than most Western police forces, including establishing the guilt of criminals – trials are used only for deciding the sentence of the accused (though this is changing and China now has the beginnings of an independent judiciary). If the culprit is deemed to show proper remorse, this will result in a more lenient sentence. Laws are harsh, with execution – a bullet in the back of the head – the penalty for a wide range of serious crimes, from corruption to rape.

The PSB also have the job of looking after foreigners, and you'll most likely have to seek them out for **visa extensions** (see p.22), reporting theft or losses (see opposite) and obtaining permits for otherwise closed areas of the country (mostly in Tibet). On occasion, they might seek you out; it's fairly common for the police to call round to your hotel room if you're staying in an out-of-the-

Emergencies

In mainland China dial the following numbers in an emergency:
Police ⓣ110
Fire ⓣ119
Ambulance ⓣ120

In Hong Kong and Macau, dial ⓣ999 for any of the emergency services.

way place that sees few foreigners – they usually just look at your passport and then move on.

While individual police can be very helpful and go out of their way to help foreigners, the PSB itself has all the problems of any police force in a country where corruption is widespread, and it's best to minimize contact with them.

Crime and petty theft

Violent crime is on the increase in China, and while there is no need for obsessive paranoia, you do need to take care. Wandering around cities late at night is as bad an idea in China as anywhere else; similarly, walking alone across the countryside is extremely ill-advised, particularly in remote regions. Both situations have resulted in the murder of foreign tourists in recent years. Hard-seat carriages on long-distance trains can also get pretty rough at times, and robberies at knifepoint on trains are not unknown. If anyone does try to rob you, try to stay calm but don't resist.

Less dangerously, you may also see a fair number of **street confrontations**, when huge crowds gather to watch a few protagonists push each other around – though such fights rarely result in violence, just a lot of shouting. Mostly they're just caused by stress, and tend to occur where the crowds are at their most overwhelming, such as at bus stations. Another irritation, particularly in the southern cities, are gangs of **child beggars**, organized by a nearby adult. They target foreigners and can be very hard to shake off; handing over money usually results in increased harassment.

Theft

As a tourist, and therefore someone far richer than anyone else around, you are an obvious target for **petty thieves**. Passports and money should be kept in a concealed money belt; a bum bag offers much less protection and is easy for skilled pickpockets to get into. Be wary on **buses**, the favoured haunt of pickpockets, and **trains**, particularly in hard-seat class and on overnight journeys. Take a chain and padlock to secure your luggage in the rack.

Hotel rooms are on the whole secure, dormitories much less so, though often it's your fellow-travellers who are the problem here. Most hotels should have a safe, but it's not unusual for things to go missing from these. It's a good idea to keep around US$200 separately from the rest of your cash, together with your traveller's-cheque receipts, insurance policy details, and photocopies of your passport and visa.

On the street, try not to be too ostentatious. Flashy jewellery and watches will attract the wrong kind of attention, and try to be discreet when taking out your cash. Not looking obviously wealthy also helps if you want to avoid being ripped off by traders and taxi drivers, as does telling them you are a student – the Chinese have a great respect for education, and much more sympathy for foreign students than for tourists.

If you do have anything stolen, you'll need to get the PSB (addresses are given throughout the guide) to write up a **loss report** in order to claim on your insurance. Though most PSB offices have English speakers around, take a Chinese speaker with you if possible, and be prepared to pay a small fee. Make sure they understand that you need a loss report for insurance purposes, otherwise you could spend hours in the station as the police fill out a crime sheet, which is no use either to you or them.

Offences to avoid

Sandwiched as it is between opium growing areas in Burma and Laos and the major Southeast Asian distribution point, Hong Kong, China has a growing **drug** problem. The Chinese are hard on offenders, with dealers and smugglers facing execution, and users forced into rehabilitiation. Even so, heroin use has become fairly widespread in the south, particularly in depressed rural areas, and ecstasy is used in clubs and discos – which explains the periodic police raids on these places. In the past, the police have turned a blind eye to foreigners with drugs, as long as no Chinese are involved, but you don't want to test this out. On the official UN anti-drugs day in 2001 and 2002, China held mass executions of convicted drug offenders.

Visitors are not likely to be accused of **political crimes**, but foreign residents, including teachers or students, may find themselves expelled from the country for talking about politics or religion. The Chinese they talk to will be treated less leniently. In Tibet, and at sensitive border areas, censorship is taken much more seriously; **photographing** military installations (which can include major road bridges), instances of police brutality or gulags is not a good idea.

Sexual attitudes and behaviour

Women travellers usually find incidences of **sexual harassment** much less of a problem than in other Asian countries. Chinese men are, on the whole, deferential and respectful. A much more likely complaint is being ignored, as the Chinese will generally assume that any man accompanying a woman will be doing all the talking. White women may get some hassles, however, in Dongbei, where Chinese men may take you for a Russian prostitute, and in Muslim Xinjiang. Women on their own visiting remote temples or sights definitely need to be on their guard – don't assume that all monks and caretakers have impeccable morals. As ever, it pays to be aware of how local women dress and behave accordingly: miniskirts and heels may be fine in the cosmopolitan cities, but fashions are much more conservative in the countryside.

Prostitution, though still illegal and harshly punished, has made a big comeback – witness all the new "hairdressers", saunas and massage parlours, every one of them a brothel. Single foreign men are likely to be approached inside hotels; it's common practice for prostitutes to phone around hotel rooms at all hours of the night. Bear in mind that China is hardly Thailand – consequences may be dire if you are caught – and that AIDS is on the increase.

Homosexuality is officially regarded as a foreign eccentricity, and gay sexual activities are technically illegal, though increasingly tolerated. Gay Chinese men often approach foreigners, partly because they are much less likely to shop them to the police.

Cultural hints

Some of the culture shock which afflicts foreign visitors to China comes from false expectations, engendered through travel in other parts of Asia. The Chinese are not a "mellow" people. Profoundly irreligious, they are neither particularly spiritual nor gentle, nor are they deferential to strangers. However, many of the irritations experienced by foreigners – the sniggers and the unhelpful service – can almost invariably be put down to nervousness and the formidable language barrier, rather than hostility. But however abused you may feel, remember that foreigners are still treated far better in China than are the Chinese themselves.

Communication between foreigners and locals is never a problem once you get beyond the language barrier. Visitors who speak Chinese will encounter an endless series of delighted and amazed interlocutors wherever they go, invariably asking about their age and marital status before anything else. Even if you don't speak Chinese, you will regularly run into locals eager to practise their English.

If such encounters lead to an invitation to someone's home, a **gift** might well be expected, though people will not open it in front of you, nor will they express profuse gratitude for it. The Chinese way to express gratitude is through reciprocal actions rather than words. Indeed, elaborate protestations of thanks can be taken as an attempt to avoid obligation. If you are lucky enough to be asked out to a restaurant, you will discover that **restaurant bills** are not shared out between the guests but instead people will go to great lengths to claim the honour of paying the whole bill by themselves. Normally that honour will fall to the person perceived as the most senior, and as a foreigner dining with Chinese you should make some effort to stake your claim, though it is probable that someone else will grab the bill before you do. Attempting to pay a "share" of the bill may cause serious embarrassment.

Another factor that foreign tourists need to note is that the Chinese have almost no concept of **privacy**. People will stare at each other from point-blank range and pluck letters or books out of others' hands for close inspection. Even toilets are built with partitions so low that you can chat with your neighbour while squatting. All leisure activities including visits to natural beauty spots or holy relics are done in large noisy groups and the desire of some Western tourists to be "left alone" is variously interpreted by locals as eccentric, arrogant or even sinister.

With privacy an almost unknown luxury, exotic foreigners inevitably become targets for **blatant curiosity**. People stare and point, voices on the street shout out "helloooo" twenty times a day, or – in rural areas – people even run up and jostle for a better look, exclaiming loudly to each other, *laowai, laowai* ("foreigner"). This is not intended to be aggressive or insulting, though the culminative effects of such treatment can be very alienating. One way to render yourself human again is to address the onlookers in Chinese, if you can. Otherwise, perhaps you should just be grateful that people are showing an interest in you.

Various other forms of behaviour perceived as antisocial in the West are considered perfectly normal in China. Take the widespread habit of **spitting**, for example, which can be observed in buses, trains, restaurants and even inside people's homes. Outside the company of urban sophisticates, it would not occur to people that there was anything disrespectful in delivering a powerful spit while in conversation with a stranger. **Smoking**, likewise, is almost universal among men and any attempt to stop others from lighting up is met with incomprehension. As in many countries, handing out cigarettes is a basic way of establishing goodwill and non-smokers should be apologetic about turning down offered cigarettes.

Although China would not normally be described as a liberal country, these days restraints on public behaviour are disappearing remarkably fast. **Skimpy clothing** in summer is quite normal in all urban areas, particularly among women (less so in the countryside), and even in potentially sensitive Muslim areas, such as the far west, many Han Chinese girls insist on wearing miniskirts and see-through blouses. Although Chinese men commonly wear short trousers and expose their midriffs in hot weather, Western men who do the same should note that the bizarre sight of hairy flesh in public – chest or legs – will instantly become the focus of giggly gossip. The generally relaxed approach to clothing applies equally when visiting temples, though in **mosques** men and women alike should cover their bodies above the wrists and ankles. As for beachwear, bikinis and briefs are in, but nudity has yet to make its debut.

Skimpy clothing is one thing, but **scruffy clothing** is quite another. If you want to earn the respect of the Chinese – useful for things like getting served in a restaurant or checking into a hotel – you need to make some effort with your appearance. While the average Chinese peasant might reasonably be expected to have wild hair and wear dirty clothes, for a rich foreigner to do so is likely to arouse a degree of contempt. Another good way to ease your progress is to have a name or business card to flash around – even better if you can include your name in Chinese characters on it.

Shaking hands is not a Chinese tradition, though it is now fairly common between men. Bodily contact in the form of embraces or back-slapping can be observed between same-sex friends, and these days, in cities, a boy and a girl can walk round arm-in-arm and even kiss without raising an eyebrow. **Voice level** in China seems to be pitched several decibels louder than in most other countries, though this should not necessarily be interpreted as a sign of belligerence.

Work and study

There are increasing opportunities to work or study in China. Many foreign workers are employed as English-language teachers, and most universities and many private colleges now have a few foreign teachers.

It's worth noting that except in Shanghai, Hong Kong and Macau, foreigners are technically allowed to **reside** only in certain areas. Housing rents in these districts are expensive, usually at least US$2000 a month. Increasingly, many foreigners live with locals and in Chinese neighbourhoods, though it's not strictly legal. Officially, you're the guest of the landlord, and it can be worth registering with the PSB as such.

Useful organizations and resources

Chinatefl Ⓦwww.chinatefl.com. Gives a good overview of English-teaching opportunties in the Chinese public sector.
Council on International Educational Exchange Ⓦwww.ciee.org. Exchange programmes for US students of Mandarin or Chinese studies, with placements in Beijing, Nanjing or Shanghai.
Earthwatch Ⓦwww.earthwatch.org. An organization which runs environmental projects overseas; volunteers who wish to participate need to contribute funds to the project – a ten-day project in China, for example, requires about £1000 – as well as pay for their own flights and transport to the site.
VSO (Voluntary Service Overseas) UK Ⓣ020/8780 7200, Ⓦwww.vso.org.uk. Highly respected charity that sends qualified professionals out to developing countries – China among them – to work on projects. Remuneration is paid at local rates.
Worldteach Ⓦwww.worldteach.org. US-based organization enabling individuals to work as voluteer teachers in China and other developing countries.
Zhaopin Ⓦwww.zhaopin.com. A huge jobs site, in Chinese and English.

The education sector

There are schemes in operation to place **foreign teachers** in Chinese educational institutions – contact your nearest Chinese embassy (see p.22 for addresses) for details, or check the list of organizations given above. Some employers ask for a TEFL qualification, though a degree, or simply the ability to speak the language as a native, is usually enough.

Teaching at a **university**, you'll earn about ¥1500 a month, more than a Chinese worker earns, but not enough to allow you to put any aside. The pay is bolstered by on-campus accommodation – a room in a foreigners' dormitory, usually without a phone. Contracts are generally for one year. Foreign university teachers have a workload of between ten and twenty hours a week – a lot more than their Chinese counterparts have to do. Most teachers find their students keen, hard-working, curious and obedient, and report that it was the contact with them that made the experience worthwhile. That said, avoid talking about religion or politics in the classroom as this can get you into trouble. You'll earn more – up to ¥150 per hour – in a **private school** in Beijing or Shanghai, though be aware of the risk of being ripped off by a commercial agency. For teaching vacancies, look in the expat magazines or on websites such as Ⓦwww.chinatefl.com, or approach the universities directly.

Universities welcome Western **students** for the extra revenue they bring. Courses cost about US$3500 a year, or US$1000 a semester. Accommodation costs around US$10 a day. Most courses are in the Chinese language, but it's possible to study just about anything. Be aware, however, that if you want to study acupuncture, martial arts or Chinese medicine, courses run in the West are often better. Write to the embassy for a list of universities, then contact the colleges themselves, but it's best not to sign up for a course until you've visited the campus and be wary of paying up front, as you won't get a refund.

Commercial opportunities

There are plenty of other **white-collar jobs** available for foreigners in mainland China, mostly with foreign firms, though some facility with Chinese is usually required; it's best to turn up in Beijing and Shanghai and trawl around offices or through expat magazines. The job market in Hong Kong is tighter, and specialist skills are usually required if you're going to land employment there; for more information, check the *Rough Guide to Hong Kong and Macau*.

China's opening, vast markets and recent WTO membership present a wealth of **business opportunities**, usually in joint-venture operations where the Chinese have a controlling interest. However, anyone wanting to do business in China is advised to do some thorough research. The difficulties are formidable – red tape and corrupt and shady business practices abound. Remember that the Chinese do business on the basis of mutual trust and personal connection and pay much less attention to contractual terms or legislation. Copyright and trademark laws are often ignored. You'll need to cultivate the virtues of patience and bloody mindedness, and develop your *guanxi* – connections – assiduously.

Travellers with disabilities

Mainland China makes few provisions for disabled people. With the country undergoing an economic boom, many cities resemble building sites at present, with uneven, obstacle-strewn paving, intense crowds and vehicle traffic, and few access ramps. Public transport is also generally inaccessible to wheelchair users, though some airlines, as well as a few of the upmarket hotels in Beijing, Shanghai, Guangzhou and even Ürümqi, have experience in assisting disabled visitors; in particular, the *Holiday Inn* and *Hilton* chains often have rooms designed for wheelchair users.

Hong Kong is about the only place in China where widespread provision is made for disabled travellers, as detailed in the Hong Kong Tourist Association's excellent free booklet, *Hong Kong Access Guide for Disabled Visitors*. **Macau**, too, has some facilities, though they're more limited.

Given the situation in most of China, it may be worth considering an **organized tour** – the contacts given below will be able to help you arrange this or assist you in researching your own trip. If you want to be more independent, it's important to become an authority on where you must be self-reliant and where you may expect help, especially regarding transport and accommodation. Make sure you take spares of any specialist clothing or equipment, extra supplies of drugs (carried with you if you fly), and a prescription including the generic name – in English and Chinese characters – in case of emergency. If there's an association representing people with your disability, contact them early on in the planning process.

Contacts for travellers with disabilities

UK and Ireland

Irish Wheelchair Association Blackheath Drive, Clontarf, Dublin 3 ⓣ01/818 6400, ⓕ833 3873, ⓦwww.iwa.ie. Useful information provided about travelling abroad with a wheelchair.

Tripscope Alexandra House, Albany Rd, Brentford, Middlesex TW8 0NE ⓣ08457/585641, ⓕ020/8580 7021, ⓦwww.tripscope.org. Advice on transport for those with a mobility problem.

US and Canada

Access-Able Ⓦwww.access-able.com. Online resource for travellers with disabilities.
Directions Unlimited 123 Green Lane, Bedford Hills, NY 10507 Ⓣ1-800/533-5343 or 914/241-1700. Travel agency specializing in bookings for people with disabilities.
Disability Travel Ⓦwww.disabiltytravel.com. Arranges all aspects of travel for the mobility-impaired, including tours to major sights in China.
Mobility International USA 451 Broadway, Eugene, OR 97401 Ⓣ541/343-1284, Ⓕ343-6812, Ⓦwww.miusa.org. Information and referral services, access guides, tours and exchange programmes. Annual membership $35 (includes quarterly newsletter).
Society for the Advancement of Travelers with Handicaps (SATH) 347 5th Ave, New York, NY 10016 Ⓣ212/447-7284, Ⓦwww.sath.org. Non-profit educational organization that has actively represented travelers with disabilities since 1976.

Australia and New Zealand

ACROD (Australian Council for Rehabilitation of the Disabled) PO Box 60, Curtin ACT 2605; Suite 103, 1st floor, 1–5 Commercial Rd, Kings Grove 2208; Ⓣ02/6282 4333, TTY Ⓣ02/6282 4333, Ⓕ6281 3488, Ⓦwww.acrod.org.au. Provides lists of travel agencies and tour operators for people with disabilities.
Disabled Persons Assembly 4/173–175 Victoria St, Wellington, New Zealand Ⓣ04/801 9100 (also TTY), Ⓕ801 9565, Ⓦwww.dpa.org.nz. Resource centre with lists of travel agencies and tour operators for people with disabilities.

Directory

Addresses Chinese street names often indicate the section of the street concerned, usually by adding the cardinal direction – *bei*, *nan*, *xi* or *dong* for north, south, west and east, respectively, or sometimes *zhong* to indicate a central stretch. *Jie* means street; *da* before it simply means big. Thus Jiefang Bei Dajie literally refers to the north section of Liberation Big Street. While street names aren't hard to figure out, the numbering of premises along streets is so random in most Chinese cities that it's little help in finding the address. Note that within buildings, street level is the "First Floor", the next storey is the "Second Floor", and so on.

Admission charges Virtually all tourist sights attract some kind of admission charge, often no more than a few yuan. Usually there is a special student price which you can qualify for if you have a student card.

Airport departure tax Currently ¥50 for internal flights, and ¥90 if you're leaving the country.

CDs, VCDs, and DVDs Just about every market and bookstore in China has a range of music CDs of everything from Beijing punk to Louis Armstrong, Vivaldi and Bob Dylan, plus VCDs and DVDs of martial art movies (often subtitled – check on the back), Hollywood blockbusters, instructional tai ji or language courses, and computer software. While extremely cheap at ¥2–15, note that most films, foreign music and software are pirated (the discs may be confiscated at customs when you get home). Note also that Chinese DVDs may be region-coded for Asia, so check the label and whether your player at home will handle them. There are no such problems with CDs or VCDs.

Cigarettes Most foreign brands are available for a fraction of the price they cost in the West, though look out for fakes. The cheaper, Chinese brands have some great packaging and names, but tend to be rough.

Contraceptives Condoms are easy to get

hold of, with imported brands available in all the big cities.

Electricity The current is 220V on the mainland (this is also the voltage used in most of Macau), and 200V in Hong Kong. Plugs come in a wide range with either two or three differently shaped prongs, so a travel conversion plug can be useful, as is a flashlight, given the erratic power supply.

Laundry Most tourist hotels have a laundry service, though it's usually not cheap. Clothes will be returned the following day.

Left luggage Some hotels will store luggage, and there are always guarded, moderately secure luggage offices at train and bus stations (sometimes open only from dawn to dusk, however) where you can leave your possessions for a few kuai.

Photography Photography is a popular pastime among the Chinese, and all big mainland towns and cities have plenty of places to buy and process 35mm film. In Hong Kong there's likely to be at least as big a range as wherever you've come from; elsewhere, colour print stock is the most widely available. Mainland Chinese brands cost about ¥10 for 36 exposures, scarcer Western varieties are around ¥20. Slide film costs about ¥60 a roll. Processing is very variable for prints – sometimes good, often mediocre – and costs about ¥15 per roll. Camera batteries are fairly easy to obtain in big city department stores. Hong Kong has every imaginable type, but it's best to bring a supply with you. Many photo stores in Hong Kong, Macau and the mainland can download images from a digital camera onto disc.

Tampons Tampons can be hard to find, but good sanitary towels are widely available in supermarkets and department stores, and are reasonably cheap.

Things to take Unless you're a big fan of nineteenth-century literature – just about all that is available in English translation – take a few meaty books for the long train rides. Coins and stamps from your country are a good idea – they will cause much excitement and curiosity and make good small presents. Another aid to bridging the language gap is a few photos of your family and friends, even where you live. China is rarely a quiet place, and for the sake of your sanity as well as comfort, earplugs are a good idea, especially if you're contemplating long bus journeys. It's also advisable to take a set of your own chopsticks, for hygiene reasons. Also worth taking are: a universal plug adaptor and universal sink plug; a flashlight; a multipurpose penknife; a needle and thread; and a first-aid kit (see p.27). If you'll be travelling in the sub-tropical south or at high altitudes, bring high-factor sun block and good-quality sunglasses.

Time China occupies a single time zone, eight hours ahead of GMT, sixteen hours ahead of US Pacific Standard Time, thirteen hours ahead of US Eastern Standard Time and two hours behind Australian Eastern Standard Time.

Tipping Not expected on the mainland, but in Hong Kong you might want to tip in restaurants where they don't already levy a ten-percent service charge.

Toilets Chinese toilets can take a lot of getting used to. Apart from the often disgusting standard of hygiene, the lack of privacy can be very off-putting – squat toilets are separated by a low, thin partition or no partition at all. The public kind are typically awful, though any staffed by an attendant should be fairly clean, and you'll have to pay a few jiao before you enter. Probably the best bet is to find a large hotel and use the toilets in the lobby. Most hotel toilets have a wastepaper basket by the side for toilet paper. Don't put paper down the loo as it blocks the primitive sewage system, and staff will get irate with you.

Guide

Guide

CHAPTER 1

Highlights

✱ **Lüsongyuan Hotel** Characterful places to stay are rare in China, but this cosy and affordable converted courtyard mansion is a welcome exception. See p.89

✱ **Forbidden City** Imperial magnificence on a grand scale and the centre of the Chinese universe for six centuries. See p.99

✱ **Qianmen area** This tangle of chaotic alleys is a brash and earthy shopping zone, one of the last remnants of the old city. See p.102

✱ **Temple of Heaven** The classic Ming-dynasty building. See p.105

✱ **Baiyunguan Si** Still functioning, this Taoist temple is ignored by tour groups but is in its way more rewarding than the flashier religious sites. A must during New Year and on festival days, when it's thronged with worshippers. See p.108

✱ **Summer Palace** Escape the city in this serene and elegant park, dotted with imperial architecture. See p.118

✱ **Hotpot** A northern Chinese classic, a stew of sliced lamb, tofu, cabbage and anything else you fancy, boiled up at your table. Specialist restaurants abound, but *Neng Ren Ju* is one of the best. See p.125

✱ **Great Wall** One of the world's most extraordinary engineering achievements, the old boundary between civilizations. See p.138

1

Beijing and around

The brash modernity of **BEIJING** (the name means "northern capital") comes as a surprise to many visitors. Traversed by freeways (it's the proud owner of more than a hundred flyovers) and spiked with high-rises, this vivid metropolis is China at its most dynamic. For the last thousand years, the drama of China's **imperial history** was played out here, with the emperor sitting enthroned at the centre of the Chinese universe, and though today the city is a very different one, it remains spiritually and politically the heart of the country. Between the swathes of concrete and glass, you'll find some of the lushest temples, and certainly the grandest remnants of the Imperial Age. Unexpectedly, some of the country's most pleasant scenic spots lie within the scope of a day-trip, and, just to the north of the city, is one of China's most famous sights, the old boundary line between civilizations, the **Great Wall**.

First impressions of Beijing are of an almost inhuman vastness, conveyed by the sprawl of identical apartment buildings in which most of the city's population of twelve million are housed, and the eight-lane freeways that slice it up. It's an impression that's reinforced on closer acquaintance, from the magnificent **Forbidden City**, with its stunning wealth of treasures, the concrete desert of **Tian'anmen Square** and the gargantuan buildings of the modern executive around it, to the rank after rank of new office complexes that line its mammoth roads. Outside the centre, the scale becomes more manageable, with parks, narrow alleyways and ancient sites such as the **Yonghe Gong**, **Observatory** and, most magnificent of all, the **Temple of Heaven**, offering respite from the city's oppressive orderliness and rampant reconstruction. In the suburbs beyond, the two **Summer Palaces** and the **Western Hills** have been favoured retreats since imperial times.

Beijing is an invaders' city, the capital of oppressive foreign dynasties – the Manchu and the Mongols – and of a dynasty with a foreign ideology – the Communists. As such, it has assimilated a lot of outside influence, and today it is perhaps the most cosmopolitan part of China, with an international flavour reflecting its position as the capital of a major commercial power. As the front line of China's grapple with **modernity** it is being ripped up and rebuilt at a furious pace – attested by the cranes that skewer the skyline and the white character *chai* ("demolish") painted on old buildings. Students in the latest baggy fashions while away their time in Internet cafés and *McDonald's*, drop outs spike their hair and mosh in punk clubs, businessmen are never without their laptops and schoolkids carry mobile phones in their lunchboxes. Red-light districts and gay bars are appearing as the city hits its own sexual revolution. Rising incomes have led not just to a consumer-capitalist society

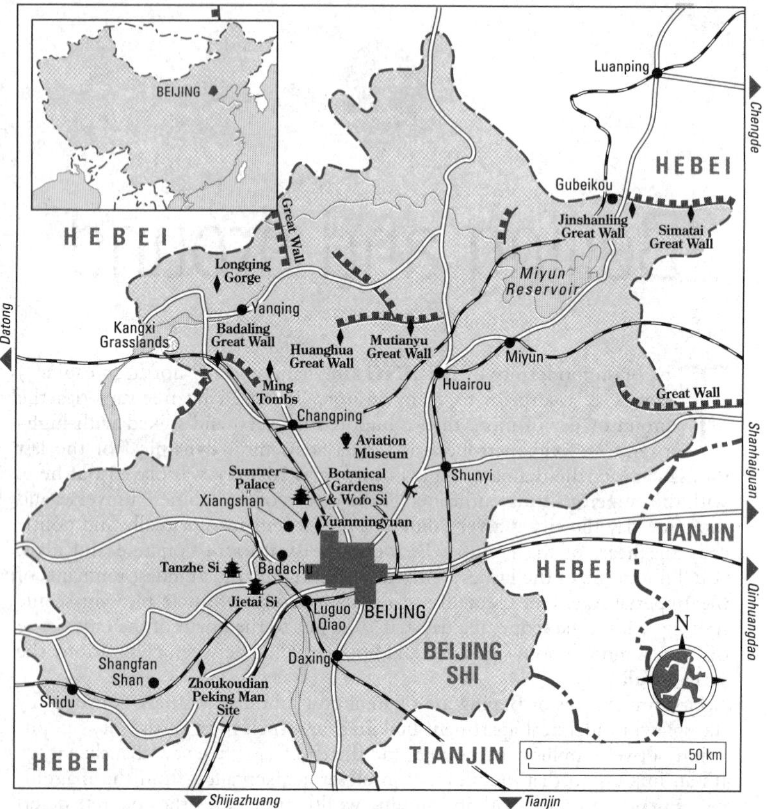

Westerners will feel very familiar with, but also to a revival of older **Chinese culture** – witness the re-emergence of the teahouse as a genteel meeting place and the interest in imperial cuisine. In the evening you'll see large groups of the older generation performing the *yangkou* (loyalty dance), Chairman Mao's favourite dance universally learned a few decades ago, and in the *hutongs*, the city's twisted grey stone alleyways, men sit with their birds and pipes as they always have done.

Beijing is a city that almost everyone enjoys. For new arrivals it provides a gentle introduction to the country and for travellers who've been roughing it round outback China, the creature comforts on offer are a delight. It's home to a huge expat population, and it's quite possible to spend years here eating Western food, dancing to Western music, and socializing with like-minded foreigners. Beijing is essentially a private city, and one whose surface is difficult to penetrate; sometimes it seems to have the superficiality of a theme park. Certainly there is something mundane about the way tourist groups are efficiently shunted around, plugged from hotel to sight, with little contact with everyday reality. To get deeper into the city, wander what's left of the labyrinthine *hutongs*, "fine and numerous as the hairs of a cow" (as one Chinese guidebook puts it), and check out the little antique markets, the residential shopping districts, the smaller, quirkier sights, and the parks, some of the best in China, where you'll see Beijingers performing *tai ji* and hear birdsong – just – over the hum of traffic. Take advantage, too, of the city's burgeoning nightlife and see just how far the Chinese have gone down the road of what used to be called spiritual pollution.

If the Party had any control over it, no doubt Beijing would have the best **climate** of any Chinese city; as it is, it has one of the worst. The best time to visit is in autumn, between September and October, when it's dry and clement. In winter it gets very cold, down to minus 20°C, and the mean winds that whip off the Mongolian plains feel like they're freezing your ears off. Summer (June–August) is muggy and hot, up to 30°C, and the short spring (April & May) is dry but windy.

Getting to Beijing is no problem. As the centre of China's **transport** network you'll probably wind up here sooner or later, whether you want to or not, and to avoid the capital seems wilfully perverse. On a purely practical level, it's a good place to stock up on visas for the rest of Asia, and to arrange transport out of the country – most romantically, on the Trans-Siberian or Trans-Mongolian trains. To take in its superb sights requires a week, by which time you may well be ready to move on to China proper. Beijing is a fun place but, make no mistake, it in no way typifies the rest of the nation.

Some history

It was in Tian'anmen, on October 1, 1949, that Chairman Mao Zedong hoisted the red flag to proclaim officially the **foundation of the People's Republic**. He told the crowds (the square could then hold only 500,000) that the Chinese had at last stood up, and defined liberation as the final culmination of a 150-year fight against foreign exploitation.

The claim, perhaps, was modest. Beijing's **recorded history** goes back a little over three millennia to beginnings as a trading centre for Mongols, Koreans and local Chinese tribes. Its predominance, however, dates to the mid-thirteenth century, and the formation of **Mongol China** under Genghis and later **Kublai Khan**. It was Kublai who took control of the city in 1264, and who properly established it as a capital, replacing the earlier power centres of Luoyang and Xi'an. Marco Polo visited him here, working for a while in the city, and was clearly impressed with the level of sophistication:

> So great a number of houses and of people, no man could tell the number . . . I believe there is no place in the world to which so many merchants come, and dearer things, and of greater value and more strange, come into this town from all sides than to any city in the world . . .

The **wealth** came from the city's position at the start of the Silk Road and Polo described "over a thousand carts loaded with silk" arriving "almost each day", ready for the journey west out of China. And it set a precedent in terms of style and grandeur for the Khans, later known as emperors, with Kublai building himself a palace of astonishing proportions, walled on all sides and approached by great marble stairways.

With the accession of the **Ming dynasty**, who defeated the Mongols in 1368, the capital temporarily shifted to present-day Nanjing, but Yongle, the second Ming emperor, returned, building around him prototypes of the city's two greatest **monuments** – the Imperial Palace and Temple of Heaven. It was in Yongle's reign, too, that the basic **city plan** took shape, rigidly symmetrical, extending in squares and rectangles from the palace and inner-city grid to the suburbs, much as it is today.

Subsequent, post-Ming history is dominated by the rise and eventual collapse of the Manchus – the **Qing dynasty**, northerners who ruled China from Beijing from 1644 to the beginning of the twentieth century. The capital was at its most prosperous in the first half of the eighteenth century, the period in which the Qing constructed the legendary **Summer Palace** – the world's most extraordinary royal garden, with two hundred pavilions, temples and palaces, and immense artificial lakes and hills – to the north of the city. With the central Imperial Palace, this was the focus of endowment and the symbol of Chinese wealth and power. However, in 1860, the **Opium Wars** brought British and French troops to the walls of the capital, and the Summer Palace was first looted and then burned by the British, more or less entirely to the ground.

While the imperial court lived apart, within what was essentially a separate walled city, conditions for the civilian population, in the capital's suburbs, were starkly different. Kang Youwei, a Cantonese visiting in 1895, described this dual world:

> **No matter where you look, the place is covered with beggars. The homeless and the old, the crippled and the sick with no one to care for them, fall dead on the roads. This happens every day. And the coaches of the great officials rumble past them continuously.**

The indifference, rooted according to Kang in officials throughout the city, spread from the top down. From 1884, using funds meant for the modernization of the nation's navy, the empress Dowager Cixi had begun building a new Summer Palace of her own. The empress's project was really the last grand gesture of **imperial architecture** and patronage – and like its model was also badly burned by foreign troops, in another outbreak of the Opium War in 1900. By this time, with successive waves of occupation by foreign troops, the empire and the imperial capital were near collapse. The **Manchus abdicated** in 1911, leaving the Northern Capital to be ruled by warlords. In 1928 it came under the military dictatorship of Chiang Kaishek's **Guomindang**, being seized by the **Japanese** in 1939, and at the end of **World War II** the city was controlled by an alliance of Guomindang troops and American marines.

The **Communists** took Beijing in January 1949, nine months before Chiang Kaishek's flight to Taiwan assured final victory. The **rebuilding of the capital**, and the erasing of symbols of the previous regimes, was an early priority. The city that Mao Zedong inherited for the Chinese people was in most ways primitive. Imperial laws had banned the building of houses higher than the official buildings and palaces, so virtually nothing was more than one storey high. The roads, although straight and uniform, were narrow and congested, and there was scarcely any industry. The new plans aimed to reverse all except the city's sense of ordered planning, with Tian'anmen Square at its heart – and initially, through the early 1950s, their inspiration was Soviet, with an emphasis on heavy industry and a series of poor-quality high-rise housing programmes.

In the zest to be free from the past and create a modern, people's capital, much of **Old Peking was destroyed**, or co-opted: the Temple of Cultivated Wisdom became a wire factory and the Temple of the God of Fire produced electric lightbulbs. In the 1940s there were eight thousand temples and monuments in the city; by the 1960s there were only around a hundred and fifty.

Even the city walls and gates, relics mostly of the Ming era, were pulled down and their place taken by ring roads and avenues.

Much of the city's **contemporary planning policy** was disastrous, creating more problems than it solved. Most of the traditional courtyard houses which were seen to encourage individualism were destroyed. In their place went anonymous concrete buildings, often with inadequate sanitation and little running water. In 1969, when massive restoration was needed above ground, Mao instead launched a campaign to build a network of subterranean tunnels as shelter in case of war. Millions of man-hours went into constructing a useless labyrinth, built by hand, that would be no defence against modern bombs and served only to lower the city's water table. After the destruction of all the capital's dogs in 1950, it was the turn of sparrows in 1956. A measure designed to preserve grain, its only effect was to lead to an increase in the insect population. To combat this, all the grass was pulled up, which in turn led to dust storms in the windy winter months.

Today, massive urban regeneration projects are under way to prepare the city for the **Olympic games** in 2008. Attempts have been made to battle pollution, and factories that can't modernize have been closed. Open spaces have been revitalized with a massive tree-planting campaign. The filthy canals are being dredged. Two more ring roads are being built. And to help with problems of overcrowding, there are ambitious plans for a series of satellite cities. But the city is also fast losing what character it has; in the mania for development, gleaming but shoddily built towers are popping up like mushrooms after rain. Now the city's main problems are the pressure of migration and traffic – car ownership has rocketed, contributing to the appalling air quality, and the streets are nearing gridlock.

Orientation, arrival and information

There's no doubt that Beijing's initial culture shock owes much to the artificiality of the city's **layout**. The main streets are huge, wide and dead straight, aligned either east–west or north–south, and extend in a series of widening rectangles across the whole thirty square kilometres of the inner capital.

The pivot of the ancient city was a north–south road that led from the entrance of the Forbidden City to the walls. This remains today as **Qianmen Dajie**, though the main axis has shifted to the east–west road that divides Tian'anmen Square and the Forbidden City, and which changes its name, like all major boulevards, every few kilometres along its length. It's generally referred to as **Chang'an Jie**.

Few traces of the old city remain except in the **street names**, which look bewilderingly complex but are not hard to figure out once you realize that they are compounds of a name, plus a direction – *bei*, *nan*, *xi*, *dong* and *zhong* (north, south, west, east and middle) – and the words for inside and outside – *nei* and *wai* – which indicate the street's position in relation to the old city walls which enclosed the centre. Central streets often also contain the word *men* (gate), which indicates that they once had a gate in the wall along their length.

The **three ring roads**, freeways arranged in concentric rectangles centring on the Forbidden City, are rapid-access corridors. The second and third, Erhuan Lu and Sanhuan Lu, are the most useful, cutting down on journey times but extending the distance travelled and therefore much liked by taxi drivers. While most of the sights are in the city centre, most of the modern

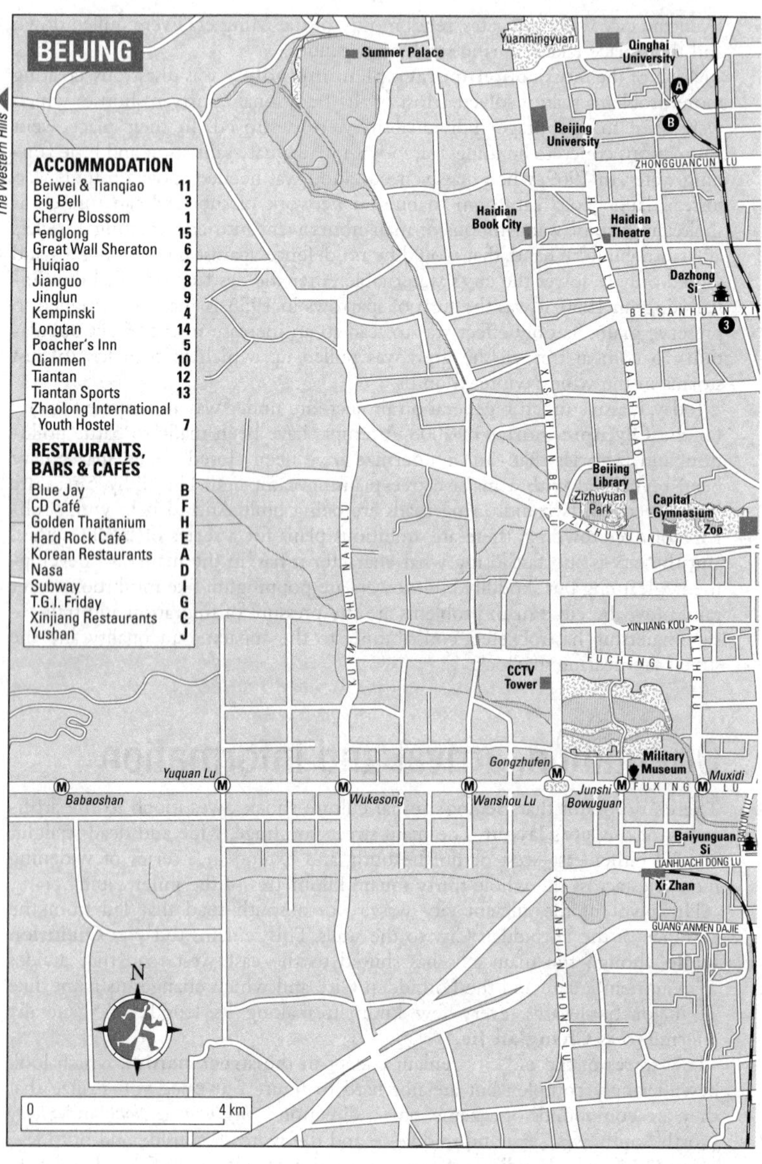

buildings – hotels, restaurants, shopping centres and flashy office blocks – are along the ring roads.

You'll soon become familiar with the experience of barrelling along a freeway in a bus or a taxi while identical blocks flicker past, not knowing which direction you're travelling in, let alone where you are. To get some sense of orientation, take fast mental notes on the more obvious and imposing landmarks:

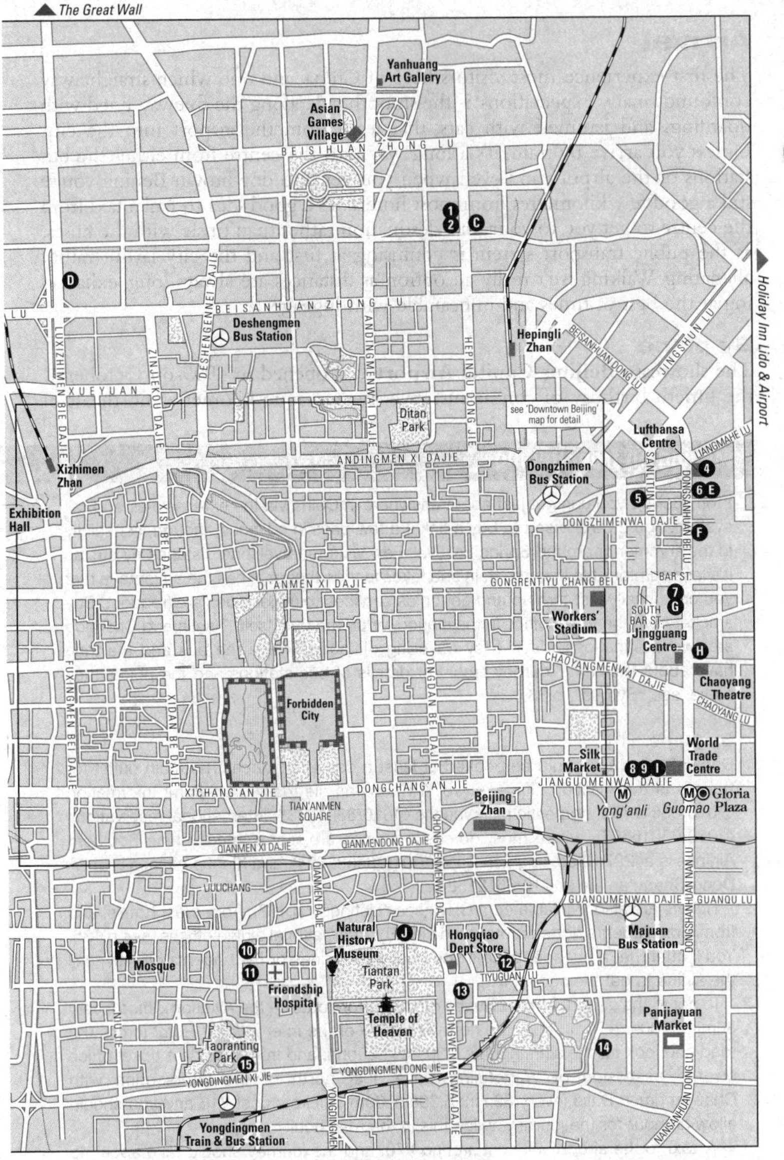

the Great Hall of the People in Tian'anmen Square; the seventeen-storey *Beijing Hotel* on Dongchang'an Jie; and, farther east on the same road, the Friendship Store and World Trade Centre. At the western intersection of the second ring road and Chang'an Jie, the astronomical instruments on top of the old observatory stand out for their oddness, as does the white dagoba in Beihai Park, just north and west of the Forbidden City.

Arrival

The first experience most visitors have of China, and one which straightaway confounds many expectations, is the smooth ride along the freeway, lined with hoardings and jammed with cars, that leads from the airport into the city. Unless you arrive by train, it's a long way into the centre from either the bus stations or the airport, and even when you get into downtown Beijing you're still a good few kilometres from most hotels. It's a good idea to hail a taxi from the centre to get you to your final destination rather than tussle with the buses, as the public transport system is confusing at first and the city layout rather alienating. Walking isn't really an option as distances are always long, exhausting at the best of times and unbearable with luggage.

By plane

The showcase **Beijing Capital Airport** was opened in 1999 on October 1, the fiftieth birthday of communist rule. Twenty-nine kilometres northeast of

Moving on from Beijing

From Beijing you can get just about anywhere in China via the extensive air and rail system. You'd be advised to buy a ticket a few days in advance, though, especially in the summer or around Spring Festival. Few visitors travel long distance by **bus** as it's less comfortable than the train and takes longer, though it has the advantage that you can usually just turn up and get on as services to major cities are frequent. Buy a ticket from the ticket office in the station, or on the bus itself. Tianjin and Chengde are two destinations within easy travelling distance, where the bus and the train have about the same journey time. For details of bus stations and the points they serve, see "By bus", p.83.

By plane

Domestic **flights** should be booked at least a day in advance. The main outlet for **tickets** is the Aviation Office, at 15 Xi Chang'an Jie (daily 7am–8pm; information ⓣ010/66017755, domestic reservations ⓣ010/66013336, international reservations ⓣ010/66016667), where most domestic airlines are represented. China Southern Airlines is at 227 Chaoyangmen Dajie (ⓣ010/65533624), and Xinhua Airlines is at 2A Dong Chang'an Jie (ⓣ010/65121587).

Tickets are also available from CITS (see "Listings", p.137), from most hotels, and from airline agents dotted around the city. For international airline offices, see p.135. You'll often get a cheaper price if you deal with airlines or their agents directly; call the airline to get their agent list.

To get to the airport, **airport buses** run daily from outside the Aviation Office (every 30min; 5.30am–7pm), from the northwest side of the *International Hotel* (cross the road and look for the sign; hourly; 6.30am–4.30pm), and from outside a ticket office on the east side of Wangfujing Dajie, just north of the intersection with Chaoyangmen Dajie (every 30min; 5.30am–6pm). Tickets cost ¥16 and you should allow an hour for the journey, twice this in the rush hour.

A **taxi** to the airport will cost around ¥70, and the journey should take about 45 minutes, at least half an hour longer in rush hour. You'll be expected to pay the ¥15 expressway toll fare. The information desk at the airport is open 24 hours for enquiries (ⓣ010/64563604).

By domestic train

Trains depart from either **Xi Zhan**, if you're heading south or west, for example to Chengdu or Xi'an, or **Beijing Zhan**, if you're heading north or east, for example to Shanghai or Harbin. You can buy **tickets** with an added surcharge of around ¥40

Beijing: Arrival

Beijing	北京	***běijing***
Beijing Capital Airport	北京首都机场	*běijīng shǒudū jīchǎng*
Bus stations		
Deshengmen	德胜门公共汽车站	*déshèngmén gōnggòng qìchēzhàn*
Dongzhimen	东直门公共汽车站	*dōngzhímén gōnggòng qìchēzhàn*
Haihutun	海户屯公共汽车站	*hǎihùtún gōnggòng qìchēzhàn*
Train stations		
Beijing Zhan	北京站	*bēijīng zhàn*
Xi Zhan	西站	*xī zhàn*
Xizhimen Zhan	西直门站	*xīzhímén zhàn*
Yongdingmen Zhan	永定门站	*yǒngdìngmén zhàn*

from large hotels or CITS, though it's little hassle to do it yourself direct. Tickets for busy routes should be booked at least a day in advance, and can be booked up to four days ahead. Buy tickets at Beijing Zhan; the Foreigners' Ticket Booking Office is at the back of the station, on the left side as you enter, and is signposted in English. It's open daily 5.30–7.30am, 8am–6.30pm and 7–11pm. There's a timetable in English on the wall. You can also get tickets from separate ticket outlets – as these are little known, there are never any queues. There's one on the first floor in the Wangfujing Department Store at 225 Wangfujing Dajie (daily 9–11am & 1–4pm) and another in the Air China ticket office in the China World Trade Centre at 1 Jianguomenwai Dajie (daily 8am–6pm). For train information (in Chinese only) phone ⓣ010/65129525.

Trans-Siberian and Trans-Mongolian trains

The International Train Booking Office (Mon–Fri 8.30–12am & 1.30–5pm; ⓣ010/65120507) is the best thing about the *International Hotel* at 9 Jianguomenwai Dajie. Here you can buy tickets to Moscow and Ulan Batur with the minimum of fuss. Out of season, few people make the journey, but in summer there may well not be a seat for weeks. Allow yourself a week or two for dealing with embassy bureaucracy. After putting down a ¥100 deposit on the ticket at the booking office, you'll be issued with a reservation slip. Take this with you to the embassy when you apply for visas and the process should be fairly painless. A Russian transit visa, valid for a week, costs around US$50, with a surcharge for certain nationalities (mostly African and South American). Transit visas for Mongolia are valid for one week and cost US$30; tourist visas valid for a month cost US$40.

Chinese train #3 to Moscow via Ulan Batur leaves every Wednesday and takes five and a half days. A bunk in a second-class cabin with four beds – which is perfectly comfortable – costs ¥1602. First class is ¥2306 (four beds) or ¥2786 (two beds). The Russian train #19, which follows the Trans-Siberian route, leaves on Saturdays and takes six days. The cheapest bunk here is ¥1888; first class is ¥3014. A Mongolian train leaves for Ulan Batur every Tuesday and costs ¥606 for one bed in a four-bed berth. Travelling on train #3 is slightly cheaper.

The tour company Monkey Business will organize your trip, if you don't mind paying an extra US$150 for the privilege of having your visas sorted out for you. Their office is in the *Hidden Tree Bar* on Nan Sanlitun Lu (ⓣ010/65916519, ⓦwww.monkeyshrine.com). A second-class ticket costs US$385 (not including visas), for which you also get an info pack and a ride to the station. Their other packages include stopovers in Ulan Batur, Lake Baikal and Irkutsk.

the centre, it serves both international and domestic flights. There are a couple of banks and an ATM on the right as you exit through customs, and commission rates are the same as everywhere else. Get some small change if you're planning to take any buses. The CAAC office sells tickets for onward domestic flights.

An expressway connects the airport to the city and is one of the best and freest-flowing roads in China. Directly in front of the main exit is the **airport bus** stand, from which comfortable, though rather cramped, air-conditioned buses leave regularly (¥16). There are two routes, A and B. **Route A buses** leave every fifteen minutes from 8am until the last flight arrives, and are the most useful to travellers, stopping at the *Hilton*, the Lufthansa Centre, Dongzhimen subway stop, *Swissotel*, and Chaoyangmen subway stop before terminating outside the *International Hotel*, just north of Beijing Zhan, the central train station, where there's a taxi rank and a subway station. **Route B buses** leave every hour, from 9.30am until the last flight, and make stops on the north and western sections of the third ring road, Sanhuan Lu, including the *SAS Royal Hotel*, Asian Games Village, *Friendship Hotel* and Foreign Language University, before terminating at the *Xinxing Hotel*, at the intersection of Chang'an Jie and Xisanhuan Bei Lu, close to the Gongzhufen subway stop.

Taxis from the airport into the city leave from the taxi rank just outside the main entrance, on the left; don't go with the hustlers who approach new arrivals. Make sure your taxi is registered; it should have a red sticker in the window stating the rate per kilometre and an identity card displayed on the dashboard. A trip to the city centre costs around ¥80 and takes about fifty minutes.

By train

Beijing has two main **train stations**. **Beijing Zhan**, the central station, just south of Dongchang'an Jie, is where trains from destinations north and east of Beijing arrive. There are **left-luggage** lockers as well as a main luggage office here (see p.137 for details). From Beijing Zhan the only hotel within walking distance is the uninspiring *International* and, more importantly, the new *International Youth Hostel* behind it. Most arrivals will need to head straight to the **bus terminus**, about 100m east of the station, the **subway stop** at the northwestern edge of the concourse, or to the **taxi rank**, over the road and 50m east. The waiting taxis are supervised by an official with a red armband who makes sure the queue is orderly and that drivers flip their meters on. Don't get a cab from the station concourse, as none of the drivers here will use their meters.

Travellers from the south and west of the capital will arrive at the new west station, **Xi Zhan**, Asia's largest rail terminal at the head of the Beijing–Kowloon rail line. A prestige project, the new station is ten times the size of Beijing Zhan. The left-luggage office is on the second floor, but at ¥5 an hour, it's expensive. Bus #122 runs between the two main stations, or, if you're heading south to the budget hotels, you can take bus #52 to Qianmen and get another bus from there. However, it's probably easier to take a **taxi** from the taxi rank.

Beijing does have more stations, though you are unlikely to arrive at them unless you have come on a suburban train from, for example, the Great Wall at Badaling or Shidu. Beijing North, also known as **Xizhimen Zhan**, is at the northwestern edge of the second ring road, on the subway. Beijing South, or **Yongdingmen Zhan**, is in the south of the city, just inside the third ring road, a short walk from the *Qiaoyuan Hotel*, with a bus terminus outside.

By bus

The **bus system** in Beijing is extensive, but complicated, as there are many terminuses, each one serving buses from only a few destinations. **Dongzhimen**, on the northeast corner of the second ring road, connected by subway, is the largest bus station and handles services from Shenyang and the rest of Dongbei. **Deshengmen**, also called Beijiao, the north station serving Chengde and Datong, is 1km north of the second ring road, on the route of bus #55, which will take you to Xi'anmen Dajie, west of Beihai Park. **Haihutun**, in the south, at the intersection of the third ring road, Nansanhuan Lu, and Yongdingmenwai Dajie, is for buses from Tianjin and cities in southern Hebei. **Private minibuses** are more likely to terminate outside one of the two main train stations.

Information and maps

A large fold-out map of the city is vital. There is a wide variety available at all transport connections and from street vendors, hotels and bookshops. The best map to look out for, labelled in English and Chinese, and with bus routes, sights and hotels marked, is the Beijing Tour Map. In general, the tourist maps, available in large hotels and printed inside tourist magazines, don't go into enough detail. The free map handed out by CITS offices also isn't much use, but it does have good magnified sections showing the shopping areas, with many of the individual shops marked. Fully comprehensive A–Z map books are available from bookshops and street vendors outside Beijing Zhan subway stop, but only in Chinese.

Here, as elsewhere in China, there are no actual tourist information offices but there are a number of English-language publications which will help you get the best out of the city. The *China Daily* (¥0.8), available from the Friendship Store, the Foreign Language Bookstore and the bigger hotels, has a listings section detailing cultural events. The rest of the paper is propaganda written in turgid prose, though the headlines occasionally have an unintentional deadpan humour to them. *Beijing This Month* covers the same ground, with light features aimed at tourists.

Much more useful, though, are the free magazines aimed at the large expat community, which contain up-to-date and fairly comprehensive entertainment and restaurant listings. *City Edition* and *Metro* are aimed at the more upmarket sections of the foreign community, but by far the best is the irreverent and informative monthly *That's Beijing* (Ⓦwww.thatsbeijing.com). The giant listings section includes club nights, art happenings and the more underground gigs, with addresses written in *pinyin* and Chinese. You can pick up copies of all three magazines in most bars and other expat hangouts. Anyone coming here to live should get hold of the fat *Beijing Guidebook* by Middle Kingdom Press, which includes information on finding housing and doing business.

Bogus art students

Spend any time in tourist areas of the capital and you will inevitably be approached by youths claiming to be art students. They aren't, of course; mostly they are ex-students from teacher training schools putting their language skills to dubious use. Their aim is to get you to visit a bogus art gallery, and pay ridiculous prices for prints purporting to be paintings, and they'll go to huge lengths to befriend foreigners. They're not aggressive though, and they can be useful if you need directions.

City transport

The scale of the city militates against taking bus #11 – Chinese slang for walking – almost anywhere, and most of the main streets are so straight that going by foot soon gets tedious. The **public transport system** is extensive but somewhat over-subscribed; most visitors tire of the heaving buses pretty quickly and take rather more taxis than they'd planned. The **metro** is speedy but not extensive. **Cycling** is a good alternative, though, with plenty of rental outlets in the city.

Buses

Even though every one of the city's 200-odd **bus and trolleybus services** runs about once a minute, you'll find getting on or off at busy times hard work (rush hours are from 7–9am & 4.30–6pm). Forget about trying to see much of the city from the window, as views tend to be limited to the backs of necks. In

Useful bus routes

Bus routes are indicated by red or blue lines on all good maps; a dot on the line indicates a stop. Next to the stop on the map you'll see tiny characters; that's the stop's name and you need to know it for the conductor to work out your fare. Trying to show the poor man a dot on a map in a swaying, crammed bus is nigh impossible; fortunately, the Beijing Tour Map has stops marked in *pinyin*. The following are some of the most useful services:

Bus #1 and double-decker #1 From Xi Zhan east along the main thoroughfare, Chang'an Jie.

Double-decker #2 From the north end of Qianmen Dajie, north to Dongdan, the Yonghe Gong and the Asian Games Village.

Double-decker #4 From Beijing Zoo to Qianmen via Fuxingmen.

Bus #5 From Deshengmen, on the second ringroad in the northwest of the city, south down the west side of the Forbidden City and Tian'anmen to Qianmen Dajie.

Bus #15 From the zoo down Xidan Dajie past Liulichang ending at the Tianqiao area just west of Yongdingmennei Dajie, close to Tiantan Park.

Bus #17 From Tian'anmen down Qianmen Dajie to the intersection of Yongdingmenwai Dajie and Nansanhuan Zhong Lu, 1km east of the *Jinghua Hotel*.

Bus #20 From Beijing Zhan to Yongdingmen Zhan, a short walk from the *Qiaoyuan Hotel*.

Bus #52 From Xi Zhan east to Lianhuachi Qiao, Xidan Dajie, Tian'anmen Square, then east along Chang'an Jie.

Bus #66 From Yang Qiao – the bridge just west of the *Jinghua Hotel* – to Qianmen.

Trolleybus #103 From Beijing Zhan, north up the east side of the Forbidden City, west along Fuchengmennei Dajie, then north up Sanlihe Lu to the zoo.

Trolleybus #104 From Beijing Zhan to Hepingli train station in the north of the city, via Wangfujing.

Trolleybus #105 From the northwest corner of Tiantan Park to Xidan Dajie, then west to the zoo.

Trolleybus #106 From Yongdingmen Zhan to Tiantan Park and Chongwenmen, then up to Dongzhimennei Dajie.

Bus #300 Circles the third ring road

Bus #332 From Beijing Zoo to Beida (University and the Summer Palace).

Luxury bus #808 From just northwest of Qianmen to the Summer Palace.

winter buses are notable for their distinct aroma, something like garlic and boiled cabbage. The **fare** for ordinary buses depends how far you are going but never exceeds ¥2 and is usually ¥0.5 – watch how the Chinese wrap up a one-fen coin in two two-fen notes to make a little origami package to give the conductor. Less aromatic and a little more comfortable, if slower, are the **minibuses**, which ply the same routes as the buses and charge ¥2 per journey. There are also five comfortable double-decker bus services, costing ¥2 a trip. Services generally run from 5.30am to 11pm everyday, though some are 24-hour. Buses numbered in the 200s only provide night services. Routes are efficiently organized and easy to understand – an important factor, since stops tend to be a good kilometre apart. Buses numbered in the 800s are modern, air-conditioned, and actually quite pleasant, but more expensive, with fares starting at ¥3 and going up to ¥10.

A word of warning – be very wary of **pickpockets** on buses. Skilful thieves target Westerners, and especially backpackers, looking not just for money but coveted Western passports.

The subway

Clean, efficient, graffiti-free and very fast, the **subway** is an appealing alternative to the bus, though again be prepared for enforced intimacies during rush hours. Mao Zedong ordered its construction in 1966, and more than 20km were open within three years, but until 1977 it was reserved for the use of senior cadres only, apparently because it was too close to the underground defence network.

The subway operates daily from 5.30am to 11pm and entrances are marked by a logo of a square inside a "C" shape. **Tickets** cost ¥3 per journey; buy them from the ticket offices at the top of the stairs above the platforms. It's worth buying a few at once to save queuing every time you use the system. The tickets are undated slips of paper and an attendant at the station takes one from you before you get on to the platform. All stops are marked in *pinyin*, and announced in English and Chinese over an intercom when the train pulls in, though the system is not taxing to figure out as there are only two lines.

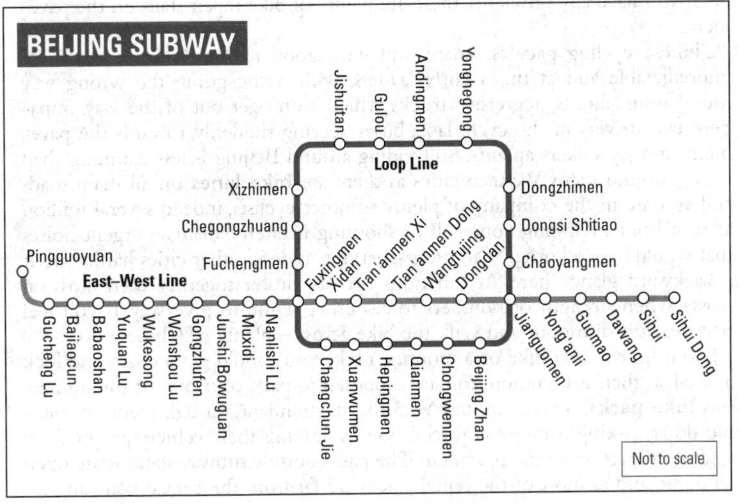

A **loop line** runs around the city, making useful stops at Beijing Zhan, Jianguomen (under the flyover, close to the Ancient Observatory and the Friendship Store), Yonghe Gong (50m north of the temple of the same name) and Qianmen, at the northern end of Qianmen Dajie. The **east–west line** runs from the western to the eastern suburbs; useful stops are at the Military Museum, Tian'anmen (west and east) and Wangfujing. There are interchanges at Fuxingmen and Jianguomen.

Taxis

Taxis come in all shapes and sizes, but all have a sticker in the back window which indicates the rate per kilometre. Luxury sedans are the most expensive, at ¥2 per kilometre with a minimum fare of ¥12; the common red "bullet-heads" charge ¥1.2 or ¥1.4 per kilometre with a minimum of ¥10. Using a taxi after 11pm will incur a surcharge of twenty percent. Drivers are generally honest (except the ones who hang around transport links) but if they don't put the meter on, you can insist by saying "*dá biǎo*". If you're concerned about being taken on an expensive detour, have a map open on your lap.

Rickshaws

Cycle-rickshaws should be treated with caution. Although they are good for short trips (they will travel a good couple of kilometres for ¥5), drivers can be hard to barter down and may demand more money when you get out. Make sure you both agree on the fare, and the currency you're negotiating in, before you set off. Around tourist sites, particularly in the *hutongs* around the Bell and Drum towers, the rickshaw drivers have reinvented themselves as tourist attractions, now that their day-to-day role has been usurped by taxis. Be prepared for frilly seat covers and silly prices.

Bike rental

As a positive alternative to relying on public transport, it's worth **renting a bike**. Many of the cheaper hotels rent out bikes on a daily basis and will negotiate weekly rates. Figure on a daily charge of ¥10–50 and a deposit of ¥200–500. Always test the brakes before riding off, and get the tyres pumped up. If you have any problems, there are plenty of bike repair stalls on the pavement.

Chinese cycling pace is sedate, and with good reason. Chinese roads are unpredictable and at times fairly lawless, with traffic going the wrong way round roundabouts, aggressive trucks which won't get out of the way, impatient taxi drivers in the cycle lane, buses veering suddenly towards the pavement, and jaywalkers aplenty. Still, riding around Beijing is less daunting than riding around many Western cities as there are **bike lanes** on all main roads and you are in the company of plenty of other cyclists, indeed several million at rush hours. Ringing your bell or shouting is rarely effective; urgent noises that would have all other road users scurrying aside in other cities hardly merit a backward glance here. At junctions cyclists cluster together then cross en masse when strength of numbers forces other traffic to give way. If you feel nervous, just dismount and walk the bike across – plenty of Chinese do.

If you have a new bike or a mountain bike you should get a chain and lock as well, as theft is common. You are supposed to park your bike at the numerous **bike parks**, where you pay ¥0.3 to the attendant, though plenty of people don't, risking a rarely enforced fine by leaving their vehicle propped up against railings or on the pavement. The parks outside subway stations are open all night, and as most of the rental places are far from the centre you can save yourself a lot of cycling by arranging to rent a bike for several days at a time and instead of cycling back and forth, leave the bike at one of these parks for the night.

Tours

Organized tours of the city and its outskirts offer a painless if expensive way of seeing all the sights quickly. CITS offers a wide variety of one- and two-day tour packages, which you can book from their offices or from the information desk in the Friendship Store. However, these tours aren't cheap, at around ¥300 a day. One good, inexpensive tour that's more imaginative than most is the *hutong* tour (see p.113), which offers the opportunity to see a more private side of the city. The one-day tours offered by the classier hotels also tend to be expensive; you'll get better value from the cheaper hotels, and you don't have to be a guest to join their tours. Worth considering is the day-trip organized from the *Fenglong* which also picks up at all the other budget hotels. It takes you to Jinshanling Great Wall and picks you up later at Simatai (see p.141). They'll also arrange trips to the acrobatics and the opera.

Accommodation

Affordable **accommodation** options in Beijing have much improved of late. There are now several well-run, cheap, well-located hotels and youth hostels – budget travellers no longer have to congregate in soulless suburban dormitories but can stay right in the **centre of town**. At the cheapest places you can expect a bed in a clean but cramped dorm, and all the facilities will be communal. Double rooms almost always come with attached bathrooms. In three-star places and above, rooms are more spacious, and there are usually facilities such as satellite TV, swimming pools and saunas. Pretty much every hotel has a hairdresser, a restaurant and a business centre.

Outer Beijing places are almost all on or near the third ring road, which makes them a long way out in what is inevitably a dull area, but there are good transport connections into the centre, and these places are usually less expensive. Beijing being the size it is, proximity to a subway station is a big advantage.

Except at the cheapest places, you should always haggle politely for a room – rack rates are only an indication, and hardly anyone pays those any more. You can often get a worthwhile discount if you book on the Internet (try Ⓦwww.sinohotels.com or www.egochina.com) a few days in advance, or try the airport reservations counter when you arrive.

All of the following hotels are keyed on our maps – you may need to look at the local maps for Qianmen, Wangfujing and Xidan to locate them.

Budget accommodation

Hoteliers have woken up to the potential offered by **budget travellers**, which means that, if you don't mind sharing a room, you can get a bed for a cheaper price than you would pay in most other Chinese cities. A group of centrally located clean new youth hostels has opened, so budget travellers no longer have to stay in shoddy dives such as the *Jinghua*, with its prostitutes, dirty sheets and rotten egg stench. The nearby *Seastar* and *Jingtai* are just as bad. Bafflingly, these places are still full of foreigners; presumably they don't know what else is available.

Beijing: Accommodation

Bamboo Garden	竹园宾馆	*zhúyuán bīnguǎn*
Beijing	北京饭店	*běijīng fàndiàn*
Beiwei	北纬饭店	*běiwěi fàndiàn*
Big Bell	大钟寺饭店	*dàzhōngsì fàndiàn*
Cherry Blossom	樱花宾馆	*yīnghuā bīnguǎn*
Chongwenmen	崇文门饭店	*chóngwénmén fàndiàn*
Far East International Youth Hostel	远东国际青年旅舍	*yuǎndōng guójìqīngnián lǚshè*
Fenglong	凤龙宾馆	*fènglóng bīnguǎn*
Fuhao	富豪宾馆	*fùháo bīnguǎn*
Great Wall Sheraton	长城饭店	*chángchéng fàndiàn*
Hademen	哈德门饭店	*hādémén fàndiàn*
Haoyuan	好园宾馆	*hǎoyuán bīnguǎn*
Holiday Inn Crowne Plaza	国际艺苑皇冠饭店	*guójìyìyuàn huángguān fàndiàn*
Huiqiao	惠乔饭店	*huìqiáo fàndiàn*
International Youth Hostel	国际青年旅舍	*guójìqīngnián lǚshè*
Jianguo	建国饭店	*jiànguó fàndiàn*
Jinglun	京伦饭店	*jīnglún fàndiàn*
Kempinski (Lufthansa Centre)	凯宾斯基饭店	*kǎibīnsījī fàndiàn*
Longtan	龙潭饭店	*lóngtán fàndiàn*
Lüsongyuan	侣松园宾馆	*lǚsōngyuán bīnguǎn*
Minzu	民族饭店	*mínzú fàndiàn*
New Otani	长富宫饭店	*chángfùgōng fàndiàn*
Palace	王府饭店	*wángfǔ fàndiàn*
Poacher's Inn	友谊青年酒店	*yǒuyíqīngnián jiǔdiàn*
Qianmen	前门饭店	*qiánmén fàndiàn*
Red House	瑞秀宾馆	*ruìxiù bīnguǎn*
Ritan	日坛宾馆	*rìtán bīnguǎn*
SCITECH	赛特饭店	*sàitè fàndiàn*
St Regis	国际俱乐部饭店	*guójìjùlèbù fàndiàn*
Tiantan	天坛饭店	*tiāntán fàndiàn*
Tiantan Sports	天坛体育宾馆	*tiāntántǐyù bīnguǎn*
Yuan Dong	远东饭店	*yuǎndōng fàndiàn*
Zhaolong International Youth Hostel	兆龙青年旅舍	*zhàolóngqīngnián lǚshè*

Another cheap option, mostly used by students studying Chinese visiting from other cities, is to stay in a university dormitory. These places aren't hotels and you're not guaranteed a room – if they're not full, as is often the case, the person in charge may simply not fancy the look of you or can't be bothered with the hassle of checking you in – but if you can get one they're very good value.

Note that the excellent *Lüsongyuan* and the *Red House* (see "Mid-range hotels" below) also have a couple of good-value dorms.

Central Beijing

Far East International Youth Hostel 113 Tieshuxie Jie, Qianmenwai ⓣ010/63018811, ⓕ63018233, ⓦwww.courtyard@elong.com. A great little place, in a traditional courtyard house. The four- and six-bed dorms are clean and have sinks. There's a kitchen, washing machine and an elegant lounge. Other facilities are limited, as in all courtyard houses – there's only one toilet block for the whole place. Staff are friendly, if a little bumbling. The location is fantastic, sunk in one of the city's last earthy *hutong* districts, a kilometre from

Qianmen. Check in at the *Far East Hotel* opposite (if you need to ask directions – and you will – ask for this place). The easiest way to find the hostel yourself is to walk south from Hepingmen subway stop and turn left at the second *hutong* after Liulichang's marble bridge. Then follow the *hutong* round – left, right, left. ¥10 discount for international youth hostel members. Dorm beds ¥45–55.
International Youth Hostel 9 Jianguomennei Dajie ⓣ010/65126688 ext 6146, ⓕ010/65229494, ⓦwww.iyhf-cn.net. Just north of Beijing Zhan subway stop, on the tenth floor of the building behind the *International Hotel* – look for the youth hostel sign. New, wel run, clean, very centrally located and with great views. Offers washing machines and bike rental but no cooking facilities. The only detriment is a dearth of cheap places to eat in the area. ¥10 discount with an international youth hostel card. Six-bed dorms ¥60.

Outer Beijing

Fenglong 5 Yongdingmen Dong Jie ⓣ010/63536413, ⓔsuyuling@etang.com. Best of the old-style backpacker motherships, with a wide range of dorm rooms – ask to see a selection, as quality, relative fustiness and prices vary widely. Those on the second floor are best. Offers bike rental and even photo developing. Staff are slack but the tourist information office is excellent – this is the nerve centre from which the tours from all the other budget places are run. Take bus #122 from Beijing Zhan. Dorm beds ¥25–50, ❸–❹
Poacher's Inn Off Sanlitun Lu ⓣ010/64172632, ⓕ010/64156866, ⓦwww.poachers.com.cn. A tempting prospect – one of Beijing's best cheap hotels abuts its best cheap bar. This place is new and well run, though staff are a bit stand-offish. There are a few dorms, but most of the rooms are doubles. All facilities are communal but spotless. There's free laundry and the price includes breakfast in the bar. To find it, head north up Sanlitun Lu and turn left after 200m, at the sign for the *Cross Bar*. Then follow the road round to the left and it's on the right. The location is great, with not just bars but some great restaurants within short walking distance, and its not as noisy as you might expect. Dorm beds ¥70, ❹
Zhaolong International Youth Hostel 2 Gongrentiyuchang Bei Lu ⓣ010/65972299, ⓕ65972288, ⓦwww.zhaolonghotel.com.cn. Behind the swanky *Zhaolong Hotel*. Another clean and ably managed hostel, a short stumble from the bars on Sanlitun Lu. Offers free laundry, bike rental and Internet access, and you can use the luxury facilities in the *Zhaolong*, such as the pool and the gym. You get a ¥10 discount with a youth hostel card. Dorm beds ¥60–70.

Mid-range hotels

Again, "mid-range" options have much improved, and no longer means anything you might only consider if you're outrageously wealthy or your company is paying. It's common to get discounts of as much as thirty percent on the rack rates.

Central Beijing

Bamboo Garden 24 Xiaoshiqiao Hutong ⓣ010/64032229, ⓦwww.bbgh.com.cn. A quiet, charming but rather rickety courtyard hotel in a *hutong* close to the Drum and Bell towers. Old-fashioned service standards complete the archaic atmsophere. Was being renovated at the time of writing, so it probably looks a lot better now. ❻
Chongwenmen 2 Chongwenmen Xi Dajie ⓣ010/65122211, ⓕ65122122. This hotel is a little cramped for space, but well located, close to the Chongwenmen subway stop on the loop line. Rack rates are comparatively high, so barter. ❼
Fuhao 45 Wangfujing Dajie ⓣ010/65231188, ⓕ65131188. A newish three-star place, more affordable than most in the area. ❼
Hademen 2a Chongwenmenwai Dajie ⓣ010/67012244, ⓕ67016865. This two-star place is a little rambling, and staff speak no English, but as one of the few moderately priced, central hotels, close to the Chongwenmen subway stop, it's worth considering. ❻
Haoyuan 53 Shijia Hutong ⓣ010/65125557, ⓕ65253179. A sedate little courtyard hotel just half a kilometre from Wangfujing but very quiet. Rooms are small but cosy and with Ming-style furniture. Head north up Dongdan Bei Dajie and take the last alley to the right before the intersection with Dengshikou Dajie. The hotel is 200m down here on the left, marked by two red lanterns. ❻
Lüsongyuan 22 Banchang Hutong ⓣ010/64040436, ⓕ64030418. A charismatic courtyard hotel converted from a Qing-dynasty mansion. Stylish and elegant rooms in a wide

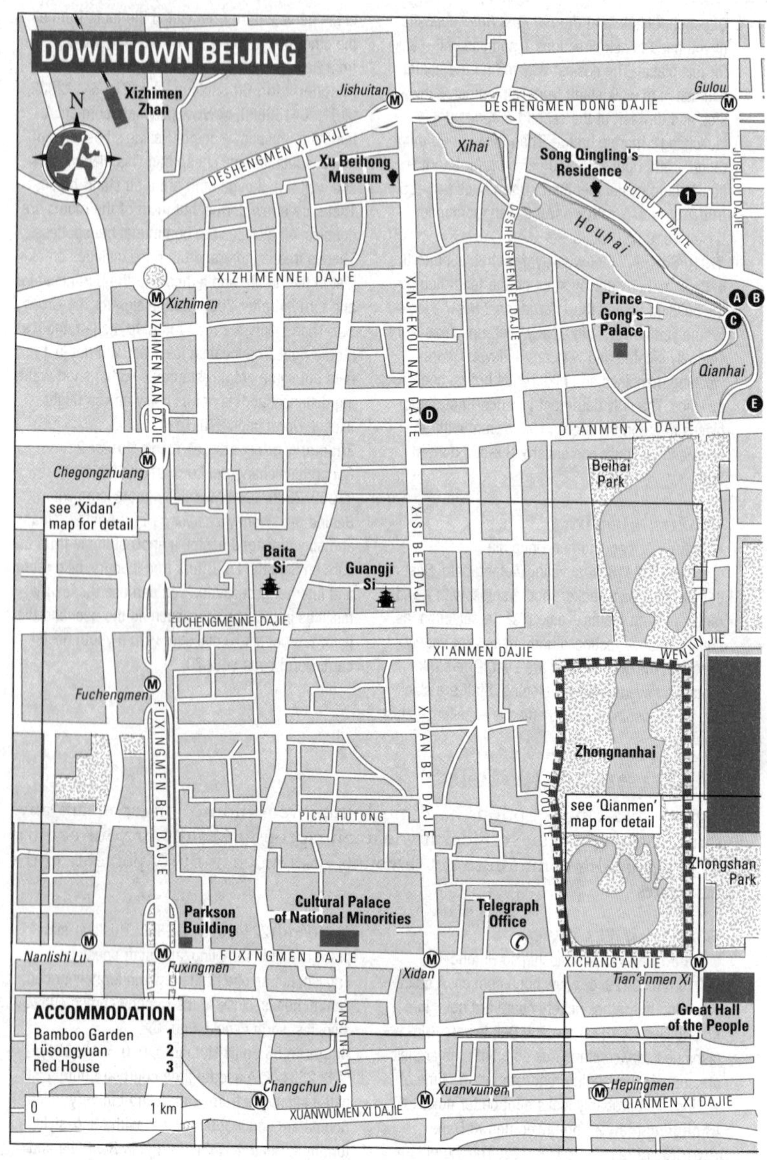

range of categories, including a basement dorm. Pleasant gardens, too. It's popular with tour groups, so you'll probably have to book ahead in season (April–September). The alley is just off Jiaodaokou Nan Dajie. Take bus #104 from the station and get off at Beibingmasi bus stop. Walk south for 50m and you'll see a sign in English pointing down an alley to the hotel. Dorm beds ¥80. ❻

Minzu 51 Fuxingmen Dajie ⓣ010/66014466, ⓕ66014849. Well appointed and close to some attractive parts of the city, midway between

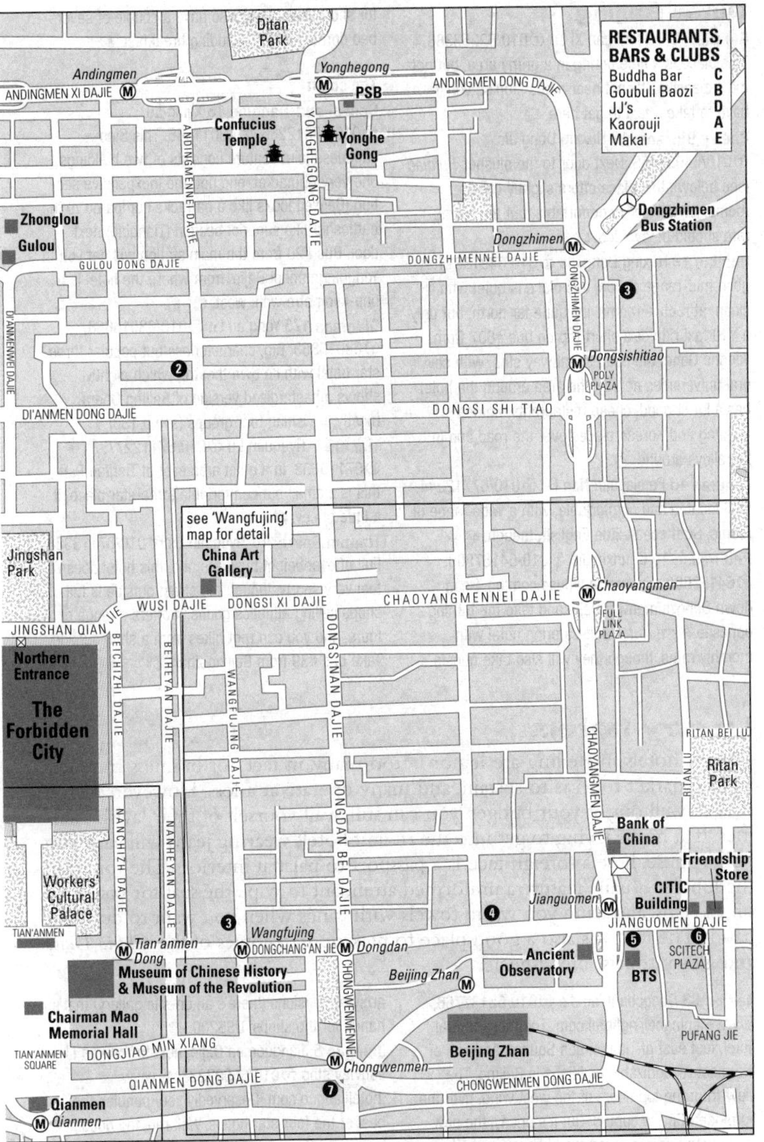

Fuxingmen and Xidan subway stops. The first-floor restaurant is good. Only worth it, though, if you can get a discount. ❽

Ritan 1 Ritan Lu ⓣ010/65125588. This small place offers a slightly more affordable alternative to the nearby lavish palaces of Jianguomenwai, but with none of their style. ❽

Yuan Dong 90 Tieshu Xiejie ⓣ010/63018811, ⓕ63018233. Squatting in a charming, ramshackle *hutong* just ten minutes' walk from Qianmen, this place is superbly located though the rooms are a little stale. ❺

Outer Beijing

Big Bell 18 Beisanhuan Xi Lu ⓣ010/62253388. This place is a little boring in a grimy area, but not too expensive. It's not near a bus stop so you'll have to take a taxi to get here. ⑤

Cherry Blossom 17 Huxing Dong Jie ⓣ010/64934455. Next door to the plusher *Huiqiao* (see below), this place offers slightly cheaper rooms. It's perfectly comfortable, but the restaurant should be avoided. ⑤

Huiqiao 19 Huxing Dong Jie ⓣ010/64918811. A good mid-range option, this place is quiet with clean, attractive rooms. It's quite far north, but only a ¥10 taxi ride or a short trip on bus #807 from Yonghe Gong, the nearest subway stop. With several universities nearby, the area around the hotel has a lot of good, cheap restaurants, notably Xinjiang and Korean places over the road and in the alleys around. ⑤

Longtan 15 Panjiayuan Nan Lu ⓣ010/67712244. Well located and comfortable, with a wide range of rooms. Staff speak little English, though. ⑤

Red House 10 Chunxiu Jie ⓣ010/64167500, ⓕ64167600, ⓦwww.redhouse.com.cn. Head down Dongzhimenwai Dajie and take the turning opposite *Pizza Hut*. A self-catering hotel with monthly rates, though they will also take guests for short stays. They also have a couple of seven-bed dorms for ¥95 including breakfast. ⑦

The south

Beiwei and Tianqiao 13 Xijing Lu ⓣ010/63012266, ⓕ63011366. This Sino-Japanese joint venture consists of two buildings, one very upmarket, one not; the inexpensive section (Beiwei) looks like a barracks compared to the battleship-like superior section (Tianqiao) next door. Bus #20 from the main station will get you to Yongdingmennei Dajie, from where the hotel is a one-kilometre walk west. ⑥–⑨

Qianmen 175 Yong'an Lu ⓣ010/63016688, ⓕ63013883. Big, characterless but popular three-star hotel with its own theatre, which nightly shows a bastardized version of Beijing Opera, mostly to visiting tour groups (see p.130). ⑦

Tiantan 1 Tiyuguan Lu ⓣ010/67112277, ⓕ67116833. In a quiet area east of Tiantan Park, this is a small but comfortable three-star place, if a little pricey. ⑧

Tiantan Sports 10 Tiyuguan Lu ⓣ010/67113388. Full of overweight businessmen, this hotel doesn't feel very sporty, though the street outside is full of shops selling athletics goods. It offers a range of tours, and you can rent bikes from a shop outside. Take bus #39 from Beijing Zhan. ⑥

Luxury hotels

Luxury hotels in Beijing are legion – too many, in fact, for business travellers and upmarket tourists to sustain, and many operate at a loss. However, even if they're well out of your budget, you can still avail yourself of their lavish facilities. If at home trying to get into the ritziest hotels wearing jeans will earn you polite abuse, here a foreign face is a passport to palatial interiors. The toilets in the lobbies usually feature a uniformed attendant to wipe the seat for you, turn on the taps, and hand you warm towels with tongs when you want to dry your hands. The lobby is also a good place to pick up free copies of the *China Daily* and glossy tourist broadsheets.

Beijing 33 Dongchang'an Jie ⓣ010/65137766, ⓦwww.chinabeijinghotel.com. The most central hotel, just east of Tian'anmen Square, and one of the most recognizable buildings in Beijing. The view from the top floors of the west wing, over the Forbidden City, is superb. But it's pricey, the new renovation has expunged the historic feel and service is not up to scratch. The cheapest rooms are US$160. ⑨

Great Wall Sheraton 6 Dongsanhuan Bei Lu ⓣ010/65005566, ⓕ65001919. A very swish, five-star modern compound out on the third ring road. US$220. ⑨

Holiday Inn Crowne Plaza 48 Wangfujing Dajie ⓣ010/65133388. Well-established hotel with artsy pretensions (there's an on-site gallery) that's handy for the shops. US$200. ⑨

Jianguo 5 Jianguomen Dajie, next to Yong'an Li subway stop ⓣ010/65002233, ⓦwww.hoteljianguo.com. Deservedly very popular, the best of the four-star hotels. Well run and good looking, with many of the rooms arranged aorund cloistered gardens. The restaurant, *Justine's*, has the best French food in the city. US$190. ⑨

Jinglun (Hotel Beijing–Toronto) 3 Jianguomenwai Dajie ⓣ010/65002266, ⓕ65002022. Bland-looking from the outside, this Japanese-run place is very comfortable and plush inside. A standard double is US$190. ⑨

Kempinski Lufthansa Centre, 50 Liangmaqiao Lu

Ⓣ010/64653388, Ⓦwww.kempinski-beijing.com. Off the third ring road on the way to the airport, this five-star place is a little out of the way, though with a huge shopping complex attached and an expat satellite town of bars and restaurants nearby there's no shortage of diversions on site. ❾

New Otani 26 Jianguomenwai Dajie Ⓣ010/65125555, Ⓕ65139810. You can get seriously pampered in this five-star, modern, Japanese-run mansion, one of the most luxurious in Beijing, though the fee for the privilege, at least US$212 a night, is hefty. ❾

Palace 8 Jingyu Hutong Ⓣ010/65128899, Ⓕ65129050. A discreet and well-located upmarket place with a good shopping centre that once boasted China's only Armani store. US$300. ❾

SCITECH 22 Jianguomenwai Dajie Ⓣ010/65123388, Ⓕ65123542. A business-like hotel conveniently located opposite the Friendship Store, though on an unflattering site, tucked at the back of a car park among a cluster of office buildings. Take the loop line to the Jianguomen subway stop and walk east. ❾

St Regis 21 Jianguomen Wai Dajie Ⓣ010/64606688, Ⓕ64603299. The best and most expensive hotel in the city, choice of visiting US dignitaries such as President George W. Bush. Rooms start at US$225. ❾

The City

Beijing requires patience and planning to do it justice. Wandering aimlessly around without a destination in mind will rarely be rewarding. The place to start is **Tian'anmen Square**, geographical and psychic centre of the city, where a cluster of important sights can be seen in a day, although the **Forbidden City**, at the north end of the square, deserves a day, or even several, all to itself. The **Qianmen** area, a noisy market area south of here, is a bit more alive, and ends in style with one of the city's highlights, the **Temple of Heaven**. The giant freeway, **Chang'an Jie**, zooming east–west across the city, is a corridor of high-rises with a few museums, shopping centres and even the odd ancient site worth tracking down. Scattered in the **north** of the city, a section with a more traditional and human feel, are some magnificent **parks, palaces and temples**, some of them in the *hutongs*. An expedition to the outskirts is amply rewarded by the **Summer Palace**, the best place to get away from it all.

Tian'anmen Square and the Forbidden City

The first stop for any visitor to Beijing is **Tian'anmen Square**. Physically at the city's centre, symbolically it's the heart of China, and the events it has witnessed have shaped the history of the People's Republic from its inception. Chairman Mao lies here in his marble **mausoleum**, with the **Great Hall of the People** to the west and the **Museum of the Chinese Revolution** to the east. Monumental architecture that's much, much older lies just to the north – the **Forbidden City of the Emperors**, now open to all.

Tian'anmen Square

Covering more than forty hectares, **Tian'anmen Square** must rank as the greatest public square on earth. It's a modern creation, in a city that tradition-

Beijing: The city

Ancient Observatory	古观象台	*gǔguānxiàngtái*
Asian Games Village	亚运村	*yàyùncūn*
Baita Si	白塔寺	*bátǎ sì*
Baiyunguan	白云观	*báyúnguàn*
Beihai Park	北海公园	*běihǎi gōngyuán*
Beijing Planetarium	北京天文馆	*běijīng tīanwénguǎn*
Beijing University	北京大学	*běijīng dàxúe*
Beijing Zoo	北京动物园	*běijīng dòngwùyuán*
China Art Gallery	中国美术馆	*zhōngguó měishùguǎn*
Confucius Temple	孔庙	*kǒngmiào*
Cultural Palace of the National Minorities	民族文化宫	*mínzú wénhuàgōng*
Dazhong Si	大钟寺	*dàzhōng sì*
Ditan Park	地坛公园	*dìtán gōngyuán*
Exhibition Hall	展览馆	*zhǎnlǎn guǎn*
Forbidden City	故宫	*gùgōng*
Former Residence of Lu Xun	鲁迅博物馆	*lǚxùn bówùguǎn*
Great Hall of the People	人民大会堂	*rénmín dàhuìtáng*
Guangji Si	广济寺	*guǎngjì sì*
Gulou (Drum Tower)	鼓楼	*gǔlóu*
Jingshan Park	景山公园	*jǐngshān gōngyuán*
Mao Memorial Hall	毛主席纪念堂	*máozhǔxí jìniàntáng*
Military Museum	军事博物馆	*jūnshì bówùguǎn*
Museum of Chinese History	中国历史博物馆	*zhōngguó lìshǐ bówùguǎn*
Museum of the Chinese Revolution	中国革命博物馆	*zhōngguó gémìng bówùguǎn*
Natural History Museum	自然博物馆	*zìrán bówùguǎn*
Niu Jie	牛街	*níujiē*
Prince Gong's Palace	恭王府	*gōngwángfǔ*
Qianmen	前门	*qiánmén*
Qinghua University	清华大学	*qīnghuá dàxué*
Ritan Park	日坛公园	*rìtán gōngyuán*
Song Qingling's Residence	宋庆龄故居	*sòngqìnglíng gùjū*
Summer Palace	颐和园	*yíhéyuán*
Taoranting Park	陶然亭公园	*táorántíng gōngyuán*
Temple of Heaven	天坛	*tiāntán*
Tian'anmen	天安门	*tiānānmén*
Tian'anmen Square	天安门广场	*tiānānmén guǎngchǎng*
TV Tower	电视塔	*diànshì tǎ*
World Trade Centre	国际贸易中心	*guójìmàoyì zhōngxīn*
Xu Beihong Museum	徐悲鸿纪念馆	*xúbēihóng jìniànguǎn*
Yonghe Gong	雍和宫	*yōnghé gōng*
Yuanmingyuan	圆明园	*yuánmíng yuán*
Zhonglou (Bell Tower)	钟楼	*zhōnglóu*
Zhongnanhai	中南海	*zhōngnán hǎi*
Zizhuyuan Park	紫竹院公园	*zǐzhúyuàn gōngyuán*

ally had no squares, as classical Chinese town planning did not allow for places where crowds could gather. Tian'anmen only came into being when imperial offices were cleared from either side of the great processional way that led south from the palace to Qianmen and the Temple of Heaven. The ancient north–south axis of the city was thus destroyed and the broad east–west thoroughfare, Chang'an Jie, that now carries millions of cyclists every day past the front of the Forbidden City, had the walls across its path removed. In the words of one of the architects: "The very map of Beijing was a reflection of the feudal society, it was meant to demonstrate the power of the emperor. We had to transform it, we had to make Beijing into the capital of socialist China." As the square is lined with railings (for crowd control) you can enter or leave only via the exits at either end or in the middle. Bicycles are not permitted, and the

Dissent in Tian'anmen Square

Blood debts must be repaid in kind – the longer the delay, the greater the interest.

Lu Xun, writing after the massacre of 1926.

Chinese history is about to turn a new page. Tian'anmen Square is ours, the people's, and we will not allow butchers to tread on it.

Wuer Kaixi, student, May 1989.

It may have been designed as a space for mass declarations of loyalty, but in the twentieth century Tian'anmen Square was as often a venue for expressions of popular dissent: against foreign oppression at the beginning of the century, and, more recently, against its domestic form. The first **mass protests** occurred here on May 4, 1919, when three thousand students gathered in the square to protest at the disastrous terms of the Versailles Treaty, in which the victorious allies granted several former German concessions in China to the Japanese. The Chinese, who had sent more than a hundred thousand labourers to work in the supply lines of the British and French forces, were outraged. The protests of May 4, and the movement they spawned, marked the beginning of the painful struggle of Chinese modernization. In the turbulent years of the 1920s the inhabitants of Beijing again occupied the square, first in 1925, to protest over the massacre in Shanghai of Chinese demonstrators by British troops, then in 1926, when the public protested after the weak government's capitulation to the Japanese. Demonstrators marched on the government offices and were fired on by soldiers.

In 1976, after the death of popular premier **Zhou Enlai**, thousands of mourners assembled in Tian'anmen without government approval, to voice their dissatisfaction with their leaders, and again in 1978 and 1979 groups assembled here to discuss new ideas of democracy and artistic freedom, triggered by writings posted along Democracy Wall on the edge of the Forbidden City. In 1986 and 1987, people gathered again to show solidarity for the students and others protesting at the Party's refusal to allow elections.

But it was in **1989** that Tian'anmen Square became the venue for a massive expression of popular dissent when, from April to June, nearly a million protesters demonstrated against the slowness of reform, lack of freedom and widespread corruption. A giant statue, the Goddess of Liberty, a woman carrying a torch in both hands, was created by art students and set up facing Mao's portrait on Tian'anmen. The government, infuriated at being humiliated by their own people, declared martial law on May 20, and on June 4 the military moved in. The killing was indiscriminate; tanks ran over tents and machine guns strafed the avenues. No one knows how many died in the massacre – probably thousands. Hundreds were arrested afterwards and many are still in jail. The problems the protesters complained of have not been dealt with, and many, such as corruption, have worsened.

streets either side are one way; the street on the east side is for traffic going south, the west side for northbound traffic.

The square has been the stage for many of the epoch-making mass movements of modern: the first calls for democracy and liberalism by the students of May 4, 1919, demonstrating against the Treaty of Versailles; the anti-Japanese protests of December 9, 1935, demanding a war of national resistance; the eight stage-managed rallies that kicked off the Cultural Revolution in 1966, when up to a million Red Guards at a time were ferried to Beijing to be exhorted into action and then shipped out again to shake up the provinces; and the brutally repressed Qing Ming demonstration of April 1976, in memory of Zhou Enlai, that first pointed towards the eventual fall of the Gang of Four. But the square is best-known to contemporary visitors for the horrific events of 1989, when students and workers peacefully protesting for democracy were savagely suppressed (see box on p.27). The square was repaved in time for the fiftieth anniversary of the founding of the People's Republic in 1999, and so was conveniently closed during the tenth anniversary of the uprising.

Tian'anmen Square unquestionably makes a strong impression, but this concrete plain dotted with worthy statuary and bounded by monumental buildings can seem inhuman. Together with the bloody associations it has for many visitors it often leaves people cold, especially Westerners unused to such magisterial representations of political power. For many Chinese tourists, though, the square is a place of **pilgrimage**. Crowds flock to see the corpse of Chairman Mao; others quietly bow their heads before the **Monument to the Heroes**, a thirty-metre-high obelisk commemorating the victims of the revolutionary struggle. Among the visitors is the occasional monk, and the sight of robed Buddhists standing in front of the uniformed sentries outside the Great Hall of the People makes a striking juxtaposition. Others come just to hang out or to fly kites, but the atmosphere is not relaxed and a ¥5 fine for spitting and littering is rigorously enforced. At dawn, the flag at the northern end of the square is raised in a military ceremony and lowered again at dusk, which is when most people come to see it, though foreigners complain that the regimentation of the crowds is oppressive and reminds them of school. After dark, the square is at its most appealing and, with its sternness softened by mellow lighting, it becomes the haunt of strolling families and lovers.

The buildings

At the centre of the centre of China lies a corpse that nobody dare remove.

Tiziano Terzani, *Behind the Forbidden Door*

The square was not enlarged to its present size until ten years after the Communist takeover, when the Party ordained the building of ten new Soviet-style official buildings in ten months. These included the three that dominate Tian'anmen to either side – the Great Hall of the People, and the museums of Chinese History and Revolution. In 1976 a fourth was added in the centre – Mao's mausoleum, constructed (again in ten months) by an estimated million volunteers. It's an ugly building, looking like a school gym, which contravenes the principles of *feng shui* (geomancy), presumably deliberately, by interrupting the line from the palace to Qianmen and by facing north. Mao himself wanted to be cremated, and the erection of the mausoleum was apparently no more than a power ploy by his would-be successor, Hua Guofeng. In 1980 Deng Xiaoping said it should never have been built, although he wouldn't go so far as to pull it down.

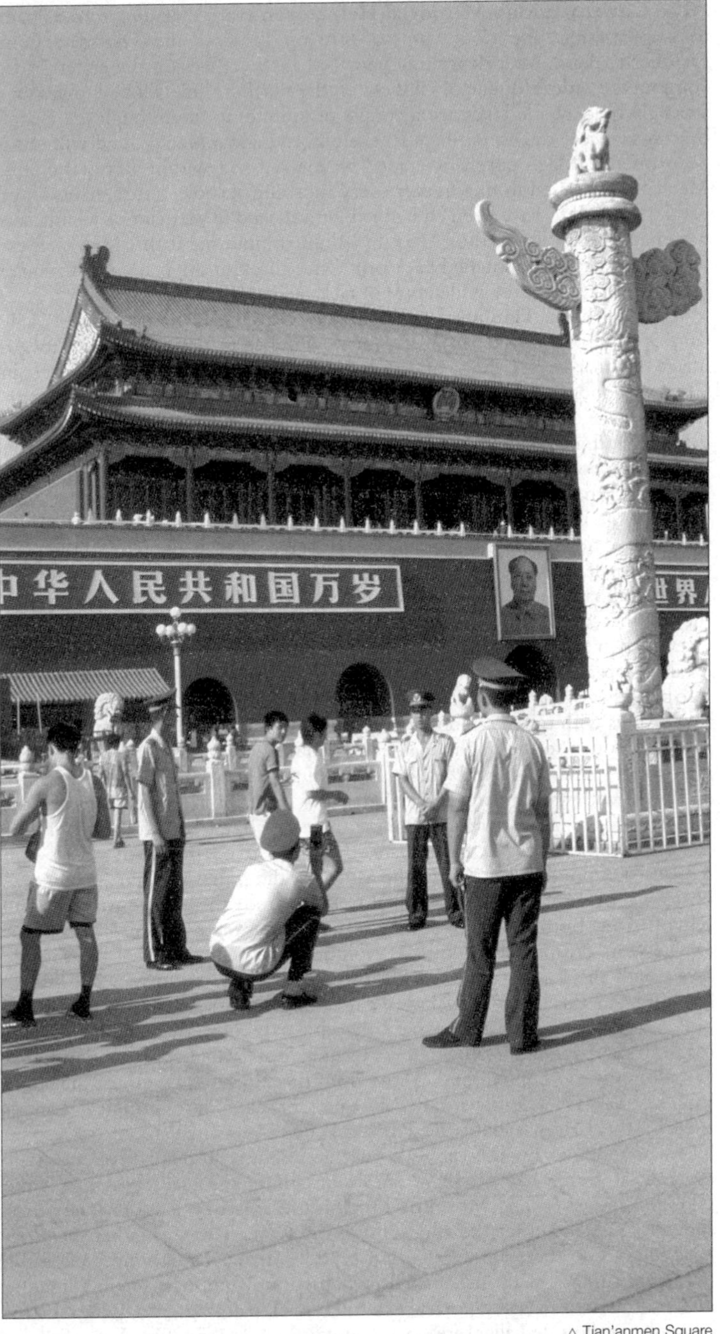

△ Tian’anmen Square

The **Chairman Mao Memorial Hall** is open every morning from 8.30am to 11.30am, and also from 2pm to 4pm on Tuesdays and Thursdays from October to April. After depositing your bag at the offices on the eastern side, you join the orderly queue of Chinese on the northern side. This advances surprisingly quickly, and takes just a couple of minutes to file through the chambers in silence – the atmosphere is reverent, and any joking around will cause deep offence. Mao's corpse is draped with a red flag within a crystal coffin. Mechanically raised from a freezer every morning, it looks unreal, like wax or plastic. It is said to have been embalmed with the aid ofVietnamese technicians who had recently worked on Ho Chi Minh (rumour has it that Mao's left ear fell off and had to be stitched back on). Once through the marble halls, you're herded past a splendidly wide array of tacky Chairman Mao souvenirs.

North of here, **Tian'anmen** itself, the Gate of Heavenly Peace (daily 8am–5pm; ¥30, students ¥10), is the main entrance to the Forbidden City. An image familiar across the world, Tian'anmen occupies an exalted place in Chinese iconography, appearing on banknotes, coins, stamps and indeed virtually any piece of state paper you can imagine. As such it's a prime object of pilgrimage, with many visitors milling around waiting to be photographed in front of the large portrait of Mao (one of the very few still on public display), which hangs over the central passageway. From the reviewing platform above, Mao delivered the liberation speech on October 1, 1949, declaring that "the Chinese people have now stood up". For an exorbitant fee you can climb up to this platform yourself where security is tight – all visitors have to leave their bags, are frisked and have to go through a metal detector before they can ascend. Inside, the fact that most people cluster around the souvenir stall selling official certificates of their trip reflects the fact that there's not much to look at.

Taking up almost half the west side of the square is the **Great Hall of the People**. This is the venue of the National People's Congress and hundreds of black Audis with tinted windows are parked outside when it's in session. When it isn't, it's open to the public (daily 8.30–3pm; ¥20). What you are shown is a selection, usually 6, of the 29 reception rooms – each named after a province and filled with appropriate regional artefacts. Actually, it's rather boring – the place just looks like a standard Chinese three-star hotel, but built for giants.

On the other side of the square, there are two **museums** (Tues–Sun 8.30am–4.30pm; ¥3) housed in the same building: the Museum of Chinese History, covering everything up to 1919, and the **Museum of the Revolution**. Both are full of propaganda; the latter often closing for refits (for twelve years during the Cultural Revolution, for example) as its curators are faced with the Kafkaesque dilemma of constantly having to reinvent history according to the latest Party line. At the time of writing, however, the vast building was open, displaying some rather dull exhibits of documents and photos from the twentieth century (these terminate at 1949, post-liberation history being just too contentious). Those from the nineteenth century, including such oddments as a contract signed by a peasant selling his wife and "Weapons used by the British against the Tibetan People" are much more interesting. There are copious English captions, but you might wish there weren't, as they are full of terms like "foreign aggression" and "colonial oppressors"; the Chinese is harsher. The **Museum of Chinese History** is more interesting, though it's intended for the education of the Chinese masses rather than foreign tourists, so there are few English captions. It was being renovated at the time of writing – with luck they'll do something about the terrible lighting and mustiness – but temporary exhibitions, of paintings and porcelain for example, in the side halls were open and worthwhile (¥5–20).

For an overview of the square, head to the south gate, **Zhenyangmen** (daily 9am–4pm; ¥3), similar to Tian'anmen and 40m high, which gives a good idea of how much more impressive the square would look if Mao's mausoleum hadn't been stuck in the middle of it. A diorama inside shows what the area looked like in 1750.

The Forbidden City

The Gugong, or Imperial Palace, is much better known by its unofficial title, the **Forbidden City**, a reference to its exclusivity. Indeed, for the five centuries of its operation, through the reigns of 24 emperors of the Ming and Qing dynasties, ordinary Chinese were forbidden from even approaching the walls of the palace. Today the complex is open to visitors daily 8.30am–5pm, with last admission at 3.30pm in winter, 4pm in summer (¥40, ¥60 including the special exhibitions). Note that the entrance is quite a way after Tian'anmen; just keep on past the souveir stalls till you can't go any further. As well as the main entrance under Tian'anmen you can also come in through the smaller north and east gates. You have the freedom of most of the hundred-hectare site, though not all of the buildings, which are labelled in English. If you want detailed explanation of everything you see, you can tag on to one of the numerous tour groups or buy one of the many specialist books on sale. The audio tour (¥30), available by the main gate, is also worth considering. You're provided with a cassette player and headphones and suavely talked through the complex by Roger Moore – though if you do this, it's worth retracing your steps afterwards for an untutored view. Useful **bus routes** serving the Forbidden City are #5 from Qianmen, and #54 from Beijing Zhan, or you could use #1, which passes the complex on its journey along Chang'an Jie. You can get to the back gate on buses #101, #103 or #109. The nearest **subways** are Tian'anmen west and east. If you're in a **taxi**, you can save yourself the walk across Tian'anmen Square by asking to be dropped at the east gate.

Some history

After the Manchu dynasty fell in 1911, the Forbidden City began to fall into disrepair, exacerbated by heavy looting of artefacts and jewels by the Japanese in the 1930s and again by the Nationalists, prior to their flight to Taiwan, in 1949. A programme of **restoration** has been under way for decades, and today the complex is in better shape than it was for most of the last century, in the interests of more than two million visitors a year. It's big enough to fill several separate visits, and its elegance on such a massive scale is extraordinary.

The complex, with its maze of eight hundred buildings and reputed nine thousand chambers, was the symbolic and literal heart of the capital, and of the empire too. From within, the **emperors**, the Sons of Heaven, issued commands with absolute authority to their millions of subjects. Very rarely did they emerge – perhaps with good reason. Their lives, right down to the fall of the Manchu in the twentieth century, were governed by an extraordinarily developed taste for luxury and excess. It is estimated that a single meal for a Qing emperor could have fed several thousand of his impoverished peasants, a scale obviously appreciated by the last influential Manchu, the Empress Dowager Cixi, who herself would commonly order preparation of one hundred or more dishes. Sex, too, provided startling statistics, with Ming-dynasty harems numbering a population of only just below five figures.

Although the earliest structures on the Forbidden City site began with Kublai Khan during the Mongol dynasty, the **plan** (and originals) of the Imperial

Palace buildings are essentially Ming. Most date to the fifteenth century and the ambitions of the Emperor Yongle, the monarch responsible for switching the capital back to Beijing in 1403. The halls were laid out according to geomantic theories – in accordance to the *yin* and *yang*, the balance of negative and positive – and since they stood at the exact centre of Beijing, and Beijing was considered the centre of the universe, the harmony was supreme. The palace complex constantly reiterates such references, alongside personal symbols of imperial power such as the dragon and phoenix (emperor and empress) and the crane and turtle (longevity of reign).

Entering the complex

Once through Tian'anmen, you find yourself on a long walkway, with the moated palace complex and massive Wumen gate directly ahead (this is where you buy your ticket). The two parks either side, Zhongshan and the People's Culture Park (both daily 6am–9pm) are great places to chill out away from the rigorous formality outside. The **Workers' Culture Palace** (¥5), on the eastern side, which was symbolically named in deference to the fact that only with the Communist takeover in 1949 were ordinary Chinese allowed within this central sector of their city, has a number of modern exhibition halls (sometimes worth checking) and a scattering of original fifteenth-century structures, most of them Ming or Qing ancestral temples. The hall at the back often holds prestigious art exhibitions. The western **Zhongshan Park** (¥1) boasts the remains of the Altar of Land and Grain, a biennial sacrificial site with harvest functions closely related to those of the Temple of Heaven (see p.105).

The **Wumen** (Meridian Gate) itself is the largest and grandest of the Forbidden City gates and was reserved for the emperor's sole use. From its vantage point, the Sons of Heaven would announce the new year's calendar to their court and in times of war inspect the army. It was customary for victorious generals returning from battle to present their prisoners here for the emperor to decide their fate. He would be flanked, on all such imperial occasions, by a guard of elephants, the gift of Burmese subjects.

Passing through the Wumen you find yourself in a vast paved court, cut east–west by the **Jinshui He**, the Golden Water Stream, with its five marble bridges, decorated with carved torches, a symbol of masculinity. Beyond is a further ceremonial gate, the **Taihemen**, Gate of Supreme Harmony, its entrance guarded by a magisterial row of lions, and beyond this a still greater courtyard where the principal imperial audiences were held. Within this space the entire court, up to one hundred thousand people, could be accommodated. They would have made their way in through the lesser side gates – military men from the west, civilian officials from the east – and waited in total silence as the emperor ascended his throne. Then, with only the Imperial Guard remaining standing, they prostrated themselves nine times.

Inside the palace

The main **ceremonial halls** stand directly ahead, dominating the court. Raised on a three-tiered marble terrace is the first and most spectacular of the three, the **Taihedian**, Hall of Supreme Harmony. This was used for the most important state occasions, such as the emperor's coronation or birthdays and the nomination of generals at the outset of a campaign, and last saw action in an armistice ceremony in 1918. It was proposed, though not carried through, that parliament should sit here during the Republic. A marble pavement ramp, intricately carved with dragons and flanked by bronze incense burners, marks the path along which the emperor's chair was carried. His golden dragon throne stands within.

Eunuchs and concubines

For much of the **imperial period**, the Inner Court of the palace was the home of more than six thousand members of the royal household, around half of this number **eunuchs**. The castrated male was introduced into the imperial court as a means of ensuring the authenticity of the emperor's offspring and as a radical solution to the problem of nepotism. In daily contact with the royals, they often rose to considerable power, but this was bought at the expense of their dreadfully low standing outside the confines of the court. Confucianism held that disfiguration of the body impaired the soul, and eunuchs were buried apart from their ancestors in special graveyards outside the city. In the hope that they would still be buried "whole", they kept and carried around their testicles in bags hung on their belts. They were usually recruited from the poorest families – attracted by the rare chance of amassing wealth other than by birth.

Scarcely less numerous were the **concubines**, whose status varied from wives and consorts to basic whores. They would be delivered to the emperor's bedchamber, wrapped in yellow cloth, and carried by one of the eunuchs, since with feet bound they could hardly walk.

Moving on, you enter the **Zhonghedian**, Hall of Middle Harmony, another throne room, where the emperor performed ceremonies of greeting to foreigners and addressed the imperial offspring (products of several wives and numerous concubines). The hall was used, too, as a dressing room, for the major Taihedian events, and it was here that the emperor examined the seed for each year's crop.

The third of the great halls, the **Baohedian**, Preserving Harmony Hall, was used for state banquets and imperial examinations, graduates from which were appointed to positions of power in what was the first recognizably bureaucratic civil service. Its galleries, originally treasure houses, display various finds from the site, though the most spectacular, a vast block carved with dragons and clouds, stands at the rear of the hall. This is a Ming creation, reworked in the eighteenth century, and it's among the finest carvings in the palace. It's certainly the largest – a 250-tonne chunk of marble transported here from well outside the city by flooding the roads in winter to form sheets of ice.

To the north, paralleling the structure of the ceremonial halls, are the three principal palaces of the **imperial living quarters**. Again, the first chamber, the **Qianqinggong**, Palace of Heavenly Purity, is the most extravagant. It was originally the imperial bedroom – its terrace is surmounted by incense burners in the form of cranes and tortoises (symbols of immortality) – though it later became a conventional state room. Beyond, echoing the Zhonghedian in the ceremonial complex, is the **Jiaotaidian**, Hall of Union, the empress's throne room, and finally the **Kunninggong**, Palace of Earthly Tranquillity, where the emperor and empress traditionally spent their wedding night. By law the emperor had to spend the first three nights of his marriage, and the first day of Chinese New Year, with his wife. This palace is a bizarre building, partitioned in two. On the left is a large sacrificial room with its vats ready to receive offerings (1300 pigs a year under the Ming). The wedding chamber is a small room, off to one side, painted entirely in red, and covered with decorative emblems symbolizing fertility and joy. It was last pressed into operation in 1922 for the child wedding of Pu Yi, the final Manchu emperor, who, finding it "like a melted red wax candle", decided that he preferred the Mind Nurture Palace and went back there.

The Mind Nurture Palace, or **Yangxindiang**, is one of a group of palaces to the west where emperors spent most of their time. Several of the palaces retain their furniture from the Manchu times, most of it eighteenth-century, and in one, the **Changchundong**, is a series of paintings illustrating the Ming novel, *The Story of the Stone*. To the east is a similarly arranged group of palaces, adapted as **museum galleries** for displays of bronzes, ceramics, paintings, jewellery and Ming and Qing arts and crafts. The atmosphere here is much more intimate, and you can peer into well-appointed chambers full of elegant furniture and ornaments, including English clocks decorated with images of English gentlefolk, which look very odd among the jade trees and ornate flywhisks.

Head over to the other side of the complex to the eastern palace quarters where an extraordinary **Clock Museum** (¥5) is housed, displaying the result of one Qing emperor's collecting passion. Most are English and French explosions of Baroque ornament, though perhaps the most arresting is a rhino-sized Chinese water clock.

Moving away from the palace chambers – and by this stage something of a respite – the Kunningmen leads out from the Inner Court to the **Imperial Garden**. There are a couple of cafés here (and toilets) amid a pleasing network of ponds, walkways and pavilions, the classic elements of a Chinese garden. At the centre is the **Qinandian**, Hall of Imperial Peace, dedicated to the Taoist god of fire, Xuan Wu. You can exit here into Jingshan Park, which provides an overview of the complex – see p.112.

South of Tian'anmen

The **Qianmen** area, to the south of Tian'anmen, offers a tempting antidote to the prodigious grandeurs of the Forbidden City – and a quick shift of scale. The lanes and *hutongs* here comprise a **traditional shopping quarter**, full of small, specialist stores which to a large extent remain grouped according to their particular trades. It's a part of the city to browse in, and a good place to eat, with one of the best selections of snacks available in the capital. Down Qianmen Dajie, once the Imperial Way, now a clogged road clustered with small shops, the **Museum of Natural History** contains a gruesome surprise and **Tiantan**, the ravishing Temple of Heaven, perfectly set in one of Beijing's best parks, is an example of imperial architecture at its best.

Qianmen

The entry to this quarter is marked by the imposing, fifteenth-century, double-arched **Qianmen Gate** just south of Tian'anmen Square. Before the city's walls were demolished, this sector controlled the entrance to the Inner City from the outer, suburban sector. Shops and places of entertainment were banned from the former in imperial days, and they became concentrated in the Qianmen area. The gate marks a major intersection on the public transport network: as well as a subway stop, a bus terminus here provides connections to the southern districts and tourist buses also leave from here to attractions outside the city, including the Great Wall at Badaling and Shisan Ling.

Qianmen Dajie, the quarter's biggest street, runs immediately south from the gate. Off to either side are trading streets and *hutongs*, with intriguing traditional pharmacies and herbalist shops, dozens of clothes shops, silk traders and an impressive array of side-stalls and cake shops selling fresh food and cooked snacks. On the western side of the gate, you'll find *KFC* and *McDonald's*, but a

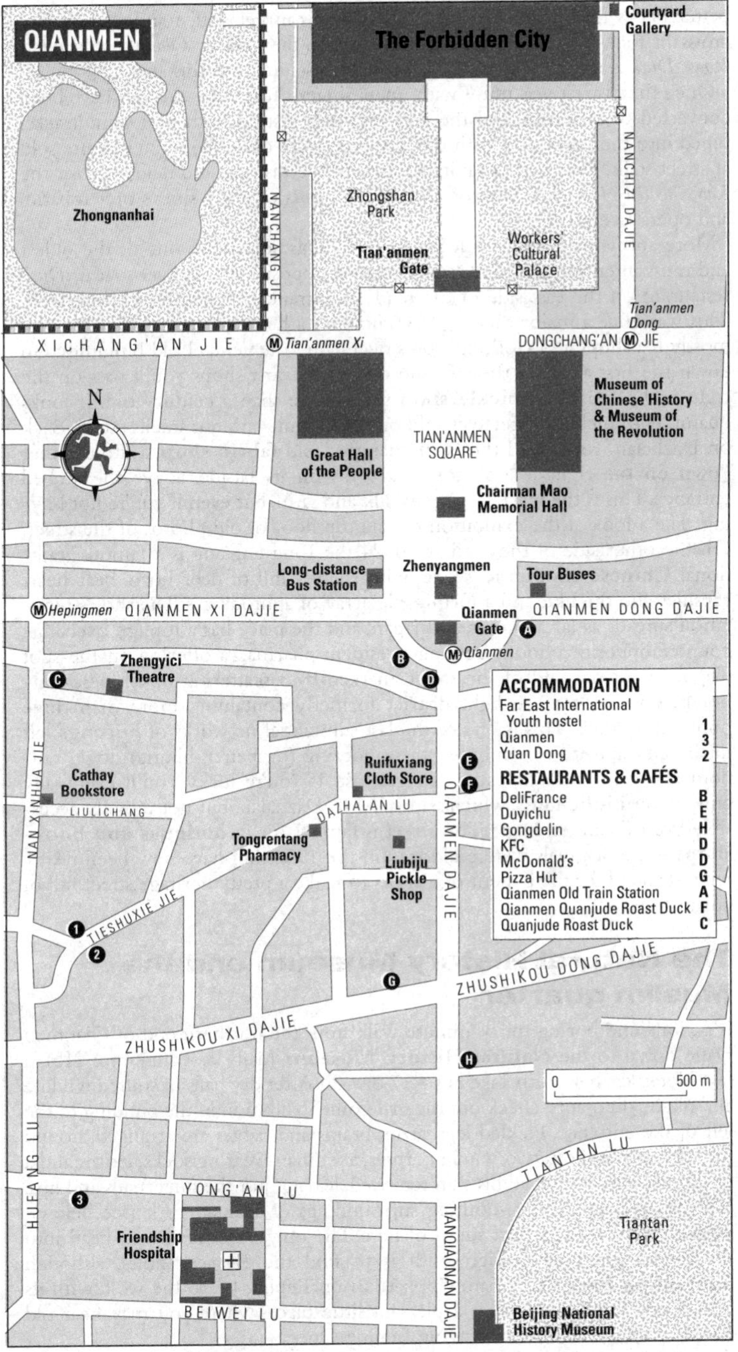
QIANMEN
The Forbidden City
Courtyard Gallery
Zhongnanhai
Zhongshan Park
Tian'anmen Gate
Workers' Cultural Palace
NANCHANG JIE
NANCHIZI DAJIE
Tian'anmen Dong
XICHANG'AN JIE
Tian'anmen Xi
DONGCHANG'AN JIE
Great Hall of the People
TIAN'ANMEN SQUARE
Museum of Chinese History & Museum of the Revolution
Chairman Mao Memorial Hall
Long-distance Bus Station
Zhenyangmen
Tour Buses
Hepingmen
QIANMEN XI DAJIE
Qianmen Gate
QIANMEN DONG DAJIE
Qianmen
Zhengyici Theatre
Cathay Bookstore
LIULICHANG
NAN XINHUA JIE
Ruifuxiang Cloth Store
DAZHALAN LU
Tongrentang Pharmacy
Liubiju Pickle Shop
QIANMEN DAJIE
TIESHUXIE JIE
ZHUSHIKOU DONG DAJIE
ZHUSHIKOU XI DAJIE
0
500 m
TIANTAN LU
HUFANG LU
YONG'AN LU
Friendship Hospital
TIANQIAONAN DAJIE
Tiantan Park
BEIWEI LU
Beijing National History Museum
ACCOMMODATION
Far East International Youth hostel 1
Qianmen 3
Yuan Dong 2
RESTAURANTS & CAFÉS
DeliFrance B
Duyichu E
Gongdelin H
KFC D
McDonald's D
Pizza Hut G
Qianmen Old Train Station A
Qianmen Quanjude Roast Duck F
Quanjude Roast Duck C

better bet is the small *DeliFrance*, where you can get coffee and a chocolate croissant for ¥13. For something more ample, the famous *Qianmen Quanjude Roast Duck* is at no. 32 (see p.123 for more restaurants in this area).

Once the district was noisy with opera singers. Today the theatres have been converted to **cinemas** and the area resounds instead with film soundtracks, piped into the street, and with the bips and beeps of the computer games sold at street stalls. For a rather sanitized taste of the district's old delights, visit the *Lao She Tea House* just west of *KFC*, which puts on daily shows of acrobatics and opera (see p.131).

More authentic is the hustle of cramped **Dazhalan Lu**, one of the oldest and most interesting of the Qianmen lanes, opposite the *Qianmen Roast Duck* restaurant on the east side of the road, its entrance marked by a white arch. This was once a major theatre street, now it's a hectic shopping district, with mostly tea shops and clothing stores occupying the genteel old buildings. Go down the first alley on the left, and one of the first shops you'll pass on the right is the Liubiju, a **pickle shop** that's more than a century old. It looks quaint, with pickled vegetables sold out of ceramic jars, but smells awful. Back on Dazhalan, you'll find the Ruifuxiang, an old **fabric shop**, a little farther down on the right – look for the storks on its facade, above the arched entrance. This is the place to get raw silk and satin, but even if you're not buying, take a look at the exhibition on the top floor of old photos of the street. On the other side of the road at no. 24 the Tongrengtang is a famous traditional **Chinese medicine store**, with shelves full of deer horn, bear heart capsules and the like, and a formidable array of aphrodisiacs. The shop's reputation spreads as far as Korea and Japan, and the place has a foreign exchange counter, opposite a booth holding a resident pharmacist offering on-the-spot diagnoses. At the end of the street, marked by a scattering of Chinese-only hotels, was the old red-light district formerly containing more than three hundred brothels. This is one of the last substantial networks of **hutongs** left in the city, and it's certainly worth wandering (or, better, biking) down random alleyways, though expect to get lost. If you're lucky you'll eventually emerge on **Liulichang**, which is parallel to Dazhalan, but not directly accessible from Qianmen Dajie. This street is famous for its **antiques and bookshops** – the originals were bulldozed in the 1950s but have now been neatly reconstructed for the benefit of visitors to make a pretty heritage street full of curio shops.

The Natural History Museum and the Muslim quarter

It's a long and boring thirty-minute walk from the northern end of Qianmen Dajie down to the **Natural History Museum** (daily 8.30am–5pm; ¥15), a few blocks farther south; take bus #17 or #20. After dry halls of stuffed wildlife and plastic dinosaurs, check out the gruesome exhibition in the building to the left of the entrance. Pickled legs, arms, brains and babies are arranged around the stars of the show, two whole corpses, a woman wearing socks, gloves and a hood, and a man with all his skin removed, leaving just the fingernails and lips. You can recover in the soothing surroundings of Tiantan Park (see below), whose western gate is just south of here. The only other reason to head into the rambling sprawl farther south is to find the *Fenglong* hotel, although **Taoranting Park** (daily 6am–7pm; ¥0.2) on Taiping Jie, to the west, with its hills, woods and pavilions, is a pleasant little place, where you may hear old people passing the time by singing Beijing Opera.

Niu Jie (Ox Street), the city's **Muslim quarter**, is a long diversion into the ugly zone west of here. The street, a *hutong* leading off Guang'anmenwai Dajie, on the route of bus #6 from the north gate of Tiantan Park, is a cramped thoroughfare lined with offal stalls and vendors selling fried dough rings, rice cakes and *shaobang* (muffins). The white hats and the beards worn by the men are what most obviously set these Hui minority people apart from the Han Chinese – there are nearly two hundred thousand of them in the capital. The focus of the street is the **mosque** (daily 8am–5pm; ¥10) at its southern end, an attractive building colourfully decorated in Chinese style with abstract decorations and text in Chinese and Arabic over the doors. You won't get to see the hand-written copy of the Koran written in the Yuan dynasty without special permission, or be allowed into the main prayer hall, but you can inspect the courtyard, where a copper bowl used for cooking for the devotees sits near two graves of Persian imams who came here to preach in the thirteenth century.

The Temple of Heaven - Tiantan

Set in its own large and tranquil park about 2km south of Tian'anmen along Qianmen Dajie, the **Temple of Heaven** is widely regarded as the high point of Ming design (daily 8.30am–8pm, buildings close at 5pm; ¥30 for a ticket that includes access to all buildings; just the park ¥10). For five centuries it was at the very heart of imperial ceremony and symbolism, and its architectural unity and beauty remain for most modern visitors more appealing – and on a much more accessible scale – than the Forbidden City. There are various bus routes to Tiantan: bus #106 runs from Dongzhimen to the north entrance; #54 passes the west gate on its way from Beijing Zhan; #17 passes the west gate on its way from Qianmen; and #41 from Chongwenmen stops close to the east gate.

The temple was begun during the reign of Emperor Yongle and completed in 1420. It was conceived as the prime meeting point of Earth and Heaven, and symbols of the two are integral to its plan. Heaven was considered round, and Earth square, thus the round temples and altars stand on square bases, while the whole park has the shape of a semicircle sitting beside a square. The intermediary between Earth and Heaven was of course the Son of Heaven, the emperor, and the temple was the site of the most important ceremony of the imperial court calendar, when the emperor prayed for the year's harvests at the winter solstice. Purified by three days of fasting, he made his way to the park on the day before the solstice, accompanied by his court in all its panoply. On arrival, he would meditate in the Imperial Vault, ritually conversing with the gods on the details of government, before spending the night in the Hall of Prayer of Good Harvests. The following day, amid exact and numerological ritual, the emperor performed sacrifices before the Throne of Heaven at the Round Altar.

It was forbidden for the commoners of old Beijing to catch a glimpse of the great annual procession to the temple and they were obliged to bolt their windows and remain, in silence, indoors. The Tiantan complex remained sacrosanct until it was thrown open to the people on the first Chinese National Day of the Republic in October 1912. Two years after this, the infamous General Yuan Shikai performed the solstice ceremonies himself, as part of his attempt to be proclaimed emperor. He died before the year was out.

The temple buildings

Although you're more likely to enter the actual park from the north or the west, to appreciate the religious ensemble it's best initially to skirt round in order to follow the ceremonial route up from the south entrance, the Zhaohen Gate. The main pathway leads straight to the **Round Altar**, consisting of three marble tiers representing Man, Earth and (at the summit) Heaven. The tiers themselves are composed of blocks in various multiples of nine, which the Chinese saw as cosmologically the most powerful odd number, representing both Heaven and Emperor. The top terrace now stands bare, but the spot at its centre, where the Throne of Heaven was placed, was considered to be the middle of the Middle Kingdom – the very centre of the earth. Various acoustic properties are claimed for the surrounding tiers, and from this point it is said that all sounds are channelled straight upwards. To the east of the fountain, which was reconstructed after fire damage in 1740, are the ruins of a group of buildings used for the preparation of sacrifices.

Directly ahead, the **Imperial Vault of Heaven** is an octagonal structure made entirely of wood, with a dramatic roof of dark blue, glazed tiles. It is preceded by the so-called **Echo Wall**, said to be a perfect whispering gallery, although the unceasing cacophony of tourists trying it out makes it impossible to tell.

The principal temple building – the **Hall of Prayer for Good Harvests**, at the north end of the park – amply justifies all this build-up. It is, quite simply, a wonder. Made entirely of wood, without the aid of a single nail, the circular structure rises from another three-tiered marble terrace, to be topped by three blue-tiled roofs of harmonious proportions. Four compass-point pillars support the vault (in representation of the seasons), enclosed in turn by twelve outer pillars (for the months of the year and the watches of the day). The dazzling colours of the interior, surrounding the central dragon motif, make the pavilion seem ultra-modern; it was in fact entirely rebuilt, faithful to the Ming design, after the original was destroyed by lightning in 1889. The official explanation for this appalling omen was that it was divine punishment for a sacrilegious caterpillar which was on the point of reaching the golden ball on the hall's crest. Nonetheless, 32 court dignitaries paid with their heads.

These days, the park is a popular venue for Chinese to sit, drink tea and play, but it's also easy to find peaceful seclusion in the large areas of park away from the temple proper, which vary from semi-wilderness to formal lawns. Old men gather with their caged birds and crickets, while from dawn onwards, the park is dotted with exponents of various forms of *tai ji*, some learning swordplay in organized classes while others are lost in solitary concentration among the groves of five-hundred-year-old thuja trees.

Along Chang'an Jie

Chang'an Jie, the freeway which runs dead straight east–west across the city, changing its name four times along its length, is downtown Beijing at its most grandiose and unreal. A showcase street, it is lined with the headquarters of official and commercial power, which rub shoulders with the glitziest hotels and malls. Architectural styles are jumbled together, with international modernism, post-modern whimsy and brute Stalinism all in evidence and a couple of ancient sites looking utterly lost amid this parade of gargantuan robots. Heading west from Tian'anmen Square, the tone is mostly official, dominated by the **Communist Party Headquarters** and two **museums**, though there's a pretty good shopping district, **Xidan**, where you can rub shoulders with the locals, and the pleasant **Baiyuguan Si** to chill out in. East is more glamorous, with heavy lashings of shopping, and flashy hotels and restaurants. In this direction, the **Observatory** provides respite from all this fun but ultimately rather exhausting consumerism. Along Chang'an Jie, you'll find most of the facilities you need: the post office, Aviation Office, central train station and plenty of banks. For a quick fix of the whole experience, take bus #1, which travels the entire length of the freeway.

West: Xichang'an Jie and beyond

The **Communist Party Headquarters**, the **Zhongnanhai**, is the first major building you pass – on the right – heading west from Tian'anmen. It's not hard to spot as armed sentries stand outside the gates, ensuring that only invited guests actually get inside. This is perhaps the most important and historic building in the country, base since 1949 of the Central Committee and the Central People's Government, and Mao and Zhou Enlai both worked here. Before the Communist takeover it was home to the Empress Dowager Cixi.

At the next junction, the **Beijing Telecommunications Centre** rears above you – like the buildings around Tian'anmen Square, it's another of the "ten years of liberation" construction projects, and suitably grand. Just west, the **Aviation Office**, the place to buy tickets and catch the airport bus, stands on the site of Democracy Wall, and over the road looms the **Beijing Concert Hall**, recessed a little from the street, another uninspiring construction.

Xidan, the street heading north from the next junction, is worth exploring, at least along its initial few blocks, though not at weekends, when it's heaving with people. This is where the locals shop, and the area is a dense concentration of **department stores**. The choice is less esoteric, and the shopping experience less earthy, than in Qianmen.

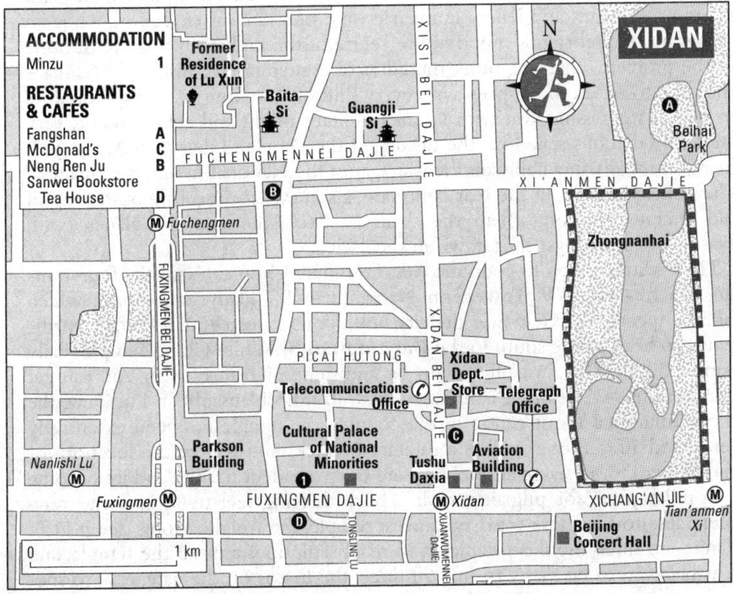

Within walking distance of the Xidan junction, the **Cultural Palace of National Minorities** (Mon–Sat 9am–4.30pm, though it's often closed for trade fairs; ¥5) is an exhibition centre for the crafts and costumes of the nation's non-Han Chinese. Reduced to statistics, these minorities account for only six percent of the Chinese population, but inhabit some sixty percent of the country's territory, establishing a political significance well above their numbers. The slant of the museum is, naturally enough, one of integration, with all the minority regions presented as moving from a divided feudal past to a common future. It could all be a little more imaginatively and less dogmatically displayed, though the exhibits (including brilliant-coloured ethnic clothing, jewellery and artefacts) make a strong impression, and the cases contrasting peasant and noble wear make their point.

It takes persistence to continue much beyond this point, though you might be spurred on by the sight of the trio of distant **skyscrapers**, bizarre buildings which look like erect, ornamented hypodermics. The first one is the pink **Beijing Radio and TV Building**, looking like a parody of the original, Soviet-style construction, over which it towers like a protective big sister. The others are foreign office buildings. On the way, you'll pass the **Parkson Building** on the north side of the next junction, a shopping centre for seriously rich Chinese. On the fifth floor of the south building is an exhibition hall (daily 9.30am–4.30pm; ¥15, students ¥4) with the air of an exclusive private collection, showing "masterpieces" from the craftwork factories across China – similar to the stuff you'll see in the Friendship Store but of much better quality. Though it's all terribly kitsch – a Red Army meeting in ivory, for example – the craftsmanship in evidence is astonishing. In case you're peckish, there's a *KFC* on the ground floor and a giant food court on the sixth.

Two kilometres west of here, another stern Soviet-style building on Fuxing Lu suits its purpose as the **Military Museum** (daily 8am–4.30pm; ¥5), more exciting than its name suggests. Catch bus #1, which terminates close by, or the subway to Junshi Bowuguan. On entering you are confronted with giant paintings of Marx and fellow luminaries, and of a nuclear explosion, while an enormous rocket stands proud at the centre of the high main hall. With none of the problems that dog other museums of contemporary history in China – the need to tweak the displays with every shift of Party line – the museum does its job of impressing you with China's military might and achievements very well. The exhibits stake out the history of the People's Liberation Army, with heavy emphasis, inevitably, on the war against the Nationalists and the Japanese. Curiosities include, in the rear courtyard, a somewhat miscellaneous group of old aircraft – among them the shells of two American spy planes (with Nationalist markings) shot down in the 1950s.

There's little reason to continue west from here – you can visit the four-hundred-metre-high **TV Tower** on Nansanhuan Lu (daily 8am–5pm), which offers a spectacular view over the city, but it costs a steep ¥50. It's more worthwhile to head a little south to the **Baiyunguan Si**, White Cloud Temple (daily 8am–5.30pm; ¥10), just off Baiyun Lu and signposted in English. You can get here on bus #212 from Qianmen, or bus#40 from Nansanhuan Lu. Once the most influential Taoist centre in the country, the temple has been extensively renovated after a long spell as a military barracks and is now the location for the China Taoism Association. There are thirty resident monks, and it's become a popular place for pilgrims, with a busy, thriving feel to it, in some ways preferable to the more touristy Lamaist temple, the Yonghe Gong (see p.115). There are three monkeys depicted in relief sculptures around the temple, and it is believed to be lucky to find all three: the first is on the gate, easy to spot as it's been rubbed black, and the other two are in the first courtyard. Though laid out in a similar way to a Buddhist temple, it has a few unusual features, such as the three gateways at the entrance, symbolizing the three worlds of Taoism – Desire, Substance and Emptiness. Each hall is dedicated to a different deity, whose area of speciality is explained in English outside, with the thickest plumes of incense emerging from the hall to the gods of wealth. The eastern and western halls hold a great collection of Taoist relics, including some horrific paintings of hell with people being sawn in half and the like. An attached bookshop has only one text in English, the *Book of Changes*, but plenty of tapes and lucky charms. The place is at its most colourful during the New Year temple fair (see "Festivals", p.59). If you're on a bike or are a very committed temple tourist, you could continue south about a kilometre from Baiyunguan to see the **Tianning Si Ta**, Heavenly Repose Pagoda, a beautiful building stranded to great effect amid heavy industrial plant, though the factories prevent you actually getting close to it.

East from Tian'anmen – Dongchang'an Jie and Jianguomen Dajie

Everything on the eastern half of Chang'an (initially called **Dongchang'an Jie**) takes its bearings from the *Beijing Hotel*, though perhaps a better marker for the abrupt transition from the political zone of Tian'anmen and around to this commercial sector is the first big billboard, opposite **Wangfujing**, Beijing's most famous shopping street.

Jianguomen Dajie, the strip beyond the second ring road, is Beijing's rich quarter, a ritzy area given much of its international flavour and distinctive atmosphere of casual wealth by a large contingent of foreigners, upmarket tourists and staff from the weird Jianguomen embassy compound. Eating and staying around here will soon sap most travellers' budgets (first-time tourists can be heard here expressing disappointment that China is as expensive as New York), but the wide variety of shopping offered – good clothes markets, the best Friendship Store in China, and plazas that wouldn't look out of place in Hong Kong – will suit all pockets. The main street is about as far away from traditional China as you can get, but the **Ancient Observatory** and quiet little **Ritan Park** nearby offer less packaged experiences.

Dongchang'an Jie, Wangfujing and around

Wangfujing, heading north from the *Beijing Hotel* on Dongchang'an Jie, is where the capital gets down to the business of **shopping** in earnest, though it's no longer the city's premier consumer cornucopia. But it does have some good stuff, even some history, and it's short enough to stroll along its length. For a century the haunt of quality stores, before the Communist takeover it was called Morrison Street. On the western side of the street are plenty of small stores selling clothes. You'll also find the China Photo Studio about halfway up at no. 228, which will produce passport photos as well as develop film. A medical instrument store just to the north provides some of the few real bargains you can get in China – Western suppliers come here to buy in bulk. Past it, just before the crossroads with Dong'anmen Jie, is the Foreign Language Bookstore, the largest in China and a good resource for travellers (see p.133 for more details). On the other side of the street, the Sun Dong'an Plaza is a glitzy mall; you're better off going here for a snack – the place is home to *McDonald's* (first floor) and a *DeliFrance* (second floor) – or to change money at the Bank of China (ground floor; Mon–Fri 9am–noon & 1.30–5pm) than to buy any of

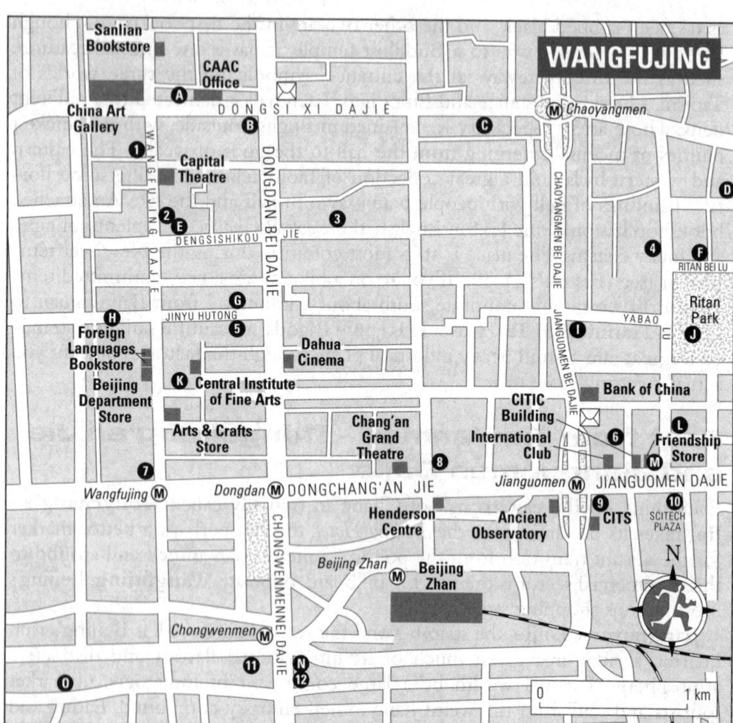

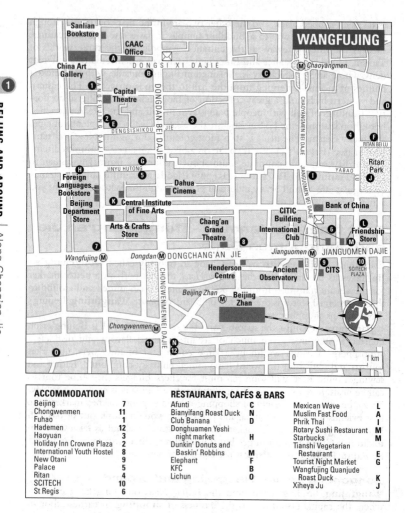

ACCOMMODATION	
Beijing	7
Chongwenmen	11
Fuhao	1
Hademen	12
Haoyuan	3
Holiday Inn Crowne Plaza	2
International Youth Hostel	8
New Otani	9
Palace	5
Ritan	4
SCITECH	10
St Regis	6

RESTAURANTS, CAFÉS & BARS	
Afunti	C
Bianyifang Roast Duck	N
Club Banana	D
Donghuamen Yeshi night market	H
Dunkin' Donuts and Baskin' Robbins	M
Elephant	F
KFC	B
Lichun	O
Mexican Wave	L
Muslim Fast Food	A
Phrik Thai	I
Rotary Sushi Restaurant	M
Starbucks	M
Tianshi Vegetarian Restaurant	E
Tourist Night Market	G
Wangfujing Quanjude Roast Duck	K
Xiheya Ju	J

the very pricey, mostly designer, clothes on sale, though the basement stalls are worth a browse if you're after tea or souvenirs.

On the eastern side of the street a number of **hutongs** lead into a quiet area well away from the bustle of the main street. The ten brothers of a Ming-dynasty emperor used to live here, so that he could keep a wary eye on them, and you can still see their palace at the end of Shuaifuyuan Hutong, now converted into a medical college. Continuing east through the *hutongs*, you'll reach **Dongdan Bei Dajie**, parallel to Wangfujing, which is rapidly becoming a shopping centre to rival it, full of clothing boutiques. The architectural medley on Dongchang'an Jie continues with the chunky Women's Activity Centre, thrown up in time for the Women's Conference in 1995, past the *International Hotel* just north of Beijing Zhan, until you reach the giant concrete knot of the Jianguomen intersection, at the limit of the old walls.

Jianguomen Dajie and the Ancient Observatory

An unexpected survivor marooned amid the highrises, the **Ancient Observatory** (Mon–Fri 9–11.30am & 1–4.30pm;¥10) is a delightful surprise, tucked in the southwest corner of the Jianguomen intersection, beside the Jianguomen subway stop. The first observatory on this site was founded under the orders of Kublai Khan, the astronomers' commission being to reform the then faulty calendar. Later it came under Muslim control, as medieval Islamic science enjoyed pre-eminence, but, bizarrely, in the early seventeenth century it was placed in the hands of Jesuit Christian missionaries. The Jesuits, a small group led by one Matteo Ricci, arrived in Beijing in 1601 and astonished citizens and emperor by a series of precise astronomical forecasts. They re-equipped the observatory and remained in charge through to the 1830s. Today the building is essentially a shell, and the best features of the complex are the garden, a placid retreat, and the eight Ming-dynasty astronomical instruments sitting on the roof, stunningly sculptural armillary spheres, theodolites and the like. The small **museum** attached, displaying early astronomy-influenced pottery and navigational equipment, is an added bonus.

North along Chaoyangmen Dajie, you come to the **International Post Office** and **Bank of China**. Heading east beyond the Jianguomen intersection, the **International Club** is the first sign that you're approaching the capital's diplomatic sector. It's a restrained building, dwarfed by the SCITECH building across the street, a 36-storey monolith with a speedy and efficient bank on the first floor which offers a comprehensive service to visitors. Turn left at the *International Club* up Ritan Lu and you'll hit the **Jianguomenwai Diplomatic Compound**, the first of two embassy complexes (the other is at Sanlitun, well northeast of here). It's a funny place, a giant toytown with neat buildings in ordered courtyards and frozen sentries on red and white plinths. **Ritan Park** is just one block back north from the *International Club*, a five-minute walk from Jianguomen Dajie. As with most of the capital's parks, it's not big on grass, but it's popular with embassy staff and courting couples, who make use of its numerous secluded nooks.

Back on Jianguomen Dajie, beyond the SCITECH building, you'll reach the **Friendship Store** (daily 9am–8.30pm), China's best. Its top floors are devoted to the usual range of goods – clothes, jewellery and paintings – but its lower floor is perhaps of more immediate and compelling use, with a carpet section, a foreign exchange (open every day), a supermarket selling plenty of foreign goodies, an information desk where you can pick up the *China Daily*, and a bookshop. There's also a photo booth for your visa photographs. Outside is a string of upmarket **coffee bars and restaurants**, the best and cheapest of which is the 24-hour *Dunkin' Donuts*, though watch your bags here as it's a favoured hangout for thieves. There's also the pricey *Starbucks* just around the corner, ideal if you're missing decent coffee. On the other side of the road, the SCITECH Plaza (daily 9am–9pm) is a more modern shopping centre with five floors of clothes and accessories. There's a food court in the basement and a Bank of China on the first floor.

A kilometre east of the Friendship Store, the **Silk Market** runs north off Jianguomen Dajie. Again, it's mostly clothes, though there are a few antique stalls as well, and a couple of stalls selling ethnic clothing and bedsheets. Again, you'll need to bargain, though it's harder here as there are more tourists around – aim to knock at least two-thirds off the starting price. Good buys are silk dressing gowns, ties and scarves. Most of the designer labels are fake, although some of the Nike, North Face and J.Crew gear is the genuine article. Youths hang around the market, illicitly selling CD-ROM computer games and music

CDs (they can be knocked down to ¥10) – they're good quality but tend to miss off the last track.

It's a long way, and you may be all shopped out by now, but dedicated consumers who continue to the **World Trade Centre**, just before the intersection with Dongsanhuan Bei Lu, about 3km east of here, are rewarded with Beijing's most exclusive mall, four shining storeys of pricey consumables. As well as boutiques there's a post office (Level B1), a Bank of China (Level 2), another *Starbucks* (Level 1) and a *Sparkice* Internet café (Level 2; see p.136). The basement has a Wellcome Supermarket (the Hong Kong brand), one of the best supermarkets in the city, though it's not cheap. As well as shopping here, foreign residents advertise flats and jobs on the noticeboard.

North of Tian'anmen

The area north of Tian'anmen Square has a scattered collection of sights, many of them remnants of the imperial past, when this area was the home of princes, dukes and monks. The finest remaining palace is **Prince Gong's**, buried in Beijing's best-preserved *hutongs* north of **Beihai Park**, the imperial pleasure park, while the finest temple, the **Yonghe Gong**, is in the northern outskirts of the centre. Other illustrious residents are more recent; in the northwest, the twentieth-century homes of the writer **Lu Xun** and the artist **Xu Beihong** are open as museums. For a general picture of the state of the Chinese arts, visit the **China Art Gallery** just north of Wangfujing.

Jingshan and Beihai parks

Visiting **Jingshan Park** (daily 6am–10pm; ¥3) is a natural way to round off a trip to the Forbidden City. An artificial mound, it was created by the digging of the palace moat and served as a windbreak and a barrier to malevolent spirits (believed to emanate from the north) for the imperial quarter of the city. It takes its name, meaning Coal Hill, from a coal store once sited here. Its history, most momentously, includes the suicide of the last Ming emperor, Chong Zhen, in 1644, who hanged himself here from a lotus tree after rebel troops broke into the imperial city. The spot, on the eastern side of the park, is easy to find as it is signposted everywhere (underneath signs pointing to a children's playground), though the tree that stands here is not the original.

It's the views from the top of the hill that make this park such a compelling target. They take in the whole extent of the Forbidden City, a revealing perspective, and a fair swathe of the city outside, a deal more attractive than at ground level. To the west is Beihai with its fat snake lake, in the north Gulou and Zhonglou (the Drum and Bell towers), and to the northeast the Yonghe Gong.

Beihai Park (daily 6am–8pm; ¥5, buildings ¥10), a few hundred metres west of Jingshan on the route of bus #13 from the Yonghe Gong or #5 from Qianmen, is almost half lake in extent, and it's a favourite skating spot in the frozen winter months. It was supposedly created by Kublai Khan, long before any of the Forbidden City structures were conceived, and its scale is suitably ambitious: the lake was man-made, an island being created in its midst with the excavated earth. Emperor Qianlong oversaw its landscaping into a classical garden and Mao's widow, the ill-fated Jiang Qing, was a frequent visitor here. Today its elegance is marred by funfairs and shops among the willows and red-columned galleries, though it's still a grand place to retreat from the city and recharge. Most of the buildings (daily 6am–4pm) lie on the central island, whose summit is marked by a white dagoba, built in the mid-seventeenth century to celebrate a visit by the Dalai Lama, a suitable emblem for a park which contains a curious mixture of religious buildings, storehouses for cultural relics and imperial garden architecture.

Just inside the south gate, the **Round City** encloses a courtyard which holds a jade bowl, said to have belonged to Kublai Khan. The white jade Buddha in the hall behind was a present from Burma. The **island** is accessible by a walkway from here. It's dotted with religious architecture, which you'll come across as you scramble around the rocky paths, including the **Yuegu Lou**, a hall full of steles, and the giant **dagoba** sitting on top with a shrine to the demon-headed, multi-armed Lamaist deity, Yamantaka, nestling inside. An exclusive restaurant, the *Fangshan*, where decor, food and prices are imperial, sits off a painted corridor running round the base of the hill. There's a boat dock near here, where you can rent rowing **boats**, or you can get duck-shaped pedal boats from near the south gate – good ways to explore the lake and its banks. On the north side of the lake an impressive **dragon screen**, in good condition, is one of China's largest at 27m long. The Five Dragon Pavilions nearby are supposedly in the shape of a dragon's spine. Over on the other side of the lake, the gardens and rockeries here were popular with Emperor Qianlong, and it's easy to see why – even when the place is crowded at weekends, the atmosphere is tranquil.

The lake area

The area north of Beihai Park has been subject to very little modernization, and the street plan remains a tangle of alleys, centring on the three artificial **Shisha lakes**, created during the Yuan dynasty, and the port for a canal network that served the capital. The choked, grey alleys show Beijing's other, private, face: here you'll see cluttered courtyards and converted palaces, and come across small open spaces where old men sit with their birds. There are also two giant old buildings, the Bell and Drum towers, hidden away among the alleys. The area has recently been prettified, with touristy venues being built and rickshaw tours running from outside the bell tower, but it retains its charm, at least for the moment. It's also become one of Beijing's hipper hangouts, with a string of low-key bars along the lakeside (see p.126). The best way to get around by yourself is certainly by bike. Traffic is light and you're free to dive into any alley you fancy, though you're almost certain to get lost – in which case cycle around until you come to the lake, the only big landmark around. The best point of entry is the *hutong* nearest the northern entrance to Beihai Park – to get here by bus, take trolleybus #111 from Dondan Bei Dajie, or bus #13 from the Yonghe Gong.

One destination to head for is **Prince Gong's Palace** (daily 9am–4.30pm; ¥10), residence of the last Qing emperor's father and the best-kept courtyard house in the city. Follow the curving alley north from Beihai Park's north entrance – Qianhai Hu (the southernmost lake) will be on your right – then take the first left, then the first right on to Qianhai Xi Jie. If you're trying to reach the palace directly by bus, you'll have to get off on Dianmen Xi Dajie and walk the same route. The attractive, leafy garden of the palace, split into discreet compounds and imaginatively landscaped, is host to irregular performances of Beijing Opera – though you'll have to time your arrival with that of the tour groups, at around 11am and 4pm to witness these. There are plenty of other **old palaces** in the area, as this was once something of an imperial pleasure ground and home to a number of high officials and distinguished eunuchs. The Palace of Tao Beile, now a school, is just west of here on Liuyin Jie. Doubling back and heading north along the lake side, you'll come to a hump-back bridge at the point where the lake is narrowest. Over the bridge is the excellent *Kaorouji Restaurant* (see "Restaurants", p.125), which boasts good views over the lake. Opposite you'll find the *Buddha Bar* (among others), a great place to sit outside with a coffee.

To get here from the east, take the first *hutong* on the right walking south from the Drum Tower. Keep going along the south side of the lake and you'll find a little park about 500m farther up with a bird market in it and beyond that the ramshackle Houhai **antique market**, signposted in English, just before Deshengmennei Dajie. If you're exploring by bike you could consider a diversion out west to the Xu Beihong Museum (see opposite) from here. Back in the *hutongs*, head north along the lakeside and loop around to the east and you'll reach **Song Qingling's Residence** (Tues–Sun 9am–4.30pm; ¥8), another Qing mansion, with a delicate, spacious garden. Song Qingling, the wife of Sun Yatsen, commands great respect in China and an exhibition inside details her busy life in a dry, admiring tone. From here, an alley will take you on to Gulou Xi Dajie, a major street, at the eastern end of which squats the **Gulou** or Drum Tower (daily 9am–4.30pm; ¥6), a fifteenth-century Ming creation. From this vantage point drums were beaten to mark the hours of day and night and to call imperial officials to meetings. In the gloomy interior is a small exhibition on *hutongs* and a drum you can beat for ¥10. Its twin, the **Zhonglou**, or Bell Tower (daily 9am–4.30pm; ¥6), is visible from here – at the end of a short *hutong*. Originally Ming, it was destroyed by fire and rebuilt in the eighteenth century. It still has its original bell. Both buildings are formidable structures, but a little shabby on close inspection. They stand on the city's main north–south axis – head directly south, going round Jingshan Park, and past the Forbidden City, and you'll eventually come to Qianmen Dajie, a route followed by bus #5.

The northwest

You're more likely to pass through the area northwest of Tian'anmen than stop, as it's on the way to the deservedly popular Summer Palace. The few attractions scattered around here are small scale, but make good points to break a journey farther afield.

Heading west from the south end of Beihai Park along Wenjin Dajie, you'll come to **Fuchengmennei Dajie**, just off Xidan Dajie, the area's shopping district. A couple of places along here make it worth a nose around. Bus #101 from the north exit of the Forbidden City, and #13 from the Yonghe Gong, traverse the street. The **Guangji Si**, headquarters of the China Buddhist Association, is a working Buddhist temple near its eastern end, on the north side of the road, with an important collection of painting and sculpture. There's no entrance fee and visitors are free to look around. Farther west along the street you'll come to a temple on the north side that's been converted into a school – the spirit wall now forms one side of a public lavatory – and at no. 133 is China's first sex shop, the Adam and Eve Health Store, where a formidable array of sex aids is sold by white-coated attendants. Farther on, the massive white dagoba of the **Baita Si** (Tues–Sun 9am–5pm; ¥10) becomes visible, rising over the rooftops of a labyrinth of *hutongs*; the only access is from Fuchengmennei Dajie. Shaped like an upturned bowl with an ice-cream cone on top, the 35-metre-high dagoba was built to house relics in the Yuan dynasty and designed by a Nepalese architect. The temple, currently under restoration, is worth a visit just for the collection of small Buddha statues, mostly Tibetan, housed in one hall. Another hall holds a collection of bronze *lohans*, including one with a beak, small bronze Buddhas and other, weirder Lamaist figures, together with silk and velvet priestly garments, which were unearthed from under the dagoba in 1978. Just outside the temple there's a tasty pancake stall.

Continue west and, just before the giant intersection with Fuchengmen Bei Dajie, you'll see Xisantiao Hutong to the north, which leads to the **Former Residence of Lu Xun** (Tues–Sun 9am–4pm; ¥10), a large and extensively renovated courtyard house. Lu Xun (1881–1936) is widely accepted as the greatest modern Chinese writer, who gave up a promising career in medicine to write books (see p.401). A hater of pomposity, he might feel a little uneasy in his house now, where the atmosphere is of uncritical admiration. His possessions have been preserved like relics, incidentally giving a good idea of what Chinese interiors looked like at the beginning of last century, and there's a photo exhibition of his life lauding his achievements. A bookshop in the eastern building sells English translations of his work, including his most popular work, *The True Story of Ah Q*.

Not far from here, at 53 Xinjiekou Bei Dajie, on the route of bus #22 from Qianmen or #38 from the east end of Fuchingmennei Dajie, the **Xu Beihong Museum** (Tues–Sun 9–11am & 1.30–4.30pm; ¥1) is definitely worth the diversion. It is dedicated to a contemporary of Lu Xun who did for Chinese art what Lu Xun did for literature. Son of a wandering portraitist, Xu Beihong (1895–1953) had to look after his whole family from the age of 17 after his father died, and spent much of his early life in semi-destitution before receiving the acclaim he deserved. His extraordinary facility is well in evidence here in seven halls which display a huge collection of his work, including many of the ink paintings of horses he was most famous for, but also oil paintings in a Western style, which he produced when studying in France, and large-scale allegorical images which allude to events in China at the time. But the images it is easiest to respond to are his delightful sketches and studies, in ink and pencil, often of his son.

The northeast

The most exciting sight in the north of the city is the **Yonghe Gong**, Tibetan Lama Temple (daily 9am–5pm; ¥15), northeast of the Forbidden City and just south of the Yonghe Gong subway stop. If you've time for just one temple in the city, make it this – you won't see many more colourful temples in Beijing, though it is a little touristy.

It was built towards the end of the seventeenth century as the residence of Prince Yin Zhen. In 1723, when the prince became the Emperor Yong Zheng and moved into the Forbidden City, the temple was retiled in imperial yellow and restricted thereafter to religious use. It became a lamasery in 1744, housing monks from Tibet and also from Inner Mongolia, over which it had a presiding role, supervising the election of the Mongolian Living Buddha, who was chosen by lot from a gold urn. After the civil war in 1949, the Yonghe Gong was declared a national monument and for thirty years was closed; remarkably it escaped the Cultural Revolution.

Visitors are free to wander through the prayer halls and gardens, though the experience is largely an aesthetic rather than a spiritual one. As well as the amazing *mandalas* hanging in side halls, there is some notable statuary. In the Third Hall the draped statues are **nandikesvras**, Buddhas having sex, which earned the lamasery its reputation as China's most illustrious sex manual – the statues were once used to educate emperors' sons. The Hall of the Wheel of Law, behind it, has a gilded bronze statue of the founder of the Yellow Hat Sect and paintings which depict his life, while the thrones next to it are for the Dalai Lamas when they used to come here to teach. In the last, grandest hall, the **Wanfu Pavilion**, an eighteen-metre-high statue of the Maitreya Buddha is made from a single trunk of sandalwood, a gift for Emperor Qianlong from the seventh Dalai Lama. The wood is Tibetan and it took three years to ship it to Beijing.

The lamasery is not just a beautiful building – and, with its gardens, a refuge – but it also functions as an active **Tibetan Buddhist centre**, for propaganda purposes, to show China guaranteeing and respecting the religious freedom of the minorities. It's questionable how genuine the monks are. This is where, in 1995, the puppet Panchen Lama chosen by the Chinese state was officially sworn in, the Dalai Lama's choice of soul boy, a 6-year-old child, having disappeared (see box, p.1161).

Next to the Yonghe Gong, on the west side, is a quiet **hutong** lined with little shops selling religious tapes, incense and images. This street, one of the city's oldest, has been home to scholars since the Yuan dynasty and is lined with *pailous*, decorative arches, which once graced many of Beijing's streets – they were torn down in the 1950s as a hindrance to traffic. On the right, about 100m down, the **Confucius Temple** (daily 8.30am–5pm; ¥10) is a rather dry place, used for decades as a museum. In the courtyard, steles record the names of those who studied here and passed the civil service exams. The last few steles are Qing, paid for by the scholars themselves as the emperor refused to fund them. The Main Hall is a dark, haphazard **museum** holding incense burners and musical instruments. Another, new museum in a side hall holds a diverse range of artefacts – the Tang pottery, which includes images of pointy-faced foreigners, is the most diverting. At the back, a warehouse-like building holds stele texts of the thirteen Confucian classics, calligraphy which once formed the standard to be emulated by all scholars. But perhaps the best thing to do here is sit on a bench in the peaceful courtyard, among ancient, twisted trees, and enjoy the silence.

Returning to the Yonghe Gong and heading north, **Ditan Park** (daily 6am–9pm; ¥1, buildings ¥5) is just 100m away, more interesting as a place to wander among the trees and spot the odd *tai ji* performance than for its small **museum** (¥5) holding the emperor's sedan chair and the enormous altar at which he performed sacrifices to the earth.

Heading back to the centre from the Yonghe Gong by bus or bike you could look in at the **China Art Gallery** (Tues–Sun 9am–4pm; entrance fee varies, ¥2–20), at the top end of Wangfujing, on the route of bus #2 which runs north–south between Qianmen and Andingmen Dajie, or trolleybus #104, which runs between Andingmennei Dajie and Beijing Zhan. A huge and draughty building, it usually holds a couple of shows at once, though there's no permanent collection. Shows in the past have included specialist women's and minority exhibitions, even a show of socialist realist propaganda put up not to inspire renewed vigour but as a way to consider past follies. Revolutionary imagery has long had its day and Chinese painting is enjoying something of a renaissance, with some very interesting work emerging from the Beijing art colleges. You can check their work out in July, when they hold their degree shows here, and it's also a good place to meet some of the most boho Chinese, the art students. Check the listings magazines for what's on.

The outskirts

The most compelling sights on the outskirts of the city are the lakeside gardens and pavilions of the **Summer Palace** – a recommended escape, summer or winter. The presence of two universities near here is not in itself of much note but they have spawned plenty of cheap **restaurants** and some of the more underground **bars**. It's generally true that all the decent **nightlife** is in the city's northern outskirts, while on the eastern edge you'll find a plethora of bars serving the city's foreign community and well-to-do Chinese (see "Drinking and dancing", p.58).

The Zoo, Big Bell Temple and the Summer Palaces

Beijing Zoo (daily 7.30am–5pm; ¥7), on Xizhimenwei Dajie, marks the edge of the inner city. There's a subway stop, Xizhimen, 1km east of the zoo, and a bus terminus just south of it; bus #7, which you can catch from Fuchingmen Dajie, terminates here. Xizhimen Zhan (Beijing North train station) is north of the subway stop. The zoo itself, flanked on either side by the monumental Capital Gymnasium and Soviet-built Exhibition Centre, is not a great attraction unless you really need to see a panda. You can join the queues to have your photo taken sitting astride a plastic replica, then push your way through to glimpse the living variety – kept in relatively palatial quarters and highly familiar through ritual diplomatic mating exchanges over the last decades. While the pandas lie on their backs in their luxury pad, waving their legs in the air, other animals, less cute or less endangered, slink, pace or flap around their miserable cells. Much the best part of the rest of the zoo is the new aquarium, though it's a bit pricey (¥100, ¥50 children).

The **Dazhong Si** (Great Bell Temple; Tues–Sun 8am–4.30pm; ¥5), is actually one of Beijing's most interesting little museums, though it's stuck out on Beisanhuan Lu, the north section of the third ring road, a long way from anywhere; you could visit on the way to or from the Summer Palace if you're travelling by taxi. Displayed to good effect in a converted temple, the exhibits, several hundred **bronze bells** from temples all over the country, are considerable works of art, their surfaces enlivened with relief texts in Chinese and Tibetan, abstract patterns and images of storks and dragons. The odd creature perching on their tops is called a *pulao*, a legendary creature which shrieks when attacked by a whale (the wooden poles with which the bells were struck are carved to look like whales). The smallest bell is the size of a wine cup, the largest, hanging in the back hall, is the size of a house. A Ming creation, called the **King of Bells**, at fifty tonnes it's the biggest and oldest bell in the world and reputedly can be heard up to 40km away. You can climb up to a platform above it to get a closer look at some of the 250,000 characters on its surface, and join Chinese visitors in trying to throw a coin into the small hole in the top. Its method of construction, and the history of Chinese bell making, are explained in side halls. Tapes on sale of the bells in action are more interesting than they might appear; the shape of Chinese bells dampens vibrations, so they can be effectively used as instruments.

It's not an obvious tourist attraction, but the whole of **Haidian district**, north of the zoo, bears mentioning – here you'll find the more underground bars and clubs, plenty of Internet cafés, and on Zhongguangcun Lu, nicknamed Electronics Street, a hi-tech zone of computer shops. In the north of the area, on the way to the Summer Palace, you'll pass **Beijing Daxue** (Beida), the capital university. Originally established and administered by the Americans at the beginning of this century, it stood on Coal Hill in Jingshan Park and was moved to its present site in 1953. Now busy with new contingents of foreign students from the West, two decades ago it was half-deserted when the Cultural Revolution saw students and teachers alike dispersed for "open schooling" or re-education. Today, Chinese applicants are still required to spend a year in the army first. It's the most prestigious university in China, with a pleasant campus – old buildings and quiet, well-maintained grounds make it nicer than most of the city's parks. The technical college, Qinghua, is not far from here, to the east. Around the gates of both universities you'll find small, inexpensive **restaurants**, **bars** and **Internet cafés** catering for the students.

Yuanmingyuan

Beijing's original Summer Palace, the **Yuanmingyuan** (daily 9am–6pm; ¥15), is a thirty-minute walk north of Beida, on the route of bus #375, which you catch from a terminus just north of Xizhimen subway stop, or bus #322, which leaves from a terminus outside the zoo. Built by the Qing Emperor Kangxi in the early eighteenth century, the palace, nicknamed China's Versailles by Europeans, once boasted the largest royal gardens in the world – with some two hundred pavilions and temples set around a series of lakes and natural springs. Marina Warner recreates the scene in *The Dragon Empress*:

> **Scarlet and golden halls, miradors, follies and gazebos clustered around artificial hills and lakes. Tranquil tracts of water were filled with fan tailed goldfish with telescopic eyes, and covered with lotus and lily pads; a superabundance of flowering shrubs luxuriated in the gardens; antlered deer wandered through the grounds; ornamental ducks and rare birds nestled on the lakeside.**

Today, however, there is little enough to hang your imagination upon. In 1860 the entire complex was burnt and destroyed by British and French troops, ordered by the Earl of Elgin to make the imperial court "see reason" during the Opium Wars. There are plenty of signs around to remind you of this, making the park a monument to Chinese xenophobia. Of course they've got a point, but it is annoying, especially when fired up locals confront visiting foreigners. The park extends over 350 hectares but the only really identifiable ruins are the **Hall of Tranquillity** in the northeastern section. The stone and marble remains of fountains and columns hint at how fascinating the original must once have been, with its marriage of European Rococo decoration and Chinese motifs. The government is jazzing the place up with a programme of restoration and construction, but this remains an attraction wholly eclipsed by the new Summer Palace.

The Summer Palace

Yiheyuan, usually just referred to as the **Summer Palace** (daily 8am–7pm, buildings close at 4pm; ¥40), is certainly worth the effort to seek out. Take the same buses that go to Yuanmingyuan and get off a few stops later, at the terminus, or take bus #808 from Qianmen. The quickest route is to take a taxi from Xizhimen subway stop (¥15). This is one of the loveliest spots in Beijing, a vast public park, two-thirds lake, where the latterday imperial court would decamp during the hottest months of the year. The site is perfect, surrounded by hills, cooled by the lake and sheltered by garden landscaping. Surviving another bout of European aggression in 1900, the impressive buildings are spread out along the lakeside and connected by a suitably majestic gallery.

There have been summer imperial pavilions at Yiheyuan since the eleventh century, although the present layout is essentially eighteenth-century, created by the Manchu Emperor Qianlong. However, the key character associated with the palace is the **Empress Dowager Cixi**, who ruled over the fast-disintegrating Chinese empire from 1861 until her death in 1908. Yiheyuan was very much her pleasure ground. She rebuilt the palaces in 1888 and determinedly restored them in 1902 – her ultimate flight of fancy being the construction of a magnificent marble boat from the very funds intended for the Chinese navy. Whether her misappropriations had any real effect on the empire's path is hard to determine, but it certainly speeded the decline, with China suffering heavy naval defeats during the war with Japan.

The **palaces** are built to the north of the lake, on and around Wanshou Shan (Longevity Hill) and many remain intimately linked with Cixi – anecdotes about whom are staple fare of the numerous guides. To enjoy the site, however, you need know very little. Like Beihai, the park, its lake and pavilions form a startling visual array, like a traditional landscape painting brought to life.

Most visitors enter through the **East Gate**, where the buses stop, above which is the main palace compound, including the **Renshoudian** (Hall of Benevolence and Longevity), a majestic hall where the empress and her predecessors gave audience. It contains much of the original nineteenth-century furniture, including an imposing throne. Beyond to the right is the **Deheyuan** (Palace of Virtue and Harmony), dominated by a three-storey **theatre**, complete with trap doors for the appearances and disappearances of the actors. Theatre was one of Cixi's main passions and she sometimes took part in performances, dressed as Guanyin, the goddess of mercy. With a neat sense of irony, the next main building, the **Yulantang** (Jade Waves Palace) on the lakeside, was for ten years the prison of the Emperor Guangxu – kept in captivity here, as a minor, while Cixi exercised his powers. Just to the west is the dowager's own principal residence, the **Leshoutang** (Hall of Joy and Longevity).

From here to the northwest corner of the lake runs the **Long Gallery**, the nine-hundred-metre covered way, painted with mythological scenes and flanked by various temples and pavilions. It is said that no pair of lovers can walk through without emerging betrothed. Near the west end of the gallery is the infamous **marble boat**, completed by Cixi with the purloined naval cash and regarded by her acolytes as a suitably witty and defiant gesture. Close by, and the tourist focus of this site, is a jetty with **rowing boats** for rent (¥10 per hour). Boating on the lake is a popular pursuit, with locals as much as foreigners, and well worth the money. You can dock again over below Longevity Hill and row out to the two **bridges** – the Jade Belt on the western side and Seventeen Arched on the east. In winter, the Chinese skate on the lake here, an equally spectacular sight, and skates are available for rent.

Eating, drinking, entertainment and shopping

You're spoilt for choice when it comes to food in Beijing. Splurging in classy **restaurants** is a great way to spend your evenings, as prices in even the most luxurious places are very competitive and a lot more affordable than their equivalent in the West. Beijing has a great deal of entertainment options, too, and it's well worth seeking them out; remember you won't have much opportunity outside the capital. There is a promising **bar and club scene** worth sampling, if just for the strange cultural juxtapositions it throws up. If you want to check out a Chinese disco or indigenous rock band, this is the place to do it and, again, a night on the town won't break your budget. **Shopping** is another diverting pastime, with the best choice of souvenirs and consumables in the country. In particular, Beijing still has a collection of intriguing little markets offering an appealing and affordable alternative to the new giant malls.

Eating

Nowhere on the Chinese mainland has the culinary wealth of Beijing, with every style of **Chinese food** available, just about any Asian, and most world cuisines. Amongst all this abundance it's sometimes easy to forget that **Beijing** has its own culinary tradition – specialities well worth trying are **Beijing duck** (*Beijing kaoya*) and **Mongolian hotpot**. Beijing duck appears in Chinese restaurants worldwide and consists of small pieces of meat which you dip in plum sauce, then wrap with chopped onions in a pancake. It's very rich and packs a massive cholesterol count. Mongolian hotpot is healthier, a poor man's fondue, involving a large pot of boiling stock, usually heated from underneath the table, into which you dip strips of mutton, cabbage and noodles, then, if you're really committed, drink the rest as soup.

There's ample opportunity to eat **Western food** in Beijing, though it generally costs a little more than Chinese. French food is fashionable, though it's pretty mediocre. An exception is the excellent *DeliFrance* chain, which has good cheap pastries. German and Italian food are better, though again expensive, with a number of outlets in the more exclusive parts of town. If you really want the comforts of the familiar, try international places such as the *Hard Rock Café* – everything just like at home, including the prices. **Japanese** and **Korean** cuisine is mainly available from restaurants in upmarket hotels, though it's possible to eat both without breaking your budget, and they're well worth trying.

Fast food comes in two forms: the Chinese version, a canteen-style serving, usually of noodles in a polystyrene packet, which you find in department stores or buy from street stalls; and Western imports such as *Pizza Hut, McDonald's* and *KFC*, which have made a considerable impact and are greatly imitated.

Beijing restaurants

Afunti	阿凡提	*āfántí*
Be There Or Be Square	不见不散	*bújiàn búsàn*
Berena's Bistro	伯瑞娜	*bóruì nà*
Bianyifang Roast Duck	便宜坊烤鸭店	*piányìfǎng kǎoyādiàn*
DeliFrance	大磨坊面包	*dàmòfáng miànbāo*
Donghuamen Yeshi	东华门夜市	*dōnghuámén yèshì*
Duyichu	都一处烧麦馆	*dōuyíchù shāomàiguǎn*
Elephant	大笨象	*dàbènxiàng*
Fangshan	仿膳饭店	*fǎngshàn fàndiàn*
Golden Elephant	金象苑东方餐厅	*jīnxiàngyuán dōngfāng cāntīng*
Golden Thaitanium	泰合金	*tàihéjīn*
Gongdelin	功德林素菜馆	*gōngdélín sùcàiguǎn*
Goubuli Baozi	狗不理包子铺	*gǒubùlǐ bāozipù*
Hard Rock Café	硬石餐厅	*yìngshí cāntīng*
Kaorouji	烤肉季	*kǎoròujì*
KFC	肯德基家乡鸡	*kěndéjī jiāxiāngjī*
Lichun	利群烤鸭店	*lìqún kǎoyādiàn*
Makai	吗凯餐厅	*mǎkǎi cāntīng*
McDonald's	麦当劳餐厅	*màidāngláo cāntīng*
Mexican Wave	墨西哥风味餐	*mòxīgē fēngwèicān*
Neng Ren Ju	能仁居饭庄	*néngrénjū fànzhuāng*
Old Character Hakka	老汉子客家菜馆	*lǎohànzi kèjiācàiguǎn*
One Thousand and One Nights	一千零一夜	*yīqiān língyīyè*
Phrik Thai	泰辣椒	*tàilàjiāo*
Pizza Hut	必胜客	*bìshèngkè*
Qianmen Quanjude Roast Duck	前门全聚德烤鸭店	*qiánmén quánjùdé kǎoyādiàn*
Quanjude Roast Duck	全聚德烤鸭店	*quánjùdé kǎoyādiàn*
Saigon Inn (Gloria Plaza Hotel)	凯莱大酒店	*kǎilái dàjiǔdiàn*
Shenglinfu	盛林府	*shènglínfǔ*
Sichuan	四川酒楼	*sìchuān jiǔlóu*
Tianshi	绿色天食	*lǜsè tiānshí*
Wangfujing Quanjude Roast Duck	王府井全聚德烤鸭店	*wángfǔjǐng quánjùdé kǎoyādiàn*
Xiheya Ju	羲和雅居	*xīhé yǎjū*
Yushan	御膳饭店	*yùshàn fàndiàn*

McDonald's arrived in 1992 and there are now more than fifty branches, often so packed that getting served is an experience not unlike that of buying a train ticket (*McDonald's* Chinese nickname is Mc-wait-a-minute). Prices are cheaper than in the West, but expensive by Chinese standards. **Street food**, mostly noodle dishes, is widely available, though not in the centre, where vendors are shooed away by the police; your best bet is at one of the designated night markets. Avoid the ice-cream vendors who hang around the parks as their home-made wares are often of a dubious standard.

If you want to get a picnic together, or have the facilities to try some self-catering, the capital is well stocked with **supermarkets**. The Wellcome Supermarket – part of the Hong Kong chain – in the basement of the World

Trade Centre is the most impressive, though everything costs about fifty percent more than you would pay in Hong Kong. The supermarket on the first floor of the Friendship Store is not nearly as good, but it does sell butter, cheese and Western beers, as do the supermarkets in the basements of the Parkson Store and the SCITECH shopping centre. Head for Sanlitun to find speciality shops catering to homesick Westerners; Jenny Lou's on Gongrentiyu Bei Lu is renowned, but not cheap.

Breakfast, snacks and fast food

Many visitors find the Chinese **breakfast** of dumplings and glutinous rice served in canteens bland and unappealing, but *jian bing guozi*, the classic Beijing breakfast snack – vegetables wrapped in an omelette wrapped in a pancake – deftly assembled by street vendors in thirty seconds, is definitely worth trying (¥2). Most hotels offer some form of Western breakfast or, alternatively, head for a branch of *DeliFrance* for cheap croissants, *Dunkin' Donuts* for muffins or *Starbucks* for cake and a caffeine jolt. Beijing is one of the few places in China you can get a decent cup of **coffee**, but it's strictly a drink of the Western-aping elite – most Chinese can't stand it, so coffee shops are clustered in expensive areas. For cheap and filling **suppers**, try street food like *huntun*, basically wonton soup, and *xianr bing* – stuffed pancake – or the diverse varieties of noodles. You'll find plenty of street food at the **night markets**, which begin operating around 5pm and start to shut down around 10pm. They're at their best in summer.

DeliFrance Qianmen Xi Dajie (by *McDonald's*); basement of the Lufthansa Centre; Level 2, Sun Dong'an Plaza, Wangfujing. This good little French bakery chain has affordable pizzas, fresh croissants and cakes.

Donghuamen Yeshi night market At the intersection of Wangfujing and Jinyu *hutong*, on the same street as the *Palace Hotel* – find it by heading west off Wangfujing close to Donghuamen Dajie. Stalls set up along the street offering *xiaochi* (literally, "small food") from all over China. Nothing is more than a few kuai, except the odd delicacy such as scorpion on a stick for ¥10.

Dunkin' Donuts and Baskin' Robbins Jianguomen Dajie, next to the Friendship Store. These stores share their premises and are open 24hr. Watch your bags here as it's a popular place for thieves. There's another *Dunkin' Donuts* on Wangfujing, north of the intersection with Donganmen Dajie.

Duyichu 36 Qianmen Dajie. This restaurant has been in business for more than a century, though you'd never guess from the bland modern decor, and has built up an enviable reputation for its steamed dumplings, which you can eat on the spot or take away. One of the best places in the area for a light lunch.

Goubuli Baozi 155 Dianmenwai Dajie, just south of the Drum Tower. A branch of the Tianjin institution, this place sells delicious dumplings (*baozi*) for a few yuan. You can eat them here – the downstairs canteen is cheaper than upstairs – or take them home, as most of the customers do.

KFC Qianmen Xi Dajie, just south of Qianmen Gate. Opened in 1987, this was the first Western fast-food chain to colonize China, and has long been overtaken for verve and style by its nearby competitors. There's another branch in the Parkson Centre west of Xidan.

McDonald's Qianmen Xi Dajie (by the *KFC*); Xidan Bei Dajie (200m north of Fuxingmen Dajie); Nansanhuan Xi Lu (200m west of the *Jinghua Hotel*); Jianguomen Dajie (opposite the CITIC Bank); and more than fifty other branches across the city. The ever-popular, fashionable haunt for Beijing's bright young things.

Pizza Hut 33 Zhushikou Xi Jie; Jianguomen Dajie (just west of the Friendship Store); 29 Haidian Rd; 27 Dongzhimenwai Dajie. Everything you might expect at home. The quietest branch is the one on Zhushikou.

Qianmen Old Train Station Qianmen Dong Dajie. Look for the building with the clocktower. The basement foodcourt here has a range of specialities from all over China, most for less than ¥10.

Starbucks First Floor, China World Trade Centre, 1 Jianguomenwai Dajie (just round the corner from the Friendship Store); COFCO building, 8 Jianguomennei Dajie. The caffeine imperialists offer the best, and some of the dearest, coffee in the city – a regular filter coffee costs ¥12, with fancier varieties more expensive.

Subway Jianguomen, between the *Jinglun Hotel* and the *China World*; the Henderson Centre (opposite the *International Hotel*); 52 Liangjiu Lu (opposite the *Kempinski Hotel*); China World Trade Centre NB209. An American chain that opens till midnight and offers filling but pricey sandwiches.

Tourist Night Market Jinyu Hutong, off Wangfujing, opposite the *Palace Hotel* on the east side. Some of Beijing's classiest restaurants have set up stalls here, offering an upmarket version of street food – everything from sushi to spaghetti – in a pleasant garden setting. Prices between ¥10 and ¥100.

Restaurants

All the expensive **hotels** have several well-appointed restaurants, where the atmosphere is sedate but prices are sometimes not as high as you might expect; look out for their special offers, advertised in the city's listings magazines. Local restaurants, though, are cheaper and livelier. Expect to eat earlier than you would in Western cities: lunch is around noon and dinner around 6 or 7pm. Few places stay open after 11pm. Restaurants usually have two, sometimes more, **dining rooms**, which are priced differently – though the food comes from the same kitchen. The cheapest one is usually the open-plan area on the first floor. It's rarely worth phoning ahead to book a table; if you do, you will always end up in the most expensive sections. Telephone numbers have been included in the reviews below only for the more expensive and popular restaurants.

Qianmen and farther south

Gongdelin 158 Qianmen Nan Dajie. This odd vegetarian restaurant serves Shanghai dishes with names like "the fire is singeing the snow-capped mountains". The food comprises mostly meat imitations which taste eerily genuine. Try the fish dishes and "dragons' eyes" made of tofu and mushroom. Service and surroundings are lacklustre, but the place doesn't need to try too hard as it's reputation is assured.

Lichun 11 Bei Xiang Hutong ⓣ010/67025681. Deep in a *hutong*, this place is tough to find but offers good duck at half the price of the chains (¥80). From Qianmen subway stop walk east along Qianmen Dong Dajie and take the first right into Zhengyi Lu, and at the end turn right. Then follow the English sign to the "Lijun Roast Duck Restaurant" – left, left and it's on the left. You'll probably have to ask. The restaurant is in a shabby old courtyard house, and it's small, so you'd be wise to reserve beforehand.

Qianmen Quanjude Roast Duck 32 Qianmen Dajie ⓣ010/67011379. "The Great Wall and Roast Duck, try both to have a luck," says a ditty by the entrance to this Beijing institution. It's massive, professional and proficient, if obvious and touristy, though there's nothing wrong with the food. Tour groups are shepherded upstairs, but the ground floor is more atmospheric. A whole duck (which feeds two) costs ¥168.

Quanjude Roast Duck 14 Qianmen Xi Dajie ⓣ010/63018833. The size of this giant eatery – seating more than two thousand – has earned it its "Super Duck" moniker. Prices the same as at the Qianmen branch.

Yushan 87 Tiantan Lu, 100m west of the north gate of the Temple of Heaven ⓣ010/67014263. A second branch of the *Imperial Restaurant* in Beihai Park, with the same grand-sounding dishes and banquet set-up, but without such an imperial atmosphere. The food, though, is a little cheaper, with the set meals starting at ¥150.

Jianguomen Dajie and around

Afunti 2A Houguaibang Hutong, off Chaoyangnei Dajie. A boisterous place serving Xinjiang food – kebabs, nan and the like – and featuring belly dancing and a Uighur band. Popular with expats.

Be There Or Be Square Floor 2, Henderson Centre, north of Beijing Zhan. Despite the awful name, there's something to be said for this artsy 24-hour place with its simple, fast Hong Kong-style Chinese food. The patterns of beans under glass on the tables are diverting, and there's an amusing English menu, which includes such items as cream on toast – probably best avoided. It's cheap and popular with chic mobile toters. The brown-shirted staff can be a bit saucy. Certainly the best place to eat close to the train station.

Elephant 17 Ritan Bei Lu. Home to a Yugoslavian restaurant downstairs and a Russian one upstairs. The Russian restaurant serves a wide variety of soups and salads and the obligatory borscht. Each main dish comes with a generous side of mashed potato. Expect to pay about ¥80 per person, more if you hit the page-long vodka list.

Justine's *Jianguo Hotel*, 5 Jianguomenwai Dajie. A simple and elegant diner with the best wine list in the capital. The food is mostly Western – try the lobster soup or grilled lamb. Around ¥150 per person.

Mexican Wave Dongdaqiao Lu. This cosy bistro with a relaxed atmosphere is aimed at, and deservedly popular with, the expats from the embassy compounds nearby. The ambience is very Western, and about the only thing to remind you that you are in China is the barman's accent. The set lunch menu (¥50) changes daily, is tasty and good value, as are the many pizza options.

Nadaman Floor 3, *China World Hotel*, World Trade Centre. Discreet, simple and seriously expensive Japanese restaurant with a set menu priced at ¥300 per person. Most of the ingredients are flown in from Japan.

Phrik Thai Gateway Building, 10 Yabao Lu. Elegant Thai restaurant popular with expats. Try the red curry and chicken satay.

Rotary Sushi Restaurant Jianguomen Dajie. Cheap and idiot-proof Japanese fast-food restaurant just outside the Friendship Store: simply choose dishes (colour-coded according to price ¥5–25) from the conveyor belt as they glide past.

Saigon Inn Floor 3, *Gloria Plaza Hotel*, 28 Jianguomenwai Dajie. This restaurant specializes in Vietnamese cuisine, and is pleasingly cheap considering its opulence. You can eat well for less than ¥150 per person, and the set lunch, at ¥50 per person, is very good value.

Sichuan Restaurant Level 2, World Trade Centre, 1 Jianguomenwai Dajie. A plush place serving Sichuan cuisine. The hotpot, at ¥170 per person, comes recommended.

Xiheya Ju Inside Ritan Park, at the northeast corner. Sichuan and Guangdong food in an imitation Qing-dynasty mansion. Try the *ganbian rou si*, dried beef fried with celery and chilli. There's also a Western menu. You'll pay aound ¥60 per head.

Sanlitun and around

Berena's Bistro 6 Gongti Dong Lu. English-speaking waiters, good service and excellent Sichuan food make this a favourite with local expats. Try *gongbao jiding* – pepper chicken. The easiest way to find it is to head south down Nan Jiuba Jie (see p.126) – it's just after the bars.

Golden Elephant Off Sanlitun Jiu Ba Jie. Head north up the west side of the street and turn left after about 200m, at the sign for the *Cross Bar*, and you'll see it. This pleasant place, the haunt of diplomats from the subcontinent, serves Indian and Thai dishes and is recommended if you fancy a change. The menu is in English and has pictures. Try the *palak paneer* and *aloo gobi* with *tandoori* chicken and garlic *nan*. The beer is cheaper here than in the bars around. Figure on about ¥80 per person.

Old Character Hakka Restaurant Off Sanlitun Jiu Ba Jie, next to the *Cross Bar*. Head north up the west side of Sanlitun, turn off after 200m and follow the signs for the *Cross Bar*. Make sure you don't end up in the pale imatiation next door – the real place has a black doorway. Very in at the time of writing, and deservedly so – it's cramped but atmospheric and the food, Hakka dishes from the south, is delicious and not expensive. There's one English menu. Staff are a bit loud, though.

One Thousand and One Nights 21 Gongrentiyuchang Bei Lu, 200m west of Sanlitun Jiu Ba Jie. Beijing's first Middle Eastern restaurant, this place is deservedly popular, a favourite both with Western big noses who come here to fill up on kebabs after hitting the nearby bars and homesick diplomats who toke hookahs on the pavement outside. Try the houmus as a starter and the baked chicken for a main course, but leave enough room for some baklava, which you can also buy at their sweet shop 100m east of the restaurant. It's open till very late, but some dishes sell out early on.

Shenglinfu Taiwan Restaurant Off Sanlitun Jiu Ba Jie. Head north up the west side of the street and after 200m you'll see a sign for "orthodox Taiwan food" pointing you down an alley. Go down the alley, turn right and look for the place with the red lanterns outside. Inside is an elegant and affordable little restaurant with classical Chinese decor, attentive service and a good claypot chicken in wine. You can also take part in a tea ceremony in an anteroom. A meal will set you back about ¥30 per person.

Wangfujing and around

Bianyifang Roast Duck 2 Chongwenmenwai Dajie ☎010/67112244. The cheapest of the roast duck outlets – head through the first dining hall into the second, less pricey one, where a whole duck is only ¥80. It's always busy, so arrive early.

Muslim Fast Food Head up Wangfujing and just past the crossroads with Wusi Dajie there's a *hutong* full of clothes stalls on the east side of the road. Walk down here about 200m and you'll come to a little square – the restaurant is on the south side, opposite a *McDonald's* (look for the white writing on a green background). This technicolour canteen might not look much, but the food is both delicious and cheap. Point to the dishes that take your fancy from the wide selection on display

at the counters, plenty of vegetarian options among them. The sweets are also especially good.
Tianshi Vegetarian Restaurant 57 Dengshi Xikou, just off Wangfujing. All dishes in this bright, modern restaurant are tuber-, legume- or grain-based, low in calories and cholesterol-free, although, this being China, most of it is presented as a meat imitation: try the "chicken" or "eel". About ¥50 per head. No alcohol is served.
Wangfujing Quanjude Roast Duck 13 Shuaifuyuan Hutong ⓣ010/65253310. Smaller than the others in the chain, this one earned its unfortunate nickname, the "Sick Duck", thanks to the proximity of a hospital.

The north

Fangshan Beihai Park, near the south gate ⓣ010/64011879. Superbly situated on the central island in Beihai Park, there is no better place to sample imperial cuisine in Beijing. Book first, arrive hungry and splash out on the set banquet menu. Prices range from ¥100 to ¥500 per person as exotica such as camel paw and bird's nest soup appear.
Golden Thaitanium Dongsanhuan Bei Lu, next to the Chaoyang Theatre. Tasty, very spicy and inexpensive Thai food in a relaxed setting. There's a picture menu. Combine with a trip to the acrobatics at the theatre next door (see p.131) for a pleasant evening out; they stay open after the performance finishes at 9pm.
Hard Rock Café 8 Dongsanhuan Bei Lu. American restaurant, with a bar and a disco, the same as every other one, selling T-shirts for the stylistically challenged. A meal will set you back about ¥100. Beers ¥35.
Kaorouji 37 Shichahai. In the northern *hutongs*, close to the Drum Tower, this Muslim place takes advantage of its great location on the shore of Qianhai Hu, with big windows and balcony tables in summer. From the Drum Tower head south down Dianmenwai Dajie, and take the first *hutong* on the right. The restaurant is a short walk down here, just before the bridge. There's no English menu, though there are a few pictures on the Chinese version. Prices are moderate and you get a sesame roll instead of rice. Dishes arrive labelled with the name of the chef. After you've eaten, check out the cosy bars nearby (see p.128).
Korean restaurants Wudaokou, Haidian district, outside the Beijing Language and Culture Insititute. Beijing's large population of Korean expats are amply catered for in this strip of restaurants, shops and bars. Prices are pretty cheap, around ¥30 per head. The other Koreatown, opposite the *Kempinski Hotel*, is a little more upmarket. Pick a busy place and order *nayng myon*, cold noodles, and *bibimbap*, a claypot of rice, vegetables, egg and beef.
Lufthansa Centre Beisanhuan Dong Lu. There are plenty of upmarket restaurants in this shopping complex including the *Trattoria* (ⓣ010/64653388 ext 5707) for Italian food, or the *Brauhaus* (ⓣ010/64653388 ext 5732) for German fare – their pork and sauerkraut meal for two for ¥135 is about as cheap a meal as you'll get around here. In the basement, *Sorabol* (ⓣ010/64651845) specializes in Korean cuisine.
Makai 3 Di'anmenwai Dajie. This big place serving Hunan cuisine is a little too tourist-friendly to feel very authentic. Nothing wrong with the food, though, and it's not too expensive; around ¥50 per head.
Neng Ren Ju 5 Taipingqiao, close to the Baita Temple. An elegant little place, perhaps the best in the capital to sample Mongolian hotpot. There's a lot on the menu, but stick to the classic ingredients – mutton, cabbage, potato and glass noodles – for a guaranteed good feed. It gets quite hot and steamy in here in the evening but it's not geared around the portly banqueting crowd, and tables are small enough for conversation.
T.G.I. Friday Dongsanhuan Lu, 300m south of the *Zhaolong Hotel*. Bland American food in an atmosphere that's a little more sedate than the *Hard Rock Café*. Expect to pay about ¥100 per person. Draught beer is ¥20.
Xinjiang restaurants They were once widespread, but following demolitions, and fears that they served as a hotbed for separatist thought, there are now only two clusters left in the capital. The one at Weicongguan, in Haidian, is more atmospheric, while the one opposite and south of the *Cherry Blossom Hotel* probably has the edge in terms of food, notably at the *Tulufan* and *Alibaba* restaurants. Flat noodles, hot nan and more mutton than you can shake a skewer at. Cheap and cheerful.

Nightlife and entertainment

Beijing's **nightlife** and **entertainment** scene has now recovered from the moral clampdown following the Communist takeover, when "bourgeois" bars and teahouses disappeared and were replaced by an artificial emphasis on traditional Chinese culture, often worthy to the point of tedium. Nowadays nobody is much interested in this sort of stuff, and modern Beijingers, who suddenly find themselves with a disposable income, living through comparatively liberal times, just want to have fun.

Beijing these days also offers much more than the karaoke and bland hotel bars you'll find in many other Chinese cities. A trend for huge **discos** swept the city in the late 1980s, and they are still popular, packed every night with young, affluent Chinese. For foreigners, the interest probably lies in observing as much as participating. The formula is always the same: a few hours of cheesy techno, followed by the slushy half-hour, when a singer comes on stage and dancers pair off, followed by a more raucous last hour or two when only the serious clubbers are left and the mood becomes much less restrained. Recently, more sophisticated **Western-style nightclubs** have opened, which feature the latest DJs flown in from the West or Japan.

The fashion for modern urbanites, however, is for **bars**. In 1995 there was one bar at the south end of **Sanlitun**, and it was losing money. A new manager bought it, believing the place had potential but that the *feng shui* was wrong – the toilet was opposite the door and all the wealth was going down it. He changed the name, moved the loo, and so revolutionized the city's nightlife. Now the area is choked with bars, with new ones opening all the time. Many are rip-offs of their popular neighbours – if one does well, soon four more will open around it with nearly the same name. Originally aimed at the city's foreign community, they are now patronized as much by locals. For Western visitors, the scene around Sanlitun can look eerily familiar – pretty much everything is just like home, including the prices. An alternative bar scene exists in **Haidian**, around the university district in the northwest. With a largely student clientele, the bars here are cheaper and hipper, with a little more edge to them.

The bars have given a huge boost to the city's **music scene**, providing much needed venues. You can now hear classical zither or bamboo tunes, jazz, deep house, or head-banging grindcore on most nights of the week. Meanwhile, most visitors take in at least a taste of **Beijing Opera** and the superb Chinese **acrobats** – highly recommended – both of which seem pretty timeless. In contrast, the contemporary theatrical scene is changing fast. A recent development has been a fashion for Chinese translations of Western **plays**, such as *The Mousetrap*, or home-grown dramatists experimenting with foreign forms.

Cinemas these days are dedicated to feeding a seemingly insatiable appetite for kung fu movies rather than edifying the populace, although there is plenty of opportunity to catch the serious and fairly controversial movies emerging from a new wave of younger film makers.

Drinking and dancing

Most of the **bars** are clustered **around Sanlitun Lu**, also called Jiu Ba Jie (literally "Bar Street"), and Nan Jiu Ba Jie ("South Bar Street"), a *hutong* south and just to the west, all within staggering distance of one another. They all offer draught beer at Western prices, and many have live music. **Haidian**, in the university district, is known for its low-key speakeasies and underground edge. For a quiet drink in chilled surroundings, head to **Houhai lake**, where a new bar zone is in its infancy. Phone numbers for those bars that have regular gigs have been included below.

Beijing's **discos** are a long way from the centre, and the only practical way to get to most (or certainly back) is by taxi. They may not be the hippest ven-

Beijing bars and discos

Blue Jay	蓝雀 酒吧	*lánquè jiǔbā*
Buddha Bar	不大	*búdà*
CD Cafè	CD 咖啡屋	*CD kāfēiwū*
Club Banana	巴那那俱乐部	*bānànà jùlèbù*
Get Lucky Bar	豪运	*háoyùn*
Hidden Tree	隐蔽的树	*yǐnbìde shù*
Jam House	芥末房	*jièmò fáng*
JJ's	JJ迪斯科	*JJ dísīkē*
Nasa	NASA迪斯科	*NASA dísīkē*
Nashville	乡谣	*xiāngyáo*
Nightman	莱特曼	*láitèmàn*
Poachers Bar	友谊青年酒店	*yǒuyí qīngnián jiǔdiàn*
Success	赛克思	*sàikèsī*
Vics	威克斯	*wēikèsī*

ues on the planet but they're certainly spirited, and cheaper than a night out in a Western capital, particularly as many let foreigners in free – reputedly because they know how to have a good time, but probably because they spend more at the bar.

Bars

Sanlitun's rash of bars lies just inside the third ring road – take the subway to Dongzhimen, then get bus #113 east. The selection of bars below are the most deserving, but there are plenty more. Strategically placed around them, small cafés offer sobering blasts of coffee and munchies. To reach **Haidian** in the northwest take bus #322, which leaves from a terminus outside the zoo. This area is more diffuse, and you'll need to know where you're headed. Most bars out here are open till well after midnight. Be aware that the mayfly lifecycle of the Beijing bar means that some of these places may be closed by the time you read this – for the latest haunts check the expat mags.

Sanlitun

Durty Nellies Irish Pub Sanlitun Nan. About as Irish as *jiaozi*, but always lively.

Hidden Tree Sanlitun Nan Lu. Cosy and relaxed, with a pleasant garden and a gnarly oak growing through the bar.

Jam House Sanlitun Nan ☎010/65063845. Go past *Nashville* for about 100m and look for the sign that points you down an alley. This little place is one of Sanlitun's hippest, largely thanks to Mimi, the colourful manageress. Popular both with young expats and trendy locals, who usually talk to each other in Chinese. Live music on weekends with jam sessions afterwards. If the raucous downstairs bar gets too heavy on your ears, head up to the rooftop seating.

Minders Bar Sanlitun Lu. Another of the originals, with an in-house Filipino band that covers seventies and eighties pop and rock.

Nashville Sanlitun Nan Lu. One of the oldest places, where you can hear both kinds of music, country and western. The in-house band plays Wednesdays to Saturdays. A wide variety of draught beers, including Hoegaarten (¥35) and Boddingtons (¥50).

Poachers Bar Off Sanlitun Lu ☎010/64172632 ext 8506. Head north up Sanlitun, then turn left after 200m at the sign for the *Cross Bar* and follow the road round. The most popular expat bar, and the only place in the area you can get a beer for ¥5. The dance floor gets busy most nights, and there's live music on Saturdays. See *Poacher's Inn* under "Accommodation".

Public Space Sanlitun Lu. Sanlitun's first bar and still one of the most pleasant. Draught beer ¥20.

Haidian and the rest

Blue Jay 44 Chengfu Lu, just west of the Language and Culture University. A two-storey warehouse popular with students, who get in free. Come on Friday or Saturday when there's a pretty good hip-hop DJ. Shots are good value at ¥10.

Cover charge for non-students ¥20.

Buddha Bar Shicha Hai, facing the *Kaorouji Restaurant* (see p.125). Charming and trendily ramshackle, with outside seating so you can relax by the lake over a cold one (¥15). Just one of a number in the area.

CD Café Dongsanhuan Bei Lu, 300m south of the *Great Wall Sheraton Hotel* ☎010/65018877 ext 3032. The new hot place to hear decent live rock and indie music on the weekends, when there's usually a cover charge of around ¥30. Check expat magazines for listings.

Get Lucky Bar Tai Yang Gong ☎010/64299109. Miles out of the way and impossible to find, but you have to go here if you want to know what's going on in the local indie music scene – live bands most weekends, though ring to check. It's 500m east of the south gate of the Business and Economics University (Jing Mao Da Xue Nan Men) – look for the neon sign.

Discos

Club Banana Top floor of the Sea Sky Shopping Centre, 12 Chaoyangmenei Dajie. Hot, dark, smoky and packed with an up for it local crowd with steam to let off. Like the nineties never happened. Daily 8.30pm–2am. Cover ¥50.

JJ's 74–76 Xinjiekou Bei Dajie. This cavernous club has lasers and a sci-fi theme. Silver-clad go-go girls show a high-street crowd how it's done. Take bus #22 from Qianmen. Daily 8pm–2am. Cover ¥20–50.

Nasa At the corner of Xueyuan Lu and Xitucheng Lu, just north of Sanhuan Bei Lu in Haidian district. The most alternative of Beijing's aircraft hangar-style discos, where you can watch Chinese girls playing air guitar and teenagers breakdancing to Chinese rap. The decor, which includes an army jeep and a helicopter, is more eclectic than the music, a fairly predictable set of pop, grunge, rap and hardish techno. Beers are ¥20, but no one seems to mind if you take your own. Daily 8pm–2am. ¥30, Sat ¥50, free for foreigners.

Nightman Junction of Qishen Nan Lu and Xibahe Zhong Jie, 100m south of the *SAS Royal Hotel*. This megadisco attracts a lot of fairly unsophisticated young locals and a few foreign students. Daily 8pm–2am. Cover ¥35, Sat ¥60.

Success 4 Gongti Dong Lu, just west of the Sanlitun intersection. An irony-free monument to spiritual pollution and kitsch excess. An awful band plays Mandopop to a smug crowd of conspicuous consumers. Get one of the slick hostesses to light your cigarette for you and feel like you've made it. Maybe Mao had it right after all. No cover charge though.

Vics Inside the Worker's Stadium North Gate, next to the *Outback* steakhouse. Eighties LA decor, cheap drinks, a sweaty dance floor, and a "Less Than Zero" ambience of numb dissipation. Come and see where blank-faced embassy kids waste their time and be glad you didn't spend your teens here. No cover.

Live music, film and cultural events

There's always a healthy variety of events taking place in the city. Check the *China Daily* for listings on officially approved events. For the best rundown of street-level happenings, though, including gigs, try to track down a copy of *Beijing Scene*. You should see a copy in most of the bars.

Live music

The **Beijing Concert Hall** (☎010/66055812), at 1 Beixinhua Jie, just off Xichang'an Jie, sates the considerable appetite in the capital for **classical music**, with regular concerts by Beijing's resident orchestra, and visiting orchestras from the rest of China and overseas. Ticket prices vary. You can get tickets at the box office or at the SCITECH Plaza. Other, smaller venues include the Music Hall at Zhongshan Park (☎010/66056059).

Local legend Cui Jian – the Chinese Bob Dylan – performs frequently in bars, and seems to fill the rest of his time hanging out in them. The new **local bands** worth looking out for are Underbaby, the father of Beijing's punk scene, garage rockers The Fly and No, indie popsters New Pants, and Flower, teenagers whose best song is a thrash metal cover of the anthem of the "Young

Beijing entertainment

Beijing Concert Hall	音乐厅	*yīnyuè tīng*
Capital Theatre	首都剧场	*shǒudū jùchǎng*
Chang'an Theatre	长安大剧场	*chángān dàjùchǎng*
Chaoyang Theatre	朝阳剧场	*cháoyáng jùchǎng*
Courtyard Gallery	四合院画廊	*sìhéyuàn huàláng*
Dahua Cinema	大华电影院	*dàhuá diànyǐngyuàn*
International Club	国际俱乐部	*guójì jùlèbù*
Jiguge Teahouse	汲古阁茶苑	*jígǔgé cháyuàn*
Lao She Teahouse	老舍茶馆	*lǎoshě cháguǎn*
National Library	北京图书馆	*běijīng túshūguǎn*
Puppet Theatre	中国木偶剧院	*zhōngguó mùǒujùyuàn*
Red Gate Gallery	红门画廊	*hóngmén huàláng*
Sanlian Bookstore	三联书店	*sānlián shūdiàn*
Sanwei Bookstore	三味书屋	*sānwèi shūwū*
Sino Japanese Youth Centre	中日青年交流中心	*zhōngrì qīngnián jiāolíu zhōngxīn*
Tian Hai Teahouse	天海茶苑	*tiānhǎi cháyuàn*
Tianqiao Teahouse	天桥乐茶园	*tiānqiáolè cháyuán*
Wanfung Art Gallery	云峰 画廊	*yúnfēng huàláng*
Workers' Stadium	工人体育场	*gōngrén tǐyùchǎng*
Zhengyici Theatre	正义祠剧场	*zhèngyìcí jùchǎng*
Zhonghe Theatre	中和剧场	*zhōnghé jùchǎng*

Pioneers" (the Chinese scouts). The punk bands are always good value, making up in energy what they lack in musicianship. The best places to hear new music are at *Get Lucky* and the *CD Café* (see "Bars", p.128). If you want it on tape, look for the *Modern Sky* label. **Jazz** is perenially popular; venues you can catch it include the *Jam House*, *CD Café*, and *Poachers*.

Giant gigs are held at the **Workers' Stadium**, in the northeast of the city, off Gongren Tiyuchang Bei Lu (bus #110 along Dongdaqiao), mostly featuring Chinese pop stars, though Vanessa Mae and Bjork have played here.

Film

There are plenty of **cinemas** showing Chinese films and dubbed Western films, usually action movies. Around ten Western films are picked by the government for national release every year, and are shown in Beijing first; *Titanic* remains the biggest hit ever in the People's Republic. All foreign films are dubbed into Chinese.

Some of the **largest screens** are the Capital Cinema at 46 Chang'an Jie, near Xidan (Ⓣ010/66055510), the Dahua Cinema at 82 Dongdan Bei Dajie (Ⓣ010/65274420) and the Shengli Movie Theatre at 55 Xisi Dong Dajie (Ⓣ010/66013130). Tickets cost ¥5–30 and you'll find film listings in *That's Beijing*.

For **art films**, try the Tuxin Cinema (Ⓣ010/68415566) at 33 Zhongguancun Nan Dajie in Haidian. To see the best in **Chinese films**, with English subtitles, visit the Cherry Lane Cinema (Ⓣ010/64615318, Ⓦwww.cherrylanemovies.com.cn), at the Sino Japanese Youth Exchange Centre, 40 Liangmaqiao Lu, 2km east of the *Kempinski Hotel*. Screenings are held every other Friday at 8pm, with a discussion, often featuring the director or actors, afterwards. Tickets cost ¥50.

Opera

Beijing Opera (*jing xi*) is the most celebrated of the country's three hundred and fifty or so regional styles – a unique combination of song, dance, acrobatics and mime, with some similarities to Western pantomime. It is highly stylized and to the outsider can often seem obscure to the point of absurdity and ultimately tedious, since performances can last up to four hours, punctuated by a succession of crashing gongs and piercing, almost discordant songs. But it's worth seeing once, and if you can acquaint yourself with the plot beforehand, there's a definite fascination. Most of the **plots** are based on historical or mythological themes – two of the most famous titles, which any Chinese will explain to you, are "The White Snake" and "The Water Margin" – and they're rigidly symbolic. Moral absolutes begin with the costumes – red signifies loyalty; yellow, slyness; blue, cruelty; and black, evil – and with the patterns painted on faces. An interesting, if controversial, variation on the traditions, highly instructive if you know enough to work out what's going on, are operas dealing with contemporary themes – like Mao's first wife, or the struggle of women to marry as they choose.

The most accessible place to see Beijing Opera is at the **Liyuan Theatre** (☎010/63016688 ext 8860) on the first floor of the *Qianmen Hotel*, 175 Yong'an Lu, where nightly performances begin at 7.30pm. There's a ticket office in the front courtyard of the hotel (daily 9–11am, noon–4.45pm & 5.30–8pm). Tickets cost ¥30–150; the more expensive seats are at tables at the front where you can sip tea and nibble pastries during the performance. In season you'll need to book tickets a day or two in advance. You won't see many Chinese faces here as the opera shown, which lasts for just an hour, is a tourist-friendly bastardization, jazzed up with some martial arts and slapstick. A display board at the side of the stage gives a senseless English translation of the few lines of dialogue. Alternatively, visit a teahouse for your opera fix and slurp tea or munch on a duck while you're being entertained (see "Teahouses", opposite). For the most authentic performances visit the **Zhengyici Theatre** at 220 Xiheyan Dajie in Qianmen (☎010/63033104), the only surviving wooden Peking opera theatre left, and worth a visit just to check out the architecture. Nightly performances begin at 7.30pm, last two hours and cost ¥150. Dinner – duck, of course – costs an additional ¥110. Check the *China Daily* for listings. Enthusiasts should also consider the big **Chang'an Theatre**, at 7 Jianguomennei Dajie (☎010/65101309), which sells tickets from ¥20 up to ¥800 for front seats and a duck dinner.

Theatre, song-and-dance and puppet shows

Spoken drama was only introduced into Chinese theatres this century. The **People's Art Theatre** in Beijing became its best-known home and, before the Cultural Revolution, staged European plays which had a clear social message – Ibsen and Chekhov were among the favourites. But in 1968, Jiang Qing, Mao's third wife, declared that "spoken drama is dead". The theatre, along with most of China's cinemas, was closed down for almost a decade, with a corpus of just eight plays, deemed socially improving, continuing to be performed. Many of the principal actors, directors and writers were banished too, generally to hard rural labour. The last decade has seen a total turnabout with the People's Art Theatre reassembled in 1979, establishing its reputation with a performance of Arthur Miller's *Death of a Salesman*. More recent works include *The Club*, about a football team, performed during the World Cup. Look out for them, and other companies, at the **Capital Theatre**, at 22 Wangfujing Dajie (☎010/65253677). The Experimental Theatre For Dramatic Arts

(☎010/64031099), at 45 Mao'er Hutong, just north of the Bell Tower, is known for putting on modern and avant-garde performances.

Though a little glitzy for many foreigners' tastes, it can't be denied that the Chinese put on good old-fashioned **song-and-dance** extravaganzas with the sort of gusto long gone in the West. Most evenings, you can catch one by turning the TV on, but if you want the live experience, try the Beijing Exhibition Theatre at 135 Xizhimenwai Dajie (☎010/68354455). Other venues occasionally hold imported shows such as *The Sound of Music*, which at ¥50–100, are a lot cheaper than at home.

Chinese **puppetry** has a lineage of two thousand years, and you can check it out at the Puppet Theatre, A1 Anhua Xi Lu (☎010/64243698), which hosts daily shows at 6.30pm for ¥20.

Acrobatics

Certainly the most accessible and exciting of the traditional Chinese entertainments, **acrobatics** covers anything from gymnastics and animal tricks to magic and juggling. Professional acrobats have existed in China for two thousand years and the tradition continues at the main training school, Wu Qiao in Hebei province, where students begin training at the age of 5. The style may be vaudeville, but performances are spectacular, with truly awe-inspiring feats.

The easiest place to see a display is at the **Chaoyang Theatre** at 36 Dongsanhuan Bei Lu (☎010/65072421), which has a show every night (7.15–9pm; ¥80; it can be cheaper if you book through your hotel). The theatre fills nightly with tour groups and Chinese tourists – at the end, the Chinese rush off as if it's a fire drill, leaving the tour groups to do all the applauding. There are plenty of souvenir stalls in the lobby – buy after the show rather than in the interval, as prices go down. An alternative venue is the Auditorium of Chinese Acrobats, in Room 232 at the Workers' Stadium (Gongren Tiyuguan). Nightly performances begin at 7.15pm.

Teahouses

A few **teahouses**, places to sit and snack and watch performances of Beijing Opera, sedate music and martial arts, have recently reappeared in the capital. You can watch a variety show of opera, martial arts and acrobatics (¥40–130), at the *Lao She Teahouse*, 3rd Floor, Dawancha Building, 3 Qianmen Xi Dajie. Performances are at 2.30pm and 7.40pm and last an hour and a half; the afternoon performance's are cheaper. More of the same is available at the *Tianqiao Happy Teahouse* at 113 Tianqiao Nan Dajie (closed Mon), though at higher prices (¥180). Both are tourist traps that give a colourful taste of the surface aspects of Chinese culture. For a more authentic atmosphere, pop into the Sanwei Bookstore at 60 Fuxingmennei Dajie (☎010/66013204), opposite the *Minzu Hotel*, which is more the haunt of expats and arty Chinese, where you can hear light jazz and Chinese folk music (8.30–10pm). Meanwhile, tucked in an alley east off Sanlitun Jiu Ba Jie, the *Tian Hai Teahouse* offers an elegant respite from the hedonism outside. Traditional music is played here on Friday and Saturday nights.

Art exhibitions

There are relatively few places to see good **contemporary art** in Beijing. A lot of the more challenging exhibitions are quickly thrown together in alternative spaces and are not always listed in the free magazines – you'll really have to put your ear to the ground to find out what's happening inside the city's rather cliquey avant garde. The best venue for mainstream contemporary art is the **Courtyard Gallery** at 95 Donghuamen Dajie (ⓣ010/65268882; ⓦwww.courtyard-gallery.com), in an old courtyard house opposite the east gate of the Forbidden City. There's also a cigar shop and a very classy restaurant here. The Red Gate Gallery (ⓣ010/65022266), at the *China World Hotel* on Jianguomenwai Dajie, and the Wanfung (ⓣ010/65233320), at 136 Nanchizi Dajie, in the old archive building of the Forbidden City, show established contemporary artists, sometimes from abroad.

Shopping

Beijing has a good reputation for **shopping**, with the widest choice of anywhere in China. **Clothes** are particularly inexpensive, and are one reason for the city's high number of Russians, as smuggling them across the northern border is a lucrative trade. There's also a wide choice of **antiques and handicrafts**, but don't expect to find any bargains or particularly unusual items as the markets are well picked over. Be aware that much that is passed off as antique is fake. Good souvenir buys are **art materials**, particularly brushes and blocks of ink, chops carved with a name, small **jade** items and handicraft items such as **kites**, painted snuff bottles and papercuts.

There are four main shopping districts: **Wangfujing**, popular and mainstream (see p.109); **Xidan**, characterized by giant department stores (see p.107); **Dongdan**, which mainly sells brand-name clothes (see p.110); and **Qianmen**, perhaps the area that most rewards idle browsing, with a few oddities among the cheap shoes and clothes stores (see p.102). In addition, and especially aimed at visitors, **Liulichang** is a good place to get a lot of souvenir buying done quickly (see p.104), or head to **Jianguomenwai Dajie** if it's clothes you're after (see p.111). In the **markets**, you have much less guarantee of quality, but you can (and should) barter, so prices are cheaper. For general goods check the **department stores**, which sell a little of everything, and provide a good index of current Chinese taste. The Beijing Department Store, on Wangfujing, and the Xidan Department Store on Xidan Dajie are prime examples, or check out the newer Landao Store, on Chaoyangmenwai Dajie. The Parkson Building, west of Xidan on Chang'an Jie, is the plushest. Rising living standards for some are reflected in the new giant **malls**, where everything costs as much as it does in the West. Try the Sun Dong'an Plaza, on Wangfujing, the Sea-Sky Plaza, on

Beijing: Shopping

Dazhalan	大栅栏街	*dàzhàlán jiē*
Foreign Languages Bookstore	外交书店	*wàijiāo shūdiàn*
Friendship Store	友谊商店	*yǒuyí shāngdiàn*
Full Link Plaza	丰联广场	*fēnglián guǎngchǎng*
Henderson Centre	恒基中心	*héngjī zhōngxīn*
Hongqiao Department Store	红桥百货中心	*hóngqiáo bǎihuò zhōngxīn*
Liulichang	琉璃厂	*liúlí chǎng*
Panjiayuan	潘家园	*pānjiā yuán*
Parkson Building	百盛购物中心	*bǎishèng gòuwù zhōngxīn*
Silk Market	秀水市场	*xiushuǐ shìchǎng*
Sun Dong'an Plaza	新东安	*xīndōng ān*

Chaoyangmenwai Dajie, or the SCITECH, COFCO or World Trade Centre plazas on Jianguomen if you don't get enough of this at home.

Shops are open daily from 8.30am to 8pm (7pm in winter), with large shopping centres staying open till 9pm. Beijing is one Chinese city where the night markets are poor, forced out by the abundance of goods in the stores.

Antiques and curios

If you're a serious antique hunter, go to Tianjin, where the choice is more eclectic and prices cheaper (see p.157). That said, there's no shortage of **antique stores** and **markets** in the capital. Most of the stuff is fake, and it can be hard even for experts to tell what's genuine and what's not, so just buy what looks attractive and stay away from jewellery or precious stones (including jade) unless you really know what you're doing. **Carpets**, made in Xinjiang, Tibet, and Tianjin, aren't cheap, but if you're looking to spend at least several hundred dollars, they're pretty good value. Antiques that date from before 1795 are forbidden for export. Technically, those that date from before 1949 should come with a small red seal and a certificate for export issued by the Cultural Relics Bureau (BCRB), which also serves to authenticate the item. In practice, however, you'll only find these available in shops; anything bought from a stall won't have one – in which case, you can get this service at the Friendship Store (Mon & Fri 2–5pm). Take the object and a receipt along.

Arts and Crafts Store 293 Wangfujing. A good if predictable selection of expensive *objets d'art*.

Beijing Curio City Dongsanhuan Nan Lu, west of Huawei Bridge. A giant mall of more than 250 stalls. Visit on a Sunday, when other antique traders come and set up in the streets around. The mall includes a section for duty-free shopping; take your passport and a ticket out of the country along and you can buy goods at the same reduced price as at the airport. Daily 9.30am–6.30pm.

Friendship Store Jianguomenwai Dajie. Tourist souvenirs with a wide range of prices, but generally more expensive than in the markets. Large carpet section.

Hongqiao Department Store Opposite the northeast corner of Tiantan Park. The giant, cramped and humid Hongqiao Department Store can be wearying but you're more likely to find bargains here than in the similar Silk Market (see p.111). The top floor sells antiques and curios; one stall is given over solely to Cultural Revolution kitsch. The stalls share space, oddly, with a pearl and jewellery market. The second floor sells clothes and accessories and the first is the place to go for small electronic items, including such novelties as watches that speak the time in Russian when you whistle at them.

Liulichang East of Qianmen Dajie (see p.104). This has the densest concentration of curio stores, with a great choice, particularly of art materials, though prices are steep.

Lufthansa Centre Liangmaqiao Lu. A section in this giant mall sells expensive antiques and carpets.

Panjiayuan Market On Panjia Lu, just south of Jinsong Zhong Jie. Beijing's biggest antique market, well worth browsing around, even if you have no intention to buy, for the sheer range of second-hand goods, sometimes in advanced stages of decay, on sale. Open weekdays, but it's at its biggest and best at weekends between 6am and 3pm.

Books

Beijing can claim a better range of **English-language literature** than anywhere else in China. If you're starting a trip of any length, stock up here or you'll get very sick of classic English novels after a few months. The expensive hotels all have bookstores with fairly decent collections, though at off-putting prices. You'll also find copies of foreign **newspapers and magazines**, such as *Time* and *Newsweek*, sold for around ¥40.

Cathay Bookstore 115 Liulichang. An enormous selection including specialist texts, dusty tomes and lavish coffee-table and art books, though not much in English. Mon–Sat 9am–6pm.

Foreign Languages Bookstore 235 Wangfujing Dajie. The largest in China. There's an information desk on the right as you go in which sells listings magazines, and on the other side of the entrance a counter sells maps, including an enormous wall map of the city (¥80), which would be great if you could get it home. Among the English books on offer, which include fiction, textbooks on Chinese medicine, and translations of Chinese classics, the *Pocket Interpreter*, produced by Beijing Foreign Language Press, is a good practical phrasebook, well worth picking up. It's worth checking the upper floors, too, which have more fiction in English, magazines, wall-hangings, and Japanese *manga*. Sometimes you'll find the same book is cheaper upstairs than it is downstairs. Mon–Sat 9am–7pm.

Friendship Store Jianguomenwai Dajie. As well as a wide variety of books on all aspects of Chinese culture, the bookshop within the store sells foreign newspapers (¥80), a few days out of date. It's all very expensive, though. Daily 9am–8.30pm.

Sanlian Bookshop Wangfujing Dajie (100m beyond the intersection with Chaoyangmennei Dajie, on the east side of the road; look for a blue glass building slightly recessed from the street). This is the most pleasant bookshop in Beijing, though its selection of English fiction, in the basement, is much less extensive than that of the Foreign Languages Bookstore to the south. Upstairs there's a huge variety of art books and, at the back, a cosy little café, with Internet access (see p.136). Mon–Sat 9am–6pm.

Tushu Daxia Xichang'an Jie. Beijing's biggest bookshop, with the feel of a department store. English fiction is on the third floor. Mon–Sat 9am–7pm.

Cameras, computers and electrical equipment

There's a string of good **camera** shops on the south side of Xichang'an Jie around the intersection with Hepingmen Dajie. Beijing's Today Photo shop offers professional, reliable slide film development. It's on the west side of Dongsi Bei Dajie – near Wangfujing – just south of the Ping An intersection.

The area around Zhongguancun Jie, in the northwest just beyond the zoo, is not really up to its hype as China's Silicon Valley, but as well as hi-tech start-ups the streets are full of stores selling **electronics** and **computer equipment**.

Clothes

Clothes are a bargain in Beijing; witness all the Russians buying in bulk. The best place to go is Jianguomen Dajie, where the Silk Market, the Friendship Store and the SCITECH Plaza offer something for every budget (see p.111). If you're tall, you'll have difficulty finding clothes to fit you, and no store has shoes above UK size 12 – for bigger clothes, head to the Silk Market. For Chinese street fashion, head to Dongdan and for designer creations, to the malls (see p.132).

Army Surplus Store 188 Qianmen Dajie. A wide selection of hats and coats, plus sleeping bags and tents, are sold by the downright abusive staff here.

Fou Clothing Company 85 Wangfujing Dajie. Designer *qipaos*; they'll also do custom tailoring.

Mingxing Clothing Store 133 Wangfujing Dajie. Well-made traditional Chinese women's clothing – *cheongsams* and *qipaos* – for slender figures only.

Ruifuxiang Store 5 Dazhalan (see p.104). Raw silk and cotton.

Sanlitun Market Sanlitun Lu. During the day the west side of the street, opposite the bars, is lined with clothing stalls, pretty similar to the stuff you get at the Silk Market.

Snowbird Outdoor Equipment 68 Deshengmen Xi Dajie ☎010/62253630. Quality hiking and mountaineering gear.

Yuanlong Silk Corporation 15 Yongnei Dong Jie, 200m west of the south gate of the Temple of Heaven. A good selection of silk clothes, competitively priced.

Music

For the latest underground Chinese **music** on CD, visit the shop of popular local DJ Youdai at 78 Yude Hutong (☎010/66181701). For **musical instruments**, head to the marble bridge at the west end of Liulichang, on Hepingmen Dajie, and walk south; you'll find some nice little instrument shops that aren't touristy.

Listings

Airline offices Air China, 15 Xi Chang'an Jie ⓣ010/66013336 for domestic flights, ⓣ66016667 international; Aeroflot, *Hotel Beijing Toronto*, Jianguomenwai Dajie ⓣ010/65002980; Air France, Floor 5, Full Link Plaza, 18 Jianguomenwai Dajie ⓣ010/65881388; Alitalia, Rm 503B, China World Trade Centre, 1 Jianguomenwai Dajie ⓣ010/65056670; All Nippon Airways, Rm 1510, World Trade Centre, 1 Jianguomenwai Dajie ⓣ010/65053311; Asiana Airlines, Rm 102, Lufthansa Centre ⓣ010/64684000; Austrian Airlines, *Kempinski Hotel*, 50 Donghua Bei Lu ⓣ010/646262161; British Airways, Rm 210, SCITECH Tower, 22 Jianguomenwai Dajie ⓣ010/65124070; Canadian Airlines, Rm 201, 50 Liangmaqiao Lu, Chaoyang ⓣ010/64630576; Dragonair, 1710 Henderson Centre, 18 Jianguomenwai Dajie ⓣ010/65182533; El Al, Rm 2906, Jing Guang Centre ⓣ010/65014512; Finnair, Rm 204, SCITECH Tower, 22 Jianguomenwai Dajie ⓣ010/65127180; Garuda Indonesia, Poly Plaza, 14 Dongzhimen Nan Dajie ⓣ010/64157658; Japan Airlines, Changfugong Office Building, 26A Jianguomenwai Dajie ⓣ010/65130888; Korean Air, Rm C401 World Trade Centre, 1 Jianguomenwai Dajie ⓣ010/65050088; Lufthansa, Rm S101, Lufthansa Centre, Dong Sanhuan Bei Lu ⓣ010/64654488; Malaysia Airlines, Lot 115A/B, Level 1, West Wing Office Block, World Trade Centre, 1 Jianguomenwai Dajie ⓣ010/65052681; Mongolian Airlines, China Golden Bridge Plaza, 1A Jianguomenwai Dajie ⓣ010/65079297; Northwest Airlines, Rm 501, West Building, World Trade Centre ⓣ010/65053505; Pakistan Airlines, Rm 617, World Trade Centre, 1 Jianguomenwai Dajie ⓣ010/65051681; Qantas, Lufthansa Centre, 50 Liangmaqiao Lu ⓣ010/64674794; SAS Scandinavian Airlines, 1403 Henderson Centre, 18 Jianguomennei Dajie ⓣ010/65183738; Singapore Airlines, L109, World Trade Centre, 1 Jianguomenwai Dajie ⓣ010/65052233; Swissair, Rm 608, SCITECH Tower, 22 Jianguomenwai Dajie ⓣ010/65123555; Thai International, Lufthansa Centre, 50 Langmaqiao Lu ⓣ010/64608899; United Airlines, Lufthansa Centre, 50 Liangmaqiao Lu ⓣ010/64631111.

Banks and exchange The Commercial Bank (Mon–Fri 9am–noon & 1–4pm) in the CITIC Building at 19 Jianguomenwai Dajie, next to the Friendship Store, offers the most comprehensive service: Visa cards, traveller's cheques and cash can be used to obtain yuan or US dollars. The main branch of the Bank of China (Mon–Fri 9am–noon & 1.30–5pm) is at 8 Yabuo Lu, off Chaoyangmen Dajie, just north of the International Post Office, but it doesn't do anything the smaller branches can't. You'll find other branches in the SCITECH Plaza (Mon–Fri 9am–noon & 1–6.30pm), the World Trade Centre (Mon–Fri 9am–5pm, Sat 9am–noon), the Sun Dong'an Plaza (Mon–Fri 9.30am–noon & 1.30–5pm), and the Lufthansa Centre (Mon–Fri 9–noon & 1–4pm). A foreign exchange office (daily 9am–6.30pm) inside the entrance to the Friendship Store is one of the few places you can change money at the weekend at the standard rate. If you have applied for a visa and only have a photocopy of your passport, some hotels and the Hong Kong and Shanghai Bank in the *Jianguo Hotel* will reluctantly advance cash on traveller's cheques; most banks won't. If you want to wire money, or have it wired to you, go to the International Post Office or the China Courier Service Company at 7 Qianmen Dajie ⓣ010/63184313. There are ATM machines in the Bright China Chang'an Building, 8 Jianguomen Dajie, in the Dong'an Shopping Centre on Wangfujing, on the east side of Qianmen next to *McDonald's*, on Floor 2 of the Hong Kong-Macau Centre on Chaoyang Bei Dajie and at many other locations.

Bike rental Pretty much all the hotels rent out bikes, at ¥20–50 a day, depending on how classy the hotel is.

Car rental BCNC Car Rental, with seven offices in the city including one at the airport, is open 24hr (ⓣ010/8008109001).

Courier service DHL has a 24hr office at 45 Xinyuan Jie ⓣ010/64662211, in Chaoyang district.

Embassies Visa departments usually open for a few hours every weekday morning (phone for exact times and to see what you'll need to take; you'll need a Chinese speaker on standby as not all will have someone who speaks English). Remember that they'll take your passport off you for as long as a week sometimes, and it's very hard to change money without it, so stock up on cash before applying for any visas. You can get passport-size photos from an annexe just inside the front entrance of the Friendship Store. Some embassies require payment in US dollars; you can change traveller's cheques for these at the CITIC Building (see "Banks and exchange" above). Most embassies are either around Sanlitun in the northeast or in Jianguomenwai compound, north of and parallel to Jianguomenwai Dajie: Australia, 21 Dongzhimenwai Dajie, Sanlitun ⓣ010/65322331; Azerbaijan, 7-2-5-1 Tayuan Building ⓣ010/65324614; Canada, 19 Dongzhimenwai Dajie, Sanlitun ⓣ010/65323536; France, 3 Dong San Jie, Sanlitun ⓣ010/65321331; Germany, 5 Dongzhimenwai Dajie, Sanlitun ⓣ010/65322161; India, 1 Ritan Dong Lu, Sanlitun ⓣ010/65321856; Ireland, 3 Ritan Dong Lu, Sanlitun ⓣ010/65322691; Japan, 7 Ritan Lu, Jianguomenwai ⓣ010/65322361; Kazakhstan, 9 Dong Liu Jie, Sanlitun ⓣ010/65326183; Kyrgyzstan, 2-4-1 Tayuan Building ⓣ010/65326458; Laos, 11 Dong Si Jie, Sanlitun ⓣ010/65321224; Mongolia, 2 Xiushui Bei Jie, Jianguomenwai ⓣ010/65321203; Myanmar (Burma), 6 Dongzhimenwai Dajie, Sanlitun ⓣ010/65321425; New Zealand, 1 Ritan Dong'er Jie, Sanlitun ⓣ010/65322731; North Korea, Ritan Bei Lu, Jianguomenwai ⓣ010/65321186; Pakistan, 1 Dongzhimenwai Dajie, Sanlitun ⓣ010/65322660; Russian Federation, 4 Dongzhimen Bei Zhong Jie, south off Andingmen Dong Dajie ⓣ010/65322051; South Korea, Floors 3 & 4, World Trade Centre ⓣ010/65053171; Thailand, 40 Guanghua Lu, Jianguomenwai ⓣ010/65321903; UK, 11 Guanghua Lu, Jianguomenwai ⓣ010/65321961; Ukraine, 11 Dong Lu Jie, Sanlitun ⓣ010/65324014; USA, 3 Xiushui Bei Jie, Jianguomenwai ⓣ010/65323831; Uzbekistan, 7 Beixiao Jie, Sanlitun ⓣ010/65326305; Vietnam, 32 Guanghua Lu, Jianguomenwai ⓣ010/65321155.

English corner Sundays in Zizhuyuan Park.

Football The Chinese were deliriously happy at qualifying for the World Cup in 2002, and made the team's Yugoslavian coach a national hero. Shame they didn't score a goal. Beijing's team, Guo An, play at the massive Workers' Stadium in the north-east of the city, off Gongren Tiyuchang Bei Lu (bus #110 along Dongdaqiao), about every two weeks, usually on Sunday afternoon at 3.30pm. There's a timetable outside the ticket office, which is just east of the north gate of the stadium. Tickets are cheap (¥15), and you buy them at the ground on the day. More interesting to watch are the dynamic Shenyang team, who play at the Olympic Stadium next to the Asian Games village (same times as above) at least until they've sorted out a ground nearer home.

Hospitals and clinics Most big hotels have a resident medic. If you need a hospital, the following have foreigners' clinics where some English is spoken: Sino-Japanese Friendship Hospital on Heping Dajie ⓣ010/64221122 (daily 8–11.30am & 1–4.30pm); Friendship Hospital at 95 Yongan Lu, west of Tiantan Park ⓣ010/63014411; Beijing Hospital at 15 Dahua Lu. For a service run by and for foreigners, try the International Medical Centre at S106 in the Lufthansa Centre, Dong Sanhuan Bei Lu ⓣ010/64651561, or the Hong Kong International Clinic on the third floor of the Swissotel Hong Kong Macao Centre, Dongsishitiao Qiao ⓣ010/65012288 ext 2346 (daily 9am–9pm). For real emergencies, the AEA International offers a comprehensive and expensive service at 14 Liangmahe Lu, not far from the Lufthansa Centre (clinic ⓣ010/64629112, emergencies ⓣ010/64629100).

Internet access In addition to hotel business centres, where you don't have to be a guest to use their computers, there are also plenty of Internet cafés, which are usually cheaper and more relaxing places to be. Sparkice offers the most pleasant environment; they have cafés at Level 2 of the World Trade Centre, Jianguomenwai Dajie (24hr; ¥8–12 per hour) and another (8am–1am) in the east wing of the Lufthansa Centre. Recommended is the cosy Net café at the back of the second floor in the Sanlian Bookshop (see p.134), on Wangfujing Dajie, near the China Art Gallery (daily 8am–8pm; ¥20 per hour). But if you really want to save money when you're online, head north to the university districts, where a computer in a cramped shop, usually full of youths playing *Counterstrike*, can cost as little as ¥2 per hour, and they're usually open through the night. Haidian also has plenty of Internet cafés; if you're out here for the night, you can round the evening off by sending drunken messages home. Beijing Login Tech is among the cheapest, charging ¥8 per hour, with branches at 38 Haidan Lu, 31 Xueyuan Lu (both in Haidian) and 75 Chengfulu Dajie (near the south gate of Qinghua University). If you're living in the city and want to apply for installation, go to the Telegraph Office on Xi Chang'an Jie (see "Telecommunications" below).

Language courses You can do short courses in Chinese at Beijing Foreign Studies University on Erhuan Xi Lu, at the Bridge School in Jianguomenwai (ⓣ010/64940243), which offers evening classes, or the Cultural Mission at 7 Beixiao Jie in Sanlitun (ⓣ010/65323005), where most students are diplomats. A cheap and easy way to study basic Mandarin, though, is to find a Chinese student of English – try hanging around English corner (see above) – and get them to teach you. You'll have to negotiate a fee, but they don't charge very much, maybe ¥15 an hour. For six-month to year-long courses in Chinese, apply to Beijing International School at Anzhenxili,

Chaoyang (☎010/64433151), Beijing University in Haidian (☎010/62751230), Beijing Foreign Studies University, at 2 Xi Erhuna Lu (☎010/68468167), or Beijing Normal University, at 19 Xinjiekouwai (☎010/62207986). Expect to pay around ¥10,000 tuition fees for a year.

Left luggage There's a left-luggage office in the foreigners' waiting room at the back of Beijing Zhan, with lockers for ¥5 or ¥10 a day depending on size, though as these are often full you are better off going to the main left-luggage office (daily 5am–midnight; ¥5 a day) at the east side of the station. The left luggage office at Xi Zhan is downstairs on the left as you enter and costs ¥10 a day.

Libraries The Beijing National Library, at 39 Baishiqiao Lu, just north of Zizhuyuan Park (Mon–Fri 8am–5pm; ☎010/68415566), is one of the largest in the world, with more than ten million volumes, including manuscripts from the Dunhuang Caves and a Qing-dynasty encyclopedia. The oldest texts are Shang dynasty inscriptions on bone. You'll need to join before they let you in. To take books out, you need to be resident in the city, but you can turn up and get a day pass that lets you browse around. An attached small cinema shows Western films in English at weekends; phone for details. The Library of the British Embassy, on Floor 4 of the Landmark Building at 8 Dong Sanhuan Bei Lu, has a wide selection of books and magazines and anyone can wander in and browse.

Mail The International Post Office is on Chaoyangmen Dajie (Mon–Sat 8am–6pm), just north of the intersection with Jianguomen Dajie. This is where post restante letters end up, dumped in a box; you have to rifle through them all and pay ¥1.5 for the privilege. They won't let you take out a letter unless you show your passport. Letters are kept only for one month, after which the post office is quick to send them back; turn up a few days late and officious staff will derive amusement from your distress. It's also possible to rent a PO Box here and there's a packing service for parcels and a wide variety of stamps on sale, but again staff are not very helpful. There are other post offices in the basement of the World Trade Centre, on Xi Chang'an Jie, just east of the Concert Hall, on Wangfujing Dajie near *Dunkin' Donuts*, and at the north end of Xidan Dajie. All are open Mon–Sat from 9am to 5pm. Express mail can be sent from a counter in the International Post Office or from the EMS office at 7 Qianmen Dajie ☎010/65129948.

Pharmacies There are large pharmacies at 136 Wangfujing and 42 Dongdan Bei Dajie, or you could try the famous Tongrentang Pharmacy on Dazhalan (see p.104). For imported non-prescription medicines, try Watsons at the *Holiday Inn Lido*, Shoudujichang Lu.

PSB The Foreigners' Police, at 2 Andingmen Dong Dajie (Mon–Fri 8–noon & 1.30–4pm; ☎010/84015292), will give you a first visa extension for a fee of ¥160. It will take them up to a week to do it, so make sure you've got plenty of cash before you go as you can't change money without your passport. Apply for a second extension and you'll be told to leave the country: don't, just leave Beijng and apply elsewhere. The nearest place with a friendly PSB office, where your visa will be extended on the spot, is Chengde (see p.169). You can make it there and back in a day. If you have an emergency and require urgent assistance, dial ☎110 or ☎010/550100, and have a Chinese speaker handy to help you.

Swimming pool Try the Olympic-size pool in the Asian Games Village, Anding Lu (daily 8am–9pm; ¥50), on the route of trolleybus #108 from Chongwenmennei Dajie, which also boasts some of the city's fiercest showers.

Telecommunications There are 24-hour telecommunication offices in the Telegraph Office at 11 Xi Chang'an Jie, about 300m from the intersection with Xidan Bei Dajie, and by the International Post Office, on Chaoyangmen Dajie. The orange coin and card phones on the street can be used for international calls. You can buy cards at most hotels, plazas and at the Telegraph Office. You can call the operator on ☎114 but have a Chinese speaker handy to help you.

Travel agents CITS is at 103 Fuxingmennei Dajie (daily 8.30–11.30am & 1.30–4.30pm; ☎010/66011122). They offer expensive tours, a tour guide and interpreter service, and advance ticket booking for trains, planes and ferries (from Tianjin), with a commission of around ¥30 added. Other CITS offices are at 103 Fuxingmennei Dajie (☎010/66011122), in the *Beijing Hotel*, 33 Dongchang'an Jie (☎010/65120507) and the *New Century Hotel* (☎010/68491426), opposite the zoo. Good private alternatives to the state monolith, geared at corporate groups, include Sunshine Travel, at 2 Nan Dong Sanhuan Lu (☎010/65868069), and the R&R Travel Company, in Room B04, 9 Ritan Dong Lu, inside Ritan Park (☎010/65868069). The Tourism Hotline (☎010/65130828) is open 24hr for enquiries and complaints; all its staff are English-speaking.

Around Beijing

There are plenty of scenic spots and places of interest scattered in the plains and hills around the capital, and no visit would be complete without a trip to the **Great Wall**, accessible in three places within easy journey time of Beijing. In addition, the Western Hills in particular shouldn't be overlooked and, if you're in the capital for any length of time, they provide an invigorating breather from the pressures of the city. Other spots such as the excavations at **Zhoukoudian** or the **Aviation Museum** will probably be of most appeal to those with a special interest, and scenic places like the Kangxi Grasslands to long-term residents.

The Great Wall

This is a Great Wall and only a great people with a great past could have a great wall and such a great people with such a great wall will surely have a great future.

Richard M. Nixon

Stretching 6000km in a dotted line across China, the **Great Wall** was begun in the fifth century BC and was still being built up to the sixteenth century. Today's surviving sections, placed end to end, would link New York with Los Angeles, and if the bricks used to build it were made into a single wall 5m high and 1m thick it would more than encircle the earth. Even at ground level, and along the small, most-visited section at Badaling, constantly overrun by Chinese and foreign tourists, Wan Li Changcheng (The Long Wall of Ten Thousand Li), is clearly the PRC's most spectacular sight.

The Chinese have walled their cities since earliest times and during the Warring States period, around the fifth century BC, simply extended the practice to separate rival territories. The Great Wall's **origins** lie in these fractured lines of fortifications and in the vision of **Qin Shi Huang** who, unifying the empire in the third century BC, joined and extended the sections to form one continuous defence against barbarians. Under subsequent dynasties – the Han, Wei, Qi and Sui – the wall was maintained and, in response to shifting regional threats, grew and changed course. It did lose importance for a while, with Tang borders extending well to the north, then shrinking back under the Song, but with the emergence of the Ming it again became a priority, and military technicians worked on its reconstruction right through the fourteenth to the sixteenth century.

For much of its history, the wall was hated. Qin Shi Huang's wall, particularly, was a symbol of brutal tyranny – he wasted the country's wealth and worked thousands to death in building it. It is estimated that he mobilized nearly a million people to construct it, but other dynasties surpassed even that figure. Many of the labourers were criminals, but in the Sui dynasty, when there weren't enough men left for the massive project, widows were pressed into service. A Song-dynasty poem expresses a common sentiment:

The wall is so tall because it is stuffed with the bones of soldiers
The wall is so deep because it is watered with the soldiers' blood.

Around Beijing

Aviation Museum	航空博物馆	*hángkōng bówùguǎn*
Badachu	八大处	*bādàchù*
Badaling Great Wall	八达岭	*bādálǐng*
Biyun Si	碧云寺	*bìyún sì*
Botanical Gardens	植物园	*zhíwù yuán*
Great Wall	长城	*chángchéng*
Huanghua Great Wall	黄花长城	*huánghuā chángchéng*
Huairou	怀柔	*huáiróu*
Jietai Si	戒台寺	*jiètái sì*
Jinshanling Great Wall	金山岭长城	*jīnshānlǐng chángchéng*
Kangxi Grasslands	康西草原	*kāngxī cǎoyuán*
Longqing Gorge	龙庆峡	*lóngqìng xiá*
Lugou Qiao	卢沟桥	*lúgōu qiáo*
Miyun Reservoir	密云水库	*mìyún shuǐkù*
Mutianyu Great Wall	慕田峪	*mùtiányù*
Shisan Ling	十三陵	*shísān líng*
Simatai Great Wall	司马台	*sīmătái*
Tanzhe Si	潭柘寺	*tánzhé sì*
Western Hills	西山	*xīshān*
Wofo Si	卧佛寺	*wòfó sì*
Xiangshan Park	香山公园	*xiāngshān gōngyuán*
Zhoukoudian	周口店	*zhōukǒu diàn*

The irony, of course, is that the seven-metre-high, seven-metre-thick wall, with its 25,000 battlements, did not work. Successive invasions crossed its defences (Genghis Khan is supposed to have merely bribed the sentries), and it was in any case of little use against the sea powers of Japan and later Europe. But the wall did have significant functions. It allowed the swift passage through the empire of both troops and goods – there is room for five horses abreast most of the way – and, perhaps as important, it restricted the movement of the nomadic peoples in the distant, non-Han minority regions.

During the Qing dynasty, the Manchus let the wall fall into disrepair as it had proved no obstacle to their invasion. Slowly the wall crumbled away, useful only as a source of building material. Now, though, the Great Wall, as Nixon might have added, is great business. At the restored sections, **Badaling**, and to a lesser extent, **Mutianyu**, the wall is daily besieged by masses of visitors. Distant **Simatai**, **Jiugulou** and **Jinshanling** are much less crowded, and far more beautiful. To see the wall in all its crumbly glory, head out to **Huanghua**, as yet untouched by development. Other places to see the wall are at Shanhaiguan (see p.165), Zhangye (see p.1041) and Jiayuguan (see p.1043).

Badaling

The best-known section of the wall, and the one most people see, is at **BADALING** (daily 9am–4.30pm; ¥35), 70km northwest of Beijing. It was the first section to be restored, in 1957, and opened up to tourists. Here the wall is 6m wide with regular watchtowers dating from the Ming dynasty. It follows the highest contours of a steep range of hills, forming a formidable defence, and this section was never attacked directly but taken by sweeping around from the side.

It's the easiest part of the wall to get to but it's also the most packaged, and to get the best out of it you need to escape the paths along which visitors are herded. A giant tourist circus greets you at the entrance, including a plethora of restaurants, rank after rank of souvenir stalls, a bank and post office. On the wall, flanked with guardrails and metal bins and accompanied by hordes of other tourists, it's hard to feel that there's anything genuine about the experience. Indeed, the wall itself is hardly original here, being a modern reconstruction on the ancient foundations. From the entrance you can walk along the wall to the north (left) or south (right). Few people get very far, which gives you a chance to lose the crowds and, generally, things get better the farther you go. Unfortunately, the authorities have recently wised up to the attempts of tourists to enjoy themselves here, and it's possible that guards will turn you back from unreconstructed sections.

If you head south, which most people do, you'll come to a cable car (¥50), after about 2km, which will take you down to a car park, and a zoo full of sad, mad bears. Keep going past the cable car and you'll reach an unreconstructed section that in parts is quite hard to climb around.

Head north from the main entrance and you'll shake off the crowds fairly quickly. After about 1km you come to the end of the reconstructed section, and from here you can climb down onto the old wall and keep going. It's on this ruined section that you get a much better impression of the wall's real, more frightening, character – a lonely road plodding on and on through a silent landscape.

Practicalities

All the more expensive Beijing hotels and a few of the cheaper ones, as well as CITS, run **tours** to Badaling, with prices that are often absurd. If you come with a tour you'll arrive in the early afternoon, when it's at its busiest, spend an hour or two, then return, which really gives you little time for anything except the most cursory of jaunts, a few photo opportunities, and the purchase of an "I climbed the Great Wall" T–shirt. It's just as easy, and cheaper, to travel under your own steam, and with more time at your disposal you can make for the more deserted sections. The easiest way to get here is on one of the **tourist buses** (¥36–50), which also go to the Ming Tombs (see p.142). They look like ordinary buses but their numbers are written in green. Tourist buses #1 and #5 go from the north side of Qianmen Dong Dajie, opposite *McDonald's*. Bus#2 goes from Beijing Zhan, bus#4 from Xizhimen, by the zoo. The buses run daily 6–10am, departing every twenty minutes, and the journey takes about two hours. Much cheaper (¥10) is bus #919 from Deshengmen (a two-minute walk east from Jishuitan subway stop).

Mutianyu

Mutianyu Great Wall (daily 8am–4pm; ¥10), 90km northeast of the city, is somewhat less developed. A two-kilometre section of the wall, well endowed with guard towers, built in 1368 and renovated in 1983, it passes along a ridge through some lush, undulating hills. From the entrance, steep steps lead up to the wall; most people turn left, which leads to the cable car (¥30 one way, ¥50 round trip) for an effortless trip down again. Turn right and you can walk along the wall for about 1km until you come to a barrier – you can't get on to the unreconstructed sections. The atmospheric *Mutianyu Great Wall Guesthouse* (Ⓣ010/69626867; ❹), situated in a reconstructed watchtower 500m before this barrier, is a good place for a quiet break, if you don't mind the basic facilities; there's no plumbing, so bring some bottled water.

To get to Mutianyu, take tourist bus #6 from Xuanwumen, outside the south cathedral (¥50) which also stops at a dull temple and amusement park on the way back. Buses run daily 7–8.30am between April 15 and October 15. Otherwise take a minibus to Huairou from Dongzhimen Station, and change there for a tourist minibus (¥20). Returning to the city isn't a hassle provided you don't leave it too late, as plenty of minibuses wait in the car park to take people to Beijing. If you can't find a minibus back to Beijing, get one to Huairou, from where you can get regular bus #918 back to the capital – the last bus leaves at 6.30pm.

Simatai and Jinshanling

Simatai (daily 8am–4pm; ¥20), 110km northeast of the city, is the most unspoilt section of the Great Wall around Beijing, though it seems about to gear up for mass tourism, with a cable car and toboggan ride. But, with the wall snaking across purple hills that resemble crumpled velvet from afar, and blue mountains in the distance, it's still beautiful. Peaceful and semi-ruined, it fulfils the expectations of most visitors more than the other sections, though it gets a little crowded at weekends. Be aware that it's pretty steep with some vertiginous drops. Most of this section is unrenovated, dating back to the Ming dynasty, and sporting a few late innovations such as spaces for cannon, with its inner walls at right angles to the outer wall to thwart invaders who have already breached the first defence. From the car park, a winding path takes you up to the wall, where most visitors turn right. Regularly spaced watchtowers allow you to measure your progress uphill along the ridge. The less energetic can take the new cable car to the eighth tower (¥20). The walk over the ruins is not an easy one, and gets increasingly precipitous after about the tenth watchtower, with sheer drops and steep angles. The views are sublime, though. After about the fourteenth tower (2hr), the wall peters out and the climb becomes quite dangerous, and there's no point going any farther. If you turn left onto the wall, you come to a chain bridge where you're charged an annoying ¥30 toll. Walk three hours in this direction and you come to Jinshanling, though most people who do this start from Jinshanling as it's easier to get a lift back to Beijing from Simatai.

Practicalities

The journey out from the capital to Simatai takes about three hours. **Tours** runs from all the backpacker hotels and hostels for around ¥80, generally once a week in the off season, daily in the summer. Most other hotels can arrange transport too, though expect to pay more. To travel here independently, catch a direct bus from Dongzhimen (¥20) or take a bus to Miyun and then start negotiating for a minibus or taxi to take you the rest of the way (don't pay more than ¥20). The last bus back to Beijing from Miyun is at 4pm. Between April 15 and October 15 tourist bus #12 leaves for Simatai from the #42 bus station south of Domgsishitiao subway stop between 6 and 8am (¥50); buses return between 4 and 6pm. A rented **taxi** will cost about ¥300 there and back, including a wait. There's a small guesthouse just inside the ticket gate (Ⓣ010/69931095; ❺).

Jinshanling

Jinshanling (¥25), 10km west of Simatai, is one of the least-visited and best-preserved parts of the wall, with jutting obstacle walls and oval watchtowers, some with octagonal or sloping roofs. It's presently being reconstructed so expect tourist buses out here some time soon, but for the moment it's not easy to reach without your own transport. Take a bus to Miyun (see above), from where a taxi to the wall will cost around ¥100. It's a three-hour walk from here to Simatai, where you'll have to pay a toll and they'll try and charge you a second entrance fee (refuse). A popular day-trip from the backpacker haunts (¥80 excluding the entrance fee and bridge toll) takes you here and picks you up at Simatai.

Huanghua and Jiugulou

The section at **Huanghua**, northeast of the capital, is unreconstructed, no one will try to sell you a T-shirt, and you can hike along the wall for as long as you feel like, though some sections, among them the first, are a little tricky for the leaden-footed. If you want to camp out, this is the section to head for. It's not too hard to get here: take bus #916 to the town of **Huairou** (¥8) from Dongzhimen bus station, and from there catch a minibus taxi the remaining 25km, which should cost ¥20, but ask around as drivers charge foreigners a lot more. You'll be dropped off on a road that cuts through the wall. Most people head right, over the little reservoir. Locals attempt to charge for the use of ladders and paths but can be ignored. The wall here shouldn't present too many hazards and gets easier, levelling off along a ridge before becoming abruptly precipitous again as it climbs "camel's back" ridge. Most people turn back here but if you continue over the ridge for about another 500m you come to a path that leads back to the road. You can ascend the left side by heading back down the road about 200m, where you'll find a twisting path that gets you onto the wall.

To get back to Huairou, walk back along the road for five minutes to a bridge where local taxis congregate (¥10), or take a bus from the roadside bus stop. The last bus from Huairou to Beijing is at 6.30pm.

You can see another wild and rarely visited section at **Jiugulou**, about 40km north of Huairou. A taxi from Huairou will cost about ¥60.

The Ming Tombs and around

Thirteen of the sixteen Ming-dynasty emperors were entombed in and around the Shisan Ling Valley, 40km northwest of Beijing. Two of these **Ming Tombs** (daily 8.30am–4.30pm; ¥20 per tomb), Chang Ling and Ding Ling, were restored in the 1950s and the latter was also excavated, yielding up various treasures to the capital's museums. They are very much on the tour circuit, conveniently placed on the way to Badaling. However, the fame of the tombs is overstated in relation to the actual interest of the sites and, unless you've a strong archeological interest, this isn't a trip worth making for its own sake. If you want to come, the easiest way to get here is to take any of the tourist buses that visit Badaling (see p.140), which visit the tombs on the way back to Beijing. On public transport, take bus #845 from Xizhimen to Changping, then bus #314 to the tombs. Buses drop you at a car park just before Ding Ling, where you buy your ticket.

The third Ming emperor, **Yongle**, who shifted the capital back from Nanjing to Beijing, chose this site for its landscape and it's undeniably one of the loveliest around the capital. Its scenic appeal has also caught the eye of Beijing's tourist planners, and the area is currently under development as a "tourist park" with hotels, amusement centres and even a golf course. Fortunately, at present only the two principal tombs have had much notice taken of them – the other eleven stand neglected and very beautiful amid former gardens, with grass and weeds breaking through their tiled roofs and marble foundations. They make a nice place to picnic if you just feel like a break from the city and its more tangible succession of sights. To get the most out of the place, plan to spend a day here and hike around the smaller tombs farther into the hills rather than sticking to the tourist route between Ding Ling and the car park. You'll need a **map** to do this and you'll find one on the back of some Beijing city maps, or you can buy one at the site.

The approach to the Ming Tombs, the seven-kilometre **Spirit Way**, is Shisan

Ling's most exciting feature. This commences with the Dahongmen (Great Red Gate), a triple-entranced triumphal arch, through the central opening of which only the emperor's dead body could be carried. Beyond, the road is lined to either side with colossal stone statues of animals and men. Startlingly larger than life, the statues all date from the fifteenth century and are among the best surviving examples of Ming sculpture. The sequence begins with groups of animals, real and mythological, including the *qilin*, a reptilian-like beast with deer's horns and a cow's tail, and the horned, feline *xiechi*. The avenue then changes alignment slightly and you are met by the first, stern human figures of military mandarins. The precise significance of the statues is unclear, although it is assumed they were intended to serve the emperors in their next life.

Animal statuary reappears at the entrances to several of the tombs, though the structures themselves are something of an anticlimax. **Chang Ling**, Yongle's tomb and the earliest at the site, stands at the end of the avenue. There are plans to excavate it, an exciting scheme since it is contemporary with some of the finest building of the Imperial Palace in the capital. At present the enduring impression is mainly one of scale: vast courtyards and hall buildings approached by terraced white marble. Its main feature is the Hall of Eminent Flowers, supported by huge columns of single tree trunks which it is said were imported all the way from Yunnan along frozen roads, slippery with ice.

The main focus of the tour, however, is **Ding Ling**, the underground tomb-palace of the Emperor Wanli. Wanli ascended the throne in 1573 at the age of 10 and reigned for almost half a century. He began building his tomb when he was 22, in line with common Ming practice, and hosted a grand party within on its completion. The mausoleum was opened in 1956 and found to be substantially intact, revealing the emperor's coffin, flanked by those of two of his empresses, and floors covered with the remains of scores of trunks containing imperial robes, gold and silver, and even the imperial cookbooks. Some of the treasures are displayed in the tomb, a huge musty vault, undecorated but impressive for its scale, and others have been replaced by replicas. It's a cautionary sight of useless wealth accumulation, as pointed out by the tour guides.

Miyun, Longqing Gorge and the Aviation Museum

The town of **MIYUN** lies some 65km northeast of Beijing, at the foot of the long range of hills along which the Great Wall threads its way. Buses run here from Dongzhimen bus station in the city. The area's claim to fame is the reservoir built in the flat, wide valleys behind the town. Supplying more than half the capital's water, it's a huge lake, scattered with islets and bays, backed by mountains and the deep blue of the Beijing sky. The reservoir has become a favourite destination for Beijing families, who flock out here at weekends to go swimming, fishing, boating and walking. Joining them is half the fun; however, if you're here for a little solitude, it's easy enough to wander off on your own. Behind the reservoir, in the hills, you'll find rock pools big enough to swim in, streams, trees, flowers and a rushing river – and on the hill tops there are outposts of the Great Wall, still in ruins. To make a weekend of it, and perhaps combine your trip with a visit to Simatai, 50km to the northeast, you can stay the night at the three-star *Miyun Yunhu Holiday Resort* (ⓣ010/69044587; ❼), on the shores of the reservoir.

Longqing Gorge is another reservoir and local recreation and beauty spot, 90km northwest of the capital. It's accessible by tourist bus #8 from the #328 bus station near Andingmen subway stop (summer only) or on train #575, which leaves Xizhimen Zhan at 8.30am, arriving two and a half hours later.

The main attraction here is the **ice festival**, similar to the one in Harbin, held in late January and February, sometimes into March. The ice sculptures, with coloured lights inside for a gloriously tacky psychedelic effect, look great at night; unfortunately, the few hotel rooms here are expensive. Not too far from here, the **Kangxi Grasslands**, accessible by train from Beijing North station (Xizhimen Zhan) or by minibus from the gorge, is an established summer resort, where you can go horse riding. The nearest decent hotel in this area is the *Yanqing Guesthouse* (ⓣ010/69142363; ❻) in **Yanqing.**

For something different, the **Aviation Museum** (daily 8.30am–5.30pm; ¥40, students ¥20), out in the sticks 60km north of the city, is a fascinating place, though it's probably only worth the awkward journey for real enthusiasts. Take bus #345 from Deshengmen bus station, close to the subway stop, and tell the conductor where you want to go. After about ninety minutes, you'll need to get off, cross the freeway, and get bus #912 for the last few kilometres. The enormous museum has a decidedly military feel, with more than three hundred aircraft displayed in a giant hangar and on a concourse, from the copy of the Wright brothers' plane flown by Feng Ru in 1909, to helicopter gunships used in the Gulf War. As well as plenty of fighters, many that saw action in the Korean War, the bomber that dropped China's first atom bomb is here, as is Mao's personal plane and the plane that scattered Zhou Enlai's ashes, which is covered with wreaths and tributes.

South and west of Beijing

The Western Hills are not far out of the city but, with swathes of wooded parkland dotted with temples, they feel a lot farther – except on weekends when the crowds are dense. The places of note south of Beijing are Zhoukoudian, where Peking Man was discovered, and on the way there or back you could make a quick stop at the Luguo Qiao.

The Western Hills

Like the Summer Palace, the **Western Hills**, 20km west of the city, are a place to escape urban life for a while, though more of a rugged experience. Because of its relative coolness at the height of summer, the area has been long favoured as a restful retreat by religious men and intellectuals, as well as politicians in this century – Mao lived here briefly, and the Politburo retreated here in 1989. West of the Summer Palace, it takes about an hour to get here by public transport from the city. The hills are divided into three parks, the closest of which is the Botanical Gardens, directly west of the Summer Palace. Two kilometres farther west, Xiangshan is the largest and most impressive park, but Badachu, south of here, a collection of temples strung out along a hillside, is just as pretty. A day gives you ample time to explore each of the three areas, if your legs are willing.

The **Botanical Gardens** (daily 6am–8pm; ¥10) are accessible by bus #333 from the Summer Palace (see p.118). Two thousand varieties of trees and plants are arranged in formal gardens which are pretty in the summer, though the terrain is flat and the landscaping is not as original as in the older parks. The main path leads after 1km to the **Wofo Si** (daily 8am–4.30pm; ¥2), whose main hall houses a huge reclining Buddha, more than 5m in length and cast in copper. With two giant feet protruding from the end of his painted robe, and a pudgy, baby face, calm in repose, he looks rather cute, although he is not actually sleeping but dying, about to enter nirvana. Huge shoes, presented as offerings, are on display around the hall. Behind the temple is a bamboo garden, from which paths wind off into the hills. One heads northwest to a pretty cherry valley, just under 1km away, where Cao Xueqiao is supposed to have written *The Dream of Red Mansions*.

Deservedly the most popular is **Xiangshan Park** (daily 7am–6pm; ¥5), whose main, eastern entrance is 2km west of the Botanical Gardens, also on the route of bus #333. The park is a carefully landscaped range dominated by Incense Burner Peak in the western corner. It's at its best in the autumn (before the sharp November frosts), when the leaves turn red in a massive profusion of colour. At weekends the park is busy, but it's too big to be swamped and it's always a good place for a hike and a picnic. Close to the main entrance, the **Xiangshan Hotel** (☎010/62591166; ❼), one of the city's most innovative buildings, comes as an unexpected sight. Designed by Bei Yuming, who also designed the pyramid at the Louvre in Paris, the light and airy building is somewhere between a temple and an airport lounge, and a great location to escape the smoke for a weekend. Northeast from here, the **Zhao Miao** (Temple of Brilliance), one of the few temples in the area that escaped vandalism by Western troops in 1860 and 1900, was built by Qianlong in 1780 in Tibetan style, designed to make visiting Lamas feel at home. From here, follow the path west up to the Peak (1hr) from where, on clear days, there are magnificent views down towards the Summer Palace and as far as distant Beijing. You can hire a horse to take you down again for ¥20, the same price as the cable car (¥20). Both drop you on the northern side of the hill, by the north entrance, a short walk from the superb **Biyun Si** (Azure Clouds Temple), just outside the park gate. A striking building, it's dominated by a north Indian-style dagoba and topped by extraordinary conical stupas. Inside, rather bizarrely, a tomb holds the hat and clothes of Sun Yatsen – his body was held here for a while before being moved in 1924. The giant main hall is now a maze of corridors lined with *arhats*, five hundred in all, and it's a magical place. The benignly smiling golden figures are all different – some have two heads or sit on animals, one is even pulling his face off – and you may see monks moving among them and bowing to each.

Badachu, or the Eight Great Sights (daily 8am–5pm; ¥10), is a forested hill 10km south of Xiangshan Park and accessible on bus #347 from the zoo. Along the path that snakes around the hill are eight **temples**, fairly small affairs, but quite attractive on weekdays, when they're not busy. The new pagoda at the base of the path holds a Buddha tooth, which once sat in the second temple. The third, a nunnery, is the most pleasant, with a teahouse in the courtyard. There's a statue of the rarely depicted thunder deity inside, boggle-eyed and grimacing. As well as the inevitable cable car, it's also possible to slide down the hill on a metal track.

The Tanzhe Si and Jietai Si

Due west of Beijing, two temples sit in the wooded country outside the industrial zone that rings the city. Between April 15 and October 15 tourist bus #7 from Qianmen head out to both temples; buses leave between 7 and 8.30am and cost ¥20 return trip. Getting to and from the area by public transport is a hassle, though you can get close without too much difficulty – bus #307 from Qianmen goes to the Hetan terminal, from where you'll need to find an unnumbered bus to the Tanzhe Si. From here a taxi to the Jietai Si should be around ¥20, but there's no transport back from here.

Forty kilometres west of the city, the **Tanzhe Si** (daily 8am–6pm; ¥20) occupies the most beautiful and serene temple site anywhere near the city. It's the largest, too, and one of the oldest, first recorded in the third century as housing a thriving community of monks. Wandering through the complex, past terraces of stupas, you reach an enormous central courtyard, with an ancient towering gingko that's more than a thousand years old (christened the "King of Trees" by Emperor Qianlong), at its heart. Across the courtyard, a second, smaller tree is known as "The Emperor's Wife" and is supposed to produce a new branch every time a new emperor is born. From here you can take in the other temple buildings, on different levels up the hillside, or look round the lush bamboo gardens, whose plants are supposed to cure all manner of ailments. The spiky zhe (Cudrania) trees near the entrance apparently "reinforce the essence of the kidney and control spontaneous seminal emission".

Twelve kilometres back along the road to Beijing, in complete contrast to the Tanzhe Si, the **Jietai Si** (daily 8am–6pm; ¥20) sits on a hillside looking more like a fortress than a temple, surrounded by forbiddingly tall, red walls. It's famous for its venerable pines, eccentric-looking trees growing in odd directions. Indeed, one, leaning out at an angle of about thirty degrees, is pushing over a pagoda on the terrace beneath it. In the main hall is an enormous Liao-dynasty platform of white marble, 3m high and intricately carved with figures – monks, monsters (beaked and winged) and saints – at which novice monks were ordained. Another, smaller hall, holds a beautiful wooden altar that swarms with dragons in relief.

Zhoukoudian and around

Fifty kilometres south of Beijing is **ZHOUKOUDIAN** village, terminus of bus #914, which leaves from a station on Beiwei Lu, just south of the *Beiwei Hotel*. The main attraction is an excavation site (daily 9am–4pm; ¥20) in the limestone hills to the south of town (¥10 by meterless taxi from the bus station). This is where the first relic – a single tooth – of **Peking Man**, who lived here between 500,000 and 230,000 years ago, was uncovered in 1921. Excavations began in earnest after archeologists realized they had found a new genus, a link between Neanderthal and modern man, and they christened it *homo erectus Pekinensis*. Excavations revealed the remains of more than forty individuals, as well as tools and ornaments and parts of animals too. The top of a skull was found in 1929 but lost again during the chaos of the Anti-Japanese War. As well as wandering around the site – a nice walk but not exactly revealing – you can visit the **museum**, which displays just enough to ignite the imagination. The first room contains the archeologists' digging tools, contrasting with Peking Man's flint tools, shown later on together with his bone needles and ornaments. No weapons were found – it seems Peking Man lived on nuts and tubers and only occasionally hunted. He was pretty short, with three-quarters of the brain capacity of modern man. Copious explanations in English, diagrams and paintings, make up for the limited nature of the objects shown – tools and fragments of bone. Much more dramatic are the remains of fearsome beasts now extinct, found at the site, which are accompanied by models or paintings of what they would have looked like. As well as the teeth of a sabre-toothed tiger, there's the whole skeleton of a huge panther-like creature, and the skull of a deer-like animal with bony plates on its head and thick antlers with a two-metre spread. The last bus back to the city is around dusk.

The **Luguo Qiao**, Reed Moat Bridge (daily 8am–6pm; ¥4), is on the route of bus #339 from the Liuli flyover in the city; ask the conductor to tell you when to get off. It's not really worth a special visit, but it can be combined with a trip to Zhoukoudian if you are in a taxi. Built in 1192, with 250 grey marble balustrades emblazoned with carved lions, each of which wears a different expression, this bridge was described in the writings of Marco Polo, earning it its alternative name, Marco Polo Bridge. Today, substantially preserved, including the elephants holding it up at either end, it's still remarkable, although the area around is pretty shabby and the river has dried up, leaving a dusty expanse used as a practice ground by the capital's driving schools.

WANPING, on the river bank by the bridge, is a small country village, and the site of the first shot fired in the war between China and Japan in 1937, prompted by the illegal Japanese occupation of a rail junction nearby. After that it was only a short step to a full-scale assault on Beijing. The Anti-Japanese War is commemorated by a **museum** (Tues–Sun 8am–5pm; ¥5) in the village, whose declared message of international friendship seems at odds with its gruesome dioramas of executions and medical experiments, and photos of dead babies.

Travel details

Trains

Beijing Zhan to: Baotou (daily; 14hr); Beidaihe (3 daily; 5hr); Changchun (daily; 14hr); Chengde (4 daily; 4hr); Dalian (2 daily; 18hr); Dandong (daily; 20hr); Datong (2 daily; 7hr); Fuzhou (daily; 35hr); Hangzhou (daily; 22hr); Harbin (daily; 18hr); Hohhot (2 daily; 12hr); Ji'nan (3 daily; 8hr); Nanjing (daily; 20hr); Qingdao (daily; 18hr); Shanghai (2 express daily; 14hr; otherwise 20hr); Shanhaiguan (3 daily; 8hr; take a 5hr fast train to Qinghuangdao instead); Shenyang (4 daily; 10hr); Tai'an (2 daily; 8hr); Tianjin (frequent; 2hr); Yantai (daily; 20hr).
Xi Zhan to: Changsha (daily; 24hr); Chengdu (2 daily; 35hr); Chongqing (2 daily; 40hr); Guangzhou (3 daily; 30hr); Guiyang (daily; 35hr); Kunming (daily; 60hr); Lanzhou (daily; 35hr); Luoyang (daily; 14hr); Nanchang (daily; 25hr); Nanning (daily; 40hr); Shijiazhuang (daily; 4hr); Taiyuan (daily; 10hr); Ulan Batur (Mongolia; weekly; 90hr); Ürümqi (daily; 70hr); Xi'an (5 daily; 16hr); Yichang (daily; 23hr); Yuncheng (daily; 18hr); Zhanjiang (daily; 40hr); Zhengzhou (2 daily; 10hr).
As well as the above, there are weekly services from Xi Zhan to Moscow and Ulan Batur; see p.81 for details.

Buses

There is little point travelling to destinations far from Beijing by bus; the journey takes longer than the train and is far less comfortable. The following destinations are within bearable travelling distance. Services are frequent, usually hourly during the day, with a few sleeper buses travelling at night.
Deshengmen bus station to: Chengde (4hr); Datong (10hr).
Dongzhimen bus station to: Shenyang (18hr).
Haihutun bus station to: Shijiazhuang (10hr); Tianjin (3hr).
Majuan bus station to: Beidaihe (9hr); Shanhaiguan (9hr; express service takes 5hr).

Flights

Beijing to: Baotou (2 daily; 1hr 30min); Changchun (6 daily; 1hr 45min); Changsha (5 daily; 2hr); Chaoyang (4 weekly; 1hr 20min); Chengdu (7 daily; 2hr 30min); Chifeng (3 weekly; 3hr); Chongqing (4–6 daily; 2hr 40min); Dalian (7–9 daily; 1hr 20min); Fuzhou (4 daily; 2hr 50min); Guangzhou (11 daily; 3hr); Guilin (2–5 daily; 3hr); Guiyang (2–3 daily; 4hr 45min); Haikou (7 daily; 3hr 45min); Hailar (3 weekly; 2hr 20min); Hangzhou (5 daily; 1hr 50min); Harbin (5–8 daily; 2hr); Hohhot (0–9 daily; 1hr 10min); Hong Kong (12 daily; 3hr); Huangyan (3 weekly; 2hr 40min); Jilin (4 weekly; 1hr 50min); Ji'nan (2–3 daily; 1hr); Jinzhou (2 weekly; 1hr 20min); Kunming (6 daily; 3hr 30min); Lanzhou (2–3 daily; 2hr 20min); Lhasa (2 weekly; 4hr) Liuzhou (2 weekly; 2hr 45min); Luoyang (weekly; 1hr 40min); Mudanjiang (1 daily; 1hr 50min); Nanchang (2–4 daily; 2hr); Nanjing (4 daily; 1hr 45min); Nanning (2–3 daily; 3hr 30min); Nantong (1 daily; 2hr 30min); Nanyang (2 weekly; 1hr 30min); Ningbo (daily; 2hr 20min); Qingdao (2–3 daily; 1hr 15min); Qiqihar (4 weekly; 2hr); Quzhou (weekly; 2hr 30min); Sanya (2 daily; 5hr 20min); Shanghai (16 daily; 1hr 50min); Shantou (2 daily; 3hr); Shenyang (8 daily; 1hr); Shenzhen (15 daily; 3hr 10min); Taiyuan (2–4 daily; 1hr 10min); Tianjin (1 weekly; 30min); Tongliao (2 weekly; 1hr 45min); Ürümqi (2–4 daily; 3hr 50min); Wenzhou (2 daily; 2hr 20min); Wuhan (4 daily; 2hr); Wulanhot (2 weekly; 3hr 20min); Xiamen (5 daily; 2hr 50min); Xi'an (10 daily; 1hr 30min); Xiangfan (2 weekly; 2hr); Xilinhot (4 weekly; 1hr 40min); Xining (4 weekly; 2hr 30min); Yanji (1–3 daily; 2hr); Yantai (2–3 daily; 1hr); Yinchuan (1–3 weekly; 2hr); Zhangjiajie (2 weekly; 3hr); Zhanjiang (2 daily; 3hr 30min); Zhengzhou (4 daily; 1hr 20min); Zhuhai (1–2 daily; 3hr 30min).

CHAPTER 2 **Highlights**

* **Tianjin** Glimpse antiquated architecture from the port's past as a foreign concession, now being rapidly razed, and wander Ancient Culture Street, whose alley bazaar is among China's best for atmosphere. **See p.151**

* **Beidaihe beach resort** Once the pleasure preserve of colonists, then Communists, the summer sands are now chock-a-block with the bikinis of the masses. **See p.160**

* **Shanhaiguan** A dusty relic of a walled city on the Beihai Gulf, where you can follow the Great Wall to where it disappears dramatically into the sea, and sleep near the First Pass Under Heaven. **See p.165**

* **Chengde** The summer playground of emperors, whose many palaces and temples have been restored, to the delight of Beijing day-trippers. **See p.169**

* **Cangyan Shan Si** Make the two-hour walk up to this ancient monastery nestled into the cleft of a mountain. **See p.183**

2

Hebei and Tianjin

Hebei is a somewhat anonymous province, with two great cities, Beijing and Tianjin, at its heart but administratively outside its borders, and split into two distinct geographical areas. In the south, a landscape of flatlands is spotted with heavy industry and mining towns – China at its least glamorous – which are home to the majority of the province's sixty million inhabitants. Most travellers pass through here, on their way to or from the capital, though few stop. However, the bleak, sparsely populated tableland rising from the Bohai Gulf in the north of the province has more promise. For most of its history this marked China's northern frontier, and was the setting for numerous battles with invading forces; both the Mongols and the Manchus swept through here. The mark of this bloody history remains in the form of the **Great Wall**, winding across lonely ridges.

The first wall was built in the fourth century AD, along the Hebei–Shanxi border, in an attempt by the small state of Zhongshan to fortify its borders against its aggressive neighbours. Two centuries later, Qin Shi Huang's Wall of Ten Thousand Li (see p.138) skirted the northern borders of the province. The parts of the wall still visible today, though, are the remains of the much later and more extensive Ming-dynasty wall, begun in the fourteenth century as a deterrent against the Mongols. You can see the wall where it meets the sea at **Shanhaiguan**, today a relaxing little fortress town only a day's journey from Beijing and well worth a visit. While you're there, don't miss the strange seaside resort of **Beidaihe**, just to the south, in summer less appealing to foreign travellers for its beaches than for its garish atmosphere and its history as the holiday home of the Party elite. Well north of the wall, the town of **Chengde** is the province's most visited attraction, an imperial base set amid the wild terrain of the Hachin Mongols, and conceived on a grand scale by the eighteenth-century emperor Kangxi, with temples and monuments to match. All three towns are popular spots with domestic tourists, particularly Beijingers snatching a weekend away from the capital's bustle and stress, and part of the interest of going is in seeing the Chinese at their most carefree. Though the Chinese like their holiday spots the way they like their restaurants, *renao* (hot and noisy), it's easy to beat the crowds and find some great scenery, and each town makes a rewarding visit.

Tianjin, an industrial giant, has outgrown its role as the region's capital to become a separate municipality. An ex-concession town with a distinctly Western stamp, it's worth a day-trip from Beijing to see its unique streetscapes, a striking medley of nineteenth-century European architecture and Chinese modernism. Hebei's new capital, **Shijiazhuang**, in the south, is a major rail

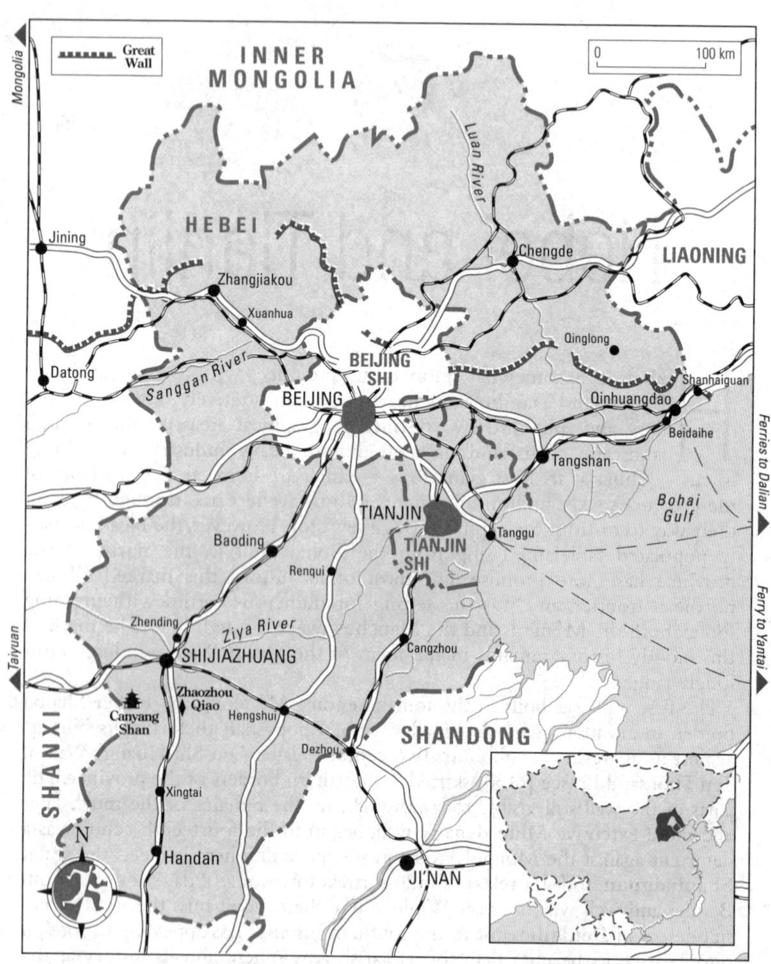

junction but a rather dull town, though you may well find yourself passing through, in which case it's worth checking out the few historical sites scattered in the countryside around.

There are good roads linking towns in Hebei with Tianjin and Beijing, making long-distance buses a viable alternative to trains; for instance, the express bus from Beijing to Qinhuangdao, a port town near Shanhaiguan, is actually faster and more convenient than the train.

Tianjin

And there were sections of the city where different foreigners lived – Japanese, white Russians, Americans and Germans – but never together, and all with their own separate habits, some dirty, some clean. And they had houses of all shapes and colours, one painted in pink, another with rooms that jutted out at every angle like the backs and fronts of Victorian dresses, others with roofs like pointed hats and wood carvings painted white to look like ivory.

Amy Tan, *The Joy Luck Club*

Tianjin

Tianjin	天津	***tiānjīn***
Ancient Culture St	古文化街	*gǔwénhuà jiē*
Antique Market	旧货市场	*jiùhuò shìchǎng*
Catholic Church	西开教堂	*xīkāi jiàotáng*
Dabei Yuan	大悲院	*dàbēi yuàn*
Earthquake Memorial	抗震记念碑	*kàngzhèn jìniànbēi*
Fine Art Museum	艺术博物馆	*yìshù bówùguǎn*
Mosque	清真寺	*qīngzhēn sì*
Museum of Science and Technology	科技术馆	*kējìshù guǎn*
Notre Dame des Victoires	望海楼教堂	*wànghǎilóu jiàotáng*
Passenger Ferry Booking Office	港客轮运输	*gǎngkèlún yùnshū*
Quanye Bazaar	劝业场	*quànyè chǎng*
Zhongxin Park	中心公园	*zhōngxīn gōngyuán*
Zhou Enlai Memorial Hall	周恩来纪念馆	*zhōuēnlái jìniànguǎn*
Accommodation		
Astor Hotel	利顺德饭店	*lìshùndé fàndiàn*
Friend	富蓝特大酒店	*fùlántè dàjiǔdiàn*
Friendship	友谊宾馆	*yǒuyí bīnguǎn*
Hyatt	凯悦饭店	*kǎiyuè fàndiàn*
Jinfang Hotel	津纺宾馆	*jīnfǎng bīnguǎn*
Longmen Guesthouse	龙门招待所	*lóngmén zhāodàisuǒ*
Nankai University	南开大学	*nánkāi dàxué*
Sheraton	喜来登大酒店	*xǐláidēng dàjiǔdiàn*
Tianjin Number One	天津第一饭店	*tiānjīn dìyī fàndiàn*
Tianjin University	天津大学	*tiānjīn dàxué*
Eating		
Erduoyan Fried Cake Shop	耳朵眼炸糕店	*ěrrduōyǎn zhágāodiàn*
Goubuli Stuffed Dumpling Restaurant	狗不理包子铺	*gǒubùlǐ bāozipù*
Guifaxiang Shop	桂发祥麻花	*guìfāxiáng máhuā*
Haihe River Palace	海河皇宫	*hǎihé huánggōng*
Quanjude Roast Duck	全聚德烤鸭店	*quánjùdé kǎoyādiàn*
Suiyuan	随园酒家	*suíyuán jiǔjiā*
Tanggu	塘沽	***tánggū***
International Seamens' Club	国际海员俱乐部	*guójì hǎiyuán jùlèbù*

China's third largest city, the commercial centre of **TIANJIN**, on the coast some 80km east of Beijing, is a dynamic and modern city, but for visitors its most attractive feature is its legacy of **colonial buildings** reflecting an assortment of foreign styles. See them while you can, however, as wide swaths of the city are being redeveloped. Locals say, not altogether with pride, that the city has become a massive construction site, requiring a new map to be printed every three months. Feng Jicai, one of China's best-known writers and a Tianjin resident, has led a campaign to preserve the old city, noting, "Once a nation has lost its own culture, it faces a spiritual crisis more dreadful than brought on by material poverty. If you regard a city as having a spirit, you will respect it, safeguard it, and cherish it. If you regard it as only matter, you will use it excessively, transform it at will, and damage it without regret." Contemporary Tianjin is an illustration of the latter.

Still, Tianjin has architecture and shopping opportunities, especially for antiques, that make it well worth a day-trip from Beijing, just over an hour away by train. Along the comfortable ride, you may be joined by young Beijingers coming to shop for clubwear, older residents in search of curios, and businesspeople shuttling between deals. A longer trip will prove expensive as there is no budget accommodation in the city.

Though today the city is given over to industry and commerce, it was as a **port** that Tianjin first gained importance. When the Ming emperor Yongle moved the capital from Nanjing to Beijing, Tianjin became the dock for vast quantities of imperial tribute rice, transported here from all over the south through the Grand Canal. In the nineteenth century the city caught the attention of the seafaring Western powers, who used a minor infringement – the boarding of an English ship by Chinese troops – as an excuse to declare war. With well-armed gunboats, they were assured of victory, and the Treaty of Tianjin, signed in 1856, gave the Europeans the right to establish nine concessionary bases on the mainland, from where they could conduct trade and sell opium.

These separate **concessions**, along the banks of the Hai River, were self-contained European fantasy worlds: the French built elegant chateaux and towers, while the Germans constructed red-tiled Bavarian villas. The Chinese were discouraged from intruding, except for servants, who were given pass cards. Tensions between the indigenous population and the foreigners exploded in the **Tianjin Incident** of 1870, when a Chinese mob attacked a French-run orphanage and killed the nuns and priests, in the belief that the Chinese orphans were being kidnapped for later consumption. Twenty Chinese were beheaded as a result, and the prefect of the city was banished. A centre for secretive anti-foreign movements, the city had its genteel peace interrupted again by the **Boxer Rebellion** in 1900 (see p.1183), after which the foreigners levelled the walls around the old Chinese city to enable them to keep an eye on its residents.

Arrival and city transport

Tianjin's large international **airport**, 15km east of the city, is served by regular shuttle buses, terminating outside the CAAC office on Heping Lu or Nanjing Lu, just west of the *Friendship Hotel*. A taxi into the centre should cost around ¥30. If you arrive by **ferry**, you'll find yourself in the port of **Tanggu**, a dull and very expensive appendage of the city. Buses that take you the 50km into the city centre congregate around the passenger ferry terminal, and drop you at the **South bus station** near Shuishang Park. The train is quicker, taking just under an hour, but Tanggu South station is inconveniently situated about 2km west of the ferry terminal.

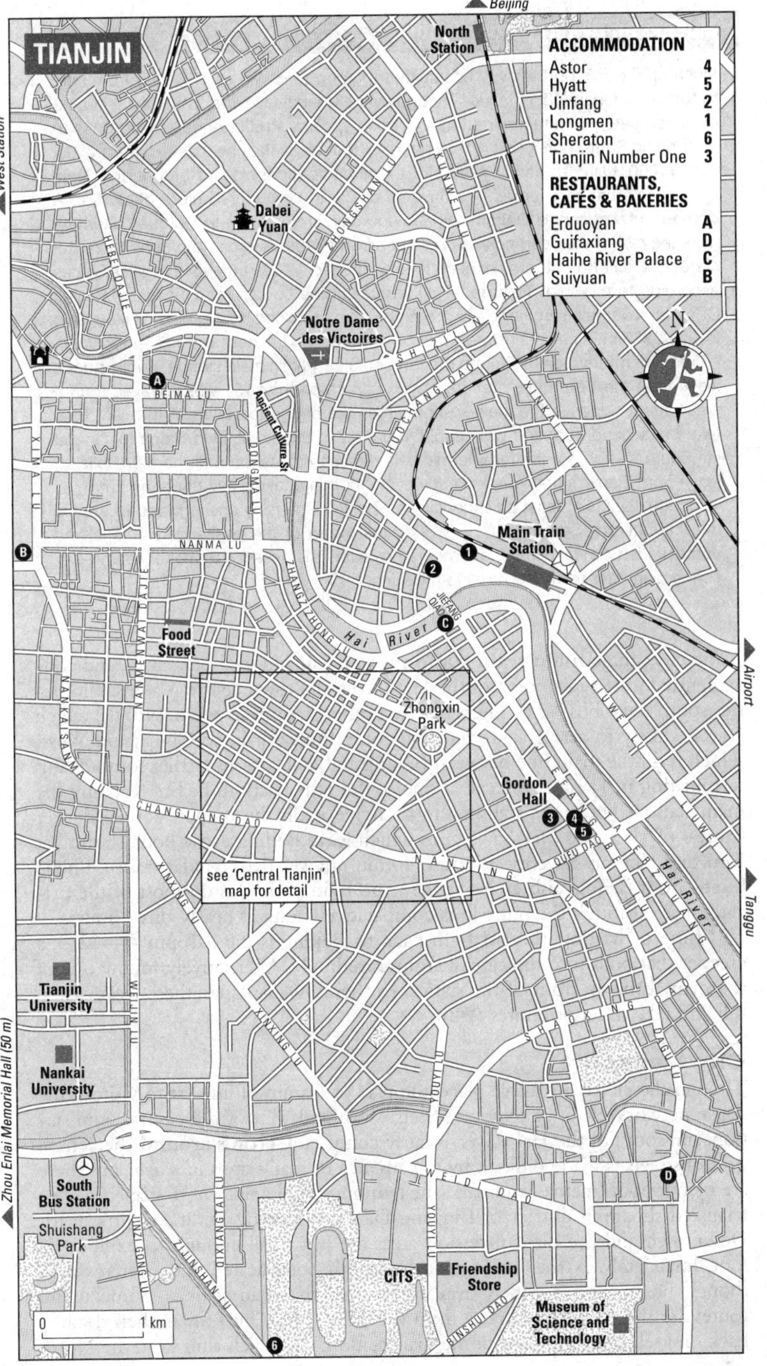
TIANJIN
Beijing
West Station
North Station
ACCOMMODATION
Astor 4
Hyatt 5
Jinfang 2
Longmen 1
Sheraton 6
Tianjin Number One 3
RESTAURANTS, CAFÉS & BAKERIES
Erduoyan A
Guifaxiang D
Haihe River Palace C
Suiyuan B
Dabei Yuan
Notre Dame des Victoires
Ancient Culture St
Main Train Station
Food Street
Zhongxin Park
Gordon Hall
Hai River
Airport
Tanggu
see 'Central Tianjin' map for detail
Tianjin University
Nankai University
Zhou Enlai Memorial Hall (50 m)
South Bus Station
Shuishang Park
CITS
Friendship Store
Museum of Science and Technology
0
1 km

Moving on by ferry from Tanggu

Much of Tianjin's port activity has shifted to **Tanggu**, 50km east. A ferry from here to **Kobe**, in Japan (48hr), leaves Tanggu every Monday evening. The cheapest ticket, which gets you a *tatami* mat in a dormitory, costs ¥1600. Another ferry goes to **Inch'on**, in South Korea (28hr), leaving every four days; the cheapest tickets are just over ¥1000, rising to nearly ¥2000 for the most comfortable two-bed berths. Note that for international ferries you have to check in two hours before departure. A **domestic ferry** serves **Dalian** from Tanggu daily from March to October, alternate days the rest of the year; tickets begin at around ¥100. Another ferry runs to **Yantai** about six times a month; expect to pay around ¥100, though the price varies according to the ship. **Tickets** for all ferries can be bought from Tianjin or Beijing CITS for a small surcharge, or from the ferry booking office at 1 Pukou Dao (Ⓣ022/23399573), a small street west off Taierzhuang Lu, near Tianjin's *Astor Hotel*.

Frequent **minibuses** to Tanggu run from outside Tianjin main station. Public **buses** leave from the South bus station, or you can catch the #151 which leaves from a small street opposite the main station: cross the bridge to the west, turn left, then take the second right and walk about 100m down the street. Two **trains** to Tanggu (its South station, for the ferry terminal, is the second station that the train calls at) leave from Tianjin's main station early every morning, taking just under an hour.

Tanggu itself is at least as expensive as Tianjin. One fairly cheap **place to stay** is the *International Seamen's Club* (¥300), just north of the passenger terminal. As domestic ferries leave in the afternoon, however, it is possible to make a same-day connection after travelling here from Beijing.

The city's huge **main train station** is well run and well organized, and conveniently located just north of the Hai River; the town centre is a few kilometres south (take bus #24). There are two other stations in town: **North**, which you are likely to arrive at if you have come from northeast China; and **West**, which is on the main line between Beijing and destinations farther south. Trains terminating in Tianjin may call at one of the other stations before reaching the main station. The most stylish way to arrive is on the orange double-decker express (T-class; ¥30 one way) trains which leave Beijing every hour, starting at 7am, and take just seventy minutes (40min quicker than regular trains). Public **buses** from Beijing also arrive at the main train station, as do most of the private ones – though the bus trip is comparatively long at nearly three hours.

At time of writing, the last train back to Beijing is the 9.16pm #4412/3, a creeper that pulls into the capital around midnight. Alternatively, follow one of the many touts in front of the station to their VW Santanas; these leave when full and take ninety minutes (¥40).

City transport

Though the city is a massive place, the part of Tianjin of interest to visitors, the dense network of ex-concession streets south and west of the central train station, and south of the Hai River, is fairly compact. **Getting around** the central grid of streets is made difficult by the absence of many signs in *pinyin*, but there are plenty of distinctive landmarks, first among them being the T-shaped pedestrianized shopping district of Binjiang Dao and Heping Lu at Tianjin's heart. Downtown and the old concession areas are just small enough to explore on foot, fortunately, as the **bus** network is both complicated and overcrowded, though bus maps are widely available around the train stations. Some useful routes are the #24, which runs from the West station into town, then doubles back on itself and terminates at the main station; #1, which runs from the North station into town, terminating at Zhongxin Park, the northern tip of the downtown area; and #50, which meanders into town from the main train station and takes you close to the Catholic Church. Bus fares around the centre are ¥0.5.

An alternative to the fiendish bus system is the L-shaped **subway** line (¥2 per journey), which was being renovated and extended at the time of writing. Yellow *miandi* **taxis** are plentiful (minimum ¥5, which is sufficient for most journeys around town).

Accommodation

Tianjin is a rotten place to stay if you're travelling on a budget, with no cheap hotels on offer, though you may be able to talk your way into a dormitory at one of the two universities, Tianjin and Nankai, in the south of town (reached by bus #8 from the main train station). A handful of cut-rate flophouses, the best of which is the *Longmen Guesthouse*, line the back of the shopping center on the train station's western concourse, with signboards in Chinese. Most accept foreigners, though ask to see the room before you pay the ¥40–80 rate. A cluster of expensive hotels is located in the south of the city – bus #4 from the centre will get you within walking distance – though given that these are within a grimy area (a couple of parks notwithstanding), you might as well try to stay within the centre. Be sure to ask for a discounted rate and keep pressing until you get one, as Tianjin's hotels regularly slash their prices – alternatively, head to Beijing for the night. For the locations of the hotels reviewed below, see the general Tianjin map on p.150, or the map of the centre on p.156.

Hotels

Astor 33 Tai'erzhuang Lu Ⓣ022/23311688, Ⓕ23316282. The best of Tianjin's luxury hotels, centrally located in a stylish British mansion more than 100 years old. The management misses no opportunity to remind you of its history: there are museum-style displays everywhere, including such priceless items as the first Chinese-made light bulbs the hotel ever used. ❾

Friend 231 Xinhua Lu Ⓣ022/3125445, Ⓕ3121454. Very friendly, clean, and a bargain by Tianjin standards. Across the street from the *Friendship*'s East Building, and much more welcoming. ❺

Friendship 94 Nanjing Lu Ⓣ022/23310372, Ⓕ23310616. A modern, somewhat banal building opposite the earthquake memorial south of the town centre. The cheapest rooms, though rather bland, are around the corner in the East Building on Xinhua Lu. From the main building's entrance turn left, walk to the first intersection, turn left, and the East Building is 50m ahead on the left. ❺ (main building ❼)

Hyatt Jiefang Bei Lu Ⓣ022/23318888, Ⓕ23311234. A four-star modernist mansion overlooking the Hai River. Feels faded and not up to Hyatt's usual poshness. ❾

Jinfang 10 Sanjing Lu Ⓣ022/24463555. Basic, tidy and inexpensive hotel across the street from the Main station's west concourse. Walk along the rear of the shopping center and cross the street; *KFC* will be to the left, the hotel directly in front. Beds from ¥70, ❹

Sheraton Zijinshan Lu Ⓣ022/23343388, Ⓕ23358740. Tianjin's nicest hotel, with all the expected five-star comforts, though inconveniently located in the south of town. That said, it's next to the pleasant Yanyuan Park. ❾

Tianjin Number One Jiefang Bei Lu Ⓣ022/3309988, Ⓕ3123000. A rather nice, rambling old colonial building with high ceilings, wide halls and Art Deco touches. ❽

The City

Tianjin has few actual sights, and it's the city's streetscapes, an assemblage of nineteenth- and early twentieth-century foreign architecture, mostly European, juxtaposed with the concrete and glass monoliths of wealthy contemporary China, which are its most engrossing attraction. The **old city** was strictly demarcated into national zones, and each section of the city centre has retained a hint of its old flavour. The area northwest of the main train station, on the west side of the Hai River, was the old Chinese city. Running from west to east along the north bank of the river were the Austrian, Italian, Russian and Belgian concessions, though most of the old buildings here have been destroyed. Unmistakable are the chateaux of the French concession, which now make up the downtown district just south of the river, and the haughty mansions the British built east of here. Farther east, also south of the river, the architecture of an otherwise unremarkable district has a sprinkling of stern German constructions. For a waterside view of the entire town all the way to its port, there are marathon daily **boat rides** – popular with Chinese tourists who don't seem to mind the duration – departing in the morning from the kiosk across from the main train station, just west of Jiefang Bridge (8hr; ¥78).

Downtown Tianjin

The majority of Tianjin's colonial buildings are clustered in the grid of streets on the southern side of the river. Coming from the main train station, Liberation Bridge (Jiefang Qiao), built by the French in 1903, leads south to an area given an oddly Continental feel by the pastel colours and wrought-iron scrollwork balconies of the French concession, which is at its most appealing around the glorified roundabout known as **Zhongxin Park**. At 12 Chengde Dao, the pink **Fine Art Museum** (daily 8.30–12am & 1.30–5pm; ¥5), a slightly pompous old building, has a broad collection of paintings, kites, Chinese New Year prints and *ni ren,* literally "mud men", clay figurines which became a popular local craft in the nineteenth century. Their greatest exponent was a skilled caricaturist called Zhang who made copies of opera stars and other notables, and some of his work is on display; unfortunately none of his depictions of Tianjin's foreigners, which got him into trouble with the authorities, is here.

Zhongxin Park marks the northern boundary of the main **shopping district**, an area bounded by Dagu Lu, Jinzhou Dao and Chifeng Dao; Heping Lu and Binjiang Dao are the two busiest streets. Though stuffed with intrepid shoppers (as fashionably dressed as a Beijing crowd), the tree-lined narrow streets have a

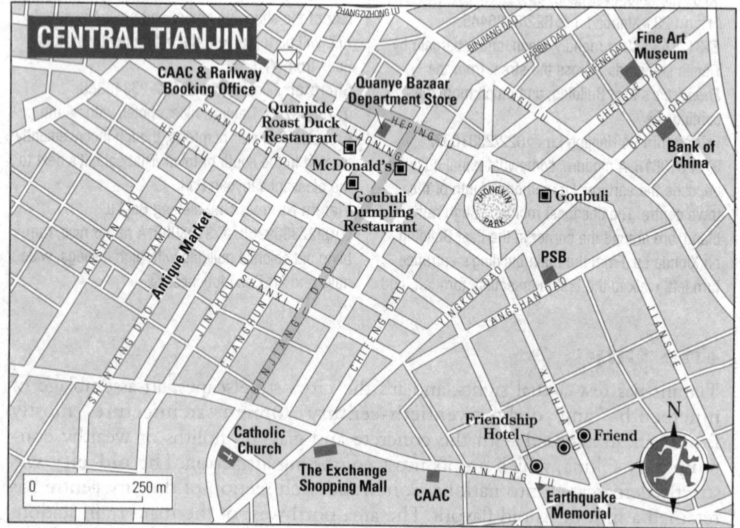

pleasingly laid-back feel, as traffic is light, and Heping Lu and Binjiang Dao are pedestrianized and lined with sculptures and benches. The **Quanye Bazaar Department Store**, a nine-storey turquoise fortress on the corner of Binjiang Dao and Heping Lu, has an enormous selection of goods and attracts more than 200,000 visitors a day. Persevere to the upper floors to find a range of fast-food restaurants, video games and a pool hall. A wider selection of cheaper clothes is available from a massive **street market** that stretches the length of Binjiang Dao, terminating at the cathedral. There are plenty of other places for a snack hereabouts; *McDonald's* and *KFC* are right on Binjiang Dao, and a more traditional form of fast food is available at *Goubuli's* (see "Eating and drinking", p.159). Electric trolleybuses run the length of the shopping area (¥2).

The antique market

Just west of here is a shopping district of a very different character, the **antique market** (daily 8am–5pm), centred on Shenyang Jie but spilling over into side alleys. A great attraction even if you have no intention of buying, the alleys are lined with dark, poky shops, pavement vendors with their wares spread out in front of them on yellowed newspapers, and stallholders waving jade and teapots in the faces of passersby. The market is open daily and expands and contracts according to the time of year (small in winter, big in the summer) but it's always at its largest on Sundays, swelled by Beijingers here for the weekend – it's generally cheaper than any in the capital. That said, the shopkeepers know the value of everything they are selling and you will have to look hard for a bargain.

The variety of goods on display is astonishing: among the standard jade jewellery, ceramic teapots, fans and perfume bottles are Russian army watches, opium pipes, snuff boxes, ornate playing cards, old photographs, pornographic paintings, and rimless sunglasses. Look out for the stalls selling picture postcards of revolutionary dramas depicting synchronized ballet dancers performing graceful mid-air leaps with hand grenades. Bargaining is mandatory, and be aware that some of the stuff is fake.

Around Nanjing Lu

At the southern end of Binjiang Lu, the **Catholic Church** (Sun only) is a useful landmark and one of the most distinctive buildings in the city, with its odd facade of horizontal brown and orange brick stripes topped with three green domes. The diffuse zone of unremarkable buildings east of here, around Nanjing Lu, is notable only for the **Earthquake Memorial** opposite the *Friendship Hotel*. More tasteful than most Chinese public statuary, this hollow pyramid commemorates the 25,000 people who died in the Tangshan earthquake of 1976.

Heading northeast back towards the river from here, you'll pass more nineteenth-century architecture – the most notable of which is **Gordon Hall**, a fortress-like building that used to house the British administrative offices; it's on Dagu Lu, just west of the *Astor Hotel*.

North of the centre

The main sight in the northern part of the city, best reached by taxi, is the **Dabei Yuan**, on a narrow alleyway off Zhongshan Lu (daily 9am–4.30pm; ¥4). Tianjin's major centre for Buddhist worship, it's easy to find as the alleys all around are crammed with stalls selling a colourful mix of religious knick-knacks: incense, tapes of devotional music, mirror-glass shrines, and ceramic Buddhas with flashing lights in their eyes. Large bronze vessels full of water stand outside the buildings, a fire precaution that has been in use for centuries.

Outside the first hall, built in the 1940s, the devout wrap their arms around a large bronze incense burner before lighting incense sticks and kowtowing. In the smaller, rear buildings – seventeenth-century structures extensively restored after the Tangshan earthquake – you'll see the temple's jovial resident monks, while small antique wood and bronze Buddhist figurines are displayed in a hall in the west of the complex. Before you leave the area, be sure to wander the rapidly diminishing district of alleyways behind the temple.

The stern cathedral, **Notre Dame des Victoires**, stands over Shizilin Dajie, just south of here, on the north bank of the river. Built in 1904, it's the third to stand on this site – the first was destroyed in the massacre of 1870, a year after it was built, and the second was burnt down in 1900 in the Boxer Rebellion. The dark stone and rigorous formality of its lines give the cathedral an austere presence, in contrast to the Catholic Church farther south. It is open to the public only on Sunday, when a morning service is held.

Ancient Culture Street

A short walk southwest of the cathedral, the more prosaic **Ancient Culture Street** runs off the southern side of Beima Lu, its entrance marked by a colourful arch. Like Liulichang in Beijing, this is a re-creation of a nineteenth-century Chinese street, minus beggars and filth and plus neon "OK Karaoke" signs, designed as a tourist shopping mall. It's all false, but with carved balconies and columns decorating the facade of red and green wooden shops topped with curling, tiled roofs, it's undeniably pretty. The shops sell pricey antiques and souvenirs, and there's an especially large range of teapots. The first shop on the right after the arch sells fifteen-centimetre-high clay figurines, in the style of Tianjin's master Zhang (see p.156). Look out, too, for the stalls selling *chatang*, soup made with millet and sugar; the stallholders attract customers by demonstrating their skill at pouring boiling soup from a long dragon-shaped spout into four bowls all held in one hand. About halfway down the street is the entrance to the heavily restored **Sea Goddess Temple** (daily 8am–4.30pm; ¥3), built in 1326 and the oldest building in Tianjin. There's an exhibition of local crafts in the side halls.

West of Ancient Culture Street

Rather more genuine streets lie in the old city, a rectangular block bounded by the four horse (*ma*) streets – **Beima**, **Nanma**, **Dongma** and **Xima**. The area is characterized by quiet, grey courtyards off intimate alleyways, and it's a good place to wander, an essentially private quarter of small shops and houses, appealing for its human scale in a city with so much grand architecture. The excellent **Erduoyan Fried Cake Shop** is located here (see opposite), and there are plenty of small noodle and dumpling places around.

The **mosque**, farther west, off Dafeng Lu, is an active place of worship, and you're free to wander around, but not to enter, the buildings. It's a fine example of Chinese Muslim architecture, with some striking wood carvings of floral designs in the eaves and around the windows.

South of the centre

South of the centre, Tianjin becomes just another sprawling Chinese metropolis, but if you have the time it's worth a diversion down here to check out the new **Science and Technology Museum**, on Longcheng Lu (daily 9am–5pm; ¥15). The shiny new building houses plenty of hands-on exhibits demonstrating scientific principles, as well as displays on acupuncture and physiology, and models of China's "Long March" rockets. It's fun playing with the ball bearings in the section on gravity, and you should look at the section on optics, perhaps designed by someone with their tongue in their cheek – distorted images of Mao and Marx are used as demonstrations. Atop the building is a 360° projection room, where you can lie back surrounded by a film on astronomy. The museum is set in an amusement park which isn't as melancholy as most – there's a go-kart track, merry-go-rounds, a Ferris wheel and mechanical sculptures that nod and honk at the entrance. To get here, take bus #20 from Zhongxin Park.

A ten-minute walk north of the museum takes you to the **Guifaxiang Shop**, an excellent place to stock up on dough twists (see below). For more prosaic items and pricier souvenirs, try the four-storey Friendship Store, which has a good supermarket; it's not far away at 21 Youyi Lu, opposite CITS.

Zhou Enlai Memorial Hall

Southwest of the centre, Tianjin's most famous resident is paid tribute at the massive **Zhou Enlai Memorial Hall** (daily 9am–5pm; ¥10). A bunker perched on the northern edge of Shuishang Park, the hall features a few wax figures, his airplane and limousine, and scattered English explanations of his achievements, though it's not so much an analysis of the difficulties in being Chairman Mao's right-hand man as a paean to his marriage to fellow comrade Deng Yingchao. Try not to crack up when reading the description of the couple's bond: "Cherishing the same ideals, following the same path, and comrade-in-arms affection tied them in love relations." The events around the Cultural Revolution, from which Zhou's legacy derives most of its strength, are curtly summarized thus: "He frustrated the attempts of the Gang of Four." To get here, take bus #8 from the station and get off at Shuishang Park near the statue of Nie Zhongjie, a general who is depicted on horseback.

Eating and drinking

Tianjin is well known for its **food** – make sure you don't leave without sampling some of its speciality cakes and pastries. Familiar multinational chains are here too: *KFC* and *McDonald's* have branches on the western side of the train-station concourse, along Binjiang Dao and in the Exchange shopping centre (Jili Dasha) on Nanjing Lu; the last of these is also home to a *Starbucks*.

Erduoyan Fried Cake Shop Beima Lu. A century-old institution that specializes in rice-powder cakes fried in sesame oil. Don't be put off by the name, which means "ear hole".

Food Street Off Nanmenwai Dajie and south of Nanma Lu. A cheerful two-storey mall, this is still the best place to eat in Tianjin, though standards have slipped a little over the years, and a *McDonald's* now anchors the ground floor. Yet with fifty or so restaurants on each level, there's something to suit all budgets and tastes. Upstairs try the *Zhejiang Restaurant* for Zhejiang cuisine, the *Da Jin Haiwei* for Tianjin seafood, and *Penglaichun* for Shandong dishes. There are two reasonably priced Sichuan restaurants, *Sichuan Xiaoguan* and *Gujing*, downstairs and a bustling branch of *Goubuli* for *baozi*. In between the restaurants are stalls and shops selling cakes, biscuits, dried fruit, nuts, chocolates and dead ducks.

Goubuli Stuffed Dumpling Restaurant 77 Shandong Lu. Handy if you're shopping around Binjiang Dao, this famous Tianjin restaurant has grown from a poky little store to the flagship of a chain with branches in the US and across Asia. There's a dining room upstairs, but locals eat in the fast-food restaurant on the ground floor, where you get a lot of dumplings plus assorted condiments in an airline-food-style tray for a very reasonable ¥13. The name, which means "dogs wouldn't believe it", is thought to be a reference either to the ugliness of the original proprietor or to the low-class status of dumplings. Branches at the main train station, and at 324 Heping Lu.

Guifaxiang Shop 568 Dagu Nan Lu. Another Tianjin institution, this cake shop is renowned for its fried dough twists (*mahua*), a delicious local speciality which makes a good gift – the assistants will wrap and box them for you.

Haihe River Palace Built on a pontoon on the Haihe River, just east of Jiefang Qiao and south of the train station. An expensive, upmarket restaurant built in classical Chinese style, and specializing in Cantonese food.

Quanjude Roast Duck Heping Lu. A branch of the famous Beijing restaurant; duck and all the trimmings should come to around ¥200 for two people.

Suiyuan Huanghe Dao, just west of Xima Lu. A good selection of Shandong-style dishes for around ¥50 per head.

Listings

Airlines The main CAAC office – signed Air China – is at 242 Heping Lu (Mon–Sat 8.30am–6pm; ⓣ022/27234353). The airport bus service runs from outside here. Shuttle buses and taxis to Tianjin (¥30) and Beijing (¥70) airports leave from the CAAC at 103 Nanjing Lu (Mon–Sat 8am–8pm), just west of the *Friendship Hotel*; domestic tickets are sold downstairs (ⓣ022/23301543), international upstairs (ⓣ022/23393497).

Banks and exchange The main office of the Bank of China is in a grand colonial edifice at 80 Jiefang Bei Lu (Mon–Fri 9am–noon & 1.30–5pm).

Bookshops The Foreign Language Bookstore is at 130 Chifeng Dao.

Internet access A branch of Sparkice, the popular Beijing internet café, is located in the *Sheraton Hotel* (daily 10am–10pm; ¥8/hr).

Mail The post office is In a building on the east side of the train station (Mon–Fri 8am–7pm).

PSB At 30 Tangshan Dao.

Shopping As well as the clothes and antique markets in the city centre, Tianjin is renowned for its handmade rugs and carpets, featuring bright, complex, abstract patterns. They're not cheap, and are best bought directly from the factories in the suburbs of the city; try Factory Number Two on Heiniucheng Lu, in Hexi District (ⓣ022/28331920). Tianjin is also noted for its kites and its bright woodblock prints of domestic subjects, pinned up for good luck at Chinese New Year; the latter are made and sold at the Yangliuqing Picture Studio on Sanhe Dao, and there's also an outlet on Ancient Culture Street. The Tianjin Cultural Relics Company, located fairly centrally at 161 Liaoning Lu (ⓣ022/27110434), has a wide selection of antique jade, embroidery, calligraphy and carvings.

Telephones The 24hr telecommunications office is in the same building as the post office.

Trains The majority of trains leave from the main station. A few trains to the northeast leave only from the North station, and some trains to southern destinations, such as Shanghai, that don't originate in Tianjin, call only at the West station. Tickets for Beijing are on sale at a special English-labelled kiosk to the right of the escalators of the main station. You can also buy your return ticket on the train from Beijing. To avoid the queues when buying train tickets from the main station, try the soft-sleeper ticket office – go up the escalator, turn left towards the soft-sleeper waiting room, and the office is discreetly located on the left. Alternatively, buy your tickets from the ticket office at 244 Heping Lu (Mon–Fri 8am–noon & 1.30–5pm).

Travel agents CITS is at 22 Youyi Lu (ⓣ022/28358479), opposite the Friendship Store. They don't impart much information, but they will book train and boat tickets for onward travel.

Beidaihe to Shanhaiguan

On the **Bohai Gulf**, 300km east of Beijing, lies the rather bizarre seaside resort of **Beidaihe**. Reminiscent of the Mediterranean, its coastline – rocky, sparsely vegetated, erratically punctuated by beaches – was originally patronized by European diplomats, missionaries and businessmen a hundred years ago, who can only have chosen it out of homesickness. They built villas and bungalows here, and reclined on verandas sipping cocktails after indulging in the new bathing fad. After the Communist takeover, the village became a pleasure resort for Party bigwigs, reaching its height of popularity in the 1970s when seaside trips were no longer seen as decadent and revisionist. Though you'll still see serious men in uniforms and sunglasses licking lollipops, and black Audis with tinted windows (the Party cadre car) cruising the waterfront, most of Beidaihe's visitors nowadays

Beidaihe to Shanhaiguan

Beidaihe	北戴河	***běidàihé***
Lianfengshan Park	联峰山公园	*liánfēngshān gōngyuán*
Pigeon Nest Park	鸽子窝公园	*gēziwō gōngyuán*
Accommodation and eating		
Diplomatic Missions Guesthouse	外交人员宾馆	*wàijiao rényuán bīnguǎn*
Friendship Hotel	友谊宾馆	*yǒuyí bīnguǎn*
Jinshan Hotel	金山宾馆	*jīnshān bīnguǎn*
Kiesslings	起士林餐厅	*qǐshìlín cāntīng*
Tiger Rock Hotel	老虎石宾馆	*lǎohǔshí bīnguǎn*
Nandaihe	南戴河	***nándàihé***
Qinhuangdao	秦皇岛	***qínhuángdǎo***
Haiyue Hotel	海岳大厦	*hǎiyuè dàshà*
International Hotel	国际饭店	*guójì fàndiàn*
Jialun Hotel	佳伦酒店	*jiālún jiǔdiàn*
Shanhaiguan	山海关	***shānhǎiguān***
First Pass Under Heaven	天下第一关	*tiānxià dìyīguān*
Great Wall Museum	长城搏物馆	*chángchéng bówùguǎn*
Jiao Shan	角山	*jiǎo shān*
Lao Long Tou	老龙头	*lǎolóng tóu*
Longevity Mountain	长寿山	*chángshòu shān*
Mengjiangnü Miao	孟姜女庙	*mèngjiāngnǚ miào*
Yansai Hu	燕塞湖	*yànsài hú*
Accommodation		
Dongfang	东方宾馆	*dōngfāng bīnguǎn*
Jingshan	京山宾馆	*jīngshān bīnguǎn*
North Street	北街招待所	*běijiē zhāodàisuǒ*

are ordinary, fun-loving tourists, usually well-heeled Beijingers. In season, when the temperature is steady around the mid-20s Centigrade and the water warm, it's noisy and crowded, and a fun place to spend the day. Everyone is here simply to enjoy themselves, and you'll see the Chinese looking their most relaxed.

Only 25km or so to the northeast, **Shanhaiguan** is a popular half-day destination with Chinese frolicking at Beidaihe, but doesn't seem to be much on the backpacker circuit, which is odd, as it's well worth a visit. Small enough to walk around, the town is peaceful and pretty and has two good hotels, and the surrounding countryside contains some fine sturdy fortifications and remnants of the **Great Wall**.

Midway between Beidaihe and Shanhaiguan is **Qinhuangdao**, an industrial city and charmless modern port; the only reason to visit is to make arrangements to leave – on the passenger-ferry service to Dalian.

To reach this part of the Bohai Gulf **from Beijing**, the express-bus service to Qinhuangdao is quicker and easier than the trains. Once you're in the area, it's straightforward to get around by **bus** rather than wait for the train; local bus services are frequent, usually hourly during the day. Buses #6 and #34 shuttle between Beidaihe and Qinhuangdao (¥2), while buses #24 and #33 run the Qinhuangdao–Shanhaiguan route (same fare). There are also frequent **tourist minibuses**, which you can catch from any major road, linking Qinhuangdao and Beidaihe (¥4) throughout the day until 6pm.

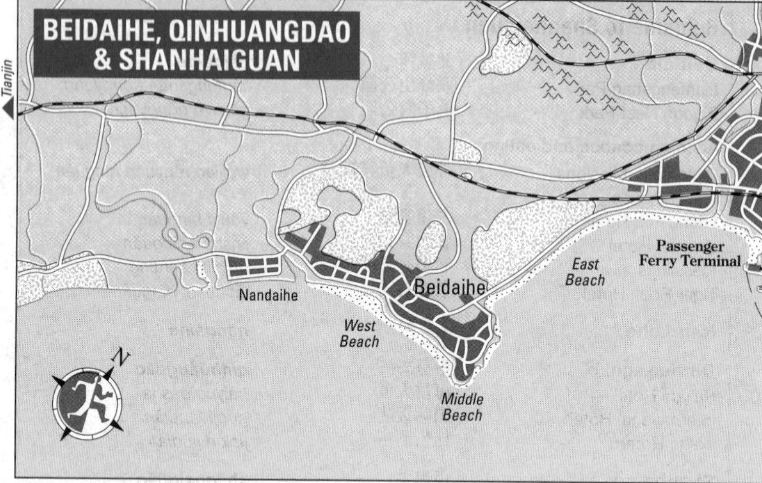

Beidaihe and around

It wasn't so long ago that **BEIDAIHE** had strict rules ordering where individuals could bathe, according to their rank. West Beach was reserved for foreigners after they were let in in 1979, with guards posted to chase off Chinese voyeurs interested in glimpsing their daringly bourgeois swimming costumes; the Middle Beach was demarcated by rope barriers and reserved for Party officials, with a sandy cove – the best spot – set out for the higher ranks. Dark swimsuits were compulsory, to avoid the illusion of nudity. These days the barriers have gone, along with the inhibitions of the urban Chinese (skimpy bikinis are fashionable now), and the contemporary town is a fascinating mix of the austerely communist and the gaudy kitsch of any busy seaside resort.

The Town

The streets along the seafront are the liveliest – most buildings are either restaurants, with crabs and prawns bobbing about in buckets outside, or shops selling Day-Glo swimsuits, inflatables, snorkels, souvenirs, even sculptures of chickens made of shells and raffia. Moving away from the sea, up the hill, the tree-lined streets are much quieter, and many of the buildings are guesthouses, though this is also where you find the **villas** of the Party elite, guarded by discreet soldiers. It's rumoured that every Politburo member once had a residence here, and probably many still do. All around are huge, chunky buildings, often with absurd decorative touches – Roman columns, fake totem poles, Greek porticoes – grafted onto their ponderous facades. These are work-unit hotels and sanatoriums for heroes of the people – factory workers, soldiers and the like – when they are granted the privilege of a seaside holiday.

On the far western side of town, 500m back from the beach, **Lianfengshan Park**, a hill of dense pines with picturesque pavilions and odd little caves, is a good place to wander and get away from the crowds for a while. On top of the hill is the **Sea Admiring Pavilion**, which has good views of the coast. There are also a couple of unexciting historical sites and the quiet temple, **Guanyin Si**.

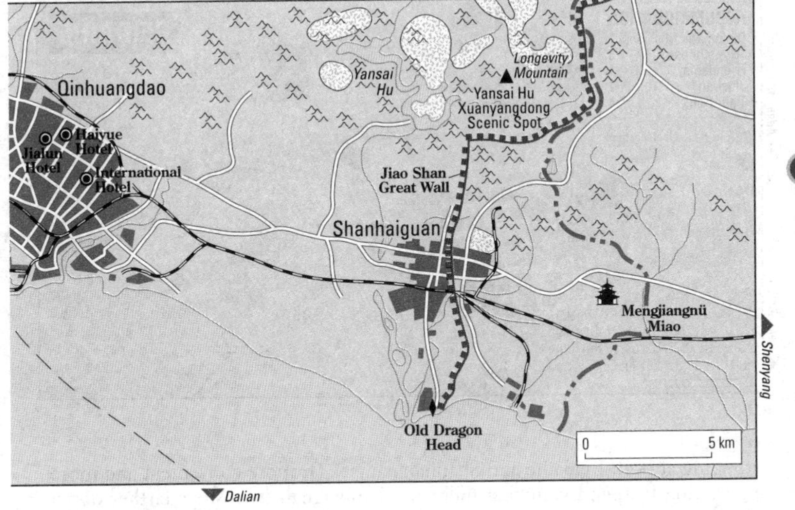

The beaches

On Beidaihe's three beaches, stirring revolutionary statues of lantern-jawed workers and their wives and children stand among the throngs of bathers. **Middle Beach**, really many small beaches with rocky outcrops in between, is the most convenient and popular. The promenade at the back is lined with soft-drink vendors, photo stalls, hoopla games, and bathing huts that look like moon dwellings from a 1950s science-fiction movie. You can get your photograph taken on top of a stuffed tiger or in a cardboard speedboat, or dressed up like an emperor. **West Beach** is more of the same, but a little quieter. East of the resort, stretching 15km to Qinhuangdao, is **East Beach** (take bus #6 or #34), popular with cadres and sanatorium patients for its more sedate atmosphere. The beach is long enough for you to be able to find a spot where you can be alone, though much of the muddy shoreline isn't very attractive. At low tide its wide expanse is dotted with seaweed collectors in rubber boots.

At the western tip of East Beach is **Pigeon Nest Park** (bus #21 from Zhonghaitan Lu), a twenty-metre-high rocky outcrop named for the seagulls fond of perching here, obviously by someone who wasn't hot on bird identification. It's a popular spot for watching the sunrise. Mao sat here in 1954 and wrote a poem, "Ripples sifting sand/Beidaihe," which probably loses something in translation. Just before Pigeon Nest Park, the bus stops near the dock for Beidaihe's **sightseeing boats**, which in season leave regularly during the day to chug up and down the coast, which isn't really that spectacular (2hr; ¥30). The highlight of the trip is passing the strange **Biluo Pagoda**, a hotel on the coast south of the dock, and resembling a seven-storey concrete conch shell.

Practicalities

Beidaihe **train station** is inconveniently located 15km north of the town; bus #5 will take you from here into the centre. If you arrive at night (likely if you're coming from Beijing), there'll be private minibuses and taxis waiting, but you'll have to barter hard to get the fare down below ¥40. If you intend

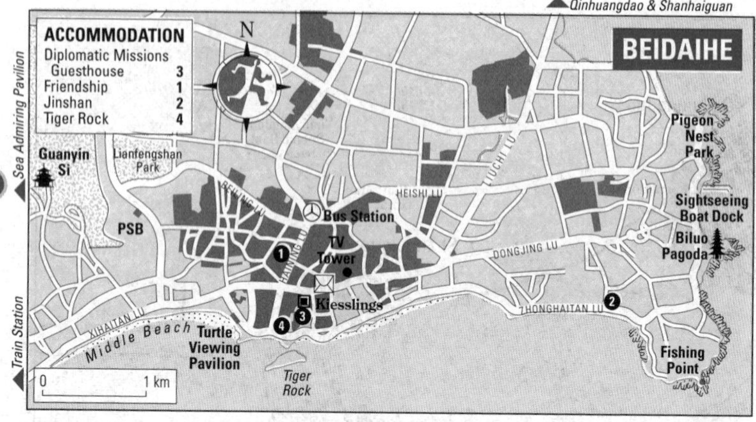

stopping at both Beidaihe and Shanhaiguan, it's far more convenient and more interesting to spend your first night in Shanhaiguan (two stops farther down the line, but check, as some trains don't stop there), where the station is close to the hotels. From Beidaihe's **bus station**, it's a fifteen-minute downhill walk from here to Middle Beach. Taxis around town cost ¥10, but Beidaihe is small enough to get around easily on foot. **CITS**, located in the *Tiger Rock Hotel*, are unhelpful, being more attuned to burgeoning domestic tourism.

Accommodation and eating

Beidaihe's accommodation is most sought between May and August, outside of which period room prices are slashed to half their summer high. That said, few of Beidaihe's many **hotels** are open to foreigners, anyway. Of those that are, one of the best is the *Diplomatic Missions Guesthouse* at 1 Baosan Lu (Ⓣ0335/4041287, Ⓕ4041807; ❽), a quiet street ten minutes' walk north of Middle Beach. It's a stylish complex of thirteen villas set among gardens of cypress and pine, with a karaoke bar, a nightclub, a tennis court, a gym and a good outside restaurant where barbecues are held in the summer. Other good options include the *Tiger Rock* (Ⓣ0335/4041373; ❹, dorm beds ¥80), well located right next to the beach, but a little bland and characterless; and the small *Friendship*, farther north on Haining Lu (Ⓣ0335/4041613; ❹, dorm beds ¥100). Out of the way in a pleasant, quiet cove on Zhonghaitan Lu is the *Jinshan*, a three-star complex with pool (Ⓣ0335/4041678; ❺).

Beidaihe is noted for its crab, cuttlefish and scallops. Try one of the innumerable small **seafood** places on Haining Lu, where you order by pointing to the tastiest looking thing scuttling or slithering around the bucket, or *Kiesslings*, on Dongjing Lu near the *Diplomatic Missions Guesthouse*. Originally Austrian, this restaurant has been serving the foreign community for most of the last century, and still has a few Western dishes on its reasonably priced menu – Western diners are even issued with knives and forks. It's an ideal place for breakfast, offering good pastries and bread.

Around Beidaihe

Fifteen kilometres west along the coast, **NANDAIHE** is a new tourist resort constructed to take advantage of Beidaihe's popularity. With 3km of beach and a few parks and viewpoints, it's the same sort of thing as Beidaihe but more regimented and artificial, and is thus best visited as a day-trip; frequent minibuses come here from the Beidaihe bus station. The main attraction in Nandaihe is **Golden Beach** to the west, where you can go "sand sliding" down the steep sand dunes on a rented sledge – great fun, but remember to keep your feet and elbows in the air. Foreigners can stay here at the expensive *Nandaihe Beach House* resort complex (Ⓣ0335/442807; ❺).

The countryside around Beidaihe has been designated as a **nature reserve** and is a stopping-off point for Siberian and red-crowned cranes migrating to Dongbei in May. Ask at CITS in Beidaihe for details of the best places to see them, and tour prices.

Qinhuangdao

Ferries to Dalian leave from **QINHUANGDAO**, 15km northeast of Beidaihe, from July to September on even-numbered days, taking thirteen hours – a lot faster than the train. Tickets can be bought from the travel agents in the *International Hotel* at 330 Wenhua Beilu, and cost from ¥140 for a seat to ¥370 for a bed in a double cabin. **Buses** and minibuses can be caught around the **train station** and **passenger ferry terminal**; bus #8 runs between the two.

The best budget place to stay is near the **train station**, at the two-star *Haiyue Hotel*, 159 Yingbin Lu (Ⓣ3065760; ❸); walk south from the station concourse and the hotel is on the west side of the road. Next door, at no. 181, is the three-star *Jialun Hotel* (Ⓣ3065888; ❼), where guests gather in the lobby to ogle the fountain. Qinhuangdao's shopping center, at the V-shaped intersection of Wenhua Beilu and Haiyang Lu (buses #6 and #34 stop here), includes a *McDonald's* and *KFC*, plus loads of Chinese restaurants. Book air and boat tickets at **CAAC**, 169 Yingbin Lu.

Shanhaiguan and beyond

A town at the northern tip of the Bohai Gulf, **SHANHAIGUAN**, "The Pass Between the Mountains and the Sea", was originally built as a fortress in the Ming dynasty, to defend the eastern end of the **Great Wall**. The wall crosses the Yanshan Mountains to the north, forms the east wall of the town and meets the sea a few kilometres to the south. Far from being a solitary castle, Shanhaiguan originally formed the centre of a network of defences, and smaller forts, now nothing but ruins, existed to the north, south and east, and beacon towers were dotted around the mountains.

Despite the Great Wall, beach, scenic grandeur and historic importance, Shanhaiguan inexplicably remains a sleepy, dusty little place of low buildings and quiet streets – even buying a train ticket out is pretty stress-free. The best thing to do here is to rent a bike and spend a few days exploring, sunning, and relaxing.

The Town

Shanhaiguan is still arranged along its original plan of straight boulevards following the compass points, intersected with a web of alleys. Dominating the town is a fortified gatehouse in the east wall, the **First Pass Under Heaven**, which for centuries was the entrance to the Middle Kingdom from the barbarian lands beyond. An arch topped by a two-storey tower, the gate is the biggest structure in town, and makes the surrounding buildings look puny in comparison. It must have looked even more formidable when it was built in 1381, with a wooden drawbridge over a moat 18m wide, and three outer walls

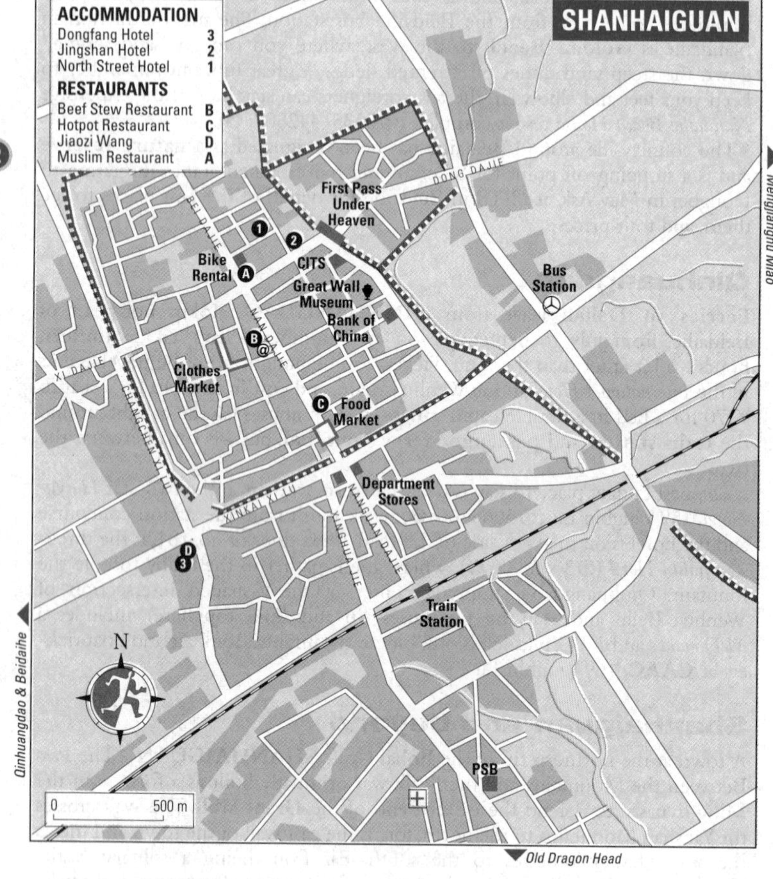

for added defensive strength. The arch remained China's northernmost entrance until 1644, when it was breached by the Manchus.

These days, the gate (daily 7.30am–5.30pm; ¥42) is overrun by hordes of marauding tourists, and is at its best in the early morning before most of them arrive. The gate's name is emblazoned in red above the archway, calligraphy attributed to Xiao Xian, a Ming-dynasty scholar who lived in the town. A steep set of steps leads up from Dong Dajie to the impressively thick wall, nearly 30m wide. The tower on top, a two-storey, ten-metre-high building with arrow slits regularly spaced along its walls, is now a **museum**, appropriately containing weapons, armour and costumes, as well as pictures of the nobility, who are so formally dressed they look like puppets. It's possible to stroll a little way along the wall in both directions; an enterprising man with a telescope stands at the far northern end, and through it you can watch tourists on the Great Wall at Jiaoshan several kilometres to the north, where the wall zigzags and dips along vertiginous peaks before disappearing over the horizon. There's plenty of tat for sale at the wall's base, including decorated chopsticks, hologram medallions and jade curios, while in a courtyard to the northern side, a statue of Xu Da, the first general to rule the fort, frowns sternly down on the scene.

Follow the city wall south from the gate, past CITS, and you come to the **Great Wall Museum** (daily 7.30am–6pm; ¥5). This modern imitation Qing building has eight halls, showing the history of the region in chronological order from Neolithic times. Though there are no English captions, the exhibits themselves are fascinating and well displayed. As well as the tools used to build the wall, the vicious weaponry used to defend and attack it are on display, including mock-ups of siege machines and broadswords that look too big to carry, let alone wield. The last three rooms contain dioramas, plans and photographs of local historic buildings – the final room's model of the area as it looked in Ming times gives an idea of the extent of the defences, with many small outposts and fortifications in the district around. It's much better than any CITS map or glossy brochure and should inspire a few bike rides. An annexe outside the museum holds temporary art exhibitions.

Practicalities

Whether you arrive at the **train** or **bus station**, respectively south and east outside the walls, you'll be greeted by an eager mob of drivers. The ¥5 flagfall covers a taxi or motor-rickshaw to any destination in town. **Local buses** from Qinhuangdao and Beidaihe don't use the bus station, but collect and deposit passengers just outside the southern gate of the city. **CITS** is just south of the First Pass Under Heaven, but there never seems to be anyone there. However, buying tickets at the train station is straightforward, so you'll have little need of them anyway. **Bikes** can be rented from the affable man who runs an English-signed shop on the eastern side of Bei Dajie (daily 8am–7pm; ¥10 per day, plus ¥100 deposit), just north of the intersection of the walled city's four roads.

Shanhaiguan has two great **hotels**, ideally located next to the First Pass Under Heaven. The small, friendly *North Street Hotel*, at 2 Mujia Hutong (ⓣ0335/5051680; dorm beds ¥20, ❸), feels like a temple: metal lions guard the gates, and inside, rooms lead off cloisters around a courtyard and garden. The rooms are large, though staff are perhaps a little too laid-back. Reception is the little shed inside the gate to the left. Note that the dorms do not have locks on the door, and you'll have to knock at the main gate to enter after 10pm. Nearby on Dong Dajie, the *Jingshan Hotel* is palatial (ⓣ0335/5051130; ❺), built to imitate a Qing mansion, with high ceilings, decorative friezes, curling roofs and red-brick walls and balconies. Rooms with TV and fan are off a series of small courtyards. If you can't get into either of these, try the *Dongfang*, offering four-person dorms and doubles on Xinkai Lu (ⓣ0335/5051376; ❺, dorm beds ¥25), outside the city's south wall. It's friendly and adequate, but not a patch on the other two, and a long way from the interesting part of town.

Food in Shanhaiguan is very good if you find the right places – which invariably are those that don't have English menus. Avoid the *Jingshan's* fancy restaurant, which overcharges foreigners, and head for the small canteens on Dong and Nan Dajie. There's a great hotpot place at 33 Nan Dajie, though the owner's brand of home brew – *baijiu* with snakes and lizards marinating in it – is perhaps best avoided. Another friendly place is at 78 Nan Dajie – try their tasty beef stew (*niurou duen tudou*). Four doors east of the main crossroads on Nan Dajie is a tiny Muslim place that's good for breakfast – go for the crispy dumplings, *shao mai*. Across from the bike-rental shop on Bei Dajie is another Muslim canteen, serving excellent vegetable-stuffed fried dumplings (*shucai guotie*). For delicious, plump, steamed dumplings, there's *Jiaozi Wang*, next to the *Dongfang Hotel*.

The Great Wall beyond Shanhaiguan

You'll see plenty of tourist **minibuses** grouped around the major crossroads in town and at the station, all serving the sights outside Shanhaiguan. Public **buses** also travel these routes, but if you have the time you're best off travelling by **bike**, as the roads are quiet, the surrounding countryside is strikingly attractive and there are any number of pretty places off the beaten track where you can escape the crowds.

Intrepid hikers could try and make it to **Yangsai Hu**, a lake in the mountains directly north of Shanhaiguan, or to **Longevity Mountain**, a hill of rugged stones east of the lake, where many of the rocks have been carved with the character *shou* (longevity). There's also a pool here, a good place for a quiet swim.

Lao Long Tou

Follow the remains of the Great Wall south and after 4km you'll reach **Lao Long Tou** (Old Dragon Head, after a large stone dragon's head that used to look out to sea here), the point at which the wall hits the coast. **Bus** #24 heads here from Xinghua Jie, near Shanhaiguan's train station. The admission charge is ¥37 (daily 7.30am–5.30pm), though note you can simply climb up onto the wall from the beach, reached by taking the first fork to the left before the car park.

A miniature fortress with a two-storey temple in the centre stands right at the end of the wall; unfortunately, everything here has been so reconstructed it all looks brand new, and the area is surrounded by a rash of tourist development, so it's not very atmospheric. The rather dirty beaches either side of the wall are popular bathing spots. Walk a few minutes past the restaurants west of Lao Long Tou and you'll come to the old British Army **barracks**, on the right; this was the beachhead for the Eight Allied Forces in 1900, when they came ashore to put down the Boxers. A plaque here reminds visitors to "never forget the national humiliation and invigorate the Chinese nation." Do your part by taking care not to trample the lawn.

Mengjiangnü Miao

Some 6.5km northeast of town is **Mengjiangnü Miao**, a temple dedicated to a legendary woman whose husband was press-ganged into one of the Great Wall construction squads. He died from exhaustion, and she set out to search for his body to give him a decent burial, weeping as she walked along the wall. So great was her grief, it is said, that the wall crumbled in sympathy, revealing the bones of her husband and many others who had died in its construction. The temple is small and elegant, with good views of the mountains and the sea. Statues of the lady herself and her attendants sit looking rather prim inside. To get here, take bus #23 from outside Shanhaiguan's south gate.

Jiao Shan

A couple of kilometres to the north of Shanhaiguan, it's possible to hike along the worn remains of the Great Wall all the way to the mountains. Head north along Bei Dajie and out of town, and after about 10km you'll come to a reconstructed section known as **Jiao Shan** (daily 8am–6pm; ¥17), passing the ruins of two forts – stone foundations and earthen humps – along the way. The further along the wall you go the better it gets – the crowds peter out, the views become grander, and once the reconstructed section ends, you're left standing beside – or on top of – the real, crumbly thing. Head a few kilometres further east and you'll discover a trio of passes in the wall, and a beacon tower that's still in good condition. You can keep going into the mountains for as long as you like, so it's worth getting here early and making a day of it. A pedicab or taxi back into town from Jiao Shan's parking lot costs ¥5.

A steep path from the reconstructed section takes you through some dramatic scenery into the Yunshan Mountains, or you can cheat and take the cable car (¥10).

Chengde

CHENGDE, a small country town 250km northeast of Beijing, sits in a river basin on the west bank of the Wulie River, surrounded by the Yunshan mountain range. It's a quiet, unimportant place, rather bland in appearance, but on its outskirts are remnants from its glory days as the **summer retreat** of the Manchu emperors – these include some of the most magnificent examples of imperial architecture in China. Gorgeous temples punctuate the cabbage fields around town, and a palace-and-park hill complex, **Bishu Shanzhuang**, covers an area nearly as large as the town itself. In recent years it has once more become a summer haven, filling up at weekends with Beijingers escaping the hassles of the capital.

Some history

Originally called "Rehe", the town was discovered by the Qing-dynasty emperor **Kangxi** at the end of the seventeenth century, while marching his troops to the Mulan hunting range to the north. He was attracted to the cool summer climate and the rugged landscape, and built small lodges here from where he could indulge in a fantasy Manchu lifestyle, hunting and hiking like his northern ancestors. The building programme expanded when it became

Chengde

Chengde	承德	***chéngdé***
Anyuan Miao	安远庙	*ānyuǎn miào*
Arhat Hill	罗汉山	*luóhàn shān*
Bishu Shanzhuang	避暑山庄	*hámá shí*
Frog Crag	蛤蟆石	*bìshǔ shānzhuāng*
Palace	正宫	*zhèng gōng*
Pule Si	普乐寺	*pǔlè sì*
Puning Si	普宁寺	*pǔníng sì*
Puren Si	溥仁寺	*pǔrén sì*
Putuozongcheng Miao	普陀宗乘之庙	*pǔtuó zōngchéng zhīmiào*
Shuxiang Si	殊像寺	*shūxiàng sì*
Sledgehammer Rock	棒锤山	*bàngzhōng shān*
Xumifushouzhi Miao	须弥福寿之庙	*xūmífúshòu zhīmiào*
Accommodation		
Chengde Binguan	承德宾馆	*chéngdé bīnguǎn*
Chengde Dasha	承德大厦	*chéngdé dàshà*
Huilong	会龙大厦	*huìlóng dàshà*
Shanzhuang	山庄宾馆	*shānzhuāng bīnguǎn*
Xinhua	新华饭店	*xīnhuá fàndiàn*
Yiwanglou	倚望楼宾馆	*yǐwànglóu bīnguǎn*
Yunshan	云山饭店	*yúnshān fàndiàn*

△ A ruined section of the Great Wall

diplomatically useful to spend time north of Beijing, to forge closer links with the troublesome Mongol tribes. Kangxi, perhaps the ablest and most enlightened of his dynasty, was known more for his economy – "The people are the foundation of the kingdom, if they have enough then the kingdom is rich" – than for such displays of imperial grandeur. Chengde, however, was a thoroughly pragmatic creation, devised as an effective means of defending the empire by overawing Mongol princes with splendid audiences, hunting parties and impressive military manoeuvres. He firmly resisted all petitions to have the Great Wall repaired, as an unnecessary burden on the people, and as a poor means of control, too, no doubt, as it had imposed no obstacle to the founders of his dynasty only a few years before.

Construction of the first palaces started in 1703; by 1711 there were 36 palaces, temples, monasteries and pagodas set in a great walled park, its ornamental pools and islands dotted with beautiful pavilions and linked by bridges. Craftsmen from all parts of China were gathered to work on the project, with Kangxi's grandson, **Qianlong** (1736–96), adding another 36 imperial buildings during his reign, which was considered to be the heyday of Chengde.

In 1786, the **Panchen Lama** was summoned from Tibet by Qianlong for his birthday celebrations. This was an adroit political move to impress the followers of Lamaist Buddhism. The Buddhists included a number of minority groups who were prominent thorns in the emperor's side, such as Tibetans, Mongols, Torguts, Eleuths, Djungars and Kalmucks. Some accounts (notably not the Chinese) tell how Qianlong invited the Panchen Lama to sit with him on the Dragon Throne, which was taken to Chengde for the summer season. He was certainly feted with honours and bestowed with costly gifts and titles, but the greatest impression on him and his followers must have been made by the replicas of the Potala and of his own palace, constructed at Chengde to make him feel at home – a munificent gesture, and one that would not have been lost on the Lamaists. However, the Panchen Lama's visit ended questionably when he succumbed to smallpox, or possibly poison, in Beijing and his coffin was returned to Tibet with a stupendous funeral cortege.

The first **British Embassy** to China, under Lord Macartney, also visited Qianlong's court in 1793. Having suffered the indignity of sailing up the river to Beijing in a ship whose sails were painted with characters reading "Tribute bearers from the vassal king of England", they had been somewhat disgruntled to discover that the emperor had decamped to Chengde for the summer. However, they made the 150-kilometre journey – in impractical European carriages – arriving at Chengde in September 1793. They were well received by the emperor, despite Macartney's refusal to kowtow, and in spite of Qianlong's disappointment with their gifts, supplied by the opportunist East India Company. Qianlong, at the height of Manchu power, was able to hold out against the British demands, refusing to grant any of the treaties requested and remarking, in reply to a request for trade: "We possess all things. I set no value on objects strange or ingenious, and have no use for your country's manufactures." His letter to the British monarch concluded, magnificently, "O king, Tremblingly Obey and Show No Negligence!"

Chengde gradually lost its imperial popularity when the place came to be seen as unlucky after emperors Jiaqing and Xianfeng died here in 1820 and 1860 respectively. The buildings were left empty and neglected for most of the twentieth century, but largely escaped the ravages of the Cultural Revolution. Restoration, in the interests of tourism, began in the 1980s and is ongoing.

Arrival and transport

The train journey from Beijing to Chengde takes four and a half hours through verdant, rolling countryside, passing the Great Wall before arriving at the **train station** in the south of town. Surprisingly, travelling from Beijing by bus is slightly quicker as the route is more direct; buses terminate at the **long-distance bus station** just off Wulie Lu in the centre of town. Touts wait in ambush at both stations, and can be useful if you already have a hotel in mind, as you won't be charged for the ride there; however, they will hassle you throughout the journey to take a minibus tour with them, and might unceremoniously dump you should you refuse. Onward train tickets can be booked from **CITS** at 6 Nanyuan Lu (ⓣ0314/2026827), near the *Yunshan Hotel*, or from any of the hotels, for a surcharge of around ¥30.

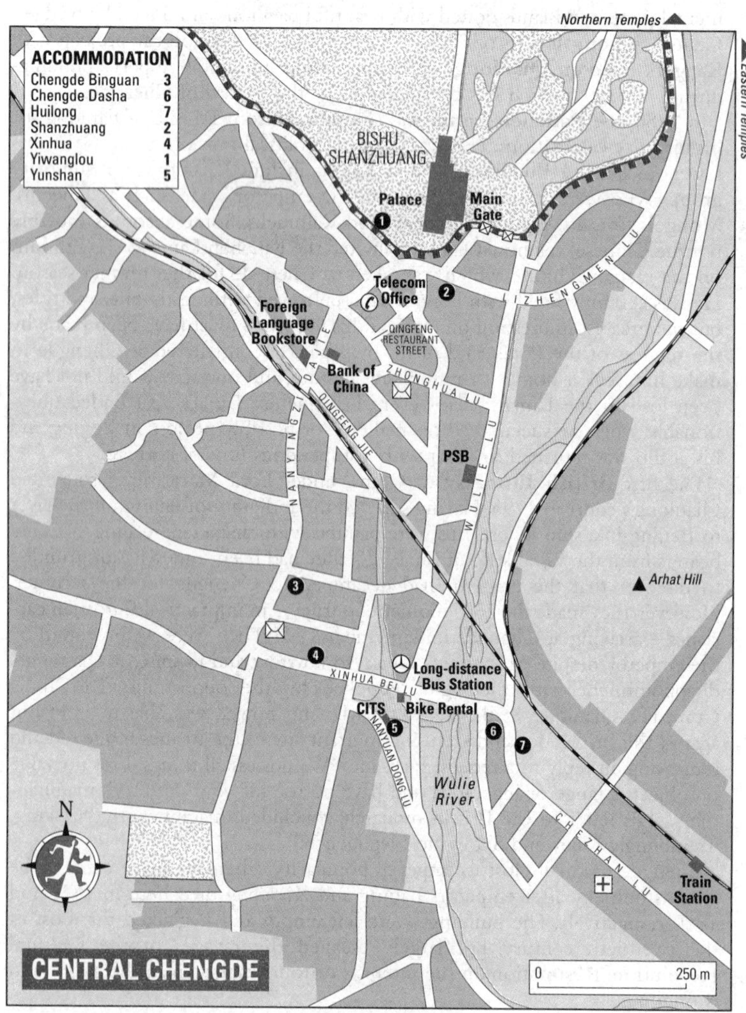

Getting around Chengde by public transport isn't easy, as **local buses** are infrequent and are always crammed. Buses #2 and #3, which go from the train station to Bishu Shanzhuang, and bus #6, from there to the Puning Si, are the most useful. **Taxis** are common, but the drivers are unwilling to use their meters – a ride around town should cost ¥5, to an outlying temple ¥10. At peak hours during the summer season (June–Sept), the main streets are so congested that it's quicker to walk. The town itself is just about small enough to cover on foot.

If your time is limited, a minibus **tour** is worth considering as a way to cram in all the sights. English-speaking tours can be arranged through CITS or through the larger hotels; expect to pay around ¥50 for a day. Chinese tours, which leave sporadically from outside the train station, are slightly cheaper. A one-day organized tour, to the resort in the morning and the biggest temples in the afternoon, is something of a trial of endurance, however, and they do tend to overlook the less spectacular temples, which is a shame, as these are also the most peaceful. Probably the best way to see everything in a short time, without going down with temple fatigue, is to take a minibus or a bike around the temples one day and explore the mountain resort the next. If you're travelling in a group you can rent a taxi or a minibus for around ¥150 a day (barter hard) and make up your own itinerary. There are also longer tours on offer from here, stretching to four and five days and taking in a section of the Great Wall at Jinshanling, 113km southwest, and the Eastern Tombs in Zunhua County 150km east – expect to spend a lot of time on a bus.

Accommodation

There are plenty of hotels in Chengde town itself, plus a couple of expensive places inside Bishu Shanzhuang, although none of them are worth getting excited about. Rates are highly negotiable; the price codes below are based on the peak summer season and weekends. At other times you can get discounts of up to two-thirds.

Chengde Binguan 33 Nanyingzi Dajie ⓣ0314/2023157, ⓕ2021341. Threadbare and gloomy, this place is only worth it if you can get one of their cheap doubles, which they would rather not tell you about. ❸

Chengde Dasha Chezhan Lu ⓣ0314/2088808, ⓕ2024319. This fifteen-storey block is convenient for the station, but in an uninteresting area of town. ❼

Huilong Chezhan Lu ⓣ0314/2085369, ⓕ2082404. Opposite the *Chengde Dasha*, and the better of the two. Twelve storeys high, with a grand lobby, but the rooms are rather small and merely adequate. ❻

Shanzhuang 127 Lizhengmen Lu ⓣ0314/2023501. This grand, well-located complex, with huge rooms, high ceilings and a cavernous, gleaming lobby, is good value, and with a wide range of rooms it's Chengde's best bet for most budgets. The large rooms in the main building are nicer but a little more expensive than those in the ugly building round the back. Buses #2 or #3 from the train station will get you here. Dorm beds ¥40, ❹

Xinhua 4 Xinhua Bei Lu ⓣ0314/2063181. Simple, standard, cheapish accommodation, in a rather ugly building that's showing its age. However, it has a good restaurant specializing in Shandong food. They have dorms, but probably won't let you stay in them. Bus #7 gets you here. Dorm beds ¥45, ❹

Yiwanglou Inside Bishu Shanzhuang, just to the left of the front entrance ⓣ0314/2023528. A well-run three-star hotel in a pleasing imitation Qing-style building. ❽

Yunshan 6 Nanyuan Dong Lu ⓣ0314/2024551. This modern block is the most luxurious place to stay in town, and is popular with tour groups. The second-floor restaurant is good, the plushest in town, and not too expensive. Bus #9 from the train station passes the door, or it's a 10min walk. ❽

The Town

The majority of Chengde's one-million-strong population live in a semi-rural suburban sprawl to the south of the centre, leaving the city itself fairly small-scale, its new high-rises yet to obscure the view of distant mountains and fields. However, the surrounding area's buildings, parks and lakes attract hundreds of thousands of visitors a year and, on summer weekends especially, the town is packed with tourists and its main artery, **Nanyingzi Dajie**, clogged with traffic. The street is much more pleasant in the evening, when a night market stretches all the way down it. As well as snacks, many vendors sell antiques and curios which are generally cheaper than in either Beijing or Tianjin, but you'll have to bargain hard (and don't expect everything to be genuine). Bishu Shanzhuang lies in the north of the town, while farther north and to the east, on the other side of the river, stand Chengde's eight imposing **temples**.

Bishu Shanzhuang

Surrounded by a ten-kilometre wall and larger than the Summer Palace in Beijing, **Bishu Shanzhuang** (also referred to as the **Mountain Resort**) occupies the northern third of the town's area (daily 5.30am–6.30pm; ¥50 combined ticket for the park and the palace). This is where, in the summer months, the Qing emperors lived, feasted, hunted, and occasionally dealt with affairs of state. The palace buildings just inside the front entrance are unusual for imperial China as they are low, wooden and unpainted; simple, but elegant,

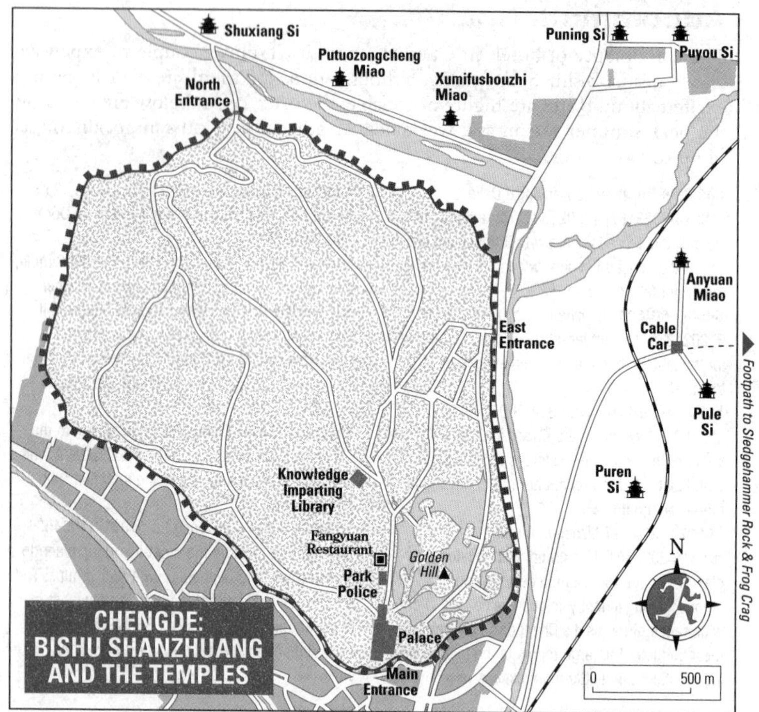

in contrast to the opulence and grandeur of Beijing's palaces. It's said that Emperor Kangxi wanted the complex to mimic a Manchurian village, to show his disdain for fame and wealth, though with 120 rooms and several thousand servants he wasn't exactly roughing it. The same principle of idealized naturalness governed the design of the park. With its twisting paths and streams, rockeries and hills, it's a fantasy re-creation of rough northern terrain and southern Chinese beauty spots that the emperors would have seen on their tours of inspection. The whole is an attempt to combine water, buildings and plants in graceful harmony. Lord Macartney, visiting in 1793, noted its similarity to the "soft beauties" of an English manor park of the Romantic style.

The **main gate**, Lizhengmen, is in the south wall, off Lizhengmen Dajie. Covering the whole park and its buildings takes at least a day, and an early start is recommended. It's at its nicest in the early morning anyway, when a vegetable market sets up just outside the front gate, and old people practise *tai ji* or play Go by the palace. The park is simply too big to get overcrowded, and if you head north beyond the lakes, you're likely to find yourself alone.

The palace

The **palace quarter**, just inside the complex to the west of the main gate, is built on a slope, facing south, and consists of four groups of dark wooden buildings spread over an area of 100,000 square metres. The first, southernmost group, the Front Palace, where the emperors lived and worked, is the most interesting, as many of the rooms have been restored to their full Qing elegance, decked out with graceful furniture and ornaments. Even the everyday objects are impressive: brushes and ink stones on desks, ornate fly whisks on the arms of chairs, little jade trees on shelves. Other rooms house displays of ceramics, books, and exotic martial-art weaponry. The Qing emperors were fine calligraphers, and examples of their work appear throughout the palace.

There are twenty-six buildings in this group, arranged south to north in nine successive compounds which correspond to the nine levels of heaven. The main gate leads into the **Outer Wumen**, where high-ranking officials waited for a single peal of a large bell, indicating that the emperor was ready to receive them. Next is the **Inner Wumen**, where the emperor would watch his officers practise their archery. Directly behind, the **Hall of Frugality and Sincerity** is a dark, well-appointed room made of cedar wood, imported at great expense from south of the Yangzi by Qianlong, who had none of his grandfather Kangxi's scruples about conspicuous consumption. Topped with a curved roof, the hall has nine bays, and patterns on the walls include symbols of longevity and good luck. The **Four Knowledge Study Room**, behind, was where the emperor did his ordinary work, changed his clothes and rested. A vertical scroll on the wall outlines the four knowledges required of a gentleman, as written in the Chinese classics: he must be aware of what is small, obvious, soft and strong. It's more spartanly furnished, a little more intimate and less imposing than the other rooms.

The main building in the **Rear Palace** is the **Hall of Refreshing Mists and Waves**, the living quarters of the imperial family, where Emperor Xianfeng signed the humiliating Beijing Treaty in the 1850s, giving away more of China's sovereignty and territory after their defeat in the Second Opium War. The **Western Apartments** are where the notorious Cixi, better known as the Dowager Empress (see p.119), lived when she was one of Xianfeng's concubines. A door connects the apartments to the hall, and it was through here that she eavesdropped on the dying emperor's last words of advice to his ministers, intelligence she used to help to force herself into power. The courtyard of the Rear Palace has a good **souvenir shop**, inside an old Buddhist tower which you reach by climbing a staircase by the rockery.

The other two complexes are much smaller. The **Pine and Crane Residence**, a group of buildings parallel to the front gate, is a more subdued version of the Front Palace, home to the emperor's mother and his concubines. In the **Myriad Valleys of Rustling Pine Trees**, to the north of here, Emperor Kangxi read books and granted audiences, and Qianlong studied as a child. The group of structures southwest of the main palace is the **Ahgesuo**, where during the Manchurian rule, male descendants of the royal family studied; lessons began at 5am and finished at noon. A boy was expected to speak Manchu at 6, Chinese at 12, be competent with a bow by the age of 14, and married at 16.

The grounds

The best way to get around the **lake area** of the park – a network of pavilions, bridges, lakes and waterways – is to rent a **rowing boat** (¥20 an hour). Much of the architecture here is a direct copy of southern Chinese buildings. In the east, the **Golden Hill**, a cluster of buildings grouped on a small island, is notable for a hall and tower modelled after the Golden Hill Monastery in Zhenjiang, Jiangsu Province. The **Island of Midnight and Murmuring Streams**, roughly in the centre of the lake, holds a three-courtyard compound which was used by Kangxi and Qianlong as a retreat, while the compound of halls, towers and pavilions on **Ruyi Island**, the largest, was where Kangxi dealt with affairs of state before the palace was completed.

Just beyond the lake area, on the western side of the park, is the grey-tiled **Wenjinge**, or Knowledge Imparting Library, surrounded by rockeries and pools for fire protection. The structure seems to have two storeys from the outside; in fact there are three – a central section is windowless to protect the books from the sun. A fine collection is housed in the building, including *The Four Treasures*, a 36,304-volume Qing-dynasty encyclopedia, but sadly you can't go inside.

A vast expanse of **grassland** extends from the north of the lake area to the foothills of the mountains, comprising Wanshun Wan (Garden of Ten Thousand Trees) and Shima Da (Horse Testing Ground). Genuine Qing-dynasty **yurts** sit here, the largest an audience hall where Qianlong received visiting dignitaries from ethnic minorities.

The hilly area in the northwest of the park has a number of rocky valleys, gorges and gullies with a few tastefully placed lodges and pagodas. The deer which graze here have been reintroduced after being wiped out by imperial hunting expeditions.

The temples and Sledgehammer Rock

The **temples** (daily: May–Sept 8am–6.30pm; Oct–April 8am–5pm) in the foothills of the mountains around Chengde are now in varying states of repair, after being left untended for decades. Originally there were twelve, but two have been destroyed and another two are dilapidated. They are built in the architectural styles of different ethnic nationalities, so that wandering among them is rather like being in a religious theme park. This is not far from the original intention, as they were constructed by Kangxi and Qianlong less to express religious sentiment than as a way of showing off imperial magnificence, and also to make envoys from anywhere in the empire feel more at home. Though varying in design, all the temples share **Lamaist features** – Qianlong found it politically expedient to promote Tibetan and Mongolian Lamaism as a way of keeping these troublesome minorities in line. Present restoration work is being paid for by the high entrance fees charged in the large temples.

The best way to see the temples is to **rent a bicycle**: the roads outside the town are quiet, it's hard to get lost and you can dodge the tour groups. One workable itinerary would be to see the northern cluster in the morning, returning to town for lunch (it's impossible to cross the river to the eastern temples from outside town); in the afternoon, head east for the Pule Si, then take the cable car up to **Sledgehammer Rock**, a bizarre hilltop protuberance that dominates the eastern horizon of the town. Before you head back to the centre, you may want to check out the small, peaceful Anyuan and Puren temples, good places to chill out with a book. For details of temple tours, see p.173.

The northern temples

Just beyond the northern border of Bishu Shanzhuang, these five temples were once part of a string of nine. The **Puning Si** (Temple of Universal Peace; ¥30) is a must, if only for the statue of Guanyin, the Goddess of Mercy, the largest wooden statue in the world. It's the only working temple in Chengde, with shaven-headed Mongolian monks manning the altars and trinket stalls, though the atmosphere is not especially spiritual. Undergoing major restoration at the time of writing, the temple is usually clamorous with day-trippers, some of whom seem to take outrageous liberties, judging by the sign that says "No shooting birds in the temple area." There are rumours that the monks you see are really paid government employees working for the tourist industry, though the vehemence with which they defend their prayer mats and gongs from romping children suggests otherwise.

The Puning Si was built in 1755 to commemorate the Qing victory over Mongolian rebels at Junggar in northwest China, and is based on the oldest Tibetan temple, the Samye. Like traditional Tibetan buildings, it lies on the slope of a mountain facing south, though the layout of the front is typically Han, with a gate hall, stele pavilions, a bell and a drum tower, a Hall of Heavenly Kings, and the Mahavira Hall. In the **Hall of Heavenly Kings**, the statue of a fat, grinning monk holding a bag depicts Qi Ci, a tenth-century character with a jovial disposition who is believed to be a reincarnation of the Buddha. Four gaudy *devarajas* (guardian demons) here glare down at you with bulging eyeballs from niches in the walls. In the **West Hall** are statues of Buddha Manjusri, Avalokiteshvara and Samantabhadra. In the **East Hall**, the central statue, flanked by *arhats*, depicts Ji Gong, a Song-dynasty monk who was nicknamed Crazy Ji for eating meat and being almost always drunk, but who was much respected for his kindness to the poor.

The rear section of the temple, separated from the front by a wall, comprises 27 Tibetan-style rooms laid out symmetrically, with the **Mahayana Hall** in the centre. Some of the buildings are solid, with false doors, suggesting that the original architects were more concerned with appearances than function. The hall itself is dominated by the awe-inspiring, 23-metre-high wooden **statue of Guanyin**. She has 42 arms with an eye in the centre of each palm, and three eyes on her face which symbolize her ability to see into the past, the present and the future. The hall has two raised entrances, and it's worth looking at the statue from these higher viewpoints as they reveal new details, such as the eye sunk in her belly button, and the little Buddha sat on top of her head.

On the thirteenth day of the first lunar month (Jan or Feb), the monks observe the ritual of "**catching the ghost**", during which a ghost made of dough is placed on an iron rack while monks dressed in white dance around it, then divide it into pieces and burn it. The ritual is thought to be in honour of a ninth-century Tibetan Buddhist, Lhalung Oaldor, who assassinated a king who had ordered the destruction of Tibetan Buddhist temples, books and priests. The wily monk entered the palace on a white horse painted black, dressed in a white coat with a black lining. After killing the king, he washed the horse and turned the coat inside out, thus evading capture from the guards who did not recognize him.

The **Xumifushouzhi Miao** (Temple of Sumeru Happiness and Longevity; ¥25), just southwest of Puning Si, is being restored and much of it is closed to the public; the parts that are open are not in a good state of repair. The temple was built in 1780 for the ill-fated sixth Panchen Lama (see p.171) when he came to Beijing to pay his respects to the emperor. Built in Mongolian style, its centrepiece is the **Hall of Loftiness and Solemnity**, its finest feature the eight sinuous gold dragons, each weighing over a thousand kilograms, sitting on the roof.

Next door to the Xumifushouzhi Miao, the magnificent **Putuozongcheng Miao** (Temple of Potaraka Doctrine; ¥25) was built in 1771 and is based on the Potala Palace in Lhasa. Covering 220,000 square metres, it's the largest temple in Chengde, with sixty groups of halls, pagodas and terraces. The grand red terrace forms a Tibetan-style facade screening a Chinese-style interior, although many of the windows on the terrace are fake, and some of the whitewashed buildings around the base are merely filled-in shapes. Inside, the West Hall is notable for holding a rather comical copper statue of the Propitious Heavenly Mother, a fearsome woman wearing a necklace of skulls and riding side-saddle on a mule. According to legend, she vowed to defeat the evil demon Raksaka, so she first lulled him into a false sense of security – by marrying him and bearing him two sons – then swallowed the moon and in the darkness crept up on him and turned him into a mule. The two dancing figures at her feet are her sons; their ugly features betray their paternity. The Hall of All Laws Falling into One, at the back, is worth a visit for the quality of the decorative religious furniture on display. Other halls hold displays of Chinese pottery and ceramics and Tibetan religious artefacts, an exhibition slanted to portray the gorier side of Tibetan religion and including a drum made from two children's skulls. The roof of the temple has a good view over the surrounding countryside.

The **Shuxiang Si** (Temple of Manjusri; ¥3), a short walk west, is Han in style, simple and unspectacular and, for that reason, quiet. Built in 1744, it consists of towers and pavilions set in somewhat overgrown gardens and rockeries, and is a loose copy of a temple in the Wutai Mountains in Shanxi. The statue of Manjusri, the Wenshu Buddha, in the main hall, apparently looks suspiciously like Qianlong himself. Closed for renovation at the time of writing, it should be open and gleaming by the time you read this.

The eastern temples

The three **eastern temples** are easily accessible off a quiet road that passes through dusty, rambling settlements, 3–4km from the town centre. From Lizhengmen Lu, cross over to the east bank of the river and head north.

The **Puren Si** (Temple of Universal Benevolence; ¥2), is the first one you'll reach and the oldest in the complex; it too was closed for renovation at time of writing. The temple was built by Kangxi in 1713, as a sign of respect to the visiting Mongolian nobility, come to congratulate the emperor on the occasion of his sixtieth birthday. The temple is a four-courtyard compound in the Han style, with a gate and three halls arranged on a central axis, and a drum and bell tower. Although architecturally unimpressive, it contains some interesting sculpture. The Hall of Generous Shade of the Cloud, the main building, has some Ming-style gilded lacquer statues of Sakyamuni and his disciples, but the best thing in the temple is the collection of *arhats* in a side hall. The most striking of these is the almost life-size image of an old man – his lined face seems to radiate benevolence – being carried on a young disciple's back.

The **Pule Si** (Temple of Universal Happiness; ¥25), farther north, was built in 1766 by Qianlong as a place for Mongol envoys to worship, and its style is an odd mix of Han and Lamaist elements. The Lamaist back section, a triple-tiered terrace and hall, with a flamboyantly conical roof and lively, curved surfaces, steals the show from the more sober, squarer Han architecture at the front. The ceiling of the back hall is a wood and gold confection to rival the Temple of Heaven in Beijing. Glowing at its centre is a mandala of Samvara, a Tantric deity, in the form of a cross. The altar beneath holds a Buddha of Happiness, a life-size copper image of sexual congress. More cosmic sex is depicted in two beautiful mandalas hanging outside. In the courtyard, prayer flags flutter while prayer wheels sit empty and unturned. Just north of the temple is the path that leads to **Sledgehammer Rock**, and the cable car (see below).

The **Anyuan Miao** (Temple of Appeasing the Borders; ¥10), the most northerly of the group, was built in 1764 for a troop of Mongolian soldiers who were moved to Chengde by Qianlong. It's not spectacular nor was it in great shape in recent times, though it may be worth a look once it reopens after renovation.

Sledgehammer Rock and beyond

Of the scenic areas around Chengde, the one that inspires the most curiosity is **Sledgehammer Rock**. Thinner at the base than at the top, the towering column of rock is more than 20m high, and is skirted by stalls selling little metal models of it and Sledgehammer Rock T-shirts. According to legend, the rock is a huge dragon's needle put there to plug a hole in the peak which was letting the sea through. The rock's obviously phallic nature is tactfully not mentioned in tourist literature, but is acknowledged in local folklore – should the rock fall, it is said, it will have a disastrous effect on the virility of local men.

Sledgehammer Rock (¥15) is a couple of kilometres on foot from the Pule Si, or there's a cable car up (15min; ¥20 return), offering impressive views. On the south side of the rock, at the base of a cliff, is **Frog Crag**, a stone that vaguely resembles a sitting frog – the two-kilometre walk here is pleasant, if the frog itself disappoints. Other rocky highlights within walking distance are **Arhat Hill**, on the eastern side of the river, supposed to look like a reclining Buddha, and **Monk's Headgear Peak**, 4km south of town, the highest point in the area and best reached by bike – head south down Chezhan Lu.

Eating and drinking

Chengde is located in Hebei's most fertile area, which mainly produces maize and sorghum but also yields excellent local chestnuts, mushrooms and apricots. This fresh produce, plus the culinary legacy of the imperial cooks, means it is possible to eat very well here. The town is also noted for its **wild game**, particularly deer (*lurou*), hare and pheasant (*shanji*), and its medicinal **juice drinks**: almond juice is said to be good for asthma; date and jujube juice for the stomach; and *jinlianhua* (golden lotus) juice for a sore throat. Date and almond are the sweetest and most palatable. Local **cakes**, such as the glutinous Feng family cakes, once an imperial delicacy but now a casual snack, can be found in the stalls on Yuhua Lu and Qingfeng Jie. Rose cakes – a sweet, crisp pastry cake and a particular favourite of Qianlong – are sold in Chengde's department stores.

There are plenty of **restaurants** catering to tourists on Lizhengmen Lu, around the main entrance to the mountain resort. The small places west of the *Shanzhuang* hotel are fine, if a little pricey, and lively on summer evenings, when rickety tables are put on the pavement outside. A meal for two should be about ¥60, and plenty of diners stay on drinking well into the evening. For a cheap feed, try *shaguo* – a mini-hotpot – at the night market – a veggie one costs ¥6, a meat-based one ¥10. For pricier fare, head down Lizhengmen Lu to **Qingfeng Restaurant Street**, an alley signposted in English. Just about every building here is a restaurant, and there's enough variety to suit most budgets and palates. Inside Bishu Shanzhuang, the *Fangyuan* offers imperial cuisine, including such exotica as "Pingquan Frozen Rabbit", in an attractive environment.

Shijiazhuang and around

Three hours by express train southwest from Beijing, but at least five years behind in development, the capital of Hebei, **SHIJIAZHUANG**, is a major rail junction that you may find yourself passing through if you're heading south to the Yellow River. At the beginning of the last century Shijiazhuang was hardly more than a village, but the building of the rail line made it an important junction town, and by the 1920s it had a population of ten thousand. Having industrialized rapidly, it's now an unglamorous, sprawling place that keeps adding parks, squares and department stores as flourishes. It's known as a centre for medicine and, besides being home to China's largest pharmaceutical factory, is reputedly a good place to study traditional **Chinese medicine**.

For tourists, the grave of Canadian surgeon Norman Bethune and the city museum are worth a look, but the best sights – Zhengding's **Longxing Si**, the **Cangyan Shan Si** and **Zhaozhou Qiao** – are out of town, though accessible by tourist minibuses which leave in the mornings from a park about 100m northeast of the train station.

The City

Downtown Shijiazhuang is laid out on a grid with long axial roads, which change their names several times along their course, running north–south and

Shijiazhuang and around

Shijiazhuang	石家庄	*shíjiāzhuāng*
Hebei Hotel	河北市宾馆	*héběi shì bīnguǎn*
Hebei Museum	河北省博物馆	*héběi shěng bówùguǎn*
Hebei Teachers' University	河北师范大学	*héběi shīfàn dàxué*
Martyrs' Memorial	烈士陵园	*lièshi língyuán*
People's Square	人民广场	*rénmín guǎngchǎng*
Yanchun Garden Hotel	燕春花园酒店	*yànchūnhuāyuán jiǔdiàn*
Zhongjing Grand Hotel	中京大酒店	*zhōngjīng dàjiǔdiàn*
Zhengding and the monasteries		
Cangyan Shan Si	苍岩山寺	*cāngyánshān sì*
Longxing Si	隆兴寺	*lóngxīng sì*
Zhaozhou Qiao	赵州桥	*zhàozhōu qiáo*
Zhengding	正定	*zhèngdìng*

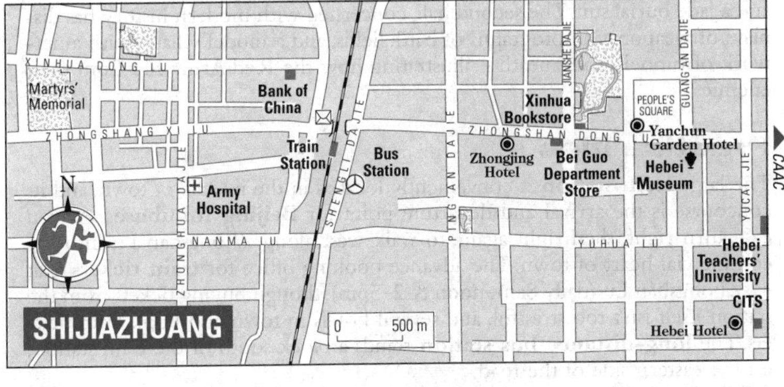

east–west. The main street running east–west across town, just north of the train station and served by the #5 bus, is one of the most interesting. Five (rather long) blocks west of the station, along a section called Zhongshan Lu, you'll find the **Martyrs' Memorial** (daily 6am–5pm), an ordered, sober-looking park, containing the graves of the only two foreigners to be honoured as heroes of the Revolution. On the west side of the park, the grave of **Norman Bethune**, a Canadian doctor, is marked by an ornate sarcophagus, a photo exhibition, and a statue, identical to one standing in Bethune Square, Montréal. Bethune (1890–1939), whose remains were moved here from Canada at the request of the Chinese government in 1953, was a brilliant, idealistic surgeon, who came to China to help the Communists in the fight against the Japanese after working on the Republican side in the Spanish Civil War. He was present at most of the major battles of the era, and became a close confidant of Mao when the Red Army was holed up in Yan'an after the Long March. Mao was so impressed with Bethune's devotion to his work that he later exhorted the Chinese to "learn selflessness from Dr Bethune". As one of the most well-known foreigners in China, Bethune is one reason why many Chinese are well disposed towards Canadians. On the east side of the park, identical treatment is given to **Dwarkanath Kotnis** (1900–42), one of five Indian doctors who came to China in the 1930s. Staying in the country for nearly a decade, he joined the Communist Party just before his death. Both doctors are celebrated in a small **museum** at the back of the park; items on display include the exercise books in which they practised writing in Chinese and the crude surgical implements they had to work with. Among the large number of photographs are pictures of Bethune operating by torchlight and chatting with Mao.

East of the station (and confusingly, behind it), the road becomes Zhongshan Dong Lu, the city's commercial sector, with a few department stores, the largest of which, the ostentatious five-storey **Bei Guo Department Store**, at the intersection with Bei Dajie, is the biggest in Hebei. Overstaffed and full of window shoppers, it's was once the city's premier tourist attraction. Now that honour falls to **People's Square**, one block east, a jumble of plaques, shrubbery and kites.

Two blocks farther east is the unexpectedly good **Hebei Museum** (daily 8.30–11.30am & 2.30–5.30pm; ¥10). The downstairs rooms hold temporary exhibitions of local products, while the two rooms upstairs display a fascinating hotchpotch of historic artefacts. The first hall includes a complete mammoth skull and tusk, a miniature terracotta army unearthed in a nearby tomb and a jade burial suit. The second hall, concerned with modern history, has displays of weaponry, photographs of battlefields, and a model village with a network of tunnels underneath – illustrating how the Red Army hid from their enemies.

Practicalities

The large **train station** is conveniently located in the middle of town, and its concourse is the arrival and departure point for **Beijing minibuses**. As you exit, turn right, then right again, to walk west along Zhongshan Lu into the commercial heart of town. The advance booking office for **train tickets** is at 47 Zhongshan Lu (daily 8am–noon & 2–5pm), though buying tickets from the station itself isn't too stressful, and several hotels in town also book train tickets. The **long-distance bus station** stands a block south of the train station, on the eastern side of the road.

Shijiazhuang **airport**, 45km northeast of the city, is served by an airport bus (¥15) which takes you to the **CAAC** office at 471 Zhongshan Lu (toll-free ⓣ0311/8027140), far from the centre. If you need to buy air tickets, it's more convenient to do so from an office next to the Hualian Commercial Building, opposite the train station.

Getting around town by bus is straightforward; buses #5 and #6, which run east and west across town, are the most useful. **Taxis** around town have a ¥5 minimum charge, with each subsequent kilometre costing around ¥1.4. Staff at **CITS**, 171 Yucai Jie (ⓣ0311/5827777), opposite the *Hebei Hotel*, speak some English and can provide information about the whole province, including tours to the surrounding monasteries.

For **changing money**, the Bank of China is at 136 Xinhua Dong Lu (Mon–Fri 8.30am–noon & 2–4.30pm). The **post office** (daily 7am–9pm) and a 24-hour **telephone office** are located in the same building on Gongli Jie, opposite the west side of the train station. **Bikes** can be rented from a stall on the southeast side of the train-station concourse, opposite the Hualian Commercial Building, at the back of a large bike park (daily 8am–8pm; ¥5 per day, plus ¥50 deposit). The Xinhua Bookstore on the second floor of 13 Jiefang Lu (with a branch opposite the train station's square) sells classic English-language novels on the second floor.

Accommodation and eating

There's not a great choice of hotels in Shijiazhuang, but with Beijing only a few hours' journey away, it's unlikely you'll need to stay more than a night here anyway. For **eating**, the stretch of Zhongshan Dong Lu, between People's Square and the Hebei Museum, features a good mix of Chinese eating places and Western fast food.

Hebei 168 Yucai Jie ⓣ0311/5815961, ⓕ5814092. This three-star, eight-storey block in the quiet eastern side of town dominates the surrounding low buildings. The hotel has two restaurants, a nightclub and a karaoke lounge, and they can book train tickets for you. ❻

Hebei Teachers' University Yuhua Lu ⓣ0311/6049941. The foreign teachers' dormitory is a cheap and friendly place to stay, offering well-maintained double rooms. Go through the main gate, take the first left and the building is on the right, signposted in English. Take bus #6 from the train station. There are plenty of small restaurants and street stalls in the vicinity. Dorm beds ¥15, ❷

Yanchun Garden Hotel 195 Zhongshan Donglu ⓣ0311/6671188, ⓕ6048689. Shijiazhuang's newest and nicest hotel with all mod cons, beside People's Square on the main drag. ❼

Zhongjing 176 Zhongshan Donglu ⓣ0311/6032551, ⓕ6032069. This stylish, low-key place has helpful staff and a good location on the main thoroughfare. ❺

Zhengding

Though it has since slipped into rural obscurity, the small town of **ZHENGDING**, 15km northeast of Shijiazhuang, was an important county town and religious centre until the eighteenth century. The finest remnant of its mystic past is the **Longxing Si** (daily 8am–5pm; ¥30), a large complex on the eastern outskirts of the town, and said to be the oldest monastery in China. **Minibuses** (¥10) from Shijiazhuang's train station to Zhengding terminate right opposite the monastery; walking from here, around the pagodas and back to the bus stop should take about two hours.

The monastery halls now serve as a **museum** (the monks disappeared after the Communist takeover) holding a few excellent and varied examples of large-scale Buddhist sculpture. Outstanding are a richly embellished bronze statue of four Buddhas on a lotus throne, supporting four smaller Buddhas, who in turn support four more; and a colourful wooden image, awash with rococo curves, of Guanyin sitting in a grotto. A hall on the west side is filled with a huge wooden machine described as a "movable bookshelf". Reminiscent of a mill, it's a giant spinning wheel whose revolving sides would once have held written sutras. The finest artefact is at the centre of the Main Hall (Da Bei Ge), where a 22-metre-high bronze image of multi-armed Guanyin is a rare and magnificent example of Song-dynasty craftsmanship, nearly 1000 years old.

All that remains of the Zhengding's many temples are four **pagodas** dotted around the town. Entrance is just a few yuan, and you can climb to at least the second storey of each; the attendants rent out flashlights as it's very dark inside. The forty-metre-high brick **Lingxiao Pagoda**, originally built in the Tang dynasty but renovated in the Ming, stands a kilometre to the west of the monastery. You can climb to the fourth floor on the inside, then continue to the top on an external wooden staircase that winds around a wooden pillar supporting the pagoda's iron tip. One block southwest of here, the simple, chunky **Xumi Pagoda** is unusually austere and geometrical in design. It was built in 540 AD and, though it has been renovated often since, its original form has been retained, providing an insight into typical Tang architecture. A belfry outside contains a three-metre-tall Tang-dynasty bronze bell. The **Chengling Pagoda**, a fifteen-minute walk south, is thin, knobbly with ornament and topped with an elaborate iron spike. It was built to honour Yixuan, a ninth-century Buddhist monk who lived in a former monastery on this site. He was a highly original teacher – famous for shouting at and hitting his pupils to surprise them – and was one of the founders of the style of Buddhism that came to be known as Zen. Today, the pagoda is a popular site with Japanese tourists and pilgrims. Finally, the **Hua Pagoda**, a short walk south of here, is a rare Jin-dynasty structure – China has only a handful of similar buildings. Its finest feature is the fourth-storey section, just under the tip, which swarms with carvings of elephants, Buddhas and whales. The lower half of the pagoda is in pretty bad shape, however.

Cangyan Shan Si and Zhaozhou Qiao

Thirty kilometres southwest of Shijiazhuang, **Cangyan Shan Si** (daily 8am–5pm; ¥32), conceived in the Sui dynasty and rebuilt by the Qing, is an elegant monastic complex made beautiful by its dramatic location. Hundreds of feet up, on the steep rocky side of a mountain, the monastery perches on top of a bridge spanning a cleft in the almost vertical face of Cangyan Shan.

The two main buildings are Sui in design, with colourful double roofs and attached gardens, and are reached by a pleasant two-hour walk along a twisting cliff path. In summer, **minibuses** run daily from Shijiazhuang to the monastery (¥10; 2hr 30min). Out of season you'll have to make your own way here: take a bus from the long-distance bus station in Shijiazhuang to Gingxing County, then hire a motor-rickshaw to take you the last ten kilometres. In winter, the path up to the monastery is sometimes impassable due to snow.

Zhaozhou Qiao (daily 8am–5pm; ¥18), 40km southeast of Shijiazhuang, just outside the town of Zhaoxiang, is a simple, elegant bridge that will impress architects and engineers. Built at the beginning of the seventh century, its builder, Li Chun, had to solve some tricky problems. The bridge had to be flat enough for the chariots of the imperial army to pass over it, yet not so low that it would be destroyed by the frequent floods. It had to rest on soft river banks but still be strong enough to withstand the military and trading convoys. The result of Li's deliberations was a single flattened arch, spanning over 36m, with a rise of just 7m. It's still in use, one of the masterpieces of Chinese architecture, and the model for dozens of northern Chinese stone bridges.

Travel details

Trains

Beidaihe to: Beijing (7 daily; 5–7hr); Qinhuangdao (9 daily; 30min); Shanhaiguan (6 daily; 1hr); Shenyang (6 daily; 5hr); Tianjin (4 daily; 5–6hr).
Chengde to: Beijing (4 daily; 4hr 30min); Dandong (daily; 30hr); Shenyang (4 daily; 7hr); Tianjin (2 daily; 5hr).
Qinhuangdao to: Beidaihe (9 daily; 30min); Beijing (3 daily; 5hr 30min–7hr 30min); Shanhaiguan (3 daily; 30min); Shenyang (daily; 5hr 30min); Tianjin (3 daily; 6hr 30min).
Shanhaiguan to: Beidaihe (daily; 1hr); Beijing (3 daily; 7hr); Qinhuangdao (daily; 30min); Shenyang (daily; 6h); Tianjin (3 daily; 7hr).
Shijiazhuang to: Beijing (many daily; 3–5hr); Ji'nan (4 daily; 3hr); Taiyuan (2 daily; 8hr); Tianjin (4 daily; 5–7hr); Zhengzhou (2 daily; 6hr).
Tianjin to: Beidaihe (3 daily; 6hr); Beijing (15 daily; 1–2hr, including hourly express services); Chengde (4 daily; 5hr); Guangzhou (3 daily; 26–32hr); Jilin (5 daily; 4hr); Qinhuangdao (4 daily; 6hr); Shanghai (3 daily; 18–20hr); Shanhaiguan (5 daily; 6hr 30min); Shijiazhuang (4 daily; 4–6hr); Xi'an (2 daily; 18–20hr).

Buses

Beidaihe to: Beijing (5hr); Qinhuangdao (20min); Shanhaiguan (40min); Tianjin (3hr 30min).
Chengde to: Beijing (3hr); Tianjin (4hr).
Qinhuangdao to: Beidaihe (20min); Beijing (5hr); Shanhaiguan (20min); Tianjin (4hr).
Shanhaiguan to: Beidaihe (40min); Beijing (5hr 20min); Qinhuangdao (20min); Tianjin (4hr 30min).
Shijiazhuang to: Beijing (4hr).
Tianjin to: Beidaihe (3hr 30min); Beijing (2hr); Chengde (4hr); Qinhuangdao (4hr); Shanhaiguan (4hr 20min).

Ferries

Qinhuangdao to: Dalian (every other day in summer; 13–15hr).
Tianjin to: Dalian (March–Oct 1 daily; rest of year every other day; 13–15hr); Inch'on, South Korea (every 4 days; 28hr); Kobe, Japan (weekly; 48hr); Yantai (6 times monthly; 18hr).

Flights

Qinhuangdao to: Changchun (2 weekly; 1hr 10min); Dalian (4 weekly; 50min); Harbin (2 weekly; 1hr 30min); Shanghai (2 weekly; 2hr); Taiyuan (7 weekly; 1hr 10min).
Shijiazhuang to: Beijing (daily; 30min); Chongqing (2 weekly; 2hr); Dalian (3 weekly; 1hr 10min); Guangzhou (5 weekly; 2hr 30min); Hohhot (daily; 50min); Kunming (4 weekly; 4hr); Nanjing (2 weekly; 1hr 15 min); Shanghai (daily; 1hr 40min); Shenzhen (2 weekly; 4hr 45min); Wenzhou (2 weekly; 2hr 15min); Xiamen (2 weekly; 3hr 25min); Xi'an (daily; 1hr 10min); Yinchuan (3 weekly; 1hr 20min).
Tianjin to: Changsha (2 weekly; 2hr); Chengdu (5 weekly; 3hr 25min); Dalian (1 or 2 daily; 1hr);

Fuzhou (5 weekly; 2hr 30min); Guangzhou (2 daily; 2hr 50min); Guilin (2 weekly; 4hr 30min); Haikou (3 weekly; 3hr 45min); Hangzhou (5 weekly; 1hr 35min); Harbin (daily; 3hr); Hong Kong (daily; 3hr); Kunming (8 weekly; 3hr); Nanjing (2 weekly; 1hr 40min); Ningbo (5 weekly; 2hr 50min); Qingdao (daily; 1hr 20min); Shanghai (5 daily; 1hr 35min); Shantou (2 weekly; 2hr 45min); Shenyang (4 weekly; 1hr 10min); Shenzhen (7 weekly; 3hr); Taiyuan (daily; 1hr); Ürümqi (2 weekly; 3hr 20min); Wuhan (3 weekly; 2hr); Xiamen (5 weekly; 2hr 15min); Xi'an (7 weekly; 1hr 40min); Xishuangbanna (4 weekly; 5hr 15min); Zhengzhou (2 weekly; 50min).

CHAPTER 3

Highlights

- **The Imperial Palace, Shenyang** Pre-empting Beijing's Forbidden City, this was the seat of the Manchus before they seized the capital. **See p.194**
- **Old Yalu Bridge, Dandong** Walk halfway to North Korea on what's left of this old structure. **See p.204**
- **Puppet Emperor's Palace, Changchun** The second act of the "last emperor" Puyi's life was played out here, where he was installed by the Japanese as leader of Manchuria. **See p.208**
- **Jilin in winter** Famous in China, the town's river promenade becomes a winter wonderland when frost forms on trees. **See p.209**
- **Changbai Shan** The northeast's loveliest nature preserve is also its least developed. Root around for wild ginseng, though beware of North Korean border guards. **See p.211**
- **Russian architecture in Harbin** Prettiest in winter, but enjoyable year-round. **See p.215**
- **Winter ice festivals** Most Manchurian metropolises have one, but Harbin's is the biggest and best, where millions pour in to admire ice carvings by international artists. **See p.220**
- **Zhalong Nature Reserve** Bird-watchers flock to the reedy lakes west of Harbin, where the rare red-crowned crane breeds. **See p.223**
- **Yabuli** China's finest ski resort. **See p.224**

3

Dongbei

Dongbei, or more evocatively Manchuria, may well be the closest thing to the "real" China that visitors vainly seek in the well-travelled central and southern parts of the country. Not many foreign tourists get up to China's northernmost arm, however, due to its reputation as an inhospitable wasteland: "Although it is uncertain where God created paradise," wrote a French priest when he was here in 1846, "we can be sure he chose some other place than this." Yet, with its immense swaths of fertile fields and huge resources of **mineral wealth**, Dongbei is metaphorically a treasure house, and this area has been fiercely contested for much of its history by Manchus, Nationalists, Russians, Japanese and Communists. Today the region, comprising **Liaoning**, **Jilin** and **Heilongjiang** provinces, forms an industrial heartland, producing more than a third of the country's heavy machinery, half its coal and oil and most of its military equipment. Economically, Dongbei is perhaps the most important region of China, and with four thousand kilometres of sensitive border territory alongside North Korea and Russia, it's strategically one of the most vulnerable.

People up here are very glad to see visitors; the closing of state-owned factories has resulted in massive lay-offs, and tourism has become one of Dongbei's leading growth industries. A **Manchurian makeover** is underway as the area cashes in on its colourful history. In Liaoning, the thriving port of **Dalian** sports cleaned-up beaches, a cliffside drive and China's best football club. China's window on North Korea, **Dandong** features a promenade on the Yalu River and an incredible Korean War Museum. China's other Forbidden City – the restored Manchu Imperial Palace – and the tombs of the men who established the Qing dynasty draw tourists to Liaoning's otherwise bland capital, **Shenyang**. To the north in Jilin Province, **Jilin** city's riverfront showcases ice-coated trees in winter, and improved ski resorts in the outskirts of town. In the provincial capital, **Changchun**, the Puppet Emperor's Palace memorializes Puyi's reign as "emperor" of the Japanese state Manchukuo. Evidence of Heilongjiang Province's border with Russia can be seen throughout its capital, **Harbin**. A restored central shopping district preserves the city's old architecture, while a history museum set in an Orthodox cathedral makes China's northernmost metropolis known for reasons other than its world-famous **ice lantern festival**.

Dongbei's geography, a terrain of fertile plains, rugged mountains and forests (a third of Heilongjiang is covered in trees), is its other attraction. The region is home to several protected reserves, most famously the mountainous **Changbai Shan Nature Reserve** in Jilin Province near the Korean border, where Lake Tian is nestled in jaw-dropping scenery. **Zhalong Nature**

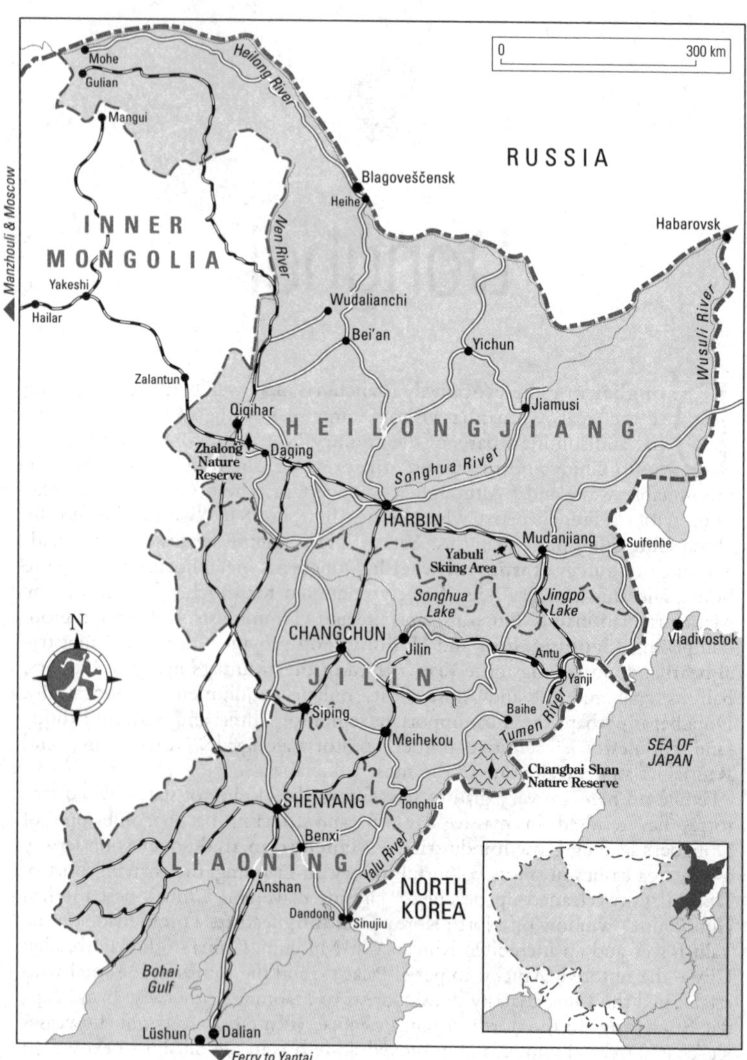

Reserve, in Heilongjiang, is a summer breeding ground for thousands of species of birds, including the rare red-crowned crane.

Visitors to these parts tend to come for quite specific reasons: foreign **students** find an environment free of thick accents and perfect for practising Chinese; **steam-train buffs** will find plenty of trains to get excited about; and keen **hunters**, **hikers** and **bird-watchers** will all find places to indulge their passions. Fans of recent Chinese **history** couldn't choose a better place to visit: Dongbei's past one hundred years of domestic and international conflicts heavily influenced the shape of the PRC today. Those interested in the **Russo-Japanese War** can follow the route of the Japanese advance; if you can find them, bring copies of Jack London's *Reports*, which contains the columns he wrote on assignment for the *San Francisco Examiner*; and *Thirty Years in Moukden* by Dugald Christie. **Puyi**'s autobiography, *From Emperor to Citizen*, lends insight to Manchukuo, and Ha Jin's recent *Ocean of Words* shows what life was like patrolling the Heilongjiang–Siberian border in the tense 1970s. Independent tour companies in each region provide better service and selection, but CITS provides details of their **special-interest tours** to the region; see also Basics, pp.13–14, for more information.

Dongbei's **climate** is one of extremes. In summer it is hot, and in winter it is very, very cold, with temperatures as low as -30°C, and howling Siberian gales. But if you can stand the cold, a trip up here in January has the added attraction of **ice festivals** in Jilin and Harbin, and the whole of winter brings excellent, cheap **skiing**, **sledding** and **skating**. As for **transport**, there's an efficient rail system between the cities and an extensive highway network due to Dongbei's export-based economy. **Hotel prices** used to be outrageous, but with the present attitude towards foreign tourists, cheap, clean dorms and rooms exist in every town. Dongbei **food** is diverse, from fresh crabs in Dalian, to the local river fish *lu zi yu* in Dandong, to mushroom dishes and fresh bread in Harbin, to silkworms in the countryside (a mushy, pasty-tasting local delicacy). Cuisine here is also heavily influenced by neighbouring countries, and every town has a cluster of Korean, Japanese and, up north, Russian restaurants. *KFC* has landed in every major city, as well.

Some history

The history of Manchuria proper begins with **Nurhaci**, a tribal leader who in the sixteenth century united the warring tribes of the northeast against the corrupt central rule of Ming-dynasty Liaoning. He introduced an alphabet based on the Mongol script, administered Manchu law and, by 1625, had created a firm and relatively autonomous government that was in constant confrontation with the Chinese. His successor, Dorgun, the regent of his grandson, Shunchih, went a stage further and with the help of the defeated Ming general, Wu Sangui, marched on Beijing, proclaiming the **Qing dynasty** in 1644 and becoming the first of a long line of Manchu emperors.

Keen to establish the Qing over the whole of China, the first **Manchu emperors** – Shunchih, Kangxi and Qianlong – did their best to assimilate Chinese customs and ideas. They were, however, even more determined to protect their homeland, and so the whole of the northeast was closed to the rest of China. This way they could guard their monopoly on the valuable **ginseng trade**, and keep the Chinese from ploughing up their land and desecrating the graves of their ancestors. But it was a policy that could not last for ever, and the eighteenth century saw increasing migration into Manchuria. By 1878, the laws had been rescinded and the Chinese were moving into the region by the million, escaping the flood-ravaged plains of the south for the fertile land of the northeast.

All this time, Manchuria was much coveted by its neighbours. The **Sino-Japanese War** of 1894 left the Japanese occupying the Liaodong Peninsula in the south of Liaoning Province, and the only way the Chinese could regain it was by turning to **Russia**, also hungry for influence in the area. The deal was that the Russians be allowed to build a rail line linking Vladivostok to the main body of Russia, an arrangement that in fact led to a gradual and, eventually, complete occupation of Manchuria by the imperial Russian armies. This was a bloody affair, marked by atrocities and brutal reprisals, and followed in 1904 by a Japanese declaration of war in an attempt to usurp the Russians' privileges for themselves. The Russo–Japanese War ended in 1905 with a convincing Japanese victory. Japan's designs on Manchuria didn't end there; their population had almost doubled in the last sixty years, and this, coupled with a disastrous economic situation at home and an extreme militaristic regime, led to their invasion of the region in 1932, establishing the puppet state of **Manchukuo**. This regime was characterized by instances of horrific and violent oppression – not least the secret germ warfare research centre in Pingfang, where experiments were conducted on live human subjects. Rice was reserved for the Japanese, and it was a crime for the locals to eat it.

It was only with the establishment of a united front between the **Communists** and the **Guomindang** that Manchuria was finally rid of the Japanese, in 1945, although it was some time (and in spite of a vicious campaign backed by both Russia and the USA against the Communists) before Mao finally took control of the region. Recent history is dominated by relations with Russia. In the brief romance between the two countries in the 1950s, Soviet experts helped the Chinese build factories and workshops in exchange for the region's agricultural products. The efficient, well-designed **Soviet factories**, such as the plant that produces the Liberation Truck in Changchun, remain some of the best in the area today. In the 1960s relations worsened, the Soviets withdrew their technical support, and bitter **border disputes** began, notably around the Ussuri, where hundreds of Russian and Chinese troops died fighting over an insignificant island in the world's first military confrontation between communist states. In addition, an extensive network of nuclear shelters was constructed in northeastern cities. Following the collapse of the Soviet Union, military build-ups around the border areas and state paranoia have lessened, and the shelters have been turned into underground shopping centres. Russian faces can again be seen on the streets, often not as tourists or foreign advisers but **traders**, legal and otherwise, buying up consumer goods to take over the border now that Russia's own manufacturing industry has almost collapsed.

Shenyang

SHENYANG, the capital of Liaoning province and unofficial capital of the northeast, is both a railway junction and banking centre that's served as host to the Manchus, the Russians, the Japanese, the Nationalists and then the Communists. An hour's flight or nine-hour train ride from Beijing, the city likens itself to the capital. As any cabby here will tell you: "We have the only other Imperial Palace in China." Shenyang does resemble the capital, but only in its wide, characterless avenues walled by Soviet-style matchbox buildings.

In fact, the most remarkable thing about Shenyang is that it isn't remarkable at all. All the ingredients for an interesting visit are here: a shopping district known for fashion; the country's most famous dumpling restaurant; China's other Forbidden City, constructed by Manchus before their takeover of the Ming dynasty in the seventeenth century; a stunning monument to Chairman Mao built during the frenzied height of the Cultural Revolution; tombs of two former emperors; architecture left over from Japan's occupation. The list goes on and on. And a list is what Shenyang feels like; a collection of curios out of context in their industrial surroundings.

Though well known in China as an important power base for the more radical hardline factions in Chinese politics (Mao's nephew, Yuanxin, was deputy

Shenyang

Shenyang	沈阳	***shěnyáng***
East Tomb	东陵	*dōng líng*
Imperial Palace	沈阳故宫	*shěnyáng gùgōng*
Liaoning Provincial Museum	辽宁省博物馆	*liáoníngshěng bówùguǎn*
Long-distance bus station	快速客运站	*kuàisù kèyùnzhàn*
North Pagoda	北塔	*běi tǎ*
North Tomb	北陵	*běi líng*
Pagoda of Buddhist Ashes	舍利塔	*shèlì tǎ*
Zhongshan Square	中山广场	*zhōngshān guǎngchǎng*
Accommodation and eating		
Courtyard New World	新世界	*xīnshì jiè*
Dongbei Hotel	东北饭店	*dōngběi fàndiàn*
Holiday Inn	假日饭店	*jiàrì fàndiàn*
Laobian Eating House	老边饺子馆	*lǎobiān jiǎoziguǎn*
Liaoning Hotel	辽宁宾馆	*liáoníng bīnguǎn*
Liaoning Tiyuguan Binguan	辽宁体育馆宾馆	*liáoníng tǐyùguǎn bīnguǎn*
Peace Hotel	和平宾馆	*hépíng bīnguǎn*
Phoenix	凤凰饭店	*fènghuáng fàndiàn*
Traders Hotel	商贸饭店	*shāngmào fàndiàn*

party secretary here until he was thrown in jail in 1976), Shenyang had its real heyday in the early seventeenth century. The city (then known as Mukden) was declared first **capital** of the expanding **Manchu empire** by Nurhaci. He died in 1626, as work on his palace was just beginning, and was succeeded by his eighth son, Abahai, who consolidated and extended Manchu influence across northern China. When the Manchus, having defeated the resident Ming, moved to Beijing in 1644, and established the Qing dynasty, Shenyang became a secondary power centre of steadily declining importance. The city began to take on its modern, industrial role with the arrival of the Russians in the nineteenth century, who made it the centre of their rail-building programme. Years later, the puppets of the Japanese state also set up shop here, exploiting the resources of the surrounding region and building an industrial infrastructure whose profits and products were sent home to Japan. Unlike in the province's secondary cities, Dalian and Dandong, however, little attempt has been made to showcase Shenyang's absorbing history, and the city offers not much to detain you for more than a brief stop.

Arrival and transport

Shenyang **airport**, the busiest in the northeast with flights to Irkutsk, Osaka and Seoul plus daily domestic connections to all major Chinese cities, lies 20km south of the city. It's linked to the CAAC office in the centre by an airport bus (¥15), while a taxi costs ¥80.

Five lines converge on Shenyang's two main **train stations**. You'll arrive first at the **South station**, the larger and more central one, if you've come from Beijing or farther south. The newer **North station**, serving destinations to the north of Shenyang (and the terminus for Beijing trains, which continue here

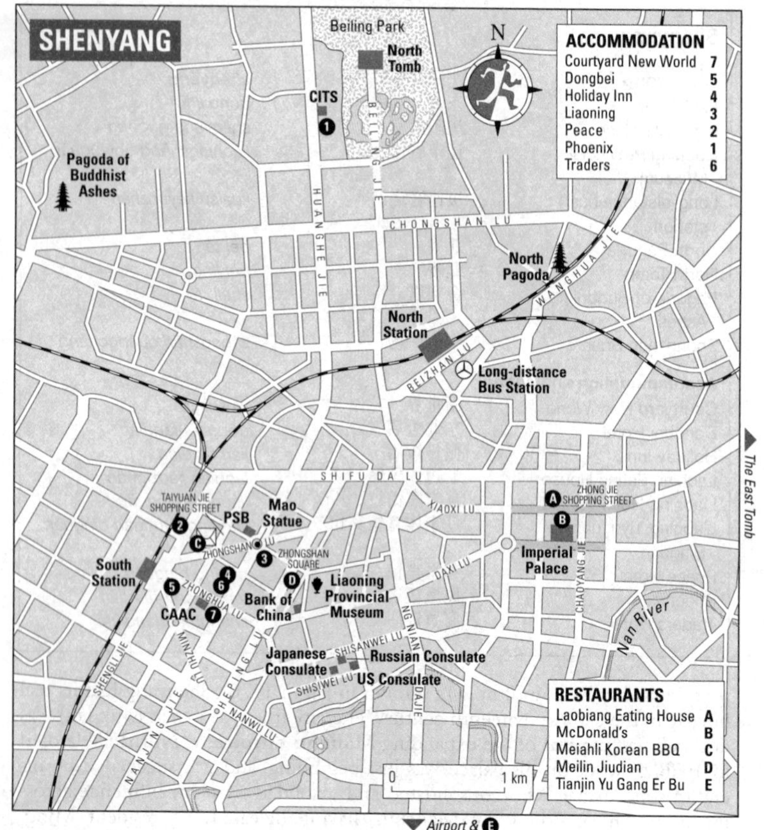

from the South station), is out of the centre; take trolley bus #5 from here to Zhongshan Square and the South station. Bus #203 connects the two stations. Tickets for trains leaving from the North station can be bought from the South station, and vice versa. The North station has an upstairs ticket booth, while the booking office for the South station is in a large hall to the left as you face the station. Make sure you check which station your train leaves from when you buy a ticket. The gleaming, futuristic **long-distance bus station** (referred to locally as the express-bus station) is near the North Station. To get into the centre from here, catch one of the many minibuses plying the route, or take a cab (¥10).

If you're entering the city by train and planning on **moving on** immediately to a major city by bus, get off at the North station, where coaches wait on the east side of the concourse to depart for Beijing (7–8hr; ¥189) and Dalian (5hr; ¥99). To Jilin (4hr 30min; ¥96), Changchun (3hr; ¥71) and Harbin (7hr; ¥130), walk one block south to the long-distance bus station.

Shenyang is very spread out and trying to walk anywhere is frustrating. **Taxis** are widely available, comprised of new VW Santanas. Flagfall is ¥7 for 3km, ¥1 per km thereafter; a taxi to or between most of the sights is around ¥10, though getting to the East Tomb from the South station costs about ¥35. Alternatively, the **local bus** and trolley bus system is extensive and not too crowded. Bus maps can be bought outside the stations.

Accommodation

Several **hotels**, mostly serving tour groups and gangs of businessmen, are clustered around Beiling Park, well out of the centre. It's a quiet area, with few shops around, served by bus #205 from the South station and bus #220, which passes the west side of the North station. The hotels in the city centre are more convenient, though downtown Shenyang is no beauty spot. Several no-frills travellers' hotels are gathered around Zhonghua Lu in front of the South station.

Courtyard New World 2 Nanjing Nanjie Ⓣ024/23869888, Ⓦwww.courtyard.com. Plush four-star hotel near Taiyuan Jie. ❼

Dongbei Fandian 6 Zhonghua Lu Ⓣ024/3839402. Tattered, but in a good location, next to *KFC*. If they won't take you, inquire at the neighbouring facilities, which are similar. Dorm beds from ¥20, ❶

Holiday Inn 204 Nanjing Beilu Ⓣ024/23341888, Ⓕ23341188. New highrise in the heart of town, and featuring Sheyang's best health club. In winter months, rates are slashed in half. ❾

Liaoning Hotel 97 Zhongshan Lu Ⓣ024/23839104, Ⓕ23839103. Shenyang's historic lodging, constructed by the Japanese in 1927 and overlooking the Chairman Mao statue and Zhongshan Square. Rooms are spacious and light. Stop over if only for a look at the furnishings and wood accents – this is the closest thing Shenyang has to a museum. ❾

Peace Hotel 104 Shengli Beijie Ⓣ024/23498888, Ⓕ23837389. The best backpacker place in town. Conveniently near the South train station; turn left at the statue topped by a tank as you exit the station's square, and the hotel is a 5min walk ahead on your left. Staff are very friendly, and you can buy train and plane tickets here. Breakfast included with room. Dorm beds from ¥40, ❸

Phoenix 109 Huanghe Nan Dajie Ⓣ024/86105858, Ⓕ86105340. Plush behemoth near Beiling Park, with a gym, sauna, coffee bar, beauty parlour and a good Western-style pastry shop. They can book transport for guests, and there's a twenty percent discount if you have a student card. ❻

Traders 68 Zhonghua Lu0 Ⓣ024/23412288, Ⓦwww.shangri-la.com. The nicest place to stay in Shenyang; rates include laundry, airport transport and breakfast. Doubles from ¥1400. ❾

The City

Shenyang has some great examples of uncompromising Soviet-style building, and you may well find yourself staying in one. The giant **Mao statue** in **Zhongshan Square** at the city's centre, erected in 1969, is by far the most distinctive landmark, its base lined with strident, blocky peasants, Daqing oilmen, PLA soldiers and students, though the Little Red Books they were waving have mostly been chipped off. Above them, the monolithic Mao stands wrapped in an overcoat, a bald superman whose raised hand makes him look as if he's directing the traffic which swarms around him. Head in the direction he's facing (today, he surveys ads for cell phones, Coke, and Golden Golf "foreign investors villa area"), and you'll hit the city's shopping district, centred around Zhongshan Lu, Zhonghua Lu and Taiyuan Jie, which abound with department stores.

The **Liaoning Provincial Museum** (Tues–Sun 8–11.30am & 1–4.30pm; ¥8), in the heart of the downtown area, is one of the largest museums in the northeast. The three thousand or so exhibits within include embroidery, painting, copperware, pottery and porcelain. Perhaps most interesting are the fragments of polished bone inscribed with characters and used for divination, which are some of the earliest extant examples of written Chinese. South of here, the Nan River marks the southern boundary of the downtown area, with the larger Hun River just farther south.

The Imperial Palace

More rewarding than the city centre are the Manchu structures on the outskirts of Shenyang, starting with the **Imperial Palace** (daily: May, June, Sept & Oct 8.30am–5pm; July & Aug 8.30am–5.30pm; Nov–April 9am–4pm; ¥35), begun in 1626, a miniature replica of Beijing's Forbidden City; it's located at the centre of the old city in the east of town (trolley bus #13 comes here from the South station). The complex divides into three sections: the first, the Cong Zhen Dian, is a low, wooden-fronted hall where the emperor first proclaimed the Qing dynasty and which was used by ministers to discuss state affairs. Beyond here, in the second courtyard, stands the Phoenix Tower, most formal of the ceremonial halls, and the Qing Ning Lou, which housed bedrooms for the emperor and his concubines. In the eastern section of the complex, the Da Zheng Dian is a squat, octagonal, wooden structure in vivid red and lacquered gold, with two pillars cut with writhing golden dragons in high relief. Here the emperor Shunchih was crowned before seizing Beijing – and the empire – in 1644. Just in front stand ten square pavilions, the Shi Wang, once used as offices by the chieftains of the Eight Banners (districts) of the Empire, and now housing a collection of bizarrely shaped swords and pikes. Shenyang's other good shopping area can be found just east of here, at the pedestrian-only **Zhong Jie**. Dating back to 1636, when it was known as Siping Jie, the street is now fronted by department stores selling Western clothing and also features a branch of the *Laobian Jiaozi* (meat dumplings) chain of restaurants.

The Tombs

From the palace, bus #213 will get you to the **North Tomb** (daily 7.30am–5pm; ¥10) in **Beiling Park** (park entry ¥2), or you can take bus #220 or trolley bus #6 direct from the South station. Abahai is buried here and, though it was his father who was the real pioneering imperialist, Abahai certainly got the best tomb. The well-preserved complex, constructed in 1643, is entered through a gate to the south, either side of which are pavilions; the easternmost was for visiting emperors to wash and refresh themselves, the westernmost for sacrifices of pigs and sheep. A drive flanked with statues of camels, elephants, horses and lions leads to the Long En Hall, which contains an altar for offerings and the spirit tablets of the emperor and his wife. Their tree-covered burial mounds are at the rear, where you'll also see a fine dragon screen. Winter in Beiling Park sees snow sculptures and ice skates for rent (¥5), as well as *pali* (¥30 for large ones), wooden sleds with blades on the bottom that you move while seated using two metal ski poles.

The more restrained **East Tomb**, built in 1629 as the last resting place of Nurhaci, is set among conifers in **Dongling Park** (daily 8am–4pm; ¥12), in the east of the city, reached by bus #218 from its stop one block north and one block east of the Imperial Palace. The tomb is less monumental in layout and shows more signs of age than the North Tomb, but it's still impressive, with fortified walls and a three-storey tower. One hundred and eight steps (the number of beads on a Buddhist rosary) lead into the main gate, while all around the tomb are walking trails into the woods covering Mount Tianzhu – a hill, really.

The rest of the city

Shenyang's other sights are hardly worth tracking down unless you have time to spare or are in the area. There were formerly four pagodas and four temples at the limits of the city, one on each side. The only one that remains in a reasonable state is the **North Pagoda** (daily 9am–3pm; ¥5), which contains a sky and earth Buddha (Tiandifu), a carnal image of twin Buddhas rarely seen in Chinese temples. The pagoda is just to the south of the long-distance bus station, though to see the Buddhas you'll have to trouble the lone attendant to unlock the gate.

Also in the north of the city is the **Pagoda of Buddhist Ashes** (daily 8.30am–4pm; ¥4), a thirteen-storey, fifty-metre-high hollow brick pagoda constructed in 1044 AD during the Liao dynasty. It's in good shape, though stained from pollution. On display inside are relics that were found when the pagoda was restored, including a fine, gold-plated, copper Buddha. Bus #205 from the South station will get you nearby; get off when you see the river and walk across the bridge.

Eating

Sadly, eating in Shenyang is a bit of a let-down – there aren't nearly enough places where you can sample fine northeastern cuisine. Ironically, it's perfectly straightforward to get Western fast food. Of the many *KFC*s here, the closest one to the South station is 100m away on Zhonghua Lu, with another one around the corner on Taiyuan Jie. *McDonald's* is on Zhong Jie, next door to yet another *KFC*.

Laobian Eating House 6 Zhong Jie ⓣ024/24843956 ext 621. Shenyang's most famous restaurant, whose noted *jiaozi* cost ¥50 for a *jin*, though you can order a fraction of that and pay accordingly, prior to arrival of your food. The restaurant may be famous, but its decor and service are terrible. The branch at 55 Shengli Beijie, across from the *Peace Hotel*, is better.

Meiahli Korean BBQ 62 Kunming Beijie. They serve *zaocha* here, a sweet, fruity tea that goes well with platefuls of beef and bottles of beer. Excellent service and inexpensive – dinner for two costs around ¥50. It's easily spotted as it's next door to a *USA Beef Noodle King*, signed in English.

Meilin Jiudian 109 Heping Beidajie. Specializes in Shanghai-style vegetarian dishes, with pleasant staff and decor.

Tianjin Yu Gang Er Bu Inside the *Liaoning Tiyuguan Binguan*, 284 Qingnian Lu. Shenyang's most popular fish restaurant; dinner for two here comes to around ¥100.

Listings

Airlines CAAC is at 117 Zhonghua Lu (daily 8am–6pm). Plane tickets can also be bought from hotels or from CITS (see below).

Banks and exchange Bank of China, 75 Heping Bei Dajie (Mon–Fri 8.30am–12pm & 1–5.30pm, Sat & Sun 9am–3.30pm).

Bike rental Turn left as you exit the South station and there's a stand renting operable clunkers for ¥10 per day, with a ¥100 deposit.

Consulates The Japanese, North Korean and US consulates are all in the same road, Shisiwei Lu, in the south of the city. At time of writing, the Russian consulate (Tues–Thurs 9am–11.30am & 1.30–5pm; ⓣ024/23221198) was moving nearby to Shisanwei Lu from its old haunt in the *Phoenix Hotel*. Reports on the ease with which Russian visas can be obtained here are mixed, so it's better to apply in Beijing.

Internet access Walk from the South train station down Zhonghua Lu, and a block past KFC on the opposite side is a 24hr Internet cafe (¥3/hr) – look for the orchid sign reading *wangba*, then head upstairs to the second floor.

Mail and telephones Shenyang's main post office is at 32 Zhongshan Lu (Mon–Fri 8am–6pm), and there's a 24hr telecoms service inside.

PSB On Zhongshan Lu, by the Mao statue (Mon–Fri 8am–5pm).

Travel agents The CITS office at 113 Nan Huanghe Lu (ⓣ024/86809383, ⓕ86808772), in the same compound as the *Phoenix Hotel*, is the central branch for Liaoning Province, though they offer speciality tours of the northeast only to large groups (twenty or more people). The travel service in the *Peace Hotel* is friendlier and more accommodating.

Dalian and around

Clean, modern and rich **DALIAN** is a large, sprawling city on the Yellow Sea. It's one of China's most cosmopolitan cities, partly because it has changed hands so often; as the only **ice-free port** in the region it was eagerly sought by the foreign powers who held sway over China in the nineteenth century. The Japanese gained the city in 1895, only to lose it a few years later to the Russians, who saw it as an alternative to ice-bound Vladivostok. In 1905, after decisively defeating the Russian navy, the Japanese wrested it back and remained in control for long enough to complete the construction of the port facilities. After World War II, the Soviet Union occupied the city for ten years, finally withdrawing when Sino–Soviet relations improved. Today Dalian is busier than ever, the funnel for Dongbei's enormous natural and mineral wealth and an industrial producer in its own right, specializing in petrochemicals and shipbuilding. The city is booming as fast as any in China and, though the "foreign devils" are still here, they're now invited: Dalian has been designated a Special Economic Zone, one of China's "open-door" cities with regulations designed to attract overseas investment.

Still, Dalian manages to be a leisurely place, popular with tourists who come here for the scenic spots and **beaches** outside the city, to recover their health in sanatoriums and to stuff themselves on seafood. The city is also known for **soccer**, which explains the large sculptures of footballs you'll see around – Dalian's team, Shide (formerly Wanda), has been the champion of the Chinese league more times than not in recent years, and contributed six players to the country's World Cup squad. The city holds two **festivals**: the Locust Flower Festival in spring is the time to visit the city's parks, and the International

Dalian and around

Dalian	大连	***dàlián***
Black Coral Reef	黑石礁	*hēishí jiāo*
People's Square	人民广场	*rénmín guǎngchǎng*
Sun Asia Ocean World Aquarium	圣亚海洋世界	*shèngyà hǎiyáng shìjiè*
Tiger Beach	老虎滩	*lǎohǔ tān*
Zhongshan Square	中山广场	*zhōngshān guǎngchǎng*
Lüshun	旅顺	***lǚshùn***
Japanese Russian Imperial Prison Site	日俄监狱旧址	*rì é jiānyù jiùzhǐ*
Accommodation and eating		
Dalian Binguan	大连宾馆	*dàlián bīnguǎn*
Everyday Fishing Port Restaurant	天天渔港酒楼	*tiāntiānyúgǎng jiǔlóu*
Friendship Hotel	友谊饭店	*yǒuyì fàndiàn*
Furama	富丽华大酒店	*fùlìhuá dàjiǔdiàn*
Golden Plaza	大连天富大酒店	*dàlián tiānfù dàjiǔdiàn*
Huanan Youth Hostel	华南国际青年旅舍	*huánéng guójìqīngnián lǚshè*
Huaneng	华能饭店	*huánéng fàndiàn*
Ramada	九州华美达酒店	*jiǔzhōu huáměidá jiǔdiàn*
Yaduda Fandian	亚都大饭店	*yàdū dàfàndiàn*

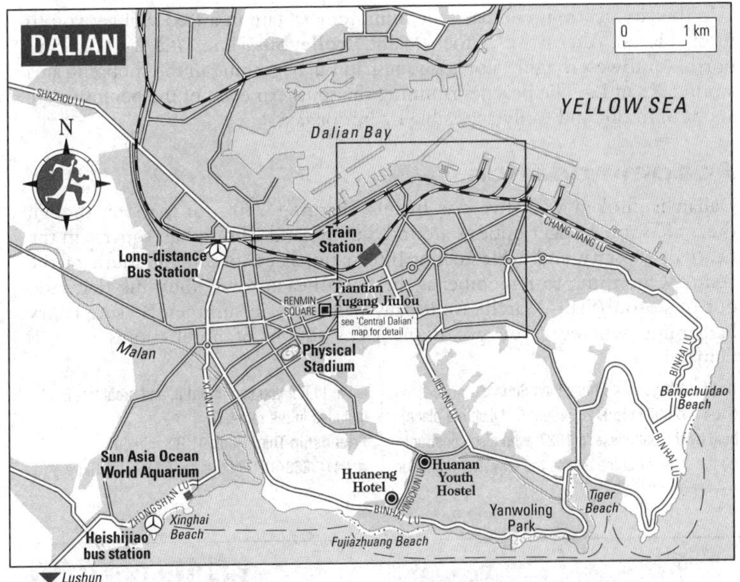

Fashion Festival around September 10 sees fashion models parading in the streets. Dalian's brand-new scenic drive, **Binhai Lu**, hugs the cliffs of the Yellow Sea, winding 40km past the villas of Party bigwigs as well as Shide stars. The city also boasts a large **aquarium**, a new **zoo** and easy connections to the town of **Lüshun**.

Tourists looking for relics from Dalian's colonial past will be disappointed, however: unlike other treaty ports such as Shanghai, Dalian is looking firmly forward to the future. Plans for a history museum have been tabled, a topic that your taxi driver will be sure to comment on once he's finished heralding Shide or the former mayor, Bo Xili, whose modernizing handiwork won him promotion to the provincial government.

Arrival and transport

The city sits at the southern tip of the Liaodong peninsula, filling a piece of land that's shaped like a tiger's head – the result, local legend has it, of a mermaid flattening the animal into land as punishment for eating the fiancé of a beautiful girl. The city has four main sections: **Zhongshan Square**, at the tiger's eye, **Renmin Square**, at his ear, the **beaches**, at his mouth and throat, and **Heishijiao** (Black Coral Reef) across the Malan He (Horse Fence River) to the west of town.

A taxi to or from the **airport**, 10km northeast of the city, should cost ¥25, or there's a regular airport bus (¥10) to and from the CAAC office. The main **train station** (there are three in total) and **ferry terminal** are within 1km of Zhongshan Square. The **long-distance bus station**, served by ancient provincial buses, is located at the terminus of bus #201 west from the train station; if you're on an express bus from Beijing, you'll probably be dropped at train station. There's also a bus station, on Zhongshan Lu, near Xinghai Beach in Heishijiao, from where buses to Lüshun depart.

As the city centre is compact, the minimum ¥8 fare in a **taxi** will get you to most places. Alternatively, the quaint **trolleybus** line, #202 (¥2), runs north–southwest roughly along Zhongshan Lu, beginning in the shopping area around Xi'an Lu. The beaches rimming the southern edge of the peninsula are about 5km out and easily accessible by bus or taxi.

Accommodation

Dalian is choked with five-star **hotels** charging ¥800 for a room, though there are some budget options around Shengli and Zhongshan squares in the heart of the city, and a Hostelling International establishment south of the centre. One thing to remember is that it's a beach town, meaning that rates out of season (Sept–March) are usually half those in summer. Be sure to try bargaining wherever you go, as the city's supply of hotel rooms exceeds demand.

Dalian Binguan 4 Zhongshan Square ⓣ0411/2633111, ⓕ2634363. A stylish old place, built by the Japanese in 1927, who also constructed the Bank of China across the way. The grandeur is worth it if you can afford it, and breakfast is included in the rates. ❻

Friendship Third Floor, 91 Renmin Lu ⓣ0411/2634121. Above the Friendship Store.

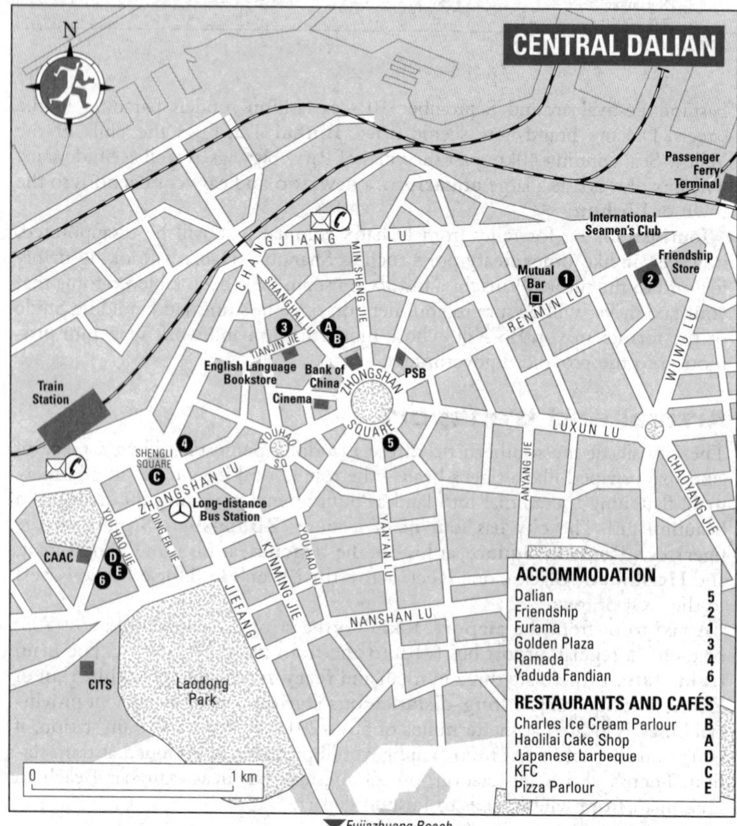

Nobody here speaks English and the place isn't very efficiently run, but the rooms are nice enough. The closest mid-range accommodation to the ferry terminal. Dorm beds ¥160, ❺

Furama 60 Renmin Lu ⓣ0411/2630888, ⓕ2804455. A very upscale Japanese hotel on Renmin Lu, this place has every imaginable facility, a lobby big enough for Shide to play in and palatial rooms. ❽

Golden Plaza 189 Tianjin Jie ⓣ0411/2813188, ⓕ2648288. Nice three-star hotel right in the heart of the shopping area. Indoor pool and gym. ❽

Huanan Youth Hostel 1 Yingchun Lu ⓣ0411/2496830, ⓕ2494665. Dalian's new HI entry is 4km from the centre, tucked away in a valley near the zoo and Fujiazhuang Beach. To get here, take bus #702 from the train station and get off at Nanshidao Jie stop; the hostel is on the south side of the road. A taxi costs ¥12 from the centre or ¥16 from the port. Rooms in the hostel range from singles to quads and feature carpeting, a/c, TV, hot water and bathroom. They also provide Internet access facilities, a laundry room and bike rental. Dorm beds from ¥40, ❺

Huaneng 2 Binhai Lu ⓣ0411/2401945, ⓕ2400873. Two-star hotel overlooking Fujiazhuang Beach. ❻

Ramada 18 Shengli Square ⓣ0411/2808888, ⓦwww.ramada-dalian.com. Four-star luxury in the heart of town next to the train station, overlooking Shengli Square. ❾

Yaduda Fandian 126 Zhongshan Lu ⓣ0411/3633560. Clean, inexpensive and conveniently located near Shengli Square and the train station, with half-price discounts in the winter. Clean bathrooms with good hot water in the doubles. Dorm beds ¥50, ❹

The City

The hub of Dalian is Zhongshan Square (really a circle) and its spokes are some of the most interesting streets in the city. Japanese and Russian buildings, German cars, *KFC* and *McDonald's*, girls in miniskirts and Western dance music blaring from the shops give the area an international flavour. The main **shopping** streets are Shanghai Lu and Tianjin Jie, just to the northwest, where you'll find designer-label clothes and shoes, as well as stalls selling a wide range of pop music, Chinese and Western. The English Language Bookstore, at 178 Tianjin Jie, has novels in English on the first floor and Japanese magazines on the second. There are two Friendship Stores, both on Renmin Lu; the newer one, next to the *Furama Hotel,* is huge.

Follow Zhongshan Lu west past **Shengli Square**, the train station, and the meandering shopping lanes of Qing Er Jie to reach Renmin Square, large, grassy and lit with footlights at night. The neighbourhoods to the south retain their colonial architecture and narrow, tree-lined streets, making for excellent wandering. East of Renmin Square is **Laodong Park**, an open, meadowy area on the route of buses #2, 5 and 403. Across from the park gate is a good **night market** (daily 5–9.30pm).

The beaches

Dalian's main attraction, its **beaches**, are clean, sandy and packed in the summertime. All are free except for **Xinghai** and **Fujiazhuang** beaches, where you'll need to buy an inexpensive entrance ticket. To reach them, take bus #801 (spring & summer only; ¥20), which leaves from the train station, and circles the entire town, with multiple stops along the way. Alternatively, a taxi will cost between ¥20 and ¥30, depending on which beach you go to.

Bangchuidao and Tiger beaches

From east to west around the coast on Binhai Lu, the first beach is **Bangchuidao**, next to the golf course, and formerly reserved for cadres but now open to the public. Highly developed **Tiger Beach**, next, can be reached on buses #2, #4, #402 or #801. The funfair here, which includes a waterborne dodgem ride, has a whopping ¥80 entrance charge, which doesn't include any rides but includes admission to the new **Arctic aquarium**, a navy ship you can board and, west on Binhai Lu, an **aviary** (daily: May–Oct 8am–5pm; Nov–April 8.30am–4.30pm). Tandem and mountain bikes are for rent along the waterfront for ¥20 an hour, and there are boat trips out to Bangchui Island and beyond (from ¥40); routes and prices are posted at ticket kiosks.

Yanwoling Park and Fujiazhuang Beach

From Tiger Beach, it's a beautiful, if strenuous, seven-kilometre hike along Binhai Lu to Fujiazhuang Beach. The turquoise sea stretches before you to the south, while the north side of the road is green year-round with trees and new grass. You'll cross Beida Bridge, a suspended beauty, before winding 3km up to **Yanwoling Park** (daily dawn–dusk; ¥10). Once you're past the statue made of shells of a little boy with seagulls, there's a profusion of maintained trails and stairs to take you down to the sea. One particularly nice hike, signed in English, ends up at Sunken Boat Rock, a cove where starfish cling to rocks and the only sounds are those of the waves. Don't attempt to swim here, however, as a strong current 50m out has claimed lives.

Continuing 4km west on Binhai Lu, you wind downhill to **Fujiazhuang Beach** (daily dawn–dusk; ¥5), less developed than Tiger Beach and more secluded, sheltered from the wind in a rocky bay. You can charter speedboats from here to take you to outlying islands – a trip to Xinghai Beach farther west and back costs ¥40. Prices are flexible, however, and bargaining is accepted. The beach has the usual complement of kitsch stalls and hawkers, as well as tents on the sand which you can rent by the hour. At the back of the beach are plenty of good, open-air seafood restaurants; expect to pay around ¥80 for a meal for two.

Xinghai Beach and beyond

Binhai Lu continues 5km west to the Ma Lan River, where it merges into busy, wide Zhongshan Lu. **Xinghai Beach,** part of a large new park, is 3km beyond the rivermouth. Coming from downtown, trolleybus #202 begins on Xi'an Lu, north of the Changjiang Lu intersection. This new line, aimed at tourists, is the nicest way of getting to **Xinghai Park** (daily 7am–9pm; ¥10). Besides a Ferris wheel, rides, souvenir stands and restaurants, it features **Sun Asia Ocean World** (Mon–Fri 9am–4pm, Sat & Sun until 4.30pm; adults ¥80, children ¥40), a New Zealand/Hong Kong/Chinese joint venture boasting more than two hundred species of marine life and a moving observation platform within an 118-metre underwater tunnel in the main tank. West of the park is **Heishijiao**, a part of the city undergoing a massive modernizing facelift.

Eating, drinking and entertainment

Dalian is full of **restaurants** and **fast food** places, especially around Tianjin Jie, where you'll also find cheap food stalls. Qing Er Jie, leading south from the train station, has lots of Hong Kong and Shanghai-style snack places, and the intersection of Youhao Jie and Zhongshan Lu features a pizza parlour and Japanese barbecue; both have bright signs in English. Down Shanghai Lu, ice cream costs ¥4 a scoop at the *Charles Ice Cream* Parlour, while a coffee here is ¥5 – it's a good place to hang out and write letters, and there's a no-smoking policy. Also along the road, at no. 15, is a branch of the *Haolilai Cake Shop*.

For **seafood** head down to the beaches or try the pricey hotel restaurants, but don't miss *Tiantian Yugang Jiulou* (*Everyday Fishing Port Restaurant*) at 3 Gao Er Ji Lu, near Renmin Square (☎0411/3643779). There are two parts to the restaurant: choose the cosier, older section with the red brick facade. A pound of fresh steamed crab costs ¥45, but be warned, you'll have to shell and eat the thing with chopsticks – wear old clothes. A dinner for two with drinks comes to around ¥150. If this doesn't appeal, you might want to check out a stretch of **Korean BBQ joints** two blocks west – simply follow the smoke and bustle, and the touts out front will wave you in like a taxing 747.

For **nightlife**, Dalian has lots of bars in all parts of the city. You might start at the *Mutual Bar*, on the corner of Renmin Lu and San Sheng Jie, east of Zhongshan Square, which has tattooed, English-speaking bartenders, live music, and bottled beers from around the world. *Noah's Ark Bar and Café*, across the street from the southern edge of People's Square, is also a favourite with locals. Look for the wooden wagon at the entrance, beside a flower market.

Listings

Airlines CAAC is at 143 Zhongshan Lu (Mon–Sat 7.30am–4.30pm; Ⓣ0411/6665558). The new Friendship Store, Renmin Lu, also has an airline booking office.
Banks and exchange The Bank of China is at 9 Zhongshan Square (Mon–Fri 8.30am–noon & 1–5pm). Outside office hours you can change money and traveller's cheques at the *Dalian Binguan* opposite. The new Friendship Store on Renmin Lu also has a money exchange.
Buses Local buses leave from the bus station between 5am and 9am, and tickets can be bought the night before to avoid queues. If you're moving on to a major city by bus, head to Shengli Square, opposite the train statin, where luxury buses depart throughout the day from the north and east sides of the square; tickets can be bought on the bus. For the service to Beijing (9hr; ¥210), you can buy tickets from the kiosk in front of the post office, on the west side of the train-station concourse.
Ferries The ferry service to Yantai and Qingdao is cheaper and much faster than the train. Tickets can be bought in advance from the passenger-ferry terminal on Yimin Jie in the northeast of the city. CITS will only book first- and second-class tickets, but third class is comfortable enough and worth considering. The best service is the express to Yantai (daily; 3hr; ¥189).
Internet access Walk south on Yan'an Lu from Zhongshan Square, or take bus #23, #29 or #901 to the intersection of Nanshan Jie, where the E Bar is one of many Internet cafés in this area.
Mail and telephones The post office (Mon–Sat 8am–6pm) is next to the main train station, and there's a 24hr telecommunications office next door.
PSB Centrally located right on Zhongshan Square.
Soccer The Physical Stadium, just southwest of Renmin Square on Wu Si Lu, is the venue for Dalian Shide matches from late March until October, with good seats going for ¥40 – buy tickets at the stadium itself.
Trains Tickets are easy to buy at the main train station, located north of Shengli Square. The ticket windows are on the ground floor, outside and to the left of the station's main entrance.
Travel agents The CITS office on the fourth floor at 1 Changtong Jie (daily 8.30–11.30am & 1–4.30pm; Ⓣ0411/3687868, Ⓕ3637631) will book tickets for onward travel. They're also at 35 Yan'an Lu.

Lüshun

The port city of **LÜSHUN**, a forty-kilometre bus ride south of Dalian, makes up for the latter's lack of attention to the past. It was near Lüshun that the Japanese shocked the world by defeating the Russians in a naval battle in 1904. This was the beginning of a bloody campaign that ended in Shenyang, where the tsar at last surrendered in 1905. Northeast China was subsequently in the hands of the Japanese, who ruled the region for the next forty years. The main

> As the authorities have sometimes been known to treat Lüshun as a closed military zone, detaining visiting foreigners, it's essential to **ask the PSB** in Dalian about the current situation before deciding whether to visit Lüshun.

reason tourists interested in the **Russo-Japanese War** come is to visit the town's prison camp turned museum, commemorating those who were interned here.

The Town

Lüshun today is a quiet place, largely unchanged from its colonial past as Port Arthur, with one main square fronted by Japanese-style buildings. The main highlight is the **Japanese Russian Imperial Prison Site**, on a small hill in the north of town (daily 8am–4.30pm; ¥15), a five-minute taxi ride from the bus station. Half of the camp was built by the Russians in 1902 as a prison for Chinese; from 1905 to 1945 it was enlarged by Japan, who used it to hold Chinese, Russians and dissidents from Japan opposed to the emperor; finally, the Communists used the prison to hold Chinese – you can still read, under the neat squares of burgundy paint attempting to block it out, "Mao Ze Dong Live Forever!" Other slogans of the Cultural Revolution have been painted over throughout the camp. The prison also has a torture room, a gallows with skeletons of victims on display, and a 1914 Model T Ford that belonged to the Japanese warden, in front of which you can have your picture taken for ¥14. There's a tour of the compound and photographs on display, though note that the commentary is in Chinese only.

Lüshun also has a **Tomb for Russian Martyrs**, in memory of the soldiers who died to liberate the city in 1945, located west of the prison. Rows of cannon and other fortifications left by the Japanese sit atop **Baiyun Shan**, a hill overlooking the Yellow Sea near the centre of town. It's not a long walk from the bus station but involves a considerable hike uphill to the battlements.

Practicalities

Buses from Dalian's Heishijiao bus station make the run to Lüshun in an hour (every 15min; ¥7). From Dalian's centre, take trolleybus #202 or buses #28 or #406, and get off at the *KFC* on the north side of Zhongshan Lu; the bus station is across the road, 50m ahead on your left. The road between the towns is lined with old Japanese villas since turned into farmhouses or stables, and you can see the sea for some of the ride. From Lüshun, buses return to Dalian from the bus station in the centre of town frequently. Buy your ticket from the window in the station (¥8). **Taxis** around Lüshun charge a minimum of ¥5, covering the trip from the bus station to the prison, for example, while a trip up to Baiyun Shan is ¥16. There are no **restaurants** near Lüshun's sights; however, fruit and noodles can be bought around the bus station and the area fronting the town's central square.

Dandong

An obscure port tucked away in the corner of Liaoning province at the confluence of the Yalu River and the Yellow Sea, **DANDONG** is of interest to travellers for its proximity to North Korea – the Korean city of **Sinuiju** (Xinyizhou in Chinese) lies on the other side of the Yalu River – and its convenience as a departure point for the Changbai Shan Nature Reserve (see p.211).

The place is a sort of Hong Kong of the northeast, all things being relative, and as such a tourist centre. South Koreans come here to look across at their

Dandong		
Dandong	丹东	***dāndōng***
Culture Square	文化广场	*wénhuà guǎngchǎng*
Museum to Commemorate Aiding Korea Against US Aggression	抗美援朝纪念馆	*kàngměi yuáncháo jìniànguǎn*
Old Yalu Bridge	鸭绿断桥	*yālù duànqiáo*
Yalu River Park	鸭绿江公园	*yālùjiāng gōngyuán*
Accommodation, eating and drinking		
Dantiedasha Hotel	丹铁大厦	*dāntiě dàshà*
Donghai Yucun	东海渔村	*dōnghǎi yúcūn*
Guolü Hotel	国旅宾馆	*guólǚ bīnguǎn*
Hong Kong Coffee House	香港咖啡厅	*xiānggǎng kāfēitīng*
Jinfangzhou Hotel	金方舟酒店	*jīnfāngzhōu jiǔdiàn*
Taiba Shaokao Dian	太白烧烤店	*tàibá shāokǎodiàn*
Wooden Guitar Bar	木吉它酒吧	*mùjíta jiǔbā*
Yalu River Guesthouse	鸭绿江大厦	*yālùjiāng dàshà*
Zhonglian Hotel	中联大酒店	*zhōnglián dàjiǔdiàn*

northern neighbour, and it's the first stop on the North Korean tourist trail through China. The Chinese come here just to see the border of their country. A strong **Korean** influence can be felt in the city, from shops to eateries. The promenade of the Yalu River is packed with games, parks, modern restaurants and even a coffee house that shows North Korean TV as entertainment. This little city may soon have its day as it's intended that an ambitious new highway and undersea tunnel network will pass through, allowing trains to travel from Beijing, through Korea, all the way to Tokyo. In September 2002 there was even talk of making Sinuiju – which is planned to become a free-market enclave within North Korea – accessible to foreigners without requiring visas, though this had yet to materialize at time of writing; if you've an interest in visiting the place, it's best to check the current situation with CITS, who run their own tours into North Korea (see p.206).

The City

Dandong is small enough to feel human in scale, and the tree-lined main streets are uncrowded, clean and prosperous, making it a worthwhile weekend trip out of Beijing or a stopover while touring the sooty northeast. Recent development, however, is impinging on this tranquility as domestic tourists pour in to stare at North Korea. Its presence just over the water is the city's most intriguing diversion, and vendors along the riverfront promenade sell North Korean stamps, with slogans in Korean like "Become human gun bombs!" North Korean TV, which you can pick up on hotel sets, consists of a string of programmes dedicated to reporting the superhuman achievements of the country's leaders, with a continuing obsession for its president-for-life, Kim Il Sum, dead since 1994.

It used to be that the nearest you could get to the Hermit Kingdom without a visa was halfway across the river on the **Old Yalu Bridge** (¥15) in the south

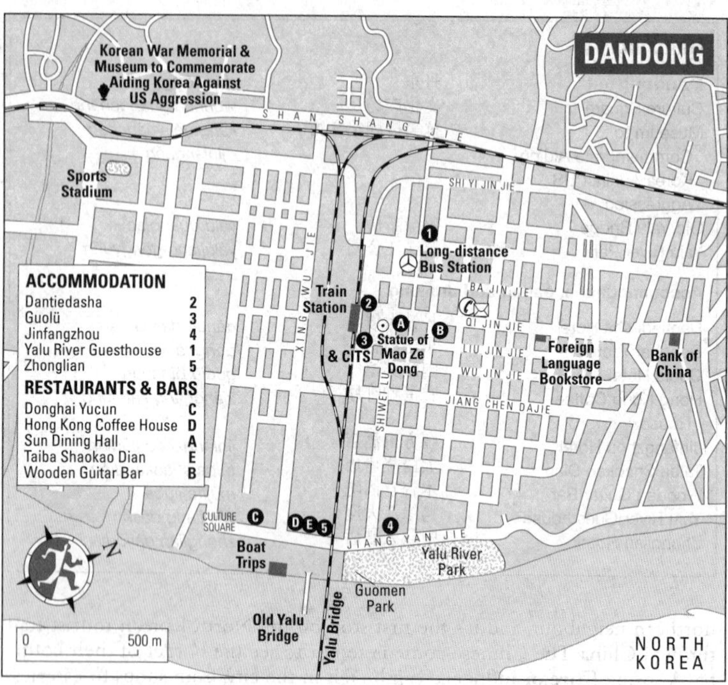

of town, next to the new bridge. The Koreans have dismantled their half but the Chinese have left theirs as a memorial, replete with thirty framed photos of its original construction by the Japanese in 1911, when the town was called Andong. The bridge ends at a tangled mass of metal resulting from the American bombing in 1950 in response to the Chinese entering the Korean War. Several viewing platforms, with picnic tables, are on site, along with Chinese entrepreneurs who charge ¥1 for a few minutes' staring at Sinuiju through a telescope. You can also take a **boat trip** across the river; boats (¥8 for a large one that leaves when full, ¥18 per person for a zippy two-seater) set out from all along Dandong's promenade by the bridge from 8am onwards. The boats take you into North Korean waters to within a metre of shore, where you can do your part for international relations by waving at the teenage soldiers shouldering automatic rifles. Photography is allowed, but most foreign tourists keep their camera lenses closed for shame of the sad plight of Sinuiju's shore: there isn't much to see, save for some rusting ships and listless civilians pointing at their stomachs.

The Dandong side of the river looks like a boomtown in comparison. The riverside by the bridges is the most scenic area, full of strolling tourists, particularly in the early evening. Nearby is **Yalu River Park** where you can drive bumper cars and pay ¥1 to sit on a patch of downy green grass. At the western end of the riverside promenade, **Culture Square** is the well-lit and more cheerful local hangout in the evening, with kids riding around in buggies and young guys playing hacky sack.

The Museum to Commemorate Aiding North Korea

Due to its tourist trade as the keyhole of North Korea, Dandong is a city of contradictions, and nowhere is this more evident than at the huge, macabre **Museum to Commemorate Aiding Korea Against US Aggression** (daily: summer 8am–4pm; winter 8.30am—3.30pm; ¥20; ⓣ0415/2150510) in a compound in the northwest of the city. You can get here on buses #1, #3, #4 or #5 from the station; get off by the sports stadium and walk north for five minutes. At the entrance to the compound, next to President Jiang Ze Min's large plaque of calligraphy swearing eternal North Korean–Sino friendship, ice-cold Coca-Colas are for sale. The gleaming museum, built in 1993, has nine exhibition halls on the **Korean War**, full of maps, plans, dioramas, machine guns, hand grenades, gory photographs and sculptures of lantern-jawed Chinese and Korean soldiers. Everything is labelled in Chinese; the only English in evidence is on Chinese propaganda which was dropped behind the American lines, in which worried wives wonder what their husbands are fighting for, and on the United Nations official declaration of war, in the first hall, which is the only written record in the entire museum of the trifling historical detail that the North Koreans kicked off the war by invading the South.

The whole place feels like a relic of the Cold War. The opening hall has the catchy ditty "Defeat Wolf-Hearted America" spelled out on marble. Hall five is a trench simulation, while in hall eight an impressive revolving panorama shows Korean and Chinese soldiers hammering American aggressors. Next door is a display of North Korean folk art, including dolls and distinctive children's shoes. The final hall is a memorial to individual Chinese soldiers, sanctified national heroes, whose photographs are printed next to descriptions of their deeds. A couple of MiGs and some Red Army tanks sit in a compound to the side of the museum.

A gleaming structure on **Huaiyuan Shan**, behind the museum, marks a graveyard containing the remains of more than 10,000 Chinese soldiers, and close by the museum is an inscribed square column, the **Resist-America, Aid Korea Memorial** (¥2 allows you access to the grounds of the monument).

Practicalities

Arriving at Dandong **train station**, or at the **long-distance bus station** just to the north, puts you right in the centre of town, a gleaming marble-paved square featuring a statue of Mao Zedong, close to the least expensive hotels and about 1km north of the Yalu River. Dandong has a small **airport**, and there's a **ferry terminal** 38km away, where vessels from South Korea dock. **Taxis** in Dandong charge a minimum of ¥5, which is sufficient for rides in town.

Most facilities, including the **Bank of China** and **post and telecommunications offices** (daily 8am–5.30pm) are on Qi Jin Jie, the main road running east from the station and site of a bustling **night market**. There are branches of the bank and post office at Culture Square as well. You can also change US, Hong Kong and Japanese money at the *Yalu River Hotel*.

Accommodation

Among the most convenient **places to stay** in Dandong is the *Guolü* (ⓣ0415/2122166; ❸, dorm beds ¥40), right next to the train station. It's old but ordered, though the staff could try a bit harder. Skip the downstairs restaurant. Budget options in Dandong are many, starting with the clean *Dantiedasha* (ⓣ0415/2131031 ext 320; ❷, dorm beds ¥25) in the train station itself. If you

Moving on from Dandong

CITS (Ⓣ0415/2135854), in front of the *Guolü Hotel*, runs a ten-day **tour** which takes in Sinuiju, Pyongyang and Mount Kumgang in **North Korea**. Going on such rigidly organized tours is probably the only way you'll ever get into the country, but they aren't cheap – figure on spending at least ¥6000, or ¥2100 for three days in Pyongyang. Day-trips into Sinuiju go from ¥450, but they're not really worth bothering with – you see little more than a listless factory town, introduced by a paranoid North Korean guide unwilling to answer questions. CITS will help you sort out your **visa**, but they need at least two weeks' notice. Note that, at time of writing, applications by US citizens for North Korean visas are not granted.

Dandong is well connected to northeast China, with **trains** arriving and departing daily. Train tickets are easy enough to get from the train station, and can also be booked through CITS. There are twice-weekly **flights** to Beijing, Chengdu, Sanya, Shanghai and Shenzhen; book tickets via CITS or call Ⓣ0415/2123427 to reach the ticket counter of the airport. If you're planning to head off to the **Changbai Shan Nature Reserve**, you'll need to spend the night in Dandong and then get the 6.30am bus (#804) to **Tonghua** (8hr; ¥40). Alternatively, bus #909 leaves at 8.50am (¥45). Buy a ticket the night before from the efficient booking office at the bus station. VW Santanas heading to **Shenyang** ply for passengers on the west side of the station concourse (¥50).

By ferry

A Korean company runs the *Oriental Pearl* ferry between Seoul, South Korea and Dandong. **Tickets** for the two-day voyage can be booked via Dandong Ferry Company (Ⓣ0415/3152666, Ⓕ3156131). A taxi to the ferry terminal takes half an hour (¥40). Note that there is a ¥30 departure tax.

want a little more luxury, the best bet is the friendly *Jinfangzhou* at 2 Shi Wei Lu (Ⓣ0415/2162009; ❹, dorm beds ¥30), well located next to the Yalu Bridge, with a view of the river and North Korea (ask for an odd-numbered room on the fourth floor or above, as these look out over the river and North Korea). The three-star *Yalu River Guesthouse* at 87 Jiu Wei Lu (Ⓣ0415/2125901, Ⓕ2126180; ❻) is a Sino-Japanese hotel that's seen better days; staff can help with train tickets. Head due north from the station and you'll see the turning on the right; the hotel is a few hundred metres down the road.

The poshest place in town faces North Korea and the bombed bridge: the *Zhonglian Hotel* (Ⓣ0415/3170666, Ⓕ3170888; ❻), at no. 1, District A2 of the riverfront promenade. The lobby travel service is exceedingly helpful in booking tickets.

Eating

Food in Dandong is surprisingly good, with freshwater fish and Korean dishes the local speciality. Try the local *lu zi yu* at *Donghai Yucun* west of the Yalu Bridge, no. 42, Block E (Ⓣ0415/3155678). All dishes are served with glutinous rice, soup, bread and dumplings, and a feast for two is a bargain at ¥60–70. Also along the promenade, Korean barbecue is plentiful and cheap (¥10) at *Taiba Shaokao Dian*, no. 15, Block B (Ⓣ0415/3120778). Opposite the train station, the *Sun Dining Hall #2* is a great experience, hot and boisterous, with excellent, inexpensive noodles and other dishes.

Start your mornings with the latest North Korean TV news at *Hong Kong Coffee House*, no. 32, Block D, where strong Korean coffee is ¥20. For a **beer**, the old standby *Wooden Guitar Bar*, around the corner on Qi Jin Jie across from the post office, features microbrewed draughts (¥15) and frequent live performances.

Changchun and Jilin

The cities of **Jilin province** took the brunt of Japanese, Russian and Chinese communist planning more than anywhere in China. This was a result of Jilin's vast mineral reserves, deposits of coal and iron ore that transformed the area into a network of sprawling industrial hubs, and, for thirteen years, the seat of the Manchukuo government. The closing of state-owned factories has resulted in massive lay-offs, but not all is glum, as tourism has crept in as one of the few growth industries in Jilin. Roads have been improved, the rail network is thorough and easy to use, almost all hotels are delighted to see foreigners, and winter brings low-cost **skiing and sledding**. Popular with both domestic and South Korean tourists is the **Changbai Shan Nature Reserve** (see p.211), a swath of mountain and forest boasting breathtaking scenery in the far eastern section of the province along the North Korean border. The most convenient jumping-off point for Changbai Shan is **Jilin**, a pleasant little city with little by way of sights, but great cheap winter sports. Some 90km to the west is **Changchun**, the provincial capital, an agreeable, well-planned place, with straight boulevards and squares throughout, though the few sights are spread far apart.

Jilin province is famous in its own country for **er ren zhuan**, a form of theatre closer to vaudeville than Beijing opera, incorporating dancing, singing, baton-twirling, costume changes and soliloquies. A typical performance sees a

Changchun and Jilin

Changchun	长春	***chángchūn***
Changchun Hotel	长春宾馆	*chángchūn bīnguǎn*
Chunyi Hotel	春谊宾馆	*chūnyí bīnguǎn*
Culture Square	文化广场	*wénhuà guǎngchǎng*
Maxcourt Hotel	吉隆坡大酒店	*jílóngpō dàjiǔdiàn*
Puppet Emperor's Palace	伪皇宫	*wěihuáng gōng*
Rail Station Hotel	铁路宾馆	*tiělù bīnguǎn*
Shangri-La Hotel	香格里拉饭店	*xiānggélǐlā fàndiàn*
Xiangyangtun Restaurant	向阳屯饭店	*xiàngyángtún fàndiàn*
Jilin	吉林	***jílín***
Beidahu Ski Park	北大湖滑雪场	*běidàhú huáxuěchǎng*
Beishan Park	北山公园	*běishān gōngyuán*
Catholic Church	天主堂	*tianzhǔ táng*
Dongguan Hotel	东关宾馆	*dōngguān bīnguǎn*
Jiangbei Park	江北公园	*jiāngběi gōngyuán*
Jiangnan Park	江南公园	*jiāngnán gōngyuán*
Jilin Fandian	吉林饭店	*jílín fàndiàn*
Jilin International Hotel	吉林国际大酒店	*jílín guójì dàjiǔdiàn*
Rosefinch Mountain	朱雀山	*zhūquè shān*
Songhua Lake	松花湖	*sōnghuā hú*
Songhuahu Ski Park	松花湖滑雪场	*sōnghuā hú huáxuěchǎng*
Yinhe Hotel	银河大厦	*yínghé dàshà*

man and woman regaling the audience with a humorous tale of their courtship and love. Tape recordings of the genre are available at stores, and you may be able to get into a performance with translation via CITS, or you could just ask a cabby or local to point you to a theatre.

Changchun

CHANGCHUN has a historical notoriety deriving from its role as Hsinking, capital of Manchukuo, the Japanese-controlled state from 1932 to 1945 that had Xuantong, better known as Puyi, as its emperor. Now a huge, sprawling industrial city based on coal, petroleum and iron, it's also renowned for its many colleges, its movie studio and the **Number One Automobile Factory**, producer of the ubiquitous Liberation Truck and Red Flag automobile, recently reintroduced, though this time without a wooden interior and aimed not at cadres but at China's new car-crazy middle class.

A stroll south from the train station down the main artery, Renmin Dajie, to Renmin Guangchang (People's Square) and then west to Wenhua Guangchang (Culture Square) is a good, but long, introduction to the city. **Culture Square** is the second-largest in the world (after Tian'anmen), and was to be the site of a Japanese palace. Today it's a large patch of grass with statues of a muscular naked man, standing with his arms raised in liberation, and a reclining naked woman marking its centre.

The Puppet Emperor's Palace

Changchun's only notable attraction is the **Puppet Emperor's Palace** (daily 9am–4.30pm; ¥20), in the east of the city on the route of bus #10 from the train station, where the last Chinese emperor, Puyi, was established as a powerless figurehead by the Japanese. In 1912, at the age of 8, Puyi ascended to the imperial throne in Beijing, at the behest of the dying Dowager Cixi. Although forced to abdicate that same year by the Republican government, he retained his royal privileges, continuing to reside as a living anachronism in the Forbidden City. Outside, the new republic was coming to terms with democracy and the twentieth century, and Puyi's life, circumscribed by court ritual, seems a fantasy in comparison. In 1924, he was expelled by Nationalists uneasy at what he represented, but the Japanese protected him and eventually found a use for him here in Changchun as a figure who lent a symbolic legitimacy to their rule. After the war he was re-educated by the Communists and lived the last years of his life as a gardener. His story was the subject of Bernardo Bertolucci's lavish film, *The Last Emperor* (probably more engrossing than a visit to this palace).

Like its former occupant, the palace is really just a shadow of Chinese imperial splendour, a poor miniature of Beijing's Forbidden City, with two badly maintained courtyards and a garden. Photos of Puyi line the walls, captioned in Chinese only, but you can surmise the tone of the presentation by looking at the mannequins of Puyi and his wife: she reclines on a sofa smoking opium while her husband gleefully confers with a Japanese general down the hall. Additional photo exhibits in the rear building document Japan's brutal invasion and rule. Next door, the **Jilin Provincial Museum** (daily except Sat 8.30am–4.30pm; ¥5) is a bland collection of artefacts and maps – you need to read Chinese to appreciate them fully.

Practicalities

Numerous flights connect Changchun daily to every major city in China. A bus from the **airport**, 10km northwest of town, drops you outside the **CAAC** office (Ⓣ0431/2988888), next to the train station. Both the **train** and the **bus stations** are in the north of town, with frequent connections to the rest of the northeast. Jilin is two hours away by bus or train and Shenyang and Harbin are four hours. There are also VWs for hire at the bus station – negotiate a price and wait for the car to fill with passengers, and you're off. Fares aren't that much higher than taking the bus, and you'll arrive at least an hour earlier. Do expect, however, to be have to change vehicles at some point on the journey. Taxis within the city have a ¥5 flagfall, and after 3km charge ¥1.3 for each kilometer thereafter.

The **Bank of China** (Mon–Fri 8.30am–4pm) lies near the *Changchun* and *Shangri-La* hotels, at 1 Tongzhi Lu. **CITS** (Ⓣ0431/5388784) is nearby, at 31 Dong Chaoyang Lu. The **PSB** is at 99 Renmin Dajie. The **post office** (daily, 8.30am-4.30pm) is next to CAAC, just to the left as you exit the train station. A good **Internet** cafe is on the fifth floor of the building opposite the *Shangri-La* hotel on Xi'an Dalu.

Accommodation, eating and drinking

The most convenient **place to stay** is the *Rail Station Hotel,* right at the train station (Ⓣ0431/2703630; ❸, dorm beds ¥25). Across the concourse to the left as you exit the station, the *Chunyi Hotel* (Ⓣ0431/2799966, Ⓕ8960171; ❹) is good value for its cleanliness, location and price. Rooms have cable TV, hot water and breakfast included. Southeast of here and best reached by taxi, the *Changchun Hotel,* 18 Xinghua Lu (Ⓣ0431/8929920), is a large compound with a good travel service and different rates for the double rooms in its two blocks (building no. 3 ❺, building no. 2 ❻). The *Shangri-La* (Ⓣ0431/8981818, Ⓕ8981919; ❾), at 9 Xi'an Da Lu, serves as the five-star option in town. They take credit cards and keep free maps of Changchun's sights in the lobby. One block west on Xi'an Dalu, the *Maxcourt* has a swimming pool, as well (Ⓣ0431/8962688, Ⓕ8986288; ❼).

For **eating**, wander the area south of the *Shangri-La* and Xi'an Dalu. Directly across from the hotel, *Weiduoqian Lamian* has excellent hand-pulled noodles. Consider, too, *Xiangyangtun*, a branch of the Beijing Cultural Revolution nostalgia-cuisine franchise. From the *Shangri-La*, walk south on Tongzhi Jie and turn left at Dong Chaoyang Lu; the restaurant is on the left-hand side, at no. 3. Try the fried scorpions and battered leaves. There's a *KFC* at the intersection of Chongqing Lu and Renmin Dajie, and, for **nightlife**, a *Bowling Beer House* on the western edge of Culture Square, on Xi Minzhu Dajie.

Jilin and around

Known as Kirin during the Manchukuo time, **JILIN** is split in two by the **Songhua River**, with the downtown area spread along its northern shore. The **promenade** along the river was finished in 1998, making for a pretty walk, especially in winter, when the trees are coated in frost. This phenomenon, known as *shugua* in Chinese, is the result of condensation from the city's hydroelectric dam at Songhua Lake, east of town. It's Jilin's claim to fame, along with an **ice festival** in January and three neighbouring **skiing and sledding** parks. This makes winter the ideal time to visit Jilin, though its **parks** – Beishan, Jiangnan and Jiangbei – are nice enough in summer. Beishan, in the west of town at the terminus of bus route #7, is the best known of the three (¥2). It's filled with pathways and temples, the most interesting of which is **Yuhuangge** (Jade Emperor's Temple), where rows of fortune tellers gather out front.

Jilin's prettiest building and a reminder of the town's past, the **Catholic church** was built in the 1920s at 3 Songjiang Lu, the road bordering the river promenade. Next door is a hospice for the elderly, which explains why the median age of a Jilin Catholic appears to be 75.

Practicalities

Bus #38 goes to and from the **airport** in the northwest of town to the fairly central **train and bus station** near the northern bank of the river. If you're going to Changbai Shan, it's worthwhile talking to the **CITS office** (Ⓣ0432/2492978, Ⓕ2430690) in front of the *Dongguan Hotel*. The Yintong Tourist Company (Ⓣ0432/4842256, Ⓕ4842296), on the fifth floor of the *Milky Way* hotel, is even more helpful, with train and airline schedules posted – they'll photocopy one for you for ¥1. They also organize tours to the surrounding area. The main **Bank of China** (daily 8am–5pm) and **post office** are across from each other on opposite sides of Jilin Dajie, just north of the bridge, church and *Dongguan Hotel*. For **Internet access**, Chongqing Jie, a road that runs diagonally northeast from the post office to the train station, has several places to choose from near the intersection with Shanghai Lu.

Accommodation and eating

The *Dongguan* **hotel**, at 2 Jiang Wan Lu (Ⓣ0432/2454272; ❹), along the river, is cavernous and frayed but puts you smack in the city centre. In terms of comfort, a better option, at 20 Zhongxing Jie right in front of the train station, is the *Jilin International*, which takes credit cards (Ⓣ0432/2929818, Ⓕ2556161; ❻). The most luxurious place in town, with its own dance hall, is the *Yinhe*, to the west at 97 Songjiang Lu (Ⓣ0432/4841780, Ⓕ4841621; ❻). It's also convenient, with a Bank of China branch just next door. Be warned, however, that this establishment fills up with raucous tour groups.

There's also a string of **guesthouses** in front of the train station, and most will be happy to have your business, though some will say it's "not safe" to put you in a dorm. One yielding establishment is the *Jilin Fandian* (no phone; ❷, dorm beds ¥30), next door to the *International Hotel* and above the seedy *Artist Bar*, whose entrance is lined with nude photographs. Apparently any artists in residence have been busy hanging Christmas decorations and spray painting "I love you" on the windows. Chongqing Jie is lined with good **restaurants**, including a dumpling place at *Dongfang Jiaozi Wang*, south of the *International Hotel* and north of the massive Fu Mart warehouse shopping and *KFC*.

Around Jilin

Twenty kilometres east of Jilin is **Songhua Hu**, a deep, very attractive lake, set in a large forested park and surrounded by hills. A taxi to this popular local beauty spot should cost about ¥40, and there are rowing boats for rent for ¥5 an hour. In 1992 an off-duty soldier reported being attacked by a dragon while boating here – it's a risk you'll just have to take. Unlike most Chinese scenic attractions, Songhua Hu seems big enough to absorb the impact of all its visitors, and even on weekends it's possible to escape to some quiet, peaceful spot.

At the lake's southern end is the huge **Fengman Dam**, a source of great local pride. Although in recent years the Songhua River's level has dropped by half – a result of extensive tree felling in its catchment area – the river floods every year, and at least a couple of the dam's four sluice gates have to be opened. With ruthless Chinese pragmatism, cities in Dongbei have been graded in order of importance in the event that the annual floods ever become uncontrollable. Jilin, as it has a hydroelectric power station, is judged to be more important than Harbin, so if the river does ever flood disastrously, all four sluice gates will be opened, Jilin will be spared, and Harbin will be submerged.

Local ski areas

In winter, the area around the lake is great for skiing and sledding. Closest to Jilin city, on bus route #338, is **Zhuque Shan** (Rosefinch Mountain), a park long known for its hiking and temples but now also for its skiing. A taxi here from the city, using the meter, will cost ¥35 from the train station. After you're dropped off, you have to walk 1km to the park, though entrepreneurs on horseback or dogsleigh will take you in for ¥10. You then buy an entrance ticket (daily dawn–dusk; ¥5). There are two small slopes here, one for sledding and one for skiing. The sleighs are two downhill skis nailed together with a piece of raised plywood, and really fly if you get a running start and bellyflop. It's ¥20 for a day of sledding, or ¥30 for skiing, equipment included (¥100 deposit required). There's a good **restaurant** here that seats guests on a *kang*, a raised heated platform which provides a nice vantage point over the hill. Foreigners are a rarity here, and the staff and patrons are a lot of fun. Skiing lessons are free; just look helpless and a staffer will come to the rescue.

Jilin also has two first-class ski areas, replete with chairlifts – though transport and lift tickets plus rental will set you back double and triple the cost of Zhuque Shan – respectively, at **Songhua Hu Hua Xue Chang** and **Beida Hu Hua Xue Chang**. To get to Songhua Hu, take bus #338 to the small district of **Fengman** (30min; ¥3), from where you'll have to take a short taxi ride to the ski resort. A taxi here from Jilin city (26km) is about ¥50. Transport to the biggest ski area, Beida Hu, 56km southeast of Jilin, is best served by taxi. A one-way trip to this resort will be around ¥100. Packages and transport are also available through Jilin's tourist agencies.

Changbai Shan Nature Reserve

The Changbai mountains run northeast to southwest along the Chinese–Korean border for about a thousand kilometres. With its long, harsh winters and humid summers, this is the only mountain range in east Asia to possess alpine tundra, and its highest peak, Baitou Shan is, at 2744m, the tallest mountain on the eastern side of the continent. The huge lake, **Tian Chi**, high in the Changbai mountains, is one of the highlights of Dongbei, and the area around, the **Changbai Shan Nature Reserve**, with jagged peaks emerging from swaths of lush pine forest, is beautiful and wild. This is remote, backwater China, difficult to get to even with the recent growth of a tourist infrastructure to shuttle people from the nearby cities to the lake and back again. Heading a little off the tourist track into the wilderness is the way to get the most out of the area, though you'll need to come well prepared.

Established in 1961, the nature reserve centres on the magnificent waters of Tian Chi, at the summit of Changbai Shan, and covers more than 800 square kilometres of luxuriant forest, most of which lies between 500m and 1100m above sea level. At the base of the range, the land is dense, with huge Korean pine trees which can grow up to 50m tall, and mixed broadleaf forest. The rare Manchurian fir is also found here. Higher altitudes are home to the Changbai Scotch pine, recognizable by its yellow bark, and the Japanese yew. As the climate becomes colder and damper higher up, the spruces and firs get hardier before giving way to a layer of sub-alpine grassland with colourful alpine plants

Changbai Shan Nature Reserve

Changbai Shan	长白山	***chángbái shān***
Baihe	白河	*báihé*
Changbaishan Hotel	长白山大酒店	*chángbáishān dàjiǔdiàn*
Tian Chi	天池	*tiānchí*
Tonghua	通化	*tōnghuà*
Yalin Hotel	雅林宾馆	*yǎlín bīnguǎn*
Yanji	延吉	*yánjí*

and tundra. Animal species on the reserve include the leopard, lynx, black bear and **Siberian tiger**, all now protected, though decades of trapping have made them a rarity. Notable bird species include the golden-rumped swallow, orioles and the ornamental red crossbill. The area is rich in medicinal plants, too, and since the eleventh century has been a focus of research. The Chinese regard the region as the best place in the country for **ginseng** and deer antlers, both prized in traditional remedies, and the reserve's rare lichens have recently been investigated as a treatment for cancer.

Visitors, mostly domestic tourists, South Koreans and Japanese, come here in great numbers, and a tourist village has grown up, with the result that the scenery is somewhat marred by litter, souvenir stalls and hawkers. Not all visitors are here for the scenery; plenty come to search for herbs, and many of the Japanese are here to catch butterflies (to keep) and ants (to eat). When the day-trippers have left, though, it's peaceful, and there are plenty of opportunities to hike around far from the crowds.

Reaching the reserve

Changbai Shan is a long way from anywhere, and the easiest way to get there is probably by booking one of the three-day, two-night **tours** arranged through CITS or the Yintong agency in Jilin, costing ¥450–600. These include park entrance fees and accommodation, and stop at all the major must-sees, including Tian Chi.

Alternatively, you can make your approach from any number of directions by **public transport**. Jilin Province is rife with rail lines and highways, and most places are well served by train, bus and long-distance taxi. Among the options is a new service from the eastern Jilin city **Yanji**, a four-and-a-half hour **bus** ride north of the mountain (this is the route the CITS tour out of Jilin follows). However, the roads can still be rough. You can also travel in by **train** to Yanji or as far as **Baihe** (see p.214), a village at the base of the mountain. The most convenient approach is from the north via bus **from Jilin** to Baihe (6hr; ¥50). If you're coming **from Changchun**, get an overnight train east to Yanji, then catch the three-hour bus onwards to Baihe.

You can also approach **from Dandong** to the south: two buses depart daily for **Tonghua** at 6.30am and 8.50am (8hr; ¥40–45). The bus zigzags through rural China along roads that are little better than dirt tracks, a rough but engrossing ride. Tonghua is a bore, so as soon as you arrive buy a ticket for the train to Baihe. Train K952/953 leaves Tonghua at 10.31pm and gets to Baihe at 5.03am; additionally, train #4241 leaves at 8.10am and arrives at in Baihe at 2.39pm. If you're coming straight **from Beijing**, you can take an overnight train to Tonghua (18hr), or do what many Chinese tourists do, and fly Beijing–Yanji (5 daily, 1hr 50min) and then take a bus on to Baihe (3hr; ¥20).

The train is the best overland route **back out** of the Changbai Shan region,

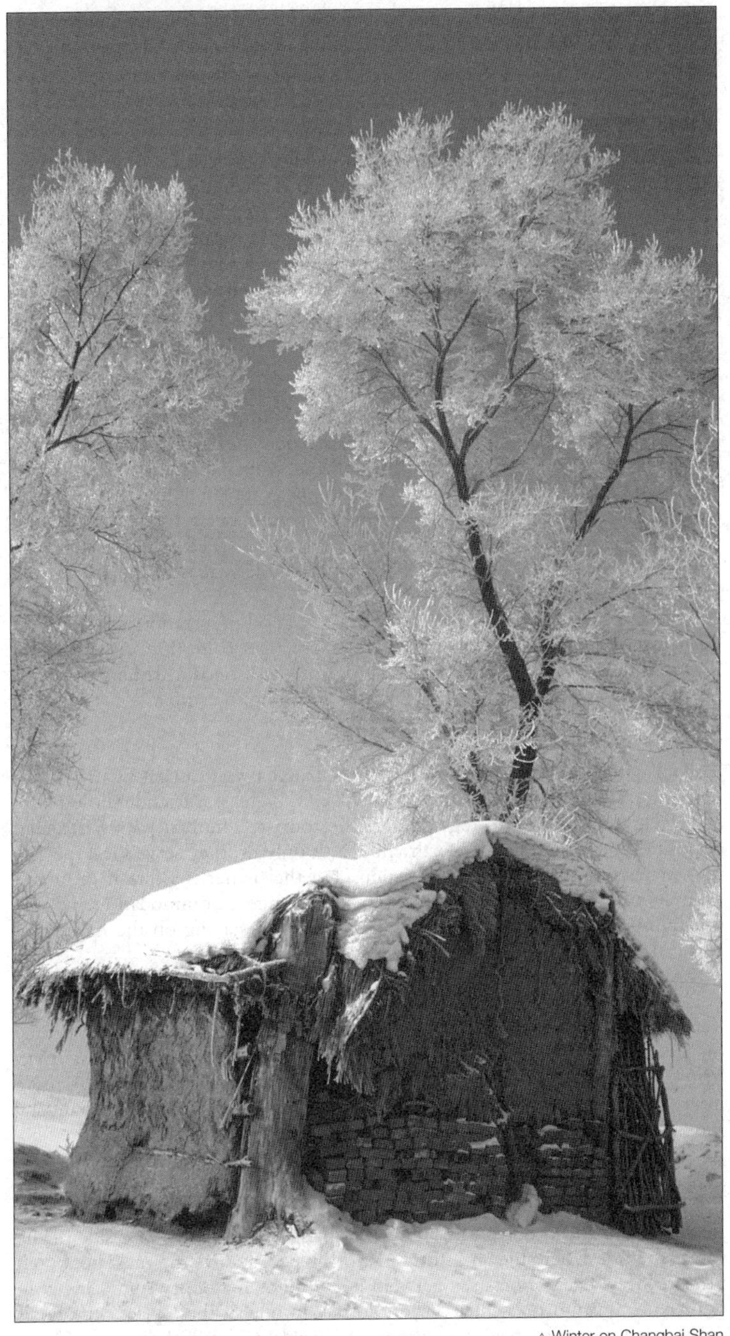

△ Winter on Changbai Shan

although there is an unreliable bus service from Baihe, which supposedly leaves every morning at 6.30am for Jilin (7hr; ¥45) and then on to Changchun (9hr; Y60).

The reserve

Changbai Shan rewards detailed exploration. Head any distance from the obvious paths, and you're quickly swallowed up in the wilderness. Settlements are few and far between, though, and the only roads are dirt tracks, so don't wander too far unless you know what you're doing. Be **especially careful** when hiking around Tian Chi, as the lake straddles the Chinese–North Korean **border**. At the height of patriotism during the Cultural Revolution, Chairman Mao ordered that the line be demarcated – the catch, however, is that the line isn't clearly marked by signs. Be sure to ask around in the Baihe for the latest information on the situation.

The **weather** in the region is not kind and can change very suddenly. In summer, torrential rain is common, mist makes it impossible to see far and the buildings at the summit often lose their electricity supply. That said, a trip is really only practical in the summer months as winter temperatures can drop very low, and snow makes the roads in and out completely impassable. Public transport is restricted to the June–September period, but before going it's wise to get a local weather report by asking at a branch of CITS, as heavy rains may flood roads and trap you on the mountain. At other times of the year, you'll have to rent a jeep.

If you're planning to stay any length of time, good preparation and the right **equipment** are essential. Bring insect repellent, tiger balm (for bites), walking boots, waterproof clothing and a sweater. You'll also need a flashlight, a good sleeping bag and all-weather gear if you're planning to camp.

Baihe

The village of **BAIHE** is the farthest into Changbai you can get by train; from here on, it's buses, dirt roads and dusty villages. Baihe is a friendly little place, and village life carries on regardless of the tourists. The *Yanleyuan Restaurant*, opposite the train station, is worthwhile. Not only do they serve local specialities such as mushrooms and rare fungus, but the owner is a one-man tourist office – he can get tickets for onward travel, arrange accommodation and sort out transport around the reserve. If you don't plan staying on the mountain, you can leave your bags at the restaurant.

To **stay** the night in Baihe, the *Yalin Hotel* (Ⓣ0433/5710526; ❸) has adequate doubles. The backpacker option is the *Changbaishan Hotel* (Ⓣ0433/5716983; dorm beds ¥50), though they can only accept independent travellers, not people on an organized tour. Tour groups get corralled into the *Baishan Hotel* (Ⓣ0433/571877), and a night here is included in the package price. A more interesting alternative, however, is to ask around the little family restaurants by the station. Many of them have rooms at the back where you can stay for as little as ¥10 per person. Rooms here have a *kang* – a raised wooden platform constructed over a pipe that leads from the oven in the kitchen – a feature of cold northern China. During the day the platform is used as a dining area, and at night mattresses are rolled out on it. The platform is always on the west side of the room, the side where the ancestors are worshipped, and it's the most honoured place to sleep. These rooms can get very hot at night, full of dry, stuffy air, but in winter the warmth is essential. If you do stay in one of these places, the locals appreciate it if you keep as low a profile as possible, as the PSB disapproves.

Tian Chi and around

Dramatic and beautiful **Tian Chi** (Heaven Pool) is a deep volcanic crater lake 5km across, surrounded by angular peaks, with waterfalls gushing around it and blue, snow-capped mountains in the distance. The Baihe–Tian Chi bus trip takes two hours (¥35), and regular tourist buses run up and down the mountain during the summer months; **jeep taxis** from Baihe to the lake are ¥100.

At the reserve entrance, everyone pays ¥80 to enter, regardless of nationality. The bus from Baihe drops you off in a car park higher up, from where a road leads to the lake; the walk up the main path takes about an hour. There's a longer western path branching off from the car park, which is more scenic but more dangerous with jagged rocks everywhere. There's a pretty waterfall 500m off to the east from the car park. A bathhouse just south of the car park offers hot spring baths for ¥40 per person. Once you've seen the lake, tracks leading off into the mountain offer the chance of further exploration but, again, don't risk wandering into North Korea.

The last buses return to Baihe around 4pm. Officially, camping is against the rules, but it's been done.

Harbin and beyond

The last major city before you hit the sub-Siberian wilderness and its scattering of oil and mining towns, **HARBIN** is the capital of Heilongjiang province and probably the northernmost location that's of interest to visitors. It's worth a visit for its **winter ice festival** alone, but it's also one of the few northern cities with a distinctive character, the result of colonialism and cooperation with nearby Russia.

Harbin was a small fishing village on the Songhua River – the name means "where the fishing nets are dried" – until world history intervened. In 1896 the Russians obtained a contract to build a rail line from Vladivostok through Harbin to Dalian, and the town's population swelled. More Russians arrived in 1917, this time White Russian refugees fleeing the Bolsheviks, and many stayed on for the rest of their lives. In 1932, the city was briefly captured by the Japanese forces invading Manchuria, then in 1945 it fell again to the Russian army, who held it for a year before Stalin and Chiang Kaishek finally came to an agreement. The city reverted to the Chinese, though when the Russians withdrew, they took with them most of the city's industrial plant. Things haven't been totally peaceful since – Harbin was the scene of fierce factional fighting during the Cultural Revolution, and when relations with the Soviet Union deteriorated, the inhabitants looked anxiously north as fierce border skirmishes took place.

Not surprisingly, the city used to be nicknamed "**Little Moscow**", and though much of the old architecture has been torn down and replaced with sterile blocks and skyscrapers, the place still looks a little like the last threadbare outpost of imperial Russia. Leafy boulevards are lined with European-style buildings painted pastel shades, and bulbous onion domes dot the skyline. It's possible to eat in Russian restaurants, and the locals have picked up on some of their neighbour's customs: as well as developing a taste for ice cream and pastries, Harbin's residents have a reputation as the hardest drinkers in China. The city's past is celebrated with the restored shopping street, **Zhongyang Dajie**, at the heart of town, as well as in a Russian cathedral that

Harbin and around

Harbin	哈尔滨	***hāěrbīn***
Flood Control Monument	防洪纪念碑	*fánghóng jìniànbēi*
Harbin Architecture and Art Centre	哈尔滨建筑艺术馆	*hāěrbīn jiànzhù yìshùguǎn*
Harbin's Provincial Museum	黑龙江省博物馆	*hēilóngjiāngshěng bówùguǎn*
Songhua River	松花江	*sōnghuā jiāng*
Stalin Park	斯大林公园	*sīdàlín gōngyuán*
Sun Island	太阳岛	*tàiyáng dǎo*
Zhaolin Park	兆林公园	*zhàolín gōngyuán*
Zhongyang Dajie	中央大街	*zhōngyāng dàjiē*
Zoo	动物园	*dòngwù yuán*
Accommodation and eating		
Beibei	北北大酒店	*běiběi dàjiǔdiàn*
Guocai	果菜大厦	*guǒcaì dàshà*
Holiday Inn	哈尔滨万达假日饭店	*hāěrbīn wàndájiàrì fàndiàn*
Huamei	华梅饭店	*huáméi fàndiàn*
Jiachangcai	家常菜饭店	*jiāchángcài fàndiàn*
Liangmao	粮贸饭店	*liángmào fàndiàn*
Longmen	龙门大厦	*lóngmén dàshà*
Longyun	龙运宾馆	*lóngyùn bīnguǎn*
Modern	马达尔宾馆	*mǎdáěr bīnguǎn*
Riyuetan	日月潭	*rìyuè tán*
Youlian	友联宾馆	*yǒulián bīnguǎn*
Daqing	大庆	*dàqìng*
Jingpo Lake	镜泊湖	*jìngbó hú*
Mudanjiang	牡丹江	*mǔdān jiāng*
Pingfang	平方	*píngfēng*
Qiqihar	齐齐哈尔	*qíqíhāěr*
Yabuli Ski Resort	亚布力滑雪场	*yàbùlì huáxuěchǎng*

now serves as the **Harbin Art and Architecture Center**, housing a photo history of the city.

Attractions beyond here are limited, and journeys can be arduous, though new highways and trains have shortened travel times. Ornithologists will be interested in the **Zhalong Nature Reserve**, home of the rare red-crowned crane, and roughnecks will enjoy **Daqing**, "Big Celebration", home of China's largest petroleum field. Beyond that sits **Qiqihar** and the volcanic spa at **Wudalianchi**, the latter an unattractive place that draws mostly elderly Chinese to its supposedly medicinal hot springs. The scenic waters of **Jingpo Hu** aren't especially worth going out of your way for, but if you're keen on skiing, you'll find **Yabuli** certainly the best place in the country to flaunt your skills.

During the summer the **climate** is quite pleasant, but in winter the temperature can plummet to well below -30°C. Local people are accustomed to the cold, however, and it is during winter that the city is most alive, with skiing and ice festivals in December and January. Outside the Ice Lantern Festival, foreigners don't get up here much and, in general, local residents are friendly and helpful.

Arrival and transport

Downtown Harbin, the most interesting part for visitors, is laid out on the southern bank of the Songhua River, with the liveliest streets between here and the train station. The urban sprawl farther south is best avoided. A good starting point is in Daoli District northwest of the train station and around

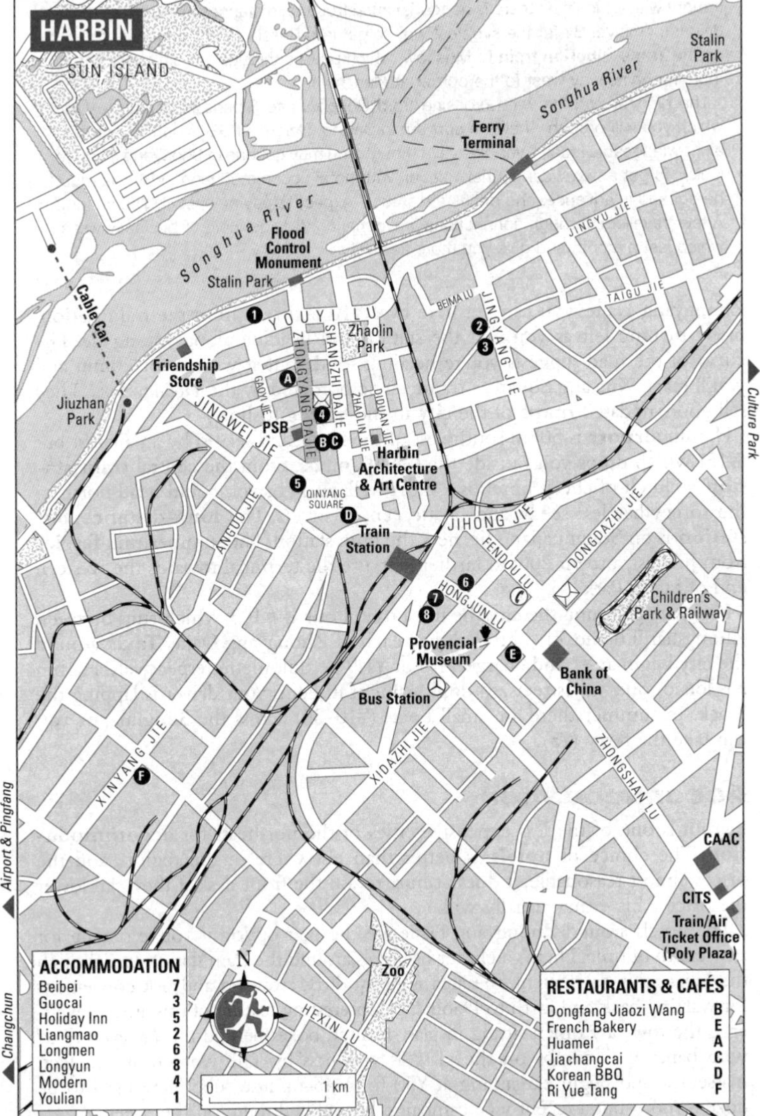

Crossing into Siberia

From northern Heilongjiang, there are a number of crossing points **into Siberia**, of which **Heihe**, a large border town that sees a lot of traffic with the Russian town of Blagoveshchensk, is the best option. From Harbin, take train K485 to Heihe (departs 6.54pm; 12hr) – Russia is a few strides and a mountain of paperwork away. Train K486 returns to Harbin daily, leaving Heihe at 6.53pm. A train connection also exists between Harbin and **Suifenhe** (train K622/623, leaving at 11.28pm; 12hr), from where it's a four-hour bus ride to Vladivostok. In practice, however, these routes are fraught with difficulties; there is no tourist infrastructure, distances are long and conditions primitive. By far the simplest way to get into Russia from Dongbei is to hop on the **Trans-Siberian train** to Moscow, which passes through Harbin every Friday morning on its way west to the border at Manzhouli.

The biggest problem with crossing from Dongbei into Siberia is getting a **visa**, which you will probably have to sort out in Beijing (Harbin's PSB is, in the words of a knowledgeable local, "worthless"), although you may get one in Shenyang if you're lucky. To get a two-week tourist visa, all your hotel accommodation in Russia must be booked in advance, and prices are steep – expect to pay at least US$50 a night. A few travellers, through connections, have managed to get hold of business visas, which last a month and give you more flexibility.

Zhongyang Dajie; you can get here by a ¥10 taxi ride from the train station, or by turning left as you exit the station and heading along Jihong Jie. The curve of the road suggests you're heading south, but stay on it for 20min and you'll reach Xinyang Square, a traffic circle bordered by the *Holiday Inn*. (They sell good, updated **maps** of the city in the hotel gift shop.)

Harbin **airport** is 50km southwest of the town, and served by an airport bus (¥15) which drops you outside the CAAC office. From the central **train station**, a clutch of cheap hotels is a short walk away, or you could head north to the somewhat less seedy and hectic central streets. The **long-distance bus station** is on Songhuajiang Jie, near the train station. The summertime **ferries** from Jiamusi, a town 200km farther east, use the terminal towards the western end of Stalin Park.

For getting around the city, the most useful **bus** is #103, which runs between Zhongshan Lu and Zhaolin Park just each of Zhongyang Dajie. **Taxis** around the city begin at ¥7 and charge ¥1.6 or ¥1.9 per kilometre respectively. Harbin has lots of one-way streets, so don't panic if it seems your driver is lapping the block. In summer there are small boats (¥10–30) across the Songhua, or you can take the ferry (¥5).

Accommodation

Harbin is one of the less expensive cities of the northeast for **accommodation**. The choice of **hotels** is better than elsewhere in the region, and the prices almost reasonable; it doesn't hurt to ask the front desk if they can lower the price a bit – they usually will.

The hotels around Zhongyang Dajie are the best option if you're staying for any length of time. There's a cluster of hotels around the train station but, though the location is convenient, the area is noisy, dirty, crowded and not convenient for walking back and forth to Daoli. One interesting feature of this area, however, is the row of women sitting in glass-fronted boxes behind the *Longyun Hotel* who bang their combs on the glass as you pass by. The women are, in fact, masseuses, and begin bargaining at ¥50 for a 45-minute rub. There used to be dozens more, but a recent vice campaign has rubbed them off the street.

Beibei Directly across from the train station ⓣ0451/3642200. Formerly a seedy dive called the *Beiyuan*, the Beibei is a refurbished reincarnation under new management. The Russian prostitutes remain in the lobby, however. ❹

Guocai 42 Beima Lu ⓣ0451/8307977. Located a bit far out and away from the action in the north-east of town, this small hotel offers light, quiet rooms. The staff are pleasant, and the second-floor restaurant is excellent. To get here, turn left out of the train station and walk to the roundabout, then get bus #107 or #109 down Jingyang Jie. If you're travelling on your own, staff may be persuaded to give you a room for half the price. ❸

Holiday Inn 90 Jingwei Jie ⓣ0451/4226666, ⓕ4221661. Worth every *jiao*, with big fluffy beds, hot baths, CNN and in-house movies as well as the best location in town and very helpful English-speaking staff. A breakfast buffet is included in the room price, and you should enquire about special year-round discounts which can lower rates by as much as a third. ❾

Liangmao 11 Beima Lu ⓣ0451/8326503. Directly opposite the *Guocai*, this budget option features dorm beds for ¥40 and single rooms for ¥100.

Longmen 85 Hongqi Jie ⓣ0451/6426810, ⓕ3639701. Built in 1901 as the *Chinese Eastern Railway Hotel*, this restored gem is a snapshot of Harbin's bicultural past. If you don't stay here, pop in to admire the woodwork, sculptures, and English-language captions on the photographs, and ask to see the suite used by the warlord Zhang Xueliang and then by Chairman Mao. The ordinary rooms are pleasant though not of five-star quality, and the staff are top-notch. ❽

Longyun ⓣ0451/3634528. A clean and modern place on the right and behind the *Beibei* as you exit the train station. Rooms are good value if you have a student card, as there's a thirty percent discount. There's also a travel service here (ⓣ0451/3634578 ext 306) which runs a tour to the Yabuli ski area for ¥260 (one day) and ¥500 (two days). Dorms from ¥37, ❸

Modern 89 Zhongyang Dajie ⓣ0451/4615846, ⓕ4614997. The name is a misnomer, as it was actually built in 1906 and survives as Harbin's oldest hotel. An elegant building on one of the city's busiest streets, it's bursting with character, with European- and Russian-style restaurants and 160 rooms. The staff are helpful and speak English. From Zhongyang Dajie, enter the reception via a shop vending leather handbags. ❺

Youlian 225 Youyi Lu ⓣ0451/4686106. The friendliest, best-located budget place in Harbin, right near the river and Zhongyang Dajie. Dorms ¥30, ❸

The City

The place to head for is Daoli District's **downtown area**, a triangle outlined by Diduan Jie and Jingwei Jie, where there are plenty of brand-name clothing boutiques, fur shops and department stores. The smaller streets and alleys around here are the best places to see the city's **Russian architecture**, with its decaying stucco facades and elegant balconies. Shops along **Zhongyang Dajie** have all been restored, with plaques out front in English detailing their past lives as colonial homes and stores. Make sure you go in the department store at no.107, if only to see its spectacular skylight and rendition of a section from Michelangelo's Sistine Chapel mural, which hangs on the back wall. Across the street is another beautiful structure, the Jiaoyu Bookstore, well worth exploring. There are numerous good restaurants and bars along Zhongyang Dajie, which is paved with cobblestones and closed to cars, the result of a city beautification project in 1998. In winter, ice sculptures line the street, while summer sees pavement cafés set up.

The cathedral and around

The finest sight in Harbin has to be the old Russian Orthodox **cathedral** (formerly St Sofia's) on Zhaolin Jie. Turn east off Zhongyang Dajie on to Xi Shi Er Dao, and carry on until you hit Government Square; the church is right behind the new department store. Restored to all its onion-domed glory, the cathedral now houses the **Harbin Architecture and Art Centre** (daily 8.30am–5pm; ¥20), with a permanent photographic survey of Harbin's history as a Russian railway outpost. Additional photos are available via touch-screen computers, although the captions, like those throughout the hall, are in Chinese.

Due to frosty relations with the Soviet Union in the 1960s and 1970s (subject of Ha Jin's excellent *Ocean of Words*, a book of short stories in English), Harbin also boasts a network of underground **bomb shelters-turned-marketplaces**. You can enter from the train station and walk all the way up to the provincial museum and beyond. The markets sell a huge selection of goods, from pirated VCDs to leather jackets. Southeast of the train station along Hongjun Lu, Harbin's **Provincial Museum** (Tues–Sun 9am–4pm; ¥12), opposite the *International Hotel*, has a dull permanent collection of dusty relics without English captions.

Along the river

The **riverbank** area is another worthwhile district to explore, starting from the **Flood Control Monument** at the bottom of Zhongyang Dajie. Built in 1958, the monument commemorates the many thousands who have died in the Songhua floods, and includes an added-on "1989" and "1998" to commemorate the horrible floods during the summer of those years. The square here is a popular hangout for local people, as is **Stalin Park**, a strip of land along the river. People come to what must be China's last public memorial to Stalin in order to wash their clothes, meet and chat, and even bathe – not a good idea, as mercury levels in the water are so high fish can no longer survive in it. Others cluster around palm-readers and storytellers, who relate old Chinese folk legends. Just southeast of the monument, **Zhaolin Park**, unremarkable in summer, is host to the spectacular winter Ice Festival.

In winter, the **Songhua River** freezes solid and you can take a horse carriage, rent a go-kart or walk across. In summer, ferries will take you across to the northern bank and **Sun Island** (daily 8.30am–4.30pm; ¥5), with lakes for boating, swimming pools, fairground rides and an arms museum. It's unpleasantly busy on summer weekends, and getting around takes a lot of walking. You can also access Sun Island by **cable car** during warm months (¥30 one way).

Out from the centre

There are some nice old working **churches** in the Nangang District, at nos. 252 and 268 Dong Dazhi Jie and one at Shike (ask the cab driver to take you to *nangang jiaotang*). At the **zoo** (daily 8am–5pm; ¥5) in the south of the city, on the route of bus #81 from Xidazhi Jie or #338 from the train station, you can see the rare Manchurian tiger – only about thirty are left in the wild. The tigers have bred successfully here, saving them from extinction, though being kept in a Chinese zoo is not much of a life.

Harbin festivals

The annual Ice Lantern Festival, centred on Zhaolin Park, is held from January 5 to February 5 – though with the influx of tourists (2.5 million in 2002), the dates extend each year. At this time, the park becomes a fairytale landscape with magnificent sculptures – sometimes entire buildings, complete with stairways, arches and bridges – made of ice, carved with chainsaws and picks, and often with coloured lights inside them to heighten the psychedelic effect. Sculptors, some of them teenagers, work in -20°C December weather, earning ¥20 for a twelve-hour day. Highlights of past festivals have included detailed replicas of St Paul's Cathedral and life-size Chinese temples, though these days cartoon characters outnumber more traditional subject matter. Over on Sun Island, a snow sculpture display is held. During the festival, plenty of other cultural events take place, and its end is marked by fireworks. In summer, Harbin hosts a classical and traditional music festival from the middle to the end of July, during which orchestras and smaller groups play in the city's eight theatres.

Eating, drinking and nightlife

Influenced by **Russian** cuisine, local cooking is characterized by the exceptionally heavy use of garlic and a lot of potato. Expensive regional specialities include bear paw and deer muzzle, available in the upmarket hotels. Staying away from the delicacies, however, food in Harbin is good value with some decent restaurants and, at the fast food end, seven *KFCs*, two of which are located on Zhongyang Dajie. The Russian-style **cafe** at the corner of Zhongyang Dajie and Xi Toudao Jie is a nice place to sit over tea or coffee, or try the *French Bakery* at 174 Zhongyang Dajie, which does inexpensive espresso, cappuccino, ice cream and pizza, and is a good place to chat with locals. For **nightlife**, try the *Kiss Pub*, at Shi San Dao Jie, a little lane off Zhongyang Dajie, or whatever new place is testing its wings on Zhongyang Dajie itself.

Restaurants

Dongfang Jiaozi Wang 39 Zhongyang Dajie. The place to be seen in Harbin, with a wait often required for a table. The dumplings here are so good, you may be loathe to leave. Everyone else seems to linger for another draught beer, another plate of food.

Huamei 142 Zhongyang Jie. Patronized chiefly by tourists, this is Harbin's only authentic Russian restaurant, and the fairly Western food is eaten with knives and forks. Though a little pricey – expect to pay at least ¥100 per person – the meals (especially the stroganoff) are good, and make a change from local cuisine. You can even indulge yourself with caviar.

Jiachangcai Off Zhongyang Dajie and across from the post office, this 24hr restaurant serves cheap eats and beer.

Korean BBQ Corner of Zhongyang Dajie and Xi Badaojie. Pricey, but clean and sumptuous.

Ri Yue Tan 502 Xinyang Lu. Formerly the *KK* disco, now Harbin's most popular restaurant. Laden with local meat-and-mushroom concoctions, such as *xiao ji dun mo gu* (chicken and mushrooms).

Listings

Airlines CAAC is at 87 Zhongshan Lu (Ⓣ0451/2651188). In summer Shanghai Airlines, at 224 Zhongshan Lu (Ⓣ0451/2637953), sometimes sells tickets at half price to anyone with a student card on certain flights to Beijing and Shanghai. If you're leaving the city by plane, allow an hour to get to the airport through the traffic. An airport bus runs from outside the CAAC office every 20min (¥15).

Banks and exchange The Bank of China is on Hongjun Jie (Mon–Fri 8am-noon & 1pm–5pm). The office for traveller's cheques and credit-card advances is just round the corner. You can also change money at its branch at 37 Zhaolin Jie (same hours).

Internet access The portal near the *Modern Hotel* at 129 Zhongyang Dajie leads down to a fast and friendly café. There's another nearby at the intersection of Zhongyang Dajie and Wudao Jie, in the pool hall downstairs.

Mail The main post office is at 51 Jianshe Jie (Mon–Sat 8am–6pm).

PSB Shi San Dao Jie, off Zhongyang Dajie (Mon–Fri 8–11am & 2–5pm).

Telephones There's a telecom office (24hr) on Fendou Lu, east of the train station.

Travel agents Don't bother with CITS, far out at 82 Yiman Jie, which is focused on domestic tourists. More convenient and useful is the Heilongjiang Overseas Tourist Corporation at 235 Huayuan Jie, in Nangang District (Ⓣ0451/3633613, Ⓕ3621022), and also Swan Travel (Ⓣ0451/2367621), in the grounds of the *Swan Hotel*, 95 Zhongshan Lu. Both organizations arrange ski trips and tours to areas farther north, including specialist hunting, fishing, skiing and bird-watching tours. The *Longyun Hotel* does packages to Yabuli. The Heilongjiang New Century International Travel Service, at 49 Hong Xiajie (Ⓣ0451/4672888, Ⓕ4612143), runs four- and five-day trips to and over the Russian border. Check with them for visa information. At 93 Zhongshan Lu, in the Poly Plaza building, a small agency based out of a booth sells train and airline tickets. Patient and helpful, they have free timetables, too.

West of Harbin

Harbin's most notorious and macabre attraction is outside the city proper, about 30km southwest, in the tiny village of **PINGFANG**, near the terminus of bus #338 (¥2), which you can catch at the train station. This was the home of a secret Japanese research establishment during World War II and is now open to the public as a grisly **museum** (daily 8.30–11.30am & 1–4pm; ¥10). Here prisoners of war were injected with deadly viruses, dissected alive and frozen or heated slowly until they died. More than three thousand people from China, Russia and Mongolia were murdered by troops from unit 731 of the Japanese army. After the war, the Japanese tried to hide all evidence of the base, and its existence only came to light through the efforts of Japanese investigative journalists. It was also discovered that, as with scientists in defeated Nazi Germany, the Americans gave the Japanese scientists immunity from prosecution in return for their research findings. The museum's collection comprises mostly photographs labelled in Chinese. Looking at the displays, including a painting of bound prisoners being used as bomb targets, you understand why many Chinese mistrust Japan to this day.

Daqing

About two hours' bus journey (¥35) west of Harbin via sleek National Highway 301 (also known as the "Ha Da Expressway"), sprawls the boom-town of

Dongbei's minority communities

After forcing **minority communities** to embrace official communist culture during the 1950s and 1960s, the Chinese government now takes a more enlightened, if somewhat patronising, approach to the minority nations of the north. The **Manchu** people, spread across Inner Mongolia and Dongbei, are the most numerous and assimilated. Having lived so long among the Han they are now almost identical, though they tend to be slightly taller and men have more facial hair. They are noted for an elaborate system of etiquette and will never eat dog, unlike their Korean neighbours who love it. The "three strange things" that the southern Chinese say are found in the northeast are all Manchu idiosyncrasies: paper windows pasted outside their wooden frame, babies carried by their mothers in handbags and women smoking in public (the latter, of course, can be a habit of Han and every other ethnicity in large cities).

In the inhospitable northern margins of Dongbei live small communities such as the **Hezhen**, one of the smallest minority nations in China, with an estimated 1400 members, who inhabit the region where the Songhua, Heilong and Ussuri (Wusuli) rivers converge. They're known to the Han Chinese as the fish tribe, and their culture and livelihood centre around fishing. Indeed, they're the only people in the world to make clothes out of fish skin: the fish is gutted, descaled, then dried and tanned and the skins sewn together to make light, waterproof coats, shoes and gloves. More numerous are the **Daur**, 120,000 of whom live along the Nenjiang River. They are fairly seamlessly assimilated these days, but still retain distinctive marriage and funerary traditions, and have a reputation for being superb at hockey, a form of which they have played since the sixth century.

However, perhaps the most distinctive minority are the **Oroqen**, a tribe of nomadic hunters living in patrilineal clan communes called *wulileng* in the northern sub-Siberian wilderness. Although they have recently adopted a more settled existence, their main livelihood still comes from deer-hunting, while household items, tools and canoes are made by Oroqen women from birch bark. Clothes are fashioned from deer hide, and include a striking hat made of a roe deer head, complete with antlers and leather patches for eyes, which is used as a disguise in hunting.

DAQING, home of China's largest oil reserve and now Heilongjiang's second city. Daqing is a nice place in which to spend a day and is certainly unique in China, not least because it recently has been the site of massive labour protests over unpaid pensions. The town is interesting in a quirky way, with road names such as "Calgary Street" and oil pumps, called *ketouji* (literally, "kowtowing machines"), everywhere. China's oil wells are owned by the government, but Western companies have a stake here as vendors of drilling equipment, so foreigners aren't that rare a sight. The town has an older western half and a new, gleaming eastern portion, with a billboard of Deng Xiaoping gracing the entrance to the government offices. Buses #23 and #30 go from the train station to the new section of town, where the *Daqing Hotel* (Ⓣ0452/4662073, Ⓕ6103195; ❺) lives up to the boom-town image of overpriced rooms, liquor and prostitutes. There's no skyline in Daqing, save for some cooling towers, but folks are friendly and the connections on to Qiqihar and Harbin are constant; trains are many and buses leave every fifteen minutes from outside the train station.

Qiqihar and the Zhalong Nature Reserve

Two-and-a-half hours' train or bus journey (¥20) west of Daqing, **QIQIHAR** is one of the northeast's oldest cities, and still a thriving industrial centre. Alas, it's more fun to say the city's name aloud than to stay here for more than a day. The only place of marginal interest is a big park, **Longsha Gongyuan** (¥2), in the south of town, accessible via the main north–south artery, Longhua Lu, which begins in front of the train station; buses #1 and #2 ply the route. There's also a small **mosque** dating from the seventeenth century, located in the maze of alleyways west of Bukui Dajie. To get there head down Longhua Lu until it hits the park at Gongyuan Lu. Near the hospital and PSB office on Gongyuan Lu, turn west into Hefa Hutong, and ask for the *qingzhensi*.

However, the main reason to come to Qiqihar is to visit the **Zhalong Nature Reserve**, 30km outside town. This marshy plain abounds in shallow reedy lakes and serves as the summer breeding ground of thousands of species of birds, including white storks, whooper swans, spoonbills, white ibis and – the star attractions – nine of the world's fifteen species of **cranes**. Most spectacular of these is the endangered red-crowned crane, a lanky black and white bird over a metre tall, with a scarlet bald patch. It has long been treasured in the East as a paradigm of elegance – the Japanese call it the Marsh God – and it's a popular symbol of longevity, as birds can live up to sixty years. The birds mate for life, and the female only lays one or two eggs each season, which the male stands guard over. Vociferous defenders of their young, cranes have been known to stab eagles to death with their sharp beaks. The best time to visit the reserve is from April to June, when the migrants have just arrived. Walking around the reserve, although not forbidden, is not encouraged by the keepers or the murderous swarms of mosquitoes – come prepared. Binoculars are a good idea, too. Dedicated ornithologists might like to spend a few days here, but for most people an afternoon crouched in the reedbeds is enough.

Practicalities

Buses to the reserve (45min; ¥10) leave from Qiqihar's bus station, 1km south down Longhua Lu, on the left, and also from outside the train station. Splendid though the birds are, it can be difficult to fill the time you're obliged to spend in Qiqihar by the bus timetable and a better bet might be to take one of the flat-bottomed-boat **tours** run by CITS, which leave from the reserve entrance.

Visitors to Zhalong have to stay in nearby Qiqihar. The two tourist **hotels** are the two-star *Hecheng* (Ⓣ0452/2722540, Ⓕ2713367; ❺) and *Hubin*

(☎0452/2713121 ext 5241; ❹). They're in the same compound at 4 Wenhua Dajie, on the route of trolley bus #15 from the train station. In the *Hubin Hotel*, CITS (☎0452/2713121 ext 5243 or 5390) can book a tour for you, in addition to selling air tickets for flights to Beijing, Shenyang, Shanghai and elsewhere. Good **food** can be had at the *Hui Min Fan Dian*, across the street from the station on the left as you exit, where a bowl of noodles is ¥3 (there's also very grotty hostel next door, with doubles from ¥15). Frequent connections out mean you won't get stuck in Qiqihar for a night unless you choose to be.

East of Harbin

Regarded as the premier ski resort in China, **YABULI** is the place to be for **Heilongjiang's International Ski Festival** from December 5 to January 5. The resort's 3800-metre piste spreads across the southern side of Guokui (literally pot-lid) Mountain (1300m), 180km southeast of Harbin. There's also a 2.5-kilometre steel **toboggan run**, built in 1996 when the resort hosted the Asian Winter Games.

A free bus from the *Swan Hotel* in Harbin makes the four-hour trip here at 8.40am and 1.40pm, though you'll be expected to stay at *Windmill Villa* (☎0451/3455168 or 3455088; ❺, villa from ¥540, dorms often available). Equipment rental and lift tickets start at ¥100 for two hours or ¥240 for the day. You may well find it easiest to come here on one of the tours offered by the *Longyun* and other hotels in Harbin (see p.219).

Jingpo Hu

Jingpo Hu (Mirror Lake), 350km east of Harbin, is one of Heilongjiang's prettiest spots. At 45km long, set deep among forested hills, it's a good place to go fishing, boating and hiking, or just to sit and eat fruit, as many of the Chinese visitors seem to do, if they're not feasting on carp, Jingpo Lake fish soup, pine nuts and ginseng. There's a rash of development concentrated at the northern end, which most people stick to, and mile after mile of virgin countryside beyond. To get here, take a train or bus to **Mudanjiang** (4hr) and then a tourist bus (3hr) to the lake itself. It's possible to stay in Mudanjiang at the *Mudanjiang Hotel*, 188 Majia Jie (☎0451/3638488; ❺), or on the north side of the lake at the *Jingpo Hu Binguan* (☎0453/6270091; ❻). There are plenty of Chinese-only guesthouses around that are a lot cheaper, but you'll need to do some persuading to convince them to take you.

Travel details

Trains

Changchun to: Beijing (4 daily; 11hr); Dandong (daily; 10hr); Harbin (4 daily; 4hr); Jilin (6 daily; 2hr); Shenyang (20 daily; 4hr); Tonghua (2 daily; 9hr).
Dalian to: Beijing (3 daily; 10hr); Dandong (daily; 11hr); Harbin (2 daily; 10hr); Shenyang (15 daily; 5hr).
Dandong to: Beijing (2 daily; 14 hr); Changchun (daily; 10hr); Dalian (daily; 11 hr); Qingdao (daily; 26hr); Shenyang (4 daily; 4hr).
Harbin to: Beijing (3 daily; 14hr); Changchun (4 daily; 3hr); Daqing (12 daily; 2 hr); Jilin (4 daily; 2hr); Moscow (weekly; 6 days); Mudanjiang (12 daily; 5hr); Qiqihar (12 daily; 4hr); Shenyang (20 daily; 8hr).
Jilin to: Beijing (daily; 13hr); Changchun (6 daily; 2hr); Dalian (daily; 15hr); Harbin (4 daily; 6hr); Shenyang (daily; 10hr); Tianjin (daily; 17hr).
Qiqihar to: Bei'an (2 daily; 4hr); Beijing (2 daily; 16hr); Hailar, Inner Mongolia (daily; 10hr).
Shenyang to: Beijing (7 daily; 9hr); Changchun (20 daily; 4hr); Dalian (15 daily; 6hr); Dandong (7 daily; 4hr); Harbin (20 daily; 8hr); Jilin (4 daily;

7hr); Tianjin (10 daily; 9hr); Tonghua (2 daily; 7hr).
Tonghua to: Baihe (2 daily; 7hr); Beijing (daily; 17hr); Changchun (2 daily; 9hr); Shenyang (2 daily; 7hr).

Buses

Bus connections are comprehensive and can be picked up to all major towns from the bus station or in front of the train station. For some stretches, buses are faster and more convenient than trains, especially from Harbin to the west and south; Changchun to Jilin and Shenyang; and Shenyang to Dalian. Away from the major cities, however, roads turn rough and the journeys arduous.

Ferries

Besides the domestic services listed, some useful international connections serve this part of China, including flights from Changchun to Seoul and Vladivostok; from Dalian to Osaka, Seoul and Tokyo; and from Shenyang to Bangkok, Osaka, Seoul and Tokyo.
Dalian to: Qinhuangdao (summer; alternate days; 18hr); Shanghai (7 monthly; 40hr); Tianjin (4 weekly; 20hr); Weihai (daily; 3hr 30min to 8hr); Yantai (daily; 3hr to 8hr).
Dandong to: Inchon, South Korea (2 weekly; 20hr).
Harbin to: Jiamusi (daily in summer; 18hr).

Flights

Changchun to: Beijing (6 daily; 1hr 20min); Chengdu (10 weekly; 4hr 15min); Chongqing (3 weekly; 4hr 45min); Dalian (daily; 1 hr 5min); Fuzhou (2 weekly; 4hr 20min); Guangzhou (daily; 5hr); Haikou (2 weekly; 5hr 20min); Hangzhou (3 weekly; 2hr 20min); Hong Kong (2 weekly; 4hr 30min); Ji'nan (3 weekly; 1hr 45min); Kunming (5 weekly; 5hr 30min); Nanjing (daily; 2hr); Qingdao (daily; 2hr); Shanghai (2 daily; 2hr 40min); Shenzhen (2 daily; 4hr 50min); Wenzhou (2 weekly; 4hr); Wuhan (3 weekly; 4hr 25min); Xiamen (10 weekly; 3hr); Xian (4 weekly; 3hr); Yantai (4 weekly; 1hr 30min).
Dalian to: Beijing (14 daily; 1hr 10min); Changchun (daily; 1hr); Changsha (daily; 3hr 15min); Chengdu (daily; 2hr 50min); Chongqing (daily; 3hr); Fuzhou (daily; 3hr 30min); Guangzhou (2 daily; 2hr 50min); Guilin (4 weekly; 4hr 5min); Haikou (daily; 5hr); Hangzhou (daily; 2hr); Harbin (5 daily; 1hr 20min); Hefei (6 weekly; 1hr 30min); Hong Kong (daily; 3hr 30min); Ji'nan (2 daily; 1hr 40min); Kunming (daily; 5hr); Luoyang (3 weekly; 1hr 40min); Nanjing (daily; 1hr 30min); Ningbo (3 daily; 2hr 45min); Qingdao (2 daily; 1hr); Qinhuangdao (4 weekly; 1hr); Shanghai (7 daily; 1hr 30min); Shenyang (2 daily; 1hr); Shenzhen (4 daily; 4hr 40min); Taiyuan (daily; 3hr 30min); Tianjin (2 daily; 1hr); Ürümqi (2 weekly; 6hr 30min); Wenzhou (daily; 2hr 5min); Wuhan (daily; 2hr 15min); Xiamen (daily; 3hr 45min); Xi'an (daily; 2hr 20min); Yanji (2 daily; 2hr 30 min).
Dandong to: Beijing (3 weekly; 1hr 20min); Chengdu (3 weekly; 4hr 35min); Sanya (3 weekly; 6hr 25min); Shanghai (3 weekly; 2hr 25min); Shenzhen (3 weekly; 5hr 25min).
Harbin to: Beijing (10 daily; 1hr 40min); Changsha (2 weekly; 3hr 10min); Chengdu (daily; 4hr 15min); Chongqing (4 weekly; 4hr 20min); Dalian (5 daily; 1hr 10min); Fuzhou (6 weekly; 3hr 20min); Guangzhou (2 daily; 4hr 10min); Haikou (4 weekly; 5hr 30min); Hangzhou (9 weekly; 2hr 50min); Hohhot (weekly; 2hr); Hong Kong (3 weekly; 4hr 40min); Ji'nan (8 weekly; 2hr); Kunming (daily; 5hr); Nanjing (6 weekly; 3hr); Ningbo (2 weekly; 3hr 30min); Qingdao (2 daily; 1hr 40min); Shanghai (4 daily; 2hr 45min); Shenyang (2 daily; 1hr 20min); Shenzhen (2 daily; 5hr 20min); Tianjin (daily; 2hr 50min); Ürümqi (2 weekly; 6hr 35min); Wenzhou (6 daily; 3hr 10min); Wuhan (daily; 3hr 50min); Xiamen (daily; 4hr); Xi'an (daily; 4hr 20min); Yantai (daily; 1hr 45min); Zhengzhou (daily; 3hr 40min).
Jilin to: Beijing (daily; 1hr 20min); Guangzhou (2 weekly; 5hr 25min); Shanghai (2 weekly; 2hr 30min).
Qiqihar to: Beijing (5 weekly; 2hr); Guangzhou (2 weekly; 6hr 10min); Shanghai (2 weekly; 3hr 15min); Shenyang (2 weekly; 1hr 20min); Taiyuan (2 weekly; 3hr 10min).
Shenyang to: Beijing (12 daily; 1hr 20min); Changsha (daily; 3hr 50min); Chengdu (2 daily; 5hr); Chongqing (4 weekly; 3hr 15min); Dalian (2 daily; 55min); Fuzhou (6 weekly; 3hr 10min); Guangzhou (2 daily; 2hr 45min); Guilin (2 weekly; 5hr 15min); Haikou (daily; 6hr); Hangzhou (daily; 2hr 30min); Harbin (2 daily; 1hr 25min); Hohhot (7 weekly; 1hr 50min); Hong Kong (4 weekly; 4hr 15min); Ji'nan (daily; 1hr 20min); Kunming (daily; 5hr 20min); Lanzhou (3 weekly; 2hr 50min); Nanjing (3 weekly; 2hr); Ningbo (6 weekly; 1hr 50min); Qingdao (2 daily; 1hr 30min); Qiqihar (2 weekly; 1hr 20min); Sanya (daily; 7hr 30min); Shanghai (5 daily; 2hr); Shantou (3 weekly; 4hr 25min); Shenzhen (2 daily; 6hr); Shijiazhuang (daily; 1hr 35min); Taiyuan (daily; 4hr); Tianjin (4 weekly; 1hr 10min); Ürümqi (10 weekly; 6hr 25min); Wenzhou (daily; 3hr 45min); Wuhan (15 weekly; 2hr 15min); Xiamen (daily; 4hr 35min); Xi'an (daily; 2hr 30min); Yanji (daily; 1hr); Yantai (7 daily; 1hr); Zhengzhou (daily; 1hr 50min); Zhuhai (3 weekly; 6hr 20min).

CHAPTER 4 **Highlights**

* **Yungang Caves** See glorious Buddhist statuary from the fifth century, nestling in grottoes near Datong. **See p.239**
* **Walking Wutai Shan** The least developed of China's four Buddhist mountains is actually five flat peaks, perfect for independent exploration. **See p.243**
* **Pingyao** A Ming-era walled city that's also home to one of China's most atmospheric hotels. **See p.255**
* **The Terracotta Army** No visit to China is complete without a peek at these warrior figurines, guarding the tomb of Qin Shi Huang near Xi'an. **See p.287**
* **Longmen caves, Luoyang** Walk along a riverside promenade past caves peppering limestone cliff faces, containing more than 100,000 Buddhist carvings. **See p.305**

4

The Yellow River

The central Chinese provinces of **Shanxi**, **Shaanxi**, **Henan** and **Shandong** are linked and dominated by the **Yellow River** (*huánghé*), which has played a vital role in their history, geography and fortunes. The river is often likened to a dragon, a reference not just to its sinuous course, but also to its uncontrollable nature, and its behaviour, by turns benign and malevolent. It provides much-needed irrigation to an area otherwise arid and inhospitable, but, as its popular nickname, "China's Sorrow", hints, its floods and changes of course have repeatedly caused devastation, and for centuries helped to keep the delta region in Shandong one of the poorest areas in the nation.

The river's modern name is a reference to the vast quantities of yellow silt – **loess** – it carries, which has clogged and confused its course throughout history, and which has largely determined the region's geography. Loess is a soft soil, prone to vertical fissuring, and in Shanxi and northern Shaanxi it has created one of China's most distinctive landscapes, plains scarred with deep, winding crevasses, in a restricted palette of browns. In southern Shaanxi and Henan, closer to the river, the landscape is flat as a pancake and about the same colour. It may look barren, but where irrigation has been implemented the loess becomes **rich and fertile**, easily tillable with the simplest of tools. It was in this soil, on the Yellow River's flood plain, that Chinese civilization first took root.

Sites of **Neolithic habitation** along the river are common, but the first major conurbation appeared around three thousand years ago, heralding the establishment of the Shang dynasty. For the next few millennia, every Chinese dynasty had its capital somewhere in the area and most of the major cities, from Datong in the north, capital of the Northern Wei, to Kaifeng in the east, capital of the Song, have spent some time as the centre of the Chinese universe, however briefly. With the collapse of imperial China the area sank into provincialism, and it was not until late in the twentieth century that it again came to prominence. The old capitals have today found new leases of life as industrial and commercial centres, and thus present two sides to the visitor: a static history, preserved in the interests of tourism, and a rapidly changing, and sometimes harsh, modernity. It is the remnants of **dynastic history** that provide the most compelling reason to visit, but the region also has much to offer in the way of scenery, with more than its fair share of holy mountains.

Shanxi province is the poor relation of the set, relatively underdeveloped and with the least agreeable climate – temperatures hit -15°C in winter – and geography, a swath of mountain plateau. But it does have some great attractions, most notably the stunning **Yungang cave temples**, and one of the most beautiful –

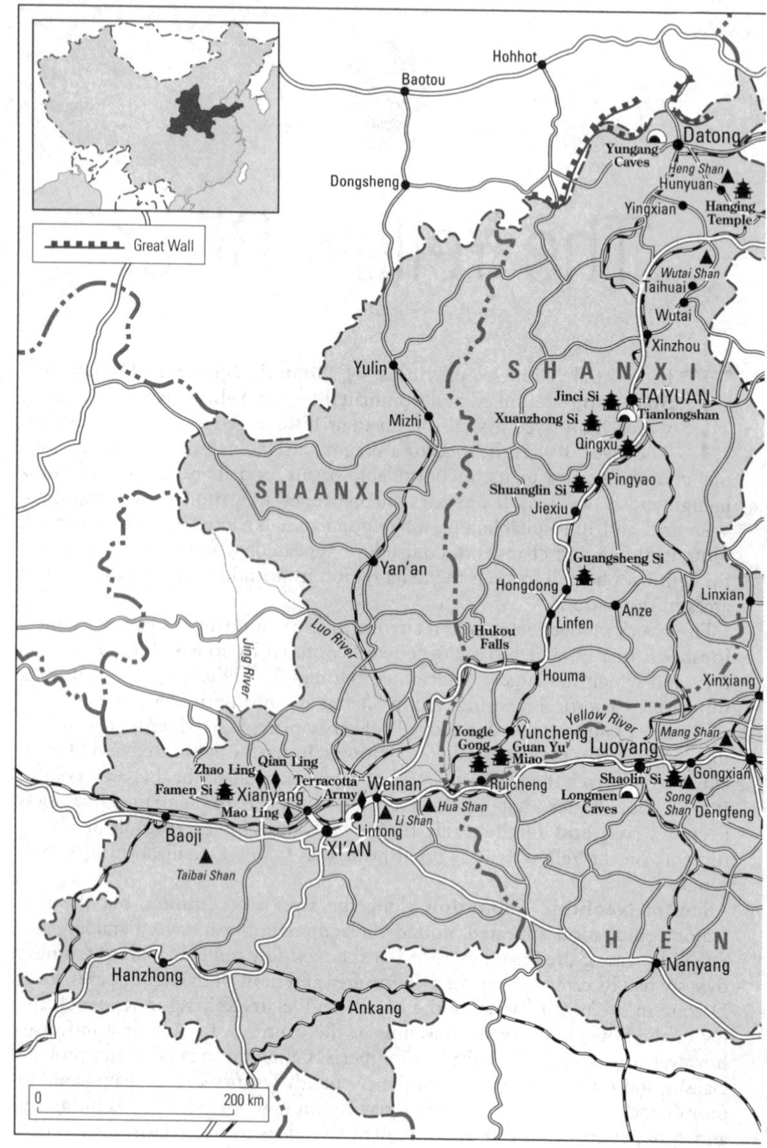

and inaccessible – holy mountains, **Wutai Shan**. Dotted around the small towns along the single rail line leading south to the Yellow River plain are quirky temples and villages that seem stuck in the nineteenth century. In contrast, wealthy **Xi'an**, capital of low-lying, fertile Shaanxi Province, has as many temples, museums and tombs as the rest of the province put together, with the **Terracotta Army** deservedly ranking as one of China's premier sights. It's also the home of

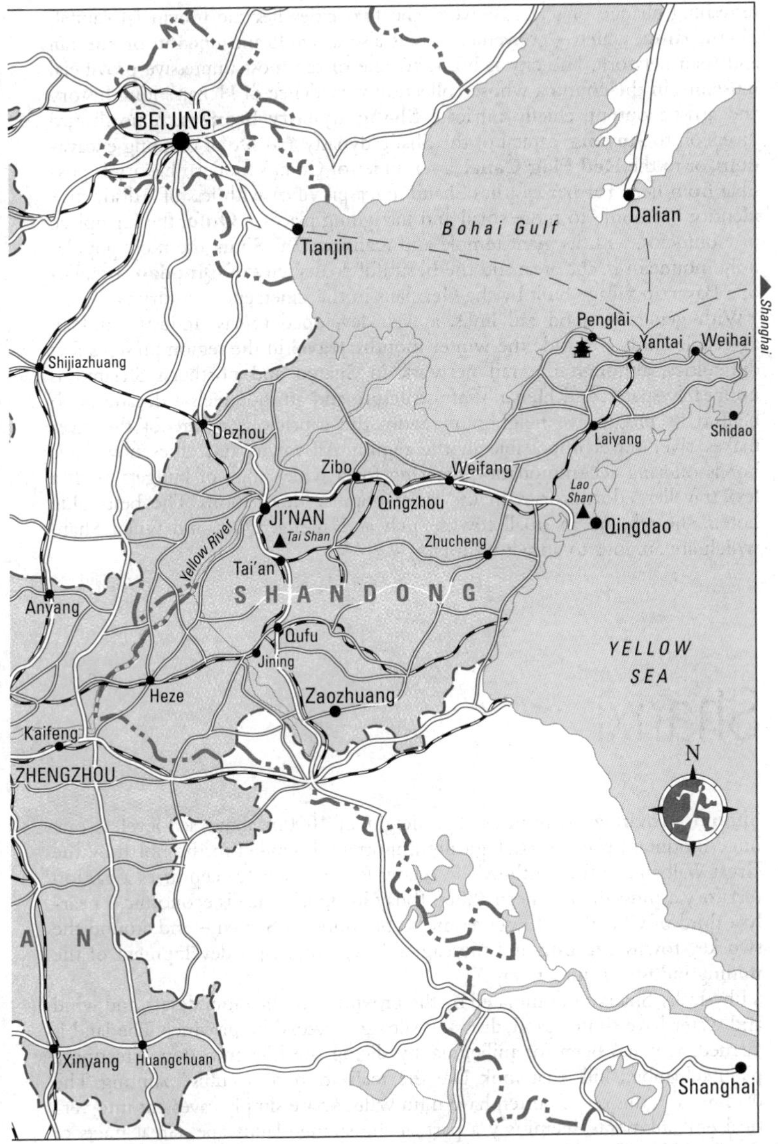

a substantial Muslim minority, whose cuisine is well worth sampling. Within easy travelling distance of here, following the Yellow River east, are two more holy mountains, **Hua Shan** and **Song Shan** (home of the legendary Shaolin monks), and the city of **Luoyang** in Henan, with the superb **Longmen cave temples** and **Baima Si** just outside. Continuing east brings you to the little-visited but appealing town of **Kaifeng**, a mellow lakeside city that provides a refreshing change of scale. Between the two cities lies the provincial capital, **Zhengzhou**, which – conveniently – is also a significant junction on the rail and road network. The city is home to one of the most impressive provincial museums in the country, whose collection is evidence of Henan's long history and artistic output, chiefly intricate **Shang dynasty bronzes**. A northward diversion to **Anyang**, capital of the Shang dynasty and site of ongoing excavations, or to the **Red Flag Canal**, a reminder of China's modern history, is possible from here. Farther east lies Shandong, a province with less of a distinctive identity, but home to more small and intriguing places – **Qufu**, the birthplace of Confucius, with its giant temple and mansion; **Tai Shan**, the most popular holy mountain in the area; and the beautiful coastal city of **Qingdao**, a replica of a Bavarian village built by the Germans in the nineteenth century.

With generally good rail links, a well-developed tourist industry and an agreeable climate outside the winter months, **travel** in the region presents few difficulties, although the rail network in Shanxi and northern Shaanxi is noticeably sparse, and Henan's infrastructure and attitude feels a decade or so behind its progressive neighbours. Sadly, the capricious nature of the river makes river travel impossible in the region. All towns and cities now have hotels offering accommodation catering for a wide range of budgets, with a few travellers' dormitories in the most popular destinations. The best-value hotels, though, are in small towns, such as Kaifeng, Qufu and Wutai Shan, which are anxious to attract visitors.

Shanxi

Shanxi province, with an average height of 1000m above sea level, is one huge mountain plateau. Strategically important, bounded to the north by the Great Wall and to the south by the Yellow River, it was for centuries a bastion territory against the northern tribes. Today its significance is economic – nearly a third of China's coal reserves are to be found in Shanxi – and around the two key towns, **Datong** and the capital **Taiyuan**, major development of the mining industry is under way.

Physically, Shanxi is dominated by the proximity of the Gobi desert, and wind and water have shifted sand, dust and silt right across the province. The land is farmed, as it has been for millennia, by slicing the hills into steps, creating a plain of ribbed hills that look like the realization of a cubist painting. The dwellings in this terrain often have mud walls, or are simply caves cut into vertical embankments, seemingly a part of the strange landscape. Great tracts of this land, though, are untillable, due to soil erosion caused by tree felling, and the uncertainty of rainfall, which has left much of the province fearsomely barren, an endless range of dusty hills cracked by fissures. Efforts are now being made to arrest erosion and the advance of the desert, including a huge tree-planting campaign. Sometimes you'll even see wandering dunes held in place by immense nets of woven straw.

Tourist workers in the province call Shanxi a "museum above the ground", a reference to the many unrestored but still intact **ancient buildings** that dot

Cave houses

A common sight among the stern folds and fissures of the dry loess plain of northern Shanxi (and neighbouring Shaanxi) are **cave dwellings**, a traditional form of housing that's been in use for nearly two thousand years. Hollowed into the sides of hills terraced for agriculture, they house more than eighty million Chinese people, and are eminently practical – cheap, easy to make, naturally insulated (they are warm in winter and cool in summer) and long-lasting. In fact, a number of intact caves in Hejin, on the banks of the Yellow River in the west of the province, are said to date back to the Tang dynasty. Furthermore, in a region where flat land has to be laboriously hacked out of the hillside, caves don't take up land that could be cultivated.

The **facade** of the cave is usually a wooden frame on a brick base. Most of the upper part consists of a wooden lattice – designs of which are sometimes very intricate – faced with white paper, which lets in plenty of light, but preserves the occupants' privacy. Tiled eaves above protect the facade from rain damage. Inside, the **single-arched chamber** is usually split into a bedroom at the back and a living area in front, furnished with a *kang* (stove) whose flue leads under the bed to heat it, then outside to the terraced field that is the roof. Sometimes the first visible indication of a distant village is a set of smoke columns rising from the crops.

Such is the popularity of cave homes that prosperous cave dwellers often prefer to build themselves a new courtyard and another cave rather than move into a house. Indeed, in the suburbs of towns and cities of northern Shaanxi, new **concrete apartment buildings** are built in imitation of caves, with three windowless sides and an arched central door. It is not uncommon even to see soil spread over the roofs of these apartments with vegetables grown on top.

the region, some from dynasties almost unrepresented elsewhere in China, such as the Song and the Tang. In the same breath they call neighbouring Shaanxi a "museum under the ground", an unfair comment no doubt engendered by that province's greater popularity as a tourist destination. Shanxi's unpopularity, despite its rich crop of historical buildings, can be put down to the grimness of its cities, dominated by the coal industry, and the relative inaccessibility of most of the province's fine constructions. Visitors usually restrict themselves to the main attraction, the **Yungang cave temples** at Datong, seven hours from Beijing, which are easily taken in en route to Hohhot in Inner Mongolia, or Xi'an farther south. Anyone who has time to explore the province further, however, is richly rewarded at **Wutai Shan**, a holy mountain in the northeast on the border with Hebei. Formerly difficult to reach (the journey can now be done in four hours by private minibus from Taiyuan, the nearest city), Wutai Shan's combination of ancient temples and breathtaking scenery make it one of the best mountain sites in the country, though Jiang Zemin's call to entrepreneurs – made on his visit in 2001 – to "make Wutai famous" is already compromising this serenity. Although **Taiyuan** itself has few historic sights to boast of, the city is commercially developing, accustomed to tourists, and thus is a good base from which to move around the region. Farther south, all within a bus ride of the towns spread along the rail line between Taiyuan and Xi'an, are obscure little places, well off the predictable China trails, full of memorable sights. Particularly fine are a couple of superb temples, stuck out in the middle of nowhere, such as the **Shuanglin Si** outside Taiyuan, with its amazing sculptures, and the striking murals of the **Yongle Gong** at Ruicheng. At **Pingyao**, the walled town seems stuck in a time warp, its alleys lined with charming Qing-dynasty architecture. Once you venture far off the arterial rail line, travel becomes hard work, as roads and bus connections aren't good. You'll need to keep this in mind if you wish to make a diversion to the banks of the Yellow River, which runs down the western margin of the province. It's here, at **Hukou Falls**, that the river presents its fiercest aspect, which so impressed the Chinese that they put a picture of the torrent on the back of their fifty-yuan notes, though it's now been replaced by an image of Lhasa's Potala Palace.

Datong and around

Don't be put off by first impressions of contemporary **DATONG**, the second largest city in Shanxi province, situated in the far north, near the border with Inner Mongolia. Amid blasted landscape of modern industrial China – coal mines, power stations and a huge locomotive factory – are some marvellous ancient sites, remnants of the city's glory days as the capital city of two non-Han Chinese dynasties.

The Turkic Toba people took advantage of the internal strife afflicting central and southern China to establish their own dynasty, the **Northern Wei** (386–534), taking Datong as their capital in 398 AD, by which time they had conquered the whole of the north. Though the period was one of strife and warfare (and elsewhere the Wei never fully consolidated their hold on power), the Northern Wei, who became fervent Buddhists, made some notable cultural achievements. The finest of these was a magnificent series of **cave temples** at Yungang, just west of the city, still one of the most impressive sights in northern China. Over the course of almost a century, more than one thousand grottoes were completed, containing over fifty thousand statues, before the capital

Datong and around

Datong	大同	***dàtóng***
Datong Binguan	大同宾馆	*dàtóng bīnguǎn*
Hongqi Hotel & Restaurant	红旗大饭店	*hóngqí dàfàndiàn*
Huayan Si	华严寺	*huáyán sì*
Locomotive Factory	大同机车工厂	*dàtóng jīchē gōngchǎng*
Nine Dragon Screen	九龙壁	*jiǔlóng bì*
Railway Binguan	火车宾馆	*huǒchē bīnguǎn*
Shanhua Si	善化寺	*shànhuà sì*
Tianjin Baozi	天津包子	*tiānjīn bāozi*
Yonghe Restaurant	永和大酒店	*yǒnghé dàjiǔdiàn*
Yungang Binguan	云冈宾馆	*yúngāng bīnguǎn*
Around Datong		*Around Datong*
Yungang Caves	云冈石窟	*yúngāng shíkū*
Hunyuan	浑源	***húnyuán***
The Hanging Temple	悬空寺	*xuánkōng sì*
Hengshan	恒山	*héngshān*
Hengshan Binguan	恒山宾馆	*héngshān bīnguǎn*
Yingxian	应县	***yìngxiàn***
Jincheng Binguan	金城宾馆	*jīnchéng bīnguǎn*
Yingxian Pagoda	应县木塔	*yìngxiàn mùtǎ*

was moved south to Luoyang (see p.298), where construction began on the similar Longmen Caves.

A second period of greatness came with the arrival of the Mongol **Liao dynasty**, also Buddhists, who made Datong their capital in 907. They were assimilated into the Jin in 1125, but not before leaving a small legacy of statuary and some fine temple architecture, notably in the **Huayan and Shanhua temples** in town, and a **wooden pagoda**, the oldest in China, in the nearby town of Yingxian. Datong remained important to later Chinese dynasties for its strategic position just inside the Great Wall, south of Inner Mongolia, and the tall city walls date from the early Ming dynasty. Though most visitors today are attracted by the Buddhist sites, Datong is also the closest city to **Heng Shan**, one of the five holy mountains of Taoism, whose most spectacular building, the almost unbelievable **Hanging Temple**, is firmly on the tour agenda. It's also possible to use Datong as the jumping-off point for an excursion to the Buddhist centre of **Wutai Shan** (see p.243).

Datong now produces a third of all China's **coal**, enough to fuel the two power stations on the city's outskirts, one of which supplies electricity for Beijing, the other for the whole of Shanxi Province. Coal dominates the modern city – it sits in the donkey carts and lorries that judder up and down the main roads, it stains the buildings black and it swirls in the air you breathe, making Datong one of the most polluted cities in China. Once you have seen the caves and temples there's no reason to stay around, and a day or two here is enough. The city is well connected by rail, and by travelling on the evening sleeper trains, Datong's major sights can be seen as a day-trip from Beijing (7hr) and Taiyuan (7hr), or as a stop off en route between Beijing and Xi'an.

Arrival, information and transport

Downtown Datong, bounded by square walls, is split by **Da Bei Jie** and **Da Xi Jie**, two dead straight streets on north–south and east–west axes, which intersect at the heart of the city, just north of the old Bell Tower. The tourist sights are all within walking distance of the crossroads, while the two main tourist hotels are considerably farther south. The de facto town center is at **Hongqi** (Red Flag) **Square**, on the corner of Da Xi Jie and Xinjian Nan Lu.

Datong's **train station** is in the city's northern outskirts, at the end of Da Bei Jie, far from any of the sights. A major railhead at the intersection of a line to Xi'an and the line between Beijing and Baotou, this is the first stop in China for trains from Mongolia, and it makes a harsh, disorientating introduction to the country for passengers stepping off the train from Ulan Batur. Grimy and cavernous, the station is usually thronged with passengers, many of them peasants migrating in search of construction work, their possessions tied up in grain sacks. Hotel touts wave signs at the crush of arriving passengers emerging from the platform gates on the station's west side. They mostly represent places which won't accept foreigners, though often they'll tell you they do. More usefully, you may be grabbed by a representative of the extremely helpful **station CITS office**, at first indistinguishable from the pushy touts and taxi drivers. If he misses you, the office, inside the station, on the west side, is a recommended first stop, a good place to get your bearings and meet other travellers and, unusually, to receive advice and information. **Long-distance buses** terminate just south of the train station on Xinjian Bei Lu. The airport, south of town, was not operating commercial flights at the time of writing, although a service may be up and running soon.

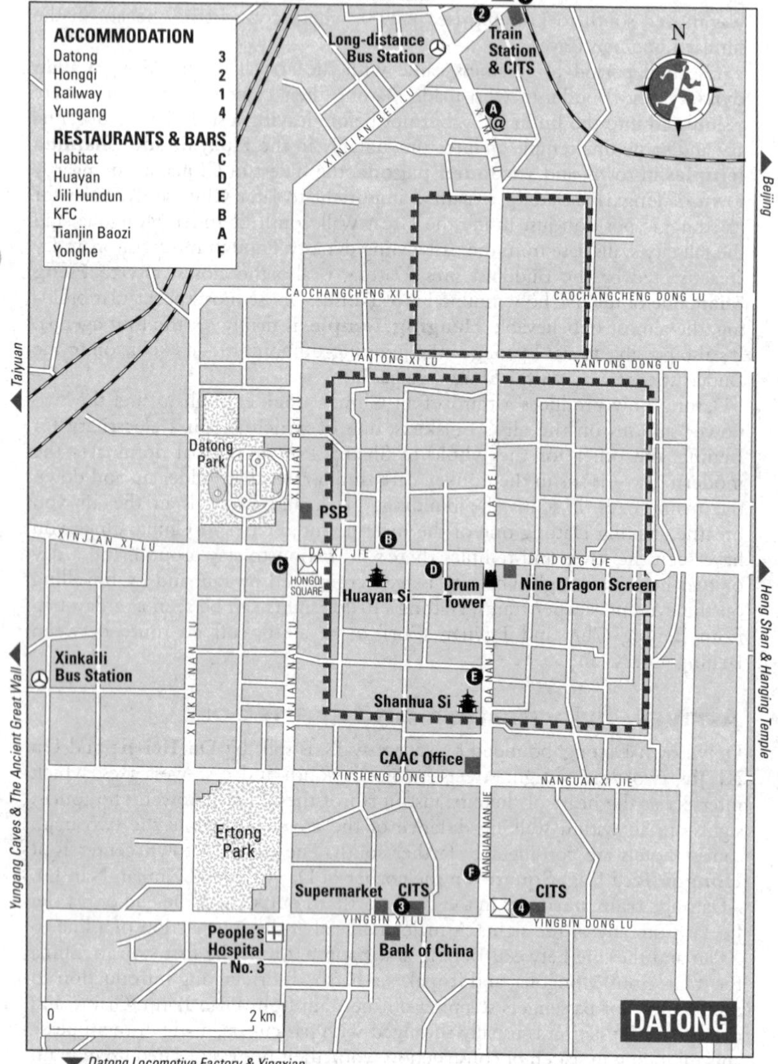

City transport

The train station is the origin of Datong's clutch of **bus routes** (¥1). Annoyingly, no single bus travels the length of the city's north–south axis, along which most places of interest to visitors are located. Bus #4 will get you from the station to the main crossroads, where it turns west, past the Huayan Si and Hongqi Square before terminating just outside the old city walls. To get from the crossroads to the southern hotels, take bus #17 from its terminus on the east side of Xiao Nan Jie. To get to these hotels direct from the train station, take bus #15, which travels south down Xinjian Nan Lu, then turns east on to

Yingbin Xi Lu. **taxi** For details of buses to places in the vicinity of Datong, see p.238.

Taxis cruise the streets; flagfall is ¥5, and either ¥1.8 or ¥1.2 per km after that. A ride within town should be under ¥10. **Walking** around the city is tiring, as it's quite spread out – over 8km from the station to the hotels – and roads are tediously straight and (air and noise) pollution astounding. Keep to the main streets after dark; at night Datong is not always a friendly city.

Accommodation

Budget accommodation is scarce in Datong, and your best bet is to book through the train station CITS (ⓣ0352/5101326), who offer a discounted rate. Most convenient of the budget options, though overpriced for what you get, is the CITS-run *Railway Binguan*, 750m north of the station, with dorm beds as well as some musty doubles (❸, dorm beds ¥40). The *Hongqi Hotel* (ⓣ0352/2816823; ❸–❺), 11 Zhanqian Jie, has a few rooms that are in the same price bracket as the *Railway Binguan* and boasts 24-hour hot water. The rate includes three meals per day in its restaurant, where locals and cadres are drawn to dine. The hotel is the neon-topped tower across the square and to the right as you exit the station.

Two more upmarket hotels are both in the south of the city, a long way from the centre. The refitted *Yungang Binguan*, at 21 Yingbin Dong Lu (ⓣ0352/5021601, ⓕ5024927; ❻), is the most comfortable, and there's a foreign exchange, a post office and a coffee shop on the premises; there's also an old east wing which, while it remains unrenovated, offers cheaper rooms (❸). Also refurbished, the *Datong Binguan* (ⓣ0352/2032476; ❼) is farther west on Yingbin Xi Lu and has similar facilities, catering to Yungang cave tourists. It has nicer surroundings than the *Yungang*, as it borders a new park and is across the street from a grocery store, bookseller, and several inexpensive restaurants.

The City

The yellow earthen **ramparts** that once bounded the old city are still quite impressive, though they have been heavily cut into and demolished in places as modern Datong has expanded. The best stretches are in the east of the city. Inside the walls, the few treasures that remain of Datong's considerably more prestigious past are off sombre streets lined with utilitarian buildings and walls painted with propaganda slogans. Outside the centre, the streets, along which Mao-suited men ride donkey carts brimming with coal, have a gritty, Dickensian feel which those who don't have to live here might just find appealing.

Downtown

Just south of the crossroads of Da Xi Jie and Da Bei Jie, at the heart of the city, Datong's three-storey **Drum Tower** dates back to the Ming dynasty. You can't go inside but it makes a useful landmark. A little way east from the crossroads, on the south side of Da Dong Jie, the **Nine Dragon Screen** (daily 8am–6pm; ¥3) stands in a courtyard a few metres back from the road, looking a little out of place without the palace it once stood in front of, which was destroyed by fire in the fifteenth century. Originally the eight-metre high screen would have stood directly in front of the entrance, an unpassable obstacle to evil spirits which, it was thought, could only travel in straight lines. The raised relief of nine sinuous dragons depicted in 426 glazed tiles along its 45-metre surface, rising from the waves and cavorting among suns, is lively and colourful.

Underneath, the dragons and other animals, real and imaginary, are depicted in a separate, much smaller relief. A long, narrow pool in front of the screen is meant to reflect the dragons and give the illusion of movement when you look into its rippling surface.

About a kilometre west of here, the **Huayan Si** (daily 8.30am–5pm; ¥6), originally a large temple dating back to 1062 AD during the Liao dynasty, is reached by an alley leading south off Da Xi Jie across from *KFC*; look for the temple's roofs, visible above the surrounding low shops. The remaining buildings, mostly Qing, are split into two complexes. The **Upper Temple**, the first one you come to, is a little shabby, but with some interesting details, and it seems to be at least semi-working, with the odd monk wandering around. Look for the unusual roof decoration on the first building – elephants carrying pagodas on their backs – and the small handmade shrines that have been placed in the temple courtyard by modern worshippers. Set on a four-metre-high platform and recently restored, the huge twelfth-century **Main Hall** is one of the two largest Buddhist halls in China, and is unusual for facing east – it was originally built by a sect that worshipped the sun. The design at the end of the roof ridge curves inwards like a horn, a rare design peculiar to the region. Inside, five Ming Buddhas, made of stucco or wood and painted gold, sit on elaborate painted thrones, attended by twenty life-size guardians, some of whom look Indian in appearance, gently inclined as if listening attentively. Qing-dynasty frescoes on the walls, depicting Buddha's attainment of nirvana, and nearly one thousand roof panels depicting flowers, Sanskrit letters and dragons, have been repainted in their original gaudy hues. Turn right out of the entrance to this complex and you come to the **Lower Temple**, notable for its rugged-looking hall, a rare Liao-dynasty construction from 1038, according to an inscription on a roof beam. Inside, a varied collection of 31 stucco Buddhas and Bodhisattvas, with elegantly carved drapery and delicate features, also Liao, sit gathering dust in the gloom. The walls are lined with bookcases for holding scriptures, made to look like little houses.

From Huayan Si, it's an enjoyable twenty-minute meander past clubs, shops and restaurants along Da Nan Jie to the **Shanhua Si** (daily 8.30am–5pm; ¥10). A temple has stood here since the Tang dynasty, though what you see is a Ming restoration of a Jin building. The two halls, with little decoration, thick russet walls and huge, chunky wooden brackets in the eaves, have a solid presence very different from the delicate look of later Chinese temples. The Jin-dynasty statues in the main hall, five Buddhas in the centre with 24 *lokapalas* (divine generals) lined up on either side, are exceptionally finely detailed. Look for the Mother of Ghosts, a matronly woman of benign expression, with a small green, impish figure with long teeth, carrying a child on its shoulder, standing at her feet. According to myth, the Mother of Ghosts was an evil woman who ate children until Buddha kidnapped her son. She was so racked with grief that when Buddha returned the child she agreed to devote her life to good deeds; the imp is a depiction of her evil side. A wooden building, in the west of the complex, is Tang in style, with three storeys and a double roof, and is impressive just for its longevity – an inscription on a beam inside records its construction in 1154.

The Locomotive Factory

An attraction in keeping with the character of the contemporary city is the **Datong Locomotive Factory**, 3km southwest of the city. This was the last steam locomotive factory in the world until it switched from steam to diesel production in 1988. To get here, take bus #27 from the train station, or hop in a cab (¥17). From the main entrance on Wenhua Jie, it's a long walk through the grounds to the factory itself – continue straight until the T-junction, turn left, then right at the guardhouse, topped by a yellow propaganda billboard. You shouldn't be stopped, and if you are, say you're going to the museum. Once inside, you're faced with a city-unto-itself. You can wander for hours – and for kilometres – though if it's the museum you fancy, take the first right after the guardhouse (at the billboard showing photos of model workers), then left 150m ahead at the propaganda announcement which, at time of writing, was "work hard today, or tomorrow you'll be looking hard for work". The open-air museum (daily 9am–11.30am & 2–5.30pm; ¥10) is ahead on the right. Look for the six locomotives and enter through the fence, where an ancient woman will issue your ticket, then leave you to wander and climb on the artefacts as you like. Before you leave, pick up a Datong Locomotive Factory faceplate (¥40) from her.

You can also take the **CITS tour**, which has to be arranged at least a few hours (preferably a day) in advance, (¥100 per person, with a preferred minimum of five people in the party). Tours run only on weekdays when the factory is open – it is sometimes shut down for short periods when business is slack. After a talk from the guide in stilted English, you're led through the giant plant, impressive for its scale – it has nearly nine thousand staff, all working with a horrifying lack of safety provisions – before being shown round the museum. The climax of the tour is a short ride in a steam train which was made here in 1987. All in all, it's more fun to explore the site on your own.

Eating and drinking

Datong is far enough north for mutton hotpot to figure heavily in the local cuisine, along with potatoes, which you can buy, processed into a starchy jelly and seasoned with sauces, from street stalls. Other typically northern dishes available are *zongyi* (glutinous rice dumplings) and *yuanxiao* (sweet dumplings). **Snacks** made from oatmeal are on sale from friendly buskers around Hongqi Square and Da Xi Jie. There are also plenty of cheap eating places north of the train station, serving bowls of noodles and steaming meat dumplings, the best among these being *Tianjin Baozi*, south from the station on the eastern side of Xima Lu.

You won't find any gourmet food in Datong, but you can sample local fare at the *Huayan Restaurant*, one block east of the temple on Da Xi Jie. *KFC* is nearby, on the same road. Other options in the vicinity are found south of the Drum Tower on Da Nan Jie, where near the Hualin Supermarket there are noodle and wonton shops, including *Jili Hundun*. Further south on Nanguan Nan Jie, the *Yonghe Restaurant*, 2km south of the Drum Tower, is vibrant and plush; expect to pay around ¥30 for two dishes with rice, tea and beer. On the west side of the train station concourse, the restaurant at the *Hongqi* hotel is well worth a visit, though try to get a table away from the private rooms, whose residents may break into karaoke in the evening. A meal for two should be about ¥50. Wherever you eat, make sure you get there early – restaurants begin closing around 9pm. For a pint and **pub food**, try the expat-oriented *Habitat* on Xinjian Nan Lu, across from Hongqi Square. Datong's latest **clubs** can be found near the Drum Tower on Da Nan Jie and Da Xi Jie.

Listings

Airlines The CAAC office (☎0352/2044039) is on 1 Nanguan Nan Jie (daily 8.30am–5pm), with another office in the *Yungang Binguan*. Note, however, that flights leave from Taiyuan, well to the south.

Banks and exchange The only place to cash traveller's cheques is at the main Bank of China (Mon–Fri 8am–6.30pm) on Yingbin Xi Lu opposite the *Datong Binguan*. If you're staying at either *Datong Binguan* or the *Yungang Binguan*, you can exchange money or cash traveller's cheques until 8pm – non-guests can only exchange cash.

Buses Buses for local towns, including Yingxian and Hunyuan, leave from the bus station on Xinjian Bei Lu about 1km from the train station. Xinkaili bus station, in the west of town, is the place to catch the #3 bus to the Yungang Caves. For Taiyuan and Wutai Shan, look for the touts working the train station concourse – you'll spot them perched in the doorways of minibuses.

Hospital People's Hospital No. 3 is in the south of the city on Yingbin Xi Lu, just west of the cross-roads with Xinjian Nan Lu.

Internet access Downtown, Internet cafés can be found on Da Nan Jie, and on the eastern side of Hongqi Square. There are also several shops offering Net access near the train station: there's a Net café next to *Tianjin Baozi*, while on Xinjian Bei Lu near the bus station is another Net café, sharing premises with a Korean BBQ.

Left luggage There's a left-luggage office outside the train station on the western side of the concourse (¥5).

Mail and telephones The large Russian-looking stately building fronting Hongqi Square, south of Da Xi Jie, houses both the post office (daily 8am–6pm), and a 24hr telecom office. Droves of laid-off women stand about selling cut-rate IC and IP phone cards.

PSB The police station (Mon–Sat 8.30–noon & 2.30–6pm) is on Xinjian Bei Lu, 200m north of the post office; take along a Mandarin speaker since they're not particularly heedful to traveller needs. If you have anything stolen insist on getting a loss report.

Shopping There's an antiques mall across from Nine Dragon Screen. Clothing shops line Da Xi Jie.

Trains Tickets are straightforward enough to buy. Check the same-day window (labelled "today" in Chinese) for the slow night train to Taiyuan (#4463; ¥65), which takes seven hours and saves you the expense of a hotel in Datong. At the back of the station opposite the door, there's a comfortable waiting room (¥5 for 2hr) featuring armchairs and TV; it's minded by a stern lady who tells you when your train arrives.

Travel agents The main CITS office (daily 6.30am–6pm; ⓣ0352/5024176), on the eastern side of the concourse of the *Yungang Binguan*, deals with tour groups and provides guides. The more useful train station CITS office (daily 6.30am–6:30pm; ⓣ0352/5101326), inside the station itself, is particularly helpful and worth a visit for information on the city and the area. They'll book same-day train tickets for a ¥40 charge. Their tours of the major sights out of town are worth considering.

Around Datong

The sights outside the city are far more diverting than those within. Apart from the glorious **Yungang Caves**, the ancient buildings dotted around in nearby country towns are worth checking out, if you have time to spare. Roads in the area are not good (and are often blocked in winter, when transport times can be as much as doubled), but at least journeys are enlivened by great views: the lunar emptiness of the fissured landscape is broken only occasionally by villages whose mud walls make them look like they have grown out of the raw brown earth. Some of the villages in the area still have their beacon towers, left over from the time when this really was a wild frontier.

To help explore the area around the city, buy a **map** of Datong (¥4) from outside the bus station, as this includes maps of Hunyuan and Yingxian, together with train timetables on the back. Getting around by yourself on the teeth-rattling buses can be time-consuming, so if your Chinese isn't up to speed and time is tight, consider taking a CITS **tour**. They run a combined day excursion from Datong to the **Yungang Caves** and the **Outer Great Wall** for ¥50–100, depending upon group size. They also do a daily tour of the caves and, depending on the weather, the **Hanging Temple** or the **Yingxian Wooden Pagoda**. This leaves daily at 9am and returns in the evening, and will pick up and drop off at your hotel. During the tour, the minibus also stops briefly in a village of squat, mud-walled houses and cave dwellings. Costs vary depending on numbers, but expect to pay around ¥100 including an English-speaking guide and lunch but excluding tickets at each sight, or ¥210 including tickets as well. If you want to sign up, it's better to do so at the more helpful of Datong's two CITS offices, at the train station (see "Listings", p.238).

The Yungang Caves

Just 25 minutes by bus from Datong, the monumental **Yungang Caves** (daily 9am–5pm; ¥50), a set of Buddhist grottoes carved into the side of a sandstone cliff 16km west of the city, are a must. Built around 400 AD at a time of Buddhist revival, the caves were the first and grandest of the three major Buddhist grottoes (the latter two being the Longmen Caves in Luoyang and the Mogao Caves: see p.305 and p.1050); they also remain the best preserved. Access is straightforward: take **bus** #4 from the train station or bus #17 from Yingbin Xi Lu to the Xinkaili bus station in the west of the city; bus #3 (¥1.5) from here terminates at the caves.

In style and design the caves are influenced by similar Indian structures, and they may also have been inspired by earlier cave art in Afghanistan. Certainly many of the craftsmen who worked on the project came from India and Central Asia, and there is much foreign influence in the **carvings**: Greek motifs (tridents and acanthus leaves), Persian symbols (lions and weapons), and bearded figures, even images of the Hindu deities Shiva and Vishnu, are incorporated among the more common dragons and phoenixes of Chinese origin. The soft, rounded modelling of the **sandstone Datong figures** – China's first stone statues – lining the cave interiors has more in common with the terracotta carvings of the Mogao Caves near Dunhuang in Gansu, begun a few years earlier, than with the sharp, more linear features of Luoyang's later limestone work. In addition, a number of the seated Buddhas have sharp, almost Caucasian noses.

The artistry on show is unsurpassed in China, and the labour involved is no less impressive, requiring as many as forty thousand workmen. **Construction** began in 453 AD, when Datong was the capital of the Wei dynasty, and petered out around 525, after the centre of power moved to Luoyang. The caves were made by first hollowing out a section at the top of the cliff, then digging into the rock, down to the ground and out, leaving two holes, one above the other. Their present condition is misleading as originally the cave entrances would have been covered with wooden facades, and the sculptures would have been faced with plaster and brightly painted; the larger sculptures are pitted with regular holes which would once have held wooden supports on which the plaster face was built. Over the centuries, some of the caves have inevitably suffered from weathering, though there seems to have been little vandalism, certainly less than at Luoyang.

Arranged in three **clusters** (east, central and west) and numbered east to west from 1–51, the caves originally spread across an area more than 15km long. What you see today is but a small fragment site stretching 1km. If it's spectacle you're after, just wander at will, but to get an idea of the changes of style and the accumulation of influences, you need to move between the three clusters. The earliest group is caves 16–20, followed by 7, 8, 9 and 10, then 5, 6 and 11 – the last to be completed before the court moved to Luoyang. Then followed 4, 13, 14 and 15, with the caves at the eastern end – 1, 2 and 3 – and cave 21 in the west, carved last. Caves 22–50 are smaller and less interesting.

The eastern caves

The **late caves**, 1–4, are slightly set apart from, and less spectacular than, the others. **Caves 1 and 2** are constructed around a single square central pillar, elaborately carved in imitation of a wooden stupa, but now heavily eroded, around which devotees perambulated. **Cave 3**, 25m deep, is the largest in Yungang; an almost undecorated cavern, it may once have been used as a lecture hall. The three statues at the west end, a ten-metre-high Buddha and his two attendants, are skilfully carved and in good condition. The rounded fleshiness of their faces, with double chins and thick, sensuous lips, hints at their late construction as they are characteristic of Tang-dynasty images. In **Cave 4**, which again has a central pillar carved with images of Buddha, there's a well-preserved, cross-legged Maitreya Buddha on the west wall.

The central caves

The most spectacular caves are numbers 5–13, dense with **monumental sculpture**. Being suddenly confronted and dwarfed by a huge, seventeen-metre-high Buddha as you walk into **cave 5**, his gold face shining softly in the half light, is an awesome, humbling experience. His other-worldly appearance is helped by blue hair and ruby red lips. Other Buddhas of all sizes, a heavenly gallery, are massed in niches which honeycomb the grotto's gently curving walls, and two Bodhisattvas stand attentive at his side.

Cave 6, though very different, is just as arresting. A wooden facade built in 1652 leads into a high, square chamber dominated by a thick central pillar carved with Buddhas and Bodhisattvas in deep relief, surrounded by flying Buddhist angels and musicians. The vertical grotto walls are alive with images, including reliefs depicting incidents from the **life of the Buddha** at just above head height, which were designed to form a narrative when read walking clockwise around the chamber. Easy-to-identify scenes at the beginning include the birth of the Buddha from his mother's armpit, and Buddha's father carrying the young infant on an elephant. The young prince's meeting with a fortune-teller – here an emaciated man with a sharp goatee, who (the story goes) predicted he would become an ascetic if confronted by disease, death and old age – is shown on the north side of the pillar. In an attempt to thwart this destiny, his father kept him in the palace all through his youth. Buddha's first trip out of the palace, which is depicted as a schematic, square Chinese building, is shown on the east wall of the cave, as is his meeting with the grim realities of life, in this case a cripple with two crutches.

Caves 7 and 8 are a pair, both square, with two chambers, and connected by an arch lined with angels and topped with what looks like a sunflower. The figures here, such as the six celestial worshippers above the central arch, are more Chinese in style than their predecessors in caves 16–20, perhaps indicating the presence of craftsmen from Gansu, which the Wei conquered in 439 AD. Two figures on either side of the entrance to cave 8 are some of the best carved and certainly the most blatantly foreign in the complex: a five-headed, six-armed Shiva sits on a bird on the left as you enter, while, on the right, a three-headed Vishnu sits on a bull. These Indian figures have distinctly Chinese features, however, and the bird, a garuda in Hindu mythology, is identical to the Chinese phoenix.

The columns and lintels at the entrances of **caves 9, 10 and 12** are awash with sculptural detail in faded pastel colours: Buddhas, dancers, musicians, animals, flowers, angels and abstract, decorative flourishes (which bear a resemblance to Persian art). Parts of cave 9 are carved with imitation brackets to make the interior resemble a wooden building. The tapering columns at the entrance to cave 12 are covered with tiny Buddhas, but look out for the cluster of musicians with strange-looking instruments depicted behind them.

The outstretched right arm of the fifteen-metre-high Buddha inside **cave 13** had to be propped up for stability, so his sculptors ingeniously carved the supporting pillar on his knee into a four-armed mini-Buddha. The badly eroded sculptures of **caves 14 and 15** are stylistically some way between the massive figures of the early western caves and the smaller reliefs of the central caves.

The western caves

Compared with the images in the central caves, the figures in these, the **earliest caves** (nos. 16–20), are simpler and bolder and, though they are perhaps more crudely carved, they are at least as striking. The **giant Buddhas**, with round faces, sharp noses, deep eyes and thin lips, are said to be the representations of five emperors. Constructed between 453 and 462, under the supervision of the monk Tan Hao, all are in the same pattern of an enlarged niche containing a massive Buddha flanked by Bodhisattvas. The Buddha in **cave 16**, whose bottom half has disintegrated, has a knotted belt high on his chest, Korean-style. The Buddhas were carved from the top down, and when the sculptors of the Buddha in **cave 17** reached ground level they needed to dig down to fit his feet in. The same problem was solved in **cave 18** by giving the Buddha shortened legs. Despite the stumpy limbs, this is still one of the finest sculptures in the complex, in which charming details, including the rows of tiny Bodhisattvas carved into his robe, are set off by strong sweeping forms, such as the simplified planes of his face. The fourteen-metre-high Buddha in **cave 20**, sitting open to the elements in a niche that once would have been protected by a wooden canopy, is probably the most famous, and certainly the most photographed. The figure is characteristic of Northern Wei art, with the folds of his garments expressed by an ordered pattern, and his physiognomy and features formed by simple curves and straight lines. His huge ears almost touch his shoulders.

The small caves 20–50, the least spectacular of the set, are not much visited, but the ceiling of **cave 50** is worth a look for its flying elephants, which also appear in cave 48, and in caves 50 and 51 there are sculptures of acrobats.

The Ancient Great Wall

The two sections of the **Great Wall** around Datong are in fact older and longer than the section at Badaling, and both sites, still devoid of the tourist nests that plague the sections around Beijing, offer a more authenticate and scenic experience.

Imperial Datong was tactically positioned between the Inner and Outer Great Walls. The purpose of the latter was to blockade entry from invading nomadic tribes, while the former formed the second line of defence. If you want to get to the **Outer Wall** independently, take bus #4 from the train station or bus #17 from Yingbin Xi Lu to the Xinkaili bus station in the west of the city; bus #3 from here terminates at the caves. From the eastern caves, continue walking east for about 15 minutes and you'll see remnants of the wall in a field. At the time of writing there was no entry fee and the site was deserted of any local entrepreneurs. The **Inner Wall** is on the eastern side of Heng Shan, 100km east of Datong, and can be approached either by bus or taxi from Hunyuan or as part of a trip to the Hanging Temple.

Heng Shan and the Hanging Temple

Heng Shan, a 250-kilometre-long range curling east to west around northern Shanxi Province, comprises one of the five holy Taoist mountains in China, whose history as a religious centre stretches back more than two thousand years. Plenty of emperors have put in an appearance here to climb the highest peak, Xuanwu (2000m), a trend begun by the very first emperor, Qin Shi Huang.

Contemporary pilgrims usually set out from **Hunyuan**, 75km southeast of Datong and also just 5km north of the **Hanging Temple** (Xuankong Si; daily 9am–5pm; ¥17). Heng Shan's most impressive building, this temple clinging perilously halfway up the side of a sheer cliff face (its name literally translates as "Temple Suspended in the Void") is propped up on long wooden stilts anchored to ledges. There's been a temple on this site since the Northern Wei, though the present structure is mostly Qing. Periodically, the temple buildings were destroyed by the flooding of the Heng River at the base of the cliff (now no longer there, thanks to a dam farther upstream), and at each successive rebuilding, the temple was built higher and higher. At its best from a distance, when its dramatic, gravity-defying location can be more fully appreciated, the temple reveals itself as a bit of a tourist trap as you get closer, with the usual gauntlet of souvenir stalls; in summer, dense crowds turn the Hanging Temple into a claustrophobe's nightmare. Tall, narrow stairs and plank walkways connect the six halls – natural caves and ledges with wooden facades – in which, uniquely, shrines exist to all three of China's main religions, Confucianism, Buddhism and Taoism, all of whose major figures are represented in nearly eighty statues in the complex, made from bronze, iron and stone. In the Three Religions Hall, at the top of the complex, statues of Confucius, Buddha and Lao Zi are seated happily together.

Practicalities

Buses (¥7) run to the small country town of **HUNYUAN** from the Datong long-distance bus station and take about an hour, terminating just opposite the expensive *Hengshan Binguan* (Ⓣ0352/8322045; ❹), where you'll find some mouldy doubles. The town hasn't much to recommend itself other than some appealing Ming street architecture. To get **to Hengshan**, you can catch a tourist bus from the town to the base of the mountain, from where a path leads up to the summit, passing a number of small temples on the way. Minibus touts at Datong's train station who say they're headed **to the Hanging Temple** will most likely drop you at Hunyuan, where there are also frequent minibuses (¥3) to the gravel road at the temple entrance; the ticket office is 100m away across the bridge. To return to Hunyuan from the Hanging Temple, be prepared to haggle with the vehicles for hire – ¥5 should be more than enough, though walking back the same way you came from leads you through friendly villages where it's easier to negotiate a ride.

The last bus back to Datong leaves Hunyuan at 5pm, though note that it's possible to stay the night in Hunyuan and get a ride on to Wutai Shan on the 9am bus from Datong.

Yingxian Pagoda

At the centre of the small town of **YINGXIAN**, 75km south of Datong, the stately **Yingxian Pagoda** (daily 8am–5pm; ¥16), built in 1056 in the Liao dynasty, is the oldest wooden building in China, a masterful piece of structural engineering that looks solid enough to stand here for another millennium. The "Woody Tower," as the English sign explains, reaches nearly 70m high and is octagonal in plan, with nine internal storeys, though there are only six layers of eaves on the outside. You can climb up as far as the fifth storey, and it's definitely worth going inside as this is where the almost unornamented structure is at its most impressive.

The first storey is taller than the rest with extended eaves held up by columns forming a cloister around a mud-and-straw wall. Everything from here up is made of wood – in fact the original pagoda was constructed without a single metal nail, though there are plenty in the floors now. The ceilings and walls of the spacious internal halls are networks of beams held together with huge, intricate **wooden brackets**, called *dougongs*, of which there are nearly sixty different kinds. Interlocking, with their ends carved into curves and layered one on top of another, these give the pagoda a burly, muscular appearance, and as structural supports they perform their function brilliantly – the building has survived seven earthquakes.

Originally each storey had a statue inside, but now only one remains, an eleven-metre-tall Buddha. During a recent renovation a cache of treasures was found buried underneath the pagoda, including Buddhist sutras printed by woodblocks dating back to the Liao dynasty.

Local **buses** to Yingxian from Datong (¥10) take two hours and leave from the long-distance bus station. Yingxian's **bus station** is on the western section of the town's main east–west road, about 1km southwest of the pagoda. You can stay the night in Yingxian at the *Jinchen Binguan* (❷), about 2km south of the pagoda on the main north–south road. From Yingxian, there are buses to Hunyuan, about 50km away, for Heng Shan and the Hanging Temple; these leave every hour until 5pm – also the time of the last bus back to Datong. Alternatively, if you start early you can just about manage to see both the Hanging Temple and Yingxian pagoda by public transport in one day.

Wutai Shan

One of China's four Buddhist mountains, the five flat peaks of **Wutai Shan** – the name means "Five-terrace Mountain" – rise around 3000m above sea level in the northeast corner of Shanxi province, near the border with Hebei. An isolated spot, it rewards the long bus ride it takes to get here with fresh air, superb alpine scenery, some of the best temple architecture in China, decent accommodation and – at its best – a peaceful, spiritual tone, though these days development is beginning to have a noticeable impact.

Wutai Shan was one of the earliest sites where Buddhism took hold in China, and it's been a religious centre at least since the reign of Emperor Ming Di (58–75 AD) when, according to legend, an Indian monk arrived at the mountain and had a vision in which he met the **Manjusri Buddha**. Each Buddhist mountain is dedicated to a particular Bodhisattva, and Wutai Shan became dedicated to Manjusri (also known as the Wenchu Buddha), god of wisdom, who is depicted riding a lion and carrying a manuscript (to represent a sutra) and a sword to cleave ignorance. By the time of the Northern Wei, Wutai Shan was a prosperous Buddhist centre, important enough to be depicted on a mural at the Dunhuang Caves in Gansu. The mountain reached its height of popularity in the Tang dynasty, when there were more than two hundred temples scattered around its peaks, in which monks devoted themselves to the study of the Avatamsaka sutra, which contained references to "a pure and fresh mountain in the northeast" where Manjusri once resided, thought to be Wutai Shan. The number of temples declined in the late Tang, when Buddhism was persecuted, but the mountain enjoyed a second upsurge of popularity in the Ming dynasty, when it found imperial favour; Emperor Kangxi was a frequent visitor. In the fifteenth century, the founder of the Tibetan **Yellow Hat** sect, which emphasizes austerity and rigour over the more indulgent, less doctrinaire, earlier Red Hat sect, came to the area to preach; the Manjusri Buddha is particularly

Wutai Shan

Wutai Shan	五台山	***wǔtái shān***
Bishan Si	碧山寺	*bìshān sì*
Dailuo Ding	黛螺顶	*dàiluó dǐng*
Falei Si	法雷寺	*fǎléi sì*
Foguang Si	佛光寺	*fóguāng sì*
Jifu Si	集福寺	*jífú sì*
Jinge Si	金阁寺	*jīngé sì*
Lingying Si	灵应寺	*língyìng sì*
Longquan Si	龙泉寺	*lóngquán sì*
Luohou Si	罗侯寺	*luóhóu sì*
Nanchan Si	南禅寺	*nánchán sì*
Nanshan Si	南山寺	*nánshān sì*
Puji Si	普济寺	*pǔji sì*
Pusa Ding	菩萨顶	*púsà dǐng*
Qifo Si	七佛寺	*qīfó sì*
Shancai Dong	善财洞	*shàncái dòng*
Shuxiang Si	数象寺	*shùxiàng sì*
Tayuan Si	塔院寺	*tǎyuàn sì*
Wanfo Hall	万佛阁	*wànfó gé*
Wanghai Si	望海寺	*wànghǎi sì*
Xiantong Si	显通寺	*xiǎntōng sì*
Yanjiao Si	演教寺	*yǎnjiào sì*
Zhenhai Si	镇海寺	*zhènhǎi sì*
Taihuai	台怀	***táihuái***
Friendship Hotel	友谊宾馆	*yǒuyì bīnguǎn*
Jinxiu Villa	锦绣山庄	*jǐnxiù shānzhuāng*
Moral Moon Restaurant	德月饭店	*déyuè fàndiàn*
Number Five Hostel	第五招待所	*dìwǔ zhāodàisuǒ*
Railway Hostel	铁路招待所	*tiělù zhāodàisuǒ*
Taihuai Hotel	台怀宾馆	*táihuái bīnguǎn*
Yunfeng Binguan	云峰宾馆	*yúnfēng bīnguǎn*

important in Tibetan and Mongolian Buddhism, and Wutai Shan became an important pilgrimage place for Lamaists.

The mountain's inaccessibility has always given it a degree of protection during purges, and many of the temples survived the Cultural Revolution intact. Most of the forty temples remaining today are in the monastic village of **Taihuai**, which sits in a depression surrounded by the five holy peaks. Highlights are the ninth-century **revolving bookcase** of the Tayuan Si and the two **Tang-dynasty halls** in the Foguan and Nanchan temples, two of the four extant Tang buildings left in China. All the temples today are working, and shaven-headed monks in orange and brown robes conducting esoteric ceremonies or perambulating around the stupas are a common sight – as, increasingly, are tour buses and cadres lumbering into watch them. Developers have taken heed of Jiang Zemin's call to "make Wutai famous" (an order since posted next to an image of the president on a towering billboard at the entrance to Taihuai) by starting to build massive villas along the valley. So, too, has the local Party branch, which installed a **Mao Zedong Memorial Hall** – housing a ceramic bust of the sworn atheist – at the heart of the main temple.

With the increasing emphasis on tourism, the best way to avoid the crowds is to visit between October and April, when the weather turns cold and domestic tour buses head elsewhere. This does, however, mean banking on the weather holding up. Wutai Shan's remote alpine location means a **winter** trip could well be uncomfortable, and even in **spring**, temperatures can fall well below freezing and transport times can double due to treacherous roads (blizzards occur well into April). Even if you keep a close eye on conditions, you'll need to be prepared for unpredictable weather whatever the time of year. Climbing the peaks shouldn't present many difficulties as there are paths everywhere, but do allow plenty of time for journeys as the paths are hard to find in the dark and the temperature drops sharply at sundown.

Travel practicalities

Plenty of tourist minibuses now ply the route into Wutai Shan, a long and bumpy trip across winding mountain passes. You can approach **Taihuai**, the mountain's tourist and pilgrim settlement, from either Datong (see p.232) or Taiyuan (see p.249). Cheap local **buses** cover both routes, but the slightly more expensive tourist buses (¥45) are worth the extra price as they go direct. Wutai Shan is on the Beijing–Taiyuan **rail** line, but if you're arriving from Beijing on the overnight train, you'll be dropped before dawn in the village of **Shahe**, where a waiting minibus (¥10) takes you to Taihuai.

The road trip **from Taiyuan**, 240km to the southwest of Wutai Shan, is much easier than from Datong, taking four hours up the lower, southern approach road, and passing close to the remote and superb Nanchan and Foguang temples. The least painful trip is from the town of **Xinzhou**, which lies on the rail line between Datong and Taiyuan, from where buses take two to three hours, travelling up the southern route. Departing from Taiyuan, your bus may slingshot passengers here, transferring you to another bus for the final approach. The bus trip south **from Datong** takes six hours and involves travelling south over some of the highest ground, passing close to the northern peak and Wanghai Si; in winter this road is usually impassable, and almost always bumpy and delayed. Ask advice from Datong CITS before you leave. It's worth considering taking the overnight #4463 train from Datong to Taiyuan

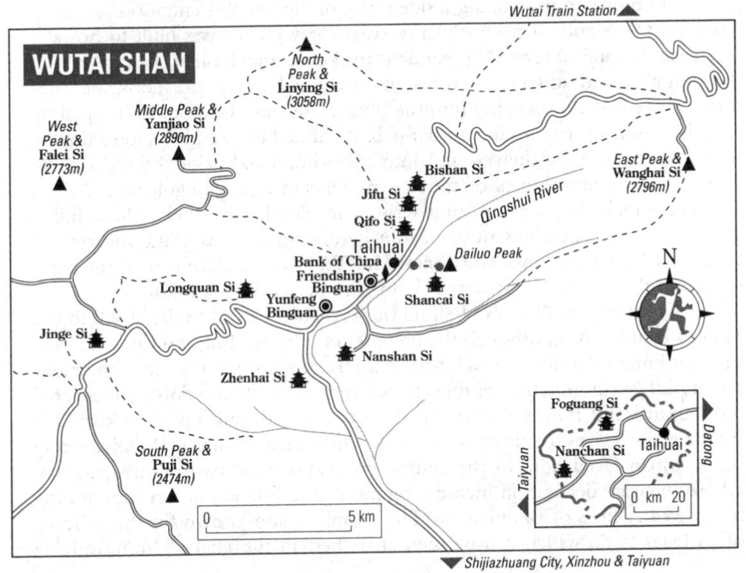

(7hr; ¥65), then immediately hopping on a bus bound for Wutai from the station concourse. This saves a night's accommodation and puts you at Wutai well before noon.

All tourists are charged a mandatory ¥48 **admission fee** to Wutai Shan. Your bus tout may claim he can sell you a discounted entrance ticket as part of your fare, but you'll invariably be charged the fee again by police boarding the bus at Wutai.

Taihuai and around

An unusual and attractive little place, **TAIHUAI** is a strip of tourist facilities and temples set along the west bank of a river, surrounded by green hills which rise to the blue mountains on the horizon. Gently curling grey roofs, decorative double eaves and pagodas are so thick on the ground that it's hard to tell where one temple ends and another begins. The streets are busy with stallholders hectoring passing tourists, clusters of slow-moving monks, wandering pilgrims and fortune-tellers sitting at the roadside.

The village temples

Reached via a stone staircase of 108 steps (the number of beads on a Buddhist rosary), the **Pusa Ding** (¥5), a Ming and Qing complex in which emperors Kangxi and Qianlong once stayed, sits on a hill in the centre of Taihuai, an ideal vantage point from which to survey the town and plan a jaunt around it. To get in, follow the English signs to Yuanzhao Si, which is part of the complex. The fifty-metre-high, Tibetan-style pagoda of the **Tayuan Si** (¥4), a short walk south of Pusa Ding, is Taihuai's most distinctive feature, and used as a symbol of the village. Its bulbous, whitewashed peak, sitting on a large square base, rises high above the grey roofs, and the chimes of the 250 bells hung from its bronze top can be heard across the town when the wind is strong. The largest of many such bottle-shaped pagodas on Wutai Shan, it testifies to the importance of the mountain to Tibetan and Mongolian Lamaism, which is also represented by the tall wooden poles with bronze caps standing inside many of the temple's entrances.

Behind the pagoda, a Ming-dynasty, two-storey library was built to house a bizarre and beautiful revolving wooden **bookcase**, much older than the rest of the complex and still in use today. A hexagonal tower, the bookcase rises through the first-floor ceiling into the library's second storey and is topped by a conical roof; it turns around a narrow base painted to resemble a lotus flower. Thirty-three layers of shelves, split into cubbyholes and painted with decorative designs, hold volumes of sutras – in Tibetan and Mongolian as well as Chinese – including a Ming sutra written in blood, and others whose ink is made of crushed precious stones. From here, English signs point you toward the new **Chairman Mao Memorial Hall** (¥2), whose placement at the heart of one of Buddhism's most sacred sights is in decidedly poor taste.

The **Xiantong Si** (¥6), also behind the Tayuan Si, is said to date back to the Eastern Han (52 AD), although the present complex is Ming and Qing. Among the four hundred rooms is a hall made entirely of bronze, complete with brackets and hinges in imitation of fine timberwork. Its walls and doors are covered with animal and flower designs on the outside and rank upon rank of tiny Buddhas on the inside, along with an elegant bronze Manjusri Buddha sitting on a human-faced lion. In the central courtyard stand two bronze pagodas, whose intricate decoration includes figures riding fish and horses through the sea as well as lines of Bodhisattvas. The temple is also known for the delicacy of its brickwork, which can be seen at its best in the Hall of Immeasurable

Splendour, whose eaves are built in imitation of wooden brackets. The open-air stage here occasionally hosts an opera performance by the wandering Shanxi troupe, when Mao-suited locals can be seen singing along, the lyrics projected onto ribbons of hanging silk.

Just east of the Tayuan Si, the **Luohou Si**, a Ming-dynasty reconstruction of a Tang temple, is notable for a round wooden altar in the main hall with a wave design at its base supporting a large wooden lotus with movable petals. A mechanism underneath opens the petals to reveal four Buddhas sitting inside the flower.

Continuing south of here, you come to the **Wanfo Hall**, once a part of the Tayuan Si, which contains a huge number of Buddhist statues. Outside it sit two Tibetan-style stone pagodas. Farther south, the **Shuxiang Si** (¥4) is the largest in Wutai Shan, a Qing restoration of a Tang building, notable for a bronze Manjusri Buddha flanked by five hundred *lohans*.

Practicalities

Buses arrive in the centre of Taihuai, not at the shuttered bus station, but at a parking area a short walk from the Pusa Ding. Outbound buses to Datong (¥40) and Taiyuan (¥40) leave from the main street between 7am and 2pm. Useful town **maps** in English, some printed on paper, others on handkerchiefs, can be picked up for ¥3. A branch of the Bank of China (daily 8am–noon & 2–6pm) is on the main road, about 1km north from the *Friendship Hotel*.

A good budget **place to stay** near the bus stop is the *Number Five Hostel* (❷), across the road and one block north off the main drag. Also across the road from the bus park is the *Taihuai Hotel* (ⓣ0350/6542731; ❸), where foreign tour groups are billeted. A complex of single-storey grey buildings with upturning eaves, it's supposed to resemble a monastery, though there's nothing monastic about the carpeted rooms with armchairs and TV. Nearby, too, is the *Railway Hostel* (ⓣ0350/6542041; ❷), a comfortable and quiet place tucked away from the masses; to get here from the bus stop, walk towards Pusa Ding and, a few metres on from its entry steps, the lane bends right towards the hotel. Alternatively, head into the alleys around Pusa Ding, where there's a flurry of small guesthouses, almost all of which are happy to take foreigners; a comfortable room can be bargained down to ¥40. Many of the pilgrims stay in the temples themselves, most of which have rudimentary facilities for guests, and this may also be possible for foreigners. It's likely you'll also be offered a homestay, which is technically illegal, but no one seems to mind.

Out of town, the *Friendship Hotel* (ⓣ0350/6542678, ⓕ6542123; ❺) and the *Yunfeng* (ⓣ0350/6542566; ❺), which has a **CITS** office, are representative of both Taihuai's past and future. Formerly the only places sanctioned to accept foreigners, they now cater to well-heeled domestic visitors. They're comfortable, typically Chinese-style places 1.5km and 2km south of town respectively.

Though **restaurants** are in abundance in Wutai, food here is almost universally expensive and mediocre – expect to pay ¥10 for a vegetarian dish, double that for meat, while rice and tea cost extra. The throng of street stalls aren't especially hygienic, and it's best to stick to the dining halls of the hotels or opt for a lively-looking restaurant like the *Fudeyuan*, across from the Monk's Fashion Factory in the alley leading from the main road to the steps of Pusa Ding.

Into the mountains

Few of the local tourists get very far out of Taihuai; it's certainly worth the effort, however, as not just the temples, but also the views and the scenery, are gorgeous. The following are all within an easy day's hike from Taihuai.

The **Nanshan Si** (¥4) sits in a leafy spot halfway up the Yangbai Mountain 5km south of Taihuai. It's approached by a steep flight of stairs, its entrance marked by a huge screen wall of cream-coloured brick. More decorated brickwork inside, including fake brackets and images of deities in flowing robes, is the temple's most distinctive feature. Eighteen Ming images of *lohans* in the main hall are unusually lifelike and expressive; one gaunt figure is sleeping with his head propped up on one knee, his skin sagging over his fleshless bones. Two kilometres southwest of here, the **Zhenhai Si**, sitting in a beautiful leafy spot at an altitude of 1600m just off the road, seems an odd place to build a temple celebrating the prevention of floods, although legend has it that Manjusri tamed the water of the spring that now trickles past the place. During the Qing dynasty a monk called Zhang Jia, reputed to be the living Buddha, lived here; he is commemorated with a small pagoda south of the temple.

The **Longquan Si** is on the west side of the Qingshui River, 5km southwest of Taihuai, just off the main road, and easily accessible by bus from town. Its highlight is the decorated marble entranceway at the top of 108 steps, whose surface is densely packed with images of dragons, phoenixes and foliage buried in a mass of abstract pattern. The rest of the temple seems sedate in comparison, though the Puji Pagoda inside is a similar confection – a fat stupa carved with guardians, surmounted by a fake wooden top and guarded by an elaborate railing. Both structures are fairly late, dating from the beginning of the twentieth century.

The **Bishan Si** (¥4), 2km north of the town, was originally used as a reception house for monks and *upasaka* (lay Buddhists). The Ming building holds many Qing sculptures, including a white jade Buddha donated by Burmese devotees.

For an excellent view of Taihuai, **Dailuo Peak**, 3km northeast from the bank of the river, can be reached by cable car (¥11 ascent, ¥10 descent). Once you get off, climb up the flight of stairs and you'll arrive at **Shancai Si**, where there's a small cluster of stalls and telescope stands; for ¥1 you can peer through the latter and get a beautiful view of the mountain range.

The far temples and the peaks

Too far to reach on foot, the following temples and peaks are all served by minibuses which assemble at Taihuai bus station, or run direct from the larger hotels. Preserved from vandalism by their inaccessibility, the temple complexes include some of the oldest buildings in the country.

The **Jinge Si** is 10km southwest of Taihuai, and worth the trip for an impressive seventeen-metre-tall Guanyin inside, the largest statue at Wutai Shan. Some of the original Tang structure remains in the inscribed base of the pillars. It's worth inquiring if you stay in their pilgrims' accommodation, as it's a useful base from which you can walk the trails behind the complex.

The superb Nanchan Si and Foguang Si require a considerable diversion to reach. The **Nanchan Si** (¥7) is about 60km south of Taihuai, a little way off the road from Taiyuan, near the town of **Wutaixian**. Tour buses sometimes stop here on their way into Taihuai; otherwise you can catch a bus to Wutaixian, then get a motor-rickshaw to the village of **Dong Ye**. A large sign here points the way, but it's another 7km along a rough road to the complex. The temple's small main hall, built in 782, is the oldest wooden hall in China, a perfectly proportioned building whose columns and walls slope gently inwards, the sturdiness given by its thick, carved, wooden brackets nicely offset by the slight curves of its wide, flaring roof. Two inward-curving peaks sit at the ends of the roof ridge – all features characteristic of very early Chinese architecture. The hall of the Jin-dynasty **Yanqing Si**, accessible by a short path behind the Nanchan Si, is somewhat dilapidated but notable for quirky architectural detail, particularly the carved demons' heads which sit atop the two columns on either side of its main entrance.

The **Foguang Si** (¥7), 40km west of Taihuai, is a museum complex of more than a hundred buildings, mostly late, but including Wutai Shan's second Tang-dynasty hall, built in 857, whose eaves are impressive for the size and complexity of their interlocking *dougongs*. The walls inside the hall are decorated with lively Tang and Song paintings of Buddhist scenes; most of the images are of saintly figures sitting sedately, but a few ferocious demons are shown, dragging emaciated bodies behind them. To get here, catch a morning bus from Taihuai to **Doucun** (¥7), where you'll be dropped at the junction near a large sign pointing the way to Foguang. It's a five-kilometre walk from here along a dusty road to the temple, or you can negotiate an onward round-trip with a vehicle for around ¥10.

The five flat **peaks** around Taihuai, north, south, east, west and middle, are all approximately 15km away and considerably higher than Taihuai at 3000m above sea level. On the summit of each sits a small temple, and pilgrims endeavour to visit each one, a time-consuming process even with help of minibuses which go some way up each mountain. In the past, the truly devout took up to two years to reach all the temples on foot, but today, most visitors make do with looking at the silhouette of the summit temples through the telescopes of entrepreneurs in town. Set off in any direction out of town for a rewarding walk, although the South Peak is regarded as the most beautiful, its slopes described in a Ming poem as "bedecked with flowers like a coloured silk blanket".

Taiyuan and around

TAIYUAN, industrial powerhouse and the capital of Shanxi province, lies midway on the rail line between the more appealing Datong (see p.232) and Xi'an (see p.267), and is the most convenient starting point for a trip to Pingyao (see p.255) and the temples of Wutai Shan (see p.243). The glossy new hotels, imposing banks and classy restaurants of **Yingze Dajie**, the showcase street, are perhaps in part an enticement to get travellers to linger a while, and indeed the downtown area, compact enough to explore on foot, rewards wandering with some intriguing alleys and a bustling, pedestrianized food street. If you're breaking your journey here to head for Wutai, there's also a scattering of ancient buildings outside town worth a diversion.

A city never far from shifting frontiers, Taiyuan, or Jinyang as it was originally called, sits in a valley next to the Fen River in the invasion corridor between the barbarian lands to the north and the Chinese heartland around the Yellow River to the south. As a result it has suffered even more than most Chinese cities from invaders and the strife that accompanies dynastic collapse. The Mongolian Huns invaded first in 200 BC, ousted when the Tobas, a nomadic Turkish people, swept south in the fourth century and established the Northern Wei dynasty. During the Tang dynasty, the city enjoyed a brief period of prosperity as an important frontier town on the edges of Han Chinese control and the barbarian lands, before becoming one of the major battlefields during the Five Dynasties (907–79), a period of strife following the Tang's collapse. In 976 the expanding Song dynasty razed the city to the ground.

Taiyuan and around

Taiyuan	太原	***tàiyuán***
Chongshan Si	崇善寺	*chóngshàn sì*
Shuangta Si	双塔寺	*shuāngtǎ sì*
Wuyi Square	五一广场	*wǔyī guǎngchǎng*
Yingze Park	迎泽公园	*yíngzé gōngyuán*
Accommodation and eating		
Bingzhou	并州饭店	*bìngzhōu fàndiàn*
Hotpot City	川妞火锅城	*chuānniū huǒguō chéng*
Kaile Binguan	凯乐 宾馆	*kǎilè bīnguǎn*
Shanxi Grand	山西大酒店	*shānxī dàjiǔdiàn*
Shanxi Huayuan	山西华苑	*shānxī huáyuàn*
Shipin Jie	食品街	*shípǐn jiē*
Tianwaitian	天外天宾馆	*tiānwàitiān bīnguǎn*
Yingze Binguan	迎泽宾馆	*yíngzé bīnguǎn*
Yunshan	云山宾馆	*yúnshān bīnguǎn*
Around Taiyuan		
Jinci Si	晋祠寺	*jìncí sì*
Shuanglin Si	双林寺	*shuānglín sì*
Tianlong Shan	天龙山	*tiānlóng shān*
Xuanzhong Si	玄中寺	*xuánzhōng sì*

In more recent history, the city was the site of one of the worst massacres of the Boxer Rebellion (see p.1183), when all the city's foreign missionaries and their families were killed on the orders of the provincial governor. This wasn't enough, though, to put off the English, French and Russians, who over the next two decades stepped up their exploitation of the city's mineral reserves begun at the end of the eighteenth century. A habit of playing host to warlike leaders continued when Taiyuan was governed by Yan Xishan between 1912 and 1949. One of the Guomindang's fiercest warlords, he treated the city as a private empire. According to Carl Crow's contemporaneous *Handbook for China*, Xishan's city was a reform-minded place, well known for the suppression of opium and its anti-foot-binding movement. His rule did not stop the city's gradual development by foreign powers, however, and extensive coal mines were constructed by the Japanese in 1940. Industrialization began in earnest after the Communist takeover and today it is the factories that dominate, relentlessly processing the region's coal and mineral deposits.

Arrival, transport and accommodation

Local officials are so proud of Taiyuan's **airport**, 15km southeast of the city (a ¥30 ride away by taxi) that a model of the modernist building sits in Yingze Park in the city centre. The **train station**, on the Beijing–Xi'an line, is likewise the focus of local pride, judging by the number of camera stalls lined up outside catering to those who want to get their photograph taken in front of it. As Chinese stations go, it's a pleasant one: clean, new and efficient, though with the usual chaos of buses and stalls outside. It's conveniently located at the eastern end of **Yingze Dajie**, the city's main thoroughfare, from where bus #10 runs the full length of the street. The **long-distance bus station** is just west of the train station, also on Yingze Dajie.

Although it's a sprawling place, Taiyuan is easy to get around as the majority of places of interest are on or near Yingze Dajie. The street runs east–west across town, passing the south side of Wuyi Square, the heart of the city, and most sights, hotels and restaurants are within walking distance. Most city **bus routes** begin from a terminal at the northeastern corner of Wuyi Square. Bus #328, which heads west down Yingze Dajie, then turns left on to Xinjian Nan Lu, may be of use. There are also five **tram** routes, which mostly travel north–south. Tram #102, which begins from a terminus on the west side of Jianshe Bei Lu, just north of the train station, travels west to Wuyi Square, then turns north up Wuyi Lu. **Taxis** are cheap, with a ¥7 minimum fare, and plentiful.

Accommodation

Most **hotels** are located along Yingze Dajie; the western end is less interesting and farther from the sights, while the eastern end, near the train station, is livelier but noisier.

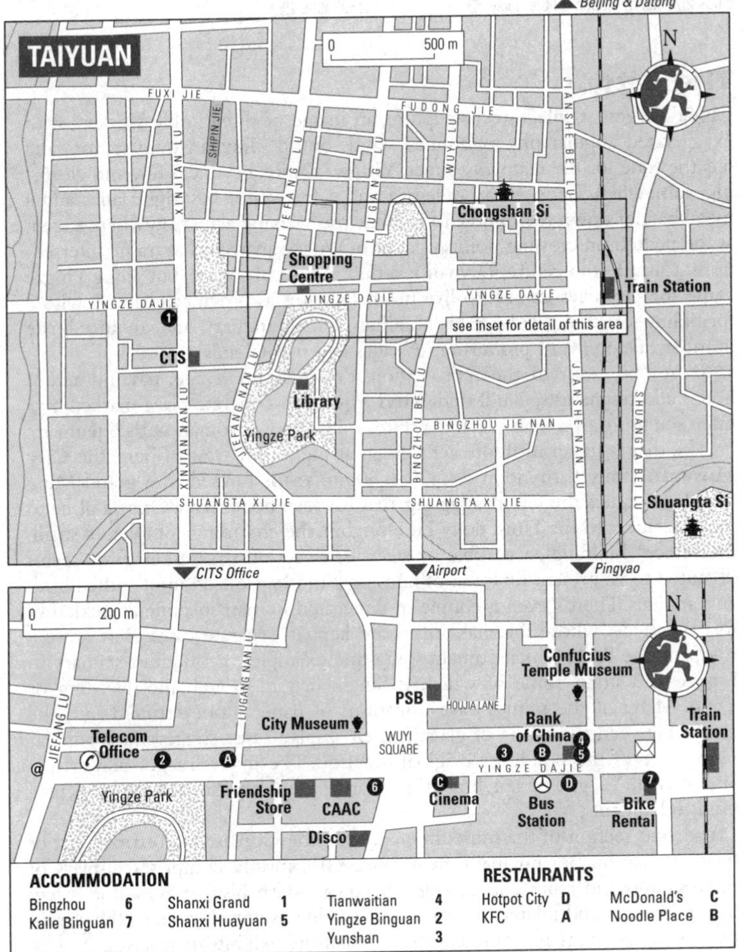

Bingzhou, 32 Yingze Dajie ⓣ0351/4041004, ⓕ4033540. Three-star place, one of the best mid-range options, with a good location opposite Wuyi Square. The cheapest rooms are in a claustrophobic basement – it's worth paying a little more for one of the spacious rooms upstairs. ❺

Kaile Binguan 2 Yingze Dajie ⓣ0351/4060011. Situated opposite the train station, this hotel is well run and convenient. ❹

Shanxi Grand 5 Xinjian Nan Lu ⓣ0351/4043901, ⓕ4043525. The poshest place in town, where tour groups end up, though it's a little far west. Oddly decorated in a mish-mash of styles, but very comfortable. ❽

Shanxi Huayuan 9 Yingze Dajie ⓣ0351/4046201, ⓣ4646980. Rooms are spacious and clean, though a little noisy. ❹

Tianwaitian 23 Yingze Dajie ⓣ0351/4041097. It may not look like much, but this budget hotel near the station has the largest selection of rooms – though most don't have windows. Clean and friendly. Descend the red-carpeted staircase from the alley off Yingze Dajie. Dorms from ¥15, ❷

Yingze Binguan 189 Yingze Dajie ⓣ0351/4043211, ⓕ4043784. This stylish four-star hotel consists of two buildings: the western wing is the upmarket section, with excellent facilities; the eastern wing is more down to earth and affordable, but may not take foreign guests. Western wing ❼, eastern wing ❻

Yunshan 99 Yingze Dajie ⓣ0351/4041351. A pleasant and agreeably low-key place with a good location and staff. Singles, doubles and triples available. ❸

The City

China's largest stainless steel sculpture, an image of three noble workers with exaggerated angular physiognomies, stands outside Taiyuan train station, and sets the tone for the main city street, **Yingze Dajie**, beyond. New and gleaming, somewhere between a boulevard and a freeway, it has eight lanes and a metal barrier down the middle to prevent you walking across anywhere except at the pedestrian crossing point just east of Wuyi Square and at traffic intersections. Outside the centre, Taiyuan is a dull industrial sprawl, but along Yingze Dajie the city tries its best to live up to its status as provincial capital, with a sprinkling of neon, flashy new buildings, garish statuary and an inordinate number of storefronts proffering massages and marital aids.

About 1km west of the train station, down Yingze Dajie, past numerous hotels and restaurants, you'll find **Wuyi Square**, a concrete plaza marked by a huge sculpture of a man playing a flute, a deer and a woman with pneumatic breasts, that is lit up in fluorescent green at night. Just west of here, the **City Museum** (daily 9am–noon & 2.30–6.30pm; ¥5) is housed in a grand Ming temple complex, the Chunyanggong, that has seen better days. Once a place to offer sacrifices to the Taoist deity Lu Dongbin, the charming complex of small, multistorey buildings, accessible by steep stairways off small courtyards, seems ill-suited to its present function of housing a motley collection of stuffed birds and animals. There's even a couple of desiccated human specimens pickled in formaldehyde, whose internal organs are kept in separate cases. Best are the rooms at the back, which contain some fine examples of Buddhist statuary in bronze and stone, some of which is Sui in origin, though mostly Ming or Qing. Many of the statues have donations of paper money stuffed into the cracks between the panes of glass in their display cases, suggesting a popular resurgence of the building's original function. The many images of warriors and of Guan Yu, god of war, hint at the martial preoccupations of the city's previous inhabitants.

A second section of the museum, housed in the **Confucius Temple** east of here off Jianshe Bei Lu (daily 8am–5pm; ¥10), mostly comprises displays of photographs and relics concerning Shanxi's modern history, as well as a few Shang bronzes and a large collection of Buddhist sutras. However, the attractive Ming buildings are more engrossing than the exhibits themselves.

Northeast of Wuyi Square, reached along alleys that grow shabbier the farther you go, the **Chongshan Si** (Temple of Veneration of Benevolence; daily 8am–5pm; ¥4) is worth the fifteen-minute walk – look for the fortune-tellers who congregate outside. Though there's nothing extraordinary about the architecture, the main hall is well maintained and full of the paraphernalia of worship: offerings, painted sheets hanging from the pillars and prayer mats stitched together out of discarded packaging. The temple also contains a display of scrolls and books – sutras printed in the Song, Yuan and Ming dynasties, some in Tibetan, and a number of woodcut illustrations. Directly south of the temple, with an entrance at its southern end, the monastery complex that it was once attached to has been converted into workshops and warehouses. You can poke around, but most of the buildings are fairly dilapidated.

The focus for a wander around sparse **Yingze Park** is provided by a Ming-dynasty library (daily 8am–5pm; ¥10) south of the park entrance on Yingze Dajie. You can't go inside, but there is some nice eave decoration, including images of pandas. A tour of the city's ancient buildings is completed with a look at the two fifty-metre-tall pagodas of the **Shuangta Si** (Twin Pagoda Temple; daily 8am–5pm; ¥6), south of the train station off Shuangta Bei Lu. These were built by a monk called Fu Deng in the Ming dynasty, under the orders of the emperor, and today have become a symbol of the city. You can climb the thirteen storeys for a panoramic view of Taiyuan.

Eating, drinking and nightlife

Yingze Dajie has a good smattering of **restaurants**, many catering for tourists. The best place to head is **Shipin Jie** (Food Street) which is parallel to and west of Jiefang Lu, and north of Yingze Dajie. The pleasant, pedestrianized row is packed with eating places, from cheap, fast-food style noodle shops to quiet, upmarket restaurants, as well as stalls selling nuts and fruit, and karaoke bars and hairdressers; it's very busy in the evening. Pick the busiest place to eat at as it's a good sign of its quality.

On **Yingze Dajie**, try *Hotpot City* at no. 16, which looks more expensive than it is – a meal for two here should come to no more than ¥50. It's just west of the train station on the south side of the road, and is easily identifiable by its steamed-up windows. The noodle restaurant at no. 73 is very popular and unusual for serving no rice. Food comes in deep bowls, and last to arrive is a bowl of noodles which you add to the remains of your other dishes. Best of the hotel restaurants is the first-floor place in the west wing of the *Yingze Binguan*, which is not too expensive (about ¥50 per person). The atmosphere is unintimidating and there are cosy tables and friendly, attentive staff. If money isn't a problem, the upmarket Chinese or Western restaurants at the *Shanxi Grand* are worth a try – expect to pay around ¥80 per person. As ever, there are branches of *McDonald's* and *KFC*, respectively on Wuyi Square and on the western section of Yingze Dajie.

For **nightlife**, try the *Chinatown Disco* (daily 8–12pm; ¥30) at 49 Bingzhou Bei Lu, not far from the intersection with Yingze Dajie. Don't let the unfortunate spelling mistake on the sign ("pisco") put you off, as this huge place is surprisingly slick for a provincial city, with Western DJs and an impressive interior including a laser, a giant bat and a spacecraft hanging from the ceiling. The high entrance charge means the clientele is more chic than bohemian, and generally too cool to pay much overt attention to foreigners on the dance floor.

Listings

Airlines CAAC is at 158 Yingze Dajie (Mon–Sat 8am–8pm; ☎0351/4042903). Check also at the Shanxi Dong Air Service, in the lobby of the *Bingzhou Hotel*'s south building.
Banks and exchange The Bank of China is at 55 Yingze Dajie (Mon–Fri 8am–noon & 2–6pm, Sat 8.30–noon).
Bike rental Bikes can be rented from a ramshackle bike park stall (daily 8am–8pm) at the eastern end of Yingze Dajie, opposite the station, for ¥5 a day, with a ¥100 deposit.
Buses Buses to nearby towns, including Pingyao, leave from outside the train station.
Cinema Catch the latest dubbed Hollywood blockbusters at 20 Yingze Dajie (¥40). Also on the west side of Wuyi Square.
Internet access Ask around the station for the latest nearby café, otherwise try the unnamed lane one block north of Yingze Dajie and east of Wuyi Square, on the route of trolley bus #102. The net café on the west side of Jiefang Lu (¥2/hr), near the intersection with Yingze Dajie, offers good connections and coffee.
Mail and telephones The white building opposite the train station on the northern side of Yingze Dajie houses an impressively modern and efficient post office (daily 8am–8pm). There's a branch office at 215 Yingze Dajie (daily 8am–6pm). The telecom office, open 24hr, is at 213 Yingze Dajie.
PSB The PSB office is at 9 Houjia Lane (daily 8am–noon & 2.30–5.30pm) on the northeastern corner of Wuyi Square.
Shopping The Friendship Store at 45 Yingze Dajie has the usual selection of jade handicrafts and art materials. For a less predictable – though still pricey – selection of souvenirs, try the Arts and Crafts Store at 54 Yingze Dajie, or the Antique Store at 15 Jiefang Lu.
Trains There's a booking office on the south side of the station. Dozens of north–south trains pass through Taiyuan daily, and getting a sleeper is usually not a problem even at the last minute. If need be, opt for *wuzuo* (unreserved) ticket and upgrade on the train, or hang around the returns window and hope your destination becomes available.
Travel agents A friendly CTS office at 8 Xinjian Nan Lu will book train tickets (daily 8am–noon & 2–6pm; ☎351/4049270). Another office in the Guolu building at 38 Ping Yang Lu (daily 8am–noon & 2.30–6pm; ☎351/7242162) is well worth the effort to get to, since the helpful English-speaking manager can arrange discounts on accommodation and a variety of excursions. To get there, continue south on Xinjian Nan Lu – the office is on the left-hand side.

Around Taiyuan

Easily reached in the flat countryside around Taiyuan is the very touristy temple complex of **Jinci Si**, though further afield the little town of **Pingyao**, which is something of a relic from the Qing dynasty, and the **Shuanglin Si**, full of breathtaking sculpture, make a more interesting day-trip (see p.255). To the west, **Tianlong Shan**'s Buddhist grottoes deserve investigation if you're not heading to the caves near Datong or the Longmen site at Luoyang.

Jinci Si

Although **Jinci Si** contains perhaps the finest Song-dynasty buildings in the country, neglect, and its extensive development as a tourist resource, means it is not as impressive as it could be. From Taiyuan, bus #308 from the train station or #804 from the Jinci terminal west of Wuyi Square will take you the 25km to the site (daily 8am–5pm; ¥20). First impressions don't augur well – after a juddering ride through a stark industrial zone, the bus drops you at the park outside the temple, a charmless fair of souvenir stalls and ragged camels, by a river at the base of a mountain.

A temple has stood on the site since the Northern Wei, and today's buildings are a diverse collection from various dynasties. The open space just inside the gate was once used as a theatre, with the richly ornamented Ming stage, the **Water Mirror Platform**, at its centre. Beyond here, a small river channelled across the complex, now ruined with litter, must have been one of its most pleasant features. Over the bridge behind the stage, four Song-dynasty iron figures of warriors, apparently guardians of the river, stand on a platform looking furious. Inscriptions on their chests record their dates of construction, though parts have been replaced since.

The **Hall of Offerings** beyond and, behind that, the **Hall of the Holy Mother** were originally constructed in the Jin dynasty as places to worship the mother of Prince Shuyu, who founded the dynasty and was attributed with magical powers. They were rebuilt in the Song and today are two of the largest buildings from that dynasty still extant. The Hall of the Holy Mother, one of the earliest wooden halls in China, is the highlight of the complex, its facade a mix of decorative flourishes and the sturdily functional, with wooden dragons curling around the eight pillars that support the ridge of its upward-curving roof. The hall's interior is equally impressive, with some fine, delicate-looking Song-dynasty female figures, posed naturalistically, some with broomsticks, jugs and seals, attendants to a central image of a gracious-looking Holy Mother. Turn right out of the hall and you come to a smaller temple, a Ming tower, and a hot spring, as well as an infuriatingly tacky waxwork show. The buildings beyond are hardly interesting in themselves, though one has been converted into an art gallery. Among the buildings to the right of the Hall of the Holy Mother, a Tang-dynasty stele records the visit of Emperor Tai Zong in 647 AD.

Tianlong Shan and Xuanzhong Si

Fifty kilometres south of Taiyuan, **Tianlong Shan** is host to a small cluster of Buddhist cave temples (daily 8.30am–4.30pm; ¥15). The caves on its eastern and western sides were carved between 534 and 907 AD, from the Eastern Wei to the Tang dynasties. Much less impressive than anything at Datong or Luoyang, the cave sculptures are badly weathered, though the large exposed Buddha in Cave 9, bare-chested and sitting regally as if on a chair, is a fine image, distinctive for his chubby face and bulging eyes. The eastern caves are protected by a Ming-dynasty wooden facade built across the cliff face. To get here, take **bus** #103 from the northeast corner of Wuyi Square (in front of the *Jinyang Fandian*) to **Qingxu**, then hire a motor-rickshaw for the last 3km.

The **Xuanzhong Si**, 80km southwest of Taiyuan, is famous as one of the birthplaces of Zen Buddhism – the priests Daochuo and Shandao, two of its founders, taught here – and has a history stretching back over 1500 years. Most of the present buildings, however, built on tiers up the side of a hill, are Ming or Qing. A thriving place of worship, today it's a popular pilgrimage spot for the Japanese, some of whom come to hear the contemporary masters preach. Tourist **minibuses** run direct from outside the train station in Taiyuan (¥15), or you can take a **bus** from the bus station to **Jiaocheng**, a town 4km northeast of the temple, and hire a motor-rickshaw from there.

Pingyao and Shuanglin Si

The small town of **Pingyao**, 100km south of Taiyuan, and the **Shuanglin Si** nearby, two of the most impressive places in the area, are certainly worth making an effort to visit. Despite a burgeoning tourist trade, Pingyao is one of the few places in this part of China that has retained more than a token of its traditional infrastructure and the buildings of its nineteenth-century heyday. Some of these have been converted into hotels – indeed Pingyao boasts one of the most atmospheric places to stay in China. Spring Festival is an exceptionally good time to visit, when the streets are illuminated by hundreds of red

Pingyao and Shuangli Si

Pingyao	平遥	***píngyáo***
Chenghuang Daoist Temple	城隍庙	*chénghuáng miào*
Former County Yamen	旧县衙	*jiùxiàn yá*
Former Residence of Lei Lütai	雷履泰故居	*léilǚtài gùjū*
Kuixing Tower	奎星楼	*kuíxīng lóu*
Rishengchang	日升昌	*rìshēng chāng*
Tian Ji Xiang Museum	天吉祥	*tiānjí xiáng*
Accommodation		*Accomodation*
Dejuyuan Folk-style Guesthouse	德居源民风宾馆	*déjūyuán mínfēng bīnguǎn*
Yunjincheng Folk Custom Hotel	云锦成民风宾馆	*yúnjǐnchéng mínfēng bīnguǎn*
Zhongdu Binguan	中都宾馆	*zhōngdū bīnguǎn*
Shuanglin Si	双林寺	***shuānglín sì***

lanterns. Some 5km outside the town walls, Shuanglin Si has a hoard of wood and terracotta sculptures, some lifelike, some ghostly, some comical, which are unparalleled in the region.

Buses to Pingyao from Taiyuan's long-distance bus station leave every half hour (¥10), and the trip – along good roads – takes two hours. Regular **trains** also come here from Taiyuan and Xi'an throughout the day and are slightly quicker than the bus.

Pingyao

PINGYAO reached its zenith in the Ming dynasty, when it was a prosperous banking centre, one of the first in China, and its wealthy residents constructed luxurious mansions, adding square walls around the city to defend them. In the course of the twentieth century, however, the town slid rapidly into provincial obscurity, which has kept it largely unmodernized. Inside the town walls, Pingyao's narrow streets, lined with elegant Qing architecture – no neon, no white tile, no cars – are a revelation, harking back to Pingyao's nineteenth-century heyday. Few buildings are higher than two storeys; most are small shops much more interesting for their appearance than their wares, with ornate wood and painted glass lanterns hanging outside, faded paintings on their eaves, and intricate wooden latticework holding paper rather than glass across the windows. The similarly designed Qiao family compound thirty minutes' drive away was used as a setting by Zhang Yimou for his film *Raise the Red Lantern*, in which the labyrinthine layout of of the place symbolizes the woman's restricted life.

Arrival and transport

The plan of Pingyao is very simple. Square walls, each 1500m long, enclose four main streets arranged along the compass points, a typical *feng shui*-influenced design that the Chinese compare to the markings on a tortoise shell. Nan Dajie, these days clogged with lookalike souvenir stalls, actually slopes downward ever so slightly, as it used to transport the city's sewage out the figurative turtle's rear end.

Buses terminate outside the tiny **train station** in the north of town, which is also where you can catch a **minibus** to Taiyuan. En route to Xi'an, you can break your journey in Pingyao for the day and then pick up one of the two evening trains that pass through on their way south. The ticket office at the station opens thirty minutes before the train's arrival. Note that the only tickets on sale here are for unallocated hard seats; once on the train, however, you should be able to upgrade (less likely at weekends). Luggage can be left behind the counter at the station shop.

Taxis are forbidden from entering the walled town. From the train station or West Gate, you can catch a **bicycle rickshaw** for ¥5, though resist your driver's exhortations that your intended hotel is most certainly full – he's looking for commission to get you to stay elsewhere. The rickshaws aren't allowed in certain parts of the city, which should account for any winding journeys through dark and narrow alleys.

Accommodation

Staying overnight in Pingyao is recommended, as after twilight the town becomes tranquil after a frenetic day of souvenir selling. Furthermore, Pingyao boasts one of the most delightful **hotels** in the country, the *Yunjincheng Folk Custom Hotel*, 62 Nan Dajie (Ⓣ & Ⓕ0354/5680944; ❷). Occupying a superb location in a restored 200-year-old home near the Bell Tower, the place boasts mahogany window screens, quaint furniture and beds which are raised up on wooden platforms behind screens. They have a range of rooms, so ask to see several before selecting. If they're full (reservations are advised), staff can suggest alternatives in nearby traditional-style lodging – *Yunjincheng* imitators sprout along Nan Dajie like mushrooms. A safe bet is the *Dejuyuan Folk-style Guesthouse*, 43 Xi Dajie (Ⓣ0354/5685266, Ⓕ5685366). If you're staying else-

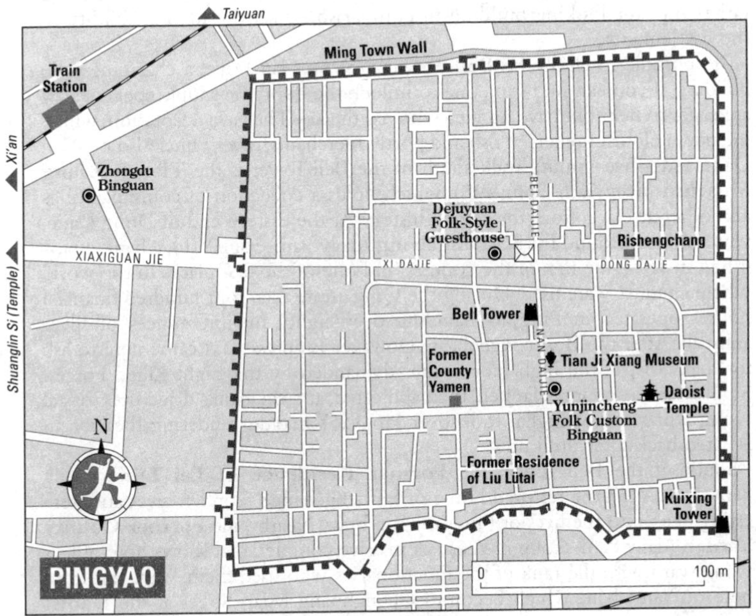

where, it's worth ask to see the room before paying, and note that some places may try to stick you in an austere modern room. Sadly, many tour groups still get shunted into the bland *Zhongdu Binguan* (☎0354/5626618; ❹), opposite the train station. The rooms here are clean, but staying here takes away most of Pingyao's charm.

The Town

If you arrive at the train station, Pingyao looks like any other dusty midsized Chinese city at first. Walk straight ahead and turn left at the first intersection onto Xiaxiguan Jie, a market street over which the West Gate looms 300m ahead. Through the gate, Xi Dajie leads into the heart of the **old city**, with the buildings becoming lovelier the deeper in you go. In between the slender main streets, a lattice of even narrower alleyways links courtyards which are well worth exploring, even by night when the glow from nearby houses shows the way – though small kids stay off the street after dark, haunted by their parents' tales of returning Ming-era ghosts who, it's said, navigate the unchanged alleys with ease. The ghosts of another era can be glimpsed in the derelict entrance architecture over old homes and the faded "Long live Chairman Mao" slogans on the walls – Pingyao, the locals say, had "a very bad Cultural Revolution".

Just inside the arch of the West Gate are steps leading up to the Ming **town walls** (daily 8am–6.30pm; ¥15), 12m high and crenellated, with a watchtower along every 50m of their 6km length. You can walk all the way around them in two hours, and get a good view into some of the many courtyards inside the walls (and at an army training base outside them, where you can watch recruits practising drill and throwing fake hand grenades). The structures where the wall widens out are *mamian* (literally, horse faces), where soldiers could stand and fight. At the southeast corner of the wall, the **Kuixing Tower**, a tall fortified pagoda with a tiled, upturned roof, is a rather flippant-looking building in comparison with the martial solidity of the battlements.

It's possible to climb the **Bell Tower** (¥5) on Nan Dajie, a charming little building, if you can find someone to unlock the door; the shopkeepers nearby are eager to help, but have no idea who has the key. The eave decoration, which includes colourful reliefs of fish and portly merchants, is very fine. Also on Nan Dajie and a five-minute walk south of the Bell Tower is the **Tian Ji Xiang Museum** (daily 9am–5pm; ¥10), which holds a collection of coins, paintings and other artefacts from the town's history. At the eastern end of Dong Dajie, you can look around the **Rishengchang** (daily 9am–5pm; ¥10), a bank established in 1824, the first in the country and one of the first places in the world where cheques were used. During the Qing, more than four hundred financial houses operated in Pingyao, handling over eighty million ounces of silver annually. After the Boxer Rebellion, Dowager Empress Cixi came here to ask for loans to pay the high indemnities demanded by the Eight Allied Forces. Soon after, the court defaulted, then abdicated, and the banks dried up. Coastal Hong Kong and Shanghai took over Pingyao's mantle, rendering the city an isolated backwater until now.

South of the Bell Tower, the **Former Residence of Lei Lütai** (daily 8am–7pm; ¥15), the restored home of Rishengchang's founder, gives an interesting peek into the lives of Pingyao's top brass. Nearby, the **Former County Yamen** (daily 8am–6.30pm; ¥20) is a massive complex that shows how offices would vary with the rank of the functionaries who used them. Walk east from here on Yamen Jie, which becomes Chenghuang Miao Street at the **Daoist**

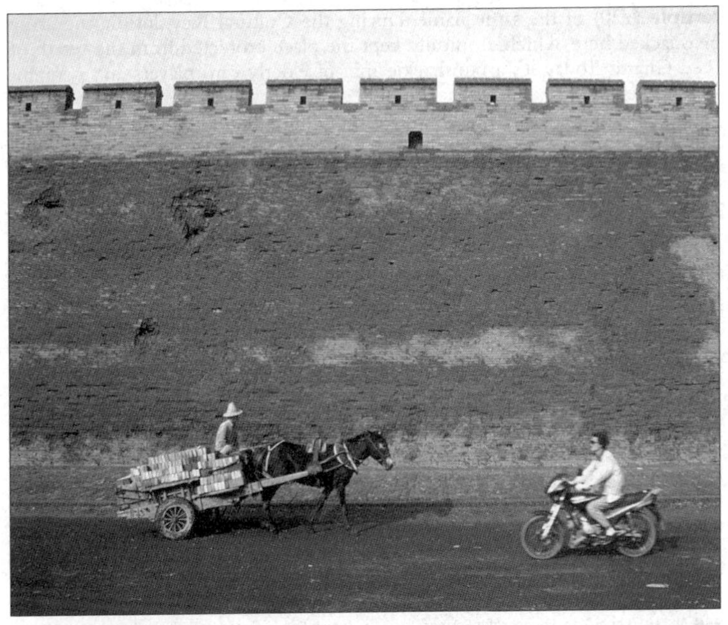

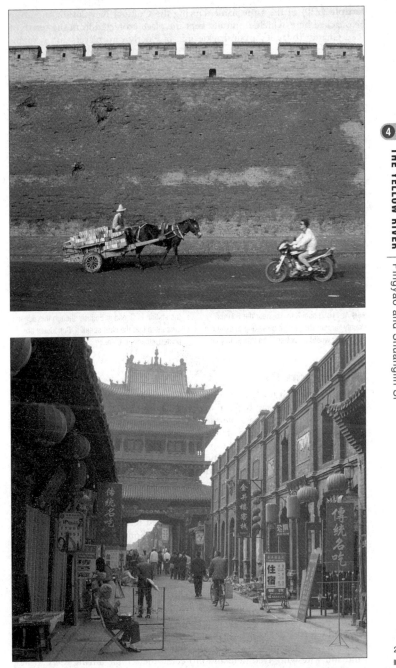

△ Two views of quaint Pingyao

temple (¥20) of the same name. During the Cultural Revolution, the army bivouacked here, which, ironically, kept the place protected from the wrath of Red Guards. Today it's a ramshackle mix of elderly card players and penitent worshippers.

Eating

By far the best place to eat is the *Yunjincheng* hotel's **restaurant**, which has an ornate wooden interior complete with red lanterns. Its chefs prepare superb traditional Pingyao cuisine, including *ca ge dou*, noodles with tomato; *suan cai chao dou fu*, bean curd with pickles; and *yiya cai*, cold pickled vegetables. Be sure to try the *sanxie shaomai*, an interesting and delicious dumpling variation. A **meal** for two here should cost around ¥40. For cheap eats, head to any one of the places that cluster south of the Bell Tower.

Listings

Banks The Bank of China is at 64 Xi Dajie (daily 8.30am–6pm, summer until 7pm).
Bike rental Bikes are available from most guesthouses, including the *Yunjincheng*, for ¥5–10 per day.
Clinics There is a helpful clinic at 43 Dong Dajie (☎5683732).
Mail The post office is at 1 Xi Dajie (daily 8am–6.30pm).
PSB At 110 Zhoubi Nan Jie, near the Former County Yamen. They might be willing to extend a visa, but it would be better to do this in Taiyuan.
Tours For a guided tour of the locality in English, including a trip to Shuanglin Si, book the services of Wu Qiulian (Julia) at the *Yunjincheng Folk Custom Hotel* (©wu_qiu_lian@sina.com). She works with international academic institutions and tour operators to provide educational overviews of her town. Highly recommended.
Trains Sixteen trains pass through Pingyao each day, bound north or south. An information desk in the station is signed in English, though this doesn't guarantee that the staff speak it. Schedules are posted, clearly, in Chinese.

Shuanglin Si

The **Shuanglin Si** (daily 8am–6pm; ¥12), with its extraordinary collection of Buddhist sculpture, stands 5km southwest of Pingyao in a stretch of quiet countryside, accessible via a pleasant walk or bike ride along a flat road or by a ten-minute taxi ride (¥15) from the train station or West Gate. Originally built in the Northern Wei, the present buildings, ten halls arranged around three courtyards, are Ming and Qing. Unfortunately, increased levels of industrial pollution have coated the structures and their occupants with coal dust, and much of the complex is undergoing restoration.

The complex looks more like a fortress from the outside, being protected by high walls and a gate. Once you're inside, the fine architecture pales beside the contents of the halls, a treasury of coloured terracotta and wood **sculptures**, more than 1600 in all, dating from the Song to the Qing dynasties. They're literally arranged behind bars, in tableaux, with backgrounds of swirling water or clouds, turning the dusty wooden halls into rich grottoes. Some of the figures are in bad shape but most still have a good deal of their original paint, although it has lost its gaudy edge. The halls are usually kept padlocked, either for the protection of the figures or simply because visitors are uncommon, and you'll be shown around them one by one by an earnest caretaker who will tell you all about the figures, whether or not you understand his Chinese. It's worth hiring a guide (see "Listings" above), as each hall and each row of statues has intriguing elements, such as the statue of the husband and wife who lived here and protected the temple during the Cultural Revolution.

The horsemen dotted in vertical relief around the **Wushung Hall**, the first on the right, illustrate scenes from the life of Guan Yu, the god of war, but the figures in most of the halls are depictions of Buddha or saints and guardians. The eighteen *arhats* in the second hall, though unpainted, are eerily lifelike, and somewhat sinister in the gloom with their bulging foreheads, long tapering fingernails and eyes of black glass that follow you round the room. In the third hall, the walls are lined with elegant twenty-centimetre-high Bodhisattvas inclined towards a set of larger Buddha figures at the centre. The Bodhisattvas are like so many roosting birds, ranked on shelves carved to represent the levels of existence, with demons on the bottom, clouds and angels at the top. In the **fourth hall**, look out for the monsters hanging above the Buddhas, and in the **fifth**, for a superb figure of many-armed Guanyin.

Between Pingyao and Xi'an

The small towns between Pingyao and Xi'an, north of the Yellow River, are largely ignored by foreign travellers, though there are some interesting places tucked away here, which should attract anyone who wants to break their journey with a little exploration off the beaten track. About 140km south of Pingyao, **Linfen** is popular with domestic tourists who come here in order to pick up a connection to **Hukou Falls**, which, though regarded by the Chinese as one of their premier beauty spots, falls short of the hype. The less-visited **Guangsheng Si**, not far from here, is another possible excursion, and its magnificent glazed pagoda makes up for the hassle of getting there. Farther south, the town of **Yuncheng** is an access point for the **Guan Yu Miao**, a fine late temple popular with the Taiwanese, and for the town of **Ruicheng** and the nearby **Yongle Gong**, a Taoist temple with some excellent murals, from where Xi'an is only a four-hour bus ride away.

Between Pingyao and Xi'an

Linfen	临纷	***línfēn***
Pingyang Hotel	平阳宾馆	*píngyáng bīnguǎn*
Hongdong	洪洞	***hóngdòng***
Feihong Ta	飞红塔	*fēihóng tǎ*
Guangsheng Si	广胜寺	*guǎngshèng sì*
Susan Prison	苏三囚牢	*sūsān qiūláo*
Hukou Falls	壶口瀑布	***húkǒu pùbù***
Yuncheng	运城	***yùnchéng***
Guan Yu Miao	解州关帝庙	*jiězhōu guāndì miào*
Huanghe Hotel	黄河大厦	*huánghé dàshà*
Xinfeng Hotel	鑫丰大酒店	*xīnfēng dàjiǔdiàn*
Jixian	吉县	***jíxiàn***
Hukou Guesthouse	壶口招待所	*húkǒu zhāodàisuǒ*
Ruicheng	芮城	***ruìchéng***
Ruicheng Binguan	芮成宾馆	*ruìchéng bīnguǎn*
Yongle Gong	永乐宫	*yǒnglè gōng*

Linfen and around

A provincial town, **LINFEN** is not unpleasant, though there's no point in hanging around. The city is being remade into a mini-Beijing, with a replica Tian'anmen Square at its heart and a massive amusement park, Yaodu Square, at its edge. There are replicas of Beijing's architectural wonders too, including the Temple of Heaven and the Great Wall, and even a park containing a topographic model of the whole country, to scale, where visitors can play Godzilla, stomping on towns they dislike.

The town's few taxis (¥4 minimum fare) congregate around the **train station**, in the west of town. The **bus station**, for connections to Hongdong and Hukou Falls, is on the other side of town. There are frequent buses north to Pingyao (3hr; ¥28). **Accommodation** is available at the *Pingyang Hotel*, at 58 Jiefang Nan Lu (Ⓣ0357/2012760; ❸), whose rooms ranging from the very basic to quite plush. The dining hall of the hotel, which serves reasonable **food**, is getting on for the size of an aircraft hangar, with round tables big enough to park a car on.

Hongdong and the Guangsheng Si

The village of **HONGDONG** lies 28km northeast of Linfen, about an hour's bus ride away (¥8). The bus may drop you at a crossroads, from where you'll have to hail a taxi or walk the remaining 4km into town. The reason to come is to pick up a connection to the Guangsheng Si, but while you're passing through you might be interested in the **Susan Prison** (daily 8am–5pm; ¥13), 1km west of the bus station. China's earliest surviving prison, this Ming-dynasty squat black and white brick building consists of cloisters off which the cells, surprisingly spacious with curved ceilings, compare favourably to a cheap Chinese hotel room. They now hold displays of torture instruments and grisly dioramas demonstrating their use. A typically illustrative English caption includes the one for the Prison Guards' House: "It is the place where prison guard lived. In ancient times, prison guards were those who guarded prisoners." The stele in the back courtyard contains a list of inmates.

Guangsheng Si

From Hongdong bus station you can take bus #5 (¥2) or charter a taxi (¥30 there and back with an hour's wait) to get the extra 15km to the **Guangsheng Si**, which sits on a hilltop in a rural area dotted with small kilns for brickmaking. You're likely to have the place almost to yourself, with just a couple of monks, who look after the temple, and a few locals, who man the obligatory souvenir stall, to keep you company. The complex is in three parts – the Upper Temple, Lower Temple, and Temple of the God of Water – most of it dating back to the early fourteenth century, when the complex, established in the Eastern Han, was rebuilt after a fire. The buildings, with roof-ridge decorations which turn inwards (a characteristic of early temple architecture), and chunky wooden brackets atop sturdy walls, have a blocky, barn-like feel. As you walk in you are confronted by the dazzling **Feihong Ta** (Flying Rainbow Pagoda), built in 1527 and covered with glazed tiles of green, blue and yellow which glisten in the sunlight. Each of the thirteen storeys is so heavily decorated with glazed figures – guardians, lions, birds, mythical animals, people riding dragons – that not much of the wall is left visible. Inside the first room steps lead up into the pagoda behind the large Buddha figure. You can climb to the ninth storey, but it isn't easy, or safe, as it's pitch black inside, and the unusual staircase comprises a series of perilous ledges winding round the edge of a vertical shaft.

The **Lower Temple** (¥10) is a sadly neglected complex built in 1309, behind the pagoda. It's exhilarating to push open the heavy doors yourself and step into the hall containing three Buddhas, their thrones finely carved, with lions and elephants depicted around them. The eave decoration, which includes images of fish and birds, is impressively detailed. Beside it, separated by a wall, the **Temple to the God of Water** contains graphic and lively murals painted in 1324, some still in good condition. Their realism and attention to detail make them invaluable to scholars, particularly the rare depiction on the south wall of ten actors on a temple stage, which provides an insight into the nature of ancient drama. The actors are in ritual dress, and some are playing instruments, while a girl peeks at them from behind the stage curtain. On the upper part of the east wall, a painting shows what the temple looked like in the Yuan dynasty.

Leaving Guangsheng Si, it's better to get dropped at the junction with the Linfen–Pingyao road, where you can flag down a passing bus, than to go back into Hongdong and negotiate its ponderous bus station.

Hukou Falls

Poetically described by CITS as "giant dragons fighting in a river", **Hukou Falls**, 150km west of Linfen, is the Yellow River at its most impressively turbulent. At Jinshan Gorge the 400-metre-wide river is suddenly forced into a twenty-metre gap and tumbles down a cliff, where the fierce torrent squirts spray high into the air; the hiss of the water can be heard 2km away, which is what gives it the name "hukou", meaning kettle spout. It's best in the summer when the river level is highest. A popular spot with the Chinese, the falls are undoubtedly magnificent, but it's a long way to go, and, with souvenir stalls aplenty, is not exactly a wilderness experience. If you've seen a waterfall or a riotous river, then skip it.

To get here from Linfen, take a taxi to what's known as the 309 bus station in town, from where a minibus will take you the remaining 30km to the falls. Alternatively, catch a **tourist minibus** (summer only; ¥20) from outside Linfen or Yuncheng train stations. The bus trip takes between four and six hours, so unless you charter a taxi (¥800 there and back from Linfen) you'll probably have to stay the night; the *Hukou Guesthouse* (❸) is new and quite adequate.

Yuncheng and the Guan Yu Miao

YUNCHENG, 140km south of Linfen, is the last major town before Xi'an on the train line south from Datong. Besides being a possible base from which to visit the Hukou Falls, it's the starting point for bus trips west and south to the Guan Yu Miao, Ruicheng and the Yongle Gong (see p.264). The **train station**, with a statue of Guan Yu outside glaring at the townspeople, is in the northwest of town, at the north end of Zhan Nan Lu, while the **bus station** is a little farther south on the western side of the same road. Buses for Xi'an (3–4hr; ¥40–60) depart from the train-station concourse or from the bus station. There's an **Internet café** beside the #11 bus stop, opposite the train-station concourse.

For a **place to stay**, walk east from the station concourse to the end of Zhan Dong Lu and you'll come to the *Huanghe Hotel* (Ⓣ0359/2023135; ❻), a friendly establishment with a wide range of rooms and a decent restaurant. On the left as you exit the station, and bordering the concourse, the *Xinfeng Hotel* (Ⓣ0359/2067666; ❸, dorm beds from ¥18) is clean and accepts foreigners.

About 20km west of Yuncheng, the **Guan Yu Miao** (daily 8am–5pm; ¥25), the finest temple to the god of war in China, sits in the small country town of **JIEZHOU**, accessible by bus #11 (¥2) from opposite the station concourse. Contemporary Jiezhou doesn't look like much – the bus drops you in a muddy square lined with a few stalls and pool tables, which makes the massive temple complex on its western side look quite out of proportion. However, this was the birthplace of **Guan Yu** (also called Guan Di), a general of the Three Kingdoms period (220–280 AD; see box, p.509). Something of a Chinese King Arthur, Guan Yu was a popular folk hero who, like many Chinese historical figures who became the stuff of legend, was later deified. As god of war, his temple (founded in 589 AD, though the present structure is eighteenth century), is appropriately robust, looking more like a castle, with high battlements and thick wooden doors. Among the images on the wooden arch at the entrance is a victorious jouster gleefully carrying off the loser's head. The martial theme is carried into the interior, with much smiting of enemies going on in the superb Qing-dynasty friezes and stone carvings in the eaves, and on the pillars of the three halls. Guan Yu is a very popular figure in Taiwan, and many Taiwanese come here in winter for the temple fair held between October 18 and 28.

Ruicheng and the Yongle Gong

The bus journey from Yuncheng to **RUICHENG**, 90km south, a village just north of the Yellow River, is an engrossing if hair-raising trip across the Zhongtiao Mountains, an ochre landscape of utter desolation. Occasionally the bus stops at some lonely peak and, astonishingly, people get off. Though the sense of travelling through a wilderness leaves when you pull into Ruicheng, you are still very much in an isolated and backward part of China, and foreigners attract a lot of attention: courteous strangers may offer you their seat on a bus or canteen owners insist that your meal is on the house. The bus pulls in just east of the crossroads of Ruicheng's four streets, not far from the *Ruicheng Binguan* (❸) on the north side of the west road.

The **Yongle Gong**, Palace of Eternal Joy (daily 8am–5pm; ¥30), is a major Taoist temple, 4km south of the village, most notable for its excellent wall paintings. Its name derives from the position it once held in the village of Yongle, farther south on the banks of the Yellow River. It was moved brick by brick in 1959, when the dam at Sanmenxia was built and Yongle disappeared beneath the water.

There are three halls, three sides of which are covered in vivid **murals**. In the **first hall**, the three major gods of Taoism, sitting on thrones, are surrounded by the pantheon of minor deities, looking like emperors surrounded by courtiers. Each figure is over 2m tall, brightly painted and concisely outlined, but although great attention is paid to an exact rendering of the details of facial expression and costume, the images have no depth. The figures, four deep, are flat, like staggered rows of playing cards. Some have the faces of monsters, others have beards which reach almost to their waists and in which every hair is painted; one man has six eyes. In the **second hall**, elegant, robed figures disport themselves in finely observed walled courtyards and temple complexes set among misty, mountainous landscapes. These are images from the life of **Lu Dongbin**, one of the eight Taoist immortals who was born at Yongle, and are arranged in panels like a comic strip. The murals in the **third hall**, showing the life of a Taoist priest, are unfortunately damaged and little remains visible.

Shaanxi and Henan

The provinces of **Shaanxi** and **Henan** are both remarkable for the depth and breadth of their history. The region itself is dusty, harsh and unwelcoming, with a climate of extremes; in winter, strong winds bring yellow dust storms, while summer is hot and officially the rainy season. But, thanks to the Yellow River,

The Yellow River

The **Yellow River** flows for 6000km through nine provinces, from the Tibetan plateau in the west, through Inner Mongolia, turning abruptly south into Shanxi and then east through the flood plains of Shaanxi, Henan and Shandong to the Bohai Gulf. The upriver section provides much-needed irrigation and power (see p.1007), but in the latter half of its journey the river causes as much strife as it alleviates. The problem is the vast quantity of **silt** the river carries along its twisted length – 1.6 billion tonnes a year – whose choking nature has confused its course throughout history. Sometimes the river has flowed into the sea near Beijing, at others into the lower Yangzi valley, and its unpredictable swings have always brought chaos. From 1194 to 1887 there were fifty major Yellow River **floods**, with three hundred thousand people killed in 1642 alone. In 1855, the river's mouth moved from the north to the south of the Shandong peninsula, a distance of more than 350km, a shift which can partly be blamed on corrupt officials, who embezzled funds intended for flood control. A disastrous flood in 1933 was followed in 1937 by another – this time man-made – tragedy when Chiang Kaishek used the river as a weapon against the advancing Japanese, breaching the dykes to cut the rail line. A delay of a few weeks was gained at the cost of hundreds of thousands of Chinese lives.

Attempts to enhance the river's potential for creation rather than destruction began very early, at least by the eighth century BC, when the first **irrigation canals** were cut. In the fifth century BC the Zheng Guo Canal irrigation system stretched an impressive 150km and is still in use today. But the largest scheme was the building of the 1800-kilometre **Grand Canal** in the sixth century, which connected the Yellow and the Yangzi rivers and was used to carry grain to the north. It was built using locks to control water level, an innovation that did not appear in the West for another four hundred years.

Dykes, too, have been built since ancient times, and today in some eastern sections the river bottom is higher than the surrounding fields, often by as much as 5m. Dyke builders are heroes around the Yellow River, and every Chinese knows the story of Da Yu (Yu the Great), the legendary figure responsible for battling the capricious waters. It is said that he mobilized thousands of people to dredge the riverbed and dig diversionary canals after a terrible flood in 297 BC. The work took thirteen years, and during that period Yu never went home. At work's end, he sank a bronze ox in the waters, a talisman to tame the flow. A replica of the ox guards the shore of Kunming Lake in Beijing's Summer Palace. Today **river control** continues on a massive scale. To stop flooding, the riverbed is dredged, diversion channels are cut and reservoirs constructed on the river's tributaries. Land around the river has been forested to help prevent erosion and so keep the river's silt level down.

For most of its course, the river meanders across a flat flood plain with a horizon sharp as a knife blade. Two good places to see it are at the **viewpoint in Kaifeng** or from the **Yellow River Park** outside Zhengzhou. To see the river in a more tempestuous mood, take a diversion to **Hukou Falls** (see p.263), farther north on the border between Shaanxi and Shanxi provinces.

this was the cradle of Chinese history, and for millennia the centre of power for a string of dynasties, the remains of whose capital cities are strung out along the southern stretch of the plain.

Traces of Neolithic settlements are thick along the river – the homes of farmers, fishermen and excellent potters – but there was no large-scale building until the time of the Shang dynasty (1600–1066 BC), the rulers of which left behind written records. For the next three thousand years this small strip of the Yellow River basin saw the development of the Chinese state and civilization – a development constantly threatened by tribes from the north and by the perils of the river itself, but steady nonetheless. The Zhou dynasty, masters of north China from about 1000 BC, established a capital near Xi'an, moving on to Luoyang after this had been sacked. After them came the great emperor Qin Shi Huang, who by 221 BC had established a dominion which stretched from the Great Wall in the north to regions far south of the Yellow River. The next dynasty, the Han, also had their capital near Xi'an. This was a period in which the establishment of the **Silk Road** through Central Asia to Syria, and the rich trade with the West which followed, greatly strengthened the Yellow River area. Other influences came down the road too, most importantly **Buddhism**. At Xi'an, magnificent capital of the Tang dynasty (618–907), there were more than a hundred temples alone, and five of the ten main schools of Buddhism in China originated here. It was under the Tang that the cities of the Yellow River basin appeared to reach the zenith of their prosperity and power, but with hindsight it's clear that the economic balance had long been shifting to the south. The **Grand Canal**, completed in 608, linking the Yangzi and the Yellow rivers, strengthened the Yangzi basin's position as China's food bowl and the main source of the empire's finances. Kaifeng was the last imperial capital on the Yellow River, achieving that status in 960: in 1127 a further wave of invasions forced the imperial court to retreat to the south.

Of these ancient capitals, none is more impressive today than thriving **Xi'an**, the capital of Shaanxi province, and perhaps the most cosmopolitan city you will find in China outside the eastern seaboard. At the same time, it retains copious evidence of its former glories, most spectacularly in the tomb guards of Qin Shi Huang, the renowned **Terracotta Army**, but also in a host of temples and museums. The whole area is crowded with buildings which reflect the development of Chinese Buddhism from its earliest days; one of the finest is the Baima Si in **Luoyang**, a city farther east, thought by the ancient Chinese to be the centre of the universe. The temple is still a Buddhist centre today, and the last resting place of monks who carried sutras back along the road from India. The **Longmen Caves**, just outside the city, are among the most impressive works of art in China, but also rewarding are excursions in the area around, where two holy mountains, **Hua Shan** and **Song Shan**, one Buddhist, one Taoist, offer a welcome diversion from the monumentality of the cities. **Zhengzhou**, farther east, the capital of Henan, has an excellent new provincial museum exhibiting the fruits of ongoing archeological excavations, mostly Shang dynasty bronzes. East of here, the town of **Kaifeng**, the Song-dynasty capital, is a pretty and quiet little place, though scant remains of its past thanks to its proximity to the treacherous Yellow River. North of Kaifeng, near the border with Hebei, the city of **Anyang** remains a backwater with an impressive archeological heritage – you can inspect the current finds from the Shang era in the museum here. If you've had enough of the relics of ancient cultures, get a glimpse of recent history at **Yan'an** in high northern Shaanxi, the isolated base high in the loess plateau to which the Long March led Mao in 1937, or at the **Red Flag Canal** – a flagship project of Mao's self-reliant China of the 1960s – at Linxian in northern Henan.

Xi'an

The capital of Shaanxi province, **XI'AN** is a manufacturing town of five million inhabitants and holds a key position in the fertile plain between the high loess plateau of the north and the Qingling Mountains to the south. It's one of the more pleasant of Chinese cities, more prosperous than any other city in inland China except Chengdu, with streets full of Japanese cars, stores flooded with consumer goods, and stylish locals in the new discos. As the de facto capital of China's west, Xi'an is also the base of the government's Xibu Da Fazhan (Develop the West) campaign that's sputtering along. Its tourism industry, of course, means Xi'an already is far more developed than the surrounding area, a fact suggested by the large numbers of rural migrants who hang around at informal labour markets near the city gates. The city is also a primer in Chinese history, as between 1000 BC and 1000 AD it served as the **imperial capital** for eleven dynasties. You'll find a wealth of important sites and relics hereabouts: Neolithic Banpo, the Terracotta Army of the Qin emperor, the Han and Tang imperial tombs (see p.282), and in the city itself, the **Goose Pagodas** of the Tang, the **Bell and Drum towers** and **Ming city walls**, as well as two excellent **museums** holding a treasury of relics from the most glamorous parts of Chinese history. Despite the drawbacks of **pollution** (many of the locals walk around with white face masks on) and congestion, common to all rapidly industrializing Chinese cities, Xi'an is very popular with **foreign residents**, and many come here to study, as the colleges are regarded as some of the best places to learn Chinese.

Some history

This area has been the site of some of the oldest cities in the world's oldest civilization. Its history begins in the Bronze Age, three thousand years ago, when the western Zhou dynasty, known for their skilled bronzework, built their capital at **Fenghao**, a few miles west. Nearby, one of their chariot burials has been excavated. When Fenghao was sacked by northwestern tribes, the Zhou moved downriver to **Luoyang** and, as their empire continued to disintegrate into warring chiefdoms, the nearby Qin kingdom expanded. In 221 BC the larger-than-life Qin Shi Huang (see p.288) united the Chinese in a single empire, the Qin, with its capital at **Xianyang**, just north of Xi'an. The underground **Terracotta Army**, intended to guard his tomb, are this tyrant's inadvertent gift to today's tourist prosperity.

His successors, the Han, also based here, ruled from 206 BC to 220 AD. Near-contemporaries of Imperial Rome, they ruled an empire of comparable size and power. Here in Xi'an was the start of the Silk Road (see box, p.990), along which, among many other things, Chinese silk was carried to dress Roman senators and their wives at the court of Augustus. There was also a brisk trade with south and west Asia; Han China was an outward-looking empire. The emperors built themselves a new, splendid and cosmopolitan capital a few miles northwest of Xi'an which they called **Chang'an** – Eternal Peace. Its size reflected the power of their empire, and records say that its walls were 17km round with twelve great gates. When the dynasty fell, Chang'an was destroyed. Their tombs remain, though, including Emperor Wudi's mound at **Mao Ling**.

It was not until 589 that the Sui dynasty reunited the warring kingdoms into a new empire, but their dynasty hardly lasted longer than the time it took to build a new capital near Xi'an called **Da Xingcheng** – Great Prosperity. The Tang, who replaced them in 618, took over their capital, overlaying it with their own buildings. This city was in its day the capital of a great empire and

Xi'an

Xi'an	西安	***xī'ān***
Baxian Gong	八仙宫	*bāxiān gōng*
Bell Tower	钟楼	*zhōng lóu*
Big Goose Pagoda	大雁塔	*dàyàn tǎ*
Century Ginwa Department Store	世纪金花百货商店	*shìjì jīnhuābǎihuò shāngdiàn*
Daci'en Si	大慈恩寺	*dàcí'ēn sì*
Daxingshan Si	大兴善寺	*dàxīngshàn sì*
Drum Tower	鼓楼	*gǔ lóu*
Great Mosque	大清真寺	*dàqīngzhēn sì*
Relifeixing Internet	热力飞行网吧	*rèlìfēixíng wǎngbā*
Shaanxi Beilin Museum	陕西碑林博物馆	*shǎnxī bēilín bówùguǎn*
Shaanxi History Museum	陕西历史博物馆	*shǎnxī lìshǐ bówùguǎn*
Small Goose Pagoda	小雁塔	*xiǎoyàn tǎ*
Tang Dynasty Arts Museum	唐代艺术馆	*tángdài yìshùguǎn*

Accommodation, eating and drinking

Ana Grand Castle Hotel	长安城堡大酒店	*chángān chéngbǎo dàjiǔdiàn*
Baohua Jiujia	宝华酒家	*bǎohuá jiǔjiā*
Bell Tower	钟楼饭店	*zhōnglóu fàndiàn*
Didi's Disco	帝者迪斯科	*dìzhě dísīkē*
Dongya Fandian	东亚饭店	*dōngyà fàndiàn*
Dynasty	秦都酒店	*qíndū jiǔdiàn*
Flats of Renmin Hotel	人民大厦公寓	*rénmín dàshà gōngyù*
Foreign Language University Guesthouse	西安外语学院外事服务中心	*xī'ān wàiyǔxuéyuàn wàishì fúwù zhōngxīn*
HYATT	凯悦饭店	*kǎiyuè fàndiàn*
Jiefang	解放饭店	*jiěfàng fàndiàn*
Laosunjia	老孙家	*lǎosūnjiā*
Lemon-tree West	柠檬树西餐咖啡厅	*níngméngshù xīcān kāfēitīng*
New World	古都大酒店	*gǔdū dàjiǔdiàn*
Renmin	人民大厦	*rénmín dàshà*
Royal	皇城宾馆	*huángchéng bīnguǎn*
Shanxi Local Food	西安饭店	*xī'ān fàndiàn*
Shuyuan Hostel	属院青年旅舍	*shǔyuàn qīngnián lǚshè*
Sichuan Fandian	四川饭店	*sìchuān fàndiàn*
Sushi Restaurant	回转寿司店	*huízhuǎn shòusīdiàn*
Tang Dynasty	唐乐宫	*tánglè gōng*
Twenty One Disco	龙都二十一世纪迪斯科	*lóngdū èrshíyīshìjì dísīkē*
Victory	胜利饭店	*shènglì fàndiàn*
Weizhong Co Ltd	维众网吧	*wéizhòng wǎngbā*
Wuyi Fandian	五一饭店	*wǔyī fàndiàn*
Xi'an	西安宾馆	*xī'ān bīnguǎn*
Xiang Xiang Da Pan Ji	香香大盘鸡	*xiāngxiāng dàpánjī*
Xianghelou Roast Duck	祥和楼烤鸭店	*xiánghélóu kǎoyādiàn*
Xijing	西京饭店	*xījīng fàndiàn*
Zhiyuan	止园饭店	*zhǐyuán fàndiàn*

one of the biggest conurbations in the world, with more than a million people housed in a magnificent city whose **plan** was so rational that it was taken as the model for the building of many other Chinese cities and for the Japanese capital, Nara, in 710. The huge rectangle enclosed by walls nearly 10km long was divided by further walls into 108 districts, crisscrossed by a grid plan of streets. These walled-in quarters had no communication with each other except by a single gate which led to the main street; the gates were closed at sunset and reopened at dawn. Only top officials were allowed doors giving directly on to the street. The preoccupation with order and compartmentalizing society became even more apparent in the Imperial City, enclosed by more walls, and the palace, further enclosed, inside that.

The Tang period was a **golden age** for the arts, and ceramics, calligraphy, painting and poetry all reached new heights. You can get some idea of the quality from the Tang horses and camels in Xi'an's Shaanxi History Museum, the Classics of Filial Piety at the Shaanxi Beilin Museum, the wall paintings in the Tang tombs and the relics buried as offerings to the Buddha's fingerbone in the Famen Si. The Roman glassware found here testifies to the flourishing trade along the Silk Road at the time, as do the many foreign coins in the museum. The open society was reflected in its religious tolerance – not only was this a great period for Buddhism, with monks at the Jianfu Si busy translating the sutras the adventurous monk Xuan Zong had brought back from India, but the city's Great Mosque dates from the Tang, and one of the steles in the Provincial Museum bears witness to the founding of a chapel by Nestorian Christians.

After the fall of the Tang, Xi'an went into a long **decline**. It was never again the imperial capital, though the Ming emperor Hong Wu rebuilt the city as a gift for his son; today's great walls and gates date from this time. Occasionally, though, the city did continue to provide a footnote to history. When the Empress Dowager Cixi had to flee Beijing after the Boxer Rebellion, she set up her court here for two years. In 1911, during the uprising against the Manchu Qing dynasty, the Manchu quarter in Xi'an was destroyed and the Manchus massacred. And in 1936, Chiang Kaishek was arrested at Huaqing Hot Springs nearby in what became known as the Xi'an Incident (see p.286).

Orientation, arrival and city transport

Xi'an is easy to get around as the layout of today's city closely follows the ordered grid map of the ancient one, with straight, wide streets running along the compass directions. The **centre** is bounded by square city walls, with a bell tower marking the crossroads of the four main streets, Bei Dajie, Nan Dajie, Dong Dajie and Xi Dajie – north, south, east and west streets. Another major street runs south from the train station, where it's called Jiefang Lu, across the city, crosses Dong Dajie where it changes its name to Heping Lu, then to Yanta Lu outside the walls and continues all the way to the Big Goose Pagoda in the **southern outskirts**, where many of the city's sights are. The only exception to the grid plan of the central streets is the **Muslim quarter**, northwest of the Bell Tower, around whose unmarked winding alleys it's easy (and not necessarily unpleasurable) to get lost.

The **modern city**, extending far beyond the confines of the walls, in general adheres to the same ordered pattern, with two large highways forming ring roads, the innermost of which goes around the outside of the city walls.

Arrival

The arrivals gate at **Xi'an airport**, outside the town of Xianyang, 40km northwest of the city, is thronged with taxi drivers, who should charge ¥120

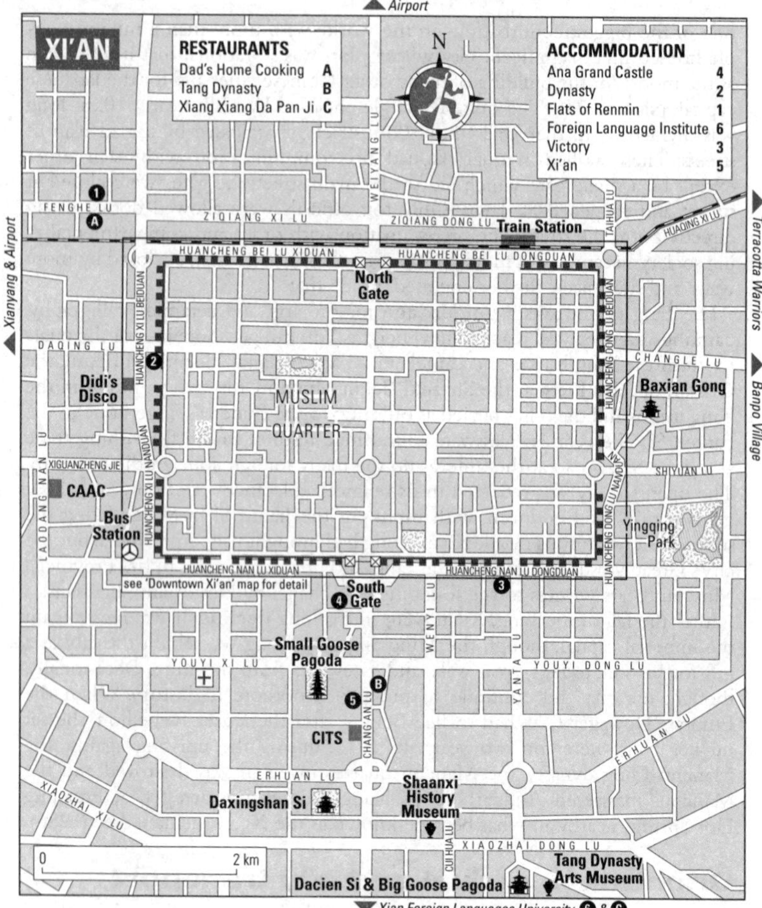

for a ride into town, but you're better off getting the **airport bus** (¥25; buy tickets from an office on the right of the main airport entrance as you exit). The bus journey takes an hour and leaves you outside the CAAC office on Laodong Lu, west of the city wall's Anding Gate. If you hail a taxi to get into the centre, be sure that it has a working meter, or you might get ripped off.

The busy **train station**, in the northeast corner of town, just outside the city walls, is a major terminus on a west–east line which splits just east of the city, one branch going north to Beijing, the other east to Shanghai. City buses leave from the tangled north end of Jiefang Lu, just south of the station, and taxis congregate on the western side of the concourse outside.

Buses supposedly arrive in Xi'an at either the bus station just south of the train station or at the terminus at the southwest corner of the city walls, but in practice where you arrive depends a lot on the bus company, the direction you approach from and the whim of the driver. As most buses arrive at night, and you are as likely to find yourself standing at the side of a main road somewhere as in the terminus, it's best to have a destination in mind and hail a taxi.

City transport

The largest concentration of **city buses** is found outside the train station at the northern end of Jiefang Lu. There are other clusters just outside the South Gate, and at the southern end of Yanta Lu, just north of the Big Goose Pagoda. Normal buses cost ¥1, fancier ones with air conditioning ¥2.

The city also has five **trolleybus** lines, which all run east–west across the city; most useful is the #101, which runs south from a terminus outside the station, down Jiefang Lu, then turns west on to Dong Dajie, runs past the Bell Tower, and continues through the west gate on to Fenghao Lu, coming close to the CAAC office. Double-decker bus #603 leaves from the station and goes through the centre of town, stopping at the Bell Tower and South Gate before terminating in the far south of town at the Foreign Language Institute.

Plentiful red **taxis** cruise the streets and can be hailed anywhere. Most destinations within the city come inside the ¥6 minimum rate.

As the streets are wide and flat, **cycling** is a good way to get around Xi'an. All the major streets have cycle lanes, controlled at major intersections by officials with flags. There are, however, few bike parks, and most people run the risk of a (rarely enforced) ¥10 fine by leaving their bikes padlocked to railings. Make sure you have a good security chain, especially if your bike is anything other than a downbeat Flying Pigeon. For rental places, see p.281.

The yellow city **maps** available everywhere (¥3) are generally reliable and hold a lot of information, including bus and tram routes. It's worth picking up one immediately, as bus routes are continually amended.

Useful bus routes

#9 Train station–*Flats of Renmin Hotel*.
#41 Train station–Heping Lu–Big Goose Pagoda.
#215 South Gate–Chang'an Lu.
#501 Huangcheng Xi Lu, 200m east of the *Flats of Renmin Hotel*–Nan Dajie–Big Goose Pagoda.
#601 Big Goose Pagoda–Dong Dajie–Bell Tower–Bei Dajie.
#603 Train station-Jiefang Lu–Bell Tower–Chang'an Lu and Foreign Language Institute.
#606 Train station–Jiefang Lu—Dong Dajie–Bell Tower.

Accommodation

Xi'an is firmly on the tourist itinerary, and **hotels** abound. The train-station touts offering budget rooms are best avoided, particularly as they may bring you to a place that doesn't take foreigners; if you do decide to go with them, be sure to bargain.

There's no shortage of international luxury hotels, with glossy five-star structures both inside and outside the city walls. Most sights are located around the city centre so, if your budget will stretch to it, it's much more convenient and atmospheric to stay inside the walls, in the thick of things. The mid-range category is also well catered for within the city walls, too.

Inside the walls

Bell Tower 110 Nan Dajie ⓣ029/7279200, ⓕ7218767. Opposite the southwest corner of the Bell Tower, right in the centre of town, this Holiday Inn-run hotel has a great location and is very comfortable. ❽

Hyatt 158 Dong Dajie, just by the intersection with Heping Lu ⓣ029/7231234, ⓕ7216799. This plush steel-and-concrete fortress full of amenities is the most luxurious place in Xi'an, and is where most tour groups end up. ❾

Jiefang 181 Jiefang Lu ⓣ029/7428946,

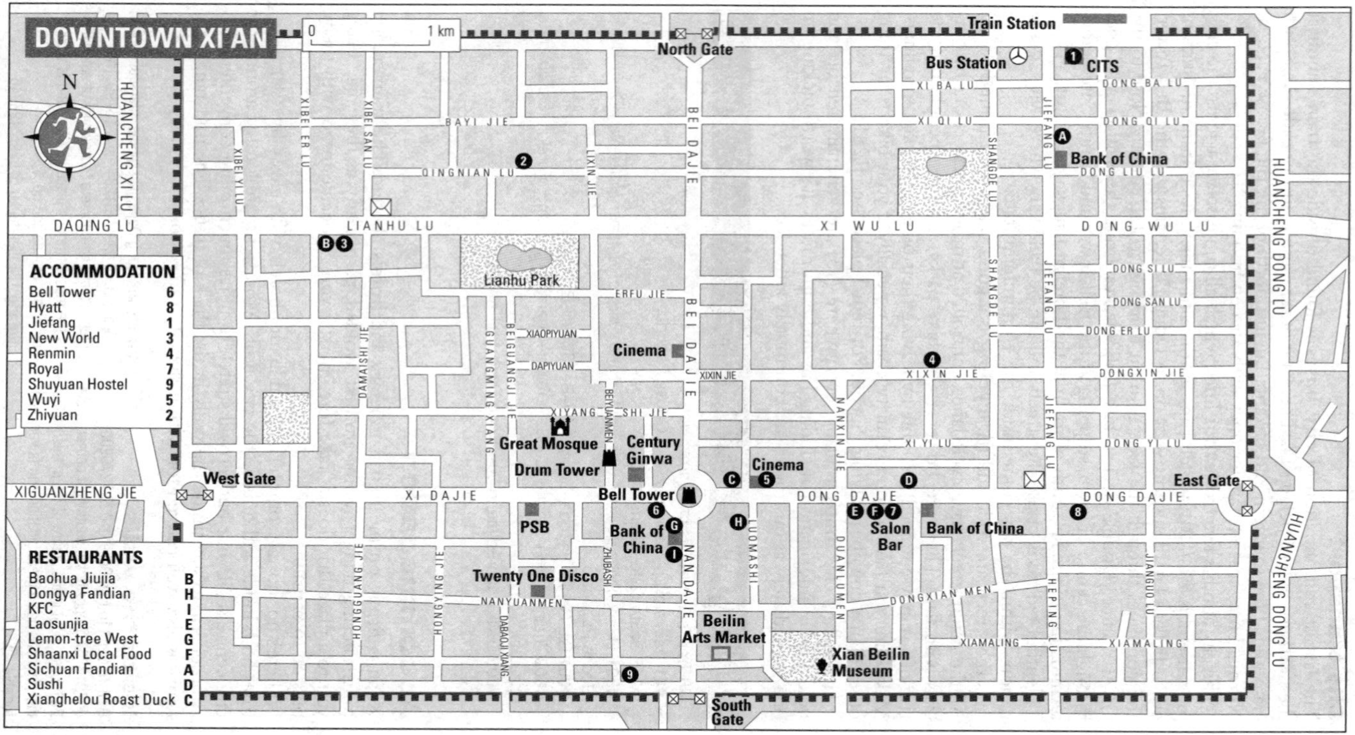

DOWNTOWN XI'AN

0 — 1 km

N

ACCOMMODATION

Bell Tower	6
Hyatt	8
Jiefang	1
New World	3
Renmin	4
Royal	7
Shuyuan Hostel	9
Wuyi	5
Zhiyuan	2

RESTAURANTS

Baohua Jiujia	B
Dongya Fandian	H
KFC	I
Laosunjia	E
Lemon-tree West	G
Shaanxi Local Food	F
Sichuan Fandian	A
Sushi	D
Xianghelou Roast Duck	C

Train Station
North Gate
Bus Station
CITS
Bank of China
XI BA LU
DONG BA LU
XI QI LU
DONG QI LU
DONG LIU LU
BAYI JIE
QINGNIAN LU
LIXIN JIE
BEI DAJIE
SHANGDE LU
JIEFANG LU
HUANCHENG XI LU
HUANCHENG DONG LU
XIBEI YI LU
XIBEI ER LU
XIBEI SAN LU
DAQING LU
LIANHU LU
XI WU LU
DONG WU LU
Lianhu Park
ERFU JIE
DONG SI LU
DONG SAN LU
DONG ER LU
DONGXIN JIE
XIXIN JIE
Cinema
XIAOPIYUAN
DAPIYUAN
DAMAISHI JIE
GUANGMING XIANG
BEIGUANGJI JIE
XIYANG SHI JIE
BEIYUANMEN
NANXIN JIE
XI YI LU
DONG YI LU
Great Mosque
Century Ginwa
Drum Tower
Cinema
West Gate
East Gate
XIGUANZHENG JIE
XI DAJIE
Bell Tower
DONG DAJIE
PSB
Bank of China
Salon Bar
Bank of China
LUOMASHI
DUANLUMEN
ZHUBASHI
NAN DAJIE
Twenty One Disco
HONGGUANG JIE
HONGYING JIE
NANYUANMEN
DABAOJI XIANG
DONGXIAN MEN
HEPING LU
JIANGUO LU
XIAMALING
Beilin Arts Market
Xian Beilin Museum
South Gate

Ⓕ7422617. As it's outside the train station, this hotel is especially convenient for a short stay, with a good range of services including a CITS office, bike rental and tours on offer. Staff are on the ball and it's reasonably priced. ❺

New World 48 Lianhu Lu Ⓣ029/7216868, Ⓕ7219754. The grand entrance leads to a lobby that's a bare plain of marble with an air of spare elegance. Quite luxurious with a price tag to match, but in rather a grey part of town. ❽

Renmin 319 Dongxin Jie Ⓣ029/7215111, Ⓕ7218152. The bulbous facade of this quirky building, built in the 1950s to house Russian advisers, looks vaguely eastern European. The inside has been renovated and now looks like everywhere else in this price bracket. ❼

Royal 334 Dong Dajie Ⓣ029/7235311, Ⓕ7235887. This de-luxe Japanese–Chinese joint venture is well located. ❾

Shuyuan International Youth Hostel Just inside the city wall's south gate Ⓣ029/7287720, Ⓕ7287238. From the train station, take buses #603, #608 or #239 to the South Gate, where a sign in English points the way. Its location and price are unrivalled, as is the setting around a quiet courtyard, though avoid the overflow basement rooms, which are damp, windowless cells. There's a great, if basic, restaurant, staff are helpful and they organize daily tours to the major sights in the locality. Dorm beds from ¥50, ❹

Wuyi (aka May 1) 351 Dong Dajie Ⓣ029/7210804, Ⓕ7213824. In a superb location tucked behind its dumpling shop in the centre of town, this little hotel has character and is good value, as well as housing an excellent restaurant. Deservedly popular and often full. Take bus #606 or trolleybus #101 from the station. ❺

Zhiyuan Qingnian Lu Ⓣ029/7336688. Go down the driveway of this tranquil complex and turn left for building no. 6, which is the hotel. A car park full of Toyota jeeps and black cars with tinted windows flying red flags on the bonnet indicates the semi-official character of this cadre hangout. Just asking for a room in the steel-grey lobby full of Party members takes some nerve. Foreigners can stay in buildings 5, 6 and 8. ❺

Outside the walls

Ana Grand Castle Hotel 12 Xi Duan Cheng Nan Lu Ⓣ029/7231800, Ⓕ7231500. Five-star concrete parody of the Big Goose Pagoda, situated just outside the South Gate. The cavernous atrium-lobby sets the somewhat impersonal tone; caters mainly to tour groups. ❾

Dynasty 55 Huancheng Xi Lu Ⓣ029/8626262, Ⓕ8627728. This four-star hotel, whose most striking feature is a bronze emperor Qin Shi Huang glaring at guests in the lobby, is aimed mainly at homesick Chinese businessmen, with luxurious karaoke rooms in the style of different regions – including a northern farmhouse, complete with fake *kang*. ❽

Flats of Renmin Hotel/International Youth Hostel 11 Fenghe Lu Ⓣ029/6240349. Most backpackers end up here, in an uninteresting area nine stops west on bus #9 from the train station. Look for the hotel's name in English on a pink sign on the west side of Xinhuo Lu; the hotel is 200m west down the next side road, over the rail line. If you're getting a taxi (¥10 from the station), make sure the driver doesn't take you to the *Renmin Hotel* in the centre of town. The older south block is much tattier and only marginally cheaper than the plusher north block; both buildings have dorms and double rooms. Ask to see your room before you pay, as there are dozens of choices. Beds in the new IYHF-sanctioned section are nicest. *Kane's* and *Dad's*, the two restaurants opposite (see p.280), which offer laundry, bike rental and information (as well as pretty good food), are a big plus. Dorms ¥25, ❹

Foreign Language Institute Guesthouse Chang'an Nan Lu Ⓣ029/5309532, Ⓕ5262221. Located on the leafy, hip campus popular with expats for Chinese studies. Internet cafés, phone offices, cheap restaurants and good shopping keep the area bustling well after dark. To get here, take bus #603, turn into the lane leading to campus, pass through the gate and turn right at the T-junction, then left with the road. The guesthouse is the white-tiled building past the playing fields. Student discounts available. ❸

Victory Heping Lu Ⓣ029/7856051. Mid-range place nicely located just outside the South Gate in the city wall, but staff are uncooperative. The hotel offers daily tours. Take bus #14 or #41 from the station. ❺

Xi'an 36 Chang'an Lu Ⓣ029/5261351, Ⓕ5261796. A large, comfortable place with a huge brown lobby, but a little too far south to warrant the cost. ❾

The City

Xi'an successfully integrates its architectural heritage with the modern city, its imposing walls and ancient geometric street plan, centring on the Bell Tower, giving it a distinct identity missing in the sprawl of most Chinese cities.

Downtown Xi'an, inside the walls, is just about compact enough to get around on foot, with enough sights to fill a busy day. And it is here that the city's new prosperity is most in evidence, in the variety and prices of goods in the shops on **Dong Dajie**, the main shopping street, where you'll also find the best hotels and restaurants, and in the number of cars that choke it during rush hour. **Nan Dajie**, to the south, is another shopping district at the end of which you'll find the **Provincial Museum**, which holds a massive collection of steles, next to the **city walls**, more imposing remnants of imperial China. Contrast is provided by the **Muslim quarter** off Xi Dajie, which preserves a different side of old China in its labyrinth of alleys centring on the **Great Mosque**.

The suburban area south of town holds more ancient buildings than the centre, as the city in Han and Tang times was considerably more extensive than in the Ming dynasty, when the walls were built. The excellent **Shaanxi History Museum** and the small **Daxingshan Si** sit between the two **Goose pagodas** and their temples, which are some of the oldest – and certainly the most distinctive – buildings in the city.

Downtown Xi'an

In the heart of town, the **Bell Tower** (daily 8.30am–6pm; ¥15) stands at the centre of the crossroads where the four main streets meet. The original building, built in 1384, stood two blocks west of here, at the centre of the Tang-dynasty city; the present triple-eaved wooden structure standing on a brick platform was built in 1582 and restored in 1739. You can enter only via the subway on Bei Dajie, in which you buy your ticket and where you must leave your bags (¥2). Inside is an exhibition of chimes and a bronze bell (not the original). A balcony all the way around the outside provides a view of the city's traffic. **Dong Dajie**, east of here, is the main downtown street, along which you can pick up a pizza, post a letter, get film developed or buy the latest jeans or trainers from clothes outlets and department stores such as the Century Ginwa (see "Shopping", p.278). There are a couple of restaurants worth checking out along here, *Laosunjia* and the *Xi'an Restaurant* (see p.280), plus plenty of fast-food and noodle places if you just want to snack: pop into the market, entered under an arch opposite the *Royal Hotel*, where you'll find captive delicacies such as snakes and toads.

The Muslim quarter

Head north off Xi Dajie, a street of small traders west of the Bell Tower, and suddenly the scale of the streets constricts to create the intimacy of a village, the narrow, unsurfaced alleys lined with cramped brown, two-storey buildings, half-timbered and with verandas. This is the **Muslim quarter**, for centuries the centre for Xi'an's Hui minority who today number around thirty thousand, a people said to be descended from eighth-century Arab soldiers. The winding streets are rewarding places to wander around; a good entry point is Damaishi Jie at the district's western extremity, the main market street, marked at the intersection with Xi Dajie by a green arch sporting Arabic calligraphy. Walk north up this street – it's often too packed to cycle up – and you pass poky little dumpling shops with rows of street stalls in front, many of which sell offal. Look out for the sheep skulls – when you buy one the vendor scoops the brains out with a chopstick and wraps them up in paper for you. More palatable, and definitely worth sampling, are the sweets, some stamped with good luck messages, the mutton cooked on skewers while you wait, and the nuts and seeds heaped on plates outside tiny shopfronts.

Head east of here at a junction about 200m up the street, walk for about 700m, then take the winding alley south and you come to the heart of the district, the **Great Mosque** (daily 8am–6.30pm; ¥12). The largest mosque in China, it was originally established in 742, then rebuilt in the Qing dynasty and heavily restored. An east–west-facing complex which integrates Arabic features into a familiar Chinese design, it's a calm place, unpenetrated by the hectic atmosphere of the streets outside, and is a rare public place where simply sitting and reading doesn't draw attention. On either side of the stone arch at the entrance are two **steles** by two of the most famous calligraphers in China, Mi Fei of the Song dynasty and Dong Qichang of the Ming. The attractive courtyard beyond, which holds a minaret in the form of an octagonal pagoda at its centre, is lined with wooden buildings featuring abstract eave decorations – the usual figurative designs being inappropriate for a mosque. Also here are free-standing steles bearing inscriptions in Chinese, Persian and Arabic. The **main prayer hall**, just beyond the two fountains, has a turquoise roof and some fine carvings on the doors and eaves; you can enter (take your shoes off) when it's not being used for prayers.

A short walk east of here is Beiyuanmen, a street lined with souvenir shops at least as interesting for their ancient trees and attractive wooden architecture as their wares. Head south along it and you come to the **Drum Tower** (daily 8.30am–6pm; ¥12), which marks the limit of the Muslim quarter. It's a triple-eaved wooden building atop a fifty-metre-long arch straddling the road. You enter up steps on the western side, though there's not much to see when you're up there, as the building no longer holds the drum which used to be banged at dusk, a complement to the bell in the Bell Tower which heralded the dawn.

The Shaanxi Beilin Museum

Heading south from the Bell Tower along Nan Dajie, a street of department stores and offices, you come to the huge **South Gate**, an arch in the wall topped with a triple-eaved wooden building, not open to the public. Turning east on to Shuyuanmen, a cobbled street of souvenir shops dressed up to look like Qing buildings, walk for 500m alongside the wall to reach the **Shaanxi Beilin Museum** (daily 9am–5pm; ¥30, students ¥15), a converted Confucian temple. Most of the exhibits are steles, from the Han to the Qing dynasties, which you don't need to understand Chinese to find fascinating – many are marked with maps and drawings.

An annexe on the west side holds an exhibition of small stone **Buddhist images**, a wealth of which have been discovered in Shaanxi. Exhibited chronologically, the sculptures demonstrate the way the physiognomy of Buddha images changed over the centuries. The earliest, from 420 AD, are of plump, Indian-style Buddhas; later images become much more Han-looking, as Buddhism developed Chinese characteristics and absorbed the influence of Confucianism and Taoism. The Sui and Tang figures are particularly good, bearing the most recognizably Chinese characteristics.

The rest of the museum collection consists of six halls containing more than a thousand **steles**. The first hall contains the twelve Confucian classics – texts outlining the Confucian philosophy – carved onto 114 stone tablets, a massive project ordered by the Tang emperor Wenzong in 837 as a way of ensuring the texts were never lost or corrupted by copyists' errors. Like most of the steles in the museum, these are set in a stone wall or secured in a steel frame. The second hall includes the **Daqing Nestorian tablet**, on the left as you go in, recognizable by a cross on the top, which records the arrival of a Nestorian priest in Chang'an in 781 and gives a rudimentary description of Christian doctrine.

Condemned as heretical in the West for its central doctrine of the dual nature of Christ, both human and divine, and for refusal to deify the virgin mother, Nestorianism spread to Turkey and the East as its priests fled persecution, and was the first Christian doctrine to appear in China. In the third hall, one stele is inscribed with a **map of Chang'an** at the height of its splendour, when the walls were extensive enough to include the Big Goose Pagoda within their perimeter. Rubbings are often being made in the fourth hall, where the most carved drawings are housed; thin paper is pasted over a stele and a powdered ink applied with a flat stone wrapped in cloth. Among the steles is an image called the "God of Literature Pointing the Dipper", with the eight characters which outline the Confucian virtues – regulate the heart, cultivate the self, overcome selfishness and return propriety – cleverly made into the image of a jaunty figure. "To point the dipper" meant to come first in the exams on Confucian texts which controlled entry to the civil service. Other tablets hold lively line drawings of local scenic spots. At the back of the hall, a stele records the harsh recriminations taken by the Qing government against a village which massacred foreign missionaries in 1903. The other three halls contain mainly texts, but notable is a stele inscribed with the large character "Hu", meaning tiger, written in a dynamic single stroke by the Qing calligrapher, Ma Dezhao.

The city walls

Largely intact and imposing enough to act as a physical barrier between the city centre and the suburbs, Xi'an's **walls** were originally built of rammed earth in 1370 on the foundation of the walls of the Tang-dynasty imperial, though they took their modern form in 1568, when they were faced with brick. Recently restored, the walls are the most distinctive feature of the modern city, forming a twelve-metre-high rectangle whose perimeter is 12km in length. Some 18m wide at the base, they're capped with crenellations, a watchtower at each corner and a fortress-like gate in the centre of each side. Originally the city would have been further defended with a moat and drawbridges, but today the area around the walls is a thin strip of parkland, created after a major restoration in 1983. Few roads which cross the walls, and traffic often has to circle around the outside for some distance before it can gain entry.

You can climb the walls (daily: summer 7am–10.30pm; rest of year 8am–6pm; ¥10) from the inside at steps 200m east of the South Gate and at the West Gate. Unrestored sections, mostly in the north and west, mean you can't walk all the way around; you can get farthest if you ascend at the West Gate and walk south, descending when you come to the road, then climbing back up at the south entrance. Locals sometimes use the wall as a nifty shortcut if traffic is bad, though you'll have to pay the fee to do so.

The Small Goose Pagoda and the Daxingshan Si

The **Xiaoyan Ta** (Small Goose Pagoda; daily 8am–6pm; ¥10) is southwest of the South Gate on Youyi Lu – from the train station, take bus #603 or #14 and get off at the crossroads with Chang'an Lu. A 45-metre-tall, delicate construction, founded in the Tang dynasty in 707 to store sutras brought back from India, the pagoda sits in what remains of the Jianfu Si. Two of the pagoda's original fifteen storeys were damaged in an earthquake, leaving a rather abrupt jagged top to the roof, to which you can ascend for an extra ¥10 for a view of the city. A shop at the back of the complex sells Shaanxi folk arts.

Just south of here on Xingshan Xijie, in Xinfeng Park, accessible down a narrow market street, the small **Daxingshan Si** (daily 8am–6pm; ¥10) is usually overlooked by visitors, but is worth a visit. It was destroyed in the Tang persecution of Buddhism, and thus today's small, low buildings are mainly Qing and Ming. This is the only working Buddhist temple in Xi'an, and monks in baggy orange trousers will write your name on a prayer sheet in the main hall for a donation.

Shaanxi History Museum

One of the city's major highlights, the **Shaanxi History Museum** (daily 9am–5.30pm, last entrance 4.30pm; ¥35, students ¥18; bags and cameras must be left outside) is an impressive modern building opened in 1992, on the route of buses #5 and #610 from the station, and within walking distance of the Daxingshan Si and the Big Goose Pagoda. The exhibition halls are spacious, well laid out, and have English captions, displaying to full advantage a magnificent collection of more than three thousand relics.

The **lower floor**, which contains a general survey of the development of civilization until the Shang dynasty, holds mostly arrowheads and simple ornaments – most impressive is a superb set of Western Zhou and Shang **bronze vessels** covered in geometric designs suggestive of animal shapes, used for storing and cooking ritual food. A small **upstairs section** displays relics from the Han to the Northern Zhou; notable are the Han ceramic funerary objects, particularly the model houses.

Back on the lower floor, two **side halls** hold themed exhibitions, the western one of bronzes and ceramics, in which the best-looking artefacts are Tang. Large numbers of ceramic **funerary objects** include superbly expressive and rather vicious-looking camels, guardians, dancers, courtiers and warriors, glazed and unglazed. There's even an ostrich and a rhinoceros, gifts from foreign ambassadors. The eastern hall holds a display of Tang **gold and silver**, mainly finely wrought images of dragons and tiny, delicate flowers and birds, and an exhibition of Tang **costume and ornament**. The hall's introduction states that Tang women led "brisk and liberated lives", though it's hard to imagine how when you see the wigs arranged to show their complex, gravity-defying hair-dos, with names like "frightened swan coil", and the tall, thin wooden soles on their shoes.

The Daci'en Si, Dayan Ta and Tang Dynasty Arts Museum

The **Daci'en Si** (Temple of Grace; daily 8am–5pm; ¥20), in the far south of town, 4km from the city wall on the route of buses #5 or #41 from the station, is the largest temple in Xi'an, though when it was established in 647 it was much larger, with nearly two thousand rooms, and a resident population of more than three hundred monks. The original was destroyed in 907, and the present buildings are Qing, as are the garishly repainted figures of *lohans* in the main hall. Other rooms hold shops and exhibitions of paintings. All around the temple you'll see rubbings from a Qing stele in the Xingjiao Si of images of the Tang-dynasty monk **Xuan Zang**, the temple's most famous resident, who spent fifteen years collecting Sanskrit sutras in India before translating them here into 1335 volumes. He is shown with the largest bamboo-frame backpack you're likely to see on your travels.

At Xuan Zang's request, the **Dayan Ta** (Big Goose Pagoda; daily 8am–5pm; ¥20) was built at the centre of the temple as a fireproof store for his precious sutras. No one seems to know where the name "Goose" comes from – perhaps from the tale in which Xuan Zang and Monkey, heroes of the popular classic *Xi You Ji* (*Journey to the West*), are saved by a goose when they get lost in the desert. More impressive than its little brother, the Big Goose Pagoda, in comparison, is sturdy and angular, square in plan, and more than 60m tall. It has been restored and added to many times, though the current design is not far from the original. On the first floor is an exhibition of different pagoda styles, and, at either side of the south entrance, stone tablets hold calligraphy by two Tang emperors, surrounded by bas-relief dragons and flying angels, also Tang, as is a fine carving of Buddha and his disciples sitting in a Chinese building over the lintel of the west door. The pagoda has seven storeys, each with large windows (out of which visitors throw money for luck). The view from the north windows is the most impressive for the rigorous geometry of the streets below, though it's hard to believe that when built the temple was at least 3km inside the Tang city, a great beauty spot dotted with pavilions and praised by poets.

A short walk east of here, the **Tang Dynasty Arts Museum** (daily 8am–5pm; ¥15) is not as good as it could be, considering the wealth of relics from this age, regarded as the high point of Chinese arts. Nevertheless, it does contain some excellent pieces, mostly pottery horses and camels and tri-coloured glazed figures, including among the usual range of warriors and courtiers a couple of stuffy-looking bureaucrats in elaborate costumes. The exhibits are dated but have no English captions.

The Baxian Gong

The **Baxian Gong** (also known as Baxian An), at the centre of a shabby area outside the East Gate, is the only Taoist temple in Xi'an, home to around a hundred monks and nuns. Containing an interesting collection of steles, including pictures of local scenic areas and copies of complex ancient medical diagrams of the human body, the temple is the setting for a popular religious festival on the first and fifteenth day of every lunar month. However, it is probably of most interest to visitors for the **antique market** that takes place outside every Wednesday and Sunday (see "Shopping" below).

Shopping

Xi'an is an excellent place to pick up souvenirs and antiques, which are generally cheaper and more varied than in Beijing, though prices have to be bartered down and the standard of goods, especially from tourist shops, is sometimes shoddy. Be aware that many of the antiques sold are fake. Shopping is also an enjoyable night-time activity since the markets and department stores are open until 10pm.

The most recent, and glitziest, addition to Xi'an's shopping scene is the **Century Ginwa Department Store**. Located on Xi Dajie just in front of the Drum Tower, it offers the usual array of designer labels and has franchises of *DeliFrance* and *Kenny Rogers Roasters* – there's also a good coffee bar on the ground floor. The basement supermarket is one of the best in China, with a good selection of reasonably priced imported goods. The **Xi'an Department Store**, opposite the *Wuyi Hotel* on Dong Dajie, and the **Guangren Department Store**, just east of the Bell Tower, sell a wide variety of household goods, sports equipment and stationery. For camping equipment or music on CD, take bus #603 to the **University District**, where dozens of campuses border Chang'an Lu. Get off at the massive Home Club store and cross the street into the warren of stalls.

The **night markets** in both the Muslim quarter and Beilin make for an entertaining stroll under the stars, where the nocturnal hawkers sell everything from dinner to souvenir silk paintings. There's also a night market on the eastern section of Dongxin Jie, with a lively atmosphere, but little to buy that's of interest to visitors – it's mostly plastic kitchenware.

Artwork

The city is something of an art centre, and the **paintings** available here are much more varied in style than those you see elsewhere. As well as the line and wash paintings of legendary figures, flowers and animals that you see everywhere, look for bright, simple folk paintings, usually of country scenes. A traditional Shaanxi art form, appealing for their decorative, flat design and lush colours, these images were popular in the 1970s in China for their idealistic, upbeat portrayal of peasant life – many villagers, especially from the town of Huxian, 20km south of Xi'an, have made a career of producing them. A good selection of these paintings is sold in a shop just behind the Small Goose Pagoda and in the temple compound, as well as outside the Banpo Museum (see p.284) together with bright folk art papercuts and flour figures. There are a number of painting shops on Beiyuanmen, north of the Drum Tower; try no. 144. For **rubbings** from steles, much cheaper than paintings and quite striking, try the Big Goose Pagoda and the Provincial Museum. The underground pedestrian route at the South Gate includes an interesting diversion down an old bomb shelter tunnel to Nan Shang Jie, where **papercuts** are for sale.

Strong competition means you can pick up a painting quite cheaply if you're prepared to **bargain** – a good, sizeable work can be had for less than ¥150. However, beware the bright young things who introduce themselves as art students whose class happens to be having an exhibition. They're touts who will lead you to a room full of mediocre work at inflated prices.

Souvenirs

Beiyuanmen is also the place to go for small souvenirs, engraved chopsticks, teapots, chiming balls and the like. Another strip of tourist shops lies along the pedestrianized Shuyuanmen, a cobbled street just east of the South Gate, where an attempt has been made to prettify the shops by making them look like Qing-dynasty buildings. Clusters of stalls and vendors swarm around all the tourist sights, and are often a nuisance, though the stalls around the Great Mosque are worth checking out – you'll see curved Islamic *shabaria* knives among the Mao watches and other tourist knick-knacks. Some stalls sell small figures of terracotta soldiers in a mesh basket; you can bargain them down to just a few yuan, but the figures aren't fired properly, and will leave your hands black whenever you touch them. For better quality, buy them from the Century Ginwa department store. They are also available from stalls outside the station – be sure to check them carefully and to bargain hard.

For a personalized souvenir, try the seal engraver at 22 Heping Lu or similar shops in Beilin, the official artist quarter; here you'll also find a variety of **artists' materials** – calligraphy sets and the like.

Antiques

There is a touristy antique shop at 14 Nanxin Jie, but the best place to go for **antiques** is the market outside the Baxian Gong, held every Wednesday and Sunday, and more of a local affair than a tourist bonanza, so prices are cheaper. Many vendors are villagers from the outlying regions who look as if they are clearing out their attics. You can find much more unusual items here than you will see in the stores, such as books and magazines dating from the Cultural Revolution containing rabid anti-Western propaganda, Qing vases, opium pipes, even rusty guns.

Clothes and books

A wide range of expensive **clothes** are sold on Dong Dajie, with a good selection of name-brand stores. For cheaper stuff try the street market in the first alley on the right as you go down Dong Dajie from the Bell Tower. Head right to the bottom of the alley, past the stores selling fake DKNY bomber jackets and the like, and on the west side you'll find a shop that sells practical, hard-wearing clothes such as hooded sweatshirts.

For **books** on Xi'an, try the Shaanxi Historical Museum or the shop behind the Small Goose Pagoda. Most are expensive, with more glossy pictures than text, but there are a couple of reasonably priced, well-illustrated paperbacks on sale. Xinhua Bookshop next door has a decent selection of books and music, in Chinese and in English. The Foreign Language Bookstore at 347 Dong Dajie has little in English except Agatha Christie novels.

Eating

With such a diverse range of ethnic cuisine on offer, it's impossible not to feast in Xi'an. There's a fine selection of restaurants in the centre of town, as well as excellent street food, such as *hele* (buckwheat noodles) and *mianpi* (flat noodles made of refined wheat dough), available from numerous stalls. Try the Muslim quarter, particularly Damaishi Jie (see p.274) or the **night market** on the eastern end of Dongxin Jie. **Muslim cuisine**, featuring skewered kebabs and delicious mutton and beef dishes, is widely available in restaurants, and it's generally true that a restaurant with Arabic above the door can be relied on to be more sanitary than most. Inevitably, there's also the usual **Western fast food**; *KFC* on Nan Dajie, just south of the Bell Tower, is so vast it always seems empty.

Restaurants

Baohua Jiujia Lianhu Lu. Just west of the *New World Hotel*, this is a popular local place – with an English menu – to suit all budgets. At the pricier end of the menu, try the braised pork or the fish with chrysanthemum. The side rooms are more pleasant than the narrow front hall.

Dad's Home Cooking Fenghe Lu. Opposite the *Flats of Renmin Hotel*, and in fierce competition with *Kane's* next door. A backpacker haunt, with the usual sweet-and-sour pork, chocolate pancakes, and chips; try the apple dipped in caramel. Check the restaurant's book for travellers' news and tips.

Dongya Fandian 46 Luoma Shi. A large, expensive Shanghai restaurant founded in 1916 that serves Wuxi and Suzhou cuisine, but it's a little uninspiring, with an English menu that doesn't give you many options.

Laosunjia 364 Dong Dajie. Highly recommended Muslim restaurant, where foreigners are escorted up to the third floor. Most of the customers eat the house speciality, *paomo*, meat stew (¥20). First you're given two cakes of bread, which you break into little pieces with your fingers and drop into a bowl – a time-consuming process, but it gets you hungry. Then the bowl, marked with a numbered clothes peg, is taken to the kitchen and piled with shredded meat, noodles and sauces. The beef and oxtail here is also very good. Wash your food down with "Eight Treasures Tea", a mixture of tea, nuts, fruit and crystallized sugar.

Lemon-tree West Nan Dajie. If you're craving a better class of Western fast food than you'll get in most of China, this mock-diner should satisfy your taste buds. To get there from the Bell Tower, walk down Nan Dajie and turn right by the Agricultural Bank of China into an alleyway. A meal for two should cost about ¥120 (including pricey drinks).

Pavilion At the *Hyatt Regency*, Dong Dajie. Elegantly decorated Cantonese restaurant, the most exclusive place in town. The food is up to standard: delicacies include abalone and shark, and there's a speciality tea list. A meal for two costs around ¥350.

Shaanxi Local Food Restaurant Dong Dajie. Formerly the *Xi'an Restaurant*, this Xi'an institution is a huge place with four dining floors; the best views over Dong Dajie are from the second floor. The atmosphere is pretty good, as is the food, but it's not cheap, with a meal for two costing at least ¥100.

Sichuan Fandian 151 Jiefang Lu. Tucked away above an unpromising-looking canteen; the stairs are on the north side. Excellent food and very popular, though they tone down the spices for foreigners.

Sushi Restaurant 223 Dong Dajie. Authentic and reasonably priced sushi bar. You can either sit and select from the conveyor belt, or order pricier options from one of the booths.

Tang Dynasty 75 Chang'an Dajie ⓣ029/5261633. Speciality dumplings and a daily Cantonese lunch buffet. Dinner is a imperial-style banquet (6.30–8.15pm) followed by a 90min cultural show, which will set you back ¥410, or ¥200 if you only want a cocktail with the performance. Tickets can be bought in advance from the theatre lobby on the ground floor.

Wuyi Fandian 351 Dong Dajie. Offers steamed buns and dumplings (¥1) which you buy on the street, then take inside to the canteen. The third floor of the hotel upstairs has a restaurant with a more sedate atmosphere specializing in Jiangsui and Anhui cuisine. The speciality Banpo fish is highly recommended.

Xiang Xiang Da Pan Ji Chang'an Nan Lu, opposite the Home Club store. For years this understated eating place, usually packed, has been serving Xi'an's signature dish, *dapanji* (literally "big plate chicken"): an entire chicken is chopped, roasted and served on a plate with hand-pulled noodles poured over the top and an aromatic sauce. Not to be missed, it's especially good with their draught beer.

Xianghelou Roast Duck 365 Dong Dajie. The entrance to this second-floor place is on the west side of an alleyway just off Dong Dajie. They specializes in Beijing duck, good value at ¥80 for a set meal for two.

Drinking and nightlife

Though not as lively as Beijing or Shanghai, Xi'an's large student population and general prosperity make it more exciting at night than most other Chinese cities. By night, red lanterns are lit across the city, and the perimeter of neon along the city walls adds to the evening ambience. Particularly worthwhile the University District (on the route of bus #603), or the **Bar Street** area on **Defu Lu**, behind the *Shuyuan Hostel* and inside the South Gate. The popularity of Xi'an with budget travellers means that there are a couple of **backpacker cafés**, some open only in the season (May–Aug), offering the familiar attractions of banana pancakes, beer late into the night and fake student cards. For an inexpensive drinking session, you're best bet is to head for Dafu Lu, the University District, or one of the the many hotel bars, where you should be wary of unsolicited advances from women drinking alone.

Tuesday is the most popular night to go out, when women get in free to all the **discos**. Foreigners who enter are likely to attract a lot of attention at first, and can live out all their *Saturday Night Fever* fantasies on the dance floor, but if you just want to watch you'll be left alone. A favourite spot with foreign students is *Didi's* on Huangcheng Xi Lu (daily 8pm–midnight; ¥20), where foreigners get in free, presumably because they are exotic and buy drinks (¥15 for a beer). It's a relatively small place and fairly alternative – the music is a mix of hip-hop, dance, rap and slushy love songs from a live singer. Things are a lot livelier after 10.30pm, when the music gets faster and only the serious clubbers are left. *Twenty One* on Nanyuanmen is a bigger, glitzier version (daily 8pm–midnight; ¥20).

The restaurant in the *Tang Dynasty Hotel* (see review above) has a lavish nightly dinner and **cultural show**, worthwhile if you've not already seen one in Beijing – highlights include opera, acrobatics and classical recitals.

Listings

Airlines CAAC is on the southeast corner of the crossroads with Fenghao Lu (Mon–Sat 8am–9pm; ⓣ029/8708450). The airport bus leaves from the bus stop outside every thirty minutes between 5am and 6pm daily.

Bike rental Bikes cost ¥5 a day, with a deposit of up to ¥100. You can rent a Flying Pigeon from the *Flats of Renmin Hotel*, the *Jiefang Hotel* and the *Shuyuan Hostel*. *Kane's* and *Dad's* restaurants also have a few bikes for rent.

Banks and exchange Branches of the Bank of China (Mon–Fri 9am–5pm, Sat 9am–3pm) are at 318 Dong Dajie and 233 Jiefang Lu; the branch on Nan Dajie next to *KFC* is open on Sun (10am–2pm). An ATM here accepts Western debit cards. You can also exchange cash at the business centres of the larger hotels.

Buses The bus station serves Hua Shan, Yan'an, Ruicheng and Luoyang, among other destinations. Another station just outside the southwest corner of the city walls has a regular service to destinations south and west of the city.

Cinema You can watch Bruce Willis speaking Mandarin at the picture houses at 379 Dong Dajie, where they show the occasional dubbed foreign action movie, a change from all the home-grown action movies. The streets around the Foreign Language Institute have several DVD parlors showing what's playing in America's theatres.

Hospital The Provincial Hospital is on Youyi Xi Lu, just west of the intersection with Lingyuan Lu.

Internet access The cheapest place to get online is the Foreign Languages University – there are dozens of 24hr Net cafés in the area. Take bus #603 from outside the Bell Tower on Chang'an Lu and get off at the Home Club warehouse mart. The best is at the intersection of Chang'an Lu and Shida Lu (the university road), where the second floor houses the Reli Feixing Internet Café (¥3/hr).

Mail and telephones The central post office faces the Bell Tower. There's also one opposite the *Hyatt*, at 161 Dong Dajie (Mon–Fri 9am–7pm), and another opposite the *New World Hotel* on Lianhu Lu (Mon–Fri 9am–noon & 2–5pm). A 24hr telephone service is available in the same building as the central post office; you can also make international phone calls from the business centres of large hotels.

PSB At 138 Xi Dajie (Mon–Sat 8am–noon & 3–5pm).

Trains Xi'an's train station is a frustrating zoo, and – bizarrely – tickets never seem to be available there. There is a Foreigners' Booking Office on the second floor of the train station booking hall (daily 10.30am–12.30pm & 2.30–4.30pm), but it's of limited use – staff ask you where you want to go and when, then write it in Chinese and tell you which of the other windows you should queue up at to buy the ticket. It's better to buy tickets from the *Kane's* or *Dad's* or the tour agency in the back of the *Jiefang Hotel*. The Advance Ticket Booking Office on Lianhu Lu, marked in English on some maps, often won't sell tickets to foreigners.

Travel agents The main office of CITS is at 48 Chang'an Lu (daily 8am–6pm; ⓣ029/5262066, ⓕ5261558), but the friendly pair who staff the small office (daily 8am–9pm; ⓣ029/7431023) at the back of the *Jiefang Hotel* (walk through the lobby and turn left; the office is in a small room off the hallway past the lift) are more approachable, and sell tickets for onward travel by train and plane, for the airport bus and for Yangzi River cruises. They are renowned for getting train tickets when the station staff have stonewalled. Also use the helpful agents at the two hostels.

Around Xi'an

You could spend days on excursions around Xi'an; look at any tourist map and the area is dense with attractions. Most people see the justifiably famous **Terracotta Army**, **Banpo Museum** and the **Imperial Tombs** at least. Other recommended attractions off the tour-group itinerary are the **Famen Si**, with a superb museum attached, which is a little too remote for most visitors, and **Hua Shan**, the holy mountain (see p.293).

The easiest way to see the sights around Xi'an is to take one of the many **tours** on offer. There are two routes: the popular **eastern route** covers the Huaqing Pool, the Terracotta Army, Qin Shi Huang's tomb and the Banpo Museum; the **western route**, going to the Imperial Tombs and the Famen Si, is less popular as more travelling is involved, and it's more expensive (it's also hard to find anyone running it off season). Local **tour buses** run by private operators leave from outside the train station every morning; get there early as most of the buses have left by 9am. Look for the ticket booths, with boards outside showing the route and the price – these are located outside the bus station and on the east side of Jiefang Lu. Tours should cost about ¥40 per person. Tour operators on the western route often skip the remote Famen Temple despite advertising it on their signs.

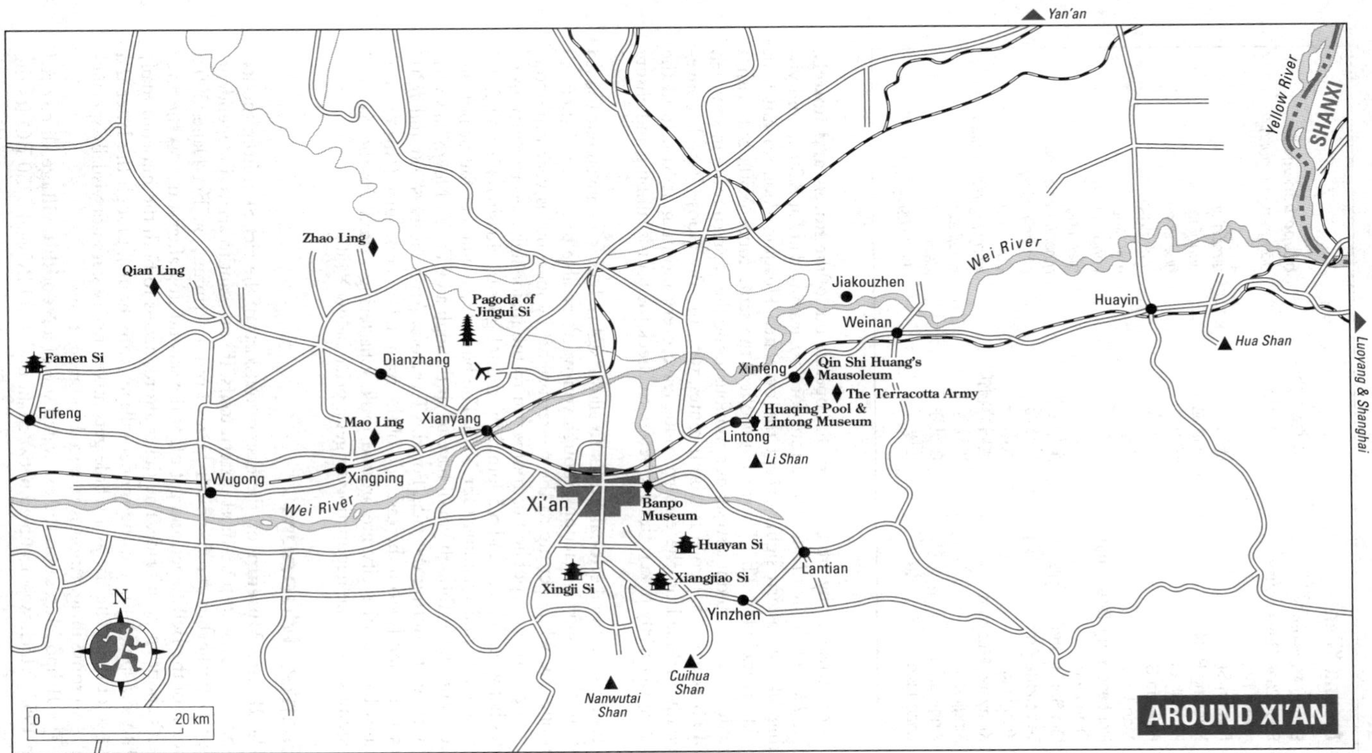
AROUND XI'AN
Yan'an
Yellow River
SHANXI
Luoyang & Shanghai
Wei River
Jiakouzhen
Huayin
Hua Shan
Weinan
Xinfeng
Qin Shi Huang's Mausoleum
The Terracotta Army
Huaqing Pool & Lintong Museum
Lintong
Li Shan
Zhao Ling
Qian Ling
Pagoda of Jingui Si
Famen Si
Dianzhang
Fufeng
Mao Ling
Xianyang
Wugong
Xingping
Wei River
Xi'an
Banpo Museum
Huayan Si
Xiangjiao Si
Xingji Si
Lantian
Yinzhen
Cuihua Shan
Nanwutai Shan
N
0
20 km

Around Xi'an

Banpo Museum	半坡博物馆	***bànpō bówùguǎn***
East Peak Guesthouse (Hua Shan)	东峰宾馆	*dōngfēng bīnguǎn*
Famen Si	法门寺	*fǎmén sì*
Huaqing Pool	华清池	*huáqīng chí*
Hua Shan	华山	*huá shān*
Huayan Si	华严寺	*huáyán sì*
Mao Ling	茂陵	*mào líng*
Princess Yong Tai's Tomb	永泰墓	*yǒngtài mù*
Qian Ling	乾陵	*qián líng*
Qin Shi Huang's Tomb	秦始皇陵	*qínshǐhuáng líng*
Terracotta Army	兵马俑	*bīngmǎ yǒng*
Xianyang	咸阳	*xiányáng*
Xianyang Museum	咸阳博物馆	*xiányáng bówùguǎn*
Xingjiao Si	兴教寺	*xìngjiào sì*
Xingji Si	香积寺	*xiāngjī sì*
Zhao Ling	昭陵	*zhāo líng*

More trustworthy are the tours that operate out of the **hotels and hostels**. The *Flats of Renmin Hotel* runs a tour for ¥50, leaving daily at 8.30am and visiting all the eastern sights except the overrated Huaqing Pool; no lunch or guide is included. The *Victory Hotel* offers the same route (¥50), but with a guide included, and it also sends a minibus along the western route in summer. **CITS tours** (¥55) covering both routes, with the Big Goose Pagoda conveniently included on the eastern route, leave every morning at 8am from the *Jiefang Hotel*; buy tickets the day before to check the tour is running and ensure a seat.

It's possible to take **local buses** to all the sights. This is a convenient way to get to the eastern attractions, though you won't be able to go round them all in one day, while getting to the western sights by local bus is very time-consuming. Two new public bus routes run to the major sights every thirty minutes between 7.30am and 5.30pm daily: the #1 goes to Huashan (2hr; ¥18); #2 to Famen Si and Qianling (3hr; ¥18). The buses leave whether full or not, and are comfortable, though you'll have to sit through a VCD of a New Year's variety program during the ride. For the Terracotta Army, buses #306 and #307 leave frequently from the east side of the train station concourse (1hr; ¥5). Last buses back to the city are around dusk. Chartering a **taxi** for the day will require some agile negotiating to get a price below ¥450.

Banpo Museum

The **Banpo Museum**, on the eastern outskirts of the city, 8km from the station, is the first stop on most eastern tours. If you want to arrive independently, take trolleybus #105, which leaves from a terminus on Bei Dajie, 300m north of the Bell Tower, and get off at the second stop after you cross the river – it's about an hour's ride. The ticket affords access to both the museum (daily 9am–5.30pm; ¥40) and the model village (same hours), though the latter is a waste of time. The site as a whole gets mixed reviews; it's not visually spectacular, so some imagination is required to bring it alive.

The Banpo Museum is the excavated site of a **Neolithic village**, discovered in 1953, which was occupied between around 4500 BC and 3750 BC. It's the biggest and best-preserved site so far found of **Yangshao culture**, and is named after the village near the eastern bend of the Yellow River where the first relics of this culture were found. A history written around 300 BC states that the Yangshao people "knew their mothers but not their fathers. Living together with the deer they tilled the earth and wove cloth and between themselves there was no strife." This, and the fact that the women's graves have more objects in them than the men's, has led to the Chinese contention that the society was **matriarchal**, and the somewhat questionable claim that theirs was "a primitive communist society", as tourist literature states. From bone hooks and stone tools unearthed, it is more securely known that they farmed, fished and kept domestic animals.

You can walk around the covered excavation site, a lunar landscape of pits, craters and humps, on raised walkways, but it can be hard to relate these to the buildings and objects described on the signs in whimsical English. The village is divided into three areas; the first is a **residential section** bounded by a surrounding trench for defence, which includes the remains of 46 houses, round or pyramid-shaped and constructed half underground around a central firepit with walls of wood faced with mud and straw. Around the houses are pits, used for storage, and the remains of pens which would have held domestic animals. A larger, central building was used as a communal hall.

North of here was a **burial ground**, around which are exhibitions of skeletons and funerary objects, mostly ceramic bowls and jade or bone ornaments. One grave, of a young girl, buried in an earthenware jar, contained 76 objects, including jade earrings and stone balls. Other ceramics found at the site, which were made in **six kilns** here, are displayed in the **museum wing**, They are surprisingly sophisticated, made by hand of red clay and decorated with schematic images of fish, deer and heads, or with abstract patterns, sometimes with marks on the rim which appear to be a form of writing. Also in the museum you can see barbed fish hooks with weights, stone tools, spindles and bone needles.

A compound of huts outside the museum, the **Culture Village** is a crude attempt to reconstruct the original village – a Neolithic theme park entered through the nether regions of an enormous fibreglass woman. Little attempt is made at authenticity beyond trying to cover the fire extinguishers with leaves.

Huaqing Pool and the Lintong Museum

Huaqing Pool (daily 8am–7pm; ¥40, students ¥20) is at the foot of Li Shan, 30km east of Xi'an on the road to the Terracotta Army (take bus #306 or #307 from the train station). Its springs, with mineral-rich water emerging at a constant and agreeable 43°C, have been attracting people for nearly 2500 years, including many emperors. Qin Shi Huang had a residence here, as did the Han emperors, but its present form, a complex of **bathing houses and pools**, was created in the Tang dynasty. The first Tang emperor, Tai Zong, had a palace at Huaqing, but it was under his successor, **Xuan Zong**, who spent much of the winter here in the company of his favourite concubine, **Yang Guifei** (see box, p.287), that the complex reached its height of popularity as an imperial pleasure resort.

Nowadays Huaqing is a collection of classical buildings, a little less romantic than it sounds – the buildings are nothing special, and the site is always thronged with day-trippers. The old **imperial bathhouses**, at the back of the complex, must once have looked impressive, but today they just resemble half-ruined, drained swimming pools. The largest is Lotus Pool, more than a hundred metres

The Xi'an Incident

Huaqing Pool's modern claim to fame is as the setting for the **Xi'an Incident** in 1936, when **Chiang Kaishek** was arrested by his own troops and forced to sign an alliance with the Communists. The story is a little more complicated than this, however. As Japanese troops continued to advance into China, Chiang insisted on pursuing his policy of national unification – meaning the destruction of the Communists before all else. In December 1936 he flew to Xi'an to overlook another extermination campaign. The area was under the control of **Marshall Zhang Xueliang** and his Manchurian troops. Although GMD supporters, they, like many others, had grown weary of Chiang's policies, a disillusionment fuelled by the failure to make any real impression on the Red Army and by the fact that the Manchurian homeland was now occupied by the Japanese. In secret meetings with Communist leaders, Zhang had been convinced of their genuine anti-Japanese sentiments, and so, on the morning of December 12, Nationalist troops stormed Chiang's headquarters at the foot of Li Shan, capturing most of the headquarters staff. The great leader himself was eventually caught halfway up the slope in a house at the back of the complex, behind the pools – a neo-Grecian pavilion on the lower slopes of the mountain marks the spot. Still in his pyjamas and without his false teeth, he had bolted from his bed at the sound of gunfire. Chiang was forced to pay a heavy ransom but was otherwise unharmed, his captors allowing him to remain in control of China provided that he allied with the Communists against the Japanese. Nowadays, tourists line up at the pavilion to don GMD uniforms and have their snapshots taken.

square, once reserved for the use of Xuan Zong; a little smaller is Crabapple Pool, for his concubine Yang. As well as the pools, there are a few halls, now housing souvenir shops, and a small **museum**, where fragments of Qin and Tang architectural detail – roof tiles and decorated bricks – hint at past magnificence. A **marble boat**, at the edge of Jiulong Pond, on the left as you enter, was constructed in 1956. The **Huaqing Hot Spring Bathhouse** behind it offers you the chance to bathe in the waters; for a steep ¥70 you are shut in a room that looks like a mid-range hotel room (complete with a photo of a glossy tropical paradise on the wall and little plastic bottles of shampoo) with a bath and a shower. Better is the public bathhouse at the front of the complex, on the left of the gate as you go in, where you can bathe in a communal pool for ¥20; you'll need to take your own towel and soap.

Tours can spend as long as two hours here, much more time than the place really warrants. Fortunately, the **Lintong Museum** (daily 8am–5.30pm; ¥20) nearby provides a rewarding diversion; turn right out of the Huaqing Pool complex, then run a gauntlet of souvenir sellers for 150m and you'll see the museum on your right. Though small and relatively expensive, it's worth it for a varied collection that includes silver chopsticks and scissors, a bronze jar decorated with human faces, a crossbow and numerous Han funerary objects, including ceramic figures of horses, dogs, ducks and pigs. The best exhibit, a **Tang reliquary** unearthed nearby, is in the second of the three rooms. Inside a stone stupa about a metre high, decorated with images of everyday life, was found a silver coffin with a steep sloping roof, fussily ornamented with silver spirals, strings of pearls and gold images of monks on the side. Inside this, a gold coffin a few inches long held a tiny glass jar with a handful of dust at the bottom. These delicate relics, and the dust, optimistically labelled "ashes of the Buddha", though crudely exhibited in what look like perspex lunchboxes, are more interesting than anything at Huaqing Pool.

Xuan Zong and Yang Guifei

The tale of Emperor Xuan Zong and his concubine Yang Guifei is one of the great Chinese **tragic romances**, the equivalent to the Western Antony and Cleopatra, and is often depicted in art and drama, most famously in an epic by the great Tang poet Bai Juyi. Xuan Zong took a fancy to Yang Guifei – originally the concubine of his son – when he was over 60, and she was no spring chicken (indeed, accounts of the time describe her as somewhat portly). They fell in love, but his infatuation with her, which led to his neglect of affairs of state, was seen as harmful to the empire by his officials, and in part led to the rebellion of the disgruntled General An Lushan. As An Lushan and his troops approached the capital, the emperor's guards refused to take arms against the invaders unless he order the execution of Yang Guifei; in despair, she hanged herself.

The Terracotta Army and Tomb of Qin Shi Huang

The Terracotta Army – probably the highlight of a trip to Xi'an – and the Tomb of Qin Shi Huang which it guards, are 28km east of Xi'an, just beyond Huaqing Pool. Plenty of tours come here, giving you two hours at the army and twenty minutes at the tomb. Alternatively, it's easy enough to get here by yourself on **bus** #306 or #307 from the car park on the east side of Xi'an train station; the journey, on minor roads, through villages, takes an hour. Slightly more expensive, but a little quicker, are the **minibuses** which leave from right outside the station and take the direct highway. The buses run only to the site of the Terracotta Army; if you want to see the tomb you'll have to walk from there.

Beware of a stop en route to the "Amusement Park of Emperor Qin and the Terracotta Army", 1km before the real thing. Buses sometimes pull in here, and tourists, not seeing the words "amusement park" in small print, hand over ¥18 before realizing they've entered a hall of photographs and torture displays. It's better to remain on the bus until the group finishes its brief, grumbling walkthrough.

The Terracotta Army

No records exist of the **Terracotta Army** (daily 8am–6pm; ¥65, students ¥35, though this is not always honoured) which was set to guard Qin Shi Huang's tomb, and it was only discovered by peasants sinking a well in 1974. Three rectangular vaults were found, built of earth with brick floors and timber supports. Today, hangars have been built over the excavated site so that the ranks of soldiers – designed never to be seen, but now one of the most popular tourist attractions in China – can be viewed in situ. If you feel the guided tour (¥200) is too expensive, rent an electronic headset (¥40) at the entrance – the commentary covers the same topics, and won't badger you to stop taking photographs (despite signs to the contrary, everyone uses their cameras, and most staff have ceased trying to police the flashbulbs).

Vault 1

Vault 1 is the largest, and about a fifth of the area has been excavated, revealing more than a thousand figures (out of an estimated eight thousand) ranked in battle formation. Facing you as you enter the hangar, this is one of the most memorable sights in China; you can inspect the static soldiers at closer range

Qin Shi Huang

Though only 13 when he ascended the throne of the western state of Qin in 246 BC, within 25 years **Qin Shi Huang** had managed to subjugate all the quarrelsome eastern states, thus becoming the first emperor of a **unified China**. "As a silkworm devours a mulberry leaf, so Qin swallowed up the kingdoms of the Empire", or so the first-century BC historian Sima Qian put it. During his eleven years as the sole monarch of the Chinese world, Qin Shi Huang set out to transform it, hoping to create an empire that his descendants would continue to rule for "ten thousand years". His reign was marked by centralized rule, and often **ruthless tyranny**. As well as standardizing weights and measures (even the width of cart wheels) and ordering a unified script to be used, the First Emperor decreed that all books, except those on the history of the Qin and on such practical matters as agriculture, be destroyed, along with the scholars who produced them. It was only thanks to a few Confucian scholars, who hid their books away, that any literature from before this period has survived. Qin Shi Huang himself favoured the strict philosophy of "legalism", a system of thought which taught that human nature was intrinsically bad, and must be reined in by the draconian laws of the state.

As well as overseeing the construction of roads linking all parts of the empire, mainly to aid military operations, Qin Shi Huang began the construction of the **Great Wall**, a project that perhaps more than any of his harsh laws and high taxes turned the populace, drummed into constructing it, against him. Ambitious to the end, Qin Shi Huang died on a journey to the east coast seeking the legendary island of the immortals and the secret drug of longevity they held. His entourage concealed his death – easy to do as he lived in total seclusion from his subjects – and installed an easily manipulated prince on the throne. The empire soon disintegrated into civil war and within a few years, Qin Shi Huang's capital had been destroyed, his palace burnt and his tomb ransacked.

It is possible that Qin Shi Huang, seen as an archetypal tyrant, has been harshly judged by history, as the story of his reign was written in the Han dynasty, when an eastern people whom he subjugated became ascendant. They are unlikely to have been enamoured of him, and the fact that the Terracotta Army faces east, the direction that Qin Shi Huang thought threats to his empire would come from, indicates the animosity that existed. The outstanding artistry of the terracotta figures has revised the accepted view of the Qin dynasty as a time of unremitting philistinism, and his reign has been reassessed since their discovery. Mao Zedong, it is said, was an admirer of his predecessor in revolution.

via raised walkways. Averaging 1.8m in height, the figures are hollow from the thighs up; head and hands were modelled separately and attached to the mass-produced bodies. Each soldier has different features and expressions and wears marks of rank; some believe that each is a portrait of a real member of the ancient Imperial Guard. Their hair is tied in buns and they are wearing knee-length battle tunics; the figures on the outside originally wore leather armour, now decayed. Traces of pigment show that their dress was once bright yellow, purple and green, though it's grey now. Originally the troops carried real bows, swords, spears and crossbows, more than ten thousand of which have been found. The metal weapons, made of sophisticated alloys, were still sharp when discovered, and the arrowheads contained lead to make them poisonous.

A central group of terracotta **horses** is all that remain of a set of chariots. These wore harnesses with brass fittings and have been identified as depicting a breed from Gansu and Xinjiang. Each has six teeth, an indication that they are in their prime.

Vaults 2 and 3

Vault 2 is a smaller, L-shaped area, still under excavation; it's thought to hold more warriers than Vault 1. The four groups here – crossbowmen, charioteers, cavalry and infantry – display more variety of posture and uniform than the figures in the main vault, though a large number of smashed and broken figures make the scene look more like the aftermath of a battle than the preparation for one. Four exceptional figures found here are exhibited at the side: a kneeling archer, a cavalryman leading a horse, an officer with a stylish goatee and the magnificent figure of a general, 2m tall, wearing engraved armour and a cap with two tails. Also on show are some of the weapons found at the site, including a huge bronze battle-axe.

The much smaller **vault 3**, where 68 figures and a chariot have been found, seems to have been battle headquarters. Armed with ceremonial *shu*, a short bronze mace with a triangular head, the figures are not in battle formation but form a guard of honour. Animal bones found here provide evidence of ritual sacrifices, which a real army would have performed before going into battle. A photo exhibition of plaster replicas gives some idea of how the figures would have been painted.

The rest of the site

At the side of vault 2 is a small **museum** where two magnificent **bronze chariots**, found in 1982 near Qin Shi Huang's tomb, are displayed in glass cases. They're about half actual size. The front one, depicting the Imperial Fleet leader's chariot, has four horses and a driver, and is decorated with dragon, phoenix and cloud designs, with a curved canopy and a gold-and-silver harness. Behind the driver is a large compartment featuring a silver door-latch and windows that open and close. The chariot at the back was the emperor's and has seats and beds in the rear. Both chariots were made with astonishing attention to detail; even the driver's knuckles, nails and fingerprints are shown. Another museum holds small artefacts found around the area, including a skull with an arrowhead still embedded in it, and a few kneeling pottery attendants, the only female figures depicted.

The complex around the Terracotta Army is a tourist circus, with a souvenir city of industrial proportions; the most popular goods are postcards and slides, as you are not allowed to take pictures inside the halls. They also sell miniature terracotta figures, fur coats and folk crafts. The food is diabolical, and it's best to eat before you go. The shops inside the halls sell souvenirs of slightly better quality, including full-size terracotta figures (¥36,000). At times you'll find a bemused-looking peasant signing postcards in the shop at Vault 2. Supposedly, it's Yang Zhifa, the man who discovered it all in 1974.

The Tomb of Qin Shi Huang

The **Tomb of Qin Shi Huang** (daily 8am–5.30pm; ¥26) is now no more than an artificial hill, nearly 2km west of the Terracotta Army. The burial mound was originally at the southern end of an inner sanctuary with walls 2.5km long, itself the centre of an outer city stretching for 6km, none of which remains. There's not much to see here; hassled at every step by souvenir sellers, you can walk up stone steps to the top of the hill, where you have a view of fields scraped bare for agriculture. According to accounts by Sima Qian in his *Historical Records*, written a century after the entombment, 700,000 labourers took 36 years to create an imperial city below ground, a complex full of wonders: the heavens were depicted on the ceiling of the central chamber with pearls and the geographical divisions of the earth were delineated on a floor of bronze, with the seas and rivers represented by pools of mercury and made to flow with machinery. Automatic crossbows were set to protect the many gold and silver relics. Abnormally high quantities of mercury have recently been found in the surrounding soil, suggesting that at least parts of the account can be trusted. Secrecy was maintained, as usual, by killing most of the workmen. The tomb has yet to be excavated; digs in the surrounding area have revealed the inner and outer walls, ten gates and four watchtowers.

North and west of the city

Except for the museum at **Xianyang**, the tombs, temples and museums in the north and west of Xi'an are a little far out to be visited conveniently. Trying to get around yourself is a hassle, as **local buses** are slow, routes complex and the country roads which pass through a stark loess plain, where coloured paper fluttering from the odd grave provides the only bright touches in the brown landscape, aren't good. At least it's easy to get back into Xi'an – just stand by a road and wave down a minibus. **Tours** start early and get back late, with the sights thinly spread out in a long day of travelling, but the museums are stimulating and it's good to get the feel of the tombs from which so many museum treasures come, even though most are little more than great earth mounds. The farthest, most obscure sight, the **Famen Si**, is also the most rewarding.

Xianyang

Most travellers who see anything of **XIANYANG**, a nondescript city eclipsed by Xi'an 60km southeast, usually do so only from the window of the CAAC bus, as this is the site of Xi'an's airport. A good highway connects Xi'an and Xianyang, so the bus journey from Xi'an takes only about ninety minutes.

Today the city is a pale shadow of its southern neighbour, but a couple of millennia ago, this was the centre of China, the site of the capital of **China's first dynasty**, the Qin. Little evidence remains of the era, however, except a flat plain in the east of the city that was once the site of Qin Shi Huang's palace. Relics found on the site, mostly unspectacular architectural details of more interest to archeologists – roof tiles, water pipes, bricks and so on – are in the city **museum** on Zhongshan Lu, a converted Confucian temple (daily 8am–5.30pm; ¥10). From the Xianyang bus station the museum is about 2km away: turn left on to Xilan Lu, then immediately left on to Shengli Anding Lu, which turns into Zhongshan Lu when it crosses Leyu Lu – the museum is on Zhongshan Lu, on the left. Star of the collection is a miniature terracotta army unearthed from a tomb, probably of a high official, 20km away, a lot less sinister than the real thing as each of the nearly three thousand terracotta figures is about 50cm high. The mass-produced figures are of two types, cavalry and infantry, some of which have heavy armour and a cap; others have light armour and a bun hairstyle. Some also still have traces of their original bright paint scheme, which show that the designs on their shields varied widely. The warriors are fairly crude, but the horses are well done.

The Imperial Tombs

Mao Ling (daily 8am–5pm; ¥30), 40km west of Xi'an, the resting place of the fifth Han emperor Wu Di (157–87 BC), is the largest of more than twenty **Han tombs** in the area. It's a great green mound against the hills, which took more than fifty years to construct and contains, among many treasures, a full **jade burial suit** – jade was believed to protect the corpse from decay and therefore enhanced the possibilities of longevity of the soul. A dozen smaller tombs nearby belong to the emperor's court and include those of his favourite concubine and his generals, including the brilliant strategist Huo Qubing who fought several campaigns against the northern tribes (the Huns) and died at the age of 24. A small **museum** displays some impressive relics, including many massive stone sculptures of animals which once lined the tombs' spirit ways, simplified figures that look appealingly quirky; look for the frogs and a cow, and the horse trampling a demonic-looking Hun with its hooves, a macabre subject made to look almost comical.

Qian Ling

Qian Ling is 80km northwest of Xi'an (daily 8am–5pm; ¥30), and usually the second tomb tour after Mao Ling. To get here under your own steam, take tour line #2 (3hr; ¥18) at the Xi'an train station, from across the concourse on the east side in front of the *Jiefang Hotel*. From Xi'an's long-distance bus station, you can go to **Qianxian**, then hire a rickshaw the rest of the way. This hill tomb, on the slopes of Liang Shan, is where **Emperor Gao Zong** and his empress **Wu Zetian** were buried in the seventh century.

The **Imperial Way** is lined with carved stone figures of men and flying horses, and by two groups of now headless mourners – guest princes and envoys from tribute states, some with their names on their backs. The tall stele on the left praises Gao Zong; opposite is the uninscribed Wordless Stele, erected by the empress to mark the supreme power that no words could express.

Seventeen **lesser tombs** are contained in the southeast section of the area. Among the five excavated since 1960 here is the tomb of Prince Zhang Huai, second son of Gao Zong, forced to commit suicide by his mother. At this tomb you walk down into a vault frescoed with army and processional scenes, a lovely tiger with a perm in the dip on either side. One fresco shows the court's welcome to visiting foreigners, with a hooknosed Westerner depicted. There are also vivid frescoes of polo playing and, in the **museum** outside, some Tang pottery horses.

Princess Yong Tai's tomb (¥20) is the finest here – she was the emperor's granddaughter, who died at the age of 17. Niches in the wall hold funeral offerings, and the vaulted roof still has traces of painted patterns. The passage walls leading down the ramp into the tomb are covered with murals of animals and guards of honour. The court ladies are still clear, elegant and charming after 1300 years, displaying Tang hairstyles and dress. At the bottom is the great tomb

Empress Wu Zetian

The rise to power of Empress Wu Zetian, in a society that generally regarded women as little better than slaves, is extraordinary. Originally the **concubine** of Emperor Gao Zong's father, she emerged from her mourning to win the affections of the son, bear him sons in turn, and eventually marry him. As her husband ailed, her power over the administration grew until she was strong enough, at his death, to usurp the throne. Seven years later she was declared empress in her own right, and ruled until her death in 705 AD. In later years her reign became notorious for intrigue and bloodshed, but that may be the result of historical bias, as a woman in the position of supreme power (her title was "Emperor", there being no female equivalent for so exalted a position) offended every rule of China's increasingly ossified society. Subsequently, one historian described her as a whore for taking male lovers (while any male emperor would be expected to number his concubines in the hundreds), and the stone mourners along the Imperial Way leading to her tomb were decapitated by unknown later generations.

in black stone, lightly carved with human and animal shapes. Some 1300 gold, silver and pottery objects were found here and are now in Xi'an's museum. At the mouth of the tomb is the traditional **stone tablet** into which the life story of the princess is carved – according to this, she died in childbirth, but some records claim that she was murdered by her grandmother, the empress Wu. The **Shun mausoleum** of Wu Zetian's own mother is small, but it's worth a look for the two unusually splendid granite figures that guard it, a lion 3m high and an even bigger unicorn.

Zhao Ling

At **Zhao Ling**, east of Qian Ling and 70km northwest of Xi'an, nineteen **Tang tombs** include that of Emperor Tai Zong. Begun in 636 AD, this took thirteen years to complete. Tai Zong introduced the practice of building his tomb into the hillside instead of as a tumulus on an open plain. From the main tomb, built into the slope of Jiuzou, a great cemetery fans out southeast and southwest, which includes 167 lesser tombs of the imperial family, generals and officials. A small **museum** displays stone carvings, murals and pottery figures from the smaller tombs.

The Famen Si

The extraordinary **Famen Si** (daily 8am–6pm; ¥60), 120km west of Xi'an, home of the fingerbone of the Buddha, and the nearby **museum** containing an unsurpassed collection of Tang-dynasty relics, are worth the long trip it takes to get here. The easiest way is to catch tour bus #2 (3hr; Y18) at the Xi'an train station, across the concourse on the east side in front of the *Jiefang Hotel*. It also stops at Qian Ling. Otherwise, take the hourly bus to **Fufeng**, a small country town of white-tile buildings and cave houses, from Xi'an's long-distance bus station (4hr). From Fufeng bus station take a minibus to the temple (20min).

In 147 AD, King Asoka of India, to atone, it is said, for his warlike life, distributed precious **Buddhist relics** (*sarira*) to Buddhist colonies throughout Asia. One of the earliest places of Buddhist worship in China, the Famen Si was built to house his gift of a **finger**, in the form of three separate bones. The temple enjoyed great fame in the Tang dynasty, when Emperor Tuo Bayu began the practice of having the bones temporarily removed and taken to the court at Chang'an at the head of a procession, repeated every thirty years. The procession to bear the finger to Emperor Tai Zong in 873 was reputed to be more than 100km long. After the emperor had paid his respect to the Buddha, the fingerbones were closed back up in a vault underneath the temple stupa, together with a lavish collection of offerings, with each emperor attempting to outdo the last in pious generosity. After the fall of the Tang, the crypt was forgotten about and the story of the Buddha's finger was dismissed as a legend until 1981, when the stupa collapsed, revealing the crypt beneath, full of the most astonishing array of Tang precious objects, and at the back, concealed in box after box of gold, silver, crystal and jade, the legendary finger of the Buddha.

Today the temple is a popular place of pilgrimage. The stupa has been rebuilt with a large **vault** underneath, around the original crypt, with a shrine holding the finger at its centre. A praying monk is always in attendance, sitting in front of the finger, next to the safe in which it is kept at night (if it's not being exhibited elsewhere, as happens periodically). Indeed, the temple's monks are taking no chances, and the only entrance to the vault is protected by a huge metal door of the kind usually seen in a bank. You can see into the original crypt, at 21m long the largest of its kind ever discovered in China, though there's not much to see in there now.

The museum

The **museum** west of the temple houses the well-preserved Tang relics found in the crypt, and is certainly one of the best small museums in China. Exhibits are divided into sections according to their material, with copious explanations in English. On the lower floor, the **gold and silver** is breathtaking for the quality of its workmanship; especially notable are a silver incense burner with an internal gyroscope to keep it upright, a silver tea basket, the earliest physical evidence of tea-drinking in China, and a gold figure of an elephant-headed man. Some unusual items on display are twenty **glass plates and bottles**, some Persian, with Arabic designs, some from the Roman Empire, including a bottle made in the fifth century. Glassware, imported along the Silk Road, was more highly valued than gold at the time. Also in the crypt were a thousand volumes of Buddhist sutras, pictures of which are shown, and 27,000 **coins**, the most unusual of which, made of tortoiseshell, are on display here. An annexe holds the remains of the silk sheets all the relics were wrapped up in, together with an exhibition on its method of manufacture.

At the centre of the main room is a gilded **silver coffin** which held one of the fingerbones, itself inside a copper model of a stupa, inside a marble pagoda. Prominent upstairs is a gold and silver monk's staff which, ironically, would have been used for begging alms, but the main display here is of the **caskets** the other two fingerbones were found in – finely made boxes of diminishing size, of silver, sandalwood, gold and crystal, which sat inside each other, while the fingerbones themselves were in tiny jade coffins.

South of the city

In the wooded hilly country south of Xi'an, a number of important **temples** serve as worthy focal points for a day's excursion. The **Xingjiao Si**, 24km southeast of the city on a hillside by the Fan River, was founded in 669 AD to house the ashes of the travelling monk Xuanzang (see p.1072), whose remains are underneath a square stupa at the centre of the temple. The two smaller stupas either side mark the tombs of two of his disciples. Beside the stupa a pavilion holds a charming and commonly reproduced stone carving of Xuan Zang looking cheery despite being laden down under a pack. Little remains of the **Huayan Si**, on the way to the Xingjiao Si, except two small brick pagodas, one of which holds the remains of the monk Dushun, one of the founders of Zen Buddhism. The **Xingji Si**, 5km west of here, has a ten-storey pagoda which covers the ashes of Shandao, founder of the Jingtu sect.

No tours visit the temples, but the sites are accessible on **bus** #215, which leaves from just outside the South Gate. Ride right to the last stop, then take a rickshaw to the temples; you'll have to negotiate a return trip.

Hua Shan

The five peaks of **Hua Shan**, 120km east of Xi'an, are supposed to look like a five-petalled flower, hence the name, Flowery Mountain. Originally it was known as Xiyue, Western Mountain, because it is the westernmost of the five mountains that have been sacred to Taoism for more than two thousand years. It's always been a popular place for pilgrimage, though these days people puffing up the steep, narrow paths or enjoying the dramatic views from the peaks are more likely to be tourists.

There's a Chinese saying, "There is one path and one path only to the summit of Hua Shan", meaning that sometimes the hard way is the only way. This path (¥60 entrance fee) has since been made much easier. The new way begins at the new **east gate**, which leads to a **cable car** (¥100 return, though note that the ride goes only halfway up the mountain). The arduous old route starts at **Yuquan Si** (Jade Fountain Temple), dedicated to the tenth-century monk Xiyi who lived here as a recluse. Starting from here, every few hundred yards you'll come across a wayside refreshment place offering stone seats, a burner, tea, soft drinks, maps and souvenirs – the higher you go, the more attractive the knobbly walking sticks on sale seem. In summer you'll be swept along in a stream of Chinese, mostly young couples, dressed in their fashionable, but often highly impractical, holiday finest, including high-heeled shoes.

Known as the "Eighteen Bends", the deceptively easy-looking climb up the gullies in fact winds for about two hours before reaching the flight of narrow stone steps which ascend to the first summit, **North Peak**. The mountain was formerly dotted with temples, and there are still half a dozen. Many people turn back at this point, although you can continue to Middle Peak next, then East, West and South peaks, which make up an eight-hour circuit trail.

Though the summits aren't all that high, the gaunt rocky peaks, twisted pines and rugged slopes certainly look like genuine mountains as they swim in and out of the mist trails. It's quite possible to ascend and descend the mountain in a single day, especially if you use the cable car. The going is rough in places, but chain handrails have been attached to the rock at difficult points, such as the evocatively named Thousand Feet Precipice and Green Dragon Ridge, where the path narrows to a ledge along a cliff face. Some people arrive in the evening and climb by moonlight in order to see the sun rise over the Sea of Clouds from Middle or East Peak.

Practicalities

As Hua Shan is a stop on the rail line to Luoyang (see p.278), you can take in the mountain en route between the two cities, or as an excursion from Xi'an or on the way to Xi'an from Ruicheng in Shanxi (see p.264). A couple of direct **trains** from Xi'an leave every morning, with one in the evening (2hr 30min), or you can take one of the more frequent trains to **Menyuan** station, from where minibuses cover the remaining 20km to Hua Shan. Simplest is to travel by **bus** to the mountain; tour bus #2 from Xi'an's train-station concourse, as well as bus #1, takes two hours to get to the new east gate (¥18), from where you can catch a bus (15min; ¥10) to the trailhead. The last buses back to Xi'an go at around 5.30pm, but walk to the main road and you'll find private minibuses leaving as late as 8pm, the last train a little earlier.

From the **train station** at Hua Shan **village**, buses go to the trailheads for ¥3, or it's a twenty-minute walk; head south to the bottom of the road, turn right on to the main road, and take the next road on the right to the west trailhead. The **bus station** is a little closer, on the main road itself. Buy a map (¥2), and if you have tender hands, gloves (¥3), both of which will be pushed at you by vendors. If you plan to climb at night, be sure to take some warm clothes and a flashlight with spare batteries.

There are several **places to stay** (typically ❸, dorm beds ¥40) grouped around the east gate. There are also basic hotels about every 5km along the circuit route, where a bed should cost about ¥30, but you'll have to bargain. Don't expect light or heat at these places, and if you plan to stay the night on the mountain it's a good idea to take your own sleeping bag. These places are at least easy to find, and hotel touts waylay travellers along the route. There's a more upmarket place on top of the East Peak, the *East Peak Guesthouse* (❼), catering to the sun watchers.

The nicest thing to be said about the **food** in the village and on the mountain is that it's palatable. It's also more expensive the higher you go. If you're on a tight budget, stock up before you go. The *Jixiang Kuaican*, a noodle restaurant near the east gate's bus park, dishes up vegetarian fried noodles, tasty if overpriced at ¥10.

Yan'an

The town of **YAN'AN**, set deep in the bleakly attractive dry loess hills of northern Shaanxi, has very little in common with the other cities of this province. By appearance and temperament it belongs with the high industrial cities of Shanxi rather than the ancient capitals of the Yellow River plain; however, the only easy way to get here is on the train or bus from Xi'an, 250km to the south. The town is a quiet backwater, and as you walk its dour streets it's hard to imagine that, as the headquarters of the Communist Party in the 1930s and early 1940s, this was once one of China's most popular tourist spots, a major revolutionary pilgrimage site second only to Mao's birthplace at Shaoshan (see p.562). In the changed political climate, with enthusiasm for the Party waning (and no longer compulsory), it's now hardly different from any other northern town, rarely visited except by groups of PLA soldiers and the odd ideologue.

There's nothing spectacular about the sights, unless the fact that Mao and Co were once here is enough to inspire awe by itself. Some insight into China's modern history is given not just by the **Revolutionary Museum**, but by the town centre, built during the tourist boom, an example of utilitarian 1950s and 1960s **architecture**, and by the slopes around, which are full of traditional Shaanxi **cave houses**. There is something perversely attractive in the town's grimness, which, together with the beauty of the surrounding countryside, makes it worth a day-trip from Xi'an; you could take the overnight train up and a bus back.

The Town

After the ride here through the ribbed loess hills, one of China's most glorious landscapes, arrival is a disappointment as Yan'an presents a Stalinist frown to the visitor. Arranged in a Y-shape around the confluence of the east and west branches of the Yan River, the town is a narrow strip of brutalist breeze-block

Yan'an

Yan'an	延安	***yán'ān***
Baota Pagoda	延安塔	*yánān tǎ*
Fenghuangshan Revolutionary Headquarters	凤凰山革命旧址	*fènghuángshān gémìng jiùzhǐ*
Wangjiaping Revolution Headquarters Site	王家坪革命旧址	*wángjiāpíng gémìng jiùzhǐ*
Yan'an Binguan	延安宾馆	*yán'ān bīnguǎn*
Yan'an Jiaoji Binguan	延安交际宾馆	*yán'ān jiāojì bīnguǎn*
Yan'an Revolutionary Museum	延安革命纪念馆	*yán'ān gémìng jìniànguǎn*

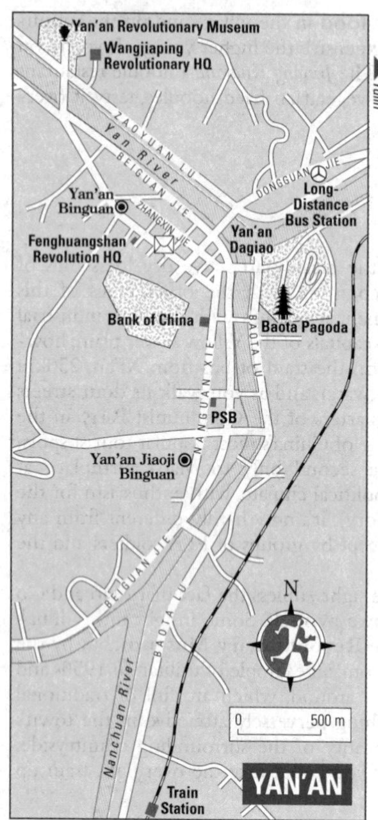

architecture, about 7km long, hemmed in by steep hills. Ironically, the centre conforms to Cold War clichés of communist austerity, with streets lined with identical apartment buildings of crumbling grey concrete, plagued by frequent electricity cuts and water shortages. The town's margins are much more attractive, as the dour buildings give way to caves, and windowless houses built to look like caves, on the slopes around.

The Revolutionary Museum

In the northeast corner of town, the **Revolutionary Museum** (daily 8am–5.30pm; ¥10), has something of the aura of a shrine, and a sculpture depicting revolutionary struggle inside, opposite the entrance, has offerings of money in front of it. The huge halls hold a massive collection of artefacts; curatorial policy seems to be that anything that was in the town between the years of 1935 and 1949 is now worth exhibiting. Relics include deflated footballs, sewing machines, rusty mugs and hundreds of guns and hand grenades. There is a stuffed white horse that is said to have once carried Mao, and translations of books by Lenin, Stalin and Trotsky in Chinese. Nothing is labelled in English though; the things of most interest to non-Chinese speakers are probably the propaganda pictures, which include wood- and papercuts of Red Army soldiers helping peasants in the fields. The walls of the halls are covered with photographs taken at the time, and sinologists can amuse themselves by trying to match the portraits of awkwardly posed, youthful, fresh-faced figures, identically dressed in Mao suits, to the octogenarian leaders of late twentieth-century China. More interesting is the **Lao Ganbu Menqiu Chang** (Old Cadre Croquet Pitch) to the left of the museum entrance, where codgers shoot the breeze with anyone who will listen.

The two revolutionary headquarters

Also more worthwhile than the museum is the **Wangjiaping Revolutionary Headquarters** (daily 8am–5pm; ¥9), just around the corner, but it can be hard to find even if you do follow the massive blue sign pointing the way. Turn immediately left as you leave the museum compound and walk 200m down a small path that seems to lead into a village. The headquarters, a compound of low buildings, is on the right, marked by a faded

The Communists of Yan'an

The arrival of the Communists in Yan'an in October 1935 marked the end of the **Long March**, an astonishing and now semi-mythical journey in which eighty thousand men, women and children of the Red Army fled their mountain bases in Jiangxi Province to escape encirclement and annihilation at the hands of the Nationalists and in a year marched 9500km across some of the world's most inhospitable terrain (see box, pp.584–585).

When Mao finally arrived in Yan'an there were only about five thousand still with him, but here they met up with northern Communists who had already established a soviet. Gradually stragglers and those who had been sent on missions to other parts arrived to swell their numbers. The **Yan'an soviet** came to control a vast tract of the surrounding country, with its own economy and banknotes to back the new political system. Soldiers in China usually lived parasitically off the peasants unfortunate enough to be in their way; but Mao's troops, trained to see themselves as defenders of the people, were under orders to be polite and courteous and pay for their supplies. Mao said victory would only be achieved "with guns and millet", that is, by co-opting peasants to the cause, and in the following years the Communists instigated land reform and organized peasants into co-operatives, while conducting a campaign of guerrilla warfare against the Japanese. **Mao** wrote some of his most important essays here, including much that was later included in the Little Red Book. As well as most of the major political personalities of Communist China, a number of distinguished foreigners came here, too, including Edgar Snow, whose book *Red Star Over China* includes descriptions of life in Yan'an, and Norman Bethune, the Canadian surgeon who died in the service of the Red Army (see p.181). Both are memorialized at the Fenghuangshan Revolutionary Headquarters.

signpost. It's a remarkably low-key approach to what was not long ago one of the most visited tourist spots in the country, the place where Mao, Zhou Enlai and Zhu De, among others, lived and worked. More worthwhile than the museum, the simple, low buildings of white plaster over straw, mud and brick, typical of traditional local architecture, are elegant structures, with wooden lattice windows faced with paper, sometimes incorporating the communist star into their design. Even with its English-language displays explaining the history, the complex has a rather monastic feel. The arched rooms, with cups sitting on the table and bedding still on the beds, as if their inhabitants will soon return, have the simplicity of monks' cells, and the main hall, an unadorned timber building with wooden benches lined up in rows before a platform, is reminiscent of a prayer hall. Occasionally the place is host to groups of PLA soldiers, who start their tour by marching into the courtyard, unfolding collapsible chairs, and listening to a lecture. The snooty attendants sell a book with plenty of photos from the period (¥10).

Proceed across the river towards the train station to get to the **Fenghuangshan Revolutionary Headquarters** (daily 8am–5.30pm; ¥8). At the end of a side road off Zhangxin Jie between the post office and *Yan'an Binguan*, this served as the initial residence of the Communists. In 1937 and 1938, the two main rooms in the western courtyard functioned as Mao's bedroom and study, and still house his wooden bed, desk with chairs and a latrine – as well as a collection of letters and photos of Communist officers, all of which are labelled in Chinese only. Two souvenir shops sell reproductions of anything to do with the period – mostly tacky offerings including singing Mao lighters.

Baota Pagoda

Standing on a hill in the southeast corner of town on the east bank of the river, the Ming-dynasty **Baota Pagoda** (daily 8am–5.30pm; ¥20, plus ¥3 to ascend the nine flights of stairs) is sometimes used as a symbol of the Communist Party. High above the town and reached by a twisty road, the pagoda commands an impressive view of its angular planes and the ragged hills, pocked with caves, beyond. Outside, tourists can pose for photographs dressed up in the blue and grey military uniforms of the first Communist soldiers, complete with red armband and wooden gun. From the hill it's possible to see other revolutionary sites dotted around town – look for the red flags – but they're mainly bridges and the sites of buildings since disappeared.

Practicalities

Yan'an lies on a branch rail line that begins in Xi'an and winds around the mountainous terrain of northern Shaanxi, a stark, beautiful landscape of raw earth with few touches of colour, just the odd red flag flying above villages. The **train station** is in the far south of town, a long way from anything interesting. Bus #1 goes from the station, up the east fork of Yan'an's Y-shape; bus #2 travels up the west fork, past the *Yan'an Binguan* and the museum. A few taxis, with a ¥5 minimum fare, also cruise the streets. Long-distance **buses**, which are much faster than the train, arrive either at the train-station concourse or the **bus station**, about 1km east of the town centre. A service from Linfen in Shanxi and Yulin in the north, close to the border with Inner Mongolia, also arrives here.

To **move on to Xi'an**, there are two daily trains, one in the morning and, more popular, one in the evening (#4762; 8hr; ¥76). Hard-sleeper tickets are sold only from the first window of the station ticket office (officially daily 6–7am, 3.30–5pm & 8–9.30pm, but they're often closed). If you arrived from Xi'an by train or are heading for Xi'an for the first time, consider getting the bus, as the views of loess and cave dwellings en route are incredible. Express services to Xi'an leave from the bus station at 9.15am and noon (6hr; ¥69). There are long-distance **buses** to destinations such as Baotou in Inner Mongolia (a rough but captivating ride), and one bus daily to Hukou Falls (see p.263), a ten-hour trip.

Accommodation is available at the four-star *Yan'an Binguan* on Yan'an Lu (ⓣ0911/2113122; ❼), in the centre of town just south of the river's fork, whose uncompromising facade belies a cosy interior. It's on the river's western bank, a short walk south of the bridge. A cheaper alternative is the austere concrete *Yan'an Jiaoji Binguan* (ⓣ0911/2113862; ❸), which is 3km north of the train station on Zhongxin Jie and has triples with shared bath as well as doubles. Other hotels around town may take foreigners; business has been bad of late. Forget about shopping or nightlife; even **eating** out presents problems if you want anything more sophisticated than a bowl of noodles. Your best bets are probably the restaurant in the *Yan'an Binguan* or the Sichuan dumpling shops along Zhongxin Jie.

Luoyang and around

LUOYANG, in the middle reaches of the Yellow River valley, has two sides. There is industrial Luoyang – established in the 1950s, drab and of little interest except in April when visitors flock to see the peony blossom – and there is

Luoyang and around

Luoyang	洛阳	***luòyáng***
Arts and Crafts Building	工艺美术楼	*gōngyì měishùlóu*
Luoyang Museum	洛阳博物馆	*luòyáng bówùguǎn*
Wancheng Park	王成公园	*wángchéng gōngyuán*
Accommodation and eating		
Aviation	航空大厦	*hángkōng dàshà*
Dongbei Fengwei Jiaozi	东北风味饺子	*dōngběi fēngwèi jiǎozi*
Guangzhou	广州酒家	*guǎngzhōu jiǔjiā*
HM	弘棉大酒店	*hóngmián dàjiǔdiàn*
Luoyang Lüshe	洛阳旅社	*luòyáng lǚshè*
Luoyang Restaurant	洛阳酒店	*luòyáng jiǔdiàn*
Luoyang Ying Binguan	洛阳迎宾馆	*luòyáng yíngbīnguǎn*
New Friendship	友谊宾馆	*yǒuyì bīnguǎn*
Peony	牡丹大酒店	*mǔdān dàjiǔdiàn*
Tianxiang	天香旅社	*tiānxiāng lǚshè*
Xuangong	旋宫大厦	*xuángōng dàshà*
Around Luoyang		
Baima Si	白马寺	*báimǎ sì*
Cloud Reaching Pagoda	齐云塔	*qíyún tǎ*
Guanlin Miao	关林庙	*guānlín miào*
Longmen Caves	龙门石窟	*lóngmén shíkū*

the ancient "City of Nine Capitals", occupied from Neolithic times through to 937 AD and now relegated to a few sites on the fringe of the modern city. Though ancient Luoyang holds an important place in Chinese history, with many finds in the museum to prove it, there is little to be seen on the grounds of the once glorious palaces and temples, and the city bears a resemblance to other formerly significant provincial cities such as Zhengzhou and Shijiazhuang, in hot pursuit of modernization. Away from the glossy main boulevards, the streets are rutted and lined with piles of rubble and stacks of identical brown apartment buildings, a marked contrast that illustrates how rapid and uneven the city's development has been.

Beyond the city limits, though, you can still see the **Longmen Caves**, whose Buddhist carvings provide one of the most important artistic sites in China, and the venerable **Baima and Guanlin temples**. The city also makes a good base for an exploration of **Song Shan**, the holy mountain, and the **Shaolin Si**, home of martial arts.

Some history

Much of Luoyang's history was revealed only by the rebuilding of the city in the 1950s and by the terracing and irrigation work in the surrounding countryside, which brought to light some sixty sites and a thousand tombs. By 5000 BC this area was already heavily populated – the Neolithic site discovered to the west of Luoyang in 1921, at **Yangshao**, proved to be just one of a whole series of sites along the Yellow River plain. Luoyang's site is a fine strategic one, guarded on three sides by hills and cut across by four rivers. Bronze Age Shang-dynasty remains have been found here, but the first real development seems to have been a walled city built by the Zhou around 1000 BC. When their rulers were forced to retreat from Xi'an in 771 BC, this became their capital – tradition claims that Confucius studied here and that Lao Zi was keeper of the archives. Under the Qin emperor and his early Han successors, Xi'an regained its title but later Han emperors (between 25 and 220 AD) were once again obliged to withdraw to Luoyang, building their city east of the Baima Si.

Luoyang's trade and communications with the West along the **Silk Road** grew rapidly: Buddhism was introduced here in 68 AD; the Imperial College was founded with thirty thousand students and a great library; Cai Lun invented paper; and Zhang Hen, the imperial astronomer, invented the armillary sphere, demonstrating that the Chinese knew the movement of the heavens long before the West. In the turbulent years after the fall of the Han, Luoyang remained, for a time, the capital of a series of dynasties and the centre of Chinese culture. Here the poet Zuo Si wrote a series of poems, *The Three Capitals*, which were so popular that people copying them caused a paper famine.

When the northern **Toba Wei** invaders decided to move their capital from Datong into the Chinese heartland, Luoyang was the site they chose, probably because it was believed to be the centre of the world. In 493, at the command of Emperor Xiao Wendi, they moved almost overnight to Luoyang and constructed a new capital. In thirty years it had grown to a city of half a million people, with markets selling goods from all over Asia and with more than 1400 Buddhist temples. The great carvings at **Longmen** were begun in this period. In 543, at the command of another Wei emperor and even more suddenly than it had been taken up, Luoyang was again **abandoned** and its people forced to move to **Yeh**. An account written thirteen years later described the city walls in a state of collapse and overgrown with artemisia, the streets full of thorn trees, and millet planted between the ceremonial towers of the ruined palace.

Luoyang lay in ruins once more for seventy years until under the **Sui dynasty** it was rebuilt west of the Wei ruins on a grid pattern spreading across both banks of the Luo River. Two million men were conscripted for the work, and the new city rapidly became the most important market centre in China, a magnet for foreign traders, with a population of a million, three separate major markets within the walls, more than three thousand shops and stalls and around four hundred inns for merchants. To feed the crowds, grain was brought up the Grand Canal from the Yangzi basin and stored in enormous barns: the Hanjia granary, discovered in 1971 west of the old city, held 250,000 tons and protected against damp, mildew, rats and insects. Emperor Yang Di also brought three thousand musicians to live at court and surrounded himself with scholars, scientists and engineers.

Under the **Tang**, Luoyang was only the secondary capital. It's said that in 800 AD Empress Wu Zetian, enraged that the **peonies**, alone among flowers, disobeyed her command to bloom in the snow, banished them from her capital at Chang'an. Many were transplanted to Luoyang where they flourished, and have since become one of the city's most celebrated attractions, the subject of countless poems and cultivation notes. Several times drought forced the court to follow the peonies to Luoyang, where the empress commissioned some of the most important carvings at Longmen.

With the decline of the Tang, Luoyang finally lost its importance for good; the capital moved to **Kaifeng**, and gradually the whole balance of the nation shifted south. Luoyang never recovered, and by 1920 there was only a run-down settlement of some twenty thousand people here. The first Five Year Plan earmarked the city for **industrial development**, and its new incarnation has not looked back since. Growth has been rapid ever since the early 1950s, helped by its position astride the east–west rail line and the southern spur to Yichang. Once again Luoyang is a thriving metropolis, if a lot less attractive and more polluted than the city of old.

Arrival and city transport

Luoyang is spread east–west between the Luo River and the rail line, with the old city in the east, the more modern conurbation of factories and residential blocks in the west. **Zhongzhou Zhong Lu** is the main thoroughfare, crossing the length of the city. A T-junction is formed at the centre of town where this street meets the main road heading south from the train station, Jinguyuan Lu.

Luoyang **airport**, 20km north of town, is tiny and served by a bus (¥15) that drops you off at the CAAC office behind the train station. The massive, upgraded **train station**, a busy junction on the line between Xi'an and Zhengzhou, is a centre of operations for most visitors: the **bus station** is opposite, tours to the sights leave from the concourse, and the budget hotels are nearby. However, it's situated in the town's northern extremity, a long walk to anywhere exciting or to the prettier parts of town.

The train station is the place to pick up most **city buses**. From here, trolleybus #102 and bus #2 go south down Jinguyuan Lu, turning west along Zhongzhou Zhong Lu at the central T-junction; bus #5 from the station turns east, passing the Xiguan roundabout in the east of the city. Another clutch of routes begins from the roundabout, too far out to be handy for much, although you can get to the Baima Si from here. **Taxis**, which can be hailed on the streets, are plentiful, with a ¥6 flagfall.

Accommodation

Basing yourself around the train station is not the bad idea it usually turns out to be in most Chinese cities, as in Luoyang, most of the attractions are outside the city anyway, and at least here you're conveniently located for all the transport connections. But if you're staying any length of time, and can afford it, stay in town; it's less noisy and cleaner.

Aviation Junction of Fanglin Lu and Kaixuan Xi Lu ⓣ0379/3385599. Take bus #8 from the train station and get off on Wancheng Lu. Staff at this nine-storey place wear the most stylish uniforms of any Luoyang hotel, and the guests – plenty of pilots and flight attendants – are pretty chic, too. The lobby, appropriately, looks like an airport lounge. It's a shame it's stuck in a drab part of town. ❻

Luoyang Lüshe ⓣ0379/3935181. A shabby building opposite the train station on your left as you exit, this is one of the better budget options. Although it's big, basic and in a noisy place, it's clean inside, and staff are pleasant. Try to get a room at the back, out of earshot of the chiming station clock, and be sure to see your room before paying for it, as some could use upkeep. The cosy four-bed dormitories are a bargain. Dorm beds from ¥15, ❷

Luoyang Ying Binguan 6 Renmin Xi Lu ⓣ0379/3935414. A well-located new place on quiet grounds in the city centre. One of the best mid-range options, with its own air ticket office. ❺

New Friendship 6 Xiyuan Lu ⓣ0379/4686666, ⓕ4912328. Bus #8 from the train station. This pleasant red-brick building with a chocolate-coloured lobby is stylish and rather elegant, but perhaps a little far west to be convenient. Faces a park abloom with peonies in springtime. There's a less expensive wing next door, though it's often full with tour groups. Cheaper wing ❺, main wing ❻

Peony 15 Zhongzhou Zhong Lu ⓣ0379/4913699, ⓕ4913668. The most upmarket place in town, charging up to ¥1000 for the most luxurious rooms. All mod cons provided, and there's a CITS office and a good, though expensive, restaurant. ❼

Tianxiang 56 Jinguyuan Lu ⓣ0379/2561135. Arguably Luoyang's best budget option, with a wide variety of clean and comfortable – if concrete – rooms. One of Luoyang's best restaurants is downstairs. Across the street from the train and bus stations, so ask for a quieter room at the back. Dorm beds from ¥20, ❶

Xuangong 275 Zhongzhou Zhong Lu ⓣ0379/3222226. Well located in the thick of things, this is a comfortable hotel with a good restaurant attached; you can't miss it at night when the front door is lit up by neon arches. ❺

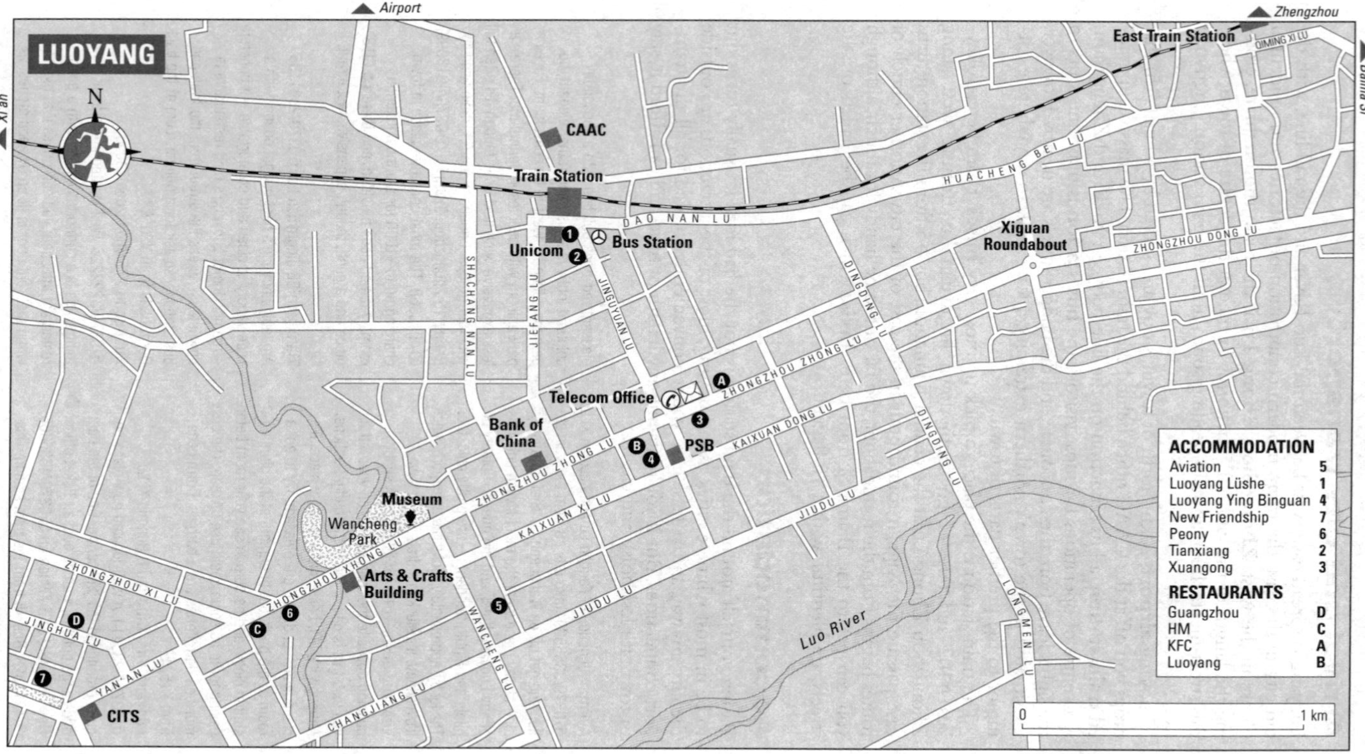
LUOYANG
N
Xi'an
Airport
Zhengzhou
Baima Si
Longmen Caves
East Train Station
QIMING XI LU
CAAC
Train Station
DAO NAN LU
HUACHENG BEI LU
Unicom
Bus Station
Xiguan Roundabout
ZHONGZHOU DONG LU
SHACHANG NAN LU
JIEFANG LU
JINGUYUAN LU
DINGDING LU
ZHONGZHOU ZHONG LU
Telecom Office
Bank of China
PSB
KAIXUAN DONG LU
KAIXUAN XI LU
JIUDU LU
Museum
Wancheng Park
Arts & Crafts Building
ZHONGZHOU XHONG LU
ZHONGZHOU XI LU
JINGHUA LU
YAN'AN LU
CITS
WANCHENG LU
CHANGJIANG LU
LONGMEN LU
Luo River
ACCOMMODATION
Aviation 5
Luoyang Lüshe 1
Luoyang Ying Binguan 4
New Friendship 7
Peony 6
Tianxiang 2
Xuangong 3
RESTAURANTS
Guangzhou D
HM C
KFC A
Luoyang B
0
1 km

The City

There's nothing much to detain you in Luoyang itself; but if you've got time between trips to the attractions outside town, there are a few nice restaurants, a museum and the old city to poke around in.

The main downtown area is around the T-junction where Jinguyuan Lu meets Zhongzhou Zhong Lu. Here you'll find the Department Store, six storeys of shopping with a café in the basement, next door to the *Xuangong Hotel*. Head west down tree-lined Zhongzhou Zhong Lu for a kilometre, or take bus #9, #2, or trolleybus #102, and you come to **Wancheng Park** (daily 8am–6pm; ¥3), at its best in April when the peonies are blooming. Luoyang's **peonies** have been intensively cultivated and collected so that the city now boasts over 150 varieties, which have found their way on to every available patch or scrap of ground – a splendid sight. The peony motif is also everywhere in the city, from trellises to rubbish bins.

Out of season, Wancheng is just another park, with a melancholy zoo, and the river dries up and smells in winter. However, **excavations** undertaken in the park have revealed much of the Zhou capital of 771 BC, including walls, palaces, temples and a marketplace, though none of this can be seen by the public. Across the suspension bridge in the northwest corner of the park there are also two **Han tombs**, which have yet to open to the public, apparently with some good early murals.

Otherwise, almost all that has been left of the ancient cities has been gathered into the **museum** (daily 9am–5.30pm; ¥10), just east of the park. There are five halls arranged chronologically, which look uninspiring at first – there's a surfeit of the bronze vessels that seem to characterize all provincial museum collections, and no English captions. It gets much better as you go on, though. In Hall 2, look for the **Shang bronzes** and an endearing **jade tiger** from the Zhou; Hall 4 has some Indian-influenced **Wei statuary**, as well as a model farm from a Han tomb with a sow and her row of piglets. In Hall 5 you'll find some comical **Tang polychrome figures**, including camels and a travelling merchant keeling over under the weight of his pack. Upstairs is an excellent new hall in which well-presented relics, copiously captioned in English, are grouped by material – bronze, silver and jade – rather than by dynasty, an unusual system that here works very well, allowing direct comparisons across the centuries. As usual, the Tang wins hands down in the pottery section with their expressive camels and a hooknosed, pointy-chinned foreigner, and in **gold and silver**, where their ornate decorative objects show the influence of Persian and Roman styles. There are some strange little animal sculptures in the **jade** section that belong to the Xia and Shang, and in the **bronze** section – particularly extensive as the area around Luoyang entered the Bronze Age before the rest of China – a horse's harness from a Shang chariot.

East of the Xiguan roundabout, the alleyways of the **old city** are a rewarding area to browse around, preferably by bicycle as it's fairly spread out. The best alleys are those south of Zhongzhou Dong Lu, where whitewashed, half-timbered buildings house small family shops whose wares include seals (engraved with your name while you wait), tea and art materials.

Eating and drinking

Among the dim, poky noodle places around the train station is a quite decent place just on the left as you come out of the *Tianxiang Hotel*, signed *Foreigner Restaurant* in English. It's trying to cater to backpackers, and musters an

English-language menu and a variety of Western snacks. For dumplings, turn right as you exit the station, cross Jiefang Lu, and walk past the dodgy guesthouses on the left to find *Dongbei Fengwei Jiaozi*, where a full plate costs ¥10. Also opposite the station you'll find plenty of snacks – oranges, apples and nuts – sold from wooden stalls that set up every evening, near the long line of shoe shiners.

Guangzhou Jinghua Lu. Out of the way but worth the trip, with an English sign so it's easy to spot. Don't walk into the grotty canteen on the lower floor; the real restaurant, boisterous and lively and serving Cantonese food, is upstairs. No English is spoken, nor is there any on the menu, but the staff are friendly. They'll do half portions for half price, so if there's only one or two of you, you can still have four or five dishes for less than ¥100.

HM Zhongzhou Zhong Lu, opposite the intersection with Zhongzhou Xi Lu. There's an intimate atmosphere, with small tables, and an English menu is provided. A good range of dishes is on offer, but the highlight for homesick palates must be the soufflé and the delicious banana rolls. At around ¥50 per head, it's not cheap though.

Luoyang Zhongzhou Zhong Lu, near the intersection with Jinguyuan Lu. A quiet place where you can eat cheap, basic dishes.

Tianxiang 56 Jingyuyuan Lu. Sumptuous Sichuan cuisine here at inexpensive prices. Part of the hotel of the same name, and packed out with local diners in the evenings.

Xuangong Zhongzhou Zhong Lu, next to the *Xuangong Hotel*. Though they only have big tables for serving large groups, this place has a friendly atmosphere and staff are eager to please. The English menu offers standard dishes at reasonable prices. Arrive early as it's is very popular.

Listings

Airlines The main CAAC office is at 196 Dao Bei Lu (☎0379/3335301), 200m north of the station. You can also buy air tickets from the CITS office in the *Peony Hotel* or the CAAC office in the *Luoyang Ying Binguan*.

Banks and exchange The Bank of China is tucked slightly back from the street at 268 Yan'an Lu (Mon–Fri 8am–5pm, Sat 8am–noon).

Bookshops The Xinhua Bookshop, next door to the *Xuangong Hotel* on the western side of Zhongzhou Zhong Lu, has a few novels in English and a good selection of art books.

Buses Luoyang's long-distance bus station is next to the train station on the eastern side of Jinguyuan Lu. Tickets can be bought from the office (daily 8am–5pm) or on the bus itself. Buses for Zhengzhou and Xi'an leave from the lot on the west side of the train station concourse. Minibuses to local tourist destinations and Shaolin Si leave from the concourse outside the train station.

Mail The post office is tucked on the north side of Zhongzhou Zhong Lu, near the junction with Jinguyuan Lu (Mon–Sat 8am–6pm).

Shopping Locally made tricolour ceramic copies of Tang sculptures are on sale at the Arts and Crafts Building, at 90 Yan'an Lu. For domestic goods try the Bai Luo Hou Department Store, next to the *Xuangong Hotel* on Zhongzhou Zhong Lu.

Telephones There's a 24hr telecom building around the corner from the post office, on Jinguyuan Lu. For international calls, the Unicom shop across from the train station and next to the *Luoyang Lüshe* charges quite low rates.

Travel agents and tours The main CITS office (☎0379/4325061) is situated on Yan'an Lu. Another more accessible office is in the *Peony Hotel* (daily 8am–6.30pm; ☎0379/4913699). They can arrange day-tours to sites in the area and will obtain train tickets for you. A standard day-tour of the sights in the vicinity of town, including Baima Si and Shaolin Si, costs around ¥35, and can be booked at the *Tianxiang* hotel.

Visa extensions The PSB is at 1 Kaixuan Xi Lu (Mon–Sat 8am–noon & 2–6pm), with gory pictures of traffic accidents displayed outside.

Around Luoyang

The **Longmen Caves** and the **Guanlin Miao** and **Baima Si** can all be visited from Luoyang by **public transport**, and you could just about pack all three into a single day's excursion if you don't have the time to explore at a more leisurely pace. Additionally, tours to **Song Shan** and the **Shaolin Si** (see p.308) usually stop at Baimi Si on the way back. If you're travelling independently to Song Shan, it makes sense to break the four-hour trip at the temple. All the sights are also served by private **tourist minibuses**, which run from outside the station. If you have limited time, the Buddhist carvings at Longmen are the place to head first: however little you know about Buddhism or about sculpture, you cannot help but be impressed by the scale and complexity of the work here and by the extraordinary contrast between the power of the giant figures and the intricate delicacy of the miniatures.

The Longmen Caves

A UNESCO World Heritage Site, the **Longmen Caves** have been beautifully renovated and features English labelling. You can get to the site (daily 7am–6.30pm; ¥60), 13km south of town, on bus #81, which leaves from a terminus at the north end of Jinguyuan Lu; there's also a stop en route just west of the *Xuangong Hotel*. Bus #60 also goes to the caves from a stop outside the *Friendship Hotel*, and bus #53 from the Xiguan roundabout. The site is very busy in the summer, overrun with tourists posing in the empty niches for photos of themselves the lotus position, and clambering over the sculptures. The best times to visit are in the early morning, at lunchtime or in the evening. It's worth spending the extra ¥5 for an audio-guide, available past the ticket window.

The **caves** are recesses in the cliffs where the Yi River cuts through a cleft called the Dragon Gate. Legend has it that this was formed when the Great Yu, Tamer of Floods, split the mountain to release an imprisoned dragon which was causing havoc. From a distance the multi-veined cliffs, decked with green cypresses, look like a vast slab of gorgonzola cheese, and close up the different rocks provide some spectacular effects, giving an extra dimension of expressiveness to the figures.

Over the years, man has added 1350 caves, 750 niches and 40 pagodas containing 110,000 statues carved out of the sheer **limestone cliffs** bordering the river. The carvings, stretching 1km and mostly found on the west bank, were commissioned by emperors, the imperial family, other wealthy families wanting to buy good fortune, generals hoping for victory and religious groups. The **Toba Wei** began the work in 492 AD, when they moved their capital to Luoyang from Datong, where they had carved the Yungang Caves (see p000). At Longmen they adapted their art to the different requirements of a harder, limestone surface. Three sets of caves, **Guyang**, **Bingyang** and **Lianhua**, date from this early period. Work continued for five hundred years and reached a second peak under the **Tang**, particularly under Empress Wu Zetian, a devoted adherent of Buddhism.

There's a clearly visible progression from the early style brought from Datong, of simple, rounded, formally modelled holy figures, to the complex and elaborate, but more linear, Tang carvings, which include women and court characters. In general the Buddhas are simple, but the sculptors were able to let their imagination go and show off their mastery with the attendant figures and the decorative flourishes around the edges of the caves. Also discernible are traces of vandalism and looting (lots of missing heads and hands) which began with the anti-Buddhist movement in the ninth century, was continued by souvenir-hunting Westerners in the nineteenth and twentieth centuries, and culminated in (surprisingly muted) attacks by Red Guards during the Cultural Revolution.

Starting from the entrance at the northern end and moving south down the group, the following are the largest and most important carvings, which stand out due to their size. The three **Bingyang** caves are early; the central one, commissioned by Emperor Xuan Wu to honour his parents, has an inscription recording that 802,336 men worked from 500 to 523 AD to complete it. The eleven statues of Buddha inside show northern characteristics – long features, thin faces, splayed fishtail robes – and traces of Greek influence. The side caves, completed under the Tang, are more natural and voluptuous, carved in high relief. **Wanfo** (Cave of Ten Thousand Buddhas), just south of here, was built in 680 by Gao Zong and his empress Wu Zetian, and has fifteen thousand Buddhas carved in tiny niches, each one different and the smallest less than 2cm high. **Lianhua** (Lotus Flower Cave) is another early one, dating from 527, and named after the beautifully carved lotus in its roof. **Fengxian** (Ancestor Worshipping Cave) is the largest and most splendid of all. Made in 672 for Empress Wu Zetian, it has an overwhelming seated figure of Vairocana Buddha, 17m high with two-metre-long ears. On his left a Bodhisattva wears a crown and pearls, and a divine general grinds a malevolent spirit underfoot. This is the highest development of Tang carving and worth studying carefully. **Medical Prescription Cave**, built in 575, details several hundred cures for everything from madness to the common cold. **Guyang** is the earliest of all, begun in 495. Here you can still see traces of the vivid paintwork that originally gave life to these carvings. There's a central Buddha and nineteen of the "Twenty Pieces", important examples of ancient calligraphy.

From the end of the west bank you can cross the bridge to the east bank, for a good view of the caves peppering the opposite bank like rabbit warrens. Up the hill is the **Tomb of Bai Juyi**, the famous Tang poet, who spent his last years in Luoyang as the Retired Scholar of the Fragrant Hill.

The Guanlin Miao

Buses to the Longmen Caves pass through the town of **GUANLIN**, 7km south of the city, and the temple here makes a convenient stop on the way to or from the caves. From Luoyang, don't get off at the main stop in the centre of town, but go to the next stop along, at the end of the red crenellated wall on the east side of the road. The temple is a five-minute walk away at the end of Guanlin Nan Lu, which leads east off from the main road through a wooden archway, by this bus stop.

The Guanlin temple (daily 8am–5.30pm; ¥25) is dedicated to **Guan Yu**, a hero of the Three Kingdoms period (see box, p.509) and loyal general of Liu Bei, King of Shu. He was defeated and executed by the King of Wu who sent his head to Cao Cao, King of Wei, hoping in this way to divert on to the Wei any revenge that might be coming. Cao Cao neatly sidestepped this grisly game of pass-the-parcel by burying the head with honour in a tomb behind the temple.

Despite its military theme, the temple is strikingly beautiful, the elegant Ming buildings highly carved and richly decorated. Especially fine are the carved stone lionesses lining the path to the Main Hall. Each has a different expression and a different cub, some riding on their mother's back, some hiding coyly behind her paws. In the first hall, look carefully at the eaves for rather comical images of Guan Yu fighting – he's the one on the red horse – and leading an army engaged in sacking a city engulfed by carved wooden flames. Inside stands a seven-metre-tall statue of the general, resplendent in technicolour ceremonial robes with a curtain of beads hanging from his hat. More images of the general are in the second and third halls, whose decoration includes frescoes of warriors jousting and men playing Go. In side halls are exhibitions of art and some fine carved tombstones and massive stone animals – the sheep are excellent, the lions almost unrecognizable. It's a quiet place, well restored and brilliantly coloured against the grey and green background of stone and the many twisted cypresses.

The Baima Si

Historic, leafy **Baima Si** (White Horse Temple; daily 8am–5pm; ¥35), 12km east of Luoyang place, is attractive for its ancient buildings and devotional atmosphere. You can get to the site on bus #56 from the Xiguan roundabout or on a minibus from outside the station. You'll be dropped either on the side of the road or at the carpark, from where it's a dash through a gauntlet of souvenir shops to the ticket window.

Founded in 68 AD, the Baima Si has some claim to be the first Buddhist temple in China. Legend says that the Emperor Mingdi of the Eastern Han dreamed of a golden figure with the sun and moon behind its head. Two monks sent to search for the origin of the dream reached India and returned riding white horses with two Indian monks in tow, and a bundle of sutras. This temple was built to honour them, and its layout is in keeping with the legend: there are two stone horses, one on either side of the entrance, and the tombs of the two monks, earthen mounds ringed by round stone walls, lie in the first courtyard.

Once inside the temple, out of earshot of the highway and the pushy souvenir sellers with their glazed pottery, you'll find this a placid place, its silence only pricked by the sound of gongs or the tapping of stonemasons carving out a stele. Beyond the Hall of Celestial Guardians, the **Main Hall** holds a statue of Sakyamuni flanked by the figures of Manjusri and Samantabhadra. Near the Great Altar is an ancient bell weighing more than a tonne; in the days when there were over ten thousand Tang monks here it was struck in time with the chanting. The inscription reads: "The sound of the Bell resounds in Buddha's temple causing the ghosts in Hell to tremble with fear." Behind the Main Hall is the Cool Terrace where, it is said, the original sutras were translated. Offerings of fruit on the altars, multicoloured cloths hanging from the ceilings, and lighted candles in bowls floating in basins of water, as well as the heady gusts of incense issuing from the burners in the courtyards, indicate that, unlike other temples in the area, this is the genuine article. This is also suggested by the presence of flocks of finches in the well-maintained gardens at the side of the halls – real temples, with their population of pacifists, are a haven to birdlife.

Home to a thriving community of monks, the Baima Si is primarily a place of worship, and over-inquisitive visitors are tactfully but firmly pointed in the right direction. The monks' daily midday perambulation around the Great Altar may have a timeless look to it, but photos of Jiang Zemin's and other leaders' visits greet you as you step inside the complex, and contemporary life intrudes here in more than just the presence of tourists – the abbot has a TV in his quarters to remain in touch with the political swings of an unsympathetic regime, and all the monks must carry red identity cards, a bit like a student card.

Southwest of the temple, in a separate compound to where the monks live, is the **Qiyun Ta** (Cloud Reaching Pagoda; no admission), built in the tenth century and restored several times since. To reach the pagoda, cross the new landscaped square and bridge to the left as you exit Baima Si. The exit gates from this part of the temple are locked, however, so you'll have to backtrack to leave the site.

Song Shan

The seventy peaks of the **Song Shan** range stretch over 64km across Dengfeng County, midway between Luoyang and Zhengzhou. When the Zhou ruler Ping moved his capital to Luoyang in 771 BC, it was known as Zhong Yue, Central Peak – being at the axis of the **five sacred Taoist mountains**, with Hua Shan to the west, Tai Shan to the east, Heng Shan to the south and another Heng Shan to the north. The mountains, thickly clad with trees, rise from narrow, steep-sided rocky valleys and appear impressively precipitous, though with the highest peak, Junji, at just 1500m, they're not actually very lofty. When the summits emerge from a swirling sea of cloud, though, and the slopes are dressed in their brilliant autumn colours, they can certainly look the part.

You can visit Song Shan on a **day-trip** from either **Luoyang** or **Zhengzhou**. It's better to visit the area en route from Luoyang to Zhengzhou, though note that the latter offers a much better selection of places to stay. Tours leave from outside both cities' train stations early every morning and take in at least the **Shaolin Si** (see p.309) and the **Zhongyue Miao** (see p.312), though you won't see much of the mountain itself. Tours from Luoyang (¥35 return) usually take in the Baima Si (see p.307) on the way back, too. Alternatively you could stay at **Dengfeng**, a town at the centre of the range, from where there's plenty to occupy two or three days' walking, with numerous paths meandering around the valleys, passing temples, pagodas and guard towers, and some wonderful views. Unlike at other holy mountains, there is no single set path, and as the slopes are not steep and the undergrowth is sparse you can set out in any direction you like. The sights aren't close to one another, so you won't be able to do more than one or two a day to count on getting back to Dengfeng before nightfall. **Maps** of the area are included on the back of maps of Zhengzhou, or can be bought for ¥2 from shops around Dengfeng and Shaolin.

Dengfeng and around

The ideal base for exploring the area is **DENGFENG**, a little town stretched along a valley at the heart of the Song Shan range, 13km from Shaolin and 4km from the Zhongyue Miao. There's nothing much here; it's basically one main street, unusual for having the name and function of every shop written neatly in English under the Chinese characters. Probably the most offbeat outlet is the Dengfeng Legendary Kungfu Weapon Shop, selling curvy swords, pointed sticks, throwing stars and the like, and cheaper than those at the Shaolin Si.

Song Shan

Song Shan	嵩山	***sōngshān***
Observatory	观星台	*guānxīng tái*
Shaolin Si	少林寺	*shàolín sì*
Shaolin Martial Arts Hotel	少林武术宾馆	*shàolín wǔshù bīnguǎn*
Songyang Academy	嵩阳书院	*sōngyáng shūyuàn*
Songyue Temple Pagoda	嵩岳寺塔	*sōngyuèsì tǎ*
Zhongyue Miao	中岳庙	*zhōngyuè miào*
Dengfeng	登封	***dēngfēng***
Shaolin International Hotel	少林国际大酒店	*shàolín guójì dàjiǔdiàn*

Dengfeng is not on the rail line. **Buses** from Luoyang and Zhengzhou both take two to three hours and arrive at the bus station at the western end of the main street. Here there are local buses (¥1) to the temples of Shaolin, or you could flag down a passing minibus on the the main road, Zhongyue Dajie. The only Western-style **hotel** is the *Shaolin International*, 16 Dong Shaolin Lu (Ⓣ0371/2861446, Ⓕ2861448; ❺), which offers decent rooms a fifteen-minute walk southeast of the bus station. Head east on Zhongyue Dajie, turn right at the canal, and Dong Shaolin Lu will be on the left; the hotel is on the north side of the road.

The Songyang Academy, Songyue Temple Pagoda and Gaocheng Observatory

Three kilometres north of Dengfeng and a good focus for a walk, the **Songyang Academy** consists of a couple of lecture halls, a library and a memorial hall, founded in 484 AD, which was one of the great centres of learning under the Song. Many famous scholars from history lectured here, including Sima Guang and Cheng Hao. In the courtyard are two enormous cypresses said to be three thousand years old, as well as a stele from the Tang dynasty. The path beyond climbs to Junji Peak and branches off to the **Songyue Temple Pagoda**, 5km north of Dengfeng. Built at the beginning of the sixth century by the Northern Wei, this 45-metre structure is the oldest pagoda in China, rare for having twelve sides.

Just within a day's walk of Dengfeng, the **Gaocheng Observatory** is 7km southeast of the town. Built in 1279 and designed by Gui Shou Jing to calculate the solstices, it's a fascinating, sculptural-looking building, an almost pyramidal tower with a long straight wall marked with measurements running along the ground behind it, which would originally have been used to calculate the solstices.

Shaolin Si

Venerable and deadly monks are today in pretty short supply at the **Shaolin Si** (daily 8am–6pm; ¥42), the famous home of kung fu (*wushu*), and you're more likely to meet tour groups of the voluble and doddery. However, this tourist black spot can still be interesting as the prime pilgrimage site of the cult of kung fu that has swept contemporary China.

The approach to the temple, through bleak, mountainous countryside, does nothing to prepare you for the crowds of visitors when you arrive, swarming along the kilometre-long road – jammed with touts, cinemas, food stalls and souvenir shops – that leads from the car park to the temple itself. Most of the shops are full of weapons, everything from throwing stars to cattle prods, or tracksuits, though unfortunately you can't buy the blue tracksuit tops you see worn by the students from the numerous *wushu* schools in the area, which say "Shaolin Monastery" in English and Chinese on the back. You'll forget any plans to steal one when you see them practising at the side of the road, kicking and punching straw-filled dummies. However, if you don't see any kung-fu kicking taking place, there's plenty of evidence of it around in the broken and splintered bark of many of the trees. In September the place is particularly busy, filling up with martial arts enthusiasts from all over the world who come to attend the international **Wushu Festival**.

The original Shaolin Si was built in 495 AD. Shortly afterwards, according to tradition, **Boddhidarma**, an Indian monk credited with the founding of Zen Buddhism, came to live here, after visiting the emperor in Nanjing, then crossing the Yangzi on a reed (depicted in a tablet at the temple). Very little remains

Shaolin Kung Fu

Kung fu was first developed at the Shaolin Si as a form of gymnastics to counterbalance the immobility of meditation. The monks studied the movement of animals and copied them – the way snakes crawled, tigers leapt and mantises danced. As the temple was isolated in fairly lawless territory, it was often prey to bandits, and gradually the monks turned their exercises into a form of self-defence.

The monks owed their strength to rigorous **discipline**. From childhood, monks trained five hours a day, every day. To strengthen their hands, they thrust them into sacks of beans, over and over; when they were older, into bags of sand. To strengthen their fists, they punched a thousand sheets of paper glued to a wall; over the years the paper wore out and the young monks punched brick. To strengthen their legs, they ran around the courtyard with bags of sand tied to their knees, and to strengthen their heads, they hit them with bricks. In the Hall of Wen Shu in the temple, the depressions in the stone floor are caused by monks standing in the same place and practising their stance kicks, year after year.

Only after twenty years of such exercises could someone consider themselves a fully fledged Shaolin monk, by which time they were able to perform incredible feats, examples of which you can see illustrated in the murals at the temple and in photographs of contemporary *wushu* masters in the picture books on sale in the souvenir shops. Apart from such commonplaces as breaking concrete slabs with their fists and iron bars with their heads, the Shaolin monks of old could balance on one finger, take a sledgehammer blow to the chest, and hang from a tree by the neck. Contemporary *wushu* masters are as proficient. Just as impressive to watch, though, are the **katas**, a series of movements of balletic grace incorporating kicks and punches, in which the art's origins in animal movements can be clearly seen. Most striking are the exercises called "Drunken Monkey", performed with a pole, and "Praying Mantis", performed almost entirely on one leg.

However, the monks were not just fighters, and their art was also intended as a technique to reach the goal of inner peace, with monks spending as many hours **meditating and praying** as practising. They obeyed a moral code, which included the stricture that only fighting in self-defence was acceptable, and killing your opponent was to be avoided if possible. These rules became a little more flexible over the centuries as emperors and peasants alike sought their help in battles, and the

today of the temple's long history, as it has been burnt down on many occasions. The last time was in 1928, when the warlord Shi Yousan ordered its destruction, so the present complex is fairly newly restored and gaudily repainted, with most of the halls now housing souvenir shops. A few shaven-headed kids wander around and man the shops, and will demonstrate their flexibility for a foreign coin.

The first courtyard of the temple holds **steles**, one of which celebrates, in English, the visit of American kung-fu masters. The **murals** in two of the halls at the back are one of the few things here that haven't been repeatedly restored, and they are delightful, though the monks depicted look more comic than frightening. The pictures in the **White Robe Hall**, an illustration of the Rescue of Emperor Tai Zong By Thirteen Monks, are Qing depictions of typical kung-fu moves. In the **Thousand Buddha Hall** is a well-known Ming-dynasty mural of five hundred *arhats*.

Your ticket also gets you into all the other attractions in the area, such as the cinema showing educational films and a hall of modern *arhats*. Most worthwhile is the **Forest of Dagobas**, 200m farther up the hill from the temple, where there are hundreds of stone memorials erected between the ninth and

Shaolin monks became legendary figures for their interventions on the side of righteousness. Well-known Chinese tales include the story of the monk who fought a thousand enemies with a stick while pretending to be drunk, and the tale of the cook who kept a horde at bay with a poker at the temple gates while the other monks continued their meditations undisturbed.

The monks were at the height of their power in the Tang dynasty, though they were still a force to be reckoned with in the Ming, when **weapons** were added to their discipline. The monks did not put up much of a fight in the Cultural Revolution, though, when Red Guards sacked the temple and arrested many of them; others escaped to become peasants. Though their art lived on abroad in **judo**, **karate** and **kendo**, all of which acknowledge Shaolin kung fu as their original form, the teaching of kung fu in China was **banned** for many years until the 1980s, when, partly as a result of the enormously popular film *Shaolin Temple*, there was a **resurgence** of the art. The old masters were allowed to teach again, and the government realized that the temple was better exploited as a tourist resource than left to rot.

Evidence of the popularity of kung fu in China today can be seen not just at the tourist circus of the Shaolin Si, but in any cinema, where **kung-fu films**, often concerning the exploits of Shaolin monks, make up a large proportion of the entertainment on offer. Many young Chinese today want to study kung fu, and to meet demand numerous **schools** have opened around the temple. Few of them want to be monks, though – the dream of many is to be a movie star. It's possible to study at the Shaolin Si itself, but such a distinction does not come cheap; one day of training costs ¥300 – the price for a month at most schools elsewhere in the country.

Though they are undoubtedly skilled fighters, the present residents of the temple cannot be called genuine Shaolin monks as the religious, spiritual side of their discipline is absent. Indeed, the present abbot of the monastery has a reputation for aggression which seems entirely at odds with the Shaolin way, and the temple is vigorously pursuing efforts to trademark the very name "Shaolin", presumably to stop its unauthorized use by everything from martial-arts outfits to beer companies. Genuine Shaolin monks do still exist, however, but they keep a low profile; the last place you will find one is in the Shaolin Si.

the nineteenth centuries. Up to 10m tall, and with a stepped, recessed top, each one commemorates an individual monk and is inscribed with the names of his disciples. These golden stone structures look particularly impressive against the purple mountain when snow is on the ground, or when the students from the temple are practising here in their orange robes (one of their exercises involves fighting while balanced halfway up the almost vertical sides of the dagobas).

Beyond here the mountain can be ascended by cable car or stone steps, but there is not much to see except the **cave** where Boddhidarma supposedly passed a nine-year vigil, sitting motionless facing a wall in a state of illumination (the mystic knowledge of the Nothingness of Everything). You can save yourself some effort by paying a few yuan to look at it from the road through a high-powered telescope.

Practicalities

Besides minibuses from Dengfeng, it's easy to get here on one of the regular **tourist minibuses** from Zhengzhou or Luoyang (2–3hr; ¥10). They arrive at the top of the market road, where it's a five-minute downhill walk to the temple. Consider hiring a pedicab (¥2), as along the way you will be badgered by middle-aged women as fierce as the *wushu* disciples kicking bricks around you. The women will promise to sneak you in the back of the temple in exchange for the honour of finding you a **room** – for which, of course, they earn a commission. Most will take you east of the temple, up a steep hill to the *Shaolin Wushu Binguan* (Ⓣ0371/2749599, Ⓕ2749017; ❸), a typical Chinese behemoth befitting a tourist trap, though decent enough as a place to stay.

Zhongyue Miao

The **Zhongyue Miao** (daily 8am–6pm; ¥6), 4km east of Dengfeng on the route of bus #8, is a huge Taoist temple founded as long ago as 220 BC, and subsequently rebuilt and considerably extended by the Han emperor, Wu Di. It was rebuilt again in the Ming, then again in 1986, when damage caused by Japanese bombs was repaired. Don't be put off by the stuffed tigers and fairground games at the gate – inside it's an attractive place, its broad open spaces and brilliantly coloured buildings standing out against the grey and green of the mountain behind. Though it's a bit shabby in places, this is a working Taoist monastery, staffed by friendly monks in characteristic blue robes, their long hair tied tightly on the top of the head, sticking through a topless blue hat. They live and worship at the rear of the temple, in old barn-like buildings, while the front is given over to stallholders.

A series of gateways, courtyards and pavilions lead to the **Main Hall** where the emperor made sacrifices to the mountain. The Junji Gate, just before the hall, has two great sentries, nearly 4m high, brightly painted and flourishing their weapons. The courtyard houses gnarled old cypresses, some of them approaching the age of the temple itself, and there are four great iron statues dating from the Song on the eastern side. The Main Hall itself has 45 separate compartments with red walls and orange tiles, and a well-preserved relief carving of dragons on the terrace steps. The **Bedroom Palace** behind is unusual for having a shrine that shows a deity lying in bed. Other deities, whose blue skin, spiky red hair and eyebrows to their knees make them look to Western eyes like punks or superheroes, sit in a long line in halls on either side. Contemporary worshippers tend to gravitate to the back of the complex, where you may see people burning what look like little origami hats in the iron burners here, or practising *qi gong*, exercises centring around control of the breath.

If you go right to the back of the complex, past the monks' quarters on the right, you come to the temple's back exit, where you are charged ¥2 for the privilege of walking 200m up stone steps to a little **pagoda** on a hill behind the temple. From here paths take you through pine woods to the craggy peaks of the mountain, a worthwhile afternoon's excursion and a rare chance for solitude; the only other person you are likely to see is the odd shepherd.

Zhengzhou and around

Close to the south bank of the Yellow River, **ZHENGZHOU** lies almost midway between Luoyang in the west and Kaifeng to the east. The walled town that existed here 3500 years ago was probably an early capital of the Shang dynasty. Excavations have revealed bronze foundries, bone-carving workshops and sacrificial altars, though there is little evidence of any history above ground except a stretch of the old city walls and artefacts on display in the fantastic provincial museum. Nowadays Zhengzhou is the capital of Henan province, though this owes nothing to its past and everything to a position astride the meeting of the

Zhengzhou and around

Zhengzhou	郑州	***zhèngzhōu***
Chenghuang Miao	城隍庙	*chénghuáng miaò*
Erqi Pagoda	二七塔	*èrqī tǎ*
Henan Provincial Museum	河南省博物馆	*hénánshěng bówùguǎn*
Accommodation and eating		
Caolaowu Restaurant	曹老五泡馍馆	*cáolǎowǔ pàomóguǎn*
Golden Sunshine	金阳光大酒店	*jīnyángguāng dàjiǔdiàn*
Holiday Inn Crowne Plaza	中州皇冠假日酒店	*zhōngzhōu huángguān jiàrì jiǔdiàn*
Muslim Restaurant	穆斯林饭店	*mùsīlín fàndiàn*
Shaolin Restaurant	少林饭店	*shàolín fàndiàn*
Sofitel	索菲特国际饭店	*suǒfēitè guójì fàndiàn*
Zhengzhou	郑州饭店	*zhèngzhōu fàndiàn*
Zhongyuan	中原大厦	*zhōngyuán dàshà*
Around Zhengshou		*Around Zhengzhou*
Gongxian	巩县	*gǒngxiàn*
Gongxian Grottoes	巩县石窟寺	*gǒngxiàn shíkū sì*
Song Tombs	宋陵	*sòng líng*
Yellow River Park	黄河公园	*huánghé gōngyuán*

north–south (Beijing–Guangzhou) and west–east (Xi'an–Shanghai) rail lines. As the most important **rail junction** in China, Zhengzhou has a population of more than three million – and the industry to match.

A World War II bomb target and archetypal post-1949 boom town, Zhengzhou makes up in vitality what it lacks in beauty. The modern city is basically a business and transport centre, with no major tourist sights outside the museum, which is worth a day's tour. There is also a good range of hotels and restaurants, fortunately as the place is difficult to avoid if you're travelling in central China. From here, Kaifeng (see p.321) and Luoyang (see p.298) are easily accessible, and you can take bus trips to Song Shan (see p.308).

Arrival and city transport

The **Erqi Pagoda** stands at the heart of the modern city, a roundabout east of the station from which the main roads radiate off. Zhengzhou **airport** lies well to the east of the city. A taxi into the centre should cost ¥70, while hourly CAAC buses cost ¥15 and drop you at the Aviation Building on Jinshui Lu. The **train station**, in the southwestern corner of the city, is fronted by a bustling square dominated by a huge screen that entertains waiting passengers with TV programmes, mostly American, such as compilations of amusing home videos. Contrasted with the scene below, of food stalls, migrant workers and families camping out with their luggage, it gives the whole area something of a surreal atmosphere. Most travellers who don't intend spending a lot of time in the city probably won't stray far beyond this area, as the cheap hotels, post and telecom offices and **long-distance bus station** are all located around here. Some buses from western towns, including Luoyang, arrive at the small **western bus station** in the suburbs of the city, from where bus #24 or an ¥8 cab ride will get you to the train station.

There are two clusters of **city bus** terminuses on either side of the square outside the train station. Bus #2, from the southern side, goes to the Erqi

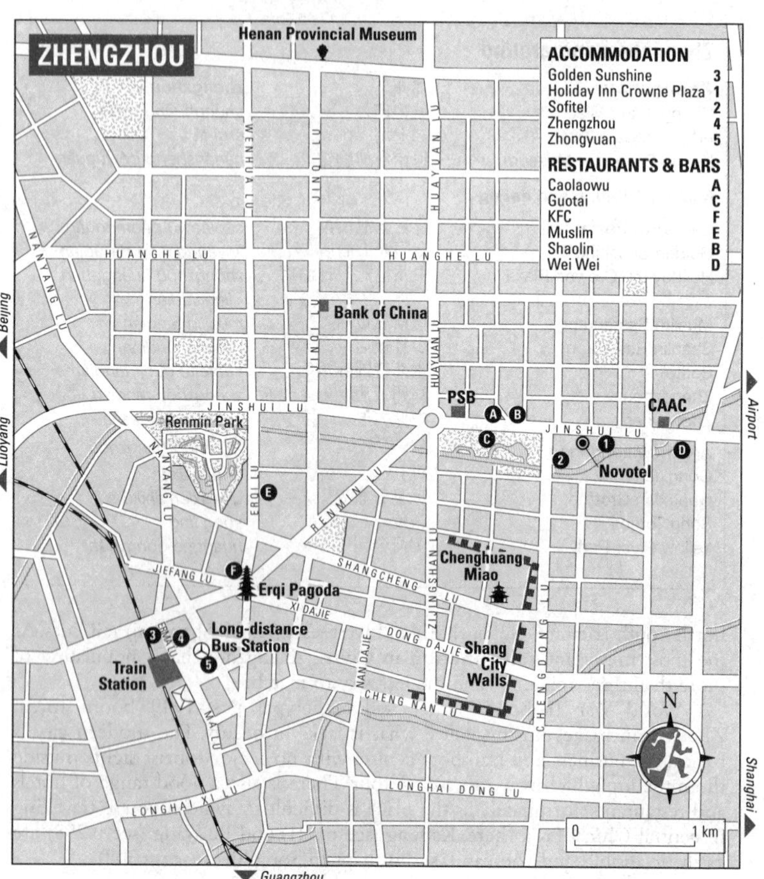

Pagoda, then up Erqi Lu; bus #10, from the northern side, goes up Renmin Lu, then Huayan Lu. **Taxis** are plentiful, and have a ¥7 minimum charge, but they aren't allowed to enter the square in front of the station; you can hail them everywhere else. **Maps** in Chinese with details of bus routes are available outside the train station (¥3); for English labelling, you'll have to buy a map from the *Holiday Inn* or *Sofitel* (¥10).

Accommodation

Zhengzhou has a wide range of accommodation to suit all price ranges. If you are just here for a night to pick up a transport connection, the hotels around the **train station** are adequate – the area is convenient and clean, but noisy. The entire block opposite the station is **dorm accommodation**, where clean rooms can be had for as little as ¥50. Talk to the middle-aged women manning the sidewalk stands opposite the station, as they can get you into a room for as little as ¥10 a night for a bed, though you should ask to see the room first. Otherwise head into town, or up to Jinshui Lu if you're not on a tight budget. Wherever you go, ask for a discount as the glut of rooms in town mean rates are often half what's posted.

Golden Sunshine North of the train station at 6 Erma Lu ⓣ0371/6969999, ⓕ6999534. New, upmarket place but with a variety of rooms to suit most budgets, from windowless singles to de luxe suites. ❷

Holiday Inn Crowne Plaza 115 Jinshui Lu ⓣ5950055, ⓔhicpzz@public.zz.ha.cn. A lobby of cream-coloured marble gives the hotel a palatial look. All mod cons imaginable, including a pool. Located in the east of town in an uninteresting cluster of five-star lodging. ❾

Sofitel 289 Chengdong Lu ⓣ0371/5950088, ⓕ5950080. The most comfortable, and newest, of Zhengzhou's five-stars. ❾

Zhengzhou 8 Xinglong Jie ⓣ0371/6760111. On the left as you leave the station. A huge building, rather bare looking, with staff who require persuasion to allow you the privilege of staying in one of their cheap rooms. ❻

Zhongyuan ⓣ0371/6768599. This multistorey warren directly opposite the train station has a very small front door set among the shops selling fruit and bags. There's an enormous stack of budget rooms with an eccentric atmosphere and a wide variety of prices. Huge, cheap doubles come complete with fly swat and spittoon. ❹

The City

Today Zhengzhou is an almost entirely modern city, rebuilt virtually from scratch after suffering heavily in the war against Japan. Its main streets have the slick look of prosperous Chinese cities, but there's still a little catching up to do – some of the citizens, dressed in Mao suits even now, don't look entirely comfortable with the new China, and plenty of the streets, including some small, useful roads in the centre, are narrow, muddy tracks that regularly get blocked by cars. Although there are plenty of modern facilities, the town's few old sights are neglected – and one was torn down, making Zhengzhou one of the few cities to raze its statue of Chairman Mao in favour of a lovely lawn fronting the park at the intersection of Jinshui Lu and Zijingshan Lu.

At the hub of downtown Zhengzhou, the **Erqi Pagoda** (daily 8.30am–6pm; ¥5) is a seven-storey structure built to commemorate those killed in a 1923 Communist-led rail strike that was put down with great savagery by the warlord Wu Pei Fu. As the exhibition of photos inside is badly maintained and has no English captions, the pagoda is best thought of as a landmark. The streets that lead off it are modern, store-lined boulevards, the largest and most interesting being **Erqi Lu** and **Renmin Lu**, which lead north to the east–west **Jinshui Lu**, the most exclusive district. East of the huge and complex roundabout at the junction of Jinshui Lu and Renmin Lu (and a host of smaller streets) is a string of classy restaurants and hotels.

The Henan Provincial Museum

A giant glass pyramid at the northern end of Jing Qi Lu, the new **Henan Provincial Museum** (daily 8.30am–6pm; ¥20; ⓦwww.chnmus.net) boasts an outstanding collection of relics unearthed in the region, dating from the Shang dynasty, when Henan was the cradle of Chinese civilization. Of the more than 1.3 million artefacts catalogued here, just a fraction are displayed on three floors, elegantly laid out and labelled in English (the fourth floor is reserved for the incongruous rubber reptiles of Dinosaur World). The audioguide (¥30, plus ¥400 or your passport as a deposit) takes you through Neolithic pottery, oracle bones, Shang bronzes, Silk Road coins, Tang glazed pottery, jade jewellery, and models of Henan's walled cities at the height of their affluence. Ancient musical instruments – some pulled from the ground months before – are displayed in the Huaxia Concert Hall, an additional wing where performances on replicas are often held. Check at the entrance gate for the schedule.

The old city

East of the Erqi pagoda, the **old city** is cut through by the **Shang city walls**, rough earthen ramparts 10m high, originally built more than two thousand years ago, though frequently repaired since. They were made by constructing a wooden frame, filling it with earth, pounding it down, then removing the frame, a technique that is still used in domestic architecture. There's a path along the top, and you can walk for about 3km along the south and east sections (the west section has been largely destroyed by development). The south section is open to the street, so you can scramble up anywhere. You have to descend to cross Nan Dajie, then walk through an alleyway to pick up the path again, and repeat the process at Shangcheng Lu. Planted with trees, the walls are now used by the locals as a short cut and a park, and in the early evening the path is full of courting couples, kids who slide down the steep sides on metal trays, and old men who hang their cagebirds from the trees and sit around fires cooking sweet potatoes. Some people grow vegetables at the wall's base, others throw their rubbish here. Indeed, the charm of the wall comes from the way it has been incorporated by the inhabitants – it doesn't seem to occur to anyone to treat the walls as a historical monument.

A short walk from the eastern wall, on the north side of Shangcheng Lu, the **Chenghuang Miao** (Temple of the City God; daily 9.30am–5.30pm; ¥6) is worth a look around. The attendants regard visitors as an interruption to their day's knitting and usually keep the doors closed; you have to shout through the gap to gain admittance. Though the temple has the look of an abandoned warehouse, it retains a glimmer of its past glory in the roof decoration. Well-observed images of birds decorate the eaves of the first hall, underneath roof sculptures of dragons and phoenixes. The East Hall now contains a small art gallery; upstairs is one of those exhibitions of African body art that the Chinese seem so fascinated by. The interior of the Main Hall is modern, with a mural on three walls whose style owes much to 1950s socialist realism. In the centre a sculpture of a stern-looking Chenghuang, magisterial defender of city folk, in a judge's costume, sits flanked by two attendants.

Eating, drinking and entertainment

The best food in town is available from the dense concentration of stylish **restaurants** on Jinshui Lu. Though they look a little intimidating on the outside, prices aren't as expensive as you might expect, due to fierce competition, and a meal for two should be around ¥100 at most. The *Guotai* and *Shaolin* are both good, and the *Caolaowu*, which serves Muslim cuisine, is a little cheaper than the others, and worth checking out at lunchtime for the buffet. The *Muslim Restaurant* on Erqi Lu is a little more upmarket, at around ¥50 per person; for something unusual try the tofu in toffee. If you're missing Western food, go along to either the *Holiday Inn* or *Sofitel*, both of which have reasonably priced coffee shops and lavish weekend brunches (¥150–200). *Dicos* is the fast-food representative around the concourse, both on the northwest and eastern edges. There's a *KFC* northwest of the Erqi Pagoda roundabout.

Around the train station there are plenty of small **dumpling canteens**, all much the same, and enormous numbers of shops selling travellers' nibbles – walnuts, oranges and dates – which testify to the great number of people passing through here every day.

For a fun **night out**, head to *Wei Wei* on Jinshui Lu (cover charge ¥30), across from the CAAC. It has a romping disco and hosts live music weekly, with such Beijing luminaries as Cui Jian and Flower having graced its stage recently.

Listings

Airlines The main CAAC office is at 3 Jinshui Lu (Mon–Sat 8am–6pm; ⓣ0371/5991111). You can also buy tickets from a small office next to the main post office (Mon–Sat 8am–10pm) and from most hotels.

Banks and exchange The Bank of China is on Jing Qi Lu (Mon–Fri 8am–noon & 2–5.30pm). The *Novotel International Hotel* also changes traveller's cheques and staff don't ask you if you're staying at the hotel.

Bookshops The Foreign Language Bookstore is just west of the Erqi Pagoda on Jiefang Lu.

Buses Zhengzhou's long-distance bus station, opposite the train station, has a computerized ticket office (daily 7am–6pm), which seems to cut down on queues, though it's easier to wander in, read the bold pinyin signs stating destinations, size up which class bus you want to take and when it departs, and board. The driver will get your ticket for you.

Mail and telephones The main post office is next to the train station on the south side (Mon–Fri 8am-8pm). There's a 24hr telecom office next door to the post office.

PSB For visa extensions, apply at 10 Jinshui Lu (Mon–Fri 8am–11pm). For other matters, there's an office at 70 Erqi Lu.

Shopping The Friendship Store is on Erqi Lu, at the north end of Renmin Park. There are also a few pricey antique stores at the eastern end of Jinshui Lu.

Trains The train station has a huge two-storey booking office that can be confusing, with more than thirty windows to choose from, and everyone scrambling to press up against them. You can also buy tickets from an advance booking office at 131 Erqi Lu (Mon–Fri 8am–noon & 1.30–3.30pm).

Travel agents and tours CITS is situated at 15 Jinshui Lu (Mon–Sat 8am–5pm; ⓣ0371/5952072) and has a branch in the *Novotel International Hotel*, 114 Jinshui Lu. There are Chinese-language tours to Song Shan (¥35) leaving every morning between 8am and 10am from a compound on the south side of the train-station concourse.

Around Zhengzhou

The most diverting attractions in the area are covered under Song Shan (see p.308), but a couple of locations within an easy bus ride of the capital deserve a mention here. You'd have to be very interested in cave temples to make it to **Gongxian**, but the shabby **Yellow River Park** at least provides the opportunity of seeing the river if you haven't already caught sight of it through a bus or train window.

Gongxian and around

The town of **GONGXIAN** (also marked on maps and schedules as Gongyishi), midway between Luoyang and Zhengzhou, on the rail line to Shanghai, is an unremarkable place, though if you do wind up here, there are some Song-dynasty tombs and a few Buddhist cave temples to visit outside the town.

The **tombs**, spread over a thirty-kilometre area southeast of the town, have the same layout as the Tang tombs near Xi'an, though the Song emperors had very different funerary practices from their predecessors. In particular, each emperor's tomb was built for him by his successor and had to be completed within seven months of the emperor's death. Not surprisingly, the results are considerably less grandiloquent than the tombs that earlier emperors had spent their own lifetimes preparing. There are seven tombs, each with a spirit way in varying states of repair. To get to them you will have to charter a **taxi** from Gongxian, though tour buses on their way from Zhengzhou to Song Shan sometimes stop here briefly. Look out for the tombs if you're travelling between Luoyang and Zhengzhou by bus.

Eight kilometres north of Gongxian are a set of five **Buddhist grottoes** from the Northern Wei dynasty (daily 8am–6pm; ¥10). The carving is cruder than at Longmen, the figures are sturdier and blockier, but there is a lot of variety, with musicians, dancers and imperial processions, even a couple of figures with rabbit and monkey heads, among the seated Buddhas. The caves have a central pillar around which worshippers perambulated. Few people get here, so this is still not a big tourist sight, though the man who looks after the place has a few books for sale. Behind the caves is a village, and beyond that the dramatic rugged landscape of stepped loess hills is a rewarding place to get lost for an afternoon.

The Yellow River Park

Twenty-eight kilometres north of the city at the terminus of bus #16, which leaves from Minggong Lu just outside Zhengzhong's train station, the **Yellow River Park** (daily 8am–6pm; ¥25) is really a stretch of typical Chinese countryside, incorporating villages and allotments, that you have to pay to get into because it has a view of the Yellow River. There's a pretty hill, Mang Shan, but none of the sights listed on the map which you can buy at the entrance – dilapidated temples and statues, including a huge image of Yu the Great – is worth it. You can spend an afternoon here walking around the hills at the back of the park, or riding – there are plenty of men hiring out horses, and an escorted trot around the hills for an hour or two should cost about ¥20. From the hilltops you have a good view over the river and the plain of mud either side of it. It's hard to imagine that in 1937, when Chiang Kaishek breached the dykes 8km from the city to prevent the Japanese capturing the rail line, the Yellow River flooded this great plain, leaving more than a million dead and countless more homeless.

Anyang and around

The city of **ANYANG**, 200km north of Zhengzhou, is the site of the Shang-dynasty capital and one of the most important archeological sites in China. As the ancient city lies under the ground, however, and the contemporary one is too small for glamour and too big to have much character, it hardly justifies a stop unless you have a special interest or want to break a trip to or from Beijing. Most of the town is south of the Huan River, but the ancient sites, the **Yinxu Ruins** and the **Yuan Forest** are just north of it, in a grey industrial zone.

Jiefang Lu and **Honqi Lu** are the liveliest districts of the modern city, with a night and weekend market on Honqi Lu. The most rewarding excursion you can take in central Anyang is a wander around the **old city**, the area around the Bell Tower at the south end of Honqi Lu, with dusty, unpaved streets and alleyways mostly too narrow for cars or lorries, but full of people and carts. From the streets you see only the long, whitewashed walls of the compounds with their tiled roofs. Direct entrance to the courtyards from the street is blocked by further walls, a traditional defence against evil spirits. Inside the old city, southwest of the Bell Tower, you'll find the **Wenfeng Pagoda** (daily 8am–5pm; ¥5), built in 925 AD and unusually shaped; it gets larger towards the top, ending with a dagoba-shaped peak atop a flat roof – and added Christmas lights. Behind it, a new zone of shops has torn out the heart of the old city, and it's worth perambulating around the remaining alleys before they, too, are razed.

Southeast of the Bell Tower, the **Chenghuang Miao** (daily 8am–4.30pm; ¥10), built in 1451, is an attractive building with stone carvings of dragons and lions around its entrance, well suited to its present purpose as a gallery displaying the work of local artists. On show are papercuts, masks and calligraphy – many of the local calligraphers use the Shang script.

Anyang and around		
Anyang	安阳	***ānyáng***
Anyang Gueshouse	安阳招待所	*ānyáng zhāodàisuǒ*
Anyang Hotel	安阳宾馆	*ānyáng bīnguǎn*
Chenghuang Miao	城隍庙	*chénghuáng miào*
Tomb of Yuan Shikai	袁世恺墓	*yuánshìkǎi mù*
Wenfeng Pagoda	文峰塔	*wénfēng tǎ*
Yinxu Ruins	殷墟博物院	*yīnxū bówùyuàn*
Zhongyuan Hotel	珠泉宾馆	*zhūquán bīnguǎn*
Linxian	林县	***línxiàn***
Red Flag Canal	林县红旗运河	*línxiàn hóngqí yùnhé*

The ancient sites

The **Yinxu Ruins** (daily 8am–6.30pm; ¥21) are all that is left of ancient Anyang, a city that vanished into the dusty fields so long ago its very existence had been forgotten. The historian Sima Qian, writing in the first century BC, mentioned the ruins of an early city on the banks of the Huan River, but this and its ruling houses were thought to be mere legend until, in 1899, quantities of oracle bones were found. Later, in the 1920s and 1930s, excavations proved beyond doubt that this had been the capital of a historical dynasty, the **Shang**, which flourished from 1711 to 1066 BC, and which is known today for its large decorated bronze vessels – you can see these in most large Chinese museums.

To visit the ruins, take bus #5 from the train station and get off at the first stop on Tie Xi Lu; the driver will probably ask if you want to get off here. Then walk back up the road to Angang Lu, head west for 100m, cross the rail line and follow the track northwest for about a kilometre. A taxi here from the station costs ¥6. At the site, a rough stretch of wasteland, the highlight is a new wing showcasing **six chariots** in pits, the skeletons of horses still attached to them. The find was unearthed in 2000, and is but a sliver of what archeologists believe is a vast trove beneath the soil. Beside this recent booty, there's little to see as the more obviously impressive relics have long since been looted or are now in the Beijing History Museum. Past excavations uncovered the city of Yin, with royal tombs containing horses, chariots and sacrificial victims; houses and workshops with tools; splendid bronze vessels, one inscribed with the name of the royal consort Fu Hao and still bearing soot marks from the fire; jade and pottery of fine design; and most importantly of all – tens of thousand of **oracle bones**, which are the only relics still on display here, in two imitation Yin buildings, held up by thin columns and topped with thatched roofs. Peasants had been digging up these chunks of bone covered with markings and selling them as dragon bones for use in medicine before they were recognized as script and excavations started. The bones were used in divination – the priest or shaman applied heated sticks to them and interpreted the cracks that appeared – and they have provided all sorts of useful information about hunting, war, the harvest and sacrifices as this was scratched on to the bone afterwards. The bones were also used for keeping records and reveal a great deal about the complicated organization of the Shang city, the names of its rulers, the titles and functions of its officials and the collection and spending of tribute money. The bones are displayed with a translation into modern Chinese, and the Shang characters they bear are recognizably the more pictorial ancestors of those used today.

There are some more Shang exhibits in the small, crusty museum in the **Yuan Forest** (daily 8am–6.30pm; ¥21), also in the north of the city, on the route of bus #8, which you can catch outside Renmin Park. Bus #2, from the station, will get you to the bridge over Shengli Lu, from which it's a short walk. You would probably have to be an expert, though, to get excited about the displays of pottery fragments and yellowing photographs. The best exhibit is a bronze horse's bridle.

Behind the museum, a grassy mound with a stone wall around its base is the **Tomb of Yuan Shikai** (¥5), a Qing warlord. His brief moment of glory was in 1915, when he declared himself emperor after taking over from Sun Yatsen as president of the Republic. He died shortly after completing the ritual ceremonies at the Temple of Heaven.

Practicalities

Anyang's **bus and train stations** are at the western end of Jiefang Lu, the town's main east–west thoroughfare, at the terminus of a clutch of bus routes. Bus #3 goes east along the street's length to Renmin Park, while bus #2 goes east, then turns north up Hongqi Lu, the main north–south road. Continuing on south **to Zhengzhou** or north **to Shijiazhuang** is easy, as buses and trains ply the route throughout the day. Train #T90 connects all three cities, costing ¥38 for a hard seat. Alternatively, catch a bus (4hr; ¥34) from the bus station. For rides **to Beijing**, there are zippy luxury coaches (6hr; ¥60) from the start of the expressway out of town (*gaosu lukou*).

Bus #3 or #4 will get you to the comfortable, though not pretty, *Anyang Hotel*, on Jiefang Lu just east of the crossroads with Zhangde Lu (☎0372/5922244; ❹). Better is the massive *Zhongyuan Hotel* (☎0372/5923235; ❸, dorm beds ¥60), a little further east down Jiefang Lu and off an alley to the right, past Hongqi Lu. The *Anyang Guesthouse*, 23 Xi Huancheng Lu (☎0372/5922266; ❷), is most friendly and central, located at the western approach to Wenfeng Pagoda. For food, try the **night market** on Honqi Lu, the line of **restaurants** along Jiefang Lu, or the restaurant at the *Anyang Hotel*. **Internet access** is widely available in the alleys around the *Zhongyuan Hotel*, and also at a second-floor shop overlooking the Bell Tower.

The Red Flag Canal

For anyone who has had more than enough pagodas to be going on with, the side-trip from Anyang to the **Red Flag Canal**, in the Taihuang Mountains in the far northwest of Henan Province, makes an unusual diversion. Like Yan'an in the north of Shaanxi, it's one of the holy sites of Communism and is fascinating not just in itself but for the glimpse it gives of more ideological times. The jumping-off point for the canal is **Linxian**, 70km west of Anyang. Frequent **buses** (¥10) come here from Anyang's bus station, dropping you off in Linxian town centre. Alternatively, you can go by slow **train** along a branch line, though the station is a forty-minute bus ride from the centre of town. From Linxian you can negotiate a jeep tour to the canal – the drivers will find you quickly enough – for about ¥50.

While most of the province lives under the threat of devastating floods, the problem in this area has been severe **drought**. The acute water shortage, allied to stony, infertile hills, condemns the local peasants to a hard life, labouring to scrape a living from the mountain dust. The ambitious plan to irrigate the area by taking water from the Zhang River in Shanxi, begun in 1960, took more than twelve years to complete and is undoubtedly a triumph of the human spirit, one of the massive engineering feats the Chinese have always excelled at, from the Great Wall onward. All the work was done by volunteers with picks and panniers – to complete one section, men even abseiled down the mountain to hack away at overhangs. Chinese pamphlets for visitors proudly state the figures: over 1000km of channel dug, 1250 hills blasted into, 143 tunnels excavated, thousands of acres of barren land made fertile. They don't mention that more than 130 people died during construction, or the criticisms of the canal – it's been said that the same result could have been achieved by laying a single irrigation pipe.

Visitors today are given **tours** that begin at the Youth Tunnel, where the water arrives in the valley through the ridge of a mountain. You then climb up to follow the course of the canal clinging to the hillside high above the valley, where you can see it winding endlessly across spurs running down from the mountain ridges – an impressive sight. The rest of the tour takes in a dam and one of the main aqueducts, with names redolent of the 1960s, among them Hero Branch Canal and Seizing Bumper Harvest Aqueduct. At one time a visit to the canal was almost obligatory for young cadres and students; key political figures and VIPs from other countries were also brought here in limousines to scramble up the hillside, admire the work and have their picture taken alongside local dignitaries. Few come here now, those that do freely admitting that such a venture, built on the optimism and spirit of volunteers, would not be possible in contemporary China. Now the heroic slogans beside the canal have faded, and the provinces it passes through have begun squabbling over water rights.

Kaifeng

Located on the alluvial plains in the middle reaches of the Yellow River, 70km east of Zhengzhou, lakeside **KAIFENG** is an ancient capital with a history stretching back over three thousand years. But its situation, repeatedly exposed to northern invaders and to flooding from the unpredictable Yellow River just to the north, has left few relics to conjure any past glory. However, unlike other ancient capitals in the area, the city hasn't grown into an industrial monster, and remains pleasingly compact, with all its sights in a fairly small area within the walls. It's been spruced up a lot recently, and today Kaifeng is a thriving town, not at all the sleepy place you might expect, with an ongoing beautification campaign underway to attract tourists. On the downside, this means tourist resources, theme parks and the like have been constructed which, together with the mass influx of visitors, may destroy the charm of the place, but on the plus side the PSB takes a relaxed attitude towards foreign visitors, which means there are no restrictions on where foreigners can stay, and visas can be extended with little hassle. A great night market, a sprinkling of sights – some pretty temples and pagodas – and a calm atmosphere make this a worthwhile place to spend a few days, especially if you've grown weary of the scale and pace of most Chinese cities.

The city's heyday came under the Northern Song dynasty between 960 and 1127 AD. First heard of as a Shang town around 1000 BC, it served as the capital of several early kingdoms and minor dynasties, but under the Song the city became the political, economic and cultural centre of the empire. A famous five-metre-long horizontal scroll by Zhang Azheduan, *Riverside Scene at the Qingming Festival*, now in the Forbidden City in Beijing, unrolls to show views

Kaifeng		
Kaifeng	开封	***kāifēng***
Fan Pagoda	繁塔	*fán tǎ*
Iron Pagoda Park	铁塔公园	*tiětǎ gōngyuán*
Kaifeng Museum	开封博物馆	*kāifēng bówùguǎn*
Memorial Temple to Lord Bao	包公祠	*bāogōng cí*
Millennium City	清明上河园	*qīngmíng shànghéyuán*
Shanshanguan Guild Hall	陕山甘会馆	*shǎnshān gānhuì guǎn*
Xiangguo Si	相国寺	*xiàngguó sì*
Yanqing Si	延庆观	*yánqìng guàn*
Yellow River Park	黄河公园	*huánghé gōngyuán*
Yu Terrace	古吹台	*gǔchuī tái*
Yuwangtai Park	禹王台公园	*yǔwángtái gōngyuán*
Accommodation and eating		
Bianjing	汴京饭店	*biànjīng fàndiàn*
Dajintai	大金台旅馆	*dàjīntái lǚguǎn*
Diyi Lou	第一楼	*dìyīlóu*
Dongjing	东京大饭店	*dōngjīng dàfàndiàn*
Gulou Dumplings	鼓楼饺子馆	*gǔlóu jiǎoziguǎn*
Kaifeng	开封宾馆	*kāifēng bīnguǎn*
Number One	第一大饭店	*dìyī dàfàndiàn*
Shao'e Huang	烧鹅皇酒店	*shāo'é huáng jiǔdiàn*
Yingbin Fandian	迎宾饭店	*yíngbīn fàndiàn*

of the city at this time, teeming with life, crammed with people, boats, carts and animals. It was a great age for painting, calligraphy, philosophy and poetry, and Kaifeng became famous for the quality of its textiles and embroidery and for its production of ceramics and printed books. It was also the home of the first mechanical clock in history, Su Song's astronomical clock tower of 1092, which worked by the transmission of energy from a huge water wheel.

This Golden Age ended suddenly in 1127 when Jurchen invaders overran the city, looting palaces and temples and putting everything else to the torch. The emperor and his court were led away as prisoners. Just one royal prince escaped to the south, to set up a new capital out of harm's reach at Hangzhou beyond the Yangzi, but Kaifeng itself never recovered. Nor did much survive. What did has been damaged or destroyed by repeated flooding since – between 1194 and 1887 there were more than fifty severe incidents, including one fearful occasion when the dykes were breached during a siege and at least three hundred thousand people are said to have died.

Orientation, arrival and city transport

Central Kaifeng, bounded by walls roughly 3km long at each side, is fairly small, and most places of interest are within walking distance of one another. **Zhongshan Lu** is the main north–south thoroughfare, while **Sihou Jie**, which changes its name to Gulou Jie at the centre and Mujiaqiao Jie in the east, is the main east–west road. Kaifeng's heart is the **crossroads** of Sihou Jie and Shudian Jie, where the night market sets up. The town is crisscrossed by canals, once part of a network that connected it to Hangzhou and Yangzhou in ancient times.

The **train station**, on the Xi'an–Shanghai line, is in a grotty area outside the walls, about 2km south of the centre. The main long-distance **bus station** is next to the train station, and there's a smaller bus station, for buses to or from western destinations, notably Zhengzhou, on Yingbin Lu, just inside the walls.

Most of the city's **bus routes** begin outside the train station. Bus #1 goes from here north up Yingbin Lu, then along Zhongshan Lu, skirts Panjia Hu and continues to the north section of the wall, terminating on Beimen Dajie at a second, small bus terminus. To get to the centre from the station, take bus #4, which runs up Yingbin Lu, then traverses the length of the town along Sihou Jie. Bus #3 is also useful, travelling from Iron Pagoda Park down the

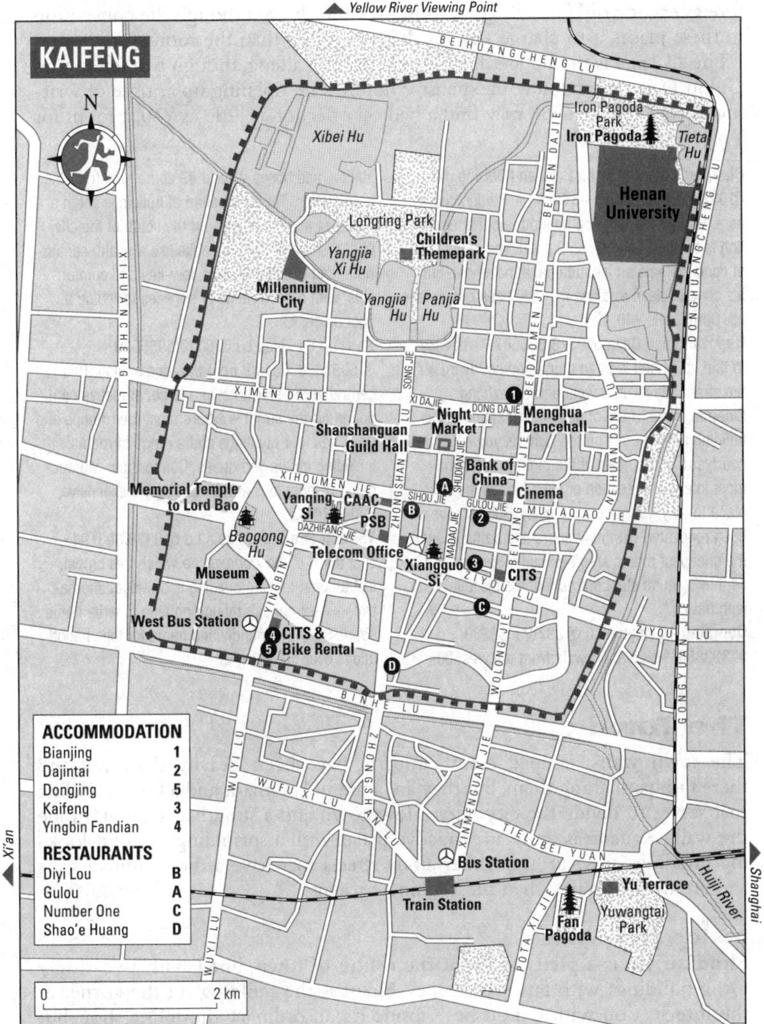

street that begins as Beimen Dajie, and ending up at the train station. For a relatively small place, there are a lot of **taxis** cruising the streets and used to dealing with tourists. The minimum fare of ¥5 is sufficient for rides in town. **Cycling** is an ideal way to get around as the streets are wide and flat, but the only rental shop is outside the *Yingbin Hotel* in the far south of town, so unless you're staying nearby it's a long walk back to your hotel once you've returned the bike. You can get a **map** of town (¥3) at the bus station.

Accommodation

Despite Kaifeng's small size, it has a wealth of good, cheap **hotels**. As there's no bar here on foreigners staying in Chinese-style hotels, lone travellers may wish to take advantage: staff are generally reluctant to put a Chinese in a room with foreigners, so you'll usually get a room to yourself even though the convention in these places is to charge you for the bed, rather than the room.

The *Dajintai* is the budget hotel of choice in Kaifeng, though further east on Gulou Dajie, several new, inexpensive hotels were opening up at time of writing. If they survive, you may find a bed on offer for as little as ¥40, a room for ¥90.

Bianjing Corner of Dong Dajie and Beixing Jie ⓣ0378/2886699. Bus #3 from the station comes here. Go into the large compound and the reception is the first building on the left. The abundance of concrete sets an institutional atmosphere, but it's central, clean and has recently been redecorated. Dorm beds ¥40, ❸

Dajintai Gulou Dajie ⓣ0378/5956677. Not easy to find, this hotel is in an unmarked courtyard off the street, about 50m west of the Dazhong Cinema, on the route of bus #4. Reception is the building immediately on the right as you enter the courtyard. In the heart of the night market and most interesting section of town, this is the best place to stay, yet not unduly noisy. Rooms have been renovated with new floors and baths, though the cheapest rooms aren't en suite. Haggle hard as they're quite stubborn as regards discounts. ❶, with bath ❹

Dongjing 14 Yingbin Lu ⓣ0378/3989388, ⓕ3938861. It's a short walk from the west bus station, and buses #1 and #9 come here from the train station. This compound of buildings set in a park just inside the walls in the south of the city, on the shore of Bao Hu, looks like a health sanatorium, and is suitably quiet, low-key and comfortable, with a good range of services including a post office. ❹

Kaifeng 64 Ziyou Lu ⓣ0378/5955589, ⓕ5953086. Bus #9 from the train station. This central, three-star hotel in a large, attractive compound off the street is where most tour groups end up. It has four buildings and a range of rooms, including triples and quads. Comfortable without being ostentatious and surprisingly inexpensive. Beds ¥70, ❹

Yingbin Fandian Yingbin Lu ⓣ0378/3931943. Just north of the *Dongjing*, to which this brown, institutional-looking building is a budget alternative, decent enough though nothing to write home about. Staff are friendly and game for long negotiations over the price. ❷

The Town

The town **walls**, tamped earth ramparts, have been heavily destroyed and there's no path along them, but they are a useful landmark and a boundary line that serves to divide the city into a downtown and a suburban section. Inside the walls, Kaifeng is quite an attractive place, with a sprinkling of good-looking buildings close to each other along streets that have a more human scale and are freer of traffic than most Chinese towns.

Inside the walls

Shudian Jie is a pretty street at the centre of town, lined with two-storey Qing buildings with fancy balconies. Finest is the building on the corner at the intersection with Gulou Jie – inside it's an ordinary dumpling shop, but the architectural detail outside, particularly the stone reliefs at the base, are very fine. Come here in the evening to see this sedate street transformed into a busy **night market**, when brightly lit stalls selling mostly underwear, cosmetics and plastic kitchenware line its length. You may find the odd trinket worth bartering for, especially if you collect novelty lighters, but it's really a place to wander in your best clothes, which is what most of the locals do. The stalls on Gulou Jie sell books with lurid covers, some of which sport curious English titles, such as *She Married A Foreigner*. Of most interest, though, are the food stalls that set up around the crossroads, huge numbers of them, where for a few yuan you can get food to make the back of the legs quiver (see p.327).

Shanshanguan Guild Hall

An alley, Xufu Jie, too narrow to be marked on some maps, leads west off the northern end of Shudian Jie to the **Shanshanguan Guild Hall** (daily 8am–6.30pm; ¥10), which is worth the effort needed to find it, as it's a superb example of Qing-dynasty architecture at its most lavish. It was established by merchants of Shanxi, Shaanxi and Gansu provinces to provide cheap accommodation and a social centre for visiting merchants. In more recent history, it was part of the school next door, though now it's being pushed as a tourist site and undergoing restoration. With a spirit wall, drum and bell tower, and the Main Hall flanked by smaller side halls, it has the structure of a flashy, ostentatious temple. The wood carvings on the eaves are excellent, including lively and rather wry scenes from the life of a travelling merchant, lots of portly figures playing instruments, sitting in boats or riding horses; look for the man being dragged along the ground by his horse on the Eastern Hall. In the eaves of the Main Hall, gold bats (a symbol of luck) sport beneath accurate images of animals and birds frolicking among bunches of grapes. Inside is a model of the modern town next to one of the Song city, and in a side hall is the usual exhibition of tribal body art.

Xiangguo Si and Yanqing Si

Head back on to Shudian Jie and walk south, past the crossroads, and you'll come to Madao Jie, signposted, in English, as "The Street of Insurance Service for Preventing Disaster" – bizarrely, it's full of clothing boutiques. At the bottom of this street, turn right and you'll come to the **Xiangguo Si** (daily 8am–6pm; ¥20), which was originally built in 555 AD, though the present structure dates back to 1766. The simple layout of the three buildings is pleasing, though the front courtyard now holds an amusement park. Things get better the farther in you go. At the back of the Main Hall is a colourful, modern frieze of *arhats*, and the Daxiong Baodian (Great Treasure House) has a good early Song bronze Buddha. In an unusual octagonal hall at the back you'll see a magnificent four-sided Guanyin carved in gingko wood and covered in gold leaf, about 3m high.

A kilometre west, along Ziyou Lu, is the **Yanqing Si** (daily 8am–6pm; ¥10), whose rather odd, knobbly central building, the **Pavilion of the Jade Emperor**, is all that remains of a larger complex built at the end of the thirteenth century. The outside of this octagonal structure of turquoise tiles and carved brick is overlaid with ornate decorative touches, such as imitation *dougong* (wooden brackets); inside, a bronze image of the Jade Emperor sits in a room that is by contrast strikingly austere. The rest of the complex at first looks just as old, though the images of kangaroos among the animals decorating the eaves give a clue to its recent construction.

Baogong Hu

Within walking distance ofYanqing Si is **Baogong Hu**, one of the large bodies of water inside Kaifeng whose undisturbed space helps give the town its laid-back feel. On a promontory on the western side, and looking very attractive from a distance, the **Memorial Temple to Lord Bao** (daily 7.30am–7pm; ¥20) is a modern imitation of a Song building holding an exhibition of the life of this legendary figure who was Governor of Kaifeng during the Northern Song. Judging from the articles exhibited, including modern copies of ancient guillotines, and the scenes from his life depicted in paintings on the walls, Lord Bao was a harsh but fair judge, who must have had some difficulty getting through doors if he really wore a hat and shoes like the ones on display. A substantial mansion on the south side of the lake, the **Kaifeng Museum** (daily 8.30am–11.30am & 2.30–5.30pm; ¥10) holds steles recording the history of Kaifeng's Jewish community that used to stand outside the synagogue, but not much else.

Song Jie, Yangjia Hu and Longting Park

Heading back in the general direction of Shanshanguan Guild Hall, you can turn north up Zhongshan Lu and continue on to **Song Jie**, on the site of the Song-dynasty Imperial Palace. This is now a street of tourist shops built to look like Song buildings, and is entered through an arch at the southern end. The shops look impressive from a distance but they're pretty shabbily made, especially the Fan Tower, an entertainments centre at the northern end, which is marked as a major attraction on tourist maps. The shops sell antiques and curios, and there are two good art shops on the eastern side. In the winter, when most of the tourists have gone, many of the shops switch to selling household goods.

At the northern end of Song Jie, **Yangjia Hu** was originally part of the imperial park but is now at the centre of a large warren of carnival-like tourist traps, including an amusement park based on Zhang Zeduan's *Riverside Scene at Qingming Festival*, one China's best-known paintings, a Song-dynasty scroll depicting the city. At **Millennium City** (daily 9am–5.30pm; ¥30), west of the lake, you can walk through the scenery Zhang painted, wandering to your

Kaifeng's Jews

The origins of Kaifeng's **Jewish community** are something of a mystery. A Song-dynasty stele now in the town museum records that they arrived here in the Zhou dynasty, nearly three thousand years ago, which seems doubtful. It's more likely their ancestors came here from central Asia around 1000 AD, when trade links between the two areas were strong, a supposition given some weight by the characteristics they share with Persian Jews, such as their use of Hebrew alphabet with 27 rather than 22 letters. The community was never large, but it seems to have flourished until the nineteenth century, when – perhaps as a result of disastrous floods, including one in 1850 which destroyed the synagogue – the Kaifeng Jews almost completely died out. The synagogue, which stood at the corner of Pingdeng Jie and Beixing Jie, on the site of what is now a hospital, was never rebuilt, and no trace of it remains today.

A number of families in Kaifeng trace their lineage back to the Jews, and, following the atmosphere of greater religious tolerance in contemporary China, have begun practising again. You can see a few relics from the synagogue in Kaifeng Museum, including three steles that once stood outside it, but most, such as a Torah in Chinese now in the British Museum, are in collections abroad.

heart's content past costumed courtesans and ingratiating shopkeepers. Children will enjoy the theme-park rides at **Longting Park** (daily 6am–6pm; ¥25), on the northern shore of Yangjia Hu and reachable via a raised path.

Iron Pagoda Park

From the northern end of Song Jie, bus #1 goes to the far northeast corner of the rough square formed by the city walls, to **Iron Pagoda Park** (daily 8am–6pm; ¥20), just north of Henan University, and only accessible off Beimen Dajie. At the centre of this leafy park you'll find the 13-storey, 56-metre-high Iron Pagoda that gives it its name, a striking Northern Song (1049 AD) construction so named because its surface of glazed tiles gives the building the russet tones of rusted iron. Its base, like all early buildings in Kaifeng, is buried beneath a couple of metres of silt deposited during floods. Most of the tiles hold relief images, usually of the Buddha, but also of Buddhist angels, animals and abstract patterns. You can climb up the inside, via a gloomy spiral staircase, for an extra ¥5.

Outside the walls

Two kilometres south of town, about 1km east of the train station, you'll find the pleasant **Yuwangtai Park**; buses #8 and #15 will get you close, otherwise it's a long and dusty walk through the most rundown part of town. It's main feature is the **Yu Terrace** (daily 8am–6pm; ¥10), an earthen mound now thought to have been a music terrace, that was once the haunt of Tang poets. The park, dotted with pavilions and commemorative steles, is pleasant in summer when the many flower gardens are in bloom.

Not far from here, its top visible from the park, the **Fan Pagoda** is not in a park as maps say, but sits between a car repair yard and a set of courtyards in a suburbia of labyrinthine alleyways. The only approach is from the western side. The fact that the local inhabitants tie their washing lines to the wall around the base and peel sweetcorn in the courtyard adds to the charm of the place. Built in 997 AD and the oldest standing building in Kaifeng, this dumpy hexagonal brick pagoda was once 80m tall and had nine storeys; three remain today, and you can ascend for a view of rooftops and factories. The carved bricks on the outside are good, though the bottom few layers are new after vandalism in the Cultural Revolution.

From a bus station on the west side of Beimen Dajie, opposite the entrance to the Iron Pagoda Park, it's worth catching bus #6 to the **Yellow River Viewing Point**, 11km north of town, especially if you haven't seen the river before. From the pavilion here you can look out on to a plain of silt that stretches to the horizon, across whose dramatic emptiness the syrupy river meanders. Beside the pavilion is an iron ox, which once stood in a now submerged temple. It's a cuddly-looking beast with a horn on its head that makes it look like a rhino sitting on its hind legs. An inscription on the back reveals its original function – a charm to ward off floods, a tradition begun by the legendary flood-tamer Da Yu (see p.265).

Eating, drinking and nightlife

The best place to eat is the **night market** on Shudian Jie (see p.325), where the food as well as the ambience is much better than in the few sit-down canteens. Here you'll find not just the usual staples such as *jiaozi*, made in front of you, and skewers of mutton cooked by Uigur pedlars, but also a local **delicacy** consisting of hot liquid jelly, into which nuts, berries, flowers and fruit are poured. You can spot jelly stalls by the huge bronze kettle they all have with a spout in the form of a dragon's head. Another delicious sweet on sale here is slices of banana covered with pancake mix then deep-fried. Wash it all down with a bottle of local Bianjing Beer.

On the south side of Gulou Jie are a couple of **fast-food places**, such as *Dicos*, which has decent coffee. For **dumplings**, don't miss the *Gulou Jiaozi Guan* in the restored wood structure at the corner of Gulou Jie and Nan Shudian Jie. In terms of location, this is probably China's prettiest dumpling shop and, though its sterile, white-tiled interior may not look like much, people-watching out of the windows is great, as are the plump dumplings. The **restaurant** in the *Kaifeng Hotel* is pretty good, and opposite the hotel, a little farther west on Ziyou Lu, the *Number One Restaurant* is fairly inexpensive with reasonable food, but the decor, with chickens trussed up just inside the door and empty aquariums, could be improved. The swanky *Shao'e Huang Restaurant*, at 214 Zhongshan Lu, is where the local elite hang out. There's no English menu, but you can select a variety of vegetable, fish and meat dishes from the display downstairs; expect to pay ¥80 for a meal for two. A traditional Chinese ensemble plays nightly at the *Diyi Lou Restaurant*, 43 Sihou Jie; dinner for two with drinks should come to around ¥60.

Evening **entertainment** prospects, aside from the night market, are poor. Try the Dazhong Cinema at the eastern end of Gulou Jie, or the Menghua Dancehall, on the south side of Dong Dajie, which is very popular with the students, though they only play slow numbers.

Listings

Airlines Buy air tickets at the CAAC office at the southwest corner of Zhongshan Lu and Sihou Jie (☎0378/5955555). The nearest airport is at Zhengzhou (see p.313).

Banks and exchange The Bank of China is on the north side of Gulou Jie (Mon–Fri 8am–noon & 2–4pm).

Bike rental You can rent decent bikes for ¥5 a day, with a ¥100 deposit, from a small cigarette and public-phone kiosk outside the *Yingbin Hotel* (daily 8am–11pm). You'll have to ask, as though a sign in Chinese announces the service, bikes are kept inside, making the stand easy to miss.

Bookshops The Xinhua Bookstore on the east side of Shudian Jie, not far from the intersection with Xi Dajie, has a limited selection of English books, but they do sell good maps. More fun is perusing the publications at the large night market that fills the Gulou area.

Buses The long-distance bus stations are pretty seedy-looking, and big noses will attract a lot of attention. Both Anyang and Zhengzhou (¥15) are only about ninety minutes away. The west station sells tickets to destinations west of the city such as Luoyang and Xi'an; the main station farther south serves all other destinations. You can buy tickets from the booking offices (daily 7am–6pm) or on the bus itself.

Mail and telephones There's a large, efficient post office on Ziyou Lu (Mon–Fri 8am–noon & 2.30–6pm), with a 24hr telecom office next door.

PSB The main police station is on Zhongshan Lu. The section that deals with visas is windows #3 and #4, where the staff are so laid-back they're almost hip; a visa extension (¥120) can take ten minutes.

Shopping Kaifeng is a good place to pick up art materials, among the best buys in China. Apart from the shops on Song Jie, there's a good, cheap art shop on the corner of Sihou Jie, not far from the intersection with Shudian Jie. For souvenirs, try Song Jie.

Trains The train station is small and not too hard to figure out. You can buy tickets at the station booking office or at the advance booking office at 70 Sihou Jie (Mon–Fri 8.30am–12.30pm & 2.30–4.30pm).

Travel agents Staff in the CITS office on 56 Ziyou Lu (☎0378/5666456) can be reluctant to help – your reception seems to depend on how much or how little you're willing to spend. They offer one- and two-day tours, sell train tickets (¥40 surcharge) and have a free map in English that is pretty inaccurate. It's east past the *Kaifeng Hotel*; head up an alley leading north and lined with tradesmen advertising their services – the office will 20m on your right.

Shandong

Shandong province, a fertile plain through which the Yellow River completes its journey, is shaped like an eagle launching itself into the sky – an appropriate image for a province beginning to assert itself after a fraught and stagnant past. For centuries Shandong languished as one of the poorest regions of China, over-populated and at the mercy of the Yellow River, whose course has continually shifted, its delta swinging over time from the Bohai Gulf in the north to the Yellow Sea in the south, bringing chaos with every move.

However, the fertility of the flood plain means that human settlements have existed here for more than six thousand years, with **Neolithic remains** found at two sites, Dawenkou and Longshan. Relics such as wheel-made pottery and carved jade indicate a surprisingly highly developed agricultural society. In the Warring States Period (720–221 BC) Shandong included the states of Qi and Lu, and the province is well endowed with **ancient tombs and temples**, the best of which are to be found on **Tai Shan**, China's holiest Taoist mountain near the centre of the province, and its most spectacular tourist site. A second major religious site is at **Qufu**, home of the province's most illustrious son, **Confucius**. Although he was ignored during his lifetime, the esteem in which he was held by later generations, and the power of his descendants, who were regarded as almost equal in status to the emperor, are graphically illustrated in the little town by the magnificence of the temple and the mansion in which his clan, the Kong, lived.

Shandong's modern history, though, is dominated by **foreign influence** and its ramifications. In 1897 the Germans arrived, occupying the port of **Qingdao** in the south of the province. They made themselves at home and today the city's streetscapes, which look transplanted from Bavaria, presiding over the best beaches in northern China, make it one of the finest-looking of all Chinese cities. The province's ugly contemporary capital, **Ji'nan**, soon followed, and German influence spread as they built a rail system across the province. Their legacy is still visible in the Teutonic forms of many of Shandong's train stations. At the beginning of the last century, resentment at foreign interference, exacerbated by floods and an influx of refugees from the south, combined to make Shandong the setting for the **Boxer Rebellion** (see p.1183).

Behind Qingdao's German facade is evidence of a new side to Shandong, and a sprawling mass of factories testifies to the rapid pace of modernization and industrialization. Qingdao is the main industrial town, with Ji'nan second, and most trade is done through the port of **Yantai**. The new **Shengli oilfield**, in the northeast, is China's second largest, and as large oil reserves in the Bohai sea bed have only just begun to be exploited, a massive economic resurgence seems on the cards. Shandong's **tourist industry** is also kicking off. Although the rail network is sparse, travelling around the province is made much easier by new highways which connect the major cities. One welcome feature of the province is the relative laxity of the rules on where foreigners are allowed to stay, and budget travellers will find the main sites, Tai Shan and Qufu, agreeably inexpensive. Another bonus is the friendliness of the people, who are proud of their reputation for hospitality, a tradition that goes right back to Confucius, who declared in *The Analects*, "Is it not a great pleasure to have guests coming from afar?"

Ji'nan

The capital of Shandong and a busy industrial city with three million inhabitants, **JI'NAN** is the province's major transit point and communication centre, which anyone travelling in the area is bound to visit at some point. It's possible to kill a day here, but tourist sights are unspectacular and the hotel situation is poor, the city is best thought of as a stop on the way to or from Qufu and Tai'an, a few hours south.

Though you'd never guess it, the city has an illustrious past. It stands on the site of one of China's **oldest settlements**, and pottery unearthed nearby has been dated to over four thousand years ago. The present town dates from the fourth century AD when Ji'nan was a military outpost and trading centre. The town expanded during the Ming dynasty, when the city walls were built – they're no longer standing but you can see where they were on any map by the moats that once surrounded them. Present development dates back to 1898, when the Germans obtained the right to build the Shandong rail lines. Track was laid from Qingdao, another German concession town, and the line completed in 1904. The city was opened up to foreign trade in 1906, and industrialized rapidly under the Germans, English and Japanese.

Ji'nan is famous in China for its **natural springs**, though these are presently showcased in typical Chinese city parks, and thus actually rather dull. Some of the nineteenth-century German and Japanese architecture remains, but Ji'nan's buildings aren't pretty: the fashion for facing buildings with white bathroom-style tiling seems to have reached its zenith here, and to Western eyes the city looks like an enormous complex of public conveniences. Outside the centre, one of the most rewarding ways to spend any time in the city is to stroll

Ji'nan

Ji'nan	济南	***jǐ'nán***
Black Tiger Spring	黑虎泉	*hēihǔ quán*
Daming Hu	大明湖	*dàmíng hú*
Longtan Park	龙潭公圆	*lóngtán gōngyuán*
Quancheng Square	泉城广场	*quánchéng guǎngchǎng*
Shandong Provincial Museum	山东省博物馆	*shāndōng shěng bówùguǎn*
Shandong Teachers' University	山东师范大学	*shāndōng shīfàn dàxué*
Thousand Buddha Mountain	千佛山	*qiānfó shān*
Accommodation and eating		
Guidu Hotel	贵都宾馆	*guìdū bīnguǎn*
Huiquan	汇泉饭店	*huìquán fàndiàn*
Ji'nan Hotel	济南大酒店	*jǐnán dàjiǔdiàn*
Ji'nan People's Market	人民商场	*rénmín shāngchǎng*
Ji'nan Roast Duck	济南烤鸭店	*jǐ'nán kǎoyādiàn*
Oriental Gourmet	东方美食城	*dōngfāng měishíchéng*
Qilu Hotel	齐鲁宾馆	*qílǔ bīnguǎn*
Sofitel	索菲特银座大酒店	*suǒfēitè yínzuò dàjiǔdiàn*
Railway Hotel	铁道大酒店	*tiědào dàjiǔdiàn*
Xibei'er Hotel	喜贝尔宾馆	*xǐbèiěr bīnguǎn*
Xuelin	学林大酒店	*xuélín dàjiǔdiàn*

through the **parks** with their attractive lakes, or slog your way up **Thousand Buddha Mountain** in the south.

Arrival, city transport and information

Ji'nan's **airport**, with international connections to Japan, South Korea and Hong Kong, is 40km east of the city, and served by an airport bus which drops you outside the CAAC office in the *Aviation Hotel*. Taxis from the airport into the city cost ¥150. The large and noisy main **train station**, at the junction of the north–south line between Beijing and Shanghai, and the line that goes east to Yantai and Qingdao, is in the northwest of town; you shouldn't have any problems buying tickets out at the train station itself. The long-distance **bus station** is nearly 2km due north of the train station. A parking lot-cum-station across the street from the train station is the place to hop on the **express bus** to **Qingdao** (4hr 30min; ¥95).

Most of the city's **bus routes** begin from the train station: bus #3 is the most useful, heading east into town along Quancheng Lu; #K54 goes south from the station to Daming Hu and the provincial museum. The mob of **taxi drivers** at the station are some of the most aggressive in China – it's better to walk some distance away and hail one yourself. Taxis are cheap, the ¥6 basic fare just about covering trips around the city centre. **CITS**, on Jingshu Lu southeast of the centre, can provide English-language **maps** and glossy brochures detailing the attractions of the city and province.

Accommodation

Ji'nan's **hotel** situation is awful, unless you have a generous budget. Most of the hotels that are allowed to take foreigners are inconveniently located and pricey. It's pretty hard find a room for less than ¥150, which is the same price as a taxi to Tai'an, a much nicer place altogether. The middle-aged women touting outside the station can be trusted to find you a cheap room, though note that this may well be at the *Xibei'er*, where some rooms were once used for karaoke – and have the decor to prove it.

Guidu 1 Shengping Lu ⓣ0531/6900888, ⓕ6900099. A rather ordinary ten-storey place, very close to the train station; not great value. ❹

Ji'nan 240 Jing San Lu ⓣ0531/7938981. At least this solid, characterless place has a good location. ❹

Qilu 8 Qianfoshan Lu ⓣ0531/2966888, ⓕ2967676. One of Ji'nan's plusher places, in the south of the city near the universities. The staff are friendly and speak English. Breakfast included. ❻

Railway Hotel Train Station ⓣ0531/6012118. Three-star, comfy place attached to the station front, convenient for transport but a long way from the interesting part of town. ❺

Sofitel Silver Plaza 66 Luoyuan Dajie ⓣ0531/606888, ⓕ6066666. The pinnacle of luxury in Ji'nan, right in the heart of the city overlooking Quanshi Square. The Sunday brunch (¥228 for two) includes use of the pool. Rates often discounted by a third. ❾

Xibei'er Hotel Jin'er Lu ⓣ0531/7933238. A popular deposit point for station touts, this place passes as Ji'nan's budget option. It's near the station, in a quiet neighborhood with some old-fashioned architecture. Ask to see the room first, as some are converted karaoke salons without windows – but with padding on the walls and a disco ball. The attached restaurant is good. Beds ¥60, ❷

Xuelin Hotel 80 Wenhua Dong Lu ⓣ0531/2963388. On the main bustling strip of the University District, southeast of the centre. The best mid-range choice. ❹

The City

Ji'nan is frustratingly spread out, and there's no real downtown shopping district. The biggest shopping streets are to be found just south of Daming Hu,

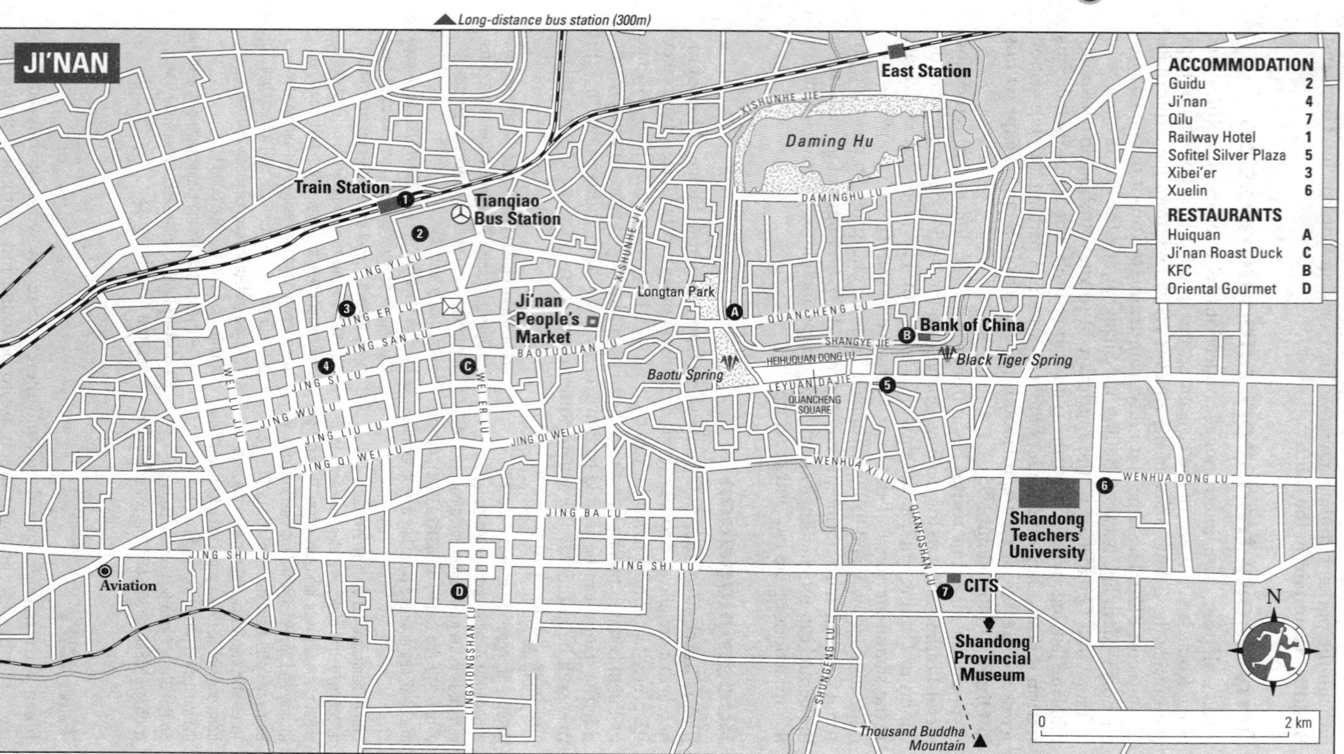
JI'NAN
ACCOMMODATION
Guidu 2
Ji'nan 4
Qilu 7
Railway Hotel 1
Sofitel Silver Plaza 5
Xibei'er 3
Xuelin 6
RESTAURANTS
Huiquan A
Ji'nan Roast Duck C
KFC B
Oriental Gourmet D
Long-distance bus station (300m)
East Station
Daming Hu
XISHUNHE JIE
DAMINGHU LU
Train Station
Tianqiao Bus Station
JING YI LU
JING ER LU
JING SAN LU
JING SI LU
JING WU LU
JING LIU LU
JING QI WEI LU
WEI LU JIU
WEI ER LU
Ji'nan People's Market
BAOTUQUAN LU
Longtan Park
QUANCHENG LU
Bank of China
SHANGYE JIE
HEIHUQUAN DONG LU
Black Tiger Spring
Baotu Spring
LEYUAN DAJIE
QUANCHENG SQUARE
WENHUA XI LU
WENHUA DONG LU
Shandong Teachers' University
JING BA LU
JING SHI LU
QIANFOSHAN LU
CITS
Shandong Provincial Museum
Aviation
LINGXIONGSHAN LU
SHUNGENG LU
Thousand Buddha Mountain
N
0
2 km

Ji'nan's springs

The area south of Daming Hu is bounded by streams and fed by the **springs** which, bafflingly, are regarded as the city's main attraction – a case of historical precedent overriding reality. Always synonymous with Ji'nan, the springs were once impressive sights, and acquired their romantic names around the tenth and eleventh centuries, when they were compared by poets to pearls arising from the earth and tigers springing from their lairs; the poet Li Fenggao wrote of Qing-era Ji'nan, "Waterlilies on four sides, willows on three, half the city is a mountain, half is a lake." Though they once earned the town a reputation for cleanliness and health, these days the springs resemble little more than muddy pools. Some don't even seem to exist any more, others are slyly assisted with hoses; pollution and droughts seem to have caused the drying up. The most famous is **Black Tiger Spring** on Heihuquan Dong Lu, which rises from a subterranean cave and emerges through tiger-headed spouts. The stone pools here are a popular bathing spot.

while a little further south, the enormous rectangular Quancheng Square, easily identiable on maps, marks the city centre. The ordered blocks west of here, south of the train station, are among the oldest in town and vaguely atmospheric, though most of the attractions are in the southern suburbs.

There are a few sights in Ji'nan worth checking out while you're waiting for connections. The **park** around Daming Hu (daily 6am–6pm; ¥10), on the route of bus #11 from the train station, is quite pleasant, containing some quaint gardens, pavilions and bridges, and the lake is edged with willow trees and sprinkled with water lilies. On an island in the centre, the **Li Xia Pavilion** holds portraits of the Tang poet Du Fu and the calligrapher Li Yong, who were supposed to have met here. To the south is the **Memorial Hall** to Xin Qiji, a famous Song poet banished for his political views and his poems criticizing the monarch for failing to resist the Jin invasion from the north. A pleasant and restrained building, it has a couple of courtyards and exhibition halls displaying calligraphy.

Longtan Park (6am–6pm; ¥5), southwest of here on the route of bus #3 from the train station, is nice enough, though little remains of its three springs, which were mentioned in the *Spring and Autumn Annals*, government texts of 694 BC. **Luoyuan Pavilion** on the north side was originally constructed in the Song dynasty, and is inscribed with a couplet by Zhao Mengfu, a thirteenth-century artist, which reads: "Clouds and mist in wet vapours, glory unfixed; the sound of the waves thunders in the Lake of Great Brightness." In the east of the park, next to the trickle that is "Gushing from the Ground Spring", is the **Hall to Commemorate Li Qingzhao**, one of China's most famous woman poets, born in 1084 in Ji'nan. The modern hall contains portraits, extracts from her work, and poems and paintings by well-known contemporary artists.

Thousand Buddha Mountain and the provincial museum

The other scenic spot worth a trip is **Thousand Buddha Mountain** (daily 8am–6pm; ¥10), to the south of the city, on the route of bus #K54, which leaves from a terminus in the southwest corner of Daming Park; the journey is about 5km. The mountainside is leafy and tracked with winding paths, the main one lined with painted opera masks. Most of the original statues that once dotted the slopes, free-standing images of Buddhas and Bodhisattvas, were destroyed by Red Guards, but new ones are being added, largely paid for by donations from overseas Chinese. The new statues, though, tend not to have the simplicity and purity of the old. It's quite a climb to the summit (2hr), but the sculptures, and the view, get better the higher you go. Behind the **Xingguo Si** near the top are some superb sixth-century Buddhist carvings. The temple courtyard contains a sculpture of the mythical Emperor Shun, supposed to have reigned around 2000 BC, who, legend has it, ploughed the soil in Ji'nan, as well as inventing the writing brush.

Near the mountain, and accessible on the same bus, the **Shandong Provincial Museum** (daily 8.30–noon & 1.30–5.30pm; ¥10) contains a number of fine Buddhist carvings as well as exhibits from the excavations at Longshan and Dawenkou, two nearby Neolithic sites noted for the delicate black pottery unearthed there. The remains date back to 5000–2000 BC and consist mostly of pottery and stone and shell farming implements. The society is judged to have been agricultural, settled and fairly sophisticated, practising ancestor worship. Also on display is China's earliest extant book, found at a Han tomb nearby. Preceding the invention of paper, the book was written with brush and ink on thin strips of bamboo which were then sewn together. It includes a full calendar for the year 134 BC, and a number of military and philosophical texts, including Sun Bin's *Art of War*. Though these exhibits are historically very important, it does take a degree of imagination to find them impressive in themselves.

Eating and drinking

To fill up inexpensively, head for **Wenhua Dong Lu**, the road cleaving the University District. Tell the cab driver to take you to the *Shifan Daxue*, the gate of the Teachers' University, around which are a slew of great dumpling and home-style eating places, along with music and book shops; *KFC* and *McDonald's* are also nearby. The area gets boisterous at night, when vendors set up on the sidewalks. West of the centre, the Ji'nan People's Market, a shopping mall on Baotuquan Lu, is well stocked with flash restaurants and fast-food places.

If you want to eat out in style, the glitzy *Ji'nan Roast Duck Restaurant*, at 10 Wei Er Lu, is a candidate, serving excellent Beijing-style roast duck, not cheap at ¥100 per person. The *Oriental Gourmet Restaurant*, at 188 Yingxiongshan Lu, is also pricey, serving Shandong specialities such as carp and scorpion. The same dishes are available for a little less outlay at the *Huiquan Restaurant*, at 22 Baotuquan Lu.

Listings

Airlines The main CAAC office is at the *Aviation Hotel* on Jing Qiwei Lu (☎0531/6018145). It's easier is to get your tickets from the tour offices surrounding and inside the *Sofitel* on Luoyan Dajie.

Banks and exchange The Bank of China is at 10 Shangye Jie, just east of the centre (Mon–Fri 8.30am–noon & 2–4.30pm).

Bookshops The Foreign Language Bookstore is on Quancheng Lu, opposite the Baihua building and very near Ji'nan People's Market (see above).

Buses Ji'nan's main long-distance bus station has services to Beijing, Tai'an and Qufu. Minibuses for the latter destinations also leave from in front of the train station. For Qingdao, board one of the luxury coaches (4hr 30min; ¥95) from the terminus across from the train station – look for the green-uniformed attendants.

Mail and telephones Ji'nan's main post office is on Wei Er Lu at the intersection with Jing Er Lu (Mon–Sat 8am–6pm). There's a 24hr telecom office inside.

Shopping The most impressive department store is the Ji'nan People's Market, an enormous mall on Baotuquan Lu. There's also an arts and crafts store on 88 Jing Shi Lu. At night, go to Wenhua Dong Lu, in the University District, where there's a boisterous market purveying bric-a-bric, CDs and the like.

Travel agents Dealing mainly with tour groups, CITS is at 86 Jing Shi Lu %0531/2965858, close to the *Qilu Hotel*.

Tai'an and Tai Shan

Tai Shan is not just a mountain, it's a god. Lying 100km south of Ji'nan, it's the easternmost and holiest of China's five holy Taoist mountains (the other four being Hua Shan, the two Heng Shans and Song Shan), and has been worshipped by the Chinese for longer than recorded history. It is justifiably famed for its scenery and the ancient buildings strung out along its slopes. Once host to emperors and the devout, it's now Shandong's biggest tourist attraction. The walk up is sometimes tacky, often engrossing, occasionally beautiful – and always hard work.

The town of **Tai'an** lies at the base of the mountain, and for centuries has prospered from the busy traffic of pilgrims coming to pay their respects to the mountain. You'll quickly become aware just how popular the pilgrimage is – on certain holy days ten thousand people might be making their way to the peak, and year round the town sees over half a million visitors.

Tai'an

TAI'AN is unremarkable, but it's not unpleasant. There's a small-town atmosphere, with buildings that are not too grand and streets not too wide. It's just

Tai'an and Tai Shan

Tai'an	泰安	***tà'iān***
Dai Miao	岱庙	*dài miào*
Puzhao Si	普照寺	*pǔzhào sì*
Accommodation		*Accommodation*
Liangmao Dasha	粮贸大厦	*liángmào dàshà*
Longtan	龙潭宾馆	*lóngtán bīnguǎn*
Overseas Chinese Hotel	华侨大厦	*huáqiáo dàshà*
Taishan Binguan	泰山宾馆	*tàishān bīnguǎn*
Tai Shan	泰山	***tàishān***
Bixia Si	碧霞祠	*bixiá cí*
Black Dragon Pool	黑龙潭	*hēilóng tán*
Bridge of the God	仙人桥	*xiānrén qiáo*
Cable Car	索道站	*suǒdào zhàn*
Cloud Bridge	云步桥	*yúnbù qiáo*
Dou Mu Convent	斗母宫	*doùmǔ gōng*
Five Pines Pavilion	五松亭	*wǔsōng tíng*
Hongmen Gong	红门宫	*hóngmén gōng*
Jade Emperor's Summit	玉皇	*yùhuáng*
Nantianmen	南天门	*nántiān mén*
Pavilion of the Teapot Sky	壶天阁	*hútiān gé*
Sheng Xian Fang	升仙房	*shēngxiān fáng*
Stone Sutra Ravine	泾石谷	*jīngshí gǔ*
Sun Viewing Point	日观峰	*rìguān fēng*
Tower of Myriad Spirits	万仙楼	*wànxiān lóu*
Wangmu Chi	王母池	*wángmǔ chí*
Yitianmen	一天门	*yītiān mén*
Yuhuang Ding	玉皇顶	*yùhuáng dǐng*
Zhanlu Terrace	占鲁台	*zhànlǔ tái*
Zhongtianmen	中天门	*zhōngtiān mén*
Zhongtianmen Hotel	中天门宾馆	*zhōngtiānmén bīnguǎn*

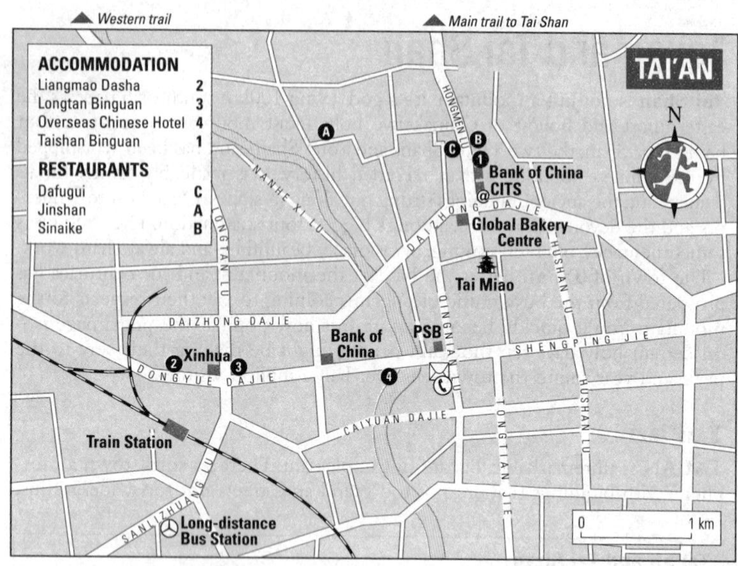

small enough to cover on foot, though few people pay it much attention; the town is overshadowed, literally, by the great mountain just to the north.

Dongyue Dajie is the largest street, a corridor of new highrises running east–west across town. Qingnian Lu, the main **shopping street**, leads north off its eastern end. The trailhead is reached on Hongmen Lu, which is flanked by a string of souvenir shops selling gnarled walking sticks made from tree roots, and shoes. Just south of Daizhong Dajie, in the north, are some busy **market streets** selling medicinal herbs which grow on the mountain, such as ginseng, the tuber of the multiflower knotweed, and Asian puccoon, along with strange vegetables, bonsai trees and potted plants.

Dai Miao

Tai'an's main sight is the **Dai Miao** (daily 7.30am–6pm; ¥20), the traditional starting point for the procession up Tai'an, where emperors once made sacrifices and offerings to the mountain. It's a magnificent structure, with yellow-tiled roofs, red walls and towering old trees, one of the largest temples in the country and one of the most celebrated. Though it appears an ordered whole, the temple complex is really a blend of buildings from different belief systems, with veneration of the mountain as the only constant factor.

The Main Hall, **Tiankuangdian** (Hall of the Celestial Gift), is matched in size only by halls in the Forbidden City and at Qufu. The hall's construction started as early as the Qin dynasty (221–206 BC), though construction and renovation have gone on ever since, particularly during the Tang and Song dynasties. Completed in 1009, it was restored in 1956 and is in an excellent state of preservation. Inside is a huge mural fully covering three of the walls. This Song-dynasty masterpiece depicts the God of Tai Shan on an inspection tour and hunting expedition. It's really a massive ego trip as the painting was produced to celebrate the deification of the mountain by Emperor Zhen Zong, who also built the temple, and there is a strong resemblance between the God of the Mountain in the painting and Zhen Zong himself. These days the mural isn't in great shape, but some of its original glory remains and you can still see most of the figures of its cast of thousands, each rendered with painstaking attention to the details of facial expression and gesture. There is also a statue of the God of Tai Shan, enthroned in a niche and dressed in flowing robes, holding the oblong tablet which is the insignia of his authority. The five sacrificial vessels laid before him bear the symbols of the five peaks.

Today the courtyards and the temple gardens are used as an open-air museum for **steles**. It's an impressive collection, covering a timespan of over two thousand years. The oldest, inside the Dongyuzuo Hall, celebrates the visit of Emperor Qin and his son in the third century BC. Many of the great calligraphers are represented, and for aesthetically inclined Chinese this place is unmissable. Calligraphy is an art of great subtlety and refinement, but even the untrained Western eye can find something to appreciate here. Charcoal rubbings of the steles can be bought from the mercifully discreet souvenir shops inside the temple complex. The courtyard also contains ancient cypresses, gingkos and acacias, including five cypresses supposedly planted by the Han emperor Wu Di.

The other temple halls are also used as **museums**. One houses a collection of early sacrificial vessels and some exquisite Tang pottery, while another is given over to the Chinese art of cutting and polishing tree roots. The art lies not in what is done to the root, but in its selection; the roots are picked for their abstract beauty and figurative connotations.

In a side courtyard at the back of the complex is the Temple of Yanxi. A Taoist resident on the mountain, Yanxi was linked with the mountain cult of the Tang dynasty. A separate Taoist hall at the rear is devoted to the Wife of the Mountain, a deity who seems somewhat of an afterthought, appearing much later than her spouse.

Practicalities

Arriving at the **train station**, a modern affair on the line south from Ji'nan to Shanghai, you'll be greeted by a mob of eager taxi drivers. The minimum fare of ¥5 is sufficient for rides in town, with no more than ¥7 required to reach the mountain. If you're here on a day-trip, drop your bag at the **left-luggage stand** (¥3) aside the ticket office. Bypass the tourist office advertising in English on your right as you exit; they don't speak English and have little by way of maps or lodging advice. Buses from Ji'nan and Qufu terminate at the long-distance **bus station** on Sanlizhuang Lu, south of the train station.

The town's four **bus routes** all leave from or stop at a terminus just north of the train station. Bus #3 is the most useful, looping from the beginning of the main Tai Shan trail head to the train station and north again to the beginning of the western trail route. Bus #2 goes from the south to the north of the town, from Hongmen Lu to Dongyue Dajie, while buses #1 and #4 traverse the east–west axis, both travelling along Shengping Jie.

The **post office** is on Dongyue Dajie (Mon–Fri 8am–6pm), near the junction with Qingnian Lu, and the **Bank of China** is located on Hongmen Lu (Mon–Fri 8am–noon & 1.30–6pm), near the *Taishan Binguan*, though you can also change money in the hotel. A helpful English-speaking branch of **CITS** is just a few doors down from the hotel at 22 Hongmen Lu (Ⓣ0538/8223259, Ⓦwww.taishan-cits.com). It's not easy to find as there's no nameplate outside; go through the arch into the courtyard and CITS occupies the building directly in front.

Moving on from Tai'an, buses congregate on the east side of the train-station concourse. During daylight hours, minibuses leave every half-hour for Qufu (¥13) and every twenty minutes for Ji'nan (¥12.5). Trains to either of these destinations are also readily available, though Tai'an is a better place to spend the night than dull Ji'nan.

Accommodation

It's worth considering staying at the hotels **on the mountain** (see p.340), if you can stand slogging up there with your gear, as the surroundings are more pleasant and the prices not unreasonable. Arguably the most worthwhile place to stay in Tai'an itself is the *Taishan Binguan* (Ⓣ0538/8224678, Ⓕ8221432; ❺), a five-storey place conveniently located at the beginning of the main Tai Shan trail on Hongmen Lu. The hotel has a good restaurant, and most of the services you could want, including the Bank of China, CITS and souvenir shops, are nearby. Another option, the *Liangmao Dasha* (Ⓣ0538/8228212; ❸, beds ¥30), is conveniently situated near the train station and offers a range of rooms.

For rock-bottom, no-frills accommodation, try the two-star *Longtan Binguan* on the corner of Longtan Lu and Dongyue Dajie (Ⓣ0538/8293688, ❹). At the other end of the scale, the four-star *Overseas Chinese Hotel* on Dongyue Dajie is the most exclusive place to stay in town (Ⓣ0538/8228112, Ⓕ8228171; ❼), gleaming like a tiara but with as much character as a plastic cup. It's nineteen storeys high, with a gym, sauna and swimming pool.

Uniquely for a tourist mecca, the **PSB** on Qingnian Lu (Ⓣ0538/8224004) doesn't seem to care where you stay, so if your budget is really tight, try some of the grotty places round the **station**. They don't have English signs, so look for the characters for *binguan* (see p.1263). You should get a room for around ¥50, less for a dorm, but don't expect anyone to speak English.

Eating and drinking

A speciality of **Tai'an cuisine** is red-scaled carp, fresh from pools on the mountain and fried while it's still alive. Other dishes from the mountain include chicken stewed with *siliquose pelvetia* (a fungus only found within 2m of the ancient pine trees around the Nine Dragon Hill), coral herb and hill lilac. The best **restaurants** are in the *Taishan Binguan* and *Overseas Chinese Hotel*, which serve Western dishes as well as the local specialities; a meal for two at either place, with vegetable and meat dishes as well as drinks, should come to around ¥80. The *Overseas Chinese Hotel* even has an Italian restaurant (among fifteen others), but you're better off sticking to the first-floor Chinese one, which is more reasonably priced.

There are some other good places to eat along Hongmen Lu, including the *Sinaike Restaurant*, a cheap diner that serves generous portions, and the *Dafugui Restaurant* over the road, a classy place with equally classy prices. For seafood try the colourfully decorated *Jinshan Restaurant* in the north of town. Stock up on picnic staples for the ascent of the mountain at the *Global Bakery Centre*, at 7 Hongmen Lu.

Tours

Apart from trips up the mountain, which you'd be better off doing under your own steam, CITS runs two **tours** that are worth considering. The **Buyang Village Tour** is a chance to visit a real, dusty, ramshackle Chinese village and get a taste of rural life. You can go fishing with the locals or try your hand at making dumplings, and if you're really interested you can stay the night at a farmer's house. You'll need to get a group of four or five together, and the tour costs ¥120 per person, dinner included.

Another tour (¥50 per person) is by taxi to the **Puzhao Si** to see a venerable old Taoist monk, a *qi gong* master who can apparently swallow needles and thread them with his tongue. Don't expect a performing clown – he only does his stuff when he feels like it. This tour gets mixed reactions, and some visitors have reported feeling intrusive.

Tai Shan

More so than any other holy mountain, **Tai Shan** was the haunt of emperors, and owes its obvious glories – the temples and pavilions along its route – to the patronage of the imperial court. From its summit, a succession of emperors surveyed their empires, made sacrifices and paid tribute. Sometimes their retinues stretched right from the top to the bottom of the mountain, eight kilometres of pomp and ostentatious wealth. In 219 BC, Emperor Qin Shi Huang had **roads** built all over the mountain so that he could ride here in his carriage under escort of the royal guards when he was performing the grand ceremonies of *feng* (sacrifices to heaven) and *chan* (offerings to earth). Participating in such ceremonies was seen as the greatest possible honour a court official could be granted. When the historiographer Sima Tan discovered he could not accompany the emperor to the summit he was said to be so distressed he was still weeping over it on his deathbed. Various titles were offered to the mountain by emperors keen to bask in reflected glory. In 725, the mountain was granted the title of King Equal to the Sky, and in 1101, it was promoted to Emperor. As well as funding the temples, emperors had their visits and thoughts recorded for posterity on steles here, and men of letters carved poems and tributes to the mountain on any available rockface. The path up the mountain is like a huge open-air museum of religion and rule spanning the whole length of Chinese history.

It's also a giant **tourist attraction**. The twentieth century's contribution to the mountain's illustrious architectural history has been its mutation into a religious theme park, and the path is now thronged with a constant procession of tourists. There are photo booths, souvenir stalls, soft-drinks vendors and teahouses. You can get your name inscribed on a medal, get your photograph taken and buy fungus and ginseng from vendors squatting on walls. Halfway up there's a **bus station** and **cable car**. Yet somehow, despite all this, Tai Shan still retains an atmosphere of grandeur; the buildings and the mountain itself are magnificent enough to survive their trivialization.

It is surprising, though, to see that numbering among the hordes of tourists are a great many genuine **pilgrims**. Taoism, after a long period of Communist proscription, is again alive and flourishing, and you're more than likely to see a bearded Taoist monk, or an ancient Shandong peasant woman shuffling up by inches with bound feet. Women come specifically to pray to **Bixia Yuan Jun**, the Princess of the Rosy Clouds, a Taoist deity believed to be able to help childless women conceive. As well as its central position in the official imperial religion, Tai Shan plays an important role in the **folk beliefs** of the Shandong peasantry. In villages in the area, the first stone in the foundations of a house is inscribed with the name of the mountain as a protection against it falling down, and blind alleys have a Tai Shan stone to deter evil spirits. Tradition has it that anyone who has climbed Tai Shan will live to be 100.

The other figures you will see are the streams of **porters**, balancing enormous weights on their shoulder poles, moving swiftly up the mountain and then galloping down again for a fresh load. They carry supplies and building materials for the hotels, restaurants and temples at the top. It's a traditional job, handed down from father to son, and well paid, but the job takes its toll and most workers past their 30s have distorted backs. It's impossible not to admire their stamina; they may make three trips a day, six days a week.

For ordinary mortals, once is tiring enough. There are more than 6,000 steps; to begin with the path is wide and not too steep, but after the midway point climb endless narrow staircases. (You can save your legs by taking the cable car from the midway point to the peak.) The trip down is even more wearying on the legs, and though it's possible to go up and down by foot in one day, the next will probably find you in bed for the duration. The seriously fit can take part in the annual **Tai Shan Race**, held in early September (check with CITS for dates), which has a prize for the best foreigner competing.

Mountain practicalities

Tai Shan looms at 1545m high, and it's about 8km from the base to the top. There are two main **paths** up the mountain: the grand historical central route, and a quieter, more scenic western route. There's a charge of ¥80 to use each path from February through to October, inclusive or ¥60 from November to January. The walk up takes about four or five hours, half that if you rush it, and the trip down takes two to three hours. Offically, both path gates are open 24 hours, though evening hikers should bring torches and head up by the central route – which is in fact the one most walkers use for the ascent – while descending by the western route; this is the circuit we've assumed in the account that follows. For the central route, walk uphill on Hongmen Lu from the Taishan Binguan, or catch bus #3 or #9 along the way or from the train station. To reach the western route, take bus #3 (¥1) to the last stop, Tianwaicun, or a taxi (¥5). Cross the street, ascend the stairs dotted with decorated columns, then descend to the bus park.

The paths converge at **Zhongtianmen**, the midway point (more often than not, climbers using the western route actually take a **bus** to Zhongtianmen, costing ¥16). The truly sedentary can then complete the journey by **cable car** (¥45 one-way). You can also head up to Zhongtianmen with a CITS **tour** (¥100).

Whatever the **weather** is in Tai'an, it's usually freezing at the top of the mountain and always unpredictable. The average **temperature** at the summit is 18°C in summer, dropping to -9°C in winter. The summit conditions are posted outside the ticket windows at the west route. You should take warm clothing and a waterproof and wear walking shoes, though indomitable Chinese tourists ascend dressed in T-shirts and plimsolls, even high heels. The best time to climb is in spring or autumn, outside the humid months. If you can tolerate the cold and want to miss the hordes, there are a number of clear winter days, though fewer hours of daylight in which to climb.

There are plenty of affordable eating places along the first leg up to Zhongtianmen, but it's a good idea to take your own **food** as well, as the fare on offer past the midway point is unappealing and gets more expensive the higher you go.

If you want to see the sunrise, you can stay at the **guesthouses** on the mountain, or risk climbing at night – take a flashlight and warm clothes. Don't be fooled by the floodlights lining the path – only some of them are ever lit, and in the winter months sunset can be as early as 4.30pm.

The ascent

If you're using the central route, your ascent will begin from **Daizhong Fang**, a stone arch just to the north of the Dai Miao in Tai'an. North of the arch and on the right is a pool, **Wangmu Chi**, and a small and rather quaint-looking nunnery, from where you can see the whimsically named Hornless Dragon Pool and Combing and Washing River. In the main hall of the nunnery is a

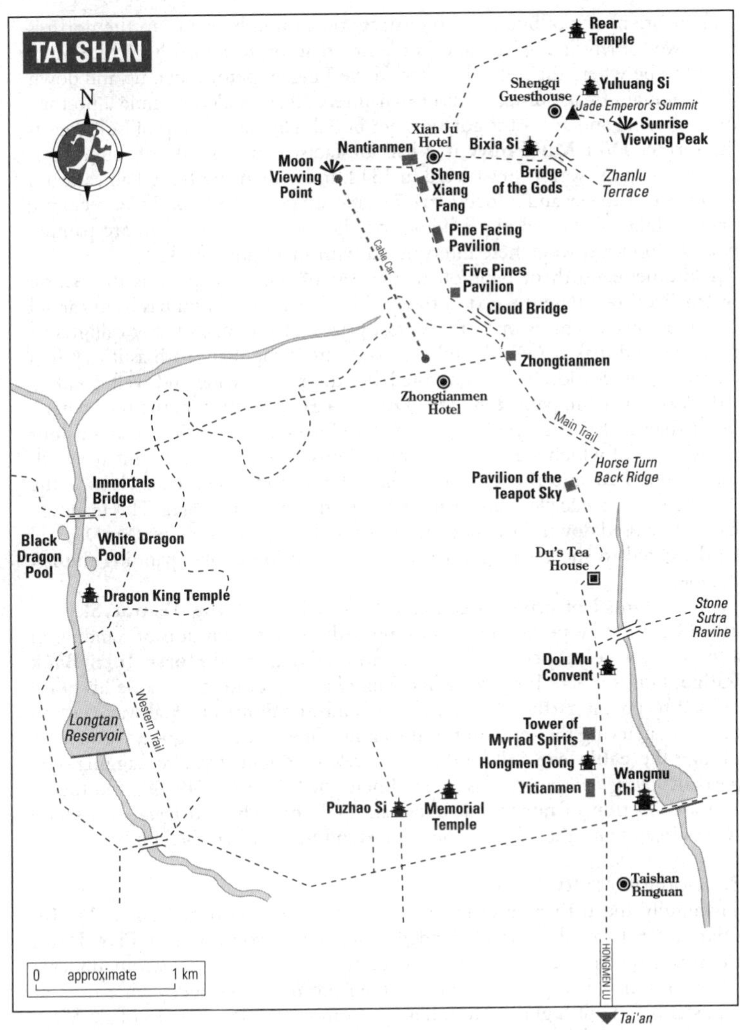

statue of Xiwang Mu, Queen Mother of the West, the major female deity in Taoism.

Yitianmen to Zhongtianmen

About 500m up is the official start of the path at **Yitianmen** (First Heavenly Gate). This is followed by a Ming arch, said to mark the spot where Confucius began his climb, and the **Hongmen Gong** (Red Gate Palace), where emperors used to change into sensible clothes for the ascent, and where you buy your ticket, which includes insurance. Built in 1626, Hongmen Gong is the first of a series of temples dedicated to the Princess of the Rosy Clouds. It got its name from the two red rocks to the northwest, which together resemble an arch.

There are plenty of buildings to distract you around here. Just to the north is the Tower of Myriad Spirits, and just below that the Tomb of the White Mule is said to be where the mule that carried the Tang emperor Xuan up and down the mountain finally dropped dead, exhausted. Xuan made the mule a posthumous general and at least it got a decent burial. The next group of buildings is the former **Dou Mu Convent**, a hall for Taoist nuns. Its date of founding is uncertain, but it was reconstructed in 1542. Today there are three halls, a drum tower, a bell tower and a locust tree outside supposed to look like a reclining dragon. Like all the temple buildings on the mountain, the walls are painted with a blood-red wash, here interspersed with small grey bricks.

A kilometre north of here, off to the east of the main path, is the **Stone Sutra Ravine** where the text of the Buddhist Diamond Sutra has been carved on the rockface. This is one of the most prized of Tai Shan's many calligraphic works, and makes a worthwhile diversion from the main path as it's set in a charming, quiet spot. It's unsignposted, but the path is wide and well trodden.

Back on the main path, don't miss **Du's Tea House**, built on the spot where, more than a thousand years ago, General Cheng Yao Jing Tang planted four pines, three of which are still alive. The teahouse and everything in it was built out of polished tree roots, which makes the interior look a fairyland – the "maiden tea" is excellent and a speciality of this mountain area. The teahouse has been passed down through generations, and the present owner, Mr Du, will be delighted to show you photos of tourists and log books spanning the last decade.

After a tunnel of cypress trees, and the **Pavilion of the Teapot Sky** (so called because the peaks all around supposedly give the illusion of standing in a teapot), you see a sheer cliff rising in front of you, called **Horse Turn Back Ridge**. This is where Emperor Zhen Zong had to dismount because his horse refused to go any farther. Not far above is **Zhongtianmen** (Halfway Gate to Heaven), marking the midpoint of the climb. There are some good views here, though the **cable car** will be the most welcome sight if you're flagging. The pleasant *Zhongtianmen Hotel* is situated here (☎0538/8226740; ❺), and there's also a collection of rather dull restaurants. Confusingly, you have to descend two staircases and then follow the road round to continue the climb.

Zhongtianmen to the top

Thankfully the path is level for a while after this. The next sight is **Yunbu Qiao** (Step Over the Clouds Bridge), after which you arrive at **Five Pines Pavilion**, where the first Qin Emperor took shelter from a storm under a group of pines. The grateful emperor then promoted the lucky pine trees to ministers of the fifth grade. From here you can see the lesser peaks of Tai Shan: the Mountain of Symmetrical Pines, the Flying Dragon Crag and Hovering Phoenix Ridge.

Farther up you pass under **Sheng Xian Fang** (the Archway to Immortality), which, according to mountain myth, assures your longevity and provides the viewpoint that inspired Tang poet Li Bai to write: "In a long breath by the heavenly gate, the fresh wind comes from a thousand miles away", though by this point most climbers are long past being able to appreciate poetry, let alone compose it.

The **final section** of the climb is the hardest, as the stone stairs are steep and narrow, climbing almost vertically between two walls of rocks. Each step, often through thick white mist, towards Nantianmen standing black against the sky at the top, calls for great effort, and pairs of fit young men offer rides on homemade sedan chairs to the exhausted.

On reaching the top you enter **Tian Jie** (Heaven Street), and the Tai Shan theme park, where you can buy an "I climbed Tai Shan" tie-dyed T-shirt or a plastic necklace, slurp a pot noodle and get your picture taken dressed as an emperor. There are a couple of **restaurants** here, **hotels** and a few **shops**. This thriving little tourist village on the top of a mountain represents a triumph of the profit motive over the elements; the weather is really not hospitable up here in the clouds, and often it's so misty you can hardly see from one souvenir stall to the next. In the middle of the street is Elephant Trunk Peak, which, it's planned, will become the terminal station of a funicular railway. If you want to stay the night, the best option is the three-star *Shenqi Guesthouse* (☎0538/8223866; ❻, beds ¥140) above the Bixia Si. There's a pricey restaurant, and an alarm bell that tells you when to get up for the sunrise. At no. 2 Tian Jie is the *Xian Ju Hotel* (☎0538/8226877; ❺, dorm beds ¥100).

The **Bixia Si**, on the southern slopes of the summit, is the final destination for most of the bona fide pilgrims, and offerings are made to a bronze statue of the princess in the main hall. It's a working temple, not a tourist trap, and its guardians enforce strict rules about where the merely curious are allowed to wander. It's also a splendid building, the whole place tiled with iron to resist wind damage, and all the decorations are metal, too. The bells hanging from the eaves, the mythological animals on the roof, and even the two steles outside are bronze. From 1759 until the fall of the Qing, the emperor would send an official here on the eighteenth day of the fourth lunar month each year to make an offering. Just below is a small shrine to Confucius, at the place where he was supposed to have commented, "the world is small".

At the **Yuhuang Si** (Jade Emperor Temple), you have truly arrived at the highest point of the mountain, and a rock with the characters for "supreme summit" carved on it stands within the courtyard. In Chinese popular religion, which mixes Taoism and Confucianism with much earlier beliefs, the Jade Emperor is the supreme ruler of heaven, depicted in an imperial hat with bead curtains hanging down his face. Outside the temple is the **Wordless Monument**, thought to have been erected by Emperor Wu, more than two thousand years ago. The story goes that Wu wanted to have an inscription engraved that would do justice to his merits. None of the drafts he commissioned came up to scratch, however, so he left the stele blank, leaving everything to the imagination of posterity.

Southeast of here is the peak for **watching the sunrise**, where hundreds of visitors gather every morning before dawn. It was here that the Song emperor performed the *feng* ceremony, building an altar and making sacrifices to heaven, in 1008. On a clear day you can see 200km to the coast, and at night you can see the lights of Ji'nan. "From the pinnacle," the Tang poet Du Fu said, "all eight corners under the sky are in view." There are numerous trails from here to fancifully named scenic spots – Fairy Bridge, Celestial Candle Peak, and the like. If the weather is good, it's a great place for aimless wandering.

The descent

The best way to descend is down the **western trail**, which is longer, quieter and has some impressive views. It starts at Zhongtianmen, loops round and joins the main trail back at the base of the mountain. Midway is the **Black Dragon Pool**, a dark, brooding pond, home of the Tai Shan speciality dish, red-scaled carp, once so precious that the fish was used as tribute to the court. Near the bottom, the **Puzhao Si** (Temple of Universal Clarity) is a pretty complex, mostly Qing, though there has been a temple on this site for more than 1500 years. It's east of the western trail, though access is via the road which runs around the base of the mountain.

Qufu and around

QUFU, a dusty rural town in the south of Shandong, easily accessible by bus or train from Tai'an, 100km north, and Ji'nan, 180km away, is quiet and pretty with an agreeably sluggish feel, but of great historical and cultural importance. **Confucius** was born here around 551 BC, taught here – largely unappreciated – for much of his life, and was buried just outside the town, in what became a sacred burial ground for his clan, the Kong. All around the town, despite a flurry of destructive zeal during the Cultural Revolution, is architectural evidence of the esteem in which he was held by successive dynasties – most monumentally by the Ming, who were responsible for the two dominant sights, the **Confucius Mansion** and the **Confucius Temple**, whose scale seems more suited to Beijing.

Qufu is a great hassle-free place to stop over for a few days, with plenty to see concentrated in a small area. It's small enough to walk everywhere, along unpolluted streets with little traffic – there are even benches to sit on, and trees full of singing birds. The compactness of the centre, however, also means that it's hard to blend in with the crowd, and you may be the object of the usual tourist hustle. If it all gets too much, remember the words of the master himself: "A gentleman understands what is moral, a base man understands only what is profitable." You could always escape to the Confucius Forest nearby, where you can lose yourself amid the eerie, twisted cypresses. Around the end of September, on Confucius's birthdate in the lunar calendar, the pace of the town picks up when a **festival** is held here and reconstructions of many of the original rituals are performed at the temple.

The Town

Orientation is easy, as the centre of town lies at the crossroads of Gulou Dajie and Zhonglou Jie, just east of the temple and mansion. There's not much reason to leave this area except to visit the **Confucian Forest** in the northern suburbs. The centre is a Confucius theme park, with a mass of shopping oppor-

Qufu and around

Qufu	曲阜	***qǔfù***
Bell Tower	钟楼	*zhōng lóu*
Confucian Forest	孔林	*kǒng lín*
Confucius Temple	孔庙	*kǒng miào*
Drum Tower	鼓楼	*gǔlóu*
Yanhui Temple	颜庙	*yán miào*
Zhou Miao	周公庙	*zhōugōng miào*
Accommodation		*Accommodation*
Confucius Mansions	孔府	*kǒng fǔ*
Dongfang	东方宾馆	*dōngfāng bīnguǎn*
Gold Mansion	金府宾馆	*jīnfǔ bīnguǎn*
Queli	阙里宾舍	*quèlǐ bīnshè*
Yingshi Binguan	影视宾馆	*yǐngshì bīnguǎn*

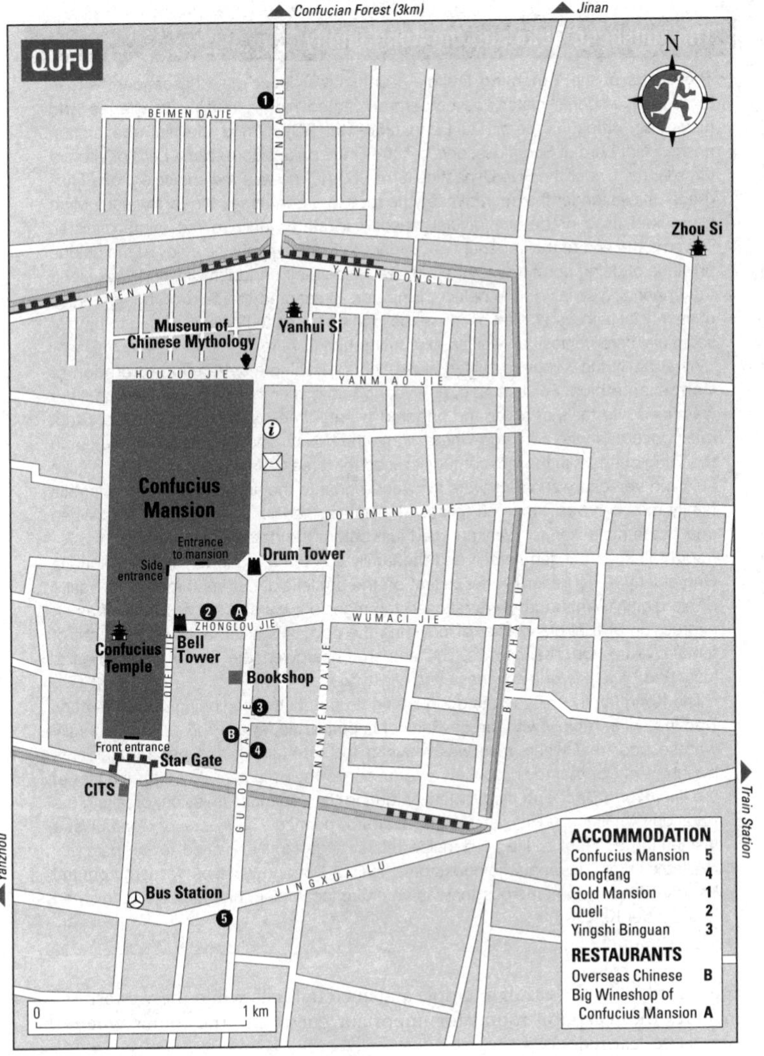

tunities clustered between the sights. Everything here is packed tight enough together to make using public transport unnecessary.

Confucius Mansion

The First Family Under Heaven – the descendants of Confucius – lived continuously at the **Confucius Mansion**, accessible off Queli Jie in the centre of town (daily 8am–5pm; ¥30), for more than 2500 years, spanning 77 generations. The opulence and size of the mansion testifies to the power and wealth of the **Kong clan** and their head, the Yansheng Duke. Built on a north–south axis, the mansion is loosely divided into living quarters, an administrative area

The Yansheng Duke and the Kong family

The status of the **Yansheng Duke** – Confucius's direct male descendant – rose throughout imperial history as emperors granted him increasing **privileges and hereditary titles**. Emperor Liu Bang (256–195 BC) named the ninth-generation descendant Lord of Sacrifices, and in 739 AD the duke also became Lord of Literary Excellence. Under the Five Dynasties (907–960 AD) he was the equivalent of a fifth-grade official, under the Yuan dynasty he rose to grade three, and by the early Ming he ranked as a grade-one official, second in status only to the prime minister. Towards the end of the imperial age, under the Qing dynasty, he enjoyed the unique privilege of being permitted to ride a horse inside the Forbidden City and walk along the Imperial Way inside the palace. Emperors presented the duke with large areas of sacrificial fields (so called because the income from the fields was used to pay for sacrificial ceremonies), as well as exempting him from taxes.

As a family the Kongs remained close-knit, practising a **severe interpretation of Confucian ethics**. For example, any young family member who offended an elder was fined two taels of silver and battered twenty times with a bamboo club. Strict rules governed who could go where within the house, and when a fire broke out in the living quarters in the last century it raged for three days as only twelve of the five hundred hereditary servants were allowed to go into the area to put it out. A female family member was expected to obey her father, her husband and her son. When one of the male Kongs, Wenxun, died just before the date of his wedding, his distraught fiancée hanged herself and the family erected a stone tablet in her honour. One elderly Kong general, after defeat on the battlefield, cut his throat for the sake of his dignity. When the news reached the mansion, his son hanged himself as an expression of filial piety. After discovering the body, his wife hanged herself out of female virtue. On hearing this, the emperor bestowed the family with a board, inscribed "A family of faithfulness and filiality".

The Kong family enjoyed the good life right up until the beginning of this century. **Decline** set in rapidly with the downfall of imperial rule, and in the 1920s the family was so poor that when wine was required for entertaining a guest, the servants bought it out of their own pocket, as a favour to their masters. In 1940, the last of the line, **Kong Decheng**, fled to Taiwan during the Japanese invasion, breaking the tradition of millennia. His sister, **Kong Demao**, penned *The House of Confucius*, a fascinating account of life lived inside this strange family chained to the past; it's available in foreign-language bookstores. Half of Qufu now claims descent from the Kongs, who are so numerous there is an entire local telephone directory dedicated to the letter K.

and a garden. In the east is a temple and ancestral hall, while the western wing includes the reception rooms for important guests and the rooms where the rites were learned.

Intricate and convoluted, this complex of twisting alleyways and over 450 rooms (most of them sixteenth century) has something decidedly eccentric about it. Inside the complex lies a central courtyard lined with long, narrow buildings, which were once administrative offices; now they hold a few trinket shops. The one English book they all sell is worth a look for its colour reproductions of portraits of the fancily dressed Yansheng dukes through the centuries. The **Gate of Double Glory** to the north was opened only on ceremonial occasions or when the emperor dropped in. To its east and west are old **administrative departments**, modelled after the six ministries of the imperial government, and an odd collection by any contemporary standard: the Department of Rites was in charge of ancestor worship; the Department of Seals concerned with jurisdiction and edicts; then followed Music, Letters and

Archives, Rent Collection and Sacrificial Fields. Beyond the Gate of Double Glory, the **Great Hall** was where the Yansheng duke sat on a wooden chair covered with a tiger skin and administered the family and proclaimed edicts. The flags and arrow tokens hanging on the walls are symbols of authority. Signs next to them reading "Make way!" were used to clear the roads of ordinary people when the duke left the mansion.

The next hall was where the duke held examinations in music and rites, and beyond it lies the **Hall of Withdrawal**, where he took tea. The hall contains two sedan chairs; the green one was for trips outside the mansion, the red one for domestic use.

The residential apartments

The **residential apartments** of the mansion are to the north, accessible through gates which would once have been heavily guarded; no one could enter of their own accord under pain of death. Tiger-tail cudgels, goose-winged pitchforks and golden-headed jade clubs used to hang here to drive the message home. Even the water-carrier was not permitted, and emptied the water into a stone trough outside that runs through the apartment walls. On a screen inside the gates is a painting of a *tan*, an imaginary animal shown eating treasures and greedily eyeing the sun. Feudal officials often had this picture painted in their homes as a warning against avarice.

The first hall is the seven-bay **Reception Hall**, where relatives were received, banquets held and marriage and funeral ceremonies conducted. Today, the only remnants of its once-salubrious past are several golden throne chairs and ornate staffs. Directly opposite the Reception Hall, the central eastern room contains a set of furniture made from tree roots, presented to the mansion by Emperor Qianlong – an original imperial decree lies on the table. Elsewhere in the central eastern room, check out the dinner service; it contains 404 pieces, including plates shaped like fish and deer, for consumption of the appropriate animals. Banquets for honoured guests could stretch to 196 courses.

Past the outbuildings and through a small gate, you reach the **Front Main Building**, an impressive two-storey structure in which are displayed paintings and clothes. The eastern central room was the home of Madame Tao, wife of Kong Lingyi, the seventy-sixth duke. Their daughter, Kong Demao, lived in the far eastern room, while Kong Lingyi's concubine, Wang, originally one of Tao's handmaids, lived in the inner western room. It doesn't sound like an arrangement designed for domestic bliss; indeed, whenever the duke was away, Madame Tao used to beat Wang with a whip she kept for the purpose. When Wang produced a male heir, Tao poisoned her. A second concubine, Feng, was kept prisoner in her rooms by Tao until she died.

The duke himself lived in the **rear building**, which has been left as it was when the last duke fled to Taiwan. Behind that is the garden where, every evening, flocks of crows come to roost noisily. Crows are usually thought to be inauspicious in China, but here they are welcome, and said to be the crow soldiers of Confucius, who protected him from danger on his travels. To the southeast of the inner east wing is a four-storey building called the **Tower of Refuge**, a planned retreat in the event of an uprising or invasion. The first floor was equipped with a movable hanging ladder, and a trap could be set in the floor. Once inside, the refugees could live for weeks on dried food stores.

The temple

In the east of the complex you'll find the family temple, the Ancestral Hall and residential quarters for less important family members. The **temple** is dedicated to the memory of Yu, wife of the seventy-second duke, and daughter of Emperor Qianlong. The princess had a mole on her face which, it was predicted, would bring disaster unless she married into a family more illustrious than either the nobility or the highest of officials. The Kongs were the only clan to fulfil the criteria, but technically the daughter of the Manchu emperor was not allowed to marry a Han Chinese. This inconvenience was got around by first having the daughter adopted by the family of the Grand Secretary Yu, and then marrying her to the duke as Yu's daughter. Her dowry included twenty villages and several thousand trunks of clothing.

Confucius Temple

The **Confucius Temple** (daily 8am–4.30pm; ¥50) ranks with Beijing's Forbidden City and the summer resort of Chengde as one of the three great classical architectural complexes in China. It's certainly big: there are 466

Confucianism

Confucius lived in poverty, largely ignored, all his life. A minor official in the Lu state court, he failed in his ambition to achieve real power, and began to travel from state to state, trying to convince rulers to accept his code of morals. His ideas were widely disseminated only after his death, when his students collected his teachings together in *The Analects*.

Confucianism is a philosophy; it was never intended as a religion, though that is how it was spread. Confucius taught gentlemanly conduct, ethics and the principles of government. He believed individuals and states should be placid, moderate and law-abiding, and should avoid extremes and excess. The state should serve the people, gathering the virtuous to it, and rulers should be well educated, humane and behave with courtesy, diligence, good faith and kindness. Peasants should be good peasants, rulers should be good rulers, and everyone should be happy with their position in society. Altruism was of fundamental importance: "Do not impose on others what you yourself do not desire." Confucius was a child of his time, and his ideas reflected the opinions and ideals of the ruling class of a static, feudal society. His ideal form of government was **benevolent despotism**; the correct structure of society and the family, he believed, was a rigid hierarchy.

Confucian ethics were adopted by rulers as a suitable system to keep the population in line, and the cult of Confucius began in earnest immediately after his death in 479 BC. Confucianism has since had an enormous impact on Chinese culture, and his stress on education formed the basis of the **civil service exams** right up until the twentieth century. When the **Communists** came to power they saw Confucianism as an archaic, feudal system and an anti-Confucius campaign was instigated, with much Confucian culture being destroyed in the Cultural Revolution. Now, however, it is making something of a **comeback**. Conservatives, perhaps frightened by the pace of change, the growing generation gap, and the new materialism of China, are calling for a return to Confucian values of respect and selflessness, just as their nervous counterparts in the West preach a return to family values. Confucian social morality – obeying authority, regarding family as the seat of morality and emphasizing the mutual benefits of friendship – is sometimes hailed as one of the main reasons for the success of East Asian economies, just as Protestantism provided the ideological complement to the growth of the industrialized West.

Most of the Confucian buildings in Qufu have been recently renovated, but this is strictly in the interests of **tourism**, not worship. Confucianism as a religious force was thought to have died, yet the ability of Chinese traditions to survive modernization and suppression always surprises observers. As one Chinese visitor commented, "Confucius is the one Chinese leader who never let the people down."

rooms, and it's over a kilometre long, laid out in the design of an imperial palace, with nine courtyards on a north–south axis. It wasn't always so grand, first established as a three-room temple in 478 BC, containing a few of Confucius's lowly possessions: some hats, a zither and a carriage. In 539, Emperor Jing Di had the complex renovated, starting a trend, and from then on, emperors keen to show their veneration for the sage – and ostentatiously to display their piety to posterity – renovated and expanded the complex for more than two thousand years. Most of the present structure is Ming and Qing.

Though there is an entrance on Queli Lu, just west of the mansion, the temple's main approach is in the southern section of the temple wall, and this is a better place to enter if you want an ordered impression of the complex. Through the gate, flanked by horned creatures squatting on lotus flowers, first views are of clusters of wiry cypresses and monolithic steles, some sitting on the backs of carved *bixi*, stoic-looking turtle-like creatures, in an overgrown courtyard. A succession of gates leads into a courtyard holding the magnificent **Kui Wen Pavilion**, a three-storey wooden building constructed in 1018 with a design unique in Chinese classical architecture – a triple-layered roof with curving eaves and four layers of crossbeams. It was renovated in 1504 and has since withstood an earthquake undamaged, an event recorded on a tablet on the terrace. To the east and west the two pavilions are abstention lodges where visiting emperors would fast and bathe before taking part in sacrificial ceremonies.

The **thirteen stele pavilions** in the courtyard beyond are worth checking out, containing 53 tablets presented by emperors to commemorate their visits, and gifts of land and funds for renovations made to the Kong family. The earliest are Tang and the latest are from the Republican period. Continuing north, you come to five gates leading off in different directions. The eastern ones lead to the hall where sacrifices were offered to Confucius's ancestors, the western to the halls where his parents were worshipped, while the central Gate of Great Achievements leads to a large pavilion, the **Apricot Altar**. Tradition has it that Confucius taught here after travelling the country in search of a ruler willing to implement his ideas. The cypress just inside the gate was supposed to have been planted by Confucius himself, and its state of health is supposed to reflect the fortunes of the Kongs.

The **Hall of Great Achievements**, behind the altar, is the temple's grandest building, its most striking feature being 28 **stone pillars** carved with bas-relief dragons, dating from around 1500. Each pillar has nine gorgeous dragons, coiling around clouds and pearls towards the roof. There is nothing comparable in the Forbidden City in Beijing, and when emperors came to visit the columns were covered with yellow silk to prevent imperial jealousy. Originally the temple was solely dedicated to the worship of Confucius, but in 72 AD, Emperor Liu Zhuang offered sacrifices to his 72 disciples, too. Five hundred years later, Zhen Guan of the Tang dynasty issued an edict decreeing that 22 eminent Confucians should also be worshipped. Emperors of later dynasties (not wishing to be outdone) added more, until by this century there were 172 "eminent worthies".

Behind the main hall is the inner hall for the worship of Confucius's wife, **Qi Guan**, who also, it seems, merited deification through association. The phoenixes painted on its columns and ceiling are symbols of female power, in the same way as the dragon symbolizes masculinity.

Beyond is the **Hall of the Relics of the Sage**, where 120 carved stone plates made in the sixteenth century from Song paintings depict scenes from Confucius's life. They begin with Confucius's mother praying for a son, and end with his disciples mourning at his grave. The workmanship is excellent but the light in the room is dim and you'll have to squint.

The **eastern axis** of the temple is entered here, through the Gate of the Succession of the Sage next to the Hall of Great Achievements. Here is the **Hall of Poetry and Rites** where Confucius was supposed to have taught his son, Kong Li, to learn poetry from the *Book of Odes* in order to express himself, and ritual from *The Book of Rites* in order to strengthen his character.

A solitary wall in the courtyard is the famous **Lu Wall**, where Kong Fu, a ninth-generation descendant of Confucius, hid the sage's books when Qin Shi Huang, the first emperor (see p.288), persecuted the followers of Confucius and burned all his books. Several decades later, Liu Yu, prince of Lu and son of the Emperor Jing Di, ordered Confucius's dwelling to be demolished in order to build an extension to his palace, whereupon the books were found, which led to a schism between those who followed the reconstructed version of his last books, and those who followed the teachings in the rediscovered originals.

The **western section** is entered through the Gate of He Who Heralds the Sage, by the Hall of Great Achievements. A paved path leads to a high brick terrace on which stands the five-bay, green-tiled Hall of Silks and Metals and the Hall of He Who Heralds the Sage, built to venerate Confucius's father, Shu Lianghe. He was originally a minor military official who attained posthumous nobility through his son. Behind is, predictably, the Hall of the Wife of He Who Heralds the Sage, dedicated to Confucius's mother.

In the east wall of the temple, near the Lu Wall, an unobtrusive gate leads to the legendary site of **Confucius's home**, sandwiched between the spectacular temple and the magnificent mansion, a tiny square of land, just big enough to have held a couple of poky little rooms.

The rest of town

Not far to the east of the gate of the Confucius Mansion is the Ming **Drum Tower**, which forms a pair with the **Bell Tower** on Queli Lu. The drum was struck to mark sunset, the bell to mark sunrise, and at major sacrificial ceremonies they would be sounded simultaneously. You can't go inside either.

A little way northeast of the Confucius Temple is a smaller complex dedicated to **Yanhui**, who was regarded as Confucius's greatest disciple and sometimes called "The Sage Returned". A temple has been situated here since the Han dynasty, though the present structure is Ming. It's attractive, quieter than the Confucius Temple, and contains some impressive architectural details, such as the dragon pillars on the main hall, and a dragon head embedded in the roof. The eastern building now contains a display of locally excavated Neolithic and Zhou pottery.

The **Zhou Miao** in the northeast of the town is dedicated to a Zhou-dynasty duke, a statue of whom stands in the main hall, together with his son Bo Qin and Bo Qin's servant. Legend has it that Bo Qin was a rasher man than his father, and the duke, worried that his son would not act sensibly in state matters, inscribed a pithy maxim from his own political experience on a slate and directed the servant to carry it on his back. Whenever Bo Qin was about to do something foolish, the ever-present servant would turn his back and Bo Qin, after reading his father's warning, would check himself. The open terrace before the hall, where sacrifices were made to the duke, contains a striking stone incense burner carved with coiling dragons.

Qufu's contemporary attractions don't compare with its historical wealth. The **Palace of Chinese Mythology** (daily 8am–8pm; ¥20), behind the mansion on Houzuo Jie, provides ten minutes of comic relief with its tacky fairground-style show of mechanical dioramas operated by listless guides. One room, the Chinese idea of hell, is quite amusing, with lots of plastic skulls and fake gore. "Heaven" is a room full of half-naked shop-window dummies.

The Confucian Forest

The **Confucian Forest** is in the suburbs 3km north of the town centre (daily 8am–6pm; ¥20), reachable by cycle-rickshaw (¥5), though it's pleasant to walk. On the way, look out for stone-masons chiselling away at sculptures – dragons, lions, eagles, women in bikinis – at the side of the road. The forest is the **burial ground** of the Kongs and, like the temple, it expanded over the centuries from something simple and austere to a grand complex, in this case centring around a single grave – the tomb of Confucius. In the Song dynasty, the place was planted with trees and in 1331 a wall was built around it. Pavilions and halls were added in the Ming dynasty and large-scale reconstructions made in 1730 when Yong Zhen constructed some impressive memorial archways. Confucian disciples collected exotic trees to plant here, and there are now more than a hundred thousand different varieties. Today it's an atmospheric place, sculptures half concealed in thick undergrowth, tombstones standing aslant in groves of ancient trees and wandering paths dappled with sunlight. This is a real, wild forest, with real wild animals and, be warned, real wild oriental insects with nasty stings. A great place to spend an afternoon, it's one of the few famous scenic spots in China that it's possible to appreciate unaccompanied by crowds. Just inside the entrance you can board a tram (¥4) to the main sites. There was no bike rental service at time of writing, which is a shame because the forest is really too large to explore on foot.

Running east from the chunky main gate, the imperial carriageway leads to a gateway and an arched stone bridge, beyond which is the spot where Confucius and his son are buried. The **Hall of Deliberation**, just north of the bridge, was where visitors put on ritual dress before performing sacrifices. An avenue, first of chop carvers and souvenir stalls, then of carved stone animals, leads to the **Hall of Sacrifices**, and behind that to a small grassy mound – the **grave**. Just to the west of the tomb a hut, looking like a potting shed, was where Confucius's disciples each spent three years watching over the grave. Confucius's son is buried just north of here. His unflattering epitaph reads: "He died before his father without making any noteworthy achievements."

According to legend, before his death Confucius told his disciples to bury him at this spot because the *feng shui* was good. His disciples objected, as there was no river nearby. Confucius told them that a river would be dug in the future. After the first Qin emperor, Qin Shi Huang, unified China, he launched an anti-Confucian campaign, burning books and scholars, and tried to sabotage the grave by ordering a river to be dug through the cemetery, thus inadvertently perfecting it.

Shopping

There are plenty of touristy **shops** in the centre of town, and a **night market** on Wumaci Dajie. Unsurprisingly the Confucian connection has been exploited to the hilt, with offerings of Confucius fans, Confucius beer, Confucius sweets and something called the "Confucius Treasure Box", which includes an acorn from the Confucian Forest and sand from the great sage's grave – basically a box of very expensive and lovingly packaged earth. The T-shirts on sale at the Confucius Mansion gift shop feature the sage's home on front (which changes colour when exposed to heat), and "*PRI esta bien para tu familia*" on the back – clearly leftovers from the Mexican political party's losing presidential campaign a few years back. Pick up a book of translated **Confucian sayings** at the *Queli Hotel*. If you're steering clear of Confucian paraphernalia, check out the **chops** (which they will carve with your name in a couple of minutes), rubbings taken from the steles in the temple and locally crafted pistachio carvings.

There's also a charming traditional Chinese **medicine store** on Zhonglou Jie, near the *Queli Hotel*; look for the herbs drying on the pavement. Get your scorpion essence – a local product, advertised as a general tonic – in the department stores on Wumaci Jie.

Practicalities

Qufu's tiny **train station** is marooned out on the outskirts of town, as building one closer was thought to disturb the sage's grave. The direct overnight train from Beijing drops you here, as do three other routes from Tai'an and Jinan. From the station, take bus #5 (¥1) into town, which stops at both the bus station and the Confucius Temple. Other trains stop at Yanzhou, 16km west, on the Beijing–Shanghai line, and regular buses (¥4) run between the two towns, arriving in Qufu at the **bus station** to the south of the Confucius Mansion. This is also where long-distance buses pull in, after rattling across flat fertile land where aubergines, beans and potatoes are farmed.

Local transport is by **cycle-rickshaw**, whereby the passenger is slung low in the front, giving an uninterrupted dog's-eye view of the street. A ride anywhere in town should cost ¥5 or less. There are also horse-drawn gypsy-style carts, strictly for tourists, so not cheap. A **taxi** in town will cost the flagfall of ¥5.

From Qufu's bus station it's easy to get to anywhere in the area. If you want to travel further afield by train, go to Ji'nan (see p.330), which has a wider selection of lines – though nowhere near Qufu's charm.

Accommodation

Qufu has an abundance of good, inexpensive **hotels**. The following are the most conveniently located.

Confucius Mansions Hotel 1 Datong Lu ⓣ0537/4411783. Opposite the bus station at the bottom of Gulou Dajie, this place has a laid-back atmosphere and friendly staff, and is popular with budget travellers. Dorm beds ¥60, ❸

Dongfang 30 Gulou Nan Dajie ⓣ0537/4412794. Clean and good value, with pleasant, if rather small rooms. Dorms ¥25, ❷

Gold Mansion 1 Beimen Dajie ⓣ0537/4413469, ⓕ4413209. A comfortable, partially foreign-owned hotel a little way out of the centre on the way to the forest. It's not as nice as the *Queli*, but is very popular with overseas Chinese. ❺

Queli 1 Queli Jie ⓣ0537/4411300, ⓕ4412022. Located right next to the Confucius Temple and the Mansion. If you can afford it, stay in this impressive modern building, one of the few Chinese hotels at the slicker end of the market that manages to harmonizes with its surroundings. There's satellite TV, 24hr hot water and the staff speak English. CITS on site. ❺

Yingshi Binguan 22 Gulou Nan Dajie ⓣ0537/4412422. Perfectly acceptable, though not quite as good value as the *Dongfang*. Dorms ¥20, ❸

Eating, drinking and nightlife

Local specialities include fragrant rice and **scorpions**, boiled in salt and soaked in oil. The Kong family also developed its own cuisine, featuring dishes such as Going to the Court with the Son (pigeon served with duck) and Gold and Silver Fish (a white and a yellow fish together). It's possible to sample this refined cuisine at the *Queli Hotel*, which does a special **Confucian Mansion Banquet** for (mostly tourist) groups, at a rather extortionate ¥200 per head.

For simpler fare, there are a few **restaurants** on Gulou Dajie, including the friendly *Overseas Chinese Restaurant* at no. 85. The *Big Wineshop of Confucius Mansion*, likewise signposted in English, near the *Queli Hotel*, is good but a little pricey at around ¥80 for a blow-out meal. It's very popular with well-heeled visitors, and conditions in the small, elegant room can get quite cramped. At night, Wumaci Dajie fills up with open-air **food stalls**, offering tasty-looking hotpots and stews. The food's not bad and the atmosphere is lively, though make sure you know the price before you order anything.

For **nightlife**, you'll have to make do with the nightclub – karaoke and expensive drinks – on the corner of Gulou Dajie and Zhonglou Jie. The **bowling alley** here can also be a hoot. Think hard before going to the gawdy **Confucius Six Arts City** to see the atrocious revue *Confucius' Dream* (daily April–Oct 8pm; ¥40), advertised all over town. It's doubtful the great sage's mind was filled with feather-headdress-wearing dancing girls and fan-waving martial arts experts as he slept, as this show depicts.

Qingdao and around

The port city of **QINGDAO** in the east of Shandong province makes a remarkable first impression. Emerging from the train station and walking north with your eyes fixed on the skyline, you could almost believe you had got off at the wrong continent – it's like stepping into a replica of a nineteenth-century Bavarian village, nestling on the Yellow Sea. With its Teutonic shapes and angles – red roofs, cobbled streets, intricate iron balconies – this area, the old **German concession**, provokes an eerie sense of dislocation. The marriage of German architecture and contemporary China has created bizarre juxtapositions, with oriental stone lions sitting in discreet European gardens, and grand, pompous facades now fronting little shops and laundries.

Qingdao's distinctive Teutonic stamp dates back to 1897, a legacy of **Kaiser Wilhelm**'s industrious attempts to extend a German sphere of influence in the East. The kaiser's annexation of Qingdao, along with the surrounding Jiazhou peninsula, was justified in terms typical of the European actions of the time. It was prompted by concern for "safety", following the murder of two German missionaries by the **Boxer movement** (see p.1183). The kaiser raised the incident to an international crisis, making a near-hysterical speech (which coined the phrase "yellow peril") demanding action from the feeble Manchu government. He got his concession, the Chinese ceding the territory for 99 years, along with the right to build the Shandong rail lines. Qingdao had previously been an insignificant fishing village, but the German choice was carefully calculated, the ubiquitous Baron von Richtofen having carried out a survey and found it ideal for a deep-water naval base. The town was split into a European, a Chinese and a business section, with a garrison of two thousand soldiers to protect its independence. A brewery was built in 1903, the rail line to Ji'nan (another concession town) was completed in 1904, and the town prospered. It was to remain German until 1914 when the **Japanese**, anxious to acquire a foothold in China, and emboldened by the support of their British allies, bombarded Qingdao. The town was taken on November 7, and five thousand prisoners were carted off to Japan. In the Treaty of Versailles, the city was ceded to Japan, which infuriated the Chinese, and led to demonstrations in Beijing – the beginning of the May Fourth Movement (see Contexts, p.1184). The port was eventually returned to China in 1922.

Qingdao and around

Qingdao	青岛	***qīngdǎo***
Brewery	青岛啤酒厂	*qīngdǎo píjiǔ chǎng*
Catholic Church	天主教堂	*tiānzhǔ jiàotáng*
Huilange Pavilion	回澜阁	*huílán gé*
Lao Shan	崂山	*láoshān*
Lu Xun Park	鲁迅公园	*lǔxùn gōngyuán*
Museum of Marine Products	海产博物馆	*hǎichǎn bówùguǎn*
Naval Museum	海军博物馆	*hǎijūn bówùguǎn*
Passenger ferry terminal	港客运站	*gǎngkè yùnzhàn*
Qingdao Museum	青岛市博物馆	*qīngdǎo shì bówùguǎn*
Qingdaoshan Park	青岛山公园	*qīngdǎoshān gōngyuán*
Xiaoqingdao Isle	小青岛	*xiǎo qīngdǎo*
Xiaoyushun Park	小鱼山公园	*xiǎoyúshān gōngyuán*
Xinhaoshan Park	信号山公园	*xìnhàoshān gōngyuán*
Ying Hotel	迎宾馆	*yíng bīnguǎn*
Zhanqiao Pier	栈桥	*zhàn qiáo*
Zhongshan Park	中山公园	*zhōngshān gōngyuán*
Accommodation and eating		
Chunhelou	春和楼饭店	*chūnhélóu fàndiàn*
Dulaishun	都来顺大酒店	*dūláishùn dàjiǔdiàn*
Friendship	友谊宾馆	*yǒuyì bīnguǎn*
Holiday Inn	颐中假日酒店	*yí zhōng jiàrì jiǔdiàn*
Huiquan Dynasty	汇泉王朝大酒店	*huìquán wángcháo dàjiǔdiàn*
International Seamen's Club	国际海员俱乐部	*guójì hǎiyuán jùlèbù*
Nanhai	南海饭店	*nánhǎi fàndiàn*
Oceanwide Elite	泛海名人酒店	*fànhǎi míngrén jiǔdiàn*
Qingdao	青岛饭店	*qīngdǎo fàndiàn*
Railway	铁道大厦	*tiědào dàshà*
Shangri-La	青岛香格里拉大酒店	*qīngdǎo xiānggélǐlā dàjiǔdiàn*
Tianqiao	天桥宾馆	*tiānqiáo bīnguǎn*
Xinhao Hill	信号山迎宾馆	*xìnhàoshān yíngbīnguǎn*

Modern Qingdao is still a very important **port**, China's fourth largest, and behind the old town is an area with a very different character, a sprawling industrial **metropolis** of highrises and factories. One of China's first "open door" cities, with an excellent geographical position and transport facilities, Qingdao has a rapidly growing industrial base. Perhaps most importantly, at least from a visitor's point of view, it continues to produce the world-renowned **Tsingtao Beer** (Tsingtao is the old transliteration of Qingdao) which owes its crisp, clean flavour to the purity of the spring water from Lao Shan, an attractive mountain area east of the city, with which it is brewed.

Qingdao is a relaxed and hedonistic place, with an atmosphere that's mellower than in most Chinese cities – even the pace at which people walk is slower. Despite the city's size, the parts you'd actually want to visit are all within manageable walking distance, and the atmosphere at the waterfront is more small-town pleasure zone than anonymous metropolis, thanks mainly to the white-sand **beaches** dotted along the shoreline, among the best in northern

China; indeed, the city has been chosen to host the sailing events of the **2008 Summer Olympics**. Though the authorities seem more interested in constructing new skyscrapers and beach hotels than in restoring old buildings, the speedy development has not yet impinged upon the area's charm, as modern hotels have largely been restricted to the eastern coast. The **season** runs from June to September, though many visitors come in late April and early May, when the cherry trees are blooming in Zhongshan Park. Fans of the local brew may be interested in the annual **Beer Festival** (mid- to late Aug).

A straightforward excursion from Qingdao is **Lao Shan**, one of China's famous peaks, appearing in Chinese mythology as the home of the Immortals; hiking here is certainly more invigorating than sitting around on the beach all day.

Arrival, information and city transport

The old concession area and the beachfront are easy to get to know and to get around. Zhongshan Lu, running north–south, is the modern, glitzy shopping district and the heart of the concession district; on the east–west axis, Taiping and Laiyang Lu follow the coastline.

The large city **airport**, 30km north of the city, is served by a regular CAAC bus which drops passengers on Zhongshan Lu. Arriving in Qingdao by **train** is the easiest option. The station, which is on a single line that splits, one fork leading to Ji'nan, the other to Yantai, is a grand German edifice at the heart of the old town, within walking distance of the beach and the seafront hotels. The **long-distance bus station** is just behind and to the west of the train station; the expressway has now cut the journey time from Ji'nan to four and a half hours (¥95). The **passenger ferry terminal**, with services from Dalian and Shanghai, is in the grotty north of town, with a few cheap hotels nearby. To get **to the seafront** from here, take bus #215 south, get off halfway down Shenxian Lu, opposite Xiaogang Port, walk east to the end of Zhongshan Lu and catch a #6. Or go to the last stop of the #215 route, walk south down to Guizhou Lu and catch bus #25 east. Get off just after Huilange Pavilion, before it turns up Daxue Lu. As this is pretty involved, it's a lot easier just to get a taxi if you are arriving with luggage.

The **Tourist Service Center** (Ⓣ0532/2968663), downstairs in the train-station concourse (to the left as you exit the station) has helpful staff, touch-screen computers introducing the area and free maps.

Bus #6 is a useful service, going from the top of Zhongshan Lu down towards the train station, then heading east along the seafront, getting close to Number 1 beach and terminating near the entrance to Zhongshan Park. Other

Ferries from Qingdao

From Qingdao, there is a twice-weekly ferry to Inchon, South Korea (Tues & Thurs; 21hr; ¥1330–2490) and also to Shimonoseki, Japan (Thurs; 39hr; ¥3400). **Tickets** can be bought in advance from the passenger ferry terminal close to the Friendship Store on Xinjiang Lu. There are five classes (special, first, second, third and fourth), with severe gradations in price as you move down the scale. Third class is about the same level of comfort as hard sleeper on a train and is probably best unless you're particularly loaded or skint.

For **Dalian** and **Shanghai**, you'll need to get a ferry from Yantai, three hours' north by bus (see p.363). You can buy tickets in advance from the kiosks on the train-station concourse.

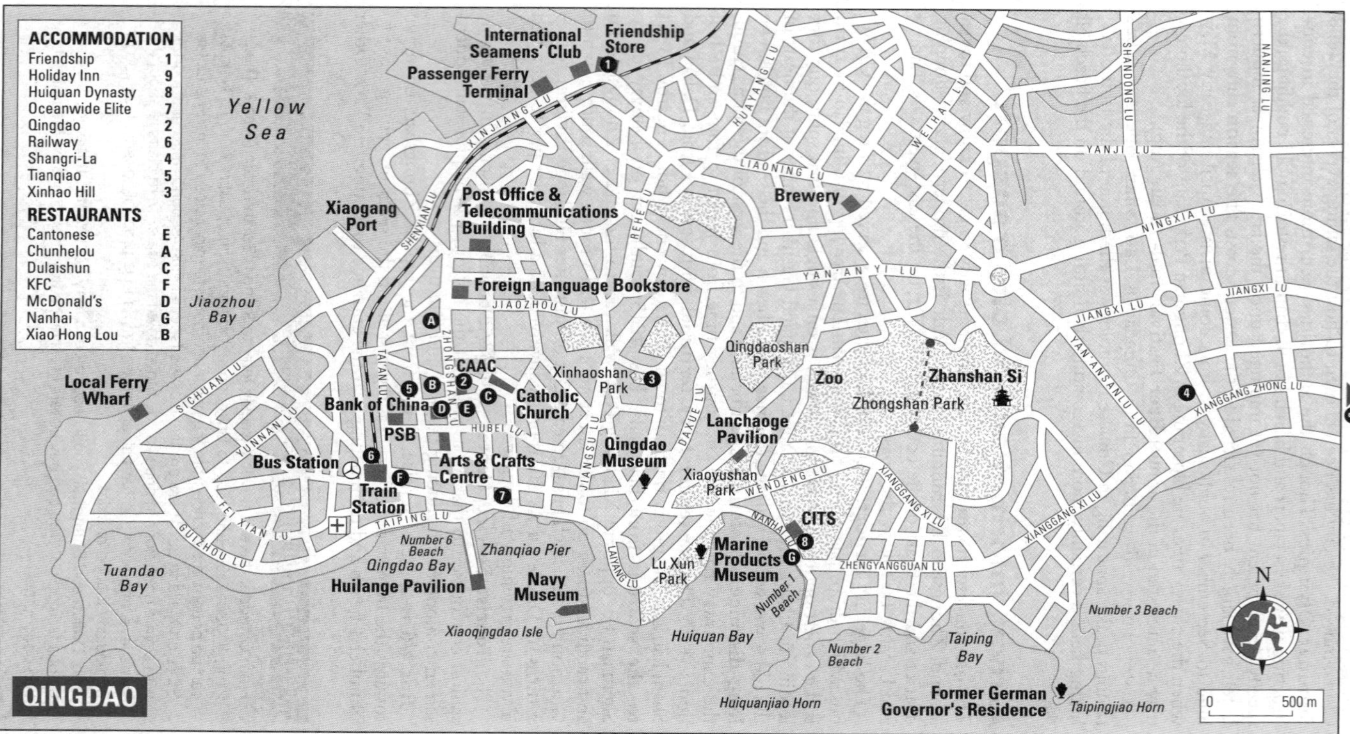
QINGDAO
ACCOMMODATION
Friendship 1
Holiday Inn 9
Huiquan Dynasty 8
Oceanwide Elite 7
Qingdao 2
Railway 6
Shangri-La 4
Tianqiao 5
Xinhao Hill 3
RESTAURANTS
Cantonese E
Chunhelou A
Dulaishun C
KFC F
McDonald's D
Nanhai G
Xiao Hong Lou B
Yellow Sea
Jiaozhou Bay
Tuandao Bay
Qingdao Bay
Huiquan Bay
Taiping Bay
International Seamens' Club
Friendship Store
Passenger Ferry Terminal
Xiaogang Port
Post Office & Telecommunications Building
Foreign Language Bookstore
Brewery
Local Ferry Wharf
Bank of China
PSB
CAAC
Catholic Church
Xinhaoshan Park
Bus Station
Train Station
Arts & Crafts Centre
Qingdao Museum
Lanchaoge Pavilion
Qingdaoshan Park
Zoo
Zhanshan Si
Zhongshan Park
Xiaoyushan Park
CITS
Marine Products Museum
Lu Xun Park
Number 1 Beach
Number 2 Beach
Number 3 Beach
Number 6 Beach
Zhanqiao Pier
Huilange Pavilion
Navy Museum
Xiaoqingdao Isle
Huiquanjiao Horn
Former German Governor's Residence
Taipingjiao Horn
NANJING LU
SHANDONG LU
YANJI LU
WEIHAI LU
HUAYANG LU
LIAONING LU
NINGXIA LU
YAN'AN YI LU
JIANGXI LU
YAN'ANSANLU LU
XIANGGANG ZHONG LU
XIANGGANG XI LU
ZHENGYANGGUAN LU
XINJIANG LU
SHENXIAN LU
REHE LU
JIAOZHOU LU
ZHONGSHAN LU
TAI'AN LU
HUBEI LU
JIANGSU LU
DAXUE LU
WENDENG LU
NANHAI LU
LAIYANG LU
TAIPING LU
SICHUAN LU
YUNNAN LU
FEI XIAN LU
GUIZHOU LU
N
0 500 m
9

useful routes are the **#300 series** (#304, #311, #312 & #316), which go between Zhanqiao Pier near the train station along the coast to the eastern sector. Private **minibuses** also run on most bus routes. They're more common, faster, but a little more expensive. **Taxis** to most destinations within the city cost the minimum fare of ¥10, though expect to pay double this to get to the eastern strip.

Accommodation

Qingdao is probably the most expensive city in Shandong, though outside the season hotel rooms can be cheaper and it's worth bargaining. That said, most hotels offer a reduced rate at weekends. Finding a room here is easy if you don't mind paying for luxury, or the view, as there are plenty of top-class international **hotels** well located on the seafront. If you're travelling on a budget, your choices are much more limited, and you'll probably end up some way from the picturesque parts of town. You can trust the touts at the train station to find you a good room in the centre – just tell them how much you want to spend, ask to see the room, then bargain. Good-value places to stay can be found in the area just northeast of the station, on the lanes between Zhongshan Lu and Tai'an Lu.

Friendship Xinjiang Lu ⓣ0532/2824686. This hotel is a long way out in the same building as the Friendship Store, next to the passenger-ferry terminal. The building is bare and ragged, but the rooms are pleasant and popular with budget travellers. It's also notable for having a helpful, English-speaking manager. Try to avoid the fourth floor as there's a nightclub here which blasts out old Euro-pop till 2am. Dorms ¥50, ❸

Holiday Inn 76 Xianggang Zhong Li ⓣ0532/571888, ⓕ5777513. Luxury highrise on the modern east side of town, with all mod cons. ❾

Huiquan Dynasty 9 Nanhai Lu ⓣ0532/2886688, ⓕ2871122. A well-located four-star hotel – the beach is directly across a narrow lane. If you're not staying here, you can use the pool for ¥35. ❽

Oceanwide Elite 29 Taiping Lu ⓣ0532/2886699, ⓕ2886699. In an excellent location opposite Zhanqiao Pier, this new four-star hotel has an impressive interior and all the facilities you'd expect. ❽

Qingdao 53 Zhongshan Lu ⓣ0532/2891888. A glitzy tower bang in the middle of town, offering substantial reductions if you plead. ❸

Railway 2 Tai'an Lu ⓣ0532/2869963. Right next door to the train station, this spartan place is clean though noisy. ❺

Shangri-La 9 Xianggang Zhong Lu ⓣ0532/3883838, ⓕ3886868. Another glossy tower, situated 5min from the beach in the plush part of town. It offers all the expected five-star luxuries, and an excellent weekend rate. Bus #223 or #501 come here from the train station. ❾, ❽ at weekends

Tianqiao Hotel 47 Feicheng Lu ⓣ0532/2808475. This hotel (and its neighbour the *Jindaiyuan*) has clean rooms that the train-station touts recommend. Beds from ¥50, ❹

Xinhao Hill 26 Longshan Lu ⓣ0532/2866209, ⓕ2861985. Modern building next to the beautiful old German mansion of the same name, nestling among the trees in Xinhaoshan Park. ❼

The City

Qingdao has plenty of diversions to offer, but the main thing to do here is stroll. The **waterfront** is a place to see and be seen, with the same indolent, flirtatious atmosphere common to beach resorts the world over, while the faster-paced **downtown** streets are the haunt of the well-heeled inhabitants and have a definite cosmopolitan feel. Unusually for a city outside Beijing, there's even evidence of the new Chinese youth culture: buskers work the crowds on the esplanade, beach bums recline elegantly on the sands and skateboarders weave down the hills, all adding to the Qingdao's generally mellow, trendy feel. As well as the **beaches** and **old German town**, some very pleasant **parks** are an added bonus, ensuring that Qingdao is easily one of the most charismatic of Chinese cities.

The German concession and the brewery

Zhongshan Lu is the main shopping drag, awash with shoe shops and designer clothing stores. Take a right opposite the *Qingdao Hotel* and follow the steep cobbled street round to the fine **Catholic Church**, a German relic whose distinctive double spires can be seen from all over the city. Services are held here on Sunday mornings, which seems to be the only time you can get inside. The streets east of here, some cobbled, many lined with pink buildings with black iron balconies overlooking the street, are a good place to wander and take in the flavour of the old German town.

The **Qingdao Museum** on Daxue Lu is worth a diversion (Tues–Sun 8.30am–5pm; ¥15). This beautiful building, constructed in 1931, was originally a welfare institute, the headquarters of the sinister-sounding but actually benign Red Swastika Association. There's a collection of paintings here from the Yuan through to Qing dynasties, and an archeological section in the courtyard which contains four large standing **Buddhas** dating back to 500–527 AD. They're slim, striking figures with bulbous, smiling heads, one hand pointing upward to heaven, the other down to the earth. The heads were cut off in 1928 by the Japanese and taken away to museums in Japan, though they've now been restored to their rightful shoulders – you can hardly see the join. The museum staff seem proudest, however, of a souvenir collected by Qingdao sailors during the 1985 Chinese expedition to the South Pole – a simple lump of rock – which sits proudly in a specially constructed pavilion in the courtyard.

Fans of **Tsingtao Beer** can take a trip into the industrial zone to see the **brewery**. It's on the route of bus #25 and easy enough to spot, but the only way to get inside is to take a tour with CITS (see p.362), which are sporadic. Free samples are available, including an unusual dark brown stout, but you'll have to sit through a lot of statistics first.

The beaches and the waterfront

Qingdao's **beaches**, with fine white sand, are active from very early in the morning, when *tai ji* exponents and beachcombers turn out, to well into the evening, when holiday-makers come for the bars and cafés on the beach and esplanade or just to sit and look out to sea against a backdrop of black Japanese pine trees. Off Nanhai Lu, **Number 1 beach**, flanked by skyscrapers on one side, red-tiled roofs on the other, is the biggest (580m long) and best. In season it's a lively, crowded place, swarming with ice-cream vendors, trinket stalls selling carved shells and a rash of photographers. Fortunately, unlike Beidaihe, the other northern beach resort (see p.160), it doesn't feel overloaded with kitsch. The whole place is very organized, with odd, beachball-shaped changing huts, shower facilities, multicoloured beach umbrellas, and designated swimming areas marked out with buoys and protected by shark nets. The water, however, is like Chinese soup – murky and warm, with unidentifiable things floating in it – so swimming is not recommended. Sit down and you're not likely to remain alone for long as there are plenty of people around who want to practise their English.

If Number 1 beach feels too crowded, head east to the more sheltered **number 2 and 3 beaches**. These are more sedate, and popular with the older, sanatorium-dwelling crowd. For the liveliest social scene, head to the illogically named **Number 6** beach, at the bottom of Zhongshan Lu; in addition to good swimming, there are plenty of shops here should you choose to stay dry.

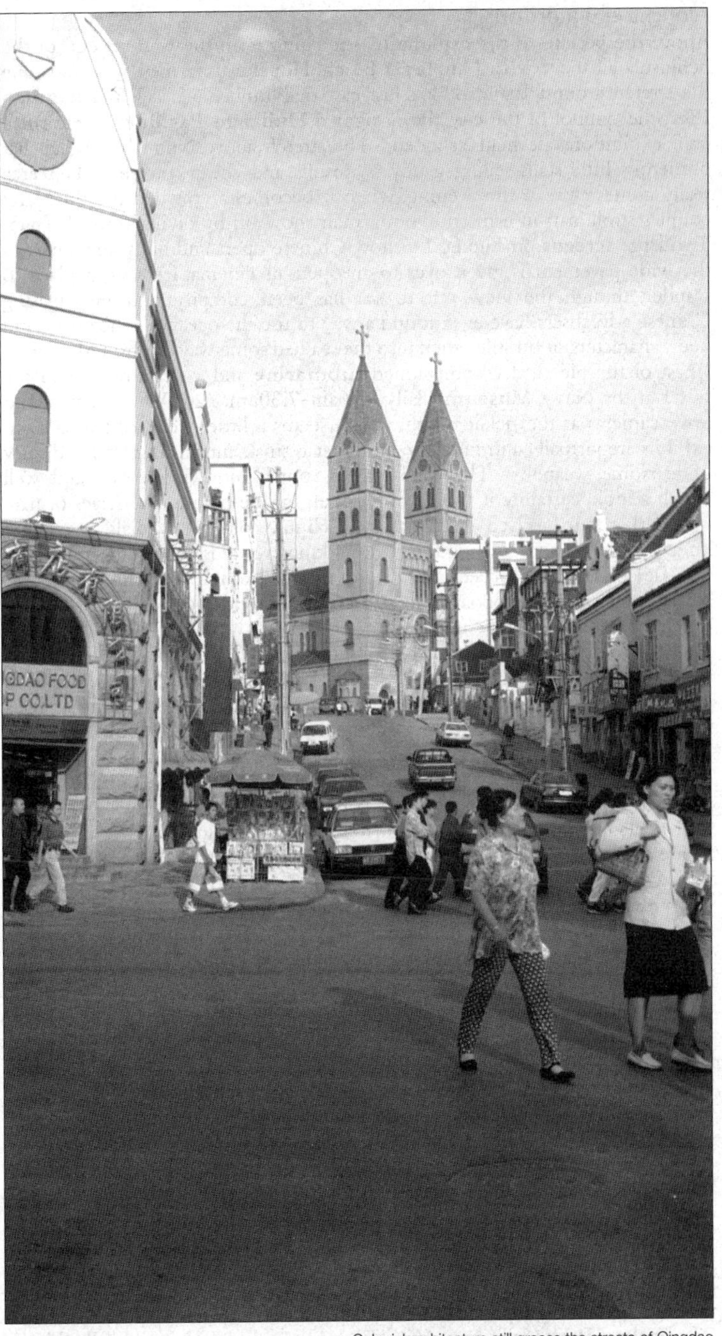

△ Colonial architecture still graces the streets of Qingdao

Along the waterfront

Above the beaches is the **esplanade**, stretching from the western end of the peninsula all the way to Number 1 beach. Hopeful fishermen with rods line the stretch around Tuandao Bay. Just east of Number 6 beach is **Zhanqiao Pier**, the symbol of the city, the octagonal **Huilange Pavilion**, where small craft exhibitions are held, at its end. The stretch above Number 6 beach has numerous little stalls selling gaudy swimsuits and cheap souvenirs. This area really comes alive in the evening, when it becomes a crowded thoroughfare: couples stroll arm in arm and young men show off by diving from the pier. Two large **screens** on Taiping Lu show Chinese opera and films, and a part of the wide pavement is given over to an open-air cinema. It's a great place to wander, though the view out to sea has been compromised; enterprising Chinese advertisers have even found a way to use the ocean as a hoarding and neon characters sit on stilts stuck into the sea bed some way out from the shore.

East of the pier, a decommissioned **submarine** and a **destroyer** sit in the water at the **Navy Museum** (daily 8.30am–7.30pm; Y20). You're required to leave cameras at the ticket booth, which seems a little over-sensitive as both exhibits are virtually antiques. The destroyer is small and rusting, with a display of fearsome weaponry. The submarine is much more interesting and well worth a look, certainly if you've never been in one before. The series of narrow, dark rooms arrayed with masses of chunky old valves, dials, levers and knobs, many of them bearing Russian markings, rewards detailed examination. You descend in the torpedo launch room, go through the sailors' quarters, hardly larger than a cupboard though they still found room for their flasks of tea, and ascend from the engine room.

Next to the sub, you can tour the military aircraft on display or follow the sandbank leading to **Xiaoqingdao Isle** (¥10). There's a pleasant little park here, a few cafés with good views, and a surprisingly lascivious statue of a sea nymph playing a violin. A white beacon stands at the highest point.

Around the bend is **Lu Xun Park** (daily 6am–7pm; ¥10), a good approach to Number 1 beach. It has green pine trees and cypresses, little winding paths, pavilions, benches and tables, full of couples indulging in what must be the well-heeled Chinese tourists' favourite hobby, photographing your spouse. Inside the park is the **Museum of Marine Products** (daily 7.45am–6pm; ¥15), consisting of two buildings, an aquarium shaped like a castle and a two-storey exhibition hall, with a seal pool in between. Founded in 1932, it's billed as the first aquarium in China, though to Western eyes it's pretty unexciting – lots of exotic marine life swimming about in tanks make it look like the average Chinese restaurant.

The farther east you go, the grander and more exclusive the buildings get. Past the *Huiquan Dynasty Hotel* is the **Badaguan area**, a health resort of sanatoriums and classy guesthouses set among trees. It's a pretty place with a suburban feel, each street lined with a different tree or flower – there are peach blossoms on Shaoguan Lu, crab apples on Ningwuguan Lu, and crab myrtle on Zhengyangguan Lu – and unlike most of the old gardens in Qingdao, the ones here are well looked after. At the eastern end of Number 2 beach stands the former German Governor's Residence, a grand castle looking out to sea.

Zhongshan Park and around

Qingdao's **parks**, dotted above the waterfront and serving as a buffer zone between the interesting parts of the city, the waterfront, and the boring industrial bits, are among the best in China. The largest is the 800-square-kilometre **Zhongshan Park** (daily 6am–6pm; ¥5), on the side of Taiping Hill. Within its boundaries sits the Buddhist **Zhanshan Si**, the zoo, a couple of theme parks, a teahouse and the TV Tower, looking as if it's just landed from outer space. A cable car runs from near the entrance to the top of the hill. It's a good place to lose the crowds and hike around, but as it's so enormous you'll need a whole day to explore it thoroughly. The park is famed for its **cherry trees**, which turn the park into a pink forest when they're in bloom in late April and early May; thousands of visitors come just to see the spectacle.

Just west of Zhongshan Park, **Qingdaoshan Park** (daily 6am–6pm; ¥3) contains the small Jingshan Fort. Farther west, near the museum, the steep but very pleasant **Xinhaoshan Park** holds the **Ying Hotel** (daily 8.30am–4.30pm; ¥10) a restored, grand old mansion built in 1905. It's worth a tour, as the German Governor-General, the warlord Yuan Shikai and Chairman Mao have lodged here in their time. The highest point of the park, reached by tortuous winding paths, is a good place to get an overview of the city. **Xiaoyushun Park**, on the top of a hill by the side of Huiquan Bay, is styled like a classical Chinese garden. The main three-storey, octagonal structure at the summit is the **Lanchao Ge**, a pavilion traditionally used for watching the tide.

Fans of modern Chinese literature should divert their walk down the hill towards the waterfront past 12 Huangxian Lu. A small plaque in Chinese outside this rundown, inhabited home denotes it as the site where the writer **Lao She** lived from 1934 to 1937.

Eating, drinking and nightlife

Qingdao has plenty of **restaurants** to choose from. The speciality is, unsurprisingly, seafood; mussels and crabs here are particularly good, and not expensive. There are plenty of small **seafood places** along Laiyang Lu, particularly near Lu Xun Park. They're all small, noisy and busy, but competition means that standards are high and, with some exceptions, the food is reasonably cheap. The expensive hotels also have restaurants, and although they're pricey, the food is very good and the setting is often palatial. The first-floor restaurant in the *Huiquan Dynasty Hotel* is one of the best.

Pick of the seafront places is the *Nanhai*, 14 Nanhai Lu, opposite the *Huiquan Dynasty Hotel*. The food is excellent, though the portions are a little small, and the beer comes in real pint mugs. Expect to pay about ¥60 per person. On and around Zhongshan Lu, try the renowned *Chunhelou*, 146 Zhongshan Lu, a quiet little place with discreet service, small tables and ambient lighting which gives it a Continental feel. The food is very good, and portions are more than generous – the spicy chicken is highly recommended. Just off the main drag, the *Cantonese Restaurant*, Qufu Lu, has good *dim sum* and seafood. For hotpot, Sichuan dishes, draught microbrew and an unbeatable view, seat yourself on the second floor of *Dulaishun*, opposite the cathedral. Cheap home-style cooking packs out the *Xiao Hong Lou*, west off Zhongshan Lu at 17 Kunming Lu. There's a *KFC* on Feixian Lu, across the road at the southern end of the train station. There's also a *McDonald's* on Zhongshan Lu, and a couple good, inexpensive sushi places across the lane.

Strangely, **nightlife** isn't as exciting here as might be expected, and it's hard to find a pub with draught beer – though you'll pass dozens of Tsingtao ads on your search for one. A lot of Chinese visitors end up in karaoke bars or expensive hotel nightclubs such as the amazingly named *Wonderful Groggery*, near the *Huiquan*. The best place to be in the early evening is around Zhanqiao Pier, where everyone goes for a stroll after eating. There's a good American-style **bar** here, shaped like a boat, at the back of Number 6 beach.

Listings

Airlines The main CAAC office is at 29 Zhongshan Lu (☎0532/2870057); there's another office in the Aviation Building on the east side of town at 30 Xianggang Zhong Lu (☎0532/5775555). Buses to the airport go to/from here (¥15).

Banks and exchange The main Bank of China at 62 Zhongshan Lu (Mon–Fri 8am–noon & 2–5.30pm) doesn't change traveller's cheques. A separate office directly opposite the front of the Catholic Church, with the same hours, deals with credit-card advances and traveller's cheques.

Boats Discoverer Kayak Club (☎0532/2889948), across from the Huiquan Hotel at Number One Beach, rents kayaks by the hour (¥20 single, ¥30 double).

Bookshops The Foreign Language Bookstore on Zhongshan Lu, near the intersection with Jiaozhou Lu, stocks all the usual dusty old novels.

Buses Qingdao's shambolic long-distance bus station is just west of the train station. Aside from Ji'nan (4hr 30min; ¥95), Yantai is the only interesting destination within easy reach by bus.

Internet access At a basement café on the western side of the cathedral.

Mail and telephones The main post office and telecom building is at the northern end of Zhongshan Lu (Mon–Sat 8am–6pm).

PSB The PSB is at 29 Hubei Lu (Mon–Sat 8am–noon & 2–7pm), not far from the train station.

Shopping There's an antiques store at 40 Zhongshan Lu and a large Arts and Crafts Centre at the northern end of the road, no. 212. A music store across the lane from the Zhongshan Lu *McDonald's* has an extraordinary selection of CDs.

Travel agents CITS is in a separate building at the back of the *Huiquan Dynasty Hotel*, at 9 Nanhai Lu (☎0532/2861513). As usual, it caters more for domestic groups than independent foreign travellers, but you can try to arrange a brewery tour here (at least ¥200 per head, with a minimum of four people required).

Lao Shan

The **Lao Shan** area, 400 square kilometres of rugged coast 40km east of Qingdao, is an easy day-trip from the city. **Minibuses** (¥10) and public buses #304 & #801 (¥8) leave frequently from outside the train station, dropping you off at the foot of Lao Shan itself; they head back to Qingdao from the same location, or you can hail a minibus from any of the three roads inside the area. There are also minibuses travelling between each of the temples and the mountain, so it's not hard to travel from one of the popular scenic spots to another. **Maps** of the area are included on all city maps, and it's a good idea to get one before you set out.

In the Tang dynasty there were 72 Taoist temples in the area; now time, neglect and the Cultural Revolution have reduced most to ruins. It's a good place to hike around – the whole area is dotted with caves, springs and waterfalls amid striking scenery – and, with a bit of effort, it's possible to lose the crowds and trinket stalls. The area is also known for being the source of **Lao Shan mineral water**, which gives Tsingtao beer its taste; from Jiushui Valley, to the northeast of the mountain, it's one of the few Chinese mineral waters that doesn't taste of swimming pools.

On a clear day, the **coastal road route** from Qingdao is spectacular, winding somewhat precariously along cliff tops. On the way you'll pass the **Stone Old Man**, a ten-metre-high rock standing in the sea, not far from the beach. Legend has it that long ago a beautiful local girl, Mudan, was kidnapped by Longwang, the King of the East Sea. Her distraught father stood so long looking out to sea for his missing daughter that he eventually turned to stone.

Around the mountain

You'll be charged ¥30 entrance near Lao Shan village, after which there are three **roads**, each route taking in some magnificent views. The southern road takes you past the Taiqing Gong, Mingxia Cave and Longtan Waterfall. The eastern route goes to Taiping Gong, and the middle road going southeast takes you to a village at the foot of Lao Shan. From the village, a pathway of stone steps, constructed a century ago by the enterprising German Lao Shan Company to cater for their compatriots' weakness for alpine clambering, runs all the way to the summit and then back down a different route on the other side. The **path** climbs past gullies and woods, streams and pools, and the ascent takes about two hours. There's a temple halfway up, where you can fortify yourself with fruit and tea for the final haul. At the summit, 1133m above sea level, a ruined temple now houses a meteorological station. The view inspires superlatives, and gets even better as you descend by the alternative route back to the village.

Other scenic spots have a religious connection. On **Naloyan Shan**, 2km northeast of Lao Shan, is a cave in which the Naloyan Buddha was said to have meditated, and on the coast just north of here the **Baiyun Cave** was once the home of a famous monk, Tian Baiyun. Ever since, it has been seen as an auspicious place to meditate. **Mingxia Cave**, 3km farther south down the coast on the slopes of Kunyu Shan, was written about by a famous Taoist, Qiu Changchun. Inside the cave are stones which reflect the rays of the morning sun, and the flat area outside is a good vantage point to watch the sunset.

Well worth a visit is the **Taiqing Gong** (¥15), a temple to the south of Lao Shan, by the coast, and close to the boat dock. It's the oldest and grandest of Lao Shan's temples, consisting of three halls set amid attractive scenery. Outside the first hall are two camellias about which Pu Songling wrote a story. It's a photogenic, leafy place, containing some rare flowers and trees, including Hanbai paleo-cypresses, planted in the Han dynasty, and Tangyu elms dating back to the Tang. There are nine temples nearby, which, though smaller, are quiet, peaceful places.

Writers have been inspired by the scenery for centuries – *Strange Stories at Liao's House*, by the Qing-dynasty author Pu Songling, was written here – and have left noble graffiti in the form of poems and sage reflections, cut into rocks all round the area. Throughout the locality you might also see large, distinctive, oddly shaped granite **stones** named after an often tenuous resemblance to an animal or person. They're interesting forms but you need plenty of imagination – or Tsingtao Red – to get the allusion.

Yantai and around

YANTAI, on the Yellow Sea in northern Shandong, 240km northeast of Qingdao, is a somewhat battered-looking seaside town, with a burgeoning port and a tourist industry based around its rather average beaches. It's the poor relation of Qingdao (see p.353), and consequently lost out in the bidding to stage the 2008 Olympic sailing competition despite having better maritime conditions. The best reason to visit is to check out the **temple of Penglai**, 70km west of the city, or to pick up a transport connection; **ferries** leave to Tianjin, Dalian and Shanghai in the northeast, while pleasant **Weihai**, where you can catch a ferry to South Korea, is a bus ride away.

Yantai means "smoke mound", the name deriving from the ancient practice of lighting wolf-dung fires on the headland to warn of imminent Japanese invasion or (more likely) approaching pirates. Prior to 1949, it was a fishing port called Chefoo, and its recent history, like that of Qingdao, is closely bound up with European adventurism. In 1862, Chefoo was made a **British treaty**

Yantai and around

Yantai	烟台	*yāntái*
Number One Bathing Beach	第一海水浴场	*dìyī hǎishuǐ yùchǎng*
Number Two Bathing Beach	第二海水浴场	*dìèr hǎishuǐ yùchǎng*
Yantai Museum	烟台博物馆	*yāntái bówùguǎn*
Yantaishan Park	烟台山公园	*yāntáishān gōngyuán*
Accommodation		*Accommodation*
Gangcheng	港城宾馆	*gǎngchéng bīnguǎn*
International Trade Hotel	国际海员俱乐部	*guójìhǎiyuán jùlèbù*
Shandong Pacific Hotel	太平洋大酒店	*tàipíngyáng dàjiǔdiàn*
Yantai Marina Hotel	滨海假日酒店	*nánhǎi fàndiàn*
Penglai	蓬莱	*pénglái*
Weihai	威海	*wēihǎi*
Passenger ferry terminal	港客运站	*gǎngkè yùnzhàn*
Qing Quan Hotel	清泉大酒店	*qīngquán dàjiǔdiàn*
Weihaiwei Hotel	威海威大酒店	*wēihǎiwēi dàjiǔdiàn*

port as a prize of the Opium War. Thirty years later the **Germans** arrived, wishing to extend their influence on the peninsula. After World War I it was the turn of the **Americans**, who used the port as a summer station for their entire Asian fleet, then the **Japanese**, who set up a trading establishment here. However, all this foreign influence has not left a distinctive architectural mark, there has never been a foreign concession, and though you will see the odd incongruous nineteenth-century grand European building, most of the town is of much more recent origin, a product of the rapid industrialization that has taken place since 1949. The **port** has been expanded, and Yantai is now a Shandong industrial heavyweight. In the early years of the last century, the main exports were beancake, vermicelli, groundnuts and silks – and a hundred thousand coolies a year, bound for Siberia. Now the area produces and exports large amounts of apples, peanuts, fish and shrimp, as well as wooden clocks. It's also known for its more than passable **wine**, produced in vineyards set up by Singaporean Chinese in 1893, who learned their skills from French soldiers stationed here.

The City

Plenty of foreigners come to Yantai on the ships that call in at the huge port in the north of town. Mostly Russian sailors, they seldom get much farther than the International Seamen's Club opposite the train station – whose bar is probably the city's most popular attraction – or the well-stocked Friendship Store just around the corner from here, where you can stock up on local wine and brandy. They're not missing much, as there's nothing spirited about the rest of the city, although the museum is worth checking out (the building more so than the exhibits).

Wandering the **seafront** is the most pleasant way to spend any time here. A large, modern fishing fleet is based in Yantai, and fishermen can be seen repairing their nets (and drinking and playing cards) around the headland at the eastern end of town, while the promenade is lined with optimistic anglers. **Yantaishan Park** (¥2) stands at the western end of the seafront, marking the eastern edge of the port area. This steep hill, latticed with twisting paths, is where the locals used to keep an eye out for pirates. It has a modern beacon (¥5), which offers an impressive overview of the port from the top. There are also a few pavilions, a couple of former European consulates and an old Japanese military camp scattered about. The city's two **beaches** are both east of here, but they're not great – littered, windy and hemmed in by unattractive buildings. Number 2 beach, the farther of the two, is the better, though the water is very polluted. Binhai Lu, along the waterfront, has a number of small seafood restaurants.

Yantai Museum

The one sight you shouldn't miss is the **Yantai Museum** on Nan Dajie (daily 8am–5pm; ¥10), housed in the largest and most beautiful of the city's old guild halls, set up for the use of merchants and shipowners. The entrance hall is startling, decorated with an ensemble of more than a hundred stone and wood carvings. The beams are in the shape of a woman lying on her side nursing a baby, and beneath the eaves are Arab figures playing musical instruments. Other panels to the north show scenes from the *Romance of the Three Kingdoms* (see p.509), the story of the Eight Immortals who Crossed the Sea, and the story of the second-century General Su Wu, condemned to look after sheep for nineteen years as a punishment for refusing to go over to the Huns.

The main building here is the **Temple to the Goddess of the Sea**. This goddess started out as a real person, the sister of four brothers who were fishermen. It is said that she fell into a deep trance while her brothers were out on a long fishing trip. Her parents, fearing that she was dead, woke her, whereupon she told them that she had dreamed of her brothers caught in a violent storm. Later, the youngest brother returned and reported that the others had been drowned. He had been saved by a woman who had appeared in the sky and towed his boat to safety. Generations of sailors in trouble at sea reported being guided to safety by the vision of a woman. Under the Ming and Qing

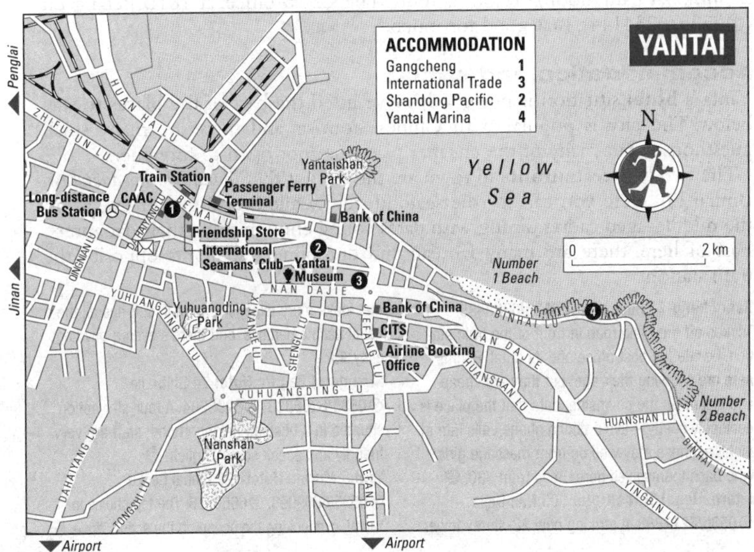

she became an official deity, and temples in her honour proliferated along the coast. The temple itself, in the style of imperial buildings of the Song dynasty, was brought from Fujian by ship in 1864 and is a unique and beautiful example of southern architecture in northern China, with its double roof and sweeping horns to the eaves, fancifully ornamented with mythical figures in wood, stone and glazed ceramics. Below are stone columns, their deep dragon motif carvings among the finest to be seen in China. The whole temple complex is set in a little garden with pools and a stage (the goddess is said to have been fond of plays). The museum in the side galleries houses a number of Stone Age cooking pots, axes and arrow heads, believed to be 6000 years old, and some fine seventeenth- and eighteenth-century porcelain.

Practicalities

Yantai's **airport** is 15km south of the city. Taxis into the centre from here cost around ¥50, while the CAAC bus (¥10) drops you at its office on Da Haiyang Lu (ⓣ0535/6245851), near the train station. The **train station**, in the northwest of town, is at the terminus of two lines, one to Qingdao and one to Ji'nan. Ferries arrive at the **passenger-ferry terminal** in the northwest of town, which is packed in summer with peasants beginning their annual migration to Manchuria for the harvest. There are ferries to Dalian, Shanghai and Tianjin, but note that if you want to be on one of the express services to Dalian, you'll only be able to buy tickets on the day of travel. For a ¥20 surcharge, a window at the main booking hall beside the train station sells onward train tickets from Dalian. The bus from Qingdao rockets along an expressway and terminates at the **long-distance bus station** on Qingnian Lu, southwest of the train station

Taxis are plentiful and cost ¥5, with ¥15 enough to journey to the far eastern beaches. Bus #2 is the most useful around the city, travelling east from the train station along Nan Dajie, the main street, then turning south down Jiefang Lu. Bus #17 travels from the train station east along the coast. Both the **post office** (Mon–Fri 8am–6pm) and the **Bank of China** (Mon–Fri 8am–noon & 2–5pm, Sat 8am–noon) are on its route. The **CITS** office, at 181B Jiefang Lu (ⓣ0535/6234144), isn't good for much.

Accommodation and eating

Yantai's **hotel** situation is not good; we've listed the best of the places to stay below. The city is popular with Chinese tourists and there are many small guesthouses, but many of the cheaper places are not open to foreigners.

The two best **restaurants** in town are the ones at the *Yantai Marina Hotel* on Binhai Lu. Here you can try the seafood stew while averting your eyes from the middle-aged cadres dining with dates young enough to be their daughters. East of here, there are many Korean and dumpling restaurants opposite the train station.

Gangcheng 72 Beima Lu ⓣ0535/6283888. Tucked off the main road in front of the train station, beside the post office and its hotel. Rooms here are showing their age, but they are cheap and clean. On the downside, note that the place is decidedly seedy – avoid taking phone calls late at night, as these may well be from massage girls who base themselves here. Beds from ¥30, ❷

International Trade Hotel 303 Nan Dajie ⓣ0535/6217888. A striking new 28-storey tower that looks more expensive than it is. It has all the usual flash amenities, and there's even a bowling alley. ❺

Shandong Pacific Hotel 74 Shifu Jie ⓣ0535/6206888, ⓕ6205204. A four-star option situated in a bustling neighborhood; staff are very friendly and speak some English. ❽

Yantai Marina Hotel 128 Binhai Bei Lu ⓣ0535/6669999, ⓕ6669770. The top choice in Yantai, overlooking the ocean on the scenic drive. ❼

Penglai

A temple on a hilltop 70km west of the city, **Penglai** makes for a worthwhile day-trip, as it holds more excitement than anything Yantai can muster. Tourist **minibuses** leave irregularly from outside Yantai's train station (45min; ¥10), or you can get a local bus to Penglai (2hr) town from the long-distance bus station. The temple is 3km beyond the town, but there are plenty of minibuses that ply the last leg of the journey.

Over 1000 years old and in a good state of repair, the temple (¥40) is a strikingly attractive complex brooding over the cliff face, dominated by a lighthouse-like tower. With crenellated walls making it look more like a castle, it has six main buildings, which have been extensively restored and added to. The Main Hall contains a fine gilt Sea Goddess, behind whose dais is a spectacular mural of sea and cloud dragons disporting themselves. You can swim or catch crabs in the sea – which is a little cleaner here than in Yantai – while you wait for the return bus.

The temple is famous for the **Penglai mirage**, which locals claim appears every few decades. Accounts of it vary widely, from a low-lying sea mist to an island in the sky, complete with people, trees and vehicles. The phenomenon lasts about forty minutes, and if you're not lucky enough to witness it you can watch it on TV in a room set aside for the purpose inside the temple. Staff declare ignorance of any correlation between an increased drive for tourist revenues and the increasing frequency of the apparation.

Weihai

The port of **WEIHAI**, 88km east of Yantai, has nothing specific to recommend it to tourists, but it is a sunny town in which to stroll while waiting for a boat. Weihai's **long-distance bus station** is about ten minutes south of the Bank of China, or 25 minutes' walk from the port. There are sleeper buses to Beijing (¥150 one way) and Shanghai (¥200 one-way) every afternoon, and frequent services to Yantai (1hr; ¥17) and Qingdao. A thrice-weekly **passenger ferry** leaves Weihai for **Inchon** in South Korea; tickets (¥750–1380) can be booked at the terminal, at the eastern terminus of Kunming Lu, or from the business centre at the *Weihaiwei Dasha*, a **hotel** at the corner of Kunming Lu and Xinwei Lu (Ⓣ0631/5285888, Ⓕ5285777; ❽). Cheaper accommodation is offered two blocks west at the *Qing Quan Hotel*, 5 Gongyuan Lu (Ⓣ0631/5224112; ❹). The **Bank of China**, where you can change traveller's cheques, is a few minutes farther west along Kunming Lu from the *Weihaiwei Dasha*.

Travel details

Trains

Anyang to: Beijing (11 daily; 7hr); Linxian (1 daily; 2hr); Shijiazhuang (3 daily; 3–5hr); Zhengzhou (12 daily; 2–3hr).
Datong to: Baotou (4 daily; 8hr); Beijing (4 daily; 7hr); Hohhot (24 daily; 5hr); Lanzhou (daily; 25hr); Linfen (daily; 12hr); Taiyuan (2 daily; 7hr); Xi'an (daily; 20hr); Xinchou (1 daily; 2hr).
Hua Shan to: Xi'an (4 daily; 2hr); Yuncheng (2 daily; 5hr).
Ji'nan to: Beijing (4 daily; 9hr); Qingdao (6 daily; 6hr); Shanghai (daily, 14hr); Tai'an (4 daily; 1hr); Yantai (4 daily; 8hr); Yanzhou (for Qufu; daily; 2hr).
Kaifeng to: Shanghai (6 daily; 12hr); Xi'an (daily; 5hr); Yanzhou (2 daily; 6hr); Zhengzhou (3 daily; 2hr).
Linfen to: Taiyuan (1 daily; 5hr); Xi'an (2 daily;

9hr); Yuncheng (3 daily; 4hr).
Luoyang to: Beijing (daily; 13hr); Shanghai (3 daily; 18hr); Xi'an (4 daily; 6 hr); Zhengzhou (6 daily; 2 hr).
Qingdao to: Beijing (2 daily; 15hr); Ji'nan (5 daily; 6hr); Shenyang (daily; 25hr); Tianjin (2 daily, 17hr); Yantai (3 daily; 5hr).
Tai'an to: Beijing (daily; 10hr); Ji'nan (4 daily; 1hr); Yanzhou, for Qufu (5 daily; 1hr).
Taiyuan to: Beijing (4 daily; 12hr); Datong (5 daily; 7hr); Linfen (daily, 7hr); Luoyang (2 daily; 12hr); Pingyao (4 daily; 2hr); Shijiazhuang (6 daily; 6hr); Xi'an (4 daily; 14hr); Yuncheng (daily; 9hr); Zhengzhou (2 daily; 13hr).
Xi'an to: Baoji (11 daily; 4hr); Beijing (5 daily; 16–18hr); Datong (2 daily; 22hr); Guangzhou (2 daily; 40hr); Hua Shan (4 daily; 3hr); Lanzhou (8 daily; 12hr); Linfen (2 daily; 6hr); Luoyang (14 daily; 6hr); Shanghai (5 daily; 24hr); Taiyuan (5 daily; 12hr); Ürümqi (daily; 60hr); Xining (4 daily; 16hr); Yan'an (2 daily; 10hr); Yuncheng (3 daily; 10hr); Zhengzhou (14 daily; 10hr).
Yantai to: Beijing (daily; 18hr); Ji'nan (3 daily; 7hr); Qingdao (6 daily; 4hr).
Yuncheng to: Linfen (3 daily; 4hr); Taiyuan (1 daily; 8hr); Xi'an (2 daily; 4hr).
Zhengzhou to: Anyang (4 daily; 2–3hr); Beijing (frequent services daily; 6–12hr); Guangzhou (2 daily; 33hr); Luoyang (8 daily; 2hr); Shanghai (3 daily; 13hr); Taiyuan (3 daily; 9hr); Xi'an (5 daily; 8–11hr).

Buses

With so many services operating in the region, bus frequencies have not been included. To most of the following destinations buses leave at least hourly during the day, with a few buses leaving in the evening and travelling through the night.
Anyang to: Kaifeng (4hr); Linxian (3hr); Zhengzhou (3hr).
Datong to: Taiyuan (7hr). Wutai Shan (6hr);
Dengfeng to: Gongxian (2hr); Luoyang (3hr); Zhengzhou (2hr).
Gongxian to: Dengfeng (2hr); Luoyang (3hr); Zhengzhou (3hr).
Ji'nan to: Beijing (8hr); Qingdao (4.5hr); Qufu (3hr); Tai'an (1.5hr).
Kaifeng to: Anyang (4hr); Zhengzhou (2hr).
Linfen to: Pingyao (1hr 45min); Taiyuan (3hr); Yuncheng (4hr).
Luoyang to: Anyang (4hr); Dengfeng (3hr); Gongxian (3hr); Ruicheng (4hr); Xi'an (6hr); Yuncheng (5hr); Zhengzhou (2hr).
Pingyao to: Linfen (1hr 45min); Taiyuan (2hr)
Qufu to: Ji'nan (3hr); Qingdao (6hr); Tai'an (1.5hr).
Tai'an to: Beijing (9hr); Ji'nan (1.5hr); Nanjing (9hr); Qufu (1.5hr); Zhengzhou (10hr).
Taiyuan to: Datong (6hr); Pingyao (2hr); Shijiazhuang (3hr); Wutai Shan (4hr); Yuncheng (7hr).
Weihai to: Beijing (13hr); Qingdao (4hr); Shanghai (16hr); Yantai (1hr).
Xi'an to: Hua Shan (1.5hr); Luoyang (6hr); Ruicheng (4hr); Yan'an (6hr); Yuncheng (5hr); Zhengzhou (7hr).
Yantai to: Beijing (12hr); Ji'nan (5hr); Qingdao (3.5hr); Weihai (1hr).
Yuncheng to: Linfen (5hr); Ruicheng (4hr); Taiyuan (7hr); Xi'an (5hr).
Zhengzhou to: Anyang (3hr); Dengfeng (2hr); Gongxian (3hr); Luoyang (2hr).

Ferries

Qingdao to: Inchon, South Korea (2 weekly; 21hr); Shimonoseki, Japan (1 weekly; 39hr).
Weihai to: Inchon, South Korea (3 weekly; 24hr).
Yantai to: Dalian (14 daily, though only four express; 4hr); Shanghai (2 weekly; 35hr); Tianjin (every 2 days; 7hr).

Flights

Among international connections from this part of China, there are flights from Qingdao to Osaka and to Seoul, and from Xi'an to Seoul.
Ji'nan to: Beijing (1 or 2 daily; 1hr); Changchun (3 weekly; 1hr 30min); Chengdu (daily; 3hr); Chongqing (daily; 2hr); Dalian (daily; 1hr 10min); Fuzhou (daily; 2hr); Guangzhou (1–3 daily; 3hr); Haikou (daily; 5hr 50min); Harbin (8 weekly; 2hr); Hong Kong (4 weekly; 2hr 30min); Kunming (daily; 3hr); Nanjing (2 weekly; 1hr 30min); Shanghai (4 daily; 1hr 40min); Shenyang (daily; 4hr); Shenzhen (daily; 3hr); Ürümqi (daily; 6hr); Wenzhou (3 weekly; 2hr); Wuhan (daily; 1hr 30min); Xiamen (daily; 3hr); Xi'an (daily; 1hr 30min); Yantai (weekly; 1hr).
Luoyang to: Beijing (daily; 1hr 40min); Chengdu (3 weekly; 1hr 40min); Dalian (3 weekly; 1hr 30min); Shanghai (daily, 2hr 10min); Xi'an (daily; 1hr)).
Qingdao to: Beijing (8 daily; 1hr 15min); Changchun (daily; 1hr 30min); Changsha (daily; 2hr); Chengdu (daily; 2hr 30min); Chongqing (6 weekly; 2hr); Dalian (6 daily; 40min); Fuzhou (4 daily; 2hr); Guangzhou (3 daily; 3hr); Guilin (6 weekly; 4hr); Haikou (daily; 6hr); Hangzhou (daily; 1hr 20min); Harbin (daily; 2hr); Hefei (4 weekly; 2hr 5min); Hong Kong (daily; 3hr 5min); Kunming (daily; 3hr); Lanzhou (3 weekly; 4hr 10min); Nanjing (daily; 1hr); Ningbo (daily; 1hr 30min); Shanghai (8 daily; 1hr 15min); Shenyang (daily;

2hr); Shenzhen (daily; 2hr 50min); Ürümqi (5 weekly; 6hr); Wenzhou (daily; 2hr); Wuhan (daily; 1hr 30min); Xiamen (daily; 3hr 10min); Xi'an (6 weekly; 2hr 20min); Zhengzhou (5 weekly; 1hr 30min).

Taiyuan to: Beijing (3 daily; 50min); Changsha (daily; 2hr); Chengdu (4 weekly; 2hr 20min); Chongqing (5 weekly; 2hr); Dalian (daily; 2hr 30min); Fuzhou (2 weekly; 3hr); Guangzhou (3 daily; 2hr 40min); Haikou (2 weekly; 4hr 30min); Hangzhou (daily; 2hr 5min); Hohhot (daily, 40min); Nanjing (6 weekly; 2hr); Shanghai (daily; 2hr); Shenyang (daily; 1hr 40min); Shenzhen (2 weekly; 3hr 15min); Tianjin (daily; 1hr); Wenzhou (2 weekly; 4hr 15min); Wuhan (daily; 3hr 20min); Xiamen (2 weekly; 3hr 15min); Xi'an (4 daily; 1hr); Zhengzhou (daily; 55min).

Xi'an to: Baotou (daily; 1hr 25min); Beijing (12 daily; 1hr 30min); Changsha (daily; 1hr 50min); Chengdu (4 daily; 1hr 15min); Chongqing (3 daily; 1hr 30min), Dalian (daily; 2hr); Dunhuang (5 daily; 2hr 20min); Fuzhou (daily; 2hr); Guangzhou (4 daily; 2hr 30min); Guilin (6 daily; 1hr 35min); Haikou (daily; 3hr); Hangzhou (daily; 1hr); Harbin (daily; 4hr 45min); Hong Kong (daily; 2hr 30min); Ji'nan (daily; 1hr 30min); Kunming (daily; 2hr 15min); Lanzhou (6 daily; 1hr 10min); Nanjing (daily; 2hr); Ningbo (daily; 2hr 40min); Qingdao (6 weekly; 1hr 45min); Shanghai (6 daily; 2hr); Shenyang (daily; 2hr 20min); Shenzhen (4 daily; 2hr 20min); Shijiazhuang (daily; 1hr); Taiyuan (4 daily; 1hr); Tianjin (daily; 1hr 30min); Ürümqi (1–3 daily; 3hr 20min); Wenzhou (4 daily; 3hr); Wuhan (1–3 daily; 2hr 20min); Xiamen (daily; 3hr); Xining (2 daily; 1hr 20min), Yantai (5 weekly; 1hr 45min); Yinchuan (4 daily; 50min).

Yantai to: Beijing (4 daily; 1hr); Changchun (5 weekly; 1hr 40min); Chengdu (4 weekly; 4hr); Guangzhou (5 weekly; 2hr 25min); Harbin (daily; 1hr 30min); Hong Kong (2 weekly; 3hr); Ji'nan (weekly; 1hr 10min); Kunming (2 weekly; 4hr); Nanjing (4 weekly; 1hr 45min); Shanghai (3 daily; 1hr 30min); Shenyang (6 weekly; 1hr); Shenzhen (6 weekly; 3hr 30min); Wenzhou (2 weekly; 2hr); Wuhan (8 weekly; 1hr 50min); Xiamen (4 weekly; 2hr 40min); Xi'an (4 weekly; 2hr 5min).

Zhengzhou to: Beijing (4 daily; 1hr 20min); Changsha (daily; 1hr 30min); Chengdu (daily; 1hr 45min); Chongqing (daily; 1hr 50min); Dalian (daily; 2hr 30min); Fuzhou (2 daily; 1hr 40min); Guangzhou (3–4 daily; 2hr 20min); Haikou (daily; 4hr); Harbin (7 weekly; 2hr 20min); Hong Kong (4 weekly; 2hr 40min); Kunming (daily; 2hr 15min); Lanzhou (6 weekly; 2hr 10min); Nanjing (4 weekly; 1hr 5min); Qingdao (5 weekly; 1hr 20min); Shanghai (3 daily; 1hr 20min); Shenyang (daily; 1hr 50min); Shenzhen (daily; 2hr 5min); Taiyuan (daily; 1hr 20min); Ürümqi (daily; 4hr); Wenzhou (daily; 2hr 30min); Wuhan (5 weekly; 1hr 30min); Xiamen (daily; 1hr 40min); Xi'an (daily; 15min).

CHAPTER 5

Highlights

* **Peace Hotel** Drop by for a cocktail and check out the Art Deco interior and the open-air views from the roof. See p.383
* **The Bund** Fusty colonial architecture and brash modernity stare each other down over the Huangpu River. See p.387
* **Huangpu boat trip** Get out on the river, either on a tourist trip or crowding on the local ferries, for a sense of the maritime industry that's the heart of the city's success. See p.391
* **Nanjing Lu** One of China's premier consumer cornucopias. See p.393
* **Shanghai Museum** Candidate for the best museum in the country and a lovely building too. See p.394
* **Cloud 9 Café** Sublime views from the top floor of Shanghai's tallest building. See p.407
* **Nightclubbing** Glamorous, raucous, vacuous and often very decadent. See p.407

5

Shanghai

After forty years of stagnation, the great metropolis of **SHANGHAI** is currently undergoing one of the fastest economic expansions that the world has ever seen. While shops overflow and the skyline fills with skyscrapers, Shanghai now seems certain to recapture its position as East Asia's leading business city, a status it last held before World War II. And yet, for all the modernization Shanghai has retained deep links with its **colonial past**.

Shanghai is still known in the West for its infamous role as the base of **European imperialism** in mainland China – its decadence, illicit pleasures, racism, appalling social inequalities, and Mafia syndicates. The intervening fifty years have almost been forgotten, as though the period from when the Communists arrived and the foreigners moved out was an era in which nothing happened. To some extent this perception is actually true: for most of the Communist period into the early 1990s, the central government in Beijing deliberately ran Shanghai down, siphoning off its surplus to other parts of the country to the point where the city came to resemble a living museum, frozen in time since the 1940s, and housing the largest array of **Art Deco architecture** in the world.

Yet the Shanghainese never lost their ability to make waves for themselves and, in recent years, China's central government has come to be dominated by individuals from the Shanghai area, who look with favour on the rebuilding of their old metropolis. In the mid 1980s, the decision was made to push Shanghai once again to the forefront of China's drive for **modernization**, and an explosion of **economic activity** has been unleashed. In the last two decades, city planners have been busy creating a subway network, colossal highways, flyovers and bridges, shopping malls, hotel complexes and the beginnings of a "New Bund" – the Special Economic Zone across the river in Pudong, soon to be crowned with the **world's tallest building**. Significantly, China's main money-printing mint is near here, hence the high proportion of shiny new coins and bills in circulation in the city. The Shanghainese are by far the most highly skilled labour force in the country, renowned for their ability to combine style and sophistication with a sharp sense for business, and international in outlook. Thanks to them their city is riding high.

Not that the **old Shanghai** is set to disappear overnight. Although the pace of redevelopment has quickened, parts of the city still resemble a 1920s vision of the future; a grimy metropolis of monolithic pseudo-classical facades, threaded with overhead cables and walkways, and choked by vast crowds and rattling trolley buses. Unlike other major Chinese cities, Shanghai has only recently been subjected to large-scale rebuilding. Most of the urban area was

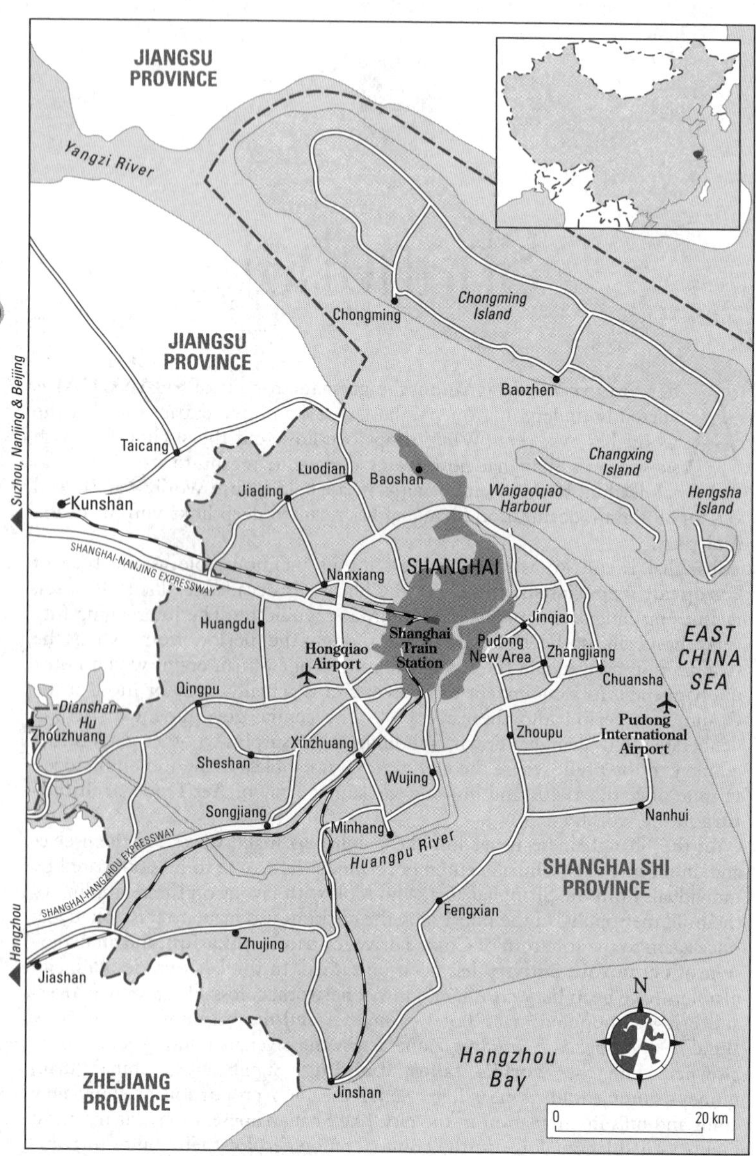

partitioned between foreign powers until 1949, and their former embassies, banks and official residences still give large areas of Shanghai an early-twentieth-century European flavour that the odd Soviet-inspired government building cannot overshadow. It is still possible to make out the boundaries of what used to be the foreign concessions, with the bewildering tangle of alleyways of the old Chinese city at its heart. Only along the Huangpu waterfront, amid the stolid grandeur of the Bund, is there some sense of space – and here you feel the past more strongly than ever, its outward forms, shabby and battered, still very much a working part of the city. Today, strolling the Bund is a required attraction for any visitor to Shanghai, and it's ironic that relics of hated foreign imperialism such as the Bund are now protected as city monuments.

Like Hong Kong, its model of economic development, Shanghai does not brim with obvious attractions to see. Besides the Shanghai Museum, the Suzhou-reminiscent Yu Yuan Gardens, and the Huangpu River Cruise, there are few sights with broad appeal – many travellers leave the city with a sense of letdown. But the beauty of visiting Shanghai lies not so much in scurrying from attraction to attraction, but in less obvious pleasures: strolling the Bund, exploring the pockets of colonial architecture in the old French Concession, sampling the exploding restaurant and nightlife scene, or wandering the shopping streets and absorbing the rebirth of one of the world's great cities.

Inevitably, many of the **social ills** that the Communists were supposed to have eliminated after 1949 are making a comeback. Unemployment, drug abuse and prostitution are rife. But the dynamic contrast that Shanghai presents with the rest of China is one that even the most China-weary of travellers can hardly fail to enjoy.

Some history

When the Communists marched into Shanghai in May 1949, they took control of the most important business and trading centre in Asia, an international port where vast fortunes were made while millions lived in absolute poverty. Whichever side you were on, life in Shanghai was rarely one of moderation. China's most prosperous city, in large part European- and American-financed, it introduced Asia to electric light, boasted more cars than the rest of the country put together, and created for its rich citizens a world of European-style mansions, tree-lined boulevards, chic café society, horse racing and exclusive gentlemen's clubs. Alongside, and as much part of the legend, lay a city of singsong girls, warring gangsters and hungry millions in thrall to their daily bowl of rice.

Inevitably, after the Communist takeover, the bright lights dimmed – the foreign community may have expected "Business as usual", but the new regime was determined that Shanghai should play its role in the radical reconstruction of China. The worst slums were knocked down to be replaced by apartments, the gangsters and whores were taken away for "re-education", and foreign capital was ruthlessly taxed if not confiscated outright (although Chiang Kaishek did manage to spirit away the gold reserves of the Bank of China to Taiwan, leaving the city broke). For 35 years Western influences were forcibly suppressed.

Contrary to Western interpretations, Shanghai's history did not begin with the founding of the British Concession in the wake of the First Opium War. Located at the confluence of the Yangzi River, the Grand Canal and the Pacific Ocean, Shanghai served as a major commercial port from the Song dynasty, channelling the region's extensive cotton crop to Beijing, the hinterland and Japan. By the Qing dynasty, vast **mercantile guilds**, often organized by trade and bearing superficial resemblance to their Dutch counterparts, had established economic and, to some extent, political control of the city. Indeed, the British only chose to set up a treaty port in Shanghai because, in the words of East India Company representative Hugh Lindsay, the city by the 1840s had become "the principal emporium of Eastern Asia".

After the **Opium Wars**, the British moved in under the Treaty of Nanking in 1842, to be rapidly followed by the French in 1847, and these two powers set up the first **foreign concessions** in the city – the British along the Bund and the area to the north of the Chinese city; the French in an area to the southwest on the site of a cathedral a French missionary had founded two centuries earlier. Later the Americans, in 1863, and the Japanese, in 1895, came to tack their own areas on to the British Concession which expanded into the so-called International Settlement. Traders were allowed to live under their own national laws, policed by their own armed forces, in a series of privileged enclaves which were leased indefinitely. By 1900 the city's favourable position, close to the main trade route to the major silk- and tea-producing regions had allowed it to develop into a sizeable port and manufacturing centre, largely controlled by the "Green Gang", the infamous syndicate founded in the 1700s by unemployed boatmen, which by the 1920s controlled the city's vast underworld. Businessmen and criminals who flouted the Green Gang's strict code of behaviour were subject to "knee-capping" punishment – having every visible tendon severed with a fruit knife before being left to die on a busy sidewalk.

Shanghai's cheap workforce was swollen during the Taiping Uprising (see box, p.458) by those who took shelter from the slaughter in the foreign settlements, and by peasants attracted to the city's apparent prosperity. Here, China's first urban proletariat emerged, and the squalid living conditions, outbreaks of unemployment and glaring abuses of Chinese labour by foreign investors made Shanghai a natural breeding ground for **revolutionary politics.** The Chinese Communist Party was founded in the city in 1921, only to be driven underground by the notorious massacre of hundreds of strikers in 1927.

Even since 1949, the city has remained a centre of radicalism – Mao, stifled by Beijing bureaucracy, launched his Cultural Revolution here in 1966. Certain Red Guards even proclaimed a Shanghai Commune, before the whole affair descended into wanton destruction and petty vindictiveness. After Mao's death, Shanghai was the last stronghold of the Gang of Four in their struggle for the succession, though their planned coup never materialized. Today, many key modernizing officials in the central government are from the Shanghai area, including President Jiang Zemin and Premier Zhu Rongji, both former mayors of the city.

As well as an important power-base for the ruling party, Shanghai has always been the most fashion-conscious and **outward-looking** city in China. The Shanghainese are renowned for their quick wit and entrepreneurial skills. Many fled to Hong Kong after 1949 and oversaw the colony's economic explosion, while a high proportion of overseas Chinese successful in business elsewhere in the world originally emigrated from this area. Even during the Cultural Revolution, Western excesses like curled hair and holding hands in public survived in Shanghai. Despite the incomprehensibility of the local Shanghainese dialect to other Chinese, it has always been easier for visitors to communicate with the locals here than anywhere else in the country, because of the excellent level of English spoken and the familiarity with foreigners and foreignness. The city's relative wealth has also allowed a greater interest in **leisure** activities and **nightlife**, with a wide variety of public entertainment on offer as well as a host of new bars and clubs. Not only is Shanghai still the nation's premier industrial base, it is also the major consumer centre, and the variety and quality of goods in the shops attract people from all over China.

Some problems remain, however, and above all Shanghai continues to suffer acute **overcrowding**. Although the housing stock has soared in recent years, even official statistics give the average inhabitant living space little larger than a double bed, and in practice this often means three generations of a family sleeping in one room. Everywhere you look, there are too many people, and the resultant stress frequently surfaces in outbreaks of bad temper and sometimes public brawling. As a centre of huge oil refineries, chemical and metallurgical plants, Shanghai is also afflicted by air **pollution** in the form of sulphurous clouds pouring from the factory chimneys. About four million tons of untreated industrial and domestic waste flow daily into the Huangpu River, the city's main source of drinking water, while the Suzhou Creek is black and foul-smelling. Finally, the **unemployment** rate is noticeably higher than that of other major cities. The problem of outsiders without Shanghai residence papers (and hence without accommodation) pouring into the city in search of riches has the potential to lead to serious social unrest. Today, though nominally closed to internal migration, and despite the one-child policy and 300,000 abortions annually, Shanghai continues to grow – to the point where a population of more than thirteen million makes it one of the largest (and most congested) cities in the world.

Orientation and arrival

Shanghai is a surprisingly compact place, considering its enormous population, and although its layout is less obviously geometrical than that of Beijing, it's not hard to find your way around on foot – though you'll certainly need buses or taxis for crossing from one quarter to the next. The area of most interest to visitors is bordered to the east by the **Huangpu River** (which flows from south to north), and to the north by the **Suzhou Creek** (which flows from west to east). A good place to get your bearings is at the southwestern corner of the junction of these two rivers, at the entrance to the small Huangpu Park. To the north, across the iron Waibaidu Bridge over Suzhou Creek, is the area of the old Japanese Concession. South from Huangpu Park, along the western bank of the Huangpu River, runs **the Bund** – in Chinese, officially Zhongshan Lu, unofficially Wai Tan. The Bund is in turn overlooked from the east bank by the Oriental Pearl TV Tower, the city's most conspicuous landmark. A lot of hotels, including some of the only dormitory accommodation, are in the Bund area. A hundred metres south from Huangpu Park, the Bund is met by **Nanjing Lu**, one of the city's premier shopping streets, which runs west, past the northern edge of Renmin Park in the centre of the city. Like all east–west routes, Nanjing Lu takes its name from that of a city; north–south roads are named after provinces. A few blocks to the south of Nanjing Lu is another major east–west thoroughfare, Yan'an Lu, which, to the east, leads into a tunnel under the Huangpu River. South of here, just west of the Bund, is the oval-shaped area corresponding to the **Old City**. The most important of the north–south axes is Xizang Lu, cutting through the downtown area just east of **Renmin Park**. Heading south, Xizang Lu runs down to an intersection with **Huaihai Lu**, Shanghai's other main shopping boulevard, which heads west into the heart of the **old French Concession**. In Shanghai, as in many other Chinese cities, long streets are divided into sections for the purpose of naming. For example Yan'an "East" Street (Yan'an Dong Lu), Yan'an "Middle" Street (Yan'an Zhong Lu) and Yan'an "West" Street (Yan'an Xi Lu). This convention is very useful when looking for an address. North and south are *bei* and *nan* respectively.

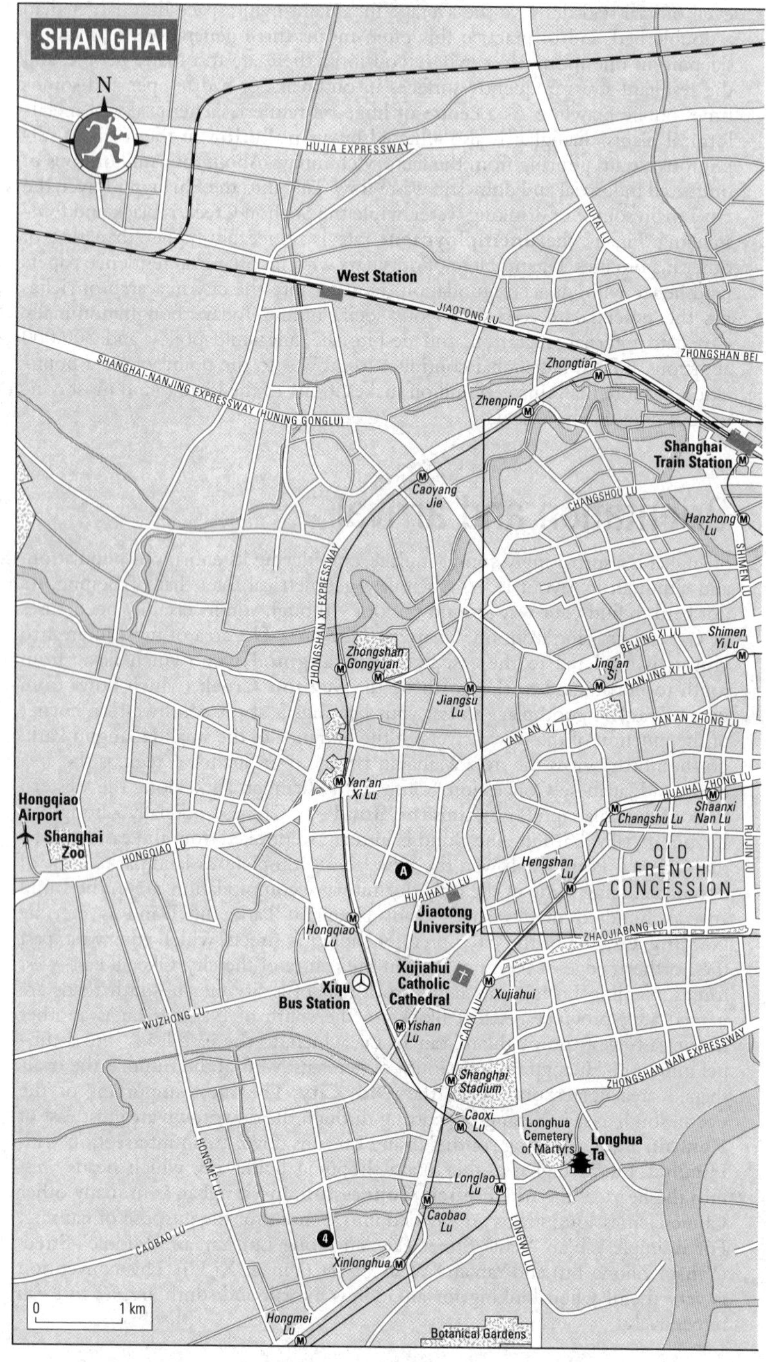

5 SHANGHAI | Orientation and arrival

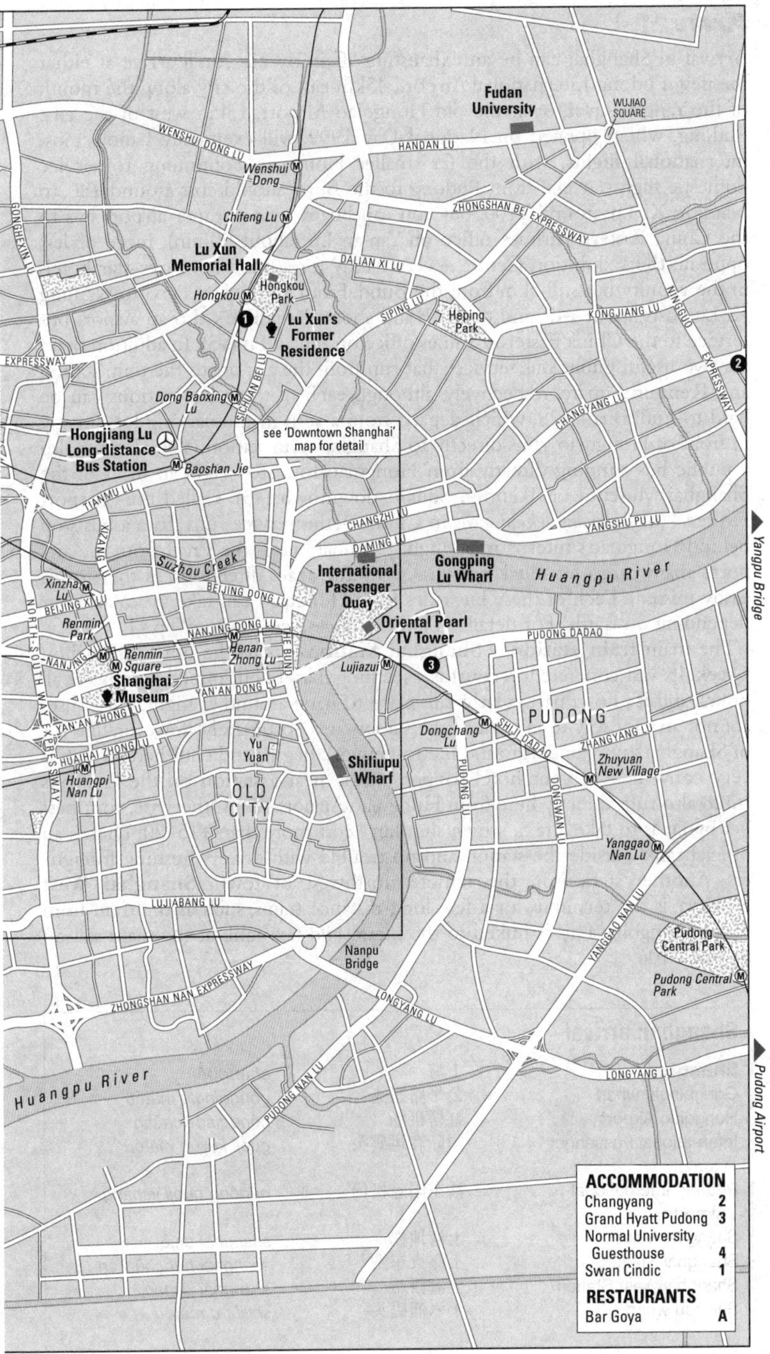

ACCOMMODATION

Changyang	2
Grand Hyatt Pudong	3
Normal University Guesthouse	4
Swan Cindic	1

RESTAURANTS

Bar Goya	A

Arrival

Arrival in Shanghai can be an exhausting affair. By **air** you'll arrive at either the new Pudong International Airport, 45km east of the city along the mouth of the Yangzi River, or at the old Hongqiao Airport, 15km west of the city. Pudong, which opened on National Day 1999, will eventually handle most international flights, with the far smaller Hongqiao continuing to service domestic flights. A taxi from Pudong to the Bund should cost around ¥80, to Nanjing Xi Lu around ¥100, but you can board a far cheaper airport bus to the China Eastern Airlines office on Yan'an Lu (about 90min), more or less opposite the Exhibition Centre – very handy for a number of five-star hotels in the vicinity, but still 3km from the Bund. From Hongqiao, a taxi to Nanjing Xi Lu costs about ¥45, and to the Bund about ¥60; there's also an airport bus service to the China Eastern Airlines office on Yan'an Lu (¥5). In addition there are two useful public bus services that run from the airport to the train station and Renmin Square, respectively, although each of these bus stations can be hard to find. Bus #328, which departs from a stop in the parking lot directly in front of Hongqiao, runs directly to Shanghai train station (¥2). There is also a public bus running directly from Hongqiao to a stop right in front of the Shanghai Museum on Renmin Square, downtown (¥3). Called the "Airport Express" (or *feijichang tekuai qiche* in Chinese), this service runs from a bus stop behind Hongqiao's international flight terminal, across the street from the airport's main cargo terminal (ask passers-by for exact directions, as the stop is easily missed). Each of these bus rides from Hongqiao can take up to an hour depending on traffic. For details of airline offices, see "Listings", p.411.

The main **train station** – **Shanghai Station** – is to the north of Suzhou Creek. Its vast concrete forecourt is a seething mass of encamped peasants at all hours, and it's not a particularly safe place to hang around at night. City buses are not an easy way to get out of the station area; fortunately, however, line #1 of Shanghai's new underground metro network begins and ends here, which is very convenient if your hotel happens to be near a station on the line. Bus #328 also runs directly here from Hongqiao Airport (¥2) Otherwise, your best bet by far is to take a taxi, which shouldn't cost more than ¥15–20. There's an official rank outside the station and no trouble with drivers hustling foreigners. Another station in the remote northwest of town, **Shanghai West Station**, is the terminus for a few long-distance trains, such as the train from Inner Mongolia. This is linked to the metro and taxi rank at the main station by bus #106.

Shanghai: arrival

Shanghai	上海	***shànghǎi***
Gongpinglu wharf	公平路码头	*gōngpínglù mǎtóu*
Hongqiao Airport	虹桥机场	*hóngqiáo jīchǎng*
International Passenger Quay	国际客运码头	*guójì kèyùn mǎtóu*
Pudong International Airport	浦东国际机场	*pǔdōng guójì jīchǎng*
Shanghai Metro	上海地铁	*shànghǎi dìtiě*
Shanghai Station	上海火车站	*shànghǎi huǒchēzhàn*
Shanghai West Station	上海西站	*shànghǎi xīzhàn*
Shiliupu wharf	十六浦码头	*shíliùpù mǎtóu*

Moving on from Shanghai

The soft seat waiting room in the main **train station** (enter from the forecourt, near the eastern end; there's an English sign) has an office that sells same-day and next-day tickets only, hard seat and sleeper as well as soft (daily 7am–9pm). Alternatively, the *Longmen Hotel,* a couple of minutes west of the station square, has a foreigners' ticket office (daily 7am–5.30pm & 6–9pm) in the lobby which sells tickets for up to four days in advance – mainly seats to Nanjing and Hangzhou, though it does also sell sleepers to a few important destinations such as Beijing or Guangzhou. To book further in advance (up to a week) you can buy tickets (with a 10–15 percent mark-up) from CTS in the *Pacific Hotel* on Nanjing Xi Lu, from the CITS office in the Shanghai Centre, or from the CITS office at 2 Jinling Dong Lu (all daily 8.30–11.30am & 1–4.45pm).

Tourists rarely travel by **bus** into or out of Shanghai, though for a few destinations buses might offer a convenient way to leave the city, because they are slightly cheaper than trains and it is easy to get a seat. In the western part of the train station square several private operators offer tickets, up to a day in advance, for destinations in Jiangsu and Zhejiang provinces, but their prices are nearly as expensive as the train. A kiosk between the Shanghai Museum and the Yan'an Lu elevated expressway sells tickets for buses leaving from the train station up to a week in advance. The Qiujiang Lu bus station, just west of Henan Bei Lu, has more reasonable prices, yet less comfortable buses, mainly leaving for Hangzhou and towns in Jiangsu. For a few destinations outside the city (see p.402), but inside the Shanghai Municipality, services leave from the **Xiqu bus station** (bus #113 from the train station) or a nameless bus stop on Shaanxi Nan Lu, outside the Wenhua Guangchang, just south of Fuxing Lu. For these buses, you pay on board.

Leaving by boat also deserves serious consideration, with tickets cheaper and travelling conditions sometimes better than the trains. You can buy tickets from any travel service for an added fee, or go to the **boat ticket office** (daily 7–11.30am & 12–5pm) at the southwest corner of Jinling Dong Lu and the Bund, which sells every kind of boat ticket out of Shanghai. The office has no English sign, but the entrance is directly across the Bund from the riverside pyramid-shaped *Diamond Restaurant*. The downstairs windows sell tickets for the coastal routes. Foreigner surcharges have been abolished, and therefore prices are fairly low. Sample first- to fifth-class fares include Dalian ¥120–387, Qingdao ¥138–345, Ningbo ¥46–170, Putuo Shan ¥68–200, Wenzhou ¥90–265 and Mawei (for Fuzhou) ¥104–317. First class generally means a double room with nice mattresses and a washbasin, while fifth class patrons can expect 32-berth compartments, lights on all night and noisy surroundings. For **Putuo Shan** there is also a special ticket window belonging to a private operator – for details, see Putuo Shan (p.493). **Yangzi River** boat tickets are sold upstairs, now also with no foreigner surcharge (ticket window open Mon–Fri 8.30–11.15am & 1–4pm). Sample fares include: Nanjing ¥56–128, Wuhan ¥130–409 and Chongqing ¥306–994.

Finally, if you go right through the upstairs hall and follow the corridor around to the right, there are two offices on the left (Mon–Sat 8.30am–noon & 1–4pm) selling tickets to **Japan and Korea**. (The long-running Hong Kong service has been discontinued with the construction of the Shanghai–Kowloon direct rail service.) For Japan there are connections to Osaka and Kobe. Each boat has berths ranging from ¥1300 (for a tatami mat on a floor) to ¥6500 (for a first-class cabin). A return ticket costs half as much again. The frequency of each boat varies according to season, but generally there are departures weekly in winter and twice-weekly in summer. The voyage takes about two days. To South Korea, there is a boat to Inch'on, Seoul's port, once a week in winter and twice a week in summer. The journey takes around 38 hours, and prices range from ¥600 to ¥1600. Onboard all boats the conditions are pretty luxurious, with steam baths, discos and clean, comfortable berths, though take some food as the restaurants are expensive.

Hardly any tourists arrive in Shanghai by **bus**, and one good reason to avoid trying to do this is that you might be dropped somewhere in the remote outskirts of the city. Some services use the **bus station** on Qiujiang Lu, just west of Henan Bei Lu, next to the Baoshan Lu metro station, a few private buses terminate at the train station itself, or you may arrive at Hengfeng Station over the road from the Hanzhong Lu metro station, but generally speaking it's pot luck where you end up.

Probably the nicest way to arrive in Shanghai is by **boat**, whether from Japan, Korea or the towns along the coast or inland up the Yangzi. The Yangzi ferries and coastal boats to and from Ningbo, Wenzhou and Putuo Shan sail south right past the Bund to the **Shiliupu wharf**, linked by bus #55 to the northern end of the Bund. Coastal boats to and from Qingdao, Dalian and Fuzhou use the **Gongping Lu wharf**, which is only about twenty minutes' walk to the northeast of the Bund or a short ride on bus #135, while boats from Japan and South Korea dock at the **International Passenger Quay**, about five minutes' walk east from the *Pujiang Hotel*.

Information and city transport

For **information** in English, call the tourist hotline ⓣ021/62520000 (daily 8am–10pm). At Hongqiao Airport dial ⓣ021/62688899 ext 56750 (daily 10am–9.30pm). At the north entrance of the Renmin Square metro station, there's also a tourist kiosk with free English maps, brochures and advice. An elderly gentleman here speaks excellent English and is a gold mine for information on Shanghai's recent history and architectural wonders.

A vital source of English-language information about current events in the city is the excellent and free expatriate-run monthly **That's Shanghai** (ⓦwww.thatsshanghai.com) available at most hotels, bars and upmarket restaurants. There are plenty of others; *ShanghaiScene* and *Shanghai Talk* are also pretty good, offering frank advice on the latest happenings. The same sort of information is available online at ⓦwww.shanghai-ed.com. The tourist bureau publishes the English-language newspapers, *Travel China: Shanghai Edition* and *Shanghai Today*, both with a heavier emphasis on current events articles and less emphasis on restaurant and nightlife listings.

Various glossy English-language **maps** are also available, with clear information on streets and sights – including the Shanghai Official Tourist Map, which is paid for by advertising and is issued free in hotels and in the Renmin Square subway station. Additionally, bus routes can be found on the Shanghai Communications Map, though this map has street names in Chinese only. English maps are available in the large hotels, bookshops and the tourist kiosk at the north end of the Renmin Square subway station. Street vendors all over town sell Chinese maps.

City transport

The clean, efficient **Shanghai metro** currently comprises three lines, with more under construction. Its futuristic design sharply resembles Hong Kong's MTR metro; both systems were created by the same company. Line #1 runs from the main train station in the north, by Renmin Park and the Shanghai Museum, and then turns west along Huaihai Lu. Line #2, which opened on October 1, 1999, the fiftieth anniversary of the founding of the People's Republic, starts in Zhongshan in the west (where it connects to line #3),

Useful Shanghai bus routes

North–south

#18 (trolley) From Hongkou Park, across the Suzhou Creek and along Xizang Lu.

#41 Passes Tianmu Xi Lu, in front of the train station and goes down through the French Concession to Longhua Park.

#64 From the train station, along Beijing Lu, then close to the Shiliupu wharf on the south of the Bund. The best bus to take from the train station to the *Pujiang Hotel* – get off at the Jiangxi Nan Lu stop.

#65 From the top to the bottom of Zhongshan Lu (the Bund), terminating in the south at the Nanpu Bridge.

East–west

#19 (trolley) From near Gongping Lu wharf in the east, passing near the *Pujiang Hotel* and roughly following the course of the Suzhou Creek to the Jade Buddha Temple just before the terminus.

#20 From Jiujiang Lu (just off the Bund) along Nanjing Lu, past Jing'an Si, then on to Zhongshan Park.

#42 From Guangxi Lu just off the Bund, then along Huaihai Lu in the French Concession.

#135 From Yangpu Bridge via the Bund to the eastern end of Huaihai Dong Lu.

intersects with the first line at Renmin Park, and travels under the Huangpu River to Pudong. Line #3 (aka the Pearl Line) runs overground southwest to northeast, skirting the northwest of the city centre en route. Tickets cost ¥3–4 depending on the distance travelled and are bought from ticket machines, which also sell a ¥50 card. The metro opens daily at 5.30am and closes at 11pm.

Local buses run everywhere, but suffer from three serious defects: they are unbelievably crowded, especially during the early morning and late evening rush hours; they are extremely slow owing to the grotesque traffic congestion; and few lines run the long distances needed to travel from one side of the city to the other. They operate from around 4am to 10.30pm, although each line has its own schedule. Bus maps, available from hotels, CITS offices and most subway stations, mark the widely separated stops with a small dot. Fares are generally ¥1 for regular buses and ¥2 for air-conditioned ones; buy your ticket from the conductor on the bus. Carrying exact change will eliminate a lot of hassle.

Taxis are very easy to get hold of and, if you're not on a very tight budget, they are often the most comfortable way to get around – fares usually come to between ¥20 and ¥40 for rides within the city. Few drivers speak English, so it will help to have your destination written in Chinese. The only kind of hassle you're likely to suffer is from drivers who take you on unnecessarily long detours, but if you sit in the front seat and hold a map on your lap they will usually be persuaded to behave themselves. However, very late at night, conventions change – meters are often switched off and you may have to negotiate the fare, or at least tell the driver "da biao", meaning turn on the meter. Starting fares between 11pm and 5am are about thirty percent higher than at other times.

To cross the Huangpu River over to the Pudong, the cheapest way is to take the very frequent double-decker **ferry** from the central part of the Bund, next to the prominent riverside *Diamond Restaurant*. The lower deck gives a more interesting feel of how crowded these waterways are. Buy a plastic token for ¥0.8 at the jetty. A **tunnel** also runs from the Bund to Pudong but costs ¥20 – you ride in a car and are treated to a light show.

Accommodation

Accommodation in Shanghai is plentiful, and in places highly stylish, but prices are generally higher than elsewhere in China. The **grand old-world hotels** that form so integral a part of Shanghai's history cost at least US$120 per room these days, though a short stay in, for example, the famous *Peace Hotel* will give you a memorable flavour of how Shanghai used to be. Even if you're not a resident, however, there's nothing to stop you strolling in to admire some of the finest Art Deco interiors in the world.

Many travellers arrive in Shanghai assuming there is only one really **budget option** in the entire city, the *Pujiang*, which not surprisingly fills up rapidly in peak season. However, don't overlook the other quality, inexpensive choices – the guesthouses at the *Shanghai Conservatory of Music* and *Normal Teachers' University* in the southwest of the city, and the new *Captain Hostel* on the Bund all have beds available for less than ¥80, and often have vacancies even into the summer.

Meanwhile, brand-new **skyscraper hotels** are going up all the time, especially in the business district of Pudong, where the tallest hotel in the world is situated on the top floors of the 421-metre-high Jin Mao Building. There are also a number of top-class hotels, including a *Sheraton* and a *Hilton*, in the western part of town, mainly along Nanjing Xi Lu. Prices are often quoted in US dollars, though you can always pay in renminbi.

Shanghai accommodation

Captain Hostel	船长酒店	*chuánzhǎng fàndiàn*
Changyang	长阳饭店	*chángyáng fàndiàn*
Chun Shen Jiang	春申江宾馆	*chūnshēnjiāng bīnguǎn*
Dong Hu	东湖宾馆	*dōnghú bīnguǎn*
Garden	花园酒店	*huāyuán jiǔdiàn*
Grand Hyatt Pudong	浦东金茂凯悦大酒店	*pǔdōng jīnmàokǎiyuè dàjiǔdiàn*
JC Mandarin	锦沧文华大酒店	*jǐncāngwénhuá dàjiǔdiàn*
Jinjiang	锦江饭店	*jǐnjiāng fàndiàn*
Metropole	新城饭店	*xīnchéng fàndiàn*
New Asia	新亚大酒店	*xīnyà dàjiǔdiàn*
Normal University Guesthouse	师范大学外宾楼	*shīfàn dàxué wàibīnlóu*
Pacific	金门大酒店	*jīnmén dàjiǔdiàn*
Park	国际饭店	*guójì fàndiàn*
Peace	和平饭店	*hépíng fàndiàn*
Portman Ritz-Carlton	波特曼丽思卡尔顿酒店	*bōtèmàn lìsīkǎěrdùn jiǔdiàn*
Pujiang	浦江饭店	*pǔjiāng fàndiàn*
Ruijin Guesthouse	瑞金宾馆	*ruìjīn bīnguǎn*
Seagull	海鸥饭店	*hǎiōu fàndiàn*
Shanghai Conservatory Guesthouse	音乐学院招待所	*yīnyuèxuéyuàn zhāodàisuǒ*
Shanghai Mansions	上海大厦	*shànghǎi dàshà*
Swan Cindic	天鹅宾馆	*tiāné bīnguǎn*

During the off-season (Nov–April) some good discounts are offered. For example, foreign students studying in Chinese universities can procure rooms in many three- and four-star Shanghai hotels for around ¥300 just by showing their red *liuxuesheng zheng* (foreign student ID card) at the front desk – check the various English-language periodicals for ads featuring the latest offers. Even if you're not a student, you can buy a realistic-looking student card in many back alleys for around ¥50. Most of the accommodation listed below is fairly central and so appears on the Downtown Shanghai map (pp.386–387).

The Bund and around

Captain Hostel 37 Fuzhou Lu ⓣ021/63235053, ⓕ63219331, ⓔcaptain@captainhostel.com.cn. A new youth hostel that will soon be challenging the *Pujiang* just down the road – service standards are high and it's very good value. Facilities are communal, but very clean, and there's a kitchen and washing machines. There's an English sign outside. The nautical theme is carried through with admirable thoroughness – the dorms are made to look like cabins, with portholes for windows, and there's even sand under glass in the tables. Dorm beds ¥50, ❸

Chun Shen Jiang 626 Nanjing Dong Lu, near Fujian Lu ⓣ021/63515710. The sign is in Chinese characters only. Slightly musty and spartan rooms, but the location – almost halfway between Renmin Park and the Bund – is hard to beat, and the prices are not astronomical. ❺

Metropole 180 Jiangxi Lu ⓣ021/63213030, ⓕ63217365. Just off the Bund and dating from 1931, this is one of the more affordable of the "old" hotels. A great lobby, but the rooms are plain. ❻

New Asia 422 Tian Tong Lu ⓣ021/63242210, ⓕ63566816. Located to the north of Suzhou Creek, a couple of blocks west of the Shanghai Mansions, this is good value for its location. ❻

Peace Junction of the Bund and Nanjing Dong Lu ⓣ021/63216888, ⓕ63290300. Formerly the *Cathay Hotel*, the most famous hotel in Shanghai, occupying both sides of the road and home to the *Jazz Bar* (see "Entertainment", p.408). Well worth a visit to see the Art Deco interiors of the lobby. Despite its high prices, however, the service in this hotel is definitely not five-star standard. Doubles start at US$160, de luxe suites with original decor from US$520. ❾

Pujiang 15 Huangpu Lu ⓣ021/63246388, ⓕ63243179. Located across the Waibaidu Bridge north of the Bund and slightly to the east, opposite the blue Russian Consulate building. From the train station, take bus #64 to the Jiangxi Nan Lu stop, walk east to the Bund, then across the Waibaidu. Formerly the *Astor Hotel*, and dating back to 1846, this is a nice, stylish old place with creaky wooden floors and high ceilings and the fusty look of an English public school. Dormitory accommodation is available here, and conditions are not at all bad: each dorm has an adjoining bathroom and toilet, as well as communal shower rooms on another floor. Dorm beds ¥55, ❹

Seagull 60 Huangpu Lu ⓣ021/63251500, ⓕ63241263. On the north bank of the Suzhou Creek, just east of the blue Russian Consulate, this is a smart, modern Chinese hotel. ❼

Shanghai Mansions 20 Suzhou Bei Lu ⓣ021/63246260, ⓕ63065147. This is the huge ugly lump of a building on the north bank of the Suzhou Creek, visible from the north end of the Bund. Originally a residential block built in the 1930s, it now offers excellent rooms, larger than the *Peace* and with superb views along the length of the Bund. Its most illustrious resident was Jiang Qing (wife of Mao Zedong) who issued a decree during the Cultural Revolution banning barges and sampans from travelling up the Huangpu or Suzhou while she was asleep. If you're not staying here, you can appreciate the views by taking the lift to the eighteenth floor. Rooms get pricier the higher up you go. ❼

Western Shanghai: Nanjing Xi Lu and the old French Concession

Dong Hu 70 Donghu Lu ⓣ021/64158158, ⓕ64157759. One block north of Huaihai Zhong Lu. Clean, spacious rooms giving no indication that the hotel served as an opium warehouse and the centre of Mafia operations in the 1920s and 1930s. ❼

Garden 58 Maoming Lu ⓣ021/64151111, ⓕ64158866. Japanese-managed and probably the best hotel in Shanghai, constructed on the grounds of the former, ultra-exclusive French Club, in the French Concession. Doubles from US$165. ❾

JC Mandarin 1225 Nanjing Xi Lu ⓣ021/62791888, ⓕ62791822. Two blocks east of the Shanghai Centre. Modern five-star hotel with plush rooms and all the amenities. Doubles from US$128. ❾

Jinjiang 59 Maoming Lu ⓣ021/62582582, ⓦwww.jinjianghotelshanghai.com. A vast place in the French Concession, with many wings, much history, and some of the best facilities in the city. Richard Nixon stayed here on his famous visit in 1972, signing the Shanghai Communiqué in the second-floor auditorium (since renovated). Doubles from US$130. ⑨

Normal University Guesthouse 100 Guilin Lu ⓣ021/64701860, ⓕ64369249. Far away in the southwest of the city, but well connected via the subway to the centre of town and the train station, this is a quiet and reasonably priced place to stay, offering clean dorm beds and comfortable doubles. To reach it, take the metro to Shangtiguan Station, then take bus #43 to the terminus. The guesthouse is through the university's main gate to the left. Dorms ¥45, ⑤

Pacific 108 Nanjing Xi Lu ⓣ021/63276226, ⓕ63723634. Another historic place, virtually in the centre of the city, with an extremely grand entrance and lobby. ⑦

Park 170 Nanjing Xi Lu ⓣ021/63275220, ⓕ63276958. Very central, right opposite Renmin Park; for many years this was the tallest building in Shanghai. Although the hotel dates back to the 1930s, the interiors have been modernized. ⑧

Portman Ritz-Carlton 1376 Nanjing Xi Lu ⓣ021/62798888, ⓕ62798999. One of the best hotels in Shanghai. Part of the luxury Shanghai Centre complex, which includes restaurants, airline offices and extremely expensive bars and restaurants. Doubles from US$250, with discounts off season. ⑨

Ruijin Guesthouse 118 Ruijin Er Lu ⓣ021/64725222, ⓕ64732277. Entrance on Fuxing Lu. Comprising eight Tudor-style villa complexes, complete with a Japanese-style garden and lawn tennis, this hotel was the home of the editor of the *North China Daily News* in the 1920s. Great location a couple of blocks south of Huaihai Lu. Doubles from US$100. ⑨

Shanghai Conservatory Guesthouse 20 Fen Yang Lu ⓣ021/64372577. Off Huaihai Lu, close to Changshu metro station, the college guesthouse offers around thirty dorm beds and eight very inexpensive, comfortable but basic doubles, some with their own shower. Right inside the grounds of the college and surrounded by music students, it's nearly always full in summer, but in winter it shouldn't be too hard to get a place. Beds ¥40, ④

Outer Shanghai and Pudong

Changyang 1800 Changyang Lu ⓣ021/65434890. A long way out, but this is an excellent, modern place. The very reasonably priced doubles make it another budget option. It's in the university district in the northeast, and there are a lot of cheap student bars and eateries nearby in Wujiaochang. Bus #22 running from just north of Suzhou Creek passes very close; get off at Linqing Lu bus stop. ③

Grand Hyatt Pudong Jin Mao Tower, 177 Lujiazui Lu, Pudong ⓣ021/50491111, ⓦshanghai.grand.hyatt.com. Across the street from the Oriental Pearl TV Tower. Occupying the top 36 floors of one of the tallest buildings in the world, this brand-new luxury hotel features a 29-storey atrium. The building is so tall that guests often have to phone down to the front desk to see if it's raining that day. Doubles priced from US$200. ⑨

Swan Cindic 2211 Sichuan Bei Lu ⓣ021/56665666, ⓕ63248002. A very smart place in a quiet, pleasant area away from the centre, across from Lu Xun Park. ⑦

The City

Although most parts of Shanghai that you are likely to visit lie to the west of the **Huangpu River** and its classic colonial riverfront, the **Bund**, by far the most easily recognizable landmark in the city is the rocket-like Oriental Pearl TV Tower on the east side, in the **Pudong** Special Economic Zone. The best way to check out both banks of the Huangpu River and their sights is to take the splendid **Huangpu River Tour** (see p.391).

Nanjing Lu, reputedly the busiest shopping street in China, runs through the heart of downtown Shanghai headed at its eastern end by the famous **Peace Hotel** and leading west to **Renmin Park**, which today houses Shanghai's excellent new **museum**. Shanghai's other main sights lie about 1.5km south of Nanjing Lu in the **Old City**, the longest continuously inhabited part of the city,

Shanghai: The City

Botanical Gardens	植物园	*zhíwù yuán*
Bund	外滩	*wàitān*
Chenghuang Miao	城皇庙	*chénghuáng miào*
Children's Palace	少年宫	*shàonián gōng*
Customs House	海关楼	*hāiguān lóu*
Dongtai Lu Market	东台路市场	*dōngtáilù shìchǎng*
First National Congress of CCP	一大会址	*yīdà huìzhǐ*
Flower and Bird Bazaar	花鸟市场	*huāniǎo shìchǎng*
Great World Entertainment Centre	大世界	*dàshì jiè*
Hongkou Park	红口公园	*hóngkǒu gōngyuán*
Huangpu River	黄浦江	*huángpǔ jiāng*
Huangpu River Tour	黄浦江旅游	*huángpǔjiāng lǚyóu*
Huxinting	湖心亭	*húxīn tíng*
Jing'an Si	静安寺	*jíngān sì*
Longhua Cemetery Of Martyrs	龙华烈士陵园	*lónghuá lièshì língyuán*
Longhua Si	龙华寺	*lónghuá sì*
Lu Xun Memorial Hall	鲁迅纪念馆	*lǔxùn jìniànguǎn*
Lu Xun's Former Residence	鲁迅故居	*lǔxùn gùjū*
Mu'en Tang	沐恩堂	*mù'ēn táng*
The Old City	南市区	*nánshì qū*
Oriental Pearl TV Tower	东方明珠广播电视塔	*dōngfāng míngzhū guǎngbō diànshìtǎ*
Pudong New Area	浦东新区	*pǔdōng xīnqū*
Renmin Park	人民公园	*rénmín gōngyuán*
Renmin Square	人民广场	*rénmín guǎngchǎng*
Shanghai Art Museum	美术展览馆	*měishù zhǎnlǎnguǎn*
Shanghai Centre	上海商城	*shànghǎi shāngchéng*
Shanghai Exhibition Centre	上海展览中心	*shànghǎi zhǎnlǎn zhōngxīn*
Shanghai Grand Theatre	上海大剧院	*shànghǎi dàjùyuàn*
Shanghai Museum	上海博物馆	*shànghǎi bówùguǎn*
Shanghai zoo	上海动物园	*shànghǎi dòngwùyuán*
Song Qingling's Former Residence	宋庆龄故居	*sòngqìnglíng gùjū*
Sun Yatsen Memorial Residence	孙中山故居	*sūnzhōng shān gùjū*
Tung Feng Hotel	东风饭店	*dōngfēng fàndiàn*
Waibaidu Bridge	外白渡桥	*wàibáidù qiáo*
World Link International Medicine Centre	瑞新国际医疗中心	*ruìxīn guójì yīliáo zhōngxīn*
Xujiahui Cathedral	徐家汇天主教堂	*xújiāhuì tiānzhǔ jiàotáng*
Yu Yuan	豫园	*yùyuán*
Yufo Si	玉佛寺	*yùfó sì*
Zhou Enlai's Former Residence	周恩来故居	*zhōuēn lái gùjū*

with a fully restored classical Chinese garden, the **Yu Yuan**, neighbouring bazaars and the traditional Huxinting Tea House at its heart. To the southwest of here lies the marvellous **old French Concession**, with its cosmopolitan cooking traditions,

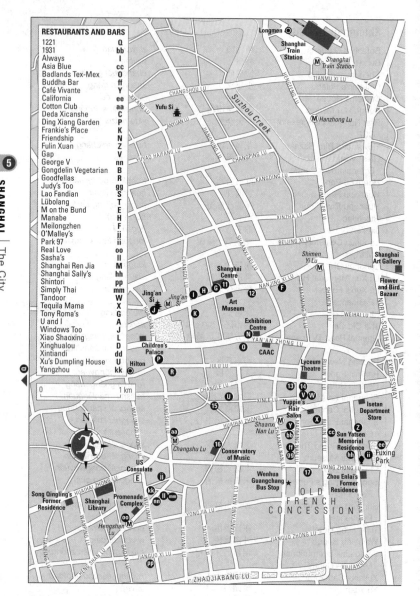

RESTAURANTS AND BARS

1221	Q
1931	bb
Always	I
Asia Blue	cc
Badlands Tex-Mex	O
Buddha Bar	ff
Café Vivante	Y
California	ee
Cotton Club	aa
Deda Xicanshe	C
Ding Xiang Garden	P
Frankie's Place	K
Friendship	N
Fulin Xuan	Z
Gap	V
George V	nn
Gongdelin Vegetarian	B
Goodfellas	R
Judy's Too	gg
Lao Fandian	S
Lübolang	T
M on the Bund	E
Manabe	H
Meilongzhen	F
O'Malley's	jj
Park 97	ii
Real Love	oo
Sasha's	ll
Shanghai Ren Jia	M
Shanghai Sally's	hh
Shintori	pp
Simply Thai	mm
Tandoor	W
Tequila Mama	X
Tony Roma's	G
U and I	A
Windows Too	J
Xiao Shaoxing	L
Xinghualou	D
Xintiandi	dd
Xu's Dumpling House	U
Yangzhou	kk

European-style housing and revolutionary relics. The energetic eating and nightlife centre of Shanghai, **Huaihai Lu**, serves as the area's main artery.

Farther out from the centre remains a scattering of sights. North of Suzhou Creek is the interesting **Hongkou Park**, with its monuments to the great twentieth-century writer, Lu Xun. Finally, in the far west are two of Shanghai's most important surviving religious sites, the **Longhua Si** and the **Yufo Si.**

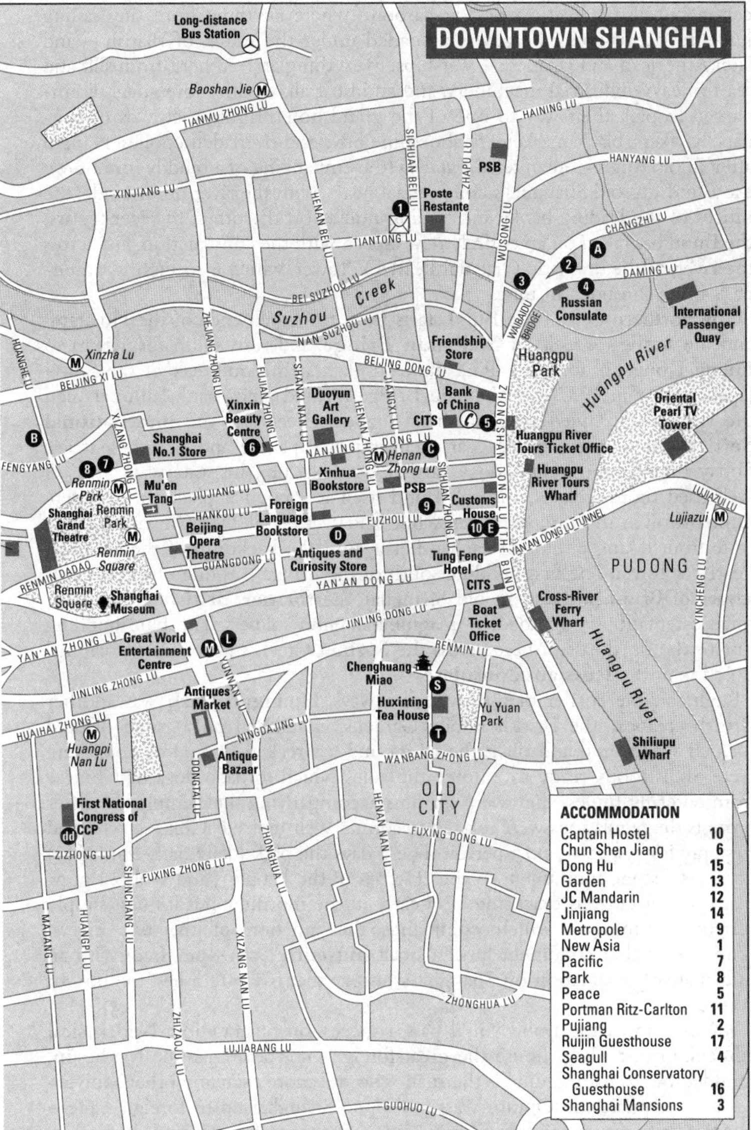

The Bund and the Huangpu River

A combination of Liverpool and 1920s Manhattan, the most impressive street in Shanghai has always been the **Bund**, since 1949 known officially as Zhongshan Lu, but better known among locals as Wai Tan (literally "outside beach"). During Shanghai's riotous heyday it was not only the city's financial centre but also a hectic working harbour, where anything from tiny sailing junks to ocean-going freighters unloaded under the watch of British – and later American and Japanese – warships. Everything arrived here, from silk and tea to heavy industrial machinery, and amidst it all, wealthy foreigners disembarked to pick their way to one of the grand hotels through crowds of beggars, hawkers, black marketeers, shoeshine boys and overladen coolies. Named after an old Anglo-Indian term, *bunding* (the embanking of a muddy foreshore), the Bund was old Shanghai's commercial heart, with the river on one side, the offices of the leading banks and trading houses on the other. In recent years, the Bund has taken on an entirely new aspect, with the construction, just across the river, of the dramatic Oriental Pearl TV Tower, which is so high its antenna is often shrouded in mist.

The northern end of the Bund starts from the confluence of the Huangpu and the Suzhou Creek, by **Waibaidu Bridge**, and runs south for 1.5km to Jinling Dong Lu, formerly Rue du Consulat. At the outbreak of the Sino–Japanese War in 1937 the Waibaidu Bridge formed a no-man's-land between the Japanese-occupied areas north of Suzhou Creek and the **International Settlement** – it was guarded at each end by Japanese and British sentries. Today though, most ships dock farther downstream, the waterways are still well-used thoroughfares, and the Bund itself is a popular place for an after-dinner stroll or morning exercises, while tourists from all over China patrol the waterfront taking photos of each other against the backdrop of the Oriental Pearl TV Tower. The first building south of the bridge was one of the cornerstones of British interests in old Shanghai, the **former British Consulate**, once ostentatiously guarded by magnificent Sikh soldiers. The blue building just to the northeast of here across the Suzhou Creek still retains its original function as the **Russian Consulate**.

Right on the corner of the two waterways, **Huangpu Park** was another British creation, the British Public Gardens, established on a patch of land formed when mud and silt gathered around a wrecked ship. Here, too, there were Sikh troops, ready to enforce the rules which forbade dogs or Chinese from entering (unless they were servants accompanying their employer). After protests the regulations were relaxed to admit "Well-dressed" Chinese, who had to apply for a special entry permit. These days the park (daily 5am–9pm; free) contains a stone monument to the "Heroes of the People", and is also a popular spot for citizens practising *tai ji* early in the morning; but it's best simply for the promenade which commands the junction of the two rivers. Underneath the monument lurks a small **museum** (9am–4pm; free) with an informative presentation on Shanghai's history that is worth a few minutes of your time.

Walking down the Bund you'll pass a succession of grandiose Neoclassical edifices, once built to house the great foreign enterprises. Jardine Matheson, founded by William Jardine – the man who did more than any other individual to precipitate the Opium Wars and open Shanghai up to foreign trade – was the first foreign concern to buy land in Shanghai. Their former base (they lost all of their holdings in China after 1949), just north of the *Peace Hotel*, is now occupied by the China Textiles Export Corporation.

Just south of here, straddling the eastern end of Nanjing Lu, is one of the most famous hotels in China, the **Peace Hotel,** formerly the *Cathay Hotel*. The main building (on the north side of Nanjing Lu) is a relic of another great trading house, **Sassoon's**, and was originally known as Sassoon House. Like Jardine's, the Sassoon business empire was built on opium trading, but by the early years of last century the family fortune had mostly been sunk into

△ Downtown Shanghai

Shanghai real estate, including the *Cathay*, which was the place to be seen in prewar Shanghai. It offered guests a private plumbing system fed by a spring on the outskirts of town, marble baths with silver taps and vitreous china lavatories imported from Britain. Noel Coward is supposed to have stayed here while writing *Private Lives*. Sassoon lived long enough to see his hotel virtually destroyed by the Japanese, including his rooftop private apartment, with 360° views and dark oak panelling (it has recently been restored), but also long enough to get most of his money away to the Bahamas. The *Peace* today still caters to the rich, but it's well worth a visit for the **bar** with its legendary jazz band (see p.408), and for a walk around the lobby and upper floors to take in the faded Art Deco elegance. The smaller wing on the south side of Nanjing Lu was originally the *Palace Hotel*, built around 1906; its first floor now holds the Western-style *Peace Café*, a much used city-centre rendezvous.

Next door to the *Peace*, at 19 Zhongshan Lu (the Bund), the **Bank of China** was designed in the 1920s by Shanghai architectural firm Palmer & Turner, who brought in a Chinese architect to make the building "more Chinese" after construction was complete. The architect placed a Chinese roof onto the Art Deco edifice, creating a delightful juxtaposition of styles. The idea is being endlessly and much less successfully copied across the nation today.

Carrying on down the Bund, the **Customs House** is one of the few buildings to have retained its original function, though its distinctive clock tower was adapted to chime *The East is Red* at six o'clock every morning and evening during the Cultural Revolution (the original clockwork has since been restored). The clock tower was modelled on Big Ben and, after its completion in 1927, local legend had it that the chimes which struck each fifteen minutes confused the God of Fire. Believing the chimes were a firebell, the god decided Shanghai was suffering from too many conflagrations, and refused to send any more. You can step into the downstairs lobby for a peek at some faded mosaics of maritime motifs on the ceiling.

Right next to this, and also with an easily recognizable domed roofline, the former headquarters of the **Hong Kong and Shanghai Bank** (built in 1921) is one of the most imposing of all the Bund facades. Each wall of the marble octagonal entrance originally boasted a mural depicting the Bank's eight primary locations: Bangkok, Calcutta, Hong Kong, London, New York, Paris, Shanghai and Tokyo. After 1949 it was taken over and turned into the local Shanghai government headquarters, until 1995 when they relocated to a site off Renmin Park in the centre of the city. This has opened the way for negotiations leading to the probable reoccupation of the building by its original owners, who would in all likelihood re-install the bronze lions – noses and paws rubbed gold by superstitious locals – that guarded the bank until 1966 (they are currently hibernating in the basement of the Shanghai Museum).

At the corner of the Bund and Yan'an Dong Lu you'll come to the *Tung Feng Hotel*, which until 1949 was home to a bastion of white male chauvinism, the *Shanghai Club*. There's still a strong feel here of the Shanghai of the 1920s and 1930s. The club's showpiece, the 33-metre mahogany Long Bar, where the wealthiest of the city's merchants and their European guests propped themselves at cocktail hour, is unfortunately no more, although the second-floor Seaman's Club, founded in the early 1900s, still functions as a meeting place for sailors.

Several blocks south of the old *Tung Feng* stands the site of the **Cornucopia Tea House**, today a huddle of nondescript office buildings. The most important associate of the **Green Gang** (the Shanghai Mafia), French Concession detective squad head Huang Jinrong, nicknamed "Pockmarked Huang", often held court here in the 1920s and 1930s. Huang represented the key link between the police force and the underworld, both of which he manipulated to strengthen his considerable business interests, mostly in the illegal opium trade. Huang thought of himself as a Robin Hood figure, doling out justice and money to those whom he felt deserved it. At this teahouse, he would receive payments for fixes or favours, and decide whether felons should be handed over to the international police squad.

The Huangpu River Tour

One highlight of a visit to Shanghai, and the easiest way to view the edifices of the Bund, is to take a **Huangpu River Tour** along what remains, even in this age of freeway projects and a sophisticated metro system, Shanghai's primary artery. The Huangpu is still a vital resource for Shanghai, and the sixty-kilometre round trip down to its confluence with the Yangzi and back will introduce you to the vast amount of shipping which still uses the port. One-third of all China's trade passes through here, and you'll also be able to inspect all the paraphernalia of the shipping industry, from sampans and rusty old Panamanian-registered freighters to sparkling Chinese navy vessels. On the way up the river, you'll also get an idea of the colossal construction that is taking place on the eastern shore, before you reach the mouth of the Yangzi River itself, where the wind kicks in and it feels like you're almost in open sea. The Huangpu is also Shanghai's chief source of drinking water, although, thick and brown, it contains large quantities of untreated waste, including sewage and high levels of mercury and phenol. At least it no longer serves as a burial ground – in the 1930s Chinese too poor to pay for the burial of relatives would launch the bodies into the river in boxes decked in paper flowers.

The **river tours**, which last 3hr 30min, leave from Shiliupu wharf, several blocks south of Huangpu Park, across the Bund from Yan'an Dong Lu. You can book tickets at the jetty (daily 8am–4.30pm). The hour-long round trip to the Yanpu Bridge costs ¥25–35; the slightly longer trip to Nanpu Bridge costs ¥45 and takes two hours. The classic cruise, though is the sixty-kilometre journey to the mouth of the Yangzi and back. **Five classes** are available on this: the two lower classes (¥35–45) give you crowds of local tourists, a hard seat and a great deal of noise; the two middle classes (¥55–70) entitle you to a plastic table outside with endless tea and sweets; while first class (¥100) affords a lounge furnished with great overstuffed armchairs, and usually entertainment in the form of a Chinese juggling act. There are weekday departures in all classes year round at 9am and 2pm; on Saturday and Sunday boats leave at 11am and 3.30pm. Given that there are sometimes several boats leaving at each of these times you should check your booking carefully. There are also special two-hour-long luxury cruises that include a buffet dinner; these boats depart at 7.30pm on weekdays, 8pm on Saturdays and Sundays (¥98–118; ¥53 without buffet). In foggy or windy weather, the tours do not run (for information call ⓣ021/63744461).

The east bank of the Huangpu: Pudong district

Historically, **Pudong** has been known as the "wrong side of the Huangpu" – before 1949, the area was characterized by unemployed migrants, prostitution, murders, and the most appalling living conditions in the city. It was here that bankrupt gamblers would *tiao Huangpu*, commit suicide by drowning themselves in the river. Shanghai's top gangster, Du Yuesheng, more commonly known as "Big-eared Du", learned his trade growing up in this rough section of town. In 1990, however, fifteen years after China's economic reforms had

The Shanghai Financial Centre

No project has better epitomized Shanghai's drive to pass Hong Kong and become the financial capital of China than the construction of the US$625-million **World Financial Centre**. At 94 storeys and 1,509 feet tall, the 3.6 million-square-foot tower is slated to be the tallest building on earth on completion, symbolizing the rising commercial might of Pudong.

Bur problems wracked the project from the beginning, when architects at Kohn Pederson Fox in New York City proposed their initial plans. They had designed a circular "moon gate" at the top of the tower to reflect Chinese notions of unity and harmony (not to mention the issue of wind resistance), as well as mirroring the pearl sphere on top of the Oriental Pearl TV Tower, currently the most recognizable landmark in the city. However, the Chinese saw the gate completely differently – as a representation of the rising sun, the emblem on the Japanese flag. The architects planned a walkway to bisect the moon gate. Shanghai officials were pleased, but then the Asian financial maelstrom of 1997 landed, leading to a glut of commercial real estate in Pudong and a further contraction of the Japanese banking system, which was responsible for financing much of the project. Building recommenced in 2000 and now the estimated completion date has been pushed back to 2005 at the earliest.

first started, it was finally decided to grant the status of Special Economic Zone (SEZ) to this large tract of mainly agricultural land across the river. This decision, more than any other, is now fuelling Shanghai's rocket-like economic advance into the new century.

With widespread confidence that Pudong will eventually be one of the major business centres of Asia, and perhaps of the world, US$70 billion of investment has already been pumped into the area. In less than ten years, the skyline has been completely transformed from a stream of rice paddies, to a sea of cranes, and ultimately a maze of skyscrapers that seemingly stretch east as far as the eye can see. The idea is to create a city of the twenty-first century to match, or preferably excel, the largely foreign-inspired city of the twentieth. There was a temporary hiccup in this vision when, in the wake of the 1997 Asian currency crisis fallout, vacancy rates in many of these buildings reached more than fifty percent. However, they have started gradually to recover as prime minister (and Shanghai ex-mayor) Zhu Rongji steers more investment into the area.

Pudong is, above all, an area of **commerce**, with few activities to interest the visitor besides giving your neck a good workout as you gaze upwards at the skyline. The 421-metre-high Jin Mao Centre stands aloof several blocks away from the site of what will be the **tallest skyscraper in the world**, the Shanghai Financial Centre (see box above), while directly across the street rises the 457-metre-high **Oriental Pearl TV Tower** (daily 8am–9.30pm; ¥40–100). Ascending the tower to admire the giddying views has become a mandatory pilgrimage for most Chinese visitors to Shanghai, despite the ridiculously high entrance fee and long queue for the lift. At the top of the tower are souvenir stands, while down on the first floor there's a resident jazz band, a café, a display of other great world cities and some quality toilets. You can get a better view for a lot less by having a coffee in *Cloud 9*, the top-floor café of the *Hyatt Hotel* (see "Eating", p.407) in the nearby Jinjiang Building.

Getting to Pudong has become very convenient in recent years. The simplest way is to catch the subway which whooshes passengers from Renmin Square to downtown Pudong in less than three minutes; otherwise, several minibuses cross under the river from the south side of Renmin Square, near the Shanghai Museum. For a more picturesque trip, catch the cross-river ferry from the Bund opposite the eastern end of Jinling Lu, then walk north for about fifteen minutes. There's also a tourist tunnel (entrance in the subway opposite Beijing Dong Lu) which takes you in a car past a silly light show and costs ¥20.

Nanjing Lu and around

Stretching west from the Bund through the heart of Shanghai lie the main commercial streets of the city, among them one of the two premier shopping streets, **Nanjing Lu**, with its two major parallel arteries, **Fuzhou Lu** and Yan'an Lu. In the days of the foreign concessions, expatriates described Nanjing Lu as a cross between Broadway and Oxford Street. Even after 1949, Nanjing Lu remained a centre for theatre and cinema as well as one of the most crowded shopping streets in the world.

Nanjing Dong Lu

On its eastern stretch, **Nanjing Dong Lu**, garish neon lights and expensive window displays of foreign and luxury goods are as prominent as they have ever been, and if any street in mainland China resembles downtown Hong Kong, this is it. Take a stroll among the crowds before things close up in late evening (9–10pm), and check out the mass of fast-food outlets, fashion boutiques, cinemas, hotels and particularly the huge department stores. Before 1949, Nanjing Dong Lu and Fuzhou Lu housed numerous teahouses which functioned as the city's most exclusive brothels. Geisha-like *shuyu* (singer-storyteller girls) would saunter from teahouse to teahouse, performing classical plays and scenes from operas, and host banquets for guests. In a juxtaposition symbolic of prewar Shanghai's extremes, just two blocks north of Nanjing Dong Lu, running along Suzhou Creek, lay strings of the lowest form of brothel, nicknamed *dingpeng* ("nail sheds" because the sex, at ¥0.3, was "as quick as driving nails"). The street was dubbed "Blood Alley" for the nightly fights between sailors on leave who congregated here.

Off the circular overhead walkway at the junction between Nanjing and Xizang Lu, just northeast of Renmin Park, is the grandest of the district's department stores, the venerable **Shanghai No.1 Store** (formerly the Sun Department Store). This, the largest store in the country, is visited by a hundred thousand Chinese each day, many of whom are country folk venturing to Shanghai for the first time. Another feature of Nanjing Lu is the innumerable **beauty salons**, where customers are beautified in shop windows for the entertainment of the public on the pavement outside. One of the most famous of these is the Xinxin Beauty Centre, just west of Fujian Lu, which employs no fewer than eighty stylists and masseurs.

Renmin Park and Renmin Square

Immediately west of the junction with Xizang Lu – where Nanjing Dong Lu becomes Nanjing Xi Lu – lies **Renmin Park** and a newly remodelled **Renmin Square** to the south. This whole area was originally the site of the Shanghai racecourse, which so satisfied the Chinese passion for gambling that by the 1920s the Shanghai Race Club was the third wealthiest foreign corporation in China. It was later converted into a sports arena by Chiang Kaishek who had decided it was unwise to pander to this passion. During the war the stadium served as a holding camp for prisoners and as a temporary mortuary. Afterwards, most of it was levelled, and while the north part was landscaped with grass and trees to become the surprisingly intimate Renmin Park, the rest was paved to form a dusty concrete parade ground for political rallies. Only the racecourse's clock tower survives to this day, on the southeast edge of the square. The former area of paving has now been turned over to green grass, fountains and pigeons, while what used to be the bomb shelters beneath have become some of the city's premier shopping malls. On the square's northwest corner lies the new and impressive **Shanghai Grand Theatre**, distinguished by its convex roof. Its state-of-the-art acoustics and large central hall were designed to accommodate all art forms, from Western drama, opera and chamber music recitals to Chinese opera and classical poetry readings. You can stroll around the lobby, stage, auditorium and rehearsal rooms on your own (daily 9–11am & 1–4.30pm; ¥20), or you can take one of the excellent hour-long tours, given in Chinese and English (Ⓣ021/63276562 or 63728702; tours ¥60; see "Entertainment" on p.409 for more information).

The views from Renmin Square are novel, offering an unexpected panorama of the developing city but, more importantly, the city's brand-new showpiece **Shanghai Museum** (Mon–Fri 9am–5pm, Sat 9am–8pm; ¥20, students free Sat 5–7pm, ¥5 at other times) is located here. The museum ranks high on the short must-do list of Shanghai sights. From the outside, the building, shaped like an early Tang vessel, is one of the most impressive new constructions in the city, and inside the presentation, labelling (in English as well as Chinese) and lighting are first class. Consider the English-language audio-guide (¥35) for a more in-depth presentation. The displays give you an excellent introduction into the development of all facets of Chinese art and culture, from ceramics to sculpture and seals. Highlights include watching a live demonstration (seven times daily) of ancient pottery-making techniques, as well as a collection of colourful lacquered opera masks of Guizhou minority groups and a salmon skin suit, as worn by the Oroqen of Dongbei. There is also an insightful exhibition on the history of Chinese painting, from military souvenirs during the Warring States through literary expressionism during the Song to Westernization under the Qing. You can access the museum's excellent art library by calling ahead and arranging an appointment (Ⓣ021/63723500).

From Renmin Park, a small detour south down Xizang Lu will bring you to the **Mu'en Tang** (Baptized with Mercy Church), a couple of blocks down on the left. Visiting a church in Shanghai is an extraordinary experience, and Mu'en is the closest to the heart of the city. Although the service is in Chinese only, visitors are more than welcome and you'll be given a seat in the balcony overlooking the packed congregation – a cross section of Shanghai society from cross old Communists to girls in silver miniskirts. There are services throughout the week – check the Chinese-only board outside. In contrast, the neon-lit **Great World Entertainment Centre** (see p.410) squats a block farther south, just under the Yan'an Dong Lu flyover.

Nanjing Xi Lu

On the western section of Nanjing Lu, **Nanjing Xi Lu**, opposite Renmin Park, stand the historic **Pacific** and **Park hotels**. The *Park Hotel*, for many years the tallest building in Shanghai, once had a reputation for superb food as well as for its dances, when the roof would be rolled back to allow guests to cavort under the stars. Latterly, Mao Zedong always stayed here when he was in Shanghai. Today, however, it has been stripped of most of its old-world charm. The *Pacific*, by contrast, a few metres to the east of the *Park*, is still worth having a look at, both for its mighty and ostentatious facade and for the fabulous plaster reliefs in the lobby. On a small lane called Jiangyin Lu, just to the south of here and parallel to the main road, Shanghai's permanent **Flower and Bird Bazaar** is a superbly earthy little corner, crowded with locals looking at puppies, kittens, goldfish, cagebirds, crickets and a host of plants.

The western end of Nanjing Xi Lu was known to "Shanghailanders" (the Europeans who made their homes here) as Bubbling Well Road, after a spring that used to gush at the far end of the street. Then, as today, it was one of the smartest addresses in the city, leading into tree-lined streets where Westerners' mock-Tudor mansions sheltered behind high walls. Now it's also the location of a number of luxury hotels, including the **Shanghai Centre**, an ultra-modern complex of luxury shops, restaurants and residential flats centred around the five-star *Portman Hotel*. Opposite, Shanghai's newly relocated and revamped **Art Museum** (daily 9–11am & 1–4pm; ¥10, special exhibits ¥5 extra) resides in a building that used to be part of the racecourse before becoming the city library. Inside is an extensive collection of staid, traditionally minded, contemporary Chinese art.

Also at this end of Nanjing Lu, a few hundred metres west of the Shanghai Centre, **Jing'an Si** (daily 5am–5pm; ¥5), a small though active temple, nestles beside the tiny Jing'an Park and under looming highrises. Building work first began on the temple during the Three Kingdoms Period, and its apparent obscurity belies its past as the richest Buddhist foundation in the city, headed by legendary abbot Khi Vehdu, who combined his abbotly duties with a gangster lifestyle. The abbot and his seven concubines were shadowed by White Russian bodyguards, each carrying a leather briefcase lined with bulletproof steel to be used as a shield in case of attack. Today the temple is the primary place of ancestral worship in the city, although an equal amount of people come to pray for more material reasons – worshippers eagerly throw coins into incense burners, in the hope that the gods will bestow financial success. Bus #20 runs here from Renmin Square, while the terminus for the metro line #2 lies underneath.

One block southwest of the temple, at the corner of Wulumuqi Bei Lu and Yan'an Zhong Lu, lies the grandiose yet slightly run-down **Children's Palace**. Originally known as Marble Hall, the sprawling estate was built in 1918 as a home by the Kadoories, a Sephardic Jewish family and one of the principal investors in pre-World War II Shanghai. The drab, worn exterior belies the mansion's current function as a children's art centre, with frequent singing and dancing performances on weekday afternoons and at weekends. The only official way to see them is by arranging a tour with CITS but, if you come here on your own, you might find the back gate along Nanjing Xi Lu ajar. West of the Children's Palace, along Yan'an Zhong Lu, you'll find the flamboyantly Gothic former residence of the KMT minister of transportation.

A block south of the Shanghai Centre on Yan'an Lu the gigantic, Stalinist wedding cake that is the **Shanghai Exhibition Centre** is worth seeing for its colossal ornate entrance, decorated with columns patterned with red stars and capped by a gilded spire. Constructed by the Russians in 1954, it was originally known as the *Palace of Sino–Soviet Friendship* and housed a permanent exhibition of industrial produce from the Shanghai area – proof of the advances achieved after 1949. In recent years it has become a vast and vulgar shopping mall selling over priced furniture and trinkets.

The Old City

The **Old City** never formed part of the International Settlement and was known by the foreigners who lived in Shanghai, somewhat contemptuously, as the **Chinese City**. Based on the original **walled city** of Shanghai, which dated back to the eleventh century, the area was reserved in the nineteenth and early twentieth centuries as a ghetto for vast numbers of Chinese who lived packed in conditions of appalling squalor, while the foreigners carved out their living space around them. Today it still covers an oval-shaped area of about four square kilometres, circumscribed by Renmin Lu (to the north) and Zhonghua Lu (to the south) and coming to within a couple of hundred metres of the southern Bund on its northeastern side. In modern times it has been slashed down the middle by the main north–south artery, Henan Lu. The easiest approach from Nanjing Dong Lu is to walk due south along Henan Lu or Sichuan Lu.

Tree-lined ring roads had already replaced the original walls and moats as early as 1912, and sanitation has obviously improved vastly since the last century, but to cross the boundaries into the Old City is still to enter a different world. The twisting alleyways are a haven of free enterprise, bursting with makeshift markets selling fish, vegetables, cheap trinkets, clothing and food. Two of Shanghai's best **antique markets** are also located in or near the Old City (see opposite). Ironically, for a tourist entering this area, the feeling is like entering a Chinatown in a Western city.

The centre of activity today is an area known locally as **Chenghuang Miao** (after a local temple) surrounding the two most famous and crowded tourist sights in the whole city, the Yu Yuan and the Huxinting Tea House, both located right in the middle of a new, touristy bazaar which caters to the Chinese tourists who pour into the area. "Antiques", scrolls and kitschy souvenirs feature prominently, and there are also lots of good places to eat *dian xin*, Shanghai *dim sum*, some more reasonable than others (see "Restaurants", p.406). The **Yu Yuan** (Jade Garden; daily 8.30am–5pm; ¥25) is a classical Chinese garden featuring pools, walkways, bridges and rockeries, created in the sixteenth century by a high official in the imperial court in honour of his father. Despite fluctuating fortunes, the garden has surprisingly survived the passage of the centuries. It was spared from its greatest crisis – the Cultural Revolution – apparently because the anti-imperialist "Little Sword Society" had used it as their headquarters in 1853 during the Taiping Uprising. Garden connoisseurs today will appreciate the whitewashed walls topped by undulating dragons made of tiles, and the huge, craggy and indented rock in front of the Yuhua Tang (Hall of Jade Magnificence). During Lantern Festival, on the fifteenth day of the traditional New Year, 10,000 lanterns (and an even larger number of spectators) brighten up the garden. The Yu Yuan is less impressive than the gardens of nearby Suzhou (see p.419), but given that it predates the relics of the International Settlement by some three centuries, the Shanghainese are understandably proud of it.

After visiting the garden, you can step into the delightful **Huxinting** (Heart of Lake Pavilion; downstairs daily 5.30–noon & 1.30–5pm; upstairs daily 8.30am–5pm & 8.30–10pm), where practically every visitor who has ever been to Shanghai, including the Queen of England, has dropped in for tea. The teahouse is reached across a zigzag bridge spanning a small ornamental lake, just across from the entrance to Yu Yuan. In the downstairs section, you buy a ticket for ¥10 and can then enjoy endless refills while watching the elderly locals, who sit for hours amid the wood panelling, playing cards, chatting, or dozing to the traditional music of a venerable Chinese orchestra that occasionally plays here. Upstairs, during the daytime the cost is at least ¥25, but you get air conditioning and quails' eggs with your tea, while in the evening (¥65) the waitresses perform traditional tea ceremonies. Whenever you come, though, the tea is excellent and the china used is the dark and distinctive Yixing ware (see p.438).

If you're in Chenghuang Miao early on Sunday morning (8–11am is the best time though trade continues to mid-afternoon), you can visit a great **Sunday market** on Fuyu Lu, the small street running east to west along the northern edge of Yu Yuan. The market has a raw, entrepreneurial feel about it; all sorts of curios and antiques – some real, some not – ranging from jade trinkets to Little Red Books can be found here, though you'll have to bargain fiercely if you want to buy. Just outside the Old City, in a small alley called Dongtai Lu leading west off Xizang Nan Lu, is the largest permanent **antique market** in Shanghai (daily 10am–4pm), and possibly in all China. Even if you're not interested in buying, this is a fascinating area to walk around. The range is vast, from old Buddhas, coins, vases and teapots, to mahjong sets, renovated furniture and Cultural Revolution badges. Much is fake, but many of the traders are serious, respectable people with reputations to maintain.

The former French Concession

Established in the mid-nineteenth century, the **former French Concession** lay to the south and west of the International Settlement, abutting the Chinese City. Despite its name, it was never particularly French: before 1949, in fact, it was a low-rent district mainly inhabited by Chinese and White Russians. Other Westerners looked down on the latter as they were obliged to take jobs that, it was felt, should have been left to the Chinese. Certain French characteristics have lingered here, however, in the local chic, and in a taste for bread and sweet cakes – exemplified in **Huaihai Lu**, the main street running through the heart of the area. Not as crowded as Nanjing Lu, Huaihai Lu is considerably more upmarket, particularly in the area around **Maoming Lu** and **Shaanxi Lu**, where fashion boutiques, extremely expensive department stores and excellent cake shops abound.

The two plushest hotels in town, the *Garden* and the *Jinjiang*, are on Maoming Lu just north of Huaihai Lu, and are worth a visit for glimpses of past luxuries. The *Jinjiang* compound includes the former **Grosvenor Residence** complex, the most fashionable and pricey address in pre-World War II Shanghai. The Grosvenor has recently been modernized, but the VIP Club still retains much of its 1920s architecture and *Great Gatsby* ambience. Non-guests might be able to sneak a peek by taking the elevator to the top floor of the Old Wing of the *Jinjiang*, where the Club is located, although gaining entrance to one of the twenty US$800-a-night VIP mansion rooms on the floors directly below, with astonishingly beautiful, refurbished Art Deco architecture, might prove slightly more difficult.

Some more excellent examples of **Palladian**, **Art Deco** and other early twentieth-century **architecture** survive several blocks south, in the private residences along Changle Lu and Julu Lu, which run parallel to and several blocks north of Huaihai Zhong Lu. Most notably, the former Russian Orthodox Mission Church still proudly features its blue dome along nearby Xinle Lu, although a securities exchange and disco called "St Peter's" now inhabit the premises.

The French may have long disappeared from the French Concession, but this area's acute sense of style lives on. Nowhere is this more obvious than in the multitude of fashionable boutiques and hair salons lining Huaihai Lu, which burst with business in the 1990s, among them the aptly named **Yuppie's Hair Salon** (Ⓣ021/64456640), at no. 819, just east of Maoming Lu. Yuppie's attention to detail and pampering of the customer would put most Western salons to shame. You can be inexpensively spoiled with two (pre- and post-haircut) shampoos, extended half-body massage, and a haircut, all for around ¥70.

The French Concession was equally notorious for its lawlessness and the ease with which police and officials could be bribed, in contrast with the relatively staid, well-governed areas dominated by the British. This made it ideal territory for gangsters, including the king of all Shanghai mobsters, Du Yuesheng, the right-hand man of Huang Jinrong. For similar reasons, **political activists** also operated in this sector – the first meeting of the Chinese Communist Party took place here in 1921, and both Zhou Enlai and Sun Yatsen, the first provisional President of the Republic of China after the overthrow of the Qing dynasty, lived here. The preserved former homes of these two in particular (see below) are worth visiting simply because, better than anywhere else in modern Shanghai, they give a sense of how the Westerners, and the Westernized, used to live.

Moving west, the **First National Congress of the Chinese Communist Party** (daily 9am–5pm, last admission 4pm; ¥4) is the first preserved 1920s relic that you'll come across, south of Huaihai Lu, at the junction of Xingye Lu and Huangpi Nan Lu. The official story of this house is that on July 23, 1921, thirteen representatives of the Communist cells which had developed all over China, including its most famous junior participant Mao Zedong, met here to discuss the formation of a national party. The meeting was discovered by a French police agent (it was illegal to hold political meetings in the French Concession) and on July 30 the delegates fled to Zhejiang Province, where they resumed their talks in a boat on Nan Hu. Quite how much of this really happened is unclear, but it seems probable that there were in fact more delegates than the record remembers – the missing names would have been expunged according to subsequent political circumstances. The site today, preserved in its original condition since 1949, contains a little exhibition hall downstairs with the usual propaganda, detailing instances of the oppressions that inspired the Communist movement in the first place. More interesting is the waxwork diorama of Mao and his mates.

A few hundred metres west of here, beyond the gigantic north–south flyover and very close to **Fuxing Park** (daily 5am–5pm, ¥1), is Sinan Lu, where two of the heroes of modern China lived. At no. 39 is the **Sun Yatsen Memorial Residence** (Mon–Sat 9am–4.30pm; ¥8), with its large British-style lawn in the back garden, screened by mature trees and high walls. Sun Yatsen lived here from 1918 to 1924, and inside the house you can see his books, a gramophone, fireplaces and verandahs – all fantastically disorienting in contemporary Shanghai. Sun's widow, Song Qingling (see below), stayed in the house until 1937. Just south of Fuxing Lu is **Zhou Enlai's Former Residence** (Tues, Wed & Fri–Sun 8.30–11am & 1–4pm, Mon & Thurs 1–4pm; ¥2), at 73 Sinan Lu. This delightful house has a terrace at the back with rattan chairs and polished wooden floors, and its garden, with hedges and ivy-covered walls, could easily be a part of 1930s suburban London.

Several blocks west rises the stately **Ruijin Guesthouse**, on the corner of Fuxing Zhong Lu and Shanxi Nan Lu. This Tudor-style country manor was home to the Morriss family, owners of the *North China Daily News*. Mr Morriss raised greyhounds for the Shanghai Race Club and the former Canidrome dog track across the street. Having miraculously escaped severe damage during the Cultural Revolution because certain high-ranking officials used it as their private residence, the house has now been turned into a pleasant inn. Even if you're not a guest, you are free to walk around the spacious, quiet grounds, where it's hard to believe you are in the middle of one of the world's most hectic cities.

A good deal farther west, at 1843 Huaihai Xi Lu, about twenty minutes' walk northwest from the Hengshan Lu metro station, is **Song Qingling's Former**

Residence (daily 9–11am & 1–4.30pm; ¥8). She lived here on and off from 1948 until her death in 1981. As the wife of Sun Yatsen, Song Qingling was part of a bizarre family coterie – her sister Song Meiling was married to Chiang Kaishek and her brother, known as "TV Soong", was finance minister to Chiang. Song Qingling herself was to remain loyal to China throughout her life, latterly as one of the honorary "Presidents" of the People's Republic, while Meiling – now reviled in the People's Republic – is still alive today, having made her permanent home in New York City. Once again the house is a charming step back into a residential Shanghai of the past, and although this time the trappings on display – including her official limousines parked in the garage – are largely post-1949, there is some lovely wood panelling and lacquerwork inside the house.

Western Shanghai

In the west of the city, sights are too distant to walk between. The main attractions are two **temples**, the rambling old Longhua Si to the southwest, and Yufo Si, which has superb statuary, to the northwest. Due west from the city there is less to see; if you follow Nanjing Lu beyond Jing'an Si, it merges into Yan'an Lu, which (beyond the city ring road) eventually turns into Hongqiao Lu, the road that leads to the airport. Shortly before the airport it passes **Shanghai Zoo** (daily 6.30am–4.30pm; ¥20), a massive affair with more than two thousand animals and birds caged in conditions which, while not entirely wholesome, are better than in most Chinese zoos. The star, inevitably, is a giant panda. The zoo grounds used to serve as one of pre-1949 Shanghai's most exclusive golf courses. Next door, at 2409 Hongqiao Lu, stands the mansion that once served as the **Sassoons' home**, and which originally boasted a fireplace large enough to roast an ox. The central room, since renovated, resembled a medieval castle's Great Hall. Victor Sassoon, who used this mansion as a weekend house (his other house was on the top floor of the *Peace Hotel*), only allowed for the design of two small bedrooms because he wanted to avoid potential overnight guests. It has served since as a Japanese naval HQ, a casino and as the private villa of the Gang of Four, but now suffers the relative ignominy of being rented out as office space. Bus #57 from the western end of Nanjing Lu will bring you out here. The side gate is sometimes open if you wish to take a peek.

The southwest

The **southwestern** limits of the city offer a few points of interest. First is the **Xujiahui Catholic Cathedral**, one of many places of public worship which have received a new lease of life in recent years. Built in 1846 on the grave of Paul Xu Guangqi, Matteo Ricci's personal assistant and first Jesuit convert, it was closed for more than ten years during the Cultural Revolution, reopening in 1979. Most of the cathedral library's 200,000 volumes, as well as the cathedral's meteorological centre (built at the same time as the cathedral and now housing the Shanghai Municipal Meteorology Department) still survive on the grounds. The congregations are remarkable for their size and enthusiasm, especially during the early Sunday morning services and at Christmas or Easter. If you're up in time, take a metro train to Xujiahui station, a short walk from the cathedral. The first service on weekdays starts at 6.30am, while on Sundays it begins at 8am.

About a kilometre to the southeast of Xujiahui is Longhua Park, now officially named the **Longhua Cemetery of Martyrs** (daily 6.30am–4pm; ¥1 for the cemetery, ¥5 for the exhibition hall) to commemorate those who died fighting for the cause of Chinese Communism in the decades leading up to the final victory of 1949. In particular, it remembers those workers, activists and students massacred in Shanghai by Chiang Kaishek in the 1920s – the site of the cemetery is said to have been the main execution ground. The area contains a glass-windowed, pyramid-shaped exhibition hall in the centre with a bombastic memorial to 250 Communist martyrs who fought Chiang's forces. Large numbers of commemorative stone sculptures, many bearing a photo and a name, dot the park, including one directly behind the exhibition hall with an eternal flame flickering in front. The fresh flowers brought daily testify to the power these events still hold. The cemetery is a short walk south from the terminus of bus #41, which you can take here from Huaihai Lu near Shanxi Lu or from Nanjing Xi Lu near the Shanghai Centre.

Right next to the Martyrs' Cemetery is one of Shanghai's main religious sites, the **Longhua Si** (daily 5.30am–4pm; ¥5), and its associated seventeen-hundred-year-old pagoda. The pagoda itself is an octagonal structure, about 40m high, its seven brick storeys embellished with wooden balconies and red lacquer pillars. In 977, a monk installed bronze wind chimes that could be heard on the Huangpu River into the nineteenth century. Until the feverish construction of bank buildings along the Bund in the 1910s, the pagoda stood as the tallest edifice in Shanghai. What you see today has been restored after a long period of neglect – Red Guards saw the pagoda as a convenient structure to plaster with banners. In recent years, an ambitious re-zoning project has spruced up the pagoda and created the tea gardens, greenery, and shop stalls that now huddle around it. The temple complex is slightly later in date than the pagoda (345 AD) and is now the most active Buddhist site in the city, with large numbers of new monks being trained. Although it has also been reconstructed, it is regarded as a prime specimen of Southern Song architecture. On the right as you enter there's a bell tower, where you can strike the bell for ¥10 to bring you good luck. On Chinese New Year, a monk bangs the bell 108 times, supposedly to ease the 108 "mundane worries" of Buddhist thought.

An extra kilometre south (bus #56 down the main road, Longwu Lu, just to the west of the Longhua Si site) will bring you to the **Botanical Gardens** (daily 7am–4pm; ¥6), whose leafy trees and chirping birds can serve as a respite from the city hubbub. Among the more than nine thousand plants on view are two pomegranate trees said to have been planted in the eighteenth century during the reign of Emperor Qianlong, and still bearing fruit despite their antiquity. Take a look as well at the orchid chamber, with more than a hundred different varieties on show. In spring 1999 the gardens hosted the World Plant Expo.

The northwest

Just south of the Suzhou Creek, **northwestern** Shanghai boasts the second of the city's most important religious sites, the **Yufo Si** (Temple of the Jade Buddha; daily 8.30am–4.30pm; ¥10), a monastery built in 1882 to enshrine two magnificent statues from Burma. Each of these Buddhas is carved from a single piece of white jade: the larger statue, a reclining figure, is displayed downstairs, while the smaller, but far more exquisite, sitting statue is housed in a room upstairs as part of a collection of sutras and paintings. Although the temple was closed from 1949 until 1980, it is now large and active. A hundred or so monks are in residence, training novices to repopulate the monasteries reopening throughout China and keeping an eye on tourists (photos are not allowed). The temple is on Anyuan Lu, just south of the intersection of Changzhou Lu and Jiangning Lu. Bus #112 from Renmin Square passes here, as does #24 from Huaihai Lu (along Shaanxi Lu); alternatively you can walk from the train station in about 25 minutes.

North of Suzhou Creek

North across the Waibaidu Bridge from the Bund, you enter an area that, before the War, was the Japanese quarter of the International Settlement, and which since 1949 has been largely taken over by housing developments. The obvious interest lies in the Hongkou Park area (also known as Lu Xun Park), and its monuments to the political novelist Lu Xun, although the whole district is lively and architecturally interesting.

Lu Xun Park (daily 6am–7pm; ¥1) is one of the best places for observing Shanghainese at their most leisured. Between 6 and 8am, the masses undergo their daily *tai ji* workout. Later in the day, amorous couples frolic on paddle boats in the park lagoon and old men teach their grandkids how to fly kites. The park is also home to the pompous **Tomb of Lu Xun**, complete with a seated statue and an inscription in Mao's calligraphy, which was erected here in 1956 to commemorate the fact that Lu Xun had spent the last ten years of his life in this part of Shanghai. The tomb went against Lu Xun's own wishes to be buried simply in a small grave in a western Shanghai cemetery. The novelist is further memorialized in the Lu Xun Memorial Hall (daily 9–11am & 1.30–4pm; ¥5), also in the park, to the right of the main entrance. Exhibits include original correspondence, among them letters and photographs from George Bernard Shaw.

A block southeast of the park on Shanyin Lu (Lane 132, House 9), you can also visit **Lu Xun's Former Residence** (daily 9am-4pm; ¥4). It's definitely worthwhile going out of your way to see this place, especially if you have already visited the former residences of Zhou Enlai and Sun Yatsen in the

Lu Xun

The man known by the literary pseudonym **Lu Xun** (his real name was Chou Shujian) was born in 1881 in the small city of Shaoxing. His origins were humble, but he would eventually come to be revered as the greatest of twentieth-century Chinese authors. Writing in a plainer, more comprehensible prose-style than any Chinese writer before him – and considered by the Communists as a paragon of Socialist Realism – he sought to understand and portray the lives of the poor and downtrodden elements of Chinese society.

He had not always intended to write. His first chosen career had been as a **doctor** of medicine, which he studied in Japan, under the impression that medicine would be the salvation of humanity. Later, however, horrified at the intractable social problems that beset China, he turned to writing, and published his *Diary of a Madman*, modelled on the work of Gogol, in 1918. This Western-style short story, the first ever written in Chinese, was in reality a scathing satire of Confucian society. Three years later Lu Xun then published his most famous short story, **The True Story of Ah Q**, which features a foolish, Panglossian illiterate whose only remedy against the numerous evils which befall him is to rationalize them into spiritual victories – once again, the logic of Confucianism. Lu Xun's writings soon earned him anger and threats from the ruling Guomindang, and in 1926 he fled his home in Beijing to seek **sanctuary** in the International Settlement of Shanghai. The last ten years of his life he spent living in the then Japanese quarter of the city, where he worked to support the Communist cause. The fact that he refused actually to join the Party did not stop the Communists from subsequently adopting him as a posthumous icon.

French Quarter (see p.398). Lu Xun's sparsely furnished house offers a fascinating glimpse into typical Japanese housing of the period – on the outside, its staid brick facade, tightly packed in among similar houses, strongly resembles the Back Bay District of Boston. Japanese housing of the time was a good deal smaller than European, but still surprisingly comfortable. Lu Xun lived in this house with his wife and son from 1933 until his death in 1936.

Outside the city

Shanghai Shi (Shanghai Municipality) covers a huge area of approximately two thousand square kilometres, comprising ten counties and extending far beyond the limits of the city itself. To the north it includes three islands in the Yangzi River delta, the largest of which, Chongming Island, is nearly 100km long. To the northwest and southwest are the provinces of Jiangsu and Zhejiang respectively, while to the east the municipality abuts the East China Sea. Surprisingly, very little of this area is ever visited by foreign tourists, though there are a couple of interesting sights.

The most obvious of these is **She Shan** (She Hill), about 30km southwest of the city. The hill only rises about 100m, but such is the flatness of the surrounding land that it is visible for miles around. It's crowned by a huge and thoroughly impressive **basilica**, a legacy of the nineteenth-century European missionary work. The hill has been under the ownership of a **Catholic** community since the 1850s, though the present church was not built until 1925. Services take place only on Christian festivals; nevertheless, it's a pleasant walk up the hill at any time of year (or you can take the cable car if you prefer), past bamboo groves and the occasional ancient pagoda. Most of the peasants in this area are fervent Catholics and welcoming towards Westerners. Also on the hill is a meteorological station and an old observatory, which contains a small exhibition room displaying an ancient earthquake-detecting device – a dragon with steel balls in its mouth which is so firmly set in the ground that only movement of the earth itself, from the vibrations of distant earthquakes, can cause the balls to drop out. The more balls drop, the more serious the earthquake.

To reach She Shan, take a bus from the Wenhua Guangchang bus stop, or the Xiqu bus station (see box p.379). If there are no direct buses, you can catch any bus to Songjiang and get off a few stops before the terminus – you'll have to ask. You then need to take a motor-rickshaw (¥15) the remaining distance to She Shan (daily 7.30am–4pm; ¥5).

Another twenty or so kilometres west of here, in Qingpu County, is **Dianshan Hu** and the **Grand View Garden**. For local tourists, the area around the southeastern shore of Dianshan Hu is being turned into a holiday resort, with opportunities for boating, swimming, fishing and even golf. The Grand View Garden is unashamedly intended for tourists, having been modelled on the famous garden from the eighteenth-century Chinese novel *Dream of the Red Chamber*. To get here, take a bus to Qingpu, and then hire a motor-rickshaw (¥5) for the short ride to the lake.

Zhouzhuang

Another 20km west, just across the border in Jiangsu Province, is the huddle of Ming architecture that comprises the small canal town of **ZHOUZHUANG**. Lying astride the large Jinghang Canal connecting Suzhou and Shanghai, Zhouzhuang grew prosperous from the area's brisk grain, silk and pottery trade during the Ming dynasty. Many rich government officials, scholars and artisans moved here and constructed beautiful villas, while investing money into developing the stately stone bridges and tree-lined canals that now provide the city's main attractions. Chinese tour groups invade Zhouzhuang in droves on weekends, but if you come on a weekday you should be able to appreciate the town in its serene, original splendour. **Minibuses** make the three-hour run from Shanghai Beizhan bus station twice daily (6.20am & 3.30pm), from Hongkou Gongyuan once daily (2pm) and from the Xinzhuang metro station twice daily (9.30am & 10.30am). There is also the intriguing possibility of travelling by speedboat from here to another canal town farther in Jiangsu, **Tongli** (see p.431), from where frequent buses complete the journey to Suzhou.

Eating, drinking and entertainment

As with so many other aspects of life, Shanghai is on China's cutting edge where leisure activities are concerned. Despite the fact that most Shanghainese have never been to a theatre or restaurant in their lives, there is now a sufficiently large class of people for whom dining out and evening entertainments are a serious option. **Restaurants** in particular have improved enormously in recent years, in terms of quality and variety. It is hard to believe that up until the early 1990s, simply getting a table was a cut-throat business. The sheer diversity of food on offer, representing all regions of China and every continent, is a reflection both of the openness of the city, and of the presence of an increasing expatriate population. There has been a similar explosion in the variety of other types of evening entertainment, which range from **English pubs** to **Beijing Opera** and from **discos** to **traditional folk music**.

Restaurants

The traditions of Shanghai's cosmopolitan past are still dimly apparent in the city's **restaurants**. Many of the old establishments have continued to thrive and although the original wood-panelled dining rooms are succumbing to modernization year by year, the growth of private enterprise ensures that the choice of venues is now wider than ever. If you are arriving from other areas of China, be prepared to be astounded by the excellent **diversity** of food in the city, with most Chinese regional cuisines represented, as well as an equally impressive range of foreign cuisine including Brazilian, Indian, Japanese and European. You will also find that restaurants serving both Chinese and international cuisine are more expensive in Shanghai than elsewhere, although **prices** remain reasonable by international standards. Despite locals' grumbles about how quickly prices are approaching Hong Kong's level, most dishes at Chinese restaurants range from US$3 to 4, and even many upmarket Western restaurants have meal specials that come to less than US$10. Compared to, for example, Sichuan or Cantonese cuisine, **Shanghai cuisine** is not particularly well known or popular among foreigners; nevertheless, there are some interesting dishes, especially if you enjoy exotic seafood. Fish and shrimps are considered basic to any respectable meal, and if possible eels and crab will appear as well. In season – between October and December – you may get the chance to try *dazha* crab, the most expensive and supposedly the most delicious. Most cooking is done with added ginger, sugar and Shaoxing wine, but without heavy spicing. One general warning about restaurant dining in Shanghai is the need to establish with absolute clarity – in advance – the prices of the dishes

Shanghai restaurants and cafés

1221	一二二一酒家	*yīèryī jiǔjiā*
1931	一九三一饭店	*yījiǔsānyī fàndiàn*
Always	奥维斯	*àowéi sī*
Badlands Tex-Mex	百岚	*bǎilán*
Bonomi	波诺米	*bōnuò mǐ*
Deda Xicanshe	德大西餐社	*dédà xīcānshè*
Ding Xiang Garden	丁香花苑	*dīngxiāng huāyuàn*
Frankie's Place	法兰奇餐厅	*fǎlánqī cāntīng*
Fulin Xuan	福临轩	*fúlín xuān*
Gap Café	锦亭酒家	*jǐntíng jiǔjiā*
Gongdelin	功德林素食馆	*gōngdélín sùshíguǎn*
Huanghe Lu	黄河路	*huánghé lù*
Hubin Mei Shilou	湖滨美食楼	*húbīn měi shí lóu*
Lao Fandian	老饭店	*lǎo fàndiàn*
Lübolang	绿波廊餐厅	*lǜbōláng cāntīng*
M on the Bund	米氏西餐厅	*mǐshì xīcāntīng*
Manabe	真锅咖啡	*zhēnguō kāfēi*
Meilongzhen	梅龙镇酒家	*méilóngzhèn jiǔjiā*
Sasha's	萨莎	*sàshā*
Shanghai Ren Jia	上海人家	*shànghǎi rénjiā*
Shashi Xiaochi Shijie	沙市小吃世界	*shāshì xiǎochī shìjiè*
Shintori	新都里餐厅	*xīndūlǐ cāntīng*
Shu Di la Zi Yu Guan	蜀地辣子鱼馆	*shǔdìlàzǐ yúguǎn*
Simply Thai	天泰餐厅	*tiāntài cāntīng*
Tandoor	锦江孟买餐厅	*jǐnjiāngmèngmǎi cāntīng*
Tony Roma's	多力罗马	*duōlì luómǎ*
U and I	亚拉餐厅	*yàlā cāntīng*
Xiao Shaoxing	小绍兴	*xiǎo shàoxīng*
Xinghualou	杏花楼	*xìnghuā lóu*
Xu's Dumpling House	许家小吃	*xǔjiā xiǎochī*
Yunnan Lu	云南路	*yúnnán lù*
Zhapu Lu	乍浦路	*zhàpǔlù*
Zhejiang Zhong Lu	浙江中路	*zhèjiāng zhōnglù*

you are ordering. Shanghai restaurateurs are notoriously unscrupulous when it comes to billing foreign tourists.

The Bund, Nanjing Dong Lu and around

The highlight of this area is the presence of a number of specialist **food streets**. In order of proximity to the top end of Nanjing Lu, the first of these is **Shashi Xiaochi Shijie**, a small lane leading south off Nanjing Dong Lu, just west of Jiang Xi Lu. It contains a number of cheap restaurants, good for hot-pots or noodle-soup snacks. North of the Suzhou Creek, and just a few minutes' walk west of the *Pujiang Hotel*, runs **Zhapu Lu** – at night it is entirely neon-lit and easily recognizable. There are large numbers of Shanghainese restaurants along here, many of them serving good food, but foreigners need to be very careful not be over-charged. **Yunnan Lu** is perhaps the most interesting of the food streets, with a number of speciality restaurants, and a huge crowd of outdoor stalls selling snacks at night; it leads south from Nanjing Lu a block to the east of Renmin Park. **Zhejiang Zhong Lu**, just north of Fuzhou Lu, is home to several **Muslim** snack shops offering delicious and filling noodle soups. Finally **Huanghe Lu**, due north of Renmin Park – and in particular the section north of Beijing Lu – contains another large concentration of restaurants, many of them open 24hr.

Nanjing Dong Lu is your best bet for baked goods, confectioneries and pastries. The **Bund** itself has few decent options for eating, although this situation is changing quickly with the recent opening of several upmarket restaurants in some of the old Art Deco buildings, most notably *M on the Bund*. The few eateries right along the waterfront are overpriced and undertasty.

Gongdelin Vegetarian 445 Nanjing Xi Lu, between Chengdu Lu and Huangpi Lu. Probably the best vegetarian restaurant in town – the "fish", "meat" and "crab" are actually all made of vegetables and tofu. The "squid" is recommended.

M on the Bund Floor 7, 5 Wai Tan, entrance at Guang Dong Lu ⑦021/63509988. Worth eating at for the extraordinary view overlooking the Bund, the Huangpu traffic and Pudong's skyline alone. The Mediterranean-style cuisine isn't half bad either – some of the classiest (and most expensive) food in town. Service could be better, and some complain that it's not all it's cracked up to be, but the set lunch (¥88) is good value. Reservations recommended.

Meilongzhen No. 22, Lane 1081, off the 800s of Nanjing Xi Lu by Jiang Ning lu. Locals flock to this cavernous, excellent Shanghainese restaurant specializing in seafood, with its simple, tasteful decor giving little overt indication that the place served as one of the most notorious Mafia dens in the 1920s. The eel and squid dishes are especially tasty.

Shanghai Ren Jia 41 Yunnan Zhong Lu. Huge, bustling restaurant, with interesting twists on the standard Shanghainese fare. Best to come in a large group so you can share multiple dishes.

Xiao Shaoxing Yunnan Lu (east side), immediately north of Jinjiang Lu. Famous in Shanghai for its "white cut chicken" (*bai qie ji*), although adventurous diners might wish to sample the blood soup or chicken feet.

Xinghualou Fuzhou Lu, a couple of blocks west of Henan Lu. Another long-established Cantonese restaurant, but less expensive than the *Ding Xiang Garden*.

The French Concession and western Shanghai

This is the area where most expatriates eat and correspondingly where prices begin to approach international levels. The compensation is that you'll find menus are almost certainly in English, and English will often be spoken, too. For travellers tired of Chinese food, Huaihai Lu and Maoming Lu brim with **international cuisine** – all-you-can-eat **buffets**, for example, are offered by some of the large hotels, of which the *Hilton*'s (at 505 Wulumuqi Bei Lu) is generally reckoned to be the best, though the *Portman* buffet is much cheaper. Many excellent **Shanghainese** and **Sichuanese restaurants** also cluster in the alleys around Huaihai Lu, at prices much lower than for international food. The *Hilton* houses an outstanding Cantonese *dim sum* restaurant with per-person bills often no higher than ¥100. **Fast-food** joints, **bakeries** and **snack stalls** line Huaihai Lu, while the best baked goods are made in the Japanese Isetan Department Store Bakery, at the eastern end of Huaihai Dong Lu. At the junction of Nanjing Xi Lu and Shaanxi Lu is the so-called **Food Theatre**, which is, in fact, a mall of immaculately clean fast-food outlets. North of the French Concession, **Xintiandi** is a recently renovated "olde worlde" area of fancy cafés and restaurants, a kind of dining theme park for yuppies.

1221 1221 Yan'an Xi Lu. A little out of the way – a taxi is your best bet, although bus #71 stops right outside – this is one of the city's best and most creative Shanghainese restaurants, attracting a mix of locals and expatriates. The drunken chicken and *xiang su ya* (fragrant crispy duck) are excellent, as are the onion cakes.

1931 112 Maoming Nan Lu, just south of Huaihai Zhong Lu. The right mix of Shanghainese, Japanese and Southeast Asian cuisines. Reasonably priced, good-sized portions.

Badlands Tex-Mex Yan'an Lu, right opposite the Shanghai Exhibition Centre. Good and cheap all-you-can-eat buffet of Mexican food for lunch and dinner; cheap booze available anytime.

Ding Xiang Garden 849 Hua Shan Lu ⑦021/62511166. The best Cantonese place in Shanghai, with scrumptious *dim sum* lunch and pleasant, if cavernous, decor. In warmer weather, you can dine alfresco in the garden, a rarity for a Cantonese restaurant. A dinner for two comes to around ¥120, drinks included, per head. Reservations recommended.

Frankie's Place 1477 Gubei Nan Lu. Reasonable Singaporean place serving excellent curries and barbecued sting ray.

Friendship Inside the Shanghai Exhibition Centre. Chinese cuisine, slightly oriented to Western tastes; popular among expatriates.

Fulin Xuan 37 Sinan Lu, two blocks south of Huaihai Lu. Typically massive Cantonese place with an English menu and a good reputation among locals. The abalone and shark's fin are almost like Hong Kong's. Most dishes come to ¥100 each. Run by Macau Chinese.

Gap 127 Maoming Nan Lu, just north of Huaihai Zhong Lu; 8 Hengshan Lu, by Wulumuqi Nan Lu; & 8 Zunyi Lu, by Hongqiao Friendship Store. This Shanghainese chain now has six branches – a testament to the superior quality of their cuisine. Specializes in seafood, although the *dim sum* is quite good, too. The Maoming Nan Lu branch has live music and fashion shows nightly.

Park 97 On the western edge of Fuxing Park three blocks south of Huaihai Lu. Home of Shanghai's best tapas bar, with big portions at reasonable prices and good pizzas. Weekend brunches and a weekly chocoholics bar keep things interesting. At night, the bar is one of the hottest places in the city to hang out.

Shintori 288 Wulumuqi Nan Lu, three blocks south of Hengshan Lu ⓣ021/64672459. Nouvelle-Japanese trendsetter. The *Keiseki*-style buffet will set you back around ¥300–400, but its entertaining presentation and excellent taste will give you something to talk about. Reservations recommended.

Simply Thai 5-C Dong Ping Lu. The best of the city's Thai joints, with eclectic dishes, impressive service, inexpensive and delicious food and a relaxing outdoor courtyard setting. Try the stir-fried asparagus and fish cakes and *tub kim krob* – coconut syrup – for dessert.

Tandoor *Jinjiang Hotel*, New South Building, just north of the Huaihai Lu and Maoming Lu intersection ⓣ021/64725494. First-class but very expensive Indian food, from ¥150 to ¥250 per head, drinks included (although at lunchtime there is a ¥96 set-menu available). Reservations recommended.

Tony Roma's Shanghai Centre, next to the *Portman Ritz-Carlton*. Probably the most American place in China, famous for spare-ribs and barbecue sauce, but the high prices make this a choice for only the truly homesick.

Sasha's 9 Dong Ping Lu, at Hengshan Lu ⓣ021/64746166. Good Continental European cuisine served in a charming wooden mansion. The set lunch is the best deal at ¥99. Reservations recommended.

Shu Di La Zi Yu Guan 187 Anfu Lu, on the corner with Wulumuqi Zhong Lu. Very good Sichuan and Hunanese cuisine. Try the *mala dofu* and spicy pepper chicken. There's an English menu and it's not too pricey.

Xu's Dumpling House No. 1, Lane 142, just off Xinle Lu. Hole-in-the-wall serving excellent, inexpensive *jiaozi* and other dumplings.

Yangzhou 72 Nanjing Xi Lu. Crammed with locals jostling to order the excellent Shanghainese seafood specialities. The *ju hua xie* (chrysanthemum crab) is sublime.

The Old City

The **Yu Yuan** area has traditionally been an excellent place for snack eating – *xiao long bao* and the like, eaten in unpretentious snack-bar style surroundings. Although the quality is generally excellent and prices very low, the drawback is the long lines which form at peak hours. Try to come to these places mid-morning or mid-afternoon, outside the main eating times of 11.30am to 1.30pm, and after 5.30pm. There are a number of snack bars in the alleys around the Yu Yuan, though the *Lübolang* (Green Wave) immediately west of the Huxingting Tea House is perhaps the best, with a large variety of dumplings and noodles. Very close to the Yu Yuan entrance is the *Hubin Mei Shilou*, which serves a delicious sweet bean *changsheng zhou* (long-life soup). The *Lao Fandian* (Old Restaurant), just north of the Yu Yuan on Fuyou Lu, is one of the most famous restaurants in town serving local Shanghai food, though prices are slightly inflated. For quick bites, check out the satay, noodle and corn-on-the-cob stands lining the street bordering the western side of Yu Yuan bazaar.

Cafés, bakeries and fast-food places

Finding a good **breakfast** remains the only problem of Shanghai's food scene. The best choices include going for the delicious yet very expensive (¥100–150) breakfast buffets at most luxury hotels, sampling the excellent Japanese and Chinese bakeries along Huaihai Zhong Lu or Nanjing Dong Lu, or finding a *Starbucks*.

Cheap **snack food** is easily available in almost any part of the city at any time of night or day – try *xiao long bao*, a local dumpling speciality. Most hotels also have respectable restaurants which serve **dim sum** at breakfast and lunch. Shanghai has taken to Western fast food in a big way, with ubiquitous *McDonald's*, *Pizza Hut* and especially *KFC*, the latter with a whopping 51 branches.

Unlike many other Chinese, the Shanghainese are famous for their sweet tooth, which is indulged by more than 1800 **bakeries, coffee and pastry shops** – a tradition that dates back to the period of the International Settlement – selling more than two thousand tons of pastries and confectionery each week.

Besides the places listed here, we've given details of snacks and fast food in specific areas of the city in the "Restaurants" section above.

Always 1528 Nanjing Xi Lu. A local institution and very popular, largely thanks to the lunchtime special (served 11.30am–5pm) which costs only ¥20 and includes unlimited coffee.

Bonomi Rm 112, Ground Floor Shanghai Centre, 1376 Nanjing Xi Lu, Rm 226, 12 Zhongshan Dong Yi Lu (on the Bund), 242 Fuyou Lu. A local chain with pastries and coffee.

Cloud 9 Floor 54, *Grand Hyatt Pudong*, Jin Mao Tower, Pudong. The highest café in China. Sit over an Asian tapas, cocktail or coffee and admire the view. Cover ¥95 per person.

Deda Xicanshe Sichuan Lu, just south of Nanjing Dong Lu. A traditional coffee bar, famous for chocolate buns and the like. Also serves Western- and Japanese-style meals.

Manabe 85 Huating Lu, 638 Huashan Lu & 1005 Huaihai Zhong Lu. A superior Taiwanese chain, with smoking and non-smoking sections and an enormous variety of coffees chosen from a picture menu.

Starbucks 1376 Nanjing Xi Lu, House 18, North Block Xintiandi & 189 Nanjing Xi Lu. Everything you'd expect from the coffee colonizers. Good for breakfast.

Subway 479 Nanjing Dong Lu, 555 Biyun Lu, 268 Shui Cheng Nan Lu. Expensive but filling sandwiches.

U and I 108 Daming Lu. A diner with a ¥16 set Western breakfast – the only such affordable place close to the *Pujiang Hotel*.

Nightlife

Shanghai has a jumping **nightlife**, although many places have a sleazy side to them. Western-style **bars** are legion, especially in the Huaihai Lu area, nearly all of which serve food, and some of which have room for dancing. The streets north of Huaihai Lu and south of Yan'an Zhong Lu, most notably Julu Lu and Maoming Lu, have the greatest concentration of bars in the city, although pockets also exist around Fudan University and Hengshan Lu. You'll find the full range of drinks available in Shanghai bars, though beer is usually bottled rather than draught and prices are on the high side; reckon on ¥30–60 per drink in most places, which is a lot more than what you'll pay in many restaurants. If it's Chinese rock you're after, **live music** can certainly be found, though don't bet on the quality. For up-to-date information about current events, as well as the newest bars, check the latest edition of the expat periodical *That's Shanghai* (see p.380).

Bars and clubs

Asia Blue 18 Gao Lan Lu, by Si Nan Lu. A gay bar but it's straight-friendly. Run by a famous local drag queen and his partner. Drinks around ¥30. Daily 8pm–2am.

Buddha Bar 172 Maoming Nan Lu. At the time of writing, the hippest venue in the city. Looks like a brothel in a temple thanks to ambient red lighting and Buddhist statuary. Comfy chairs aid passive observation. Only terminal show-offs will glory in the raised dance floor, but there are plenty of those around. Voted best place to pull in an expat magazine, though don't buy anyone too many drinks as they're not cheap (¥30). Raucous parties all night long to hypnotic trance. It can't last; it probably hasn't. Daily 9pm–2am, till 7am at weekends.

Café Vivante 82 Maoming Nan Lu, just south of Huaihai Zhong Lu. In the middle of a lively nightlife district, this is an intimate 24hr café to escape the clubbing and bar-hopping crowds.

California 2 Gao Lan Lu (in Fuxing Park). Dress up and come to be seen in the company of Shanghai's moneyed set, most of whom sit around this posh nightclub trying to look like they own the place. No cover though and it does get rocking later on. Mon–Thurs & Sun 7pm–2am, Fri–Sat 9pm–late.

Cotton Club 1428 Huaihai Zhong Lu. *The* place to head for live jazz and blues, played every night except Mondays and of a very high quality. Occasional open-mike nights. Requisite stop for all the big names doing pan-Asian tours. Cover charge varies from ¥25 to ¥100 depending on the act. Daily 7.30pm–2am.

Face *Ruijin Guesthouse*, 118 Rui Jin Er Lu. The only hotel bar that's cool. Sip very slowly at your ¥55 cocktail (the cheapest) and admire the busy beautiful people and the old Shanghai decor. Daily 2pm–2am.

George V 1 Wulumuqi, directly across from the US Consulate. Laid-back, fun place with pool table, dartboard and Boddington's bitter on draught. Jazz three times weekly; R&B and classical violin concerts once weekly each. Mon–Fri 9am–2am, weekends 6pm–2am.

Goodfellas 907 Julu Lu. One of many intimate, friendly bars with reasonably priced beers in the area. Daily 2pm–2am.

Goya 359 Xin Hua Lu. Sophisticated martini bar with comfy couches for practising one eyebrow raising and jiggling your ice suggestively. Fifty kinds of martini available, from iced to fruit-flavoured. Daily 7pm–2am.

Judy's Too 176 Maoming Nan Lu. German draught beer, food and dancing. Wednesday is latin, Thursday is retro, and Friday and Saturdays is your standard Shanghai disco and bar-girl combo. Daily 6pm–2am.

O'Malley's 42 Tao Jiang Lu. Typically cartoony Irish theme pub, with the expected expat contingent, but also a sizeable local patronage. Daily 11am–2am.

Peace Hotel Jazz Bar Junction of the Bund and Nanjing Dong Lu. A dark and cavernous pub inside the north building of the *Peace Hotel*, legendary for its eight-piece dance band whose members played here in the 1930s, suffered persecution during the Cultural Revolution, then re-emerged in the twilight of their years to fame and fortune. Their younger successors now play stately instrumental versions of Fats Domino and Elvis Presley standards, while portly tourists swirl to the nostalgic rhythms and sip cocktails amidst the original 1930s decor. Cover charge ¥60. Daily 8pm–1.30am.

Pegasus Floor 2, Golden Bell Plaza, 98 Huai Hai Zhong Lu. The best of the big clubs, with guest Western DJs and lively decor. No cover charge and drinks are ¥25. Closed Mondays and Tuesdays. Open till 2am in the week, a little later at weekends.

Real Love 10 Heng Shan Lu, in the Promenade Complex. Long-running disco. Not as fashionable as it was, so cover charges have dropped to a comparatively reasonable ¥40. Ladies get in free on Monday and Wednesdays. Daily 8pm–2am.

Shanghai Sally's Corner of Sinan Lu and Xiangshan Lu opposite Sun Yatsen's Memorial Residence (south of Huaihai Lu). Attempts an approximation of Britishness, including pool, darts and retro posters, though few Brits would stand paying this much for drinks at home (Guinness ¥55). The tube themed disco underneath – Underground – is as atmospheric as the Northern Line. Tues–Sat 4pm–late, Sun 11am–late.

Tequila Mama 24 Ruijin Lu, just south of Huaihai Lu. Mexican-flavoured bar/dance club with often-mediocre music selection, but the frequent drink offers make this one of the cheaper places for serious drinking – at the time of writing, beer was free before 9pm and after 1.30am Examine your life and start to make some changes if you come here more than once. Mon–Thurs & Fri–Sun 7pm–2am.

Windows Too J104, Jingan Si Plaza, 1699 Nanjing Xi Lu, by Hua Shan Lu. ¥10 beers, loud music, a laid-back atmosphere and it's open very late. Not much class but a lot of fun. Daily 6.30pm–2am.

Entertainment

It's not hard to run away with the impression that, in Shanghai, self-expression means shopping and culture is something that happens to pearls. There is a cultural scene of sorts out there though, with cinemas showing foreign and Chinese films, and theatres featuring opera, dance, drama, acrobatics and puppets.

To find out what's on and where, look in the expat magazines. Otherwise ask CITS to check the listings in a local newspaper for you. For many events it's worth either booking at the relevant venue in advance (try to have your requirements written out in Chinese) or getting CITS to do it for you for a fee, although you may be lucky just turning up on the night.

Shanghai's stately new glass ballet, drama, opera and symphony house, the **Grand Theatre** (300 Renmin Da Dao), was designed by the same architects who created the Bastille Opera House in Paris. The Shanghai Grand Theatre has pretensions of being a truly world-class theatre, on a par with Milan's La Scala and, based on the quality of recent interpretations of an Ibsen play and several Wagner operas, it stands a good chance of succeeding. There are two smaller theatres that host Chinese opera and chamber music productions (ticket hotline ⓣ021/63728701 or 63723833).

The huge, new multipurpose theatre (ⓣ021/62798663) in the **Shanghai Centre** on Nanjing Xi Lu hosts concerts, ballet, opera and acrobatics of international standard. The nightly acrobatics show by the famous **Shanghai Acrobatics Troupe** is a superb spectacle – in Western terms it's more of a circus, including tumbling, juggling, clowning, magic and animal acts. Some of these skills – sword swallowing, fire eating and the amazing balancing acts – were developed as long ago as the Han dynasty, others have taken on a more trashy look featuring motorbikes, spectacular costumes and even a giant panda driving a car. Tickets (¥70 per show) can be bought on the same day from a window outside the theatre or up to three days in advance at a ticket booth in front of the Shanghai Centre (daily 9am–8pm; ⓣ021/62798663). Performances begin at 7.30pm.

Shanghai is well represented by both Western and Chinese opera. The Tianchan Yifu Theatre at 701 Fuzhou Lu (south side), one block east of Renmin Park, puts on twice-daily performances of **Chinese opera**, with Sunday matinees of **Beijing opera** (daily 1.30pm & 7.15pm; ¥20–100; Chinese speakers can call ⓣ021/63514668). The **Grand Stage Theatre**, at 1111 Cao Xi Bei Lu, also holds occasional performances of traditional Chinese operas and plays (ⓣ021/64384952). Both Western and Chinese opera, as well as the occasional **magic shows**, take place at the imperial-era Lyceum Theatre, now better known as the **Lan Xin Theatre** (ⓣ021/62178530), home of that mainstay of colonial life, the British Amateur Dramatic Society, located just opposite the *Jinjiang Hotel* on the northeast corner of Changle Lu and Maoming Lu. The local expatriates' dancing school performed a wildly popular "Follies" revue every year here until 1933, once featuring a promising young ballerina called Margaret Hookham – who grew up to become Margot Fonteyn.

There are plenty of **cinemas** in Shanghai, some of them dating back to the pre-1949 days, though most foreign films are dubbed into Chinese. There is, however, a rapidly growing number of cinemas playing films in English, to satisfy expats and local English students alike, such as the Shanghai Film Art Centre, at 160 Xinhua Lu (ⓣ021/62804088), which regularly shows the latest American blockbusters; and the Yong Le Gong Cinema (Paradise Theatre), at 308 Anfu Lu, which screens more arty films (ⓣ021/64312961). Many bars have regularly scheduled "movie nights"; check the listings section of *That's Shanghai* for details.

Of the venues where you can hear **classical music**, one of the most pleasant has to be the **Shanghai Conservatory of Music** at 20 Fenyang Lu, south of Huaihai Lu, quite near the Changshu Lu metro station. Established in 1927 as a college for talented young musicians, it continues to train many of China's infant prodigies. There are performances here every Sunday evening at around 7pm. To find the ticket office, go in through the main entrance and turn immediately right, until you come to a noticeboard; the office is on the third floor of the building opposite here. It's best to book a day or two in advance to be sure of a seat. Tickets are incredibly cheap – just a few yuan (Chinese speakers can call ⓣ021/64310334 to make enquiries). Other theatres for classical music include the **Shanghai Concert Hall** at 523 Yan'an Dong Lu (ⓣ021/64604699), and the **Jingan Hotel Auditorium**, at 371 Huashan Lu, with chamber music concerts every Friday evening (ⓣ021/62481888 ext 687; ¥20). For **jazz**, the most popular venues are the **Cotton Club** (the locals' choice), the **Jingan Hotel**, at 371 Huashan Lu, and the touristy **Peace Hotel Jazz Bar**.

For a little taste of everything, the **Great World Entertainment Centre** is unbeatable. Standing in neon-lit splendour at 1 Xizang Nan Lu, just south of the elevated Yan'an Dong Lu expressway and characterized by its white-and-beige steeple, it began life in the 1920s as an even bigger complex of buildings putting on every conceivable kind of entertainment, from love-letter booths to *fan tan* tables and earwax extractors. It now consists of four floors with two auditoriums on each, surrounding a central well with an open-air stage. Staircases fly off in all directions; supposedly one used to have a dummy doorway at the top, through which ruined gamblers could step to their deaths as the climax to an unsuccessful evening. Peripheral amusements include dodgems, a Hall of Mirrors, snooker, bowling and video games, but in addition there are simultaneous performances of Beijing Opera, a large-scale puppet theatre, at least one movie, talent shows, gyrating pop singers and discos, while the main stage features non-stop acrobatics, clowning and comedy. You can wander at will from one room to another, walking to the front for example to examine the opera orchestra at close range and then leaving when the plot gets too complicated (daily 9am–8.30pm; ¥20 includes admission to everything within the complex).

Shopping

Although Shanghai cannot yet hope to compete with places such as Hong Kong or Bangkok where shopping is concerned – mainly because imported goods are a lot more expensive here – the city's old mercantile and consumerist traditions are reviving fast and there are now many goods worth picking up. **Tailored clothes** represent one of the best bargains in the city. Due to low labour and fabric costs, tailors can make male and female suits, shirts, cashmere, jackets and trousers for twenty percent or less than their counterparts along Savile Row, with the quality of the workmanship often equally stellar. However, few of the tailors speak English – you should bring a Chinese speaker along. Some of the best tailors include Aijian, at 45 Xianggang Lu (just west of the Bund; ⓣ021/63299993), 454 Handan Lu in the north of town near Wujiaochang (Five Corner Square), and No. 3 Lane 471 Miyun Lu in Hongkou (ⓣ021/65523473).

Antiques shopping can also yield fruitful, inexpensive results. The two antique markets at Dongtai Lu and Fuyou Lu in the Old City area (see p.395) are the best places for browsing though be aware that the majority of stuff is fake. If you don't like the risks associated with bargaining you might be better off visiting the city's government antique stores, the largest of which, the

Shanghai Antique and Curio Store at 218–226 Guang Dong Lu, has a large array of modern arts and crafts as well as some large antiques. There's also a much better-value private store, G. E. Tang Antique and Curio Shop, with its head office at 85 Dongtai Lu, which sells extremely attractive restored Chinese furniture and other larger pieces. For **Chinese art**, pay a visit to the Duoyun Art Gallery, on Nanjing Dong Lu just west of Shanxi Lu, or to the several galleries along Maoming Bei Lu just north of Yan'an Zhong Lu. Some superb scrolls (watercolours and calligraphy) are on sale here, as well as art books and all the equipment for producing traditional Chinese art. For **stationery**, the Bai Fu Stationery Store at 428 Fuzhou Lu offers an extensive selection of pens, papers, calligraphy brushes, and other supplies (daily 9am–5.30pm).

Another area where Shanghai has pretensions to compete with Hong Kong is in **clothing**. Some of the low-price (but good-quality), Hong Kong-owned, brand-name chain stores such as Giordano have a presence in the city, though large-sized Westerners may have difficulty finding clothes which fit. Every evening Huashan Lu, next to Wujiaochang in the north of the city near Fudan, fills with a **night market** brimming with inexpensive (but still decent-quality) clothing and souvenirs. To get here from downtown, take bus #55 or #910 from the Bund. **Silk** products, particularly traditional Chinese ladies' wear, are also good value; for these you might try department stores such as the monumental but basic No. 1 Store at the junction of Nanjing Lu and Xizang Lu, or – much more upmarket – the swish Huaihai Lu department stores, Shanghai Paris Printemps at the junction with Shaanxi Lu and the Japanese-run Huating-Isetan Department Store just east of Chengdu Lu. Finally, the **Friendship Store** (daily 9am–10pm) at 40 Beijing Lu, close to the *Peace Hotel,* is always worth a visit given its wide range of goods. The first floor is full of food, Chinese medicines, leather goods and consumer durables, while the second and third floors contain arts, handicrafts and clothing, as well as every type of silk. It's a fun place to browse but don't expect any bargains.

Listings

Airlines China Eastern Airlines (domestic ☎021/62471960; international ☎021/62472255) is at 204 Yan'an Xi Lu, while Shanghai Airlines (☎021/62681551) is at 555 Yan'an Zhong Lu. The following foreign carriers also have offices; most are in the Shanghai Centre, at 1376 Nanjing Xi Lu: Aeroflot, *Donghu Hotel*, Donghu Lu ☎021/64158158; Air France, Rm 1301, Novel Plaza, 128 Nanjing Xi Lu ☎021/63606688; All Nippon Airways, Shanghai Centre ☎021/62797000; Austrian Airlines, Rm 303, *Equatorial Hotel*, 65 Yan'an Xi Lu ☎021/62491202; Canadian, Floor 6, New Jinjiang Tower ☎021/64153091; Dragonair, Rm 202, Shanghai Centre ☎021/62798099; Japan Airlines, Floor 2, Ruijin Building, 205 Maoming Lu ☎021/64723000; Korean Air, Rm 104–5, *Hotel Equatorial*, 105 Yan'an Xi Lu ☎021/62481777; Lufthansa, *Hilton Hotel*, 250 Huashan Lu ☎021/62481100; Malaysian Airlines, Rm 209, Shanghai Centre ☎021/62798657; Northwest, Rm 207, Shanghai Centre ☎021/62798088; Qantas, Rm 203A, Shanghai Centre ☎021/62798660; SAS ☎021/62407003; Singapore Airlines, Rm 208, Shanghai Centre ☎021/62798008; Swissair, Rm 203, Shanghai Centre ☎021/62797381; United Airlines, Rm 204, Shanghai Centre ☎021/62798009.

American Express Rm 206, Shanghai Centre, 1376 Nanjing Xi Lu (Mon–Fri 9am–5.30pm; ☎021/62798082).

Banks and exchange Traveller's cheques can be exchanged at most hotels and at all branches of the Bank of China, the head office of which is at 23 Zhongshan Lu, next to the *Peace Hotel* (The Bund; Mon–Fri 9am–noon & 1.30–4.30pm, Sat 9am–noon). Next door lies a Citibank ATM machine with 24hr banking service.

Bike rental Only residents are allowed to ride bikes in Shanghai's crowded streets. If you have a bike you won't be stopped, but there is nowhere for visitors to rent them.

Bookshops The Foreign Language Bookstore, 390 Fuzhou Lu, is by far the best place to check in the city, as it has a good selection of modern and classic English-language fiction and non-fiction, as well as a collection of specialist translated Chinese literature around the corner at 201 Shandong Zhong Lu (open daily 9am–5.30pm). Most other places along Fuzhou Lu (nicknamed "Book Street" for its multitude of bookstores) have very limited English sections. Western paperbacks and periodicals can be found at all major hotels and at the Friendship Store.

Consulates Australia, 17 Fuxing Xi Lu ⓣ021/64334604; Austria, Qihua Building, 1375 Huaihai Zhong Lu ⓣ021/64712572; Canada, Rm 604 West Tower, Shanghai Centre, 1376 Nanjing Xi Lu ⓣ021/62798400; Denmark, Floor 6, 1375 Huaihai Lu ⓣ021/64314301; France, Suite 7A 21/F, Qihua Tower, 1375 Huaihai Zhong Lu ⓣ021/64377414; Germany, 181 Yongfu Lu ⓣ021/64336951; Holland, #1403, 250 Hua Shan Lu ⓣ021/62480000; India, Rm 1008, Shanghai International Trade Center, 2200 Yan'an Lu ⓣ021/62758885; Israel, #55, Floor 7, Lou Shan Guan Lu ⓣ021/62783075; Italy, Floor 11, Qihua Tower, 1375 Huaihai Zhong Lu ⓣ021/64716980; Japan, 517 Huaihai Zhong Lu ⓣ021/62780788; New Zealand, Floor 15, Qihua Mansion, 1375 Huaihai Lu ⓣ021/64332230; Poland, 618 Jianguo Lu ⓣ021/64339288; Russia, 20 Huangpu Lu ⓣ021/63242682; Singapore, 400 Wulumuqi Zhong Lu ⓣ021/64331362; South Korea, Floor 4, 2200 Yan'an Lu ⓣ021/62196420; Sweden, 6A Qihua Mansion, 1375 Huaihai Zhong Lu ⓣ021/64741311; Thailand, 7 Zhongshan Dong Lu ⓣ021/63219371; UK, Rm 301, Shanghai Centre, 1376 Nanjing Xi Lu ⓣ021/62797650; USA, 1469 Huaihai Zhong Lu ⓣ021/64336888.

Football The Shanghai Shenhua Club were the champions of China in 1996 and the runners-up from 1997 to 1999. During the football season (winter), you can see a game in the gleaming 35,000-seat Hongkou Football Stadium, at 444 Dongjianwan Lu in the north of town. Tickets are ¥30 and you can buy them at the ground on the day. They play every other Sunday at 3.30pm.

Hospitals A number of the city's hospitals have special clinics for foreigners, including the Huadong Hospital at 221 Yan'an Xi Lu (ⓣ021/62483180) and the 19th floor of the Hua Shan Hospital at 12 Wulumuqi Lu (ⓣ021/62489999). You'll find top-notch medical care at World Link Medical and Dental Centres (ⓣ021/62797688) in Suite 203 of the Shanghai Centre at 1376 Nanjing Xi Lu, but they are pricey at ¥700 per consultation. World Link also has an office in Hongqiao near the airport at 778 Hong Xu Lu (ⓣ021/6405 5788).

Internet access The cheapest Internet hook-up is in the basement of the Shanghai Library at 1555 Huaihai Zhong Lu (daily 8.30am–8pm; ¥6/hr; take your passport as ID). Other cafés are on the second floor of the Shanghai Bookstore at 465 Fuzhou Lu (Mon–Fri 9.30am–6.30pm, Sat & Sun 9.30am–9pm; ¥14/hr); Hong Tai on the second floor at 507 Sichuan Zhong Lu (daily 1–10.30pm; ¥18/hr); and Worldwide Network Club at 555 Jiangsu Lu (daily 8am–midnight; ¥12/hr). There are also several Net places dotted around Fudan University and other college campuses; ask local students for specifics as new places are always opening.

Mail There are post office branches all over the city. The main office is at 1761 Sichuan Lu, just north of and overlooking Suzhou Creek. A stately fin-de-siecle Art Deco edifice, the post office offers a very efficient parcel service; the express option can send packages to England or the USA within two days. Poste restante arrives at the Bei Suzhou Lu office across the street – each separate item is recorded on a little slip of cardboard in a display case near the entrance. Most hotels, including the *Pujiang*, also accept and hold mail. PO and poste restante open daily 9am–5pm. Branches dot the city, with convenient locations along Nanjing Dong Lu, Huaihai Zhong Lu, the Portman Centre, and near the Huangpu River ferry jetties at the corner of Jinling Dong Lu and Sichuan Bei Lu.

PSB 210 Hankou Lu, near the corner of Henan Zhong Lu. For visa extensions go to 333 Wusong Lu (daily 8.30am–11am & 2–5pm).

Telephones International calls are most easily and cheaply made with phone cards that can be bought and used in hotels and at street stalls. Otherwise they can be made from the second floor of the main post office at 1761 Sichuan Bei Lu, or at the China Telecom office three stores down from the north building of the *Peace Hotel* on 30 Nanjing Dong Lu (open 24hr). A large, English-speaking staff can deal with most requests.

Travel agents CITS has a helpful office several stores down from the north building of the *Peace Hotel* at 66 Nanjing Dong Lu (ⓣ021/63233384, ⓕ63290295), providing travel and entertainment tickets, with a small commission added on. There's another CITS branch at 1277 Beijing Xi Lu (ⓣ021/62898899), as well as a ticket office (but not travel agency) just off the Bund at 2 Jinling Dong Lu, opposite the boat ticket office (all branches daily 8.30am–11.30am & 1–4.45pm). Most if not all hotels have travel agencies offering the same services.

Travel details

Trains

The list below is only meant as an approximation. Train schedules change four times a year and the Transportation Agency is constantly adding new trains. Check the ticket window for the latest.

Shanghai Station to: Beijing (4 express daily; 14hr; 8 regular daily; 22hr); Changsha (3 daily; 19hr); Changzhou (17 daily; 2–3hr); Chengdu (2 daily; 40–45hr); Chongqing (daily; 44hr); Fuzhou (2 daily; 21hr); Guangzhou (3 daily; 24hr); Guilin (3 daily; 27hr); Hangzhou (16 daily; 2–3hr); Harbin (daily; 33hr); Hefei (5 daily; 9hr); Hong Kong (3–5 weekly; 28hr); Huangshan (daily; 12hr); Kunming (daily; 48–58hr); Lanzhou (2 daily; 30hr); Lianyungang (daily; 14hr); Nanchang (daily; 12hr); Nanjing (19 daily; 3–4hr); Nanning (2 daily; 15hr); Ningbo (6 daily; 6–9hr); Qingdao (1 daily; 20hr); Shaoxing (6 daily; 3–5hr); Shenyang (1 daily; 28hr); Suzhou (23 daily; 1hr); Tai'an, for Qufu (4 daily; 11hr); Tianjin (4 daily; 16hr); Ürümqi (daily; 64hr); Wuxi (16 daily; 2hr); Xiamen (daily; 26hr); Xi'an (2 daily; 21hr); Xining (daily; 41hr); Xuzhou (7 daily; 9hr); Zhenjiang (16 daily; 3hr).

Shanghai West Station to: Baotou (2 daily; 34hr); Hohhot (2 daily; 31hr).

Buses

There is little point travelling to destinations far from Shanghai by bus; the journey takes longer than the train and is far less comfortable. To destinations near Shanghai, however, journey times and price, though not necessarily comfort, are comparable to the train, thanks to massive amounts of freeway construction in the past several years.

Shanghai to: Hangzhou (45 daily; 3hr); Lianyungang (5 daily; 8hr); Nanjing (27 daily; 4hr); Shaoxing (6 daily; 4hr); Suzhou (53 daily; 1hr); Wenzhou (3 daily; 12hr); Wuxi (35 daily; 3hr); Yangzhou (13 daily; 5hr).

Ferries

Shanghai to: Chongqing (daily; 6 days); Dalian (weekly; 48hr); Fuzhou/Mawei (3 weekly, 36hr); Kobe, Japan (seasonal, weekly; 38hr); Nanjing (6 weekly; 16hr); Ningbo (twice daily; 4–8hr); Osaka, Japan (seasonal, two weekly; 36hr); Putuo Shan (twice daily; 4–12hr); Qingdao (weekly; 26hr); Wenzhou (four weekly; 24hr); Wuhan (4 daily; 56hr).

Flights

Shanghai to: Baotou (2 weekly; 2hr 50min); Beijing (16 daily; 1hr 50min); Changchun (3 daily; 2hr 45min); Chengdu (5 daily; 2hr 45min); Chongqing (4 daily; 2hr 30min); Dalian (5 daily; 1hr 30min); Fuzhou (1 daily; 1hr 30 min); Guangzhou (10 daily; 2hr); Guilin (2 daily; 2hr 20min); Haikou (4 daily; 3hr); Harbin (2–4 daily; 2hr 40min); Hohhot (3 weekly; 2hr 20min); Hong Kong (19 daily; 2hr 10min); Huangshan (3 weekly; 1hr); Kunming (1–3 daily; 3hr); Lanzhou (1–2 daily; 3hr); Macau (2 daily; 2hr 20 min); Nanning (daily; 3hr); Ningbo (daily; 40min); Qingdao (daily; 1hr 20min); Shenzhen (10 daily; 2hr); Taiyuan (daily; 2hr); Tianjin (daily; 1hr 30min); Ürümqi (5 weekly; 5hr); Wenzhou (1–3 daily; 1hr); Wuhan (3 daily; 1hr); Xiamen (3 daily; 1hr 30min); Xi'an (6 daily; 2hr 15min).

CHAPTER 6

Highlights

* **The Grand Canal** Original source of the region's wealth and a construction feat to rival the great wall. See p.418
* **Suzhou** A striking medley of tree-lined canals, ramshackle homes, old stone bridges and hi-tech factories. See p.419
* **Tongli** A quiet, charming town of winding lanes and canals. See p.431
* **The cable car at Zhenjiang** The ride from this sleepy town to the verdant island of Jiao Shan offers a unique view of the Yangzi. See p.442
* **Fuzi Miao, Nanjing** A bustling consumer cornucopia, hot, noisy and earthy. See p.457
* **Cycling around Xi Hu** A leisurely way to appreciate the great vistas offered by Hangzhou's beautiful lake. See p.477
* **Shaoxing** Charismatic backwater, once home to some cultural heavyweights, such as the writer Lu Xun, whose elegant mansion, now a museum, offers a glimpse into a vanished world. See p.483
* **Putuo Shan** A tranquil island of Buddist temples and beaches. See p.493

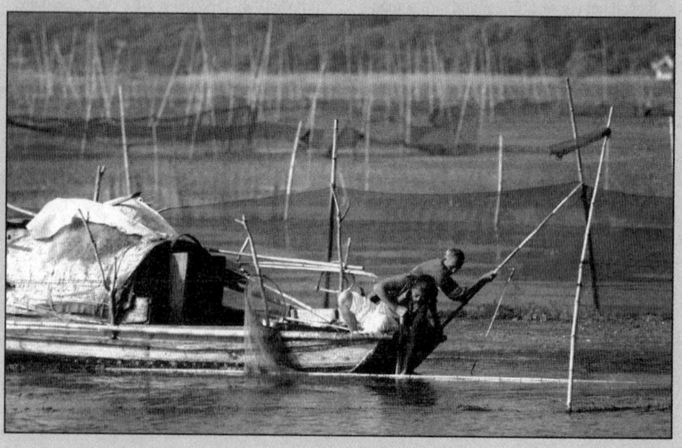

6

Jiangsu and Zhejiang

China's original heartland may have been the dusty Yellow River basin, but it was the greenness and fertility of the **Yangzi River estuary** that drew the Chinese south, and provided them with the wealth and power needed to sustain a huge empire. The provinces of **Jiangsu** and **Zhejiang**, which today flank the metropolitan area of Shanghai to the north and south, have been playing a vital part in the cultural and economic development of China for the last two thousand years. No tour of eastern China would be complete without stopovers in some of their classic destinations.

The story begins in the sixth century BC when the area was part of the state of Wu and had already developed its own distinct culture. The flat terrain, the large crop yield and the superb communications offered by coastal ports and navigable waterways enabled the principal towns of the area to develop quickly into important **trading centres**. These presented an irresistible target for the expanding Chinese empire under the Qin dynasty, and in 223 BC the region was annexed, immediately developing into one of the economic centres of the empire. After the end of the Han dynasty in the third century AD, several regimes established short-lived capitals in southern cities; however, the real boost for southern China came when the Sui (589–618 AD) extended the **Grand Canal** to link the Yangzi with the Yellow River and, ultimately, to allow trade to flow freely between here and the northern capitals. With this, China's centre of gravity took a decisive shift south. Under later dynasties, Hangzhou and then Nanjing became the greatest cities in China.

Visiting the region, you find yourself in a world of **water**. The whole area is intensively drained, canalized, irrigated and farmed, and the rivers, canals and lakes which web the plain give it much of its character. The traditional way to travel here was by **boat**, and today ferries continue to ply the Yangzi, while the major sea ports – Shanghai, Ningbo, Wenzhou – are also linked by coastal passenger services. There are even still a few local services inland, such as those between Suzhou, Wuxi and Hangzhou, along the canals in among silk farms and tea plantations.

The powerful commercial cities of the waterways have long acted as counterweights to the bureaucratic tendencies of Beijing. Both **Hangzhou** and **Nanjing** have served as the capital of China, the latter having been Sun Yatsen's capital during the brief years of the Chinese Republic after the overthrow of the Qing dynasty. Marco Polo called Hangzhou "the most beautiful and magnificent city in the world", and its Xi Hu (West Lake), still recognizable from classic scroll paintings, is deservedly rated as one of the most scenic spots in China. **Suzhou** and **Yangzhou**, too, should not be missed, for the bustle of life along the canals that crisscross their centres, and the peace of their famous

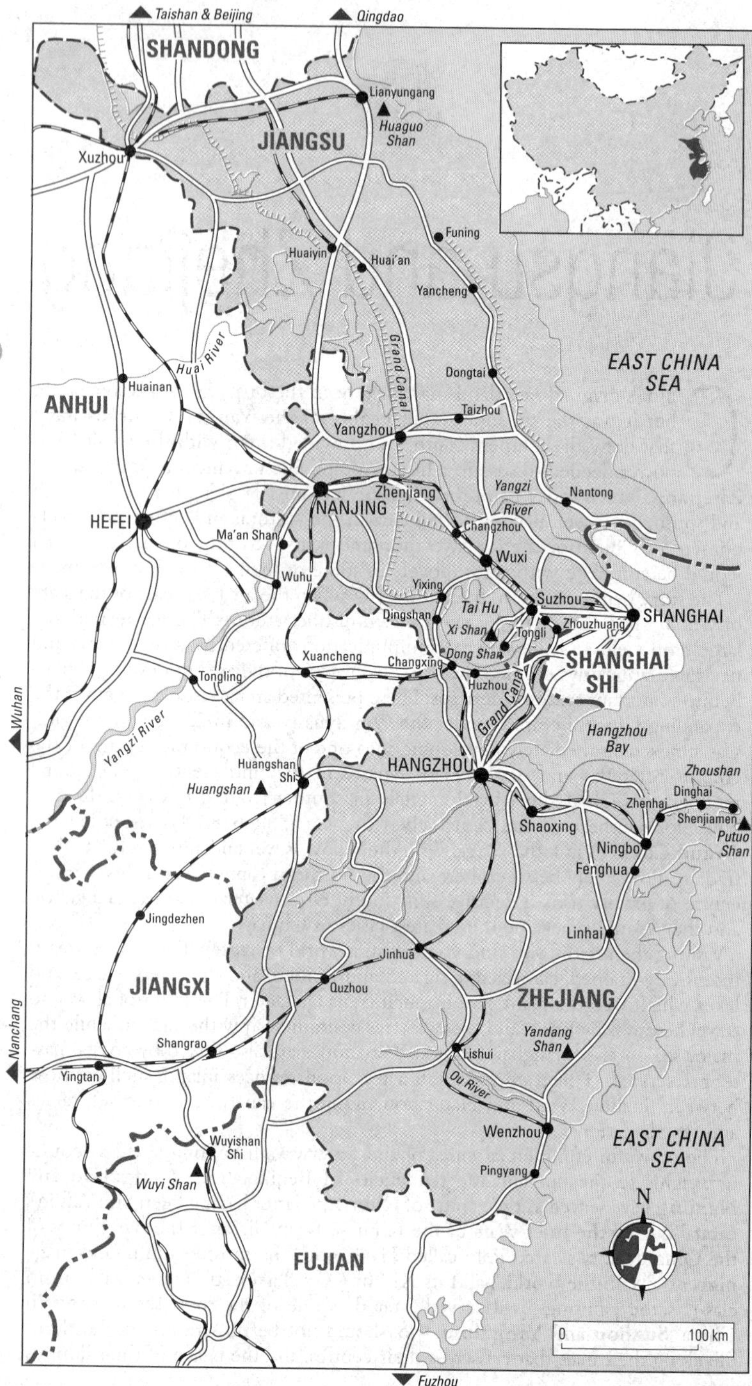

6 JIANGSU AND ZHEJIANG

gardens. These and other cities – **Zhenjiang**, **Wuxi**, **Ningbo** – have also developed as manufacturing centres, enjoying the boom which has put Jiangsu and Zhejiang to the forefront of economic development in China. Indeed, southern Jiangsu's per capita income is the highest in China outside Shanghai, southern Guangdong and Hong Kong.

The downside to relative prosperity in China is chronic over-population. Well over 135 million people live in Jiangsu, Shanghai and Zhejiang and it can seem when crossing the area by train that it has been built over from end to end. You will be hard-pressed to find much that might be classed as countryside here, with the exceptions of the area around the charming **Shaoxing**, and, above all, the sacred Buddhist island of **Putuo Shan**, where superb beaches and monasteries are set deep in wooded hillsides.

For visitors, perhaps the most important point is that most foreign tourists who come here are on expensive package tours, and there are few facilities, such as foreigners' dormitories, for independent travellers. **Accommodation** is almost uniformly on the expensive side, with the cheapest hotels rarely dipping below ¥200 for a double room – often university accommodation is the only budget possibility. As for the best **season** to visit, you should note that the area around the Yangzi, despite being low-lying and far from the northern plains, is unpleasantly cold and damp in winter, and unbearably hot and sticky during the summer months when most people choose to visit – Nanjing's age-old reputation as one of the "three furnaces" of China is well justified. If possible, you should try to visit during the spring (mid-April to late May; many residents claim if you blink, you'll miss it), during which a combination of rain-showers, sunshine and low humidity gives the terrain a splash of green as well as putting smiles on the faces of residents emerging from the harsh winter.

Jiangsu

Jiangsu is a long, narrow province hugging the coast south of Shandong. Low-lying, flat and wet, it is one of the most fertile and long-inhabited areas of China, dense in population and with plenty of sights of interest. The provincial capital, **Nanjing**, one of the great historical cities of China, was until only fifty years ago the nation's capital. **Suzhou** and **Yangzhou** are ancient cities famous throughout China for their gardens and silk production, while **Wuxi** attracts thousands of tourists to the shores of **Tai Hu** for its scenery, fruit trees and fish, and for the caves of **Yixing** across the lake.

The traditional route across Jiangsu is the **Grand Canal**, which was once navigable all the way from Hangzhou in Zhejiang Province to Beijing, and is still very much alive in the sections that flow through southern Jiangsu. In addition to Suzhou, Yangzhou and Wuxi, **Zhenjiang** is another classic trading centres full of the bustle of canal life. The province's other great water highway – the **Yangzi River** – connects Nanjing with the seaport of Shanghai, ensuring that trade from both east and west continues to bring wealth to the region.

The northwest has traditionally been the poor and backward part of the province, but even here **Xuzhou** is now a major rail junction with modern

The Grand Canal

The **Grand Canal** (Da Yun He), at 1800km the longest canal on earth, ranks alongside the Great Wall of China as the country's greatest engineering achievement. The first sections were dug about 400 BC, probably for military purposes, but the historic task of linking the Yellow and the Yangzi rivers was not achieved until the early seventh century AD under the Sui emperor Yang Di, when as many as six million men may have been pressed into service for its construction.

Locals like to point out that whereas the Great Wall was designed to stop contact and communication, the canal was made to further it. The original function of the canal was specifically to join the fertile rice-producing areas of the Yangzi with the more heavily populated but barren lands of the north, and to alleviate the effects of regular crop failures and famine. Following its completion, however, the canal became a vital element in the expansion of **trade** under the Tang and Song, benefiting the south as much as the north. Slowly the centre of political power drifted south – by 800 AD the Yangzi basin was taking over from the Yellow River as the chief source of the empire's finances, a transformation that would bring an end to the long domination of the old northern capitals, and lead to Hangzhou and Nanjing becoming China's most populous and powerful cities. A Japanese monk, Ennin, who travelled in China from 836 to 847 AD, described the traffic on the water then (in places you might find similar scenes today):

Two water buffalo were tied to more than forty boats, with two or three of the latter joined to form a single raft and with these connected in line by hawsers. Since it was difficult to hear from head to stern there was great shouting back and forth . . . Boats of the salt bureau passed laden with salt, three or four or five boats bound side by side and in line, following one another for several tens of *li*.

By the twelfth century, the provinces of Jiangsu and Zhejiang had become the economic and political heart of China. The Song dynasty moved south and established a capital at **Hangzhou** and the Ming emperors subsequently based themselves in **Nanjing**. During this period, and for centuries afterwards, the canal was constantly maintained and the banks regularly built up. A Western traveller, Robert Morrison, journeying as late as 1816 from Tianjin all the way down to the Yangzi, described the sophisticated and frequent locks and noted that in places the banks were so high and the country around so low that from the boat it was possible to look down on roofs and treetops.

Not until early in the twentieth century did the canal seriously start falling into **disuse**. Contributing factors included the frequent flooding of the Yellow River, the growth of coastal shipping and the coming of the rail lines. Unused, much of the canal rapidly silted up. But since the 1950s its value has once more been recognized, and renovation undertaken. The stretch **south of the Yangzi**, running from Zhenjiang through Changzhou, Wuxi and Suzhou (and on to Hangzhou in Zhejiang Province), is now navigable all year round, at least by flat-bottomed barges and the cruisers built for the tourist trade. Although most local **passenger boat services** along the canal have been dropped, the surviving services from Hangzhou to Suzhou or Wuxi will probably give you enough of a taste. It's fascinating rather than beautiful – as well as the frenetic loading and unloading of barges, you'll see serious pollution and heavy industry. **North of the Yangzi**, the canal is seasonably navigable virtually up to Jiangsu's northern border with Shandong, and major works are going on to allow bulk carriers access to the coal-producing city of Xuzhou. Beyond here, towards the Yellow River, the canal sadly remains impassable.

coal mines to supplement the fame of its early Han origins. The central parts of Jiangsu have a coast too shallow for anchorage, but ideal for salt panning, traditionally the source of its income. Among these flat lands dotted with small towns and lakes, and seamed with canals, the highlight is **Huai'an**, the attractive hometown of Zhou Enlai.

Suzhou and around

Famous for its gardens, beautiful women and silk, the ancient and moated city of **SUZHOU**, just sixty minutes from Shanghai by train, lies at the point where the rail line meets the Grand Canal, about 30km to the east of Tai Hu (see p.432). The town itself is built on a network of interlocking canals whose waters feed the series of renowned **classical gardens** which are Suzhou's pride and glory. Though Suzhou is now a boom town, with industrial towns springing up all round the outskirts, its centre is crisscrossed with water and dotted with greenery, and retains enough traces of its original character to merit a visit of at least several days.

He Lu, semi-mythical ruler of the Kingdom of Wu, is said to have founded Suzhou in 600 BC as his capital, but it was the arrival of the **Grand Canal** more than a thousand years later that marked the beginning of the city's prosperity. The **silk trade**, too, was established early here, flourishing under the Tang and thoroughly booming when the whole imperial court moved south under the Song. To this day, silk remains an import source of Suzhou's income.

With the imperial capital close by at Hangzhou, Suzhou attracted an overspill of scholars, officials and merchants, bringing wealth and patronage with them. In the late thirteenth century, Marco Polo reported "six thousand bridges, clever merchants, cunning men of all crafts, very wise men called Sages and great natural physicians". These were the people responsible for carving out the intricate gardens that now represent Suzhou's primary attractions. When the first Ming emperor founded his capital at Nanjing, the city continued to enjoy a privileged position within the orbit of the court and to flourish as a centre for the production of wood block and the weaving of silk. The business was transformed by the gathering of the workforce into great sheds in a manner not seen in the West until the coming of the Industrial Revolution three centuries later.

Until recently, Suzhou's good fortune had been to avoid the ravages of history, despite suffering brief periods of occupation by the Taipings in the 1860s and by the Japanese during World War II. The 2,500-year-old city walls, however, which even in 1925 were still an effective defence against rampaging warlords, were almost entirely demolished after 1949, and the parts of the **old city** that still survive – moats, gates, tree-lined canals, stone bridges, cobblestoned streets and whitewashed old houses – are disappearing fast. Soon there may be little more than the famous gardens themselves to provide testimony to the city's past.

Arrival and transport

Lying within a rectangular moat formed by canals, the historic town's clear grid of streets and waterways makes Suzhou a relatively easy place in which to get your bearings. **Renmin Lu**, the main street, bulldozes south through the centre from the **train station**, which is just to the north of the moat. The traditional commercial centre of the city lies around **Guanqian Jie**, halfway down Renmin Lu, an area of cramped, animated streets thronged with small shops,

Suzhou and around

Suzhou	苏州	***sūzhōu***
Beisi Ta	北寺塔	*běisì tǎ*
Canglang Ting	沧浪亭	*cānglàng tíng*
Feng Qiao	枫桥	*fēng qiáo*
Hanshan Si	寒山寺	*hánshān sì*
Huqiu Shan	虎丘山	*hǔqiū shān*
Liu Yuan	留园	*liú yuán*
Museum of Opera and Theatre	戏曲博物馆	*xìqǔ bówùguǎn*
Ou Yuan	藕园	*ǒuyuán*
Pan Men	盘门	*pánmén*
Ruiguang Ta	瑞光塔	*ruìguāng tǎ*
Shi Lu shílù	石路	*shílù*
Shizi Lin	狮子林	*shīzi lín*
Shuang Ta	双塔	*shuāng tǎ*
Silk Museum	丝绸博物馆	*sīchóu bówùguǎn*
Wangshi Yuan	网师园	*wǎngshī yuán*
Wumen Qiao	吴门桥	*wúmén qiáo*
Xi Yuan	西园	*xīyuán*
Xuanmiao Guan	玄妙观	*xuánmiào guàn*
Yi Yuan	怡园	*yíyuán*
Zhuozheng Yuan	拙政园	*zhuózhèng yuán*
Accommodation and eating		
Canglang	沧浪宾馆	*cānglàng bīnguǎn*
Korean Restaurant	汉城韩国料理	*hànchénghánguó liàolǐ*
Lexiang	乐乡饭店	*lèxiāng fàndiàn*
Nanlin	南林饭店	*nánlín fàndiàn*
Nanyuan	南园宾馆	*nányuán bīnguǎn*
New Century	新世纪大酒店	*xīnshìjì dàjiǔdiàn*
Renjia	人家	*rénjiā*
Sakura Gawa	樱川	*yīngchuān*
Sheraton	喜来登大酒店	*xǐlàidēng dàjiǔdiàn*
Shiquan Ren Jia	十全人家	*shíquán rénjiā*
Sicily	西西里餐厅	*xīxīlǐ cāntīng*
Songhelou Caiguan	松鹤楼	*sōnghè lóu*
Suzhou	苏州饭店	*sūzhōu fàndiàn*
Yingfeng	迎枫饭店	*yíngfēng fàndiàn*
Yonghe Doujiang	永和豆浆小吃	*yǒnghé dòujiāng xiǎochī*
Youyi	友谊宾馆	*yǒuyí bīnguǎn*
Around Suzhou		
Baodai Qiao	宝带桥	*bǎodài qiáo*
Lingyan Shan	灵岩山	*língyán shān*
Tianchi Shan	天池山	*tiānchí shān*
Tianping Shan	天平山	*tiānpíng shān*
Tongli	同里	*tónglǐ*

teahouses and restaurants. A newer, smarter shopping area has also developed outside the northwestern part of the moat around **Shi Lu**, while the area of town due west of the moat is the modern, ugly **Xincheng**.

Nearly all travellers arrive by **train**, Suzhou being on the main Shanghai–Nanjing rail line and served by frequent trains to and from both cities. Perhaps because Suzhou is a major tourist destination, hotel touts here are much more aggressive than elsewhere in China – the best strategy to shake them off is to ignore them completely. Buses #1 and #20 take you into town from just east of the train station. Some private **minibuses** also use the train station square as their terminus, for example services to and from Wuxi and points on Tai Hu.

Suzhou has two main bus stations. The **Beimen bus station**, which has half-hourly connections with Shanghai and Wuxi, as well as a frequent service to Zhouzhuang, is directly to the east of the train station. The **Nanmen bus station**, with buses to points south including Hangzhou and Wenzhou, is at the southern end of Renmin Lu (take bus #1 to get into the centre). Very near the Nanmen bus station is the **passenger dock** for canal boats to and from Hangzhou. A third bus station travellers might use is the **Wuxian bus station** in the far south of the town, one large block south of the moat (city bus #1 also passes here). This is the base for buses to and from local towns such as Tongli and Zhouzhuang. There's no airport at Suzhou (the nearest is at Shanghai, accessible in about an hour by taxi), though there is a CAAC office for bookings (see "Listings", p.430).

Opposite the train station's soft-seat waiting room is a small jetty where you can sign up for two-hour **boat tours** along the Grand Canal, either south to Pan Men or northwest to Hu Qiu (¥30 per person for groups; entire boat for about ¥150 for lone travellers).

Accommodation

The main **hotel** area, and the heaviest concentration of gardens and historic buildings, is in the south of the city, around **Shiquan Jie**. Out of season (Oct–May), you should be able to get rooms in all the hotels listed below at a discount of ten to twenty percent if you bargain at the front desk.

Bamboo Grove 168 Zhuhui Jie ⓣ0512/65205601, ⓦwww.bg-hotel.com. The new favourite of tour groups, an efficient Japanese-run four-star hotel that emulates local style with black and white walls and abundant bamboo in the garden. There are a couple of good restaurants on site. ❾

Canglang Hotel/Suzhou Medical School Guesthouse 53 Wuqueqiao Jie ⓣ0512/65201557, ⓕ65103285. A drab exterior but the rooms are clean and en suite, with matching velvet curtains and bedcovers. No English is spoken and staff will assume you want the one of more expensive rooms until firmly told otherwise. Dorm beds ¥60, ❹

Dongwu Shiquan Jie ⓣ0512/65194437, ⓕ65194590. By far the best budget place, this large compound run by Suzhou University is central but quiet and offers clean rooms either in the main building or – the cheaper option – in the pleasant foreign students guesthouse at the back. There's a very cheap canteen on site too. Single rooms are available for ¥80. ❸

Huayuan Suzhan Lu ⓣ0512/67225510. Dilapidated and mosquito-infested, but okay as a last resort, with grotty doubles, some of which have an attached bathroom. It's about a 15min walk north of the train station: turn right as you emerge from the station, then right again through a tunnel under the rail line. Follow the road to the T-junction, and the hotel is on your right, just past the corner (no English sign). ❶

Lexiang 18 Dajin Xiang, the third lane south of Guanqian Jie, east off Renmin Lu ⓣ0512/65222890, ⓕ65244165. A very good, friendly, central hotel, one of the best mid-range options, with CITS next door and convenient for some good restaurants. The three- or four-bed rooms can work out fairly cheap if you bring enough friends to fill them. ❻

Nanlin Shiquan Jie ⓣ0512/65194641 ext 8830, ⓕ65191028. A big three-star garden-style affair with an immaculate lobby. The new wing has luxury rooms, while the old wing still offers reasonably priced doubles and triples. ❺–❽

Nanyuan Shiquan Jie ⓣ0512/65227661, ⓕ65238806. Right opposite the *Nanlin*, this is a smart, well-appointed place with spacious grounds, nice for an evening stroll. Staff are a bit snooty though. ❻

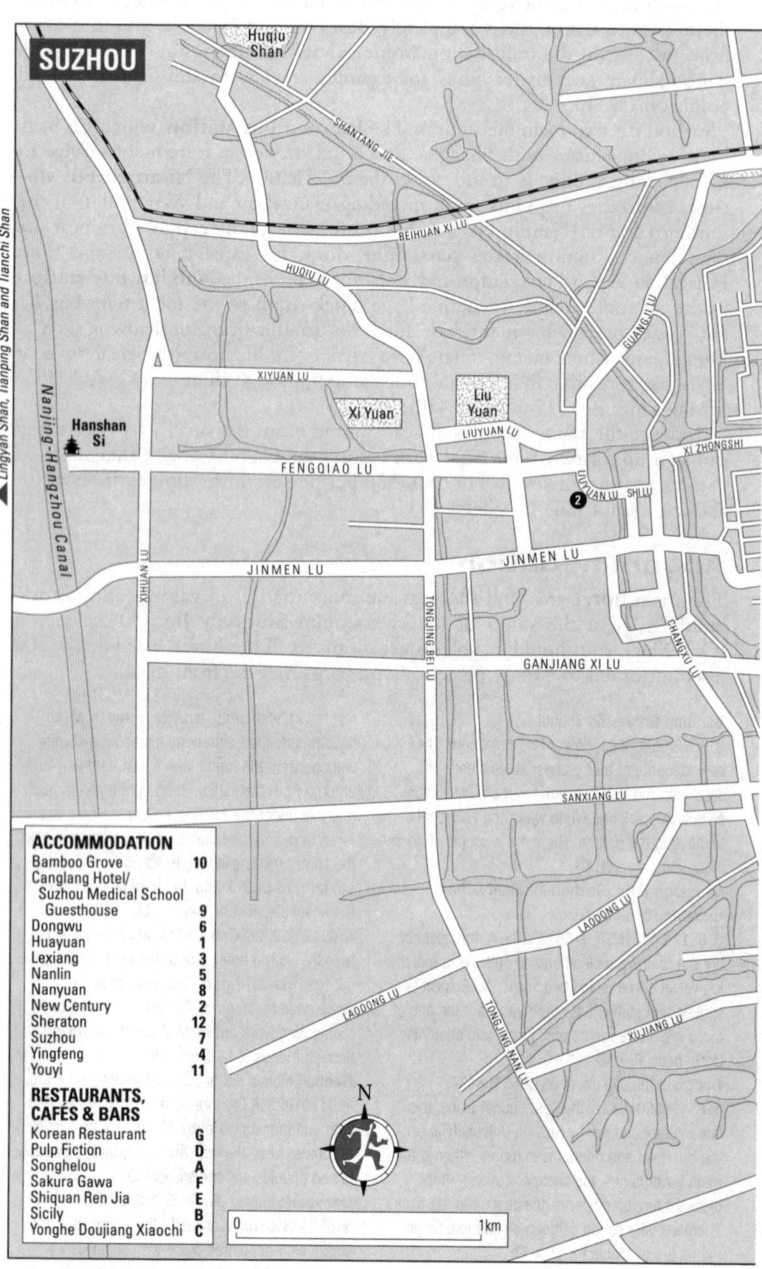
SUZHOU
Huqiu Shan
SHANTANG JIE
BEIHUAN XI LU
HUQIU LU
GUANGJI LU
XIYUAN LU
Liu Yuan
Xi Yuan
LIUYUAN LU
Hanshan Si
Nanjing-Hangzhou Canal
XI ZHONGSHI
FENGQIAO LU
LIUYUAN LU
SHILU
JINMEN LU
JINMEN LU
XIHUAN LU
TONGJING BEI LU
CHANGXU LU
GANJIANG XI LU
SANXIANG LU
LAODONG LU
LAODONG LU
TONGJING NAN LU
XUJIANG LU
N
0
1km
Lingyan Shan, Tianping Shan and Tianchi Shan
ACCOMMODATION
Bamboo Grove 10
Canglang Hotel/ Suzhou Medical School Guesthouse 9
Dongwu 6
Huayuan 1
Lexiang 3
Nanlin 5
Nanyuan 8
New Century 2
Sheraton 12
Suzhou 7
Yingfeng 4
Youyi 11
RESTAURANTS, CAFÉS & BARS
Korean Restaurant G
Pulp Fiction D
Songhelou A
Sakura Gawa F
Shiquan Ren Jia E
Sicily B
Yonghe Doujiang Xiaochi C

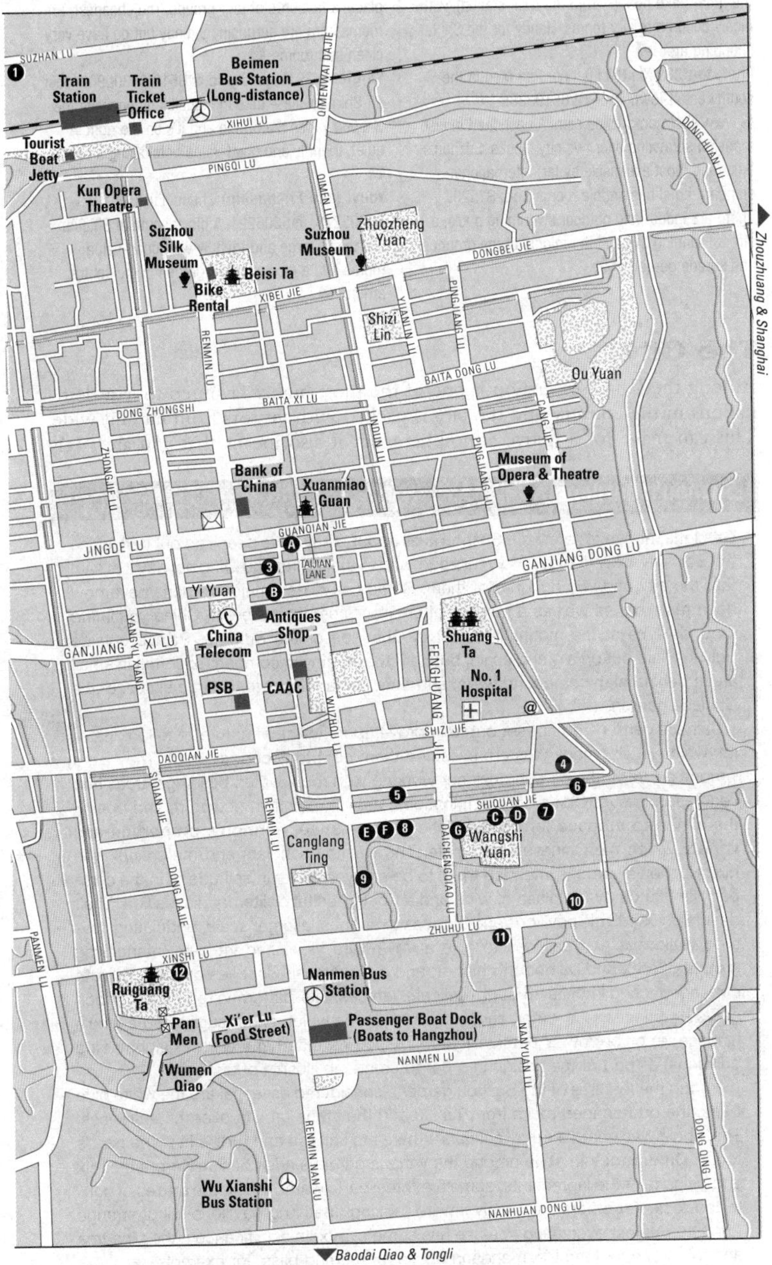

1
Train Station
Train Ticket Office
Beimen Bus Station (Long-distance)
Tourist Boat Jetty
Kun Opera Theatre
Suzhou Silk Museum
Beisi Ta
Bike Rental
Suzhou Museum
Zhuozheng Yuan
Shizi Lin
Ou Yuan
Museum of Opera & Theatre
Bank of China
Xuanmiao Guan
Taijian Lane
Yi Yuan
Antiques Shop
China Telecom
PSB
CAAC
Shuang Ta
No. 1 Hospital
Wangshi Yuan
Canglang Ting
Ruiguang Ta
Pan Men
Xi'er Lu (Food Street)
Nanmen Bus Station
Passenger Boat Dock (Boats to Hangzhou)
Wumen Qiao
Wu Xianshi Bus Station
Zhouzhuang & Shanghai
Baodai Qiao & Tongli

SUZHAN LU
XIHUI LU
PINGQI LU
QIMENWAI DAJIE
QIMEN LU
DONG HUAN LU
DONGBEI JIE
XIBEI JIE
RENMIN LU
YUANLIN LU
PINGJIANG LU
BAITA DONG LU
BAITA XI LU
DONG ZHONGSHI
LINDUN LU
CANG JIE
ZHONGJIE LU
GUANQIAN JIE
JINGDE LU
GANJIANG DONG LU
GANJIANG XI LU
YANGYU XIANG
FENGHUANG JIE
WUZHOU LU
SHIZI JIE
DAOQIAN JIE
SIQIAN JIE
SHIQUAN JIE
DAICHENGQIAO LU
DONG DAJIE
ZHUHUI LU
PANMEN LU
XINSHI LU
NANMEN LU
NANYUAN LU
RENMIN NAN LU
DONG QING LU
NANHUAN DONG LU

A B C D E F G
3 4 5 6 7 8 9 10 11 12

New Century 23 Guangji Lu ⓣ0512/65338888, ⓕ65337788. Out in the west of the city, beyond the moat (take bus #7 from the train station), with nicely decorated, airy rooms. Handy for the Shi Lu shopping area. ❼

Sheraton 388 Xin Shi Lu, near Pan Men in the southwest of town ⓣ0512/65103388, ⓦwww.sheraton-suzhou.com. A pastiche Chinese mansion sprawling over two city blocks, Suzhou's best (and most expensive by far) international-standard hotel has double rooms from $1520. There are indoor and outdoor swimming pools, a stream running through the middle of the grounds and serene gardens. ❾

Suzhou Shiquan Jie ⓣ0512/65204646, ⓕ65204015. A huge but relatively characterless place, a favourite of tour groups. The cheapest rooms here are surprisingly dingy but do have very clean bathrooms. ❻

Yingfeng 39 Wuya Chang ⓣ0512/65300907. Just off Shiquan Jie – take the small lane opposite the *Suzhou*, cross the bridge and it's on the right. A quiet, friendly and good-value hotel along a canal. ❺

Youyi (aka Friendship) Zhuhui Lu ⓣ0512/65205218, ⓕ5206221. A block south of Shiquan Jie, this is large and friendly with good-value rooms and a nice open-air garden in the central atrium. ❺

The City

Among the Chinese, Suzhou is one of the most highly favoured tourist destinations in the country, and the city is packed with visitors from far and wide. This can make for a festive atmosphere, but it also means that you are rarely

Suzhou's gardens

Gardens, above all, are what Suzhou is all about. They have been laid out here since the Song dynasty, a thousand years ago, and in their Ming and Qing heyday it is said that the city had two hundred of them. Some half-dozen major gardens have now been restored, as well as a number of smaller ones. Elsewhere in China you'll find grounds – as at the mountain resort of Chengde or the Summer Palace outside Beijing – laid out on a grand scale, but here they're tiny in comparison, often in small areas behind high compound walls, and thus are far closer to the true essence of a Chinese garden.

Chinese gardens do not set out to improve upon a slice of nature or to look natural, which is why many Western eyes find them hard to accept or enjoy. They are a serious art form, the garden designer working with rock, water, buildings, trees and vegetation in subtly different combinations; as with painting, sculpture and poetry, the aim is to produce for contemplation the **balance, harmony, proportion** and **variety** which the Chinese seek in life. The wealthy scholars and merchants who built Suzhou's gardens intended them to be enjoyed either in solitude or in the company of friends over a glass of wine and a poetry recital or literary discussion. Their designers used little pavilions and terraces to suggest a larger scale, undulating covered walkways and galleries to give a downward view, and intricate interlocking groups of rock and bamboo to hint at, and half conceal, what lies beyond. **Effects** depended on glimpses through delicate lattices, tile-patterned openings, moon gates or reflections in water, cunning perspectives which either suggested a whole landscape, or borrowed outside features (such as external walls of neighbouring buildings) as part of the design in order to create an illusion of distance.

Among the features of the Suzhou gardens considered essential are the white pine trees, the odd-shaped rocks from Tai Hu and the stone tablets over the entrances. The whole was completed by animals – there are still fish and turtles in some ponds today. **Differences in style** among the various gardens arise basically from the mix and balance of the ingredients; some are three-parts water, others are mazes of contorted rock, yet others are mainly inward-looking, featuring pavilions full of strange furniture. Almost everything you see has some symbolic significance – the pine tree and the crane for long life, mandarin ducks for married bliss, for example.

able to appreciate the **gardens** in the peace for which they were designed. The three most famous gardens – Wangshi Yuan, Shizi Lin and Zhuozheng Yuan – are on everyone's itinerary, attracting a stream of visitors year round, but many of the equally beautiful yet lesser-known gardens, notably Canglang Ting and Ou Yuan, are comparatively serene and crowd-free. The best strategy is to visit as much of the three popular gardens as possible before 10am and spend the rest of the day in the smaller gardens. If you can, choose a day with blue sky and a hint of cloud – the gardens need contrast, light and shade, clear shadow and bold reflection. Seasons make surprisingly little difference as the gardens can be appreciated at any time of year, although springtime brings more blossom and brighter colours. **Entrance fees** for the gardens (most of which are open daily: summer 7.30am–5.30pm, winter 8am–5pm) vary from ¥5 to ¥40. If you intend to visit all the three most popular gardens, the combined ¥100 ticket works out cheaper and also gets you into Tiger Hill.

It is possible to overdo the gardens: the mannered and artificial combination of nature, art and architecture may seem cluttered and pedantic, and the brief flourish of spring blossom apart, they can appear colourless and muted – so don't feel you need to see them all. Besides, Suzhou is one of the more enjoyable cities in China for simply **roaming** without special purpose. Stray from the main streets and you'll come across pagodas, temples, lively shopping districts and hectic canal traffic. Distances are too large to rely purely on walking, but **cycling** is an excellent alternative as the terrain is pretty flat (see "Listings", p.430 for bike rental).

Within the moat

A few minutes' walk south down Renmin Lu from the train station, the **Beisi Ta** (North Temple Pagoda; daily 8am–5pm; ¥15) looming up unmistakably. On the site of the residence of the mother of Wu Kingdom king Sun Quan, the Beisi Ta was first built in the third century AD, and rebuilt in 1582. The Ta retains only nine of its original eleven storeys, but it is still, at 76m, the highest Chinese pagoda south of the Yangzi. Climbing it gives an excellent view over some of Suzhou's more conspicuous features – the Shuang Ta, the Xuanmiao Guan and, in the far southwest corner, the Ruiguang Ta. There's also a very pleasant teahouse on the site.

Virtually opposite, also on Renmin Lu, is the **Suzhou Silk Museum** (daily 9am–5.30pm; ¥7), one of China's better-presented museums, clearly marked in English throughout. Starting from the legendary inventor of silk, Lei Zu, the concubine of the equally legendary Emperor Huang Di, it traces the history of silk production and its use from 4000 BC to the present day, and includes a collection of reproductions of early silk patterns, as well as actual fragments. There's a display of early looms and weaving machines, complete with demonstrations of how to use them, and a section on the science of sericulture, but the most riveting display, and something of a shock, is the room full of silkworms munching mulberry leaves and spinning cocoons, and copulating moths.

Suzhou Museum, the Zhuozheng Yuan and Shizi Lin

Turning east immediately south of Beisi Ta, along Xibei Jie (which shortly becomes Dongbei Jie) and beyond the first large intersection, brings you to the **Suzhou Museum** and the **Zhuozheng Yuan** (Humble Administrator's Garden). The museum (daily 8.15am–4.15pm; ¥10), housed in the former residence of Taiping leader Li Xiucheng, contains a rather obscure collection of dusty ceramics with no English labels, but the garden next door (¥40) is compulsory visiting. By far the largest of the Suzhou gardens, covering forty thousand square metres, the Zhuozheng Yuan is based on water and set out in three linked sections: the eastern part (just inside the entrance) consists of a small lotus pond and pavilions; the centre is largely water, with two small islands connected by zigzag bridges; while the western part has unusually open green spaces. Built at the time of the Ming by an imperial censor, Wang Xianchen, who had just resigned his post, the garden was named by its creator as an ironic lament on the fact that he could now administer nothing but gardening.

A couple of minutes south of the Zhuozheng Yuan is another must-see garden, the **Shizi Lin** (Lion Grove; ¥15). Tian Ru, the monk who laid this out in 1342, named it in honour of his teacher, Zhi Zheng, who lived on Lion Rock Mountain, and the rocks of which it largely consists are supposed to resemble lions in all shapes and sizes. Once chosen, these strange water-worn rocks were submerged for decades in Tai Hu to be further eroded. Part of the rockery takes the form of a convoluted labyrinth, from the top of which you emerge occasionally to gaze down at the water reflecting the green trees and grey stone. Qing emperors Qianlong and Kangxi were said to be so enamoured of these rockeries that they had the garden at the Yuanmingyuan Palace in Beijing modelled on them.

Xuanmiao Guan and Yi Yuan

Moving south from here, you arrive at the Taoist **Xuanmiao Guan** (Temple of Mystery), just north of Guanqian Jie and rather incongruously at the heart of the modern city's consumer zone. Founded originally during the Jin Dynasty in the third century AD, the temple has been destroyed, rebuilt, burnt down and put back together many times during its history. For centuries it was the scene of a great bazaar where travelling showmen, acrobats and actors entertained the crowds. Nowadays the complex, still an attractive, lively place, consists basically of a vast entrance court full of resting locals with, at its far end, a hall of Taoist deities and symbols; it's all encircled by a newly constructed park.

A few minutes south of Guanqian Jie, on the northwest corner of the Renmin Lu and Ganjiang Lu junction, is one of the lesser gardens, **Yi Yuan** (Joyous Garden; ¥5), laid out by official Gu Wenbin. Late Qing-dynasty, and hence considerably newer than the others, it is supposed to encompass all the key features of a garden (see box, p.424). Unusually, it also has formal flower beds and arrangements of coloured pebbles.

The Museum of Opera and Theatre, and Ou Yuan

A ten-minute walk along narrow lanes due east from Guanqian Jie, the unusual and memorable **Museum of Opera and Theatre** stands on Zhongzhangjia Xiang (daily 8.30am–4.30pm; ¥5). The rooms are filled with costumes, masks, musical instruments, and even a full-sized model orchestra, complete with cups of tea, though the building itself is the star, a Ming-dynasty theatre made of latticed wood. The stage is raised up on the second floor of a large pavilion, beneath a spiralling wooden dome, with an open-air "pit", and galleries to all sides.

The Suzhou area is the historical home of the **Kun Opera** style which, at 5000 years old, is China's oldest operatic form – Beijing Opera has existed for a mere 3000 years. Kun is distinguished by storytelling and ballad singing, though it can be hard to follow as it is performed in the all-but-unintelligible (even if you speak Chinese) Suzhou dialect. The Kun Operatic Society still puts on occasional **performances** in the museum, which the curators, many of whom are former opera stars, will gladly tell you about. The curators are also goldmines of information on the art form as well as on the degradation that opera performers had to endure during the Cultural Revolution – but you'll need to speak Chinese to engage them in conversation. You'll certainly be able to trace the history of the Kun style from a century of photographs on display at the museum, though there are no English captions; look for the interlude in the years of lavish costumes and spectacular productions, when the disgruntled company can be seen performing revolutionary operas, dressed in drab denim, in a vast steelworks. The teahouse next door holds daily performances of Kun-style opera and music, beginning around 1pm, for the edification of elderly locals.

A five-minute walk northeast of the museum, abutting the outer moat and along a canal, is the relatively untouristed **Ou Yuan** (daily 8am–4.30pm; ¥15). Here a series of hallways and corridors open out to an intimate courtyard, with a pond in the middle surrounded by abstract rock formations and several relaxing teahouses. Ou Yuan's greatest asset is its comparative freedom from the loudhailer-toting tour groups that crowd the other gardens. The surrounding area houses some of the loveliest architecture, bridges and canals in Suzhou and is well worth an hour-long stroll.

Shuang Ta, Canglang Ting and Wangshi Yuan

Several blocks east of Renmin Lu and immediately south of Ganjiang Lu, the **Shuang Ta** (Twin Pagodas; daily 7am–4.30pm; ¥10) are matching slender towers built during the Song dynasty by a group of successful candidates in the imperial examinations who wanted to honour their teacher. Too flimsy to climb, the pagodas sprout from a delightful patch of garden dotted with bits of statuary like a scene from classical Greece, and featuring a gardener's cottage at one end, teeming with chrysanthemums in pots and lovingly tended bonsai trees. At the other end is a teahouse crowded with old men fanning themselves against the heat in summer.

A kilometre or so farther south of here, just beyond Shiquan Jie, are two more gardens. The undervisited but intriguing **Canglang Ting** (Dark Blue Wave Pavilion; daily 8am–4.30pm; ¥8), at the corner of Renmin Lu and Zhuhui Lu, is the oldest of the major surviving gardens, originally built in the Song dynasty by scholar Su Zimei around 1044 AD. There is no enclosing wall on the northern side and the garden was supposed to "borrow" features from outside, which then became integral parts of the overall effect. You approach through a grand stone bridge and ceremonial marble archway; inside the garden, the central mound is designed to look like a forested hill. In the south of the garden (away from the entrance) stands the curious Five Hundred Sage Temple lined with stone tablets recording the names and achievements of great statesmen, heroes and poets of Suzhou.

The nearby **Wangshi Yuan** (Master of the Nets Garden; ¥15), on Shiquan Jie, is a short walk west from the *Suzhou Hotel* and down a narrow alleyway on the left. So named because the owner, a retired official, decided he wanted to become a fisherman, this tiny and intimate garden was started in 1140, but later abandoned and not restored to its present layout until 1770. Considered by garden connoisseurs to be the finest of them all, it boasts an attractive central lake, minuscule connecting halls, pavilions with pocket-handkerchief courtyards and carved wooden doors – and rather more visitors than it can cope with. Aficionados of Chinese gardens should enquire at CITS about the possibility of visiting the garden in the late evening, after the nightly performances of the eight major forms of **Chinese opera**, including the local Kun style (see p.430). The garden is said to be best seen on moonlit nights anyway, when the moon can be seen three times over from the Moon-watching Pavilion – in the sky, in the water and in a mirror. The garden's other main features are its delicate latticework and fretted windows through which you can catch a series of glimpses – a glimmer of bamboo, dark interiors, water and a miniature rockery framed in the three windows of a study.

Pan Men and around

In the far southwestern corner of the moated area is one of the city's most pleasant areas, centred around **Pan Men** (Coiled Gate) and a stretch of the original city wall, built in 514 BC by King Helu of the Wu Kingdom; the gate is the only surviving one of eight that once surrounded Suzhou. The best approach to this area is from the south, via **Wumen Qiao**, a delightful high-arched bridge (the tallest in Suzhou) with steps built into it; it's a great vantage point for watching the canal traffic (bus #7 from the train station passes the southern edge of the moat). Walking north from the bridge brings you to Pan Men, where you can climb up and walk east along the 300m of city wall (daily 8am–5pm; ¥20). Just to the northeast of the wall sits the dramatic **Ruiguang Ta** (¥6), a thousand-year-old pagoda now rebuilt from ruins, once housing a rare Buddhist pearl stupa (since moved to the Suzhou Museum). More diverting than the attractions, however, are the cobbled alleyways around, cobwebbed with washing lines, and the walk along the canal.

West of the moated city

If you're relying on public transport, the gateway to sites west of the moated city is the train station. Otherwise the following sites can all be taken in as part of a pleasant half-day bicycle trip.

Liu Yuan and Xi Yuan

There are two elegant gardens not far to the west of Shi Lu, on the route of bus #2 from the train station. The **Liu Yuan** (Garden to Linger In; ¥16) was originally called Dong Yuan (East Garden) as a foil to Xi Yuan (West Garden) across the street. Destroyed by the Japanese and restored in 1953, it was built during Ming times by Xu Taishi, a doctor who wanted his patients to recuperate in a pleasant environment. Its four scenic areas, and their buildings, are connected by a 700-metre-long winding corridor which assiduously follows the changing landscapes. Qing poets, as well as some of Xu's patients, recorded their impressions of the park on the stone tablets hanging along the corridor. Among the attractions is the largest of all the Tai Hu rocks, a single lump weighing around five thousand kilos and known as the **Cloud-crowned Peak**.

Just a couple of hundred metres to the west of here is the **Xi Yuan** (West Garden; ¥10), constructed by Xu Taishi to attest to his ardent love of Buddhism and, more temple than garden, its great sweeps of yellow-ochred walls contrasting richly with the charcoal-grey roof tiles and the red woodwork. The main hall of the temple here has a striking ceiling, and a wing to one side contains ranks of impressively sculpted *arhats*. Despite the droves of tourists it's a pleasant spot, with giant carp and soft-shelled turtles cruising in the pond.

Huqiu Shan

Due north of these gardens rises **Huqiu Shan** (Tiger Hill; daily 7am–6pm; ¥30), the legendary site of the tomb of He Lu, a king of Wu and supposed founding father of Suzhou. Legend has it that the hill was named after a mythical white tiger who began to guard the tomb on the third day of the burial ceremony and refused to leave.

The haphazard and asymmetrical design of this sprawling park stands in direct contrast to the intricate, balanced organization of the gardens downtown. There are terraces laid out with shrubs and trees, a teahouse, and everywhere rocks and pools each with their own name and hoary legend. They include the **Thousand Men Rock**, where the men who built the tomb were supposedly executed to keep its whereabouts secret, and the **Sword Pond**, which is said to conceal the treasures of the king's tomb – including three thousand swords. At the summit stands Suzhou's very own leaning tower, the **Yunyan Ta** or Cloud Rock Pagoda. Octagonal, with seven brick storeys, it leans more than two metres and needs constant attention to prevent it from toppling altogether; during one such operation, in 1965, workmen found a box containing tenth-century Buddhist sutras wrapped in silk. Despite conservationists' best efforts, the tower lists north a further centimetre every year. Archeologists suspect that one reason for the subsidence of the tower is the presence of underground passages, which may hold the secrets of the legendary tomb.

Huqiu Shan is on the route of buses #1 and #2, both of which originate at the train station. If you're coming by bike, one fascinating (albeit bone-shaking) option is the direct route, following the cobbled towpaths lining the small Shantang canal, past the splendour of the former merchants' houses with their imposing facades and watergates.

Hanshan Si

Hanshan Si (Cold Mountain Temple; daily 8am–5pm; ¥10), punctuated by the seven-storey, eleventh-century Puming Ta, also lies in the suburbs, about 5km west of town. Take bus #3 from the train station to the stop by the temple, then walk straight ahead, past the temple wall, until you reach the canal (you can also sometimes reach the site along the canals, on a tour boat from Pan Men). Here the main entrance to the temple is to your right, and you'll get a view of the superb, arched **Feng Qiao**, built in 1557 by Emperor Jiaqing to defend against the invading Japanese. Today the bridge offers good views of the barges chugging along the canal.

Dating from around 500 AD, the temple is particularly famous in both China and Japan because the celebrated Tang poet **Zhang Ji** wrote a poem about it which is inscribed on a stone stele inside:

Moonset; through the freezing air the caw of a crow;
By Feng Qiao, breaking my rest, the fishing lamps glow;
To me as I lie in my boat the dark hour brings
The plangent repeated sound as the temple bell rings
At Han Shan beyond Suzhou.

Zhang Ji's bronze statue reposes in a small memorial to the poet (with some well-crafted dioramas of Tang-era Suzhou) next to the archway in front of Hanshan Si (daily 8am–4pm; ¥5). At New Year, Hanshan and the memorial are crammed with Japanese visitors who come to hear the midnight bell. So wealthy has the temple now become through donations, that large-scale additions – including new halls and pagodas – are currently being built to the east of the original site.

Eating, drinking and entertainment

Suzhou's cooking, with its emphasis on fish culled from the nearby lakes and rivers, is justly renowned; specialities include *yinyu* ("silver fish") and *kaobing* (grilled pancakes with sweet filling). The town is well stocked with **restaurants** for all budgets (our selection appears on p.430), though it holds little in the way of **nightlife** – the city's younger set escape to Shanghai for serious nights out. That said, there are a slew of touristy bars scattered along Shiquan

Jie near Wangshi Yuan; the best are *Pulp Fiction*, 200m west of the Suzhou Hotel, and the much smaller *Pub Bar*, 50m further west.

The best entertainment in town is the nightly **opera extravaganza** at Wangshi Yuan, featuring eight displays of the most prominent forms of Chinese performance arts, from Beijing Opera to folk dancing and storytelling. Shows run from 7.30pm to 10pm and cost ¥60. In addition, occasional performances of the Kun operatic style still take place in the Museum of Opera and Theatre (see p.426), as well as in their own **theatre** on Renmin Lu just south of the Pingsi Lu intersection (near the train station; ☎0512/67533268).

Restaurants

Korean Restaurant Daichengqiao Lu, just south of Shiquan Jie. One of the best of a host of unimaginatively named Korean restaurants, with good barbecued beef, cooked on your table.

Sakura Gawa Shiquan Jie, west of the *Nanyuan Hotel*. Elegant Japanese dining, not as pricey as it looks – the set meal for one is ¥50.

Shiquan Ren Jia Shiquan Jie, just west of the *Sakura Gawa*. Not a bad little place to try the local dishes, and it won't cost you much.

Sicily Restaurant and Pub 1 Shaomozhen Xiang. Dark, comfy bar serving Western food. The spaghetti isn't up to much though the French fries are good.

Songhelou Caiguan South side of Guanqian Jie, 200m east of Renmin Lu. The most famous restaurant in town – it claims to be old enough to have served Emperor Qianlong. The menu is elaborate and long on fish (crab, eel, squirrel fish and the like). An interesting place to eat, though not cheap at around ¥150 a head.

Taijian Lane Restaurants Off Guanqian Jie opposite the Xuanmiao Guan. A short street that contains four restaurants of repute, all more than 100 years old – the *Dasanyuan* is at no. 8, *Deyuelou* at no. 27, *Wangsi* at no. 23, and *Laozhengxing* at no. 19. They're all big, busy and a little expensive but good for a splurge on local dishes, with foreigner-friendly staff and menus.

Yonghe Doujiang Xiaochi In front of the entrance to Wangshi Yuan. Inexpensive snacks, dumplings, noodle soups and soybean milk. Open 24hr.

Listings

Airlines The main CAAC reservations and ticketing office is at 120 Renmin Lu, a few minutes' walk south of Gangjiang Lu (☎0512/5222788; daily 8–11.30am & 1–5.15pm).

Banks and exchange The Bank of China head office is on Renmin Lu right in the centre of town, just north of Guanqian Jie (Mon–Fri 8.30–11.30am & 1.30–4.30pm, Sat 8am–11.30pm). You can change traveller's cheques in any of the upmarket hotels if you're a guest.

Bike rental Rental outfits abound along Shiquan Jie; most of them are just west of the *Suzhou Hotel*. They charge ¥20 for a day but can be bargained down to ¥10–15. There's also a rental place opposite the Silk Museum.

Boats Connecting Suzhou and Hangzhou, there is one boat service daily in both directions, taking around thirteen hours, with a bar and karaoke on board. The incoming boat arrives in the early morning at around 7am, and the outbound boat leaves at 5.30pm; fares range from ¥20 (hard seat) to ¥180 for a private cabin, while a bunk in a four-person cabin is ¥60. Buy tickets at the dock at the southern end of Renmin Lu or at the ticket office on 556 Renmin Lu (second floor).

Bookshops The Xinhua bookstore at 166 Guanqian Jie has a small selection of classic novels.

Hospital The No. 1 Hospital is in the east of town, at the junction of Fenghuang Jie and Shizi Jie.

Internet access The most pleasant place to get online, on Shizi Jie east of the hospital (daily 9am–11pm), is also the cheapest at ¥1.5 an hour; alternatively, try China Telecom at 333 Renmin Lu (daily 9.30am–9pm; ¥4/hr) or the Internet café just west of and opposite the *Nanlin Hotel* (foreigners are charged ¥5/hr). Places are constantly opening and closing along Shiquan Jie, so check with your hotel for the latest information.

Mail Suzhou's main post office is at the corner of Renmin Lu and Jingde Lu.

PSB On Renmin Lu, at the junction with the small lane Dashitou Xiang.

Shopping There are numerous opportunities to shop for silk in Suzhou, although be aware of outrageous prices, especially in the boutiques along Shiquan Jie and Guanyin Jie and the night market on Shi Lu. Bargain hard as these sellers can quote prices up to ten times the going rate. The King Silk Store next to the Silk Museum has a good selection, including great duvets starting at just over ¥300. The Antique Store (daily 10am–5.30pm) along Renmin Lu and Ganjiang Dong Lu is the place to find old furniture, while paintings and embroidery are on hand in a pavilion near the corner of Renmin Lu and Baita Xi Lu and in the shops along Shiquan Jie.

Tours If you're in a hurry, a one-day tour can be an excellent way to get round all the main sights. Minibus tours depart from the train station square at 7.30am and return at 4.30pm, and cost ¥10 exclusive of admission charges. Tours in air-conditioned buses specially geared for foreign tourists can be booked at CITS (or other travel services) for around ¥260, which includes lunch and all admission fees.

Trains The train ticket office is located in a separate building to the left of the station as you walk out. There's also a ticket office at 556 Renmin Lu (second floor). CITS and most hotels will book tickets for a commission.

Travel agents CITS is next to the *Lexiang Hotel* on Dajing Xiang (☎0512/65155199). Nearly all hotels have their own travel agencies.

Around Suzhou

In the immediate vicinity of the city are a number of places which make easy day- or half-day-trips by bike or local bus. A short bike ride **south** of the city, out along the canals to the main section of the Grand Canal where it heads off towards Hangzhou, is **Baodai Qiao** (Precious Belt Bridge). With 53 arches, this Tang-dynasty structure is named after Wang Zhongshu, a local prefect who selflessly sold his precious belt to raise money for his subjects. It's not wildly exciting, but with traffic now rerouted over a newer crossing, it does make a tranquil spot to sit and contemplate the boats and the local anglers. To reach it, pedal south along Renmin Lu, south of the inner moat, through Suzhou's southern suburbs, over a roundabout with a re-creation of the Eiffel Tower in the middle, cross the wide Grand Canal, then at Shihu Lu, the first major intersection south of here, turn left (east) and head straight for 2 or 3km, until the next major junction, where you turn left along a canal.

Much farther south of the bridge, 23km from Suzhou, is the little town of **TONGLI**, a superb example of a town built on water – every house backs on to canals, there are 49 stone bridges and nearly all movement takes place by boat. You can reach Tongli by minibus from the Xianshi bus station, south of the moat, for ¥5. Tongli's main street has become rather touristy, with overpriced souvenir stands and restaurants, but a little exploration along the back alleys will reveal canals shaded by stately bridges, overhanging willows, lazing elderly folk, put-putting barges and rural splendour. The top sights here include **Tuisi Yuan** (daily 8am–4.15pm; ¥8), a late Qing garden that vaguely resembles Suzhou's Ou Yuan, and **Jiayin Hall** (daily 9am–5.15pm; ¥2), the two-storey austere home of Liu Yazi, a Nationalist actor and entertainer renowned for his eccentric collection of gauze caps. Speedboats ply the route from Tongli to the canal town of Zhouzhuang (see p.402), across Tongli Lake, for around ¥80-100 per boat (45min). For an interesting if long day-trip from Suzhou, take the bus to Tongli in the morning, the boat over to Zhouzhuang around noon, and return to Suzhou by bus in the late afternoon.

There's more of interest to the **west**, towards Tai Hu. Fifteen and eighteen kilometres respectively from Suzhou, **Lingyan Shan** and **Tianping Shan** lie close to each other in the low hills, and both offer tremendous views. Together they make a good day's outing on a bicycle, following Sufugong Lu away from the southwestern corner of the moat. (Alternatively, you can take bus #16 from in front of the train station to Lingyun Shan.) At Lingyun Shan (Divine Cliff Hill; daily 6.30am–5.30pm; ¥11) you climb stone steps past a bell tower to reach a walled enclosure with a temple hall, a seven-storey pagoda and a well. Tianping Shan (Sky Level Hill; daily 6.45am–4.45pm; ¥6), 3km beyond, was already a well-known beauty spot under the Song, the hillside cut with streams and dotted with strange rock formations. Wooded paths meander up to the summit past pavilions and small gardens, and in autumn the maples which cover the slopes seem to blaze. Adventurous types can hike from Tianping Shan along a three- to four-kilometre trail that follows a hillcrest to **Tianchi Shan**, another temple complex set in more remote, scenic surroundings.

Tai Hu and around

One of the four largest freshwater lakes in China, constantly replenished by heavy rains, **Tai Hu** is liberally sprinkled with islands and surrounded by wooded hills. With an average depth of just 2m, it's a natural reservoir of

Tai Hu and around

Tai Hu	太湖	***tàihú***
Dong Shan	东山	***dōngshān***
Longtou Shan	龙头山	*lóngtóu shān*
Zijin An	紫金庵	*zǐjīn ān*
Xi Shan	西山	***xīshān***
Donghe	东河	*dōnghé*
Linwu Cave	林屋古洞	*línwūgǔdòng*
Wuxi	无锡	***wúxī***
City of Water Margin	水浒景区	*shuǐhǔ jǐngqū*
Lingshan Buddha	灵山大佛	*língshān dàfó*
Mei Yuan	梅园	*méiyuán*
Miaoguang Pagoda	妙光塔	*miàoguāng tǎ*
Tang Dynasty World	唐朝景区	*tángcháo jǐngqū*
Three Kindoms Worlds	三国景区	*sānguó jǐngqū*
Xihui Park	锡惠公园	*xīhuì gōngyuán*
Yuantou Zhu	鼋头渚	*yuántóuzhǔ*
Accommodation		
CTS Grand	中旅大酒店	*zhōnglǚ dàjiǔdiàn*
Jinhua	锦华大饭店	*jǐnhuá dàfàndiàn*
Lakeview Park	太湖花园度假村	*tàihúhuāyuán dùjiàcūn*
Milido	美丽都	*měilìdū*
Qinggongye University Foreign Experts Hotel	轻工业大学专家楼	*qīnggōngyè dàxué zhuānjiālóu*
Taihu Hotel	太湖饭店	*tàihú fàndiàn*
Yuquan Hill View	玉泉山庄	*yùquán shānzhuāng*
Yixing Town	宜兴市	***yíxīng shì***
Beisite Guoji	贝斯特国际大酒店	*bèisī tèguójì dàjiǔdiàn*
Huating Hotel	华亭大酒店	*huátíng dàjiǔdiàn*
Yixing Hotel	宜兴宾馆	*yíxīng bīnguǎn*
Yixing County	宜兴县	***yíxīngxiàn***
Dingshan (Dingshu)	丁山	*dīngshān*
Linggu caves	灵谷洞	*línggǔ dòng*
Shanjuan caves	善卷洞	*shànjuǎn dòng*
Zhanggong caves	张公洞	*zhānggōng dòng*

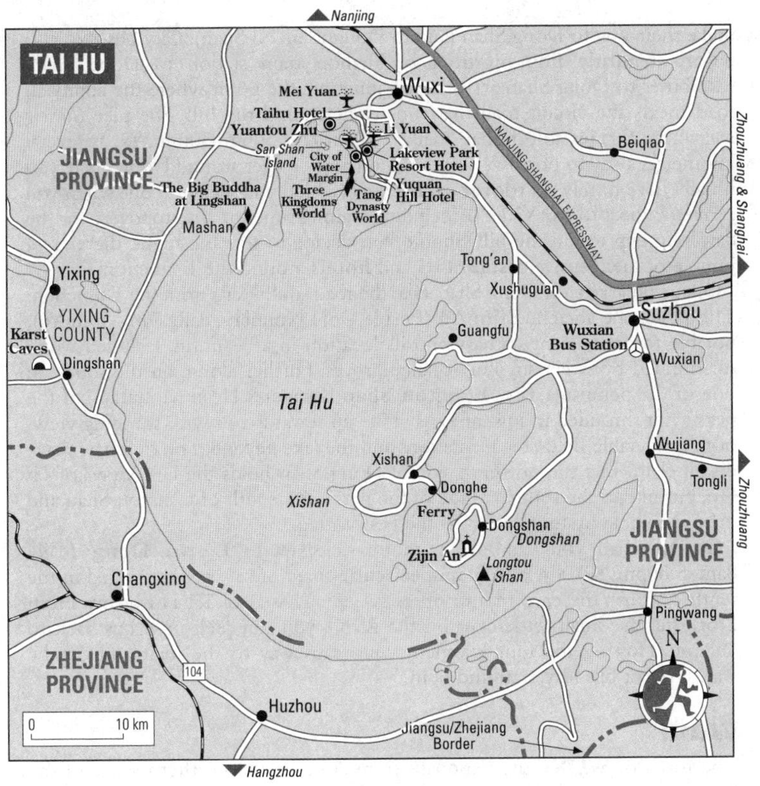

relatively unpolluted water, where fish are bred, and lotus and water chestnut grown in ideal conditions on the islands. Other plant- and wildlife is rich, too, and the shores are clad with tea plantations and orchards of loquat, pear, peach, apricot and plum, particularly on the western side among the caves and potteries of **Yixing County**. The southeastern shore of the lake, particularly the charming rural areas of **Dong Shan** and **Xi Shan**, are most easily visited from Suzhou, but the most famous and popular Tai Hu scenic area, **Yuantou Zhu**, is best visited from the town of **Wuxi**, set in a landscape of water, fertile plains and low hills some 40km northwest of Suzhou.

Dong Shan and Xi Shan

Some 35km from Suzhou, and within easy reach of the city, lie two green fingers of land projecting into Tai Hu, known as **Dong Shan** (East Hill) and **Xi Shan** (West Hill) respectively; the latter is actually an island, joined to the mainland via an artificial causeway. This area of Tai Hu is entirely rural, with small villages of friendly people, green hillsides, fragrant fruit orchards and hardly a trace of industry.

One possible long day-trip from Suzhou, described below, is to ride out to Dong Shan by minibus, cross to Xi Shan by boat in the afternoon, then return to Suzhou's Wuxian bus station by minibus. From the west side of the train station square in Suzhou and from Wuxian bus station, frequent private **minibuses** make their way to Dong Shan (and to Donghe on Xi Shan). City bus #20 also departs regularly from in front of Suzhou train station to Dong Shan. Minibuses to Dong Shan arrive at a T-junction, the point where the approach road meets the circuit road that runs right around the hill. The pier (*lugang matou*) for **ferries** to Xi Shan (daily 7.30am & 2.30pm; 30min; ¥5) is several kilometres away to northwest of the T-junction. To get around Dong Shan, you usually have to rely on **motor-rickshaws** (which will seek you out when you arrive). Expect to pay ¥30–40, including waiting time for any stopovers, for the day-long trip round the hill. Should you decide to stay the night, there are a jumble of inexpensive **restaurants** and **hotels** around the T-junction.

Once you arrive on Dong Shan, take the road south (left) from the T-junction. This passes the ancient **Zijin An** (Purple Gold Nunnery; daily 7am–5pm; ¥6), notable for its ancient statuary and its location in a beautiful, secluded wood surrounded by sweet-smelling orange groves. Further along, on the southern side of the peninsula, rises **Longtou Shan** (Dragon's Head Mountain); if the peak's not shrouded in mist, the easy hike up rewards you with stunning views of the vegetable fields, tea plantations and the lake beyond. The rickshaw drivers all claim that the northern side of Dong Shan holds the best views of Tai Hu, but in fact the southern side of the peninsula, south of Longtou Shan and only accessible by foot, harbours the best vantages.

On Xi Shan you can take a motor-rickshaw to **Linwu Dong** (daily 8am–5.30pm; ¥9), a relatively unspectacular chain of caverns discovered in the tenth century; the cave mouth offers sweeping vistas of Tai Hu below. From **Donghe**, the small settlement on the island, you can pick up a bus back to Suzhou, crossing the four-kilometre-long causeway to the mainland on the way. The last bus leaves around 6pm.

Wuxi

The town of **WUXI**, the regional centre close by the northern shore of the lake, is not particularly attractive, but it is the most convenient place to base yourself for a visit to the Tai Hu beauty spots. Wuxi was allegedly established more than 3500 years ago as the capital of the Wu Kingdom. It served as the Wu capital for over 600 years until the Han Dynasty, when the neighbouring tin mines were exhausted. At this point, the Wu capital shifted further west to Wuhan (Wuxi means "without tin"). It was the construction of the Grand Canal centuries later that brought importance to local trade and industry, as it did for so many other canal towns. These days Wuxi is surpassed as a lakeside city by Hangzhou, and as a canal town with traditional gardens by Suzhou. In an effort to siphon tourists away from its more famous neighbours, Wuxi boosters have constructed many "instant tourism" sights in the past few years, most notably a slew of theme parks and the world's **tallest Buddha**, which smack of revenue-minded artificiality. Local Chinese come here in droves to sample the lakeside scenery and marvel at the statue, but foreign travellers will not miss much if they confine their investigations to the lake itself.

The City

The old city of Wuxi is roughly oval-shaped, and surrounded by a ring of canals. The main branch of the Grand Canal runs outside this ring (but well inside the modern city) about 1km to the southwest. Inside the canal ring, the ring road, Jiefang Lu, is cut from north to south by Zhongshan Lu, and from east to west by Renmin Zhong Lu. The junction of Renmin Zhong Lu and Zhongshan Lu forms the approximate centre of downtown Wuxi.

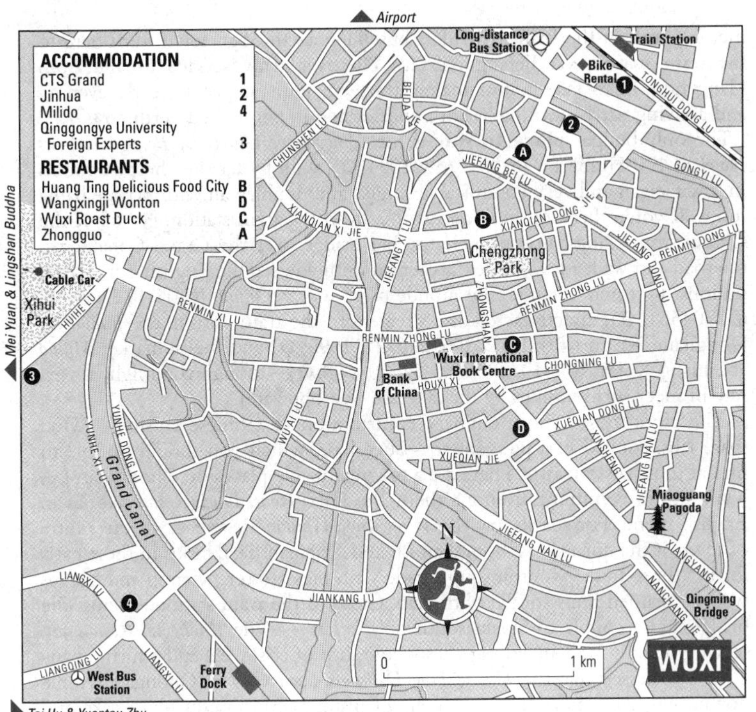

One place in town to pass a few hours amid trees and small paths is **Xihui Park** (daily 7am–7pm; ¥4; bus #2 through town from the train station), west of the centre and allegedly once visited by Emperor Qin Shi Huang. The path from the main entrance on Huihe Lu leads up to the Dragon Light Pagoda on top of **Xi Shan**; more interesting, though, is the **cable car** (¥25) whose long, slow trajectory links with another peak on neighbouring **Hui Shan**. The cable-car ride is definitely worth the panoramic views over to Tai Hu on a clear day, though you'll need a good head for heights. Hui Shan itself is the source of a special black clay used for the ugly painted figurines sold all over Wuxi, and which have been made here since at least the Ming dynasty.

Practicalities

All trains running between Shanghai and Nanjing stop at Wuxi **train station**, which is outside the canal ring to the northeast. Bus #11 goes right across town from the stop to the the east of the *CTS Grand Hotel*, opposite the station. The main **long-distance bus station** is a couple of minutes' walk to the west of the train station, and is served by buses from most nearby cities, including Shanghai, Suzhou and Nanjing, and a number of remoter destinations such as Yangzhou and Wenzhou. Diametrically on the other side of the city from here, across the Liangxi Bridge over the Grand Canal, is a smaller bus station from where there are frequent connections with Yixing. Bus #20 and frequent minibuses cross the city from here on their way to the train station. You may even arrive by boat at the **ferry dock** on the Grand Canal, a few hundred metres south of the Liangxi Bridge; bus #1 goes through town from here to the train station, via Jiefang Xi Lu). There's a daily service to and from Hangzhou; boats take approximately thirteen hours, departing early evening and arriving early morning at both ends. A bed in a four-bed berth costs ¥82.

The only budget **place to stay** is the *Qinggongye University Foreign Experts Hotel*, at 170 Huihe Lu (Ⓣ0510/5861034; ❸), with by far the cheapest rooms in town, clean and very comfortable singles and doubles, all with private bathroom. If you're heading here on bus #2 from the train station, get off at the second stop (Qingshanwan) after the big bridge over the Grand Canal, cross the road and walk a few metres farther on until you see the English sign. Other options in town include the nondescript *CTS Grand* (Ⓣ0510/2300888, Ⓕ2304561; ❽), directly across the street from the train station; the *Jinhua* on Dongliang Xi Lu (Ⓣ0510/2720612, Ⓕ2711092; ❺) and the upmarket *Milido* at 2 Liang Xi Lu (Ⓣ0510/5865665, Ⓕ5801668; ❼) – though you might as well stay in nicer surroundings by the lakeside (see opposite).

The city's most famous culinary contribution to Chinese cuisine is Wuxi spare ribs, cooked in a pungent soy-sauce base, which you should be able to find at most **restaurants**. There are a few reasonable places on Zhongshan Lu, just south of Renmin Lu; among them, the *Wuxi Roast Duck Restaurant* has an English menu. For snacks, try the *Wangxingji Wonton Restaurant*, in the centre of town at the corner of Zhongshan Lu and Xueqian Jie, famous in these parts for its "three-fresh" wonton soup (made with pigs' trotters, shrimp and egg) as well as steamed buns stuffed with crab. Close to the train station – across the bridge and a couple of blocks south on the left – is the *Zhongguo Restaurant*, serving Jiangsu food, including a tasty cold dish of crispy eel and a turnip pancake. For dessert, try the *Huang Ting Delicious Food City* in Chongan Temple downtown, with more than 120 years of history, scrumptious plum cake and Yulan pastry.

Around Wuxi

The shores of Tai Hu closest to Wuxi, fringed with gardens, woods, pagodas and waterside hotels, boast two parks, **Mei Yuan** and **Yuantou Zhu**, where you can spend half a day rambling, though they are expensive to get into and full of tour groups. This part of the lake is also where you'll see the results of much of the construction boom that has gripped Wuxi in the last several years, which has been devoted to building tacky **theme parks** in the hopes of attracting tourists away from nearby Suzhou and Hangzhou. Although most visitors **stay** in Wuxi, it's worth noting that a building boom along Tai Hu in recent years has resulted in a glut of rooms and, consequently, reasonable prices when compared with downtown Wuxi.

Further afield, on the Ma Shan peninsula 10km southwest of Wuxi by the shores of Tai Hu, stands a monument to cynicism, the pointless **Lingshan Fo** (The Ling Mountain Buddha). At 88m high, this bronze-plated giant is the tallest Buddha in the world, built for the record books and to extract yuan from tourists at a spot with no religious significance. You can get here on bus #14 from just east of Wuyi's train station (daily 8am–4.30pm; ¥35).

Mei Yuan and Yuantou Zhu

You can **arrive** either on the shore due west from town (for Mei Yuan) or, slightly farther away, on the northern end of a peninsula extending into the lake (Yuantou Zhu). The two areas are linked by boat, and a circular trip from town taking in both is perhaps the best way to go.

On the slopes of a small hill, looking down through the woods to the spread of fishponds fringing the lake, sits **Mei Yuan** (Plum Garden; daily 8am–5pm; ¥15). Originally established in 1912, the park now offers a springtime sea of blossom from four thousand plum trees, best appreciated from the pagoda at the highest point. In autumn you can enjoy the heady scent of osmanthus blossom, used to flavour the local delicacy, honeyed plums.

From just south of Mei Yuan there are small boats (¥15) to and from **Yuantou Zhu** (Turtle Head Isle; daily 6.30am–5pm; ¥50), the principal Tai Hu pleasure spot and a relaxing place to stroll around for a few hours, though not worth the steep entrance fee. The huge park covers the northwestern end of the peninsula jutting into the lake (which bears little obvious resemblance to a turtle's head), is capped by a small lighthouse at the western tip, and is scattered with teahouses and pavilions, the former summerhouses of the wealthy.

From a pier on Yuantou Zhu, a little north of the lighthouse, a ferry shuttles tourists regularly to and from the tiny former bandits' lair of **San Shan** (Three Hills Island), comprising a central knob of land linked by causeways to minuscule outcrops on either side. Neat paths lead up to a teahouse, pavilion and pagoda giving views of tree-clad islands, winding inlets, fishing boats under sail and – if you're lucky enough to catch a sunny day – blue waters.

From another pier, on the northern edge of Yuantou Zhu and facing the mainland, you can catch small, fast boats to the Mei Yuan area, near the #2 bus terminus. Buy your ticket from the kiosk (¥6), not on the boat. You arrive at an obscure pier apparently in the middle of nowhere – walk straight ahead, cross a small bridge, then walk along a canal with an entertainment park on the other side, and you'll emerge more or less opposite Mei Yuan.

The theme parks

The two historically themed amusement parks at the southern end of Yuantou Zhu are somewhat better than their counterparts elsewhere around the lake. The **Tang Dynasty World** is a re-creation of a typical Chinese city in that period, complete with kung-fu displays and attendants dressed in period costume (daily 9am–10pm; ¥20). **City of Water Margin** comprises a reproduction of a medieval fortified city and an ersatz Ming canal village (daily 8.30am–10.30pm; ¥36). Owned by a television station, both parks often serve as the set for made-for-TV kung-fu epics or period pieces.

Practicalities

Bus #1 to Yuantou Zhu and #2 to Mei Yuan both run through Wuyi from the train station square; otherwise it's a pleasant hour's bicycle ride to Mei Yuan following Liang Xi Lu west out of town. The **hotels** here offer great opportunities for enjoying some peace and quiet, particularly after the rush of day-trippers has subsided. Twenty minutes' walk south of the #2 bus terminus, the *Taihu Hotel* (Ⓣ0510/5517888; ❻) stands among the fish ponds just south of Mei Yuan. It's a great, secluded place to stay, surrounded by flame trees, with birdsong and green fireflies in the gardens. The hotel restaurant serves excellent Lotus Leaf Chicken, a local speciality of chicken braised in soy sauce and steamed in a lotus leaf wrapping. More luxurious and beautifully located is the opulent *Lakeview Park Resort* (Ⓣ0510/5555888, Ⓕ5556909; ❽), just south of the entrance to Yuantou Zhu on 8 Qitang Lu, with a player-piano in the very stately lobby and an Internet connection in each room. Directly across from the *Lakeview*, the *Yuquan Hill View Hotel* (Ⓣ0510/5559999, Ⓕ5551599; ❼), is good value for money, with airy, comfortable rooms and a curious emphasis on table tennis – five tables fill the lobby and bronze statues of Jiangsu Province table-tennis champions decorate the front lawn.

Yixing County

On the western shores of Tai Hu about 60km from Wuxi, **Yixing County** is a mild, fertile plain crisscrossed by canals and with a smattering of small lakes, making it ideal for the cultivation of tea and bamboo. The most important and traditional of all the local products, however, is the **pottery** from the small town of **Dingshan** (aka Dingshu). The other main attractions of the area are the underground caves that have formed, hollowed out of the karst hills in a skein running southwest from Yixing Town. The whole area can be visited on a hectic day trip from Wuxi (see p.434), though you might choose to spend a night in Yixing Town, perhaps en route from Nanjing to Wuxi or Hangzhou.

Although there's precious little to see in **YIXING TOWN** itself, you'll almost certainly have to pay it a visit, as it's the regional transport and accommodation centre. Travellers arrive by either at the **Shi** (Town) **bus station**, or at the smaller **Sheng** (Provincial) **bus station**, both of which are in the far northwest of town. Frequent minibuses (¥3) in and out of the stations make the connection with Dingshan to the south.

If you're looking for **accommodation** in Yixing, walk east along Taige Lu from either station, in the direction of the tall Bank of China building, the top of which is clearly visible. About fifteen minutes' walk along here is the *Beisite Guoji Hotel* (Ⓣ0510/7908866, Ⓕ7906412; ❻) offering large, smart doubles. Alternatively, turn south across the bridge (before reaching the *Beisite Guoji*) down the main street, Renmin Lu. A little way down here, on Jiefang Lu to the left, is the *Huating Hotel* (Ⓣ0510/7911888, Ⓕ7903364; ❻), which has similarly upmarket rooms. Finally, virtually in the centre of the city, farther south down Renmin Lu and on the left through an imposing archway, is the clean, efficient *Yixing Hotel* (Ⓣ0510/7916888, Ⓕ7900767; ❼). Just inside the archway here are a couple of travel services which will book tours for you and rent cars with drivers.

Dingshan

If you're interested in pottery, or if you simply want to buy a Chinese tea set, head for **DINGSHAN**, a thirty-minute **minibus** ride south of Yixing. There's nothing to see here beyond pots and ceramic artefacts, but it's fascinating to find the products of the **pottery factories** literally crammed into every nook and cranny. Ceramic lampposts line the road into town, pottery shards crunch under your feet on the main street and the walls of buildings are embedded with broken tiles.

Incredibly, this obscure town has been producing pots since the beginning of recorded history. Primitive unglazed pots have been found here which date back to the Shang and Zhou periods, some three thousand years ago. Since the Han dynasty at least, around 200 BC, this has been the most renowned site for glazed wares in China – Dingshan can take a lot of the credit for our use of the word "china" to mean ceramics. In terms of wealth, Dingshan had its heyday under the Ming from the fourteenth century, but manufacturing is still going strong today, in the town's thirty or so ceramics factories. A sandy local clay is used to produce the **purple sand pottery**, a dull brown unglazed ware, heavy in iron, whose properties of retaining the colour, fragrance and flavour of tea supposedly make for incomparable teapots. If you buy one, don't wash it between brews – eventually it will become so thoroughly imbued that you'll never need to add tea leaves again.

All along Dingshan's main street you'll find stalls and pavement displays with **tea sets** on offer at very low prices. If you're interested in buying, first see that the spout, body, knob, handle and lid are all balanced. Check that the lid fits snugly and that there is a clear sound when the pot is tapped. Feel the texture; a rough texture does not indicate poor quality – in fact pots should be rough, especially on the inside. Also ask to put some water in the teapot; the water should shoot out of the spout, not dribble, when poured. Lastly, don't forget to bargain – as a general rule, you should not pay any more than half the shopkeeper's first offer.

Dingshan is also where replacement **roof tiles** and ornamental rocks are manufactured for use in the vast work of reconstructing China's temples. The enormous pots decorated with writhing dragons are extremely fine, as are the round, heavy, blue-glazed tables found in so many Chinese gardens. In the **Pottery Exhibition Centre**, 2km north up the main street from the spot where minibuses arrive, you can see both artistic pieces – from delicate Song-dynasty teapots to flamboyant modern lamps – as well as lavatory bowls and spark-plug insulators.

The Yixing Caves

South and west of Yixing Town and Dingshan are delightful hills, woods, tea plantations and, below ground, several collections of **karst caves** that are worth seeing if you're in the area. All the caves can be reached by buses from Yixing Town – you'll have to ask around both bus stations – and are often connected to each other by private minibuses, so it's easy to spend a pleasant day trundling independently around the area. Alternatively, you can join a group tour, either from Yixing or from Wuxi. Sturdy shoes and some form of waterproof protection against dripping stalactites are a good idea. The caves are all open daily until around 4.30pm and charge varying entrance fees up to ¥30.

The nearest and most interesting set of caves, **Zhanggong**, is just forty minutes by bus from Yixing, and only ten minutes north of Dingshan. It consists of 72 separate caves, connected on two levels by more than 1500 steps; you actually climb a hill, but on the inside. Although the stalactites, stalagmites and other rock formations are all named for their resemblance to exotic beasts or everyday objects, you'll need a powerful imagination to work out which is which. Legend has it that Zhang Daolin, the father of Chinese Taoism, and Zhang Guolao, one of the legendary Eight Immortals, both practised their theory here. The real highlight is the **Hall of the Sea Dragon King** where the rock soars upwards in strange contortions and emerges on to the green hillside far above – look up and you'll see an eerie patch of swirling, dripping mist.

A further fifteen minutes on the bus south of the Zhanggong caves takes you through tea plantations to the most recently discovered group, the **Linggu caves**, which feature an underground waterfall. This series of large interlinked caverns has yet to be fully explored, though ancient human remains have been found here along with Tang inscriptions, many supposedly left by Lu Guimeng, the Tang poet, who allegedly stumbled upon the cave when he was searching for the perfect tea leaves. The mouth of the cave has great views of Taihu, bamboo groves, tea fields, and lush, verdant hills. Near the Linggu Caves lies the **Yanxian Tea Plantation**, with large expanses of green stretching from the road far off into the hilly distance. The tea here is overpriced, but the views are sublime.

The third group, **Shanjuan**, is the most popular cave site, located 25km southwest (an hour on the bus) from Yixing, about halfway on the road to Dingshan. The caves are set on three interconnecting levels, including the snail-shell-shaped upper cave and the more interesting lower Water Cave. From here a boat ferries you through subterranean passages formed by limestone dissolution, the boatman picking out highlights with his flashlight all the way to the exit, humorously named "Suddenly See the Light".

Zhenjiang

Northwest of Changzhou and Wuxi, and east of Nanjing, **ZHENJIANG** isn't the most beautiful of cities but does offer three intriguing temples to explore, each perched on top of a hill from which there are some excellent vistas of the Yangzi River. The city is worth a stopover either as a day-trip from Nanjing or, more realistically, as an overnight stop en route between Shanghai or Suzhou and Nanjing. Tourists flock to the temples on weekends, but at most other times you'll feel blissfully free of the herds that characterize Suzhou and other tourist draws in the area.

For more than two thousand years, Zhenjiang has provided a safe harbour and a strong defensive position at the junction of two of the world's greatest trade routes, the **Yangzi River** and the **Grand Canal**, and protected on three sides by low hills. During the Three Kings period, a Wu ruler built a walled city on this site as his capital; it grew rapidly, boosted over the centuries by the southern branch of the Grand Canal, and by proximity to the Ming capital at Nanjing. Marco Polo remarked on the richness of the local **silks** and gold fabrics, and these are still renowned, as are, less romantically, Zhenjiang vinegar and pickles. After the Opium Wars the British and French were granted **concessions** here, intriguing traces of which remain today around the site of the former British Consulate.

Now on the main Shanghai–Nanjing rail line, and still an important Yangzi anchorage, Zhenjiang is an outward-looking city whose prosperity remains assured, with yet more expansion on the way as a new **bridge** across the river – a cornerstone in Jiangsu's massive transportation development plans – creates further trade links with northern Jiangsu. The bridge is the third crossing over the Yangzi (after the Nanjing Daqiao, built in the 1960s) and is soon to be followed by two more bridges, one near Nanjing and one connecting Shanghai with the northern bank of the Yangzi.

Zhenjiang

Zhenjiang	镇江	*zhènjiāng*
Beigu Shan	北固山	*běigù shān*
Jiao Shan	焦山	*jiāo shān*
Jin Shan	金山	*jīn shān*
Accommodation and eating		
Dantuxian	丹徒县招待所	*dāntúxiàn zhāodàisuǒ*
Guoji Fandian	国际饭店	*guójì fàndiàn*
Jingkou	京口饭店	*jīngkǒu fàndiàn*
Yanchun Jiulou	宴春酒楼	*yànchūn jiǔlóu*
Zhenjiang Binguan	镇江宾馆	*zhènjiāng bīnguǎn*
Zhenjiang Dajiudian	镇江大酒店	*zhènjiāng dàjiǔdiàn*

The City

Although sheer size means that walking is rarely a practical way of getting around Zhenjiang, it is a relatively easy place to get your bearings. Across the north flows the Yangzi; in the south, the rail line forms another barrier; and down through the middle, meandering approximately north–south across the city centre, is the Grand Canal. The modern downtown area centres on **Dashi Kou**, the junction of Zhongshan Lu and Jiefang Lu, about 3km east of the train station, and 2km south of the Yangzi. The temples are all close to the riverbank, and can be reached by city buses #2 and #4, both of which leave from the square in front of the train station.

The oldest section of town, due north of the train station and just south of the river, around Daxi Lu and Boxian Lu, is a fascinating area for a stroll; it's crowded with ancient architecture, dozens of small shops and tiny alleys running off in all directions. You can reach Daxi Lu is on the #2 bus which runs here from the train station via Dashi Kou. West along Daxi Lu is the curious red brick of the former **British Consulate** – part British colonial, part Qing-dynasty – now housing the local **museum** (daily 9am–4.30pm; ¥10). It's definitely worth dropping in, for the building if not for the museum contents; if you're on the bus, get off immediately after you see the building on the right, just as the bus is making a sharp left curve. Built in the 1890s, the creaky staircases, wooden floorboards, and balconies offering views over the river are delightfully reminiscent of another era. A few minutes' walk farther south from here brings you to another bizarrely improbable facade, the crumbling **Dahuangjia Hotel**, formerly the *Royal Hotel*. The building is a highly unexpected anachronism, with columns and caryatids on the outside, and a lobby from the 1920s. Its main boast, surprisingly in the People's Republic, is that Chiang Kaishek once stayed here. Disused now, it was until recently a sleazy karaoke bar. Carry on past here and you get to the pleasantly delapidated Boxian Park (¥2), which has more than the usual complement of old folk. If you're lucky you'll catch an open-mike Chinese opera slam at the teahouse, fascinating more to observe, frankly, than to listen to.

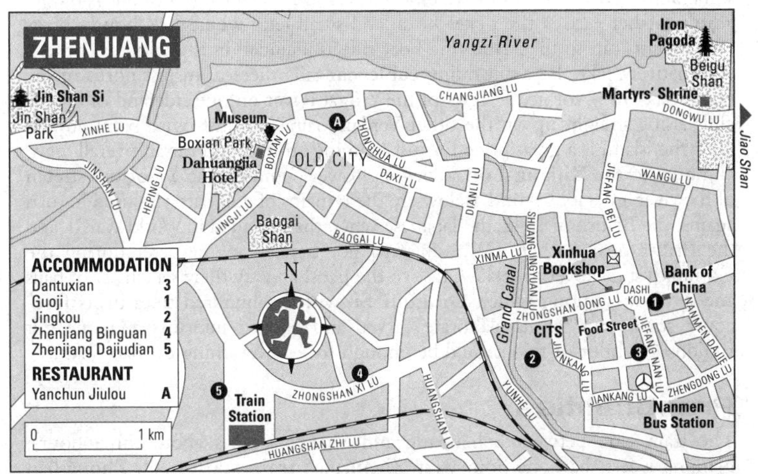

Jin Shan Park

Jin Shan Si, a temple scenically located in its own **Jin Shan Park** (daily 8am–8pm; ¥10) in the far northwest of the city at the terminus of bus #2, is a pleasant riverside spot worth a couple of hours of your time. At one time a small island in the Yangzi, Jin Shan has silted up over the years to create a low-lying peninsula, with a series of rectangular fishponds overlooked by a small hill. The temple buildings wrap themselves dramatically around this hill behind a series of heavy yellow-ochre walls. Twisting stairways lead past them to the **Cishou Pagoda** (daily 8.30–6pm; ¥4), built more than 1400 years ago and renovated in 1900 at great expense to celebrate the Dowager Empress Cixi's sixty-fifth birthday. From the top of this seven-tiered octagonal tower you get a superb view down to the jumbled temple roofs, and across the ponds to the river. The temple itself, with a 1500-year history and a former complement of three thousand monks, has recently been restored to something of its former glory and is packed with the usual unselfconscious mix of tourists and worshippers. There are also four **caves** at the top of this hill, two of which – Fohai (Buddhist Sea) and Bailong (White Dragon) – feature prominently in the classic fairy tale *Baishe* (White Snake), which every Chinese is supposed to have read as a child. From a canal in the park you can catch an imitation dragon boat (¥10) around the corner to the **First Spring Under Heaven** at the edge of a small lake. The spring itself is of no special interest, but it's nice to get out on the water.

Beigu Shan and Jiao Shan

To the northeast of town and on the route of bus #4, **Beigu Shan** is a refreshing hilltop (daily 7am–7pm; ¥8), named 1400 years ago by an enthusiastic emperor as the "Best Hill in the World above a River". From the entrance, climb the stairs on the right, then turn left along the rampart to come to the lightning-damaged remains of the 900-year-old **Iron Pagoda** and, on top of the hill, the exquisite **Lingyun Ting** (Soaring Clouds Pavilion), where you can sit in the shade and enjoy the commanding views over the river. Immediately south of Beigu Shan is the modern **Martyrs' Shrine** for victims of the wars which brought communism to China.

Farther east, a few more stops along the bus #4 route, is the most interesting place in Zhenjiang, **Jiao Shan** (daily 7.30am–4.45pm; ¥7), still a genuine island, some 5km downstream from the city centre. From the terminus of bus #4, walk a little farther east to the ticket kiosk and small jetty where half-hourly boats take tourists out to the island (the boat ride is included in the entrance ticket). Alternatively, take the exhilarating **cable-car** ride there from just north of the boat dock (¥15), for great views of the Yangzi River on one side and of craggy cliffs rising straight up on the other. Verdant, rural and lush with bamboo and pine, the island is a great place for just roaming around, and for an overall view, climb up to the **Xijiang Lou**, a viewing tower commanding a glorious stretch of the river and city beyond. Below are the remains of gun batteries used in turn against the British in 1842, the Japanese when they invaded in World War II, and the British again, when *HMS Amethyst* got trapped in the river during the Communist takeover in 1949. Close to the Jiaoshan jetty there's a cluster of halls and pavilions, among which **Dinghui Si**, with six hundred trees in its forecourt, stands out for its elaborate carved and painted interiors and fine gilt Buddha. An hour or two should be enough to see everything on Jiao Shan.

Practicalities

The train ride between Zhenjiang and Shanghai takes about three hours; Nanjing is less than one hour west. Zhenjiang's **train station**, on Zhongshan

Lu, is in the southwest of the city. From here, buses #2 and #4 run to Dashi Kou and then head north, while buses #10 and #12 run to Dashi Kou and turn south. Points of arrival by bus are harder to predict: some buses stop very close to the train station, others at the **bus station** on Jiefang Nan Lu, 500m south of Dashi Kou. There are frequent minibuses to Nanjing from the train-station square, and from the bus station there are buses to Nanjing, Huai'an, Yangzhou and Lianyungang. Most facilities are in the Dashi Kou area, including the **Bank of China** (Mon–Fri 8–11.30am & 1.30–4pm), just to the east on Zhongshan Lu, and the **post office** immediately to the north on Jiefang Bei Lu. There's a **CITS** office at 92 Zhongshan Xi Lu.

Accommodation

Hotel accommodation isn't cheap in Zhenjiang. However, on weekdays and during the September–June off-season, you should be able to negotiate a ten to thirty percent discount on your room, depending on how hard you bargain with the front desk.

Dantuxian Shuilusi Xiang ⓣ0511/5011666. On a small lane a little south of Dashi Kou, this friendly place is signposted in English from the main road, and offers pretty cheap singles, doubles and triples. Convenient for the bus station on Jiefang Lu. ❹

Guoji 218 Jiefang Lu, at the corner of Zhongshan Dong Lu in the centre of town ⓣ0511/5021888, ⓕ5021777. The only four-star hotel in town, it offers spacious, clean doubles and attentive service. ❼

Jingkou Binhe Lu ⓣ0511/5224866, ⓕ5230056). A quiet, attractive complex centrally located down a small lane running south from Zhongshan Lu, immediately east of the Grand Canal. From the train station take bus #15; walk right through to the back for the reception. You'll find a very wide range of rooms here, from some of the cheapest in town to the most expensive. ❸

Zhenjiang Binguan 92 Zhongshan Xi Lu ⓣ0511/5233888 ext 511, ⓕ5231055. A 10min walk east of the station square, this is one of the most upmarket places in the city, a little heavy on the marble, with a couple of travel agents based in the lobby. ❼

Zhenjiang Dajiudian Zhongshan Xi Lu ⓣ0511/5236666, ⓕ5230145. A smart, modern place, conveniently located right in the train station square – it's to the left as you emerge from the station. ❺

Eating

Among the locals, the most famous **restaurant** in town is the *Yanchun Jiulou*, on an alley just north of Daxi Lu, a short way east of the former British Consulate and opposite a bank of China. Specialities here include little appetizers of cold dishes brought round on a trolley – salads, stuffed buns and diced rectangles of pork which have been tenderized so that they literally melt in the mouth. Downstairs is a cheap canteen. This area of the old town also contains numerous noodle and dumpling shops. For fast food – Chinese style – try the **food street** down a small alley one block south of and parallel to Zhongshan Dong Lu to the west of the *Guoji Hotel*; it usually goes from 5pm until around 2am every night.

Yangzhou

Straddling the Grand Canal north of the Yangzi, an hour by bus north of Zhenjiang and a couple of hours from Nanjing, **YANGZHOU** is a leafy and relaxing city. Today its proud boast is of having produced President Jiang Zemin, though its origins go back to around 500 BC when the Wu rulers had channels dug here which were later incorporated into the Grand Canal. Thanks to its

Yangzhou

Yangzhou	扬州	***yángzhōu***
Daming Si	大明寺	*dàmíng sì*
Ershisi Qiao	二十四桥	*èrshísì qiáo*
Ge Yuan	个园	*gèyuán*
He Yuan	何园	*héyuán*
Shi Kefa Memorial	史可法纪念馆	*shīkěfǎ jìniànguǎn*
Shi Ta	石塔	*shítǎ*
Shou Xihu	瘦西湖	*shòuxī hú*
Tomb of Puhaddin	普哈丁墓	*pǔhādīng mù*
Wenfeng Ta	文峰塔	*wénfēng tǎ*
Wuting Qiao	五亭桥	*wǔtíng qiáo*
Xianhe Mosque	仙鹤寺	*xiānhè sì*
Accommodation and eating		
Dongyuan	东园饭店	*dōngyuán fàndiàn*
Fuchun Tea House	富春茶社	*fùchūn cháshè*
Hongqiao	红桥宾馆	*hóngqiáo bīnguǎn*
Qionghua	琼花大厦	*qiónghuā dàshà*
Shita	石塔宾馆	*shítǎ bīnguǎn*
Xiyuan	西园饭店	*xīyuán fàndiàn*
Yangzhou Binguan	扬州宾馆	*yángzhōu bīnguǎn*

position on the Grand Canal and sandwiched between the Yangzi and the Huai rivers, Yangzhou rapidly developed into a prosperous city, aided by a monopoly of the lucrative **salt trade**. Under the Tang and later, many foreign merchants, including a community from Persia, lived and traded here, leaving behind a twelfth-century **mosque** and a much-quoted (though wholly unsubstantiated) tale that Marco Polo governed the city for three years. It was a city renowned too for its culture, its storytellers and oral traditions, with stories being handed down through the generations. As such, it frequently attracted the **imperial court** and its entourage, as well as artists and officials moving here in retirement, who endowed temples, created enclosed gardens and patronized local arts.

Despite the industrial belt which now stretches round the south and east of the city, there's still a faint sense of a cosmopolitan, cultured past here, evident in the **gardens**, in the Islamic relics and in the layout of roads, waterways and bridges in the city centre. Out on the northwest edge of town are Yangzhou's two main sights, **Shou Xihu** and **Daming Si**, a lake and a temple which were part of Emperor Qianlong's regular tourist itinerary in the eighteenth century.

The City

Gardens and temples are scattered thinly throughout the city, though there is a concentration of sights around the canal to the north and northwest, where you'll find a snaking greenbelt that houses **Shou Xihu** and **Daming Si**, the lakeland area and temple that constitute the two main sights. Much of the rest of town can be explored on foot, though you'll need city buses for trips right across town. Yangzhou is mobbed by day-trippers from nearby Nanjing on weekends and holidays; you'll find things far less hectic if you visit on a weekday.

Shou Xihu and Daming Si

It makes sense to visit Yangzhou's two key attractions in conjunction, taking in lesser sights west or north of the centre on the way there or back. If you enter Shou Xihu at the southern end (near bus routes #1, #3, #4, #5 and #15) and then exit through the northern end, you're halfway to Daming Si; you can pick up bus #5 from here for the remaining distance, or take a rickshaw. The other way to get around both sights is by **tourist boat** – south of the Shou Xihu the canal runs east to Qianlong's old imperial barge landing-place, in front of what is now the *Xiyuan Hotel*. In recent years a jetty has been built here so that tourists can travel by mock dragon boats, complete with plush yellow furnishings, through the Shou Xihu and right up as far as Daming Si. The high prices make this only really practicable for large groups, however – reckon on several hundred yuan to rent a twenty-person boat for a couple of hours.

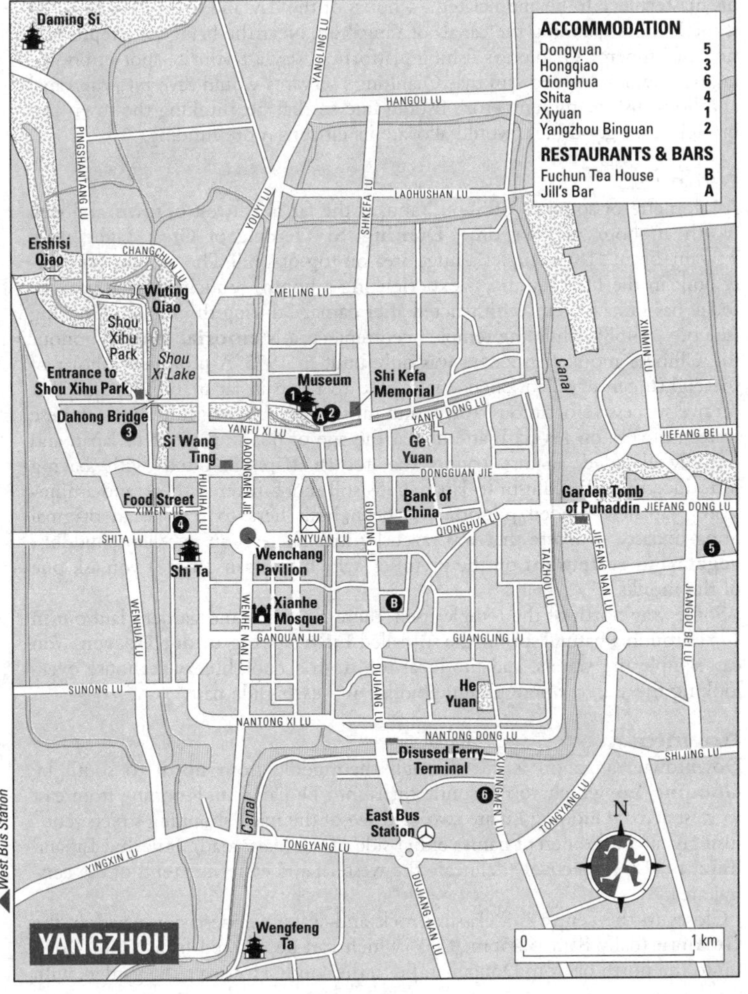

The **Shou Xihu**, which winds, snake-like, through an elongated park area (daily 6.45am–5.30pm; ¥30), literally translates as "Thin West Lake" – so named to recall the original "fat" West Lake at Hangzhou. In some respects it's a typical Chinese park, full of water and melancholy weeping willows, though it does also contain an array of interesting structures, follies in the romantic sense: a plain white **dagoba**, modelled after the one in Beihai in Beijing; the **Chui Tai** (Happiness Terrace), whose three moon gates each frame a different scene; and in particular the much-photographed **Wuting Qiao** (Five Pavilion Bridge), an eighteenth-century construction with massive triple-arched and yellow-tiled roofs. If you walk about fifteen minutes west from the Wuting Qiao, along the north bank of the lake, you'll also come to another bridge, the spectacular **Ershisi Qiao** (Twenty-four Bridge), its single hump so high and rounded as to form a virtual circle through which boats could pass. The bridge is so named because there are 24 archways in the design; the designer wanted his masterpiece to be appreciated 24 hours of the day, and there used to be 24 stone bridges spanning the canals of Yangzhou. Near the bridge is a reproduction of Emperor Qianlong's fishing platform, today a favourite spot of photo-taking couples. Legend says that Qianlong's servants would dive into the canal and hook fish to the emperor's fishing line so that he, thinking the town had brought him good luck, would allocate its citizens more funding.

Daming Si

A kilometre or so north of Shou Xihu, in the far northwest of town, and well worth an hour of your time, **Daming Si** (Temple of Great Light; daily 7.30am–5pm; ¥18) occupies a huge area on top of a hill. The temple, originally built in the fifth century, is experiencing a boom – much of what you see today has in fact been reconstructed after damage during the Taiping Uprising (see box, p.458), while the temple's centrepiece, a **Memorial Hall** to honour the Chinese monk Jian Zhen, was only built in 1973. A profound scholar of the eighth century, Jian Zhen was invited to teach in Japan, only to find that on five successive occasions storms and misfortune drove him back to Chinese waters. Finally, on his sixth attempt, at the age of 66, he made it to Japan and sensibly decided against trying the return trip. Credited with having introduced *ritso* Buddhism to Japan, he is still much revered there, and a nine-storey Japanese-funded **pagoda** has been built here to replace an original Song-dynasty structure that was razed by fire. There is an excellent Buddhist **vegetarian restaurant** on the premises, which you can eat at if you ask one of the monks.

Some way north of the temple itself, there are parks and gardens laid out in 1751 around a natural spring, the so-called **Fifth Spring under Heaven**. You can sample the waters, and the local tea, from a cool, breezy teahouse overlooking the water, where plump goldfish and carp glide past.

Downtown

Downtown Yangzhou is cut through the middle from north to south by **Guoqing Lu**, which, to the south, turns into Dujiang Lu. Running from east to west across Guoqing Lu are two or three of the main shopping streets (confusingly, all with different names either side of the main road). **Huaihai Lu** and **Taizhou Lu** respectively delineate the western and eastern extents of the central area.

Closes to the centre is a classical rock-and-water Chinese composition, the **Ge Yuan** (daily 8am–4.45pm; ¥15), which can be entered from Yanfu Dong Lu to the north or from Dongguan Jie to the south. However, the garden, with its ponderously styled pavilions and landscaped rockery supposedly suggesting the four seasons, is in a state of some neglect and relatively free of visitors; more attractive is He Yuan to the south. A rather more promising line of exploration here is to cross the canal immediately north of Ge Yuan and walk a few minutes west from the top of Guoqing Lu, as far as the **Museum** (daily 8.30am–5.30pm; ¥12), overlooking the canal near the *Xiyuan Hotel*. A delightful group of assorted old pavilions set in large grounds, this is one of China's more interesting provincial museums, featuring a 1000-year-old wooden boat recovered from the Grand Canal, as well as an extraordinary Han dynasty funeral suit made of five hundred pieces of jade, and two wooden tombs from the Han and Song dynasties. Right next to the museum, to the east, in charming grounds full of flowers and plum trees, is the **Shi Kefa Memorial** (daily 8.15–11.30am & 2–5.30pm; ¥10), a temple devoted to the memory of a local hero who in the last days of the Ming dynasty gave his life resisting the advancing Qing armies. The victorious Qing subsequently raised this memorial to him in recognition of his courage. West from the museum is a strip along the canal now gearing up to become a tourist centre, with "traditional" architecture and souvenir shops, while in front, right on the canal itself, stands a small jetty from where tour group boats run up to Shou Xihu and Daming Si.

West of the centre

Moving west of the central area, you'll find the main surviving testament to the presence of Persian traders in the city in the Middle Ages, the **Xianhe (Crane) Mosque**, just north of Ganquan Lu, on the small turning to the east of Wenhe Lu. Small and austere, its main feature is one wall covered entirely with Arabic script. You may have to sign your name in the book before being admitted.

The streets in this western quarter conceal several more sights, a seemingly haphazard selection of survivors from different eras of history, scattered thinly in among the traffic and the modern shopping streets. One is the **Shi Ta**, a diminutive Tang-dynasty stone pagoda standing in the shade of a 1000-year-old gingko tree, on Shita Lu just west of Huaihai Lu. Right in the middle of the junction between Shita Lu and Wenhe Lu you'll come across the round Ming-dynasty **Wenchang Ge** (Flourishing Culture Pavilion), resembling a mini Temple of Heaven, and, one block north, there's the thirteenth-century **Si Wang Ting** (Four View Pavilion), a three-storeyed octagonal pavilion.

East and south of the centre

For more evidence of the early Muslim presence in Yangzhou, take a look to the east of the centre, just past the canal on Jiefang Nan Lu. From the west bank of the canal, or from the Jiefang Bridge, just to the north, you'll see a wooded hill and, behind it, a jumble of Muslim architecture. This rather sad, dusty relic from the most cosmopolitan era of China's history is actually the **Garden Tomb of Puhaddin** (or Bulhanding; daily 7.15am–4.30pm; ¥7), a descendant of the Prophet Mohammed, who came to China in the thirteenth century, spent ten years in Yangzhou and adopted the city as his home, to the extent that he insisted on being buried here. Labelled in Chinese, paintings and artefacts in a small exhibit hall next door chronicle his life.

There are a couple more attractions in the **south** of the city, though again rather randomly scattered. A short way north of the canal, in an old, quiet part of town, is the exquisite **He Yuan** (daily 8am–6pm; ¥15). Designed in the nineteenth century, this tiny garden uses trees, shrubs and a raised walkway to give an ingenious illusion of variety and depth – it's a beautiful little place for a stroll on a sunny morning. The He Yuan also contains a couple of charming teahouses.

In the far south of the city, on Wenfeng Lu, is the conspicuous seven-storey **Wengfeng Ta** (daily 6.30am–5.30pm; ¥2), standing by a bend in the Grand Canal in a small plot crammed with hollyhocks. Built in 1582, it was intended to bring luck to local candidates in the imperial examinations, though its main interest now is as a vantage point over the intense activity on the water. Walk up alongside the canal and wharves for a closer view of the heavy river traffic and the small family boats queuing in vast jams to be laden with anything from grain and bottled drinks to gravel and truck tyres. There is no bus connection to the pagoda, so you'll either have a rather ugly thirty-minute trek southwest from the long-distance bus station, or you can take a rickshaw.

Practicalities

Generally speaking, the very frequent buses to and from Zhenjiang and Nanjing use the remote **West bus station** in the southwest, while buses serving destinations further afield, including long-distance sleepers, use the **East station** on Dujiang Nan Lu in the south of the city; bus #3 from the West station runs to Huaihu Lu, while bus #8 runs between the two stations. It's possible to visit Yangzhou on a day-trip from Nanjing or Zhenjiang, but you'll be stranded here if you don't head out by sunset, when both stations close. It's usually possible to book **train tickets** (the nearest train station is at Zhenjiang) at the East bus station and at the disused canal-ferry terminal to the north, on the northern bank of the canal. The nearest airport is at Nanjing, with plane tickets available at major Yangzhou hotels. At time of writing, a **CITS** office located between the *Xiyuan* and *Yangzhou* hotels was about to open. There's a **Bank of China** on Qionghua Lu, while the **post office** is on Sanyuan Lu.

Accommodation

Yangzhou is a rather expensive place to stay unless you can get a room in the *Hongqiao*, the guesthouse of Yangzhou Normal University, or want to stay east of the centre at the *Dongyuan*.

Dongyuan 25 Lixin Lu, close to the corner of Jiangdu Bei Lu ⓣ0514/7233003, ⓕ7221705. Slightly remote, out in the east of the city, but bus #12 from the centre of town stops right outside. Quiet, decent-quality rooms at reasonably prices. ❸

Hongqiao Yangzhou Normal University campus ⓣ0514/7365275. t's just south of the entrance to Shou Xihu Park: from the West bus station, take bus #3 to the corner of Yanfu Lu and Huaihai Lu; from the East bus station, take bus #1 to the terminus, then take a right onto Huaihai Lu. Head a little way north and turn onto Dahongqiao Lu, which is the first left north of Yanfa Lu; once you've walked over the large stone bridge, take the first left again, then the first right through the main gate. The spartan but clean doubles here are among the best deals in town. ❸

Qionghua 1 Pifang Lu, on the corner with Xuningmen Lu. ⓣ0514/7811321 ext 8811, ⓕ7812079. The only place within walking distance (about 20min) of the bus station. Fairly smart, good-value singles and doubles. ❺

Shita 18 Shita Lu ⓣ0514/7344467, ⓕ7314125. Just west of Huaihai Lu, the *Shita* offers very smart and comfortable rooms; on bus routes #7 and #13 from the bus station. ❻

Xiyuan 1 Fengle Shang Jie ⓣ0514/7344888, ⓕ7233870. In large grounds located just north of the museum on Yanfu Xi Lu, this hotel has a wide range of rooms and is very convenient for the sights. Various travel agents have their offices here. ❺

Yangzhou Binguan 5 Fengle Shang Jie ⓣ0514/7342611, ⓕ7343599. An upmarket, high-rise tower located in the north of the city, next to the museum. ❻

Eating and drinking

Eating is a real pleasure in Yangzhou if you know where to look. The best-known restaurant in town is the *Fuchun Tea House*, down a small alley called

Dexingqiao running east off Guoqing Lu – there's a big sign suspended over the alley entrance. A plate of ten different kinds of dumpling here costs ¥28; other specialities include *doufu gansi* (dried shreds of tofu) and *qingshao xiaren* (fried shrimps). There's another branch beside the Ge Yuan. The restaurant in the *Qionghua Hotel* is also worth trying, and there's plenty of noodles and dumplings on offer in the area around Ganquan Lu. Every night until 2am street vendors set up a **food street** along Ximen Jie just off Huaihai Lu, offering everything from hotpot to skewered beef and puddings. Yangzhou fried rice has become a staple on restaurant menus countrywide, but tastes surprisingly like ordinary fried rice – you can find it at eating places throughout town. There's a slither of **nightlife** by the canal near the *Xiyuan* and *Yangzhou Binguan*. Of the bars, *Jills*, equidistant between the two hotels, is the best and the most foreigner-friendly; the *Banana Disco* outside the Yangzhou is very provincial.

Nanjing and around

NANJING, formerly known in the West as Nanking, is one of China's greatest cities. Its very name, "Southern Capital", stands as a direct foil to the "Northern Capital" of Beijing, and the city is still considered the rightful capital of China by many Overseas Chinese, particularly those from Taiwan. Today, it's a wealthy, prosperous city, benefiting both from its proximity to Shanghai and from its gateway position on the **Yangzi River**, which stretches away west deep into China's interior. With its broad, tree-lined boulevards and balconied houses within Ming walls and gates, Nanjing is also one of the most attractive of the major Chinese cities and, although it has become rather an expensive place to visit, it offers a fairly cosmopolitan range of tourist facilities, as well as a wealth of historic sites that can easily fill several days' exploration.

Some history

Occupying a strategic site on the south bank of the Yangzi River in a beautiful setting of lakes, river, wooded hills and crumbling fortifications, Nanjing has had an important role from the earliest times, though not until 600 BC were there the beginnings of a walled city. By the time the Han empire broke up in 220 AD, Nanjing was the capital of half a dozen local dynasties, and when the Sui reunited China in 589, the building of the **Grand Canal** began considerably to increase the city's economic importance. Nanjing became renowned for its forges, foundries and weaving, especially for the veined **brocade** made in noble houses and monasteries. During the Tang and Song periods, the city rivalled nearby Hangzhou as the wealthiest in the country, until in 1368 the first emperor of the Ming dynasty decided to establish it as the **capital** of all China.

For centuries thereafter, although Nanjing's claims to be the capital would be usurped by the heavily northern-based Qing dynasty, anti-authoritarian movements always associated themselves with movements to restore the old capital. For eleven years in the mid-nineteenth century, the **Taiping rebels** (see box, p.458) set up the capital of their **Heavenly Kingdom** at Nanjing. The siege and final recapture of the city by the foreign-backed Qing armies in 1864 was one of the saddest and most dramatic events in China's history. After the Opium War, the **Treaty of Nanking**, which ceded Hong Kong to Britain, was signed here in 1841, and Nanjing itself also suffered the indignity of being a

Nanjing

Nanjing	南京	***nánjīng***
Bailuzhou	白鹭洲	*báilù zhōu*
Chaotian Gong	朝天宫	*cháotiān gōng*
City Wall	城市墙	*chéngshì qiáng*
Dujiang Jinianbei	渡江纪念碑	*dùjiāng jìniànbēi*
Fuzi Miao	夫子庙	*fūzǐ miào*
Gugong Park	故宫	*gùgōng*
Gulou	鼓楼	*gǔlóu*
Jinghai Si	静海寺	*jìnghǎi sì*
Linggu Si	灵谷寺	*línggǔ si*
Meiyuan Xincun	梅园新村	*méiyuán xīncūn*
Memorial to Nanjing Massacre	南京大屠杀纪念馆	*nánjīngdàtúshā jìniànguǎn*
Ming Xiaoling	明孝陵	*míngxiào líng*
Mochou Hu Park	莫愁湖公园	*mòchóuhú gōngyuán*
Nanjing Museum	南京博物馆	*nánjīng bówùguǎn*
Qinhuai River	秦淮河	*qínhuái hé*
Qixia Si	栖霞寺	*qīxiá sì*
Shixiang Lu (Stone Statue road)	石象路	*shíxiàng lù*
Taiping Heavenly Kingdom History Museum	太平天国历史博物馆	*tàipíngtiānguólìshǐ bówùguǎn*
Tianchao Gong	天朝宫	*tiāncháo gōng*
Xinjiekou	新街口	*xīnjiē kǒu*
Xuanwu Hu Park	玄武湖公园	*xuānwǔhú gōngyuán*
Yangzi River Bridge	长江大桥	*chángjiāng dàqiáo*
Yuhuatai Park	雨花台公园	*yǔhuātái gōngyuán*
Zhonghua Men	中华门	*zhōnghuá mén*
Zhongshan Ling	中山陵	*zhōngshān líng*
Zhongshan Men	中山门	*zhōngshān mén*
Zhongyang Men	中央门	*zhōngyāng mén*
Zijin Shan	紫金山	*zǐjīn shān*
Accommodation		
Central	中心大酒店	*zhōngxīn dàjiǔdiàn*
Daqiao	大桥饭店	*dàqiáo fàndiàn*
Future Inn	明日大酒店	*míngrì dàjiǔdiàn*
Heyuan	和园饭店	*héyuán fàndiàn*

treaty port. Following the overthrow of the Qing dynasty in 1911, however, the city flowered again and became the provisional capital of the new Republic of China, with Sun Yatsen as its first president. Sun Yatsen's mausoleum, **Zhongshan Ling**, on the edge of modern Nanjing, is one of the great centres of pilgrimage of the Chinese.

In 1937, the name of Nanjing became synonymous with one of the worst atrocities of World War II, after the so-called **Rape of Nanking**, in which invading Japanese soldiers butchered an estimated three hundred thousand civilians. Subsequently, Chiang Kaishek's government escaped the Japanese advance by moving west to Chongqing, though after Japan's surrender and Chiang's return, Nanjing briefly resumed its status as the official capital of China. Just four years later, however, in 1949, the victorious Communists decided to abandon Nanjing as capital altogether, choosing instead the ancient

Hongqiao	虹桥饭店	*hóngqiáo fàndiàn*
Jinling	金陵饭店	*jīnlíng fàndiàn*
Longpan	龙蟠大厦	*lóngpán dàshà*
Mandarin Garden	状元大酒店	*zhuàngyuán dàjiǔdiàn*
Nanjing	南京饭店	*nánjīng fàndiàn*
Nanjing University Foreign Students' Residence	南京大学外国留学生宿舍	*nánjīng dàxué wàiguóliúxuéshēng sùshè*
Normal University (Nanshan Hotel)	师范大学南山宾馆	*shīfàn dàxué nánshān bīnguǎn*
Shuangmenlou	双门楼宾馆	*shuāngménlóu bīnguǎn*
Xihuamen	西华门饭店	*xīhuámén fàndiàn*
Xinli	信力酒店	*xìnlì jiǔdiàn*
Xuanwu	玄武饭店	*xuánwǔ fàndiàn*
Yuehua	悦华大酒店	*yuèhuá dàjiǔdiàn*
Zhongshan	中山大厦	*zhōngshān dàshà*
Eating and drinking		
The Answer	答案酒吧	*dáàn jiǔbā*
Black Cat	黑猫餐馆	*hēimāo cānguǎn*
Chaozhou	潮州饭店	*cháozhōu fàndiàn*
Daniang Dumplings	大娘水饺	*dàniáng shuǐjiǎo*
Fusheng Yuan	福盛缘酒店	*fúshèngyuán jiǔdiàn*
Gold & Silver	金银餐厅	*jīnyíng cāntīng*
Haitian Ge	海天阁	*hǎitiān gé*
Hefeng	和风日膳	*héfēng rìshàn*
Henry's	亨利之家	*hēnglìzhījiā*
Jack's	杰克餐厅	*jiékè cāntīng*
Jiangsu	江苏饭店	*jiāngsū fàndiàn*
Jiaozi Wang	饺子王	*jiǎozi wáng*
Jinzhu	金竹居	*jīnzhú jū*
Lao Zhengxing	老正兴菜馆	*lǎozhèngxīng càiguǎn*
Musilin Noodles	穆斯林餐厅	*mùsīlín cāntīng*
Orgies Bar	奥杰酒吧	*àojié jiǔbā*
Red Balloon Bar	红色气球酒吧	*hóngsè qìqiú jiǔbā*
Scarlet's	乱世佳人	*luànshì jiārén*
Shanghai Tan	上海滩	*shànghǎi tān*
Swede & Kraut	老外乐	*lǎowài lè*
Tianyuan Longjuan	天缘龙娟	*tiānyuán lóngjuān*
Xiao Ren Ren	小任任饭店	*xiǎorènrèn fàndiàn*
Yinghua Yuan	樱花园菜馆	*yīnghuāyuán càiguǎn*

– and highly conservative – city of Beijing in which to base the country's first "modern" government. Nowadays capital of Jiangsu Province, Nanjing remains an important rail junction – a great 1960s bridge carries the Beijing–Shanghai line over the Yangzi – and a major river port for large ships.

Orientation, arrival and city transport

The city's broken and meandering Ming walls are still a useful means of orientation, and the main streets run across town between gates in the city wall. The big gate in the north, now marked by a huge traffic circle and massive flyovers, is **Zhongyang Men**. To the northeast of here, outside the city wall, is the **train station**, while inside the wall, running due south from Zhongyang Men, the city's main street (called Zhongyang Lu, then

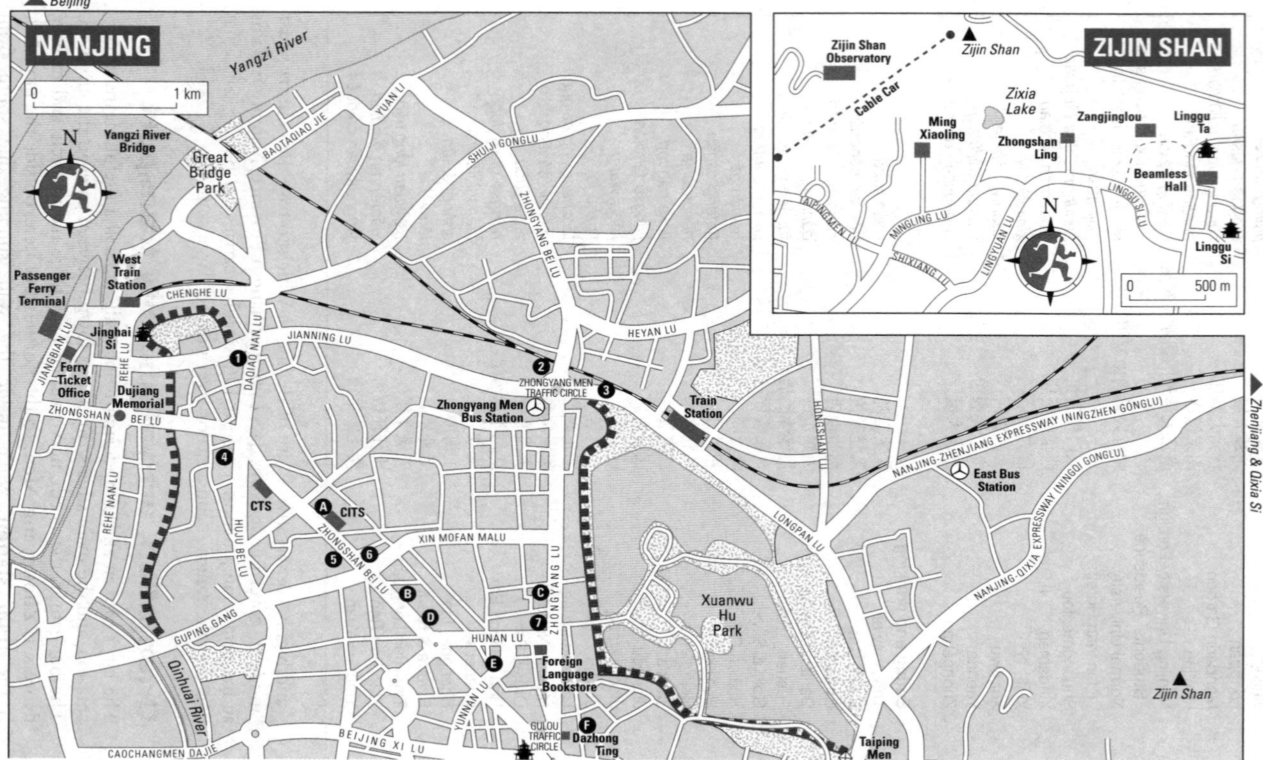
NANJING
Beijing
Yangzi River
0 1 km
N
Yangzi River Bridge
Great Bridge Park
BAOTAQIAO JIE
YUAN LI
SHUIJI GONGLU
ZHONGYANG BEI LU
West Train Station
Passenger Ferry Terminal
CHENGHE LU
Jinghai Si
JIANGBIAN LU
REHE LU
DAQIAO NAN LU
JIANNING LU
HEYAN LU
Ferry Ticket Office
Dujiang Memorial
ZHONGSHAN BEI LU
ZHONGYANG MEN TRAFFIC CIRCLE
Zhongyang Men Bus Station
Train Station
HONGSHAN LU
CTS
CITS
REHE NAN LU
HUJU BEI LU
XIN MOFAN MALU
ZHONGYANG LU
GUPING GANG
HUNAN LU
Foreign Language Bookstore
Qinhuai River
YUNNAN LU
BEIJING XI LU
CAOCHANGMEN DAJIE
GULOU TRAFFIC CIRCLE
Dazhong Ting
Taiping Men
Xuanwu Hu Park
LONGPAN LU
NANJING-ZHENJIANG EXPRESSWAY (NINGZHEN GONGLU)
NANJING-QIXIA EXPRESSWAY (NINGQI GONGLU)
East Bus Station
Zhenjiang & Qixia Si
Zijin Shan
A
B
C
D
E
F
1
2
3
4
5
6
7
ZIJIN SHAN
Zijin Shan Observatory
Zijin Shan
Cable Car
Zixia Lake
Ming Xiaoling
Zhongshan Ling
Zangjinglou
Linggu Ta
Beamless Hall
Linggu Si
LINGGU SI LU
TAIPINGMEN LU
MINGLING LU
SHIXIANG LU
LINGYUAN LU
N
0 500 m

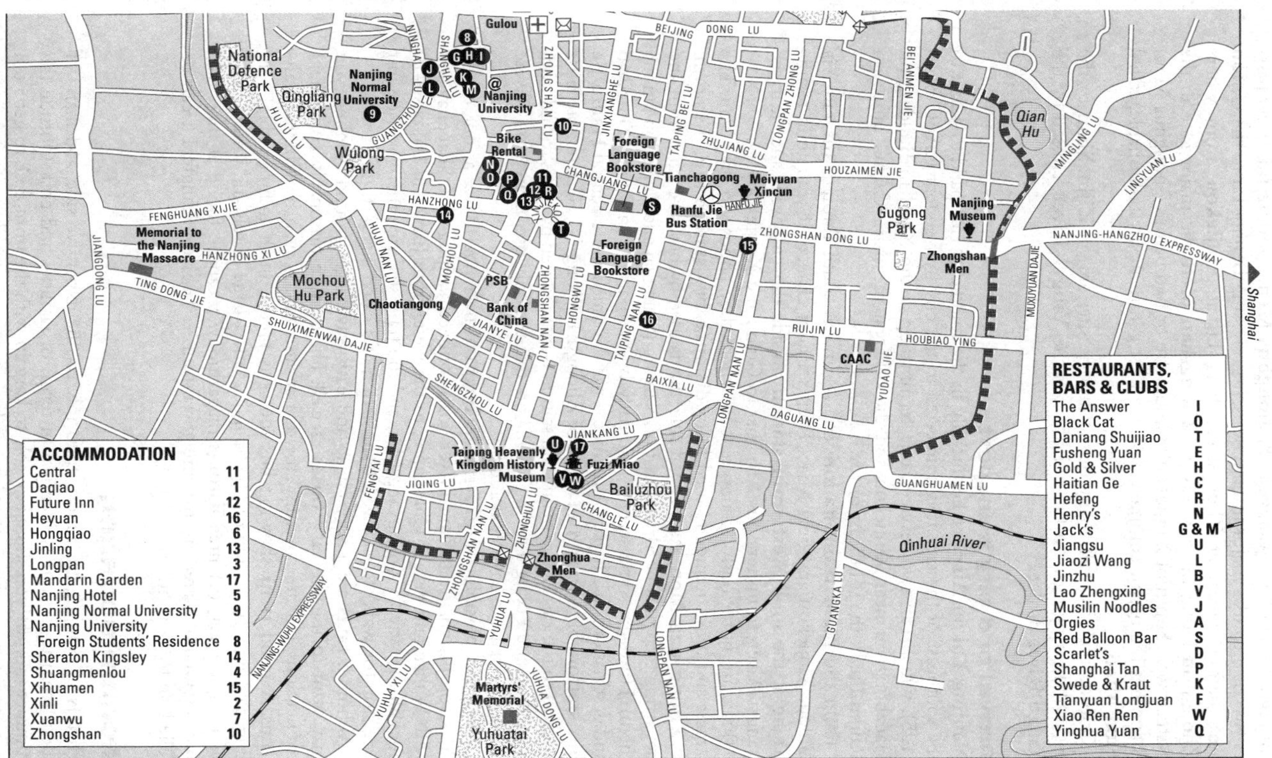
Shanghai
Airport
ACCOMMODATION
Central 11
Daqiao 1
Future Inn 12
Heyuan 16
Hongqiao 6
Jinling 13
Longpan 3
Mandarin Garden 17
Nanjing Hotel 5
Nanjing Normal University 9
Nanjing University
Foreign Students' Residence 8
Sheraton Kingsley 14
Shuangmenlou 4
Xihuamen 15
Xinli 2
Xuanwu 7
Zhongshan 10
RESTAURANTS, BARS & CLUBS
The Answer I
Black Cat O
Daniang Shuijiao T
Fusheng Yuan E
Gold & Silver H
Haitian Ge C
Hefeng R
Henry's N
Jack's G & M
Jiangsu U
Jiaozi Wang L
Jinzhu B
Lao Zhengxing V
Musilin Noodles J
Orgies A
Red Balloon Bar S
Scarlet's D
Shanghai Tan P
Swede & Kraut K
Tianyuan Longjuan F
Xiao Ren Ren W
Yinghua Yuan Q
Gulou
National Defence Park
Qingliang Park
Nanjing Normal University
Nanjing University
Wulong Park
Bike Rental
Foreign Language Bookstore
Tianchaogong
Meiyuan Xincun
Hanfu Jie Bus Station
Gugong Park
Nanjing Museum
Zhongshan Men
Qian Hu
Memorial to the Nanjing Massacre
Mochou Hu Park
Chaotiangong
PSB
Bank of China
CAAC
Taiping Heavenly Kingdom History Museum
Fuzi Miao
Bailuzhou Park
Zhonghua Men
Martyrs' Memorial
Yuhuatai Park
Qinhuai River
BEIJING DONG LU
BEI'ANMEN JIE
MINGLING LU
LINGYUAN LU
NANJING-HANGZHOU EXPRESSWAY
MUXUYUAN DAJIE
HOUZAIMEN JIE
ZHUJIANG LU
LONGPAN ZHONG LU
TAIPING BEI LU
JINXIANGHE LU
ZHONGSHAN LU
SHANGHAI LU
NINGHAI LU
GUANGZHOU LU
HUJU LU
HANZHONG LU
CHANGJIANG LU
HANFU JIE
XINJIEKOU
ZHONGSHAN DONG LU
FENGHUANG XIJIE
HANZHONG XI LU
JIANGDONG LU
TING DONG JIE
HUJU NAN LU
MOCHOU LU
ZHONGSHAN NAN LU
HONGWU LU
TAIPING NAN LU
RUIJIN LU
HOUBIAO YING
YUDAO JIE
SHUIXIMENWAI DAJIE
JIANYE LU
BAIXIA LU
LONGPAN NAN LU
DAGUANG LU
SHENGZHOU LU
JIANKANG LU
GUANGHUAMEN LU
FENGTAI LU
JIQING LU
ZHONGHUA LU
CHANGLE LU
GUANGKA LU
NANJING-WUHU EXPRESSWAY
YUHUA LU
YUHUA XI LU
YUHUA DONG LU

Zhongshan Lu, then Zhongshan Nan Lu), runs for 8km before emerging through the southern wall west of **Zhonghua Men**. En route, this street passes two of the city's major intersections, first crossing Beijing Lu in the **Gulou** area, before traversing Zhongshan Dong Lu at **Xinjiekou**, from where Zhongshan Dong Lu runs east to **Zhongshan Men**, the major gate in the eastern wall. South of Xinjiekou (a kilometre or two before Zhonghua Men) is another important commercial and tourist centre, newly fashionable, called **Fuzi Miao**.

Outside the city wall, many of the historic sites are on **Zijin Shan** to the east, while fringing it to the northwest is the **Yangzi River**, crossed by the Yangzi River Bridge.

Arrival and city transport

Nanjing Lukou Airport lies literally in the middle of rice paddies 42km to the southeast of the city. It is connected to the city by frequent CAAC buses (¥25), which run two services, one terminating at the Xinghan Building on Hanzhong Lu near Xinjiekou and the other at the main CAAC office on Ruijin Lu, in the southeast of town.

From the **main train station**, bus #1 travels south through the city, via Gulou, Xinjiekou and Fuzi Miao. There's a faint chance of your train terminating at the small **West train station** outside the city walls and near the Yangzi River; from here bus #16 goes to Gulou and Xinjiekou.

Buses are notoriously inconsistent in where they choose to drop you. The largest and most frequently used **long-distance bus station** is in the north, at **Zhongyang Men**; as a general rule, this is used by buses coming from and departing to points north and east of Nanjing (Shanghai and Yangzhou among them). However, some services – usually buses to and from Yixing, Dingshan and destinations in Zhejiang province – use the much more central **Hanfu Jie bus station**, on a small road north of Zhongshan Dong Lu). The remote **East station** to the east of the main train station is mainly used by buses to and from Yangzhou and Yixing. Leaving town, note that the only **bus tickets** on sale are for same- or next-day departures.

The other possibility is to arrive by **boat** on the Yangzi River at one of the docks on Jiangbian Lu. Yangzi river boats connect Nanjing with Shanghai, and with Wuhan and distant Chongqing to the west. From Jiangbian Lu, bus #10 goes all the way to Zhongyang Men and the train station; otherwise ride just one stop (or walk) to the West train station and catch bus #16 into town.

Although **taxis** are a very cheap and easy way to get around Nanjing, you may want to use the **city buses** as well. These make reasonably convenient connections, but are absurdly crowded at rush hours, even by Chinese standards. A good **map** showing bus routes is pretty much indispensable – an English-language version can be bought at most large hotels and some tourist sights. The expat-oriented **listings** magazine *Map* can be found at most bars and restaurants geared up for foreign custom – *Jack's* on Wangfu Lu can be relied on to carry it.

Accommodation

Hotels in Nanjing are almost uniformly on the expensive side, and many of them seem to be almost identical in terms of facilities and cost. Outside the summer months, you should be able to bargain with the front desk to get a ten to twenty percent discount on rooms. For cheap accommodation, however, the only options are the two universities which house foreign students.

Hotels

Central 75 Zhongshan Lu, west side ⓣ025/4733888, ⓕ4733999. A 5min walk north of Xinjiekou and recently renovated, this is one of the most luxurious places in town. ⑨

Daqiao 255 Jianning Lu, at the junction with Daqiao Nan Lu ⓣ025/8801544, ⓕ8809255. A friendly place just over 1km from the ferry terminal, and offering single and double rooms; bus #10 comes here from the train station or Zhongyang Men. ⑤

Future Inn 34 Guanjia Qiao, one block west of Zhongshan Lu ⓣ025/4700999, ⓕ4700123. Right next to the *Central*, this is a newish place with great service and clean rooms. The location is excellent, very near Xinjiekou and several excellent restaurants. ⑥

Heyuan 305 Taiping Nan Lu, about halfway between Fuzi Miao and Xinjiekou ⓣ025/4405561, ⓕ4417848. A pleasant place to stay in one of the quieter downtown districts. ④

Hongqiao 202 Zhongshan Bei Lu, just north of Xinmofan Malu ⓣ025/3400888, ⓕ6635756. Bus #13 from the train station. A pleasant hotel with very comfortable and clean doubles. ⑥

Jinling Hanzhong Lu ⓣ025/4711999, ⓕ4711666. A few steps west of Xinjiekou, this is one of the city's premier hotels, boasting satellite TV, a fitness centre, swimming pool, shops and a choice of restaurants. ⑨

Longpan 250 Longpan Lu, next to the city bus depot and a 5min walk west of the train station. No English signs, and not a place you would expect to take foreigners, but it does, offering decent if slightly grotty rooms at decent prices. Under renovation at the time of writing. Beds ¥80, ④

Mandarin Garden 9 Zhuang Yuan Jing ⓣ025/2202555, ⓕ2201876. A stylish place to stay with hundreds of rooms and five-star amenities. In a great location, right in the heart of lively Fuzi Miao, situated on a small lane facing the southern end of Taiping Lu. ⑦

Nanjing 259 Zhongshan Bei Lu ⓣ025/3411888. Right opposite the *Hongqiao*, this is a slightly old-fashioned, stately hotel set in large secluded gardens. ⑥

Sheraton Kingsley 185 Hanzhong Lu, two blocks west of Xinjiekou ⓣ025/6509478, ⓕ6519990. As plush and luxurious as its sister hotels all over the world. Doubles priced from ¥1600. ⑨

Shuangmenlou 185 Huju Bei Lu, near the intersection with Zhongshan Bei Lu ⓣ025/8805961 ext 280, ⓕ8801421. Not a bad place, it offers some of the cheapest rooms in Nanjing in the as yet unrenovated wing, and is surrounded by large gardens. ⑤

Xihuamen Zhongshan Dong Lu, south side ⓣ025/4596221 ext 2888. Just west of a small canal about 2km east of Xinjiekou. Quite an attractive place set in gardens, and relatively cheap with perfectly decent rooms. ⑤

Xinli Jianning Lu ⓣ025/5504688 ext 281. Immediately north of the main long-distance bus station, and offering clean, airy, recently renovated rooms. ⑤

Xuanwu 193 Zhongyang Lu, just north of Hunan Lu ⓣ025/3358888, ⓕ3366777. A huge place with good views over Xuanwu Hu Park, this place has pretentions to being a luxury hotel and almost makes it. ⑦

Zhongshan 200 Zhongshan Lu, at the corner of Zhujiang Lu ⓣ025/3361888 ext 0008, ⓕ3377228. Very centrally located, midway between Gulou and Xinjiekou. Rooms are spacious and elegantly furnished. A disco and an airline office on the premises. ⑥

University rooms

Nanjing Normal University (Nanshan Hotel) Ninghai Lu, off Guangzhou Lu ⓣ025/3716440, ⓕ3738174. From Beijing Lu (served by bus #13 from the train station), walk south down Shanghai Lu, then cut west down one of the small alleys to Ninghai Lu. Walk into the university campus through the imposing gate and straight ahead to the grassy oval, then bear left up a slope; the *Nanshan* is at the top. This student accommodation is actually a very pleasant, relaxing place to stay, though it's sometimes full (particularly during the summer), so make a reservation in advance – the telephone operators speak English. Beds ¥70, ③

Nanjing University Foreign Students' Residence Shanghai Lu ⓣ025/3593589, ⓕ3594699. Take bus #13 from the train station to Beijing Lu, then it's a short walk south; you'll see the high-rise building on your left, entered via a small lane. Excellent two-bed rooms with or without attached bath. ③–⑤

The City and around

Nanjing is huge, and a thorough exploration of all its sights would take several days. The **downtown** area actually comprises three main focal points, **Gulou**, **Xinjiekou** and **Fuzi Miao**. Of these Xinjiekou and Fuzi Miao are the most interesting areas for simply wandering, with historic buildings, pedestrianized shopping streets, canals, some good restaurants and the interesting Museum of the Taiping Uprising. It's a long five-kilometre walk to take in all three centres, though a number of bus routes, including #1, #16, #26 and #33, pass through or near all of them.

The **north** of the city takes in the enormous **Xuanwu Hu Park** and the **Yangzi River** area, while to the **west** are a number of smaller parks, including the Ming **Chaotian Palace** and the **Memorial to the Victims of the Nanjing Massacre**. The **east** and the **south** contain some of the best-preserved relics of Nanjing's mighty Ming **city wall**, as well as the excellent **Nanjing Museum**. However, the most interesting area of all for tourists is the green hill beyond the city walls to the east of the city, **Zijin Shan**, with its wealth of historical and cultural relics. If you only have a day or two to spare, you should at least try and see Zijin Shan, the Nanjing Massacre Museum, the city wall and the **Tianchao Palace**, the former seat of government under both the nineteenth-century Taipings and the Nationalists. With more time, you'll find the imposing **Qixia Si**, 22km northeast, well worth a day-trip from the city.

Gulou

The **Gulou** area, around the junction between Zhongyang Lu, Zhongshan Lu and Beijing Lu, is the administrative centre in the heart of old Nanjing. When Nanjing became a Treaty Port in the mid-nineteenth century, the foreign consulates were all based here, though today it comprises mostly traffic jams overlooked by offices. There are just a couple of relics from earlier times, both rather lost in the bustle. One, immediately west of the main traffic circle, is the six-hundred-year-old Gulou itself (daily 8am–midnight; ¥5), a small, solid **drum tower** on a grassy mound in the road, entered through a traditional-style gateway and surrounded by vendors of rain flower pebbles (see p.456). Historically, a drum used to call the watch from here seven times a day, and sound warnings at times of danger; now the interior holds exhibits of amateur paintings, while the tower itself has been semi-converted into a teahouse. A ghastly legend surrounds the fourteenth-century bell sitting outside – it's said that the emperor ordered the bell be fused by the blood of a virgin. The two daughters of the city's blacksmith apparently threw themselves into the furnace so that their father could obey the emperor and escape the penalty of death. The large stone stele in the middle of the teahouse commemorates the reign of Emperor Kangxi in the seventeenth century.

The other sight by Gulou is the **Dazhong Ting** (Great Bell Pavilion), immediately northeast of the junction behind the China Telecom building, sitting in a well-kept garden and also home to a pleasant teahouse.

Xinjiekou

Nearly 2km due south of Gulou along Zhongshan Lu lies the main commercial and geographical centre of Nanjing, **Xinjiekou**. Adorned by a statue of Sun Yatsen, the huge traffic circle at its heart does not contain any specific sights, but the streets teem with banks, hotels and department stores, and quite major sights lie within walking distance.

Shortly to the east, about fifteen minutes' walk from Xinjiekou and a short block north, on Changjiang Lu (running into Hanfu Jie), are a couple of fascinating buildings. The first of these is an otherwise obscure government building at 292 Changjiang Lu, the **Tianchao Gong** (Palace of the Heavenly Kingdom; daily 8am–5pm; ¥10), located in the Suzhou-esque **Xu Yuan**

Garden. From a historical point of view, this is one of the most interesting buildings in China. Tianchao Gong and Xu Yuan were both built more than six hundred years ago as the private residence and gardens of a Ming prince, and were subsequently turned into the seat of the provincial governor under the Qing. In 1853 the building was seized by the armies of the Taiping Heavenly Kingdom and converted into the headquarters of Taiping leader Hong Xiuquan. Later, after the overthrow of the Qing, it became the Guomindang Government's Presidential Palace. It was from here, in the early decades of the twentieth century, that first Sun Yatsen and later Chiang Kaishek governed China. Visiting the palace today, you'll see exhibitions of the Taiping Uprising and of the life and times of Sun Yatsen. Even the hated Chiang Kaishek appears in a few photos. The surrounding garden is a favourite destination of Nanjing families and can get very crowded at weekends.

A short walk east is the **Meiyuan Xincun** (daily 8am–5pm; ¥8), the former office of the Chinese Communist Party, headed by Zhou Enlai, who was based here during the time of the Guomindang government. The Communists and the Guomindang held a failed series of peace talks here in 1946 and 1947, which broke down soon thereafter into civil war. Now a museum, it's worth a visit of only to observe the bitterly anti-GMD slant of the explanations (most of which are in English.) There are one or two fascinating photos, including a little-known snap of Chiang Kaishek and Mao Zedong standing chatting together.

In the other direction from Xinjiekou – about 1km to the southwest – on Jianye Lu (bus route #4 from Fuzi Miao), is the former Ming palace, the **Chaotian Gong**, now containing the **Municipal Museum** (daily 8am–5pm; ¥15 including the court rites show). The large square that houses the palace, bounded by a high vermilion wall on one side and a gateway protected by tigers on the other, is supposedly the site of the ancient Ye Cheng (Foundry City), built in the fifth century BC. During the Han dynasty, the square also served as a meeting place where peasants could gather to offer sacrifices to the heavens or ask for a fruitful harvest. The palace was subsequently built here in 1384 by the Ming, and used by nobles to worship their ancestors, as well as for audiences with the emperor – hence the name Chaotian, meaning Worshipping Heaven. Later it became a seat of learning and a temple to Confucius, before becoming a tiny museum, which contains a few excellent bronzes. In the palace square, there is additionally a display of **Ming-dynasty court rites** (daily 11.15am–12.15pm), showing the emperor's entrance surrounded by courtiers, eunuchs, guards and dancing girls. It's touristy and amusing rather than seriously educational, but quite an elaborate show.

Fuzi Miao

Another 2km farther south of Xinjiekou, near the terminus of bus #1, is the Fuzi Miao (Temple of Confucius) area, which begins south of Jiankang Lu, around the bottom end of Taiping Lu, and harbours a noisy welter of street vendors, boutiques, arcades and restaurants. On a hot day, nothing beats slurping on a *lüdou shatou*, a drink made of green beans with shaved ice (¥3), sold by the streetside stalls.

The central **Temple of Confucius** itself, which resembles a Disney Confucian theme park inside, complete with mannequins in fancy dress, is hardly worth bothering about, but there's also an attractive waterfront area (where the Tang poet Liu Yuxi composed his most famous poem, *Wuyi Lane*), along which you can pick up canal **leisure boats** (¥10) that trundle south to Zhonghua Men. Cross the canal in front of the temple, and a short walk southeast brings you to

The Taiping Uprising

One of the consequences of the weakness of the Qing dynasty in the nineteenth century was the extraordinary **Taiping Uprising**, an event that would lead to the slaughter of millions, and has been described as the most colossal civil war in the history of the world. The Taipings were led by **Hong Xiuquan**, failed civil-service candidate and Christian evangelist, who, following a fever, declared himself to be the younger brother of Jesus Christ. In 1851, he assembled twenty thousand armed followers at **Jintian village**, near Guiping in Guangxi Province, and established the **Taiping Tianguo**, or Kingdom of Heavenly Peace. This militia then routed the local Manchu forces, and by the following year were sweeping up through Hunan into central China. They **captured Nanjing** in 1853, but though the kingdom survived another eleven years, this was its last achievement. Poorly planned expeditions failed to take Beijing or win over western China, and Hong's leadership – originally based on the enfranchisement of the peasantry and the outlawing of opium, alcohol and sexual discrimination – devolved into paranoia and fanaticism. After a gigantic struggle, **Qing forces** finally managed to unseat the Taipings when Western governments sent in assistance, most notably in the person of Queen Victoria's personal favourite, Charles "Chinese" Gordon.

Despite the rebellion's ultimately disastrous failure and its overtly Christian message, the whole episode is seen as a precursor to the arrival of communism in China. Indeed, in its fanatical rejection of Confucianism and the incredible damage it wrought on buildings and sites of historic value, it finds curious echoes in Mao Zedong's Cultural Revolution.

a small park, **Bailuzhou** (Egret Isle). This ancient corner of the city remained the Chinese quarter after the arrival of the Manchu Qing dynasty in the seventeenth century, and the area is still full of traditional houses.

Ten minutes' walk west of the Temple of Confucius and right on the small Zhanyuan Lu, just east of Zhonghua Lu, is the **Taiping Heavenly Kingdom History Museum** (daily 7am–5pm; ¥10), located in the former residence of Xu Da, a Ming prince, and well worth a visit. The sad but fascinating story of the Taiping Uprising (see box), which culminated in the occupation of Nanjing by rebels from 1853 to 1864, is told here in pictures and relics, with English captions. The building itself was the residence of one of the rebel generals during the uprising.

Xuanwu Hu Park

North of the centre, to the east of Zhongyang Lu and south of the train station, the enormous **Xuanwu Hu Park** (daily 5am–9pm; ¥15) comprises mostly water, with hills on three sides and the city wall skirting the western shore. Formerly a resort for the imperial family and once the site of a naval inspection by Song emperor Xiaowu, it became a park in 1911 and is a pleasant place to stroll and mingle with the locals who come here en masse to relax at weekends. The lake is 5km long and contains five small **islets** linked by causeways and bridges, with restaurants, teahouses, pavilions, rowing boats, paddle boats with awnings, places to swim, an open-air theatre and a zoo. The most scenic of the islands is **Yingzhou**, in a part of the inner lake covered with lily pads and surrounded by fantastical trees with trunks shaped like corkscrews. The most convenient point to enter the park is through Xuanwu Gate, on Zhongyang Lu about 1km north of Gulou (bus #1). The southern end of the park contains one of the better-preserved reaches of the city wall. There is a ticket booth on Jiwusi Lu (daily

6.30am–7pm; ¥5), but you can climb up for free by continuing farther east to the end of the wall.

Around the Yangzi River

The far northwest of town in the area of the **Yangzi River** offers a modicum of interest. The **Nanjing Treaty Museum** (daily 8am–4.30pm; ¥4), located in **Jinghai Si**, lies very near the West train station off Rehe Lu; it's on a narrow alley through an archway directly opposite Longjiang Lu. It was here in this temple that the British and Chinese negotiated the first of the many unequal treaties in the wake of the Opium War in 1843 (the treaty was later signed on a British naval ship in Nanjing harbour). Unfortunately, the museum's detailed exposition of fractious Sino–British relations throughout the nineteenth and twentieth centuries is in Chinese only, but the temple is a very pleasant place to stroll around nonetheless. It was originally built in the Ming Dynasty by Emperor Chengzu to honour the fourteenth-century naval hero Zhenghe, who led the Chinese fleet on exploratory voyages to East Africa and the Persian Gulf.

The streets around Jinghai Si, the **West train station** (bus #16 from Gulou and Xinjiekou) and the port, just beyond the city wall, are quite atmospheric and a good place to wander, with their crumbling alleys and smelly fish markets. Marking the junction between Rehe Lu and Zhongshan Bei Lu, the huge stone monument, **Dujiang Jinianbei**, was erected in memory of the crossing of the river from the north and the capture of Nanjing by the Communists in 1949.

If you're in this area you should definitely take a look at the 1.5-kilometre-long **double-decker bridge** over the Yangzi, still a source of great pride to the Chinese who built it under their own steam after the Russians pulled out in 1960. Before the bridge was built, trains and road vehicles took an hour and a half to ferry across the river. For a great view of the structure and the banks of the Yangzi, head for **Great Bridge Park** (daily 7am–4.30pm) on the eastern bank; you can ride in an elevator up to a raised platform above the upper (road) deck of the bridge, for ¥4. To reach Great Bridge Park, take bus #15 from Zhongyang Men or Gulou.

West of the centre

The west and southwest of the city have a few minor and one major sights to offer. Between Caochangmen Dajie and Hanzhong Lu, an impressive bastion of the city wall towers high above the small Qinhuai River. This is part of the original city wall, around two thousand years old. Although it was constantly strengthened and eventually became part of the Ming defences, the original structure, of red rock in places, is still plainly visible along a three-hundred-metre section of the wall. You can see it from bus #18, which runs outside the walls between Xinjiekou and the West train station. Inside the wall is a sprinkling of small parks, most of which are mobbed by locals at weekends but which still offer, in places, a sense of open space. Arguably the best of these is the tiny **Wulong Park** (daily 7am–5.30pm; ¥2), to the south, often full of old musicians who gather to sing opera and play traditional instruments.

Farther south, just across the narrow Qinhuai River, lies the entrance to **Mochou Hu Park** (daily 6.30am–midnight; ¥12; bus ¥7 from Fuzi Miao), which is only worth the rather steep entrance fee during uncrowded weekdays – at weekends, this park is invaded by hordes of loud schoolchildren. An open-air stage juts out into the lake here, with a substantial teahouse behind. A clutch of pavilions and walkways includes the **Square Pavilion**, with a statue of the

Nanjing's city walls

Nanjing was walled as many as 2500 years ago, and traces of the original red stone wall can still be seen at Stone City in the west of the city. The present **city wall**, however, is basically the work of the first Ming emperor, who extended and strengthened the earlier walls in 1369–73. Built of brick and more than 32km long, his wall followed the contours of the country, skirting Xuanwu Hu in the north, fringing Xijin Shan in the east, and tracing the Qinhuai River (which doubled as a moat) to the west and south. The wall was mainly paid for by rich families resettled here by the emperor: one third of it was "donated" by a single native of Wuxiang in Zhejiang Province. Its construction employed two hundred thousand conscripts, who ensured that the bricks were all the same size and specification, each one bearing the names of the workman and overseer. They were held together, to an average height of twelve metres and a thickness of seven, by a mixture of lime and glutinous rice paste.

legendary maiden, Mochou, after whom the lake is named: her name means "sorrow-free" because her sweet singing could soothe away all unhappiness. Ming emperor Zhu Yuanzhang once played a pivotal game of chess with his first general in the **Winning Chess Building**, next to the Square Pavilion.

West of the park is the must-see **Memorial to the Nanjing Massacre** (daily 8.30am–4.30pm; ¥10; bus ¥7). A visit to this grim, gravelly garden includes a gruesome display of victims' skulls and bones, half-buried in the dirt, as well as a clearly marked (in English) pictographic account of the incredible sufferings endured by the Chinese at the hands of the Japanese army during World War II. The last room displays contrite letters written by Japanese schoolchildren.

South of the centre

Another excellent place to see fortifications is at **Zhonghua Men** in the far south, now bereft of its wall and isolated in the middle of a traffic island, just inside the river moat on the bus #16 route from Xinjiekou and Gulou. This colossal gate actually comprises four gates, one inside another, and its seven enclosures were designed to hold three thousand men in case of enemy attack, making it one of the biggest of its kind in China. Today you can walk through the central archway and climb up two levels, passing arched recesses which are used for displays and snack stalls and are beautifully cool in summer. Up above, there's a tremendous view of the gates with the city spread out beyond.

The road south, across the Qinhuai River, between Zhonghua Men and Yuhuatai Park, is an interesting stretch lined with two-storey wooden-fronted houses, many with balconies above, while below are small shops and workshops. The all-purpose trees lining the pavement provide shade as well as room to hang birdcages, pot plants and laundry. Just beyond, the road reaches a small hill, now a park known as **Yuhuatai** (daily 6am–6.45pm; ¥8). In legend it was here that a fifth-century Buddhist monk delivered sermons so moving that flowers rained down from the sky upon him. You still see Chinese tourists grubbing around here for the multicoloured pebbles called *yuhuashi* (literally rain-flower stones), associated with the legend. Sadly, however, the hill also has other very much less pleasant connotations. After 1927 it was used as an execution ground, and the Guomindang is said to have murdered vast numbers of people here. The spot is now marked by a **Martyrs' Memorial**, a colossal composite of nine thirty-metre-high figures, well worth seeing as a prime example of gigantic Chinese Socialist Realism. The park itself is pleasantly laid out on a slope thickly forested with pine trees, where you can witness locals giving their cagebirds an airing in the cool of the morning, while they gossip and play cards underneath. You can climb the four-storey pagoda on the hillock behind the memorial for excellent views of Nanjing, despite the persistent pollution, to the north.

East of the centre

On Zhongshan Dong Lu, about 3km east of Xinjiekou (buses #5 and #9 from Xinjiekou; #20 from Gulou), the huge **Nanjing Museum** (daily 9am–4.45pm; ¥20) is one of the best provincial museums in China, especially in terms of clarity of explanations – nearly everything is labelled in English. Its highlights include some superb examples of silk-embroidered sedan chairs and several heavy cast bronzes, dating from as early as the Western Zhou (1100–771 BC). The jade and lacquerwork sections, as well as the model Fujian trading ships, are also well worth seeing.

A short walk east of the museum is **Zhongshan Men**, the easternmost gate of the ancient city walls. You can climb up to the top of the wall here, and walk along a little way to the north before the structure crumbles into a small lake, Qian Hu. It's surprisingly spacious and peaceful on the top and affords excellent views. In the morning, you can watch many of Nanjing's elders doing their daily exercises on the top of the wall.

Zijin Shan

Not far outside Zhongshan Men is **Zijin Shan** (Purple Gold Mountain), named after the colour of its rocks. Traditionally, the area has been a cool and shady spot to escape the furnace heat of Nanjing's summer, with beautiful fragrant woods and stretches of long grass, but here also are the three most visited sites in Nanjing. Of these, the centrepiece, right in the middle of the hill, is **Zhongshan Ling**, the magnificent mausoleum of China's first president, Sun Yatsen. To the east of Zhongshan Ling is the **Linggu Si** complex, and to the west are the ancient **Ming Xiaoling**, tombs of the Ming emperors who ruled China from Nanjing.

Visiting the three main sites on Zijin Shan can easily take a full day, though access to and from the hill is not difficult. Large numbers of private **minibuses** run along Zhongshan Dong Lu on the way to Zijin Shan; most terminate at Zhongshan Ling (¥3) but some go via one of the other two sites. Bus #9 goes to Zhongshan Ling via Linggu Si from Xinjiekou, while bus #20 heads to Ming Xiaoling from Gulou. Private minibuses and a host of private operators also make the trek from the train station square. Perhaps the best way to visit all three is to catch a bus from town to either Ming Xiaoling or Linggu Si, and then walk to the other two sites – this enables you to avoid backtracking. Various half-day **bus tours** are also available from town; ask at any travel service or upmarket hotel.

If you're interested in an overview of the whole mountain, you can ride a **cable car** to the peak from a station about 1km east of Taiping Men, the gate by the southern end of Xuanwu Hu Park (one-way ¥25, return ¥40).

Linggu Si

Starting from the eastern side of the hill, farthest from the city, the first, if least interesting sight on Zijin Shan, is the collection of buildings around **Linggu Si** (daily 8am–5pm; ¥15 entry to the whole site). If you arrive here by bus, the main building in front of you is the so-called **Beamless Hall**. Completed in 1381, and much restored since, it's unusual for its large size, but particularly for

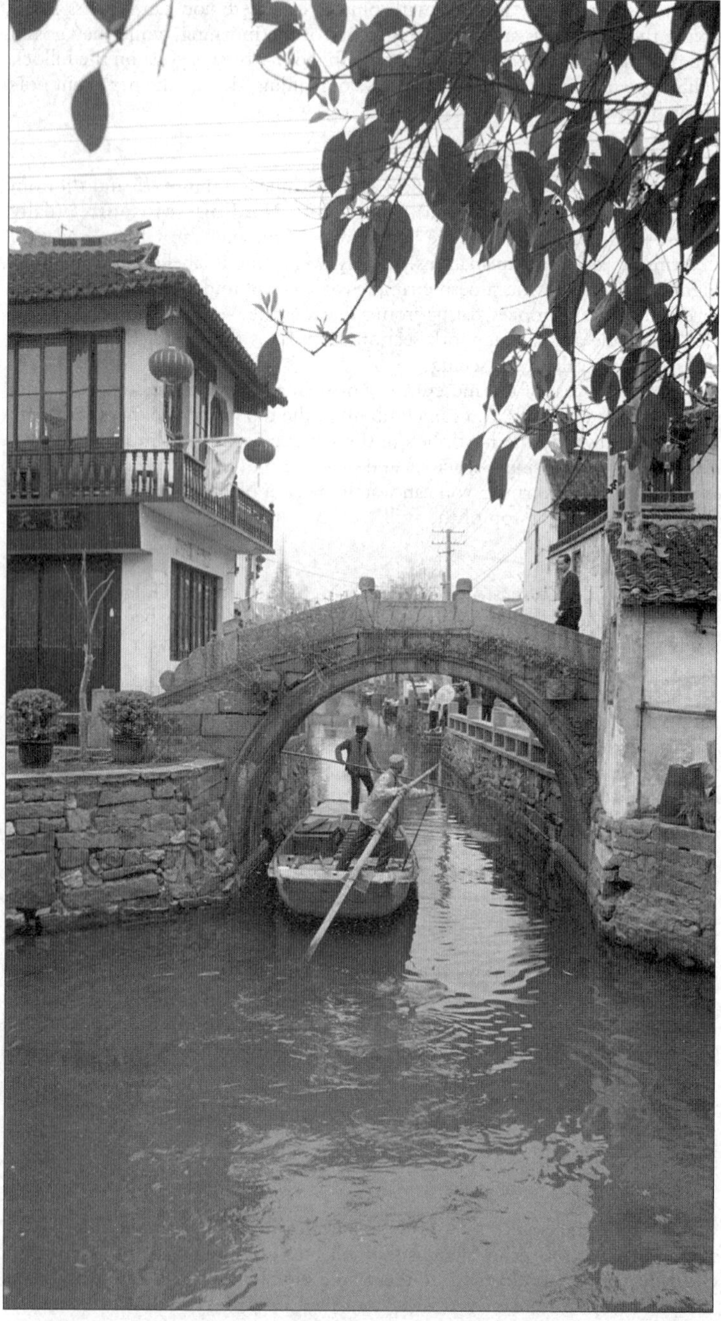

△ The atmospheric old canals of Suzhou

its self-supporting brick arch construction with five columns instead of a central beam. The hall was used to store Buddhist sutras before the Taiping rebels made it a fortress; now it's an exhibition hall.

A couple of minutes' walk east from the Beamless Hall is the Linggu Si itself, a very much smaller, and much restored, version of its original self, but still a thoroughly active temple attended by monks in yellow robes. North of the hall stands a small pavilion surrounded by beautiful cypresses and pines, and north of this again is the **Linggu Ta**, an octagonal, nine-storey, sixty-metre-high pagoda, dating back to the 1930s and built, rather extraordinarily, as a monument to the Guomindang members killed in the fighting against insurgent Communists in 1926–27. It's well worth climbing up for the views over the surrounding countryside.

Although the Linggu buildings and Zhongshan Ling are connected by a shuttle bus (¥1), there's also a delightful and fairly clear footpath through the wood between the two, leading northwest from the Linggu buildings. On the way, you'll pass one or two more buildings, including the **Zangjinglou** (Buddhist Library) at the top of a grand stairway, which now houses the rather dull **Sun Yatsen Museum** – a collection of pictures with explanations in Chinese only.

Zhongshan Ling

Dr Sun Yatsen, the first president of post-imperial China and the only hero revered by Chinese jointly on both sides of the Taiwan Straits, is, if anything, growing in status as China gropes towards a post-communist future and closer relations with Taiwan. This is reflected in the incredible pulling power of the former leader's mausoleum, the **Zhongshan Ling** (daily 6.30am–6.30pm; ¥25; compulsory bag deposit) which, with its famous marble stairway soaring up the green hillside, is one of the most popular sites for Chinese tourists in the entire country. Walking up the steps (you can instead ride a sedan chair for ¥50) is something that every tourist to Nanjing has to do once, if nothing else for the great views back down the stairs and across the misty, rolling hills to the south.

An imposing structure of white granite and deep blue tiles (the Nationalist colours), set off by the dark green pine trees, the mausoleum was completed in 1929, four years after Sun Yatsen's death. From the large bronze statue at the bottom, 392 marble steps lead up to the Memorial Hall, dominated by a five-metre-tall seated white marble figure of the great man himself. Beyond the marble figure is the burial chamber with another marble effigy lying on the stone coffin, from where, according to unsubstantiated rumours, the bones were removed to Taiwan by fleeing Guomindang leaders in 1949. The Guomindang ideals – Nationalism, Democracy and People's Livelihood – are carved above the entrance to the burial chamber in gold on black marble.

Ming Xiaoling

A thirty-five-minute walk along the road west from Zhongshan Ling brings you to the **Ming Xiaoling** (daily 8am–5.30pm; ¥15), the burial place of Zhu Yuan Zhang, founder of the Ming dynasty and the only one of its fourteen emperors to be buried at Nanjing (his thirteen successors are all buried in Beijing; see p.142). So colossal was the task of moving earth and erecting the stone walls that it took two years and a hundred thousand soldiers and conscripts to complete the tomb in 1383. Although the site was originally far larger than the Ming tombs near Beijing, its halls and pavilions, and 22-kilometre-long enclosing vermilion wall, were mostly destroyed by the Taipings. Today what remains is a walled collection of beautiful trees, stone bridges and dilapidated gates leading to the lonely wooded mound at the back containing the (as yet unexcavated) burial site of the emperor and his wife, as well as the fifty courtiers and maids of honour who were buried alive to keep them company.

The Ming Xiaoling actually comprises two parts, the tomb itself and the approach to the tomb, known as Shandao (Sacred Way) or, more commonly, **Shixiang Lu** (Stone Statue Road; daily 8am–6.30pm; ¥10) – which leads to the tomb at an oblique angle as a means of deterring evil spirits, who can only travel in straight lines. It's a strange and magical place to walk through, the road lined with twelve charming pairs of stone animals – including lions, elephants and camels – and four pairs of officials, each statue being carved from a single block of stone. The pairs of animals here are grouped together on a central grass verge, with the road passing either side, while the officials stand among the trees farther off. Most people visit the tomb first and the approach afterwards, simply because the road from Zhongshan Ling arrives immediately outside the tomb entrance. To reach the Sacred Way from the tomb entrance, follow the road right (with the tomb behind you) and then round to the left for about fifteen minutes.

Next to Ming Xiaoling is the entrance to **Zixia Hu** (daily 7am–6pm; ¥10), a small lake whose wooded surroundings are perfect for a comfortable stroll at any time of year. In summer, the lake is open for swimming, although you should avoid the weekends when the place is full of Nanjing residents escaping the heat of the city.

One more sight 2 or 3km to the north of the Ming Xiaoling is the **Zijin Shan Observatory** (¥10), built in 1929 high on one of the three peaks where the Taipings formerly had a stronghold. For fresh air and good views of Nanjing, try to find a minibus heading this way.

Around Nanjing: Qixia Si

Built by the fifth-century monk Shao Shezhai, **Qixia Si** (daily 7am–5.30pm; ¥10) is today one of China's largest Buddhist seminaries, reposing in wooded hillside northeast of Nanjing. There are two main temple halls, the front one housing two whole walls of flying *apsaras* and a statue of a cross-legged Maitreya Buddha, the latter a statue of a standing Vairocana Buddha. Directly behind the temple stretch the so-called **Thousand Buddha Cliffs**, featuring 515 statues carved directly into the rockface. Many of the Buddhas' heads are missing, victims of the Cultural Revolution, but the ones who escaped intact carry an amusing variety of expressions, from sombre to jovial. Several of the reliefs date from the fifth-century Qi dynasty, but most were created in the Song and Tang. The woods behind the cliffs make for a pleasant day-long stroll, with tiny pavilions seemingly marking every other turn in the trail. Qixia is easily reached by public bus or private minibus from the train station square on a sign in the front of each bus); the journey takes 45 minutes or less.

Eating

Nanjing has a wide selection of local, regional Chinese and foreign foods, often at much more reasonable prices than their counterparts in nearby Shanghai. It's an especially great place to sample **Jiangsu cuisine**, most notably *yanshui ya* (salted duck), so renowned that it has now become a country-wide favourite. The duck is first pressed and salted, then steeped in brine and baked – the skin should be creamy-coloured and the flesh red and tender. Other Jiangsu dishes worth trying include *majiang yaopian* (pig's intestines), *jiwei xia* (a lake crustacean vaguely resembling a lobster, but much better tasting, locals affirm) and *paxiang jiao* (a type of vegetable that resembles banana leaves). The best areas of town to sample Jiangsu food are in the north of town, north of Gulou along Zhongyang Lu and northwest along Zhongshan Bei Lu.

The presence of a heavy contingent of foreign students in the city, as well as a growing population of expatriate and home-grown business people, ensures a scattering of highly **Westernized restaurants and bars**, which are not always that expensive. There are, in particular, a number of places around the Nanjing University Foreign Students' Residence that cater to Western palates. Otherwise Xinjiekou and Fuzi Miao are generally good districts to browse for restaurants. For standard **Chinese snacks** – noodles, Sichuan hotpot, *jiaozi* and *wonton* soup – promising areas include Ninghai Lu, just north from the main entrance of the Normal University; the area just west of Fuzi Miao; and the area immediately southeast of Xinjiekou.

Restaurants

Black Cat Along an alley near the junction of Hanzhong Lu and Mochou Lu. A tall metal telephone pole marks the mouth of the alley. The decor's not great, but you can get a good meal of steak, chips and as much salad as you can eat here for just ¥40. There is another branch around the corner in the Great Eagle Building.

Chaozhou In the *Nanjing Hotel* compound on Zhongshan Bei Lu. Expensive, banquet-style Chaozhounese cuisine, such as the delicious *chongcao* (a vegetable whose shape vaguely resembles an insect) and *jiayu* (a member of the tortoise family). There's a saucy floorshow of Russian dancers at 7pm.

Daniang Shuijiao In the basement of the Xinjiekou Department Store, on the traffic circle. More than forty varieties of cheap and filling dumplings on offer here, most for under ¥5 each.

Fusheng Yuan Yunnan Lu, just off Hunan Lu. Dishes up Nanjing and Yangzhou specialities in pleasant surroundings. Locals especially go for the excellent hotpot.

Gold and Silver Jinying Lu, just off Shanghai Lu. The best of a number of Chinese restaurants catering to especially Nanjing University students. Their *mantou* – served fried and doused in condensed milk – makes an excellent dessert.

Haitian Ge 179 Zhongyang Lu, just north of the Hunan Lu intersection and opposite Xuanwu Hu. Jiangsu and Beijing fare, especially salted duck, are the specialities, but the kitchen also makes several Macanese dishes that are well worth trying. Reasonable prices and very popular with locals; it's packed from 5pm onwards.

Hefeng 75 Zhongshan Lu, in the *Central Hotel*. Wonderfully presented and deliciously inexpensive Japanese food. You could eat your fill of sushi here for under ¥50.

Henry's 33 Huaqiao Lu. Tasty pasta, salad, steak and burger dishes, most for under ¥25.

Jack's Corner of Jinying Lu and Shanghai Lu, directly across from the Nanjing University foreign students' dormitory. Western and Japanese food in a backpacker-friendly setting, plus good coffee, though they don't usually open early enough for breakfast. There's another branch directly across the street from the Nanjing Normal University main gate and an upmarket branch, specializing in Italian food, 35 Wangfu Jie.

Jiangsu 26 Jiankang Lu, just east of Zhonghua Lu in Fuzi Miao near the Taiping Museum. One of the most upmarket places to try local food – *yanshui ya* is a speciality.

Jiaozi Wang Ninghai Lu near the intersection with Guangzhou Lu near the Normal University. Another excellent-value dumpling place, with every imaginable type of *jiaozi* available. A student favourite.

Jinzhu 204 Zhongshan Bei Lu, on the north side between Xin Mofan Malu and the Hunan Lu traffic circle. Locals pack this family joint offering Jiangsu specialities at very reasonable prices – most dishes, even specials, are under ¥30. Ask about the excellent seafood specials, which are constantly changing.

Lao Zhengxing 119 Gongyuan Jie, near Fuzi Miao. A traditional, lively place with interesting local dishes, backing onto the river. A favourite of Kuomintang officials in the 1930s.

Musilin Noodles Ninghai Lu, near Hankou Xi Lu and the Normal University front gate. Cheap, filling Xinjiang-style *lamian* (pulled noodles). A student favourite.

Shanghai Tan On a small alley directly behind the *Central Hotel* off Guanjia Qiao, near Xinjiekou. Excellent Shanghainese cuisine with the odd Jiangsu dish (notably *yanshui ya*) thrown in. The seafood is especially good. Very popular with locals.

Swede and Kraut 14 Nan Xiui Cun – an alley off Shanghai Lu – the restaurant is signposted. By far the best western food in the city and not too pricey. The pasta and bread are all homemade – the lasagna and fettucini especially are scrumptious, and the ciabatta is essential. Managed by a genteel European couple, who also run a bakery, Skyways, at 3–6 Hankou Xi Lu.

Tianyuan Longjuan Gaolou, one block northeast of Gulou. Small, family-run restaurant with an incredible deal on Beijing duck at ¥30 for two people, including soup and garnishes on the side.

Xiao Ren Ren 97 Gongyuan Jie, in Fuzi Miao. Friendly place designed in the style of a traditional teahouse, with musicians serenading patrons. You can try a smorgasbord of local delicacies for just ¥38.

Yinghua Yuan Just off Hanzhong Lu, in the basement (a staircase from the pavement leads down to it). Intimate decor and tasty, reasonably priced Jiangsu and Shanghainese food make this one of the most popular restaurants in town with locals. The wild rabbit stew is a perennial favourite.

Drinking and entertainment

Nanjing **nightlife** is nowhere near as varied as Shanghai's, but there are some pretty good bars and discos – our pick appears below – with a mixed clientele of foreigners, most of them students, and Chinese. A night out is inexpensive as cover charges are generally waived for foreigners and beers can be as cheap as ¥10 per bottle.

Nanjing's cultural life, however, is sadly lagging far behind Shanghai's, though your visit might coincide with infrequent acrobatics or Chinese opera performances somewhere in town. The lecturers and foreign students at the *Nanjing University Foreign Student's Residence* are often in tune with the latest happenings. Upmarket hotels might also have the latest information on hand.

The Answer Jinying Lu, near the Nanjing University Foreign Students' Residence. Popular with foreign students and artsy locals, this intimate bar has frequent live music. Daily 8pm–2am.

Casablanca *Xuanwu Hotel* second floor, 193 Zhongyang Lu. Hotel disco that's more classy than hip. Daily 8pm–2.30am.

Orgies 202 Zhingshan Bei Lu. Dancers in leopard-skin bikinis followed by a raffle; only in China, surely. Popular with a young Chinese crowd, who shake their heads to artless techno. Daily 9pm–2am.

Red Balloon Bar 118 Chengxian jie, by the junction of Taiping Bei Jie and Zhongshan Dong Lu, in an alley behind a derelict hotel. Bohemian hangout with art films and live music. Daily 8pm–2am.

Scarlet's 29 Chezhan Dong Xiang, on a small lane just off Zhongshan Bei Lu several blocks west of Gulou. Two-storey bar with a western DJ playing playing dance and rock. Venue of choice for most of Nanjing's foreigner residents, who generally arrive late. Daily 6.30pm–2am.

Listings

Airlines The main CAAC reservations and ticketing office is at 52 Ruijin Lu (daily 8am–noon & 1.30–5.30pm; ⓣ025/4408583) in the southeast of town. China Eastern Airlines' head office is at the corner of Changbai Jie and Zhongshan Dong Lu (daily 8.30–6pm; ⓣ025/4400102). Smaller offices of both airlines are dotted all over town.

Banks and exchange The Bank of China head office (Mon–Fri 8am–5pm, Sat 8am–12.30pm) is a few hundred metres due south of Xinjiekou on Zhongshan Nan Lu, and there's a 24hr ATM on site. You can change traveller's cheques in any of the smaller branches, as well as at upmarket hotels if you are a guest.

Boats Buy ferry tickets to Shanghai, Wuhan, Chongqing or points in between in the large, yellow terminal directly across from the no. 4 dock on Jiangbian Lu next to the river. Alternately, CITS or CYTS will buy your tickets for you, for a small commission.

Bookshops The best selection of English-language books is in the Foreign Language Bookstore on Zhongshan Dong Lu, one block east of Xinjiekou. They also have a very large branch near Xuanwu Hu Park, on Hunan Lu just south of Zhongyang Lu.

Hospitals The most central hospital is the Gulou Hospital, on Zhongshan Lu just south of the Gulou intersection.

Internet access A multitude of Internet places serving the needs of students have sprung up along Shanghai Lu near Nanjing University and the Normal University. Laiba, inside the *Nanjing University Foreign Students' Residence* on Jinying Lu near Shanghai Lu, is one of the roomier ones.

Mail and telephones Nanjing's main post office (daily 8am–6.30pm), offering international phone and fax calls as well as postal services, is at 2 Zhongyang Lu, immediately north of Gulou. There's also a post office at 19 Zhongshan Lu, just north of Xinjiekou.

Travel agents Nearly all hotels have their own travel agencies. In addition, CITS is at 202 Zhongshan Bei Lu (daily 9am–4.30pm; Ⓣ025/3421125, Ⓕ3421960), a couple of kilometres northwest of Gulou. CTS, whose staff speak good English, is nearby at 309 Zhongshan Bei Lu (daily 8am–noon & 1.30–5.30pm; Ⓣ025/8801502, Ⓕ8801533). CYTS is at 160 Hanzhong Lu (daily 8.30am–5pm; Ⓣ025/523344) and next to the *Nanjing University Foreign Students' Residence* at 20 Jinying Jie (daily 8.30am–4.30pm; Ⓣ025/594902, Ⓕ3594904). All these firms can supply train, boat and plane tickets, and also organize local tours.

Northern Jiangsu

There's considerably less of interest once you get away from the historic canal towns in the south of Jiangsu Province. Although the canal north of the Yangzi is – in season – navigable all the way to the borders of Shandong, and occasionally even as far as the Yellow River, the only thing people are likely to be transporting in this area is coal. There is no tourist traffic along here, and frankly not a great deal to see, though you might want to break a journey between Nanjing and Qingdao here. For the most part, the country is flat and wet, ideal for **salt panning** but little else. Of the towns in the area, none positively demands attention: tiny, rural **Huai'an**, birthplace of Zhou Enlai, is an attractive old place; and heavily industrial **Xuzhou** is home to the excellent Han Dynasty Tomb..

Huai'an

HUAI'AN was already settled five thousand years ago, and has been a walled town for 1600 years, but these days it's famous throughout China as the birthplace of the much-loved Premier Zhou Enlai. The town has preserved his

Northern Jiangsu

Huai'an	淮安	***huái'ān***
Liu E's Former Residence	刘鹗故居	*liúè gùjū*
Wu Cheng'en's Former Residence	吴承恩故居	*wúchéngēn gùjū*
Xiao Hu	肖湖	*xiāohú*
Zhou Enlai's Former Residence	周恩来故居	*zhōuēnlái gùjū*
Zhou Enlai Memorial	周恩来纪念馆	*zhōuēnlái jìniànguǎn*
Accommodation		
Huai'an Binguan	淮安宾馆	*huái'ān bīnguǎn*
Jingdu	静都大酒店	*jìngdū dàjiǔdiàn*
Youdian	邮电宾馆	*yōudiàn bīnguǎn*
Xuzhou	徐洲	***xúzhōu***
Guishan Hanmu	龟山汉墓	*guīshān hànmù*
Hanhua Stone Engravings Museum	汉画像石馆	*hànhuàxiàng shíguǎn*
Heroes Hotel	茴圣楼宾馆	*huíshènglóu bīnguǎn*
Terracotta Army Museum	兵马俑博物馆	*bīngmǎyǒng bówùguǎn*

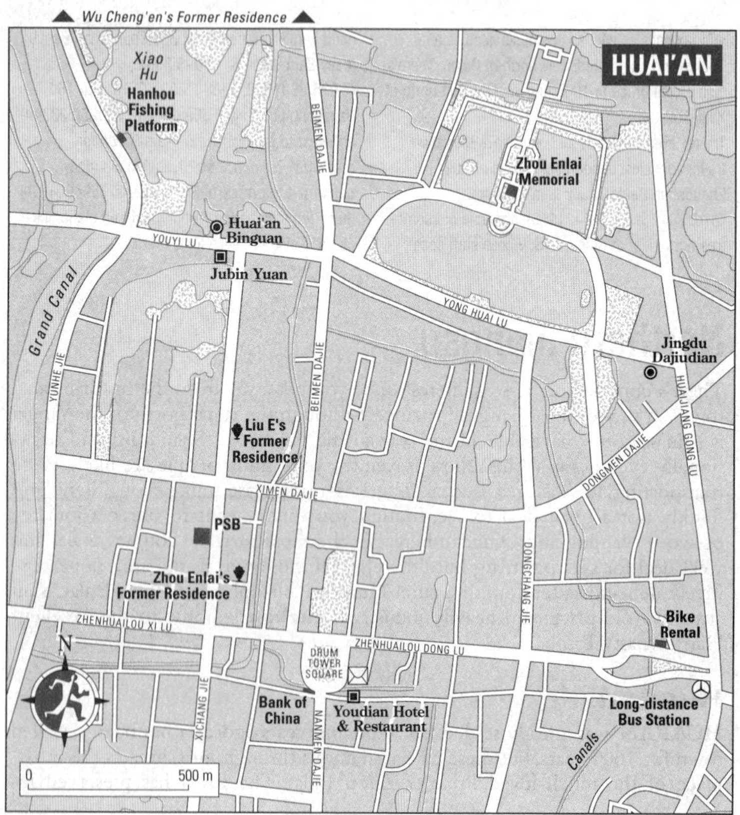

home as a national monument, as well as constructing a huge mausoleum in his honour. Apart from this, Huai'an is a quiet, attractive town of parks and lakes with a large amount of old housing, located in a fertile and agriculturally productive part of Jiangsu. Relatively few tourists make it to Huai'an, and this gives the town most of its charm.

The Town

Huai'an is one of those pleasant places where you can get around entirely on foot, and orientation is unproblematic. The main street, Zhenhuailou Lu, cuts from east to west across the middle of the city, with the central **Drum Tower Square** along it; the town's other important commercial street, Nanmen Dajie, leads south from here. The older part of town lies to the north and northwest of Drum Tower Square, with streets crammed full of little shops, restaurants, fortune-tellers, *daixie* (those who write letters on behalf of illiterate people), and interesting architecture.

Zhou Enlai's Former Residence is the main attraction in the centre of town (daily 7am–6pm; ¥10), signposted up an alley off Zhenhuailou Lu. An attractive house of black brick and heavy roof tiles, it was where Zhou was born in 1898, and has been lovingly restored to its original splendour.

Considering the several courtyards within the walls, and the separate rooms for Zhou's stepmother and wet nurse, the family were obviously well-off. As well as some interesting old wooden furniture, the house contains a small photo exhibition documenting Zhou's life, and also that of his wife, Deng Yingchao, who occupies a similarly high place in the Chinese people's affections.

Continuing north another ten minutes up the main Xichang Jie brings you to another former residence, this time of a local intellectual **Liu E**, who died in 1909. The former occupant, known in China for his achievements both as a scientist and novelist, may seem obscure to outsiders, but his house (daily 7.45am–5pm; ¥2) is a delightful place. On some afternoons you'll find traditional storytelling performances going on in the courtyards, the spoken word accompanied by a small drum. Here, amid the bamboos and goldfish ponds, you can catch an insight into the very peaceful, cultured world of old China.

The **Zhou Enlai Memorial** (daily 7.30am–6.30pm; ¥15) stands to the northeast of the centre. There are two possible entrances, one due north of the bus station along Huaijiang Gong Lu, and the other just east off Beimen Jie, about 1km north of the Drum Tower. The park, and the memorial itself, built on a small lake, seems to have been modelled on a certain presidential memorial in Washington DC – the seated statue of Zhou is remarkably similar to that of Abraham Lincoln. The craftsmanship and quality of stone, however, are sadly inferior. There is a small museum downstairs with Chinese-only explanations detailing the life of this remarkable man.

Northwest of the centre

The west of Huai'an is delineated along its entire length by the **Grand Canal**. There's a good two-hour **circular walk** here which will take you through areas almost wholly untouched by modern life. You begin by heading north along the canal from the area just west of the *Huai'an Binguan*. Along the waterway you'll be able to watch the bustle of canal life, with barges manoeuvring for position and people loading and unloading by hand. Shortly, **Xiao Hu** will appear to your right; a stone gateway by this little lake signifies that you've reached **Hanhou Fishing Platform**, an attractive walking area by the lakeside amid trees and long grass. Back on the road, and farther north from here, a right turn just where the canal begins bending round to the west takes you into an interesting old area of stone-tiled houses. If you walk approximately northeast through here along country lanes – you'll need to ask the locals for directions – you'll reach the **Former Residence of Wu Cheng'en** (daily 7.30am–4.30pm; ¥6), the sixteenth-century author of the famous classic *Journey to the West*. It's another charming old house of black brick, with colonnaded walkways and clumps of bamboo in the courtyards. From here, head east along more country lanes, through allotments and vegetable patches, before coming out on the main Beimen Jie, where you can catch a rickshaw back into town for ¥3.

Practicalities

The **bus station** is at the far eastern end of Zhenhuailou Lu. There are **Banks of China** all over town, including one on the southwestern edge of the Drum Tower Square (Mon–Fri 8–11.30am & 1.30–5pm); across the square from here is the **post office**.

Despite its few visitors, Huai'an has a handful of **accommodation** options for foreigners. Just southeast of Drum Tower Square is the friendly and clean *Youdian Hotel* (Ⓣ0517/5919501; ❸), with its own perfectly decent restaurant. The *Jingdu Hotel* is a comfortable place 1km north of the bus station, just to the southeast of the Zhou Enlai Memorial along Yonghuai Lu (❹). There's similar though more upmarket accommodation at the *Huai'an Binguan* in the north of town on Xichang Jie (❹).

There are a few places to **eat** around the downtown area; the jumble of lanes around Zhou Enlai's former residence hides several inexpensive, filling family restaurants where a huge bowl of *pingchao dofu* – delicious tofu cooked with black pepper and coriander – costs just a few yuan. Otherwise, try the *Jubin Yuan* opposite the *Huai'an Binguan* along Xichang Jie, which has a good selection of local and Sichuan hotpot dishes.

Xuzhou

At the intersection of the Beijing–Nanjing–Shanghai and Lianyungang–Zhengzhou rail lines, **XUZHOU** is primarily a coal-mining and food-processing centre, but it hides some interesting attractions that can keep visitors entertained for at least half a day, most notably the Gui Mountain Han Dynasty Tomb, where a first-century BC duke is buried. Xuzhou's other claim to fame is that, more than 2000 years ago, it was the home of Han Dynasty Emperor Liu Bang, of whose stay here little unfortunately remains.

The **train station** lies in the east of town and has connections to places as far-flung as Guangzhou and Ürümqi. Local **bus** #1 runs from here to the centre of town at the intersections of Huaihai Dong Lu and Zhongshan Lu, from where you can pick up bus #37 to take you several kilometres northwest to **Guishan Hanmu**, the tomb of Liu Zhu – the third Duke of Chu – and his wife, and certainly one of provincial China's better-displayed sights (daily 8am–5.30pm; ¥15). The couple (and the slaves who worked for them) went through much trouble to ensure that their treasures would remain with them in the afterlife: the entrance to the mausoleum was cleverly built into the contours of the neighbouring turtle-shaped hills (Guishan means Turtle Mountain) and was only discovered in the 1980s by quarrying peasants. Excellent English captions explain the purpose of each of the twenty-plus caverns, ranging from the stable where live horses were supplied with feed by servants sealed in here with the duke's body, to the squat toilet which bears an uncanny resemblance to those in China today, the treasure room (today filled with replicas), and the coffin rooms themselves.

South of town are two more sights worth your time. In the southeast stands the three-thousand-strong brigade of the **Xuzhou Terracotta Army Museum** (daily 8.30am–4.30pm; ¥14), a miniature (both in size and number) version of its more famous Xi'an counterpart. The army is believed to have protected the grave of a local prince from the Han Dynasty or earlier. Four pits are home to a myriad of archers, foot soldiers, clay horses, chariots and servants, each of whose postures and facial expressions is different. Bus #5 runs here from downtown. On the other side of town, the **Hanhua Stone Engravings Museum** (daily 8.30am–5pm; ¥5), along the eastern shore of Yunlong Hu, has a rather extensive collection of Han Dynasty stone carvings, many from Liu Bang's era. The art provides a fascinating glimpse into market life, transportation options and entertainment in that period, although there are no English captions. Bus #22 runs from the sportsground just to the south of downtown all the way here.

Xuzhou's **accommodation** options for foreigners are limited. One of the best bets is the centrally located *Heroes Hotel* on Jiahe Jie (Ⓣ0516/5730001; ❻); it's off Zhongshan Bei Lu, two blocks north of the Huaihai Lu intersection and the square marking the centre of town.

Zhejiang

ZHEJIANG, one of China's smallest provinces but also one of the wealthiest, is made up of two quite different areas. The northern part shares its climate, geography, history and the Grand Canal with Jiangsu – the land here is highly cultivated, fertile and netted with waterways, hot in summer but cold in winter. The south, however, mountainous and sparsely populated in the interior, thriving and semi-tropical on the coast, has much more in common with Fujian Province. Even the dialect spoken in the area around Wenzhou has many similarities to Fujianese.

Recent excavations have shown, contrary to expectations, that the Yangzi delta had Neolithic settlements every bit as old as those in the Yellow River valley. At Hemudu on the Shaoxing–Ningbo plain, settled farmers were growing cultivated rice and building solid, precisely structured two-storey houses as long as seven thousand years ago, when rhinoceros and elephant still roamed the land. For millennia thereafter, the region remained prosperous but provincial, politically in the shadow of the more populous Yellow River basin in northern China. The eventual economic shift to the south slowly worked to the region's advantage, however. The Grand Canal was built, and finally, in the twelfth century AD, the imperial court of the Song moved south and set up capital in Hangzhou. For over two centuries, northern Zhejiang enjoyed a spell of unprecedented power, which ended only when the capital moved back to Beijing.

The whole province has an attractive, prosperous air, but most of the tourist destinations are in the north. **Hangzhou**, the terminus of the Grand Canal, once a great capital and still a centre for silk, tea and paper-making, is one of the greenest, most attractive cities in China, with a famous lake, former resort of emperors. Nearby **Shaoxing**, a charming small town threaded by canals, offers the chance to tour its beautiful surroundings by boat, while **Ningbo**, although long superseded by Shanghai as an industrial port, is mainly of interest as a launching pad to the Buddhist island of **Putuo Shan**, offshore from Ningbo. With more temples than cars, the island is as fresh, green and tranquil as eastern China ever gets. Finally, in the south of the province, the former treaty port and current economic boomtown of **Wenzhou**, although rather isolated and individual, serves as the gateway to the lush **Yandangshan**, a nature park filled with waterfalls, pagodas and hiking possibilities.

Hangzhou

HANGZHOU, capital of the province, southern terminus of the Grand Canal, and one of China's leading tourist attractions, lies in the north of Zhejiang at the head of Hangzhou Bay. The canal has been the instrument of the city's prosperity and fortunes, establishing it for more than a thousand years as a place of great wealth and culture. As is often the case in China, the modern city is not of much interest in itself, but **Xi Hu** – the lake around which Hangzhou curls – and its shores still offer wonderful Chinese vistas of trees, hills, flowers, old causeways over the lake, fishing boats, pavilions and pagodas – all within a walk of the city centre. No tour of China would be complete without appreciating the lake's stunning natural beauty – still largely intact

Hangzhou

Hangzhou	杭州	***hángzhōu***
Art Institute	美术学院外事招待所	*měishùxuéyuàn wàishì zhāodàisuǒ*
Bai Di	白堤	*báidī*
Baopu Daoist Compound	包朴道院	*bāopǔ dàoyuàn*
Baoshu Ta	保淑塔	*bǎoshū tǎ*
Feilai Feng	飞来峰	*fēilái fēng*
Gu Shan	孤山	*gūshān*
Huanglong Dong Park	黄龙洞公园	*huánglóngdòng gōngyuán*
Hupaomeng Quan	虎跑梦泉	*hǔpǎomèng quán*
Huqingyu Tang Museum of Chinese Medcine	胡庆余堂中药博物馆	*húqìngyútáng zhōngyào bówùguǎn*
Jinci Si	净慈寺	*jìngcí sì*
Lingyin Si	灵隐寺	*língyǐn sì*
Liuhe Pagoda	六和塔	*liùhé tǎ*
Longjing	龙井	*lóngjǐng*
Nine Creeks and Eighteen Gullies Road	九溪十八涧	*jiǔxī shíbājiàn*
Santanyinyue	三潭印月	*sāntán yìnyuè*
Su Di	苏堤	*sūdī*
Xi Hu	西湖	*xīhú*
Xiling Seal Engravers' Society	西泠印社	*xīlíng yìnshè*
Yuefei Mu	岳飞墓	*yuèfēi mù*
Zhejiang Museum	浙江博物馆	*zhèjiāng bówùguǎn*
Zhongshan Park	中山公园	*zhōngshān gōngyuán*
Accommodation		
Dahua	大华饭店	*dàhuá fàndiàn*
Dongpo	东坡宾馆	*dōngpō bīnguǎn*
Haihua Novotel	海华大酒店	*hǎihuá dàjiǔdiàn*
Hangzhou University	杭州大学	*hángzhōu dàxué*
Huaqiao	华侨饭店	*huáqiáo fàndiàn*
Qingbo	青波饭店	*qīngbō fàndiàn*
Shangri-la	香格里拉饭店	*xiānggélǐlā fàndiàn*
Taipingyang	太平洋大酒店	*tàipíngyáng dàjiǔdiàn*
Xi Hu	西湖饭店	*xīhú fàndiàn*
Xinqiao	新桥饭店	*xīnqiáo fàndiàn*
Xinxin	新新饭店	*xīnxīn fàndiàn*
Zhejiang	浙江宾馆	*zhèjiāng bīnguǎn*
Zhejiang University Gusthouse	浙江大学招待所	*zhèjiāng dàxué zhāodàisuǒ*
Zhonghua	中华饭店	*zhōnghuá fàndiàn*
Eating		
Bafangyuan	八方缘	*bāfāng yuán*
Kuiyuan Guan	奎元馆	*kuíyuán guǎn*
Louwailou	楼外楼	*lóuwài lóu*
Tianwaitian	天外天	*tiānwài tiān*
Zhiweiguan	知味观	*zhīwèi guàn*

despite the ever-increasing flood of tourists – and its subsequent impact on the evolution of Chinese literature and culture.

The city is particularly busy at weekends and in summer, when it's packed with trippers escaping from the concrete jungle of Shanghai. This has pushed up hotel prices, but it also brings advantages: there are plenty of restaurants, the natural environment is being protected and the bulk of the Taiping destruction on the lakeside has been repaired (the temples rebuilt and the gardens replanted). Most of the places to see can be visited on foot or bicycle; for attractions farther afield city buses are very convenient.

Some history

Apart from the fact that **Yu the Great**, tamer of floods, is said to have moored his boats here, Hangzhou has little in the way of a legendary past or ancient history, for the simple reason that the present site, on the east shore of Xi Hu, was originally under water. Xi Hu itself started life as a wide shallow **inlet** off the bay, and it is said that Emperor Qin Shihuang sailed in from the sea and moored his boats on what is now the northwestern shore of the lake. Only around the fourth century AD did river currents and tides begin to throw up a barrier of silt which eventually resulted in the formation of the lake.

However, Hangzhou rapidly made up for its slow start. The first great impetus came from the building of the **Grand Canal** at the end of the sixth century, and Hangzhou developed with spectacular speed as the centre for trade between north and south, the Yellow and Yangzi river basins. Under the **Tang dynasty** it was a rich and thriving city, but its location between lake and river made it vulnerable to the fierce equinox tides in Hangzhou Bay. When Tang-dynasty governors were building locks and dykes to control the waters round Hangzhou, a contemporaneous writer, describing the beginning of a sea wall in 910 AD, explained that "archers were stationed on the shore to shoot down the waves while a poem was recited to propitiate the King of Dragons and Government of the Waters; the waves immediately left the wall and broke on the opposite bank so the work could go on." The problem of **floods** – and the search for remedies – was to recur down the centuries.

During the **Song dynasty**, Hangzhou received its second great impetus when the encroachment of the Tartars from the north destroyed the northern capital of Kaifeng and sent remnants of the imperial family fleeing south in search of a new base. The result of this upheaval was that from 1138 until 1279 Hangzhou became the **imperial capital**. There was an explosion in the silk and brocade industry, and indeed in all the trades that waited upon the court and their wealthy friends. When Marco Polo wrote of Hangzhou towards the end of the thirteenth century, he spoke of "the City of Heaven, the most beautiful and magnificent in the world. It has ten principal market places, always with an abundance of victuals, roebuck, stags, harts, hares, partridge, pheasants, quails, hens and ducks, geese . . . all sorts of vegetables and fruits . . . huge pears weighing ten pounds apiece. Each day a vast quantity of fish is brought from the ocean. There is also an abundance of lake fish." So glorious was the reputation of the city that it rapidly grew overcrowded. On to its sandbank Hangzhou was soon cramming more than a million people, a population as large as that of Chang'an (Xi'an) under the Tang, but in a quarter of the space – tall wooden buildings up to five storeys high were crowded into narrow streets, creating a ghastly fire hazard.

After the Southern Song dynasty was finally overthrown by the Mongols in 1279, Hangzhou ceased to be a capital city, but it remained an important centre of commerce and a place of luxury, with **parks and gardens** outside the ramparts and hundreds of boats on the lake. In later years, the Ming rulers repaired the city walls and deepened the Grand Canal so that large ships could go all the way from Hangzhou to Beijing. Two great Qing emperors, Kangxi and Qianlong, frequented the city and built villas, temples and gardens by the lake. Although the city was largely destroyed by the **Taiping Uprising** (1861–63), it recovered surprisingly quickly, and the **foreign concessions** which were established towards the end of the century – followed by the building of rail lines from Shanghai and Ningbo – stimulated the growth of new industries alongside the traditional silk and brocade manufacturers. Since 1949 the city has grown to attain a population of around one million, much the same as under the Song.

Arrival, information and transport

Hangzhou has two halves; to the east and north is **downtown**, with its shops and tourist facilities, while to the west and south the **lake** offers greenery and

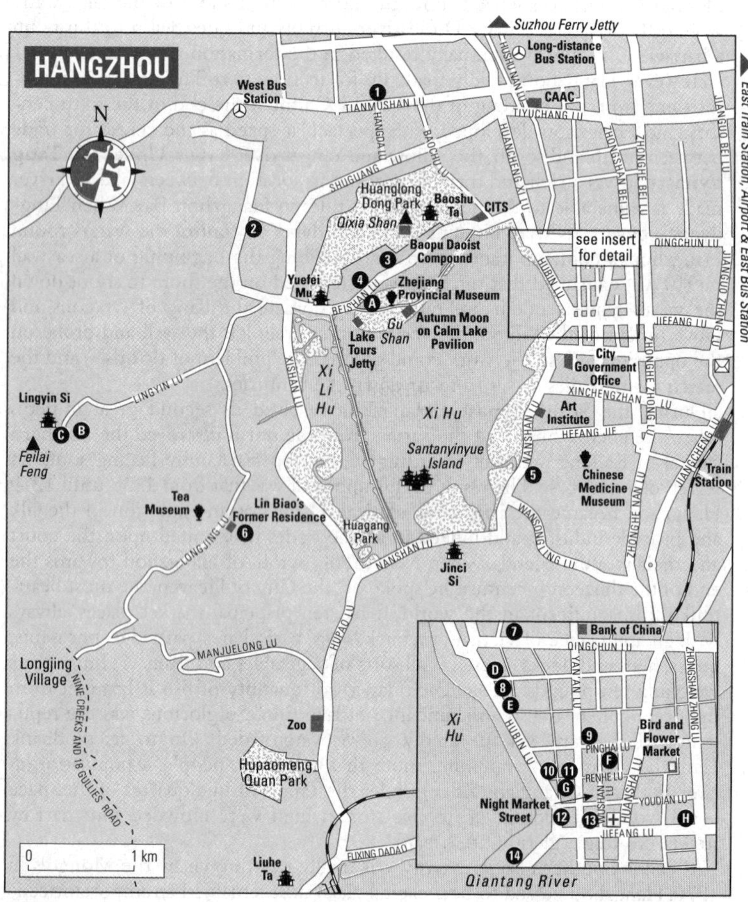

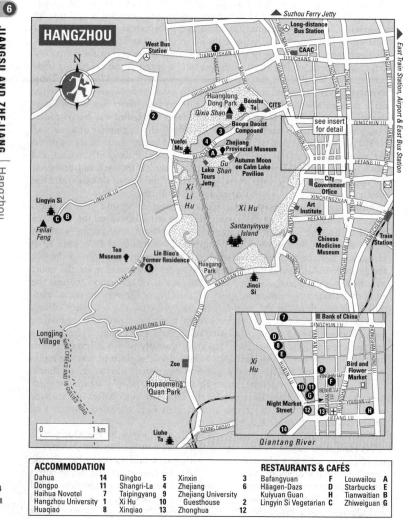

ACCOMMODATION

Dahua	14	Qingbo	5	Xinxin	3
Dongpo	11	Shangri-La	4	Zhejiang	6
Haihua Novotel	7	Taipingyang	9	Zhejiang University Guesthouse	2
Hangzhou University	1	Xi Hu	10	Zhonghua	12
Huaqiao	8	Xinqiao	13		

RESTAURANTS & CAFÉS

Bafangyuan	F	Louwailou	A
Häagen-Dazs	D	Starbucks	E
Kuiyuan Guan	H	Tianwaitian	B
Lingyin Si Vegetarian	C	Zhiweiguan	G

scenic spots. The main east–west street, **Jiefang Lu**, runs from just north of the train station in the east to the lake, with major north–south streets crossing it, including Zhongshan Lu, and, closer to the lake, Yan'an Lu. The area around the Jiefang Lu/Yan'an Lu intersection (including the lake front and the small streets just to the north) is the commercial centre of town where you can shop, stay, eat and catch buses round the lake. On the outskirts of the city, the **Qiantang River**, Hangzhou's gateway to the sea, flows well to the south and west, while the **Grand Canal** runs across to meet it from the north; many travellers to Hangzhou never see either of them.

Hangzhou's **airport** is 15km north of town, and connected by CAAC bus (¥5) to the main booking office on Tiyuchang Lu, just east of Hushu Lu. The **train station** is just 2km east of the city centre. To reach the lake from here on foot takes about forty minutes if you walk straight ahead out of the station and keep bearing right until you hit Jiefang Lu, which heads due west. Otherwise, take bus #7 direct to the lake or #151 or #152 as far as Yan'an Lu. Occasional trains only stop at the remote **East train station**; from here, while #518 goes to the centre of town.

The main **long-distance bus station** lies in the north of town, on Hushu Nan Lu, just north of Huancheng Lu; bus #151 through town to and from the train station passes here. Most long-distance buses arrive at this station, except for those from Shaoxing, Ningbo and Fuzhou, which use the **East bus station** in the northeast of town, the latter connected by bus #502 to the long-distance bus station and #503 to the train station. To reach town from here go to the long-distance bus station first, then head south on #151. Frequent private buses use the train-station square, connecting with nearby cities such as Suzhou, Shanghai and Wenzhou. There are West and South bus stations, though you're highly unlikely to arrive at these as they serve small provincial towns.

Since the Grand Canal has been so important for Hangzhou, it would seem appropriate to arrive here by **boat** – and there are still daily passenger services connecting Hangzhou with Suzhou and Wuxi, both arriving in the morning and leaving in the early evening. The dock is on the Grand Canal in the far northeast of town, and bus #305 into town passes very near here. There is also an irregular boat service connecting Hangzhou with Huangshan in Anhui Province via the Xin'an River and Thousand Island Lake; enquire at the ferry jetty for the latest on its availability. For tickets and more detailed information on the canal boats, consult a travel service (see "Listings", p.483).

Hangzhou is one of not many Chinese cities blessed with a **tourist office**, the Hangzhou Tourist Information Centre on the northern corner of Jiefang Lu and Hubin Lu (daily 8am–4pm; ⓣ0571/7012003). Staff here speak English and enthusiastically dispense maps, brochures and advice. As for getting around town, it shouldn't be a problem to flag down one of the comfortable red **taxis** (¥10 to most destinations within Hangzhou).

Accommodation

There are some excellent **hotels** in Hangzhou, particularly those around the lake, but the only good budget accommodation is available at the two universities – they fill up quickly in the summer, so you may want to reserve in advance. At the time of writing the Art Institute at 218 Nanshan Lu was being renovated; when it reopens it will also have a guesthouse.

Dahua 171 Nanshan Lu ⓣ0571/7011901, ⓕ7061770. On the lakeside, several blocks south of Jiefang Lu. Spacious grounds with comfortable rooms and attentive service. High prices, but actually better value than many other options in the city. Mao Zedong and Zhou Enlai stayed here whenever they visited Hangzhou. ❼

Dongpo 52 Renhe Lu ⓣ0571/7069769, ⓕ7024266. Smart new rooms and friendly, attentive staff make this just about the best deal in town. Beautiful six-storey atrium in the middle. Doubles from ¥200. ❺

Haihua Novotel 298 Qingchun Lu ⓣ0571/7215888, ⓕ7215108. One of the more upmarket offerings from this international hotel chain, with luxurious and tastefully designed rooms. The grand lobby features an imposing staircase. Rooms overlooking the lake command a premium. ❽–❾

Hangzhou University Tianmushan Lu. Located at the northern end of Hangda Lu, in the north of town (bus #11 or #153 from the train station, or bus #28 from the East train station). There are two options here. Slightly to the east of the main university entrance is the *Foreign Experts' Hotel*, which has double rooms of hotel standard. Much cheaper is the *Foreign Students' Dormitory* in Building #3; once inside the main gate, turn right, then walk straight ahead for about 5min. There are sometimes a few spare beds or even double rooms, with communal showers, available. ❷

Huaqiao (aka Overseas Chinese Hotel) 15 Hubin Lu ⓣ0571/7074401, ⓕ7074978. On the lakefront near the western end of Changsheng Lu, this four-star offering has nice, though slightly overpriced rooms, in a great location. ❼

Qingbo 109 Qingbo Lu, along Xi Hu ⓣ0571/7079988. Reasonably priced, comfortable rooms in this conveniently located mid-range hotel. Be sure to ask if one of the few lake-view rooms is available; you may get a good discount out of season. ❺

Shangri-La Beishan Lu, next to the Yuefei Mu ⓣ0571/7077951, ⓦwww.shangri-la.com. Total air-conditioned luxury in beautiful, secluded grounds, overhung by trees, on the northern shore of the lake. Expensive but scrumptious breakfast buffet. ❾

Taipingyang (aka Pacific Hotel) 52 Pinghai Lu, just east of Yan'an Lu ⓣ0571/7077666, ⓕ7063638. Fairly anonymous, but clean and comfortable. ❻

Xi Hu 80 Hubin Lu ⓣ0571/7066933. Perfectly located on the lake front, with slightly ropey but inexpensive rooms, some with attached bathroom. Take bus #7 from the train station. ❹

Xinqiao 176 Jiefang Lu, on the corner of Yan'an Lu ⓣ0571/7076688, ⓕ7022768. An absolutely central location, and one of the plushest of the town-based hotels. ❼

Xinxin 58 Beishan Lu ⓣ0571/7987101, ⓕ7053263. Standard, mildly worn rooms, but surprisingly good value considering the great location overlooking the northern shore of the lake. ❺

Zhejiang 53 Longjing Lu ⓣ0571/7977988, ⓕ7971904). Remote, but peaceful and rural, down to the southwest of the lake, set amid the tea plantations (see p.480), with slightly downtrodden doubles. Take bus #27 from Pinghai Lu. ❼

Zhejiang University Guesthouse Zheda Lu ⓣ0571/7951207. Just off Yugu Lu next to the *Lingfeng Hotel*; take bus #16 from the lakeside. Go through the north gate (*beimen*), walk about a hundred metres and the building will be on the right. The accomodation here, in clean new rooms, is excellent value and there's a good canteen too. ❸

Zhonghua 55 Youdian Lu ⓣ0571/7027094, ⓕ7029574. Very central, between the lake front and Yan'an Lu, this place offers nice new single and double rooms in a pleasant setting. ❺

The City

The municipality of Hangzhou is unusual for a Chinese city in that it encompasses large areas of greenery which might normally be classified as countryside. This is mainly thanks to Xi Hu itself – so central and dominant a role has the lake played in the city's history that even today a trip right round its shores does not feel like an excursion out of the city.

Within the lake are various **islands** and causeways, while the shores are home to endless **parks**, which hold Hangzhou's most famous individual sights, ranging from the extravagant and historic **Yuefei Mu** (Temple and Tomb of Yuefei) to the ancient hillside Buddhist carvings of **Feilai Feng** and its associated temple, the **Lingyin Si**, one of China's largest and most renowned. Farther afield, beautiful tea plantations nestle around the village of **Longjing** and the bizarre former home of the disgraced leader **Lin Biao**, while south down to the **Qiantang River** are excellent walking opportunities.

With most of Hangzhou's sights located on or near the lake shore, you'll find that an ideal way to get between them is by **bike**, otherwise you can use the local buses or simply walk. It's possible to walk round the lake's entire circumference in one day, but you wouldn't have time to do justice to all the sights en route.

Xi Hu

A voyage on this lake offers more refreshment and pleasure than any other experience on earth...

Marco Polo

Xi Hu forms a series of landscapes with rock, trees, grass and lakeside buildings all reflected in the water and backed by luxuriant wooded hills. The lake itself stretches just over 3km from north to south and just under 3km from east to west, though the surrounding parks and associated sights spread far beyond this. On a sunny day the colours are brilliant, but even with grey skies and choppy waters, the famous lake views are delicate, soothing and tranquil; for the Chinese they are also laden with literary and historic associations. Although the crowds and hawkers are sometimes distracting, the area is so large that it is possible to find places to escape the hubbub. A good time to enjoy the lake is sunrise, before the crowds have woken up, when mellow *tai ji* practitioners serenely hone their craft to the backdrop of early morning mists slowly dissipating across the lake.

As early as the Tang dynasty, work was taking place to control the waters of the lake with dykes and locks, and the two **causeways** which now cross sections of the lake, Bai Di across the north and Su Di across the west, originated in these ancient embankments. Mainly used by pedestrians and cyclists, the causeways offer instant escape from the noise and smog of the built-up area to the east. Strolling the causeways at any time of day or night, surrounded by clean, fresh water and flowering lilies, is a real pleasure and a favourite pursuit of Chinese couples. The western end of Bai Di supposedly offers the best vantage point of the lake, especially on autumn nights when the moon is full.

Bai Di and Gu Shan

The northern **Bai Di** causeway is the shorter and more popular of the two, about 1500m in length. Starting in the northwest of the lake near the *Shangri-La Hotel*, it runs along the outer edge of Gu Shan (Solitary Island) before crossing back to the northeastern shore, enclosing a small strip known as Beili Hu (North Inner Lake). The little island of **Gu Shan** in the middle of the Bai Di

Boat trips on Xi Hu

One of the pleasantest elements of a visit to Hangzhou is a boat trip on Xi Hu, offering a chance to visit the **islands**. The small canopied boats which are poled around the lake can be picked up at various points, including the jetty on Gu Shan, near the museum, and on Hubin Lu. The boat owners charge a fixed fee per hour, which is posted at the jetties, but watch out for tourist rip-offs. For a cheaper, less intimate ride, go to the jetty in front of the Yuefei Mu on the northern shore from where there are regular departures for the islands for ¥35 (including entrance fee). A round trip back to the jetty via some of the islands and the Three Flags, in a fancy twin-roofed dragon boat, takes just over an hour.

causeway is one of Hangzhou's highlights, a great place to relax under a shady tree. Bursting with chrysanthemum blossoms in the spring and sprinkled with pavilions and pagodas, this tiny area was originally landscaped under the Tang, but the present style dates from the Qing, when Emperor Qianlong built himself a palace here, surrounded by the immaculately green and quiet **Zhongshan Park**. Part of the palace itself, facing south into the centre of the lake, is now the **Zhejiang Provincial Museum** (Tues–Sun 8.45am–4.15pm; ¥10), a huge place with clear English captions throughout and a number of different wings. The main building in front of the entrance houses historical relics, including some superb bronzes from the eleventh to the eighth century BC. Another hall centres on coin collections and has specimens of the world's first banknotes, dating to the Northern Song; you'll get an appreciation of the deep conservatism of Chinese society from its coinage, which remained fundamentally unchanged for two thousand years from the Han to the Qing dynasties. New galleries outisde hold displays of painting and Tibetan Buddha statues.

The curious **Xiling Seal Engravers' Society** (daily 9am–4.30pm; ¥3), founded in 1904, occupies the western side of the hill, next to the *Louwailou Restaurant*. Its tiny park encloses a pavilion with a pleasant blend of steps, carved stone tablets, shrubbery, and nearby a small early Buddhist stupa; drop in here in summer and you can often see the engravers at work. On the southeastern side of the hill by the water is another of Qianlong's buildings, the **Autumn Moon on a Calm Lake Pavilion**, which is the perfect place to watch the full moon. It's a teahouse now, very popular after sunset and full of swooning honeymooners.

From the causeway just east of Gu Shan you can rent paddle boats which are fun in the cool of the evening (¥20 per hour, ¥200 deposit). The low stone **Duan Qiao** (Broken Bridge), at the far eastern end of the causeway, gets its name because winter snow melts first on the hump of the bridge, creating the illusion of a gap.

Su Di and Santanyinyue Island

The second, longer causeway, **Su Di**, named after the Song-dynasty poet-official Su Dong Po, who was governor of Hangzhou, starts from the southwest corner of the lake and runs its full length along the west side to the northern shore close to Yuefei Mu. Consisting of embankments planted with banana trees, weeping willows and plum trees, linked by six stone-arch bridges, the causeway encloses a narrow stretch of water, **Xili Hu** (West Inner Lake). East of the causeway, also in the southern part of the lake, is **Xiaoying Island**, better known as **Santanyinyue** (Three Flags Reflecting the Moon) after the three "flags" in the water – actually stone pagodas, said to control the evil spirits lurking in the deepest spots of the lake. The largest of the islands here, and roughly circular, Santanyinyue was built up in 1607. Bridges link across from north to south and east to west so that the whole thing seems like a wheel with four spokes and a central hub just large enough for a pavilion, doubling as a shop and a restaurant. You pay a ¥20 admission fee to get onto the island.

The lake shore

The account here assumes you start from the northeast of the lake on Beishan Lu, and head anticlockwise, in which case the seven-storey **Baoshu Ta** on Baoshi Shan is the first sight you'll encounter. Looming up on the hillside to your right, the pagoda is not original – it's a 1933 reconstruction of a Song-dynasty tower – but it's a nice place to walk to along hillside tracks. From Beishan Lu a small lane leads up behind some buildings to the pagoda. Tracks continue beyond and you can climb right up to **Qixia Shan** (Mountain Where Rosy Clouds Linger) above the lake. About halfway along this path you will see a yellow-walled monastery with black roofs lurking below to your left, the **Baopu Daoist Compound** daily (7am–4pm; ¥4), well worth a stop if only to witness the numerous traditional activities taking place, most often in the late afternoon near and after official closing hours. You might catch one of the frequent ancestral worship ceremonies that are held here, full of priests clad in colourful garb and widows clutching long black necklaces to pay tribute to their husbands. If you climb up the stairs, you will find several smaller halls where old men practice their calligraphy and young women play the *pipa*. As always, tourists should remain discreet and be sensitive to the privacy of those taking part, as many of the people are rather shy.

Back on the path along the ridge above the monastery, you can stroll past **Chuyang** (Sunrise Terrace), which is traditionally the spot for watching the spring sun rise over the lake, Gu Shan and the northern shore. If you continue west, you'll eventually reach some steep stone stairs which will bring you back down to the road, close to the Yuefei Mu at the northwest end of the lake, next to the *Shangri-La Hotel*.

Yuefei Mu and Huanglong Dong Park

The **Yuefei Mu** (Temple and Tomb of Yuefei; daily 7.30am–5.30pm; ¥20) is one of Hangzhou's big draws, the twelfth-century Song general Yuefei being considered a hero in modern China thanks to his unquestioning patriotism. Having emerged victorious from a war against barbarian invaders from the north, Yuefei was falsely charged with treachery by a jealous prime minister, found guilty and executed at the age of 39. However, twenty years after his execution, the next emperor annulled all charges against him and had him reburied here with full honours, thus guaranteeing his name to posterity. Walk through the temple to reach the tomb itself – a tiny bridge over water, a small double row of stone men and animals, steles, a mound with old pine trees and four cast-iron statues of the villains, kneeling in shame with their hands behind their backs. On the front wall of the tomb the calligraphy reads, "Be loyal to your country."

Immediately west of Yuefei's Tomb is a lane leading away from the lake and north into the hills behind. Thirty minutes' walk along here eventually leads to the **Huanglong Dong Park** (Yellow Dragon Cave Park; daily 6.30am–4pm; ¥5), to the north of Qixia Shan. The park can also be approached from the roads to the north of here, south of Hangzhou University. The main area of the park is charmingly secretive, sunk down between sharply rising hills with a pond; some teahouses; a shrine to the Chinese god of arranging marriages, Yue Lao; cherry blossoms that flower in the early spring; and a pavilion with musicians performing traditional music – you can even choose a tune if you like, for ¥10.

Huagang Park, Jinci Si and the Museum of Chinese Medicine

On a promontory in the southwestern corner of the lake, the small Song-era **Huagang Park** contains a pond full of enormous fish, and there are also wonderful stretches of grass and exotic trees under which to relax. East of here, by the southern shore of Xi Hu, is another temple, **Jinci Si** (daily 6am–4.30pm; ¥10), housing an impressively large Buddha. Although the temple is nowhere near as active and busy as Lingyin Si, it has been fully restored; buses #308 and #315 to and from town run past.

Finally, just east of the lake down a small alley called Dajing Xiang, off Hefang Jie, is the impressive **Huqingyu Tang Museum of Chinese Medicine**, which traces the complicated history of Chinese medicine from its roots several thousand years ago. The museum is housed in an authentic traditional medicine shop, a setting fast disappearing from modern China (Mon–Wed & Fri–Sun 8am–4.30pm, Thurs 1–4.30pm; ¥5).

Feilai Feng and Lingyin Si

Three kilometres west, away from the lake (bus #7 from Yuefei Mu to its terminus) are Hangzhou's most famous sights, scattered around **Feilai Feng** (daily 7am–4.30pm; ¥15). The hill's bizarre name – "The Hill that Flew Here" – derives from the Indian Buddhist devotee named Hui Li, who, upon arrival in Hangzhou, thought he recognized the hill from one back home in India, and asked when it had flown here. Near the entrance is the **Ligong Pagoda**, constructed for him. If you turn left shortly after entering the site, you'll come to a surprisingly impressive group of fake rock carvings, replicas of giant Buddhas from all over China. To the right of the entrance you'll find a snack bar and beautiful views over the neighbouring tea plantations rolling up the hill.

The main feature of Feilai Feng, other than the crowds of tourists, is the hundreds of **Buddhist sculptures** carved into its limestone rocks. These date from between the tenth and fourteenth centuries and are the most important examples of their type to be found south of the Yangzi. Today the little Buddhas and other figurines are dotted about everywhere, moss-covered and laughing among the foliage. It's possible to follow trails right up to the top of the hill to escape the tourist hubbub.

Deep inside the Feilai Feng tourist area you'll eventually arrive at **Lingyin Si** (Temple of the Soul's Retreat; daily 7.30am–4.45pm; ¥12; entrance only from within the Feilai Feng site), one of the biggest temple complexes in China. Founded in 326 AD by Hui Li, who is buried nearby, it was the largest and most important monastery in Hangzhou and once had three thousand monks, nine towers, eighteen pavilions and 75 halls and rooms. Restored at least sixteen times, the complex was said to be among those protected by Zhou Enlai during the Cultural Revolution, and today it is an attractive working temple with daily services, usually in the early morning or after 3pm.

So badly riddled with woodworm was the temple in the 1940s that the main crossbeams collapsed onto the statues, but in 1956 a replica was produced of the eighteen-metre-high Tang statue of Sakyamuni, carved from 24 pieces of camphorwood. Elsewhere in the temple, the old frequently brushes against the new – the **Hall of the Heavenly King** contains four large and highly painted Guardians of the Four Directions made in the 1930s, while the Guardian of the Buddhist Law and Order, who shields the Maitreya, was carved from a single piece of wood eight hundred years ago.

Southwest of the lake

Down in the southwestern quarter of the lake, in the direction of the village of **Longjing**, the dominant theme is **tea production**. Gleaming green tea bushes sweep up and down the land, and old ladies pester tourists into buying fresh tea leaves. Fittingly, this is where you'll find the worthwhile **Tea Museum** (daily 8am–4.15pm; ¥10), a new, very smart place with lots of captions in English, tracing the history of tea, from its early medicinal uses through to the etiquette of tea drinking and its close relationship with Buddhism. There are displays on different varieties of tea, techniques of growing, the development of special teaware, and finally, reconstructed tearooms, in various ethnic styles, such as Tibetan and Yunnanese. Bus #27 from Pinghai Lu in the town centre comes here; get off more or less opposite the *Zhejiang Hotel*, then head southwest to the museum along a small lane just to the north of, and parallel to, the main road.

The nearby **Zhejiang Hotel** houses one of China's oddest attractions, connected with the hotel's most famous former resident, the disgraced **Marshal Lin Biao**. Formerly Mao Zedong's anointed number two, in 1971 Lin Biao mysteriously died, along with his family, in an alleged plane crash over Mongolia, while attempting to defect to the Soviet Union. Somebody with a sense of humour has decided to capitalize on Lin Biao's sinister reputation by setting up a rather absurd **chamber of horrors** (¥8) of monsters, skeletons and other ghouls, in the once secret underground rooms to which Lin had access. You can also visit the rooms above ground where he lived and worked with his wife – your guide will dwell on Lin's cowardice and paranoia, pointing out the padded lamp shades, which could do no injury if dislodged from above, and the triple-reinforced, bulletproof one-way windows. To find a guide (Chinese-speaking only), enquire at the reception beside the driveway into the hotel; one of the bored security guards there will usually show you round. The hotel complex sprawls across several acres, and there are no signs directing you to this attraction – ask passers-by to point you to Building #1.

A couple of kilometres further southwest, the village of **LONGJING** ("Dragon Well"), with tea terraces rising on all sides behind the houses, is famous as the origin of **Longjing Tea**, perhaps the finest variety of green tea produced in China. Depending on the season, a stroll around here affords glimpses of leaves in different stages of processing – being cut, sorted, or dried. You'll be pestered to sit at an overpriced tea house or to buy leaves when you get off the bus – have a good look around first as there is a very complex grading system and a huge range in quality and price. The **Dragon Well** itself is at the end of the village, a group of buildings around a spring, got up in a rather touristy fashion. Bus #508 runs to Longjing once an hour from the northwestern lake shore, near Yuefei Mu; alternatively, you can actually hike up here from the Qiantang River (see below).

South of the lake

The area to the south and southwest of Xi Hu, down to the Qiantang River, is full of trees and gentle slopes. Of all the parks in this area, perhaps the nicest is the **Hupaomeng Quan** (Tiger Running Dream Spring; daily 6.30am–5.45pm; ¥10). Buses #308 and #315 both run here from the city centre, down the eastern shore of the lake, while bus #508 ambles down from Longjing. The spring here – according to legend, originally found by a ninth-century Zen Buddhist monk with the help of two tigers – is said to produce the purest water around, the only water that serious connoisseurs would use for brewing the best Longjing teas. For centuries, this has been a popular site for hermits to settle and is now a large forested area dotted with teahouses, shrines, waterfalls and pagodas.

A few more stops south on bus #308 takes you to the 1000-year-old **Liuhe Ta** (daily 6.45am–5.30pm; ¥10), a pagoda occupying a spectacular site overlooking the Qiantang River, a short way west of the rail bridge. The story goes that a Dragon King used to control the tides of the river, wreaking havoc on farmers' harvests. Once a particularly massive tide swept away the mother of a boy named Liuhe, to the Dragon King's lair. Liuhe figured the easiest way to bring his mother back was by throwing pebbles into the river, shaking the Dragon Palace violently and forcing the Dragon King into an agreement to return his mother to him, and to promise to never again manipulate the tides. In appreciation, villagers built the pagoda, a huge, impressive structure of wood and brick, hung with 104 large iron bells on its upturned eaves. Today, ironically, the pagoda is the most popular vantage point from which to view the dramatic **tidal bores** during the autumn equinox.

Twenty minutes' walk upriver west from the pagoda, at the #2 bus terminus, a lane known as **Nine Creeks and Eighteen Gullies** runs off at right angles to the river and up to Longjing. This is a delightful narrow way, great for a bike ride or a half-day stroll, following the banks of a stream and meandering through paddy fields and tea terraces with the hills rising in swelling ranks on either side. Halfway along the road, a restaurant straddles the stream where it widens into a serene lagoon. It's an exquisite spot with a tiny pavilion nestling into the woody slope above, and it serves excellent tea and food. From here, you continue north up a bumpy rock and cobbled track, constantly crisscrossed by streams with neat stepping stones, to Longjing.

Eating and drinking

As a busy resort for local tourists, Hangzhou has plenty of good **places to eat**, though there is nothing like the cosmopolitan range of either Shanghai or Nanjing. Cheap Yangzi and Northern Zhejiang cuisine abounds along Wushan Lu, one block east of and parallel to Yan'an Lu; as well as on Huabin Lu and Pinghai Lu, both on the eastern edge of the lake.

Many Chinese tourists make it a point to visit one of the famous historical restaurants in town. Both *Louwailou* (*Tower Beyond Tower*), on Gu Shan Island, or *Tianwaitian* (*Sky Beyond Sky*), near Lingyin Si, serve local specialities at reasonable prices. A third, *Shanwaishan* (*Mountain Beyond Mountain*), has garnered a bad reputation over the years. All three restaurants were named after a line in Southern Song poet Lin Hejin's most famous poem: "Mountain beyond mountain and tower beyond tower/Could song and dance by West Lake be ended anyhow?"

There's a Häagen-Dazs on Huibin Lu, but it's ridiculously expensive; the nearby *Starbucks* on Xueshi Lu is a better bet if all you're after is a snack and a coffee. For a touch of **nightlife**, try the *Phoenix Fire* at 103 Nanshan Lu, opposite the Art Institute Guesthouse; it's one of a strip of bars, popular with foreign students from nearby Hangzhou University and tourists alike.

Restaurants

Bafangyuan Pinghai Lu. In the middle of town, two blocks east of Yan'an Lu, this is a popular, clean and efficient Taiwanese-owned snack bar serving a slew of drinks (including the delicious Taiwanese *naizhu cha* (aka bubble tea, a milky drink containing crunchy bits of tapioca flour), desserts, hotpots (including a dogmeat version), and full set meals.

Kuiyuan Guan Jiefang Lu, just west of Zhongshan Zhong Lu (second floor; go through the entrance with Chinese lanterns hanging outside, and it's on the left). Specializes in more than forty noodle dishes for all tastes, from the mundane (beef in noodle soup) to the acquired (pig intestines and kidneys). Also offers a range of local seafood delicacies.

Lingyin Si Vegetarian Lingyin Si. Excellent lunchtime-only fare; full meals come to around ¥50 per person.

Louwailou, Gu Shan Island. The best-known restaurant in Hangzhou, on the southern shore of Gu Shan Island, very near the museum. Specialities include *dongpo* pork, fish shred soup and beggar's chicken (a whole chicken cooked inside a ball of mud, which is broken and removed at your table). Lu Xun and Zhou Enlai, among others, have dined here. Standard dishes cost ¥30–45.

Tianwaitian Lingyin Si, upstairs from the vegetarian restaurant. Chinese tourists flock here to sample the fresh seafood (supposedly caught from Xi Hu, and reasonably priced). Dishes are ¥40–55 each. Not as good as *Louwailou* though.

Zhiweiguan Renhe Lu, half a block east of the lake. One of the nicest places in town for lunch. In a very urbane atmosphere, with piped Western classical music, you can eat assorted *dian xin* by the plate for around ¥20, including *xiao long bao* (small, fine stuffed dumplings) and *mao erduo* (fried, crunchy stuffed dumplings). The *huntun tang* (wonton soup) and *jiu miao* (fried chives) are also good.

Listings

Airlines The main CAAC reservations and ticketing office is at 160 Tiyuchang Lu in the north of town (daily 8.15am–6pm; ⓣ0571/5154259 domestic flight schedules, ⓣ0571/5152575 reservations). CAAC buses to the airport (¥10) leave here approximately 2hr 30min before each flight's departure.

Banks and exchange The Bank of China head office is at 140 Yan'an Bei Lu (Mon–Fri 8am–4.30pm & Sat 8am–12.30pm), immediately north of Qingchun Lu. You can change traveller's cheques in any of the smaller branches as well, and at upmarket hotels if you're a guest.

Bike rental Most of the big hotels now also rent bikes – the *Huaqiao Hotel* rents for ¥5 an hour, with a ¥200 deposit. Tandems are ¥20 an hour.

Buses For Ningbo and Shaoxing, there are frequent private buses from the main train station's square; for Shanghai and points in Jiangsu, buses arrive at and leave from the North bus station, isolated in the far north of town on Mogan Shan Lu. For Huangshan, use the West bus station located west of Hangzhou University on Tianmu Shan Lu. Wenzhou and Fujian province buses leave from the South bus station on the corner of Dong Bao Lu and Qiushou Lu, a 5min walk south of the main train station. To all destinations except perhaps Shaoxing and Ningbo, the train is more convenient, more comfortable and often cheaper.

Hospitals The most central is the Shengzhong Hospital, on Youdian Lu three blocks east of the lake (ⓣ0571/70688001). Hangda Hospital, inside the Hangzhou University campus, is most convenient for the northern part of town (ⓣ0571/7072524), with Zhejiang Hospital best located for those on the western side of the lake (ⓣ0571/7987373).

Internet access There are a number of poky little places outside the gates of both universities.

Mail The main post office is just north of the train station on Huancheng Dong Lu.

PSB For visa extensions, enquire at the City Government office in the centre of town, on the southwest corner of the junction between Jiefang Lu and Yan'an Lu.

Shopping There is a night market on Wushan Lu running parallel one block east of Yan'an Lu between Pinghai Lu and Youdian Lu, with street sellers peddling the usual jumble of wares ranging from Yixing teapots to daggers and seals. On Nanshan Lu across the street from the Art Institute, there are several art galleries worth poking around. The Hangzhou Silk and Brocade Shop and the retail shop of Wangxingji Fan Factory, at nos. 1 and 8 Hubin Lu respectively, on the northeast shore of the lake, have some of the best selection and prices for silk in the city.

Trains The main train station contains a very convenient soft-seat ticket office for foreigners (Mon–Sat 8–11.30am & 1–4.30pm) on the left as you enter the station. For hard seats or hard sleepers, queue inside the station at window no. 1 or 2.

Travel agents CITS is on the north shore of the lake, on a hillock above the junction of Beishan Lu and Baoshu Lu. Walk through the main gate and the office is 80m ahead to the left (daily 8.30am–5pm; ⓣ0571/5152888, ⓕ5156667). Nearly all Hangzhou hotels have their own travel agencies.

Shaoxing and around

Located south of Hangzhou Bay in the midst of a flat plain crisscrossed by waterways and surrounded by low hills, **SHAOXING** is one of the oldest cities in Zhejiang, having established itself as a regional centre in the fifth century BC. During the intervening centuries – especially under the Song, when the imperial court was based in neighbouring Hangzhou – Shaoxing remained a flourishing city, though the lack of direct access to the sea has always kept it out of the front line of events.

For the visitor, Shaoxing is a quieter and more intimate version of Suzhou, combining some attractive little sights with great opportunities for boating round classic Chinese countryside. It's a small city that seems to have played a disproportionately large role in Chinese legend and culture – some of China's more colourful characters came from here, including the mythical tamer of floods Yu the Great, the wife-murdering Ming painter Xin Wei, the female

Shaoxing and around		
Shaoxing	绍兴	***shàoxīng***
Bazi Qiao	八子桥	*bāzī qiáo*
Fushan Park	府山公园	*fŭshān gōngyuán*
Lu Xun's Former Residence	鲁迅故居	*lŭxùn gùjū*
Lu Xun Memorial Hall	鲁迅纪念馆	*lŭxùn jìniànguăn*
Qingteng Shuwu	青滕书屋	*qīngténg shūwū*
Qiu Jin's Former Residence	秋瑾故居	*qiūjĭn gùjū*
Sanwei Shuwu	三味书屋	*sānwèi shūwū*
Yingtian Pagoda	应天塔	*yìngtiān tă*
Accommodation		
Jiaoyundasha Luguan	交运大厦旅馆	*jiāoyùn dàshà lǚguăn*
Jinyu	金鱼宾馆	*jīnyú bīnguăn*
Shaoxing Dasha	绍兴大厦	*shàoxīng dàshà*
Shaoxing Fandian	绍兴饭店	*shàoxīng fàndiàn*
Dong Hu	东湖	*dōnghú*
Lanting	兰亭	*lántíng*
Yu Ling	禹陵	*yŭlíng*

revolutionary hero Qiu Jin, and the great twentieth-century writer Lu Xun, all of whom have left their mark on the city.

Shaoxing lies near **Jian Hu**, whose water's unusual clarity have made the city known throughout China for its alcohol. Most famous are the city's sweet **yellow rice wine**, a favourite of so many Chinese recipe books worldwide; and its ruby-coloured **nu'er hong wine**, traditionally the tipple brides sipped to toast their new husbands – it was bought when the bride was born and buried in the backyard to age. Although Shaoxing is sometimes recommended as a day-trip from Hangzhou, a single day is definitely not enough to do justice to the town and its surroundings. And, if any added incentive is needed, hotel accommodation in Shaoxing is cheap.

The City

Although Shaoxing's immediate centre comprises a standard shopping street, elsewhere there are running streams, black-tiled whitewashed houses, narrow lanes divided by water, alleys paved with stone slabs, and back porches housing tiny kitchens that hang precariously over canals lined with old ladies doing their daily washing. You can easily explore all of this by bicycle (see p.487 for information on bike rentals). **Fushan Park** (daily 7am–10pm; ¥8), in the west of town south of the *Shaoxing Hotel*, is as good a place as any to get your orientation. There's a large temple here near the entrance, a number of small pavilions as you climb the hill, and from the top you can see out over the town's canals and bridges, not to mention the large numbers of amorous couples who gather in the park, especially after sunset. The main entrance to the park is on Fushanhen Jie, a small street easily found by the prominent archway guarding its eastern end next to the north–south thoroughfare, Jiefang Lu. In the afternoons and evenings Fushanhen Jie transforms into a frenetic marketplace selling everything from vegetables to bootleg CDs.

Along Jiefang Lu are a number of famous people's former residences. The exquisitely tranquil **Qingteng Shuwu** (Green Vine Study; daily 8am–4.30pm; ¥2), a perfect little sixteenth-century black-roofed house, hides 100m south of the Renmin Lu intersection on a small alley, Houguan Xiang, west off the main road. The house is rather hard to find as there are no signs along Jiefang Lu, but passers-by, many unused to seeing foreigners, are eager to help. The serenity of the place belies the fact that it was once the home of the eccentric Ming painter and dramatist Xu Wei (1521–93), who among other violent acts in his life is notorious for having murdered his wife. Xu led a particularly colourful existence, serving as the emperor's principal calligrapher, battling Japanese pirates, and eventually, at the end of his life, becoming a destitute vagrant selling his calligraphy anonymously. Some of his brushes, paintings and calligraphy are still on display in the house.

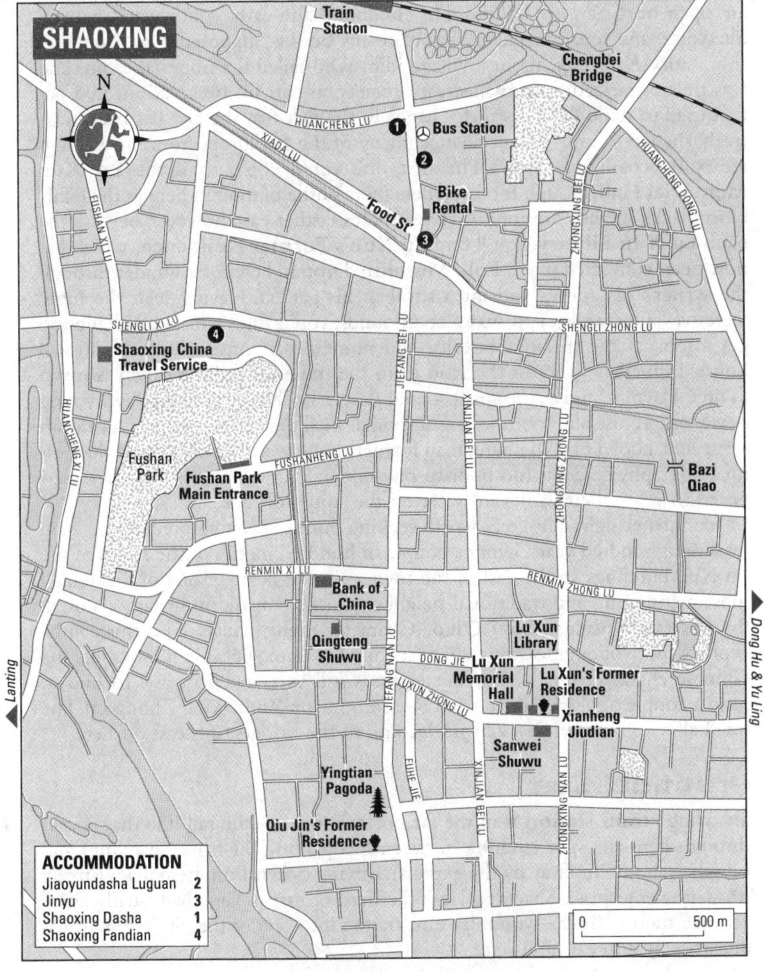

Another 500m south down Jiefang Lu from here, the **Yingtian Pagoda** (daily 8am–5pm; ¥2) crowns a low hill, Tu Shan. Part of a temple founded by the Song, burnt down by the Taiping rebels and subsequently rebuilt, the pagoda repays the stiff climb with splendid views over the canals of the town. The black roof tiles, visible a block to the south, belong to the former **residence** of the early radical woman activist **Qiu Jin**, which is situated on a small lane, Hechang Tang (daily 8am–4pm; ¥2). Born here in 1875, Qiu Jin went to study in Japan before returning to China to work as a teacher and join Sun Yatsen's clandestine revolutionary party. After working as editor of several revolutionary papers in Shanghai, and taking part in a series of abortive coups, she was captured and executed in Hangzhou in 1907 by Qing forces. The house is full of background material on her life and, although there's no explanation in English, the photographs and paintings convey some of the atmosphere of the time.

East off Jiefang Lu, down Luxun Lu, are several sights associated with the writer **Lu Xun** (see box, p.401). A combined ticket for all three is ¥30, and all are open from 8am to 4.30pm. His childhood and early youth were spent in Shaoxing, and local characters populate his books. Supposedly, he based his short story *Kong Yi Ji*, about a village idiot who failed the imperial exams and was thus ostracized from mainstream society, in part on observations in a bar that used to stand on this street. Thanks to the fact that the city has been relatively sheltered from violent change, many of the backdrops from his writings are still recognizable today. The first one you'll come to is the **Lu Xun Memorial Hall**, though for foreigners there's little of interest here as the exhibition lacks English captions. A few minutes farther east, however, beyond the plain **Lu Xun Library**, you'll find **Lu Xun's Former Residence**, which has now been converted into a **Folk Museum**. Drop in here for a wander through the writer's old rooms and for a stroll in his garden. Having seen the high, secretive outer walls of so many compounds, you'll find it makes a change to get a look at the spacious interior and numerous rooms inside a traditional house. Immediately across the road from the museum is the **Sanwei Shuwu** (Three Flavour Study), the small school where Lu Xun was taught as a young boy. There is just one room to see, and on a small desk to the right is a smooth stone and a bowl of water, which, in former times, were the only available tools for calligraphy students too poor to buy ink and paper. Visitors today are supposed to write their names in water on the stone for luck.

One further sight definitely worth seeking out in Shaoxing predates Lu Xun by several hundred years. Lying a couple of hundred metres to the north of the Lu Xun buildings, in the east of the town – in the heart of one of Shaoxing's most picturesque and traditional neighbourhoods – is the most famous of all the town's old bridges, **Bazi Qiao** (Character Eight Bridge). This thirteenth-century piece of engineering, which acquired its name because it looks like the Chinese character for the number eight, is still very much in use. To find it, head a couple of blocks north from Renmin Lu, up Zhongxing Zhong Lu. The small alley called Baziqiao Zhi Jie, leading to the bridge, runs east off here.

Practicalities

Shaoxing's **train station** is in the far north of town – the rail line that comes through here is a spur running between Hangzhou (1hr from Shaoxing) and Ningbo (about 2hr away by the express). Buying tickets from here is a relatively stress-free enterprise. Shaoxing lacks the herd of map-sellers that usually characterize train stations – you'll have to traipse into one of the city's downtown department stores to find one.

The **long-distance bus station** is south of the train station at the junction of Jiefang Lu and Huancheng Lu. If you're arriving from Hangzhou or Ningbo by bus, you might be deposited in a nameless depot in the far north of town – in which case look for the private bus operator just outside that will drive you to the main bus terminal. From the train station, buses #1, #2, #3 and #4 all run past the bus station, while #2 and #4 continue on to the southern end of Jiefang Lu.

There are impromptu **bike-rental shops** on the west side of the pavement along Jiefang Bei Lu between the train station and the Shaoxing Dasha. The main **Bank of China** is on Renmin Dong Lu just east of Jiefang Lu (daily 8.30am–5pm), but there are branches that can change traveller's cheques all over town. The friendly and English-speaking staff of **Shaoxing CTS**, 360 Fushan Lu (Ⓣ0575/5155888), a few minutes west of the *Shaoxing Hotel,* can arrange tours of the surrounding area as well as book onward travel connections.

Accommodation and eating

There appear to be no restrictions on where foreigners can **stay** in Shaoxing. Among the few options clustered round the northern end of Jiefang Lu, easily the best of which is the *Jinyu* (❸), five minutes south of the bus station, with semi-luxurious singles and doubles. Immediately south of the bus station, the *Jiaoyundasha Luguan* is far from salubrious, but does have very cheap doubles, with (❸) or without (❶) bath. Across Jiefang Lu, opposite the bus station, is the *Shaoxing Dasha,* with reasonable air-conditioned doubles (❸). The most upmarket hotel in town is the Ming-styled *Shaoxing Fandian* on Shengli Lu (Ⓣ0575/5155888; ❻), a huge and charming place in grounds so large that you can travel around them by boat. It's a couple of hundred metres west of Jiefang Lu – bus #3 heads there from the train station.

You'll find a few **restaurants** around the northern half of Jiefang Lu, including a small **food street** on an alley near the stone bridge one block south of the *Jinyu Hotel.* The restaurant in the *Jinyu Hotel* is quite good, serving several dishes in the local Shaoxing *mei* (charcoal grilled) style, but the menu is in Chinese only. Dried freshwater fish is a great speciality in Shaoxing, as is the **yellow rice wine** which they claim to have been making round here for over two thousand years. It's made from locally grown glutinous rice and (most importantly) water from Jian Hu, a substantial lake to the southwest. These days the wine is more commonly used for cooking than drinking, *shaoxing ji* (Shaoxing chicken – cooked in the wine) being a classic dish prepared thus. While walking around town you might be struck by the huge number of stalls selling that malodorous staple of Chinese street life, *chou doufu* (smelly tofu). The recipe, since disseminated all over China, was allegedly created by a Shaoxing woman who, tired of her limited cooking prowess, decided to experiment by throwing a variety of spices into a wok with some tofu. If you dare to try it, you will find, surprisingly, that the taste doesn't stink.

Around Shaoxing

Much of the reason for coming to Shaoxing is to experience the charm and beauty of its outlying sights. Beyond Shaoxing, but still easily accessible from town, **Dong Hu** (East Lake; daily 7am–5.30pm; ¥15) is an attractive twenty-minute ride away on the #1 bus route (ask the conductor to tell you when to get off). Despite appearances, the lake is not a natural one. In the seventh century the Sui rulers quarried the hard green rock east of Shaoxing for building and, when the hill streams were dammed, the quarry became a lake, to which, for picturesque effect, a causeway was added during the Qing. The lake is highly photogenic (Emperor Qin Shi Huang commented on its beauty when he visited here more than 2000 years ago), with the massive cliff edge of the quarry leaning over its whole length, the colours and contortions of the rock face reflected in the water. The cliff face and lake are now surrounded by a maze of streams, winding paths, pagodas and stepping-stone bridges. Once inside the site, you can rent a little boat (three people maximum; ¥30) to take you around the various caves, nooks and crannies in the cliff face. You can choose to be dropped on the opposite shore, from where a flight of steps leads up to a path running to the clifftop, offering superb views over the surrounding paddy fields. The last bus back to Shaoxing leaves around 5.30pm.

There's also plenty of water transport around the area. You can take a **boat** back to Shaoxing instead of returning on the bus (45min; ¥45 per boat after bargaining), or continue on to Yu Ling (see below), threading through the network of waterways. This is a great trip (1hr 20min; ¥65 per boat after bargaining) on long, slim, flat-bottomed boats with a curved awning where you can sit in the shade as you glide past the paddy fields, the peace broken only by the occasional goose or duck. In the stern, the boatman steers with a paddle and propels the boat with his bare feet on the loom of the long oar.

Yu Ling and Lanting

Yu Ling (Tomb of Yu; daily 8am–4pm; ¥15), 6km southeast of Shaoxing and linked to town by bus #2, is a heaped-up chaos of temple buildings in a beautiful setting of trees, mossy rocks and mountains. Yu, the legendary founder of the Xia dynasty, around 2000 BC, earned his title "Tamer of Floods" by tossing great rocks around and dealing with the underwater dragons who caused so many disasters. It took him eight years to control a great flood in the Lower Yangzi, after which he settled, and died, here. The first temple was probably built around the sixth century AD, while the actual tomb, which seems to predate the temple, may be Han dynasty. The temple today, most recently restored in the 1930s, contains a large painted figure of Yu and scores of inscribed tablets. Outside, the tall, roughly shaped tombstone is sheltered by an elegant open pavilion. The vigorous worshipping you'll see inside the temple shows what a revered figure Yu still is in modern China.

Another wonderfully rural excursion from Shaoxing is 11km southwest to **Lanting**, the Orchid Pavilion (daily 7.30am–5pm; ¥10), named when Goujian, a Yue Kingdom king, planted an orchid here almost three thousand years ago. The fourth-century poet and calligrapher Wang Xizhi allegedly composed the *Orchid Pavilion Anthology* here, today considered one of the masterpieces of Chinese poetry. Wang held a party with 41 friends, sitting along a creek and floating cups full of wine along it. When a cup stopped, the person sitting nearest either had to drink from the cup or compose a poem. Wang later composed the *Anthology* as a preface to all the poems. Today Lanting is considered a shrine, a place of resonance for all Chinese serious about calligraphy and poetry. Inside Wang's ancestral shrine, located on a small island in the middle of spacious gardens, you can watch artists and calligraphers work. There's also some classic Chinese countryside around here, with paddy fields and green hills on all sides, while inside the Lanting site you'll find geese, bamboo thickets, ferns, lakes and teahouses, as well as small exhibition halls. Lanting is on the #3 bus route from Jiefang Lu (45min), but you'll have to ask locals where to get off.

Ningbo and beyond

The rail spur from Hangzhou through Shaoxing ends at **NINGBO** (Calm Waves), an important economic hub and ocean-going port in the northeast corner of the province. Despite being a port, the city is actually set some 20km inland, at the point where the Yuyao and Yong rivers meet to flow down to the ocean together. All around you'll see flat watery plains and paddy fields and, along the heavily broken and indented shoreline, the signs of local salt-panning and fishing industries. These would hardly make Ningbo worth a special journey, though the city has one or two features of interest, in the striking Tianyige Library and in the monasteries in the countryside beyond. More importantly, the city is a vital staging post for the trip to the nearby island of **Putuo Shan** (see p.493).

Ningbo possesses a short but eventful history. Under the Tang in the seventh century, a complicated system of locks and canals was first installed to make the shallow tidal rivers here navigable, and at the end of the twelfth century a breakwater was built to protect the port. From that time onwards, **trade** with Japan and Korea began to develop massively, with silk shipped out in exchange for gold. Under the Ming, Ningbo became China's most important port. There was early European influence, too: by the sixteenth century the Portuguese were using the harbour, building a warehouse downstream and helping to fight pirates, while in the eighteenth century the East India Company began pressing to set up shop. Eventually, in 1843, after the Opium War, Ningbo became a **treaty port** with a British Consulate.

The town was swept briefly into the Taiping Uprising in 1861, but thereafter lost ground to Shanghai very rapidly. Only since 1949 has it begun to expand once more, and the river has been dredged, passenger terminals and cargo docks built, bridges completed and facilities generally expanded to handle the

Ningbo and beyond

Ningbo	宁波	***níngbō***
Catholic Church	天主教堂	*tiānzhǔ jiàotáng*
Dongmen Kou	东门口	*dōngmén kǒu*
Jiangsha Bridge	江厦桥	*jiāngshà qiáo*
Tianfeng Pagoda	天封塔	*tiānfēng tǎ*
Tianyige Library	天一阁图书馆	*tiānyīgé túshūguǎn*
Xinjiang Bridge	新江桥	*xīnjiāng qiáo*
Yue Hu	月湖	*yuè hú*
Zhongshan Park	中山公园	*zhōngshān gōngyuán*
Accommodation		
Asia Garden	亚洲华园宾馆	*yàzhōuhuáyuán bīnguǎn*
Dongya	东亚饭店	*dōngyà fàndiàn*
Huagang	华港宾馆	*huágǎng bīnguǎn*
Jinlong	金龙饭店	*jīnlóng fàndiàn*
Tianyi	天一大酒店	*tiānyī dàjiǔdiàn*
Beyond Ningbo		
Ayuwang Si	阿育王寺	*āyùwáng sì*
Baoguo Si	保国寺	*bǎoguó sì*
Tiantong Si	天童寺	*tiāntóng sì*
Xikou (Chiang Kaishek's Birthplace)	溪口(蒋介石故居)	*xīkǒu (jiǎngjièshí gùjū)*

output of the local chemicals, food-processing, and metallurgy industries. However, despite the fact that Ningbo today is considered one of the boom areas of China, it still wears a dilapidated, provincial air.

The City

Downtown Ningbo is divided in three by the confluence of its two rivers. Connecting the western part of town, the area of the original walled city, with the northern part, the former foreign concession, is the **Xinjiang Bridge**. The neighbourhoods flanking each side of the bridge are the best places in town to soak up a bit of atmosphere; take bus #1 here from the train station. Just south of the bridge, on its west side, is an interesting dried-fish market, while on the northern bank, you'll find fishing boats, sailors and all the trappings of a busy harbour. Also on this side, but east of the bridge, a few of the elaborate porticos and verandas of the old **treaty port** still survive, flanked by impromptu waterside fish markets, while directly south of the ferry terminal stands a seventeenth-century **Portuguese church**, which today serves the local Christian community. The inside is nothing special, with stained-glass depictions of the Twelve Stations of the Cross, but one of the caretakers should be more than willing to take you around on a short tour (daily 6am–6.30pm; free). Viewed from afar, the church steeple and the

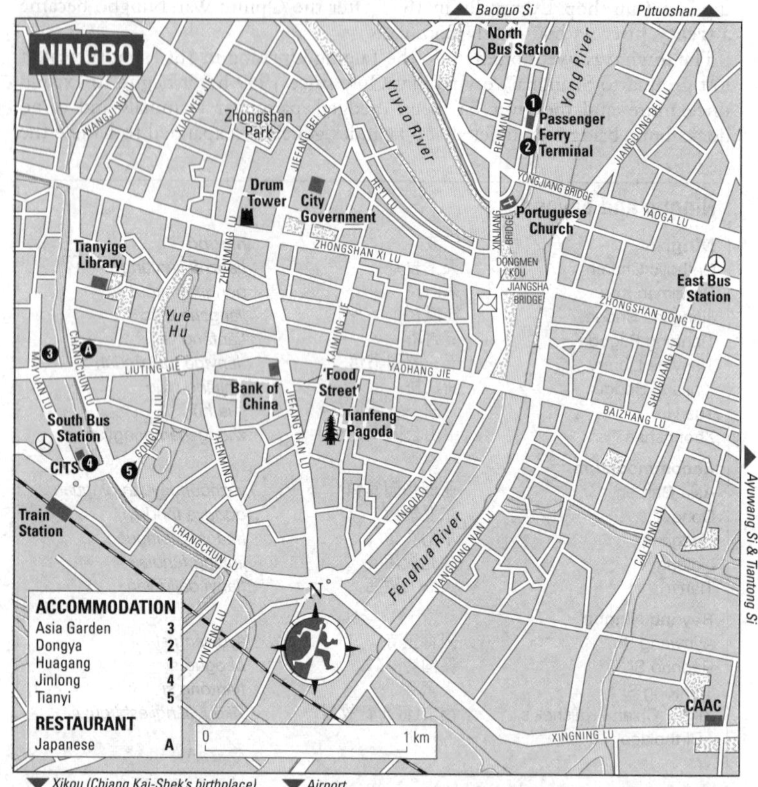

surrounding low-rise Mediterranean-style houses would not look out of place in Southern Europe.

The modern town, similar in sights and scale to other Chinese cities, stretches out south of the Xinjiang Bridge. Two blocks south of the bridge, the main commercial street, **Zhongshan Lu**, cuts across the big **Dongmen Kou** junction from east to west. The eastern section, across the **Jiangsha Bridge**, is an upmarket shopping area complete with several American fast-food restaurants, but it's the western stretch that's the heart of the modern city, a broad avenue lined with modern buildings housing Ningbo's big department stores. Half a kilometre west of Dongmen Kou, it's worth taking a walk down Kaiming Jie, which runs south off Zhongshan Lu. This street is crowded with little shops and stalls, and has some of the better places to eat local seafood. About 1km down here, near the junction with Jiefang Lu, you'll find the fourteenth-century **Tianfeng Pagoda**, which you can climb for views. West of here, and about 1km west of Dongmen Kou, Zhenming Lu is a street full of half-timbered houses and arched trees. It leads north past the **Drum Tower** to **Zhongshan Park**, a small open space which teems with martial-arts enthusiasts in the early mornings.

The oldest part of town is an area to the southwest around **Yue Hu** (Moon Lake); bus #20 comes here from just south of the Xinjiang Bridge. Little more than a large version of a village pond, the lake has an enclosed area for swimming and the usual crowd of people doing their washing on the stone steps. Much of the area's charm has recently been razed, with the construction of a sprawling new park on the western shores, but Ningbo's best tourist attraction, the **Tianyige Library** (daily 8am–4.30pm; ¥12), survives in the middle. Built in 1516 and said to be the oldest surviving library building in China, it was founded by Ming official Fan Qin, whose collection went back to the eleventh century and included woodblock and handwritten copies of the Confucian classics, rare local histories and lists of the candidates successful in imperial examinations. Nowadays you can visit the library's garden and outhouses, some of which contain small displays of old books and tablets. It's quite a charming place, and the gold-plated, wood-panelled buildings, their bamboo groves, pool and rockery still preserve an atmosphere of seclusion, contemplation and study.

Practicalities

Ningbo's **airport**, with flights to many Chinese cities including Hong Kong, is 25km south of the city and connected to the CAAC office in the southeast of downtown via an airport bus (#10). Bus #10 connects the **train station**, in the southwest of the city, with both the CAAC office and the centre of the city, via the eastern part of town. Minibuses and bus #1 run from the train station through the town centre, north over Xinjiang Bridge and close to the ferry terminal and the **North bus station** across the street. Some buses from Hangzhou, Shaoxing or Wenzhou might arrive at the North bus station, but most long-distance bus services operate out of the **South bus station**, just next to the train station. The **East bus station**, across the Jiangsha Bridge at the corner of Shuguang Lu and Ningbo Lu (buses #514 and #604 run here from the ferry terminal and Dongmen Kou), operates suburban services to the temples and pagodas outside town.

The **ferry terminal**, for boats to and from Putuo Shan and Shanghai, is in the northern part of town, north of the Xinjiang Bridge, on Waima Lu; frequent minibuses and bus #1 head to the town centre. If approaching by bus, get off north of Xinjiang Bridge, just after passing beneath an overpass, then walk a couple of minutes northeast. The main **ticket office** here (daily 5.45am–6pm) sells tickets for the daily departures to Putuo Shan and Shanghai, and for some irregular summer services to Suzhou. Note that only slow boats – including the 9am Putuo Shan departure (5hr) – depart from Ningbo itself, leaving from just behind the ticket office; the fast, comfortable services to Shanghai and Putuo leave from the docks at **Zhenhai**, to which there's a connecting bus from the terminal (1hr; included in the price of ferry ticket). The exact schedule changes seasonally; for more details on Putuo Shan boats, see p.495.

Most of the city's facilities are in the town centre right at the Dongmen Kou junction, including the main **post office** and a branch of the **Bank of China**. The main Bank of China office (Mon–Fri 8–11.15am & 1.30–4.15pm) is on Jiefang Lu, just south of Liuting Lu; there's also a convenient branch across from the train station near the *Jinlong Hotel*. For **visa extensions**, enquire at the City Government headquarters east off Jiefang Bei Lu. The best **travel service** to help with tickets is located on the fifth floor of the *Jinlong Hotel*, right across from the train station (Room 507; daily 8am–5pm; ⓣ0574/7329381).

Accommodation and eating

There are two **hotel** areas to consider in Ningbo, one near the train station, and one near the ferry terminal. Take your pick according to which is most convenient. **Food** in Ningbo is dominated by **seafood**, and neon-lit Food Street, between Kaiming and Jiefang streets, is one of the best places to look, as are the streets south of the ferry terminal. The restaurant in the *Jinlong Hotel* serves stupendous crab, and a decent Japanese restaurant at 70 Changchun Lu, north of the train station, offers reasonable lunchtime set menus.

Hotels

Asia Garden, Mayuan Lu ⓣ0574/7116888, ⓕ7116554. Ningbo's premier place to stay, with a luxurious lobby and rooms almost as impressive. A 10min walk from the train station. ❾

Dongya (aka East Asia Hotel) 88 Zhongma Lu ⓣ0574/7356224, ⓕ7353529. Right near the ferry terminal in a characterful old part of town. Although the hotel doubles as a brothel, the soundproofed walls and comfortable rooms make it a fairly pleasant place to stay – a good alternative if the nearby *Huagang* is full. From the train station, take bus #1 and get off at the first stop (*lunchuan matou*) after Xinjiang Bridge. Walk to the ferry terminal and take the first alley on the right (south). ❹

Huagang 146 Zhongma Lu ⓣ0574/7691888, ⓕ7691001. Right next to the ferry terminal and the best option if you're taking the morning ferry to Putuo Shan. The rooms are comfortable, without ostentatious decorations. For some excitement, there's a bowling alley next door. ❹

Jinlong (aka Golden Dragon) Gongqing Lu ⓣ0574/7318888 ext 7114, ⓕ7312288. An excellent place to stay, with comfortable rooms and a great location right opposite the train station. ❻

Tianyi Gongqing Lu ⓣ0574/7316595 ext 40. Situated on the corner with Changchun Lu, just a few minutes' walk northeast from the train station. If you're in a group, you might be able to talk yourselves into the five-bed dorms. There are also doubles and triples available, and there's a boat-ticketing office in the lobby. ❺

Beyond Ningbo

There are numerous temples and pagodas to be visited in the countryside around Ningbo but, unless you have an extra day to fill here, they offer few contrasts with their counterparts elsewhere in China. Perhaps the most interesting is **Baoguo Si** (daily 7am–4.30pm; ¥5), some 15km northwest of town, one of the oldest wooden buildings in China – it's certainly the oldest wooden building south of the Yangzi. Buses #331 and #332 run here from just north of Xinjiang Bridge (every 30min; 40min), out into a landscape of endless green paddy fields broken only occasionally by villages with their obligatory duck-ponds. Nestling on a hill, the temple itself was built in 1013 and restored under the Qing, but is left bare so that its structure can be clearly seen. The entire hall was originally constructed without nails, relying on its interlocking structure to stay upright, although every Ningbo schoolchild knows the workmanship has started to fall apart in recent years and nails have been drilled in. Beyond the temple, you can continue up the steps to a pavilion from where the view of the temple is half-concealed by trees, but there's a fine vista of the flat lands beyond the ridge, with ribbons of water threading through the paddies into the distance.

Southeast of the city are a couple more sites which can be combined into a single excursion. **Ayuwang Si**, the temple of king Asoka, is about 20km east of town, on the slopes of Tai Ba Shan. Built in the fifth century, it's notable for its miniature stupa which allegedly contained a cranium bone of Sakyamuni, the founder of Buddhism, until the Cultural Revolution, when Red Guards spirited it away. One of the monks shuffling around can give a heartfelt, tearful recount of this tragic episode. The architecture is rightly renowned too, a spectacular blend of orange tile and dark red wood against the green of the hill, with cool grey steps and a refreshingly shadowy interior (daily 6.30am–4.30pm; ¥3). Bus #82 runs out here from near the ferry terminal, but it might be more comfortable and quicker to take a minibus from Ningbo's East bus station – they leave the station every ten minutes nonstop to the temple, while the public bus is overcrowded and makes frequent stops. Buses #514 and #604 run from Xinjiang Bridge and Dongmen Kou to East station. You can also rent a private car and driver from a travel service to see these sights, although this option is far more expensive.

A few kilometres farther on from Ayuwang Si, the **Tiantong Si** (Children of Heaven Temple; daily 5am–5.30pm; ¥3) is a splendid collection of buildings at the base of a group of hills, set deep in the forest. Founded in the third century AD, this is one of the largest monasteries in China, with 963 halls and many important Buddhist works of art – the Zen Buddhist sect considers this their second most important pilgrimage site in the country. At the centre of it all there's a very large, very fat Buddha with an enormous smile. You may also see crowds of Japanese visitors – the Japanese monk Dogen came here to study in 1223 and on his return home founded the Sotoshu sect, which now has some eight million adherents in Japan. From Ayuwang Si, there are frequent minibuses that go directly to Tiantong Si.

A little farther afield, **Chiang Kaishek's birthplace** sits in the delightful small town of **XIKOU**, 35km south of Ningbo, characterized by verdant paddy fields and (increasingly) flotillas of Taiwanese tour groups. The house where Chiang was born no longer stands, but some of his childhood haunts, including his grade school and his ancestral graveyard, still remain. To get here, take a bus from the East station bound for **Fenghua** (ask the driver where to get off).

Putuo Shan

A few hours by boat north of Ningbo and south of Shanghai lies the island of **Putuo Shan**, just twelve square kilometres in area and divided by a narrow

Putuo Shan

Putuo Shan	普陀山	***pǔtuóshān***
Chaoyang Dong	潮阳洞	*cháoyáng dòng*
Chaoyin Dong	潮音洞	*cháoyīn dòng*
Dasheng An	大乘庵	*dàshèng ān*
Duobao Pagoda	多宝塔	*duōbǎo tǎ*
Fanyin Dong	梵音洞	*fányīn dòng*
Fayu Si	法雨寺	*fǎyǔ sì*
Foding Shan	佛顶山	*fódǐng shān*
Guanyin Leap	观音跳	*guānyīn tiào*
Huiji Si	慧济寺	*huìjì sì*
Puji Si	普济寺	*pǔjì sì*
Ten Thousand Step Sands	百步沙	*bǎibù shā*
Thousand Step Sands	千步沙	*qiānbù shā*
Zizhu Si	紫竹寺	*zǐzhú sì*
Accommodation		
Baotuo	宝陀饭店	*bǎotuó fàndiàn*
Fu Quan	福泉山庄	*fúquán shānzhuāng*
Putuoshan Hotel	普陀山大酒店	*pǔtuóshān dàjiǔdiàn*
Putuo Shanzhuang	普陀山庄宾馆	*pǔtuóshānzhuāng bīnguǎn*
Ronglai Yuan	融来院	*rónglái yuàn*
Sanshengtang	三圣堂饭店	*sānshèngtáng fàndiàn*
Xilai Xiao Zhuang	息来小庄宾馆	*xīlái xiǎozhuāng bīnguǎn*
Xilai Yuan	息来院饭店	*xīláiyuàn fàndiàn*
Xilin	锡麟饭店	*xīlín fàndiàn*

channel from the much larger Zhoushan Island. Sometimes called "the fairy-like land of the Immortals" by the Chinese, Putuo Shan is also one of the four Chinese mountains sacred to Buddhism, a peak which rises to 300m at one end of the island. Undoubtedly one of the most charming places in eastern China, the island has no honking cars or department stores, only endless vistas of blue sea, sandy beaches and lush green hills dotted with ancient monasteries, making it an ideal place to escape and to recuperate from the noise, traffic and dirt of the big cities, with endless opportunities for walking. Although bursts of local tourists at weekends and in summer threaten the serenity, and despite a recent declaration by the Chinese travel industry to lure visitors by greatly improving the tourist infrastructure, you should still be able to avoid the hordes if you schedule your visit on a weekday or in the off-season; the best times to come are April, May, September and October, when the weather is still warm and the island isn't especially busy.

Putuo has been attracting Buddhist pilgrims from all over northeast Asia for at least a thousand years, and there are many legends to account for the island's status as the centre of the **cult of Guanyin**, Goddess of Mercy. According to one, the goddess attained enlightenment here; another tells how a Japanese monk named Hui'e travelling home with an image of the goddess took shelter here from a storm and was so enchanted by the island's beauty that he stayed, building a shrine on the spot. Over the years, more than a hundred monasteries and shrines were built, with magnificent halls and gardens to match. At one time there were four thousand monks squeezed onto the island, and even as late as 1949 the Buddhist community numbered around two thousand. Until that date indeed, secular structures were not permitted on the island, and nobody lived here who was not a monk.

Although there was a great deal of destruction on Putuo during the Cultural Revolution, many treasures survived, some of which are in the Zhejiang Provincial Museum in Hangzhou. Restoration continues steadily, and from only 29 monks in the late 1960s there are now several hundred. Three principal monasteries survive – **Puji**, the oldest and most central; **Fayu**, on the southern slopes; and **Huiji**, at the summit. There are also large numbers of lesser temples and monuments. You'll notice when touring Putuo that the crowds of Chinese tourists carry identical yellow cotton bags which are stamped with symbols of Guanyin at each temple, sometimes in exchange for donations. With the old beliefs on the rise again, many people come specifically to ask the goddess for favours, often to do with producing children or grandchildren.

Access to the island

The island has become far easier to reach in the last several years as local officials realize the huge potential of tourism on the island, but more convenient transport links are somewhat of a mixed blessing because a greater number of tourists now have easy access to the island.

The only way in or out of Putuo Shan is by **boat**. Many fast ferries arrive here from **Ningbo** every day (last one departs at 3pm; 2hr; ¥55) and one slow boat (at 9am; 5hr; ¥22). Three to four fast ferries to and from **Shanghai** arrive every day (4hr; ¥243) and one or two slow overnight boats (14hr; ¥72–350). Second class on the overnight Shanghai boat affords a tolerably comfortable three- or four-bed cabin with a washbasin and costs ¥96. Tickets for both ferries are sold on the first floor of the boat ticket office at Jinling Dong Lu in Shanghai; the fast boat has a special booth by the window).

A cheaper and potentially more interesting route to or from Putuo Shan is via **Shenjiamen** on the neighbouring island of Zhoushan. The two islands are linked by at least seven boats per day (30min; ¥15). Shenjiamen is in itself an interesting place to spend a few hours, and from here you can get frequent bus connections to Ningbo crossing on the recently constructed bridge linking Zhoushan with the mainland.

Arrival

The island is long and thin, with the **ferry jetty**, where all visitors arrive, in the far south of the island; you'll be required to pay a rather steep ¥60 fee to enter the island. About 1km north from here is the main "town", a tiny collection of hotels, shops and restaurants, with a recognizable central square around three ponds, dotted with trees and faced to the north by the island's principal temple, Puji Si. There are only a few roads, travelled by a handful of minibuses which connect the port with Puji Si and other sights farther north.

Upon arrival, you can reach the town by following either the road heading west or the one heading east from the jetty (20min), or by picking up a bus from the car park just east of the arrival gate. The westerly route is slightly shorter and takes you past most of the modern buildings and facilities on the island, including the **Bank of China** (daily 8–11am & 1–4.30pm) and **CITS** next to the *Baotuo Hotel* directly opposite. A little farther north, up a small lane to the left just before the *Xilin Hotel*, is the **post office**, while in the central square, at the northwestern corner, you'll find a **ticket booking office** where you can book domestic flights out of Ningbo or Shanghai. The alternative eastern route from the jetty takes you through a ceremonial arch symbolizing the

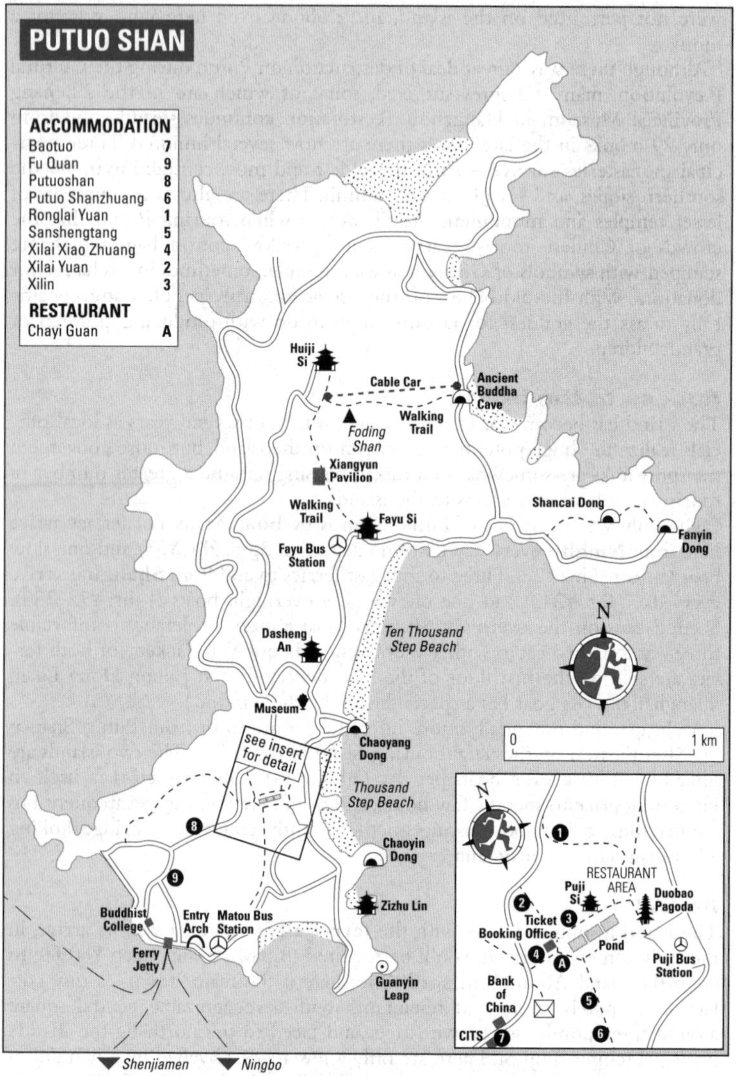

PUTUO SHAN

ACCOMMODATION

Baotuo	7
Fu Quan	9
Putuoshan	8
Putuo Shanzhuang	6
Ronglai Yuan	1
Sanshengtang	5
Xilai Xiao Zhuang	4
Xilai Yuan	2
Xilin	3

RESTAURANT

Chayi Guan	A

entrance to the mountain and then on to a path that cuts away to the left a few minutes later, with the imposing statue of Guanyin standing on a promontory point straight ahead.

When you need to **move on** from Putuo Shan, you can buy tickets for outbound boats from any of the island's hotels or at the jetty office (daily 6am–6pm). Note that the jetty's departure point is 200m to the east of the arrival point; signs in Chinese point the way. The slow boat back to Shanghai is worth considering, chugging into the city just after sunrise and providing an absorbing and memorable view of the awakening metropolis.

Accommodation

There are several delightful **hotels** on Putuo, including a number of converted monasteries, but be warned that in the peak summer months, and especially during the weekend stampede out of Shanghai, you may face a trek around town before you find an empty room, not to mention very expensive prices once you've found something. Another option, often the only one for budget travellers, is to stay in a private house; note that although this is standard practice for Chinese tourists on Putuo, it's technically illegal for foreigners, so use your discretion. It shouldn't be too hard to find people with houses to let – they congregate at the jetty pier, and you should be able to bargain them down to around ¥100–150 a person, depending on the season. A third option, pursued especially by younger foreign travellers, is to crash on one of the island's two beaches for the night.

Baotuo On the main road between the pier and the town ⓣ0580/6092090, ⓕ6091148. Nicely furnished rooms in pleasant surroundings. The front desk attendants speak some English and are very eager to please. ❻

Fu Quan A bit down the path from the *Sanshengtang*; the sign is only in Chinese and easy to miss ⓣ0580/6092069. Basic but agreeable rooms; one of the cheaper places on the island. ❺

Putuoshan Hotel On the main west road from the jetty to the town ⓣ0580/6092828, ⓕ6091818. Very easy to spot, thanks to its spacious grounds and opulent design. Managed by Hong Kong investors, this is the best hotel on the island, with prices to match. ❾

Putuo Shanzhuang Just south of the *Sanshengtan* ⓣ0580/6091666, ⓕ6091667. A beautiful, relatively isolated and extremely comfortable option. ❻

Ronglai Yuan Guesthouse In the middle of town ⓣ0580/6091262. Walk past Puji Si to its eastern end, through an arch, then turn left (north) up the first alley. The alley first bends slightly to the right, then seriously to the left (the hotel is actually directly behind Puji Si). The main building, a converted ancient monastery overhung by giant trees, no longer accepts foreigners, but the front desk will kindly lead you to the small annex across the street with comfortable, if a little cramped, rooms. The incredibly genteel owner speaks no English but is always ready to help you. ❸

Sanshengtang ⓣ0580/6091277. On the eastern route from the jetty to town, this is just a couple of minutes due south of the centre on a small path. Quite an attractive place, styled like a temple, but note that they have an annoying habit of attempting to surcharge foreigners by fifty percent. ❹

Xilai Xiao Zhuang ⓣ0580/6091812 ext 501, ⓕ6091023. Though not in a terribly attractive building, it's a very comfortable hotel that is first choice for many of the Chinese tour groups. You'll pass it at the northern end of the west route just before you reach the centre of town. ❽

Xilai Yuan At the end of a tiny lane immediately west of Puji Si ⓣ0580/6091119 ext 3568. One of a number of former monasteries converted into hotels, with some good, cheap two- and four-bed rooms here. ❹

Xilin Right on the central square, to the west of Puji Si ⓣ0580/6091303. A great location with an entrance that makes it look like a temple, plus a good restaurant. Foreigners are usually surcharged here, but with a little persuasion you can get around this. ❻

The island

All of the three main temples on the island are in extremely good condition, recently renovated, with warm yellow-ochre walls offsetting the deep green of the mature trees in their forecourts. This is particularly true of **Puji Si** (daily 6am–9pm; ¥5), right in the centre of the island, built in 1080 and enlarged by successive dynasties. It stands among magnificent camphor trees and boasts a bridge lined with statues and an elegantly tall pagoda with an enormous iron bell.

South of here, the **Duobao Pagoda**, just to the east of the square ponds, was built in 1334 and is five storeys tall with Buddhist inscriptions on all four sides. The stones for its construction were all brought over from Tai Hu in Jiangsu Province. Twenty minutes' walk farther south down on the southeastern corner of the island, the cave **Chaoyin Dong** is remarkable for the din of the crashing waves, thought to resemble the call of Buddha (and hence a popular spot for monks to commit suicide in earlier days). The neighbouring **Zizhu Si** (Purple Bamboo Temple; daily 6am–6pm; ¥5 including admission to Chaoyin Dong) is one of the less-touristed temples on the island and, for that reason alone, a good spot to observe the monks' daily rituals.

On the island's southern tip is Putuo's most prominent sight, the **Guanyintiao** (Guanyin Leap; daily 7am–5pm; ¥6), a headland from which rises a spectacular 33-metre-high bronze-plated statue of the Goddess of Mercy, visible from much of the island. In her left hand, Guanyin holds a steering wheel, symbolically protecting fishermen (not to mention travelling monks like Hui'e) from violent seastorms. Fisherfolk and seaside villagers view Guanyin as a saviour, who has traditionally guarded them from the worst of the sea's fury. In a pavilion at the base of the statue hangs a small exhibit of wooden murals recounting how Guanyin aided Putuo villagers and fishermen over the years, while in a small room directly underneath the statue sit 400 statues representing the various spiritual incarnations of Guanyin. The view from the statue's base over the surrounding islands and fishing boats is sublime, especially on a clear day. A small memorial plaque on the coast between Guanyintiao and Chaoyin Dong marks the spot where Hui'e, the Japanese founder of the Putuo sect, made landfall while escaping a violent storm.

△ Suzhou, Jiangsu

North of the town

The two temples in the northern half of the island, Huiji Si and Fayu Si, make for a pleasant day-trip from the town. They're conveniently connected to the southern half via minibuses (¥6) departing from the bus stop just southeast of the central square, though it's also possible to make the journey by foot (see below).

Huiji Si stands near the top of **Foding Shan**, whose summit provides some spectacular views of the sea and the surrounding islands. A **cable car** makes the journey from the minibus stand (daily 7am–5pm; ¥22 up, ¥12 down), although it's also possible to walk up the mountain. The temple itself (daily 6.30am–5pm; ¥7), although not as old as Puji – it was mainly built between 1793 and 1851 – occupies a beautiful site just to the northwest of the summit surrounded by green tea plantations. Its halls stand in a flattened area between hoary trees and bamboo groves, with the greens, reds, blues and gold of their enamelled tiles gleaming magnificently in the sunshine. There's also a vegetarian restaurant here. You can then head down along a marked path leading south towards the third major temple, Fayu Si, the whole walk taking about an hour. Shortly after setting off, you'll see a secondary track branching away to the left towards the **Ancient Buddha Cave**, a delightfully secluded spot by a sandy beach on the northeastern coast of the island; give yourself a couple of hours to get there and back. Back on the main path, the steep steps bring you to the **Xiangyun Pavilion** where you can rest and drink tea with the friendly monks.

Thirty minutes farther on you'll reach the **Fayu Si** (daily 6.30am–5.30pm; ¥6), another superb collection of over two hundred halls amid huge green trees, built up in levels against the slope during the Ming. With the mountain behind and the sea just in front, it's a delightful place to sit in peaceful contemplation. The Daxiong Hall has recently been brilliantly restored, and the Dayuan Hall has a unique beamless arched roof and a dome, around the inside of which squirm nine carved wooden dragons. This hall is said to have originally stood in Nanjing, being moved here by Emperor Kangxi in 1689. Its great statue of **Guanyin**, flanked by monks and nuns, is the focal point of the goddess's birthday celebrations in early April, when thousands of pilgrims and sightseers crowd onto the island for chanting and ceremonies which last all evening. Bus services from directly outside the temple link it to Puji and to the ferry jetty. There are also occasional minibuses heading out along the promontory immediately east of Fayu Si to **Fanyin Dong** (daily 8am–4.30pm; ¥5), a cave in the rocky cliff with a small shrine actually straddling a ravine. The cave was named after the resemblance of the sound of crashing waves to Buddhist chants. Legend says that Guanyin's image is sometimes visible from the cave mouth looking out to sea if the timing of the waves is just right. From here, you can follow a path up through beautiful scenery in a northwesterly direction to another cave, the **Shancai Dong** (daily 8.30am–4.30pm; ¥5). Walking around anywhere on the promontory is a pleasure given the absence of crowds and the difficulty of getting seriously lost.

You will appreciate Putuo's beauty much more by making the trip to Huiji Si and Fayu Si **on foot** via the two excellent **beaches** that line the eastern shore, Qianbu Sha (Thousand Step Sands; ¥10 until 5pm, free afterwards) and Wanbu Sha (Ten Thousand Step Sands; ¥15 until 5pm, free afterwards). In summer, it is possible to bring a sleeping bag and camp out on either beach – be sure to bring all your supplies from town as there are no convenience stores or restaurants nearby. The beaches are separated by a small headland hiding the **Chaoyang Dong**. Just inside this little cave there's a teahouse and a seating area overlooking the sea, while from the top of headland itself you'll get great views. One kilometre south of Fayu Si and directly across from Wanbu Sha is the **Dasheng An** (daily 8am–5.30pm; ¥1), a nunnery notable for the reclining Buddha downstairs in the main hall, and the thousands of tiny seated Buddhas upstairs. Just south of here, the rather forlorn **museum** offers a little collection of cultural artefacts from the island's history (daily 8.30am–4pm; ¥1).

Eating and drinking

Eating and drinking is not likely to be the highlight of your trip to Putuo Shan – most food must be brought in from the mainland, and is therefore expensive and not too fresh – but there are a few options, mostly in the hotels. The lane running northeast away from Puji Si as well as the road between the jetty departure and arrival points both have a string of dingy-looking eating houses which specialize in **seafood** ranging from fish to molluscs and eel, but also have standard dishes and noodles. For a more upmarket eating experience in very pleasant surroundings, try the *Chayi Guan*, in the central square, southwest from Puji Si. As well as excellent tea here, you can get *dim sum* for breakfast or lunch, and full meals in the evening.

Wenzhou and beyond

Tucked away on the southeastern coast of Zhejiang Province, **WENZHOU** appears at first glance to be an obscure provincial backwater. However, despite its lack of historical associations, its location on the sea is crucial. The inhabitants of southern Zhejiang, along with Fujian to the south – hemmed in on the coast by the mountainous interior – have for centuries looked out to the sea rather than the mainland for their livelihood. Shipping, fishing and trading have been the mainstay of the economy, while politically the tendency has been to ignore the rest of China altogether, an inclination that can still be seen today both in the notoriously eccentric local dialect and in the free-market economy gone wild. Smuggling and the pirating of brand-named products have always been popular sidelines down here. Now, with the city attracting significant amounts of overseas (mainly Taiwanese) investment, local entrepre-

Wenzhou

Wenzhou	温洲	***wēnzhōu***
Christian Church	基督教堂	*jīdū jiàotáng*
Jiangxin Park	江心孤屿	*jiāngxīn gūyǔ*
Ou River	瓯江	*ōujiāng*
Yandang Mountain	雁荡山	*yàndàng shān*
Accommodation and eating		
Awailou	阿外楼餐馆	*āwàilóu cānguǎn*
Dong'ou	东瓯大厦	*dōngōu dàshà*
Dongwailou	东外楼餐馆	*dōngwàilóu cānguǎn*
Huaqiao	华侨饭店	*huáqiáo fàndiàn*
Hubin	湖宾饭店	*húbīn fàndiàn*
Jiaoyu Guesthouse	教育招待所	*jiàoyù zhāodàisuǒ*
Shuichan	水产招待所	*shuǐchǎn zhāodàisuǒ*
Wenzhou Dajiudian	温洲大酒店	*wēnzhōu dàjiǔdiàn*
Wenzhou Restaurant	温州饭店	*wēnzhōu fàndiàn*

neurial skills have made this a boom town like no other in China – many locals attribute their business know-how to their eleventh-century Jewish trader ancestors.

Quite apart from the difficulty of getting here, the effect of this economic maelstrom on **tourism** is questionable. Although Wenzhou has plenty of hotels, its attractions are mainly confined to **Jiangxin Park** in the middle of the Ou River, a moderately interesting waterfront, and a surprisingly well-preserved old city, dating to the days when it was a prosperous **foreign treaty port**, from the 1870s onwards. Farther afield lies the **Yandang Shan** nature park, with excellent walking opportunities, pagodas and lush scenery.

The Town

The old town centre corresponds roughly to the area facing onto the broad **Ou River** to the north, bounded by the two important shopping streets, Xinhe Lu and Jiefang Lu, to the west and east respectively. To the south, the area is bordered approximately by Renmin Lu, although you'll see that the bulldozers and architects of the modern city are encroaching steadily. The city has been subject to an extensive facelift recently, and the main shopping street, the pedestrianized **Wuma Jie**, has been transformed from a charming jumble

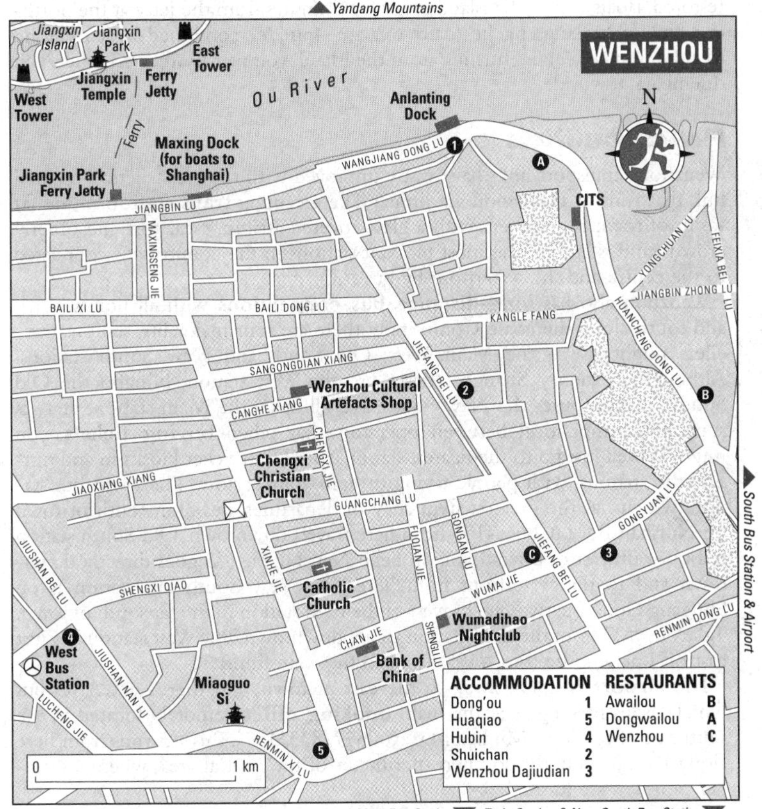

of mom-and-pop shops into a mix of modern boutiques. Farther towards the river, though, life is still much as it has always been, with some unexpected old stone facades above the shop entrances.

There are also a few specific sights worth searching out. Right in the middle of the old town area, on Canghe Xiang, is the **Wenzhou Cultural Artefacts Shop**, where all kinds of art-related objects (including brushes, paints, scrolls and some antiques) are on sale in an interesting old building. Just south on Cheng Xi Jie, looms an incongruous **Christian Church**, a gothic building of black brick dating back to 1778, originally built by a British missionary. A few minutes south, on Zhouzhaisi Xiang running east from Xinhe Jie, is the rather larger but less attractive **Catholic Church**, dating to 1888 during the treaty port era. One rather more typically Chinese sight is the **Miaoguo** on Renmin Xi Lu (daily 8am–5pm; ¥3), on the southern side of Songtai Hill. Originally constructed in the Tang dynasty, more than a thousand years ago, this temple has been rebuilt many times, most recently in 1984.

The major tourist sight of Wenzhou, however, is **Jiangxin Park**, an island located a few minutes offshore in the Ou River to the north of town. The park – where no cars are allowed – contains a number of pavilions, towers and gardens, and is well worth two or three hours for a stroll or a picnic among the huge old trees. The most notable features of the island's skyline are its two **towers**; the one to the east is old and decrepit, but the western one has been fully restored. Boats run to the island every few minutes from the jetty at the northern end of Maxingseng Jie (daily 6.30am–4pm; ¥7 combined boat ride and island entrance fee). Returning from the island, you pay another ¥3 when you disembark townside.

Practicalities

Wenzhou's transport links have vastly improved with the construction of a rail link that runs to Hangzhou via Jinhua. The gleaming **train station** in the far south of town is complete with a glass-covered atrium, escalators and orderly crowds, and is among the most pleasant stations in the country; it's connected to the centre and the waterfront by bus #33.

Wenzhou also has **long-distance bus connections** with all points north and south along the coast. Confusingly, there are four major bus stations travellers might use – the Main, West, Old South and New South stations. Although in theory Shanghai buses use the West station, Ningbo the Old South, Fuzhou buses the New South, and all buses the Main station, there is such hot competition between operators that when **buying tickets**, you might as well just go to the nearest station. You'll find ticket kiosks in and outside the stations, with people trying to grab your custom. The Main bus station, which has the greatest frequency of departures, lies 3km south of town on Niushan Bei Lu; bus #103 from here travels downtown. Old South station is 1km southeast of downtown, on Feilu Nan Lu; bus #3 goes directly downtown and to the waterfront from here. The New South bus station is on Shugang Gong Lu, two blocks west of the train station in the far south of town. Take bus #27 from the train station to get downtown. The West station lies just east off Lucheng Jie (bus #105 heads to the waterfront).

The **airport** is 25km away to the east of town, and there's a CAAC bus which drops passengers at the main **booking office** remotely located in the southeast of town on Minhang Lu (Ⓣ0577/8333197). Bus #5 runs from here along Renmin Lu, the southern perimeter of the central area, where a number of hotels are located.

The other possibility is to arrive by **ferry** from Shanghai, in which case you'll find yourself at Anlanting dock in the northeastern part of town, on the Ou River. Bus #4 passes here running west along Wangjiang Dong Lu and then heads south along Jiefang Lu. The ferry **ticket office** is located on a small alley just to the east off the northern end of Maxingseng Jie (daily 8–11.30am & 1–4.30pm). There are departures every day and tickets range from ¥275 (special class) through ¥158 (first class) to ¥53, though be warned that this is no luxury cruise – even first class is very functional and the lower ones can be hellish. Despite the proud ferry-route map on the wall of the office, all boat routes other than that to Shanghai are now defunct. Wenzhou's **Bank of China** is at 113 Chan Jie (Mon–Fri 8-11.30am & 1.15–4.45pm), while the main **post office** (daily 8am–5.30pm) is off Xinhe Jie.

Accommodation and eating

There's plenty of accommodation in Wenzhou, some of it surprisingly cheap, though you may have some trekking to do as it is widely scattered. Away from the hotels are a number of **restaurants** worth trying out which specialize, unsurprisingly, in **seafood**. One of the liveliest and most popular is the *Wenzhou Restaurant* at the junction of Wuma Jie and Jiefang Lu. Low-budget dishes are served on the first floor; go upstairs for Wenzhou-style *dian xin* and Shanghainese seafood, as well as smarter service. The *Awailou Restaurant*, on Huaicheng Lu in the east of town, with its sister restaurant *Dongwailou* on Huaicheng Lu near the Anlanting dock, are both good places to sample local seafood specialities, or simply to admire the incredible variety and size of some of the fish on display in the fishtanks. For a fun night out, head to *Wumadihao* – a disco/coffee bar complex on the corner of Wuma Jie and Shengli Jie.

Hotels

Dong'ou 1 Wangjiang Lu ⓣ0577/8187901. This is the tall building right on the waterfront opposite the docking point for the Shanghai ferries. Slightly shabby singles and doubles. ❹

Huaqiao Xinhe Jie ⓣ0577/8222406, ⓕ8229656. Located at the southern end of Xinhe Jie, near Renmin Xi Lu, in a busy commercial area, this is one of Wenzhou's best-established and biggest hotels. ❻

Hubin Youyongqiao Lu ⓣ0577/8227961, ⓕ8210600. A couple of minutes' walk east from the West bus station. Comfortable and upmarket. ❻

Shuichan Jiefang Lu ⓣ0577/8292929 ext 3188. In the heart of the old town, a couple of blocks north of Guangchang Lu, this place has a grotty lobby, but the rooms are tolerable. ❷

Wenzhou Dajiudian Gongyuan Lu ⓣ0577/8235991, ⓕ82221333. One of the bigger, smarter hotels, with standard facilities. ❻

Beyond Wenzhou

The Wenzhou vicinity is host to some superb mountain scenery, most notably in the **Yandang Shan**, an area of soaring cliffs and stunning verdant slopes some 80km to the northeast of town, in Leqing County. From Wenzhou's West bus station, you can get there on a bus to Baixi or "Leqing Yandangshan" (but ask to be dropped off in Baixi). Outside Baixi, there are several interesting hikes you can undertake to monasteries and scenic spots in the area, including the **Dalongqiu Pubu** (Da Long Qiu Waterfall), at 190m high one of the tallest in China. Although very few Western tourists have been to this area, it's not exactly undiscovered as Chinese tour groups have been coming here for a while and a tourist infrastructure is firmly in place. The **inn**, with adjoining restaurant, next to the **Lingfeng Si** (Lingfeng Temple), 2km from Baixi, has basic rooms and accepts foreigners (❶).

Travel details

Trains

Hangzhou to: Beijing (4 daily; 16hr); Guangzhou (3 daily; 22–24hr); Nanchang (daily; 12hr); Nanjing (8 daily; 5–7hr); Ningbo (8 daily; 3–4hr); Shanghai (22 daily; 2–3hr); Shaoxing (8 daily; 1hr 30min); Suzhou (9 daily; 3–4hr); Wenzhou (5 daily; 8–11hr); Wuxi (8 daily; 5hr).
Lianyungang to: Beijing (daily; 14hr); Nanjing (2 daily; 8hr); Shanghai (daily; 14hr); Xuzhou (7 daily; 5hr).
Nanjing to: Beijing (9 daily; 11–17hr); Chengdu (2 daily; 34–40hr); Fuzhou (2 daily; 19hr); Hangzhou (8 daily; 7–9hr); Lianyungang (daily; 8hr); Qufu (6 daily; 13hr); Shanghai (20 daily; 3–5hr); Suzhou (15 daily; 3–4hr); Wuhu (4 daily; 3hr); Wuxi (15 daily; 2–3hr); Xi'an (2 daily; 17hr); Xuzhou (5 daily; 5hr); Zhenjiang (17 daily; 1hr).
Ningbo to: Hangzhou (8 daily; 3–4hr); Shanghai (6 daily; 5–7hr); Shaoxing (8 daily; 2hr).
Shaoxing to: Hangzhou (8 daily; 1hr 30min); Ningbo (8 daily; 3–4hr); Shanghai (6 daily; 3–4hr).
Suzhou to: Hangzhou (9 daily; 3–4hr); Nanjing (15 daily; 3–4hr); Shanghai (18 daily; 1hr); Wuxi (17 daily; 1hr); Zhenjiang (16 daily; 2–3hr).
Wenzhou to: Hangzhou (7 daily; 8–11hr); Nanjing (daily; 16hr); Shanghai (4 daily; 10–12hr).
Wuxi to: Hangzhou (6 daily; 5hr); Nanjing (14 daily; 2–3hr); Shanghai (14 daily; 2hr); Suzhou (16 daily; 1hr); Zhenjiang (17 daily; 2hr).
Xuzhou to: Beijing (7 daily; 8–11hr); Ji'nan (4 daily; 7hr); Kaifeng (6 daily; 5hr); Lianyungang (7 daily; 5hr); Nanjing (6 daily; 5hr); Qufu (3 daily; 5hr); Shanghai (13 daily; 9hr); Zhengzhou (12 daily; 6hr).
Zhenjiang to: Nanjing (17 daily; 1hr); Shanghai (13 daily; 3–4hr); Suzhou (16 daily; 2–3hr); Wuxi (16 daily; 2hr).

Buses

Vast numbers of bus companies operate throughout the Jiangsu/Zhejiang region and beyond, so it should be convenient to find a bus to your destination, though if your trip is of any great length turn up at the bus staion before midday. The construction of new freeways between Shanghai and Nanjing, and Lianyungang and Nanjing, has greatly reduced travel times in the region in the past few years.
Hangzhou to: Huang Shan (5hr); Lianyungang (9hr); Nanjing (6hr); Ningbo (3hr); Shanghai (2hr); Shaoxing (1hr); Suzhou (4hr); Wenzhou (10hr); Wuxi (4hr); Yangzhou (6hr).
Huai'an to: Lianyungang (2 daily; 3hr); Nanjing (4hr); Shanghai (8hr); Xuzhou (4–5hr); Yangzhou (2 daily; 3hr); Zhenjiang (2 daily; 5hr).
Lianyungang to: Hangzhou (10hr); Huai'an (3hr); Nanjing (5hr); Qingdao (6hr); Shanghai (8hr); Xuzhou (4hr); Yangzhou (5hr); Zhenjiang (7hr).
Nanjing
East station to: Yangzhou (2hr); Yixing (4hr).
Hanfu Jie station to: Hangzhou (5hr); Huang Shan (5hr); Ningbo (8hr); Wenzhou (12hr); Wuhan (19hr).
Zhongyangmen station to: Hefei (7hr); Huai'an (3–4hr); Lianyungang (4–5hr); Qingdao (12hr); Shanghai (4–5hr); Suzhou (3–4hr); Wuxi (2–3hr); Xuzhou (5–6hr); Zhenjiang (1hr).
Ningbo to: Hangzhou (3hr); Nanjing (8hr); Shaoxing (2hr); Wenzhou (7hr).
Shaoxing to: Hangzhou (1hr); Ningbo (2hr).
Suzhou
Beimen station to: Hangzhou (4hr); Nanjing (3hr); Shanghai (1–2hr); Wuxi (1hr); Yangzhou (5hr).
Nanmen station to: Dingshan (3hr); Tongli (1hr); Yixing (3hr), Zhouzhuang (2hr).
Wenzhou to: Fuzhou (8hr); Guangzhou (36hr); Hangzhou (9 daily; 10hr); Nanjing (13hr); Ningbo (7hr); Shanghai (12hr); Suzhou (12hr); Wuxi (13hr); Xiamen (13hr).
Wuxi
North station to: Hangzhou (4hr); Lianyungang (8h); Nanjing (2hr); Shanghai (2hr); Suzhou (1hr); Yangzhou (2hr 30min); Zhenjiang (1hr 30min).
South station to: Yixing (2hr).
Xuzhou to: Huai'an (4–5hr); Lianyungang (4hr); Nanjing (5–6hr); Yangzhou (5hr).
Yangzhou
East station to: Hangzhou (7hr); Huai'an (5hr); Shanghai (6hr); Suzhou (5hr); Wuxi (2hr 30min).
West station to: Nanjing (2hr); Zhenjiang (1hr).
Yixing to: Hangzhou (4hr); Nanjing (4hr); Wuxi (2hr); Zhenjiang (3hr).
Zhenjiang to: Huai'an (3hr); Lianyungang (6hr); Nanjing (1hr); Yangzhou (1hr 30min); Yixing (3hr).

Ferries

Hangzhou to: Suzhou (2 daily; 13hr); Wuxi (daily; 14hr).
Nanjing to: Chongqing (2 daily; 5 days); Shanghai (2 daily; 14hr); Wuhan (5 daily; 2 days).
Ningbo to: Putuo Shan (9 daily; 2–4hr); Shanghai (3 daily; 6–9hr).
Putuo Shan to: Ningbo (10–13 daily; 2–4hr); Shanghai (3 or 4 daily; 4-12hr).

Suzhou to: Hangzhou (daily; 13hr).
Wenzhou to: Shanghai (daily; 18hr).
Wuxi to: Hangzhou (daily; 14hr).

Flights

Hangzhou to: Beijing (daily; 2hr); Chengdu (6 daily; 2hr 30min); Fuzhou (3 daily; 1hr); Guangzhou (4 or 5 daily; 2hr); Guilin (daily; 1hr 45min); Hong Kong (2 daily; 2hr 30min); Kunming (2 daily; 2hr 30min); Qingdao (daily; 1hr 30min); Shanghai (daily; 25min); Shenzhen (daily; 2hr); Singapore (3 weekly; 6hr); Wenzhou (2 daily; 50min); Xiamen (2 daily; 1hr 20min); Xi'an (daily; 2hr 20min).
Lianyungang to: Beijing (5 weekly; 1hr 35min); Guangzhou (6 weekly; 2hr 20min); Shenzhen (3 weekly; 2hr 10min).
Nanjing to: Beijing (7 daily; 1hr 50min); Chengdu (1 or 2 daily; 2hr 25min); Chongqing (daily; 2hr 20min); Dalian (daily; 1hr 30min); Fuzhou (2 daily; 1hr 40min); Guangzhou (6 daily; 2hr 5min); Guilin (6 weekly; 2hr); Haikou (4 weekly; 3hr 15min); Hong Kong (5 daily; 2hr 35min); Kunming (daily; 2hr 40min); Ningbo (2 weekly; 1hr); Qingdao (2 daily; 1hr); Shenzhen (2–4 daily; 2hr); Ürümqi (2 weekly; 4hr 45min); Wenzhou (daily; 1hr 20min); Xiamen (2–4 daily; 1hr 45min); Xi'an (daily; 2hr).
Ningbo to: Beijing (4 daily; 2hr); Guangzhou (2 daily; 2hr); Hong Kong (2 daily; 2hr 15min); Nanjing (2 weekly; 1hr); Shanghai (4 daily; 40min); Shenzhen (2 daily; 2hr 10min); Wenzhou (daily; 50min); Xiamen (daily; 1hr).
Wenzhou to: Beijing (4 daily; 2hr 30min); Fuzhou (5 weekly; 40min); Guangzhou (4 daily; 2hr); Hangzhou (4 daily; 1hr); Hong Kong (4 weekly; 2hr 15min); Nanjing (6 weekly; 1hr 20min); Ningbo (daily; 50min); Shanghai (5 daily; 1hr 5min); Shenzhen (2 daily; 1hr 55min); Xiamen (daily; 55min); Xi'an (6 weekly; 2hr 30min).

CHAPTER 7

Highlights

* **Yixian** Amazing collection of antique Ming villages, used atmospherically in Zhang Yimou's film *Raise the Red Lantern*. **See p.524**
* **Huang Shan** Arguably China's most scenic mountain, wreathed in narrow stone staircases, contorted trees, and cloud-swept peaks. **See p.525**
* **Hubei Provincial Museum** On show here are 2000-year-old relics from the tombs of aristocrats, including a lacquered coffin and an orchestra of 64 giant bronze bells. **See p.538**
* **Shennongjia Forest Reserve** Wild and remote mountain refuge of the endangered golden monkey and (so it's said) the enigmatic *ye ren*, China's yeti. **See p.547**
* **Wudang Shan** Temple-covered mountains at the heart of Taoist martial art mythology; it's said this is where *tai ji* originated. **See p.551**
* **Jingdezhen** China's porcelain capital for the last six centuries, with a fine ceramic history museum and busy street markets. **See p.581**

7

The Yangzi basin

Having raced out of Sichuan through the narrow Three Gorges, the **Yangzi** (here known as the **Changjiang**) widens, slows down, and loops through its flat, low-lying middle reaches, swelled by lesser streams and rivers which drain off the highlands surrounding the four provinces of the Yangzi basin: **Anhui**, **Hubei**, **Hunan** and **Jiangxi**. As well as watering one of China's key rice- and tea-growing areas, this stretch of the Yangzi has long supported trade and transport; back in the thirteenth century, Marco Polo was awed by the "innumerable cities and towns along its banks, and the amount of shipping it carries, and the bulk of merchandise that merchants transport by it". The fact that rural fringes away from the river – including much of Anhui and Jiangxi provinces – remain some of the least developed regions in central China will hopefully be redressed by the completion around 2008 of the mighty **Three Gorges Dam** on the border between Hubei and Chongqing, whose estimated hydroelectric output will power a local industrial economy to rival that of the east coast.

The river basin itself is best characterized by the flat expanses of China's two largest freshwater lakes: **Dongting**, which pretty well marks the border between Hunan and Hubei, and **Poyang**, in northern Jiangxi, famed for porcelain produced at nearby **Jingdezhen**. Riverside towns such as **Wuhu** in Anhui are also interesting as working ports, where it's still possible to see traditional river industries – fish farming, grain, rice and bamboo transport – existing alongside newer ventures in manufacturing. Strangely enough, while all four regional capitals are located near water, only **Wuhan**, in Hubei, is actually on the Yangzi itself, a privileged position which has turned the city into central China's liveliest urban conglomeration. By contrast, the other provincial capitals – **Changsha** in Hunan, Anhui's **Hefei** and Jiangxi's **Nanchang** – seem somewhat dishevelled, though long settlement has left a good deal of **history** in its wake, from well-preserved Han-dynasty tombs to whole villages of Ming-dynasty houses, and almost everywhere you'll stumble over sites from the epic of the **Three Kingdoms**, making the tale essential background reading (see box, p.509). Many cities also remain studded with hefty European buildings, a hangover from their being forcibly opened up to foreign traders as **Treaty Ports** in the 1860s, following the Second Opium War. Perhaps partly due to these unwanted intrusions, the Yangzi basin can further claim to be the **cradle of modern China**: Mao Zedong was born in Hunan; Changsha, Wuhan and Nanchang are all closely associated with Communist Party history; while the mountainous border between Hunan and Jiangxi was both a Red refuge during right-wing purges in the late 1920s and the starting point for the subsequent Long March to Shaanxi.

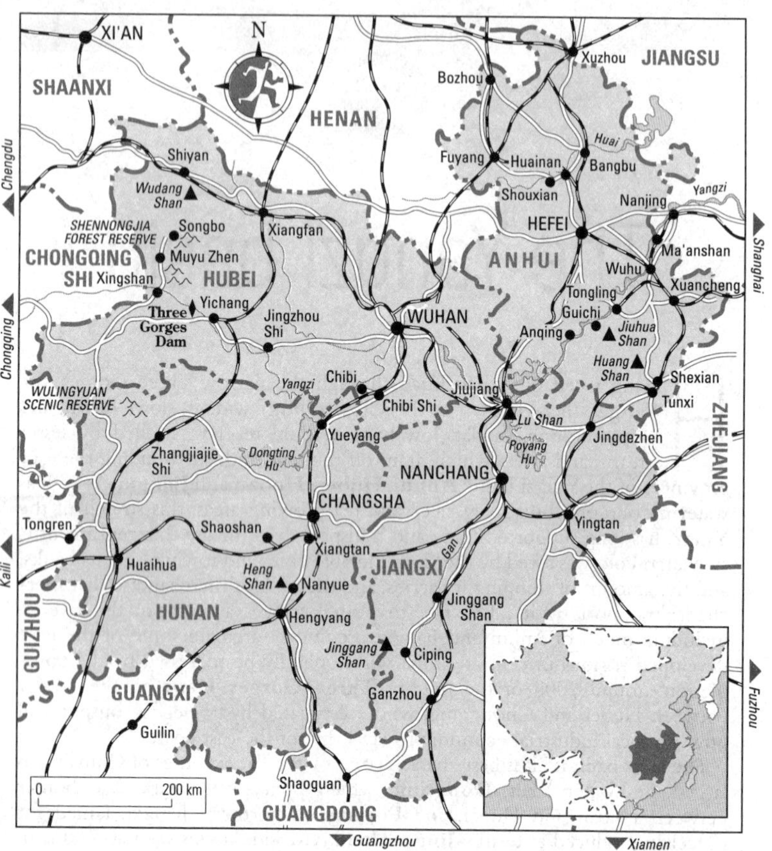

Away from the river, wild mountain landscapes make for some fine **hiking**, the pick of which is undoubtedly at **Huang Shan** in southern Anhui, followed by Hubei's remote **Shennongjia Forest Reserve**, and **Zhangjiajie** in Hunan's far west. Pilgrims also have a selection of Buddhist and Taoist **holy mountains** to scale on seemingly unending stone-flagged staircases – Hubei's **Wudang Shan** is outstanding – and less dedicated souls can find pleasant views at the mountain resort town of **Lu Shan** in Jiangxi.

In theory, **getting around** isn't a problem. **Ferries** remain an interesting, if slow, way to explore the river, with **rail** lines from all over China crossing the region, and a choice of **buses** and swifter, pricier minibuses linking cities to the remotest of corners. Autumn is probably the most pleasant time of year, though even winters are generally mild, but near-constant rains and consequential lowland **flooding** plague the summer months (June–Aug). In 1998, the worst floods in living memory claimed four thousand lives, wiped out entire villages, isolated cities and destroyed millions of hectares of crops, with a similar disaster only narrowly averted in 2002.

Sanguo: The Three Kingdoms

The empire, long divided, must unite; long united, must divide. Thus it has ever been.

So, rather cynically, begins one of China's best-known stories, the fourteenth-century historical novel **Romance of the Three Kingdoms**. Covering 120 chapters and a cast of thousands, the story touches heavily on the Yangzi basin, which, as a buffer zone between the Three Kingdoms, formed the backdrop for many major battles and key events. Some surviving sites are covered both in this chapter and elsewhere in the guide.

Though well founded in fact, the *Three Kingdoms* is – like King Arthur – essentially the stuff of legend. Opening in 168 AD, the tale recounts the decline of the Han empire, how China was split into three states by competing warlords, and the subsequent (short-lived) reunification of the country in 280 AD under a new dynasty. The main action began in 189 AD. At this point, the two protagonists were the villainous **Cao Cao** and the virtuous **Liu Bei**, whose watery character was compensated for by the strength of his spirited sworn brothers **Zhang Fei** and **Guan Yu** – the latter eventually becoming enshrined in the Chinese pantheon as the red-faced god of war and healing. Having put down the rebellious Yellow Turbans in the name of the emperor, both Cao and Liu felt their position threatened by the other; Cao was regent to the emperor **Xian**, but Liu had a remote blood tie to the throne. Though both claimed to support the emperor's wishes, Cao and Liu began fighting against each other, with Cao being defeated in Hubei at the **Battle of the Red Cliffs** (208 AD) after Liu engaged the aid of the wily adviser **Zhuge Liang**, who boosted Liu's heavily outnumbered forces by enlisting the help of a third warlord, **Sun Quan**.

Consolidating their positions, each of the three formed a private kingdom: Cao Cao retreated north to the Yellow River basin where he established the state of **Wei** around the ailing imperial court; Sun Quan set up **Wu** farther south along the lower Yangzi; while Liu Bei built a power base in the riverlands of Sichuan, the state of **Shu**. The alliance between Shu and Wu fell apart when Sun Quan asked Guan Yu to betray Liu. Guan refused and was assassinated by Sun in 220 AD. At this point Cao Cao died, and his ambitious son, **Cao Pi**, forced the emperor to abdicate and announced himself head of a new dynasty. Fearing retaliation from the state of Shu after Guan Yu's murder, Sun Quan decided to support Cao Pi's claims while, over in Shu, Liu Bei also declared his right to rule.

Against Zhuge Liang's advice, Liu marched against Wu to avenge Guan Yu's death but his troops mutinied, killing Zhang Fei. Humiliated, Liu withdrew to **Baidicheng** in the Yangzi Gorges and died. With him out of the way, Cao Pi attacked Sun Quan, who was therefore forced to renew his uncomfortable alliance with Shu – now governed by Zhuge Liang – to keep the invaders out of his kingdom. By 229 AD, however, things were stable enough for Sun Quan to declare himself as a rival emperor, leaving Zhuge to die fighting against the armies of Wei five years later. Wei was unable to pursue the advantage, as a coup against Cao Pi started a period of civil war in the north, ending around 249 AD when the **Sima clan** emerged victorious. Sun Quan died soon afterwards, while Shu abandoned all claim to the empire. Wei's Sima clan founded a new dynasty, the **Jin**, in 265 AD, finally overpowering Wu and uniting China in 280 AD.

Anhui

Despite government hopes that it will one day become a wealthy corridor between the coast and interior, **Anhui** largely lives up to its tradition as eastern China's poorest province. It has a long history, however, not all of it bad: million-year-old remains of the proto-human *Homo erectus* have been found here, while Shang-era copper mines in southern Anhui fuelled China's Bronze Age. The province later became well known for its artistic refinements, from decorative Han tombs through to Song-dynasty porcelain and Ming architecture.

All this, however, has been a struggle against Anhui's unfriendly geography. Arid and eroded, the north China plains extend into its upper third as far as the **Huai River**, and while the south is warmer and wetter, allowing for tea and tobacco cultivation, the fertile wooded hills soon climb to rugged mountains, and not much in the way of food can be grown there. But it is the **Yangzi** itself that ensures Anhui's poverty by regularly inundating the province's low-lying centre, which would otherwise produce a significant amount of crops. Until recently, a lack of bridges across the river also created a very physical division, separating the province's mountainous south from its more settled regions. Despite improvements in infrastructure since the 1990s, including the expansion of highways and railways, development remains muted, and Anhui seems to remain, rather unfairly, as economically retarded as ever.

For the visitor, this isn't all bad news. While neither the provincial capital, **Hefei**, nor the north have much beyond their history, there are compensations for Anhui's lack of development south of the Yangzi. Here, superlative mountain landscapes at **Huang Shan** and the collection of Buddhist temples at **Jiuhua Shan** have been pulling in droves of sightseers for centuries, and there's a strong cultural tradition stamped on the area, with a substantial amount of antique rural architecture surviving intact around **Tunxi**. Also here is a riverside reserve near **Xuancheng**, protecting the **Chinese alligator**, one of the World's most endangered animals, though another local rarity, the **Yangzi river dolphin**, is heading rapidly towards extinction.

Flooding aside – and there's a near guarantee of this affecting bus travel during the summer months – the main problem with finding your way around Anhui is that many towns have a range of aliases, and can be differently labelled on maps and timetables. **Rail lines** connect Hefei to Nanjing through Wuhu – Anhui's major port and a stop for Yangzi ferries – with other lines running west towards Changsha, north to Xi'an and Beijing, and south from Tunxi to Jiangxi.

Hefei

Nestled in the heart of the province but generally overlooked in the rush to cross the Yangzi and reach Huang Shan, Anhui's capital, **HEFEI**, gets few chance visitors. An unimportant backwater until being developed as a modest industrial base after 1949, Hefei's sole points of interest are a couple of **historical sites** and an unusually thorough **museum**. However, it's a comfortable

Hefei

Hefei	合肥	***héféi***
Bao Gong Ci	包公祠	*bāogōng cí*
Baohe Park	包河公园	*bāohé gōngyuán*
Li Hongzhang Ju	李鸿章居	*lǐhóngzhāng jū*
Mingjiao Si	明教寺	*míngjiào sì*
Provincial Museum	省博物馆	*shěng bówùguǎn*
Three Kingdoms	三国	*sān guó*
Xiaoyao Jin Park	逍遥津公园	*xiāoyáojīn gōngyuán*
Accommodation and eating		
Ao Xing	澳星宾馆	*àoxīng bīnguǎn*
Fuhao Fandian	富豪饭店	*fùháo fàndiàn*
Hao Xiang Lai	豪享来	*háoxiáng lái*
Holiday Inn	古井假日饭店	*gǔjǐng jiàrì fàndiàn*
Huaqiao Fandian	华侨饭店	*huáqiáo fàndiàn*
Jinli Yinlu	金利银路	*janlì yínlù dàjijdiàn*
Jinxin Jiujia	金新酒家	*jīnxīn jiǔjiā*
Luzhou	庐州	*lúzhōu*
Xinya	新亚大酒店	*xīnyà dàjiǔdiàn*
Zhongxi Kafei	中西咖啡	*zhōngxī kāfēi*

place to spend a couple of days, relatively untouched by the ugly building mania sweeping the rest of the country and dignified by a number of important science and technology colleges.

The City

Ringed by parkland and canals – the remains of Ming-dynasty moats – downtown Hefei resembles a suburban high street more than a provincial capital. Nothing is too far away to reach on foot, although the main roads are travelled by frequent **buses** – including claustrophobic double-deckers – and plenty of **taxis** prowl the centre, costing around ¥5 to hire.

The **Provincial Museum**, on Mengcheng Lu (Mon–Fri 8.30–10.40am & 2–4pm, Sat & Sun 8.30–11.40am & 2–5pm; ¥10), provides sound evidence for Anhui's contributions to Chinese culture. A walk-through plaster cave leads on to a cast of the **Homo erectus cranium** from Taodian in the south of the province, proudly displayed in an oversized glass case, while splinters of more immediate history emerge in a few Stone Age items and an exceptional Shang bronze urn decorated with tiger and dragon motifs. Also interesting are the carved blocks taken from **Han-dynasty mausoleums** – Chinese-speakers might be able to decipher the comments about the Cao family (of *Three Kingdoms* fame) incised into the bricks of their Bozhou tomb by construction labourers. Farther on, there's a special exhibition of the "**Four Scholastic Treasures**" for which the province is famed: high-quality ink sticks, heavy carved ink stones, weasel-hair writing brushes and multicoloured papers.

Across town, hyper-modern shopping plazas along the busy, pedestrian eastern half of Huai He Lu seem an unlikely location for **Mingjiao Si** (¥5), a sixteenth-century temple last restored in 1991, whose fortress-like walls front the unpretentious halls and peach garden. The temple occupies a Three Kingdoms site where the northern leader **Cao Cao** drilled his crossbowers during the winter of 216–217 AD. Earlier, his general Zhang Liao had routed Wu's armies at the bloody battle of **Xiaoyaojin** – the site is now an unexciting

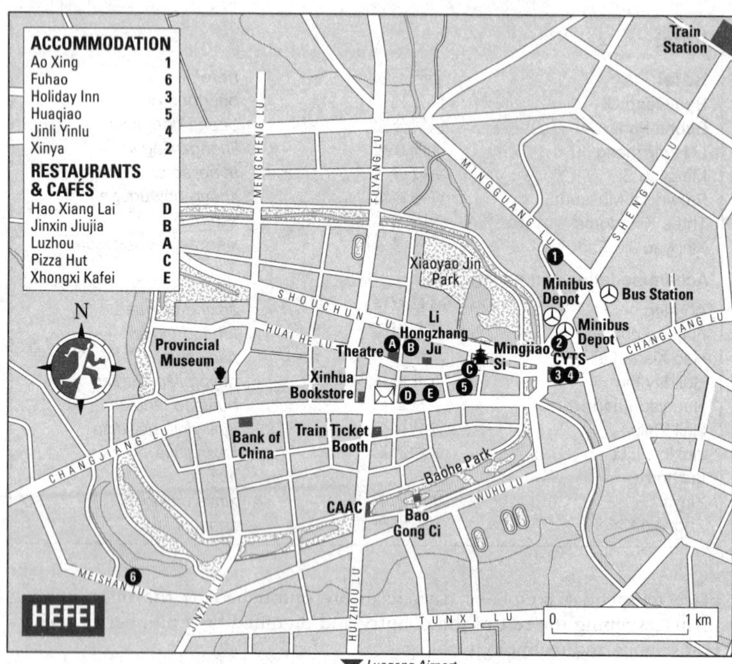

park directly north of the temple – where Sun Quan, the leader of Wu, had to flee on horseback by leaping the bridgeless canal. A glassed-in **well** in the temple's main courtyard reputedly dates from this time, and definitely looks ancient – a worn stone ring set close to the ground, deeply scored by centuries of ropes being dragged over the rim. Just west of Mingjiao Si, **Li Hongzhang Ju** (daily 8.30am–5.30pm; ¥15) is a similarly anachronistic Qing-era mansion, whose surrounding grey brick wall hides a series of tastefully decorated courtyards and halls embellished with opulently carved wooden furniture.

Down at the southeastern side of town, **Baohe Park** is a nice strip of lakeside willows and arched bridges off Wuhu Lu, where the **Bao Gong Ci** (Lord Bao Memorial Hall; ¥10) identifies Hefei as the birthplace of Bao, the famous Song-dynasty administrator, later governor of Kaifeng. Lord Bao's ability to uncover the truth in complex court cases, and his proverbially unbiased rulings, are the subject of endless tales – he also often appears as a judge in paintings of Chinese hell. Along with gilded statues, a **waxworks** brings a couple of well-known stories to life: look for Lord Bao's dark face, improbably "winged" hat, and the **three choppers** – shaped as a dragon, tiger and dog – he had made for summary executions; the implement used was chosen according to the status of the condemned.

Practicalities

Luogang airport is about 7km due south of the city, and connected by an airport bus to the **CAAC office** on Huizhou Lu, whose entrance doubles as a florist's (daily 8am–10pm; Ⓣ0551/2886626, Ⓕ2885553). The **train station** is 3km northeast of the centre at the end of Shengli Lu – bus #119 runs down

Shengli Lu and into town along Changjiang Lu – with lines servicing Bozhou, Shanghai, Guangzhou, Chengdu, Xiamen and Beijing. Aside from the station, you can also buy **train tickets** at a booth on Huizhou Lu, just south of the Changjiang Lu intersection.

Hefei's **main bus station**, on Minguang Lu, handles traffic to all over Anhui and to adjacent provincial capitals, though there are just as many services from the chaotic clutch of **minibus depots** nearby on Shengli Lu – leaving, you'll have to hunt around stations for the right vehicle.

Changjiang Lu is Hefei's high street, with all essential services in its vicinity: various **department stores**; a huge **Bank of China** (foreign exchange Mon–Fri 8.30am–4.30pm); and a **post office** (8am–6pm) with telephones, copies of the *China Daily*, and upstairs **Internet bar** (¥2 per hour). For **information** and **tours** concerning Anhui's highlights, the friendly and bilingual **CYTS** (Ⓣ0551/4291999, Ⓕ4291666) is housed on the ground floor of the Scitech Plaza, next to the *Holiday Inn*. The Xinhua Bookstore on Changjiang Lu has a good range of **books** in English – including translated Chinese novels – on the second floor, as does the Foreign Languages Bookshop on Huai He Lu.

Accommodation

Hefei's **hotels** are mostly mid-range or upmarket, although spoken Chinese may get you into one of the budget **hostels** (dorm beds ¥35 or so) around the long-distance bus stations.

Ao Xing Mingguang Lu Ⓣ0551/4298183. Fairly inexpensive, if not wonderfully furnished, with single and double rooms. ❹

Fuhao Fandian Meishan Lu Ⓣ0551/2811818, Ⓕ2817583. The budget wing of the four-star *Anhui Fandian*, located around the back. Rooms are bare but well looked after, and the rates are reasonable. ❹

Holiday Inn Changjiang Dong Lu Ⓣ0551/4291188, Ⓕ4291166. Usual range of facilities, along with a surprisingly inexpensive 24hr noodle bar. Foreign exchange counter for guests only. ❾

Huaqiao Fandian 98 Changjiang Lu Ⓣ0551/2652221, Ⓕ2542861. Seriously overpriced, but with decent facilities and a light breakfast included in the room price. ❺

Jinli Yinlu Dajiudian Shouchun Lu Ⓣ0551/4296255. Newly renovated and reasonably priced, though the staff are none too helpful. ❹

Xinya Dajiudian Near the bus stations on Shengli Lu Ⓣ0551/4292929, Ⓕ4296067. Upmarket lobby hides worn furnishings upstairs, but the rooms are large, everything works, and the staff are happy to have you. ❹

Eating, drinking and entertainment

There are plenty of cheap **stalls and canteens** where you can fill up on stir-fries, noodle soups and **river food** – especially little crabs and snails – east of the museum on Huai He Lu. Near the post office on Changjiang Lu, *Hao Xiang Lai* offers a good, inexpensive range of regional snacks – soups, buns, noodles, cold vegetable and meat dishes – all laid out for you to order by pointing. A few streets back on Suzhou Lu, near the intersection with Huai He Lu, are a couple of excellent places to tuck in with noisy local crowds: *Luzhou* is a barely furnished roast duck restaurant, but so popular you generally have to queue to get in; while *Jinxin Jiujia* is a smarter affair specializing in dumplings and light meals. For **Western-style** fare, there's a *Pizza Hut* and 24-hour café across from Mingjiao Si, or *Zhongxi Kafei* on Changjiang Lu, a café with set meals of steak or pasta from ¥30.

For an evening out, Hefei has something of a reputation for **stage productions** – there are at least two indigenous opera styles and a local acrobatic troupe – and there's a **theatre** west of Mingjiao Si on Huai He Lu. Consult the ticket office, local papers or CYTS for performance information.

Northern Anhui

Cynics say that northern Anhui's high points are the roads, which run on flood-proof embankments a few metres above the green, pancake-flat paddy fields. Certainly, about the only geographic features are **rivers** such as the **Huai He**, setting for the rather drab industrial and grain centre of **BANGBU**. The **battle of Huai Hai** took place nearby in 1948, when a million Guomindang and PLA combatants fought a decisive encounter in which the guerrilla-trained Communists overran Chiang Kaishek's less flexible forces. A demoralized GMD surrendered in Beijing in January the next year, and though war resumed when the two sides couldn't agree on terms, it was largely a mopping-up operation by the Communists against GMD bastions.

All this is mainly background for what you'll see along the way, but historians, town planners and anyone interested in Traditional Chinese Medicine will find a smattering of attractions at **Shouxian** – feasible as a day-trip from the capital – and **Bozhou**, which is worth a day's scrutiny on the long haul into or out of the province. There are **minibuses** through the day from Hefei's Shengli Lu depots to Bozhou or Shouxian; make sure with the latter that you don't end up getting herded aboard a bus bound for the more familiar tourist destination of Shexian (the local pronounciation is very similar). Less conveniently, the daily **train** from Hefei to Bozhou leaves at around 3am.

Shouxian

About 100km and two hours north of Hefei, **SHOUXIAN** was a regional capital back in 241 BC, during the Warring States Period, and is now a small country seat surrounded by over 6km of dykes and Ming-era **stone walls** which can be climbed for views. Minibuses from Hefei drop you at the virtually defunct bus station about 700m south of the walls; the road bends around to enter the town through the **south gate**'s triple arch and then you're following Shouxian's die-straight main road through the best surviving example of a Song-dynasty street plan in China. There are a couple of specific sights – an old **theatre** on the eastern axis, and the ruinous **Bao'en Monastery** hidden in the southwestern quarter – but there's more fun in just wandering the tiny back lanes, where you frequently come across buildings with dated wood-

Northern Anhui

Bangbu	蚌埠	***bàngbù***
Bozhou	亳州	***bózhōu***
Chinese Medicinal Products Marketplace	中药材交易中心	*zhōngyàocái jiāoyìzhōngxīn*
Cuiwei Dajiudian	翠微大酒店	*cuìwēi dàjiǔdiàn*
Dixia Yunbing Dao	地下运兵道	*dìxià yùnbīndào*
Gujing Dajiudian	古井大酒店	*gǔjǐng dàjiǔdiàn*
Gu Qian Zhuang	古钱庄	*gǔqián zhuāng*
Hua Xi Lou	花戏楼	*huāxì lóu*
Fuyang	阜阳	***fǔyáng***
Huainan	淮南	***huáinán***
Shouxian	寿县	***shòuxiàn***
Bao'en Monastery	报恩寺	*bàoēn sì*

en lintels and bronze detailing on doors. Shouxian was also the home of the Han-dynasty philosopher **Liu An**, who supposedly invented bean curd, and there's an annual September **Tofu Festival** in his honour.

A couple of inexpensive **guesthouses** (❷) lie along Shouxian's main street, but foreigners are a rare sight in town and attract so much attention that you may feel more comfortable **moving on**. For destinations further afield than Hefei, catch a minibus-taxi (¥2) from outside the bus station 20km east to the monochrome coal-mining centre of **Huainan**, from where there are irregular buses to Nanjing, Shanghai, Wuhan, and **Fuyang**, on the way to Bozhou.

Bozhou

BOZHOU lies in Anhui's northwestern corner, around five hours from Hefei or three from Shouxian, the journey taking in scenes of river barges loading up with coal, red-brick villages surrounded by polled willows, and a level horizon pierced by kiln chimneys. The city's fame rests on its being the largest marketplace in the world for **traditional medicines**; as the birthplace of **Hua Mulan**, heroine of Chinese legend and Disney animation (though there are no monuments to her here); and as the ancestral home of the Three Kingdoms warlord, **Cao Cao**. Portrayed in the tale as a self-serving villain whose maxim was "Better to wrong the world than have it wrong me", he was nonetheless a brilliant general and respectable poet, whose claims to rule China were just as legitimate as his arch rival, Lu Bei. At any rate, nobody in Bozhou seems ashamed of the connection.

Bozhou's frankly grimy, squalid main streets may initially have you wondering why you made the journey, but it's worth perservering. About 3km southeast of the centre, the eastern end of Zhan Qian Lu (the train station approach road) sets up from Monday to Friday as a **medicinal market**, attracting something in the region of 60,000 traders daily from all over China and Southeast Asia. The main **Chinese Medicinal Products Marketplace** here is a huge building on the south side of the road, packed to the roof in places with bales of dried plants, fungi – including the bizarre caterpillar fungus, or *cordyceps* – and animals (or bits of them), the rest of the space taken up by enthusiastic crowds. The market's activity and strangely reassuring smell is alone justify the trip to town.

The rest of Bozhou is for history buffs. On the south side of Renmin Zhong Lu, **Dixia Yunbing Dao** (¥5) is a 100m-long subterranean **tunnel** Cao Cao had installed so his troops could take an invading army by surprise; the arched, claustrophobic brick passages are totally unexpected at street level. North from here, Renmin Bei Jie forms the congested heart of Bozhou's **Muslim** community, full of noodle, bread and mutton kebab vendors, and containing a couple of small **mosques**; the street ends by passing through the city's solid stone **north gate**. Beyond, the area between Heping Lu and the river is filled by a quiet net of nineteenth-century lanes, a procession of small whitewashed shops and home industries. **Gu Qian Zhuang** (Old Bank; ¥5) on Nanjing Gang here served its original function between 1825 and 1949 and provides great views of surrounding grey-tiled roofs from an upstairs balcony, though otherwise it's rather bare.

Bozhou's architectural masterpiece is **Hua Xilou** (¥12), a seventeenth-century guild-temple **theatre** some 500m north of Gu Qian Zhuang at the river end of Nanjing Gang. Sporting skilfully carved brick and wood embellishments, the theatre is named after the Han-dynasty doctor **Hua Tuo**, the first person credited with using anaesthetics during surgery, who was bumped off by Cao Cao after refusing to become the warlord's personal physician. Check out the painted friezes surrounding the stage, where several well-known *Three Kingdoms* set-pieces are depicted, including Zhuge Liang's celebrated "Empty City Stratagem": having no troops to defend the key stronghold of Xicheng, Zhuge opened the gates and sat in surrender on the battlements while his men swept the road below; but knowing his cunning the invading general, Sima Yi, suspected some elaborate trap and fled. The theatre's rear hall contains a collection of neolithic stone axes and Eastern Han artefacts unearthed nearby, including a **jade burial suit** made of 2400 tiles belonging to Cao Cao's father, Cao Song, who was ignominiously killed by rebels while hiding in a toilet.

Practicalities

Bozhou's centre is a two-kilometre-wide grid just south of the slow-flowing **Wo He**, the main roads being east–west Renmin Lu, and north–south Qiaoling Lu, which intersect on the eastern side of town. The **train station** is about 3km southeast – best reached by taxi – but the only useful connection on this minor track is an early-morning departure back to Hefei. An alternative rail option is to catch a minibus south to **Fuyang** (around 1hr 30min), which is on the Beijing–Jiujiang and Hefei–Zhengzhou lines. The two adjacent **bus stations** on Qiaoling Lu mostly serve Hefei, Fuyang, or local destinations, with a few battered and elderly (if cheap) long-distance buses to adjoining provinces.

The intersection of Renmin Lu and Qiaoling Lu, about 500m south of the bus stations, marks a heap of **accommodation** options. *Cuiwei Dajiudian* is an ordinary urban hotel (Ⓣ0558/5516604; ❸), while across the road *Gujing Dajiudian* (Ⓣ0558/5521274; ❹) has some pretentions to comfort – there are plenty of others if these two don't appeal. The **Bank of China** is also on the crossroads, with the main **post office** 500m west on Renmin Zhong Lu. Hotpot and noodle stalls abound, and the *Cuiwei Dajiudian*'s **restaurant** is extremely popular with local dignitaries.

The Yangzi River towns

The Yangzi flows silt-grey and broad for 350km across Anhui's lower third, forming a very visible geographic boundary – once across, hills and mountains are always in view, if you're not actually among them. An indication of the province's chronic underdevelopment is the fact that as recently as 1995 the only way to cross the river was by ferry, though it's now bridged east at **Wuhu** and roughly halfway along at **Tongling**. Most of the riverside towns are unashamedly functional and don't really justify special trips, but you'll pass by on ferries or minibuses while transiting the province; Wuhu and **Xuancheng** are also on the Hefei–Tunxi (Huang Shan) **rail line**.

Ma'anshan, Wuhu and Xuancheng

Powering up the Yangzi from Nanjing into eastern Anhui, you immediately pass **MA'ANSHAN**, an industrial centre notable for cliffside scenery 7km south at **Cuiluo Shan**. Here, a series of halls and pavilions comemorate the itinerant romantic Tang poet **Li Bai**, who drowned nearby in 762 AD after drunkenly falling out of a boat while trying to touch the moon's reflection.

A more likely stop is at south-bank **WUHU**, Anhui's major ferry port and trading post. In treaty-port days this was as far upstream as steamers could nav-

The Yangzi River towns

Yangzi River	长江	***chángjiāng***
Anqing	安庆	***ānqìng***
Guichi	贵池	***guìchí***
Ma'anshan	马鞍山	***mǎ'ān shān***
Cuilou Shan	翠螺山	*cuìlúo shān*
Tongling	铜岭	***tónglǐng***
Wusong Shan Binguan	五松山宾馆	*wǔsōngshān bīnguǎn*
Yangzi river dolphins	白鳍	*báijì*
Wuhu	芜湖	***wúhú***
Jing Hu	镜湖	*jìnghú*
Tieshan Binguan	铁山宾馆	*tiěshān bīnguǎn*
Zheshan Park	赭山公园	*zhěshān gōngyuán*
Zhongjiang Pagoda	中江塔	*zhōngjiāng tǎ*
Xuancheng	宣城	***xuānchéng***
Chinese Alligator Breeding Centre	扬子鳄养殖场	*yángzìè yǎngzhíchǎng*
Xuanzhou Binguan	宣州宾馆	*xuānzhōu bīnguǎn*

igate, and the shipyards were kept busy turning out smaller rafts for carrying coastal wares farther along the Yangzi and its tributaries. Today, despite the rail and road taking much of this business away, you can still see barges from Anhui's north unloading their coal, bamboo, timber and gravel down at Wuhu's wharves, though the city's focus has shifted to textile manufacture and other light industries. These include **wrought-iron pictures**, possibly China's most pointless handicraft, an artistic technique said to have resulted from an argument between a painter and a blacksmith in the seventeenth century.

Given the convergence of transport routes here it's almost impossible to avoid Wuhu, and it's not a bad place to break your journey for an hour or two. The **train station** is in the northeastern quarter of town, facing the **bus station** across a huge empty field; there are minibuses through the day to Hefei, Nanjing, Shanghai, Tunxi, and Jiuhua Shan. Bus #4 runs from here down Dazhai Lu past hilly **Zheshan Park** on the right – where you can clamber up a semi-ruinous three-storey pagoda for views over the town – before terminating at the **ferry terminal**, about 1km north of the five-storey, mid-stream **Zhongjiang Pagoda**. Not far from here, through the leafy, narrow streets of the old town centre, is **Jing Hu** (Mirror Lake), which is little more than an overgrown pond and small pavilion. For a **place to stay**, the three-star *Tieshan Binguan* on Gengxin Lu (Ⓣ0553/3835981, Ⓕ3830240; ❹) is nicely located on the west side of Zheshan Park, or you can try hostels near the bus and ferry terminals for budget beds.

Xuancheng

Chinese-speakers interested in wildlife should make the trip to **XUANCHENG**, two hours by bus to the southeast of Wuhu across low hills patterned by tea plantations – confusingly, you pass another Wuhu, the county town, halfway there. An untidy but friendly place, Xuancheng is associated with the production of high-quality handmade art paper (though this actually comes from **Jiangxian**, 55km to the southwest), and is also the site of a **Chinese alligator breeding centre**, several kilometres south of town. It's worth the effort to reach because wild populations of these timid alligators are few and confined to Anhui, though since the 1990s a worldwide project co-ordinated by the US Bronx Zoo has boosted their captive numbers to several thousand. Getting to the breeding centre can be impossible after rain – you're likely to find the road under water and locals paddling between their houses in wooden tubs – otherwise, negotiate with the minibus drivers at the crossroads near the bus station. If you can't speak Chinese, try asking travel companies at Tunxi or Hefei to phone ahead and arrange a visit for you.

Surrounded by small rivers, Xuancheng is about 2km across, with the **train station** on the eastern side and the main **bus station** to the southwest. For **accommodation**, food and information, there are several hostels close to transit points, or the more upmarket *Xuanzhou Binguan* (Ⓣ0553/3022957; ❹) near the bus station on Zhuangyuan Lu.

Tongling and around

Connected by road to Wuhu and Qingyang, and by an expressway to Hefei, **TONGLING** – Anhui's "Copper Capital" and surrounded by industrial complexes and power stations – marks the halfway point in the Yangzi's journey across the province. In recent years Tongling has been at the forefront of efforts to save the light grey *baiji*, or **Yangzi river dolphin**, from oblivion. The *baiji*'s catastrophic decline – there were only an estimated two dozen animals left in 1997, though they were common as recently as the 1970s – has been directly linked to the growth of industrial pollution, river traffic and net fishing on the Yangzi. A reserve was belatedly created southwest of town but attempts to locate a breeding pair of dolphins have so far failed and it remains vacant. Unless recent reports of attempted **cloning** can be trusted, the species seems doomed, lingering on only in Tongling's **Baiji beer**, which has the dolphin's Latin name, *Lipotes vexillifer*, stamped on the bottle cap. Tongling is not a hard place to navigate: most of the town stretches for a couple of kilometres along **Yi'an Lu**, which runs south from the main **bus station**, past the westerly T-junction with Huai He Lu, down to a **country minibus depot** for departures to Qingyang and Jiuhua Shan (see below). For **accommodation**, there's the *Wusong Shan Binguan* across from the bus station (Ⓣ0562/2864487, Ⓕ2862937; ❹) – don't confuse it with the adjacent, very run-down guesthouse of the same name.

Further upstream towards the border with Jiangxi and Hubei, **Guichi** is the next stop for river traffic, with plenty of minibuses from here to Qingyang and Jiuhua Shan, clearly visible off to the south. Not much farther on, the last port of call within Anhui is the northern bank town of **Anqing**, both a Taiping rebel stronghold during the late 1840s, and a cultural centre famed nationally for its **Huangmei opera style**. Beyond here the boat takes half a day to reach Jiujiang and Poyang Hu in Jiangxi Province (see p.576).

Jiuhua Shan

As an alternative to the better-known Huang Shan (see p.525), **Jiuhua Shan** (Nine Glorious Mountains) has many advantages: it's lower (the highest peak is a little over 1300m), the walking is considerably easier, and there's plenty of

Jiuhua Shan		
Jiuhua Shan	九华山	***jiǔhuá shān***
Baisui Gong	百岁宫	*bǎisuì gōng*
Cable-car station	索道站	*suǒdào zhàn*
Dabei Lou	大悲楼	*dàbēi lóu*
Fenghuang Song	凤凰松	*fènghuáng sōng*
Funicular Railway	缆车站	*lǎnchē zhàn*
Huacheng Si	化城寺	*huàchéng sì*
Julong Dajiudian	聚笼大酒店	*jùlóng dàjiǔdiàn*
Longquan Fandian	龙泉饭店	*lóngquán fàndiàn*
Taihua Shanzhuang	太华山庄	*tàihuá shānzhuāng*
Tiantai Zhengding	天台正顶	*tiāntái zhèngdǐng*
Yingke Song	迎客松	*yíngkè sōng*
Zhiyuan Si	执园寺	*zhíyuán sì*
Qingyang	青阳	***qīngyáng***

interest beyond the scenery. A place of worship for fifteen hundred years, this has been one of China's **sacred Buddhist mountains** ever since the Korean monk **Jin Qiaojue** (believed to be the reincarnation of the Bodhisattva Dizang, whose doctrines he preached) died here in a secluded cave in 794 AD. Today there are more than sixty temples – some founded back in the ninth century – containing a broad collection of sculptures, religious texts and early calligraphy, though there are also plenty of visitors (many of them overseas Chinese and Koreans) and some outsized building projects threatening to overwhelm Jiuhua Shan's otherwise human scale. Even so, an atmosphere of genuine devotion is clearly evident in the often austere halls with their wisps of incense smoke and distant chanting.

Practicalities

Though it's remote from major transport centres 60km south of the Yangzi, Jiuhua Shan is straightforward to reach, with direct **buses** at least from Hefei, Tangkou, Taiping (Huang Shan), Tongling and Guichi. Other traffic might drop you 25km to the northeast at **Qingyang**, from where mountain minibuses (¥6) leave when full throughout the day; in case you arrive late, there's a **hotel** (¥75) attached to the bus station here.

The twisting Jiuhua Shan road passes villages scattered through the moist green of rice fields and bamboo stands, white-walled houses built of bricks interlocked in a "herringbone" pattern, with some inspiring views of bald, spiky peaks above and valleys below. The road ends at picturesque **JIUHUA SHAN village**, where the mountain's accommodation, and the most famous temples, huddle around a couple of cobbled streets and squares, all hemmed in by encircling hills. On arrival at the village **gates** you'll have to pay Jiuhua Shan's **entry fee** (Mar–Nov ¥60, Dec–Feb ¥50). From here the road runs up past a host of market stalls selling postcards, trinkets, and waterproof **maps** and umbrellas for the frequently sodden weather.

About 100m along, the road divides around the village in a two-kilometre circuit; a booth selling onwards **bus tickets** is just down on the right here, while the core of the village lies straight ahead. Long-distance transport to Hefei, Nanjing, Tangkou, Taiping, Tunxi and Shanghai congregates first thing

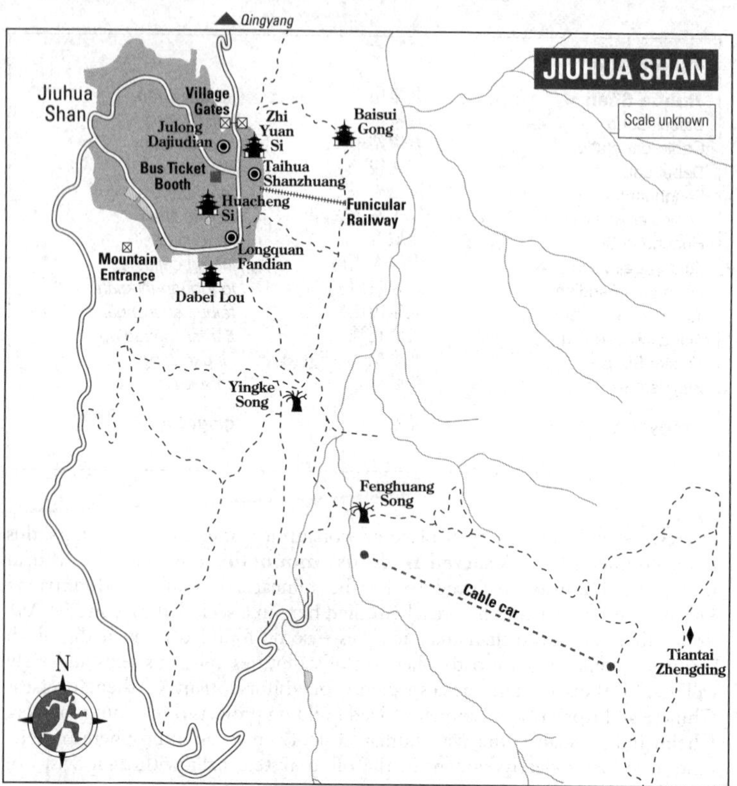

in the morning near the booth, or you can pick up frequent minibuses to Qingyang and look for connections there.

You'll be grabbed on arrival and offered all manner of **accommodation**, most of it decent value. For upmarket facilities try *Julong Dajiudian* (Ⓣ0566/5011368, Ⓕ5011022; ❺) to the right of the village gates behind an illuminated fountain, although they won't bargain and rooms are damp. Directly opposite, Zhiyuan Si has extremely bare beds (¥30) designed for itinerant monks, which may be available to tourists. Up the main street on the left, look for steps and an English sign above a parking lot for *Taihua Shanzhuang* (Ⓣ0566/5011340, Ⓕ5012888; ❸), a hospitable guesthouse with constant hot water; further along on the right you'll find clean rooms and plenty of Chinese tourists at *Longquan Fandian* (Ⓣ0566/5011320; ❸). Numerous **places to eat** offer everything from cheap buns to expensive game dishes.

On Jiuhua Shan

Just inside the village gates, **Zhiyuan Si** (¥5) is an imposing Qing monastery built with smooth, vertical walls, upcurving eaves and yellow-tiled roof nestled up against a cliff. Despite a sizeable exterior, the numerous little halls are cramped and stuffed with sculptures, including a fanged, bearded and hooknosed thunder god bursting out of its protective glass cabinet just inside the gate. Head for the main hall, in which a magnificently gilded **Buddhist trinity** sits solemnly on separate lotus flowers, blue hair dulled by incense smoke, and ringed by *arhats*. This makes quite a setting for the annual **temple fair**, held in Dizang's honour on the last day of the seventh lunar month, when the hall is packed with worshippers, monks and tourists. Make sure you look behind the altar, where Guanyin statuettes ascend right to the lofty wooden roof beams.

If you follow the main road around through the village, the next temple of note you come to is the new and garish **Dabei Lou** (¥5), which sports some hefty carved stonework; more or less opposite, **Huacheng Si** (¥5) is the mountain's oldest surviving temple, in part possibly dating right back to the Tang, though comprehensively restored. The stone entrance is set at the back of a large cobbled square whose centrepiece is a deep pond inhabited by some gargantuan goldfish. Inside, Huacheng's low-ceilinged, broad main hall doubles as a **museum**, with paintings depicting the life of Jin Qiaojue from his sea crossing to China (accompanied only by a faithful hound) to his death at the age of 90, and the discovery of his miraculously preserved corpse three years later.

To the peaks

The mountain's official "entrance" is marked by a huge ornamental gateway and temple about 500m past Dabei Lou on the main road, though well-concealed, smaller flagstoned paths ascend from behind Zhiyuan Si and at the corners of the main road in the village. There's also a **funicular railway** from the main street near *Longquan Fandian* to the ridge above Zhiyuan Si (¥32). Using these points, you can make a good, easy **circuit walk** on the ridges just above the village in about an hour, or extend this to a full **day's hike** up around Jiuhua's higher peaks – though again, you can save time by using minibuses and the cable car for part of the way. For the circuit, walk past Dabei Lou to where the road bends sharply right. Steps ascend from here to a moderately sized temple complex whose entrance-hall atrium contains some gruesomely entertaining, life-size sculptures of **Buddhist hell**. These are so graphic that it's hard not to feel that the artists enjoyed their task of depicting sinners being skewered, pummelled, strangled, boiled and bisected by demons, while the virtuous look down, doubtless exceedingly thankful for their salvation. Past the temple, a few minutes' walk brings you to a meeting of several paths at **Yingke Song** (Welcoming Guest Pine); bear left and it's a couple of kilometres past several pavilions and minor temples to steep views down onto the village at **Baisui Gong** (¥5), a plain, atmospheric monastery. The interior is far from weatherproof, with clouds drifting in and out of the main hall. A rear room contains the mummy of the Ming priest **Wu Xia**, best known for compiling the **Huayan sutras** in gold dust mixed with his own blood; his tiny body is displayed seated in prayer, grotesquely covered in a thick, smooth skin of gold leaf. Steps descend from Baisui Gong to Zhiyuan Si, or you can take the **funicular railway** down to the main street. To reach the upper peaks, turn right at Yingke Song, and you've a two-hour climb ahead of you via **Fenghuang Song** (Phoenix Pine), more temples, wind-scoured rocks, and superb scenery surrounding the summit area at **Tiantai Zhengding** (Heavenly Terrace). There's also a **cable car** from Fenghuang Song to just below the peaks (¥55 up, ¥45 down); the truly indolent can catch a minibus to the Fenghuang Song terminus from opposite Dabei Lou in the village (¥5). Witnessing the sunrise from here, **Li Bai**, the Tang man of letters, was inspired to bestow Jiuhua Shan with its name by the sight of the major pinnacles rising up out of clouds. In future years, this will also be the place to follow the progress of China's most grandiose religious building project: a 99-metre-high **statue of Dizang** is planned for the mountain, which if completed will be the largest Buddha sculpture in the world.

Tunxi and around

The most obvious reason to stop in **Tunxi**, set down near Anhui's southernmost borders, is because of the town's transport connections to Huang Shan, 50km off to the northwest (see p.525): Tunxi has the closest **airport** and **train station** to the mountain, while many long-distance buses pass through here as well. However, if you've the slightest interest in classical Chinese **architecture**, then Tunxi and its environs are worth checking out in their own right. Anhui's isolation has played a large part in preserving a liberal sprinkling of seventeenth-century monuments and homes in the area, especially around **Shexian** and **Yixian**, just short bus-rides away.

Tunxi

An old trading centre, **TUNXI** (aka **Huang Shan Shi**) is set around the junction of two rivers, with the original part of town along the north bank of the **Xin'an Jiang** at the intersection of Huang Shan Lu and Xin'an Lu, and a newer quarter focused around the train and bus stations a kilometre or so to the northeast. If you've time to spare, try tracking down two **Ming-dynasty houses** in Tunxi's eastern backstreets (neither is well marked). The more easterly house – that of the mathematician Cheng Dawei – is in a sorry state of repair, but both are classic examples of the indigenous **Huizhou style**, of which you'll find plenty more at Shexian or Yixian. Their plan, of two floors of galleried rooms based around a courtyard, proved so popular that it became the benchmark of urban domestic architecture in central and eastern China.

Tunxi and around

Tunxi	屯溪	***túnxī***
Cheng Dawei's House	程大位居	*chéngdàwèi jū*
Cheng Family House	程氏三宅	*chéngshì sānzhái*
Huaxi Fandian	花溪饭店	*huāxī fàndiàn*
Jingwei Jiudian	经纬酒店	*jīngwěi jiǔdiàn*
Lao Jie	老街	*lǎojiē*
Tunxi Fandian	屯溪饭店	*túnxī fàndiàn*
Shexian	歙县	***shèxiàn***
Doushan Jie	斗山街	*dǒushān jiē*
Nan Lou	南楼	*nánlóu*
Tangyue Archway	堂越牌坊	*tángyuè páifāng*
Xuguo Archway	许国石坊	*xǔguó shífāng*
Yanghe Men	阳和门	*yánghé mén*
Yixian	黟县	*yíxiàn*
Hongcun	宏村	*hóngcūn*
Nanping	南屏村	*nánpíng cūn*
Xidi	西递	*xīdì*

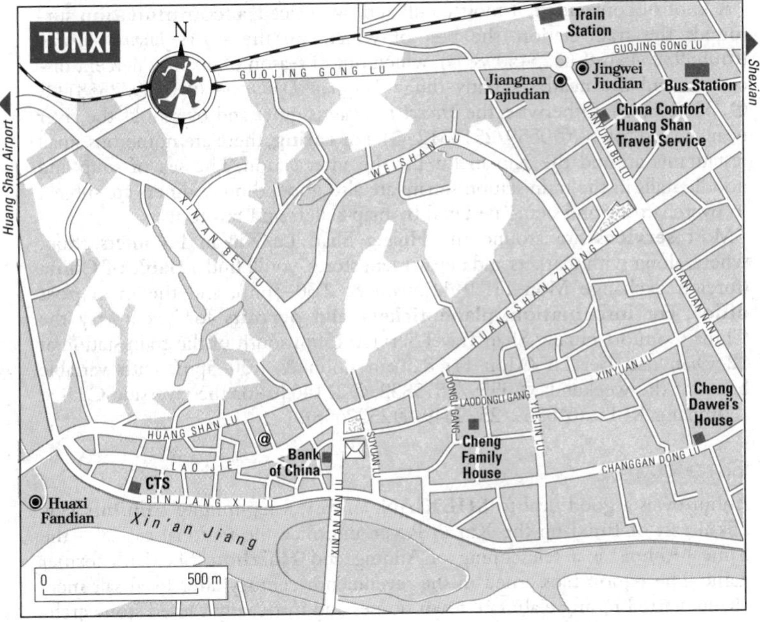

For more, head down to Tunxi's historic, flagstoned **Lao Jie** (Old Street), a westerly continuation of Huang Shan Lu. Here, 500m of **Ming shops** running parallel to the river have been nicely restored for visitors, selling local teas, medicinal herbs and all manner of artistic materials and "antiques" – ink stones, brushes, Mao badges, decadent advertising posters from the 1930s, and carved wooden panels prised off old buildings. A few genuine businesses stand out, notably an apothecary sporting 1920s timber decor, and several small **dumpling houses** filled with local clientele. You'll also see characteristic **horse-head gables** rising out below the rooflines in steps. These originated as fire baffles between adjoining houses, stopping the spread of flames from building to building, but eventually became somewhat decorative affairs.

Practicalities

Busy **Huang Shan airport** is around 10km west of town, with an **airport bus** (¥5) delivering to train and bus stations. The **train station** is at the northern city limits on the end of Qianyuan Bei Lu, which runs 250m south to Huang Shan Lu; there are connections to Hefei (via Xuancheng and Wuhu), Nanchang, Shanghai, Xiamen and Beijing, along with a useful – though ploddingly slow – daily train southwest to Jingdezhen in Anhui (see p.581). Tangkou minibuses prowl the station forecourt, while Tunxi's **bus station** occupies an entire block 250m east off Guojing Gong Lu, with frequent services for Shexian, Yixian, Tangkou and Taiping, and long-distance departures to Jiuhua Shan, Wuhu, Hefei, Shanghai, Jiujiang, Nanchang and even Guangzhou. A couple of **city buses** run around Tunxi: from the train station, #6 takes a back road into town, while #1 and #2 follow Huang Shan Lu southwest from the bus station – either route is a twenty-minute walk.

A knot of convenient, if mostly dull and overpriced, **accommodation** surrounds the train station, the best of which are the smart *Jingwei Jiudian* (Ⓣ0559/2345188, Ⓕ2345098; ❻), which out of season offers fifty percent discounts; and the nearby, slightly dingy *Jiangnan Dajiudian* (Ⓣ0559/2358111, Ⓕ2358248; ❹). Otherwise, the *Huaxi Fandian* is quiet and overlooks the river near the old town (Ⓣ0559/2514312; ❹). For **eating**, there are numerous small restaurants around the Xin'an Lu/Lao Jie intersection. The sea of soup and noodle stalls in the train station square are also good, though diners are subject to overcharging and being pestered by map-sellers and bus touts.

Most **services** are around the Huang Shan Lu/Xin'an Lu intersection, where, along with markets and department stores, you'll find a **Bank of China** (foreign exchange Mon–Fri 9–11.30am & 2.30–5pm), and the main **post office**. For **information**, **plane tickets**, and **permits** for Yixian, try the China Comfort Huang Shan Travel Service 150m south of the train station at 12 Qianyuan Bei Lu (Mon–Fri 8.30am–noon & 1.30–5pm, with variable hours at the weekend; Ⓣ0559/2515832, Ⓕ2114040) or the riverside CTS at 1 Binjiang Xi Lu (Ⓣ0559/2522649, Ⓕ2522635).

Shexian

Anhui owes a good deal to **SHEXIAN**, an easy, forty-minute **minibus** ride 25km east of Tunxi up the Xin'an River and once the regional capital – the name "Anhui" is a telescoping of Anqing and **Huizhou**, Shexian's former name. The region blossomed in the seventeenth century after local salt merchants started raising elaborate town houses and intricately carved stone archways, some of which survive today, in a showy display of their wealth. The province's opera styles were formalized here, and the town became famous for *hui* ink stones and fine-grained *she* ink sticks, the latter still considered China's best.

Shexian's **bus station** is out on the highway, where arrivals are accosted by "guides" and motor-rickshaw drivers. You don't need them: take the bridge over the river and carry straight on past 100m of uninspiring, concrete-and-tile buildings; at the end of the road turn right, then first left, and you're walking up **Jiefang Jie**, off which run the narrow lanes that comprise the older part of town. To the sides you'll see the restored **Nan Lou** and **Yanghe Men** gate towers; straight ahead, however, Jiefang Jie runs under the smaller but highly decorative **Xuguo archway**, one of the finest in the region. Nearby are souvenir stalls and a **bookshop**, where you should pick up a **map** of Shexian (about ¥3) with all the streets and points of interest marked. Though by no means every building is an architectural wonder, one of Shexian's charms is that most are still in everyday use, not tarted up for tourism, and there's a genuinely dated ambience to soak up. You could just walk at random, snacking on traditional "pressed buns" but, for a detailed look, seek out **Doushan Jie**, a street full of well-preserved Huizhou style homes, around which you can tour with a Chinese-speaking guide (¥8). When you've had enough, return to the station and get a Tunxi-bound minibus to drop you off around 5km down the highway, then walk or catch a motorbike-rickshaw for the last 3km to where the **Tangyue archway** (¥20) forms a strange spectacle of six ornamental gates standing isolated in a row in a field.

Yixian

For reasons that have nothing to do with architecture, you need a **police permit** (arranged through agents in Tunxi for about ¥50) to stop off in

YIXIAN, 60km due west of Tunxi. The town itself is a stepping stone to surrounding villages, for which you'll have to charter a minibus (about ¥30 per stop) and pay for compulsory guides to tour each site (¥20). **Xidi** is the pick, a particularly attractive place comprising some 120 eighteenth-century houses set along a riverbank, now turned into a large antiques market. There are endless examples of carved gilded wooden screens and panels inside the houses, as well as thin line paintings on front walls showing pairs of animals or "double happiness" characters. Mirrors placed above the three-tiered door lintels reflect bad luck or reveal a person's true character – a useful tool for judging the nature of strangers. **Hongcun** is another fine spot, whose street plan (with some imagination) resembles the body of a buffalo, complete with horns, body, and legs, while **Nanping** was used as a set in Zhang Yimou's film *Judou*.

Huang Shan

Rearing over southern Anhui, **Huang Shan** – the Yellow Mountains – are among eastern China's greatest sights. It's said that once you've ascended their peaks you will never want to climb another mountain, and certainly the experience is staggeringly scenic, with pinnacles emerging from thick bamboo forests, above which rock faces dotted with ancient, contorted pine trees growing from narrow ledges disappear into the swirling mists. These views seem often familiar, for Huang Shan's landscape has left an indelible impression on Chinese art, and painters are a common sight on the paths, huddled in padded jackets and sheltering their work from the incipient drizzle beneath umbrellas – the more serious of them spend months at a time up here.

As a pilgrimage site trodden by emperors and Communist leaders alike, Huang Shan is regarded as sacred in China, and it's the ambition of every Chinese to conquer it at least once in their lifetime. Consequently, don't expect to climb alone: noisy multitudes swarm along the neatly paved paths, or crowd out the three cable-car connections to the top. All this can make the experience depressingly like visiting an amusement park, but then you'll turn a corner and come face to face with a huge, smooth monolith topped by a single tree, or be confronted with views of a remote square of forest growing isolated on a rocky platform. Nature is never far away from reasserting itself here.

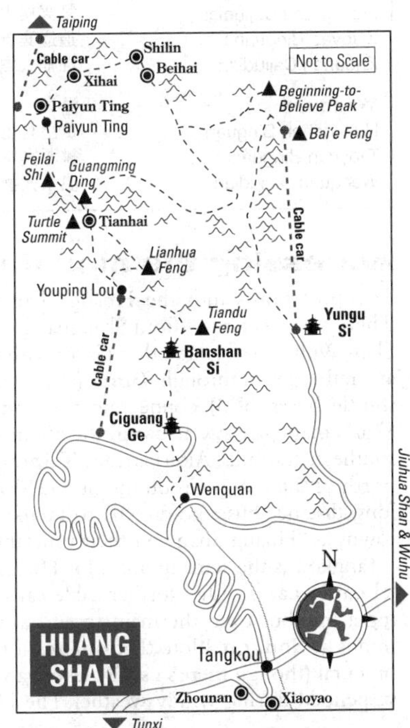

Huang Shan

Huang Shan	黄山	***huángshān***
Bai'e Feng	白鹅峰	*bái'é fēng*
Banshan Si	半山寺	*bànshān sì*
Beginning-to-Believe Peak	始信峰	*shǐxìn fēng*
Cable-car station	索道站	*suǒdào zhàn*
Ciguang Shi	慈光阁	*cíguāng gé*
Feilai Shi	飞来石	*fēilái shí*
Guangming Ding	光明顶	*guāngmíng dǐng*
Jiyu Bei	鲫鱼背	*jìyú bèi*
Paiyun Ting	排云亭	*páiyún tíng*
Tiandu Feng	天都峰	*tiāndū fēng*
Yingke Song	迎客松	*yíngkèsōng*
Yungu Si	云谷寺	*yúngǔ sì*
Yuping Lou	玉屏楼	*yùpíng lóu*
Accommodation and eating		
Beihai Binguan	北海宾馆	*běihǎi bīnguǎn*
Paiyun Ting Binguan	排云亭宾馆	*páiyúntíng bīnguǎn*
Shilin Dajiudian	石林大酒店	*shílín dàjiǔdiàn*
Tianhai Binguan	天海宾馆	*tiānhǎi bīnguǎn*
Xihai Fandian	西海饭店	*xīhǎi bīnguǎn*
Taiping	太平	***tàipíng***
Tangkou	汤口	***tāngkǒu***
Dacong Fandian	大众饭店	*dàzhòng fàndiàn*
Fuxing Lou Dajiudian	复兴楼大酒店	*fùxīng lóu jiǔdiàn*
Xiaoyao Binguan	逍遥宾管	*xiāoyáo bīnguǎn*
Zhounan Dajiudian	洲楠大酒店	*zhōunán dàjiǔdiàn*
Wenquan	温泉	***wēnquán***
Huangshan Binguan	黄山宾馆	*huángshān bīnguǎn*
Taoyuan Binguan	桃源宾馆	*táoyuán bīnguǎn*
Wenquan Dajiudian	温泉大酒店	*wēnquán dàjiǔdiàn*

Accessing the mountains

Transport pours into the Huang Shan region from all over eastern China. There are direct buses from Shanghai, Hangzhou and Nanjing, as well as Jiuhua Shan, Wuhu, Hefei and other places within Anhui. Much of this, and all rail and air traffic, passes through **Tunxi** (aka Huang Shan Shi; see p.522), with regular shuttle buses (¥13) connecting the train and bus stations here with Huang Shan's main gateway at **Tangkou**, 50km northwest of Tunxi on the mountain's southern foothills. Alternatively, **Taiping** is a lesser-used access point to the north of the mountain on the Jiuhua Shan–Tangkou road. Be aware that some long-distance buses go directly to Tangkou or Taiping, and might refer to these towns as "Huang Shan" on their timetables.

Tangkou is the starting point for Huang Shan's two **hiking trails** and parallel **cable cars**, with a further cable car (¥65) accessed from Taiping by catching a minibus from the main-street bus station for the 22km ride to the terminus at **Songgu**. Note that **queues** for peak-bound cable cars can be monumental (though there's usually less of a wait to go down), and that services are suspended during windy weather. The Huang Shan **entry fee**, payable at the start of the trails or at the cable-car ticket offices, is ¥62, or ¥55 for concessions. Cable cars to the summit area take upwards of twenty minutes, or you'll need between two and eight hours to walk up, depending on whether you follow the easier **eastern route**, or the lengthy and demanding **western route**. Once at the top, there's a half-day of relatively easy hiking around the peaks. Ideally, plan to spend two or three days on the mountain to allow for a steady ascent and circuit, though it's quite feasible to see a substantial part of Huang Shan in a full day. There's **accommodation** (mostly fairly expensive) and **food** available in Tangkou, Taiping and on the mountain itself, but you'll need to come prepared for steep paths, rain and winter snow – all an essential part of the experience. Hiring guides and porters is something of an extravagance, as paths are easy to follow and accommodation in Tangkou and Taiping will store surplus gear; just bring a day-pack, strong shoes and something warm for the top.

Tangkou and Wenquan

Two hours and 50km from Tunxi, **TANGKOU** is an unattractive jumble of narrow lanes, hotels and restaurants on the **Taohua Gully**, where roads from Wuhu, Tunxi and Jiuhua Shan meet. Most Huang Shan buses terminate here, though another road runs up the mountain to further accommodation 3km along at **Wenquan** where it divides and continues to the two trailheads.

Minibuses from Tunxi and Jiuhua Shan collect and drop off at Tangkou's central bridge, while the **long-distance bus stop** is 1km up the Wenquan road by Huang Shan's official entrance. Tangkou's **places to stay** are of most interest to cheapskates and late arrivals; down in the gully, the gloomy facade of the *Xiaoyao Binguan* (Ⓣ0559/5562571; ❹, dorm beds ¥35) hides dilapidated rooms and bored staff; while, just off the main road, the *Zhounan Dajiudian* (Ⓣ0559/5562387; ❺) is modern and comfortable, and readily offers discounts. Alternatively, ask around to find the Chinese-oriented *Dacong Fandian* (Ⓣ0559/5562453; ❹, dorm beds ¥50) or *Fuxing Lou Dajiudian* (Ⓣ0559/5563588; ❹).

The cheapest places to **eat** a filling noodle or *baozi* breakfast are at tables under the bridge, with a host of canteens all around the town, whose owners will drag you in as you walk past. Some have bilingual menus offering arresting delights such as squirrel hotpot and scrambled mountain frog, and more conventional soya-braised bamboo shoots and fungi – agree a price in advance to avoid being ripped off. You can also pick up umbrellas, walking sticks and **mountain maps** from hawkers and stalls around Tangkou. **Heading up** the mountain, minibuses wait on the Wenquan road, where you'll have to bargain hard for reasonable fares – current rates are ¥5 to Wenquan and ¥10 to the eastern route and at Yungu Si.

Wenquan

About 3km uphill from Tangkou where the mountain's two main ascent routes diverge, **WENQUAN** is altogether a nicer prospect, surrounded by pine and bamboo forest and perched above the clear blue **Taoyuan Stream** and a noisy waterfall. The first thing you'll see here is the arched bridge over the gully, where the road heads on 8km to the eastern route's trailhead; follow the footpath upstream and it's about half an hour to **Ciguang Ge**, the Merciful Light Pavilion, at the start of the western route (a minibus here from Wenquan costs ¥5).

Wenquan's **places to stay** are on either side of the stream. The smartest is the near-side *Taoyuan Binguan* (Ⓣ0559/5562666, Ⓕ5562888; ❼), while below the bridge, the *Wenquan Dajiudian* (Ⓣ0559/5562198, Ⓕ5562788; ❻) is fine if you avoid the damp cheaper rooms. Across the bridge, the red-roofed *Huangshan Binguan* (Ⓣ0559/5585818, Ⓕ5585816; ❻) has tiny rooms but is relatively inexpensive and amenable to bargaining. Near the *Huangshan Binguan*, the trail-weary can take advantage of a **thermal bathhouse** (¥30, or ¥50 for a private spa), though it's a bit grotty. **Eat** at your accommodation or head down to Tangkou.

Huang Shan hikes

Huang Shan barely rises above 1870m, but as you struggle up either of the staircases it can begin to feel very high indeed. The **eastern route** is by far the easiest; the road from Wenquan ends at **Yungu Si** (Cloud Valley Temple), where a **cable car** (daily 9am–3.30pm; ¥66) can whisk you to the summit area at **Bai'e Feng** in twenty minutes – once you've queued two hours for your turn. Alternatively, you can climb the steps to Bai'e Feng in under three hours, though the forest canopy tends to block views and the path is thick with **porters** ferrying laundry, garbage, and building materials up and down the slopes.

In contrast, the exceptional landscapes on the fifteen-kilometre **western route** are accompanied by up to eight hours of exhausting legwork – though you can shorten things by catching another gondola between the trailhead at Ciguang Ge and Yuping Lou (daily 9am–3.30pm; ¥40). There are around two thousand steps from the Ciguang Ge to **Banshan Si**, the misleadingly named Midway Monastery, after which things start to get interesting as you continue up an increasingly steep and narrow gorge, its sides overgrown with witch hazel, azaleas and wild plum. The rocks are huge, their weirdly contorted figures lending some creedence to the usual gamut of bizarre names, and the broken hillside is riddled with caves. A steep, hour-long detour from Banshan – not a climb for those nervous of heights – follows steps cut into the cliffs up to **Tiandu Feng** (Heavenly City Peak), where **Jiyu Bei** (Kingfish Ridge), a narrow, ten-metre-long path extending over a precipice towards distant pinnacles surrounded by clouds, provides Huang Shan's most spectacular views.

Back on the main track, the beautifully positioned **Yuping Lou** (Jade Screen Pavilion), is the true halfway house at around three hours into the journey. The vegetation thins out here, exchanged for bare rocks with only the occasional wind-contorted tree, one of which, **Yingke Song** (Welcoming Pine), has been immortalized in countless scroll paintings, photographs, cigarette packets and beer labels. The steps wind on up to a pass where more strange rocks jut out of the mist; bear right for the climb to Huang Shan's apex at **Lianhua Feng** (1864m) or press on to **accommodation** at *Tianhai Binguan* (Ⓣ0559/5562201; ❻). From here, it's just a short climb to where you finally reach the peak circuit at **Guangming Ding** (Brightness Summit), with a TV tower and weather station off to the right and **Feilai Shi** (Far-flying Rock) ahead.

The peak circuit

However you've arrived, it takes around three hours to **circuit the peaks**. North (anticlockwise) from the eastern steps and Bai'e Feng cable-car terminus, the first stop is where a side track leads out to **Shixin Feng**. This cluster of rocky spires makes a wonderful perch to gaze down to lowland woods and rivers, with white-rumped swifts and pine and rock silhouettes moving in and out of shifting silver clouds. Tour groups concentrate on the higher levels, so the lower stairs are more peaceful.

From here, the path continues round to the comfortable *Beihai Binguan* (ⓣ0559/5582555, ⓕ5581996; ❼), where there's also a **Bank of China** with, incredibly, an ATM. Crowds congregate each morning on the terrace nearby to watch the **sunrise** over the "northern sea" of clouds, one of the most stirring sights on the mountain. Views are still good even without the dawn, and the area tends to be busy all day. Straight ahead, a side track leads to the cosy *Shilin Dajiudian* (ⓣ0559/5584040, ⓦwww.shilin.com/eindex.htm; ❽), which even has copies of the *China Daily*; while another thirty minutes on the main path brings you to the luxurious *Xihai Fandian* (ⓣ0559/5588987, ⓕ5588988; ❼), the perfect spot to sip drinks on the terrace and watch, in its turn, the sun setting over the "western cloud sea".

It's another ten minutes or so from *Xihai* to where the track splits at the mountain's least expensive accommodation, the *Paiyun Ting Binguan* (ⓣ0559/5581558, ⓕ5583999; ❼, dorm beds ¥120). Ahead is the **Taiping cable-car station** down to Songgu. Stay on the main track for **Paiyun Ting**, the Cloud-dispelling Pavilion; on a clear day you'll see a steep gorge squeezed between jagged crags below, all covered in pine trees and magnolias. More views await further around at the lonely tower of **Felai Shi**, which after rain looks across at cascades dropping off lesser peaks into infinity. Beyond here, the path undulates along the cliff edge to where the western steps descend on the right (below the TV tower and weather station), then winds back to the Bai'e Feng cable car.

Hubei

HUBEI is Han China's agricultural and geographic centre, mild in climate and well watered. Until 280 BC this was the independent state of **Chu**, whose sophisticated bronzeworking skills continue to astound archeologists, but for the last half-millennium the province's eastern bulk, defined by the low-lying **Jianghan plain** and spliced by waterways draining into the Yangzi and Han rivers, has become an intensely cultivated maze of rice fields, so rich that (according to tradition) they alone are enough to supply the national need. More recently, Hubei's central location and mass of transport links by rail, road and river into neighbouring regions saw the province becoming the first in the interior to be heavily industrialized. Once the colossal **Three Gorges hydroelectric dam** upstream from **Yichang** is completed as planned (see p.547), car manufacturing – already up and running with the help of foreign investment – and long-established iron and steel plants, will provide a huge source of income for central China.

As the "Gateway to Nine Provinces", skirted by mountains and midway along the Yangzi between Shanghai and Chongqing, Hubei has always been of great strategic importance, and somewhere that seditious ideas could easily spread to the rest of the country. The central regions upriver from the capital, **Wuhan**, feature prominently in the legends of the *Three Kingdoms* (see box, p.509), with the ports of **Jingzhou** and **Chibi** retaining their period associations, while Wuhan itself thrives on industry and river trade, and played a key role in

China's early twentieth-century revolutions. In the west, the ranges that border Sichuan contain the holy peak of **Wudang Shan**, alive with Taoist temples and martial-arts lore, and the remote and little-visited **Shennongjia Forest Reserve**, said to be inhabited by China's yeti.

Wuhan

One way or the other, almost anyone travelling through central China has to pass through **WUHAN**, Hubei's sprawling capital, most likely cruising in along the Yangzi from Sichuan or Shanghai, or rattling in by rail. The name is a portmanteau label for the original settlements of **Wuchang**, **Hankou** and **Hanyang**, separate across the junction of the Han and Yangzi rivers, but given some sense of unity by three great interconnecting bridges. The city's sheer size, bustle and obvious regional economic importance lend atmosphere, even if Wuhan is more of an administrative and social centre than a tourist magnet. Nonetheless it's an upbeat, characterful metropolis, and Hankou's former role as a **foreign concession** has left a whole quarter of colonial European heritage in its wake, while the **Provincial Museum** in Wuchang is one of China's best. There are also a couple of temples and historical monuments to check

Wuhan

Wuhan	武汉	***wǔhàn***
Hankou	汉口	*hànkǒu*
Hanyang	汉阳	*hànyáng*
Wuchang	武昌	*wǔchāng*
The City		
Botanical Gardens	植物园	*zhíwù yuán*
Changchun Guan	长春观	*chángchūn guàn*
Customs House	武汉海关	*wǔhàn hǎiguān*
Dong Hu Scenic Area	东湖风景区	*dōnghú fēngjǐngqū*
Electric special #1	电一专路	*diànyī zhuānlù*
Flood Control Monument	防洪纪念碑	*fánghóng jìniànbēi*
Great Changjiang Bridge	长江大桥	*chángjiāng dàqiáo*
Guishan Park	龟山公园	*guīshān gōngyuán*
Guiyuan Si	归元寺	*guīyuán sì*
Guqin Ta	古琴塔	*gǔqíntǎ*
Hong Ge	红阁	*hónggé*
Hubei Provincial Museum	湖北省博物馆	*húběishěng bówùguǎn*
Jiu Nudun	九女墩	*jiǔnǚ dūn*
Mo Shan	磨山	*móshān*
She Shan	蛇山	*shéshān*
Tianhe airport	天河飞机场	*tiānhé fēijīchǎng*
Workers' Cultural Palace	工人文化宫	*gōngrén wénhuàgōng*
Wuhan Museum	武汉博物馆	*wǔhàn bówùguǎn*
Wuhan University	武汉大学	*wǔhàn dàxué*
Yangzi ferry terminal	武汉港客运站	*wǔhàn gǎngkè yùnzhàn*
Yellow Crane Tower	黄鹤塔	*huánghè tǎ*
Zhongshan Park	中山公园	*zhōngshān gōngyuán*

out, some connected to the **1911 revolution** which ended two thousand years of Imperial rule. On the down side, Wuhan has a well-deserved reputation – along with Chongqing and Nanjing – as one of China's three summer "furnaces": between May and September you'll find the streets melting and the gasping population surviving on a diet of watermelon and ice lollies.

Arrival and city transport

Wuhan spreads more than 10km across, and, with a choice of transit points all over the place – there are two separate train stations and at least three long-distance bus stations, it's important to know where you're arriving before you get here; train and bus timetables usually spell out the district where services arrive, rather than just "Wuhan". Most people stay on the northern bank of the Yangzi in **Hankou**, which, as the city's trade and business centre, contains the best of the services and accommodation. South across the smaller Han River is lightly industrial **Hanyang**, while **Wuchang**, receding southeast of the Yangzi into semi-rural parkland, harbours most of the sights.

Tianhe airport lies 30km to the north of Wuhan along a good road, with a **bus link** from here to the China Southern airline office on Hangkong Lu in Hankou. **Rail** services from the north tend to terminate at Hankou's train station, up in the north of the city along Fazhan Dadao, while those from the

Accommodation

Guansheng Yuan	冠生园大酒店	*guānshēngyuán dàjiǔdiàn*
Hanghai	航海宾馆	*hánghǎi bīnguǎn*
Holiday Inn	天安假日酒店	*tiānānjiàrì jiǔdiàn*
Jianghan	江汉饭店	*jiānghàn fàndiàn*
Kunlun Victory	昆仑胜利饭店	*kūnlún shènglì fàndiàn*
Linjiang	临江饭店	*línjiāng fàndiàn*
Mingtian Hu	明天湖宾馆	*míngtiānhú bīnguǎn*
New Oriental Empire	新东方帝豪酒店	*xīndōngfāng dìháo jiǔdiàn*
Ramada Plaza	华美达天禄酒店	*huáměidá tiānlù jiǔdiàn*
Shengli	胜利饭店	*shènglì fàndiàn*
Xingang	新港饭店	*xīngǎng fàndiàn*
Xuangong	璇宫饭店	*xuángōng fàndiàn*

Eating and drinking

Blue Sky Café	蓝色天空酒吧	*lánsètiānkōng jiǔbā*
Bordeaux Bar	波尔图酒吧	*bōěrtú jiǔbā*
Changchun Sucai Guan	长春素菜馆	*chángchūn*
Da Zhonghua	大中华	*dà zhōnghuá*
Dehua Jiulou	德华酒楼	*déhuá jiǔlóu*
Dezhuang Huoguo Guangchang	德庄火锅广场	*dézhuāng huǒguō guǎngchǎng*
Dong Lai Shun	东来顺	*dōnglái shùn*
Lao Huibin	老会宾	*lǎohuì bīn*
Lao Tongcheng	老通成	*lǎotōng chéng*
Si Li Mei	四李美	*sìlìměi*
Yonghe Dawang	永和大王	*yǒnghé dàwáng*
Yuan Ye Jiaozi Guan	原野饺子馆	*yuányě jiǎoziguǎn*

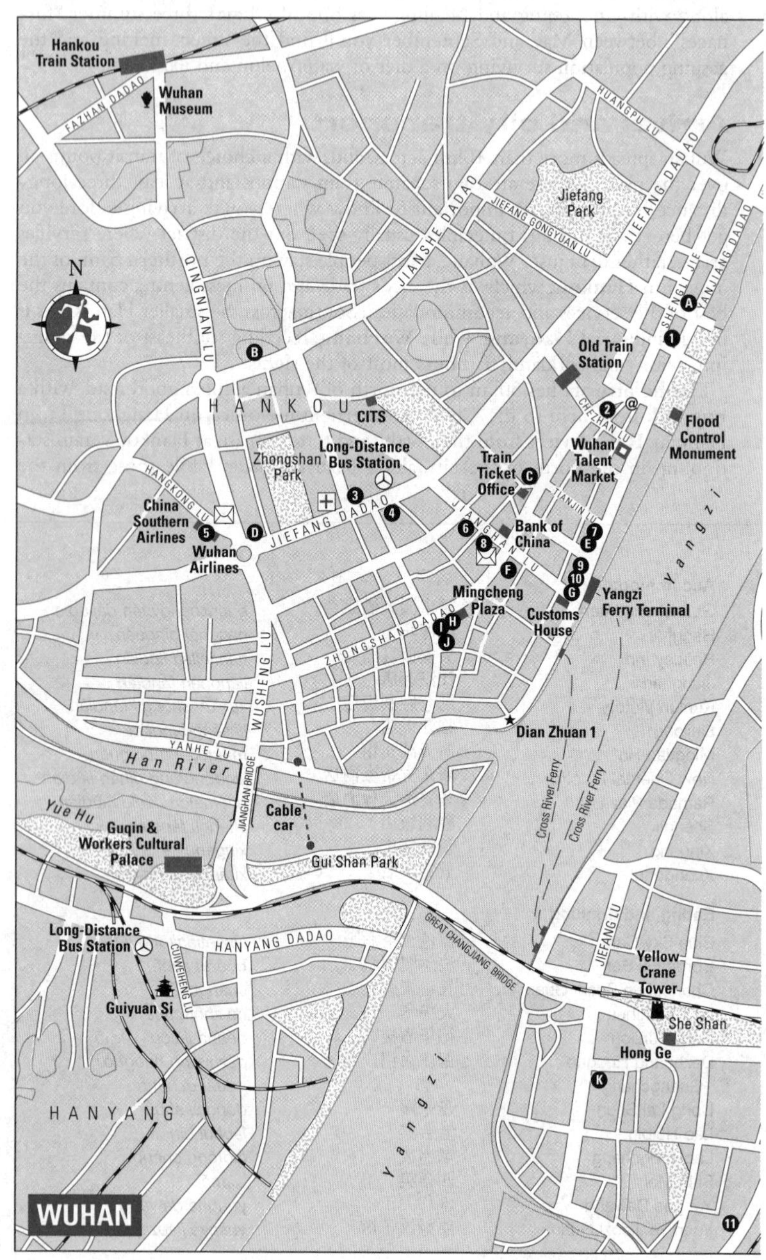
WUHAN
Hankou Train Station
Wuhan Museum
FAZHAN DADAO
HUANGPU LU
JIEFANG DADAO
Jiefang Park
JIEFANG GONGYUAN LU
JIANSHE DADAO
QINGNIAN LU
YANJIANG DADAO
SHENGLI JIE
N
Old Train Station
HANKOU
CITS
CHEZHAN LU
Flood Control Monument
Wuhan Talent Market
Train Ticket Office
Zhongshan Park
Long-Distance Bus Station
HANGKONG LU
China Southern Airlines
Wuhan Airlines
JIEFANG DADAO
TIANJIN LU
Bank of China
JIANGHAN LU
Yangzi
Mingcheng Plaza
Customs House
Yangzi Ferry Terminal
ZHONGSHAN DADAO
WUSHENG LU
Dian Zhuan 1
YANHE LU
Han River
JIANGHAN BRIDGE
Cable car
Yue Hu
Guqin & Workers Cultural Palace
Gui Shan Park
Cross River Ferry
Cross River Ferry
Long-Distance Bus Station
HANYANG DADAO
CUIWEIHENG LU
GREAT CHANGJIANG BRIDGE
JIEFANG LU
Yellow Crane Tower
She Shan
Hong Ge
Guiyuan Si
HANYANG
Yangzi

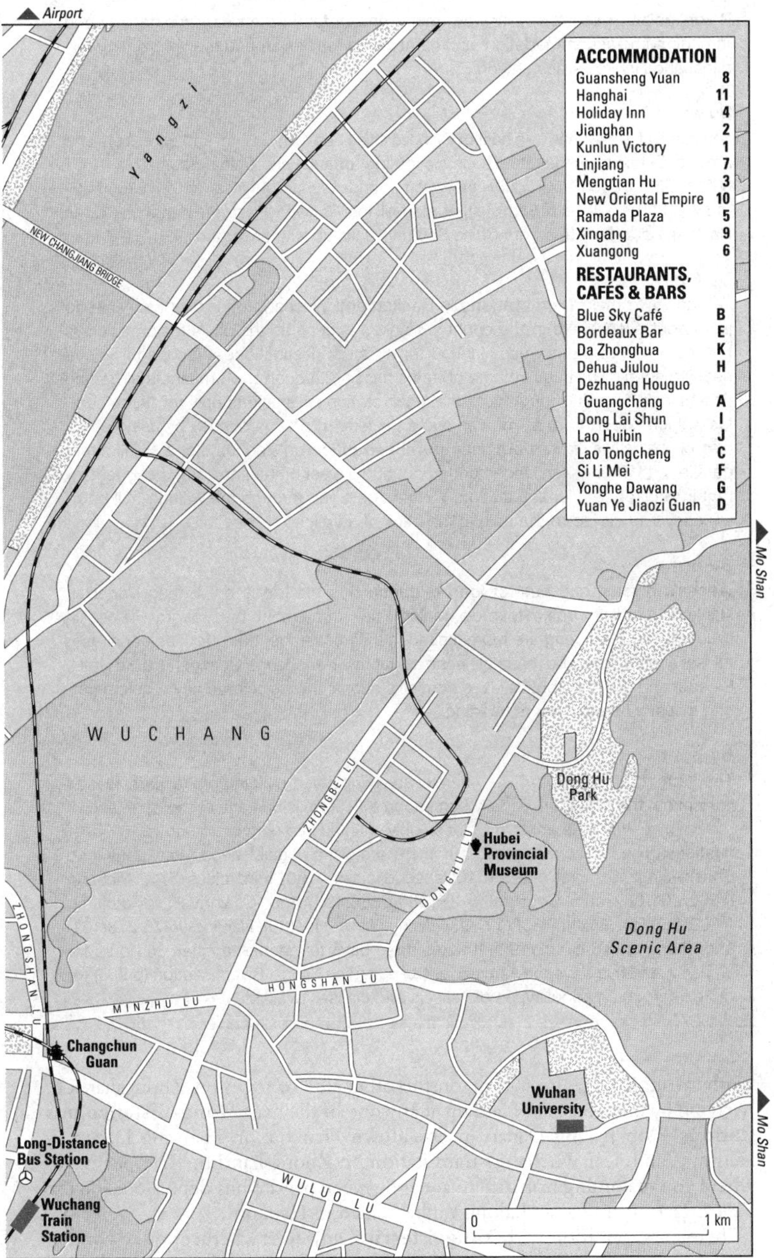
Airport
ACCOMMODATION
Guansheng Yuan 8
Hanghai 11
Holiday Inn 4
Jianghan 2
Kunlun Victory 1
Linjiang 7
Mengtian Hu 3
New Oriental Empire 10
Ramada Plaza 5
Xingang 9
Xuangong 6
RESTAURANTS, CAFÉS & BARS
Blue Sky Café B
Bordeaux Bar E
Da Zhonghua K
Dehua Jiulou H
Dezhuang Houguo Guangchang A
Dong Lai Shun I
Lao Huibin J
Lao Tongcheng C
Si Li Mei F
Yonghe Dawang G
Yuan Ye Jiaozi Guan D
Yangzi
NEW CHANGJIANG BRIDGE
Mo Shan
WUCHANG
ZHONGBEI LU
Dong Hu Park
Hubei Provincial Museum
DONGHU LU
Dong Hu Scenic Area
ZHONGSHAN LU
HONGSHAN LU
MINZHU LU
Changchun Guan
Wuhan University
Mo Shan
Long-Distance Bus Station
WULUO LU
Wuchang Train Station
0
1 km

Moving on from Wuhan

Before going miles out of your way, train, plane, or ferry tickets can also be arranged through some accommodation, and numerous agencies around the Yangzi ferry terminal and Hankou's bus station.

By air

You can **fly** from Wuhan to a host of Chinese cities between Urumqi and Shenzhen, and also to Fukuoka in Japan. The main **airline offices** are China Southern (Ⓣ027/83611756, Ⓕ83632265; daily 8am–9pm), and Wuhan Airlines (Ⓣ027/83646425, Ⓕ83641320; daily 8am–8pm), either side of the *Ramada Plaza* on Hangkong Lu in Hankou. An **airport bus** from China Southern links up with departures.

By train

Wuhan's two main **train stations** in Hankou and Wuchang offer direct services to just about everywhere in the country. Hankou is seen as the city's major terminus but, as a rule of thumb, use Hankou for northern destinations, Wuchang if you're heading south. The huge volume of traffic passing through town means that getting tickets isn't difficult, though note that each station sells tickets only for those services which depart from it. You can avoid the lengthy station queues by using agencies or the railway's own **advance purchase office** on Baohua Jie, a small street parallel with Zhongshan Dadao and about 500m west of the *Lao Tongcheng* restaurant in Hankou. At Hankou station, ¥5 extra gets you through the waiting-hall barriers early and carted to the train in the back of a trailer.

By bus

Wuhan's biggest and busiest **long-distance bus station** is on Jiefang Dadao in Hankou, handling traffic to most major cities throughout the country. Those in Wuchang and Hanyang are more limited in their coverage, but offer additional useful services south and east at least as far as Nanchang, Changsha and Hefei. Sleeper and standard buses leave from all stations; there's seldom any problem getting a seat wherever you're heading.

By boat

The **Yangzi ferry terminal** is an unmissable white tiled building on Yanjiang Dadao in Hankou: the ticket office (daily 9am–noon & 2–5pm) is upstairs at the north end of the building with timetables in Chinese only, divided into upriver and downriver destinations. The schedule varies, but there are usually daily departures upriver to Shashi–Jingzhou (first class ¥310; second class ¥160; third class ¥71), Yichang (¥392/201/88) and Chongqing (¥1080/588/249); and downriver to Jiujiang (¥200/117/56), Guichi (¥338/197/93), Wuhu (¥418/244/116), Nanjing (¥476/278/131) and Shanghai (¥698/408/192). It takes three days to reach Shanghai, 36 hours for Yichang, and five days to Chongqing. Consult "The Yangzi River" section (p.965) for more information about types of vessels and classes available.

south favour Wuchang's station, on the other side of town on Zhongshan Lu. Arriving by bus, you could end up at any one of the major **long-distance bus stations** – on Jiefang Dadao in downtown Hankou, on Hanyang Dadao in Hanyang, and near Wuchang's train station on Zhongshan Lu – irrespective of where you're coming from; there are also several private bus depots outside the Yangzi ferry terminal and along Yanhe Dadao in Hankou.

There's no confusion with **Yangzi ferries**, however: whether you're coming upstream from Shanghai or downstream from Yichang or Chongqing, they all call in at the ferry **terminal** on Yanjiang Dadao in Hankou.

Useful bus routes

The most convenient bus for sightseeing is the **Dian Zhuan** (Electric Special) **#1**, not to be confused with any other #1 bus or trolleybus – the characters for *dian zhuan* are displayed either side of the number. It runs from Yanhe Dadao in Hankou, via Hanyang and the Great Changjiang Bridge, and then links the Yellow Crane Tower with Changchun Guan, the Provincial Museum, and the entrance to Dong Hu Scenic area.

#9 Connects Hankou train station with the Yangzi ferry terminal.

#10 Runs between Hankou and Wuchang train stations, via Qingnian Lu, Wusheng Lu and the Great Changjiang bridge – not through downtown Hankou – in 45–90 minutes, depending on the traffic.

#38 Runs from Hankou train station through the downtown concession area, terminating along the river on Yanjiang Dadao near the Flood Control Monument.

#503, 507 Run from Wuluo Lu, about 500m north of Wuchang's train and bus stations, to the ferry terminal in Hankou.

City transport

Wuhan is too large to consider walking everywhere, though the overloaded **bus and trolley bus** system seldom seems to be much quicker, and stops can be widely spaced. The main **city-bus terminuses** are at Hankou and Wuchang train stations, and beside the Yangzi ferry terminal on Yanjiang Dadao. Staff are on hand at each of these to help you find the right vehicle. Services are at least regular and cheap – it only costs ¥2 between Wuchang and Hankou stations – crawling out to almost every corner of the city between around 6am and 10pm. Ubiquitous **taxis** are pretty convenient and, at ¥8 for the first 2km, not too expensive. For short hops, haggle with **motorbike** and **motor-rickshaw** drivers who prowl the bus and train depots. **Bicycles** are difficult to rent and not overly used, partly because of Wuhan's size, but also because of unpredictably enforced regulations banning them from being ridden across the bridges. During daylight hours, there are **passenger ferries** across the Yangzi between the southern end of Hankou's Yanjiang Dadao and Wuchang's city-bus terminus, below and just north of the Changjiang Bridge; trips cost ¥1 and take about thirty minutes.

Maps of Wuhan showing transport routes can be picked up at bus and train stations, but shop around first as many are either painfully detailed or almost abstract.

Accommodation

Much of Wuhan's **hotel** accommodation is upmarket, but there are a couple of cheap options, and mid-range places can be good value. The biggest selection – a sprinkling of which are reviewed below – is in **Hankou**. In Wuchang, the noisy *Hanghai* (❸), in Zhongshan Lu opposite the train station, is only recommended if you arrive late; buses #507 and #10 to Hankou run past the door.

Guansheng Yuan 117 Jianghan Lu ⓣ027/82779069, ⓕ82778151. Beside a department store of the same name, and just south of the *Xuangong* hotel. Nothing glamorous, but clean, central and the right price. Often full. ❹

Holiday Inn 868 Jiefang Dadao ⓣ027/85867888, ⓕ85845353. Reliable comforts and service – and surprisingly low rates – in this smart international hotel. ❼

Jianghan 245 Shengli Jie ⓣ027/82811600, ⓕ82814342. Wuhan's best, a renovated French colonial mansion, with porphyry floors and wooden panelling through the lobby, fairly luxurious rooms and bilingual staff. Polite enquiries often get non-guests the use of banking, mail and telephone facilities. ❽

Kunlun Victory 11 Siwei Lu ⓣ027/82732780, ⓕ82721106. Hidden away behind a high wall so difficult to locate; otherwise a modern, five-storey block with much the same facilities as the nearby *Jianghan*, but none of the panache. ❻

Linjiang 1 Tianjin Lu ⓣ027/82818830, ⓕ82832056. Army-owned hotel with colonial facade (in 1924, this was the Asian Kerosene Company building), just up the road from the Yangzi ferry terminal. Reasonably priced rooms for town, and good service; immediate discounts if asked. ❺

New Oriental Empire 136 Yanjiang Dadao ⓣ027/82211881, ⓕ82813132. Another colonial front and mid-range urban hotel interior; a notch above the nearby *Linjiang* but more expensive too. ❻

Mengtian Hu West of the bus station, Jiefang Dadao ⓣ85776595. It's quite easy to miss this slightly seedy operation, though rooms are all right and staff relaxed about having foreigners stay. ❷

Ramada Plaza 5 Qingnian Lu ⓣ027/83630888, ⓕ83630849, ⓦwww.ramadaplaza-tianlu.com. Spotless international hotel, though in a poor location on a busy road near a big intersection and flyover. ❾

Xingang Opposite the mid-section of the ferry terminal on Yanjiang Dadao, between two travel agencies ⓣ82834552. No frills but a bargain if they'll take you; the cheapest deal in town likely to accept foreign custom. ❷

Xuangong 57 Jianghan Lu, entrance in westerly side street ⓣ027/68822330, ⓦwww.xuangonghotel.com. Gloomy but very atmospheric 1920s concession building, nicely central with comfortable rooms. Advertised rates are often hugely reduced. ❼

Hankou

Now the largest of Wuhan's districts, **Hankou** was a simple fishing harbour until being opened up as a **treaty port** in 1861 – a move greatly resented by the Chinese, who took to stoning any foreigners bold enough to walk the streets. Consequently, the Chinese were barred from the riverside concession area, which over the following decades was developed in a grand style, complete with a racetrack and a **Bund** (flood-preventing embankments built by the British in the 1860s) lined with Neoclassical European architecture housing banks, embassies, and company headquarters.

The twentieth century was not kind to the city, however. On October 10, 1911, a **bomb** exploded prematurely at the Hankou headquarters of a revolutionary group linked to **Sun Yatsen**'s Tongmen Hui, a society pledged to dismantling Imperial rule in China and replacing it with a democratic government. Imperial troops executed the ringleaders, sparking a savage, city-wide **uprising against the Manchus** which virtually levelled Hankou and soon spread across China. The last emperor, Pu Yi, was forced to abdicate and a Republican government under Sun Yatsen was duly elected in Nanjing the following year. The foreign concession was rebuilt, but anti-Western riots broke out in 1925, which were suppressed by the British navy, though they erupted again in 1927, leading to the **handing back** of Hankou's concession areas to China. A few months afterwards the Guomindang stormed through on their Northern Expedition, and returned briefly in 1937 to establish a national government in town before being forced farther west by the Japanese. Thirty years later Hankou saw more fighting, this time between the PLA and various Red Guard factions, who had been slugging it out over differing interpretations of Mao's Cultural Revolution.

The district

Bursting with traffic and crowds, today Hankou is a place to walk, shop, eat, spend money and watch modern Chinese doing the same. The main thoroughfare is **Zhongshan Dadao**, a packed, three-kilometre-long stretch of restaurants, stores, and shopping plazas. Surprisingly, given the city's history, Hankou's **colonial quarter** survives almost in its entirety, restored during a big clean-up project in 2001. Aside from the racetrack, now watery **Zhongshan Park** (¥2) near the corner of Jiefang Dadao and Qingnian Lu, the colonial core lies mostly between the eastern half of Zhongshan Dadao and the river. The best sections are along the former Bund, renamed **Yanjiang Dadao**, and pedestrianized **Jianghan Lu**, which converge at the mighty **Customs House** – a solid Renaissance edifice, with imposing grey-stone portico and Corinthian capitols. The Bund itself is still visible, with the Communists adding a **Flood Control Monument** in 1954 up in Binjiang Park, a tall obelisk embellished with Mao's portrait. Many buildings in the area have plaques in English outlining their history; some to look for include the unusual seven-storey Art Deco/modernist exterior of the former **Siming Bank** at 45 Jianghan Lu, and the brick "Wuhan Talent Market" on Yanjiang Dadao – once the **US Consulate**. The **Bank of China**, at the intersection of Jianghan Lu and Zhongshan Dadao, retains its period interior of wooden panelling and chandeliers; while Hankou's **old train station** on Chezhan Lu sports a derelict French Gothic shell surrounded by a seedy mass of shops and stalls.

If you're up near Hankou's train station, drop in to the **Wuhan Museum** (Tues–Sun 8.30am–4.30pm; ¥10), whose collections of antique bronzes, porcelain, jade, and scrolls of painting and calligraphy are so outstanding you can begin to appreciate what the Chinese see in these things. In particular, there's a wonderful Ming-dynasty painting of the Yueyang Tower in Hunan (p.566), with a view of gnarled pines and boats riding a turbulent Yangzi; and a 1700-year-old, 15-centimetre-wide bronze mirror decorated with scenes from the Han-dynasty collection of Chinese mythology, the *Book of Songs*.

Hanyang

From Hankou, you cross over the Han River into Hanyang either by bus over the short Jianghan Bridge, or the **cable car** (¥15) between Yanhe Dadao and eastern Hanyang's **Gui Shan Park**. Settled as far back as 600 AD, Hanyang remained insignificant until the late nineteenth century when the viceroy **Zhang Zhidong** built China's first large-scale steel foundry here as part of the "Self-Strengthening Movement" – a last-ditch effort to modernize China during the twilight years of the Qing dynasty.

Hanyang remains Wuhan's principal manufacturing sector, its distinctly shabby streets dotted with small-scale industries. The Jianghan Bridge runs south to a huge **roundabout** below the western end of Gui Shan Park, from whose hills the Xia king Yu is said to have quelled floods four thousand years ago. East of the roundabout, **Guqin Tai** (Ancient Lute Platform; ¥5) was the haunt of legendary strummer **Yu Boya**, who played over the grave of his friend Zhong Ziqi and then smashed his instrument because the one person able to appreciate his music was dead. Infrequent gatherings at the adjacent Workers' Cultural Palace are worth a look, the band performing traditional tunes to a slumbering, elderly audience.

Guiyuan Si (daily 8.30am–5pm; ¥5) is a busy Buddhist monastery a couple of streets southwest of the roundabout on Cuiweiheng Lu, behind Hanyang's long-distance bus station. There's an authoritarian atmosphere to the place, emphasized by blocky, black-and-white brick buildings, though the temple's **scripture collection** – which includes a complete seven-thousand-volume set of the rare *Longcan Sutra* – has made Guiyan famous in Buddhist circles. Of more general interest are several hundred individually styled saintly statues in the Arhat Hall, and the statue of Sakyamuni in the main hall, carved from a single block of white jade, a gift from Burma in 1935.

Wuchang

Wuchang, on the right bank of the Yangzi, was founded as Sun Quan's walled capital of Wu during the Three Kingdoms period. Tang rulers made the city a major port, which, under the Mongols, became the administrative centre of a vast region covering present-day Hunan, Hubei, Guangdong and Guangxi provinces. Wuchang hosted appaling scenes during the 1910 insurrection, when ethnic Han troops mutinied under a banner proclaiming "Long live the Han, Exterminate the Manchu" and accordingly slaughtered a Manchu regiment and over eight hundred civilians here. The city and its bureaucracy survived though, and today Wuchang comprises government offices and the huge **Wuhan University** campus, with a good part of its outskirts taken up by **Dong Hu Scenic Area**, a five-kilometre-wide expanse of greenery and water which makes an excellent escape from Hankou's crowds. Other draws out this way are the **Provincial Museum**, along with the Taoist retreat of **Changchun Guan** and the **Yellow Crane Tower**, the greatest of the Yangzi's many riverside pavilions.

Yellow Crane Tower and around

The road from Hanyang to Wuchang crosses the **Great Changjiang Bridge**, before whose construction in 1957 all traffic – rail included – had to be ferried 1500m across the river. On the far side, Wuluo Lu curves around She Shan (Snake Hill) which, along with the river, is overlooked by the bright tiles and red wooden columns of the fifty-metre-high **Yellow Crane Tower** (¥30), no less magnificent for being an entirely modern Qing-style reproduction sited 1km from where the original third-century structure burned down in 1884. Legend has it that She Shan was once home to a Taoist Immortal who paid his bills at a nearby inn by drawing a picture of a crane on the wall, which would fly down at intervals and entertain the guests. A few years later the Immortal flew off on his creation, and the landlord, who doubtless could afford it by then, built the tower in his honour. Climb the internal staircases to the top floor and see Wuhan and the Yangzi at their best.

On the southern slopes of She Shan, **Hong Ge** is a handsome colonial-style red-brick mansion which housed the Hubei Military Government during the 1910 uprising. A bronze statue of Sun Yatsen stands in front, though at the time of the uprising he was abroad raising funds. Follow Wuluo Lu east for 1km from here and you'll be standing outside the russet walls of **Changchun Guan** (¥5), a Taoist complex which made its name through the Yuan-dynasty luminary **Qiu Chuzi**, who preached here and later founded his own sect. Only partially open to the public, the halls are simply furnished with statues of the Three Purities, the Jade Emperor, and other Taoist deities. A side wing has been co-opted as a pharmacy, where Chinese speakers can have their vital signs checked by a traditonal doctor and buy medicines collected, according to the staff, on Wudang Shan. There's also a martial-arts training area, with rusty poleaxes and swords displayed on racks. Next door, Changchun's **vegetarian restaurant** is well worth visiting at lunch time (see p.540).

Hubei Provincial Museum

It takes around twenty minutes by bus from the Yellow Crane Tower to **Hubei Provincial Museum** (daily 8.30am–noon & 1.30–5pm; ¥30) on Donghu Lu, whose display of items unearthed from the Warring States Period's **tomb of**

the Marquis Yi deserves a good hour of your time – especially if you're planning on visiting similar collections at Jingzhou (see p.544) and Changsha (see p.560).

The Marquis died in 433 BC and was buried in a huge, multiple-layered, wooden lacquered coffin at nearby Suizhou, then a major city of the state of **Zeng**, accompanied by fifteen thousand bronze and wooden artefacts, twenty-one women and one dog. The museum's comprehensive English explanations of contemporary history and photos of the 1978 excavation put everything in perspective. Don't miss the impressive orchestra of **64 bronze bells**, ranging in weight from a couple of kilos to a quarter of a tonne, found in the waterlogged tomb – the largest such set ever discovered – along with the wooden frame from which they once hung in rows. Clapperless (they are played with hand-held rods), each bell can produce two notes depending on where it is struck. The knowledge of metals and casting required to achieve this initially boggled modern researchers, who took five years to make duplicates. More than a hundred other musical instruments are also on show, including stone chimes, drums, flutes and zithers, along with spearheads and a very weird brazen crane totem sprouting antlers – an inscription suggests that this was the Marquis's steed in the afterlife. Souvenir shops outside sell pricey **recordings** of period tunes played on the bells, and there are brief **performances** held every hour or so in the museum's auditorium.

Around Dong Hu

Up the road from the museum and laid out as a park in 1949, **Dong Hu Scenic Area** occupies some 73 square kilometres of winding lake shore and green open spaces, somewhere to relax in relative peace among picnicking families and courting couples. Walking along the shore from the entrance with the water on your right, you pass a series of **pavilions and gardens** whose evocative names – Billow Listening House and Poem Reciting Hall, for example – compensate for their scruffy modern construction. Farther on, **Jiu Nüdun** (Nine Heroines Tomb) is the resting place of nine women who fought in the Taiping Army during the great rebellion of 1851–64. From here, a five-kilometre-long causeway – covered by bus #54 – crosses to a mid-lake pavilion (where you can have lunch) and over to the far shore at **Mo Shan**, site of Wuchang's **Botanical Gardens**, an over-elaborate attempt to re-create a "traditional" garden. From Mo Shan, bus #36 will take you round the southern shore and back to the east side of the Changjiang Bridge past **Wuhan University** on Luojia Hill, whose intriguing campus, built in 1913 in pagoda-style, was the setting for a fierce battle in 1967 between revolutionary forces and the PLA.

Eating and drinking

Cooking in Wuhan reflects the city's position midway between Shanghai and Chongqing, and restaurants here offer a good balance of eastern-style steamed and braised dishes – particularly **fish and shellfish** — along with some seriously spicy Sichuanese food. There's also a strong **snacking** tradition in town, and many places specialize in designer dumplings: various types of *shaomai*; *tangbao*, soup buns stuffed with jellied stock which burst messily as you bite them, much to the amusement of other diners; and *doupi*, a sticky rice packet stuffed with meat and rolled up in a beanpaste skin.

Hankou has the best of the **restaurants**, which are concentrated along

Zhongshan Dadao and its offshoots. Even formal places are inexpensive, and many have first-floor canteens where you can eat local staples very cheaply; the train stations have some good budget places too, serving mostly vegetable and fish dishes.

An increasing number of Western-style **cafés and bars** – many livening up after dark – are springing up along Yanjiang Dadao and Jianghan Lu, and plague proportions of Western fast-food chains can be found throughout the city. The *Holiday Inn*'s ground-floor **coffee shop** offers chocolate and cream confections at ¥15 a piece, or it's ¥38 per person for afternoon tea and cakes; there's also a stack of **cake shops** at the river end of Jianghan Lu. Don't expect to find many English signs or menus.

Restaurants

Hankou

Blue Sky Café Jianshe Dadao. Favourite hangout for Wuhan's substantial expat community, a restaurant-bar with excellent Asian and Western food, air-conditioning, a huge TV screen and long hours. The bar is stocked to overflowing; spirits are about ¥20 a shot and drinks are generous.

Bordeaux Bar Just west of the *Linjiang* hotel on Yanjiang Dadao. One of many such café-bars in the area, this place has a bit of character, with pavement tables and nicely dimmed lighting inside. Western-style pasta and steak dishes, along with an eclectic range of Chinese fare, are expensive; best stick to the coffee or beer.

Dehua Jiulou Zhongshan Dadao. Inexpensive buns and dumplings – *tangbao* are the thing to go for – along with first-rate regional cuisine, not too pricey.

Dezhuang Huoguo Guangchang Cnr of Yanjiang Dadao and Sanyang Lu. If you're craving northern-style hotpot, this is the place – big, bright, noisy and inexpensive.

Dong Lai Shun Zhongshan Dadao. Famous Muslim restaurant chain, founded in 1903 but rather modern and smart for a rapid-turnover joint dolling out bowls of spicy *lamian*, kebabs and lamb hotpots at budget prices.

Lao Huibin Cnr of Sanmin Lu and Sanquan Lu – look for the statue of Sun Yatsen at the intersection. A typically chaotic first-floor dumpling house, with more formal arrangements upstairs. Good for everything from spring rolls, buns and noodles (under ¥5 a dish) through to classy fish dishes (over ¥25).

Lao Tongcheng Cnr Zhongshan Dadao and Dazhi Lu. Enter through a mobile-phone emporium and head upstairs to this canteen-style institution, renowned for its *doupi*, costing around ¥3 a portion. "Three flavoured" are considered best, stuffed with tongue, heart and bamboo shoots, but there are also shrimp and chicken fillings for those not addicted to offal. Order off cards scrawled in Chinese at the front counter.

Si Li Mei Zhongshan Dadao. It's easy to miss the entrance of this place, which is small and buried behind steamed-bun vendors. Another place to try river food and *tangbao*.

Yonghe Dawang Across from the ferry terminal on Yanjiang Dadao, and elsewhere. Open around the clock, this restaurant chain's logo looks suspiciously like *KFC*'s but the food is very different: big bowls of beef noodle soup or *doujiang*, steamed buns, and fried rice – inexpensive Chinese breakfast staples.

Yuan Ye Jiaozi Guan Just west of Zhongshan Park, Jiefang Dadao. It's no trouble identifying the long glass windows of this extremely popular, comfortable snack house, which offers *jiaozi* by the *jin* (around ¥10), preserved eggs, and cold Sichuan-style vegetable and meat dishes.

Wuchang

Changchun Sucai Guan Changchuan Guan, Wulou Lu, Wuchang. Vegetarian restaurant with Ming decor and resolutely Chinese menu; "beef" and "chicken" are made from beancurd sheets, "prawns" from beanstarch, and so on. Portions are huge (ask for small servings if you want to try a variety), liberally laced with chillies and aniseed, and very tasty. Mains from ¥15 or so.

Da Zhonghua Pengliuyang Lu, Wuchang. Four-storey establishment, long known for its classic and innovative ways with fish – try the lake fish with red berry sauce. Noodles and soups on the first floor, general dining room on the third, tea house on top. Most dishes under ¥30.

Listings

Banks and exchange Bank of China, Zhongshan Dadao, Hankou (Mon–Sat 8.30am–4.30pm, Sun 9am–noon).

Bookshops The Xinhua bookstore, just west of the

Jianghan Lu/Zhongshan Dadao intersection, Hankou, has plenty of maps and some English titles, including abridged texts of Chinese classics. Stalls on Hangkong Lu also have the odd foreign-language item, and the post office here stocks the *China Daily*.

Cinema There are screens in Hankou at the Mingcheng Plaza on Zhongshan Dadao, and near the former US Consulate on Yanjiang Dadao.

Hospitals The Tongji, east of the Jiefang Dadao/Qingnian Lu crossroads in Hankou, is considered Wuhan's best. Another good place to go for acupuncture and massage is the hospital attached to the Hubei Traditional Medicine College, just north of She Shan, Wuchang.

Internet access In Hankou, there are Net bars near the junction of Zhongshan Dadao and Shengli Jie, not far from the *Jianghan* hotel; and east of the *Holiday Inn* on Jiefang Dadao. In Wuchang there's one on Wulou Lu, west of Zhongshan Lu.

Left luggage There are booths charging ¥5 a bag at the bus and train stations, open from around 5am to 9pm.

Mail and telephones The main post offices, with IDD phones, are on Zhongshan Dadao and at the junction of Hangkong Lu and Qingnian Lu, Hankou (daily 8am–6pm). There is no GPO as such, so ensure that poste-restante mail addresses use the street name and "Hankou", or it could end up anywhere in the city.

Markets and shopping Coin and stamp collectors congregate outside the post office on Hangkong Lu, Hankou; for larger "antique" souvenirs, try the shops at the Hubei Provincial Museum, Wuchang. Hankou's old concession area, north of Zhongshan Dadao, has the liveliest market activity, mostly revolving around fruit and vegetables. Like most Chinese cities, Hankou is a very good place to buy clothes – try the new Galaxy Plaza, halfway along Zhongshan Dadao, or numerous smaller shops nearby.

Pharmacies In addition to smaller places elsewhere, Hankou's Hangkong Lu has a string of pharmacies stocking traditional and modern medicines, the biggest of which is the Grand Pharmacy, or, according to the English sign, the "Ark of Health".

Travel agents These abound around the Yangzi ferry terminal and Hankou long-distance bus station. Alternatively, CITS here are an informed, English-speaking agency geared up to organizing Three Gorges cruises, and trips to Shennongjia and Wudang Shan; they're set back from the road on Floor 7 of a 1980s-style office block on Taibei Lu, Hankou (Ⓣ027/85784100, Ⓕ85784089).

Up the Yangzi to Yichang

The flat, broad river plains west of Wuhan don't seem too exciting at first, but historic remains lend solid character to towns along the way. It takes around 36 hours to navigate upstream from Wuhan via **Chibi** and **Jingzhou** to **Yichang**, from where the exciting journey through the Yangzi Gorges and on to Chongqing in Sichuan begins. As most boats don't stop along the way, however, if you want to see anything it's more convenient – and anyway far quicker – to use the Wuhan–Jingzhou–Yichang **expressway**, which bypasses Chibi but cuts the journey time to Yichang down to less than four hours.

Chibi

The first place of any significance along the river, about 80km southwest of Wuhan, **CHIBI** (Red Cliffs) was the setting for the most important battle of the Three Kingdoms period, the confrontation at which the competing states defined their final boundaries. It was here in 208 AD that the northern armies of Wei, led by Cao Cao, descended on the combined southern forces of Liu Bei and Sun Quan. Though heavily outnumbered, the southerners had brought two remarkable strategists along – **Zhuge Liang** and **Pang Tong** – who took full advantage of Cao's decision to launch a naval assault across the river. Misled by Pang Tong's spies, Cao chained his ships together on the north bank while preparing for the attack, and Zhuge Liang – using, it's said, Taoist magic - created an unseasonal southeasterly wind and sent a flotilla of burning hulks across

△ Pottery from Jingdezhen

Up the Yangzi to Yichang

Chibi	赤壁	***chìbì***
Baifeng Terrace	拜风台	*bàifēng tái*
Feng Chu An	风雏庵	*fēngchú ān*
Nanping Shan	南屏山	*nánpíng shān*
Wangjiang Pavilion	望江亭	*wàngjiāng tíng*
Wuhou Palace	武侯宫	*wǔhóu gōng*
Jingzhou	荆州	***jīngzhōu***
Jingzhou Museum	荆州博物馆	*jīngzhōu bówùguǎn*
Kaiyuan Guan	开元观	*kāiyuán guàn*
Puqi	蒲圻	***púqí***
Shashi	沙市	***shāshì***
Yichang	宜昌	***yíchāng***
Dagong Bridge Transit Terminal	大公桥水路客运站	*dàgōngqiáo shuǐlù kèyùnzhàn*
Dagong Fandian	大公饭店	***dàgōng fàndiàn***
Dongxin Dajiudian	东鑫大酒店	*dōngxīn dàjiǔdiàn*
Gezhou Dam	葛洲坝	*gězhōu bà*
Hydrofoil port	高速客轮中心	*gāosù kèlún zhōngxīn*
Liujin Suiyue Kafei	流金岁月咖啡	*líujīn suìyuè kāfēi*
Sanxia airport	三峡机场	*sānxiá jīchǎng*
Taohualing Binguan	桃花岭宾馆	*táohuālǐng bīnguǎn*
Three Gorges Dam site	三峡大坝区	*sānxiá dàbàqū*
Yichang International Hotel	宜昌国际大酒店	*yíchāng guójì dàjiǔdiàn*

the Yangzi, completely incinerating Cao's armada and permanently imprinting the colour of flames on the cliffs. Despite Cao Cao's defeat, neither of the other armies had the strength needed to pursue him, nor to take on each other in a final engagement which might have seen China unified instead of plunged into civil war for most of the following five centuries.

To reach Chibi, clearly visible from the river, take a train or bus to **Chibi Shi** (also known as **Puqi**) about two-thirds of the way between Wuhan and Yueyang in Hunan, from where it's a ninety-minute local bus ride to the site, locally known as **Sanguo Chibi** to distinguish it from Chibi Shi. A flight of steps on the right near the bus stop leads up Jinluan Hill to **Feng Chu An**, a whitewashed hall where Pang Tong studied military strategy and so conceived the plan that defeated Cao. Back below, following the main road to the left brings you to **Nanping Shan**, where two stone lions up on the hill flank the entrance to **Wuhou Palace** and **Baifeng Terrace**. Four statues here commemorate Zhuge Liang and Liu Bei, along with Liu Bei's oath brothers, Guan Yu and Zhang Fei (see box, p.509). Further on towards the river, the small **Wangjiang Pavilion** is a former guard post which still commands broad views of the terraced paddy fields below. Spears, arrowheads and pottery shards in a gloomy museum nearby offer proof that the legends have a historical basis. The cliffs overlooking the Yangzi's southern bank just outside town are carved with the two characters for "*chibi*", supposedly by the triumphant Wu general, **Zhou Yu**.

Jingzhou Shi and around

Around 240km west of Wuhan on the highway to Yichang, or the best part of a day upstream by ferry from Chibi, **JINGZHOU SHI** lies on the north bank of the Yangzi, where the Wuhan–Yichang expressway joins the highway up to Xiangfan in northern Hubei (see p.550). The city is divided into two separate districts: while the easterly section of **Shashi** is an indifferent modern port, the **Jingzhou** district, 10km west, is ringed by around 8km of moats and well-maintained, seven-metre-high **battlements**, built by the *Three Kingdoms* hero Guan Yu, who commanded Shu's eastern defences here. Even earlier, the now vanished city of **Jinan**, immediately north of Jingzhou, was the capital of the state of Chu until its destruction by the Qin armies around 278 BC.

From Shashi's long-distance bus station on Taqiao Lu, city bus #1 runs west into Jingzhou through the **east gate**, trundles down past Jingzhou's own long-distance bus station on Jing Nan Lu, turns in to **Jingzhong Lu**, and finally terminates by the **west gate**. Walls aside, there's not much to be impressed with in this forty-minute trawl, but walk 100m back along Jingzhong Lu from the bus stop and you'll be outside **Jingzhou Museum** (Tues–Sun 8am–4pm; ¥8). Skip the lifeless main building, full of dusty cases of unidentified pots and blurred photos, and instead walk around to the back, where ¥10 gets you in to the "Treasure Display" (same hours), a fantastic collection of Western Han **tomb remains**. These were found a few kilometres north at **Fenghuang Shan**, the site of Jinan, which former residents turned into a cemetery after the city's destruction, in order to be buried alongside their ancestors. More than 180 tombs dating from the Qin era to the end of the Western Han (221 BC–24 AD) have been found, an impressive range for a single site; the exhibition here focuses on Tomb 168, that of a court official named **Sui**. In many regards the items on display are similar to those in Wuhan's provincial museum (p.539) – the house-like sarcophagi and copious lacquerwork, for example – but the bonus here is Sui's astoundingly well-preserved **corpse**, along with some comfortingly practical household items and wooden miniatures of his servants; either he wasn't powerful enough to have his real attendants buried with him, or else this trend had gone out of style. *Three Kingdoms* aficionados should go next door to **Kaiyuan Guan**, a tiny, elderly temple dedicated to Guan Yu set among overgrown gardens.

There are buses both ways along the expressway until early evening from either Jingzhou's or Shashi's **long-distance bus stations**, with at least eight additional services north to Xiangfan through the day. There's also **accommodation** (❸) in the vicinity of either bus station if you get caught here for the night.

Yichang

You might well end up spending a night at **YICHANG**, a transport terminus on the Yangzi 120km west from Jingzhou; Yichang marks the start of routes north to Shennongjia, and is positioned on the rail line between Xi'an and Hunan. A commercial centre under the Han, it later became an important, if remote, treaty port, fading during the twentieth century. The recent blossoming of Yangzi tourism and the building of the **Three Gorges dam** upstream has got the place kicking over again, though activities are limited to touring the dam site or tracking down scattered remnants of the colonial era (for

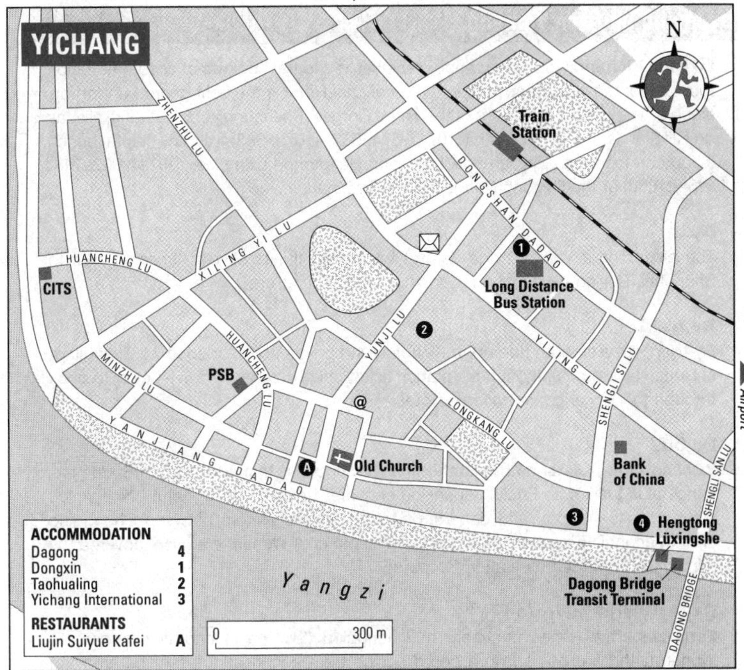

instance, the **church** just east off Yujin Lu). Otherwise, animated evening river scenery adds a bit of life to the place, with water traffic moored up and crowds flying kites, gorging themselves on shellfish at nearby street restaurants, or just cooling off with an ice cream.

Practicalities

Yichang stretches along the Yangzi's northern bank for around 5km, directly below the relatively small **Gezhou dam**. Arriving at **Sanxia airport**, 10km east of town, you'll need to catch a taxi into the centre (¥50). The **train station** is at the north side of town atop a broad flight of steps leading down to the intersection of Dongshan Dadao and **Yunji Lu**, while the main **long-distance bus station** is 500m east. Buses might also terminate south across town at the riverside **Dagong Bridge Transit Terminal**, which is also where **Yangzi ferries** pull in – the bridge in question is an unmistakable spray of suspension cables and blue concrete. Arrival by **hydrofoil** from Chongqing lands you about 5km northwest of town where bus #3 awaits. The train station and Dagong Bridge area are connected by buses #3 and #4 down Yunji Lu and the waterfront. A **taxi** costs a fixed ¥5 in the city centre.

For **accommodation**, the *Dagong Fandian* (❸) offers clean if dreary rooms close to the ferry terminal; a better bet is the friendly *Dongxin Dajiudian* (Ⓣ0717/6453449, Ⓕ6443525; ❹), between the bus and train stations on Dongshan Dadao. More upmarket options include the *Yichang International Hotel* on the corner of Yanjiang Dadao and Shengli Si Lu (Ⓣ0717/6222888,

Moving on from Yichang

Leaving Yichang, you can arrange plane, ferry, and train **tickets** at accommodation tour desks; the one at the *Yichang International Hotel* is the best geared up for foreigners. They also book **tours** of the Three Gorges, Shennongjia, and Zhangjiajie, as do CITS at 40 Yanjiang Dadao (Ⓣ0717/6746582, Ⓕ6731683) – a fairly helpful bunch if you can locate an English-speaker – and Hengtong Lüxingshe (Ⓣ0717/6222714, Ⓕ6224860) at the Dagong Bridge Transit Terminal.

By air

The **airport** is a ¥50 taxi ride east of town, with flights several times a week to Shanghai, Beijing, Guangzhou, Chongqing and Zhangjiajie.

By train

By **train**, it's a smooth ride up to Xiangfan and points north, or south to Zhangjiajie in Hunan (see p.569), though the station ticket office can be a brawl – better to book through the *Yichang International Hotel*.

By bus

Yichang's **long-distance bus station** has better buses than the Dagong Bridge terminal, plus there's an English-speaking enquiries desk, a **left luggage** office which stays open until 8pm, and departures to almost everywhere between Chongqing and Shanghai. Xingshan, Xiangfan, Jingzhou and Wuhan are also covered by minibuses from the bus-station forecourt.

By ferry and hydrofoil

Ferry departure times upstream to Chongqing (four days) and downstream to Wuhan (24hr) are posted on a board beside the Dagong bridge terminal booking office – see p.962 for more about classes and conditions. The **hydrofoil** up through the Three Gorges to Chongqing (¥380; 11 hr) departs daily at 7am from above the Gezhou Dam, 5km northwest of town – catch bus #3 or a taxi.

Ⓔwebmaster@ycinthotel.com; ❻), which has its own brewery, a revolving restaurant, and 24-hour café; and the *Taohualing Binguan* off Yunji Lu (Ⓣ0717/6236666, Ⓕ6238888; ❼), set in quiet grounds. All hotels have **places to eat**, and there are some good, cheap establishments around the Dongshan Dadao/Yunji Lu junction; the Western-style *Liujin Suiyue Kafei* at the river end of Yujin Lu does awful food and good coffee.

The Three Gorges Dam site

The **Three Gorges Dam site**, where you can watch the progress of the world's most ambitious construction project, is about 35km west of town at **Sandouping**. The dam wall, a huge grey monolith surrounded by mud, vehicles, and people, is already well underway across the western end of the Yellow Ox Gorge. At the time of writing, preparations were being made to divert the river for a second time (the first was in 1997) in order to start building the hydroelectric station – river traffic is currently diverted through a four-kilometre-long, 350-metre-wide artificial channel, something you'll have noticed if you arrived in Yichang from upstream.

To get there, catch bus #4 from just west of the train station on Dongshan Lu for four stops, then bus #8 to the site – all in all, this takes about an hour. Minibuses are on hand (¥10), or you can just walk out to the viewing area from the bus stop.

The Three Gorges Dam

Through the centuries, the Yangzi's unruly nature has been a source of trauma for China, and conquering the river's tendency to flood extravagantly once a decade has been the dream of many Chinese rulers. So far this has only been achieved by the mythical Xia emperor Yu, but by 2009 the river may finally come under human control. After almost a century of planning (the idea was first mooted by Sun Yatsen), the **Three Gorges Dam** will be the largest of its kind in the world, the 1983-metre-long, 185-metre-high wall creating an artificial lake extending back 670km through the Three Gorges to Chongqing.

Investment in the project has been promoted on the back of the dam's **hydro-electric potential** – the eventual output of its 26 generators will be 18.2 million kilowatts, ten percent of all China's power needs – and the income that the region would receive from both using the generated power and selling it abroad. Financial returns would undoubtedly bring considerable improvements in infrastructure to an otherwise poorly developed part of the country. Yet it's the dam's **flood-controlling** capabilities that blunt-speaking Communist Party front-man Zhu Rongji is using to counter protests against the project, though dissenters point out that it will probably do little to relieve flooding – which occurs along downstream tributaries as much as the Yangzi itself – and say it would be more effective and cheaper to build a string of lesser dams along these other rivers.

Meanwhile the project continues. Eventual costs are estimated at around ¥205 billion and rising, partly due to developers pocketing funds and then employing inferior materials to make up the shortfall – a practice which resulted in **cracks** appearing in the incomplete wall and locks in winter 2001, necessitating expensive repairs. In addition, increased water levels of up to 115m through the Three Gorges will submerge dozens of communities, requiring the **relocation** of millions of people, a highly controversial programme which has already cost ¥28 billion and led to clashes where transmigrants have been resettled on other people's lands. Untold **historic relics** and sites will disappear beneath the rising waters, and archeologists are frantically scrambling to excavate as much as possible before the dam begins to fill in 2008. **Ecologically** the project is indefensible – Chongqing, one of China's most heavily industrial cities, will be pouring its effluent directly into the new lake, while even the Chinese government admit that **siltation** will make the dam unusable within seventy years unless they come up with a solution.

Shennongjia Forest Reserve

Hidden away 200km north of Yichang in Hubei's far west, **Shennongjia Forest Reserve** encloses a rough crowd of mountains rising to the 3053-metre-high **Da Shennongjia**, the tallest peak in central China. Botanically, this is one of the country's richest corners, famed for its plant life ever since the Taoist immortal and legendary Xia king **Shennong** – also credited with introducing mankind to farming, medicine, and tea – scoured these heights for herbs. More recently, the botanist **Ernest Wilson** found several new species for London's Kew Gardens here in the early twentieth century. Intriguingly, Shennongjia has since hosted sightings of the **Chinese wild man**, whose existence seems far from impossible in this stronghold of ancient plants – and even if these elude you, there's a good chance of seeing endangered **golden monkeys** here.

On few tourist agendas, Shennongjia is nonetheless easy to reach from Yichang – three days is enough for a quick return trip – though most of the

Shennongjia Forest Reserve		
Muyu Zhen	木鱼镇	***mùyú zhèn***
Songbo	松柏	*sōngbǎi*
Xingshan	兴山	*xīngshān*
Yumingshan Binguan	玉名山宾馆	*yùmíngshān bīnguǎn*
Shennongjia Forest Reserve	神农架林区	***shénnóngjià línqū***
Banbi Yan	板壁岩	*bǎnbì yán*
Dalong Tan	大龙潭	*dàlóng tán*
Fengjing Ya	风京垭	*fēngjīng yà*
Jinhou Ling	金猴岭	*jīnhóu lǐng*
Reserve Gates	鸭子口	*yāzi kǒu*
Xiaolong Tan	小龙潭	*xiǎolóng tán*
Wildlife		
Giant Salamander	娃娃鱼	*wáwá yú*
Golden Monkey	金丝猴	*jīnsīhóu*
Golden Pheasant	红胸锦鸟	*hóngxiōng jǐnniǎo*
Temminck's tragopan	红胸角雉	*hóngxiōng juézhì*

region is actually **off-limits to foreigners**. Chinese maps highlight the central **Shennongjia town** (known locally as **Songbai**) as an access point: go here and you will be arrested, fined and booted out by the PSB. As all transport beyond Muyu travels via Songbai, it is not possible to continue north to Shiyan and Wudang Shan, however easy this appears on a map. Neither Yichang's PSB nor CITS are clued up to the situation, and will blithely suggest travelling through the restricted zone. If you stick to the open area around the village of **Muyu Zhen**, however, you'll have a trouble-free trip; just remember that its altitude makes the region very cold in winter, and the reserve can be **snowbound** between November and May.

To Muyu Zhen and the reserve

Minibuses from outside Yichang's bus station leave every thirty minutes between dawn and mid-afternoon for the four-hour run to **XINGSHAN** (¥45), most of this on a decent road climbing through well-farmed, increasingly mountainous country overloaded with hydroelectric stations. Xingshan itself is an unpleasant industrial town; turn right out of the bus station and walk 100m up to a crossroads and you'll find battered **minibuses** to Muyu Zhen (¥10) waiting to fill up with passengers for the final two-hour stretch up the Songbai road.

MUYU ZHEN – also known as **Muyu** or **Yuzhen** – is a service centre 17km south of the reserve, a 500-metre-long street of small stores, guesthouses and canteens leading off the main road. It's a good base for a quick visit, though there's cheaper accommodation inside the reserve if you're planning on staying a while. Muyu's **hotels** are surprisingly upmarket: at the far end of the street, the *Yumingshan Binguan* (Ⓣ0719/3453088; ❸) has spacious, clean doubles and a fair restaurant. The exclusive *Shenlong Resort* (❹) is clearly visible on the hill above. For **maps and tours** of the reserve, drop in on Muyu's **Forestry Office Travel Service** (Ⓣ0719/3452303, Ⓕ3452335) about 100m before *Yumingshan Binguan* – look for the "Shennongjia Natural Reserve" sign on the left. Some staff here speak English, and can advise on the best places to find unusual plants and animals – hiring a car and interpreter for the day will cost ¥400. To **reach the reserve** on your own, either flag down Songbai-bound buses on the main road (note that the reserve gates here are as far as foreigners are allowed to travel) or bargain with the Xingshan minibus drivers for a charter (about ¥50 to the reserve gates, or ¥300 for the day), who otherwise run **back to Xingshan** until the afternoon.

Around the reserve

The steep and twisting Songbai road continues north of Muyu to a checkpoint marking the **reserve gates**, where you hand over the ¥60 entry fee and add your name to the list of the few foreigners who make it here each year. Beyond, 6km of gravel track runs southwest up a once-logged valley to the couple of wooden Forestry Department buildings that comprise **XIAOLONG TAN**, a source of **beds** (¥50), meals and close-up views of golden monkeys if any have been brought in to the "animal hospital" here. There's also a **Wild Man museum**, where paintings, newspaper clippings, maps and casts of footprints document all known encounters with the gigantic, shaggy, red-haired *ye ren*, first seen in 1924.

There are some good **walking tracks** around Xiaolong Tan, though you'll need advice from Forestry staff on current conditions. One route (much of it along a vehicle track) climbs south, in around 2.5km, to a forest of China firs on the slopes of **Jinhou Ling** (Golden Monkey Peak), the prime spot to catch family groups of **golden monkeys** foraging first thing in the morning. Favouring green leaves, stems, flowers and fruit, the monkeys live through the winter on **lichen** and moss, which the trees here are covered in. The males especially are a tremendous sight, with reddish-gold fur, light blue faces, huge lips and no visible nose. A far rougher trail continues to the top of the mountain in four hours, which you'd be ill-advised to tackle without a guide. Alternatively, a relaxed 3km north of Xiaolong Tan is **Dalong Tan**, a cluster of run-down huts by a stream (reputedly inhabited by giant salamanders), from where there's an undemanding eight-kilometre walk up the valley to **Guanyin Cave**. Most of this is through open country with plenty of wildflowers in spring, and the chance for birders to flush out **golden pheasants** and the splendidly coloured, grouse-like **tragopans**.

For scenery alone, the gravel road from Xiaolong Tan curves westwards up the valley, climbing almost continually along the ridges and, in clear weather, allowing for spectacular views. On the way you cross Da Shennongjia, though the rounded peak is barely noticeable above the already high road. Better are the cliffscapes about 10km along at **Fengjing Ya** and **Jinzi Yanya**, and the "forest" of limestone spires where the road finally gives up the ghost 17km due west of Xiaolong Tan at **Banbi Yan**.

Northwestern Hubei

Hubei's river plains extend well into the province's northwest, where, 300km from Wuhan, you'll find the gateway town of **Xiangfan**, central China's car-manufacturing capital, busy turning out indigenous Volkswagens. A few hours farther west, the flatlands reluctantly cede to mountain ranges butting up against Henan, Shaanxi and Sichuan, steeped in legends surrounding **Wudang Shan**, the Military Mountain, known for its Taoist temples and fighting style. An easy ascent coupled with the mountain's splendid scenery really make the

Northwestern Hubei		
Shiyan	十堰	***shíyàn***
Wudang Shan Town	武当山市镇	***wǔdāngshān shìzhèn***
Taishan Miao	泰山庙	*tàishān miào*
Xuanwu Jiudian	玄武酒店	*xuánwǔ jiǔdiàn*
Yuxu Gong	玉虚宫	*yùxū gōng*
Wudang Shan	武当山	***wǔdāng shān***
Feisheng Rock	飞升岩	*fēishēng yán*
Huangjing Hall	皇经堂	*huángjīng táng*
Huanglong Dong	黄龙洞	*huánglóng dòng*
Jindian Gong	金殿宫	*jīndiàn gōng*
Lang Mei Xian Ci	榔梅仙祠	*lángméi xiānci*
Nanyan Gong	南岩宫	*nányán gōng*
Nanyuan Binguan	南岩宾馆	*nányán bīnguǎn*
San Tianmen	三天门	*sāntiān mén*
Taihe Binguan	太和宾馆	*tàihé bīnguǎn*
Taihe Gong	太和宫	*tàihé gōng*
Zixiao Gong	紫霄宫	*zǐxiāo gōng*
Xiangfan	襄樊	***xiāngfán***
Dico's	德克士	*dékè shì*
Landun Binguan	蓝盾宾馆	*lándùn bīnguǎn*
Railway Grand Hotel	铁路大酒店	*tiělù dàjiǔdiàn*
Tiege Jiaozi Guan	铁哥饺子馆	*tiěgē jiǎoziguǎn*

journey worthwhile, with direct transport from Wuhan and Yichang – including the Hubei–Xi'an **rail line** – crossing the region.

Xiangfan

XIANGFAN, a friendly manufacturing and transport hub on the upper reaches of the **Han River**, has a long history. It was at the hill resort of **Longzhong**, 30km southwest, that the *Three Kingdoms* warlord Liu Bei first sought the advice of the reclusive genius **Zhuge Liang** in his struggles against Cao Cao. Though Liu was dismissed three times without meeting Zhuge, his patience finally gained him an interview: in the novel's famous "Reply at Longzhong" episode, Zhuge outlined the philosophy which was to enable Liu to defeat Cao's superior forces, and Zhuge was persuaded to join Liu's war effort as his chief adviser. A more recent relic is Xiangfan's Ming-dynasty **city wall** – you can take a round trip on bus #13 or #14 from the train station and over the river, where some sections have been fully restored.

None of this necessitates a stop here, but transport connections may see you staying overnight. Most of Xiangfan is north of the river; the **train station** is on Qianjin Lu and faces up Zhongyuan Lu, 200m along which you'll find the **long-distance bus station**. There are useful buses to Jingzhou, Yichang, and Wuhan, and trains to Xi'an, Chengdu, Chongqing, Yichang, Wuhan and beyond – aside from the station, rail tickets can be bought at the Railway International Travel Service, next to the *Railway Grand Hotel* on Qianjin Lu. For **Wudang Shan**, there's a slow dawn train which gets in around noon, or a midday service that only takes around two hours; alternatively, catch a Shiyan **minibus** (¥30; 3hr) from outside Xiangfan's bus station, which can drop you off at Wudang Shan en route.

Both the train station and long-distance bus station have a **place to stay** opposite: the *Railway Grand Hotel* (Ⓣ0710/3220043, Ⓦwww.railway-hotel.com; ❺), which is an upmarket place except for a couple of budget rooms (❹); and railway-police-run *Landun Binguan* (Ⓣ0710/3254377; ❷, beds ¥50) respectively. The area is thick with inexpensive **restaurants** – down a plate of *jiaozi* and a bottle of beer at the good-value *Tiege Jiaozi Guan* past the *Railway Grand* on Qianjin Lu, or there are countless anonymous *lamian* joints and a branch of *Dico's Burgers* between the bus and train stations. The **Bank of China** is a ten-minute ride on bus #11 from the train station to Changzheng Lu, with the **post office** a few more stops along on Jiefang Lu. There's also a small **Internet bar** just down from *Tiege Jiaozi Guan*.

Wudang Shan

Peaking at its 1600-metre **Tianzhu summit**, Wudang Shan's 72 pinnacles have, since Tang times, been liberally covered in **Taoist temples**. Those that survived a wave of thirteenth-century revolts were restored following proclamations for the development of religion under the Ming emperor **Cheng Zi** in 1413 – the work took three hundred thousand labourers ten years to complete – and the mountain is currently enjoying another bloom of religious fervour, with many of the temples emerging fabulously decorated and busy after decades of neglect.

Wudang Shan is also famous for its **martial arts**, which command as much respect as those of Henan's Shaolin Si (see p.309). It's said that the Song-dynasty monk **Zhang Sanfeng** developed Wudang boxing – from which *tai ji* is derived – after watching a fight between a snake and a magpie, which revealed to him the essence of *neijia*, an internal force used (in typical Taoist manner) to control "action" with "non-action". Fighting skills would also have come in handy considering the vast number of **outlaws** who've inhabited these mountains over the centuries. The rebel peasant **Li Zicheng** massed his forces and rose to depose the last Ming emperor from here, and there's a tablet recording the suppression of the Red Turbans on the mountain by Qing troops in 1856. More recently, the Communist **Third Front Army** found sanctuary here in 1931, after their march from Hong Lake in southern Hubei.

On a more peaceful note, Wudang Shan was also the retreat of emperor **Zhen Wu**, who cultivated his longevity in these mountains during the fifteenth century, and whose portly statue graces many local temples – his **birthday** is celebrated locally on the third day of the third lunar month, a good time to visit the mountain. Wudang's valuable plants later attracted the attention of the sixteenth-century pharmacologist **Li Shizhen**, who included four hundred local species among the 1800 listed in his *Materia Medica*, still a source work on the medicinal use of Chinese herbs.

Wudang Shan town

About 120km west of Xiangfan, rail and road converge at the small market town of **WUDANG SHAN**, with the mountain range rising immediately to the south. There are buses here until late afternoon and two trains daily from Xiangfan, or you can leave transport 25km farther west at the city of **Shiyan** and catch a minibus back to Wudang Shan (¥10) from opposite Shiyan's train station. Wudang Shan town is just a few muddy backstreets south of the 500-metre-long main road; opposite the bus station, the *Xuanwu Jiudian* is the pick of places **to stay** (Ⓣ0719/5666013; ❸). Looking south into the backstreets beside the bus station, you'll see a road which passes under a railway arch;

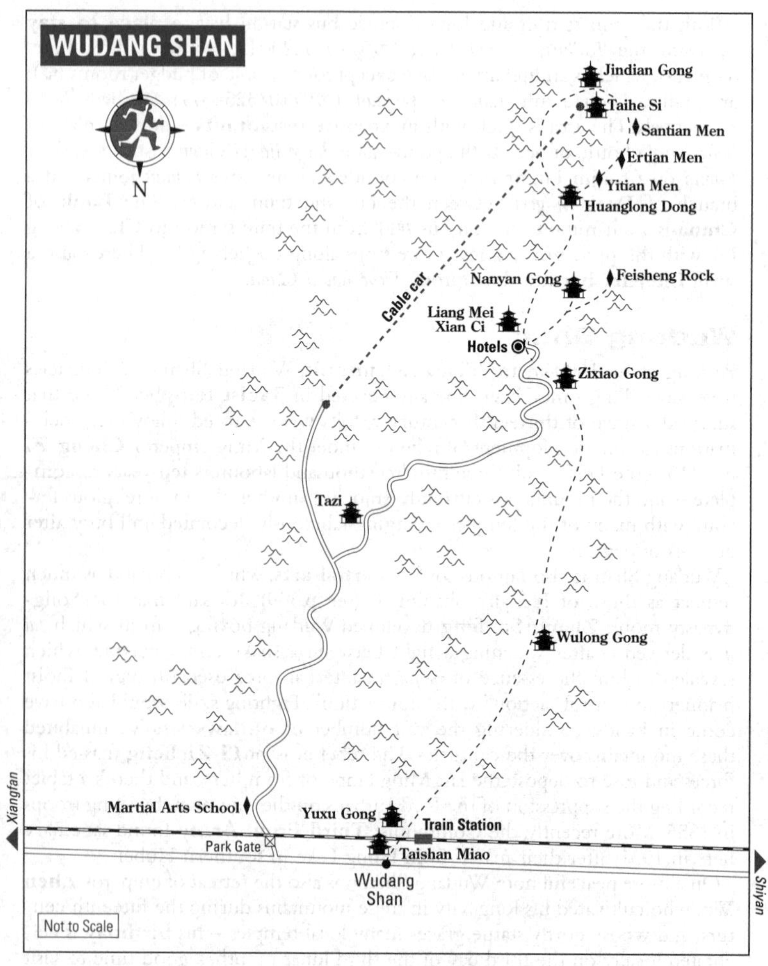

follow it down and on the left before the arch you'll find **Taishan Miao** (¥2), a small temple museum whose eccentric exhibits include a hefty bronze model of Jindian Gong (see opposite), and an illustrated medical scroll describing how the phases of the moon affect different organs. Heading on under the railway arch brings you to **Yuxu Gong** (¥2), the largest temple complex at Wudang Shan before burning down in 1745; it's now just a few vegetated pavilions, staircases and wells scattered around a flagstoned area the size of a couple of soccer pitches.

The mountain

Heading up the mountain, it's possible to **hike** from town to the summit in about eight hours – the footpath starts near the train station – though most people catch one of the ubiquitous **minibuses** (¥10) to the roadhead three-quarters of the way up at Nanyan Gong. There's a stop at the **park gates** outside town to pay the inevitable entrance fee (¥31), then drivers tear up past stark fields, outlying temples and martial-arts schools to where the road ends among a cluster of hotels, sword shops and parked vehicles.

Accommodation is expensive for what's on offer, and you'll need to thoroughly check out the room and availability of hot water before commencing bargaining. The current best deal is at *Nanyan Binguan* (❶); another similar option is the *Taihe Binguan* (❷). All places to stay serve **meals**, generally not bad value.

Nanyan Gong and Zixiao Gong

A path from the hotel area leads, via several Tang-dynasty ruins and long views down onto the plains, to **Nanyan Gong** (¥10), perched fortress-like on a precipice. The halls are tiny and austere, carved as they are out of the cliff face, but the main sight here is **Dragon Head Rock**, a two-metre-long slab sculpted with swirls and scales which projects straight out over the void. Countless people lost their lives trying to walk to the end with a stick of incense before it was walled off. Carry on past the temple to **Feisheng Rock** for far safer views of the scenery.

About 3km downhill from the end of the road – you'll have seen it in passing – is **Zixiao Gong**, the Purple Cloud Palace (¥10), an impressively huge early Ming temple complex whose pattern of successively higher platforms appears to mimic the structure of the hills above. Pleasantly active with monks, tourists and the occasional mendicant traveller, the place is becoming the mountain's most important single monastery. Through the gates, a broad stone staircase climbs between boxy Tang pavilions housing massive stone tortoises to the **main hall**, whose exterior is lightened by the graceful sweep of its tiled roof. Inside is a rare wooden spiral cupola and a benevolent statue of the Yellow Emperor; surrounding courtyards are sometimes used for martial-arts displays.

Tianzhu

It takes around two hours to walk from the hotel area to the top of **Tianzhu Peak** along a comfortably paved path (a waterproof or umbrella may come in handy as protection against Wudang Shan's famously changeable weather). One way to keep your mind off the flights of steps is by watching out for boisterous red-billed magpies, with graceful blue tails, in the forest. Almost immediately you arrive at **Lang Mei Xian Ci** (¥2), a small shrine dedicated to Zhang Sanfeng and his contribution to Chinese martial arts – there's a statue of him along with a cast-iron halberd in one hall, and Chinese-only accounts of his development of Wudang boxing in adjoining rooms.

Halfway up to Tianzhu the path divides at **Huanglong Dong** (Yellow Dragon Cave) to form an eventual circuit via the peak; continue straight ahead for the least taxing walk and superb views through the canopy of cloud-swept, apparently unscalable cliffs. A surprisingly short time later you'll find yourself on top of them, outside the encircling wall which has turned Tianzhu and its temples into a well-defended citadel. Inside, the Ming-dynasty **Taihe Gong** is impressive for the atmosphere of grand decay enclosed by the thick green tiles and red walls of **Huangjing Hall**, where monks stand around the cramped stone courtyards or pray in the richly decorated, peeling rooms squeezed inside. For a further ¥10 you can ascend the unbelievably steep **Jiuliandeng** (Nine-section Staircase) to where the mountain is literally crowned by **Jindian Gong**, the Golden Palace Temple, a tiny shrine decorated with a gilded bronze roof embellished with cranes and deer, whose interior is filled by a statue of armour-clad Zhen Wu sitting behind a desk in judgement. Views from the front terrace (clearest in the morning) look down from the top of the world, with sharp crags dropping away through wispy clouds into the forest below. There's a **hostel** (dorm beds ¥25) just outside Tianzhu's gates; Chinese-speakers will find the monks' company well worth enduring the hostel's spartan facilities. For an alternative descent, follow the stairs off Jiandian Gong's rear terrace, which return to Huanglong Dong down some very rickety steps via **Santian Men**, the Three Sky Gates.

Hunan

For many travellers, their experience of **Hunan** is a pastiche of the tourist image of rural China – a view of endless muddy tracts or intensely farmed paddy fields rolling past the train window, green or gold depending on the season. But the bland countryside, or rather the lot of the peasants farming it, has greatly affected the country's recent history. Hunan's most famous peasant son, **Mao Zedong**, saw the crushing poverty inflicted on local farmers by landlords and a corrupt government, and the brutality with which any protests were suppressed. Though Mao is no longer accorded his former god-like status, monuments to him litter the landscape around the provincial capital **Changsha**, which is a convenient base for exploring the scenes of his youth. By contrast, the history-laden town of **Yueyang** in northern Hunan, where the Yangzi meanders past **Dongting Hu**, China's second largest lake, offers more genteel attractions. Both Hunan and Hubei – literally "south of the lake" and "north of the lake" respectively – take their names from this vast expanse of water, which is intricately tied to the origins of **dragon-boat racing**. Farther afield, there's a pleasant group of mountain temples a day's journey south of Changsha at **Heng Shan**, and some inspiringly rugged landscapes to tramp through far to the west at **Wulingyuan Scenic Reserve**.

Changsha and around

There's little evidence to show that the site of **CHANGSHA**, Hunan's tidy, nondescript capital, has in fact been inhabited for three thousand years, though it has long been an important river town and, prior to Qin invasions in 280 BC, was the southern capital of the kingdom of **Chu**. Changsha was declared a treaty port in 1903, though Europeans found that the Hunanese had a very short fuse (something other Chinese already knew), and, after the British raised the market price of rice during a famine in 1910, the foreign quarter was totally destroyed by rioting. The bulk of the remainder was torched by the Guomindang in 1938, following their "scorched earth" policy as they fled the Japanese advance, and recent modernizations have claimed the rest. While ancient sites and objects occasionally surface nearby – such as Shang-era

Changsha and around

Changsha	长沙	***chángshā***
Aiwan Ting	爱晚亭	*àiwǎn tíng*
First Teachers' Training School	第一师范	*dìyī shīfàn*
Hunan Provincial Museum	湖南省博物馆	*húnánshěng bówùguǎn*
Hunan University	湖南大学	*húnán dàxué*
Jiezi Dao	桔子岛	*júzi dǎo*
Martyrs' Park	烈士公园	*lièshì gōngyuán*
Qingshui Tan	清水潭	*qīngshuǐ tán*
Wangxiang Pavilion	望乡亭	*wàngxiāng tíng*
Yuelu Academy	岳麓书院	*yuèlù shūyuàn*
Yuelu Shan	岳麓山	*yuèlù shān*
Accommodation		
Civil Aviation	民航大酒店	*mínháng dàjiǔdiàn*
Cygnet	小天鹅大酒店	*xiǎotiāné dàjiǔdiàn*
Didu	地都大酒店	*dìdū dàjiǔdiàn*
Dolton	通程国际大酒店	*tōngchéng guójì dàjiǔdiàn*
Purple Gold Dragon	紫金龙大酒店	*zǐjīnlóng dàjiǔdiàn*
Sanjiu Chunyun	三九楚云大酒店	*sānjiǔchǔyún dàjiǔdiàn*
University Guesthouse	湖南大学专家楼	*húnán dàxué zhuānjiālóu*
Eating		
Beijing Jiaozi Guan	北京饺子馆	*běijīng jiǎozi guǎn*
Chaozhou Caiguan	潮州菜馆	*cháozhōu càiguǎn*
Dong Lai Shun	东来顺	*dōnglái shùn*
Fire Palace	火宫饭店	*huǒgōng fàndiàn*
Juyuan Jiujia	聚远酒家	*jùyuǎn jiǔjiā*
Ludao Kafei Guan	绿岛咖啡馆	*lùdǎo kāfēiguǎn*
Shangdao	上岛	*shàngdǎo*
Xinhua Lou	新华楼	*xīnhuá lóu*
Zhiwei Kafei Niupai	之味咖啡牛排	*zhīwèikāfēi níupái*
Shaoshan	韶山	***sháoshān***
Dripping Water Cave	滴水洞	*dīshuǐ dòng*
Mao Ancestral Temple	毛氏宗祠	*máoshì zōngcí*
Mao Zedong Exhibition Hall	毛泽东纪念馆	*máozédōng jìniànguǎn*
Mao's Family Home	毛泽东故居	*máozédōng gùjū*
Shaofeng Binguan	韶凤宾馆	*sháofèng bīnguǎn*
Shaoshan Binguan	韶山宾馆	*sháoshān bīnguǎn*

bronze wine jars, and the magnificently preserved contents of three **Han burial mounds** – their presence is swamped by busy clover-leaf intersections, grey concrete facades, and other trappings of modern urban China.

Primarily, though, Changsha is known for its links with **Mao**. Aged 18, he arrived here from his native Shaoshan as nationwide power struggles erupted following the Manchu dynasty's fall in 1911, and soon put aside his university studies to spend six months in the local militia. After he returned to the classroom in 1913, Changsha became a breeding ground for secret political societies and intellectuals, and by 1918 there was a real movement for Hunan to become an independent state. For a time, this idea found favour with the local warlord **Zhao Hendi**, though he soon violently turned on his supporters. Mao, then back in Shaoshan heading a Communist Party branch and leading peasant protests, was singled out and fled to Guangzhou in 1925 to take up a teaching post at the Peasant Movement Training Institute (see p.633). Within three years he would return to Hunan to organize the abortive **Autumn Harvest Uprising**, and would be establishing guerilla bases in rural Jiangxi.

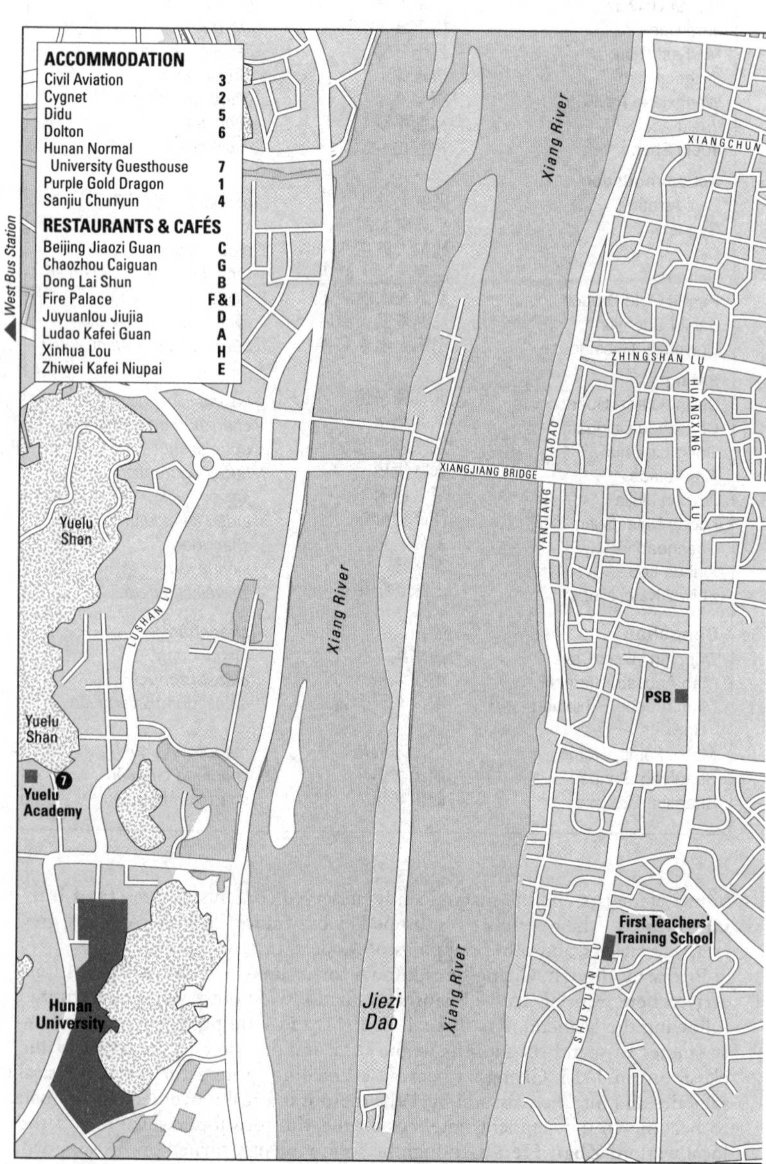

Mao was by no means the only young Hunanese caught up in these events, and a number of his contemporaries later surfaced in the Communist government: **Liu Shaoqi**, Mao's deputy until he became a victim of the Cultural Revolution; four Politburo members under Deng Xiaoping, including the former CCP chief, **Hu Yaobang**; and **Hua Guofeng**, Mao's lookalike and briefly empowered successor. Today, several of Changsha's formal attractions involve

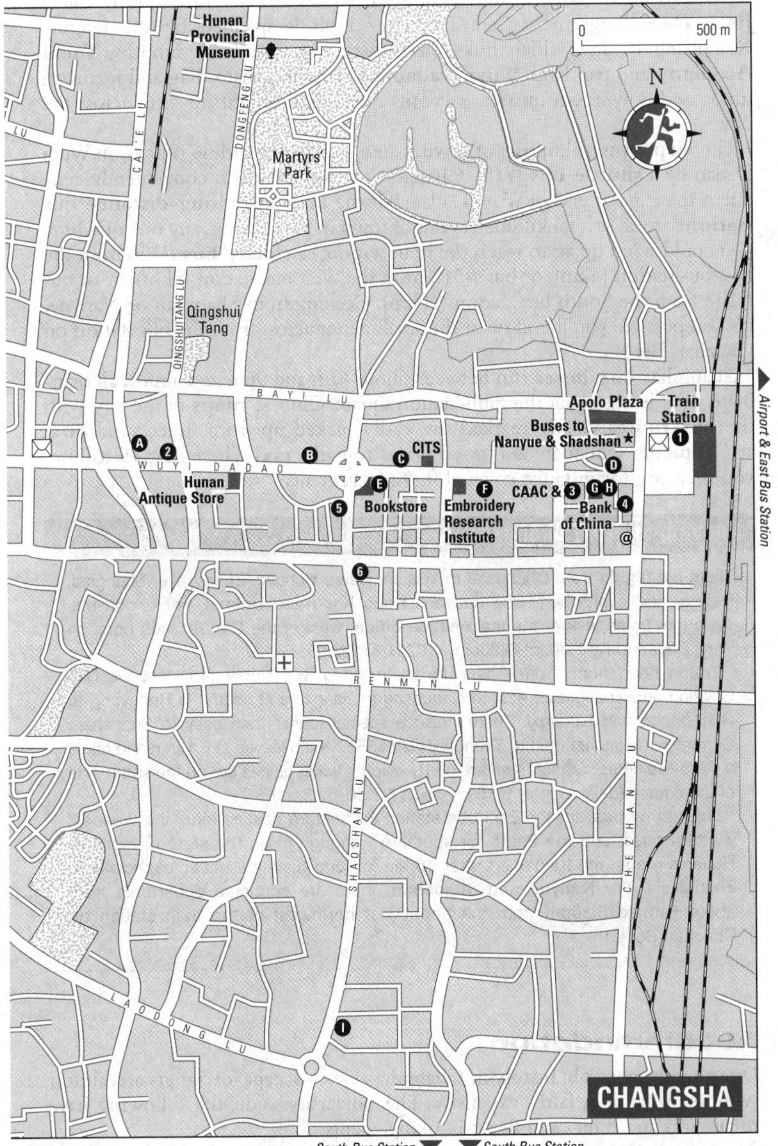

the Chairman, though there are also a couple of parks to wander around, and a fascinating **Provincial Museum**. The only real day trip from Changsha is out to Mao's birthplace at **Shaoshan**, 90km to the southwest, a very pleasant excursion made easy by local rail.

Arrival and city transport

The bulk of Changsha is spread east of the **Xiang River**, and the city's name – literally "Long Sand" – derives from a narrow midstream bar, now called **Jiezi Dao**, Tangerine Island. The river itself is spanned by the lengthy Xiangjiang Bridge, which links the city to the west bank suburbs, **Yuelu Academy** and parkland. **Wuyi Dadao** is Changsha's main drag and forms an unfocused downtown district as it runs broad and straight for 4km across the city.

The **airport** is 15km east of town, connected to the airline offices on Wuyi Dadao by a **shuttle bus** (¥15). Changsha's **train station** is conveniently central at the eastern end of Wuyi Dadao, but the three main **long-distance bus stations** are all several kilometres out of town in the suburbs, any one of which you could wind up at: to reach the train station, catch **city bus** #126 from the East bus station (4km), or bus #312 from the West bus station (8km), or or bus #107 from the South bus station (10km). Coming from Shaoshan or Nanyue, it's also possible you'll end up at the small depot across from the bus station on Chezhan Bei Lu.

Changsha's **city buses** run between about 6am and 9pm and almost all originate, or at least stop, at the train-station square. Chinese **maps** of the city, with the **bus routes** clearly marked, are easily picked up from street vendors at arrival points, which are also good places to hail a **taxi**. These cost ¥5 to hire; you then pay for distance covered in ¥2 increments.

Moving on from Changsha

There are **flights** from Changsha to Wuhan, Hefei, Yichang, Zhangjiajie, Shanghai, Beijing, and everywhere else between Hong Kong and Ürümqi. For airport-bus departure times, ask at the main **airline office**, west of the *Civil Aviation* hotel on Wuyi Dadao (daily 7.30am–9.30pm; ⓣ0731/4112222).

Trains head north from Changsha to Yueyang and Hubei province; west to Guizhou and Zhangjiajie; east to Nanchang in Jiangxi; and south via Hengyang to Guangdong and Guangxi. There's also a special tourist train daily to Shaoshan. Currently, the fastest train to Zhangjiajie is #T358, which leaves at 6.15am and takes a mere five hours. Station staff are pretty helpful; ticket offices are on the south side of the square (daily roughly 8.15am–noon & 2.30–5.45pm).

Leaving by **bus**, try the East bus station for eastern destinations, the West for western ones, and the South for southern – though given the state of many of Hunan's roads, the train is a better option for long-distance travel, especially to Zhangjiajie. For **Nanyue** and **Shaoshan**, there are continual departures from about 8am to 5.30pm from the depot just northwest of the train station on Chezhan Bei Lu.

Accommodation

Due to tight controls, **hotels** in Changsha able to accept foreigners are, almost without exception, fairly expensive. The university aside, the following have restaurants and train- and flight-booking agents.

Civil Aviation 75 Wuyi Dadao ⓣ0731/4170228, ⓕ4170388. A well-run and tidy airlines operation, though reception staff are harassed and brusque. ❺

Cygnet 178 Wuyi Dadao ⓣ0731/4410400, ⓕ4423698. This large multistorey complex, designed to lure international business folk, has a cabaret nightclub, swimming pool and gym. ❺

Didu Jiudian 80 Shaoshan Bei Lu ⓣ0731/4451555, ⓕ4454483; buses along Wuyi Dadao stop nearby. Inexpensive lodgings in a tatty, renovated 1930s building. Not listed as a foreigners' hotel but – at time of writing – had no qualms about letting them stay. ❹

Dolton 149 Shaoshan Bei Lu ⓣ0731/4168888, ⓕ4169999, ⓦwww.dolton-hotel.com. Changsha's height of luxury, a hugely opulent sprawl of marble, chandeliers and five-star service. ❾

Hunan Normal University Guesthouse Below Yuelu Shan in western Changsha ⓣ0731/8872211. Catch bus #202 from the train station, or #305 from the West bus station to its bridge-side terminus, where you can pick up a #202 or #106. The area you need is actually north of the main campus, and it's a good ten-minute walk uphill to the guesthouse once you're in the grounds. After all this, rooms are cheap but often full, so phone ahead. ❸

Purple Gold Dragon Northeast corner of the train station square, right next to the arrivals exit ⓣ0731/2293366, ⓕ2295412. This popular place is good value and usually full – hang around mid-morning to snap up rooms as they appear. Be firm if the staff try to foist their most expensive rooms on you. ❸

Sanjiu Chunyun Just southwest of the train station, on Chezhan Lu ⓣ0731/4191999, ⓕ4191399. New three-star venture, as yet untarnished and with enthusiastic staff. ❺

The City

While there's little in Changsha to absorb between the sights, it's a clean, well-ordered city and people are noticeably friendly – don't be surprised if you acquire a guide while walking around. If the city's streets seem unusually empty and you're wondering where Changsha's crowds hang out, head down to the main **shopping district** west of the centre at the junction of Wuyi Dadao and **Huangxing Lu**. The latter is being pedestrianized at present, but the area is already loaded with shopping plazas, Western fast-food chains, and groups of teenagers orbiting between the two.

Qingshui Tang

North of Wuyi Dadao, on Bayi Lu, is **Qingshui Tang** (Clearwater Pool; daily 8.30am–5pm; ¥8; bus #1 stops outside), Mao's former home in Changsha and the site of the first local Communist Party offices. A white marble statue of Mao greets you at the gate, and the garden walls are covered with stone tablets carved with his epigrams. Near the pool itself is a scruffy vegetable patch and the reconstructed room in which Mao and his second wife, **Yang Kaihui** (daughter of Mao's stoical and influential teacher, Yang Chang Qi), lived after moving here from Beijing following their marriage in 1921. There's also a display of peasant tools – a grindstone, thresher, carrypole and baskets – and a short history of Chinese agriculture. In the same grounds, a brightly tiled **museum** contains a low-key but interesting collection of historical artefacts, including a clay tomb figurine of a bearded horseman and a cannon used for defending the city against Taiping incursions in 1852. These pieces lead through to a depressing photographic record of Guomindang atrocities and eulogies to Mao, Zhou Enlai, and others. The three red flags here are those of the Party, the PLA and the nation.

Martyrs' Park and Hunan Provincial Museum

From Qingshui Tang, follow Qingshuitang Lu north and then turn east for 500m to the gates of **Martyrs' Park** (free). Though it's often crowded, plenty of shade and lakes complete with ornamental gardens, bridges and pagodas make the park a nice place to stroll. But the main reason to head up this way is to visit **Hunan Provincial Museum** (Tues–Sun 8am–noon & 2.30–5pm; ¥20; bus #203, from the station via Wuyi Dadao, stops outside), whose entrance is on Dongfeng Lu above the park's northwestern corner. Though run-down, the museum is one of Changsha's high points, dedicated solely to the Han-era tomb of **Xin Zui**, the Marquess of Dai. Xin Zui died around 160 BC, and her subterranean tomb – roughly contemporary with similar finds at Jingzhou (see p.544) and Wuhan (see p.530) – was one of three discovered in 1972 during construction work at **Mawangdui**, about 4km northeast (the others contained her husband and son). Thanks to damp-proof rammed walls of clay and charcoal, a triple wooden sarcophagus, and wrappings of linen and silk, the Marquess' **body** was so well preserved that modern pathologists were able to establish that when she died, aged 50, she suffered from tuberculosis, gall stones, arteriosclerosis and bilharzia. The sarcophaguses are in a side hall, while access to the mummy (after sealing your dusty shoes in plastic bags) is through a basement display of **embroideries**, lacquered bowls and coffins, musical instruments, wooden tomb figures and other funerary offerings. Taoist texts written on silk were also found in the tomb, and one piece illustrating **qigong postures** is on display. Xin Zui herself lies in a fluid-filled tank below several inches of perspex, a gruesome white doll decently covered from chin to thigh, with her internal organs displayed in jars.

Around the river

A couple of kilometres south of the Xiangjiang Bridge on Shuyuan Lu, the grey and white **First Teachers' Training School** is where Mao completed his formal education and later taught during the 1920s; bus #139 comes here from the train station. Historical associations aside, there's nothing to see and the school is, in fact, a reconstruction after the original burned down in the 1930s.

Crossing the river, gaze down on semi-rural midstream **Jiezi Dao**, which was settled by the local European community after the events of 1910. Some of their former homes are still standing, though one-time mansions are now partitioned into family apartments. Legend has it that Mao used to swim regularly to shore from the southern tip of the island, a feat he repeated on his 65th birthday as one of his famous river crossings.

Over the river, **Hunan University**'s campus sits south of **Yuelu Shan**, a famous breezy hilltop and beauty spot, reached from the train station by bus #202, which runs along Wuyi Dadao, crosses the bridge and heads south to terminate at a square dominated by a Mao statue below **Yuelu Academy**. Paths flanked by food and souvenir stalls lead from here to the park gates (¥2), then meander uphill, making for forty minutes' stroll through pleasant woodland to **Wangxiang Ting**, a pavilion with views over the city. On the way, the small **Aiwan Ting** (Loving the Dusk Pavilion) was one of Mao's youthful haunts (there's a tablet here bearing his calligraphy), whose name derives from the verse *Ascending the Hills* by the soulful Tang poet Du Mu:

A stony path winds far up cool hills
Towards cottages hidden deep amongst white clouds
Loving the maple trees at dusk I stop my cart
To sit and watch the frosted leaves
Redder than February flowers

Eating, drinking and entertainment

A predilection for strong flavours and copious chillies places **Hunanese food** firmly inside the Western Chinese cooking belt – Mao himself claimed that it was the fiery food that made locals so (politically) red. Pungent **regional specialities** include air-cured and **chilli-smoked meat**; *dong'an* chicken, where the shredded, poached meat is seasoned with a vinegar-soy dressing; *gualiang fen*, a gelatinous mass of cold, shaved rice noodles covered in a spicy sauce; *chou dofu* (literally "stinking tofu"), a fermented bean-curd dish which actually tastes good; and a mass of less spicy snacks – preserved eggs, pickles, buns and dumplings – that form the regular fare in town. Canteens around the train station are unusually good for these things, as are several upmarket but still inexpensive restaurants.

For **Western-style cafés** with the usual run of set meals and fresh brews, try *Zhiwei Kafei Niupai*, near the Xinhua bookstore on Wuyi Dadao; the *Shangdao*, west of the *Civil Aviation* hotel; or the above-average *Ludao Kafei Guan* near the Cai'e Lu/Wuyi Dadao intersection. There's also the *New Mario* **cake shop**, outside the *Sanjiu Chunyun* hotel, which has biscuits, cakes, sponges, and Portuguese-style baked custard tarts.

For unknown reasons, tropical **betel nut** (the areca palm's stimulating seed pod) is a popular pick-me-up here, sold either boiled and sliced for chewing, or powdered in cigarettes.

Restaurants

Beijing Jiaozi Guan Wuyi Dadao. As the name suggests, *jiaozi* are what to order here, and they come with various meat and vegetable fillings – beef is best. The decor is army mess-hall, with forcibly intimate long wooden benches and tables – this is somewhere to fill your belly rather than dine.

Chaozhou Caiguan Wuyi Dadao. Big, mid-range southern Chinese restaurant with a bias towards seafood.

Dong Lai Shun Wuyi Dadao. Muslim restaurant specializing in lamb hotpot served with pickled garlic dip; their meat is meticulously selected and pretty tasty.

Fire Palace There are at least two branches of this riotously good restaurant: on Shaoshan Lu (bus #7, #202 or #104 from outside the train station), and Wuyi Dadao. The original on Shaoshan Lu is the best, and a busier, noisier, and more thoroughly enjoyable place to wolf down Hunanese food would be hard to imagine. Get an order card off the waitress, request some dark Baisha beer, and stop trolleys loaded with small plates of goodies as they pass – you could eat here a dozen times and not get through the selection. Stay off the à la carte menu and you'll only pay ¥2–12 a plate at either branch.

Juyuan Jiujia Eastern end of Wuyi Dadao. A friendly restaurant specializing in river food, though it also has some original meat dishes – try *wuxiang* (five-spiced) beef, where thin slices of meat are stir-fried with garlic, chilli, ginger, onion and whole cumin seeds.

Xinhua Lou Eastern end of Wuyi Dadao. Another excellent place for local dishes, with trolleys of smoked tofu and meats, crisp cold vegetables dressed in sesame oil, black-skinned-chicken soup, preserved eggs, and a huge range of dumplings being wheeled around between 6.30am and 2am. ¥2–10 a dish.

Listings

Banks and exchange The Bank of China is near the train station on Wuyi Dadao (Mon–Sat 8am–noon & 2.30–5.30pm). Upmarket hotels such as the *Dolton* and *Cygnet* also change traveller's cheques, and might not mind whether you're staying or not.

Bookshops Xinhua Bookstore, at the Wuyi Dadao/Shaoshan Lu intersection, has a good art section including books on painting techniques, but slim pickings in English.

Hospital Changsha Number 2 Medical College, Renmin Lu ⓣ0731/5550400 or 5550511.

Internet access There's a mass of Internet cafés southwest of the train station along Chezhan Zhong Lu, all charging ¥3 an hour; a convenient option here is on the third floor of the *Sanjiu Chunyun* hotel.

Left luggage There are left-luggage offices at the train and bus stations, though you'll need an onward ticket to use them.

Mail and telephones The most convenient post office – with parcel post and international phones – is in the train station square.

PSB The Foreign Affairs Department of the PSB is on Huangxing Lu (Mon–Fri 8.30am–5pm; ⓣ0731/4413851).

Shopping As you'll appreciate after visiting the Provincial Museum, Changsha has long had a reputation for silk embroidery, which you can buy at various stores along Wuyi Dadao. At the Hunan Embroidery Research Institute shop, expect to pay from ¥50 for a token handkerchief, to ¥2000 or more for a top-notch, towel-sized design. The Hunan Antique Store on Wuyi Dadao has a host of old wood carvings, porcelain, ink stones, chops and tourist souvenirs. The Apolo Plaza, on eastern Bayi Lu, is a mid-range department store which, along with others around the junction of Chezhan Lu and Wuyi Dadao, can supply all you'll need for daily living.

Travel agents CITS are at 170 Wuyi Dadao (air tickets ⓣ0731/4469991, tours ⓣ4469992, ⓕ4469990). You can also book Chinese-oriented tours to Heng Shan (1 day; ¥280) and Zhangjiajie (2–5 days, ¥600–900) at the small bus depot on Chezhan Bei Lu.

Shaoshan

Mao Zedong's birthplace, the hamlet of **SHAOSHAN**, lies 90km to the southwest of Changsha, a fine day-trip from the capital through the mild Hunanese countryside. Established as a pilgrimage site for idolatrous Red Guards during the Cultural Revolution, Shaoshan today seethes with Chinese tourists, who – following a low point in Mao's reputation through the 1980s – have started to flock back to visit the Great Helmsman's home town. The best way to get here is on the **special train** from Changsha, which departs daily at 7.05am for the three-hour journey (¥15 each way; returns from Shaoshan around 4.55pm). Alternatively, **tour buses** leave from the square outside the train station ticket office at 6am (guided day-tour ¥185).

Shaoshan is two settlements: a knot of hotels and services that have sprung up around the railhead and long-distance bus depot, and **Shaoshan Dong**, the village itself, some 6km distant. Patriotic jingles and a large portrait of Mao greet **arrivals** at the train station, as do **minibuses** heading up to the village (¥1). Unless you're planning to stay overnight or are hungry – in which case there's a cheap **hotel** (❷) and several **restaurants** ahead and round to the right near the bus depot – you should hop straight on board the first minibus. The first place to disembark is just before the village proper outside **Mao's Family Home** (daily 8am–5pm; free), a compound of bare adobe buildings next to a lotus-filled pond, where Mao was born on December 26, 1893. The home is neatly preserved, with a few pieces of period furniture, the odd photograph, and wonderfully turgid English explanations completing the spartan furnishings. Here he led a thoroughly normal childhood, one of four children in a relatively wealthy peasant household which comfortably survived the terrible famines in Hunan during the first decade of the twentieth century. Though a rebellious youth, it was not until he moved to Changsha in his late teens that he became politicized.

Just up the road is the huge **village square** where, next to a bronze statue of an elderly Mao and a swarm of souvenir stalls selling fairground-quality trinkets, stands the **Mao Zedong Exhibition Hall** (daily 8am–5pm; ¥15). Photos and knick-knacks here chart Mao's career, though today there's a great distinction between Mao the heroic revolutionary and the character who inflicted the Great Leap Forward – the disastrous movement which was meant to bring Chinese industrial output up to Western levels – and Cultural Revolution on his country. The exhibition reflects this: noticeable omissions include the *Little Red Book*, and just about any mention of the years between 1957 and his funeral in 1976. A newly opened **extension** portrays Deng Xiaoping as Mao's natural successor, and ends with the handover of Hong Kong and portrait of a very statesman-like Jiang Zemin. Next door to the museum is the former **Mao Ancestral Temple** (¥5), now a memorial to the leader's early work among the peasants here.

After his Great Leap Forward had begun to falter, Mao returned to Shaoshan in 1959, interviewing peasants here about the movement's shortcomings. He can't have liked what he heard; on his final visit in 1966 at the start of the Cultural Revolution, he kept himself aloof near the reservoir in a secret retreat, poetically named **Dishui Dong** (Dripping Water Cave), to which you can catch a minibus. Alternatively, the elegant pavilion atop of **Shaoshan peak** overlooks the local landscape – not really typical, given the amount of tourist revenue, but a nice scene of healthy fields and bamboo thickets.

There are a few restaurants and **places to stay** in Shaoshan village around the square, including the *Shaoshan Binguan* in the square itself, with a jumble of indifferent rooms around an ornamental pool (Ⓣ0732/5682309; ❸), and the welcoming *Shaofeng Binguan* (Ⓣ0732/5685073, Ⓕ5685241; ❸, dorm beds ¥30), about 100m up a side road from the square.

Heng Shan

Some 120km south of Changsha, the **Heng Shan region** is one of China's most holy sites. Spread over 80km or so, the ranges form scores of low peaks dressed in woodland with a smattering of **Buddhist and Taoist temples**, some of which were established more than 1300 years ago. It's somewhere to relax and admire the scenery (frosted in winter, golden in autumn and misty year-round), either tackling the easy walks between shrines on foot, or resorting to local transport to ascend the heights.

Confusingly, it's **Nanyue**, not the nearby town of Hengshan, that marks the starting point up into the hills. Early-morning **buses** from Changsha or Shaoshan take around five hours to reach Nanyue via **Xiangtan**, where you might have to change both bus and stations (the two are next door to each

Heng Shan

Heng Shan	衡山	***héngshān***
Danxia Si	丹霞寺	*dānxiá sì*
Huangting Si	黄庭寺	*huángtíng sì*
Nongye Binguan	农业宾馆	*nóngyè bīnguǎn*
Shangfeng Si	上封寺	*shàngfēng sì*
Xiufeng Binguan	秀风宾馆	*xiùfēng bīnguǎn*
Xuandu Si	玄都寺	*xuándū sì*
Zhurong Gong	祝融殿	*zhùróng diàn*
Zushi Gong	祖师宫	*zǔshī gōng*
Nanyue	南岳	***nányuè***
Nanyue Damiao	南岳大庙	*nányuè dàmiào*
Nongye Binguan	农业宾馆	*nóngyè bīnguǎn*
Xiufeng Binguan	秀风宾馆	*xiùfēng bīnguǎn*
Zhusheng Si	祝圣寺	*zhùshèng sì*
Hengyang	衡阳	***héngyáng***

other). If you're coming up from the south by road or rail from Shaoguan in Guangdong Province, or Guilin in Guangxi, the nearest city is **Hengyang**, where minibuses to Nanyue leave for the hour-long trip from the depot on Jiefang Lu – bus #1 connects Hengyang's nightmarishly busy **train station** with this depot, which is across the river. Alternatively, leave the train farther on at **Hengshan Town**, where regular minibuses cover the twenty-kilometre trip west to Nanyue.

Nanyue

Banners strung across the highway welcome visitors to **NANYUE** (South Mountain), a small but expanding village of old flagstoned streets and new hotels set around Nanyue Damiao and Zhusheng Si, the two largest and most architecturally impressive temple complexes in the area. The Changsha–Hengyang highway runs along the eastern side of the village, with the **bus station** at its southern (Hengyang) end, where map sellers, rickshaw drivers and hotel touts descend on new arrivals. Midway along the highway an ornamental **stone archway** forms the "entrance" to the village proper and leads through to the main street, Dongshan Lu. Here you'll find a mass of **restaurants**, whose staff will call you over as you pass – as always, avoid over-charging by establishing prices as you order. Many of these places also offer basic **accommodation** for about ¥35 a bed, or there are plenty of **hotels** in the vicinity, such as the *Nongye Binguan* (☎0734/5666491; ④) or *Xiufeng Binguan* (☎0734/5666111; ④).

Off Dongshan Lu, streets lead through the old village centre to **Nanyue Damiao** (¥15). There's been a place of worship at this site since 725 AD at least – some say that it was sanctified in Qin times – but the older buildings succumbed to fire long ago and were replaced in the nineteenth century by a small version of Beijing's Forbidden City. It's a lively place, freshly painted, echoing with bells and thick with smoke from incense and detonating firecrackers – there are actually furnaces in the courtyards to accommodate the huge quantities offered up by the crowds. Seventy-two pillars, representing Heng Shan's peaks, support the massive wooden crossbeams of the **main hall**'s double-staged roof, and gilt phoenixes loom above the scores of kneeling worshippers paying homage to Taoist and Buddhist deities. Other halls in the surrounding gardens are far more humble, but sport detailed carvings along their eaves and exterior alcoves.

Far quieter, with fewer tourists and more monks in evidence, is the monastery, **Zhusheng Si**, a short walk left out of the temple gates. A purely Buddhist site originating around the same time as Nanyue, the entire monastery – whose name translates as "Imperial Blessings" – was reconstructed for the anticipated visit of **Emperor Kangxi** in 1705, but he never showed up. The smaller scale and lack of pretension here contrast with Nanyue's extravagances, though there's a series of five hundred engravings of Buddhist *arhat*s set into the wall of the rear hall, and a fine multi-faced and many-handed likeness of **Guanyin** to seek out among the charming courtyards.

In the hills

There's a good day's walking to be had between Nanyue and **Zhurong Gong**, a hall perched 15km from town on Heng Shan's 1290-metre apex. Even major temples along the way are small and unassuming, requiring little time to investigate, and tracks are easy, so around eight hours should be enough for a return hike along the most direct route – though you'd need at least ten hours to see everything on the mountain. **Minibuses** run between Nanyue and Shangfeng Si, below the summit, in under an hour (¥10). **Food stalls** lurk at strategic points, so there's no need to carry much beyond something to keep out any seasonally inclement weather at the top.

Take the main road through Nanyue to the park gates behind Nanyue Damiao, where the **admission fee** (¥45) covers entry to all temples and includes a bilingual **map** of the mountain. The first two hours are spent passing occasional groups of descending tourists and black-clad Taoist mendicants, as the road weaves past rivers and patches of farmland before reaching the temple-like **Martyrs' Memorial Hall**, built to commemorate those killed during the 1911 revolution. Entering pine forests shortly after, you'll find **Xuandu Si** marks the halfway point – it's also known as the Midway Monastery – and is Hunan's Taoist centre, founded around 700 AD. Even so, an occasional Buddhist saint graces side shrines, but the best feature is the unusually domed ceiling in the second hall, watched over by a statue of Lao Zi holding a pill of immortality.

The rest of the ascent is past a handful of functioning, day-to-day temples with monks and nuns wandering around the gardens – **Danxia Si** and **Zushi Gong** are larger than most – before arrival outside **Shangfeng Si**'s red timber halls, which mark the minibus terminus. Overpriced **hotels** here cater for those hoping to catch the dawn from the **sunrise-watching terrace**, a short walk away below a radio tower. On a cloudy day, it's more worthwhile pushing on a further twenty minutes to the summit, where **Zhurong Gong**, a tiny temple built almost entirely of heavy stone blocks and blackened inside from incense smoke, looks very atmospheric as it emerges from the mist. For the descent, there's always the bus, or an alternative track (shown on local maps) from Xuandu Si which takes in Lingzhi spring, the Mirror Grinding Terrace and the bulky Nantai Monastery, before winding back to town past the quiet halls of **Huangting Si**, another sizeable Taoist shrine.

Yueyang and Dongting Hu

YUEYANG, a major riverside city and stop for Yangzi ferries on the Beijing–Guangzhou rail line, lies 120km north of Changsha on the eastern shores of **Dongting Hu**, the second largest freshwater lake in the land, covering a crescent-shaped area of 2500 square kilometres. Fringed with reeds and lotus ponds, the lake is surrounded by villages farming rich cane and paddy fields; many locals also earn a livelihood from fishing. Despite accelerating tourism and an unpleasantly down-at-heel new city springing up in the background, the impressive **Yueyang Tower** and little **Junshan Dao**, an island famed for its tea – not to mention historical links to the nationwide sport of **dragon-boat racing** – make Yueyang a good place to spend the day in transit between Changsha and Wuhan, either only a few hours away.

The City

Yueyang's main street, **Baling Lu**, runs west for 5km, bare, broad and numbingly straight right up to **Nanyuepo docks** on the lake shore. Here it's crossed by **Dongting Lu**, with the Yueyang Tower and most of the services close to this junction.

Yueyang and Dongting Hu

Yueyang	岳阳	***yuèyáng***
Chenglingji	城陵矶	*chénglíng jī*
Cishi Pagoda	慈氏塔	*císhì tă*
Junshan Dao	君山岛	*jūnshān dăo*
Miluo River	汨罗江	*mìluó jiāng*
Nanyue Docks	南越码头	*nányuè mătóu*
Yueyang Binguan	岳阳宾馆	*yuèyáng bīnguăn*
Yueyang docks	岳阳楼客运站	*yuèyánglóu kèyùnzhàn*
Yueyang Tower	岳阳楼	*yuèyáng lóu*
Yueyanglou Binguan	岳阳楼宾馆	*yuèyánglóu bīnguăn*
Yunmeng	云梦宾馆	*yúnmèng bīnguăn*
Dongting Hu	洞庭湖	***dòngtínghú***

Frequently packed with Chinese tourists, the **Yueyang Tower** (¥30) on Dongting Bei Lu rises from walled ramparts overlooking Dongting Hu. Originally, this was a mere platform where the *Three Kingdoms* general **Lu Su** reviewed his troops; it was through Lu's diplomacy that the armies of his native Wu and those of Shu were united against the overwhelming forces of Wei, who were subsequently defeated in 208 AD at the Battle of the Red Cliffs (p.509). A tower was first built here in 716, but the current timber edifice, last restored in 1983, is of Qing design. Twenty metres tall, three upward-curving, yellow-glazed roofs are supported by huge blood-red pillars of *nanmu* ("southern-wood"); screens, eaves and crossbeams are decorated with animal carvings, and the tower makes a striking and brilliant spectacle. For an additional ¥5 you can climb up and take in grand views of the lake, which quickly whips up into a stormy sea scene at the first breath of wind. Flanking the tower are two lesser

Dragon boats

The former state of **Chu**, which encompassed northern Hunan, was under siege in 278 BC from the first stirrings of the ambitious Qin armies, who were later to bring all of China under their thumb. At the time, Dongting was the haunt of the exiled poet-governor **Qu Yuan**, a victim of palace politics but nonetheless a great patriot of Chu. Hearing of the imminent invasion, Qu picked up a heavy stone and drowned himself in the nearby **Miluo River** rather than see the state he loved conquered. Distraught locals raced to save him in their boats, but were too late. They returned later to scatter *zongzi* (packets of meat and sticky rice wrapped up in reeds and lotus leaves) into the river as an offering to Qu Yuan's spirit.

The **Dragon-boat Festival**, held throughout China on the fifth day of the fifth lunar month (June or July), commemorates the rowers' hopeless rush – though many historians trace the tradition of food offerings and annual boat races to long before Qu's time. At any rate, it's a festive rather than mournful occasion, with huge quantities of steamed *zongzi* eaten and keen competition between local dragon-boat teams, who can be seen practising in their narrow, powerful crafts months before the event, to the steady boom of a pacing drum. Locally staged on the Miluo River south of Yueyang, it's a lively spectator sport, with crowds cheering their rowers along, and you need to be up early to get the most from the ceremonies – catching, for example, the dedication of the dragon-headed prows – as the race itself lasts only a few minutes. Contact either the CITS or your hotel for transport details.

pavilions: **Xianmei Ting** (Immortal's Plum) – named after the delicately etched blossom design on a Ming stone tablet within – and **Sanzui Ting** (Thrice Drunk). This recalls the antics of **Lu Dongbin**, one of the Taoist Eight Immortals, who regularly visited the pavilion to down a wine gourd or two; there's a comic painting of this inside, warts and all, and an overflowing votive box. Lu is also credited with populating Dongting Hu with shoals of silvery fish by tossing woodshavings into the water. **Xiao Qiao**, the wife of another historic general, lies buried at the northern end of the surrounding gardens, the grassy mound honoured by a tablet bearing the calligraphy of the renowned Song-dynasty poet, **Su Dongpo**.

Dongti Hu was once a common haunt of the **Yangzi river dolphin** (see p.518), whose decline here was partly due to **siltation** – itself caused by flood preventative dykes built through the 1980s – and subsequent **land reclamation** for farming, measures which saw the lake shrink by almost sixty percent after 1949. But following the awful 1998 floods, the government resettled about 300,000 farmers and pulled down the dykes to encourage greater water flow through the lake, and it is slowly expanding in surface area each year. Earlier attempts at regulating the Yangzi saw the construction of **Cishi Ta**, a stone pagoda built in 1242 to evict flood-inducing demons, and now quietly crumbling away beneath a mane of vegetation about 1km south of the Yueyang Tower off Dongting Nan Lu.

Junshan Dao

Once a Taoist retreat and now an isolated city park covering barely more than a square kilometre, **Junshan Dao** (Monarch's Island; ¥35) lies a thirty-minute boat ride from Yueyang across the lake's placid brown waters (it's not worth the trip in bad weather). **Ferries** depart four times daily from 7.30am to 3.30pm from both the Yueyang docks – follow the alley downhill to the water immediately north of the tower – and the Nanyuepo docks at the western end of Baling Lu (¥15 return from either); the last boat back is at 4.30pm. Private **speedboats** make regular crossings, too, but you'll have to negotiate fares with the touts.

Paths lead up from the concrete jetty around the **terraces** which cover much of the island, source of the famed **silver needle tea** which is said to impart longevity and once paid in tribute to the emperor. It's incredibly expensive – stores in Yueyang sell a spoonful for around ¥5 – with tips that look like pale green twists; pour boiling water over them, inhale the musty vapour and watch them bob up and down in the glass. Aside from tea, the island has a vast store of sites built around carefully contrived legends, such as the **grave** of the mythical Emperor Shun's two widows, whose tears stained surrounding groves of speckled bamboo as they lamented his death; and a **bell**, looking distinctly foolish wedged halfway up a tree, which was supposedly used by the twelfth-century rebel **Yang Yao** to summon meetings.

Practicalities

Yueyang's **bus and train stations** are on opposite sides of a huge, multilevel roundabout 3km east down Baling Lu, along which you can catch **city bus** #22 to the lake and then north along Dongting Bei Lu to the Yueyang Tower – pick up a current **map** on arrival. When it comes to leaving, note that long-distance sleeper train tickets are very hard to book from Yueyang; go first to Changsha or Wuhan and look for a service originating there. **Yangzi ferries** stop 17km north of the city at **Chenglingji**, where bus #1 connects with the train station.

The English-speaking **CITS** (daily 9–11.30am & 2–5pm; ⓣ0730/8232010) is inside the grounds of the *Yunmeng* hotel and can arrange tours to lakeside sights. There's a **post office** on Baling Lu towards the bus and train stations (daily 8am–6pm), but for **foreign exchange**, you're better off trying the *Yueyang Binguan*.

Yueyang's **places to stay** aren't outstanding. Options include the touristy *Yueyang Binguan* overlooking the lake on Dongting Bei Lu (ⓣ0730/8320011, ⓕ8320235; ❹), the clean but increasingly threadbare *Yueyanglou Binguan* (ⓣ0730/8321288; ❸), in the side street opposite the southern entrance to the Yueyang Tower; and the slightly downbeat *Yunmeng*, at 25 Cheng Dong Lu (ⓣ0730/8221115; ❸) – look for the huge overpass on Baling Lu and follow Cheng Dong Lu south for 300m. For **food**, the hotels have restaurants with menus based around lake produce, and there are plenty of other eating places along Dongting Bei Lu.

Wulingyuan (Zhangjiajie)

Hidden away in the northwestern extremities of Hunan, **Wulingyuan Scenic Reserve** (widely known as **Zhangjiajie**) protects a mystical landscape of sandstone shelves and fragmented limestone towers, often misted in low cloud and scored by countless streams, with practically every horizontal surface hidden under a primeval, subtropical green mantle. Among the 550-odd tree species (twice Europe's total) within its 370 square kilometres are rare dove trees, gingkos and **dawn redwoods**, these last identified by their stringy bark and feathery leaves; a now-popular ornamental tree, until 1948 they were believed extinct. The **wildlife** list is impressive, too, including civets, giant salamanders, monkeys and gamebirds, and the region is home to several million ethnic **Tujia**, said by some to be the last descendants of western China's mysterious prehistoric Ba kingdom. On the down side, despite UNESCO World

Wulingyuan (Zhangjiajie)

Wulingyuan Scenic Reserve	武陵源风景区	***wŭlíngyuán fēngjĭngqū***
Bewitching Terrace	迷魂台	*míhún tái*
Black Dragon Village	黑龙寨	*hēilóng zhài*
Huangshi Village	黄石寨	*huángshí zhài*
Suoxi Village	索溪峪镇	***suŏxīyù zhèn***
Baofeng Hu	宝峰湖	*băofēng hú*
Huanglong Cave	黄龙洞	*huánglóng dòng*
Immortal's Bridge	仙人桥	*xiānrén qiáo*
Shentangwan	神堂湾	*shéntáng wān*
Ten-li Corridor	十里画廊	*shílĭ huàláng*
Tianzi Feng	天子峰	*tiānzĭ fēng*
Zhangjiajie	张家界	***zhāngjiājiè***
Jinyan Fandian	金岩饭店	*jīnyán fàndiàn*
Wuling Binguan	武陵宾馆	*wŭlíng bīnguăn*
Xiangdian Shanzhuang	香殿山庄	*xiāngdiàn shānzhuāng*
Zhangjiajie Binguan	张家界宾馆	*zhāngjiājiè bīnguăn*

Heritage listing, a total fire ban (smoking included) and a generous number of erosion-resistant paths, Wulingyuan is definitely beginning to suffer from its popularity – more accessible parts of the reserve are often almost invisible under hordes of litter-hurling tour groups.

Practicalities

Most visitors base themselves on the southern boundaries of the reserve at **Zhangjiajie village**, where there's certainly enough to keep you occupied for a few days. It's also possible to organize extended walks north to **Tianzi Mountain**, or east to the **Suoxi Valley**. There are villages and stalls along the way supplying accommodation and food, but take water and snacks on long journeys. You'll need comfortable walking shoes and the right seasonal dress – it's humid in summer, cold from late autumn, and the area is often covered in light snow early on in the year.

Note that **accommodation prices** double at weekends and holidays, when crowds are at their worst and train tickets will be in short supply – try and avoid these times. If you're on a Chinese package **tour** to Wulingyuan, watch out if they try to sting you an extra ¥50–100 based on a supposedly higher foreigners' entrance fee to the reserve: there's no discriminatory pricing here. If the tour staff won't back down, tell them you'll pay the surcharge yourself at the gates.

Zhangjiajie Shi

ZHANGJIAJIE SHI is the regional hub, 33km south of the reserve. The **bus station** is pretty central, but the **train station** and ticket office are a further 9km south, and the **airport** is a similar distance to the west. **Minibuses** prowl arrival points for the hour-long journey to the reserve at either Zhangjiajie village or Suoxi (¥10). If you get stuck overnight at Zhangjiajie Shi, there's a **hostel** with reasonable doubles at the train station (❷), and a host of hotels to choose from in town – the *Wuling Binguan* (Ⓣ0744/82226302; ❺) is good, if fairly expensive.

Leaving, it's a slog to get anywhere by bus – Changsha is twelve hours away on the far side of the province. **Trains** are better; there are direct services east to Changsha, north to Yichang in Hubei, and south to Liuzhou in Guangxi. For Guizhou and points west you'll have to change trains at the junction town of **Huaihua**, six hours to the southwest – sleeper tickets out of Huaihua are virtually impossible to buy at the station, but you can usually upgrade on board. You can also **fly** from Zhangjiajie Shi to Changsha and a half-dozen other provincial capitals.

Zhangjiajie village and around

ZHANGJIAJIE village is simply a couple of streets in the valley at the reserve entrance, overflowing with **map** and souvenir retailers, pricey restaurants (meat dishes are particularly expensive), a **post office** and **places to stay**. The best value of these is the *Zhangjiajie Binguan* (Ⓣ0744/5712388; ❹), with comfy doubles in the new wing, and clean but damp rooms in the older section, arranged around an ornamental pond. Cheaper dorms exist but are inevitably "full". Otherwise try the more comfortable and expensive *Xiangdian Shanzhuang* (Ⓣ0744/5712266; ❺) up past the bridge, or *Jinyan Fandian* near the bus compound (❹). The *Zhangjiajie Binguan*'s travel service is fairly helpful with general hiking advice, and can arrange **white-water rafting** day tours (¥250 per person) in the Suoxi Valley.

The reserve

With a closely packed forest of tall, eroded karst pinnacles splintering away from a high plateau, Zhangjiajie's scenery is awesomely poetic – even Chinese tour groups are often hushed by the spectacle. The road through the village leads downhill to the **reserve entrance** (¥55), past a throng of Tujia selling medicinal flora and cheap plastic ponchos. There are also **bicycles** for rent – of dubious value for many of the tracks. The left path here follows a four-hour circuit along a short valley up to **Huangshi village**, on the edge of a minor, island-like plateau surrounded by views of the area. The right path offers several options, the shortest of which (again, around 4hr) runs along **Golden Whip Stream**, branching off to the right and returning to base through a particularly dense stand of crags below two facing outcrops known as the **Yearning Couple** (engraved tablets along the path identify many other formations). Alternatively, bearing left after a couple of kilometres – consult a map – takes you up past **Bewitching Terrace** into the **Shadao Valley**. From here, basic trails continue through magnificent scenery around the western edge of the plateau to **Black Dragon village**, then circuit back to the park gates. This is a lengthy day's walk, and you won't see many other tourists along the way.

Suoxi Valley and Tianzi Shan

With much the same facilities as Zhangjiajie, **SUOXI village** makes a good base for exploring the east and north of the reserve. Set in the **Suoxi Valley**, it's 10km as the crow flies from Zhangjiajie but the better part of a day on foot, though it's possible to get between the two by local bus. Attractions here include groups of rhesus monkeys and relatively open riverine gorges where it's possible to **cruise** – or even go whitewater rafting – between the peaks. Around the two-kilometre-long **Baofeng Hu**, a lake accessed by a ladder-like staircase from the valley floor, there's a chance of encountering golden pheasants, the grouse-like tragopans and **giant salamanders** – secretive, red-blotched monsters which reach 2m in length; considered a great delicacy, they're sometimes seen in the early mornings around Baofeng's shore. There's also **Huanglong Dong** (Yellow Dragon Cave), a few kilometres east of Souxi, a mass of garishly lit limestone caverns linked by a subterranean river, and **Hundred Battle Valley**, where the Song-dynasty Tujia king, Xiang, fought imperial forces.

The **Tianzi Shan** region, which basically covers the north of the park, is named after an isolated 1250-metre-high peak, and contains most of Wulingyuan's caves. It's probably best visited from Suoxi village, where there's a possible circuit of 30km setting off along the **Ten-li Corridor**. High points include the mass of lookouts surrounding **Shentangwan**, a valley thick with needle-like rocks where Xiang is said to have committed suicide after his eventual defeat, and **Immortals' Bridge**, next to the peak itself, an unfenced, narrow strip of rock bridging a deep valley. Instead of returning to Suoxi, it's feasible to continue past the mountain to **TIANZI SHAN village**, spend the night in the guesthouse there, and then either hike south to Zhangjiajie, or leave Wulingyuan by catching a bus first to Songzhi (45km) and then on to Dayong (another 60km).

Jiangxi

Stretched between the Yangzi in the north and a mountainous border with Guangdong in the south, **Jiangxi Province** has always been a bit of a backwater. Though it has been inhabited for some four thousand years, the first major influx of settlers came as late as the Han dynasty, when its interior offered sanctuary for those dislodged by warfare. The northern half benefited most from these migrants, who began to farm the great plain around China's largest freshwater lake, **Poyang Hu**. A network of rivers covering the province drains into Poyang, and when the construction of the Grand Canal created a route through Yangzhou and the lower Yangzi in the seventh century, Jiangxi's capital, **Nanchang**, became a key point on the great north–south link of inland waterways. Then the region enjoyed a long period of quiet prosperity, until coastal shipping and the opening up of treaty ports took business away in the 1840s. The next century saw a complete reversal of Jiangxi's fortunes: the population halved as millions fled competing warlords and, during the 1920s and 1930s, there was protracted fighting between the Guomindang and Communist forces concentrated in the southern **Jinggang Shan** ranges, which eventually led to an evicted Red Army starting on their **Long March** across China.

Despite the troubles, things picked up quickly after the Communist takeover, and a badly battered Nanchang licked its wounds and reinvented itself as a revolutionary city and centre of modern heavy industry. More traditionally, access provided by Poyang and the Yangzi tributaries benefits the hilly areas to the east, where **Jingdezhen** retains its title as China's porcelain capital. North of the lake, **Jiujiang** is a key Yangzi port on the doorsteps of Anhui and Hubei, while the nearby mountain area of **Lu Shan** offers a pleasant reminder of Jiangxi's better days, having long been a summer retreat for Chinese literati and colonial servants.

Nanchang

Hemmed in by hills, **NANCHANG** sits on Jiangxi's major river, the **Gan Jiang**, some 70km south of where it flows into Poyang Hu. Built on trade, today Nanchang has its position as a rail hub for central-southern China to thank for its character; unfortunately, this mostly reflects its steel and chemical industries and an overbearing, incomplete reconstruction since the 1950s. Initially it seems a grey and noisy place afflicted by the usual stifling summer temperatures; first impressions are slightly moderated by the handful of resurrected older monuments, and the sheer enthusiasm with which locals have grasped free-market principles, crowding every alley with stalls.

Nanchang saw little action until the twentieth century, when the city was occupied by the Guomindang army in December 1926. At the time, the military was still an amalgam of Nationalist and Communist forces, but when Chiang Kaishek broke his marriage of convenience with the Communists the following year, any left-wing elements were expelled from the Party. On August 1, 1927, **Zhou Enlai** and **Zhu De**, two Communist GMD officers, mutinied in Nanchang and took control of the city with thirty thousand

Nanchang

Nanchang	南昌	***nánchāng***
August 1 Uprising Museum	八一纪念馆	*bāyī jìniànguǎn*
Bada Shanren Museum	八大山人纪念馆	*bādàshānrén jìniànguǎn*
Bayi Monument	八一纪念塔	*bāyī jìniàntǎ*
Bayi Park	八一公园	*bāyī gōngyuán*
Provincial Museum	省博物馆	*shěng bówùguǎn*
Renmin Square	人民广场	*rénmín guǎngchǎng*
Shengjin Ta	绳金塔	*shéngjīn tǎ*
Taxia Si	塔下寺	*tǎxià sì*
Tengwang Pavilion	滕王阁	*téngwáng gé*
Xiangtan airport	香檀飞机场	*xiāngtán fēijīchǎng*
Youmin Si	佑民寺	*yòumín sì*
Zhu De's Former Residence	朱德旧居	*zhūdé jiùjū*
Accommodation		
Gloria Plaza	凯莱大酒店	*kǎilái dàjiǔdiàn*
Jiangxi Fandian	江西饭店	*jiāngxī fàndiàn*
Jiaotong	交通宾馆	*jiāotōng bīnguǎn*
Jiujiu Long	九九隆大酒店	*jiǔjiǔlónā dàjiǔdiàn*
Xiangshan	象山宾馆	*xiàngshan bīnguǎn*
Youzheng Dasha	邮政大厦	*yōuzhèng dàshà*
Eating and drinking		
Baden Bar Street	巴登酒吧街	*bādēng jiǔbājiē*
Caigenxiang	菜根香	*càigēng xiāng*
Fengwei Xiaochi Cheng	风味小吃城	*fēngwèi xiǎochīchéng*
Fukuoka Japanese	福冈日本饭店	*fúgāng rìběn fàndiàn*
Guhan Feng	古汉风	*gǔhàn fēng*
Jiangnan Fandian	江南饭店	*jiāngnán fàndiàn*
Hao Xiang Lai	豪享来	*háoxiǎng lái*
Hunan Wangcai Guan	湖南王菜馆	*húnánwáng càiguǎn*
Manhattan Bar	曼哈顿酒吧	*mànhādùn jiǔbā*
Xiangcancun	香餐村	*xiāngcān cūn*

troops. Though they were soon forced to flee into Jiangxi's mountainous south, the day is celebrated as the foundation of the **People's Liberation Army**, and the red PLA flag still bears the Chinese characters "8" and "1" (*bayi*) for the month and day.

Arrival, transport and accommodation

Nanchang sprawls away from the east bank of the Gan Jiang into industrial complexes and wasteland, but the centre is a fairly compact couple of square kilometres between the river and **Bayi Dadao**, which runs north through the heart of the city from the huge **Fushan roundabout** and past **Renmin Square**, becoming **Yangming Lu** as it turns east over the Bayi Bridge.

Arriving at **Xiangtan airport**, 28km to the south, you'll need to take a taxi into town (¥100). Other transit points are more central. Nanchang's **train station** is 700m east of the Fushan roundabout at the end of Zhanqian Lu; locals consider the huge square hole through the station facade bad *feng shui*, allowing the city's wealth to escape down the tracks. Some buses from Lu Shan, Jinggang

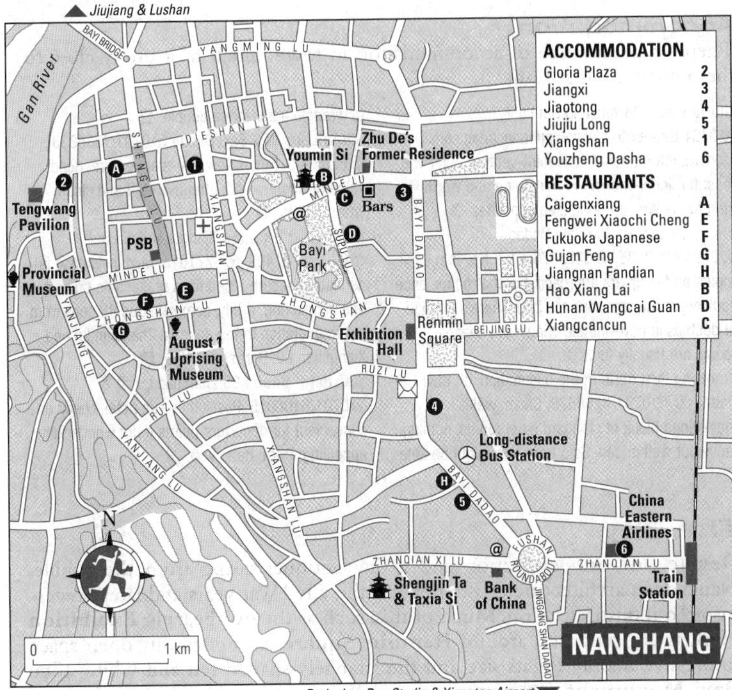

Shan and farther afield terminate here, but the main **long-distance bus station** is 1km away on Bayi Dadao. **Taxis** (¥6 standing charge) and motor-rickshaws cruise downtown arrival points, while **city bus** #2 runs from the train station along Bayi Dadao, and then makes a circuit of the central area, either passing or coming close to all the hotels.

Moving on from Nanchang

You can **fly** from Nanchang to Beijing, Shanghai, Guangzhou and a handful of other cities. Zhanqian Lu is thick with airline agents, including China Eastern (ⓣ0791/6100009, ⓕ6104789), next to the *Youzheng Dasha*.

Nanchang lies on the Kowloon–Beijing **train** line, and just off the Shanghai–Kunming line, with connections through easterly Yingtan down into Fujian Province. Sleeper tickets are pretty easy to obtain, but prepare yourself for some mighty queues; alternatively, there's a railway **ticket booth** (daily 8am–4pm) at the eastern entrance to Bayi Park on Supu Lu, and airline agents on Zhanqian Lu also sell train tickets at a slight mark-up. If you're heading to southern Jiangxi, note that "Jinggang Shan" railhead is not Ciping, but a small town 120km further east.

The **bus** station looks huge and crowded, but the ticket office is user-friendly and there's no problem in getting seats. Minibuses and smart coaches run through the day along fast expressways to Jiujiang, Lushan, and Jingdezhen, with daily services within Jiangxi to Jinggang Shan and Ganzhou, and further afield to Wuyi Shan in Fujian and destinations across central China.

Accommodation

There's a good range of accommodation in town, much of it pretty close to the train and bus stations.

Gloria Plaza 88 Yanjiang Bei Lu ⓣ0791/6738855, ⓦwww.gphnanchang.com. Modern, international-style joint-venture hotel, the most foreigner-friendly in Nanchang and worth visiting for its Western food (see opposite). ❾

Jiangxi Fandian 356 Bayi Dadao ⓣ0791/6212135, ⓕ6202176. Staff flee into back rooms as foreigners approach, but the rooms, once you've got one, are none too bad. There's a range of doubles in new and old wings; the cheaper rooms are usually full. ❸

Jiaotong Just north of the bus station, on Bayi Dadao ⓣ/ⓕ0791/6268578. Clean, well-maintained block of standard hotel rooms, nothing fancy but well priced. Solo travellers might be able to wrangle a half-price double. ❸

Jiujiu Long 122 Bayi Dadao ⓣ0791/7036333, ⓕ6295299. Smart new two-star venture; good value for money, with attentive staff and clean, warm rooms. ❹

Xiangshan Binguan Xiangshan Bei Lu ⓣ0791/6781402, ⓕ6771015. Mild insistence is needed to secure a bed for a reasonable price in this uninspiring, if tidy, complex. Bus #5 goes from the train station to the door via Zhanqian Lu and Xiangshan Lu. Dorm beds ¥60, ❸

Youzheng Dasha 86 Zhanqian Lu ⓣ & ⓕ0791/6106015. Post-office-run hotel, cheap and convenient for departure points if not wonderfully appealing. Dorm beds ¥50, ❸

The City

Despite slow modernization and a few antiques rising from the rubble, Nanchang's architecture mostly reflects the Civil War years and later Soviet-inspired industrialization. Much of this, such as the overbearing **Exhibition Hall**, is concentrated around **Renmin Square**, an enormous open space impressive mainly for its size and the strangely shaped red and white stone **Bayi Monument** at the southern end. West of here, **Zhongshan Lu** runs through the core of Nanchang's bustling shopping district, with the water and greenery of **Bayi Park** to the north and, further along, the **August 1 Uprising Museum** (daily 8am–5.30pm; ¥5). Formerly a hotel, this was occupied by the embryonic PLA as their 1927 General Headquarters, and is now of interest mainly as the most complete example of Nanchang's colonial architecture. As a museum, however, it's dull – three floors stuffed with period furniture, weapons, and maps labelled in Chinese. Facing north from here, **pedestrianized** Shengli Lu provides more opportunities to window-shop.

Opposite the top end of Bayi Park and set back off Minde Lu, **Youmin Si** (¥2) is a Buddhist temple dating back to 503 AD, which – perhaps because of the city's revolutionary associations – Nanchang's Red Guards were especially diligent in wrecking during the 1960s. The three restored halls include a striking, ten-metre-high **standing Buddha statue**, which rises out of a lotus flower towards a cupola decorated with a coiled golden dragon. East of the here, the austere-looking traditional grey brick house on the corner of Huayuanjiao Jie is **Zhu De's former residence**, although it's presently closed to the public.

Tengwang Pavilion and the Provincial Museum

The mighty **Tengwang Pavilion** (summer 7.30am–5.30pm; winter 8am–4.30pm; ¥30) overlooks the river on Yanjiang Lu, 1km or so west of Youmin Si. There have been 26 multistoreyed towers built on this site since the first was raised more than a thousand years ago in memory of a Tang prince; the current "Song-style" building was only completed in 1989. It's impressive to look at, nonetheless, a huge pile isolated by a square of flat, grey paving and a monumental stone base, each floor lightened by a broadly flared roof supported by interlocking wooden beams. Disappointingly, the six-storeyed interior is a let-down, the upper-level balconies only offering sweeping views of a very drab cityscape. However, it's worth catching the lift (¥1) to the top floor at weekends, when a tiny indoor **theatre** hosts traditional dances and music sessions, and with luck, there may even be a performance of local opera.

South of the pavilion, bridges off Yanjiang Lu cross an inlet to the **Provincial Museum** (Tues–Sun 8.30am–5.30pm; ¥10), a weird, futuristic-looking construction with green glass towers and knife-like side wings. There's an ambitious plan to create a cultural research centre here, but at present the buildings feel almost deserted, though the collection covers everything from dinosaurs to Jingdezhen **porcelain**. Future exhibits might include the contents of **Qing-dynasty tomb** discovered outside Nanchang in 2001, which contained a trove of gold and silk artefacts and a well-preserved noblewoman's corpse.

Southern Nanchang

West of the Fushan roundabout off Zhanqian Lu (bus #5 passes by on its route between the roundabout and Xiangshan Lu), the gates to the partially restored **Taxia Si** are frequently locked, barring entry to **Shengjin Ta**, perhaps because a legend says that the city will fall if the seven-storey pagoda is ever destroyed. The warning is still taken fairly seriously, despite the fact that Shengjin has been knocked down several times, the last time being in the early eighteenth century. At any rate, the pagoda itself is only of moderate interest, but the looking-glass logic needed to find the entrance will see you thoroughly exploring the neighbourhood, which is a pleasure. A few of the **teahouses** for which Nanchang was once famous – down-to-earth, open-fronted establishments patronized by gregarious old men watching the world go by – linger on in this market quarter, as do some equally archaic barber shops.

For an easy reprieve from the city, catch bus #20 from Yanjiang Lu 5km south to **Bada Shanren Museum** (Tues–Sun 8.30am–4pm; ¥15), a whitewashed Ming-era compound set in parkland. This was the haunt of the painter Zhu Da, also known as Bada Shanren, a wandering Buddhist monk of royal descent who came to live in this former temple in 1661 and was later buried here. He is said to have painted in a frenzy, often while drunk, and his pictures certainly show great spontaneity. There are a number of originals displayed inside, and some good reproductions on sale.

Eating, drinking and nightlife

Nanchang's **eating** opportunities cover quite a broad range, from dumpling houses and spicy Hunanese restaurants to the regional **Gan cooking** – lightly sauced fresh fish, crayfish, snails, and frogs. **Soups** are something of a Jiangxi favourite – egg and pork soup is a typical breakfast – along with communal affairs served up in huge pots at the table. Restaurants are spread all over the city, though the streets around Bayi Park seem to have the highest concentration. The best **Western-style food** in Nanchang is at the *Gloria Plaza* – serving lunch or dinner buffets where you can stuff your face for ¥80, and coffee and cakes in their *Atrium Café* (¥33).

For **nightlife**, the eastern end of Minde Lu hosts several **bars and nightclubs**, a bit too upmarket to attract students but pretty popular all the same. Try *Baden Bar Street* for drink, KTV and dance, while *Manhattan* is more upmarket, somewhere to be seen paying ridiculous prices for booze and companionship.

Restaurants

Caigenxiang Dieshan Lu. Mock-antique restaurant with dark wooden furniture and huge frosted glass front. Authentically spicy Sichuanese cuisine but not too expensive, with mains such as strange-flavoured chicken around ¥35.
Fengwei Xiaochi Cheng Shengli Lu. Bustling dumpling house, one of several in the area. You order from the range of plastic cards behind the cashier, or point to whatever others are eating. Individual clay-pot casseroles, cold meats, buns and vegetables from around ¥5 a serving.
Fukuoka Japanese Zhongshan Lu. Relatively expensive, with most dishes ¥30 or more, but very good – the vegetable *tempura* or *norimaki* rolls are best.
Guhan Feng Western end of Zhongshan Lu. Another modernized "olde worlde" restaurant with reproduction Ming crockery and heavy chairs, this time specializing in local cuisine. Separate snack-tearoom and proper sit-down dining area.
Jiangnan Fandian Bayi Dadao. The big bronze cauldron standing outside marks this down as a Jiangxi-style soup restaurant, and you really need about three people to cope with the generously-sized pot which gets delivered to your table for the diners to ladle out their own portions. Around ¥30 a pot.
Hao Xiang Lai Minde Lu. Good-value, sizzling pepper steaks for ¥25; also trolleyfuls of delicious Chinese snacks, biscuits and dumplings wheeled around *dim sum*-style from ¥2 a plate. One of the few places in town with an English menu.
Hunan Wangcai Guan Supu Lu. Popular, mid-range hotpot restaurant with front window overlooking Bayi Park.
Xiangcancun Minde Lu. Inexpensive three-storey canteen and restaurant where you can tuck in with the local crowds.

Listings

Bank and exchange The main Bank of China is just off the Fushan roundabout on Zhanqian Xi Lu (foreign exchange Mon–Fri 9–11.30am & 2–5pm).
Hospital First City Hospital, Xiangshan Lu.
Internet access Three useful net bars (¥2 an hour) are across from the Bank of China on Zhanqian Xi Lu; west of Youmin Si on the south side of Minde Lu; and in the lane between the *Xiangshan Binguan* and Shengli Lu.
Left luggage Offices at train and bus stations open roughly 6am–7pm.
Mail and telephones The main post office and the telecommunications building (both daily 8am–8pm) are near each other at the corner of Bayi Dadao and Ruzi Lu.
PSB On Shengli Lu, just north of Minde Lu.
Shopping Nanchang Department Store, the city's largest and best-stocked department store, hides behind a 1950s frontage west of Renmin Square along Zhongshan Lu. Zhongshan Lu itself and the pedestrianized southern stretch of Shengli Lu are thick with clothing stores and boutiques. For a big range of porcelain, chops and paintings, try the Jiangxi Antique Store on Minde Lu.
Travel agents Most accommodation places have travel desks where you can book train and plane tickets.

Jiujiang and Lu Shan

Set on the Yangzi 150km north of Nanchang, **Jiujiang** had its heyday in the nineteenth century as a treaty port, and now serves mostly as a jumping-off point for tourists exchanging the torrid lowland summers for nearby cool hills at **Lu Shan**. Yangzi ferries stop at Jiujiang, as do trains on the Kowloon–Beijing line, while fast buses from Nanchang run through the day to both Jiujiang and Lu Shan. On the way, you might consider stopping where the Gan Jiang enters Poyang at the hamlet of **Wucheng**. Between November and March the adjacent **Hou Niao Baohu Reserve** attracts 160 varieties of wintering wildfowl, notably mandarin ducks, storks and a flock of two thousand rare **Siberian cranes**.

Jiujiang

JIUJIANG (Nine Rivers) is well named, sited on the south bank of the Yangzi where Poyang Hu disgorges itself in a generous maze of streams. Small but

RECIPE IDEA

CHINESE BEEF WITH MUSHROOMS

Preparation time: 10 minutes
Cooking time: 10 minutes SERVES 2

- 250g Rump steak, thinly sliced
- 2 tbsp Dry sherry
- 2 tbsp Vegetable oil
- 4 Spring onions, trimmed, cut on the diagonal into 2.5cm
- 2 tsp Minced garlic
- 2 tsp Minced ginger
- 25g Blue Dragon Dried Black, Shiitake or Oyster Mushrooms soaked in 150ml boiling water for 30 minutes
- 1 Large carrot, cut into fine strips
- 1 Sachet Blue Dragon Oyster and Spring Onion Stir Fry sauce

1. Toss together the steak and sherry. Cover and leave to stand while preparing the remaining ingredients.

2. Heat the oil in a large wok or deep frying pan and stir-fry the spring onion, garlic and ginger for 1-2 minutes until softened slightly but not coloured. Drain the mushrooms and squeeze to remove any excess liquid, add to the wok with the carrots and stir-fry for 3 minutes over a high heat.

3. Stir in the steak and sherry and stir-fry for 2 minutes until the steak is tender. Pour over the Blue Dragon Oyster and Spring Onion sauce and cook for 1-2 minutes until hot and bubbling. Season to taste and serve with plain boiled rice.

Appetite suitably whetted? For more information or other mouth-watering recipes simply visit our website:
www.bluedragon.com

Jiujiang and Lu Shan

Jiujiang	九江	***jiŭjiāng***
Bailu Binguan	白鹿宾馆	*báilù bīnguăn*
Gantang Hu	甘棠湖	*gāntáng hú*
Kuanglu Binguan	匡庐宾馆	*kuānglú bīnguăn*
Nengren Si	能仁寺	*néngrén sì*
Xinhua Binguan	新华宾馆	*xīnhuá bīnguăn*
Xunyang Lou	寻阳楼	*xúnyáng lóu*
Yanshui Pavilion	烟水亭	*yānshuĭ tíng*
Guling	牯岭	***gŭlĭng***
Guling Fandian	牯岭饭店	*gŭlĭng fàndiàn*
Lulin	芦林饭店	*lúlín fàndiàn*
Lushan Binguan	庐山宾馆	*lúshān bīnguăn*
Lushan Dasha	庐山大厦	*lúshān dàshà*
Lushan Villas	庐山别墅	*lúshān biéshù*
Meilu Villa	美庐别墅	*mĕilú bié shù*
Lu Shan	庐山	***lúshān***
Botanical Garden	植物园	*zhíwù yuán*
Five Immortals' Peak	五仙人山	*wŭxiānrénshān*
Lulin Hu	芦林湖	*lúlín hú*
People's Hall	人民剧院	*rénmín jùyuàn*
Ruqin Hu	如琴湖	*rúqín hú*
San Diequan	三叠泉	*sāndié quán*
Xianren Dong	仙人洞	*xiānrén dòng*
Wucheng Bird Reserve	误成鸟保护区	***wùchéng niăo băohùqū***

always an important staging post for river traffic, the town grew wealthy during the Ming dynasty through trade in Jingdezhen's porcelain, which was distributed all over China from here. Largely destroyed during the Taiping Uprising, Jiujiang was rebuilt as a treaty port in the 1860s, and today – despite catastrophic flooding through the town centre in 1998 – it's enjoying a low-scale renaissance, the docks and adjacent streets busy from dawn to dusk.

The west side of town between the Yangzi and **Gantang Hu** is the most interesting area, a collection of narrow streets packed with small stores selling bright summer clothing, porcelain and home-made hardware utensils. Completely occupying a tiny islet in the lake is the picturesque **Yanshui Pavilion** (¥5), its tastefully proportioned Ming pavilion commemorating the Tang poet-official **Li Bai**, who was responsible for the causeway and the much restored moon-shaped sluice gate. A ten-minute walk southeast of here down Yuling Lu leads to the red walls and flower beds outside the **Nengren Si** (¥2), whose five-storey pagoda rises over three plain halls, the largest barely big enough to contain a looming, blue-haired Buddha statue.

Much more fun is **Xunyang Lou** (daily 9am–late; ¥6), an "antique" wooden winehouse facing Anhui and Hubei provinces across the Yangzi on Binjiang Lu, about 1500m east of the ferry port. Built in 1986 to replace a previous Tang-dynasty structure, it was the setting – in literature – for a scene in **Outlaws of the Marsh** (aka *The Water Margin*), China's own Robin Hood legend. This lively story, set mostly farther east in Zhejiang Province, involved 108 rebel heroes who were often more bloodthirsty than the oppressive Song-dynasty officials they fought – the tale was one of Mao's favourites. The winehouse was where the future outlaws' leader Song Jiang imprudently wrote some revolutionary verses on the back wall after downing too much wine; condemned to death, he was rescued dramatically at the last moment. Those familiar with the tale will recognize porcelain figurines of Song Jiang, "Black Whirlwind" Liu Kei (the original axe-wielding maniac) and the other heroes in the lobby. The upstairs **restaurant** is worth visiting at lunch for *dongpo rouding* (steamed and braised pork belly), river fish, "Eight Treasure" duck, scrambled eggs and green pepper, or *sunyang dabin* (a pancake invented by one of the outlaws). Just east again is another elderly **pagoda**, with more fine views of the river once you've climbed the seven flights of wobbly wooden stairs.

Practicalities

Jiujiang's centre is laid out in the narrow space between the north shore of Gantang Hu and the Yangzi: **Xunyang Lu** runs west from the top of the lake out to the highway, while parallel **Binjiang Lu** is 100m further north and follows the river bank.

The **Yangzi ferry port** is on the western end of Binjiang Lu, with the ticket office (daily 8.30–11am & 2.30–5pm) and timetables at the far side of the building, and departure hall in the middle. Jiujiang's **train station** is 3km southeast at the bottom end of Gantang Hu – catch #17 to the ferry port, or #1 to the bus station – and has quick links to Wuhan, Nanchang and Hefei. The **long-distance bus station** is 1500m east down Xunyang Lu, with buses back to Nanchang or on to Lu Shan until 7pm, and others to Wuhan and Nanjing; between here and the lake you'll find a **Bank of China** (Mon–Fri 8.30–11am & 1.30–5pm), and Nanchang's most convenient **accommodation**. The best deal is at the *Xinhua Binguan* (Ⓣ0792/8989222, Ⓕ8989999; ❹), though you can find cheaper beds nearby at the shabby *Kuanglu Binguan* (Ⓣ0792/8228893; ❷), and more upmarket rooms at *Bailu Binguan* (Ⓣ0792/8222818, Ⓕ8221915; ❹), a flashy place patronized by well-heeled tour groups.

Summer evenings are too close to spend indoors and everyone heads down Xunyang Lu to window-shop and eat at one of the **pavement cafés** on Gantang's north shore, admiring views of Lu Shan and gorging on fish and crayfish hotpots, sautéed frogs and piles of freshwater snails. If you like Chinese spirits, crack open a bottle of *Jiuling Jiu*, the local firewater, which comes with a clay seal – once opened, you'll have to drink the lot.

Lu Shan

Lu Shan's cluster of wooded hills rises to a sudden 1474m from the level shores of Poyang Hu, its heights a welcome relief from the Yangzi basin's steamy summers. Once covered in temples, Lu Shan was developed in the mid-nineteenth century by **Edward Little**, a Methodist minister turned property speculator, as a resort area for European expatriates. After the Europeans lost their grip on the region, the Chinese elite moved in; **Chiang Kaishek** built a summer residence and training school for Guomindang officials up here in the 1930s, and Lu Shan hosted one of the key meetings of the Maoist era twenty years later. Nowadays the place is overrun with proletariat holiday-makers who pack out the restaurants and troop along the paths to enjoy the clean air, and former mansions have been converted into hotels and sanatoriums for their benefit. Crowds reach plague proportions between spring and autumn, so winter – though very cold – can be the best season to visit, and a weekend's walking is enough for a good sample of the scenery.

Guling

The thirty-kilometre trip from Jiujiang takes two hours on the sharply twisting road, with sparkling views back over the great lake and its junction with the Yangzi. There's a pause at the top gates for passengers to pay an **entry fee** (¥50), then it's a short way to **GULING** township in Lu Shan's northeastern corner, whose handful of quaintly cobbled streets, European stone villas and bungalows are the base for further exploration. The one "sight" in town is the **Meilu Villa** on Hexi Lu, former residence of Chiang Kaishek and of interest simply because its exhibition is one of the few in China to so much as mention the Generalissimo (though it's named after his wife, Song Meiling). Other than this, there are some nice views around the centre of Guling's mosaic of red roof tiles and grey buildings nestled among the fir trees.

Buses arrive on He Dong Lu immediately after emerging from a tunnel into town (though minibuses from Jiujiang might terminate anywhere). Fifty metres downhill on the right is a pedestrian mall leading through to Guling Lu. Most essential services are either in the mall or on Guling Lu: souvenir shops selling **maps**, a post office, Bank of China (though larger hotels are a better bet for exchanging traveller's cheques) and a **market** selling vegetables, bananas, peaches and lychees.

Leaving Lu Shan is fairly simple, though due to the one-way road system in Guling, departing buses and their **ticket offices** are located on Guling Lu, separate from the arrival points. It's essential to book long-distance tickets the day before departure. Regular buses head to Jiujiang, Nanchang and beyond; if you can't find direct services, go first to Jiujiang for Wuhan and points east, and Nanchang for southern or westerly destinations.

Accommodation and eating

Summers are very busy – arrive early on in the day to make sure of a room – and expensive, with accommodation raising their prices and refusing to bargain. Winters see tumbling room rates and fewer tourists but are cold enough for snow, so check out the availibility of heating and hot water. Prices quoted in the listings below are for summer.

There are plenty of **restaurants** in Guling, mostly good value despite the numbers of tourists, and some post their menus and prices outside. For local flavours – mountain fungus and fish – try the stalls and open restaurants around the market, or the *Wurong Canting*, above a teashop in the mall.

Guling Fandian 104 He Dong Lu Ⓣ0792/8282200, Ⓕ8282209. The two wings face each other across the road about 100m downhill from the bus stop. There's an older, cheaper section, while the rooms in the newer building are much smarter. ❻

Lushan Binguan 446 He Xi Lu Ⓣ0792/8282060, Ⓕ8282843. Ten minutes farther on past the *Guling*, this is a heavy stone mansion with slightly ordinary cheaper rooms, good-value suites and a fine restaurant. ❹

Lushan Dasha 506 He Xi Lu Ⓣ0792/8282178. A regimental exterior betrays this hotel as the former Guomindang Officers' Training Centre; rooms are well furnished and comfortable. ❼

Lushan Villas Ⓣ0792/8282927, Ⓕ8282275. Nice quiet location off He Xi Lu in a group of recently renovated cottage villas named after different historic figures. Two excellent restaurants on site. ❼

Into the hills

Covering some 300 square kilometres, Lu Shan's **highlands** form an elliptical platform tilted over to the southwest, comprising a central region of lakes surrounded by pine-clad hills, with superb rocks, waterfalls and views along the vertical edges of the plateau. Freelance minibuses cruise Guling Lu and usually charge a flat fee of ¥10 per person to any site in Lu Shan, while tour buses cover a variety of places on day-trips from the long-distance bus arrival stop.

For an easy walk out from town (3hr round trip), follow the road downhill to the southwest from Guling Lu and the Jiexin Garden to the far end of **Ruqin Hu**, where you can pick up the **Floral Path**. This gives impressive views of the Jinxui Valley as it winds along Lu Shan's western cliff edge past **Xianren Dong**, the Immortal's Cave, once inhabited by an ephemeral Taoist monk and still an active shrine, complete with a slowly dripping spring.

The most spectacular scenery is found on Lu Shan's southern fringes. A full exploration makes a fair day's hike, and even hardened walkers will probably take advantage of transport into the area. About an hour's stroll down He Xi Lu and then left takes you past the unpleasantly crowded **People's Hall** (daily 8am–5pm; ¥15), site of the 1959 Central Committee meeting at which Marshal Peng Dehui openly criticized the Great Leap Forward, and was subsequently denounced as a "Rightist" by Mao – events which ultimately sparked the Cultural Revolution. Next is **Lulin Hu**, a nice lakeside area with its attractive Dragon Pools and elderly Three Treasure trees over to the west. Due east of here – about 5km by road but less along walking tracks – is China's only sub-alpine **botanical garden**, the finest spot in Lu Shan to watch the sunrise. Admittedly, clear days are a rare commodity on Lu Shan, whose peaks are frequently obscured by mist – the local brew is suitably known as "Cloud Fog Tea".

Jingdezhen and Yingtan

From Nanchang, road and rail lines head northeast towards **Jingdezhen**, which lies diagonally across the far side of Poyang Hu from the capital on the border with Anhui Province. Following the Jiujiang expressway clockwise around the lake, it's only three hours to Jingdezhen from Nanchang; alternatively, you can take the much slower road eastwards via the untidy copper-mining town of **YINGTAN** (you might have to stop here to catch trains heading southeast to Fujian Province), 180km from Nanchang, locally famed for the nearby Taoist retreat of **Longhu Shan** (Dragon-Tiger Mountain), 20km south. Yingtan's train and bus stations face each other on Sihai Lu, with

Jingdezhen and Yingtan

Jingdezhen	景德镇	***jĭngdézhèn***
Ancient Porcelain Workshop	古窑瓷厂	*gŭyáo cíchăng*
Changcheng Binguan	长城宾馆	*chángchéng bīnguăn*
Jingdezhen Joint Venture Hotel	景德镇合瓷宾馆	*jĭngdézhèn hécí bīnguăn*
Jinsheng Dajiudian	金盛大酒店	*jīnshèng dàjiŭdiàn*
Longzhu Ge	龙珠阁	*lóngzhū gé*
Museum of Ceramic History	陶瓷历史博物馆	*táocí lìshĭ bówùguăn*
Zhongjin Dajiudian	中锦大酒店	*zhōngjĭn dàjiŭdiàn*
Yingtan	鹰潭	***yīngtán***
Changcheng Binguan	长城宾馆	*chángchéng bīnguăn*
Longhu Shan	龙虎山	*lónghŭ shān*

adjacent hostels (¥80) and the *Changcheng Binguan* (❹) providing beds. It's a further five hours or so by bus from Yingtan to Jingdezhen, half this for the train.

Jingdezhen

JINGDEZHEN was producing ceramics at least two thousand years ago, and, due to local geography and national politics, ceramics remain the city's chief source of income. The town lies in a river valley rich not only in clay suitable for firing but also in the feldspar needed to turn it into **porcelain**, and when the Ming rulers developed a taste for fine ceramics in the fourteenth century, Jingdezhen's location was conveniently close to the original capital at Nanjing. An **imperial kiln** was built in 1369, and its wares became so highly regarded – "as white as jade, as thin as paper, as bright as a mirror, as tuneful as a bell" – that Jingdezhen retained official favour even after the Ming court shifted to Beijing fifty years later.

As demand grew, workshops experimented with new **glazes** and a classic range of decorative styles emerged: *qinghua*, blue and white; *jihong*, rainbow; *doucai*, a blue and white overglaze; and *fencai*, multicoloured *famille rose*. The first examples reached Europe in the seventeenth century, and became so popular that the English word for China clay – kaolin – derives from its source nearby at **Gaoling**. Factories began to specialize in **export ware** shaped and decorated in European-approved forms, which reached the outside world via the booming Canton markets: the famous **Nanking Cargo**, comprising 150,000 pieces salvaged from the 1752 wreck of the Dutch vessel *Geldermalsen* and auctioned in 1986, was one such shipment. Foreign sales on this scale petered out after European ceramic technologies improved at the end of the eighteenth century, but Jingdezhen survived by sacrificing innovation for a more production-line mentality, and today the town's scores of private and state-owned kilns employ some fifty thousand people.

The Town

Surrounded by paddy fields and tea terraces, Jingdezhen is a thoroughly scruffy city whose streets labour under the effects of severe pollution caused by the numerous porcelain factories dotted throughout the centre. The only available vistas of Jingdezhen are from the four-storey **Longzhu Ge** (Dragon Pearl Pavilion) on Zhonghua Bei Lu, a pleasant construction in wood and orange tile along the lines of Hunan's Yueyang Tower (see p.566). From the top, the town's smoggy horizon is liberally pierced by tall, thin smokestacks, which fire up by late afternoon.

But porcelain, not views, is the reason Jingdezhen figures on tourist itineraries, and the town is geared towards **selling**. There are a few tourist shops, but it's more fun – and much cheaper – to head down to the **markets** south of Guangchang on Jiefang Lu, where you'll find pavements clogged by stacks of everything that has ever been made in porcelain, in or out of fashion: metre-high vases, life-sized dogs, Western- and Chinese-style crockery, antique reproductions including yellow and green glazed Tang camels, ugly statuettes of Buddhist and historical figures, and simple porcelain pandas for the mantelpiece. It's a surreal sight, as are the Chinese visitors buying by the cartload.

The Museum of Ceramic History

To experience the manufacturing side of things, either try to join a CITS **factory tour**, or visit the **Museum of Ceramic History** (daily 9am–5pm; ¥15 entry for each area). Normally the museum is a bit quiet, but if a big tour party is expected, the workshops get fired up and it's much more entertaining. The museum is out of town on the west side of the river – take bus #3 from Zhushan Lu to its terminus on Cidu Dadao, then cross the road and head under the ornamental arch opposite. A fifteen-minute walk through fields leads to a surprising collection of antique buildings divided into two sections. A Ming mansion houses the **museum** itself, and its ornate crossbeams, walled gardens and gilt eave screens are far more interesting than the second-rate **ceramics display**, though this covers everything from thousand-year-old kiln fragments through to the Ming's classic simplicity and overwrought, multi-coloured extravagances of the late nineteenth century. Next door, another walled garden conceals the **Ancient Porcelain Workshop**, complete with a Confucian temple and working pottery, where the entire process of throwing, moulding and glazing takes place. Out the back is a rickety two-storey **kiln**, packed with all sizes of the unglazed yellow pottery sleeves commonly seen outside local field kilns – these shield each piece of porcelain from damage in case one explodes during the firing process.

Practicalities

The town is concentrated on the east bank of the **Chang Jiang** – not the Yangzi, but a lesser river of the same name. **Zhushan Lu** runs east from the river for a kilometre through to where roads converge at central **Guangchang**, a broad, paved public square where children fly kites in windy weather.

The **train station** is 1500m southeast of Guangchang on Tongzhan Lu, while the new **long-distance bus station** is 3km northwest across the river – bus #28 (¥1) connects the two via Zhushan Lu and Guangchang. **Leaving**, there are trains northeast to Tunxi in Anhui, Nanjing, and Shanghai, and southwest to Yingtan and Nanchang; the train station can be complete chaos so allow time to buy a ticket, and don't expect anything better than hard seat. Buses can get you to Yingtan, Nanchang, and Jiujiang. Tongzhan Lu is where you'll also find the **Bank of China**; the main **post office** is west of the river on Zhushan Lu, and there are several small **Internet bars** (¥2) near Longzhu Ge on Zhonghua Bei Lu.

Jingdezhen's **accommodation** prospects are mediocre. The best option near the station is *Zhongjin Dajiudian* on Tongzhan Lu (Ⓣ0798/7020888; ❸); around Guangchang, there's the *Changcheng Binguan* (Ⓣ0798/8226727, Ⓕ8214246; ❸) at the northwest corner of Guangchang on Xinshu Xi Lu, and the grubby but welcoming *Jinsheng Dajiudian* (Ⓣ0798/8232728; ❹). The *Jingdezhen Joint Venture Hotel* is the most upmarket place in town (Ⓣ0798/8225012, Ⓕ8226416; ❻), nicely located 1km due north of Guangchang along Lianshi Bei Lu in **Lianhuata Park**, with a CITS office on site. **Food stalls** offering hotpots and stir fries can be found east of Guangchang along Tongzhan Lu.

Southern Jiangxi

When Zhou Enlai and Zhu De were driven out of Nanchang after their abortive uprising, they fled to the **Jinggang Shan** ranges, 300km southwest in the mountainous border with Hunan. Here they met up with Mao, whose **Autumn Harvest Uprising** in Hunan had also failed, and the remnants of the two armies joined to form the first real PLA divisions. Their initial base was

Southern Jiangxi		
Ciping	茨坪	***cípíng***
Former Revolutionary Headquarters	革命旧居群	*gémìng jiùjǔqún*
Jinggang Shan Binguan	井岗山宾馆	*jǐnggǎngshān bīnguǎn*
Jinggang Shan Fandian	井岗山饭店	*jǐnggǎngshān fàndiàn*
Martyrs' Tomb	烈士纪念堂	*lièshì jìniàntáng*
Revolutionary Museum	井岗山博物馆	*jǐnggǎngshān bówùguǎn*
Jinggang Shan	井岗山	***jǐnggāng shān***
Wulong Tan	五龙潭	*wǔlóng tán*
Wuzhi Feng	五指峰	*wǔzhǐ fēng*
Ganzhou	赣州	***gànzhōu***
Bajing Park	八境公园	*bājìng gōngyuán*
Ji'an	吉安	***jí'ān***

near the country town of **Ciping**, and, though they declared a Chinese Soviet Republic in 1931 at the Fujian border town of **Ruijin**, Ciping was where the Communists stayed until forced out by the Guomindang in 1934.

Jinggang Shan is reasonably accessible thanks to new roads, though it doesn't seem to be attracting a great number of tourists – probably because it is so far from anywhere else. This makes it a pleasant proposition, as there is some good forest scenery and a few hiking trails. Ciping is an eight-hour **bus** trip from Nanchang via the ancient river town of **Ji'an**, whose landmark **Yunzhang Ge** (Cloud Sect Pavilion) is built out on a wooded mid-stream island. You can also get into the region **by train**, disembarking either at the southern city of **Ganzhou**, or east at the Jinggang Shan railhead – either way, you've still got at least 120km to cover by bus.

Ciping and Jinggang Shan

Also known as Jinggang Shan Shi, **CIPING** is, at least in scale, nothing more than a village. Completely destroyed by artillery bombardments during the 1930s, it was rebuilt after the Communist takeover as one enormous revolutionary relic, though recent greening projects have lightened the heavily heroic architecture and monuments, giving the place a dated rural charm. The main streets form a two-kilometre elliptical circuit, the lower half of which is taken up with a lake surrounded by grassy gardens – much appreciated by straying cattle – and a tiny amusement park, complete with a real MiG-style fighter plane to play on.

Ciping's austere historical monuments can be breezed through fairly quickly, as it's the surrounding hills which better re-create a feeling of how the Communist guerrillas might have lived. Five minutes west of the bus station at the top end of town is the squat, angular **Martyrs' Tomb**, positioned at the top of a broad flight of stairs and facing the mountains that the fighters it commemorates died defending. Farther round at the **Revolutionary Museum** (daily 8am–4pm; ¥12), where signs ban smoking, spitting and laughter, the exhibition consists almost entirely of maps showing battle sites and troop movements up until 1930 – after this the Communists suffered some heavy defeats. Paintings of a smiling Mao preaching to peasant armies face cases of the spears, flintlocks and mortars which initially comprised the Communist

The Long March

In 1927, Chiang Kaishek, the new leader of the right-wing Nationalist Guomindang government, began an obsessive war against the six-year-old Chinese Communist Party, using a union dispute in Shanghai as an excuse to massacre their leadership. Driven underground, the Communists set up half a dozen remote rural bases, or soviets, across central China. The most important of these were the **Fourth Front army** in northern Sichuan, under the leadership of **Zhang Guotao**; the **Hunan soviet**, controlled by the irrepressible peasant general **He Long**; and the main **Jiangxi soviet** in the Jianggan Mountains, led by Mao and Zhu De, the Communist Commander-in-Chief.

Initially poorly armed, the Jiangxi soviet successfully fought off Guomindang attempts to oust them, acquiring better weapons in the process and swelling their ranks with disaffected peasantry and defectors from the Nationalist cause. But they over-estimated their position and, abandoning Mao's previously successful guerrilla tactics in 1933, were drawn into several disastrous pitched battles. Chiang, ignoring Japanese incursions into Manchuria in his eagerness to defeat the Communists, blockaded the mountains with a steadily tightening ring of bunkers and barbed wire, systematically clearing areas of guerrillas with artillery bombardments. Hemmed in and facing eventual defeat, the **First Front army**, comprising some eighty thousand Red soldiers, decided to break through the blockade in October 1934 and retreat west to team up with the Hunan soviet – the beginning of the **Long March**.

Covering a punishing 30km a day on average, the Communists moved after dark whenever possible so that the enemy would find it difficult to know their exact position – even so, they faced daily skirmishes. One thing in their favour was that many putative Guomindang divisions were, in fact, armies belonging to local warlords who owed only a token allegiance to Chiang Kaishek and had no particular reason to fight the Communists once it became clear that the Red Army was crossing, not invading, their territory. But after severe losses incurred during a battle at the **Xiang River** near Guilin in Guangxi, the marchers found their progress north impeded by massive Guomindang forces determined to prevent their joining up with the Hunan soviet, and were obliged to continue west to Guizhou where they took the town of **Zunyi** in January 1935. With their power structure in disarray and with no obvious options left to them, an emergency meeting of the Party hierarchy was called. This was the **Zunyi Conference**, from which **Mao** emerged as the undisputed **leader** of the Chinese Communist Party with a mandate to "go north to fight the Japanese" by linking up with Zhang Guotao in Sichuan. During the following months they circled through Yunnan and Guizhou, trying to shake off the Guomindang, routing twenty regiments of the Guangxi provincial army at the **Loushan Pass** in the

arsenal, perhaps suggesting that righteousness will prevail against all odds. On a more mundane level, a group of mud-brick rooms across the park at the **Former Revolutionary Headquarters** (daily 8am–4pm; ¥12) gives an idea of what Ciping might have originally looked like and, as the site of where Mao and Zhu De co-ordinated their guerrilla activities and the start of the **Long March**, is the town's biggest attraction as far as visiting cadres are concerned.

Practicalities

Ciping's **bus station** is on the northeastern side of the circuit, served by buses from Nanchang and Ganzhou, and also Hengyang in Hunan Province, from where there are transport links into southern and central China. About 100m downhill from the bus station, on the left past a gauntlet of **restaurants**, the process; they then suddenly moved up into Sichuan to cross the Jinsha River and, in one of the most celebrated and heroic episodes of the march, took the **Luding Bridge** across the Dadu River (see p.979). Now they had to negotiate **Daxue Shan** (Great Snowy Mountains), where hundreds died from exhaustion, exposure and altitude sickness before the survivors met up on the far side with the Fourth Front army.

The meeting between these two major branches of the Red Army was tense, with Mao and Zhang Guotao quarrelling over supreme military command. Mao, with Party backing, wanted to start resistance against the Japanese, but Zhang, who felt that his better-equipped forces and better education gave him superiority, wanted to found a Communist state in Sichuan's far west. Zhang eventually capitulated, and both he and Mao took control of separate columns in order to cross the last natural barrier they had to face, the **Aba Grasslands** in northern Sichuan. But here, while Mao was bogged down with swamps, hostile nomads and dwindling food reserves, Zhang suddenly retreated with his column to **Garzê**, where he set up an independent government. Mao and what remained of the First Front managed to struggle through southern Gansu, where they suffered further losses through Muslim supporters of the Guomindang, finally arriving in Communist-held **Yan'an**, Shaanxi Province, in October 1935. While the mountains here were to become a Communist stronghold, only a quarter of those who started from Jiangxi twelve months before had completed the 9500-kilometre journey. Zhang was soon harried out of western Sichuan by Chiang's forces, however, and after meeting up with He Long, he battled his way through to Shaanxi to add another twenty thousand followers to the Communist ranks. Here he made peace with Mao in October 1936, but later defected to the Guomindang.

Mao summed up the Long March immediately afterwards, admitting that in terms of losses and the Red Army's failure to hold their original positions against the Nationalists, the Guomindang had won. Yet in a more lasting sense, the march was an incredible success, uniting the Party structure under Mao and defining the Communists' aims, while creating a **legend** which changed the Communists' popular image from simply another rebel group opposing central authority into one of a determined, honest and patriotic movement. After Zunyi, Mao turned the march into a deliberate propaganda mission to spread the Communist faith among the peasantry, opening up prisons in captured Guomindang towns and promoting tolerance and co-operation with minority groups (though not always successfully). As Mao said, "Without the Long March, how could the broad masses have learned so quickly about the existence of the great truth which the Red Army embodies?"

Jinggang Shan Fandian (Ⓣ0791/6552328; ❷, dorm beds ¥45) is a comfy Chinese **hotel** whose seemingly limitless wings and floors contain a huge number of beds, including three-bed dorms with private facilities. Alternatively, take the first street down the hill on the right from the bus station, which leads through Ciping's **tourist market**, a collection of white-tiled shops selling local teas, cloud-ear fungus and bamboo roots carved into faces. Straight through the market is the *Jinggang Shan Binguan* (Ⓣ0791/6552272, Ⓕ6552221; ❹), favoured by visiting officials but otherwise a bit grey.

Farther along from the *Jinggang Shan Fandian*, just past the Former Revolutionary Headquarters, is a large **Bank of China** only too happy to change traveller's cheques (Mon–Fri 9–11.30am & 2–5pm). The **CITS** office at the *Jinggang Shan Binguan* (no fixed opening times; Ⓣ0791/6522504) might be able to arrange a local tour with an English-speaking guide, or offer some explanation for the inadequate **maps** of walking trails available from the bus station and outside the museum.

Jinggang Shan

Having waded through the terribly serious displays in town, it's nice to escape from Ciping into Jinggang Shan's surprisingly wild **countryside**. Some of the peaks provide glorious views of the sunrise, or more frequent mists, and there are colourful plants, natural groves of pine and bamboo, deep green temperate cloud forests, and hosts of butterflies and birds. If you want a day-tour of all the local sights, ask CITS to arrange a jeep and driver or use the minibuses which leave from the station.

One problem with **walking** anywhere is that maps of the footpaths are pretty vague, and locals can be shy of foreigners, running off should you stop to ask directions. Relatively easy to find and also one of the nicest areas for its own sake, **Wulong Tan** (Five Dragon Pools) is about 8km north along the road from the Martyrs' Tomb. A footpath follows from the roadhead past where some poetically pretty waterfalls drop into the pools (of which there are actually eight) between a score of pine-covered peaks. The same distance south is **Jinggang Shan** itself, also known as **Wuzhi Feng**, apex of the mountains at 1586m. Follow the road out of town past the Bank of China, then turn right and take the concrete "driveway" uphill past company housing and on to a dirt road. About ten minutes later this forks; go left down to the bridge, cross over and carry on past a huge quarry, where machinery turns boulders into gravel, and on to a **tunnel** leading into the hillside. Ignore the tunnel and follow the steps above up through a small patch of forest full of ginger, ferns and moss-covered trees, to more stairs ascending to Wuzhi Feng's sharp and lightly wooded summit. The last bit of the track is slippery and not overly used, giving a rare opportunity to be on your own, musing on how the Communists must have found things and watching the trees and waterfalls below sliding in and out of the clouds. Examine the bushes and you'll find that some extraordinary insects congregate up here: multicoloured crickets, scarabs with orange antennae and huge, bushy caterpillars.

Ganzhou

Six hours south of Jinggang Shan, **GANZHOU** lies on the sub-tropical side of Jiangxi's mountain ranges, only a short hop from the Guangdong border. A stop on the Kowloon–Beijing rail line, Ganzhou makes an interesting few hours' break in your journey, and is very different in feel from elsewhere in Jiangxi.

The Town

Ganzhou is a small place by Chinese standards, with a centre only a couple of kilometres across. The town's focus is **Nanmen Guangchang**, South Gate Square: from here, **Wenqing Lu** runs north through the centre to Bajing Park and the river, lined with clothes shops and restaurants, while **Hongqi Lu** is the town's east–west transport artery.

The town sits on a triangular peninsula where two rivers, the Gong Shui and Zhang Shui, combine to form the **Gan Jiang**, which flows north from here all the way to Nanchang and Poyang Hu. Ganzhou was formerly a strategic port guarding the routes between central and southern China – during the 1930s, Chiang Kaishek's son was governor here, doubtless keeping a close watch on the events at Jinggang Shan. A surprising amount survives from these times. The peninsula's northern end is enclosed by several kilometres of **stone battlements**: at the very tip, **Bajing Park** (¥8) is an untidy arrangement of willows and ponds enlivened by **Bajing Tai**, a platform and tower whose rusting cannon no longer threaten barges negotiating the river junction below. Exiting the park, you can follow the walls southeast down Zhongshan Lu through 1930s streets to the old **east gate**, still with a functioning portcullis; on the far side is a small market, people mid-stream fishing with cast nets and **cormorants** (see p.795), and villagers wheeling their bicycles to the far bank across a low **pontoon bridge**. Originally built by chaining punts across the river and laying a wooden decking on top (though mid-section floats here are steel), these bridges were common through the region until the 1950s, being cheap to make and easily removed in times of flooding or war. Look back from the middle at the steep walls and appreciate Ganzhou's defences – it wouldn't have taken much time to cut the bridge, drop the portcullis and load the cannon.

Back inside the city, if you head more or less southwest you'll come to more elderly architecture, including narrow side streets of Qing houses, colonial-style colonnaded shop-fronts along the main roads, a couple of small temples, and a pagoda – nothing of great importance, but atmospheric all the same, though demolitions are edging closer all the time.

Practicalities

The **long-distance bus station** is on Bayi Si Dadao 3km from the centre at the southeastern corner of town, a relentlessly unappealing area. The **train station** is further out in the same direction; from either, bus #2 will get you to Nanmen Guangchang. **Leaving**, trains head to Jinggang Shan, Nanchang, Jiujiang, Wuhan, Hefei and well beyond, with useful buses south to Shaoguan and Guangzhou in Guangdong Province.

The main **Bank of China** is halfway up Wenqing Lu, with a **post office** on Nanmen Guangchang. For a **place to stay**, there are a few cheap hotels north of the bus station on Bayi Si Dadao, but you're better off forking out for a decent room at the *Ganzhou Fandian*, near Nanmen Guangchang at 29 Hongqi Dadao (Ⓣ0797/8280118, Ⓕ8280128; ❹) – it's not as expensive as you'd think from the exterior. As regards **eating**, head up Wenqing Lu: there's Western-style food and coffee upstairs at *Spring of Taipei*, about 100m along on the west side; 500m along at the intersection with Qingnian Lu you'll find a branch of *Dicos* and extremely popular hot-pots at *Wuzhou Kuaican* on the left, and buns, soya milk and snacks at *Yonghe Doujiang* on the right.

Travel details

Trains

Changsha to: Beijing (30 daily; 16hr); Guangzhou (30 daily; 7–10hr); Guiyang (2 daily; 15hr); Hengyang (14 daily; 4hr); Nanchang (5 daily; 7hr); Shaoshan (1 daily; 3hr); Shenzhen (3 daily; 9hr 30min); Wuhan (30 daily; 3hr 30min–5hr); Yueyang (30 daily; 1hr 30min–2hr); Zhangjiajie (4 daily; 5–7hr).

Ganzhou to: Beijing (1 daily; 22hr); Guangzhou East (3 daily; 8–10hr); Hefei (1 daily; 14hr); Jinggang Shan (1 daily; 1hr 40min); Jiujiang (7 daily; 8hr); Nanchang (11 daily; 5–7hr); Shenzhen (3 daily; 9hr); Wuchang (1 daily; 14hr).

Hefei to: Beijing (3 daily; 12hr); Bozhou (1 daily; 4hr); Ganzhou (1 daily; 14hr); Jingdezhen (1 daily; 10hr); Jiujiang (3 daily; 4hr); Nanchang (3 daily; 8hr); Nanjing (2 daily; 6hr); Shanghai (2 daily; 9hr);

Tunxi (4 daily; 8hr); Wuhan (1 daily; 9hr); Wuhu (4 daily; 2hr); Xi'an (2 daily; 17hr).

Jingdezhen to: Hefei (1 daily; 10hr); Nanchang (4 daily; 6hr); Shanghai (1 daily; 17hr); Tunxi (6 daily; 3–5hr)

Jiujiang to: Ganzhou (7 daily; 8hr); Hefei (3 daily; 4hr); Nanchang (9 daily; 2–5hr); Shanghai (2 daily; 15hr); Wuhan (6 daily; 4hr).

Nanchang to: Beijing (4 daily; 14–19hr); Changsha (5 daily; 7hr); Fuzhou (3 daily; 13hr); Ganzhou (11 daily; 5–7hr); Guangzhou (5 daily; 12–15hr); Hefei (3 daily; 8hr); Jingdezhen (4 daily; 6hr); Jinggang Shan (7 daily; 3hr); Jiujiang (9 daily; 2–5hr); Shanghai (4 daily; 11hr); Shenzhen (2 daily; 13hr); Tunxi (1 daily; 9hr); Wuhan (6 daily; 9hr); Xiamen (1 daily; 20hr); Yingtang (6 daily; 2hr 30min).

Tunxi to: Beijing (1 daily; 20hr); Hefei (4 daily; 8hr); Jingdezhen (6 daily; 3–5hr); Nanchang (1 daily; 9hr); Nanjing (6 daily; 9hr); Shanghai (2 daily; 11hr).

Wuhan to: Beijing (10 daily; 12–15hr); Changsha (30 daily; 3hr 30min–5hr); Ganzhou (1 daily; 14hr); Guangzhou (15 daily; 12hr 30min–16hr); Hefei (1 daily; 9hr); Jiujiang (6 daily; 4hr); Nanchang (6 daily; 9hr); Shiyan (8 daily; 5–8hr); Wudang Shan (1 daily; 7hr); Xi'an (8 daily; 16hr); Xiangfan (9 daily; 3–6hr); Yueyang (30 daily; 2–4hr).

Wuhu to: Hefei (4 daily; 2hr); Nanjing (2 daily; 4hr); Shanghai (2 daily; 8hr).

Xiangfan to: Shiyan (15 daily; 2–6hr); Wudang Shan (2 daily; 2–5hr); Wuhan (9 daily; 3–6hr); Yichang (5 daily; 4hr); Zhangjiajie (1 daily; 7hr 30min).

Yichang to: Beijing (5 daily; 22hr); Xi'an (1 daily; 12hr); Xiangfan (5 daily; 4hr); Zhangjiajie (2 daily; 6hr).

Yueyang to: Changsha (30 daily; 1hr 30min–2hr); Wuhan (30 daily; 2–4hr).

Zhangjiajie to: Changsha (4 daily; 5–7hr); Huaihua (for connections to Guiyang or Changsha; 7 daily; 5hr); Xiangfan (1 daily; 7hr 30min); Yichang (2 daily; 6hr).

Buses

Changsha to: Heng Shan (4hr); Jiujiang (13hr); Nanchang (10hr); Wuhan (9hr); Yichang (10hr); Yueyang (4hr); Zhangjiajie (14hr).

Ciping (Jinggang Shan) to: Ganzhou (6hr); Hengyang (8hr); Jinggang Shan Station (2hr); Nanchang (8hr).

Hefei to: Bozhou (6hr); Huainan (2hr); Jiuhua Shan (5hr); Jiujiang (8hr); Nanchang (12hr); Nanjing (4hr); Shouxian (2hr); Tongling (2hr); Tunxi (4hr); Wuhan (8hr); Wuhu (2hr).

Jingdezhen to: Jiujiang (1–2hr); Nanchang (3hr); Yingtan (2hr 30min).

Jiuhua Shan to: Hefei (5hr); Qingyang (1hr); Taiping (3hr); Tangkou (4hr 30min); Tongling (2hr); Wuhu (6hr).

Jiujiang to: Changsha (13hr); Hefei (8hr); Jingdezhen (1–2hr); Lu Shan (2hr); Nanchang (2hr); Wuhan (6hr).

Nanchang to: Changsha (10hr); Hefei (12hr); Jingdezhen (3hr); Jinggang Shan (8hr); Jiujiang (2hr); Lu Shan (4hr); Wuhan (12hr); Yingtan (2hr 30min).

Tunxi to: Hefei (4hr); Jingdezhen (5hr); Jiuhua Shan (5hr); Nanjing (6hr); Shanghai (12hr); Shexian (1hr); Tangkou (1hr 30min); Tongling (4hr); Wuhu (2hr); Yixian (2hr).

Wuhan to: Changsha (9hr); Hefei (8hr); Jingzhou (2hr 30min); Jiujiang (6hr); Nanchang (12hr); Xiangfan (8hr); Yichang (4hr); Yueyang (5hr).

Wuhu to: Hefei (2hr); Jiuhua Shan (6hr); Nanjing (3hr); Tongling (2hr); Tunxi (3hr); Xuancheng (2hr).

Xiangfan to: Jingzhou (4hr 30min); Wudang Shan (3hr); Wuhan (8hr); Yichang (6hr).

Yichang to: Changsha (10hr); Jingzhou (1hr 30min); Jiujiang (12hr); Wuhan (4hr); Xiangfan (6hr); Xing Shan (4hr).

Ferries

Jiujiang to: Guichi (for Jiuhua Shan and Huang Shan; daily; 12hr); Nanjing (daily; 24hr); Shanghai (daily; 48hr); Wuhan (8 daily; 12hr).

Wuhan to: Chongqing (daily; 5 days); Jiujiang (18hr); Nanjing (daily; 48hr); Shanghai (daily; 3 days); Wuhu (daily; 30hr); Yichang (daily; 36hr).

Yichang to: Chongqing (daily; 2–3 days); Wuhan (daily; 22hr).

Flights

Changsha to: Beijing (5 daily; 3hr); Chongqing (1 daily; 1hr 45min); Guangzhou (3 daily; 1hr); Hefei (1 daily; 1hr 35min); Hong Kong (7 weekly; 1hr 30min); Shanghai (4 daily; 1hr 30min); Shenzhen (2 daily; 1hr 10min); Wuhan (8 weekly; 1hr 10min); Zhangjiajie (1 daily; 45min).

Hefei to: Beijing (2 daily; 1hr 40min); Changsha (1 daily; 1hr 35min); Guangzhou (2 daily; 1hr 45min); Nanchang (2 weekly; 1hr); Shenzhen (2 daily; 2hr); Tunxi (1 daily; 1hr); Xiamen (1 daily; 1hr 10min); Xi'an (1 daily; 1hr 30min).

Nanchang to: Beijing (3 daily; 2hr 20min); Ganzhou (4 weekly; 1hr 15min); Guangzhou (2 daily; 1hr 10min); Hefei (2 weekly; 1hr); Shanghai (4 daily; 1hr); Tunxi (2 weekly; 50min); Wuhan (2 weekly; 50min).

Tunxi (Huang Shan) to: Beijing (5 weekly; 2hr); Guangzhou (1 daily; 1hr 40min); Hefei (1 daily; 1hr); Nanchang (2 weekly; 50min); Shanghai (6 weekly; 50min); Wuhan (2 weekly; 1hr).
Wuhan to: Beijing (4 daily; 1hr 50min); Changsha (8 weekly; 1hr 10min); Guangzhou (7 daily; 1hr 15min); Hong Kong (daily; 1hr 50min); Nanchang (2 weekly, 50min); Shanghai (4 daily; 1hr); Tunxi (2 weekly; 1hr); Zhangjiajie (2 weekly; 50min).
Yichang to: Beijing (3 weekly; 2hr); Chongqing (10 weekly; 50min); Guangzhou (4 weekly; 1hr 45min); Shanghai (4 weekly; 1hr 10min); Zhangjiajie (6 weekly; 50min–4hr).
Zhangjiajie to: Changsha (1 daily; 45min); Wuhan (2 weekly; 50min); Yichang (6 weekly; 50min–4hr).

CHAPTER 8

Highlights

* **Wuyi Shan** Take a bamboo raft through dramatic gorges or explore hiking trails in this mountain park. **See p.598**

* **Gulangyu Island** Uniquely relaxing island sporting vehicle-free streets, European-style colonial mansions, and sea views. **See p.613**

* **Hakka Mansions** These circular mud-brick homes housing up to five hundred people are China's most distinctive traditional architecture. **See p.615**

* **Cantonese food** Sample China's finest cuisine, from *dim sum* to roast goose, in one of Guangzhou's restaurants. **See p.640**

* **Chaozhou** Old town with Ming-dynasty walls, some great street life, the famous Kaiyuan temple, and more good food. **See p.671**

8

Fujian, Guangdong and Hainan Island

There's something very self-contained about the provinces of **Fujian**, **Guangdong** and **Hainan Island**, which occupy 1200km or so of China's convoluted southern seaboard. Though occasionally taking centre stage in the country's history, the provinces share a sense of being generally isolated from mainstream events by the mountain ranges which surround Fujian and Guangdong, physically cutting off the rest of the empire. Forced to look seawards, the coastal regions have a long history of contact with the outside world, continually importing – or being forced to endure – foreign influences and styles. This is where Islam entered China and porcelain and tea left it along the **Maritime Silk Road**; where the mid-nineteenth-century theatricals of the Opium Wars, colonialism, the Taiping Uprising and the mass overseas exodus of southern Chinese were played out; and where today you'll find China's most Westernized cities. Conversely, the interior mountains enclose some of the country's wildest, remotest corners, parts of which were literally in the Stone Age within living memory.

Possibly because its specific attractions are thinly spread, the region receives scant attention from visitors. Huge numbers do pass through Guangdong in transit between the mainland and Hong Kong and Macau, but only because they have to, and few look beyond the overpowering capital, **Guangzhou**. Yet while the other two regional capitals – **Fuzhou** in Fujian, and Hainan's **Haikou** – share Guangzhou's modern veneer, all three also hide temples and antique architecture that have somehow escaped developers, while other cities and towns have managed to preserve their old, character-laden ambience intact. The pick of these are the Fujian port of **Xiamen**, its streets almost frozen in time since the start of the twentieth century, and **Chaozhou** in eastern Guangdong, a staunchly conservative place consciously preserving its traditions in the face of the modern world.

Indeed, a sense of local tradition and of being different from the rest of the country pervades the whole region, though this feeling is rarely expressed in any tangible way. **Language** is one difference you will notice, however, as the main dialects here are Cantonese and Minnan, whose rhythms are recognizably removed from Mandarin, even if you can't speak a word of Chinese. Southern pronunciation is also very distinct: "h" and "k" replace "f" and "j" respectively, for instance, so that "Fujian" comes out as "Hokkian" in local parlance. Less

obvious are specific **ethnic groups**, including the **Hakka**, a widely spread Han sub-group whose mountainous Guangdong–Fujian heartland is dotted with fortress-like mansions; the Muslim **Hui**, who form large communities in Guangzhou, coastal Hainan and in **Quanzhou** in Fujian; and the **Li**, Hainan's animistic, original inhabitants.

While a quick look around much of the coastal areas here leaves a gloomy impression of uncontrolled development and its attendant ills (some cities seem to consist of nothing but beggars and building sites), most of this is actually contained within various **Special Economic Zones** (SEZs), specifically created in the mid-1980s as a focus for heavy investment and industrialization. Beyond their boundaries lurk some respectably wild – and some nicely tamed – corners where you can settle back and enjoy the scenery. Over in western Guangdong, the city of **Zhaoqing** sits beside pleasant lakes and hills, while the **Wuyi Shan** range in northeastern Fujian contains the region's lushest, most picturesque mountain forests. Way down south, the country's best **beaches** have encouraged the tourist industry to hype Hainan as "China's Hawaii", and there's also a limited amount of hiking to try through the island's interior highlands.

Anyone wanting to stop off and explore will find plentiful local and long-distance **transport**, though **accommodation** can be expensive and suffers additional seasonal price hikes in Guangzhou. The **weather** is nicest in spring and autumn, as summer storms from June to August bring daily doses of heavy humidity, thunder and afternoon downpours on the coast, while the higher reaches of the Guangdong–Fujian border can get very cold in winter.

Fujian

FUJIAN, on China's southeastern coast, is well off the beaten track for most Western travellers, which is a pity because the province possesses not only a wild mountainous interior, but also a string of old ports, including **Xiamen**, China's most attractive and interesting coastal city. From Hong Kong the well-trodden routes head directly west towards Guilin, or north to Shanghai, but a detour to Xiamen makes an excellent introduction to mainland China – boats from Hong Kong come here, as does a spur of China's rail network.

Culturally and geographically, the province splits into distinct halves. One is made up of large, historical seaports and lush, semi-tropical coastal stretches, whose sophisticated population enjoy warm sun and blossoming trees even in January. The other is a rugged, mountainous and largely inaccessible interior, freezing cold in winter, home to around 140 different local dialects and with a history of poverty and backwardness: when the Red Army arrived in the 1960s they found communities unaware that the Qing dynasty had been overthrown; and even today, the area is wild enough to harbour the last few populations of **South China tiger**. However, while inland Fujian knew very little of China, contacts between the coastal area and the outside world had been flourishing for centuries. In the Tang dynasty, the port of **Quanzhou**, considered on a par with Alexandria as the most international port in the world, teemed with Middle Eastern traders, some of whose descendants still live in the area today. So much wealth was brought into the ports here that a population explosion led to mass emigration, and large parts of the Malay Peninsula, the Philippines and Taiwan were colonized by Fujianese. In the early eighteenth century this exodus of able-bodied subjects became so drastic that the imperial court in distant Beijing tried, ineffectually, to ban it.

Today the interior of Fujian remains largely unvisited and unknown, with the exception of the scenic **Wuyi Shan** area in the northwest of the province, and the **Hakka regions** around southwesterly **Yongding**. The coast, however, is booming, with colossal investment pouring in from both Hong Kong and, in particular, neighbouring **Taiwan**, many of whose citizens originate from the province and speak the same dialect, Minnan Hua. The cities of **Fuzhou** and **Xiamen** are among the wealthiest in the country, particularly Xiamen, whose clean beaches, charming streets and shopping arcades, it's hoped, represent the face of Chinese cities to come. The proximity of Taiwan to Xiamen accounts not only for the rapid economic development and the proliferation of first-class tourist facilities, but also for the occasional outbreak of tension, such as during the 1996 Taiwanese presidential election when the mainland authorities suddenly decided to hold large-scale military exercises just off the Taiwanese coast, as a gentle reminder to the Taiwanese people not to vote for separatist candidates.

Getting around Fujian has improved considerably in recent years, with an extremely fast **coastal expressway** linking the main cities with neighbouring Zhejiang and Guangdong provinces. For reaching the interior wilds of Wuyi Shan you're better off catching a **train**, with separate lines from Fuzhou, Quanzhou and Xiamen; Fuzhou also has a decent link through to Jiangxi province, and there's another track west to Meizhou in Guangdong from Xiamen and Quanzhou. Otherwise, train travel within or beyond the province is circuitous and very slow.

Fuzhou

Capital of Fujian province, **FUZHOU** is comfortably modern and clean city, with shiny business highrises looming over the main roads. There's precious little to detain casual visitors though, and the city is probably best seen as a springboard for reaching the wilds of Wuyi Shan.

Fuzhou has been an important trading centre for over a thousand years, and was visited by Marco Polo during the Yuan dynasty. In the fifteenth century, Fuzhou shipbuilders earned themselves the distinction of having built the world's largest ocean-going ship, the *Baochuan*, sailed by the famous Chinese navigator Zheng He, who used it to travel all around Asia and Africa. One thing Polo noted when he was here was the high-profile presence of Mongol armies to suppress any potential uprisings, and, by coincidence, the city is no less well defended today, forming the heart of Fujian's military opposition to Taiwan – even as Taiwan's proximity has contributed to the enormity of Fuzhou's recent economic boom.

Fuzhou

Fuzhou	福州	***fúzhōu***
Bai Ta	白塔	*báitǎ*
Changle Airport	长乐机场	*chánglè jīchǎng*
Fuzhou Provincial Museum	福建省博物馆	*fújiànshěng bówùguǎn*
Gu Shan	鼓山	*gǔshān*
Lin Zexu Memorial Hall	林则徐纪念馆	*línzéxú jìniànguǎn*
Mao Statue	毛塑像	*máo sùxiàng*
Min River	闽江	*mǐnjiāng*
Wu Ta	乌塔	*wūtǎ*
Wuyi Square	五一广场	*wǔyī guǎngchǎng*
Xi Hu Park	西湖公园	*xīhú gōngyuán*
Yu Shan	于山	*yúshān*
Accommodation and eating		
Foreign Trade Centre	外宾中心酒店	*wàibīnzhōngxīn jiǔdiàn*
Galaxy Garden	银河花园大饭店	*yínhéhuāyuán dàfàndiàn*
Hao Ke Lai	豪客来	*háokè lái*
Haoyun	好运宾馆	*hǎoyùn bīnguǎn*
Huoguo Cheng	火锅城	*huǒguō chéng*
Minhang	民航大厦	*mínháng dàshà*
Nanyang	南洋饭店	*nányáng fàndiàn*
Wenquan	温泉大饭店	*wēnquán dàfàndiàn*
Yu San Mei Canyuan	于三美餐园	*yúsānměi cānyuán*

Arrival and accommodation

Flowing east–west through the city, the **Min River** roughly delineates the southern border of Fuzhou. The five-kilometre-long main north–south axis, called **Wusi Lu** in the north and **Wuyi Lu** farther south, cuts right through the city, intersecting with Dong Jie, and farther south with Gutian Lu, marking the centre of the city at **Wuyi Square**. The main shopping areas are **Bayiqi Lu** (parallel with Wuyi Lu), the area around Gutian Lu, and one more much farther south, almost at the river on Rongcheng Gujie.

Changle airport is 50km south of the city, from where an **airport bus** (¥18) runs to the CAAC office on Wuyi Lu, a few minutes north of Guohuo Lu. From the **train station**, in the far northeast of town, bus #51 runs straight down Wusi and Wuyi roads to the Min River, while bus #17 runs down Bayiqi Lu. Arriving **by bus**, you'll almost certainly end up at either the **North station**, a few minutes' walk south of the train station, or the **South station** at the junction of Guohuo Lu and Wuyi Lu – both handle arrivals from just about everywhere.

Fuzhou's **PSB** is opposite the sports complex on Beihuan Zhong Lu (☎0591/7821104). The main **post office** is at the southeastern intersection of Dong Jie and Bayiqi Bei Lu. There's an **Internet bar** in a lane south off Dong Jie, near Wuyi Lu.

Accommodation

Most of Fuzhou's accommodation is upmarket, but there are a few budget options which can usually be persuaded to take foreigners, most notably around the train and North bus stations.

Moving on from Fuzhou

For booking **tours** to Wuyi Shan, or tickets for trains, planes, or luxury buses to Xiamen, Guangzhou and Shenzhen, approach either CITS (☎0591/7552052) or CTS (☎0591/7536250), either side of the *Minjiang* hotel.

By air

You can **fly** from Fuzhou to Wuyi Shan and a host of major cities, including Hong Kong and Macau; the CAAC **ticket office** is on Wuyi Lu (daily 8am–8pm; ☎0591/3340268). Travelling to the **airport**, pick up the bus from inside the courtyard of the *Fujian Civil Aviation Hotel*, next door – the journey takes an hour and you'll need to get to the airport at least an hour before your departure.

By train

Fuzhou is the terminus for a couple of fairly remote **rail lines**. Heading northwest, trains run to Wuyi Shan, and through into Jiangxi and the rest of China; be aware that most trains to Guangdong province also travel this way and so take much longer than you'd expect. The new line west from Fuzhou via Longyan to Meizhou in eastern Guangdong has sparse services at present, and it may well be faster to take a bus for these destinations. The **ticket office** is west of the station (the left as you face it); you'll almost certainly need to reserve sleeper berths a day in advance.

By bus

Long-distance buses to everywhere in Fujian and neighbouring provinces leave from both bus stations. There are several sleepers daily to Wuyi Shan, and constant departures along the coastal expressway to Quanzhou, Xiamen and Guangdong; just remember that, if you've a choice, there's a huge price discrepancy between standard and luxury buses.

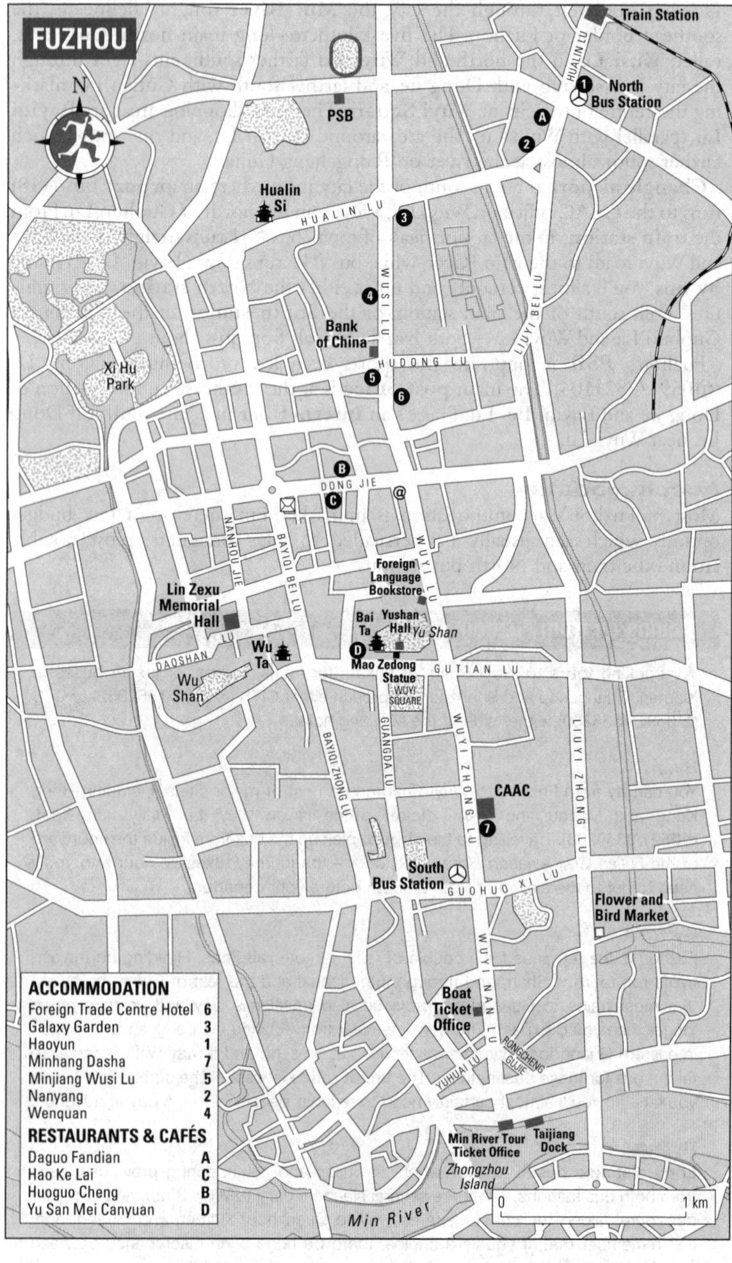
FUZHOU
N
Train Station
HUALIN LU
North Bus Station
PSB
Hualin Si
HUALIN LU
WUSI LU
LIUYI BEI LU
Bank of China
HUDONG LU
Xi Hu Park
DONG JIE
NANHOU JIE
BAYIQI BEI LU
WUYI LU
Foreign Language Bookstore
Lin Zexu Memorial Hall
Bai Ta
Yushan Hall
Yu Shan
Wu Ta
DAOSHAN LU
Mao Zedong Statue
GUTIAN LU
Wu Shan
WUYI SQUARE
BAYIQI ZHONG LU
GUANGDA LU
WUYI ZHONG LU
LIUYI ZHONG LU
CAAC
South Bus Station
GUOHUO XI LU
Flower and Bird Market
Boat Ticket Office
WUYI NAN LU
RONGCHENG GUJIE
YUHUAI LU
Min River Tour Ticket Office
Taijiang Dock
Zhongzhou Island
Min River
0
1 km
ACCOMMODATION
Foreign Trade Centre Hotel 6
Galaxy Garden 3
Haoyun 1
Minhang Dasha 7
Minjiang Wusi Lu 5
Nanyang 2
Wenquan 4
RESTAURANTS & CAFÉS
Daguo Fandian A
Hao Ke Lai C
Huoguo Cheng B
Yu San Mei Canyuan D

Foreign Trade Centre Hotel, Wusi Lu ⓣ0591/7523388, ⓕ7550358. Undoubtedly the best hotel in town, but so large it tends to feel rather lonely and empty most of the time. ❾

Galaxy Garden Cnr of Hualin Lu and Wusi Lu ⓣ0591/7831888, ⓕ7843662. New business-oriented hotel with smart furnishings and attentive staff. ❻

Haoyun Right beside the North bus station ⓣ0591/7578208. One of many budget hotels in the vicinity. Beds from ¥35, ❷

Minhang Dasha Next to CAAC, Wuyi Zhong Lu ⓣ0591/3343988, ⓕ3341978. Brand new hotel run by CAAC, with spacious, clean rooms, a fair deal for the price. ❻

Minjiang Wusi Lu ⓣ0591/7557895, ⓕ7551489. Mid-range hotel with ageing but sound rooms, well placed just south of Hu Dong Lu on the way into the centre from the train station. CITS are based here. ❻

Nanyang Hualin Lu ⓣ0591/7579699, ⓕ7577085. A convenient location near the train and North bus stations. Rooms a bit frayed for the price, but staff are helpful. ❹

Wenquan (aka Hot Spring) Wusi Lu ⓣ0591/7851818, ⓦwww.hshfz.com. A smart hotel with a cavernous interior full of Pierre Cardin shops and the like. Service is excellent, as you'd expect for the price. ❾

The City

Almost totally devoid of formal sights – though many small, nondescript temples are secreted away between more modern structures – Fuzhou is centred around **Wuyi Square**, an open expanse dominated by a statue of Mao Zedong looking south. This statue commemorates the Ninth Congress of the Chinese Communist Party in 1969, an event that ratified Maoism as the "state religion" of China, and named the mysterious Lin Biao (subsequently disgraced) as official heir to Mao's throne. Just behind Mao's statue, the large modern building is Yushan Hall, sometimes used for exhibitions, while climbing up a path to the west of the hall lands you at the gates of **Yu Shan** (Jade Hill; daily 8am–6pm; ¥5). The main sight here is the thousand-year-old **Bai Ta**, a whitewashed pagoda located beside a temple and a small exhibition of the contents of a local Song-dynasty tomb, which includes the preserved bodies of a man and a woman and some silk garments.

West from Yu Shan is **Bayiqi Lu**, a busy, crowded avenue at the heart of Fuzhou's shopping district. On the far side is another small hill, Wu Shan, currently isolated by a sea of demolitions and roadworks. The flat summit, fringed in banyan trees, is capped by a small temple and **Wu Ta**, a black granite pagoda dating back to the same era as the White Tower and containing some attractive statuary. North from here on Aomen Lu, you'll find the **Lin Zexu Memorial Hall** (daily 8am–5pm; ¥5), a quiet, attractive couple of halls and courtyards with funereal statues of animals. Lin Zexu (1785–1850) is fondly remembered as the patriotic Qing-dynasty official who fought against the importation of opium by foreigners – even writing persuasive letters to Queen Victoria on the subject – though his destruction of thousands of chests of the drug in 1840 sparked the first Opium War and, rather unfairly, he was exiled to Xinjiang.

The northwest of the city is dominated by **Xi Hu Park** (daily 7am–9pm; ¥4), whose entrance is along southerly Hu Bin Lu – you can get here on buses #1 or #2 from the southern end of Bayiqi Lu, or #810 from the train station. The park, mostly comprising an artificial lake formed by excavations some seventeen hundred years ago, is a good spot to go boating or stroll with the masses on a hot day. Within the grounds, the **Fuzhou Provincial Museum** used to include a 3500-year-old coffin-boat removed from a Wuyi Shan cave, though it's currently closed for rebuilding.

The south

The southern part of the city, down towards the river, contains another dusting of sights. Awkwardly located just east off Liuyi Lu, the north–south express road to the east of Wusi/Wuyi Lu, is the **flower and bird market** (bus #8 from Gutian Lu), packed at weekends with people buying caged birds and puppies. Farther south, right by the river, several pedestrianized streets are crammed with shoppers, especially the small, old-style streets between the southern ends of Bayiqi Lu and Wuyi Lu, and Rongcheng Gujie just east of Wuyi Lu.

On the riverfront itself, facing the southern end of Wuyi Lu, you'll find Taijiang dock and a kiosk (daily 8.30am–4.30pm) selling tickets for the **Min River boat tour**. This is a great trip, in which the boat proceeds slowly to the mouth of the river and back again, offering views of barges, freighters and all the paraphernalia of river life. The tour lasts from 7.30am to 5pm and costs ¥53 but runs only when there is sufficient demand – most probable during the summer and at weekends. The ticket office will know the afternoon before if boats will be running for the following day.

The area **south** of the river, including the small mid-river island Zhongzhou (reached from Jiefang Bridge), is worth a wander if you're in the vicinity. The **former foreign concession** was based here and some of the old banks, consulates, residences and churches can still be seen. A random stroll along the south bank and the neighbouring streets will uncover any number of buildings in the colonial style with verandas and shuttered windows. Bus #1 coming down Bayiqi Lu from Xi Hu Park crosses to the south bank.

Gu Shan

Fuzhou's most-touted tourist attraction is **Gu Shan** (Drum Mountain), about 9km east of the city. To get here, catch one of the regular **minibuses** from the Nanmen terminus on Guangda Lu, just west of Wuyi Square (¥8); it's an attractive 45-minute journey through forested hills, with sweeping views as the road starts climbing. The Gu Shan area offers walks through the woods as well as scattered sights, including the 1000-year-old, heavily restored **Yongquan Si**, which gets phenomenally crowded at weekends. One way to escape the crowds is to climb the 2500 stone steps behind the temple to the wooded summit of Gu Shan.

Eating and drinking

For such a major city, Fuzhou suffers a serious lack of **restaurants** outside the hotels, though Western and Chinese fast-food chains are omnipresent. For **snacks**, street vendors pedal small, bagel-like "cut buns" (*gua bao*), stuffed with vegetables or a slice of spiced, steamed pork, and hole-in-the-wall operations surround transit points; otherwise, the highest concentration of places to eat is along downtown Dong Jie. One of the best places here for inexpensive, tasty and varied food in a comfortable setting is *Hao Ke Lai*, which serves Sichuan-style cold spiced meats and vegetables, along with soups, noodles, spring rolls and local buns, all at a few yuan a serve – look for the yellow and green sign spelling out "Houcaller". Across the road, the huge *Huoguo Cheng* is a full-on noisy and busy hotpot restaurant with two-person pots from ¥38. North off Wuyi Square on Gutian Lu, *Yu San Mei Canyuan* has an inexpensive first-floor canteen for snacks and an upstairs formal restaurant specializing in fish dishes – two can eat well here for ¥50.

Wuyi Shan

Away in the northeast of the province, 370km from Fuzhou and close to the Fujian–Jiangxi border, the **Wuyi Shan** scenic district contains some of the most unspoilt and picturesque scenery in southern China. It's the only inland

Wuyi Shan		
Wuyi Shan Scenic District	武夷山风景区	***wǔyíshān fēngjǐng qū***
Chishi	赤石	*chìshí*
Chongyang Stream	崇阳溪	*chóngyáng xī*
Dawang Feng	大王峰	*dàwáng fēng*
Jiuqu River	九曲溪	*jiǔqū xī*
Shuilian Cave	水帘洞	*shuǐlián dòng*
Tianyou Feng	天游峰	*tiānyóu fēng*
Wuyigong	武夷宫	*wǔyí gōng*
Wuyishan Shi	武夷山市	*wǔyíshān shì*
Yingzui Yan	鹰嘴岩	*yīngzuǐ yán*
Accommodation		
Jiuqu	酒曲宾馆	*jiǔqū bīnguǎn*
Wuyi Shan Manting Villa	武夷山幔亭山房	*wǔyíshān màntíng shānfáng*
Wuyishan Shi Work Hotel	武夷山市劳动宾馆	*wǔyíshān shìláodòng bīnguǎn*

area of Fujian regularly visited by tourists and consists of two principal parts, the **Jiuqu River** which meanders at the feet of the mountains, and the **Thirty-six Peaks** that rise up from the river, mostly to its north. With peaks protruding from low-lying mists, the scenery is classic Chinese scroll-painting material, and the reserve, dotted with small, attractive villages, can be a tremendous place to relax for a few days, offering clean mountain air and leisurely walks through scenery of lush green vegetation, deep red sandstone mountains, soaring cliff faces, rock pools, waterfalls and caves. Despite the remoteness, Wuyi is surprisingly full of tourists – especially Taiwanese – in high summer, so a visit off-season might be preferable, when you'll also see the mountain tops cloaked with snow. Note that all tourists here are regarded as fair game for some serious overcharging.

Practicalities

The sixty-square-kilometre site is bordered by the **Jiuqu** (Nine-Twisting) **River** to the south, which runs its crooked course for some 8km between **Xingcun** village to the west, and the main village in the area, **WUYIGONG** to the east – where it joins the **Chongyang Stream** running from north to south and bordering the area to the east. Wuyigong, which contains the bus stop and some hotels, lies in the cleft between the junction of these two waterways.

Most transport arrives 15km north of the scenic area at **WUYISHAN SHI**, the regional town. You can get here by **train** from Fuzhou, Quanzhou or Xiamen, or by **sleeper bus** (¥104) from Fuzhou. The alternative is to **fly** from Fuzhou (¥380 each way), Xiamen and other cities across China; **Wuyi airport** is at the village of Chishi, a few kilometres to the northeast of the scenic area and to the south of Wuyishan Shi. Minibuses connect Wuyishan Shi and the airport with Wuyigong. Fuzhou's CITS and CTS (see box on p.595) also run **tour buses** direct to Wuyigong.

Accommodation and eating

The *Jiuqu* is perhaps the most scenically located **hotel** (Ⓣ0599/5252528, Ⓕ5252863; ❹), on the north bank of the river and at the head of many walking

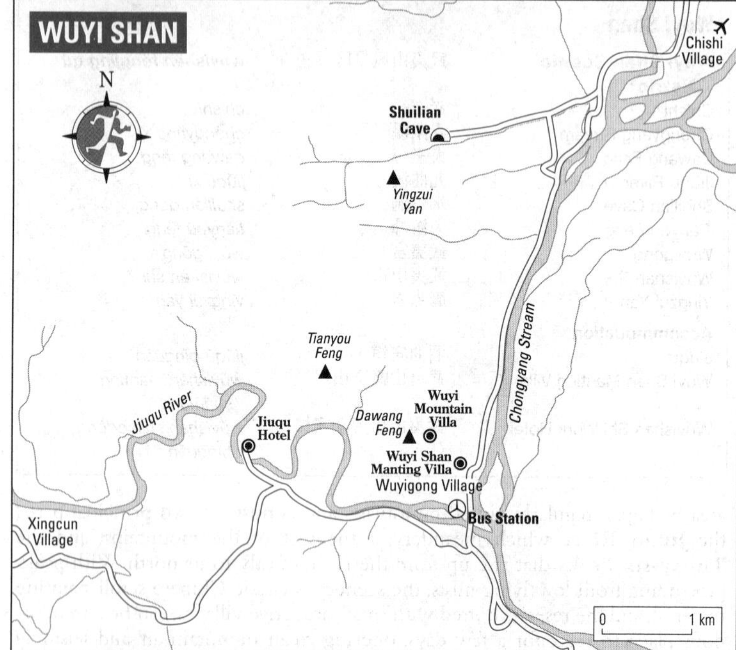

trails into the hills. Cycle-rickshaws and minibuses run between here and the village of Wuyigong. Alternatively, you can stay at the luxury hotels in Wuyigong itself, where the *Wuyi Shan Manting Villa* (❼), just north of the village, has a branch of CITS and a Western-style nightclub complex with bar, dance hall and plush restaurant. The *Wuyi Mountain Villa* (Ⓣ0599/5251888, Ⓕ5252567; ❻) nearby is even smarter, with a marvellous location, resting hard under Dawang Feng and built round a Suzhou-style ornamental garden. There are also much cheaper hotels in Wuyigong which periodically take foreigners. In Wuyishan Shi, the *Wuyishan Shi Work Hotel* has comfortable doubles (❻).

Foodwise, it's the local Shilin frogs which make **Wuyi cuisine** special; along with other popular dishes such as bamboo shoots and fungus, they're served almost everywhere. To get out of the hotel restaurants and eat with the locals, try the takeaway stalls in the villages.

The Thirty-six Peaks

There are a series of trails heading north into the mountains from the main trailhead area behind the *Jiuqu Hotel* (about halfway between Xingcun and Wuyigong). It costs a ruinous ¥62–91 to enter the trails here, depending on how much of the area you want to see, though it is possible to avoid this charge by walking a little downstream and looking for a path cut into the rock. The **mountains** look quite large and imposing, but in fact are relatively easy to climb. The summit of **Tianyou Feng** (Heavenly Tour Peak) is no more than a thirty-minute clamber away from the *Jiuqu Hotel*. The best time to get up here is early morning, when you can catch the sunrise and watch the early-

Bamboo-raft trips

The traditional, and still the best, way to appreciate the Wuyi Shan area is to take a leisurely two-hour **bamboo-raft trip** along the Jiuqu River. The rafts leave daily between 7.30am and 2pm all year round, and you can pick one up more or less anywhere on the river. From the first crook in the meandering river right up to the ninth, you'll have stupendous gorge scenery all the way. The odd boat-shaped **coffins** in caves you can glimpse above the fourth crook are said to be 4000 years old, and appear similar to those in Gongxian and along the Little Three Gorges in Sichuan (see p.956 and p.968). The fee for a six-passenger raft along all nine twists is ¥425 – if you're on your own, join a group and negotiate your fare as a fraction of the total cost.

morning mists clear to reveal a good view of the nine crooks in the Jiuqu River. There are a number of tiny pavilions and **tea gardens** on the lower slopes should you need sustenance on the way up. **Tea** is a huge institution in Fujian, and Wuyi Shan is famous as the original home of **Oolong**, one of the few types known by name in the West. Leaves for Oolong are picked when mature, then processed by alternately bruising, fermenting and airing before being fire-dried; one of the best varieties is the widely available *tie guanyin cha*, or Iron Buddha Tea.

Another peak well worth the ascent is **Dawang Feng** (King of Peaks) at the easternmost end of the river, north of Wuyigong, more of a gentle walk than a climb (2hr). If you have time, try to get to the **Shuilian Cave**, about 6km north of the river; you can walk along easy trails or take a minibus from the *Jiuqu Hotel* area or from Wuyigong. The cave is about halfway up a cliff of red sandstone, down which a large waterfall cascades in the summer months. You can sit in the adjacent teahouse, cut out of the rock, while the waterfall literally crashes down beside you (watch out for a heavy charge at the entrance to the cave, though). The walk between the cave and river passes tea plantations, more teahouses and all kinds of little sights, including **Yingzui Yan** (Eagle Beak Crag), whose point of interest is the walkways leading to a set of caves where, during the Taiping Uprising, local bigwigs fled to escape persecution.

Quanzhou and around

I tell you that for one shipload of pepper which may go to Alexandria or to other places, to be carried into Christian lands, there come more than one hundred of them to this port.

Thus wrote Marco Polo when he visited **QUANZHOU**, then called Zaytoun (from the Arabic word for olive, symbol of peace and prosperity), in the late thirteenth century. At this time, Quanzhou was a great port, one of the two largest in the world, exploiting its deep natural harbour and sitting astride trade routes which reached southeast to Indonesian Maluku, and west to Africa and Europe. It became uniquely cosmopolitan, with tens of thousands of Arabs and Persians settling here, some of them to make colossal fortunes – the Arabs of Quanzhou are also believed responsible for introducing to the West the Chinese inventions of the compass, gunpowder and printing.

Quanzhou and around

Quanzhou	泉州	***quánzhōu***
Fuwen Miao	府文庙	*fŭwén miào*
Guandi Miao	关帝庙	*guāndì miào*
Kaiyuan Si	开元寺	*kāiyuán sì*
Maritime Museum	海外交通史博物馆	*hăiwàijiāotōngshĭ bówùguăn*
Qingjing Mosque	清净寺	*qīngjìng sì*
Qingyuan Shan	清源山	*qīngyuán shān*
Sheng Mu	伊斯兰教圣墓	*yīsī lánjiào shèngmù*
Tianhou Gong	天后宫	*tiānhòu gōng*
Accommodation, eating and drinking		
Chongqing Huoguo	重庆火锅	*chóngqìng huŏguŏ*
Coffee Language	尚典啡茶语	*shàngdiănfēi cháyŭ*
Great Wall	长城宾馆	*chángchéng bīnguăn*
Gucuo Chadian	古厝茶店	*gŭcuò chádiàn*
Huaqiao Zhijia	华侨之家	*huáqiáo zhījiā*
Jinquan	金泉酒店	*jīnquán jiŭdiàn*
Jinzhou	金州大酒店	*jīnzhōu dàjiŭdiàn*
Lanbai	蓝白餐厅	*lánbái cāntīng*
Qiwei Yazai	奇味鸭仔	*qíwèi yāzăi*
Quanzhou	泉州酒店	*quánzhōu jiŭdiàn*
Shishi Ming Xiaochi	石狮名小吃	*shíshīmíng xiăochī*
Zhonglou	钟楼旅社	*zhōnglóu lǚshè*
Anping Bridge	安平桥	***ānpíng qiáo***
Chongwu	崇武古城	***chóngwŭ gŭchéng***
Shishi	石狮	***shíshī***
Sisters-in-law Tower	姑嫂塔	*gūsăo tă*

The Song and Yuan dynasties saw the peak of Quanzhou's fortunes, when the old Silk Road through northwestern China into Central Asia was falling prey to banditry and war, deflecting trade seawards along the **Maritime Silk Road**. Polo was by no means the only European to visit Quanzhou around this time: the Italian **Andrew Perugia**, Quanzhou's third Catholic bishop, died here in 1332 having supervised the building of a cathedral; and fourteen years later the great Moroccan traveller **Ibn Battuta** saw the port bustling with large junks. But by the Qing era, the city was suffering from overcrowding and a decaying harbour, and an enormous **exodus** began, with people seeking new homes in Southeast Asia. According to Chinese government statistics, there are more than two million Quanzhounese living abroad today – as compares with just half a million remaining in the entire municipal area. Despite these depredations of history, Quanzhou today retains several reminders of its glorious past, and it's certainly worth a stopover between Fuzhou and Xiamen.

The Town and around

Quanzhou is a small town, located entirely on the northeast bank of the Jin River, and the majority of its sights can be reached on foot. The two major north–south streets are Zhongshan Lu and Wenling Lu. The town centre falls mainly between these two, with the oldest part of town to the west, and up along the northern section of Zhongshan Lu where you'll find attractively restored colonial-era arcaded streets, lined with trees and packed with pedestrians and cyclists. As in Fuzhou, there are plenty of minor temples scattered around, perhaps the best of which is **Tianhou Gong** (¥4), a large airy hall at the southern end of Zhongshan Lu crammed with worshippers asking help from southeastern China's most popular deity, the Heavenly Empress.

One of the town centre's most interesting areas lies north off **Tumen Jie**, Quanzhou's main east–west street, which sports a surprisingly well-integrated collection of genuine antique buildings and modern shops with traditional flourishes. Heading northwest up Tumen Jie from its junction with Wenling Lu, you'll first encounter **Guandi Miao**, a splendid temple dedicated to the Three Kingdoms hero-turned-god of war and healing, Guan Yu (see p.509). The temple's roofline is typically florid and curly, and the atmospheric interior – guarded by life-sized statues of soldiers on horesback – features low-ceilinged halls, smoke-grimed statues and wall engravings showing scenes from Guan Yu's life.

Almost the next building along, the granite-built **Qingjing Mosque** (daily 8am–5pm; ¥3) provides firm evidence of just how established the Arabs became in medieval Quanzhou. Founded by Arab settlers in 1009 and rebuilt by Persian Muslims three centuries later, Qingjing ranks as one of the oldest mosques in China and is highly unusual in being Middle Eastern in design, though only parts of the original buildings survive. The tall gate tower is said to be an exact copy of a Damascus original, its leaf-shaped archway embellished with fourteenth-century Arabic calligraphy and designs, while parts of

the walls and supporting pillars of the original prayer hall stand alongside. A side room has a detailed account of the Arab presence in Quanzhou, with an English translation; the small tiled building next door is the modern prayer hall.

West between Qingjing and Zhongshan Lu, an ornamental gateway leads north to a broad paved square, at the back of which is a Confucian temple, **Fuwen Miao**. This isn't of great importance, but the square is dotted with freshly restored examples of Quanzhou's **traditional domestic architecture**, all built of granite blocks and characteristic red bricks marked with dark chevrons, the roof ridges pulled up into projecting forks. At present this display is rather unfocused, though presumably an open-air museum is being planned.

Kaiyuan Si

Quanzhou's most impressive historical remains are at **Kaiyuan Si**, a huge, restful temple dotted with magnificent trees in the northwest of town on Xi Jie (¥7). Bus #2 runs up here from the long-distance bus station, but it's much more interesting to follow the backstreets from the Tumen Jie/Zhongshan Lu intersection, through narrow lanes lined with elderly homes. Founded in 686 AD, Kaiyuan was built, legend has it, after the owner of a mulberry grove dreamed of a Buddhist monk who asked him to erect a place of worship on his land. "Only if my mulberry trees bear lotus flowers," replied the owner dismissively – whereupon the lotus flowers duly appeared. In memory of this, an ancient mulberry in the temple courtyard bears the sign "Mulberry Lotus Tree". The two five-storey **stone pagodas** were added in the thirteenth century, apart from which the whole complex was rebuilt during the Ming dynasty after being destroyed by fire.

The temple is highly regarded architecturally, not least for its details which include a hundred stone columns supporting the roof of the **main hall**, most of which are carved with delicate musicians holding instruments or sacrificial objects. Surviving everything from earthquakes to the Red Guards, the unimaginably solid pagodas are also carved on each of their eight sides with two images of the Buddha; inside, one of them has forty Buddhist stories inscribed on its walls. The temple grounds also hold a special **exhibition hall** (¥2) housing the hull of a twelfth- or thirteenth-century **wooden sailing vessel** found in 1974 (a series of photos detail the stages of the excavation), still with the herbs and spices it had been carrying preserved in its hold.

The Maritime Museum

Across on the northeast side of town on Dong Hu Lu, the **Maritime Museum** (Tues–Sun 8.30am–5.30pm; ¥10; bus #19 from the long-distance bus station) recalls Quanzhou's trading history and illustrates how advanced Chinese shipbuilders were compared to their European contemporaries. Two floors of exhibits track the development of Chinese boatbuilding, reaching as far back as the Warring States period (around 500 BC). A corner devoted to the "Recovery of Taiwan from the Greedy Grasp of the Dutch Invaders and the Development of Foreign Trade" reinterprets **Koxinga**'s exploits (see p.607) in a modern light, but the museum's heart is hundreds of lovingly made **wooden models**, illustrating everything from small coastal junks to Zheng He's mighty *Baochuan* – possibly the largest wooden vessel ever made – and ornate pleasure boats used by the wealthy for touring China's famous lakes and rivers.

While you're here, don't miss the first-floor collection of **tombstones** dating back to Quanzhou's heyday. Most of these are Muslim, but you'll also find those of Italians and Spaniards, Nestorian Christians from Syria, and the fourteenth-century Bishop, Andrew Perugia. In the back, stone pillars, lintels and statues show that there were also Hindus and Manicheans (followers of a Persian religion that drew on Christianity, Jainism and Buddhism) in Quanzhou, each with their own places of worship – further proof of Quanzhou's cosmopolitan heritage.

Qingyuan Shan and Sheng Mu

A few sites just outside the town warrant the effort of reaching them on local buses. The **Qingyuan Shan** scenic area is 3km to the north, with good views over Quanzhou from small crags and pavilions – though most people come out here for the huge stone **Laojun Yan**, a Song-dynasty sculpture of Laozi which is said to aid longevity if you climb onto its back and rub noses. Bus #3 comes up here from Tumen Jie and Zhongshan Zhong Lu.

East of the town centre on Donghu Jie, **Sheng Mu** is a Muslim cemetery housing the graves of two of Mohammed's disciples sent to China in the seventh century to do missionary work – and so presumably the first Muslims in China. There's little to see but it's a peaceful, semi-forested place; catch bus #7 from Wenling Lu to the Sheng Mu stop. The entrance can be seen to the south of the road – when you glimpse a stone archway, take the alley leading towards it.

Around Quanzhou

You'll need to use the **local bus station** on Wenling Lu to reach a handful of sights some way out of town. About 60km east of Quanzhou, **CHONGWU** is an old walled city built entirely of stone, now nicely restored as a huge museum piece. The adjacent new town has one of southern China's largest fishing fleets, with just about every man employed in this industry – the women work in local stone quarries, carting huge rocks around on carrypoles and wearing characteristic blue jackets and wide-brimmed straw hats. Slightly closer to the southeast is the town of **SHISHI** (Stone Lion), from where you can pick up a ride for the 5km to the beautiful **Sisters-in-law Tower**, another Song-dynasty monument, overlooking the sea. Finally, 30km south, just off the expressway to Xiamen and outside the town of Anhai, the spectacular two-kilometre-long **Anping Bridge**, also 800 years old, actually crosses a section of sea.

Practicalities

You'll most likely arrive in Quanzhou **by bus** along the coastal expressway between Xiamen and Fuzhou. The **long-distance bus station** is down in the newer, southeastern part of town, just east of Wenling Lu. From here there are frequent minibus connections between 8am and 5.30pm with Xiamen (¥15–40) and Fuzhou (¥35–70), as well as long-distance buses for practically anywhere in southern China, from Ningbo and Hangzhou in the north, to Guangzhou and Shenzhen in the south. Quanzhou's new **train station** is about 5km east down Dong Hu Jie; bus #23 from outside will get you to the long-distance bus station. There's an evening departure to Wuyi Shan, and slow services to Longyan, Yongding and Meizhou; a couple of **ticket offices** in town, just north of the *Great Wall* hotel on Wenling Lu and opposite the *Jinquan* hotel, save trekking out to the station. There's also a recently constructed **airport** about 20km southeast of town, from which you'll need to take a taxi. For all bookings, either try your accommodation or the **CTS office** near the *Jinquan* hotel on Daxi Jie. There are several **Internet cafés** in the lane north of the Qingjing mosque.

Accommodation

There's only one real budget accommodation option in Quanzhou (the *Zhonglou*, below) but the following hotels all offer a good deal.

Great Wall Wenling Lu ⓣ0595/2298081, ⓕ2288965. Excellent value, good location and friendly staff in this new hotel. ❸

Huaqiao Zhijia Southern end of Wenling Lu ⓣ0595/2283559, ⓕ2283560. Standard, fairly smart rooms. ❸

Jinquan (aka Golden Fountain) Baiyuan Lu ⓣ0595/2285078, ⓕ2281676. Situated on a small road leading south from Daxi Jie, this is the budget wing of the adjacent *Huaqiao Dasha*. The rooms have recently been renovated. ❹

Jinzhou Around from the bus station on Quanxiu Lu ⓣ0595/2586788. The exterior appears too decrepit to bother with, the lobby looks too upmarket, but rooms are good value, and they immediately discount if you haggle. ❸

Quanzhou Zhuangfu Xiang ⓣ0595/2289958, ⓦwww.quanzhouhotel.com. Semi-luxurious establishment right in the centre of town, just west of Zhongshan Lu. Old wing ❻, new wing ❾

Zhonglou Xi Jie ⓣ0595/2373433. About the cheapest place in town, in a lively, central area close to Kaiyuan Si at the junction with Zhongshan Lu. Beds from ¥20, ❷

Eating and drinking

For **food**, northern Zhongshan Lu, the area around Kaiyuan Si, and backstreets off Tumen Jie are thick with cheap noodle stalls and canteens. Light meals can be had at the good-value *Lanbai* canteen, next to the *Jinzhou* hotel, for around ¥10, or try *Chongqing Huoguo*, near the *Great Wall* hotel on Wenling Jie, for hotpot. For something slightly more upmarket, head north of the Bank of China on Nanjun Lu to *Qiwei Yazai*, a roast-duck restaurant, or *Shishi Ming Xiaochi*, which specializes in local snacks and buns. The *Jianfu* hotel serves weekend all-you-can-eat breakfast *dim sum* (¥15 a person) on the fifth floor.

Tumen Jie hosts several **cafés** serving Western sandwiches and grills, including a branch of *Coffee Language* at the corner with Wenling Lu, while the *Quanzhou* hotel has a Western-style restaurant and the *Jinquan* hotel has a coffee bar in the lobby. For something more traditional, *Gucuo Chadian* is a **teahouse** in an old brick home, in the lane directly behind Qingjing Mosque.

Xiamen

XIAMEN, traditionally known in the West as **Amoy**, is smaller and much prettier than the provincial capital Fuzhou, and offers a lot more to see, its streets and buildings, attractive shopping arcades and bustling seafront boasting a nineteenth-century European flavour. One of China's most tourist-friendly cities, Xiamen is in addition the cleanest and, perhaps, most tastefully renovated city you'll see anywhere in the country, giving it the feel of a holiday resort, despite the occasional seedy, fishy backstreet. Compounding the resort atmosphere is the wonderful little island of **Gulangyu**, a ten-minute ferry ride to the southwest, the old colonial home of Europeans and Japanese whose mansions still line the island's traffic-free streets – staying here is highly recommended.

A little history

Xiamen was founded in the mid-fourteenth century and grew in stature under the Ming dynasty, becoming a **thriving port** by the seventeenth century, influenced by a steady and rather secretive succession of Portuguese,

Xiamen and around

Xiamen	厦门	***xiàmén***
Bailu Dong	白鹿洞	*báilù dòng*
Huli Shan Paotai	胡里山炮台	*húlǐ shān pàotái*
Huxiyan	虎溪岩	*hǔxī yán*
Jinmen	金门	*jīnmén*
Nanputuo Si	南普陀寺	*nánpǔtuó sì*
Overseas Chinese Museum	华侨博物馆	*huáqiáo bówùguǎn*
Wanshi Botanical Gardens	万石植物馆	*wànshí zhíwùguǎn*
Xiamen University	厦门大学	*xiàmén dàxué*
Gulangyu	鼓浪屿	***gǔlàng yǔ***
Gulangyu Guesthouse	鼓浪屿宾馆	*gǔlàngyǔ bīnguǎn*
Haoyue Garden	皓月园	*hàoyuè yuán*
Koxinga Memorial Hall	郑成功纪念馆	*zhèngchénggōng jìniànguǎn*
Lizhi Dao	丽之岛酒店	*lìzhīdǎo jiǔdiàn*
Luzhou	绿洲酒店	*lǜzhōu jiǔdiàn*
Shuzhuang Garden	菽庄花园	*shūzhuāng huāyuán*
Statue of Koxinga	郑成功塑像	*zhèngchénggōng sùxiàng*
Sunlight Rock	日光岩	*rìguāng yán*
Underwater World	海底世界	*hǎidǐ shìjiè*
Yingxiong Shan	英雄山	*yīngxióng shān*
Jimei School Village	集美学校村	***jíměi xuéxiàocūn***
Ao Park	鳌园	*áoyuán*
Chen Jiageng (Tan Kahkee)	陈嘉庚	*chénjiā gēng*
Downtown accommodation and eating		
Donghai	东海大厦酒店	*dōnghǎi dàshà jiǔdiàn*
Gongde Caiguan	功德菜馆	*gōngdé càiguǎn*
Holiday Inn	假日皇冠海景大酒店	*jiàrì huángguān hǎijǐng dàshàjiǔdiàn*
Huangzehe Huashengtang Dian	黄则和花生汤店	*huángzéhé huāshēng tāngdiàn*
Jiaotong	交通大厦酒店	*jiāotōng dàshà jiǔdiàn*
Lujiang	鹭江宾馆	*lùjiāng bīnguǎn*
Xiamen Guesthouse	厦门宾馆	*xiàmén bīnguǎn*
Xiamen Spring Sunlight	厦门春光酒店	*xiàmén chūnguāng jiǔdiàn*
Xin Nan Xuan Jiujia	新南轩酒家	*xīnnánxuān jiǔjiā*
Xinqiao	新桥酒店	*xīnqiáo jiǔdiàn*

Spanish and Dutch fortune-hunters. When invading Manchu armies poured down from the north in the seventeenth century, driving out the Ming, Xiamen became a centre of resistance for the old regime. The pirate and self-styled **Prince Koxinga** (also known as Zheng Chenggong) led the resistance before being driven out to set up his last stronghold in Taiwan – incidentally deposing the Dutch traders who were based there – where he eventually died, before Taiwan too was taken by the Manchus. Koxinga's exploits have been heavily romanticized and reinterpreted over the years, and today his recapturing of Taiwan from unfriendly forces is used both to justify China's claims on its neighbour, and also to provide an example of how to pursue those claims.

A couple of hundred years later the **British** arrived, increasing trade and establishing their nerve centre on Gulangyu; the manoeuvre was formalized with the Treaty of Nanjing in 1842. By the start of the twentieth century, Xiamen, with its offshore foreigners, had become a relatively prosperous community, supported partly by a steady turnover in trade and by the trickle of wealth back from the city's emigrants, who over the centuries had continued to swell in numbers. This happy state of affairs continued until the **Japanese invasion** at the beginning of World War II.

The end of the war did not bring with it a return to the good old days, however. The **arrival of the Communists** in 1949, and the final escape to Taiwan by Chiang Kaishek with the remains of his Nationalist armies, saw total chaos around Xiamen, with thousands of people streaming to escape the Communist advance in boats across the straits. In the following years the threat of war was constant, as mainland armies manoeuvred in preparation for the final assault on Taiwan, and more immediately, on the smaller islands of Jinmen and Mazu (known in the West as Quemoy and Matsu) which lie only just off the mainland, within sight of Xiamen.

Today the wheel of history has come full circle. Although Jinmen and Mazu are still in the hands of the Nationalists, the threat of conflict with Taiwan has been subsumed by the promise of colossal economic advantage. In the early 1980s Xiamen was declared one of China's first **Special Economic Zones** and, like Shenzhen on the border with Hong Kong, the city has entered a period of unprecedented boom. Things seem only to be getting better: Spring Festival 2001 saw the first **direct passenger ferry** between Taiwan and the mainland for fifty years – though this was a one-off event – and in early 2002 irregular freight services started up.

Arrival and transport

Joined to the mainland by a five-kilometre-long causeway, the island on which Xiamen stands is located inside a large inlet on the southeastern coast of Fujian. The built-up area occupies the western part of the island, which faces the mainland, while the eastern part faces onto Taiwanese Jinmen island. The areas of most interest are the **old town** in the far southwest, and **Gulangyu Island** just offshore. The remainder of the city is the Special Economic Zone, which stretches away to the east and the north, and to the causeway back to the mainland. There's little to detain you here, though the small town of **Jimei**, on the mainland just beyond the causeway, has the attraction of its **School Village**.

The main north–south road, passing through the centre of the old town, is Siming Lu, which is crossed from east to west by Zhongshan Lu, the main shopping street. Xiamen's **train station** is on **Xiahe Lu**, about 4km east from the seafront end of Zhongshan Lu, to which it's connected by city buses #1, #3 and #4. There are several **long-distance bus stations**; you'll most likely end up either 2km northeast of the centre on Hubin Lu (exit the station, turn right and it's 100m to the stop for city bus #23 to the seafront), or about 200m north of the train station (bus #27). The most central arrival point, the **Heping Ferry Terminal**, served weekly by boats from Hong Kong, is fifteen minutes' walk south along the seafront from the *Lujiang Hotel*. Twelve kilometres to the north of town, Xiamen's **airport** is connected to the waterfront area by bus #27.

Buses cover the city and are fast, regular, and cheap – rides cost ¥1–2. **Taxis** are also plentiful, costing upwards of ¥8 to hire. **Maps** of the city (¥5) are sold by vendors near the Gulangyu ferry terminal.

Moving on from Xiamen

Xiamen is well placed for bus and plane connections; rail lines – as usual in Fujian – are a bit unsatisfactory, though you've also the option of catching a boat to Hong Kong.

By air

Flights link Xiamen with Wuyi Shan, Fuzhou, Guangzhou, and several other cities in eastern China. CAAC (ⓣ0592/2208866, ⓕ2139216) have an agency outside the *Lujiang* hotel; see "Listings", p.615, for airline offices.

By train

Rail lines run north from Xiamen to **Wuyi Shan** and **Jiangxi Province**, and west into **Guangdong Province** via **Longyan**. Services to Fuzhou are very circuitous; it's much faster to take the bus. Buying tickets is not too problematic, though queues are often lengthy (ticket office daily 8.10am–noon, 1.40–6.10pm & 7.20–9.30pm).

By bus

Both bus stations have frequent departures to **Fuzhou** and **Quanzhou** between about 6am and 10pm; several daily to **Longyan** and **Yongping**; and services at least daily to **Guangzhou** and **Shantou**. It's possible that your bus might leave from a station other than the one where you buy your ticket; if this is the case, your ticket will be stamped on the back with a message to that effect in Chinese, and a free shuttle bus will be laid on around half an hour before departure.

By boat

There's a weekly service to **Hong Kong** from the Heping Ferry Terminal. The ticket office is in an anonymous white tiled building on waterfront Tongwen Lu (ⓣ0592/2022517; daily 8–11.15am & 2.30–5.15pm); berths for the eighteen-hour trip cost anything from ¥385 to ¥2180 depending on whether you want a dorm bed, shared cabin, or private suite. As yet, there's no regular service to Jinmen Island in Taiwan; group vessels are chartered as necessary and the option isn't open to Westerners.

Accommodation

There's a good range of accommodation in Xiamen, ranging from mid-range to luxurious. Some of the nicest hotels (and the cheapest one which takes foreigners) are on Gulangyu Island, although you'll have to carry your own luggage here as there are no buses or taxis. The wonderful peace and quiet of the island more than compensate for this, however. Wherever you stay, make a point of bargaining – off-season discounts can slash forty percent off advertised rates.

Downtown Xiamen

Donghai (aka East Ocean) Zhongshan Lu ⓣ0592/2021111, ⓕ2033264. One block east of the *Lujiang*. An excellent location and nice rooms. ❼

Holiday Inn Zhenhai Lu, at the junction with Siming Nan Lu ⓣ0592/2023333, ⓦwww.hi592.com. This has all the usual international facilities. ❾

Huaqiao Xinhua Lu ⓣ0592/2025602, ⓕ2038236. Very smart, modern and well-serviced hotel, with airline agents and CTS conveniently located outside. ❾

Jiaotong Siming Bei Lu ⓣ0592/2024403, ⓕ2022928. Just opposite the small bus station a little south of Xiahe Lu, there's a garage-like entrance with the reception on the right. It may not look like a hotel, but it's a homely, friendly place that has some quite acceptable doubles with private bathroom. ❺

Lujiang Zhongshan Lu ⓣ0592/2022922, ⓔlujihtl@public.xm.fj.cn. Occupying a prime site

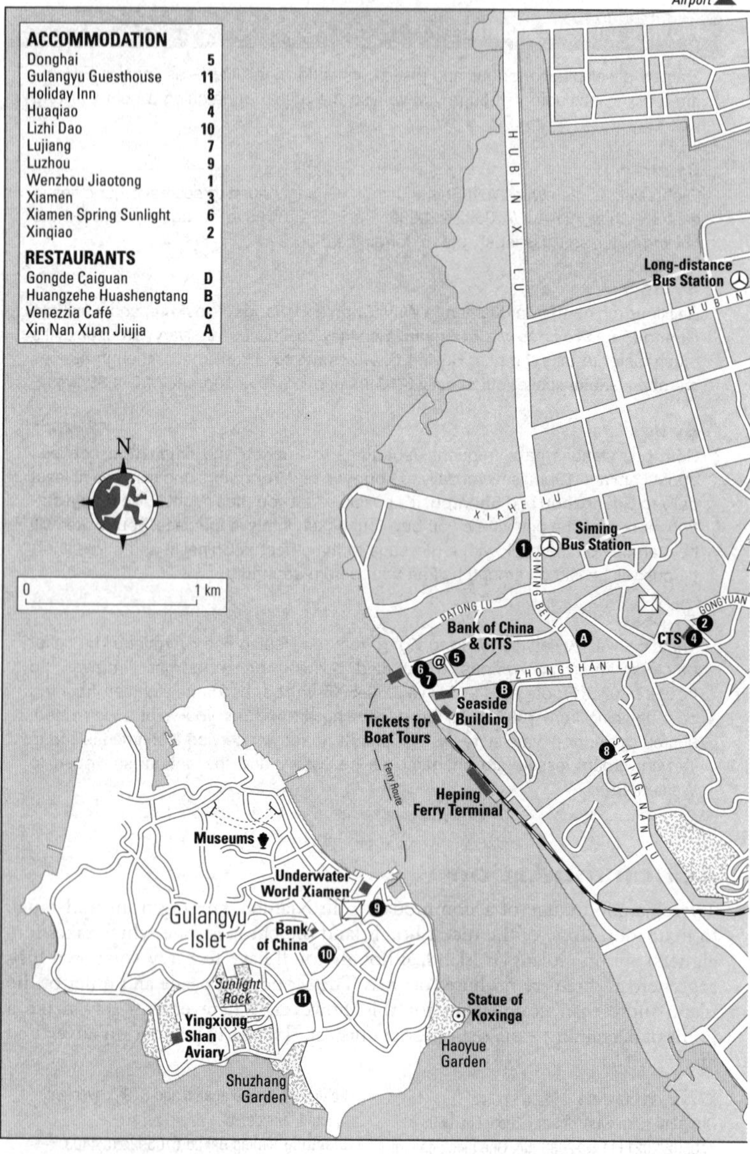

on the seafront in a well-maintained colonial building, this is the ideal place to stay for views over Gulangyu Island. Cheaper twins are rather small; otherwise an excellent hotel. 7

Xiamen Huyuan Lu ⓣ0592/2022265, ⓕ2021765. Overhung by lots of trees and built up a hillside without being too remote, this is a modern place to stay, though somewhat gloomy. Bus route #4 from the train station comes this way. 7

Xiamen Spring Sunlight Directly opposite the Gulangyu ferry terminal, Haihou Lu ⓣ0592/2021793, ⓕ2071665. Colonial-faced building, though interior is blandly modern and spotlessly clean. Good value given the location. 6

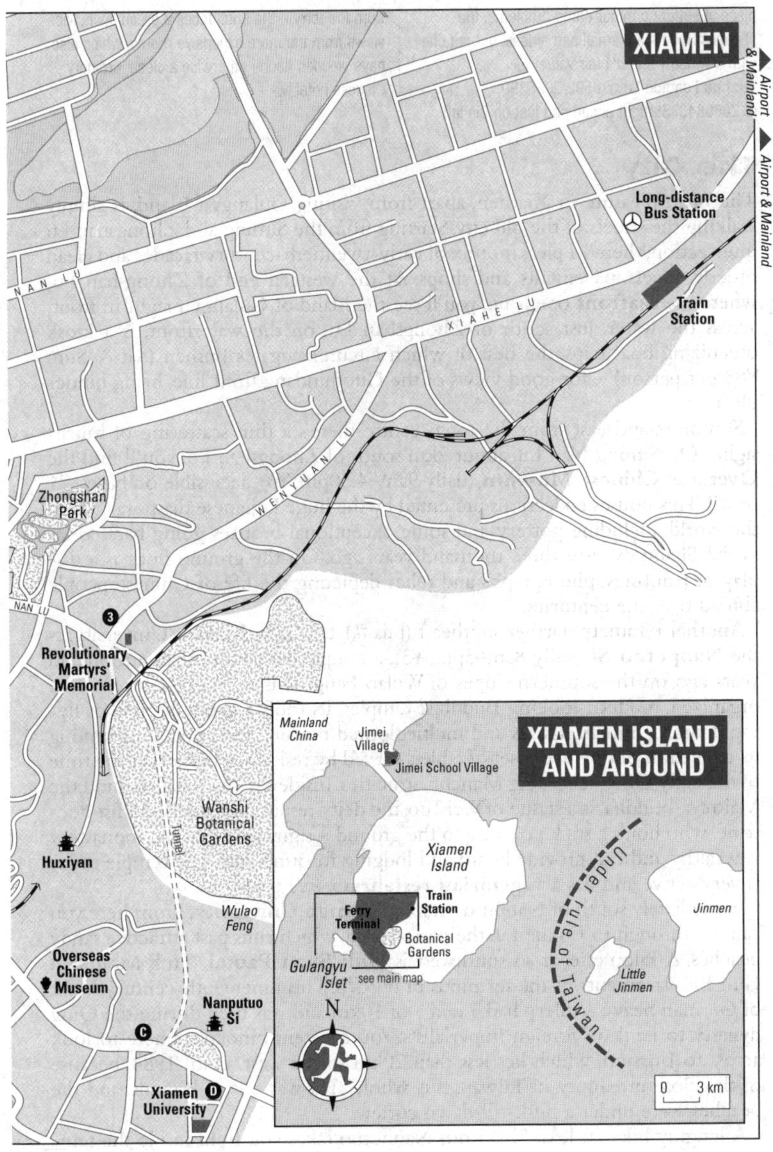

Xinqiao Xinqiao Lu ⓣ0592/2038883, ⓕ2038765. A nice hotel at the junction with Zhongshan Lu, mainly frequented by business people. ❻

Gulangyu Island

Gulangyu Guesthouse Huangyan Lu ⓣ0592/2066050. A 15min walk from the jetty (you need to cut southwest through a maze of streets to get here), this former colonial mansion is a tourist attraction in itself. Rooms are adequate and clean, though overpriced for the generally elderly furnishings. ❺

Lizhi Dao (aka Beautiful Island) 133 Longtou Lu ⓣ0592/2063309, ⓕ2063311. Very convenient place, if suffering minor damp problems; the cheapest rooms are small and airless, but get one with a window and it's fair value. ❸

Luzhou Longtou Lu ⓣ0592/2065390, ⓕ2065843. Straight ahead and just on the left from the ferry – the hotel faces a green lawn. Nice views from the more expensive rooms, which also have wooden floors; otherwise a clean, ordinary Chinese hotel. ❺

The City

The main pleasure in Xiamen, apart from visiting Gulangyu Island, is simply walking the streets of the old city. Starting from the Siming and Zhongshan Lu intersection, there's a pleasant mix of early-twentieth-century facades and clean orderly streets, pavements and shops. At the western end of Zhongshan Lu, where the **seafront** opens up, you'll see the island of Gulangyu right in front, across the water. Just south of Zhongshan Lu, on the waterfront, is a kiosk organizing boat trips, the best of which circumnavigates Jinmen (Sat & Sun; ¥88 per person) – for good views of the Guomindang front line, bring binoculars.

Southeast and east from the town centre there's a thin scattering of tourist sights. On Siming Nan Lu, about 2km south of Zhongshan Lu, you'll find the **Overseas Chinese Museum** (daily 9am–4.30pm; ¥6), accessible on buses #1 or #2. This houses collections presented by the huge Fujianese diaspora around the world, including pottery and some exceptional bronzes going back as far as the Shang dynasty, three thousand years ago. On the ground floor is a display of paintings, photographs and relics depicting the life of Chinese people abroad over the centuries.

Another kilometre farther southeast (bus #1 to Xiada, Xiamen University) is the **Nanputuo Si** (daily 8am–5pm; ¥3), a temple built more than a thousand years ago on the southern slopes of Wulao Feng. This is one of China's most organized, modern-looking Buddhist temples, its roofs a gaudy jumble of flying dragons, human figures and multicoloured flowers, and containing among its collection of treasures a set of tablets carved by resistance fighters at the time of the early Qing, recording Manchu atrocities. Inside the main hall, behind the Maitreya Buddha, is a statue of Wei Tuo, the deity responsible for Buddhist doctrine, who holds a stick pointing to the ground – signifying that the monastery is wealthy and can provide board and lodging for itinerants. The temple today is very active and has a **vegetarian restaurant** (see p.614).

Immediately south of Nanputuo stands **Xiamen University**. From here you can cut through to Daxue Lu, the coastal road, which runs past attractive sandy beaches. A kilometre or so southwest is **Huli Shan Paotai** (Huli Mountain Gun Emplacement), at the terminus of bus #2. This nineteenth-century hunk of German heavy artillery had a range of 10km and was used during the Qing dynasty to fend off foreign imperialists. You can rent binoculars here to look across to **Jinmen**, which lies less than 20km to the west. Until 1984, because of the close proximity of Taiwan, this whole area was out of bounds, and the beaches were under a dusk-till-dawn curfew.

A lengthy hike (at least 2hr) from Nanputuo takes you from inside the temple grounds, up and over the forested Wulao Shan behind the temple – otherwise, catch bus #17 from the little street outside Nanputuo's entrance. Either way, you'll arrive at **Wanshi Botanical Gardens** (daily 6.30am–6.30pm; ¥5), where a stock of four thousand varieties of plant life includes a redwood tree brought here by President Nixon on his official visit to China. From the botanical gardens' north (main) gate, you cross a rail line to reach the Revolutionary Martyrs' Memorial, about 1500m west of the town centre, near the #4 bus route. Southwest of here, along the rail line, is the **Huxiyan** (Tiger

Stream Rock) on your right, built up high on a rocky hillside. If you climb up you'll find a great little temple nestling here amid a pile of huge boulders, and you can actually slip through a cave to one side and climb rock-hewn steps to the top of the largest boulder. Right up on the hilltop, a second small temple called **Bailu Dong** commands spectacular views over the town and the sea.

Gulangyu Island

Gulangyu Island was Xiamen's foreign concession until World War II, and architecturally it remains more or less intact from that time. In summer and at weekends the island and its accommodation are packed but, with battery-powered golf-buggies the only vehicles allowed on the island, the atmosphere is always restful, and exploring can easily fill up a day of your time. Gulangyu's narrow tangle of streets can be a confusing place to find your way around, but the compactness of the island (it's less than two square kilometres in size) means this isn't really a problem. The various sights are scattered around the island and any stroll through the streets will uncover plenty of architectural attractions – especially along Fuzhou Lu and Guxin Lu – overhung with flowers and blossom at all times of the year.

The **boat** to the island runs from early morning to midnight from the pier across from the *Lujiang Hotel*, the short ride offering delightful views of the waterways. On the outbound journey the lower deck is free while the upper deck is ¥1, and on the way back the lower and upper decks cost ¥3 and ¥4 respectively. The **island centre** – a knot of small shopping streets with a bank (unable to change traveller's cheques), a post office, a few **restaurants** and shops – is ahead as you disembark from the ferry. Diagonally to your right is a splendid bronze sculpture of giant octopus, complete with suckers and beak, marking the entrance to **Underwater World Xiamen** (daily 9am–4.30pm; adults ¥70, children ¥40), with walk-through aquariums, seal displays, penguins, turtles and a massive whale skeleton. Past here, follow Sanming Lu northwest and you'll come to the mouth of a **tunnel**, built in the 1950s when the threat of military confrontation with Taiwan seemed imminent, which burrows right underneath the hill to Gulangyu's northern end on Neicuo Ao Lu. From here, try and find your way back to the jetty through the backlanes – an excellent half-hour walk. It's not worth walking a complete circumference of the island though, as the northwest is very exposed and has nothing to see.

If you head southeast from the jetty, you'll pass a number of grand old buildings, including the former British and German consulates. The road continues on to the island's rocky eastern headland, now enclosed by **Haoyue Garden** (¥25), containing a gigantic granite **statue of Koxinga** dressed in grand military attire and staring meaningfully out towards Taiwan, the island he once heroically recaptured from foreign colonialists. Shortly beyond the garden, the road heads west towards the middle of the island, bringing you to a sports ground, with the old colonial **Gulangyu Guesthouse** facing onto it. President Nixon stayed here on his 1972 trip, and it's still the haunt of Chinese VIPs. You can have a peep inside, though for security reasons you might be chased away if you're not a guest. Inside the middle building the original 1920s decor and furniture are intact, with dark wooden panelling, a billiard hall and a terrace with rattan chairs.

Due south, on the southern shore, is the **Shuzhuang Garden** (daily 7am–8pm; ¥20), full of flowers and boasting some nicely shady areas for taking tea right by the sea, as well as a music saloon. The clean, sandy **beach** running west from the park is very tempting for swimming when it's not too packed out. It's overlooked to the north by the **Sunlight Rock** (daily 8.30am–5pm;

¥50 includes cable-car ride), the highest point on Gulangyu (93m) and something of a magnet for the large numbers of local tourists who take a cable car up to the platform for the views right over the entire island. At the foot of the rock (and covered by the same entrance ticket) is the **Koxinga Memorial Hall**, which contains various relics including Koxinga's own jade belt and bits of his "imperial" robe; unfortunately there are no English captions. Follow the path along the coast from here – a beautiful walk on a bright day – and you pass below **Yingxiong Shan**, the top of which is enclosed in netting as an open-air **aviary** (¥15), thick with tropical pigeons, egrets and parrots.

Jimei School Village

Some 15km north of Xiamen proper on the mainland, across the bridge, is the **Jimei School Village**, a site of huge significance for the local Chinese and the Fujianese in particular, as a model of what Overseas Chinese patriots are capable of when they return their money to the motherland. **City bus #18** runs from outside Nanputuo Si to Jimei via the train station, and takes between half an hour and an hour depending on traffic. From the Jimei bus stop you can hire a cycle-rickshaw to take you around the whole site for about ¥40, otherwise it's a pleasant two-hour walk; the sights are about twenty minutes' walk east from the main gate to the village (very close to the Jimei bus stop).

Having earned his millions in Malaysia, **Chen Jiageng**, or **Tan Kahkee** as he is known in the local dialect (1874–1961), is Fujian's most famous "returnee"; he started endowing educational institutions in the Xiamen area after the establishment of the Republic in 1911, and continued to do so for the next fifty years. As well as Xiamen University itself, Tan Kahkee's most enduring legacy is here at Jimei, where the **Jimei High School** is set in a beautiful park on the seafront – it's the huge building, a grand Chinese-Gothic arrangement of patterned bricks and fancy windows, facing onto the lake. Past the front of the school, bear left through a small park containing Tan Kahkee's statue and across a street at the northern end you'll see his **former residence**. The wing on the left contains a photographic record of his life, his business achievements and his patriotism, with captions in English. The ideological complications of a communist state accepting money from a millionaire capitalist are not addressed. A short walk farther east from the residence is **Ao Park**, projecting right into the sea, and entered through a corridor lined with a series of stone engravings telling the stories of China's mythic ancient history.

Eating and drinking

Food is one of Xiamen's assets, with plenty of fresh **fish and seafood**, particularly oysters, crabs and prawns. The best place to try some is in restaurants around Gulangyu's market area, but make sure you establish a price in advance: the seafood is usually sold by weight, not per portion. Otherwise the city centre is thick with places to eat: for **peanut buns and soups** (another regional speciality) check out *Huangzehe Huasheng Tangdian*, a crowded, noisy canteen on Zhongshan Lu. More local snacks – everything, in fact, from spring rolls, noodle soups and dumplings to whole baked crabs – are on offer at *Xin Nan Xuan Jiujia* on Siming Lu. Nanputuo Si's **vegetarian restaurant** is expensive for what you get, with set meals at ¥30–80, depending on the number of dishes you want; across from the temple and near the University, *Gongde Caiguan* is another, cheaper, vegetarian option. Also in the area, the *Venezzia* **café** is a nice spot with outdoor tables, cheapish beer and slightly overpriced Westernized meals; for more in this line, the *Lujiang* hotel on Gulangyu Island has a very pleasant rooftop café-restaurant upstairs, overlooking the sea, while it also serves excellent *dim sum* breakfasts and lunches on the lower floor. The *Holiday Inn* also has a lobby café charging ¥32 a pot, with accompanying cakes from ¥6.

Listings

Airlines Air China, Huguang Dasha building, Hubin Dong Lu ⓣ0592/5084376; Dragon Air, 8 Jianye Lu ⓣ0592/5117702; China Eastern, 311 Siming Nan Lu ⓣ0592/2028936; Philippine Airlines, 837 Xiahe Lu ⓣ0592/5094551; Silk Air, *Holiday Inn* ⓣ0592/2053257.

Banks and exchange There are branches of the Bank of China on Guluangyu Island – note that traveller's cheques can't be cashed here – and on Zhongshan Lu, back from the seafront (Mon–Fri 8.30am–noon & 2.30–5pm, Sat 8am–12.30pm).

Consulates Philippines, near the geographic centre of Xiamen on Lianhua Bei Lu (ⓣ0592/5130355).

Internet access There are several Net bars in the lane directly north of the *Donghai* hotel, parallel with Datong Lu.

Mail and telephones Xiamen's main post office, where IDD telephone calls can also be made, is on Xinhua Lu, south of the junction with Siming Dong Lu.

PSB Across from the Post Office on Gongyuan Nan Lu ⓣ0592/2262203.

Travel agents CITS, upstairs in the building immediately west of the Bank of China building on Zhongshan Lu ⓣ0592/2103911; CTS, *Huaqiao* hotel, Xinhua Lu ⓣ0592/2025617.

Southwestern Fujian: the Hakka homelands

Fujian's hilly southwestern border with Guangdong is an area central to the **Hakka**, a Han sub-group known to locals as *kejia* (guest families) and to nineteenth-century Europeans as "China's gypsies". Originating in the Yangzi basin during the third century and dislodged ever southward by war and revolution, the Hakka today form large communities both here and in Hong Kong and Hainan Island. They managed to retain their original languages and customs by remaining aloof from their neighbours in the lands which they settled, a habit that caused resentment and led to their homes being well defended. While towns up this way are mostly unattractive, the countryside is pretty in spring, and villages and hamlets around the focal city of **Yongding** sport fortress-like **Hakka mansions** built of stone and adobe, the largest of which are three storeys high, circular and house entire clans.

Southwestern Fujian

Yongding	永定	***yǒngdìng***
Dongfu	东府酒店	*dōngfǔ jiǔdiàn*
Jiari	假日旅馆	*jiàrì lǚguǎn*
Tianhe	天河旅馆	*tianhé lǚguǎn*
Chengqi	乘启	***chéngqǐ***
Gaotou Lou	高头楼	*gāotóu lóu*
Hukeng	湖坑	***húkēng***
Zhencheng Lou	振城楼	*zhènchéng lóu*
Longyan	龙岩	***lóngyán***

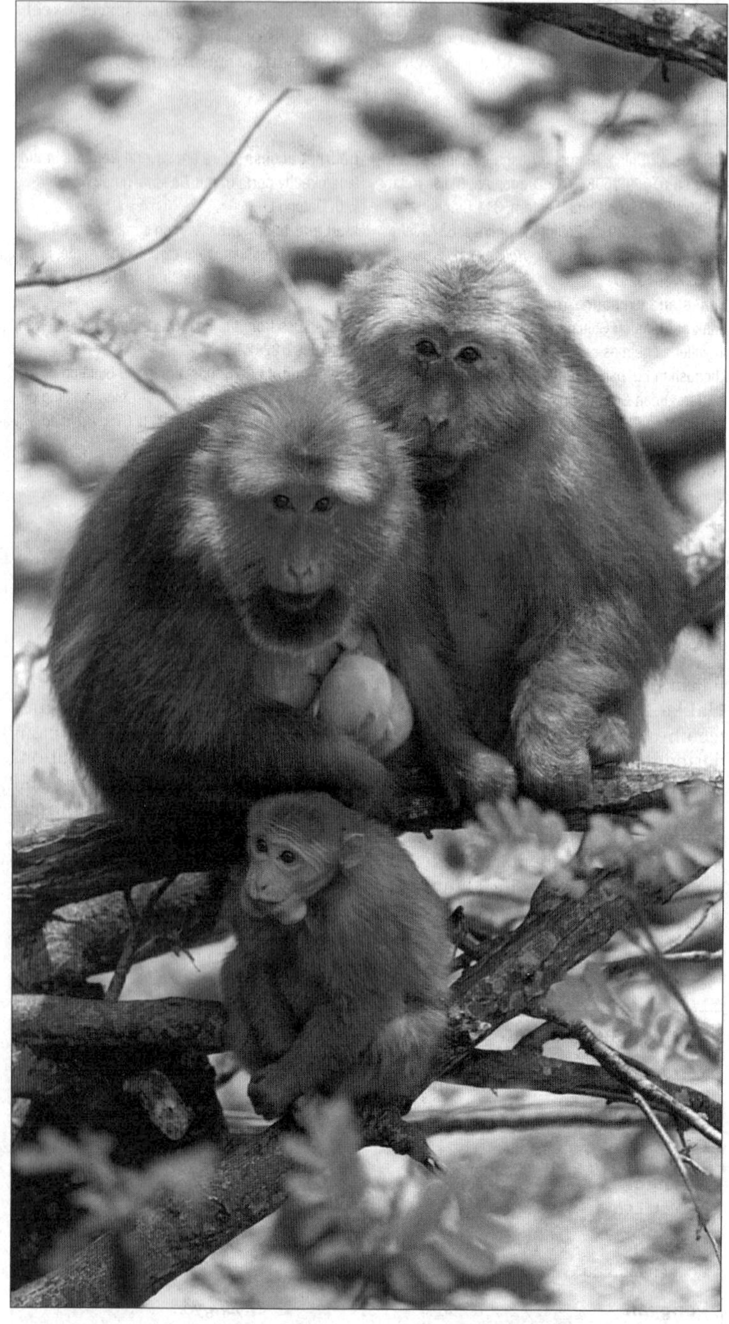

△ Monkeys at Wuyi Shan

If you can't find direct transport from coastal Fujian, aim first for **LONGYAN**, a small city 170km northwest of Xiamen where roads and separate rail lines from Fuzhou, Quanzhou, and Xiamen converge to head west to Meizhou in Guangdong (see p.675). From the **train station** on the eastern edge of town, catch bus #14 over three bridges to Longzhou Xi Lu and the **long-distance bus station**, 2km away and just south of Longyan's centre. Here you'll be mobbed by minibus drivers for the final sixty-kilometre, hour-long run southwest to Yongding (¥10), through several Hakka towns marked by large, mud-brick mansions and inevitably surrounded by cement factories.

Yongding and around

Set on the edge of a flat river basin, **YONGDING** is an old town today recast as a heavily built-up, typically ugly place, whose residents are nevertheless very friendly towards the few foreigners who make it up here. The road from Longyan ends up at a **roundabout** where you'll find the **bus station** and decent, if forgettable, **accommodation** options: the *Jiari Lüguan* (❷), *Tianhe Lüguan* (❶) and *Dongfu Jiudian* (❷). From here, the main street runs north over the river and into town; immediately on the far bank, Huangcheng Dong Lu forks left into a market area, while steps on the right climb a ridge to a **park**, with views across town and the countryside. **Places to eat** surround the bus station area and main streets; you'll find all sorts of rice noodles, snacks, and **kourou**, a Hakka dish made from slices of soya-braised pork belly on a bed of bitter kale. **Leaving**, there are daily buses to Meizhou in Guangdong, and minibuses through the day back to Longyan, and at least as far east as Hukeng village.

Hukeng and Zhencheng Lou

An hour's bus ride east of Yongding via the crossroads town of **Zhiling**, you'll find what is considered the most perfect **Hakka roundhouse** 5km north of **HUKENG** village. Known as **Zhencheng Lou**, this century-old home is now a well-maintained if slightly sterile tourist attraction (¥20): plain and forbidding on the outside, the huge outer wall encloses three storeys of galleried rooms looking inwards to a central courtyard, where guests were entertained and containing the clan shrine. The galleries are vertically divided into eight segments by thick **fire walls**, a plan that intentionally turns the building into a giant **bagua**, Taoism's octagonal symbol. This powerful design occurs everywhere in the region, along with demon-repelling **mirrors** and other Taoist motifs. An almost disastrous consequence of roundhouse design – which from above looks like a ring – was that (so locals say) the first US satellite photos of the region identified the houses as missile silos.

The hamlet surrounding Zhencheng is quite attractive in itself, with other, more "authentic" houses (all still lived in) laid out along a small stream. Those worth investigating include an 1920s schoolhouse; **Fuyu Lou**, the old *yamen* building; **Rushen**, one of the smallest multistorey roundhouses; and **Kuijiu**, a splendid, 160-year-old square-sided Hakka mansion, its interior like a temple squeezed into a box. There's also a small, white-tiled roundhouse **hotel** clearly visible near Zhencheng Lou (❸), and you might ask about getting 20km farther north to **Chengqi**, where **Gaotou Lou** is the largest roundhouse of them all, built in 1709 and currently home to more than a thousand people in its six hundred rooms.

Heading on **to Guangdong** from Hukeng, catch transport back to Zhiling, which lies on the junction of roads to Guangdong from Longyan and Yongding, from where you should be able to flag down buses for the five-hour trip to Meizhou (see p.675) or Dapu (see p.675) until mid-morning.

Guangdong

Halfway along **Guangdong**'s eight-hundred-kilometre coastline, rivers from all over the province and beyond disgorge themselves into the South China Sea through the tropically fertile **Pearl River Delta**, one of China's most densely cultivated areas. Perched right at the delta's northern apex and adjacent to both Hong Kong and Macau, the provincial capital **Guangzhou** provides many travellers with their first taste of mainland China. It's not everyone's favourite city, but once you've found your bearings among the busy roads and packed shopping districts, Guangzhou's world-famous **food** merits a stop, as does an assortment of museums, parks and monuments. The Pearl River Delta itself has a few patches of green and some history to pick up in passing, but the major targets are the cities of **Shenzhen** and **Zhuhai**, modern, purpose-built economic buffer zones at the crossings into Hong Kong and Macau.

Farther afield, the rest of the province is more picturesque, with a mass of sights from Buddhist temples to Stone Age relics – and the seasonal thrill of white-water rafting – to slow you down around **Shaoguan**, up north by the Hunan and Jiangxi borders. Over in the east near Fujian, the former colonial treaty port of **Shantou** is the springboard for journeying up through some beautiful countryside to the ancient towns of **Chaozhou** and **Meizhou**. On the way west into Guangxi Province, **Zhaoqing** sports pleasant formalized lake and hill landscapes, while those heading towards Hainan need to aim for the disjointed, bland ferry port of **Zhanjiang**, down in Guangdong's southwestern extremities.

Guangdong has a generous quantity of rail and road traffic, and **getting around** is none too difficult, though often requiring some advance preparation. **Rail lines** run north through Shaoguan and up into Hunan and central China, east to Meizhou, Shantou and Fujian, and west through Zhaoqing to Zhanjiang and Guangxi. **River travel** was, until recently, a highlight of the province, though the only easy excursions left are the fast hydrofoils between the Pearl River Delta towns and Hong Kong, and a day-cruise from the northern town of **Qingyuan** to some riverside temples. As for the **climate**, summers can be sweltering across the province, with typhoons along the coast, while winter temperatures get decidedly nippy up in the northern ranges – though it's more likely to be miserably wet than to snow, except around the highest mountain peaks.

Guangzhou

GUANGZHOU, once known to the Western world as **Canton**, was only a decade ago dismissed by many visitors as a nightmare caricature of Hong Kong, one of the most dizzyingly overcrowded, polluted and chaotic places to daunt a newcomer to the country. While the city is still hardly somewhere to come for peace and relaxation, recent improvements have wrought great **changes**: an expanding **metro network** and multiple-layered flyovers are relieving traffic congestion; the waterfront area has been paved and flowerbeds dug wherever possible; old buildings have been scrubbed and restored to public view by demolishing the badly constructed 1950s concrete boxes which obscured them; and the city's **nightlife** is snowballing.

True, Guangzhou's **sights** remain relatively minor, though a fascinating 2000-year-old tomb and palace site complement the obligatory round of temples, and the city is an enjoyable place simply to observe the Chinese being themselves. The Cantonese are immediately upfront, and pleasantly indifferent to foreign faces after two thousand years of contact with the outside world. They're also compulsively garrulous, turning Guangzhou's two famous obsessions – **eating** and **business** – into social occasions, and filling streets, restaurants and buildings with the sounds of *Yueyu*, the Cantonese language. And while the newer districts pass as a blur of chrome and concrete from the inside of your taxi, make your way around on foot through the back lanes and you'll discover a very different city, one of flagstoned residential quarters, tiny collectors' markets, laundry strung on lines between buildings, and homes screened away behind barred wooden gates. Guangzhou has also long been the first place where foreign influences have seeped into the country, often through returning Overseas Chinese, and this is where to watch for the latest fashions and to see how China will interpret alien styles.

It may seem, what with the **biannual Trade Fair**, that the emphasis here is towards business rather than tourism – and it's certainly true that commerce is Guangzhou's lifeblood, a religion inspiring train-station pickpockets and company CEOs alike. In purely practical terms, however, while the city is expensive compared with some parts of China, it's often far **cheaper** than Hong Kong, particularly in regard to **onward travel**. Airfares into China are considerably less from Guangzhou than what you'd pay just south of the border, allowing big savings even after you factor in transport from Hong Kong and a night's accommodation.

Some history

Legend tells how Guangzhou was founded by **Five Immortals** riding five rams, each of whom planted a sheaf of rice symbolizing endless prosperity – hence Guangzhou's nickname, **Yang Cheng** (Goat City). Myths aside, a settlement called **Panyu** had sprung up here by the third century BC, when a rogue Qin commander founded the **Nanyue Kingdom** and made it his capital. Remains of a contemporary **shipyard** uncovered in central Guangzhou during the 1970s suggest that city had contact with foreign lands even then: there were merchants who considered themselves Roman subjects here in 165 AD, and from Tang times vessels travelled to Middle Eastern ports, introducing **Islam** into China and exporting porcelain to Arab colonies in distant Kenya and Zanzibar. By 1405 Guangzhou's population of foreign traders and Overseas Chinese was so large that the Ming emperor Yongle founded a special quarter for them, and when xenophobia later closed the rest of China to outsiders, Guangzhou became the country's main link with the world.

Restricted though it was, this contact with other nations proved to be Guangzhou's – and China's – undoing. From the eighteenth century, the **British East India Company** used the city as a base from which to purchase silk, ceramics and tea, but became frustrated at the Chinese refusal to accept trade goods instead of cash in return. To even accounts, the company began to import **opium** from India: addiction and demand followed, making colossal profits for the British and the **Co Hong**, their Chinese distributors, but rapidly depleting imperial stocks of silver. In 1839 the Qing government sent the incorruptible Commissioner **Lin Zexu** to Guangzhou with a mandate to stop the drug traffic, which he did by blockading the foreigners into their waterfront quarters and destroying their opium stocks. Britain declared war and, with a navy partly funded by the opium traders, forced the Chinese to cede five ports (including Guangzhou and Hong Kong) to British control under the **Nanking Treaty** of 1842.

Unsurprisingly, the following century saw Guangzhou develop into a revolutionary cauldron. It was here during the late 1840s that Hong Xiuquan formulated his **Taiping Uprising** (see p.458), and sixty years later the city hosted a premature attempt by **Sun Yatsen** to kick out China's Qing rulers. When northern China was split by warlords through the 1920s, Sun Yatsen chose Guangzhou as his **Nationalist capital**, while a youthful Mao Zedong and Zhou Enlai flitted in and out between mobilizing rural peasant groups. At the same time, anger at continuing colonial interference in China was channelled by **unionism**, the city's workers becoming notoriously well organized and prone to rioting in the face of outrages perpetrated by the Western powers. However, many of Guangzhou's leftist youth subsequently enrolled in militias and went north to tackle the warlords in the **Northern Expedition**, and so became victims of the 1927 **Shanghai Massacre**, Chiang Kaishek's suppression of the Communists (see p.399). A Red uprising in Guangzhou that December failed, leaving the city's population totally demoralized. Controlled by the Japanese during the war and the Guomindang afterwards, they were too apathetic to liberate themselves in 1949, and had to wait for the PLA to do it for them.

Few people would today describe the Cantonese as apathetic, at least when it comes to **business** acumen. Unlike many large, apparently modern Chinese cities, Guangzhou enjoys real wealth and solid infrastructure, its river location and level of development making it in many ways resemble a grittier, rougher-around-the-edges version of Shanghai. Hong Kong's downturn since the handover and Asian financial crisis of the late 1990s has also encouraged southern businesses and wealthy entrepreneurs to relocate to Guangzhou, taking advantage of the mainland's lower costs and better work opportunities. At the same time, Guangzhou is thick with China's mobile rural community, often living below the poverty line: at any one time, a staggering one million **migrant workers**, many from the backblocks of Jiangxi and Anhui provinces, are based in Guangzhou – one fifth of the city's total population.

Orientation

For a city of five million people, Guangzhou is compact and easy to navigate, and readily divides into five uneven areas. **Central** and **Northern Guangzhou** comprise the original city core – still pretty much the geographic centre – north of the river between Renmin Lu in the west and Yuexiu Lu in the east. A modern urban landscape predominates, cut by the city's main arterial roads: **Zhongshan** and **Dongfeng** run east–west, and **Jiefang** and **Renmin** run north–south. These streets are divided up into north, south, east, west and central sections, with the exception of Zhongshan Lu, whose segments are numbered. It's not all relentless modernity and traffic, however: most of Guangzhou's historical sites are located here, along with two sizeable parks, **Yuexiu** and **Liuhua**.

Western Guangzhou, the area west of Renmin Lu, is a thriving shopping and eating district centred on Changshou Lu. This formed a Ming-dynasty overflow from the original city and retains its former street plan, though the narrow back lanes, old houses and markets are also ringed by main roads, such as waterfront **Liuersan Lu**. Right on the river here is the former foreigners' quarter of **Shamian Island**. Over on the south bank, **Honan** was a seedy hotspot during the 1930s, though nowadays it's a smaller version of the Changshou Lu districts, and beginning to grow in popularity.

East of Yuexiu Lu the city opens up, and Zhongshan Lu and Dongfeng Lu are joined by Huanshi Lu as, lined with glassy corporate offices, they run broad and straight through **Eastern Guangzhou** to culminate in the vast, open square and sports stadium at the centre of **Tianhe**. Nightlife is the east's biggest draw – many of Guangzhou's bars are out this way – while a few kilometres to the north is **Baiyun Shan**, a formalized string of hills and parkland just beyond the city proper.

Arrival

Baiyun international airport lies 6km north of the city centre – there's an **airport bus** to the China Southern offices on Huanshi Dong Lu for ¥8, a nearly completed metro link, and taxis into the centre (¥30). This will all change at some point in 2004, when Guangzhou's **new airport**, around 20km north of town, is expected to open. Ferries **from Hong Kong** dock at least a twenty-minute taxi ride southwest of Guangzhou at **Nanhai** (aka Pingzhou) – a metro link is planned for 2005.

The city has two major train stations. At the northern end of Renmin Lu, **Guangzhou train station** is the most confrontational place to arrive in town, the vast **square** outside perpetually seething with passengers, hawkers and hustlers. Main-line services from most central, northern and western destinations terminate here. New arrivals exit on the west side of the square, while taxis and most **city buses** wait over on the east side; bus #31 will take you down to the

Guangzhou: Arrival and downtown metro stops

Guangzhou	广州	***guǎngzhōu***
Arrival		
Baiyun airport	白云机场	*báiyún jīchǎng*
East train station	东方火车站	*dōngfāng huǒchēzhàn*
Guangfo bus depot	广佛车站	*guǎngfó chēzhàn*
Guangzhou Train Station	广州火车站	*guǎngzhōu huǒchēzhàn*
Liuhua bus station	流花车客运站	*liúhuā chē kèyùnzhàn*
Nanhai (Pingzhou) ferry terminal	南海（平洲）码头	*nánhǎi (píngzhōu)mǎtóu*
Provincial bus station	省汽车客运站	*shěngqìchē kèyùnzhàn*
Tianhe bus station	天河客运站	*tiānhé kèyùnzhàn*
Downtown metro stops		
Changshou Lu	长寿路	*chángshòu lù*
Chen Jia Ci	陈家祠	*chénjiā cí*
Dongshan Kou	东山口	*dōngshān kǒu*
Gongyuan Qian	公园前	*gōngyuán qián*
Guangzhou Dongzhan	广州东站	*guǎngzhōu dōngzhàn*
Huang Sha	黄沙	*huángshā*
Lieshi Lingyuan	烈士陵园	*lièshì língyuán*
Nongjiang Suo	农讲所	*nóngjiǎng suǒ*
Ximen Kou	西门口	*xīmén kǒu*
Tiyu Xilu	体育西路	*tǐyù xīlù*
Tiyu Zhongxiao	体育中小	*tǐyù zhōngxiǎo*
Yangji	杨箕	*yángjī*

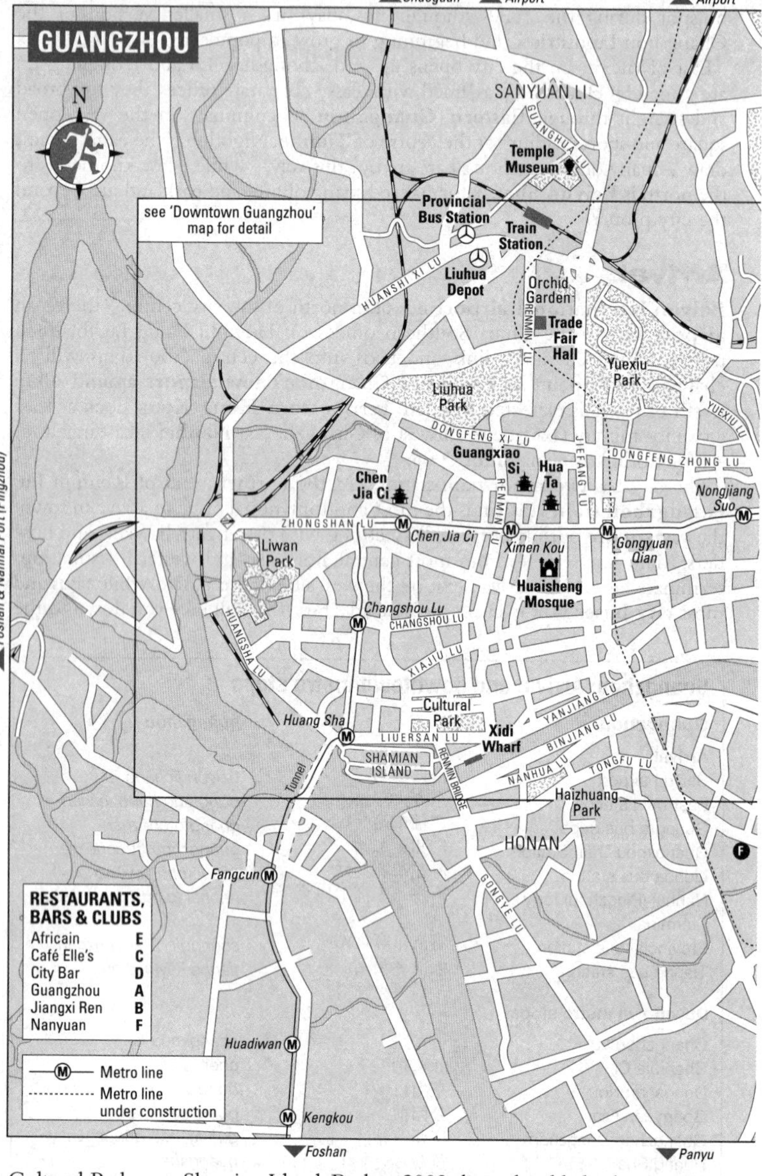

Cultural Park near Shamian Island. By late 2003 there should also be a **metro** stop at the station; for Shamian, take it south three stops to Gongyuan Qian interchange, then catch line #1 south to Huang Sha.

Guangzhou's second rail terminus is **Guangzhou East train station**, 5km east of the centre at Tianhe. This is where trains from Shenzhen terminate, along with the Kowloon Express, services from Shantou, Meizhou and western Fujian, and a growing quantity of traffic from central China. From the

basement, catch metro line #1 direct to the Huangsha stop for Shamian Island; for Guangzhou train station, take bus #271 or, once the line has opened, the metro, changing at Gongyuan Qian. A taxi to the centre costs ¥30–40.

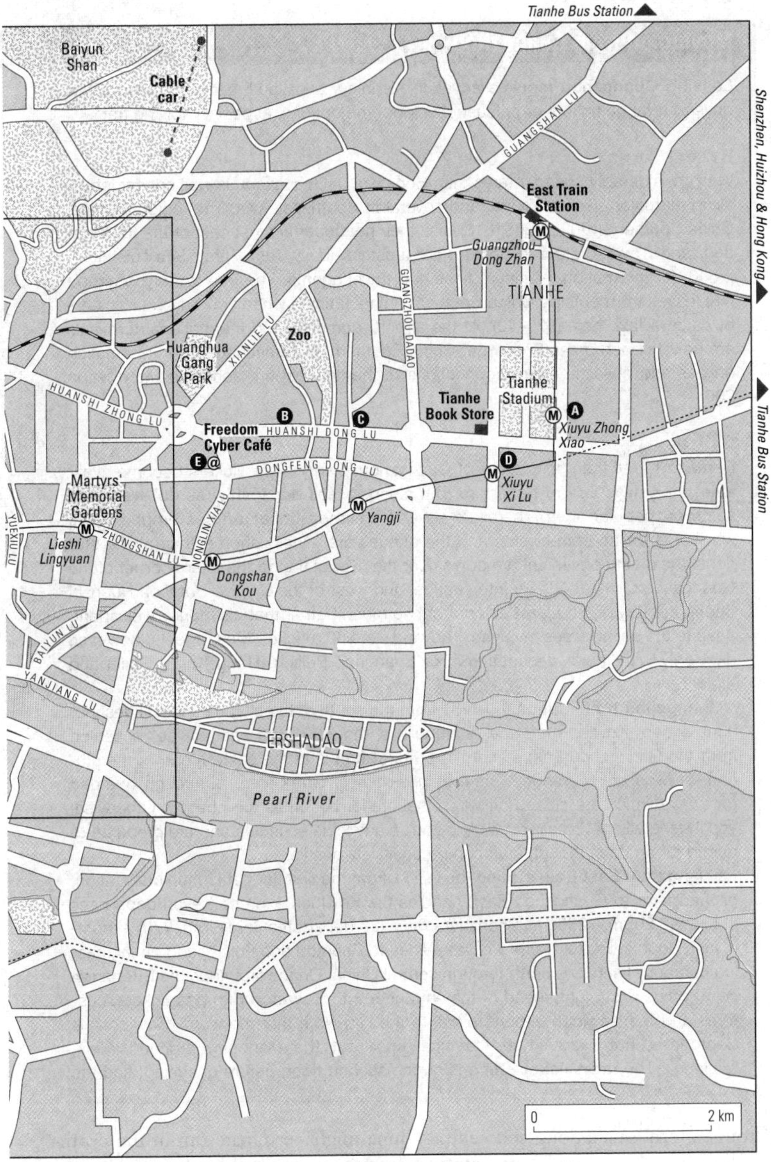

There are several major long-distance bus stations. West of Guangzhou train station on Huanshi Xi Lu, the **provincial bus station** handles arrivals from almost everywhere in the country, with more local traffic often winding up across the road at one of the number of depots which comprise **Liuhua station**. Buses

Moving on from Guangzhou

Leaving Guangzhou requires advance planning, and you'll generally need a few days to arrange tickets or at least check out the options, especially for the train.

By air

With considerably cheaper fares than Hong Kong, Guangzhou is well connected by air to all major cities in China, and several in Southeast Asia. The regional airline, China Southern (Ⓣ020/86681818), has their headquarters just east of the train station, and a well-organized ticket office upstairs (daily 7am–7pm). See "Listings", p.646, for international airline offices and travel agents. The bus to Baiyun airport (¥8) leaves from outside China Southern – check times when you buy your ticket – or catch a taxi there (¥30–40). At the airport, domestic and international terminals are next to each other. Enquire at China Southern or a travel agent for information on bus and possible metro connections to the new airport, scheduled to open in 2004.

By train

Demand for all train tickets out of Guangzhou is very high. Tickets become available three days before departure, but sleepers sell out swiftly, as do even hard seats on popular lines. There are several **advance-ticket offices** around town, where there's no commission and the queues are usually shorter than at the stations: the most convenient are down near the river at the northeastern corner of the Guangzhou Qiyi Lu/Yide Lu intersection; and west of the *Garden Hotel* on Huanshi Zhong Lu. Paying an **agent** can cut out so much bother that it's money well spent, despite the service fees involved – upwards of ¥50 a ticket. Most agents, however, deal only with major destinations like Shanghai, Beijing, Hong Kong, Guilin and Xi'an.

Guangzhou train station (bus #31 from the south of the city) handles all destinations except Kowloon and the Shantou line, though points east are better served from the Guangzhou East station. The **ticket hall** is at the eastern end of the station; crowds are horrendous here at peak times, when entry is through guarded gateways which are closed off when the interior becomes too chaotic. Otherwise, you'll generally get what you want if you've a flexible schedule and are prepared to queue for an hour, though staff can be positively hostile.

Guangzhou East train station (bus #271 from the first floor at Liuhua bus station, or the metro to Guangzhou East) handles the Kowloon express (seven departures 8.30am–5.20pm; ¥265), all Shenzhen traffic (39 departures 6am–9pm; ¥70) – mostly fast, double-decker trains – eastern lines to Shantou and Fujian, and an increasing number of services north through central China. On the first floor, the **Shenzhen** ticket office is straight ahead of the entrance, with **Kowloon Express** tickets, customs and the Kowloon departure hall to the left. Note that the word "Kowloon" is Cantonese, but signs in the terminal spell out the Mandarin pronounciation, "Jiulong". The **main ticket office** is on the second floor; before queueing, find the

from eastern Guangdong and central China might terminate out in the northeastern suburbs at **Tianhe bus station**; from here your best bet for reaching the centre is to catch either the shuttle bus to the provincial bus station, or a taxi to Guangzhou East train station and city transport from there – though Tianhe bus station will ultimately also be on a metro line.

City transport and information

Getting around Guangzhou isn't difficult, though the city is too big to walk everywhere, and bicycles are not recommended because of heavy traffic. Most train number from the Chinese timetable on the wall, then match this with the number displayed above each ticket window. The main departure areas are on the third and fourth floors.

At the time of writing, a new **high-speed rail** track was being laid from Guangzhou East to Yichang, Chengdu, Nanyang, and Guiyang, which is expected to knock a third to a half off current journey times when it's completed some time in 2006.

By bus

Leaving Guangzhou by bus can be the cheapest of all exit options, and more comfortable than the average hard-seat experience if you have any distance to travel. Fast, relatively expensive **express buses** are very much the rage at present – especially around the Pearl River Delta and along the expressway to eastern Guangdong – so if money is your prime consideration, check to see whether there are any ordinary buses to your destination.

The **provincial bus station** on Huanshi Xi Lu is always full of people, but tickets are easy to get – once you've found the right window out of the forty or so available – and there are at least daily departures to everywhere in Guangdong, and as far afield as Guizhou, Anhui, Hainan and Fujian provinces.

Destinations within 100km or so of Guangzhou – including all Delta towns, Qingyuan and Huizhou – are covered from the **Liuhua bus station**, also on Huanshi Xi Lu. In fact, this is a series of depots strung out for 500m along the road; the **main ticket office** is on the second floor at the eastern end of it all, though your bus might leave from anywhere – you'll be herded towards the correct departure point. For Foshan, minibuses leave frequently from the **Guangfo depot** at the western end of Zhongshan Lu – catch the metro to the Chenjia Ci stop and walk the last 250m.

Buses for Shantou, Meizhou and points east mostly depart from the new **Tianhe bus station**, about 7km east of town. You can buy tickets for these at the provincial bus station – they'll stamp your ticket on the back for a free shuttle bus to the Tianhe station, which takes around thirty minutes.

Express buses to **Hong Kong** and **Macau** run by CTS and others depart from various hotels between 7.45am and 5pm; buy tickets at the departure points. For **Kowloon** – either Hong Kong Airport or Kowloon Tong MCR (3hr; around ¥115) – try the *China* (11 daily), *Dongfang* (10), *Landmark* (9) or *White Swan* (2). For **Macau** (3hr 30min; ¥55), the *Landmark* has five departures daily to the border at Zhuhai (see p.658), though you can also catch any bus heading this way from the Liuhua station.

By boat

Guangzhou's **ferry port** is southwest of the city at **Nanhai** (Pingzhou), about halfway to Foshan (see p.655), with two daily speedboats to the China–Hong Kong City Terminal in Hong Kong (2hr; ¥170). At time of writing, the big problem is getting to the terminal without a taxi, though there's a plan to extend Guangzhou's metro line #1 out here by 2005.

often, you'll find yourself using Guangzhou's cheap and slow **bus and trolleybus** network, which covers most of the city from ¥1 a ride.

Where possible, it's better to plump for Guangzhou's speedy **metro**. At the time of writing, only **line #1** was in operation, running diagonally across the city from Guangzhou East train station at Tianhe, through the centre along Zhongshan Lu, then turning south at Chenjia Ci, past Shamian Island and across the river. **Line #2**, which will put all of Central Guangzhou within a few minutes' walk of a station, is due to open in 2003; it will run south via Sanyuanli and Guangzhou train station, interchange with line #1 at Gongyuan

Qian, then cross the river and head east; at the same time, line #1 will be extended to link up with Tianhe bus station. There's also talk of building new lines out to Foshan (see p.654) via the ferry port at Nanhai by 2005. **Metro stations** can be hard to locate at street level; keep an eye out for the logo, rather like a "Y" made up of two red lines on a yellow background. **Fares** are ¥2–6 according to the number of stops from your starting point; ticket machines take ¥1 coins only, with change available from booths at each station. Carriages have bilingual route maps, and each stop is announced in Mandarin and English. For an **update** on the metro situation, check out Ⓦwww.gzmtr.com.

Taxis are plentiful and can be hailed in the street. Fares start at ¥7, but larger vehicles charge more – all have meters. Drivers rarely try any scams, though the city's complex traffic flows can sometimes make it seem that you're heading in the wrong direction.

Maps of varying detail and quality are sold for around ¥5 by hawkers at the train and bus stations, and at numerous bookshops, hotels and stalls around the city. The current favourite is called *The Tour Map of Guangzhou*, which has many of the sights marked in English, and is kept fairly up to date – though no maps illustrate all of Guangzhou's two-hundred-plus bus routes. For the latest in food, events, music and clubs – or anything else to do with Guangzhou – pick up a copy of *That's Guangzhou* (or check out Ⓦwww.thatsguangzhou.com), an invaluable free monthly **magazine** aimed at foreign residents, with extensive reviews and listings, plus some interesting features on contemporary life in the city; some hotels and most bars listed below should have copies.

Accommodation

Guangzhou's business emphasis means that budget accommodation is limited – even Hong Kong has a better range – so resign yourself to this and plan your finances accordingly. Prices can more than **double** during the three-week Trade Fairs each April and October, when beds will be in short supply, and

Guangzhou: Accommodation

Aiqun	爱群大酒店	*àiqún dàjiǔdiàn*
Baigong	白宫酒店	*báigōng jiǔdiàn*
Beijing	北京大酒店	*běijīng dàjiǔdiàn*
China Marriott	中国大酒店	*zhōnggúo dàjiǔdiàn*
Customs	海关会议接待中心	*hǎiguānhuìyì jiēdàizhōngxīn*
Dongfang	东方宾馆	*dōngfāng bīnguǎn*
Garden	花园酒店	*huāyuán jiǔdiàn*
Guangdong Guesthouse	广东宾馆	*guǎngdōng bīnguǎn*
Guangdong Tourist Hotel	广东旅游	*guǎngdōng lǚyóu*
Guangzhou Youth Hostel	广州青年招待所	*guǎngzhōu qīngnián zhāodàisuǒ*
Holiday Inn	文化假日酒店	*wénhuà jiàrìjiǔdiàn*
Landmark	华厦大酒店	*huáxià dàjiǔdiàn*
Liuhua	流花宾馆	*liúhuā bīnguǎn*
Shamian	沙面宾馆	*shāmiàn bīnguǎn*
Shengli	胜利宾馆	*shènglì bīnguǎn*
White Swan	白天鹅宾馆	*báitiāné bīnguǎn*
Yishu	艺术宾馆	*yìshù bīnguǎn*

tend to be lower in winter, when fewer visitors are about. Every hotel has some sort of travel-booking service, while smarter places have their own banks, post offices, restaurants and shops, and are likely to accept international credit cards.

For anything more than an overnight stop, **Shamian Island** is the best place to hole up, whatever your budget: it's a pleasant spot with well-tended parks, a bit of peace, and plenty of good places to eat. Otherwise, there are several relatively inexpensive Chinese-style hotels in **central Guangzhou**, mostly near the riverfront; and the bulk of the city's upmarket accommodation in the city's **north and eastern** quarters – though there are two budget options here, near Guangzhou train station.

Shamian Island

The places reviewed below are marked on the map on p.638.

Bank of China Shamian Dajie ⓣ020/81885913. Very under-patronized, they're eager for business and try hard to please. Furnishings are pretty straightforward, in keeping with its reasonable price. ❹

Customs Hotel Shamian Dajie ⓣ020/81102388, ⓕ81918552. A new, upmarket venture aimed at Chinese businessmen, inside a former Customs House – though the interior is strictly modern. ❼

Guangzhou Youth Hostel Shamian Si Jie ⓣ020/81884298, ⓕ8884979. Across from the lavish *White Swan* is one of Guangzhou's cheapest options – there's usually a waiting list for spare beds here, which are distributed at noon. The dorms are a bit damp, but other rooms are modern and clean. There's an expensive left-luggage office, and a transport booking service. Despite the name, not an actual IYHF hostel. Dorm beds ¥50, ❹

Shamian Shamian Nan Jie ⓣ020/81912288, ⓕ81911628. Rooms are small and mostly windowless, but otherwise this is a very snug and comfortable option, just around the corner from the youth hostel. ❺

Shengli (aka Victory) Shamian Si Jie and Shamian Bei Jie ⓣ020/81862622, ⓦwww.gd-victory-hotel.com. Formerly the *Victoria* in colonial days, this is a good-value upmarket choice, with two separate buildings, good restaurant and store with a coffee bar and trove of imported Western foods. Bei Jie building ❻, Si Jie building ❺

White Swan Shamian Nan Jie ⓣ020/81886968, ⓦwww.whiteswanhotel.com. Once Guangzhou's most upmarket place to stay, this government-funded hotel is probably still the city's most famous and prestigious, and a favourite with US citizens in town to adopt Chinese orphans. You'll find a waterfall in the lobby, river views, an on-site bakery and countless other services – some reserved for the use of guests alone. ❾

Central Guangzhou

Aiqun Yanjiang Lu ⓣ020/81866668, ⓕ81883519. Slightly gloomy (or possibly atmospheric) 1930s monumental mansion block with good river views and snooty staff; this was the tallest pre-liberation building in Guangzhou. Fair-value doubles and singles available. ❻

Baigong Renmin Nan Lu ⓣ020/81882313, ⓕ81889161. Absolutely classic urban hotel. Can be noisy, but it's also tidy, friendly and well priced for the location. ❺

Beijing Xihao Er Lu ⓣ020/81884988, ⓕ81861818. Another typical inner-city Chinese hotel – smart lobby, slightly tarnished rooms, huge restaurant and, of course, a karaoke hall. ❺

Guangdong Guesthouse Jiefang Bei Lu ⓣ020/83332950, ⓦwww.ggh.com.cn. A huge complex of square concrete wings, Sinicized with green tiling and flared eaves and best known for its twenty different dining rooms. Quite comfortable, but fading around the edges. ❼

Landmark Yanjiang Lu ⓣ020/83355988, ⓕ83336197, ⓦwww.hotel-landmark.com.cn. Four-star business centre between a busy roundabout and the river. ❼

Northern and eastern Guangzhou

China Marriott Liuhua Lu ⓣ020/86666888, ⓕ86677014, ⓦwww.marriotthotels.com/CANMC. Five-star labyrinth of red marble corridors right opposite the Export Commodities Hall, with upmarket shopping malls and places to eat. You almost need a map to get around and are expected to pay in foreign currency, but rooms are good despite a stiff price tag. Guangzhou's *Hard Rock Café* is in

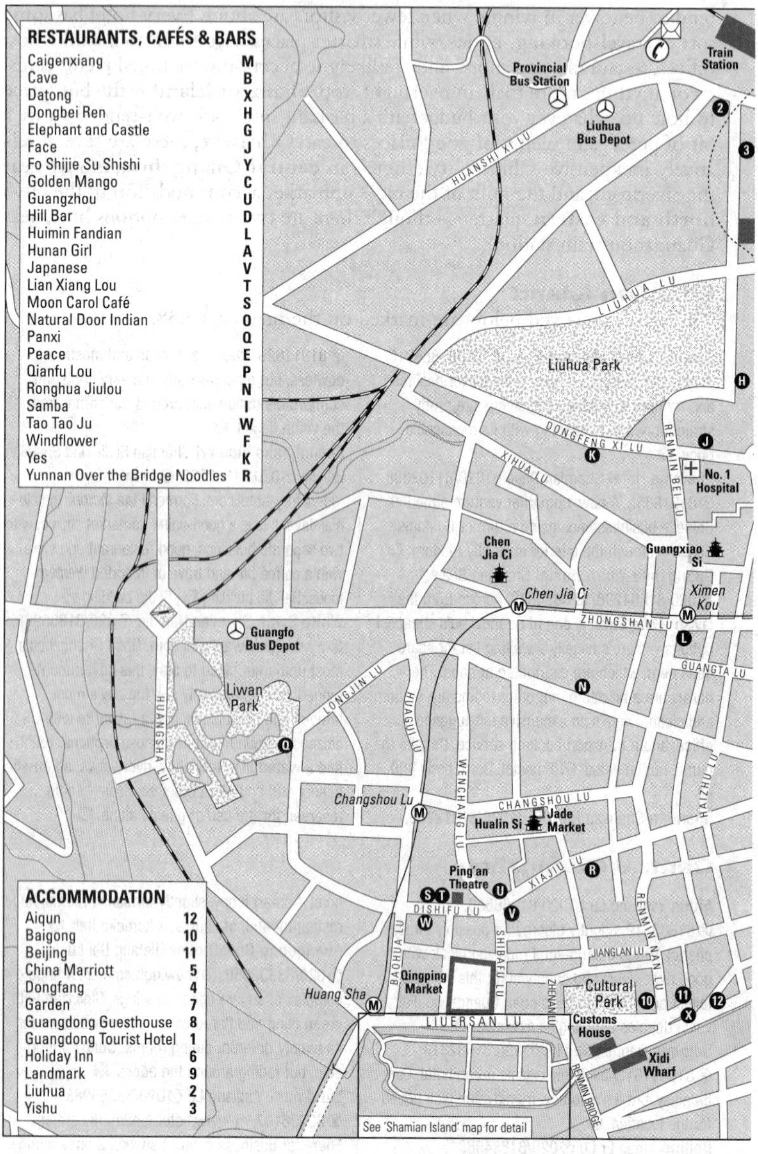

the basement. 9

Dongfang Liuhua Lu ⓣ020/86669900, ⓕ86662775. Literally in the *China*'s shadow, this is another self-contained five-star maze with a ridiculous number of restaurants housed in smartly remodelled 1950s buildings around a nice garden. 9

Garden Huanshi Dong Lu ⓣ020/83338989, ⓕ83350467, ⓦwww.gardenhotel-guangzhou.com. The city's most opulent accommodation, this private-enterprise version of the *White Swan* – there's even a waterfall – is its superior in every respect but the setting. Pool, gym and sauna all free for guests. 9

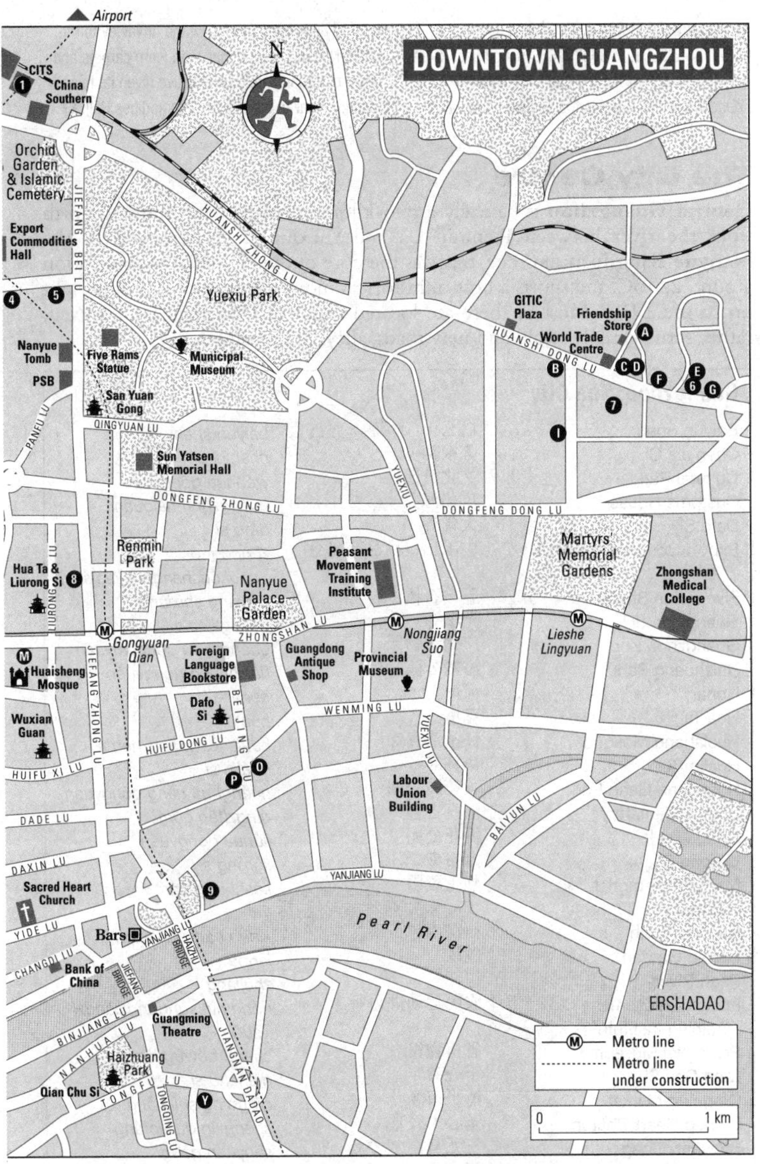

Guangdong Tourist Hotel Huanshi Xi Lu ⓣ020/86666889, ⓕ86679787. Right next to the China Southern office and Guangzhou train station, this budget CITS-managed, IYHF-affiliated affair is an excellent deal, offering clean, good-value facilities and a fine restaurant. Often full. Dorm beds ¥50, ❹

Holiday Inn Guangming Lu ⓣ020/87766999, ⓦwww.holiday-inn-guangzhou.com. Usual international-standard facilities, including a cinema. ❾

Liuhua Huanshi Xi Lu ⓣ020/86668800, ⓦwww.lh.com.cn. Trusty but ageing hotel close to the train station, with a broad range of rooms – the cheaper ones are not such good value, however. ❻

Yishu (aka Art Hotel) Renmin Bei Lu ⓣ020/86670255, ⓕ86670266. Tucked back from the street just north of the undistinguished *Friendship Hotel*; look for the English name on a gateway out front and follow the driveway to the hotel. Nothing exceptional, with worn carpets and basic bathrooms, but inexpensive given its busy location near to the Export Commodities Hall. ❹

The City Centre

Central Guangzhou is basically a two-kilometre-wide band running north from the river between Renmin Lu and Yuexiu Lu. As remnants of the **Nanyue Kingdom** illustrate, this was the core of the city from its foundation around 220BC, and sports a host of historical monuments from this time right up to the 1930s. Most of these are located south of Dongfeng Lu, a mixed, rather scruffy mesh of old and new roads, alleys and businesses.

Guangzhou: The City

Baiyun Shan	白云山	*báiyún shān*
Chen Jia Ci	陈家祠	*chénjiā cì*
Cultural Park	文化公园	*wénhuà gōngyuán*
Customs House	广州海关	*guǎngzhōu hǎiguān*
Dafo Si	大佛寺	*dàfó sì*
Export Commodities Hall	中国出口商品交易会	*zhōngguó chūkǒushāngpǐn jiāoyìhuì*
Five Rams Statue	五羊石像	*wǔyáng shíxiàng*
Guangxiao Si	光孝寺	*guāngxiào sì*
Guangzhou Zoo	广州动物园	*guǎngzhōu dòngwùyuán*
Haizhuang Park	海幢公园	*hǎizhuàng gōngyuán*
Honan	河南	*hénán*
Hua Ta	花塔	*huātǎ*
Huaisheng Mosque	怀圣清真寺	*huáishèng qīngzhēn sì*
Hualin Si	华林寺	*huálín sì*
Huanghua Gang Park	黄花岗公园	*huánghuā gǎng gōngyuán*
Islamic Cemetery	清真古墓	*qīngzhēn gǔmù*
Liuhua Park	流花公园	*liúhuā gōngyuán*
Liurong Si	六榕寺	*liùróng sì*
Martyrs' Memorial Gardens	烈士陵园	*lièshì língyuán*
Nanyue Tomb	西汉南越王墓	*xīhàn nányuèwángmù*
Orchid Garden	兰圃	*lánpǔ*
Pearl River	珠江	*zhūjiāng*
Peasant Movement Training Institute	农民运动讲习所	*nóngmín yùndòng jiǎngxí suǒ*
Provincial Museum	省博物馆	*shěng bówùguǎn*
Qian Chu Si	千处寺	*qiānchù sì*
Qingping Market	清平市场	*qīngpíng shìchǎng*
Sacred Heart Church	圣心大教堂	*shèngxīn dàjiàotáng*
Sanyuan Gong	三元宫	*sānyuán gōng*
Sanyuan Li	三元里	*sānyuán lǐ*
Shamian Island	沙面岛	*shāmiàn dǎo*
Shamian Park	沙面公园	*shāmiàn gōngyuán*
Sun Yatsen Memorial Hall	中山纪念堂	*zhōngshān jìniàn táng*
Wuxian Guan	五仙观	*wǔxiān guàn*
Xidi Wharf	西堤码头	*xīdī mǎtóu*
Yuexiu Park	越秀公园	*yuèxiù gōngyuán*
Zhenhai Lou	镇海楼	*zhènhǎi lóu*

Around the Pearl River to Wuxian Guan

Yanjiang Lu, the northern promenade along the **Pearl River**, was paved in 2001 as part of a civic smartening campaign coinciding with Guangzhou hosting the China National Games. Lined with trees and a smattering of colonial-era buildings – such as the **Customs House** and **Aiqun Hotel** – it's a good place just to mill about on hot summer evenings.

North from the river, **Yide Lu** is stuffed with small shops selling toys, dried marine produce – jellyfish, sharks' fin, fish maw and whole salted mackerel – along with sacks of nuts and candied fruit. Set north off the road at the back of a court, the **Sacred Heart Church** – also known as the Stone House – is a Gothic-style cathedral completed in 1888, impressive for its size and unexpected presence, though it's not generally open to the public. Three streets up from here on Huifu Xi Lu is **Wuxian Guan** (Five Immortals' Temple; daily 9am–noon & 1.30–5pm; ¥2). Dating from 1377, the original wooden building is nonfunctional and dusty, but some obviously ancient statues pop up around the place: weathered guardian lions flank the way in, and there are some stylized Ming sculptures out the back, looking like giant chess pieces. The Five Immortals – three men and two women – are depicted too, riding their goatly steeds as they descend through the clouds to found Guangzhou. Also impressive is a fourteenth-century **bell tower** behind the temple, in which hangs a three-metre-high, five-tonne bronze bell, silent since receiving the blame for a plague which broke out shortly after its installation in 1378, and named the "Forbidden Bell" ever since.

Pearl River cruises

Oily grey and second only to the Yangzi in importance as an industrial channel, the **Pearl River** (Zhu Jiang) originates in eastern Yunnan province and forms one of China's busiest waterways, continually active with ferries and barges loaded down with coal and stone. Its name derives from a legend about a monk named Jiahu who lost a glowing pearl in its waters, and although it shone on the riverbed night after night, nobody was ever able to recover it.

Eight **evening cruises** depart daily between 6.30pm and 9.50pm from **Xidi Wharf**, roughly opposite the Customs House on Yanjiang Lu – tickets cost upwards of ¥35 depending on how much you want to eat. Seated downstairs at the karaoke bar, or eating your meal on the upper deck, you sit back and watch the lights of the city slip slowly past your table, with fine views en route of Guangzhou's busy waterfront, flanked by ever-higher buildings. It all lasts a bit less than two hours, taking you past the *White Swan Hotel* on Shamian Island and then back under Renmin Bridge, past Haizhu Bridge and down to the grand Guangzhou suspension bridge at the far end of Ershadao. The largest of the river's mid-stream islands, Ershadao houses the city's former **boat dwellers** – outcasts who lived on the Pearl River until Liberation, forbidden to settle ashore or marry anyone who lived on land – in a purpose-built estate known as New Riverside Village. From the island, on a clear moonless night, you'll be able to see the lights of international freighters at anchor far downstream in **Huangpu**, once the site of a Military Academy where Mao studied under Chiang Kaishek, his future arch enemy and leader of the Guomindang.

Huaisheng Mosque, Liurong Si and Guangxiao Si

A few blocks north of Wuxian Guan, the modern thoroughfare of **Zhongshan Lu** runs within striking distance of three of Guangzhou's most important **temples** – Ximen Kou or Gongyuan Qian are the closest **metro** stops. South of Zhongshan Liu Lu on Guangta Lu, **Huaisheng Mosque** and its grey, conical tower, **Guangta**, loom over a surrounding wall which bars entry to non-Muslims. Looking like a lighthouse, Guangta is possibly the world's oldest minaret outside Mecca and something of a stylistic fossil, said by some to have been built by Abu Waqas in the seventh century (see p.636). During the fifteenth century, Huaisheng's environs were known as **Fanfang**, the foreigners' quarter; today there's a smattering of halal canteens and restaurants in the vicinity, including the famous *Huimin Fandian* (see p.643).

Liurong Si (Temple of the Six Banyan Trees; daily 8.30am–5.15pm; ¥6) lies north of the mosque on Liurong Lu, and is associated with the dissident poet–governor **Su Dongpo** (see p.687), who named the temple on a visit in 1100 and drew the characters for "Liu Rong" on the two stone steles just inside the gates. Very little of the temple itself survives, and the site is better known for the 57-metre-high **Hua Ta** (Flower Pagoda), a contemporary structure enshrining relics brought from India by Emperor Wu's uncle. Carvings of lions, insects and birds adorn the pagoda's wooden eaves; of its seventeen storeys, nine have balconies and the rest are blind. At the top is a gigantic bronze pillar covered with over a thousand reliefs of meditating figures rising up through the roof, solid enough to support the five-tonne begging bowl and pearl that you can see from ground level.

A narrow lane along Liurong Si's northern boundary leads west through a street market on to Haizhu Bei Lu. Turn south and then west again along

Chan Buddhism

Chan – known in Japan as **Zen** – believes that an understanding of the true nature of being can be achieved by sudden **enlightenment**, sparked by everyday, banal conversations or events. In this it differs from other forms of Buddhism, with their emphasis on the need for years of study of ritual and religious texts; though also using meditation and little parables to achieve its ends, Chan therefore puts enlightenment within the grasp of even the most secular individual.

The founder of Chan was **Bodhidarma** (known as **Damo** in China), who arrived in Guangzhou from India around 520 AD intending to enrich China's rather formal, stodgy approach to Buddhism with his more lateral slant. After baffling the emperor with his teachings, Bodhidarma ended up at **Shaolin Si** in Henan, where exercises he taught monks to balance their long hours of meditation are believed to have formed the basis of Chinese **kung fu** (see pp.309 & p.311). Shaolin subsequently became the centre for Chan Buddhism, spreading from there across China and into Japan and Korea.

Chan's most famous exponent was its Sixth Patriarch, **Huineng** (638–713). Huineng was from Guangzhou, but as a youth heard a wandering monk reciting sutras and was so impressed that he went to **Huangmei** in central China specifically to study Chan under the Fifth Patriarch, Hong Ren. Scorned by his fellow students for his rough southern manners, Huineng nonetheless demonstrated such a deep understanding of Chan that within a mere eight months he had achieved enlightenment on hearing the **Diamond Sutra** (which teaches how to recognize and dispense with illusions) and had been elected by Hong Ren to succeed him as patriarch, though the matter was kept secret at the time. Returning south to Guangzhou, in 676 Huineng settled incognito at **Guangxiao Si**, where one day he heard two monks watching a flag and debating whether it was the wind or the flag that was moving. As they couldn't reach a decision, Huineng volunteered that neither was right, it was the mind that moved. His statement so stunned everyone present that he was invited to lecture, thereby revealing himself as the Sixth Patriarch (Hong Ren having died in the meantime). Huineng apparently spent his later years at **Nanhua Si** near Shaoguan in northern Guangdong – see p.664 for more.

Jinghui Lu for the entrance to the spacious and peaceful **Guangxiao Si** (daily 8am–5pm; ¥2), the oldest of Guangzhou's Buddhist temples. In 113 BC this was the residence of **Zhao Jiande**, last of the Nanyue kings (see p.635), becoming a place of worship only after the 85-year-old Kashmiri monk **Tanmo Yeshe** built the first hall in 401 AD. The temple was later visited by Buddhist luminaries such as the sixth-century monk Zhiyao Sanzang, who planted the fig trees still here today; the Indian founder of Chan (Zen) Buddhism, **Bodhidharma**; and Chan's Sixth Patriarch, **Huineng** (for more on whom, see the box opposite). Though again none of the original buildings survive, the grounds are well ordered and enclose pavilions concealing wells and engraved tablets from various periods, while three halls at the back contain some imposing Buddha images; the westerly one is unusually reclining, while a more ordinary trinity fills the central hall.

The Provincial Museum and around

Around 1500m east of Wuxian Guan on Wenming Lu is the **Provincial Museum** (daily 9.30am–4.30pm; ¥8); walking here from Wuxian Guan, you'll pass the small and unassuming **Dafo Si**, the Big Buddha Temple, and the frenetically crowded shopping district along **Beijing Lu**; coming straight up from the river, look for the yellow, 1920s **Labour Union Building** on Yuexiu Lu, later appropriated, somewhat cynically, as the Guomindang headquarters.

The similar-looking buildings inside the Provincial Museum grounds are those of the former **Zhongshan University**; the writer **Lu Xun** lectured here and his life is outlined in photographs. A more modern structure houses the museum proper, whose best features are a **natural history display**, incorporating an innovative walk-through "jungle" with spotlit creatures hidden in the undergrowth; and several rooms of exquisitely fine porcelain, carved jade and Ming household ornaments. The lack of visitors and explanatory notes somewhat deadens it all, but it's remarkable to see such a high standard of exhibits.

Thanks to the subsequent career of its dean, Mao Zedong, Guangzhou's **Peasant Movement Training Institute**, on Zhongshan Lu (daily 8.15–11.30am & 2–5pm; ¥10), is the city's most frequented revolutionary site. It still looks like the Confucian Academy it was for six hundred years, before **Peng Pai**, a "rich peasant" from Guangdong, established the Institute in 1924 with Guomindang permission and 38 students. The school lasted just over two years, with Mao, Zhou Enlai and Peng Pai taking the final classes in August 1926, eight months before the Communist and Guomindang alliance ended violently in Shanghai. There's actually little to see; most poignant are the photographs of alumni who failed to survive the Shanghai Massacre and the subsequent **1927 Communist Uprising** in Guangzhou.

The scene of the latter event lies farther east along Zhongshan Lu at the **Martyrs' Memorial Gardens** (daily 8am–7pm; ¥3). It was near here, on December 11, 1927, that a small Communist force under **Zhang Teilai** managed to take the Guangzhou Police Headquarters, announcing the foundation of the **Canton Commune**. Expected support never materialized, however, and on the afternoon of the second day Guomindang forces moved in; five thousand people were killed outright or later executed for complicity. The grounds contain a small lake, some trees and a lawn, and a strange rifle-like monument beside the grassy mound where the insurgents lie buried.

The Nanyue Palace Garden

About 500m west of the Peasant Movement Training Institute on Zhongshan Si Lu, the **Nanyue Palace Garden** (daily 9am–noon & 2.30–5.30pm, last entry 45min before closing; ¥15) is – while rather cryptic in appearance – one of the most extraordinary historical sites in China. The **Nanyue Kingdom** was founded by Zhao Tuo, a Qin general from Hebei Province who was ordered down here in 214 BC to subjugate China's unruly southern tribes. Following the collapse of the Qin empire, Zhao, backed by his army, declared himself head of an independent state. China's new Han dynasty initially acknowledged his position and even granted him the title of "Emperor Wu" during his 67-year reign. But by the time of his grandson the Nanyue Kingdom was in decline, and in 111 BC the Han sacked the capital and reclaimed the territory for central China.

The gardens are the partially excavated site of **Zhao Tuo's palace grounds**, the full extent of which is believed to continue several blocks north of the area on view. It's very complex: on show is part of the **garden** which surrounded the palace buildings, superimposed over which are remains of an even earlier shipyard, along with later sewers, wells, a tenth-century palace, and a Song-era college to further muddle the picture. You're first shown an English-language **video** of the excavations during the 1990s, followed by a trot through a small **museum**: stone slabs and pillars from the site predominate, beside spiky ceramic rooftiles and the largest fired brick found in China, all decorated with designs or characters – including that for "**Pan**", an abbreviation of "Panyu", Guangzhou's original name. A half-fused pile of bronze coins and charred beams support the account given by Sima Qian, the Han-dynasty historian, of the palace's **destruction** by the Han armies.

Outside, the actual **excavated site** covers about five thousand square metres, protected from the elements by a corrugated iron roof, with a raised boardwalk linking key items. The main feature here is the corner of a **paved lake** to the northeast, from which the bed of an ornamental **stream** follows a curved path westwards. Passing through a crescent **pond**, it's lined with pebbles and ramps, presumably placed to cause ripples, swirls and noise as the water flowed through. Seeds and leaves found preserved in the muddy riverbed show that lotuses and trees were also part of the garden, along with turtles, whose carapaces were found in the crescent pond. At the far southwestern corner, a tantalizing fraction of a **Qin-dynasty shipyard** has been left as discovered in 1975, the oldest evidence for ocean-going vessels in China. Like Zhao Tuo's palace itself, which test digs have located northwest of the garden under a department store and park, this all awaits further excavation.

Northern Guangzhou

The area north between Dongfeng Lu and Guangzhou train station is primarily occupied by two huge **parks**, Liuhua and Yuexiu, with a sole momento of a colonial-era confrontation further out beyond the station at **Sanyuan Li**.

Yuexiu Park

Yuexiu Park is China's biggest spread of urban greenery (daily 7am–7pm; ¥5), encompassing over ninety hectares of sports courts, historic monuments, teahouses and shady groves. On the way here you'll pass a couple of notable buildings, most visibly the large rotunda and blue tiled roof of the **Sun Yatsen Memorial Hall** on Dongfeng Zhong Lu (daily 8am–6pm; ¥5), built on the spot where the man regarded by Guomindang and Communists alike as the father of modern China took the presidential oath in 1912. Inside it's a plain auditorium with seating for two thousand people, occasionally used as a concert hall. Far less obvious is **Sanyuan Gong** (Three Purities Temple; ¥1) just west of here, whose entrance is virtually unmarked below a broad stone staircase. This is actually the largest Taoist temple in Guangzhou, and the oldest too – it was first consecrated in 319 – though the current arrangement of dark, spartan halls occupied by statues of Taoist deities is Qing. Gloomy furnishings aside, it's a busy place of worship, and there are a few splashes of red and gold in the painted bats, cranes, and other Taoist motifs scattered around.

The park

While there are entrances at all points of the compass, Yuexiu's **front gate** is on Jiefang Bei Lu, a ten-minute walk north of San Yuan Gong. To the north of the porcelain dragons here are **Beixiu Hu** and the **Garden of Chinese Idiom**, where many strange stone and bronze sculptures lurk in the undergrowth, illustrating popular sayings. Head south, and you'll wind up at the much photographed **Five Rams Statue**, commemorating the myth of Guangzhou's foundation – at least one of these is definitely not a ram, however.

Roughly in the middle of the park atop a hill, paths converge at **Zhenhai Lou**, the "Gate Tower Facing the Sea", a wood and rendered-brick building which once formed part of the Ming city walls. Today it houses the **Municipal Museum** (Tues–Sun 9am–4pm; ¥8), three floors of locally found exhibits ranging from Stone Age pottery fragments and ivory from Africa found in a Han-dynasty tomb, to fifth-century coins from Persia, a copy of *Good Words for Exhorting the World* (the Christian tract which inspired the Taiping leader, Hong Xiuquan), and nineteenth-century cannons tumbled about in the courtyard (two made by the German company, Krupp). A statue of Lin Zexu and letters from him to the Qing emperor documenting his disposal of the British opium stocks always draws big crowds of tongue-clicking Chinese. Your ticket includes tea on the top floor, where you can gaze south across Guangzhou's sprawl.

The Nanyue Tomb and Liuhua Park

Five hundred metres north of Yuexiu Park's Jiefang Bei Lu entrance (and reachable on bus #5) is the looming red sandstone facade of the **Nanyue Tomb** (daily 9.30am–5.30pm, last admission 4.45pm; ¥12, plus ¥5 to enter the tomb itself). Discovered in 1983 during foundation digging for a residential estate, this houses the 2000-year-old site of the tomb of **Zhao Mo**, grandson of the Nanyue Kingdom's founder Zhao Tuo (see p.634), and really deserves an hour of your time – there's another English-language **video** and a mass of exhibits.

Zhao Mo made a better job of his tomb than running his kingdom, which disintegrated shortly after his death: excavators found the tomb stacked with gold and priceless trinkets. They're on view in the museum, including a **burial suit** made out of over a thousand tiny jade tiles (jade was considered to prevent decay), and the ash-like remains of slaves and concubines immured with him. Several artefacts show Central Asian influence in their designs, illustrating how even at this early stage in Guangzhou's history there was contact with non-Chinese peoples. It's all fascinating and expertly presented, particularly worthwhile if you plan to visit contemporary grave sites in the Yangzi Basin or at Xi'an. Incidentally, Zhao Tuo's tomb still awaits discovery, though rumours of its fabulous treasures had eager excavators turning Guangzhou inside out as long ago as the Three Kingdoms period (220–280 AD).

West of the Nanyue Tomb between Liuhua Lu and Renmin Bei Lu, **Liuhua Park** (daily 7am–7pm; ¥2) is a large expanse of lakes, purpose-built in 1958 and pleasant enough during the week, though hellishly crowded at weekends.

Liuhua means "Flowing Flowers", a name said to date back to the Han period when palace maids tossed petals into a nearby stream while dressing their hair.

To the train station

About 1km south of the train station and surrounded by business hotels on Liuhua Lu and Renmin Lu, the **Export Commodities Hall** is the venue each April and October for the city's **Trade Fair**, first held in 1957 to encourage Western investments. This isn't the most pleasant area of town but there is one oasis of peace and quiet, Guangzhou's delightful, though fairly small, **Orchid Garden**, off Jiefang Bei Lu (daily 8am–5pm; ¥8, entry includes tea in the central pavilion). Besides orchids, there are ponds surrounded by tropical ferns and lilies, winding stone paths, palms and giant figs with drooping aerial roots, and pink-flowering azaleas. Apart from the filtered traffic noise, it's hard to believe that the city lies just outside. Along the western edge of the garden, Guangzhou's **Islamic Cemetery** contains the tomb of **Abu Waqas**, a seventh-century missionary who brought Islam to China. The details are a little sketchy, however, as Abu Waqas supposedly died around 629, three years before Mohammed, and the Quran wasn't collated for another generation afterwards. The cemetery was recently closed to non-Muslims, though it can be glimpsed from inside the garden through a screen of bamboos.

Sanyuan Li

For a return to earth after the Orchid Garden, continue up Jiefang Bei Lu for a kilometre after it crosses Huanshi Lu – take bus #58 rather than walk, as there's a lot of traffic to dodge. You're now north of the train station in **Sanyuan Li**, an untidy district due for development, currently something of a migrant workers' quarter. This was where the **Sanyuan Li Anti-British Movement** formed in 1841 after the British stormed into the area during the First Opium War. Following months of abuse from the invaders, local workers and peasants rose under the farmer **Wei Shaoguang** and attacked the British camp, killing around twenty soldiers in an indecisive engagement before being dispersed by heavy rain. A **temple** 250m along on the south side of Guanghua Lu, built in 1860 on the sight of the battle, is now a **museum** (daily 9–11.30am & 2–4pm; ¥2) housing the peasants' armoury of farm tools and ceremonial weapons, though don't take captions – the turgid product of later propaganda – too seriously.

Western Guangzhou

Western Guangzhou, the area west of Renmin Lu and south of Dongfeng Xi Lu, features a charismatic warren of back roads and lanes around Changshou Lu, all stuffed to overflowing with market activity, restaurants and shops, which empty down near the waterfront opposite **Shamian Island**, a quiet haven of colonial mood and huge trees. North of the river, Zhongshan Lu continues westwards through the area, cut by a score of roads running south to parallel **Liuersan Lu**, along the river; south, the main roads are Nanhua Lu and Tongfu Lu. There are several **metro** stops through this area.

Chen Jia Ci

Zhongshan Lu's western arm cuts through a new, relatively tidy district before eventually heading over a tributary of the Pearl River and out of the city towards Foshan. About 2.5km from the Jiefang Lu intersection, a pedestrian walkway across the road leads to gardens outside **Chen Jia Ci** (Chen Clan

Academy; daily 8.30am–5.30pm; ¥10). The story of its founding is unusual; subscriptions were invited from anyone named **Chen** – one of the most common Cantonese surnames – and the money raised went to build this complex, part ancestor temple where Chens could worship, part school where they could receive an education. Though belittled today by tea rooms and souvenir stalls, the buildings remain impressive, forming a series of rooms arranged around open courtyards, all decorated by the most garish tiles and gorgeously carved screens and stonework that money could buy in the 1890s. Have a good look at the extraordinary brick reliefs under the eaves, both inside and out. One of the first, on the right as you enter, features an opera being performed to what looks like a drunken horse, who lies squirming on the floor with mirth. Other cameos feature stories from China's "noble bandit" saga, *Outlaws of the Marsh*, and some of the sights around Guangzhou.

Changshou Lu and around

Below Zhongshan Lu, the ring of part of the old city walls can be traced along **Longjin Lu** in the north, and **Dishifu Lu** and others to the south – you'll actually cross a low mound marking their foundations if you enter the area off Zhongshan Lu down Huagui Lu. Though a couple of wide, modern main roads barge through, most of this district, with east–west **Changshou Lu** at its core, retains its Ming dynasty street plan and a splash of early-twentieth-century architecture, making for excellent random walks. In addition to some of Guangzhou's biggest shopping plazas and a crowd of markets spreading into each other south from Changshou Lu right down to the river, several **famous restaurants** are here, and the area is particularly busy at night.

Southwest of the Changshou Lu/Kangwang Lu intersection, shops almost conceal the narrow lanes through into Guangzhou's **jade market** – it's not up to Hong Kong's, but is still worth a browse. The market surrounds an auspiciously red-painted gateway, behind which is the Buddhist temple of **Hualin Si** (daily 8am–5pm; free), founded as a modest nunnery by the Brahman prince **Bodhidarma** in 527 (see box, p.632). After his Chan teachings caught on in the seventeenth century, the main hall was enlarged to house five hundred *arhat* sculptures ranged along the cross-shaped aisles, and Hualin remains as the most lively temple in the city – during festivals you'll be crushed, deafened and blinded by the crowds, firecrackers and incense smoke.

From here, the best thing you can do is throw away your map and roam unaided southwards through the maze of alleys and Qing-era homes (some of which are protected historic relics), most likely emerging in the vicinity of the *Guangzhou* restaurant. Two streets lined with restored 1920s facades and pedestrianized at the weekends lie here – **Dishifu Lu** to the west and **Xiajiu Lu** to the east – and places to eat and shop are legion, the pavements always crammed to capacity. South again off Xiajiu Lu, you enter the upper reaches of the infamous **Qingping Market**, with each intersecting east–west lane forming dividing lines for the sale of different goods: dried medicines, spices and herbs, fresh vegetables, livestock, bird and fish. Once one of China's most confronting – not to say gory – markets, this has been scaled down considerably in recent years with the removal of rare animals and large-scale streetside butchering, though it remains a lively and busy affair, amply illustrating the Cantonese demand for fresh and unusual food.

You exit Qingping onto **Liuersan Lu**, a recently widened road given a stack of flyovers to relieve chronic traffic congestion, lined with palms, flowerbeds, and fake colonial frontages mirroring the real thing opposite on Shamian Island. "Liuersan" means "6, 23", referring to June 23, 1925, when fifty people were shot by colonial troops during a demonstration demanding, among other things, the return of Shamian Island to Chinese control. East along Liuersan, the **Cultural Park** (daily 6am till late; ¥3) is a rather bland area of paving and benches where gangs of children queue for their turn on arcade games and fairground rides, and theatre and sound stages host weekend performances of anything from local rock to opera.

Shamian Island

It's only a short hop across Liuersan Lu and a muddy canal (or head to Huang Sha metro, then cross the bridge) on to **Shamian Island**, but the pace changes instantly, and Guangzhou's busiest quarter is exchanged for its most genteel. A tear-shaped sandbank about 1km long and 500m wide, Shamian was leased to European powers as an Opium War trophy, the French getting the eastern end and the British the rest. Here the colonials re-created their own backyards, planting the now massive **trees** and throwing up solid, Victorian-style **villas**, banks, embassies, churches and tennis courts – practically all of which are still standing. Iron gates on the bridges once excluded the Chinese from Shamian (as the Chinese had once forbidden foreigners to enter within Guangzhou's city walls), leaving the Europeans in self-imposed isolation from the bustle across the water. Shamian retains that atmosphere today, a quiet bolt hole for many long-term travellers in the city. There's restricted traffic flow, and the well-tended architecture, greenery and relative peace make it a refreshing place to visit, even if you're not staying or sampling the restaurants and bars.

The main thoroughfare is east–west **Shamian Dajie**, with five numbered streets running south across the island. Wandering around, you'll find buildings have largely been restored to their original appearance – most were built between the 1860s and early twentieth century – with plaques sketching their history. Though sharing such a tiny area, the British and French seemingly kept

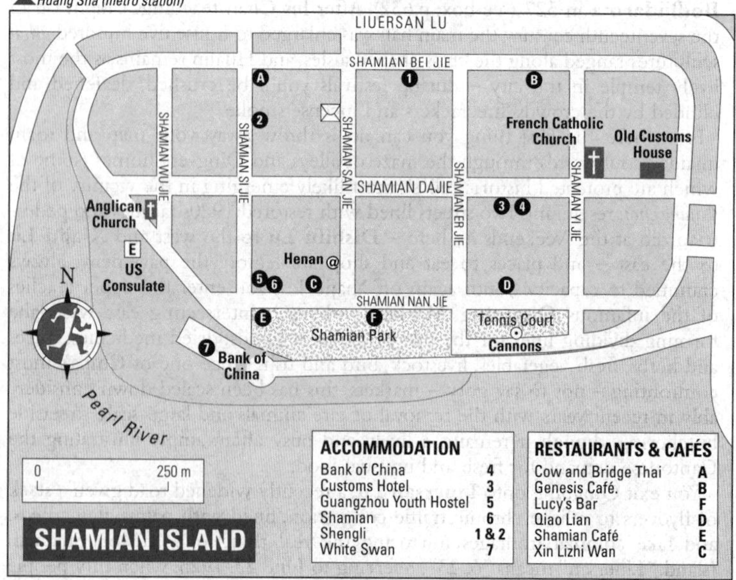

themselves to themselves, building separate bridges, churches and customs houses; nothing is particularly worth searching out, but it's all great browsing. Next to the atypically modern *White Swan* hotel on the **Shamian Nan Jie** esplanade, a focus of sorts is provided by **Shamian Park**, where two **cannons**, cast in nearby Foshan during the Opium Wars, face out across the river, and you might catch Cantonese opera rehersals here on Saturday afternoons. The island's waterfront area is also the venue for Guangzhou's major Spring Festival **fireworks display**, held on the first night at around 9pm; the best seats are at the *White Swan*'s riverside buffet at ¥400 a head, failing which you can join half of the city in the surrounding streets – or watch from your room at the *Youth Hostel*.

Honan

Honan, the area immediately south of the river between westerly **Gongye Dadao** and **Jiangnan Dadao**, 1500m further east, can be reached on any of **three bridges**: Renmin bridge, which connects Liuersan Lu with Gongye Dadao; and the closely spaced Jiefang and Haizhu bridges off Yanjiang Lu, which become Tongqing Lu and Jiangnan Dadao respectively. Metro line #2 will, when completed, have several stations along Jiangnan Dadao; until it opens it's easiest just to walk across the nearest bridge and explore on foot.

Prior to 1949, Honan was Guangzhou's red-light district, crawling with opium dens, brothels and gambling houses, none of which survived the Communist takeover. Indeed, in 1984 Honan was chosen as a model of **Hu Yaobang**'s "Civic Spirit" campaign, which called on residents to organize kindergartens, old folks' clubs, and to keep their communities clean and safe. It's still a surprisingly calm and quiet corner of the city, the small flagstoned alleys off Nanhua Lu and Tongfu Lu kept litter-free and lined with austere, wooden-gated homes. During the **spring flower festival** (a southern Chinese tradition originating in Guangzhou) however, florist stalls along riverfront Binjiang Lu attract crowds from all over the city to buy blooms of every colour and shape for good luck in the coming year. There's also another big Cantonese-style **market** here – a rather more spirited affair than Qingping – in the backstreets southwest off the Nanhua Lu/Tongqing Lu junction.

Honan's sole formal sight is in **Haizhuang Park** (¥1.5), sandwiched between Nanhua Lu and Tongfu Lu, about ten minutes' walk from Renmin Bridge. The buildings here have recently been returned to their original purpose as **Qian Chu Si**, a sizeable Buddhist monastery. Renovations have spruced up the broad south hall with its fine statuary and interlocked wooden beam roof, so typical of south China's early Qing temple buildings – the flashing coloured "halos" surrounding several of the statues are less traditional touches.

Eastern Guangzhou and Baiyun Shan Park

Hemmed in on all other flanks by rivers and hills, Guangzhou inevitably expands east to accommodate its ever-growing population, and it's here you'll find the most "modern" parts of the city, shadowed by highrises housing corporate headquarters and cut by several expressways. **Huanshi Lu** and **Dongfeng Lu** are the biggest of these, converging out in the northeastern suburbs at the vast open-plan district of **Tianhe**. Much of the city's **expat community** is based out this way, and there are numerous Western-oriented **restaurants and bars** – if few actual sights – to recommend a visit. One exception is **Baiyun Shan Park**, which lies immediately to the north and offers an unexpectedly thorough escape from the city.

Northeast off Huanshi Dong Lu along Xianlie Lu, **Huanghua Gang Park** (daily 8am–5pm; ¥2) recalls Sun Yatsen's abortive 1911 Canton Uprising in the **Mausoleum to the 72 Martyrs**, a very peculiar monument reflecting the nationalities of numerous donors who contributed to its construction – Buddhist iconography rubbing shoulders with a Statue of Liberty and Egyptian obelisk. Of more general appeal is **Guangzhou Zoo**, about a kilometre farther out along Xianlie Lu (daily 9am–4pm; ¥10; take bus #6 from Dongfeng Lu, one block east of the Sun Yatsen Memorial Hall). This is the third largest in the country, with the animals kept in relatively decent conditions – though far below what you'll probably consider pleasant. Among the rarities are clouded leopards, several species of wildfowl and, of course, pandas.

You'll most likely find yourself out at **Tianhe**, the area surrounding the train station 2km due east of the zoo, en route to Guangzhou East train station. A planned area of vast spaces of concrete paving, broad roads and glassy towers, where pedestrians are reduced to insignificant specks, Tianhe has as its showpiece a huge **sports stadium** built for the 1987 National Games (Xiuyu Zhong Xiao metro), all revamped when Guangzhou was the Games' host for the second time in 2001.

Baiyun Shan Park

Just 7km north of downtown, **Baiyun Shan** (White Cloud Mountain) is close enough to central Guangzhou to reach by city bus, but open enough to leave all the city's noise and bustle behind. Once covered with numerous monasteries, Baiyun's heavily reforested slopes now offer lush panoramas out over Guangzhou and the delta region. A **park** here encloses almost thirty square kilometres (¥15), its entrance a thirty-minute ride on bus #24 from the south side of Renmin Park, immediately northeast of the Jiefang Lu/Zhongshan Lu crossroads.

It's a good three-hour walk from the entrance off Luhu Lu to **Moxing Ling** (Star-touching Summit), past strategically placed teahouses and pavilions offering views and refreshments. There's also a **cable car** (¥20) from the entrance as far as the **Cheng Precipice**, a ledge roughly halfway to the top, which earned its name when the Qin-dynasty minister **Cheng Ki** was ordered here by his emperor to find a herb of immortality. Having found the plant, Cheng nibbled a leaf only to see the remainder vanish; full of remorse, he flung himself off the mountain but was caught by a stork and taken to heaven. Sunset views from the precipice are spectacular.

Eating

Eating out is the main recreation in Guangzhou, something the city is famous for and caters to admirably. Guangzhou's restaurants, the best to be found in a province famed for its food, are in themselves justification to spend a few days in the city, and it would be a real shame to leave without having eaten in one of the more elaborate or famous **Cantonese** places – there's nothing to match the experience of tucking into a Cantonese spread while being surrounded by an enthusiastic horde of local diners. Locals are so proud of their cuisine that a few years ago it was hard to find anywhere serving anything else, though now you can also track down a good variety of **Asian**, **European**, and even **Indian** food – not to mention **regional Chinese**. Some canteens open as early as 5am and breakfast – including traditional **dim sum** – is usually served from 7am to 10am, later on Sundays or if the restuarant has a particularly good reputation.

Guangzhou: Eating

Banana Leaf Curry House	蕉叶饮食	*jiāoyè yǐnshí*
Caigenxiang	菜根香	*càigēn xiāng*
Cow and Bridge Thai	泰国牛桥	*tàiguó niúqiáo*
Datong	大同大酒家	*dàtóng dàjiǔjiā*
Dongbei Ren	东北人	*dōngběi rén*
Fo Shijie Su Shishe	佛世界素食社	*fóshìjiè sùshíshè*
Genesis Café	创世纪	*chuàngshì jì*
Guangzhou	广州酒家	*guǎngzhōu jiǔjiā*
Huimin Fandian	回民饭店	*huímín fàndiàn*
Hunan Girl	湘妹子	*xiāngmèi zi*
Japanese	大禾会日本饭店	*dàhéhuì rìběn fàndiàn*
Jiangxi Ren	江西人	*jiāngxī rén*
Lian Xiang Lou	莲香楼	*liánxiāng lóu*
Lucy's Bar	露丝吧	*lùsī bā*
Nanyuan	南园酒店	*nányuán jiǔdiàn*
Natural Door Indian	自然门印度餐厅	*zìránmén yìndù cāntīng*
Panxi	泮溪酒家	*pànxī jiǔjiā*
Qianfu Lou	千福楼	*qiānfú lóu*
Qiao Lian	侨联餐厅	*qiáolián cāntīng*
Ronghua Jiulou	荣华酒楼	*rónghuá jiǔlóu*
Samba	森巴西餐厅	*sēnbāxī cāntīng*
Shamian Café	沙面咖啡屋美食	*shāmiàn kāfēiwū měishí*
Tao Tao Ju	陶陶居	*táotáo jū*
Xin Lizhi Wan	新荔枝湾酒楼	*xīnlìzhīwān jiǔlóu*
Yunnan Over The Bridge Noodles	云南过桥米线坊	*yúnnán guòqiǎo mǐxiàn fang*

Lunch is on offer between 11am and 2pm, and dinner from 5pm to 10pm, though most people eat early rather than late.

Restaurants are pretty evenly spread across the city, though Dishifu Lu in the west, and Shamian Island, have a ridiculous quantity and variety between them. Ordering is a bit easier here than in the average Chinese city, as many restaurants have an **English menu** tucked away somewhere, even if these omit dishes that they believe won't appeal to foreigners. **Prices** have actually fallen somewhat in recent years, though the sociable Cantonese fashion of entertaining (and impressing) family or wealthy clients with food means that you'll pay upwards of ¥40 a head for a good Chinese meal, and ¥60 if you're after more exotic Asian or Western fare.

You can, of course, eat for a fraction of this cost day or night at the city's numerous **food stalls** which, like the restaurants, are never far away (streets off Beijing Lu have the best selection). The usual fare at these places is a few slices of roast duck or pork on rice, meat and chicken dumplings, or noodle soups, and rarely exceed ¥8–10 a plate. Be sure to try a selection of **cakes** and the fresh tropical **fruits** too; local lychees are so good that the emperors once had them shipped direct to Beijing.

If Chinese dining just isn't for you, there are Western fast-food outlets throughout the city, though there's no need to resort to them – **bars** and **cafés** listed below serve grills, sandwiches, and counter meals as good as anything you'll get at home. Tourist **hotels** have restaurants used to dealing with foreign palates, too, and some are worth checking for special sittings. The daily dessert buffet at the *China* (3–5pm; ¥40 per person), for example, features an

Guangdong cooking

Guangdong cooking is one of China's four major regional styles and, despite northern critics decrying it as too uncomplicated to warrant the term "cuisine", it's unmatched in the clarity of its flavours and its appealing presentation. The style subdivides into **Cantonese**, emanating from the Pearl River Delta region; **Chaozhou**, from the city of the same name in the far east of Guangdong; and **Hakka**, from the northeastern border with Fujian, named after the Han subgroup with whom it originated. Though certain Chaozhou and Hakka recipes have been incorporated into the main body of Guangdong cooking – sweet-and-sour pork with fruit, and salt-baked chicken, for instance – it's Cantonese food which has come to epitomize its principles. With many Chinese emigrants leaving through Guangzhou, it's also the most familiar to overseas visitors, though peruse a menu here and you'll soon realize that most dishes served abroad as "Cantonese" would be unrecognizable to a local resident.

Spoiled by good soil and a year-round growing season, the Cantonese demand absolutely **fresh ingredients**, kept alive and kicking in cages, tanks or buckets at the front of the restaurant for diners to select themselves. Westerners can be repulsed by this collection of wildlife, and even other Chinese comment that the Cantonese will eat anything with legs that isn't a piece of furniture, and anything with wings that isn't an aeroplane. The cooking itself is designed to keep **textures** distinct and **flavours** as close to the original as possible, using a minimum amount of mild and complementary seasonings to prevent dishes from being bland. **Fast stir-frying** in a wok is the best known of these procedures, but **slow-simmering** in soy sauce and wine and **roasting** are other methods of teasing out the essential characteristics of the food.

No full meal is really complete without a simple plate of rich green and bitter **choi sam** (*cai xin* in Mandarin), Chinese broccoli, blanched and dressed with oyster sauce. Also famous is **fish and seafood**, often simply steamed with ginger and spring onions – hairy crabs are a winter treat, sold everywhere – and nobody cooks **fowl** better than the Cantonese, always juicy and flavoursome whether served crisp-skinned and roasted or fragrantly casseroled. Guangzhou's citizens are also compulsive snackers, and outside canteens you'll see **roast meats**, such as whole goose or strips of *cha siu* pork, waiting to be cut up and served with rice for a light lunch, or burners stacked with **sandpots** (*sai bo*), a one-person dish of steamed rice served in the cooking vessel with vegetables and slices of sweet *lap cheung* sausage. **Cake shops** selling heavy Chinese pastries and filled buns are found everywhere across the region. Some items like **custard tartlets** are derived from foreign sources, while roast-pork buns and flaky-skinned **mooncakes** stuffed with sweet lotus seed paste are of domestic origin.

Perhaps it's this delight in little delicacies that led to the tradition of **dim sum** (*dian xin* in Mandarin) really blossoming in Guangdong, where it's become an elaborate form of breakfast most popular on Sundays, when entire households pack out restaurants. Also known in Cantonese as **yum cha** – literally, "drink tea" – it involves little dishes of fried, boiled and steamed snacks being stuffed inside bamboo steamers or displayed on plates, then wheeled around the restaurant on trolleys, which you stop for inspection as they pass your table. On being seated you're given a pot of tea which is constantly topped up, and a card which is marked for each dish you select and later surrendered to the cashier. Try *juk* (rice porridge), spring rolls, buns, cakes and plates of thinly sliced roast meats, and small servings of restaurant dishes like spareribs, stuffed capsicum, or squid with black beans. Save most room, however, for the myriad types of little fried and steamed **dumplings** which are the hallmark of a *dim sum* meal, such as *har gau*, juicy minced prawns wrapped in transparent rice-flour skins; and *siu mai*, a generic name for a host of delicately flavoured, open-topped packets.

unbelievable array of cakes served with tea or coffee; the *White Swan* does endless coffee refills (¥36) as well as a buffet breakfast (¥96) before 11am – and has the best riverside views in Guangzhou.

Central Guangzhou

Caigenxiang Zhongshan Lu. Mid-range vegetarian restaurant, with dumpling house downstairs and menu-dining above. A bit grubby round the edges with decidedly offhand service, but the food is extremely good; try the gluten "roast honey pork", "fried eel" (battered curls of dried mushroom) or needle mushroom and *bok choi* casserole. Around ¥30 a person.

Datong 63 Yanjiang Xi Lu. If you're after an authentically noisy, crowded *dim sum* session with river views, head here to floors 2, 5 or 6 between 7am and noon. They pride themselves on their roast suckling pig. Window seats are in high demand, so arrive early.

Huimin Fandian (aka Five Rams) Southeast corner of the Renmin Lu/Zhongshan Lu crossroads. The city's biggest and most popular Muslim restaurant, serving lamb hotpots, roast duck, lemon chicken and spicy beef, with a cheaper canteen downstairs dolling out spicy noodle dishes. Inexpensive to moderately priced.

Natural Door Indian Small lane off the east side of Beijing Lu. Small and under-patronized Southern Indian and Malay restaurant, with roti, *rendang*, samosas, dhal, biryanis and fish cakes in banana leaves. Set meals from ¥20, individual dishes under ¥40.

Qianfu Lou Beijing Lu. Full-on Cantonese restaurant on three floors, with a take-away roast-meat shop and canteen downstairs, plus more formal arrangements above.

Northern and eastern Guangzhou

Banana Leaf Curry House World Trade Centre, Huanshi Dong Lu. Good, eclectic mix of Thai, Malaysian and Indonesian fare, all authentically spiced. Not cheap though; expect upwards of ¥70 a head.

Dongbei Ren Opposite Liuhua Park on Renmin Bei Lu. Nationwide chain serving Manchurian food in comfortable surroundings; sautéed corn kernels with pine nuts, steamed chicken with mushrooms, or eggs and black fungus are all good. Portions from ¥20.

Hunan Girl Taojin Lu. Hunanese restaurant more popular with Guangzhou's expats than Chinese residents – the interior even looks like an average Chinese restaurant overseas – though the cooking is good and prices are reasonable.

Jiangxi Ren 475 Huanshi Dong Lu. It's easy to spot the huge earthernware jars outside this one, and the second-floor restaurant is decked out in Chinese "folksy" furnishings. The main thing to try here is the Jiangxi-style giant soups, enough for three or four people, at around ¥35–60; the duck and pear variety is excellent.

Samba Restaurant Bar Jianshe Lu. Excellent evening atmosphere here, with South American music (live, courtesy of the Brazillian staff), a colossal selection of imported booze, and various all-you-can-eat deals for about ¥50–70 – if you're not tempted by the juiciest beef ribs in town. Lieshe Lingyuan metro.

Western Guangzhou

Guangzhou Corner of Wenchang Nan Lu and Xiajiu Lu; other branches citywide. The oldest, busiest and most famous restaurant in the city, with entrance calligraphy by the Qing emperor Kangxi and a rooftop neon sign flashing "Eating in Guangzhou". The menu is massive, and you won't find better fragrant oil chicken or crisp-skinned pork anywhere – bank on ¥80 a person for a decent feed. Service is offhand though.

Japanese Shibafu Lu, just south of the *Guangzhou* restaurant. Sit around a central bar and pick up plates of sushi as they pass on a conveyor belt; good fun and very popular. Plates are colour coded according to an ¥8–22 pricing scheme, and staff tot up your empties at the end.

Lian Xiang Lou Dishifu Lu. Established in 1889 and famous for its mooncakes, baked dough confections stuffed with sweet lotus paste and shaped as rabbits and peaches, which you can buy from the downstairs shop. The upstairs restaurant does commendable roast suckling pig, brown-sauced pigeon, and duck fried with lotus flowers for about ¥30 a portion.

Moon Carol Café Dishifu Lu. Western-style grills, including mighty New Zealand T-bone steaks at ¥78, or set meals with coffee from ¥28.

Panxi Longjin Xi Lu, Liwan Park. The best thing about this Cantonese restaurant – a teahouse of poor repute in the 1940s – is the lakeside location and interesting *dim sum* selection. Main meals are undistinguished, however, and the English-language menu is disappointingly perfunctory. Inexplicably popular with tour groups, who apparently haven't discovered the far superior *Tao Tao Ju*.

Ronghua Jiulou Longjin Dong Lu. Two restaurants: a cheap, rice-pot outlet on the north side of the road, and a pricier, new branch opposite offering everything from standard Cantonese stir-fries to ¥500 banquets. No English menu, but they try hard to help out.

Tao Tao Ju Dishifu Lu. Looks upmarket, with huge chandeliers, wooden shutters and coloured lead-light windows, but prices are mid-range and very good value. Roast goose is the house speciality, and they also do cracking seafood – plain boiled prawns or fried crab are both excellent – along with crisp-skinned chicken, lily-bud and beef sandpots, and a host of Cantonese favourites. Comprehensive English menu; mains ¥20–80.

Yunnan Over the Bridge Noodles Shangjiu Lu. Authentic Yunnanese food at very reasonable prices in a bright, modern restaurant. The house dish, Over the Bridge Noodles, is a meal in itself: a huge bowl of scalding soup full of noodles, shreds of meat, and vegetables, available in various combinations. Also try chicken steamed in a bamboo tube, and truly delicious *qiguo*, chicken soup delicately flavoured with medicinal herbs. Most dishes ¥10–20.

Shamian Island

Cow and Bridge Thai Shamian Dajie. Very formal place to dine on what is unquestionably the finest Thai food in Guangzhou, if not all China. The food is beautifully presented and the service impeccable, though expect to pay ¥120 a head.

Genesis Café Shamian Dajie. Guangzhou's first Mediterranean restaurant is a smart place with an authentic-tasting selection of treats from southern France, north Africa and the Middle East. If you can't decide, go for the bass with pine nuts, or roast chicken with honey and mint. Set meals from ¥50 are good value, otherwise expect to pay ¥100 each for a three-course dinner.

Lucy's Bar Shamian Nan Jie. Sit outside in the evening at this Westerner-oriented place and eat decent Mexican-, Thai- and Indian-style dishes, along with burgers, pizza, and grills – their fish and chips is also nostalgically good. Mains ¥25–70; cheap beer at ¥22 a pint; and afternoon tea for ¥20 per person.

Qiao Lian Opposite the tennis court, Shamian Nan Jie. Whitewashed walls and rickety furniture make a plain setting for inexpensive and good quality Cantonese food – "tiger skin" stuffed chilli peppers; sliced chicken and ham rolls; fish baked in wine, served flaming at the table; lemon pigeon; and roast meats aplenty. Dishes upwards of ¥10; full English menu.

Shamian Café Outside the *White Swan* hotel, Shamian Nan Jie. An inexpensive Chinese canteen with good rice-noodle and pork soups, fried rice, and bowls of *jiaozi* – nothing to cross town for but offering the cheapest food on the island.

Shengli Hotel Shamian Si Jie. Worth a visit for good, if pricey, *dim sum* eaten among the usual cheerful throngs. Daily 6.30am–2.30pm.

Xin Lizhi Wan Shamian Nan Jie. One of the most highly regarded seafood restaurants in the city, always busy with a mostly upmarket clientelle. Not too expensive, however; you can eat well here for ¥80 a head.

South of the river

Fo Shijie Su Shishe South off Tongfu Lu – look for the yellow sign with red characters and green-tiled, temple-like flourishes. Scrumptious vegetarian fare, and huge portions; crispy chicken drumsticks in sweet-and-sour sauce, salt-fried prawns, chicken-ball casserole and the rest are all made from beancurd, with heaps of straightforward vegetable dishes too. Full English menu; most dishes under ¥30.

Nanyuan 142 Qianjin Lu. Possibly the best restaurant in Guangzhou, serving cheapish *dim sum* until about 10am, when it transforms into an upmarket establishment. Superb stewed Chaozhou-style goose, Maotai chicken (steamed in the famous sorghum spirit of that name) and fish with pine nuts. Bus #35 from Haizhu Square on Yanjiang Zhong Lu, or metro line #2 when completed.

Drinking, nightlife and entertainment

By Chinese standards, Guangzhou has good **nightlife**. A scattering of **clubs** in the central and eastern parts of the city range from warehouse-sized discos to obscure, almost garage-like affairs; aimed at a mostly Chinese student and yuppie crowd, some have a **cover charge**, though most get their money through higher than average prices for drinks. Expats favour the bars located in Guangzhou's eastern reaches, where the booze is cheaper (around ¥25 a pint), pub-style meals can be had for ¥20–40, and the music is for listening to rather than dancing. Club hours are from 8pm to 2am, bars are open anytime from lunch to 2am, but don't expect much to be happening before 9pm at either. As usual, places open and close without notice, or swing in and out of popularity;

Guangzhou: Drinking and nightlife

Bars and clubs		
Africain	非洲吧	*fēizhōu bā*
Café Elle's	木子吧	*mùzǐ bā*
Cave	墨西哥餐厅酒吧	*mòxīgē cāntīng jiǔbā*
Face	菲私俱乐部	*fēisī jùlèbù*
Peace	和平路西餐酒廊	*hépínglù xīcānjiǔláng*
City Bar	城市酒吧	*chéngshì jiǔbā*
Elephant and Castle	大象堡酒吧	*dàxiàngbǎo jiǔbā*
Golden Mango	金芒果酒吧	*jīnmángguǒ jiǔbā*
Hill Bar	小山吧	*xiǎoshān bā*
Opera venues		
Guangming	光明剧院	*guāngmíng jùyuàn*
Ping'an	平安大戏院	*píng'ān dàxìyuàn*

one promising up-and-coming area is waterfront **Yanjiang Lu**, where the classy *1920 Café* and wonderfully named *Deep Anger Music Power House* are the pick of new places to go for live music and drinks. At any rate, but the places reviewed below should be good starting points – check out *That's Guangzhou* for the latest.

Cantonese opera is superficially similar to Beijing's, but more rustic. Virtually extinct by the 1990s, it has recently bounced back in popularity, and two theatres have been resurrected, hosting several performances monthly (¥10–50) when not doubling as cinemas: the Ping'an on Dishifu Lu in western Guangzhou (Ⓣ020/81395329); and Guangming, south of the river at the junction of Baogang Dadao and Nanhua Lu in Honan (Ⓣ020/84499721). You might also catch amateur groups performing in the parks at the weekends – Shamian Park on Shamian Island is a good place to look.

Clubs

Africain Floor 2, Zidong Hua Dasha, 707 Dongfeng Dong Lu, just west of Nonglin Xia Lu. Popular dance venue – though more hip-hop than reggae or African – with a big bar and surprisingly few foreigners.

Café Elle's Floor 2, Huaxin Dasha, northeast corner of Huanshi Lu and Shuiyin Lu. Best jazz and blues venue in the city, with regular international bands and a nightly mix of Latin and dance. It's not easy to find the right entrance, which is the small one on the eastern side of the building.

Cave Huanshi Dong Lu, west from the *Garden Hotel*. Tex-Mex cantina and sports bar, hidden down in a basement, with live music most nights.

Face Dongfeng Xi Lu. Just up the road from rival *Yes* and just as crowded, though dishing up more run-of-the-mill dance mixes.

Hard Rock Café *China Hotel*, Liuhua Lu. Disco with expensive cover charge and beer, the music either DJ-driven or live – the latter more likely at weekends.

Peace Heping Lu. Nightly live music on two floors – everything from Canto-pop to Chinese rock and more offbeat local bands. At the time of writing, *Peace 2* was in the making at 358 Huanshi Dong Lu, near the *Cave*, and promised more of the same.

Windflower Huanshi Dong Lu. Pub with beer garden and stage, hosting nightly DJ and jazz-powered dance sessions.

Yes Dongfeng Xi Lu, south of Liuhua Park. Huge, popular, full-on house experience at maximum decibels. The place of the moment for a night's rave.

Bars

City Bar City Plaza, Tianhe Lu, Tianhe. Relaxed place to spend an hour or two over a *Heineken* before your train goes from Guangzhou East. Hard to find, the building is east of the better-signed Teem Plaza.

Elephant and Castle Huanshi Dong Lu. Dim corners and cramped bar make this a favourite with barfly foreigners, though has a good beer garden and typically gets loud and busy as the evening progresses. Variable happy hours. Opens late afternoon.

Golden Mango Huanshi Dong Lu. Current pick of bars catering to Guangzhou's large and generally jaded expat community. Cosy and laid-back atmosphere, welcoming staff and fine beer garden.

Hill Bar Hanshi Dong Lu, across from the *Garden Hotel*. Third choice in the trinity of adjacent expat bars; a bit of a pick-up joint, but it opens early and has cheap beer at ¥23 a pint.

Shopping

Guangzhou's **shopping** ethos is very much towards the practical side of things. The **Changshou Lu** area in western Guangzhou is a mass of shopping plazas, designer clothes shops and boutique stores, with **Beijing Lu** a similar, more central version; both have sections which are pedestrianized at weekends. To see where Guangzhou – and China – is heading, however, make your way over to the shockingly modern and upmarket **Friendship Store**, five floors of expensive imported designer gear and some good-value, domestic formal wear; it's on easterly Taojin Lu, just off Huanshi Dong Lu.

For functional memorabilia, the streets running east off the southern end of Renmin Lu might give you some ideas. Yide Lu has several huge wholesale warehouses stocking **dried foods** and **toys** – action figures from Chinese legends, rockets and all things that rattle and buzz. Other shops in the area deal in home decorations, such as colourful tiling or jigsawed decorative wooden dragons and phoenixes, and at New Year you can buy those red and gold good-luck posters put up outside businesses and homes.

For out-and-out tourist souvenirs, head first to the *White Swan Hotel* on Shamian Island. Their batiks and clothing, carved wooden screens and jade monstrosities are well worth a look, if only to make you realize what a good deal you're getting when you buy elsewhere – such as the shops in the vicinity of the *Shamian Island Hostel*, just outside on Shamian Si Jie. The Guangdong Antique Store, just south of Zhongshan Lu on Wende Lu, and various small shops in the streets between Dishifu Lu and Liuersan Lu, have varying selections of authenticated **antiques**, jade, lacquerwork, scrolls, chops and cloisonné artefacts, identical to what you'll find in the Yue Hua stores in Hong Kong, but at half the price.

For **Western groceries**, the Beatrice Supermarket, attached to the *Shengli* hotel on Shamian Si Jie, is a treasure trove of imported cheese, olives, pasta, and biscuits – and there's also a coffee bar with hearty brews at ¥10 a cup.

Listings

Acupuncture Anyone interested in receiving cheap acupuncture preceded by massage by a blind masseuse should head for the clinic attached to the Zhongshan Medical College, Zhongshan Lu, where students practise.

Airlines Malaysia Airlines (Ⓣ020/83358828, Ⓕ83358898), Thai Airways (Ⓣ020/83824333, Ⓕ83823986) and Vietnam Airlines (Ⓣ020/83867093, Ⓕ83827187) all have offices at the *Garden Hotel*, Huanshi Dong Lu. Japan Airlines are in the *China Hotel* (Ⓣ020/86696688). China Southern Airlines is at 181 Huanshi Dong Lu (Ⓣ020/86681818), two doors east of the North train station.

Banks and exchange Two major branches of the Bank of China are in the south of the city on Changdi Lu and outside the *White Swan* hotel, Shamian Island (both open for currency exchange Mon–Fri 9–11.30am & 1.30–5pm). Counters at the *Liuhua*, *China*, *Landmark* and *Garden* hotels change currency for non-guests; the *White Swan* does not.

Bookshops The Xinhua bookstore on Beijing Lu has an unexciting range of English literature and translated Chinese classics. The city's biggest bookstore, Guangzhou Bookbuying Centre, is at the southwest corner of Tianhe square, Tianhe Lu – four storeys of technical manuals, computer texts, and university tomes, but little in English. Otherwise, the main source of reading material is the comprehensive and expensive range of everything from potboilers to coffee-table works and contemporary Chinese fiction paperbacks – along with international newspapers and magazines – available at the *White Swan.*

Consulates Australia, Room 1509, GITIC Plaza, Huangshi Dong Lu ⓣ020/83350909, ⓕ83350718; Canada, Rm 801, *China Hotel* ⓣ020/86660569, ⓕ86672401; France, Room 803, GITIC Plaza ⓣ020/83303405, ⓕ83303437; Germany, Floor 19, GITIC Plaza ⓣ020/83306533, ⓕ83317033; Italy, Room 5207, CITIC Plaza, 233 Tianhe Bei Lu ⓣ020/38770556, ⓕ38770270; Japan, *Garden Hotel*, Huanshi Dong Lu ⓣ020/83338999, ⓕ83878835; Malaysia, Floor 19, CITIC Plaza, Tianhe Bei Lu ⓣ020/38770766, ⓕ38770769; Netherlands, Room 905, *Guangdong International Hotel*, 339 Huanshi Dong Lu ⓣ020/83302067, ⓕ83303601; Philippines, Room 427, *White Swan Hotel*, Shamian Island ⓣ020/81886968, ⓕ81862041; Thailand, *Garden Hotel*, Huanshi Dong Lu ⓣ020/83338989, ⓕ83889567; UK, Floor 2, GITIC Plaza ⓣ020/83351354, ⓕ83327509; US, Shamian Nan Lu, Shamian Island ⓣ020/83354269, ⓕ83354764; Vietnam, Floor 2, *Landmark Hotel*, Yanjiang Lu ⓣ020/83306801). Note that consulates' visa sections are usually open only from around 9am to 11.30am and getting served isn't always easy.

Hospitals There's an English-speaking team at SOS, Guangdong Provincial Hospital of Traditional Chinese Medicine, 261 Datong Lu, Er Sha Dao, Guangzhou (Mon–Fri 9am–6pm; ⓣ020/87351051). Other options include Guandong Provincial People's Hospital, 96 Dongchuan Lu (ⓣ020/83827812) and the Red Cross Hospital, 396 Tongfu Zhong Lu (ⓣ020/84446411). A recommended English-speaking dentist is Dr Xin Shaoqin (ⓣ020/84403983). For anything serious, though, you're better off heading to Hong Kong.

Internet access Henan Internet, at the south end of Shamian San Lu, Shamian Island, charges a steep ¥20 an hour (daily 9am–11pm). For better value, try Freedom Cyber Cafe, at the Dongfeng Dong Lu/Nonglin Xia Lu crossroads (open after 2pm), and the Net bar on floor 3 of the southern-most *Xinhua* bookstore, Beijing Lu – both charge around ¥8 an hour. Some of the cafés and bars opening up west of the Haizhu bridge on Yanjiang Lu might have Net access at lower prices than these places, but note that hotel Net services are very expensive.

Interpreters The major hotels can organize interpreters for around ¥250 per day – you're also expected to cover all additional incidental costs such as meals and transport.

Left luggage Offices at the train and bus stations open approximately daily 8am to 6pm.

Mail and telephones There are major post offices (daily 8am–6pm) with IDD telephones, parcel post and poste restante, on the western side of the square outside Guangzhou train station, and across from the Cultural Park entrance on Liuersan Lu. Shamian Island's post counter is open 9am–5pm for stamps, envelopes and deliveries. All hotels have postal services and international call facilities.

Police For all police matters, such as reporting theft, head to the PSB.

PSB The self-styled "Section of Aliens' Administration of Guangzhou Municipal PSB" is on Jiefang Bei Lu (ⓣ020/83116688 or 83331949; Mon–Fri 8–11.30am & 2.30–5pm, Sat 8–11.30am).

Travel agents Try the following if hotels can't help with tours and transport reservations. CITS/STA Travel, beside the *Guangdong Tourist Hotel*, immediately east of the North train station square on Huanshi Dong Lu (ⓣ020/86671455, ⓦwww.statravel.com.cn), is also the agent for numerous international airlines; CTS, at the *Landmark Hotel* (ⓣ020/83355988, ⓦwww.chinatravelone.com). X-Pat Travel, east of the Friendship Store at Floor 20, Regent House (Lizhen Dasha), 50 Taojin Lu (ⓣ020/83586961, ⓔxpats@public.guangzhou.gd.cn), is a very friendly, English-speaking organization worth seeing for all air tickets and tour bookings – though their office takes some finding.

The Pearl River Delta

The **Pearl River Delta** seems initially entirely a product of the modern age, dominated by industrial complexes and the glossy, high-profile cities of **Shenzhen**, east on the crossing to Hong Kong, and westerly **Zhuhai**, on the Macau border. Back in the 1980s these were marvels of Deng Xiaoping's reforms, rigidly contained **Special Economic Zones** whose officially sanctioned free-market activities were anathema to Communist ideologies. Their incredible success inspired an invasion of the delta by foreign and domestic companies, obscuring an economic history dating back to the time of Song

The Pearl River Delta

Cuiheng	翠亨村	***cùihēng cūn***
Sun Yatsen's Residence	孙中山故居	*sūnzhōngshān gùjù*
Dongguan	东莞	***dōng guǎn***
Keyuan	可园	*kěyuán*
Foshan	佛山	***fóshān***
Green Garden	健康素食馆	*jiànkāng sùshíguǎn*
Huaqiao Dasha	华侨大厦	*huáqiáo dàshà*
Liang Yuan	梁园	*liángyuán*
Pearl River Hotel	珠江大酒店	*zhūjiāng dàjiǔdiàn*
Renshou Si	仁受寺	*rénshòu sì*
Zu Miao	祖庙	*zǔmiào*
Humen	虎门	***hǔmén***
Jiangmen	江门	***jiāng mén***
Duyuan	杜院	*dùyuàn*
Little Bird's Paradise	小鸟天堂	*xiǎoniǎo tiāntáng*
Xinhui	薪会	*xīnhuì*
Nancun	南村	***náncūn***
Yuyin Shanfang	余英山房	*yúyīng shānfáng*
Panyu	番禺	***pānyú***
Lianhua Shan	莲花山	*liánhuā shān*
Shajiao	沙角	***shājiǎo***
Shajiao Paotai	沙角炮台	*shājiǎo pàotái*
Lin Zexu Park	林则徐公园	*línzéxú gōngyuán*
Shenzhen	深圳	***shēnzhèn***
Folk Culture Village	民俗文化村	*mínsú wénhuàcūn*

engineers who constructed irrigation canals through the delta's **five counties** – Nanhai, Panyu, Shunde, Dongguan and Zhongshan. From the Ming dynasty, local crafts and surplus food were exported across Guangdong, artisans flourished and funded elaborate guild temples, while gentlemen of leisure built gardens in which to wander and write poetry.

Today, it's easy to hop on high-speed transport and cut through the delta in a couple of hours, seeing little more than the unattractive urban mantle which surrounds the highways. But spend a little longer on your journey or dip into the region on short trips from Guangzhou, and there's a good deal to discover about China here, especially in the way that everything looks hastily built and temporary – development is clearly happening too fast for any unified planning. The past survives too. Don't miss **Foshan**'s splendid **Ancestral Temple**, or **Lianhua Shan**, a landscaped ancient quarry; historians might also wish to visit **Humen**, where the destruction of British opium in 1839 ignited the first Opium War, and **Cuiheng**, home village of China's revered revolutionary elder statesman, **Sun Yatsen**.

The delta has China's highest density of **expressways**, including the 175-kilometre **Guangshen Expressway**, which runs southeast from Guangzhou to Shenzhen. The delta's western side is covered by a mesh of roads which you

Lizhi Park	荔枝公园	*lìzhī gōngyuán*
Luohu	罗湖	*luóhú*
Minsk World	明思克航空世界	*míngsīkè hángkōng shìjiè*
Shekou	蛇口	*shékǒu*
Splendid China	锦绣中华	*jǐnxiù zhōnghuá*
Accommodation		
Airlines	航空大酒店	*hángkōng dàjiǔdiàn*
Dongnan	东南大酒店	*dōngnán dàjiǔdiàn*
Dragon	港龙大酒店	*gǎnglóng dàjiǔdiàn*
Far East	远东酒店	*yuǎndōng jiǔdiàn*
Landmark	深圳富苑酒店	*shēnzhèn fùyuán jiǔdiàn*
Nanyang	南洋大酒店	*nányáng dàjiǔdiàn*
Shunde	顺德	***shùndé***
Fengling Park	风岭公园	*fēnglǐng gōngyuán*
Qinghui Gardens	清晖园	*qīnghuī yuán*
Xishan Gumiao	西山古庙	*xīshān gǔmiào*
Xinhui	新会	***xīnhuì***
Xiqiao	西樵	***xīqiáo***
Zhongshan	中山	***zhōngshān***
Zhuhai	珠海	***zhūhǎi***
Changan	昌安酒店	*chāngān jiǔdiàn*
Gongbei	拱北	*gǒngběi*
Hualigong	花丽宫酒店	*huálìgōng jiǔdiàn*
Huasha Shijie	华夏食街	*huáxià shíjiē*
Jida	吉大	*jídà*
Lianhua	莲花大厦	*liánhuā dàshà*
Minan	民安酒店	*mínān jiǔdiàn*
Xiangzhou	香州珠海度假村	*xiāngzhōu zhūhǎi dùjiàcūn*
Yuehai Jiudian	粤海酒店	*yuèhǎi jiǔdiàn*

can follow more or less directly south between sights to Zhuhai, 155km from Guangzhou. Buses from Guangzhou's Liuhua and provincial bus stations cover all destinations in the locality. There's also the **Guangzhou–Shenzhen train**, though services don't tend to stop along the way, and there should be a **metro link** to Foshan by 2005 – see the accounts below for further transport details.

It's worth noting that both Shenzhen and Zhuhai SEZs are surrounded by electric fences and inspection posts to deter smugglers – one of the few times you're likely to see armed police in China – and you'll need to show **passports** to get through, whether you're coming in by bus or, to Shenzhen, by train. Don't confuse these checks with actual border formalities; you'll still have to fill out forms and get your passport inspected again to cross into Macau or Hong Kong from the SEZs.

Southeast to Shenzhen

An hour southeast of Guangzhou down the expressway, **DONGGUAN** is the administrative seat of the delta's most productive county, its factories churning out textiles, electronic components and pirated VCDs and computer software – an industry which, controlled as it is by the military, Beijing has had no suc-

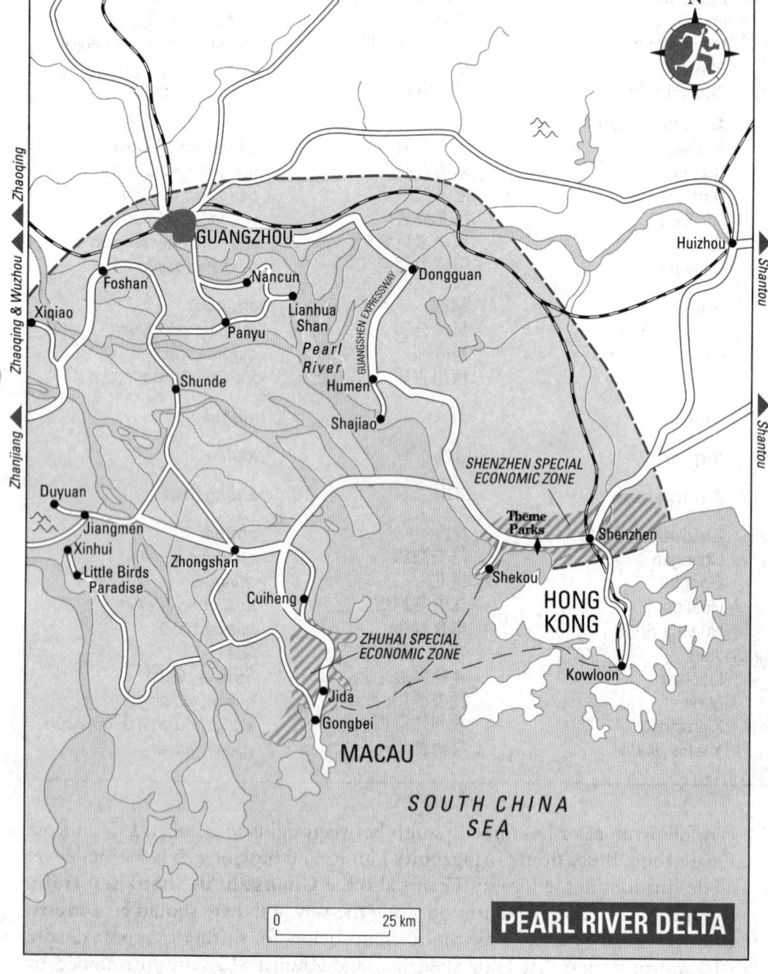

cess in suppressing despite periodic US threats of trade sanctions.

If you're heading to Dongguan's port, **Humen**, famous for its role in the nineteenth-century **Opium Wars**, you may need to stop in Dongguan to change buses, in which case you could take the time to have a look at **Keyuan** (daily 8am–4pm; ¥8), once one of Guangdong's "Four Famous Gardens". Walk north from the **bus station** up Wantai Dadao for 250m, turn west along Keyuan Nan Lu, and it's about 1km away across the river. Laid out for the Qing minister, Zhang Jingxiu, Keyuan puts its very limited space to good use, cramming an unlikely number of passages, rooms, pavilions and devious staircases inside its walls, all built in distinctive, pale blue bricks. There are a few flowerbeds and trees, but Keyuan's most striking aspect is the way it shuts out the rest of the city at ground level – though Dongguan's motorways are only too obvious from the upper storey of the main **Yaoshi Pavilion**.

Humen and Shajiao

Minibuses from Guangzhou or Dongguan land at **HUMEN** (pronounced "Fumen" locally), though some transport drops you 5km short on the Guangshen Expressway, where shuttle buses wait to carry you into town. In 1839, after a six-week siege of the "Foreign Factories" in Guangzhou, the British handed over 1200 tons of **opium** to **Lin Zexu**, the Qing official in charge of stopping the opium trade. Lin brought it to Humen, mixed it with quicklime, and dumped it in two 45-metre pits on the beach 4km south of Humen's centre at **Shajiao**; after three weeks the remains were flushed out to sea. Incensed at this destruction of their opium, the British massacred the Chinese garrisons at Humen and on nearby **Weiyun Island**, and attacked Guangzhou. Lin got the blame and was exiled to the frontier province of Xinjiang, only to be replaced by the ineffectual Yi Shan, a nephew of the emperor, later a signatory to the humiliating Guangzhou Treaty.

These events are recounted in Chinese documents and heroic sculptures at the **Lin Zexu Park Museum** on Jiefang Lu (daily 9am–4pm; ¥12), a twenty-minute walk between the skyscrapers northwest of Humen's bus station. It's more rewarding, however, to catch a minibus to Shajiao where the opium pits remain, along with a fortress, **Shajio Paotai** (daily 9am–5pm; ¥10). The whole place is thick with poinsettias, banyans and butterflies, all making for a nice couple of hours on the beach.

Shenzhen

If **SHENZHEN** had been around in classical times, poets would doubtless have compared its gleaming downtown towers to mountain peaks, each rising higher than the other. Incredibly, in 1979 this metropolis was a simple rural hamlet and train station called **Baoan**, the first office foundations yet to be dug in its alluvial plains on the Hong Kong border. Within six years, delegations from all over China were pouring in to learn how to remodel their own businesses, cities and provinces on Shenzhen's incentives-based economy. By 1990 the city had four harbours and its manufacturing industries alone were turning over US$2 billion a year, necessitating the construction of a nuclear power station to deal with local energy needs; eleven years later, output stood at US$238 billion a year, and another new power station was under way. Today, a third of Shenzhen's income comes from exporting hi-tech products, and almost half the world's watches are made in town.

Shenzhen may not have been the cause of capitalism in the People's Republic, but it was a glorious piece of propaganda for those who promoted its virtues. It's no coincidence that, on his landmark 1992 "**Southern Tour**", Deng Xiaoping chose Shenzhen as the place to make his memorable statement: "Poverty is not Socialism: to get rich is glorious", voicing the Party's shift from Communist dogma to a pragmatic, results-driven approach to economics – and opening the gate for the start of China's financial boom.

Having said all this, Shenzhen isn't so amazing these days, what with similar skylines rearing up all over China; the border area is also a bit grubby, and overrun by beggars. So, after a quick sniff around, there's little reason to stay any longer than it takes to organize your next move into or out of the mainland.

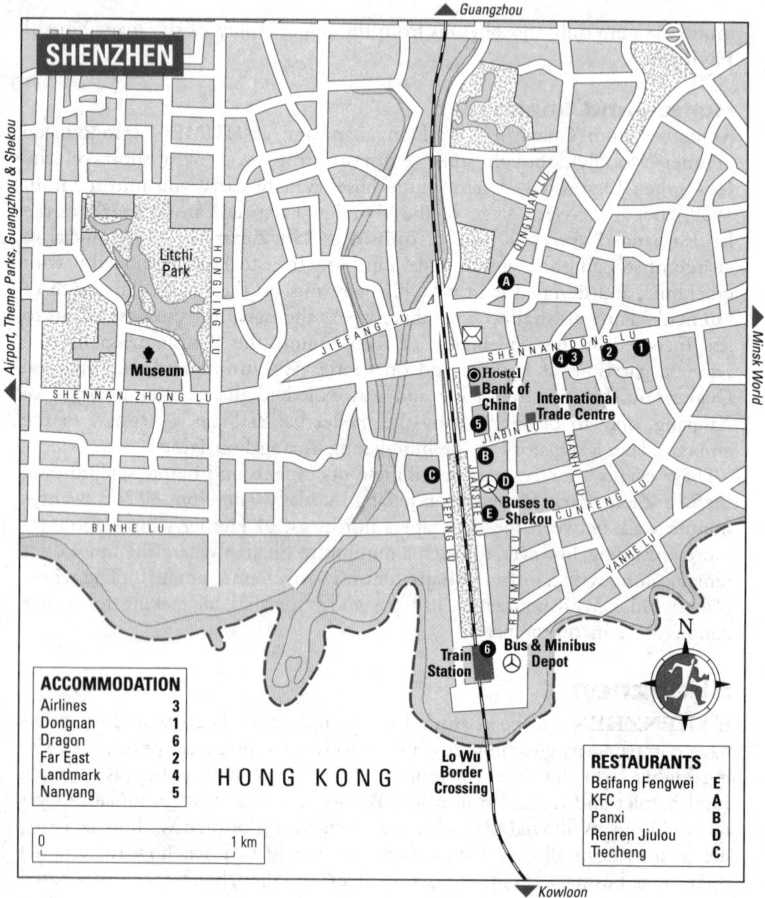

The City

For a good glimpse of the city's extremes of wealth and poverty, spend an hour strolling along Renmin Lu, which runs northeast from the train station and **Lo Wu border crossing** (you might see the *pinyin* rendering, Luo Hu, on signs) through the centre. The **International Trade Centre** is a three-storey block on the corner of Jiabin Lu, full of people browsing through stocks of upmarket jewellery and perfume. Push on over Jiefang Lu and you're in the tangle of narrow lanes which formed the **old town** of Baoan, now a downmarket selection of stalls selling cheap clothes, shoes and gadgets. There's a historic monument of sorts here in a squat, blue-roofed diner on Qingyuan Lu – China's original *McDonald's* restaurant, now a *KFC* outlet.

For a shot of greenery, walk 1500m west from the centre along Shennan Zhong Lu to **Lizhi Park**, a surprisingly refreshing, open space, with a nice lake and modern **opera house**, worth checking out for occasional performances of Chinese theatre. More reliably, hop on bus #204 from Jianshe Lu for the thirty-minute ride west to Shenzhen's three very professional **theme parks**, next to each other on the Guangshen Expressway (daily 8am–5.30pm; ¥100–120 for each park with various joint entry discounts) – look for a miniaturized Golden Gate Bridge spanning the road. Amid limitless souvenir stalls, **Splendid China** and **Window on the World** are a collection of scale models of famous monuments such as the Great Wall and Eiffel Tower, while the **Folk Culture Village** is an enjoyably touristy introduction to the nation's ethnic groups – there are yurts, pavilions, huts, archways, rock paintings, and mechanical goats, with colourful troupes performing different national dances every thirty minutes.

If you're after something completely different, jump aboard bus #220 from Jianshe Lu about 8km east to Luogong Lu, then change for bus #202 for another 8km out to **Shatoujiao** district. Here you'll find **Minsk World** (¥88), a whole Russian aircraft carrier – complete with aircraft – moored up at the docks for your entertainment; allow at least half a day for a full exploration.

Practicalities

A five-kilometre-wide semicircle immediately north of the Hong Kong border, central Shenzhen is evenly bisected by the **rail line** which descends straight down Jianshe Lu to the Lo Wu crossing. The border area itself is defined by the massive Lo Wu **bus station** to the east and similarly sized **train station** to the west; if you've just crossed from Hong Kong, these are ahead and to your right and left respectively.

The **international airport** is 20km west of town, with a shuttle bus (¥15) operating between here and the *Airlines Hotel* on Shennan Dong Lu. The **port** lies 15km west at **Shekou**, where ferries from Macau, Zhuhai and Hong Kong pull in, and is served thrice hourly by the #204 bus (¥6) to Jianshe Lu. Taxis and minibuses roam everywhere, and the city has an enviably efficient bus service, with a **metro** under construction. There are **banks** at the border crossing, the airport, ferry terminal and some hotels, and a suitably oversized Bank of China on Jianshe Lu (Mon–Fri 9am–5pm).

Accommodation and eating

The cheapest places to **eat** are in the streets immediately north of Jiefang Lu, where Chinese canteens can fill you up with good dumplings, soups and stir-fries for around ¥18 per person. There are dozens of smarter options all through the centre, such as inexpensive casseroles at *Renren Jiulou*, east of the

Moving on from Shenzhen

The **Hong Kong border** is open daily 7am–9pm. There's a lack of directional signs in the vicinity; you need to get on to the overpass from upstairs at the train station and then head south past souvenir stalls, roasted meat vendors, and pet shops. Border formalities on both sides are streamlined, and it shouldn't take more than an hour to find yourself waiting for the **KCR** (Kowloon–Canton Railway) train into Hong Kong.

Double-decker **trains** to Guangzhou East take less than ninety minutes on the the new high-speed track; they run between 6am and 10pm and tickets cost ¥70. The **ticket office**, at street level, also sells tickets on direct services to dozens of destinations between Shenzhen and Beijing.

Buses leave regularly from the Lo Wu bus station for the delta, Guangzhou, the rest of Guangdong, and many places in central China. **Ferries** depart direct to Macau, Hong Kong, Zhuhai and Guangzhou through the day; catch bus #204 from Jianshe Lu to the port at Shekou. For **flights** into the rest of China, contact CAAC at the *Airlines* hotel.

Airlines Hotel on Shennan Dong Lu; mantis shrimps, stonefish and other seafood at the *Panxi*, on the corner of Jianshe Lu and Jiabin Lu; fine northern cooking and an ornate red and gold exterior at the *Beifang Fengwei*, farther down Jianshe Lu; and upmarket snake, cat and wildfowl delights at the *Tiecheng*, west of the tracks on Heping Lu. The **hotels**, a selection of which are reviewed below, have good restaurants, too, along with karaoke bars, interpreters and postal services.

Airlines Shennan Dong Lu ⓣ0755/2237999, ⓕ2237866. Ordinary rooms, with just enough space to be comfortable. Good seafood restaurant and expensive coffee shop. ❺

Dongnan Shennan Dong Lu ⓣ0755/2288688, ⓕ2291103. A reasonably priced, low-frills hotel with the usual complement of places to eat and drink. ❺

Dragon At the train station, Jianshe Lu ⓣ0755/2329228, ⓕ2334585. Rooms are smartly furnished, but staff are disinterested. The huge Cantonese restaurant has good *dim sum*. ❻

Far East Shennan Dong Lu ⓣ0755/2205369, ⓕ2200239. Well-organized business venue advertising its rooms, billiard hall, Sichuanese restaurant and dance hall as "environmentally friendly". ❻

Landmark Nanhu Lu, corner of Shennan Dong Lu ⓣ0755/2172288, ⓕ2290473. Rightly claims to be the best hotel in Shenzhen, boasting a beautifully furnished neo-colonial interior and "Banquet Halls" instead of restaurants. ❾

Nanyang Jianshe Lu ⓣ0755/2224968, ⓕ2238927. Tidy, spacious rooms, all with balcony views of Shenzhen's skyline, though becoming a bit worn. ❺

The western delta: Foshan

Twenty-five kilometres southwest of Guangzhou and today a satellite suburb of the city, **FOSHAN** historically was very much a town in its own right, with a history dating back to the seventh century. Along with the nearby village of **Shiwan**, Foshan became famous for its ceramics, silk, metalwork and woodcarving – a reputation it still enjoys – and the splendour of its **temples**, two of which survive on **Zumiao Lu**, a kilometre-long street shaded by office buildings and set in the heart of what was once the old town centre. At the southern end, **Zu Miao** (Ancestral Temple; daily 8.30am–8pm; ¥20) is a masterpiece of southern architecture, founded in 1080 as a metallurgist's guild temple. Ahead and to the left of the entrance is an elevated garden fronted by some locally made Opium War **cannons** – sadly for the Chinese, poor casting techniques and a lack of rifling made these inaccurate and liable to explode. Nearby, magnificent glazed **roof tiles** of frolicking lions and characters from local tales were made in Shiwan for temple restorations in the 1830s. The temple's **main hall** is on the left past here, its interior crowded with minutely carved wooden screens, oversized guardian gods leaning threateningly out from the walls, and a three-tonne **statue of Beidi**, God of the North, who in local lore controlled low-lying Guangdong's flood-prone waters – hence this shrine to snare his good will. Opposite the hall is the elaborate masonry of the **Lingying archway**, similar to those at Shexian in Anhui Province (see p.524). Foshan is considered the birthplace of Cantonese opera, and beyond the archway you'll find the highly decorative **Wanfu stage**, built in 1685 for autumnal performances given to thank the Divine Emperor for his bountiful harvests.

A few blocks north, **Renshou Si** (Benevolent Longevity Temple) is a former Ming monastery whose southern wing, graced by a short seven-storey pagoda, is still consecrated. The rest has been cleaned out and turned into the **Foshan Folk Arts Studio**, a good place to look for souvenirs including excellent **papercuts** with definite Cultural Revolution leanings, showing the modernizing of rural economies. Around the Spring Festival, side halls are also full of celebratory lions, fish and phoenixes constructed from wire and coloured crepe paper.

About 1km due north of here on Songfeng Lu – continue up Zumiao Lu to its end, turn right and then first left – **Liang Yuan** (¥10) is another of the delta's historic **gardens**, built between 1796 and 1850 by a family of famous poets and artists of the period. There are artfully aranged ponds, trees and rocks, and the tastefully furnished residential buildings are worth a look, but the real gem here is the **Risheng Study**, a perfectly proportioned retreat looking out over a tiny, exquisitely designed pond fringed with willows.

Practicalities

Fenjiang Bei Lu forms the western boundary of the old town, running south for about 2km from the **train station**, over a canal, past the **long-distance bus station** and through to where the highrises, which constitute Foshan's business centre, cluster around a broad roundabout. **Minibuses** from Guangzhou's Guangfo bus depot (¥10) deposit you just west of the roundabout on Chengmentou Lu; walk 50m east and you're at the bottom end of Zumiao Lu. To reach Zumiao Lu from the stations, catch bus #1, #6 or #11, or walk down Fenjiang Bei Lu for about 700m, then east for a couple of minutes along tree-lined Qinren Lu to the intersection with Zumiao Lu. At the time of writing there was no news of where the proposed **metro** from Guangzhou will terminate; it's due for completion around 2005. Foshan's main **Bank of China** (Mon–Fri 9–11.30am & 1–5pm) is between the two temples.

Foshan's **accommodation** prospects include the swish *Huaqiao Dasha* (Ⓣ0757/2223828, Ⓕ2227702; ❻), across from Renshou Si on Zumiao Lu; and the *Pearl River Hotel* next door, where an IYHF-run wing offers **budget dorms** (Ⓣ0757/2221624, Ⓕ2292263; ❺, dorm beds ¥53). Both have **restaurants** and bars, and there are Western-style fast-food outlets scattered through the centre; for something better at ¥30 or so a dish, try the *Green Garden* **vegetarian restaurant** next to the *Huaqiao Dasha* – their "nest of gems" (a taro basket filled with stir-fried vegetables), vegetarian chicken and ham rolls, and mushrooms with black-hair fungus are works of art.

Around Panyu

A couple of attractive sights surround the town of **PANYU**, about 50km east of Foshan. It's roughly the same distance by road from Guangzhou, with buses departing from the Liuhua station, and there are also direct **ferries** from Hong Kong.

Overlooking the Pearl River 15km east of Panyu, **Lianhua Shan** (daily 8am–4pm; ¥35) is an odd phenomenon, a mountain quarried as long ago as the Han dynasty for its red stone, used in the tomb of the Nanyue king, Zhao Mo. After mining it in such a way as to leave a suspiciously deliberate arrangement of crags, pillars and caves, Ming officials planted the whole thing with trees and turned it into a pleasure garden laid with lotus pools, stone paths and pavilions. A fifty-metre-high pagoda was built in 1612, and the Qing emperor Kangxi added a fortress to defend the river. Still a popular excursion from Guangzhou, it's an interesting spot to while away a few hours, though frequently crowded.

A twenty-kilometre drive north of Panyu is Nancun, a fair-sized village where you'll find **Yuyin Shanfang** (daily 8am–5pm; ¥8), a retreat founded by the Qing dynasty scholar Wu Yantian. He spent a fortune hiring the biggest names in contemporary landscape gardening and created an artificial mountain, a lake, bamboo clumps, calligraphy walls and an octagonal pavilion. Here Wu sat listening to flocks of cagebirds, and the muted tones of stringed *zheng* and *pipa*, played upstairs in the ladies' quarters (now a teahouse). The music has gone, and the former ancestral temple has been converted into a dance hall for wedding receptions, but the gardens remain as a nicely nostalgic tribute to a more refined time.

Shunde

Yet another antique garden is one reason to pause in the county town of **SHUNDE**, also known as **Daliang Zhen**, 50km south of Guangzhou on the most direct route to Zhuhai (¥15 from Guangzhou's Liuhua bus station). The other highlight here is the *Qinghui Yuan* restaurant, revered by the gastronomically inclined as the epitome of classic Cantonese cooking. Both are in the grounds of **Qinghui Gardens**, in the middle of town on Qinghui Lu (¥8), where osmanthus, mulberry bushes and bamboo are arranged around square fish ponds. The restaurant (daily 7–9am, 11am–2pm & 5–7pm) is expensive – count on at least ¥75 a person – but the dishes are superb, with mild, fresh flavours which have to be taken slowly to be properly appreciated; their roast pork, or steamed scorpion fish with ginger and spring onions, just melts in the mouth. After eating, you can walk off your meal in the restored colonial-style streets behind the gardens off Hua Lu, where the old town centre forms a miniature version of Guangzhou's back lanes, with flagstones, hectic markets and a fully restored street of colonial-era architecture. Alternatively, it's about a kilometre north across a huge open square and Wenxiu Lu to wooded and hilly **Feng Ling Park**, with the old **Xishan Gumiao** temple on the east side.

Shunde's new **long-distance bus station** is about 3km south of the centre on the highway; catch bus #3 from here to Qinghui Lu and the gardens. For a **place to stay**, there's the plush *Marriott Courtyard* hotel opposite the gardens on Qinghui Lu (Ⓣ0765/2218333, Ⓦwww.courtyard.com; ❾); budget travellers should head to Feng Ling Park (also bus #3 from the station) and take the steps from Wenxiu Lu up to the temple, where at the top on the right is a small hotel (❸). **Moving on**, if you can't find necessary long-distance transport at the bus station, head to Guangzhou or Zhongshan and pick up services there.

Jiangmen and around

Halfway between Guangzhou and Zhuhai, but slightly off to the west, **JIANGMEN** was formerly a pleasant town on the busy Jiangmen River, birthplace of the Ming poet **Chen Baisha**, and later dressed in cobbled streets and rows of nineteenth-century European-style mansions. Sadly, these have all but vanished, and the city has well and truly sold its soul to the ugliest side of urban development, retaining only its reputation for gymnastic excellence. You'll pass through if you're on the bus between Foshan and Zhuhai; on the way, a fifteen-kilometre stretch of wholesale **furniture warehouses** displaying chairs, beds and tables of every possible shape, style and colour adds a surreal touch to the journey.

While Jiangmen itself holds little appeal, the surrounding countryside might inspire you to stop off long enough to pick up a local minibus from beside the bus station on Jianshe Lu. There are a few very dilapidated Ming villages in the vicinity, some sporting two-storey towers built early last century by returning Overseas Chinese to parade their riches. About 15km southwest, at a spot reached via the town of **Xinhui**, flocks of cranes and waterfowl roost in the huge sprawl of a 500-year-old fig tree in the middle of the Tianma River, known locally as Xiaoniao Tiantang, the **Little Birds' Paradise**; here there are walkways around the tree, and paddle boats for rent. **Duyuan**, 10km west of Jiangmen, sits at the bottom of **Guifeng Shan**, a nicely formalized mountain offering a day's pleasant hiking between temples, trees and waterfalls on the way up to the windswept **Chishi Crag**.

Zhongshan and Cuiheng

Almost every town in China has a park or road named **Zhongshan**, a tribute to China's first Republican president, the remarkable **Dr Sun Yatsen** – "Yatsen" is the Cantonese pronunciation of "Zhongshan". Unless you need to change buses, there's no need to visit Zhongshan itself, a characterless county town 100km from Guangzhou, but 30km east of here on the coastal road to Zhuhai is the good doctor's home village of **CUIHENG**, now the site of a **memorial garden** (daily 8.30am–5pm; ¥15) celebrating his life and achievements. Transport from Zhongshan town and from Zhuhai (35km south) sets you down right outside, where there are also a few cheap **places to eat** and buy ice creams; when you need to move on, you'll find that public transport heads in both directions along the highway until at least 6pm.

Along with a banyan tree supposedly brought back from Hawaii and planted by Sun, the grounds incorporate a comprehensive museum of photographs, relics (including the original Nationalist flag) and biographical accounts in

Sun Yatsen

Born in 1866, **Sun Yatsen** grew up during a period when China laboured under the humiliation of colonial occupation, a situation justly blamed on the increasingly feeble Qing court. Having spent three years in Hawaii during the 1880s, Sun studied medicine in Guangzhou and Hong Kong, where he became inspired by that other famous Guangdong revolutionary, Hong Xiuquan (see p.458), he began to involve himself in covert anti-Qing activities. Back in Hawaii in 1894, he abandoned his previous notions of reforming the imperial system and founded the **Revive China Society** to "Expel the Manchus, restore China to the people and create a federal government." The following year he incited an uprising in Guangzhou under **Lu Haodong**, notable for being the first time that the green Nationalist flag painted with a white, twelve-pointed sun (which still appears on the Taiwanese flag) was flown. But the uprising was quashed, Lu Haodong was captured and executed, and Sun fled overseas.

Orbiting between Hong Kong, Japan, Europe and the US, Sun spent the next fifteen years raising money to fund revolts in southern China, and in 1907 his new Alliance Society announced its famous **Three Principles of the People** – Nationalism, Democracy and Livelihood. He was in Colorado when the Manchus finally fell in October 1911; on returning to China he was made provisional president of the Republic of China on January 1, 1912, but was forced to resign in February in favour of the powerful warlord, **Yuan Shikai**. Yuan established a Republican Party, while Sun's supporters rallied to the Nationalist People's Party – **Guomindang** – led by **Song Jiaoren**. Song was assassinated by Yuan's henchmen following Guomindang successes in the 1913 parliamentary elections, and Sun again fled to Japan. Annulling parliament, Yuan tried to set himself up as emperor but couldn't even control military factions within his own party, who plunged the north into civil war on his death in 1916. Sun, meanwhile, returned to his native Guangdong and established an independent Guomindang government, determined to unite the country eventually. Though unsuccessful, he died in 1925 greatly respected by both the Guomindang and the 4-year-old Communist Party for his life-long efforts to enfranchise the masses.

English emphasizing the successful aspects of Sun Yatsen's career. There's also the solid, Portuguese-style family home where he lived between 1892 and 1895, "studying, treating patients and discussing national affairs with his friends". Out the back of Sun's home are some rather more typical period buildings belonging to the peasant and landlord classes, restored and furnished with wooden tables and authentic silk tapestries.

Zhuhai

ZHUHAI is an umbrella name for the Special Economic Zone encompassing three separate townships immediately north of **Macau** (Aomen): **Gongbei** on the border itself, and **Jida** and **Xiangzhou**, the port and residential districts 5–10km farther up along the coast. Full of new offices, immensely wide roads and tasty economic incentives, Zhuhai has yet to blossom in the way that Shenzhen has – probably because Zhuhai's neighbour is Macau, not Hong Kong. Sights are also few; the coastline hereabouts is pretty enough on a warm day, but there are no true beaches and most people have come for the border

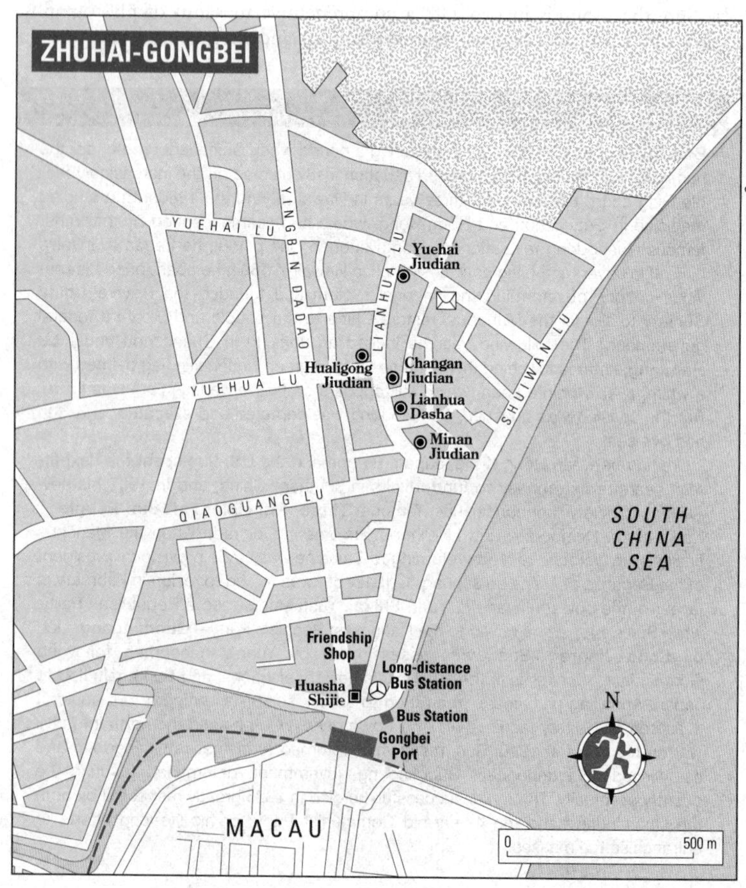

crossing, or to take advantage of what amounts to a **duty-free enclave** aimed at Macanese day-trippers in Gongbei's back streets. **Lianhua Lu** is Gongbei's main drag, a kilometre of hotels, restaurants, and shops selling cheap clothes, household goods and trinkets you never realized you needed. South across a paved square, the **crossing into Macau** is itself concealed inside a huge shopping plaza – labelled "Gongbei Port" in gold on the red roof – where you can buy more of the same.

Practicalities

If you've just **walked across the border** – which is open 7am to 8pm – into Zhuhai from Macau, you exit the customs building at Gongbei with Lianhua Lu and the two adjacent **bus stations** 250m diagonally across to the right. Buses go from both stations to the delta, Guangzhou, and beyond, with the last bus to Guangzhou leaving at 8.30pm (¥55; 2hr). **Jiuzhou ferry port** is 5km up the road at Jida, with twice-hourly services to Shenzhen between 8am and 6pm (1hr; ¥70), and frequent departures to Hong Kong from 8am to 9.30pm (1hr 10min; ¥90). Bus #4 (daily 6.30am–9.30pm) runs up to the port from Gongbei, or you can hail a taxi.

For **accommodation**, there are literally dozens of mid-range places in Gongbei with almost identical facilities and prices: on Lianhua Lu, the *Changan Jiudian* (Ⓣ0756/8118828), *Hualigong Jiudian* (Ⓣ0756/8131828), and *Minan Jiudian* (Ⓣ0756/8131168) are all in the ❻ bracket. There's also the more upmarket *Yuehai Jiudian* (*Guangdong Hotel*; Ⓣ0756/8888128, Ⓕ8885063; ❼) on Yuehai Dong Lu, whose exterior glass lift offers an ear-popping vantage of Macau. The sole budget option is the *Lianhua Dasha* on Lianhua Lu (Ⓣ0756/8885637; ❸), though they're not keen on taking foreigners.

Of the numerous **places to eat**, a canteen opposite the *Lianhua Dasha* on Lianhua Lu serves excellent **Hakka chicken**, baked in salt and displayed outside wrapped in paper (¥35 for a whole bird); while *Huasha Shijie*, which faces the border, has upstairs views into Macau and a dizzying choice of Chinese, Macanese, Indian and Southeast Asian food which you order direct off the chefs by pointing (try *jiuhua yu*, chrysanthemum fish) – portions are colossal and prices reasonable.

Northern Guangdong

Guangdong's hilly northern reaches form a watershed between the Pearl River Valley and the Yangzi Basin, guarding the main route through which peoples, armies and culture flowed between central China and the south – there are even remains of the physical road, broad and paved, up near **Meiling** on the Jiangxi border. Its strategic position saw the region occupied as long ago as the Stone Age, and it was later used by the Taiping rebels and the nineteenth-century Wesleyan Church, who founded numerous missions in northern Guangdong. Today, **Qingyuan** and its pretty riverside temples lie only an hour northwest of Guangzhou by bus, while a host of offbeat attractions farther north around the rail town of **Shaoguan** include the Buddhist shrine of **Nanhua Si**; **Danxia Shan**, a formalized mountain park; and even **white-water rafting** down the Wu River. For those not continuing up into central China, Shaoguan is also a jumping-off point for a backwoods trip west **into Guangxi Province** through ethnic Yao and Zhuang territories.

Northern Guangdong		
Lechang	乐昌	***lèchāng***
Liannan	连南	***liánnán***
Lianzhou	连州	***liánzhōu***
Pingshi	坪石	***píngshí***
Jinji Ling	金鸡岭	*jīnjī lǐng*
Nine Torrents and Eighteen Shoals	九泷十八滩漂流	*jiǔlóngshíbā tānpiāoliú*
Qingyuan	清远	***qīngyuǎn***
Bei River	北江	*běijiāng*
Docks	水陆客运站	*shuǐlù kèyùnzhàn*
Feilai	飞来古寺	*fēilái gǔsì*
Feixia	飞霞古寺	*fēilxiá gǔsì*
Huaqiao Dasha	华侨大厦	*huáqiáo dàshà*
Nandamen Jiudian	南大门酒店	*nándàmén jiǔdiàn*
Qiaolian Dasha	侨联大厦	*qiáolián dàshà*
Tianhu Dajiudian	天湖大酒店	*tiānhú dàjiǔdiàn*
Zhiwei Guan	之味馆	*zhīwèi guǎn*
Shaoguan	韶关	***sháoguān***
Dajian Chan Si	大鉴禅寺	*dàjiànchán sì*
Danxia Shan	丹霞山	*dānxiá shān*
Fengcai Lou	风采楼	*fēngcǎi lóu*
Nanhua Si	南华寺	*nánhuá sì*
Qujiang (Maba)	曲江（马坝）	*qūjiāng(mǎbà)*
Renhua	仁化	*rénhuà*
Shizi Yan	狮子岩	*shīzi yán*
Wu River	武江	*wǔjiāng*
Zhen River	浈江	*zhēnjiāng*
Accommodation and eating		
Dongjiang Fandian	东江饭店	*dōngjiāng fàndiàn*
Guest's Hotel	迎宾馆	*yíngbīn guǎn*
Shaoguan Jiulou	韶关酒楼	*sháoguān jiǔlóu*
Shaohua Jiudian	韶华酒店	*sháohuá jiǔdiàn*
Xinxing Lüguan	新兴旅馆	*xīnxīng lǚdiàn*
Yuelai Jiudian	悦来酒店	*yuèlái jiǔdiàn*
Sanpai	三排	***sānpái***

Qingyuan and around

Surrounded by countryside thick with rice fields and mud-brick villages, **QINGYUAN** is a busy back-road market town on the north bank of the **Bei River**, about 80km northwest of Guangzhou by bus from the Liuhua station (¥35). Ringed by grimy manufacturing complexes, Qingyuan's centre is none too bad, if crowded by narrow streets and hordes of pedestrians. Its attraction lies in its position as a departure point for day-trips 20km upstream to the poetically isolated, elderly temple complexes of **Feilai and Feixia**, which can be reached only by boat.

Qingyuan's **bus station** is about 3km south of the river in an ugly residential area alongside the highway; from here there are several daily buses to

Shaoguan, and masses to Guangzhou, Foshan, and Shenzhen. Heading into the centre, orange bus #6 runs over the Beijiang Bridge and into town, whose kilometre-wide core is centred on the intersection of north–south **Shuguang Lu** and east–west **Xianfeng Lu**. Qingyuan's interesting, older quarter is southwest of here along **Beimen Jie** and its disjointed southern extension, **Nanmen Jie**, which runs down to the water. The **docks** – labelled in English "Go to Feilai and Feixia" – are east off the bottom end of Nanmen Jie, with two **accommodation** options in the vicinity: *Huaqiao Dasha*, at 70 Nanmen Jie (Ⓣ0763/3337118, Ⓕ3334300; ❹), and *Qiaolian Dasha* right next door (Ⓣ0763/3337783; ❸, dorm beds ¥60). There's also the new and pricey *Tianhu Dajiudian* (Ⓣ0763/3820168, Ⓕ3820333; ❻), on the Shuguang Lu/Xianfeng Lu intersection. Hotels aside, Nanmen Jie and Beimen Jie have the best **places to eat**; options include river food at *Nandamen Jiudian*, a café and restaurant in various sections near the dock; or at *Zhiwei Guan*, a Cantonese diner on Beimen.

Feilai and Feixia

Ferries to Feilai and Feixia depart daily at 8am from the dock off Nanmen Jie if enough customers show – it's a popular weekend outing with locals – and leave Feixia to return at about 3pm. The ferry costs ¥27 per person, or you can hire a private, six-person boat for ¥200.

The Bei River runs shallow in winter, and the boats oscillate from bank to bank along navigable channels. For the first hour it's a placid journey past a few brick pagodas, bamboo stands screening off villages and wallowing water buffalo being herded by children. Hills rise up on the right, and then the river bends sharply east into a gorge and past the steps outside the ancient gates of **Feilai Gusi** (¥8), a charmingly positioned Buddhist temple whose ancestry can be traced back 1400 years. Wedged into the base of steep slopes, the current cramped halls date from the Ming dynasty, and manage to look extremely dignified. You'll only need about forty minutes to have a look at the lively ridge tiles and climb up through the thin pine forest to where a modern pavilion offers pretty views of the gorge scenery. If you have time to spare before your boat heads on, the temple gates are a good place to sit and watch the tame cormorants sunbathing on the prows of their owners' tiny sampans, or you can bargain with the local women for freshwater mussels and carp – you'll have a chance to get these cooked for you at Feixia.

Feixia

Some 3km farther upstream from Feilai at the far end of the gorge, **Feixia Gusi** (¥15) is far more recent and much more extensive in the scale and scope of its buildings. The name covers two entirely self-sufficient Taoist monasteries, founded in 1863 and expanded fifty years later, were built up in the hills in the Feixia and Cangxia grottoes, with hermitages, pavilions and academies adorning the 8km of interlinking, flagstoned paths in between. Chinese visitors initially ignore all this, however, and head straight for the huge collection of **alfresco restaurant shacks** on the riverbank, where they buy and organize the preparation of river food with the numerous, eager wok-wielding cooks – a nice way to have lunch.

A couple of hours is plenty of time to have a look around. A broad and not very demanding set of steps runs up from the riverfront through a pleasant woodland where, after twenty minutes or so, you pass the minute Jinxia and Ligong temples, cross an ornamental bridge, and encounter **Feixia** itself. Hefty surrounding walls and passages connecting halls and courtyards, all built of stone, lend Feixia the atmosphere of a medieval European castle. There's nothing monumental to see – one of the rooms has been turned into a **museum** of holy relics, and you might catch a weekend performance of **traditional temple music** played on bells, gongs and zithers – but the gloom, low ceilings and staircases running off in all directions make it an interesting place to explore. If you walk up through the monastery and take any of the tracks heading uphill, in another ten minutes or so you'll come to the short **Changtian Pagoda** perched right on the top of the ridges, decorated with mouldings picked out in pastel colours, with views down over Feixia and the treetops. Another small temple next door offers food, drink and basic accommodation (¥50).

Five minutes' walk east along the main track from Feixia brings you to the similar but smaller complex of **Cangxia**. Restorations began here in 1994, but Cangxia remains in a semi-ruinous state, though monks hounded out during the 1960s are back in attendance, and many of the statues and shrines are smudged with incense soot. Look for the garden with its fragrant white magnolia tree, an unusual, life-sized statue of the Monkey God Sun Wu Kong, and some wonderful **frescoes** – an immortal crossing the sea on a fish, storm dragons and two golden pheasants.

Shaoguan

Just about any train from the Guangzhou train station calls in at **SHAOGUAN**, 200km north, and expresses take a mere three hours – not a bad hard-seat experience (¥40). An ancient city, Shaoguan was unfortunately the target of Japanese saturation bombing during the 1930s, which robbed the town of much of its heritage. Since the 1950s, textile mills and steelworks have ensured a moderate prosperity, if not a pretty skyline, but there's plenty to do in the immediate area.

Shaoguan's downtown area fills a south-pointing **peninsula** shaped by the **Zhen River** on the east side and the **Wu River** on the west, which merge at the peninsula's southern tip to form the Bei River. The pedestrianized main street, Fengdu Lu, runs vertically through the centre to bald, paved Zhongshan Park, crossed by Fengcai Lu at the north end of town, and Jiefang Lu in the south. While there's plenty of activity in the clothing and trinket **markets** which fill the side streets off Fengdu Lu, and some crumbling colonial architecture, most of the town is functional and modern. The city sights, such as they are, comprise **Fengcai Lou**, a 1930s reconstruction of the old eastern city gate

West into Guangxi

Though the main transport routes run north and south from Shaoguan, if you're looking for an unusual way into Guangxi Province, consider heading west through the mountainous strongholds of Guangdong's **Yao** and **Zhuang** population, a corner of the province virtually untouched by tourism. An early-morning bus leaves Shaoguan's long-distance station daily and takes about five hours to cover the 185km to **Lianzhou**, a Han town established by Emperor Wudi in 111 BC and containing an ancient **hexagonal pagoda** whose base is of Song vintage. Another 15km southwest from Lianzhou is **Liannan**, from where you can catch minibuses 10km out to **Sanpai**, a predominantly Yao village, and 35km beyond Liannan you'll find **Lianshan**, surrounded by Yao and Zhuang hamlets. Continuing through to Guangxi, the road from Lianshan runs a farther 100km over the mountains to **Hezhou**, a small town in Guangxi province from where you can get onwards transport to Wuzhou or Guilin.

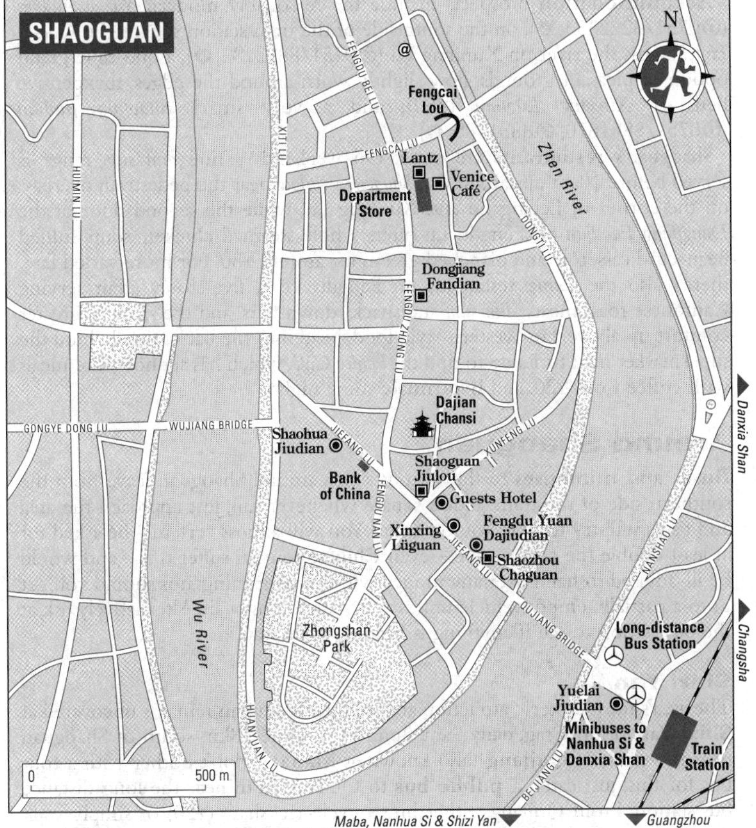

tower, up along Fengcai Lu; and **Dajian Chansi**, an insubstantial monastery with ancient heritage – it was founded in 660 AD, and Huineng (see p.632) taught here – just east off the bottom end of Fengdu Lu.

Practicalities

Both **arrival points** are immediately east of the centre over the Zhen River, linked to Jiefang Lu by the Qujiang Bridge: the **train station** sits at the back of a big square here, while the **long-distance bus station** is just north of the bridge on the square's edge. Onward train tickets are in short supply, as this is the main line north out of Guangdong and, despite a continuous stream of trains passing through, it's perpetually overcrowded, as is the train station itself. Long-distance buses – heading north to Pingshi, Jiangxi and Hunan, east to Meizhou and Shantou, south to Guangzhou and west to Lianshan – leave throughout the day. **Taxis** cruise the streets (¥5 within town), with **minibuses** out to nearby attractions leaving from the train-station square. There's a **Bank of China** on Jiefang Lu (Mon–Fri 9–11.30am & 1–5pm), a **post office** on the south side of the train station square, and several **Internet bars** just north of Fengcai Ta on Dongti Lu.

Accommodation prospects include the reasonably modern *Yuelai Jiudian* (ⓣ0751/8222333; ❺), on the south side of the train station square; the *Guest's Hotel* across the river on Xunfeng Lu (ⓣ0751/8882282; ❹), a one-time grand option in pleasant grounds, now slightly worn around the edges; inexpensive beds at *Xinxing Lüguan* (¥50); and a very smart *Shaohua Jiudian* (ⓣ0751/8881870, ⓕ8881988; ❺).

Shaoguan's **restaurants** are good. On weekends a fine *dim sum* range is served before 10am upstairs at the *Shaoguan Jiulou*, near the pedestrian overpass on the corner of Jiefang Lu and Xunfeng Lu, while the second floor of the *Dongjiang Fandian* on Fengdu Lu offers whole steamed chicken, soup, stuffed bean-curd casserole and blanched greens for around ¥80. For more varied fare, there's also the *Lantz* restaurant on Fengdu Lu, a five-storey affair serving Cantonese roast meats, *dim sum* and snacks downstairs, and the same in greater comfort up above. For Western-style food, head into the back lanes behind the supermarket next to *Lantz* to find the *Venice Café*, which has set hot-plate meals with coffee from ¥20, and **live music** some nights.

Around Shaoguan

Buses and minibuses to the various sights around Shaoguan leave from the southern side of the train station square whenever full; just approach the area and touts will try to drag you on board. You will almost certainly be asked for at least double the correct fare – even Chinese tourists suffer this – and would be ill-advised to hand over any money without bargaining; nor should you get onto a partially empty vehicle unless you want a long wait. Alternatively, ask at the bus station to see if anything is heading your way.

Shizi Yan

The area's most esoteric attraction are prehistoric human remains uncovered at **Shizi Yan** (Lion Crag; daily 9am–4pm; ¥15), some 18km south of Shaoguan near the town of **Qujiang** (also known as **Maba**) – don't bother with a tour bus for this, just catch a **public bus** to Qujiang from near the long-distance bus station. From Qujiang, either hire a cycle-rickshaw (¥20) or simply walk the final 3km – head west along Fuqian Zhong Lu, then turn south down Jiangshe Nan Lu, over a corroded metal footbridge, and follow the rutted main road off into the country.

Once clear of the town you'll see Shizi Yan not far off, a short limestone hill projecting out of the ground like a tooth; the entrance is marked by a stone archway on the roadside. The crag turns out to be hollow and surrounded by caveman statues, and a Chinese-speaking guide takes you through the small caverns and explains how human remains were first found by the Guomindang when they were caching silver here during the 1930s. More comprehensive investigations twenty years later uncovered animal and human bones in quantities, suggesting that the cave was regularly occupied by *Homo erectus* (here nicknamed Maba Man), our immediate ancestors. A further ¥3 gets you into the **museum** back near the main gate, where there's a second-floor exhibition of stone axes, arrowheads, pottery and other artefacts unearthed from more recent Neolithic burials found in the surrounding fields in 1977. Unfortunately, labelling is scanty and in Chinese only.

Nanhua Si

Nanhua Si (Southern Flower Temple; ¥10) lies southeast of Qujiang, a 25-kilometre, thirty-minute minibus ride from Shaoguan (¥5). Founded in 502

AD by the Indian monk Zhiyao Sanzang, the temple became famous through the activities of the Sixth Patriarch of Chan Buddhism, **Huineng** (see box, p.632), who sat in meditation here for 36 years. The seven halls are rather stark, but look for the **bell tower**, in the atrium on the far side of the first hall, whose massive bronze bell was cast in 1167; the room beyond houses a riot of *arhats* and Bodhisattvas cavorting with sea monsters in a sea of papier-mâché. Pick of the sculptures here are those of **Ji Gong**, the Song beggar-monk with a tatty pandanus-leaf fan who became a sort of Robin Hood to China's poor, and an unidentified fat priest waddling on improbable stilts at the back. A collection of fine **wooden sculptures** and a seventh-century cast-iron statue of a levitating spirit grace another room, dedicated to Guanyin, while in the back of the final hall is a **model of Huineng** – which some maintain was cast from his corpse – who sits with pendulous earlobes and sunken eyes, staring at a bhodi tree.

Danxia Shan

Danxia Shan, a formation of vivid red sandstone cliffs lining the **Jin River**, 50km northeast of Shaoguan near the town of **Renhua**, makes a hugely enjoyable day-trip. Buses from Shaoguan's train station square (¥15) drop you by the main road gates, where you pay the ¥55 **entry fee**, which includes all minibus rides into and around the park – note that these stop around 5pm, and that the **last bus** back to Shaoguan passes the gates in the late afternoon.

The first place to aim for is **Yuan Shan Jing**, 2km inside the gates across the Jin, famous for **Yangyuan Shi**, a rock which – though the description is less suitably applied to outcrops all over China – really does look like the male member. It's a tough climb to the summit of neighbouring (and less phallic) Yuan Shan, after which you can charter a **boat** (¥10 a person) or catch the bus for another couple of kilometres to Danxia Shan itself. The surrounding area is covered in 12km of paths, which rise steeply through woodland, past cliff-side nunneries and rock formations, and up the various summits; Chinese tourists stay overnight in the handful of **hotels** here (❷ and up) and rise early to catch the sunrise from the pavilion at the mountain's apex, **Changlao** – only an hour's climb – though the views are great all day long.

Pingshi to Lechang: rafting the Nine Torrents

In 1986, after many attempts and much loss of life, the Chinese Academy of Sciences finally succeeded in shooting the entire length of the Yangzi River on rubber rafts, thereby sparking nationwide interest in the sport and a new tourist industry at **PINGSHI**, a small, functional town 100km northwest of Shaoguan on the Wu River. Though not part of the Yangzi system, the 103-kilometre flow between Pingshi and southerly **Lechang** – not entirely fancifully described as comprising "**Nine Torrents and Eighteen Shoals**" – is well suited to recreational rafting, and there's a month-long **rafting festival** in Lechang each July, when Chinese tour groups from all over the country come to ride these rapids. You can either organize a round trip with accommodation in Shaoguan, or go to Pingshi and make all arrangements there. There's at least one bus daily from Shaoguan to Pingshi (5hr; ¥35), or several trains can get you there in about three hours. The **rafting ticket office** (daily 9–11am & 1.30–5pm; tickets ¥210 per person) is opposite Pingshi's train station, and if there are no tickets left here for the next day, try the CITS at the nearby *Jinji Ling Binguan*, with reasonably maintained doubles and some grotty dorms (❹, dorm beds ¥35).

Ideally, give yourself the best part of a day in Pingshi and climb **Jinji Ling** (Golden Rooster Ridge) which sits 1km to the north. While it peaks at a modest 350m, the rock formations and vegetation here are interesting, especially the vertical tower of **Yizi Ling**. Previews of the forthcoming rapids can be had from the rather more accessible, flatter humps at Yizi's base, where a handful of modern pavilions and a statue reveal that during the 1850s this was the training ground for **Hong Xuanjiao**, a female commander of the Taiping army.

Downstream to Lechang

There are two morning and two afternoon rafting sessions daily. You meet up at the ticket office to be fitted with a life jacket and then board your vessel, a motorized, inflatable, heavyweight rubber dinghy seating nine or ten people. As you speed downstream past a gamut of strangely contorted crags, keep your eyes peeled for holes worn deep into the rocks on either side of the river, where pilots of the less manoeuvrable wooden boats, which regularly used to haul cargo and passengers along this stretch, tried to gain purchase for their bamboo poles. Back in the Tang dynasty, one of these crafts carried **Han Yu**, the disgraced prime minister of Emperor Xuanzong, into distant exile at Chaozhou, and there's a **temple** on the right bank to commemorate his sad trek.

There are other natural and historic sites along the way at which the raft might stop for a while, and sometimes **mishaps** do occur, but it generally takes about seven hours to reach **LECHANG**. You could either stay the night in one of Lechang's guesthouses, or catch one of the frequent **minibuses to Shaoguan** (¥10) or a train on the Guangzhou–Hunan line.

Eastern Guangdong

All in one go, it's an arduous six-hundred-kilometre journey east from Guangzhou to Xiamen in Fujian province, but there's a wealth of intrinsically interesting territory to explore on the way. Only three hours away, **Huizhou**'s watery parkland makes it an excellent weekend bolthole from Guangzhou, while over near the Fujian border, the seedy splendour of the former treaty port of **Shantou** is just an hour from **Chaozhou**, famed for its own cooking style and splendid Ming-era architecture. With enough time, you could spend a few days farther north in the hilly country around **Meizhou**, investigating ethnic **Hakka culture** in its heartland. Getting around is easy: **expressways** from Guangzhou or Shenzhen run via Huizhou along the coast to Shantou and on into Fujian, while the **rail line** from Guangzhou's East train station bends northeast from Huizhou to Meizhou – where a new extention runs up to Yongding in Fujian – then down to Chaozhou and Shantou.

Huizhou and Xi Hu

HUIZHOU, 160km from Guangzhou, is a place of water, caught between five lakes and the confluence of the Dong and Xizhi rivers. It was settled over two thousand years ago and later became capital of the Southern Han court. What saves Huizhou from being just another small, run-of-the-mill Chinese town is the genteel scenery surrounding the two-square-kilometre **Xi Hu** (West Lake). First laid out as a park by Song-dynasty engineers, the lakeside is a pleasant place to spend a day or a few hours strolling around the constructed landscapes and watching crowds of locals do the same.

Huizhou isn't a large place, and Xi Hu covers about the same area as the centre of town. There are several **entrances** open from 6am until after dark (¥16), but the main one is next to the *Huizhou Binguan* on Huangcheng Lu. The path here crosses the lake over a five-hundred-metre causeway, whose two sections are joined by a small humpbacked bridge made of white marble. It was built in 1096 by a monk named Xigu and funded by the Sichuanese poet-official **Su Dongpo**, then Huizhou's governor and composer of a famous verse extolling the beauty of the full moon seen from this spot. On the far shore there's a thirteen-storey brick pagoda from 1618, whose wobbly wooden stairs can be climbed for fine views north and south across the waters. Next door is a noble statue of Su Dongpo, with an adjacent museum displaying a battered ink stone said to have belonged to this ubiquitous man of letters.

The main path heads off across the lake again from here, this time via a zigzagging bridge and a series of strategically placed islets, thick with bamboo groves, to the northern shore forecourt of **Yuan Miao**, an old Taoist nunnery. It's a bizarre place, with an improbable number of tiny rooms and atriums decorated with Taoist symbols and auspicious carvings of bats, tigers and cranes; one hall at the back is dedicated to the Three Kingdoms hero and war god Guan Yu, and a side wing contains a pit full of live tortoises. Walking back down Huangcheng Lu from here, there are a few more islands linked to the footpath, the favoured haunt of weekend street performers who keep crowds entertained with theatre and martial arts displays.

Practicalities

Huizhou's town centre sits immediately below a kink in the 500-metre-wide Dong River, a proportionately thin strip of land hemmed in by the smaller Xizhi River to the east, and Xi Hu to the west. The **train** pulls in about 3km west, from where a taxi or bus #9 will get you to Huizhou's **long-distance bus station**. This is on a roundabout 1km south of the lake on Eling Bei Lu, which runs north, away from the roundabout, to Huangcheng Lu, which in turn follows Xi Hu's eastern shore. Take any of the small side streets east off Huangcheng Lu and you'll end up on parallel Shuimen Lu, Huizhou's functional shopping precinct. The town's hotels can **change money**, and there's a huge Bank of China five minutes' walk east of the bus station roundabout along Eling Dong Lu (Mon–Fri 9am–noon & 1.30–5pm).

For inexpensive **accommodation**, stick around the bus station, where noisy hostels such as the *Huiyun Zhaodaisuo* offer basic facilities (❷, dorm beds ¥40), or walk up Eling Bei Lu to the clean and quiet *Fei'e Lou* (Ⓣ0752/2288999; ❸). But it's better to splash out for a nicer room near the lake, particularly if you're here for a break from Guangzhou. Best is the *Huizhou Binguan*, a very comfortable affair with spacious doubles (Ⓣ0752/2232333, Ⓕ2231439; ❻); it's right on Xi Hu's eastern shore on Huangcheng Lu. Alternatively, try the *Xihu Dajiudian* just across the road (Ⓣ0752/2226666, Ⓦwww.hzwestlakehtl.com; ❼), or the more ordinary but good-value *Dongjiang Jiudian* farther up Huangcheng Lu (Ⓣ0752/2233848; ❸). For **food**, there are canteens near the bus station and inexpensive restaurants along Huangcheng Lu and Shuicheng Lu. Try the hotels for more upmarket meals – the *Huizhou Binguan* might even be able to rustle up an English menu.

Moving on, you can book train tickets through the *Huizhou Binguan*'s travel service (daily 8am–8pm); buses run back to Guangzhou and Shenzhen between 6am and 6pm, with several daily onwards least as far as Chaozhou and Shantou.

Eastern Guangdong

Huizhou	惠州	***huìzhōu***
Dongjiang Jiudian	东江酒店	*dōngjiāng jiǔdiàn*
Huiyun Zhaodaisuo	惠运招待所	*huìyùn zhāodàisuǒ*
Huizhou Binguan	惠州宾馆	*huìzhōu bīnguǎn*
Xi Hu	西湖	*xīhú*
Xihu Dajiudian	西湖大酒店	*xīhú dàjiǔdiàn*
Yuan Miao	元庙	*yuánmiào*
Shantou	汕头	***shàntóu***
Qhaolian Dasha	侨联大厦	*qiáolián dàshà*
Chaozhou Caiguan	潮洲莱馆	*cháozhōu càiguǎn*
Huaqiao Dasha	华侨大厦	*huáqiáo dàshà*
Piaoxiang Xiaocidian	飘香小吃店	*piāoxiāng xiǎochīdiàn*
Shipaotai Gongyuan	石炮台公园	*shípàotái gōngyuán*
Tianhou Gong	天后宫	*tiānhòu gōng*
Tuodao Binguan	舵岛宾馆	*tuódǎo bīnguǎn*
Xinhua Binguan	新华宾馆	*xīnhuá bīnguǎn*
Zhongshan Park	中山公园	*zhōngshān gōngyuán*
Chaozhou	潮州	***cháozhōu***
Confucian Academy	海阳县儒学宫	*hǎiyángxiàn rúxuégōng*
Fenghuang Pagoda	凤凰塔	*fènghuáng tǎ*
Guangji Gate	广济门	*guǎngjì mén*
Hanwen Gong	韩文公	*hánwén gōng*
Kaiyuan Si	开元寺	*kāiyuán sì*
Xiangzi Qiao	湘子桥	*xiāngzǐ qiáo*
Xihu Park	西湖公园	*xīhú gōngyuán*
Xufu Mafu	许驸马府	*xǔfù mǎ fǔ*

Shantou

SHANTOU sits in a well-protected marine harbour at the mouth of the stunted Rong River, where eastern Guangdong's major waterway, the **Han River**, disgorges into the South China Sea through a complex estuary. This strategic access to the south's mountainous interior, not to mention a useful position between Guangzhou and Xiamen in Fujian, was overlooked until Shantou was first opened to foreigners in 1858 following the post-Opium War **Tianjin Treaty**. The mainly British entrepreneurs who moved in called the town **Swatow** after the local pronunciation, followed the Han River upstream to establish church missions, built a city in grand colonial style and, by 1900, had turned Shantou from a fishing village into a major trading port. It remained so for half a century, but the Communist takeover saw the city's interests gradually shifting towards light industries, which were greatly expanded after Shantou's 1980 elevation to one of Guangdong's Special Economic Zones. Today the old waterfront district is neglected, as a new, modern business city of over a million inhabitants expands steadily east. While incredibly crowded and noisy, the crumbling old quarter and a few nice traditional buildings make Shantou a decent place to pause before continuing east into Fujian, or north to Chaozhou.

The City

Overall, Shantou is a huge, sprawling city, but everything of interest is in the western end, a stubby, three-kilometre-broad thumb of land bounded south by

Accommodation and eating		
Chaozhou Binguan	潮州宾馆	*cháozhōu bīnguǎn*
Ciyuan Jiujia	瓷苑酒家	*cíyuàn jiǔjiā*
Hongyun Jiudian	鸿运酒家	*hóngyùn jiǔjiā*
Hu Rong Quan	胡荣泉	*húróng quán*
Taiwan Binguan	台湾宾馆	*táiwān bīnguǎn*
Xin Banhu Jiulou	新板湖酒楼	*xīnbǎnhú jiǔlóu*
Meizhou	梅州	***méizhōu***
Dongshan Bridge	东山桥	*dōngshān qiáo*
Lingguang Si	灵光寺	*língguāng sì*
Meijiang Bridge	梅江桥	*méijiāng qiáo*
Mei River	梅江	*méijiāng*
Qianfo Si	千佛寺	*qiānfó sì*
Renjinglu	人境庐	*rénjìng lú*
Wenhua Park	文化公园	*wénhuà gōngyuán*
Yinna Shan	阴那山	*yīnnà shān*
Accommodation and eating		
Huaqiao Dasha	华侨大厦	*huáqiáo dàshà*
Huayun Dajiudian	华运大酒店	*huáyùn dàjiǔdiàn*
Huihua Jiudian	晖华酒店	*huīhuá jiǔdiàn*
Keji Fan	客家饭	*kèjiā fàn*
Meizhou Dasha	梅州大厦	*méizhōu dàshà*
Shang's Meatball Store	尚记肉丸店	*shàngjì ròuwándiàn*
Dapu	大埔	***dàpǔ***
Gongyuan Binguan	公园宾馆	*gōngyuán bīnguǎn*
Hu Shan	虎山	*hǔshān*

the harbour and farther west and north by various trailing outflows descending from the Han River estuary. One of these, the **Mei Canal**, surrounds **Zhongshan Park** (¥2) on the northern side of the "thumb" – the entrance is east off Dahua Lu. The park, the nicest place in Shantou to start the day in relative calm among ballroom dancers and martial arts experts training with swords, has a small outdoor **theatre** on the eastern side (where Chaozhou opera gets an airing most weekends), and plenty of trees and water.

Five minutes southwest of the park along Minzu Lu is a large, pavilion-centred **roundabout**. Turning east along Shengping Lu, you can seek out **Tianhou Gong**, built in 1879 and now beautifully restored. The main courtyard can barely contain twenty people, but the statues and decorations are extraordinarily opulent, with guardian spirits handpainted on the wooden doors, beams carved into dragons and animals, and roof tiles showing scenes from the lives of the red-faced warrior Guan Yu, and a local heroine and her tiger.

Back at the roundabout, Anping Lu runs southwest for more than a kilometre towards the waterfront between mouldering **colonial facades** and block upon block of three-storeyed town houses and warehouses, all with elaborate, decaying plaster decor and fluted columns flanking windows and doorways. Though the area is decidedly downmarket and claustrophobic – many of the buildings look as if they're about to keel over on top of you – it's easy to spend a couple of absorbing hours poking around. When you've had enough, make your way back over to Waima Lu and catch bus #3 for about 3km east along

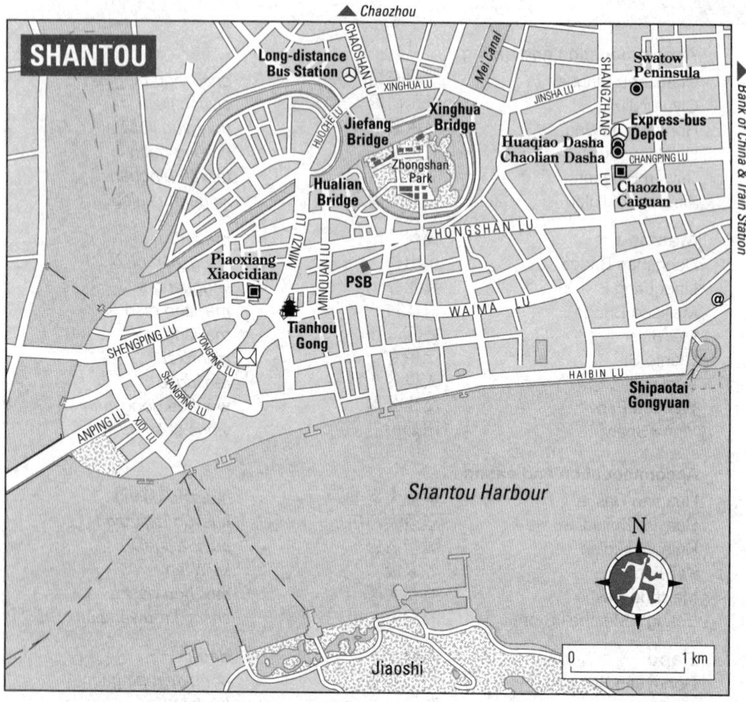

Haibin Lu to **Shipaotai Gongyuan** (Stone Gun Emplacement Park; ¥6). Surrounded by a moat, his large, fortified ring was built in the 1870s to protect the city from seaborne invasion, the blocks for its six-metre-high sloping walls made of rammed earth, granite, glutinous rice, sugar and lime. Inside, you can walk right around in between the inner and outer walls, and climb to the top of the fort where several of the original eighteen cannons face south.

Practicalities

The excellent **Shenshan expressway** between Huizhou and Shantou makes for fast and furious driving, and it's not unusual for buses to cover the 300km in a respectable four hours – even faster than the train. Shantou's **long-distance bus station** is in the north of town, at the bottom of Chaoshan Lu; the **train station** is 10km away on the eastern side of the new city, connected to the bus station by city buses #11 or #4. Plenty of **taxis** haunt arrival points; watch out for pickpockets on local buses.

The long-distance bus station has very helpful staff, regular shuttles to Chaozhou (¥15) – faster than the train – and long-distance departures at least as far afield as Xiamen, Guangzhou and Meizhou. There's also an **express bus depot** near the hotels on Shangzhang Lu, with express services to Guangzhou, Shenzhen, Macau, Meizhou, Xiamen and Fuzhou. Rather than making the long haul out to the train station, you can buy **train tickets** to Chaozhou, Meizhou, Huizhou and Guangzhou through your accommodation, or at the special window in the bus station, or from the agent next door to the luxury bus depot.

The huge **Bank of China** is in the new city on Jinsha Dong Lu (foreign exchange Mon–Fri 9am–5pm) – bus #2 from Zhongshan Lu stops outside. The **PSB** are on Gongyuan Lu (ⓣ0754/8423592).

Accommodation and eating

The pick of Shantou's **accommodation** lies about 2km east of the bus station – bus #4 comes closest. The *Swatow Peninsula*, Jinsha Lu (ⓣ0754/8316668, ⓦwww.pihotel.com; ❻) and *Huaqiao Dasha* on Shanzhang Lu (ⓣ0754/8629888, ⓕ8252223; ❺) are both fairly upmarket tourist hotels; *Chaolian Dasha* on the corner of Shanzhang and Changping roads is a friendly budget alternative (ⓣ0754/8259109; ❷).

Shantou and Chaozhou share a distinctive **cooking style** (for more of which see p.674), and the city has a good reputation for seafood and rice-flour dumplings. Cheap stalls and canteens fill the old quarter's back lanes; make sure you eat at *Piaoxiang Xiaocidian*, a scruffy, inexpensive **dumpling house** serving local snacks and light meals from inside a former temple 70m north off the Shengping Lu roundabout (oyster omelettes are a speciality here); and *Chaozhou Caiguan*, near the hotels on the corner of Changping Lu, which offers similar fare in more comfort.

Chaozhou

Just 40km north of Shantou on the banks of the Han River, **CHAOZHOU** is one of Guangdong's most culturally significant towns, yet manages to be overlooked by tourist itineraries and government projects alike – principally through having had its limelight stolen during the nineteenth century by its noisy southern sister. In response, Chaozhou has become staunchly traditional, proudly preserving the architecture, superstitions and local character which Shantou, a recent, foreign creation, never had, making it a far nicer place to spend some time.

Founded back in antiquity, by the Ming dynasty Chaozhou had reached its zenith as a place of culture and refinement, and the originals of many of the town's monuments date back to this time. A spate of tragedies followed, however. After an anti-Manchu uprising in 1656, only Chaozhou's monks and their temples were spared the imperial wrath – it's said that the ashes of the hundred thousand slaughtered citizens formed several fair-sized hills. The town managed to recover somehow, but was brought down in the nineteenth century by famine and the Opium Wars, which culminated in Shantou's foundation. Half a million desperately impoverished locals fled Chaozhou and eastern Guangdong through the new port, many of them **emigrating** to European colonies all over Southeast Asia, where their descendants comprise a large proportion of Chinese communities in Thailand, Malaysia, Singapore and Indonesia. Humiliatingly, Shantou's rising importance saw Chaozhou placed under its administration until becoming an independent municipality in 1983, and there's still real rivalry between the two.

For the visitor, Chaozhou is a splendid place. Among some of the most active and manageable street life in southern China, there are some fine historic **monuments** to tour, excellent shopping for local **handicrafts**, and a nostalgically dated small-town ambience to soak up. Chinese speakers will find that Chaozhou's **language** is related to Fujian's *minnan* dialect, different from either Mandarin or Cantonese, though both of these are widely understood.

Arrival and accommodation

Laid out on the western bank of the Han River, Chaozhou comprises an oval, 1500-metre-long **old town centre**, enclosed by Huangcheng Lu, which,

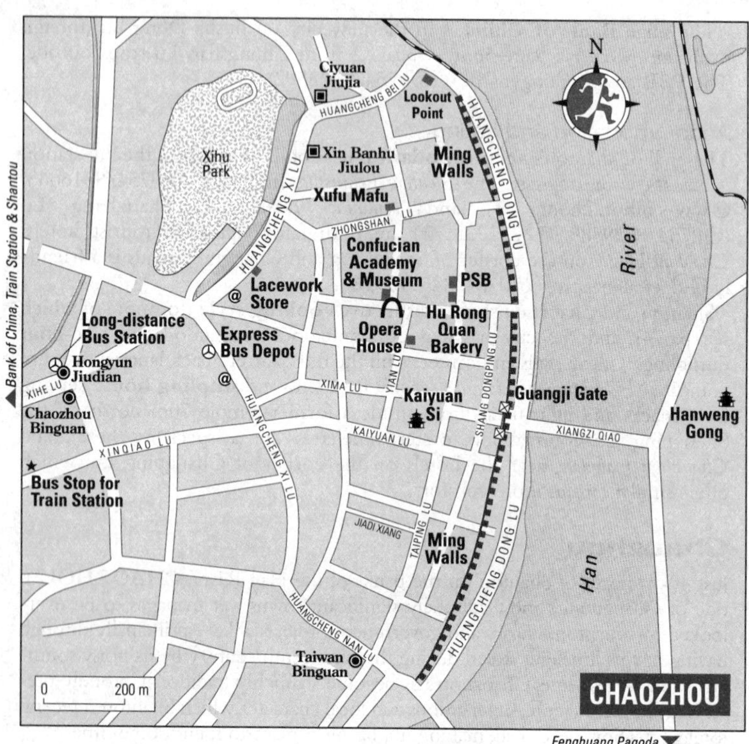

divided into north, south, east and west sections, follows the line of the **Ming-dynasty stone walls.** A stretch of these still faces the river on the centre's eastern side, while Chaozhou's modern fringe spreads west of Huangcheng Lu. The old town's main thoroughfares are Taiping Lu, orientated north–south, crossed by shorter Zhongshan Lu, Xima Lu, and Kaiyuan Lu, which all run east from Huangcheng Lu, through arched gates in the walls, and out to the river.

Chaozhou's **long-distance bus station** is just west of the centre on Xihe Lu; shuttles from Shantou wind up here too. The **train station** is about 5km northwest; from here, you can walk 100m to the main road and catch city bus #2 (daily 6.30am–8.30pm; ¥2) to Xinqiao Lu, a western extension of Kaiyuan Lu. **Motor-rickshaws** – the only vehicle able to negotiate the old town's back streets – are abundant, though once in town everything is within walking distance. The **Bank of China** is about 2km west of the bus station on Chaofeng Lu; catch any public bus heading this way.

Moving on from Chaozhou, there are **buses** to Meizhou, Shantou, Guangzhou, Shenzhen and Fujian from the long-distance bus station, and **express coaches** east and west along the coastal road from a private depot on Huangcheng Xi Lu. **Trains** (station ticket office daily 6–11.30am & 1.30–5.30pm) run down to Shantou or back to Guangzhou via Meizhou and Huizhou. Shantou is quickest reached by bus, Meizhou by train.

Places to stay are mostly clustered around the bus station. The best deal is at the bus station itself, whose *Hongyun Jiudian* has clean and tidy doubles

(Ⓣ0768/2206052; ❹); across the road, the touristy *Chaozhou Binguan* (Ⓣ0768/2261168, Ⓕ2264298; ❻) is overpriced but better than badly ageing competition nearby. Otherwise, head to the *Taiwan Binguan* (Ⓣ0768/2232050, Ⓕ2233029; ❺), a smart business hotel 1500m south on Huangcheng Nan Lu.

The Town

Chaozhou's old centre has none of Shantou's decrepitude. Instead you'll find an endlessly engaging warren of narrow streets packed with a well-maintained mixture of colonial and traditional buildings. In the quieter residential back lanes, look for old wells, Ming-dynasty stone archways, and antique family mansions, protected from the outside world by thick walls and heavy wooden doors, and guarded by mouldings of gods and good luck symbols. Out on the main streets, motorbikes and cycle-rickshaws weave among the shoppers, who are forced off the pavement and into the roads by the piles of goods stacked up outside stores. If you need a target, **Xufu Mafu** is a decaying mansion guarded by stone lions on Zhongshan Lu, with a Ming-style memorial archway and a former **Confucian academy** – now a **museum** full of prewar photos of town – one block away. Down in the south of town, **Jiadi Xiang**, a lane west off Taiping Lu, is an immaculate Qing period piece, its flagstones, ornamental porticos and murals (including a life-sized rendition of a lion-like *qilin* opposite no. 16) restored for the benefit of residents, not tourists. For a bit of space, head up to **Xihu Park** (¥5), just north of the old town across a "moat" on Huangcheng Xi Lu, where there's a dwarf pagoda, hillocks, and some vegetated sections of the town walls.

If you bother with only one sight, however, make it **Kaiyuan Si** (daily 8am–6pm; ¥5), a lively Buddhist temple founded in 738 AD, at the eastern end of Kaiyuan Lu. Here, three sets of solid wooden doors open onto courtyards planted with figs and red-flowered phoenix trees, where a pair of Tang-era **stone pillars**, topped with lotus buds, symbolically support the sky. The various halls are pleasantly proportioned, with brightly coloured lions, fish and dragons sporting along the sweeping, low-tiled roof ridges. Off to the west side is a **Guanyin pavilion** with a dozen or more statues of this popular Bodhisattva in all her forms. Another room on the east side is full of bearded Taoist saints holding a *yin-yang* wheel, while the interior of the **main hall** boasts a very intricate vaulted wooden ceiling and huge brocade banners almost obscuring a golden Buddhist trinity. At the time of writing, the complex was being expanded by the construction of a new, eastern wing.

The town walls and the east bank

About 250m east past the temple down Kaiyuan Lu you run up against the **old town walls**. Seven metres high and almost as thick, these were only ever breached twice in Chaozhou's history, and more than 1500m still stand in good condition. At the main **Guangji Gate**, there's a set of steps up to a rickety guard tower and a walking track along the top of the wall. Pass through the gate and you're standing by the river next to the five-hundred-metre-wide **Xiangzi Qiao**, a bridge whose piles were sunk in the twelfth century. Until the 1950s the central section was spanned by a row of wooden punts, now replaced by an ordinary concrete construction, closed to heavy traffic and popular with hawkers selling cheap clothes. Crossing over, you can see the shrub-covered shell of the ancient **Fenghuang Pagoda** a couple of kilometres downstream, while on the far bank a short street bears left to the gate of **Hanwen Gong** (¥5), a temple complex built in 999 in memory of Han Yu, a

Confucian scholar who a century earlier had denounced Buddha as a barbarian and cleared the river of troublesome crocodiles. A flight of broad, steep granite stairs here leads up to three terraces, each with a hall; the uppermost one has numerous ancient stone proclamation tablets and a painted statue of Han Yu.

Eating, drinking and entertainment

Chaozhou's cooking style is becoming ever more popular in China though, thanks to emigrants from the region, it has long been unconsciously appreciated overseas. Seafood is a major feature, while local roast goose, flavoured here with sour plum – the use of fruit is a characteristic feature of the style, as is a garnish of fried garlic chips, a Southeast Asian influence – rivals a good Beijing duck. A string of **restaurants** overlook Xihu Park on Huangcheng Xi Lu: the *Xin Banhu Jiulou* here serves a decent cold chopped goose and green vegetables, but the *Ciyuan Jiujia* is superb. Indicate how much you're prepared to spend and staff at the *Ciyuan* will arrange a meal for you – four people pay around ¥50 each for roast goose, crispy-fried squid, steamed crab, fishball soup, fried spinach and a selection of *dim sum*. For **snacking**, *Hu Rong Quan*, a bakery specializing in mooncakes on Taiping Lu, makes the best spring rolls you'll ever eat, stuffed with spring onions, yellow bean, mushrooms and a little meat. Unusually for China, very fresh goat's **milk** can be bought from the farmer who tethers his animals around the junction of Xihe Lu and Huangcheng Xi Lu in the afternoons – bring your own bottle.

The local **tea** ritual is called *gongfu cha*, and Chaozhou's residents perform it on the slightest pretext – if nobody offers you a cup, most places to eat serve tea at a couple of yuan a session. First, the distinctive tiny pot and cups arrive on a deep ceramic tray with a grid on top for drainage; the pot is stuffed to the brim with large, coarse Oolong tea leaves, filled with boiling water, and immediately emptied – not into the cups, but the tray. Then the pot is topped up and left to steep for a moment before the cups are filled with a rapid movement which delivers an equal strength brew to all. For all this effort you have a thimbleful of tea, which has to be swiftly downed before it goes cold, more of a social activity than a source of refreshment.

For **entertainment**, try and track down a performance of *chaoju*, the indigenous **opera style**. It's quite listenable, with little of the warlike clanging and falsetto singing of Beijing's theatre; the plots tend to involve witty cautionary tales about lax sexual morality. Your best bet now are infrequent shows in Xihu Park, most likely during festivals. There's actually an old opera house on Yian Lu, parallel with Taiping Lu and one block west, though this has been converted into a **cinema**, sometimes screening videotaped opera performances.

Shopping

Adherence to the past has made Chaozhou a centre for **traditional arts and crafts**, and a great place to buy souvenirs. For something a bit unusual, the **hardware market**, just inside the Guangji Gate along Shangdong Ping Lu, has razor-sharp cleavers, kitchenware and old-style brass door rings. **Temple trinkets**, from banners to brass bells, ceramic statues – made at the nearby hamlet of Fengxi – and massive iron incense burners, are sold at numerous stores in the vicinity of Kaiyuan Si, also a good area to find ceramic **tea sets** and **silk embroideries**. The best place to buy **lacework** is at the large store on Huangcheng Xi Lu, opposite Xihu Park. While not dirt cheap, prices for all these items are very reasonable and the quality is high.

Meizhou and around

In the foothills of the Fujian border, 200km north of Chaozhou where rail lines from Guangzhou, Shantou, and Fujian converge, **MEIZHOU** is the ancestral home of a huge number of Overseas Chinese, whose descendants have begun to pump an enormous quantity of money back into the region. While not a pretty city, Meizhou is ethnically **Hakka** (see p.615) and is thus a fine place to pick up local background before heading off into their Fujian heartlands, just up the train line around Yongding – if you can't make it out that far, a nearby mountain temple makes a good excuse for a quick trip.

The Town and around

Meizhou is a lightly industrial town producing handbags and clothing, surrounded by hills and set in the fertile bowl of a prehistoric lake bed through which flows the convoluted **Mei River**. The scruffy centre is a two-square-kilometre spread on the north bank, connected to the neat, newer southern suburbs by the **Meijiang** and **Dongshan bridges**. As in Chaozhou, almost everything is within walking distance or the range of cycle-rickshaws.

Meizhou's social focus and main shopping district surrounds the open **square** at the junction of various main roads immediately north of the **Meijiang Bridge**. The colonial-style shopfronts on Lingfeng Lu, which runs west along

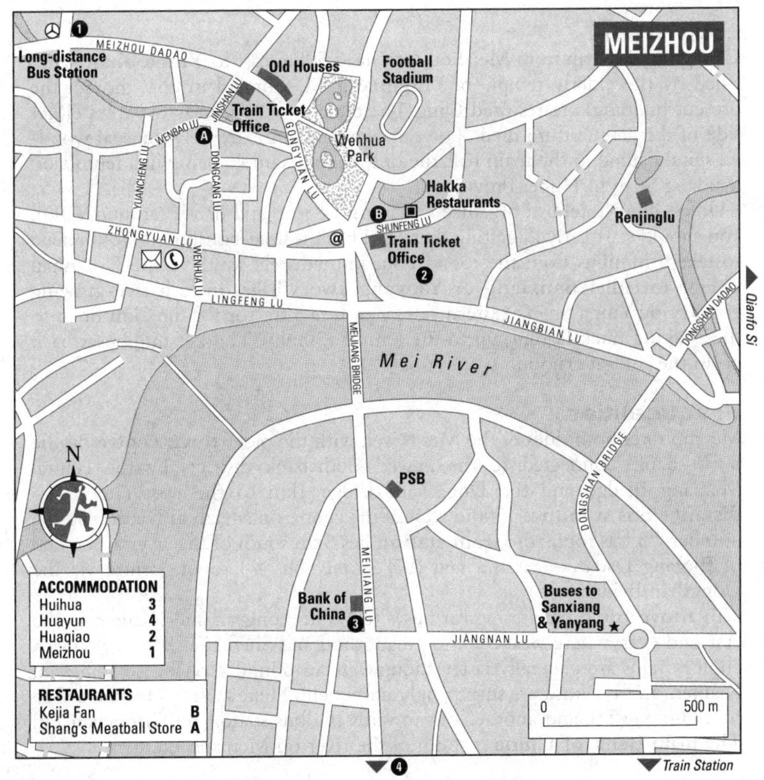

the riverfront, are worth a wander, but the tone is set by a billboard at the Tian'anmen Square-like entrance to **Wenhua Park** (¥1), advertising the next **football match** at the stadium here. You'll certainly know when a game is on: the entire town descends on the park, the merrymaking kept in order by police. At other times the park isn't up to much, though at night older houses in nearby streets look very atmospheric, lit by tapers and red paper lanterns.

For more local culture, head northeast off the square up Shunfeng Lu, and then follow the lanes and Chinese signs five minutes east to some scummy ponds outside **Renjinglu** (open around 3pm; ¥2), former home of Meizhou's nineteenth-century poet and diplomat, **Huang Zunxian**. The building is the most ornate of several around the ponds, the others being classically austere **Hakka town houses**, with high central gateways and square-sided walls and windows.

Somewhat more attractive, **Qianfo Si** (Thousand Buddha Temple; ¥5) overlooks Meizhou 1km east of the Meijiang Bridge – take Jiangbian Lu east along the river for 700m to the Dongshan Bridge, follow Dongshan Dadao north for another 100m, then bear right over the rail lines and uphill to the gates. Just before you arrive, there's an excellent vegetarian **restaurant** off to the right (see opposite). Above on the hill, the original temple and pagoda were demolished in 1995 in order to be totally rebuilt with expatriate funding and an attention to detail which has to be seen to be believed. The stonework is particularly accomplished, the temple pillars carved in deep relief with heroes and coiling dragons, while the base of the pagoda has finely executed scenes from Buddha's life.

Lingguang Si

One good day-trip from Meizhou is to head 50km east to **Yinna Shan**, sanctified by the elderly temple of **Lingguang Si**, founded in 861, though the present buildings are restored Qing. There are two 1000-year-old trees either side of the gate (a third died 300 years ago), and an extremely unusual wooden spiral ceiling in the main hall, the only other example being in a temple on Wudang Shan in Hubei Province.

Unless your hotel can organize you a private jeep and driver (around ¥300), you should start early as getting there and back is time-consuming. You'll need to take a minibus from the roundabout immediately south of the Dongshan Bridge to either **Sanxiang** or **Yanyang**, two villages in lush rice-growing country on Yinna Shan's eastern side, then hire a tractor for the 7km or so to the walking track leading up to the temple (30min). The last minibuses back go in the mid-afternoon.

Practicalities

Meizhou lies both sides of the Mei River, with the older **town centre** on the north bank, connected to the newer south-bank districts by the central Meijiang Bridge and the Dongshan Bridge 1km to the east. The **long-distance bus station** is 1500m west of the centre on Meizhou Dadao and the number #3 bus route; the **train station** lies 5km south of the river at the end of Binfang Dadao – catch a taxi (¥7) or city bus #4 to the centre via the Dongshan Bridge.

To **move on**, there are regular buses to Dapu, Longyan and Xiamen in the east, and everywhere west back to Guangzhou and Shenzhen. Where you've a choice, trains are generally faster, though Fujian-bound services (to Longyan, Xiamen, and Fuzhou) are surprisingly infrequent. There's a small **ticket office** on Shunfeng Lu, and another out towards the bus station on Gongyuan Lu. The main **Bank of China** is south of the river on Meijiang Lu.

Accommodation and eating

Places to stay are distributed both sides of the river. South of the Meijiang Bridge on Meijiang Lu, *Huihua Jiudian* is inexpensive though its furnishings are tatty (Ⓣ0753/2256988; ❷); further down the street, the unkempt exterior of *Huayun Dajiudian* hides surprisingly clean and spacious rooms (Ⓣ0753/2240338; ❷). Over the river on Jiangbian Lu, *Huaqiao Dasha* (Ⓣ0753/2232388, Ⓕ2210008; ❺) is an overpriced, upmarket affair, while opposite the bus station, the basic *Meizhou Dasha* has large, basic doubles and is perfect for early morning departures (Ⓣ0753/2235705; ❷).

Make sure you **eat** at the vegetarian restaurant at Qianfo Si, serving outstanding meals daily at noon, including imitation meat dishes which are virtually indistinguishable from the real thing – it's ¥48 for four dishes, ¥78 for five, and so on. Also try the **Hakka specialities** sold at the smart *Kejia Fan* and numerous family-run restaurants east of the square on Shunfeng Lu – juicy salt-baked chicken, wrapped in greaseproof paper (around ¥30 for a whole bird); little doughy rissoles made with shredded cabbage; and quick-fried cubes of bean curd, stuffed with pork and served in a gluey, rich sauce. For a takeaway, hunt down *Shang's Meatball Store* on Wenbao Lu in the western backstreets. **Hakka wine** is pretty nice by Chinese standards, similar to a sweet sherry and often served warm with ginger – most places to eat can provide a bottle.

Dapu and beyond

To learn more about the Hakka you need to head out to settlements north and east of Meizhou, surrounded in summer by some very attractive countryside. The small, dishevelled town of **DAPU**, two hours and 100km east, is a good place to start. A fraction of the size of Meizhou, the town shares the same river valley setting and an unexciting centre, but in the fields just outside, next to a modern sports stadium (another gift from an expatriate investing in his homeland), there's a huge square-sided **weiwu**, a three-storeyed Hakka house with walls as solid as any castle's. The residents, amazed to see a foreign face, will come out to chat if you walk over for a look. Elsewhere are some very nicely constructed low-set family compounds, whose walls enclose several temple-like halls, all with decorated roofs, and at least two small, traditionally circular homesteads. The largest, most highly regarded Hakka mansions anywhere in China, however, are three hours away over the Fujian border around **Yongding** (see p.617) – there are daily buses from Dapu.

The **bus station** is on the northern edge at the corner of Renmin Lu and Hu Shan Lu, which runs south right through Dapu, terminating below steps ascending to the tidy parkland of **Hu Shan** (Tiger Hill). There's **accommodation** at the relatively garish *Gongyuan Binguan* (❸) near the park on Tongren Lu, and plain beds (¥50) in the peeling hostel 50m west off Hushan Lu on Yanhua Lu.

Western Guangdong

While it's not an unpleasant area, there's very little to delay your passage across western Guangdong on the way to Guangxi or Hainan Island. Buses are best for the former route, while the rail line is the quickest way to cover the 450km between the capital and **Zhanjiang**, where boats to Hainan depart. Either way, consider stopping off for a day or two at **Zhaoqing**, a pleasant resort town also

Western Guangdong

Zhaoqing	肇庆	***zhàoqìng***
Chongxi Ta	崇禧塔	*chóngxī tǎ*
Dinghu Shan	鼎湖山	*dǐnghú shān*
Mosque	清真寺	*qīngzhēn sì*
Plum Monastery	梅庵	*méiān*
Qingyun Si	清云寺	*qīngyún sì*
Qixing Yan Park	七星岩公园	*qīxīngyán gōngyuán*
Accommodation and eating		
Dinghu Shan Youth Hostel	鼎湖山国际青年旅馆	*dǐnghúshān guójì qīngnián lǚguǎn*
Huaqiao Dasha	华侨大厦	*huáqiáo dàshà*
Jinye Dasha	金叶大厦	*jīnyè dàshà*
Jiuli Xiang Shaoya	九里香烧鸭	*jiǔlǐxiāng shāoyā*
Seven Stars Crags Youth Hostel	七星岩国际青年旅馆	*qīxīngyán guójì qīngnián lǚguǎn*
Zhanjiang	湛江	***zhànjiāng***
Canton Bay Hotel	华侨宾馆	*huáqiáo bīnguǎn*
Chikan	赤坎	*chìkǎn*
Cuiyuan Binguan	翠园宾馆	*cuìyuán bīnguǎn*
Hai'an	海安	*hǎi'ān*
Xiashan	霞山	*xiáshān*

connected by a direct ferry to Hong Kong, whose scenery has been a tourist attraction for more than a thousand years.

Zhaoqing and Dinghu Shan

Road, rail and river converge 110km west of Guangzhou at **ZHAOQING**, a smart, modern city founded as a Qin garrison town to plug a gap in the line of a low mountain range. The first Europeans settled here as early as the sixteenth century, when the Jesuit priest **Matteo Ricci** spent six years in Zhaoqing, using Taoist and Buddhist parallels to make his Christian teachings palatable. Ricci was eventually invited to Beijing by emperor Wanli, where he died in 1610 having published numerous religious tracts. Since the tenth century, however, the Chinese have known Zhaoqing for the limestone hills comprising the adjacent **Qixing Yan**, the Seven Star Crags. Swathed in mists and surrounded by lakes, they lack the scale of Guilin's peaks, but make for an enjoyable wander, as do the surprisingly thick forests at **Dinghu Shan**, just a short local bus ride away from town.

There's quite a bit to see in Zhaoqing itself, though the sights are widely scattered and not of great individual importance. Produced for more than a thousand years, Zhaoqing's **ink stones** are some of the finest in China, and there's a **factory** on Gongnong Lu which turns out some wonderfully executed pieces – you can buy them here and at several craft stores at the start of the causway at the Duanzhou Lu/Tianning Lu intersection.

Overlooking the river, **Chongxi Ta** (daily 8am–5.30pm; ¥5) is a Ming pagoda at the eastern end of riverfront Jiangbin Lu. Looking much like Guangzhou's Liurong Ta, at 57.5m this is the highest pagoda in the province; views from the top take in sampans, cargo boats and red cliffs across the river surmounted by two more pagodas of similar vintage. A few aged buildings lurk in the backstreets west of here behind Jiangbin Lu – and there's an excellent **market** north off Zhengdong Lu – but Zhaoqing's most interesting quarter is a thirty-minute walk west beyond Renmin Lu. Solid sections of the **ancient city walls** still stand here on Jianshe Lu, which you can climb and follow around to Chengzong Lu; head north from here along Kangle Zhong Lu and enter a tight knot of early-twentieth-century lanes, shops and homes – all typically busy and noisy – along with a brightly tiled **mosque**. A further kilometre out on the western edge of town, the **Plum Monastery** (daily 7am–5.30pm; ¥5), on Mei'an Lu, was established in 996 and has close associations with **Huineng**, founder of Chan Buddhism (see p.632), who is remembered in various paintings and sculptures here.

Arranged in the shape of the Big Dipper and said to be fallen stars, the seven peaks which make up **Qixing Yan Park** (daily 8am–5pm; ¥50) rise 2km north of town on the far side of **Xin Hu**. To get here, go to the top end of Tianning Lu and cross over busy Duanzhou Lu to the paved area on the lakeshore, from where a **causeway** continues north across Xin Hu. Towards the opposite shore it forks at the park gates. The crags themselves are quite modest, named after objects they imaginatively resemble – **Chanchu** (Toad), **Tianzhu** (Heavenly Pillar), **Shizhang** (Stone Hand). An interlocking network of arched bridges, pathways, graffiti-embellished caves and willows all make for a pleasantly romantic two-hour stroll – even if the entry fee is absurdly high.

Practicalities

Set on the north bank of the Xi, Zhaoqing is squashed between the river and the northerly lakes bordering Qixing Yan Park. Jianshe Lu and Duanzhou Lu run right across town east to west in numbered sections, crossed by **Tianning Lu**, which is oriented north–south between Qixing Yan Park's boundaries and the river. Zhaoqing's **train station** lies 5km away to the northwest; the **long-distance bus station** is on Duanzhou Lu, 100m east of the northern end of Tianning Lu; while the **ferry port** lies on the southeastern side of town at the junction of Jiangbin Lu and Gongnong Lu, near Chongxi Ta. **Taxis** can be hailed everywhere (¥5), but otherwise there isn't

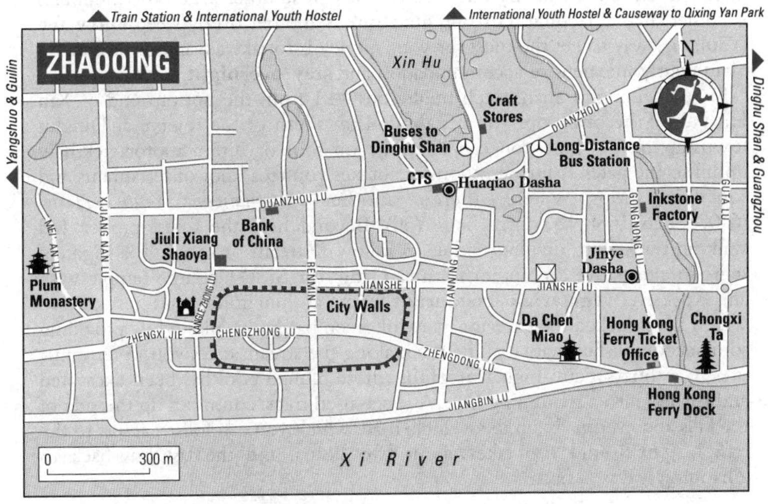

much in the way of public transport; Zhaoqing is, anyway, somewhere to get about on foot.

There are onward buses to Qingyuan, Shaoguan, Zhanjiang and just about everywhere between Guilin and Guangzhou – check which of Guangzhou's bus stations you're headed for before you board. Trains go to Nanning, Zhanjiang, Guangzhou and through to Shenzhen. Ferries for **Hong Kong** leave from near the ticket office (daily 8–11.30am & 2–5pm) on the corner of Gongnong Lu and Jiangbin Lu west of Chongxi Ta. If you need help booking any of the above, try the **CTS**, upstairs and just west of the *Huaqiao Dasha*. The main **Bank of China** is 500m to the west (Mon–Fri 9–11.30am & 2.30–5.30pm), and there's a **post office** on Jianshe Lu.

Accommodation and eating

The town has abundant **accommodation**, and there are also places to stay out at Dinghu Shan. Reasonable-value options include the *Huaqiao Dasha* on Duanzhou Lu (Ⓣ0758/2232650, Ⓕ2231197; ❻) and the cosy *Jinye Dasha* on Gongnong Lu (Ⓣ0758/2221338, Ⓕ2221368; ❹). Just outside the northern edge of Qixing Yan Park – best reached by taxi from arrival points – *Seven Stars Crags International Youth Hostel* (Ⓣ0758/2226688, Ⓕ2224155; ❹, dorm beds ¥30) is a well run if elderly place whose manager speaks good English.

There's a shortfall of **restaurants** outside the hotels – where it's worth indulging in *dim sum* at the *Jinye Dasha*'s popular third-floor restaurant – though numerous places along eastern Jianshe Lu and all through the centre sell local *zongzi* (conical rice packets wrapped in a bamboo leaf), sandpots and light Cantonese meals. There's also *Jiuli Xiang Shaoya*, a great **roast-duck shop** on Kangle Lu; it's not a restaurant, but you could buy a bird and then head up to the park for a picnic.

Dinghu Shan

Twenty kilometres east of Zhaoqing, the thickly forested mountains at **Dinghu Shan** were declared China's first national park way back in 1956, and have since been incorporated into the UNESCO biosphere program. With well-formed paths giving access to a waterfall, temple and plenty of trees, the small area open to the public gets crowded at the weekends, but at other times Dinghu Shan makes an excellent half-day out – particularly in summer, when the mountain is cooler than Zhaoqing. The one drawback is another overly steep **entry fee** (¥50); one way to get the most for your money is to take advantage of Dinghu Shan's fairly inexpensive accommodation and **stay overnight**.

To reach Dinghu Shan, catch public bus #21 from the bottom end of Xin Hu (¥3.6); the bus drops you off about 1km south of the reserve at Dinghu township, from where you can continue on foot or hire a motor-rickshaw uphill to the gates. A further kilometre brings you to a knot of restaurants and souvenir shops, where there's another *International Youth Hostel* (Ⓣ0758/2621688; ❹, dorm beds ¥30). Beyond here the forest proper and walking track start, dividing either to follow a stream or to climb a flight of stairs to alternative accommodation at **Qingyun Si** (❸), a large temple with an expensive **vegetarian restaurant** open at lunchtime, and restorations which have decked the exterior in awful green bathroom tiles while providing some accomplished statuary. The track along the stream takes you in ten minutes to a thirty-metre-high **waterfall**, whose plunge pool has been excavated and turned into a swimming hole. A lesser-used track continues up the side of the falls and eventually up to a vehicle road, which you can follow across to the temple. The round trip takes about two hours, and the last bus back to Zhaoqing leaves at 5pm.

Zhanjiang

The only reason to make the long haul to **ZHANJIANG**, 400km from Guangzhou on the province's southwestern coastline, is to catch onward transport to Hainan Island. Otherwise the town, though a major port, is without interest. The French obtained a lease here in 1898, and today they've been joined by US and British prospectors, who since 1975 have poured capital and labour into Zhanjiang as they scour sites in the South China Sea for **oil**. Signs of Western money are everywhere – especially in the huge docking facilities designed to accommodate large tankers, and a heliport to ferry workers out to the rigs – but the town remains a dull place, with everyone still waiting for the first major strikes.

Zhanjiang is curiously split into two equal but well-separated halves. There's no need to visit northerly **Chikan** unless your bus terminates here, in which case catch the #11 or #10 city bus to the port area at **Xiashan**, 10km south along straight and empty Renmin Dadao. Xiashan is a two-kilometre-wide grid of streets, with Renmin Dadao and Jiefang Lu the main axes. Much of Xiashan was built by the French, and there are some fairly grand blocks here along with broad, tree-lined avenues, but nothing is particularly attractive. The huge, modern **train station** – terminus of the line to Zhaoqing and Guangzhou – is right at the western end of Jiefang Lu, where taxis await new arrivals; the main **long-distance bus station** is just south of here on Jianshe Lu. Right at the very end of Renmin Dadao are the **Hainan ferry** and ticket office (daily 9am–5pm), from where twice-daily passenger ferries can whisk you over to Hainan's capital, Haikou, in three hours (¥43 standing, ¥122 for a seat). If you miss these, or if services have been cancelled because of rough weather, catch a bus 120km south to the port of **Hai'an** (3hr; ¥35), where there are departures for the ninety-minute run to Haikou through the day (¥34) – you can book combined bus/ferry tickets at the bus station.

Zhanjiang's **accommodation** is pretty average; the best places to stay are the *Canton Bay Hotel* on Minzhi Lu (Ⓣ0759/2281966, Ⓕ2281347; ❺), and the friendly *Cuiyuan Binguan*, also on Minzhi Lu (Ⓣ0759/2286633; ❹). The hotel **restaurants** are good, and there are plenty of cake shops, canteens, and formal places to dine strung out along Jiefang Lu between Renmin Dadao and the station. The **Bank of China** is on Renmin Dadao, just north of the Jiefang Lu intersection (Mon–Fri 9–11.30am & 1.30–5pm).

Hainan Island

Rising out of the South China Sea between Guangdong and Vietnam, **Hainan Island** marks the southernmost undisputed limit of Chinese authority, a 300-kilometre-broad spread of beaches, mountain scenery, history, myth and – most of all – the effects of **exploitation**. Today a province in its own right, Hainan was historically the "Tail of the Dragon", an enigmatic full stop to the Han empire and – in the Han Chinese mind – an area inhabited by unspeakably backward races, only surfacing into popular consciousness when it could be of use. Han settlements were established around the coast in 200 AD, but for millennia the island was only seen fit to be a place of exile. So complete was Hainan's isolation that, as recently as the 1930s, ethnic **Li**, who first settled here more than two thousand years ago, still lived a hunter-gatherer existence in the interior highlands.

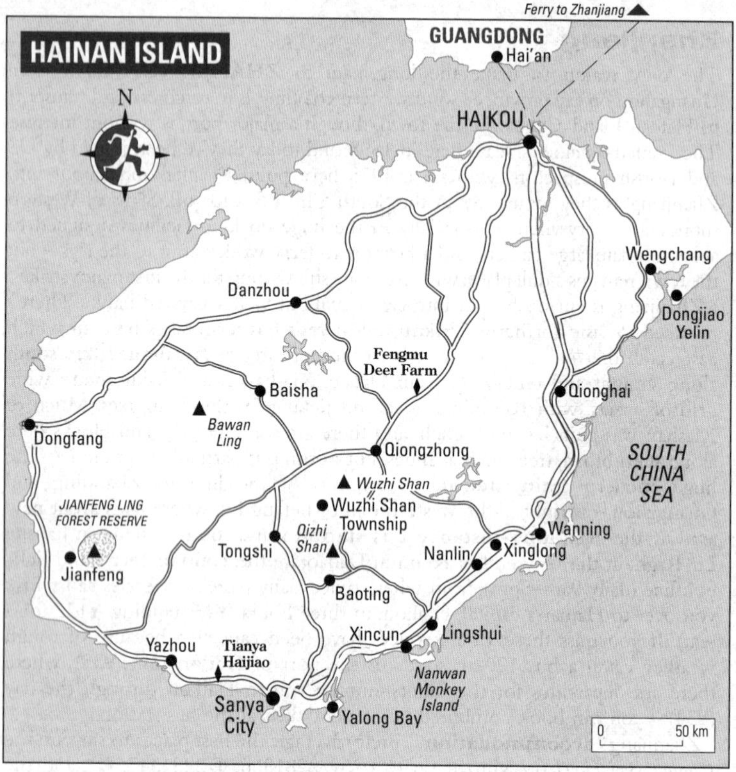

Modern Hainan is no primitive paradise, however. After two years of naval bombardments, the island was occupied by the Japanese in 1939, and by the end of the war they had executed a full third of Hainan's male population in retaliation for raids on their forces by Chinese guerrillas. **Ecological decline** began in the 1950s during the Great Leap Forward, and escalated through the 1960s when large numbers of Red Guards were sent over from the mainland to "learn from the peasants", and became involved in the first large-scale **clearing of Hainan's forests** to plant cash crops. Successive governments have continued the process of stripping the island's natural resources and abandoning the inhabitants to fend for themselves, in an appalling example of **economic mismanagement**: while there are skyscrapers and modern factories around the cities, you'll also see country people so poor that they live in lean-tos made of mud and straw, which have to be rebuilt after each wet season. With the exception of ragged remnants clinging to the very tips of Hainan's mountains, rainforest has ceded to eroded plantations given over to experimentation with different crops – rubber, mango, coconuts and coffee – in the hope that a market will emerge. **Tourism** seems to be the sole reliable source of income, and everyone is desperate to be involved. Persistent marketing has made Hainan the place that all Chinese want to come for a holiday, but investment has been wildly over-optimistic, with numerous hotels and entertainment complexes around the place standing empty, unfinished or never used.

For foreign and domestic tourists alike, the most obvious reason to come to Hainan is to flop down on the warm, sandy **beaches** near the southern city of **Sanya** – as a rest cure after months on the mainland, it's a very good one. Initially there doesn't seem much more to get excited about. **Haikou**, Hainan's capital, bears evidence of brief colonial occupation, but its primary importance is as a transit point, while Han towns along the **east coast** have only slightly more character and scenic appeal. Spend a little time and effort elsewhere, however, and things start to get more interesting: the highlands around the town of **Tongshi** are the place to start looking for **Li culture**, and the mountainous southwest hides some forgotten **nature reserves**, where what's left of Hainan's indigenous flora and fauna hangs by a thread. There are even a handful of underwater sites off the southern coast, the only place in provincial China where those with the necessary qualifications can go **scuba diving**.

Hainan's extremely hot and humid **wet season** lasts from June to October. It's better to visit between December and April, when the climate is generally dry and tropically moderate, sunny days peaking around 25°C on the southern coast. **Getting to Hainan** is straightforward, with flights from all over the country to Haikou and Sanya, and regular ferries from Guangzhou and Zhanjiang in Guangdong Province, and Beihai in Guangxi.

Once here, **getting around** is easy: Hainan's highways and roads are covered by a prolific quantity of **local transport**; high-speed buses link Haikou and Sanya in just three hours, while you can easily hop around the rest of the island by bus and minibus. As you move around you'll find that many of Hainan's towns have different local and Mandarin **names**; as the latter occur more frequently on maps and bus timetables, Chinese names are used below in the main text and character boxes, with local names indicated in brackets. Also note that, as a recognized tourist destination, Hainan is more **expensive** than the adjacent mainland – even Chinese tourists grumble about being constantly overcharged.

Haikou and the east coast

Haikou is Hainan's steamy capital, set at the north of the island and separated from Guangdong Province by the thirty-kilometre-wide Qiongzhou Channel. Haikou is by no means a bad place to spend a day in transit, and certainly feels more spacious and friendly than the average provincial capital, but nobody would pretend there is much to see or do here. If you can resist heading straight on to Sanya to work on your tan, spend a couple of days hopping down between the towns along Hainan's **east coast**. This is the part of Hainan longest under Han dominion, and it's a good way to get the feel of the island.

Haikou

Business centre, main port and first stop for newly arrived holiday-makers and hopeful migrants alike, **HAIKOU** has all the atmosphere of a typical Southeast Asian city. There's a smattering of French colonial architecture, a

Haikou and the east coast

Haikou	海口	***hǎikǒu***
Central bus station	总站	*zǒngzhàn*
East bus station	汽车东站	*qìchē dōngzhàn*
Hai Rui Mu	海瑞墓	*hǎiruì mù*
Haikou Park	海口公园	*hǎikǒu gōngyuán*
New Port	海口新港	*hǎikǒu xīngǎng*
West bus station	汽车西站	*qìchē xīzhàn*
Wugong Ci	五公祠	*wǔgōng cí*
Xiuying Battery	秀英古炮台	*xiùyīng gǔpàotái*
Xiuying Wharf	秀英港	*xiùyīng gǎng*
Accommodation		
Civil Aviation	海南民航宾馆	*hǎinán mínháng bīnguǎn*
Haikou	海口宾馆	*hǎikǒu bīnguǎn*
Haikou International Financial	海口国际金融大酒店	*hǎikǒu guójì jīnróng dàjiǔdiàn*
Haiyang	海洋大厦	*hǎiyáng dàshà*
Huaqiao	华侨大厦	*huáqiáo dàshà*
Overseas Post and Telecommunications	邮电大厦	*yōudiàn dàshà*
Songtao	松涛大厦	*sōngtāo dàshà*
Eating		
Aincientry of Noodle Reflection	面点世家	*miàndiǎn shìjiā*
Ganghai Canting	港海餐厅	*gǎnghǎi cāntīng*
Haikou Fandian	海口饭店	*hǎikǒu fàndiàn*
Japanese	香寿司	*xiāngshòu sī*
Kuaihuolin	快活林	*kuàihuó lín*
Shuihou Doujiang Dawang	水和豆浆大王	*Shuǐhé dòujiāng dàwáng*
Xianzong Lin	仙踪林	*xiānzōng lín*
Lingshui	陵水	***língshuǐ***
Puli Binguan	普利宾馆	*pǔlì bīnguǎn*
Yiyuan Binguan	怡园宾馆	*yíyuán bīnguǎn*
Nanlin	南林	***nánlín***
Qionghai	琼海	***qiónghǎi***
Dongshen Dasha	东什大厦	*dōngshén dàshà*
Fushan Coffee House	福山咖啡厅	*fúshān kāfēitīng*
Liangchang Jiudian	良昌酒店	*liángchāng jiǔdiàn*
Wanning	万宁	***wànníng***
Dongshan Ling	东山岭	*dōngshān lǐng*
Wenchang	文昌	***wénchāng***
Dongjiao Yelin	东郊椰林	*dōngjiāo yēlín*
Xiange Binguan	仙阁宾馆	*xiāngé bīnguǎn*
Yunshan Binguan	云山宾馆	*yúnshān bīnguǎn*
Xincun	新村	***xīncūn***
Nanwan Monkey Island	南湾猴岛	*nánwān hóudǎo*
Xinglong	兴隆	***xīnglóng***

few parks and monuments, modern highrises, broad streets choked with traffic and pedestrians, and the all-pervading spirit of wilfully glib commerce. An indication of the ethos driving Haikou is that nobody seems to be a local: officials, businessmen and tourists are all from the mainland, while Li, Miao and Hakka flock from southern Hainan to hawk trinkets, as do the Muslim Hui women selling betel-nut – all drawn by the opportunities that the city represents. More than anything, Haikou is a truly tropical city: humid, laid-back, pleasantly shabby, and complete with palm-lined streets, something particularly striking if you've just arrived from a miserable northern Chinese winter.

Arrival, city transport and information

Haikou's downtown area forms a compact block south of the waterfront Changti Dadao. The centre is marked by a busy circuit of wide one-way traffic flows and pedestrian overpasses surrounding **Haikou Park**, where much of the accommodation is located, with the most interesting shopping districts in the northerly **old colonial quarter** around Jiefang Lu and Bo'ai Bei Lu.

The **airport** is 2km south of town on Jichang Lu; bus #10 runs up to Haikou Park from outside, or catch the shuttle (¥15) to the China Southern office on Haixiu Dong Lu. The **New Port** is north off Changti Dadao on Xingang Lu, where most ferries from Hong Kong and the mainland pull in;

Moving on from Haikou

Flying is the easiest way out of Haikou, with the city connected to Sanya and mainland locations between Harbin, Kunming, and Hong Kong. Tickets for all airlines can be reserved at agents (see "Listings", p.689) or the China Southern office (Ⓣ0898/66763166, Ⓕ66723460; daily 8am–10.30pm), next to the *Civil Aviation Hotel* on Haixiu Dong Lu.

Ferries leave Haikou's New Port for Zhanjiang (¥43) and for Hai'an (¥34) at Guangdong's southernmost tip, where buses meet ferries for the 150-kilometre run to Zhanjiang. There are also ferries from the New Port (and sometimes from the Xiuying Wharf) for Beihai (seat ¥60; cabin ¥136 per person), on which it's worth paying for a cabin rather than spending the trip surrounded by seasick hordes watching non-stop kung fu flicks. Ticket offices at the ports open daily from 9am to 4pm, and there's usually no trouble getting a seat, though rough seas can suspend services. Your accommodation will be able to make bookings for boats and planes if you give them at least a day's notice.

The practicalities of getting out by **bus** depend on where you're heading. All **mainland traffic** leaves from the central bus station, where you'll find standard and luxury buses to destinations as far afield as Chongqing, Nanning, Jiujiang, Shenzhen and Guangzhou; tickets include ferry costs. **Sanya** and the **east coast** are served by the east bus station, from where there are also a few buses to Tongshi; a normal bus to Sanya is ¥49 and takes six hours, while an express is ¥78 and takes three. The west bus stations deals mostly with **central and western** destinations, though you can also get to Sanya from here.

There's no public railway on Hainan, but you can book **train tickets** out of Zhanjiang at any of the bus stations, or from a rail office at the New Port, next to the ferry ticket windows.

those from Beihai in Guangxi sometimes use the **Xiuying Wharf**, 5km farther east along Binhai Dadao – take bus #6 to the centre from either. Buses from the mainland wind up at the **central bus station** south of Haikou Park on Jichang Dong Lu; those from elsewhere on the island use the **east bus station** 2km down Haifu Dadao (bus #1 or minibus #217 to the Haifu Dadao/Haixiu Dong Lu junction), or the **west bus station** way out on Haixiu Xi Lu (bus #2 or minibus #217 go to Haixiu Dong Lu from here).

Haikou's **city bus service** is comprehensive and cheap, with more frequent and crowded private minibuses running the same routes. The **taxis**, inevitably driven by northerners from Heilongjiang Province, are so absurdly plentiful that you have only to pause by the kerb for one to pull up instantly, but they're expensive at ¥10 standing charge – New Port to central Haikou costs around ¥20.

There's a total lack of **information** about the island in Haikou, with hotel tour agents only geared to getting you to Sanya as fast as possible. If you plan to explore Hainan's backwaters, pick up a **map** of the island from hawkers or kiosks; some include spreads of Haikou, Sanya and Tongshi, along with detailed road maps of the island including even minor sights marked in English.

Accommodation

There's plenty of central accommodation in Haikou, much of it conveniently located around Haikou Park. Room rates are always flexible; in summer, ensure that air-conditioning is part of the bargain. All hotels handle transport bookings and have their own coffee shops and restaurants.

Civil Aviation Haixiu Dong Lu ⓣ0898/6772608, ⓕ6772610. Smart hotel, very central and not bad value for its price. ❼

Haikou Daying Houlu ⓣ0898/65351234, ⓕ65350232. Formerly Haikou's most prestigous accommodation, now self-conciously past its prime – and their "Standard Lovers Rooms" says nothing flattering about guests' abilities. They do have a good restaurant, however. ❼

Haikou International Financial Datong Lu ⓣ0898/6773088, ⓕ6772113. Luxury, international-standard business affair with all the trimmings. ❾

Haiyang Jichang Dong Lu ⓣ0898/66519200. Inexpensive, friendly and spotless hotel, with vases of silk flowers beside the TV as a nice touch. ❸

Huaqiao Datong Lu ⓣ0898/6772623, ⓕ6772094. A three-star business centre built in the early 1990s and beginning to look a bit threadbare. ❻

Overseas Jichang Dong Lu ⓣ0898/65365999, ⓕ65365333. Fairly decent three-star venture, with tubs in each room taking advantage of a hot spring located 800m below the hotel. ❼

Post and Telecommunications Nanbao Lu ⓣ0898/66778251, ⓕ66772452. Hidden away in the backstreets, this hotel offers fair value, though the spruced-up lobby is not a reflection of the rooms. ❸

Songtao Jichang Dong Lu ⓣ0898/6778016. Cheap and often full, though in need of maintainance. ❸

The City

The **old quarter**, boxed in by Bo'ai Bei Lu, Datong Lu, and pedestrianized Deshengsha Lu, is the best area to stroll through, with its grid of restored colonial architecture functioning as stores and businesses. **Jiefang Lu** and **Xinhua Lu** are the main streets here, especially good in the evening when they're brightly lit and bursting with people out shopping, eating and socializing; there's also a busy **market** west off Xinhua. Otherwise, **Haikou Park** (¥2) is small but quite pleasant, a venue for extensive early-morning martial art sessions and with shrubberies concealing cracked stone statues, reputedly from a vanished Ming-dynasty temple.

Haikou has just three formal sights, any of which will fill you in on Hainan's position in Han Chinese history. Southeast of the centre along Haifu Lu, **Wugong Ci** (Five Officials' Memorial Temple; daily 8.30am–5pm; ¥15; bus #1 or minibus #217 down Haifu Lu), is a brightly decorated complex built in 1889 to honour Li Deyu, Li Gang, Li Guang, Hu Chuan and Zhao Ding, Tang men of letters who were banished here after criticizing their government. Another hall in the grounds commemorates Hainan's most famous exile, the poet **Su Dongpo**, who lived in the island's northwest between 1097 and 1100 and died on his way back to the imperial court the following year. A **museum** in a new building opposite has photos and Chinese-only captions of historical sites around the island, though a group of weathered Song-style **stone statues** of horses and scholars, almost lost in vegetation outside, are more interesting.

About 5km west of the centre, **Xiuying Battery** (daily 8am–7pm; ¥15) offers a different take on the island – to get there, catch bus #1 from Longhua Lu to its terminus on Jinmao Zhong Lu, then follow it on for ten minutes. Built after the Chinese had apparently beaten off an attempted invasion by the French in the latter part of the nineteenth century, Xiuying was part of a string of coastal defences designed to deter foreign incursions along south China's coastline. A huge fortification, now maintained as a park, it's surrounded by basalt block walls concealing six twenty-centimetre naval cannon set in concrete bunkers, all connected by subterranean passageways. The bunkers are now camouflaged by fig trees and lit by bare bulbs, with the squat-barrelled, bezel-mounted guns pointing at high rises to the north. It must be said that Xiuying's design and weaponry look suspiciously European – perhaps they were modernized in 1937 when the fort was dusted off to resist the Japanese.

A kilometre or so southwest of Xiuying off Haixiu Zhong Lu, a park and stone sculptures of lions surround **Hai Rui Mu**, tomb of the virtuous Ming-dynasty official Hai Rui (daily 9am–4pm; ¥15) – bus #2 from central Haixiu Dong Lu comes closest, though again you'll need to walk the last bit. Hai Rui's honesty, which earned him exile during his lifetime, caused a furore in the 1960s when historian **Wu Han** wrote a play called *The Dismissal of Hai Rui*, a parody of events surrounding the treatment of Marshall Peng Dehui, who had criticized Mao's Great Leap Forward. The play's suppression and the subsequent arrest of Wu Han, who happened to be a friend of Deng Xiaoping, are generally considered to be the opening events of the Cultural Revolution.

Eating

Perhaps because Haikou is essentially a mainland Chinese colony, food here is not as exotic as you'd hope. The ingredients on display at market stalls are promising: green, unhusked coconuts (sold as a drink, but seldom used in cooking); thick fish steaks, mussels, eels, crab and prawns; mangoes, pineapples, bananas, watermelons, guavas, plums, starfruit and jackfruit; and, everywhere, piles of seasonal green vegetables. But Hainan's most famous dishes – Wenchang "white-cut" chicken, steamed duck and glutinous rice, and Dongshan mutton – are nothing extraordinary, though tasty. Compounding this is a current craze for Cantonese and Western-style food, with hotel restaurants trying to out-compete each other in these lines.

Restaurants

The highest concentration of **restaurants** are in the old quarter along Jiefang Lu, with grilled chicken wings, kebabs and other snacks sold outside the cinema and in the market east off Xinhua Lu.

Aincientry of Noodle Refection Jiefang Lu. You'll come here for the name, and stay for the cheap and tasty noodles, dumplings and *baozi.*

Cocowind At the *Haikou Binguan*. Best of the hotel restaurants for local favourites, including steamed chicken in coconut milk, and seafood rolls in coconut sauce. Not too expensive either – a whole chicken or duck costs around ¥60, with other dishes starting at ¥20.

Ganghai Canting Jiefang Lu. Locals-oriented teahouse with tiled floor, dated wooden furniture and great *dim sum.*

Haikou Fandian Xinhua Lu, just north of Jiefang Lu on the west side, and signed in Chinese. Hainan's famous dishes dished up in authentically noisy, busy surroundings; Wenchang chicken is ¥25 a serving, with duck a steal at ¥30 per bird.

Japanese Floor 3, Tailongcheng building, Datong Lu. Sushi at ¥5–10 per plate, with set one-dish meals from ¥20.

Kuaihuolin Next door to the *Haiyang* hotel, Jichang Dong Lu. Plates of Cantonese roast meats and steamed chicken, Sichuanese cold spiced noodles, preserved eggs, and pickles wheeled around on trolleys for you to point and choose. They also have more complex dishes such as twice-cooked fish, and an English menu to boot. Smart and inexpensive – two can eat well for ¥20–30.

Shuihe Doujiang Dawang Jichang Dong Lu. Open 24hr for excellent *shujiao*, rice packets, *baozi* and soya milk in fast-food-café surroundings.

Xianzong Lin Jiefang Lu. A cute place with swings instead of chairs and a Western–Chinese menu which includes pizza and some weird cold drinks – black sesame-seed milkshakes for one.

Listings

Banks and exchange There are branches of the Bank of China opposite the *Huaqiao* hotel, next to the *Hainan* hotel, and in the same building as the *International Financial Hotel*. Banking hours are approximately Mon–Sat 8am–6pm.

Books There's a big Xinhua bookstore on Jiefang Lu, east of the post office; the discount bookstore upstairs at the Mingzhu Guangchang shopping centre on Haixiu Dong Lu, west of the bus station, has maps and guides to Hainan, mostly Chinese-only.

Cinema There's a popular screen and entertainment complex behind the snack stalls on Jiefang Lu.
Hospital Hainan Provincial People's Hospital, Longhua Lu ⓣ0898/6225933.
Internet access The cinema on Jiefang Lu has a Net café upstairs on the western side (¥2/hr).
Mail and telephones The main post office, with parcel post service and IDD phones, is opposite the cinema on Jiefang Lu (daily 8am–6pm).
PSB The Foreign Affairs Department is on Changti Dadao, just west of the junction with Longhua Lu.
Shopping Pearls are a good thing to buy while on Hainan, but Sanya is a much better place to find a bargain. Department stores along Haixiu Dong Lu such as Mingzhu Guangchang sell indigenous products such as coconut coffee, coconut powder, coconut wafers, coconut tea, palm sugar and betel-nut; clothing sections also stock Hainan shirts, which differ from their Hawaiian counterparts in their use of dragons instead of palm trees on bright backgrounds. Whole shark skins – like sandpaper – dried jellyfish and other maritime curiosities in the shops along Jiefang Lu are also worth a look.
Travel agents *China Travel Air Service*, next to to the *Huaqiao* hotel (ⓣ0898/66781735, ⓕ66706281), are agents for a vast array of domestic and international carriers, including China Southern, Dragonair, Hainan Air, Cathay Pacific, Japan Airlines, Malaysia Airlines and Singapore Airlines. CTS are next to the *Haikou* hotel on Haifu Lu (ⓣ0898/65351623, ⓕ65331872), with a branch about 50m further east (ⓣ0898/65379966), both offering coach tours of the island and transport bookings.

The east coast

Most east-coast communities comprise small settlements of ethnic subgroups such as the Hakka, who were shuffled off the mainland by various turmoils, or returning Overseas Chinese deliberately settled here by the government, and many live by fishing, farming cash crops or pearl cultivation. Nowhere here takes more than half a day to look round, with the pick of the bunch being **Lingshui**, a hamlet with a long history, unexpected Communist connections and a nearby wildlife reserve. Everywhere has accommodation and places to eat, and **minibuses** are the best way to get around, with shuttle services running between towns from sunrise until after dark. Bear in mind that there are **no banks** capable of foreign currency transactions along the way, so carry enough cash to last until Sanya.

Wenchang and Qionghai

WENCHANG, a decent-sized county town 70km southeast of Haikou, is known to the Chinese as the ancestral home of the sisters **Song Qingling** and **Song Meiling**, wives to Sun Yatsen and Chiang Kaishek respectively. Built up as a commercial centre in the nineteenth century by the French, it has now rather gone to seed, but you could usefully make a quick detour from here to **Dongjiao Yelin**, Hainan's first **coconut plantation**. This area is becoming developed in a haphazard way, with a handful of hotels under construction, but remains a nice place to laze for a few hours, the trees forming a nice backdrop to acres of beachfront.

Walking downhill into town along Wenxin Lu from the **main bus station**, on the northern outskirts, you'll quickly pass the reasonably priced *Yunshan Binguan* (ⓣ0898/3222579; ❸) and *Xiange Binguan* (ⓣ0898/3221401; ❸) on the left, before coming to an acute kink in the road over a **canal** with well-constructed stone embankments. For Dongjiao Yelin, cross over the canal and turn left, and some 500m straight ahead is the **new town** and a far more modern bridge, where you can catch minibuses out to the coastal village of **Qinglan** (20min), then the ferry here across a small inlet, and it's another brief ride to the plantation.

Back in Wenchang, the road from the modern bridge continues uphill to the outskirts of town and another minibus depot with services 60km south to **QIONGHAI** (Jiaji), where China's **first Communist cell** was formed in 1924. It's a busy place, unusually tidy and with a healthy glut of markets specializing in locally made cane furniture. Qionghai's most famous resident was **Huang Sixiang**, a female guerrilla leader on Hainan during the Japanese occupation. The main road through town is Dongfeng Lu, where you'll find the **bus station** and, nearby, air-conditioned rooms at the *Dongshen Dasha* (Ⓣ0898/2822338; ❸). For food, there are plenty of places to eat in the streets around the heroic revolutionary sculpture which marks the town centre – try the *Liangchang Jiudian*, or the *Fushan Coffee House* on Wenming Lu.

Wanning, Xinglong and Nanlin

Another 50km south of Qionghai is **Wanning** (Wancheng), from where motorbike taxis with sidecars can take you 3km southeast to coastal vistas at **Dongshan Ling**, a formation of strangely sculpted and delicately balanced rocks, traced with paths and steps linking strategically placed pavilions and drink vendors. Further south along the highway from town, it's about 20km to **Xinglong**, a dusty little village of interest for its **Tropical Agricultural Research Station**, set up by expatriate Chinese from Vietnam, Malaysia and Indonesia and famed for its coffee, as well as the nearby **hot springs** resort, 3km from town. The cheapest beds in the area are in Xinglong itself, while the Research Station and hot springs are expensive (❺ and up). If you fancy something wilder, try heading 15km south again to **Nanlin** village, which lies just northwest of a small but protected area of **native forests**, with some good hiking potential through the low hills.

Lingshui

Ninety minutes south of Wanning, **LINGSHUI** (Lingcheng) has been around for a long time. They were forging iron tools and making pottery here as far back as the Han dynasty, while uncovered silver tomb ornaments point to the town being an important commercial centre by the Ming dynasty. Lingshui played a part in modern history when, having shifted south from Qionghai, China's **first Communist government** convened here in 1928; it was still functioning when the Japanese stormed Hainan in February 1939, whereupon its members retreated into the hills to wage guerrilla war on the invaders with the help of the local Li population (for more on the Li, see the box on p.700). The Communists never forgot this, and once in power granted the district nominal self-rule as **Lingshui Li Autonomous County**.

Today, Lingshui's dozen or so narrow streets are set back off the highway where it bends sharply past town near the bus station. Around town you'll see remains of a **Qing-dynasty monastery**, the interior still decorated with original frescoes, but now used to store video-game machines; a **Communist Museum** in another building of similar vintage (there's a cannon outside); and several 50-year-old shops with what look like their original fittings. Wander off to Lingshui's fringes and you could be stepping back a hundred years with lanes twisting into the countryside between walls surrounding family compounds, houses sporting decorative columns topped with lotus-bud motifs, and courtyards thickly planted with slender **areca palms**, often with conical buckets strapped around the trunks. These catch falling **betel nuts** (*binlang*), a crop cultivated as a stimulant by the Li since at least Ming times. Women are the biggest users, but just about everyone in Lingshui seems to have stained their lips and teeth from chewing slices of the palm seed, wrapped inside a heart-shaped pepper vine leaf.

Practicalities

Lingshui's main **bus station**, on a bend in the highway, is where most minibuses from Wanning drop off and where Sanya- and Haikou-bound vehicles depart. If you're arriving from the south, you might end up at the **minibus depot** about 1km down the road on the Sanya side of town; this is where you'll also find onward **transport to Xincun**. For **accommodation**, try the rooms at the *Puli Binguan* (☎0898/3323968; ❸) or basic doubles at the *Yiyuan Binguan* (☎0898/3323500; ❸), near each other on the highway just north of the bus station. The best places to **eat** are around here too, with numerous bustling **teahouses** along the highway and backstreets.

Xincun and Nanwan Monkey Island

About 10km south of Lingshui, **XINCUN** is a small market town with a large Hakka population – you'll see plenty of black-clad women with broad hats and gold and jade jewellery. **Ferries** ply from here across to **Nanwan Monkey Island**, actually a peninsula without overland access. The **research station** based here studies local groups of macaques, small, bronze-haired monkeys with pale eyelids and red backsides, and there's a **visitors' centre** where you can feed them.

Minibuses from Lingshui leave you on Xincun's main street. Having pushed your way between market stalls and down to the water, you'll be grabbed by sampan owners to negotiate the cost of the ten-minute ride over to Nanwan – ¥5 per person is a decent price for the return trip, though locals pay far less. The inlet here is crammed with Hakka houseboats, all linked by boardwalks, with posts and nets marking their **pearl farms**, a major source of income for the town. When you land on the island, tractors can take you up to the visitors' centre for a small fee, or it's a thirty-minute walk along a well-maintained road – a good option, as you'll almost certainly get your best views of completely wild monkeys along the way. Those that hang out at the visitors' centre itself (¥20) are technically wild too, but seeing them here can be an awful experience, mainly because Chinese tourists like to intimidate them with big sticks and thrash any monkey they can catch, and the animals have become understandably hostile as a result. Buy peanuts at the gate if you want to feed them, but you'll be mobbed if you show any food and it's much better just to walk through the grounds and climb the hillside for views of family troups crashing around in the treetops.

Sanya and the south coast

Across the island from Haikou on Hainan's central south coast (320km direct down the expressway), **SANYA** is, sooner or later, the destination of every visitor to the island. Though relics at the westerly town of **Yazhou** prove that the area has been settled for close on a thousand years, Sanya City itself is entirely modern, a scruffy fishing port and **naval base** maintained for monitoring events (and staking China's claims) in the South China Sea. These unexpectedly came to international attention in 2001, when a **US spyplane** made a forced landing here after colliding with a Chinese fighter jet. Generally, though, what pulls in the crowds – an increasing number of whom are Russian and Korean – are Sanya's surrounding sights, especially easterly **Dadonghai beach**, one of the few places in China where you can unwind in public. The Chinese also flock to associated legendary landmarks atop the **Luhuitou**

Sanya and the Southern Coast		
Sanya	三亚	***sānyà***
Dadonghai	大东海	*dàdōng hǎi*
Luhuitou Peninsula	鹿回头	*lùhuí tóu*
Yalong Bay	亚龙湾	*yàlóng wān*
Accommodation and eating		
Cactus Resort	仙人掌度假酒店	*xiānrénzhǎng dùjiàjiǔdiàn*
Chezhan Lüguan	车站旅馆	*chēzhàn lǚguǎn*
Chuanya	川亚宾馆	*chuānyà bīnguǎn*
Dongbei Wang	东北王	*dōngběi wáng*
Dongjiao Yelin Seafood	东郊椰林海鲜城	*dōngjiāoyēlín hǎixiānchéng*
Gloria Resort	凯莱度假酒店	*kǎilái dùjià jiǔdiàn*
Hawaii	夏威夷大酒店	*xiàwéiyí dàjiǔdiàn*
Hengyun	横云酒家	*héngyún jiǔjiā*
Holiday Inn	假日酒店	*jiàrì jiǔdiàn*
International Youth Hostel	青年旅馆	*qīngnián lǚguǎn*
Landscape Beach	丽景海湾酒店	*lìjǐng hǎiwān jiǔdiàn*
Pearl Seaview	明珠海景酒店	*míngzhū hǎijǐng jiǔdian*
Sanya	三亚宾馆	*sanyà bīnguǎn*
Seaside Holiday Inn	海滨度假村	*hǎibīn dùjiàcūn*
South China	南中国大酒店	*nánzhōngguó dàjiǔdiàn*
Dongfang	东方	***dōngfāng***
Jianfeng	尖峰	***jiān fēng***
Jiangfeng Ling Forest Reserve	尖峰岭热带原始森林自然保护区	*jiānfēnglǐng rèdài yuánshǐ sēnlín zìránbǎohùqū*
Tianya Haijiao	天涯海角	***tiānyá hǎijiǎo***
Yazhou	崖州	***yázhōu***

Peninsula, a huge granite headland rising immediately south of the city, and west at the scenic spot of **Tianya Haijiao**, while foreigners generally find the day-trip out to tiny inhabited **coral islands** off Dadonghai more interesting.

Farther afield, the coastal arc between Sanya and the western industrial port of **Dongfang** sees few visitors. While Dongfang itself doesn't justify a trip, it's emphatically worth getting as far as **Jianfeng Ling**, the most accessible surviving fragment of Hainan's indigenous mountain rainforest. If this doesn't appeal, there's plenty of transport north from Sanya to the Li stronghold of Tongshi, and on into the central highlands.

It must be said that though the beaches here are very pleasant, a trip to Sanya can also involve a few **irritations**, especially for those on a budget: rooms are expensive and often poor value; you'll have to watch for scams at cheaper restaurants; and foreign pedestrians are continually mobbed by taxi drivers and touts.

Arrival

The **Sanya area** comprises four sections: Sanya City, Dadonghai, the Luhuitou Peninsula – all fairly closely grouped – and Yalong Bay, a distant satellite tourist development. **Sanya City** occupies a three-kilometre-long peninsula bounded west by the Beibu Gulf and east by the Sanya River. Aligned north–south,

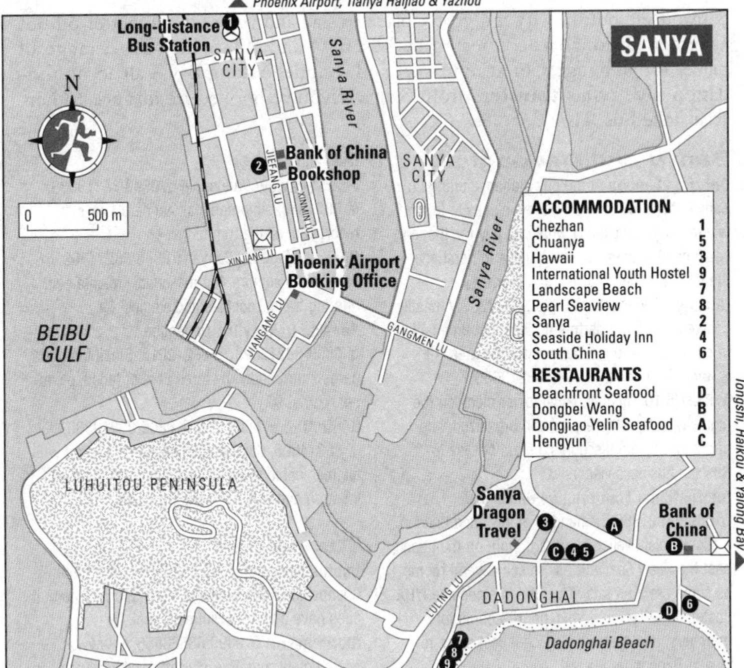

Jiefang Lu is the main road, forking at its southern end to run briefly southwest to the cargo wharves as Jiangang Lu, and east to form busy Gangmen Lu. Changing its name several more times, this extends 4km out to **Dadonghai**, a kilometre-long spread of hotels, restaurants and shops backing on to Dadonghai beach, beyond which are the start of routes to Haikou and Tongshi. Accessible by road from Dadonghai, the **Luhuitou Peninsula** is separated from the cargo wharves by the harbour, while **Yalong Bay** is a cluster of insular resorts and nice beaches 20km east of town.

Phoenix **airport** is about 15km to the west, from where you'll need to catch a taxi into the city (¥40). Sanya's main **long-distance bus station** is at the northern end of Jiefang Lu; coming from Haikou, you'll first pass through Dadonghai, so if you're planning to stay there, ask to be set down en route. The bus station handles normal and luxury buses to Haikou), and normal services to just about everywhere on the island, including Dongfang (aka Basuo; 11.45am–6pm only), Tongshi and Wenchang. For **getting around**, there's the usual overload of taxi cabs and some motorcycle-and-sidecar assemblies as well as **public buses** – #2 and #4 run regularly from 6am until well after dark between the long-distance bus station and Dadonghai, while bus #102 runs hourly to Yalong Bay, via Jiefang Lu and the highway at Dadonghai.

Accommodation

Sanya's accommodation is pretty well polarized between being expensive and good value, or mid-range and poor, though bargaining can often get substantial reductions on advertised rates. There are a couple of cheapish options in

Sanya itself, but the city is a grotty place to stay and you're much better off out at either Dadonghai (connected by buses #4 and #2), which has a range of places for all budgets, or at upmarket and secluded Yalong Bay – all accommodation here offers **transfers** from Sanya if you've booked in advance (otherwise, take bus #102).

Sanya and Dadonghai

Chezhan Lüguan At the bus station, Jiefang Lu, Sanya. Basic, but one of the few places in town where you'll get exactly what you pay for, though you'll need to speak some Chinese to persuade the management to give you a room. ❷

Chuanya Dadonghai ⓣ0899/88227333. A hastily cobbled-together apartment block, but amenable to bargaining and inexpensive for the area. ❺

Hawaii Dadonghai ⓣ0899/88213666, ⓕ88212210. Unimaginative tower block on the highway, but pretty relaxed and organized, and offers immediate discounts; caters heavily to Russian business visitors. ❼

International Youth Hostel Dadonghai ⓣ0899/88213665. A handful of low, tiled units in a slightly dishevelled courtyard, right on the beach past the *Pearl Seaview*; ask to see several rooms as some are a bit tatty. Though it's a genuine IYHA hostel, there are no dorms, nor discounts for members; it is, however, the cheapest place to stay in Dadonghai. ❹

Landscape Beach Dadonghai ⓣ0899/88228666, ⓦwww.sanyaliking.com. A real rarity for China: a hotel which is more than just somewhere to stay, and has its own character – in this case, a stylish atmosphere enhanced by thoughtful use of slate tiling and wood. ❽

Pearl Seaview Dadonghai ⓣ0899/88213838, ⓕ88215822. International standard four-star resort with all the trimmings. ❽

Sanya Jiefang Lu, Sanya ⓣ0899/88274703. Elderly and sombre, but reasonably maintained, offering triples, doubles and singles. ❸

Seaside Holiday Inn Dadonghai ⓣ0899/88213898, ⓕ88212018. Small forecourt garden surrounded by three tiers of faded, pleasant rooms. ❻

South China Dadonghai ⓣ0899/88219888, ⓕ88214005. Comfortable, beachfront resort with all imaginable facilities, including pool, gym and Western and Oriental restaurants. ❾

Yalong Bay

Cactus Resort ⓣ0899/88568866, ⓕ88568867. Cheapskate's alternative to sister *Gloria*, though it does have a better swimming pool. ❽

Gloria Resort ⓣ0899/88568855, ⓦwww.gloriahotels.com. Five-star affair with private beach, host of restaurants, pool, bike rental, water-sports hire, travel agent and airport transfers. ❾

Holiday Inn ⓣ0899/88565666, ⓦwww.holiday-inn-sanya.com. Another international effort, with all facilities. ❾

The City

Despite the area's holiday image, **Sanya city** itself is not a tourist attraction but a noisy and grubby port, complete with neatly uniformed navy recruits scooting around on bicycles. It has atmosphere though, and for sheer sleaziness you can't beat the **wharf area** along Jiangang Lu, where dubious characters, scantily clad women and an air of lazy indifference fill the untidy teahouses and back alleys. Sanya's **main market**, held in streets parallel and east of southern Jiefang Lu, is an interesting place to snack on local seafood and shop around the open-fronted stores, many so full that their wares overflow on to tables set up outside. Night or day, you can buy all manner of tropical fruits here, along with clothes, boiled sweets by the kilo, kitchen hardware from coconut graters to giant cleavers and woks, and expensive imported toiletries, cigarettes and spirits smuggled in through Vietnam.

Dadonghai and the Luhuitou Peninsula

Only 150m from the main road, often crowded and seasonally blistering hot, three-kilometre-long **Dadonghai** has pretty well everything you could ask for in a tropical beach: palm trees, white sands, and warm, blue water – a fair reward for making the journey to Hainan. A beachside bar and kiosks renting out beach umbrellas, jet skis, catamarans and rubber rings complete the scene, but on the whole the Chinese appear strangely bemused by beach life, as if they know it should be fun but are unsure of sure how to go about enjoying themselves. Swimming out farther than waist-deep water is sure to draw disbelieving looks from holidaying mainlanders, who seem uncomfortably self-concious in swimwear and hardly dare get their ankles wet. While it's all very relaxed for China, don't mellow too much, as unattended valuables will vanish, and women going topless, or any nudity, will lead to arrests.

The **Luhuitou Peninsula** shouldn't take up much of your time. You can catch a motorcycle combi – or bus #101 – from outside the *Hawaii Hotel* at Dadonghai to the summit entrance, where ¥30 gains access to a ponderous granite statue depicting a Li legend about a deer transforming into a beautiful girl as it turned to face a young hunter – Luhuitou means "deer turns its head".

Eating and drinking

Given Sanya's tropical climate and location at China's southernmost point, there's something perverse about the bias towards northern and western Chinese food – probably explained by the fact that most of the restauranters are migrants from Sichuan and Dongbei. Places of note are all at **Dadonghai** – we've reviewed a selection below – with the best over towards the east; a host of budget places with translated menus lurk west of the *Seaside Holiday Inn*, with staff who leap out and try to drag you inside.

Like accommodation, eating here can be an expensive business, though the excellent **seafood** (almost all from Indonesia and the Philippines – Sanya's marine fauna is long fished out) is reasonably priced. Don't eat anywhere – especially cheaper spots – without getting solid confirmation of **prices**, or you'll end up paying ¥30 for a bowl of noodles.

Beachfront seafood Just above the beach near the *South China* hotel. A surprisingly romantic place to eat in the evening: select fish, crabs, lobster, prawns and other seafood from the live tanks and say how you want it cooked, order a couple of beers, and kick back at outdoor tables under the coconut trees. A *jin* of prawns is about ¥40.

Dongbei Wang On the highway. Lively, enjoyable Manchurian restaurant, with a menu illustrated with photos to help smooth linguistic problems. Portions are huge and the service good. The fried whole fish with pine nuts is a treat, as are cold beef shreds with aniseed, and a stir-fried mix of peas, pine nuts, and corn kernels. ¥60 will feed two.

Dongjiao Yelin Seafood On the highway. A warehouse of a restaurant, offering a glut of seafood and Hainanese dishes in an opulent setting. Expensive.

Hengyun Near the *Seaside Holiday Inn*. Outdoor tables under an awning, with a tree growing through the roof, mark this relatively inexpensive Sichuanese stir-fry place, one of many in the area.

Listings

Airlines Most hotels have airline agents on hand. The Phoenix airport booking office is at the junction of Gangmen Lu and Jiefang Lu, Sanya (Ⓣ0899/88278221 or 88277409; Mon–Sat 9am–noon & 1.30–5pm). There's also a major Hainan Air booking office beside the bus station (Ⓣ0899/88267988, Ⓕ88252168).

Banks and exchange The main Bank of China, on Jiefang Lu in Sanya (Mon–Fri 8am–noon & 2.30–6pm), is excruciatingly understaffed and slow. There's also a Dadonghai branch, but it has been known to refuse to cash traveller's cheques.

Internet access There's a Net café upstairs at the Xinhua bookstore, near the Bank of China on Jiefang Lu, Sanya; and another one just north of the bus station entrance.

Mail There are post offices on Xinjiang Lu, Sanya, and on the highway at Dadonghai (daily 7.30am–7.30pm).

Scuba diving Low visibility and maximum depths between 10m and 30m don't make Hainan the most exciting location for this, but it can be good fun and there's always the novelty of having dived in China. The three areas are at Yalong Bay, east of

Sanya (best for its moderate coral growth, and a variety of fish and lobster); Tianya Haijiao, over to the west (good for molluscs, but extremely shallow); and the coral islands, also west (these are the deepest sites). Staff are NAUI/PADI qualified, hire gear is of reasonable quality, and you'll be expected to flash a C-card or make do with an introductory "resort" dive (¥280). Two shore dives cost ¥380, two boat dives ¥560. Make bookings at the office by the *South China* hotel's pool, or with the beachfront office at the *International Youth Hostel*.

Shopping Sanya is an good place to pick up pearls, white, pink, yellow or black. The best buys are from local hawkers on Dadonghai beach, who sell strings of "rejects" for ¥40 or less with hard bargaining. Most of these pearls are perfectly genuine, just not of good enough colour, shape or size for commercial jewellery. If in doubt, scratch the surface – flaking indicates a thinly coated plastic bead. If you're after any supplies from food to toiletries, there's a good store on the highway at Dadonghai, just on the corner with the road down to the *South China* hotel.

Travel agents Upmarket hotels have their own travel desks, or try Sanya Dragon Travel, west past the *Hawaii Hotel* on Luling Lu, Dadonghai (Ⓣ88213526, Ⓕ88213799; daily 8.30am–5pm). They speak some English, and can arrange scuba diving, mountain bike rental (¥40 a day), coral island or fishing trips, airport transfers and bookings, and day tours to Tongshi.

Around Sanya

Of the many coral islets south of Sanya, two – **Xizhou** and **Dongzhou**, the West and East islands – are deemed of no military significance, and can make an enjoyable trip in good weather. You're really doing this for the ninety-minute journey, which takes in some beautiful views of the coastline and mountains rising to the north, and the sight of long lines of grey destroyers powering west to patrol China's maritime boundaries. Once on the islands, you'll find the beaches mediocre and the inhabitants, who live in houses built from coral blocks, not particularly friendly; there's little to do except try out the local seafood and sit around waiting for the boat home. An academic attraction is that the islands mark the southernmost limit of China's unquestioned political authority – though there are ongoing attempts to stretch this as far as the **Spratly Islands**.

If you can speak Mandarin, boat owners might approach you on Dadonghai beach and offer their services. You can usually negotiate the cost down to ¥250

The South China Sea Islands

Chinese maps of the country always show a looped extension of the southern borders reaching 1500km down through the South China Sea to within spitting distance of Borneo, enclosing a host of reefs and minute islands. These sit over what might be major **oil and gas reserves**, and are consequently claimed by every nation in the region – China, Malaysia, the Philippines, Taiwan and Vietnam have all put in their bids, based on historical or geographic associations. Occupied by Japan during the 1940s but unclaimed after World War II, the **Spratly and Paracel islands** are perhaps the most contentious groups. Vietnam and China both declared ownership of the Paracels in the 1970s, coming to blows in 1988 when the Chinese navy sank two Vietnamese gunboats. Then the Philippines stepped in in 1995, destroying Chinese territorial markers erected over the most westerly reefs in the Spratly group and capturing a nearby Chinese trawler. Continuing minor brawls encouraged the nations of the region – including China – to hammer out a landmark agreement in November 2002, which basically allows access for all while territorial disputes are settled one by one. This is likely to be a relief to companies such as the US conglomerate Exxon, who – despite the fact that guaranteed oil reserves have yet to be found – are already investing in the region.

or less for a four-person boat, and pilots seem strangely willing to accept payment after the trip. Booking through an agent costs about twenty percent more, cash upfront. Either way, pack a bottle of drinking water, a sunscreen, hat and sunglasses, as there's scant shade on the islands and the boats are open-topped. The whole excursion lasts from about 8.30am to 5.30pm.

Tianya Haijiao and Yazhou

Any westbound bus from Sanya, or tourist bus #101 from the roundabout at the base of the Luhuitou Peninsula at Dodonghai, can cart you 20km out of the city to **Tianya Haijiao** (¥35), a long beach strewn with curiously shaped boulders, whose name roughly translates as the "ends of the earth". This isn't as fanciful as it sounds, as for Hainan's scholarly political exiles this was just about as far as you could possibly be from life's pinnacle at the imperial court. The modern world has unfortunately descended very heavily on the area, however, and a new township with expensive accommodation and restaurants, ever-escalating entry fees to the beach itself and overly persistent hawkers make for an irritating experience. Chinese come in their thousands to have their photographs taken next to rocks inscribed with big red characters marking them as the "Sweetheart Stones", or "Limit of the Sky, Edge of the Sea".

Another 15km west of here on local transport, past a luxurious golf course, is **YAZHOU**, formerly one of Hainan's biggest towns but now more of a bottleneck for through traffic. It's chiefly known as the place where the thirteenth-century weaver **Huang Daopo** fled from her native Shanghai to escape an arranged marriage. After forty years living with the coastal Li, she returned to northern China in 1295 and introduced their superior textile techniques to the mainland. Get out when you see the reconstructed **Ming city gate**, and walk through it to a tiny **temple museum**, which includes traditional Li clothing and a **Muslim Hui** headstone and mosque oil lamp. The Hui have been on Hainan for centuries – some say they were originally Song-dynasty refugees from Vietnam, others that they're a relict of the old Maritime Silk Road – and the countryside hereabouts is peppered with their distinctive cylindrical graves. Walk back onto the main road and continue a kilometre or so west out of town, and you'll find a 400-year-old, seven-storey brick **pagoda** leaning at a rakish angle next to a school – one of the few genuinely old structures on the island. The last direct transport back to Sanya leaves in the late afternoon.

West to Jianfeng and Dongfang

There are departures until after midday from Sanya's long-distance bus station for the 165-kilometre run to the western port of **Dongfang**, up the coast beyond Yazhou, though you can also travel there in stages by minibus until later on in the day. This side of the island is incredibly poor and undeveloped compared with the east, partly because it's too far out of the way to benefit from tourism, also because the main sources of income here are various forms of **mining**, an industry that sees little financial return for local communities.

The real reason to head out this way is to spend a day at **Jianfeng Ling Forest Reserve**, a small indication of what the whole of southwestern Hainan looked like before the 1960s. Head first for **JIANFENG** township, which lies at the base of the distinctively peaked Jianfeng range some 10km east of the coastal road, about 115km from Sanya. Dongfang-bound transport can drop you at the turning, from where you can walk or wait for the next passing vehicle to pick you up. A dusty little hollow where pigs and dogs roam the streets between the market, Jianfeng has two teahouses and around a hundred homes. The sole

guesthouse (❸) is a friendly place with a fine **restaurant** (try the chicken with locally grown cashew nuts), functioning plumbing and electric power.

The reserve itself is in the mountains 18km beyond Jianfeng, reached daily by a single scheduled minibus (¥10), although it's possible to hire one (¥70 up, ¥50 down). **Jianfeng Ling** – the mountain range itself – was aggressively logged until 1992, when a UNESCO survey found 400 types of butterfly and 1700 plant species up here and persuaded the Chinese government to establish the reserve, leaving a sharp-edged forested crown above bare lowland slopes. Though commercial timber stands have since been planted, locals have been left without a livelihood for the time being, a problem slightly eased by aid packages from the Asian Development Bank. The dirt road to the summit ends on the forest's edge at a group of stores, a small restaurant, a botanical research station, and a little-frequented **hotel** (¥150), whose staff will be most surprised to see you. A tiled gateway marks the reserve entrance about 100m back up the road, from where partially paved paths lead off uphill for an hour-long circuit walk taking in some massive trees, vines, orchids, ferns, birds, butterflies and beautiful views from the 1056-metre ridge. After dark, if you're armed with a flashlight and some caution, it's a good place to look for small mammals and reptiles.

Dongfang

Four hours from Sanya, **DONGFANG** (Basuo) is an industrial port with unfortunate associations. During the 1940s, the Japanese took Dongfang as their Hainan headquarters, developing mining operations inland, building the goods rail line which still runs between here and Sanya, and executing thousands of Li who are buried in a mass grave on a nearby hill. Arms smuggling and a large floating population of Vietnamese, Malay and Filipino "merchants" and boat crews on shore leave have given the town something of a wild reputation today, with tales of gun battles and banditry surrounding freelance gold mines in the area. However Dongfang is friendly enough, though definitely dull. Should you end up here, there's one grey, overly long main street, a few places to eat and, next to the bus station, the best-value **hotel** (❸). Plenty of onward traffic covers the roads back to Sanya or northeast to Haikou via Danzhou.

Tongshi and the highlands

Occupying the island's central core, **Hainan's highlands** get scant attention from visitors, despite evidence of long association with **Li and Miao** peoples. Just 100km north of Sanya, **Tongshi**'s quiet pace and large concentration of Li make it the favoured place to start delving into the region, while farther out, **Baisha** and **Qiongzhong** are less obvious alternatives, though shot through with scenic and historic appeal. Tongshi and Qiongzhong lie on the main inland route between Haikou and Sanya, while Baisha is more remotely positioned on a less-frequented road in Hainan's central west.

Tongshi and around

Two hours north of Sanya, **TONGSHI** (Tongza, also known as **Wuzhi Shan Shi**) was voted China's most liveable modern town in 1995, and it still deserves the accolade. Pocket-sized and surrounded by pretty countryside, a lack of heavy traffic or industry make it a pleasantly unpolluted spot to hang out for a day or two. The town has a well-presented **museum**, and there's the possibility of making local contacts in Tongshi itself, while energetic hikers might want

Tongshi and the highlands

Tongshi (Wuzhi Shan Shi)	通什(五指山市)	***tōngshì (wǔzhǐ shān shì)***
Jinyuan Dajiudian	金源大酒店	*jīnyuán dà jiǔdiàn*
Nationality Museum	民族博物馆	*mínzú bówùguǎn*
Qiongzhong University	琼州大学	*qióngzhōu dàxué*
Shang Cheng Chazhuang	山城茶庄	*shānchéng cházhuāng*
Tongshi Guolü Binguan	通什国旅宾馆	*tōngshíguólǚ bīnguǎn*
Baisha	白沙	***báishā***
Bawang Ling	坝王岭	*bàwáng lǐng*
Baoting	保亭	***bǎotíng***
Qizhi Shan	七指山	*qīzhǐ shān*
Qiongzhong	琼中	***qióngzhōng***
Fengmu Deer Farm	枫木养鹿场	*fēngmù yǎnglùchǎng*
Wuzhi Shan	五指山	***wǔzhǐ shān***

to go scrambling up nearby **Qizhi Shan** and **Wuzhi Shan**, whose summits are both steeped in local lore.

Before 1987, Tongshi was also capital of Hainan's autonomous Li government, until it blew a billion-yuan road grant by importing luxury goods from Hong Kong and Vietnam, and building the literally palatial offices, now **Qiongzhou University**, on the hill above town. When Beijing caught up with what was going on they sacked the government and put the region under their direct control, a move which, while entirely justified, was greatly resented by the Li.

The Town

Reached via a street running uphill just past the bus station, the **Nationality Museum** (Tues–Sun 8am–5pm; ¥10) affords views across town to the aptly named **Nipple Mountain**, 5km away to the west, while the collection itself is excellent. **Historical exhibits** include prehistoric stone tools and a bronze drum decorated with sun and frog motifs, similar to those associated with Guangxi's Zhuang; Ming manuscripts about island life; Qing wine vessels with octopus and frog mouldings; and details of the various modern conflicts culminating in the last pocket of Guomindang resistance being overcome in 1950. Artefacts and photos illustrate Hainan's **cultural heritage**, too – Li looms and textiles, traditional weapons and housing, speckled pottery from Dongfang, and pictures of major festivals. The museum is also near to the **university** – have a look at the latter's absurdly ostentatious green-tiled architecture.

Back across the river, the town centre is a far less pretentious handful of streets and modern concrete-and-tile buildings which you can tour in around thirty minutes. **Henan Lu** runs west along the waterfront from the bridge; one block back, Tongshi's **public square** is a sociable place to hang out after dark and meet people, full of tables serviced by drink and snack vendors, crowds watching open-air table-tennis tournaments and queuing for the cinema. Nearby, on **Jiefang Lu**, there's a chance to see dark-dressed Miao and the occasional older Li women with tattoos at the daily **market**, whose wares include sweet, milky-white spirit sold in plastic jerrycans, deer and dog meat, and also **rat**, split open like a French roll and grilled.

You can see more of the Li by catching a minibus 2km south to the tacky displays at **Fanmao Mountain Fortress Village**, but there's more to be said for

Li and Miao

Hainan's million-strong **Li** population take their name after the big topknot (*li*) which men once wore. Archeological finds and traditions shared with other southwestern Chinese peoples point to their arriving on Hainan from Guangxi about 200 BC, when they occupied the coast and displaced the aboriginal inhabitants. Driven inland themselves by later Han arrivals, the Li finally settled Hainan's central highlands (though a few remained on the coast) and spent the next two thousand years as rice farmers and hunters, living in villages with distinctive tunnel-shaped houses, evolving their own shamanistic religion, and using poisoned arrows to bring down game. **Li women** have long been known for their **weaving** skills, and the fact that, until very recently, many had their faces heavily **tattooed** with geometric patterns – apparently to make them undesirable to raiding parties of slavers from the coast, or rival **clans**. The latter form five major groups – Ha, Qi, Yun, Meifu and Cai – and they have never coexisted very well, quarrelling to this day over territorial boundaries and only really united in their dislike of external rulers.

Though actively supporting Communist guerrillas against the Japanese, the Li have no great affection for the Han as a whole, and there were fourteen major rebellions against their presence on the island during the Qing era alone. Superficially assimilated into modern China, the Li would probably revolt again if they felt they could get away with it. They are, however, pretty friendly towards outside visitors, and though traditional life has all but vanished over the last half-century, there are still a few special events to watch out for. Best is the **San Yue San festival** (held on the third day of the third lunar month), the most auspicious time of the year in which to choose a partner, while in more remote corners of the highlands, **funerals** are traditionally celebrated with gunfire and three days of hard drinking by male participants.

Touted as Hainan's second "native minority" by the tourist literature, the **Miao** are in fact comparatively recent arrivals, forcibly recruited from Guizhou Province as **mercenaries** to put down a Li uprising during the Ming dynasty. When the money ran out the Miao stopped fighting and settled in the western highlands, where today they form a fifty-thousand-strong community. Though they apparently now intermarry with the Li, the US adventurer, Leonard Clark, who traversed the highlands in 1937, reported them as living apart in the remotest of valleys (for more on the Miao, see p.700).

just heading off into the countryside on foot. From the north side of the bridge, follow Hebei Xi Lu west along the river for 150m to a grossly patronizing **statue** of grinning Li, Miao and Han characters standing arm in arm. Take the road uphill from here and keep going as far as you want to, through vivid green fields and increasingly poor villages, ultimately built of mud and straw and surrounded by split bamboo pickets to keep livestock in. Among these you'll see more substantial barns with traditional tunnel shapes and carved wooden doors.

Practicalities

Set at the base of low hills, Tongshi's tiny centre sits on the southern bank of a horseshoe bend in the generally unimpressive **Nansheng River**. The main road comes up from the coast as **Haiyu Lu**, bypasses the centre, crosses over the river, turns sharply left past the **bus station**, and bends off north through the island towards Qiongzhong and Haikou. Buses from the station head to Baoting, Baisha, Qiongzhong, Haikou and Sanya; for Wuzhi Shan, you need to ask about minibuses which leave irregularly through the morning from the street two streets back from the market. There are a couple of **internet cafés** around the bus station, but there's no Bank of China in town.

Tongshi's very reasonable **accommodation** prices are a relief after Sanya. Opposite the bus station, *Jinyuan Dajiudian* has clean, tiled rooms

(Ⓣ0899/86622434; ❷), as does the slightly more upmarket *Tongshi Guolü Binguan* (Ⓣ0899/86633158; ❷). Another option, the *Minzhu Binguan* (Ⓣ0899/86622962) commands an excellent position on the hill above the bus station, but was closed indefinitely at the time of writing.

Teahouses near the market fill with sociable crowds on most mornings, which is also a good time to eat *dim sum* in *Shan Cheng Chazhuang* on Jiefang Lu – an extraordinary institution whose men's-club atmosphere is compounded by a card-gaming hall out the back; *hainan gau* here are sticky rice packets with coconut and banana. Probably the best **restaurants** are the canteens around the bus station.

Wuzhi Shan and Qizhi Shan

Several Li myths explain the formation of **Wuzhi Shan** (Five-Finger Mountain) whose 1867-metre summit rises 30km northeast of Tongshi at Hainan's apex. In one tale the mountain's five peaks are the fossilized fingers of a dying clan chieftain, while another holds that they represent the Li's five most powerful gods. Either way, Wuzhi Shan was once a holy site drawing thousands of people to animist festivals. Though the mountain is rarely a place of pilgrimage for the Li today, remoter villages in this part of Hainan maintain the old religion, raising archways over their gates which are occasionally embellished with bull or chicken heads. It's still possible to climb the mountain – take a bus from Tongshi to **Wuzhi Shan township**, then local transport to the *Wuzhi Shan Binguan* (Ⓣ86622981; ❸). From here it's a steep and slippery three-hour scramble to the peak, initially through jungly scrub, then pine forests. Although it's often clouded over, the summit offers further contorted pines, begonias and views.

Qizhi Shan (Seven-Finger Mountain), representing seven lesser Li immortals being vanquished by Wuzhi's five, lies about 40km by road southeast of Tongshi via **Baoting** (Baocheng). A sleepy place, Baoting is another good place to wander aimlessly off into the countryside from, and you can get to the base of the mountain by catching available transport 10km east to **Shiling**, and thence 11km north to **Ba Cun**. The climb is said to be shorter than that at Wuzhi Shan, but much harder.

Baisha and Qiongzhong

The sixty-kilometre journey from Tongshi north to **Baisha**, along a turning off the main road, takes in some splendid views as the road weaves up Hainan's denuded central ranges. Passing a couple of abandoned, ruinous blockhouses which were the headquarters of Hainan's Communist forces during the Japanese occupation, the bus eventually reaches a ridge from where, on a clear day, you can see the remarkable peaks of **Hong Mo Shan**, the Red Mist Mountains, away to the northeast. Thirty minutes later you rumble into **Baisha**, an unattractive sugar town with a large but not obvious Li population. At one end of a high, fertile valley covered in patchy remnant forests and various plantations, Baisha's surroundings make very appealing walking country, however, overlooked by the broodingly romantic **Bawang Ling** mountain range, 20km away to the west, whose jungles are home to Hainan's last **black gibbons**. The animals were remorselessly hunted for their long forearm bones, which were turned into chopsticks valued for their rumoured ability to turn black if dipped in poisoned food. Now only an estimated nineteen survive.

The road from Tongshi to **QIONGZHONG** (Yinggen) bears east around the base of Wuzhi Shan, with viewing points along the roadside to take in the spectacle of **Baihua Waterfall** tumbling off the peak, a spot said to be inhabited by several Li goddesses. Qiongzhong itself is an intensely busy, thoroughly scruffy three-street market centre, with no shortage of places to eat and good-value **accommodation** in the white-tiled transport building downhill from the bus station – look for the circular bus symbol on the roof (Ⓣ86222615; ¥90). About 25km northeast along the Haikou road, the entrance to **Fengmu Deer Farm** (daily 9am–4pm; ¥15) is marked by an unmissable stylized concrete deer and a reception centre hoping to tap interest in another rare beast, the **Hainan deer**. On the shores of a small reservoir, the farm was established as a breeding centre in 1964 after the Hainan deer became extinct in the wild, and has since reintroduced populations to reserves in the west of the island. At the small paddock at the back, visitors can stroke the animals and be deafened by their shrill whistles. There's plenty of passing traffic throughout the day in both directions along the main road.

Travel details

Trains

Chaozhou to: Guangzhou (4 daily; 7–12hr); Huizhou (5 daily; 7–8hr); Meizhou (4 daily; 1–3hr); Shantou (5 daily; 30min).
Fuzhou to: Beijing (1 daily; 33hr); Guangzhou (2 daily; 36hr); Kunming (2 daily; 38hr); Longyan (1 daily; 10hr); Meizhou (1 daily; 13hr); Nanchang (7 daily; 14hr); Shanghai (1 daily; 29hr); Shenzhen (2 daily; 21hr 30min); Wuyi Shan (4 daily; 7hr); Yongding (1 daily; 11hr).
Guangzhou to: Beijing (8 daily; 23hr); Changsha (30 daily; 7–10hr); Chaozhou (5 daily; 7–12hr); Chengdu (3 daily; 30hr); Foshan (8 daily; 45min); Fuzhou (2 daily; 36hr); Guilin (3 daily; 18hr); Guiyang (5 daily; 32hr); Huizhou (7 daily; 2–3hr); Kowloon (7 daily; 2hr); Kunming (3 daily; 30hr); Meizhou (4 daily; 9hr); Nanchang (5 daily; 12–15hr); Nanning (3 daily; 18hr); Shanghai (7 daily; 24hr); Shantou (5 daily; 7–12hr); Shaoguan (many daily; 3–5hr); Shenzhen (2 hourly; 50min–2hr); Wuhan (20 daily; 10–15hr); Xiamen (1 daily; 15hr); Xi'an (2 daily; 27hr); Zhaoqing (8 daily; 2hr).
Huizhou to: Chaozhou (5 daily; 7–8hr); Guangzhou (7 daily; 2–3hr); Meizhou (5 daily; 5hr 30min); Nanchang (2 daily; 18hr); Shanghai (1 daily; 36hr); Shantou (3 daily; 9hr); Wuhan (2 daily; 23hr).
Meizhou to: Chaozhou (3 daily; 1–2hr); Fuzhou (1 daily; 13hr); Guangzhou (3 daily; 9hr); Huizhou (3 daily; 5hr 30min); Longyan (2 daily; 3hr); Quanzhou (1 daily; 13hr); Shantou (4 daily; 3–4hr).
Quanzhou to: Longyan (1 daily; 10hr); Meizhou (1daily; 13hr); Wuyi Shan (1 daily; 13hr).
Shantou to: Chaozhou (5 daily; 30 min); Guangzhou (5 daily; 7–12hr); Huizhou (3 daily; 9hr); Meizhou (4 daily; 3–4hr).
Shaoguan to: Changsha (many daily; 5hr); Guangzhou (many daily; 3–5hr); Hengyang (many daily; 5hr).
Shenzhen to: Changsha (2 daily; 15hr); Fuzhou (2 daily; 21hr 30min); Guangzhou (2 hourly; 50min–2hr); Shanghai (2 daily; 36hr); Shantou (2 daily; 11hr); Shaoguan (3 daily; 6hr); Wuhan (3 daily; 15hr).
Wuyi Shan to: Fuzhou (4 daily; 7hr); Quanzhou (1 daily; 13hr); Xiamen (1 daily; 13hr).
Xiamen to: Guangzhou (1 daily; 15hr); Nanchang (4 daily; 11hr); Nanjing (1 daily; 18hr); Shanghai (1 daily; 25hr); Wuyi Shan (1 daily; 13hr); Xi'an (1 daily; 16hr).

Buses

Chaozhou to: Guangzhou (7hr); Huizhou (5hr); Meizhou (8hr); Shantou (1hr); Shenzhen (7hr).
Fuzhou to: Guangzhou (16hr); Longyan (9hr); Ningbo (20hr); Quanzhou (2hr 30min); Shantou (10hr); Shenzhen (16hr); Wenzhou (11hr); Wuyi Shan (7hr); Xiamen (4hr); Yongding (10hr).
Guangzhou to: Beihai (24hr); Changsha (20hr); Chaozhou (7hr); Dongguan (1hr); Foshan (1hr); Fuzhou (16hr); Ganzhou (11hr); Guilin (13hr); Haikou (20hr); Huizhou (3hr); Jiangmen (3hr); Kowloon (3hr); Macau (several daily; 3hr); Meizhou (12hr); Nanning (30hr); Panyu (1hr); Qingyuan (1hr); Shantou (6hr); Shaoguan (6hr); Shenzhen (3hr); Shunde (1hr 30min); Xiamen (9hr); Zhangjiang (13hr); Zhaoqing (3hr); Zhuhai (3hr).
Haikou to: Guangzhou (20hr); Lingshui (6hr); Qionghai (3hr 30min); Qiongzhong (5hr); Sanya (3–7hr); Shenzhen (20hr); Tongshi (5hr); Wanning (5hr); Wenchang (2hr); Zhanjiang (7hr).
Huizhou to: Chaozhou (5hr); Guangzhou (3hr);

Meizhou (10hr); Shantou (3hr); Shenzhen (4hr).
Meizhou to: Chaozhou (8hr); Dapu (4hr); Guangzhou (12hr); Longyan (7hr); Shaoguan (12hr); Shantou (9hr); Shenzhen (12hr); Xiamen (9hr); Yongding (5hr).
Quanzhou to: Fuzhou (2hr 30min); Longyan (5hr); Xiamen (1hr 30min).
Qingyuan to: Guangzhou (1hr); Shaoguan (4hr); Zhaoqing (5hr).
Sanya to: Baisha (4hr); Baoting (90min); Dongfang (4hr); Haikou (3–7hr); Lingshui (2hr); Qionghai (4hr 30min); Qiongzhong (4hr); Tongshi (2hr); Wanning (3hr); Wenchang (6hr); Yazhou (1hr).
Shantou to: Chaozhou (1hr); Fuzhou (10hr); Guangzhou (7hr); Huizhou (4hr); Meizhou (9hr); Shaoguan (12hr); Shenzhen (7hr); Xiamen (5hr).
Shaoguan to: Ganzhou, Jiangxi Province (6hr); Guangzhou (10hr); Huizhou (4hr); Meizhou (12hr); Pingshi (4hr); Qingyuan (8hr); Shantou (12hr).
Shenzhen to: Chaozhou (7hr); Dongguan (2hr); Fuzhou (16hr); Guangzhou (3hr); Hong Kong (2hr); Meizhou (12hr); Shantou (7hr).
Xiamen to: Fuzhou (4hr); Guangzhou (20hr); Longyan (5hr); Meizhou (9hr); Quanzhou (1hr 30min); Shenzhen (20hr); Wenzhou (18hr).
Zhanjiang to: Guangzhou (13hr); Haikou (7hr); Zhaoqing (10hr).
Zhaoqing to: Guangzhou (3hr); Guilin (10hr); Qingyuan (5hr); Yangshuo (8hr 30min); Zhanjiang (10hr).
Zhuhai to: Cuiheng (1hr); Foshan (4hr); Guangzhou (3hr); Jiangmen (2hr); Shunde (2hr 30min); Zhongshan (1hr).

Ferries

Guangzhou to: Hong Kong (2 daily; 2hr).
Haikou to: Beihai (3 daily; 11hr); Hai'an (10 daily; 1hr 30min); Hong Kong (2 weekly; 25hr); Zhanjiang (2 daily; 3hr).
Shenzhen to: Hong Kong (7 daily; 45min); Macau (daily; 2hr); Zhuhai (30 daily; 1hr).
Xiamen to: Hong Kong (1 weekly; 17hr).
Zhanjiang to: Haikou (2 daily; 3hr).
Zhaoqing to: Hong Kong (daily; 5hr).
Zhuhai to: Macau (5 daily; 20min); Shenzhen (30 daily; 1hr).

Flights

Besides the domestic flights listed here, Guangzhou (and to a lesser extent, Xiamen and Shenzhen) is linked by regular services to major Southeast Asian cities.
Fuzhou to: Beijing (4 daily; 3hr); Guangzhou (4 daily; 1hr 30min); Haikou (6 weekly; 2hr); Hong Kong (5 daily; 1hr 30min); Macau (1 daily; 1hr 20min); Shanghai (7 daily; 1hr 10min); Shenzhen (2 daily; 1hr); Wuyi Shan (4 weekly; 30min); Xiamen (2 daily; 35min).
Guangzhou to: Beihai (3 daily; 50min); Beijing (11 daily; 2hr 45min); Changsha (2 daily; 1hr); Chengdu (5 daily; 1hr 45min); Chongqing (7 daily; 1hr 30min); Dalian (1–3 daily; 3hr); Fuzhou (4 daily; 1hr 30min); Guilin (6 daily; 40min); Guiyang (3 daily; 1hr 15min); Haikou (7–10 daily; 1hr); Hangzhou (3 daily; 1hr 30min); Harbin (2 daily; 4hr); Hefei (1–2 daily; 1hr 30min); Hohhot (2 weekly; 5hr); Hong Kong (12 daily; 30min); Kunming (3 daily; 2hr); Lanzhou (1 daily; 3hr); Meizhou (2 daily; 30min); Nanchang (3 daily; 1hr); Nanjing (5 daily; 2hr); Nanning (4 daily; 50min); Qingdao (2 daily; 2hr 30min); Sanya (2 daily; 1hr 10min); Shanghai (11 daily; 2hr); Shantou (4 daily; 40min); Tianjin (daily; 2hr 30min); Urumqi (2 daily; 5hr); Wuhan (8 daily; 1hr 20min); Xiamen (2 daily; 1hr); Xi'an (3 daily; 2hr); Zhengzhou (4 daily; 1hr).
Haikou to: Beihai (2 daily; 30min); Beijing (4 daily; 3hr); Changsha (1–2 daily; 2hr); Chengdu (1 daily; 2hr); Fuzhou (6 weekly; 2hr); Guangzhou (7–10 daily; 1hr); Guilin (2 weekly; 1hr 20min); Hong Kong (2 daily; 1hr 30min); Kunming (1 daily; 1hr 20min); Nanjing (5 weekly; 2hr 40 min); Sanya (2 daily; 1hr); Shanghai (2–4 daily; 2hr); Shenzhen (4 daily; 50min); Wuhan (1–2 daily; 2hr); Xiamen (5 weekly; 2 hr); Xi'an (6 weekly; 4hr); Zhanjiang (1–2 daily; 30min); Zhuhai (6 weekly; 1hr).
Sanya to: Beijing (5 weekly; 5hr); Guangzhou (2 daily; 1hr 10min); Haikou (2 daily; 1hr); Hong Kong (6 weekly; 1hr 30 min); Macau (2 weekly; 1hr 20min); Shanghai (5 weekly; 2hr 30min); Shenzhen (4 weekly; 1hr 15min).
Shenzhen to: Beihai (2 daily; 1hr 30min); Beijing (7 daily; 3hr); Changsha (6 weekly; 1hr); Chengdu (2 daily; 2hr 20min); Chongqing (5 daily; 2hr 20min); Fuzhou (2 daily; 1hr); Guilin (3 daily; 50min); Guiyang (1 daily; 1hr 20min); Haikou (4 daily; 50min); Hangzhou (1 daily; 1hr 40min); Harbin (2 daily; 5hr); Kunming (2 daily; 2hr 40min); Meizhou (3 weekly; 45min); Nanchang (2 daily; 1hr); Nanjing (5 daily; 1hr 50min); Sanya (4 weekly; 1hr 15 min); Shanghai (5 daily; 2hr); Shantou (1 daily; 40min); Wuhan (4 daily; 1hr 30min); Xiamen (2 daily; 1hr 10min); Xi'an (daily; 2hr).
Wuyi Shan to: Fuzhou (4 weekly; 30min), Shanghai (3 weekly; 1hr); Xiamen (5 weekly; 40min).
Xiamen to: Beijing (3 daily; 2hr 30min); Fuzhou (2 daily; 35 min); Guangzhou (3–5 daily; 50min); Hong Kong (3 daily; 50min); Macau (3 daily; 1hr); Shanghai (7 daily; 1hr 10min); Shenzhen (2 daily; 1hr 10min); Wuyi Shan (5 weekly; 40min).

CHAPTER 9

Highlights

* **Hong Kong Island trams** The best way to travel the north shore is by rattling double-decker tram. Ride from North Point to Western, upstairs and at night for the full effect. **See p.718**

* **Star Ferry** The crossing from Tsim Sha Tsui to Hong Kong Island is the cheapest harbour tour on earth, and one of the most spectacular. **See p.719**

* **Harbour view from the Peak** Just before dusk, watch the city's dazzling lights slowly brighten across Hong Kong, the harbour and Kowloon. **See p.734**

* **Seafood restaurants** Spend a day hiking the Dragon's Back before tucking in to honey squid at one of Shek O's seafood restaurants. **See p.737**

* **Dim sum** Book in advance for an authentic *dim sum* lunch alongside enthusiastic families – try the chicken's feet and barbecue pork buns. **See p.751**

* **Old Macau** Hunt for bargain rosewood furniture and traditional clothing in central Macau's cobbled streets. **See p.771**

* **Taipa and Coloane** Rent a bike and explore Macau's green retreats and colonial secrets. **See p.777**

* **Coffee** Macau's coffee shops offer authentic ink-black Portuguese coffee – a rarity in China. **See p.779**

9

Hong Kong and Macau

The handover of **Asia's last two European colonies**, Hong Kong in 1997 and Macau in 1999, opened new eras for both places. While the vestiges of their colonial eras are still obvious – the buildings, the names, the food and the use of European languages – and among their greatest attractions, subtle changes are already underway, as these two "Special Administrative Regions of China" seek to establish identities and roles for themselves.

Under colonial rule such soul-searching was never an issue. The populations in both places had little say in their futures, so they concentrated their efforts on other things, notably making money. Of course, they were not the only ones in Asia to take this path, but their economic success – at least Hong Kong's – simply highlighted their anachronistic position as dependent territories, decades after most other colonies had achieved self-rule.

That, understandably, was one of the reasons for the delay in resolving their status. Independence was never a serious proposition for either place, but the alternatives were not attractive. In the end, the situation was forced by two things: in Hong Kong's case, the approach of 1997, when the treaty on the New Territories ran out, while in Macau's, the desire of the post-revolutionary Portuguese government to get rid of the place. Both entities now find themselves in a unique position – subject to the ultimate rule of Beijing, they form two semi-democratic capitalist enclaves under the control of an unaccountable communist state.

This is not to say that the people of Hong Kong and Macau were not glad to see the end of colonialism – an overwhelming majority in both places supported the transfer of power, something shown by the way the handover produced remarkably little emotion or nostalgia among local people. They are, after all, thoroughly **Chinese** (the population of the two territories is 97 percent Chinese), and very largely Cantonese (although that doesn't mean there isn't tension and mutual suspicion between them and people from other parts of China). The overwhelming majority of the people speak only the Cantonese dialect, eat only Cantonese food, pray in Chinese temples and enjoy close cultural and blood relations with the Cantonese population that lives just over the border, in the southern provinces of mainland China.

Indeed, it is hard to overstate the symbolic importance that the handovers had for the entire Chinese population – sealing the end of the era of foreign dom-

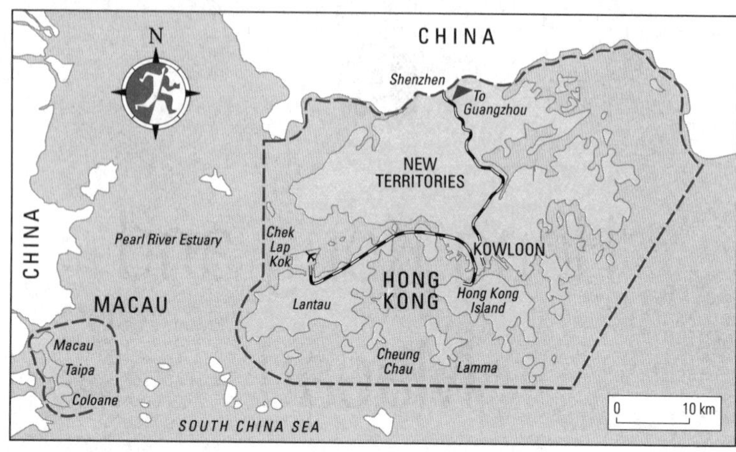

ination, with the return of the last piece of occupied soil to the motherland. However, worrying questions remain, notably whether the One Country/Two Systems policy dreamed of by Deng Xiaoping will work in the longer term, in particular if China's own economic progress begins to falter.

Amid the uncertainty, however, life continues as normal in many ways for both territories. **Hong Kong** continues to offer the densest concentration and greatest variety of **shops and shopping malls** of any place on earth, and the vistas of sea and island, green mountains and futuristic cityscapes remain. The **range and variety of cuisines** available – from Nepali snackbars to British pubs – is also ongoing. An excellent infrastructure, including the **airport** at Chek Lap Kok, the efficient underground trains, the helpful tourist offices and all the other facilities of a genuinely international city, make this an extremely soft entry indeed into the Chinese world.

While Hong Kong is a place to do business, **Macau** is known in the region as a Chinese playground, a haven for **gambling** and other sins, a mini Las Vegas of the East. The marks of its colonial past are more immediately obvious than they are in Hong Kong, in its **Portuguese architecture**, old churches and (almost) Mediterranean seafront promenade. It can even boast its own indigenous population, the Macanese, a tiny mixed-blood minority, whose origins in the colony date back centuries and who are often bilingual in Portuguese and Cantonese. The cheap Portuguese wine and **Macanese cooking** – an interesting marriage of Chinese and Mediterranean influences – are further reminders of colonial heritage, as is the faintly Latin lifestyle, altogether less hectic and mellower than in other parts of southern China. South of the main city, on the tiny islands of Taipa and Coloane, are beaches and quiet villages where you can eat fish and drink wine in relative peace.

Visitors to this part of southern China can expect to spend more **money** here than in other parts of the country, though not necessarily as much as you might expect considering the often huge differential in terms of quality of service compared to the mainland. **Public transport** in both Hong Kong and Macau is still incredibly cheap. Travellers on a tight budget who stay in dormitory accommodation can get by on US$25 a day, though at the other end of the market in hotels, restaurants and shops, prices quickly rise to international levels.

Hong Kong

In its multifaceted role as a repository of traditional Chinese culture, the last jewel in the crown of the British Empire and one of the key economies of the Pacific Rim, **HONG KONG** is East Asia's most extraordinary city. The territory's per capita GNP, for example, has doubled in a decade, overtaking that of the former imperial power. Yet the inequality of incomes is staggering: the conspicuous consumption of the few hundred super-rich (mostly Cantonese) for which Hong Kong is famous tends to mask the fact that most people work long hours and live in crowded, tiny apartments (Kwun Tong district reputedly possesses the highest population density in the world at 50,080 people per square kilometre). In spite of this, the population of almost seven million is generally sophisticated and well informed compared with their mainland cousins, the result of a vibrant and free press (although self-censorship is a constant and growing concern). The **Hong Kong Special Administrative Region** (HK SAR) is currently the largest source of external investment in the People's Republic of China. And the view of sky-scrapered Hong Kong Island, across the harbour from Kowloon, is one of the most stunning urban panoramas on earth.

The territory of Hong Kong comprises an irregularly shaped peninsula abutting the Pearl River Delta to the west, and a number of offshore islands, which cover in total 1,100 square kilometres. The bulk of this area, namely the land in the north of the peninsula as well as most of the islands, is semi-rural and is known as the **New Territories** – this was the land leased to Britain for 99 years in 1898. The southern part of the peninsula, known as **Kowloon**, and the island immediately south of here, **Hong Kong Island**, are the principal urban areas of Hong Kong. They were ceded to Britain in perpetuity, though the British government in 1984 saw no alternative but to agree to hand back the entire territory as one piece, so that from midnight on June 30, 1997, it became the Hong Kong Special Administrative Region of China.

The island of Hong Kong offers not only traces of the **old colony** – from English place names to ancient, double-decker trams trundling along the shore – but also superb **modern architecture** and bizarre cityscapes of towering buildings teetering up impossible slopes, as well as unexpected opportunities for **hiking** and even bathing on the **beaches** of its southern shore. Kowloon, in particular its southernmost tip, **Tsim Sha Tsui**, is where many visitors end up staying. This is not only the budget accommodation centre of Hong Kong, but also the most cosmopolitan area of perhaps any Chinese city, with a substantial population of immigrants from the Indian subcontinent. And, as the territory's principal tourist trap, it boasts more shops offering a greater variety of goods per square kilometre than anywhere in the world (not necessarily at reasonable prices, though). North of Tsim Sha Tsui, Kowloon stretches away into the New Territories, an area of so-called **New Towns** as well as ancient villages, secluded beaches and rural tranquillity. In addition, there are the **offshore islands**, which are well worth a visit for their seafood restaurants, scenery and, if nothing else, for the experience of chugging about on the **inter-island ferries**. The islands of **Lamma** and **Lantau**, in particular, offer a relatively rural and traffic-free contrast to the hubbub of downtown Hong Kong.

Some visitors dislike the speed, the obsessive materialism and the addiction to shopping, money and brand names in Hong Kong. As in many a Western city, the locals are reserved towards strangers and, with its perennial massive engineering projects (something else which hasn't been changed by the handover), downtown is certainly not a place to recover from a headache. On the other hand, it's hard not to enjoy the sheer energy of its street- and commercial life, which continues to thrive despite uncertainties over the long-term future of the city and the current economic downtown.

Some history

While the Chinese may argue, with justification, that Hong Kong is Chinese territory, the development of the city only began with the **arrival of the British** in Guangzhou in the eighteenth century.

The **Portuguese** had already been based at Macau, on the other side of the Pearl River Delta, since the mid-sixteenth century, and as Britain's sea power grew, so its merchants, too, began casting envious eyes over the Portuguese trade in tea and silk. The initial difficulty was to persuade the Chinese authorities that there was any reason to want to deal with them, though a few traders did manage to get permission to set up their warehouses in Guangzhou – a remote southern outpost, from the perspective of Beijing – and slowly trade began to grow. In 1757 a local Guangzhou merchants' guild called the **Co Hong** won the exclusive rights to sell Chinese products to foreign traders, who were now permitted to live in Guangzhou for about six months each year.

In the meantime, it had not escaped the attention of the foreigners that the trade was one-way only, and they soon began thinking up possible products the Chinese might want to buy in exchange. It did not take long to find one – **opium** from India. In 1773 the first British shipload of opium arrived and an explosion of demand for the drug quickly followed, despite an edict from Beijing banning the trade in 1796. Co Hong, which received commission on everything bought or sold, had no qualms about distributing opium to its fellow citizens and before long the balance of trade had been reversed very much in favour of the British.

The scene for the famous **Opium Wars** was now set. Alarmed at the outflow of silver and at the rising incidence of drug addiction among his population, the emperor appointed Lin Zexu as Commissioner of Guangzhou to destroy the opium trade. Lin, later hailed by the Chinese Communists as a patriot and hero, forced the British in Guangzhou to surrender their opium, before ceremonially burning it. Such an affront to British dignity could not be tolerated, however, and in 1840 a naval expeditionary force was dispatched from London to sort the matter out once and for all. After a year of gunboat diplomacy – blockading ports and seizing assets up and down the Chinese coast – the expeditionary force finally achieved one of their main objectives, through the **Treaty of Nanking** (1842), namely the ceding to Britain "in perpetuity" of a small offshore island. The island was called Hong Kong. This was followed eighteen years later, after more blockades and a forced march on Peking, by the **Treaty of Peking**, which granted Britain the Kowloon peninsula, too. Finally, in 1898, as the Qing dynasty was entering its terminal phase, Britain secured a 99-year lease on an additional one thousand square kilometres of land to the north of Kowloon, which would be known as the New Territories.

The twentieth century saw Hong Kong grow from a seedy merchants' colony to a huge international city, but progress was not always smooth. The drug trade was voluntarily dropped in 1907 as the Hong Kong merchants began to make the transfer from pure trade to manufacturing. Up until World War II, Hong

Kong prospered as the growing threat of both civil war and Japanese aggression in mainland China increasingly began to drive money south into the apparently safe confines of the British colony. This confidence appeared glaringly misplaced in 1941 when **Japanese forces** seized Hong Kong along with the rest of eastern China, though after the Japanese defeat in 1945, Hong Kong once again began attracting money from the mainland, which was in the process of falling to the Communists. Many of Hong Kong's biggest tycoons today are people who escaped from mainland China, particularly from Shanghai, in 1949.

Since the beginning of the **Communist era**, Hong Kong has led a precarious existence, quietly making money while taking care not to antagonize Beijing. Had China wished to do so, it could have rendered the existence of Hong Kong unviable at any moment, by a naval blockade, by cutting off water supplies, by a military invasion – or by simply opening its border and inviting the Chinese masses to stream across in search of wealth. That it has never wholeheartedly pursued any of these options, even at the height of the Cultural Revolution, is an indication of the huge **financial benefits** that Hong Kong brings to mainland China in the form of its international trade links, direct investment and technology transfers.

In the last twenty years of British rule, the spectre of **1997** loomed large in people's minds. In 1982 negotiations on the future of the colony began, although during the entire process that led to the **Sino-British Joint Declaration** nerves were kept on edge by the public posturings of both sides. The eventual deal, signed in 1984, paved the way for Britain to hand back sovereignty of the territory (something the Chinese would argue they never lost) in return for Hong Kong maintaining its capitalist system and way of life for at least fifty years.

Almost immediately the deal sparked controversy. It was pointed out that the lack of democratic institutions in Hong Kong – which had suited the British – would in future mean the Chinese could do what they liked. Fears grew that repression and the erosion of freedoms such as travel and speech would follow the handover. The **Basic Law**, which was published by the government in 1988, in theory answered some of those fears. It served as the constitutional framework, setting out how the "One Country, Two Systems" policy would work in practice. But it failed to restore confidence in Hong Kong, and a brain-drain of educated, professional people leaving for other countries began to gather pace.

The 1989 **crackdown in Tian'anmen Square** seemed to confirm the Hong Kong population's worst fears. In the biggest demonstration seen in Hong Kong in modern times, a million people took to the streets to protest what had happened. Business confidence was equally shaken, as the Hang Seng index, the performance indicator of the Stock Exchange, dropped 22 percent in a single day.

The 1990s were a roller-coaster ride of domestic policy dramas: the arrival of tens of thousands of **Vietnamese boat people** (ironically, refugees from communism), the rise of the **democracy movement** and arguments about whether Britain would give **passports to the local population**. When **Chris Patten** arrived in 1992 to become the last governor, he walked into a delicate and highly charged political situation. By means of a series of reforms, Patten quickly made it clear that he had not come to Hong Kong simply as a makeweight: first, much of the colonial paraphernalia was abandoned, and then – much to the fury of Beijing – he broadened the voting franchise for the 1995 **Legislative Council elections** (Legco) from around 200,000 to around 2.7

million people. Even though these and other changes he introduced guaranteed that the run-up to the 1997 handover would be a bumpy ride, they won the governor significant popularity among ordinary Hong Kong people, although the tycoons and business community had far more mixed feelings.

After the build-up, the **handover** itself was something of an anticlimax. The British sailed away on HMS Britannia, Beijing carried out its threat to disband the elected Legco and reduce the enfranchised population, and Tung Che Hwa, a shipping billionaire, became the **first chief executive** of the Hong Kong Special Administrative Region. But if local people had thought that they would be able to get on with "business as usual" post-handover, they were wrong. Within days the **Asian Financial Crisis** had begun, and within months Hong Kong was once again in the eye of a storm. While the administration beat off attempts to force a devaluation of its currency, the stock and property markets suffered dramatic falls, tourism collapsed, unemployment rose to its highest levels for fifteen years, and the economy officially went into recession. While the administration characterized these as temporary setbacks – part of a global economic downturn – there was undoubted dismay amongst official circles in both Hong Kong and Beijing at the increasing – and unprecedented – level of criticism of officials and their policies in newspapers, on radio phone-ins and among ordinary people – not to mention the enduring and not unrelated popularity of the democratic parties. A couple of years into the new century, the sluggish economy continues with record **unemployment** of over seven percent, problems of negative equity, controversial treatment of illegal immigrants from mainland China and a shift in emphasis towards investing and doing business in Guangzhou.

Post-1997

Just as Hong Kong citizens have retained their right to visa-free travel to most countries of the world, so most foreigners have continued to be allowed to enter Hong Kong without prior permission for up to three months. This includes nationals of the USA, Australia and New Zealand; British nationals can currently stay on a tourist visa for six months. For detailed information, contact your local HKTB office.

Hong Kong has retained its own separate currency, the **Hong Kong dollar**, which is pegged at around $7.80 to the US dollar. Coincidentally, one Hong Kong dollar is a little more than one Chinese yuan, though yuan and Hong Kong dollars cannot (officially) be used interchangeably in either territory. In this chapter, the symbol $ refers to Hong Kong dollars throughout unless stated.

Be warned that regulations introduced in 2002 have initiated $600 on-the-spot fines for spitting, littering, not cleaning up dog waste, and fly-posting, which are being enthusiastically enforced.

Orientation, arrival and information

Orientation for new arrivals in the main urban areas is relatively easy: if you are "**Hong Kong-side**" – on the northern shore of Hong Kong Island – **Victoria Harbour** lies to your north, while to your south the land slopes upwards steeply to the **Peak**. The heart of this built-up area on Hong Kong Island is known, rather mundanely, as **Central**. Just across the harbour, in the area known as **Tsim Sha Tsui**, you are "**Kowloon-side**", and here all you

Hong Kong phone numbers have no area codes. From outside the territory, dial the normal international access code + ⓣ852 (the "country" code) + the number. However, **from Macau** you need only dial ⓣ01 + the number. To call Hong Kong from mainland China, dial ⓣ00 + 852 + the number.

really need to recognize is the colossal north–south artery, **Nathan Road**, full of shops and budget hotels, that leads down to the harbour, and to the phenomenal view south over Hong Kong Island. Two more useful points for orientation on both sides of Victoria Harbour are the **Star Ferry terminals** where the popular cross-harbour ferries dock, in Tsim Sha Tsui (a short walk west of the south end of Nathan Road) and in Central.

Arrival

Public transport is so convenient and efficient that even first-time arrivals are unlikely to face any particular problems in reaching their destination within the city – apart from the difficulty of communicating with taxi drivers or reading the destinations on minibuses. All signs are supposed to be written in English and Chinese (although the English signs are sometimes so discreet as to be invisible) and travel times from the main international arrival points are reasonable, though road traffic is often heavy.

By plane

The Hong Kong International Airport opened in 1998 in **Chek Lap Kok** on the outlying island of Lantau as part of a $155.3 billion engineering project. Although a good deal farther out from the downtown areas than the old **Kai Tak** airport, the excellent rail and road links that were built with it mean that the travel times are not much longer. However, one thing the Hong Kong International Airport cannot match is the hair-raising approach that made the old Kai Tak airport so unique – swooping between apartment buildings, and with a dramatic last-minute turn, dropping onto a runway right in the central harbour.

The most efficient way to get into town from the airport is by the high-speed **Airport Express (AEL)** rail service (ⓣ2881 8888). The station platforms are joined directly to both the arrival and departure halls. Air-conditioned trains whisk you to Central in 23 minutes ($100) with stops on the way at Tsing Yi (12min; $60) and Kowloon (19min; $90). Services operate daily every eight minutes between 5.50am and 1am. There are taxi ranks, bus stops and hotel shuttle bus stops (operating every twenty minutes) at the AEL stations, and a left-luggage service at Hong Kong and Kowloon stations operates daily from 6am to 1am (ⓣ2868 3190).

Running alongside the AEL line for much of the way is the **Tung Chung Line**, which also offers services every eight minutes. This is designed as a slower commuter line, stopping at five other stations in addition to the AEL stops. It's handy if you're heading for certain destinations in the New Territories, or as a cheaper means into the centre ($23), but you need to take bus #S51 or #S61 from the airport to Tung Chung first ($4).

Another way into the city (and to most hotels) is by **bus**. There are six Airbus routes, and their departure points are clearly signposted in the terminal; the airport customer-service counters sell tickets and give change, while if you pay on the buses themselves you need to have the exact money. All six routes have very regular departures between 6am and midnight, and there's plenty of room

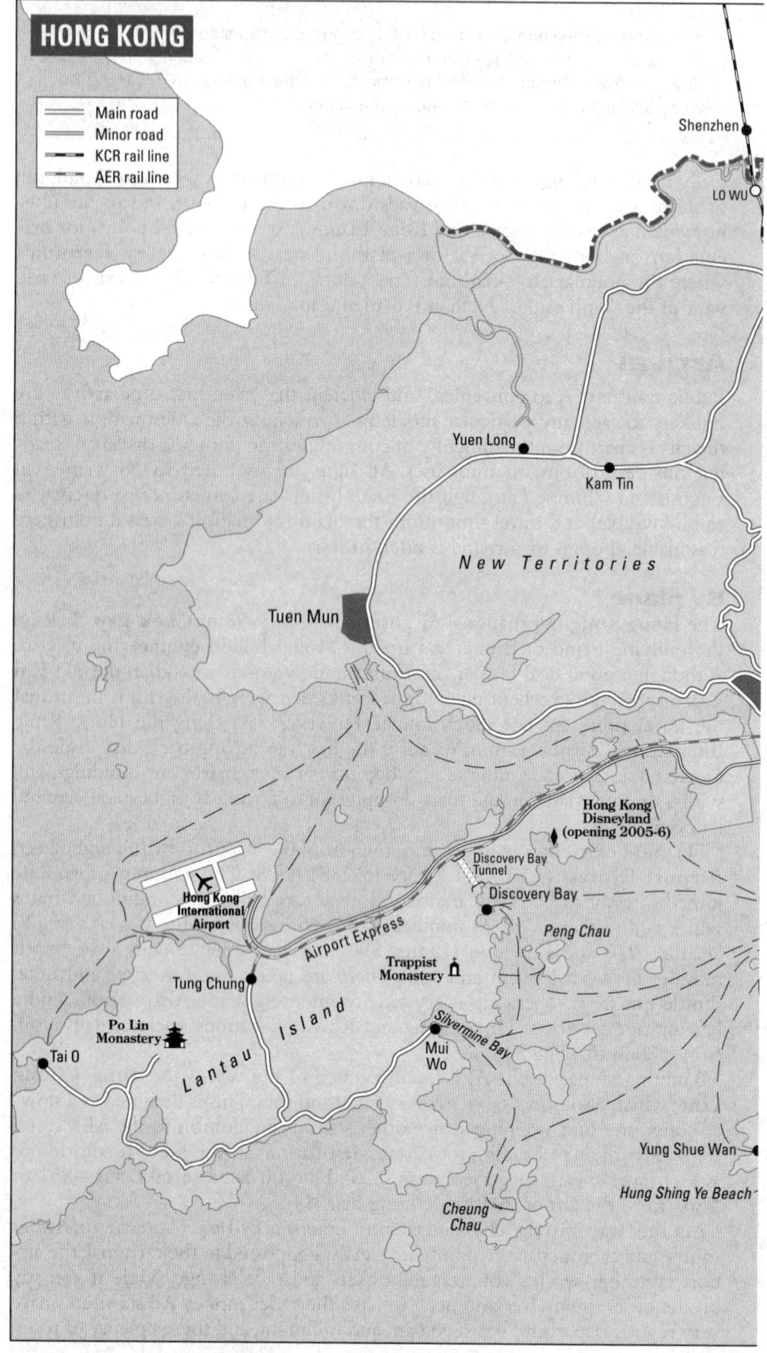
HONG KONG
Main road
Minor road
KCR rail line
AER rail line
Shenzhen
LO WU
Yuen Long
Kam Tin
New Territories
Tuen Mun
Hong Kong
Disneyland
(opening 2005-6)
Discovery Bay
Tunnel
Discovery Bay
Hong Kong
International
Airport
Airport Express
Peng Chau
Trappist
Monastery
Tung Chung
Lantau Island
Silvermine Bay
Mui
Wo
Po Lin
Monastery
Tai O
Yung Shue Wan
Hung Shing Ye Beach
Cheung
Chau

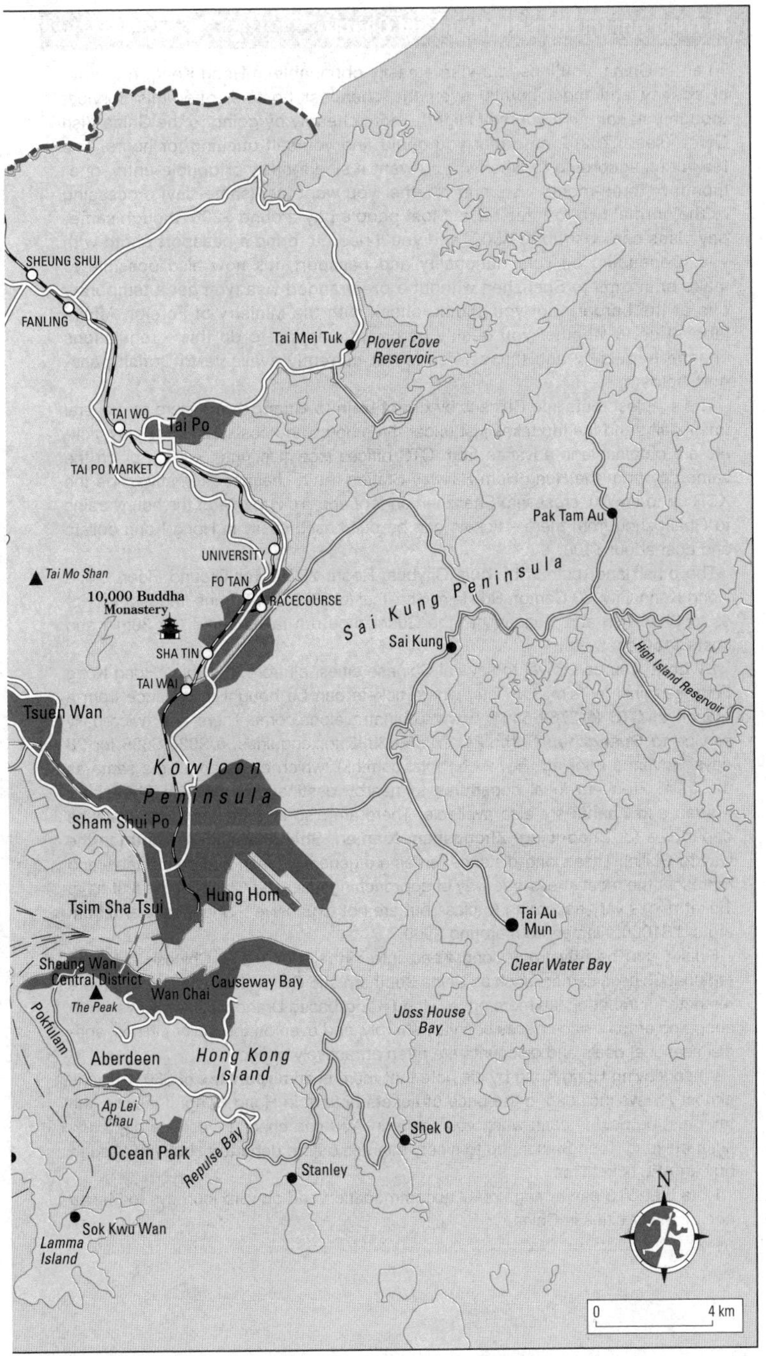
SHEUNG SHUI
FANLING
Tai Mei Tuk
Plover Cove Reservoir
TAI WO
Tai Po
TAI PO MARKET
Pak Tam Au
UNIVERSITY
Tai Mo Shan
FO TAN
10,000 Buddha Monastery
RACECOURSE
Sai Kung Peninsula
Sai Kung
SHA TIN
High Island Reservoir
TAI WAI
Tsuen Wan
Kowloon Peninsula
Sham Shui Po
Hung Hom
Tsim Sha Tsui
Tai Au Mun
Sheung Wan
Central District
Clear Water Bay
Causeway Bay
Wan Chai
The Peak
Pokfulam
Joss House Bay
Aberdeen
Hong Kong Island
Ap Lei Chau
Shek O
Ocean Park
Repulse Bay
Stanley
N
Sok Kwu Wan
Lamma Island
0
4 km

Moving on: routes into mainland China

To enter China, you'll need a **visa** – easily obtainable in Hong Kong. Any travel agency and most hotels, even the cheapest hostels, offer this service, though you can do it yourself slightly more cheaply by going to the China Visa Office (see p.762) – note that you could find yourself queuing for hours. The fee varies according to whether you want a single-entry or double-entry, one-month or three-month visa, and whether you want fast (same-day) processing or the normal two to three days. Most people pay around $200, though same-day visas can cost up to $500, and you'll need to bring a passport photo with you. Depending on your nationality and passport, it's now also possible to make brief trips to Shenzhen without a prearranged visa (you get a temporary one at the border), but you should check with the Ministry of Foreign Affairs (above) as to whether you qualify before attempting to do this – regulations change frequently and this service is not currently available to British passport-holders.

The simplest route into China is by **direct train to Guangzhou**. There are several trains daily, and the trip takes just under three hours and costs $230 one way; tickets are obtainable in advance from CTS offices (see "Listings", p.764), or on the same day from the Hung Hom Railway Station. As a cheaper alternative, ride the KCR up to Lo Wu, cross into Shenzhen on foot and pick up one of the hourly trains to Guangzhou from there – tickets can be purchased easily in Hong Kong dollars and cost about $100.

The other land route is by **bus**. Citybus, Room 28, Lower Ground Floor, China Hong Kong City, 33 Canton Rd, Tsim Sha Tsui (Ⓣ2873 0818), runs frequent services to Shenzhen and Guangzhou; the Guangzhou run takes about 3hr 30min and costs $150 one way.

By **boat**, you can travel to several Chinese cities, all from the China Hong Kong Ferry Terminal in Tsim Sha Tsui, where tickets can be bought in advance from a branch of **CTS** (Ⓣ2789 5401, Ⓦwww.chinatravelone.com). There is a twice-daily service to **Guangzhou** (TurboJet; Ⓣ2859 3333 for enquiries, Ⓣ2921 6688 for 28 days' advance booking, Ⓦwww.turbojet.com.hk), which costs about the same as the train. Frequent local departures to nearby destinations such as **Shenzhen**, **Macau** and **Zhuhai** are also available. There are also less frequent long-distance departures for **Zhaoquing**, **Zhongshan**, **Xiamen**, **Shanghai** and **Wuzhou** (on the way to Guilin). These long-distance ferries are generally clean and comfortable and represent the most stress-free way of approaching mainland China for the first time. Ticket prices vary according to class but are not expensive – Shanghai starts from around $1000, Xiamen from around $500.

Finally, you can **fly** from Hong Kong into virtually all major Chinese cities on regional Chinese carriers such as China Southern and China Northwest, or to a more restricted number on the more pricey Hong Kong-based Dragonair. It's always worth shopping around since prices can vary sharply, and even on the major airlines, special seasonal deals and discounts are often attractively priced.

When leaving Hong Kong by air, note that there is an **airport tax** of $80, which is almost always included in the price of tickets bought in Hong Kong. If it's not, the tax must be paid in cash when you check in. You can check in for your departing flight at Hong Kong Station, up to ninety minutes before departure, but you need to buy an AEL ticket first.

Note that CTS can arrange hotel accommodation and onward journeys to Macau and all major cities in China.

for luggage. The #A11 and #A12 go to Causeway Bay on Hong Kong Island via Sheung Wan, Central, Admiralty and Wan Chai; the #A12 continues to Fortress Hill, North Point Quarry Bay and Tai Koo. Bus #A21 goes to Kowloon KCR station via Tsim Sha Tsui, Jordan, Yau Ma Tei and Tai Kok Tsui (and stops off at Chungking Mansions); #A22 to Kowloon and Lam Tin MTR station via Kwung Tong, Ngau Tau Kok, Kowloon Bay, Kowloon City, To Kwa Wan, Hung Hom and Jordan; #A31 and #A41 go to the New Territories, with #A31 calling at Tsuen Wan MTR station, Kwai Chung Road, Kwai Fong, Tsing Yi Road, and #A41 going to Sha Tin. The average journey time is about an hour. There are also 21 cheaper **city bus** routes, used mainly by local residents, some of which run 24-hour services.

Taxis into the city are metered and reliable (see p.719, for more details). You might want to get the tourist office in the Buffer Hall to write down the name of your destination in Chinese characters for the driver, though they should know the names of the big hotels in English. It costs roughly $290 to get to Tsim Sha Tsui, about $350 for Hong Kong Island. There may be extra charges for luggage and for tunnel tolls – on some tunnel trips the passenger pays the return charge, too. **Rush-hour traffic** can slow down journey times considerably, particularly if you're using one of the cross-harbour tunnels to Hong Kong Island.

The new airport is open 24 hours, unlike Kai Tak, but transport for **early or late flights** can be a problem. Between midnight and 5.50am the rail connections are closed. There are four night bus services, but otherwise you'll have to take a taxi.

By train and bus

The main land route into Hong Kong is by **train**. Express trains from Guangzhou arrive at **Hung Hom Railway Station** (train enquiries ⓣ2602 7799), east of Tsim Sha Tsui, also known as the **Kowloon–Canton Railway Station (or KCR)**. Signposted walkways lead from here to an adjacent bus terminal, taxi rank and – ten minutes around the harbour – the Hung Hom Ferry Pier: for Tsim Sha Tsui, take bus #5C to the Star Ferry; for Hong Kong Island, take the cross-harbour ferry to Wan Chai or Central.

A cheaper alternative is to take a **local train** from Guangzhou to the Chinese border city of Shenzhen, from where you walk across the border to Lo Wu on the Hong Kong side and pick up the regular KCR trains to Kowloon. However, bear in mind that you are likely to queue for anything from ten minutes to two and a half hours before passing through PRC customs, with the longest delays on Fridays, at weekends and public holidays. It's then a fifty-minute ride into central Hong Kong, the trains following the same length of track to Hung Hom station. By **bus** there are regular daily services from Guangzhou and Shenzhen operated by CTS and Citybus (see box); these take about one hour longer than the direct train and arrive in downtown Tsim Sha Tsui (tickets from $100).

By ferry

Arriving by sea is a great way to approach Hong Kong for the first time. There are two important long-distance ferry terminals, one for Macau ferries and one for ferries from other Chinese ports. The **Hong Kong–Macau Ferry Terminal** is in the Shun Tak Centre, on Hong Kong Island, from where the Sheung Wan MTR station is directly accessible (for details on travel to and from Macau, see p.768). The vast, gold-coloured **Hong Kong China Ferry Terminal**, where ferries from Shanghai, Xiamen, Guangzhou, Shekou and

Zhuhai (and a few from Macau) dock, is in the west of Tsim Sha Tsui, just ten minutes' walk from Nathan Road. There is also a berth for international cruise liners at Ocean Terminal in Tsim Sha Tsui.

Information and maps

The **Hong Kong Tourism Board** (HKTB) issues more leaflets, pamphlets, brochures and maps than the whole of the rest of China put together – and you don't have to pay for most of them. They have offices in the arrivals area, buffer halls and transfer area of the airport (daily 8am–6pm) and a 24/7 Cyberlink providing access to their very helpful City of Life website, ⓦwww.DiscoverHongKong.com; HKTB staff walk round trying to find new arrivals even before you find them. In downtown Hong Kong, there are two more offices, for personal callers only, one in Tsim Sha Tsui at the Star Ferry concourse (daily 8am–6pm) and one on the ground floor of The Centre, at 99 Queen's Road Central on Hong Kong Island (daily 8am–6pm, plus a 24/7 cyberlink). The offices are staffed by helpful, trained English speakers, and there's also an HKTB multilingual **visitor hotline** (daily 8am–5pm; ⓣ2508 1234). Check out their monthly programme, promoting the eighteen HKSAR districts in rotation, and *Meet the people*, their publication offering free courses on *feng shui*, Chinese tea and pearl grading, among others.

HKTB **maps**, and the maps in this book, should be enough for most purposes, though more detailed versions such as the paperback *Hong Kong Guide*, which includes all major bus routes, can be bought from English-language bookstores (see "Listings", p.762). HKTB **listings magazines** include the useful *Hong Kong Now!* and *Essential: The Official Hong Kong Guide*, both of which cover all events for the current month, as well as guides to walks, heritage tours, gourmet dining and shopping. Among the unofficial listings magazines, the trendy *HK Magazine* and *BC Magazine* are both free and available in hotels, cafés and restaurants: *HK Magazine* in particular contains excellent, up-to-date information on restaurants, bars, clubs, concerts and exhibitions and offers a free weekly e-mail newsletter (ⓔhk-weekend@asia-city.com.hk).

City transport

Hong Kong's public transport system has been designed to serve virtually the entire population, with the result that it is efficient, fast, comfortable, extremely extensive and relatively cheap.

Trains

The **MTR** (Mass Transit Railway) is Hong Kong's underground train system, comprising four lines, which operate from 6am to 1am. The Island Line (marked blue on maps) runs along the north shore of Hong Kong Island, from Sheung Wan in the west to Chai Wan in the east, taking in important stops such as Central, Wan Chai and Causeway Bay. The Tsuen Wan Line (red) runs from Central, under the harbour, through Tsim Sha Tsui, and then northwest to the new town of Tsuen Wan. The Kwun Tong Line (green) connects with the Tsuen Wan Line at Mong Kok in Kowloon, and then runs east in a circular direction, eventually coming back down south under the harbour to join the Island Line at Quarry Bay. Finally, the Tung Chung Line (yellow) follows much of the same route as the Airport Express, linking Central and Tung Chung.

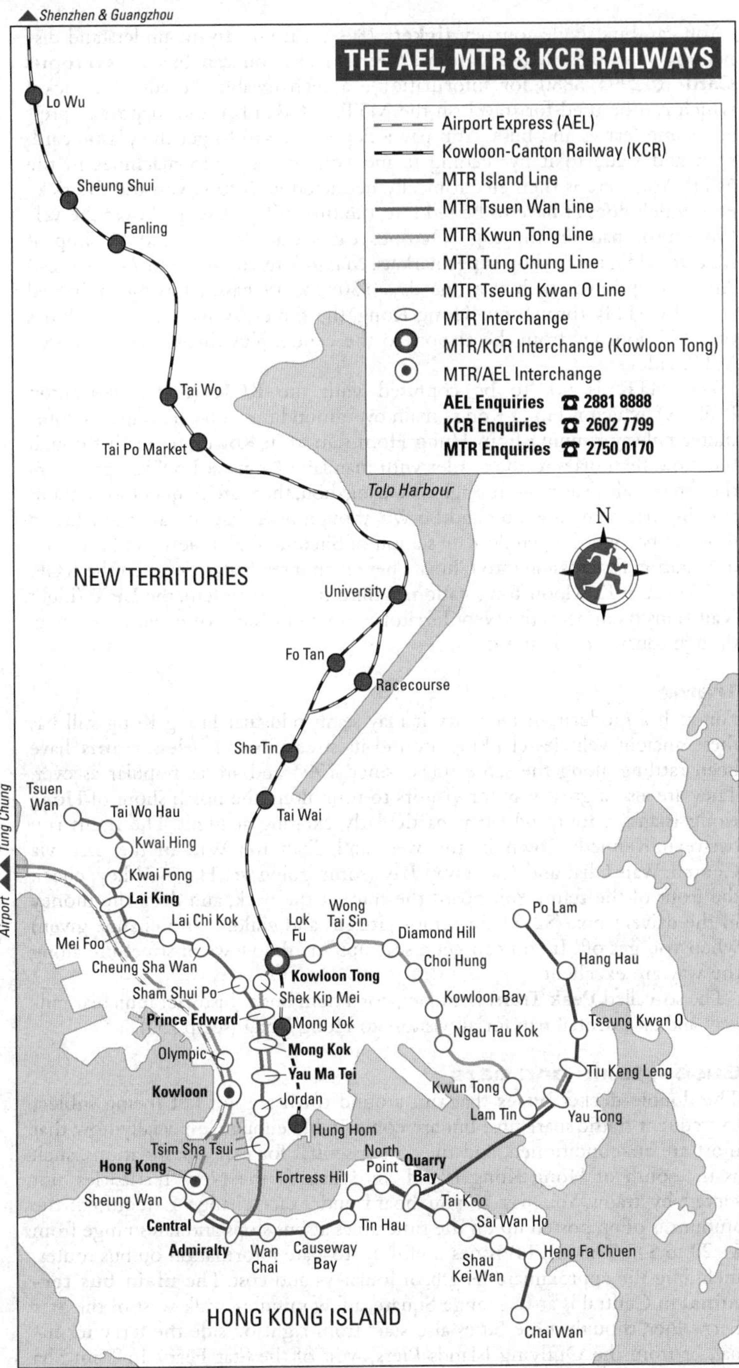
Shenzhen & Guangzhou
THE AEL, MTR & KCR RAILWAYS
Airport Express (AEL)
Kowloon-Canton Railway (KCR)
MTR Island Line
MTR Tsuen Wan Line
MTR Kwun Tong Line
MTR Tung Chung Line
MTR Tseung Kwan O Line
MTR Interchange
MTR/KCR Interchange (Kowloon Tong)
MTR/AEL Interchange
AEL Enquiries 2881 8888
KCR Enquiries 2602 7799
MTR Enquiries 2750 0170
Lo Wu
Sheung Shui
Fanling
Tai Wo
Tai Po Market
Tolo Harbour
N
NEW TERRITORIES
University
Fo Tan
Racecourse
Sha Tin
Tai Wai
Tsuen Wan
Tai Wo Hau
Kwai Hing
Kwai Fong
Lai King
Lai Chi Kok
Mei Foo
Cheung Sha Wan
Sham Shui Po
Prince Edward
Olympic
Kowloon
Tsim Sha Tsui
Hong Kong
Sheung Wan
Central
Admiralty
Wan Chai
Causeway Bay
Tung Chung
Airport
Lok Fu
Wong Tai Sin
Diamond Hill
Choi Hung
Kowloon Bay
Ngau Tau Kok
Kwun Tong
Lam Tin
Kowloon Tong
Shek Kip Mei
Mong Kok
Mong Kok
Yau Ma Tei
Jordan
Hung Hom
Po Lam
Hang Hau
Tseung Kwan O
Tiu Keng Leng
Yau Tong
North Point
Quarry Bay
Fortress Hill
Tin Hau
Tai Koo
Sai Wan Ho
Shau Kei Wan
Heng Fa Chuen
Chai Wan
HONG KONG ISLAND

You can buy single-journey **tickets** ($4–11) from easy-to-understand dispensing machines in the stations. Alternatively, you can buy an **Octopus Card** (☎2993 8880 for information), a rechargeable stored-value ticket which can be used for travel on the MTR, KCR, LRT, the Airport Express and some ferries and buses. You pay a deposit of $50 to get the plastic card, then add value to it by feeding it and your money into machines in the MTR. Your fare is then electronically deducted each time you use the ticket – which doesn't have to be fed into the turnstile, just swiped over the yellow sensor pad on the top. (Octopus cards can also be used to shop at MacDonald's, Parkn'shop supermarkets, Maxim's restaurants and 7-11 stores.) Another option is to buy a one-day ($50) tourist pass, allowing unlimited travel by MTR throughout Hong Kong; the three-day pass ($220) includes one AEL journey from the airport to the centre, plus three days' unlimited MTR rides.

The MTR is not to be confused with the **KCR** (Kowloon–Canton Railway), which is Hong Kong's main overground train line, serving as a commuter railway running from Hung Hom station in Kowloon, north through the New Territories to the border with mainland China at Lo Wu. Apart from the direct trains running through to Guangzhou, there are frequent local trains running between Kowloon and Lo Wu, though note that you are not allowed to travel beyond the penultimate station of Sheung Shui, unless you have documentation for crossing into China. There is an interchange between the KCR and MTR at Kowloon Tong station. A third transport system, the **LRT** (Light Rail Transit) connects the New Territories towns of Tuen Mun and Yuen Long, though tourists rarely use it.

Trams

For such a modern, hi-tech city it may seem odd that Hong Kong still has these ancient vehicles clanking around its streets. Nevertheless, **trams** have been rattling along the same tracks since 1904 and are as popular as ever. They are also a great way for visitors to tour along the north shore of Hong Kong Island, a route which is particularly exciting at night. The trams run between Kennedy Town in the west and Shau Kei Wan in the east, via Central, Wan Chai and Causeway Bay (some going via Happy Valley; check the front of the tram). You board the tram at the back, and drop the money in the driver's box ($2, $1 for senior citizens and children, no change given) when you get off. If you can get a seat upstairs the views of street life along the way are excellent.

The so-called **Peak Tram** is, in fact, not a tram but a (historic) funicular railway and an essential trip for all visitors to Hong Kong (see p.733).

Buses, taxis and cars

The double-decker **buses** that run around town are not fast (being subject to frequent traffic snarl-ups) but are comfortable enough, especially now that most are air-conditioned, and they are essential for many destinations, such as the south of Hong Kong Island, and parts of the New Territories, not served by trains. You pay as you board and exact change is required; the amount is often posted up on the timetables at bus stops and fares range from $1.20 to $45. The HKTB issues useful up-to-date information on bus routes, including the approximate length of journeys and cost. The **main bus terminal** in Central is at Exchange Square, a few minutes' walk west of the Star Ferry Pier, though some buses also start from right outside the ferry terminal, or from the Outlying Islands Piers, west of the Star Ferry. In Tsim Sha

A few important local bus routes

From Central:
#6 and #6A to Stanley via Repulse Bay
#15 to the Peak
#70 to Aberdeen
#90 to Ocean Park

From Tsim Sha Tsui Star Ferry:
#8A and #5C to Hung Hom station
#1 and #1A to Mongkok
#6A to Lei Cheng Uk Han Tomb Museum
#1, #1A, #2, #6, #7 and #9 to Temple Street Night Market

Tsui, Kowloon, the main bus terminal is right in front of the Star Ferry Terminal.

As well as the big buses, there are also ubiquitous cream-coloured **minibuses** and **maxicabs** that can be stopped almost anywhere on the street (not on double yellow lines), though these often have the destination written in Chinese only. They cost a little more than regular buses, and you usually pay the driver as you disembark; change – in small amounts – is only given on the minibuses (which have a red rather than a green stripe). The drivers of either are unlikely to speak English.

Taxis in Hong Kong are not expensive, with a minimum fare of $15, although they can be hard to get hold of in rush hours and rainstorms. Note that there is a toll to be paid (around $5–15, but the amount varies according to the tunnel) on any trips through the cross-harbour tunnel between Kowloon and Hong Kong, and drivers often double this – as they are allowed to do – on the grounds that they have to get back again. Many taxi drivers do not speak English so be prepared to show the driver the name of your destination written down in Chinese. If you get stuck gesture to the driver to call his dispatch centre on the two-way radio; someone there will speak English. It is also obligatory to wear seat belts in Kowloon and on Hong Kong Island.

Car rental is theoretically possible, though unnecessary and highly inadvisable in Hong Kong. Taxis are far cheaper and more convenient, unless you simply have to fork out for a chauffeur-driven limo.

Ferries

One of the most enjoyable things to do in Hong Kong is to ride the humble **Star Ferry** between Kowloon and Hong Kong Island. The views of the island are superb, particularly at dusk when the lights begin to twinkle through the humidity and the spray. You'll also get a feel for the frenetic pace of life on Hong Kong's waterways, with ferries, junks, hydrofoils and larger ships looming up from all directions. You can ride upper deck ($2.20) or lower deck ($1.70). Ferries run every few minutes between Tsim Sha Tsui and Central (an eight-minute ride; daily 6.30am–11.30pm), and between Tsim Sha Tsui and Wan Chai. There are also similarly cheap and fun ferry crossings between Hung Hom and Central and between Wan Chai and Hung Hom (both $5.30).

In addition, a large array of other boats run between Hong Kong and the outlying islands, most of which use the piers immediately north of Exchange Square; see p.747 for details.

Accommodation

Hong Kong boasts a quite colossal range of **hotels and guesthouses**, particularly in the Tsim Sha Tsui area of Kowloon, and you will never fail to find a room if you are prepared to do some traipsing around. At the upper end of the market, you'll find some of the best hotels in the world, such as the legendary *Peninsula*, which is a tourist sight in its own right. At the lower end, most of the options are squeezed into one or two giant blocks on Nathan Road, principally the **Chungking Mansions** and the somewhat more salubrious **Mirador Mansions**. Many of the guesthouses in these buildings have recently been renovated, and most are perfectly clean inside (with TV and air conditioning), in spite of what you might think from the appallingly dirty stairwells and questionable health and safety conditions in the Chungking Mansions. Always check the room to see its size (many rooms are minuscule), whether the shower is separate, whether it has a window and whether you have to pay extra for the use of air conditioning.

Even budget hotel accommodation is not that cheap, however – you'll be lucky to find a room for less than $200, and only if you are willing to sleep in shared **dormitory accommodation** at one of the crowded travellers' hostels will you get down as low as $70–80 a night for a bed. Among the cheapest options is to stay at one of Hong Kong's seven official **youth hostels**, all of which offer excellent conditions and very reasonable dormitory accommodation at around $30–55 if you've got an IYHF membership card, slightly more if you haven't. The most popular of these hostels is the *Mount Davis Youth Hostel* on Hong Kong Island (see p.723); there are four more hostels in the New Territories and two on Lantau Island. The charm of the hostels lies in their rural locations, but the drawback is getting to them in the first place – advance booking, especially at weekends, is essential to avoid wasted journeys. For detailed information on all of them, pick up the free *Member's Handbook* from the head office at Room 225-7, Block 19, Shek Kip Mei Estate, Sham Shui Po, Kowloon (Ⓣ2788 1638, Ⓕ2788 3105, Ⓦwww.yha.org.hk). Otherwise, the Hong Kong Hotels Association (Ⓦwww.hotels-in-hong-kong.com) features deals, packages and offers for all HKHA properties and licensed hostels.

Kowloon

Most of the accommodation listed below is within fifteen minutes' walk of the Tsim Sha Tsui Star Ferry Terminal – conveniently central, though very touristy.

Accommodation price codes

Hong Kong accommodation has been graded according to the following price codes, which represent the **cheapest double room** available to foreigners, except where the text refers specifically to dorm beds when the actual price per person is given. Most places have a range of rooms, and staff will usually offer you the more expensive ones – it's always worth asking if they have anything cheaper. The more upmarket hotels will levy an additional ten percent service charge on top of their quoted room rates. Our price codes are based on the pre-tax rates.

- ❶ Under $80
- ❷ $80–200
- ❸ $200–300
- ❹ $300–500
- ❺ $500–800
- ❻ $800–1200
- ❼ $1200–2000
- ❽ $2000–3000
- ❾ Over $3000

For a less claustrophobic atmosphere you might choose to stay slightly farther out. Places listed represent a fraction of the total on offer, and it is always worth having a look at several options.

Anne Black GuestHouse (YWCA) 5 Man Fuk Rd ⓣ2713 9211, ⓕ2761 1269, ⓔannblack@ywca.org.hk. Not far from the Yau Ma Tei MTR, this YWCA pension is surprisingly smart, light and airy. ❺

Booth Lodge 11 Wing Sing Lane, Yau Ma Tei ⓣ2721 9266, ⓕ2385 1140, ⓦ222.boothlodge.salvation.org.hk. Run by the Salvation Army, immaculately clean and comfortable, with discounts for families and senior citizens. No alcohol allowed on the premises. ❶–❷

Holiday Inn Golden Mile 50 Nathan Rd, Tsim Sha Tsui ⓣ2369 3111, ⓕ2369 8016, ⓦwww.goldenmile.com. A few steps from the Tsim Sha Tsui MTR, this hotel offers the usual excellent facilities from this international chain, including a roof-top swimming pool. The entire hotel was renovated in 1997. Doubles start at around $2000 if you walk in off the street. Telephoning in advance should produce a much better rate. ❼–❾

New King's Hotel 473–473A Nathan Rd, Yau Ma Tei ⓣ2780 1281, ⓕ2782 1833, ⓔnewkings@netvigator.com. Immediately south of the Yau Ma Tei MTR. More than a guesthouse – it occupies the whole building – the *King's* is probably the cheapest "real" hotel in town. On-site coffee shop. Single and double rooms. ❹

The Peninsula Salisbury Rd, Tsim Sha Tsui ⓣ2920 2888, ⓕ2722 4170, ⓦwww.peninsula.com. One of the classiest hotels in the world, which has been overlooking the harbour and Hong Kong Island for nearly seventy years. If you want to be picked up at the airport by a green Rolls-Royce, make a booking here. If not, at least pop in for afternoon tea (see p.755). Rooms start at $2500, but if you really want to stay in this piece of history try checking out some upmarket package tours for a better deal. ❽–❾

The Salisbury YMCA 41 Salisbury Rd, Tsim Sha Tsui ⓣ2268 7000, ⓦwww.ymcahk.org.hk. The location could not be better, right next door to the *Peninsula* and with views over the harbour and Hong Kong Island. There's a very wholesome atmosphere here, though it's slightly sterile compared to the Chungking Mansions. Facilities include indoor pools, fitness centre and a squash court. Four-bed dorms with attached shower are also available, but cannot be reserved in advance. Open to both men and women. A ten percent service charge is added to all room rates. Dorms $210, rooms ❷

Star Guesthouse Flat B, Floor 6, 21 Cameron Rd, Tsim Sha Tsui ⓣ2723 8951. Very clean and friendly, with good English spoken. The rooms with windows and own bath are bright but slightly pricey for what they are; the cheaper rooms have shared bath. Under the same management as the *Lee Garden*. ❸

STB Hostel (HK) Floor 2, Great Eastern Mansion, 255–261 Reclamation St, Yau Ma Tei ⓣ2710 9199, ⓦwww.hkst.com.hk. On the corner of Reclamation and Dundas streets, a few minutes northwest of Yau Ma Tei MTR station. This clean hostel is pleasantly located out of Tsim Sha Tsui, but the dormitories (salubrious three-and-four-bed rooms with attached shower) aren't exactly cheap. Dorms $280, rooms ❸–❹

Victoria Hostel Floor 2, 33 Hankow Rd, Tsim Sha Tsui ⓣ2376 1182. Just west of Nathan Road. If you can cope with his brusqueness and rigid rule-keeping, the Sri Lankan owner of this hostel is honest, very helpful and understanding of budget travellers' needs. He also personally cooks superb low-cost meals for guests. Dorm beds decrease in price the more days you commit yourself to staying. Dorms $130, rooms ❸

Chungking Mansions

Occupying one of the prime sites towards the southern end of Nathan Road at No 40, the Chungking Mansions is an ugly monster of a building, as deep and wide as it is tall, looking just about fit for demolition. The arcades on the lowest two floors are an exotic warren of tiny shops and restaurants mostly patronized by residents from the Indian subcontinent, while the remaining sixteen floors are crammed with budget guesthouses. Above the second floor, the building is divided into five blocks, lettered A to E, each served by two tiny lifts which can carry only a few people at a time. The lifts for blocks A and B in particular, which contain the largest concentration of guesthouses, are often attended by long queues. If you decide to use the stairs instead, be warned that the stairways are dark, damp and dirty. Overall, the guesthouses in the Chungking Mansions are pleasant and cheap, and the atmosphere is a very characterful Sino-Indian mixture, but bear in mind that the whole building is not only claustrophobic, with its endless dingy stairwells and gloomy interiors, but also an undoubted fire and safety hazard. The guesthouses listed below are just a handful of the total.

Chungking House Floors 4 & 5, A Block ⓣ2366 5362, ⓕ2721 3570. The most upmarket place in the whole building, just like a proper hotel, with carpets, air conditioning, TV and even bath tubs. ❹

New Carlton Guesthouse Floor 15, B Block ⓣ2721 0720. Friendly, with good English spoken and spotlessly clean, refurbished rooms on offer. ❷–❸

Payless Guesthouse Flat 2, Floor 7, A Block ⓣ2723 0148. Quite friendly with English spoken. Has clean, tiny doubles with bath. ❷

Rhine Guest House Block A, Floors 11 & 13 ⓣ2367 1991 or 2721 6863. Very friendly, family-run place offering two singles and basic doubles with and without bath. ❷

Tom's Guesthouse Flat 5, Floor 8, A Block ⓣ2722 4956. Under very friendly management, the double and triple rooms here are reasonably bright and very good value. *Tom's* has another branch at Flat 1, Floor 16, C Block ⓣ2722 6035, ⓕ2366 6706, where the rooms are positively salubrious. ❷ & ❸ respectively.

Welcome Guest House Block A, Floor 7 ⓣ2721 7793. A recommended first choice, offering air-conditioned doubles with and without shower. Nice clean rooms, luggage storage, laundry service and China visas available. ❷

Yan Yan Guest House Block E, Floor 8 ⓣ2366 8930. Helpful staff renting out doubles with all facilities; you could sleep three in some at a squeeze, making them pretty good value. ❷

Mirador Mansions

This is the big block at 54–64 Nathan Road, on the east side, in between Carnarvon Road and Mody Road, right next to the Tsim Shat Sui MTR station. Dotted about in among the residential apartments are large numbers of guesthouses. The advantage of Mirador over the Chungking Mansions is that the stairwells and corridors are a lot cleaner, brighter and quieter, and there is no queue for the lifts.

Garden Hostel Flat F4, Floor 3 ⓣ2311 1183. A scruffy but friendly travellers' hang-out, with washing machines, lockers and even a patio garden. Mixed and women-only dorms; beds get cheaper if you pay by the week. Dorms $70.

Man Hing Lung Flat F2, Floor 14 ⓣ2722 0678 or 2311 8807. Run by a helpful, friendly man with good English, this is a clean and recently furbished place, offering both singles and doubles, although the rooms are very small. ❷

Mei Lam Guest House Flat D1, Floor 5 ⓣ2721 5278. The nice, very helpful, English-speaking owner here has very presentable singles and doubles, all spick-and-span and with full facilities. Worth the higher-than-usual prices. ❸

Hong Kong Island

Accommodation on the island is nearly all of the upmarket variety, with just one budget option, the delightful *Mount Davis Youth Hostel*. The *Noble Hostel* in Causeway Bay is another relative bargain.

Bishop Lei International House 4 Robinson Rd, Mid-Levels ⓣ2868 0828, ⓦwww.bishopleihtl.com.hk. A short hop from the escalator, this is one of the few mid-priced hotels in the centre; although the rooms are small, there's a swimming pool. ❻

Garden View International House 1 Macdonnell Rd, Central ⓣ2877 3737, ⓦwww.ywca.org.hk. This YWCA-run place is just off Garden Road, north of the Zoological and Botanical Gardens. Bus #12A from the Admiralty bus terminal runs past. Very salubrious, and the cheapest place in this area of Central. ❻

Grand Hyatt 1 Harbour Rd, Wan Chai ⓣ2588 1234, ⓦwww.hongkong.hyatt.com. Part of the Convention and Exhibition Centre complex (along with the neighbouring, cheaper, *Renaissance Harbour View*). The sumptuous lobby needs to be seen to be believed – luxurious rather than tasteful. Regarded by people in the know as one of the poshest places in town. Doubles from $2600. ❽–❾

Harbour Plaza North Point 665 King's Rd, North Point ⓣ2187 8888, ⓦwww.harbour-plaza

.com/hpnp. This very friendly four-star hotel is opposite the Quarry Bay MTR station, exit C, some twenty minutes by MTR from Central. Excellent value, with kitchenettes in each room, large pool and gym – and they offer visitors a goldfish in their rooms, for company. ❻

Harbour View International House 4 Harbour Rd, Wan Chai ⓣ2802 0111, ⓦwww.harbour.ymca.org.hk. Very close to the Wan Chai Ferry Terminal, and next door to the Arts Centre, this is an excellent place to stay, with good-value rooms starting at the bottom of this category. ❺

Mandarin Oriental 5 Connaught Rd, Central ⓣ2522 0111, ⓦwww.mandarinhotel.com. Considered to be one of the best hotels in the world, the service here is unmatched. The location is also excellent, and the hotel lobby is a great place to people-watch – anyone who's anyone in Hong Kong eats or drinks at the *Mandarin*. The published full room rate is $3200, but seasonal discounts can cut this by half. ❾

Mount Davis Youth Hostel (Ma Wui Hall) Mt Davis Path, Mt Davis ⓣ2817 5715. If you're sick and tired of the hustle of Hong Kong, this is the perfect escape. Perched on the top of a mountain, it has superb views over the harbour and the atmosphere is unbelievably peaceful. The only catch is that getting here is a major expedition: take bus #47A from Admiralty, or minibus #54 from the Outlying Islands Ferry Terminal in Central and get off near the junction of Victoria Road and Mount Davis Path; walk back 100m from the bus stop and you'll see Mt Davis Path branching off up the hill. You can walk up here to the hostel, but it's a long hot walk of around 45 minutes. The sensible alternative if you have luggage is to get off the bus in Kennedy Town and catch a taxi from there (around $50 plus $5 per item of luggage). There is also a hostel shuttle bus ($10) from the bus terminal next to the ground floor of the Shun Tak Centre at the Macau Ferry Terminal, near Sheung Wan MTR station. The shuttle leaves the Shun Tak Centre at 9.30am, 7pm, 9pm, 10.30pm; the return service leaves Ma Wui Hall at 7.30am, 9am, 10.30am, 8.30pm. Conditions in the hostel are excellent, though all guests are expected to carry out one small cleaning task daily. IYHA members pay less. Dorms $95, doubles/family rooms ❶–❷

Noble Hostel Floor 17, Patterson Building, 27 Paterson St, Causeway Bay ⓣ2576 6148, ⓦwww.noblehostel.com. A great place to stay, right in the middle of Causeway Bay, one of the most attractive eating and shopping areas in Hong Kong. Rooms are air-conditioned, immaculately clean and good sizes with private bathrooms, and are available as singles, doubles, triples and quads. ❸–❹

Park Lane 310 Gloucester Rd, Causeway Bay ⓣ2293 8888, ⓦwww.parklane.com.hk. Located slap bang on Victoria Park, the plush *Park* is conveniently sited for the shopping and eating delights of Causeway Bay. ❾

The Wesley 22 Hennessy Rd T2866 6688, ⓦwww.grandhotel.com.hk. A quiet and comfortable, modern hotel with cheap rates for its location. The restaurant isn't great – eat elsewhere. ❻

The New Territories and Outlying Islands

The point of staying in these outer regions is to escape into rural tranquillity where the hubbub is less and prices cheaper. Be warned, though, that at weekends these places are likely to double in price, and may be booked solid anyway. Advance planning is always necessary. However, it's worth contacting the HKTB for information about reliable holiday flats in the Outlying Islands.

Six of Hong Kong's seven official **youth hostels** are here, two on Lantau Island, and four in the New Territories (see p.742). Don't imagine, however, that you can use them as a base for exploring the rest of Hong Kong – they are far too remote, and you are even advised to take your own food with you.

Bradbury Lodge Tai Mei Tuk, Tai Po, New Territories ⓣ2662 5123. Of all the hostels this is about the easiest to get to. Take the KCR train to Tai Po, then bus #75K to Tai Mei Tuk Terminal. Walk south a few minutes, with the sea on your right. Lots of boating, walking and cycling opportunities right by the scenic Plover Cove Reservoir (see p.745). Dorms $85, rooms ❶–❷

Concerto Inn 28 Hung Shing Ye Beach, Yung Shue Wan, Lamma Island ⓣ2982 1668, ⓕ2836 0022, ⓦwww.concertoinn.com.hk. On a relatively isolated and quiet beach, with a delightful terraced restaurant. ❼

Lamma Vacation House 29 Main St, Yung Shue Wan, Lamma Island ⓣ2982 0427. A few minutes' walk from the ferry pier, with Chungking Mansions-sized rooms offering a very cheap way of staying on the island. ❹

Pak Sha O Hostel Pak Sha O, Hoi Ha Rd, Sai Kung, New Territories ⓣ2328 2327. Take bus #94 from Sai Kung (see p.746). Get off at Ko Tong, walk 100m farther on and take Hoi Ha Road on the left – from here it's a forty-minute walk. Great for access to Hong Kong's cleanest, most secluded beaches. Dorms $90

Regal Airport Hotel 9 Cheong Tat Road, Hong Kong International Airport, Chek Lap Kok ⓣ2286 8688, ⓕ2286 8686, ⓦwww.RegalHotel.com. Over eleven hundred sound-proofed rooms with a direct airbridge link to the airport, express check-in, pools and a health club. Look out for special meal and accommodation offers; they often throw in free airport express tickets. ❻–❾

Regal Riverside 34–36 Tai Chung Kiu Rd, Sha Tin ⓣ2649 7878, ⓕ2637 4748, ⓦwww.RegalHotel.com. The New Territories' best hotel – though there's not a lot of competition – right in the centre of Sha Tin, where a double will cost you $680. This comfortable place often appears in holiday packages; there's a fine Asian lunch buffet served here and a free shuttle bus to Tsim Sha Tsui, too. ❺

S. G. Davis Hostel Ngong Ping, Lantau Island ⓣ2985 5610. From Mui Wo (see p.749) take bus #2 to the Ngong Ping Terminal and follow the paved footpath south, away from the Tian Tan Buddha and past the public toilets. It's a ten-minute walk and well signposted. This is a great base for hill walking on Lantau, and you can eat at the nearby Po Lin Monastery. It's cold on winter nights, though – bring a sleeping bag. Dorms $85

Silvermine Beach Hotel 648 Silvermine Bay, Mui Wo, Lantau Island ⓣ2984 8295, ⓕ2984 1907, ⓦwww.asiatravel.com/hongkong/silvermine/reserve.html. Superbly located right on the beachfront, a few minutes' walk from the Mui Wo Ferry Pier. The rooms here are comfortable, quiet and good value – even more so during the week when they are discounted (without the discount, a double will cost you $800). The restaurant spilling out onto the terraces offers popular barbecues and Thai grub. ❹–❻

Warwick East Bay, Cheung Chau ⓣ2981 0081, ⓕ2981 9174, ⓦwww.workshop.com.hk/warwick. Overlooking Tung Wan Beach, this is the most upmarket – if also most expensive – place to stay, with a swimming pool and modest restaurant. Singles and doubles have balconies, private baths, cable TV. There's a forty percent discount on rooms weekdays and during winter. ❾

Hong Kong Island

As the oldest colonized part of Hong Kong, its administrative and business centre, and site of some of the most expensive real estate in the world, **Hong Kong Island** is naturally the heart of the whole territory. Despite its tiny size, just 15km from east to west and 11km from north to south at the widest points, and despite the phenomenal density of development on its northern shore, the island offers a surprising range of **mountain walks** and attractive **beaches** as well as all the attractions of a great city.

On the northern shore of Hong Kong Island, overlooking **Victoria Harbour** and Kowloon on the mainland opposite, are the major financial and commercial quarters of **Central** and **Wan Chai**, which in the last two decades have sprouted several of Asia's tallest and most interesting skyscrapers. To the east is **Causeway Bay**, a shopping and entertainment area, while to the west is **Kennedy Town**, one of the most traditionally Chinese parts of the city, where streets are lined with shops selling dried fish and ancient Chinese medicines. A cliche it certainly is, but whether it be a smoky temple squatting among skyscrapers, or Chanel-dressed shoppers jammed into a smelly fish market, the built-up areas of Hong Kong are a fascinating blend of East and West.

The southern shore of the island, on the other hand, is more notable for its beaches, greenery and small towns, among them **Aberdeen**, in whose harbour you'll still see the traditional barrel-shaped fishing boats (junks) and the smaller sampans, as well as Hong Kong's famous floating restaurants. Meanwhile, the centre of the island rises steeply to a series of wooded peaks. Of these, the most famous, **Victoria Peak**, immediately south of Central district and accessible on the one-hundred-year-old **Peak Tram**, commands superb views of the city and the harbour below.

Central

The area known as **Central** takes in the core of the old city, which was originally called Victoria, after the Queen. It extends out from the Star Ferry Terminal a few hundred metres in all directions, east to the Admiralty MTR, west to the Central Market and south, up the hill, to the Zoological and Botanical Gardens. Starting from the Star Ferry Terminal, the first things you'll see as you emerge are a number of ancient hand-pulled rickshaws and their equally ancient runners who pre-date the time when the last licences were issued. Now they are just there for the tourists, so if you take photos expect to pay for them.

The busy streets of Central are not ideal for walking. Moving inland from the shore, the main west–east roads are Connaught Road, Des Voeux Road and Queen's Road respectively, though pedestrians are better off concentrating on the extensive system of **elevated walkways**. To reach this system from the Star Ferry Terminal, climb the slightly grotty stairs to the west (the right as you come out). Ahead, on the seafront, you will see the newly built **ferry piers for the Outlying Islands**, and beyond them a vast ongoing reclamation project to win yet more precious real estate from the steadily shrinking harbour. Just behind the piers is the **International Finance Centre** building, which also houses the station for the **Airport Express** rail link. Before reaching the International Finance Centre, if you take the walkway to the left and follow it inland, you'll pass right between **Jardine House** (the tall building full of portholes) on your left and **Exchange Square** on your right. Jardine House contains a branch of the HKTA in its basement, while Exchange Square is home to the three gloriously opulent marble-and-tinted-glass towers which house the Hong Kong Stock Exchange. The Exchange Square bus station is located underneath the square. A further branch of the elevated walkway runs northwest from here, parallel with the shore and along the northern edge of Connaught Road, past Exchange Square and all the way to the Macau Ferry Terminal and Sheung Wan MTR; follow this for some great views over the harbour. Otherwise continue across Connaught Road into the heart of an extremely upmarket shopping area, around Des Voeux Road.

Easily recognizable from the tramlines that run up and down here, **Des Voeux Road** used to mark Hong Kong's seafront before the days of reclamation, hence the name of the single smartest shopping mall in the area, the **Landmark**, on the corner with Pedder Street. Of all the shops around here, one definitely worth a visit is **Shanghai Tang**, across Pedder Street from the Landmark, for pricey silver, glass and silk collectibles, and superb designer garments recalling traditional Chinese wear.

The stretch of Des Voeux Road running west from the Landmark is connected by a series of lanes running south to the parallel Queen's Road. Two of these, Li Yuen Street East and Li Yuen Street West, are **markets**, packed out with clothes and fabrics stalls. About 300m from the Landmark, you'll reach the **Central Market** – worth dropping in on during the morning business (if you're not squeamish) for some incredible photo opportunities of poultry, fish and meat being hacked about on a huge scale. Just Southwest of Central Market, leading uphill from Queen's Road Central, is **Graham Street**, one of the great fruit and vegetable markets which still manage to survive and flourish in downtown Hong Kong. Also leading uphill from Queens Road, immediately south of Central Market, is the fantastic **Central-Mid-Levels Escalator**, basically a giant series of twenty escalators which runs 800m straight up the hill as far as Conduit Road servicing the expensive **Mid-Levels**

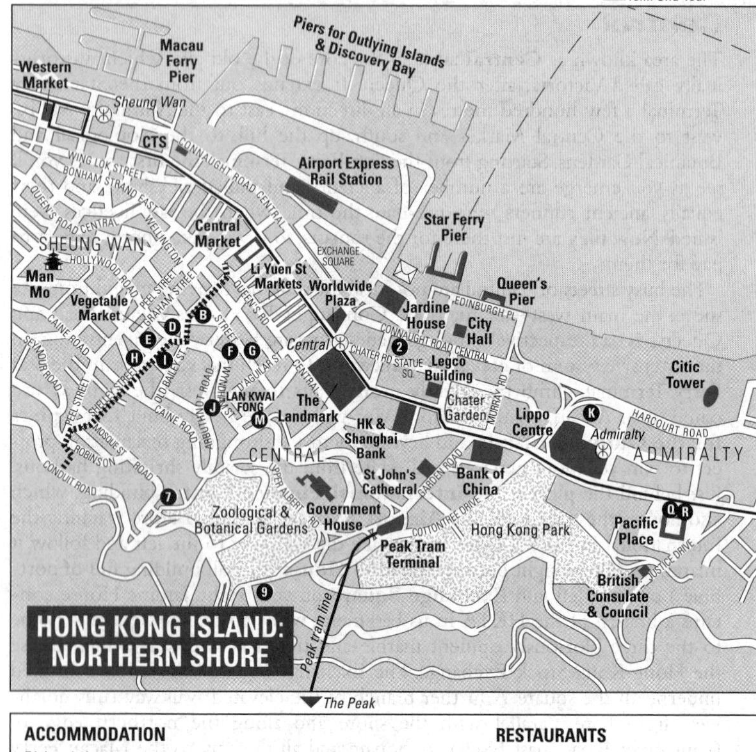

ACCOMMODATION				RESTAURANTS	
Bishop Lei International House	7	Harbour View International House	6	2 Sardines	H
Garden View International House	9	Mandarin Oriental	2	Aqua	D
Grand Hyatt	4	Noble Hostel	5	Banana Leaf Curry House	N
Harbour Plaza North Point	1	Park Lane	3	Chee Kee Wonton Noodle Shop	O
		The Wesley	8	The Chilli Club	S
				Dan Ryan's Chicago Grill	Q

residential area and moving up to 40,000 people a day; it's also given birth to its own "escalator culture", with the blossoming restaurant, bar and café district of **SoHo**. During the morning rush hour (6am–10am), when people are setting out to work, the escalators run downwards only; from 10.20am to midnight they run up. It's well worth riding up to the top to appreciate this quite unique piece of urban public transport. It's also a great way to explore the old streets that run east and west from the escalator.

In the opposite direction from the Landmark, east along Des Voeux Road, you'll find **Statue Square** on your left towards the shore. This is an oddly redundant empty piece of land, divided from east to west in the middle by Chater Road, which was the heart of the late-nineteenth-century colony. Today it is principally used as a picnic area by Hong Kong's tens of thousands of Filippina maids on Sundays, their weekly day off. The ninety-year-old domed, granite building to the east of the square, dwarfed and overlooked by the gigantic modern buildings immediately to the south, is the home of the Legislative Council, Hong Kong's equivalent of a parliament – hence its name, the 1898 **Legco Building**.

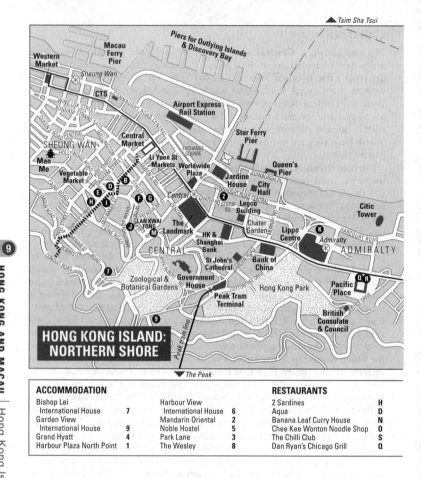

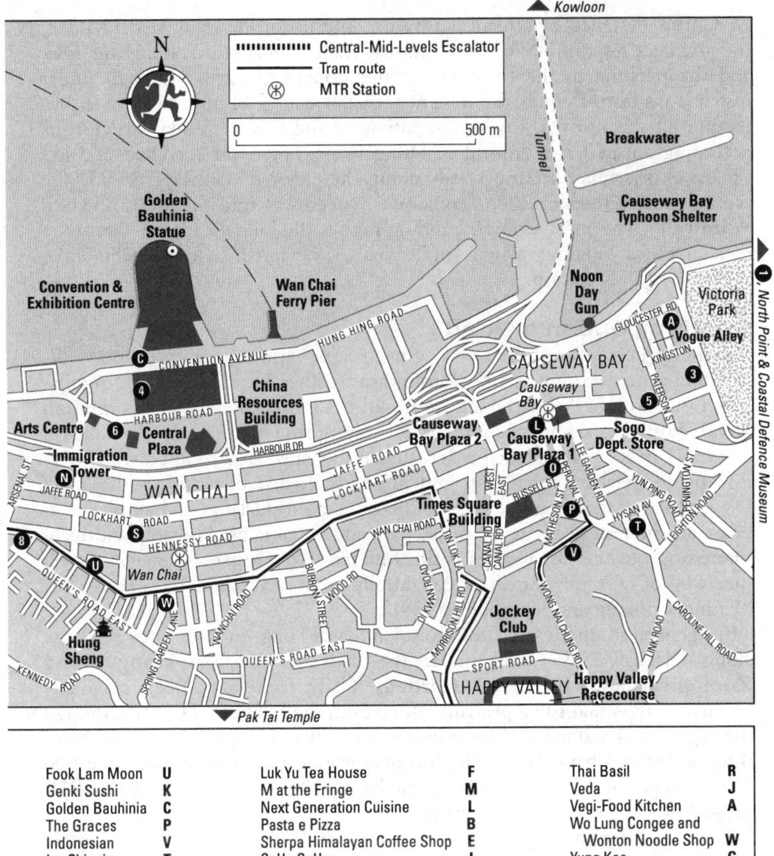

Seawards, the north of Statue Square contains the **Cenotaph** war memorial. An underground walkway connects the square to the Star Ferry concourse to the north.

Immediately south of Statue Square is the magnificently hi-tech **HSBC** building designed by Sir Norman Foster. At the time of its construction in 1985 it was reputedly one the most expensive buildings ever, at a cost of over US$1 billion. At ground level you can see that the whole building is supported on groups of giant pillars and it's possible to walk right under the bank and come out on the other side – a necessity stipulated by the old *feng shui* belief that the centre of power on the island, Government House, which lies directly to the north of the bank, should be accessible in a straight line by foot from the main point of arrival on the island, the Star Ferry. From under the bank the building's insides are transparent, and you can look up, through the colossal glass atrium, into the heart of the building.

East, a couple of hundred metres down the road from the Hong Kong and Shanghai Bank, is the three-hundred-metre, 74-floor blue-glass and steel **Bank**

of China, designed by a team led by the internationally renowned I.M. Pei, the architect responsible for the National Gallery of Art in Washington, DC, and the pyramid in the forecourt of the Louvre in Paris. Although under instructions from Beijing, the designers of this bank had no hesitation in by-passing all the normal *feng shui* sensitivities, and this knife-like structure is accordingly feared and disliked in Hong Kong. For more attractive, and less offensive, skyscraper wizardry, walk along the elevated walkways, or ride the tram, another 200m or 300m east down Queensway into the area known as **Admiralty**. The most striking building here is the bulging **Lippo Centre**, a general office building which you'll pass to the north before reaching the Admiralty MTR station.

South of Queen's Road

South of Queen's Road the land begins to slope seriously upwards, and walking can become extremely laborious in hot weather. Head south up D'Aguilar Street (just west of Pedder Street) from Queen's Road, and you'll enter the **Lan Kwai Fong** area, the main focus for eating and particularly drinking in Central. Lan Kwai Fong itself is actually an L-shaped lane jammed with over-flowing theme bars, restaurants and flower stalls that branches southeast off D'Aguilar Street, though several of the neighbouring lanes and small streets boast an interesting range of snack bars and restaurants. Probably the most interesting of these for visitors is the **Luk Yu Tea House** on Stanley Street (just west of D'Aguilar Street), a delightfully traditional Chinese tea house (see "Eating, drinking and nightlife", p.754).

In a general southerly direction from Lan Kwai Fong – a short but steep walk along Glenealy Street and under the flyover – are the **Hong Kong Zoological and Botanical Gardens** (daily 6am–7pm; free), originally opened in 1864 and still a pleasant refuge from the hubbub of Central, though the caged birds and animals are nothing spectacular. The gardens are cut down the middle by Albany Street, but an underground walkway connects the two halves. To get here direct from the Star Ferry Terminal area, catch buses #3B or #12 heading east along Connaught Road.

North of the gardens, just across Upper Albert Road, **Government House** was the official residence of fifteen Hong Kong governors from 1855 until 1997. Although the present chief executive has chosen not to live here, and uses it only for official entertaining, the house is not open to the public, and the gardens are only open one weekend a year – usually in March. A few hundred metres to the east, and rather more impressive than the Botanical Gardens, is **Hong Kong Park** (daily 6.30am–11pm; free). From the eastern exit of the Botanical Gardens you can walk to the park in about ten minutes along Garden Road. There's also an entrance just to the east of the Peak Tram terminal (see p.733). Otherwise, the main entrance to the park is from the north, on Supreme Court Road; follow signs from Admiralty MTR station, through the Pacific Place shopping mall. The highlight here is the excellent **Edward Youde aviary** which, if you are at all interested in birds, is well worth a visit (daily 9am–5pm, free). Walk around the raised walkways inside the superbly re-created natural environment, and you'll find yourself surrounded by rare birds swooping about, nesting and breeding. At the south (highest) end of the park, there is also a *tai ji* court, while in the north is the **Museum of Tea Ware** (daily except Wed 10am–5pm; free), housed in Hong Kong's oldest surviving colonial building, Flagstaff House, constructed 1844–46, and today incongruously located right in the shade of the Bank of China tower. It's stuffed with 3,000 Chinese artefacts related to tea making.

One other relic of the earliest days of Hong Kong's colonial past is the Anglican **St John's Cathedral**, a little farther north down Garden Road from the Peak Tram terminal. Dating back to 1849, the church is now located in a hillside grove of trees in the lee of skyscrapers.

Wan Chai and Causeway Bay

Stretching away east of Central, the built-up area on the north shore runs for at least 6km and comprises a number of localized centres, of which the two most visited by tourists for nightlife, dining and shopping are **Wan Chai** and **Causeway Bay**. The street layout of both districts is similar to Central, with a number of east–west streets running parallel to the shore. The main street, **Hennessy Road**, is a continuation of Queensway from Central, and carries the tramlines right through the whole area (apart from where they temporarily divert south to Johnston Road). Immediately north of Hennessy Road, and parallel with it, is **Lockhart Road**, while farther north still is the principal east–west highway, **Gloucester Road**, a continuation of Connaught Road. South of Causeway Bay the low-lying area known as **Happy Valley** is home to Hong Kong's racecourse.

MTR trains and trams connect Central with both Wan Chai and Causeway Bay, as do numerous buses, including #2 and #11. Wan Chai is additionally accessible by ferry from Tsim Shat Sui.

Wan Chai

In the 1950s and 1960s **Wan Chai** was known throughout east Asia as a thriving red-light district, catering in particular to the needs of US soldiers on leave from Korea and Vietnam. Hong Kong's most famous fictional character, Suzy Wong, a prostitute from Richard Mason's novel *The World of Suzy Wong*, resided and worked here. Nowadays, however, the soldiers have gone and Wan Chai has lost most of its raunchy air. Nevertheless, the **restaurants** and **bars**, **Chinese shops** and **wet markets** are still certainly worth a visit, but as there aren't any real sights to see, it's probably most interesting to come in the evening.

In the far west of the area, just north of Gloucester Road on the corner of Fenwick Street and Harbour Road, is the **Hong Kong Arts Centre** (ten minutes' walk from Wan Chai MTR), which is worth dropping in on for its art galleries, films and other cultural events. You can pick up a free copy of the monthly magazine *Artslink* here, which has a detailed diary and reviews of what's happening on the art scene in Hong Kong. There are also two good cafés here, both with harbour views.

Immediately to the east of the Arts Centre stands a vast new set of gleaming modern buildings that have changed the face of Wan Chai beyond all recognition. The **Hong Kong Convention and Exhibition Centre** on the seafront at 1 Harbour Road is probably the biggest and best of its kind in Asia and was designed to resemble a soaring hawk. When there are no events going on, you can visit the centre's extraordinary interior, which includes the hall where the official handover ceremonies took place. The centre's extension (the part with the curving roof) was originally designed to be completed for the annual meeting of the World Bank and International Monetary Fund, in September 1997, but the opening date was brought forward to accommodate the handover ceremonies in June 1997. Note that there is a daily flag-raising and -lowering ceremony on **Golden Bauhinia Square** opposite, at 8am and 6pm respectively.

Two upmarket hotels, the *Grand Hyatt* and the *Renaissance Harbour View*, are part of the same complex. Immediately inland, across Harbour Road, soars one of the (currently) tallest edifices in Hong Kong, the 78-storey **Central Plaza**, the golden, glowing cladding of which is visible from far away to the north in Kowloon and which changes colour every fifteen minutes from 6am to 6pm. Catch the lift to the (free) public viewing area on the forty-sixth floor for splendid 360 degree views over the city. You can reach Central Plaza and the Exhibition Centre by walking along raised walkways from Wan Chai MTR station exit A, or from the ferry terminal immediately in front.

In contrast to these hi-tech marvels near the seafront, inland Wan Chai is a solidly functional area packed with residential highrises and shopping streets with just a scattering of curiosities. On 129 Queen's Road East, south of the tramlines on Johnston Road, is the little **Hung Shing Temple**, built into a hillside and alwys open. This old brick building, smoke-blackened and hung with ancient draperies, was once a shrine by the sea; now, rather sadly, it has been marooned far inland by reclamation. There's a tiny flower and bird market opposite the temple, on Tai Wong Road West. A couple of hundred metres east of the Hung Sheng Temple, you'll pass the quaint, whitewashed and unexpectedly ancient **Wan Chai Post Office**, built in 1912 and only closed finally in 1992. A short walk from here, along Stone Nullah Lane running south from Queen's Road East, is the **Pak Tai Temple**, at 2 Lung On Street (daily 8am–6pm), where you can see craftsmen making fantastic little burial offerings out of bamboo and coloured paper, including cars, houses and aeroplanes.

Causeway Bay

Causeway Bay derives its name from the fact that it used to be a bay, until reclamation in the 1950s. Now it is thoroughly earth-based, a colourful, upmarket district packed with shops and restaurants centred around the area between the eastern end of Lockhart Road and the western edge of Victoria Park. Trams run just to the south of here along Yee Wo Street, a continuation of Hennessy Road from Wan Chai. Causeway Bay has an MTR station and is also the point of arrival of the original **cross-harbour tunnel** which carries vehicle traffic over from Kowloon.

The main preoccupation in Causeway Bay is definitely shopping and consumption. Within a couple of minutes of the MTR station you'll find a number of ultra-modern **Japanese department stores**, including Sogo and Mitsukoshi, while slightly to the north is **Vogue Alley**, a lane to the east of and parallel with north–south Paterson Street, which comprises, as its name suggests, a group of fashion boutiques, as well as some restaurants and bars. South of Yee Wo Street the atmosphere is slightly more downmarket, but just as busy, particularly around Jardine's Bazaar and Jardine's Crescent, two alleys almost immediately south of Causeway Bay MTR.

Bang on Causeway Bay MTR (exit A) at Matheson Street lies **Times Square** (Ⓦwww.timessquare.com.hk), two towers constructed in 1993 and packed with themed shopping over sixteen floors. These range from computers to haute couture, a cinema multiplex and four floors of eateries. Look out for the giant outdoor video screen in the piazza, a popular meeting place, offering daily news and weather reports.

Specific tourist sights are thin on the ground here, though you might stroll up to the waterfront to see the **Noon Day Gun** – immortalized in Noel Coward's song *Mad Dogs and Englishmen* – which is fired off with a loud report every day at noon. The Noon Day Gun overlooks the Causeway Bay Typhoon Shelter, which is always jammed full of boats.

The eastern part of Causeway Bay is dominated by **Victoria Park**, a surprisingly extensive space by Hong Kong's standards, which contains swimming pools and other sports facilities. In recent years, this has become the location for the annual candle-lit vigil held on June 4 to commemorate the victims of Tian'anmen Square, in addition to hosting one of Hong Kong's largest lunar New Year fairs. Come early in the morning and you'll see dozens of people practising their *tai ji*. Down at the southeastern corner of the park, right by the Tin Hau MTR (exit A), is the two-hundred-year-old **Tin Hau Temple**, a rather dark, gloomy place surrounded unhappily by highrises (daily 7am–7pm). Tin Hau is the name given locally to the Goddess of the Sea, and her temples can be found throughout Hong Kong, normally in prominent positions by the shore where they were frequented by fishermen and sailors. The fact that temples such as this one have now been submerged in development is a reflection of priorities in modern Hong Kong. You can also reach this Tin Hau Temple on any tram heading for North Point; get off immediately after passing Victoria Park on your left.

Happy Valley

The low-lying area extending inland from the shore south of Wan Chai and Causeway Bay and known as Happy Valley (or Pau Ma Dei) really means only one thing for the people of Hong Kong: horse racing, or, more precisely, gambling. The **Happy Valley Racecourse**, which dates back to 1846, was for most of Hong Kong's history the only one in the territory, until a second course was built at Sha Tin in the New Territories. Hong Kong is gripped by serious gambling fever during the racing season, which runs from September until June, with meetings once or twice a week at Happy Valley. If you're interested in witnessing Hong Kong at its rawest and most grasping, entrance to the public enclosure is just $10 with races almost every Wednesday. Otherwise, enquire at HKTB about their "Come Horse-racing Tour" ($490), which includes transportation to and from the track, entry to the Members' Enclosure and a buffet meal at the official Jockey Club – and tips on how to pick a winner. Happy Valley can be reached from Central or Causeway Bay on a spur of the tramline, or on bus #1 from Central.

Western District

West of Central lies a district rather older and more exotic in character than other parts of Hong Kong. An almost entirely Chinese-inhabited area, its crowded residential streets and traditional shops form a characterful contrast to Central, though the atmosphere has been somewhat diluted by the building of the road network for the **Western Harbour Crossing**, the third cross-harbour road tunnel from Kowloon. Sheung Wan is the largest sub-zone within this area, and like Central it comprises straight east–west roads near the shore, and increasingly meandering roads up the hill away from the harbour. Kennedy Town in the far west is squeezed up against the shore by sharply rising hills and served by tramlines which extend from Central along Des Voeux Road, Connaught Road West, Des Voeux Road West, and finally Kennedy Town Praya.

Sheung Wan, immediately adjacent to Central, spreads south up the hill from the seafront at the modern Shun Tak Centre, which houses the Macau Ferry Terminal (for details of travel to Macau, see p.768) and the Sheung Wan MTR station, for the time being still the last stop on this line. You can reach the Shun Tak Centre by a pleasant fifteen-minute walk along the elevated walkway from Exchange Square in Central, though you'll get more flavour of the district by following the tramlines along Des Voeux Road, west from

Central Market (see p.725). A number of interesting lanes extend south from this stretch of Des Voeux Road, such as Wing Sing Street, which specializes in preserved eggs, and Man Wa Lane very near the Sheung Wan MTR, where Chinese character chops (name stamps) are carved from stone or wood. Another couple of minutes along Des Voeux Road from here brings you to the back end of **Western Market** (daily 10am–7pm), a delightful brick Edwardian-style building on the outside, and since 1991 no longer a stinking market but a mall full of small kitschy kiosks, Chinese food joints, arts, crafts and fabric shops.

A short walk south, up the hill from the harbour, is **Bonham Strand**, which specializes in Chinese medicinal products, teas and herbs. This is a fascinating area for poking around, with shop windows displaying items such as snakes (alive and dead), snake-bile wine, birds' nests, shark fins, antlers and crushed pearls, as well as large quantities of expensive ginseng root. You'll find medicinal shops scattered along an east–west line extending from Bonham Strand to the small **Ko Shing Street** – the heart of the trade – which is adjacent to, and just south of, Des Voeux Road West. This section of Des Voeux Road boasts another long line of extremely exotic shops specializing in every kind of dried food, including sea slugs, starfish, shark fins, snakes and flattened ducks, as well as reeds, sacking and salted fish.

A short but stiff walk up from Bonham Strand leads to the scenically located **Hollywood Road**, running west from Wyndham Street in Central (immediately south of Lan Kwai Fong; see p.728) as far as the small Hollywood Park in Sheung Wan, where it runs into Queen's Road West. Bus #26 takes a circular route from Des Voeux Road in Central to the western end of Hollywood Road, then east again along the whole length of the road. The big interest here is the array of **antique, arts and crafts and curio shops**, and you can pick up all sorts of oddities, from tiny embroidered women's shoes to full size traditional coffins. The antique shops extend into the small alley, Upper Lascar Row, commonly known as **Cat Street**, which is immediately north of the western end of Hollywood Road and due south of the Sheung Wan MTR. Here you'll find wall-to-wall curiosity stalls with coins, ornaments, jewellery, Chairman Mao badges and chops all on sale. There's even an air-conditioned mall, the Cat Street Galleries, offering more serious antiques in more salubrious surroundings.

Another attraction in the Cat Street area is **Ladder Street**, which runs north–south across Hollywood Road and is, almost literally, as steep as a ladder. This is a relic from the nineteenth century when a number of such stepped streets existed to help sedan-chair carriers get their loads up the steep hillsides. On 170 Hollywood Road adjacent to Ladder Street, the 150-year-old **Man Mo Temple** (daily 10am–6pm) is notable for its great hanging coils of incense suspended from the ceiling. The two figures on the main altar are the Taoist gods of Literature (Man, or Cheung) and the Martial Arts (Mo, also known as Kwan Tai). Located as it is in a deeply traditional area, this is one of the most atmospheric small temples to visit in Hong Kong.

You'll find a group of smaller temples a few minutes southwest of Hollywood Road on **Tai Ping Shan Street**, which you can reach by climbing a little way south up Ladder Street and taking the second lane on the right. This was one of the first areas of Chinese settlement in Hong Kong, and the temples are still very much part of the fabric of the neighbourhood, and are in daily use.

Kennedy Town, oddly named after an early governor of the colony, is the farthest west point of the built-up area on the northern shore and was for many years a busy town of crumbling old streets facing an old harbour jammed with green and red painted barges. There are still traces of character in

Kennedy Town, though land reclamation and development has removed the old markets and the junks which used to moor in the harbour. The final terminus of the tramline from Central is here.

The Peak

The uppermost levels of the 552-metre Victoria Peak that towers over Central and Victoria harbour have always been known as **the Peak** and, in former colonial days, the area was populated by upper-class expats, mostly living in expensive houses paid for by their employers or (in the case of civil servants) the government. Meanwhile, the vast mass of the population lived down below, where the climate was hotter, more humid and less healthy. The story of the colonization of what was originally a barren, treeless rock is an extraordinary one. Before 1859, when the first path up to the Peak was carved out, it was barely possible to get up here at all, let alone put houses on it. And yet within twenty years, a number of summer homes had been built for a wealthy minority of British merchants, who sought out the higher levels as a way of escaping the heat and malaria of the seafront in summer. Incredible though it is to imagine now, everything – from human beings to building materials – was carried laboriously up the hill by coolies.

The idea of building a rail link to the top of the Peak was originally scoffed at when first proposed, because the gradients were considered impossibly steep. In 1888, however, this all changed with the successful opening of a **funicular railway** known as the Peak Tram, which allowed speedy and regular connections to the harbour. The mountain began to be transformed with the planting of trees as well as the construction of a regular summer village. By 1924, when the first road to the Peak was built, permanent homes had begun to appear, though Chinese were not allowed to set up home here until much later. Now, anyone can live here who can afford it – and these days that usually means Chinese tycoons. Aside from its exclusive residential area, the Peak is still a cool, peaceful retreat from the rigours of downtown and a vantage point offering some extraordinary panoramic views over the city and harbour below.

Ascending the Peak

Ascending the Peak is half the fun, assuming you plan to ride the **Peak Tram**. The track is incredibly steep and at times you'll feel that you are practically lying on your back in your seat as the tram climbs the 386 vertical metres to its terminus. The journey takes about eight minutes, and there are actually some intermediate stations on the way, in Mid-Levels, though tourists are not likely to bother with these.

To find the Peak Tram terminal in Central, the easiest solution is to catch the free shuttle bus (Mon–Sat 10am–8pm, Sun 10am–9pm) from outside the Star Ferry Terminal. On foot it's not a particularly convenient place to get to – it's on Garden Road a little way south of St John's Cathedral (see p.729). The Peak Tram itself (daily 7am–midnight; $20 single, $30 return; you can also pay with your Octopus card) runs every ten to fifteen minutes, and you can also use the shuttle bus back to the Star Ferry afterwards, provided you still have your Peak Tram ticket.

If you have an irrational fear of funicular railways, you can catch **bus** #15 or #15B to the Peak from Exchange Square and Tin Hua MTR respectively – the views are just as good, but it takes a lot longer. Fitness fanatics can **walk** up if they wish, though for most people walking down is a more realistic option. See below for routes.

On and around the Peak

The Peak Tram drops you right below the wok-shaped **Peak Tower**, featuring the Peak Galleria shopping mall full of souvenir shops and pricey bars and cafés with spectacular view and several terraces commanding a vast panorama. There's also a range of indoor entertainments, should the heavens open. These include a high-tech virtual reality show, the Peak Explorer, plus branch of Madame Tussauds with about one hundred wax models, from Arnie Schwarzenegger to Jacky Chan, and Ripley's Believe-It-Or-Not! Odditorium. There's also a Moevenpick Marche restaurant offering decent self-service grub in addition to the view. Virtually opposite here is the historic **Peak Lookout**, a traditional place with rattan chairs and fans that, despite changing hands and undergoing some modernization, still has a great outdoor terrace where you should definitely enjoy at least one cold beer (see "Eating, drinking and nightlife", p.754).

From the Peak Tram terminal area, you'll see four roads leading off to the west and north. Of these, the middle one, Mount Austin Road, leads up to the very top of the Peak where you'll find the Victoria Peak Garden, formerly the site of the governor's residence. Two of the other roads, however, make a much more attractive walk, since they form a circuit around the Peak that takes about an hour on foot. Harlech Road (leading due west) is a delightfully shady, rural stroll through trees with a picnic area en route. After half an hour the road runs into Lugard Road, which heads back towards the terminal around the northern rim of the Peak, giving magnificent views over Central and Kowloon. The fourth road, Old Peak Road, leads down to the May Road tram station.

An excellent way to descend the Peak is to walk, along one of a number of possible **routes down**, the simplest being to follow the sign pointing to Hatton Road, from opposite the picnic area on Harlech Road. The **walk** is along a very clear path all the way through trees, eventually emerging in Mid-Levels, after about 45 minutes, near the junction between Kotewall Road and Conduit Road. Catch bus #13 from Kotewall Road to Central, or you can walk east for about 1km along Conduit Road until you reach the top end of the Mid-Levels Escalator (see p.725), which will also take you into Central. Another good route down is to take a road leading from Harlech Road, not far from the Peak Tram, signposted to **Pokfulam Reservoir**, a very pleasant spot in the hills. Beyond the reservoir, heading downhill, you'll eventually come out on Pokfulam Road, from where there are plentiful buses to Central, or south to Aberdeen.

Hong Kong Island: the southern and eastern shores

On its south side, Hong Kong Island straggles into the sea in a series of dangling peninsulas and inlets. The atmosphere is far quieter here than on the north shore, and the climate reputedly warmer and sunnier. You'll find not only separate towns such as **Aberdeen** and **Stanley** with a flavour of their own, but also beaches such as that at **Repulse Bay** and, much farther east, at the remote little outpost of **Shek O**. Especially if you're travelling with children you should consider a visit to **Ocean Park**, a huge adventure theme park with a wonderful aquarium, just beyond Aberdeen. Buses are plentiful to all destinations on the southern shore, and Aberdeen is linked to Central by a tunnel under the Peak. Nowhere is more than an hour from Central.

Aberdeen

Aberdeen is the largest separate town on Hong Kong Island, with a population of more than sixty thousand, a dwindling minority of whom still live on

sampans and junks in the narrow harbour – and typhoon shelter – that lies between the main island and the island of Ap Lei Chau. The boat people who live here are following a tradition that certainly preceded the arrival of the British in Hong Kong, though, sadly, it now seems that their ancient way of life is facing extinction. In the meantime, a time-honoured and enjoyable tourist activity in Aberdeen is to take a tour around the harbour on one of the surviving sampans.

You won't get lost in Aberdeen. From the bus stop just head in the direction of the shore and cross over the main road using the footbridge, where women will be waiting to solicit your custom for a **sampan tour**. Either do a deal with one of these private entrepreneurs, or walk along the ornamental park by the waterfront until you reach a sign advertising "Water Tours" ($50 per head for a thirty-minute ride, irrespective of the number of travellers). The trip offers great photo opportunities of the old houseboats jammed together, complete with dogs, drying laundry and outdoor kitchens, as well as endless rags, nets and old tyres. Along the way you'll also pass boat yards and the three **floating restaurants**, which are especially spectacular when lit up at night (though they are really better for admiring from the outside than for eating in; see "Eating, drinking and nightlife", p.753).

To reach Aberdeen, catch **bus** #70M or #970 from Exchange Square, in Central (15min) or Admiralty bus terminus (20min). There's also a **boat** connection between here and nearby Lamma Island (see p.747).

Ocean Park

Ocean Park, a gigantic theme and adventure park (daily 10am–6pm; $180, children aged 3 to 11 $90, children under 3 free; ⓣ2552 0291, ⓦwww.oceanpark.com.hk), covers an entire peninsula to the east of Aberdeen. The price of the ticket is all-inclusive, and once you're inside all rides and shows are free. You could easily spend the best part of a day here, and at weekends in summer you may find yourself frustrated by queues at the popular attractions, so make sure you arrive early in order to enjoy yourself at a relaxed pace. The park is divided into a number of sections joined together by wacky transportation facilities, and new attractions are being added all the time. One of the most popular is a pair of Giant Pandas, An-An and Jia-Jia, for whom a special $80-million, 2,000-square-metre complex has been created, complete with kitchen, clinic, fake mountain slopes and misting machines to mimic a mountain atmosphere.

The first section you will reach is the Lowland section, which is devoted to the wonders of nature – and includes some superb life-size, moving dinosaur models and a butterfly house – there's a peaceful 1.5-kilometre **cable car ride** to the Headland section at the tip of the peninsula. This is the area where you'll find one of the fastest and longest **roller coasters** in the world and other scary rides such as the **Abyss** turbo drop. There's also an **aquarium** where you can view **sharks** nose-to-nose through glass, and the so-called Ocean Theatre, where trained **dolphins and whales** perform, plus the **Atoll Reef**, a huge coral reef aquarium, which contains more than five thousand fish. From the Headland you can then ride an enormous escalator down to **Middle Kingdom**, actually a separate park though covered by the same ticket, which aims to re-create five thousand years of Chinese history through architecture, crafts, theatre and opera. In addition, Ocean Park offers evening dinner shows, "The Glory of the Forbidden City" three times a week. All in all it's great value for an extraordinary amount of entertainment.

A special bus service runs from the Star Ferry Pier in Central and from Admiralty MTR to Ocean Park approximately every fifteen minutes from 9am to 6.30pm daily (the all-inclusive ticket covering the return bus ride and the park entrance fee is $204, children $102, with one child free for each adult). If you prefer local buses, the #6 minibus runs from the Star Ferry to Ocean Park (Mon–Sat); otherwise take bus #70 or #90 from Central, or #72 from Causeway Bay, and get off immediately after the Aberdeen Tunnel and follow the signs. On Sundays, buses #90 from Central and #73 from Stanley/Repulse Bay stop right by the park.

Deep Water Bay, Repulse Bay and beyond

Two bays with names ringing of adventure on the high seas, **Deep Water Bay** and **Repulse Bay**, line the coast east of Ocean Park. Unfortunately the water in this area can be quite polluted, while on summer weekends and public holidays the beaches are jam packed with tens of thousands of people. Of all the bays on the south coast, Repulse Bay is the most popular, partly because it contains a number of shops and restaurants, but also because of its Tin Hau Temple which has a longevity bridge, the crossing of which is said to add three days to your life. The backdrop to Repulse Bay is slightly bizarre with an enormous, garish tower silhouetted against verdant hills. In front of it is what remains of the *Repulse Bay Hotel*. Sadly this historic hotel was torn down in the 1980s; what carries the name now is in fact a restaurant and shopping complex. South of Repulse Bay, you'll find **Middle Bay** and **South Bay**, fifteen and thirty minutes farther along the coast. These offer more secluded but narrower beaches.

You can reach Repulse Bay on **buses** #6, #61 or #260 from Exchange Square, in Central. Between Aberdeen (to the west) and Stanley (to the east) there are frequent buses that pass all of the bays mentioned above; sit on the right hand side of the upper deck for an exhilarating ride along the twisting roads.

Stanley

Straddling the neck of Hong Kong's most southerly peninsula, **Stanley** is a moderately attractive residential village, of which perhaps the main draw is the bustling covered market, the clutch of pubs and restaurants catering to expatriates and colonial **Murray House**. However, the annual Dragon Boat Races on the fifth day of the fifth month of the lunar calendar are Hong Kong's largest and are great fun. Stanley's a tiny place – walk downhill from the bus stop and you'll soon find **Stanley Market** (selling a mish-mash of beaded and sequinned outfits, cheap clothing, bedlinen, prints and tourist souvenirs), while a little way to the north of here is **Stanley Beach** which, although not suitable for swimming, has a little row of great seafront restaurants. If you continue walking beyond the restaurants, you'll come to another **Tin Hau Temple**, built in 1767, on the western side of the peninsula. Inside there is a large tiger skin, the remains of an animal shot near here in 1942 – there could hardly be a more poignant symbol of how the area has changed. The temple is surrounded by Stanley Plaza, replete with shops, a village square and **Murray House** on the shoreline. One of Hong Kong's oldest colonial buildings, this two-storey mansion was dismantled and removed from its original site in Central to make way for the Bank of China. Today, its colonnades house stylish stores, bars and restaurants, as well as a basement exhibition about its history. In the opposite direction, south down the peninsula along Wong Ma Kok Road, it's about a ten-minute walk to the fairly pleasant St Stephen's Beach, accessible by steps down to the right immediately after a playing field. Beyond here is **Stanley Military Cemetery**, on Wong Ma Kok Road, containing the graves of many of those killed fighting the Japanese in World War II, and also the top-security Stanley Prison. The southern part of the peninsula is a closed military zone. Stanley is accessible on **buses** #6 and #260 from Central, or #73 from Aberdeen or Repulse Bay.

Shek O

In the far east of the island, **Shek O** is Hong Kong's most remote settlement and, incredibly, it still gives the feeling of being "undiscovered", if such a thing is possible in Hong Kong. There's a strong surf beating on the wide, white **beach**, which has a shady area of vine trellises at one end for barbecues and, during the week, is more or less deserted. Come for sunbathing and lunch at one of the cheap local restaurants. It's also a popular hiking spot with breathtaking views; if you're interested, the HKTB can provide you with information about walking part of the Hong Kong Trail along the D'Aguilar peninsula.

You can't miss the beach – it's just a few minutes' walk east from the bus stop, beyond a small roundabout. For a small detour through the village, however, stop at the excellent Thai restaurant with outdoor tables and chairs that you see on your left just before the roundabout. If you take the small lane left running right through the restaurant area, you'll pass first the local temple and then a variety of shops and stalls.

Reaching Shek O in the first place is one of the best things about it. First you need to get to **Shau Kei Wan** on the northeastern shore of Hong Kong Island, either by tram or MTR. From the bus terminal outside the MTR station, catch bus #9 to Shek O, a great journey over hills (30min) during which you'll be able to spot first the sparkling waters of the Tai Tam Reservoir, then Stanley (far to the southwest) and finally Shek O itself, appearing down below like a Mediterranean village on the shore. Shau Kei Wan MTR is also the stop-off for the splendid **Coastal Defence Museum**, located at the 1887 Lei Yue Mui Fort (exit B1, walk ten minutes up Shau Kei Wan Street East, then along Tun Hei Road; daily except Wed 10am–5pm). This offers a history of Hong Kong's coastal defence from the Ming dynasty to the handover; there are also good walks around the rocks and to the shore.

Kowloon

A four-kilometre strip of the mainland grabbed by the British in 1860 to add to their offshore island, **Kowloon** was part of the territory ceded to Britain "in perpetuity" and was accordingly developed with gusto and confidence. With the help of land reclamation and the diminishing significance of the border between Kowloon and the New Territories at Boundary Street, Kowloon has over the years just about managed to accommodate the vast numbers of people who have squeezed into it. Today, areas such as Mong Kok, jammed with soaring tenements, are among the most densely populated urban areas in the world.

While Hong Kong Island has mountains and beaches to palliate the effects of urban claustrophobia, Kowloon has just more shops, more restaurants and more hotels. It's hard to imagine that such an unmitigatedly built-up, crowded and commercial place as this could possibly have any cachet among the travelling public – and yet it does. One of the reasons is that this is the best place for viewing Hong Kong Island. The **view** across the harbour to the island, wall-to-wall with skyscrapers, is one of the most unforgettable city panoramas you'll

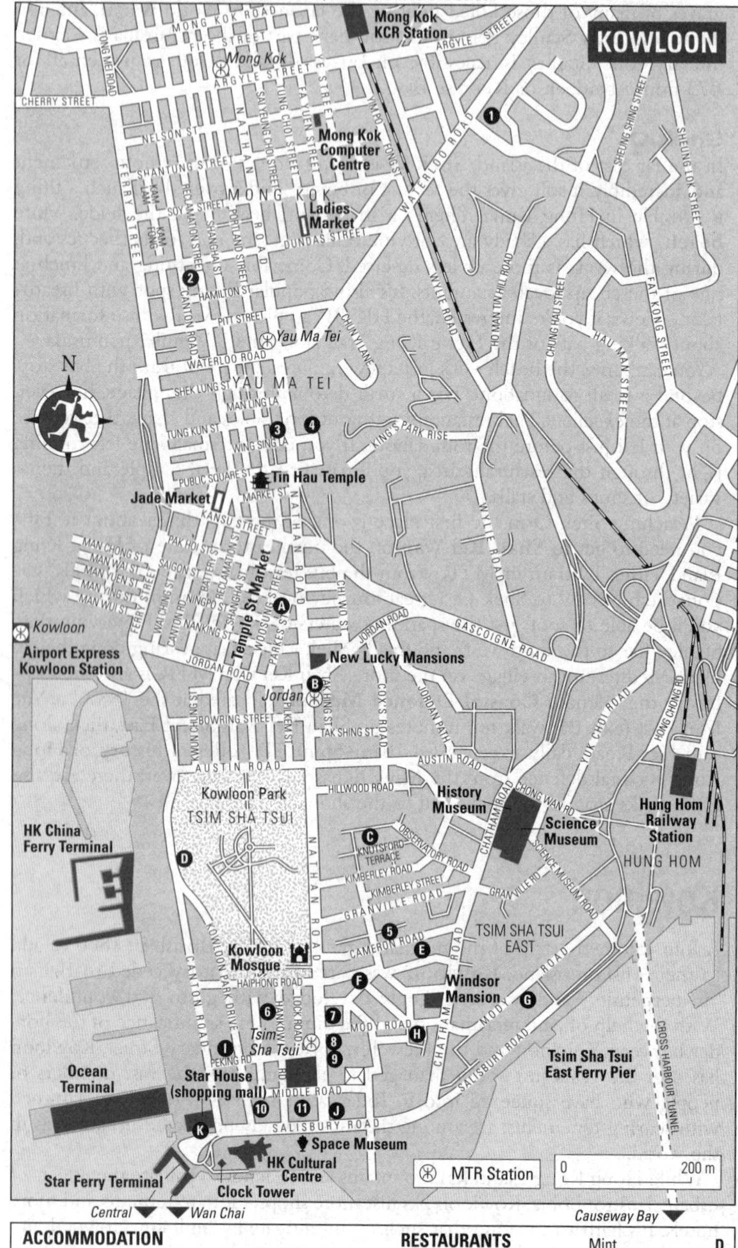

ACCOMMODATION

- Anne Black Guesthouse (YWCA) 1
- Booth Lodge 4
- Chungking Mansions 9
- Holiday Inn Golden Mile 8
- Mirador Mansions 7
- New King's Hotel 3
- Peninsula 11
- Salisbury YMCA 10
- Star Guesthouse 5
- STB Hostel (HK) 2
- Victoria Hostel 6

RESTAURANTS

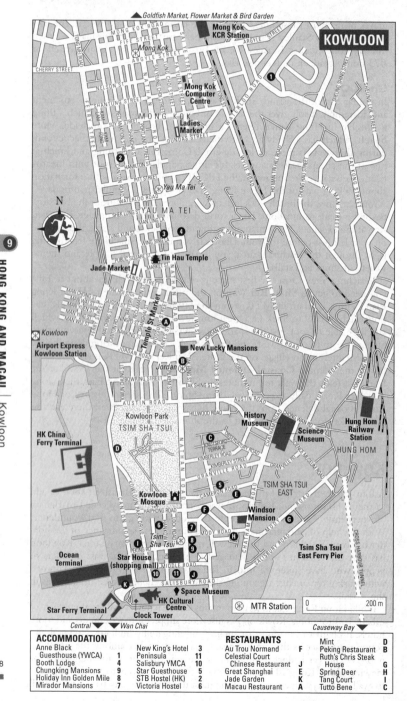

- Au Trou Normand F
- Celestial Court Chinese Restaurant J
- Great Shanghai E
- Jade Garden K
- Macau Restaurant A
- Mint D
- Peking Restaurant B
- Ruth's Chris Steak House G
- Spring Deer H
- Tang Court I
- Tutto Bene C

see anywhere, especially at night. This, and its ritzy neon-lit streets full of hotels and restaurants in the couple of square kilometres at the tip of the peninsula that make up **Tsim Sha Tsui** are enough to keep drawing in the crowds. A further attraction of Tsim Sha Tsui is the presence of a very visible community of immigrants from the Indian subcontinent. Their great stronghold is the **Chungking Mansions**, which, as well as being a **budget accommodation** haven, is a superbly atmospheric shopping arcade where the great cultures of Asia mingle in a haze of spices and incense.

North, into **Yau Ma Tei** and **Mongkok**, you'll find less touristy districts teeming with local life, while farther north still, beyond Boundary Street – technically just outside Kowloon – is a scattering of sights including one of Hong Kong's busiest temples, the **Wong Tai Sin**.

Tsim Sha Tsui and beyond

The tourist heart of Hong Kong, **Tsim Sha Tsui**, is an easy place to find your way around. The **Star Ferry Terminal**, for ferries to Hong Kong Island, is right on the southwestern tip of the peninsula. East of here, along the southern shore, facing Hong Kong Island, are a number of hi-tech, modern museums and galleries built on reclaimed land, while the main road just to the north of these is **Salisbury Road**, dominated by the magnificently traditional **Peninsula Hotel**. Running south to north right through the middle of Tsim Sha Tsui, and on through the rest of Kowloon, is Hong Kong's most famous street, **Nathan Road**, jammed with shops and shoppers at all hours of the day and night. All the streets immediately to the east and west of here are likewise chock-a-block with small traders.

Given the brash speed of change in this area, it's almost a miracle to find anything more than a few years old here. Nevertheless, there are a handful of relics surviving from earlier times, one of these being the **Clock Tower**, about 100m east of the Star Ferry Terminal. The tower is the only remaining piece of the original Kowloon Railway Station which was demolished in 1978. In the old days, you could take a train from here all the way back to Europe, via Mongolia and Russia. The seafront **promenade** runs east from here, giving fantastic views over Hong Kong Island, particularly popular at night when people come to stroll, sit, roller-skate and fish.

Between the western section of the promenade and Salisbury Road to the north, is a series of buildings which cynics might regard as Tsim Sha Tsui's desperate attempt to acquire a more cultured image. The distinctive winged, ski-slope roofline of the **Hong Kong Cultural Centre**, which occupies the former site of the Kowloon Railway Station, is unmissable. Inside there are concert halls, theatres and galleries including, in an adjacent wing, the **Hong Kong Museum of Art** (Mon–Wed, Fri & Sat 10am–6pm, Sun 1–6pm; $20), which is definitely worth a visit. As well as calligraphy, scrolls and an intriguing selection of paintings covering the history of Hong Kong, the museum houses an excellent Chinese antiquities section which has far more informative English labels than comparable museums in China. For up-to-date information on events in the Cultural Centre, pop into the foyer for a brochure.

Immediately to the east of the Cultural Centre, the domed **Hong Kong Space Museum** (Mon & Wed–Fri 1–9pm, Sat & Sun 10am–9pm; $10) houses some highly user-friendly exhibition halls on astronomy and space exploration. The highlight here, however, is the planetarium, known as the **Space Theatre**, which presents amazing wide-screen space shows for an additional fee ($32, concessions $16; call ⓣ2734 2722 for show times).

Salisbury Road, running east–west immediately north of the Cultural Centre, is patrolled by Rolls Royces, many of them belonging to the chauffeur-driven fleet of the **Peninsula Hotel**. Before reclamation pushed the shore a couple of hundred metres south, the *Peninsula* commanded a view directly across the harbour to the island. By way of compensation for having lost its view, however, the *Peninsula* became the first building in Kowloon to exceed the old twenty-storey height limit imposed on development, with its new wing towering up at the back. Needless to say, rooms are pricey, but it's worth dropping by for lunch or afternoon tea in the foyer if you are not looking too scruffy.

Immediately east of the *Peninsula*, running north from Salisbury Road, is the neon-lit **Nathan Road**, which dominates the commercial heart of Kowloon. While by no means a beautiful street, it's one you'll find yourself drawn to again and again for Hong Kong's most concentrated collection of electronics shops, tailors, jewellery stores and fashion boutiques. The variety of goods on offer is staggering, but the southern section of Nathan Road, known as the Golden Mile for its commercial potential, is by no means a cheap place to shop these days, and tourist rip-offs are all too common (for more details, see "Shopping", p.757). One of the least salubrious but most exotic corners of Nathan Road is the gigantic **Chungking Mansions** (see "Accommodation", p.721), a couple of hundred metres north of the junction with Salisbury Road. The shopping arcades here on the two lowest floors are a steaming jungle of ethnic shops, curry houses and dark corners which seem to stretch away into the impenetrable heart of the building, making an interesting contrast with the antiseptic air-conditioned shopping malls that fill the rest of Hong Kong.

A few hundred metres north of Chungking Mansions, **Kowloon Park** (daily 6am–midnight) is marked at its southeastern corner by the white-domed **Kowloon Mosque and Islamic Centre**, which caters to the substantial Muslim population of the area – tourists are not allowed in without special permission (call ⓣ2724 0095). The park itself provides welcome green respite from the unremitting concrete of Tsim Sha Tsui, though strangely you can't see it from the street and have to climb steps up from Nathan Road. There's also an indoor and outdoor swimming pool complex, with Olympic-size facilities (daily 8am–noon, 1.30–6pm & 7.30–10pm; $19), plus an aviary, sculpture walk and piazza in the grounds.

A few blocks to the east of Nathan Road at no. 100 Chatham Road, you'll find the **Hong Kong Museum of History** (Mon & Wed–Sat 10am–6pm, Sun 10am–7pm, $10), which features the Hong Kong Story, a permanent history about the SAR's life and times, as well as numerous history-related temporary exhibitions.

Beyond Chatham Road, the area known as **Tsim Sha Tsui East** is built on entirely reclaimed land and comprises exclusive hotels and shopping malls. From the Star Ferry Terminal an excellent walk follows the seafront promenade east and then north past this area as far as **Hung Hom**, which is the site of the Kowloon–Canton Railway Station. The **Hong Kong Science Museum** can also be found in this district, at 2 Science Museum Road (Tues–Fri 1–9pm, Sat, Sun & public holidays 10am–9pm; $25). Opened in 1998, its best feature is probably the twenty-metre Energy Machine, although there's also a good children's zone.

Yau Ma Tei and Mong Kok

In some ways, the part of Kowloon north of the tourist ghetto of Tsim Sha Tsui is more rewarding to walk around, with more authentic Chinese neighbourhoods and interesting markets. **Yau Ma Tei**, whose name, meaning "Place of Sesame Plants", rather belies its present appearance, is jammed with high-rise tenements and busy streets. The area begins north of Jordan Road, and most of the interest lies in the streets to the west of Nathan Road. You can walk up here from Tsim Sha Tsui in about twenty minutes, otherwise take the MTR or, if you're coming from Central, take the cross-harbour ferry to the Jordan Road Ferry Pier.

Temple Street, running north off Jordan Road a couple of blocks west of Nathan Road, becomes a fun-packed **night market** after around 7pm every day, although the market actually opens in the early afternoon. As well as shopping for cheap clothing, watches, CDs, tapes and souvenirs, you can get your fortune told here, eat some great seafood from street stalls, and sometimes listen in on impromptu performances of Chinese opera. A minute or two to the north of here is the local **Tin Hau Temple**, just off Nathan Road, tucked away between Public Square Street and Market Street, a couple of minutes south of Jordan MTR. Surrounded by urban hubbub, this old little temple devoted to the sea sits in a small concreted park, usually teaming with old men, playing mahjong under the banyan trees. East of the Tin Hau Temple, just under the Gascoigne Road flyover at the junction of Kansu and Battery streets, the **Jade Market** (daily 9am–6pm) has 450 stalls in two different sections offering an amazing variety of items from souvenir trinkets to family heirlooms in jade, crystal, quartz and other stones – it's another good place for a browse.

Nearby on Tung Choi Street, between Argyle Street and Dundas Street, is the **Ladies Market**, flogging piles of cheap clothes, jewellery, toys and bags between noon and 10.30pm every day.

To the east of Nathan Road, at the corner of Nelson Street and Fa Yuen Street, a specialist market of a rather different flavour, the **Mong Kok Computer Centre**, offers some incredible bargain software on CD, though be warned that much of this is pirated and, strictly speaking, illegal – exercise caution when importing such material into your own country. Not far from here is the **Goldfish Market**, on Fa Yuen Street and Bute Street, where you can find aquaria, corals, exotic fish and even some dubiously exotic breeds of snake, lizard and turtle. A few hundred metres from here in the direction of Mong Kok MTR, just to the north of Prince Edward Road, are two delightful markets, the **Flower Market** (daily from 10am), in Flower Market Street, and the **Bird Garden** (daily 7am–8pm), at the eastern end of the same street, where it meets the KCR flyover. The flower market is at its best on Sundays and in the run up to Chinese New Year, when many people come to buy narcissi, orange trees and plum blossom to decorate their apartments in order to bring good luck. In 1997, the bird market moved from some rather fetid lanes off Nathan Road in Mong Kok to its purpose-built site here. Over seventy songbird stalls are set in a Chinese-style garden, with trees, seats and elegant carved marble panels showing birds in the wild. As well as the hundreds of birds on sale here, along with their intricately designed bamboo cages, there are also live crickets – food for the birds. Many local men bring their own songbirds here for an airing, and the place gives a real glimpse into a traditional area of Chinese life which is spiritually a thousand miles from Tsim Sha Tsui.

Outer Kowloon

Head a few hundred metres north of Mong Kok and you reach **Boundary Street**, which marks the border between Kowloon and the New Territories – though these days this distinction is pretty meaningless. By far the busiest tourist attraction in this area is well to the northeast at the **Wong Tai Sin Temple** (daily 7am–5.30pm; small donation expected), a huge, thriving Taoist, Buddhist and Confucian temple that's packed with more worshippers than any other in Hong Kong. Big, bright and colourful, it's interesting for a glimpse into the practices of modern, popular Chinese religion: vigorous kneeling, incense burning and the noisy rattling of joss sticks in canisters, as well as the presentation of food and drink to the Taoist deities. Large numbers of fortune-tellers, some of whom speak English, have stands to the right of the entrance and charge around $200 for palm-reading, about half that for a face-reading. The temple can be reached directly from the Wong Tai Sin MTR station, using exit B.

Northwest from Mongkok, in the opposite direction from Wong Tai Sin, are a couple of places worth a visit. The **Lei Cheng Uk Branch Museum** (Mon–Wed, Fri & Sat 10am–1pm & 2–6pm, Sun 1–6pm; free), part of the main Museum of History, has been constructed over a two-thousand-year-old Han-dynasty tomb which was unearthed by workmen in 1955. By far the oldest structure discovered in Hong Kong, the tomb offers some rare proof of the ancient presence of the Chinese in the area. What is really interesting, however, is to compare photos of the site from the 1950s (paddy fields and green hills) with the high-rises that surround the area today. You can reach the museum from Chang Shan Wan MTR; take exit A2, walk for five minutes along Tonkin Street and the museum is on your left.

Further afield, Kowloon also boasts the **Chi Lin Nunnery**, five minutes' walk from exit 2 of the Diamond Hill MTR (daily 9am–3.30pm, free; gardens 6.30am–7pm, free; however, small donation expected). Constructed according to traditional Chinese methods, this elegant wooden temple was built without nails in Tang-dynasty style and features pavilions, flower gardens and seven halls over a 30,000 square metre area.

The New Territories

Many people fly in and out of Hong Kong without even realizing that the territory comprises anything more than the city itself. The mistake is an unfortunate one, for it is in the **New Territories** that some of the most scenic and traditionally Chinese areas of Hong Kong can be found. Comprising 794 square kilometres of land abutting the southern part of China's Guangdong province, the New Territories come complete with country roads, water buffalo, old villages, valleys and mountains – as well as booming New Towns which now house well over three million people.

It's the country areas that hold most appeal, and there is a whole series of designated **country parks**, including the amazingly unspoilt **Sai Kung Peninsula** to the east, offering excellent hiking trails and secluded beaches. For serious extended hikes, the **MacLehose Trail** extends right across the peninsula and beyond. Some of the towns are also interesting in their own right, either as ordinary residential districts, or as gateways to relics from the past such as the **walled villages** near Kam Tin or the **Heritage Museum** in Sha Tin.

Getting around the New Territories is simplicity itself – frequent buses connect all towns, while the MTR reaches as far as Tsuen Wan and the KCR runs north through Sha Tin, the Chinese University and Tai Po. There are also a number of boats from Central, including the fast hoverferries that connect with Tuen Mun in only thirty minutes. Tuen Mun is the terminus of the LRT rail line that runs north to Yuen Long. You can get a flavour of the New Territories in just one day's independent exploration, or it's worth considering a **HKTB tour** ($385, children $335). These run every day, take six hours and include lunch. Covering such a large distance, this is probably one of their best tours in terms of convenience and value. It's also worth checking their website (Ⓦwww.DiscoverHongKong.com) for details of their ongoing "**City of Life: Hong Kong is it**!" campaign, covering all eighteen Hong Kong districts with recommendations of the month for festivals, eating out and trips.

By **public transport**, a satisfying do-it-yourself tour can be made in a few hours along the following route, starting from the Jordan Road Ferry bus terminus in Kowloon (accessible by bus #8 from Tsim Sha Tsui): take bus #60X to Tuen Mun bus terminal, then from here ride the LRT north to its terminus at Yuen Long. From Yuen Long, take bus #76K to Sheung Shui bus terminal in the north. Finally ride the KCR train south back to Kowloon.

The west

Tsuen Wan in the west of the New Territories is one of Hong Kong's **New Towns** – a satellite town, built from scratch in the last 25 years to absorb some of the overflow from Hong Kong's burgeoning population. With getting on for a million inhabitants, Tsuen Wan now has all the amenities of a large, modern city in its own right, and is easily reached from downtown Hong Kong by MTR or by hoverferries from Central. If you are interested in seeing a New Town (and the way most Hong Kong people live), this is the perfect place to start.

One very attractive sight virtually in the middle of Tsuen Wan is the **Sam Tung Uk Museum** (daily except Tues 9am–5pm; free), which is essentially a restored two-hundred-year-old walled village of a type typical of this part of southern China. The village was founded in 1786 by a Hakka clan named Chan, who continued to live here, incredibly, until the 1970s. Now the houses have been restored with their original furnishings, and there are various exhibitions on aspects of the lives of the Hakka people. You can reach the museum by following signs out of Tsuen Wan MTR station – it's about a ten-minute walk.

A couple of blocks south of the MTR station (in the direction of the shore), on Shiu Wo Street, maxicab #81 runs up to the nearby Lo Wai Village, where the **Yuen Yuen Institute** is located. This is a large temple complex dedicated to the three main religions practised in Hong Kong – Buddhism, Taoism and Confucianism – and its main structure is a copy of the Temple of Heaven in Beijing. Its chief attractions, however, are the beautiful hillside location and an excellent vegetarian restaurant.

Moving on from Tsuen Wan, you can either catch bus #60M or #68M from the bus terminal opposite the MTR to **Tuen Mun** – another huge New Town whose main boast is that it holds the Gold Coast development, featuring Hong Kong's largest shopping mall, a resort hotel, a marina club and convention centre – or, from an overpass just north of the MTR, catch bus #51 north to Kam Tin. The ride to Kam Tin is a spectacular one, running right past Hong Kong's highest peak, **Tai Mo Shan**, which at 957m is nearly twice the height of Victoria Peak on Hong Kong Island. If you want to climb up to the top of the mountain, there's a bus stop on a pass right under the peak – get off here and follow a signposted path up to the top. The excellent **MacLehose Trail** runs right through here, and this is as good a place as any to join it. For detailed information on the trail, which in all runs 100km across the New Territories from Tuen Mun in the west to the Sai Kung Peninsula in the east, contact the HKTB (see p.716) or the Country and Marine Parks Branch, Floor 12, 393 Canton Rd, Tsim Sha Tsui, Kowloon (Mon–Fri 9am–5pm, Sat 9am–noon; ⓣ2733 2132).

Kam Tin

This small town is famous in Hong Kong as the site of **Kat Hing Wai**, one of Hong Kong's last inhabited **walled villages**. Dating back to the late seventeenth century when a clan named Tang settled here, the village ($1 donation to enter) still comprises thick six-metre-high walls and guard towers, although most traces of the moat have gone. Inside the walls, there's a wide lane running down the middle of the village, with tiny alleys leading off it. A few souvenir sellers and old Hakka ladies in traditional hats pester visitors with cameras for more donations, but the atmosphere is as different from Hong Kong as you can possibly imagine. To get here, get off bus #51 in Kam Tin, walk a few minutes farther west (the same direction as the bus), and it's on your left, visible from the main road.

North: the KCR route

There is a whole series of possible outings to be made from the stops dotted along the **Kowloon–Canton Railway** as it wends its way north from Kowloon to the border with mainland China. As well as booming New Towns, you can still find traces of Hakka communities, the women dressed in conspicuous black baggy trousers and heavy fringed hats. If you're on a day-trip, visits to the New Towns of **Sha Tin** and **Sheung Shui** might be all you have time for, though if you're really keen on getting out into some countryside, the excellent walks around **Plover Cove Country Park** will need a day in themselves.

Sha Tin

The first important stop is at the booming New Town of **Sha Tin**, best known to Hong Kongers as the site of the territory's second **racecourse**, which is packed with fanatical gamblers on race days during the season (for details on the HKTB horse-racing tour, see "Happy Valley", p.731). For tourists, however, the main attraction of Sha Tin is the **Heritage Museum** at 1 Man Lam Road (ⓣ2180 8188, ⓦwww.heritagemuseum.gov.hk; Mon & Wed–Sat 10am–6pm, Sun & public holidays 10am–7pm; $10; free admission on Wed). About fifteen minutes' walk from the New Town Plaza at Sha Tin KCR station (there's a good location map, or pick up the museum newsletter with location maps at the customer service centre of Seiyu in New Town Plaza phase III), you can reach it by following signs through the Sha Tin Park. The museum is packed with permanent and temporary exhibitions; one of the best covers life in the New Territories across the ages and features a mock-up of a traditional fishing village.

Another popular attraction is the **Ten Thousand Buddhas Monastery** (daily 9am–5pm; free), dating back to the 1960s, which is probably the single most interesting temple in the whole of the New Territories, if not in all Hong Kong, and the **Po** (or Bo) **Fook Ancestral Worship Halls** (9am–5pm; free). Unfortunately, there are illegal structures within the monastery, rendering it unsafe; tourists are therefore currently advised not to visit and the – actually around thirteen thousand – Buddhas may be re-housed in another monastery at some point. From the monastery you can also follow a path farther up the mountain to another terrace containing some smaller temples, although recently this has been closed by landslides caused by monsoon rain.

Tai Po and the Plover Cove Country Park

Tai Po, a few KCR stops north of Sha Tin, is not in itself an enormously exciting place but it does offer opportunities for escaping into some serious countryside. To reach **Plover Cove Country Park**, take bus #75K from outside Tai Po Market KCR station to its terminus at the small village of **Tai Mei Tuk**, right by the Plover Cove Reservoir. The signposted circular walk around the park takes about an hour. Alternatively, you can stroll or ride a rented bike ($35–60 per day from rental shops in Tai Mei Tuk) along the road to **Bride's Pool**, an attractive picnic and camping site beside pools and waterfalls, or follow on foot the five-kilometre **Pat Sin Leng Nature Trail**, a highly scenic, if slightly circuitous, route from Tai Mei Tuk to the pool. The pool area is very crowded at weekends, but during the week it can be pretty quiet. For more details about the many walks in this area, contact the HKTB.

Sheung Shui

Unless you're planning to cross the border into mainland China, **Sheung Shui** is as far as you can get on the KCR – in fact, it lies just 3km south of the border. There are no special tourist sights as such, but of all the towns in the New Territories, this is one of those least affected by modern development, and casual exploration in the Shek Wu Hui area just outside the KCR station will reward you with a great old market full of haggling Hakka women. Sheung Shui is also linked by bus #77K to Yuen Long and Kam Tin in the west of the region.

The east

The eastern part of the New Territories, around **Clear Water Bay** and the **Sai Kung Peninsula**, is where you'll find the most secluded beaches and walks in Hong Kong, though at weekends they do begin to fill up. The best way to appreciate the seclusion is to come during the week and bring a picnic – you'll need to put aside a whole day to visit either place. The starting point for buses into both areas is Diamond Hill MTR station.

Clear Water Bay

The forty-minute ride on bus #91 from Choi Hung MTR to Clear Water Bay already gives an idea of the delightful combination of green hills and sea that awaits you. Around the terminus at **Tai Au Mun**, overlooking Clear Water Bay, are a couple of excellent, clean **beaches**, and to the south is the start of a good three- to four-hour walk around the bay. First, follow the road south along the clifftop, as far as the Clear Water Bay Golf and Country Club (to use the tennis, swimming and golf facilities of this luxury club, visitors must join HKTB's "Sports and Recreation Tour", which costs $430 plus pay-as-you-play charges). From the car park outside the club entrance, follow signposts on to the wonderfully located **Tin Hau Temple** in **Joss House Bay**. There is thought to have been a temple to the Taoist goddess of the sea here for more than eight hundred years, and although today's temple dates back only to its last major restoration in 1962, there is a venerable feel about the place. As one of Hong Kong's few Tin Hau temples actually still commanding the sea, it's of immense significance, and on the 23rd day of the third lunar month each year (Tin Hau's birthday) a colossal seaborne celebration takes place on fishing boats in the bay.

Heading back up the slope, you can take another path which starts from the same car park outside the Golf and Country Club down past **Sheung Lau Wan**, a small village on the western shore of the peninsula. The path skirts the village, and continues on, forming a circular route around the headland back to the Clear Water Bay bus terminal.

Sai Kung Peninsula

Some way to the north of Clear Water Bay, the irregularly shaped Sai Kung Peninsula, jagged with headlands, bluffs and tiny offshore islands, is the least developed area in the whole of Hong Kong, and a haven for hikers and beach lovers.

The only sizeable town in the area, **Sai Kung Town**, accessible on bus #92 from Diamond Hill MTR, lies slightly to the south of the peninsula but is nevertheless the jumping-off point for explorations of Sai Kung. It's now being developed fairly fast, though it still retains some of the pleasant features of a fishing town, with a promenade packed with seafood restaurants and fishermen offering their fairly exotic wares, plus additional seafood restaurants, arts and crafts shops, cafes and bars on bustling Sai Kung Hoi Pong Square. Small boats also run from the quayside to the various islands, the nearest and most popular of which is **Kiu Tsui Chau** (or Sharp Island), boasting a beach and a short hike to its highest point, although **Tai Long Wan** is also clean, quiet and beautiful.

The highlights of Sai Kung, however, are the **country parks** that cover the peninsula with virgin forest and grassland leading to perfect sandy beaches, where you can even go snorkelling. Although it is possible to see something of these on a day-trip, the best way really to appreciate them is to bring a tent, rent a junk for the day with a group of friends, join an HKTB junk tour ($350 a day) or consider staying at the youth hostel on Sai Kung (see "Accommodation", p.723). Access to the parks is by bus #94 from Sai Kung Town and #96R (Sundays only) from Diamond Hill MTR, which pass through **Pak Tam Chung** on their way to Wong Shek pier in the north of the peninsula. Buses depart once an hour during daylight. Don't come to Pak Tam Chung expecting a town – all you'll find is a **visitors' centre** (daily except Tues 9.30am–4.30pm; ⓣ2792 7365), which supplies hikers with maps (some are free) and vital information about the trails.

Of the many possible hikes, the MacLehose Trail, liberally dotted with campsites, heads east from here, circumventing the **High Island Reservoir** before heading west into the rest of the New Territories. If you want to follow the trail just a part of the way, the **beaches** at Long Ke, south of the reservoir, and Tai Long, to the northeast, are Hong Kong's finest, though to walk out to them and back from Pak Tam Chung takes several hours. The last bus back from Pak Tam Chung is at 7.30pm.

The Outlying Islands

Officially part of the New Territories, the **Outlying Islands** of Hong Kong, numbering over 260, offer weary visitors a chance to escape if the urban hubbub has become too claustrophobic. Covering twenty percent of the land area of the territory but containing just two percent of the population, the islands offer a delightful mix of seascape, old fishing villages and relative rural calm, almost entirely free of motor vehicles, except for the taxis and buses on Lantau

Ferries to the islands

The following is a selection of the most useful island ferry services. Schedules differ slightly on Saturdays and Sundays, when prices also rise. You can pay by Octopus, or you might want to consider buying an Island-Hopping Pass, offering unlimited rides to Mui Wo, Cheung Chau and Peng Chau (@www.nwff.com.hk).

To Cheung Chau

From Outlying Islands Ferry Piers – first boat out 6.25am, last boat back 12.30am (at least hourly; 1hr; fast ferries 30min). There are also six hoverferries daily from the same piers.

To Sok Kwu Wan, Lamma Island

From Outlying Islands Ferry Piers – first boat out 7.20am, last boat back 11.40pm (10 daily; 50min; fast ferries 35 min).
From Aberdeen – first boat out 6.45am, last boat back 10.40pm (8 daily; 30min).

To Yung Shue Wan, Lamma Island

From Outlying Islands Ferry Piers – first boat out 6.45am, last boat back around 12.30am (at least hourly; 40min; fast ferry 25min).

To Discovery Bay, Lantau Island

From Outlying Islands Ferry Pier 3 – 24-hour departures (at least every 30min between 6.50am and 12.30am; 25min).

To Mui Wo (Silvermine Bay), Lantau Island

From the Outlying Islands Ferry Piers – first boat out 7am, last boat back 12.20am (at least hourly; 1hr). Early and late sailings go via Peng Chau. There are also four hoverferries daily, all via Peng Chau.
From Peng Chau – first boat out 5.40am, last boat back midnight (approximately every 2hr; 25min).

To Peng Chau

From the Outlying Islands Ferry Piers – first boat out 7am, last boat back 12.20am (approximately hourly; 50min).

Island. The islands are conveniently connected to Central by plentiful **ferries** and other boats. By comparison with other areas, development has been relatively restrained, although the opening of the Hong Kong International Airport at **Chek Lap Kok** on the northern shore of the largest and emptiest island, Lantau, means that this is likely to change.

Although most tourists come on day-trips, there is some **accommodation** on the islands (see p.723), and **restaurants** of the fishy variety are also numerous.

Lamma

Lamma is the closest island to Hong Kong Island and the third-largest in the SAR, lying just to the southwest of Aberdeen, and conspicuous for the giant chimneys protruding from its power station on the western shore. The tiny population of roughly five thousand includes a number of Western expatriates who have come here in search of a more laid-back existence – although their numbers have dwindled since the introduction of tougher visa restrictions in 1997 and the end of the airport building project the following year. Despite the power station and the island's quarrying industry, the air is cleaner than in the main urban areas, and there are lots of cheap, interesting restaurants, no cars and you can walk across green hills to sandy beaches.

There are two possible points of **arrival** on Lamma, either by ferry from Central to Yung Shue Wan, or to Sok Kwu Wan either from Central or from Aberdeen. By far the nicest way to appreciate the island is to take a boat to either Yung Shue Wan or Sok Kwu Wan, then walk to the other and catch the boat back from there.

Yung Shue Wan is a pretty little tree-shaded village where the bulk of the island's residents live, with one or two hotels and a clustering of small grocery stores, bars and eating places catering for both Chinese and Western palates. There's a very relaxed feel to the place in the evening when people sit out under the banyan trees. To walk to Sok Kwu Wan from here (1hr), follow the easy-to-find cement path that branches away from the shore by the *Light House Bar*, shortly before the Tin Hau Temple. Make your way through the rather grotty apartment buildings on the outskirts of the village and you'll soon find yourself walking amid butterflies, long grass and trees. After about fifteen minutes you'll arrive at **Hung Shing Yeh Beach**, a nice place if you stick to its northern half; stray a few metres to the south, though, and you'll rapidly find your horizon filling up with power station. There are a couple of places to get a drink or rent a room, including one proper hotel with restaurant (the *Concerto Inn*, see p.723), where you can sit on the outdoor terrace and eat relatively inexpensive sandwiches, noodles and rice dishes. One of Lamma's best restaurants, the *Han Lok Yuen* is just up the hill behind the beach – its speciality is roast pigeon. On from the beach, the path climbs quite sharply up to a little summit with a pavilion commanding views over the island. Continue on for another hour or so and you'll reach **Sok Kwu Wan**, which basically comprises a row of seafood restaurants with terraces built out over the water. The food and the atmosphere are good, and consequently the restaurants are often full of large parties of locals enjoying lavish and noisy meals. Some of the larger places also operate their own boat services for customers. Many people get the ferry over to Sok Kwu Wan in the evening for dinner, but, if you're not taking a restaurant service, make sure you don't miss the last scheduled boat back at 10.50pm, because there's nowhere to stay here – your only option would be to hire a sampan back to Aberdeen.

Cheung Chau

Another great little island where you can spend a couple of hours strolling around and then have dinner, hour-glass-shaped **Cheung Chau** is just south of Lantau, an hour from Hong Kong by ferry and refreshingly vehicle-free. Despite its minuscule size of just 2.5 square kilometres, Cheung Chau is nevertheless the most crowded of all the outer islands, with a population of some 23,000. Historically, the island is one of the oldest settled parts of Hong Kong, being notorious as an eighteenth-century base for pirates who enjoyed waylaying the ships that ran between Guangzhou and the Portuguese enclave of Macau. Today, it still gives the impression of being an economically independent little unit, with Pak She Praya Road, the narrow strip between its two headlands, jam-packed with tiny shops, markets and seafront seafood restaurants. As well as romantic dinners and late-night ferry rides home, the island offers some nice **walks** around the old fishing ports and views of traditional junk building. It also has some interesting temples, the most important being the two-hundred-year-old **Pak Tai Temple**, a few hundred metres northwest of the ferry pier, along the interesting Pak She Street, lined with old herbalists and shops selling religious trinkets. Fishermen come to the temple to pray for protection, and beside the statue of Pak Tai, the god of the sea, is an ancient iron sword, discovered by fishermen and supposedly symbolizing good luck. For a few days in late April or early May the temple is the site of one of Hong Kong's liveliest and most spectacular festivals, the so-called **Tai Chiu (Bun) Festival**.

The main beach on the island, the scenic but crowded **Tung Wan Beach**, is due west of the ferry pier. Windsurfers are available for rent at the southern end of the beach, from a centre run by the family of Hong Kong's Olympic medal-winning windsurf champion, Lee Lai Shan, who won a gold at the 1996 Atlanta games. The centre also serves beer and snacks on a terrace with a nice sea view.

The southern headland of Cheung Chau contains more walking possibilities, although it can be quite a scrabble up and down rocks and through bays. You can follow the path around the island, with marked trails to the nearby **Tin Hau Temple** and then the **Cheung Po Tsai Cave**, named after Cheung Chau's most famous pirate who used the cave as a hide-out in the early part of the nineteenth century. Legend aside, however, the cave is nothing special and you'll need a torch to see pretty much anything. The walk back from the cave area to the main ferry pier is an attractive one that takes about an hour, although it's not suitable for small children.

Lantau

It comes as something of a surprise that **Lantau Island** (also known as Big Fish Mountain) is actually twice as big as Hong Kong Island – and, despite the new towns of Discovery Bay and Tung Chung, there is clearly considerable scope for getting off the beaten track as more than half the island has been designated a country park. With wild countryside, monasteries, old fishing villages and seriously secluded beaches, Lantau offers the best quick escape from downtown Hong Kong – more than half the island is designated as "country park". However, this tranquillity is unlikely to last, at least along the northern and northeastern shores, as Hong Kong's airport at Chek Lap Kok and its associated transport links are spawning a range of new commercial and residential developments, plus Disney World, slated to open in 2005–6.

The tranquillity of other parts of the island shouldn't be fatally disturbed, and serious hikers might want to take advantage of the seventy-kilometre **Lantau Trail**, which links up the popular scenic spots on the island in twelve stages and is dotted along its length by campsites and youth hostels; for detailed information on this, pay a call to the Country Parks Authority in Kowloon (see p.744). Even if you intend doing only a short hike or a quick whip round the main sights, try to set aside a full day for Lantau, or plan to pay two or more visits, as the sights are scattered. If you're pressed for time, you could catch the Lantau Explorer Bus trip, operated by New World Fast Ferry ($130 per person, including return ferry trip, bus and guide; lasts five hours and covers the main sights).

The main point of arrival for visitors to Lantau Island is **Mui Wo**, otherwise known as **Silvermine Bay**, about one hour from the Outlying Islands Ferry Piers. Some of the Mui Wo boats stop at the small island of Peng Chau en route. There are also a few ferries daily which connect Mui Wo with Cheung Chau. The other point of arrival is **Discovery Bay**, a residential area connected by frequent high-speed ferries (24hr) from Outlying Islands Ferry Pier 3.

From Mui Wo to Discovery Bay

Mui Wo itself is not much to speak of, although it has some decent, low-key seafood restaurants near the ferry pier. Having disembarked at the ferry pier, most people head straight for the bus station right outside. There are, however, some excellent walks that can be made directly from Mui Wo, one of which, the trail to Discovery Bay (2hr), is reasonably straightforward. From the pier you need to head northwest towards the attractive, curving, sandy bay you'll see from the ferry as you approach the island. Keep following the bay around to the end of the beach and continue past the end of the village, until you reach a signposted path bearing steeply uphill to the left. This climbs up through open land to a lookout point with superb views over the mountains, then drops downhill, taking you through more open land and some jungle until you reach the **Trappist Monastery** on your right. Most of the buildings are closed to the public, but it's a pleasant, cool spot – albeit mosquito heaven. The normal access to the monastery, if not on foot, is by an infrequent kaito service from nearby Discovery Bay and Peng Chau Island to the pier about fifteen minutes' walk from the monastery, on the broad path that leads down the hill. If you want to go on from the monastery to **Discovery Bay** (known as "**DB**" to the locals), follow the same road down towards the pier, and a little way down on your left you'll see a sign post pointing you in the right direction. After about thirty minutes, you'll arrive at a series of sandy bays, a cluster of shanty houses and then Discovery Bay itself, which with its condominiums, a shopping mall, blonde kids and golf buggies will leave you wondering whether you've stepped through a time warp into some Orwellian version of middle-America. This is the main settlement on the island, inhabited by Chinese and expatriate families. From Discovery Bay you can catch ferries back to Mui Wo and Peng Chau, or direct to the Outlying Islands Ferry Piers in Central; you can also catch airport buses and local shuttle buses to Tung Chung, which operate every fifteen minutes.

Western Lantau

The road west from Mui Wo passes along the southern shore, which is where Lantau's best beaches are located. **Cheung Sha Upper and Lower Beaches**, with a couple of cafés and a hotel, are the nicest, and buses #1, #2, #4 and #5 all pass by here.

Beyond the beaches, there are a couple more interesting sights in the western part of the island that can also be reached by direct bus from Mui Wo. The first of these is the **Po Lin (Precious Lotus) Monastery** (daily 10am–6pm; free), which is by far the largest temple in the whole territory of Hong Kong. Located high up on the Ngong Ping Plateau, this is not an ancient site, indeed it was only established in 1927. Nevertheless, it is very much a living, breathing temple, and busloads of locals arrive here by the hour, in particular to pay their respects to the bronze **Tian Tan Buddha**, the largest seated bronze outdoor Buddha in the world and weighing in at 200 tonnes, and to eat in the huge vegetarian **restaurant** (daily 11.30am–5pm; meal tickets $60 for the "deluxe" meal, $25 for a "snack"; tickets from the office at the bottom of the steps to the Buddha). The Po Lin Monastery, which is often referred to in bus schedules as Ngong Ping, is reached by bus #2 from Mui Wo, and it's a spectacular forty-minute ride through the hills. The last bus back to Mui Wo leaves at 7.30pm. Alternatively, you can catch buses #23 or #11 from Tung Chung town centre.

Right on the far northwestern shore of Lantau is the interesting little fishing village of **Tai O**. This remote place, constructed over salt flats and a tiny offshore island, has become a popular tourist spot (the government has plans for further development) particularly at weekends, but still retains much of its old character. There are some interesting local temples, wooden houses built partially on stilts, caged animals, and a big trade in dried fish. You can reach it by bus #41 from Mui Wo (last bus back 1.30am) and also by the relatively infrequent bus #21 from the Po Lin Monastery (last service at 3pm).

Eating, drinking and nightlife

As one of the great culinary capitals of the world, Hong Kong can boast not only a superb native cuisine – **Cantonese** – but also perhaps the widest range of **international restaurants** of any city outside Europe or North America. This is due in part to the cosmopolitan nature of the population, but also, perhaps more importantly, to the incredible seriousness attached to dining by the local Chinese.

As well as the joys of **dim sum** – another Hong Kong speciality – the city offers the full gamut of Chinese restaurants from Beijing to Shanghai to Sichuan (and many smaller localities). It also offers excellent **curry houses** from the Indian subcontinent, surprisingly reasonable **Japanese** sushi bars, **British** pub-style food and endless cheap outlets of the noodle-and-dumpling variety, which are often the best value for money of all. However, the big hotels also offer great-value buffet lunches – check local listings for special offers and themed feasts. You'll also find the local Chinese **fast-food** chains, *Café de Coral* and *Maxim's*, alongside *McDonald's, Pizza Hut, Pret A Manger, Haagen Dazs* and *KFC*. The choice is endless, and all budgets are catered for. Travellers arriving after a long stint in mainland China are in for the gastronomic blow-out of their lives. The places listed below are a mere fraction of the total, with an emphasis on the less expensive end of the market. Serious gourmets should consult HKTB's *Best of the Best Culinary Guide, Hong Kong Tatler's* website, Ⓦwww.hkbestrestaurants.com and the independent free weekly, *HK Magazine*.

Hong Kong sometimes seems to have more **nightlife** than the rest of China put together. In the **pubs** and **bars** you'll sometimes find **live music and dancing**, but the clutch of restaurant-, bar- and pub-crammed streets known as **Lan Kwai Fong** remain the heart of Hong Kong's party scene and drinking-culture nightlife. Despite its image as a cultural desert, **classical concerts** appear increasingly frequently at several venues and there are a number of art, jazz and other **festivals** year round (check the listings magazines detailed on p.716).

Most of the main English-language films find their way to Hong Kong's **cinemas** soon after release, and they are usually shown in the original language, sometimes with Chinese subtitles (although the local audience prefers dubbed versions, which usually hit the screen soon afterwards). Some Chinese-language films are also shown with English subtitles. See "Listings", p.762 for details of the main screens.

Breakfast and snacks

All the bigger hotels serve expensive buffet breakfasts with vast quantities of Chinese and European food. For cheaper, traditional Western breakfasts, head for any of the cafés listed (all open daily throughout the day), although *dim sum* with tea or *congee* is a more authentic way to start the morning (see

"Restaurants" below). Local chains include *DeliFrance*, *Pacific Coffee*, *Starbucks*, *MiX* and *Pret A Manger*, all of which offer muffins, breakfast dishes and sandwiches throughout the day and can be found in most MTR concourses.

Ge Ming Café 48 Staunton St, SoHo. All-day breakfasts in a cosy, red-walled and tiled hang-out. Fish and veggies also served; cheap and friendly.
Kiku Express Basement of Jardine House, Connaught Rd, Central. All kinds of breakfasts, from big English fry-ups to bowls of noodles.
MiX Floor 1, Hong Kong Station, Central. Good, healthy wraps and salads, groaning with veggies and fresh produce, plus more smoothies and vitamin drinks than you can shake a stick at. Thirty minutes' free Internet access for patrons. Inexpensive. Daily 7am–7pm.
Movenpick Marché Levels 6 & 7, The Peak Galleria. Good fresh food from this Swiss chain. Salads, sandwiches, soups and daily hot dishes, plus Swiss ice cream. The seventh-floor café has an outside terrace. (There is another branch, using the name *Delicious* at Century Square, D'Aguilar St, Central.) Daily 11am–11pm. Inexpensive.
Ngan Ki Heung Tea Co Ltd 290 Queens Rd, Central. A source of a vast range of Chinese teas to drink and buy. The owner is only too happy to serve you teas in the traditional manner and talk you through their various properties.
Oliver's Super Sandwiches Many branches including: Shop 104, Exchange Square II, 8 Connaught Place, Central; Shop 201–205, Prince's Building, 10 Chater Rd, Central; Tower One, Lippo Centre, Admiralty; Shop A, Fleet House, 38 Gloucester Rd, Wan Chai; *Repulse Bay Hotel*, 109 Repulse Bay Rd, Repulse Bay; Ocean Centre, Tsim Sha Tsui. Popular chain offering excellent sandwiches, salads, baked potatoes, cooked breakfasts and fresh juices.

Restaurants

Eating is an enormously large part of life in Hong Kong, and restaurant dining in particular is a sociable, family affair. The authentic Chinese restaurants are large, noisy places where dining takes place under bright lights – not as discreet as the candle-lit ambiences so beloved in the West but much more fun. Don't be intimidated by the speed with which you will be rushed to your seat: service is brisk as a rule. Menus in all but the cheapest restaurants should be in English as well as Chinese (although you many not get the full menu translated, and prices have also been known to vary between the two versions). In the very cheap noodle-and-dumpling shops, order by pointing at other people's dishes.

The busiest, brightest restaurants of all are often those serving **dim sum** for breakfast or lunch – snack-sized portions of savoury dumplings, rolls and buns served in bamboo baskets or on small plates from trolleys which are pushed around the restaurant. In these places you simply request items from passing trolleys, and a card on your table will be marked with the item. Keep picking things up until you are full and the bill will rarely come to $100 per head.

Eating in Chungking Mansions

African Food Palace Floor 11, Block E. Tasty African dishes in a friendly place.

Delhi Club Floor 3, C Block. A curry house par excellence, once you ignore the spartan surroundings and slap-down service. The ludicrously cheap set meal would feed an army.

Khyber Pass Floor 7, E Block. Consistently good food, with friendly and efficient service. One of the best in Chungking Mansions.

Sher-E-Punjab Floor 3, B Block. Excellent food with friendly service in clean surroundings. Slightly more expensive than some of its neighbours.

Taj Mahal Club Floor 3, B Block. Excellent Indian food and good value if you avoid the relatively expensive drinks.

It's worth trying seasonal dishes: abalone, garoupa and dried seafood in March–May; melon greens, mushrooms and beancurd from June to August; green, giant, soft-shell and hairy crabs between September and November; and casseroles and hotpots from December to February.

The largest concentration of restaurants in Hong Kong Island is probably in the **Wan Chai–Happy Valley** area, bordering on **Causeway Bay**. The streets around D'Aguilar Street in **Central**, just a couple of minutes' walk south from the MTR, are particularly popular with young people and yuppie expatriates. This area is known as **Lan Kwai Fong**, after the small lane branching off D'Aguilar Street to the east, which is chock-a-block with bars and restaurants. The newest restaurant area is known as **SoHo**, meaning South of Hollywood Road. In fact, expansion means it now starts at Lyndhurst Terrace, and clusters around the Mid-Levels escalator as far up the slope as Mosque Street. Restaurants here come and go very quickly, but in general they tend to be rather less flashy and more civilized than in Lan Kwai Fong, and the clientele is a mix of the more cosmopolitan locals and expats. On the south side of the island, **Stanley** and **Aberdeen** are also popular spots for tourists on dining excursions; while, in the New Territories **Sai Kung**, **Cheung Chau** and **Lei Yue Mun** are famous for their seafood restaurants.

In Kowloon, the choice of eateries is hardly less than on the island, though watch out for the possibility of tourist rip-offs in the Chinese restaurants in the **Tsim Sha Tsui** area, such as heavy charges on unasked-for side dishes. For Indian food, many of the best-value places are secreted away in the recesses of Chungking Mansions, 36–44 Nathan Road (see box opposite).

Opening hours are long, to accommodate the long working day, and while many of the traditional Chinese restaurants start to wind down around 9.30pm, you'll have no trouble getting served something late. Don't worry too much about **tipping** either. Expensive restaurants will add on their own service charge, usually ten percent, while in cheaper places it's customary just to leave the small change. Generally **prices** are comparable to those in the West: a full dinner without drinks is unlikely to cost less than $100 per head, and that figure can climb to $500 or more in the plushest venues. We have included phone numbers where booking is advisable.

Aberdeen

Jumbo Floating Restaurant Shun Wan Pier, Aberdeen Harbour (Ⓣ2553 9111, Ⓦwww.jumbo.com.hk. This famous floating restaurant serves *dim sum* from breakfast onwards, as does its neighbouring sister ship, the *Jumbo Palace*. Their lights shining on the water are one of Hong Kong's night-time landmarks. Shuttle boats carry customers to and from the quayside Unfortunately both restaurants are now horribly touristy, and the food quality reflects that – few locals eat there. Daily 7am–5pm. Buses #70 or #75 from Admiralty bus terminal.

Central

2 Sardines 43 Elgin St, SoHo Ⓣ2973 6618. Small restaurant which has built itself a big reputation for reliable, reasonably priced French food.

Aqua 49 Hollywood Rd, Central Ⓣ2545 9889. A sumptuously elegant, colonial-style restaurant, decorated with Chinese lanterns and offering clever, international dishes at suitably steep prices. Reservations recommended.

Café Deco Level 1 & 2, 118 Peak Rd, The Peak Ⓣ2849 5111. Superbly located restaurant with unrivalled views and a stylish Art Deco interior that extends to the rest rooms. The menu ranges over gourmet pizzas, curries, Thai noodles, grilled meats and oysters; prices, surprisingly, are not too high, and the portions are vast. Or just call in for a drink, or cake and coffee; the bar stays open an hour or so after the kitchen closes (around 11.30pm), and there's often live jazz. Book if you want window seats.

Dan Ryan's Chicago Grill 114 Pacific Place, 88 Queensway; Shop 200 Ocean Termainal, Tsim Sha Tsui; L2-28 Festival Walk, Kowloon Tong. American restaurant serving classic breakfasts at weekends (Sat & Sun 7.30–11am) – plus mammoth steaks, salads and pasta in American-size portions.

Great Basement, SEIBU, Pacific Place. A top-notch deli and supermarket, fast-food joint and restaurant rolled into one, Great offers Korean, Thai, Cantonese, Japanese and Italian dishes, freshly made and at very reasonable prices.

Luk Yu Tea House 24–26 Stanley St, just west of D'Aguilar St ⓣ2523 5464. A living museum with spittoons, sixty-year-old furniture and geriatric waiters, this is possibly the most atmospheric restaurant in Hong Kong. Tea and *dim sum* as well as full meals are available, though the prices are somewhat tourist-inflated. The service is also authentically brusque and reservations are essential.

M at the Fringe 2 Lower Albert Rd, Central ⓣ2877 4000, ⓦwww.m-atthefringe.com. Stylish, high-priced restaurant much favoured by the glitterati for its boldly flavoured, health-conscious dishes – meat, fish and veggie – whose influences range the world.

Man Wah Floor 25, *Mandarin Oriental Hotel*, 5 Connaught Rd, Central ⓣ2522 0111. Superb Cantonese food at connoisseurs' prices, and offering a beautiful view. You might also want to try the *Clipper Lounge* for afternoon tea or the famous *Mandarin Grill*.

Pasta e Pizza Basement, 11 Lyndhurst Terrace. Cheap and cheerful Italian-ish joint – ideal for a good-value set lunch after trawling the shops and stalls around Hollywood Road.

The Peak Lookout 121 Peak Rd ⓣ2849 1000. For years this has been *the* place to dine on the Peak, and remains in traditional colonial style. South-facing views from the terrace are superb, and the food, with an Asian–Indian slant, is still reasonable value for brunch, or al fresco dining at night; reckon on around $200 per head for a full meal.

Sherpa Himalayan Coffee Shop 11 Staunton St, SoHo ⓣ2973 6886. Friendly restaurant with an interesting range of dishes, and beers to go with them. Food is good and inexpensive, and both vegetarians and chilli addicts will find something to suit. If they send you over the road to another restaurant, don't worry, it's the same management and kitchen.

SoHo SoHo 9 Old Bailey St, Central ⓣ2147 2618. Excellent Modern British cooking offering traditional ingredients with a twist. The menu changes regularly, according to what is fresh in the markets. Friendly staff. The set lunch is very reasonably priced at $95 for two courses. Regular comedy nights.

Thai Basil Pacific Place, 88 Queensway ⓣ2537 4682. In addition to 23 Asian-inspired ice creams, this offers deftly prepared modern Thai cuisine, at around $50–75 a dish, and a casual-chic atmosphere. Booking advised unless you want to queue for twenty minutes.

Veda 8 Arbuthnot Rd, Central ⓣ2868 5885. Hong Kong's first contemporary Indian eatery, replete with upstairs restaurant, ground-floor lounge and basement wine cellar. The creative, fresh dishes are wildly popular.

Yung Kee 32–40 Wellington St, on the corner with D'Aguilar St. An enormous place with bright lights, scurrying staff and seating for a thousand, this is one of Hong Kong's institutions. Roast meats are a speciality, and the *dim sum* is also good. Highly recommended for the prize-winning seafood dishes, too.

Shek O

Shek O Chinese Thai Seafood Shek O. On the way from the main bus stop to the seafront. Laid-back atmosphere with outdoor tables under a trellis. The food here is excellent. The perfect place for lunch if you are on a day trip to Shek O.

Stanley and Repulse Bay

The Boathouse 86–88 Stanley Main St ⓣ2813 4467. Very popular and stylish hang-out in a snazzy waterfront house; booking essential.

The Curry Pot Floor 6, 90B Stanley Main St. Very friendly little restaurant with ocean views from its sixth-floor windows and delicately judged Indian food from all regions. The set lunch is remarkable value, but you can't go wrong choosing *à la carte* either.

El Cid Caramar 102, Murray House, Stanley; also 14 Knutsford Terrace, Tsim Sha Tsui ⓣ2312 1898. Tapas, fine wines, luscious paella and seafood in one of Hong Kong's best Spanish restaurant, which spills out onto the colonnaded balcony wrapped around colonial Murray House.

Thai Thai Floor 5, 90B Stanley Main St. Friendly Thai restaurant, which also does takeaways.

The Verandah The Repulse Bay, 101 Repulse Bay Rd ⓣ2812 2722. Pricey, but the perfect place for a splurge, romantic dinner or indolent Sunday brunch. Jazz, candlelight and views across the bay in a mock-colonial retreat.

Tsim Sha Tsui

Au Trou Normand 6 Carnarvon Rd ⓣ2366 8754. A fine place to escape the hustle of Hong Kong if you want to imagine yourself in rural France for a night. For a good dinner with wine reckon on $200–300 per head.

Celestial Court Chinese Restaurant Level 2, *Sheraton Hong Kong Hotel and Towers*, 20 Nathan Rd ⓣ2369 1111, ext. 3991–2. The winner of

HKTB's gold with distinction award for perfect *dim sum* – especially the shrimp dumplings, egg tarts, spring rolls and steamed barbecue buns. Worth a splurge if you don't mind parting with well over $100 a head.

Felix Floor 28, *Peninsula Hotel* ⓣ2315 3188. This possibly ranks as Hong Kong's most exclusive restaurant. The restaurant was designed by Philippe Starck, and the incredible views of Hong Kong Island in themselves warrant a visit here. The food is Eurasian and understandably expensive, but you can just come for a Martini, or try the early-bird menu (orders between 6 and 7pm) at $350–380 per head for three courses.

Great Shanghai 26 Prat Ave ⓣ2366 8158. One of the most reliable of Hong Kong's Shanghai restaurants, with well-presented food (fine fish and seafood) served in small or large portions. A good choice for a first Shanghai meal.

Jade Garden Floor 4, Star House, 3 Salisbury Rd, by the Star Ferry Pier ⓣ2730 6888. Part of the *Maxim* chain, serving *dim sum*, with harbour views. There's another branch, also with reasonable *dim sum*, at 25–31 Carnarvon Rd ⓣ2369 8311.

Macau Restaurant Ground Floor, 119–127 Parkes St, Jordan MTR ⓣ2270 9166. Dirt cheap, authentic Macanese cooking; packed out at lunchtime with local workers and office staff.

Mint 122–126 Canton Rd ⓣ2735 5887. Reasonably priced Australian grub. Although lamb and seafood are their specialities, it's worth trying the fourteen-course set dinner, sluiced down with cocktails and Ozzie wine.

Peking Restaurant 227 Nathan Rd, Jordan MTR ⓣ2730 1316. Just north of the main Tsim Sha Tsui area. Don't be put off by the fairly glum decor: this place serves some of the best Beijing food in Hong Kong. The Beijing duck is particularly good.

Peninsula Hotel Lobby *Peninsula Hotel* ⓣ2366 6251. The set tea served in the lobby and accompanied by a string quartet comes to around $150 plus ten percent service. As well as a lot of food, you also get a chance to hang out in the most beautiful lobby in Hong Kong, serenaded by live music. It's a good way to get a glimpse of a more elegant, civilized and relaxed Hong Kong.

Ruth's Chris Steak House Ground Floor, Empire Centre, 68 Mody Rd; also at Ground Floor, Lippo Centre, Admiralty. Fab sauces accompany luscious matured US steaks for a carnivorous meal out.

Spring Deer First Floor, 42 Mody Rd ⓣ2723 3673. Long-established place noted for its barbecued Peking duck (carved at the table), among a barrage of authentic dishes such as shark's fin and baked fish on a hot plate. Try the smoked chicken, and the bean curd with minced pork.

Tang Court First Floor, *Great Eagle Hotel*, 8 Peking Rd ⓣ2375 1133, ext 2250. This seafood restaurant offers splendid prawn and crab dishes; it's not the cheapest but the cooking is extraordinarily good – ask for sautéed prawns with pork and crab meat puffs.

Tutto Bene 7 Knutsford Terrace ⓣ2316 2116. Located on a small lane just north of Kimberly Road, off the main tourist beat, this is a popular expatriate hang-out. Good Italian food in a pleasant atmosphere, with tables spread out on the pavement.

Wan Chai and Causeway Bay

Banana Leaf Curry House 440 Jaffe Rd, Wan Chai. One of a number of branches of this highly popular Malaysian–Singaporean restaurant, offering great mild curries full of cream and coconut.

Chee Kee Wonton Noodle Shop Ground Floor, 52 Russell St, Causeway Bay. Noodles are a Hong Kong speciality; this low-key haunt serves some of the best wonton noodles in town.

The Chilli Club 88 Lockhart Rd, Wan Chai ⓣ2527 2872. A shade too popular for its own good these days, full of in-the-know *gweilos*, the *Chilli Club* continues to knock out splendid meals on the spicy side. Booking ahead – especially at night – is wise.

Fook Lam Moon 35–45 Johnston Rd, Wan Chai ⓣ2866 0663. One of the best places in Hong Kong, if not the world, to eat Cantonese food. Expensive.

Genki Sushi Around thirty branches across Hong Kong, including 376 Lockhart Rd, Wan Chai; 22 Stanley St, Central; 733 Nathan Rd, Tsim Sha Tsui. Efficient chain of restaurants offering one of the cheapest ways to eat Japanese food. Either take away by ticking items on a form, or sit inside picking up dishes from a conveyor belt. Portions of any sushi are around $15–20 each.

Golden Bauhinia Hong Kong Convention & Exhibition Centre, Golden Bauhinia Square ⓣ2582 7728. Award-winning *dim sum* and poultry-based dishes – especially the roast chicken with garlic sauce – cheek by jowl with the conference centre.

The Graces Restaurant Floor 29, Lee Theatre Plaza, 99 Percival St, Causeway Bay ⓣ2882 1889. A few minutes' walk from Times Square, this vast and airy eatery has views over Causeway Bay and is always packed to the gunwales with Chinese families hovering up good *dim sum*, rice, noodle and seafood dishes. Booking essential at weekends.

Indonesian 28 Leighton Rd, Causeway Bay ⓣ2577 9981. Recommended place with canteen-style surroundings and staff who will help you get the best out of the extensive menu – the curries and spicy eggplant are great

Ivy Chinoise 4 Sun Wui Road ⓣ3162 3922. Cantonese cuisine with a Western spin, by a chef known as the King of Cookery, in an attractive, understated room.

Next Generation Cuisine Ground Floor, 478 Lockhart Rd, Causeway Bay ⓣ2911 0119. Luscious Modern Cantonese cooking. The chicken poached in superior soy sauce scooped the HKTB's Best of the Best award.

Vegi-Food Kitchen 8 Cleveland St, Causeway Bay. On a small street a couple of blocks east of Paterson Street at its northern end. The sign informing customers not to "bring meat of any kind into this restaurant" says it all. Classy, strictly vegetarian Chinese food.

Wo Lung Congee and Wonton Noodle Shop 49–51 Lee Tung St, Wan Chai ⓣ2893 7721. Not the poshest place on the block, but one that proffers perfect dumplings, *congee* (like soupy porridge with savoury items sprinkled in) and noodles. Closed on public holidays.

Bars, pubs and clubs

The most concentrated collection of bars is in the **Lan Kwai Fong** area on Hong Kong Island. A stroll along Lan Kwai Fong Lane, and neighbouring streets, will take you past any number of possibilities (with new places constantly opening) for late-night carousing, with drinkers spilling out on to the street. Just up the hill from Lan Kwai Fong, the bars of **SoHo** are also becoming increasingly popular, and are slightly less raucous. **Wan Chai** is another busy area after dark, though not so convenient for browsing as the various locations are more thinly scattered. **Tsim Sha Tsui** is not generally known for its nightlife, though in fact there is something of a scene here, too, catering for both travellers and expats. Hart Avenue and Prat Avenue, west from Chatham Road South, are the best places to look for a drink, with several alternatives very close together. For up-to-the-minute listings consult the latest issue of *HK Magazine* or other listings publications.

Some venues charge an entrance fee on certain nights (generally Fridays and Saturdays), which ranges from around $50 to as much as $200 in the flashest clubs. In the early evening, on the other hand, a lot of places run **happy hours** – some lasting several hours – serving two drinks for the price of one. Opening times often extend well into the small hours. **Live music**, and sometimes even **raves**, can be found if you look hard, though they are unlikely to match what you're used to back home. For details, consult *HK Magazine*. The **gay scene**, while hardly prominent, is at least more active than in other Chinese cities, given that laws on homosexuality are more liberal here than on the mainland.

Hong Kong Island

Alibi 73 Wyndham St, Central. Rather mellow, thanks to plush red curtains, organic nosh and a laid-back bar.

Blue Door Floor 5, 37 Cochrane St, Central ⓦwww.bluedoor.com.hk. Sadly Hong Kong's only jazz club, following the close of the eponymous club on D'Aguilar Street. Top quality live music and jazz at weekends.

Caledonia Ground Floor, Hutchinson House, 10 Harcourt Rd, Admiralty. British beer, pub grub and the stuffed heads of various hairy beasts nailed to the walls in a cavernous, clubby pub – plus a "Wall of Whisky".

Carnegie's 53–55 Lockhart Rd, Wan Chai. Noise level means conversation here is only possible by flash cards, and once it's packed hordes of punters keen to revel the night away fight for dancing space on the bar. Regular live music.

C-Club Basement, California Tower, 30–32 D'Aguilar St, Lan Kwai Fong. Sinfully comfortable basement bar boasting VIP zones, velvet and fur decoration, heaped up cushions and a ground-floor bar dishing out shorts and long drinks.

The Fringe Club 2 Lower Albert Rd, Central ⓦwww.hkfringeclub.com. Live acts, drinks, exhibitions and generally alternative culture in a rather bohemian hang-out in the red and white Fringe building. One of the cheaper places, with a regular happy hour.

Mad Dogs 1 D'Aguilar St, Lan Kwai Fong. A few metres south of Stanley St (with another branch at 32 Nathan Rd). Always packed out with expats tucking into pub grub and beer, who can get fairly riotous by the late evening. Occasionally has live bands.

Music Room Floor 2, California Entertainment Building, 34–36 D'Aguilar St, Lan Kwai Fong Ⓦwww.lankwaifong.com. Booze, live R&B, percussion, soloists in a popular, cooler-than-cool venue.

Petticoat Lane 1 Tung Wah Lane, Central. Stylish wine bar under the escalator just above Lyndhurst Terrace. Baroque hangings, topiary, candles and good snacks give it a great atmosphere. Also patronized by the local gay community.

Post '97 9 Lan Kwai Fong, Central. A disco downstairs and a vaguely arty, bohemian atmosphere in the bar upstairs with a strong gay presence on Friday nights. Serves fry-ups, sandwiches and all-day breakfasts.

Staunton's Bar and Café 10–12 Staunton St, SoHo. Right by the escalator, this rather cavernous bar and fusion-food restaurant quickly fills up in the evening; a good place to gather before checking out neighbouring joints.

Stormy Weather Ground and First Floor, 46–50 D'Aguilar St, Lan Kwai Fong. Comfort food – wings and calamari – when you can't face another bowl of noodles, in the heart of raucous Lan Kwai Fong.

Kowloon

Bahama Mama's 4–5 Knutsford Terrace, just north of Kimberly Rd. A good atmosphere with a vibrant mix of nationalities, and plenty of space for pavement drinking. There's a beach-bar theme and outdoor terrace that prompts party crowd antics. On club nights there's a great range of mixed music.

Delaney's Basement, Mary Building, 71–77 Peking Rd. Friendly Irish pub with draught beers, including Guinness; features Irish folk music most nights.

Ned Kelly's Last Stand 11A Ashley Rd. Very popular with both travellers and expats. Features a nightly performance from an excellent ragtime jazz band.

Shopping

Visitors are still coming to Hong Kong to go **shopping** despite the fact that the cost of living in the territory has risen above that of most other countries in the world. The famed **electronic goods** of Nathan Road, for example, are by no means cheap any more and when you consider the high possibility of some form of rip-off, you are probably best advised to buy your cameras and other gadgets at home. What is special about Hong Kong, however, is the enormous range of goods on offer – and all in such a tiny area of land. And some things are indeed cheap, particularly **clothes**, **silk**, **jewellery**, **Chinese arts and crafts**, some **computer accessories** and **pirated goods**. Many of these are made in the People's Republic. As a general rule you'll find that the farther you are from touristy Tsim Sha Tsui, the cheaper your shopping becomes. Shops stay open late and are open daily. In Tsim Sha Tsui, Causeway Bay and Wan Chai, general hours are 10am–10pm; in Central it's 10am–7pm. For more detailed shopping listings, consult the HKTB shopping guide for the latest and greatest or browse Ⓦwww.qtshk.com for shops and stores listed under the HKTB's Quality Tourism Services Scheme or check their shopping guide (listed under "Things to do" at Ⓦwww.DiscoverHongKong.com).

Antiques, arts and crafts

You are unlikely to find any bargain **antiques** in Hong Kong, but you may find it pleasanter making your purchase here than in aggressive mainland China. You'll also find a larger selection of items and a wider range of quality. The main area for antiques is Hollywood Road in Central, where there are dozens of shops, selling everything from embroidery to burial ceramics. Even if you have no intention of buying, it's fun to look and you can learn a lot about ancient Chinese culture in a couple of hours. If you are interested, note that "antique" doesn't always mean more than 100 years old – ask to be sure. Vincent Choi's guide, *Collecting Chinese Antiquities in Hong Kong*, is also worth a read (available at Dragon Culture, 184 & 231 Hollywood Rd, Sheung Wan Ⓣ2545 8098, Ⓦwww.dragonculture

△ Old postcards and prints on sale at Hollywood Road

.com.hk). If you're more interested in modern **arts and crafts**, there are also a number of stores specializing in goods from China and elsewhere in the region. The best is probably Chinese Arts and Crafts, which has branches at the China Resources Building, 26 Harbour Rd, Wan Chai; 230 The Mall, Pacific Place, 88 Queensway, Admiralty; Star House, 3 Salisbury Rd, Tsim Sha Tsui; and the *Nathan Hotel*, 378 Nathan Rd, Kowloon. Each has a huge selection of fabrics, porcelain, cashmere, clothes and other Chinese-made items, although some of the silks and household linens can be bought cheaper in Stanley Market. They also stock jewellery and jade – for more of the latter the Jade Market in Mong Kok is a good place to look (see p.741) – and it's sensible to take everything the stallholders here tell you with a heavy pinch of salt. Otherwise, if you're after Chinese furniture and home decorations, it's worth trekking out to Horizon Plaza at Ap Lei Chau, for 200,000 square feet of shops such as Banyan Tree and Shambala. Some more specific stores include:

Banyan Tree 214–218 Prince's Building, Chater Rd, Central (also at 257 Ocean Terminal, Canton Rd, Tsim Sha Tsui, and Horizon Plaza, Ap Lei Chau). Antique and reproduction furniture, and handicrafts from around Asia. Pricey for what it is.

Dynasty Antiques Ground Floor, 48–50 Hollywood Rd, Central ⓣ 2851 1389, ⓦ www.dynasty-antiques.com. Finely restored classic Chinese and Tibetan antique furniture in a cavernous store.

Eu Yan Sang Ground Floor, 152–156 Queens Rd, Central ⓣ 2544 3308, ⓦ www.euyansang.com. One of the most famous medicine shops in town, said to have been around for over ninety years, this is your source of teas, herbs and Chinese medicines, all carefully weighed and measured.

Friendship Trading Company 105–107 Hollywood Rd ⓣ 2548 3830. Wholesale and retail antiques, arts and crafts. They also organize shopping trips to mainland China, if you're keen; goods can either be taken home on the spot or exported once they've been renovated.

Karin Weber Gallery 32A Staunton St, SoHo ⓣ 2544 5004. Large selection of mid-price items. Also organizes furniture-buying trips to warehouses on the mainland.

L&E 188 Hollywood Rd ⓣ 2546 9886. New decorative porcelain and old Chinese furniture. They have a warehouse in Sheung Shui full of old furniture and china. Packing and shipping can be arranged.

Museum Shop Hong Kong Arts Centre, Cultural Centre, Salisbury Rd, Tsim Sha Tsui. Art books and supplies, calligraphy materials, prints, postcards, gifts and stationery. Unfortunately the staff are not very helpful.

Palette Collections Gallery Floor 5, 23 D'Aguilar St, Lan Kwai Fong ⓣ 2522 5928, ⓦ www.palettecollections.com. Authentic paintings from all over China and the US, in addition to porcelain and antique Chinese furniture.

Shanghai Tang Pedder Building, Pedder St, Central. As well as clothes they also stock a small selection of upmarket craft and household items – linen, notebooks, photo frames, and the ever-popular Mao and Deng watches.

Teresa Coleman 79 Wyndham St ⓣ 2526 2450, ⓦ www.teresacoleman.com. One of Hong Kong's best-known dealers, with an international reputation for Chinese textiles. In addition, they have a good selection of pictures and prints.

The Tibetan Gallery 55 Wyndham St ⓣ 2530 4863. This has an interesting – if expensive – selection of Tibetan furniture, rugs, silverware and religious paintings.

Wah Tung China Ltd Floors 14–17, Grand Marine Ind. Buildings, 3 Yue Fung St, Aberdeen ⓣ 2873 2272. A 30,000 square foot showroom, groaning with antique porcelain and reproductions.

Clothes

These can be good value in Hong Kong, particularly the local fashion brand names such as Gordiano, U2, G2000, Jessica, Episode and Bossini, which have branches all over the city. Big-name foreign designer clothes can also be found with remarkable ease, although they are often significantly more expensive than back home because of the extra cachet attached to foreign upmarket brands. But the sales are worth checking out.

Another interesting and potentially very cheap way to buy clothes (including designer clothes without the labels) is from **factory outlets**. These places can open and close very quickly so consult the HKTB brochure, *Factory Outlets*, for addresses, or pick up a locally published guide like *The Smart Shopper in Hong Kong* or *The Complete Guide to Hong Kong Factory Bargains*. Be sure to try things on before you buy – marked sizes mean nothing. If you just want to browse, good places to start include **Granville Road** in Tsim Sha Tsui, the **Pedder Building** on Pedder St in Central and, just round the corner, **Wyndham St** and **D'Aguilar St**. If you're a fan of high fashion the **Joyce Warehouse** in the Hing Wai Centre, Aberdeen, is a must – it's where Hong Kong's smartest boutique sends last season's (or last month's) stuff that didn't sell – discounts up to eighty percent. Other places to look include:

Blanc De Chine Floor 2, Pedder Building, 12 Pedder St, Central. Elegant designs loosely based on traditional Chinese clothes, mostly in silk or cashmere.

Joyce Boutique 16 Queen's Rd, Central; Shop 226 & 344 Pacific Place, 88 Queensway, Admiralty. Hong Kong's most fashionable boutique offers its own range of clothing, as well as many top overseas designer brands.

Shanghai Tang Ground Floor, Pedder Building, 12 Pedder St, Central. A must visit store, beautifully done up in 1930s Shanghai style. It specializes in new versions of traditional Chinese styles like the *cheongsam* split-sided dress – often in vibrant colours – and they can also make to order, although items are far from cheap (see below). The sales are regular and good.

Walter Ma Century Square, 1 D'Aguilar St, Central. One of the best-known local designers, who designs for foreign figures as well as local people. He is particularly well known for his formal wear.

Tailor-made clothes

Tailor-made clothes are a traditional speciality of the Hong Kong tourist trade and wherever you go in Tsim Sha Tsui you'll be accosted by Indian tailors offering this service. But you may find better work elsewhere, in residential areas and locations like hotels or shopping arcades where the tailors rely on regular clients. Western women in particular should look for someone who understands the Western body shape. Prices are relatively low here, but not rock bottom. Have a long chat with your tailor before committing yourself, and make sure you know exactly what's included. And don't ask for something in 24 hours – it either won't fit or will fall apart, or both. Expect at least two or three fittings over several days if you want a good result. You'll need to pay about fifty percent of the price as deposit.

The best-known tailor in town is probably **Sam's Tailors**, at 94 Nathan Rd, Tsim Sha Tsui. Sam is famous as much for his talent for self-publicity as for his clothes. Others include:

Johnson & Co 44 Hankow Rd, Kowloon. Does a lot of work for military and naval customers. Mostly male clientele.

Linva Tailor 38 Cochrane St, Central. Well-established ladies' tailor, popular with locals who want *cheongsams* for parties. They work a lot with embroidery.

Margaret Court Tailoress Floor 8, Winner Building, 27 D'Aguilar St, Central. She has lots of local Western female clients, and a solid reputation for good work, although it doesn't come cheaply. A shirt costs around $300 plus fabric.

Pacific Custom Tailors Floor 3, 322 Pacific Place, 88 Queensway, Admiralty. Upmarket suits with a price to match, in one of Hong Kong's snazziest shopping malls.

Shanghai Tang Pedder Building, 12 Pedder St, Central ⓦwww.shanghaitang.com. This boutique also has a tailoring service turning out Chinese-style garments for men and women, and a fabulous selection of fabrics. They are used to helping visitors – and can arrange quick fittings and posting of finished garments.

Computers

Both hardware and software can work out very cheap in Hong Kong, though if you are buying hardware check that it is compatible with your country's electrical mains voltage, and make sure you get the right kind of warranty. Without an international warranty you won't be able to have your computer repaired or replaced once you have left Hong Kong. It's often wise to patronise local chains, such as Fortress, if you want to avoid the risk of taking home shoddy goods. A good place to check the latest prices and special offers is the Technology supplement in the *South China Morning Post*, published every Tuesday. **Pirated computer software** is also big business, though these days it's more discreet. As with all pirated goods the risk is yours. You pay very little but it may not work and you may even have difficulty importing it into your own country.

298 Computer Zone 146 Fuk Wa St, Sham Shui Po, Kowloon (Sham Shui Po MTR exit C2). Ranging from dodgy pirated stuff to top-notch brands.

Golden Shopping Centre 156 Fuk Wah St, Sham Shui Po, Kowloon (Sham Shui Po MTR exit D2). Lots of cheap computer goods, including pirated software.

Mongkok Computer Centre, at the corner of Nelson St and Fa Yuen St, Mongkok. One of the best places for pirated CDs.

Wan Chai Computer Centre 298 Hennessy Rd, Wan Chai (Wan Chai MTR, ext A4). Warren-like place, full of shops selling new, second-hand, official and pirated computer gear.

Department stores

You probably never intended to while away your time in China walking around department stores, but in a shoppers' paradise like Hong Kong the chances are you will go to one at some point. In summer particularly their air conditioning is attractive, and most have nice cafés to boot. You should also give a few of Hong Kong's glossy shopping malls a whirl; some of the best include Times Square (Causeway Bay MTR), Pacific Place (Admiralty MTR), Lee Gardens (Causeway Bay MTR) and Festival Walk (Kowloon Tong MTR).

CRC Department Store Chiao Shang Building, 92 Queen's Rd, Central; Lok Sing Centre, 31 Yee Wo St, Causeway Bay. At the cheaper end of the spectrum, but a good supply of Chinese specialities like medicines, foods, porcelain and handicrafts.

Lane Crawford 70 Queen's Rd, Central; One Pacific Place, 88 Queensway, Admiralty; Times Square, 1 Matheson St, Causeway Bay. Hong Kong's oldest Western-style department store.

Mitzukoshi Hennessy Centre, 500 Hennessy Rd, Causeway Bay. If you've never been to Japan, try this place at least. Possibly the smartest of all the Causeway Bay stores.

SOGO East Point Centre, 555 Hennessy Rd, Causeway Bay. Another of the Japanese contingent. Immaculately presented goods over ten floors, including a Japanese supermarket.

Wing On 26 Des Voeux Rd, Central (and other branches). Another long-established store, with branches throughout Hong Kong SAR. Standard, day-to-day goods rather than luxuries.

Yue Hwa Chinese Products Emporium 54–64 (main branch) and 301–309 Nathan Rd, Yau Ma Tei (and other locations). Chinese department store particularly strong on silk clothing, medicines and foodstuffs.

Jewellery

Hong Kongers – both men and women – love **jewellery**, the flashier and more sparkling the better. Consequently, there are literally thousands of jewellers. Some offer pieces which look remarkably like the more popular designs of the famous international jewellery houses. Prices are low, so if you've always coveted something like that, it's worth having a look. But shop around, as different shops may ask wildly different prices for the same design. Most places will bargain a little. The HKTA's free *Shopping Guide to Jewellery* is helpful. Some places to start include:

Gallery One 31–33 Hollywood Rd, Central. A huge selection of semi-precious stones and jewellery – amber, amethyst, tiger's eye, crystal and much more. They will string any arrangement you want.

Kai-Yin Lo Ltd Floor 3 Pacific Place; Shop 11A, *Peninsula Hotel*. Hong Kong's best-known jewellery designer, who uses old jade, carved and semi-precious stones. Expensive, but nice to look.

Opus Collections Ground Floor, Tak House, 5–11 Stanley St, Central ☎2868 2801. Classy jewellery, watches and ink pens.

Peter Choi Gems & Jewellery Shop 224A, *Hong Kong Hotel*, 3 Canton Rd, Kowloon. This shop is just inside the main entrance to Ocean Terminal. It has a lot of nice, simple designs, including some classics, and a wide range of prices. Peter Choi will bargain a little.

Listings

Airlines Air India, Rm 3008–9, The Centre, 99 Queen's Rd, Central ☎2522 1176; British Airways, Floor 24, Jardine House, Exchange Square, Central ☎2822 9000; Cathay Pacific, Floor 35, Two Pacific Place, 88 Queensway, Admiralty ☎2747 1888; Dragonair, Rm 601–3 Wheelock House, 20 Pedder St, Central ☎2590 1188; JAL, Floor 20, Gloucester Tower, Pedder St, Central ☎2523 0081; KLM, Rm 2201–3, World Trade Centre, 280 Gloucester Rd, Causeway Bay ☎2808 2111; Korean Air, Floor 11, Tower Two, South Seas Centre, 75 Mody Rd, Tsim Sha Tsui East ☎2368 6221; Malaysia Airlines, Central Tower, Queens Rd, Central ☎2521 8181; Qantas, Rm 3701, Jardine House, 1 Connaught Place, Central ☎2842 1438; Singapore Airlines, Floor 17, United Centre, 95 Queensway, Admiralty ☎2520 2233; Thai International, Floor 24 United Centre, 95 Queensway, Admiralty ☎2876 6888; United Airlines, Floor 29, Gloucester Tower, The Landmark, 11 Pedder St, Central ☎2810 4888.

American Express Ground Floor, New World Tower, 16–18 Queen's Rd, Central (Mon–Fri 9am–5.30pm, Sat 9am–noon; ☎2801 7300; report stolen cheques on ☎2885 9331).

Banks and exchange Banks generally open Mon–Fri 9am–4.30pm, Sat 9am–12.30pm, though there is quite a hefty commission on traveller's cheques in many banks; among those who generally don't charge commission are the Hang Seng, Wing Lung Bank and the Wing On. The licensed moneychangers, on the other hand, which open all hours including Sundays, may not charge commission but sometimes give very poor rates; signs saying "No Commission" may only apply if you're selling Hong Kong dollars. Especially avoid moneychangers with windows looking onto Nathan Road, and always ask around before changing large sums as there are significant variations in rates. There are also ample ATMs throughout the SAR.

Bookshops For such a cosmopolitan city, Hong Kong has a rather poor selection of decent foreign-language bookshops. The Swindon Book Company has what is probably the largest centrally located English-language bookstore at 13–15 Lock Rd, Tsim Sha Tsui; it has another branch at the Star Ferry concourse, Tsim Sha Tsui, which is particularly good for books on Hong Kong and for glossy art books. Dymock's bookshop at the Star Ferry, Central, is good for paperbacks and travel guides. Some of the shopping malls also have reasonable outlets, in particular Page One in Festival Walk, Kowloon Tong, in Times Square, the Taikoo Shing mall in Quarry Bay, Causeway Bay, and Bookazine at 89 Queensway, Admiralty. The Government Publications Centre, at Tower Block, Ground Floor, 66 Queensway, Admiralty, has Hong Kong maps, and all kinds of books on local politics and the local environment.

Cinema The major cinemas include UA Pacific Place at 88 Queensway, Central, and also at Times Square, Causeway Bay. For alternative or art films, including Chinese, try the Hong Kong Arts Centre at 2 Harbour Rd, Wan Chai ☎2582 0200; Broadway Cinematheque, at Prosperous Garden, 3 Public Square St, Yau Ma Tei ☎2388 3188; or the Cine-Art House, Sun Hung Kai Centre, 30 Harbour Rd, Wan Chai ☎2827 4820.

Embassies and consulates Australia, Floor 23, Harbour Centre, 25 Harbour Rd, Wan Chai ☎2827 8881; Britain, 1 Supreme Court Rd, Admiralty ☎2901 3000; Canada, Floor 14, 1 Exchange Square, Central ☎2810 4321; China Visa Office, China Resources Bldg, Lower Block, 26 Harbour Rd, Wan Chai ☎3413 2300; India, 504 Admiralty Centre, Tower One, 18 Harcourt Rd, Admiralty ☎2528 4028; Japan, Floor 46, One Exchange Square, Central ☎2522 1184; Korea, Floor 5, Far East Financial Centre, 16 Harcourt Rd, Central ☎2529 4141; Malaysia, Floor 23, Malaysia Building, 50 Gloucester Rd, Wan Chai ☎2527 0921; New Zealand, Rm 2705, Jardine House, Connaught Rd, Central ☎2877 4488; Philippines, Floor 6, United Centre, 95 Queensway, Admiralty ☎2823 8500; Taiwan, Floor 4, East Tower, Lippo Centre, 89 Queensway, Admiralty ☎2525 8315; Thailand, Floor 8, Fairmont House, 8 Cotton Tree Drive, Central ☎2521 6481; USA, 26 Garden Rd, Central ☎2523 9011; Vietnam, Floor 15, Great Smart Tower, 230 Wan Chai Rd, Wan Chai ☎2291 4510.

Festivals Festivals specific to Hong Kong include the Tin Hau Festival, in late April or May, in honour of the Goddess of Fishermen. Large seaborne festivities take place, most notably at Joss House Bay on Sai Kung Peninsula (see p.746). Another is the Tai Chiu Festival (known in English as the Bun Festival) held on Cheung Chau Island during May. The Tuen Ng (Dragon-boat) Festival takes place in early June, with races in various places around the territory in long, narrow boats. Other Chinese festivals, such as New Year and Mid-Autumn, are celebrated in Hong Kong with as much, if not more, gusto than on the mainland.

Hospitals Government hospitals have 24-hour casualty wards, where treatment is free. These include the Princess Margaret Hospital, Lai King Hill Rd, Lai Chi Kok, Kowloon ⓣ2990 1111 and the Queen Mary Hospital, Pokfulam Rd, Hong Kong Island ⓣ2855 3111. For an ambulance dial ⓣ999.

Internet access Thanks to free local phone calls throughout Hong Kong and competitive broadband Internet services, it's hardly surprising that you'll be able to access the Internet for next to nothing throughout Hong Kong. Indeed, cafés such as *MiX* and *Pacific Coffee* provide 15–30 minutes' free use, provided you purchase something from them.

Laundry There is a cheap laundry service on the ground floor of the Golden Crown Court on Nathan Rd (one block north of the Mirador Mansions) – use the red entrance; you'll see a sign at the end of the corridor. Same-day service for three kilos of clothes costs $30. Mirador Mansions, Floor 13, has a similar place called Posh Wash.

Left luggage There's an office in the departure lounge at the airport (daily 6.30am–1am), and at the Central and Kowloon stations for the Airport Express. Alternatively you can usually leave luggage at your guesthouse or hotel – but ensure you're happy with the owners and general security before leaving anything valuable. There are also coin-operated lockers in the HK China Ferry Terminal in Tsim Sha Tsui.

Library The main English-language library is in the City Hall High Block, Edinburgh Place, Central (Mon–Fri 10am–9pm, Sat 10am–5pm, Sun 10am–1pm). The British Council, 1 Supreme Court Rd, Admiralty, also has a library which includes a selection of UK newspapers, videos and talking books (Mon–Fri noon–8pm, Sat 10.30am–5.30pm; ⓣ2913 55005.

Lost property For belongings left in taxis call ⓣ2389 8288; however they charge a steep fee in advance to search for lost items, and they don't have a very good record for finding anything. See also the police general enquiries number below.

Mail The general post office is at 2 Connaught Place, Central (Mon–Fri 8am–6pm, Sat–Sun 8am–2pm; ⓣ2921 2222), just west of the Star Ferry and north of Jardine House (the tower with porthole windows). Poste restante mail is delivered here (you can pick it up Mon–Sat 8am–6pm), unless specifically addressed to "Kowloon". The Kowloon main post office is at 10 Middle Rd, Tsim Sha Tsui ⓣ2366 4111. Both have shops which sell boxes, string and tape to pack any stuff you want to send home.

Police Crime hotline and taxi complaints ⓣ2527 7177. For general police enquiries call ⓣ2860 2000.

Sport For horse racing, see "Happy Valley", p.731. Every Easter, Hong Kong is host to an international Rugby Sevens tournament (information from Hong Kong Rugby Football Union ⓣ2504 8300). The following activities are also available in the territory: sailing (information from the Hong Kong Yachting Association ⓣ2504 8158); windsurfing (try the Windsurf Centre on Kwun Yam Wan Beach, Cheung Chau, for rentals and instruction); martial arts (*tai ji* takes place in all public parks; for more general information, call the HK Chinese Martial Arts Association ⓣ2394 4803); marathon-running (the Hong Kong marathon takes place in January; to enter, call the HK Amateur Athletic Association ⓣ2504 8215). Public tennis courts are available in Victoria Park (ⓣ2570 6186), at the Hong Kong Tennis Centre on Wong Nai Chung Gap Road (ⓣ2574 9122) and at King's Park (ⓣ2388 8154) in Kowloon. Courts are around $40 per hour. Private coaching (ask at the courts) is around $350 per hour. The easiest way to get a round of golf on the crowded local links is probably by taking the HKTA's golfing tour, which provides transport and entry for around $500. Alternatively, try ringing the Clearwater Bay Golf & Country Club ⓣ2719 1595.

Swimming pools One of the most conveniently located public pools is in Kowloon Park on Nathan Rd, Tsim Sha Tsui (daily 6.30am–9pm; adults $19, children $8). Another is in Victoria Park, Causeway Bay (daily 6.30am–10pm; adults $19, children $8). All public pools tend to be very crowded, and the water is sometimes not that clean.

Telephones All local calls are free, and you can usually use any phones in hotel lobbies and restaurants for no charge. Payphones require $1 for five minutes. For IDD calls, use a payphone or go to a Hong Kong Telecom office; there's one at Hermes House, 10 Middle Rd, Tsim Sha Tsui (24hr), and also at Telecom House, 3 Gloucester Rd, Wan Chai (Mon–Fri 8am–9pm, Sat 8am–3pm). For directory enquiries in English call ⓣ1081 and for emergency services call ⓣ999.

Thomas Cook Traveller's cheques service available at Floor 18, Vicwood Plaza, 199 Des Voeux

Rd, Central (Mon–Fri 9am–5.30pm, Sat 9am–1pm; ⓣ2544 4986) or Room 602, Tern Plaza, 5 Cameron Rd, Tsim Sha Tsui.

Tours The HKTB runs a series of interesting theme tours, such as the "Sports and Recreation Tour" (see "Clear Water Bay", p.745) and the "Come Horse-racing Tour" (see "Happy Valley", p.731). These tours are fun, but are really for those in a hurry and with plenty of money. Consult HKTB's brochures for details. Other operators offering numerous tours – the harbour, shopping trips to Shenzhen, the New Territories, Kowloon, the Mai Po Wetlands, Hong Kong Dolphinwatch – are advertised in brochures available around the Star Ferry ticket windows. Helicopter flightseeing and heli-hiking trips to the New Territories are also available (ⓣ2802 0200, ⓦwww.heliservices.com.hk), or you might consider hiring a junk for a short-term charter, affordable if you split the cost between a group of ten (ⓦwww.panaoceans.com).

Travel agents Hong Kong is full of budget travel agents including Shoestring Travel Ltd, Flat A, Floor 4, Alpha House, 27–33 Nathan Rd (ⓣ2723 2306, ⓕ2721 2085) and Hong Kong Student Travel Ltd, Hang Lung Centre, Yee Wo St, Causeway Bay (ⓣ2833 9909). The cheaper hostels often have useful up-to-date information and contacts for budget travel as well, or look in the classified ads of the *South China Morning Post*. For train tickets, tours, flights and visas to mainland China, try the Chinese state travel agency, CITS, Rm 1213–15, Floor 13, Tower A, New Mandarin Plaza, 14 Science Museum Rd, Tsim Sha Tsui East (ⓣ2732 5888, ⓕ2721 7204) or, alternatively, the more friendly CTS, whose main office is on Floor 4, CTS House, 78–83 Connaught Rd, Central (ⓣ2522 0450).

TV, radio and the media English-language television channels include Pearl and ATV, although many hotels show satellite and cable TV channels. The BBC World Service is available in Hong Kong on 675kHz AM. Hong Kong's main newspapers include the *South China Morning Post* (plus the *Sunday Morning Post*) broadsheet, *The Standard* (a business-focused tabloid) and *China Daily*, with a mainland slant.

Macau

Sixty kilometres west across the Pearl River estuary from Hong Kong lies the tiny former Portuguese enclave of **MACAU**. A mere sliver of mainland and a couple of islands covering just twenty-six square kilometres in total (a considerable proportion of which is reclaimed land), the territory is geographically and economically a midget compared with its booming cousin across the water, and the Macanese transfer of sovereignty back to China in 1999 – two years after Hong Kong's – had none of the drama or controversy that surrounded that of Hong Kong. As in its larger neighbour, Hong Kong, the majority of Macau's population are Cantonese-speaking Chinese, some of whom still ply the waters as fishermen. However, this has not prevented the territory from developing an atmosphere distinct not only from Hong Kong but from other parts of southern China. With outdoor cafés, charming Portuguese place names, public squares, the odd palm tree and numerous Portuguese restaurants, there is a definite whiff of southern Europe in the air.

However, by the millions of gambling fanatics living in nearby Hong Kong (and increasingly Shenzhen and Guangzhou as well), Macau, with its liberal gambling laws, is seen as little more than one giant **casino**, although the 2002 liberalization of its gambling laws is seeing Dr Stanley Ho's monopoly challenged by two huge US investors from Las Vegas. It is largely as a spin-off from the colossal gambling trade that money is being pumped in, allowing large-

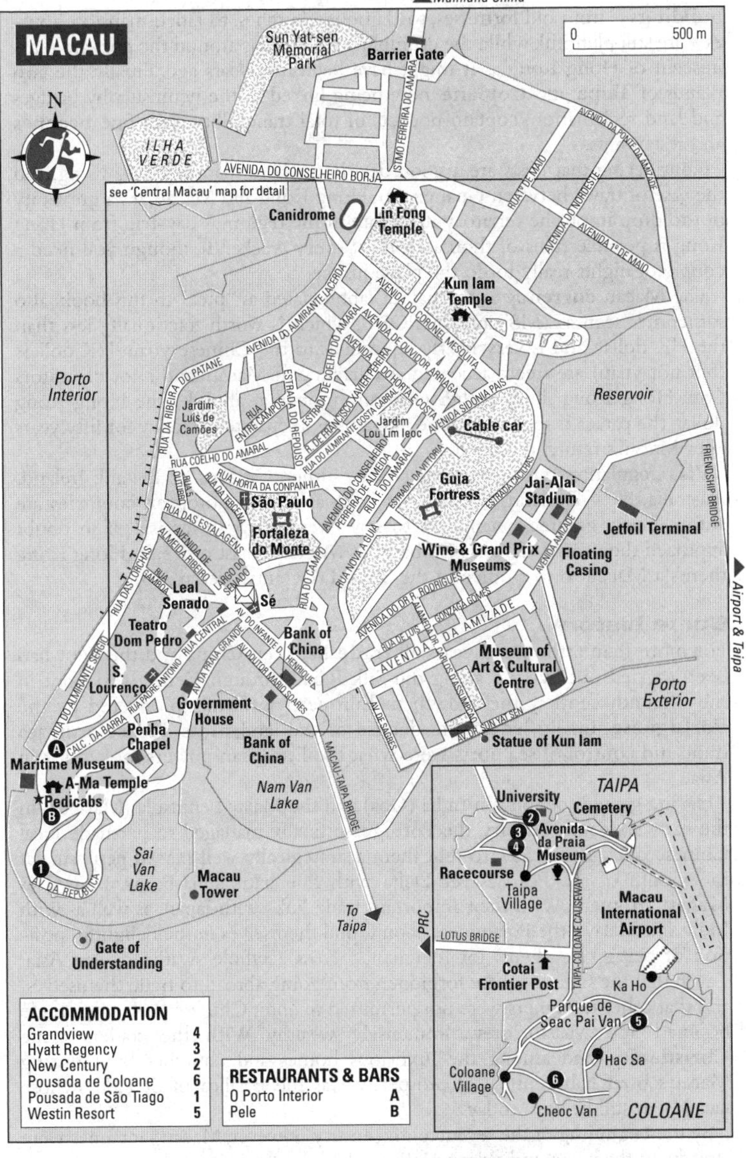

scale construction to take off, including that of Macau's own (underused) **international airport** on the island of Taipa. New highrise hotels, highways and bridges are appearing, and even Hong Kong-style land reclamation has taken place en masse.

Nevertheless, temptations for non-gamblers remain. With a colonial past pre-dating that of Hong Kong by nearly three hundred years, Macau's **historic**

buildings – from old fortresses, to Baroque churches, to faded mansion houses – are still plentiful, while the crumbling backstreets around the port are reminiscent of Hong Kong as it might have been fifty years ago. Finally, the two islands of **Taipa** and **Coloane**, now being linked to the peninsula by bridges and land reclamation, contain pockets of total tranquillity with fine **beaches** and restaurants.

Considering that costs are a good deal lower here than in Hong Kong, and the ease of travel between Guangzhou, Hong Kong and Macau, it's a great pity not to drop in on the territory if you are in the region. A day-trip from Hong Kong is possible (tens of thousands do it every weekend), though you need a couple of nights really to do the place justice.

The Macau **currency** is the pataca (abbreviated as "ptca" in this book; also sometimes seen as "M$" and "MPO$"), which is worth fractionally less than the HK dollar, and is very nearly equivalent to the Chinese yuan. HK dollars (but not yuan) are freely accepted as currency in Macau, and a lot of visitors from Hong Kong don't bother changing money at all. Like the Hong Kong dollar, the pataca is set to continue its status as a separate currency for fifty years after Macau's return to China.

Visa regulations are not set to change either. Citizens of Britain, Ireland, Australia, New Zealand, Canada, the USA and most European countries are automatically granted permission to stay twenty days on arrival. If in doubt approach the nearest Chinese Embassy or Macau tourist office. In Hong Kong there's a Macau tourist office in the Shun Tak Centre (see p.715).

Some history

For more than a thousand years all **trade** between China and the West had been carried out by land along the Silk Road through Central Asia, but in the fifteenth century the growth in European seafaring, pioneered by the **Portuguese**, finally led to the demise of the land route. Henceforth, sea trade and control of sea ports were what the European powers looked for in Asia.

Having gained toeholds in India (Goa) and the Malay Peninsula (Malacca) in the early sixteenth century, the Portuguese finally managed to persuade local Chinese officials, in 1557, to rent them a strategically well-placed peninsula at the mouth of the Pearl River Delta with fine natural harbours, known as **Macao** (Aomen). With their important trade links with Japan, as well as with India and Malaya, the Portuguese soon found themselves in the delightful position of being sole agents for merchants across a whole swathe of east Asia. Given that the Chinese were forbidden from going abroad to trade themselves, and that other foreigners were not permitted to enter Chinese ports, their trade boomed and Macau grew immensely wealthy. With the traders came **Christianity**, and among the luxurious homes and churches built during Macau's brief half-century of prosperity was the Basilica of St Paul, whose facade can still be seen today.

By the beginning of the seventeenth century, however, Macau's fortunes were already on the wane, and a slow decline, which has continued almost ever since, set in. A combination of setbacks for the Portuguese, including defeats in war against the Spanish back home, the loss of trading relations with both Japan and China, and the rise of the Dutch as a trading power, saw Macau almost wiped off the map by mid-century.

In the eighteenth century, fortunes looked up somewhat, as more and more non-Portuguese European traders came looking for opportunities to prise open the locked door of China. For these people, Macau seemed a tempting base from which to operate, and eventually they were permitted to settle and build homes in the colony. The British had greater ambitions than to remain forever as guests in someone else's colony and when they finally seized their own piece of the shore to the east in 1841, Macau's status – as a backwater – was definitively settled. Despite the introduction of **licensed gambling** in the 1850s, as a desperate means of securing some kind of income, virtually all trade was lost to Hong Kong.

Over the last century, Macau's population has increased massively to roughly 450,000 as repeated waves of **immigrants** have flooded the territory, whether fleeing Japanese invaders or Chinese Communists, but, unlike in Hong Kong, this growth has not been accompanied by the same spectacular economic development. Indeed, in 1974, with the end of the fascist dictatorship in Portugal, the Portuguese attempted unilaterally to hand Macau back to China; the offer was refused, as it had been previously in the 1960s at the time of the Cultural Revolution. Only after the 1984 agreement with Britain over the future of Hong Kong did China agree to negotiate the formal return of Macau as well. In **1999**, the final piece of Asian soil still in European hands was surrendered.

When they departed, however, the Portuguese left one rather low-profile legacy – the **Macanese**, offspring of mixed Chinese–Portuguese parentage, many of whom are entirely rooted in the fundamentally Chinese world of Macau, but still maintain Portuguese traditions and speak Portuguese.

Arrival, information and transport

Macau comprises three distinct parts: the **peninsula**, which is linked by bridge to the island of **Taipa**, which is in turn linked by bridge to a second island, **Coloane**. The peninsula of Macau, where the original old city was located and where most of the historic sights still are (as well as the city amenities), is entirely developed right up to the border with China in the north, though the islands, Coloane in particular, contain some quiet rural patches.

The peninsula is not large and it's possible to get around much of it on foot, though you'll need buses for the longer stretches. Macau's Jetfoil Terminal, for boats to and from Hong Kong, is in the southeast of the peninsula. The most important road, **Avenida Almeida Ribeiro**, cuts across from east to west, taking in the *Hotel Lisboa*, one of Macau's most famous landmarks, and exits on its western end at the Inner Harbour, near to the docking point for ferries from Guangzhou. The western part of Almeida Ribeiro is also the budget hotel area.

In Macau, all boats from **Hong Kong** and **Shenzhen** use the same terminal, usually referred to on bus schedules and maps as the **Jetfoil Terminal** (Nova Terminal in Portuguese), in the southeast of town by Avenida da Amizada. This is connected to the *Hotel Lisboa* and the budget hotel area on Almeida Ribeiro by a number of buses including #3 and #3A.

> **Macau phone numbers** have no area codes. From outside the territory, dial the normal international access code + ☎853 (country code) + the number. **To call Hong Kong from Macau** dial ☎01 + the number. To call Macau from mainland China, dial ☎00 + 853 + the number.

Getting to Macau and getting away

Access to and from Macau is chiefly by **boat** from Hong Kong. Large numbers of competing vessels make the one-hour journey between Macau and Hong Kong's Shun Tak Centre daily, departing roughly every fifteen minutes, including jetfoils (marginally the fastest at 55 minutes, and the most frequent, even running through the night), catamarans and high-speed ferries (roomy and cheap, but infrequent and much slower than the others). There are also less frequent catamaran services from the HK China Ferry Terminal on Canton Road in Tsim Sha Tsui. **Tickets** vary slightly in price according to type of boat, time and class of travel; reckon on paying HK$95–140 each way, though about half that for the high-speed ferry (ticket prices all include a government departure tax of HK$19). Unless you're planning to travel at peak times, such as weekends, it is not normally necessary to book in advance, though you should do so if you are on a tight schedule. In Macau, advance tickets are available from the Jetfoil Terminal in the Outer Harbour. Otherwise, for travel in either direction, simply show up at the pier half an hour before, purchase a ticket for the next sailing, clear passport control and board.

By **air**, you can fly to and from Beijing, Shanghai, Guangzhou, Taiwan, Bangkok and Singapore and a rapidly increasing list of other Chinese cities. It's hoped that destinations will soon include direct flights from Europe and North America.

By land, you can **walk** across the border (daily 7am–midnight) at the Barrier Gate, into the Zhuhai Special Economic Zone. Alternatively, there are two daily **bus** services which go direct to Guangzhou, taking two and a half hours. The MTIB can give details; tickets are available from China Travel Service (CTS) at Avenida Dr Joao IV, 13, Centro Commercial. There's a second land connection (by bus) at the Lotus Bridge that links Macau to the city of Zhuhai and on to Guangzhou (costing around 50ptca).

For those arriving at the international **airport** on Taipa Island, the airport bus #AP1 goes to the *Hotel Lisboa* and the Jetfoil Terminal while, if you've walked across the border, in the far north of the peninsula from Zhuhai in China, you can ride bus #5 from there to Almeida Ribeiro and Rua da Praia Grande. There are now also frequent direct **buses** from Guangzhou right into Macau; these deposit passengers at the Inner Harbour, near the Guangzhou Ferry Pier.

Information

The **Macau Government Tourist Office** (MGTO; Ⓦwww.macautourism.gov.mo) is a helpful organization well worth your time. They provide various leaflets on Macau's fortresses, museums, parks, churches and outlying islands as well as a good city **map**, and a free monthly **newspaper** called *Macau Travel Talk* which contains listings of all current happenings in the cultural world of the territory, as well as information on hotels and restaurants.

You can find MTIB even before you leave Hong Kong, in the Macau Ferry Terminal, Room 1303, Shun Tak Centre (Mon–Fri 9am–1pm & 2–6pm, Sat 9am–1pm; Ⓣ2549 8884). Otherwise, drop by their friendly Visitor Information Centre (daily 9am–6pm; Ⓣ5726 416) on arrival in the Jetfoil Terminal, or their main office at Largo do Senado 9 (daily 9am–6pm; Ⓣ3315 566).

Transport

Being such a tiny place, you'll have little difficulty getting around Macau. Many, if not all, places can be reached on foot or even pedicab (costing 60–80ptca from the Au Ma Temple to Senado Square), and many of the locals buzz around on scooters. If you get tired, try the cheap **taxis**, bearing in mind that trips to Taipa or Coloane will attract a surcharge on top of the meter reading of 5ptca from Macau, and 2ptca between the two islands. Otherwise, hop onto one of the many **buses** – important bus interchanges include the Jetfoil Terminal (referred to as Nova Terminal), the *Hotel Lisboa*, Almeida Ribeiro, Barra (near the A-Ma Temple), Praça Ponte e Horta (near the Guangzhou Ferry Pier on the Inner Harbour), Barra (near the Maritime Museum on the Inner Harbour), the Barrier Gate (referred to as Porto do Cerco) and the islands Taipa and Coloane. As in Hong Kong, change is not given on buses, but fares are low. There are two main bus companies; useful routes include **#3 and #3A** from the Jetfoil Terminal to *Hotel Lisboa* and Almeida Ribeiro; **#5** from Barra to Almeida Ribeiro to the Barrier Gate; **#21**, **#21A**, **#26A** and **#28A** from Almeida Ribeiro to Taipa Village and Coloane; **#28B** from the Jetfoil Terminal to *Hotel Lisboa* and Rua de Praia Grande.

Finally, **cycling** is a possibility, on the islands at least, though note that you are not allowed to cycle over the causeway from the mainland to Taipa. For details on rental, see p.778.

Accommodation

Accommodation is a good deal cheaper in Macau than in Hong Kong. For the same money that would get you a tiny box in Chungking Mansions, you can find quite a spacious room with private shower and a window here. At the bottom end, furthermore, there are one or two ancient **Chinese hostels** of a type that probably don't exist anywhere else in the Chinese world, though foreigners are not always particularly welcome at the cheaper places.

Be warned, however, that at weekends **prices** shoot up everywhere, and you are advised to come during the week if you can. Other times to avoid if possible are Chinese holidays, the Macau Grand Prix (third weekend in November) and generally the summer season, which is more expensive than the winter.

The densest concentration of hotels occurs around the western end of Almeida Ribeiro, spreading out from the Inner Harbour, though one or two places can also be found in remote, tranquil places such as the island of Coloane. Note that addresses are written with the number after the name of the street.

Western Macau

East Asia Rua da Madeira 1 ⓣ922 433, ⓕ922 430; Hong Kong reservations ⓣ2540 6333. A couple of blocks north from the western end of Almeida Ribeiro. One of Macau's oldest hotels, and a very smart, comfortable place, with great views from some of the upstairs windows. Friendly staff and very good value. ❻

Accommodation price codes

All the accommodation in this book has been graded according to price codes, which represent the cheapest double room available. Accommodation in Macau has been given codes from the categories below. Note that accommodation is generally cheaper on weekdays, unless stated otherwise.

❶ Under 75ptca
❷ 75–100ptca
❸ 100–150ptca
❹ 150–200ptca
❺ 200–300ptca
❻ 300–500ptca
❼ 500–700ptca
❽ 700–1000ptca
❾ Over 1000ptca

Hou Kong Travessa das Virtudes 1 ⓣ937 555, ⓕ338 884. Just off Rua Felicidade, down Travessa do Auto Novo. More welcoming than most along here, a real hotel with clean, balconied rooms. ❻

Kou Va Rua da Felicidade 71 ⓣ375 599. A reasonably pleasant hotel on one of Macau's most interesting streets. Although a bit run down, the rooms are large, making this one of the most attractive budget choices. ❸–❻

Hotel London Praça de Ponte e Horta 4 ⓣ937 761. A nice place offering single, double and triple rooms. ❸–❺

New World Emperor Rua de Xangai ⓣ781 888, ⓦwww.nweh.ctm.net. A centrally located, mid-price hotel, with en-suite bathrooms, evening jazz band and Chinese-style breakfasts. Forty percent discounts on weekdays, ten percent at weekends. ❹–❻

Hotel Peninsula Rua das Lorchas, Ponte Cais 14 ⓣ318 899, ⓕ344 933. Modern, clean rooms, with air conditioning. Also some good-value suites. ❹–❻

Pension Diamante Rua Nova do Comercio 11 ⓣ923 118. Slightly fancier than the guesthouses on the other side of the avenue. ❹–❺

Sun Sun Praça de Ponte e Horta 14–16 ⓣ939 393, ⓕ938 822, Hong Kong reservations ⓣ2517 4273. Immaculate, with an anonymity reminiscent of new hotels on the mainland, but good value. No weekend hike in prices. ❻

Vila Universal Rua Felicidade 73 ⓣ573 247. South of Almeida Ribeiro, this is a fairly large place, very clean and comfortable with spacious rooms. Highly recommended. ❸–❺

Vong Kong Hospedaria Rua das Lorchas 45 ⓣ574 016. On the seafront road, opposite the Gulf service station, this place offers a glimpse into the lost world of sailor life on the South China seas. Dingy and dirty, with ancient furniture and wooden partitions, but it certainly has atmosphere. Singles and doubles available. ❶–❸

Southern and eastern Macau

Lisboa Avenida de Lisboa 2–4 ⓣ377 666, Hong Kong reservations ⓣ2546 6944, ⓦwww.hotelisboa.com. This is the bizarre orange-coloured, cylindrical building you pass on the way into town from the ferry – Macau's major architectural landmark. As well as Macau's most popular casino, the *Lisboa* also houses a shopping arcade, an over-the-top exhibition of casino mogul Dr Stanley Ho's jade and porcelain gifts and numerous restaurants. Double rooms are around 900ptca on weekdays and up to 1,400ptca at weekends; it's often cheaper to stay as part of a package tour. ❽–❾

Metropole Avenida Praia Grande 493–501 ⓣ388 166, ⓕ330 890. A few hundred metres west of the *Lisboa*, well located and smartly fitted out. ❻–❼

Pousada de São Tiago Avenida da República ⓣ378 111, ⓕ552 170, Hong Kong reservations ⓣ2739 1216. Constructed from an old fortress on the southern tip of the peninsula, with walled stairways lined by gushing streams, huge stone archways and 22 delightfully furnished rooms. Popular for local wedding parties. Expect to pay 1650ptca for a double room. ❾

Taipa

Grandview Estrada Governador Albano de Oliveria ⓣ837 788, ⓕ837 736. Glitzy establishment, near the racecourse. Lots of facilities and a shuttle bus to the piers. ❻

Hyatt Regency 2 Estrada Almirante Marques Esparteiro ⓣ831 234, ⓕ830 195, ⓦwww.macau.hyatt.com, Hong Kong reservations ⓣ2559 0168. Just over the bridge from Macau (all the Taipa buses run past it), it has all the standard *Hyatt* chain facilities, including a casino, spa and landscaped swimming. Doubles from 1580ptca ❾

New Century Av. Padre Tomas Pereira 889 ⓣ831 111, ⓕ832 222, ⓔnch@macau.ctm.net. Reachable via the free shuttle service from the Macau Pier, this five-star pile features its own casino, a slew of spa and sports facilities and karaoke and mahjong rooms. ❾

Coloane

Pousada de Coloane Praia de Cheoc Van ⓣ828 143, ⓕ882 251. Great scenery, if somewhat remote, situated by Cheoc Van Beach on the far south shore of the island of Coloane. All rooms have balconies overlooking the beach, there's a swimming pool and an Italian restaurant, and if you want a relaxing holiday experience this is the place for it. ❼–❽

Westin Resort Estrada de Hac Sa ⓣ871 111, ⓕ871 122, Hong Kong reservations ⓣ2803 2015. At the far end of Hac Sa's fine beach, this is good for a quiet day or two mid-week, although it fills up with Hong Kong families at the weekend. Three restaurants and excellent sports facilities, including an eighteen-hole golf course, two pools and a Jacuzzi. Doubles from 1625ptca – although keep your eyes peeled for good weekend special offers. ❾

Macau Peninsula

The town of Macau was born down in the south of the peninsula, around the bay-front road known as the **Praia Grande**, and grew out from there. More rewarding is the main road that cuts the Praia from east to west, called **Avenida do Infante d'Henrique** to the east and **Avenida de Almeida Ribeiro** to the west. At the eastern end of the road rises the extraordinarily garish *Lisboa Hotel*, though most of the interest lies in the section west of the Praia, particularly in the beautiful **Largo do Senado** (Senate Square), which marks the downtown area and bears the unmistakeable influence of southern Europe, not only in its architecture, but also in its role as a place for people to stroll, sit and chat in the open air.

At the northern end of Largo do Senado, away from the main road, is the beautiful honey-and-cream-coloured seventeenth-century Baroque church, **São Domingos**, adjoined by Macau's **Religious Museum**, containing a treasury of sacred art under a stunning timbered roof while, to the south, facing the square from across the main road, stands the **Leal Senado** (Mon–Sat 1–7pm; free), generally considered the finest Portuguese building in the city. Step into the interior courtyard here to see wonderful blue and white Portuguese tiles around the walls, while up the staircase from the courtyard, you reach first a formal garden and then the richly decorated **senate chamber** itself. In the late sixteenth century this hall used to be packed out with the entire citizenry of the colony, who gathered to debate issues of importance. The senate's title *leal* (loyal) was earned during the period when Spain occupied the Portuguese throne and Macau became the final stronghold of loyalists to the true king. Today the senate chamber is still used by the municipal government of Macau, though it's hardly the democratic chamber of old. Adjacent to the chamber is the wood-carved **public library**, whose collection includes a repository of many fifteenth- and sixteenth-century books which you can still see on the shelves; you're free to go in and browse.

A couple of hundred metres west from Largo do Senado, Almeida Ribeiro emerges onto the so-called **Inner Harbour** (Porto Interior), which overlooks, and is sheltered by, the mainland just across the water. Ferries to Guangzhou still use this harbour, and it used also to be the location of the **Floating**

Gambling

The eleven official Macau **casinos** (of which ten are open to the general public), although numerous and always packed, have none of the glamour of casinos in places such as Las Vegas or Monte Carlo. You are free to enter any casino at any time of the day or night, dressed in any attire, with the only restriction being that you should be 18 years of age, and your cameras should be deposited at the entrance. Once inside, another restriction you should note is that there is a **minimum bet** on many games, varying between 10 and 100ptca.

The glittering four-storey casino in the *Hotel Lisboa* is the largest and probably the most interesting for a visit. For information on how to play the various games, ask MTIB for a leaflet. Be warned, however: signs in tiny print at the entrances to the casinos politely suggest that punters should engage in betting for fun only, and not as a means of making money. Revenues from the gambling trade in Macau are thought to approach half a billion US dollars annually, although this could all change due to the ending of Dr Stanley Ho's monopoly on gambling in 2002 and the entry of big fish from Las Vegas, likely to start operations around 2005.

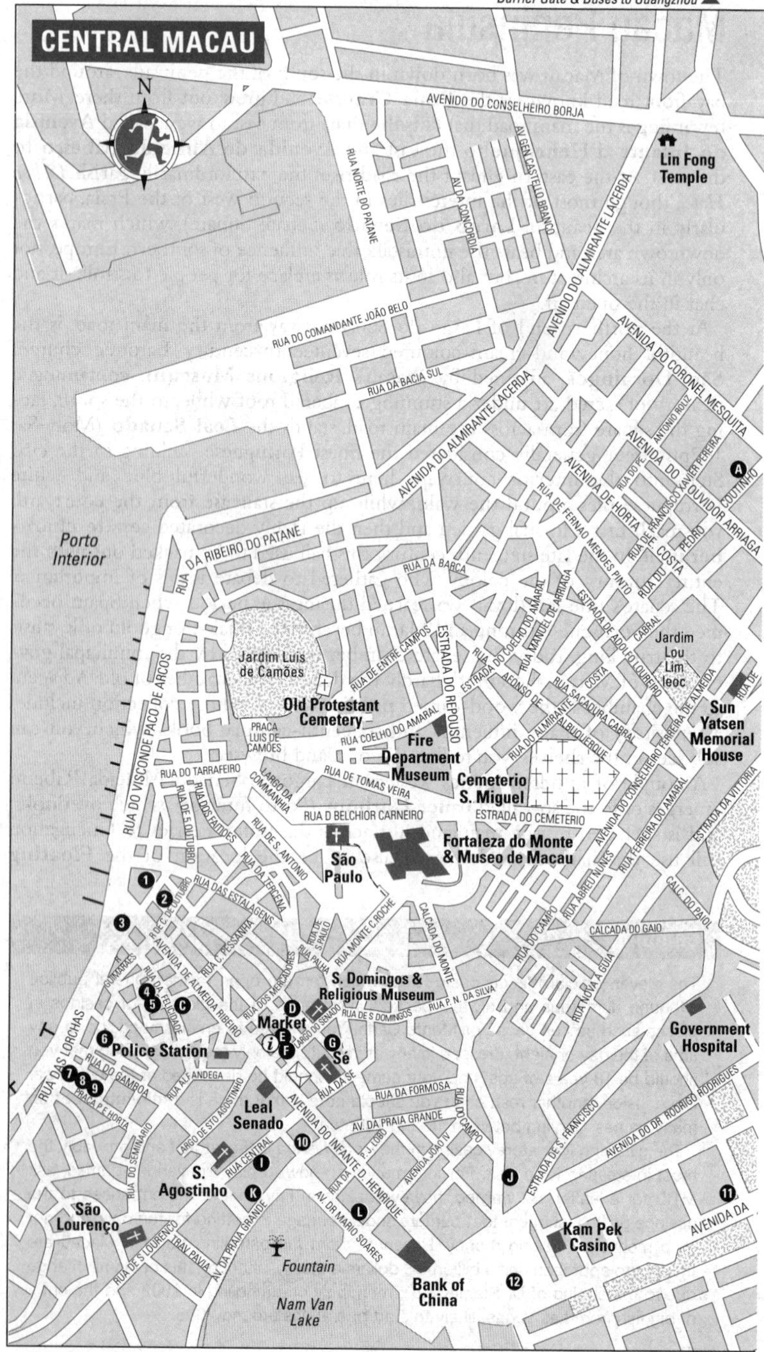

Barrier Gate & Buses to Guangzhou
CENTRAL MACAU
N
AVENIDO DO CONSELHEIRO BORJA
RUA NORTE DO PATANE
AV. DA CONCORDIA
AV. GEN CASTELLO BRANCO
AVENIDO DO ALMIRANTE LACERDA
Lin Fong Temple
RUA DO COMANDANTE JOÃO BELO
RUA DA BACIA SUL
AVENIDA DO ALMIRANTE LACERDA
AVENIDA DO CORONEL MESQUITA
AVENIDA DO OUVIDOR ARRIAGA
AVENIDA DE HORTA E COSTA
RUA DE FERNAO MENDES PINTO
RUA DE FRANCISCO XAVIER PEREIRA
RUA DO PEDRO COUTINHO
Porto Interior
RUA DA RIBEIRO DO PATANE
RUA DA BARCA
Jardim Luis de Camões
Old Protestant Cemetery
PRACA LUIS DE CAMÕES
RUA DE ENTRE CAMPOS
ESTRADA DO REPOUSO
RUA COELHO DO AMARAL
Fire Department Museum
ESTRADA DE ADOLFO LOUREIRO
RUA SACADURA CABRAL
Jardim Lou Lim Ieoc
Sun Yatsen Memorial House
RUA DO VISCONDE PACO DE ARCOS
RUA DO TARRAFEIRO
RUA DE TOMAS VEIRA
Cemeterio S. Miguel
ESTRADA DO CEMETERIO
AVENIDA DO CONSELHEIRO FERREIRA DE ALMEIDA
RUA FERREIRA DO AMARAL
ESTRADA DA VITORIA
RUA D BELCHIOR CARNEIRO
São Paulo
Fortaleza do Monte & Museo de Macau
RUA DAS ESTALAGENS
RUA DE S. ANTONIO
CALCADA DO MONTE
CALCADA DO GAIO
CALC. DO PAIOL
RUA DO CAMPO
RUA NOVA A GUIA
AVENIDA DE ALMEIDA RIBEIRO
RUA DA FELICIDADE
S. Domingos & Religious Museum
Market
Police Station
Sé
RUA DAS LORCHAS
Leal Senado
AVENIDA DO INFANTE D. HENRIQUE
RUA DA FORMOSA
AV. DA PRAIA GRANDE
Government Hospital
ESTRADA DE S. FRANCISCO
AVENIDA DO DR RODRIGO RODRIGUES
S. Agostinho
São Lourenço
Fountain
Nam Van Lake
AV. DR MARIO SOARES
Bank of China
Kam Pek Casino
AVENIDA DA

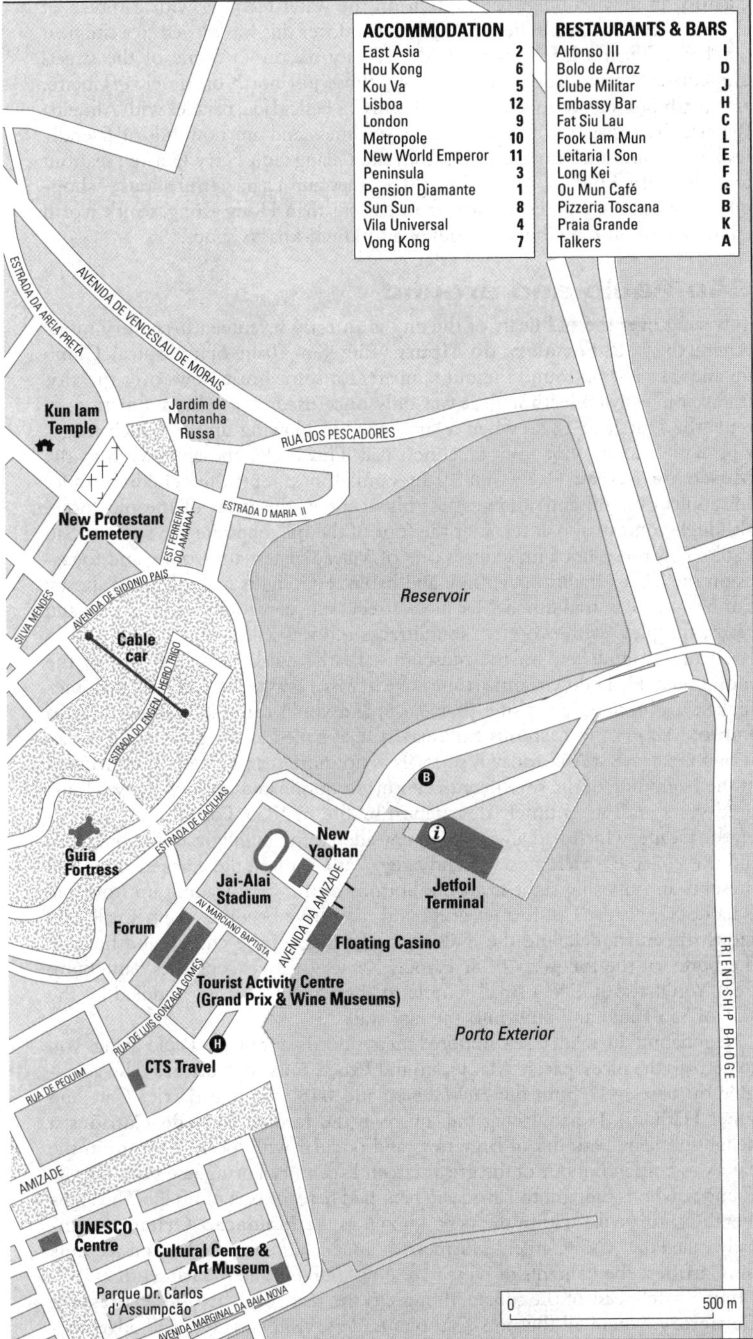
ACCOMMODATION
East Asia 2
Hou Kong 6
Kou Va 5
Lisboa 12
London 9
Metropole 10
New World Emperor 11
Peninsula 3
Pension Diamante 1
Sun Sun 8
Vila Universal 4
Vong Kong 7
RESTAURANTS & BARS
Alfonso III I
Bolo de Arroz D
Clube Militar J
Embassy Bar H
Fat Siu Lau C
Fook Lam Mun L
Leitaria I Son E
Long Kei F
Ou Mun Café G
Pizzeria Toscana B
Praia Grande K
Talkers A
ESTRADA DA AREIA PRETA
AVENIDA DE VENCESLAU DE MORAIS
Kun Iam Temple
Jardim de Montanha Russa
RUA DOS PESCADORES
ESTRADA D MARIA II
New Protestant Cemetery
EST FERREIRA DO AMARAL
AVENIDA DE SIDONIO PAIS
SILVA MENDES
Reservoir
Cable car
ESTRADA DO ENGENHEIRO TRIGO
ESTRADA DE CACILHAS
Guia Fortress
New Yaohan
Jai-Alai Stadium
AVENIDA DA AMIZADE
Jetfoil Terminal
Forum
AV MARCIANO BAPTISTA
Floating Casino
Tourist Activity Centre (Grand Prix & Wine Museums)
RUA DE LUIS GONZAGA GOMES
Porto Exterior
FRIENDSHIP BRIDGE
CTS Travel
RUA DE PEQUIM
AMIZADE
UNESCO Centre
Cultural Centre & Art Museum
Parque Dr. Carlos d'Assumpcão
AVENIDA MARGINAL DA BAIA NOVA
0
500 m
Airport, Taipa & Coloane

Casino, an ugly wooden contraption on the water teeming with gamblers at all hours. (A few months before Macau's handover this was moved to a site near the Jetfoil Terminal, for unspecified "security reasons".) Some of the streets immediately inland from here, especially those just north of Almeida Ribeiro, are worth poking around. Streets such as Rua Felicidade, parallel with Almeida Ribeiro, have shaken off their former seediness and are now full of friendly restaurants and small hotels. South from the Guangzhou Ferry Pier the seafront road, Rua das Lorchas, is lined by old arcades and characterful shops – shopping is about sixty percent cheaper in Macau than Hong Kong, so it's worth taking a look in the Chinese antiques and knick-knacks shops.

São Paulo and around

Towering over the old heart of the city is an early seventeenth-century monument, the 1618 **Fortaleza do Monte** (Tues–Sun 10am–6pm; 15ptca). Climb up and take a stroll round the old ramparts for some great views over the city. It's an impressive pile, though it was only once used in a military function, to repel the Dutch in 1622, when it succeeded in blowing up the Dutch magazine with a lucky shot from a cannon ball. This is also the entrance into the **Museo de Macau** (Tues–Sun 10am–6pm; 15ptca, 8ptca for children under 11, adults over 60 and students) as this occupies the ruins of the old fort – although you can also access it at the foot of the hill, opposite the ruins of Sao Paolo. This three-floor museum is one of Macau's latest attractions, and focuses on the SAR's traditions, culture and habits. Highlights include video shows, a mock-up of a traditional Macanese street, and depictions of local arts and crafts, complete with evocative soundtracks of local sellers' cries.

On the ground floor of the museum, take the escalator to the foot of the monument. Head down some stone steps across a grassy slope dotted with picnickers and retirees practising their *tai ji*, and you'll reach the church of **São Paulo**, Macau's most famous landmark. Once hailed as the greatest Christian monument in east Asia, today it survives as no more than a facade. Constructed at the beginning of the seventeenth century, it dominated the city for two hundred years until its untimely destruction by fire in 1835. Fortuitously, however, the facade, which had always been considered the highlight of the building, did not collapse – richly carved and laden with statuary, the cracked stone still presents an imposing sight from the bottom of the steps leading up from the Rua de São Paulo. The former crypt and nave have become a very small religious **museum**, detailing the building and design of the church and holding the bones of the followers of St Francis Xavier (daily except Tues 9am–6pm; free). You'll also notice a small temple to the child god Raja, huddled by the side of Sao Paulo and built into the city walls.

Negotiating the roads a few hundred metres northwest of São Paulo brings you to perhaps the nicest part of Macau, around **Praça Luís de Camões** (also accessible on buses #17 from the *Hotel Lisboa* and #18 from the Barrier Gate and Inner Harbour). North, facing the square, is the **Jardim Luís de Camões**, a delightful shady park full of large trees and popular with locals. A grotto in the park was built in honour of the great sixteenth-century Portuguese poet, Luís de Camões, who is thought to have been banished here for part of his life. The eighteenth century villa within the park, known as the **Fundacao Oriente** (originally called the "Casa Garden") formerly housed a museum, the **Museu de Luís de Camões**, the contents of which are now found in the Art Museum.

Immediately east of the square, though, is the real gem, the **Old Protestant Cemetery**, where all the non-Catholic traders, visitors, sailors and adventurers who happened to die in Macau were buried. The gravestones have all been restored and are quite legible. In this quiet garden, under the shade of trees, the last testaments to these mainly British, American and German individuals, who died far from home in the early part of the last century, make incredibly poignant reading.

The east

About 1km northeast of the Fortaleza do Monte is another area worth walking around (buses #12 and #22 run up here from the *Hotel Lisboa* along the Avenida do Conselheiro Ferreira de Almeida). At the junction with Estrada de Adolfo Loureiro, the first site you'll reach, screened off behind a high wall, is the scenic **Jardim Lou Lim Ieoc** (daily dawn–dusk; free), a formal, Chinese garden full of bamboos, pavilions, birds in cages and old men playing mahjong. A couple of minutes around the corner from here stands the **Sun Yatsen Memorial House** (daily except Tues 10am–5pm; free) at the junction of Avenida de Sidonia Pais and the Rua de Silva Mendes. There isn't that much to see – basically it's an attractive, rambling old mansion scattered about with mementoes of Sun Yatsen, who spent some time living in Macau in the years before he turned to revolutionary activities. Drop by to see the turn-of-the-century interior decor if nothing else.

The sharp hill to the east of here is Macau's highest, and its summit is crowned by the seventeenth-century **Guia Fortress**, the dominant feature of which is a charming whitewashed lighthouse, added in the last century and reputed to be the oldest anywhere on the Chinese coast. It's also worth visiting the de Guia chapel, discovered in 2001, which contains original Christian paintings featuring Chinese characters and dragons. You can take a leisurely hike along a path up to the fort in about an hour, or at the other end of the Colina da Guia there's a **cable car** which connects to the Flora Garden below. At the top there are some superb views over the whole peninsula, including, on a clear day, a glimpse of Lantau Island far to the east. There's a tourist information counter and coffee bar (daily 9am–4pm; free) up here as well. In the harbour below the Colina da Guia you'll see the **Floating Casino**, a rickety but atmospheric wooden structure, packed with hard-faced Chinese gamblers. Nearby is the **Tourist Activity Centre** containing the **Grand Prix Museum** (daily except Tues 10am–6pm; 10ptca) and the **Wine Museum** (daily except Tues 10am–6pm; 15ptca), which, respectively, celebrate the history of the Macau Grand Prix and offer a glimpse into the history of winemaking – with a free glass of wine thrown in. To the north, on a small artificial island near the Culture Centre and linked to the seafront by a short causeway, another feature of the Outer Harbour (Porto Exterior) is the twenty-metre-high **bronze statue of Kun Iam**, the Goddess of Mercy (free). The lotus-flower-shaped base serves as an ecumenical centre, open to all.

Close by lies the **Macau Museum of Art**, one of the SAR's newest landmarks (Tues–Sun 9am–7pm, 15ptca; 8ptca for children under 11, adults over 60 and students). Its four cavernous levels of gallery space house permanent exhibitions of Chinese calligraphy, China Trade paintings, Shiwan ceramics and historical documents inherited from the Luís de Camões museum, plus a number of temporary exhibitions.

Further round the harbour, you can find the spanking-new and altogether rather elegant **Macau Tower** Convention and Entertainment Centre, located at the southwestern tip of the peninsular. Topping 338 metres, it boasts a 223-metre observation lounge, a decidedly classy revolving restaurant and numerous glossy restaurants and boutiques at ground and basement level. New Zealand bungee-jumping company AJ Hackett operates the Skywalk and numerous other activities on and around the tower (daily 10am–9pm; 45 ptca, observation lounge at level 58; 35ptca, outdoor observation deck; 70ptca, access to both; Ⓦwww.macautower.com.mo).

The north

The northern part of the peninsula up to the border with China is largely residential, though it has a couple of points of interest. It's possible to walk the 3km from Almeida Ribeiro to the border, but the streets at this end of town are not particularly atmospheric, so it makes sense to resort to the local buses.

On Avenida do Coronel Mesquita, cutting the peninsula from east to west about 2km north of Almeida Ribeiro, is the enchanting **Kun Iam Temple** (daily 7am–6pm), accessible on bus #12 from the *Hotel Lisboa*. The complex of temples here, dedicated to the Goddess of Mercy, is around four hundred years old, but the most interesting fact associated with the place is that here, in 1844, the United States and China signed their first treaty of trade and co-operation – you can still see the granite table they signed it on. Inside the complex, shaded by banyan trees, are a number of small shrines, with the main temple hall approached via a flight of steps. Around the central statue of Kun Iam herself, to the rear, are a crowd of statues representing the eighteen wise men of China, among whom, curiously, is Marco Polo (on the far left), depicted with a curly beard and moustache. The worshippers you'll see here shaking bamboo sticks in cylinders are trying to find out their fortunes.

From the Kun Iam Temple you can catch bus #18 direct to the Portas do Cerco, or **Barrier Gate** (open 7am to midnight), the nineteenth-century stuccoed archway marking the border with China. These days unfortunately the old gate itself is redundant – people actually cross the border through a customs and immigration complex to one side or choose to cross at the new border gate on the Lotus Bridge. This does at least mean that you can examine the monument from close quarters as it is no longer a restricted area. A short walk to the west of the gate is **Sun Yatsen Memorial Park**, which gives interesting views over Zhuhai on the mainland, immediately across a small canal. Buses #3 or #10 will get you back to Almeida Ribeiro and the *Hotel Lisboa* from the gate.

The south

The small but hilly tongue of land south of Almeida Ribeiro is a highly interesting place to stroll, with colonial mansions and their gardens looming up round every corner. The best way to start exploring this area is to walk up the steep Rua Central leading south from Almeida Ribeiro just east of Largo do Senado. After five minutes you can detour off down a small road to your right, which contains the pastel-coloured early nineteenth-century church of **Santo Agostinho**. Back along Rua Central again will lead you to another attractive church of the same era, the cream and white **São Lourenço**, standing amid palm trees.

Continuing several hundred metres farther south you'll reach the seafront on the southwestern side of the peninsula, which is known as the **Barra district**. As you face the sea, the celebrated **A-Ma Temple** is immediately to your right. Situated underneath Barra Hill overlooking the Inner Harbour, this temple may be as old as six hundred years in parts, and certainly predates the arrival of the Portuguese on the peninsula. Dedicated to the goddess A-Ma, whose identity blurs from Queen of Heaven into Goddess of the Sea (and who seems to be the same as Tin Hau in Hong Kong), the temple is an attractive jumble of altars and little outhouses among the rocks.

Immediately across the road from here, on the seafront, stands the twentieth century's votive offering to the sea, the **Maritime Museum** (daily except Tues 10am–5.30pm; 10ptca, 5ptca at weekends). This is an excellently presented, modern museum, covering old explorers, seafaring techniques, equipment, models and boats. For an additional charge, you can even join a boat tour (daily 10.30am, 11.30am, 3.30pm & 4.30pm; 10ptca) on one of the junks moored just outside the museum. This gives you a chance to sail around the Inner Harbour hearing details of the lives of local fishermen in English.

A short walk south along the shore from the museum brings you to the very tip of the peninsula, which is today marked by the *Pousada de São Tiago*, an incredible hotel built into the remains of the seventeenth-century Portuguese fortress, the **Fortaleza de Barra**. Enter the front door and you find yourself walking up a stone tunnel running with water – it's well worth climbing up to the *Pousada*'s verandah café for a drink overlooking the sea. Continuing the walk around the southern headland, and back to the north again, you'll pass a beautiful cream colonial-style building high up on the headland. This used to be the *Bela Vista*, the finest hotel in the territory, but at the handover it was given to Portugal's representative in Macau as a residence. The road north from here up to the Praia Grande, near the *Hotel Lisboa*, takes about another ten minutes on foot. The wonderful pink building on your left shortly before the *Praia Grande* restaurant is the nineteenth-century **Palácio do Governo** (Government House), which is not open to visitors.

The islands

Macau's two islands, **Taipa** and **Coloane**, are just dots of land which traditionally supported a few small fishing villages, though now, with the opening of the new airport on Taipa, a second bridge from the mainland and a large reclamation programme, that old tranquillity is on the way out. Indeed, Taipa is fast acquiring the characteristics of a city suburb. For the time being, life seems to remain relatively quiet, particularly on Coloane, and the two islands are well worth a visit, either by bus or by rented bicycle.

Buses #11, #32, #33 and #34 go to Taipa Village from Almeida Ribeiro, while buses #21, #21A, #26 and #26A stop outside the *Hyatt Regency* on Taipa before going on to Coloane.

Taipa

Until the eighteenth century **Taipa** used to be two islands separated by a channel, the silting up of which subsequently caused the two to merge into one. In an interesting repetition of history, the same fate is now befalling Taipa and Coloane, except that this time it is not silt which is the culprit, but land reclamation – the two islands are being deliberately fused into one, to make space for new development.

Although Taipa's northern shore is hardly worth a stop now that it is being subsumed into the general Macau conurbation, **Taipa Village** on the southern shore, with its old colonial promenade, makes a pleasant stop for an extended lunch, especially on Rua do Cunha (or "food street"), lined with souvenir stalls and eateries. The Tai Yao Lai shop is particularly noted for its famous pork sandwiches – with roughly 5,000 sold daily. There isn't much more than a few streets to the modern village, where the buses stop, though there are some great restaurants (see opposite) along the central north–south alley, Rua do Cunha, and to the west – the right as you face the shore – a couple of temples in the vicinity of a quiet old square. If you prefer to travel around the islands under your own steam, there are three or four bicycle shops at the roundabout at Largo Governador Tamagnini Barbosa renting kids and adults' bikes for 8–18ptca an hour.

The real interest lies a few minutes' walk to the east of Taipa Village, at the old waterfront area. Here, as though frozen in time, remains a superb old colonial promenade, the **Avenida da Praia**, complete with its original houses, public benches and street lamps. Great, peppermint-green mansions with verandahs overlook the water which has now receded almost out of sight and is smothered in lotuses. These form the **Taipa House Museum** (Tues–Sun 10am–6pm; 5ptca allows entry to all five) and reveal details of early nineteenth-century domestic life for the resident Macanese families: highly religious, well-to-do and high-ranking civil servants, but not enormously wealthy. Unsurprisingly, the furniture is a Eurasian hybrid, combining features such as statuettes of saints with Chinese dragon motifs on the sofas. House 1 can be hired for receptions; No. 2 features an exhibition gallery and archive photographs; No. 3, the House of the Portugal Regions, showcases traditional costumes; No. 4, the House of the Islands, is stuffed with info about Taipa and Coloane but also serves as a temporary exhibition hall; and No. 5 is decorated as a traditional, bourgeouis Macanese house.

Coloane

Coloane is considerably bigger than Taipa at nine square kilometres and, although it has no outstanding attractions, it's a pleasant place to spend a few hours. After crossing the bridge from Taipa, which also links Macau SAR to mainland China, the buses pass the **Parque de Seac Pai Van** (daily except Mon 9am–7pm; free), a large park with pleasant walks. On top of the hill is a white marble statue of the goddess A-Ma, at 19.99m high the tallest in the world. Once past the park the buses all stop at the roundabout in pretty **Coloane Village** on the western shore, overlooking mainland China just across the water and home to a fair number of expats. There's no beach, just mud, in which you'll see old men fishing with nets. To the north of the village are a few junk-building sheds, while the street leading south from the village roundabout, one block back from the shore, contains a couple of interesting old shops and the unexpected yellow and white **St Francis Xavier Chapel**, where a relic of the saint's arm bone is venerated. A couple of hundred metres beyond this is the **Tam Kung Temple**, housing a metre-long whale bone carved into the shape of a ship. Another highlight is Lord Stow's Bakery, offering irresistible Portuguese egg tarts, at 1 Rua da Tassara.

On the north side of the village roundabout there's a small shop where you can rent bicycles for 12ptca an hour, although you can also rent these from the *Westin Resort*. Cycling is a good way to travel the 3km farther round to **Hac Sa Beach** on the eastern shore (otherwise take bus #21A, #26 or #26A), perhaps dropping in on **Cheoc Van Beach** to the south on the way as well. The beach at Hac Sa, though, tree-lined and stretching far off round the bay, is without doubt the best in Macau, despite the black colour of its sand, and has good facilities including cafés, bars, showers and toilets as well as some fine restaurants nearby (see opposite). There's also a sports and swimming pool complex here (Mon–Fri 9am–9pm, Sat & Sun until midnight; 15ptca) although it all gets pretty crowded at weekends. Otherwise, try the **Parque Natural da Barragem de Hac-Sa**; a short hop from Hac-Sa Beach, this features BBQ pits, a kids' playground and maze, boating on a small reservoir and various short trails in the hills (Tues–Fri 2pm–7pm, Sat, Sun & public holidays 10am–7pm; 10–40ptca for boat rental).

Eating, drinking and nightlife

Despite comparison with the overwhelming variety on offer in Hong Kong, there is nevertheless plenty of good food to be had in Macau, with a particular emphasis on the territory's native cuisine, **Macanese food** – a fascinating blend of Portuguese and Asian elements. The Portuguese elements include fresh bread, cheap imported wine and coffee, as well as an array of dishes ranging from *caldo verde* (vegetable soup) to *bacalhau* (dried salted cod). Macau's most interesting Portuguese colonial dish is probably **African chicken**, a concoction of Goan and east African influences, comprising chicken grilled with peppers and spices. Straightforward **Cantonese restaurants**, often serving *dim sum* for breakfast and lunch, are also plentiful, though you'll find wine on the menus even here. Alongside the local dumplings and noodles, Macau's numerous snack bars often offer fresh-milk products such as fruit milkshakes and milk puddings, unusual for China. Thanks to the 24-hour casinos, you'll be able to find something open at any hour of the day or night. Costs, however, are nearly always lower, with bills even in smart venues usually not exceeding 150–250ptca per head.

Bars and nightlife include ubiquitous karaoke bars, nightclubs, discos and massage parlours in Macau, as most of the drinking is done in restaurants or in the thirty or so bars in the "Macau Lan Kwai Fong", located along the waterfront facing the Outer Harbour and offering live music and streetside tables.

Restaurants and cafés

Alfonso III Rua Central 11 ☎586 272. Genuine and excellent Portuguese food in a Portuguese environment, though the waiters speak English. Centrally located, not far from Largo do Senado.

Bolo de Arroz Travessa de São Domingos 11. Near the Largo do Senado, this is a great place for Portuguese pastries and some of the best coffee in town.

Clube Militar Avenida de Praia Grande 795 ☎714 009. Although this is a private club, the dining room is open to the public. A great way to see inside one of Macau's colonial buildings – which has been beautifully restored – although the food doesn't match the surroundings.

Fat Siu Lau Rua da Felicidade 64 ☎573 585. A very popular, traditional old restaurant in an area busy with cafés and restaurants. Pigeon is the speciality.

Fook Lam Mun Avenida Dr Mario Soares 259. Excellent Cantonese seafood, although expensive.

Leitaria I Son Largo do Senado 7. Virtually next door to *Long Kei*, this is an excellent milk bar offering milk with everything – fruit, chocolate, eggs, ice creams, puddings and breakfasts.

Long Kei Largo do Senado 7B. A one-hundred-year-old, traditional, but inexpensive and excellent Cantonese restaurant, on the left side as you face the square from Almeida Ribeiro. Unsurprisingly, recently granted a tourism award.

Ou Mun Café This sells home-made Portuguese cakes and coffee, as well as soups and salads.

Pele Rua de São Tiago da Barra 25 ☎969 000. A short walk south of the Maritime Museum and offering excellent Macanese dishes in a friendly atmosphere.

Pizzeria Toscana Avenida da Amizade. Genuine Italian food and not just pizzas, though these are superb, as is the coffee.

O Porto Interior Rua da Almirante Sergio 259-B ☎967 770. Just by the A-Ma Temple, this features antique Chinese screens, superb old Macanese cuisine, such as African chicken, or grilled sardines, plus a splendid wine cellar.

Praia Grande Praca Lobo D'Avila, Rua Praia Grande ☎973 022. One of Macau's best restau-

rants, just outside the city centre. Pleasant staff, excellent food, good value.
Star East Club Macau Tower. Owned by a bevy of Hong Kong stars – including Jacky Chan – this is located at the foot of the tower and offers a wide range of international cuisines.

Taipa

Galo Rua da Cunha 45 ☎827 423. Low-priced, basically international menu. Just inland from the main bus stop on Rua Correa da Silva in Taipa Village.
Mocambique Rua dos Clerigos 28A ☎827 471. Probably the most popular restaurant in Taipa Village, serving tasty Portuguese colonial food alongside various dishes from Goa and Africa.
O-Manel R. Fernao Mendes Pinto 90 ☎827 571. A small, family-run and homely restaurant with checked tablecloths, Portuguese wine and superb cooking. The *bacalhau* (cod) in olive oil and garlic is the house speciality.
Restaurante Panda Rua Direita Carlos Eugenio 4–8 ☎827 338. On a tiny alley leading east from the southern end of Rua da Cunha in Taipa Village. Reasonably priced Portuguese place, with outdoor tables in good weather.
Pinocchio's Rua do Sol 4 ☎827 128. Good Macanese food, including fish cakes, crab, prawns and crispy roast duck. On the square opposite the fire station in Taipa Village.

Coloane

Caçarola Rua das Gaivotas 8 ☎882 226. Welcoming and deservedly popular restaurant with excellent daily specials and very affordable prices. It's off the main village square.
Café Nga Tim Coloane Village. A small, very friendly cheap place ideal for lunch or an evening drink, right opposite the Chapel of St Francis Xavier.
Fernando Hac Sa Beach ☎882 531. Not far from the bus stop. *Fernando's* is an institution amongst local expats trying to escape the city pace, and its casual, cheerful atmosphere is probably the closest you will get to a Mediterranean bistro without boarding a plane. Add on great Portuguese food and you've got one of the best restaurants in the territory. You might need a taxi to get home, though – reckon on 50ptca for the ride back to the peninsula. Advance booking recommended, and a must at weekends.
Lord Stow's Bakery Coloane Town Square. One of the best places to eat Macau's creamy Portuguese egg tarts (*natas*).

Bars and clubs

Crazy Paris Show Mona Lisa Hall, *Hotel Lisboa*, Avenida da Amizade ☎577 666. Something of a Macau institution now, this vaguely naughty cabaret-style show of scantily clad dancing girls can be seen nightly at 8pm and 9.30pm (also 11pm Sat; 250ptca).
Embassy Bar *Mandarin Hotel*, Avenida da Amizade, Outer Harbour ☎567 888. Rather snazzy indeed, featuring cocktails and live bands, and good value at 30ptca to enter.
Talkers Rua de Pedro Coutinho 104. A little south of Avenida do Coronel Mesquita, just west of the Kun Iam Temple, are several bars and pubs that make up most of Macau's nightlife. *Talkers* tends to get very busy very late.

Listings

Airlines The airline situation in Macau is likely to develop fast, though as yet airline representation in the territory is thin. Air Macau is at Avenida da Praia Grande 639 ☎396 6888. For other airlines operating from Macau, including Silk Air, Singapore Airlines, China Air and EVA Airways (of Taiwan), call the airport flight enquiries ☎861 111 or contact a travel agency.
Banks and exchange Banks generally open Monday to Friday from 9am until 4 or 4.30pm, but close by lunchtime on Saturdays. There are also licensed moneychangers which exchange traveller's cheques (and which open seven days a week), including a 24-hour one in the basement of the *Hotel Lisboa*, and one near the bottom of the steps leading up to São Paulo.
Bike rental For details of bike rental possibilities on Taipa and Coloane, see p.778.
Bookshops Don't bother looking for English-language books here – go to Hong Kong.
Festivals The normal Chinese holidays are celebrated in Macau, plus some Catholic festivals introduced from Portugal, such as the procession of Our Lady of Fatima from São Domingos church annually on May 13.
Hospitals There's a 24-hour emergency department at the Centro Hospitalar Conde São Januário, Calçada Visconde São Januário ☎313 731; English spoken.
Police The main police station is at Avenida Dr Rodrigo Rodrigues ☎573 333. In an emergency call ☎999.

Mail Macau's General Post Office is in Largo do Leal Senado, on the east side (Mon–Fri 9am–6pm, Sat 9am–1pm); poste restante is delivered here. Small red booths all over the territory also dispense stamps from machines.

Telephones Local calls are free from private phones, 1ptca from payphones. Cardphones work with CTM cards, issued by the Macau State Telecommunication Company, on sale in hotels or at the back of the main post office (open 24hr), where you can also make direct calls.

Travel agencies CTS, Rua de Nagasaki (☎700 888), can sort out China visas and tickets, as can most other tour operators.

Travel details

Trains

Hong Kong to: Guangzhou (4 daily; 3hr); Lo Wu (KCR line, for Shenzhen; frequent; 50min).

Buses

Hong Kong to: Guangzhou (frequent; 3hr); Shenzhen (frequent; 1hr).

Macau to: Guangzhou (several daily; 3hr).

Ferries

Hong Kong to: Guangzhou (2 daily; 2hr); Macau (frequent; 1hr); Shanghai (weekly; 60hr); Shekou (4 daily; 45min); Shenzhen airport (6 daily; 1hr); Wuzhou (daily; 10hr); Xiamen (4 weekly; 20hr); Zhuhai (daily; 1hr 10min).

Macau to: Guangzhou (daily; 9hr); Hong Kong (frequent; 1hr); Shenzhen (1 daily; 1hr).

Flights

Hong Kong is a major international gateway for flights both within Asia and beyond. Macau offers international flights to and from Bangkok, Singapore and Taipei.

Hong Kong to: Beijing (several daily; 4hr); Chengdu (1 daily; 2hr 30min); Fuzhou (3–4 daily; 1hr 5min); Guangzhou (4 daily; 30min); Guilin (2 daily; 1hr); Haikou (2 daily; 50min); Hangzhou (2 daily; 2hr); Kunming (1 daily; 2hr); Nanjing (2 daily; 2hr); Ningbo (1 daily; 2hr); Shanghai (10 daily; 2hr); Shengyang (4 weekly; 3hr 30min); Tianjin (1 daily; 2hr 50min); Wuhan (1 daily; 1hr 30min); Xiamen (3 daily; 1hr); Xi'an (1 daily; 2hr 30min).

Macau to: Bangkok (4 weekly; 3hr); Beijing (1 daily; 2hr); Shanghai (1 daily; 2hr); Singapore (2 weekly; 4hr); Taipei (daily; 1hr 30min); Xiamen (1 daily; 1hr).

CHAPTER 10

Highlights

* **Li River** Cruise between Guilin and Yangshuo through a forest of tall, weirdly contorted karst peaks. **See p.790**

* **Dong villages** Communities of wooden houses, bridges and drum towers pepper remote rural highlands along the Guangxi–Guizhou border. **See p.801**

* **Hua Shan** Another boat trip to see a whole cliff-side of mysterious rock art flanking Guangxi's Zuo River. **See p.820**

* **Sisters' Meal festival** Exuberant showpiece of Miao culture, featuring three days of dancing, bull fighting and dragon-boat racing. **See p.839**

* **Caohai** Spend a day punting around this beautiful lake, a haven for ducks and rare black-necked cranes. **See p.847**

10

Guangxi and Guizhou

China's subtropical central southwest, comprising **Guangxi** and **Guizhou**, manages to include one of the country's most intensely visited areas while remaining largely unknown as a whole. This is entirely due to the countryside's picturesque limestone hills which, though a tourist phenomenon today, have in the past made communications virtually impossible and have created some of provincial China's worst agricultural land. So poor that they were hardly worth the trouble of invading, local tribes were left pretty much to their own devices, and the region evolved into a stronghold for **ethnic groups**. Some kept their nominal identity but more or less integrated with the Chinese, while others thoroughly resisted assimilation by occupying isolated highlands, and even today retain many of their cultural traditions. A very long way from the flow of things, the region generally remained in obscurity until the **Taiping Uprising** exploded in central Guangxi in 1850, marking the start of a century of civil conflict and famine. Harrison E. Salisbury's *The Long March* describes how Red Army soldiers passing through rural Guizhou in the 1930s found people working naked in the fields and an economy based on opium. The Communist takeover saw the minority groups enfranchized by the formation of several **autonomous prefectures**, but industry and infrastructure still remain underdeveloped and few of the cities – including **Guiyang** and **Nanning**, the provincial capitals – have much to offer except transport to more interesting locations.

Small wonder, then, that most visitors are drawn to the **landscape**, epitomized by the tall **karst** (weathered limestone) towers rising out of the plains around the city of **Guilin** in northeastern Guangxi, instantly familiar to Chinese and Westerners alike through centuries of eulogistic poetry, paintings and photographs. So famous has this become, and in all fairness quite justifiably, that it totally overshadows the rest of the region, so that in remote areas you can almost feel like a pioneer, seeing parts of the country little known in the outside world. Most rewarding is the chance of close contact with ethnic groups, particularly the **Miao**, **Dong** and **Zhuang**, whose culture is apparent not only in their daily lives but also in traces of their prehistoric past. There's also further terrain to explore, encompassing beaches, moist mountain forests and some of the country's largest waterfalls and limestone caverns.

While **travel** out to all this can be time-consuming, a reasonable quantity of buses and trains means that remoteness is not the barrier it once was. **Language** is another matter, as many rural people understand neither Mandarin nor Cantonese; since 1995 the government has, unusually,

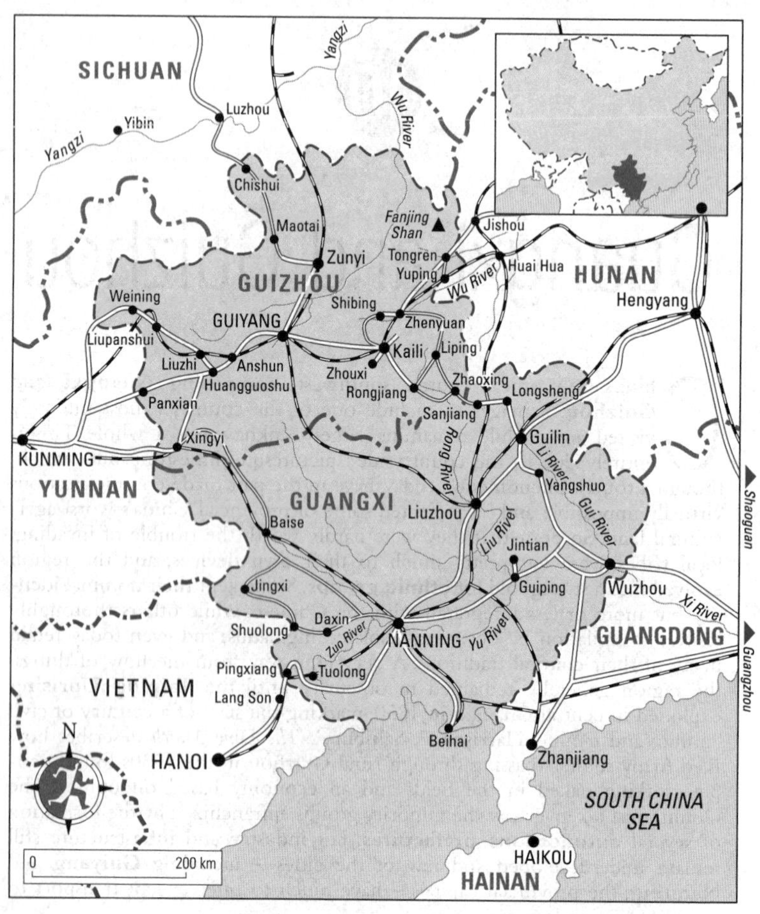

approved the use of local dialects alongside Mandarin in schools to encourage literacy. But in any case, locals rarely expect to communicate easily with foreigners, and you'll find that hand signals and patience will go a long way. With a geography that includes the South China Sea and some respectable mountains, **weather** is fairly localized, though you should expect warm, wet summers and cold winters, especially up in the hills. April and May, and September and October are probably the driest, most pleasant months to visit the region.

Guangxi

Lush and green most of the year round, **Guangxi** unfolds south from the highlands it shares with Guizhou to a tropical coast and border abutting Vietnam. The pick of the postcard-perfect limestone and paddy-field landscape is concentrated around the northeastern city of **Guilin**, which, long famous and easily accessible from Hong Kong and Guangzhou, has become a massive tourist draw. Not everyone likes the city itself, but most visitors find the scenery accompanying a trip along the **Li River** to the budget-travellers' haven of **Yangshuo** quite unforgettable, and ample compensation for the high prices and irritating commercial hype you might have to endure back in Guilin.

The one drawback to all this is that Guilin has become a hard act to follow, and, despite some equally rich material, the rest of Guangxi seems to have given up trying. Since 1958 the province has not been a province at all but the **Guangxi Zhuang Autonomous Region**, heartland of China's thirteen million-strong **Zhuang** nationality. They constitute about a third of the regional population and, although largely assimilated into Chinese life today, there's enough archeological evidence to link them with a Bronze Age culture spread throughout Southeast Asia, including prehistoric **rock friezes** surviving along the **Zuo River** near the open **border with Vietnam**. For contemporary contact, you'll find fairly traditional groups of Zhuang elsewhere along this almost untouristed western boundary, especially in the attractive region surrounding the **Detian Waterfall**, which actually pours over the Vietnamese border. Diagonally across the province, the northeastern hills around **Sanjiang** are home to the less-integrated **Dong**, whose architecture and way of life makes for a fascinating trip up into Guizhou province, hopping between villages on public buses.

The appeal of Guangxi's cities is more fleeting. A fair number of Guilin- or Yangshou-bound visitors transit the rail city of **Liuzhou**, or easterly **Wuzhou**, which is right on the border with Guangdong province. Far fewer head west to **Baise**, or south to the tropically languid capital, **Nanning**, and the coastal port of **Beihai**; those who do, cross a region whose history touches on Long March lore and the origins of the **Taiping Uprising**, nineteenth-century China's most widespread rebellion against the rotting Qing empire.

Despite its subtropical latitude, Guangxi's **weather** can be deceptive – it actually snows in Guilin about once every ten years. Another thing of note is that the **Zhuang language**, instead of using *pinyin*, follows its own method of rendering Chinese characters into Roman text. This accounts for the novel spellings you'll encounter on street signs and elsewhere – "Minzu Dadao", for example, becomes "Minzcuzdadau".

Guilin

GUILIN is one of China's worst tourist traps, entirely dependent on visitors for its income and flaunting an expensive service industry tailored to the well-heeled tour groups that are forever passing through. It is, however, a nice-looking city, with plenty of well-designed landscaping, shady avenues and rocky parkland to explore – not to mention the chance to embark on the

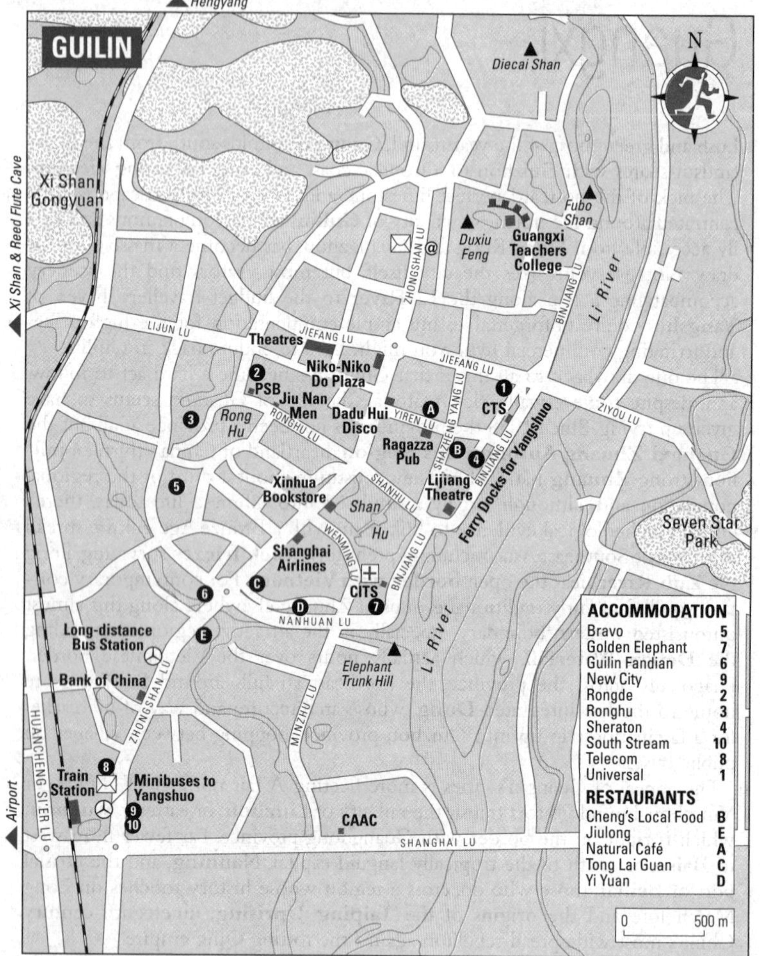

famous **Li River cruise** downstream past the host of bizarrely shaped, legend-ridden outcrops which line the river banks. Budget travellers might flounder in Guilin's mercenary atmosphere, but in that case it's simple to base yourself in the more mellow village of **Yangshuo**, just ninety minutes away to the south, and come here on a day-trip.

The capital of Guangxi from the Ming dynasty until 1914, Guilin only started to play any significant role in history after losing that rank to Nanning. Sun Yatsen planned the Nationalists' "Northern Expedition" here in 1925, the Long Marchers were soundly trounced by Guomindang factions outside the city nine years later, and the war with Japan saw more than a million refugees hiding out in Guilin, until the city was occupied by the invaders – events harrowingly recounted in Amy Tan's *Joy Luck Club*. Wartime bombing spared the city's natural monuments but turned the

Guilin

Guilin	桂林	***guìlín***
Camel Hill	骆驼山	*luòtuó shān*
Diecai Shan	叠彩山	*diécǎi shān*
Duxiu Feng	独秀峰	*dúxiù fēng*
Elephant Trunk Hill	象鼻山	*xiàngbí shān*
Fubo Shan	伏波山	*fúbō shān*
Huanzhu Dong	还珠洞	*huánzhū dòng*
Li River	漓江	*lí jiāng*
Old South Gate	旧南门	*jiù nánmén*
Reed Flute Cave	芦笛岩	*lúdí yán*
Rong Hu	榕湖	*róng hú*
Seven Star Cavern	七星洞	*qīxīng dòng*
Seven Star Park	七星公园	*qīxīng gōngyuán*
Shan Hu	杉湖	*shān hú*
Stone Forest	石林	*shí lín*
Ta Shan	塔山	*tǎ shān*
Xi Shan Park	西山公园	*xī shān gōngyuán*
Yueya Shan	月牙山	*yuèyá shān*
Accommodation and eating		
Bravo	桂林宾馆	*guìlín bīnguǎn*
Golden Elephant	金象大酒店	*jīnxiàng dàjiǔdiàn*
Guilin Fandian	桂林饭店	*guìlín fàndiàn*
Jiulong	九龙	*jiǔlóng*
Natural Café	闻莺阁	*wényīng gé*
New City	新城市酒店	*xīnchéngshì jiǔdiàn*
Rongde	榕德酒店	*róngdé jiǔdiàn*
Ronghu	榕湖饭店	*rónghú fàndiàn*
Sheraton	大宇大饭店	*dàyǔ dàfàndiàn*
South Stream	南溪饭店	*nánxī fàndiàn*
Telecom	电信宾馆	*diànxìn bīnguǎn*
Tong Lai Guan	同来馆	*tónglái guǎn*
Universal	环球大酒店	*huánqíu dàjiǔdiàn*
Yi Yuan	怡园饭店	*yíyuán fàndiàn*

centre into a shabby provincial shell, neatened up since the late 1980s by a self-conscious beautification project involving planting every available open space with flowers, and lining streets with sweet-scented osmanthus trees. All this lightens the modern, high-density architecture and heavy pedestrian and motor traffic, but it's the famous hills that are Guilin's focus of interest, not the city itself.

Arrival, information and accommodation

Central Guilin lies on the western bank of the south-flowing Li River, with its suburbs spread in all directions. Various peaks are scattered around the centre, but tall buildings render them invisible from ground level and of no use for orientation. Parallel with the river and about 500m west, Zhongshan Lu is the main street, running north for 4km or so from the train station past a knot of accommodation and services, the long-distance bus station and on through the centre. The main roads which cross it are Nanhuan Lu, Ronghu Lu and adjoining Shanhu Lu, and Jiefang Lu, all of which stretch for at least 1km west across town from Binjiang Lu, the riverside promenade.

Moving on from Guilin

Minibuses to Yangshuo leave the train station forecourt through the day whenever full. Foreigners are almost always grossly overcharged, though the correct rate is ¥5, plus ¥2 per large item of luggage. **Buses** from the long-distance station to elsewhere in the province and beyond are easy to book a day in advance: options include heading north to Sanjiang and Guizhou province (pp.798–805); to Guangzhou; or to the holy peaks at Heng Shan in Hunan. **Flying** is similarly straightforward, with Guilin linked to cities right across the mainland, as well as to Hong Kong, Korea and Japan. Agents both here and in Yangshuo can book you a taxi to the airport.

Because few **trains** actually originate in Guilin, the city has always been a notoriously difficult place to leave by rail, requiring advance planning for anything better than standing room or hard seat – inadvisable for the lengthy trips to Changsha, Guangzhou, Shanghai or Kunming. The **ticket office** opens daily 8am–5pm, with destinations and fares for all classes listed (in Chinese) above the windows. If you can't get what you want here, agents in both Guilin and Yangshuo can sort things out, though they need three days' notice and charge varying mark-ups.

Guilin's busy **Liangjiang International Airport** is 20km west of the city, connected to the CAAC office on Shanghai Lu by airport bus (¥15) and taxi (about ¥75). The **train station** is very central, set at the back of a large square off Zhongshan Lu, within striking distance of accommodation and places of interest, with the **long-distance bus station** just a couple of hundred metres further north. **Minibuses from Yangshuo** tend to drop passengers west of the long-distance bus station on Huancheng Si'er Lu, though they might also wind up at the depot in front of the train station. Most of Guilin's sights are close enough to walk to, others can be reached easily on public buses, or by taxi (a fixed ¥10–12 fare within the city limits).

The city is unusual in China in having an independent, English-speaking tourism advice service, which offers general **information** as well as making bookings for tours, transport and accommodation. They have booths at the airport, outside the train station, and at the bus station.

Accommodation

Guilin offers foreigners little budget accommodation and you'll find it better to head down to Yangshuo if you're after a choice. All the following are central and have at least one restaurant; the more expensive have post and banking facilities, and international telephones. Expect a ten percent service charge at upmarket accommodation, though this can be offset in winter with thirty to fifty percent discounts.

Bravo 14 Ronghu Nan Lu Ⓣ0773/2823950, Ⓕ2822101, Ⓔglhi@public.glptt.gx.cn. Reasonably maintained, upmarket hotel, nicely positioned near what's left of the older parts of town, with rooms starting at US$110. ❾

Golden Elephant 36 Binjiang Lu Ⓣ0773/2808888, Ⓕ2809999. Very smart and cosy three-star Korean-run affair overlooking Elephant Trunk Hill and the river. ❼

Guilin Fandian 25 Zhongshan Zhong Lu Ⓣ0773/2822754. Best of the city's budget options, clean and tidy though nothing flash. Rooms range from basic triples and doubles to more comfortable doubles. ❷–❹

New City 86 Zhongshan Nan Lu Ⓣ0773/2158888, Ⓕ2158168. Comfortable three-star option close to the bus and train stations; rooms are the standard functional design but clean and in good order, and it's always worth bargaining. ❼

Rongde 2 Yiwu Lu Ⓣ0773/2813598, Ⓕ2819996. Just around the corner from the PSB and Rong Hu, this is a tidy, inexpensive hotel in a quiet location. ❺

Ronghu 17 Ronghu Bei Lu Ⓣ0773/2823811, Ⓕ2825390. A business-meeting favourite set in huge grounds in a quiet part of town, modern though with a faintly tired atmosphere. ❼

Sheraton 9 Binjiang Nan Lu ⓣ0773/2825588, ⓕ2825598, ⓔsheraton_guilin@sheraton.com. Definitely one of the nicest hotels in town, with the best rooms (US$120) overlooking the river and across to Seven Star Park. ❾

South Stream 84 Zhongshan Nan Lu ⓣ0773/3834943, ⓕ3832633. Close to the train and bus stations, this tatty urban Chinese hotel is inexpensive for Guilin. Singles, doubles and triples with shared and own facilities. ❷

Telecom 57 Zhongshan Nan Lu ⓣ0773/3839898, ⓕ3818619. Not a bad little place with ordinary but decent rooms; very central. ❺

Universal 1 Jiefang Dong Lu ⓣ0773/2828228, ⓕ2823868, ⓔhtlunivs@public.glptt.gx.cn. Fairly swish, three-star Macau-run operation in a pleasant location, with some rooms offering river views. Substantial discounts in winter. ❽

The City

Before starting a tour of Guilin's hills, head 2km north of the train station to where Zhongshan Lu cuts between **Rong Hu** and **Shan Hu**, two lakes which originally formed the moat that surrounded the Tang city walls, and are now crossed by attractively hunchbacked stone bridges and fringed with flowerbeds, willow, and banyan trees. The only surviving remnant of the walls is **Jiu Nan Men**, the old South Gate – now an expensive teahouse.

The best views of the Li River are from along Binjiang Lu (though expect to be courted by cruise touts as you wander), which is well shaded from the summer sun by the **osmanthus trees** after which Guilin is named. From here you look south to riverside **Elephant Trunk Hill**, said to be the body of a sick imperial baggage elephant who was cared for by locals and turned to stone rather than rejoin the emperor's army. You can cross to the hill by ferry from Nanhuan Lu, or walk over via a bridge; either way it's ¥15 admission, which also gives you the chance to climb up to a crumbling pagoda, or have your photo taken holding a parasol while you sit next to a cormorant on a brightly coloured bamboo raft.

Guilin's three most central peaks are within a twenty-minute walk north of here, close to the river. Two kilometres along Binjiang Lu is **Fubo Shan**, a hill where the giant **Jie Die** fought a demon which was descending on Guilin with a vanguard of deadly animals. The demon was vanquished and the city never troubled by evil spirits again. At its foot is **Huanzhu Dong** (Returned Pearl Cave), named after the story of a guilt-stricken fisherman who returned a sleeping dragon's stolen treasure. Climb to Fubo's summit and you pass three hundred Buddha images, carved into the rock during the Tang and Song dynasties.

A further ten minutes' walk north brings you to riverside **Diecai Shan** (Folded Brocade Hill), its limestone seams eroded into a series of small peaks, supposedly resembling a pile of interlaced fabric. The same distance west of Fubo is **Duxiu Feng** (Solitary Beauty Peak), which stands within the grounds of the mansion of **Zhu Shouqian**, Guilin's fourteenth-century ruler and grandson of the emperor Hongwu. Apart from the gate, there's little of the original left; the present building once served as Sun Yatsen's office and is now the home of the Guangxi Teachers' College. Three hundred and six steps lead to the top of the peak, where views once again make the climb worthwhile.

Seven Star Park

Guilin's most extensive formations are at Qixing Gongyuan, the **Seven Star Park** (¥35), where you can spend a good half-day exploring caves and a set of seven peaks arranged in the shape of the Great Bear (Big Dipper) constellation. The main **entrance** lies east over the river, and bus #13 from Zhongshan Lu stops outside. On the way in you cross over a Song-style covered bridge, complete with palisades and tiled roof. The left-hand mass as you enter the park is **Putuo**, named after Zhejiang's famous Buddhist mountain and topped by peaks representing the Great Bear's four northern stars, Tianshi, Tianxuan, Tianji and Tianquan. The left track here leads down past a pavilion to the **Stone Forest** and the 22-storey **Putuo Si**, a temple behind which is a cave where the Bodhisattva Kumara reputedly preached; the right leads to a chain of caves culminating at the huge **Seven Star Cavern**. Over 1km long, 40m wide and almost 30m tall, it was originally a channel cut by a subterranean river (lower reaches are still flooded), and while access is restricted, what you can see is impressive enough. The remaining three stars – Yuleng, Kaiyang and Yaoguang – are atop **Yueya Shan** in the south of the park. At the foot is a pavilion where you can stop and buy drinks before climbing up to ever better views from various lookouts. Descending on the far side, you reach the **Dragon Refuge Cave**, whose walls are patterned with "scales" caused by erosion and with thousands of poems inscribed by visitors. There's more of this farther on at the **Guilin Stele Forest**, where more than two thousand stone tablets record dissertations on subjects from literature to Marxist economics.

Lutuo Shan (Camel Hill) rises east of Yueya, and looking south from the top you'll see **Chuan Shan** (Hill with the Hole) and the adjacent **Ta Shan** (Pagoda Hill), crowned by a hexagonal Ming-dynasty pagoda. It was built to imprison a centipede demon which had been harassing the city's populace, after a worthy cockerel who lived on Chuan Shan had chased it into a cave on the mountain. The people swiftly erected this demon-quelling structure, permanently sealing the centipede inside.

The Li River cruise

The **Li River** meanders south for 85km between **Guilin and Yangshuo** through the finest scenery that this part of the country can provide, and the **six-hour cruise** from the docks above Elephant Trunk Hill is, for some, the highlight of their trip to China. Others find the cost extortionate, the journey too long, and, with some two thousand people a day in peak season, the river overcrowded – the Li's banks have recently been concreted in the early stages to reduce erosion caused by the volume of cruise boats. If any of this seems likely to bother you, the Li can be explored in a cheaper and more leisurely manner from Yangshuo itself (see p.792).

You can book cruises through hotels, agents or more cheaply, direct at the **docks** in the vicinity of the *Sheraton* on Binjiang Lu. Cruise boats leave daily at 8am, and the ¥500 price tag to Yangshuo (¥460 one-way) gets you a comfortable seat, decent food, running commentary in Chinese and a bus from Yangshuo back to Guilin. Alternatively, ¥150 buys you a two-hour excursion down to **Zhujiang**, which, while missing the most impressive peaks, presents a beautiful scene in autumn, with the banks coloured red by maple trees. In winter, the river runs so low that boats for Yangshuo have to start from Zhujiang anyway, and passengers are taken there by bus.

The cruise is a generally tranquil experience despite the legend that the spirit of every sailor who ever drowned on the Li River rocks boats as they navigate the rougher shoals. Along the way you'll pass **cormorant fishermen** (see box, p.795) poling their almost submerged bamboo rafts, buffalos wallowing in the fields and, of course, scores of exotically shaped hills with romantic names. The atmosphere ends abruptly after docking at Yangshuo, when several hundred stallholders descend on passengers and desperately try to push their faked coins and glass animals before the Guilin buses arrive. Yangshuo has a far better side, but you'll need to stay overnight to appreciate it.

Xi Shan and Reed Flute Cave

Bus #3 from Zhongshan Lu heads a couple of kilometres down Lijun Lu towards **Xi Shan**, the Western Hills, an area of long Buddhist associations. Xi Shan's peaks are named after Buddhist deities, and many grottoes were once adorned with carvings, long since defaced. However, the **Xiqinglin Si** survives as one of southern China's major Buddhist halls, filled with hundreds of exquisitely executed statues ranging from ten centimetres to over two metres in height. There's also a **regional museum** in the park (daily 9am–noon & 2.30–5pm; free), which tries to animate a massive collection of ethnic clothing by using mannequins to depict key festival events – staff in the gift shop downstairs might offer to translate for you.

The #3 bus terminates another 6km north along the Peach Blossom River outside **Reed Flute Cave** (daily 8.30–11am & 12.30–3.30pm; ¥50), a huge warren eaten into the south side of **Guangming Shan** in one of the most extraordinary examples of limestone erosion in the country. The entry fee is high, and the coloured lighting is at once overpowering and crude, but the size and variety of the rock formations are impressive, even if you don't know that you're looking at "Rosy Dawn in a Lion Forest" or "Waterfall Splashing Down from a High Valley". You're meant to follow one of the tours which run every twenty minutes, but you can always linger inside and pick up a later group if you want to spend more time. The cave was developed as a tourist site only in the 1950s, before which it provided a refuge from banditry and Japanese bombs.

Eating, drinking and entertainment

Guilin's **restaurants** are famous for serving exotica, such as palm civets, turtles, snakes and rare birds. Fortunately, you can eat well here without devouring endangered species. Food is of good quality though prices can be steep – at least ¥50 per person in a proper restaurant – and it's essential to check them before ordering. Far cheaper are the mass of nondescript, clean places for sandpots, dumplings, stir-fries, roast and braised meats, located throughout the centre, especially around the bus and train stations on Zhongshan Lu; some of these go as far as offering pigeon and pheasant. Most larger establishments have English menus and open around 11am–2pm and 5.30pm–late.

Restaurants

Cheng's Local Food Shazheng Yang Lu. Cantonese roast meats, sandpots and steamed greens, with popular pavement tables for hot weather; not expensive.

Food Street Top floor of Niko-Niko Do Plaza, corner of Jiefang Lu and Zhongshan Lu. Cheap and clean canteen offering Chinese noodles, *dim sum* and Western-style pizza, pasta, coffee and tea.

Jiulong Zhongshan Lu. Stick to straightforward Cantonese and regional fare – smoked duck, chicken with bamboo shoots, taro and pork – and this multistorey place is fair value, with great food. Gourmet dishes, however, will bankrupt you, though exotic treats like scorpion and sea snake are not too outrageously priced at around ¥30 a portion.

Natural Café Yiren Lu. Eclectic "foreign" menu including spaghetti, borscht, and Southeast Asian coconut curries from ¥18, and steaks for around ¥35.

Tong Lai Guan Entry is around the side of the building in an alley off Zhongshan Lu. Hot, noisy, smoky, and an excellent place for an inexpensive *dim sum* breakfast of Cantonese and local snacks, all wheeled around on trolleys.

Yi Yuan 106 Nanhuan Lu. Real Sichuanese food, comfortable surroundings and friendly, English-speaking staff make this a nice place to dine. It's not that expensive, either; two or three can eat well for ¥80. Try the "strange-flavoured" chicken, green beans with garlic or first-rate sweet-and-sour fish.

Entertainment

Guilin's tradition of **opera and ballad singing** goes back several hundred years, though performances of these have been supplanted by "minority displays" laid on for tour groups by thirteen of the region's ethnic groups. There's actually nothing wrong with these for their own sake, though visiting Chinese audiences seem to pay scant attention and you'll probably want to avoid occasional specials such as horse fighting – not an edifying spectator sport – which traditionally conclude Lunar New Year festivities. There are several **theatres** along Jiefang Xi Lu and the surrounding streets, busiest Friday through to Sunday nights; tickets for the hour-long performances are sold at the doors (¥40–50). Western-oriented variety, operatic and acrobatic shows are also held at the Lijiang Theatre on riverfront Binjiang Lu, near the *Sheraton*.

For **nightlife**, the *Dadu Hui* disco, on the corner of Yiren Lu and Zhongshan Lu, and *Gogo*, farther east on Yiren Lu, are busy with expat teachers and trendy Chinese; expect a ¥15 cover charge. Drinkers might prefer one of a growing number of **bars** such as the *Ragazza Pub*, also near the corner of Yiren Lu, though a large beer is expensive at ¥35.

Listings

Airlines Offices open daily 9am–5pm. CAAC, Shanghai Lu ⓣ0773/2834067; Dragonair, at the *Bravo* hotel ⓣ0773/2823950, ⓕ0773/2861666; Shanghai Airlines, Zhongshan Lu ⓣ0773/2826935. Hotels and agents can also make bookings.

Banks and exchange The Bank of China on Zhongshan Lu is able to change currency and traveller's cheques (Mon–Fri 9–11.30am & 1.30–5pm). Larger hotels, such as the *Bravo*, *Sheraton* and *Hidden Hill*, may allow non-residents to use their services, too.

Bookshops There's a subterranean Xinhua bookstore just west of Shan Hu on Zhongshan Lu, with a good selection of translated Chinese classics, maps, stodgy Victorian potboilers, and even a few cookbooks, plus CDs, VCDs and DVDs.

Hospital Renmin Hospital, off Wenming Lu, is the best place to head if you get sick and your accommodation can't help out.

Internet access You can get connected for ¥2 an hour at the building opposite the Zhongshan Bei Lu post office, about 2.5km north of the train station (bus #1).

Mail and telecommunications The most convenient post office is just north of the train station on Zhongshan Nan Lu, with mail services and poste restante downstairs, telephones upstairs (daily 8am–8pm). There's also another major branch about 2.5km farther north on Zhongshan Bei Lu.

PSB Sanduo Lu, west off Zhongshan Lu, just north of Rong Hu ⓣ0773/2823334.

Shopping Zhongshan Lu is lined with well-stocked department stores, the best of which is the Niko-Niko Do Plaza on the corner with Jiefang Lu. For souvenirs – mostly outright tack and ethnicky textiles – try the shops on Binjiang Lu, though stalls in Yangshuo sell the same stuff at literally a fraction of the price.

Travel agents Hotel tour desks can help with plane, bus and boat tickets, as can the CITS, opposite the train station at 112 Zhongshan Lu (Mon–Sat 7.30am–noon, 1–6pm & 7–9pm; ⓣ0773/2999164, ⓕ0773/3840750), and the CTS, on Binjiang Lu (daily 8am–5pm; ⓣ0773/2861623, ⓕ0773/2827424).

Yangshuo and around

Nestled 70km south of Guilin in the thick of China's most spectacular karst scenery, **YANGSHUO**, meaning Bright Moon, rose to prominence during the mid-1980s, when visitors on Li River cruises from Guilin realized that beyond simply spending an hour here buying souvenirs, the village made an excellent place to settle down and get on intimate terms with the river and its peaks. Yangshuo has grown quite a bit since then, and today the newer area around the highway is as noisy, polluted and crowded as anywhere in

Yangshuo and around

Yangshuo	阳朔	***yángshuò***
Green Lotus Peak	碧莲峰	*bìlián fēng*
Hotel California	加州饭店	*jiāzhōu fàndiàn*
Hotel Explorer	文化饭店	*wénhuà fàndiàn*
Li River	漓江	*líjiāng*
Mountain View	山水旅馆	*shānshuǐ lǚguǎn*
Nation	民族饭店	*mínzú fàndiàn*
Paradise Yangshuo	阳朔百乐度假饭店	*yángshuò bǎilèdùjià fàndiàn*
Peace	和平客栈	*hépíng kèzhàn*
Si Hai	四海饭店	*sìhǎi fàndiàn*
Sunshine Spa	阳光酒店	*yángguāng jiǔdiàn*
West Street International Youth Hostel	西街国际青年旅馆	*xījiē guójì qīngnián lǚguǎn*
Yangshuo Park	阳朔公园	*yángshuò gōngyuán*
Around Yangshuo		
Black Buddha New Water Caves	黑佛新水洞	*hēifó xīnshuǐ dòng*
Black Dragon Caves	黑龙洞	*hēilóng dòng*
Camel Hill	骆驼山	*luòtuó shān*
Fuli	福利	***fúlì***
Moon Hill	月亮山	*yuèliàng shān*
Xingping	兴坪	***xīngpíng***
Yangdi	杨堤	***yángdī***

China. But in the village streets between here and the river the atmosphere remains much calmer, and with Guilin oriented firmly towards big-spending tour groups, so independent tourists – an increasing number of them Chinese – have made Yangshuo their haven instead. There are foreign-oriented restaurants and accommodation everywhere, some of which are surprisingly sophisticated. You can rent a bike and spend a day zipping between hamlets, hike around or go **rock climbing** on nearby peaks, study calligraphy or *tai ji* or just relax in the village park.

The village

A simple country marketplace before the tourists arrived, Yangshuo has little to see, but it's still a nice place to be. Nor do you have to go far to find a hill to climb, as the village is completely hemmed in by them – all nicely illuminated at night by high-wattage floodlights. West off Diecui Jie is **Yangshuo Park** (¥6), a pleasant place in summer with its colourful formal garden and breezy vantages of town from pavilions lodged on the main rise. Squeezed between the highway and the river directly opposite is **Green Lotus Peak**, the largest in the immediate area, which can be climbed from a footpath along the bank. Otherwise, just walk upstream from Yangshuo for a kilometre or two and take your pick of the rough paths which scale many other slopes to summits covered in tangled undergrowth and sharp, eroded rocks.

The presence of tourists hasn't entirely altered the daily routine of villagers, who spend hours inspecting wares in the produce market. There's a good selection of game, fruit, nuts and fungus laid out on sheets in the street here,

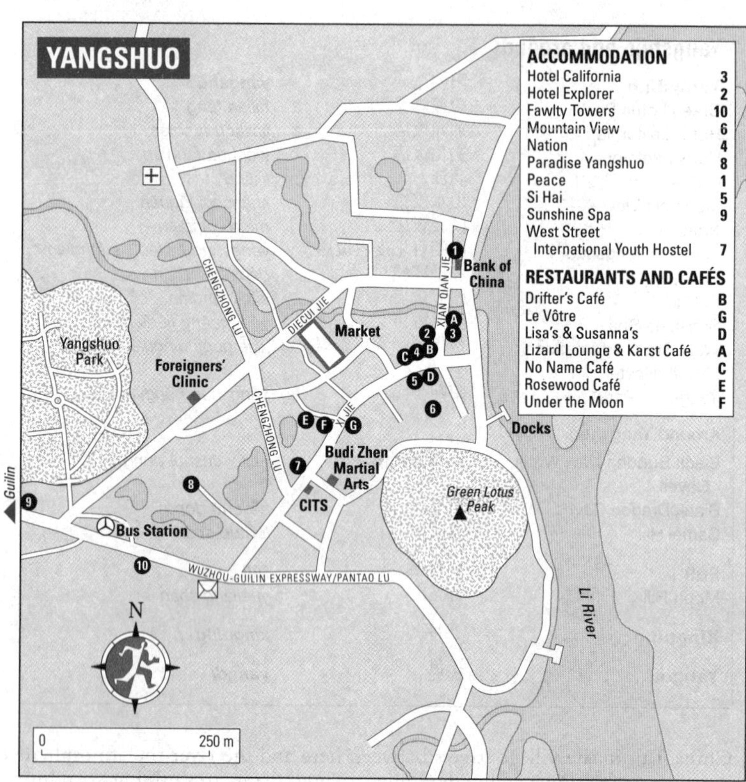

including rats and pheasants, fresh straw and needle mushrooms, and spiky water caltrops, which contain a kernel similar to a Brazil nut. Foreigners tend to save their money for the shops down at the river end of **Xi Jie** (also signposted as West Street), one of the best places in China to pick up a bargain **souvenir**: Little Red Books in English, stylish and cheap jackets and T-shirts made here (to order, if needed) from batiks or silk, Bai, Miao and Dong textiles, modern and traditional paintings turned out by art students in Guilin, chops, and heaps of elaborately carved wooden screen panels, printing blocks and grotesque theatre masks. As always in China, buy because you like something, not because it looks valuable – most articles are "new antiques". Vigorous, friendly bargaining is essential, and don't buy anything when tour boats from Guilin pull in unless you want to pay five times the going rate. Several shops also specialize in Western music CDs at around ¥15 a disc; and a couple sell factory reject brand-name designer clothing at absurdly low prices.

The village also offers a window into the more esoteric side of Chinese culture. For around ¥20–25 a session you can take **courses** in painting, calligraphy, languages, cooking, massage and many other subjects – cafés (see "Practicalities" below) have the current information. There's also the excellent **Budi Zhen martial arts school** here up an alley beside CITS, run by old Mr Gao (currently in his late 70s) and his twin sons, whose unique family style is a blend of Shaolin and Wudang techniques – the sons speak good English.

Cormorant fishing

When you've had enough scenery for one day, do something unusual and spend an evening watching **cormorant fishing** (book through cafés; ¥100 for a four-person boat and ninety-minute trip). This involves heading out in a punt at dusk, closely following a tiny wooden fishing boat or bamboo raft from which a group of cormorants fish for their owner. People still make their living from this age-old practice throughout central and southern China, raising young birds to dive into the water and swim back to the boat with full beaks. The birds are prevented from swallowing by rings or ties around their necks, but it's usual practice for the fisherman to slacken these off and let them eat every seventh fish – apparently, the cormorants refuse to work otherwise.

Practicalities

Most people arrive in Yangshuo by bus along the speedy Wuzhou–Guilin expressway, lined with stalls selling bamboo furniture and seasonal gluts of pomelos, plums and peaches. This highway bends in from the west to the **bus station**, runs east for about 500m as Pantao Lu, then kinks off due south en route to Moon Hill, Liuzhou and Wuzhou. Yangshuo's two main streets run northeast off the highway to the **Li River**; Diecui Jie extends from the bus station through the village centre, while east and parallel is pleasantly cobbled, vehicle-free Xi Jie, extending past cafés and accommodation, plus old wooden shops, down to the **docks**.

There's an unusual quantity of **information** to be had in Yangshuo. The hotels have information desks, and the helpful CITS-China Southern office on Xi Jie (daily 9am–9pm; ⓣ0773/8827103, ⓔchuyanxi@163.net) takes Visa and can organize local guides and tours to Longsheng (see p.800). However, many people make arrangements by shopping around Yangshuo's ubiquitous **cafés**. Specifically geared to Western travellers, these act as meeting places to swap news – some have noticeboards, others leave journals out for you to write in and read – and offer **book exchanges** (the best being at the *Si Hai* hotel), Internet access, and deals on everything that it's possible to do during your stay here.

English teachers for private lessons are always wanted in Yangshuo; you'll find adverts posted in accommodation and stores along Xi Jie. Payment is usually in bed and board – you could also swap your services for Chinese lessons.

There are two **banks**, on Xi Jie and on the waterfront between Xi Jie and Diecui Jie (foreign currency transactions daily 9am–noon & 1–5pm); the **post office** (daily 8am–5pm; parcel and post restante services available) is over on the highway. **Internet access** is available at net bars and many of Xi Jie's cafés – sometimes free if you have a meal too; otherwise, expect to pay ¥6 an hour. Should you get sick, there's a **foreigners' clinic** on Diecui Jie, and also a **Hospital of Traditional Chinese Medicine** on Xi Jie.

Moving on, minibuses to Guilin orbit the bus station all day long, though long-distance bookings to Guangzhou, Liuzhou, Nanning and Wuzhou have to be made through agents, as these buses originate in Guilin. If you're planning to take a sleeper to Wuzhou, go to Guilin first or put up with the worst berths – over the back wheel – as the bus will be otherwise full by the time it gets to Yangshuo. Local agents can also book flights, **taxis to Guilin airport** (¥200) and, with at least three days' warning, **train tickets** from Guilin.

Accommodation

Stiff competition means that Yangshuo's accommodation prices are good value, whether you're paying for a budget dorm bed or something a bit more upmarket. Locations aside – the highway area is pretty noisy through the night – there's little to separate **hotels** within similar price brackets; everywhere offers laundry and booking services, and most have restaurants. In addition to the places listed below, many of the cafés, such as *Lisa's*, also have dorm beds for as little as ¥15, or doubles for ¥60. Room rates drop during the winter low season, when you'll want to check the availability of heating and hot water.

Hotel California 35 Xian Qian Jie Ⓣ & Ⓕ0773/8825559, Ⓔhotelcaliforniayangshuo@yahoo.com. Budget favourite, modern, clean and well run. Dorm beds ¥20, air-con doubles with and without bathroom. ❶–❸

Hotel Explorer Xian Qian Jie Ⓣ0773/8828116, Ⓕ8827816, ⒺJimmyQin@hotmail.com. Smart new Chinese affair, though low-key and inexpensive for the fairly spacious, standard rooms. ❶

Fawlty Towers On the highway near the post office Ⓣ0773/8824309. Set back off the road, this friendly place is quiet for the location, though rooms are on the small side. Dorm beds ¥20, ❸

Mountain View In an alley off the eastern end of Xi Jie Ⓣ0773/8821603, Ⓔgreenstravelling@163.net. Quiet, no-frills option with friendly management. Dorm beds ¥20, ❶

Nation Xi Jie Ⓣ0773/8829988, Ⓔysmzjd@gi.gx.cninfo.net. Another modern, stylish Chinese place; entry is through the wood-panelled bar. ❹

Paradise Yangshuo Off Xi Jie Ⓣ0773/8822109, Ⓦwww.paradiseyangshuo.com. Yangshuo's most upmarket affair, a series of buildings set in a spacious private garden complete with pond. US$80, though you can often negotiate substantial discounts. ❾

Peace Xian Qian Jie, behind the riverfront Bank of China Ⓣ0773/8826262, ⒺJankinLuo@163.net. One of the best deals in town: large rooms with aircon, bathroom and balconies in a quiet street just off Xi Jie. ❷

Si Hai River end of Xi Jie Ⓣ & Ⓕ0773/8822013, ⒺSiHai@hotmail.com. Popular for its budget rooms with all-day hot water. The higher category rooms are comfortable but small, and come with private bathrooms and air-con. Dorm beds ¥15, ❶–❷

Sunshine Spa On the highway near the park Ⓣ0773/8828333, Ⓦwww.sunshinespa.com. Location aside, this is a very cosy mid-range option with timber floors and stylish furnishings in the rooms. ❻

West Street International Youth Hostel Xi Jie Ⓣ0773/8820933, Ⓕ8820988, Ⓔstgyp@263.net. The price is fair in this IYHA-affiliated hotel, but the place is sterile and the management loud, offhand, and pushy with tours. Dorm beds ¥15, ❶

Eating, drinking and nightlife

You'll probably while away the evenings in Yangshuo drinking beer and eating in Xi Jie's numerous **restaurants**. These are relatively upmarket, serving pretty authentic Western fare, from wood-fired pizzas and char-grilled steak, to apple pie and ice cream; others have decent Chinese menus, including local specialities such as cane rats, fresh bamboo shoots and river fish. Alternatively, **cafés** on Xi Jie and Xian Qian Jie – the latter also currently at the core of Yangshuo's **rock-climbing scene** – offer much the same things, though prices are a bit lower and the food more ordinary; most also screen films in the evenings. Both restaurants and cafés open early in the morning for Western breakfasts and coffee, and in good weather might host outdoor barbecues. Everyone finds their own favourites, and the following recommendations should be treated as a starting point. There are also plenty of inexpensive **Chinese canteens** and **food stalls** selling noodle soups and buns around the market and upper Xi Jie.

Eating aside, the **cinema** on Xi Jie is busy every night, as are countless private VCD screens easily located by the high-volume, scream-and-thud soundtracks emanating from within.

Cafés and restaurants

Drifters Café Xi Jie. Excellent apple pie, good *mapo doufu*, and possibly the best muesli, yoghurt and fruit breakfast in town. Service can be slack, though.

Le Vôtre Xi Jie. Yangshuo's poshest dining, inside

a Ming-era building complete with period furnishings. Food is French – snails, paté, onion soup, steak au poivre, chocolate mousse – or Chinese seafood. Also, excellent coffee and croissants for breakfast. Expect to pay at least ¥50 a head.

Lisa's and **Susanna's** Near to each other on Xi Jie. Two cosy, perennially popular backpacker joints. Cheap food ranges from Western to decent Chinese dishes along the lines of sweet-and-sour pork, stuffed bean curd and fried beansprouts.

Lizard Lounge and **Karst Café** Xian Qian Jie. Two climber-oriented café-bars with an average run of Chinese and Western staples and good opportunities to make contacts.

No Name Café Xi Jie. Excellent pizza and bread, along with Italian-style fare.

Rosewood Café Just off Xi Jie. Romantic ambience and extensive Western menu covering pizza, pasta, grills and salads. Have their duck in brandy sauce followed by a mango-sago pudding, and you'll forgive China for all its problems. Two can eat well for ¥100.

Si Hai Xi Jie. Toasted sandwiches, bamboo rats, vegetarian hotpots, and excellent beer-battered fish. The walls are plastered with Mao photos and Cultural Revolution iconography.

Under the Moon Xi Jie. Almost chic place, with nicely styled upstairs dining room with balcony, and slightly over-large first-floor café with the best street tables in town. Good Western and Chinese food – their lemon sorbet is excellent.

Around Yangshuo

Getting to see the countryside around Yangshuo is no problem, as the land between the hills is flat and perfect for **bicycles** – Xian Qian Jie is thick with **rental shops** if your accommodation can't help (¥10 a day, plus ¥100 deposit). Various people offer excellent and inexpensive **guided bike tours**, too, allowing close contact with villages and locals through an interpreter; costs are subject to negotiation but ¥15 an hour seems about right. **Motor-rickshaws** also cruise around, destinations listed on their windshields in Chinese, but are relatively expensive and the drivers don't speak English.

In summer, a popular way to see the **river** is by renting an **inner tube** from one of the cafés and simply drifting around. Except in very dry winters, **boats** leave all year round from the **dock** at the end of Xi Jie; the **ticket office** here advertises morning departures upstream, and you'll also be mobbed by touts. While it's not such a good idea to travel the whole way to Guilin from Yangshuo – an ultimately tedious twelve-hour journey upstream (wrap warmly in winter) – there are plenty of shorter trips to make, though as Gulin operators have a monopoly on vessels, prices are still relatively high. One way

Climbing Yangshuo's peaks

Yangshuo is one of Asia's fastest-growing **rock-climbing** centres, with an estimated 70,000 pinnacles of up to 200m in height in the area. However, there are only about fifty established climbing routes, many of them under 30m in length – though one around the arch at Moon Hill is rated as the toughest in all China – and, as most are within easy day-trips of Yangshuo, you won't need to plan any mighty expeditions (though camping out on site is fun).

The main **climbing season** lasts from October through to February, as the rest of the year can be uncomfortably hot or wet. Advance information can be found at Ⓦwww.chinaoutdoors.com/activities/climbing/yangshuo.html.

Once in Yangshuo, visit the cafés along Xian Qian Jie to make contacts; in particular, the *Lizard Lounge* can provide climbing **guides** who are useful for locating established routes and suggesting where you might find new challenges. Outdoors and climbing **equipment** (mostly clothing) is sold at China Climb, 22 Xi Jie, who also sometimes arrange climbing expeditions (Ⓦwww.ChinaClimb.com); and you can rent camping gear, including tents, from SZ Redfox on Xian Qian Jie for ¥10 a day plus ¥100 deposit.

around this is to catch an early morning minibus from Yangshuo north to **Xingping** (about ¥5), and then a boat from there upstream to **Yangdi**, past the thickest, most contorted collection of peaks (¥40; 2hr). From Yangdi, you should be able to catch transport to either Guilin or Yangshuo along the highway. Some agents in Yangshuo can arrange this for you.

In the opposite direction, **Fuli** (¥40 by boat) is a pretty village an hour's ride downstream from Yangshuo on the east bank – you could easily cycle here - whose **produce market** (every fifth day) is the best and busiest in the area. If you just want to **swim**, take the road southeast of town to **Camel Hill**, turn right down a lane and follow the track to the river – about an hour's cycling time. Villagers turn up to wash at about 6.30pm, and there are good views of Moon Hill from here (see below).

To Moon Hill

There's nothing to stop you simply picking a distant hill and heading out there – cycling along the muddy paths between villages takes you through some wonderful scenery – but for a specific target it's hard to beat the twenty-kilometre return trip out to **Moon Hill**. This lies on the highway southwest of town as it twists between the sudden peaks – some of these are negotiable for a fair height before becoming too sheer to climb. A **rifle range** about 3km from Yangshuo welcomes you to "shoot a gun in this beautiful place it makes you in madness happy", but far more interesting are the **Black Buddha New Water Caves**, a series of underground caves discovered only in 1991, accessed down a 500-metre easterly track just short of Moon Hill – highlights include an underground river, fossils and bats. Another 3km along the same track are the equally imposing **Black Dragon Caves**, where you take a boat, then have to wade and stagger through the largest regional caverns yet discovered to a fifteen-metre subterranean waterfall and swimming holes inhabited by blind fish. Only open in summer, either system costs about ¥45 for an hour's tour, or ¥65 for a three- or four-hour flashlight exploration; come prepared to get soaked, cold, and muddy.

Moon Hill itself (¥6, plus ¥1 to park your bike) requires forty minutes of effort to ascend a stone staircase rising through bamboo and brambles to the summit. A beautiful sight, the hill is named after a crescent-shaped hole that pierces the peak. Views from the top take in the whole of the Li River valley spread out before you, fields cut into uneven chequers by rice and vegetable plots.

Longsheng, Sanjiang and on to Guizhou

A hundred kilometres northwest of Guilin the road winds steeply through some fine stands of mountain bamboo, and enters the southern limit of a fascinating ethnic **autonomous region**. With a rich landscape of mountains and terraced fields as a backdrop, it's simple to hop on local transport from the county towns of **Longsheng** and **Sanjiang** and head off to tour a very rural corner of China that seemingly remains little affected by the modern world. Day-trips abound but, with five days or so to spare, you can push right through the mountainous **Dong** heartlands northwest of Sanjiang into Guizhou province, a fabulous journey which takes you to the area around **Kaili**, similarly central to the Miao people (p.832). Before starting, note that there are **no banks** capable of cashing traveller's cheques between Guilin and Kaili.

Longsheng, Sanjiang and on to Guizhou

Longsheng	龙胜	***lóngshèng***
Longsheng Hotel	龙胜宾馆	*lóngshèng bīnguǎn*
Lüyou Binguan	旅游宾馆	*lǚyóu bīnguǎn*
Longji Titian	龙脊梯田	***lóngjǐ tītián***
Huang Lo	黄洛	*huángluò*
Liqing Guesthouse	丽晴旅社	*lìqíng lǚshè*
Longji village	龙脊村	*lóngjǐ cūn*
Ping An	平安	*píngān*
Sanjiang	三江	***sānjiāng***
Chengyang Qiao Binguan	程阳桥宾馆	*chéngyángqiáo bīnguǎn*
Department Store Hostel	百货招待所	*bǎihuò zhāodàosuǒ*
Travellers' Home	行旅之家宾馆	*xínglǚzhījiā bīnguǎn*
Wind and Rain Bridge Travel Service	风雨桥旅行社	*fēngyǔqiáo lǚxíngshè*
Chengyang	程阳	***chéngyáng***
Guandong	关东	*guāndōng*
Danzhou	丹洲	***dānzhōu***
Banjiang	板江	*bǎnjiāng*
Chankou	产口	*chǎnkǒu*
Laobao	老堡	*lǎobǎo*
Zhenjiang Fandian	振江饭店	*zhènjiāng fàndiàn*
Mapang	马胖	***mǎpàng***
Bajiang	八江	*bājiāng*
Baxie	八协	*bāxié*
Dudong	独峒	*dútóng*
Gaoding	高定	*gāodìng*
Hualian	华联	*huálián*
Mengjiang	孟江	*mèngjiāng*
Tongle	同乐	*tónglè*
Zhaoxing	肇兴	***zhàoxīng***
Diping	地坪	*dìpíng*
Fulu	富禄	*fùlù*
Heli	和里	*hélǐ*
Tang An	堂安	*tángān*
Liping	黎平	***lípíng***
Baitian Zhaodaisuo	白天招待所	*báitiān zhāodàisuǒ*
Luoxiang	落香	***luòxiāng***
Jitang	纪堂	*jìtáng*
Longtu	龙图	*lóngtú*
Congjiang	从江	***cóngjiāng***
Basha	八沙	*bāshā*
Mingzhu Jiulou	明珠酒楼	*míngzhū jiǔlóu*
Rongjiang	榕江	***róngjiāng***
Qingfeng Binguan	庆丰宾馆	*qìngfēng bīnguǎn*

Longsheng and Longji Titian

Some two hours from Guilin, **LONGSHENG** sits on the torrential **Rongshui River**, known for the tiny quantities of alluvial **gold** found in its tributaries which still entice the occasional Chinese dreamer up into the hills with shovels and pans. It's also a busy marketplace for those interestingly shaped rocks that end up in miniature gardens and bonsai pots throughout the land, a trade that was illegal until the late 1990s.

Longsheng itself is unattractive, but it makes a convenient base for further explorations. The road from Guilin follows the river north into town, then kinks sharply west past the **bus station** and off towards Sanjiang. At the kink, there's a **bridge** east over the river and into Longsheng's centre, just a couple of messy market streets and high-rise buildings parallel to the riverbank. For **accommodation**, the *Riverside Tiger Hotel* (ⓣ0773/7511335; ❶) is a very basic, friendly **hostel** run by an English teacher about 100m south of the bridge on the Guilin road (there's an English sign); more central options include the comfortable *Longsheng Hotel* (ⓣ0773/7517718; ❹) and *Luyou Binguan* (ⓣ0773/7517206, ⓕ7516632; ❷). **Eating**, there are plenty of hole-in-the-wall options around the bus station; the *Riverside Tiger* does simple Chinese meals; and the *Green Food Restaurant*, north from the town side of the bridge, has an enthusiastic manager and good food.

Scores of daily **buses** run on from Longsheng to Sanjiang (daily 6am–3pm; ¥7) or to Guilin (daily 6am–6pm; ¥10); there are also luxury coaches to Guilin at twice the price. Less frequent services can get you as far south as Liuzhou, or northeast to Congjiang. **Minibuses** for the Longji Titian area (see below) leave at 9.20am, 12.40pm and 4pm (¥6.5); you can leave extra bags at Longsheng's bus station for ¥3 a day.

Longji Titian

The real reason to visit Longsheng is the chance to explore the rest of this splendidly rural county. At **Longji Titian**, a range of hills 20km to the south-east whose name translates as "Dragon's Spine Terraces", you'll find some of the most extraordinarily extreme **rice terracing** that exists in China: the steep-sided and closely packed valleys have been carved over centuries of back-breaking effort to resemble the literal form of a contour map. Most of the people up here are **Zhuang** – for more on whom, see p.785 – but there are also communities of **Yao**, some of whom still hunt for a living; more aspiring locals in town depict them as rustic savages, happy to own just a gun and a knife. Longji Titian's villages are almost exclusively built of timber in traditional styles, and electricity and telephones are very recent introductions to the region, and still available in only a couple of places.

Tourism is beginning to kick off, however, with a new road making the village of **PING AN** easily accessible in about an hour on minibuses from Longsheng's bus station. Vehicles initially follow the Guilin road south, then turn off up an ever-tightening river valley. It's possible to **hike** up to Ping An from the Yao hamlet of **HUANG LO** here, where old women will hustle you wildly, offering souvenirs and porterage for your bags; shake yourself free, cross the suspension bridge, turn left and it's a steep ninety-minute walk. Stay on the bus and the road zigzags steeply uphill to the roadhead, where you pay ¥30 to enter the region and have to walk the last 500m up stone steps to Ping An itself, a beautiful Zhuang village of wooden homes and cobbled paths squeezed into a steep fold between the terraces. Many places offer **accommodation** at around ¥15 a person in a simple room with shared toilets and showers, with meals extra; the best atmosphere is at family-run businesses such as the *Liqing Guesthouse* (☎0773/7582412; ❶), where some English is spoken, and the food is good. Ask at your accommodation about the number of excellent **walks** in the region – there's a good four-hour round trip to lookouts, or across to the ancient village of **LONGJI** – some offer guides for about ¥25 per person including lunch. Ping An's two **stores** stock only absolute basics, so bring your own snacks or luxuries. **Leaving**, minibuses head back to Longsheng at 7.30am, 10.40am, 2.10pm and 5.30pm.

Sanjiang and the Dong

Two hours west of Longsheng the road crosses a high stone bridge over the Rongshui and lands you at **SANJIANG**, the small, desperately untidy capital of **Sanjiang Dong Autonomous County**. Sanjiang's main attraction is the neat, indigo-clad **Dong** themselves, a people renowned for their wooden houses, towers and bridges which dot the countryside hereabouts, and it's well worth roving the region with the help of minibuses and converted tractors known locally as "Dong taxis". There's a scattering of simple hostels and places to eat, and villagers will sometimes offer lodgings and sustenance – characteristically sour hotpots, *douxie cha* or **oil tea** (a bitter, salty soup made from fried tea leaves and puffed rice), and home-made rice wine – though it's polite to offer payment in these circumstances. **Language** can be problematic, as many locals can't speak *putonghua*, let alone English; people are, however, very friendly.

Sanjiang's older core is north of the Rongshui, with a newer section spreading south along the Longsheng road. There are **two bus stations**, one on either side of the river; buses from Longsheng and Guilin terminate at a depot around 200m south of the bridge down the Longsheng road – look for the speed barrier at the entrance on a curve in the road, as it's not otherwise marked – while those arriving from Guizhou province wind up immediately north of the bridge in the centre of town. Sanjiang is also on the Huaihua–Liuzhou **rail line**; the train station is about 10km northwest of town with minibuses meeting arrivals.

Places to stay north of the river include the budget *Department Store Hostel* (❶) – look for the tiny English sign just across from the central bus station – and the *Chengyang Qiao Binguan* (☎0772/8613071; ❷), 100m from the bus station. South of the river and about 100m back towards Longsheng from the bus depot, the *Travellers' Home* (☎0772/8615584; ❹) is clean, comfortable and good value. For **food**, try the noodle and hotpot stalls north of the bridge, or your accommodation.

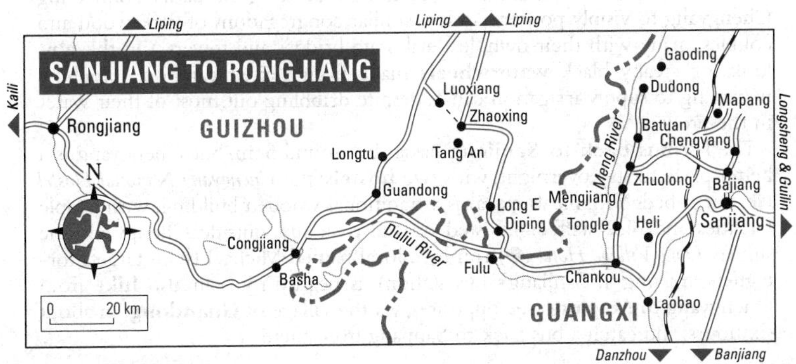

Opposite the *Travellers' Home*, the Wind and Rain Bridge Travel Service (☎0772/8617088, Ⓦwww.3jiang.com) is a particularly helpful and conscientious source of **information** as the manager, Daniel Hou, is fluent in both English and the Dong dialect. They can advise on local transport for travelling around Sanjiang and on up to Kaili in Guizhou province; otherwise give serious thought to their ¥500 full-day tour of just about every important village in the vicinity.

Leaving Sanjiang, there are buses to Longsheng, Guilin, Wuzhou and Liuzhou from the south bus station; those for local villages, Congjiang, Tongle, Zhaoxing and Liping leave from the north bus station. Minibuses to the train station, Mapang and Bajiang also leave from outside the north bus station.

Chengyang

Eighteen kilometres north of Sanjiang, **CHENGYANG** sits on the far side of the Linxi River, crossed from the main road by a splendid **wind-and-rain bridge** (**fengyu qiao** in Chinese). There are over a hundred of these in the region, but Chengyang's is the finest and most elaborate. Raised in 1916, five solid stone piers support an equal number of pavilions (whose different roofs illustrate several regional building styles) linked by covered walkways, entirely built from pegged cedar – not one nail was used in the bridge's construction. Cool and airy in summer, and protected from downpours, these bridges are perfect places to sit around and gossip, though they once served a religious purpose, too, and other examples have little shrines grimed with incense smoke in their halfway alcoves. The shrine on Chengyang's is vacant as the bridge is a protected cultural relic and no fire is allowed. Women here hawk pieces of embroidery, cotton blankets boldly patterned in black and white, and the curiously shiny blue-black Dong jackets, dyed indigo and varnished in egg-white as a protection against mosquitoes.

Across the bridge, Chengyang itself is a pretty collection of warped, two- and three-storeyed traditional **wooden houses**, overlooked by a sqaure-sided **drum tower** – both, like the wind-and-rain bridges, synonomous with the Dong. Drum towers were used as lookout posts when the country was at war, the drums inside beaten to rouse the village; today people gather here for meetings and entertainment. The Dong are not great believers in stone or concrete buildings, as traditional wooden structures can more easily be extended or even shifted as necessary. Fire is a major concern, though, and throughout the year each family takes turns to guard the village from this hazard. There's a trail from the main road up to two pavilions overlooking Chengyang, with some nice views of the dark, gloomy villages nestled among vivid green fields.

Wander out to the fields and you'll find a string of paths connecting Chengyang to visibly poorer hamlets, similar congregations of dark wood and cobbles, many with their own, less elaborate bridges and towers. On the way, look for creaky black **waterwheels** made from plaited bamboo, somehow managing to supply irrigation canals despite dribbling out most of their water in the process.

The last **bus back to Sanjiang** passes by around 5pm, but Chengyang is a better place to stay overnight, with two **hostels**: the *Chengyang National Hostel* (❶, dorm beds ¥15; meals extra) is a traditional wooden building, with simple facilities and nice staff, signposted on the river just outside Chengyang; the similar *Dong Village Hotel* (❶) run by a local named Michael (who targets foreigners arriving at Sanjiang's bus station), is nearby. You can also **hike** from Chengyang to **Mapang** (see opposite), via the village of **Guandong**, in about six hours, and catch a bus back to Sanjiang from there.

Downstream to Danzhou

The hamlet of **Danzhou** almost entirely covers a two-kilometre-long mid-river island about 60km south of Sanjiang on the **Duliu River**. It served as the regional capital from the Ming era until 1948, when the government moved to Sanjiang. The main reason for a visit is as an excuse to do some **river travel** on public ferries, though it's also possible to get most of the way here by road; the Wind and Rain Bridge Travel Service in Sanjiang can arrange a trip at around ¥80 a person for a group of ten, or you can negotiate with them for a lift to convenient departure points.

You first need to head west by road towards **Chankou** (see p.804), and catch a small ferry across the river to the couple of lanes which comprise **LAOBAO**. Inhabited by Yao, Miao and Dong, this interesting place was founded as a fortified town in the Song dynasty where the Xun and Meng rivers meet to form the Duliu, and faces a big, stony cliff upstream known as Shimen. Around three ferries – low, wooden barges seating thirty passengers – pass by Laobao between 10am and noon, and the ride down to Danzhou (¥10) amongst shy villagers and their goods takes about two hours. The scenery is best in the early stages, with bamboo tufted hills, beautifully blue water and isolated villages; the town of **Dalang** marks the return of road access, followed shortly by a **hydro-electric dam**, where the ferry has to negotiate a lock.

DANZHOU itself is about 10km downstream from here through a couple of narrow gorges, a pleasantly run-down collection of pomelo groves, abnormally quiet lanes – there are no vehicles on the island – and buildings dating back to the 1920s or earlier. Of most interest are the old walls, where you'll find a Ming-dynasty **map** of the town by the east gate; an oil-seed factory, with the presses all still operated by hand; and numerous unassuming Qing mansions, some of which were torched by the Japanese in the 1940s. There's nowhere to stay in Danzhou, but you can hire a small punt from here to the main-road town of **BANJIANG** just opposite, and either try for **food and lodgings** at *Zhenjiang Fandian* (❶), or wait for the next bus heading back to Sanjiang – there are plenty throughout the day.

Mapang and the Meng River region

Feasible as a day-trip from Sanjiang, **MAPANG** lies some 30km north of town via a change of buses in **Bajiang**, and features a huge drum tower with an unusually broad rectangular base. The last buses back to Sanjiang leave late afternoon, though it's also possible to hike from here to Chengyang in about six hours.

The most interesting corner of this land, however, lies northwest across the mountains from Bajiang along the **Meng River**, which ultimately runs down from the north to Chankou on the Sanjiang road. The daily bus from Sanjiang to **Dudong** (departs 8am) crosses these ranges, emerging 33km away above a deep valley containing the tiny, dark-roofed village of **ZHUOLONG**, where Deng Xiaoping rested up during the Long March. There are two drum towers here, but press on a couple of kilometres north to **BAXIE**, whose bright green and yellow bridge was built in 1980 (purists might notice a few nails in the decking). The cobbled village square in front of Baxie's drum tower also has a small stage carved with monkeys and lions for festival performances. The oldest surviving bridge, built in 1861, is in the next village north, **HUALIAN**, after which comes a unique two-tier example at the village of **BATUAN**, with one lane for people and one for animals. This bridge still has its shrine, a cupboard with a bearded god on a stone slab, and, at the far end, a path leads along the riverbank to where tall trees shade a small new temple.

At the end of the road, **DUDONG** was a centre for guerilla action against the Japanese during the 1940s, and its newly built drum tower is the highest in the region. There's a **guesthouse** (❶) and an excellent two-hour hike uphill from here to **GAODING**, an attractive Dong village with six towers and nothing but wooden buildings.

After a night in Dudong, either catch the 8am bus back to Sanjiang, or the **Tongle** bus as far as **MENGJIANG**, an interesting village only a few kilometres south of Zhuolong. Mengjiang is half Miao, half Dong, each community settled on opposite banks of the river. After generations of fighting over land, their leaders became reconciled in the 1940s, and together built the traditionally designed **Nationality Union Bridge** across the divide. Today it's hard to distinguish between the two communities, as both dress similarly – women wearing heavy metal earrings or a piece of white cord through their lobes – though the drum tower is, naturally enough, on the Dong side. It's a great place to wander between the large houses and out into the fields, and tractors can be hired for the run down to **TONGLE**. Here you'll find a store, a hostel and an early-morning minibus for the ninety-minute ride back to Sanjiang.

Into Guizhou: Sanjiang to Kaili

While the roads west of Sanjiang hardly swarm with tourists, an increasing number of travellers rave about the countryside and people they have encountered in the 300km between here and the Miao stronghold of **Kaili** in Guizhou province. Daily buses run from Sanjiang to **Zhaoxing** – itself a highlight – from where you can either reach Kaili on regular buses via the northerly town of **Liping**, or by continuing west to **Congjiang**, where you'll find scheduled onward transport. Note that while some direct Sanjiang–Congjiang buses go via Zhaoxing, others use the new road via Fulu, which bypasses Zhaoxing and the most interesting places; but they might come in handy for a return trip. Though distances between places are not huge, some villages are connected once a day only; miss the bus and you'll have to stay overnight. Three days is a likely minimum for the trip, though five would be more realistic and it is, anyway, not a journey to be hurried. Expect frugal facilities and food in villages, and cold, icy winters.

To Zhaoxing

About 20km west from Sanjiang, the **HELI** area is another possible day-trip from town, sporting the semi-ruined **Sanwang Gong** (Three Kings' Palace), a temple to local protective deities, next to three wind-and-rain bridges and a further two drum towers in the nearby village of **Nanzhai**. Another 10km brings you to the junction with the road from Dudong and Tongle at the riverside town of **CHANKOU**, a smattering of modern concrete-and-tile buildings with a huge **banyan tree**, social focus for villages right across tropical Asia.

An hour west of Chankou is the Guangxi–Guizhou border hamlet of **FULU**, known for its **firecracker festival** on the third day of the third lunar month. Through buses bypass the town, moving north across the border to the scruffy settlement of **DIPING**, which sports plenty of waterwheels, an excellent Dong bridge, a small drum tower, and the *Bridge Flower Hotel* (❶). Not much farther on, **LONG E** is a similarly dishevelled town with a new drum tower and the mouldy *Concerning Foreign Affairs Hotel* (❶) – really just somewhere to pull up for the night.

It's a further ninety minutes from here to **ZHAOXING**, a wonderful place set in a small valley with a generous smattering of old buildings including five square-based **drum towers**, each differently styled and built by separate clans. Some have accompanying wind-and-rain bridges and theatre stages, all decorated with fragments of mirrors and mouldings of actors and animals. Miao and Dong women in town sell embroidery and silver; houses are hung with strings of drying radishes for sour hotpots; the backstreets are full of cruising livestock and the sound of freshly dyed cloth being pounded with wooden mallets to give it a shiny patina; the only downside is a ¥5 **fee** that all visitors to Zhaoxing have to pay. Rice terraces and muddy tracks provide fine country walks; one of the best is 7km uphill from town to **Tang An**, another photogenic collection of wooden buildings.

Zhaoxing now has five **guesthouses** (❶), all offering pretty much the same comforts – hot water, flush toilets, and even **Internet** access, though this seldom seems to work. There are a couple of places to **eat**, such as the *Sanxiao Fanguan*, which has a partially translated menu, decent food and welcome braziers on a cold day. **Moving on**, several minibiuses run daily north to Liping, at least one bus goes via the Liping road to Congjiang, and there are two buses each way to Liping/Sanjiang.

Zhaoxing to Kaili

The easiest road to Kaili heads up to **LIPING** (2hr), famous as the place where the Long Marchers made up their minds to storm Zunyi. While not a traditional town it's not too unappealing, the streets are lined with trees and the *Baitian Zhaodaisuo* (❷) near the central crossroads and **bus station** offers inexpensive, comfy doubles with cable TV. The handful of daily Kaili-bound buses take about eight hours from Liping, travelling southwest through **Rongjiang** (see below); there's also traffic to Sanjiang and Congjiang, and points north on the long road to Sanhui and Zhenyuan (see p.840).

A more interesting route heads west from Zhaoxing to Congjiang, Rongjiang and Kaili. You can do this in two ways: either catch a Congjiang-bound bus from Zhaoxing (about 5hr); or walk 7km northwest to **LUOXIANG**, a small, mostly concrete-and-tile place with a big **market** every fifth day, and catch one of the morning minibuses to Congjiang from here (3hr). Either way, the journey passes attractive villages, at least seven drum towers and bridges, and a landscape of broad valleys studded with low limestone bluffs. **Longtu** and **Jitang** are the pick of the places to get off and explore, with formal lodgings at the mid-point town of **Guandong**.

CONGJIANG itself is a relatively large, modern logging town on the Duliu River, whose best accommodation prospects are at the *Mingzhu Jiulou* (doubles with air conditioning and shower ❷) near the north-bank **bus station**. There's also a department store in the same street and plenty of uncomplicated places to eat where you'll find a few stir-fries to balance the hotpot-and-noodle-soup staples. Cross the river and the original wooden Dong town is down on the right. For variety, you can catch local transport 10km west to **BASHA**, a **Miao** village whose inhabitants grow a long top-knot and seem to wear traditionally embroidered clothes, heavy metal jewellery and pleated skirts as a matter of course, not just for festivals.

Heading on, **RONGJIANG** is a reliable four hours away across the mountains, along some wild, winding country roads, very cold in winter. Rongjiang has a good Sunday **market** where you can watch villagers bargaining the last mao out of a deal, and there are comfortable **rooms** at the *Qingfeng Binguan* (❷), beside a small pavilion across from the bus station. From here it's seven hours northwest over steep, thinly settled mountains to Leishan and Kaili; for more about Kaili and the Miao, see pp.832–836.

Wuzhou

WUZHOU, 220km southeast of Guilin via Yangshuo, is an increasingly modern, prosperous trading city, its fragmentary colonial architecture a reminder of foreign influence during the late nineteenth century when British steamers puffed down the **Xi River** to Guangzhou and Hong Kong. Until 2000 the river remained a major transport artery, but today buses and the highway to Guangzhou have replaced the river ferries – a one-time favourite with travellers wanting to vary their mode of transport in China – though timber and coal barges still ply the route. While all this means that a stop in Wuzhou is no longer inevitable, the city is comfortably sized, eminently Cantonese (not surprisingly, as the Guangdong border is just east of town), and remains a good place to break the overlong journey between Guilin and Guangzhou.

The City

Everything of interest in Wuzhou is scattered through the old quarters and you can easily visit all the sights on foot. Daily life is best experienced at the many **markets**, the largest of which fills the streets north of the waterfront; the eastern end of **Dadongshang Lu** is formally pedestrianized and labelled in English as "Sauntering Street", with patched-up colonial buildings painted in pastel colours. It's all here: dried and fresh food by the sackful or slab, pet goldfish and songbirds of all descriptions, an army of cobblers, key cutters and watch repairmen, pots of ancient-looking bonsai, and a thoroughly Cantonese selection of wok-bound **wildlife** (including endangered mandarin ducks and flying squirrels). On Sunday mornings the crowds are medieval in their intensity, though everything is unusually clean and organized, and prices are clearly marked – even if they turn out merely to be a starting point in negotiations.

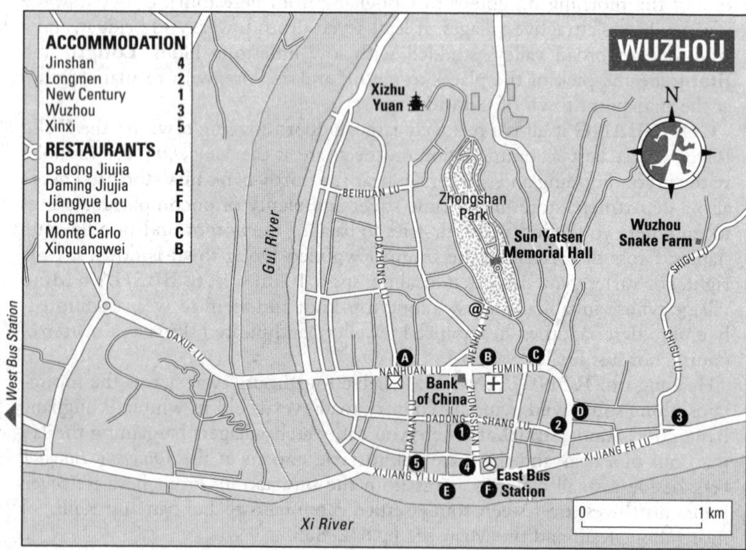

Wuzhou

Wuzhou	梧州	***wúzhōu***
Wuzhou Snake Farm	梧州蛇园	*wúzhōu shéyuán*
Xizhu Yuan	西竹园	*xīzhú yuán*
Zhongshan Park	中山公园	*zhōngshān gōngyuán*
Accommodation and eating		
Dadong Jiujia	大东酒家	*dàdōng jiǔjiā*
Daming Jiujia	大明酒家	*dàmíng jiǔjiā*
Jiangyue Lou	江月楼	*jiāngyuè lóu*
Jinshan	金山酒店	*jīnshān jiǔdiàn*
Longmen Hotel	龙门酒店	*lóngmén jiǔdiàn*
Longmen Restaurant	龙门酒楼	*lóngmén jiǔlóu*
New Century	新纪大酒店	*xīnjì dàjiǔdiàn*
Wuzhou	梧州大酒店	*wúzhōu dàjiǔdiàn*
Xinguangwei	新广卫	*xīnguǎng wèi*
Xinxi	新西酒店	*xīnxī jiǔdiàn*

North of the market area, a shady fig tree overhanging a tiny triangle of green at the intersection of Nanhuan Lu and Zhongshan Lu is a meeting point for the city's domino and chess players. Up Wenhua Lu from here, steps ascend to **Zhongshan Park** (¥1), a leafy hilltop covered in well-established, relaxing ornamental gardens. Opposite the park's north gates you'll find an alleyway winding around the hill to **Xizhu Yuan**, the Western Bamboo Nunnery, whose yellow, fortress-like walls and green-tiled roof stand proudly above the city. Restored in the 1980s and run by a handful of nuns who go about their devotions with quiet enthusiasm, the necessarily cramped halls are steeply stacked up the slope, and contain wooden Buddhist statues and a decent **vegetarian restaurant**, sometimes open to the public for an hour or two around noon.

Wuzhou Snake Farm

One of the world's largest **snake farms** is about 1.5km northeast of downtown Wuzhou along Shigu Lu (daily 9am–noon & 2.30–4pm; ¥5). Here you can find out why the southern Chinese eat, pickle and milk these creatures so enthusiastically. After being shown a video of the hapless reptiles goaded into action, there's a rather better tour round the cages to meet some of the charismatic inmates – banded kraits, cobras, leaf-nosed vipers – all fanged but handled with shocking abandon by the English-speaking tour guide. The non-venomous common rat snake is said to taste the best, while the preparation of a really fine anti-arthritic **snake wine** requires a tree snake, rat snake and cobra to be steeped in rice spirits for a year; the shop sells various by-products. It's probably best to visit in summer, when the farm is up to its half-million capacity, as during the winter stocks can get low and the inhabitants are very sluggish.

Practicalities

Wuzhou comprises two sections, both lying north of the Xi Jiang: an **older centre** with most of the accommodation, services and arrival points occupying high ground east of the Gui River; and a **modern city** expanding inexorably west. The main **west bus station** is out in the western suburbs, connected to the more central **east bus station**, on the corner of Xijiang Lu and

Zhongshan Lu in eastern Wuzhou, by a shuttle bus or public bus #3 – it takes at least fifteen minutes to cross town. **Taxis** haunt arrival points and cost ¥5 to hire; the trip between stations is around ¥10.

The *Wuzhou* hotel's **bank** handles foreign transactions (Mon–Fri 9–11.30am & 1–5pm), as does the Bank of China at the Zhongshan Lu/Nanhuan Lu intersection. The **post office**, with IDD telephones, is on Nanhuan Lu (main counter daily 8am–9pm, but customs inspections for parcels only function 9am–5.30pm), and there's an **Internet bar** (¥2/hr) on Wenhua Lu, near the southern entrance to Zhongshan Park. For **pharmacies** head up Dazhong Lu, which runs north off Nanhuan Lu from opposite the post office; the **People's General Hospital** is just west of Zhongshan Park on Jianshe Lu.

Moving on, most buses leave from the west station, but you can buy tickets and catch the free shuttle there at the east station. Luxury, normal and sleeper buses for Guangzhou, Guiping, Yangshuo, Guilin and Nanning depart between dawn and dusk, with several daily to Liuzhou, Sanjiang and Beihai. The *Wuzhou* hotel also runs luxury buses direct **to Hong Kong** (Kowloon); if you still want to do at least part of this journey by water, take a bus to Zhaoqing in Guangdong province (see p.678), and catch the daily speedboat downriver to Hong Kong from there.

Accommodation

Jinshan Opposite the east bus station, Zhongshan Lu ⓣ0774/2822965. Rooms are a bit dingy, but the price is low and everything works. The second-floor restaurant serves good *dim sum*. ❶

Longmen Corner of Fumin Lu & Dadong Shang Lu ⓣ0774/2025366. Clean and friendly place, with good-value rooms. ❷

New Century Zhongshan Lu ⓣ0774/2828222, ⓕ2824895. Newer version of the *Wuzhou*, better run and smarter. ❻

Wuzhou Xijiang Er Lu ⓣ0774/2024905, ⓕ2025971. Once the city's best-appointed hotel, now showing its age but still a reasonable option. ❺

Xinxi 11 Xijiang Yi Lu. Crumbling colonial edifice awaiting refurbishment or demolition, as long-term road-widening projects creep closer. Doubles and with bathroom. ❶

Eating and drinking

Wuzhou deals almost entirely in **Cantonese food**, with plenty of fresh fish, vegetables, and fruit – market stalls reek of tropical durian and mangosteens in season – and cake shops selling custard tarts and roast pork buns. There are cheap places to eat serving dumplings, noodle soups and rice pots all through the centre, and **medicinal tea stalls** are a big thing here, peddling pick-me-up brews by the cupful. The best place for **dim sum** is on riverside Xijiang Yi Lu, either on the third floor of the warehouse-sized *Daming Jiujia*, where the food is excellent but there are no views; or at the almost open-air *Jiangyue Lou*, across from the east bus station, the perfect place to spend a morning with relaxing scenery, hectic company, a wonderful choice of snacks, and hospitable staff.

Dadong Jiujia Nanhuan Lu, across from the post office via the pedestrian bridge. Small cake shop and formal restaurant downstairs, with a lower-key upstairs hall serving "smorgasbord" lunchtime hot-pots from ¥35 for two.

Longmen Fumin Lu. Smart, popular place to eat Cantonese food, and prices are lower than the decor suggests – two can eat their fill for ¥60.

Monte Carlo Fumin Lu. Western-style restaurant, serving steak, bamboo-rice chicken, curries, and good coffee. Set meals include main dish, plus small soup and drink, for about ¥30.

Xinguangwei Fumin Lu, just east of the Zhongshan Lu intersection. Noodle and cake shop on the ground floor, and a good morning *dim sum* hall and restaurant on the second floor.

Xizhu Yuan (Western Bamboo Nunnery). Straightforward vegetarian meals – mushrooms, bamboo shoots and tofu – for very little money; most dishes cost ¥8 or so. The only place in town with an English menu. Hours are erratic, but try 11am–noon.

Guiping, Jintian and Liuzhou

The Xi River is just a tiny section of a waterway which, under various names, runs from Yunnan, across central China, and finally flows into the Pearl River and so down to Guangzhou and Hong Kong. Approaching **Guiping**, 200km west of Wuzhou, it runs faster and deeper, dividing into the Qian River, which heads north as the Liu River to rail junctions at **Liuzhou**, while the Yu River branches down towards **Nanning**. Dredged and used as a transport artery during the colonial era, siltation and faster roads saw the end of regional river travel, and now highways provide the only easy access.

The countryside here doesn't look too badly off today, but during the 1840s this corner of China was destitute, wracked by famine and the raising of new taxes to pay off indemnities levied by Britain following the Opium War. Rebellion flared across the region, channelled by anti-dynastic societies such as the **Tiandi Hui** (Heaven and Earth Society, later known as *Sanho* or Triads), which led a prolonged revolt in the Guangxi–Hunan border regions from 1847. Nothing, however, touched on the scale of the subsequent **Taiping Uprising**, a movement which started at the village of **Jintian** near Guiping, and ultimately involved millions of participants and saw the foundation of a rebel capital at Nanjing, in Jiangsu province (see p.449). More recently, a moral famine during the 1960s saw the region involved in one of the more shocking episodes of China's recent history – see the "Cultural Cannibalism" box, p.810.

Guiping and Jintian

Though set at the junction of two major rivers, **GUIPING** is slightly disappointing; just an ordinary Chinese town three hours or so west of Wuzhou along the Wuzhou–Nanning highway, with a little industry and a lot of sugar cane. Guiping is centred around **Guangchang**, a public square at the intersection of east–west-oriented Renmin Lu and south-pointing Guinan Lu, where you'll also find the **long-distance bus station** with connections to Wuzhou, Nanning and Liuzhou. In practice, however, you may well find yourself dropped off on the main road, a couple of kilometres south of town; catch a cycle-rickshaw up Guinan Lu to the centre.

The Chinese come to Guiping to see **Xi Shan**, a typical formalized sacred mountain right on the western outskirts – catch a bus (7am–4.30pm) from Guangchang square or simply walk for twenty minutes along Renmin Xi Lu to the gates (¥15 entry). Far tamer than the country's great holy peaks, Xi Shan

Guiping, Jintian and Liuzhou

Guiping	桂平	***guìpíng***
Dianzi	电子宾馆	*diànzǐ bīnguǎn*
Guiping Binguan	桂平宾馆	*guìpíng bīnguǎn*
Guiping Fandian	桂平饭店	*guìpíng fàndiàn*
Jintian	金田	***jīntián***
Taiping Museum	太平博物馆	*tàipíng bówùguǎn*
Liuzhou	柳州	***liǔzhōu***
Liusi Park	柳寺公园	*liǔsì gōngyuán*
Liuzhou Fandian	柳州饭店	*liǔzhōu fàndiàn*
Yufeng Dasha	鱼蜂大厦	*yúfēng dàshà*

Cultural cannibalism

The apparently insignificant town of **Wuxuan**, 70km northwest of Guiping, is one of the poorest, most purely rural corners of southern China. It hardly seems credible that in the summer of 1968 – while students were demonstrating in Paris and the anti-war movement was at its height in Washington, DC – in Wuxuan they were **eating people**. The details are documented in a secret but thorough report compiled by the county government in 1987, which listed the "different forms of eating human flesh"; taboos were eroded by degrees until students ate their teachers and human flesh was being cheerfully served at banquets with wine. When news of the events reached Beijing, the army was swiftly sent in to remove Wuxuan's Red Guard factions and the **ritual cannibalism** ceased – but only after five hundred people had already been eaten. The report listed by name 27 local Party cadres who had been expelled from the Party for cannibalism, as well as a large number of peasant members, only a small proportion of whom were ever jailed. Most of the participants live and prosper in Wuxuan today.

The Chinese government has never publicly admitted that these grotesque events ever occurred, and the details first reached the outside world through the efforts of the dissident writer Zheng Yi. They've since been corroborated in the book *Real China: From Cannibalism to Karaoke* by British journalist John Gittings, who visited Wuxuan in 1995 and spoke to witnesses. These events were certainly part of the wider political conflicts that tore China apart during the Cultural Revolution, and which saw (according to the official minimum estimate) ninety thousand people killed in Guangxi alone, but, as far as is known, only in Wuxuan did this lead to the killing and eating of "class enemies" – those branded as political undesirables during the Revolution. Certainly there was a tradition, in poorer parts of China, of eating people during times of famine, and so-called "revenge cannibalism" was also noted by the philosopher Mencius in the fourth century BC, and features several times in the fifteenth-century popular novel *Outlaws of the Marsh* (see pp.577 & 1252). Whatever the answer, an open investigation of the crimes is unlikely during the lifetime of the current regime.

is a comfortable introduction to the Chinese obsession with landscaping natural phenomena to turn them into places of pilgrimage and weekend excursions. The two-hour hike to the top follows paved paths leading off into a forest of fish-tailed palms and huge pines, past the usual run of temples – near the entrance, **Xishi Si** has an excellent **vegetarian restaurant** open for lunch – and up to a summit with hazy views of the two rivers snaking across a watery flatland to join at Guiping. **Tea** aficionados should sample the famous Xi Shan brand; rumour has it that temple-bought leaves are superior to anything you'll find in Guiping's shops.

Guiping's **accommodation** includes spacious, threadbare rooms at *Dianzi Binguan* (dorm beds ¥25, rooms with bath ❷), on the west side of the square; and nondescript, elderly furnishings at either the *Guiping Binguan* (❷), or *Guiping Fandian* (❷), both east along Renmin Zhong Lu. There are heaps of wholesome places **to eat** in the area, with the ingredients laid out for you to point and choose, and staff are delighted to have foreign custom – dog is very popular in winter.

Jintian

For Taiping enthusiasts, Guiping is simply a stop on the way to **JINTIAN**, about 25km and an hour to the north. Catch a minibus (which run whenever full; ¥4) from the western side of Guangchang square; on arrival, get off at

Jintian's south gate, then head through the stone arch and down the long road leading west. You can hire a motorcycle-taxi, but it's a quiet walk once you've escaped the main road, the track crossing the fertile irrigated plain towards distant blue mountains, passing clusters of mud-brick farmhouses and village ponds. After about 4km you come to a small wooded hill and the site of the former **Taiping headquarters**. A recent reconstruction of this fort houses a small **museum** with erratic opening hours (¥10), where a few period documents, rather jolly paintings and some old weapons glorify the revolutionary zeal of Taiping leader **Hong Xiuquan** and his generals. Just north is a circular grassy bank beneath the trees, marking all that remains of the original fort. As is so often the case in China, it's the effort of travel and the site associations, rather than tangible relics, that justify the journey. The last transport back to Guiping leaves any time between 5pm and 7pm.

Liuzhou and around

Rail lines, roads and rivers from all over Guangxi and beyond converge on **LIUZHOU**, a city with morbid connotations in the Chinese mind, as its local cedar wood was once much prized for coffins. An untidy, manufacturing conglomeration between Guilin and Nanning, it doesn't have anything to keep you unless you need to change transport, though the surrounding hills theoretically harbour settlements of ethnic Yao, Miao and Zhuang. In practice, however, these communities are well integrated into the majority Han populace, and it's only during festivals (dates and places can be obtained from the CITS in Liuzhou) that you'll see much beyond the everyday rural scenes common to all of southwestern China.

In earlier times Liuzhou itself was a posting for disgraced court officials such as **Liu Zongyuan**, who was sent here as governor in 815 AD and wrote poems describing the timelessly hard lot of working people. The city's only real sight is the **temple** built in his honour in peaceful **Liusi Park**, due east of Liuzhou Square. Paths wind around a deep pond to Liu's tomb, a grander version of the circular cairns littering the fields out of town, and the temple itself, where there's a stone rubbing of his portrait and explanations in Chinese of his various good deeds as governor.

Practicalities

The city is split in two by the **Liu Jiang**, with all traffic arriving on the south side of the river; Fei'e Lu runs east–west through the southern part of town, while Longcheng Lu runs north across the river into the city centre around **Liuzhou Square**, abode of two mighty dragon sculptures – buses #4, #10 and #11 go this way. **Trains** arrive at the western end of Fei'e Lu on the city's western outskirts, while **buses** terminate at depots either towards the station on Fei'e Lu, or off the southern end of Longcheng Lu. Either depot has departures to Yangshuo, Guilin, Guiping, Nanning, Sanjiang and Wuzhou. **Taxis** await at arrival points.

At the junction of Longcheng Lu and Fei'e Lu you'll find a post office and clean **accommodation** at the *Yufeng Dasha* (Ⓣ0772/3838177; ❹). Opposite the Fei'e Lu bus station, the *Tiedao Fandian* (Ⓣ0772/3611140; ❸) is probably the cheapest option in town. About 2km away on the northeast side of town you'll find more rooms at the *Liuzhou Fandian* on Youyi Lu (Ⓣ0772/2828336, Ⓕ0772/2821443; ❻). CITS is also here (Ⓣ0772/2825669 or 2822637). For **food**, cheap places surround transit points, or try your accommodation – the *Yufeng Dasha* offers the usual Sunday *dim sum* selection.

Nanning

Founded during the Yuan dynasty, **NANNING** was only a medium-sized market town until European traders opened a river route from Wuzhou in the early twentieth century, starting a period of rapid growth which saw the city supplanting Guilin as the provincial capital. Largely untouched by the civil war and Japanese invasion, it became a centre of supply and command during the **Vietnam War**, when the **Nanning–Hanoi rail line** was used to transport arms shipments via the border town of Pingxiang, 160km away. Nanning saw particularly vicious street fighting after these weapons were looted by rival Red Guard factions during the Cultural Revolution. The military returned for a decade when China and Vietnam came to blows in 1979, but following the resumption of cross-border traffic in the 1990s the city is beginning to capitalize on trade agreements with its neighbour.

Today, Nanning is a bright, easy-going place with a mild boom town atmosphere and mix of leafy boulevards, modern architecture and a handful of narrow, colonial-era streets. Amongst all this you'll find good shopping, decent food, a **museum** strong on regional archeology, and both international and domestic transport connections. In particular, the nearby **open border with Vietnam** to the west means that Nanning is the first – or final – taste of China for an increasing number of independent travellers.

Arrival, city transport and accommodation

Well over 5km across, with its downtown area concentrated on the northern bank of the **Yong Jiang**, Nanning is a blandly user-friendly city, its streets dusty, hot and planted with exotic trees. The bulk of the city's accommodation and attractions are in the vicinity of **Chaoyang Lu**, Nanning's main thor-

Nanning

Nanning	南宁	***nánníng***
Chaoyang Lu bus station	客运总站	*kèyùn zǒngzhàn*
Chaoyang Square	朝阳广场	*cháoyáng guǎngchǎng*
Hanoi (Vietnam)	河内	*hénèi*
Nanshu Park	南湖公园	*nánhú gōngyuán*
Provincial Museum	省博物馆	*shěng bówùguǎn*
Renmin Park	人民公园	*rénmín gōngyuán*
You'ai Lu bus station	客运中心	*kèyùn zhōngxīn*
Zhonghua Lu bus station	市第二客运中心	*shìdièr kèyùnzhōngxīn*
Accommodation and eating		
Candlelight Bar	烛光水吧	*zhúguāng shuǐbā*
Chaoyang	朝阳酒店	*cháoyáng jiǔdiàn*
Civil Aviation	民航饭店	*mínháng fàndiàn*
Fengyuan	丰源海味酒楼	*fēngyuán hǎiwèi jiǔlóu*
Majestic	明园新都酒店	*míngyuán xīndū jiǔdiàn*
Meilihua	美丽花冰城	*měilìhuā bīngchéng*
Nanning	南宁饭店	*nánníng fàndiàn*
Qingzhen Canting	清真餐厅	*qīngzhēn cāntīng*
Tiedao	铁道饭店	*tiědào fàndiàn*
Xiaodulai Shijie	小嘟来食街	*xiǎodūlái shíjiē*
Ying Bin	迎宾饭店	*yíngbīn fàndiàn*

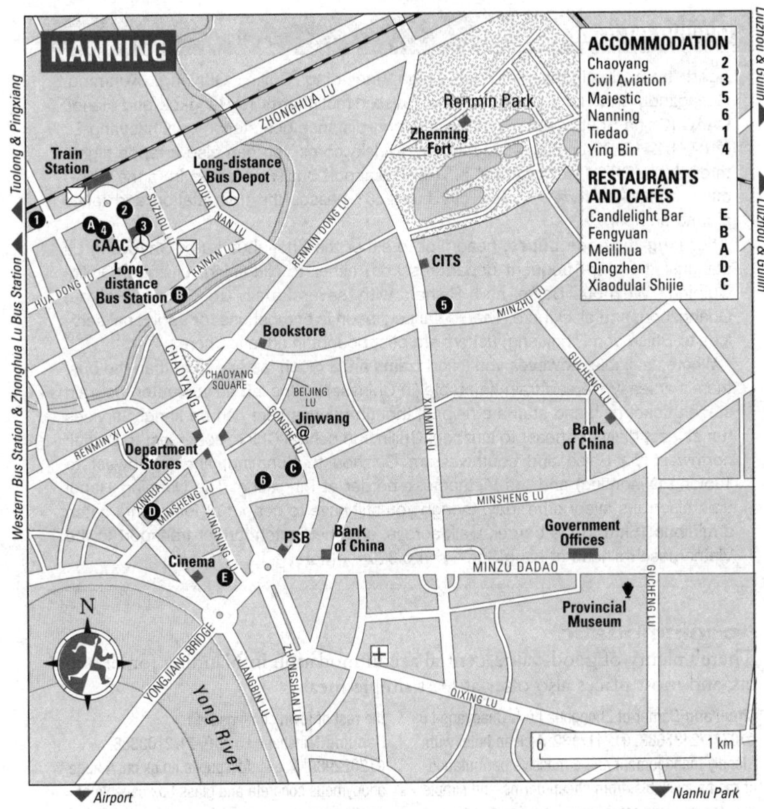

oughfare, which runs for 2km south from the **train station**, through the city centre and down to a complicated riverside traffic intersection associated with the **Yongjiang Bridge**. Roughly parallel with Chaoyang Lu but somewhat shorter, easterly **Xinmin Lu** cuts through the more modern part of town, linked to Chaoyang Lu by, amongst others, **Minzhu Lu**, **Minsheng Lu** and **Minzu Dadao**.

Nanning has two centrally located main **long-distance bus stations**, 500m apart on Zhonghua Lu and Chaoyang Lu, both handling traffic from all over the place. The smaller You'ai Nan Lu depot deals mostly in sleeper and luxury services from Guangdong, though you could end up here coming from western Guangxi. There's also a **western bus station** 3km across town on Beida Lu, where arrivals from the Yunnan/Vietnam borders might find themselves – bus #8 or #10 will get you to the train station area from here. The **international airport** is 35km southwest of Nanning, with an **airport bus** or city bus #301 (¥10) to the CAAC offices or train station respectively – taking a taxi costs around ¥100. In the city itself, a **taxi** trip shouldn't cost more than ¥10, and Chaoyang Lu is covered along its length by city bus #6.

Moving on from Nanning

Apart from destinations within China, including Guilin, Guiyang, Kunming, Guangzhou and Hong Kong, there are also direct **flights** to Bangkok and Hanoi. CAAC (China Southwest) is next to the long-distance bus station on Chaoyang Lu (ⓣ0771/2416496 or 2431459, ⓦwww.travelsky.com); you can also arrange flights through the CITS (see "Listings" p.816). The airport bus (¥10) leaves from the CAAC office and takes forty minutes; city bus #301 passes the train station and takes around an hour.

For **long-distance buses**, head first to either the Zhonghua Lu or Chaoyang Lu stations; there are frequent departures from either to Ningming, Liuzhou, Guilin, Guiping, Wuzhou, Baise and Beihai, with several daily to Sanya, Haikou, Guangzhou, and elsewhere. The You'ai Lu station is of most use for additional services to Baise and Pingxiang; tickets are best bought in advance here.

Where available, however, you'll find **trains** are a much faster option than the bus; there's an easy-to-read train timetable (in Chinese) on the left as you enter the train station ticket hall, and staff are helpful, though queues here can be tiring. Services run at least daily northeast to Liuzhou, Guilin and central China; southeast to Beihai; northwest via Baise and southwestern Guizhou to Kunming; and southwest to Tuolong (Ningming) and the Vietnamese border at Pingxiang. The Nanning–Hanoi train also runs every other day, though you still have to get out at Pingxiang, catch a minibus 15km to the border, walk across, and then catch further transport to the Vietnamese railhead at Lang Son – see p.820 for more.

Accommodation

There's plenty of good-value, central accommodation in Nanning for all budgets, and most places also offer at least simple meals.

Chaoyang Corner of Zhonghua Lu & Chaoyang Lu ⓣ0771/2437688, ⓕ2417132. A clean hotel with friendly management and a massive permutation of rooms available, from cheap dorms and simple doubles, to more comfy doubles with their own bathrooms. Dorm beds ¥20, ❶–❷

Civil Aviation Chaoyang Lu, between the bus and train stations ⓣ0771/2439014, ⓕ2425522. Looks a little dingy, but in fact is comfortable and clean. Listed prices are steep – negotiate a thirty percent discount and it's a fair deal. All rooms have their own showers and toilets, and the attached restaurant is very reasonable. ❺

Majestic 38 Xinmin Lu ⓣ0771/2830808, ⓕ2830811, ⓔmyxdhtl@public.nn.gx.cn. Part of a chain of exclusive hotels owned by an Overseas Chinese management: at ¥858 a night (though rooms are often discounted), this is self-contained, seamlessly run and offers more places to eat than the rest of town combined. ❾

Nanning Minsheng Lu ⓣ0771/2103888, ⓕ2622980, ⓔgxnnfd@public.nn.gx.cn. A huge, anonymous concrete and glass box capable of swallowing thousands of Chinese tourists and conference delegates; staff seem as lost as the guests. ❻

Tiedao Between the train and bus stations on Zhonghua Lu ⓣ0771/2438600, ⓕ2422572. Excellent value at this very clean and well-run option, with enthusiastic staff who are open to price negotiations despite the hotel's obvious popularity. ❸

Ying Bin Diagonally across from the train station, cnr of Chaoyang Lu & Zhonghua Lu ⓣ0771/2412299, ⓕ2439297. Another unpretentious budget option close to the bus and train stations, offering doubles with or without aircon. ❷

The City

To get the feel of Nanning's bustle, try wandering around the crowded markets and lanes either west or southeast of Chaoyang Lu among the remnants of the city's colonial architecture. Along with chickens, ducks, turtles and frogs, there's a mouthwatering variety of perfumed **tropical fruit**, and the city has some of China's best **longan** (a bit like a spherical lychee). **Chaoyang Lu** itself is mostly modern, full of late-opening department stores overflowing with shoes and clothing, all colourfully lit up with fairy lights at night. Halfway along at the corner of Renmin Dong Lu, **Chaoyang Square** is a nice area of tidy paving, park benches and shady trees, popular with *tai ji* enthusiasts, chess players, amateur musicians, groups dancing to country and western tunes, and anyone after a breath of air in the summer heat. West from here and parallel with Chaoyang Lu, pedestrianized **Xingning Lu** and its offshoots sport the city's most attractive older facades, all lit with red lanterns around the lunar New Year.

Better still are the waters and woodland of **Renmin Park** (¥2), a couple of square kilometres of green about a twenty-minute walk east of the train station on Renmin Dong Lu. Stone causeways zigzag across the lake between islets inhabited by willows and chess players, while, on the eastern side, steps ascend to **Zhenning Fort**, a defensive structure built in 1917 to house a 6" German naval cannon – a serious piece of firepower in such a commanding position, with clear views of the whole city. The **tropical plants garden** (¥2) below has a medicinal herb plot and a carefully constructed undergrowth of philodendrons, palms, heliconias and giant "elephant-ear" taro, bird nest ferns and cycads – its private recesses are very popular with young couples. A few kilometres southeast at the #2 bus terminus, **Nanhu Park** (¥2) is worth a look during the annual fifth-month **dragon-boat festivals** (usually early June), when a quarter of a million people turn up to watch this colourful and thoroughly joyful event. At other times the park is simply a peaceful retreat, a huge, broad stretch of canal crossed by a white humpbacked bridge.

The Provincial Museum

Essential viewing for anyone heading southwest to the Zuo River, the **Provincial Museum** on Gucheng Lu (bus #6 from Chaoyang Lu; daily 8.30–noon & 2.30–5pm; ¥8) provides an insight into the enigmatic **Dongson culture**. Sophisticated metalworkers, the Dongson flourished over two thousand years ago in the Guangxi–Yunnan–Vietnam border area, and their works were ultimately traded as far afield as Burma, Thailand and Indonesia. The characteristic Dongson artefact is a squat, narrow-waisted **bronze drum**, finely chased with lively designs of birds, mythical animals, cattle, dancers and stars, sometimes incorporating dioramas on the lid or human and **frog** figurines sitting on the rim (suitably for a drum, frogs are associated with the thunder god in Zhuang mythology). They seem to have originated as storage vessels, though according to a Ming historian, the drums became a symbol of power: "Those who possess bronze drums are chieftains, and the masses obey them; those who have two or three drums can style themselves king." Drums appeared during the Warring States period and were cast locally right up until the late Qing dynasty; their ceremonial use survives among groups of Zhao, Yi, Miao and Yao in China, and on the eastern Indonesian island of Alor.

The museum has dozens of well-preserved varieties excavated in Guangxi and elsewhere across the region, including a rather gruseome example from Yunnan whose lid sports a diorama of crowds attending what appears to be a human sacrifice – note the "king" up on the platform, surrounded by drums. Check out the museum grounds too, with bamboo and palms growing between full-sized wooden buildings in regional architectural styles: a Zhuang rural theatre, Dong bridge and Miao houses, which are all put to good use by Nanning's various communities during festivals.

Eating, drinking and nightlife

Just about every downtown corner has somewhere to **snack**, whether you're after hotpots, steamers of small, soft *baozi*, cakes – bakeries are legion – or a seasonal choice of fresh fruit. At night, swarms of low-price **street stalls** near the bus and train stations, and along Gonghe Lu, serve quick-fried shrimps, grilled chicken wings, steamed packets of lotus-wrapped *zongzi* with unusual fillings (a mix of pork, beans and sometimes shredded coconut), dog hotpot and plates of juicy snails. Formal restaurant times are around 11am–2pm and 5–8pm.

Candlelight Bar Xinning Lu. Western-style café ambience; the food is a bit pricey and ordinary, but their coffee is great.

Fengyuan Hainan Lu. Large, upmarket restaurant where you pick your meal from the tank. Big spenders may want to try a *jin* of lobster at ¥280 or crab at ¥150, but there's also a very popular ¥15 eat-all-you-can buffet served in the mornings.

Meilihua (aka Mayflower) Corner of Zhonghua and Chaoyang Lu. English menu, burgers, noodle soups, steak platters and florid desserts – including refreshing "snow ice", a Southeast Asian treat of shaved ice drizzled with luridly coloured syrups – combined with low prices make this a favourite with expats as well as locals. There's another, not quite as comfortable branch on Chaoyang Square. Most dishes under ¥15.

Qingzhen Canting Minsheng Lu. Inexpensive Muslim restaurant, with a soup-noodle canteen in the front and a dining hall behind. Their English menu is pretty comprehensive; the lemon duck, marinated cucumber and chicken soup with lily buds are tasty and well presented. Expect to pay ¥25 a head in the dining hall.

Xiaodulai Shijie East of the *Nanning Hotel*, with entrances in Gonghe Lu and Minsheng Lu. What look like temple gates front this excellent place, where you can choose from a wide range of dumplings, spiced noodles, cold meats, vegetable dishes, small meals and soups. Everything is on display, so point if you can't ask; just check your bill and change for discrepancies. Almost everything under ¥10.

Listings

Banks and exchange Bank of China, Minzu Dadao (foreign exchange Mon–Fri 8–11.30am & 2.30–5.30pm); there's a major branch being built north of the museum on Gucheng Lu too. Flasher hotels will cash traveller's cheques for their guests.

Books Nanning's Foreign Language Bookstore is on floor three of the elderly market complex overlooking Chaoyang Park on Minzhu Lu – there's a small English sign. The surprisingly large selection of pulp paperbacks, as well as English classics, some translated Chinese literature, magazines, maps and art books is above average. The rest of the floor is given over to pirated film and music CD shops.

Cinema While away a wet afternoon at the screen just northwest of the bridge on Jiangbin Lu; seats are ¥12.

Hospital The City First Hospital (Shiyi Yiyuan) is southeast of the centre along Qixing Lu.

Internet access Log on for ¥2 an hour at the hard-to-find Jinwang, Floor 2, 166 Gonghe Lu; entry is through a street-level covered car park. There's another Internet bar at the cinema on Jiangbin Lu (¥2).

Mail and telecommunications The main post office, with telephones, is more or less between the bus stations on Suzhou Lu (8am–8.30pm).

PSB On the roundabout at the south end of Chaoyang Lu. Foreign Affairs Department open Mon–Fri 9am–noon & 2–5pm.

Shopping Nanning is an excellent place to shop for clothes, with no less than three department stores full of good-quality, low-price attire at the junction of Chaoyang Lu and Xinhua Lu. Xinning Lu has nostalgically styled specialist shops if you're after musical instruments, more clothes, tea or gold. The Nanning Antique Store, next to the museum, has a touristy and expensive selection of batiks, teapots, chops, paintings and jade, on two floors.

Travel agents CITS, 40 Xinmin Lu (daily 8am–noon & 3–5.30pm; ⓣ0771/2804960, ⓕ2806025, ⓔcitsgx@public.nn.gx.cn). A whole courtyard full of CITS offices; try and track down Ms Zhou Run Ling, who speaks some English and works upstairs in the building ahead of you as you walk in off the street. Two-day Zuo River trips – including all transport, accommodation, food and a visit to Hua Shan's rock art – are ¥500 per person; you'll have to negotiate if you want an interpreter too. Vietnamese visas arranged through the consulate in Guangzhou cost ¥480 and take ten working days, or ¥650 and five days; you'll need to provide a passport and passport photo.

West to Yunnan and Vietnam

Most foreigners pass through the area **west of Nanning** without stopping, intent on crossing into Yunnan and Vietnam, though the laid-back, historic town of **Baise**, plus outstanding scenery at the **Detian Waterfall** and **Zuo River**, are major draws, deserving an extra day or two of your time. More than anything, however, the region is worth exploring for its visible **Zhuang** culture, both on a day-to-day level and in its prehistoric **rock art**. The area has reasonable transport connections: Baise, **Tuolong** (jumping-off point for the Zuo River), and the **Vietnamese border crossing** at **Pingxiang** are all easily accessible by train – and, less comfortably, by bus – from Nanning. Detian requires a bit more effort and several changes of vehicles to reach, though you'll probably manage it in a day from either Nanning or Baise.

Baise

BAISE is a pleasant, small city set on the junction of the Dengbi and You rivers 220km northwest of Nanning on the Nanning–Yunnan rail line. Historically,

West to Yunnan and Vietnam

Baise	百色	***bǎisè***
Baise Memorial	百色起义烈士纪念碑	*bǎisè qǐyì lièshì jìniànbēi*
Guixi Dajiudian	桂西大酒店	*guìxī dàjiǔdiàn*
Guizhou Fandian	桂州饭店	*guìzhōu fàndiàn*
Uprising Museum	粤东会馆	*yuèdōng huìguǎn*
You River Minorities Museum	右江民族博物馆	*yòujiāng mínzú bówùguǎn*
Zhongshan Ge	中山阁	*zhōngshān gé*
Daxin	大新	***dàxīn***
Hurun	湖润	***húrùn***
Jingxi	靖西	***jìngxī***
Ningming	宁明	***níngmíng***
Panlong	攀龙	***pānlóng***
Hua Shan	花山	*huāshān*
Longrui Nature Reserve	陇瑞自然保护区	*lóngruì zìrán bǎohùqū*
White-headed leaf monkey	白头叶猴	*báitóu yèhóu*
Pingxiang	凭祥	***píngxiáng***
Friendship Pass	友谊关	*yǒuyíguān*
Hanoi (Vietnam)	河内	*hénèi*
Jinxiang Yu Dajiudian	金祥玉大酒店	*jīnxiángyù dàjiǔdiàn*
Shuolong	硕龙	***shuòlóng***
Detian Waterfall	得天瀑布	*détiān pùbù*
Luyou Dajiudian	旅游大酒店	*lǚyóu dàjiǔdiàn*
Tuolong	驮龙	***tuólóng***
Zuo River	左江	*zuǒjiāng*
Xialei	下雷	***xiàléi***

Baise's fame dates back to 1929: no Chinese government could then seriously lay claim to this remote region, but **Deng Xiaoping** found thousands of willing converts amongst Baise's Zhuang population when he arrived in September with a CCP mandate to spread the Communist message, and on December 11 he declared the formation of the **You Jiang Soviet** here in what became known as the **Baise Uprising**. Over-ambitious attempts to raise an army and secure the province against the Nationalists, however, saw the movement falter rapidly, though survivors eventually managed to join up with Mao's Jiangxi Soviet during the Long March in 1934.

The city's **Uprising Museum** (daily 9am–noon & 3–5pm; ¥5) is just west of the river on Jiefang Jie, housed in an old Confucian academy – check out the ceramic eave friezes of court and street scenes, and murals of rigged ships in the river, painted unusually with linear perspective. Though there's a great diorama of the town as it was in 1929, the exhibits themselves are inaccessible, a dense collection of photos, weapons, documents and paintings – anything, in fact, remotely touched by the events of the time. It's more worthwhile to head east over the bridge, which overlooks a sampan boatyard and timber depot with cranes shifting cargo onto barges, and climb the broad stairway to the **Baise Memorial**, a stumpy, sharp-tipped spire surrounded by heroic sculptures and an ornamental garden, the latter offering fine views over the city and rivers. Two minutes beyond the memorial, the excellent **You River Minorities Museum** (¥3) provides insight into Zhuang settlement of the region. There are heavy stone tools and photos of cave paintings, including a strikingly fierce creature with dragon's head and cloven paws; bronze drums and an almost comical equestrian statue; textiles featuring loomed cloth and intricate embroideries and tie-dyeing; all rounded out by photos.

Practicalities

Most of Baise lies west of the Dongbi River, where a fringe of colonial architecture and leafy backstreets surround a kilometre-broad centre. The **train station** is isolated 5km east of the centre, connected to town by bus #1 (¥1). Zhongshan Lu runs west from the river through the centre of town, with Xiangyang Lu heading north off this for 500m to the long-distance **bus station**, a seething mass of scheduled departures and private operators. From here you'll find traffic through the day southeast to Nanning; minibuses every twenty minutes south to Jingxi, en route to the Detian Waterfall; and daily services to Xingyi in Guizhou province, Liuzhou, Guilin and Guangzhou.

Places to stay in Baise include the noisy rooms at the bus station hotel (❸, beds ¥25); the clean and ordinary *Guixi Dajiudian* (❷), at the junction of Zhongshan Lu and Xiangyang Lu; and tidy, motel-like lodgings at army-run *Zhongshan Ge* (☎0776/2810187; ❸), east on Zhongshan Lu. For **food**, there are the usual run of cheap eats at the bus station and backstreet canteens – *shuijiao* here come with plum sauce – and a fine Guizhou-style restaurant 150m east of the bus station on Chengbi Lu, serving up big, reasonably priced portions of crispy fish, hot-and-sour soup and whole casseroled fowl.

Detian Waterfall

Straddling the Vietnamese border 150km due west of Nanning, or the same distance south by road from Baise, **Detian Waterfall** is worth the trip not just for the falls themselves, but also because it draws you into the Zhuang heartlands – a world of fabulously shaped dark karst hills, grubby towns, water buffalo wallowing in green paddy fields, and Zhuang farmers in black, broad-sleeved pyjamas and conical hats. Roads through the area are alright, but transport operates on a leaves-if-full principle, so it's likely you'll spend longer on the trip than you planned. Expect to be the star attraction if you step into the region: even Chinese tourists are a rare sight.

The nearest settlement to the falls is **Shuolong**. Coming **from Nanning** you need to catch a bus from the west bus station to **DAXIN** (3hr; ¥15), a kilometre-long road with the **bus station** and places to eat at the north end, a mid-range **hotel** about halfway down, and a street leading east off the far end where you'll find the old south gate and **minibuses** heading to Shuolong (1hr 30min; ¥6) until early afternoon. **From Baise**, your first target is **JINGXI** (5hr; ¥15), a strangely stretched, dusty market town surrounded by flat fields and limestone hills which make for some interesting walks. Baise buses wind up at the **north bus station**, where you'll find basic **accommodation** (❶); it's a kilometre through town to the **south station** and minibuses for the ninety-minute ride to tiny **Hurun** (¥5), where you need to change vehicles again for **Xialei** (¥4), a smaller, dustier replay of Jingxi. Here you may find yourself stuck in one of two basic **guesthouses** (❶) for the night, as after midday there's little transport for the final thirty-minute run to Shuolong (¥2), though you could try chartering a minibus for about ¥40.

SHUOLONG is a large village strung along the main road, with a sealed track running 16km west to the falls just north of town, and a vertical cliff overhanging the marketplace where through traffic congregates. There are two basic **places to stay**: beds above the restaurant at the junction of the falls' road (¥15 per person); and rooms at *Lüyou Dajiudian* (❷), which also has the better food. **Moving on**, ask around at the marketplace to hitch a ride to the falls, or wait here to flag down morning traffic to Xialei or Daxin.

The falls

The **Detian falls** repay the effort of reaching them in unexpected ways. The road there winds along a wide river valley to the official entrance (¥10). Past here is a **guesthouse** (❷) with clear views across the river into Vietnam – certainly a better spot to stay than Shuolong – and then you're looking at the falls themselves, a delightful set of cataracts broader than their 30m height and at their best after the spring rains, framed by peaks and fields. Paths lead down to the base of the falls past a series of pools and bamboo groves; at the bottom you can hire a **bamboo raft** and be punted over to straddle the mid-river borderline. The best part, however, is to follow the road along the top to its end in a field, where you'll find a **stone post** proclaiming the Sino–Vietnamese frontier in French and Chinese, along with a bizarre **border market** – a simple trestle table laden with Vietnamese sweets, cigarettes and stamps in the middle of nowhere. Don't try to go any farther: you're likely to find the stall-holder is a plain-clothes border guard, and there is ongoing mine-clearing in the region.

Into Vietnam: the Zuo River and Pingxiang

The **Vietnamese border crossing** lies about 170km southwest of Nanning beyond the town of **Pingxiang**, a smooth five-hour ride on either of the morning trains (¥30) – though there are also plenty of buses through the day. Either way, it's worth spending an extra couple of days to stop off en route and catch a boat up the **Zuo River**, an area with more superb karst scenery, prehistoric **rock paintings** and a remote nature reserve.

The Zuo River trip

There are no roads into the Zuo River area, and the only access is by boat from **TUOLONG**, rail stop for the nearby hamlet of **Ningming**, about an hour short of Pingxiang. Chinese-speakers can go down to the water here and negotiate a vessel to **Panlong** village; a four-person boat should cost between ¥100 and ¥200 depending on your bargaining skills. Otherwise, arrange a tour with Nanning's CITS (see "Listings", p.816).

It's a placid ninety-minute journey up the Zuo from Tuolong to Panlong – buffalo wallow in the shallows, people fish from wooden rafts and tend family plots, and the banks are thick with spindly branched kapok trees, flowering red in April. Mountains spring up after a while, flat-faced and sheer by the river, and it's here you'll see the first painted figures, red, stick-like markings, though most are very faded or smeared with age. **PANLONG** comprises a fun group of large wooden **hotel** buildings, loosely based on traditional ethnic designs, offering good meals and three- and four-bed rooms as well as doubles (❸). From the hotel, a rough path leads up to the **Longrui Nature Reserve** in the hills above. An incredible place whose rough tracks see few visitors, Longrui's densely vegetated peaks are squeezed together to form an isolated, elevated valley inhabited by rare **white-headed leaf monkeys**, and is well worth setting a day aside for.

The most extensive series of **rock paintings** are another forty minutes upstream at **Hua Shan**, a steep cliff overhanging the river. Nobody has worked out a definitive interpretation, or even how they were painted in such inaccessible positions, but Hua Shan's 1900 sharply posed figures have been dated to two thousand years ago and include drummers and dancers, dogs and cattle, a dragon-boat race, men with arms bent upwards, a "king" with a sword, and just two women, long-haired and pregnant. The designs are similar to those decorating the Dongson drums, and there's little doubt that they were produced by the same culture, currently identified with the Zhuang people. A few Bronze Age weapons have also been found here.

Pingxiang and the border crossing

Surrounded by jutting karst hills, **PINGXIANG** is a small, bustling trading town and railhead for the Vietnamese border crossing, 15km away. The **train station** is about 3km outside town on the border road; the **bus station** is in the centre of town on mainstreet Bei Da Lu. Gaggles of motor-rickshaws descend on new arrivals, the drivers engaging in Ben-Hur-like races down to the border – try for around ¥10.

You shouldn't really need to stay in Pingxiang, but almost every building within 100m of the bus station on Bei Da Lu offers **accommodation**: hostels ask ¥15–30 per person; while the *Jinxiang Yu Dajiudian* (Ⓣ0771/8521303; ❸) is a typically clean, functional hotel, and gives massive discounts. There's a huge produce **market** behind the bus station, a **Bank of China** on Bei Da Lu, and cheap places to eat everywhere. Heading **back to Nanning**, there are two trains at 9am and 1.25pm – both stopping at Tuolong – and buses between 7am and 7pm.

The **border crossing**, known here as **Friendship Pass**, is worth a trip even if you're not heading to Vietnam. It's set in a natural gap through a series of steep cliffs and hills all wooded with conifers and bamboo, thick enough to harbour at least one **tiger** – the first spotted in thirty years was seen nearby in May 2002. The Chinese side is marked by lines of imperious black cars with tinted windows, trucks loaded with vehicle chassis, a defunct French colonial Customs House built in 1914, and a huge Chinese **gate tower**. A Ming-era

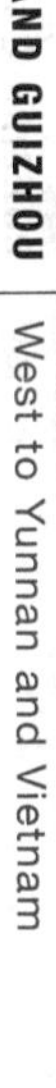

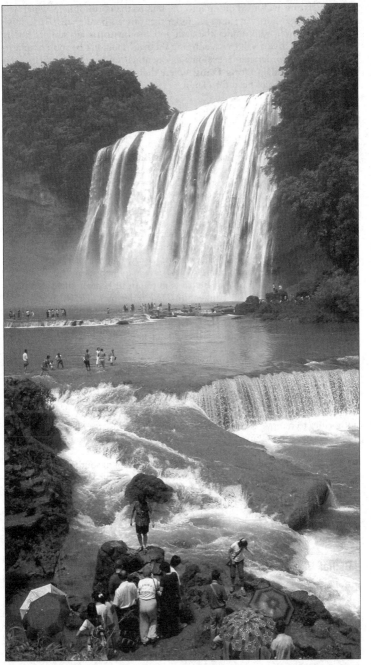

△ Huangguoshu waterfalls

defensive **stone wall** runs off up into the hills to the north of here, which you can follow for a short way; just remember that this is a border area. Back down at the gate tower, walk under the arch and the **customs** are straight ahead. Assuming you have a valid visa, entering Vietnam shouldn't be too complicated, though the border guards examine all documents minutely. The Vietnamese town on the far side is **Dong Dang**, where there's further transport 5km south to **Lang Son**, the rail head for Hanoi.

Beihai

BEIHAI, a pleasant town situated on the **Beibu Gulf** some 150km from Nanning on the south coast of Guangxi, was adopted from neighbouring Guangdong province in 1954 so that Guangxi would have a viable seaport. It got going in the late nineteenth century when the British signed the **Yantai Trading Agreement** with the Qing court, and grew swiftly as Europeans set up schools, churches, offices and banks. A bland four-hour train ride from Nanning or an overnight ride on the **ferry from Hainan Island**, attempts through the 1990s to turn Beihai into a trading centre for the southwest seem to have faltered, leaving the original core of narrow colonial lanes and buildings surrounded by a mesh of pointlessly wide new roads and vacant high-rises.

While the only reason to visit Beihai is in transit to Hainan, there's no problem filling in time between connections. The older part of town is along the seafront and on **Zhongshan Lu**, where mouldering colonial buildings add to the sleepily tropical atmosphere. It's best in the morning when the fresh catches arrive, and there's a fabulous **fish market** here selling every type and part of sea life imaginable. Hop on a #2 bus heading west down **Haijiao Lu** from the end of Zhongshan Lu and you end up a couple of kilometres away at **Waisha harbour**, packed with scores of wooden-hulled junks, motorized and sailless, but otherwise traditionally designed. Most of the vessels here belong to the community of thirteen thousand refugee "**boat people**" living in the adjacent UN-sponsored village. They were victims of an attempt by the Vietnamese authorities to remove ethnic Chinese from their territory, a major cause of the 1979 war between China and Vietnam. China's reciprocal group are the **Jing**, ethnic Vietnamese who settled islands off Beihai in the sixteenth century.

Alternatively, **Beihai Sand Beach** (¥25) is about 5km south of the centre at the end of the #3 bus route (¥3) from Sichuan Lu, a long, broad stretch of grey sand where you can organize a spin in a speedboat or a beach buggy, or just roam – swimming isn't perhaps such a good idea, given that the city lacks a sewerage treatment plant. In all, Hainan's beaches are far better – and free to enter – so don't set aside an extra day for this one if you're in transit.

Beihai

Beihai	北海	***běihǎi***
Beihai Binguan	北海宾馆	*běihǎi bīnguǎn*
Beihai sand beach	北海银滩	*běihǎi yíntān*
Hainan ferry port	北海港客运站	*běihǎigǎng kèyùnzhàn*
Taoyuan Dajiudian	桃园大酒店	*táoyuán dàjiǔdiàn*
Waisha harbour	外沙内港	*wàishā nèigǎng*
Zhongshan Park	中山公园	*zhōngshān gōngyuán*

Practicalities

A hugely sprawling grid of right-angled streets, Beihai is so positioned on a broad peninsula that the main seafront, unexpectedly enough given its location on China's southern coast, is to the north of town. The centre is marked by **Zhongshan Park**, at the intersection of north–south oriented Beijing Lu, and Beibuwan Lu, which crosses it at right angles. **Arrival points** are widely spread across the city from here: the **train station** is 3km south at the end of Beijing Lu – catch #2 to Zhongshan Park; the **Hainan ferry port** and ticket office is 4km west along Haijiao Lu, also on the #2 bus route; while the **long-distance bus station** is 500m east of the park on Beibuwan Lu (bus #7). **Taxis** cost ¥5 to hire; expect twice this to get between the train and ferry terminals.

One block west of the park, Beibuwan Lu intersects with Sichuan Lu (down which the #3 bus runs south to the beach); 100m south is the **post office**, while the same distance west is the **Bank of China**. Department stores fill the area, and a small booth at the southwestern side of the intersection sells plane, train and ferry **tickets**.

For **accommodation**, try the elderly but reasonable-value *Taoyuan Dajiudian* (Ⓣ0779/2020919, Ⓕ2020520; ❶), down a lane behind the Xinhua bookstore opposite the bus station on Beibuwan Lu; or the surprisingly inexpensive, colonial-style *Beihai Binguan* (Ⓣ0779/2080880, Ⓕ2023285; ❷), a short walk west of the bus station on Beibu Lu. Good **places to eat** include the string of cheap and filling Cantonese diners east of the bus station – look for the roast meats hanging up in the window – or try the cheap, hole-in-the-wall **seafood** restaurants beside the ferry terminal.

Leaving, there are afternoon ferries to Haikou (10hr; dorms ¥91, very basic private cabins ¥136 per person); all toilets are shared, and hot water urns and a snack shop are the only sources of refreshment. There are also daily trains to Nanning, and buses to Wuzhou, Guilin, Liuzhou, Nanning, Baise and Guangzhou.

Guizhou

A traditional saying describes **Guizhou** as a land where there are "no three days without rain, no three kilometres without a mountain, and no three coins in any pocket". Superficially this is accurate. Despite a generally mild climate and growing industrial output, Guizhou has the highest rainfall in China and a poverty ensured by more than eighty percent of its land being covered in untillable mountains or leached limestone soils. Perhaps this is why tourists scorn the province, but it is, in fact, a fascinating place, largely because of its undesirable reputation.

Chinese influence was established here around 100 BC, when farms and garrisoned towns spread along the accessible and fertile **Wu Jiang**, a tributary of the Yangzi which settlers followed down from southern Sichuan. Beyond the river valley, however, the Han encountered fierce opposition from the indigenous peoples they were displacing, and the empire eventually contented itself less with occupying the province than with extracting a nominal tribute from its chieftains. Full subjugation came as late as the Qing era, after a population explosion in central China saw waves of immigrants flooding into Guizhou's northeast. The tribes rose in rebellion but were overwhelmed, and retreated into remote mountain areas. Consisting of about thirty nationalities and forming a quarter of Guizhou's population, they remain there today as farmers and woodworkers: principally the **Miao** and **Dong** in the eastern highlands; the **Bouyei**, a Thai people, in the humid south; and the **Yi** and Muslim **Hui** over on western Guizhou's high, cool plateaus. Generally welcoming to outsiders, they indulge in a huge number of **festivals**, some of which attract tens of thousands of participants and are worth any effort to experience. There is also an accomplished artistic tradition to investigate, notably some unusual architecture and exquisite **textiles**.

While Guizhou's often shambolic towns are definitely not a high point of a trip to the region, the provincial capital, **Guiyang**, is friendly enough, and its central location makes it a comfortable base from which to plan an exploration of the province. To the north, the historic city of **Zunyi** is steeped in Long March lore, while those on a cultural quest will relish the villages, traditions and festivals of the **Miao and Dong Autonomous Region**, reached through the easterly town of **Kaili**. Northeast again from here is the atypically pleasant town of **Zhenyuan**, and a rather more ordinary **Tongren**, stepping stone for an impressively undeveloped nature reserve atop **Fanjing Shan**. A couple of hours west of the capital, **Anshun** marks the starting point for easy excursions out to the mighty **Huangguoshu Waterfall** and, rather more distant, **Caohai Lake** on the Yunnanese border, a haven for wintering birds.

Guiyang

GUIYANG lies in a valley basin right in the middle of the province it governs, encircled by a range of hills which hems in the city and concentrates its traffic pollution. Established as a capital during the Ming dynasty, Guiyang received little attention until the early 1950s, when the new Communist government repaid minority groups for their tacit help during the civil war by filling the centre with heavy monuments and extending the provincial rail line to make the city a hub for western China. This encouraged investment, though wealth arrived only recently, accelerating Guiyang from a quiet conglomerate of tumbledown town houses to a web of wide roads and twentieth-century high-rises comprising a busy downtown district. The result may not be one of China's most beautiful cities, but Guiyang is a friendly place, with a growing expat population and well-stocked shopping centres and market stalls.

Most visitors simply spend one night here in transit, though anyone planning to explore the province should seek out Guiyang's informative CITS office (see "Listings", p.829 for details), and spend a couple of hours browsing through the **Provincial Museum**'s collection. There are also a scattering of **temples and pavilions** and a **park** within easy distance of the centre.

Arrival, city transport and accommodation

Central Guiyang is a concentrated couple of square kilometres around the narrow **Nanming River**, with the downtown area focused along Zhonghua Lu, which runs south through the centre into Zunyi Lu, crosses the river and continues for another kilometre before terminating at the new **train station**. In

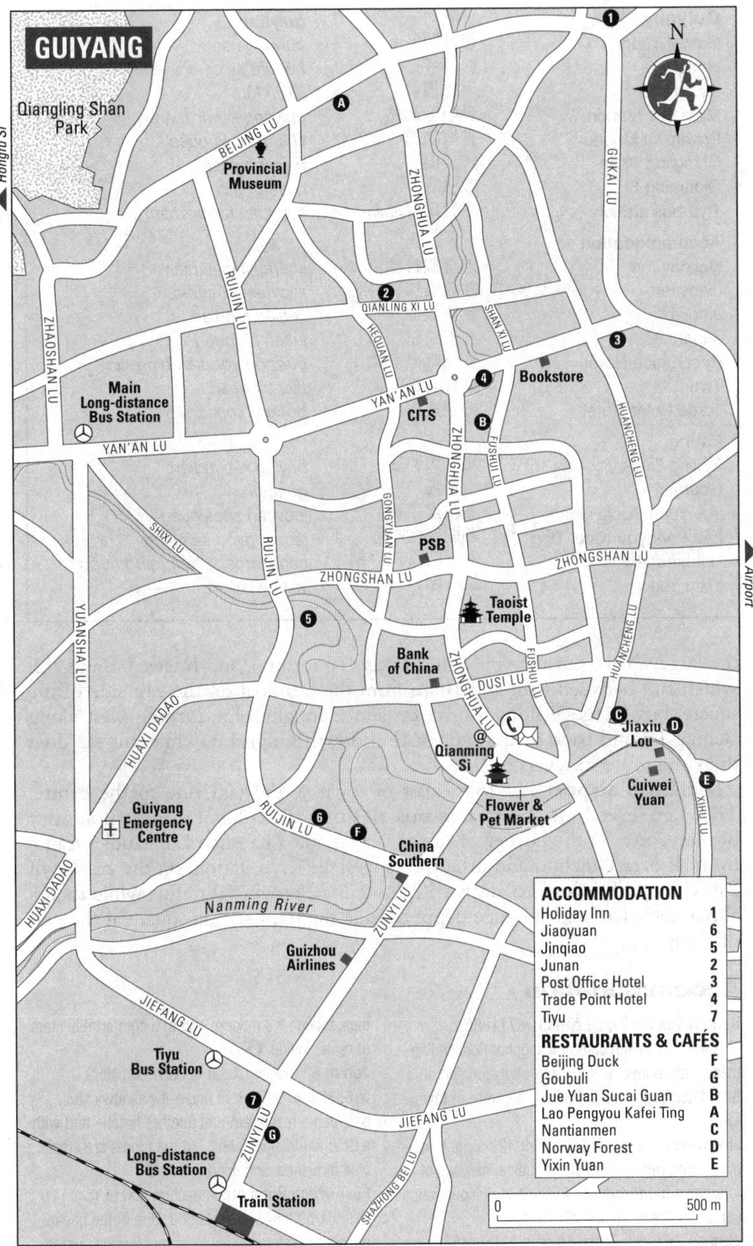
GUIYANG
Qiangling Shān Park
Hongfu Si
Provincial Museum
Beijing Lu
Zhonghua Lu
Gukai Lu
Ruijin Lu
Qianling Xi Lu
Shan Xi Lu
Heguan Lu
Zhaoshan Lu
Bookstore
Main Long-distance Bus Station
Yan'an Lu
CITS
Fushui Lu
Huancheng Lu
Gongyuan Lu
Shixi Lu
PSB
Zhongshan Lu
Airport
Yuansha Lu
Taoist Temple
Bank of China
Dusi Lu
Huaxi Dadao
Qianming Si
Jiaxiu Lou
Cuiwei Yuan
Xihu Lu
Flower & Pet Market
Guiyang Emergency Centre
China Southern
Nanming River
Zunyi Lu
Guizhou Airlines
Jiefang Lu
Tiyu Bus Station
Long-distance Bus Station
Train Station
Shazhong Bei Lu
0 500 m
ACCOMMODATION
Holiday Inn 1
Jiaoyuan 6
Jinqiao 5
Junan 2
Post Office Hotel 3
Trade Point Hotel 4
Tiyu 7
RESTAURANTS & CAFÉS
Beijing Duck F
Goubuli G
Jue Yuan Sucai Guan B
Lao Pengyou Kafei Ting A
Nantianmen C
Norway Forest D
Yixin Yuan E

Guiyang		
Guiyang	贵阳	***guìyáng***
Cuiwei Yuan	粹惟园	*cuìwéi yuán*
Hongfu Si	弘福寺	*hóngfú sì*
Jiaxiu Lou	甲秀楼	*jiǎxiù lóu*
Main bus station	贵阳客运站	*guìyáng kèyùnzhàn*
Provincial Museum	省博物馆	*shěng bówùguǎn*
Qiangling Shan	黔灵山	*qiánlíng shān*
Qianming Si	黔明寺	*qiánmíng sì*
Tiyu bus station	体育馆客运站	*tǐyùguǎn kèyùnzhàn*
Accommodation		
Holiday Inn	神奇假日酒店	*shénqí jiàrì jiǔdiàn*
Jiaoyuan	教苑宾馆	*jiàoyuàn bīnguǎn*
Jinqiao.	金桥饭店	*jīnqiáo fàndiàn*
Junan	君安宾馆	*jūnān bīnguǎn*
Post Office Hotel	贵州邮电宾馆	*guìzhōu yóudiàn bīnguǎn*
Tiyu	体育宾馆	*tǐyù bīnguǎn*
Trade Point Hotel	柏顿宾馆	*bódùn bīnguǎn*
Eating		
Beijing Duck	北京烤鸭店	*běijīng kǎoyādiàn*
Goubuli	狗不理	*gǒubùlǐ*
Jue Yuan Sucai Guan	觉园素菜馆	*juéyuán sùcàiguǎn*
Lao Pengyou Kafei Ting	老朋友咖啡厅	*lǎopéngyǒu kāfēitīng*
Nantianmen	南天门重庆火锅	*nántiānmén chóngqìng huǒguō*
Yixin Yuan	怡心园	*yíxīn yuán*

the large square outside you'll find **taxis** (¥8 to hire), and **buses** #1 and #2, which run between 6am and 10pm from the terminal on the east side of the square: bus #1 goes along Zunyi Lu and Zhonghua Lu, turning west along Beijing Lu and back to the train station down Ruijin Lu, while bus #2 does the same route in reverse.

Guiyang's **airport** lies 15km east of town, a ¥50 taxi ride to the centre. There are several **long-distance bus stations**: the colossal main station, west of the centre on the corner of Yan'an Xi Lu and Zhaoshan Lu, handles traffic from all over Guizhou and other provinces; the Tiyu station, on the corner of Zunyi Lu and Jiefang Lu, deals with more local provincial traffic; while there's also a freelance long-distance depot outside the train-station square at the end of Zunyi Lu.

Accommodation

Holiday Inn Beijing Lu ⓣ0851/6771888, ⓦwww.holiday-inn.com/guiyangchn. Reasonable place with rooms for ¥800, but badly located on a busy intersection distant from the centre of town. ❾

Jiaoyuan Ruijin Lu ⓣ0851/5840428. Bright, ordinary place with inexpensive doubles, nervous of foreigners but friendly and willing to discount once you break the language barrier. ❸

Jinqiao 34 Ruijin Zhong Lu ⓣ0851/5814872, ⓕ5813867. A bulging 1959 exterior immediately sets this mid-range hotel apart from nearby buildings, though it's modern and in a comfortable state of repair inside. ❺

Junan 62 Qianling Xi Lu ⓣ0851/6816999, ⓕ6852986. Difficult to find – it's sandwiched between a restaurant and another hotel – and with a drab and dismal lobby, but the rooms are smart, well furnished, and good value. ❹

Post Office Hotel At the eastern end of Yanan Lu ⓣ0851/5930648, ⓕ5928668. One of the cheapest places in town likely to accept foreign custom, though it's almost impossible to get a dorm bed. Dorms ¥25, ❹

Moving on from Guiyang

You'll find Guizhou Airlines (ⓣ0851/5982879 or 5981967) and China Southern (ⓣ0851/5828429) near each other on Zunyi Lu. They're open daily 8.30am–5.30pm. At the time of writing there was no airport bus, and taxis charged ¥50 to the airport. Before buying a **bus** ticket, note that it's often faster and more comfortable to get to Kaili, Zunyi or Liupanshui by train. For anywhere outside the province, and cities within, head to the main bus station on the corner of Yan'an Xi Lu and Zhaoshan Lu. The Tiyu station has more frequent luxury coaches and minibuses to Anshun, Zunyi,and Kaili; down towards the train station on Zunyi Lu, you'll find sleeper buses to Xingyi, Liupanshui and Zunyi, and minibuses to Kaili, lined up on the kerb; this is also the place to find early-morning day-trips to Huangguoshu, for which you buy tickets on the day.

Trains out of Guiyang head east into central China and beyond via Kaili; north to Zunyi and Chongqing; west to Kunming via Anshun and Liupanshui; and south to Liuzhou and other destinations in Guangxi. The train station staff are very helpful; there are plenty of signs in English and buying tickets is unproblematic (ticket offices 7am–noon & 1–7pm). If you're heading to Zunyi, Kaili or Liupanshui, the train is generally faster than bus.

Tiyu Corner of Jiefang and Zunyi Lu ⓣ0851/5798777, ⓕ5790799. Just 500m from the train station, the hotel is to the left side of the entrance to the Guiyang sports stadium. Welcoming and spacious, but tatty. ❸

Trade Point Hotel Yanan Dong Lu ⓣ0851/5827888, ⓦwww.trade-pointhotel.com. Sharp, upmarket option with local and Cantonese restaurants and all executive trimmings for ¥900 a night. ❾

The City and around

Guiyang's most interesting quarter lies immediately north of the Nanming River, around where Zunyi Lu and Zhonghua Lu meet at the enormous **Post and Telecommunications building**. Recently rebuilt, in the 1950s this was the grandest building in town, a symbol that the formerly isolated province had at last been connected to the outside world.Across the road, Guiyang's lively **flower and pet market** sets up in a lane running alongside the river, selling a mix of puppies, budgerigars, bonsais and orchids; a few stall also sell curios such as Mao-era badges, Communist commemorative crockery, pulp comics and the like. Behind all this is **Qianming Si**, a cramped and smoky collection of Ming-dynasty halls.

East of here along the riverbank – which was being extensively relandscaped at the time of writing – stands **Jiaxiu Lou** (¥2), a small, three-storeyed pavilion reached over an arched bridge of similar vintage. Both date back to 1587, when the pavilion was built to inspire students taking imperial examinations. Carefully restored, it holds a teahouse and photos from the 1930s. Continue on across the bridge to the far bank, and you're outside **Cuiwei Yuan** (¥3), a one-time Jain Buddhist temple whose halls now house a good collection of **Miao embroidery**, some of which are for sale – prices are high.

Running north from the river, **Zhonghua Lu** is Guiyang's commercial precinct, a crowded area of department stores and shops selling clothes, domestic appliances, sound systems and more. Catch bus #1 up here to the **Provincial Museum** (Tues–Sun 9–11.30am & 1–4pm; ¥10), 2.5km north along Beijing Lu. The place smells of a long-abandoned good cause; once you've woken up the surprised staff upstairs in the left wing, they'll unlock the three dusty halls of exhibits, many of which languish in the aisles in an unlabled, half-assembled state. **Ethnic groups** such as the Miao, Dong and

Bouyei are represented through costumes, festival photos, and models of their architecture. There are also a couple of items – a poster-sized manifesto, official seal, and armour – relating to the so-called **Miao Uprisings**, a string of nineteenth-century rebellions against the Han Chinese presence in Guizhou.

Qiangling Shan Park and Hongfu Si

About 1km west of the Provincial Museum, **Qiangling Shan Park** (¥2) is a pleasant handful of hills right on the edge of town, thickly forested enough to harbour some colourful birdlife and noisy groups of monkeys. There's a popular **funfair**, and a large **lake** with paddle boats to rent, but the highlight is **Hongfu Si**, an important Buddhist monastery up above – follow steps from the gates for thirty minutes to the top. You exit the woods into a courtyard containing the ornamental, four-metre-high **Fahua Pagoda** and a screen showing Buddha being washed at birth by nine dragons. On the right is a **bell tower** with a five-hundred-year-old bell, which the guardian monk might invite you to strike. The missing chunk was removed during the Cultural Revolution, when the temple was completely destroyed. Now it's the headquarters for Guizhou's Buddhist Association, rebuilt to hold a comprehensive collection of Buddhist texts. There are some older sculptures among the glossy paintwork of recent restorations, including a 32-armed Guanyin, each palm displaying an eye, facing a rather benevolent-looking King of Hell.

Eating and drinking

With its predilection for dog meat and chillies, Guizhou's cuisine comes under the Western Chinese cooking umbrella, and the capital has some good places to eat local food. Nondescript **restaurants** on Zhonghua Zhong Lu and intersecting streets all serve staples such as hot-spiced chicken, pork, vegetables and dumplings through the day, with snack stalls along **Heqing Lu** running from 6pm to 4am. One speciality are thin **crêpes** – here called *tianliao wawa*, or "stuffed dolls" – which you fill from a selection of pickled and fresh vegetables to resemble an uncooked spring roll, with the best places just outside Qiangling Shan Park. **Hotpots** are a Guizhou institution offered everywhere, with tables centred round a bubbling pot of slightly sour, spicy stock, in which you cook your own food. **Dog** is a winter dish, usually stir-fried with noodles, soya-braised or part of a hotpot – the area east of the train station along Shazhong Bei Lu has the best. For **Western food**, the *Trade Point Hotel* does a great all-you-can-eat buffet breakfast (7–10.30am; ¥60 a head), and their tiny lobby café serves real cream cakes.

Canine cuisine

Dog meat is widely appreciated not only in Guizhou, Guangxi and Guangdong, but also in nearby culturally connected countries such as Indonesia, the Philippines and Vietnam. Possibly the habit originated in China and was spread through Southeast Asia by tribal migrations. Wherever the practice began, the meat is universally considered to be warming in cold weather and an aid to male virility. As a regional speciality, Chinese tourists to Guizhou generally make a point of trying a dog dish, but for Westerners, eating dog can be a touchy subject. Some find it almost akin to cannibalism, while others are discouraged by the way restaurants display bisected hindquarters in the window, or soaking in a bucket of water on the floor. If you're worried about being served dog by accident, say "*wǒ bùchī gǒuròu*" (I don't eat dog).

Restaurants

Beijing Duck Ruijin Lu, near the *Jiaoyuan* hotel. Overlooking the river, this place isn't too expensive – about ¥80 a person for a full duck – serving exactly what you'd expect from the name.
Goubuli Zunyi Lu. Branch of the famous Tianjin dumpling house, hidden away behind stalls near the train station – there's no English sign. Good, filling, cheap and noisy.
Jue Yuan Sucai Guan 51 Fushui Bei Lu. Vegetarian temple restaurant in the town centre (the temple is out the back), whose food is liberally laced with chillies. There's no English menu, but the staff will help you order; dishes are around ¥10 or less.
Lao Pengyou Kafei Ting Beijing Lu. Despite calling itself a café, the place concentrates on inexpensive, Cantonese-style sandpots and local hotpots. Useful if you're in the area for the museum, though not worth a special visit.
Nantianmen Corner of Xihu Lu and Huancheng Lu. Popular Sichuanese-style hotpot restaurant, with set selections starting at ¥35.
Norway Forest Xihu Lu. One of Guiyang's many Western-style cafés, this snug place features (expensive) gourmet coffee, beer and snacks.
Yixin Yuan Xihu Lu. A smart, very popular mid-range restaurant near the river and Jiaxiu Lou. The manageress is friendly and speaks some English, and the food is extremely good, from snacks such as stir-fried potato shreds, crisp-fried sprats in vinegar, and cornmeal steamed in lotus leaves, through to cold sliced meats, noodles or *shuijiao* with dipping sauces, and dried ham and gingko nuts. *Zima daming* is another Guizhou speciality you'll find here: a large, circular, bread-like sweet cake.

Listings

Banks and exchange The main Bank of China is just west off Zhonghua Lu on Dusi Lu; foreign exchange is on the second floor (Mon–Fri 9–11.30am & 1.30–5pm). The *Holiday Inn* and *Trade Point Hotel* change money for guests only.
Bookshops The Foreign Language Bookshop, on Yan'an Lu, is well stocked with classics, an eclectic range of childrens' books, maps of the city and province, and Chinese guidebooks on Guizhou.
English corner Held every Sunday morning in the old Taosit temple/teahouse on Zhonghua Lu, just north of the Zhongshan Lu crossroads.
Hospital Guiyang Emergency Centre (Guiyang Shi Jijiu Zhan) is on Huaxi Dadao on Guiyang's western side.
Internet access There's an Internet bar on the fourth floor of the new commercial Telecom building, opposite the post office (¥3) – look for the external glass lifts.
Mail Guiyang's Post and Telecommunications building is at the southern end of Zhonghua Nan Lu (daily 8.30am–7pm), handling all mail, parcels and poste restante needs.
PSB The Foreign Affairs Department is in the city centre on Zhongshan Xi Lu.
Travel agents CITS is at 20 Yan'an Zhong Lu (Mon–Sat 8.30–11am & 1–5pm; ⓣ0851/5816348, ⓕ5824222). An exceptionally helpful office whose staff will happily sit down with you and a cup of tea and discuss any aspect of the province. They can also make hotel, ticket and tour bookings. Ask for Tang Yun Fang.

Zunyi and the north

Northern Guizhou is mountainous and undeveloped, the two main attractions being the historic city of **Zunyi** and an only recently accessible pocket of natural forest and waterfalls around the town of **Chishui**. Zunyi is on the main road and rail routes between Guiyang and Chongqing in Sichuan, while Chishui lies off the beaten track, right up along the Sichuanese border in the northwestern corner of the province.

Zunyi and around

Some 170km north of Guiyang, **ZUNYI** – despite being heavily industrialized of late – is historically the site of one of the most important events of China's civil war years. The Communist army arrived here on their **Long**

Zunyi and the north

Zunyi	遵义	***zūnyì***
Long March Museum	长征博物馆	*chángzhēng bówùguǎn*
Monument to the Red Army Martyrs	红军烈士纪念碑	*hóngjūn lièshì jìniànbēi*
Site of the Zunyi Conference	遵义会议址	*zūnyì huìyìzhǐ*
Accommodation		
Xiangshan Binguan	香山宾馆	*xiāngshān bīnguǎn*
Zuntie Dasha	遵铁大厦	*zūntiě dàshà*
Zunyi Binguan	遵义宾馆	*zūnyì bīnguǎn*
Chishui	赤水	***chìshuǐ***
Chishui Dajiudian	赤水大酒店	*chìshuǐ dàjiǔdiàn*
Maotai	茅台	***máo tái***
Sidonggou	四洞沟	***sìdòng gōu***
Shizhangdong Falls	十丈洞瀑布	*shízhàngdòng pùbù*
Yang Can Mu	杨粲墓	***yángcàn mù***

March in January 1935, in disarray after months on the run and having suffered two defeats in their attempts to join up with sympathetic forces in Hunan. Having taken the city by surprise, the leadership convened the **Zunyi Conference**, a decision that was to alter the entire purpose of the March and see Mao Zedong emerge as political head of the Communist Party. Previously, the Party had been led by Russian Comintern advisers, who modelled their strategies on urban-based uprisings among the proletariat. Mao felt that China's revolution could only succeed by mobilizing the peasantry, and that the Communist forces should base themselves in the countryside to do this. His opinions carried the day, saving the Red Army from certain annihilation at the hands of the Guomindang and, though its conquest still lay fifteen years away, marking the Communists' first step towards Beijing. (For more on the Long March, see p.584.)

The City

The obvious first place to head for is the **Site of the Zunyi Conference** (daily 8.30am–4.30pm; ¥10), an attractive black-brick, European-style house 5km south of arrival points and over the river on Ziyin Lu. There's a powerful feeling that this is where history was made, though there's little to see beyond a tour of the rooms – including the leaders' quarters and, of course, the Conference Hall – all of which have been restored to their 1930s condition and filled with period furniture. For more in the way of information, head a short way back east to the nineteenth-century **French Catholic Church**, now a **Long March Museum** (daily 8.30am–5pm; ¥3). Photos and maps illustrate the Communist peregrinations through Guizhou; they actually circled around to the north and captured the city again shortly after leaving it, completely disorganizing local Guomindang militias. One thing subtly absent is any mention of the actual manoeuvrings behind Mao's appropriation of the political scene, and doubtless there never will be. For a last taste of Red history, cross back over the river and up into **Fenghuang Shan Park**, where the **Monument to the Red Army Martyrs** rises to the west, a reminder that of the eighty thousand soldiers who started the Long March, only twenty thousand arrived at the Communists' final base in Shaanxi. However, it's grand rather than maudlin, with four huge red sandstone busts (vaguely resembling Lenin) supporting a floating, circular wall and a pillar topped with the Communist hammer and sickle.

Practicalities

Zunyi is set on the slopes below **Fenghuang Shan** (Phoenix Hill), with the centre concentrated along the **Xiang River**, which winds along the western side of the hill. The **bus and train stations** are on **Beijing Lu**, a very seedy area about 2.5km northeast of the centre off **Zhonghua Lu**, which runs down into town, turns north as Zhongshan Lu, then crosses west over the river to the main revolutionary sites.

The best basic **accommodation** is offered at the *Zuntie Dasha* (Ⓣ0852/8223266; rooms ❷, dorm beds ¥25), up near the bus and train stations on Beijing Lu. Alternatively, hop on a minibus into town, where there are comfortable rooms at either the conveniently placed *Zunyi Binguan* (Ⓣ0852/8222911; ❸), at the junction of Xima Lu and Shilong Lu, or the *Xiangshan Binguan* (Ⓣ0852/8225754; ❹), slightly south on Wanli Lu. The hotels can also provide **meals**.

Yang Can Mu

Zunyi has a much longer history than the city's monuments admit. Twenty-five kilometres south of town in the village of **HUANGFENZUI** is **Yang Can Mu**, the well-preserved resting place of the Song-dynasty official **Yang Can** and his wife. The Yang family ruled this region for over four hundred years, with Can holding the hereditary position of deputy defence minister until his death around 1250. The sandstone tomb is decorated with some superb relief carvings of both mythical and real beasts, plants and guardian figures – check out the character emerging from the dragon gate at the mouth of the tomb chamber.

Minibuses run out here from the city centre (¥5); ask at the *Xiangshan Binguan*'s reception desk for details. Alternatively, a taxi would cost ¥50–100, including waiting time.

On to Sichuan: Maotai and Chishui

The rail line continues smoothly north of Zunyi into Sichuan, but there's also a roundabout route out of the province by road, taking in Guizhou's second most impressive waterfalls, near **Chishui**, up on the Sichuanese border some 250–350km and at least eight hours from Zunyi on local buses. The shorter route initially follows the rail line north to **Tongzi** (where the Red Army cut through the Luoshan Pass and down to Zunyi) and then bends northwest to Chishui via the similarly named town of **Xishui**. The other circles west via the small town of **MAOTAI**, set in a valley along the Chishui River. Nobody seems to know exactly how long spirits have been produced here, but it became famous in 1704 when a travelling scholar named Zheng Zhen declared it China's finest producer. The town's **sorghum distillery** – which looks like a Disney castle – has made the Maotai brand a household word across the country, and the white porcelain bottle with its red diagonal stripe is essential at any banquet. While it certainly numbs your nervous system in a slow, creeping manner that takes you unawares, Westerners tend to be of the opinion that it's pretty indistinguishable from the contents of a cigarette lighter.

However you reach it, the town of **CHISHUI** is bang in the middle of a fabulous area of subtropical **forests** harbouring monkeys and groves of three-metre-high tree ferns. Two patches are accessible: the best is 40km due south of Chishui where the Fengxi River steps out at the **Shizhangdong Falls**, similar to the more famous Huangguoshu (see p.846) except for the refreshing lack of tourists. Closer to town, about 15km to the southwest, **Sidonggou** is simply a good place to explore the vegetation along well-formed paths, though there's an impressive twin waterfall here, too. As ever, things are at their best after rain in late summer. The *Chishui Dajiudian* (❸) is recommended for **accommodation** and, at least during the summer tourist season, regular minibuses run out to the sights.

Moving on, daily buses run from Chishui to the Yangzi River port of **Luzhou** in **Sichuan** (about 120km). If the water level is high enough it's possible to pick up a **ferry** from here along the river, otherwise Luzhou is connected by road to Chongqing and Zigong (see pp.958 & 953).

Eastern Guizhou

The journey from Guiyang into **eastern Guizhou** passes through a quintessentially Asian landscape of high hills cut by rivers, and dotted with dark wooden houses with buffalos plodding around rice terraces; women working in the fields have babies strapped to their backs under brightly quilted pads, and their long braided hair is coiled into buns secured by fluorescent plastic combs. They are Miao, and the scene marks the border of the **Miao and Dong Autonomous Prefecture**, arguably the best place in China to meet ethnic peoples on their own terms. Miao villages around the district capital, **Kaili**, are noted for their hundred or more annual **festivals**, the biggest of which attract busloads of tourists but are anyway such exuberant social occasions that there's no sign of their cultural integrity being compromised. Beyond Kaili, the adventurous can head southeast on public buses to the mountainous border with Guangxi province, where **Dong** hamlets sport their unique drum towers and bridges, or push on northeast through the pretty countryside surrounding **Zhenyuan** and the **Wuyang River** to **Tongren**, jumping-off point for a demanding ascent to cloud forests atop **Fanjing Shan**.

Even if you don't plan anything so energetic, the region is still enjoyable, the attractive home of a friendly people who take pride in their traditions. They are, however, difficult to understand: while younger villagers speak Mandarin, the older generation often know only a few phrases in addition to their own local languages. **Travelling around**, you'll find that minibuses cover more destinations and leave more frequently than long-distance buses, but to reach more remote corners you'll probably have to aim for the nearest main-road settlement and take pot luck with tractor taxis or whatever else is available – there's also scope for some excellent **hiking**.

Kaili and the Miao

Surrounded by scores of villages, some lush countryside and a couple of cooling towers for the local power plant, **KAILI**, 170km east from Guiyang, is a moderately industrialized, easy-going focus for China's 7.5 million **Miao**, though migrations and forced resettlements since the Tang dynasty have spread their population from Sichuan right down to Hainan Island. They were formerly treated as slaves by the Han, and many Miao popular heroes were rebel

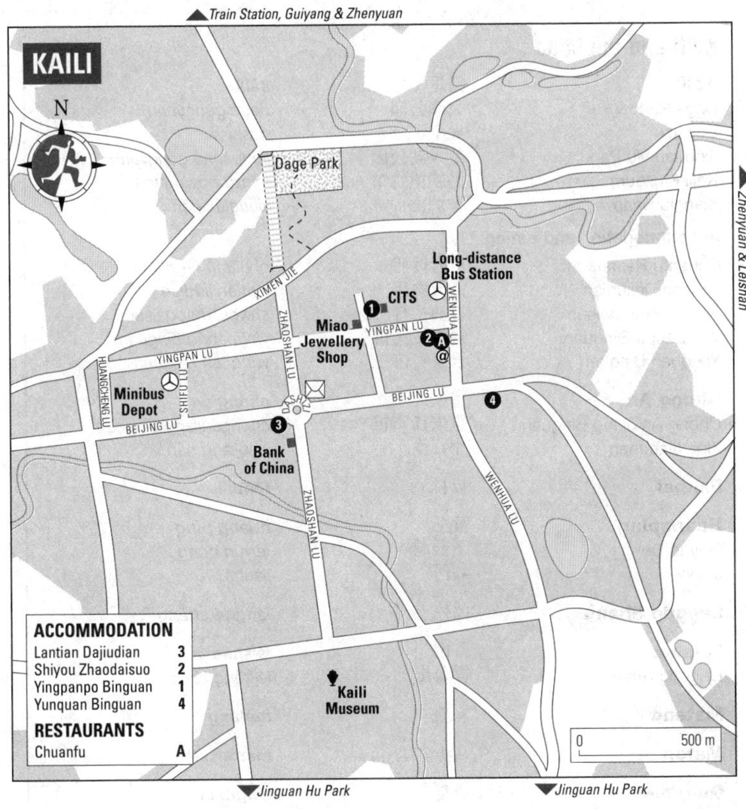

leaders such as **Zhang Xiumei**, who seeded almost twenty years of insurrection against the Qing during the mid-nineteenth century **Miao Uprisings** before being defeated outside Kaili. The Uprising's suppression left Guizhou in the desperately poor state witnessed by the Red Army sixty years later when, understandably sympathetic with the Communist cause, the Miao were rewarded for their help by being given their autonomy. The Cultural Revolution set things back, but since the late 1980s the area has received government assistance in schooling, medical services and transport, and today there's no doubt that Miao culture is flourishing.

The Town

Functional and compact, Kaili is oriented around the **Beijing Lu/Zhaoshan Lu** intersection, a crossroads generally known as **Dashizi**. Split by Dashizi into east and west sections, Beijing Lu holds most of Kaili's shops and businesses, while Zhaoshan Lu extends a short way north into the older residential end of town, and south past more shops into the countryside. At the time of writing, Kaili was undergoing major roadworks, though this didn't appear to involve altering the general street plan.

To get your bearings, head up from the crossroads to the northern end of Zhaoshan Lu, turn east along **Ximen Jie**, and then follow the backstreets through to **Dage Park**, a shady hill top inhabited by old men who gather to

Kaili and the Miao

Kaili	凯里	***kǎilǐ***
Dage Park	大阁公园	*dàgé gōngyuán*
Dashizi	大十子	*dàshí zi*
Jinquan Hu Park	金泉湖公园	*jīnquánhú gōngyuán*
Kaili Museum	民族博物馆	*mínzú bówùguǎn*
Xianglu Shan	香炉山	*xiānglú shān*
Accommodation and eating		
Chuanfu Restaurant	川府饭店	*chuānfǔ fàndiàn*
Lantian Dajiudian	蓝天酒店	*lántiān jiǔdiàn*
Shiyou Zhaodaisuo	石油招待所	*shíyóu zhāodàisuǒ*
Yingpanpo Binguan	营盘坡宾馆	*yíngpánpō bīnguǎn*
Yunquan Binguan	云泉宾馆	*yúnquán bīnguǎn*
Chong An	重安	***chóng'ān***
Chong An Jiang Binguan	重安江宾馆	*chóngānjiāng bīnguǎn*
Xiao Jiangnan	小江南	*xiǎojiāng nán*
Fanpai	反排	***fǎnpái***
Huangping	黄平	***huáng píng***
Feiyun Dong	飞云洞	*fēiyún dòng*
Jianhe	剑河	*jiànhé*
Langde Shang	郎德上	***lángdé shàng***
Leishan	雷山	***léishān***
Leigong Shan	雷公山	*léigōng shān*
Matang	麻塘	***mátáng***
Matou	马头	***mǎtóu***
Qingman	青曼	***qīngmàn***
Shibing	施秉	***shībǐng***
Shan He Dajiudian	山河大酒店	*shānhé dàjiǔdiàn*
Yuntai Shan	云台山	*yúntái shān*
Shidong	施洞	***shīdòng***
Taijiang	台江	***táijiāng***
Minghui silver factory	明晖民族工艺厂	*mínghuī mínzúgōngyìchǎng*
Wenchang Ge	文场阁	*wénchāng gé*
Youzheng Gongyu	邮政公寓	*yōuzhèng gōngyù*
Xijiang	西江	***xījiāng***
Zhouxi	舟溪	***zhōuxī***

smoke and decorate the trees with their caged songbirds. There's also a **pagoda** to climb, its wooden interior home to a mix of Buddhist and Taoist statues. From here, you can see the town spreading out on to an unusually level valley (*kaili* is a Miao word roughly translating as "prepared fields"), while **Xianglu Shan** (Incense-Burner Mountain) is the flat tableland rising off to the northwest, an important landmark for exploration farther afield.

Back down on Ximen Jie, head west for 500m and you'll end up at busy **produce markets** on Huancheng Lu and Ximen Lu, active daily but packed on

Sunday mornings with Miao, Yao and Dong in town to sell their wares. They also visit stalls near the Zhaoshan Lu/Beijing Lu crossroads, where you may be able to pick up items of clothing and jewellery, and you can't go near the *Yingpanpo Binguan* on Yingpan Lu without being accosted by Miao women hawking bundles of embroidery.

Fifteen minutes south of the crossroads at the end of Zhaoshan Lu, **Kaili Museum** (¥8) is a disappointingly lifeless array of photographs, costumes and artefacts, housed in an apparently derelict building hidden behind a wall – make enough noise and the caretaker will appear with a bunch of keys. It's probably more interesting to carry on walking for another thirty minutes south of here to **Jinquan Hu Park**, where the conical wooden **Gulou** (Drum Tower) is a full-sized Dong construction painted in blue and white – for more on these drum towers, see p.803. Built for tourists in 1985 and stuck way out here, it's fascinating nonetheless, assembled without nails and sometimes serving as a meeting place for locals.

Practicalities

Kaili's **train station** is about 3km by road to the north of town, where taxis and bus #3 meet arrivals; you can also buy train tickets at the long-distance bus station. Train is the best bet for heading direct to Guiyang or Zhenyuan.

The main **long-distance bus station** is 500m northeast of the centre on Wenhua Bei Lu, with many departures daily to Guiyang, Rongjiang, Jianhe, Leishan and Taijiang from morning to night, and less frequent services to Xijiang and Congjiang. Aside from schedule enquiries, skip the ticket office and pay on board the bus. More transport to Guiyang and some local destinations also operates out of a **minibus depot** about 500m west of Dishizi on Shifu Lu.

Kaili's **accommodation** prospects are not lavish. By far the best deal is at the *Yunquan Binguan* on Beijing Lu (Ⓣ0855/8275138; ❷), which is a clean, comfortable, motel-like affair; rooms without air conditioning are slightly cheaper but very cold in winter. For basic dorm beds and doubles, try either the *Shiyou Zhaodaisuo* on Yingpan Lu (Petroleum Guesthouse; ❶), or the *Yingpanpo Binguan* (Ⓣ0855/8223163; ❶–❷), just north of Yingpan Lu; the latter also has pricier rooms, but they're not worth it. As a last resort, the *Lantian Dajiudian* (Ⓣ0855/8222483; ❹) on Dashizi – the entrance is around the right side of the department store – has overpriced, cigarette-scented doubles which you can try bargaining down.

For **food**, side-street stalls around the markets and bus station sell light soups and noodle dishes, and stodgy fried buns. Hole-in-the-wall joints opposite the *Yingpanpo Binguan* are the cheapest places to eat indoors (don't order any chilli dishes unless you have a cast-iron stomach), with canteens along the eastern end of Beijing Lu specializing in dog hotpots. Good regional Chinese fare can be eaten in comfort up near the bus station on Wenhua Lu at the *Chuanfu* **restaurant**, which even has an English menu; most dishes are under ¥15.

The **Bank of China** is on Zhaoshan Lu (foreign exchange Mon–Fri 8.30–11am & 2–5pm) – the **last bank** until you reach Sanjiang in Guangxi province, if you're heading that way – and the main **post office** is right on Dashizi. Numerous **Internet bars** along Wenhua Lu, beside the *Chuanfu* restaurant, tend to be permanently filled with students outside of school hours.

Finally, if you're planning any local trips, call in first on Kaili's **CITS**, just inside the gates at the *Yingpanpo Binguan* (daily 8.30–11.30am & 2.30–6pm; Ⓣ0855/8256642, Ⓕ8222506, ⒺLeemqing@hotmail.com) – ask for Li Mao Qing or James, both of whom speak English and know the area backwards.

They can provide the latest information about festivals and market days, and how to get there, stock useful bilingual **maps** of Kaili and its environs, and are available as **guides** for anything from day-trips to local villages (¥450 for the car and ¥150 for an interpreter), to three-day hikes up Langde Shan (¥150 a day plus food for a group of five).

Around Kaili

The biggest problem around Kaili is deciding where to go, as there are dozens of **Miao villages** within a couple of hours' drive of town. **Markets**, which generally operate on a five-day cycle, or **festivals**, make the choice much easier – most festivals take place in early spring, early summer and late autumn, when there's little to do in the fields and plenty of food to share. The bigger ones attract as many as fifty thousand people for days of buffalo fights, dances, wrestling, singing matches and horse or boat races. Participants dress in multi-coloured finery, and the action often crosses over to the spectators – foreigners are rare treats, so don't expect to sit quietly on the sidelines. The biggest events of the year are the springtime **Sisters' Meal**, the traditional time for girls to choose a partner, and **dragon-boat races**, held for a different reason here than others in China – for more on these, see village accounts and the "Sisters' Meal" box on p.839. Major festivals are explosive occasions, while smaller events, where tourists are less expected, can be that much more intimate. If planning a trip to coincide with particular events, be careful of **dates**, as Chinese information sometimes confuses lunar and Gregorian calendars – "9 February", for instance, might mean "the ninth day of the second lunar month".

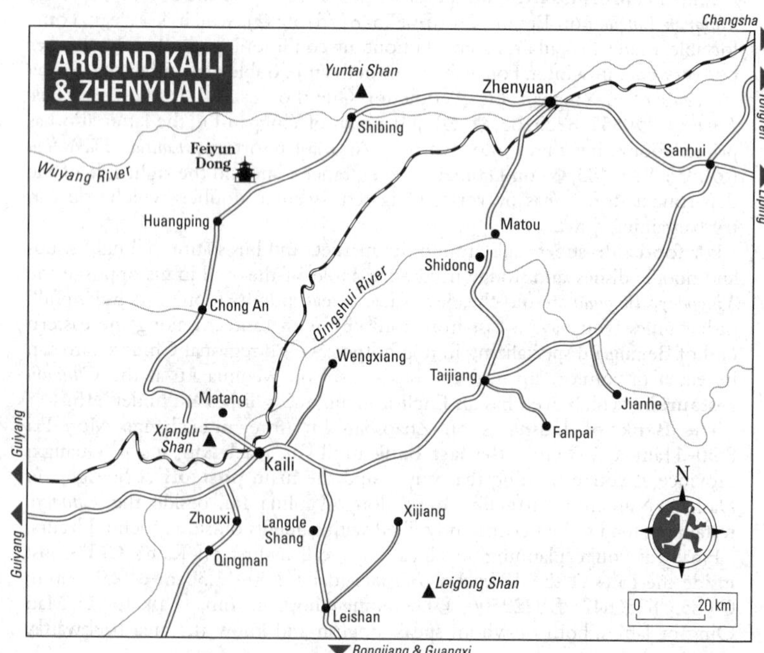

Though some Miao villages are interesting in themselves, outside of the festival season people will be working in the fields, and smaller places may appear completely deserted. With luck, however, you'll be invited to tour the village, look around the distinctive wooden homes, fed – pickled vegetables and sour chicken hotpot, with copious amounts of **no mijiu**, a powerfully soporific rice wine, to wash things down – and asked if you'd like to see some antique wedding garments or have a young woman don full festival regalia for your camera. All this will cost, but it's offered in good humour and worth the price; people sometimes have embroidery or silver to sell, for which bargaining is essential.

CITS **tours** aside, all the villages below are connected by at least daily bus or minibus services from Kaili, and also make fine stopovers on the way into the Rongjiang or Zhenyuan regions. Return transport can leave quite early, however, so be prepared to stay the night or hitch back if you leave things too late.

Northwest to Shibing

The 110-kilometre-long road northwest from **Kaili to Shibing** passes a host of interesting villages and gets you much of the way to Zhenyuan (see p.840). Buses leave from Kaili's main bus station, and the whole trip to Shibing costs ¥20 or so.

The first place to aim for is **MATANG**, a village 20km from Kaili, home of the **Gejia** (or Geyi), a Miao sub-group. Tell the bus driver where you're heading; the track to Matang heads off across the paddy fields from below square-topped **Xianglu Shan**, the mountain where the rebel leader Zhang Xiumei met his end at the hands of imperial troops in 1873 – there's a big **festival** here each August commemorating the event. It's a twenty-minute walk from the main road to the village, a cluster of muddy fields and dark wooden houses, and you'll be mobbed on arrival by old women selling jewellery, swirly **batik** cloths and characteristically orange-and-yellow embroidery. To move onwards from Matang, return to the main road and flag down a passing vehicle.

Next stop is **CHONG AN**, a pleasant riverside town about 50km north of Matang with the friendly, basic *Xiao Jiangnan* guesthouse (❶) or the plusher *Chong An Jiang Binguan* (❷), water-powered mills downstream, and a small **nunnery** just off the Kaili road, reached over a chain-and-plank bridge. Make sure you catch Chong An's fifth-day **market**, where you'll be battered and bruised by crowds of diminuative Miao grandmothers as they bargain for local crafts, or bring in clothes (everything from traditional pleated skirts to denim jeans) for dyeing in boiling vats of indigo. Children around here often wear bright blue "tiger hats", with tufted fabric ears and silver embellishments, which ward off bad luck. There are also some interesting villages near Chong An, and your accommodation may be able to organize guided **walks**.

Some 20km north again on the Shibing road, **HUANGPING** is a larger market town with a few old buildings known for its **silversmiths**, currently in an unfortunate state between being half demolished and half rebuilt. Between here and Shibing you pass **Feiyun Dong** (¥3), a pretty Taoist temple surrounded by trees and rocky outcrops, whose moss-covered main hall houses a **museum** of Miao crafts, a dragon-boat prow and a big bronze drum.

Set in a wide, humid valley 34km from Huangping, **SHIBING** is a busy, ordinary modern town laid out east–west along the south bank of the **Wuyang**

River; the bus station is at the west end. The thing to do here is organize a **river cruise** (¥120) up the **Shanmu He**, a westerly tributary of the Wuyang, which is flanked by steep limestone cliffs and thick forest. Kaili's CITS can arrange this, or try local **accommodation** – the *Shan He Dajiudian* (❸), across the river by the bridge, is your best bet, or there are cheaper beds at the bus station hostel (¥35). **Moving on**, there are buses and minibuses leaving whenever full back along the Kaili road, and east to Zhenyuan (2hr; ¥8) until late afternoon.

South to Qingman, Leishan and Guangxi

One simple trip from Kaili is out to **ZHOUXI**, an untidy but interesting collection of traditional homes and bunker-style concrete buildings about 20km southwest of Kaili on the Danzhai road, where you might see people soaking sheets in wooden vats of indigo dye. There's also a fine Sunday market where you can pick up local silk work, and a particularly big **lusheng performance** – named after the long-piped bamboo instrument which accompanies Miao dances – at the end of the Spring Festival celebrations, usually in late January/February. Nearby **QINGMAN** village has a reputation for producing the best *lusheng* players.

A broader option, which could ultimately see you ending up 200km from Kaili over the border in Guangxi province, starts 25km southeast of Kaili at **LANGDE SHANG**, a tremendously photogenic collection of wooden houses, cobbles, fields and chickens set on a terraced hillside, a twenty-minute walk from the main road. Twenty kilometres south of here is **LEISHAN**, an unself-consciously grubby town and famous tea-growing region ninety minutes from Kaili, with another highly recommended market day, and the central *Jianxin Binguan* (❷) offering the only **accommodation**. There's also some superb hiking to the east at the **Leigong Shan Nature Reserve**, featuring remote villages, forests, bears, deer and other wildlife – contact Kaili's CITS (p.835) to arrange a trip. In a valley northeast of Leishan along a dirt road is **XIJIANG**, also known as the "Thousand Miao Village" and reckoned to be the largest, most traditional Miao settlement, well worth an overnight trip – there's a basic guesthouse here (❶). Three minibuses from Kaili to Xijiang pass through Leishan in the early afternoon.

Four hours southeast of Leishan are the fringes of a remote landscape of steep mountain terraces and dark wooden villages dominated by elaborately shaped towers and bridges: **Dong country**. You can see the main features in a couple of days, but with time, patience and stamina (roads and accommodation are basic), it's very rewarding to push right through to the other side of their territory at **Sanjiang** in Guangxi province. Your first destination is the town of **RONGJIANG**, 100km southeast of Leishan and connected to Kaili by a direct daily bus: for more about the Dong, their architecture, and details of the trip, see p.801.

Northeast to Taijiang and Shidong

The small town of **TAIJIANG** lies 55km northeast of Kaili on the junction of the Sanhui and Shidong roads, its sports ground the venue for a major **Sisters' Meal Festival** held on the fifteenth day of the third lunar month (April/May – see box opposite). A collection of cheap modern buildings, the town is being targeted for tourism, with **accommodation** (❸) available at the *Youzheng Gongyu* (Ⓣ0855/5323777), the *Dishui Binguan* and *Xinghe Binguan*. There's also a more central **guesthouse** (❶), not far from the bus station. Book festival accommodation in advance, perhaps via Kaili's CITS. Ask around in Taijiang for

Sisters' Meal

Taijiang's **Sisters' Meal festival** is the one to catch. The town fills beyond capacity for the two-day event, crowds jostling between lottery stalls and markets, buying local produce and, of course, embroidery and silverwork. More of this is being worn by teenage girls from villages around Taijiang, who gamely tramp up and down the streets, sweltering under the weight of their decorated jackets and silver jewellery, jingling as they walk. By nine in the morning there's hardly standing room left in the sports ground, ready for the official opening an hour later; once the necessary speeches are out the way, things formally kick off with two hours of energetic **dancing and lusheng playing**, after which the party breaks up into smaller rings, dancers and musicians practising for bigger things later on in the festivities, or just flirting – this is a teenagers' festival after all.

Discreet **cockfighting** (not to the death) and much drinking of *mijiu* carries on through the afternoon, then at dusk the **dragon-lantern dances** get underway, a half-dozen teams carrying their wire-and-crepe, twenty-metre-long hollow dragons and accompanying model birds and butterflies into the main street. Candles are lit and placed inside the animals before things begin in earnest, the dragons animated into chasing swirls by the dancers, who charge up and down the street battling with each other; the mayhem is increased by drummers, whooping crowds and fireworks tossed at leisure into the throng.

Day two sees the action shifting a couple of kilometres west of town to a wide river valley, venue for mid-morning **buffalo fights**. Bloodless trials of strength between two bulls, these draw a good five thousand spectators who assemble around the ill-defined fighting grounds while competitors are paraded up and down, decked out with plaited caps, coloured flags and pheasant tail-feathers, and numbers painted in red on their flanks. The fights each last a few minutes, a skull-cracking charge ending in head-to-head wrestling with locked horns, bulls scrabbling for purchase; the crowds get as close as possible, scattering wildly when one bull suddenly turns tail and bolts, pursued by the victor. Back in town, the **Sisters' Meal** itself is underway, a largely personal affair where young men give parcels of multicoloured **sticky rice** to their prospective partner: a pair of chopsticks buried inside returned rice is an acceptance, a single chopstick or – even worse – a **chilli**, a firm refusal. The festival winds up that night back at the sports ground, the closing dances all held under floodlights, and followed again by much livelier, ad hoc dancing after which couples drift off into the dark.

the **Minghui silver factory**, which creates traditional pieces and replates old ones, and whose English-speaking manager, Mr Wang, will be happy to show you around – and happier still if you buy something. Easier to find is **Wenchang Ge**, a recently restored Qing temple just uphill from the central intersection, with wooden halls unexpectedly containing a collection of locally found **fossils** of Cambrian sealife.

There are several side-trips to make from Taijiang. High in the hills 30km east, the ancient village of **FANPAI** is said to be very attractive, with terraced fields and unusual dances; there are at least two minibuses a day from Taijiang. Simpler to reach either from here or direct from Kaili, **JIANHE** is 40km northeast of Taijiang off the Sanhui road, a little-touristed town whose Red-sleeved Miao incorporate decorative pieces of tin into the designs on their aprons. You can catch transport from Jianhe southeast to **Liping**, staging post for the journey to Zhaoxing and Guangxi province.

Beyond Taijiang, there are two buses daily for the final two-hour, forty-kilometre leg to Shidong, through some of the most beautiful countryside this part of China can provide. **SHIDONG** itself is a tiny farming town at the end of the road, set beside flat fields on a bend in the blue **Qingshui River**, with a single "Hotel for Foreigners" (❶) – or anybody else. The river is the setting of the region's biggest **Dragon-boat Festival**, which follows on from Taijiang's Sisters' Meal celebrations. This riotous occasion commemorates a local hero who battled Han invaders, and not, as in the rest of China, the memory of Qu Yuan's suicide in 280 BC (see box, p.566). If you're here then you'll be drunk, as a roadblock of young women in festival dress stop arrivals outside town, a draught of *mijiu* from a buffalo horn the price of passage – touch the horn with your hands and you have to drain it. Masses of transport is laid on for the festival, but at other times there are only a couple of buses a day back south from outside the hotel. To continue north **to Zhenyuan**, take a small boat across the river to the hamlet of **Matou** and wait for the midday bus – though in May and June the river may be too high to cross.

Zhenyuan and beyond

ZHENYUAN was founded two thousand years ago, though today's town, occupying a constricted valley 100km northeast of Kaili on the **Wuyang River**, sprang up in the Ming dynasty to guard the trade route through to central China. A characterful place on the Guiyang–Changsha rail line, Zhenyuan's narrow streets and tall houses pile together beside an aquamarine stretch of water, along which you can **cruise** west through a string of offshoot gorges (¥62 per person return; 5hr; book at your accommodation), though a dam prevents you from travelling all the way to Shibing by boat.

Zhenyuan itself is two lengthy streets on either side of the river, crossed by several bridges. Just east of the bus station and up a staircase to the left, **Tianhou Gong** (¥1) is a recently restored, 400-year-old Taoist complex, with a balcony overhanging the street. Continuing east, you pass the main bridge and enter Zhenyuan's nicely restored **old quarter**, about 500m of wood and stone buildings in the Qing style, backed up against stony cliffs. The street eventually crosses the river via a multiple-arch, solid stone span leading to **Qinglong Dong** (¥5), a sixteenth-century temple whose separate Taoist, Buddhist and Confucian halls appear to grow out of a cliff face. The halls are dripping wet and scattered with idols, while a mess of vines forms a curtain

Zhenyuan and beyond

Zhenyuan	镇远	***zhènyuǎn***
Lerong Binguan	乐容宾馆	*lèróng bīnguǎn*
Mingcheng Binguan	名城宾馆	*míngchéng bīnguǎn*
Qinglong Dong	青龙洞	*qīnglóng dòng*
Tianhou Gong	天后宫	*tiānhòu gōng*
Wuyang River	舞阳河	*wǔyáng hé*
Zhenyuan Binguan	镇远宾馆	*zhènyuǎn bīnguǎn*
Gaotun	高屯	***gāotún***
Jinping	锦屏	***jǐnpíng***
Liping	黎平	***lípíng***
Sansui	三穗	***sānsuì***
Tianzhu	天柱	***tiānzhù***

Moving on from Zhenyuan

There are several daily **trains** from Zhenyuan southwest to Kaili and Guiyang, and northwest via **Yuping** (1hr; jumping off point for Tongren, see below) to Huaihua (for Zhangjiajie, p.569) and Changsha. Buy tickets from the station the day before travel if you don't want to stand.

By **bus**, there's plenty of transport through the day west **to Shibing** (2hr; ¥8), and a few services to Zunyi, Kaili and Guiyang. Just one bus heads southwest **to Matou** for the Shidong–Kaili road, passing down the station road around 9–11am; note that early summer rains and flooding can halt the ferry crossing from Matou to Shidong.

It's also possible to hop in stages southeast **to Liping** and so via the Dong village of Zhaoxing into Guangxi province. You'll need two days for the trip to Liping, which takes you over steep hills and green, flat valleys, and through small wooden villages and messy market towns – the whole journey costs around ¥50 in bus fares. The first place to aim for is **Sanhui**, a nondescript town about 40km east of Zhenyuan and connected by frequent minibuses; from here catch another vehicle to **Tianzhu** (75km; 3hr), a relatively large place with a bus station at either side of town – rickshaws will ferry you between the two. Your next target is **Jinping** (50km; 2hr), where you can stay opposite the bus station at the basic but cheap and clean *Hunan Dajiudian* (¥30) – which also has a decent **restaurant** – before catching one of the frequent morning buses to Liping (90km; 2hr). About 10km from Liping, there's a scenic diversion at **Gaotun**, where a limestone arch over the Bazhou River forms a natural bridge; for Liping itself and the trip to Zhaoxing and Guangxi, see p.805.

between the overhang and pavilions, and there are some nice views along the river of rickety sampans, children swimming and (in early June) dragon-boat rehearsals. Zhenyuan's **market** is south of the river by the main bridge, and a couple of **city wall fragments** lurk in lanes between houses and the water west of here.

The **bus station** is on the north bank, while **trains** pull in at Zhenyuan's southwestern edge. Of the **accommodation**, the cheapest option is south of the river at the *Lerong Binguan* (Ⓣ0855/5721908; ❶); while about 750m east of the bus station you'll find the good-value *Zhenyuan Binguan* (Ⓣ0855/5722592; ❷) and, slightly plusher, adjacent *Mingcheng Binguan* (Ⓣ0855/5726028, Ⓕ0855/5726018; ❹). The *Mingcheng* has a good **restaurant**, and there are anonymous hotpots and noodle canteens all over the place.

Tongren and Fanjing Shan

The only settlement of any size in far northeastern Guizhou, **TONGREN** is a small, lightly industrial city, situated at a bend on the high banks of the **Jin River**, only a stone's throw from the Hunanese border. In 1981 a nature reserve was formalized at nearby **Fanjing Shan**, a Buddhist mountain long recognized for the extraordinary diversity of its plants and wildlife, and there's been a steady flow of visitors since access improved in the early 1990s. You need to be fit, but Fanjing Shan's scenery is magnificent and there's always the chance of seeing *jinsi hou*, **golden monkeys**, one of China's prettiest endangered species, whose wild population numbers only a few thousand individuals. Around 170 live on Fanjing Shan's upper reaches and it's easy to recognize their slight build, big lips, tiny nose and, in males, vivid orange-gold fur, should you be lucky enough to spot one.

Tongren is curiously isolated, best reached via **Yuping**, a stop on the Zhenyuan–Huaihua rail line, from where **minibuses** (¥20) take under two

Tongren and Fanjing Shan		
Fanjing Shan	梵净山	***fànjìng shān***
Golden Monkey	金丝猴	*jīnsī hóu*
Heiwan	黑湾	*hēiwān*
Jiankou	剑口	*jiànkǒu*
Jinding Si	金顶寺	*jīndǐng sì*
Tongren	铜仁	***tóngrén***
Dong Shan Park	东山公园	*dōngshān gōngyuán*
Dongshan Si	东山寺	*dōngshān sì*
Fanyu Dajiudian	梵宇大酒店	*fányǔ dàjiǔdiàn*
Jin River	锦江	*jǐnjiāng*
Jinlong Binguan	金龙宾馆	*jīnlóng bīnguǎn*
Qiandong Binguan	黔东宾馆	*qiánlóng bīnguǎn*

hours to reach town – exit the train station, turn right, and the minibus depot is 400m along the road.

The main part of town is east of the river, where the streets form a compact and unfocused shopping district: Minzhu Lu is a partly pedestrianized collection of clothing and department stores, with a large sculpture of a **bronze drum** halfway along. Overlooking the river to the south is **Dong Shan Park**, where a stone staircase leads up to **Dongshan Si**, China's only official **Nuo temple**. Nuo is an animistic religion, now watered down by Buddhist and Taoist influences but retaining something of its original form in open-air **theatre**, still held at festivals in villages around Tongren. Performing stylized fights to rhythmic drumming, dancers don grotesquely shaped **masks**, each of which is individually named and has a spirit that the wearer is constantly in danger of being overwhelmed by, unless it is propitiated with a sprinkle of chicken's blood. The number of masks owned by a troupe increases their reputation. The temple has more than a hundred arranged in two halls, along with local batiks, a tacky "Nuo" shrine, and other trappings of the religion. Below, riverside Shuangjiang Lu is lined with elderly wooden stores and homes.

Practicalities

Tongren's **bus station** is west of the river on **Jinjiang Lu**, with regular transport to Yuping (for the Guiyang–Huaihua **train** – ask at the bus station for departure times) and Jiangkou (for Fanjing Shan), and further afield to Zunyi, Guiyang and, for some reason, Guangzhou. There's **accommodation** opposite at the dusty *Fanyu Dajiudian* (❹); otherwise, cross the river to the *Jinlong Binguan* (❷) on Huanxi Lu, whose eccentric decor compensates for age; while up along Minzhu Lu is the fairly decent *Qiandong Binguan* (Ⓣ0856/5223636;❸, dorm beds ¥20). There are a few inexpensive **restaurants** in the centre, including a couple of cake shops serving coffee, plus a large Hui and Uigur population pedalling kebabs and grilled chicken wings. Tongren's **Bank of China** is near the *Jinlong* hotel on Huanxi Lu, with several **Internet bars** near the bronze drum on Minzhu Lu.

Fanjing Shan

Some 75km northwest of Tongren, **Fanjing Shan**'s summit rises to 2500m. You should be aware that the climb involves more than seven thousand stairs, long sections of which are narrow, steep, and in a bad state of repair – allow for one day up, one day on the top, and one day to return. There's sufficient

accommodation and **food** along the route, so copy the Chinese, who carry only a jar of tea with them. Summers are humid lower down, but cold wind and fog often tear across the upper levels, and winters are freezing – take some warm clothing.

From Tongren, minibuses go to **JIANGKOU** (2hr), a single-street town with some uppity urchins, from where jeeps and smaller minibuses bounce along the 25-kilometre dirt track leading up the valley to the mountain. Prices, speed and eventual destination of this latter stage vary according to the vehicle and disposition of the driver; ¥15 should carry you as far as the **park gates** (¥15) at **Heiwan**, a collection of basic shops, restaurants and accommodation. A red earth road runs 7km from Heiwan to the foot of the mountain, an enjoyable walk through lowland forests of bamboo and flowering trees, clouds of butterflies and a near-vertical waterfall. At the end is **Dahe** – two teahouses where porters lounge, hoping to carry you up in a bamboo litter, a souvenir shop selling walking sticks and **maps**, and a bridge over the stream – and then you're on the lower stairs, in every respect the worst on the mountain. It's a long ninety minutes to where the steps begin to follow less extreme ridges, through thinner woodland and a dwarf bamboo understorey. This continues pretty well all the way, past a halfway meal shack (they'll let you sleep here if need be) to heath country, basic lodgings and a restaurant five hours from Dahe at **Jinding Si**, the Golden Summit Monastery. The mountain's true apex is up another five hundred stairs to the right past some intriguingly piled rock formations. The general practice is to overnight around the temple and then climb up to watch the sunrise, but there's also a good day's hiking out to minor peaks.

Western Guizhou

Extending for 350km between Guiyang and the **border with Yunnan province**, Western Guizhou is a desperately poor region of beautiful mountainous country and relentlessly functional towns drenched in the fallout from coal mining, concrete and steel operations. About a third of the way along is the Bouyei town of **Anshun** and adjacent **Huangguoshu Falls**, one of China's largest, a magnet for busloads of tourists on day-trips from the capital. Anshun sits on the Guizhou–Yunnan rail line and highway, and all routes west from here can ultimately lead to Kunming, Yunnan's capital: trains head northwest to **Liupanshui**, springboard for a detour through Yi, Hui and Miao settlements to the remote wildfowl sanctuary of **Caohai** – being poled around this shallow lake on a sunny day is one of Guizhou's highlights – while the highway follows a more southerly road into Yunnan through the Yi border town of **Panxian**; and a lesser route snakes southwest from Anshun to further scenic attractions at **Xingyi**. Getting around isn't too tricky if you stick to the main routes, though buying bus tickets for travel along back roads can be occasionally problematic; note that the west has **no banks** capable of changing traveller's cheques.

Anshun and around

ANSHUN is a country town 100km from Guiyang on the rail line to Kunming, established as a garrisoned outpost in Ming times to keep an eye on the empire's unruly fringes. Later a stage for merchants treading the difficult roads between central China and Yunnan, it became a centre for distributing

Western Guizhou		
Anshun	安顺	*ānshùn*
Batik Factory	蜡染总厂	*làrăn zŏngchăng*
Huayou Binguan	华油宾馆	*huáyóu bīnguăn*
Minzu Binguan	民族宾馆	*mínzú bīnguăn*
Wen Miao	文庙	*wénmiào*
Xixiu Shan Binguan	西秀山宾馆	*xīxiùshān bīnguăn*
Xixiu Shan Ta	西秀山塔	*xīxiùshān tă*
Longgong and Huangguoshu		
Huangguoshu Binguan	黄果树宾馆	*huángguŏshù bīnguăn*
Huangguoshu Falls	黄果树瀑布	*huángguŏshù pùbù*
Longgong Caves	龙宫洞	*lónggōng dòng*
Liupanshui	六盘水	*liùpánshuĭ*
Liuzhi	六枝	*liùzhī*
Weining	威宁	*wēiníng*
Black-necked crane	黑颈鹤	*hēijĭng hè*
Caohai	草海	*căohăi*
Jiangong Binguan	建工宾馆	*jiàngōng bīnguăn*
Xingyi	兴义	*xīngyì*
Maling Canyon	马陵峡谷	*mălíng xiágŭ*
Nationalities Museum	民族婚俗博物馆	*mínzú hūnsú bówùguăn*
Panjiang Binguan	盘江宾馆	*pánjiāng bīnguăn*
Xingyi Binguan	兴义宾馆	*xīngyì bīnguăn*

opium between the 1880s and the Communist takeover in 1949, but today the emphasis is on subsistence farming, textiles and tourism, with the town acting as a base for tours to the nearby **Longgong Caves** and **Huangguoshu Falls**.

While the land around Anshun is relatively flat, the province's brittle limestone hills are never far away, and the limited spaces in between are intensely farmed by blue-skirted **Bouyei** busy planting rice or using buffalo to plough the muddy flats. Closely related to Guangxi's Zhuang nationality (see p.785), the Bouyei number 2.5 million and range throughout southwestern Guizhou, though this is their heartland. Brick kilns – so common elsewhere in rural China – are conspicuously absent from this region, as there simply isn't enough spare clay to waste on making building blocks. Instead, angular homes are skilfully constructed from stone and roofed in slate, with villages occupying wooded outcrops surrounded by neatly tended terraces.

Anshun is centred around the intersection of Nanhua Lu and Tashan Lu. Stuck in redevelopment limbo, the surrounding area is nonetheless packed with scenes typical of healthy rural commerce: horses hauling cartloads of coal, market crowds bargaining over bags of ducks and neat piles of fresh cabbages, shops selling cheap clothes and every imaginable plastic household utensil. For specific targets, seek out the **Xixiu Shan Ta**, a short Ming-dynasty pagoda on a hill above buildings northwest of the Zhonghua Lu/Tashan Lu intersection; or **Wen Miao**, a six-hundred-year-old Confucian academy with a finely restored, carved stone gateway, hidden away at the top end of town.

Anshun batik

Anshun is particularly famous for its **batik** work, a tradition said to have originated more than two thousand years ago when wax from a convenient beehive dribbled unnoticed over some linen awaiting dyeing. People were amazed at the resulting patterns and started creating them deliberately. In its pure form, molten wax is first applied with a copper "knife" on white cloth, most often in spirals and curves said to represent buffalo horns or liquorice plants, and in geometric designs. The cloth is simply dyed once in **indigo**, then boiled to fix the colour and remove the wax, leaving bold white patterns on a dark blue background.

Though batik is practised throughout southwestern China by Miao, Yao and Bai people, it was Guizhou's Bouyei who cornered the commercial ethnic textile market after Anshun's **batik factory** opened in 1953. A bold venture at the time, today their products are in demand across the country, with modern multicoloured, mass-produced designs supplementing older monochrome patterns. A dozen **shops** outside the factory near the main bus station on Nanhua Lu sell touristy banners and wall hangings in various styles. Few are strictly "traditional" designs, but many have a local feel: blue monochrome portraits of Bouyei girls in bridal finery, or banners depicting stylized figures and animals from Bouyei myths. Prices are low, but bargaining is quite acceptable.

Practicalities

The **train station** is about 1km south from the centre at the very end of Nanhua Lu, with regular trains shuffling through en route between Guiyang and Kunming, and a couple daily to Liupanshui – the only way to get there from Anshun. The town's **main bus station** is back towards the centre on Nanhua Lu, where the highway from Guiyang enters town; masses of traffic runs to Guiyang and Huangguoshu through the day, with a few services to Xingyi and Yunnan. For more traffic to Huangguoshu, head to the **west bus station**, 500m west from the central crossroads down Tashan Xi Lu.

Anshun's **accommodation** is uninspiring, and much of it is reluctant to take foreigners. The *Huayou Binguan* (Ⓣ0853/3226021; ❷), about 150m west of the central crossroads along Tashan Xi Lu, is all right but very chilly in winter. Just up from the bus station on Nanhua Lu and across the road, *Xixiu Shan Binguan* (Ⓣ0853/3223900) was closed for redevelopment at the time of writing, and looked to be aiming at the ¥200 a room bracket. Otherwise, the 1980s tourist standby, the *Minzu Binguan*, on Tashan Dong Lu (Ⓣ0853/3222500; ❸), is pretty run down. You won't find better **places to eat** than the canteens around the main bus station, which serve basic, tasty stir-fries, noodle dishes, and hotpots. **Dog** is always available (though it's not obligatory), and the best in this line is at *Gouzhenpeng*, whose English sign declares "Orthodox Dog Flesh Restaurant in China" – the restaurant is 150m from the long-distance bus station down the Guiyang road.

Longgong and Huangguoshu

The 150-kilometre return trip from Anshun out to **Longgong Caves** and **Huangguoshu Falls** is also a good opportunity to take a look at rural Guizhou. A **minibus day-tour** combining the two is the easiest way to travel, and indeed the only transport option for visiting the caves – you can pick these up from Guiyang's or Anshun's train station squares in the early morning. If just Huangguoshu is enough and you want to linger in the area, aim for **Huangguoshu township** at the top of the falls, which can be reached on direct minibuses from Guiyang and Anshun, or long-distance buses can drop you off on the highway nearby.

About an hour from Anshun, **Longgong Caves** (various fees totalling about ¥30) are flooded and have to be explored by boat. The trip lasts about an hour, the boat drifting past various stark outcrops and caverns, all draped with flashing neon lights. After Longgong, it's a further thirty minutes to **Huangguoshu Falls** (¥35), some 70km from Anshun on the Yunnan road at little **HUANGGUOSHU** township. At 68m high this may not quite rank as China's highest cataract, but in full flood after summer rains it's certainly the most spectacular, and probably the loudest – on a good day the thunder rolls way off into the distance. A staircase descends past plagues of souvenir stalls and subtropical shrubberies to the blue-green river below the falls, and the most imposing view of Huangguoshu is off to the left where the full weight of its eighty-one-metre span drops into the **Rhino Pool** – expect a good soaking from the spray. At times of low water levels it's possible to wade across here; otherwise head back to the wire **suspension bridge** downstream before ascending to the hundred-metre-long, windowed **tunnel** running behind the water curtain (¥10).

If you get stuck here for the night, there are a couple of cheap Chinese **hostels** in Huangguoshu township which might be convinced to take you; otherwise there's the relatively pricey *Huangguoshu Binguan* (Ⓣ0853/3592110, Ⓕ3592111; ❷–❹) up near the falls' entrance. **Moving on**, buses run to Anshun and Guiyang through the day. If you're Xingyi or Yunnan bound, first catch a minibus 7km west to **Guanling** and look for connections there.

The far west

Heading west from Anshun, there are **three routes** to choose between on the way into Yunnan. The Guiyang–Kunming train can get you northwest to **Liupanshui**, from where Weining and wintering birdlife at Caohai are a bus ride away. Meanwhile, the main Guizhou–Yunnan road runs due west of Anshun to the Yi-dominated border town of **Panxian** – an uneventful journey – while a less direct alternative leads down through the **Xingyi region** at Guizhou's southwestern extremities, where you can connect with the Nanning–Kunming rail line. Karst mountains and terraced fields are the backdrop wherever you head.

To Liupanshui, Weining and Caohai

The land northwest of Anshun forms a tumultuous barrier of jagged peaks and deep valleys, pretty well restricting all access to the railway, which masterfully cuts through everything via a string of tunnels and long sweeps of high, clouded track hugging the hillsides. An hour along, **LIUZHI** is a dismal place, though the surrounding area harbours villages of **Long-horned Miao**. Women of this particular group wear the strangest of headpieces, resembling bolsters made from plaited hair bound around wooden "buffalo horns" (for more on the Miao, see p.832).

Two hours from Liuzhi the train rocks in to **LIUPANSHUI** (also known as **Shuicheng**), generally regarded as the poorest city in China and such a mess of broken pavements and dilapidated buildings permanently mired in steel plant fallout and coal dust, that the train station area looks almost appealing by comparison. The **bus station** is a few streets behind (a taxi costs ¥5), with transport on **to Weining** (¥25) until mid-afternoon; there are also sleepers down **to Xingyi** (¥66), but the station staff are scared of getting reprimanded for selling foreigners tickets for this, so get someone else to do it for you.

The road to Weining takes about four hours, twisting up hills past a disproportionate number of truck wrecks – it's not that bad a road – to emerge above the clouds on the 2000-metre-high Weining Plateau, which seems to enjoy a surprisingly mild microclimate. **WEINING** is another small, run-down shell of a town immidiately north of reed-fringed **Caohai**, populated by a friendly mix of Muslim Hui, Yi and Dahua Miao, and is moderately well known for its Yi torch festival in July/August, sheep farming and **potatoes** – skewers of chilli-dusted potato "kebabs" are sold everywhere. Exit the bus station, turn right, and the only viable **accommodation** is 100m past the crossroads at the *Jiangong Binguan* (ⓣ0857/6222048; ❸, beds ¥25), whose restaurant is also inexpensive and welcoming.

A ¥1.5 motor-rickshaw ride from the town centre – or a half-hour walk – **Caohai**, the "Grass Sea", fills about twenty-five square kilometres of a shallow lake basin, the core of a regional **nature reserve**. Wintering wildfowl shelter here in huge numbers, including around 400 **black-necked cranes** – almost ten percent of the entire world population – along with golden eagles, white-tailed sea eagles, black storks, Eurasian cranes, spoonbills and assorted ducks. Walk down to the lake and you'll be approached by touts wanting to take you out on **boat trips**: you pay about ¥60 for a three-hour tour being poled around in a four-person punt after ducks. The Chinese head first for a meal at the hamlet of **Longjia** on the far shore, famed for its food. On a sunny day, Caohai's overall tranquillity is a complete break with daily life in China; wintering cranes often hang out in the shallows near the shore and are not too hard to photograph.

Moving on from Weining, you'll have to head back to Liupanshui for the train, though it's also possible to catch buses from Weining to **Zhaotong** and **Qujing** in Yunnan, for connections to Xichang (Sichuan) and Kunming respectively.

Xingyi and the Maling Canyon

The scene of sporadic fighting between the Guomindang and locally organized guerrillas before the PLA took control in 1951, **XINGYI** is a small, tidy city surrounded by occasionally dramatic limestone scenery about 250km southwest from Anshun on the Yunnanese border. It's also a stop on the **Nanning–Kunming railway**, making it a more useful place to aim for than you might guess from its otherwise remote location; the town also enjoys a year-round supply of fresh fruit and vegetables as a result.

With low hills rising all around, Xingyi's kilometre-wide centre is south of the insignificant **Wantang stream**, where a small web of lanes converge on **Panjiang Square**, a paved oval surrounded by a two-storey ring of department stores. There's not really much to see in town, though it's a relaxed place and you might spot a few Dahua Miao with boldly patterned capes in back-lane markets; mostly the attractions comprise a couple of low-key parks, and a few old teahouses populated by water-pipe-puffing patrons along the Wantang's banks. There's meant to be a **Nationalities Museum** too, but it takes some finding – ask at the hotel.

Xingyi's **train station** is about 10km east of town, connected by minibuses; most trains bound for Kunming, Baise, or Nanning pass through either late at night or very early in the morning. The **two long-distance bus stations** are just east of the centre on streamside Hunan Jie, and about a kilometre west on Xihu Lu; both handle sleepers to Anshun, Guizhou, Kunming, Baise and Nanning. For local traffic, there's a **minibus depot** just past the east bus station on Hunan Jie. The best **place to stay** is about 700m south of Panjiang

Square at the *Panjiang Binguan*, at the end of Panjiang Xi Lu (☎0859/3223456; ❸, dorms ¥25); the similar *Xingyi Binguan* (☎0859/3111111; ❸) is 1km east of the centre on Ruijin Lu. The *Panjiang*'s **restaurant** is good and even has a basic English menu, otherwise look for noodle-soup and dog hotpot kitchens around town.

The area's highlight is the **Maling Canyon**, a tortuous, fifteen-kilometre river gorge northeast of Xingyi featuring rapids, waterfalls, deep cliffs, and hanging vegetation. There are two sections: the **upper** part is 25km from town and of most interest for **white-water rafting** (arranged through accommodation); while the **lower section** is 15km away and makes for a good couple of hours' walking – catch an **Anlong**-bound minibus from the Hunan Jie depot (¥3), or charter a taxi (¥15). Entry costs ¥30, with flagstoned paths leading down into the gorge and then heading upstream, and suspension bridges link tracks along both sides of the river. It's all pretty spectacular, with the ice-blue water twisting into ribbon falls and rapids, the high gorge walls green and dripping with moisture – the only downside is agricultural runoff foaming into the gorge from the western side.

Travel details

Trains

Anshun to: Guiyang (10 daily; 2hr); Kunming (10 daily; 13hr); Liupanshui/Shuicheng (12 daily; 3hr).
Baise to: Kunming (3 daily; 11hr); Nanning (5 daily; 4hr); Xingyi (4 daily; 5hr).
Beihai to: Nanning (4 daily; 3hr 30min).
Guilin to: Changsha (5 daily; 8hr); Guangzhou (2 daily; 14hr); Guiyang (4 daily; 16hr); Kunming (2 daily; 30hr); Liuzhou (13 daily; 2hr 30min–4hr); Nanning (6 daily; 6hr 30min–8hr).
Guiyang to: Anshun (10 daily; 2hr); Beijing (2 daily; 32hr); Changsha (4 daily; 16hr); Chengdu (3 daily; 17hr); Chongqing (7 daily; 10hr); Guangzhou (6 daily; 28hr); Guilin (4 daily; 16hr); Huaihua (7 daily; 8hr); Kaili (9 daily; 4hr); Kunming (10 daily; 12hr); Liupanshui/Shuicheng (12 daily; 5hr); Liuzhou (4 daily; 14hr); Shanghai (3 daily; 35hr); Yuping (7 daily; 8hr); Zhenyuan (7 daily; 7hr); Zunyi (9 daily; 3hr).
Kaili to: Changsha (4 daily; 12hr); Guiyang (9 daily; 4hr); Huaihua (7 daily; 5hr); Yuping (7 daily; 3hr); Zhenyuan (7 daily; 3hr).
Liupanshui to: Anshun (12 daily; 3hr); Guiyang (12 daily; 5hr); Kunming (10 daily; 8hr).
Liuzhou to: Changsha (5 daily; 10hr); Guilin (13 daily; 2hr 30min–4hr); Hengyang (5 daily; 8hr); Nanning (7 daily; 4–6hr).
Nanning to: Baise (5 daily; 4hr); Beihai (4 daily; 3hr 30min); Beijing (1 daily; 29hr); Changsha (5 daily; 15hr); Guangzhou (2 daily; 15hr); Guilin (6 daily; 6hr 30min–8hr); Kunming (3 daily; 14hr 30min); Liuzhou (7 daily; 4–6hr); Pingxiang (2 daily; 5hr); Tuolong/Ningming (2 daily; 3hr); Xingyi (3 daily; 8hr 30min).
Pingxiang to: Nanning (2 daily; 5hr); Tuolong/Ningming (2 daily; 1hr).
Xingyi to: Baise (4 daily; 5hr); Kunming (3 daily; 5hr); Nanning (3 daily; 8hr 30min).
Zhenyuan to: Guiyang (7 daily; 7hr); Huaihua (7 daily; 3hr 20min); Kaili (7 daily; 3hr); Yuping (7 daily; 1hr 10min).
Zunyi to: Chongqing (7 daily; 7hr); Guiyang (9 daily; 3hr).

Buses

Anshun to: Guiyang (2hr); Xingyi (8hr).
Baise to: Jingxi (4hr); Kunming (12hr); Nanning (6hr).
Beihai to: Nanning (5hr); Wuzhou (8hr).
Guilin to: Guangzhou (22hr); Hengyang (12hr); Liuzhou (3hr); Longsheng (2hr); Nanning (8hr); Sanjiang (4hr); Wuzhou (8hr); Yangshuo (1hr 30min).
Guiping to: Jintian (1hr); Liuzhou (4hr); Nanning (4hr 30min); Wuzhou (3hr 30min).
Guiyang to: Anshun (2hr); Huangguoshu (4hr); Kaili (5hr); Kunming (24hr); Nanning (24hr); Rongjiang (10hr); Tongren (10hr); Xingyi (12hr); Zunyi (5hr).
Kaili to: Chong An (2hr); Guiyang (5hr); Leishan (1hr 30min); Rongjiang (6hr); Shibing (3hr); Shidong (4hr); Taijiang (2hr); Zhenyuan (6hr).
Liupanshui to: Weining (4hr 30min); Xingyi (12hr).

Liuzhou to: Guilin (3hr); Guiping (4hr); Nanning (5hr); Wuzhou (8hr); Yangshuo (5hr).
Nanning to: Baise (6hr); Beihai (5hr); Guangzhou (20hr); Guilin (8hr); Guiping (4hr 30min); Kunming (36hr); Liuzhou (5hr); Ningming (4hr); Pingxiang (5hr); Wuzhou (8hr); Yangshuo (7hr).
Pingxiang to: Nanning (5hr); Ningming (1hr).
Sanjiang to: Baxie (1hr 30min); Chengyang (40min); Diping (2hr); Guilin (4hr); Liping (9hr); Longsheng (2hr); Mapang (2hr); Zhaoxing (4hr).
Weining to: Liupanshui (4hr 30min).
Wuzhou to: Beihai (8hr); Guangzhou (9hr); Guilin (8hr); Guiping (3hr 30min); Liuzhou (8hr); Nanning (8hr); Yangshuo (7hr); Zhaoxing (7hr).
Xingyi to: Anshun (8hr); Guiyang (12hr); Kunming (12hr); Liupanshui (12hr).
Yangshuo to: Guilin (1hr 30min); Liuzhou (5hr); Nanning (7min); Wuzhou (7hr).
Zhaoxing to: Diping (2hr); Liping (4hr); Sanjiang (4hr).
Zunyi to: Chishui (8–12hr); Guiyang (5hr).

Ferries

Beihai to: Haikou (2 daily; 10hr).

Flights

In addition to the domestic flights listed, there are international flights out of Guilin to Korea and Japan, and from Nanning to Thailand and Vietnam.
Guilin to: Beijing (3 daily; 2hr 15min); Changsha (5 weekly; 1hr 20min); Chengdu (1 daily; 1hr 20min); Chongqing (2 weekly; 1hr); Guangzhou (3 daily; 50min); Guiyang (1 daily; 50min); Hong Kong (5 weekly; 1hr); Kunming (1 daily; 1hr 15min); Shanghai (3 daily; 2hr); Shenzhen (2 daily; 1hr); Xi'an (2 daily; 1hr 30min); Zhuhai (3 weekly; 1hr).
Guiyang to: Beijing (2 daily; 2hr 30min); Chengdu (1 daily; 1hr); Guangzhou (2 daily; 1hr 30min); Guilin (1 daily; 50min); Hong Kong (3 weekly; 1hr 30min); Kunming (1 daily; 55min); Nanning (1 daily; 1hr); Shanghai (1 daily; 2hr); Shenzhen (1 daily; 1hr 30min); Wuhan (1 daily; 1hr 20min).
Nanning to: Beijing (1 daily; 3hr); Guangzhou (2 daily; 55min); Guilin (1 daily; 50min); Guiyang (1 daily; 1hr); Haikou (1 daily; 50min); Hanoi (2 weekly; 50min); Hong Kong (3 weekly; 1hr); Kunming (at least 1 daily; 1hr); Shanghai (1 daily; 2hr 15min); Shantou (1 weekly; 1hr 20min); Shenzhen (1 daily; 55min); Xiamen (2 weekly; 2hr).

CHAPTER 11

Highlights

* **Kunming's bars** Check out the jumping nightlife of one of China's most relaxed cities. See p.863
* **Dali** An ancient town with an enjoyable, laid-back travellers' ghetto offering café society and lush scenery. See p.874
* **Lijiang** Deservedly popular Naxi town of charming winding alleyways. See p.881
* **Tiger Leaping Gorge** Relax for a few days on the top ridge of this dramatic gorge, trekking between farmstead homestays. See p.887
* **Lugu Lake** Stay with matriarchal tribal people on the banks of a turquoise mountain lake. See p.889
* **Deqin mountain** Dramatic jagged scenery in China's remote Shangri-La. See p.891
* **Ruili** A boisterous border town of traders and smugglers with lovely temples and countryside a short bike ride away. See p.898
* **Trekking in Xishuangbanna** Tramp through the jungle in a region populated by many different ethnic groups, all with their own distinctive dress and customs. See p.904

11

Yunnan

Yunnan has always stood apart from the rest of China, set high on the empire's "barbarous and pestilential" southwestern frontiers and shielded from the rest of the nation by the unruly, mountainous provinces of Sichuan and Guizhou. Within this single province, unmatched in the complexity and scope of its history, landscape and peoples, you'll find a mix of geography, climates and nationalities that elsewhere on Earth take entire continents to express. This diversity makes Yunnan as elusive a place for the modern traveller to come to grips with as it was for successive dynasties to govern, and it's rare to feel that you've done more than obtain the most superficial of impressions.

The northeast of the province is fairly flat and productive, seat of the attractive capital, **Kunming**, whose mild climate earned Yunnan its name, meaning literally "South of the Clouds". Increasingly touristed, it's nonetheless a charming area, with enjoyable day-trips to nearby scenic marvels, and easy access to a varied bag of little-visited sights southeast towards the border with **Vietnam**.

West of Kunming, the Yunnan plateau rises to serrated, snowbound peaks extending north **to Tibet** and surrounding the ancient historic towns of **Dali** and **Lijiang**, while farther west is subtropical **Dehong**, a busy trading region and unlikely Chinese holiday destination on the central **border with Burma**. Yunnan's deep south comprises a further isolated stretch of this frontier, which reaches down to the tropical forests and paddy fields of **Xishuangbanna**, a botanic, zoological and ethnic cornucopia abutting Burma and **Laos** – about as far from Han China as it's possible to be.

Dwelling in this stew of border markets, mountains, jungles, lakes, temples, modern political intrigue and remains of vanished kingdoms are 28 recognized **ethnic groups**, the greatest number in any single province. Providing a quarter of the population and a prime reason to visit Yunnan in themselves, the indigenous list includes Dai and Bai, Wa, Lahu, Hani, Jingpo, Nu, Naxi and Lisu, plus a host shared with other provinces or adjoining nations. Though much of what you'll initially glean of their cultures is put on for tourists, anyone with even a couple of days to spare in Xishuangbanna or Lijiang can begin to flesh out this image. With more time you can look for shyer, remoter groups leading lives less influenced by the modern world.

Yunnan's scale makes travel very time-consuming and, whatever your usual preferences, it's tempting to **fly** occasionally. Fortunately Yunnan Air is one of China's better airlines, and a good excuse to avoid retracing a back-wrenching, four-day bus journey. The state of country **buses and roads** is often surprisingly good, though, and whatever their condition, it's an undeniable achievement that some routes exist at all. Make sure you travel at least briefly along

the famous **Burma Road** between Kunming and the western border, built with incredible determination during the 1930s. There's a limited **rail network** inside Yunnan – one service down through the southeast to the Vietnamese border, and a line to Xiaguan, near Dali – though Kunming is well linked to the rest of the country via Sichuan and Guizhou. The **weather** is generally moderate throughout the year, though northern Yunnan has cold winters and heavy snow up around the Tibetan border, while the south is always warm, with a torrential summer wet season.

One factor confusing travel in the border regions is the oscillating open status of various areas although, technically, almost all of the province is accessible to foreigners. The causes for closures vary from dangerous roads to reported outbreaks of plague, but it's often due to the army looking for illegal cross-border traffic in cars, timber, gems and **opiates**. Most of the world's heroin originates in Burma and is funnelled through China to overseas markets. Officially, the Yunnanese government is tough on the drug trade, executing traffickers, forcibly rehabilitating addicts and intercepting around twice the quantity of heroin netted by Thai officials in any one year. All this means that, open or not, there are military **checkpoints** on many rural roads, where you'll have to show passports, and it is possible that you may be fined and turned around if you wander too far off-track. It pays to be polite, and things are often easier if you avoid appearing fluent in Chinese in these circumstances.

Some history

Yunnan has been inhabited for a very long time, with evidence reaching back through galleries of Stone Age rock art to two 1.5-million-year-old teeth found near the northern town of Yuanmou. Records of civilization, however, are far more recent. According to the Han historian Sima Qian, the Chinese warrior prince **Zhuang Qiao** founded the pastoral **Dian Kingdom** in eastern Yunnan during the third century BC, though it's probable that he simply became chief of an existing nation. The Dian were a slave society, who vividly recorded their daily life and ceremonies involving human sacrifice in sometimes gruesome **bronze models** unearthed from contemporary tombs. The kingdom was acknowleged by China in 109 BC, its ruler receiving military aid and a golden seal from the emperor **Wu**, who hoped to control the Southern Silk Road through to India. But the collapse of the Han empire in 204 AD was followed by the dissolution of Dian into private statelets which were absorbed during the eighth century by the emerging **Nanzhao Kingdom**, based around Dali.

Politically and culturally, the Nanzhao and its successors managed to dominate large parts of Southeast Asia before succumbing in the thirteenth century to the armies of **Kublai Khan**. Directly controlled by China for the first time, for a while Yunnan served as a remote dustbin for political troublemakers, thereby escaping the population explosions, wars and migrations that plagued central China. But the Mongol invasion had also introduced a large **Muslim population** to the province, who, angered by their deteriorating status under the Chinese, staged a **rebellion** in 1856, storming Kunming and briefly managing to establish an independent state at Dali. Millions died in the rebellion's suppression, and a wasted Yunnan was left to local bandits and private armies for the following half-century.

Strangely, it was the **Japanese invasion** during the 1930s that sparked a resurgence of the province's fortunes. Blockaded into southwestern China, the **Guomindang government** initiated great programmes of rail and road building through the region, though they never really controlled Yunnan. Moreover, their poor treatment of minority groups made the Red Army's cause all the more attractive when civil war resumed in 1945. Liberation came smoothly, but the **Communists**' good intentions of coexistence with minorities, better hospitals, schools and communications were badly stalled during the Cultural Revolution and then, in the 1980s, by the war with Vietnam, and it's only now that Yunnan is finally benefiting from its forced association with the rest of the country. Never agriculturally rich – only a tenth of the land is considered arable – the province looks to mineral resources, tourism and its potential as a future conduit between China and the much discussed, but as yet unformed, trading bloc of **Vietnam**, **Laos**, **Thailand and Burma**. Though political snags have slowed its formation, should these countries ever form an unrestricted economic alliance, the amount of trade passing through Yunnan would be immense – a resurrection of the old Silk Road – and highways, rail and air services have already been laid for the day the borders open freely.

Kunming and the southeast

Every visitor to Yunnan at some point finds themselves in **Kunming**, the province's comfortable, fair-weather capital and transport hub. Though the city initially appears blandly modern, its character is partially salvaged by surrounding temples and fine lake-and-limestone-hill landscapes. **Southeast**, both road and rail extend all the way down to the **Vietnamese border**, taking you within striking distance of some fine scenery, old architecture, and some offbeat sights to slow you down en route to the crossing.

Kunming

Basking 2000m above sea level in the fertile heart of the Yunnan plateau, **KUNMING** does its best to live up to its English title as the City of Eternal Spring. However, until recently it was considered a savage frontier settlement,

Kunming and around

Kunming	昆明	***kūnmíng***
Confucian Temple	文庙	*wénmiào*
Cuihu Park	翠湖公园	*cuìhú gōngyuán*
Daguan Park	大观公园	*dàguān gōngyuán*
Eastern Pagoda	东寺塔	*dōngsì tǎ*
Kunming City Museum	昆明市博物馆	*kūnmíngshì bówùguǎn*
Mosque	南城清真寺	*nánchéng qīngzhēn sì*
Pet Market	宠物市场	*chǒngwù shìchǎng*
Western Pagoda	西寺塔	*xīsì tǎ*
Yuantong Si	圆通寺	*yuántōng sì*
Yunnan Provincial Museum	云南省博物馆	*yúnnánshěng bówùguǎn*
Zoo	动物园	*dòngwù yuán*
Accommodation		
Camellia	茶花宾馆	*cháhuā bīnguǎn*
Chuncheng	春城饭店	*chūnchéng fàndiàn*
Cuihu	翠湖宾馆	*cuìhú bīnguǎn*
Golden Dragon	金龙饭店	*jīnlóng fàndiàn*
Holiday Inn	假日酒店	*jiàrì jiǔdiàn*
Kunhu	昆湖饭店	*kūnhú fàndiàn*
Kunming	昆明饭店	*kūnmíng fàndiàn*
Kunming Youth Hostel	昆明国际青年旅社	*kūnmíng guójì qīngnián lǚshè*
Eating and drinking		
Camel Bar	骆驼酒吧	*luòtuó jiǔbā*
Fuhua Yuan	福华园	*fúhuá yuán*
Hump Across the Himalayas	金马碧鸡坊金	*jīnmǎ bìjī fǎngjīn*
King Dragon Regional Cuisine Village	元龙风味城	*yuánlóng fēngwèichéng*
Mamafu's	妈妈付餐厅	*māmāfù cāntīng*
Zhen Xing	振兴	*zhènxīng*

and authorities began to realize the city's promise only when people exiled here during the Cultural Revolution refused offers to return home to eastern China, preferring Kunming's more relaxed life, better climate and friendlier inhabitants. Today, the city's immediate face is an ordinary blend of broad, monochrome main roads and glassy modern office blocks, but beneath this there's an air of satisfied wellbeing in the crowded restaurants, new bars, bustling streets and markets supplying year-round fresh produce. The people, too, are mellow enough to mix typically Chinese garrulousness with introspective pleasures, such as quietly greeting the day with a stiff hit of Yunnanese tobacco from fat, brass-bound bamboo pipes. There are other novelties – clean pavements enforced by on-the-spot fines, an orderly traffic system, and a low-profile but sizeable gay community – suggesting that Kunming's two million or so residents enjoy a quality of life above that of most urban Chinese.

Historically the domain of Yunnan's earliest inhabitants and first civilization, Kunming long profited from its position on the caravan roads through to Burma and Europe and was visited in the thirteenth century by Marco Polo, who found the locals of **Yachi Fu** (Duck Pond Town) using cowries for cash, enjoying their meat raw, and inviting guests to sleep with their womenfolk. Little of the city's wealth survived the 1856 Muslim rebellion, when most Buddhist sites in the capital were razed, or events some forty years later, when an uprising against working conditions on the **Kunming–Haiphong rail line** saw 300,000 labourers executed after France shipped in weapons to suppress the revolt. (The line, designed by the French so that they could tap Yunnan's mineral resources for their colonies in Indochina, was only completed in 1911.) Twenty-five years later, **war with Japan** brought a flock of wealthy east-coast refugees to the city, whose money helped to establish Kunming as an industrial and manufacturing base for the wartime government in Chongqing. The allies provided essential support for this, importing materials along the Burma Road from British-held Burma, and, when that was lost to the Japanese, through the volunteer US-piloted **Flying Tigers**, who flew in supplies over the Himalayas from British bases in India. The city consolidated its position as a supply depot during the Vietnam War and subsequent border clashes, though during the **Cultural Revolution** buildings that missed the attentions of nineteenth-century vandals perished at the hands of the Red Guards. Virtually all that remained were cleared when the city centre was rebuilt in its current "modern" style to impress visitors attending the **1999 World Horticultural Expo**. Survivals include a couple of temples, the long-established **university** and a **Minorities' Institute** set up in the 1950s to promote mutual understanding among Yunnan's multifaceted population.

Since the mid-1980s, Kunming has also enjoyed snowballing tourism and foreign investment. Neighbouring nations such as Thailand trace their ancestries back to Yunnan and have proved particularly willing to channel funds into the capital. The city has become ever more developed and accessible as a result, an easy place to experience the bustle of a healthy Chinese city, with good food, warm summers and tolerably cool, bright winters. It's also just a short hop to temples and landscapes surrounding the sizeable lake, **Dian Chi**, and the celebrated **Stone Forest**.

Orientation, arrival, city transport and accommodation

Kunming has few natural landmarks to help guide you around, but its layout is uncomplicated. The city hangs off two main thoroughfares: **Beijing Lu** forms the north–south axis, passing just east of the centre as it runs for 5km between the city's two train stations; while **Dongfeng Lu** crosses it halfway along, divided into east (Dongfeng Dong Lu), middle (Dongfeng Zhong Lu) and west (Dongfeng Xi Lu) sections as it cuts right through the business centre. The far end runs out of the city as **Renmin Xi Lu**, the first leg of the Burma Road. Most of the city's accommodation lies along Dongfeng Dong Lu and the southern half of Beijing Lu, while the majority of specific sights are north and west of the centre around Dongfeng Xi Lu and **Cuihu Park**. Circling most of this is the city's first highway ring road, **Huancheng Lu**, though others are planned.

Moving on from Kunming

The **airport bus** (¥5) leaves from outside the Yunnan Air headquarters on Tuodong Lu – check with them inside for bus departure times, and be prepared to take a taxi (¥15) if the bus doesn't materialize. The journey takes about thirty minutes, and it's recommended that you get to the airport with two hours to spare. As well as flights to all major Chinese cities, there are regular services to Vientiane, Rangoon, Singapore and Bangkok (see "Travel details" at the end of the chapter). Yunnan Air is very helpful and organized, and can also book you on other airlines out of Kunming.

At **Kunming train station**, you'll find the booking office on the east side of the vast station square, with windows open 6.30am–midnight. When staffed, the **ticket service desk** here is pretty helpful and will fill you in on which queue to join. Trains run **north to Chengdu** – try breaking your journey at Xichang in southern Sichuan (see p.951) – **southeast** via Xingyi to Baise and Nanning in Guangxi (pp.812–818), and **east through Guizhou**, via Liupanshui, Anshun and Guiyang (pp.824–848), into the rest of the country. Tickets are sold three days in advance and, if you plan ahead, it's not difficult to get what you're after.

Trains to **Hekou and Vietnam** leave from the **North train station**, and you have to buy tickets there – take bus #23 up Beijing Lu. Hidden away at the northeast corner of the station, the ticket office's advertised hours are 6am–10.40pm, but don't take this too literally. There's currently one afternoon train, which takes about 16 hours to reach Hekou (a seat is ¥35, berths around ¥90), and 32 hours to Hanoi (hard sleeper lower bunk ¥175, upper bunk ¥235).

At Kunming's main **long-distance bus station**, the ticket office is computerized and staff are helpful, with standard, luxury, express and sleeper buses departing for all over Yunnan and neighbouring provinces – but finding the right vehicle out the back can be a protracted business. Keep a tight hold on your luggage, as plenty of people get something pinched either at the station or in transit. You can also catch standard and sleeper buses to Dali, Jinghong and elsewhere in Yunnan from the depot across the road from the main bus station. If you're taking the long bumpy road to Jinghong, consider the luxury bus, which takes 16 hours and costs ¥152; the standard bus takes 21 hours and costs ¥119. There's also a useful luxury service to Xiaguan (for Dali), which leaves hourly from 8am to 7pm, takes four hours (two less than the regular service) and costs ¥103, and one to Lijiang which takes only nine hours and costs ¥152. These buses are new and feature hostesses and even onboard toilets. Other useful destinations covered by this this include Zhongdian, Jinghong and Hekou (11hr; ¥95).

Leaving China by road into Vietnam and Laos is also possible, through the respective crossings at Hekou in southeastern Yunnan (p.872) or Bian Mao Zhan in Xishuangbanna (p.914). At the time of writing, foreigners entering Burma had to fly in to Rangoon – no overland entry was allowed – and had to change US$200 for their stay. See p.864 for consulate and visa details.

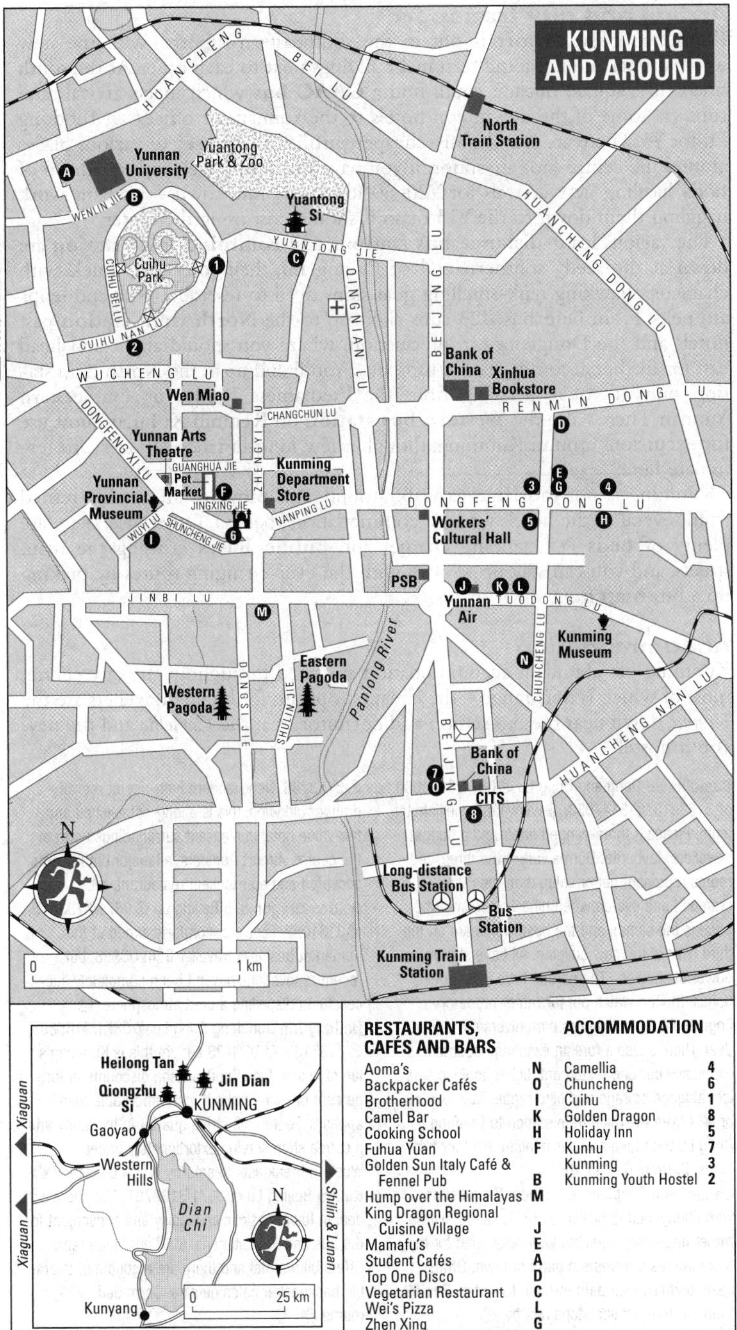
KUNMING AND AROUND
HUANCHENG BEI LU
North Train Station
Yunnan University
Yuantong Park & Zoo
Yuantong Si
YUANTONG JIE
WENLIN JIE
Cuihu Park
CUIHU BEI LU
CUIHU NAN LU
Western Bus Station
HUANCHENG DONG LU
QINGNIAN LU
BEIJING LU
Bank of China
Xinhua Bookstore
WUCHENG LU
Wen Miao
CHANGCHUN LU
RENMIN DONG LU
DONGFENG XI LU
Yunnan Arts Theatre
ZHENGYI LU
GUANGHUA JIE
Kunming Department Store
Yunnan Provincial Museum
Pet Market
JINGXING JIE
NANPING LU
DONGFENG DONG LU
WUYI LU
SHUNCHENG JIE
Workers' Cultural Hall
PSB
Yunnan Air
TUODONG LU
JINBI LU
Kunming Museum
Panlong River
CHUNCHENG LU
Eastern Pagoda
Western Pagoda
DONGSI JIE
SHULIN JIE
HUANCHENG NAN LU
Bank of China
CITS
Long-distance Bus Station
Bus Station
Kunming Train Station
N
0
1 km
Heilong Tan
Jin Dian
Qiongzhu Si
KUNMING
Gaoyao
Xiaguan
Western Hills
Dian Chi
Shilin & Lunan
Xiaguan
Kunyang
Jinghong
0
25 km
RESTAURANTS, CAFÉS AND BARS
Aoma's N
Backpacker Cafés O
Brotherhood I
Camel Bar K
Cooking School H
Fuhua Yuan F
Golden Sun Italy Café & Fennel Pub B
Hump over the Himalayas M
King Dragon Regional Cuisine Village J
Mamafu's E
Student Cafés A
Top One Disco D
Vegetarian Restaurant C
Wei's Pizza L
Zhen Xing G
ACCOMMODATION
Camellia 4
Chuncheng 6
Cuihu 1
Golden Dragon 8
Holiday Inn 5
Kunhu 7
Kunming 3
Kunming Youth Hostel 2

Arrival and city transport

Kunming's busy **airport** is out in the southeastern suburbs, with the new international and domestic terminal buildings next to each other. At the south side of the square outside you'll find a **CAAC bus** which meets arrivals and runs via some of the downtown hotels to the Yunnan Air offices on Tuodong Lu for ¥5. There are also slightly cheaper **public minibuses** to various places around the centre (not an option if you have much luggage), and squadrons of **taxis** hassling new arrivals for ¥20–80 for a ride into town – it's hard work haggling them down to the ¥15 or so it should cost using the meter.

The various **long-distance bus stations** and **Kunming train station** are down at the seedy southern end of Beijing Lu, their forecourts thick with characters hawking rank-smelling goat skins dyed to resemble tiger and leopard pelts. From here, bus #23 runs right up to the **North train station** past hotels and the Dongfeng Lu intersection, where you should alight and head east for further accommodation prospects. You'll end up at the North train station only if you're arriving from the Vietnamese border or southeastern Yunnan. There's also the **Western bus station** on Renmin Xi Lu, of most use for excursions around Kunming, though a few long-distance services also terminate here.

Kunming is not too large to walk around, and **bicycles** are readily rented from several of the hotels (see "Accommodation" below). Otherwise, there are plenty of **taxis** (¥8 standing charge) and **public buses** cruising the main streets, and you can stay up to date with the ever-changing routes by picking up a bus **map** from street sellers.

Accommodation

Kunming has abundant accommodation scattered throughout the city centre, most of which is mid-range – the cheapest options for budget travellers are the *Kunhu*, down near the bus station and dormitories at the *Camellia* and the new youth hostel.

Camellia 96 Dongfeng Dong Lu ⓣ0871/3163000 or 3162918, ⓕ3147033, ⓦwww.kmcamelliahotel.com. Pleasant three-winged affair and a budget travellers' favourite. Dorms vary – the three-bed rooms represent better value than the rather cramped and overcrowded nine-bed rooms (the price is the same), and the best rooms are on the third floor of the new building. All have shared powerful showers. The garden here is an added bonus, though watch out for rather predatory English students. Doubles are universally a good deal. There's also a foreign exchange counter, expensive bar and restaurant, ticket booking service, luggage storage and bike rental. Take bus #2 or #23 from the main train station to Donfeng Dong Lu then take any bus heading east for two stops. Dorm beds ¥35, ❸

Chuncheng Dongfeng Xi Lu, near the junction with Zhengyi Lu ⓣ0871/3633271. Faded, with a rather oppressive feel, but well positioned for the more interesting western parts of town. Offers basic doubles with bath through to suites. Bus #2 from the train station stops nearby. ❷

Cuihu Cuihu Nan Lu ⓣ0871/5158888, ⓕ5153286. New, modern high-rise at rear of drabber old wing, this is a long-established and fair-value hotel in pleasant surroundings north of the centre. Airport transfers, all major credit cards accepted and an excellent restaurant. ❺

Golden Dragon 575 Beijing Lu ⓣ0871/3133015, ⓕ3131082. Four-star comforts aimed at the upmarket business traveller from US$88, but recent renovations haven't been completely successful in dispelling a tired atmosphere. ❽

Holiday Inn Dongfeng Dong Lu ⓣ0871/3165888, ⓕ3135189. At US$125 a night this is Kunming's lap of luxury, though off-season discounts of forty percent or more make it more affordable than it appears. Features a string quartet in the lobby and a coffee shop serving extortionately priced Western breakfasts to smartly dressed visitors. ❽

Kunhu Beijing Lu ⓣ0871/3133737. The cheapest deal in town, basic, clean, noisy and convenient for the bus and train stations. Staff are indifferent. Offers bike rental and there are a couple of tolerable backpacker cafés outside. Dorm beds ¥20, rooms ❷–❸

Kunming Dongfeng Dong Lu ⓣ0871/3162063 or

3162172, ⓕ3163784. A big, standard Chinese hotel with reasonable services and Korean restaurant, also offering bikes for rent. It's not cheap, though – the less expensive rooms are in the older, south wing. ❼

Kunming Youth Hostel 94 Cuihu Nan Lu ⓣ0871/5175395, ⓕ5167131, ⓔyouthhostel.km@sohu.com. New clean, and efficient, this place will soon be giving the *Camellia* and the *Kunhu* a run for their money. Pleasantly located by Cuihu Park, and with helpful, English-speaking staff, the hostel offers not just basic, four-bed dorms but the best cheap doubles in the city. Also has kitchen facilities and bike rental. Take bus #2 from the train station, alight at Xiao Xi Men stop, and look for the YHA triangle on the *Zhengxie Hotel* – the hostel is just behind. Small discount for IYHA members. Dorm beds ¥25, ❷

The City

Kunming's public focus is the huge square outside the grandiose **Workers' Cultural Hall** at the Beijing Lu/Dongfeng Lu intersection, alive in the mornings with regimented crowds warming up on hip pivots and shuttlecock games. Later in the day it's somewhere to consult a fortune-teller, or receive a shoulder and back massage from the hard-fingered blind practitioners who pounce on passers-by; you might also catch weekend amateur theatre here, too. Rapidly being modernized, the city's true centre is west of here across the **Panlong River**, outside the modern Kunming Department Store at the **Nanping Lu/Zhengyi Lu crossroads**, a densely crowded shopping precinct packed with clothing and hi-fi stores. In getting here you'll pass beneath plenty of new high-rises, while the river itself, though black and oily, is at least nicely landscaped – the general impression is that, unlike many Chinese cities, some time, trouble and planning is behind these modernizations. The centre itself is an area of importance to Kunming's Hui population, and **Shuncheng Jie** – the last old street in the city, and an essential wander for as long as it survives – forms a **Muslim quarter**, full of wind-dried beef and mutton carcasses, pitta bread and raisin sellers, and huge woks of roasting coffee beans being earnestly stirred with shovels. Rising behind a supermarket one block north off Zhengyi Lu, **Nancheng Qingzhen Si** is the city's new **mosque**, its green dome and chevron-patterned minaret visible from afar and built on the site of an earlier Qing edifice.

Running west off Zhengyi Jie just past the mosque, **Jingxing Jie** leads into one of the more bizarre corners of the city, with Kunming's huge **pet market** convening daily in the streets connecting it with northerly, parallel Guanghua Jie. At least at weekends, this is no run-of-the-mill mix of kittens and grotesque goldfish: rare, multicoloured songbirds twitter and squawk in the wings, while furtive hawkers display geckos, monkey-like loris and other endangered oddities illegally "liberated" from Xishuangbanna's forests. There are plants here, too, along with **antique and curio** booths – this is somewhere to find dirt-cheap coins and Cultural Revolution mementoes, bamboo pipes and prayer rugs – from where backstreets continue up through to the city's northwest. Heading this way, it's worth pausing in the small **grounds of Wen Miao** (¥1.5), a vanished Confucian temple off the western end of Changchun Lu. There's an avenue of pines, an ancient pond and pavilion, and beds of bamboo, azaleas and potted palms – a quiet place where old men play chess and drink tea.

Yunnan Provincial Museum

About 500m west of the centre along Dongfeng Xi Lu and the #5 bus route, the **Yunnan Provincial Museum** (Mon–Thurs 9am–5pm, Fri 9am–2pm; last entry an hour before the museum closes; ¥15) has its moments, though the collection of clothes and simpering photographs near the entrance fails to inform on Yunnan's cultural groups. Far better are the **Dian bronzes** on the second floor, dating back more than two thousand years to the Warring States Period and excavated from tombs on the shores of Dian Chi, south of Kunming. The largest pieces include an ornamental plate of a tiger attacking an ox and a **coffin** in the shape of a bamboo house, but lids from **storage drums** used to hold cowries are the most impressive, decorated with dioramas of figurines fighting, sacrificing oxen and men and, rather more peacefully, posing with their families and farmyard animals outside their homes. A replica of the Chinese imperial **gold seal** given to the Dian king early on in the second century implies that his aristocratic slave society had the tacit approval of the Han emperor. Upstairs again is a **prehistoric museum** with enjoyably awful plaster models and casts of locally found trilobites, armoured fishes, bits of dinosaur and early human remains.

Cuihu Park, Yuantong Si and the Zoo

A twenty-minute walk north of the museum via Dongfeng Xi Lu and Cuihu Nan Lu (alternatively, take bus #5 from the museum or bus #2 from the southern end of Beijing Lu), **Cuihu Park** (open at least dawn to dusk; ¥2) is predominantly lake, a good place to join thousands of others exercising, listening to storytellers, feeding wintering flocks of **gulls**, or just milling between the plum and magnolia gardens and over the maze of bridges. Immediately northwest of the park, the **Yunnan University** campus offers a glimpse of old Kunming, its partially overgrown 1920s exterior reached up a wide flight of stone steps. **Cafés** and cheap restaurants in the vicinity are the haunt of expats and students eager to practise their English – see p.862 for details.

East from Cuihu Park along Yuantong Jie is **Yuantong Si** (daily 8am–5.30pm; ¥4), northern Yunnan's major Buddhist site and an active place of pilgrimage. Newly spruced up along with the rest of the city, the Qing-vintage temple is busy and cheerful, with gardens of bright pot plants just inside the entrance. A bridge over the central pond crosses through an octagonal pavilion dedicated to a multi-armed Guanyin and white marble Sakyamuni, to the threshold of the **main hall**, where two huge central pillars wrapped in colourful, Manga-esque **dragons** support the ornate wooden ceiling. Faded frescoes on the back wall were painted in the thirteenth century, while a new annexe out the back houses a graceful gilded bronze Buddha flanked by peacocks, donated by the Thai government. Cooks in the **vegetarian restaurant** opposite on Yuantong Jie work wonders at lunchtime.

The temple sits on the southern slope of the large **Yuantong Park** (¥4), though to reach this you have to go out and follow the main roads east and around to the north. Kunming's **zoo** (daily 8am–5pm; ¥10) is up here, too, with the entrance at the corner of Yuantong Jie and Qingnian Lu on the #4 bus route. It's not the worst in China, offering nice vignettes of children stroking and feeding the deer, along with views of the city from a hilltop planted with crab apple groves.

Kunming City Museum

The highlight of the **Kunming City Museum** (Tues–Sun 10am–5pm; ¥5), west off Beijing Lu along Tuodong Lu, is the **Dali Sutra Pillar**, a 6.5-metre-high, pagoda-like Song-dynasty sculpture in pink sandstone in its own room on the ground floor. An octagonal base supports seven tiers covered in Buddha images, statues of fierce guardian gods standing on subjugated demons, and a mix of Tibetan and Chinese script, part of which is the Dharani Mantra. The rest is a dedication, identifying the pillar as being raised by the Dali regent, **Yuan Douguang**, in memory of his general **Gao Ming**. The whole thing is topped by a ring of Buddhas carrying a ball – the universe – above them. Formerly part of the defunct Dizang temple, the pillar is a powerful work, full of the energy that later seeped out of the mainstream of Chinese sculpture.

The other exhibits are a well-presented repeat of the Provincial Museum's collection. **Bronze drum** enthusiasts can examine a range from the oldest known example to relatively recent castings, allowing you to see how the typical decorations – sun and frog designs on top, long-plumed warriors in boats around the sides, tiger handles – became so stylized (for more on bronze drums, see p.815). There are cowrie-drum lids, too, and a host of other bronze pieces worth examining for nit-picking details of birds, animals and people. Other rooms contain two excellent **dioramas** of modern and Ming-dynasty Kunming, accounts (in Chinese) of the voyages of **Zheng He**, the famous Ming eunuch admiral, and five locally found **fossilized dinosaur skeletons** – including a tyranosaurus-like allosaur, and the bulky *Yunnanosaurus robustus*.

Southern Kunming

Jinbi Lu runs roughly parallel to and south of Dongfeng Lu, reached on bus #3 from Beijing Lu. Two large Tang-dynasty **pagodas** rise in the vicinity, each a solid thirteen storeys of whitewashed brick crowned with four jolly iron cockerels. South down Dongsi Jie, past another **mosque**, the entrance to the **Western Pagoda** is along a narrow lane on the right. A few jiao gain you admission to the tiny surrounding courtyard where sociable idlers while away sunny afternoons playing cards and sipping tea in the peaceful, ramshackle surroundings. The **Eastern Pagoda** is a more cosmetic, slightly tilted duplicate standing in an ornamental garden a few minutes' walk away on Shulin Jie. The temples associated with both pagodas are closed to the public.

For a change of atmosphere, ride bus #4 from Dongfeng Lu to its terminus at **Daguan Park** (daily 7am–8pm; ¥15) on Kunming's southwestern limits. Originally laid out by the energetic seventeenth-century Qing emperor Kangxi, it has been modified over the years to include a noisy funfair, photographers, snack stalls and souvenir emporiums, and is a favourite haunt of Kunming's youth. Among shady walks and pools, Daguan's focal point is **Daguan Ge**, a square, three-storeyed pavilion built to better Kangxi's enjoyment of the distant **Western Hills** and now a storehouse of calligraphy extolling the area's charms. The most famous poem here is a 118-character verse, carved into the gateposts by the Qing scholar Sun Ran, reputed to be the longest set of rhyming couplets in China. The park is set on Daguan Stream, which flows south into **Dian Chi** (see p.866), and there are frequent hour-long cruises down the waterway, lined with willows, to points along Dian's northern shore.

Eating, drinking and entertainment

Eating out is the main pleasure after dark in Kunming. Food aside, one feature of less formal Yunnanese restaurants is that they often have a communal bamboo water pipe and tobacco for their customers. Nightlife has improved vastly of late, thanks to rising incomes and a big expat population, and there are plenty of student bars, local dives and raucous discos to explore. The city has several **operatic troupes** and indigenous entertainments which include *huadeng*, a lantern dance. Indoor performances are sadly infrequent, but there are often informal shows at the weekend outside the Workers' Cultural Hall and in Cuihu Park. Keep an eye on local newspapers (or ask at your hotel) for similar activities at the Yunnan Arts Theatre on Dongfeng Xi Lu.

Yunnanese food

Yunnanese food broadly splits into three cooking styles. In the **north**, a cold, pastoral lifestyle produces dried meats, vegetables and – very unusually for China – dairy products, infused with a Muslim cuisine, a vestige of the thirteenth-century Mongolian invasion. Typical dishes include wind-cured ham (*yuntui* or *huotui*), sweetened, steamed and served with slices of bread; toasted cheese and dried yoghurt wafers (*rubing* and *rushan*); the local version of crisp-skinned duck (*shaoya*), flavoured by painting it with honey and roasting over a pine-needle fire; and *shaguoyu*, a tasty fish casserole.

Southeastern Yunnan produces the most recognizably "Chinese" food. From here comes *qiguoji*, chicken flavoured with medicinal herbs and stewed inside a specially shaped earthenware steamer, and **crossing-the-bridge noodles** (*guoqiao mixian*), probably the most famous dish in the province. A sort of individualized hotpot, the curious name comes from a tale about a Qing scholar who retired every day to a lakeside pavilion to compose poetry. His wife, an understanding soul, used to cook him lunch, but the food always cooled as she carried it from their home over the bridge to where he studied – until she hit on the idea of keeping the heat in with a layer of oil on top of his soup. It's best sampled in Kunming, where numerous places serve a huge bowl of oily, scalding chicken stock with a platter of noodles, shredded meats and vegetables, which you add along with chilli powder and spices to taste.

Not surprisingly, Yunnan's **southwestern borders** are strongly influenced by Burmese cooking methods, particularly in the use of such un-Chinese ingredients as coconut, palm sugar, cloves and turmeric. Here you'll find a vast range of soups and stews displayed in aluminium pots outside fast-turnover restaurants, roughly recognizable as **curries**, and oddities such as purple rice-flour pancakes sold at street markets. As most of these aren't generally available outside the area, however, their description and a glossary of local names appears in the relevant section (see p.898). The southwest also produces good **coffee** and red *pu'er cha*, Yunnan's best **tea**, both widely appreciated across the province.

Restaurants, cafés and bars

Kunming is stacked with Yunnanese specialities and more ordinary Chinese fare, though there's also a smattering of upmarket restaurants serving Western dishes. Back lanes running north off **Dongfeng Xi Lu** or **Jinbi Lu** have the best stalls and cheap restaurants where you can battle with the locals over grilled cheese, hotpots, fried snacks rolled in chilli powder, loaves of excellent meat-stuffed soda bread, and rich duck and chicken casseroles. **Hotels** have the most refined surroundings, while city **restaurants** tend to focus their efforts on the food, so don't be discouraged by the outward appearance of some venues. Shuncheng Jie has endless rows of cheap **Muslim** diners with glazed ducks and fresh ingredients piled up outside; mutton stews, kebabs and *lamian* – pulled noodles – are popular.

Aoma's 20 Chuncheng Lu. Western-style food and some local dishes, in an urbane and relaxed atmosphere. Their specialities are steaks, pasta and pizzas.

Backpacker cafés Beijing Lu, south of the *Kunhu Fandian*. Two crowded backpacker hang-outs offering beer, approximately Western food, bike rental, "tourist consultancies" and earwax removers.

Brotherhood Wuyi Lu. Clean and modern-looking place close to the Provincial Museum where you choose your own stuffed bean curd, bitter melon and sliced meats and cook them in a hotpot.

Cooking School Dongfeng Dong Lu, opposite the *Camellia Binguan*. The largest of a handful of local efforts serving inexpensive, fairly ordinary Chinese meals. The food isn't bad, but the service on the ground-floor canteen is – upstairs has less abrupt

staff and more comfortable furnishings. Crossing-the-bridge noodles are ¥20–40.
Fuhua Yuan Jingxing Jie. Airy, canteen-like affair in one of the most charismatic parts of town, serving crossing-the-bridge noodles and other light meals downstairs, full meals upstairs.
Golden Sun Italy Café & Fennel Pub Cuihu Bei Lu. Western-style bars aimed at expat students and teachers. Both offer imported beers and wines, coffee (even cappuccino), and Westernized Chinese dishes along with pizza, tortillas, pasta and ice cream. Happy hours at some point between 8pm and midnight, where you'll get 3-for-1 deals on bottled beer.
King Dragon Regional Cuisine Village Tuodong Lu. Huge, multi-floored affair with stalls, canteens and sit-down restaurants offering everything from local street snacks through to Cantonese banquet cuisine. Cheaper places are on the ground floor, with posher, private restaurants on successive levels. Good fun at the weekends, when it can get very crowded.
Mamafu's Owned by the same people as *Aoma's*, this cultivated café is handy for the *Camellia Hotel*.
Student cafés Tianjundian Jie. Head north up the alleyway opposite Everbright Bank on Wenlin Jie. An alley full of bars and cafés, most of which feature ads for accommodation and teachers, European meals, and cliquey Westerners. *French Café (Lan Bai Hong)* – look for the tricolour – has the best reputation, with good pastries and cakes.
Vegetarian restaurant Opposite the Yuantong Si, Yuantong Jie. This is an excellent place, reasonably priced and with an English menu and pictures of the dishes on the wall. Serves a mix of straight vegetable and imitation meat dishes – best of the latter are coconut-flavoured "spareribs" (bamboo shoots, celery and fried bean-curd skin), "chicken" and fungus rolls (dried bean curd), and "fish" (deep fried mashed potato served in a rich garlic and vinegar sauce).
Wei's Pizza In an alley north off Tuodong Lu. Long-running, popular expat café with low prices, a book exchange, wood-fired pizzas, coffee, and some unusual Chinese food, including river moss with coriander and Hakka bean curd.
Zhen Xing (Yunnan Typical Local Food) Corner of Dongfeng Dong Lu and Baita Lu. Inexpensive, unadorned restaurant with brusque staff, mostly local clientele, and simple fare that lives up to the restaurant's name. Noodles ¥3–5; pay at the counter and give the chit to the cook.

Nightlife

Kunming residents no longer have to go to Ruili for a wild night; the city is now a great place to go out, with plenty of friendly, reasonably priced venues patronized by a good mix of locals and expats, and all within walking distance. The *Hump Over the Himalayas* on Jinbi Lu is a mall (or, after a few drinks, a maze) of interlinked bars – stumble out of one and you fall straight into another. Places move in and out of favour but *Mandalay*, which offers comparatively cheap ¥10 beers, was popular at the time of writing. There's also a coffee house, sports bar and disco. The roof is used for parties and fashion shows. Once a month, the place hosts a "street dance" – basically a big rave. However, most nights out begin and are rounded off at the *Camel Bar* on Tuodong Lu. The most well-established and polished local bar, it has a lively, mixed clientele and hosts regular gigs, jam sessions and the like. Downstairs has a dance floor and a dartboard; upstairs is more laid back and makes a good place to sit over a coffee in the day. It's jumping at weekends, and always open well into the early hours. Bottled beers are ¥10–15. The cheapest drinks are available from the sprinkling of bars around the university (see above). If you can't live without cheesy techno and flashing lights, you can join Kunming's silver-suited and platform-booted finest at the *Top One Disco* on Beijing Lu. It's free to get in – though drinks cost ¥25 – and it's open till three every night.

Listings

Airlines Yunnan Air, Tuodong Lu (daily 8am–8pm; ⓣ0871/3164270 or 3138562) sells tickets for all Chinese airlines but offers discounts only on Yunnan air flights. China Southern, 433 Beijing Lu, south of the Dongfeng Lu intersection ⓣ0871/3101831; China Southwest, north of the *King World Hotel* at 160 Beijing Lu ⓣ0871/3539702, ⓕ3539700 (daily 8.30am–noon & 2–7pm); Kunming United Airlines, 13 Dongfeng Xi Lu ⓣ0871/3628592; Shanghai Airlines, 46 Dongfeng Xi Lu ⓣ0871/3138502;

International airlines in Kunming are Dragonair at in the *Golden Dragon Hotel* on Beijing Dong Lu ⓣ0871/3138592; JAL, Floor 25, *Holiday Inn*, Dongfeng Dong Lu ⓣ0871/3161230; and Thai International, next door to the *King World Hotel*, Beijing Lu ⓣ0871/3133315, ⓕ3167351 (Mon–Fri 9am–noon & 1–5pm).

Banks and exchange The main branch of the Bank of China is at the corner of Beijing Lu–Renmin Dong Lu (Mon–Fri 9–11.45am & 2.30–5.30pm) and there's a smaller branch on Huancheng Nan Lu. Some hotels also have foreign exchange counters with identical rates.

Bike rental The *Camellia*, *Kunhu* and the *Youth Hostel* rent out bikes for ¥3 an hour.

Bookshops The Xinhua Bookstore next to the Bank of China on Renmin Dong Lu has a small selection of novels in English on the third floor.

Cinema Kunming's main screen is on the south side of the Dongfeng Lu/Zhengyi Lu intersection.

Consulates Myanmar (Burma), Room 214, *Camellia Binguan*, Dongfeng Dong Lu (Mon–Fri 8.30–12am & 1–4.30pm, closed during frequent Burmese public holidays; ⓣ0871/3176609, ⓕ3178556; 28-day tourist visa issued in three working days, ¥185). Note that you have to change at least US$200 before they let you in (flight only). Laos, Ground Floor, *Camellia Binguan*, Dongfeng Dong Lu (Mon–Fri 8.30–11.30am & 1.30–4.30pm; ⓣ0871/3176623, ⓕ3178556; 7, 14 and 28-day visas issued in three working days, cost dependent on nationality but around US$40 for a 28-day visa); Thailand, in a building in front of the *Kunming* hotel on Dongfeng Dong Lu (Mon–Fri 9–11.30am; one-month transit visa ¥70, sixty-day tourist visa ¥110; various conditions apply; note that most foreigners only require a visa if they plan to spend more than a month in Thailand). Vietnamese visas for the Hekou crossing are available in China only through consulates in Hong Kong, Nanning and Beijing.

Left luggage Your accommodation may be able to help, or there are luggage offices at both train and bus stations, open dawn to evening.

Hospital Yunnan Province Red Cross hospital and emergency centre is on Qingnian Lu.

Internet Most hotels, and foreigner-oriented cafés up near the university, have Internet access, though it's considerably cheaper at the main Telecom building, on the corner of Dongfeng Lu and Beijing Lu.

Mail and telecomunications The GPO is on the southern stretch of Beijing Lu (daily 8am–8pm); post restante can also be addressed to the *Kunhu*, *Camellia* and larger hotels with their own postal desks. There are phones at the GPO, but the main Telecom building is north at the junction with Dongfeng Lu (Mon–Fri 8am–6.30pm, Sat & Sun 9am–5pm).

PSB The main office is on Beijing Lu, but the Foreign Affairs Department is at 82 Renmin Dong Lu (daily 8–11am & 1–5pm; ⓣ0871/3166191). They speak good English and are generally helpful with visa extensions.

Shopping The antique store in the grounds of the *Camellia Binguan* on Dongfeng Dong Lu has a collection of wooden panels prised off Qing-dynasty homes, silver hairpins, porcelain and some nice inkstones. For local flavour, try bamboo pipes, home-grown tobacco, and trinkets sold in backstreet markets, such as the curio stalls at the pet market. Yunnan also has a reputation as a source of rare medicines, though prices in Kunming for many of these are grossly inflated – if you're curious, check out the handful of shops south of the Beijing Lu GPO for caterpillar fungus, dragon's blood and other weird items. A "gift pack" selection of these costs ¥680.

Travel agents CITS has counters at the *Holiday Inn* (ⓣ0871/3165888), *King World Hotel* (ⓣ0871/3138888) and at Yunnan Air (ⓣ0871/3162214), and an office at 285 Huancheng Nan Lu (ⓣ0871/3554283). The *Camellia Binguan*'s private service, and the CYTS at the *Kunhu Fandian*, are recommended for all independent travellers' needs. All can organize private tours around the city and to Shilin, Dali and Xishuangbanna, and obtain train and plane (and sometimes long-distance bus) tickets. Expect commissions of at least ¥20 for bus and ¥80 for train ticket reservations. The Tibet Tourism Office in the *Camellia Binguan* arranges flights from Deqin Airport in Zhongdian to Lhasa, and the necessary permits, for ¥2400.

Around Kunming

The countryside around Kunming has enough to keep you occupied for a good few days, shuttling around on public transport or private tours out from the capital. Extraordinary sculptures make the westerly **Qiongzhu Si** the pick of local holy sites, while immediately south of Kunming is **Dian Chi**, a spectacular 270-square-kilometre spread of deep blue water dotted with the rectangular sails of fishing junks. You can boat across to the lakeside towns, but Dian's colourful sprawl is best absorbed from the nearby heights of Xi Shan, the **Western Hills**. Further afield, **Shilin**, the spectacular Stone Forest, is one of the highlights of Yunnan's package tourist trail.

Heilong Tan, Jin Dian and Tanhua Si

Three pleasant temple parks are easily visited from Kunming on public buses. Ten kilometres north on bus #10 from the North train station, **Heilong Tan** (Black Dragon Pool; daily 8am–6pm; ¥5) is set in a garden of ancient trees, full of plum blossoms in spring. The two Ming temple buildings are modest Taoist affairs dedicated to the Heavenly Emperor and other deities, while the pool itself is said to be inhabited by a dragon forced by the Immortal, Lu Dongbin, to provide a permanent source of water for the local people. It should also be haunted by a patriotic Ming scholar who zealously drowned himself and his family as a gesture of defiance in the face of invading Qing armies; his tomb stands nearby.

The same distance to the northeast on bus #11 from the North train station, the **Jin Dian** (Golden Temple; 8am–5pm; ¥5) has a convoluted history. Built in 1602 as a copy of the Taihe Hall atop Wudang Shan in Hubei province (see p.551), the original temple was shifted to a monastery on Jizu Shan near Dali 35 years later, and the current double-eaved structure was founded by the Qing rebel general Wu Sangui in 1671. Again associated with the mystical Lu Dongbin, who apparently instigated its construction, the temple is supported on a marble base and the lattices, beams and statues in the main hall are made entirely of that thoroughly Yunnanese metal, **bronze**, and house two magical swords used by Taoist warriors. The gardens here are full of fragrant camellias and weekend picnickers, and a tower on the hill behind encloses a large Ming bell from Kunming's demolished southern gates.

Tanhua Si (¥3) is 4km east of the city at the base of the Jinma Hills, over the creek and about 1km north of where the #4 bus from Renmin Dong Lu terminates. There's little to see in the heavily restored Ming Buddhist temple, but the **ornamental gardens** are pleasant, with narrow paths winding around groves of exotic trees, bamboos, peonies and azaleas. "Tanhua" is a type of magnolia which grew here in profusion before the temple was built, though now just one slender, broad-leafed tree survives in a small courtyard next to the scripture hall.

Qiongzhu Si

A fantastic array of over-the-top sculptures makes **Qiongzhu Si**, the Bamboo Temple (¥5), an essential trip from town. Facing Kunming in hills 10km to the west, you can get here either on irregular **minibuses** (¥5.5) from the Western bus station on Renmin Xi Lu, at the end of the #5 bus route; by chartering a minibus from in front of the Yunnan Arts Theatre on Dongfeng Xi Lu (¥60 for a seven-seater); or on the 8am **tour bus** from the same place, which also visits the Western Hills (see below). A dignified building with black and red woodwork standing on Yuan-dynasty foundations, the temple has been restored continually through the ages and, late in the nineteenth century, the eminent Sichuanese sculptor **Li Guangxiu** and his five assistants were engaged to embellish the main halls with five hundred clay statues of *arhats*. This they accomplished with inspired gusto, spending ten years creating the comical and grotesquely distorted crew of monks, goblins, scribes, emperors and beggars which crowd the interior – some sit rapt with holy contemplation, others smirk, roar with hysterical mirth or snarl grimly as they ride a foaming sea alive with sea monsters. Unfortunately it all proved too absurd for Li's conservative contemporaries and this was his final commission, though it's hard to see how he could possibly have bettered this work in originality. There's also a fourteenth-century **stone tablet** to seek out in the main hall recording dealings between imperial China and Yunnan in Mongolian and Chinese script, and a good **vegetarian restaurant** open at lunchtime.

Dian Chi and the Western Hills

Kunming has always owed much of its easy living to the well-watered lands surrounding **Dian Chi** (Dian Lake), which stretches for 50km south from the city. A road circuits the shore, and you could spend a couple of days hopping around from Kunming's Western bus station, though the workers' sanatoriums and recently industrialized lakeside hamlets are not greatly appealing. One place to aim for is southerly **KUNYANG**, birthplace of China's only famous navigator, the Ming-dynasty Muslim eunuch **Zheng He**, who commanded an imperial fleet on fact-finding missions to Southeast Asia, India and Africa – one of the few times in Chinese history that its rulers showed any interest in the outside world. A hill outside Kunyang has been set aside as a **park** (Zheng He Gongyuan) in his memory, complete with a temple museum and the mausoleum of Zheng's pilgrim father, **Hadji Ma**.

Far better, however, are the views of the lake from the top of Xi Shan, the well-wooded **Western Hills**, which rise to 2500m above the shore, 16km southwest of Kunming. The easiest way to get here is by catching bus #5 from Dongfeng Dong Lu to its terminus on Renmin Xi Lu, then transferring to bus #6 for the township of **GAOYAO** (last bus back to Kunming around 6pm). From Gaoyao you can either slog up to the summit 8km south in about three hours, pausing for breath and refreshment in temples along the way, or catch a minibus up. There's also the 8am **tour bus** from outside the Kunming Arts Theatre on Dongfeng Xi Lu to the top (¥15), though walking up makes the trip far more worthwhile.

The first temple is **Huating Si**, originally designed as a country retreat for Gao Zhishen, Kunming's eleventh-century ruler, in the form of a pavilion surrounded by gardens and a small pond. Developed as a Buddhist temple from the fourteenth century, it was last rebuilt in the 1920s. Today, there are some fine **statues** – especially the two gate guardians inside the entrance hall – and a moderately priced **Yunnanese restaurant**, a handy place to break your journey. Winding on through groves of ancient trees you next reach the halfway **Taihua Si**, a monastery set up by the roving Chan (Zen) sect monk **Xuan Jian** in 1306. Best known for its carelessly arranged **botanical gardens**, there's a massive gingko tree near the entrance claimed to be almost as old as the temple itself. A couple more kilometres bring you to the Taoist complex of **Sanqing Ge**, another former royal villa set on the Western Hills' highest peak. The nine halls are stacked up the slopes in a fine display of Tao style and Qing architecture, each one dedicated to a particular patriarch.

Less than a kilometre beyond Sanqing Ge the path runs into the **Dragon Gate Grotto**, a series of chambers and narrow tunnels through the hillside which took the late eighteenth-century monk **Wu Laiqing** and his successors more than seventy years to excavate, and which replaced a set of wooden stairs morticed into the cliffs. It's incredible that anyone could conceive of such a project, far less complete it with enough flair to incorporate the sculptures of Guanyin and the gods of study and righteousness which decorate niches along the way. At the end is **Grand Dragon Gate** (¥20), a precarious balcony offering magnificent views as it overhangs the wide expanse of Dian Chi.

Shilin and Lunan

Yunnan's premier natural wonder is **Shilin**, the **Stone Forest**, an exposed bed of limestone spires weathered and split into intriguing clusters, 130km east of Kunming near the town of **LUNAN**. There are many such "forests" in southwestern China, but here the black, house-sized rocks are embellished with trees and vines, steps, paths and pavilions. An enjoyable day-trip if you can accept the fairground atmosphere and crowds dutifully tagging behind their cosmetically perfect tour guides, it takes about an hour to cover slowly the main circuit through the pinnacles to **Sword Peak Pond**, an ornamental pool surrounded by particularly sharp ridges which you can climb along a narrow track leading right up across the top of the forest. This is the most frequented part of the park, with large red characters incised into famous rocks and ethnic **Sani**, a Yi subgroup, in unnaturally clean dresses strategically placed for photographers, but paths heading out towards the perimeter are far quieter and lead out to smaller, separate stone groupings in the fields beyond. You can see a bit more by staying the night, as Shilin is surrounded by Sani villages – if you do, Wednesday is **market day** in Lunan (a thirty-minute ride on a motorbike taxi from outside the park gates), where Sani sell their wares and sport embroidered costumes.

Transport to Shilin is not a problem. A comfortable option are the **day tours** run by hotels and agents in Kunming from ¥50 upwards, and there are also early morning **tour minibuses** (about ¥30) from the corner of Huancheng Nan Lu, next to the *King World Hotel* – look for the blue, bilingual sign. Note that the latter are Chinese-oriented, and involve plenty of stops at souvenir shops along the way, giving you only about two hours at Shilin. The cheapest route is to take the tourist train (¥30 return) which leaves the south station at 8.28am and arrives at 9.50am. The *Camellia Binguan* will sell you a ticket for the train and take you to it in a free minibus at 7.50am. The train returns at 3.30pm.

Otherwise, the journey takes around three hours and ends at a mess of stalls at the park gates selling poor souvenir embroideries and excellent, reasonably priced **food** – roast duck (a local speciality), pheasant, pigeon or fish.

Entry costs ¥80, after which you cross the bridge and bear left up the hill for 50m to a basic hostel (❶) in the square. Continue round the lake and you'll find the ageing but comfortable *Stone Forest Hotel* (☎0871/7711405; ❺) and the more modern *Shilin Summer Palace Hotel* (☎0871/7711888; ❺) either side of steps which lead directly down into the forest itself. Keep going around the lake and uphill for the better-value *Yunlin Hotel* (☎0871/7711409; ❸), which offers singles, doubles and triples. All of the **places to stay** have decent **restaurants**, and the hotels host infrequent evenings of **Sani dancing**, surprisingly enthusiastic, spontaneous events which counter the tacky image portrayed by hawkers at the park.

Southeast to Vietnam

Southeastern Yunnan, the region between Kunming and Vietnam, was off-limits until the early 1990s due to the Sino-Vietnamese War, but – with the exception of remoter parts – it has now opened up to free exploration. A nicely unpackaged corner of the province, there are plenty of reasons, aside from the border, to head down this way. Closest to Kunming, **Fuxian and Qilu lakes**, while not as scenic as their northwestern sister Dian Chi, have a smat-

Southeastern Yunnan

Chengjiang	澄江	***chéngjiāng***
Fuxian Hu	抚仙湖	*fǔxiān hú*
Jiangchuan	江川	*jiāngchuān*
Gejiu	个旧	***gèjiù***
Baohua Park	宝华公园	*bǎohuá gōngyuán*
Liangyou Jiudian	良友酒店	*liángyǒu jiǔdiàn*
Shi Haolou Binguan	十号楼宾馆	*shíhàolóu bīnguǎn*
Tin Capital Restaurant	锡城饭店	*xīchéng fàndiàn*
Hekou	河口	***hékǒu***
Jianshui	建水	***jiànshuǐ***
Chaoyang Lou	朝阳楼	*cháoyáng lóu*
Confucian Academy	文庙	*wénmiào*
Garden Hotel	花园招待所	*huāyuán zhāodàisuǒ*
Lin'an Fandian	临安饭店	*lín'ān fàndiàn*
Lin'an Jiudian	临安酒店	*línān jiǔdiàn*
Zhujia Huayuan	朱家花园	*zhūjiā huāyuán*
Kaiyuan	开远	***kāiyuǎn***
Malipo	麻栗坡	*málìpō*
Tonghai	通海	***tōnghǎi***
Li Yue Fandian	礼乐饭店	*lǐyuè fàndiàn*
Nanjie Fandian	南街饭店	*nánjiē fàndiàn*
Tonghai Government Guesthouse	通海县政府招待所	*tōnghǎixiàn zhèngfǔ zhāodàisuǒ*
Tong-Print Hotel	通印大酒店	*tōngyìn dàjiǔdiàn*
Xiushan Binguan	秀山宾馆	*xiùshān bīnguǎn*
Xiushan Park	秀山公园	*xiùshān gōngyuán*
Yongjin Si	涌金寺	*yǒngjīn sì*
Wenshan	文山	***wénshān***
Xinmen	薪门	***xīnmén***
Yanzi Dong	燕子洞	***yànzi dòng***
Yuanyang	元阳	***yuányáng***

tering of historic sites focused on nearby towns, the best of which is **Tonghai**. Farther south, amiable **Jianshui** has its own complement of Qing architecture, and an unusual attraction in nearby caves; while surprisingly sophisticated **Gejiu** surrounds an artificial lake, an unintentional consequence of old mining methods. Those with more time should consider side-trips to **Malipo**, a remote Zhuang town reached via the rail town of **Kaiyuan**, or the impressive terraced landscapes of the **Hong He Valley**.

There are two ways to cover the 350km between Kunming and the border town of **Hekou**: either on the daily, narrow-gauge **Kunming–Hanoi train**, which stops at Kaiyuan along the way (see Kunming's "Moving on" box, p.856); or by road, hopping down between towns on **public buses** from Kunming's main bus station – the better option if you want to have a look around. There's a **Kunming–Hekou highway** too, reaching the border via Lunan and Kaiyuan, with a spur connecting it to Gejiu, but most of the sights lie on smaller roads. Note that you need a Vietnam visa in advance to cross the border – in China, they are currently available only in Beijing, Nanning and Hong Kong.

The lakes and Tonghai

Surrounded by green farmland and russet, mud-block villages, **Fuxian Hu** is a thinner, smaller version of Dian Chi, its blue waters plied by long wooden fishing boats. Around 70km from Kunming along winding country roads, the county capital of **CHENGJIANG** marks Fuxian's northern end, a long-established market town with a sixteenth-century Confucian temple that was used by Guangdong province's Zhongshan University as its campus during the Japanese occupation. The main road from here follows the lake's western shore 50km south via smaller **Xingyun Hu** and **Jiangchuan**, beyond which is little **Qilu Hu**, on the west side of which lies **XINMEN**. The town is home to a community of four thousand **Mongolians**, descendants of an army garrison left behind by Kublai Khan and now employed as fishermen and blacksmiths. It's hard to miss the place: by day you'll see Xinmen's huge **mosque**, and by night the town glows in the hellish light of its metal **foundries**, some factory-sized, others just backyard smithies.

Tonghai

Another half hour on the bus brings you to **TONGHAI**, a small town backed by temples arrayed up the slopes of **Xiu Shan**, which makes for a good stopover. Marking Tonghai's centre is a **drum tower**, from where the four main streets flanked by old wood-fronted shops run off to the main compass points. Wander around and you'll come across stocky ponies pulling carts, stores selling locally made silver jewellery and copperware, Mongolians upholding their reputation for metalwork by hawking home-made knives, and back-lane markets for tobacco and bamboo pipes. Follow Nan Jie south and uphill onto Wenmiao Lu for 300m, then look for an English sign directing you to **Xiushan Park** (¥15). Study the map by the entrance before going in. For its size, this is one of the most charming mountain parks in China; an easy path takes you through pine forests past half-a-dozen unpretentious **temples and pavilions**; some are inhabited, some are teahouses, but all are lovingly decked with bright paint, elegant screens and eaves, and set amidst tranquil gardens. Strangely, given the lack of foreign tourists, English signs along the way explain each building's significance; the best building is **Yongjin Si**, whose pride are 400-year-old cypress and fir trees and well-proportioned temple halls.

Tonghai's core is a 500-metre-wide square grid of streets defined by **Huangcheng Lu**, divided into north (Bei), east (Dong) and west (Xi) sections. The **bus station** is at the northwest corner of town on the junction of Huangcheng Bei Lu and Huangcheng Xi Lu, with an overflow of private operators in side lanes; between them these manage at least daily runs to Hekou, and more frequent departures to Jiangchuan, Kunming and Jianshui. There's **accommodation** at *Tonghai Government Guesthouse*, whose Chinese-only sign is 100m east of the bus station on Huangcheng Bei Lu; don't let them put you in the musty old building, but go to the new one at the back (❷, dorm beds ¥20). The *Li Yue Fandian* (Ⓣ0877/3011651; ❷), 75m south of the bus station on Huangcheng Xi Lu is slightly better value, and the communal bathrooms are very clean. The *Tong-Print* (Ⓣ0877/3021666; ❹), 200m west of the bus station, is the upmarket option, featuring a sauna and fitness room; it had an outdoor swimming pool until it got too dirty and was remodelled as a pond.

It's not as pricey as it looks, and they'll split a double for a lone traveller. There are snack stalls throughout the centre; for more substantial **meals** try the cheap portions of red-cooked mutton and vegetable stir-fries at canteens opposite the bus station, or the old-style *Nanjie Fandian*, south of the drum tower, where crossing-the-bridge noodles come in ¥5–20 helpings, and a three-dish meal for two costs around ¥40. The *Iceberg* next door has refreshing rice jelly drinks.

Jianshui and Yanzi Dong

JIANSHUI lies 80km south of Tonghai through some seriously eroded countryside full of short limestone fingers poking out of the soil – a stone forest beginning to sprout. An administrative centre for over a thousand years, first impressions of a parochial Chinese town are dispelled as the huge red **Chaoyang Lou**, the former eastern gate tower in the city's Ming-dynasty walls, looms into view – one of several historic structures that, together with a provincial, kitschy charm and a friendly populace, make Jianshui a fascinating stopover. Get here sooner rather than later though, as it's all being tarted up for tourists.

The town is full of **historic old buildings**, mostly serving as schools and offices, and you can spend an enjoyable afternoon trying to find them. The grandest are being restored and opened up to the public. Chaoyang Lou is locked and its grounds swarm with loungers, but there's a pleasant teahouse at the top. Follow Jianzhong Lu for 200m then turn north up Jianxin Jie, and you'll arrive shortly at the grand **Zhujia Huayuan**, the Zhu Clan Gardens (¥20). It's a Chinese box of interlocking halls and courtyards in good condition and brightly painted. You can stay at the hotel here (Ⓣ0873/7667988; ❺) – certainly one of China's more imaginative – in a room full of imitation Qing furniture; the four poster beds are particularly fine. Back on Jianzhong Lu, a few minutes further past more market activity and old shops brings you to the front of a **temple** – don't go in, it's a military base – followed shortly afterwards by another, grander affair, the entrance to Jianshui's venerable **Confucian Academy**. The fee here (¥20) allows you to walk around a small **lake**, haunt of kingfishers and elderly musicians, to **Dacheng Men**, the complex's actual gates behind which is a school and a series of halls with accomplished interlocking wooden eaves (very good monkeys, as usual) and fine carved screen doors, while some elderly **stone statues** of goats, lions and **elephants** stand around the grounds – the latter a recurring theme in the academy's decorations.

Practicalities

Buses wind up 100m northwest of Chaoyang Lou on Chaoyang Bei Lu. From here head back to the roundabout and take Jianzhong Lu, the town's high street, which will bring you after 250m to the *Garden Hotel* (❶–❷). Rooms with their own bathroom are the best bet as the communal ones are pungent and unlit. Third-floor rooms have balconies and are pleasant enough, but avoid the fourth floor, where the toilets are. The *Lin'an Jiudian* on Chaoyang Bei Lu (❹) is a lot more expensive, a little more classy but musty and in a dull part of town. Alternatively, and far more romantically, you can stay at the *Zhujia Huayuan* (see above).

In food circles, Jianshui's most famous product is the **qiguo** – a steampot casserole whose inverted funnel design simultaneously poaches meat and creates a soup – though it's hard either to find shops selling souvenir pots, or a restaurant serving the casserole. The town's most atmospheric **restaurant** is the

Lin'an Fandian on Jianzhong Lu, whose lower floor with beam-and-flagstone decor offers cheap soups and stir-fries; there are more formal arrangements in the balcony rooms upstairs. Otherwise, you'll fall over swarms of fruit sellers and cheap street kitchens, whose charcoal-grilled, skewered tofu, eggs, meat or veggies with chilli relish are the most popular meal in town.

Moving on from Jianshui, the bus station has regular departures to Kunming, Tonghai, Gejiu and Kaiyuan, and daily services to Hekou and Yuanyang.

Yanzi Dong

Yanzi Dong, the Swallows' Caves (¥15), are 30km east of Jianshui on the road to Kaiyuan or Gejiu – easy to reach on public buses heading this way from town, or by chartering a minibus from either of the Chaoyang Bei Lu depots. Part of karst formations along the forested **Lu River Valley**, stone tools, animal bones and freshwater mussel middens reveal the caves' use in Neolithic times, but for the last few centuries people have come to see the tens of thousands of swiftlets who nest here – the noise of wheeling birds is deafening during the early summer – and Yangzi Dong has become an enjoyable Chinese-style tourist attraction, featuring wooden walkways and underground restaurants. If you can, catch the **Bird Nest Festival** on August 8, the only day of the year that collecting the then-vacant nests is allowed – a very profitable and dangerous task for local Yi men, who scale the sixty-metre-high cliffs unaided as crowds look on. Buses either way along the main road continue until mid-afternoon.

Kaiyuan, Malipo, Gejiu and Yuanyang

KAIYUAN, a major stop on both the rail line and highway, is about 50km east of Jianshui and around the same distance north of **Gejiu** on the Hekou road. There's an interesting two-hundred-kilometre side trip by bus southeast of Kaiyuan via the city of **Wenshan** to **MALIPO**, a small town which authorities may not want you to visit owing to its proximity to a remote section of the Vietnamese border. A number of ethnic groups inhabit the region hereabouts, and there's a collection of **rock paintings** on cliffs about 1km west of town near the Chaoyang River, apparently connected with local Zhuang mythology (for more on which, see p.820).

Gejiu

A more likely target, **GEJIU** is the capital of **Honghe Hani and Yi Autonomous Prefecture** and nothing like the towns farther north, owing its character to the **tin mines** above which the city was founded during the late Qing dynasty. These collapsed during a flood in the 1950s, turning the town centre into the kilometre-long **Jin Hu**, a lake now fringed by a shiny and urbane new city whose main streets, along with remnants of the old town, are on the southern shore. There's not really anything to see, but it's a pleasant place to wander. Distant detonations and souvenir shops full of tin trinkets are reminders of the town's raison d'etre, and you'll probably see village women in semi-traditional blue embroidered clothing in town to trade. There are brilliant vistas from the upper ridges of eastern **Baohua Park** (¥2 entry; cable car ¥20 one way, ¥30 return).

Gejiu's huge **bus station** is at the north of town, handling transport to Kunming, Kaiyuan, Jianshui, Yuanyang and Hekou. From here, **Jinhu Xi Lu** and bus #3, or **Jinhu Dong Lu** and bus #2, head down the west and east sides of the lake respectively to either end of **Jinhu Nan Lu**, which follows the 300-metre-long southern shore; quickly being modernized, the town's older quarters are south off here. Gejiu's best-value **accommodation** is the *Shi Haolou Binguan* (Ⓣ0873/2122514, Ⓕ2122830; ❸), at the southern end of Jinhu Dong Lu. Of the many places **to eat**, *Liangyou Jiudian*, halfway along Jinhu Nan Lu at the southwest corner of Zhongshan Lu, has excellent all-you-can-eat **hot-pots** with sliced meat, fish, seafood and vegetables for ¥35; or try cheap steamers of filling dumplings at the noisy, grubby *Tin Capital Restaurant* on Cailu Jie. For street food, visit the railway station market on the west side of the lake on Jinhu Xi Lu.

Hong He and Yuanyang

Hong He, the **Red River**, starts life near Xiaguan in Yunnan's northwest and runs southeast across the province, enters Vietnam at Hekou, and flows through Hanoi before emptying its volcanic-soil-laden waters into the Gulf of Tonkin. For much of its journey, the river is straight, channelled by the **Ailao Shan range** into a series of fertile, steep-sided valleys. These have been **terraced** by resident **Hani** (for more on whom see p.915), whose mushroom-shaped, adobe and thatch houses pepper the hills. In spring and autumn thick mists blanket the area, muting the violent contrast between red soil and brilliant green paddy fields. Villages around **YUANYANG**, a small town 80km south of Jianshui and 110km southwest of Gejiu, are said to offer the best of the scenery, including valley after valley of 1800-metre-high terracing, reckoned by seasoned hands as the most spectacular in all Asia.

Hekou and the border

It's another 150km southeast from either Kaiyuan or Gejiu to where rail and road converge at the border town of **HEKOU**. For those who are Vietnam-bound the border post is only a few minutes' walk from the bus and train station. Over in Vietnam, **Lao Cai** has a huge game market, a few despondent hotels, and a **train station** 3km south with two services daily for the ten-hour run to Hanoi. Most travellers take a **bus** for the hill resort town of **Sa Pa**, or hop on a motorbike taxi, a *xe om* (US$5).

For arrivals from Vietnam, turn right after the border crossing and the train station is 100m away. Trains head up to Kunming at 2.15pm – remember that China is one hour ahead of Vietnam – and the station ticket office is open 11am–1.30pm (you can wait in the *International Hotel* canteen nearby). Alternatively, head 50m up the main road and the bus station is on the left. Here you can get sleepers for Kunming (14hr) or ordinary buses to Gejiu and Jianshui. To change money, walk up the main street from the border crossing and turn right after 200m and you'll arrive at the Bank of China (daily 8am–5.30pm), the only place to cash traveller's cheques (Mon–Sat only).

Northwestern Yunnan

Uplifted vigorously during the last fifty million years as the Indian subcontinent buckled up against China, **northwestern Yunnan** is a geologically unsettled region of subtropical forests, thin pasture, alpine lakes and shattered peaks painted crisply in blue, white and grey. An overnight trip from Kunming, **Xiaguan**, on the southern tip of **Er Hai Lake**, is the regional access point, the start of roads north past the Bai town of **Dali**. Though Dali is firmly on the beaten track, the lake and mountains make a splendid backdrop, while a few hours beyond Dali is the former Naxi kingdom of **Lijiang**. The Naxi are still resident, though the old town and surrounding villages endured major renovations following the terrible 1996 earthquake. Here hikers can organize themselves for a two-day trek through **Tiger Leaping Gorge**, where a youthful Yangzi cuts through the deepest chasm on Earth. East is **Lugu Hu**, lakeside home to the matrilineal Mosuo, while north again is the Tibetan town of **Zhongdian**, beginning of trips up to the Tibetan borderlands at **Deqin**, or beyond into Sichuan province. In a completely different direction, heading southwest from **Xiaguan to the Burmese border** takes you to the historic city of **Baoshan** and through the **Dehong region**, a subtropical pocket full of shady traders and ludicrous antics revolving around the border towns of **Ruili** and **Wanding**.

Heading up through Dali to Lijiang and Zhongdian, you'll find mild, even warm **weather** from spring through to autumn, though winters are extremely cold, the likelihood of snow between November and April increasing as you move north. Southwest of Xiaguan, however, temperatures are warm year-round, with heavy summer rains and only cool winter nights in the hills. **Transport** is improving: rough roads – including the famous **Burma Road** between Kunming and Wanding – are being replaced or upgraded to highways; while Kunming is directly connected by **air** to Xiaguan, Lijiang, Zhongdian and **Mangshi** in Dehong, and by **train** to Xiaguan.

To Xiaguan: Chuxiong and the Burma Road

The first 390km of the **Burma Road** runs west of Kunming to Xiaguan through a succession of valleys and mountain ranges which would well repay a few days' exploration. But for most, the lure of Dali is too great, an all-too-easy trip from Kunming on a direct bus or train via Xiaguan.

If the leisurely approach suits you, the now almost entirely modern midpoint town of **CHUXIONG** makes a good base, inhabited since the Zhou dynasty (700 BC) and today home to a substantial Yi population who celebrate their **Torch Festival** on the 24th day of the sixth lunar month with a fair and night-time revelries. The markets here are known for their silver jewellery, there are a few nearby parks and temples – most notably 20km away at **Zixi Shan**, a wooded mountain dedicated to Buddhism since the twelfth century – and, for historians and paleontologists especially, some interesting associations. In 1975 a huge Zhou mausoleum was discovered on Chuxiong's southern outskirts at **Wanjiaba**, containing farm tools and five of the oldest **bronze drums** yet discovered in Asia, now in Kunming's Provincial Museum (for more on bronze drum cultures, see p.815). Separate sites surrounding the town of **LUFENG**, 80km east, closer to Kunming, have yielded dinosaur bones and fragments of *ramapithecus* and *sivapithecus* fossils, possible hominid prototypes. For **accommodation** in Chuxiong, try the *Chuxiong Binguan* on Xinshi Jie (❷–❹) or the *Zixi Luguan* (dorms ¥15, rooms ❸) on central Zhong Da Lu, both with fair restaurants.

Xiaguan

XIAGUAN, an increasingly industrialized transport hub, lies on the southern shore of Er Hai Lake. It's also confusingly known as **Dali Shi** (Dali City), and some "Dali" buses from Kunming may actually terminate here – in which case catch public bus #4 as below. Xiaguan's main drag is **Jianshe Dong Lu**, a 500-

The Burma Road

Trade routes through northern Yunnan into **Burma** and beyond were established more than two thousand years ago by merchants carrying goods between the Han empire and Rome along the Southern Silk Road. Travelled by Marco Polo on one of his errands for the Mongol court, it became known as the "Tribute Road" following China's successful eighteenth-century annexation of eastern Burma, but later fell into disuse as the Qing court cut off ties with the outside world. When Japan invaded China during the 1930s they drove the Guomindang government to Sichuan, isolating them from their eastern economic and industrial power base. Turning west for help, the Guomindang found the **British**, who then held Burma and were none too keen to see China's resources in Japanese hands. In fact, there had been plans for a link through to Burma for forty years, and a road had already been built from Kunming to Xiaguan. Britain agreed to help extend this into a 1100-kilometre-long supply line connecting **Kunming** with the Burmese rail head at **Lashio**.

This was to become the **Burma Road**, swiftly completed by three hundred thousand labourers in 1938, an incredible feat considering the basic tools available and the number of mountains along the way. After the Japanese stormed French Indochina in 1940 and halted rail traffic between Vietnam and Kunming, the road became China's only line of communication with the allies, though it was always a tenuous one, cut frequently by landslides and summer monsoons. Lashio fell a year later, however, and the road became redundant once more, remaining so after the war ended through Burma's self-imposed isolation and the chaos of the Cultural Revolution. Now partially sealed and open again as the Yunnan–Burma Highway, the 910-kilometre Chinese stretch between Kunming and the border crossing at **Wanding** remains – like the Great Wall – a triumph of stolid persistence over unfavourable logistics.

metre-long street between Tai'an Lu in the east and Renmin Lu in the west. The **airport** is 15km east of here, for which you'll need a taxi; the **train station** is 2km east on Dianyuan Lu along the #5 and #6 bus routes. Long-distance buses stop at a number of depots along Jianshe Dong Lu, though the **main bus station** is down towards Renmin Lu. There's a cheap and basic **hotel** (❶) here, with the upmarket *Xiaguan Fandian* (Ⓣ8072/2125859; ❺), favoured by tour groups and with a CITS desk, about 100m east, and the mid-range *Xiaguan Binguan* (❹) on the Jianshe Dong Lu/Renmin Lu corner. Markets and cheap places to eat fill the backstreets, and if you've got time to kill, go for a stroll in **Erhai Gongyuan**, a green, hilly park a couple of kilometres northeast of the centre on the lakeshore.

For Dali, catch public bus #4, which passes along Jianshe Dong Lu every hour (¥7) and terminates one stop beyond the main bus station. The main bus station has daily departures west to **Baoshan**, northeast to Jizu Shan and Lugu Hu via **Binchuan**, and, for the hardened traveller only, a nerve-shattering 72-hour run south to **Jinghong** in Xishuangbanna (see p.905).

Dali and around

A thirty-minute bus ride north of Xiaguan and almost a satellite suburb, **DALI** draws swarms of tourists for various reasons. Aside from a beautiful setting, Chinese package groups come seeking some colourful history, while foreign backpackers escape China in a Westerner-friendly theme park of beer gardens, massages, language courses, day-trips and food. It might sound grim, but the

Dali and around

Chuxiong	楚雄	***chŭxióng***
Chuxiong Binguan	楚雄宾馆	*chŭxióng bīnguăn*
Dali	大理	***dàlĭ***
Apricot Flower Restaurant	杏花酒店	*xìnghuā jiŭdiàn*
Dali Museum	大理博物馆	*dàlĭ bówùguăn*
Jim's Peace Guesthouse	吉姆和平客楼	*jímŭ hépíng kèlóu*
Jinhua Binguan	金花宾馆	*jīnhuā bīnguăn*
Marley's Café	马丽咖啡馆	*mălì kāfēiguăn*
Old Dali Inn	大理四季客栈	*dàlĭ sìjì kèzhàn*
Red Camellia Hotel	红茶花宾馆	*hóngcháhuā bīnguăn*
Tibetan Café	西藏餐厅	*xīzàng cāntīng*
Xingyue Hotel	星月	*xīngyuè*
Yu'er Park	玉耳公园	*yù'ĕr gōngyuán*
Around Dali		
Butterfly Spring	蝴蝶泉	*húdié quán*
Du Wenxiu's Tomb	杜文秀之墓	*dùwénxiù zhīmù*
Er Hai Lake	洱海	*ĕrhăi*
Gantong Si	甘通寺	*gāntōng sì*
Guanyin Tang	观音堂	*guānyīn táng*
Jizu Shan	鸡足山	*jīzú shān*
San Ta Si	三塔寺	*sāntă sì*
Shaping	沙坪	*shāpíng*
Shegu Ta	蛇骨塔	*shégŭ tă*
Shizhong Shan	石钟山	*shízhōng shān*
Taihe	太河	*tàihé*
Wase	挖色	*wāsè*
Xizhou	喜洲	*xĭzhōu*
Yita Si	一塔寺	*yītă sì*
Zhoucheng	周城	*zhōuchéng*
Xiaguan	下关	***xiàguān***
Xiaguan Binguan	下关宾馆	*xiàguān bīnguăn*
Xiaguan Fandian	下关饭店	*xiàguān fàndiàn*

town and surrounding villages are both pretty and interesting, full of old houses and an indigenous **Bai** population. To the east lies the great **Er Hai Lake**, while the invitingly green valleys and clouded peaks of the fifty-kilometre-long **Cang Shan range** rear up behind town, the perfect setting for a few days' walking or relaxation.

And there's much more to Dali than its modern profile. Favouring its profitable location near the Silk Road, an aspiring eighth-century Yunnanese prince named **Piluoge** invited his rivals to dinner, set fire to the tent with them inside, and afterwards established the **Nanzhao Kingdom** here, a realm later expanded to include much of modern Burma, Thailand and Vietnam. In 937, the Bai warlord **Duan Siping** toppled the Nanzhao and set up a smaller **Dali Kingdom**, which survived until Kublai Khan and his Mongolian hordes descended in 1252, subduing the Bai and imposing Chinese rule. This persisted until 1856 when, inspired by the Taipings, **Du Wenxiu** led the **Muslim Uprising** against the Qing empire to Dali, and again declared the town capital of an independent state. But in 1873 the the rebellion was crushed with the wholesale massacre of Yunnan's Muslim population; Du

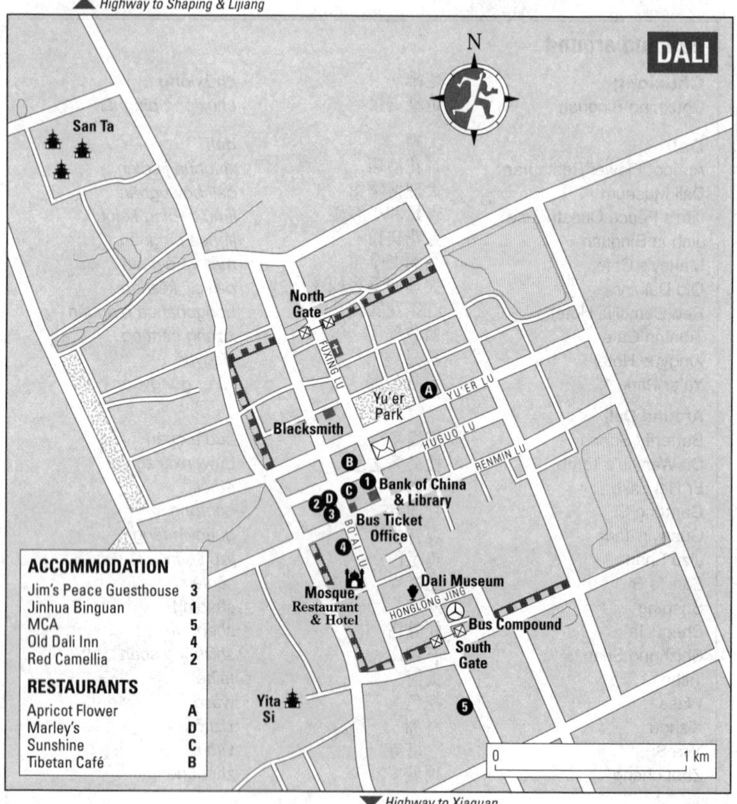

Wenxiu died and Dali was devastated, never to recover its former political position.

Muslims and Han remain today, but the majority of the regional population are still Bai. If you can, visit during the **Spring Fair**, held from the fifteenth day of the third lunar month (April or May). Originally a Buddhist festival, the event has grown into five hectic days of horse trading, wrestling, racing, dancing and singing, attracting thousands of people from all over the region to camp at the fairground just west of town. You'll probably have to follow suit, as beds in Dali will be in short supply.

Orientation, arrival and getting around

Covering only about four square kilometres, much of Dali is contained by the remains of its Ming-dynasty walls. These aside, an earthquake destroyed the town in 1925, but it was rebuilt in its former style. Cobbled and planted with cherry trees, the main axis of its grid-like street plan is **Fuxing Lu**, which runs between the old north and south gates. **Bo'ai Lu** runs parallel and to the west, while the centre hinges around **Huguo Lu**, cutting across both at right angles.

The #4 bus from Xiaguan drives through the town, but **long-distance buses** either drop off on the highway, which skirts Dali's western side, or deliver to the bus compound just inside the south gates on Fuxing Lu, where there's also a **ticket office**. There's another useful **booking office** on Bo'ai Lu, with more scattered around; **leaving**, you might have to pick up long-distance services from the main road, or even proceed to Xiaguan or Lijiang first.

You don't need them for Dali itself, but **bicycles** for trips out to nearby sites can be rented from hotels and foreigners' cafés for about ¥10 per day, plus deposit. Always check the rental policy and condition of the bike, as you are fully responsible for any damage or loss.

Accommodation

Low-pressure touts meet the buses, hoping to escort arrivals to accommodation.

Jim's Peace Guesthouse Bo'ai Lu. Thoroughly likeable owner, and new comfortable rooms above one of the town's best restaurants. ❷

Jinhua Binguan Corner of Fuxing Lu and Huguo Lu ⓣ0872/2673343, ⓕ2673846. Dali's upmarket, air-conditioned option and not bad value, right in the town centre and complete with an art gallery. Tiling makes for cold rooms in winter, however. Dorm beds ¥25, ❺

MCA Just west off the road, 100m south of the south gate outside the town. A favourite with long-term budget travellers, offering rooms in a self-contained family compound arranged around a garden. Dorm beds ¥10, ❶

Old Dali Inn (No. 5 Guesthouse) Bo'ai Lu ⓣ0872/2670382. Indifferent staff and basic toilets compensated for by very hot, powerful showers, and a courtyard surrounded by two tiers of dusty wooden "traditional Bai" rooms – check a few out, as some are better than others. Don't bother with the restaurant. Dorm beds ¥10 and ¥15, ❷

Red Camellia (No. 4 Guesthouse) Western end of Huguo Lu. Dreary, basic dorms and primitive doubles. A nice garden but lazy staff and another indifferent restaurant. Dorm beds ¥10 and ¥15, ❶

Xingyue (Mosque) Bo'ai Lu. You can't miss the minarets at the corners of this interesting variation on local options. There's a decent Muslim restaurant here, too. Rooms have TV but shared bathrooms and are spartan. Dorm beds ¥15, ❷

The Town

Dali is small enough to walk around in a morning, though you'll be slowed down by the crowds of hawkers, farmers and shoppers who descend for the Friday **market**. Most places of specific interest are along Fuxing Lu, but the narrow stone side streets are good for a wander. Get your bearings from on top of Dali's old **south gate** (¥2) where you can study Xiaguan, Er Hai Lake, the town and mountains from the comfort of a teahouse. Dali's antique **pagodas** stand as landmarks above the roof lines, **Yita Si** due west, and the trinity of **San Ta** a few kilometres north; below is a busy **artisans' quarter** where carpenters and masons turn out the heavy and uncomfortable-looking tables and chairs inlaid with streaky grey **Dali marble** that lurk in Chinese emporiums around the world. Mined up in the hills, smaller pieces of marble are worked into all sorts of souvenirs – rolling pins, chopping boards, miniature pagodas – which you can buy from shops and stalls in town.

The **Dali Museum** (Tues–Sun 9am–5pm; ¥5) is opposite the bus compound, just 50m or so inside the gate. Built for the Qing governor and appropriated as Du Wenxiu's "Forbidden City" during his insurrection, the museum takes the form of a small Chinese palace with stone lions guarding the gate and cannons in the courtyard. Historic relics include a strange bronze model of two circling dragons, jaws clenched around what might be a tree, a few Buddhist figurines from the Nanzhao period, and some lively statues of an orchestra and serving maids from a Ming noblewoman's tomb – a nice addition to the usual cases of snarling gods and warrior busts. With the mountains behind, the gardens outside are pleasant, planted with lantana and bougainvillea.

North along Fuxing Lu, young and old socialize in the square outside the **library**, playing dominoes or video arcade games according to their interests.

A few doors along is the **Bank of China** (foreign exchange daily 8am–7pm), with Dali's **international telephone counter** at the **post office** (where you have to pay for everything, even the overseas postage forms; daily 8am–9pm), a little farther on at the Huguo Lu crossroads. Huguo Lu's western arm forms the core of the budget travellers' world, a knot of **cafés**, cheap tailors, bilingual **travel agents** happy to book you on tours or long-distance buses (for a ¥20 commission), and massage clinics advertising their services with couplets like "Painful In, Happy Out". It's also the best place to purchase beautiful jewellery and embroideries (many from Guizhou's Miao), and attractive Bai tie-dyes from hawkers – asking prices are ludicrously high, dropping swiftly once bargaining commences. Don't show any interest unless you really want to buy, or you'll be mercilessly hounded.

Farther north again on the corner of Fuxing Lu and Yu'er Lu, **Yu'er Park** (entrance on Yu'er Lu; ¥1) is a peaceful refuge from Huguo Lu's hard-sell perils, frequented by locals and full of camellias, fruit trees, palms and ponds linked by tidy paths. The backstreets north of the park are some of the nicest in Dali; places to seek out include a stone **church** and a **blacksmith**, the latter decorated with inventive animal sculptures made from scrap iron. Fuxing Lu itself terminates at the **north gate** (¥2), which can also be climbed.

Eating and drinking

Sweet buns and noodle soups constitute a typical Dali breakfast and are sold by street stalls and cheap restaurants around the centre. Snacks include pickled vegetables wrapped in a fine pancake, and brittle "fans" of dried yoghurt often fried and crumbled over other dishes – much nicer than they sound. Two **specialities** are based on fish from Er Hai Lake: *shaguoyu*, where the fish is fried, then simmered with dried vegetables in a sour stock, and *youdeyu*, a casserole of small oily sprats and tofu.

Dali's **cafés** serve a mix of Western dishes, Chinese staples and even Bai specialities, and are good places to meet other foreigners and swap news. You can also use the **Internet** (around ¥15 an hour), and get in touch with the latest martial art, language or painting courses. They swing in and out of favour, but the ones listed here are good starting points.

Apricot Flower Restaurant Yu'er Lu. Despite a monastic austerity in the stone floors and well-used wooden furniture, this is the best place in town for an inexpensive, accomplished and tasty Chinese dinner. No English menus.

Café de Jacks Bo'ai Lu. Popular after dark for its bar and Chinese version of curries, pizzas, salads and chocolate cake.

Jim's Peace Café Huguo Lu, underneath *Jim's Guesthouse*. A long-termers' hang-out, with comfy sofas, a well-stocked bar and a fine yak stew. Get six people together for a Tibetan banquet, cooked by the owner's mother.

Marley's Huguo Lu. Known for its chocolate cake, good coffee and Western breakfasts, Marley's also organizes "Bai banquets" on Sunday night if they can get the numbers; book before 6pm.

Sunshine Huguo Lu. Distinctly hippie hang-out, offering baked potatoes, banana splits and hash browns.

Tibetan Café Huguo Lu. Upbeat "Tibetan" menu, featuring very tasty stews and soups, if nothing like what you'd actually get in the Himalayas.

Around Dali

Plentiful public **minibuses** shuttle between Xiaguan and the villages along Er Hai's western shore. These can be flagged down on the highway immediately west of Dali, and are a cheaper and more flexible way to get around than the **tours** offered by agents – though the latter are convenient and reasonable value. Alternatively, you could rent a bike (see p.877).

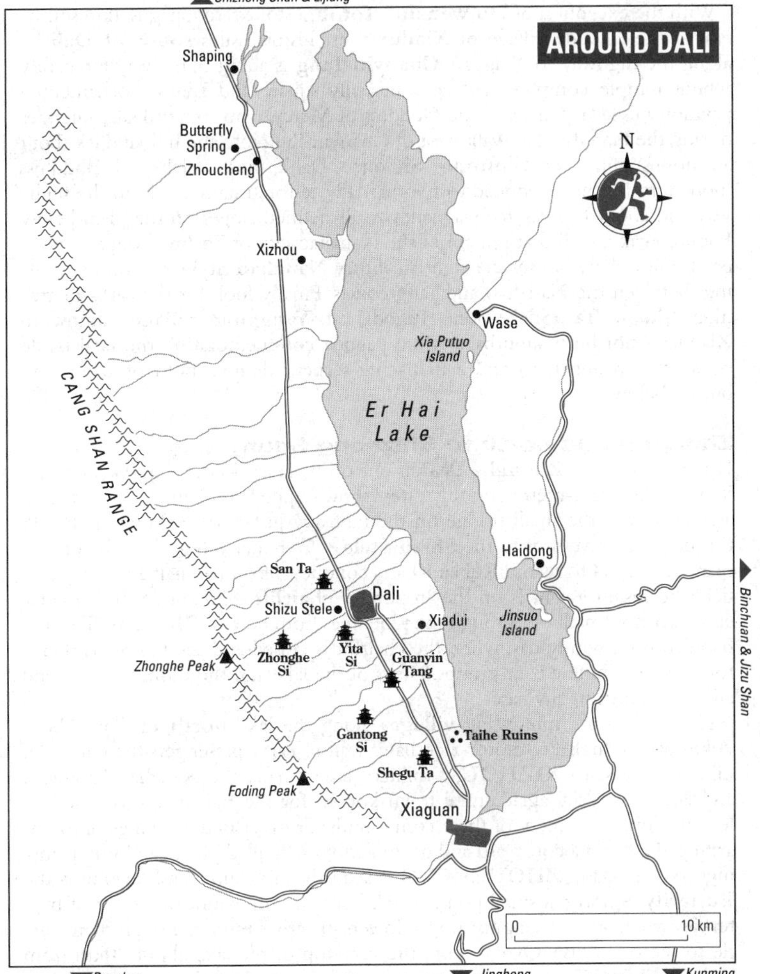

The pagodas and southern sites

Built when the region was a major Buddhist centre, Dali's distinctively tall and elegant pagodas are still standing after a millennium of wars and earthquakes. Just west of Dali's south gate is the solitary **Yita Si**, a tenth-century tower and virtually abandoned Ming temple surrounded by ancient trees. Better presented is **San Ta**, the **Three Pagodas**, a twenty-minute walk north of town in the grounds of the now vanished Chongsheng Monastery (8am–5pm; ¥32). Built around 850, the square-based **Qianxun tower** stands 69m high, some hundred years older than the two smaller octagonal pagodas behind. As the structures are sealed, San Ta really looks best at a distance – the stiff entrance fee gives you access only to souvenir stalls and a hall at the back containing religious relics discovered during renovations in the 1970s.

With the exception of **Du Wenxiu's Tomb**, a stone sarcophagus 4km southeast at the lakeside village of **Xiadui**, most historic sites **south of Dali** lie along the highway to Xiaguan. **Guanyin Tang** is about 5km away, a recently rebuilt temple complex with an unusually square and lavishly ornamented pavilion raised to Guanyin, the Goddess of Mercy, who routed Dali's enemies during the Han dynasty. Walk west of Guanyin Tang into the hills and it's about an hour's climb to **Gantong Si**, once Dali's most celebrated Buddhist monastery but now reduced to two partially restored halls. Back on the highway and about halfway to Xiaguan, two ill-defined ridges on the plain below Foding Peak are all that remain of the Nanzhao city of **Taihe**, though a modern pavilion here houses the eighth-century **Nanzhao Stele**, recounting dealings between the Nanzhao and Tang courts. Finally, look for the forty-metre-high **Shegu Ta** (Snake-bone Pagoda) at **Yangping village**, almost in Xiaguan's northern suburbs, a Ming pagoda commemorating the fatal battle between a young hero and a menacing serpent demon, both of whom are buried below.

Zhonghe and north to Shizhong Shan

Due **west** of Dali, **Zhonghe Peak** is one of the tallest in the Cang Shan range, its four-thousand-metre summit often snow-capped until June. For a partial ascent, start at the small bridge on the highway just north of town and walk through the graveyards to the **Shizu Stele**, a four-metre-high inscribed tablet planted in 1304 to record Kublai Khan's conquest ofYunnan half a century earlier. The easiest ascent is on the "ropeway" **chairlift** (¥20), but there's a fairly easy, two-hour path up through the pine trees from here to **Zhonghe Si** – best handled on a windy day, when the chairlift is closed and the temple is therefore free of Chinese tour groups. Views of the lake and the mountains beyond are stupendous in any case.

There are some interesting **villages** along the lake **north** of Dali. About 20km up the highway, motor-rickshaws wait to carry passengers the couple of kilometres east to **XIZHOU**, a military base during the Nanzhao Kingdom and later a wealthy agricultural town known for the Bai mansions raised by leading families. Ninety of these compounds survive, based on wings of rooms arranged around a courtyard and decorated with "pulled" eaves and wall paintings. North again, **ZHOUCHENG** is a tie-dyeing centre, and beyond is the **Butterfly Spring**, a small pond which becomes the haunt of clouds of butterflies when an overhanging acacia flowers in early summer, though there's little to see otherwise. Overlooking the very top of the lake about 30km from Dali, **SHAPING** is definitely worth a visit for its **Monday market**, when what seems like the entire regional population of peasants, labourers, con-men and artisans crowds on to the small hill behind town to trade in everything imaginable from livestock to hardware and bags of coriander seeds.

With a couple of days to spare, head out to the forested slopes of **Shizhong Shan**, 140km northwest of Dali via the towns of Diannan and Shaxi, where there's accommodation. A handful of temples and grottoes dating back to the Nanzhao Kingdom are ranged up the slopes, connected by a thousand-step staircase, full of very out-of-the-ordinary sculptures and frescoes. Some of these are graphically sexual, others show emissaries from India and the Middle East, and everyday scenes from the Nanzhao court.

Er Hai Lake and Jizu Shan

Heading east out of Dali's north gate, an hour's walk brings you to the shores of forty-kilometre-long **Er Hai Lake**, so called because it's shaped like an ear ("*er*"). The thing to do here is arrange a **fishing trip** or excursion out to the islets and villages around the east shore (¥25–50), most easily done through an agent in Dali; boats have small cockpits and no canopies against sun and spray, so come prepared.

A pleasant day out, there's really nothing to do on the lake beyond watching clouds constantly forming and dissipating over Cang Shan. Directly across from Dali, uninhabited **Jinsuo Island** was the summer retreat for Nanzhao royalty, while more northerly **Xia Putuo Island** is a tiny rock completely occupied by a temple whose withered guardian stumbles out after payment. The far shore settlements of **HAIDONG** and **WASE** are full of narrow back lanes with crumbling adobe homes and family mansions, their waterfronts thick with fishing gear. You can stay the night in Wase at the government guesthouse (❶) and catch the lively Saturday morning **market**, slightly smaller and less touristed than Shaping's.

From Wase there are minibuses 30km south to Xiaguan, and also 60km southeast to **BINCHUAN**, from where it's a short hop to **SHAZHI** at the foot of **Jizu Shan** (Chickenfoot Mountain), one of western China's holiest peaks after the legendary monk **Jiaye** brought Buddhism from India to China and fought here with the wicked Jizu King. By the seventh century both Buddhist and Taoist pilgrims were coming in their thousands to honour his memory. In its heyday, a hundred or more monasteries graced Jizu's heights, including the original Golden Temple transported here from Kunming, though by 1980 all but half a dozen had decayed. Things are now picking up again, and everyone who visits the mountain enthuses about the scenery, **Zhusheng Si**, and the ninth-century **Lengyan Pagoda** and accompanying **Jinding Si**, a temple splendidly positioned on a cliff edge at the summit. The track to the peak takes about half a day, with food and basic lodgings at Shazhi, Zhusheng and Jinding.

Lijiang and around

Some 150km north of Dali through numerous Bai and Yi hamlets, roads make their final descent from the ridges to a plain dominated by the inspiringly spiky and ice-bound massif of **Yulong Xue Shan**, the Jade Dragon Snow Mountain. Nestled to the southeast among green fields and dwindling pine forests is **LIJIANG**, capital of the **Naxi Kingdom**, whose centuries-old maze of winding lanes and clean streams, wooden wineshops, weeping willows and rustic stone bridges are alone worth the journey here. Lijiang is by no means an entirely traditional, undiscovered haven, however, partly due to a devastating **earthquake** which destroyed a third of the town in 1996. Having invested heavily in rebuilding, the government now aims to profit through tourist development, and while restorations have been largely tasteful where carried out, Lijiang's **Naxi** seem often marginalized as players in a cultural theme park. They deserve better: the Naxi are descended from a race of Tibetan nomads who settled the region before the tenth century, and until recently a matriarchal society, they brought with them what are still considered some of the sturdiest horses in China, and a shamanistic religion known as **Dongba**. A blend of Tibetan Bon, animism and Taoist tendencies, Dongba's scriptures are written with unique pictograms, and its pantheistic **murals** still decorate temples around Lijiang, a good excuse to explore nearby **villages** by bicycle. For some background reading before you leave home, try to find the exhaustive, two-

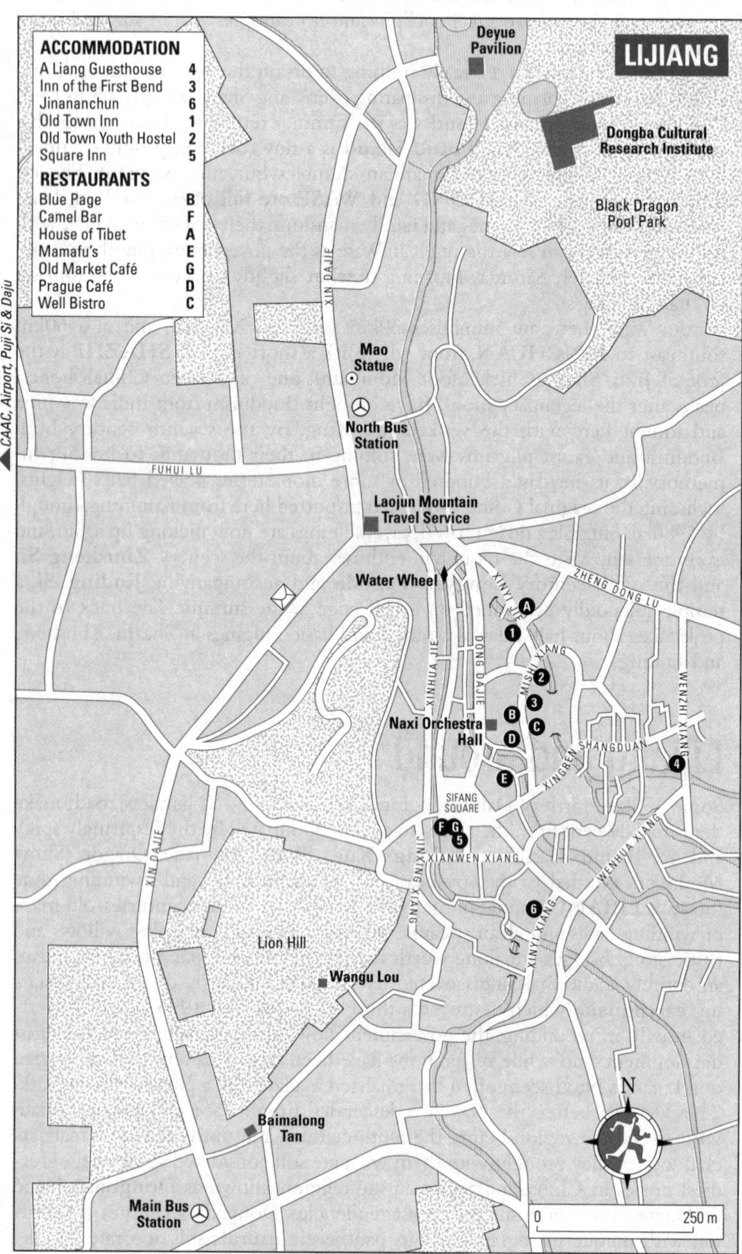

LIJIANG
ACCOMMODATION
A Liang Guesthouse 4
Inn of the First Bend 3
Jinananchun 6
Old Town Inn 1
Old Town Youth Hostel 2
Square Inn 5
RESTAURANTS
Blue Page B
Camel Bar F
House of Tibet A
Mamafu's E
Old Market Café G
Prague Café D
Well Bistro C
Deyue Pavilion
Dongba Cultural Research Institute
Black Dragon Pool Park
XIN DAJIE
Mao Statue
North Bus Station
FUHUI LU
Laojun Mountain Travel Service
Water Wheel
XINYI JIE
ZHENG DONG LU
MISHI XIANG
DONG DAJIE
XINHUA JIE
WENZHI XIANG
Naxi Orchestra Hall
XINGREN SHANGDUAN
SIFANG SQUARE
XIANWEN XIANG
JIXING XIANG
WENHUA XIANG
XINYI XIANG
Lion Hill
Wangu Lou
Baimalong Tan
Main Bus Station
N
0 250 m
CAAC, Airport, Puji Si & Daju
Dali, Shigu, Qiaotou & Zhongdian

Lijiang and around

Lijiang	丽江	***lìjiāng***
Baimalong Tan	白马龙潭	*báimǎ lóngtán*
Black Dragon Pool Park	黑龙潭公园	*hēilóngtán gōngyuán*
Dongba Cultural Research Institute	东巴文化研究室	*dōngbā wénhuà yánjiūshì*
Five Phoenix Hall	五凤楼	*wǔfèng lóu*
Lion Hill	狮子山	*shīzi shān*
Mu Clan Garden	木家院	*mùjiā yuàn*
Accommodation		
A Liang Guesthouse	阿亮客栈	*āliàng kèzhàn*
Inn of the First Bend	一湾酒店	*yīwān jiǔdiàn*
Jiannanchun	丽江剑南春文苑	*lìjiāng jiànnánchūn wényuàn*
Old Town Inn	古城客栈	*gǔchéng kèzhàn*
Old Town Youth Hostel	古城青年旅馆	*gǔchéng qīngnián lǚguǎn*
Square Inn	四方客栈	*sìfāng kèzhàn*
Around Lijiang		
Baisha	白沙	*báishā*
Dazu	大组	*dàzǔ*
Jinjiang	金江	*jīnjiāng*
La wa	落凹	*làāo*
Lugu Hu	泸沽湖	*lúgū hú*
Meilu Xue Shan	梅里雪山	*méilǐ xuěshān*
Ninglang	宁蒗	*nínglàng*
Qiaotou	桥头	*qiáo tóu*
Shigu	石鼓	*shígǔ*
Tiger Leaping Gorge	虎跳峡	*hǔtiào xiá*
Weixi	维西	*wéi xī*
Yongsheng	永胜	*yǒng shèng*
Yuhu	玉湖村	*yùhú cūn*
Yufeng Si	玉峰寺	*yùfēng sì*
Yulong	玉龙	*yùlóng*

volume *Ancient Nakhi Kingdom of Southwest China* by eccentric botanist-anthropologist **Joseph Rock**, who lived here back in the 1930s.

While Lijiang and nearby villages are good for an easy few days, there are more ambitious trips to consider west to the small towns of **Shigu** and **Weixi**, or the excellent two-day **hike** through **Tiger Leaping Gorge** due north of Lijiang. Farther afield, those heading **east into Sichuan** via the rail head at Panzhihua or remote Lugu Lake have the chance to delve deeper into regional cultures.

The Town

Oriented north–south, **Xin Dajie** is Lijiang's three-kilometre-long main street. Just about everything west of this line is modern, but east, behind **Lion Hill**'s radio mast, is where you'll find the old town, known locally as **DAYAN**. It's not easy to navigate around Dayan's backstreets, but as there are few particular sights this hardly matters. While you wander, try to peek in around the solid wooden gates of **Naxi houses**. These substantial two-storey homes are built around a central paved courtyard, eaves and screens carved with mythological figures and fish, representing good luck. Family houses are very important to the Naxi –

Naxi music

The **Naxi Orchestra** is an established part of Lijiang's tourist scene. Using antique instruments, the orchestra performs Song-dynasty tunes derived from the Daoist *Dong Jin* scriptures, a tradition said to have arrived in Lijiang with Kublai Khan, who donated half his court orchestra to the town after the Naxi chieftain helped his army cross the Yangzi. Banned from performing for many years, the orchestra regrouped after the Cultural Revolution under the guidance of **Xuan Ke**, though the deaths of many older musicians have reduced their repertoire from over 60 to just 23 pieces. To counter this, the orchestra's scope has been broadened by including traditional **folk-singing** in their performances.

The orchestra now plays nightly in Lijiang in the well-marked hall just off Dong Dajie (8pm; ¥30–50). The music is haunting, but unfortunately Xuan Ke's smug commentaries are too long, and include anti-foreigner jokes. Better to catch them practising in the afternoon in Black Dragon Pool Park, for free.

Further north on Dong Dajie, another hall called the "Inheritance and Research Base of China" hosts a song and dance troupe who put on spirited nightly performances to a small audience (8–9.30pm; ¥20).

Lijiang was formerly organized into clans – and many people spend a large part of their income maintaining and improving them.

All roads into Dayan lead to its core at **Sifang**, the main **marketplace**. Well geared up to the tourists who come to buy embroidery, hand-beaten copper pots, and wooden carvings of hawks and cockerels, cheap **restaurants** around the square make it a fine place to stop and watch for older people wearing traditional dark tunics and capes patterned in cream and blue, representing the cosmos. North from here, Dong Dajie is lined with touristy, wooden-fronted souvenir shops (though you have to admire the work that has gone into these new buildings), while heading south takes you right into Dayan's maze, where you'll encounter more locally oriented markets and characterful streets. West, cobbled lanes lead up to views of tiled roofs from the fringes of **Lion Hill**, whose forested crown is topped by wooden **Wangu Lou** (¥15), an overbuilt, 22-metre-high pavilion. Below here, the southern part of Dayan didn't survive the earthquake and has been replaced by a complex of weighty Qing-style stone pavilions and ornamental arches, all emphatically Han Chinese and totally inappropriate for the town. Less at odds with local character, the southern boundary is marked by **Baimalong Tan**, an old, dragon-headed spring and washing pool in front of a small temple and tangled garden,

When you've had enough of strolling the streets, head up to **Black Dragon Pool Park** (daily 7am–late evening; ¥20) on Lijiang's northern outskirts. Less contrived than the average public space in China, the sizeable pool is also known as **Yuquan** (Jade Spring), after the clear, pale green water which wells up from the base of surrounding hills. With Yulong Xue Shan behind, the elegant mid-pool **Deyue Pavilion** is outrageously photogenic – in the early afternoon, you can watch traditionally garbed musicians performing **Naxi music** in the western halls.

A path runs around the shore between a spread of trees and buildings, passing first the cluster of compounds which comprise the **Dongba Cultural Research Institute**. The word "dongba" relates to the shamans themselves, about thirty of whom are still alive and kept busy here translating twenty thousand rolls of the old Naxi scriptures, *dongba-jings*, for posterity. Farther around, and almost at the top end of the pool, is a group of halls imported in the 1970s from the site of what was once Lijiang's major temple, **Fuguo Si**. The best of these is Wufeng Lou, the

Five Phoenix Hall, a grand Ming-dynasty palace with a triple roof and interior walls embellished with reproductions of Baisha's temple murals (see p.886).

Practicalities

Lijiang is three hours from Dali on the new expressway, or five hours if you take the older road (likely if you get a rattletrap country bus). The **airport** lies 20km south along the highway. From the **main bus station**, a grey concrete block at the southern edge of town, a fifteen-minute walk uphill along Xin Dajie takes you past a shopping centre and the **post office**, then continues north past the **Bank of China**, the small **North bus station** and a statue of Chairman Mao, and towards Black Dragon Pool Park. Walking and cycling are the main means of getting around – ask at your accommodation about bike rental. The old town is tough to find your way around – look out for prints of the hand-drawn English map, "Roaming in Lijiang" sold in tourist stores (¥5). General **information** is provided by accommodation and tourist cafés (see below), while you can book **tours** of local sights through Laojun Mountain Travel Service (ⓣ0888/5105618), at the intersection of Xin Dajie and roads into Dayan – count on ¥300 a day for a car and driver, and from ¥140 per person for day-trips to the mountain.

As a rule of thumb, buses **leaving Lijiang** for northern destinations depart from the North bus station, while other directions are covered from the main depot. Buses head in all directions: south as far as Kunming and Baoshan; west to **Weixi**; north to **Qiatou** or **Daju** (for **Tiger Leaping Gorge**), and **Zhongdian**; and east to Lugu Hu and Panzhihua in Sichuan. While the Sichuan routes have become popular alternative trails between the provinces, the Tibetan border beyond Zhongdian is only accessible to groups on tours (see p.891). **CAAC** is in the western part of town on Fuhui Lu, or you can buy tickets from the travel agents outside the bus station; as well as frequent services to Kunming, there are also daily flights to Jinghong in Xishuangbanna.

Accommodation

Lijiang has plenty of **places to stay**, and it's one place in China where families are encouraged to open up their homes to guests, so there are some great small places in the old town. Mid-range hotels in the new town are legion, though there's no reason to stay there – even if you have an early bus, it's a very short cab ride to the station. The hotels below are all housed in Naxi-style buildings, some more authentic than others. Addresses are listed but they aren't much help – look at the map for locations.

A Liang Guesthouse 110 Wenzhi Xiang ⓣ0888/5129923. The best place to stay in Lijiang, this is simply a snug old Naxi courtyard house – one of a hundred "specially protected" buildings in Lijiang – with three upstairs rooms that the amiable family rent out at reasonable rates. ❶

Inn of the First Bend 43 Mishi Xiang ⓣ0888/5181688. An old backpacker staple. All facilities are shared and staff are friendly and professional. Rooms surround a central courtyard. Bike rental available. Dorm beds ¥20, ❷

Jiannanchun 8 Xinyi Xiang ⓣ0888/5102222. The upmarket option, a new, imitation Naxi building, in which the mostly Han staff wear Naxi costume all day. The location is good though, but it's only worth considering if you absolutely must have your own bathroom. ❼

Old Town Inn Xinyi Jie ⓣ0888/5189000, ⓕ5126618. Slightly more upmarket, a new, quiet, good-looking place offering rooms with and without a bath. ❷–❹

Old Town Youth Hostel 61 Xinhua Jie ⓣ0888/5188611. A new, accredited youth hostel, offering beds in rooms off a central courtyard. Small discount for YHA members. Offers bike rental. Dorm beds ¥15–50.

Square Inn Off Sifang Square ⓣ0888/5127487. Small, good value and well located at the heart of the old town. Dorm beds ¥25, ❷

Eating

Lijiang's **restaurants** enjoy a good standard of cooking, though local treats are limited to *baba*, a rather stodgy deep-fried flour patty stuffed with meat or vegetables. The old town's **inns** (not accommodation) around Sifang marketplace are interesting places to wolf down ricepots, pork stews and dried ham dishes with locals; some have gone to the trouble of translating their names into English, such as "Welcome to Flourish Snack". There are also plenty of **tourist restaurants** and foreign-oriented **cafés** in the vicinity of Sifang: *Old Market Café* has some good Chinese food; *Prague Café* scores for its blueberry cake, menagerie of animals and video collection; *Well Bistro* gets universal approval for its pasta, apple cake and chocolate brownies; *Blue Page Vegetarian* provides filling Western and Chinese dishes; *Mamafu's* has great outside seating by a stream; while *House of Tibet* has unusual Yak cheese pancakes with honey. The *Camel Bar* is the most conducive place for a drink. In winter, keep an eye open in the markets for the best **walnuts** in Yunnan, and bright orange **persimmons** growing on big, leafless trees around town – these have to be eaten very ripe and are an acquired taste.

Puji, Baisha and beyond

Rich pickings surround Lijiang, with numerous **temples** and villages on the lower slopes of Yulong Xue Shan well within bicycle range. Single women should be on their guard when visiting the more remote temples, as the past behaviour of some of the caretakers has been less than exemplary.

The monastery of **Puji Si** is the closest to Lijiang, and though it's difficult to find and not of great importance, in summer the journey there takes you through a valley brimming with wild flowers of all descriptions. Head west from the Mao Statue for about 1.5km, then turn left; snake around for a further couple of kilometres and you'll reach **PUJI village**. Ask here for a safe place to leave your bicycle and walk up the hill for thirty minutes or so to where an eccentric caretaker will open the monastery up for you. Inside it's new (like other temples in the area, Puji was destroyed during the Cultural Revolution) and deserted.

More ambitious is a trip to the village of **BAISHA**, about 10km north of Lijiang. From the top of Xin Dajie, take the road left just before Black Dragon Pool Park and follow it for a couple of kilometres until you reach a big reservoir. Keep straight on up the main road for 8km and then take a road left across the fields. Baisha is an attractive place, planted with willows and home to the renowned **Doctor Ho** who lives at the north end and will doubtless detect your presence, inviting you in to drink one of his cure-all herb teas and make a donation. Prise yourself away and make for the alleyway leading up from the school to **Liuli Dian**, a temple housing wonderful Ming-dynasty **murals** whose strange mix of Taoist, Tibetan and Buddhist influences was the work of local Dongbas.

It takes around an hour to reach Baisha by bike, and another ten minutes of pedalling north brings you to **YULONG village**. Nearby is **Beiyue Si**, a temple whose eighth-century origins predate the arrival of the Naxi in Lijiang, though it's been managed by descendants of the first Naxi landowners for almost a thousand years and is dedicated to one of their gods, **Sanduo**. There's a mighty statue of him inside, faced by the cringing, life-size image of a peasant – a very feudal tableau. Farther north again is another village, and here a steep path leads up from the main road to **Yufeng Si**, the Jade Peak Temple (30min). It's not of great interest in itself, but there's an ancient, intertwined

camellia tree in the top hall representing matrimonial harmony, and in spring the flower-filled courtyard with its mosaic floor is a nice spot for peaceful contemplation.

Two kilometres along the main road beyond Yufeng is **Yuhu**, the Jade Lake village where Joseph Rock based himself in the 1920s and 1930s. His house still stands and a steadily dwindling number of locals can remember him. Alternatively, Yufeng Si sits in the foothills of Yulong Xue Shan itself, and higher up are villages of **Yi** herders and woodcutters, whose women wear oversized black bonnets and three-coloured skirts. The 5596-metre-high mountain is too difficult to climb without proper equipment – though two **cable cars** to points above the snowline should be operational now – but there are endless possibilities for careful wandering around the trails across the lower slopes.

Shigu and Weixi

Seventy kilometres west of Lijiang, **SHIGU** (Stone Drum) is a small place named after a tablet raised here in the eighteenth century by one of Lijiang's Mu clan to mark a particularly bloody victory over Han Chinese armies. Broad and not too rough, the **Yangzi River** makes its first major bend here, deflected sharply to the northeast towards Tiger Leaping Gorge, having flowed uninterrupted in a thousand-kilometre arc from its source away on the Tibet–Qinghai border. Part of the Red Army chose this point to ford the Yangzi during the Long March in April 1936, breaking through Nationalist lines under the guidance of the spirited Communist general He Long. There's a small **guesthouse** (❷) in Shigu, and it's a pretty area to spend a spring day walking around.

For the adventurous, buses run 100km northwest beyond Shigu through a beautiful, little-explored area which still lacks any tourist infrastructure. The road follows the Yangzi to the halfway town of **Jiudian**, and then bears west past the slopes of **Hengduan Shan** and **Xinzhu Botanical Garden** – basically just a protected natural hillside boasting over three hundred species of trees, some of which are estimated to be a thousand years old. **WEIXI** town marks the end of the road, of interest for nearby villages inhabited by the **Pumi**, a Tibetan race forming one of China's smallest nationalities.

Tiger Leaping Gorge

About 100km north of Lijiang, and the same distance south of Zhongdian, the Yangzi River's upper reaches, the Jinsha Jiang, channel violently through **Tiger Leaping Gorge** (Hutiao Xia). The gorge is so narrow in places that legend has it a tiger once escaped pursuit by leaping across. The drama is heightened by this being the world's deepest canyon, set at an altitude of 2500 metres with the line of ash grey mountains forming its southern wall rising for a further 3km above the rapids. Statistics aside, what makes the **hike through the gorge** so compelling is that for once you are doing this entirely for its own sake: there are no temples to see, the villages along the way are quaint but minute, and the scenery is dramatic but stark – the gorge's pastoral residents have long since stripped the land of trees and shrubs.

There are **two routes** through the gorge between **Daju** in the east, and westerly **Qiaotou**, on the Lijiang–Zhongdian road, both of which are connected by daily services to Lijiang's North bus station. The forty-kilometre-long **low road** has better views of the river but follows a new vehicle track, especially built for Chinese tour buses; if this sounds unappealing, the fifty-kilometre **high road** offers a rougher and more exciting detour off this between Qiatou and the halfway point at **Walnut Garden**. Either option takes at least **two days** of walking, though there are side trips to make from Walnut Garden – one of which can take you 120km north **to Zhongdian** (see p.890). Plenty of people tackle the trek as if it was a competition, but you'll get more out of it if you take an extra day or two – there are few enough oppurtunities to stay in attractive villages in China, so take advantage.

You can tackle the trail from either direction: if you want to head onto Zhongdian afterwards, you can start at Daju – the way described below – and catch a direct bus on to Zhongdian afterwards. This is mostly uphill though. Alternatively, start from Qiaotou (which makes for easier walking) and leave your lugagge at the *Shengjian Café* (see below). Then from Walnut Garden it's easy to hitch a lift back along the low road.

Hostel **accommodation and meals** are available along the way, though you need to bring snacks, a solid pair of boots, flashlight and a first-aid kit. Winter days are often warm enough to hike in a T-shirt and shorts, but nights are cold throughout the year.

It's best not to walk alone, if only in case something goes wrong along the way. The high road is marked by red and yellow arrows but it's still possible to get lost; try and pick up the home-made **maps** floating around cafés in Lijiang and at the stops on the route, as these provide some protection against misdirection. **Landslides** are a more serious hazard and killed a party of seven hikers in 1994 – do not attempt either route in bad weather.

Daju to Walnut Garden

All things considered, the hike is superb. The early morning bus from Lijiang takes an uncomfortable three hours, skirting the base of Yulong Xue Shan and climbing up through patches of primeval forests and open pasture, before finally juddering to a halt at the dusty jumble of stone-walled houses which comprise **DAJU**. There are several restaurants and two simple guesthouses here (❶), along with similar outlying villages to explore; the **bus back to Lijiang** leaves at around 1.30pm.

From Daju, it's about an hour's walk across the open plateau to the **ferry across the Yangzi**; the departure point is just short of a small pagoda. Make enough noise and the ferry will turn up, if it isn't there already; the charge is a hefty ¥10 per foreigner, and nothing will alter this. Climb the bank on the far side and take any of the tracks towards the gorge, which is clearly visible away to the west; the next hour takes you past a couple of villages before a short, steep descent onto the main path. From here it's steadily uphill around a huge, bowl-shaped depression to rejoin the river at the gorge's mouth, which closes in abruptly, the path now running some 200m above a very fierce Yangzi. A further two hours should see you at the open valley surrounding the tiny village of **WALNUT GARDEN** where you'll be charged a ¥30 entrance fee at a ticket office. Some people try to avoid this by coming through at night; they only end up getting lost in the dark. Two establishments provide good meals, beer and warm beds. The westerly one, *Sean's* (❶) faces into the gorge and is a favourite for its English-speaking management and front porch, where you can sit after dark and watch an amazing number of satellites zipping through the clear night skies. There's a rare track down to the river here, plus a couple of **guided excursions** that you can arrange. The first is a half-day round trip to a small **cave**, the second a **three-day hike to Zhongdian**, around 120km northwest through a very untouristed part of the world; this heads initially to the villages of **Haba** (6hr) and **Baishui**, the White Water Terrace (another 6hr), where you can find irregular buses for the remaining 60km (5hr) to Zhongdian.

Walnut Garden to Qiaotou

The two routes diverge at Walnut Garden. The **low road** is the easier of the two and provides some splendid views: the gorge is tight and steep, the Yangzi fast and rough, and the road narrow, though formerly dangerous stretches now bore through a **tunnel** – but be aware, landslides do still occur along here. You are basically walking along a dusty road, however, and tourist buses will roar back and forth. Expect to take around eight hours to reach Qiaotou.

The **high road** – really a mountain path – is for most the more appealing option. It's a long hike but there are a couple of excellent places to rest up along the way, and it's worth taking your time. From Walnut Garden it's a three-hour, mostly uphill hike to the *Halfway House* (❶) in Bendiwan village, which has one of the greatest toilet views outside Tibet. You can arrange horse riding and guided walks from here. It's another five hours to the *Naxi Family Guesthouse* (❶), a homely farmhouse with tasty food. Another couple of hours of light trekking takes you to **QIAOTOU**, an ordinary market town. English signs pick out the *Gorge Village Hotel* (❶) on the roadside, but the rooms at the *Youth Hostel* (❶) opposite on the main road are better. The *Shengjian Coffee House*, just before the bridge, is good for information, and has a pleasant and helpful owner, but the food is pretty bad. There are plenty of buses from here to Zhongdian or Lijiang, either of which is about three hours away; the last bus leaves at around 6pm.

To Sichuan: Lugu Hu and Panzhihua

An increasingly popular route **into Sichuan** heads 200km due east from Lijiang over the border to **Panzhihua**, a stop on the Kunming–Chengdu **rail line**. It's about a ten-hour trip – twelve coming the other way – and you're unlikely to forget the early stages of the journey, as the road traverses an almost sheer 1200-metre cliff on the way to the Yangzi crossing and the town of **YONGSHENG**, where the bus will probably stop for lunch.

Yongsheng marks the start of a 300-kilometre trail north on public transport to **Ninglang**, and thence to **Lugu Hu**, a remote lake right on the border whose partially forested shores are inhabited by groups of **Norzu** and **Mosuo**. A branch of Yi, the Norzu were **slave owners**, and well into the 1950s would raid surrounding lowlands for captives. These were dragged off into the mountains and condemned to live in abject misery while their masters had the power of life and death over them (more of the story is told in Alan Winnington's excellent *Slaves of the Cool Mountains*). For their part, the Mosuo are a Naxi subgroup, still retaining the **matrilineal traditions** lost in Lijiang, such as *axia* marriage, sealed without a specific ceremony and freely broken by either party. Children are automatically adopted by the mother – men have no descendants or property rights. It takes five hours to get from Lijiang to **NINGLANG**, where the *Jiamei Binguan* (❷) comes recommended as somewhere **to stay**, and another two hours in a share taxi from here to lakeshore **LUOSHUI**, where you'll be charged ¥30 for a "ticket" you never see. There's plenty of accommodation in Luoshui, or, much more romantically, you can head to one of the lakeside villages where many families rent out beds in their busy farmhouses for around ¥20. The mountains and lake can be stunning, though there's little to do except hire a dugout and be ferried across into Sichuan, landing either at the north-shore village of **Dazu**, or eastern **La'ao** – nicely set at the foot of a 2800-metre peak. From either place, there's local transport east via **Yanyuan** to **Xichang**, also on the Kunming–Chengdu line (see p.950); roads are really appalling, however.

If you don't detour to Lugu, it takes about five hours to reach Panzhihua from Yongsheng, with most of the trip spent above the edges of broad irrigated valleys. **Dukou**'s barren hills and filthy industrial mess appear first, with **PANZHIHUA** – also known as **Jinjiang** – not far beyond. The bus stops right outside the station and, as Panzhihua is not somewhere you'd choose to stay for long, try and get on one of the evening trains. There's a **hostel** (❷) opposite the train station if you get stuck, and a daybreak bus back to Lijiang.

Zhongdian and Deqin

Six hours and 200km northwest of Lijiang, the road climbs out of a steadily narrowing gorge onto a high, barren plateau grazed by shaggy-tailed yaks and ringed by frosted mountains – the borderland between Yunnan, Sichuan and Tibet. First stop is **ZHONGDIAN**, an initially unprepossessing Han-style outpost with a heavy police presence and a good number of crusty looking Tibetans wandering around. It's not a bad place, however, and the splendid **Jietang Songlin Monastery** (¥10) just north of town will keep you busy for a few hours – catch a northbound bus #3 from the main street for ¥1. Destroyed during the 1960s, it is now reactivated and houses four hundred Tibetan monks; amongst butter sculptures and a forest of pillars, the freshly painted murals in the claustrophobic, windowless main hall are typically gruesome and colourful, all lit by low-wattage bulbs. Don't forget to walk clockwise around both the monastery and each hall.

Zhongdian's wide, kilometre-long main street, Changzheng Lu, points north, with the **bus station** and **post office** about halfway along, and the rest a string of markets, hardware stores, and souvenir shops selling Tibetan knives, clothes and trinkets. The best **accommodation** is 700m southeast of the centre – catch a south-bound bus #3 – at the *Tibet Long Life Hotel* (Ⓣ0887/8222448, Ⓕ8223863; ❷, dorm beds ¥20), whose nice staff and warm, conservatory dining room are unbelievably welcome in winter. Half a kilometre out of town towards the monastery you'll see the *Living Buddha Guesthouse* labelled in English on the left. It's a big local house that rents out beds (¥40) and is home to a "living Buddha" – that is, someone declared a reincarnation by llamas – who has no qualms about cashing in on his status.

Otherwise, there's not much in the way of **places to eat**, just a Sichuanese restaurant back on the main street, and a few **foreigners' cafés** on the main street and the road parallel to it. The best of them is the *Shangri La Coffee House*, where the more fashionable locals go too. Cafés and accommodation also provide information on **trips out** from Zhongdian – including the three-day hike via **Baishui** to **Tiger Leaping Gorge** (see p.887).

Moving on, there are ten buses daily back to Lijiang, and three daily services north to **Deqin**, last stop before the Tibetan border (see below), and northeast **into Sichuan**. You need to check on the latest situation, but at the time of writing foreigners were allowed to take this rough, scenic and unpredictable

Zhongdian and Deqin

Deqin	德钦	***déqīn***
Zhongdian	中甸	***zhōngdiàn***
Tibet Long life Hotel	西藏永生旅馆	*xīzàngyǒngshēng lǚguǎn*

ride. Join the wild-looking guys who reek of yak butter on the 7.30am bus to Litang. You can stay the night there at the somewhat unsanitary bus station guesthouse (❶). It will take you another day to go from there to Kangding in Sichuan (see p.981). Destinations further north are closed.

The rules on travelling **to Tibet** from this area are always in a state of flux, but the news at the time of writing was that it was again possible; you can fly from the confusingly named Deqin airport in Zhongdian to Lhasa for ¥2400 (about the same as you'll pay in Chengdu). The **tourist office** in room 306 of the *Khamba Hotel* (on the main street; Ⓣ0887/8230110; Ⓦwww.tibetmotorhome.com) will sort out your ticket and permit (the air ticket office on Wenming Jie decidedly won't). The tourist office also runs seven-day overland jeep tours to Lhasa for around ¥5000 per person (minimum two people). There's another smaller branch in the *Tibet Long Life*, and one in the *Camellia Hotel* in Kunming.

Deqin

Nine hours north of Zhongdian across some permanently snowy ranges, and only 80km from Tibet by road, **DEQIN** has traditionally been one of Yunnan's remotest corners. Recently, however, the region was seriously "identified" by the provincial government as **Shangri-la**, the fabled setting for James Hilton's classic tale *Lost Horizon* – an interesting claim considering *Lost Horizon* is fiction. Hype aside, Deqin is a Tibetan town in the Lancang River (Mekong) Valley, with a couple of temples. The main sight in the area is 30km west at **Meilu Xue Shan**, Yunnan's 6740-metre apex whose dwindling forests are home to the highly endangered **Yunnan Golden Monkey**. There are scheduled buses to Deqin from Zhongdian at 7am, 8am and 9am, though in winter the road is often closed, and the trip takes a rough eight hours. Deqin's *Tibet Hotel* (❶) is reasonable enough, but apparently there's a better place on the road towards the bridge. Getting to the mountain is not easy, involving **jeep rental** – check the noticeboards at the hotels in Deqin and talk to outlets in Zhongdian before trying it.

The route northwest to the Tibetan border is theoretically simpler – this is the main Yunnan–Tibet highway after all – but the PSB will have to approve your presence before any vehicle will have you on board, which means you'll have to go on a tour. If you make it, the road follows the dramatic upper reaches of the Lancang River to Markam, and then turns west towards Lhasa.

Xiaguan to Burma

Southwest of Xiaguan, the latter 500km of China's section of the Burma Road continues relentlessly through **Baoshan Prefecture** and into the **Dehong Dai–Jingpo Autonomous Region**, cut by the deep watershed gorges of Southeast Asia's mighty **Mekong** and **Salween rivers** (Lancang Jiang and Nu Jiang respectively). It's impressive country, almost entirely covered by tightly pinched extensions of the dark, monsoonal **Gaoligong Mountains**, and the road forever wobbles across high ridges or descends towards the green fields of rice and sugar cane which occupy the broad valleys in between. Settlements have large populations of **Dai**, **Burmese**, **Jingpo** and others, and until recently mainstream China never had a great presence here. Even after Kublai Khan invaded and left his relatives to govern from inside walled towns, the region was basketed into the "Department of

Xiaguan to Burma

Baoshan	保山	***bǎoshān***
Taibao Shan Park	太保山公园	*tàibǎoshān gōngyuán*
Wenbi Pagoda	文笔塔	*wénbǐ tǎ*
Wuhou Si	武侯寺	*wǔhóu sì*
Yu Huang Si	玉皇寺	*yùhuáng sì*
Accommodation		
Huacheng Binguan	花城宾馆	*huāchéng bīnguǎn*
Yindou	银都大酒店	*yíndū dàjiǔdiàn*
Yongchang	永昌宾馆	*yǒngchāng bīnguǎn*
Around Baoshan		
Banqiao	板桥	*bǎnqiáo*
Jihong Bridge	霁虹桥	*jìhóng qiáo*
Shuizhai	水寨	*shuǐzhài*
Wofo Si	卧佛寺	*wòfó sì*
Mangshi	芒市	***mángshì***
Ruili	瑞丽	***ruìlì***
Jingcheng Hotel	景成大酒店	*jǐngchéng dàjiǔdiàn*
Limin	利民宾馆	*lìmín bīnguǎn*
Mingrui Hotel	明瑞宾馆	*míngruì bīnguǎn*
Nanyang Hotel	南洋宾馆	*nányáng bīnguǎn*
Ruili Hotel	瑞丽宾馆	*ruìlì bīnguǎn*
Around Ruili		
Denghannong Si	召尚弄寺	*zhāoshàngnòng sì*
Jiexiang	姐相	*jiěxiàng*
Jinya Ta	金鸭塔	*jīnyā tǎ*
Nongdao Xiang	弄岛乡	*nòngdǎo xiāng*
Tengchong	腾冲	***téngchōng***
Daying Shan	打应山	*dǎyìng shān*
Heshun Xiang	和顺乡	*héshùn xiāng*
Huo Shan Kou	火山口	*huǒshān kǒu*
Laifeng Shan Park	来风山公园	*láifēngshān gōngyuán*
Mazhan	马站	*mǎzhàn*
Post Office Hotel	邮政宾馆	*yōuzhèng bīnguǎn*
Rehai	热海	*rèhǎi*
Tengchong Binguan	腾冲宾馆	*téngchōng bīnguǎn*
Tengyun Binguan	腾云宾馆	*téngyún bīnguǎn*
Tonglida Binguan	通利达宾馆	*tōnglìdá bīnguǎn*
Zhonghe	中和	*zhōnghé*
Wanding	畹町	***wǎndīng***
Longlong	弄弄	*nòngnòng*
Manbang	曼棒	*mànbàng*
Wanding Binguan	畹町宾馆	*wǎndīng bīnguǎn*
Wanding Forest Park	畹町国家森林公园	*wǎndīng guójiā sēnlín gōngyuán*
Yufeng Dajiudian	裕丰大酒店	*yùfēng dàjiǔdiàn*

Pacification and Mollification" and largely left to the pleasure of local **saubwas**, hereditary landowners. They were deposed in the 1950s, but it's still often unclear whether rules and regulations originate in Beijing or with the nearest officer in charge.

The Burma Road itself links the towns of **Baoshan**, **Mangshi** and the border crossing at **Wanding**, from where it's only an hour west to weird wonders at **Ruili**, more of a circus than a city. There's also a rougher back road between Baoshan and Ruili, taking in the tectonically unstable **Tengchong** region and some diminishing jungle. Whichever way you travel, roads tend to disintegrate during the subtropically humid **wet season** between May and October, when airports at Baoshan and Mangshi may provide the only access.

Baoshan and around

BAOSHAN, 120km from Xiaguan, may be dull but it has its share of history. The region was settled long before Emperor Wu's troops oversaw the paving of stretches of the Southern Silk Road nearby in 109 BC, and the famous third-century Sichuanese minister **Zhuge Liang** later reached Baoshan in one of his invasive "expeditions" across southwestern China. Kublai Khan fought a massive battle with the Burmese king **Narathihapade** outside the town in 1277, won by the khan after his archers managed to stampede Burmese elephants back through their own lines. Twenty years later the women and slaves of Marco Polo's "Vochan" (today's Baoshan) supported a tattooed, gold-toothed aristocracy – tooth-capping is still practised both here and in Xishuangbanna today. Baoshan was again in the front line in the 1940s, when a quarter of a million Chinese troops fought to keep the Japanese from invading through Burma, and remains garrisoned today, with young army recruits in poorly fitting green fatigues drilling around the parks and parade grounds.

The Town and around

Baoshan's centre is boxed in by **Huancheng Lu**, whose north, south, east and west sections follow the square lines of the now demolished Ming city walls. Ennobled as a city in 1983, Baoshan is nonetheless very much a provincial town, and its grubby, half-modernized streets are full of activity. In the Burma Road's heyday the shops stocked Western goods siphoned off from supply convoys heading through to Kunming, and even now they seem abnormally well provisioned with locally grown "World Number One Arabica" coffee, tins and bottles of imported luxuries, smart suits and shoes. Rural produce gets an airing in the **main marketplace** on Qingzhen Jie, somewhere to browse among Baoshan's older buildings, but it's not especially exciting. A nicer spot to spend a few hours among pine trees, butterflies and twittering birds is **Taibao Shan Park**, about 1.5km west of the centre at the end of Baoxiu Lu. Near the entrance is **Yu Huang Si**, a Ming Taoist temple whose slanted pillars support a small octagonal dome. It's no longer a place of worship, filled with photos and maps describing local engagements with the Japanese forces, but you'll have to remove your shoes to visit the five alabaster Buddhas in the tiny nunnery next door.

The path climbs farther up to pavilions offering views over town and the surrounding Baoshan Plain, until it reaches **Wuhou Si** on the flattened, wooded summit. Wuhou Si commemorates the Three Kingdoms' leader Zhuge Liang (see p.509), whose huge bearded statue sits between his ministers. Behind the hall are some respectably large trees, and fragments of stone tablets recording imperial proclamations. On the far side of Taibao Shan is the thirteen-storey **Wenbi Pagoda** – blocked off and surrounded by graves – and **Yiluo Chi**, an uninteresting walled pond below the steps leading up to Baoshan's **Teacher Training College**. If you're looking for conversation, students and the couple of overseas teachers quartered here are often glad to talk to foreigners.

Practicalities

Surrounded by dumpling, soup and noodle stalls, the **main bus station** (ticket office daily 8am–9pm) is on the corner of Huancheng Dong Lu and Baoxiu Lu, the latter of which runs due west straight through the city. About 500m along it's crossed by Zhengyang Lu, where there's a **Bank of China** (Mon–Fri 8am–6pm), department store and a tiny, well-concealed **airline office**. Gradually narrowing in its final kilometre, Baoxiu Lu is further crossed by Qingzhen Jie and Huancheng Xi Lu before ending at a staircase leading up to Taibao Shan Park.

Baoshan has plenty of **accommodation and food**. Just east of the station on Huancheng Dong Lu, *Huancheng Binguan* (℡0875/2203047; ❶–❷) is getting musty round the edges. West along Baoxiu Lu, the smarter *Yindou Dajiudian* (℡0875/2120948; ❷), right next to the bank, is a better bet, though none of its facilities, even the restaurant, ever seem to open. The rooms on the top floor are the best maintained, with good views. The *Yongchang Binguan* (℡0875/2122802; ❶–❹), in a courtyard on the south side of Baoxiu Lu just over Zhengyang Lu, has rooms ranging from spartan to bland, but at least they're clean. Not counting the hotels, there are a dozen or more restaurants turning out decent stir-fries and casseroles between the bus station and the park, with the yellow-tiled Muslim place on the corner of Qingzhen Jie the best of the bunch – look for the Arabic script.

Moving on, there are direct daily buses to all destinations east and west including Kunming, Tengchong and Ruili, and also a lengthy southern link with Jinghong in Xishuangbanna – see p.901 before undertaking this journey.

Around Baoshan

Two more historical snippets lie near the town of **BANQIAO**, thirty minutes by bus from Baoshan on the Xiaguan road. About 7km northwest of Banqiao, **Wofo Si** (Reclining Buddha Temple) is a split-level cave at the foot of Yunyan Shan, named after a graceful fifteen-metre marble statue said to date from the Tang dynasty. Fifteen kilometres northeast of Banqiao is **SHUIZHAI township**; an hour's walk short of here the heavy-duty, five-hundred-year-old chains of the **Jihong Qiao** bridge the **Mekong River**. There are infrequent minibuses to both sites from Baoshan, or you could try taking any bus to Banqiao and looking for local transport from there.

Tengchong and the back road to Ruili

The ghost of the former Southern Silk Road runs west of Baoshan, and the bus is initially slowed by police roadblocks and crowded village markets, then by steep hairpin bends as it skirts the dense undergrowth of the **Gaoligong Shan Nature Reserve**. Two valleys along the way are fertilized by the early stirrings of the Salween and **Shweli** rivers (the latter a tributary of the Irrawaddy), both of which ultimately empty into the sea several thousand kilometres away in southern Burma.

Six hours from Baoshan the bus trundles to a halt at **TENGCHONG**, an untidy, energetic town undergoing expansion. A Han-dynasty settlement which first grew wealthy on Silk Road trade, Tengchong has a high incidence of **earthquakes**, which have left it bereft of large historic monuments or tall buildings, but business still flourishes and there are some unusual geological sights nearby. The **bus station** is in the eastern outskirts along Huancheng Dong Lu. For the centre, continue south past shops selling bamboo furniture and pipes, and then bear west down either Guanghua Lu or parallel Yingjiang

Lu to where Tengchong's high street, **Fengshan Lu**, cuts across them at right angles. One kilometre farther south down Fengshan Lu takes you past a **post office** and **bank** to the junction with **Fangshou Lu**, the main road west out of town. Cycle-rickshaws wait at the station, though a walk right across town takes only thirty minutes.

Tengchong's premier market is the **Frontier Trade Bazaar**, held every morning along western Guanghua Lu. With business revolving around household goods and food, things are not quite as romantic as they sound, but there's also a **jewellery and gem market** on Fengshan Lu, and both should whet your appetite for better affairs in Ruili. For a stroll, follow Guang Xiang for twenty minutes to its end at **Laifeng Shan Park**, several square kilometres of hilly woodland immediately southwest of Tengchong. Full of family activity at weekends, paths ascend to **Laifeng Si**, a monastery-turned-museum, and a resurrected, thirteen-storey **pagoda** which will guide you to the park from town.

For **accommodation**, try the low-priced *Tonglida Binguan* offering huge doubles with bathroom (❸, dorm beds ¥30) across from the bus station; the *Post Office Hotel* (❸), next to the post office on Fengshan Lu; or the quiet *Tengchong Binguan* (Ⓣ0875/5121044; ❷, dorm beds ¥30) – walk to the western end of Fengshan Lu, cross straight over Fangshou Lu and head uphill, turn left and the hotel is about 100m farther on. Their cheapest rooms are bare, but they can arrange **tours** into the countryside, and the **restaurant** provides small set meals for the princely sum of ¥6. Other general places to eat lurk along Yingjiang Lu and Guanghua Lu, where evening stalls also sell charcoal-grilled chicken and fish. There's a tiny **Burmese bar** at the entrance to the otherwise avoidable *Tengyun Binguan* off Yingjiang Lu, marked with a tiny English sign and patronized by people claiming to be diamond merchants – you'll make friends here if you can hold your rum.

Around Tengchong

Five kilometres west of town along Fangshou Lu, **HESHUN XIANG** is a Qing-style village whose splendid memorial gateways, ornamental gardens and thousand or more houses are tightly packed within a whitewashed brick wall. It is trumpeted for the achievements of its former residents, many of whom have led profitable lives after emigrating overseas and have since ploughed money back into the village's upkeep, and you could easily spend half a day here with a camera. In particular, look for **Yuanlong Tan**, a delightful pond surrounded by pavilions and a creaky water mill.

Geological shuffles over the last fifty million years have opened up a couple of hotspots around Tengchong. Easiest to reach, **Rehai** ("Hot Sea") is 11km southwest along the Ruili Road, where the scalding **Liuhuang** and **Dagungguo** pools steam and bubble away, contained by incongruously neat stone paving and ornamental borders. Get there on minibuses (¥5 per person) from Huancheng Nan Lu, at the junction with the Ruili road. Volcano hunters should ask around at the bus station or hotels for transport 10km northwest to **Zhonghe** village and the slopes of 2614-metre-high **Daying Shan**, or 30km north to **Huo Shan Kou**, a large crater near the town of **Mazhan**. These two are the largest of many surrounding cones, dormant but covered in rubble from previous eruptions.

On to Ruili

The quickest way from Tengchong to Ruili is by taking the southeasterly road via Mangshi and Wanding (below), but there's also a direct road running west, towards and then along the Burmese border, a seven-hour trip on a good day.

This begins smoothly, cruising through a river valley where the scenery becomes less and less "Chinese" as the bus passes Dai villages with rounded wats, red-leaved poinsettias and huge, shady fig trees. Progress becomes unpredictable after a lunch stop and more officious police checks near **Yingjiang**, where the road turns south to cross the ranges above Ruili. You may well get a close look at the forests here – one downhill stretch is notorious for the house-sized boulders which crash down from the slopes above to block the road completely, causing extended delays as labourers hammer and blast away at the obstructions. If this happens, go for a walk along the road, as there's birdlife hiding in patches of vegetation and villages along the way which have seen few foreigners.

Mangshi

South of Baoshan the Burma Road makes a grand descent into the Salween River Valley on the five-hour journey to **MANGSHI** (also known as **Luxi**), Dehong's little administrative capital and the site of its airport. Surrounded by Dai and Jingpo villages, the Mangshi region has a reputation for excellent pineapples and silverwork, though the town itself holds only enough to occupy a couple of hours between connections. Hot and grey, the highway runs through as **Tuan Jie Dajie**, its eastern end marked by a large roundabout and its western end by a narrow, black canal. Just over this canal, **Yueyi Lu** points north into a jumble of quieter, older streets filled with markets and a fair complement of **Buddhist temples** raised on wooden piles in the ornate Dai style, many of them being restored.

The **airport** is about 7km south off the highway, where taxis and minibuses to Mangshi, Ruili and Wanding meet incoming flights. A minibus to Ruili takes one and a half hours and should cost ¥20. Most Mangshi vehicles will set down at the eastern end of Tuan Jie Dajie, either on the roundabout outside the **airline office** (daily 8.30–11.30am & 1.30–5pm; the bus to the airport leaves 2hr before each flight) or about 1km west at the cluster of depots where **long-distance buses and minibuses** stop. The airline office has a clean and simple **hotel** attached (❷), or there are smart rooms at *Dehong Binguan* (❷), nicely located in large grounds at the top of backstreet Yueyi Lu. The *Dehong* has a good **restaurant**, and there are countless shacks serving buns and curries in almost every lane through the town.

Wanding and around

Two hours south of Mangshi the road crosses the **Long Jiang** (Shweli River) and then finally slaloms down the slopes of a narrow valley to where the shallow Wanding Stream separates Chinese **WANDING** from **Jiugu** over in Burma. Opened in 1938 as the Burma Road's purpose-built border crossing, Wanding was immediately attacked by villagers who suspected that this customs post was connected with Guomindang units who were then busy trying to exterminate Mangshi's Jingpo hill tribes. The tension proved short-lived but, although hundreds of trucks a day passed through during the war, Wanding has never amounted to much – possibly because, aware of its showpiece status as China's official point of entry into Burma, authorities deter the illicit backroom dealings that make neighbouring Ruili such an attractive proposition for traders.

Not that Wanding is uninteresting. The **Wanding Bridge crossing** is a marvel, decked in customs houses, smartly uniformed military, barriers, barbed wire, flags and signs everywhere prohibiting unauthorized passage. The bridge itself – though ridiculously short – is a sturdy concrete span, and there's even a prominent red line painted across the road on the Chinese side. But it's all a sham. Walk 100m downstream and you'll find people rolling up their trousers and wading across a ford almost within sight of patrolling soldiers, while farther on some enterprising soul has even set up a bamboo raft (so long it's virtually a bridge) to punt customers over to the far bank. Naturally everyone knows what's happening, but this arrangement spares authorities and locals, for whom the border is more or less open, endless official bother.

Unfortunately, **foreigners wanting to cross** will find the situation very different. At the time of writing, Westerners could enter Burma only by flying to Rangoon (see "Kunming", p.856, for more details), and though some have quietly snuck across from Wanding for an hour or two, bear in mind that you'll be very conspicuous and that there's nothing to see in Jiugu apart from a large wat on the hill above.

Practicalities

Wanding stretches thinly for 1.5km along the north bank of the Wanding Stream and Minzhu Jie, both of which run west towards Ruili, with Guofang Jie descending from the hills at Minzhu's eastern end to the border checkpoint and Wanding Bridge. There's no **bus station** as such, but local transport and vehicles shuttling between Mangshi (¥10) and Ruili (¥7) stop around the Minzhu Jie–Guofang Jie intersection. Here you'll also find a couple of fairly wholesome **restaurants**, with a **bank** (Mon–Fri 8.30–11.30am & 2–5pm) and **post office** (daily 8am–6pm) nearby on Minzhu Jie. **Accommodation** prospects are limited to the cavernous but clean *Yufeng Dajiudian* on the northeast corner of the intersection (❶), and the surprisingly good *Wanding Binguan* (❷) uphill off Minzhu Jie on Yingbin Lu. Despite the border, the backstreet **markets** along Wanding Stream are small and unenthusiastic affairs except on Saturday mornings. Street hawkers sell herbs and roots and you can pick up presentation packs of **Burmese coins** from shops near the bridge.

Around Wanding: the Forest Park and the Jingpo

One of the best ways to get a good look at Burma from the Chinese side is to spend an hour in **Wanding Forest Park** (¥3) – walk uphill along Guofang Jie, take the first lane on the left and follow it upwards to the park gates. A few minutes more bring you to an amusement area, where a dirt footpath leads into scrub and pine plantations behind the dodgems, eventually ending up at a newly completed **temple**, bare inside except for prayer cushions and a large alabaster Buddha. The front entrance looks down across the border at Jiugu, undulating green hills and the red earth continuation of the Burma Road heading south of the crossing towards Lashio.

There are a number of **Jingpo villages** around Wanding. The *Wanding Binguan* sometimes organizes tours, otherwise look for minibuses at the intersection in town. Fifteen kilometres west via **Manbang** township, **LONGLONG** comes alive for the **Munao festival** on the last day of the lunar new year (usually some time in February), when hundreds of Jingpo take part in an ancient dance said to have been handed down to their ancestors by the children of the sun god. Always considered a primitive spirit-worshipping race by the Han government, and so poor that in the early twentieth century they were forced to grow opium as a cash crop (hence the Guomindang campaign against them), the Jingpo live a relatively secluded existence in the Dehong highlands, and their settlements around Wanding are some of the most accessible.

Ruili and around

Yunnan's most westerly town, **RUILI** is barely thirty minutes by road from the sober formalities and politely quiet cross-border sneaking at Wanding, but infinitely distant in spirit. Once the capital of the Mengmao Dai Kingdom but now an ostentatious boom town, Ruili revels in the possibilities of its proximity to Burma – 5km south over the Shweli – with such a heavy flow of illegal traffic pouring over the dozens of crossing points to **Mu Se**, its Burmese counterpart, that locals quip "feed a chicken in China and you get an egg in Burma". Though things along the Burmese side have tightened up considerably in recent years, trade is very much a two-way affair, and Ruili is the main conduit for Burmese **heroin** entering China, reflected in the town's high incidence of addicts and AIDS patients. Burmese, Pakistani and Bangladeshi nationals wander around in sarongs and thongs, clocks are often set to Rangoon time, markets display foreign trade goods and most Chinese in town are tourists, attracted by the chance to pick up some cut-price trinkets and the decadent thrills of commercial sex and gambling. A few years ago you couldn't move in Ruili for karaoke set-ups, even on the pavement; but now you'll hardly find one – crazes flare and die here at a furious pace. At the time of writing, street dicing was the new big thing. At each of the many back alley stalls, three giant dice, with pictures of animals instead of numbers, are rolled down a slope. Punters bet on a particular animal turning up and double their money if it does. One constant is the almost industrial scale of prostitution, centred around ill-disguised massage parlours. While all this might sound like something to avoid, here at the fringes of the Chinese empire Ruili is a surreal treat, though take the sleaze seriously – it may be exciting after dark but it's not always safe, especially for women. If the town's nightlife appalls you, the **markets** are unquestionably fascinating, and many foreign traders speak good English and make interesting company – and the surrounding countryside, studded with Dai villages and temples, is only a bike ride away.

Burmese vocabulary

Hello (polite)	*Min galaba jinbaya*
Thank you	*Jayzu tinbadé*
I'd like to eat	*Htamin saa gyinbadé*
Beef	*Améda*
Chicken	*Jeda*
Curry	*Hin, tha*
Cold drink	*A-ay*
Crushed peanuts	*Nanthaung*
Dhal (split pea soup)	*Pey hin*
Fish	*Nga*
Fish soup with banana stem and noodles	*Moh hin gha*
Fork	*Khayan*
Milk	*Nwa nou*
Noodles	*Kaukswe*
Pickled vegetables	*Lapatoh*
Rice	*Htamin*
Sticky rice (in a bamboo tube)	*Kauk nyaimn paung (tauk)*
Sour sauce	*Achin*
Spoon	*Zone*
Tea	*La pay-ee*

Numbers

One	*Did*
Two	*Nhid*
Three	*Dhong*
Four	*Lay*
Five	*Ngar*
Six	*Chauk*
Seven	*Khunik*
Eight	*Chind*
Nine	*Cho*
Ten	*Desay*
Eleven	*Say did*

The markets

Washed red and blue in the glare of competing night-time neon, by day Ruili's broad pavements and drab construction pin it down as a typical Chinese town. Fortunately, the markets and people are anything but typical, and the **Burmese stallholders** in Xingshi Jie can sell you everything from haberdashery and precious stones to birds, cigars, Mandalay rum and Western-brand toiletries. Dai girls powder their faces with yellow talc, young men ask politely whether you'd like to part with your watch and street sellers skilfully assemble little pellets of stimulating **betel nut** dabbed in ash paste and wrapped in pepper-vine leaf, which stains lips red and teeth black.

The Burmese are very approachable, and some are refugees of a sort, as upheavals in Rangoon in 1988 and 1991 saw Muslims slipping over the border to enjoy China's relative religious freedoms. Many pedal their wares at the **jade and gem market** in an alley off Xingshi Jie, where Chinese dealers come to stock up on ruinously expensive wafers of deep green jade. You'll need hard currency (prices are given in US dollars) but most of the rubies, amethysts, sapphires, moonstones and garnets on show are flawed and poorly cut. The art of buying is a protracted process here, with dealers producing their better stones only for properly appreciative customers. For the newcomer, it's safer just to watch the furtive huddles of serious merchants, or negotiate souvenir prices for coloured pieces of sparkling Russian glass "jewels", chunks of polished substandard jade and heavy brass rings. When you've filled up your pockets, Dai and Jingpo haunt Ruili's huge **produce market**, ten minutes' walk past the post office off the west end of Xingshi Lu. This has been quiet of late, but on market days the piles of deer meat and wildcat pelts, limes, palm sugar blocks (*jaggery*), coconuts, curry pastes and pickles make this a far cry from the standard Chinese effort.

Practicalities

Ruili's kilometre-long main street is **Nanmao Jie**, which runs west from a tree-shaded roundabout past the Bank of China (foreign exchange Mon–Fri 9–11.30am & 2.30–4.30pm), a **minibus depot** for transport into the immediate area, and the **long-distance bus station**, before crossing Renmin Lu. Turn north here and there's a **post office** (daily 8am–6pm) 50m away on the corner of Xingshi Jie, along which is Ruili's major market. Cross over the broad junction here and continue up Jianshe Lu for Ruili Travel Service (Mon–Sat 7.30–11.30am & 3–6.30pm) next to the *Ruili Hotel*. They don't speak English but can organize air tickets, and there's an **airport bus** from here to Mangshi every morning – book the day before. There are minibuses every hour to Wanding and Mangshi, at least daily **buses** to everywhere along the highway between here and Kunming, and one minibus south to **Nansan**, first stop on the rough, three-day haul to Xishuangbanna (for more on this journey, see p.901).

Accommodation

Jingcheng Maohai Lu, south and parallel to Nanmao Jie ⓣ0692/4159999. A new four-star place with decent rooms, a swimming pool and gym. ❻

Limin Nanmao Jie, about 300m west of the bus sation. Good-value rooms in a well-kept multi-storey block around a courtyard, though finding the staff can be difficult. Bicycles for rent. ❷

Mingrui Western end of Nanmao Jie. Budget rooms, peeling decor and indifferent staff. ❷

Nanyang Nanmao Jie, about 200m west of the bus station. Spacious, if a little mildewed, with comfy beds. Dorm beds ¥25, ❸

Ruili Corner of Jianshe Lu and Xinjian Lu ⓣ0692/4141463 or 4141269. Nice grounds with a palm garden, but overpriced rooms, all of which have shared toilets. Scruffy dorm beds ¥25, ❹

Eating and drinking

The mobile **stalls** around the market on Xingshi Jie serve fine grilled meats, hotpots, soups and buns, and you'll also come across some Burmese delicacies. Try *moongsee joh*, a sandwich made from purple glutinous rice pancakes heated over a grill until they puff up, and spread with sugar and peanut powder. Another similar confection involves bamboo tubes stuffed with pleasantly bland, sweetened rice jelly, while *niezi binfang* is a thoroughly Southeast Asian drink made from sago, coconut jelly, condensed milk, sugar, crushed ice and water – quite refreshing on a hot day.

Hotel restaurants have good Chinese fare, but since you're here try the **Burmese cafés**, which you'll find both north of the roundabout on Jiegang Lu, and in the alleys at the western end of Xinghse Jie. They don't look much, but can produce a platter of a half-dozen small pots of tasty pickles and some basic meat and rice dishes for about ¥8. But the most pleasant Burmese place is *Bobos*, on Xin'an Lu, just off Nanmao Jie (look for the English sign), which sells great juices and snacks. There's no English spoken, and not much Chinese either.

Around Ruili

Villages and Buddhist monuments dot the plains around Ruili, easy enough to explore either by renting a bicycle from the *Limin Binguan*, or by minibus from the Nanmao Jie depot – just keep repeating the name of your destination and you'll be shepherded to the right vehicle. Ruili Travel Service can also organize private transport for the day, but it tends to be expensive. Most of the destinations below are only of mild interest in themselves, really just excuses to get out into Ruili's attractive countryside. For more about the Dai, see the Xishuangbanna section (p.904).

A few sights lie within walking distance. About 5km east along the Mangshi road is the two-hundred-year-old **Jiele Jin Ta**, a group of seventeen portly **Dai pagodas** painted gold and said to house several of Buddha's bones. Nearby are some open-air hot springs where you can wash away various ailments. The same distance south takes you past the less expansive **Jinya Ta** (Golden Duck Pagoda) to the busy **bridge over the Shweli River** into Burma, though apart from the volume of traffic, there's little to see.

Heading west along the road from Jinya Ta, another 5km brings you to a small bridge with the region's largest Buddhist temple, the nicely decorated **Hansha Si**, just off to the north. Ten kilometres beyond Hansha Si is the town of **JIEXIANG** and the splendid Tang-era **Leizhuang Xiang**, where the low square hall of a nunnery is dominated by a huge central pagoda and four corner towers, all in white. Another fine temple with typical Dai touches, such as "fiery" wooden eave decorations, **Denghannong Si**, is farther west again, and though the current halls were built only during the Qing dynasty, the site is said to mark where Buddha once stopped to preach. Beyond Denghannong, about 25km in all from Ruili, **NONGDAO XIANG** is a nice place to spend the evening chatting to locals. There's a hostel (❶) next to the post office, and the town is surrounded by Dai communities.

Southwestern Yunnan

Far more so than the rest of the province, which at least backs onto other Chinese territories, southwestern Yunnan's culture and history are products of adjoining countries. **Transport** into the region has always been a problem for any external power seeking control. Even the rivers – historically so important for inter-provincial communications in central China – here run out of the country, and long-promised highways were only completed in the 1990s. Most visitors find their attention fully occupied by the ethnically and environmentally diverse corner of **Xishuangbanna**, barely an hour from Kunming on the thrice-daily flight to the regional capital, **Jinghong**. Coming by road is not such a bad option either, with sleeper buses making the twenty-four hour incarceration as comfortable as possible, but watch that your luggage doesn't disappear while you slumber – chain bags securely or rest your legs over them. There's also some interesting territory **along the Burmese border** between Yunnan's northwest and Xishuangbanna, though you'll need time and motivation to get the best from landscape and people along the way – and to be impervious to long, tortuous bus rides on extremely rough roads.

The southwest's emphatically tropical **weather** divides into just two main seasons: a drier stretch between November and May, when warm days, cool nights and dense morning mists are the norm, after which high heat and torrential daily rains settle in for the June–October **wet season**. Given the climate, you'll need to take more than usual care of any cuts and abrasions, and to guard against mosquitoes (see "Health" in Basics, p.28). The busiest time of the year here is mid-April, when thousands of tourists flood to Jinghong for the Dai **Water-splashing Festival**, and hotels and flights will be booked solid for a week beforehand. Once there, **getting around** Xishuangbanna is easy enough, with well-maintained roads connecting Jinghong to outlying districts. **Place names** can be confusing, though, as the words "*Meng-*", designating a small town, or "*Man-*", a village, prefix nearly every destination.

Along the Burmese border

There are a few things to bear in mind before tackling one of the 500-kilometre-long roads probing down **along the Burmese border** between Xiaguan, Baoshan or Ruili in Northwestern Yunnan and Jinghong in Xishuangbanna. Whichever route you take, you're in for a tough two- to five-day trip; the routes are often so poor that it can be quicker to travel via Kunming – which is what the PSB will tell you to do if you ask about access – but you'll certainly penetrate China's untouristed backwaters, zigzagging across cold, thinly inhabited mountain folds between the **Nu** and **Lancang river systems**. What makes it worthwhile is some spellbinding scenery, the chance to glimpse at least three regional ethnic groups, and simply the thrill of travelling through an area which has seen virtually no foreigners. What is certain is that you'll end up dusty or muddy, and can expect to have your passports and bags searched at regular **army checkpoints** along the way.

Along the Burmese border

Cangyuan	沧原	***cāngyuán***
Gengma	耿马	***gěngmǎ***
Lancang	澜沧	***láncāng***
Shangye Binguan	商业宾馆	*shāngyè bīnguǎn*
Mengding	孟定	***mèngdìng***
Meng A	勐阿	***mèngā***
Meng A Binguan	勐阿宾馆	*mèngā bīnguǎn*
Nansan	南伞	***nánsǎn***
Simao	思茅	***sīmáo***
Yunxian	云县	***yúnxiàn***

From Xiaguan and Baoshan

The most direct way through the region – though still a thirty-hour journey – is to catch a Jinghong-bound sleeper bus from either **Xiaguan or Baoshan** (see pp.891–894). These routes converge around 120km into the trip at **Yunxian**, from where there's something approaching a main road all the way to Jinghong. Around a third of the way into the trip, **LANCANG** is a likely overnight stop, with alternative transport west to Gengma and beyond if you want to explore (see below). Otherwise it's another day to **SIMAO**, briefly a French concession and formerly the site of Xishuangbanna's airport, where the road joins the final 150km of the main Kunming–Jinghong highway.

From Ruili

Begining at **Ruili** (p.898) is a much tougher prospect, though there's far more in the way of interest on this route, and the landscape is a spread of intensely cultivated, vastly scaled peaks and deep river valleys, dotted with tiny villages. Start by catching a bus to **NANSAN**, basically just a truck stop twelve hours away, with a very basic hostel opposite the bus station (❶). You're right on the Burmese border here, though there's a mountain in the way to stop you wandering. From Nansan, the road continues 90km southeast over a seemingly endless succession of serrated ranges to the far more animated market town of **MENGDING**, another possible stop with a range of accommodation options and a host of outlying thatched villages.

GENGMA is a further 90km along, a small, concrete and brick town in a broad valley. Minibuses from Nansan drop off at a depot on the northern edge; walk south down the 250-metre-long main street, past a **guesthouse** (❷) to a roundabout, where you'll find the **long-distance bus station** (with departures to Cangyuan, Lincang, Menghai, Menglian and Jinghong) and a **hotel** (❸) opposite. West off the main street, Gengma's large, every-fifth-day **market** is somewhere to be eyeballed by disbelieving villagers from the hills, and the town is the first place you'll encounter **Dai** in any quantity (see p.904) – there's even a five-spired Dai pagoda on a hill southeast of the roundabout. A worthwhile detour from Gengma takes you 90km south towards the Burmese border at **CANGYUAN**, a trading centre supplying everything from motorbikes to betel nut and mushrooms, and surrounded by attractive villages whose population are mostly **Wa**. Though Buddhism was introduced at some point from

Burma, several remote **rock painting sites** associated with earlier religious rituals survive in the Awa Mountains northeast of the city. As recently as the 1960s the Wa were head-hunters, also known for their sacred drums, passion for smoking and festivals involving the frenzied dismemberment of bulls – though such things are rare events today.

Back on the main Jinghong road, it's 180km to **LANCANG**, the compact, scruffy capital of **Lahu Autonomous County**. Lancang's main streets form an inverted "Y", the stem pointing north towards Gengma, the arms heading southeast to Jinghong and southwest to **Menglian**, and their junction forming the centre of town. There are scores of places to eat around the centre, and separate **long-distance bus stations** on both arms; the best **place to stay** is on the southeastern arm, right behind the Jinghong road depot at the clean and friendly *Shangye Binguan* (❷–❸). The main reason to pause in the area is to spend a day or two looking at nearby villages, some of which are **Lahu**. Hunters of legendary skill whose name loosely implies "Tiger-eaters", the Lahu probably originated in the Dali area, perhaps driven into this southern refuge by the Mongols. Though local Lahu are pastoralists and superficially resemble neighbouring Dai, traditionally both men and women hunt, shave their heads and wear turbans. **From Lancang**, it's just six hours to Jinghong on buses from either station, descending into Xishuangbanna through the westerly town of Menghai (see p.915).

Alternatively, try spending a few days 40km southwest of Lancang at **MENGLIAN**, a pleasant Dai and Lahu town reached on hourly minibuses from the Menglian road bus station. A drab, kilometre-long main street has everything of use, including the **bus station**; head west from here and it's a five-minute walk to a **bank**, and nearby comfortable *Menglian Binguan* (Ⓣ0879/8723020; ❸), next

△ Bai seamstress

to a **bridge**. Over the road, a simple **restaurant** faces the water, while around 500m south along the river there's another gold-painted Dai **pagoda**. Cross the bridge from the *Menglian Binguan* and bear right (uphill) into the **old town**, and you'll find plenty of winding streets and some fine traditional wooden buildings – including two **temples** and the **Xuanfu Shishu museum**. Menglian also has a busy **market** every fifth day patronized by **Hani** wearing porcupine quills and colourful beetles in their hair, and offers the chance to hitch tractor rides out to Wa settlements, such as **Fu'ai**, 28km northwest.

Xishuangbanna

A lush tropical spread of virgin rainforests, plantations and paddy fields nestled 750km southwest of Kunming along the Burmese and Laotian borders, **Xishuangbanna** has little in common with the rest of provincial China. Despite recent resettlement projects to affirm Han authority, thirteen of Yunnan's ethnic groups constitute a sizeable majority of Xishuangbanna's 500,000-strong population. Foremost are the **Dai**, northern cousins to the Thais, whose distinctive temples, bulbous pagodas and saffron-robed clergy are a common sight down on the plains, particularly around **Jinghong**, Xishuangbanna's sleepy capital. The region's remaining 19,000 square kilometres of hills, farms and forest are split between the administrative townships of **Mengla** in the east and **Menghai** in the west, peppered with villages of Hani, Bulang, Jinuo, Wa and Lahu; remoter tribes are still animistic, and all have distinctive dress and customs. Cultural tourism aside, there are a number of mar-

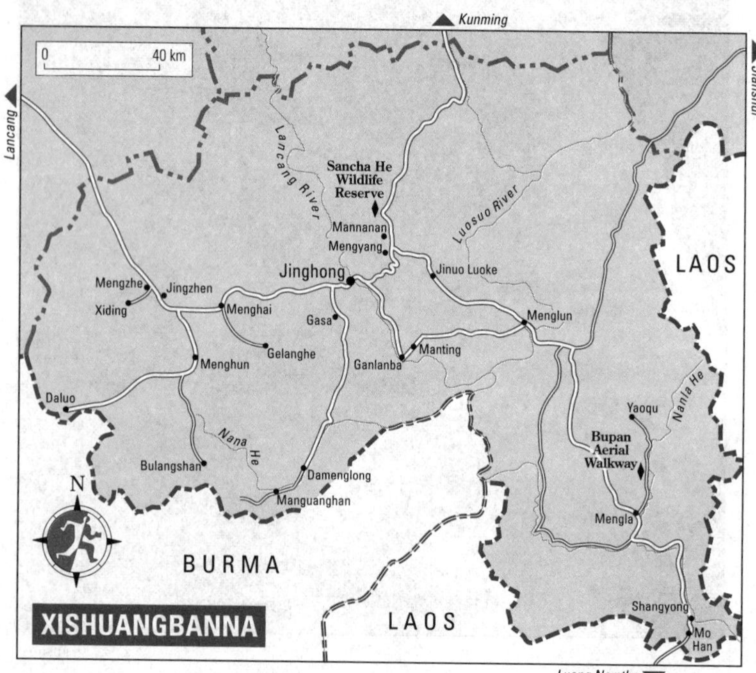

ginally developed **wildlife reserves** inhabited by elephants and other rare beasts, plenty of hiking trails, and China's **open border with Laos** to explore.

Historically, there was already a Dai state in Xishuangbanna two thousand years ago, important enough to send ambassadors to the Han court in 69 AD. Subsequently incorporated into the Nanzhao and Dali kingdoms, a brief period of full independence ended with the Mongols' thirteenth-century conquest of Yunnan. For ease of administration, the Mongols governed Xishuangbanna through Dai chieftains whom they raised in status to **pianling**, hereditary rulers, and the region was later divided into **twelve rice-growing districts** or *sipsawng pa na*, phonetically rendered as "Xishuangbanna" in Chinese. The *pianling* wielded enormous power over their fiefdoms, suppressing other minorities and treating people, land and resources as their personal property. This virtual slave system survived well into the twentieth century, when Xishuangbanna came under the thumb of the tyrannical Han warlord, **Ke Shexun**.

Not surprisingly, the **Communists** found Xishuangbanna's populace extremely sceptical of their attempts at reconciliation after taking control of the region in 1950, an attitude eventually softened by the altruistic persistence of medical and educational teams sent by Beijing. But trust evaporated in the violence of the **Cultural Revolution**, and the current atmosphere of apparent cultural freedom is undercut by resentment at what verges on colonial assimilation. More contentious aspects of religion have been banned, forests are logged to the detriment of semi-nomadic hunter groups – who then have to settle down and plant rice – and many ethnic people feel that the government would really like them to behave like Han Chinese, just dressing in colourful clothing to attract the tourists. It's certainly true that Xishuangbanna is a rather anaemic version of what lies across the border in Laos, though in fairness, Chinese administrators are the first to admit the "terrible mistakes" of the past, and feel that they are now developing the area as sensitively as possible.

Jinghong

JINGHONG, Xishuangbanna's small and easy-going "Dawn Capital", first became a seat of power under the Dai warlord **Bazhen**, who drove the Bulang

Xishuangbanna (Jinghong)

Xishuangbanna	西双版纳	***xīshuāngbǎnnà***
Jinghong	景洪	***jǐnghóng***
Chunhuan Park	春欢公园	*chūnhuān gōngyuán*
Manting	曼听	*màntīng*
Medicinal Botanic Gardens	药用植物园	*yàoyòng zhíwùyuán*
Tropical Crops Research Institute	热带作物科学研究所	*rèdàizuòwù kēxué yánjiū suǒ*
Tropical Flowers Garden	热带花卉园	*rèdài huāhuìyuán*
Wat Manting	曼听佛寺	*màntīng fósì*
Accommodation and eating		
Dai Building Inn	傣家花苑小楼	*tàijiā huāyuán xiǎolóu*
Ha'erbin Jiaoziguan	哈尔滨饺子馆	*hā'ěrbīn jiǎoziguǎn*
Mengyuan	勐园宾馆	*měngyuán bīnguǎn*
Xinmin International	新门(闵)国际大酒店	*xīnmén (mǐn) guójì dàjiǔdiàn*
Xishuangbanna Binguan	西双版纳宾馆	*xīshuāngbǎnnà bīnguǎn*

and Hani tribes off these fertile central flatlands and founded the independent kingdom of Cheli in 1180. It has been maintained as an administrative centre ever since. There was a moment of excitement in the late nineteenth century when a battalion of British soldiers marched in during a foray from Burma, but they soon decided that Jinghong was too remote to be worth the effort of defending. An attempt to forge a highway through Xishuangbanna during the 1950s (only recently completed) saw Jinghong built up in the grey edifices of the contemporary Han style. Now being slowly modernized, these make a suitably colonial backdrop for Dai women in bright sarongs and straw hats meandering along the gently simmering, palm-lined streets.

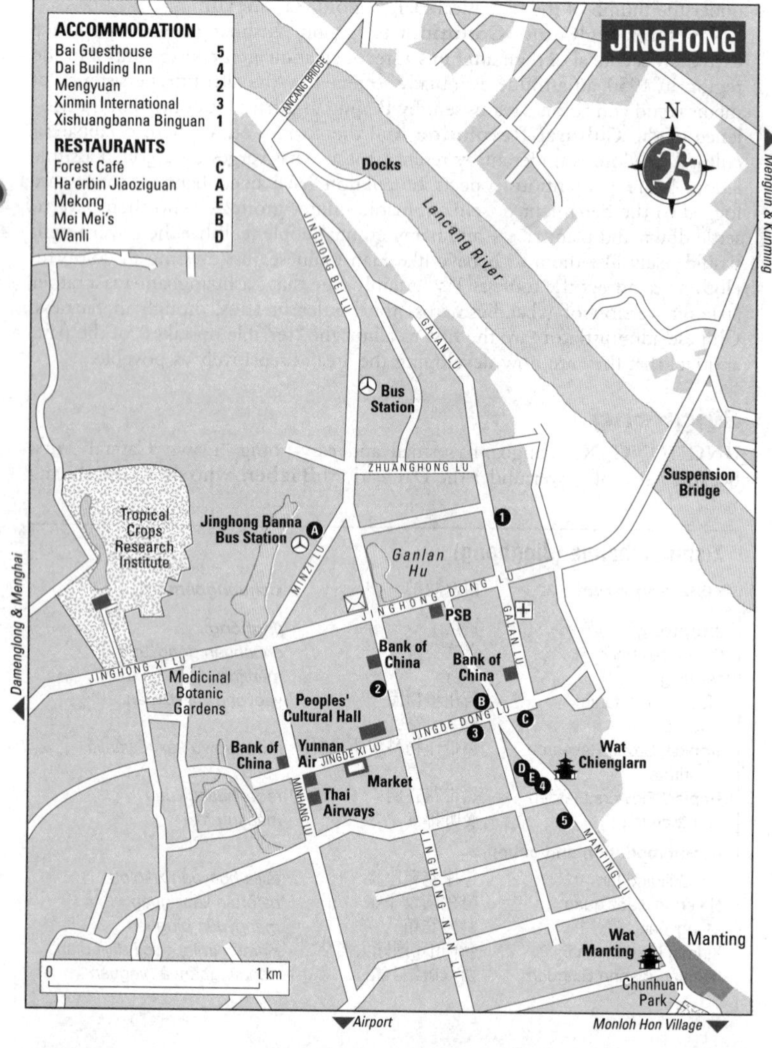

For the most part, the city is simply an undemanding place to spend a couple of days adjusting to Xishuangbanna's climate and investigating Dai culture. Aside from energetic excesses during the water-splashing festivities, you'll find the pace of life is set by the tropical heat – though the centre is often full of people, nobody bothers rushing anywhere. Once you've tried the local food and poked around the temples and villages which encroach on the suburbs, there's plenty of transport into the rest of the region. Ganlanba, only 45 minutes away on the bus, is a tempting first target; indeed, as a place to soak up atmosphere for a few days, it's preferable to Jinghong in many respects (see p.912).

Orientation, arrival and city transport

Jinghong sits on the southwestern bank of the **Lancang River**, which later winds downstream through Laos and Thailand as the Mekong. The city centre is marked by a sculpture of four elephants set where **Jinghong Lu**'s four arms radiate north (*bei*), south (*nan*), east (*dong*) and west (*xi*). A kilometre up along Jinghong Bei Lu is the **Lancang Bridge** and the top of **Galan Lu**, which runs parallel with Jinghong Bei Lu and the river; there's also a new **suspension bridge** over the river off the eastern end of Jinghong Dong Lu.

The **airport** lies about 10km southwest of the city, a ten-minute, ¥15–20 taxi ride into the centre along a new expressway, or ¥4 on the bus. There are two **long-distance bus stations**: the main one is Jinghong Banna bus station on Minzu Lu, handling services from all over Xishuangbanna and beyond, including Xiaguan, Kunming and even the Vietnamese border at Hekou (see p.872); the other depot, 500m north on Jinghong Bei Lu, concentrates on minibuses from Menghan (Ganlanba) and other places around Xishuangbanna. Central Jinghong is too small for a public bus service – nothing is more than a twenty-minute walk – but if you need to be driven anywhere there are plenty of taxis. Watch out for pickpockets at the post office and bus stations.

Accommodation

All but the smallest lodgings have restaurants and tour agencies.

Bai Guesthouse Manting Lu. Very basic rooms but the cheapest dorm beds in the city at ¥15. ❶

Dai Building Inn Manting Lu. Simple comforts in very popular, spotless bamboo stilt houses with separate toilets and showers, run by a resident Dai family. Pricey for what you get though, and it could be so much better than it is. Dorm beds ¥25, ❶

Mengyuan Minhang Lu ⓣ0691/2123028. Centrally located, tidy Chinese hotel, though nothing stylish, and cheaper rooms are minimally maintained. Try to get a room on the newly renovated third floor. A range of rooms from those with shared bath, to larger en-suite ones with air conditioning. ❶–❷

Xinmin International Jingde Dong Lu ⓣ0691/2126888, ⓕ2132880. New, luxury option with gym, sauna, restaurants and business centre, but rather distant from any local flavour. ❽

Xishuangbanna Binguan (also known as the *Banna Binguan*) Galan Lu ⓣ0691/2123679, ⓕ2126501. Large grounds and a faded air suit Jinghong's atmosphere. Dorms are a bit dingy, and the upper-range rooms don't quite make the grade, but the mid-range triples and doubles are clean and comfortable. All rooms and dorms have their own bathrooms. Dorm beds ¥40, ❸–❺

The City

Right in Jinghong's centre, **Ganlan Hu** (Peacock Lake) is an unexceptional, small, flagstoned park and pond used for early morning exercises. Much more interesting is the **Tropical Crops Research Institute**, 1.5km west down Jinghong Xi Lu (daily 8am–6pm; ¥10), where there are palms, fruit trees, and brightly flowering shrubs and vines, nicely arranged around a lake. The new tropical flower gardens – aerial flower subgarden, bougainvillea subgarden, and so on, are well worth a visit, and in the early afternoon local dancing is put on for the tour groups.

Shops outside the institute's entrance sell local herbal remedies such as **dragon's blood** (see p.913 for more details). Across the road are the **Medicinal Botanic Gardens** (daily 8am–5pm), a quiet grove of gingers and small shrubs growing in the gloom of closely planted, unidentified rainforest trees. The gardens lead through to a large **Traditional Medicine Clinic**, whose friendly staff might invite you in for a cup of tea and impromptu *qi gong* demonstration – one doctor specializes in plugging himself into a wall socket and passing electrical currents through patients' bodies.

For some more greenery and an introduction to Dai life, head about 1km southeast of the centre to **Manting**, once a separate village but now absorbed into Jinghong's lazy spread. On the way here down Manting Lu, you'll pass a brisk morning market outside the temple school of **Wat Chienglarn**. Traditionally, all Dai boys spend three years at such institutions getting a grounding in Buddhism and learning to read and write – skills denied to Dai women. Manting itself is mostly modern, though Neolithic pottery has been dug up here and a few older, two-storey wooden Dai houses still lurk in the wings (you'll see entire villages of these elsewhere in the region). Near the end of the road is **Wat Manting** (¥1), Jinghong's main **Buddhist monastery** and the largest in all Xishuangbanna, a simply furnished affair recently rebuilt with donations from Thailand – check out the glossy **jinghua murals**, an art form derived from India, and the roof rafters, full of ceremonial bits and pieces. Dai temples differ from others across the land both in their general shape and the almost exclusive use of wood in their construction, which necessitates their being raised off the ground on low piles to guard against termites and rot. Also unlike Buddhists anywhere else in China, whose Mahayana (Greater Vehicle) teachings filtered through from India, the Dais follow the **Theravada**

The Lancang River and New Year festivities

Despite its potential as a great river highway, the **Lancang River** has never seen much traffic, and today the docks in the north of town at the junction of Galan Lu and Jinghong Bei Lu are usually moribund. The only vessels you're likely to see are irregular **tour boats from Thailand**, rare barges running down to the tiny Thai port of Chiangkhong, and a biweekly workers' ferry to the hydroelectric plant 20km upstream – none of which will carry foreigners, owing to regional politics.

Where the river does come into its own, however, is during the highlights of the **Dai New Year celebrations** (also held in Dai communities all over Xishuangbanna), of which the famous **Water-splashing Festival** is just a part. Once set by the unpredictable Dai calendar, but now reliably fixed by the Han authorities for **April 13–16**, the first day sees a **dragon-boat race** on the river, held in honour of a good-natured dragon spirit who helped a local hero outwit an evil king. On the second day everybody in Jinghong gets a good soaking as water-splashing hysteria grips the town, and basinfuls are enthusiastically hurled over friends and strangers alike to wash away bad luck and, hopefully, encourage a good wet season. Manting Park also hosts cockfighting and dancing all day. The third-day finale includes **Diu Bao** (Throwing Pouches) games, where prospective couples fling small, triangular beanbags at each other to indicate their affection, and there's a mammoth **firework display**, when hundreds of bamboo tubes stuffed with gunpowder and good luck gifts are rocketed out over the river. Nightly carousing and dancing – during which generous quantities of *lajiu*, the local firewater, are consumed – take place in the parks and public spaces: look out for the **Peacock dance**, a fluid performance said to imitate the movements of the bird, bringer of good fortune in Dai lore; and the **Elephant-drum dance**, named after the instrument used to thump out the rhythm.

(Hinayana, or Lesser Vehicle) school of thought, a sect common to Sri Lanka, Thailand, Laos and Burma. As the Dai consider feet to be the most unclean part of the body, remember to **remove your shoes** before entering any temple.

Next to Wat Manting is the rather more secular **Chunhuan Park** (also known as Manting Park; daily 8am–7.30pm, ¥10; 7.30–11.30pm, ¥2), where the royal slaves were formerly kept. Official tour groups are shown water-splashing highlights every afternoon and there's also a large pen bursting with **100 peacocks**, which you can feed. Corners of the park are very pleasant, paths crossing over one of the Lancang River's tiny tributaries to full-scale copies of Jingzhen's Baijiao Ting (see p.916) and a portly, Dai-style pagoda. Continuing past the park, the road ends at **Manloh Hon village**, which gets its water through the efforts of a large bamboo waterwheel, beyond which is a ferry across the Lancang to paddy fields, more villages and banana groves.

Eating, drinking and entertainment

Jinghong is the best place in Xishuangbanna to try **authentic Dai cooking**, either in restaurants or on the street. **Sticky rice** in various guises is the staple; one type is wrapped in banana leaves, rammed into a bamboo tube and grilled, and a prized purple strain is used as the basis of pancakes, stuffed with sugar and chopped nuts. Formal menus often feature meat or fish courses flavoured with sour bamboo shoots or lemon grass, while oddities include **fried moss**, and **pineapple rice** for dessert – the fruit is hollowed out, stuffed with pineapple chunks and sweet glutinous rice, and steamed. Year-round fresh **tropical fruit** is also sold around town – try jackfruit, physically weighty and heavily scented. Sit-down stalls sell bland curries, claypot casseroles, hotpots and huge bowls of noodle soup. The area around the **night market** on Jinghong Nan Lu has a host of small, low-cost canteens specializing in stewed and simmered dishes, and there's a bigger, perpetually full affair just around the corner in Jingde Lu. As usual, **tourist cafés** are expensive, but good places to pick up local information, rent bikes and arrange tours. Pick of these are *Mei Mei's* on Jingde Dong Lu, and *Mekong*, just north of the *Dai Building Inn* on Manting Lu. For mainstream Chinese food try *Ha'erbin Jiaoziguan*, next to the Jinghong Banna bus station, on Minzi Lu. Pricey but first-rate, the house speciality is huge steamers of *jiaozi*, enough for three people.

Entertainment is unpredictable, though there's always something – anything, in fact, from traditional music to huge synchronized dance groups with fans – going on in the paved square outside the **People's Cultural Hall** between Jinghong Nan Lu and Minhang Lu. The Jinghong Nan Lu market gets going nightly around 7pm, with the general public roller-skating, playing pool and stuffing their faces at stalls. Occasionally, tour groups can trigger performances of local dances in the hall itself, and elsewhere people just seem to assemble spontaneously in the streets after dark and go through routines.

Listings

Airlines Fast and efficient, Yunnan Air is on the corner of Jingde Xi Lu and Minhang Lu (☎0691/2124774; daily 8am–8pm), selling tickets for their daily flights to Kunming and Lijiang. The office of Thai Airways, just around the corner on Minhang Lu (☎0691/2121881; Mon–Fri 8am–6pm) sells tickets for thrice weekly flights to Chang Mai and Bangkok.

Banks and exchange Three branches of the Bank of China, on Jinghong Nan Lu and Jingde Xi Lu and Galan Lu, are open for foreign exchange Monday–Friday 8am–6pm and Saturday 8–11.30am and 3–6pm. The *Xishuangbanna Binguan* and other larger hotels will cash traveller's cheques outside these hours.

Bike rental The *Xishuangbanna Binguan* and *Forest*

Café have a cluster of bikes for rent at ¥10 per day, plus whatever they decide is a reasonable deposit.
Hospital The Provincial Hospital is at the lower end of Galan Lu, and there's a clinic and pharmacy attached to the *Xishuangbanna Binguan*.
Internet access For Internet access at ¥2 an hour, visit the noisy cyber café just north of the *Dai Building Inn* on Manting Lu.
Laundry Foreigner cafés offer the least expensive laundry services in town.
Mail and telecommunications The GPO, with parcels, post restante and international telephones, is on the corner of Jinghong Bei Lu and Jinghong Xi Lu (daily 8am–8.30pm).
Massage White-robed practitioners set up along central Galan Lu in the evening, and there are afternoon foot massage sessions around Ganlan Hu.
PSB Jinghong Dong Lu, across from Ganlan Hu Park (Mon–Fri 7–11.30am & 3–5.30pm; ⓣ0691/2130366) – look for the English sign. Visa extensions and contradictory information about the region.
Shopping For everyday needs, there are plenty of well-stocked department stores around the centre. Zhuanghong Lu, a thin street between Galan Lu and Jinghong Bei Lu, has a very regulated arts and crafts market run for the most part by Burmese selling gems, jade, colourful curios and heavy wooden carvings of elephants. The City Produce Market is at the western end of Jingde Lu, near the Yunnan Air office, where there's a massive range of food and clothing, while stores along Manting Lu offer souvenir-quality Dai trinkets and jewellery.
Tour agents Hotel travel services in Jinghong offer much the same range of day-trips for ¥100–200 to: Daluo on the Burmese border; the Botanic Gardens at Menglun; Mandian Waterfall; the Menglong region; the Sunday market at Menghun; and (very rarely) Sancha He Wildlife Reserve. For something different, Lemongrass Tours (ⓣ0691/2149615; no premises at the time of writing) organizes highly recommended guided treks in the forests and hills of Menglong and Menglun districts, covering 10–15km per day through Bulang, Lahu, Ake and Hani territory. You get an English-speaking guide and all food, transport and accommodation at a cost of ¥700 a person for three days, ¥1200 for five. Ask for "Luke" Liu (ⓔluketrek@yahoo.com).

Exploring Xishuangbanna

Flowing down from the northwest, the Lancang River neatly cuts Xishuangbanna into two regions on either side of Jinghong. **East** there's a choice of roads through highland forests or more cultivated flatlands to the botanic gardens at **Menglun**, down beyond which lies **Mengla**, and the open **Laotian border**. Head **west** and your options are split between the **Damenglong** and **Menghai** regions – linked by a three-day hiking trail – with a more varied bag of ethnic groups and a firmly closed crossing into Burma. There are direct public buses and tours to most destinations from Jinghong's two bus stations, but once in an area the mass of short-range minibuses is far more convenient, with tractors picking up where these won't go. Cycling around is another possibility in the lowlands, though Xishuangbanna's hill roads are steep, twisted and long.

With the exception of Mengla, most main centres can be visited on day trips from Jinghong, but you won't see more than the superficial highlights unless you stop overnight. The towns are seldom attractive or interesting in themselves and you'll need to get out to surrounding villages, small temples and the countryside to experience Xishuangbanna's better side. Be prepared for basic accommodation and generally bland, if plentiful, food. Many people are friendly and some villagers may offer meals and a bed for the night – or yank you enthusiastically into the middle of a festival, if you're lucky enough to stumble across one – but elsewhere locals are wary of strangers, so don't force your presence while looking around. There have also been a couple of **muggings** in recent years along remoter stretches of the Burmese border – walking alone is ill advised.

East to Menglun: the northern route

The road to Menglun, 80km east of Jinghong, divides shortly after crossing the

Lancang Bridge on the outskirts of town. The **northern route** initially follows the road to Kunming, winding up through forested hills for 35km before levelling out at **MENGYANG**, a market and transport stop surrounded by a host of **Huayao** villages. The Huayao (Flower Belt) form one of three Dai subgroups, though they differ greatly from the lowland "Water Dai", who scorn them for their over-elaborate costumes and the fact that they are not Buddhists. Though you'll see plenty at Mengyang – the women wear turbans draped with thin silver chains – the village considered most typical is about 10km farther north along the main road at **MANNANAN**.

On a completely different tack, a farther 18km beyond Mannanan (still on the Kunming road) is the **Sancha He Wildlife Reserve** (¥15), a dense chunk of rainforest based around the Sancha Stream. Transport heading north from Mengyang to Dadugang, Puwen or Kunming can drop you at the large stone sign which marks the reserve entrance. There's a resident family of seven **wild elephants** at Sancha He, frequently seen at dawn from creaky wooden riverside hides, and the jungle gets interesting the farther in you go along the overgrown, partially paved trails – you're sure to encounter elephantine footprints, along with brightly coloured birds, butterflies and snakes. Give the **elephant displays** here a wide berth, however, unless you enjoy watching captive animals perform circus tricks while being jabbed with a spear. **Minibuses** heading in both directions along the Kunming road pass the reserve entrance until well into the afternoon; miss them and you'll have to stay near the reserve entrance at a newish but terminally mildewed **hotel** (❹).

The latter 45km of the northern route to Menglun misses all this, however, diverging east off the Kunming road between Mengyang and Mannanan. Twenty kilometres along is **JINUO LUOKE** (Jinuo Shan), home to the independently minded **Jinuo**, who received official recognition of their ethnicity as recently as 1979. An enigmatic group who some say are descended from the

Eastern Xishuangbanna

Northern route to Menglun		
Jinuo Luoke	基诺	
Mannanan	曼那囡	*mànnànán*
Mengyang	勐养	*mèngyǎng*
Sancha He Wildlife Reserve	三岔河自然保护区	*sānchàhé zìrán bǎohùqū*
Southern route to Menglun		
Manting	曼听	*màntīng*
Menghan	勐罕	*mènghǎn*
Menglun	勐仑	***mènglún***
Tropical Botanic Plant Garden	热带植物园	*rèdài zhíwùyuán*
Mengla	勐腊	***mènglà***
Bronze Spire Pagoda	青铜尖顶塔	*qīngtóng jiāndǐngtǎ*
Yaoqu and Laos		
Bupan Aerial Walkway	补蚌望天树空中索道	*bǔbàng wàngtiānshù kōngzhōngsuǒdào*
Mo Han	边贸站	*biānmào zhàn*
Shangyong	尚勇	*shàngyǒng*
Yaoqu	瑶区	*yáoqū*

remnants of Zhuge Liang's third-century expedition to Yunnan, the Jinuo once lived by hunting and slash-and-burn farming, but now grow tea as a cash crop. They never got on well with external rulers, describing their highlands homeland as *Youle* (Hidden from the Han), and were almost annihilated by Ke Shexun and the Dai ruling caste after they poisoned a government tax collector in 1942. Numbering about twenty thousand today, Jinuo women wear a distinctive white-peaked hood, and both sexes pierce their ears and formerly practised tattooing. Jinuo Luoke is not the most welcoming of places, but there's a **guesthouse** (❶) which might let you stay, and a fair amount of through traffic for the final 25km run to Menglun.

The southern route to Menglun

Because of the time it takes to climb the range to Mengyang, most buses between Jinghong and Menglun follow the **southern road**. This begins across the Lancang Bridge following the Lancang River Valley downstream for 30km between endless neat rows of rubber trees to **GANLANBA** (also known as **Menghan**), the main settlement of the famously fertile "Olive-shaped Flatland". This is one of Xishuangbanna's three major agricultural areas won by force of arms over the centuries and now vitally important to the Dai (the other two are west at Damenglong and Menghai). You'll see plenty of farming hamlets in the vicinity sporting **traditional wooden houses** completely covered by huge roofs, raised on stilts off the moist earth – however, under orders for "modernization" from the regional government, this style is being replaced by absurdly humid brick structures. Menghan itself is pleasantly surrounded by paddy fields and low hills bordering the flatland and is a great place to stop over and sample regional life for a few days. The well-run traveller café, the *Olive Tree,* is a good place to find out about the area and rent bikes (¥20 a day) – turn right from the bus stop, through the market, then turn left and it's on the right. The most popular **place to stay** is at the *Sarlar Restaurant,* 200m on from the bus stop, where you get a mat on the floor in a room off the dining area for ¥10. Check their visitors' book for tips. However, better value is offered by a little hotel opposite and to the left of the *Olive Tree*, which has spotless rooms for ¥40. If you can't find it (there's no sign), ask at the café. The most upmarket place in town is the *Ganlanba Hotel,* 200m west of the *Olive Tree,* but it's expensive for what you get (❻). An unusual feature of the town is the high density of Internet cafés, mostly full of lads playing *Counterstrike*. There are also plenty of day walks and cycle rides. A couple of kilometres east, at **MANTING**, there's the excellent **Manting Fo Si** (Manting Buddhist Temple) and **Da Duta** (Grand Single Pagoda), both fine reconstructions of twelfth-century buildings destroyed during the 1960s. East, paths lead off from Manting along and across the river to more pagodas and villages, somewhere to spend a couple of days of easy exploration.

Menglun

Routes from Jinghong meet at **MENGLUN**, a dusty couple of streets overlooking the broad flow of the **Luosuo River**. There's no bus station so vehicles pull up wherever convenient on the main road, usually among the restaurants and stores on the eastern side of town. Take the side street downhill through the all-day market, and within a couple of minutes you'll find yourself by a large pedestrian **suspension bridge** over the river. Here you pay ¥35 to cross into Menglun's superb **Tropical Botanic Gardens**, founded in 1959 by the botanist **Cai Xi Tau** who, having carved the gardens out of the jungle, started investigating the lives and medicinal qualities of Xishuangbanna's many little-known plant species. One of his pet projects involved the effects of resin from the

Dragon's Blood Tree, which looks like a thin-stemmed yucca with spiky leaves, used as a wound-healing agent in Chinese medicine. It was believed extinct in China since the Tang dynasty, but Cai Xi located a wild population in Xishuangbanna in 1972 and transplanted some to the gardens. You could spend a good half-day here, as there's masses to see, from Dragon's Blood trees and rainforest species to a thousand-year-old cycad and groves of palms, bamboos, vines and shrubs. You might also encounter Chinese visitors seranading the undistinguished-looking "Singing Plant", which is supposed to nod in time to music.

There's a guesthouse inside the gardens (❹), at the side of the pool, and though it's a little pricey it does offer the chance of seeing the place at its most charismatic, early in the monring and in the evening. There are plenty of cheap and unremarkable alternatives in town. You'll need to tramp back onto the main road to catch onward transport, though at the rear of the gardens, near the accommodation, is an exit on to the Mengla road, where you can flag down buses heading southeast.

Mengla

Having been a patchy affair so far, the jungle really sets in for the hundred-kilometre trip from Menglun to Mengla (4hr). The first part is slow-going uphill, then the bus suddenly turns along a ridge giving early morning passengers a clear view (best in winter) back down on to a "cloud sea" over the treetops below. Farther on are rock outcrops and small roadside settlements carved out of the forest, and though once over the mountains the trees begin to give way to rubber plantations and cultivated land, it's all pretty impressive. This is the largest of Xishuangbanna's five wildlife reserves, comprised of relatively untouched tracts which the government has set aside to be protected from development, and full of the plants you'll have seen at the Botanic Gardens up the road.

Doubtless anything would be a disappointment after this, but **MENGLA** seems a deliberately ugly town, quiet and grey. The main point of interest here lies 2km south near the river at the **Bronze Spire Pagoda**, originally founded in antiquity by two Burmese monks as a shrine for Buddha relics. With a spire donated by heaven, the pagoda's presence brought lasting peace to the land, though it eventually fell into disrepair and had to be rebuilt in 1759, when Jinghong's Dai ruler contributed thirty thousand silver pieces to cover the pagoda and temple columns in bronze. What happened next is a bit of a mystery, as Mengla was closed to foreign eyes for almost thirty years after the Cultural Revolution, but it's nowhere near this grand today; there are plenty of monks floating around Mengla itself, however, and a smaller temple pagoda on the hill to the west.

There's a proper **bus station** at Mengla's northern end (vehicles head back to Menglun throughout the day), from where Mengla's main street – with the last **bank** before Laos – runs south for 1500m to the far end of town and a **depot** for southbound vehicles. Take your pick of the dozen or so main-street noodle shops, **restaurants** and **hotels** (all ❷–❸). **Plainclothes police** are everywhere – even among the Uigur running the kebab stalls – as this is the last major town before the Laos border, 60km southeast.

Around Mengla: to Yaoqu and Laos

An afternoon bus runs from Mengla to the small town of **Yaoqu** (returning the following morning), 40km north along the beautiful farmland and forest scenery flanking the **Nanla He**. Not far off the road, just over halfway, is the **Bupan aerial walkway**, a very insecure-looking metal "sky bridge" running across the forest canopy. **YAOQU** itself is a road head for remote highland

Into Laos

Laos has been open to independent travellers since the late 1980s, and visas are available from the Lao Consulate in Kunming – see Kunming "Listings", p.864.

On the opposite side of the border from Mo Han is the Lao village of **Ban Boten**, where there's nowhere to stay or change your Chinese currency for Laotian kip, though yuan seem acceptable. The nearest banks and beds are a ¥10 truck ride away at the town of **Luang Namtha**, from where you can hitch out to the early morning markets at Muong Sing to see local people in full tribal regalia. There's also transport from Luang Namtha to **Nung Kie** via Muong Tai, and thence by boat down the Mekong to **Luang Phabang** – you can also come the whole way from the border by road. Luang Phabang was Laos's Buddhist centre and royal capital until the military took over in 1975, and there are caves and dozens of sumptuously decorated temples dating back to the eighteenth century here, as well as the former Royal Palace, now a museum. Luang Phabang also has good road and air connections to the present capital, Vientiane.

villages, with two **hostels** (❶) and all sorts of people turning up to trade, including Yao, dressed in dark blue jackets and turbans, and possibly Kumu, one of Xishuangbanna's officially unrecognized nationalities.

Heading down from Mengla's south bus station **towards Laos**, it takes about ninety minutes to reach **SHANGYONG**, the last village before the border. Shangyong is a centre for Xishaungbanna's isolated **Miao** population, more closely allied here with their Hmong relatives in Laos than with other Miao groups in China. The Hmong made the mistake of supporting US forces during the Vietnam War and were savagely repressed in its aftermath, many fleeing into China from their native regions in northern Vietnam and, after the Vietnamese army swarmed into the country in 1975, to Laos.

Not much farther, **MO HAN** township (also known as **Bian Mao Zhan**, literally "Frontier Trade Station"), is just 6km from the **border crossing**. There's basic **accommodation** at Mo Han, and transport to the relaxed customs post (closes mid-afternoon) where, assuming you already have a visa, the crossing should be free and uncomplicated.

West: Damenglong and the trail to Bulangshan

Several buses a day make the seventy-kilometre run from Jinghong's Minzu Lu depot southwest to **DAMENGLONG** (or **Menglong** as it's often marked on maps), one of the many western Xishuangbanna towns worth visiting for its **Sunday market**. It's also an area rich in Buddhism, and just about every village along the way has its own temple and pagoda. One worth closer inspection is **Manguanglong Si** near **Gasa** (15km from Jinghong), a monastery with a wonderful dragon stairway. The most impressive and famous structure in the region is **Manfeilong Bei Ta** (White Bamboo Shoot Pagoda), set up on a hill a thirty-minute walk north of Damenglong. First built in the thirteenth century and now brightly adorned with fragments of evil-repelling mirrors and silver paint, it's a regular place of pilgrimage for Burmese monks, who come to meditate and to worship two footprints left by Sakyamuni in an alcove at the base. The pagoda's unusual name derives from the nine-spired design, which vaguely resembles an emerging cluster of bamboo tips. On a separate rise closer to town, Damenglong's other renowned Buddhist monument is the disappointingly shoddy **Hei Ta** (Black Pagoda), though it looks good from a distance.

Western Xishuangbanna		
Bulangshan	布朗山	***bùláng shān***
Damenglong	大勐龙	***dàmèng lóng***
Manfeilong Bei Ta	曼飞龙笋塔	*mànfēilóng sŭntă*
Manguanglong Si	曼光龙寺	*mànguānglóng sì*
Hei Ta	黑塔	*hēită*
Gelanghe	格朗和	***géláng hé***
Jingzhen	景真	***jĭngzhēn***
Baijiao Ting	八角亭	*bājiăo tíng*
Menghai	勐海	***mènghăi***
Menghun	勐混	***mènghún***
Mengzhe	勐遮	***mèngzhē***
Manlei Fo Si	曼佛寺	*mànfó sì*
Xiding	西定	***xīdìng***

While there are plenty of cheap places to eat in Damenglong, high-volume karaoke at the new **bus station guesthouse** (❶) doesn't always make for a relaxing stay. What is attractive, however, is the three-day **hiking trail** which follows for 40km the Nana He and its tributaries to **Bulangshan** township, through a region of forests and farmland – there are villagers here who have never been to Jinghong. However, the route, once all tribal paths, is being earnestly tarmacked, so get here sooner rather than later. Food and camping gear will come in handy, though it is possible to negotiate meals and accommodation in the villages – offer a useful gift or ¥10–15 in these circumstances.

Start by taking any available transport 15km south from Damenglong to **Manguanghan**. Carry on along the road for about 1km, then look for a tractor track to the right leading shortly to **Guanmin**, a riverside Hani settlement. Another 5km takes you past a **thermal spring** to the Bulang village of **Manpo**, beyond which the track becomes a walking path only. In the next 20km you'll pass **Nuna** village before crossing the river and proceeding to **Song'er** (both of which are inhabited by Lahu), then cross back over and re-enter Hani territory at Bangnawan and **Weidong**, the latter one of the nicest villages on the trip. Here the track turns into a new road for the final 10km to the trail head at **BULANGSHAN**, mountainous headquarters of the dark-clad **Bulang** nationality. There's formal accommodation at Bulangshan (❶), and at least one bus a day 50km north to **Menghun**, on the Menghai–Daluo road (see below).

Menghai and the Hani

MENGHAI is western Xishuangbanna's principal town, centrally placed on the highland plains 55km from Jinghong. The usual grubby assemblage of kilometre-long high street and back lanes, Menghai was once a **Hani** (Aini) settlement until, as elsewhere, they were defeated in battle by the Dai and withdrew into the surrounding hills. They remain there today as Xishuangbanna's second largest ethnic group and long-time cultivators of Xishuangbanna's **pu'er tea**, the red, slightly musty brew esteemed from Hong Kong to Tibet for its fat-reducing and generally invigorating properties. There's a nice village temple about 2km east off the Jinghong road, and a tea-processing factory in Menghai (Jinghong's CITS can arrange a tour), but otherwise the town is little more than a stop on the way towards outlying Dai and Hani settlements.

The **bus station** is at the eastern end of town along with a **mosque** and Muslim canteens, while the **bank**, **post office** and attached **hotel** (❹), and the basic *Banna Hotel* (❷), are grouped around the central crossroads. The **minibus depot** for western destinations is on the far outskirts.

Beyond Menghai to the Burmese border

The main routes beyond Menghai head southwest down to **Daluo and the Burmese border**, or northwest out of Xishuangbanna towards the Lancang region (see p.902). The most celebrated Buddhist sights around Menghai are within an hour's drive along this latter road, including **Baijiao Ting** (Octagonal Pavilion), 20km away at **JINGZHEN**, and **Manlei Fo Si** (Manlei Buddha Temple), 5km farther on at **MENGZHE**. Though inferior copies of older buildings, the hilltop Baijiao Ting is a bizarre structure built in the eighteenth century to quell an angry horde of wasps, and both have important collections of Buddhist manuscripts written on fan-palm fibre. There's plenty of **minibus** transport to Mengzhe throughout the day, plus a small **guesthouse** (❶) near the marketplace if you want to stay; even better would be to overnight at similar lodgings 10km southwest at **XIDING**, whose busy Thursday **market** is less touristed than some in the region.

One of the best places to come to grips with the Hani is at **GELANGHE** township, 30km southeast of Menghai, where there's hostel accommodation (❶). In fact, many of the people here are Dai and **Ake**, a long-haired Hani subgroup spread as far afield as Menglian and Simao. In common with other Hani, unmarried women have elaborate head ornaments while wives wear cloth caps decorated with silver beads and coins. An excellent walk leads up into the hills above Gelanghe past a lake and plenty of traditional wooden Ake villages, but people are very shy.

Somewhere to meet locals on more even terms is 25km out along the Daluo road at tiny **MENGHUN**, whose **Sunday market**, starting at daybreak and continuing until noon, does a good job of lowering ethnic barriers. It's best to stay in Menghun the night before as this way you'll already have seen plenty before the mid-morning tour buses from Jinghong descend around 9am, although you'll have to decide which of Menghun's two atrocious guesthouses (❶) deserves your custom – one is on the main street (look for the English sign), the other 75m on the left down the road leading south into the fields. However, the market is worth a night's discomfort to see Hani women under their silver-beaded headdresses, Bulang in heavy earrings and oversized black turbans, and remote hill-dwellers in plain dress, carrying ancient rifles. Most common though, are the Dai, who buy rolls of home-made paper and sarongs. Take a look around Menghun itself, too, as there's a dilapidated nineteenth-century **monastery** with a pavilion built in the style of Jingzhen's octagonal effort, and a **pagoda** hidden in the bamboo groves on the hills behind town. Another temple down on the flats to the south is linked to a legend that the stream here changed course at the bidding of Sakyamuni.

Beyond Menghun, the fifty-kilometre-long road takes you past the turning south to Bulangshan (see above) and through a stretch of forest inhabited by an as-yet unnamed nomadic group who speak an unintelligible language and were only "discovered" in the late 1980s. At the end of the bitumen is the town of **DALUO** (two buses daily between here and Menghai), set just in from the Burmese border. Here there's a multi-trunked, giant **fig tree** whose descending mass of aerial roots form a "forest". You'll find **lodgings** at the newish, white hotel on the far side of the bridge (❶), and a daily **border trade market** is timed for the arrival of Chinese package tours between 11am and 1pm. Chinese nationals can also get a two-hour visa for Burma, ostensibly to shop for jade; in fact, many are really going over to catch transvestite stage shows held for their benefit – check out the photos in the windows of Jinghong's processing labs.

Travel details

Trains

Hekou to: Kaiyuan (2 daily; 8hr); Kunming (1 daily; 16hr).
Kunming to: Beijing (daily; 48hr); Chengdu (3 daily; 18–21hr); Chongqing (2 daily; 23hr); Guangzhou (2 daily; 45hr); Guilin (2 daily; 30hr); Guiyang (5 daily; 12hr); Hanoi (daily; 28hr); Hekou (1 daily; 16hr); Kaiyuan (2 daily; 8hr); Nanning (daily; 20hr); Panzhihua (3 daily; 6hr); Shanghai (2 daily; 60hr); Xiaguan (daily; 8hr); Xichang (3 daily; 12hr).

Buses

Baoshan to: Jinghong (48hr); Kunming (18hr); Lancang (40hr); Lijiang (8–12hr); Lincang (12hr); Mangshi (4hr); Ruili (6hr); Tengchong (7hr); Wanding (7hr); Xiaguan (7hr).
Dali to: Kunming (12hr); Lijiang (3hr); Shaping (1hr); Xiaguan (30min); Xizhou (30min); Zhongdian (9–12hr); Zhoucheng (45min).
Gejiu to: Hekou (6hr); Jianshui (2hr); Kaiyuan (30min); Kunming (5hr); Tonghai (4hr).
Hekou to: Gejiu (6hr); Jianshui (11hr); Kaiyuan (9hr 30min); Kunming (16hr); Tonghai (13hr).
Jianshui to: Gejiu (2hr); Hekou (11hr); Kaiyuan (2hr); Kunming (7hr); Tonghai (2hr).
Jinghong to: Baoshan (48hr); Daluo (5hr); Damenglong (2hr); Kunming (24hr); Lancang (8hr); Lincang (48hr); Menghai (2hr); Menghun (3hr); Mengla (7hr); Menglun (3hr); Xiaguan (48hr).
Kunming to: Anshun (24hr); Baoshan (18hr); Chengdu (36hr); Chuxiong (6hr); Dali (12hr); Gejiu (5hr); Guiyang (72hr); Hekou (16hr); Jianshui (5hr); Jinghong (24hr); Kaiyuan (5hr); Lijiang (11hr); Mangshi (22hr); Nanning (72hr); Panxian (12hr); Ruili (24hr); Shilin (3hr); Tonghai (2hr); Wanding (25hr); Xiaguan (10hr); Xichang (24hr); Xingyi (13hr).
Lancang to: Gengma (7hr); Jinghong (8hr); Lincang (10hr); Menglian (2hr).
Lijiang to: Baoshan (8–12hr); Daju (4hr); Dali (3hr); Kunming (11hr); Panzhihua (10hr); Shigu (2hr); Weixi (5hr); Xiaguan (6hr); Yongsheng (5hr); Zhongdian (6hr).
Ruili to: Baoshan (6hr); Kunming (24hr); Mangshi (1–2hr); Nansan (12hr); Tengchong (7hr); Wanding (30min–1hr); Xiaguan (15hr).
Tonghai to: Jianshui (2hr); Gejiu (2hr); Hekou (13hr); Kaiyuan (4hr); Kunming (2hr).
Xiaguan to: Baoshan (7hr); Binchuan (2hr); Dali (30min) Jinghong (48hr); Kunming (10hr); Lancang (48hr); Lijiang (6hr); Lincang (12hr); Ruili (14hr); Tengchong (14hr); Wanding (12hr); Zhongdian (11hr).
Zhongdian to: Deqin (9hr); Lijiang (6hr); Litang (3 days); Xiaguan (11hr).

Flights

There are international flights out of Kunming to Bangkok, Rangoon, Singapore and Vientiane, and from Jinghong to Chiang Mai and Bangkok.
Baoshan to: Kunming (3 weekly; 30min).
Dali to: Kunming (5 weekly; 30min).
Deqin to: Kunming (3 weekly; 2hr).
Jinghong to: Kunming (3 daily; 55min); Lijiang (2 weekly; 1hr 20min).
Kunming to: Baoshan (3 weekly; 30min); Beijing (6 daily; 2hr 35min); Changsha (1 or 2 daily; 1hr 30min); Chengdu (6–9 daily; 1hr 5min); Chongqing (4–7 daily; 50min); Dali (5 weekly; 30min); Deqin (3 weekly; 2hr); Guangzhou (5 daily; 1hr 20min); Guilin (1 or 2 daily; 1hr 30min); Guiyang (1 or 2 daily; 1hr 10min); Hong Kong (1 or 2 daily; 2hr 45min); Jinghong (3 daily; 55min); Lijiang (4 weekly, 40min); Mangshi (2 daily; 45min); Nanning (2 daily; 50min); Shanghai (2–3 daily; 2hr 30min); Xi'an (2–4 daily; 1hr 40min).
Lijiang to: Jinghong (daily; 1hr 20min); Kunming (4 weekly, 40min).

CHAPTER 12 **Highlights**

* **Emei Shan** A tough climb is rewarded with gorgeous scenery and monasteries that make atmospheric places to stay. **See p.942**

* **The Buddha at Leshan** You'll never forget the first time you see this gargantuan statue rearing above your boat. **See p.949**

* **The Wenshu Temple Teahouse** Discover why the Sichuanese have a reputation for being garrulous at one of Chengdu's best – and noisiest – teahouses. **See p.930**

* **Zigong** Gas-powered buses, salt and dinosaur museums and a lantern festival make this quirky, untouristy town memorable. **See p.953**

* **Cruising the Yangzi** Relax as magnificent scenery, most notably the towering Three Gorges, glides past your boat. **See p.962**

* **Wolong Giant Panda Research Base** The best place to see pandas in something resembling their natural habitat. **See p.970**

* **Horse trekking, Songpan** A chance to get really out into the wild and give your feet – though not your seat – a rest. **See p.974**

* **Langmusi** Remote Tibetan village, gritty but charming, nestled in a peaceful valley. **See p.975**

12

Sichuan and Chongqing

Ringed by mountains which proverbially made the journey here "harder than the road to heaven", **Sichuan** and **Chongqing** stretch for more than 1000km across China's southwest. Administratively divided in 1997, when **Chongqing Municipality** was carved off the eastern end of Sichuan Province, the region has long played the renegade, differing from the rest of China in everything from food to politics and inaccessible enough both to ignore central authority and to provide sanctuary for those fleeing it. Recent divisions aside, Sichuan and Chongqing share a common history, and the area splits more convincingly into very different geographic halves: a densely populated eastern plain, and a mountainous west, emphatically remote.

In the east, peaks surround one of the country's most densely settled areas, the fertile **Red Basin**, whose subtropical climate and rich soil conspire to produce endless green fields turning out three harvests a year. This bounty has created an air of easy affluence in **Chengdu**, Sichuan's capital, and the southern river towns of **Zigong** and **Yibin**. Elsewhere, visitors have the opportunity of joining pilgrims on **Emei Shan** in a hike up the holy mountain's forested slopes, or of sailing **down the Yangzi** from **Chongqing**, industrial powerhouse and terminus of one of the world's great river journeys. You'll also find that the influence of **Buddhism** has literally become part of the landscape: most notably at **Leshan**, where a giant Buddha sculpted into riverside cliffs provides one of the most evocative images of China; and farther east at **Dazu**, whose marvellous procession of stone carvings has miraculously escaped desecration.

In contrast, the west is dominated by densely buckled ranges overflowing from the heights of Tibet; a wild, thinly populated land of snow-capped peaks, where yaks roam the treeline and roads negotiate hair-raising gradients as they cross ridges or follow deep river valleys. To the northwest, the mountains briefly level out onto the high-altitude **Aba Grasslands**, while south the ranges run lower but no less severe, cloaked in the impenetrable greenery of cloud forests. Occupied but never tamed by Han China, and often excruciatingly difficult to traverse, the west has its very inacccessibility as its biggest appeal. Nearest to Chengdu, there's a chance to see giant pandas at **Wolong Nature Reserve**, while travelling north towards Gansu takes you through eth-

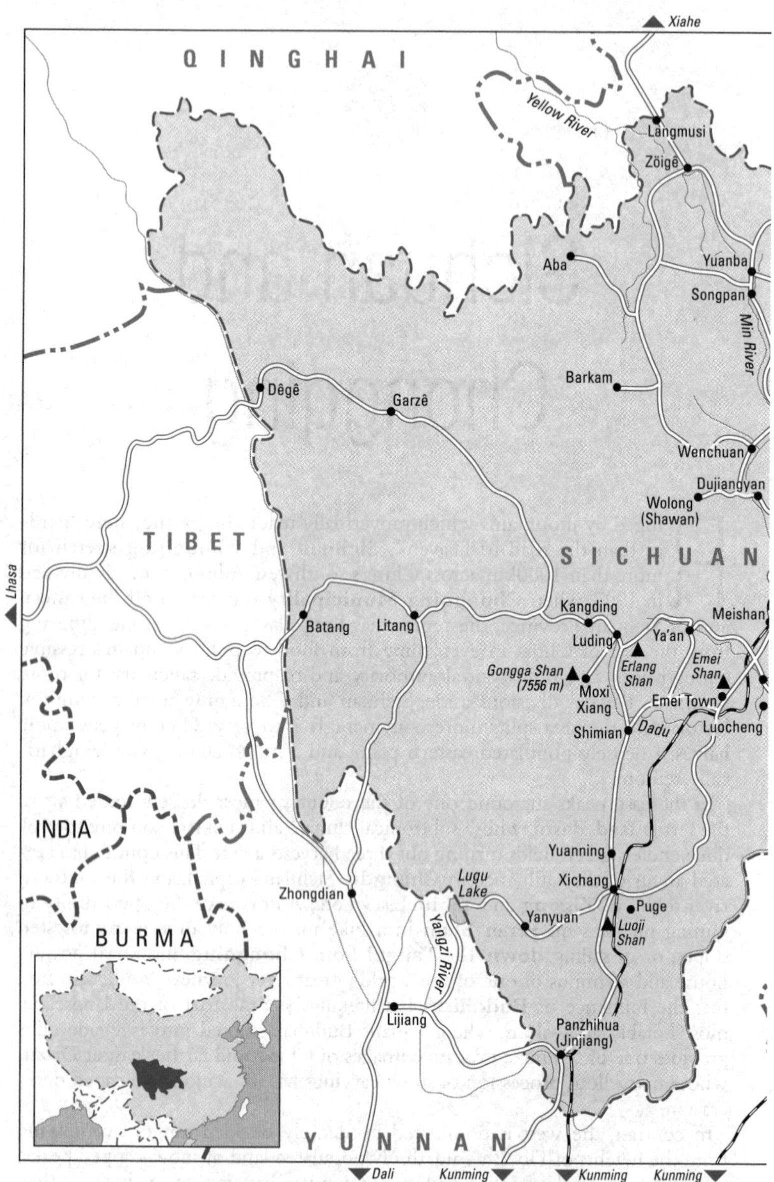

nic Hui and Qiang heartlands past the vivid blue lakes and beautiful mountain scenery of **Songpan** and **Jiuzhai Gou**, with the tranquil village of **Langmusi** the most remote of targets, right on the provincial border. Due west of Chengdu are the fringes of Tibet, including **Hailou Gou Glacier** lying in the foothills of **Gongga Shan**, Sichuan's highest peak, and predominantly Tibetan towns such as **Kangding**.

New roads and better vehicles mean that **getting around** all this is not always the endurance test it once was, though those heading westwards still need to prepare for unpredictably long and uncomfortable journeys. **Rail lines** are restricted by geography – construction was such a monumental task that Chengdu was linked to the national network only in 1956 – and most people use the train only for travel beyond regional borders; the most useful internal route is along the Xi'an–Kunming line, which runs southwest from Chengdu via Emei Shan and Xichang. As for the **weather**, expect warm and wet summers and cold winters, with the north and west frequently buried under snow for three months of the year.

Some history

In prehistoric times the region was apparently divided into the eastern **Ba** and western **Shu kingdoms**, which may have amalgamated during the Shang era (1600–1100 BC). Sites at **Sanxingdui**, near Chengdu, suggest the Ba–Shu was a slave society with highly developed metalworking skills and bizarre aesthetics (see p.938). Agricultural innovations at the end of the third century BC opened up eastern Sichuan to intensive farming, and when the Qin armies stormed through, they found an economic base which financed their unification of China in 221 BC – as did Genghis Khan's forces almost 1500 years later. In between, the area became the Three Kingdoms state of **Shu** – a name by which Sichuan is still sometimes known – and later twice provided refuge for deposed emperors.

Otherwise too distant to play a central role in China's history, the region leapt to prominence in 1911, when government interference in local rail industries sparked the nationwide rebellions that toppled the Qing empire. The next four decades saw rival warlords fighting for control, and, though some stability came when the **Nationalist government** made Chongqing their capital after the Japanese invaded China in 1937, nominally independent states persisted within the former Sichuan's borders as late as 1955: "When the rest of the country is at peace, Sichuan is the last to be brought to heel", went the saying. The province suffered badly during the Cultural Revolution – **Jung Chang**'s autobiography, *Wild Swans*, gives a firsthand account of the vicious arbitrariness of the times in Sichuan – and was left, by the early 1970s, poor and agriculturally devastated. Typically, it was the first province to reject Maoist ideals, when party leader Zhao Ziyang allowed farmers to sell produce on the free market, spearheading the reforms of his fellow native Sichuanese, **Deng Xiaoping**. So effective were these reforms that by the 1990s Sichuan was competing vigorously with the east-coast economy, a situation for which Chongqing – the already heavily industrialized gateway river port between Sichuan and eastern China – claimed a large part of the credit; Chongqing's economic weight secured separate provincial status for the city and its surrounds. Meanwhile, development continues across the region, bringing all the problems of runaway growth: appalling industrial pollution, ecological devastation, and an unbelievable scale of urban reconstruction.

Eastern Sichuan and Chongqing

One of the most pleasant areas of China to explore randomly, eastern Sichuan is focused around **Chengdu**, the relaxed provincial capital. Famed not least for its fiery cuisine, the city offers a number of worthwhile day-trips to nearby scenic and historic sights, the most unusual of which is a 2000-year-old **irrigation scheme** at **Dujiangyan**. Northeast is a little-noticed but historically important **route to Shaanxi**; southwest, both road and rail run past Buddhist landmarks at **Emei Shan** and **Leshan** and down to the Yunnanese border via **Xichang**. Southeast of the capital, the historic towns of **Zigong** and **Yibin** offer access to picturesque bamboo forests, and traces of an obscure, long-vanished society. East of Chengdu, further Buddhist sites surround the country town of **Dazu**, and beyond, western China's largest city, **Chongqing**, marks the start of the **journey down the Yangzi** to Hubei Province, with ferries exiting the region through the dramatic **Three Gorges**.

Chengdu and around

Set on the western side of the Red Basin, **CHENGDU** is a city with two faces: a modern, smoggy provincial capital whose boutique-lined streets are traversed by Japanese four-wheel-drives and fluorescent bicycles, coupled with narrow back lanes where old men play cards in noisy teahouses and pot plants crowd the porches of traditional, half-timbered homes. Whether you're an old hand or arriving through the air link with Tibet for your first taste of Han China, you'll find Chengdu a far-from-typical metropolis – it's one of the country's most mellow cities, intrinsically interesting and built on a very human scale.

Settled for more than 2400 years and once ringed by almost 20km of battlements and gates, Chengdu was styled **Brocade City** in Han times, when the urban elite were buried in elegantly decorated tombs, and its silk travelled west along the caravan routes as far as imperial Rome. A refuge for the eighth-century Tang emperor Xuan Zong after his army mutinied over his infatuation with the beautiful concubine Yang Guifei, the city later became a **printing** centre, producing the world's first paper money. Chengdu was sacked by the invading Mongols in 1271, but recovered soon enough to impress Marco Polo with its busy artisans and handsome bridges, since when it has since survived similar cycles of war and restoration to become, once again, a major industrial and business centre. Plenty of sights illustrate this chequered history, with a sprinkling of monuments and temples in and around the city well worth a few days' browsing. The **university**, founded in the 1920s, adds a lively element to the city's strong cultural tradition, and there's also an important **School of Chinese Medicine**. Backed by an embryonic nightlife, and with one of China's most outstanding cuisines to spike your taste buds on, Chengdu at the very least offers a comfortable base to organize travel into the rest of Sichuan, or to recuperate afterwards.

Chengdu and around

Chengdu	成都	***chéngdū***
Baihuatan Park	百花潭公园	*bǎihuātán gōngyuán*
Chengdu Giant Panda Breeding Research Base	成都大熊猫繁育研究基地	*chéngdū dàxióngmāo fányù yánjiū jīdì*
Chengdu Zoo	成都动物园	*chéngdū dòngwùyuán*
Cultural Palace	文化宫	*wénhuà gōng*
Du Fu's Cottage	杜甫草堂	*dùfǔ cǎotáng*
Exhibition Hall	省展览馆	*shěng zhǎnlǎnguǎn*
Hospital of Traditional Chinese Medicine College	中医药大学	*zhōngyīyào dàxué*
Jinjiang Theatre	锦江剧场	*jǐnjiāng jùchǎng*
North bus Station	北站中心站	*běizhàn zhōngxīnzhàn*
Provincial Museum	省博物馆	*shěng bówùguǎn*
Qingyang Gong	青羊宫	*qīngyáng gōng*
Renmin Park	人民公园	*rénmín gōngyuán*
Renmin Stadium	人民体育场	*rénmín tǐyùchǎng*
Shudu Theatre	蜀都剧场	*shǔdū jùchǎng*
Sichuan University Museum	四川大学博物馆	*sìchuān dàxué bówùguǎn*
Wang Jian Mu	王建墓	*wángjiàn mù*
Wangjiang Lou Park	望江楼公园	*wàngjiānglóu gōngyuán*
Wenshu Monastery	文殊院	*wénshū yuàn*
Wuhou Ci	武侯祠	*wǔhóu cí*
Ximen bus station	西门车站	*xīmén chēzhàn*
Xinnanmen bus station	新南汽车站	*xīnnán qìchēzhàn*
Zhaojue Si	照觉寺	*zhàojué sì*
Accommodation		
Holiday Inn Crowne Plaza	总府皇冠假日酒店	*zǒngfǔ huángguān jiàrìjiǔdiàn*
Jiaotong	交通饭店	*jiāotōng fàndiàn*
Jinhe	金河大酒店	*jīnhé dàjiǔdiàn*
Jinjiang	锦江宾馆	*jǐnjiāng bīnguǎn*

Arrival, information and city transport

Around 4km across, Chengdu's **downtown** area contains a warped grid of streets enclosed on three sides by the black, malodorous, canal-like **Fu** and **Jin** rivers, themselves surrounded by an ever-increasing number of ring roads. Broad and lined with plane trees, **Renmin Lu** is the main thoroughfare, divided into north, middle and south sections. The centre itself is marked by a large, grassy public square in front of the city's ponderous **Exhibition Hall**.

Shuangliu airport is 16km southwest of town, an ¥8 ride on the **airport bus** to the China Southwest Airlines office on Renmin Nan Lu (approximately 2 hourly; 30min); alternatively, a taxi costs around Y35. Four kilometres north of the city centre, the **main train station** is dwarfed by a square and roundabout out front, packed with jostling crowds of passengers, beggars and hawkers. The **city bus terminus** is just west off this square, from where bus #16 runs the length of Renmin Lu; #61 terminates at Xinnanmen bus station; and #25 can get you to Yihuan Lu near Ximen bus station in the northwest. Five kilometres south of town, Chengdu's **South train station** generally handles freight, but if you wind up here catch bus #16 to the centre.

Minshan	岷山饭店	*mínshān fàndiàn*
Railway Travel Hotel	铁旅大厦	*tiělǚ dàshà*
Rongcheng	荣城宾馆	*róngchéng bīnguǎn*
Eating and drinking		
Chen Mapo Tofu	陈麻婆豆腐	*chénmápó dòufù*
Chengdu	成都餐厅	*chéngdū cāntīng*
Guotang Yuan	郭汤圆	*guōtāng yuán*
Half Dozen Pub	半打啤酒馆	*bàndǎ píjiǔguǎn*
Highfly Cafe	高飞咖啡	*gāofēi kāfēi*
Lao Chengdu Gong Guan Cai	老成都公馆菜	*lǎochéngdū gōngcàiguǎn*
Long Chaoshou	龙抄手饭店	*lóngchāoshǒu fàndiàn*
Tianfang Lou	天方楼	*tiānfāng lóu*
White Night Bar	白夜酒吧	*báiyè jiǔbā*
Xiaocheng Xiaocan	小城小餐	*xiǎochéng xiǎocān*
Dujiangyan	都江堰	***dūjiāngyàn***
Anlan Cable Bridge	安澜索桥	*ānlán suǒqiáo*
Erwang Miao	二王庙	*èrwáng miào*
Fulong Guan	伏龙观	*fúlóng guàn*
Jingyuan Binguan	京园宾馆	*jīngyuán bīnguǎn*
Lidui Park	离堆公园	*líduī gōngyuán*
Guanghan	广汉	***guǎnghàn***
Fanghu Park	房湖公园	*fánghú gōngyuán*
Sanxingdui Museum	三星堆博物馆	*sānxīngduī bówùguǎn*
Xinxing Dajiudian	新星大酒店	*xīnxīng dàjiǔdiàn*
Qingcheng Shan	青城山	***qīngchéng shān***
Shangqing Gongsi	上青宫寺	*shàngqīnggōng sì*
Xindu	新都	***xīndū***
Baoguang Si	宝光寺	*bǎoguāng sì*

Otherwise, you'll arrive at one of Chengdu's many **long-distance bus stations**, most of them scattered around the city perimeter. The three largest are the **North bus station**, 500m west of the train station, which mostly deals in mid-range traffic from the north and northeast (buses into town as from the main train station); **Ximen bus station**, 3km northwest of the centre, with long-distance arrivals from the north and west (bus #62 heads southeast across town from Yihuan Lu); and **Xinnanmen bus station**, by the Jin River a couple of kilometres southeast of the centre, where you'll probably wind up if you arrive from Chongqing, Leshan or Emei Shan (bus #61 to the main train station).

The expat-oriented magazine *Go West*, available in bars and hotels, has a **listings** section including restaurants and nightlife, and articles about the city and its locality.

City transport

Chengdu's extensive **bus** network, including some restored, wooden-decor coaches, covers every area of the city between 6am and 10pm, for around ¥1–2 a ride. Private **minibuses** ply the same routes with the route number displayed

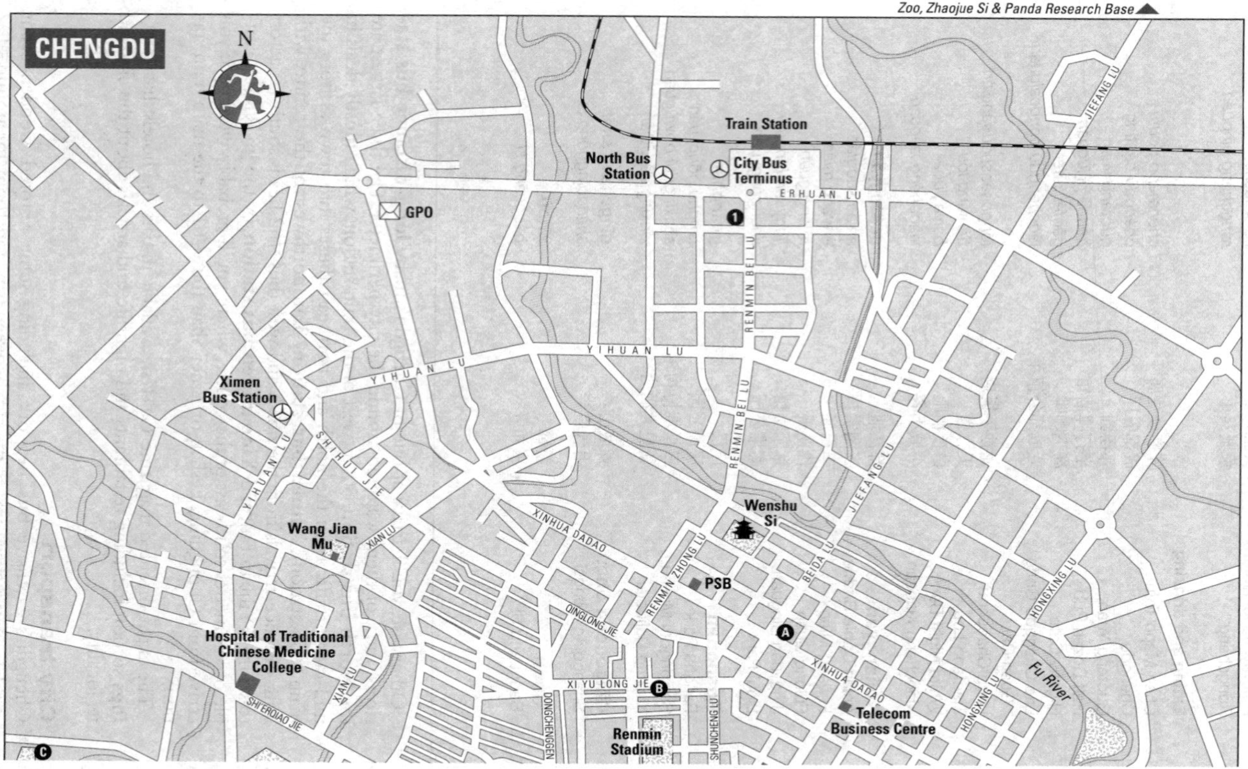

CHENGDU
N
Zoo, Zhaojue Si & Panda Research Base
Train Station
North Bus Station
City Bus Terminus
ERHUAN LU
GPO
JIEFANG LU
RENMIN BEI LU
YIHUAN LU
Ximen Bus Station
SHIHUI JIE
Wenshu Si
XINHUA DADAO
Wang Jian Mu
XIAN LU
RENMIN ZHONG LU
PSB
BEIDA LU
HONGXING LU
QINGLONG JIE
Hospital of Traditional Chinese Medicine College
XI YU LONG JIE
Fu River
SHI'ERQIAO JIE
DONGCHENGGEN
SHUNCHENG LU
Telecom Business Centre
Renmin Stadium

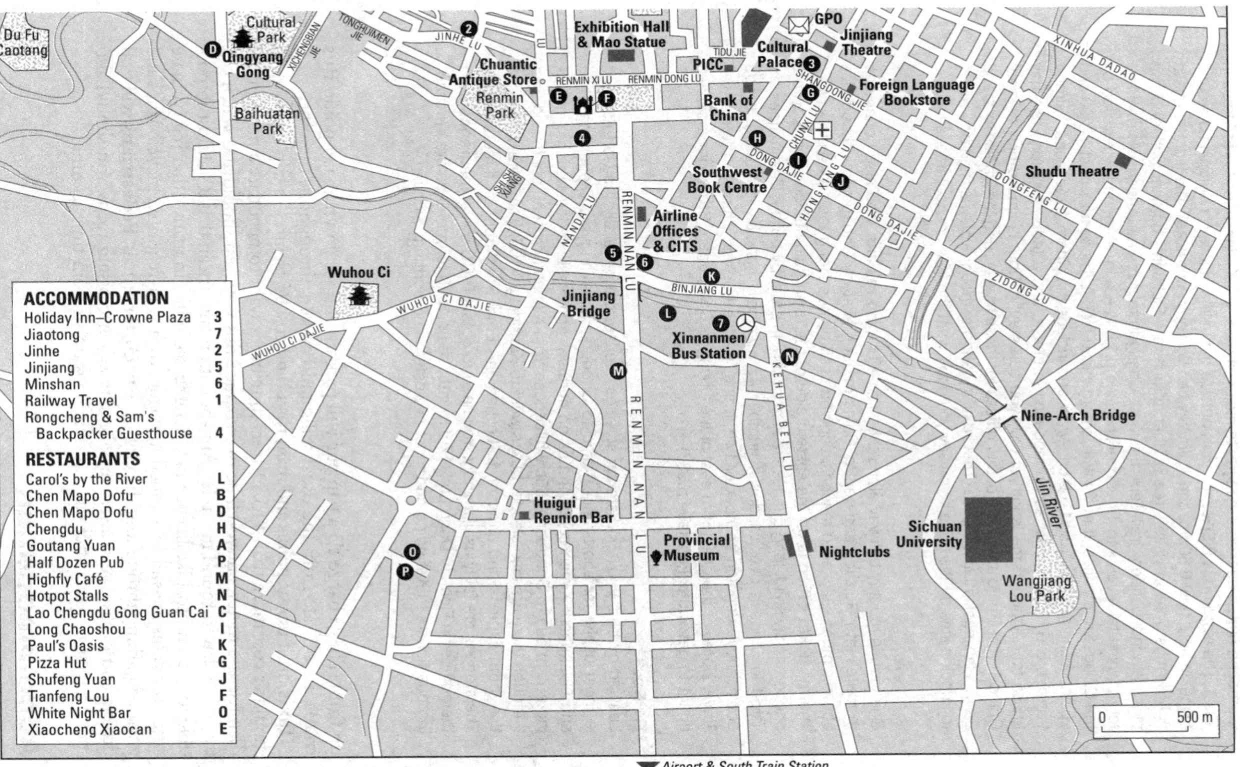
Du Fu Caotang
Cultural Park
Qingyang Gong
Baihuatan Park
XICHENGBIAN JIE
TONGHUIMEN JIE
JINHE LU
Exhibition Hall & Mao Statue
GPO
Jinjiang Theatre
Cultural Palace
TIDU JIE
PICC
Chuantic Antique Store
RENMIN XI LU
RENMIN DONG LU
Renmin Park
Bank of China
SHANGDONG JIE
Foreign Language Bookstore
XINHUA DADAO
CHUNXI LU
DONG DAJIE
Southwest Book Centre
HONGXING LU
Shudu Theatre
DONGFENG LU
SHI SHI XIANG
NANDA LU
RENMIN NAN LU
Airline Offices & CITS
ZIDONG LU
Wuhou Ci
WUHOU CI DAJIE
Jinjiang Bridge
BINJIANG LU
Xinnanmen Bus Station
KEHUA BEI LU
Nine-Arch Bridge
Jin River
Huigui Reunion Bar
Provincial Museum
Nightclubs
Sichuan University
Wangjiang Lou Park
0
500 m
Airport & South Train Station
ACCOMMODATION
Holiday Inn–Crowne Plaza 3
Jiaotong 7
Jinhe 2
Jinjiang 5
Minshan 6
Railway Travel 1
Rongcheng & Sam's Backpacker Guesthouse 4
RESTAURANTS
Carol's by the River L
Chen Mapo Dofu B
Chen Mapo Dofu D
Chengdu H
Goutang Yuan A
Half Dozen Pub P
Highfly Café M
Hotpot Stalls N
Lao Chengdu Gong Guan Cai C
Long Chaoshou I
Paul's Oasis K
Pizza Hut G
Shufeng Yuan J
Tianfeng Lou F
White Night Bar O
Xiaocheng Xiaocan E

Moving on from Chengdu

Outbound **flights** connect Chengdu to major cities across China, and also to **Lhasa** in Tibet. The airport bus (¥8) leaves from outside the airline offices on Renmin Lu around twice an hour until 6.30pm; check times when you buy your ticket. The flight to Lhasa is how most foreign visitors reach Tibet from here – Sichuan's borders with Tibet are closed to independent travellers, though a Chengdu tour operator now sells package tours which take you into Tibet overland (see p.1122) – and, as generally required by the Chinese authorities, they fly with an organized "tour". These trips cost ¥2200 and up (the flight on its own is ¥1200 one-way), and include the airfare, travel permit, airport transfer, two nights' dorm accommodation in Lhasa, and a (non-obligatory) two-day Lhasa tour – though the length of time you can stay in Tibet is limited only by your Chinese visa. There are plenty of tour offices for these trips around the *Traffic Hotel* and *Sam's Backpacker Guesthouse*. They're all in cahoots, though you may find one willing to knock a little off the price if you say you don't want the tour or accommodation.

By train

Chengdu is roughly halfway along the Xi'an–Kunming **rail line**, and also connected to routes into Guizhou and central China through easterly Chongqing – though it's actually much quicker to reach Chongqing itself by bus along the new expressway. The rail **ticket office** is on the eastern side of the main train station square, where phenomenally solid, long queues are almost kept in order by police. Destinations are listed in Chinese over windows; number #5 nominally handles foreigners. If you don't fancy spending an hour or two in line, try the booking office at the *Railway Travel Hotel*, or the one 150m east of the Chengdu Department Store, or employ an agent to get you tickets (see p.937).

By bus

Leaving by bus, you'll find station services overlap, but generally the North station is most useful for short-range traffic to Chongqing, Dujiangyan, Qingcheng Shan and Guanghan; Ximen concentrates on northern and western destinations, including a 7am bus to Songpan (¥65); while those from Xinnanmen head south and east – though there are also sleeper buses west to Kangding (¥105) from here, and shuttles (both express and ordinary) to Leshan and Emei Shan from all three stations. The stations are fairly user-friendly. You need to obtain **PICC travel insurance** from their office on Renmin Dong Lu (¥17 a month; see p.1020 for more) before purchasing bus tickets to Kangding and most of western and northern Sichuan.

up front. They charge ¥3 a trip but will pick up and set down at any point. **Bus maps** are on sale from the usual stalls and hawkers throughout the city.

Taxis orbit transit points and main roads, and cost ¥5 to hire – a trip across town shouldn't cost more than ¥15. Drivers sometimes want to negotiate a price rather than use the meter, but you'll be overcharged this way; you should also watch out for being driven round in circles. Anti-pollution laws mean that it's almost impossible to get a motorbike licence in Chengdu, so, unlike in many other big Chinese cities, **bicycles** are still very much in vogue, with well-regulated bicycle lanes and guarded parking throughout the city – see p.937 for rentals. **Pedestrians** will find drivers and cyclists very assertive: take care when crossing roads. You should also stick to well-lit roads after dark, as muggings occur from time to time.

Accommodation

Most of Chengdu's accommodation lies near Renmin Lu, in striking distance of #16 buses. All have somewhere to eat and tour-booking services, and most offer Internet connections; the more upmarket include banking, IDD and postal facilities.

Holiday Inn Crowne Plaza Zong Fu Lu ⓣ028/86786666, ⓕ86786599. Massive, solid and impressive building, faultlessly located and with all the facilities you'd expect from an international chain charging US$140 a night. ❾

Hospital of Traditional Chinese Medicine College Shi'er Qiao Jie ⓣ028/87772593, ⓕ028/84476823. Rooms here – all with their own bathroom – are fair value. The dorms are often booked up. Dorms ¥20–50, ❹

Jiaotong (Traffic) 77 Jinjiang Lu ⓣ028/85551017, ⓕ85582777. A little faded, and losing custom to *Sam's*, but good value and still Chengdu's budget mainstay. Facilities include spotless doubles and three-bed dorms with TV and shared or private bathroom, a cheap left-luggage office and a message board outside advertising travelling companions and used gear. You also get a free breakfast, though it's not up to much. Bus #16 passes close by – get off just south of Jinjiang Bridge, then walk east for 1km. Dorm beds ¥40, ❸

Jinhe 18 Jinhe Lu ⓣ028/86642888, ⓕ86632037. Multistorey tower near Renmin Park, with accommodation ranging from upmarket suites to comfortable but tiny "economy rooms" with shared bathroom. ❸–❻

Jinjiang 80 Renmin Nan Lu ⓣ028/85582222. Uninspiring Soviet-style building with red carpets and cream wallpaper. Overpriced, though rooms are decent enough. ❾

Minshan 55 Renmin Nan Lu ⓣ028/85583333, ⓕ85582154. Chengdu's top business venue, whose comfortable but fairly ordinary rooms are a bit of a letdown after the acres of granite tiling and the string quartet in the lobby. ❽

Railway Travel Hotel Renmin Bei Lu ⓣ028/83177512, ⓕ83178704. Renovations have seen a new mid-range wing added to this formerly gloomy hotel, now fair value; there are also cheap dorms, though they're rarely available to foreigners. Train-booking service to boot. ❺

Rongcheng (Sam's Backpacker Guesthouse) 130 Shaanxi Jie ⓣ028/86112933 ext 2233, ⓕ84476823. A comfortable two-star hotel with one wing – originally a nineteenth-century salt merchant's residence – leased out in some kind of backdoor arrangement to the enterprising Sam. Don't approach the hotel reception but go through the gate on the west side of the hotel and Sam's office is through the first door on your right. Rooms aren't well lit, but they are good value and the garden is lovely. Facilities include left luggage, bike rental and a café, plus they organize tours of the city and its surroundings. Dorm beds ¥20, ❸

The City

Despite sometimes overpowering pollution, Chengdu is a cheerful city, its streets and parks full of floral colour – especially during the **Spring Flower Festival** – while market stalls groan under the weight of seasonal fruit. And everywhere, **buildings** are shooting up and crashing down, demolitions carefully carried out brick by brick using muscle and sledgehammer. City expansions may be commonplace given China's snowballing economic boom, but, given its relative isolation, Chengdu seems to have attracted a disproportionate amount of investment. The shops are well stocked with imported goods, while more traditional enterprises still flourish in the backstreets, which can make reaching the city's scattered sights more interesting than the sights themselves.

Downtown Chengdu and Wenshu Si

Chengdu's centre is firmly marked by a massive white statue of **Chairman Mao**, who smiles smugly over traffic congestion as he faces south across the central **public square**, his back to the **Exhibition Hall**. Immediately west, turrets and dome mark out a huge **mosque**, built for Chengdu's sizeable Muslim community after the old Muslim quarter was demolished to make the square in 1997. East of the Exhibition Hall, Renmin Dong Lu runs east into **Dongfeng Lu** and **Dong Dajie**, through the heart of the city's shopping precinct. Running between the two is **Chunxi Lu**, a prestigious shopping

Teahouses

The Sichuanese have a reputation for being particularly garrulous, a trait best seen at one of the province's many **teahouses** (*chadian*), for which Chengdu has always been particularly famous. Traditionally, these were social clubs where people met to finalize deals, hold meetings and relax after work, listening to storytellers or watching acting troupes perform. The teahouses suffered badly during the Cultural Revolution, when such activities were labelled as bourgeois, and while they've recovered in recent times, much of the "men only" atmosphere of the older establishments is disappearing along with the backstreets and buildings that housed them. Today, you'll find teahouses in all Chengdu's parks, temple grounds and theatres, where the elderly and the idle can spend whole days chatting, or playing chess, mahjong or cards, when crowds surround good games. Elsewhere people lounge in open-backed bamboo or lilac plastic chairs smoking cheroots, chewing melon seeds and arguing with their neighbours, while a waiter moves around filling up cups from a broken-spouted teapot. They're open to all, foreigners included – somewhere to socialize over a perpetually full teacup.

street; south of here, a quiet string of walled alleys runs down behind leafy Hongxing Lu towards the river, where wooden gateways lead into the courtyards of century-old homes.

About 1500m north of Mao's statue on the route of bus #16, the entrance to **Wenshu Si** (aka the Hollow Wood Temple; daily 6am–8.30pm; ¥1) lies east off Renmin Zhong Lu down Wenshu Yuan Jie, a lane crammed with stalls selling paper money, incense and gaudy porcelain Buddha statues. Dedicated to Wenshu, God of Wisdom, the temple was founded in the seventh century and last rebuilt around 1700. The headquarters of Sichuan's Chan (Zen) Buddhist sect, it's perpetually full of Chinese posturing to shrines and showing their children how to do likewise. Five unpretentious halls within sport beautifully sweeping tiled roofs, carved eaves and painted ceilings, enclosing statues of Maitreya and Guanyin, all bathed in incense smoke. The third hall contains a row of gilt *arhats* under glass – look for the one whose eyebrows droop onto his chest – while the next houses a wonderful painting of a strange dog-like creature behind a smiling Buddha. The monastery also has a famous collection of **sutras**, some written in blood, although these are not on display. Outside in the gardens, shady rows of pine and gingko trees surround a noisy **teahouse**, jam-packed with locals clamouring for refreshment, and a very fine **vegetarian restaurant**, whose food is prepared by monk chefs – an excellent reason to visit Wenshu at lunchtime (see p.934).

Renmin Park

Ten minutes' walk west of the Exhibition Hall, **Renmin Park** (¥2, or ¥5 including tea) is typical of Chengdu's open spaces. It's best in the early morning as *tai ji* and *wushu* enthusiasts compete for space with groups of ballroom dancers circling to piped music, and old men hang up their caged songbirds. Entering from Jinhe Lu, you'll see the **Monument to the Martyrs**, a tall obelisk commemorating the 1911 rail disputes which marked the beginning of the end for the Qing empire – hence the unusual motifs of trains and spanners. There's a good **teahouse** nearby, along with **ornamental gardens**, surrounded by flowers, green lawns (elsewhere trampled to dust) and artificial rock formations. Look for vendors with little burners and a slab of marble along the paths – they execute skilful designs of the Chinese zodiac animals in **toffee**. At the eastern end of the park, there's a small **lake** where you can rent pedal boats and squeak across the waters (¥1), while the south exit leads straight into a lively produce market and narrow lanes where you can glimpse a rapidly vanishing older Chengdu in the informal street life and wooden homes with pole-frame balconies.

Qingyang Gong and around

Jinhe Lu continues due west past Renmin Park for 2km or so towards Qingyang Gong, founded in Tang times; if you don't fancy the walk, flag down bus #42, which terminates opposite the temple. Along the way the road becomes first Tonghuimen Jie and then Shi'erqiao Jie; turn off Tonghuimen Jie to head down **Xichengbian Jie**, an extraordinary street rebuilt in the Qing style. It's interesting to look at, though nowhere in China was ever this perfect and the result is more like a Western "Chinatown", full of expensive jewellery shops, restaurants and karaoke bars. At the southern end of the street you can either turn left and follow the road to Qingyang, or follow the ornamental bridge across the Jin River to **Baihuatan Park** (¥2), famous for its pretty **flower gardens** decorated with gnarled bonsai, orchids and an ancient **gingko tree**, said to date back to Tang times. Rather incongruously, there's also a dinosaur theme park, whose entrance is graced by a life-size brass band of mechanical pandas.

Sited in the southern part of the tacky **Cultural Park** (only worth a visit around the Chinese New Year when it becomes the focus for Chengdu's flower festival), **Qingyang Gong** (Green Goat Temple; ¥1) is dedicated to Taoism's mythical proponent, Laozi. The exterior of the main **Three Purities Hall** is decorated with brightly coloured animals and dragons, while two **bronze goats** in the entrance are fenced off after being worn smooth by the caresses of luck-seekers. The right-hand "goat" is somewhat odd, being the simultaneous incarnation of all twelve zodiacal animals. Inside, plaster saints lining the walls are overlooked by the golden bulks of the Three Purities themselves, representing the three levels of Taoist heaven. Behind them is a spirited carved panel of the Purities riding their assigned beasts: a crane, a tiger and a nine-headed lion. For active entertainment, head around the back of the final hall, where those after a blessing stumble with eyes shut and arms outstretched towards a large good luck symbol painted on the bricks, hoping to make contact; onlookers laugh at their efforts before trying themselves.

A ten-minute walk north along Yihuan Lu from the temple is the **Hospital of Traditional Chinese Medicine College**. Foreigners are allowed to study here, and some classes are held in English – contact *Sam's Backpacker Guesthouse* (p.929) to arrange a visit.

Du Fu Caotang

The line of minibuses pulled up outside **Du Fu Caotang** (Du Fu's Thatched Cottage; 9am–5pm; ¥5 park, ¥25 museum), located in pleasant parkland a couple of kilometres west of Qingyang on Chengdu's fringes, attests to the respect the Chinese hold for the Tang-dynasty poet **Du Fu**. Born in 712 AD, Du Fu struggled for years to obtain a minor position at the imperial court in Chang'an, succeeding only after one of his sons had died of starvation and just as a civil war was breaking out. Forced to leave the capital, he arrived in Chengdu around 759 and, as war swept the country, he holed up in a simple grass-roofed dwelling outside the city's west wall. Here he wrote some 240 of his 1400 surviving poems: direct, moving pieces about daily life, human suffering, and his longing for his home in Henan. Later forced to move on again, he spent the rest of his days wandering central China "like a lonely gull between the sea and the sky", dying on a boat in Hunan in 770.

This temple park was founded three centuries after his death, and now includes a **main hall** with a statue of Du Fu, and a **museum** wing with some marvellous early woodblock and hand-written versions of his poems. In the gardens themselves, there's the inevitable teahouse and a silly thatched pavilion meant to resemble the poet's hut.

Wuhou Ci and Wang Jian Mu

Historians will find two other sites in western Chengdu worth a look. **Wuhou Ci** (¥5 general entry, or ¥30 including all halls), south of the Jin River on Wuhou Ci Dajie (bus #1 from Renmin Nan Lu terminates nearby), is a much-restored Tang-dynasty complex set in densely planted grounds and dedicated to **Zhuge Liang**, the Machiavellian strategist of *Three Kingdoms* fame who became the first prime minister of the state of Shu in 212 AD (see p.509). Here it's worth seeking out the **temple** to Zhuge, the black **Three Wonder Tablet** of 809 AD (so called because it is considered perfect in text, calligraphy and carving), and the **Three Kingdoms Museum**, which uses models, maps and mementoes to put everything in context. A bigger pull for visiting Chinese, however, is the **Tomb of Liu Bei**, founder and emperor of Shu, who lies buried alongside his two wives under a huge grassy mound at the back. You can buy all kinds of *Three Kingdoms* souvenirs around the grounds, and a host of martial arts weapons from stalls a little farther west along Wuhou Ci Dajie.

Over in the north of town off Xi'an Lu and the #46 bus route, **Wang Jian Mu** (Tues–Sun 9am–5.30pm; ¥2) is a cleaned but otherwise unrestored tomb commemorating one of the rulers of Shu during the chaotic Five Dynasties period (907–960 AD). There's not really much to see, just a small display of tomb relics, a statue of Wang Jian himself, and the tomb chamber where twelve carved muscular gods support the coffin platform, while the walls are decorated in relief with musicians and dancers.

The Provincial Museum

Some 2km south of Mao's statue and across the Jinjiang Bridge on Renmin Nan Lu, the dusty **Provincial Museum** (Tues–Fri 9am–noon & 2–5pm, Sat & Sun 10am–4pm; ¥5), on the route of bus #16, is worth an hour's browse. English captions are few, but a map in the left-hand hall detailing Sichuan's archeological sites leaves no doubt as to Chengdu's historic importance, with local finds going right back to Shang **Ba–Shu** relics. Exhibits include a four-metre-long wooden **hanging coffin** found in a cliffside cave above the Yangzi, and casts of the extraordinary **masks** found in the Sanxingdui **sacrificial pits** – for more on which, see p.938. Later bronzework includes a fine set of fourteen clapperless **bells** from the Warring States period, contemporary with those found at Wuhan in Hubei (see p.530). Over in the right wing, a statue of the third-century BC engineer **Li Bing**, discovered in 1974 face down in the bed of his irrigation project at Dujiyangyan, stands at the far end like a giant chess piece. The rest of the room is taken up with rubbings of **Han tomb reliefs**, panels alive with wavy, elongated figures in rural and court settings depicting scenes from the deceased's life – one shows a savage toothed camel and its handlers. Similarly animated **pottery** figurines include portly animal sculptures and a grotesque model of a storyteller banging a drum.

Sichuan University and Wangjiang Lou Park

Away on Chengdu's southeastern extremity, **Sichuan University** merits a visit for its own museum and the nearby **Wangjiang Lou Park** – though there's also the possibility of meeting and talking with students. Buses #62 and #35 terminate nearby on the north bank of the Jin River at the **Nine-arch Bridge**, where Tibetans sit on the pavement selling tiger paws and dried monkey carcasses; cross over and walk east along the south bank for ten minutes to the university gates. Inside, an avenue leads down to a neatly planted garden, with the building to your right housing the excellent **University Museum** (Mon–Fri 9am–noon & 2.30–5pm; ¥10). Downstairs are more Han tomb reliefs and the fragmentary remains of some beautifully proportioned Tang **Buddhist statues**, while upstairs there are some worthy, if dry, **ethnology** exhibits, including Qiang, Yi and Miao textiles, and a room devoted to Tibetan religious artefacts – silverwork, paintings and a human thigh-bone flute. Better is a separate display of local items, including swathes of Chengdu's famous **brocades**, some made into wedding costumes and coverings for an elaborate Qing bridal sedan. At the back of the upper floor a model tearoom has cups laid out at tables in front of a **shadow-puppet theatre** (*piying shi*, or "skin-moving theatre" in Chinese). Its walls are covered with heroes, villains and mythical beasts, all of flat pieces of leather snipped and pierced like paper-cut-outs.

Just beyond the university gates, **Wangjiang Lou** (River-viewing Pavilion; daily 9am–5pm; ¥2) sits in a small park hugging the river bank. A Ming-dynasty building, this is said to be the spot where the Tang poetess **Xue Tao** lived and used the local well water to wash and dye a special kind of red paper, still available today. Three buildings are given over to displays of scrollwork and bonsai, while outside, river breezes stir the hundred or so varieties of **bamboo** which flank the paths.

Chengdu Zoo, Zhaojue Si and the Panda Breeding Centre

Out in the city's northeastern suburbs, Chengdu **Zoo** (daily 8am–6pm; ¥5) is probably best skipped, despite nice bamboo gardens and the fuss made over its **pandas**, of which there are both the giant and the smaller red species. The animals sit lethargic and flea-bitten behind bars while the public throw ice-cream sticks and rubbish at them to try and get a reaction. Far more worthy is **Zhaojue Si** (¥1), accessed through the zoo, and housing a dozen halls and more than two hundred monks from a blend of Buddhist sects. Recently refurbished, the temple was founded in Tang times and enlarged under the Qing. Its splendid **main hall** is set on a raised foundation and dominated inside by three gigantic, blue-haired, gilt Buddhas who sit gazing over a sea of brightly coloured patchwork prayer cushions, while orange and red dragon banners droop from the ceiling. The rest of the complex repays a wander, with the surrounding courtyards hiding small, smoky shrines dedicated to various pudgy deities, while monks chant and strike bells in the background. There's also a decent **vegetarian restaurant** (closes mid-afternoon), though it's a bit problematic ordering here if you can't speak Chinese.

The zoo and Zhaojue Si make a half-day excursion, which you can extend by dropping in on the **Giant Panda Breeding Research Base** 5km east (daily 8am–6pm; ¥10). Short of heading off to Wolong (p.970), the base offers the best possible views of both giant and arboreal red pandas, housed here in semi-naturalistic, spacious pens. Get to the base early – after the twelve pandas finish munching their way through piles of bamboo at around 10am, they slump into a stupor.

From just east of the train station on Erhuan Lu, **bus** #9 runs to the zoo gates in about fifteen minutes, beyond which you'll need to catch a motor-rickshaw (¥10) to the panda breeding centre. The last bus back to the centre leaves at 6.15pm. Alternatively, tour agents can organize an all-inclusive return trip from town, taking in all three places, at ¥50 a person.

Eating

Eating is one of the best reasons to prolong a stay in Chengdu – you could spend months experimenting with the food here, and you won't forget your first taste of genuinely fiery and pungent Sichuanese food. Downtown is packed with **restaurants**, most looking like greasy-spoon canteens in Western cities, but for the aromatic local dishes and dark brown, crispy fried ducks on display at the front. Out in the streets, Muslims grill chilli- and coriander-coated kebabs over open coals, peddlers trundle around selling steamed buns, noodles and spicy tofu and, at night, the kerbsides are thick with alfresco **hotpot stalls**. You'll find the best of these setting up around dusk in a side-street east off **Kehua Bei Lu**, near Xinnanmen bus station. The ingredients are largely vegetarian – lotus root, potato slices, white radish, tofu, boiled quail's eggs – check the price per skewer beforehand (from ¥0.1 each), and count on a small service charge. All Sichuanese food tastes especially good with **beer** – try the locally brewed Blue Sword. Most proper restaurants open around 10am and shut by 9pm.

Chengdu also has several **cafés** aimed at expats and backpackers, where you can restock on Western-style food and drink, use the **Internet**, browse through book exchanges, and catch up with the latest travellers' news – particularly with regard to getting to Tibet. You'll also find *KFC* and *McDonald's* outlets throughout the centre, and there's a *Pizza Hut* at the western end of Dongfeng Lu.

Restaurants and cafés

Carol's By The River 2 Linjiang Lu (along the river west of the *Jiaotong* and Xinnanmen). Part of a smart chain serving good Mexican and Italian fare (the pizzas are fine), burgers and coffee in comfortable surroundings.

Chen Mapo Dofu Xi Yu Long Jie, north of the stadium; also Yihuan Lu, opposite Qingyang Gong. The Xi Yu Long Jie branch is said to be the original home of Grandma Chen's bean curd, and, though local opinion is divided as to whether it still serves Chengdu's best *mapo dofu*, it's pretty good. ¥10 buys a bowl of tofu glowing with minced meat, chilli oil and wild pepper sauce, plus rice, tea and a thin soup to wash it down.

Chengdu 134 Shandong Dajie, a westerly extension of Dong Dajie. Reasonably priced and one of the best places to try classic Sichuanese dishes, or a filling ¥15–30 sampler of local snacks: sweet and savoury dumplings, small crispy-fried fish, shredded dry-fried beef, shaved rice-jelly noodles, and much more. Try the outside tables, livened up by caged parakeets and set around a goldfish pool, and get in early, before debris from other diners litters the floor.

Guotang Yuan Beida Lu. Traditional pillar-and-beam decor sets the scene for this ancient, inexpensive dumpling house, specializing in peanut dishes.

Highfly Café Renmin Nan Lu. Variable Western food and toned-down Chinese fare; generally sound, and with friendly service.

Lao Chengdu Gong Guan Cai By the north gate of Dufu Caotang. Fine Sichuan dining in elegant garden surroundings, though a little on the pricey side; the classic Sichuan combo of spicy chicken and *mapo dofu* will set you back around ¥50.

Long Chaoshou Chunxi Lu. A renowned dumpling house, this chaotic, canteen-style place is jammed full at lunchtime with a face-stuffing clientele making the most of the selection of local snacks, at ¥5–20 a plateful. Upstairs offers proper sit-down dining; the set meal at ¥50, which involves innumerable small dishes, is a great way to fill up.

Paul's Oasis Opposite the *Jiaotong* on Binjiang Lu. Fills nightly with backpackers and foreign students, though note that the food really isn't great, nor are the prices.

Tianfang Lou At the mosque, Jinhe Lu. Inexpensive Muslim restaurant with plenty of roast meats, breads, pulled noodles, and very spicy soups.

Xiangzhai Tang Wenshu Si. Superb, inexpensive restaurant, not to be missed. All the fare is vegetarian – "bear paw", "chicken with chilli and prickly ash", "crackling rice with sea slug" and the like are all made from gluten, bean curd, aubergine and potato. Circle your choices on a tear-off menu (in Chinese – match the characters with the English shown on a board), pay at the kiosk, then collect food from the kitchen. Or head through the garden to the slightly more expensive section, which has an English menu.

Xiaocheng Xiaocan Corner of Renmin Xi Lu and Dongcheng Gen Lu. Good, mid-range restaurant upstairs, and a selection of dumplings and small snacks to eat with tea or beer downstairs. Their smoked duck is particularly good. Staff are a bit offhand, but should be able to track down the one English menu.

Sichuan cooking

If your experience of **Sichuan cooking** outside China has been a stir-fry drowned in red food colouring and tabasco, then you're in for a shock the first time you sit down to eat in Chengdu. Dominating the Southwestern China cooking school, the Sichuanese style is also one of the most subtle – after you grasp the principles behind the use of the far-from-subtle ingredients.

The most obvious ingredient here is **chilli**, with the food often arriving glistening under a layer of bright red chilli oil. Locals explain its use as a result of climate – chillis are warming in winter and cooling in summer and, according to Chinese medicine, dispel "wet" illnesses brought about by damp or humid conditions. Unfortunately for novices, they can also be the biggest hurdle to enjoying the food, as, even by Asian standards, the Sichuanese heap a phenomenal amount on any one dish. But chillis don't simply blast the tastebuds, they stimulate them as well, and, once conditioned, you'll find flavours much more complex than they might appear at the initial, eye-watering, mouthful.

Often present in the same dish, Sichuan cuisine's two most definitive tastes are the **manifold flavour** – a blend of hot, salty, sweet and sour – and **aromatic heat** (*mala*), characterized by the use of spring onions and **Sichuan pepper** (*huajiao*, or flower pepper), with its soapy perfume and gum-numbing side-effects. Typical dishes include **hot and sour soup**, flavoured with pepper and vinegar; **tangerine chicken** – cooked with the slivered, dried peel of local fruit – and **mapo dofu**, bean curd and minced pork swamped in a chilli sauce. *Mapo dofu* also illustrates another feature of Sichuan food, where the main ingredient becomes a simple vehicle for the sauce; other classic examples are **fish-flavoured pork** (whose "seafood" sauce is made from vinegar, soy sauce, sugar, ginger and sesame oil) and **strange-flavoured chicken** – cold chicken shreds served with a dressing of sesame paste, vinegar, chilli oil, Sichuan pepper, spring onion, ginger and garlic.

As in the rest of the country, **texture** also plays an important role in Sichuanese food, with the emphasis often on a **chewy**, **dry** effect, the result of prolonged cooking. While this may sound unappealing – some people find many Sichuanese dishes unpleasantly oily – with dishes such as **dry-fried pork shreds**, the effort of chewing seems to enhance the rich flavour of the meat.

Several dishes that originated in Sichuan otherwise have little in common with the above examples. For instance, **double-cooked pork**, where a plain piece of meat is boiled, sliced thinly and then stir-fried with green chillis, is a straightforward meal invented by salt-miners in eastern Sichuan. Other favourites include **smoked duck** (especially a version using camphor wood shavings), a chilli-free cold dish, aromatic, juicy and acrid; and **crackling rice**, where a meat soup is poured over a sizzling bed of deep-fried rice crusts.

Meals here are not always a gastronomic experience, however, and much of everyday food is similar to what you'd eat elsewhere in China, though often given a Sichuanese twist. Anywhere should be able to cook up **gongbao pork**, the local version of stir-fried pork and peanuts; spiced and oily **dandan mien** ("carry-pole" noodles, named after how street vendors used to carry them around); dumplings served with chilli and garlic relish; **tiger-skin peppers**, scorched then fried with salt; and spicy aubergine slices, battered and stuffed with mince. Perhaps the most striking adaptation to local taste is the **hotpot** (*huoguo*), which, though found all over China in one form or another, has really been taken to heart by the Sichuanese. At its best eaten informally at street restaurants, hotpot here consists of skewers of meat, boiled eggs or vegetables, cooked – by you at the table – in a bubbling pot of chicken stock liberally laced with chillis and cardamom pods. You then season the cooked food in oil spiced with MSG, salt and chilli powder. The effect is powerful, and during a cold winter in Chengdu you may well find that hotpots fast become your favourite food.

Nightlife and entertainment

Chengdu's **nightlife** is growing, but venues open and close very rapidly; check in *Go West* for the latest hotspots. Definitely worth a visit is *Huigui Reunion Bar*, west of Renmin Nan Lu on Yihuan Lu; get in past the bulky Chinese bouncers for a night of serious techno on the third floor. For a more relaxed experience hobnobbing with the local literati and other creative types – invariably clad in black – try the *White Night*, west of here at 85 Yulin Xi Lu; take bus #12 and get off at the Yiguan Miao stop. The *Half Dozen Pub* at 26 Fangcao Jie, was Chengdu's first bar, and still packs them in; there's a live band most nights.

As for **entertainment**, it's well worth spending an afternoon at the theatre, soaking up at least the atmosphere, if not the plots, of one of China's main opera styles. For something different, head up to the modern **Renmin Stadium** on Renmin Zhong Lu, where **football matches** are scheduled for most weekend afternoons – pick up tickets (¥10–50) from the office outside on the day of the match. Newspapers and tour agents might have details of these and other offerings such as travelling troupes performing in parks or tea houses.

Opera and theatre

More than two hundred years old and immensely popular in Chengdu, the **Sichuan Opera** derived from local religious and folk festival perfomances blended with the Beijing style. There are five forms: **gaoqiang**, with high-pitched singing; **kunqu**, **huqin** and **tanxi**, featuring flute, violin and zither accompaniment respectively; and **denxi**, lantern-play. The main differences between Sichuan and Beijing operas involve the themes – far more rustic here, based on everyday events and local legends – and the **language**, which is not impossible for outsiders to appreciate. All local pieces are performed in Sichuanese, a distinctively rhythmic dialect well suited to theatre, which allows for puns – the Sichuanese are renowned for their sense of humour and clever wordplay – and also affects the pace of the music, closely linked as it is to speeches. The music itself is cruder than in the Beijing Opera, with a relatively basic orchestra featuring harsh-pitched oboes and heavy use of the drum, a reflection of the Sichuan Opera's humble origins.

There's an **opera school** in Chengdu, and students often appear in minor roles in theatres around the city. Performances are held daily in the city, though the best actors and biggest crowds turn out on Sundays. Don't expect Beijing-style glamour, however; shows are far lower-key and even large venues tend towards a teahouse atmosphere, with the audience relaxed and enjoying the acting. Programmes last for the whole afternoon, consisting of at least three short pieces or episodes from longer sagas, often interspersed with non-operatic skits such as **qingyin** ballad-singing or **jinqianban** "castanet" dances.

Among places to see opera is the small teahouse theatre right at the back of the **Cultural Palace** on Tidu Jie, just east of the centre. It's a very casual affair, full of octogenarians crunching sunflower seeds, slurping the complimentary tea, and occasionally breaking off from gossiping to applaud the actors' finer points. More professional efforts take place at the **Jinjiang Theatre** on Xinglong Jie (currently closed for repairs), and the **Shudu Theatre** way down Yushuang Lu. For the cheapest **tickets** (¥2.50–20, depending on seat and venue) go direct to the theatre box offices – the daily fare is chalked up outside. Alternatively, ¥50 to a travel agent (see "Listings" opposite) buys a **guide** to accompany you, translate, explain plots and get you in backstage beforehand to see the actors preparing. These tours are often well worth it, but check the guide's English and where the performance is before paying, and never buy from wandering touts – you don't want to end up in a teahouse theatre, fun though they are, for this price.

Listings

Airlines China Southwest, near the *Minshan Hotel* on Renmin Nan Lu ⓣ028/86665911; Dragonair, at CITS (see "Travel agents" below).

Banks and exchange The main Bank of China is a tall, new tower on Renmin Zhong Lu with burnished bronze doors and special counters for corporate account holders (foreign exchange and credit card transactions Mon–Fri 9–11.30am & 2–5.30pm); accommodation, and the more convenient BOC branch on Renmin Dong Lu, also change traveller's cheques.

Bike rental Bikes can be rented from the courtyard of the *Jiaotong Hotel* and at *Sam's Backpacker Guesthouse* (both ¥10 per day plus ¥200 deposit).

Bookshops The Southwest Book Centre on Dong Dajie has a good collection of novels, not all of them Victorian potboilers either.

Consulates US: 4 Lingshiguan Lu, Section 4, Renmin Nan Lu (ⓣ028/85583992, ⓕ85583520), about 1km south of the Provincial Museum on the same side of the road.

English Corner Wed and Fri at 7.30pm on the corner of Renmin Nan Lu and Binjiang Lu, by the Jinjiang bridge. Worth dropping in on for the mix of young local students, who may offer to act as guides in return for English conversation.

Hospitals People's No.1 Hospital and Chengdu Municipal Chinese Medicine Research Institute, Chunxi Lu ⓣ028/86667223; Sichuan Hospital, Yihuan Xi Lu ⓣ028/85551312 or 85551255.

Internet access A couple of places opposite *Sam's Backpacker Guesthouse* offer Internet access for ¥3/hr and are open till the early hours. Otherwise try Floor 2 at the Telecom Business Centre (daily 10am–11.30pm; ¥20 an hour), one block south from the PSB on Yusha Lu.

Left luggage The train and bus stations all have left-luggage facilities open to anyone who can produce an onward ticket. Most hotels can also look after excess gear while you're off in the wilds.

Massage Some hotels have masseurs for around ¥80 an hour; cheaper operators set up outside the *Minshan Hotel* in the evenings, or cruise the tourist restaurants along the Jin River.

Mail and telephones There are two main post offices: an unmistakeable colonial-style grey brick building on the corner of Xinglong Jie, and a newer place on the northwestern outskirts at the corner of Yihuan Lu and Shawan Lu (both daily 8am–6pm). Poste restante will probably end up at the latter, in a cardboard box kept at the EMS counter. Note that the *Jinjiang Hotel* also has a very helpful postal counter. The telecommunications office is on Renmin Dong Lu, just east of Mao's statue; it's open daily from 8am to 6pm for IDD calls.

PSB Foreigners after visas or reporting problems are directed to the compound opposite the police headquarters on Wenwu Lu.

Shopping Three interesting markets are a Sunday pet market (selling mostly kittens and puppies) across from Baihuatan Park on Yihuan Lu; the small bird market about a kilometre north over Shi'er Qiao Jie (Wed & Sun); and the antiques market opposite Du Fu Caoting (Sun). The Friendship Plaza, cnr Dong Dajie and Chunxi Lu, is one of Chengdu's biggest, best-equipped shopping centres, selling everything from toothpaste to home gym kits. More interesting, however, is the bustle down at the old, four-storey Chengdu Department Store (cnr Renmin Nan Lu and Dongyu Jie), which sells food, cameras, chess sets, teapots and everyday items – you can hardly get in here over the bicycles parked outside. For antiques and souvenirs try the Chuantic Antique Store, cnr Dongchenggen Lu and Renmin Xi Lu (daily 9am–5pm). Prices here are fairly high, but items are genuine, certified with a wax seal if more than a century old: chops from ¥100 (name carving ¥20 extra), snuff bottles, jewellery, antique birdcages, wooden screens and porcelain. Stamp and coin collectors also set up daily outside the post office along Xinglong Jie. You'll also find several competing army-surplus stores at the Xinnanmen bus station. For camera supplies and reasonable quality, 1hr print processing, try the stores on Chunxi Lu.

Travel agents Besides booking train and plane tickets, CITS, near the *Minshan Hotel* on Renmin Nan Lu (ⓣ028/86650888, ⓕ86650999), organize very expensive guided tours to Jiuzhai Gou, Emei Shan, Hailuo Gou and elsewhere. Independent travel agents at hotels and cafés are much cheaper and more flexible for all bookings, and also arrange PICC travel insurance (see p.1020) for Western Sichuan, plus local interest tours to the see the Panda Breeding Base, the Sichuan Opera, and Traditional Chinese Medicine College. There's a huge number of these agents inside and around the *Jiaotong Hotel*; otherwise, the best are Sam Yue at *Sam's Backpacker Guesthouse* (see p.929); Mr Chen, who you'll find at *Paul's Oasis*; George Zhong of George of the Jungle (Ⓣ & Ⓕ 028/85531285), out front at the *Jiaotong Hotel*; and Tray Lee (Ⓕ 028/85564952), often at the *Highfly Café*. If you've an insatiable yen to enter Tibet overland from Sichuan and the cash to spare, contact China International Everbright Travel (Ⓣ 028/86624395, Ⓦ cooleast.hypermart.net), among whose tours is a pricey trip into Tibet from here, via Kangding. The cost – US$1000 or so per person, for a party of twenty – is pretty well all-inclusive, covering permits, an English-speaking guide, accommodation and food, road transport, plus a flight back from Bangda in eastern Tibet.

Around Chengdu

The countryside around Chengdu offers some interesting day-trips, but it's perhaps not surprising that visitors, lured or sated by grander prospects at Leshan and Emei Shan, tend to give them a miss. Even so, those not yet over-dosed on temples will find **Xindu** and its Buddhist monastery worth a look, from where it's a short hop northeast to **Guanghan** and a museum stuffed with incredible prehistoric bronzes, evidence of the otherwise virtually undocumented **Ba–Shu** civilization which flourished around 1600 BC. Northwest, the town of **Dujiangyan** and nearby **Qingcheng Shan** – both possible either as day-trips or as first stops on the journeys north to Wolong or Jiuzhai Gou – offer an impressive, 2000-year-old irrigation scheme and a wooded mountain park, peppered with shrines.

Xindu

A forty-minute bus ride 16km north of Chengdu (buses every 30min from the train station forecourt; ¥4), the market town of **XINDU** lies knee-deep in summertime vegetables and locally made coloured basketware, but what draws the crowds here is the **Baoguang Si** (Monastery of Divine Light; ¥5). A lively, large and influential complex since the Tang dynasty, its treasures include a **stone tablet** from 540 AD cut with the figures of a thousand Buddhas, an unusually wide range of Ming- and Qing-era **paintings** and calligraphy, and some tiny, jewel-like gardens that hide away in secluded corners. Seek out the thirteen-storey **Sheli Pagoda**, whose upper storeys are slightly tilted off the perpendicular and, in the gloomy **Arhat Hall**, a set of five hundred comical and eerie statues sculpted in 1851. These all represent Buddhist saints but for two, which depict the emperors Kangxi and Qianlong – look for their distinctive beards, boots, and capes. For lunch, try the airy and cheap **vegetarian restaurant** in the monastery compound.

Guanghan and Sanxingdui Museum

Half an hour and 8km beyond Xindu (minibuses ¥2, or ¥6 direct from the eastern side of Chengdu's train station), **GUANGHAN** is a small, largely modern town on the south side of the **Yazi River**. The chief attraction here is the isolated **Sanxingdui Museum** (daily 9am–5pm; ¥30), a twenty-minute ride away on **local bus** #6 from south-bank Changsha Lu. Excellently presented, the museum charts the discovery, between the 1920s and 1980s, of a colossal trove of jade, ivory, bronze and gold artefacts associated with a large Shang town on the site, many of which were found deliberately broken up and buried in rectangular **sacrificial pits**. It's not just the quality of the finds here that are startling, but the actual designs themselves, products of a very alien view of the world: a two-metre-high bronze figure with a hook nose and oversized, grasping hands standing atop four elephants; metre-wide, grinning masks with obscene grins and eyes popping out on stalks; a "spirit tree" covered in ambiguous swirls and motifs. Hundreds of smaller, finely detailed pieces are on show, too, along with comprehensive accounts of the excavations.

Local buses to Guanghan drop off on the highway immediately east of town, while the **train station** is 2km away over on the western outskirts, serving the Xi'an–Chengdu–Kunming line. Heading on from Guanghan, you can catch Chengdu or Dujiangyan minibuses until late in the afternoon. For Mianyang and points north, you'll need either the train or to seek out Guanghan's **long-distance bus station**, on Zhongshan Dadao just south of the central Fanghu Park, a cramped collection of old ramparts, ponds and carefully arranged shrubs. If you want to **stay** the night in Guanghan, one central option is the *Xinxing Dajiudian* (❷) on Fanghu Lu, near the park.

Dujiangyan

There's enough to hold you for a half a day at **DUJIANGYAN** (formerly **Guanxian**), a large town 60km northwest of Chengdu reached from either Ximen or the North bus stations (¥8). It was here in 256 BC that the provincial governor, **Li Bing**, set up the **Dujiangyan Irrigation Scheme** to harness the **Min River**, a notoriously capricious tributary of the Yangzi. Li designed a three-part engineering project using a central dam and artificial islands to split the Min into an inner flow for irrigation and an outer channel for flood control. A spillway directed and regulated the water, and allowed silt to be dredged, while an opening carved through the hillside controlled the flow of oncoming water. Completed by Li Bing's son, the scheme has been maintained ever since, the present system of dams, reservoirs and pumping stations irrigating some 32,000 square kilometres. It was due to become a World Heritage Site, but this status hasn't yet been granted as it looks likely that the scheme will be destroyed when the new Zipingpu Dam, 9km upstream, starts operation in 2006.

Dujiangyan's **bus station** is south of the centre on Yingbin Dadao; turn left up Taiping Jie for a kilometre to a T-intersection, then bear left and follow the road around to **Lidui Park** (¥5), which encloses the original heart of the project. Lively eave carvings and an ancient stone statue of Li Bing grace **Fulong Guan** (Subduing Dragon View), a wooden, 1600-year-old temple, flanked with die-straight *nanmu* trees, which sits right at the tip of the first channel. The name symbolizes the taming of the river, and it's a good place to survey the scheme's layout; for even better views, take the **chairlift** (¥16) from beside Fulong Guan across the river and up to **Erwang Miao** (Two Kings' Temple; ¥15). Posthumously dedicated to Li Bing and his son, who are remembered by statues in the two main halls, this is an unspoiled complex built of heavy stone, and holds a wedge of tree trunk said to be 4000 years old. Above is a **road** – from where you can catch bus #1 back to the bus station – and a disappointingly restored **pagoda**; below, steps descend to the plank-and-wire **Anlan Cable Bridge** (¥3), where you can cross the Min and follow footpaths back to town.

For **somewhere to stay** in Dujiangyan, try the clean and helpful *Jingyuan Binguan* (❸), just up from the **bus station** on Taiping Jie. There are dozens of **places to eat** along Taiping Jie and around the entrance to Lidui Park. **Leaving**, buses head back to Chengdu and on to Qingcheng Shan through the day, with at least daily services west to Wolong and Xiaojin, and north to Wenchuan and Songpan.

Qingcheng Shan

Qingcheng Shan, the thickly wooded Green City Mountain, holy to Taoists, is an easy 15km by bus from Dujiangyan; you can also get here direct on early morning services from Chengdu's three main bus stations. Once the quietest spot under heaven, but now a popular weekend getaway, complete with a funfair with grotesque animal slide, Qingcheng still makes a good alternative if you haven't the time or energy for the higher, more distant Emei Shan (see p.942). Spartan but atmospheric temple accommodation is available at the base, at the Jianfu Temple (❶). After you've paid the ¥40 entrance fee, it's a pleasant six-kilometre hike up tree-covered slopes scattered with pavilions, bridges and temples, the best of which is **Tianshi Dong** (Grotto of the Heavenly Teacher), about halfway up, whose main hall is decorated with Ming-dynasty panels. This place also has rooms and a dormitory (❶–❷), as does the Shanqing Si at the summit (❶).

Northeast to Shaanxi

An ancient, 400-kilometre-long trade route runs northeast **from Chengdu into Shaanxi**, historically the easiest way in or out of Sichuan Province. While sights along the way are not great, you're well off tourist trails here and signs of the area's history are formidable: starting at the ancient remains at Sanxingdui (see p.938) and exiting the region bound for Xi'an, you pass several low-key mountain temple complexes; narrow passes featured in *Three Kingdoms* lore; the birthplace of the only Chinese empress, **Wu Zetian**; and the road that one of her successors, the emperor Xuan Zong, fled to Chengdu to escape rebellion in 756 AD.

You can get into the region by bus or on the Chengdu–Xi'an train. The rail line and the old Chengdu–Guangyuan road diverge about a third of the way along at **Mianyang** (though a new road, following the track, has been completed), with most of the sights laid out along the old road between here and **Guangyuan** itself, just 60km short of the Shaanxi border. Guangyuan is also a jumping-off point for routes **to Jiuzhai Gou** in northwestern Sichuan (see p.976).

To Guangyuan

From Chengdu, road and rail run together for 120km via Sanxingdui and **Deyang** to riverside **MIANYANG**, which has grown rapidly over the past

Northeast to Shaanxi

Guangyuan	广元	***guǎngyuán***
Fenghuang Shan Park	凤皇山公园	*fènghuángshān gōngyuán*
Guangyuan Binguan	广元宾馆	*guǎngyuán bīnguǎn*
Huangze Temple	皇泽寺	*huángzé sì*
Lizhou Binguan	利州宾馆	*lìzhōu bīnguǎn*
Thousand Buddha Cliff	千佛崖	*qiānfó yá*
Jiange	剑阁	***jiàngé***
Sword Gate Pass	剑门关	*jiànmén guān*
Jiangyou	江油	***jiāngyóu***
Haideng Kungfu School	海灯武馆	*hǎidēng wǔguǎn*
Mianyang	绵阳	***miányáng***
Linyuan Binguan	临园宾馆	*línyuán bīnguǎn*

decade to become Sichuan's second largest city. The **train station** is west of town; Hongxing Lu runs from here to central **accommodation** at the *Linyuan Binguan* (❷). If you're travelling by train, it's worth stopping 40km farther on at **JIANGYOU**, famed for its **Haideng kungfu school** and **Douchuan Shan**, a hilltop collection of Taoist halls 12km farther north again featuring three rocky towers, each capped by a small temple, which you can move between only across a thin wire bridge.

The old road, meanwhile, carries on to **Zitong** and **JIANGE**, a small town 135km northeast of Mianyang whose **pagoda** and **Chaotian Pass** – a dusty track flanked by ancient trees – are a reminder of this former garrison town's long strategic importance. Better yet lies 30km farther on, where the road runs up to the sheer-sided **Sword Gate Pass**, once the only way through a tall, 100-kilometre-long line of hills. Zhuge Liang's forces defended Shu from invasion here during the Three Kingdoms period, and the Sword Gate is rumoured to be the origin of the Chinese phrase "With one monkey in the way, not even a thousand men can pass" – applied nowadays to bureaucratic obstruction. In fact, you'll have to get a ride in someone's car or tractor to detour here, as the through road circuits around the hills and then meets up with the rail line for the last 50km to Guangyuan.

Guangyuan

Around 330km from Chengdu and a similar distance to Xi'an, **GUANGYUAN** is an oddly shaped, determinedly ugly town on the **Jialing River**, site of a huge weapons production facility and largely ignored as the birthplace of **Wu Zetian**, China's only empress (see box below). Carved out of the riverside cliffs 1500m south of the train station is **Huangze Temple** (¥2), dedicated to her, and also here are numerous murals and **rock sculptures** of Buddhist saints set into niches, some of them 4m high, though they're largely in a state of some disrepair. Completed between 557 and 684 AD in a static, heavily monumental style, these actually predate Wu Zetian, but her time as

Wu Zetian

Born in 624 AD to a court official, at the age of 14 **Wu Zetian** became a concubine to the Tang emperor Taizong, but was later forced into seclusion as a Buddhist nun after she was rumoured to be having an affair with Taizong's son, **Gaozong**. Restored to favour as a concubine in 652, after Gaozong's accession, Wu Zetian spent the next thirty years building up her power at court, ruthlessly eliminating anyone she saw as a threat to her position – including numerous officials, one of her sisters, several of her sons and stepsons, one grandson and four daughters-in-law. By the time Gaozong died in 683, she was secure enough to pass over his designated successor, **Li Xian**, in favour of her own son by Gaozong, Li Dan – known as emperor **Ruizong**. Ruling as Empress Dowager behind Ruizong, Wu Zetian brought her own Wu clan to the fore by virtually annihilating the old dynasty's Li family through warfare and intrigue, and in September 690 formally took power – and founded a new dynasty – as **Empress Wu of Zhou**.

Given this record, Wu Zetian's fifteen-year reign was surprisingly enlightened. Her patronage of Buddhism inspired the famous sculptures at Luoyang (see p.298), and even her critics admitted that she appointed officials based on their merits. But her new dynasty was short-lived; threatened with a revolt, she was forced to reinstate Li Xian as crown prince – later emperor **Zhongzong** – and abdicated in his favour shortly before her death in 705.

a Buddhist nun and later sponsorship of the Luoyang carvings (p.298) make the temple's dedication appropriate. The empress herself features in just two sculptures, one worn beyond recognition outside, the other a very unflattering, dumpy copy in its own room; look, too, for the carved **phoenix tablet** by the temple entrance – a symbol of female power – instead of the usual dragon. For more of the same, catch local transport 4km north of the train station to **Thousand Buddha Cliff**, where more than 600m of rockface, in places 40m high, has been decorated with Buddha figurines dating back to the Sui dynasty.

Guangyuan's **bus and train stations** are 100m apart on the west side of the river; cross over the bridge into town and it's ten minutes to **Shumen Bei Lu**, which runs south around the base of **Fenghuang Shan Park**. The park's summit is topped by a ludicrous concrete-and-tile tower, looking more like a ski lift than a pagoda, but it's an excellent landmark; you're facing south with this on your left. Not far along Shumen Bei Lu is the *Guangyuan Binguan* (Ⓣ0839/3224114; ❷), which, if they will take you, is immeasurably better than the dilapidated cells available two busy market streets over towards the river at the *Lizhou Binguan*, 21 Guangyuan Xi Lu (Ⓣ0839/3232347; ❸), Guangyuan's only official foreigner **hotel**. For **meals**, there are plenty of hotpot stalls and restaurants along Shumen Bei Lu and the backstreets. **Moving on**, there's just one bus a day for the 360-kilometre run to **Nanping**, east of Jiuzhai Gou, from where there are daily buses via Jiuzhai Gou to Songpan and Chengdu (see p.923); trains are your best bet for direct transport to Chengdu or Xi'an.

Emei Shan, Leshan and Xichang

Some 150km southwest of Chengdu lies the edge of the Red Basin and the foothills of the mountain ranges which sprawl south and west into Tibet and Yunnan. Fast-flowing rivers converge here at **Leshan**, where more than a thousand years ago sculptors created a **giant Buddha** overlooking the waters, one of the world's most imposing religious monuments; while an hour away, **Emei Shan** rises to more than 3000m, its forested slopes rich in scenery and temples. Sichuan's two most famous sights, the Buddha and Emei Shan, have become tourist black holes thanks to easy access – don't go near either at New Year, when crowds are so awful that the army is sometimes called in to sort out the chaos – and are well worth the effort; most people combine the two as part of a round trip from Chengdu. Alternatively, they could form the first part of an extended circuit out to western Sichuan, or a stopover on your way down south to Yunnan – in which case **Xichang**, home to the Yi people and China's Long March space rocket, is worth a visit. Using the horde of interconnecting buses and minibuses is the easiest way to get around the region, though Emei and Xichang are also served by the Chengdu–Kunming rail line.

Emei Shan

Emei Shan has been a place of pilgrimage for more than 1800 years, and by the sixth century it had become one of the country's four sacred Buddhist mountains. Around thirty **temples** punctuate Emei's trails today, offering food and beds to pilgrims and tourists alike – though the latter are far more numerous. Religious considerations aside, Emei is also one of China's most pristine natural regions and a wonderful place to explore, its slopes scored by numerous hiking trails set against a background of rich **animal and plant life**. The landscape changes markedly with the seasons: in the **summer**, when most

Emei Shan, Leshan and Xichang

Emei Shan	峨眉山	***éméi shān***
Baoguo Si	报国寺	*bàoguó sì*
Fu Hu Si	伏虎寺	*fúhǔ sì*
Hongzhushan Binguan	红珠山宾馆	*hóngzhūshān bīnguǎn*
Jieyin Hall	接引殿	*jiēyǐn diàn*
Jinding	金顶	*jīndǐng*
Meishan	眉山	*méi shān*
Niuxin Si	牛心寺	*niúxīn sì*
Qingyin Ge	清音阁	*qīngyīn gé*
Wanfoding	万佛顶	*wànfó dǐng*
Wannian Si	万年寺	*wànnián sì*
Xian Feng Si	仙峰寺	*xiānfēng sì*
Xixiang Chi	洗象池	*xǐxiàng chí*
Zhongling Si	中岭寺	*zhōnglǐng sì*
Leshan	乐山	***lèshān***
Dafo	大佛	*dàfó*
Lingyun Shan	凌云山	*língyún shān*
Luocheng	罗城古镇	*luóchéng gǔzhèn*
Wuyou Si	乌优寺	*wūyōu sì*
Accommodation		
Hong Li Lai	红利来	*hónglì lái*
Jiazhou	嘉州宾馆	*jiāzhōu bīnguǎn*
Jinding Dajiu Dian	金顶大酒店	*jīndǐng dàjiǔdiàn*
Jiurifeng Binguan	就日峰宾馆	*jiùrìfēng bīnguǎn*
Nanlou Binguan	南楼宾馆	*nánlóu bīnguǎn*
Taoyuan Binguan	桃园宾馆	*táoyuán bīnguǎn*
Xichang	西昌	***xīchāng***
Huang Shui	黄水	*huángshuǐ*
Liangshan Binguan	凉山宾馆	*liángshān bīnguǎn*
Luoji Shan	螺髻山	*luójì shān*
Puge	普格	*pǔgé*
Qionghai Hu	邛海湖	*qiónghǎi hú*
Red Army Museum	红军长征纪念馆	*hóngjūnchángzhēng jìniànguǎn*
Space Flight Centre	航天发射中心	*hángtiān fāshè zhōngxīn*
Wumao Binguan	物贸宾馆	*wùmào bīnguǎn*
Yanyuan	盐源	*yányuán*
Yuanning	冤宁	*yuānníng*

people come, the vegetation is a dense, lush green and the weather, though warm, is a welcome escape from higher temperatures on the surrounding plains. **Spring and autumn** bring brilliant colours and a cooler climate, while in **winter**, when a hardy few make the ascent, the light is clear and the snow lends grandeur.

Ideally, plan to spend three or four days walking the lower slopes, allowing a better chance of picking a fine day for the assault on the top and, perhaps, **Wanfoding** (Ten Thousand Buddha Peak), the highest of Emei's three summits. It's only worth climbing this high if the weather's good: for a richer bag of views, temples, streams and vegetation – everything, in fact, but the satisfaction of reaching the summit – you won't be disappointed with the lower paths.

Mountain practicalities

Access to the area is through **Emei town**, 150km southwest of Chengdu. The mountain's **trail head** is a short minibus ride away at **Baoguo Si**, and dedicated pilgrims can start a stern three-day round trip from here. Those with less time can omit the first few kilometres by taking a further bus from Baoguo to alternative starting points near either **Qingyin Ge** for the southern route (8km from Baoguo Si) or **Wannian Si** for the shorter northern route (12km). Leaving early enough, you could make it to the top in one day from either of these via **Xixiang Chi** (Elephant Washing Pool) and **Jinding**, the lowest peak,

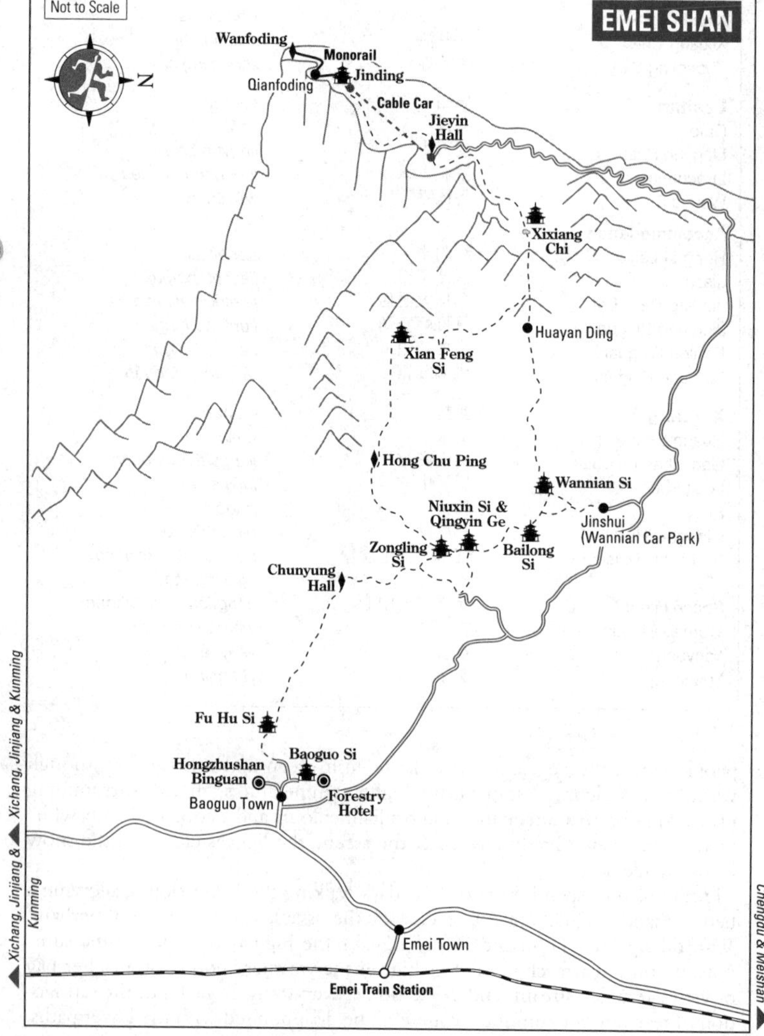

descending the next morning. If you're really pushed, you could get up and down in a single day by catching the minibus between Baoguo Si and **Jieyin Hall**, which is located a cable-car ride or an easy walk from Jinding, but this way you'll miss much of what makes Emei Shan such a special place.

Emei's **entry fee** of ¥60 is payable at the start of the trails, with a few random checkpoints along the way to make sure you don't sneak in. **Temples** also charge ¥4 or so, but there are always paths around them if you're not interested. **Accommodation** – at temples and a few private hotels – varies from around ¥20 for a mattress in a large dormitory (not often available to foreigners) to ¥45 or more per person in a double room. Temple reception offices are usually at the gates; you'll need to haggle to get a good deal and, to be sure of a bed, start looking for lodgings by mid-afternoon. There's unlikely to be running water, and electricity is often erratic (though many places do have electric blankets), so carry a **flashlight**. Temple restaurants are the best places to **eat** – vegetarian dinners cost ¥15–40 – and stalls along the way can keep you topped up with bottled drinks, snacks and hot food, such as rice gruel, garlic soup and noodles.

Footwear needs to have a firm grip; in winter, when stone steps become dangerously icy, straw sandals and even iron crampons (sold all over the mountain for a few yuan and tied onto your soles) are an absolute necessity. Don't forget **warm clothing** for the top, which is around 15°C cooler than the plains and so liable to be below freezing between October and April. You'll also want an umbrella or other protection against the near certainty of **rain**. A **walking stick** is handy for easing the pressure on thigh muscles during descent and waving at monkeys – a range are sold along the way. One thing you don't want to take is a heavy backpack – store spare gear at the lower monasteries and hotels, or in Chengdu if you're contemplating a round trip.

Meishan and Emei town

Some 75km south of Chengdu, both rail line and road pass **MEISHAN**, where Ming and Qing pavilions at **Sansu Ci** (the Three Su's Ancestral Hall; daily 8.30am–5pm; ¥5) honour this renowned local family of Song-dynasty artists. Best known is **Su Dongpo**, who reached the pinnacle of literary aspirations by securing a post at court, only to lose it and be exiled first to Hubei and then Hainan Island. Undaunted, he remained an influential poet during his lifetime, and is still known today for his atmospheric verses, his theses expounding his views on painting and, strangely, a pork banquet dish named in his honour. There isn't much to see unless you admire calligraphy, of which there's plenty, but the grounds are pleasant.

Farther on, bustling, untidy **EMEI TOWN** lies about 7km from Baoguo Si and the foot of the mountain. **Trains** pull into the station 3.5km away, while **buses** from Chengdu and Leshan terminate either in Emei's main street depot or at Baoguo Si, with minibuses constantly shuttling between the train station, town and Baoguo during daylight hours.

Baoguo and around

The fifteen-kilometre road from Emei town runs west to **BAOGUO**, one long, straight kilometre of hotels and restaurants, before fizzling out at a T-junction. Baoguo's **bus station** is about 500m before this intersection, with **minibuses** to drop-off points for Qingyin Ge, Wannian Si and Jinding, but they need at least sixteen people to run and so depart infrequently after the early morning rush. You can also get transport to Chengdu, Chongqing, Ya'an and Leshan either from here or down in Emei town – make bookings for these and the train through the *Teddy Bear Café* or the pricier *Hongzhushan Binguan*, or – a drag but far cheaper – get a bus into Emei and then a rickshaw to the station and buy the tickets yourself.

Close to the bus station is the *Teddy Bear Café*, where the food isn't up to much, though Patrick, the English-speaking proprietor, is very helpful, lending out walking sticks, looking after your excess bags and organizing outbound tickets (around ¥50, including a steep mark-up). He will get you into the hotel opposite for a discounted rate (❷), which is where many backpackers end up, though the two temple guesthouses within walking distance are much more inviting.

At the intersection, turn left for upmarket rooms, bank and booking office at the *Hongzhushan Binguan* (Ⓣ08426/525888, Ⓕ525666; ❹), or right for **Baoguo Si**, a large and busy Song-era temple. Rebuilt and enlarged during the seventeenth century, the four main halls which rise one behind the other up the slope are decorated with carved doorways, opening onto courtyards containing bonsai and flower displays. The porcelain Buddha in the **Sutra Hall** is eye-catching, with its red-lined black garments covered with tiny golden icons, and it's said that the huge Ming-dynasty **bell** here, encrusted with characters, can be heard 15km away. You can, of course, stay and eat at Baoguo Si itself, or carry on past the temple to the *Forestry Hotel*, a drab affair with languid staff and fairly basic rooms (❷, dorm beds ¥25).

Twenty minutes walk up the other road near the intersection, through a forest of *nanmu* trees, brings you to the charming **Fu Hu Si** (Taming Tiger Temple). It's a comfortable nunnery, with plenty of **accommodation** on hand. The terminus of the single local bus is quite close if you don't want to walk. Here you'll find the **Huayan Pagoda**, fourteen little storeys but only 7m tall, cast of bronze in the sixteenth century and engraved with 4700 images of Buddha.

The southern route

The southern route up the mountain from Baoguo and Fu Hu Si takes you past some minor sights to **Chunyang Hall**, where you can spend the night and take in some panoramic views of the summit. From here it's a gentle climb past **Zhongling Si** (Mid-peak Temple) to the tiny wooden **Niuxin Si**, on a rock at the hub of two streams and several paths. On the far side is the charming Qingyin Ge, the nicest place to stay on Emei; forest rises overhead, water babbles through a gorge, and you may encounter the mountain's famous **bearded frogs** (at least, the males are bearded – females make do with stripes). As well as the standard dorms, the temple has a separate wing with some good en-suite doubles (❷), where you can be lulled to sleep by the gurgle of the falls outside your window.

From here you can follow the quicker northern route to the top by pressing on for 3km to Wannian Si (see opposite), or continue along the southern route by following the path past the left side of Niuxin Si; this takes you along a river bed and past a **monkey-watching area** and swimming spot, before starting to climb pretty steeply through a series of gorges. About two hours later, **Hong Chu Ping**, the Ancient Trees Terrace, is the first possible stopover, after which it takes about the same time to tackle the often steep and narrow stairs to **Xian Feng Si** (Fairy Peaks Monastery). This is another nice place, well forested with pine and dove trees and planted with camellia and rhododendrons. Over the next two hours it's partly downhill to a dragon-headed bridge, then ever up to where the trail joins the north route at **Xixiang Chi** (see opposite).

Emei Shan flora

Of Emei Shan's three thousand or so plant species, more than a hundred are Chinese endemics. The **red nanmu tree** – straight, tall and favoured for temple pillars – is one of these; another is the **dove tree**, which has hard spherical fruit, thin pale leaves and a white, two-petalled flower said to resemble a perching dove. Most remarkable, though, is the stately **gingko** – identified by its distinctive, lobed crescent leaves -- which was found worldwide in prehistoric times. Once extinct in the wild, botanic lore has it that the gingko was unintentionally saved from oblivion by its popularity as an ornamental tree in monastery gardens, where it was perhaps grown for the medicinal qualities of its mildly poisonous fruit, said to curb desire. From these it has reintroduced itself and is now found in a semi-wild state in China's central southwest.

The gingko is not the only mountain plant to have benefited from cultivation. Most of Europe's ornamental **roses** are hybrids derived from wild Chinese stock two hundred years ago, and in summer you'll still find bushes of their small pink and white ancestors blooming on Emei's lower slopes. The region is also famous for its **tea**, with an excellent jasmine-scented variety on offer at Baoguo or Emei town for around ¥50 per kilo. In addition, the mountain provides a huge range of fungi and **medicinal herbs**, which you'll see for sale all over the place: make sure you know what you're buying and how to use it though, as some – such as the scarlet and black beans on display in glass jars outside Baoguo Si – are extremely poisonous.

The northern route

Most people start their ascent by catching a **bus** from Baoguo to various drop-off points for the **northern route**. The first of these is 15km along at **Jinshui** (¥5 by bus), start of the forty-minute path to Emei's oldest temple, **Wannian Si** (Myriad Years Monastery). Last rebuilt after a devastating fire in 1945 which claimed all but the seventeenth-century main hall, Wannian's pride is in a dumpy pavilion out the back. Here, bare whitewashed brick and thousands of tiny iron Buddhas surround a stunning **sculpture of the Bodhisattva Puxian** (also known as **Samantabhadra**), riding a gilt lotus flower astride a great six-tusked white elephant. Puxian reputedly visited the mountain in the sixth century, four hundred years after which this huge bronze statue was built on imperial orders and brought from Chengdu in pieces. The temple's **accommodation** is frugal, but the food is good and you should find that the atmosphere makes up for any discomfort. The evening stillness is punctuated by the drone of chanting chants and the tinkling of their bells.

From Xixiang Chi to the top

It's less than an hour from Wannian to Niuxin Si and the start of the southern ascent; or stick on the northern trail and a steady four hours through thick mists and groves of bamboo and pine should see you mounting the last slippery steps to **Xixiang Chi**, a pool where the elephant carrying Puxian stopped for a dip on his way up the mountain. Finely set on a hilltop, a nearby **temple** is not as imposing as Wannian but has a fantastic view, surrounded by groves of age-old trees and rhododendron bushes. It's another four hours on to Jinding from here, but if you plan to stay the night you'll find that the temple's position at the meeting of the ways makes for crowds – get in early to be sure of a bed.

Beyond here the path gets easier, but you'll encounter gangs of aggressive **monkeys** who threaten you for food with teeth bared. They tend to pick on women; showing empty hands and calling their bluff by striding on seems to work, daunting though their response can be – you'll probably feel safer with a stick or a few stones in your hand, ready to throw. Keep a good grip on your bags too. The path continues through thick woods to **Jieyin Hall**, where the fifty-kilometre-long road from Baoguo Si, which has snaked its way round the back of the mountain, ends at a **cable-car** connection to the summit (¥40 up, ¥30 down), and the area is thick with minibus tour parties fired up for their one-day crack at the peak. It's also somewhere to find a lift off the mountain on your way down, if you've run out of time or steam (¥20 back to Baguo; 1hr 30min). **Hotels** around Jieyin look good, but they have a reputation for rudeness once they've got your money.

Whether you take the cable car or spend the next couple of hours hoofing it (not to be attempted without crampons in winter), **Jinding**, the Golden Summit (3077m), is the next stop and, for many, the main reason to be up here at all. The name of this bland temple, set in a terraced complex near the cliff edge, derives from its former shiny bronze roof, replaced in 1989 with bright yellow tiles. You can **stay** the night here or in one of the rather shabby doubles at nearby *Jinding Dajiudian* (☎0833/55247045; ❺), then get up at dawn and join the swarms huddling on the terrace in the hope of catching the **sunrise**, which is marvellous on a good day, as it lights up the sea of clouds below the peak. In the afternoon, these clouds sometimes catch rainbow-like rings known as **Buddha's Halo**, which surround and move with your shadow, while in clear conditions you can even make out **Gongga Shan** (see p.979), 150km to the west. On a bad day, Jinding is wrapped in cloud, with the huge broadcasting mast looming above the temple complex the only scenery. In these conditions you certainly won't be tempted to plod on for a final hour – or to take the **monorail** (¥50) – up to **Wanfoding** (Ten Thousand Buddha Summit), Emei's true 3099-metre-high apex.

Leshan and around

Set beside the wide convergence of the Qingyi, Min and Dadu rivers, 180km from Chengdu and 50km from Emei Shan, **LESHAN** is a 1300-year-old market town, its centre decked with sleek paving and tall new offices, and its expanding suburbs sprawling continually northwards. Mostly, it's just somewhere to spend a quiet evening before taking a ferry across to the incredible **Dafo**, who faces the town from his deep niche in the cliffs.

Leshan **train station** is actually about 15km away; arriving by road will land you at one of the town's **bus stations**. The newest is 5km distant on the town's northern outskirts, but an older, more central depot is still in business, about 1km north of the downtown along **Shengshui Jie**. Under various names, this road runs south into the triangular town centre past the huge **Minjiang Bridge**, a Bank of China and an eccentric crocodile-and-maiden statue. Here Binjiang Lu splits southwest off along the riverfront and down to the **ferry terminals**. Stay on the main road to reach shopping centres at the crossroads with Dong Dajie, then turn right for the **post office** and, farther on along Yutang Jie and Baita Jie, the older quarter of town. A **taxi** is a fixed price of ¥5 for anywhere central. **Moving on**, there are buses to Chengdu and Emei town until 6pm, and less plentiful traffic to Luocheng, Xichang, Zigong, Chongqing and Ya'an.

Leshan's best cheap **place to stay** is the *Taoyuan Binguan* (☎0833/231810, Ⓕ232102; ❶, or ❷ with bathroom), in two buildings near the ferry docks on Binjiang Lu; make sure you stay in its northern building, as the southern one, with its own reception, is pretty musty. West along the Dadu River, the *Jiazhou Binguan* is a smart tour group complex with a pricey river-view restaurant

(☎0833/2139888, Ⓕ2133233; ❻). If there are three of you and you're on a tight budget, though, check out the *Hong Li Lai* (☎0833/2127137; ❶) – turn left as you exit the bus station and walk for a hundred metres – as it has good triples (¥54). Alternatively, there's mid-range accommodation at Dafo itself (see below). There are inexpensive **places to eat** past the *Jiazhou* on Baita Jie, and all along Binjiang Lu.

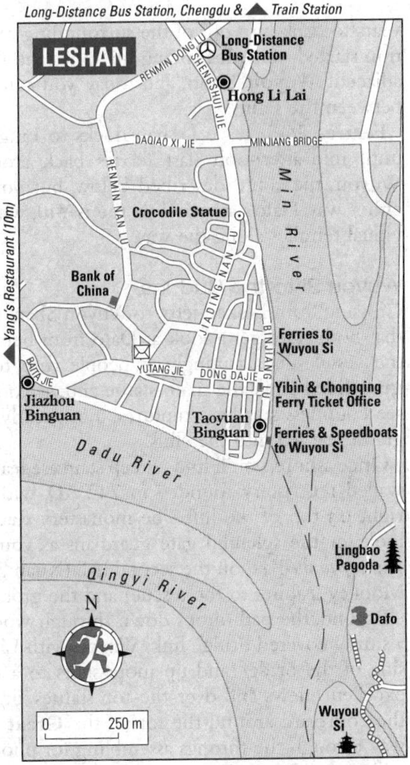

While in Leshan, you may well be tracked down by the affable Richard Yang – he checks the hotel registers – who offers his services as a booking agent and a guide for village tours around Leshan's countryside. He'll invite you back to his restaurant at 49 Baita Jie (☎0833/2112046) for food and chats about his seventy-odd years in Leshan, and to garner the obligatory effusive guestbook entry, though note that his travel packages aren't necessarily the great deals he promises.

Dafo aside, there's a good day-trip to make 60km southeast of Leshan to **LUOCHENG**. In addition to an anonymous new town, Luocheng sports an old quarter with original Qing-vintage cobbled streets, wooden and stone gateways and buildings (including a good **teahouse**), narrow lanes, a theatre pavilion where public performances were once held, and a house-lined "square" shaped as a **boat**. Buses run here from Leshan, but Luocheng has yet to feature on tourist itineraries, so prepare to be the subject of some curiosity if you visit.

Dafo

Impassive, gargantuan **Dafo** (the Great Buddha) peers out from under half-lidded eyes, oblivious to the sightseers swarming round his head, clambering over his toes and nearly capsizing their boats in their eagerness to photograph his bulk. He's touted as the world's largest Buddhist sculpture at 71m tall, though statistics alone can't convey the initial impression of this squat icon, comfortably seated with his hands on his knees, looming over you as the ferry nears. Work on Dafo was started by the monk **Haitong** in 713, who felt that the image would protect boats navigating the rough waters below Lingyun Shan. After Haitong blinded himself to convince the government to hand over funds, the project was continued by the monks **Zangchou** and **Weigao**, who designed the Buddha's robes and hair to shed water and incorporated an internal drainage system to reduce weathering. All in all it took more than ninety years to hack him out of the surrounding red sandstone cliffs. Once construction started, **temples** sprang up above the Buddha at **Lingyun Shan** and on adjacent **Wuyou Shan**, and today you can spend a good five hours walking between the sights.

Ferries (¥15) leave Leshan docks to Lingyun and Wuyou from about 8am until mid-afternoon (last ferries back around 6pm). Most people start at Wuyou, the route described below, but you'll encounter tour parties going either way. Dafo's **admission fee** is ¥40, with a further ¥2 each to enter individual temples along the way.

Wuyou Si to the Buddha

Crossing from Leshan jetty to Wuyou Shan, cruise boats turn in mid-stream so that both sides get a look at Dafo from beneath – the best view by far – and the vessel tilts alarmingly as people rush to the railings. Two much smaller **guardians** flank the main statue and, as you approach the Wuyou jetty, you'll see countless smaller sculptures, most nearly weathered to oblivion, as well as graffiti carved into the cliffs.

Once ashore, you'll find a steep staircase leads up to **Wuyou Si**, a warm pink-walled monastery founded in 742 AD, with a good **vegetarian restaurant** right on top of the hill. The monastery **decorations** are particularly good – look for the splendid gate guardians as you enter, the animated scenes from *Journey to the West* on the second hall (Xuan Zang being carried off by demons, Monkey leaping to the rescue) and the grotesque *arhat* sculptures inside.

Beyond, the path drops down through woodland to the water's edge, where a sturdy covered bridge links Wuyou with **Lingyun Shan**. Turn left on the far side of the bridge and up more stairs to a new temple complex, with more excellent views and over-the-top statues, or continue along the main path to the courtyard around the top of the **Great Buddha** himself. Elbowing your way through the throngs assembling for photos, you'll find yourself up against railings level with Dafo's ear, where you can watch lines descending the slippery **Staircase of Nine Turns** to his feet. In the vicinity of the courtyard there's **accommodation** at the clean but damp *Nanlou Binguan* (Ⓣ0833/233811; ❺), plus various teahouses and restaurants, a **museum** housing statues of Haitong and his successors, and the thirteen-storey, whitewashed **Lingbao Pagoda** out the back. The *Jiurifeng Binguan* Ⓣ0833/230827; ❺) below has further **beds** in rather ordinary rooms.

The main path descends from the Buddha to the road running along the east bank of the Min River parallel with town. On the way down have a good look at where the three rivers meet – despite Dafo's presence, there are still some vicious currents as brown and black waters mingle over low-lying shoals. Once at the bottom and through the gates, you can catch a ferry back to Leshan's jetty or tout around the **buses** for a lift back to town.

South to Xichang and Yunnan

The long train journey south from Emei town to the Yunnanese border and ultimately Kunming is famous not for the scenery itself, splendid though it is, but for the fact that you rarely catch a glimpse of it. Estimates vary, but there are more than **two hundred tunnels** along the way, some lasting seconds, others several minutes, and you'll soon get fed up trying to get a long look at the peaks and gorges passing the window. Yi villages and China's space base (note that you'll need a week to secure a permit for the latter) reward a stop in **Xichang**, from where you can either continue south by train to Kunming, or test your endurance on some remote back roads into northern Yunnan from either Xichang or farther south at **Panzhihua**.

Xichang and around

Given its otherwise remote setting in a very undernourished, infertile countryside seven hours from Emei by train, **XICHANG**'s friendly bustle and almost prosperous air are surprising. Focus for southwestern China's **Yi community**, Xichang is also the site of China's **Long March Space Programme**, which in the past has launched satellites with varying degrees of success in competition with NASA and Europe's Ariane project. Bigger things are afoot now: China is hoping to put its first manned spacecraft into space from here. This would have delighted Mao, who once commented that China "cannot even get a potato into orbit". In town itself, there's also an **older quarter** just northeast of the centre where you'll find crowded markets, reconstructed stone gateways, adobe and timber homes, and a couple of rickety teahouses on Nan Jie.

Practicalities

Xichang is about 3km across, with the **train station** another few kilometres west – catch a **minibus** into town for ¥1. The kilometre-long main street, **Chang'an Lu**, runs east, crossed part way along by **Shengli Lu** and running on to a **roundabout** and the usually dry **Dong River**. From here, Daxiangkou Jie runs north into the older part of town, while Sanchakou Xi Lu crosses southeast over the river to two branches of the **Bank of China** – the second of which changes foreign currency. The **bus station** is on the Chang'an Lu/Shengli Lu junction close to **accommodation**; north on Shengli Lu you'll find the cavernous, upmarket *Liangshan Binguan* (Ⓣ0834/3223007, Ⓕ3221370; ❺), while across the road and east along Changan Lu is the good-value *Wumao Binguan* (❶, dorms ¥35; rate includes breakfast). Snack stalls and inexpensive **restaurants** are everywhere, with tasty fare served up in hole-in-the-wall places near the *Wumao*. For **information**, there's a **CITS** office loaded with model rockets just up from the bus station on Shengli Lu, and the much better **XITS** (Ⓣ0834/3223338 or 3223061; ask for English-speaking "Kevin") hidden away in a Chinese-signed block on Xiyanjing Bei Xiang, an alley running east off Shengli Lu, south of the Chang'an Lu intersection.

Train tickets for **onward travel** are very hard to obtain yourself – better to buy through one of the information offices. Five hours down the Kunming line, **Panzhihua** (Jinjiang) is where to catch connecting buses west to Lijiang in Yunnan (see p.881). There's also a very rough, two-day **bus trip** 180km west from Xichang to **Lugu Hu** on the Yunnan border (see p.889); you first target **Yanyuan**, from where there's transport to the lake. Don't catch a bus from Xichang to Lugu, a small town 50km away in the wrong direction. Otherwise, buses run out to sights around Xichang, and also north – via some amazing scenery of dry, uplifted valleys ringed by peaks – to Shimian and Chengdu, or south to Panzhihua and Kunming.

Around Xichang

The area around Xichang, known as **Liang Shan** (the Cool Mountains), is heartland of the Yi. Minibuses from the Chang'an Lu roundabout head 5km south to **Qionghai Hu**, a large lake where a **museum** exhibits Yi festival clothing and household items, and books written in the Yi script – you'll also see this on official signs around town. For more on the Yi, head 76km south to

The Yi

Spread through the mountains of southwestern China, the **Yi** form the region's largest – and perhaps China's poorest and most neglected – ethnic group, with a population of around five million. Their shamanistic religion, language and unique, wavy script indicate that the Yi probably originated in northwestern China. Until the 1940s they were farmers with a matriarchal **slave society** divided into a landowning "black" caste, and subordinate tenants and labourers who comprised a "white" caste. Officially, such divisions are gone, but shamanism is certainly still practised and there's a chance of at least a superficial view of the old ways during occasional **festivals**. These can be riotous occasions with heavy drinking sessions, bullfights and wrestling matches interspersed with music and archery displays. Traditionally everyone dressed up, though today this is largely left to the women who don finely embroidered jackets and sometimes twist their hair into bizarre horned shapes, the married women wearing wide, flat black turbans. Best is the **torch festival** at the end of the sixth lunar month, commemorating both an ancient victory over a heavenly insect plague, and the wife of Tang-dynasty chieftain Deng Shan, who starved to death rather than marry the warlord who had incinerated her husband. The Yi new year arrives early, in the tenth lunar month.

PUGE (buses daily 7am–5pm; ¥15; 3hr), marketplace for surrounding hamlets, where you're certain to see people in traditional dress; there's at least one **guesthouse** if you want to delve deeper, though the town is frankly a dump.

To visit the **Space Flight Centre**, 65km north of Xichang, you need a week to arrange a permit and tour through the XITS (which requires your passport number, a photograph and ¥110), though they don't always accept foreigners and the centre is not always open – Long March rockets have previously crashed shortly after take-off, killing scores of people.

There's regular transport, however, to **YUANNING**, a dusty little place 60km north on the Shimian road, where a **Red Army Museum** commemorates the safe passage through Yi territory granted to the Long Marchers in 1935, after army chief Liu Bocheng drank a friendship toast of chicken's blood with a Yi leader. To really get off the beaten track, ask XITS to organize a trip 40km south of Xichang to **Luoji Shan**; you'll need horses and three days to get east from the main-road town of **Huang Shui** to the mountain's summit.

Zigong and Yibin

Surrounding the fertile confluence of the Yangzi and Min rivers 250km southeast of Chengdu, where Sichuan, Yunnan and Guizhou provinces meet, the **Zigong and Yibin districts** have some intriguing attractions. Zigong itself is a treat, with some well-preserved architecture, dinosaurs and salt mines. The town is worth a visit at any time of year, but is especially worth checking out during Spring Festival, when its streets and public spaces become the venue for huge lantern displays (though be warned that accommodation doubles in price at this time). Some 80km farther south, Yibin offers access to the aptly named **Bamboo Sea**, and some esoteric hanging coffins near the town of **Gongxian**.

Both Zigong and Yibin are easily accessible **by bus** from Chengdu, Chongqing and Leshan. Approaching from Leshan, you'll encounter yet more monumental religious sculpture at **Rongxian**, a small county seat whose scattered colonial-era architecture is being messily modernized; the south of town

Zigong and Yibin

Zigong	自贡	***zìgòng***
Dinosaur Museum	恐龙博物馆	*kǒnglóng bówùguǎn*
Salt Museum	盐业历史博物馆	*yányèlìshǐ bówùguǎn*
Shawan Binguan	沙湾宾馆	*shāwān bīnguǎn*
Wangye Miao	王爷庙	*wángyé miào*
Xiqin Guildhall	西亲会馆	*xīqīnhuìguǎn*
Zigong Luguan	自贡旅馆	*zìgòng lǚguǎn*
Yibin	宜宾	***yíbīn***
Cuiping Park	翠屏公园	*cuìpíng gōngyuán*
Daguan Lou	大观楼	*dàguān lóu*
Jingsheng Teahouse	京盛茶坊	*jīngshèng cháfáng*
Post & Telecommunications Hotel	邮电公寓	*yōudiàn gōngyù*
Xufu Binguan	叙府宾馆	*xùfǔ bīnguǎn*
Changning	长宁	***chángníng***
Bamboo Sea	竹海	*zhúhǎi*
Jiaotong Binguan	交通宾馆	*jiāotōng bīnguǎn*
Zhuhai Binguan	竹海宾馆	*zhúhǎi bīnguǎn*
Gongxian	珙县	***gǒngxiàn***
Luobiao	洛表	***luòbiǎo***
Hanging coffins	悬棺	*xuánguān*
Luzhou	泸州	***lúzhōu***
Rongxian	荣县	***róngxiàn***
Giant Buddha	荣县大佛	*róngxiàn dàfó*

is flanked by carved riverside cliffs, along with an imposing, thirty-metre-high **Giant Buddha** protected by a temple frontage. Yibin is also on the Yangzi River between Leshan and Chongqing, and is therefore accessible by **ferry** from either during high summer river levels. An interesting way out of the region is by busing east to **Luzhou**, and then over to **Chishui** in Guizhou province – see p.832.

Zigong

ZIGONG, a thriving industrial centre, has long been an important source of **salt**, tapped for thousands of years from artesian basins below the city. In the fourth century the Sichuanese were sinking 300-metre-deep boreholes here using bamboo fibre cables attached to massive stone bits, later replaced by more effective two-piece percussion drills. By the 1600s, bamboo buckets were drawing brine from wells bored almost a kilometre beneath Zigong, centuries before European technology (which borrowed Chinese techniques) could reach this deep. **Natural gas**, a by-product of drilling, was used from the second century to boil brine in evaporation tanks, and now powers city buses – look for the huge, floppy black rubber gas bags on their roofs.

As good a place to begin a city tour as any is the splendid Qing-era **Xiqin Guildhall** on central Jiefang Lu, now an absorbing **Salt Museum** (daily 8.30am–5pm; ¥5), full of photos and mining relics – including drill bits which

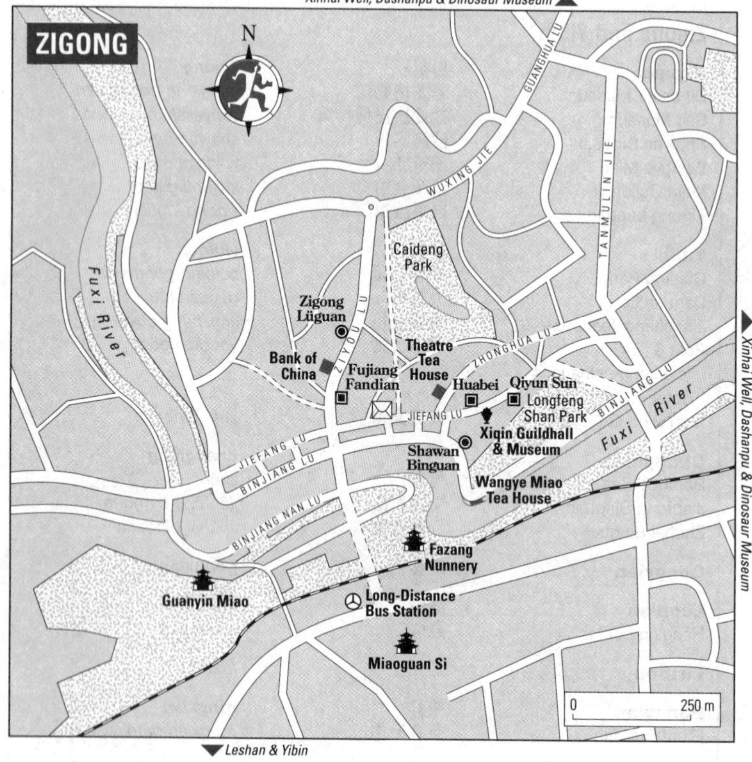

look like part of a medieval torturer's armoury. One of the best things here is the building itself, whose extravagantly curled roof corners, flagstone-and-beam halls, and finely carved woodwork were renovated in 1872 by master craftsman Yang Xuesan. Several other contemporary structures survive in Zigong, including two marvellous **teahouses** where you can gossip, lounge or play cards with locals surrounded by dated furnishings: the unmissable Wangye Miao, which sits high over the river near the *Shawan Binguan* on Binjiang Lu; and a former theatre with a beautifully carved stone gateway at the junction of Jiefang Lu and Zhonghua Lu.

Bus #3 **to Dashanpu** (¥0.5) from opposite the *Shawan Binguan* on Binjiang Lu heads 15km northeast into Zigong's suburbs, passing **Xinhai Well** (¥1), the deepest ever drilled using traditional methods at a fraction over 1000m. In use until 1966, the twenty-metre-high wooden tripod minehead still towers over the site, and you can look at the rusted evaporation tanks (gas is now used to boil the caretaker's kettle), bamboo-fibre cables, excellent stone engravings on the wall detailing the well's development (much of it using buffalo power), and the tiny well shaft itself, corked and barely 20cm across. Stay on the bus and it's about 45 minutes from Binjiang Lu to the Dashanpu terminus, from where you'll have to walk the last 500m to Zigong's **Dinosaur Museum** (daily 8.30am–5pm; ¥20), built over the site of excavations carried out during the 1980s with the help of the British Museum. Near-perfect skeletal remains of dozens of Jurassic fish, amphibians and dinosaurs – including monumental thighbones, and Sichuan's own **Yangchuanosaurus**, a lightweight velociraptor – have been left partially excavated *in situ*, while others have been fully assembled for easy viewing; the poor lighting and captions are minor quibbles.

Practicalities

Zigong's compact, hilly centre lies on the north side of the narrow **Fuxi River**. The **long-distance bus station** is on the highway south of town; turn right out of the station and head through a **tunnel**, which exits on the south bank by a bridge. Cross over and you're facing up **Ziyou Lu**, with **Binjiang Lu** running under the bridge along the north bank, and **Jiefang Lu** parallel and one block back. There's **accommodation** at the *Zigong Lüguan* (❶), up Ziyou Lu on the left, where it's hard to get anything but overpriced doubles; or at the *Shawan Binguan*, east on Binjiang Lu (Ⓣ0813/2208888, Ⓕ2201168; ❶–❺), which has three-star facilities in its new, modern block, and clean, tatty doubles in an older "vice-wing" (as it's described in their price list) – where, for some bizarre reason, the cheaper rooms are best. **Places to eat** are legion, with evening hotpots and kebab stalls along Jiefang Lu; try fiery hot, stodgy dumplings, soups, noodles, mung-bean dishes and fried or smoked meats at the inexpensive *Qiyun Sun* or *Huabei* restaurants on Jiefang Lu, or the *Fujiang Fandian*, on the right along Ziyou Lu.

Leaving, there are plenty of normal and four express buses until mid-afternoon to Chengdu, Leshan, Luzhou and Chongqing; twice-hourly departures to Yibin; and daily buses each to Gongxian and Kunming.

Yibin and around

The port city of **YIBIN** sits where the Jinsha Jiang and Min Jiang combine to form the **Chang Jiang**, the main body of the Yangzi. A well-ordered, modern place, Yibin produces two substances known for wreaking havoc – enriched plutonium and Wuliangye *bai jiu*, China's second-favourite spirit. However, there's little to do here beyond organizing transport to surrounding sights: westerly **Cuiping Park** offers a lengthy flight of steps from Zhenwu Lu up to views over the town and river junction, while **Daguan Lou**, a former gate tower on central Mazhang Lu, has been co-opted as the inevitable stylish teahouse.

Around 2km across, the town focuses on a central **crossroads**; from here Shangbei Jie runs north, Minzhu Lu runs south into Nan Jie, Zhongshan Lu heads east to the **docks**, and Renmin Lu runs west. **Beimen long-distance bus station** is 250m northwest of the centre off **Zhenwu Lu**, the highway in from Zigong which skirts the western side of the city. For somewhere **to stay**, try either the reasonable *Xufu Binguan*, at 14 Renmin Lu, just west from the crossroads (Ⓣ0831/8221582, Ⓕ8223986; ❹), or the friendly *Post and Telecommunications Hotel* (Ⓣ0831/8247388; ❶–❸), next to the **post office** on Nan Jie. If you want a change from the usual canteen fare, seek out the **Jingsheng teahouse** – more of a dumpling and light-meal restaurant – on Renhe Jie, which runs south off Renmin Lu.

Beimen station handles traffic to Chongqing, Chengdu and Zigong; for regional sights, catch a **city bus** from beside Daguan Lou south over the river to **Nan'an bus station** (15min; ¥1), from where early morning services to the Bamboo Sea and Gongxian depart. **Ferries** to Luzhou and Chongqing leave daily from the docks on the eastern side of town.

The Bamboo Sea

Around 50km southeast of Yibin via **Changning**, the extraordinary **Bamboo Sea** covers more than forty square kilometres of mountain slopes with feathery green tufts. Foreigners on the bus are turned in at the park gates to cough up the ¥15 entrance fee – there are further charges to enter each section of the park, too – from where the road follows through to the knot of buildings comprising **Wanling**. The smart *Zhuhai Binguan* (❺) is the pick of the **accommodation** here; for anything substantially cheaper, you'll need to head 1500m south to the *Jiaotong Binguan* (❶). Paths lead from both into the forest, an unusual walk given such a large expanse of just the one type of plant. It's surprisingly dark, with the tall, slender trunks reaching up 10m or more. For the best views of the "sea", however, climb the hills above to a scattering of **temples**, from where the bowed tips of bamboo ripple in waves as breezes sweep the slopes. The best of the shrines is the Buddhist–Taoist **Feiyun Dong**, which contains some really grotesque Ming-dynasty sculptures. Transport back to Yibin leaves from Changning until early afternoon.

The Bo and hanging coffins

It's 90km and around five hours from Yibin, via the dispiriting coal-mining town of **Gongxian** (where you have to change buses), to hilltop **Luobiao**, a similar, smaller place. Head downhill from where the bus stops outside some basic restaurants, and it's 2km to the broad Dengjia River valley where dozens of **Bo hanging coffins** decorate flanking limestone cliffs (¥5). The **Bo people** themselves are an enigma, having vanished during the sixteenth century, routed by imperial forces after their leader rashly declared himself emperor during a rebellion against the local governor. Though portrayed as a degenerate aboriginal race skulking along the river basins and stirring up trouble among the populace, their cliff burials show a well-developed artistic culture – the sites contain engraved and carved artefacts, and ochre paintings depicting sun symbols, animals and people. Locating the coffins high up in the open on wooden galleries, it's believed, was done to aid the return of spirits to the sky. How the coffins were actually positioned is unknown, though presumably the process involved scaffolding. Be aware that this is a very long day-trip from Yibin, and you'll have to leave Luobiao by mid-afternoon to catch connecting services all the way back.

Dazu

About 180km east of Chengdu and 90km west of Chongqing, the celebrated **cliff sculptures** of **Dazu** lie amid beautiful lush countryside of green rolling hills cut with gentle terraces. Dazu means "Big Foot", referring to a story of Buddha leaving a footprint on rocks nearby, though perhaps this is just a way of saying that the sculptures here were divinely inspired. They are certainly extraordinary, comprising some fifty thousand images carved into niches, caves and overhangs in the sides of **Bei Shan** (North Hill) and **Baoding Shan**

Dazu

Dazu	大足	***dàzú***
Baoding Shan	宝顶山	*bǎodǐng shān*
Bei Shan	北山	*běishān*
Beishan Binguan	北山宾馆	*běishān bīnguǎn*
Dazu Binguan	大足宾馆	*dàzú bīnguǎn*

(Precious Summit Hill). Begun in 892, work on them continued for more than four hundred years, and they have since avoided the ravages of weather through an ingenious internal drainage system, as well as the attentions of foreign looters and native vandals thanks to isolation and decree. Some of the sculptures are small, others huge, many are brightly painted and form comic-strip-like narratives, their characters portraying religious, moral and historical tales. While most are set fairly deeply into the rock faces, all can be viewed by natural light and are connected by walkways and paths.

Dazu town, Bei Shan and Baoding Shan

The base for exploring the sculptures is **DAZU TOWN**, 200km from Chengdu and 100km from Chongqing. A nondescript place with a centre only a few hundred metres across, Dazu is set along the north side of the mild Laixi River immediately south of Bei Shan, whose carvings can be reached on foot via Bei Jie. Baoding Shan is 16km off to the east, connected to Dazu by frequent minibuses through the day (¥2; last one back leaves Baoding Shan around 5pm).

Dazu's main **bus station** is by the bridge on the south bank, a four-hour haul from Chongqing, or eight hours from Chengdu's Xinnanmen station. **Accommodation** is expensive and limited (as far as foreigners are concerned) to the recently rebuilt and pretty good value *Dazu Binguan* (❸; includes breakfast) and the similar *Beishan Binguan* ❺), both left out of the bus station, over the bridge and down on the right. For **food**, try the hotels or the dozen or so restaurants along the main streets.

Bei Shan

A couple of kilometres' walk north from Dazu's main street brings you to a flight of steps leading up to the area's earliest carvings, begun in the ninth century, at **Bei Shan** (daily 8am–5pm; ¥25), and constituting 264 decorated recesses cut into the hillside and joined by a path. The work was started by General **Wei Junjing**, who is suitably remembered by a piece carved in his honour by a defeated Shu warlord. Other sculptures were funded by donations, some military, some given by monks and nuns whose names are recorded in inscriptions or appear on the arrangements themselves.

One of Bei Shan's most outstanding friezes is **cave 245** (they are all numbered), with more than six hundred figures and some nice details of contemporary Tang life, including ornaments, dress and musical instruments. Just north of here, though, the finest detail and craftsmanship are displayed in some **Song-dynasty** carvings. **Cave 113** has an elegant Guanyin gazing at the moon's reflection, and in **cave 125** the Bodhisattva appears again with a rosary, looking more like a shy debutante than a saint. The largest cave, **136**, depicts Sakyamuni flanked by twenty finely detailed Bodhisattvas, among them Manjusri riding a blue roaring lion, and Puxian sitting calmly in a lotus position on his sturdy elephant.

Baoding Shan

Exciting, comic and realistic by turns, the sculptures at **Baoding Shan** (daily 8am–5pm; ¥45) comprise the best of Dazu's art, funded by subscriptions collected between 1179 and 1245 by **Zhao Zhifeng**, a dedicated monk. As he alone organized the work, there's little repetition of the stories – all of which are taken from Buddhist scriptures – and the ten thousand images divide into two clear groupings. **Xiaofowan** is the earliest, carved into stone-walled grottoes supported by pillars and beams, but most people concentrate on the later and more impressive **Dafowan**, whose 31 niches are more naturally incorporated into the inner side of a horseshoe curve of hills. Here, as at Bei Shan, there's a chance to get eye to eye with some quite incredible and illuminating detail. **Fierce Tiger Descending a Mountain** greets you with superb elan, and leads to another striking group, the **Six Ways of Transmigration**, in which a brightly coloured giant holds a great segmented disc, representing one of the six courses of predestination. The path leads from here to **niche 5**, where there's a huge representation of Vairocana, Manjusri and Samantabhadra, the last holding out a stone pagoda said to weigh half a ton. No less imposing is niche 8, the **Dabei Pavilion**, where the figure of a thousand-armed Guanyin is the largest ever carved in China. Each hand is different, fanning out in glowing gold like peacock feathers. Impressive in a different way are the thirty-metre-high **reclining Buddha** in niche 11, and niche 15, **Requital of Parent's Kindness**. Here, seven Buddhas represent the stages of a man's life – praying for a son, conception, birth, feeding and washing the baby, arranging a marriage – right through to old age. By contrast, the next but one along shows **Buddha Requiting his Parents' Kindness**, with figures recalling his goodness to his parents while on the left heretics slander him as unfilial. Niche 20 houses the memorable **Eighteen Layers of Hell**, a Chamber-of-Horrors scene interspersed with delicate and amusing comic-strip cameos such as the **Hen Wife** and the **Drunkard and his Mother**. Near the exit, **niche 30** returns to a naturalistic theme, showing ten buffaloes with their herder, both a symbol of meditation and a tranquil picture of pastoral life.

Chongqing city

Based around a crowded, comma-shaped peninsula at the junction of the Yangzi and Jialing rivers, **CHONGQING** is southwestern China's dynamo, its largest city both in scale and population. Formerly part of Sichuan Province and now the heavily industrialized core of **Chongqing Municipality**, the city is also a busy **port**, whose location 2400km upstream from Shanghai, at the meeting point between eastern river traffic and overland trade routes with Tibet and Burma, has given Chongqing an enviable commercial acumen. It oozes the atmosphere of a typical waterfront city: dirty, seedy and not particularly attractive, but bursting with life.

Able to trace its history right back into legend, Chongqing was capital of the state of Ba when the mythical king **Yu**, tamer of floods, found a consort here. The current name, meaning "Double Celebration", was bestowed by former resident **Zhaodun** on his becoming emperor in 1189. The city has a long tradition as a place of defiance against hostile powers, despite being ceded as a nineteenth-century **treaty port** to Britain and Japan. From 1242, Song forces held Mongol invaders at bay for 36 years near **Hechuan**, 60km to the north, during the longest continuous campaign on Chinese soil, and it was to Chongqing that the Guomindang government withdrew in 1937, having been driven out of Nanjing by the Japanese. The subsequent influx of refugees and bombing raids did little to raise morale in the undefended wartime capital, as the Nationalists became more preoccupied with a propaganda war against the Communists than defeating the invaders. After the Japanese surrender in 1945 and the resumption of civil war following the failure of US-brokered talks in the city between Mao and Chiang Kaishek, Chongqing remained one of the

Chongqing

Chongqing	重庆	***chóngqìng***
Chaotianmen docks	朝天门码头	*cháotiānmén mǎtóu*
Chongqing Museum	重庆市博物馆	*chóngqìngshì bówùguǎn*
Guiyuan	桂园	*guìyuán*
Hongyan	红岩村	*hóngyán cūn*
Jiefang Bei	解放碑	*jiěfàng bēi*
Luohan Si	罗汉寺	*luóhàn sì*
Metropolitan Tower	大都会商厦	*dàdūhuì shāngshà*
People's Concert Hall	人民大礼堂	*rénmín dàlǐtáng*
Pipa Shan Park	枇杷山公园	*píbāshān gōngyuán*
SACO prisons	中美合作所	*zhōngměi hézuòsuǒ*
Accommodation, eating and drinking		
Chongqing	重庆宾馆	*chóngqìng bīnguǎn*
Chung King	重庆饭店	*chóngqìng fàndiàn*
Huixian Lou	会仙楼宾馆	*huìxiānlóu bīnguǎn*
Lao Shu Huoguo	老蜀火锅	*lǎoshǔ huǒguǒ*
Lao Sichuan	老四川	*lǎosì chuān*
Minzhu Meibaocheng	民主美包城	*mínzhǔ měibāochéng*
Renmin	人民宾馆	*rénmín bīnguǎn*
Shipin	食品大厦	*shípǐn dàshà*
Yizhishi	颐之时	*yízhī shí*
Zeng Xiao Rong	曾小容	*zēngxiǎo róng*

last Guomindang bastions, falling to Communist forces in November 1949. Since then Chongqing has boomed; now more than two million people rub elbows on the peninsula, with five times that number in the ever-expanding mantle of suburbs and industrial developments spreading away from the river.

Built on and surrounded by steep-sided hills, the **Mountain City** – as locals sometimes refer to Chongqing – has, in many respects, little appeal. Faster-paced and less friendly than Chengdu, the city is plagued by intense industrial pollution, compounded by winter fogs, and nowhere does the region's summer humidity feel more oppressive than on the peninsula's narrow streets. Nor is there much to illustrate Chongqing's history, though some **revolutionary sites** survive, as do **prisons** where Reds and subversives were kept and tortured. Surprisingly, then, you'll nonetheless find Chongqing an upbeat city with plenty of character, and it's a rewarding enough place simply to wander the streets, in between arranging **Yangzi river cruises**, and trips west to the Buddhist grottoes at Dazu (see p.956).

Arrival, city transport and accommodation

Beginning to resemble a miniature Hong Kong, complete with skyscrapers, hills and a profit-hungry populace, Chongqing centres on a four-kilometre-long peninsula, capped by grassy parks atop **Pipa Shan** and **Eling Shan**. The **downtown area** and most accommodation prospects surround **Victory Monument** in the eastern Jiefangbei commercial district; **Chaotianmen docks**, where Yangzi ferries (see p.962) pull in, are just a short walk away at the eastern tip of the peninsula. The seething **long-distance bus** and **train stations** are southwest across town, on a complex traffic flow near river level. From here, either flag down a minibus or bus #102 to Chaotianmen docks, or climb the covered stone stairway up to Zhongshan Er Lu, where trolleybus

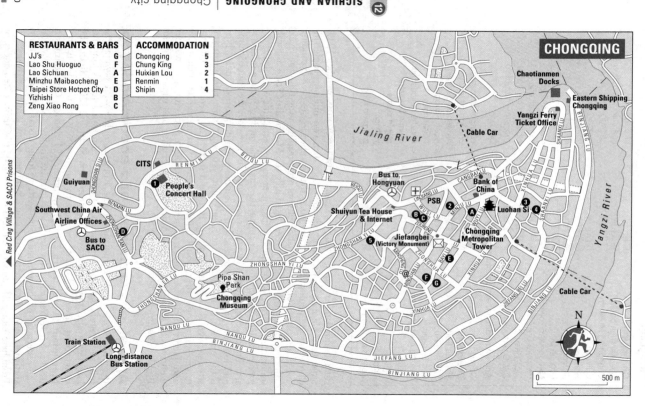

CHONGQING

RESTAURANTS & BARS	
JJ's	G
Lao Shu Huoguo	F
Lao Sichuan	A
Minzhu Maibaocheng	E
Taipei Store Hotpot City	D
Yizhishi	B
Zeng Xiao Rong	C

ACCOMMODATION	
Chongqing	5
Chung King	3
Huixian Lou	2
Renmin	1
Shipin	4

#405 runs to Jiefangbei. The airport shuttle bus (¥15) transports passengers the 30km from the **airport** to the CAAC office on Zhongshan San Lu; from here buses #104 and #105 run along Renmin Lu to the Jiefangbei terminus on Linjiang Lu).

At ¥1–2 for a ride, **buses** are the easiest way to get around if you want to give your legs a break from the serpentine stone staircases linking different levels of town. Because of the hills, **bicycles** are a rare sight. If at all possible, avoid Chongqing's piratical **taxis**, or establish the fare first and make sure you have the exact change. The peninsula is so small that it shouldn't cost much more than the cab's standing charge (¥5–10) to reach anywhere central.

Accommodation

There's little budget or mid-range accommodation for foreigners in Chongqing, though you can often bargain a discount.

Chongqing 235 Minsheng Lu ⓣ023/63845888, ⓕ63830643. Overpriced but a comfortable-enough business venue, with full facilities and two good restaurants specializing in banquets and "sizzling hot" Western food. ❼

Chung King 41–43 Xinhua Lu ⓣ023/63849301, ⓕ63843085. Interesting 1930s building housing a Hong Kong-run hotel with good rooms and a decent Sichuanese restaurant. ❻

Huixian Lou Minzu Lu (ⓣ023/63837495, ⓕ63844234). Very central with tidy furnishings and a few English-speaking staff. Doubles are quite a good deal, and the seven-bed dorms, with shared bathroom, are the cheapest option in town. Dorm beds ¥70, ❺

Luohan Si Xiao Shizi ⓣ023/63737144. The pretty Luohan temple has basic rooms available in the building next door, with or without bath. It's clean and well run and some rooms have views into the temple grounds. The temple restaurant makes a great place for lunch (you'll have to get up very early indeed to catch breakfast). Dorm beds ¥20–30, ❶–❷

Renmin 173 Renmin Lu ⓣ023/63851421, ⓕ63852076. Recent refurbishments have greatly enhanced this four-star hotel in the wings of the grandiose People's Concert Hall. Extremely popular with Chinese and Western tour groups. ❽

Shipin Shaanxi Lu ⓣ023/63847300. Fair-value Chinese hotel close to Chiaotianmen docks; an alternative to the *Huixian Lou*'s mid-range rooms. ❹

The City

Chongqing's steep slopes, back alleys and bicycle-free streets immediately set the city apart from others in China, though things have changed from the heady 1890s when **George Morrison**, an Australian journalist who later became an adviser to the mendacious warlord Yuan Shikai, described an enormously rich port with mighty walls, temples, pagodas and great public buildings – seemingly financed by the surrounding fields of **opium poppies**. Wealth is still visible, and even the basic, congested street plan seems unaltered, but the opium trade, old buildings and walls have since fallen victim to relentless expansion, and today Chongqing is best characterized by inner-city development and urban sprawl.

Jiefangbei and Luohan Si

Isolated by by a broad, paved pedestrian square and glassy offices, **Jiefangbei**, the **Victory Monument**, marks Chongqing's commercial heart, though you'd expect something better than this drab clock tower to celebrate the Communists' liberation of the city from seventy years of colonial and right-wing occupation. The area is packed with noisy, well-dressed crowds investigating the latest imports piled high at the several department stores, flitting between restaurants, and blithely disregarding the signs asking them not to litter. Nearby backstreets are busy, too: narrow pavements congested with bright, cheap clothing stalls; and the city **market** around Bayi Lu full of buckets of

Yangzi ferries from Chongqing

Chongqing is the most obvious departure point for the three-day **Yangzi river cruises** downstream through the **Three Gorges** to Yichang and Wuhan (see pp.544 & 530), but you might find that organizing a berth is the most frustrating part of your time here. Be warned, however, that with people rushing to do the trip before the Three Gorges Dam submerges the scenery, prices have increased and standards slipped. For up-to-date information on Yangzi river trips, check ⓦwww.chinahighlights.com.

It's best to arrange things in advance, but outside the autumn tourist season you shouldn't have problems finding tickets for next-day travel. The official **ticket office** is at the dock-end of Shaanxi Lu, though long before you get there you'll have been grabbed and harassed beyond endurance by freelance touts; see Chongqing "Listings" (p.965) for ticket agents, and p.966 for on-board facilities. Several ferries leave daily, and Chongqing has vague docking arangements, so establish the **boat name** and **dock number** when buying tickets, and try to locate them during daylight. You also need to check the ferry **departure time** – dawn used to be the norm, but an increasing number now leave in the evening to hit the Three Little Gorges early on the third day.Try to avoid a departure between 10am and 12am as you'll hit the first gorge too early and the third too late to see much. If you have a dawn departure, you may be able to **sleep on board** the night before; go down with your luggage after 8pm and pay the purser. Note that the charge for this is set by your ticket class, but at less than ¥50 it can be cheaper than a night in Chongqing.

Competition between agents, along with surcharges, means that the following **per-person prices** for travel from Chongqing should be used as a guide only (see p.966 for more details). Note that the bottom bunk is about ten percent cheaper, and that the Shanghai trip usually involves a change of vessel at Wuhan.

	2-berth cabin	3/4-berth	8-berth	16-berth
Yichang	¥928	¥464	¥218	¥155
Wuhan	¥1370	¥686	¥322	¥231
Shanghai	¥1968	¥1029	¥478	¥337

Luxury cruises to Wuhan are also available, departing at least daily between June and October; some of the vessels have the facilities of four-star hotels, with fares starting at around ¥2000. Tickets for these can be bought at tour agents (see p.965). Finally, there's also a daily 7am **hydrofoil** service to Yichang (arriving at 11pm; ¥400) via Wushan (5.30pm), from which you'll get daytime views of the gorges, though you won't be able to alight for a closer view en route.

frogs, cages of snakes – which vendors laughingly invite you to handle – and huge, fragrant bags of dried spices and fungi.

Moving northeast along Minzu Lu takes you past **Luohan Si** (¥2), set down an alleyway but given away by the incense and paper money sellers hanging around the gates. Beyond the unusual entrance, lined by weathered rock carvings, the best feature of this tiny, century-old temple is the **arhat hall**, where you're guided anticlockwise by a rope handrail through a maze of five hundred brightly painted, life-sized statues of Buddhist saints. All the figures are distinctive, some with grotesquely contorted features, one with five eyes and another reaching elongated arms heavenwards. Outside stands an isolated statue of a drunkard. There's a great **vegetarian restaurant** here, too, open to the public for lunch.

Across the road and around the corner from the temple, along Cangbai Lu, is the **cable-car station** from where you can ride high across the river to northern Chongqing (¥1) – there's another cable-car route to the southern suburbs from Xinhua Lu. Views from either take in river traffic, trucks collecting landfill in low-season mud, and distant hills – merely faint grey silhouettes behind the haze. However, the machinery tends to break down in the rain.

To spy on more waterfront activity, head down to **Chaotianmen docks**, a five-minute walk downhill from Luohan Si along Xinhua Lu. Built in 1999 atop a flood-proof embankment, booking offices and an observation area look down on **Yangzi ferries** and barges moored out in the centre of the river. You'll also spot heavily laden porters shifting bundles of goods on carrypoles, across seemingly random walkways laid out over the sticky seasonal mud flats between the boats and shore – a route you may well be taking, perhaps at night, if you take the ferry from here during winter.

Pipa Shan and the west end

A ten-minute ride on the #405 trolleybus west of Jiefangbei down Zhongshan Yi Lu lands you outside the gates of **Pipa Shan Park** (¥1), from where a short walk uphill leads to a pavilion perched on the airy, grassy peak. At 220m, this is the highest spot in Chongqing – below, the city labours under a haze of smog and the chink of countless construction hammers drifts up in the breeze, but at night, pollution is invisible, and the hills and river are picked out by streetlamps and industrial spotlighting. Halfway down the south side of the park, the quiet **Chongqing Museum** (daily 9am–5.30pm; ¥5) has a leaden collection of paintings and porcelain, two dynamic, dragon-draped **warrior busts** from Ya'an, a **hanging coffin** akin to those still pinioned onto cliffs near Yibin (see p.955), and a few interesting Ba–Shu pieces, including bronzes and **sword blades** finely etched with animals and some undeciphered hieroglyphics. A small **natural history** wing next door (¥2) has casts of Sichuanese **dinosaur fossils** unearthed at Zigong (p.954).

Other west-end sights are things to imbibe in passing. In the vicinity of Renmin Lu, you can't miss the green-tiled roof and monumental dimensions of the **People's Concert Hall**. Built in the 1950s along the lines of Beijing's Temple of Heaven, this lavish construction accommodates four thousand opera-goers in the circular rotunda (where you can sit for ¥3 outside performance times), while the *Renmin Hotel* occupies three adjoining wings. Hidden away to the northwest along Zhongshan Si Lu, **Guiyuan** (Osmanthus Garden) is the house where Mao stayed while in town between August 12 and October 10, 1945, toasting the victory over Japan and negotiating the **Double Tenth Treaty** with Chiang Kaishek – the famous "words on paper" which established a short-lived truce between the Red Army and Guomindang (see below).

Hongyan and the SACO prisons

About 4km from the centre through the western riverside suburbs, **HONGYAN** (Red Crag; daily 8.30am–5pm; ¥8), is the village where China's wartime government, an uneasy alliance between Chiang Kaishek's Nationalist and Mao's Communist parties, set up in 1938 – wisely remote from the Japanese bombing raids concentrated around the peninsula. Mao visited here with US Ambassador Patrick Hurley in August 1945 to negotiate a role for the Communists in a postwar government, but Chiang's insistence that the Red Army should disband led to nothing but a lukewarm agreement on political freedom, which was almost immediately wrecked by the US assisting Guomindang troop deployment in Communist-strong areas. To get here, take **bus** #104 downhill from the roundabout on Beiqu Lu to the Hongyan terminus.

For the Chinese, Hongyan is synonymous with two great twentieth-century figures, Mao and the subsequent premier **Zhou Enlai**, who spent much of the war here as secretary of the regional Communist Party (there's no mention of Chiang Kaishek). Nervous-looking cadres assemble to have their photos taken in front of the Chairman's bronze statue, which overlooks Chongqing from the forecourt. For others, however, the pleasant few acres of hilly parkland surrounding the site are likely to prove more appealing than the restored government buildings and photo collections that make up the bulk of the exhibition.

The events surrounding Hongyan ultimately led to the renewal of civil war in 1946 and the Guomindang defeat three years later. Chongqing was one of their last stands and, when it fell, the Communists found the grim **SACO prisons** (daily 8.30am–5pm; ¥4) at the foot of Gele Hill on the city's north-western limits; bus #217 comes here from Liziba Lu, near the China Southwest Airlines office. Now called the **US–Chiang Kaishek Criminal Acts Exhibition Hall**, this is where political prisoners were tortured under the baleful eye of the Guomindang's hatchet man, **General Dai Li**. SACO refers to the Sino-American Co-operation Organization of 1937, which had inadvertently provided the prison's funding. Photographs and instruments of torture from the war years make the prison a dismal place to visit, and the museum's run-down condition suggests that nobody really wants to remember those days.

Eating, drinking and nightlife

Chongqing's centre is alive with canteens and food stalls, and at meal times, already busy side streets and markets become obstacle courses of plastic chairs, low tables and wok-wielding cooks. Local tastes lean towards Sichuanese small-dish assemblies – perfect for solo diners – in which dumplings, pickled vegetables, fish, fowl and offal figure strongly. Look for snake beans with ginger, tiger-skin peppers, braised frog or spareribs, and "pearl" rice balls. Chongqing is where Sichuan's **hotpot** originated, and residents tuck into the dish even during the sweltering summers. A variation here is that the raw ingredients arrive on plates, not skewers, so the pots are divided up into compartments to prevent everyone's portions getting mixed up. Night tables along Bayi Lu are popular places to have them – fix prices per plate first. A *KFC* overlooking Jiangfangbei, and the hotels, are your best bets for non-Sichuanese fare.

Chongqing's **nightlife** is limited but quite good, with several **clubs and bars** in the Jiangfangbei area. *JJ's House Disco*, on Bayi Lu, is the pick of the moment, crowded, sweaty and pulsating with a young Chinese crowd after 9pm; the *Silver Rock* and *Rainbow* are adjacent alternatives. Foreigners get in free everywhere. Imported beers are pretty expensive, but you can get cheaper Chinese booze by the pitcherful; Chongqing Beer is the local brew, served in squat, brown-glass bottles.

Restaurants

Lao Shu Huoguo Bayi Lu. An inexpensive, off-street hotpot option, handy if the weather is foul. Friendly staff and decent portions.

Lao Sichuan Wuyi Lu. A good, long-established restaurant, offering both classic courses and side dishes such as preserved eggs, dry-fried beef, chilli-braised frogs and eels, and green beans with garlic.

Luohan Si Luohan Si Jie. Temple restaurant with first-rate vegetarian cuisine.

Minzhu Meibaocheng Bayi Lu. Busiest of many such inexpensive canteens in this street; sit in cheap plastic seats and devour great portions of *shuijiao*, spring rolls, noodles and soups.

Taipei Stone Hotpot City, 23 Zhongshan San Lu. A well-regarded self-service hotpot restaurant that gets very busy in the evening; look for the steamed-up windows.

Yizhishi Zourong Lu. A popular place for Chongqing's full range of cheap and excellent snacks – best in this line are the range of cold vegetables and chilli braised meats. Everything available is on show, so order by pointing.

Zeng Xiao Rong Zourong Lu. Similar to the nearby *Yizhishi*, but with the emphasis on steamed *jiaozi* and "potsticker" dumplings with chilli sauce, glutinous rice balls, and other dumplings also available. The decor is a strange mishmash of concrete trees, wooden booths and chirping budgies.

Listings

Airlines Dragonair, at the *Holiday Inn*, 15 Nanpin Bei Lu ☎023/62803380; China Southwest Air, Zhongshan San Lu ☎023/63660444. The airport bus (¥15) leaves from CAAC on Zhongshan San Lu (daily 8am–7pm; ☎023/63603223).

Banks and exchange Bank of China, 104 Minzu Lu (☎023/63844816) handles foreign exchange (Mon–Fri 9am–noon & 2.30–5pm, Sat 9am–noon) and has a 24hr ATM. Hotels have exchange facilities for guests.

Bookshops The Xinhua Bookstore opposite the post office on Minzu Lu has a wide selection of the usual nineteenth-century titles, with an art section in the back, used mostly as a reference library by students.

Buses Chongqing's bus station is excellent, and there should be no problems organizing tickets out to Chengdu, Leshan, Yibin, Zigong, Dazu or beyond.

Consulates The Metropolitan tower on Wuyi Lu has both a Canadian Consulate (suite 1705) and a British (suite 2802).

Hospital Sanxia Foreign Tourist Medical Consultation Centre, hidden in a lane beside the People's Concert Hall/*Renmin Hotel* on Xuetianwan Zheng Jie, is the best place to look for English-speaking doctors.

Internet access There's an Internet bar above the *Shuiyun* teahouse on Linjiang Lu (¥10/hour) and a cramped café (¥5/hr) at the south end of Minsheng Lu.

Left luggage Facilities at CAAC and all long-distance transport terminals.

Mail and telephones The post office is on Minzu Lu and has IDD phones.

PSB The foreign affairs department is on Linjiang Lu, just east of Wusi Lu (☎023/63847017).

Shopping Department stores abound around Jiangfangbei, and competition makes for some low prices – follow the crowds to the current discounts. The Chongqing Art Store on Minsheng Lu, and the highbrow Huipu on Renmin Lu, are alternatives to the hotel shops for paintings and carvings.

Trains There are departures at least daily to Chengdu (a journey that's much quicker by bus, though), Beijing, Xi'an, Guangzhou, Zunyi and Guiyang. Expect long, slow queues if you buy tickets at the station.

Travel agents All train, bus, boat and plane tickets can be arranged direct yourself, through your hotel travel desk or, for a ¥50 commission, the CITS, opposite the *Renmin Hotel*, on Renmin Lu (daily 8.30–noon & 2–5.30pm; ☎023/63850598 or 63831830). They speak good English here, but are geared towards tour groups. For ferry bookings only, try Eastern Shipping Chongqing, just east of the docks at 2 Chao Dong Lu (☎023/67871216); they'll take you on board your vessel to choose your cabin, guide you to the docks, and collect you from arrival points.

The Yangzi River

Sichuan means "Four Rivers", and of these the most important is the **Yangzi**, once virtually the only route into the province and today still a major link between Sichuan and eastern China. Its source rises in the mountains above Tibet, receiving seven hundred tributaries as it sweeps 6400km across the country to spill its muddy waters into the East China Sea, making it the third longest flow in the world. Appropriately, one of the Yangzi's Chinese names is **Chang Jiang**, the Long River, though above Yibin it's generally known as **Jinsha Jiang** (River of Golden Sands); the name applied by foreigners to the river as a whole, Yangzi, derives from a ford near Yangzhou in Jiangsu Province. Defining the border with Tibet and Yunnan, it skirts Sichuan's western ranges before running up to Chongqing, from where it first becomes navigable year-round to all vessels as it continues east towards Shanghai and the coast.

The Yangzi river

Yangzi River	长江	***cháng jiāng***
Baidicheng	白帝城	*báidì chéng*
Fengdu	丰都	*fēngdū*
Fulong	伏龙	*fúlóng*
Three Little Gorges	小三峡	*xiǎosān xiá*
Three Gorges	三峡	*sānxiá*
Wanxian	万县	*wànxiàn*
Wushan	巫山	*wūshān*
Zhongxian	中县	*zhōngxiàn*

Although people have travelled along the Yangzi for more than a thousand years, it was not, until recently, an easy route – though it was still preferable to traversing Sichuan's difficult, bandit-ridden mountains. The river's most dangerous stretch was the **Three Gorges**, 200km of rapids and sharp hairpin bends constricted between a series of vertical limestone cliffs between **Baidicheng** and Yichang in Hubei Province. Well into the twentieth century, nobody could negotiate this vicious stretch of river alone; steamers couldn't pass at all, and small boats had to be hauled literally inch by inch through the rapids by teams of **trackers**, in a journey that could take several weeks, if the boat even made it at all.

With the last of the rocks and reefs blasted away in the 1950s, today the **ferry journey** provides a respite from trains and buses, as well as the chance to cruise through some spectacular scenery, steeped in history and legend. And now is the time to see it: assuming that the **Three Gorges Dam** upstream from Yichang (p.547) is completed according to schedule, water levels are due to rise more than 100m through the gorges during the next decade, forever changing – if not submerging outright – the whole landscape. It's a full six days between Chongqing and Shanghai, but the best of the scenery – the Three Gorges themselves – is covered in the two-day cruise between Chongqing and the Hubei port of **Yichang**, though it's only a further day from Yichang to **Wuhan** if you can handle the extra time on a Chinese boat. Many of the towns along the river are also accessible by **road** from Chongqing, so you can also shorten the river trip by picking up the ferry along the way.

Practicalities

Crowded and noisy, **public ferries** are the cheapest, easiest way to see the river. Though most people board at Chongqing and take the same vessel all the way through the gorges, it's also easy enough to get off and spend an extra day or two examining towns along the way, assuming you have the time. If you're travelling at peak times, try to get a boat that reaches your destination before sunset or you may have difficulty finding a room. Whether you're buying **ferry tickets** through an agent or direct from the ticket office, foreigners are charged up to fifty percent more than the posted fares, and there's a surcharge for each day spent on the river – **prices** from Chongqing to Yichang and Wuhan are given on p.962. When using an agent, establish *exactly* what the price entails. Many brochures talk of guided tours around sights, or trips along the Three Little Gorges, as if they're part of an inclusive package, but the price is normally for your cabin only; other agents will try to sell you an all-inclusive ticket that includes tours for all the sights on the way.

Options on the ferries start with **first class** – a double cabin with bathroom – and descend in varying permutations through triples and quads with shared toilets, to a bed in 12- or 24-person cabins and, ultimately, a mat on the floor. Don't expect anything luxurious, as even first-class cabins are small and functional. It's very unusual for foreigners to be sold anything less than cabin class, but if you are, pick up a bamboo mat and get in early to claim some floor space as the stairwells, decks and toilets are awash with bodies, sacks and phlegm long before the boat pulls out.

Not all ferries pull in at all ports, and some stay longer than others – schedules can also change en route to compensate for delays, so it's possible that you'll miss some key sights. At each stop, departure times are announced in Chinese; make sure you have them down correctly before going ashore. If you're boarding anywhere except the endpoints, vessels are unlikely to arrive on time, so get to the dock early and be patient; once aboard, make haste for the purser's office on the mid-deck, where available beds are distributed. As for **facilities**, shared toilets fast become vile, and **meals** (buy tickets from the mid-deck office) are cheap, basic and only available for a short time at 7am, 10am and 6pm. Bring plenty of snacks, and in winter **warm clothing**.

Alternatively, you could travel in style on a **luxury cruise**. The vessels which do these trips (among them the *Kunlun*, formerly Chairman Mao's private transport) resemble floating hotels, with glassed-in observation decks, games rooms and real restaurants. At least double the cost of a first-class cabin on local services, they're usually booked out by tour parties, though CITS and some private agents can often get you on at short notice outside the August–November peak season.

Chongqing to Yichang

The first possible stop on the 250-odd kilometres between Chongqing and the mouth of the Three Gorges at Wanxian, **FULONG** marks the mouth of the Wu River, long a port for river traffic heading south into Guizhou Province. Beyond here, the great **Baihe ridge** sits midstream, bearing centuries-old carvings that might have served as water-level marks. Due to be submerged by rising waters, the small town of **FENGDU** comes next, glowered over by Ming Shan, the mountainous abode of **Tianzi**, King of the Dead. Shrines and absurdly huge sculptures cover the heights, now contained inside a **park** (¥60); the main temples here, crammed full of colourful demon statues, are worth a look, as are cheaper fairground-style **side-shows** around town. This is also the first place you'll see white cliffside **markers**, showing how high the water will rise after the dam is in place.

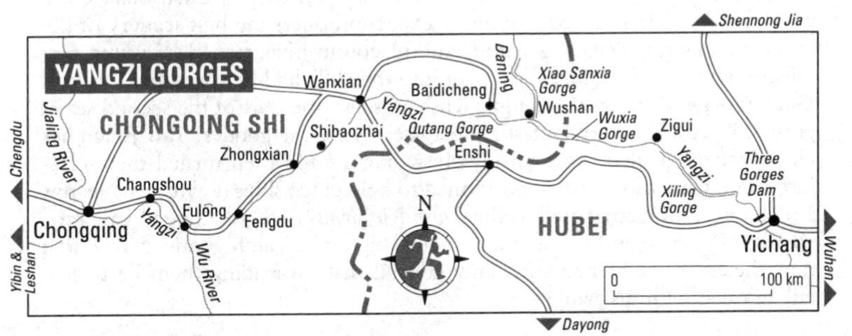

Around 70km downstream is **ZHONGXIAN**, a metropolis being rebuilt on higher ground; it's famous for its fermented bean curd and, rather more venerably, the **Hall of Four Virtuous Men** where the poet Bai Juyi is commemorated. Nearby, you'll get a good look at **Shibaozhai** (Stone Treasure Stronghold), a lumbering rock buttress on the north bank. Built into its side is the thirty-metre-high, bright red **Lanruo Dian** (Orchid-like Temple; ¥30), with circular "portholes" on each level instead of more conventional windows. It's said that there was once a tiny hole in the temple's granary wall, through which poured just enough rice to feed the monks; greedily, they tried to enlarge it, and the frugal supply stopped forever – a Chinese version of the goose with the golden eggs.

Ferries might pull in overnight at **WANXIAN**, an old trading city clinging fortress-like to the hillside at "the gateway to eastern Sichuan", with steps leading up through slits in the enormous walls. Late-afternoon arrival means there's time to get off the boat and stroll around the main street market, where visiting Chinese bargain enthusiastically for steamers, furniture and brightly coloured baskets, all woven of bamboo and rattan. Wanxian is also on a main road, with **buses** running west to Chongqing and southeast to **Enshi** in Hubei, from where there are further services down to the Hunanese town of **Zhangjiajie Shi** (see p.569).

The Three Gorges

The **Three Gorges** themselves begin at **BAIDICHENG**, a town associated with events of the *Three Kingdoms* (see box, p.509) – it was here that **Liu Bei** died after failing to avenge his sworn brother Guan Yu in the war against Wu. Both of them, and the remaining two "Four Musketeers" of the legend, Zhuge Liang and Zhang Fei, are commemorated here by colourful tableaux, featuring life-size statues, in both the **Baidi temple** (¥15) and, across the river, the **Zhang Fei temple** (¥15).

The first of the gorges, eight-kilometre-long **Qutang**, is extremely impressive, its angry, shoal-streaked waters described by the Song poet Su Dongpo as "like a thousand seas poured into one cup". The vertical cliffs are pocked by **Meng Liang's staircase**, square holes chiselled into the rock as far as the platform halfway up, where legend has it that the Song general **Yang Jiye** was killed by traitors. When his bodyguard climbed the cliff to recover the headless corpse, he was deceived by a monk whom he later up-ended and hung by the feet from the cliff face. Other man-made features include wooden scaffolds supporting four **hanging coffins**, similar to those at Gongxian near Yibin (see p.956).

WUSHAN serves as a likely half-day stopover to detour north up Xiao Sanxia, the **Three Little Gorges**, lining the **Daning River**. Once ashore, bargain with minibuses (¥15) for the ten-minute ride to the Xiao Sanxia dock, where you pay ¥150 for a seat in a modern, open-topped canal-boat. On a good day, this five-hour, 33-kilometre excursion offers the best scenery of the entire Chongqing–Yichang trip: beautiful countryside, fast, clear water, tiny villages, remains of a Qin-era path cut into the cliffs, and the awesome **Dragon Gate Gorge**. Back on the Yangzi, Wushan is also the start of the second set of gorges, **Wuxia**, 45km of fantastic precipices where the goddess **Yao Ji** and her eleven sisters quelled some unruly river dragons and then turned themselves into mountains, thoughtfully positioned to help guide ships downriver. Nearby, a rock inscription attributed to the *Three Kingdoms* strategist Zhuge Liang proclaims: "Wuxia's peaks rise higher and higher" – ambiguous words that nonetheless so frightened an enemy general that on reading them he turned tail and fled with his army.

Farther downstream in Hubei, **ZIGUI** town was the birthplace of the poet **Qu Yuan**, whose suicide a couple of millennia ago is commemorated throughout China by dragon-boat races, and it's also where **Xiling**, the longest gorge, begins. The Xiling stretch was always the most dangerous: Westerners passing through in the nineteenth century described the shoals as forming weirs across the river, the boat fended away from threatening rocks by trackers armed with iron-shod bamboo poles, as it rocked through into the sunless, narrow chasm. The scenery hasn't changed a great deal since then, but the rocks, rapids and trackers have gone and the boat passes with relative ease, sailing on to a number of smaller gorges, some with splendid names – Sword and Book, Ox Liver and Horse Lung – suggested by the rock formations. At the end, the monstrous **Three Gorges Dam** at **Sandouping** is another possible stopover, with regular minibuses (¥2) running tourists from the dock to the dam site, great if you like swathes of concrete and giant machines; see p.547 for more on the project.

Past here are the sheer cliffs and shifting currents of **Nanjin Pass**, and after that the broad gentle plain above **Gezhouba**, an enormous complex of dams, power plants, locks and floodgates. The boat squeezes through the lock, which can take some time, to dock in **Yichang**. Aside from continuing downriver from here to Wuhan, you could take a bus from Yichang to **Wudang Shan** in Hubei's mountainous north – details of this, Yichang and river travel between here and Nanjing are covered in Chapter Seven.

Western Sichuan

Very much on the fringes of modern China despite development and resettlement projects, **Sichuan's western half**, extending north to Gansu and west to Tibet, is in every respect an exciting place to travel. The countryside couldn't be farther from the Chengdu plains, with the western highlands forming some of China's most imposing scenery – dense forests, dripping with moisture, snowbound gullies and passes, and unforgettable views of mountain ranges rising up against crisp blue skies. Larger towns contain Han populations, though you'll also find **Qiang**, **Hui** and, most noticeably, **Tibetans** living among them and in the hills. The area has a strong sense of history, too, with monuments to the Communists' **Long March** during the 1930s still dotting the map.

It's a remote but certainly not an undisturbed region, with endless convoys of blue logging trucks hogging the road, decorated with Tao symbols and bulging with freshly cut timber. Western Sichuan also hides some fabulously rare **wildlife** – most notably **giant pandas** at **Wolong Nature Reserve**, only a few hours from Chengdu. In truth, these animals are so rare that your chances of seeing them are very slim – which is, in itself, an excellent reason to try.

Travel practicalities

Travel in western Sichuan has always been an endurance test, even dangerous. Traditionally, traders between China and Tibet managed to cross the mountains only by using wooden galleries hammered into sheer cliffs, and even today

Routes to Western Sichuan

There are two routes into western Sichuan **from Chengdu**. **Heading north**, buses from Ximen station follow the road via Dujiangyan – where you'll find connections west to **Wolong Nature Reserve** – to the town of **Songpan**. Here you can explore the local hills on horseback, then either continue on to the scenery at **Jiuzhai Gou**, or bus through the **Aba Grasslands** right up into Gansu province (p.974). **Heading west**, buses leave daily from Chengdu's Xinnanmen station via **Ya'an** and over the ranges to the historic town of **Luding** – where you can detour to take in **Hailuo Gou Glacier** – before heading on to **Kangding**, a former outpost on the trade route to Tibet. You can buy tickets for Chinese minibus tours to Wolong, Jiuzhai Gou, Luding, Kangding and Hailuo Gou from booths outside Chengdu train station, and tour operators in Chengdu can also arrange jeeps with English-speaking guides for ¥600–1000 per day to anywhere in the region.

From the **Emei Shan** region, there are early morning buses to Ya'an via Meishan. Jiuzhai Gou is also accessible by bus from **Guangyuan** in the northeast, on the Xi'an–Chengdu rail line (see p.941).

you'll see deep gorges spanned by no more than a spindly bridge or terrifyingly basic passenger-operated sling-and-pulley arrangement – probably as you sit on the roadside waiting for your bus to be repaired. Vehicles suffer terribly, shedding tyres and bits of chassis as they battle gradients, appalling roads, oncoming traffic and landslides. Don't count on arriving at your destination in the same bus you started in, travel light, carry enough **cash** to see you through – there are few banks – and regard the journey times we've given as a bare minimum. It's worth noting that much of the region rises above 3000m, and you might experience **altitude sickness**; see p.30 for information on this. As for the **seasons**, the area looks fantastic in spring and autumn, with rain most likely between May and October. Once the winter snows have set in, you'll need plenty of warm clothing and an infinitely flexible timetable.

Irrespective of whether you already have travel insurance, you'll almost certainly need to purchase **PICC insurance** (see p.1020) before travelling into western Sichuan, as many bus stations in the region will not sell Westerners tickets unless they can produce a PICC policy (though sometimes the fare actually incorporates the insurance). Then again, some ticket offices add a hefty surcharge or refuse to sell you a ticket even if you do produce PICC cover, and some don't care whether you have the insurance or not. Policies are available from PICC offices in Chengdu and many towns within the region.

At time of writing, all of western Sichuan – with the exception of Aba town – was open to independent travellers, including the road from Kangding to Yunnan via Zhongdian, and roads up to the Tibetan border. It must be stressed, however, that at the time of writing crossing **overland into Tibet** from Sichuan was still forbidden, and that the rules of access to western Sichuan iself change frequently: it's essential to check the latest information with the PSB before setting out.

Wolong

Covering a respectable two thousand square kilometres of high-altitude forest 140km northwest of Chengdu in the Qionglai Shan range, **Wolong Nature Reserve** was established in 1975 as the first region specifically protecting the

Wolong		
Wolong Nature Reserve	卧龙自然保护区	***wòlóng zìrán bǎohùqū***
Giant panda	大熊猫	*dàxióngmāo*
Red panda	小熊猫	*xiǎoxióngmāo*
Shawan	沙湾	*shāwān*
Wolong Binguan	卧龙宾馆	*wòlóng bīnguǎn*
Yinchang Gou	银厂沟	*yínchǎng gōu*
Yingxiong Gou	英雄沟	*yīngxióng gōu*

giant panda, black-eyed symbol of endangered species worldwide. In fact, two animals share the name panda, the other being the raccoon-sized (and probably unrelated) **red panda**, still relatively common in Sichuan. It was the latter creature to which the Nepalese term "panda" was originally applied in the West; the Chinese call the giant panda *da xiongmao*, meaning big bear-cat.

The reserve (¥20) is three hours from **Dujiangyan** (see p.939) on the daily **bus** (¥27). Once inside the highland valley which forms the bulk of the reserve, the road follows the **Pitiao River** for 35km to the **research base**, established in 1983, where you can enter pens to see red pandas (¥2) or giant pandas (¥5) surrounded by their natural habitat. Even if you *are* dedicated to tracking the creatures down in the wild, it's almost certainly the case that the captive animals here will be the only ones you encounter; researchers can spend months in the mountains at Wolong without seeing any pandas face to face.

Some 5km farther on, the road reaches **SHAWAN**, a small cluster of buildings at the park's centre. The *Wolong Binguan* (❷) here provides meals,

Panda conservation

News of **giant pandas** first reached Europe in the nineteenth century through the untiring French zoologist and traveller **Père Armand David**, who came across a skin in China in 1869. They are decidedly odd creatures, bearlike, endowed with a carnivore's teeth and a digestive tract poorly adapted to their largely vegetarian diet. Though once widespread in southwestern China, they've probably never been very common, and today their endangered status is a result of human encroachment combined with the vagaries of their preferred food – **fountain bamboo** – which periodically flowers and dies off over huge areas, leaving the animals to make do with lesser shrubs and carrion, or starve. Half of Sichuan's panda habitat was lost to logging between 1974 and 1989, which, coupled with the results of a bamboo flowering during the 1980s, has reduced the total wild population to a thousand animals, with about a hundred at Wolong and the remainder scattered through twelve other **reserves** in Sichuan, Yunnan and Guizhou.

Probably what has saved the inefficient creatures from extinction is the fact that humans find them cute – pretty much their sole evolutionary advantage. In response to the international attention their plight garnered, the Chinese government set up a panda study programme at Wolong in association with the **World Wide Fund for Nature**, accompanied by successful **breeding programmes** at Wolong and Chengdu. The government has also arrested (and sometimes executed) anyone found harming pandas. The most serious of the programmes' problems in the past have been that reserves were isolated from each other, leading to inbreeding, and were just too small to obviate the effects of the bamboo's cyclic lifestyle, though the formation of fourteen new interconnected reserves in 1995 was a step towards relieving the situation.

accommodation and basic **maps** of walking trails, while researchers at the base – who are mainly from the US – can be helpful sources of information about local conditions and hiking trails. These include fairly serious treks upstream along meagre paths through **Yingxiong Gou** (Hero Gully) or **Yinchang Gou** (Silver Mine Gully) – the latter starts some 10km from Shawan and hence is the least visited – but you shouldn't wander far from base without orienteering skills, cold-weather gear and some supplies. Once out in the wilds, **birders** can spot white- and blue-eared pheasants and the unbelievably coloured, grouse-like Temminck's tragopan; above 2000m, there are scattered groups of **golden monkeys** and near-mythical **snow leopards**, while conditions for tracking the scarce giant pandas themselves are at their best from April through to October.

To Gansu and Jiuzhai Gou

Not something to be contemplated by anyone who demands creature comforts, the trip north from Chengdu to **Songpan** and beyond to either **Gansu** Province or **Jiuzhai Gou Scenic Reserve** nevertheless offers encounters with Sichuan's lesser-known ethnic groups, as well as some superb grassland and alpine scenery. It's also true that even completing your journey can itself be something of an achievement – landslides during summer rains and winter snows are responsible for regular strandings and long detours. While Songpan is a fairly reliable eight hours from Chengdu, you should allow at least two days to reach Jiuzhai Gou, and probably a week to reach Xiahe in Gansu.

To Gansu and Jiuzhai Gou

Wenchuan	汶川	***wènchuān***
Maowen	茂汶	***màowén***
Songpan	松潘	***sōngpān***
Huanglong	黄龙	*huánglóng*
Aba Autonomous Prefecture	阿坝自治州	***ābà zìzhì zhōu***
Barkam	马尔康	*mǎěr kāng*
Langmusi	郎木寺	*lángmùsì*
Zöigê	诺尔盖	*nuòěr gài*
Jiuzhai Gou	九寨沟	***jiǔzhàigōu***
Nuorilang	诺日朗	*nuòrì láng*
Primeval Forest	原始森林	*yuánshǐ sēnlín*
Rize	日则	*rìzé*
Shuzheng	树正	*shùzhèng*
Zechawa	则查洼	*zéchá wā*
Accommodation		
Hongye Binguan	红叶宾馆	***hóngyè bīnguǎn***
Linye Binguan	林叶宾馆	*línyè bīnguǎn*
Songzhou Binguan	松州宾馆	*sōngzhōu bīnguǎn*
Yangdong Zhaodaisuo	羊峒招待所	*yángdòng zhāodàisuǒ*
Zhenzhu Binguan	真主宾馆	*zhēnzhǔ bīnguǎn*

Considering the effort involved in getting there, coupled with the hefty entrance fee, those heading to Jiuzhai Gou will also want to spend at least three days on site, and need to take its status as a "Scenic Reserve" literally. While inaccessible corners are very wild indeed, the surfaced main roads and dolled-up Tibetan villages can be something of an anticlimax – it's scenery, and not a wilderness experience, which is provided here. For the genuine thing, you may be happier skipping Jiuzhai Gou in favour of **horse trekking** around Songpan.

Chengdu to Songpan

An hour north of Chengdu the mountains rise up, forcing the road into a deep gully alongside the fast-flowing Min River. At the small town of **WENCHUAN**, a road forks northwest to the towns of **Barkam** and **Zöigê** in the Aba Grasslands (see p.975), used as an alternative, very roundabout bad-weather route to Songpan. Wenchuan itself sports strips of the old town walls above the bus station, while up on the hills you'll see the distinctive rectangular split stone houses and forty-metre-high watchtowers of the **Qiang**, who tend the apple and walnut groves lining the roadside. A close look at the houses reveals flat roofs covered in earth for winter insulation, their eaves hung with long bunches of drying corn cobs. The Qiang themselves are easily identifiable: most rural Sichuanese wear white headscarves – in mourning, they say, for the popular *Three Kingdoms* minister Zhuge Liang – but the Qiang, who were persecuted by Zhuge, generally wear black turbans instead, while the women dress in broad, embroidered jackets with split skirts. The Qiang pick Sichuan peppercorns as a cash crop off the small, spiky shrubs which grow wild in the hills here, but it's when the orchards are in bloom in May that the valley is at its best, while July brings a glut of fruit to local markets.

Back on the main Songpan road, the next substantial town is 50km farther on at **MAOWEN**, whose simple main street contains a Tibetan stupa and several Hui restaurants, recognizable by Arabic script over their doorways or paintings of an idealized Mecca on the walls, which serve breakfasts of rice porridge and buns. In fact, the town is better known as a Qiang stronghold, though there's little evidence of this. Should you get delayed here, the **hotel** at the bus depot has cheap dormitory beds, or you might be allowed to sleep aboard the bus.

North of Maowen the landscape becomes sombre; felled logs cut far upstream wash ashore or tumble in the current, while the steep slopes, long stripped of timber, are notoriously unstable despite some attempts at reafforestation and terracing. **Landslides** aside, the bus can also be held up, literally, by farmers needing help in towing their bogged tractors. Closer to Songpan, there's a sudden rash of new timber and stone houses built in an attractively loose interpretation of the local style, their red-tiled roofs proudly topped by satellite dishes.

Songpan

SONGPAN was founded as a Qing garrison town straddling the Min River, 220km north of Chengdu, and three of its massive stone gateways still stand. From up on top of the North Gate, the town's dark-tiled rooftops look rather gloomy, though over in the northeastern quarter the bright colours of the **mosque** are an exception (Songpan has a substantial Muslim population). It's not a large town, and dogs, chickens and horses roam the kilometre-long main street, which runs down to the **South Gate** past the ramshackle wooden fronts of cheap **restaurants** and shops selling Qiang and Tibetan clothes, ornate knives, horsetail switches, fox pelts, decorated ram skulls and jewellery. Tibetan couples wander around shopping, men casually dressed in capes and felt hats, women wearing silver bracelets, red scarves and chunky amber necklaces. About a third of the way down there's a **crossroads** and several department stores stocked with essentials; turn left for the **East Gate**, now pretty well worn, and out of town. Farther along the main street, the narrow Min River is spanned by the open-sided cloister of an attractive **all-weather bridge**, whose roof, corners drawn out into long points, is embellished with painted dragon, bear and flower carvings.

The reason most people stop in Songpan is to spend a few days **horse trekking** through the surrounding hills; although the horses are unevenly tempered, the experience, taking in out-of-the-way lakes, waterfalls and gorges, is certainly worth the money. There are at least two competing businesses with similar standards, and you'll probably encounter touts offering their services on the bus here. Accommodation is in tents and the guides are attentive, though prepare for extreme cold and tasteless food; some groups have bought and slaughtered a goat (¥200) to bolster rations. Expect to pay around ¥60 per person per day, which includes everything except fees to enter the reserve (around ¥70 extra); padded jackets are available for winter nights. The friendly veneer of staff at these horse-trekking companies disappears rapidly if they're presented with a complaint, so be sure to agree beforehand on exactly what your money is buying.

Practicalities

Songpan's **bus station** is at the north of town. From here, turn right onto the main street, continue on 50m and the *Songzhou Binguan* (❷) is on the right. Alternatively, follow the street opposite the bus station for similar prices and facilities at the *Linye Binguan*. Slightly better value are the dorms and basic rooms at the *Songpan Fandian* (Ⓣ0837/7232531; ❶) a further 100m past the *Songzhou*. Hot water at all these places is available for a few hours in the evening. A slightly more upmarket experience – though, like everyone else in town, you won't see hot water for much of the day – is available at the *Songpan Binguan* (❸), 200m beyond the *Linye*. Hotel **restaurants** serve meals as good as any in town, and main-street stalls sell noodle soups and highly spiced **yak**.

Moving on from Songpan, don't be too discouraged by poor weather, as this is often localized. When the roads are open, there are up to three buses weekly northwest to Zöigê, en route to Gansu, and daily buses to Jiuzhai Gou. In summer only, there's also erratic transport along poor roads to **Huanglong** – a smaller, isolated version of Jiuzhai Gou some 50km northeast of Songpan via **Yuanba**.

The Aba Grasslands, Zöigê and on to Gansu

Songpan sits just east of the vast, marshy **Aba Autonomous Prefecture**, which sprawls over the Sichuan, Gansu and Qinghai borders. Resting at around 3500m and draining directly into the convoluted headwaters of the Yellow River, the **Aba Grasslands** are the domain of the strongly independent-minded **Goloks**, a nomadic group of herders. The region enjoys infamy in China for the losses the Red Army sustained here during their Long March, at the mercy of Golok snipers and the waterlogged, shelterless terrain, but it's also a **Bonpo** stronghold (see box, opposite) and something of a corridor between Sichuan and Gansu province.

Bon

Scattered through Sichuan's northwestern reaches, the **Bonpo** represent the last adherents to Tibet's native religion, **Bon**, before it fused with Buddhist ideas to form Lamaism. A shamanist faith founded by **Gcen-rabs**, one of eighteen saints sent to clear the kingdom of demons, Bon lost influence in Tibet after 755 AD, when the Tibetan royalty began to favour the more spiritual doctrines of Buddhism. As Yellow-hat Sect Lamaism developed and became the dominant faith, the Bonpo were forced out to the borders of Tibet, where the religion survives today.

Though to outsiders Bon is superficially similar to Lamaism – so much so that it's often considered a subsect – the two religions are, in many respects, directly opposed. Bonpo circuit their stupas anti-clockwise, use black where Lamas would use white, and still have rituals reflecting **animal sacrifice**. Because of this last feature, both the Chinese government and Lamas tend to view Bon as a barbaric, backward belief, and Bonpo are often not keen to be approached or identified as such. Bon monasteries survive at Huanglong and several towns in the central Aba Grasslands.

The most direct route across the region is by road to the grasslands' northernmost edge at **Zöigê**, 150km northwest of Songpan. About 150km northwest of Wenchuan, off the Zöigê road, the regional capital, **Barkam**, sports the **Baisha Monastery**, with its splendid Sutra Hall, while 200km due west of Songpan, the simple **Gemo Temple** sits near the town of **Aba** – officially closed to foreigners – on the Qinghai border. You'll find only basic accommodation and food along the way, and irregular buses whose drivers may be reluctant to let you on board, but, especially if you're discouraged by Juizhai Gou's hype, the area is at least refreshingly uncommercialized.

Zöigê and beyond

ZÖIGÊ is a drab collection of buildings enlivened during the June/July **horse races**, when horsemen set up tents outside the town and show off their riding skills to the crowds. Markets here occasionally display **medicinal oddities**, such as deer musk, the lung- and kidney-strengthening orange caterpillar fungus, and a cough medicine derived from fritillary bulbs, but Zöigê can also be an intimidating place. Dreadlocked, knife-wielding Goloks ride motorcycles down the main street, and people trying to hitch from here to Xiahe have been threatened after turning down the outrageous prices asked by truck drivers. There are several **places to stay** – the *Liangju Binguan* (❶) is recommended – and two **bus stations** with a daily morning bus to Songpan and another to **Hezuo** in Gansu (see p.1037), a couple of hours short of Xiahe. Buy your ticket the day before and get to the station in plenty of time, as schedules are not always respected.

Langmusi

Just off the road to Hezuo, three hours from Zöigê, you'll find the beautiful village of **LANGMUSI**, populated by Huis, Goloks and Tibetans, whose mountain scenery and lamaseries are beginning to attract the attention of travellers – certainly the place gives an easy taster of Tibet. There's no direct bus service; in Zöigê, buy a ticket for "Langmu qiaotou" and the Hezuo-bound bus will drop you at an intersection where jeeps wait to take you the 3km to the village itself (¥2 after negotiation). The jeep drops you at the village square where the very basic dorms and rooms at *Langmusi Hotel* and *Langmusi Guesthouse* await (❶). The hotel has slightly better dorms and more amiable staff. Both places feature acceptable toilets, warm water in the evening, and monks and kids who show little respect for your personal space. A third place to stay, the *White Dragon Hotel*, has just opened nearby and offers the same deal (❶), though the owner claims the rooms are soon to be renovated.

With two lamaseries, a mosque and good walking in the hills around – though don't anger locals by stumbling through the **sky burial ground** to the west, where the bodies of the dead are left on hilltops for birds of prey to devour – there's plenty to keep you for a few days. Don't leave without eating at *Lesha's*, a small traveller-style **café** close to the hotels, whose owner whips up a great apple pie. Leaving, there is one direct bus to Hezuo from the village at 7am, though big noses are charged double. Otherwise you'll have to get a ride to the intersection, and hope to catch a bus going your way; one or two pass daily any time between 11am and 2.30pm.

Jiuzhai Gou

Deep in the heart of the 4500-metre-high, perpetually snow-clad Min Shan Range, **Jiuzhai Gou Scenic Reserve** encloses one of provincial China's most spectacular landscapes. It was settled centuries ago by Tibetans, whose fenced villages gave Jiuzhai Gou (Nine Stockades' Gully) its name, and legend has it that the goddess **Semo** accidentally smashed her mirror here, the shards forming the hundred or so impossibly vivid blue **lakes** which descend the valley in a series of broad steps. The park was created back in 1978 and, beneath a veneer of intense tourism, traditional life continues – yaks are still herded, prayer wheels turn in the streams, and shrines adorned with prayer flags protect unstable cliffs against further slips. **Wildlife** abounds, too, and the authorities seem keen to keep it that way, with litter bins at popular spots and signs at the park gates warning against "shooting or hitting animals". Beneficiaries of this policy include shy rarities such as giant pandas and the obscure, bison-like **takin**. More obviously, the lakes swarm with fish and birds including waterfowl, kingfishers, shrikes, wagtails, hoopoes and pheasants.

All places to stay in the reserve have some sort of restaurant either on site or nearby, though few have anything but a basin to wash in. **Supplies** – snacks, drinks and films – are expensive, and **meals** on offer at accommodation and a few simple township canteens palatable but on the small side, so bring essentials with you from Songpan or Chengdu. **Warm clothing** is a must throughout the year with daytime temperatures ranging from 16°C in July to minus 4°C in January, though it can be surprisingly hot in the valleys at midday. Don't leave marked trails without good orienteering skills, a **first-aid kit** and adequate supplies. Finally, if you're expecting a quiet commune with nature, be warned that the place is extremely popular with local tourists, so try to avoid coming here on weekends and holidays.

The scenic reserve

Jiuzhai Gou's **layout** is simple. The valleys form a north-orientated Y-shape, with the **entrance** gates at southern **Jiuzhai Gou town**. The most convenient base is in the centre of the park at **Nuorilang**, a township some 14km south of the entrance and below **Semo Shan**, where roads head off 18km or so to **Long Lake** or the **Primeval Forest**. Either option takes in some fine scenery, with a couple of villages along the way offering further basic accommodation. For the more adventurous, gullies and forests head up into the hills, and camping is certainly an option, though not officially sanctioned – mainly because of the risk of forest fires.

After the journey along the 105-kilometre Songpan–Jiuzhai Gou road with its fine mountain scenery, yaks grazing in alpine meadows, and conifers and sharp-edged ranges covered in snow, arrival at **JIUZHAI GOU** township is a huge disappointment – the surrounding hills have been clear-logged to provide materials for an ugly sprinkling of expensive concrete and tile hotels. Nor is there much joy at the **park gates**, where you're obliged to cough up the stiff **entry fee** (¥108; includes a night's dormitory accommodation) and buy the bus pass to use the local transport (¥70; valid for two days). The long-distance **bus depot** is just back off the main road, and you should buy your return tickets well in advance, before you go into the park, to be sure of a seat out on the daily service back to Songpan and Chengdu. There are kiosks selling **maps** and snacks at the gates, and regular minibuses to Nuorilang, the Primeval Forest and Long Lake. For **accommodation** here, the *Yangdong Zhaodaisuo* (❸) has pricey rooms and unreliable hot water; try the attentive, clean *Hongye* (❷) instead.

To Nuorilang

It's worth doing the four-hour **hike** from the park gates to Nuorilang. The road follows a stream uphill through groves of pine, soon passing the gateway to **Zaru Temple** on the left, a wooden structure with cliffs rising behind. Farther along is Heye village, where the stream drains out of a marshy tract known as **Reed Lake**. This in turn is fed by the more substantial **Shuzheng lakes**, the largest group in the reserve and, with **Dege Shan** rising behind, also the most impressive, particularly in autumn when red stands of **maple** contrast brilliantly with the waterfalls, pine and mountain scenery. Just over halfway along, where the twenty-metre **Shuzheng Falls** squeeze between the road and a wooded island, **Shuzheng village** is a good place to stop and play tourist – there's also a basic **hotel** here (❶). Tibetan men offer photo sessions on horseback, women and girls sell knives, jewellery and ethnic clothing, and a group of "typical" Tibetan dwellings sits on the lakeshore, the cabins crowded by a water-powered millstone and a decorative but empty **prayer wheel** – it should contain ten thousand written prayers which are "spoken" when tumbled around inside the rotating drum. Head about 500m up the road towards **Rhinoceros Lake**, however, and there's another wheel emblazoned with a *savastika*, the lack of tourists suggesting that it's not for show.

Nuorilang, the Primeval Forest and Long Lake

Another 4km from Rhinocerous Lake, **NUORILANG** consists simply of a restaurant, two stores and Jiuzhai Gou's most famous cascades, the **Nuorilang Falls**. Often dry in the late afternoon as water is redirected for other purposes, in full flow they look best from the road, framed by trees as water forks down over the strange, yellow crystalline rock faces. There's a **hostel** (❷) left at the fork and about 200m along, though accommodation twenty minutes further on at Zechawa (see p.978) is better.

The road forks east and west at Nuorilang, either direction offering a full day's return hike (around 36km). Heading east takes you to the **Primeval Forest** via **Pearl Beach Falls**, where a whole hillside has calcified into an ankle-deep cascade ending in a ten-metre waterfall similar to Nuorilang's, and to **Panda-Arrow Bamboo Lake**, a shallow affair whose optimistic name has long been out of date in such a heavily grazed valley. There's another, rather mysterious reference to pandas at the halfway point, **Rize village**, a settlement consisting of a road maintainence depot, a very under-used hostel, and a large, firmly locked hall whose dusty entrance is capped by the legend "**Panda Hospital**". As residents are apt to deny the building's very existence, it's unclear whether the facilities are for unlucky hikers or injured beasts. The scenery slacks off for a while after Rize, as the road climbs through a pass to **Grass Lake** and then follows the left-hand stream into the **Primeval Forest**, a dense and very atmospheric belt of conifers. A discreetly placed tent here would allow a full day exploring the area.

The slightly longer road from Nuorilang to **Long Lake** is, on the whole, less interesting and so less frequented by tour buses. Not far along is **Zechawa village** and the *Zhenzhu Binguan* (❷) and store. After this there's little to see until near the end at the stunning **Five-coloured Lake** which, for sheer intensity, if not scale, is unequalled in the park. Superlatives continue at the road's end, where the mundanely named **Long Lake** is both exactly that and, at 3103m, Jiuzhai Gou's highest body of water.

The far west: Chengdu to Tibet

The main road **west of Chengdu** still follows an ancient **trade route** between China and Tibet. Porters, weighed down with compressed blocks of tea, once made the three-week journey over the mountains from Ya'an to the town of Kangding, where their loads were exchanged for Tibetan wool. The first **Europeans** through here were French Catholic organizations in the 1850s, who spread Christianity among the Tibetan, Yi and Qiang populace. Many of their **churches** survive today, though by the late 1920s political instabilities had forced the foreigners away. As early as 1893, when Britain defined Tibet's borders at the **Sikkim Convention**, China's claims to rule Tibet – which it had nominally done since the Mongol invasions some six hundred years earlier – were being seriously undermined. Following the British invasion in 1904, the Chinese government sent troops into eastern Tibet, destroying monasteries and evicting the Dalai Lama. The Qing empire fell soon afterwards, however, and Lhasa regained the disputed territory. In 1929 the Nationalists tried once again to establish Chinese control by creating **Xikang**

The far west

Batang	巴塘	*bātáng*
Dêgê	德格	*dégé*
Garzê	甘孜	*gānzī*
Kangding	康定	*kāngdìng*
Anjue Si	安觉寺	*ānjué sì*
Kangding Guesthouse	康定宾馆	*kāngdìng bīnguǎn*
Paoma Binguan	跑马宾馆	*pǎomǎ bīnguǎn*
Paoma Shan	跑马山	*pǎomǎ shān*
Litang	理塘	*lǐtáng*
Luding	泸定	*lùdìng*
Moxi Xiang	磨西乡	*móxī xiāng*
Gongga Shan	贡嘎山	*gònggā shān*
Hailuo Gou Glacier Park	海螺沟公园	*hǎiluógōu gōngyuán*
Ya'an	雅安	*yǎān*

province. Stretching from Ya'an through to within 200km of Lhasa, Xikang's presence on paper did little to alter the real situation. Divided itself, China was unable to counter rival claims from Tibet or control its own unruly forces in the province. With a capital moving ever east from Batang to Kangding and finally Ya'an, Xikang remained effectively independent for over two decades, surviving until five years after the border issue was made redundant by China's annexation of Tibet in 1950.

The journey from Chengdu's Xinnanmen bus station to Kangding is long but straightforward, worth some discomfort to reach the **Hailuo Gou Glacier** in the foothills of the mighty **Gongga Shan** – you can also get here in a full day **from Xichang** via Shimian (see p.951). En route there's a tangible monument to the efforts of the Long March at **Luding**, and the monasteries, people and frontier atmosphere of **Kangding** itself. Beyond Kangding, it may well be possible to visit towns right up to the Tibetan frontier, though continuing **overland to Tibet** is not permitted for foreigners at present (see pp.1122–1124).

Roads in this region are closed frequently in winter; if open, progress will be slow, and supplies limited. After dry spells, winds can sometimes whip up clouds of dust along the valleys, ruining the views and muting colours. **Distances and times** can be confusing – Ya'an, for instance, is halfway between Chengdu and Kangding as the crow flies, but barely a third of the way as far as journey time is concerned – and downhill return legs can be considerably quicker than outward travel uphill. Prices for the same stretches can also vary from bus to bus, so fares quoted may contradict each other.

Ya'an and Luding

First stop on the journey west is the town of **YA'AN**, which sits on the banks of the Qingyi River below Erlang Shan, five hours by bus from Chengdu or Emei across the flat Red Basin. Originally a garrisoned staging post on the trail to Tibet, and briefly the capital of Xikang before its dissolution in 1955, today Ya'an has ambition. The approach road tunnels through a hillside and on to an empty plain, where an isolated colonnade of tall street lights, the first stage of a massive urban expansion project, flank the highway into town. There's nothing to see here, but buses always pull in for a meal.

Luding

For travellers heading towards Hailuo Gou Glacier, the scruffy, two-street market town of **LUDING** marks a half-day hiatus between buses, with plenty of time to soak up some history at the **Luding Bridge**, one of the great icons of the Long March. In May 1935, the Red Army reached Anshunchang on the southern side of the Dadu River but were unable to cross the rapids there. Pressured by enemy troops, they decided to head upstream to where a nominal Guomindang force, baulking at destroying the only crossing for hundreds of kilometres, had pulled the decking off the Luding suspension bridge, but left the chains intact. On a forced march, the Communists covered the 100km to Luding in just two days, where 22 **heroes** braved heavy fire to climb hand-over-hand across the chains and take Guomindang emplacements on the west bank. Official accounts say that only three men were killed.

Though substantial by local standards, the bridge is simply a series of thirteen heavy-gauge chains spanned by planks which look as if they might have been pirated from a packing crate. The Dadu flows roughly below, while temple-style gates and ornaments at either end lend the bridge an almost religious aspect. On the near side is a ticket office (¥1) and a gold-lettered tablet detailing the events of May 29, 1935, while a pavilion on the far side houses a **museum** with period photos.

There's precious little to see in the town itself, though it's full of nondescript places to **eat** and so busy in spring that an overflow of produce from stalls has to be laid out on sheets in the narrow main street. For **accommodation**, try the comfortable *Yagudu Hotel* and **restaurant** (❶), where they don't speak a word of English, despite a scattering of signs, or there's a choice of cheaper rooms, such as the polite *Luhe Zhaodaisuo* (❶), to the right of the bus station. **Moving on**, there are at least daily buses to Kangding (¥10), Shimian (for Xichang; ¥10) and Chengdu (¥90). For Moxi (for Hailuo Gou), a private service leaves from outside the bus station (¥15); you'll need to change buses at Hongqiao.

Moxi Xiang and the Hailuo Gou Glacier

Tracks etched along the cliffs between Luding and Moxi Xiang are barely wide enough for the two-way traffic that uses them, and frequent, heart-stopping encounters with logging trucks tend to focus your attention on the **scenery** far below: timber mills, people pole-net fishing in the river, deep gorges spanned by vestigial footbridges, and Qiang wandering around their stone villages, black robes set off by violent pink sashes.

Surrounded by fields of barley and maize, the upper-valley village of **MOXI XIANG** comprises a single street of closely stacked dark wooden shops selling karaoke ghetto-blasters and other modern necessities. Just left off the street, there's a small **Catholic Church** built in the 1920s, whose blue and yellow bell tower overlooks a European, box-like main building, its eaves pinched as a concession to local aesthetics. After the action at Luding, Mao and the Red Army rested up in Moxi Xiang before heading off on a 56-kilometre trek north to Xiaojin over **Jiajin Shan**, through the "land of everlasting snow". Hundreds died of exposure and altitude sickness, and Mao himself was stretcher-ridden. Few visitors today attempt anything so strenuous, most using the town simply as a base camp for the trip to **Hailuo Gou Glacier**, whose trails start immediately beyond. The bus pulls in at a pleasant **guesthouse** (❶), a creaking wooden structure with views down the valley from the upper rooms, though the toilets out back are a bit distant if they put you on the top floor; just a bit up the road, *Hailuo Gou Binguan* (❷) has decent rooms and hot water. Glacier practicalities can be arranged either at your accommodation or one of the **restaurants** up the road. Transport back to Luding leaves between 6am and noon.

Gongga Shan and the Hailuo Gou Glacier

The highest point in western China, and only 1300m lower than Everest, **Gongga Shan**, known locally as Minya Konka, rises to 7556m behind Moxi Xiang, a stunning sight on the rare mornings when the near constant cloud cover and haze of wind-driven snow above the peak suddenly clear. Hailuo Gou Glacier is the lowest of four descending the mountain, carving out **Conch Gully** as it extends right down to the treeline, some 13km from Moxi inside **Hailuo Gou Glacier Park** (¥60). With the terrain and the three-thousand-metre altitude making for slow and steady hiking, at least three days is recommended for the return trip to the glacier, though the unexpectedly thick forests and alpine scenery, not to mention the glacier itself – a tongue of blue-white ice scattered with boulders and black gravel – are spellbinding, and might make you linger. Basic **meals and accommodation** are available along the way, or you can pitch a tent at one of the three **campsites**.

Guides can be hired in Moxi Xiang from ¥50 per day, though with well-marked trails through the park they're not necessary in warmer months – your entry fee into the park includes a guide from the last camp to the glacier itself anyway. You should take some energy food, good footwear and warm, padded clothing whatever the time of the year. Just up the road from Moxi, a cluster of stalls surrounds the **park gates**. The **first camp** is 10km (3hr) farther on and there are **hot springs**, hostel accommodation and kiosks both here and 5km (2hr) up the valley at the **second camp**, where rhododendron bushes finally give way to forest proper. You could easily forget about the glacier for a while and spend a day exploring here, though it's only another 5km (two hours) to the trail head at **camp three**, a relatively substantial affair with orange, four-person "chalet" dorms (beds ¥30) offering basic protection from the elements. Here you pick up your guide for the last 2km from the camp to the **viewing platform** and out along the glacier itself, which takes several hours to explore properly.

Kangding and beyond

Even before you arrive in town, it's not hard to see why **KANGDING**, 60km west of Luding, is portrayed as one of the wildest settlements in China, nor why the government had such a tough time controlling the region until the 1950s. The walls of **Daxue Shan** (the Great Snowy Mountains) rise immediately beyond the town and, whatever the maps might say, this is where Tibet really begins.

An ugly collection of concrete apartments and dark-roofed houses carelessly arranged along the fast-flowing **Zhepuo River**, Kangding is still very much a nexus between cultures. As the capital of the **Ganzi Tibetan Region**, Kangding is thick with government staff, recently arrived Hui, and tough-looking **Khambas** – eastern Tibetan "cowboys" – here to buy supplies, while valley slopes above town are dotted with monasteries and bulbous white *chortens* (Tibetan pagodas).

Though tea is no longer the prime currency, **trade** is still Kangding's lifeblood, and the central streets bustle with activity. On the east bank, there's a produce market in the rickety alleys near the **mosque**'s blue gate, shops sell Persian rugs, religious attire and finely ornamented knives grouped around the public square on the far bank, with wares piled high on collapsible beds being scrutinized by Tibetans sporting straw hats and chunky turquoise jewellery. Over the second bridge, **Anjue Si** is a quietly busy collection of courtyards and Tibetan shrines over on the west bank, whose monks are tolerant of tourists wandering around. East above town, the upper slopes of **Paoma Shan** – look for the transmitter tower – host a couple more small temples and a **horse-race festival** in the middle of the fourth lunar month. The steps up are opposite the mosque on Dong Dajie.

Practicalities

Kangding's **bus station** is north of town. Turn right and follow the street south for a couple of minutes past several **canteens** – and yaks foraging in dustbins – to the river's east bank; a high street and an associated network of back lanes run south through town on either side of the flow, linked by three bridges.

The cheapest **place to stay** is the **hostel** attached to Anjue Si (❶); behind, on Guangming Lu, there's poor value at the blue-glassed *Kangding Binguan* (☎0836/23137; doubles with/without bathroom ❸/❶) and better facilities nearby at *Paoma Binguan* (❹). For **food** there are a couple of cake shops and plenty of canteens staffed by white-capped Hui where you can fill up on *mantou* or a bowl of *lamien* (pulled noodles) and coriander soup. The best **breakfast** is eaten early with the locals at market stalls: Tibetan **butter tea**, noodle soup, *shaomai* and fried dough coils spiced with mince and wild pepper. **Leaving**, there are early morning departures at least as far as Chengdu, Shimian, Litang and Garzê, but you'll find it hard to buy tickets at the bus station; get there at dawn and approach drivers or conductors direct. Vehicles leave for Luding throughout the day, whenever full.

Kangding to Tibet

Two routes head west from Kangding over the mountains to where the Jinsha River, the upper reaches of the Yangzi, marks China's border with Tibet. Though the roads to the border were open at the time of writing, the fact that they link up on the far side and press right **through to Lhasa** is an academic one for foreigners. Rules come and go, but for the present trying to cross the Tibetan border is a guarantee of being pulled off the bus and booted back the way you came by the PSB. Political considerations aside, authorities are not simply being obstructive: these are some of the world's most dangerous roads, high, riven by gorges and permanently snowbound, and the Chinese government is not keen to have tourists extend the list of people killed in bus crashes along the way. What might make it worth the risk is that the journey takes you within sight of the world's highest unclimbed mountain ranges, and even those hardened by stints in the Himalayas have reported the scenery as staggeringly beautiful.

There's plenty to explore without annoying the authorities, however. On the **southern route**, destinations include **Litang**, where there's a monastery and a newly opened back road south **to Zhongdian** in Yunnan (p.890); and the border town of **Batang**, once a headquarters for various Christian missions and capital of Xikang. On the longer **northern route**, **Garzê** is a valley town surrounded by mountains and chessboard fields, where the Communist leader **Zhang Guotao** formed a short-lived splinter government after differences between himself and Mao erupted during the Long March in 1935. Closer to the border, **Dêgê** is famous for its functioning **scripture printing lamasery**, where you can still watch monks mass-producing religious texts from woodblocks.

Travel details

Trains

Chengdu to: Beijing (4 daily; 36hr); Chongqing (5 daily; 12hr); Emei (6 daily; 3hr); Guangyuan (12 daily; 7hr); Guangzhou (2 daily; 46hr); Guiyang (2 daily; 18hr); Kunming (2 daily; 22hr); Mianyang (12 daily; 2hr 30min); Panzhihua (5 daily; 14hr); Shanghai (2 daily; 40hr); Xi'an (8 daily; 16hr); Xichang (6 daily; 11hr).

Chongqing to: Beijing (daily, 32hr); Chengdu (5 daily; 12hr); Guangzhou (5 daily, 40hr); Guiyang (5 daily; 12hr); Shanghai (2 daily; 35hr); Wuhan (daily; 24hr).

Emei to: Chengdu (6 daily; 3hr); Kunming (2 daily; 19hr); Panzhihua (6 daily; 11hr); Xichang (6 daily; 5hr).

Buses

Chengdu to: Chongqing (8hr); Dujiangyan (1hr 30min); Emei (5hr); Guanghan (50min); Guangyuan (10hr); Jiuzhai Gou (36hr); Kangding (14–24hr); Leshan (5hr); Luding (12–19hr); Meishan (3hr); Mianyang (5hr); Songpan (8hr); Xichang (15hr); Xindu (30min); Ya'an (5hr); Yibin (8hr); Zigong (6hr).

Chongqing to: Chengdu (8hr); Dazu (7hr); Yibin

(6hr); Zigong (4hr).
Dujiangyan to: Chengdu (1hr 30min); Chongqing (10hr); Guanghan (1hr 30min); Leshan (7hr); Qingcheng Shan (45min); Songpan (7hr); Wenchuan (4hr); Wolong (3hr).
Emei to: Chengdu (5hr); Leshan (90min); Xichang (10hr); Ya'an (3hr).
Leshan to: Chengdu (4hr); Chongqing (6hr); Emei (90min); Xichang (10hr); Yibin (6hr); Zigong (3hr 30min).
Xichang to: Chengdu (15hr); Panzhihua (6hr); Shimian (6hr).
Yibin to: Chengdu (8hr); Chongqing (6hr); Gongxian (2hr 15min); Zigong (2hr 30min).
Zigong to: Chengdu (6hr); Chongqing (4hr); Leshan (3hr 30min); Yibin (2hr 30min).

Ferries

Chongqing to: Wanxian (daily; 12hr); Wuhan (daily; 3 days); Yibin (2hr); Yichang (daily; 16hr by hydrofoil, 48hr conventional ferry).

Flights

Besides the domestic flights listed, there are flights from Chengdu to Bangkok and Singapore.
Chengdu to: Beijing (12 daily; 2hr); Chongqing (9 daily; 45min); Guangzhou (10 daily; 2hr); Guilin (3 weekly; 1hr 20min); Guiyang (1 daily; 1hr); Hong Kong (7 weekly; 2hr); Kunming (5 daily; 90min); Lhasa (2 daily; 1hr 50min); Shanghai (2 daily; 2hr 15min); Xi'an (6 weekly; 1hr 10min).
Chongqing to: Beijing (2 daily; 2hr); Chengdu (9 daily; 45min); Guangzhou (5 daily; 90min); Guilin (daily; 55min); Hong Kong (5 weekly; 1hr 50min); Kunming (1 daily; 1hr 10min); Shanghai (2 daily; 2hr); Xi'an (2 weekly; 1hr).

CHAPTER 13 Highlights

* **The grasslands** Explore the rolling green horizons of Inner Mongolia's "grass sea" on horseback, and sleep in a Mongol yurt. **See p.1000**

* **Genghis Khan's Mausoleum** A surreal Japanese-planned, Chinese-executed monument to the cult of Genghis Khan – though he probably isn't even buried here. **See p.1008**

* **Labrang Monastery** The most imposing Lamaist monastery outside of Tibet, set in a beautiful mountain valley. **See p.1034**

* **Jiayuguan Fort** Stronghold at the western end of the Great Wall, symbolically marking the end of China proper. **See p.1045**

* **Mogao Caves** Unbelievable collection of Buddhist grottoes and sculptures, carved into a desert gorge a millennium ago. **See p.1050**

* **Qinghai Hu** China's largest salt lake is a magnet for migrating and wintering waterfowl, including the rare black-necked crane. **See p.1063**

* **Turpan** Relax under grape trellises or investigate Muslim Uigur culture and ancient Silk Road relics, such as the ruins of Jiaohe. **See p.1073**

* **Tian Chi** An alpine lake surrounded by meadows and snow-covered mountains, home to a Kazakh population. **See p.1083**

* **Kashgar's Sunday Market** Join crowds bargaining for goats, carpets, knives, and exotic spices in China's most westerly city. **See p.1103**

13

The Northwest

Reaching across in a giant arc from the fringes of eastern Siberia to the borders of Turkic Central Asia, the provinces of Inner Mongolia, Ningxia, Gansu, Qinghai and Xinjiang account for an entire third of China's land area. Compressing so vast a region into a single chapter of a guidebook may seem something of a travesty – but at least it is based on a perception that originates from China itself, that these territories lie largely beyond the Great Wall. To ancient Chinese thinking the whole region is remote, subject to extremes of weather and populated by non-Chinese-speaking "barbarians" who are, quite literally, the peoples from beyond the pale – *zhai wai ren*. It is here, thinly scattered through the vast areas of steppe and grassland, desert and mountain plateau, that the bulk of China's **ethnic minorities** still live. Out of deference to these, Inner Mongolia, Ningxia and Xinjiang are officially not provinces at all, but so-called **Autonomous Regions**, for the Mongol, Hui and Uigur peoples respectively.

However, a **Chinese presence** in the area is not new. Imperial armies were already in control of virtually the whole northwest region by the time of the Han dynasty two thousand years ago and since then Gansu, Ningxia and the eastern part of Qinghai have become Chinese almost to the core. The uncultivatable plains of Inner Mongolia have been intimately bound up with China since Genghis Khan created his great empire in the early thirteenth century, and even Xinjiang has always found itself drawn back into the Chinese sphere after repeatedly breaking free.

Today the relatively unrestricted use of **local languages** and **local religions** in all these areas could be taken as a sign of China's desire to **nurture patriotism** in the minority peoples, and regain some of the sympathy lost during disastrous repressions both under communism and in previous eras. Furthermore, in economic terms, there is a clear transfer of wealth, in the form of industrial and agricultural aid, from the richer areas of eastern China to the poorer, outer fringes of the country. On the other hand, the degree of actual autonomy in the "autonomous" regions is strictly controlled, and relations between Han China and these more remote corners of the empire remain fractious in places. **Dissent** on the part of the Uigurs of Xinjiang, for example, has shown itself as recently as the 1990s, when there were large-scale city riots in Kashgar.

Organized tourism across the Northwest has boomed in recent years, focusing particularly on the **Silk Road**, a series of historic towns and ruins running from Xi'an in Shaanxi Province, through Ningxia, Gansu and Xinjiang, and eventually on into Central Asia. The Northwest also offers possibilities for enjoying the last great remaining **wildernesses** of China – the

grasslands, mountains, lakes and deserts of the interior – far from the teeming population centres of the east. For this, there is perhaps no better place to start than **Inner Mongolia**'s famous **grasslands**, on which Genghis Khan trained his cavalry and where nomads on horseback still live today. As well as visiting the supposed **tomb of Genghis Khan**, outside Dongsheng, it's also possible, in places, to catch a glimpse of the Mongols' ancient and unique way of life, packaged for tourists to a greater or lesser degree depending on how far off the beaten track you are willing to travel. You can sleep in a nomad's yurt, sample Mongol food and ride a horse across the grasslands, all within half a day's train journey from Beijing.

The other great natural feature of Inner Mongolia is the Yellow River, which detours north into the region from tiny, rural **Ningxia**. Here, at the resort of **Shapotou**, you can witness the spectacle of a mighty river running between

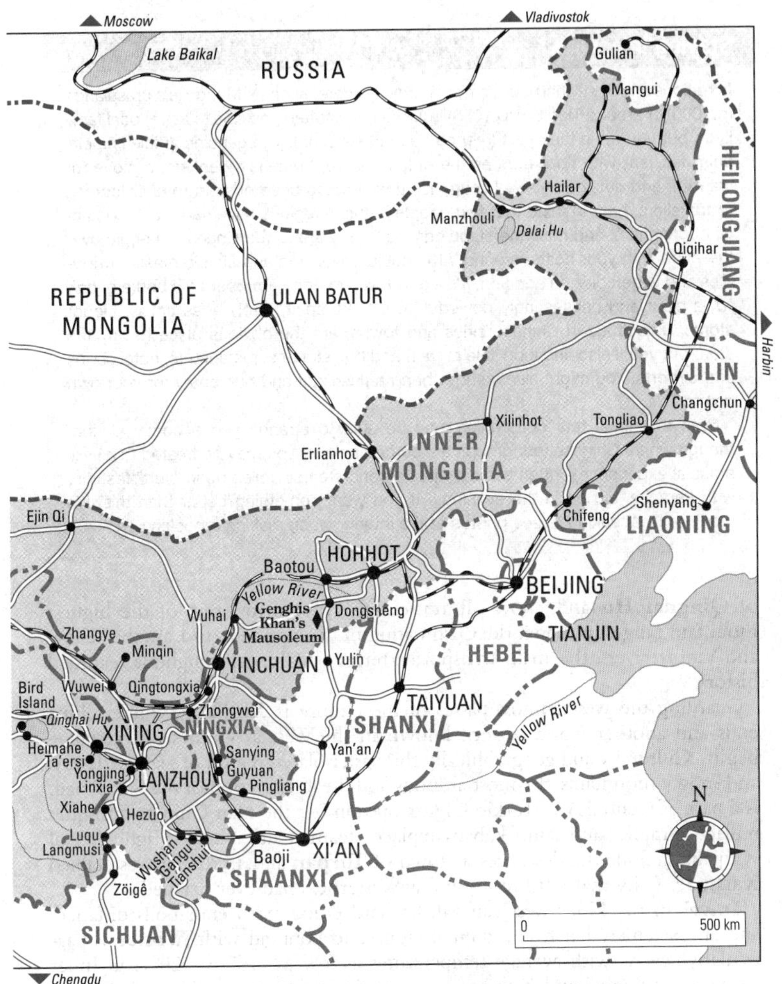

desert sand dunes. Rarely visited by foreign tourists, Ningxia also offers quiet, attractive cities and a variety of scenery ranging from terraced, abundantly fertile hillsides in the south to pure desert in the north. Extending west from here is **Gansu**, the historic periphery of ancient China. This rugged terrain of high mountains and deserts is spliced from east to west by the **Hexi Corridor**, a narrow path through the mountains, historically the only road from China to the West, and still marked along its length by the Great Wall – terminating magnificently at the fortress of **Jiayuguan** – and a string of Silk Road towns culminating in **Dunhuang**, with its fabulous Buddhist cave art.

South of the Hexi Corridor rise the mountains which extend all the way to the plains of northern India. The ancient borderland between the mountains and China proper is **Qinghai**, perhaps the least-explored province in the whole of the Northwest, which offers mountains, monasteries, the colossal lake

Staying in a yurt

In regions which still harbour semi-nomadic herders, such as Mongolia's grasslands (p.1000) or around Tian Chi (p.1083) in Xinjiang, it's often possible to ask a local family to put you up in their **yurt** (*mengu bao* in Mandarin). The genuine article is a circular felt tent with floor rugs as the only furniture, horsehair blankets, a stove for warmth, and outside toilets. Though it's a well-established custom to offer lodging to travellers, bear in mind that few people in these regions have had much contact with foreigners, and misunderstandings can easily arise. You'll need to haggle over the price with your hosts; around ¥40 should cover bed and simple meals of noodles and vegetables. In addition, it's a good idea to bring a **present** – a bottle of *baijiu*, a clear and nauseatingly powerful vodka-like spirit, rarely goes amiss. Liquor stores, ubiquitous in Chinese cities and towns, are the obvious place to buy the stuff, but you'll also find it on sale at train and bus stations, restaurants, hotel shops and airports. You might also want to bring a flashlight and bug spray for your own comfort.

Note that local tour companies may be able to arrange yurt accommodation, though where Chinese tour groups are commonplace, you may be treated to a very artificial experience – often basically just a concrete cell dolled up in "yurt" fashion, with karaoke laid on in the evenings. If you want something better than this, it's worth at least asking to see photos of the interior when making a booking.

of **Qinghai Hu** and, above all, routes **to Tibet** across one of the highest mountain ranges in the world. Originating in this province, too, are the Yellow and Yangzi rivers, the main transport arteries of China throughout recorded history.

Guarding the westernmost passes of the empire is **Xinjiang**, where China ends and another world – once known in the West as Chinese Turkestan – begins. Culturally and geographically this vast, isolated region of searing deserts and snowy mountains, the most arduous and dreaded section of the Silk Road, is a part of Central Asia. Turkic Uigurs outnumber the Han Chinese, mosques replace temples, and lamb kebabs replace steamed dumplings. Highlights of Xinjiang include the desert resort town of **Turpan** and, in the far west, fabled **Kashgar**, a city that until recently few Westerners had ever reached.

Travel in the Northwest can still be hard going, with enormous distances and an extremely harsh continental climate to contend with. **Winter** is particularly severe, with average temperatures as low as -15° or -20°C in Inner Mongolia, Qinghai and Xinjiang. Conversely, in **summer**, Turpan is China's hottest city. Despite the wild, rugged terrain and the great distances, however, facilities for tourists have developed considerably in recent years. In nearly all towns, there are now hotels and restaurants catering for a range of budgets – in general, the price of accommodation is a good deal cheaper here than in eastern China. Where rail lines have not been built, nearly everywhere is accessible by bus, and quite a few towns by plane as well. Finally there is the possibility of **onward travel** to or from China's Asian neighbours – the Republic of Mongolia, Kazakhstan, Kyrgyzstan and Pakistan can all be reached by road or rail from the provinces covered in this chapter (though remember that you may need to acquire visas for these countries in Beijing or elsewhere before setting out).

Inner Mongolia

Mongolia is an almost total mystery to the outside world, its very name being synonymous with remoteness. For hundreds of years, landlocked between the two Asian giants Russia and China, it seems to have been doomed to eternal obscurity, trapped in a hopeless physical environment of fleeting summers and interminable, bitter winters. And yet, seven hundred years ago the people of this benighted land suddenly burst out of their frontiers and for a century subjugated and terrorized virtually the entire Eurasian continent.

Visitors to the **Autonomous Region of Inner Mongolia** will not necessarily find many signs of this today, and if you come here expecting to find something reminiscent of Genghis Khan you are likely to be disappointed. The modern-day heirs of the Mongol hordes are not only placid – quietly going about their business of shepherding, herding horses and entertaining tourists – but, even in their own autonomous region, are vastly outnumbered by the Han Chinese (by seventeen million to two million). In addition, this is, and always has been, a sensitive border area, and there are still restrictions on the movements of tourists here, despite the demise of the Soviet Union.

Nevertheless, there are still traces of the "real" Mongolia out there, in terms of both landscape and people. Dotting the region are enormous areas of **grassland**, gently undulating plains stretching to the horizon and still used by nomadic peoples as pastureland for their horses. Tourists are able to visit the grasslands and even stay with the Mongols in their yurts, though the only simple way to do this is by **organized tour** out of the regional capital **Hohhot** – an experience rather short on authenticity. If you don't find what you are looking for in the Hohhot area, however, don't forget that there is a whole vast swathe of Mongolia stretching up through northeastern China that remains virtually untouched by Western tourists, and here, especially in the areas around **Xilinhot** and **Hailar**, determined independent travellers can manage to glimpse something of the grasslands and their Mongol inhabitants. Finally, Inner Mongolia offers overland connections with China's two northern neighbours, the Republic of Mongolia (Outer Mongolia) and Russia, through the border towns of **Erlianhot** and **Manzhouli** respectively.

Some history

Genghis Khan (1162–1227) was born, ominously enough, with a clot of blood in his hand. Under his leadership, the **Mongols** erupted from their homeland to ravage the whole of Asia, butchering millions, razing cities and laying waste all the land from China to eastern Europe. It was his proud boast that his destruction of cities was so complete that he could ride across their ruins by night without the least fear of his horse stumbling.

Before Genghis exploded onto the scene, the nomadic Mongols had long been a thorn in the side of the city-dwelling Chinese. Construction of the **Great Wall** had been undertaken to keep these two fundamentally opposed societies apart. But it was always fortunate for the Chinese that the early nomadic tribes of Mongolia fought as much among themselves as they did against outsiders. Genghis Khan's achievement was to weld together the warring nomads into a fighting force the equal of which the world had never seen. Becoming Khan of Khans in 1206, he also introduced the Yasak, the first **code of laws** the Mongols had known. Few details of its Draconian tenets survive

The Silk Road

The passes of Khunjerab and Torugut, linking China with western Asia – and ultimately with the whole of the western world – have only in recent years reopened to a thin and tentative trickle of cross-border traffic. Yet a thousand years ago these were on crucial, well-trodden and incredibly long trade routes between eastern China and the Mediterranean. Starting from Chang'an, the **Silk Road** curved northwest through Gansu to the Yumen Pass, where it split. Leaving the protection of the Great Wall, travellers could follow one of two routes across the terrible deserts of Lop Nor and Taklamakan, braving the attacks from marauding bandits, to Kashgar. The **southern route** ran through Dunhuang, Lop Nor, Miran, Niya, Khotan and Yarkand; the **northern route** through Hami, Turpan, Kuqa and Aqsu. High in the Pamirs beyond Kashgar, the merchants traded their goods with the middlemen who carried them beyond the frontiers of China, either south to Kashmir, Bactria, Afghanistan and India, or north to Ferghana, Tashkent and Samarkand. Then, laden with western goods, the Chinese merchants would turn back down the mountains for the three-thousand-kilometre journey home. **Oases** along the route inevitably prospered as staging posts and watering holes, becoming important and wealthy cities in their own right, with their own garrisons to protect the caravans. When Chinese domination periodically declined, many of these cities turned themselves into self-sufficient city-states, or **khanates**. Today, many of these once powerful cities are now buried in the sands.

The foundations for this famous **road to the West**, which was to become one of the most important arteries of **trade and culture** in world history, were laid over two millennia ago. In the second century BC nothing was known in China of the existence of people and lands beyond its borders, except by rumour. In 139 BC, the imperial court at Chang'an (Xi'an) decided to despatch an emissary, a man called Zhang Qiang, to investigate the world to the west and to seek possible allies in the constant struggle against nomadic marauders from the north. Zhang set out with a party of a hundred men; thirteen years later he returned, with only two other members of his original expedition – and no alliances. But the news he brought nevertheless set Emperor Wu Di and his court aflame, including tales of Central Asia, Persia and even the Mediterranean world. Further **expeditions** were soon despatched, initially to purchase horses for military purposes, and from these beginnings trade soon developed.

By 100 BC a dozen immense caravans a year were heading into the desert. From the West came cucumbers, figs, chives, sesame, walnuts, grapes (and winemaking), wool, linen and ivory; from China, jade, porcelain, lacquerware, oranges, peaches, pears, roses, chrysanthemums, cast iron, gunpowder, the crossbow, the wheelbarrow, paper and printing, and **silk**. The silkworm had already been domes-

today (though it was inscribed on iron tablets at Genghis' death), but Tamerlane, at Samarkand, and Baber the Great Mogul in India were both later to use it as the basis for their authority.

The secret of Genghis Khan's success lay in skilful **cavalry tactics**, acquired from long practice in the saddle on the wide open Mongolian plains. Frequently his armies would rout forces ten or twenty times their size. Each of his warriors would have light equipment and three or four horses. Food was taken from the surrounding country, the troops slept in the open, meat was cooked by being placed under the saddle; and when the going got tough they would slit a vein in the horse's neck and drink the blood while still on the move. There was no supply problem, no camp followers, no excess baggage.

The onslaught that the Mongols unleashed on China in 1211 was on a massive scale. The Great Wall proved no obstacle to Genghis Khan, and with his two ticated in China for hundreds of years, but in the West the means by which silk was manufactured remained a total mystery – people believed it was combed from the leaves of trees. The Chinese took great pains to protect their monopoly, punishing any attempt to export silkworms with death. It was only many centuries later that sericulture finally began to spread west, when silkworm larvae were smuggled out of China in hollow walking sticks by Nestorian monks. The first time the **Romans** saw silk, snaking in the wind as the banners of their Parthian enemies, it filled them with terror and resulted in a humiliating rout. They determined to acquire it for themselves, and soon Roman society became obsessed with the fabric which by the first century AD was coming west in such large quantities that the corresponding outflow of gold had begun to threaten the stability of the Roman economy.

As well as goods, the Silk Road carried new ideas in **art and religion**. Nestorian Christianity and Manichaeism trickled east across the mountains, but by far the most influential force was **Buddhism**. The first Buddhist missionaries appeared during the first century AD, crossing the High Pamirs from India, and their creed gained rapid acceptance among the nomads and oasis dwellers of what is now western China. By the fourth century, Buddhism had become the official religion of much of northern China, and by the eighth it was accepted throughout the empire. All along the road, monasteries, chapels, stupas and grottoes proliferated, often sponsored by wealthy traders. The remains of this early flowering of **Buddhist art** along the road are among the great attractions of the Northwest for modern-day travellers. Naturally, history has taken its toll – zealous Muslims, Western archeologists, Red Guards and the forces of nature have all played a destructive part – but some sites have survived intact, above all the cave art at **Mogao** outside Dunhuang.

The Silk Road continued to flourish for centuries, reaching its zenith under the Tang (618–907 AD) and bringing immense wealth to the Chinese nobility and merchants. But it remained a slow, dangerous and expensive route. Predatory tribes to the north and south harried the caravans despite garrisons and military escorts. Occasionally entire regions broke free of Chinese control, requiring years to be "re-pacified". The route was physically arduous, too, taking at least five months from Chang'an to Kashgar, and whole caravans could be lost in the deserts or in the high mountain passes.

There was a brief final flowering of the trade in the thirteenth century, to which **Marco Polo** famously bore witness, when the whole Silk Road came temporarily under Mongol rule. But by now the writing was clearly on the wall for the overland routes. With the arrival of sericulture in Europe and the opening of sea routes between China and the West, the Silk Road had had its day. The road and its cities were slowly abandoned to the wind and the blowing sands.

hundred thousand men he cut a swathe across northwest China towards Beijing. It was not all easy progress, however – so great was the destruction wrought in northern China that **famine and plague** broke out, afflicting the invader as much as the invaded. Genghis Khan himself died (of injuries sustained in falling from his horse) before the **capture of Beijing** had been completed. His body was carried back to Mongolia by a funeral cortege of ten thousand, who murdered every man and beast within ten miles of the road so that news of the Great Khan's death could not be reported before his sons and viceroys had been gathered from the farthest corners of his dominions. The whereabouts of his **tomb** is uncertain, though according to one of the best-known stories his ashes are in a mausoleum near Dongsheng (see p.1009), south of Baotou.

In the years after Genghis Khan's death, the fate of both China and of distant Europe teetered together on the brink. Having conquered all of Russia, the

Kublai Khan

In Xanadu did Kubla Khan
A stately pleasure dome decree . . .

Immortalized not only in the poetry of Samuel Coleridge but also in the memoirs of Marco Polo, **Kublai Khan** (1215–94) – known to the Chinese as Yuan Shizu – is the only emperor in all of China's long history popularly known by name to the outside world. And little wonder: as well as mastering the subtle statecraft required to govern China as a foreigner, this grandson of Genghis Khan commanded an **empire** that encompassed the whole of China, central Asia, southern Russia and Persia – a larger area of land than perhaps anyone in history has ruled over, before or since. And yet this king of kings had been born into a nomadic tribe which had never shown the slightest interest in political life, and who, until shortly before his birth, were almost entirely illiterate.

From the beginning, Kublai Khan had shown an unusual talent for politics and government. He managed to get himself elected **Khan of the Mongols** in 1260, after the death of his brother, despite considerable opposition from the so-called "steppe aristocracy" who feared his disdain for traditional Mongolian skills. He never learned to read or write Chinese, yet after audaciously establishing himself as **Emperor of China**, proclaiming the Yuan dynasty in 1271, he soon saw the value of surrounding himself with advisers steeped in Confucianism. This was what enabled him to set up one hundred thousand Mongols in power over perhaps two hundred million Chinese. As well as **reunifying China** after centuries of division under the Song, Kublai Khan's contributions include establishing **paper money** as the standard medium of exchange, and fostering the **development of religion**, Lamaist Buddhism in particular. Above all, under his rule China experienced a brief – and uncharacteristic – period of **cosmopolitanism** which saw not only foreigners such as Marco Polo promoted to high positions of responsibility, but also a final flowering of the old Silk Road trade, as well as large numbers of Arab and Persian traders settling in seaports around Quanzhou in southeastern China.

Ironically, however, it was his admiration for the culture, arts, religion and sophisticated bureaucracy of China – as documented so enthusiastically by Marco Polo – that aroused bitter hostility from his own people, the Mongols, who despised what they saw as a betrayal of the ways of Genghis Khan. Kublai Khan was troubled by skirmishing nomads along the Great Wall no less than any of his more authentically Chinese predecessors. The great palace of **Xanadu** (in Inner Mongolia, near the modern city of Duolun), where Kublai Khan kept his legendary summer residence, was abandoned to fall into ruin; today virtually nothing of the site remains.

Mongol forces were poised in 1241 to make the relatively short final push across Europe to the Atlantic, when a message came from deep inside Asia that the invasion was to be cancelled. The decision to spare western Europe cleared the way for the **final conquest of China** instead, and by 1276 the Mongols had established their own **Yuan dynasty**. It was the first time the Chinese had come under foreign rule. The Yuan is still an era about which Chinese historians can find little good to say, though the boundaries of the empire were expanded considerably, to include Yunnan and Tibet for the first time. The magnificent zenith of the dynasty was achieved under **Kublai Khan**, as documented in Marco Polo's *Travels*. Ironically, however, the Mongols were able to sustain their power only by becoming thoroughly Chinese, and abandoning the traditional nomadic Mongol way of life. Kublai Khan and his court soon forgot the warrior skills of their forefathers, and in 1368, less than a hundred years later, the Yuan, a shadow of their former selves, were **driven out of China** by the Ming. The Mongols returned to Mongolia, and reverted to their former ways, hunting, fighting among themselves and occasionally skirmishing with the Chinese down by the Wall. Astonishingly, history had come full circle.

Thereafter, Mongolian history moves gradually downhill, though right into the eighteenth century they maintained at least nominal control over many of the lands to the south and west originally won by Genghis Khan. These included **Tibet**, from where **Lamaist Buddhism** was imported to become the dominant religion in Mongolia. The few Tibetan-style monasteries in Mongolia that survive are an important testimony to this. Over the years, as well, came **settlers** from other parts of Asia: there is now a sizeable Muslim minority in the region, and under the Qing many Chinese settlers moved to Inner Mongolia, escaping overpopulation and famine at home, a trend that has continued under the Communists. The incoming settlers tried ploughing up the grassland with disastrous ecological results – wind and water swept the soil away – and the Mongols withdrew to the hills. Only recently has a serious programme of land stabilization and reclamation been established.

Sandwiched between two imperial powers, Mongolia found its independence constantly threatened. The Russians set up a protectorate over the north, while the rest came effectively under the control of China. In the 1930s, Japan occupied much of eastern Inner Mongolia as part of Manchuguo, and the Chinese Communists also maintained a strong presence. In 1945 Stalin persuaded Chiang Kaishek to recognize the independence of **Outer Mongolia** under Soviet protection as part of the Sino–Soviet anti-Japanese treaty, effectively sealing the fate of what then became the Mongolian People's Republic. In 1947, **Inner Mongolia** was designated the first Autonomous Region of the People's Republic of China.

Hohhot and around

There has been a town at **HOHHOT** (known as Huhehaote, or more commonly Hushi, to the Chinese) since the time of the Ming dynasty four hundred years ago, though it did not become the capital of Inner Mongolia until 1952. Until relatively modern times, it was a small town centred on a number of **Buddhist temples**. The temples are still here and, although it's now a major city, Hohhot manages to be an interesting blend of the old and the new, and a relatively green and leafy place in summer – which is fitting, as the town's Mongolian name means "green city". As well as the shiny new banks and department stores downtown, there's an extensive area in the south of the town with old, narrow streets built of black bricks and heavy roof tiles. These days Hohhot is largely a Han city, though there is also a Hui and a Mongol presence; it's worthwhile tracking down the **Mongol** areas, not least to try some of their distinctive **food**. The other reason for visiting Hohhot is its proximity to some of the famous Mongolian **grasslands** which lie within a hundred-kilometre radius of the city.

Arrival and accommodation

Hohhot is a fairly easy place to find your way around. The heart of the modern commercial city, including most hotels, lies in the blocks to the south of the **train and bus stations**, while the old city and its flamboyant temples are

Hohhot and around

Hohhot	呼和浩特	***hūhéhàotè***
Dazhao	大召	*dàzhào*
Great Mosque	清真大寺	*qīngzhēn dàsì*
Inner Mongolia Museum	内蒙古博物馆	*nèiménggǔ bówùguǎn*
Jiangjun Yashu	将军衙署	*jiāngjūn yáshǔ*
Mongolian Consulate	蒙古共和国领事馆	*ménggǔ gònghéguó lǐngshìguǎn*
Nationalities Market	民族商场	*mínzú shāngchǎng*
Qingcheng Park	青城公园	*qīngchéng gōngyuán*
Wuta Si	五塔寺	*wǔtǎ sì*
Xilituzhao	席里图召	*xílǐtú zhào*
Xinhua Square	新华广场	*xīnhuá guǎngchǎng*
Accommodation		
Beiyuan Hotel	北原饭店	*běiyuán fàndiàn*
Hohhot	呼和浩特宾馆	*hūhéhàotè bīnguǎn*
Railway Hotel	铁路宾馆	*tiělù bīnguǎn*
Tongda	通达饭店	*tōngdá fàndiàn*
Xincheng	新城宾馆	*xīnchéng bīnguǎn*
Zhaojun	昭君大酒店	*zhāojūn dàjiǔdiàn*
Eating		
Beijing Jiaozi Wang	北京饺子王	*běijīng jiǎoziguǎn*
Daxue Lu Shangchang	大学路商场	*dàxuélù shāngchǎng*
Malaqin	马拉沁饭店	*mǎlāqìn fàndiàn*
Taiwan Beef Noodle	台湾牛肉面	*táiwān niúròumiàn*
Around Hohhot		
Bai Ta	百塔	*bǎi tǎ*
Erlianhot	二连浩特	*èrlián hàotè*
Gegentala	格根塔拉草原	*gégēntǎlā cǎoyuán*
Huitengxile	辉腾锡勒草原	*huīténgxīlè cǎoyuán*
Tomb of Wang Zhaojun	昭君墓	*zhāojūn mù*
Ulan Batur	乌兰巴托	*wūlán bātuō*
Wusutu Zhao	乌素图召	*wūsùtú zhào*
Xilamuren	希拉穆仁草原	*xīlāmùrén cǎoyuán*

southwest of the central Qingcheng Park. The **airport** lies 35km east of the city, and the airport bus drops arriving passengers at the CAAC office on Xilinguole Lu, the road running south from the bus station.

Travellers arriving by train, in particular, are often subjected to furious and persistent harassment from the moment they disembark, by travel agents trying to sell them grassland tours. The only practical way to escape the melee is to get into a **taxi**. The minimum fare is ¥6, sufficient for most rides within the city.

Accommodation

Hohhot has a sprinkling of **accommodation**, all fairly good value but not in great locations.

Beiyuan 28 Chezhan Xi Lu ⓣ0471/6966211. A small, quite salubrious place just opposite the train station and a little to the right, offering a wide range of rooms and prices, including reasonably priced double rooms with bathrooom. Dorm beds from ¥25, ❸

Hohhot Yingbin Bei Lu ⓣ0471/6962200. An old-fashioned place with unspectacular rooms, not terribly welcoming to foreigners but convenient for the centre. Turn left out of the station, walk a few

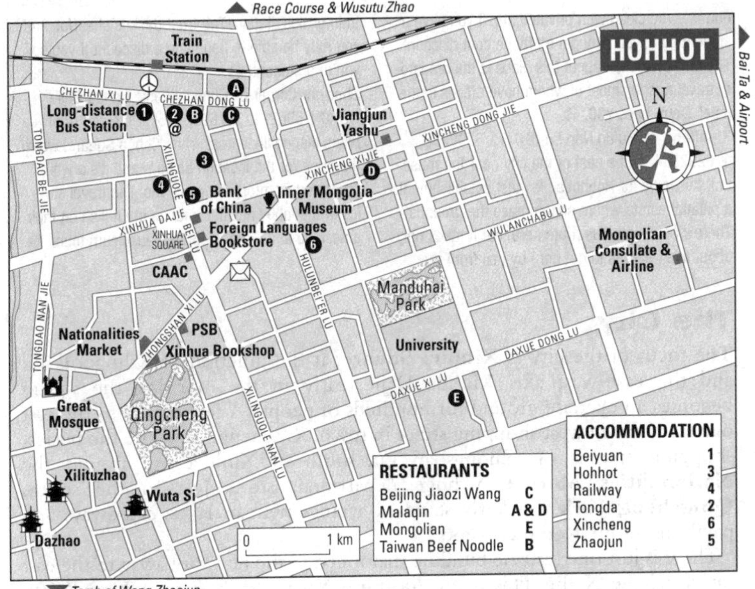

minutes and take the first turning on the right – it's about a fifteen-minute walk. ❺

Railway Hotel 131 Xilinguole Lu ⓣ0471/6933377. Standard budget hotel with attentive staff and clean facilities, far enough south of the train station to escape the attention of touts. Breakfast is included in the rate, and they'll book train tickets. ❸

Tongda Chezhan Dong Lu ⓣ0471/6968731. Very convenient for the train station – it's straight across the road, and a little to the left as you come out. All rooms – doubles and three- and four-bedded

Moving on from Hohhot

There are daily bus services from Hohhot to **Erlianhot** (see box, p.999) – Erlian on schedules – and **Xilinhot** (see p.1001). Word at the station is that you no longer need a travel permit to these destinations – though it wouldn't hurt to check in at the PSB before departure to make absolutely sure the winds of reform and openness are still blowing. You can also catch train #4602/3 to Erlian, departing Hohhot 10:50pm and arriving at 6:36am the next day.

To **Baotou**, there are buses running every thirty minutes; you can find them on the main street outside the station, attended by people with loud-hailers. Fast ones charge ¥26, slower ones ¥17. There is also at least one daily (early morning) bus to **Dongsheng** (6hr; ¥62) for Genghis Khan's Mausoleum (see p.1008), with increased frequency during the summer. In addition, sleeper buses and luxury coaches leave Hohhot in the late afternoon, bound for **Tianjin** and **Beijing** (8hr; ¥150) respectively; these buses are easier to buy tickets for and work out cheaper than the trains.

Hohhot is linked by **train** to **Lanzhou** to the west, **Beijing** to the east and **Hailar** (a sixty-hour direct journey via Beijing) to the northeast. There are also trains to **Ulan Batur** in the Republic of Mongolia (see box, p.999). Leaving Hohhot by train, you can seek the help of a travel agent to procure tickets (see "Listings", p.998) for a small commission. You'll need to give them at least 36 hours' notice for a hard sleeper – or try your luck at the station ticket office, which is sometimes hideously crowded and sometimes empty.

dorms – are clean with private bath. If you have a student card, you may get a fifty percent discount. The only drawback about this place is the predatory travel agents, most of whom have offices in the hotel. Dorm beds ¥30, ❷

Xincheng 40 Hulun Nan Lu ⓣ0471/6292288, ⓕ6292334. In the east of the city near the museum, this is by far Hohhot's plushest establishment, a palatial estate where sheep graze the grounds. There's no simple bus route here, but it takes only about five minutes to get here by taxi from the train or bus station. The front desk is cheerful, and you may be able to negotiate a discount if you say you're a student. ❺

Zhaojun Corner of Xilinguole and Xinhua Dajie ⓣ0471/6962211, ⓕ6968825. In the centre of town, diagonally across from Xinhua Square, worth the price for the location alone – and it's a well-organized, comfortable place too. The travel service in the lobby has information in English on their grassland and Genghis Khan mausoleum tours. ❺

The City

The focus of the city is **Xinhua Square**, at the junction of Xilinguole Lu and the east–west axis Xinhua Dajie; early in the morning the square becomes an exercise ground for hundreds of people. A few blocks to the east of here is the newest shopping street in town, Xincheng Lu, while the busiest shopping area is on Zhongshan Lu, south of Xinhua Lu, around the **Nationalities Market**, a huge department store. Just to the south, **Qingcheng Park** is a fairly standard arrangement of lakes, causeways and pavilions, home to the city zoo.

There is just one historic building marooned in the new city, away to the east on Xincheng Xi Jie. This is the **Jiangjun Yashu** (daily 8am–4.30pm; ¥10), actually the office of a prominent Qing-dynasty general, even though it looks like a temple. Now it's a tiny museum with some bizarre modern Buddhist art in the right wing, and some curious Qing office furniture at the back.

More centrally located, the **Inner Mongolia Museum** on the corner of Xinhua Dajie and Hulunbei'er Lu (daily 9am–5pm;¥10) – a few minutes' walk from the *Xincheng* hotel – is well worth a visit. In the downstairs exhibition, there's a large display of ethnic Mongolian items, such as costumes, saddles, long leather coats and cummerbunds, as well as hunting and sporting implements, including some very European-looking hockey sticks and balls. There's also a fascinating paleontology display, with complete fossils of a woolly rhinoceros and a sizeable dinosaur. Upstairs are interesting maps and objects detailing the exploits of Genghis Khan, and the huge Mongol empire of the thirteenth century. While there are some English explanations, if you're truly keen on grasping the significance of the display, check in at the main office behind the ticket desk, where the curator speaks English and may be willing to give you a tour.

A couple of kilometres north of the train station, and served by #13 bus from the centre of town, is a gigantic **race course**, the biggest in China, built in the shape of two circular Mongolian yurts, adjacent and connected to each other to form the elongated shape of a stadium. In the evening, displays of Mongolian singing and dancing sometimes take place here (for details of performances try enquiring at the upmarket hotels, or at CTS).

Old Hohhot

Most of the historic buildings of Hohhot are crowded into the interesting – though fast-disappearing – old southwestern part of the city, where you can enjoyably spend the best part of a day simply ambling around. The **Great Mosque**, at the southern end of Zhongshan Lu, is an attractive old building bearing traces of Chinese and Arabic style, constructed of black brick and accompanied by a Chinese-style minaret with a pagoda roof. Some of the Hui people who worship here are extremely friendly, and will probably be delighted if you ask to look round the mosque. The surrounding streets comprise the Muslim area of town, and besides a lot of old men with wispy beards and skull caps, you'll find a fantastic array of noodle and kebab shops if you head down the tight alleyway directly north of the mosque.

Walking south from the mosque for about fifteen minutes along the main road, you'll come to a couple of Buddhist temples. The biggest of these is the **Dazhao**, down a side street west of the main road (daily 8am–5pm; ¥10). Originally constructed in 1579, and recently been the subject of a typically gaudy renovation, the structure was dedicated in the late seventeenth century to the famous Qing emperor Kangxi – a gold tablet with the words "Long Live the Emperor" was set before the silver statue of Sakyamuni, and in the main hall murals depicting the visit of the Emperor Kangxi can still be seen.

Just a few minutes from Dazhao, over on the other side of the main road, is the **Xilituzhao** (daily 8am–5pm; ¥5), another temple of similar scale and layout to the Dazhao, and dating from the same era, though it too has been restored since the destruction of the Cultural Revolution. The dagoba is interesting for featuring Sanskrit writing above Chinese dragons above Tibetan-style murals. Since 1735 this has been the official residence of the reincarnation of the Living Buddha, who is in charge of Buddhist affairs in the city. Friendly and homesick Tibetan monks who speak pretty good English are happy to show you around.

Farther east, via a diverting walk along winding, narrow alleys comprising the last remains of the old city, you'll come to the most attractive piece of architecture in the city, known as the **Wuta Si** (Five Towers Temple; daily 8am–5pm; ¥10). Built in 1727, in pure Indian style, this composite of five pagodas originally belonged to the Ci Deng Temple, which no longer exists. It's relatively small, but its walls are engraved with no fewer than 1563 Buddhas, all in slightly different postures. Currently stored inside the pagoda building is a rare, antique Mongolian cosmological map which marks the position of hundreds of stars.

Eating and drinking

The highlight of eating in Hohhot is the chance to eat **Mongolian food**. Mongolian **hotpot**, or *shuan yangrou*, is a perfectly delicious dinner, best shared with friends and beer, and cooked yourself at the table: piles of thinly sliced mutton, ordered by the *jin*, are cooked by being dropped into a cauldron of boiling water at the table, then quickly removed and dipped into a spicy sauce. Tofu, glass noodles, cabbage and mushrooms are common accompaniments which all go into the pot, too. Many restaurants in Hohhot serve *shuan yangrou* – the most famous being *Malaqin Restaurant* on Xincheng Xi Jie, a few blocks east of Hulunbei'er Lu. Dinner here with plenty of beer shouldn't cost more than ¥35 per head. There's also a branch in the guesthouse of the same name east of the train station, on the north side of Chezhan Donglu.

For an even more exotic meal, however, with the focus on Mongolian dairy products, head for the Mongolian quarter in the southeast of town. Bus #4 comes down here – get off at Daxue Lu just south of the university. During term time, this area is packed with students, and restaurants stay open late. Any restaurant with Mongolian letters above the door is worth trying, in particular, the one just 200m down the small street leading south from beside the Daxue Lu Shangchang. For an excellent breakfast or lunch, order a large bowl of sugary milk tea, and *chaomi* (buckwheat), *huangyou* (butter), *nailao* (hard white cheese) and *naipi* (a sweetish, biscuit-like substance formed from the skin of boiled milk). Toss everything into the tea, and eat it with chopsticks – it's surprisingly delicious. To make this into a substantial meal, eat it with *mengu baozi* or *jianbing* – dough stuffed with ground mutton, respectively steamed or fried.

There's plenty of standard **Chinese** food in Hohhot. The hotel restaurant of the *Xincheng* is good and cheap; for a livelier atmosphere, however, stick around the train station, where you can savour the dumplings at *Beijing Jiaozi Wang*, a multi-segmented eating place 100m east of the station on the south side of Chezhan Dongjie; or try the simple *Taiwan Beef Noodle Restaurant*, whose limited menu is written in English – it's a little to the east of the *Tongda Hotel*. At the Nationalities Market, along with the inevitable *KFC*, there's a fast-food café in the wing to the left (as you face the bridge), serving passable hamburgers and fries.

Listings

Airlines CAAC, Xilinguole Lu, is just south of Xinhua Square (Mon–Sat, 8am–9pm; ⓣ0471/6964103). MIAT (the airline of the Republic of Mongolia; ⓣ0471/4953250) is in the east of the city next to the Mongolian Consulate and near to the Neimenggu Jiancai Xuexiao (Inner Mongolia Construction Materials College). To reach the MIAT office by bus, get the #2 service east to Nongwei bus stop, then walk a little farther east, and a couple of blocks south.

Banks and exchange The easiest place to change money, including traveller's cheques, is inside the *Zhaojun Hotel*, which changes money for non-guests, offers the same rates as the bank and operates at weekends. The head office of the Bank of China (Mon–Fri 8am–noon & 2–5pm, Sat am only) is actually across the road from the hotel.

Bookshops There's a Foreign Language Bookstore on Xilinguole Lu, across the road from Xinhua Square. Xinhua Bookstore is on Zhongshan Lu, across the road from (and a couple of minutes to the south of) the Nationalities Market.

Consulate The Consulate of the Republic of Mongolia is in the east of the city (Mon, Tues & Thurs 8.30am–noon; ⓣ0471/4303254), next to the MIAT office. Visas are fairly easy to obtain, though they cost ¥500 for a month and may take some time to be issued. US citizens do not need visas for stays up to thirty days.

Internet access A spanking new and very cheap Internet café is upstairs in the Telecom Office, next door to the post office (daily 8am–6pm; ¥8/hr). Walk south from the train station on the left-hand side of Xilinguole Lu, and a signboard points the way into the recesses of a building, where a grotty but friendly café has fast connections.

Mail and telecommunications The main post office is on the south side of Zhongshan Lu, just east of Xilinguole Lu (Mon–Sat 8am–7pm). The Telecom Centre is adjacent (daily 8am–6pm), with a small 24hr office.

PSB In the government building to the south of the junction between Zhongshan Lu and Xilinguole Lu.

Travel agents There are numerous travel agents in town, many of whom will find you before you find them. They nearly all have English-speaking employees, and deal in grassland tours as well as booking train tickets. CTS, on the third floor of the back building of the *Inner Mongolia Hotel* (ⓣ0471/6964233 ext 8936), has some pleasant, approachable staff. The *Tongda Hotel* also holds several tour operators, as does the helpful desk in the *Zhaojun Hotel*'s lobby.

Around Hohhot

There are a few more sights scattered around the outer suburbs of Hohhot, some of which can be reached on city buses. The **Tomb of Wang Zhaojun**, about 8km to the south of Hohhot, is the burial site of a Tang-dynasty princess sent from Chengdu to cement Han–Mongol relations by marrying the king of Mongolia. It isn't a spectacular sight – a huge mound raised from the plain and planted with gardens, in the centre of which is a modern pavilion – but the romantic story it recalls has important implications for modern Chinese politics, signifying the harmonious marrying of the Han with the minority peoples.

The road to Outer Mongolia

The Republic of Mongolia, otherwise known as **Outer Mongolia**, is now open to foreign tourists travelling independently. **Visas**, should you require them, are available in Hohhot and Beijing, and are a lot easier to obtain since the departure of the old Communists from power in Ulan Batur in 1996.

There are various ways into the country from China. Chinese airlines and MIAT, the Mongolian airline, both fly three times weekly **from Beijing** to Ulan Batur; tickets cost around ¥2000 one-way, while the direct train, which takes about 36 hours, is cheaper at ¥500. Alternatively, you can do the journey by stages, which works out a lot cheaper and is perhaps more interesting. The first stage is to get to the border at Erlianhot: take the Hohhot train as far as Jining (10hr; ¥75), then change to the Erlianhot train (8hr; ¥42). **From Hohhot**, MIAT flies twice weekly to Ulan Batur for ¥640, and there are relatively expensive direct trains to Ulan Batur as well as direct daily services to the border at Erlianhot (8hr). If you want to take the bus from Hohhot to Erlianhot (also 8hr), check with the Hohhot PSB if tourists need a permit to travel on it. Crossing the border at Erlianhot is still something of a palaver if you are not on a through train. Assuming you arrive in Erlianhot in the evening you'll certainly have to spend one night here. In the morning there's one local bus that does the seven-kilometre trip across to the Mongolian town of **Zamen Uud**, though you may wait hours for it to leave, and it will cost you an absurd US$15. From there to Ulan Batur it's an eighteen-hour train journey, which costs about US$5.

Erlianhot itself is a curious border town in the middle of nowhere, which caters to Mongolian nomads and shepherds coming to town to do their shopping. It's also a famous centre for wool production. Twice a week its train station briefly fills with foreigners as the Trans-Mongolian Express comes through on its way to or from Moscow – there's even a disco and a bar here for their entertainment. There is some very cheap accommodation available in town. Eat all you can here, because the food in Outer Mongolia is notoriously poor.

In the rose garden, among pergolas festooned with gourds, is a tiny museum devoted to Zhaojun, containing some of her clothes, including a tiny pair of shoes, plus jewels, books and a number of steles. You can reach the tomb by the #14 bus, or by walking due south along the main road from the Great Mosque in the west of town.

Not accessible by bus, but well worth the effort to reach, is the **Wusutu Zhao** complex, the only temple in Mongolia to have been designed and built solely by Mongolians. Boasting buildings in Mongolian, Tibetan and Han styles, it lies 12km northwest of Hohhot, south of the Daqing Mountain and in attractive countryside separated from the city by the new expressway. Admission to each of the four neighboring temples is ¥3, collected by an elderly monk who will probably be surprised to see you. There are no souvenir stands, no gawdy refurbishments, so take the time to scour the Ming-era murals within and the ornate woodcuts attached to sticks at the base of the Buddhas. The surrounding grasslands and trails into the mountains make for a relaxing day out. To get here from the train station, take bus #5 to its terminus and hire a taxi from there, a ride which shouldn't be come to more than ¥20, though unless you're prepared to hire the taxi for a half day, you'll probably have to walk back to the bus stop later, about an hour's hike along a busy road.

Slightly farther out is one more site that you can reach only by taxi: the **Bai Ta** (White Pagoda), about 17km east of the city, is an attractive, 55-metre-high wood and brick construction, erected as long ago as the tenth century and covered in ornate carvings of coiling dragons, birds and flowers on the lower parts of the tower. You can reach it by following Xincheng Xi Jie east out of the city – it's a possible stopoff on the way to the airport.

The grasslands

Mongolia isn't all one giant steppe, but three areas in the vicinity of Hohhot are certainly large enough to give the illusion of endlessness. These are **Xilamuren** (which begins 80km north of Hohhot), **Gegentala** (150km north) and **Huitengxile** (120km west). It's hard to differentiate among them, save to say that Xilamuren – the only one of the three that can feasibly be reached independently – is probably the most visited and Gegentala the least. Bear in mind that your grassland experience in the immediate area of the regional capital is likely to be a rather packaged affair, and you may find yourself surrounded by crowds of rowdy tourists from other parts of East Asia. A visit to a grassland in another, remoter part of the region (such as Xilinhot or Hailar – see opposite and p.1002) may well give you a more authentic flavour of Mongolia.

The most convenient way to visit the grasslands is to take one of the semi-notorious **grassland tours**, which Westerners rarely enjoy but east Asian tourists seem to love – or at least put up with in good humour. The tours always follow a similar pattern, with visitors based at a site comprising a number of **yurts**, plus a dining hall, kitchen and very primitive toilets. The larger sites, at Xilamuren, are the size of small villages. Transport, meals and accommodation are all included in the price, as are various unconvincing "Mongolian entertainments" – wrestling and spectacular horse-riding in particular – and visits to typical Mongol families in traditional dress. Only the food is consistently good, though watch out for the local *baijiu*, which you're more or less forced to drink when your Mongolian hosts bring silver bowls of the stuff round to every table during the evening banquet. The banquet is followed by a fairly degenerate evening of drinking, dancing and singing.

If you accept the idea that you are going on a tour of the grasslands primarily to participate in a bizarre social experience, then you'll get much more out of it. Besides, it is perfectly possible to escape from your group if you wish to do so. You can hire your own horse, or just walk off over the horizon into an endless expanse of grass. If your stay happens to coincide with a bright moon, you could be in for the most hauntingly beautiful experience of your life.

A two-day tour (with one night in a yurt) is definitely enough – in a group of six or seven people, this should come to between ¥250 and ¥350 each. Some travel services (such as the Inner Mongolia Lüye International Travel Company based in the *Tongda Hotel*, Room 424; ⓣ0471/6968613) can tack smaller parties onto existing groups. Bear in mind that, if you choose this option, you may find yourself sleeping crushed into a small yurt with six others who don't speak your language, and consequently that the tour may not be in English, even if you've specifically requested that it should be.

Travelling independently to the Xilamuren grassland can work out a good deal cheaper than taking a tour. Store your luggage at your hotel in Hohhot, and catch a bus from the long-distance bus station to the small settlement of **Zhaohe** (2 daily; 2–3hr; ¥8), adjacent to the grassland. When you get off you will be accosted by people offering to take you to their yurts – try to negotiate an all-inclusive daily rate of about ¥50 per person, for food and accommodation, before you accept any offer. You aren't exactly in the wilderness here, but you can wander off into the grass and soon find it.

The northeast of Inner Mongolia

The colossal area of land that comprises Inner Mongolia to the east and north of Hohhot is scarcely visited by tourists, which is reason enough to journey up here. As an area populated by nomadic sheep-herders since the beginning of history, its attractions lie not in old towns, but in the wilderness. The terrain is hilly, and the farther north you go the wetter it gets and the more trees there are. The grass on the **eastern grasslands** is accordingly longer and more lush, though for only a brief period each year. People are few and far between, the land outside the towns only occasionally punctuated by the sight of **muchang jia** – pastureland homes – comprising groups of yurts in the grass, surrounded by herds of sheep, cattle or horses. Visiting *muchang jia* is exclusively a summertime activity; during the long winters, temperatures can dip to an appalling -50°C.

For travellers the area is not an easy one to explore, given the paucity of **transport** connections. As the local authorities have in the past not been keen on foreign travellers crossing the region by **bus** (it's worth checking the current situation with the PSB), flying may turn out to be the only option if you don't want to spend ages on trains – though for rail enthusiasts, the epic train journeys are themselves a possible reason for coming here. The only rail lines are in the far north, offering access to **Hailar** and **Manzhouli** on the Russian border. Hailar lies a full sixty hours by train from the provincial capital Hohhot, the route first passing east through Datong to Beijing, then moving north back into Inner Mongolia, passing the towns of **Chifeng** and **Tongliao** – both of which are surrounded by their own grasslands which can also be visited. From here the train drifts east into Jilin province in Dongbei (see p.207). Much later the train cuts back into Inner Mongolia at Zhalantun from where it travels northwest to Hailar. For hour after hour there's barely a sign of sentient life, the train traversing hilly, grassy pastures, past mist-hung rivers and cool, wooded valleys during the last third of the journey.

Xilinhot

XILINHOT (aka Xilin in Chinese), 500km northeast of Hohhot and 600km north of Beijing, is probably the most visited town in the whole area. The joy of a place like this is that you are already in the **grasslands** – they begin at the edge of town.

As around Hohhot, there are CITS-approved grassland sites, and travel services will compete for the honour of escorting you there. **Tours** from Xilinhot are likely to be cheaper and more tranquil than those operating from Hohhot. Considering, however, that you are so close to the grasslands here, it is quite feasible if you speak a little Chinese to do a **private deal** with somebody – a travel-service employee, a hotel worker or a taxi-driver – to take you out to any *muchang jia* with which they have acquaintance. This needn't cost much; reckon on about ¥2 per kilometre. Try to arrange some all-inclusive daily rate which includes all meals and drinks, but don't be too aggressive about it – ¥50 per day is a good rate – and remember to bring a gift, such as a bottle of the local *baijiu*.

The main difficulty with Xilinhot is getting there in the first place. There is a daily **bus** from Hohhot (14hr), but check with the PSB whether you need a permit to be on this. The alternatives are either to take a train to Erlianhot (see p.999), and then try to get a bus from there; or simply to **fly** directly from Hohhot (or Beijing); at the time of writing, there were flights from Hohhot on Monday, Wednesday, Friday and Sunday (1hr). In Xilinhot, **accommodation**

The northeast of Inner Mongolia

Pastureland homes	牧场家	*mùchǎngjiā*
Chifeng	赤蜂	***chìfēng***
Hailar	海拉尔	***hǎilāěr***
Bei'er Hotel	贝尔大酒店	*bèiěr dàjiǔdiàn*
Beiyuan Hotel	北苑宾馆	*běiyuán bīnguǎn*
Hulunbeier Hotel	呼伦贝尔宾馆	*hūlúnbèiěr bīnguǎn*
Hulunbuir Grasslands	呼伦贝尔草原	*hūlúnbèiěr cǎoyuán*
Japanese army tunnels	侵华日军海拉尔要塞遗址	*qīnhuá rìjūn hǎilāěr yàosài yízhǐ*
Laodong Hotel	劳动宾馆	*láodòng bīnguǎn*
Manzhouli	满洲里	***mǎnzhōulǐ***
Dalai Hu	达赉湖	*dálài hú*
Tongliao	通辽	***tōngliáo***
Xilinhot	锡林浩特	***xīlínhàotè***

is available at the upmarket *Baima* (❹) or, just behind the bus station, at the *Xilinhot* (❸).

Hailar and the northeast frontier

In the far northeast of Inner Mongolia, **HAILAR**, with rail connections as well as an airport, is the main transport hub of the region, and a centre for grassland visits. The town of Hailar itself is of minimal interest, a small, light-industrial and agricultural place on the banks of the Heilongjiang (Amur) River with a small Muslim population as well as the usual Mongol/Han mix. The main attraction in the town itself is the recently reopened **network of tunnels** used by the Japanese army during World War II. Hailar was Japan's westernmost base during the war, the Japanese agreeing to halt their advance at Hailar in exchange for Russia's non-interference in Manchuria, which in turn allowed Russia to concentrate on battling Hitler in the west. The tunnel complex, wrought by Chinese prisoners-of-war, sits in Hailar's northwest, atop a ridge that affords an excellent vantage point of the river and grasslands. At time of writing, the site could only be reached by a bumpy taxi ride (¥12) from the train station via a rutted track in the grasslands. A plaque at the entrance explains, in English, the wartime history of the area. Enter the rebuilt bunker (¥20) to descend 40m underground into the tunnels themselves. A small Chinese-language exhibit greets you in the chilly depths, after which you're free to wander about with a torch amid the eerie echo of your footsteps. Back above ground, it's a pleasant thirty-minute walk back to the train station.

The chief reason most visitors come to Hailar, however, is to see the North Mongolian **Hulunbuir Grasslands**, an apparently limitless rolling land of plains and low grassy mountains, traced by slow rivers teeming with fish. Hundreds of thousands of sheep, cattle and horses graze this inexhaustible pasture, spread over hundreds of kilometres. In summer they occupy the higher pastures and in winter they come down to the lowlands, still often deep in snow. Transport in the area is mostly by camel and pony. Not only is the grass scattered with a variety of flowers and huge fungi, but, as you soon discover, it's also alive with little black toads (which it's virtually impossible to avoid treading on), grasshoppers, birds and insects (**mosquito repellent** is essential).

As elsewhere in Inner Mongolia, there are the CITS-approved villages of Mongol herders, who earn part of their income from occasional groups of tourists, mostly from Japan. Though you could try to strike off independently, it's worth noting that the grassland **tours** here don't attract hordes of people. A day-trip from Hailar to eat a traditional mutton banquet on the grassland, for a group of four people, costs in the region of ¥120 each. If you want to spend a night on the grasslands as well, reckon on around ¥200. Inclusion of an English-speaking guide sends the price soaring to ¥800, so you'll need to be in a large group to make this worth your while. For bookings and more information, contact CITS (Ⓣ0470/8246368, Ⓕ8221728) at their small office on the third floor of the *Beiyuan Hotel* (see below).

Practicalities

A compact place, Hailar is divided into two by the Yimin River. The **train station** is on the west bank; to reach the city centre from here, turn left as you exit, continue on for a block and then turn left again to cross the tracks via a pedestrian bridge. Once across the footbridge, you'll find buses #1 and #3 running a little way south to Zhongyang Jie, the city's main artery, passing the **long-distance bus station**, at the junction of Huochezhan Jie and Shanghua Jie, on the way. The bus station is useful only for the frequent service to the Russian border at Manzhouli (3hr; ¥25). Zhongyang Jie turns into Qiaotou Jie at the *Bei'er Dajiudian*; the area between here and Zhongyang Qiao – the river bridge – is filled with shops selling everything from pirated CDs to Mongolian saddles. The district across the bridge, where the road becomes Shengli Dajie, is of minimal interest unless you're staying at one of its cavernous hotels. **CAAC** is off Qiaotou Jie (daily 8am–5pm), on the small road leading east off the southwestern approach road to the bridge. There's a **bank** right next to the *Bei'er* hotel.

Hailar offers a range of **accommodation**, and most places welcome foreigners. One convenient place is the *Binzhou Fandian* (no phone), on the left-hand side of the train-station concourse as you exit the building. Rooms here are simple and clean, and the hot water works. Though it isn't close to the centre, its hourly (¥10) and half-day (¥30) rates make it a good pit stop if you've been out on the grasslands and want to wash up before heading out of town. In the centre, the best option is the *Bei'er Dajiudian* (Ⓣ0470/8332511, Ⓕ8334960; ❸), 36 Zhongyang Dajie, where the rate includes breakfast. The travel service here is helpful and its grassland tours cost less than those at CITS, though note that you will likely be wedged into a minibus with high-spirited (ie drunk) Chinese tourists. Across the street, at no. 35, the *Laodong Hotel* has three-person dorms as well as doubles (Ⓣ0470/8331349; ❸, dorm beds ¥50). Lurking on the east bank of the river is Hailar's throwback to the bad old days of Chinese tourism, the enormous, impersonal *Hulunbeier Hotel* (Ⓣ0470/8211000, Ⓕ8221123; ❸–❺), with a large range of bland doubles in its many wings, as well as accommodation in cement "yurts" dotting its parking lot. For a better atmosphere at similar rates, head further east to the *Beiyuan Hotel* (Ⓣ0471/8235666; ❹), 22 Shengli San Lu, north off Shengli Dajie. Its major drawback is being surrounded by the district government and police offices, meaning street and nightlife congregate elsewhere.

Eating in Hailar is a slapdash affair, with some restaurants serving excellent mutton and dumplings and others too bothered to try. The best area to eat is in the pedestrianized commercial district east of the Bei'er and north of Qiaotou Dajie. Whatever you do, be sure to study the menu (or even better, the kitchen), as Hailarites have a taste for **dog**, judging by the number of canine skeletons hanging about.

Beyond Hailar

A few hours to the west of Hailar is **MANZHOULI**, on the border with Russia. There are frequent buses here from Hailar (3hr; ¥25), along with daily trains. The Trans-Manchurian train from Beijing to Moscow also passes through once a week in each direction. The town has important steam locomotive yards, which you can visit, and not far to the south of town is the great lake **Dalai Hu** (Hulun Nur in Mongolian), a shallow expanse of water set in marshy grazing country where flocks of swans, geese, cranes and other migratory birds come to nest. The grasslands in this region are said to be the greenest in all Mongolia.

North of Hailar is a true wilderness, the final frontier of China. Here are some of the last great areas of untouched primeval forest in the country, a natural habitat for the wolf and the much-threatened Manchurian tiger. There is a rail line that meanders up as far north as Mangui, above the fifty-second parallel, but before attempting to visit this area you should check with the Hailar PSB.

Baotou and beyond

Just three hours to the west of Hohhot by train or bus lies Inner Mongolia's biggest city, **BAOTOU**. Its primary significance is as the chief iron- and steel-producing centre in China: if you're arriving at night from the direction of Yinchuan, your first glimpse of the city is likely to be of satanic fires burning in the great blast furnaces. The sky over the western half of Baotou is a more or less permanent yellow, orange and purple colour. For visitors, there can be something magnificent about ugliness on such a scale, but otherwise, apart

Baotou and beyond

Baotou	包头	***bāotóu***
Donghe	东河	*dōnghé*
Iron and Steel Works	钢铁公司	*gāngtiě gōngsī*
Kundulun	昆都仑	*kūndū lún*
Qingshan	青山	*qīngshān*
Steam Locomotive Museum	蒸汽火车博物馆	*zhēngqìhuǒchē bówùguǎn*
Accommodation		
Aviation	民航大厦	*mínháng dàshà*
Baotou	包头宾馆	*bāotóu bīnguǎn*
Beiyang	北洋饭店	*běiyáng fàndiàn*
Shenhua International	神华国际大酒店	*shénhuá guójì dàjiǔdiàn*
Tianwaitian	天外天大酒店	*tiānwàitiān dàjiǔdiàn*
Xingyuan	兴苑大酒店	*xīngyuán dàjiǔdiàn*
Dongsheng	东胜	***dōngshèng***
Genghis Khan's Mausoleum	成吉思汗陵园	*chéngjísīhàn língyuán*
Wudangzhao	五当召	***wǔdāng zhào***
Yellow River	黄河	***huánghé***

from a few minor sights, including **Wudangzhao**, an attractive Tibetan-style monastery outside the town, the city does not have much to offer. One further site of considerable romantic interest (if nothing else), **Genghis Khan's Mausoleum**, lies well to the south of Baotou near the town of **Dongsheng**.

The City

A colossal city stretching for miles in all directions, Baotou comprises three main areas: Donghe, the ramshackle, oldest part of town, to the east, and Qingshan and Kundulun to the west. Qingshan is a shopping and residential area, while Kundulun includes the iron and steel works on its western edge. The three parts of the city are well connected by frequent buses (#5 and #10),

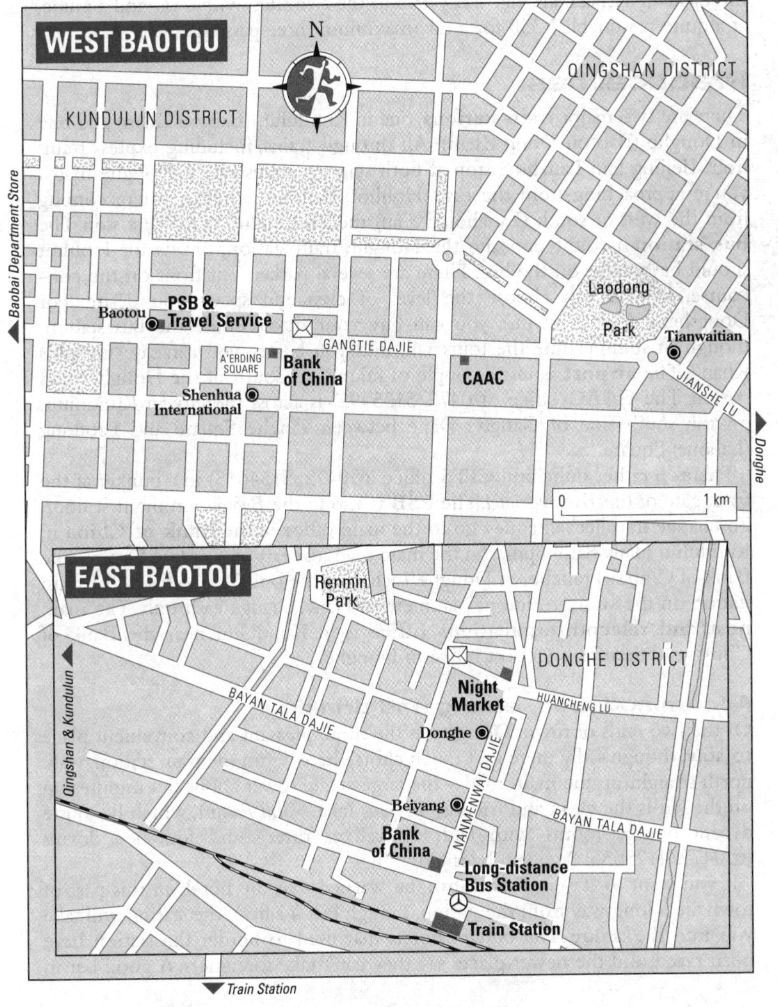

which take thirty to forty minutes to travel between the Donghe and Kundulun districts.

The only area in the whole city that could be described as remotely attractive is **Donghe** north of Renmin Park, where the tangled old streets are quite interesting to wander around. You can see a lot of old mud-brick houses here, each opening on to fascinating little courtyards full of plants and bicycles. Catch it while you can, however, as the area is being razed to resemble sterile, Westernized **Qingshan**, an expanse of malls and high-rise hotels. Along with Qingshan, **Kundulun** is mainly interesting as a monument to town-planning gone wrong – the treeless streets and squares are wide and bleak beyond belief. Even the "sights" – the **Iron and Steel Works** and the **Steam Locomotive Museum** (hours variable) – are not especially easy or cheap to visit. The museum is located in a particularly remote area, 25km out to the northwest. You may be able to visit it by yourself in a taxi, but make enquiries first; CITS in the *Baotou Hotel* can arrange a day-trip to the two sites, with a car and a guide, at a quite reasonable ¥350 for a car (maximum three passengers).

Practicalities

There are two major **train stations**, one in Kundulun (Baotou Zhan) and one in Donghe (Baotou Dong Zhan). All through-trains, including express trains from Beijing and Lanzhou, stop at both stations; trains call at Donghe first if you're approaching from the east (Hohhot, Beijing), while if you're coming from the west or south (Lanzhou, Xi'an) then Kundulun is the first stop. The **bus station** is right opposite the Donghe train station; tickets for Hohhot should be bought on the bus. There are several parked out front on the concourse, so you can choose the level of class and speed you desire. For Dongsheng (every 30min), you can buy your ticket inside the bus station, though in summertime the touts will find you before you can say "Genghis Khan". The **airport** is just a couple of kilometres south of the Donghe train station. The **CAAC** office (Ⓣ0472/5135492) is across the city in Kundulun, on the south side of Gangtie Dajie between Yinghe Square and Laodong (Labour) Square.

There's a rather unhelpful **CITS** office (Ⓣ0472/5154615) in a bunker at the front gate of the *Baotou Hotel*. The **PSB** is also in the *Baotou*, on the first floor. To change traveller's cheques, go to the main office of the **Bank of China** in Kundulun (daily 8am–6pm), on the main road just east of A'erding Square. The Bank of China's branches in Donghe, including the one 50m south of the train station on the western side of Nanmenwai Dajie, change cash only. The main **post and telecommunications office** is in Kundulun near the Bank of China, and there's also a post office in Donghe.

Accommodation, eating and drinking

Of the two ends of town, **Donghe** is the more pleasant and convenient place **to stay**, though sadly there isn't much choice here. From the train station, walk north straight up the main road – the large white tower about ten minutes up on the left is the clean and friendly *Beiyang* (aka *North Pacific*), which has quite decent double rooms with bath as well as three- and four-bed dorms (Ⓣ0472/4175656; ❷, dorm beds ¥10–20).

If you want to stay in **Kundulun**, be warned that the hotels in this part of town are a long way from the station, though bus #1 from the station will take you into the centre. The budget hotels that used to border the station have been razed, and the newer places say they can't take foreigners. A good bet in

Kundulun is the enormous *Baotou* (ⓣ0472/5156655, ⓕ5154641; ❹), on the main east–west Gangtie Dajie, a few hundred metres west of A'erding Square. It's reasonably comfortable, central and home to the city's PSB and CITS offices. The most upmarket hotel in town is the new *Shenhua International*, the tall edifice behind A'erding Square at 17 Shaoxian (ⓣ0472/2248888, ⓕ5147556; ❼), with its own pool, sauna, and gym. Also fancy, with swimming pool and fitness centre, is the older *Tianwaitian*, on the southern end of Hudemulin Dajie in Qingshan district (ⓣ0472/3137766, ⓕ3131771; ❺), though the cheaper *Aviation Hotel* (ⓣ0472/5135492; ❹), part of the CAAC office, has friendlier staff.

Baotou has a lousy array of **restaurants**. In Kundulun, tell the taxi driver to take you to Baobai, the new shopping district west on Gangtie Dajie; there's a *KFC* here, and across the street is a market with food stalls and small eateries. In Donghe, concentrate on the junction of Nanmenwai Dajie and Huancheng Lu, where a night market sets up.

Wudangzhao and the Yellow River

The one definite attraction in the Baotou area, **Wudangzhao** is the best-preserved Lamaist monastery still functioning in Inner Mongolia (daily 8am–6pm; ¥10), and is one of the results of the Mongolian conquest of Tibet in the thirteenth century. For centuries afterwards, the roads between Tibet and Mongolia were worn by countless pilgrims and wandering monks, bringing Lamaist Buddhism to Mongolia. This particular monastery, of the Yellow Sect, was established in 1749 and at its height housed twelve hundred lamas; seven generations of Living Buddhas were based here, the ashes of whom are kept in one of the halls. Today, however, the few remaining monks are greatly outnumbered by local tourists from Baotou, and sadly their main duties now seem to involve hanging around at the hall entrances to check tourists' tickets.

Set in a pretty, narrow valley scattered with pine trees about 70km northeast of the city, the monastery can be reached by catching the daily **minibus** from outside the Donghe train station in Baotou at around 8am. Otherwise, take **bus** #7 (50min; ¥4) from the east side of the station square (on the right as you exit the station) to the terminus at Shiguai. The monastery is another 25km on – if you arrive early enough there are one or two minibuses that go on to it from here, otherwise take a taxi from Shiguai (¥30). Once at the monastery, you can hike off into the surrounding hills and, if you're keen, you should be able to **stay** in the pilgrims' hostel in the monastery as well. Returning to Baotou is fairly easy as there are various minibuses and other tour vehicles plying the route, up to around 5pm.

The other main sight in the Baotou area is the **Yellow River**. It's worth having a look at, if only to ruminate on its historical significance. The whole area from Baotou to Hohhot was never automatically considered a part of China. In fact, the Chinese built the Great Wall far to the south of here, leaving the area enclosed by the loop of the river – known as the **Ordos** – to remain the dominion of the nomad. It was a simple dilemma: the Yellow River seemed like the logical northern limit of China, but the Ordos, to the south of the river, was part of the steppe and desert of Central Asia. The Qing eventually decided matters once and for all not only by seizing control of the Ordos, but also by moving north of the river into the heart of Mongolia. Today, the whole Yellow River region from Yinchuan in Ningxia Province, up to Baotou and across to Hohhot, is thoroughly irrigated and productive land – without the river, it would be pure desert. You can take a stroll along the northern bank of the Yellow River by taking **bus** #18 from in front of Donghe train station for about 6km to the new bridge. The river here is nearly a mile wide, shallow, sluggish and chocolate brown.

Genghis Khan's Mausoleum

The first thing to be said about **Genghis Khan's Mausoleum** (daily; ¥50) is that it's not all it's cracked up to be: it probably isn't the tomb of Genghis Khan, and it isn't a particularly attractive place anyway, but can nonetheless be fascinating as an insight into the modern cult of Genghis Khan.

Genghis Khan is known to have died in northern China but, while his funeral cortege may have passed through this region on its way back to Mongolia, the story that the wheels of his funeral cart got stuck in the mud here, resulting in his burial on the spot, is almost certainly apocryphal. At best, scholars believe, the site contains a few relics – perhaps weapons – of Genghis Khan. The real tomb is thought to be on the slopes of Burkhan Khaldun, in the Hentei Mountains, not far to the east of Ulan Batur in Outer Mongolia. The reason why it came to be so strongly believed that the Khan was buried here in China appears to be that the tribe who were charged with guarding the real sepulchre later drifted down across the Yellow River to the Ordos – but continued to claim the honour of being the official guardians of the tomb.

The alleged **relics** here have a murky political history. Several times they have been removed, and later returned, the most recent occasion being during World War II, when the Japanese seized them. Apparently the Japanese had plans to set up a puppet Mongol state, centred around a Genghis Khan shrine. They even drew up plans for an elaborate mausoleum to house them – plans that were then commandeered by the Chinese Communists who, having safely returned the relics from a hiding place in Qinghai, built the mausoleum for themselves in 1955 as a means of currying favour with the Mongolian people.

The site

The main part of the mausoleum is formed by three connecting halls, shaped like Mongolian yurts. The corridors connecting the halls are adorned with bizarre murals supposedly depicting the life of the Khan – though note the ladies in Western dress (1890-style). In the middle of the main hall is a five-metre-high marble **statue** of the Khan before a map of his empire. Whatever the truth about the location of his burial place, the popular view among Mongolians, both in China and in the Republic of Mongolia, is that this is a holy site: the side halls, all very pretty, have ceremonial yurts, altars, burning incense, hanging paintings and Mongolian calligraphy, and offerings as though to a god. Some bring offerings – not leave the usual apples and bread, but bottles of rotgut *baijiu* – it's on sale in the souvenir shop – and bow in penitence with prayer. Others, including several of the female staff, get drunk early and keep sipping until they're surly – or extremely affectionate; be prepared for anything as the site attracts its fair share of dodgy characters, including about fifteen "hairdressers" just outside. There's a small **museum** by the ticket office with a few relics.

Special **sacrificial ceremonies** take place here four times a year on certain days of the lunar calendar – the fifteenth day of the third lunar month, the fifteenth day of the fifth lunar month, the twelfth day of the ninth month and the third day of the tenth month. On these occasions, Mongolian monks lead solemn rituals which involve piling up cooked sheep before the statue of the Khan. The ceremonies are attended not only by local people, but by pilgrims from the Republic of Mongolia itself.

Practicalities

The mausoleum is located in the Ordos, beside a small road leading south into Shaanxi province, and is served by buses originating in **Yulin**, some 200km north of Yan'an. To reach the site from Baotou or Hohhot, take a bus first to the coal-mining town of **DONGSHENG**, 50km from the mausoleum. From Baotou there are frequent buses there (¥12) that take about two hours; from Hohhot the journey takes five hours. It would be possible, if you left Baotou very early in the morning, to reach the mausoleum and make it back the same evening – the last bus from Dongsheng to Baotou leaves at about 8pm. It's a tiring trip, though, and spending a night in Dongsheng is the most pleasant way to do it. Dongsheng is also accessible from Yinchuan in Ningxia, via Wuhai. On the way to Dongsheng, you'll pass spectacular areas of sand dune as well as grassland.

From Dongsheng to the mausoleum it takes a further one to two hours on a very rough road by bus or minibus (¥7), and outside of summer there are only a few departures a day; you should aim to catch a bus by 12.30pm, otherwise you may have to spend the night there. To return to Dongsheng from the mausoleum, simply stand in the road and flag down passing minibuses.

If you need a bed, you can **stay** either in Dongsheng or at the mausoleum itself. The best place to stay **in Dongsheng** is right by the bus station: come out of the station, turn right, then immediately right again into a cul-de-sac. On the right at the back is a pleasant hotel with "Room Dep" written in English above the door, offering double rooms with bath (❷). The square outside here holds a **night market** where you can get your dinner. A few minutes farther down the main street, away from the bus station, is the upmarket *Dongsheng Dajiudian* (Ⓣ0477/327333; ❺), which has good rooms and an elegant, not-too-pricey restaurant. There are also rooms **at the mausoleum** itself, or you can stay in a (very) fake yurt on concrete for ¥40–50 per person. Either way, there is no shower (and be warned: *baijiu* stings the eyes).

Ningxia

Covering just 66,000 square kilometres and squeezed between Inner Mongolia to the north and Gansu to the west, **Ningxia Autonomous Hui Region** is the smallest of China's provinces. Historically, the area has never been a secure one for the Chinese; almost every dynasty built its section of **Great Wall** through here and, in the nineteenth century, the Hui people played an active part in the Muslim rebellions, which were subsequently put down with great ferocity by the Qing authorities. Until recent times, Ningxia's very existence as a separate zone remained an open question; having first appeared on the map in 1928, the region was temporarily subsumed by Gansu in the 1950s before finally reappearing again in 1958. It appears that the authorities of the People's Republic could not make up their minds whether the Hui population was substantial enough to deserve its own autonomous region, in the same way as the Uigurs and the Mongols.

Hui is a vague term, applied to followers of the Muslim faith all over China who have no other obvious affiliation; Ningxia's Hui are descended from

Middle Eastern traders who arrived here over a thousand years ago. In Ningxia, as with all the autonomous regions of the Northwest, the central government has steadily encouraged **Han immigration** – or colonization – as a way of tying the area to the Chinese nation, but the situation of the Hui people is not comparable with that of the disaffected Uigurs or Tibetans. While remaining Muslim, the Hui have otherwise long since integrated with Han culture; barring a few Persian or Islamic words they speak Chinese as their mother tongue and, at present, there is little concept of a Hui nation floating round the backstreets of the provincial capital, Yinchuan. Today, the Hui make up about thirty percent of Ningxia's tiny population of four million, the remainder comprising mainly Han. Indeed, most Hui do not live in Ningxia at all, but are scattered around neighbouring regions, to the point where they often seem strangely absent within what is supposed to be their homeland.

Despite a certain degree of industrialization since the Communists came to power, and the opening of the Lanzhou to Baotou rail link in 1958, Ningxia remains an underdeveloped area. For visitors, the rural scenes are the charm of the place, but this province is one of the poorest parts of the country. Geographically, the area is dominated by coalfields and the **Yellow River**, without which the hilly south of the province, green and extremely beautiful, would be barren and uninhabitable desert. Unsurprisingly, the science of **irrigation** is at its most advanced here: two thousand years ago, the great founding emperor of China, Qin Shihuang, sent a hundred thousand men here to dig irrigation channels. To those ancient systems of irrigation, which are still used to farm cereal crops, have now been added ambitious reafforestation and desert reclamation projects. Some of these can be visited, particularly around the city of **Zhongwei**. Other sights include the regional capital **Yinchuan**, which makes a pleasant stopover, and one relic from an obscure northern branch of the Silk Road, the delightful **Xumi Shan Grottoes**, located well away from the Yellow River in the southern hills.

Yinchuan and around

The capital of Ningxia, **YINCHUAN** is a pleasantly unpolluted and leafy place to spend a couple of days. Although the bland modern city possesses little of tourist interest, from 1038 Yinchuan was capital of the **Western Xia kingdom**, an independent state which survived for two hundred years by playing off various Chinese dynasties – including the Song – against each other, before being conquered by the Mongols in 1227. So complete was their defeat that the Western Xia were virtually forgotten about until, in the early twentieth century, their archeological remains started being recognized for what they were; you should definitely make a visit to their weathered **mausoleums**, some 20km outside the city.

Orientation, arrival and accommodation

Yinchuan is another of China's spread-out cities, with its main bus and train stations at opposite ends, some 12km apart. The train station is in the western part of town, known as **Xincheng** (New City), while the bus station is in the east – **Laocheng** (Old City). There are a few hotels in Xincheng; Laocheng, however, bisected from east to west by its main street, **Jiefang Jie**, is undoubtedly the centre of things and is certainly the best place to stay.

Yinchuan and around

Yinchuan	银川	***yínchuān***
Gulou	古楼	*gŭlóu*
Hai Bao Ta	海宝塔	*hăibăo tă*
Laocheng	老城	*lăochéng*
Nanguan Mosque	南关清真寺	*nánguān qīngzhēn sì*
Nanmen	南门	*nánmén*
Regional Museum	宁夏博物馆	*níngxià bówùguăn*
Xi Ta	西塔	*xītă*
Xincheng	新城	*xīnchéng*
Yuhuang Ge	玉皇阁	*yùhuáng gé*
Accommodation		
Gulou	古楼饭店	*gŭlóu fàndiàn*
Huatian	华天 宾馆	*huátiān bīnguăn*
Labour Union	宁夏工会大厦	*níngxià gōnghuì dàshà*
Ningfeng	宁丰宾馆	*níngfēng bīnguăn*
Pijiu	啤酒饭店	*píjiŭ fàndiàn*
Railway Station Hotel	银川铁道宾馆	*yínchuān tiĕdào bīnguăn*
Rainbow Bridge Hotel	宁夏 红桥大酒店	*níngxià hóngqiáo dàjiŭdiàn*
Xincheng	新城饭店	*xīnchéng fàndiàn*
Yinchuan Fandian	银川饭店	*yínchuān fàndiàn*
Eating		
Hongyuan Shuai	红元帅	*hóngyuán shuài*
Xianhe Lou	仙鹤楼	*xiānhè lóu*
Xianhe Shuijiao	仙鹤水饺	*xiānhè shuĭjiăo*
Yingbin Lou	迎宾楼	*yíngbīn lóu*
Around Yinchuan		
108 Dagobas	一百零八塔	*yìbăilíngbātă*
Baisikou Shuang Ta	拜寺口双塔	*bàisìkŏu shuāng tă*
Gunzhong Pass	滚种口	*gŭnzhŏng kŏu*
Helan Shan	贺兰山	*hèlán shān*
Qingtongxia station	青铜峡站	*qīngtóngxiá zhàn*
Sha Hu	沙湖	*shā hú*
Suyu Kou	苏峪口	*sūyù kŏu*
Xixia Wangling	西夏王陵	*xīxià wánglíng*
Zhenbeibu	镇北堡	*zhènbĕi băo*

Yinchuan's new **airport** lies 15km southeast of Laocheng. Airport buses (¥15) connect with the CAAC office on Minzu Jie, a little north of Jiefang Jie. Long-distance **buses** from Xi'an, Lanzhou and Baotou use the Nanmen bus station in the south of Laocheng. The **train station** is located in the remote end of Xincheng, far to the west of town, serving Lanzhou in the west, and Beijing (via Inner Mongolia) in the east. Bus #1 (¥1) and private minibuses (negotiable) run from the train station – the stop is in the left part of the station square as you come out – into Xincheng and on to the bus station in Laocheng. Most of the hotels lie in the vicinity of this route – in Xincheng you should get off at Tiedong Lu, while in Laocheng you can get off along Jiefang Jie. A taxi from the train station to Laocheng costs about ¥15.

Accommodation

Accommodation in Yinchuan can be amazingly tight in midsummer: Chinese tourists flock here and you may end up doing a lot of traipsing around to find

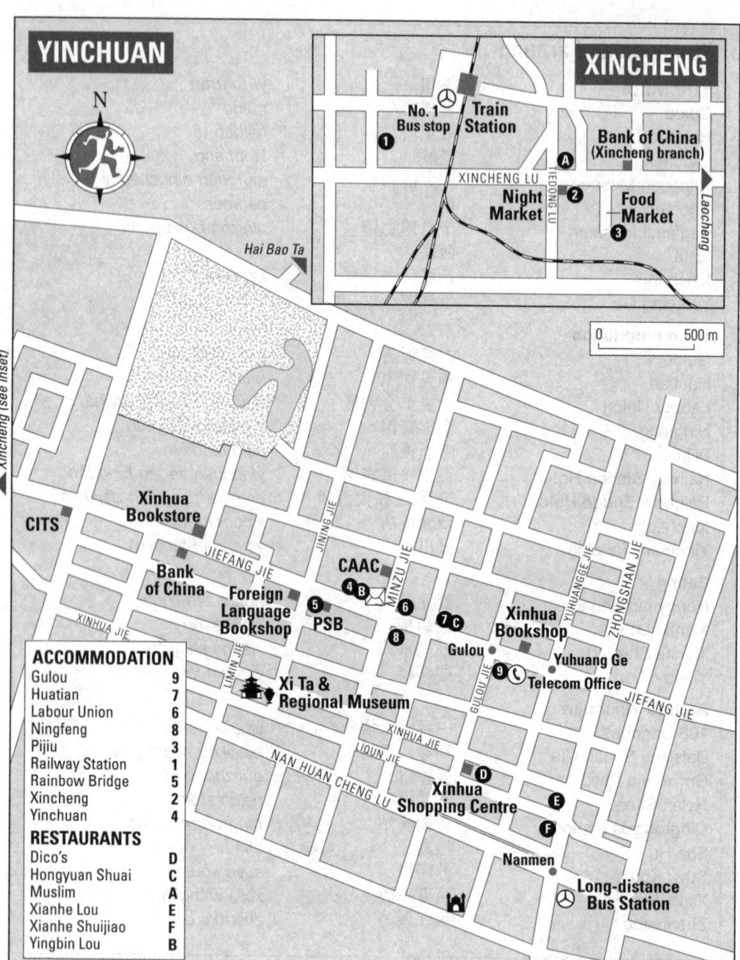

a place. Fortunately, however, there are plenty of options in both Xincheng and Laocheng. The former is more convenient for the train station and airport, but the latter is a far more pleasant place to stay.

Laocheng

Gulou Jiefang Jie ⓣ0951/6024331. Well located beside the Drum Tower, this little hotel has comfortable and affordable doubles, though they're very reluctant to rent their cheapest rooms to foreigners. ❷

Huatian West of the drum tower, on Jiefang Jie ⓣ0951/6025555. Good, cheap little place, though you'll need to speak some Chinese to negotiate a room. ❸

Labour Union Hotel Jiefang Jie ⓣ0951/6016898, ⓕ6024931. The newest and most upmarket place in town, good value and comfortable, with its own travel service, coffee shop, and Muslim restaurant. ❺

Ningfeng Jiefang Jie, at the junction with Minzu Jie ⓣ0951/6027162. This place looks very smart, but prices are affordable, and can be bartered down. Old wing ❷, otherwise ❹

Rainbow Bridge Jiefang Jie ⓣ0951/6918888,

ⓕ6918788. Though not as colourful as its name suggests, this four-star block is one of the plushest hotels in town, with a good restaurant. Rooms range from moderately priced to downright expensive. ❺

Yinchuan Fandian Jiefang Jie, a short walk east of Jining Jie ⓣ0951/6023053. Very cheap and with a wide range of rooms including doubles with and without a bath, and triples. Staff can be unhelpful though. ❶–❷

Xincheng

Pijiu (aka Beer Hotel). South down the first intersection east of Tiedong Lu if you're coming from the station, along a market street. A very cheap and simple place not used to foreigners, where a few words of Chinese will come in handy for getting a bed. ❷

Railway Station Hotel Off Xincheng Lu, close to the station ⓣ0951/3069112. What you might expect from a hotel run by the railways; staff are efficient if brusque, rooms are spartan, though reasonably well maintained. ❸

Xincheng Xincheng Lu ⓣ0951/3066010. Right on the corner with Tiedong Lu, this is one of the only hotels in the area that doesn't try to charge foreigners double. Doubles with bath. ❸

The City

Yinchuan's sights are all located in Laocheng, and can easily be visited on foot in a single day. The best place to start exploring is the centre of the city, based around the eastern part of Jiefang Jie, which is dominated by a couple of well-restored, traditionally tiered Chinese towers guarding the chief intersections. From the west, the first of these is **Gulou** (Drum Tower) at Gulou Jie, while the second, one block farther east, is the four-hundred-year-old **Yuhuang Ge** (Yuhuang Pavilion), at Yuhuang Jie, which also contains a tiny exhibition room.

Moving south from this part of Jiefang Jie towards the train station takes you through the main **downtown shopping area** of the city. The commercial heart of town centres around pedestrianized Gulou Jie, full of massive department stores and clothing boutiques and crammed to bursting on Sundays. From here it's about another kilometre southeast to the **Nanmen** (South Gate) at the southern end of Zhongshan Jie near the bus station, where a mock-up of the front gate of the Forbidden City in Beijing has been erected, complete with Mao Zedong's portrait and tiered seating for dignitaries. Fifteen minutes' walk southwest of Nanmen is the **Nanguan Mosque**, one of the few places in town you'll find Hui in any appreciable numbers. First built in 1915, it was rebuilt in 1981 after years of damage and neglect during the Cultural Revolution. The mosque is in the Arabian style with green domes and minarets, which sets it apart from the purely Chinese style of flying eaves and pagoda-style minarets of many mosques farther east.

Moving to the eastern half of Laocheng you'll find a couple more sights. On Jining Jie, a few blocks south of Jiefang Jie, are the **Regional Museum** and **Xi Ta** pagoda, together on the same site (daily 8am–5pm; site entry ¥2, museum ¥8, pagoda ¥5). One wing of the museum dryly sketches out local Hui history in photos and Chinese text, but there are also some splendid stone sculptures in the hall opposite – the best being a squat, fanged female demon pillar support from the Han dynasty – and a bronze drinking vessel of Greco-Roman origins, imported along the Silk Road two thousand years ago. Outside, Xi Ta is a classic Chinese pagoda and a place of worship for Buddhists, built around 1050 during the time of the Western Xia. You can climb the octagonal, 65-metre tower right to the top for excellent views.

Look north up Jining Jie from Jiefang Jie and you'll see another tower peering up from the horizon in the distance directly ahead – this is the 1500-year-old **Hai Bao Ta** (¥5), otherwise known as the North Pagoda. Brick-built, 54m high and of an unusual, angular shape, with protruding ledges and niches at every level, it's architecturally by far the most interesting structure in Yinchuan and well worth a visit – you can ascend the rather bare interior to the uppermost level for further views of the city. Walking there from Jiefang Jie takes forty minutes.

Eating and drinking

Of the two parts of town, it's **Laocheng** that has the better choice of **food**. Just west of the drum tower on Jiefang Jie, *Hongyuan Shuai* is a canteen with shared tables and tasty, Sichuan-style cold snacks and bowls of spicy noodle soups; you'd have to be very hungry to spend more than ¥10 here. For local flavour, *Yingbin Lou* is a smart, mid-range Muslim restaurant near the *Yinchuan Fandian*, serving lamb hotpots, kebabs, noodles and eight-treasure tea; while *Xianhe Shuijiao*, down near the bus station on Zhongshan Jie, deals in dumplings – vegetable or various meats – which you order by the *jin* and then watch being assembled by an army of cooks in the restaurant window. A half *jin* costs ¥15 and is plenty for one person. Their nearby sister restaurant, *Xianhe Lou*, offers similarly inexpensive hotpots, casseroles and more cold snacks. For Western-style fare, there's a branch of *Dico's Burgers* on Xinhua Jie, and the *Labour Union Hotel*'s coffee shop does a decent brew.

In **Xincheng**, you can get spicy grilled lamb kebabs and bowls of yoghurt at the small **night market** that sets up on the south side of the intersection between Xincheng Jie and Tiedong Jie, near the hotels. Walking east from this intersection and taking the first right brings you into a larger market street where you can buy food during the day and night. Otherwise, try the Muslim restaurant next door to the *Taoyuan Hotel* on Tiedong Lu, which serves fairly standard Chinese fare.

Listings

Airline CAAC, Minzu Jie (Mon–Sat 8am–5.30pm; ⓣ0951/6022063).
Banks and exchange The main Bank of China building is in the western part of Laocheng, on Jiefang Jie (Mon–Sat 9am–noon & 2.30–6.30pm). There is also a branch in Xincheng, on Xincheng Lu a few hundred metres east of Tiedong Lu.
Bookshops For English-language novels as well as local maps, the Foreign Language Bookstore is at the corner of Jiefang Jie and Jining Jie.
Internet access There's a Net bar on Zhongshan Jie, just north of the Jiefang Jie intersection, where you can log on for ¥2 an hour.
Mail and telephones The main post office is at the junction of Jiefang and Minzu Jie. Long-distance calls can be made from the 24hr office on Jiefang Jie.
PSB At the southeastern corner of the intersection between Jiefang Jie and Limin Jie.
Trains Outward-bound tickets can be bought easily from the station, or your hotel will almost certainly be able to arrange it for you, with around ¥30 commission, as long as you give at least 24 hours' notice. Otherwise try a travel agent.
Travel agents The China Travel Service of Ningxia is located at 150 Jiefang Jie (ⓣ0951/5044485), at Ximen in the western end of Laocheng. Ningxia CITS shares the same address (ⓣ0951/5043720). Enquire at these for tours of areas outside the city.

Around Yinchuan

A few interesting spots outside Yinchuan can comfortably be visited as day-trips. The best of these are the **Xixia Wangling** (Mausoleums of the Western Xia) about 20km west of the new city. Dotted around on the plain at the foot of the eastern slopes of the Helan Shan range, these giant tumuli stand as monuments to the twelve kings of the Western Xia, whose kingdom was based at Yinchuan from 1038 to 1227. The site is spectacular and atmospheric, with towering, haystack-shaped piles of brown mud bricks, slowly and silently disintegrating, punctuating the view for miles around. The cheapest way to reach the site is to take **bus** #17, which goes right through both Laocheng and Xincheng. Ride to the end stop and take a taxi or motor-rickshaw for the last 10km – a return trip from the bus stop to the mausoleums costs ¥30–50.

The **Helan Shan** themselves are also of interest. The **Gunzhong Pass**, about 25km west of Xincheng, is a pleasant summer-resort area, with attractive, historic buildings and plenty of opportunities for hiking around the hills and admiring the views. Six or seven kilometres north of here are the **Baisikou Shuang Ta**, a couple of twelve-metre-high pagodas guarding another pass, a few more kilometres to the east of which is the village of **Zhenbeibu** where the film *Red Sorghum*, directed by Zhang Yimou, was shot. The film depicts village life in northwest China during the period leading up to World War II – in part a rural idyll, in part a brute struggle to survive. The scenes of dry, dusty hillsides alternating with the lush fields of sorghum are a fair record of how Ningxia still looks today. Fairly extensive galleries of engraved **rock art** have also been found near here at **Suyu Kou**, mostly depicting stylized faces, figures and animals, though their meaning and age is uncertain. A tour of these places from Yinchuan costs around ¥180–200 in a car or small minivan which you can pick up in the street, or rent from one of the travel agents in town.

Farther away from town, about 57km north of Yinchuan, is the beautiful **Sha Hu** (Sand Lake). This is a developing summer resort par excellence, with swimming, sand-dunes, rafting and beautiful scenery. As yet few Western tourists have visited this place, though it is an easy ninety-minute minibus ride from Nanmen; accommodation is available at Sha Hu.

Finally, about 80km south of Yinchuan, are the **108 Dagobas**. These dagobas – Buddhist stupas of the type found in Tibetan monasteries – stand in a strange triangular pattern on a slope on the west bank of the Yellow River in Qingtongxia County. The white, bell-shaped dagobas are arranged in twelve rows, tapering from nineteen in the bottom row to a single one at the top. They are thought to have been put there in the fourteenth century during the Yuan dynasty, though their exact significance is not known. To visit the dagobas, catch the morning train from Yinchuan to **Qingtongxia station** (actually 15km southwest of Qingtongxia town; 1hr). From Qingtongxia you can catch a motor-rickshaw 7km east to the dagobas for about ¥15, or hike. The sole train from Qingtongxia station back to Yinchuan leaves in the late afternoon.

Zhongwei and Shapotou

A small country town, **ZHONGWEI** is 160km and a few hours by bus to the southwest of Yinchuan near the Yellow River. Historically, the old, walled city of Zhongwei was said to have had no north gate – simply because there was nothing more to the north of here. The city is still in a potentially awkward location, between the fickle **Yellow River** to the south and the sandy Tenger Desert to the north, but today Zhongwei is surrounded by a rich belt of irrigated fields, and the desert is kept at bay through reafforestation projects. The river outside the town, at **Shapotou**, is a splendid sight and should definitely be visited if you are in the area.

Zhongwei is based around a simple crossroads, with a traditional Gulou (Drum Tower) at the centre. It's small enough to walk everywhere, although there are cycle-rickshaws available to ferry you around. The town has one intriguing sight, the **Gao Miao** (daily 8am–6pm; ¥5), a quite extraordinary temple catering for any number of different religions, including Buddhism,

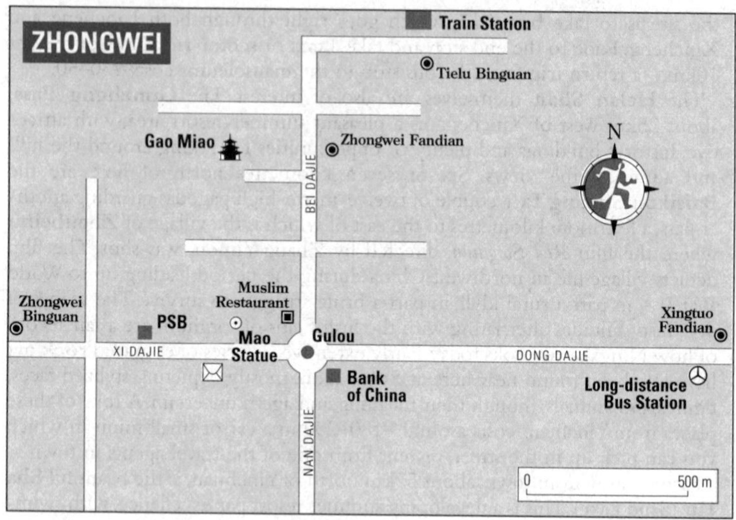

Confucianism, Taoism and even Christianity. Originally built in the early fifteenth century, and rebuilt many times, the temple is now a magnificent jumble of buildings and styles. From the front entrance you can see dragon heads, columns, stairways and rooftops spiralling up in all directions; altogether there are more than 250 temple rooms, towers and pavilions. Inside, you need a pretty expert eye to distinguish the saints of the various religions – they all look very much alike. To reach the Gao Miao, walk a few minutes north from the crossroads, and take a left turn down a small lane opposite the *Zhongwei Fandian*.

Practicalities

All trains on the main Lanzhou–Beijing (via Inner Mongolia) rail line call at Zhongwei. Branch lines also serve Wuwei in Gansu province and Baoji in Shaanxi. Zhongwei's **train station** is just off the north arm of the crossroads; the **bus station** is on the east road, with connections to Guyuan farther south and Wuwei in Gansu Province. Buses to and from Yinchuan run frequently, but stop at around 3pm.

Zhongwei and Shapotou

Zhongwei	中卫	***zhōngwèi***
Gao Miao	高庙	*gāomiào*
Tielu Binguan	铁路宾馆	*tiělù bīnguǎn*
Xingtuo Fandian	兴拓饭店	*xīngtuò fàndiàn*
Zhongwei Binguan	中卫宾馆	*zhōngwèi bīnguǎn*
Zhongwei Fandian	中卫饭店	*zhōngwèi fàndiàn*
Shapotou	沙坡头	***shāpōtóu***
Desert Research Institute	沙漠研究所	*shāmò yánjiūsuǒ*
Shapo Shanzhuang	沙坡山庄	*shāpō shānzhuāng*

If you're arriving in Zhongwei by train, you'll find **accommodation** right outside the station at the *Tielu Binguan* (*Railway Hotel*; Ⓣ0953/7031948; ❸), a nice, clean and friendly place offering double rooms with bath. From the train station, it's a short walk into town – turn right as you exit the station, and then take the first left onto Bei Dajie into the centre. Along here, you'll pass the pleasant *Zhongwei Fandian* on the left (Ⓣ0953/7102219; ❷), more or less opposite the entrance to the Gao Miao. A more upmarket option is the *Zhongwei Binguan* (Ⓣ0953/7012609, Ⓕ7012284; ❹), ten minutes' walk west from the centre along the Xi Dajie. East from the centre, on Dong Dajie near the bus station, is the *Xingtuo Fandian* (❷, dorm beds ¥30), which does not have a permit to take foreigners, but they will anyway – turn right as you come out of the station and walk for a couple of minutes. It's not as nice as the other budget hotels, and is slightly remote.

There are lots of cheap **noodle shops** along Bei Dajie near the Gao Miao and opposite the *Zhongwei Fandian*. You'll also find quite a good **Muslim restaurant** almost immediately to the northwest of Gulou in the centre – dinner here with beer will cost less than ¥20 per head. For a slightly smarter ambience (but still not expensive) try the restaurant in the *Zhongwei Binguan*.

Shapotou

Sixteen kilometres west of Zhongwei by minibus from the bus station, **SHAPOTOU** is a tourist resort of sorts by the banks of the Yellow River. Most people come on a day-trip, but you can easily spend an enjoyable night or two here. The main pleasure of the place is in the contrast between the leafy, shady banks of the river itself, and the harsh desert that lies just beyond. There's also some dramatic sand-dune scenery, and the spectacle of sandy desert actually in the process of being reclaimed: the **Shapotou Desert Research Centre** has been based here for forty years, working on ways to conquer the sands, and some of the fruits of their labour can be seen en route to the resort. Travelling either by bus or train between Zhongwei and Shapotou, you'll see the chequerboard grid of straw thatch implanted to hold the sands in place; all the trees you see along the way are the results of this work, planted into this painfully constructed grid. A new water conservancy and hydroelectric scheme just outside Shapoutou is due for completion in 2004, and will presumably help expand the work already done in providing irrigation for future fields.

Arriving at the **train station**, facing the river, turn right and walk a few hundred metres along the road to the entry point to the **tourist resort**, marked by a couple of kiosks. Stepping through the gate (¥15), you'll find yourself on the top of a gigantic dune from where you can look down onto the research institute, surrounded by an entire plain of reclaimed greenery. Reaching the resort area from here is easy – simply slide down the dune (the reverse journey can be done by a kind of ski lift; ¥10). It's quite a charming place, with shady trees, cafés and outdoor restaurants. There are also activities such as camel-riding and, more unusually, **sheepskin rafting** in traditional rafts of sewn-up sheepskins, pumped full of air like footballs with legs, and tied together. You'll see a lot of these rafts in various stages of production and maintenance.

A few minutes downstream, the *Shapo Shanzhuang* is a delightful **hotel** (Ⓣ0953/7681481; ❷) in a very cool and pleasant location, with gardens full of trees and vine trellises. It has nice doubles with bath, and the muffled roar of the neighbouring Yellow River makes for soothing ambient sound.

Southern Ningxia

Located in the remote, impoverished southern part of Ningxia, the town of **Guyuan** has seen very little tourist traffic. Only in 1995 did it finally join the rail network, with the opening of the Zhongwei–Baoji line. Aside from a ruinous stretch of the **Great Wall** 5km north of town (you'll see it in passing), the main interest here is in the Buddhist grottoes at **Xumi Shan**, a major relic of the Silk Road, curiously marooned far to the north of the main route from Lanzhou to Xi'an. The great Taoist temple Kongtang Shan at Pingliang (see p.1025) is only two hours from Guyuan, another possible day-trip. Travellers can also enjoy some lovely countryside, especially if you're coming up from relatively arid regions such as Tianshui or Pingliang in Gansu province to the south. The hills along the road from Gansu have been terraced for centuries; every inch of land in the vast landscape is under cultivation, with terraces laddering up the slopes and flowing round every tiny hillock and gully in fantastic swirls of colour.

The high pass on the border with Gansu, **Liupan Shan** (which you cross on the way to or from Tianshui), is also famous for the fact that the Long Marchers managed to elude pursuing Guomindang forces here in the 1930s; a commemorative stone marks the spot.

Guyuan

GUYUAN is a useful place to base yourself for a visit to the Xumi Shan grottoes, but is itself of no special interest – in fact tourists are so rare here that you are likely to be mobbed wherever you go. Although trains now pass through Guyuan on their way between Zhongwei and Baoji in Shaanxi Province, the **train station** is inconveniently located several kilometres from town. It's easier to rely on long-distance **buses**, connecting Guyuan with Xi'an and Luoyang to the east; and Lanzhou, Tianshui and Pingliang in Gansu to the west. There is also one daily connection to Zhongwei and Yinchuan, leaving in the morning.

Guyuan's **post office** is a short walk from the bus station: turn right out of the station and continue past the cinema to the first intersection, then turn right again. Continue walking and it's on the right just past the traffic circle. For the **Bank of China**, walk left from the bus station for a few minutes, and you'll see it on the left.

Accommodation is available at the affable *Dongfang Hotel* (❸, dorm beds ¥30). Come out of the bus station, turn left, and the hotel is about 100m down the road, on the opposite side. Though it's a little creaky, the staff are trying their best – the blankets sculpted into scallop shapes on the beds every morning is a nice touch. There's hot water in the evening. Alternatively, turn right out of the bus station and a couple of minutes' walk will bring you to the very primitive *Yongxiang Fandian* (❸, dorm beds ¥30).

Southern Ningxia

Liupan Shan	六盘山	***liùpán shān***
Sanying	三营	*sānyíng*
Xumi Shan	须弥山	*xūmí shān*
Guyuan	固原	***gùyuán***
Dongfang Binguan	东方宾馆	*dōngfāng bīnguǎn*
Yongxiang Fandian	永祥饭店	*yǒngxiáng fàndiàn*

The street in front of the bus station transforms into quite a lively **night market** in the evening, with kebabs, noodles and *hundun* soup all available. There's some excellent fruit including melons and peaches here in summer, too. The restaurant of the *East Hotel* is pretty good but gets very busy. If you get tired of the locals' friendly but overbearing curiosity, you could take refuge in the **cinema**, 200m farther down the road from the *Yongxiang*.

The Xumi Shan grottoes

The dramatic **Xumi Shan grottoes** (daily; ¥15) lie about 50km northeast of Guyuan and make a worthy day-trip. More than one hundred caves have been carved out from the cliff faces on five adjoining hillsides here, and a large number of statues survive, primarily from the Northern Wei, Sui and Tang dynasties. The natural backdrop is beautiful and secluded; at Xumi Shan, the grottoes occupy a huge site of rusty red sandstone cliffs and shining tree-covered slopes commanding panoramic views. The last stage of the journey there takes you through one of the remotest corners of rural China where, at the height of summer, you can see the golden wheat being cut by hand, then spread out over the road to be ground by passing vehicles.

The **site** takes at least two hours to walk around. After entering the cliffs area, bear left first for Cave No. 5 and the **Dafo Lou**, a statue of a giant twenty-metre-high Maitreya Buddha facing due east. Originally this Buddha used to be inside a protective wall, but the wall has long since fallen away. Head back to the entrance again and you'll see the five hillocks lined up along an approximate east–west axis, each with one key sight and a cluster of caves. After the Dafo Lou, the second major sight you come to is **Zisun Gong** (Descendants' Palace); it's followed by **Yuanguang Si**, a modern temple. From here you have to cross a bridge and bear left to reach **Xiangguo Si**, centred around the magnificent Cave No. 51 with its five-metre-high Buddhas all seated around a central pillar. Returning to the bridge, walk underneath it and up the dry river bed towards the cliff, to reach **Taohua Dong** (Peach Blossom Cave).

The cheapest way to reach Xumi Shan is first to take a public **bus** (or train) to the small town of **Sanying**. Frequent buses and minibuses (hourly; ¥2) run back and forth between the Guyuan bus station and Sanying all day until early evening. You'll then have to hire a motor-rickshaw for the thirty-minute drive to the caves; a return trip (and at least a 2hr wait while you look around) should cost about ¥40. At the grottoes' car park, there's a kiosk where you can buy **drinks and snacks**, plus a basic **hotel** in the unlikely event that you might need to stay the night, though it's also possible to stay in Sanying at the respectable *Dianli Fandian* (❸).

Gansu

Traditionally, the Chinese have regarded **Gansu** as marking the outer limit of China. During the Han dynasty (206 BC–220 AD), the first serious effort was made to expand into the western deserts, primarily as a means to ensure control over the Silk Road trade. Prefectures were established and, although Gansu

PICC insurance

Irrespective of any other insurance policies you may have, in many rural parts of China foreigners need to be covered by the state insurer, **PICC** (People's Insurance Company of China), in order to travel on buses. This has nothing to do with paying you in the event of an accident, but is a waiver to prevent the authorities from being sued. Generally, insurance for each journey is included in the ticket price, but in Gansu and Western Sichuan you're actually required to **buy** a separate PICC policy before anyone will even sell you a bus ticket. Certificates of two weeks' validity can be bought from PICC offices (in Gansu, all cities have them) for between ¥30 and ¥50, though some offices seem unaware of the regulations and can't understand what you're after. In this case, try hotels, CITS offices, or even bus stations, where you'll have to pay an additional commission.

As is always the case in China, the regulation is erratically enforced: sometimes flashing the policy at the right moment is the only way to get aboard a bus; sometimes nobody cares. If you can't get a policy and nobody will sell you a ticket, try flagging the bus down once it has left the station – often the drivers are happy to take you anyway.

did not officially become a Chinese province until the Mongolian Yuan dynasty (1279–1368), it is unquestionably a part of the Chinese heartland. At various stages over the last two thousand years Chinese control has extended well beyond here into Xinjiang. Nevertheless, right into the nineteenth century, the primarily Muslim inhabitants of this province were considered little better than the "barbarian" Uigurs of Xinjiang by central government; the great Muslim revolts of that period were ruthlessly quashed.

A harsh and barren land, subject to frequent droughts, Gansu has always been a better place for travelling through rather than settling down in. The province's geography is remarkable – from the great **Yellow River**, dense with silt, surging through the provincial capital of **Lanzhou**, to the mountains and deserts of the **Hexi Corridor**, the thousand-kilometre route between mountain ranges that narrows at times to as little as 15km wide. It's the Hexi Corridor that accounts for the curious elongated shape of the province: the Silk Road caravans came down here, the Great Wall was built through here, and today's trains chug through here as well, along what is – until the line from Golmud to Tibet is completed – the only rail line in northwestern China and the only link through Central Asia between China and the West. The towns along the Hexi Corridor are mere dots of life in the desert, sustained by irrigation using water from the mountains. Given that agriculture is barely sustainable here, central government has tried to import a certain amount of industry into the province, particularly in the east. The exploitation of mineral deposits, including oil and coal, has made a tentative beginning. But still the population is relatively small, comprising just twenty million, who continue to display an extraordinary ethnic mix, with Hui, Kazakhs, Mongols and Tibetans all featuring prominently.

The province may be wild and remote by Chinese standards, but it's of enormous historical interest. The **Mogao Caves** at **Dunhuang** in the far west house the finest examples of Buddhist art in all China, and further Silk Road sights are scattered right along the length of the province, ranging from the country's largest reclining Buddha at **Zhangye** to the stunning Buddhist caves at **Bingling Si**, near Lanzhou, and **Maiji Shan**, near **Tianshui** in the far south. The Great Wall, snaking its way west, comes to a symbolic end at the great Ming fortress at **Jiayuguan**, and, in the southwest of the province, right on the edge of the Tibetan plateau, is the fascinating **Labrang Monastery** at the Tibetan town of **Xiahe**.

Eastern Gansu

West of the border with Shaanxi, the first significant Silk Road city is **Tianshui**, with the spectacular **Maiji Shan** complex just a few kilometres to the southeast. Maiji Shan – literally "Wheatstack Mountain", a name derived from its shape – is the fourth largest Buddhist cave complex in China, after Dunhuang, Datong and Luoyang. Set amid stunning wooded hill scenery, the caves easily accessed from Tianshui, which is located about halfway along on the Lanzhou–Xi'an rail line. You will probably need to spend at least one night at Tianshui, the nearest transport hub to the caves but itself of limited interest to tourists. A little way to the west of Tianshui, towards Lanzhou, are some more fascinating Silk Road relics, in and around the towns of **Gangu** and **Wushan**.

Tianshui

The area around **TIANSHUI** was first settled back in neolithic times, though today the city is an enormous industrial spread with two distinct centres, known as **Qincheng** (West Side) and **Beidao** (East Side), situated some 20km apart. Whether you choose to stay in Beidao or Qincheng will probably be determined by whether you arrive at the Beidao train station or the Qincheng bus station. If your only interest is a trip to Maiji Shan and back, you should stay in Beidao, from where all the Maiji Shan minibuses depart, though this is the grottier of the two ends of town, with the feel of a rural backwater.

Eastern Gansu

Tianshui	天水	***tiānshuǐ***
Beidao	北道	*běidào*
Fuxi Miao	伏羲庙	*fúxī miào*
Qincheng	秦城	*qínnchéng*
Yuquanguan Park	玉泉观公园	*yùquánguān gōngyuán*
Yuquan Si	玉泉寺	*yùquán sì*
Accommodation		
Jianxin	建新饭店	*jiànxīn fàndiàn*
Tianshui	天水宾馆	*tiānshuǐ bīnguǎn*
Xihuang	天水羲皇宾馆	*tiānshuǐ xīhuáng bīnguǎn*
Yatai	天水亚太大酒店	*tiānshuǐ yàtài dàjiǔdiàn*
Gangu	甘谷	***gāngǔ***
Daxiang Shan	大象山	*dàxiàng shān*
Maiji Shan	麦积山	***màijī shān***
Pingliang	平凉	***píngliáng***
Kongtong Shan	崆峒山	*kōngtóng shān*
Wushan	武山	***wǔshān***
Lashao Temple	拉稍寺	*lāshāo sì*
Shuilian Dong	水帘洞	*shuǐlián dòng*

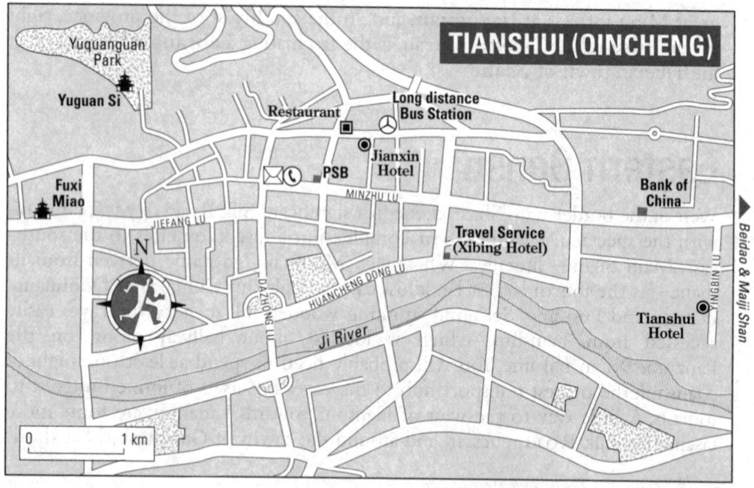

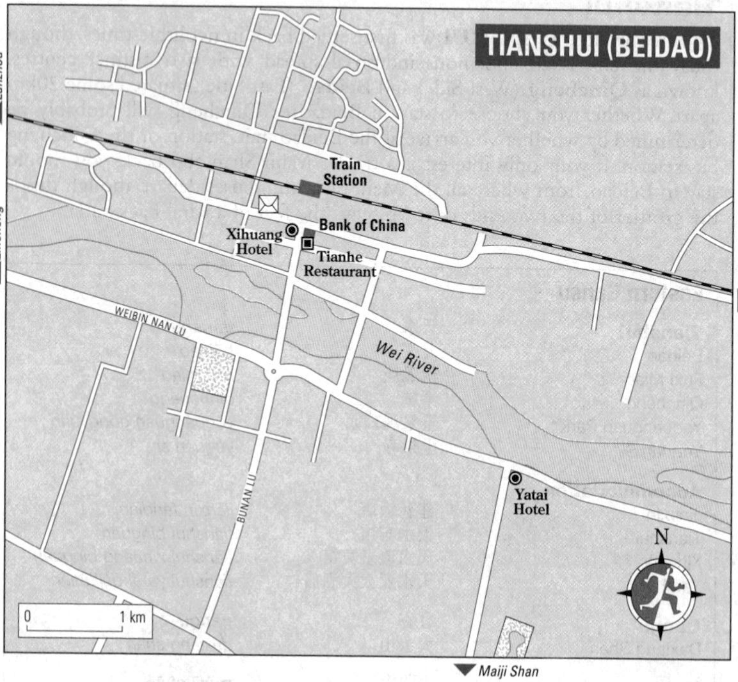

In slightly smarter Qincheng, head west from the main square (at the west end of Minzhu Lu) along Jiefang Lu and you'll almost immediately reach an area of crumbling, traditional architecture with low, upward sweeping roof eaves and heavy tiles now gathering moss. Tiny alleyways lead off in all directions. About fifteen minutes' walk along Jiefang Lu is the Ming-dynasty complex of **Fuxi Miao** commemorating the mythological Fuxi, credited with introducing the Chinese to fishing, hunting and animal husbandry – there is a statue of him, clad in leaves, in the main hall. The temple is notable for its beautiful cypress trees; as you enter, you pass a thousand-year-old tree on the right. Another interesting temple complex, **Yuquan Si**, in the western part of town, occupies **Yuquanguan Park**, up above Renmin Xi Lu. This is a 700-year-old active Taoist temple, on a hill about ten minutes' walk northwest of the main square. The temple is surrounded by attractive cypress trees and gives good views over the old city.

Practicalities

All trains stop at the **train station** in Beidao. **Buses**, including services to and from Lanzhou, Linxia, Pingliang, Guyuan (in Ningxia) and Xi'an, usually use the long-distance **bus station** in Qincheng, or stop and start in front of the train station. **City transport** between the two centres is swift and efficient, with minibuses and bus #1 between the two stations running all day – the run takes about thirty minutes and costs ¥2. Buses become scarce around 10pm at night, and the first bus in the morning leaves at around 6am. A taxi between the two should cost around ¥20.

The Beidao **post office** is just west of the train station, the **Bank of China** just east. About the only decent place to get a **meal** in Beidao is at the *Tianhe* – head south from the station to the first crossroads, then turn left and it's on the corner. The staff are very friendly, and the cook makes an effort to impress.

In Qincheng, the **Bank of China** head office is on Minzhu Lu close to the *Tianshui Hotel*. To make long-distance calls, use the main **post office** on Minzhu Lu. One useful **travel agent** worth trying in Qincheng, the China Travel Service of Tianshui (Ⓣ0938/8213621), is in the *Xibing Hotel* on Huancheng Dong Lu, facing a small river. Some of the staff here speak English and may be able to act as your guide to the Maiji Shan Caves, for a very reasonable ¥100 or so.

Accommodation

There's decent accommodation in both Qincheng and Beidao, but as there's little to detain you in town after a visit to Maiji Shan, you might consider getting a late train out.

Jianxin A 5min walk west of the bus station in Qincheng Ⓣ0938/8214900. A cheap and hospitable place, with a good restaurant right opposite. To spot it, look for an English placard saying "We welcome all distinguished guests". ❷

Tianshui Yingbin Lu, Qincheng Ⓣ0938/8212611, Ⓕ8212823. From the bus station, walk on to Minzhu Lu and catch bus #1, or any minibus, east to Yingbin Lu. You can also get here on bus #1, or minibuses from Beidao. The town's most upmarket hotel, though a bit frayed and pricey for what you get. ❺

Xihuang Binguan In the round building on the corner opposite and to the right of the station concourse, Beidao (Ⓣ0938/2734700). Cheap and unattractive, with concrete floors that the staff seem perpetually to be washing. ❶

Yatai Beidao Ⓣ0938/2727712. Exit the station, head south across the river, then take the first left and it's about 1500m further, on the right. The lobby is a little pretentious given the fairly average rooms, but rates aren't expensive and, usefully, the place is on the minibus route to the caves. ❸

Maiji Shan

The trip to the Buddhist caves on the mountain of **Maiji Shan** is the highlight of eastern Gansu. As is often the case with the Buddhist cave sites in northwest China, the natural setting itself is spectacular: although the whole area is very hilly, the sheer, rocky cliffs of Maiji Shan, rising out of the forest, make this one hill a complete anomaly. The centrepiece of the statuary, the giant **sixteen-metre-high Buddha** (complete with birds nesting in its nostril) is visible from far away, hanging high up on the rock in conjunction with two smaller figures. The combination of rickety walkways on the cliff face with the beautiful wooded, mountain scenery opposite makes this a charming site.

The cliffs were apparently split apart by an earthquake in the eighth century and there are in total 194 surviving **caves** on the eastern and western sections, dating from the northern Wei right through to the Qing. The western cliff caves are particularly well preserved, and date mainly from the fourth to the sixth century AD: cave no. 133 is considered to be the finest, containing sculptures and engraved stones. You are free to explore on your own, climbing higher and higher up the narrow stairways on the sheer face of the mountain. The caves are all locked though, and you often find yourself peering into half-lit caverns through wire grilles, but for the non-specialist the views are probably adequate – at least some of the artwork and statuary shows up clearly.

Frequent **minibuses** run to the caves from the square outside Tianshui's train station (45min–1hr); the ride costs ¥6 each way, though they usually try to charge foreigners double. According to some local maps, bus #5 also goes to the caves from Qincheng, but in fact this route is defunct. When you reach Maiji Shan (daily 8am–6pm), there is a fee of ¥10 per person to enter the mountain area. The minibuses continue for another few hundred metres, after which you have to walk up the hill past the souvenir touts to the ticket office; a ticket without guide costs ¥25. If you ask around at the site, you may be able to find an English-speaking guide to unlock the cave doors and explain the artwork. Another option is to arrange this in advance with the Tianshui CTS before you set out (see p.1023).

Gangu, Wushan and Pingliang

West of Tianshui, on the road and rail line to Lanzhou, are a couple of little-known but fascinating reminders of the Silk Road era. The attraction at **GANGU**, 65km west of Tianshui, is **Daxiang Si** (Giant Statue Temple; ¥15), which gets its name from the giant statue of an unusually moustached Sakyamuni Buddha which was carved out of a cliff during the Tang dynasty. The statue is more than 23m tall, and can be reached in about an hour by foot along a path leading uphill from the town, following a shrine-studded ridge all the way to the temple.

From **Wushan**, 45km farther west from Gangu, you can visit the **Shuilian Dong** (Water Curtain Grottoes), which contain a number of important relics, including the **Lashao Temple** as well as a Thousand Buddha Cave site. This is an extraordinary area, all the better preserved for being so inaccessible – the temple, being set into a natural cave in a cliff, is not even visible from the ground. Digging at the grottoes began during the Sixteen States period (304–439 AD) and continued through the dynasties. The Lashao Temple was built during the Northern Wei (386–534). There is a thirty-metre-high statue of Sakyamuni on the mountain cliff, his feet surrounded by wild animals, including lions and elephants. The grottoes, about 30km north of Wushan, can only be reached along a dried-up riverbed – there is as yet no proper road.

All **buses** – and all **trains** except for express services – running between Tianshui and Lanzhou stop at both Gangu and Wushan. It's also possible to visit Gangu as a day-trip from Tianshui; minibuses run from the Qincheng bus station in the morning. If you want to visit both Gangu and the grottoes in one day from Tianshui you have to rent a vehicle; to handle the rough road from Wushan, this needs to be something bigger than a taxi – more like a small minibus. It's a long, tiring excursion and will cost in the region of ¥500. It might be simpler to stay a night at either Wushan or Gangu, perhaps as a stopover on the way between Tianshui and Lanzhou. Note that access to the Water Curtain Grottoes is dependent on the weather – you won't be able to use the riverbed if it has been wet recently.

Pingliang

About 200km northeast of Tianshui, an eight-hour bus ride, lies the city of **PINGLIANG**. The surrounding area is a mountainous and very beautiful part of Gansu Province near the border with Ningxia, and little known to foreigners. The chief local attraction is **Kongtong Shan**, a Taoist monastery, one of China's most venerated, perched precariously on a clifftop, with Guyuan in southern Ningxia (see p.1018) a possible day-trip, two hours away by bus. The last bus to Guyuan is at 4pm, and there are late-night trains to Yinchuan and Xi'an.

If you arrive by bus, the most convenient **place to stay** is at the well-maintained *Jiaotong* (❷, dorm beds ¥40); come out of the bus station, turn left, and it's about 100m down on the left. Continue down the road and you come to a string of cheap restaurants. If you arrive at the train station, 2km out of town, the nearest hotel is the *Qinsanjiao* (❷, dorm beds ¥50), just south of the station, over the bridge and on the right. Continue down this road for 100m and you come to a private **bus station** with sleeper buses to Xi'an and Lanzhou.

Kongtog Shan lies 15km west of the city; a taxi there costs around ¥30. You'll be dropped at the bottom of the mountain, from where you then walk 3km up a winding road to the top, buying a ticket (¥24) on the way. On arrival you'll be rewarded with spectacular views over an azure lake, the surrounding ribbed landscape dotted with Taoist temples. Maps of the area are available from kiosks at the top, and you're free to hike off in any direction – head up for the best buildings, down towards the lake for the best scenery.

Lanzhou and around

On the map, **LANZHOU** appears to lie very much in the middle of China, though this is a misleading impression. Culturally and politically it remains remote from the great cities of eastern China, despite being both the provincial capital and the largest industrial centre in the Northwest. At the head of the Hexi Corridor, it was a vital stronghold along the Silk Road and was the principal crossing point of the mighty Yellow River. For centuries it has been a transportation hub, first for caravans, then shallow boats and now rail lines. Not until the Communist era, however, did it become a large population centre as well, in response to the city's burgeoning industry. Now there are nearly three million people in Lanzhou, the vast majority of them Han Chinese.

Lanzhou is a mellow place with an excellent **museum**, tasty food and busy downtown **shopping** areas. The Yellow River, running thick and chocolatey through the city against a backdrop of hills dim with mist, dust, and industrial pollution, is one of China's classic sights, while the major historical and artistic attraction lies just beyond the city at the **Bingling Si** Buddhist Caves. Nearly all travellers on their way to or from Xinjiang will end up stopping in Lanzhou; it's worth staying the day.

Lanzhou and around

Lanzhou	兰州	***lánzhōu***
Baita Park	白塔公园	*báitǎ gōngyuán*
Baiyi Si	白衣寺	*báiyī sì*
Baiyun Guan	白云观	*báiyún guàn*
Dongfanghong Square	东方红广场	*dōngfānghóng guǎngchǎng*
Gansu Provincial Museum	甘肃省博物馆	*gānsùshěng bówùguǎn*
Journey to the West statue	西游记塑像	*xīyóujì sùxiàng*
Lanshan Park	兰山公元	*lánshān gōngyuán*
Wuquan Park	五泉公元	*wǔquán gōngyuán*
Xiguan Traffic Circle	西关十字	*xīguān shízì*
Yellow River	黄河	*huánghé*
Arrival		
East bus station	汽车东站	*qìchē dōngzhàn*
Gongyong bus station	公用车站	*gōngyòng chēzhàn*
Lanzhou bus station	兰州汽车站	*lánzhōu qìchēzhàn*
Main bus station	市长途汽车站	*shì chángtú qìchēzhàn*
West bus station	汽车西站	*qìchē xīzhàn*
Accommodation		
Jincheng	金城宾馆	*jīnchéng bīnguǎn*
Lanshan	兰山宾馆	*lánshān bīnguǎn*
Lanzhou Dasha	兰州大厦	*lánzhōu dàshà*
Lanzhou Fandian	兰州饭店	*lánzhōu fàndiàn*
Lanzhou Legend	飞天大酒店	*fēitiān dàjiǔdiàn*
Shengli	胜利宾馆	*shènglì bīnguǎn*
Yingbing	迎宾饭店	*yíngbīn fàndiàn*
Youyi	友谊宾馆	*yǒuyì bīnguǎn*
Eating and drinking		
Boton Coffee	伯顿餐厅	*bódùn cāntīng*
Ganju Lou Huoguo Cheng	干聚楼火锅城	*gànjùlóu huǒguōchéng*
Lihua Fandian	丽花饭店	*lìhuā fàndiàn*
Miandian Wang	面点王	*miàndiǎn wáng*
Qingzhen Fandian	清真饭店	*qīngzhēn fàndiàn*
Bingling Si Caves	炳灵寺千佛洞	***bǐnglíngsì qiānfódòng***
Liujiaxia Reservoir	刘家峡水库	*liújiāxiá shuǐkù*
Yongjing	永靖	*yǒngjìng*

Arrival and accommodation

Squeezed 1600m up into a narrow valley along the Yellow River, Lanzhou stretches out pencil-thin for nearly 30km, east to west. The modern centre and most of the hotels and shops lie in the east, focused on the Xiguan Traffic Circle and Dongfanghong Square; the oldest part of the town, and the most interesting for walking, eating and shopping, is roughly in the middle; and the museum and popular *Youyi Hotel* are in the west.

Lanzhou's **airport** lies about 70km to the north of the city, at least a two-hour journey, with connections to all major Chinese cities and Dunhuang and Jiayuguan within Gansu Province. The airport buses terminate conveniently in the eastern part of the city, outside the CAAC office on Donggang Xi Lu, a few minutes west of the *Lanzhou Fandian*.

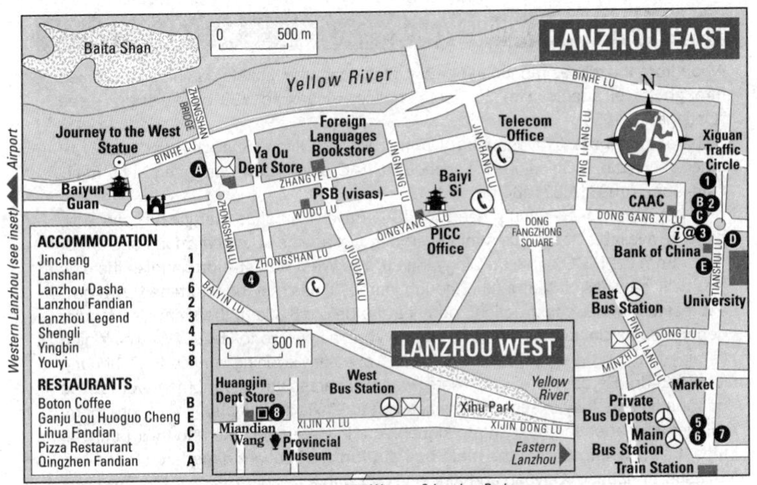

Being the main rail hub of northwest China, Lanzhou is an easy place to travel into or out of by train. Arriving this way, you will almost certainly be dropped off at the massive main **train station** – undergoing a major refit at time of writing – in the far southeast of the city, where there are a number of hotel options in the immediate vicinity. The Xiguan Traffic Circle is about 2km due north of here (buses #7, #10 or #34) while western Lanzhou, more than a dozen kilometres away, can be reached on bus #1 and trolleybus #31. **Taxis** either use meters or have set fares from ¥5 – the figure is pasted on their windscreens.

There are several **long-distance bus stations** in Lanzhou. Buses from **Xiahe** arrive at the **West bus station** on Xijin Xi Lu, about 15km from the train station and close to the *Youyi Hotel*, from where city bus #1 and trolleybus #31 run east through town. Buses from the Hexi Corridor might wind up here too, or – along with traffic from everywhere else – terminate near the train station at the **main bus station** (well hidden on lower Pingliang Lu, and actually pretty small), or at the larger **East bus station** 1km north, or at one of a handful of **private depots** nearby on Pingliang Lu.

Accommodation

Most accommodation in Lanzhou is in the vicinity of the train station – an inexpensive but grotty location – or in the eastern half of the city, though there is one good option, the *Youyi*, in the west.

Jincheng Tianshui Lu ⓣ0931/8416638. A modern and snooty place, a little way north of the Xiguan Traffic Circle, 2km due north of the train station. ❺

Lanshan Tianshui Lu ⓣ0931/8827211 ext 218. Near the station end of Tianshui Lu, the main road directly facing the station. Very shabby but friendly option with double rooms and three- and four-bed dorms. Dorm beds ¥26, ❷

Lanzhou Dasha Tianshui Lu ⓣ0931/8417210, ⓕ8417177. As you emerge from the train station, you'll see this monolithic hotel opposite and slightly to the left. Chaotic but not bad value, with hot water 7–12pm. Dorm beds ¥30, ❹

Lanzhou Fandian Donggang Xi Lu, right on the Xiguan Traffic Circle ⓣ0931/8416321, ⓕ8418608. From the train station take bus #1, #7 or #10 due north for a couple of stops. A huge complex which looks very upmarket from the front, but there's a well-maintained, inexpensive

Moving on from Lanzhou

Aside from the places mentioned below, plane and train tickets can also be booked through travel agents with 36 hours' notice, at around ¥30 commission – see "Listings", p.1030.

There are **flights** to Dunhuang, Ürümqi, Beijing, Xi'an, Shanghai and plenty of other destinations China-wide. Lanzhou's CAAC office is on Donggang Xi Lu (daily 8am–9pm; ⓣ0931/8821964).

To buy **bus** tickets, you'll need a PICC Travel Insurance Certificate (see box, p.1020), available at the bus stations, from travel agents at the *Lanzhou Fandian*, or direct from the PICC office on Qingyang Lu. The **West bus station** handles the only two daily services to **Xiahe** (8hr, though journey times may be shortened by a new expressway under construction), both leaving before 8.30am; there are also regular departures to **Linxia** between 8.30am and 4pm, as well as to Hezuo, Wuwei, Xining (a fairly fast trip on a new expressway) and one early evening service to Dunhuang (about 24hr). Be careful of touts here, who will harass you the moment you queue up for a ticket – they assume you're heading to Linxia and, should you ignore them, will get your attention by trying to kidnap your luggage and take it to their bus. The most useful services from the **main bus station** are frequent departures to Wuwei, Tianshui, Yinchuan, Guyuan and Xining, along with a sleeper to Xi'an. The **East bus station** is much bigger and busier, handling basically the same destinations plus far more long-distance traffic – fares here are slightly cheaper. **Private depots** between the two serve all destinations to the west; their buses are more expensive, but services are more frequent.

Unless you're heading to Xiahe, Linxia, or somewhere similarly remote, the **train** is probably the best way to leave Lanzhou – all main towns along the Hexi Corridor to the northwest have stations, and there are good connections east to Tianshui, north to Yinchuan in Ningxia, and west to Xining over in Qinghai. Even better, you won't need a PICC certificate. **Buying train tickets** is easy enough at the station, though you'll have to queue up; if this doesn't appeal, try a travel agency.

older wing with good value dorms and doubles, which the management often discount before you ask. Conveniently, a number of travel agents are based here. Dorm beds ¥40, ❸

Lanzhou Legend Panxuan Lu, across the road from the *Lanzhou Fandian* and on the Xiguan Traffic Circle ⓣ0931/8882876, ⓕ8887876. This is the plushest hotel in town, with international-standard rooms, three restaurants, a disco, bar and nightclub. ❼

Shengli Zhongshan Lu ⓣ0931/8465221. Right in between the east and west halves of the city, handily placed for the downtown eating areas. To get here, take trolleybus #31 from the train station (heading west) or from the West bus station (heading east). ❸

Yingbin Tianshui Lu ⓣ0931/8886552. A couple of minutes due north of the train station, on the left-hand side of the road if you're walking from the station. A friendly and quite helpful place offering cheap triples and reasonable doubles with bath. ❸

Youyi Xijin Xi Lu ⓣ0931/2333051, ⓕ2330304. A good budget option, clean, quiet and with 24hr hot water. It's located opposite the museum, a 15min walk from the West bus station – convenient for Xiahe. If you're arriving by bus from any point in western Gansu you'll pass in front of the hotel and can ask the driver to let you off. From the train station take bus #1 or trolleybus #31. Economy/standard doubles ❷/❹

The City

The best place to start a tour of Lanzhou is the main shopping district, roughly in the middle of the city, in the blocks that lie to the north and west of Zhongshan Lu (this street comes south from Zhongshan Bridge, then turns a right angle at the *Shengli Hotel* and continues east). There's a downtown feel to the place, with boutiques, Western music, fast food and smart department stores; the city's **Muslim quarter** and accompanying white-tiled mosque is also in the vicinity, at the western end of Zhangye Lu.

Immediately north of here, the city's greatest sight is the **Yellow River**, already flowing thick and fast, although it still has some 1500km to go before it finally reaches the sea at Qingdao. In summer, the water of the river is a rich, muddy brown colour, a legacy of the huge quantities of silt it picks up, and the fast flow helps to create a wind corridor through the city, which both moderates the climate and removes some of the worst effects of the pollution. For boating on the river, try the area just west of Zhongshan Bridge (city side) – there are a few motor boats operating brief viewing trips. South-bank Binhe Lu here has a paved promenade from where you can watch the mud slide by, with a large *Journey to the West* statue featuring Xuanzang, Monkey, Pigsy, Sandy and the horse (see p.1073); across the road, **Baiyun Guan** is a small, semi-ruinous Taoist temple being extensively restored. Over the bridge, **Baita Shan Park** (daily 7am–7pm; ¥5) is ranged up a steep hillside with great views down over the river from stone terraces. A seventeen-metre-high white pagoda up here officially dates back to the Ming dynasty, though some say it was erected on the orders of Genghis Khan, to commemorate a Tibetan lama who had pleased him.

Moving east from the central area takes you into the mainly modern part of the city, which has few attractions for tourists. One possible exception, a few hundred metres east of Jiuquan Lu (just east of Jingning Lu) on the north side of Qingyang Lu, is the **Baiyi Si** and an accompanying Ming-dynasty stupa. The temple is interesting more for the poignancy of its location than anything else. With huge Hongkong-style department stores looming on all sides, it looks as alien as a spaceship. **Dong Fanghong Square**, nearby, is worth checking out at dusk, when the flag in the centre is lowered in a military ceremony.

The west of the city comprises an upmarket shopping and residential area strung out along Xijin Xi Lu; from the centre of town take bus #1, #6 or trolleybus #31. The one sight worth visiting here, the **Gansu Provincial Museum** (Mon–Sat 9am–noon & 2.30–5.30pm; ¥25), occupies a boxy Stalinist edifice opposite the *Youyi* hotel; the entrance is around to the left and then upstairs. It has an interesting collection, divided between natural resources of Gansu (downstairs) and historical finds (upstairs). Apart from the four-metre-tall **mammoth skeleton**, recovered from the Yellow River basin in 1973, the natural resources exhibit is not of enormous interest, but upstairs the display is excellent, with full English explanations. There are some remarkable **ceramics** dating from the Neolithic age as well as a huge collection of **wooden tablets and carvings** from the Han dynasty – priceless sources for studying the politics, culture and economy of the period. The bronze **Flying Horse of Wuwei**, 2000 years old and still with its accompanying procession of horses and chariots, is the highlight, however – note the stylish chariots for top officials with round seats and sunshades. The fourteen-centimetre-tall horse, depicted with one front hoof stepping on the back of a flying swallow, was discovered in a Han-dynasty tomb in Wuwei some thirty years ago.

In the hills bordering the south of the city lie **Wuquan** and **Lanshan parks** (daily 8am–6pm; ¥4), just south of the terminus of bus #8 (which you can pick up anywhere on Jiuquan Lu in the centre of town). Wuquan Park is full of mainly Qing pavilions, convoluted stairways twirling up the mountainside interspersed with teahouses, art-exhibition halls and ponds. One of the oldest buildings, the **Jingang Palace**, is Ming and contains a five-metre-high bronze Buddha cast in 1370. It's a nice place to wander with the locals at weekends.

From Wuquan Park, Lanshan Park can be reached by chairlift – it's about twenty minutes to the very top.

Eating and drinking

There are good places to eat all over Lanzhou. The West bus station is surrounded by inexpensive Muslim canteens, and also in this part of town is *Miandian Wang*, west of the *Youyi* hotel, serving Chinese-style breakfasts of steamed or fried dumplings, rice porridge, and bowls of soya milk with dough sticks. Around the **centre**, *Qingzhen Fandian* is another, moderately smart, Muslim restaurant opposite the post office on Zhongshan Lu (look for the green and gold sign and Arabic script); the area east of the *Shengli* hotel is also swarming with inexpensive places to eat.

The best pickings are further **east** around the Xiguan Traffic Circle. *Lihua Fandian*, just outside the *Lanzhou* hotel on Donggang Xi Lu, is a bright, busy, cheap place serving local fare: try *jincheng niangpi*, spiced glass noodles; *suncai fentiao*, another noodle dish flavoured with pickled vegetables, chillies and aniseed; and *jing rousi*, stir-fried meat shreds in a sweet soy sauce, eaten Beijing-duck style inside pancakes. It's hard to spend more than ¥15 a head, including beer. South on Tianshui Lu, *Ganju Lou Huoguo Cheng* is the place if you like hotpots served while other diners play raucous drinking games in the background; ¥60 buys enough vegetables and meat for two.

For **Western-style food** – and a quiet, low-light environment – try *Boton Coffee*, next to the *Lanzhou* hotel, which is the only place in town with an English menu. Coffee here is ¥25 a pot, and they do pizza, sandwiches, apple pie (all around ¥18), as well as set meals and steaks (around ¥40). There's also a pizza place diagonally across the roundabout from here, very popular with students from the adjacent Lanzhou University – a medium pizza with the works is ¥20. Finally, Lanzhou is famous for its summer **fruit**; don't leave without trying the melons, watermelons, peaches or grapes.

Listings

Banks and exchange The main Bank of China is on Tianshui Lu, just south of the *Lanzhou Legend*; foreign exchange is on the second floor.

Bookshops The third floor of the Foreign Languages Bookstore, on Zhangye Lu, has a wide selection of novels in English. The entrance is not easy to find – it's on the western side of the building.

Internet access There are several net bars south of the university on Tianshui Lu, all charging about ¥3 an hour – or try the slightly pricier Lanzhou Online Net Bar, upstairs through a pool hall, more or less opposite the *Lihua* restaurant.

Mail and telephones The Post and Telecommunications Office (Mon–Sat 8am–7pm) stands at the junction of Pingliang Lu and Minzhu Dong Lu. There's also a post office at the West bus station in the western part of the city, and you can make collect calls at the Telephone and Telegram Office on the corner of Qingyang Lu and Jinchang Lu.

PSB Visas can be extended at an office on Wudu Lu, a couple of hundred metres west of Jiuquan Lu.

Shopping Good things to buy in Lanzhou include army surplus clothes – winter coats, waistcoats, hats and boots are all locally produced, tough and cheap. They're made at the local factory at 227 Yanchang Lu, north of the river, the largest such factory in China. You can even visit it if you like and buy direct from them (bus #7 from the train station).

Travel agents Just about every business remotely connected with travel, from the bus stations and hotels to the Bank of China, seem to have a counter where you can arrange train and plane tickets. The *Lanzhou* hotel's Western Travel Service is highly recommended (Ⓣ & Ⓕ 0931/8852929), with English speaking staff; or try the *Youyi* hotel's Gansu International Hope Travel Agency (Ⓣ 0931/2310637). Aside from transport bookings, both run all-inclusive day-trips to Bingling Si (around ¥200–300), and whirlwind overnight stays at Xiahe (¥510).

Bingling Si Caves

The trip out from Lanzhou to the Buddhist caves of **Bingling Si** is one of the best excursions you can make in all of Gansu province – enough in itself to merit a stay in Lanzhou. Not only does it offer a glimpse of the spectacular **Buddhist cave art** that filtered through to this region along the Silk Road, but it's a powerful introduction to the **Yellow River**.

The caves are carved into a canyon beside the **Liujiaxia Reservoir** on the Yellow River, and can be reached only by boat at certain times of the year (see below). From Lanzhou, the first stage of the expedition is a two-hour bus ride through impressively fertile loess fields to the massive **Liujiaxia Hydro-Electric Dam**, a spectacular sight poised above the reservoir and surrounded by colourful rocky mountains. At the dam you board a waiting ferry, which takes three hours to reach the caves and offers excellent views en route, of fishermen busy at work and peasants cultivating wheat, sunflowers and rice on the dark, steep banks. During the trip, the ferry enters a tall **gorge** where the river froths and churns; you'll see sections of the bank being whipped away into the waters. It's said that the Yellow River carries some 35 kilos of silt in every cubic metre of water – hence its constant murkiness and its name.

The ferry docks just below the Bingling Si Caves. Cut into sheer cliff, amid stunning scenery above a tributary of the river, the caves number 183 in all. They are among the earliest significant Buddhist monuments in China – started in the Western Jin and subsequently extended by the Northern Wei, the Tang, Song and Ming. Since their inaccessibility spared the caves the attentions of foreign devils in the nineteenth century and the Red Guards in the twentieth, most of the cave sculpture is in good condition, and some impressive restoration work is in progress on the wall paintings. The centrepiece sculpture, approached along a dizzying network of stairs and ramps, is a huge 27-metre **seated Buddha**, probably carved under the Tang. The artwork at Bingling Si reached its peak under the Song and Ming dynasties and, though the wall paintings of this period have been virtually washed away, there remain a considerable number of small and exquisite carvings.

Practicalities

The most convenient way to see the caves is on a pre-booked day-trip from Lanzhou. Before booking any tour, note that the water in the reservoir is only high enough to permit **access** between June and October. Some years, however, the caves remain out of bounds through most of the summer as well, and some tour operators have been known to take people all the way to the reservoir before "discovering" that the water level is too low – no fee is refundable. Try to check the situation at the reservoir with other travellers before you book.

Most travel services in Lanzhou can arrange **trips** to the caves (see "Listings", opposite), though if you are on your own you may have to hunt around in order to tag along with another group. For a maximum car-load of three passengers, an all-inclusive price (car, boat, entry ticket and insurance) usually comes to ¥400–500; the Gansu International Hope Travel Agency in the *Youyi* hotel work out their rates at ¥200 per person. There may also be larger (and therefore cheaper) group tours operating out of the *Shengli* – enquire here for details. The standard trip takes up to twelve hours, which includes less than two hours at the caves, but the scenery en route makes it all worthwhile. If you want a detailed guided tour, encompassing all the caves, it's worth asking about the possibility of a private trip.

Alternatively, you could consider travelling **independently** to the reservoir on a public bus. Both from the West bus station and from a special stop outside the *Shengli* hotel, there are buses to **Yongjing**, which pass the ferry departure point (if you fail to get off at the right place, you'll have to walk back thirty minutes from the bus terminus), from where you can usually charter your own motorboat to the caves (around ¥500). On the way back you may end up staying the night in Yongjing, if the last public bus back to Lanzhou (around 5pm) leaves without you.

South from Lanzhou

This mountainous and verdant area to the south and southwest of Lanzhou, bordering on Qinghai to the west and Sichuan to the south, is one of enormous scenic beauty, relatively untouched by the scars of industry and overpopulation. The people who live here are not only few in number, but also display a fascinating cultural and ethnic diversity, with a very strong **Hui** and **Tibetan** presence in the towns of **Linxia** and **Xiahe** respectively. Xiahe, in particular, is a delightful place to visit, housing as it does one of the major Lamaist temples in China, and attracting monks and pilgrims from the whole Tibetan world. South of Xiahe, it's possible to follow an adventurous route into **Sichuan** province.

From Lanzhou to Xiahe

The road southeast from Lanzhou to Xiahe passes by first Yongjing and Liujiaxia, the jumping-off points for Bingling Si (see p.1031), before traversing

South from Lanzhou

Dongxiang Autonomous County	东乡自治县	***dōngxiāng zìzhìxiàn***
Linxia	临夏	***línxià***
Longlin Hotel	龙林饭店	*lónglín fàndiàn*
Nanguan Mosque	南关大寺	*nánguān dàsì*
Shuiquan Hotel	水泉宾馆	*shuǐquán bīnguǎn*
South bus station	汽车南站	*qìchē nánzhàn*
West bus station	汽车西站	*qìchē xīzhàn*
Xiahe	夏河	***xiàhé***
Gongtang Pagoda	贡唐宝塔	*gòngtáng bǎotǎ*
Hongjiao Si	红交寺	*hóngjiāo sì*
Labrang Monastery	拉卜楞寺	*lābólèng sì*
Sangke Grasslands	桑科草原	*sāngkē cǎoyuán*
Accommodation		
Labrang	拉卜楞宾馆	*lābólèng bīnguǎn*
Tara Guesthouse	夏河县卓玛旅社	*xiàhéxiàn zhuōmǎ lǚshè*
Tibetan Guesthouse	华侨旅社	*huáqiáo lǚshè*
Youyi	友谊宾馆	*yǒuyì bīnguǎn*
Hezuo	合作	***hézuò***
Mila'erba Monastery	郎木寺	*lángmù sì*
Luqu	碌曲	***lùqǔ***

Dongxiang Autonomous County. The Dongxiang minority, numbering nearly two hundred thousand, are Muslims with Mongol origins. These days, to outsiders at least, they are indistinguishable from the Hui except at certain celebrations and festivals when ancient Mongol customs re-emerge. Beyond the pilgrimage centre of Linxia, 60km from Lanzhou, the climb up to Xiahe takes three or four hours (but only two coming down again). The area through which the route passes is potentially fascinating, a zone of cultural overlap between ancient communities of Islamic and Buddhist peoples. A couple of China's lesser-known minorities also live here, the **Bao'an** and the **Salar**. The Bao'an, who number barely eight thousand, are very similar to the Dongxiang people as they, too, are of Mongolian origins. The Salar are a Turkic-speaking people whose origins lie, it's thought, in Samarkand in Central Asia; they live primarily in Xunhua County in neighbouring Qinghai Province.

Linxia

A three-hour bus journey from Lanzhou, **LINXIA** is a very **Muslim** town, full of mosques, most of which have been restored since the depredations of the Cultural Revolution. Nearly everybody here seems to wear a white skull cap, and the women additionally wear a square-shaped veil of fine lace, black if they are married and green if they are not. Linxia is also the place where all the large, fancy eyeglasses that old men wear throughout this region are made. There's nothing much to see in town; nevertheless, it's an interesting place to stroll around for a few hours if you feel like breaking your journey from Lanzhou to Xiahe.

Linxia's main street, which runs north–south through town, is called Tuanjie Lu in the north and Jiefang Lu in the south, with a large central square in between the two. The main mosque, the **Nanguan Mosque**, is immediately to the south of the square. Jiefang Lu terminates at a large traffic circle at its southern end. There is no train station in Linxia, though there are **two bus stations**. If you're arriving from the west (Xining or Tongren), you may be deposited at the smaller one in the far northwest of the city (known as the West bus station), in which case you'll have to catch a cycle-rickshaw into town. If you arrive at the main (South) station, on Jiefang Nan Lu a couple of hundred metres south of the Jiefang Lu traffic circle, you'll be able to walk to a **hotel**. The nearest is almost immediately to the north of the station, on the right as you come out – the *Shuiquan* (Ⓣ0930/214964; ❷, dorm beds ¥38). It's the cheapest place around, with doubles and three-bed dorms, but they may want to charge foreigners double. A few minutes farther north from here, on the right at the first big roundabout, is the *Longlin* (❸), which has quite a smart **restaurant**. Otherwise, head for the pleasant **night market** centred around the top end of Jiefang Nan Lu (the next roundabout north of the *Longlin Hotel*). You can stuff yourself here on heavy round breads (*bing*) flavoured with curry powder; roast chickens are also available, as well as noodles and soups. On terraces overlooking the central square on the south side are a couple of very pleasant teahouses where you can sit out and enjoy the night air.

When trying to **leave** Linxia, be aware that the touts for the bus companies are very aggressive, seeming to stop at nothing to get you aboard their vehicles. Watch your bags carefully, or they might be grabbed off you and hurled through a minibus window. There are frequent buses to Lanzhou (via Liujiaxia, for Bingling Si; see p.1031) and several daily to Xiahe from the main bus station. There are also buses to Xining, Tianshui and Wuwei (via Lanzhou). You'll need to show your PICC insurance certificate when buying tickets in Linxia; the **PICC office** is north of the main bus station, beyond the central square, about twenty minutes' walk or one or two yuan in a cycle-rickshaw. The **Bank of China** lies a few minutes north of the *Longlin Hotel*, on the right.

Xiahe and around

A tiny, rural town tucked away 3000m up in the remote hills of southern Gansu, right on the edge of the Tibetan plateau, **XIAHE** is an unforgettable place. As well as offering glimpses into the life of the **Tibetan people** – living and working in one of the most beautiful Tibetan monasteries you are likely to see – Xiahe also offers visitors the rare chance to spend some time in open countryside, sited as it is in a sunny, fresh valley surrounded by green hills.

Xiahe is the most important Tibetan monastery town outside Tibet itself, and the **Labrang Monastery** (Labuleng Si) is one of the six major centres of the Gelugpa, or Yellow Hat Sect (of the others, four are in Tibet and one, Ta'er Si, is just outside Xining in Qinghai province). Tibetans from Tibet itself come here on pilgrimage dressed in traditional costume (equipped with mittens and kneepads to cushion themselves during their prostrations), and the constant flow of monks in bright purple, yellow and red, alongside semi-nomadic herdsmen wrapped in sheepskins and reeking of yak butter, makes for an endlessly fascinating scene.

The town is essentially built along a single street that stretches 3–4km along the north bank of the Daxia River, from the bus station in the east, through the Labrang Monastery in the middle, to the old Tibetan town and finally the *Labrang Hotel* in the west. The **eastern end** of town, where the bus station lies, is predominantly Hui- and Han-populated. It's also the commercial and administrative part of town, with a couple of banks, a post office and plenty of shops and markets. The shops round here make interesting browsing, with lots of Tibetan religious objects on sale, such as hand-printed sutras, little prayer wheels, bells and jewellery. There's also lots of riding equipment – saddles and bridles – for the nomads from the nearby grasslands who come striding into town, spurs jangling.

Beyond the monastery, at the **western end** of town, is the local Tibetan area. West of the bridge that carries all motorized traffic to the south side of the river, the road becomes a bumpy dirt track with homes built of mud and wood, and pigs and cows ambling around. There is one more religious building up here, the **Hongjiao Si**, or Temple of the Red Hat Sect; it's on the right as you walk west from town. The monks of the Red Hat sect wear red robes which include a large white band, and live in the shadow of their rich and more numerous brethren from the Yellow Hat Sect.

Labrang Monastery

About 1500m up from the bus station, the **monastery** area begins. There's no wall separating the town from the monastery – the two communities just

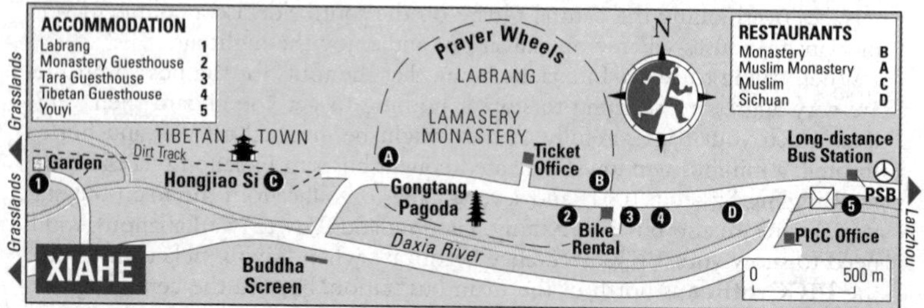

merge together and the main road goes right through the middle of both. The only markers are the long lines of roofed **prayer wheels** stretching out to the right and left of the road, which together trace a complete circle around the monastery. To the south side, in particular, along the north bank of the river, you can follow the prayer wheels almost to the other end of the monastery – the gaps that still exist along the route are being rapidly filled. It's a mesmerizing experience to walk alongside the pilgrims (clockwise around the monastery), who turn each prayer wheel they pass, sending prayers to heaven.

The monastery was founded in 1709 by a monk called E'Ang Zongzhe, who thereby became the first-generation Living Buddha, or **Jiemuyang**. Upon the death of each Jiemuyang, a new one is born, supposedly representing the reincarnation of the previous one. The present Jiemuyang, the sixth incarnation, is third in importance, in the Tibetan Buddhist hierarchy, to the Dalai Lama and Panchen Lama. Although Labrang may seem a peaceful haven today, it has not always been so. In the 1920s ferocious battles took place here between Muslim warlords and Tibetans, with atrocities being committed by both sides. Then in the Cultural Revolution came further disaster, with persecution for the monks and the virtual destruction (and closure) of the monastery. It was not until 1980 that it reopened, and although it is flourishing once again it is nevertheless a smaller place today than it used to be. For an idea of its original extent, see the painting in the Exhibition Hall, on the wall at the far end from the entrance. There are now around two thousand monks, about half their former number.

The vast majority of the important **monastery buildings** are to the north of the main road. The buildings include six colleges, as well as temple halls, Jiemuyang residences and endless living quarters for the monks themselves. The institutes, where monks study for degrees, are of Astronomy, Esoteric Buddhism, Law, Medicine and Theology (higher and lower). There are also schools for dance, music and painting. The **Gongtang Pagoda** (daily 8am–7pm; ¥5) is the only major monastery building to the south of the main road – you pass it when following the prayer wheels. It's worth climbing to the top for a spectacular view over the shining golden roofs of the monastery.

For most non-specialist visitors, however, trying to identify the individual buildings will probably be of secondary importance given the pleasure of simply imbibing the atmosphere created by the monks themselves – whether massing for collective prayers, engaging in religious discussions or larking around like schoolboys (which is actually what many of them really are). There is nothing to stop you, at any time of day or night, from wandering around the entire site by yourself. You may even be allowed to wander into the temples – be sensitive and use your discretion, and walk clockwise. On the other hand, given the bewildering wealth of architecture, art and statuary, it's a good idea to take a **guided tour** at some stage during your stay in Xiahe. This can be arranged at the ticket office – take the only sizeable turn off the north side of the road within the monastery area (the right if coming from the station). The hour-long tours, led by English-speaking monks, cost ¥23, and start around 10am and 3.30pm, more frequently in peak season.

Labrang Monastery is the site of some spectacular **festivals** which, as with Chinese festivals, take place according to the lunar calendar. The largest of these is the **Monlam Festival**, three days after the Tibetan new year (late Feb or early March). The opening of the festival is marked by the unfurling of a huge cloth adorned with a holy painting of the Buddha, measuring twenty metres by thirty, on the south side of the Daxia River. Subsequent days see processions, dances and the lighting of butter lamps. You might see activities like these, though on a smaller scale, at any season of the year if you happen to arrive on a special day.

Practicalities

Until the airport is completed around 2004, practically all travellers will arrive by **bus**, at the station at the far eastern end of town. The station is served by frequent buses from Linxia and Hezuo; there are also two buses a day to and from Lanzhou, and one for Tongren in Qinghai. For the route to Sichuan, you should take the morning bus to Hezuo and proceed south from there (see opposite for more on this route).

Most tourist restaurants and hotels offer **bikes** for hire; the *Monastery Restaurant* and the rental shop opposite have the cheapest rates (¥2/hr, or ¥10 /day) while bikes are annoyingly expensive at the *Labrang Hotel* (¥5/hr). There is no Bank of China in Xiahe (the nearest is in Linxia) and you cannot change traveller's cheques anywhere in town; only cash will do here. There are a number of **travel services** in the *Youyi Hotel* (see below).

Accommodation

The east end of town has plenty of Chinese-style hotels. However, it's more fun to try one of the charismatic Tibetan-owned guesthouses farther up the road, which attract a mixed clientele of pilgrims and budget travellers.

Labrang In the fields to the west of the town ☎09412/21849. It's 4km from the bus station and nearly 1km from the next nearest building; from the station, a cycle-rickshaw here shouldn't cost more than about ¥5, though you might have to get off and push for one or two stretches. Easily Xiahe's best hotel; accommodation ranges from simple three-bed dorms with bath, through plain doubles to rather damp concrete "Tibetan-style" cabins. Prices increase at the height of summer, while in winter the hotel may not be open at all. Dorm beds ¥20, cabins ¥320, ❸

Monastery Guesthouse In the heart of the monastery area, and run by monks who obviously have more important things on their minds than cleaning. Basic rooms with stoves, spartan as any monk's cell, are arranged around a courtyard. There's an 11pm curfew and no hot water. ❶

Tara Guesthouse Signed 50m west of the *Tibetan Guesthouse*, with its entrance a few doors down in the alley leading off to the south. Some find the eccentric Tibetan staff too much to handle, but it's a good place: the lovingly decorated rooms have stoves, some have *kangs*, and there's a stereo instead of a TV in most. The shower, shared with the *Tibetan Guesthouse*, is in a separate building a little farther down the alley and costs ¥2. ❶

Tibetan Guesthouse A clean and well-maintained building offering the cheapest dorms in town; the first good place you come to if you head west of the bus station. Dorm beds ¥15, ❶

Youyi Across the road from the bus station and a few minutes' walk west ☎09412/21593. Friendly, Chinese-style place. Dorm beds ¥40, ❷

Eating

The influx of tourists has given a huge boost to the Xiahe catering trade in recent years. In the eastern part of town there are plenty of **restaurants** offering Tibetan and traveller food – banana pancakes and the like. They usually have either "Tibet" or "Snow" in their titles, and they're all pretty much the same. You won't see many Tibetans in any of them – they tend to eat in the cheaper, unnamed places.

One of two places called *Monastery Restaurant* lies at the monastery's eastern edge; run by a family from the Gancha grasslands, it's a homely place which offers Tibetan staples such as as *tsampa*, made from yak butter and coarse flour – you add sugar and turn it into a kind of breakfast cereal. There's an English menu which includes "banana in melted sauce" (actually coated in toffee), and plenty of Wild West characters hanging around. Budget travellers, bizarrely, seem to prefer the terrible food of the depressing *Snowland* over the road. The other *Monastery Restaurant*, farther west, is a Muslim place serving some pretty decent yak-meat dishes – a lot of meat for very little money.

For Chinese food, try the small, cosy *Sichuan Restaurant* in the east of town, where you might also see monks taking time out to watch Hong Kong action movies on VCD. East along the dirt track from the *Labrang* into the old Tibetan town, the first restaurant on your right – inside a courtyard – is a Muslim place offering great breakfasts, with yoghurt and honey, pancakes, bread and even cream cheese.

Around Xiahe

Even without the monastery, Xiahe would be a delightful place to relax given its rural setting. The hills around the valley offer excellent hiking opportunities, and the views down on to the gleaming roofs of the monastery can be breathtaking. About 15km farther west up the valley are the **Sangke Grasslands**, which can be reached by motor-rickshaw (about ¥30 return), or by bicycle. If you're cycling you can follow either the dirt track north of the river, or the sealed road to the south. You'll know when you've arrived – a ticket booth (¥3) in the middle of nowhere marks the entrance, beyond which the valley opens out into a vast, grassy pasture, a lovely place to walk in summer. Nomads hang around here offering rides on their horses for ¥10 an hour. You can also stay out here in yurts affiliated to the *Labrang Hotel* – enquire at the hotel reception about these (though the associated garish pink casino labled "Nira Ethnic Paradise Resort" is not an encouraging sign for the future development of this tranquil area). The **Gancha Grasslands**, another 30km to the north, are even more vast and empty, but harder to get to – tours run in summer from the *Tara Guesthouse* (¥60 for the day).

The road to Sichuan

South of Xiahe the roads are narrow and traffic irregular; nevertheless, there is a route you can follow by public bus which leads ultimately to Chengdu in Sichuan Province. It's a rough trip, which requires several stopovers in remote towns, but a fascinating one – through one of the most beautiful parts of China. Some of the villages en route, notably Langmusi just inside Sichuan, are the most authentically Tibetan settlements most travellers are ever likely to see, given that it can be so hard to travel off the beaten track inside Tibet itself.

Hezuo

From Xiahe, the first stop is **HEZUO**, about 70km to the southeast. It's a trading post for Tibetan nomads and you'll see some fairly wild-looking types in the town. If you get the first morning bus from Xiahe, you can move on to Luqu or Langmusi the same day – there's one bus daily from Hezuo at 9.30am. However, getting stuck here for a day is no trial.

Hezuo is centred on a crossroads with a sculpture of a goat in the middle – the goat looks north. The **bus station** is on the northwest corner of the crossroads. Almost opposite, on the road leading north, is an adequate hotel, the *Gangnan* (❶), kept very clean by its Muslim staff. There's no English sign – look for the double doors and the characters for *binguan* above them. The Agricultural Bank, on the southwest corner, is the only place in town that will change foreign currency into yuan. Head east from the crossroads, and you'll find a fascinating little street with a very good two-storey Muslim **restaurant** on the right, and most **shops** selling Tibetan trinkets to the visiting nomads. The prices here will be a revelation after Xiahe – if you want to spend money on Tibetan souvenirs, this is definitely the place to do it. Astonishingly for such a one-yak town, Hezuo is the proud owner of an **Internet club**; head south from the crossroads for half a kilometre and you'll see it, signposted in English, on the right.

Hezuo also boasts one worthwhile attraction, the **Mila'erba Monastery**, in the north of the city. From the crossroads, head north for about two kilometres and you'll see it on the right; you can hardly miss it as the impressive central temple is nine storeys high. The exterior may look stern and robust, but the interior is pure chocolate box, each room gaudy with paintings and sculpture. Provided you take your shoes off at the door, you are free to ascend every storey. From the roof you can gaze at hills dotted with prayer flags.

South of Hezuo

Beyond Hezuo, the road runs **south to Sichuan** via **LUQU**, 70km from Hezuo and served by a couple of buses daily. The countryside around Luqu is beautiful and easily accessible for hiking, and a stroll up or down the river is likely to turn up one or two monasteries. In Luqu itself you can stay at the *Yinghang Zhaodaisuo* (❶); there's no English sign, but turn right out of the bus station and it's less than five minutes' walk. From Luqu, it's a further 80km south to **Langmusi**, just over the Sichuan border. Buses don't stop in Langmusi itself, but drop you off 4km away, from where jeeps will take you up the hill to the village for ¥2. For more on Langmusi, see p.975.

The Hexi Corridor

For reasons of simple geography, travellers leaving or entering China to or from Central Asia and the West have always been channelled through this narrow strip of land that runs 1000km northwest of Lanzhou. With the foothills of the Tibetan plateau, in the form of the Qilian Shan range, soaring up to the south, and a merciless combination of waterless desert and mountain to the north, the road known as the **Hexi Corridor** offers the only feasible way through the physical obstacles that crowd in on the traveller west of Lanzhou.

Historically – given the total absence of alternative routes – whoever controlled the corridor could operate a stranglehold on the fabulous riches of the Silk Road trade (see box, p.990). Inevitably the Chinese took an interest from the earliest times, and a certain amount of Great Wall-building was already taking place along the Hexi Corridor under Emperor Qin Shi Huang in the third century BC. Subsequently, the powerful Han dynasty succeeded in incorporating the region into their empire, though the influence of central government remained far from constant for many centuries afterwards, as Tibetans, Uigurs and then Mongols vied for control. Not until the Mongol conquests of the thirteenth century did the corridor finally become a settled part of the Chinese empire, with the Ming consolidating the old Great Wall positions and building its magnificent last fort at **Jiayuguan**.

Two other towns along the corridor, **Wuwei** and **Zhangye**, offer convenient means of breaking the long journey from Lanzhou to Dunhuang, and have their own share of historic sights which might justify a stopover in their own right.

Wuwei and around

Lying approximately halfway between Lanzhou and Zhangye, **WUWEI** is a small city in the uncomfortable state, rather common in China at present, of

The Hexi corridor

Hexi Corridor	河西走廊	***héxī zǒuláng***
Jiayuguan	嘉裕关	*jiāyù guān*
First Beacon Tower	第一墩	*dìyì dūn*
Fort	城楼	*chénglóu*
Great Wall Museum	长城博物馆	*chángchéng bówùguǎn*
Heishan rock carvings	黑山岩画	*hēishān yánhuà*
Overhanging Wall	悬壁长城	*xuánbì chángchéng*
Qiyi Bingchuan	七一冰川	*qīyī bīngchuān*
Xincheng Dixia Hualang	新城底下画廊	*xīnchéng dìxià huàláng*
Accommodation and eating		
Changcheng	长城宾馆	*chángchéng bīnguǎn*
Jiayuguan	嘉裕关宾馆	*jiāyùguān bīnguǎn*
Linyuan Fandian	林园饭店	*línyuán fàndiàn*
Shuangxing Lou	双兴楼	*shuāngxīng lóu*
Wumao	物贸宾馆	*wùmào bīnguǎn*
Xiongguan	雄关宾馆	*xióngguān bīnguǎn*
Mati	马蹄	***mǎtí***
Mati Si	马蹄寺	*mǎtí sì*
Minqin	民勤	***mínqín***
Wuwei	武威	***wǔwēi***
Ancient Bell Tower	大云寺古钟楼	*dàyúnsì gǔzhōnglóu*
Leitai Si	雷塔寺	*léitái sì*
Luoshi Pagoda	罗什塔	*luóshí tǎ*
South gate	南门	*nánmén*
Wen Miao	文庙	*wénmiào*
Accommodation		
Liangzhou	凉州宾馆	*liángzhōu bīnguǎn*
Tianma	天马宾馆	*tiānmǎ bīnguǎn*
Ya Ou	亚欧宾馆	*yà'ōu bīnguǎn*
Zhangye	张掖	***zhāngyè***
Dafo Si	大佛寺	*dàfó sì*
Daode Guan	道德关	*dàodé guān*
Gulou	古楼	*gǔlóu*
Mu Ta	木塔	*mùtǎ*
Tu Ta	土塔	*tǔtǎ*
Xilai Si	西来寺	*xīlái sì*
Accommodation and eating		
Ganzhou	甘州宾馆	*gānzhōu bīnguǎn*
Shibazhe Fandian	十八摺饭店	*shíbāzhě fàndiàn*
Zhangye	张掖宾馆	*zhāngyè bīnguǎn*

being half-demolished and half-rebuilt. Gansu's most famous historical relic, the Han-dynasty **Flying Horse of Wuwei**, was discovered here in 1969 underneath the Leitai Si, a temple just north of town. Now housed in the Lanzhou Museum (see p.1029), the symbol of the horse, depicted in full gallop and stepping on the back of a swallow, can be seen everywhere in Wuwei.

The city is divided into four quadrants by the main north–south road (Bei Dajie and Nan Dajie) and the east–west road (Dong Dajie and Xi Dajie), with

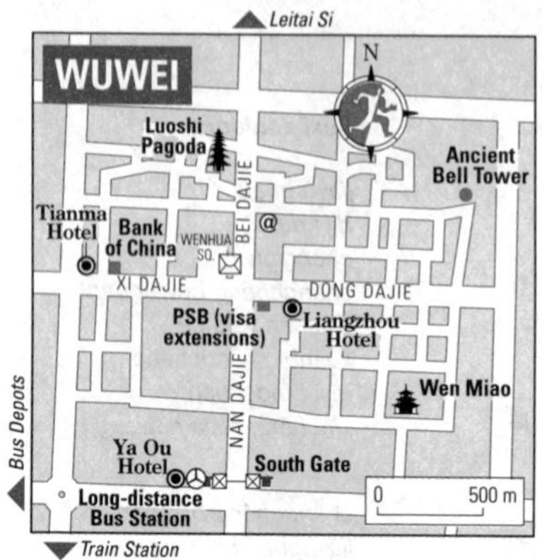

the centre of the city at the crossroads, marked by **Wenhua Square**. There's a trace of the old city near the bus station on Nan Dajie, where the original **south gate** has been impressively reconstructed. North of here, if you take the first road on the right you'll come after ten minutes to the **Wen Miao** (daily 8–11.30am & 2.30–5.30pm; ¥20), a delightful museum in the grounds of an old temple with large gardens full of oleanders and singing birds. The museum may not grab you with its contents – stone inscriptions and porcelain from the Han dynasty – but the setting is tranquil.

About twenty minutes due north of here, the **Ancient Bell Tower** (daily 8am–4.30pm; ¥5) is worth a visit mostly for its grounds, where old men play mahjong or cards and drink tea under vine trellises and enormous hollyhocks – a rare scene from old China. A further twenty minutes' walk west brings you to Bei Dajie, near the brick **Luoshi Pagoda**, from where you can catch bus #2 a few kilometres north to **Leitai Si** (daily 8am–5pm; ¥20). The temple, built high up on impressive mud ramparts and surrounded by beautiful countryside, is unfortunately being submerged by modern construction projects, but its grounds remain pleasantly calm and shady. Underneath the site, through a separate entrance, you can enter the famous Han-dynasty tomb where the Flying Horse was discovered. There's not much to see – it's a series of very low passageways, with a mock-up of the tomb contents at the back – but the 2000-year-old brickwork is still in perfect condition and amazingly modern in appearance.

If you're trying to get off the beaten track a little, consider a trip 90km north to **MINQIN** – buses there run between 7am and 7pm from Wuwei's bus station. Minqin is an oasis town between grasslands and the Tenger Desert, once an important **camel depot** for caravans to Ürümqi and Baotou in Mongolia, which ran until the late 1980s. There are still plenty of camels and sand in the area, as well as old mud-brick mansions, built like castles to defend against bandits.

Practicalities

The **bus station** lies just outside the old south gates, with several freelance depots further west. There are frequent **buses** to Zhangye and Lanzhou from 7am until late; at least one daily bus each to Dunhuang and Ürümqi; and two south to Xining. Station staff are rigid in requiring foreigners to have PICC insurance. The **train station** is 3km to the south, from where it costs a couple of yuan to take a minibus into the centre. All trains between Ürümqi and the east stop at Wuwei, and there's also a slow train to Zhongwei in Ningxia. It's easy to buy hard-seat tickets at the station – fine for the short hops to Lanzhou or Zhangye – but sleepers are best arranged through a travel agent.

Accommodation in Wuwei for foreigners is scarce and expensive. Just a few minutes west of the bus station, staff at the *Ya Ou* (Ⓣ0935/2213178; ❹) give the impression they'd be happier if you didn't stay. The *Liangzhou* on Dong Dajie (Ⓣ0935/2212450; ❹), a couple of minutes east of the central crossroads, has nice doubles with 24-hour hot water. The sole budget option is the official foreigners' hotel, the *Tianma*, west on Xi Dajie (☎0935/2212356; ❸, dorm beds ¥80), though getting one of the cheaper rooms is a struggle. For **food**, there are numerous noodle houses around the bus station and on Nan Dajie north of the south gate, serving soups and mutton dishes heavily laced with chilli; the *Liangzhou* also has a decent Chinese restaurant.

The **travel service** at the *Liangzhou* (☎0935/2212237) is the easiest place to arrange PICC insurance, and there's also a branch of the **CITS** immediately outside the hotel (☎0935/2212102). The **Bank of China**, just to the east of the *Tianma Hotel*, is open Monday to Friday. The **PSB** office that deals with visa extensions is just to the west of the *Liangzhou Hotel* – there's an English sign.

Zhangye and around

A medium-sized town, about 450km northwest of Lanzhou and 150km southeast of Jiayuguan on the edge of the Loess plateau, **ZHANGYE** has long been an important stopover for caravans and travellers on the Silk Road. Indeed, Marco Polo spent a whole year here. Today it's still worth stopping, especially if you have time for a visit to the Buddhist **Mati Si**, 60km south of the town.

During the Ming period, Zhangye was an important garrison town for soldiers guarding the **Great Wall**, and today the road from Wuwei to Zhangye is

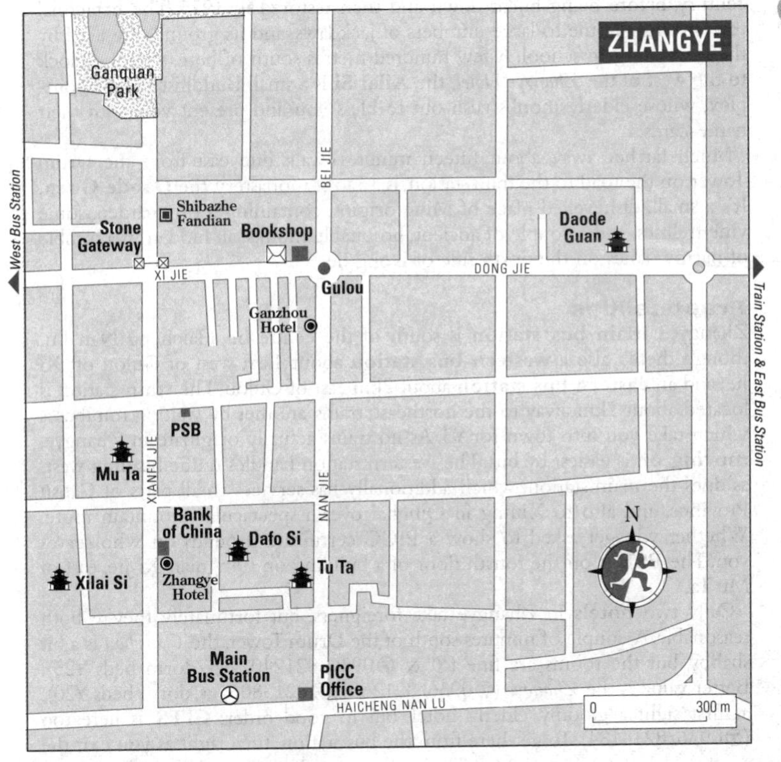

still a good place from which to view the Wall, visible for a large part of the way as a slightly sad and crumbling line of mud ramparts. Initially it runs to the north of the road, until, quite dramatically, the road suddenly cuts right through a hole in the Wall and continues on the other side.

Although Zhangye is not an especially attractive town, there are a number of places that fill at least a day of sightseeing. The centre of the town is marked, as in many Chinese towns, by a **Gulou** (Drum Tower) at the crossroads. The tower, built in 1507 during the Ming dynasty, has two tiers and houses a massive bronze bell. The four streets radiating out from here, Bei Jie, Dong Jie, Nan Jie and Xi Jie, are named after their respective compass points, and most of the sights are in the southwest of town in the vicinity of the *Zhangye Hotel*.

From east to west, the scattering of sights begins just off Nan Jie with the **Tu Ta** (Earth Tower), a former Buddhist monastery. Now in use as a local Culture Centre (*wenhua guan*), it features a single large stupa 20m in height. In the same grounds, though accessed from the west, a central smoke-grimed hall at **Dafo Si** (Big Buddha Temple; daily 7.30am–6.30pm; ¥20) houses a 34-metre-long **reclining Buddha**, easily China's largest, whose calm expression and gentle form make a powerful impression. Immediately behind the Buddha are ten disciples, and grotesque-looking *lohans* (saintly warriors) stand around in the gloom. Unusually, the hall itself, built in 1098 and restored in 1770, is almost entirely made of wood.

Just a few hundred metres north of the *Zhangye Hotel* looms the 31-metre-tall **Mu Ta** (Wooden Tower; daily 8am–5pm; ¥5), built as long ago as the sixth century, before being burnt down and then restored in 1925. The octagonal tower is now home to large numbers of jackdaws, and its grounds are used by the local kung-fu school. A few hundred metres south of here, and one block to the west of the *Zhangye Hotel*, the **Xilai Si** is a small Buddhist temple complex, whose elderly monks rush out to bless you and present you with their name-cards.

Much farther away, about fifteen minutes' walk due east from the Drum Tower on the road to the train station, is a Taoist monastery, the **Daode Guan**. It's a small, dishevelled place of Ming origins, containing a tiny garden, some vine trellises, and a couple of ancient, hospitable monks, all hidden in a jumble of narrow lanes on the north side of Dong Jie.

Practicalities

Zhangye's **main bus station** is south of the centre on Haicheng Nan Lu, though there's also a **western bus station** about 1km west of Gulou off Xi Jie; and an **eastern bus station** about 2km east of Gulou. The **train** station is located about 7km away to the northeast; trains are met by waiting minibuses which take you into town for ¥3. As no trains actually originate in Zhangye, **moving on** is easiest by bus. The western station handles traffic heading west, as does the main station, which additionally has services to all parts of Gansu Province, and also to Xining in Qinghai over a spectacular mountain route. Whether you get asked to show a PICC certificate depends on who serves you. The **PSB** is on the fourth floor of a building on Qingnian Xi Jie, east of Mu Ta.

Only two **hotels** in Zhangye take foreigners, but fortunately they're both reasonable. A couple of minutes south of the Drum Tower, the *Ganzhou* is a bit shabby, but the rooms are fine (Ⓣ & Ⓕ0936/8212402; ❷, dorm beds ¥25). Better value is the *Zhangye* (Ⓣ0936/8212601, Ⓕ8213806; ❷, dorm beds ¥20), at first sight a gloomy, elderly hotel, but in good order; **CITS** is here too (Ⓣ0936/8214184). To get here from the bus station, turn right as you exit the station, then head north for a few minutes up Xianfu Jie; the hotel is on the right.

The northern end of Xianfu Jie, beyond the stone gateway at the junction with Xi Jie, has been done up as a mock Ming-dynasty **food street** serving noodle soups, kebabs, hotpots and the like. Several places here specialize in excellent *shuijiao*, stuffed with either vegetables, seafood, beef or more exotic meats, from about ¥10 a *jin*; or try the almost smart *Shibazhe Fandian*, partway up the east side of the street, which serves an inexpensive range of casseroles, hotpots and local snacks.

Mati

The intriguing **Mati Si** – literally Horse-hoof Temple – is located in the tiny Tibetan town of **MATI** in mountains about 60km south of Zhangye. It's a complex of Buddhist caves which are carved into a cliff face and connected by a series of back-breaking passageways, tunnels, balconies and stairways. Once in Mati, finding the cave temples is easy – people will crowd around to show you the way, and the town generally is full of cheerful Tibetans offering you rides on their horses. Apart from the Mati Si, there are other temples and monasteries dotted around the area, all within walking distance; the surrounding countryside is an area of cool pine forests, mountains and grasslands.

To visit Mati, you'll need an **Alien Travel Permit**, issued in minutes without fuss from the Zhangye PSB. On summer weekends tourist minibuses costing ¥18 each way leave Zhangye for Mati at 7am, returning at 5pm. At other times, you'll need to stay a couple of nights in Mati – the only bus from Zhangye's main bus station leaves at 3pm and takes three or four hours, while the bus coming back from Mati leaves at 7am. The ride costs around ¥6 each way. You'll find cheap **accommodation** (❷) in the immediate vicinity of Mati's bus station.

Jiayuguan and beyond

One more cup of wine for our remaining happiness. There will be chilling parting dreams tonight.

Ninth-century poet on a leave-taking at Jiayuguan

To some Chinese the very name **JIAYUGUAN** is synonymous with sorrow and a ghastly remoteness. The last **fortress** of the Great Wall was built here by the Ming in 1372, over 5000km from the wall's easternmost point at Shanhaiguan, from which time the town made its living by supplying the needs of the fortress garrison. This was literally the final defence of the empire, the spot where China ended and beyond which lay a terrifying wilderness. The fort, just outside the town and perfectly restored, is one of the great sights of northwestern China, and there are also a number of other forts and beacons scattered around in the desert outside Jiayuguan.

Apart from the great fort, the city today is a bleak, lonely place, laid out in a regular grid pattern, and sliced through diagonally from east to west by the principal Gansu Highway. Its centre is a large traffic circle, overlooked by the *Jiayuguan Hotel* and the post office; Xinhua Lu is the main street leading southeast from here. One of its few attractions is the **Great Wall Museum** (daily 8am–noon & 2.30–6.30pm; ¥8), where the history of the Wall is traced from Han times right up to the last frenzied spurt of wall building which took place under the Ming. The museum lies due south of the central traffic

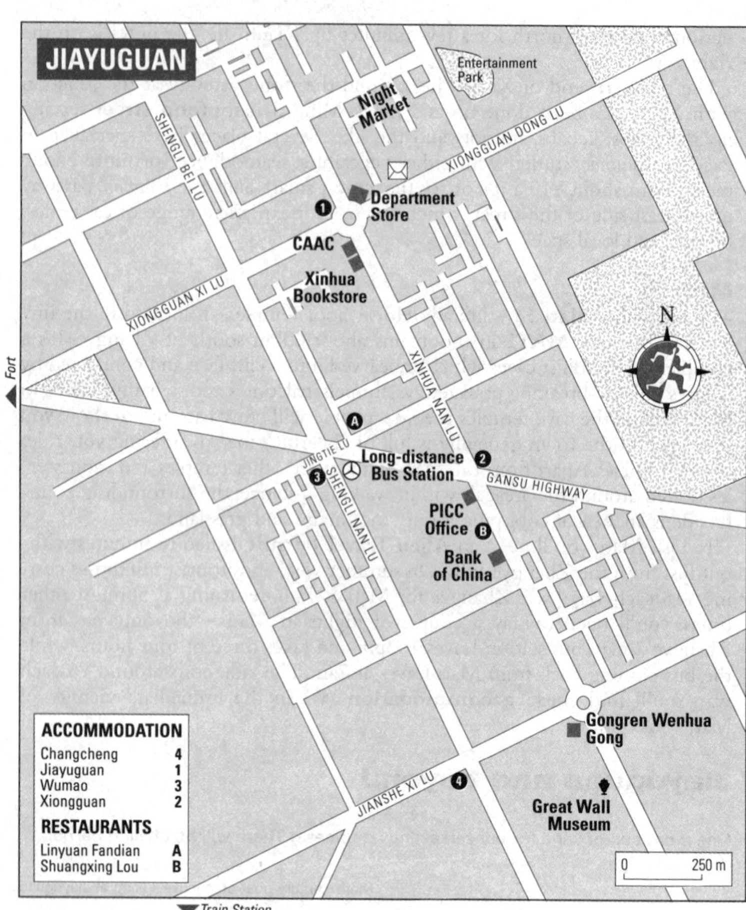

circle, on the main road, about thirty minutes' walk from the *Jiayuguan Hotel*; alternatively, take bus #1 or any minibus heading to the train station, and get off at the Gongren Wenhua Gong (Workers' Culture Palace) – the museum is just a few minutes' walk south from here. The highlights are photos of the Wall taken from points right across northern China, places that for the most part lie well away from tourist itineraries. There are also scale models of sections of wall from different areas and times, showing the materials from which they were built. The museum is on two floors; you may need to ask somebody to open the upstairs for you. It's worth making your way to the rooftop of the museum as there's a great view over the city and surrounding desert.

In the north of the town is an **Entertainment Park**, which is a good spot for an evening stroll among the crowds, giant sculptures, pagodas, pleasure boats and dodgem cars. Head north along Xinhua Bei Lu from the central traffic circle and take the first right along a narrow market street – the park lies at the far end of the street.

Practicalities

Jiayuguan's **train station** is in the far southwest of the city and linked by bus or minibus #1 to the centre. All trains running between Ürümqi and eastern China stop here. The **bus station** has a much more convenient location on the main highway, about a kilometre southwest of the central roundabout. For tourists, the most useful buses are the frequent connections with Dunhuang or Zhangye. Some services, for example the one running between Hami and Jiuquan, must be flagged down on the highway outside the station. The **airport**, 10km from town, is connected by CAAC buses to the **CAAC** office, south of the central traffic circle (Mon–Sat 8.30am–12pm & 2.30–6pm; Ⓣ0937/226237).

Jiayuguan's **CITS** (Ⓣ0937/6225083), situated in a downstairs office of the *Jiayuguan Hotel*, can supply train tickets for a ¥30 commission and offer reasonably priced tours – for example, a car carrying four passengers to the fort, the Overhanging Wall, the Heishan rock carvings and the Underground Gallery (see below) will cost about ¥50 per person. They can also arrange a day trip to the July 1st Glacier. **Train tickets** out of Jiayuguan are hard to come by – you will almost certainly need the help of a travel service, and may need to resort to soft class if you want a sleeper. When **buying bus tickets**, foreigners without PICC certificates (see p.1020) have sometimes managed to sweet-talk the station staff into letting them pay a tiny supplement for single-day cover; if you fail, you can buy certificates at the *Jiayuguan* and *Changcheng* hotels, as well as at the PICC office on Xinhua Lu, just south of the Gansu Highway.

Accommodation is all fairly central. Just west from the bus station, the *Wumao* is very worn (Ⓣ0937/6227514; ❷, dorm beds ¥40), but offers bike rental at ¥2 an hour; cleaner rooms are available a few minutes east at the friendly *Xiongguan* (Ⓣ0937/6225115, Ⓕ6225399; ❸, dorm beds ¥20). For something more upmarket, your best bet is the *Jiayuguan*, right on the central roundabout (Ⓣ0937/6226983, Ⓕ6227174; ❻), offering smart doubles and a good restaurant. The #1 bus from the train station stops here. Alternatively, there's the four-star *Changcheng*, south on Jianshe Xi Lu (Ⓣ0937/6225213, Ⓕ6226016; ❻), its architecture mimicking a martial theme.

The *Jiayuguan Hotel* **restaurant** serves bland Chinese breakfasts and much better evening meals. Staples – noodles and dumplings – are available around the bus station and at the **night market** north from the *Jiayuguan* and along the road to the Entertainment Park. If you want to sit down to standard Chinese fare in a cheerful setting, try either the *Linyuan Fandian*, pretty well opposite the bus station, or *Shuangxing Lou*, near the Bank of China on Xinhua Lu.

The fort and beyond

The **fort** (Cheng Lou; daily 8am–12.30pm & 2.30–6pm; ¥40) at the Jiayuguan Pass is the biggest sight in the Hexi Corridor. Its location, between the permanently snow-capped Qilian Mountains to the north and the black Mazong (Horse's Mane) Mountains to the south, could not be more dramatic – or more strategically valuable. Everything that travels between the deserts of Central Asia and the fertile lands of China – goods, traders, armies – has to file through this pass. The desolation of the landscape only adds to the melancholy – being forced to leave China altogether was a citizen's worst nightmare, and it was here that disgraced officials and condemned or fleeing criminals had to make their final, bitter farewells.

Some kind of fort may have occupied this site as early as the Han dynasty, but the surviving building is a Ming construction, completed in 1372. Sometimes referred to as the "Impregnable Defile under Heaven", it comprises an outer and an inner wall, the former more than 700m in circumference and about 10m high. At the east and the west of the inner wall stand symbolic gates, the Gate of Enlightenment and the Gate of Conciliation, respectively. Inside each gate are sloping walkways leading to the top of the wall, enabling horses to climb up and patrol the turrets. In between the Gate of Enlightenment and the outer wall stand a pavilion, a temple and a somewhat haunting open-air theatre which was once used to entertain troops.

The so-called **Overhanging Wall** (daily 8am–6pm; ¥8), about 6km north of the fort, is a section of the Great Wall connecting the fort to the Mazong range, originally built in the sixteenth century and recently restored. From the ramparts there are excellent views of the surrounding land, and it's actually much more atmospheric than the fort, especially if you take the scenic cycle route along the crumbling Wall.

Other desert sights

Several other desert attractions around Jiayuguan could also be combined with a trip to the fort and the Wall. About 6km south of Jiayuguan are the ruins of the **First Beacon Tower**. Built on the Great Wall in the sixteenth century, the long-abandoned tower is now crumbling on a cliff top on the northern bank of the Taolai River at the foot of the Qilian Mountains. The desert also harbours a couple of unusual collections of ancient Chinese art. One is the **Xincheng Dixia Hualang** (Underground Gallery), about 20km east of Jiayuguan. Actually a burial site from the Wei and Jin periods, more than fifteen hundred years ago, the graves are brick-laid and contain paintings depicting contemporary life. Not far beyond the fort, 9km northwest of Jiayuguan, are the **Heishan rock carvings**. These look more like our conception of real cave man's art: on the cliffs of the Heishan Mountain are carved more than a hundred pictures of hunting, horse-riding and dancing, all dating back to the Warring States Period (476–221 BC). Finally, one stupendous but rather inaccessible natural sight is the **Qiyi Bingchuan** (July 1st Glacier), located 4300m up in the Qilian Mountains, 120km from Jiayuguan – remarkably close considering what a hot place Jiayuguan is in summer.

Practicalities

The easiest way to reach both the fort and the Wall is to hire a small **minibus** (around ¥50 for the whole trip); visiting the First Beacon Tower and the two art sites in conjunction with a tour of the fort and Overhanging Wall takes a day and costs around ¥250 in a taxi. You can get to the fort itself by public transport – take one of the occasional minibuses that leave for the fort from the roundabout outside the *Jiayuguan Hotel* (¥3 one way). To **cycle** to the fort, follow the Gansu Highway west from the bus station until you cross the bridge over the rail line. A blue sign pointing right indicates the way to the fort from here. From the Fort to the Overhanging Wall, you go back 50m from the car park and follow a gravel road to your left marked by a stele. This takes you through a stripped, bleak landscape, past a graveyard and to the Wall, which you follow for about a kilometre – there's not much of a path – until you reach the ticket office for the Overhanging Wall. Returning to Jiayuguan from the Overhanging Wall, you can take a direct road into town. It's about thirty minutes to the fort, another thirty to the Overhanging Wall, and forty back into town.

CITS can take you to the glacier on an expensive and hectic day-trip, involving a three-hour drive, followed by five hours climbing up and down, and three hours driving back. Reckon on ¥500–1000 for the whole trip, including a guide.

Dunhuang and the Mogao Caves

An oasis town perched right on the outer periphery of old Chinese Turkestan, **DUNHUANG** has always been literally on the edge of the desert – from downtown you can see giant, spectacular **sand dunes** at the bottom of the street, and winds can whip up abrasive yellow sandstorms. Dunhuang's fame rests on the astonishing artwork at the nearby **Mogao Caves**, and the town has become something of a desert resort for visiting them, with inexpensive hotels, lots of English-language menus in the restaurants and friendly people.

The town itself is nothing more than a few appealing ordinary streets – the centre is marked by a traffic circle with streets radiating out to the north, east, south and west. On the main street east, Dong Dajie, there's a surprisingly interesting **souvenir night market** every summer evening, where you can stroll with no pressure to buy. Coins, jade articles, Buddhas, Tibetan bells and horns, leather shadow puppets, scroll paintings and Chinese chops are all on sale. Nearby, the mediocre **Dunhuang Museum** (¥10) houses a few of the scrolls left behind after the depredations of the archeologist and adventurer Sir Aurel Stein (see box, p.1052) – there's a much better museum at the caves themselves.

Practicalities

There is no rail line directly to Dunhuang. The nearest **train station** is at Liuyuan (usually labelled as "Dunhuang" on timetables), about 130km away; minibuses wait outside the station to carry passengers to town. The **bus station** lies right in the budget hotel area in the south of town on Mingshan Lu; diagonally opposite is a **sleeper bus station**. Dunhuang's **airport** is about 13km southeast of town; the airport bus stops at the CAAC office on Bei Dajie. Most accommodation has **travel agents**, who arrange local tours, and tickets out; the best for budget travellers are the local branch of *John's Café* (see p.1049) in the *Feitian* hotel (Ⓔjohncafe@hotmail.com); and the **CTS** is in the

Dunhuang and the Mogao Caves

Dunhuang	敦煌	***dūnhuáng***
Baima Ta	白马塔	*báimă tă*
Dunhuang Gucheng	敦煌古城	*dūnhuáng gŭchéng*
Mingsha Shan	明沙山	*míngshā shān*
Mogao Caves	莫高千佛洞	*mògāo qiānfódòng*
Xi Qianfodong	西千佛洞	*xī qiānfódòng*
Yangguan	阳关	*yángguān*
Yueya Quan	月牙泉	*yuěyá quán*
Yumenguan	玉门关	*yùmén guān*
Accommodation		
Dunhuang Binguan	敦煌宾馆	*dūnhuáng bīnguăn*
Dunhuang Fandian	敦煌饭店	*dūnhuáng fàndiàn*
Feitian	飞天宾馆	*fēitiān bīnguăn*
Five Rings	五环宾馆	*wŭhuán bīnguăn*
Guangyuan	广源大酒店	*guăngyuán dàjiŭdiàn*
International	敦煌国际大酒店	*dūnhuáng guójì dàjiŭdiàn*
Jinye	金叶宾馆	*jīnyè bīnguăn*
Xiyu	西域宾馆	*xīyù bīnguăn*
Liuyuan	柳园	***liŭyuán***

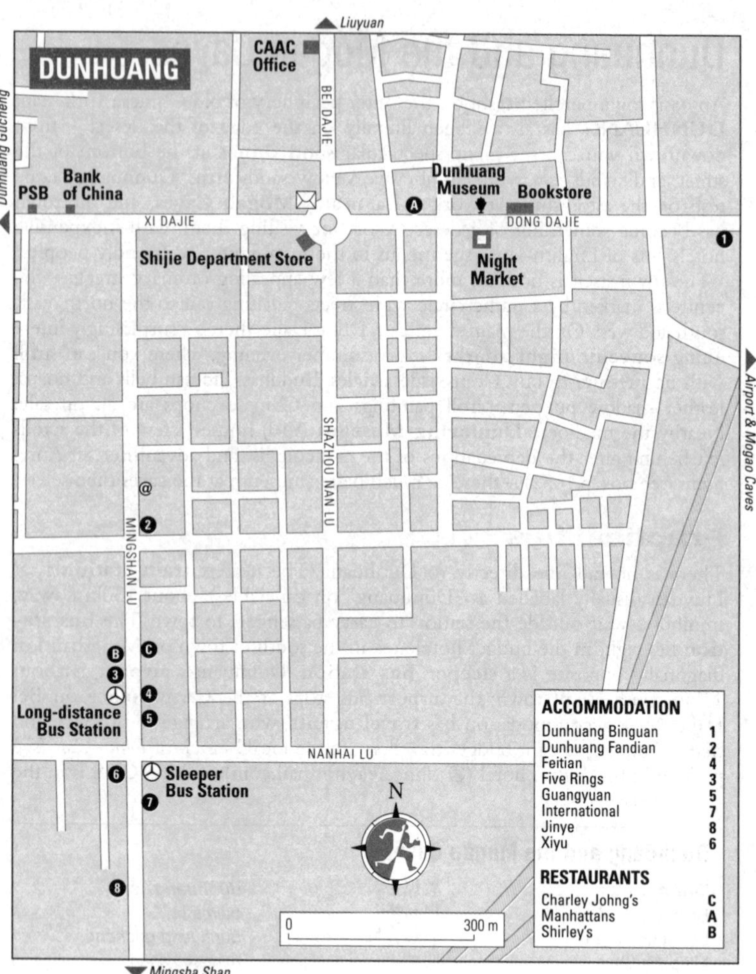

International hotel (☎0937/8822312) – an English-speaking guide from here costs ¥150 for the day; a car, from ¥300.

You can **rent bikes** from *Shirley's Café* for ¥1 an hour. **Internet bars** abound north of the bus station on Mingshan Lu, and foreign-oriented cafés often have Net access too – connections are good and cost ¥3–5 an hour.

Accommodation

There's a glut of accommodation in Dunhuang, which may go some way to explaining why it is such good value, especially at the lower end of the market. Prices rise in peak season (July and August), and are considerably discounted in winter, though you'll need to check on the availability of heating and hot water. Most places offer dorm beds; whether you'll get one depends on the management and how full the hotel is – they won't mix Chinese and Westerners in the same rooms.

Moving on from Dunhuang

Several ordinary, luxury and sleeper **buses** depart daily from both the Dunhuang bus station and sleeper bus station to Jiayuguan (about 5hr), and at least one daily to Lanzhou (24hr) and all points in between. There are also buses to Hami in Xinjiang (7hr; see p.1070). In the past, buying tickets for the fifteen-hour bus journey to **Golmud** in Qinghai Province (on the road to Tibet) was an extremely expensive affair for foreigners – a PSB-sponsored scam that involved a special ticket at five times the usual cost – though at the time of writing they were only being charged the ordinary price (¥98). Wherever you're heading, nobody seems to be interested in seeing PICC certificates.

There are **flights** three times a week to Lanzhou, and once a week each to Ürümqi and Xi'an. **CAAC** are on Bei Dajie (ⓣ0937/8825699), with a China Northwest office near *Charley Johng's Café* on Mingshan Lu. **Train tickets** are most conveniently bought at a special window in the bus station, or at the rail office at the *Dunhuang Binguan*, though other travel agents will insist this is impossible; you may be charged a ¥30 fee here per order (not per ticket), so try and get a group together. Frequent minibuses for the **train station at Liuyuan** depart from outside the bus station; the journey takes two to three hours. Note that most **accommodation** – and the local branch of *John's Café*, inside the *Feitian* hotel – can organize plane and train tickets, though commissions are a steep ¥50 per ticket.

Dunhuang Binguan Yangguan Dong Lu ⓣ0937/8822415, ⓕ8822309. Drab 1980s concrete exterior, but smart inside; rooms are comfortable, and they also have a few budget beds in two- or three-person dorms. This is the only place in town where you can change money on Sundays. Dorm beds ¥30–40, ❻

Dunhuang Fandian Mingshan Lu ⓣ0937/8822413, ⓕ8822785, ⓔdhfd@public.lz.gs.cn. Recently refurbished to mid-range comforts, though it still has dormitory beds available. Dorm bed ¥35, ❺

Feitian Mingshan Lu ⓣ0937/8822726. Very conveniently located opposite the bus station, this place has decent doubles and inexpensive dorms – though the staff often refuse to admit this. *John's Café* has a branch here too. Dorm beds ¥30, ❸

Five Rings Mingshan Lu ⓣ0937/8822620. Just north of the bus station, this hotel is good value if you go for the four-bed dorms or cheaper doubles. Dorm beds ¥30, ❷

Guangyuan Corner of Nanhai Lu and Mingshan Lu ⓣ0937/8839028, ⓕ8839008. Not outstanding from the outside, but furnishings are modern and the triples fine for the money. Triples ¥100, ❻

International Mingshan Lu ⓣ0937/8828638, ⓕ8821821, ⓔjqdhgj@public.lz.gs.cn. A modern prospect, whose rooms are a good deal considering the standard of accommodation offered. CTS are here too. Dorm beds ¥60, ❻

Jinye Mingshan Lu ⓣ0937/8821470. A couple of minutes farther to the south from the *Xiyu Hotel*, and much more upmarket though rather overpriced, offering air-conditioned doubles. Credit cards accepted. ❻

Xiyu Mingshan Lu ⓣ0937/8823017. Very convenient for the bus station, just one block to the south (turn right on emerging from the station). Very cheap dorms and fair doubles with bath. Dorm beds ¥35, ❻

Eating and drinking

There are plenty of good places for visitors to **eat** in Dunhuang, especially in the south of town along Mingshan Lu. One block south of the bus station, there are a number of foreigner-oriented places specializing in cheap Western and Chinese dishes with English menus, friendly service and tables on the pavement. *Shirley's* is most popular for its apple pie, coffee and ginger tea; their Chinese food isn't bad either.

A couple of minutes north of the *Feitian Hotel*, on the same side of the road, you'll find *Charley Johng's Café*, whose menu includes excellent pancakes, banana fritters and chicken curry. The Chinese restaurants farther up Mingshan

Lu on the east side of the road from here are more "authentic", but lack English menus and often serve inferior food.

The most atmospheric place to eat in the evening is the **night market** located through an imposing gateway off the south side of Dong Dajie, next to the souvenir market. Inside there are fountains, fairy lights and billiard tables, and you can sit on deck chairs and drink *babao* (also known as "Eight Treasures Tea"), full of delicious dried fruits, or have a full meal. Everything is cooked in front of you – just point to what you want. On the other side of Dong Dajie is the improbable *Manhattans Café*, featuring tuna fish and peanut-butter-and-jam sandwiches as well as pasta salads, at US prices. The decor is southwest USA-style – try it if you're badly homesick. The *Dunhuang Binguan* has the best of the **hotel restaurants**, including a not-too-expensive Japanese canteen.

The Mogao Caves

The **Mogao Caves**, 25km southeast of Dunhuang, are one of the great archeological discovery stories of the East. The first-known **Buddhist temples** within the boundaries of the Chinese empire, supposedly established in 366 AD by a monk called Lie Zun, they were a centre of culture on the Silk Road right up until the fourteenth century, and today contain religious artworks spanning a thousand years of history. Chinese Buddhism radiated out to the whole Han empire from these wild desert cliffs, and with it – gradually adapting to a Chinese context – came the artistic influences of Central Asia, India, Persia and the West.

Of the original thousand or more **caves**, over six hundred survive in recognizable form, but many are off-limits, either considered no longer of significant interest or else containing Tantric murals which the Chinese reckon are too sexually explicit for visitors. Of the thirty main caves open to the public, you are likely to manage only around fifteen in a single day.

Visiting the caves

Getting to the caves from Dunhuang is easy. Step on to the street between eight and nine in the morning and you will instantly be accosted by **minibus** drivers, who charge ¥5 for the one-way fare; the trip takes about twenty-five minutes. Choose a minibus that is nearly full – they won't leave until the last seat is occupied – or hire a bus for the return trip for ¥40.

The caves are open daily from 8.30am to 11.30am, and from 2.30pm to around 4pm. A half-day guided **tour** costs ¥80 (¥40 with a student card). You cannot take a **camera** into the caves without an extremely expensive permit, and all bags must be left at an office at the gate (¥2). Note that if you're caught taking photos without a permit, you may be subjected to a large fine. The caves are not lit, to avoid damage to the murals; your guide will have a **flashlight**, but you are strongly advised to bring one of your own as well – you can hire one for about ¥3 plus a deposit from the ticket office, but they are pretty anemic.

The **guides** generally speak Chinese only, though in the peak season you shouldn't have difficulty engaging an English-speaking guide (expect to pay about ¥20). The guides are well informed, though their English is not always brilliant. There is something of a set route, but you may be able to persuade the guide to unlock specific caves you want to see.

Before or after your tour, it's worth visiting the **Research and Exhibition Centre** (daily 9am–5pm; ¥25), the impressive modern building opposite the car park. Paid for by Japanese money, it holds seven replica caves – nos. 3, 217,

220, 249, 275, 285 and 419. The big advantage here is that the lights are on, the colours are fresh and you can study the murals close up. A further cave is not from Mogao at all, but from the Yulin Caves (no. 25) in nearby Anxi County. Upstairs are a few surviving silk scrolls and manuscripts, and there's a film about the Mogao site. There's also a separate **museum** at the caves which you'll visit as part of your tour, with a history in English of the site, plus more scrolls, nineteenth- and twentieth-century photos of Mogao, and reproductions of some of the plundered frescoes, now in Europe.

Getting back to Dunhuang is as simple as getting to the site: go to the car park and wait for the next minibus. The last one leaves around 4pm. If you get stuck, you could stay on site at the basic **guesthouse**.

The caves

What makes the caves so interesting is that you can trace the **development of Chinese art** over the centuries, from one dynasty to the next. Some grasp of the history of the caves is essential to appreciate them properly. but restorations and replacements in the modern era have complicated the picture, particularly where statuary is concerned – many of the statues are not original. You may hear your guide blaming the ugly replacements on the Qing dynasty – in other words on the monk Wang Yuan Lu – but some of them are a good deal newer than that. The caves are all clearly labelled with numbers above the doors.

Northern Wei

The earliest caves were hewn out in the fourth and fifth centuries AD during the **Northern Wei** (386–581). This dynasty was formed by Turkic-speaking people known as the Tobas, and as the centuries progressed there was constant friction between the forces of conservatism (who wanted to retain the ancient Toba customs) and those of change (who wanted to adapt Chinese customs).

The Wei caves are relatively small in size, and are often supported in the centre by a large column – a feature imported from India. A statue of the Buddha is usually central, surrounded in tiers on the walls by a **mass of tiny Buddhas** brilliantly painted in black, white, blue, red and green. The statues are in fact made of terracotta: the soft rock inside the caves was not suited to detailed carving, so the craftsmen would first carve a rough outline of the figure, then build it up with clay.

The style of the murals in these caves shows a great deal of **foreign influence**. Faces have long noses and curly hair, and women are large-breasted. **Cave 101**, decorated towards the end of the fifth century, provides a good example: the Buddha, enclosed by attendant Bodhisattvas, is essentially a Western figure, recognizably Christ-like, reminiscent of Greek Byzantine frescoes. In **cave 257** the Buddha seems to be dressed in a Roman toga, while the beautiful **cave 428** shows a notably Indian influence in both content (note the peacocks on the ceiling) and style. There are, however, also the beginnings of Chinese influence in the wavy, flower-like angels sometimes seen fluttering above.

Though originally designed as a focus of devotional contemplation, the murals gradually acquired a **narrative purpose** as well, and the paintings soon move towards a wider subject matter, their story sequences arranged in long horizontal strips. **Cave 135** (early sixth century) illustrates a *jataka* story – concerning a former life of Buddha – in which he gave his own body to feed a starving tigress, unable to succour her cubs. The narrative, read from right to left, is broken up by simple landscapes, a frequently used device. **Cave 254** shows the story of Buddha defeating Mara, or Illusion.

The Mogao cave treasures

The story of Mogao's development, then subsequent abandonment and rediscovery, is an intriguing one. Before the arrival of Buddhism from India, the Chinese – Taoist and Confucian – temple tradition had been mainly of buildings in wood, a material well adapted to most Chinese conditions. The idea of cave temples came to China from India, where poverty, lack of building materials and the intense heat had necessitated alternative methods.

The emergence of the complex of cave temples at **Mogao** dominated early Chinese Buddhism, as pilgrims, monks and scholars passing along the Silk Road settled and worked here, translating sutras, or holy texts. Merchants and nobles stopped, too, endowing temples to ensure the success of their caravans or to benefit their souls, as they did in varying degrees all along the Silk Road. Huge numbers of **artists and craftsmen** were employed at Dunhuang, often lying on high scaffoldings in the dim light provided by oil lamps. The workers usually lived in tiny caves in the northern section of Mogao furnished with small brick beds, and were paid a pittance – in a collection of Buddhist scriptures, archeologists have discovered a bill of indenture signed by one sculptor for the sale of his son.

Under the Tang, which saw the establishment of Buddhism throughout the Chinese empire, the monastic community reached its peak, with more than a thousand cave temples in operation. Thereafter, however, as the new ocean-going trading links slowly supplanted the Silk Road, Mogao (and Dunhuang) became increasingly provincial. At some point in the fourteenth century, the caves were **sealed and abandoned**.

Although Mogao's existence remained known to a few Buddhist scholars, it was only in 1900 that a wandering monk, **Wang Yuan Lu**, stumbled upon them by accident and decided to begin the work of excavation. He at once realized their significance, and made it his life's work to restore the site, excavating caves full of sand, touching up the murals, planting trees and gardens and building a guesthouse. This work he undertook with two acolytes and financed through begging expeditions.

The reconstructions might have gone on in relative obscurity were it not for the discovery of a bricked-up hidden chamber (cave 17), which Wang opened to reveal an enormous collection of **manuscripts**, **sutras** and **silk and paper paintings** – some 1000 years old and virtually undamaged. News of the cache soon reached the ears of the Dunhuang authorities, who, having appropriated a fair haul for themselves, decided to re-seal them in the cave on the grounds that it would be too expensive to transport them. So it remained for a further seven years, until the arrival in 1907 of the Central Asian explorer and scholar **Aurel Stein**. Stein, a Hungarian

Artistic changes, and a shift towards a more distinctive Chinese style, began to appear at the end of the Northern Wei period, around the middle of the sixth century. One of the most strikingly Chinese of the Wei murals is in **cave 120N** and shows, above the devotional niches, a series of battle scenes, interesting for their total lack of perspective. All the figures are drawn as though seen straight on, regardless of their relative positions, a favourite device throughout the history of Chinese painting.

Sui

With the founding of the short-lived but dynamic **Sui dynasty** in 581, Western influences began to decline rapidly. The Chinese empire had been torn apart by civil wars but now there followed a boom in Buddhism, and Buddhist art. In the four decades up to the emergence of the Tang, more than seventy caves were carved at Mogao.

working for the British and the Indian Survey (in other words, a secret agent), had heard rumours of the caves and been offered items for sale. In good Howard Carter tradition, he persuaded Wang to reopen the chamber. This is how Stein later described what he saw:

The sight the small room disclosed was one to make my eyes open; heaped up in layers, but without any order, there appeared in the dim light of the priest's little lamp a solid mass of manuscript bundles rising to a height of nearly 10 feet and filling, as subsequent measurement showed, close on 500 cubic feet – an unparalleled archeological scoop.

This was no understatement. Examining the manuscripts, Stein found original sutras brought from India by the Tang monk and traveller **Xuanzang**, along with other Buddhist texts written in Sanskrit, Sogdian, Tibetan, Runic-Turkic, Chinese, Uigur and other languages unknown to the scholar. Amid the art finds, hardly less important were dozens of rare Tang-dynasty paintings on silk and paper – badly crushed but totally untouched by damp.

Eventually Stein, donating the equivalent of £130 to Wang's restoration fund, left Mogao for England with some seven thousand manuscripts and five hundred paintings. Later in the year a Frenchman, Paul Pelliot, negotiated a similar deal, shipping six thousand manuscripts and many paintings back to Paris. And so, virtually overnight, and before the Beijing authorities could put a stop to it, the British Museum and the Louvre had acquired the core of their Chinese manuscript and painting collections. Not all the caves were looted however; a fresh batch of 248 were only located in 2001, though the scrolls and artefacts they contained have yet to be fully assessed.

Today, fuelled perhaps by Greek claims on the Elgin marbles, the Chinese are pressing for the **return** of all paintings and manuscripts in foreign collections. It is hard to dispute the legitimacy of these claims now, though it was only in 1961 that Mogao was declared a National Monument. Had the treasures not been removed, more would almost certainly have been lost in the chaotic years of the twentieth century. A large party of White Russians used the caves as a barracks in 1920, showing their disregard for history by scrawling their names over the frescoes. Fortunately, despite the massive loss in terms of manuscripts and scrolls, the art work and statuary at the caves themselves are still fabulously preserved. The cave art was not damaged during the Cultural Revolution – protected, it is said, on a personal order from Premier Zhou Enlai.

Structurally, they dispense with the central column, while, artistically, they show the replacement of the bold, slightly crude Wei brushwork with intricate, flowing lines and an increasingly extravagant use of colour that includes gilding and washes of silver. In **cave 150**, for example, painted in the last year of the Sui, narrative has been dispensed with altogether in favour of a repeated theme of throned Buddhas and Bodhisattvas. In terms of statuary, the Sui period also shows a change, the figures becoming stiff and inflexible and dressed in Chinese robes. **Cave 427** contains some characteristic Sui figures – short legs, long bodies (indicating power and divinity) and big, square heads.

Tang

The **Tang-dynasty** artists (618–906), under whom the caves at Mogao reached their artistic zenith, drew both from past traditions and real life. The classic Tang cave has a square floor, tapering roof and a niche for worship set into the back wall. The statuary includes **warriors** – a new theme – and all figures are carefully detailed, the Bodhisattvas above all, with their pleats and folds clinging softly to undulating feminine figures.

For sheer size, their **Buddhas** are the most famous, notably in **caves 96 and 130**. The astonishing 34-metre-high seated Buddha in cave 96 – dressed in the traditional dragon robe of the emperor – is thought by some to have been designed deliberately to remind pilgrims of the famous Tang empress Wu Zetian. In **cave 148** there is another huge Buddha, this one reclining as though dead, and surrounded by disciples.

The **Tang paintings** range from huge murals depicting scenes from the sutras – now contained within one composition rather than the earlier cartoon-strip convention – to vivid paintings of individuals. One of the most popular and spectacular Tang mural themes was that of the Visit of the Bodhisattva Manjusri to Vimalakirti. **Cave 1** contains perhaps the greatest expression of this story. Vimalakirti, on the left, is attended by a great host of heavenly beings, eager to hear the discourse of the ailing old king. Above him the plane is tilted to take in a seemingly limitless landscape, with the Buddha surrounded by Bodhisattvas on an island in the middle. Another version can be seen in **cave 51E**, in a mural that is also especially notable for the subtle shading of its portraiture, which includes a magnificently depicted Central Asian retinue. Other superb Tang murals include a very free, fluid landscape in **cave 70** and, perhaps most developed of all, **cave 139A**'s depiction of the Western Paradise of the Amitabha Buddha. This last is a supremely confident painting, working in elaborate displays of architecture and figures within a coherent whole. The theme is the Buddha's promise of paradise: the souls of the reborn rise from lotus flowers in the foreground, with heavenly scenes enclosing the Buddha above.

The later caves

Later work, executed by the **Five Dynasties, Song and Western Xia** (906–1227), shows little real progression from the Tang. Much, in any case, is simply restoration or repainting of existing murals. Song work is perhaps the most interesting, tending towards a heavy richness of colour, and with many of its figures displaying the features of minority races.

During the Mongol **Yuan dynasty** (1260–1368), towards the end of which period Mogao seems to have been abandoned, the standard niche in the back wall of the caves gave way to a central altar, creating fresh and uncluttered space for murals. Tibetan-style Lamaist (or Tantric) figures were introduced, and occult diagrams (mandalas) became fashionable. The most interesting Yuan art is in **cave 465**, slightly set apart from the main body of grottoes. You might try asking the guides if they will open this up for you, though they will probably only do so for a huge fee. In the fashion of Indian Buddhist painting, the murals include Tantric figures in the ultimate state of enlightenment, graphically represented by the state of sexual union.

Other sights around Dunhuang

A few kilometres to the south of town are the much-touted **Yueya Quan** (Crescent Moon Lake) and **Mingsha Shan** (Singing Sand Dune), set amid the most impressive sand-dune scenery anywhere in China, with dunes 200–300m high. The sands reportedly make a humming noise in windy weather, hence the name. The Crescent Moon Lake is not much to look at, but is curious for its permanence, despite being surrounded by shifting sands – it was recorded in history at least two thousand years ago. Various activities take place from the tops of the main dune, such as sand-tobogganing and paragliding. The paragliding is great fun and costs ¥30 – you get to try two or three times if your initial flight isn't successful. Tobogganing costs ¥10 and feels a little safer. Climbing the dune in the first place, however, is incredibly hot, exhausting work; if you use the wooden steps you may have to pay a small fee. Or you can ride up on a camel for ¥40.

Minibuses from Dunhuang will drop you by a gate and **ticket office** – entry is ¥50, but you can also reach the dunes by cutting round the side about 300m back from the gate. In the summer heat the only sensible time to come here is early in the morning around 7.30am, or in the evening. Between 5pm and 6pm minibuses cruise around Dunhuang looking for passengers (¥3 per person). Otherwise you can walk here in about 45 minutes, or cycle in twenty – just head south out of town. Park your bike somewhere before the entrance or you'll be charged an annoying ¥5 to put it in the bike park.

About 20km southwest of the city, right out in the desert, is the **Dunhuang Gucheng** – literally "Dunhuang Ancient City". This particular ancient city is actually a 1990s film set; nevertheless, it has become a regular feature on the Dunhuang tourist trail. From a distance it looks impressive with its dramatic backdrop of desert, but the closer you get the more tacky it seems. Inside there are a number of souvenir shops, noodle stands and even yurts to stay in. There are occasional **minibuses** here from Mingshan Lu in Dunhuang (¥10 return trip), usually around lunchtime. You can also cycle here if you can cope with the heat, or else take a taxi for ¥30.

On the way back to Dunhuang, be sure to drop in on the **Baima Ta** (White Horse Dagoba). This attractive, nine-tiered dagoba was built in honour of the horse belonging to the monk Kumarajiva from Kuqa (see p.1090), which died on this spot in 384 AD. It lies amid corn fields and the remains of the old city walls, about 4km west of town, and is a pleasant place to take a breather.

A number of other historical sites lie farther away from Dunhuang but within the scope of a day-trip. One is the **Xi Qianfodong** (Western Thousand Buddha Caves), another cave site along the lines of Mogao, if incomparably smaller and less significant. If you are a real Buddhist art buff, talk to a travel service about visiting this place: in the past it was open to groups only and individuals were turned away.

Finally, there are two Han-dynasty gates, **Yumenguan** and **Yangguan**, which for periods of Chinese history marked the western border of China. They lie to the west of Dunhuang, 80km and 75km away respectively, and were originally joined together by a section of the Great Wall before being abandoned as long ago as the sixth century. Both sites today are impressive for their historic resonance and total desolation as much as for anything else: Yumenguan comprises imposingly sturdy, if crumbling, ten-metre-high mud walls while Yangguan is little more than a ruined tower, though sandstorms have periodically exposed contemporary antiques buried in the surrounding sands. Today, the road to Yangguan is in good condition, but that to Yumenguan is extremely rough – to visit both gates by taxi would take all day and cost more than ¥600. One exciting option, however, is to visit the two gates **by camel**; to see the two gates, and bits of the Han Great Wall, takes around three days, and in the mild months of the year – early or late summer – this can be an excellent expedition. For an individual traveller, the cost of your camel, a guide, the guide's camel and a spare camel, works out at two or three hundred yuan per day (cheaper in a group). Contact *John's Café* at the *Feitian* hotel for more information.

Qinghai

Qinghai Province is for the most part a huge, empty wilderness with a population of just 4.5 million. Geographically and culturally a part of the **Tibetan plateau**, Qinghai has for centuries been a frontier zone, contested between Chinese immigrants and the Tibetans and Muslims who originally dwelt in its pastures and thin snatches of agricultural land. Today, the **minority presence** in Qinghai can still be felt strongly – as well as Tibetans, there are Hui, Salar, Tu, Mongol and Kazakh people all living here.

Only incorporated into the Chinese empire two hundred years ago – and not brought under firm Han control until 1949 when Communist armies defeated those of the Muslim warlord Ma Bufang – the area is still perceived by the Han Chinese as a frontier land for pioneers and prospectors, and, on a more sinister note, a dumping-ground for criminals and political opponents to the regime. The number of inmates held in Qinghai **prison and labour camps**, including those released but who must remain in the province because they cannot regain residency rights in their home towns, is estimated to reach four hundred thousand – almost one in ten of the population of Qinghai. Of these, a tenth are political prisoners. Several of the prison camps are actually in the outskirts of the capital, Xining, purporting to be ordinary factories.

It is only the eastern part of the province around **Xining** that has a long-established Han presence. With its lush green valleys and plentiful annual rainfall, this is also the only part of Qinghai where sustainable agriculture takes place. To the west and south of here the land rises to a three-thousand-metre plateau which, bitterly cold for half the year, can at best be used as pastureland for cattle and sheep. To the northwest, on the other hand, towards the border with Xinjiang, the land sinks into an arid basin, which was good for little until the communist era, when mineral deposits and oil were discovered. Now the area supports extensive mining.

For the traveller, the primary point of interest in Qinghai is as an access point **into Tibet**: you can fly from Xining to Lhasa; the road from Golmud to Lhasa is the only officially approved overland route for foreigners; and there's also a rail line under construction which follows this road, due for completion in 2006. Qinghai is in many respects a part of Tibet and, in addition to the substantial Tibetan minority who live here, the splendid **Ta'er Si**, one of the major Tibetan lamaseries in all China, is located just outside Xining.

The province has other attractions, too, chiefly as an unspoilt natural wilderness area. The enormous **Qinghai Hu**, China's biggest lake, in particular, offers opportunities for hikes and bird-spotting. There are also possibilities for longer treks, rafting, hunting and mountaineering. Such activities have to be arranged by local travel agents, who can sometimes manage this at just a few days' notice.

Xining and around

Qinghai's unassuming provincial capital, **XINING** contains few tourist sights in itself, and is usually regarded simply as a base from which to explore the nearby Tibetan monastery of Ta'er Si. Nevertheless, as the only sizeable city in Qinghai, Xining is an interesting place in its own right. Set in a rather extraor-

Xining and around

Xining	西宁	***xīníng***
Beishan Si	北山寺	*běishān sì*
Da Shizi	大十子	*dàshízì*
Great Mosque	清真大寺	*qīngzhēn dàsì*
Huangshui River	黄水河	*huángshuǐ hé*
Shuijing Food Market	水井香市场	*shuǐjǐngxiāng shìchǎng*
Ximen	西门	*xīmén*
Accommodation and eating		
Jiangjian	江渐宾馆	*jiāngjiàn bīnguǎn*
Minzu	民族宾馆	*mínzú bīnguǎn*
Qinghai	青海宾馆	*qīnghǎi bīnguǎn*
Xining Guest Hotel	西宁宾馆	*xīníng bīnguǎn*
Yahao Huayuan	雅豪花园宾馆	*yǎháo huāyuán bīnguǎn*
Yongfu	永副宾馆	*yǒngfù bīnguǎn*
Zangjia Ju	藏家居	*zàngjiā jū*
Ta'er Si	塔尔寺	***tǎ'ěr sì***
Ledu	乐都	***lèdū***
Qutan Si	瞿昙寺	*qútán sì*
Maduo	玛多	***mǎduō***
Mengda Nature Reserve	孟达自然保护区	***mèngdá zìrán bǎohùqū***
Guanting	官亭	*guāntíng*
Xunhua	循化	*xúnhuà*

dinary location, with stark mountains rearing up right behind, and the inhospitable terrain immediately beyond gives the city a cosy, reassuring feel. At a height of 2200m, right on the outermost edge of the Tibetan plateau, Xining experiences pleasantly cool weather in summer and bitter cold in winter.

Although definitely a centre of Han population, Xining is also full of minority nationalities, in particular Hui and rather lost-looking Tibetans. It has quite an ancient history, having been established probably as early as the Han dynasty. It even served as a stopover on a minor southern route of the Silk Road and has been a fairly important trading city for the Han since at least the sixteenth century. Today, connected by fast trains to Lanzhou and other Chinese cities, Xining is a firmly established part of the network of Han China.

The city is bordered by steep hills to the north, along the foot of which runs the Huangshui River. The major sight is the **Great Mosque**, on Dongguan Dajie, one of the most attractive in northwest China. Built in 1380, it encloses a large public square where worshippers can congregate. There is hardly a trace of Arab influence in the architecture – it is purely Chinese in style with flying eaves and colourful painted arches. There is also a local **museum** (¥5) in a charming historic building along a small market-lane just south of the *Yongfu Hotel*; it's easy to miss – you want no. 41, with a couple of pillars outside. Visitors are so rare your arrival is likely to set the attendants into a panic to find the keys, but with artefacts from most dynasties and a display of ethnic minority clothing, it's a worthy detour.

To the north of the Huangshui River, a couple of kilometres west of the train station, it is possible to climb the mountain up to the 1400-year-old **Beishan**

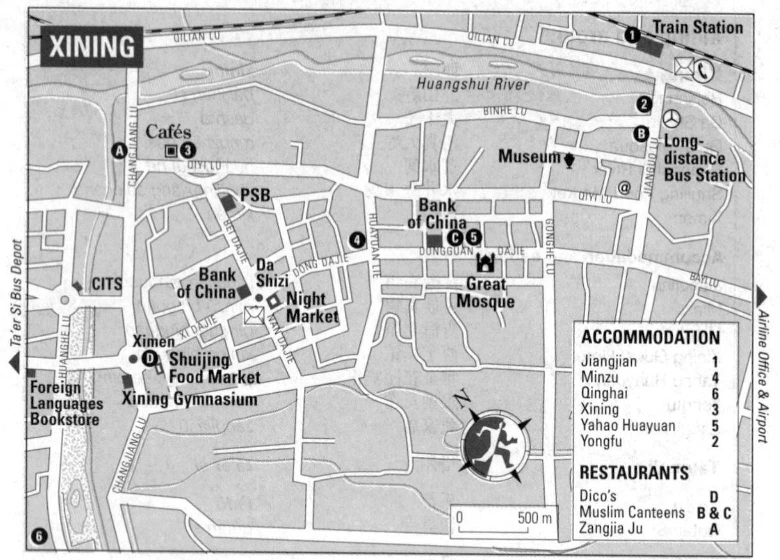

Si (North Mountain Temple). You climb hundreds of steps, then walk along a whole series of walkways and bridges connecting together little caves decorated with Taoist designs, often packed with people engaged in prayer ceremonies. At the very top is a pagoda, offering fine views over the city on a clear day. To reach Qilian Lu at the foot of the mountain, take bus #11 from the train station, or #10 from the town centre just south of the Ximen traffic circle; there is an obvious entrance just west of Changjiang Lu.

Perhaps most diverting, however, is simply strolling around the centre of town amid the crowds. Make a point of visiting the **Shuijing Food Market**, a covered market at Shuijing Gang, off Xi Dajie and very close to Ximen. There are more than three thousand fixed stalls down here, mostly dealing in mutton hotpots and kebabs. Many of the stalls are open until late at night, their stoves blazing in the dark.

Practicalities

Most of the city lies to the south of the river, though the **train station** lies immediately on the north bank, just across the bridge from the long-distance **bus station**. The centre of Xining is located about 3km to the west of here, along the main east–west streets Dong Dajie and then Xi Dajie, which connects **Da Shizi** (Big Crossroads) with the large **Ximen** traffic circle a few hundred metres farther west. Xining's **airport** is 26km east of town; a bus collects arrivals and drops them at the airline offices on Bayi Lu, about 1500m southeast of the train station – bus #2 runs west up Dongguan Dajie from here, or #28 will get you to the bus and train stations.

The main **Bank of China** is a huge building on Dongguan Dajie near the mosque, though any of the branch offices can also change traveller's cheques – there's one just east of Da Shizi. The main **post office**, where you can make IDD telephone calls, is on Da Shizi; you enter by climbing the raised pedestrian

Routes on from Xining

Xining's **airline office** is inconveniently located a few kilometres east of the centre at 85 Bayi Lu (Ⓣ0971/6146970), on the number #2 bus route. Direct flights are limited, and for most destinations locals advise taking the train to Lanzhou and flying from there. One exception is the four weekly flights from Xining **to Lhasa** as – at the time of writing – the airline office wasn't demanding that foreigners join an expensive tour, or pay for a special "Tibet permit" in order to purchase a ticket (see box, p.1121 for more on visiting Tibet). These things can change very quickly, however, and it's best to ask other travellers about the current situation. There are also eight flights a week to **Golmud**.

Direct **trains** run to and from most major cities in eastern China, including comfortable, fast double-deckers to Lanzhou in Gansu Province (3hr). There are also three services west to Golmud, for those gravitating towards Tibet; two of these are as fast as the bus (16hr), but watch out for the slow train (22hr). Buying tickets at the station is straightforward – Chinese timetables are on display and seats to Lanzhou are generally available on the morning of departure.

Aside from the obvious smooth rides to Golmud or Lanzhou on the new expressway, there are lots of interesting **bus routes** out of Xining and **tickets** are very cheap. In the direction of **Xiahe**, there is a bus to Linxia and another to the monastery town of Tongren, from both of which there are connecting services to Xiahe. There's also a bus to **Zhangye** in Gansu Province, via a spectacular ride north across the mountains. An equally exciting possibility is a bus southwest to **Maduo**. From here, very close to the source of the Yellow River, you can continue by bus along a rough route into Sichuan Province, though be aware that this route is not officially open to foreigners.

There have been recent reports of bus operators approaching foreigners in Xining offering seats on a **bus to Lhasa** for around ¥1200. While this is substantially cheaper than CITS charges for the Golmud–Lhasa run, note that foreigners are officially not allowed on the Xining–Lhasa bus; if you're caught along the way – at the checkpoint just outside Golmud, for instance – you'll be kicked off, with no refund available.

walkway. You'll find another office for making IDD calls a few minutes east of the train station. **Internet** bars are scattered around the place; there's one relatively near the bus station on Qiyi Lu, and another hidden behind stalls in a market street south of the bank off Dong Dajie – look for the vertical yellow sign. The Foreign Languages **bookstore**, west on Xiguan Dajie, has a surprisingly good selection of English-language classics and Chinese works in translation.

There are several **travel agents** in town that may come in handy for buying train or plane tickets, and for organizing trips to Qinghai Hu (see p.1063) or more remote parts of Qinghai. The most convenient are the Qinghai Jiaotong Lüxingshe (Ⓣ0971/8149504), based at the front of the long-distance bus station; Qinghai Nationalities Travel Service at the *Minzu* hotel (Ⓣ0971/8225991); and CITS, at 156 Huanghe Lu (Ⓣ0971/6133841, Ⓦwww.citsqh.com) – they also have an office outside the PSB on Bei Dajie (Ⓣ0971/8224937).

Accommodation

Foreign-friendly accommodation in Xining is sparse; the couple of budget options are both near the train station.

Jiangjian West side of the train station square Ⓣ0971/8149385. Chinese hostel with reasonable doubles and enthusiastic staff; you'll need to speak some Mandarin to negotiate a bed. ❶

Minzu (Nationality Hotel) Near the bank on Dong Dajie Ⓣ0971/8225951. Buses #1 or #2 come here from the train station. The best feature of this faded place is its central location and 24hr hot water. Dorm beds ¥60, ❸

Qinghai Huanghe Lu ☎0971/6144888. By far the most upmarket place in town, with lots of facilities including a pretty decent restaurant, far out in the southeast of the city. Take bus #32 from the train station and ask where to get off. From the bus stop head south towards the vast tower – about a 10min walk. ❺

Xining Guest Hotel Qiyi Lu ☎0971/8238701. About 1km north of Da Shizi, this is a lifeless, 1950s place which, though recently renovated, still isn't particularly attractive. To get here, take bus #9 from the station. ❺

Yahao Huayuan Just west and opposite the mosque on Dongguan Dajie ☎0971/8137994. Brand new and clean mid-range choice, though they're not always sure whether foreigners are allowed to stay. ❹

Yongfu (aka Kunlun) Jianguo Lu ☎0971/8140236. A cheap and friendly option, located in a peculiar round building directly across the road from the bus station. The reception is on the ground floor, but the hotel begins on the third floor, above a department store. Dorm beds ¥25, ❷

Eating

The hotels all have **restaurants** in keeping with their facilities, and there's a knot of cafes and **bars** around the *Xining Guest Hotel* on Qiyi Lu. Also near here, on Changjiang Lu, *Zangjia Ju* is a Tibetan restaurant, which puts on evening shows of Tibetan dancing. For Muslim food, there's a canteen near the bus station, and a large and authentic place across from the mosque on Dongguan Dajie, full of old men sipping tea and chewing their way through lamb and noodle dishes. If you're after vaguely Western fare, head for the branch of *Dico's Burgers* on the Ximen intersection.

The best places to eat in Xining, however, are the **markets** downtown; staples here are kebabs, bowls of spicy noodles, mutton hotpots and *zasui* soup, made with ox and sheep entrails. *Shaguo* – earthenware hotpots full of tofu, mushrooms and meat cooked in broth – are excellent, as are *jiaozi*, *hundun* soup and other basic dishes prepared on the spot. The covered market, Shuijing Gang (see p.1058), is a good place to head to, as are many of the side streets around Da Shizi.

Ta'er Si and beyond

Lying about 25km southeast from Xining, **Ta'er Si**, known as Kumbum in Tibetan, is one of the most important **monasteries** outside Tibet. Although not as attractive as Labrang in Xiahe (see p.1034), and rather swamped by tourists, Ta'er Si is nevertheless a good introduction for outsiders to Tibetan culture. Both as the birthplace of Tsongkhapa, the founder of the **Yellow Hat Sect**, and as the former home of the current Dalai Lama, the monastery attracts droves of pilgrims from Tibet, Qinghai and Mongolia, who present a startling picture with their rugged features, huge embroidered coats and chunky jewellery.

Aside from the hulking new **military base** built right next to the monastery, installed no doubt to ensure compliance among the monks (though not very successfully – the abbot, considered a puppet of Beijing, recently absconded to the US), the countryside around is beautiful: the views stretch away to distant mountains, and you can ramble through hills of wheat, pastures dotted with cattle or horses, and over ridges and passes strewn with wild flowers. Apart from the large numbers of Han Chinese tourists, the people you meet here are mainly Tibetan horsemen, workers in the fields who will offer an ear of roasted barley by way of hospitality, or pilgrims prostrating their way around the monastery walls.

The monastery

The monastery dates from 1560, when building was begun in honour of **Tsongkhapa**, founder of the reformist Yellow Hat Sect of Tibetan Buddhism, who was born on the Ta'er Si estates. Legend tells how, at Tsongkhapa's birth, drops of blood fell from his umbilical cord causing a tree with a thousand leaves to spring up; on each leaf was the face of the Buddha, and there was a Buddha image on the trunk (now preserved in one of the stupas). During his lifetime, Tsongkhapa's significance was subsequently borne out: his two major disciples were to become the two greatest living Buddhas, one the Dalai Lama, the other the Panchen Lama.

Set in the cleft of a valley, the walled complex (daily 8am–6pm) is an imposing sight, an active place of worship for about six hundred monks (ranging in age from 10 to 80) as well as the constant succession of pilgrims. There's a ¥30 **entrance fee**, your ticket providing access to nine temples. At the gate, furtive hawkers appear to be selling Dalai Lama pendants which you are strongly advised against buying, since possession of them is illegal and this is doubtless a set-up. A stone tablet here, detailing (in English) the restoration of Ta'er Si in the 1980s, contains the worshipful statement that repairs were needed as "400 years of exposure to the elements had taken its toll".

The complex itself defies cynicsm, however, and the most beautiful of the **temples** is perhaps the **Great Hall of Meditation** (Da Xingtang; temple no. 5 on your ticket), an enormous, very dimly lit prayer hall, colonnaded by dozens of carpeted pillars and hung with long silk tapestries (*thangkas*). Immediately adjacent to this is the **Great Hall of the Golden Roof**, with its gilded tiles, red-billed choughs nesting under the eaves, wall paintings of scenes from the Buddha's life and a brilliant silver stupa containing a statue of Tsongkhapa. The grooves on the wooden floor in front of the temple have been worn away by the hands of prostrating monks and pilgrims. This hall, built in 1560, is where the monastery began, on the site of the pipal tree that grew with its Buddha imprints. You will still see pilgrims studying fallen leaves here, apparently searching for the face of the Buddha.

Other noteworthy temples include the **Lesser Temple of the Golden Roof** (no. 1) and the **Hall of Butter Sculpture** (no. 7). The former is dedicated to animals, thought to manifest characteristics of certain deities – from the central courtyard you can see stuffed goats, cows and bears on the balcony, wrapped in scarves and flags. The Hall of Butter Sculpture contains a display of colourful painted yak-butter tableaux, depicting Tibetan and Buddhist legends. After touring the temples, you can climb the steep steps visible on one side of the monastery to get a general view over the temples and hills behind.

During the year, five major **festivals** are held at Ta'er Si, each fixed according to the lunar calendar. In January/February, at the end of the Chinese New Year festivities, there's a large ceremony centred around the lighting of yak-butter lamps. In April/May is the festival of Bathing Buddha, during which a giant portrait of Buddha is unfurled on a hillside facing the monastery. In July/August the birthday of Tsongkhapa is celebrated, and in September and October there are two more celebrations commemorating the nirvanas of Sakyamuni and Tsongkhapa respectively.

Practicalities

Buses from Xining to Ta'er Si (¥4) depart from a depot on Xiguan Dajie in the west of town; pass the Foreign Languages Bookstore, and the depot is rather well hidden about 150m further west on the north side of the road. Minibuses run frequently from around 7.20am until late afternoon; bear in mind that private tour buses start rolling up at Ta'er Si around 10am, after which the place gets crowded. The ride takes just over thirty minutes through summer scenery of wheat fields, green hills, lush woods and meadows of flowering yellow rape.

On arrival, you may be dropped at the bus station 1km short of the monastery, or taken right up to the complex itself. From the bus station, it's a twenty-minute walk uphill past the trinket stalls and rug sellers until you see the row of eight stupas at the monastery entrance. Returning to Xining, exit the monastery and hang around on the street until the bus arrives.

Most travellers just come up to Ta'er Si for a few hours, but by staying the night you can appreciate the monastery unattended by hordes of day-trippers. **Accommodation** is available at the sixteenth-century pilgrims' hostel *Kumbum Motel* (beds ¥15) just inside the monastery enterance, whose basic facilities include an ancient balcony and peeling murals, though it's often full. For something slightly smarter, there's also the *Ta'ersi Hotel* (❷), a large, newish place facing the monastery across a gully. It's to the left of the monastery entrance, as you arrive. You can get **meals** at the *Pilgrim's Hostel*; otherwise, try one of the Muslim restaurants on the road between the town and monastery. These are great value, providing huge, warming bowls of noodles with plenty of vegetables and tea for a few yuan.

Beyond Ta'er Si

Another monastery, **Qutan Si**, around 80km to the east of Xining in Ledu County is much less visited by tourists. The monastery, started in 1387 during the Ming dynasty, was once among the most important Buddhist centres in China. Today, it is still impressive, with 51 rooms of murals, exceptionally fine examples of their type, illustrating the life story of Sakyamuni. You can reach the town of **Ledu** by direct bus or local train from Xining. From Ledu you should be able to find cheap minibuses for the seventeen-kilometre ride to Qutan Si, or you could take a taxi there and back for about ¥60.

About 200km southeast of Xining lies an area of outstanding natural beauty, centred around **Mengda Nature Reserve**. This part of the province, Xunhua County, has a wet, mild climate conducive to the prolific growth of trees and vegetation. The woods here are full of wild flowers and inhabited by deer and foxes. Hardly any foreign tourists come this way but, if you want to try, you can visit it as a stopover on the way between Xining and Linxia in Gansu province. From either Xining and Linxia, you can take buses to **Guanting** or **Xunhua**, two small towns on either side of the reserve, each not more than 30km from it. Xunhua is slightly nearer, but Guanting offers easier access. From either town, hitch with a passing tractor, or take a taxi. **Accommodation** is available at the reserve.

West of Xining

West of Xining, Qinghai for the most part comprises a great emptiness. The three-thousand-metre plateau is too high to support any farming, and population centres are almost nonexistent – the only people who traditionally have managed to eke out a living in this environment have been nomadic yak-herders. Not surprisingly, this is where China decided to site its **Nuclear Weapons Research and Design Academy**, where it developed its first atomic and hydrogen bombs in the 1960s and 70s. The centre is on a road and rail line 90km from Xining at **Haiyan** (locally known as "Atom Town") and has recently been opened to visitors – enquire at Xining's travel agents to arrange a tour.

The real highlight of the area, though, is about 150km west of Xining at the huge and virtually unspoilt saline lake of **Qinghai Hu**, the size of a small sea

West of Xining

Haiyan	海宴	***hǎiyàn***
Qinghai Hu	青海湖	***qīnghǎi hú***
Bird Island	鸟岛	*niǎodǎo*
Chaka Salt Lake	茶卡盐湖	*chákǎyán hú*
Heimahe	黑马河	*hēimǎ hé*
Golmud	格尔木	***gé'ěr mù***
Cai Erhan Salt Lake	察尔汗盐湖	*cháěrhàn yán hú*
Golmud Hotel	格尔木宾馆	*gé'ěrmù bīnguǎn*
Kunlun Mountains	昆仑山	*kūnlún shān*
Quanjiafu Jiulou	全家福酒楼	*quánjiāfú jiǔlóu*
Tibet bus station	西藏汽车站	*xīzàng qìchēzhàn*

and home to thousands of birds. Beyond here, the solitary road and rail line wind their way slowly to **Golmud**, the only town of any size for hundreds of kilometres around, and an important crossroads for overland travellers, linked by bus not only to Xining, but also to Lhasa in Tibet and Dunhuang on the Silk Road.

Qinghai Hu and around

Situated 150km west of Xining, high up on the Tibetan plateau, is the extraordinarily remote **Qinghai Hu**. The lake is vast, occupying an area of more than 4,500 square kilometres and, at 3200m above sea level, its waters are profoundly cold and salty. They are nevertheless teeming with fish and populated by nesting sea birds, particularly at the so-called **Bird Island**, which has long been the main attraction of the lake for visitors. If you don't have time to stop here, you can at least admire the view while travelling between Golmud and Xining. The train spends some hours running along the northern shore; travelling by bus you will pass the southern shore, and it's well worth scheduling your journey to pass the lake during daylight hours.

Apart from a visit to Bird Island – which tends to be a rushed, hectic experience – you can also hike and camp in peaceful solitude around the lake. From the smooth, green, windy shores, grazed by yaks during the brief summer, the blue, icy waters stretch away as far as the eye can see. If you have a tent, and really want a wilderness experience in China, this may be the place to get it. Don't forget to bring warm clothes and sleeping bags, though. You can take any bus to the lake and then strike off or, alternatively, you could get off at the **Qinghai Lake Tourist Centre**, where you can stay (❸, dorm beds ¥25) and enjoy boating, fishing and horse-riding.

Bird Island

This tiny rocky outcrop, situated at the far western side of the lake, is annually nested upon by literally thousands of birds. An immense variety of seasonal birds spend time here – gulls, cormorants, geese, swans and the rare **black-necked crane**. The main **bird-watching season** is from April to July, though the giant swans are best seen from November to February.

The easiest way to reach Bird Island is on a **day-trip** from Xining. There used to be an independent tour bus, but this seems to have vanished and now your best bet is an excursion with one of Xining's **travel services** (see p.1059); foreigners are charged ¥150, excluding food and entrance tickets. It's a very long day out, leaving at 7am and getting back at around 10pm; up to ten hours of the time is spent driving and if you aren't a bird-spotter, you may find it an awfully long way to come just to see a lot of birds roosting on a rock. On the way up onto the plateau you will probably stop at the Riyue Pass, where there you can see a Tibetan prayer-flag site and a couple of Chinese towers. One of the highlights is **lunch** – delicious and very cheap fried fish – which you have at a tiny settlement just outside Bird Island, and the general backdrop of blue sky, white clouds, blue water and distant snow-capped mountains is pretty rewarding in itself.

Visiting Bird Island **independently** is something of a challenge, but it's possible, either as part of a general tour of the lake, or as a stopover between Xining and Golmud. Riding any bus between these two cities, make sure you get off at the right place by the lake – a grubby little Tibetan town called **Heimahe**, about four hours from Xining, which has a shop and a basic hotel. From here a road leads up towards Bird Island and you'll have to hitch a ride from a passing tractor or car. Fifty minutes' drive brings you to the *Bird Island Guesthouse* with clean, but very cold, double rooms with bath (❸). You'll be lucky if there's any hot water, but there's always plenty to eat.

You need to buy a **ticket** (¥20) at the guesthouse to continue the remaining 15km to the two **observation points**. The first of these is actually a beach, which you view from a hide. The second is Bird Island itself, which you observe from the opposite cliff.

Chaka Salt Lake

Not far beyond Qinghai Hu is the **Chaka Salt Lake**, which has recently become something of a tourist attraction. It's a potentially beautiful place, with its white gleaming salt crystals forming a perfect mirror-like surface from a distance. At the site, you can ride a small freight train, visit a house of salt, walk on a sixty-kilometre salt bridge – and take a hunk of the stuff home with you afterwards. At present, the only way to visit Chaka Lake is on a **tour**, usually in conjunction with Qinghai Hu. A hectic two-day visit to the two lakes (sleeping overnight at one of them) is run by the Qinghai Jiaotong Lüxingshe (see p.1059) for ¥650 per person, inclusive of all food, tickets and accommodation. The tour runs only if there are enough people.

Golmud and the road to Tibet

Nearly 3000m up on the plateau, **GOLMUD** is an incredibly isolated city, even by the standards of northwest China. A new airport provides a link to Xining, but otherwise the city lies at least sixteen hours away from the nearest sizeable population centre. In spite of this, it still manages to be the second largest city in Qinghai with around 130,000 mainly Han Chinese residents, workers at the potash plants from which Golmud earns its living. It's hard to imagine that anyone would have come to live in such a cold and arid place otherwise. Geographically, Golmud is located close to the massive **Kunlun Mountains** to the south, and to the **Cai Erhan Salt Lake** to the north. Both are very scenic in parts, though they remain as yet virtually unexplored by foreign tourists.

For travellers, the city is really only interesting as a transit point between Xining in the east, Dunhuang in the north and Lhasa in the south – Golmud is the only place in China from where foreign tourists are officially allowed to cross **by land to Tibet**. At present this means a lengthy bus trip, but the government is also hard at work extending the **rail line to Lhasa**, an incredibly

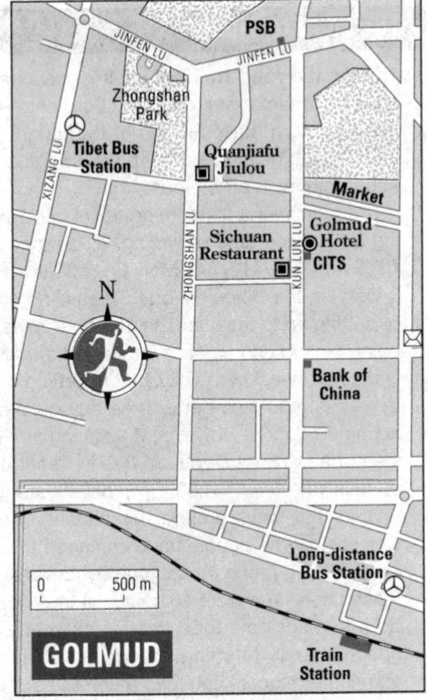

ambitious project due for completion in late 2006, which aims to lay 1118km of track, most of it on permanently frozen ground lying at over 4000m above sea level.

Practicalities

Golmud's **train** and **bus** stations sit facing each other, way down in the south of the city. The scene as you exit them is bleak almost beyond belief: a vast emptiness, rimmed by distant buildings. It's an ugly forty-minute walk to the town centre. Take a minibus (or bus #1) and it'll drop you at the only **hotel**, the *Golmud* (ⓣ0979/412066; ❹, dorm beds ¥30), not a bad place, comprising two buildings: the dorms are housed in the building on the left and the double rooms on the right.

There is some surprisingly good **food** to be had in town. Across the road from the hotel, and a few minutes to the south, is an excellent Sichuan restaurant. You can recognize it from the English words in the window, though there's no English menu – try the old Sichuan favourite, *gongbao jiding*, diced chicken with chillies and peanuts. For Western delicacies, there's an amazingly good menu at the obscurely located *Quanjiafu Jiulou* (Happy Family) restaurant, worth the walk for its thick, luscious banana pancakes (¥4). To find it, walk north from the hotel (turn right as you come out), and then head west towards Zhongshan Park at the crossroads. It's about ten minutes' walk along here, on the right-hand side, immediately after the place with a mock-pagoda entrance. There's also a market north of the hotel with some outdoor eating places at the sides of the main area; the entrance is on the right as you head north.

In the smart wing of the *Golmud Hotel*, you'll find two branches of **CITS**. One deals with tours within Golmud and Qinghai (ⓣ0979/413003); the other primarily deals with trips to Tibet (see box, p.1066), though it also arranges other tours. The most exciting of these is a journey, by four-wheel-drive, all the way to the city of Ruoqiang (see p.1094) in Xinjiang over the little-explored western edge of Qinghai. For a small group, expect to pay about US$150 each. There's a **Bank of China** south of the hotel (Mon–Fri 8.30am–noon & 2.30–6pm). Ancient **bicycles** (¥1 per hour) can be rented from a little compound just behind the hotel; go round the back of the old wing, and you'll see the doorway.

Heading on to Xining is probably easiest by rail: there are two fast trains daily (16hr) and one slow (22hr). Buy your tickets in the station; the queues are usually short here, though for same-day departures you first have to go to a second-floor office, accessible from the platform, to make a reservation. For same-day departures, you can also buy your ticket by queuing up in an office

The road to Tibet

Though the **road to Tibet** itself is reasonable and sealed to within 50km or so of Lhasa, the fact that it crosses 5000-metre-high passes and almost continually runs above 4000m makes it one of the toughest in the world for passengers. Vehicles tend to lack heating and stop very irregularly, so take plenty of warm clothing, food and drink, even on the bus.

The regulations concerning travel into Tibet **for foreigners** are constantly changing but, at the time of writing, all arrangements must be made through Golmud's **CITS** (☎0979/412764; Mon–Fri 8.30am–noon & 3–6.30pm, Sat 8.30–10.30am & 3–5pm) in the *Golmud Hotel*. There is no other official way of getting a bus ticket or of getting on to the bus. The deal here is that you are buying a "**tour**", which involves being picked up in a car from the *Golmud Hotel* and taken to the **Tibet bus station** in the northwest of the city, before setting off for the 24- to 36-hour journey to Lhasa. On arrival you also get a three-day guided tour in Lhasa for your money, without accommodation. However, if – having arrived in Tibet – you are not enticed by the idea of a CITS tour, you are free to forfeit it and set off exploring on your own. The price is ¥1700, or ¥1280 if you have a student or teacher's card.

There are ways around this situation, though you'll need to be able to speak Chinese. Some people have managed to hook up with Chinese independent travellers renting **jeeps** for the journey; drivers go like maniacs and have been known to reach Lhasa in a mere 16 hours – if they don't join the piles of vehicle wreckage that dot the roadside – for a fraction of what it costs through the CITS. The only other option is to try **hitching**, though note that this is a clandestine operation as drivers carrying foreigners can land themselves in big trouble; given the climate, you'll also have to decide whether you're up to two days exposed to the elements in the back of a truck. Basically, if you hang around the Tibet bus station, you *may* be approached by a truck driver willing to take you. You'll still pay at least ¥500, and run the risk of being caught at police road blocks on the way. In fact, any truck driver willing to risk taking you will usually only do so because he has his own deal with the police – but you can never be sure. If you *are* caught, you will either be fined substantially, or have to pay a bribe.

in the front of the *Golmud Hotel*. **Buses** to Xining take 16 hours, the same as the fast train; there's also an early morning bus to Dunhuang in Gansu Province (15hr), a little-trodden route for which you require a "registration" paper (¥20) from Golmud CITS in the *Golmud Hotel* to enable you to buy a ticket at normal price. For plane tickets to Xining, use CITS.

Xinjiang

Xinjiang Uigur Autonomous Region is one of the most exciting parts of China, an extraordinary terrain, more than 3000km from any coast, which, despite all the historical upheavals since the collapse of the Silk Road trade, still comprises the same old oasis settlements strung out along the ancient routes, many still producing the silk and cotton for which they were famed in Roman times (see box, p.990).

Geographically, Xinjiang – literally "New Territories" – occupies an area slightly greater than Western Europe or Alaska, and yet its population is just thirteen million. And with the Han population probably comprising just more than fifty percent of the whole, Xinjiang is perhaps the least "Chinese" of all parts of the People's Republic. By far the largest minority in Xinjiang is the **Uigur** (pronounced *Weeg-yur*), though there are also some dozen other Central Asian minority populations.

The land of Xinjiang is among the least hospitable in all China, covered for the most part by arid **desert and mountain**. Essentially, it can be thought of as two giant basins, both surrounded on all sides by mountains. The range lying between the two basins is the Tian Shan (Heavenly Mountains), which effectively bisects Xinjiang from west to east. The basin to the north is known as the **Junggar Basin**, or Jungaria. The capital of Xinjiang, and only major city, **Ürümqi**, is here, on the very southern edge of the basin, as is the heavily Kazakh town of **Yining**, right up against the border with Kazakhstan. The Junggar Basin has been subject to fairly substantial Han settlement over the past forty years, with a degree of industrial and agricultural development. It remains largely grassland, with large state farms in the centre and Kazakh and Mongol herdsmen (still partially nomadic) in the mountain pastures on the fringes. The climate is not particularly hot in summer, and virtually Siberian from October through to March. To the south is the **Tarim Basin**, dominated by the scorching Taklamakan Desert, where the weather is fiercely hot and dry in summer. This is where the bulk of the Uigur population lives, in strings of oases (Turpan and Kashgar among them) scattered along the old routes of the Silk Road. Some of these oasis cities are buried in the desert and long forgotten; others survive on irrigation using water from the various rivers and streams that flow from surrounding mountains. As well as forgotten cities, these sands also cover another buried treasure – **oil**. Chinese estimates reckon that three times the proven US reserves of oil are under the Taklamakan alone, which is one reason that the government is firmly establishing a Han presence in the region.

Highlights of Xinjiang include the **Tian Shan** mountain pastures outside Ürümqi, where you can hike in rare solitude and stay beside Heaven Lake with Kazakhs in their yurts; but it is the old **Silk Road** that will attract most travellers. The most fascinating of the Silk Road oasis cities are **Turpan** and **Kashgar**, both redolent of old Turkestan, and it is possible to follow not only the Northern Silk Road from Turfan to Kashgar via Aksu and Kuqa, but also the almost forgotten southern route via Khotan. The routes were established over two thousand years ago, but traffic reached its height during the Tang dynasty, when China's most famous Buddhist pilgrim, **Xuanzang**, used them on his seventeen-year voyage to India. There's still the possibility of continuing the Silk Road journey out beyond the borders of China itself – not only over

Xinjiang time

For travellers, the classic illustration of Xinjiang's remoteness from the rest of the country is in the fact that all parts of China set their clocks to Beijing time. The absurdity of this is at its most acute in Xinjiang, 3000–4000km distant from the capital – which means that in Kashgar, in the far west of the region, the summer sun rises at 9am or 10am and sets around midnight. Locally, there is such a thing as unofficial **"Xinjiang time"**, a couple of hours behind Beijing time, which is used more frequently the further west you head towards Kashgar; when buying bus, train or plane tickets, you should be absolutely clear about which time is being used.

the relatively well-established **Karakoram Highway** into Pakistan, but now also over the less well-known routes into Kazakhstan and Kyrgyzstan (see p.1102). Finally, there exists an exciting if perilous road from Kashgar into western Tibet, a route officially closed to tourists.

Some history

The region's history has been coloured by such personalities as Tamerlane, Genghis Khan, Attila the Hun and even Alexander the Great. More often, though, in counterpoint to the great movements of history, Xinjiang has been at the mercy of its isolation and the feudal warring between the rulers of its oasis kingdoms, or **khanates**.

The influence of China has been far from constant. The area – commonly referred to in the West as Eastern (or Chinese) Turkestan until 1949 – first passed under Han control in the second century BC, under Emperor Wu Di. But it was only during the **Tang dynasty** (650–850 AD) that this control amounted to more than a military presence. The Tang period for Xinjiang was something of a golden age, with the oases south of the Tian Shan largely populated by a mysterious but sophisticated Indo–European people, and the culture and Buddhist art of the oases at their zenith. Around the ninth century, however, came a change – the gradual rise to dominance of the **Uigurs**, and their conversion to **Islam**.

Subsequent centuries saw the **conquests of the Mongols** under Genghis Khan and later, from the west, of Tamerlane. Both brought havoc and slaughter in their wake, though during the brief period of Mongol rule (1271–1368) the Silk Road trade was hugely facilitated by the fact that, for the first and only time in history, east and west Asia were under a single government.

After the fall of the Mongols, and the final disappearance of the Silk Road, Xinjiang began to split into khanates and suffered a succession of religious and factional wars. Nonetheless, it was an independence of a kind and Qing **reassertion of Chinese domination** in the eighteenth century was fiercely contested. A century later, in 1862, full-scale **Muslim rebellion** broke out, led by the ruler of Kashgaria, **Yakub Beg**, armed and supported by the British who were seeking influence in this buffer zone between India and Russia (for

The Uigur

The Uigur are the easternmost branch of the extended family of **Turkic peoples** who inhabit most of Central Asia, and the language they speak is essentially a dialect of Turkish. Despite centuries of domination by China and some racial mingling along the way, the Uigur remain culturally entirely distinct from the Han Chinese, and many Uigurs look decidedly un-Chinese – stockily built, bearded, with brown hair and round eyes. For at least a thousand years they have been overwhelmingly **Muslim**, and religion remains the focus of their identity in the face of relentless Han penetration.

As the Uigurs are for the most part unable to speak Chinese and therefore unable to attend university or find well-paid work, their prospects for self-improvement inside the People's Republic are generally bleak. It is also true that many Han Chinese look down on the Uigurs as unsophisticated ruffians, and are frankly scared of their supposedly short tempers and love of knives. Perhaps as a consequence of this, Uigurs seem at times to extend their mistrust of Han Chinese to all foreigners, tourists included. Nevertheless, gestures such as drinking tea with them, or trying a few words of their language, will help to break down the barriers, and invitations to Uigur homes frequently follow.

Uigur food

Uigur food, unsurprisingly, has far more of a Central Asian than a Chinese flavour. The most basic staple – which often seems to be the only food available – is **laghman**, known in Chinese as *lamian*, literally "**pulled noodles**". Watching these being made to order is greatly entertaining: the cook grabs both ends of a roll of elastic dough and pulls it into a long ribbon by stretching his arms apart; he then slaps it down onto a floured counter, and brings his hands together to join the ends of the dough, so forming two ribbons. These are slapped again, pulled again, the cook once more rejoins his hands to make four ribbons; and the process is repeated, doubling the number of ribbons each time, until a mass of thin, metre-long noodles are strung between the cook's hands. The "handles" of surplus dough are torn off either end, and the noodles dropped into boiling water to cook for a couple of minutes. The speed at which a skilled cook transforms the raw dough into a bowlful of noodles, banging, pulling, and managing to keep all the strands separate, is incredible.

In Xinjiang, *laghman* is served with a stew of mutton, tomatoes, chilli and other vegetables; rather different from the more soupy version sold elsewhere in China. For the same spicy sauce but without the noodles, try *tohogish* (known in Chinese as *dapan ji*), a chicken served chopped up in its entirety, head, feet and all; or *jerkob*, a beef stew – both are served in smarter restaurants. **Coriander leaf** is used as a garnish on everything.

In summer, apart from *laghman,* street vendors also offer endless cold noodle soup dishes, usually very spicy. **Rice** is rare in Xinjiang, though it does appear in **pilau**, comprising fried rice and hunks of mutton coloured with saffron. More familiar to foreigners are the skewers of **grilled mutton kebabs**, dusted with chilli and cumin powder – buy several of them at once, as one skewer does not make much more than a mouthful. They are often eaten with delicious glasses of ice-cold yoghurt (known in Chinese as *suannai*), which are available everywhere in Xinjiang. **Tea** often comes flavoured with cinnamon, cardamom and rose hips.

Oven-baked **breads** are also popular in markets: you'll see bakers apparently plunging their hands into live furnaces, to stick balls of dough on to the brick-lined walls; these are then withdrawn minutes later as bagel-like bread rolls, and *nan* flat breads, or sometimes *permuda* (known in Chinese as *kaobao)*, tasty baked dough packets of mutton and onions, which can also be fried – as *samsa* – rather than baked. The steamed version, *manta*, recalls Chinese dumplings or *mantou*.

A couple of other specialities are worth trying: **madang** is nougat thick with walnuts, raisins and dried fruit, sold by pedlars who carve the amount you want (or usually, more than you want – it's sold by weight) off massive slabs of the stuff. More refreshing is that characteristic Central Asian fruit, the **pomegranate**, known as *shiliu* in Chinese. You can find them whole at markets, or buy the juice off street vendors – look for the piles of skins and the juicing machines, which resemble a large, spiky torture implement.

more of which, read Peter Hopkirk's excellent *The Great Game* – see p.1244). Ultimately the revolt failed – Beg became a hated tyrant – and the region remained part of the Chinese empire.

At the beginning of the twentieth century, Xinjiang was still a Chinese backwater controlled by a succession of brutal warlords who acted virtually independently of the central government. The last one of these before World War II, **Sheng Shizai**, seemed momentarily to be a reforming force, instituting religious and ethnic freedoms, and establishing trade with the newly emergent Soviet Union. However, he ended by abandoning his moderate positions. Slamming the door on the Soviets and on leftist influences within Xinjiang itself in 1940, he began a reign of terror resulting in the deaths of more than two hundred thousand Communists, intellectuals, students and Muslim Nationalists.

The drive towards the defeat of the Guomindang in 1949 temporarily united the conflicting forces of Muslim nationalism and Chinese communism. After the Communist victory, however, there could be only one result. The principal Muslim Nationalist leaders were quietly murdered, allegedly killed in a plane crash, and the impetus towards a separate state was lost. The last Nationalist leader, a Kazakh named Osman, was executed in 1951.

Since 1949, the Chinese government has made strenuous attempts to stabilize the region by **settling Han Chinese** from the east, into Ürümqi in particular – the number by 1996 was up to six million from just two hundred thousand forty years earlier. The Uigur population of Xinjiang, from being ninety percent of the total in 1949, had slipped to below fifty percent by 1982, and is still slipping, in spite of the minorities' exemption from the One Child Policy. Today, however, the Chinese government remains nervous about Xinjiang, especially given the enormous **economic potential** of the area, in terms of coal mining, oil exploration and tourism. In recent years there have been outbursts of **Uigur dissent**, most notably in 1992, in the city of Kashgar, when the army and air force were called in to suppress demonstrations, and the city was temporarily closed to foreigners. Bombs, allegedly set by separatists, exploded in Ürümqi in 1992 and Kashgar in 1993. Prior to that, in 1986 there had been protests in response to China's **nuclear tests** at the desert site near Lop Nor, prompted by what seemed to be numerous cases of early death from cancer and a high incidence of deformity in lambs and newborn children. In the meantime the nuclear tests go on, and in the aftermath of the break-up of the Soviet Union, the possibility of a new outbreak of violent nationalism among the Xinjiang Uigurs cannot be ruled out – though post-September 11, the Chinese government has equated dissent in the region with "terrorism", vowing to crush any displays of nationalism with extreme force.

Eastern Xinjiang: the road to Turpan

The road from Dunhuang in western Gansu as far as **Hami** and then **Turpan** – the easternmost part of Xinjiang, east of the central area dominated by the Tian Shan – comprises some of the harshest terrain in the whole of China. Little water ever reaches this area of scorching depressions – geographically an extension of the Tarim Basin – which in summer is the hottest part of the country, and which was dreaded by the Silk Road traders as one of the most hazardous sections of the entire cross-Asia trip. Even today, crossing the area is most memorable for its suffocating heat and monotonous gravel and dune landscapes, though ironically Turpan – despite the heat – can be one of the most relaxing and enjoyable places in all China.

Hami

HAMI today is the eastern gateway to Xinjiang, a rich oasis in the midst of a seemingly endless desert, and famous throughout China for its **melons**, the *hami gua*. There's not much here to detain the visitor; nevertheless, it's a convenient stopping point along the road between Dunhuang and Turpan – it lies more or less midway between the two.

Historically, Hami has always been an important part of the Silk Road, occupying one of the few fertile spots between Gansu province and Turpan.

Eastern Xinjiang		
Hami	哈密	***hāmì***
Hami Hotel	哈密宾馆	*hāmì bīnguǎn*
Hui Wang Fen	回王坟	*huíwángfén*
Jiageda Hotel	加格达宾馆	*jiāgédá bīnguǎn*
Maixiang Yuan	麦香园	*màixiāng yuán*
Turpan	吐鲁番	***tùlǔfān***
Astana Graves	阿斯塔娜古墓区	*āsītǎnà gǔmùqū*
Bezeklik Caves	柏孜克里克千佛洞	*bózīkèlǐkè qiānfódòng*
Daheyan	大河沿	*dàhéyàn*
Emin Minaret	苏公塔	*sūgōng tǎ*
Flaming Mountains	火焰山	*huǒyàn shān*
Gaochang	高昌	*gāochāng*
Grape Valley	葡萄沟	*pútáo gōu*
Jiaohe	交河	*jiāohé*
Karez irrigation site	坎儿井	*kǎnér jǐng*
Accommodation		
Jiaotong	交通宾馆	*jiāotōng bīnguǎn*
Oasis	绿洲宾馆	*lǜzhōu bīnguǎn*
Turpan	吐鲁番宾馆	*tùlǔfān bīnguǎn*
Yiyuan	颐园宾馆	*yíyuán bīnguǎn*

Xuanzang, the famous Buddhist pilgrim nearly died of thirst on his way here, while Marco Polo noted with evident pleasure the locals' habit of not only supplying guests with food and shelter but also allowing them to sleep with their wives.

Kept small by the surrounding inhospitable desert, the town centres around the northern end of Zhongshan Lu. The bus station and hotels are in this area, while the train station is farther out in the north of town. There is just one historical site in Hami – the **Hui Wang Fen**, the Tombs of the Hami Kings (daily 7am–5pm; ¥10). From 1697 until 1930, Hami was nominally controlled by kings who for a time had obediently sent tribute to the Qing court, before becoming involved in the Muslim revolts that periodically engulfed Xinjiang. Although the kings ruled until 1930, Hami was virtually destroyed at least twice during these revolts. Today the tomb complex is in the south of the city and comprises an appealingly decayed mausoleum, a renovated

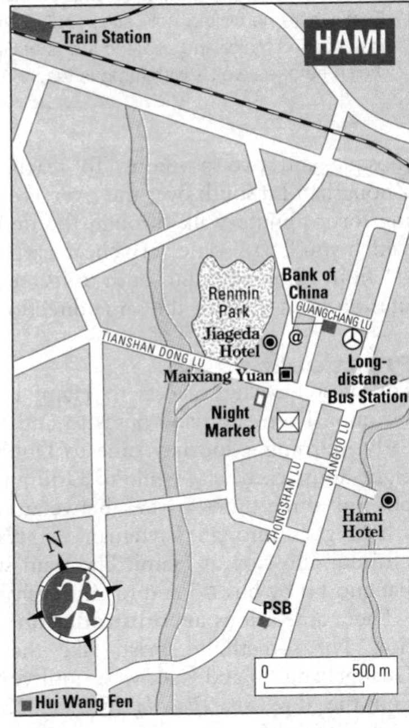

Xuanzang and the Journey to the West

Trade goods were not the only things to travel along the Silk Road; it was along this route that **Buddhism** first arrived in China at some point in the first century AD. Cities along the way became bastions of the religion (which in part explains their abandonment and desecration following the introduction of Islam after 1000) and, from early on, Chinese pilgrims visited India and brought back a varied bag of Buddhist teachings. The most famous is the Tang dynasty monk **Xuanzang**, unique for the depth of his learning and the exhaustive quantity of material with which he returned after a seventeen-year journey from the then capital of China, Chang'an (Xi'an), to India.

Born near Luoyang in 602, Xuanzang favoured **Mahayana** Buddhism, which depicts the world as an illusion produced by our senses. Having studied in Luoyang, Chengdu and Chang'an, he became confused by often contradictory teachings, and in 629 he decided to visit India to study Buddhism at its source. But China's new Tang rulers (the dynasty was established in 618) had forbidden foreign travel, so Xuanzang went without official permission, narrowly avoiding arrest in western Gansu. He almost died of thirst before reaching **Hami** and then **Turpan**, at the foot of the Flaming Mountains. Turpan's king detained him for a month to hear him preach but eventually provided a large retinue, money and passports for safe passage through other kingdoms. Despite bandits, Xuanzang reached **Kuqa** unharmed, where he spent two months waiting for the passes north over the Tian Shan to thaw – even so, a great number of his party died traversing the mountains. On the far side in modern Kyrgyzstan, Xuanzang's religious knowledge greatly impressed the Khan of the Western Turks, before he continued, via the great central Asian city of **Samarkand**, through modern-day Afghanistan, over the Hindu Kush and so down into **India**, arriving about a year after he set out. Xuanzang spent fifteen years in India, journeying from the northern mountains, through Assam down the east coast to around Madras, then crossing the centre of the country to northwestern Nasik and Baroda. Everywhere he visited holy sites (including the Ganges and places from Buddha's life), studied major and esoteric forms of Buddhism, lectured and entered debates – which he often won – with famous teachers on aspects of religious thought.

mosque and two pavilions. To reach it from the centre of town, follow Zhongshan Lu south over the river and right along to the end. It's an engrossing forty-minute walk through the dusty alleys of the Uigur quarter, during which you'll pass some very cheap carpet shops. Alternatively, you can take bus #1 from Zhongshan Lu south to its terminal and then walk another few minutes on from there in the same direction.

Practicalities

For most travellers, access to Hami is by **bus** from Dunhuang, Turpan or Ürümqi. There are daily buses to and from all three cities, all leaving in the early morning – journey time to Dunhuang and Turpan is between six and eight hours each way, while to Ürümqi it's about eleven hours. There's also a bus link three times a week between Hami and Jiuquan in Gansu Province, which goes through Jiayuguan. All **trains** running between Lanzhou and Ürümqi also stop at Hami. The train station is linked to the bus station on Jianguo Lu by bus #3 and to Zhongshan Lu by bus #1.

There are various **accommodation** possibilities in the area of the bus station. For something smart, take the side exit of the bus station onto Guangchang Lu and walk west until you come to Aiguo Bei Lu, where you'll find the three-star *Jiageda* (Ⓣ0902/2232140, Ⓔjgd-hm@xj.cninfo.net; ❻).

If he hoped to find ultimate clarity he was probably disappointed, as the interpretation of Buddhist lore in India was even more varied than in China. However, he did manage to acquire a vast collection of Buddhist statues, relics and – especially – **texts**, and in 644 decided that it was his responsibility to return to China with this trove of knowledge. Given an **elephant** to carry his luggage by the powerful north Indian king Harsha, Xuanzang recrossed the Kush and turned east to travel over the Pamirs to **Tashkurgan** (near where the elephant unfortunately drowned) before heading up to **Kashgar**, then – as now – an outpost of the Chinese empire. From here he turned southeast to the silk and jade emporium of **Khotan**, whose king claimed Indian ancestry and where there were a hundred Buddhist monasteries. Xuanzang spent eight months here, waiting for replacements of Buddhist texts lost in northern India, and a reply from the Tang emperor **Taizong**, to whom he had written requesting permission to re-enter China. When it came, permission was enthusiastic, and Xuanzang lost little time in returning to Chang'an via Minfeng, Miran, Loulan and **Dunhuang**, arriving in the Chinese capital in 645. He had left unknown, alone, and almost as a fugitive; he returned to find tens of thousands of spectators crowding the road to Chang'an. The emperor became his patron, and he spent the last twenty years of his life translating part of the collection of Buddhist texts acquired on his travels.

Xuanzang wrote a biography, but highly coloured accounts of his travels also passed into folklore, becoming the subject of plays and the sixteenth-century novel **Journey to the West**, still a popular tale in China. In it, Xuanzang (known as **Tripitaka**) is depicted as terminally naïve, hopelessly dismayed by the various disasters which beset him. Fortunately, he's aided by the Boddhisatva of Mercy, **Guanyin**, who sends him spirits to protect him in his quest: the vague character of **Sandy**; the greedy and lecherous **Pigsy**; and **Sun Wu Kong**, the brilliant Monkey King. As many of the novel's episodes are similar, varying only in which particular demon has captured Tripitaka, the best parts are the lively exchanges between Pigsy and Monkey, as they endeavour to rescue their master; a good abridgement in English is Arthur Waley's *Monkey* – see "Books", p.1252.

Rooms are pricey but fair value, especially in winter when you might get them half-price. On the other side of town is the cheaper, basic *Hami* (❸, dorm beds ¥30); to get there from the bus station, walk south from the main exit for about fifteen minutes along Jianguo Lu, or take bus #3 for two stops, then turn left down Yingbing Lu. It's sometimes possible to stay in very cheap, basic rooms at guesthouses right at the bus station itself.

For **food**, you need go no farther than the excellent **night market**, which has a host of stalls and more permanent canteens, located on the same road as the *Jiageda* – just head south from the hotel. This is one of the nicest night markets you'll find: extremely friendly, busy and clean, with great kebabs, grilled spicy freshwater fish, noodles and *hundun* soup, along with buns and Sichuanese-style hotpots. For approximately Western fare, try burgers at *Maixiang Yuan*, south and opposite from the *Jiageda*.

Turpan

The small and economically insignificant town of **TURPAN** (**Tulufan** to the Chinese) has in recent years turned itself into one of the major tourist destinations of Xinjiang. Credit for this must go largely to the residents, who have not only covered the main streets and walkways of the town with vine trellises, converting them into shady green tunnels (partly for the benefit of tourists), but have also managed to retain a relatively easy-going manner even in the heady economic climate of modern China.

Today, Turpan is a largely **Uigur-populated** area, and, in Chinese terms, an obscure backwater, but it has not always been so. As early as the Han dynasty, the Turpan oasis was a crucial point along the Northern Silk Road, and the cities of **Jiaohe**, and later **Gaochang** (both of whose ruins can be visited from Turpan), were important and wealthy centres of power. On his way to India, Xuanzang spent more time than he had planned here, when the king virtually kidnapped him in order to have him preach to his subjects. This same king later turned his hand to robbing Silk Road traffic, and had his kingdom annexed by China in 640 as a result. From the ninth to the thirteenth century, a rich intellectual and artistic culture developed in Gaochang, resulting from a fusion between the original Indo-European inhabitants and the (pre-Islamic) Uigurs. It was not until the fourteenth century that the Uigurs of Turpan converted to Islam.

The town is located in a depression 80m below sea level, which accounts for its extreme climate – well above 40°C in summer (reputedly the hottest in China), well below freezing in winter. In summer the **dry heat** is so soporific that there is little call to do anything but sleep or sip cool drinks in outdoor cafés with other tourists. This may not be what you came to China for, but quite a lot of people appreciate it by the time they reach Turpan. To ease the consciences of the indolents, there are in addition a number of **ruined cities** and **Buddhist caves** in the countryside around the city, testimony to its past role as an important oasis on the Silk Road. Turpan is also an agricultural oasis, famed above all for **grapes**. Today, virtually every household in the town has a hand in the grape business, both in cultivating the vines, and in drying the grapes at the end of the season. Every house has its own ventilated brick barn, usually on the roof, the best spot for catching the hot desiccating winds that sweep through the area. Bear in mind that Turpan is very much a summer resort; if you come out of season (Nov–March), the town itself is cold and uninspiring, with the vines cut back and most businesses closed – though surrounding sights remain interesting, and devoid of other tourists.

The Town

For some travellers, the real draw of Turpan is its absence of sights, enabling total relaxation. The downtown area doesn't amount to much, with most of the services near the bus station on Laocheng Lu; pedestrianized Qingnian Lu is protected from the baking summer sun by vine trellises. There is a **museum** on Gaochang Lu (daily 9am–8pm; ¥12), containing a smallish collection of silk fragments, boots, tools, manuscripts and preserved corpses recovered from the nearby Silk Road sites, including those from the Astana Graves which you can visit just outside Turpan (see p.1078). Other than this, the **bazaars** off Laocheng Lu, a few hundred metres east of Gaochang Lu, are worth a casual look, though they are not comparable to anything in Kashgar. You'll find knives, clothes, hats and boots on sale, while the most distinctively local products include delicious sweet green raisins, as well as walnuts and almonds.

One of the nicest ways to spend an evening after the heat of the day has passed is to **rent a donkey cart** and take a tour of the countryside south of town, a world of dusty tracks, vineyards, wheat fields, shady poplars, running streams and incredibly friendly, smiling people. You are unlikely to encounter

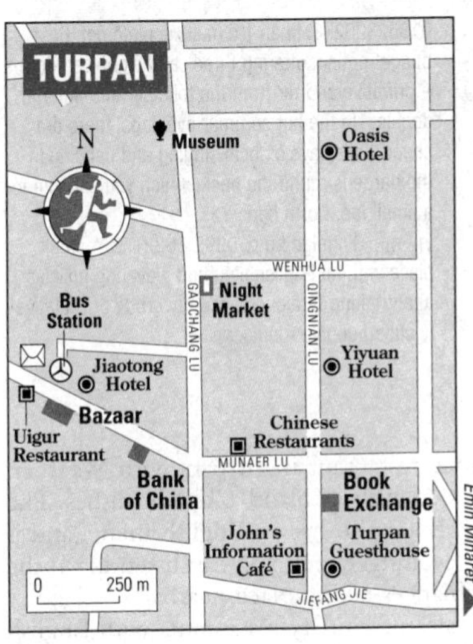

many more tranquil rural settings than this in China. It's easy to arrange a tour from any donkey-cart driver around *John's Café*; for a tour lasting an hour or more, two or three people might pay around ¥10–15 each. *John's* also offers **bike rental** for ¥3 per hour, which works out slightly cheaper than the hotels' rates.

Practicalities

The only way to arrive in downtown Turpan is by **bus**. Frequent buses run between Ürümqi and Turpan, and there's a daily bus service to and from Hami and Korla. Turpan's **train station** is 35km away at Daheyan (marked "Tulufan" on timetables) – from where it takes at least an hour to get into town by bus. From Daheyan station, turn right and walk a few hundred metres to reach the bus station, or catch a minibus from the station concourse. Unfortunately, there are no buses to Turpan after 7pm, so you'll either have to stay the night in Daheyan or get a taxi (¥50).

Getting around Turpan is best done on foot, or – given the 45°C summer heat – by bicycle or donkey cart, for which you should rarely have to pay more than ¥1 per journey. All of Turpan's accommodation, regardless of cost, has **air-conditioning** – just make sure that yours is working when you check in. If you're looking for something to read, try the **book exchange** just up from the *Turpan* hotel on Qingnian Lu.

Turpan has two **travel agents**, both of which can help out with transport bookings for around ¥30 commission (including, in the absence of an airport at Turpan, **flights** out of Ürümqi), as well as local tours. CITS (Ⓣ0995/8521352) is in the *Oasis Hotel*; or try the independent *John's Information Café* (Ⓔjohncafe@hotmail.com) outside the *Turpan Guesthouse*. "John" is a Chinese entrepreneur who has made a fortune catering to budget travellers – he also has branches of his café in Kashgar, Ürümqi, and Dunhuang. There's a rumour that he reports on travellers' activities to the authorities, however, so if you are planning anything illegal (such as crossing from Kashgar to Tibet), this is not the place to discuss it.

When you're **leaving Turpan**, the bus is your best bet to Ürümqi, a journey which takes five hours via the new highway. Otherwise, it's a dusty, gritty ten hours east to Hami or west to Korla, past views of distant snow-ridged mountains. For anything more distant, you definitely want to travel by **train**; travel agents can make bookings, though it's often possible to buy your own train tickets at Daheyan station, with sleeper reservations for the same evening if you get there by 6pm.

Accommodation

Not many places in Turpan will take foreigners, but there's still a good range of accommodation options available.

Jiaotong At the bus station. Inexpensive, though not the cleanest of places despite recent renovations. Dorm beds ¥25, ❸

Oasis Qingnian Lu ⓣ0995/8522491, ⓕ8523348, ⓦwww.the-silk-road.com. A pleasant upmarket hotel set in leafy grounds, where performances of local singing and dancing take place every evening. Staff speak English and couldn't be more helpful, and rooms have clean carpets, modern bathrooms and even mock *kangs* instead of beds. Gives major discounts out of season. ❻

Turpan Qingnian Lu ⓣ0995/8522301, ⓕ8523262, ⓔlfhan-tl@mail.xj.cninfo.net. Best budget option, offering three- and eight-bed dorms – primitive and far from the toilets – and smarter doubles. In the hot summer evenings, there are cheerful displays of local singing and dancing in the gardens round the back, which you can join for a small fee. Dorm beds ¥25, ❸

Yiyuan Qingnian Lu ⓣ0995/8522170. A small place with no English sign and wavering policies about taking foreigners; slightly grotty but relatively cheap double rooms. ❸

Eating and drinking

John's Information Café is the most visible restaurant in Turpan, with **Western breakfasts** available under the trellises, as well as bland Chinese dishes. The outdoor café at the back of the *Turpan* hotel also has an English menu, and is quite a nice place to drink beer in the evenings when you can listen in on the live Uigur singing and dancing performances taking place nearby.

For **Chinese** food, there's a whole series of touristy restaurants with English menus, to the west of the main crossroads north of the *Turpan* hotel on Munaer Lu. All have outdoor tables and chairs under the vines, and friendly service – though establish prices when ordering to avoid being overcharged. Try *liang ban hong gua*, a delicious cold cucumber salad with garlic and soya sauce. For more upmarket Chinese food, try one of the restaurants in the *Oasis Hotel*. The *Uigur Restaurant*, on Qingnian Lu just south of the intersection with Laocheng Lu, is an excellent place to sample **Uigur cuisine**, while basic, cheap Uigur staples can be picked up in the stalls and cheap restaurants in the west of town on Laocheng Lu, near the bazaar. While you're in Turpan, try to get hold of some of the **local wine** if you don't mind paying ¥30 a bottle. The red is sweet and thick like port, the white fruity and very drinkable.

Around Turpan

Nearly all visitors to Turpan end up taking the customary **tour** of the historical and natural sights outside the town. These are quite fun, as much for the chance to get out into the desert as for the sights in themselves, which usually include the two ancient cities of **Gaochang** and **Jiaohe**, the **Emin Minaret**, the **karez underground irrigation channels**, the **Bezeklik Caves** and **Astana Graves**. Sites are open daily, for most of the hours of daylight, around 8am–5pm.

Assuming you can get together a group of five people – not difficult, as the tourist hotels organize this, as does CITS – a trip to all the above sites will take the best part of a day (with a break for lunch and siesta if you choose) and cost ¥30–50 per person for the minibus. CITS can also rent you a four-passenger car at ¥200 for the day. Alternatively, for places close to town, **cycling** is a good option if you want to avoid a tour. Be aware that, however you travel, you'll be in blistering heat for the whole of the day, so sun cream, a hat, waterbottle and sunglasses are essential.

The only downside are the **entry fees**, which are not included in the cost of a tour and have become quite steep recently at ¥20–30 per site (less if you have a Chinese student card). Frankly, the only site which is unquestionably worth the money is Jiaohe: if you're looking to cut costs, the Bezeklik Caves can be skipped if you're planning to visit any other Buddhist cave art in China; and you can get good views of Gaocheng and the Emin Minaret without actually entering the sites.

The Emin Minaret, Jiaohe and karez irrigation site

Start off a tour at the eighteenth-century **Emin Minaret** (¥20) just 2km southeast of the city; you can walk there by following Jiefang Jie east out of town for about thirty minutes. Slightly bulging and pot-bellied, built of sun-dried brown bricks arranged in differing patterns layer by layer, the minaret tapers its way 40m skyward to a rounded tip. You can see all this without actually going in, though if you do you'll find the adjacent mosque has an interesting latticework ceiling held up by wooden supports, with good views from the top over the green oasis in the foreground and the distant snowy Tian Shan beyond.

About 9km east of Turpan is the ruined city of **Jiaohe** (¥30), just about within bicycle range on a hot day. Although Jiaohe was for large parts of its history under the control of Gaochang (see below), it became the regional administrative centre during the eighth century, and occupies a spectacular defensive setting on top of a two-kilometre-long, steep-sided plateau carved out by the two halves of a forking river. What sets Jiaohe apart from all other ruined cities along the Silk Road is that although most of the buildings comprise little more than crumbling, windswept mud walls, so many survive, and of such a variety – temples, public buildings and ordinary dwellings – that Jiaohe's **street plan** is still evident, and there's a real feeling of how great this city must once have been. As with Gaochang, a Buddhist monastery marked the town centre; sign-posted in English, its foundations – 50m on each side – can still be seen. Another feature is the presence of ancient wells still containing water. Make sure you walk to the far end of the site, where the base of a former tower, dated to around AD360, overlooks the rivers.

Returning from Jiaohe, minibus drivers usually drop you off at a dolled-up **karez irrigation site** (¥20), an intrinsically interesting place unfortunately turned into an ethnic theme park, complete with regular Uigur dance shows, presumably to justify the entry fee. Karez irrigation taps natural underground channels carrying water from source (in this case, glaciers at the base of the Tian Shan) to the point of use. Strategically dug wells then bring water to small surface channels which run around the streets of the town. Many ancient Silk Road cities relied on this system, including those much farther to the west, in areas such as modern Iran, and karez systems are still in use throughout Xinjiang – there are plenty of opportunities to see them for free on the way to Kashgar.

The Bezeklik Caves, Gaochang and Astana Graves and Iding Lake

For the other sites, you definitely need a minibus – they are too far to reach by bicycle. The first stop is usually the Bezeklik Caves, but on the way you'll pass the **Flaming Mountains**, made famous in the sixteenth-century Chinese novel *Journey to the West*, a highly embellished version of the story of the Chinese Buddhist Xuanzang's pilgrimage to India. The novel depicts these sandstone mountains as walls of flame, and it's not hard to see how the story arose, from the red sandstone hillsides, lined and creviced as though flickering with flame in the heat haze. The plains below are dotted with dozens of small "nodding donkey" **oil wells**, all tapping into Xinjiang's vast reserves.

The **Bezeklik Caves** (¥20), in a valley among the Flaming Mountains some 50km east of Turpan, are disappointing, offering mere fragments of the former wealth of Buddhist cave art here. The location is nonetheless strikingly beautiful, with stark orange dunes behind and a deep river gorge fringed in green below, but most of the murals were cut out and removed to Berlin by Albert Von Le Coq at the beginning of the twentieth century, and the remainder painstakingly defaced by Muslim Red Guards during the 1960s. (A good deal of the murals removed by Le Coq were subsequently destroyed by the allied bombing of Germany in World War II.) Just before the caves is a bizarre fantasy-land (¥20), featuring giant sculptures of characters from *Journey to the West* – a very surreal sight springing up out of the dessicated landscape.

South of here, the **Astana Graves** (¥20) mark the burial site of the imperial dead of Gaochang. Unfortunately, the graves have had most of their interesting contents removed to museums in Ürümqi and Turpan, and little remains beyond a couple of preserved corpses and some murals. The adjacent ruins of **Gaochang** (¥30) are somewhat more impressive, however, especially for their huge scale and despite having suffered from the ravages of both Western archeologists and the local population, who for centuries have been carting off bits of the city's ten-metre-high adobe walls to use as soil for their fields. You can walk, or take a donkey cart, from the entrance to the centre of the site, which is marked by a large square building, the remains of a monastery. Its outer walls are covered in niches, in each one of which a Buddha was originally seated; just a few bare, broken traces of these Buddhas remain, along with their painted halos. If you have time, the nicest thing you can do in Gaochang is strike off on your own and listen to the hot wind whistling through the mud-brick walls. Alternatively, there's a Muslim cemetery on a rise beside the main road out to the site, from where you can take in Gaocheng's scale without entering the site.

North of Turpan, and at the western end of the Flaming Mountains, is the so-called **Grape Valley**. There's very little point visiting this place out of season, but from mid-July to August, it's a pleasant little oasis in the middle of a stark desert, covered in shady trellises bulging with fruit (which you have to pay for if you want to eat). This could be included on your minibus tour, or you could reach it on a very hot bicycle ride, but bear in mind that the scenery here is not much different from that of downtown Turpan.

Finally, 100km south of Turpan, though not included on any tours, is the bleak but dramatic **Iding Lake**. Located in a natural depression 154m below sea level, this is the second lowest lake in the world after the Dead Sea, though you won't actually see any water here except in spring – the rest of the year the lake is a flat plain of dried salt deposits. The land around the lake is white with crusty salt and dotted with bright yellow pools of saturated water that feels like oil on the skin. Locals rub it over themselves enthusiastically, claiming that it's good for you. A car to the lake and back should cost around ¥150. Don't take your best shoes as it's very muddy.

Ürümqi and Tian Chi

ÜRÜMQI – **Wulumuqi** in Chinese – is the political, industrial and economic capital of Xinjiang, and by far the largest city in the region, with a population of well over one million, the overwhelming majority of whom are Han Chinese. Its name means "Beautiful Pastures" – a misleading description for what has become a drab and functional place, even though the skyline to the east is marked by the graceful snowy peaks of the Tian Shan.

Ürümqi and Tian Chi		
Ürümqi	乌鲁木齐	***wūlǔ mùqí***
Erdaoqiao Market	二道桥市场	*èrdàoqiáo shìchǎng*
Hongshan Park	红山公园	*hóngshān gōngyuán*
Main bus station	客运站	*kèyùn zhàn*
Renmin Park	人民公园	*rénmín gōngyuán*
South bus station	南部客运站	*nánbù kèyùnzhàn*
Xinjiang Museum	新疆博物馆	*xīnjiāng bówùguǎn*
Accommodation and eating		
Bogda	博格达	*bógé dá*
Holiday Inn	假日大酒店	*jiàrì dàjiǔdiàn*
Laiyuan	徕远宾馆	*láiyuǎn bīnguǎn*
Overseas Chinese	华侨宾馆	*huáqiáo bīnguǎn*
Ramada	屯河华美达到酒店	*túnhé huáměidá jiǔdiàn*
Shuhan Fengwei Jiulou	蜀汉风味酒楼	*shǔhàn fēngwèi jiǔlóu*
Xinjiang	新疆饭店	*xīnjiāng fàndiàn*
Ya Ou	亚欧宾馆	*yà'ōu bīnguǎn*
Moving on: foreign cities		
Almaty	啊拉木图	*ālā mùtú*
Bishkek	比什凯克	*bǐshí kǎikè*
Islamabad	伊撕兰堡	*yīsī lánbǎo*
Moscow	莫撕科	*mòsīkē*
Tashkent	塔什千	*tǎshí qiān*
Baiyang Gou	白扬沟	***báiyáng gōu***
Tian Chi	天池	***tiānchí***

For travellers arriving from western China or Central Asia, this will be the first truly Chinese city on your route, and the first chance to witness the consumer boom that is sweeping the high streets of China, in the shape of smart department stores and designer clothes boutiques. So vital has the city become as China's most westerly industrial outpost that in 1992 it was officially decreed a "port" to enable it to impose the special low rates of tax, normally permitted only in port cities such as Shanghai and Xiamen, as a means of luring in capital – an unusual distinction, to say the least, for a city located 2000km from the nearest sea.

If you're coming from eastern China, however, the city may not seem particularly exciting given its lack of historical identity, though it's strange to see so many signs written in curly Arabic script. Nevertheless, it does have lively bazaars, as well as a certain pioneering feel to it – the shiny, new highrise office buildings and hotels downtown seem to suggest a great metropolis, until you notice the barren, scrubby hillsides just around the corner and realize that the whole place has fairly recently been dropped into the desert. Apart from this, the main reason to visit Ürümqi is to arrange a trip to **Tian Chi** (Heaven Lake), three hours east of the city by bus.

Under the name of Dihua, Ürümqi became the capital of Xinjiang in the late nineteenth century. During the first half of the twentieth century the city was something of a battleground for feuding warlords – in 1916 Governor Yang Zengxin invited all his personal enemies to a dinner party here, and then had their heads cut off one by one during the course of the banquet. Later, shortly before the outbreak of World War II, **Soviet troops** entered the city to help quell a Muslim rebellion; they stayed until 1960. Ürümqi began to emerge from its extreme backwardness only with the completion of the Lanzhou–Ürümqi **rail line** in 1963. This more than anything helped to integrate the city, economically and psychologically, into the People's Republic. And with the opening of the Ürümqi–Almaty rail line in 1991, the final link in the long-heralded direct route from China through Central Asia to Europe was complete.

Arrival and city transport

Ürümqi's international **airport** is 15km northwest of the city, from where you can reach town on the CAAC airport bus (¥18), which delivers to various airline offices. Alternatively, take city bus #51 (¥5) from the main road outside the airport, which runs via Xibei Lu, Yangzijiang Lu (near the long-distance bus station), Qiantanjiang Lu (near the train station), and Xinhua Nan Lu to terminate just past the southern bus station; or a taxi (¥30).

The **train station** lies in the southwest of the city, with services arriving from as far afield as Beijing and Shanghai in the east, to Kashgar in the west, not to mention Alma Ata in Kazakhstan. Bus #8 from the southern end of Changjiang Lu runs northeast to Minzhu Lu, near much of the accommodation. The **main long-distance bus station** is a few blocks north of the train station, on Heilongjiang Lu, but just as many services end up a couple of kilometres south of the centre at the the **south bus station** on Xinhua Nan Lu (bus #1 runs north up Xinhua Lu), and private operators use their own depots, scattered across the city.

Distances within the city are fairly large, so you will need to use **taxis** (from ¥10 within the city) and **buses** (¥1–2) – pick up a map with bus routes from hawkers at arrival points.

Accommodation

Ürümqi's **accommodation** options are quite diverse, with most of the budget places around the train station.

Bogda Guangming Lu ⓣ0991/2815238, ⓕ2815769. A little bit distant from transit points and staff are a bit unhelpful, but otherwise a quiet and reasonable choice, with good-value dormitories. Dorm beds ¥25, ❺

Holiday Inn Xinhua Bei Lu ⓣ0991/2818788, ⓦwww.holiday-inn.com/hotels/urcch. Of fully international standard, with a wide range of restaurants, a disco and health club. Even if you're not staying here, foreigners are usually granted the privilege of going up to the lounge on the top floor to watch satellite TV and use the toilets. Doubles from ¥1100. ❾

Laiyuan ⓣ0991/2828368, ⓕ2825109. Located on the small lane opposite the *Holiday Inn*, just a few hundred metres down, and offering very plush doubles that can be bartered down in price. ❻

Overseas Chinese Hotel Xinhua Nan Lu ⓣ0991/2860793. Slightly remote in the south of the city, but has a pleasant, quiet atmosphere, with one old (cheaper) building and one new one. Take bus #7 south down Xinhua Bei Lu to get here. ❺

Ramada Changjiang Lu ⓣ0991/5876688, ⓕ5876685, ⓦwww.ramadahotels.com. New upmarket competition for the *Holiday Inn*, and rather more realistically priced, with a similar range of amenities. ❼

Xinjiang Corner of Changjiang Lu and Qiantangjiang Lu ⓣ0991/5852511, ⓦwww.xjfd.com.cn. Just a 10min walk from the train station is this lively place full of Pakistani traders. Rooms are classified "Normal", "OK" and "Magnificent", which roughly translate as spartan, standard and overpriced. Dorm beds ¥20, ❶–❺

Ya Ou Right in the train station square, to the far left (north) as you come out of the station ⓣ0991/5856699. Clean, modern doubles and three- and four-bed dorms. The ¥40 dorms have showers. There's no English sign. Dorm beds from ¥20, ❺

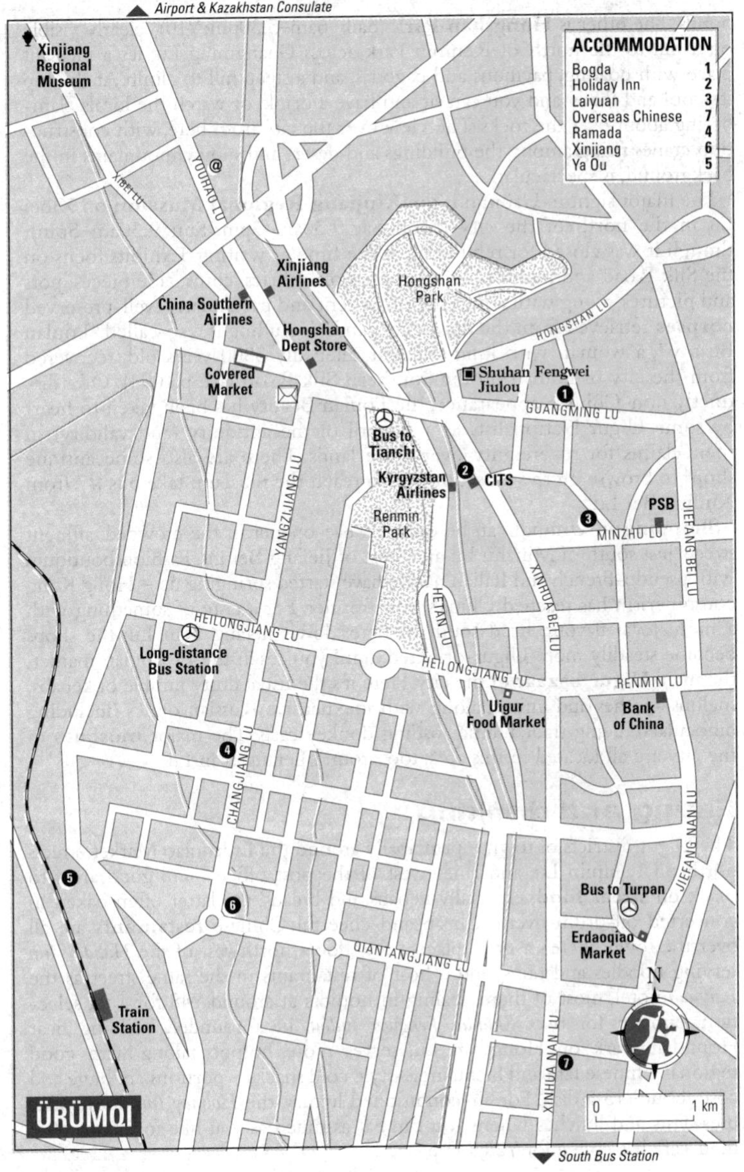

The City

Ürümqi doesn't really have a well-defined centre as such, being more a collection of districts, though a couple of parks are useful for orientation. One is **Renmin Park** (daily 8am–10.15pm; ¥5), which runs from north to south right through the geographic centre of the city, cooled by various streams and ponds. The other is **Hongshan Park** (daily 6am–5.30pm; ¥10), clearly visible on a hill to the north of Renmin Park across Guangming Lu; it's a pleasant place with boating, pavilions and pagodas, and a steep hill to climb. At the top it's cool and shady and you can sit and have a drink, or watch the locals clambering about over the rocks. The view over the city from here, with construction cranes rising among the buildings and desert and snowy mountains in the background, is spectacular.

The major sight in Ürümqi is the **Xinjiang Regional Museum** on Xibei Lu in the north of the city (Mon–Sat 9.30am–7pm, Sun 9.30am–5pm), though it was closed for rebuilding at the time of writing. Exhibits focus on the Silk Road and includes an array of tools, fabrics, coins, jade pieces, pots and pictures, along with a number of ancient and particularly well-preserved **corpses** retrieved from the dry desert sands, including the so-called "Loulan Beauty", a woman with long fair hair, allegedly 3800 years old, recovered from the city of Loulan on the Southern Silk Road (see p.1094). Of a distinctly non-Chinese appearance, the Loulan Beauty has been taken to heart by some Uigur Nationalists as a symbol of the antiquity (and validity) of their claims for sovereignty over these lands. There are also some antique shops to browse on the museum site. To reach the museum take bus #7 from Xinhua Bei Lu.

Shopping in Ürümqi can be quite an eye-opener in the crowded, affluent streets just south of Minzhu Lu and west of Jiefang Bei Lu. Fashion boutiques with pseudo-French and Italian names have started springing up – Hong Kong consumerism has reached China's final frontier. For a taste of something with a more local flavour, head south of here, down Jiefang Nan Lu; the shops become steadily more Uigur-oriented, until you reach the Erdaoqiao market, the main **Uigur bazaar** of the city. Here it's the usual dusty jumble of kebabs, melons, clothes and knives, along with inexpensive Russian optics (including binoculars), being traded amid jostling donkey carts. The major **mosques** of the city are all located in this area, too, around Jiefang Nan Lu.

Eating and drinking

The Uigur districts of town – principally around the Erdaoqiao Market, streets north off Renmin Lu, and lanes west of the post office – are good areas to snack on **street food**, especially kebabs and breads, the latter often baked in converted oil-drum ovens. Cheap and cheerful Chinese **restaurants** are all over the town: there's a great place a few doors northwest of the *Holiday Inn* serving noodles and buns; and a host of restaurants in the same street as the *Laiyuan* hotel, most of them dealing in hotpots at around ¥48 for a set selection, enough for two. *Shuhan Fengwei Jiulou*, in a rounded building near Hongshan Park on Hongshan Lu, serves more hotpots, along with good regional Chinese fare and Sichuanese-style cold snacks – portions are huge and cost about ¥15 a dish. For air-conditioned luxury, the *Holiday Inn* does buffet breakfasts and lunches where you can eat as much as you like for about ¥95; their café has coffee for ¥28 a cup.

Listings

Airlines China Southern is on Youhao Lu (☎0991/4516919 or 4516865), with Xinjiang Air opposite (☎0991/2641826); bus #101 heading west along Guangming Lu or #51 north up Changjiang Lu will get you there. Kazakh Airlines has an office in the consulate (see below). Kyrgyzstan Airlines (☎2316638 or 2316333) is in the lobby of the *Yingjisha* hotel, accessed via a lane near the *Holiday Inn*. Siberia Airlines (☎0991/2862326) has an office in the *Overseas*

Chinese Hotel on Xinhua Nan Lu.

Banks and exchange The Bank of China is at the junction of Renmin Lu and Jiefang Lu (Mon–Fri 10am–2pm & 3.30–6.30pm, Sat 1–3pm).

Bookshops The Foreign Language Bookstore on Xinhua Bei Lu has English novels, plus a few guidebooks to Xinjiang, on the second floor.

Cinema There is a cinema (Chinese-language only) in the ornate theatre building across from the Bank of China on Minzhu Lu.

Consulates The Kazakhstan consulate is at 31 Kunming Lu (visa applications and airline tickets Mon–Thurs 10.30am–1pm; ⓣ0991/3815796, ⓕ3821203, ⓔkazpass@mail.xj.cninfo.net), a small street east off Beijing Bei Lu in the north of the city; catch bus #12 from Guangming Lu and tell the driver where you want to get off.

Internet access There's a handful of smoky Internet bars charging ¥3/hr out past the airline offices on Youhao Lu.

Mail and telephones The main post office west of the northern end of Renmin Park is one place to make long-distance calls. More simply, however, you can buy and use telephone cards in the lobbies of upmarket hotels, such as the *Holiday Inn*.

Travel agents Just about all places to stay have agents who can book train, bus and plane tickets for about ¥30, though they might need a few days' notice. Ürümqi CITS is located in the building immediately south of the *Holiday Inn* and offers the same services. Independent travellers after customized tours, general information on Xinjiang and a chance to meet other travellers should contact John Hu (ⓔjohncafe@hotmail.com) for the new location of the Ürümqi branch of *John's Information Café*.

Tian Chi and Baiyang Gou

Tian Chi means "Heaven Lake", and this unspoilt natural haven 110km east of Ürümqi – the starting point ofVikram Seth's book *From Heaven Lake* – does almost live up to its name, especially for travellers who have spent long in the deserts of northwest China. At the cool, refreshing height of 2000m, the lake is surrounded by grassy meadows, steep, dense pine forests and jagged snow-covered peaks, including the mighty Bogda Feng, which soars to over 6000m, and the nicest feature of the area is that you can wander at will. There are no restrictions on accommodation (most people stay in yurts, with the semi-nomadic Kazakh population), and there is virtually limitless hiking. You need only to watch the **weather** – bitterly cold in winter, the lake is really only accessible during the summer months, May to September.

The **Kazakhs**, who lead a semi-nomadic herding existence in these hills, are organized into communes, very loosely managed by the State, which in theory owns both their land and animals and lets them out on fifteen- or thirty-year "contracts". Their traditional livelihood is from sheep, selling lambs in spring if the winter spares them. But it's a hard, unpredictable business – the State sometimes has to bail them out if the winter is a disastrous one – and revenues come increasingly from tourism. As in Inner Mongolia, the Kazakhs have taken to performing at horse shows, mostly for tourists. The extra income from providing visitors with food and accommodation is also welcome.

If you have not pre-booked your accommodation, you can simply set off to find yourself a **yurt**. Staying in one is a well-established custom, and you'll soon find people eager to cater for you. Most tourists prefer to lodge near the lake, but you can climb right up into the remote valleys of the Tian Shan – for this it's advisable to have a guide and a horse (¥50–100 per day), a service which young Kazakhs at the lakeside are happy to provide. Once up at the snowfields, the valleys are yours. Each is dotted with Kazakh yurts, and there's nearly always somewhere you can spend the night – you'll find yourself directed as soon as you ask. If you come in May – considered the most beautiful time – you may get to try the alcoholic *kumiss*, fermented mare's milk, a rare delicacy. The rest of the year the Kazakhs make do with a kind of tea, with an infusion of dried snow lily and sheep's milk.

Practicalities

Access to the lake is by **bus** from Ürümqi. The bus leaves at 9am from the northern entrance to Renmin Park, and costs ¥35 for the same-day return (double if you return another day) – try to buy your ticket the day before, from the bus stop. The hundred-kilometre journey takes around three hours, and the outward trip from Ürümqi is spectacular, initially through flat desert, then climbing through green meadows, conifer forests and along a wild mountain river. There's a ¥20 entrance fee to the lake area, where there's a small lakeside **village** comprising a bus park, some shops and souvenir stands and a guesthouse.

Communication with the Kazakhs can be problematic. Few speak Chinese, let alone English, which sometimes results in unpleasant misunderstandings – you may find yourself being charged extra for every cup of tea. One way to avoid these anxieties is to join a **pre-booked tour**, which will include yurt accommodation as well as transport between Ürümqi and the lake. Agents such as CITS in Ürümqi offer these, but are relatively expensive and of dubious quality; the best people to book through seem to be the independent operators who hang around hotels frequented by budget travellers, as most are touting their own family yurts. Recommended is a Mr Rachit, who speaks a little English and offers two-night tours for ¥100 per person. Included in the price are delightful boat rides to and from his two yurts, which are a couple of kilometres up the lake from the bus park.

Baiyang Gou

Seventy-five kilometres south of Ürümqi spreads another natural paradise, the **Baiyang Gou** (Southern Pastures), located in a spur of the Tian Shan. Basically, it's another green valley with a stream and a waterfall, and a backdrop of fir trees and snowy peaks. The Kazakhs also like to summer here and, accordingly, there are opportunities for tourists to join them. The main difficulty is transport: buses (¥53 return) run from the north end of Renmin Park in Ürümqi only if there is sufficient demand.

Yining and around

The pretty **Ili Valley** is centred around the city of **Yining** (known to the Uigurs as Kulja), just 60km east of the border with Kazakhstan, and 400km

Yining and around

Yining	伊宁	***yīníng***
Chapucha'er	察布查尔	*chábù chá'ěr*
Huiyuan	惠远	*huìyuǎn*
Sayram Lake	赛里木湖	*sàilǐmù hú*
Accommodation		
Ili	伊犁宾馆	*yīlí bīnguǎn*
Yaxiya	亚西亚宾馆	*yàxīyà bīnguǎn*
Yilite Dajiuiian	伊力特大酒店	*yīlìtè dàjiǔdiàn*
Youdian	邮电宾馆	*yōudiàn bīnguǎn*
Youyi	友谊宾馆	*yǒuyì bīnguǎn*
Ili	伊犁	***yīlí***

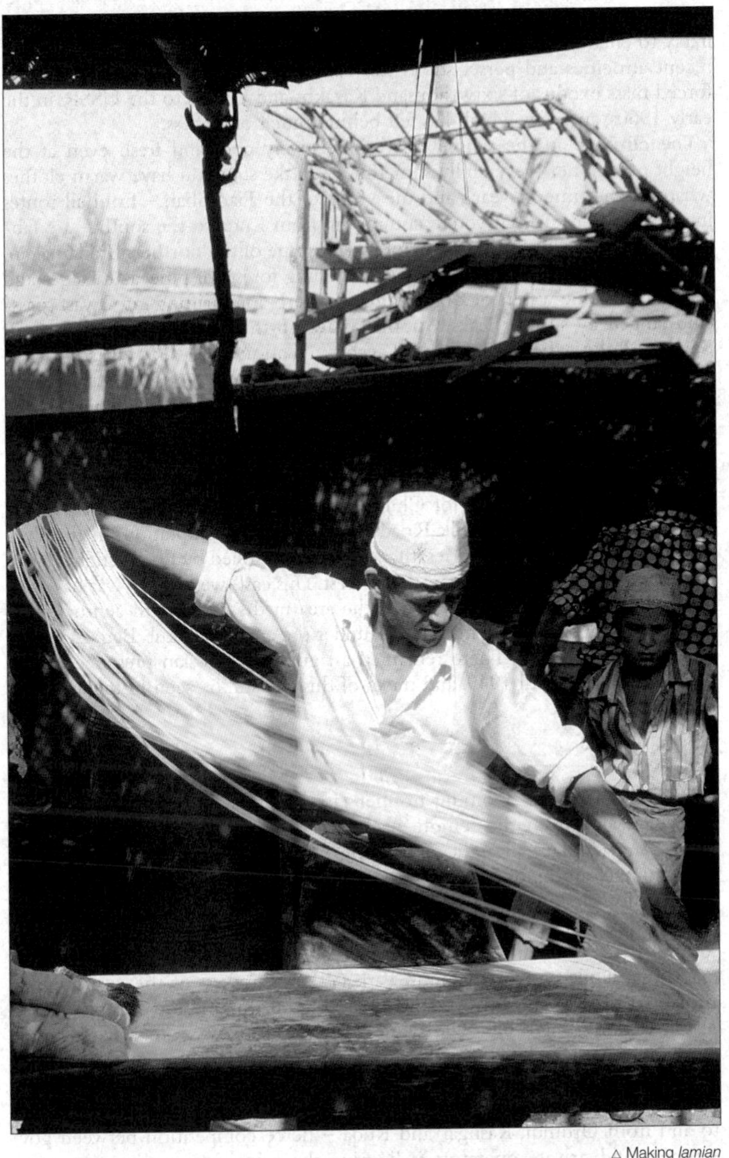

△ Making *lamian*

northwest of Ürümqi. As it is right off the principal Silk Road routes, not many travellers make the detour to get here, but if you have the time, or you're travelling to Kazakhstan, the trip is definitely worthwhile. Ili is one of the three so-called **Kazakh Autonomous Prefectures** within Xinjiang (the other two are Karamay and Altai), which form a block along the northwest frontier. Despite the nominal Kazakh preponderance, however, it is in fact the Uigurs who are the dominant group, and in this city, more than anywhere in Xinjiang, you're likely to encounter open expressions of hostility to Chinese rule. Memories of recent atrocities and persecutions still hang heavy in the air – including the forced mass exodus of sixty thousand Kazakhs and Uigurs to the USSR in the early 1960s, an event which has left behind much bitterness.

The **climate** in the whole valley is relatively cool and fresh even at the height of summer (very chilly sometimes – make sure you have warm clothes whatever the time of year), and the views of the Tian Shan – from all routes into Yining, especially if you're coming up from Kuqa to the south – are fabulous. The road climbs the harsh, rocky landscape of the northern Taklamakan, then enters pure alpine scenery with marching forests of pine, azure skies and the glorious blue waters of **Big Dragon Lake**, before drifting into a vast grassland ringed by snowy peaks. Another draw, north of Yining, is the beautiful **Sayram Lake**, where you can find accommodation in Kazakh yurts.

The **history** of the Ili Valley is one of intermittent Chinese control. At the time of the Han dynasty, two thousand years ago, the area was occupied by the **Wusun kingdom**. The Wusun people, ancestors of today's Kazakhs, kept diplomatic relations with the Han court and were responsible for introducing them to the horse. By the eighth century, however, a Tang-dynasty army had taken control of the region for China – its value as a staging post for a newly developing branch of the Silk Road was too great a temptation. In the thirteenth and fourteenth centuries, the area was controlled by first Genghis Khan from the east, then Tamerlane from the west. This east–west tug of war has gone on ever since, with the Qing seizing the area in the eighteenth century, only for the Russians to march in, in 1871, under the cover of Yakub Beg's Xinjiang rebellion (see p.1068). There remained a significant Russian presence in one form or another until 1949, and traces of this can still be seen in the architecture of Yining.

Yining

YINING today is a booming frontier city and as such has changed almost unrecognizably from the remote backwater it once was. Nevertheless, it's a small, compact place, pleasant for walking, with shady, tree-lined streets and an extraordinary amount of food for sale from street vendors. The centre of town isn't readily obvious – most of the action seems to straddle the length of **Jiefang Lu**, though the old city is centred around **Qingnian Park** to the southeast. The **Uigur bazaars**, just south of Qingnian Park, are well worth exploring, while, over in Renmin Park (¥1) in the west of the city, there's a **museum** (daily; ¥5). However, the building itself – an old Russian place, with plaster reliefs, painted blue and white – is more interesting than its contents, which number a few remains of early settlements in the region (there are no English labels).

The **bus station** is located in the northwest of the city. Many daily buses run to and from Ürümqi, Kashgar and Kuqa – fierce competition between government and private operators is keeping the prices low and service good, though be aware that private buses leave only when they are full, no matter what the drivers say. You can simply buy your ticket on the pavement outside the front of the station. Another interesting bus service out of Yining is that to Almaty across the border in Kazakhstan, though note that Kazakhstan visas, now essential, are not available here. There is no train to Yining, and the only **flights** here are from Ürümqi. Yining's **CAAC** office (Ⓣ0999/8044328) is in the *Yilite Hotel*, but their tickets are very hard to book at short notice, so you

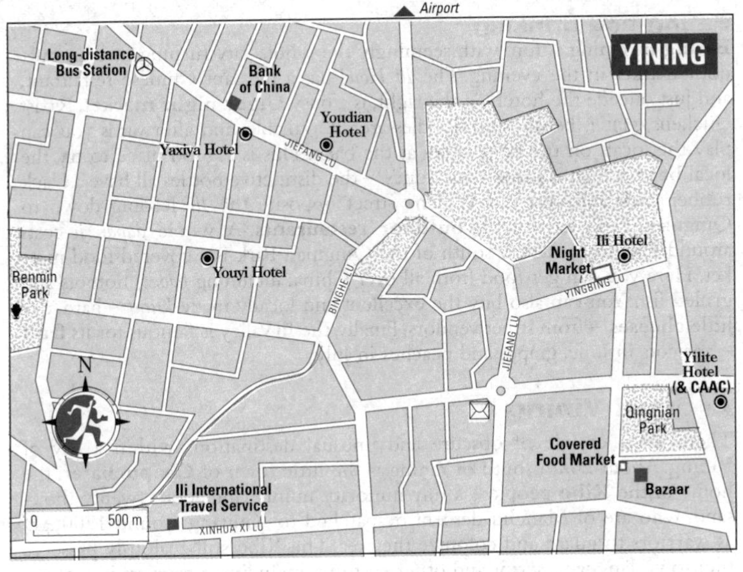

may prefer to try a **travel service** – for example, the Ili International Travel Service (Ⓣ0999/ 8023535), down on Xinhua Xi Lu (bus #2), where a little English is spoken.

Accommodation

A good **place to stay** is the *Ili* (Ⓣ0999/8023126, Ⓕ8024964; ❹), an old-fashioned hotel, in huge leafy grounds. There are a number of buildings offering varying degrees of comfort and different prices – the cheaper No. 4 building, for example, offers perfectly respectable, if small, doubles with bath. They have dorms as well but are unwilling to let foreigners into them. To reach the hotel from the bus station, take bus #1 heading east for three stops, cross over the road and it's a few minutes' walk east along Yingbing Lu.

Another long-standing hotel in Yining is the *Youyi* (Ⓣ0999/8023126, Ⓕ8024631; ❸–❻, dorm beds ¥55), with cheap doubles and three-bed dorms in the old wing and smarter singles and doubles in the new wing. However, if you are travelling on your own, they might insist you pay for all the beds in the dorm. The hotel is far from any bus route; leaving the bus station, turn right and walk until you see a sign in English pointing to the hotel. This sign will actually bring you to the back door of the hotel which you can easily miss; it's better to take the next street to the right – the front of the hotel is a fifteen-minute walk along here. On the way, you'll pass another, smaller hotel called the *Yaxiya* (Ⓣ0999/8031800; ❸). There's no English sign, but you can recognize it from the Greek columns outside. Here you'll find clean and modern doubles with bath. Back on the main road, a little farther down from the bus station, is the *Youdian* (Ⓣ0999/8023844; ❹, dorm beds ¥45), offering smart, upmarket doubles and very cheap dorm beds round at the back – not bad value, especially as each dorm has satellite TV. An alternative is the new *Yilite* (Ⓣ0999/8044328; ❹) on the crossroads just east of Qingnian Park. It's not a very interesting part of town, but the hotel is quite good value.

Eating and drinking

Eating in Yining is fun, with seemingly the whole city turning into an outdoor market in the evening. The *Ili Hotel* has a pleasant Chinese restaurant, and just outside the hotel, on the right, is a busy **Uigur night market**. Roast chickens, *samsa,* kebabs and noodles are all available, and afterwards you can play the locals on the pool tables at the back. This is a good place to try the local **beer**, which is made with honey – the distinctive bottles all have a black rubber cork and cost just ¥1. The street opposite the *Ili,* leading down to Qingnian Park, has lots of **outdoor restaurants**. A whole *dapan ji* costs around ¥35. Immediately south of the Qingnian Park is a covered food market. Here you can get food from all over China, including *baozi,* hotpots and grilled fish. You can also buy the excellent and locally made *kurut* – hard, dry little **cheeses** – from street vendors. Finally, the Ili Valley is famous for its **fruit** – apricots in June, grapes and peaches in July.

Around Yining

There are a couple of obscure and unusual destinations within a day of Yining. About 20km south of Yining is the little town of **Chapucha'er**, the home of the **Xibo** people – a tiny minority, numbering about twenty thousand, who are of Manchu descent despatched to Xinjiang around 1700 AD as warriors to guard and colonize the area. The Xibo still zealously preserve their own language, script and other customs, including a prowess in archery that is of Olympic standard. Chapucha'er is just thirty minutes by bus from Yining's long-distance bus station. From the same bus station, there are also buses to **Huiyuan**, 30km west of Yining, a small but historic town with a three-storey **drum tower** dating from the nineteenth century. Another 20km north of here is the pretty Persian-style **tomb of Telug Timur**, a fourteenth-century Muslim leader, located just outside the small town of **Qingshui**. To visit Huiyuan and the tomb of Telug Timur as a combined trip from Yining, rent a car from a travel service – a day with the car will cost about ¥300.

About 180km out of Yining, on the road east to Ürümqi, **Sayram Lake** occupies a fantastic location between mountains and grassy banks. Around 2000m above sea level and decidedly chilly for most of the year, Sayram offers tremendous opportunities for the intrepid to escape the hustle of the cities. Tourism here is still very much at a pioneering stage – there are simple **guesthouses** at the lakeside, otherwise you can try to find accommodation in a Kazakh or Mongol **yurt**. Access to and from the lake is by bus from Yining (3hr) or Ürümqi (15hr); given the frequency of the buses on this route it should be easy to pick one up if you stand on the road.

Korla to Kashgar: the Northern Silk Road

Some 300km southwest of Ürümqi, and 400km southwest of Turpan, the wealthy but dull town of **Korla** marks the start of the most direct route to Kashgar, which follows the ancient Northern Silk Road (see box, p.990). Having crossed the Tian Shan and entered the Tarim Basin, this route skirts round the northern rim of the Taklamakan Desert for more than a thousand kilometres, flanked by snowy peaks. The country is largely a barren wilderness,

The Northern Silk Road

Korla	库尔勒	***kùěrlè***
Bayangol Tian'e hotel	巴州天鹅宾馆	*bāzhōu tiāné bīnguǎn*
Bositun Hu	博斯腾湖	*bósīténg hú*
Tiemen Guan	铁门关	*tiěmén guān*
Kuqa	库车	***kùchē***
Kizil Thousand Buddha Caves	克孜尔千佛洞	*kèzīěr qiānfódòng*
Pilang	龟兹古城	*qiūcí gǔchéng*
Subashi Ancient City	苏巴什古城	*sūbāshí gǔchéng*
Tomb of Molena Ashidin Hodja	默拉纳额什丁坟	*mòlānà éshídīng fén*
Accommodation		
Kala Kuer	卡拉库尔宾馆	*kǎlākùěr bīnguǎn*
Kuqa	库车宾馆	*kùchē bīnguǎn*
Minmao	民贸宾馆	*mínmào bīnguǎn*
Qiuci	龟兹宾馆	*qiūcí bīnguǎn*

though there are occasional transitions from parched desert to green pasture in the rare places where water from the Tian Shan has found its way down to the plain. The small oasis towns west of Korla usually comprise brown mud-built houses, perhaps a few vine trellises, and thick muddy water running in trenches beside the streets; **Kuqa**, about a third of the way to Kashgar, is worth a stopover for its Old Town's traditional feel, and a couple of low-key Silk Road relics in the surrounding deserts.

The **road** is for the most part in fairly good condition, though given the vast distances involved, it makes much more sense to use the parallel **railway**, with two services daily running the full distance from Ürümqi, via Korla and Kuqa, to Kashgar. The line, completed in 2000, has completely transformed the journey; Ürümqi to Kashgar now takes 24 hours in an air-conditioned carriage, instead of at least 36 hours of dust, baking heat, and scenic vacuum in a bus seat. While epic bus journeys do have their attractions, diehards will find more of interest in the three-day trip to Kashgar via the Southern Silk Road (see p.1092).

Korla

There's been a settlement at **KORLA** (**Kuerle** in Chinese) since at least Tang times, and today the city is capital of the **Bayangol Mongol Autonomous Prefecture**, a vast region that encompasses the eastern side of the Taklamakan as well as better watered areas around the city itself. Despite all this, Mongols themselves are not much in evidence and today Korla is mostly just a base for companies – including the US conglomerate Exxon – tapping into the Taklamakan's **oil reserves**. It's also of inescapable interest as a transport nexus: the rail line and roads from Ürümqi and Turpan converge here; the Northern Silk Road heads due west; and the Southern Silk Road curves down around the eastern side of the Taklamakan via Ruoqiang (p.1094). The town is also a terminus for buses shortcutting the Southern Silk Road by crossing diagonally southwest across the Taklamakan to Minfeng and Khotan (see p.1095). There isn't anything aside from transport connections to justify a stopover here, though the grey brickwork and red tiled roof of the Ming dynasty **Tiemen Guan**, the Iron Gateway, asserts Korla's age in the face of what is otherwise a relentlessly modern city – you'll see it from the bus to the north of town. In summer, locals spend all their spare time 60km east at **Bositun Hu**, a huge artificial lake where you can cool off in the water, rent a beach umbrella, and kick back on the sand, admiring distant desert mountain ranges.

Korla's **centre** is only about a kilometre across, with main-street Renmin Lu containing a massive **Bank of China** and lined with upmarket **hotels** – including the *Bayangol Tian'e* (Ⓣ0996/2022858; ⑤) – and oil-company and mining offices. The **bus station** is just to the north on Jiaotong Dong Lu, and has frequent departures through the day to Ürümqi, Turpan and Kuqa, plus evening sleeper buses to Ruoqiang, or via Minfeng to Khotan, on the Southern Silk Road. The **train station**, on the Hami–Ürümqi–Kashgar line, is about 3km east at the end of the #1 bus route from Renmin Lu.

Kuqa and around

KUQA (pronounched "ku-cher" and known to the Chinese as **Kuche**) lies about 300km to the west of Korla, past one of the world's largest **wind farms**, a collection of futuristic-looking fan blades on twenty-metre-high poles laid out across the desert. A good place to break the long journey to Kashgar, it's a small town with a long history, and a largely Uigur population. The fourth-century linguist and scholar **Kumarajiva**, one of the most famous of all Chinese Buddhists, came from here. Having travelled to Kashmir for his education, he later returned to China as a teacher and translator of Buddhist documents from Sanskrit into Chinese. It was in large measure thanks to him that Buddhism came to be so widely understood in China and, by the early Tang, Kuqa was a major **centre of Buddhism** in China. The fantastic wealth of the trade caravans subsidized giant monasteries here, and Xuanzang, passing through the city in the sixth century, reported the existence of two huge Buddha statues, 27m high, guarding its entrances. The city even had its own Indo-European language. With the arrival of Islam in the ninth century, however, this era finally began to draw to a close, and today only a few traces of Kuqa's ancient past remain.

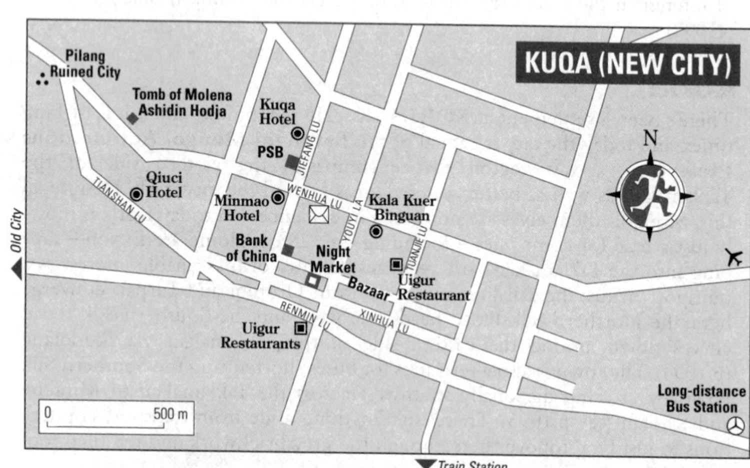

The City

There's little evidence now of Kuqa's past wealth; today the city is dusty and poor. It is effectively in two parts, the old (to the west) and the new (to the east), lying a few kilometres apart. The New City, largely Han-populated, contains all the facilities you'll need, while the Old City, largely Uigur, is peppered with mosques and bazaars and has a Central Asian atmosphere very different from Chinese towns. To reach the Old City, take any bus heading west along Renmin Lu, the main street on which the bus station is located, until you reach a bridge across the river – the old city lies beyond the river. A **Friday market**, where the Uigur population are out in force in both sections of town, buying and selling leather jackets, carpets, knives, wooden boxes, goats and donkeys, is not to be missed, though a much smaller affair than at Kashgar.

From the **New City**, a couple of sights are easily accessible. One is the remains of the ruined city of **Pilang**, otherwise known as Qiuci (the old name for Kuqa), though there is nothing really to see beyond a solid, weatherbeaten mud wall. If you follow Tianshan Lu from the new city, the ruined city is about ten minutes' walk west of the *Qiuci Hotel*. Slightly more interesting is the nearby **Tomb of Molena Ashidin Hodja**, a simple shrine and mosque, in honour of an Arab missionary who came to the city, probably in the thirteenth century. It's on Wenhua Lu, about fifteen minutes' walk west of the *Minmao Hotel*. There's also a daily **bazaar** in the lane running east for several blocks from the Bank of China, north of and parallel with Xinhua Lu, containing Xinjiang's second-largest **goldsmiths' quarters** (after Kashgar's).

The bridge leading to the **Old City** is really where the main area of interest begins. Right by the bridge, the **bazaar** is the main venue for the Friday market; cattle and sheep are traded on the river banks below. Beyond the bridge, you can soon lose yourself in the labyrinth of narrow streets and mud-brick houses. Right in the heart of this area, fifteen minutes approximately northeast of the bridge, is the **Kuqa Mosque** (¥5), built in 1923. Delightfully neat and compact, with an attractive green-tiled dome, this mosque is of wholly arabesque design, displaying none of the Chinese characteristics of mosques in more eastern parts of the country. Beyond the mosque, on Linqi Lu, is the **museum** (¥12), housing a moderately interesting collection of locally discovered pottery, coins, skeletons and a few frescoes. Opening hours depend on whether the doorman is awake or not. To reach the museum from the bridge, follow the main road through the old city to the end, then turn right and it's a few hundred metres farther on.

Practicalities

Flights connect Kuqa with Ürümqi; the **airport** is a very short taxi ride east of the new city. The **bus station** is in the far southeast of the new city, for the lengthy rides to Korla, Ürümqi and Turpan; Kashgar buses don't originate in town, so you have to stop them as they pass through (usually in the afternoon – check at the bus station) and negotiate a seat. Kuqa's **train station** is 5km southeast of the new city (¥5 in a taxi), with three trains daily west to Kashgar, and two east to Ürümqi (the other eastbound service stops in Korla). You can only buy hard-seat tickets here, and only just before the train pulls in; go to carriage 7 to upgrade on board, or pay an agent to reserve you something better. Your accommodation will know the current train timetable.

For plane and train tickets out of Kuqa, and for **booking tours** of the sites outside the city, it's worth paying a call on the friendly Kuqa **CITS** (daily 9.30am–1.30pm & 4–8pm; ⓣ0997/7122524), in the *Qiuci Hotel*. The woman here speaks some English and is delighted to help you.

There are a couple of **hotels** right outside the bus station, but this is a rather distant corner of the town to stay in. To reach the more central hotels from here, catch a bus from just in front of the station, heading west. Get off at the second stop and take the next road north, Jiefang Lu. Motor-rickshaws also operate from the station, or it's around a twenty-minute walk. The *Minmao* (ⓣ0997/7122998; budget doubles ❷, standard doubles ❺), on the southwest side of the intersection between Jiefang Lu and Wenhua Lu, is a convenient place to stay. Five minutes' walk farther north up Jiefang Lu is the *Kuqa Binguan* (ⓣ0997/7122901; ❹), a big, bright and good-value place set in its own gardens, offering 24-hour hot water and doubles with or without bath. One block east of the post office, the *Kala Kuer Binguan* is clean and neat (ⓣ0997/7122957, ⓕ7123140; ❷, dorm beds ¥40). The most upmarket accommodation in town is at the secluded *Qiuci* on Tianshan Lu (ⓣ0997/7122005, ⓕ0997/7122524; ❹), a few minutes west of the new city.

There are a number of basic **Uighur restaurants** in the new town's market area around the Renmin Lu/Youyi Lu intersection – hugely busy on Fridays – where you can tuck in to bowls of *laghman* and Uigur tea, with great rough sticks and leaves floating in the cup. Nearby stalls sell delicious baked *kaobao* and *samsa*. In the other direction, on Xinhua Lu, a little east of Jiefang Lu, is a busy, smoky **night market** full of the usual kebabs and roast chickens, as well as plenty of fresh fruit in season. For all the same things in relative comfort, try the huge restaurant on Tuanjie Lu, around from the *Kala Kuer* hotel; the *Kuqa Binguan*'s restaurant can supply Chinese food.

Around Kuqa

Around Kuqa, you can explore a whole series of ruined cities and Buddhist cave sites, testimony to the fabulous history of the area. Probably the two most significant of these are the **Subashi Ancient City**, 30km north of Kuqa along a good paved road, and the **Kizil Thousand Buddha Caves**, 75km to the west. The Kizil Caves, in particular, were once a Central Asian treasure trove, a mixture of Hellenistic, Indian and Persian styles with not even a suggestion of Chinese influence. Sadly, the caves have suffered the ravages of the German archeologist and art thief Albert Von Le Coq who, at the beginning of the twentieth century, cut out and carried away many of the best frescoes. Some of the twenty or so caves are entirely bare. Unless you're a serious student of archeology, you're unlikely to find anything here to compare with the Mogao Caves at Dunhuang in Gansu province (see p.1050). The Subashi Ancient City (¥15) is a far better prospect. Abandoned in the twelfth century, Subashi comprises fairly extensive ruins, including sections of buildings and the former six-metre-high city walls, and looks very atmospheric with the bald, pink and black mountain ranges rising up behind. Along the way there, look for the **irrigation channels** carrying runoff from the mountains to villages.

To visit either of these sites, you'll need to rent a car (the CITS can arrange this – their tour to both Subashi and Kizil costs ¥300) or simply stop a taxi and start negotiating – ¥1 per kilometre covered is a reasonable rate, so expect to pay ¥150 for the round trip to Kizil, and ¥60 for Subashi.

The Southern Silk Road

Originally, the **Southern Silk Road** split off from the northern route near Dunhuang in Gansu province, crossed to **Ruoqiang** on the eastern edge of the

The Southern Silk Road

Khotan	和田	***hétián***
Carpet factory	地毯厂	*dìtǎn chǎng*
Jade factory	玉器厂	*yùqì chǎng*
Melikawat	米力克瓦特古城	*mǐlìkèwǎtè gǔchéng*
Silk factory	丝厂	*sīchǎng*
White Jade River	白玉河	*báiyù hé*
Accommodation and eating		
Hetian	和田宾馆	*hétián bīnguǎn*
Hetian Shi	和田市宾馆	*hétiánshì bīnguǎn*
Huimin Fandian	回民饭店	*huímín fàndiàn*
Jiaotong	交通宾馆	*jiāotōng bīnguǎn*
Yurong	玉融宾馆	*yùróng bīnguǎn*
Minfeng	民丰	***mínfēng***
Qiemo	且末	***qiěmò***
Qiemo Gucheng	且末古城	*qiěmò gǔchéng*
Ruoqiang	若羌	***ruòqiāng***
Miran	米兰古城	*mǐlán gǔchéng*
Lop Nor	罗布泊	*luóbù bó*
Loulan	楼兰古城	*loúlán gǔchéng*
Yarkand	沙车	***shāchē***
Aleytun mosque	阿勤电清真寺	*āqíndiàn qīngzhēn sì*
Amannishahan tomb	阿曼尼莎汗纪念陵	*āmànníshāhàn jìniànlíng*
Shanche Binguan	沙车宾馆	*shāchē bīnguǎn*
Yecheng	叶城	***yèchéng***
Cengsa	曾萨	*céngsà*
Kudi	库地	*kùdì*
Yecheng Dengshan hotel	叶城登山宾馆	*yèchéng dēngshān bīnguǎn*
Yengisar	英吉沙	***yīngjí shā***

Taklamakan, then skirted the southern rim of the desert before rejoining the northern road at Kashgar. In modern times this route has fallen into almost total obscurity, lacking as it does any major city and connected by poor roads and minimal transport. Of the two branches, however, this route is actually the older and historically more important of the two. The most famous Silk Road travellers used it, including the Chinese Buddhist pilgrims Fa Xian and Xuanzang (see pp.1072–1073), as well as Marco Polo and, in the 1930s, the British journalist and adventurer Peter Fleming. The ancient settlements along the way were oases in the desert, kept alive by streams flowing down from the snowy peaks of the Kunlun Shan, which constitute the outer rim of the Tibetan plateau to the south.

Following what remains of this southern route opens up the prospect of travelling overland from Turpan to Kashgar one way, and returning another way, thus circumnavigating the entire Taklamakan Desert. The southern route is not to everyone's taste, in that it chiefly comprises desert interspersed by extremely dusty oasis towns, with none of the green or tourist facilities of the northern route; nor is there a rail line to fall back on if bus travel loses its appeal. Nevertheless, it represents the chance to visit an extremely little-known corner of China, where foreigners are still a rare sight.

Today, there is no road covering the eastern section of the original route between Dunhuang and Ruoqiang, though there are other roads to Ruoqiang from Korla and, less reliably, from Gansu and Qinghai provinces. Once at Ruoqiang – itself 450km from Korla – a decent road runs 1400km around the southern perimeter of the Taklamakan to Kashgar, with the ancient city of **Khotan** as the pick of places to get off the bus and explore. You can also reach Khotan more or less directly from Korla, via a road which cuts right through the Taklamakan and shaves 500km – and the slowest part of the journey – off the trip. For the truly intrepid, it's possible to leave the Southern Silk Road between Khotan and Kashgar and slip south **into Tibet** – for foreigners, an illegal (though regularly travelled) route to Lhasa, which will severely test your abilities to travel rough.

From Korla to Khotan

The most painless way to deal with the southern route is to take the road southwest from Korla **across the Taklamakan** to **Minfeng** and Khotan. Built by the oil companies in the late 1990s, this veritable 500-kilometre-long expressway traverses the very heart of the Taklamakan and should, in theory, give you a close-up of why the Uigurs call this desert the "Sea of Death". Unfortunately, buses coming either way make the crossing at night, so you don't get a view of the centre; it is, however, a very quick road, and the whole one-thousand-kilometre trip between Korla and Khotan takes a mere seventeen hours.

For a dustier, rougher, more rewarding trip to Khotan, you'll want to catch a bus southeast from Korla around the eastern edge of the Taklamakan to **Ruoqiang**. It's also theoretically possible to get here from Dunhuang or Golmud along routes which approximately parallel the original Silk Road, though foreigners trying it report being pulled off buses by policemen and kicked back in the direction they came from. This may be for their own safety (the route is a real backwater) or it might have something to do with the proximity of **Lop Nor**, a huge salty marshland covering 3000 square kilometres northeast of Ruoqiang that happens to be China's **nuclear test site**.

Ruoqiang

A small, busy place with at least one guesthouse, **RUOQIANG** (**Charkhlik** to the Uigurs) is most notable for being the jumping-off point for treks by camel or jeep out to two little-known ruined cities of Silk Road vintage. The first of these, **Miran** – subject of Christa Paula's book *Voyage to Miran* – is relatively accessible, approximately 75km northeast of Ruoqiang; a far more ambitious trip would be to **Loulan**, at least 250km from town on the western edge of Lop Nor. Loulan is particularly intriguing, as its very existence had been completely forgotten until the Swedish explorer **Sven Anders Hedin** rediscovered the site, which had been buried in sand, in the early twentieth century; it wasn't until the 1980s that the first Chinese archeological surveys were undertaken. Remains include traces of the city walls and huge numbers of collapsed wooden and adobe houses; the site was also littered with wooden bowls and plates. Foundations of a pagoda indicate a Buddhist population, graves yielded mummified corpses of non-Chinese appearance wrapped in silk and wool (see opposite), and **Han-dynasty coins** reveal the city's age. What little is known about Loulan comes from contemporary records written in Chinese and a northern Indian language found here, which mention that large numbers of people were abandoning the city in the early fourth century – why is a mystery. Certainly by 399, when the Buddhist monk Fa Xian passed through this area, Loulan was depopulated.

Qiemo and Minfeng

Back on the Kashgar road, the next settlement of any size is **QIEMO** (**Cherchen**), another small, surprisingly modern town famed for the frequency of its sandstorms, and lying some 300km southwest of Ruoqiang. There are more **ruins** about 10km to the northwest at **Qiemo Gucheng** – dated to at least 2000 years old – and the *Muzitage* hotel if you need somewhere to stay in town.

From here it's a further 300km west to **MINFENG** (**Niya**), where you meet up with the trans-Taklamakan road from Korla. Minfeng comes alive every evening, when long-distance buses converge and the main street becomes one long chaotic strip of kebab, bread and noodle vendors. On the final 300km between here and Khotan, you pass through some of the most vividly empty landscapes you will ever see, an indication of what the centre of the Taklamakan must be like: a formless expanse of sky and desert merging at a vague, dusty yellow horizon.

Khotan and around

KHOTAN (known in Chinese as **Hetian**) has for centuries been famed throughout the country for its **carpets**, **silk**, and **white jade**. A bleak and dusty grid of wide streets, the town itself is pretty ordinary, but the substantial Uigur population is hospitable, and there's ample opportunity to watch the materials for which Khotan is famed being worked in much the same way as they always have been.

Khotan's centre comprises a couple of blocks to the south and west of the junction between Nuerwake Lu (running east–west) and Gulibake Lu (north–south). The crenelated **old city walls** still stand remarkably intact – if marred by graffitti and occasional piles of garbage – either side of Nuerwake Lu, east of the river. The **museum** on Tanai Lu (irregular hours; ¥7), south of where it intersects with Nuerwake Lu, includes fragments of silk, wooden utensils, and two mummified bodies from Loulan (see opposite). Immediately to the south of the museum is the **jade factory** where you can see craftsmen bent over small lathes. The results of their labour are on sale in the shop above, with prices between ¥30 and

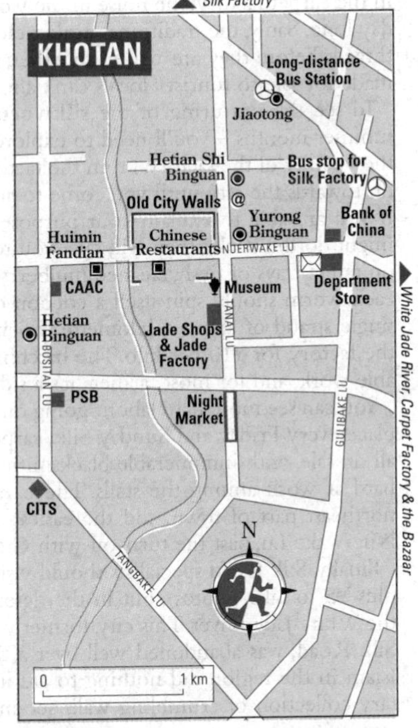

¥30,000, and in shops all over the town. The biggest concentration of stalls selling jade is at the east end of Nuerwake Lu.

About 4km to the east of town, following Nuerwake Lu, is the **White Jade River** from which, historically, so much jade has been recovered, and which still yields the odd stone for casual searchers. The river flows through a wide, stony plain; it's easy to get down here and forage, but you'll need to find one of the locals – who come here with garden forks to rake the stones – to show you what you are looking for, or you may end up with a pocketful of pretty but worthless quartz.

The town **carpet factory** stands just across the river and to the left; it's particularly worth a visit if you are interested in making a purchase. Prices here, and in the shop in town, are very cheap. The atmosphere in the factory workshop is friendly, with the workers, mostly young women, exchanging banter as they weave with incredible dexterity. They encourage visitors to take pictures, and ask to be sent copies.

If you're interested in the secrets of **silk production**, catch bus #1 right to its last stop from Gulibake Lu, five minutes' walk north of Nuerwake Lu and to the east, where the road is bisected by a small park. Walk back just a few hundred metres towards town and you'll come to the front entrance of the head office of the **silk factory**. The security man there should understand what you want. If you come during the week (avoid the 1–3pm lunch break), the chances are that you will be supplied with an English-speaking employee to show you round for free. You can see the whole process: the initial unpicking of the cocoons, the twisting together of the strands to form a thread (ten strands for each silk thread), the winding of the thread onto reels, and finally the weaving and dying. The women here have it hard compared to their sisters in the carpet factory: the noise in the workshops is immense, and they stand all day long. Sadly, the traditional **atalas cloth**, where the design is dyed into the threads before they are woven together, producing a fuzzy image, is now only made for sale to tourists; locals can't afford the ¥200 per length price tag.

To see the nurturing of the **silkworms** themselves – only possible in the summer months – you'll need to explore some of the nearby country lanes in the vicinity of the factory. From the factory, walk a few hundred metres farther on towards the city, until you come to an area of green trees and vine trellises. If you are able to explain your purpose to people (a drawing of a silkworm might do the trick), they will take you to see their silkworms munching away on rattan trays of fresh, cleaned mulberry leaves in cool, dark sheds. Eventually each worm should spin itself a cocoon of pure silk; each cocoon comprises a single strand of about a kilometre in length. The farmers sell the cocoons to the factory for ¥10 per kilo. The hatching and rearing of silkworms is unreliable work, and for most farmers it's a sideline.

You can see more hard labour going on at the fascinating **bazaar** which takes place every Friday and Sunday. Silk, carpets, leather jackets, fruit and spices are all on sale, with innumerable blacksmiths, tinsmiths, goldsmiths and carpenters hard at work among the stalls. The bazaar stretches across the whole of the northeast part of town, and the easiest way to reach it is to head east along Nuerwake Lu, past the turn-off with Gulibake Lu, then take the first left.

Finally, Silk Road specialists should visit the ruined city of **Melikawat** (¥10, plus ¥5 to take photos), out in the desert 30km to the south of town beside the White Jade River. This city, formerly an important Buddhist centre on the Silk Road, was abandoned well over a thousand years ago, and the arrival of Islam in the region did nothing to aid its preservation. The site is a fragmentary collection of crumbling walls set among the dunes and tamarisk bushes, thousands of wind-polished pot shards littering the ground – you might find odd fragments of glass or wood poking out of the ruins. For a visit to Melikawat, contact a travel service (see below) or flag down a taxi and start some hard bargaining; ¥60 is a reasonable price for the return trip.

Practicalities

Khotan's **airport**, with daily connections to Ürümqi (¥1000), lies 10km west from town. You can reach the centre either by taxi or by the airport bus that meets incoming flights. The **bus station** is in the north of the city, with daily services to Korla and Ürümqi via the trans-Taklamakan route (prices to Korla vary from ¥180 to ¥300, depending on the vehicle and your bargaining skills), and to everywhere else along the Southern Silk Road between Kashgar and Qiemo. To reach Nuerwake Lu from the bus station on foot takes about twenty minutes; turn right as you come out onto the main road. Taxis charge ¥5 to any hotel.

Right beside the bus station entrance, the *Jiaotong* (❷) is the cleanest of several **hotels** here; more central options include the rather gloomy *Hetian Shi Binguan* (ⓣ0903/2022824; ❷, dorm beds ¥20); and the friendly, unpretentious *Yurong Binguan* (ⓣ0903/2025242; ❹, dorm beds ¥20). The best place to stay in Khotan is the *Hetian Binguan* in the southwest of the city (ⓣ0903/2023564; ❹, dorms ¥30), comfortable and good value – even the dorms have their own bathrooms – with at least two large restaurants serving Chinese and Muslim food.

All hotels have **travel services** for booking plane and bus tickets and arranging **tours**. Local excursions with a guide taking in the carpet and silk factories should set you back between ¥50–100, and it's possible to organize lengthier jeep or camel trips around the region, using routes not necessarily covered by public transport. Expect to pay ¥300 per day for a jeep, ¥100 for a camel; camping gear is around ¥50 per person, and a guide will cost ¥100 a day. If your hotel can't help, try CITS (ⓣ0903/2026090, ⓕ2512846), inconveniently located on the third floor of a building at the end of Bositan Lu; better yet is the local Uigur guide Elly Umai (ⓣ0903/2516090 or 2026460), who can be slightly abrasive but is also helpful and speaks good English.

Eating in Khotan is straightforward. *Huimin Fandian*, just west of the river on Nuerwake Lu, is a large, bustling Muslim restaurant serving *laghman*, beef noodle soups, kebabs, and the like, with nothing over ¥8. There is an excellent Uigur **night market** on Tanai Lu, just south of Nuerwake Lu, where you can get roast chickens, pilau, eggs and fish, as well as the customary kebabs, sheep heads and *laghman*. For **Chinese food**, try just east of the river on Nuerwake Lu. Just pull open the curtains in the doorways, and go in; most of the proprietors here are Sichuanese in exile.

Khotan to Kashgar

The last 500km of the Southern Silk Road runs northwest from Khotan to Kashgar through a dusty wasteland interspersed with dunes, groups of camels, mountain ranges to the south, and sudden patches of willows and green marking irrigated settlements. Some 200km along, **YECHENG** (Karagilik) is a kind of giant Uigur highway service station, with flashing lights, fires, bubbling cauldrons, overhead awnings and great hunks of mutton hanging from meat hooks. The *Yecheng Deng Shan* **hotel** on Tilan Dong Jie is recommended as somewhere to stay (ⓣ0998/7282900; dorm beds ¥50).

The road divides at Yecheng, one fork running north towards Kashgar, the other southwest into **Tibet** (see box p.1098). Heading a further 60km north

Yecheng to Tibet

The road **southeast from Yecheng** follows the line of the Karakorum mountain ranges for about 1000km to the town of **Ali** in **western Tibet** (see p.1170). Though a well-used trucking route, it has never been open to travellers, but a steady trickle seem to make it through each year. Don't underestimate the physical and official **difficulties** you'll face, however, especially since not only the road but western Tibet itself is often closed to foreigners – you might make it through to Ali only to be arrested on arrival.

The Yecheng–Ali road is best tackled between July and October, but can be extremely **cold** even then – take a sleeping bag (though truck stops along the way provide beds for about ¥20) and plenty of warm, windproof clothing. The road is dusty and, in places, very rough; jeeps have made the run in two days, but trucks might take around six. You'll be travelling at over 5000m for most of the duration, with no chance of a speedy descent if you develop **altitude sickness**; bring something for headaches and as much water as you can carry. Meals are available at truck stops (about ¥15 a dish), but are basic and you'll appreciate some fruit and energy food. There will almost certainly be **police checkpoints** along the way, and if detected you may be arrested, fined, and sent back. It's best not to attempt the journey alone, as truck drivers have occasionally been known to rob Westerners. Don't pay more than half the fare money upfront, and take all your gear with you every time you have to leave the vehicle.

In Yecheng, you have several options for **finding transport**. There are separate Uigur, Tibetan and Chinese **truck depots** around town, where you'll also find **jeeps**. Getting a lift involves approaching drivers to see if they're willing to take you; make it clear to truck drivers you want to travel in the cab, not in the back (too exposed). Trucks will leave early, jeeps when they fill up. At the time of writing the going rate to Ali was around ¥400 per person; you may have to pay more in a jeep if it's not full. Alternatively, catch a **minibus** from Yecheng for about 80km down the Ali road to **Cengsa**, and from here hitch for a further 100km or so to **Kudi**, a favourite spot for Ali-bound trucks to pull up for meals and sleep. From here on, road conditions, the number of breakdowns, and for how long – or whether – your driver decides to sleep each night, will determine how long it takes to reach Ali.

lands you at **Yarkand**, a miniature version of Kashgar but with minimal tourist infrastructure. That said, the backstreets are possibly the closest you'll come in China to the Central Asia of a hundred years ago.

Yarkand and Yengisar

A strategically important staging post for at least the last thousand years, **YARKAND** (also known as **Shache**) is – now that Kashgar is becoming ever more developed and sanitized – possibly the best place to soak up the character of Muslim Xinjiang. The town centres on a crossroads, from where Xincheng Lu runs west through the Han-dominated part of town towards Kashgar, while Laocheng Lu runs east into the older, Uigur quarters. The best thing to do here is simply wander the northeastern backstreets, a warren of muddy lanes lined with willows and crowded by donkey carts, artisans' quarters, bazaars and traditional adobe homes with wooden-framed balconies. You'll find the town's major sights here too, close together on a road running north off Laocheng Lu: the **old fort**, and the **Aleytun mosque** and **Amannishahan tomb** (¥10), opposite – you'll see the fort's gates (just about all that is left) flanked by two narrow towers, well before you reach it. The mosque itself is off-limits to non-Muslims, but the tomb, built for the poet-wife of a sixteenth-century khan, is a beautiful white- and blue-tiled affair. The adjacent **cemetery** contains the mausoleums of several of Yarkand's former rulers, and is also crowded with more ordinary cylindrical Muslim tombs and truly ancient trees. Sunday would be the best time to visit Yarkand, when a huge, rustic **market** along the same lines as the more famous one in Kashgar is held in the main bazaar behind the fort – though this area is pretty good most days.

The **bus station**, with frequent departures through the day to Kashgar and Khotan, is south off Xincheng Lu. There's a **Bank of China** on the southeast side of the crossroads. The only **hotel** that accepts foreigners, the *Shache Binguan* (❹, dorm beds ¥40) is a ten-minute walk east along Xincheng Lu; it's a friendly place, but overpriced and with atrocious dorms. Uigur **restaurants** serving staples can be found north of the crossroads.

Some 120km further on up the Kashgar road, the town of **Yengisar** has for centuries been supplying the Uigur people with hand-crafted knives. Most of the knives on sale in Xinjiang these days are factory-made, but here at the **Yengisar County Small Knife Factory** a few craftsmen still ply their old skills, inlaying handles with horn or plastic. From here it's a mere 70km or so to Kashgar.

Kashgar

A large part of the excitement of **KASHGAR** lies in the experience of reaching it. Set on the western edge of the Chinese empire astride overland routes to Pakistan and Kyrgyzstan, Kashgar is fantastically remote from eastern China: as the crow flies, it's more than 4000km from Beijing, of which the thousand-plus kilometres from Ürümqi is for the most part sheer desert. As recently as the 1930s, the journey time to and from Beijing ran to a number of months. And yet Kashgar today, an oasis 1200m above sea level, is a remarkably prosperous and pleasant place, despite being, in part, an essentially medieval city.

Kashgar remains a visible bastion of old Chinese Turkestan, though gradually the more "authentic" parts of the town are being cleaned up as tourist attractions, and its residents moved to modern highrises on the city limits. Nonetheless, despite Han migration into the city, its population is still overwhelmingly Muslim, a fact you can hardly fail to notice with the great **Id Kah Mosque** dominating the central square, and the Uigur bazaars and teashops, the smell of grilled lamb and, above all, the faces of the Turkic people around you. If you can choose a time to be here, catch the Uigur Corban **festival** at the end of the Muslim month of Ramadan, and again, exactly two months later, which involves activities such as dancing and goat-tussling. And don't miss Kashgar's extraordinary **Sunday market**, for which half of Central Asia seems to converge on the city and which is as exotic to the average Han Chinese as to the foreign tourist.

Kashgar's **history** is dominated by its strategic position. There was already a Chinese miltary governor here when Xuanzang passed through on his way back from India in 644. The city was Buddhist at the time, with hundreds of monasteries; Islam made inroads around 1000 and eventually became the state religion. More recently, the late nineteenth century saw Kashgar at the meeting point of three empires – **Chinese**, **Soviet and British**. Both Britain and the Soviet Union maintained consulates in Kashgar until 1949: the British with

Kashgar		
Kashgar	喀什	***kāshí***
Hanoi ancient city	罕诺依古城	*hànnuòyī gǔchéng*
Id Kah Mosque	艾提尕尔清真寺	*àitígǎ'ěr qīngzhēnsì*
Id Kah Square	艾提尕尔广场	*àitígǎ'ěr guǎngchǎng*
Kashgar Silk Road Museum	喀什丝绸之路博物馆	*kāshí sīchóuzhīlù bówùguǎn*
Moor Pagodas	莫尔佛塔	*mò'ěr fótǎ*
Sunday Market	中西亚市场	*zhōngxīyà shìchǎng*
Tomb of Abakh Hoja	阿巴克和加墓	*ābākèhéjiā mù*
Tomb of Sayyid Ali Asla Khan	赛衣提艾里撕拉罕墓	*sàiyītíàilǐsīlāhàn mù*
Tomb of Yusup Hazi Hajup	哈撕哈吉南墓	*hāsīhā jínánmù*
Arrival and international destinations		
International bus station	国际汽车站	*guójì qìchēzhàn*
Bishkek	比什凯克	*bǐshí kǎikè*
Main bus station	客运站	*kèyùnzhàn*
Sust	苏撕特	*sūsī tè*
Accommodation, eating and drinking		
Kashgar	喀什宾馆	*kāshí bīnguǎn*
Laoding Sushi	老鼎速食	*lǎodǐng sùshí*
Nanlin Fandian	南林饭店	*nánlín fàndiàn*
Qiniwak	其尼巴合宾馆	*qíníbāhé bīnguǎn*
Seman	色满宾馆	*sèmǎn bīnguǎn*
Tiannan	天南饭店	*tiānnán fàndiàn*
Tuman River	吐蔓河大饭店	*tùmànhé dàfàndiàn*

an eye to their interests across the frontier in India, the Soviets (so everyone assumed) with the long-term intention of absorbing Xinjiang into their Central Asian orbit. The conspiracies of this period are brilliantly evoked in Peter Fleming's *News from Tartary* and Ella Maillart's *Forbidden Journey*. At the time of Fleming's visit, in 1935, the city was in effect run by the Soviets, who had brought their rail line to within two days of Kashgar. During World War II, however, Kashgar swung back under Chinese control, and with the break in Sino–Soviet relations in the early 1960s, the Soviet border (and influence) firmly closed. In the wake of the break-up of the Soviet Union, however, it seemed that Kashgar would resume its status as one of the great travel cross-roads of Asia, but this recovery sadly stalled after the events of September 11, 2001, and the ensuing conflict in Afghanistan. The town is still experiencing something of a downturn, with neither traders nor tourists as plentiful as they once were.

Orientation, arrival and accommodation

It's helpful to think of Kashgar as centred on a large cross, with a principal north–south axis, Jiefang Bei Lu and Jiefang Nan Lu, and an east–west axis, Renmin Dong Lu and Renmin Xi Lu. North of Renmin Lu lies the core of the **old town**, containing much of the accommodation, the Id Kah Mosque, former consulates, and interesting streets; south of Renmin Lu the prevailing cityscape is modern Chinese, with grey-fronted department stores and overly wide roads.

The **train station** is 7km east of town, where bus #28 to Jiefang Bei Lu, minibuses and taxis await new arrivals. Just east of centre on Tiannan Lu is the main **long-distance bus station**, handling connections from most parts of Xinjiang, including Ürümqi, Kuqa, Korla, Yarkand and Khotan. The **international bus station**, about 1500m north up Jiefang Bei Lu and just over the river beside the *Tuman River* hotel, is terminus for luxury buses from Ürümqi, as well as all traffic from Tashkurgan, Sust in Pakistan, and Bishkek in Kyrgyzstan – bus #2 runs down Jiefang Bei Lu from here. Kashgar's **airport** is to the north of town; the airport bus (¥4) drives straight down Jiefang Lu to the CAAC office.

Accommodation

There are some pleasant, inexpensive hotels in Kashgar, catering to Pakistani traders from over the Karakoram Highway and foreign tourists.

Kashgar ⓣ0998/2614954. Well out of town, 3 or 4km east of the centre and in a nice location surrounded by woods, but rather faded and neglected. Access is by bus #10, which runs along Renmin Lu and stops right outside the hotel. ❸

Qiniwak (aka Chini Bagh) ⓣ0998/2822291, ⓕ2823842. Formerly one of the best hotels in town, and the site of the former British Consulate, this was being completely refurbished at the time of writing. If you're arriving on the airport bus, the

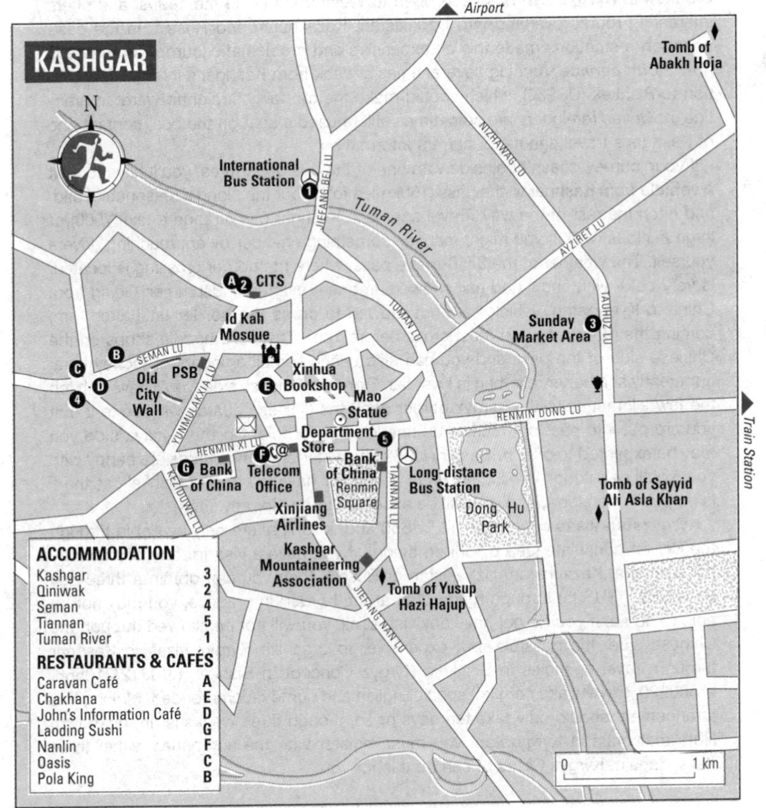

Moving on from Kashgar

There's just one daily **flight** to Ürümqi only, so book well ahead in peak season. Three **trains** leave daily, one of which terminates at Korla (where you can pick up buses to Turpan) while the other two continue to Ürümqi; if you can't handle the train station queues, buy tickets through a travel agent.

Buses from the **main bus station** head eastwards, though taking one along the Northern Silk Road via Kuqa to Korla and Ürümqi doesn't make much sense given the availability of the train. For the Southern Silk Road, there's ample traffic through the day as far as Yarkand (¥25), and less frequently to Khotan, Minfeng, and Qiemo. The bus station ticket office is computerized and pretty helpful.

The **international bus station** is where to head for all westbound traffic, via Karakul (¥43) and Tashkurgan (¥63), through the Khunjerab Pass (see p.1109) to **Sust in Pakistan** (¥270). Note that the border is open only from May until October. The other option is to travel due north over the Torugut Pass to **Bishkek**, the capital of **Kyrgyzstan**. Note that you're charged **excess baggage** rates for every kilo over 20kg on international buses, and should get the latest information about **visas** before travelling to either Pakistan or Kyrgyzstan, as they are not reliably available either in Kashgar or at the borders.

The road to Kyrgyzstan: the Torugut Pass

The 720-kilometre-long road due north from Kashgar via the Torugut Pass to **Bishkek** in **Kyrgyzstan** has been open to Westerners since the 1990s, and offers interesting routes overland into Uzbekistan, Kazakhstan and Russia. In the past, transport restrictions made this an expensive and problematic journey, but there is now a **bus service**, running several times a week from Kashgar's international station to Bishkek (US$50), which should make the trip fairly straightforward. In practice, however, foreigners are sometimes still refused a seat on the bus; contact one of Kashgar's travel agents for current information.

If your journey doesn't coincide with one of the bus departures, you'll have to **rent a vehicle** from Kashgar to the pass (160km), a four-hour trip along a reasonable road, and hitch the rest of the way. Travel agents in Kashgar can arrange a taxi (¥500) or large minibus (¥800); you might manage something cheaper by approaching drivers yourself. The weather at the 3750-metre pass, where the border crossing is located, is very cold, with snow and hail showers frequent even in midsummer. Going from China to Kyrgyzstan, vehicles are not allowed to **cross the border** until after 1pm; coming the other way, you must cross before 1pm. There are noodle shops on the Chinese side of the pass and you can also change small amounts of money here, apparently at a better rate than in Kashgar. From the Chinese side, you'll have to hitch the few kilometres to the Kyrgyz border post; the Chinese guards will see to it that you are put into passing trucks. You needn't pay for this. **On the Kyrgyz side** you may be expected to offer **bribes** (try US$20 as a starter); if the guards are happy with you, you'll be through in minutes. From here you'll have to **hitch** to Bishkek, as there is no public transport, and you will be expected to pay for any lifts.

Kyrgyzstan visas currently cost $US50 and, in China, are only available through the Beijing consulate (see p.136). In theory, if you have a visa for any CIS country (for example, Kazakhstan, Uzbekistan or Russia) then you can obtain a three-day transit visa ($US25) through Kyrgyzstan at the border; in practice, you may not be able to do so. If you do not have any visa at all, you will not be allowed through the Chinese side. It's possible, but expensive, to organize Kyrgyz visas in Kashgar through travel agencies in Bishkek; Kyrgyz Concept in Bishkek (ⓣ0312/210556, ⓕ660220, ⓦwww.akc.com.kg) speak English and come recommended. Making this arrangement should only take ten days or so, though three weeks is not unknown. Note that once in Kyrgyzstan, you must register with the authorities within three days – again, Kyrgyz Concept can do this for you.

driver can drop you on Jiefang Lu, a few minutes' walk east of the hotel. Dorms and budget doubles of various sizes with bath were previously available, along with more modern doubles. Dorms ¥20, ❸–❼

Seman Seman Lu ⓣ0998/2822129. The most popular place among budget travellers, with the proximity of a number of English-menu restaurants a big attraction. It's a huge, rambling old complex located in the west of the city, with the former Russian Consulate out the back. The three-bed dorms are excellent, especially on the top floors, as the rooms are old conservatories, with windows stretching the length of one wall. Also has tidy budget and mid-range doubles, both with bathrooms. Dorm beds ¥20, ❷–❸

Tiannan ⓣ0998/2824023. Opposite the long-distance bus station off Tiannan Lu, this is an eccentric place, with high, wood-panelled walls, recently renovated to mid-range status. ❸

Tuman River Right beside the international bus station ⓣ0998/2822912. A reasonable-value option popular with traders, though in a noisy area. Bus #2 from Renmin Square, near the Bank of China, passes by. Dorm beds ¥30, ❸

The City

There are one or two monuments of note in Kashgar, but the main attractions of this city are the ordinary streets of the old town – principally the bazaars, the restaurants, the teahouses and the people in them. Roads radiate out from the centre of the original Uigur city, which is focused on **Id Kah Square**, with its clock tower and huge mosque. A few hundred metres to the south is the modern, commercial centre of the city, at the junction between Jiefang (Bei and Nan) Lu and Renmin (Xi and Dong) Lu. The main post-liberation monument of Kashgar – the absurdly colossal **statue of Mao Zedong** hailing a taxi on Renmin Dong Lu, a towering reminder of the ultimate authority of China over the region – is just to the east of here, opposite the bald stone expanse that is Renmin Square. Finally, scattered around the fringes of the city are a number of **mausoleums** to Uigur heroes of the past, best reached by bus or bicycle.

Kashgar's Sunday Market

The mother of all bazaars takes place on a Sunday, in a huge area to the east of town. Known in Chinese as the **Zhongxiya Shichang** (Western–Central Asia Market) or, in Uigur, as the **Yekshenba Bazaar** (Sunday Bazaar), this attracts up to one hundred thousand villagers and nomads, all riding their donkey carts from the surrounding area into the city. For the sheer scale of the occasion, it's the number one sight in Kashgar, if not all Xinjiang. Considering the large numbers of minority peoples who come to trade here, all sporting their own particular headwear, it is also an anthropologist's delight. Traffic jams of thousands of donkey carts compete with horsemen and herds of sheep for space in the chaotic dusty alleys. At the animal market, horses are test-driven, sheep are picked over and cattle are paraded before potential buyers. Animals, knives, hats, pots, carpets and pans, fresh fruit and vegetables, clothes and boots and every kind of domestic and agricultural appliance – often handmade in wood and tin – are all on sale. Some produce, such as Iranian saffron – at ¥10 a gram, over three times as valuable as gold – has come a long way to be sold here. The market goes on all day and into the early evening, and food and drink are widely available on and around the site.

The market is a thirty-minute walk northeast from the town centre, crossing the minor Tuman River on the way. Otherwise, take a donkey cart for a few yuan. If you cycle you will need to find a cycle parking lot well before you reach the confines of the market itself.

Id Kah Square and around

The main historical sight in central Kashgar is the **Id Kah Mosque**, occupying the western side of Id Kah Square, off Jiefang Bei Lu. Originally built in 1442, it has been restored many times, most recently after the Cultural Revolution. It is one of the biggest mosques, and almost certainly the most active, in the country; you can even hear the call to prayer booming around the city centre – a rare sound in China. Although visitors are theoretically allowed in (there is a small entrance fee), Western tourists are often shooed away by zealous worshippers. On Fridays, the main Muslim prayer day, some ten thousand people crowd out the mosque and square; the quietest time, when your presence will cause least disturbance, is probably early to mid-morning of any other day. Inside are pleasant courtyards and tree-lined gardens where the worshippers assemble. Note that visitors of either sex should have their arms and legs fully covered when entering this (or any other) mosque.

The main Uigur bazaars are in the neighbouring streets, but while you're in the area, keep an eye open for a couple of substantial fragments of Kashgar's **old city walls**, most easily viewed south of Seman Lu and west off Yunmulakxia Lu. And don't miss out on the **old consulates** either: the British had theirs behind the *Qiniwak* hotel, which, like the hotel, was being given a major facelift at the time of writing; the Russian headquarters survive as a nicely preserved period piece in the courtyard behind the *Seman* hotel.

The bazaars

The street heading northeast from Id Kah Square is the main **carpet** area. The best carpets of the region are made in Khotan (see p.1095), but some good bargains are to be had in the Kashgar bazaars. You should be able to get a nice felt of rolled coloured wool (1.5m x 2.5m) for less than ¥300. A brightly dyed hand-knotted carpet, approximately 2m x 3m, should cost around ¥800. The carpets are relatively rough in quality and have geometric designs only, but the prices are about a third of the equivalent in Turkey. Kashgar **kilims**, produced by nomads, are highly sought after and almost impossible to find locally. You can watch people making carpets (and musical instruments) at the Handicrafts Centre 200m north of Id Kah Square on Jiefang Lu.

The small road leading south from the carpet bazaar (due east of Id Kah Square and parallel to Jiefang Lu) is the big area for Central Asian **hats**. As well as the green and white square-shaped variety, so beloved by Uigur old men, there are prayer caps, skullcaps, furry winter hats and plain workmen's caps. Following this lane south you pass the main bazaar, where all kinds of blacksmiths and carpenters are hard at work in front of their shops, and enter a world of mud-brick walls and pony carts. Items you might come across while exploring the bazaars include **knives** with decorative handles, produced in the nearby city of Yengisar, and **chests** overlaid with brightly coloured tin, purpose-built for carrying special gifts for brides-to-be (insurance against the possible loss of the husband in later years). Locally produced **musical instruments** are also of interest, particularly stringed instruments of inlaid wood, with long slender necks and round bowls. The two-stringed *dutah* is the most common. The *tanber* has an even longer stem and a round bowl shaped like half a gourd, while the *rawupu* has five strings and a snakeskin drum.

To the north of Id Kah Square is a covered **cloth market**, which also includes some of the wildest **Uigur restaurants** – huge wood fires burning, vats bubbling and TV sets blaring. In the southern part of the square is the Kashgar **night market**, while to the west – the two roads to the north and south of the Id Kah Mosque – are the bulk of the **Uigur teahouses** and small eating establishments.

About a hundred metres down the road leading south from the mosque, on the left-hand side, is the **Chakhana** (teahouse). With its upstairs veranda, rickety wooden beams, grimy plaster reliefs on the walls and old men in baggy, oily coats, this place is a fascinating glimpse into the Central Asia of another era.

The outskirts

The historic architecture remaining in Kashgar today chiefly comprises a number of mausoleums to famous Uigur personages. The most central of these is the **Tomb of Yusup Hazi Hajup** (daily 8am–5pm; ¥10), the eleventh-century Uigur poet and philosopher. It's about 1500m south of Renmin Lu, on Tiyu Lu, a small road located between Jiefang Nan Lu and Tiannan Lu – bus #8 down Jiefang Lu comes within striking distance. The mausoleum, of handsome blue and white wall tiles, was reconstructed in 1989, though with slightly shoddy workmanship – it's worth dropping by if you are in the vicinity.

To the east of the city lies the **Tomb of Sayyid Ali Asla Khan** (¥5). Bus #3 from Renmin Lu passes it, or you can cycle: follow Renmin Lu east, past Dong Hu (East Lake). The lake is a fairly standard Chinese arrangement, with bridges, islands, walkways and pleasure boats. A few hundred metres after the lake, take the main road right and, after about a kilometre, you'll see a mosque entrance on your right, amid trees. The mausoleum is a rather sad, neglected little construction behind the mosque. More interesting than the mausoleum itself is the graveyard around it, a huge area of mud-built, domed constructions with tiny dark entrances.

While you're out this way, the **Kashgar Silk Road Museum** (irregular hours; ¥6), on the #10 bus route from Renmin Lu, is worth a visit to see an iron-age **mummy** recovered from the desert hereabouts, still dressed in felt hat and fur-lined jacket, woollen trousers, leather boots, and a belt with herbs and a knife attached. (Another Silk Road tomb, this time from the eighth century, yielded mummified *jiaozi*, though these are not on display, sadly.) There are also examples of various ancient **scripts** found at Silk Road sites, including Indian-derived Kharosthi, along with the usual run of pottery, wooden and metal artefacts, some going back to 1000 BC.

The most impressive of all Kashgar's tombs is the **Tomb of Abakh Hoja** (daily 8am–5.30pm; ¥8), 8km northeast of the centre on bus #20 from Renmin Square, or forty minutes by bike through wheat fields and poplar woods. From downtown, head past the Sunday Market site and the turning for the mausoleum is signposted in English after a few kilometres. The mausoleum itself is a large mosque-like building of blue and white tiles with a green dome and tiled minarets. Built in the seventeenth century, it was the resting place for a large number of people – the most famous being Abakh Hoja and his granddaughter Ikparhan, who is known in Chinese as **Xiang Fei**, "Fragrant Concubine". Having led the Uigurs in revolt against Beijing, she was subsequently seized and married to the Qing emperor Qian Long, later being ordered to commit suicide by the emperor's jealous mother. In both commemorating a local heroine and stirring anti-Qing propaganda in the cruelty she suffered, the story serves the convenient dual purpose of pleasing both the Uigurs and the Han Chinese.

Outside Kashgar and accessible only by car are the **Moor Pagodas** at the **ancient city of Hanoi** on a rough road about 30km east of the city. The pagodas have been worn down to rough stumps about a dozen metres high, but the remains of the ruined Tang city-walls of Hanoi make quite a dramatic scene in what is a virtual desert. To reach this place, you'll need to rent a car from a travel service, or deal directly with a taxi yourself – try for ¥60 return.

Eating and drinking

Kashgar has plentiful **places to eat** for all budgets. Westerners tend to gravitate towards the foreigner-friendly restaurants on the roundabout outside the *Seman* hotel; the branch of *John's Information Café* here (see p.1075) offers their usual Sino-Western fare and beer, but is more expensive than the perfectly decent canteens opposite – the *Oasis* is recommended. A few shops east of the roundabout on Seman Lu, look for a handmade sign for *Pola King*, a tiny place with good, cheap breakfasts of tea or coffee with bagels, honey and fresh yoghurt. Similar food to *John's* (and a slightly better atmosphere) is also available at the *Caravan Café*, outside the *Qiniwak* hotel.

The best place to pick up **Uigur food** is around Id Kah Square. Street vendors sell pilau, kebabs, cold spicy noodles, *kao bao* and *jiaozi*. *Laghman* is available almost everywhere. Other street food worth sampling is the vanilla ice cream, mixed up on the spot in containers encased in lumps of ice, which is delicious if not obviously hygienic. In the filthy but picturesque *Chakhana*, southwest of the Id Kah Mosque, a plate of *laghman* costs only ¥3. For the same but without the atmosphere, try *Laoding Sushi*, a clean canteen on the corner of Renmin Xi Lu and Keziduwei Lu, selling huge bowls of beef noodle soup, along with buns, *laghman* and kebabs. For **Chinese food**, *Nanlin Fandian* is an upmarket hotpot restaurant on Renmin Xi Lu; and the lane parallel to this and behind the Bank of China is thick with stalls offering one-person casseroles, *shuijiao* and hotpots. There's also a group of Chinese places at the top of Jiefang Nan Lu, on the west side, just south of Renmin Lu. You can get a really good dinner here, with beer, for less than ¥30, though the menus are all in Chinese.

A good place to go **drinking** is at the outdoor seating area at the north end of Jiefang Nan Lu, which is usually open until the small hours. The waitresses bring you beer and nibbles, including such staples as chickens' feet.

Listings

Airline Xinjiang Airlines, 106 Jiefang Nan Lu (Mon–Fri 9.30am–8pm, Sat & Sun 10am–7.30pm; ⓣ0998/2826188).

Banks and exchange Both branches of the Bank of China, on the western side of Renmin Square and at Renmin Xi Lu (Mon–Sat 9.30am–1.30pm & 4–7pm, Sun 11am–3pm), can change foreign currency. You may have to show proof of purchase for cashing traveller's cheques.

Bike rental Bicycles can be rented from *John's Café*, *Caravan Café* and a stall at the front gate of the *Qiniwak* – all charge ¥20 per day.

Bookshops Xinhua Bookshop is at 32 Jiefang Bei Lu, on the east side of the road and just north of the intersection with Renmin Lu.

Internet access The foreigners' cafés have Internet connections, but they tend to be more expensive than the wonderfully named "Shining Pearl of the Silk Road Net Bar" (daily 10.30am–10pm; ¥8/hr), in the Telecom building on Renmin Xi Lu.

Mail The post office is at 40 Renmin Xi Lu, a short walk west of Jiefang Lu (Mon–Sat 9.30am–7.30pm).

PSB On Yunmulakexia Lu, a few minutes' walk southwest of the *Qiniwak Hotel* (10.30am–7.30pm).

Telephones Direct dial long-distance calls can be made from an office opposite the post office on Renmin Xi Lu, or from the new wing of the *Qiniwak Hotel*. Both charge by the minute.

Travel agents While there's not much in the way of day-trips around Kashgar, agents are useful for organizing train tickets (at a ¥30 commission) and longer back-road excursions, and should have the latest advice on international routes out from town. CITS have branches in front of the *Qiniwak* (ⓣ0998/2832875) and behind the *Seman* (ⓣ0998/2550130); staff at both are friendly and speak English. Independent budget travellers will be better served by the *Caravan Café* outside the *Qiniwak* (ⓔcaravan_cafe@yahoo.com), an excellent place run by Uigur-speaking expats; or *John's Café* (ⓔjohncafe@hotmail.com). A freelance operator named Elvis Ablimit (ⓔElvisablimit@yahoo.com) comes highly recommended for guided camel safaris into the Taklamakan. There's also the Kashgar

Mountaineering Association (Ⓣ0998/2523660, Ⓕ2522957, Ⓔkeyou-ks@mail.xj.cninfo.net), just across from the Yusup Hazi Hajup tomb on Jiefang Nan Lu. They're a helpful, English-speaking bunch who can arrange rafting expeditions down the Mazar river, hiking trips through the relatively low Kunlun ranges, camel treks into the Taklamakan and, of course, climbing in the Pamirs near the Pakistan border. Ask here too about trips to Shipton's Arch, the largest natural rock arch in the world and believed to have been climbed for the first time as recently as 1999.

The Karakoram Highway

For centuries the **Khunjerab Pass**, lying some 400km south of Kashgar, was the key Silk Road crossing point between the Chinese world and the Indian subcontinent – and thence to the whole of the Western world. Today the 4700-metre pass still marks the frontier between China and **Pakistan**, but, while crossing the mountains used to be a highly perilous journey undertaken on horse, camel or foot, modern engineering has blasted a highway right through the pass, opening the route to a seasonal stream of trucks and buses. The entire 1300-kilometre route from Kashgar over the mountains to Rawalpindi in northern Pakistan is known as the **Karakoram Highway**. The highway was formally opened in 1982, and foreign tourists have been travelling through in both directions since 1986. The trip is still not without its perils, but it's hard to think of a more exciting route into or out of China. If the highway is closed for any reason, note that you can also **fly** twice weekly direct from Ürümqi to Islamabad (¥2270).

En route from Kashgar, travellers have to spend a night in **Tashkurgan** on the Chinese side, before crossing over the pass to the Pakistani town of **Sust**. There is also the option of camping out for a night or two by the wintry but beautiful **Lake Karakul**, in the lee of glaciers. The road over the pass is open from the beginning of May until the end of October each year, though it can close without notice when the weather is bad, for days at a time, even in summer. The journey from Kashgar to Rawalpindi/Islamabad, or vice versa, takes a minimum of four days if there are no hold-ups. Most travellers need a **visa to enter Pakistan**; in China, the three-month tourist visas for US$45, valid from the date of issue, are available only in Beijing or Hong Kong.

Lake Karakul

Southwest of Kashgar, the road soon leaves the valley, with its mud-brick buildings and irrigated wheat and rice plantations, behind. Climbing through river gorges strewn with giant boulders, it creeps into a land of treeless, bare dunes of sand and gravel, interspersed with pastures scattered with grazing yaks and camels. The sudden appearence of **Lake Karakul** by the roadside, some 200km out of Kashgar, is dramatic. Right under the feet of the Pamir Mountains and the magnificent 7546-metre Mount Muztagata, whose vast snowy flanks have been split open by colossal glaciers, the waters of the lake are a luminous blue.

The Karakoram Highway

Karakoram Highway	喀拉昆仑	***kālā kūnlún***
Khunjerab Pass	红其拉南达坡	*hóngqílā nándápō*
Lake Karakul	喀拉湖	*kālā hú*
Tashkurgan	塔什库尔干	***tǎshí kùěrgàn***

The opportunities for **hiking** over the surrounding green pasture are virtually limitless, especially if you are equipped with a tent and warm clothing; at 3800m, the weather can be extremely cold even in summer, with snow showers normal well into June. It's possible to walk round the lake in a day, in which case you will almost certainly encounter some friendly Kyrgyz yurt-dwellers on the way – you may well be able to stay with them if you can communicate your meaning (not easy). Otherwise, if you are without your own tent, you can stay at a rather muddy and not particularly enticing tour-group yurt site just off the road, with its own restaurant and local attendants. This costs about ¥60 per head, on the basis of two people in a yurt, plus a rather steep ¥70 per person per day for all meals. The food is good and the local people are friendly. There are very rudimentary washing and toilet facilities, and fresh drinking water is available.

Transport to the lake is simple. From the Kashgar international bus station there is at least one daily **bus**, leaving at 8.30 am. From Tashkurgan you can take the Kashgar bus and get off at the lake. Leaving the lake requires slightly more ingenuity – for either direction you will need to flag down the passing buses, which may involve standing assertively in the middle of the road. Check approximate expected times of buses with the locals at the lake. For travellers heading to Pakistan, it is perfectly feasible to travel to Tashkurgan via the lake, and then book yourself onto a bus to Sust from Tashkurgan (contrary to what you may be told in Kashgar).

Tashkurgan

The last town before the border, **TASHKURGAN**, lies 280km southeast of Kashgar, and about 220km north of the Pakistani town of Sust. Its primary importance for travellers is as a staging post between Kashgar and Sust, and all travellers passing through, in either direction, must stay the night here. It's a tiny place, comprising a couple of tree-lined streets, with the bus station and two budget hotels at the western end. Chinese customs and immigration are located a few minutes round the corner from the bus station.

The town boasts a long history as well as fantastic mountain scenery. The Chinese Buddhist pilgrim and Silk Road traveller **Xuanzang** stopped over here in the seventh century, a time when, as now, it was the last outpost of Chinese rule. Today, Tashkurgan has a peculiar atmosphere. The native population is mainly Tadjik, but there are also groups of melancholy Han Chinese, thousands of miles from home, as well as intrepid Pakistanis setting up shop outside their country – plus, incredibly, a minor entertainment industry involving sex and alcohol for Pakistani tourists. Few travellers bother to stop for a day, but you could pleasantly rest up here for 24 hours. Worth a look, especially at sunset, is a brown, crumbling, mud-brick **fort**, at least 600 years old, still standing on the only hill for miles around at the edge of town. To reach it, walk east from the bus station right to the end of town, then strike off a few hundred metres to the left.

Practicalities

At the **bus station**, the *Jiaotong* (Ⓣ0998/3421192; ❶) is a pretty rudimentary **place to stay** but not too bad, though you're better off at the Pakistani-managed *Ice Mountain* (❶–❷). As you exit the bus station, turn right and walk a hundred metres to the east; it's across the road. The *Pamir* at the other end of town is slightly more upmarket (Ⓣ0998/3421025; ❶–❷), with high ceilings and eclectic decor. Rooms here are the only ones in town to have hot water, available both morning and evening.

The plentiful **beer** in Tashkurgan often comes as a relief to travellers arriving from Pakistan. For **food**, your best bet is to try one of the Chinese restaurants a couple of hundred metres east of the bus station. For delicious bread – excellent for breakfast and bus journeys – try the bakery opposite the *Ice Mountain*.

The **bank**, **post office** and **PSB office** are all at the west end of town. The immigration point also has a couple of banks where cash (and sometimes traveller's cheques) can be changed at official exchange rates. If arriving from Pakistan, you can easily change your rupees with the locally resident Pakistanis if the banks are closed.

The **entry and exit formalities** for Western tourists are straightforward to the point of being lax. You may or may not be issued with Currency and Valuables Declaration forms – but nobody seems to care what you put on them. If your bus arrives late in the evening, your passports are collected in and formalities take place the next morning. Onward connections, in both directions, will wait until everyone is through customs, so there is no need to worry about being left behind.

Travellers heading to Pakistan do not need to buy onward bus tickets – the ticket from Kashgar covers the whole route right through to Sust. Coming from Pakistan, however, you'll find that the only onward transport is the bus to Kashgar (¥70). Buying your ticket requires standing in a long and heated queue, but don't worry – sufficient transport will be laid on for however many people need it. Whichever way you're heading, note that **cyclists** are not allowed to ride their bikes through the pass, but have to bus it between Tashkurgan and Sust. If you plan to get off at Lake Karakul (see p.1107) en route to Kashgar, you may be asked to pay the full Kashgar fare anyway. The alternative to catching buses is to **hitch a ride** on a truck. These often cruise around town in the evening looking for prospective customers to Kashgar (or Karakul) for the day after. You'll pay, but it will be cheaper than travelling by bus.

The Khunjerab Pass

Khunjerab means "River of Blood" in the local Tadjik language – which may refer to the rusty colour of local rivers, or to the long traditions of banditry in these areas. The trip across the border at the **Khunjerab Pass** is not a totally risk-free affair, even today. You should be aware that if your bus departs in rainy weather, you can almost certainly expect rock slides – and people are killed almost every year by falling rocks on the Karakoram Highway.

From Tashkurgan, the road climbs into a vast, bright plain, grazed by yaks and camels, with the mountains, clad in snow mantles hundreds of metres thick, pressing in all around. Emerging onto the **top of the pass**, you're greeted by a clear, silent, wind-swept space of frozen streams, protruding glaciers and glimpses of green pasture under the sunshine. The only creatures that live here are the ginger, chubby Himalayan marmots, a kind of large squirrel or woodchuck, existing, so it's said, off a diet of snow and desert – it's easy to spot them from the bus. At these heights (the pass lies at some 4800m) a lot of travellers experience some form of **altitude sickness**, though most people simply riding up and over the pass will feel little more than a faintly feverish or nauseous sensation.

The journey time between Tashkurgan and the small town of **Sust**, where Pakistani customs and immigration take place, takes about seven hours. Travellers in both directions again have to spend a night here, and plentiful accommodation is available. From Sust there are direct daily buses to Gilgit, from where frequent buses cover the sixteen-hour route to **Rawalpindi** and **Islamabad**.

Travel details

Trains

Baotou to: Beijing (6 daily; 15hr); Hohhot (8 daily; 3hr); Lanzhou (2 daily; 19hr); Shanghai (1 daily; 43hr; Xi'an (3 daily; 27hr)); Yinchuan (3 daily; 9hr).
Daheyan (for Turpan) to: Hami (12 daily; 5–6hr); Jiayuguan (11 daily; 12–17hr); Korla (4 daily; 8hr); Lanzhou (5 daily; 20–28hr); Liuyuan (11 daily; 8–12hr); Tianshui (9 daily; 28hr); Ürümqi (11 daily; 2–3hr); Wuwei (6 daily; 17–23hr); Zhangye (11 daily; 14–16hr).
Golmud to: Xining (3 daily; 16–22hr).
Guyuan to: Lanzhou (3 daily, 10hr); Yinchuan (3 daily; 6hr); Zhongwei (4 daily; 4hr).
Hami to: Daheyan (12 daily; 5–6hr); Lanzhou (10 daily; 18–23hr); Ürümqi (11daily; 7–8hr).
Hohhot to: Baotou (8 daily; 3hr); Beijing (6 daily; 12hr); Erlianhot (1 daily; 12hr); Hailar (1 daily; 60hr); Shanghai (1 daily; 40hr); Ulan Batur (1 daily; 30hr); Xi'an (3 daily; 24hr).
Jiayuguan to: Daheyan (11 daily; 12–17hr); Lanzhou (10 daily; 11–13hr); Liuyuan (10 daily; 4hr); Tianshui (9 daily; 16hr); Ürümqi (10 daily; 14–16hr); Wuwei (6 daily; 5–7hr); Zhangye (11 daily; 2hr 30min–3hr).
Kashgar to: Korla (3 daily; 13–17hr); Kuqa (3 daily; 9–11hr); Ürümqi (2 daily; 24hr).
Korla to: Daheyan (4 daily; 8hr); Kashgar (3 daily; 13–17hr); Kuqa (3 daily; 3hr 30min–5hr); Ürümqi (3 daily; 10–11hr).
Lanzhou to: Baotou (2 daily; 15hr); Beijing (5 daily; 24hr); Chengdu (2 daily; 24hr); Daheyan (5 daily; 20–28hr); Guangzhou (1 daily; 42hr); Guyuan (3 daily, 10hr); Hami (10 daily; 18–23hr); Hohhot (2 daily; 18hr); Jiayuguan (10 daily; 11–13hr); Liuyuan (10 daily; 13–18hr); Shanghai (2 daily; 28hr); Tianshui (13 daily; 6hr); Ürümqi (9 daily; 25hr); Wuwei (10 daily; 5hr); Xi'an (9 daily; 13–15hr); Xining (4 daily; 3hr); Yinchuan (3 daily; 8hr); Zhangye (10 daily; 8–10hr); Zhongwei (6 daily; 6hr).
Liuyuan (for Dunhuang) to: Beijing (1 daily; 37hr); Daheyan (11 daily; 8–12hr); Jiayuguan (10 daily; 4hr); Lanzhou (10 daily; 13–18hr); Tianshui (10 daily; 19hr); Ürümqi (9 daily; 12hr); Wuwei (9 daily; 8hr 30min); Zhangye (9 daily; 5hr 30min).
Tianshui to: Daheyan (9 daily; 28hr); Jiayuguan (9 daily; 16hr); Lanzhou (13 daily; 6hr); Liuyuan (10 daily; 19hr); Ürümqi (10 daily; 31hr); Wuwei (7 daily; 12hr); Zhangye (9 daily; 14hr).
Ürümqi to: Almaty, Kazakhstan (2 daily; 36hr); Beijing (1 daily; 48hr); Chengdu (1 daily; 54hr); Daheyan (11 daily; 2–3hr); Hami (11daily; 7–8hr); Jiayuguan (10 daily; 14–16hr); Kashgar (2 daily; 24hr); Korla (3 daily; 10–11hr); Lanzhou (9 daily; 25hr); Liuyuan (9 daily; 12hr); Shanghai (1 daily; 51hr); Tianshui (10 daily; 31hr); Xi'an (1 daily; 53hr); Wuwei (10 daily; 19hr); Zhangye (10 daily; 16hr).
Wuwei to: Daheyan (6 daily; 17–23hr); Jiayuguan (6 daily; 5–7hr); Lanzhou (10 daily; 5hr); Liuyuan (9 daily; 8hr 30min); Tianshui (7 daily; 12hr); Ürümqi (10 daily; 19hr); Zhangye (11 daily; 3hr); Zhongwei (1 daily; 5hr 30min).
Xining to: Beijing (1 daily; 36hr); Golmud (3 daily; 16–22hr); Lanzhou (4 daily; 3hr); Shanghai (1 daily; 32hr); Xi'an (1 daily; 15hr).
Yinchuan to: Baotou (3 daily; 9hr); Beijing (3 daily; 22hr); Guyuan (3 daily; 6hr); Hohhot (3 daily; 11hr); Lanzhou (3 daily; 8hr); Xi'an (4 daily; 20hr); Zhongwei (3 daily; 2–3hr).
Zhangye to: Daheyan (11 daily; 14–16hr); Jiayuguan (11 daily; 2hr 30min–3hr); Lanzhou (10 daily; 8–10hr); Liuyuan (9 daily; 5hr 30min); Tianshui (9 daily; 14hr); Ürümqi (10 daily; 16hr); Wuwei (11 daily; 3hr); Xi'an (1 daily; 28hr).
Zhongwei to: Baotou (3 daily; 11hr); Guyuan (4 daily; 4hr); Hohhot (3 daily; 14hr); Lanzhou (6 daily; 6hr); Shapotou (3 daily; 1hr); Wuwei (1 daily; 5hr 30min); Yinchuan (3 daily; 2–3hr).

Buses

Baotou (Donghe) to: Beijing (1 daily; 17hr); Dongsheng (every 30min; 3hr); Hohhot (every 30min; 3hr).
Dongsheng to: Baotou (every 30min; 3hr); Hohhot (8 daily; 5hr); Yulin (daily; 6hr).
Dunhuang to: Golmud (15hr); Hami (6hr 30min); Jiayuguan (5hr); Lanzhou (24hr); Liuyuan (2hr 30min); Wuwei (18hr); Zhangye (13hr).
Golmud to: Dunhuang (15hr); Lhasa (36hr); Xining (16hr).
Guyuan to: Lanzhou (7hr); Luoyang (16hr); Pingliang (2hr); Sanying (1hr); Tianshui (10hr); Xi'an (10hr); Yinchuan (7hr); Zhongwei (6hr).
Hailar to: Beijing (3 weekly; 2hr 30min); Hohhot (2 weekly; 2hr 30min).
Hami to: Dunhuang (6hr 30min); Turpan (8hr); Ürümqi (11hr).
Hohhot to: Baotou (every 30min; 3hr); Beijing (2 daily; 14hr); Dongsheng (3 daily; 5hr); Erlianhot (8hr); Xilinhot (daily; 12hr); Zhaohe (2 daily; 3hr).
Jiayuguan to: Dunhuang (5hr); Lanzhou (16hr); Wuwei (12hr); Zhangye (5hr).

Kashgar to: Khotan (11hr); Korla (30hr); Kuqa (20hr); Lake Karakul (6hr); Sust (36hr); Tashkurgan (8hr); Ürümqi (35hr); Yarkand (2hr 30min); Yecheng (4hr); Yining (40hr).
Khotan to: Kashgar (11hr); Korla (17hr); Minfeng (6hr); Qiemo (12hr); Ürümqi (22hr); Yarkand (9hr).
Korla to: Kashgar (30hr); Khotan (17hr); Kuqa (12hr); Turpan (10hr); Ürumqi (5hr).
Kuqa to: Kashgar (20hr); Korla (12hr); Turpan (20hr); Ürümqi (17hr); Yining (24hr).
Lanzhou to: Dunhuang (24hr); Guyuan (7hr); Hezuo (8hr); Jiayuguan (16hr); Linxia (3hr); Tianshui (8hr); Ürümqi (44hr); Wuwei (5hr); Xiahe (8hr); Xi'an (16hr); Xining (5hr); Yinchuan (14hr); Zhangye (11hr).
Linxia to: Lanzhou (3hr); Tianshui (9hr); Wuwei (9hr); Xiahe (5hr); Xining (11hr).
Tianshui to: Guyuan (daily; 10hr); Lanzhou (8hr); Linxia (9hr); Pingliang (8hr); Xi'an (9hr).
Turpan to: Hami (6hr 30min); Korla (10hr); Kuqa (20hr); Ürümqi (5hr).
Ürümqi to: Almaty, Kazakhstan (36hr); Altai (24hr); Hami (11hr); Kashgar (35hr); Khotan (22hr); Korla (5hr); Kuqa (17hr); Lanzhou (44hr); Liuyuan (daily; 23hr); Turpan (5hr); Yining (14hr).
Wuwei to: Dunhuang (18hr); Jiayuguan (12hr); Lanzhou (5hr); Linxia (9hr); Zhangye (6hr); Zhongwei (7hr).
Xiahe to: Hezuo (2hr); Lanzhou (8hr); Linxia (4hr); Tongren (6hr).
Xining to: Golmud (16hr); Lanzhou (5hr); Linxia (11hr); Maduo (24hr); Tongren (8hr); Zhangye (24hr).
Yinchuan to: Guyuan (7hr); Lanzhou (14hr); Xi'an (12hr); Zhongwei (4hr).
Yining to: Almaty, Kazakhstan (3 weekly; 24hr); Kashgar (40hr); Kuqa (24hr); Ürümqi (14hr).
Zhangye to: Dunhuang (13hr); Jiayuguan (5hr); Lanzhou (11hr); Wuwei (6hr).
Zhongwei to: Guyuan (6hr); Shapotou (1hr); Wuwei (7hr); Yinchuan (4hr).

Flights

Besides the domestic services listed below, there are international flights linking Ürümqi with Almaty, Bishkek, Islamabad, Moscow, Novosibirsk and Sharjah.

Baotou to: Beijing (2 daily; 1hr 30min); Guangzhou (2 weekly; 4hr 30min); Shanghai (2 weekly; 2hr 50min); Wuhan (2 weekly; 3hr); Xi'an (2 weekly; 3hr 30min); Yulin (2 weekly; 2hr 40min).
Dunhuang to: Beijing (daily; 4hr); Lanzhou (daily; 2hr); Ürümqi (daily; 2hr); Xi'an (daily; 2hr 30min).
Hohhot to: Beijing (3 daily; 1hr); Chifeng (3 weekly; 3hr); Guangzhou (2 weekly; 4hr); Hailar (2 weekly; 2hr 30min); Shanghai (2 weekly; 2hr 20min); Shenzhen (1 weekly; 4hr); Shijiazhuang (1 weekly; 1hr); Wuhan (4 weekly; 2hr); Xi'an (2 weekly; 2hr 20min); Xilinhot (2 weekly; 1hr 30min).
Jiayuguan to: Lanzhou (daily; 1hr 30min).
Kashgar to: Ürümqi (daily; 1hr 20 min).
Khotan to: Ürümqi (daily; 1hr 45min).
Kuqa to: Ürümqi (2 weekly; 1hr 50min).
Lanzhou to: Beijing (3 daily; 2hr); Changsha (4 weekly; 2hr); Chengdu (daily; 1hr); Chongqing (2 weekly; 1hr 40min); Dunhuang (1 or 2 daily; 2hr); Fuzhou (2 weekly; 3hr 40min); Guangzhou (daily; 3hr); Haikou (2 weekly; 4hr); Jiayuguan (daily; 1hr 30min); Kunming (daily; 1hr 20min); Qingdao (3 weekly; 3hr 30 min); Shanghai (1 or 2 daily; 2hr 30min); Shenzhen (4 weekly; 4hr); Ürümqi (daily; 2hr 30min); Xi'an (1 or 2 daily; 1hr); Yinchuan (4 weekly; 50min).
Ürümqi to: Beijing (daily; 3hr 30min); Changsha (3 weekly; 4hr); Chengdu (daily; 3hr 20min); Chongqing (daily; 3hr 30min); Dunhuang (daily; 2hr); Guangzhou (daily; 4hr 40min); Guilin (2 weekly; 6hr); Kashgar (daily; 1hr 20min); Khotan (daily; 1hr 45min); Korla (daily; 1hr); Lanzhou (daily; 2hr 30min); Shanghai (daily; 4hr); Xi'an (daily; 2hr 45min); Xining (3 weekly; 2hr 20min); Yinchuan (4 weekly; 3hr); Yining (2 daily; 2hr).
Xining to: Beijing (daily; 2hr 10min); Chengdu (5 weekly; 1hr 20min); Guangzhou (6 weekly; 3hr); Lhasa (2 weekly; 2hr 15min); Shanghai (2 weekly; 2hr 40min); Ürümqi (3 weekly; 2hr 20min) ; Xi'an (2 weekly; 3 hr).
Yinchuan to: Beijing (2 daily; 2hr); Chengdu (1 daily; 2hr); Guangzhou (4 weekly; 4hr); Lanzhou (4 weekly; 50min); Nanjing (5 weekly; 3hr 30min); Shanghai (1 daily; 3hr 30min); Ürümqi (4 weekly; 3hr); Xian (3 weekly; 50min).
Yining to: Ürümqi (2 daily; 2hr).

CHAPTER 14 Highlights

* **The Jokhang, Lhasa** Wreathed in juniper smoke and surrounded by prostrating pilgrims, this temple must be one of the world's most venerated sites. **See p.1134**

* **Lake Namtso** Sits bright as a jewel beneath muscular peaks. **See p.1155**

* **The Friendship Highway** The bumpy winding road between Lhasa and Nepal passes some of the region's best and certainly most accessible sights. **See p.1164**

* **Mount Everest Base Camp** Breathe deep and gaze up at the jagged, snow-blown top of the world. **See p.1168**

* **Mount Kailash** The world's holiest mountain, its very remoteness part of its appeal. **See p.1170**

14

Tibet

Tibet (Bod to Tibetans, Xizang to the Chinese), the "Roof of the World", has exerted a magnetic pull over travellers for centuries. The scenery has a majesty and grandeur that are spellbinding, the religious monuments and practices are overwhelmingly picturesque and moving, and the Tibetan people are welcoming and wonderful. But look just a little below the surface and it is all too apparent that Tibet's past has been tragic, its present is painful, and the future looks bleak. Tibet today is a sad, subjugated colony of China. While foreign visitors are perhaps more worldly than to expect a romantic Shangri-la, there is no doubt that many are surprised by the heavy military and civilian Chinese presence, the modern apartments and factories alongside traditional Tibetan rural lifestyles and monasteries. All this doesn't mean you should stay away, however: though **tourism** provides legitimacy as well as foreign currency to the Chinese government, many people, the Dalai Lama among them, believe that travellers should visit Tibet to learn all they can of the country and its people.

In reaching Tibet, you'll have entered one of the most isolated parts of the world. The massive **Tibetan plateau**, at an average height of 4500m above sea level, is guarded on all sides by towering **mountain ranges**: the Himalayas separate Tibet from India, Nepal and Bhutan to the south, the Karakoram from Pakistan to the west and the Kunlun from Xinjiang to the north. To the east, dividing Tibet from Sichuan and Yunnan, an extensive series of subsidiary ranges covers almost a thousand kilometres. The plateau is also birthplace to some of the greatest **rivers** of Asia, with the Yangzi, Mekong, Yellow and Salween rising in the east, and the Indus, Brahmaputra, Sutlej and some feeder rivers of the Ganges in the west near Mount Kailash.

Tibet's isolation has long stirred the imagination of the West, yet until the British, under the command of Younghusband, invaded in 1904, only a trickle of bold eccentrics, adventurers and the odd missionary had succeeded in getting close to Lhasa, and then only at serious risk to their lives, for it was firm Tibetan policy to exclude all influence from the outside world. So great was the uncertainty about the geographical nature of the country even 150 years ago that the British in India despatched carefully trained spies, known as *pundits,* to walk the length and breadth of the country, counting their footsteps with rosaries and mapping as they went. When Younghusband's invasion force finally reached Lhasa they were, perhaps inevitably, disappointed. One journalist accompanying them wrote:

If one approached within a league of Lhasa, saw the glittering domes of the Potala and turned back without entering the precincts one might still imagine an

enchanted city. It was in fact an unsanitary slum. In the pitted streets pools of rainwater and piles of refuse were everywhere: the houses were mean and filthy, the stench pervasive. Pigs and ravens competed for nameless delicacies in open sewers.

Since the Chinese **invasion** in 1950, Tibet has become much more accessible, with approaches eased by plane links with Chengdu and Kathmandu. There has subsequently been heavy Han migration into the region, and although it is impossible to know how many Chinese live here now, it is likely that they outnumber Tibetans. The situation is most marked in the cities, where the greatest opportunities exist: not only are the numbers of Han increasing all the time, but they are becoming economically dominant too.

Today's **Tibetan Autonomous Region** (TAR), though covering a massive 1.2 million square kilometres, is but a shadow of the former Tibetan lands. The old area, sometimes referred to as Greater Tibet or Ethnographic Tibet, was carved up by the Chinese following their invasion, when the Amdo and Kham regions were absorbed into Qinghai, Sichuan, Gansu and Yunnan provinces. The TAR consists only of the West and Central (U-Tsang) regions of Greater Tibet and divides into four geographical areas. The northern and largest portion is the almost uninhabited **Chang Tang**, a rocky desert at an average altitude of 4000m, where winter temperatures can fall to minus 44°C. South of this is the **mountainous grazing area**, land that cannot support settled agriculture, inhabited by the wide-ranging nomadic people with their herds of yaks, sheep and goats. The **southern valleys**, sandwiched between this nomad area and the **Himalayas** along the southern border, are the most hospitable for human habitation. Not surprisingly, this is the most populated area and where visitors spend the majority of their time, particularly in the extensive valley system of the Tsangpo River (Brahmaputra) and its tributaries.

Lhasa, **Shigatse** and **Gyantse** offer the most accessible **monasteries** and **temples** – the Jokhang, Tashilunpo and the Kumbum respectively – and are also tourist-friendly cities with the biggest range of facilities in the region. The **Potala Palace** in Lhasa remains an enduring image of Tibet in the Western mind and should on no account be missed, and there are plenty of smaller sights in the city to keep anyone busy for several days. Farther afield, the **Yarlung** and **Chongye** valleys to the southeast boast temples and ancient monuments, and the ancient walled monastery of **Samye** is easily combined with these. The tourist corridor between Zhangmu on the Nepalese border and Lhasa is relatively well trodden these days, although by no means overcrowded, and offers side-trips to the huge Mongolian-style monastery at **Sakya** and to **Everest Base Camp**.

While the Chinese prefer easily controllable, high-rolling tour parties to the less malleable, less lucrative budget travellers, they are, for the moment, prepared to tolerate both – though the trip is likely to be expensive, as the Chinese authorities are keen to milk tourism by charging for permits to enter the region and restricting accommodation and transport options available to foreigners. **Tibetan organizations** abroad ask that visitors try, wherever possible, to buy from Tibetans and to hire Tibetan guides. At all times, you should avoid putting Tibetans – and yourself – at risk by bringing up **politically sensitive issues**; remember that you (and your emails) are monitored here. It's also advisable not to bring in Dalai Lama pictures to hand out – Tibetans found with them are in serious trouble.

Finally, remember that the situation here is not black and white. The Han Chinese in Tibet are not demons – most are poor people trying to make a life

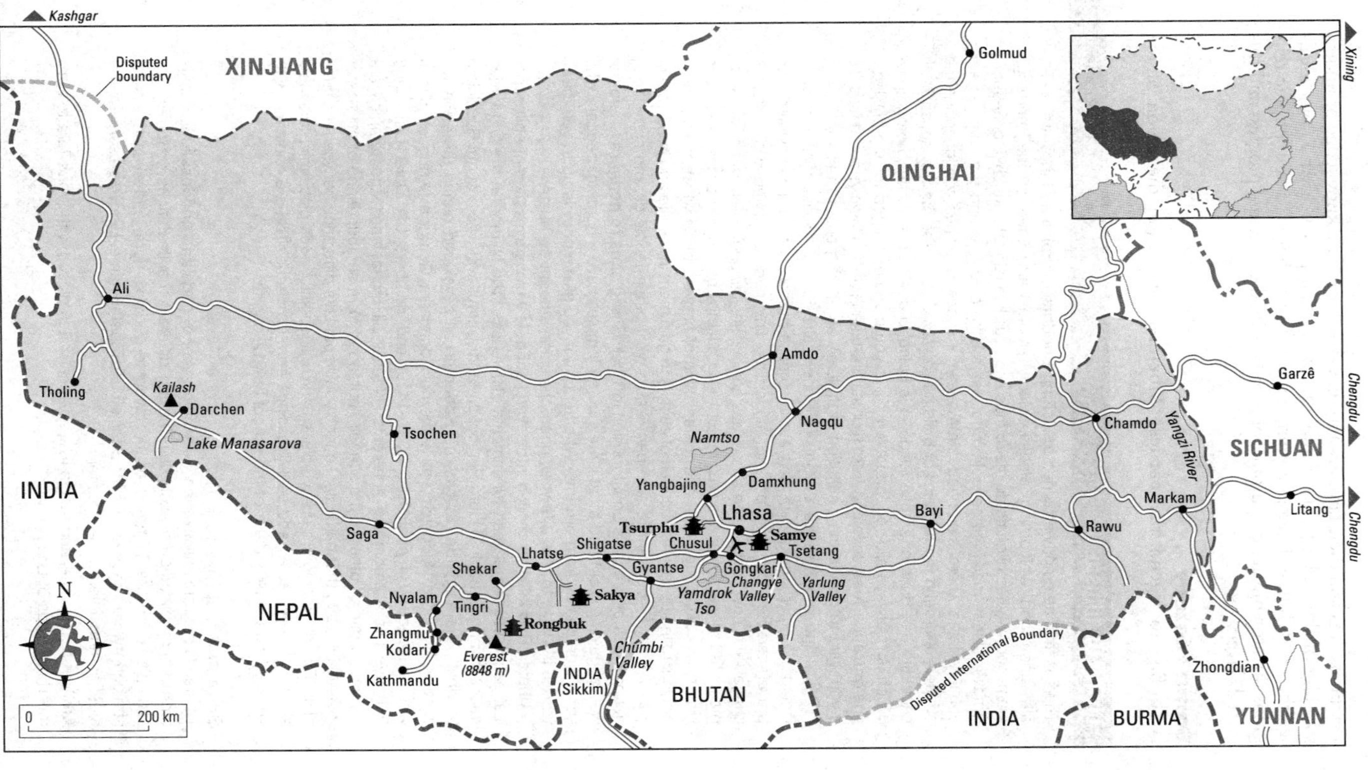
Kashgar
Xining
Chengdu
Chengdu
Disputed boundary
XINJIANG
QINGHAI
SICHUAN
YUNNAN
BURMA
INDIA
NEPAL
BHUTAN
INDIA (Sikkim)
Golmud
Garzê
Litang
Zhongdian
Yangzi River
Chamdo
Markam
Rawu
Amdo
Nagqu
Namtso
Damxhung
Yangbajing
Lhasa
Tsurphu
Samye
Chusul
Tsetang
Gongkar
Changye Valley
Yarlung Valley
Yamdrok Tso
Bayi
Shigatse
Gyantse
Sakya
Chumbi Valley
Lhatse
Shekar
Tingri
Rongbuk
Everest (8848 m)
Nyalam
Zhangmu
Kodari
Kathmandu
Saga
Tsochen
Ali
Tholing
Kailash
Darchen
Lake Manasarova
Disputed International Boundary
N
0
200 km

for themselves and their families, and they may have little knowledge or understanding of the wider political implications of their presence. And don't idealize the pre-Chinese Tibetan administration; it was, after all, a xenophobic religious dictatorship, feudal in outlook, which stifled economic progress and tolerated slavery.

Some history

According to legend, the **earliest Tibetans** came from the union of the

Living Buddhism

There is little ceremony attached to **visiting Buddhist temples** and they are generally open and welcoming places. Most temples are open in the mornings (9am–noon), when pilgrims do the rounds and usually again after lunch (2 or 3–5pm). Smaller places may well be locked but ask for the caretaker and the chances are you'll be let in. There is no need to remove your shoes, but when walking inside the chapels or around the complex or building you should proceed **clockwise**, and you shouldn't eat, drink or smoke inside. It is polite to ask before taking photographs, which isn't always allowed, and even if it is you may be charged for the privilege. The **entrance fees** collected from tourists are taken by the Chinese authorities, so if you want to give to the instiitution itself, leave an offering on an altar.

The range of **offerings** devout Tibetans make to their gods is enormous. It includes juniper smoke sent skyward in incense burners, prayer flags printed with prayers erected on rooftops and mountains, tiny papers printed with religious images and cast to the wind on bridges and passes (*lungda*), white scarves (*katag*) presented to statues and lamas, butter to keep lamps burning on altars, repetitious *mantras* invoking the gods, and the spinning of prayer wheels which have printed prayers rolled up inside. The idea of each is to gain merit in this life and hence affect your *karma*. If you want to take part, watch what other people do and copy them; nobody is at all precious about religion in Tibet. Giving **alms to beggars** is another way of gaining merit and most large Tibetan temples have a horde of beggars who survive on charity from pilgrims. Whether or not you give money is up to you, but if you do it's wise to give a few *fen* or so, the same amount as Tibetans.

Tibetan Buddhism is divided into several **schools** which have different philosophical emphases rather than fundamental differences. The **Nyingma**, the Old Order, traces its origins back to Guru Rinpoche, Padmasambhava, who brought Buddhism to Tibet. The **Kagyupa**, **Sakya** and **Kadampa** all developed during the eleventh-century revival of Buddhism, while the now dominant **Gelugpa** (Virtuous School) was founded by Tsongkhapa (1357–1419) and numbers the Dalai Lama and Panchen Lama among its adherents. Virtually all monasteries and temples are aligned to one or other of the schools, but, apart from an abundance of statues of revered lamas of that particular school, you'll spot little difference between the temples. Tibetan people are pretty eclectic and will worship in temples which they feel are particularly sacred and seek blessings from lamas they feel are endowed with special powers, regardless of the school they belong to.

Gods and goddesses

Tibetan Buddhism has an overwhelming number of **gods and goddesses** and matters are complicated by each deity having different manifestations or forms. For example, there are 21 forms of the favourite goddess Tara, and even the most straightforward image has both a Sanskrit and Tibetan name. Below are some of the most common you will encounter:

Amitayus (Tsepame) and **Vijaya** (Namgyelma), often placed with White Tara to form the Three Gods of Longevity.

ogress, Sinmo, and a monkey, reincarnation of the god Chenresi, on the mountain of Gangpo Ri near Tsetang. Ethnographers, however, think it likely the Tibetans are descended from the nomadic Ch'iang who roamed eastern Central Asia, to the northwest of China, several thousand years ago. The first Tibetan king, Nyatri Tsenpo, believed to have come to earth via a magical "sky-cord", was the first of a long lineage of 27 kings who ruled in a pre-Buddhist era when the indigenous, shamanistic **Bon religion** held sway throughout the land (see p.975). Each of the **early kings** held power over a

Avalokiteshvara (Chenresi in Tibetan, Guanyin in Chinese temples), patron god of Tibet, with many forms, most noticeably with eleven faces and a thousand arms.

Maitreya (Jampa), the Buddha of the Future.

Manjusri (Jampelyang), the God of Wisdom.

Padmasambhava, with eight manifestations, most apparent as Guru Rinpoche. You may see him with his consorts, Yeshe Tsogyel and Mandarava.

Sakyamuni, Buddha of the Present.

Tara (Dolma), Goddess of Compassion. Green Tara is associated with protection and White Tara with long life.

Festivals

Festival dates are calculated using the Tibetan lunar calendar and thus correspond to different dates on the Western calendar each year.

February/March

Driving out of evil spirits. Twenth-ninth day of the twelfth lunar month, the last day of the year.

Losar, Tibetan New Year. First day of the first lunar month.

Monlam, Great Prayer Festival, Lhasa. Eighth day of the first lunar month.

Butter Lamp Festival, on the final day of Monlam. Fifteenth day of the first lunar month.

May/June

Birth of Buddha. Seventh day of the fourth lunar month.

Saga Dawa (Buddha's Enlightenment). Fifteenth day of the fourth lunar month.

Gyantse Horse Festival. Fifteenth day of the fourth lunar month.

July

Tashilunpo Festival, Shigatse. Fifteenth day of the fifth lunar month.

July/August

Buddha's First Sermon. Fourth day of the sixth lunar month.

Drepung Festival. Thirtieth day of the sixth lunar month.

August/September

Shotun (Yoghurt Festival), Lhasa. First to the seventh day of the seventh lunar month.

Bathing Festival, Lhasa. Twenty-seventh day of the seventh lunar month.

September

Damxhung Horse Festival. Thirtieth day of the seventh lunar month.

September/October

Harvest Festival. First to the seventh day of the eighth lunar month.

November

Lhabab (Buddha's descent from Heaven). Twenty-second day of the ninth lunar month.

November/December

Peldon Lhama Festival, Lhasa. Fifteenth day of the tenth lunar month.

small area, the geographical isolation of Tibet making outside contact difficult. Nevertheless, it is apparent that as early as the seventh century there was considerable cultural exchange between Tibet and its neighbours. Pens, ink, silks, jewels and probably tea reached Tibet from China in the seventh century, and for many centuries Tibet looked to India for religious teaching.

It was in the time of King **Songtsen Gampo**, the thirty-third ruler in the dynasty, born in 617 AD, that expansionism began. Songtsen Gampo's twenty-year rule saw the unification of the country and the aggressive spread of his empire from Northern India to China. To placate their assertive neighbour, China and Nepal each offered Songtsen Gampo a wife: in 632 he married Princess Bhrikuti (also known as Tritsun) of Nepal and in 641 Princess Wencheng arrived from the Tang court sent by her father, Emperor Taizong. They both brought their Buddhist faith and magnificent statues of the Buddha which are now the centrepieces of Ramoche temple and the Jokhang in Lhasa. Songtsen Gampo himself embraced the **Buddhist faith** and established Buddhist temples throughout the country, although the indigenous Bon faith remained the religion of the ordinary people. Following his death in 650, his descendants strengthened the kingdom politically, and in 763 Tibetan armies even took the Chinese capital Chang'an (modern Xi'an). Trisong Detsen (742–797) was another champion of the new faith who invited two Indian Buddhist teachers to Tibet, Shantarakshita and the charismatic and flamboyant **Padmasambhava**. The latter, who was also known as Guru Rinpoche, is regarded as responsible for overcoming the resistance of the Bon religion and ensuring the spread of Buddhism within Tibet. Although he is closely associated with the Nyingma school of Buddhism, you'll spot his image somewhere in most temples.

In 838, the infamous **Langdarma** came to the throne, having assassinated his brother. A fervent supporter of Bon, he set about annihilating the Buddhist faith. Temples and monasteries were destroyed, monks forced to flee and the previously unified Tibet broke up into a number of small principalities. A Buddhist revival involving monastery construction, the translation of scriptures into Tibetan and the establishment of several of the schools of Tibetan Buddhism was spearheaded by the arrival of **Atisha** (982–1054), the most famous Indian scholar of the time. Politically the country was not united but the various independent principalities lived largely in harmony and there was little contact with China.

Absorbed in internal events, the Tibetans had largely neglected the outside world, where the Muslim surge across India in the twelfth and thirteenth centuries resulted in the destruction of the great Buddhist centres of teaching to which the Tibetans had looked for generations. And to the north and east of Tibet the **Mongol leader**, Genghis Khan, was beginning his assault on China. In 1207 Chingis Khan sent envoys to Tibet demanding submission, which was given without a fight, and the territory was largely ignored until Chingis Khan's grandson, Godan, sent raiding parties deep into the country. Hearing from his troops about the spirituality of the Tibetan lamas, Godan invited the head of the Sakya order, Sakya Pandita, to his court. In exchange for peace, Sakya Pandita again offered Tibetan submission and was created regent of Tibet at the Mongolian court, making the Sakya lamas the effective rulers of Tibet under the patronage of the emperor. This lasted through the generations, with Godan's son **Kublai Khan** deeply impressed by Sakya Pandita's nephew, Phagpa.

When the Chinese Ming dynasty overcame the Mongols in the fourteenth century, Tibet began a long period of independence which ended in 1642 with the Mongols intervening directly in support of the Fifth Dalai Lama, Lobsang Gyatso (1617–82), of the **Gelugpa order**. Often referred to as "**the Great Fifth**", he united the country under Gelugpa rule and within fifteen years, largely neglected by Mongol rulers, established authority from Kham to Kailash – the first time that one religious and political leader had united and ruled the country. He invited scholars to Tibet, restored and expanded religious institutions and began work on the Potala in Lhasa.

One disadvantage of the **reincarnation system** of succession (in which a new-born child is identified as the next manifestation of the dead lama) is that an unstable period of fifteen or twenty years inevitably follows a death while the next reincarnation grows up. Initially, the death of the Fifth Dalai Lama in 1682 was concealed by his regent, Sangye Gyatso, who claimed he had entered a period of solitary meditation and meanwhile raised the Sixth Dalai Lama to adulthood. The following two centuries saw no strong leadership from the Dalai Lamas, and there were repeated incursions by Mongolian factions. The most influential figures in Tibet at this time were the regents and representatives of the Manchu rulers in China, the *ambans*. During the **nineteenth century**, Tibet became increasingly isolationist, fearing Russian plans to expand their empire south and British plans to expand their empire north. Seeing themselves caught in the middle, the Tibetans simply banned foreigners from their land. But, at their borders, Tibetans continued trading with Indians and in 1904 their one-sided trading arrangements exasperated the British, who determined to forge a fair treaty on the subject. The Tibetans refused to negotiate, so an expeditionary force was sent in 1904 under Colonel Younghusband, to obtain satisfaction. Meeting with obfuscation and hostility from Tibet's rulers, the invaders marched further and further into Tibet, and fought a couple of dispiriting battles against peasant soldiers armed with scythes and charms of invulnerability – gifts from their lamas, who stood at the back yelling encouragement. Patching up their poor opponents in improvised field hospitals along the way, the British marched up to Gyantse through the Chumbi Valley and eventually on to Lhasa. A series of British Representatives in Lhasa forged good relationships with Tibet and became a window on the outside world.

The **Thirteenth Dalai Lama**, Tubten Gyatso (1876–1933), was an insightful and capable leader who realized that Tibet's political position needed urgent clarification, but he had a difficult rule, fleeing into exile twice, and was much occupied with border fighting against the Chinese and tensions with conservatives inside the country. Following his death, the **Fourteenth Dalai Lama** was identified in Amdo in 1938 and was still a young man when world events began to close in on Tibet. The British left India in 1947, withdrawing their Representative from Lhasa. In 1949 the Communists under Mao Zedong created the People's Republic of China and the following year declared their intention "to liberate the oppressed and exploited Tibetans and reunite them with the great motherland". In October 1950, the People's Liberation Army invaded the Kham region of eastern Tibet before proceeding to Lhasa the following year. Under considerable duress, Tibet signed a seventeen-point treaty in 1951, allowing for the "peaceful integration of Tibet".

The Chinese era

Initially the Chinese offered goodwill and modernization. Tibet had made little headway into the twentieth century; there were few roads, no electricity, and glass windows, steel girders and concrete were all recent introductions.

Hygiene and health care were patchy and lay education was unavailable. While some Tibetans viewed modernization as necessary, the opposition was stiff, as many within the religious hierarchy saw changes within the country and overtures to the outside world as a threat to their influence. Throughout the 1950s an underground resistance operated which flared into a public confrontation in March 1959, fuelled by mounting distrust and hostility, as refugees from eastern Tibet fled to Lhasa and told of the brutality of Chinese rule. In Lhasa the Chinese invited the Dalai Lama to a theatrical performance at the Chinese military base. It was popularly perceived as a ploy to kidnap him, and huge numbers of Tibetans mounted demonstrations and surrounded the Norbulingka where the Dalai Lama was staying. On the night of March 17, the Dalai Lama and his entourage escaped, heading into **exile** in India where they were later joined (and are still joined today) by tens of thousands of refugees.

Meanwhile the **uprising in Lhasa** was ferociously suppressed – 87,000 people were killed by the Chinese between March 1959 and September 1960. From that point on all pretence of goodwill vanished, and a huge military force moved in, with a Chinese bureaucracy replacing Tibetan institutions. Temples and monasteries were destroyed and Chinese **agricultural policies** proved particularly disastrous. During the years of the Great Leap Forward (1959–60) it is estimated that ten percent of Tibetans starved, and it wasn't until the early 1980s that the food situation in Tibet began to improve. Harrowing accounts tell of parents mixing their own blood with hot water and *tsampa* to feed their children.

In September 1965 the U-Tsang and Western areas of Tibet officially became the **Xizang Autonomous Region** of the People's Republic of China, but more significant was the **Cultural Revolution** (1966–76) during which mass destruction of religious monuments and practices took place under the orders of the Red Guards, some of them young Tibetans. In 1959 there were 2700 monasteries and temples in Tibet; by 1978 there were just eight monasteries and fewer than a thousand monks and nuns in the TAR. Liberalization followed Mao's death in 1976, leading to a period of relative openness and peace in the early 1980s when monasteries were rebuilt, religion revived and tourism was restored. By the end of the decade, repression was again in place following riots in Lhasa in 1988–9, but in the early 1990s foreigners were allowed back.

The current mood seems to be one of apparent openness, with the encouragement of tourism against a background of increased internal control of the Tibetan population. Dissent is ruthlessly quashed and there are currently between six and seven hundred political detainees, more than at any time since 1990. Estimates of three hundred thousand to one million have been given for the number of Tibetans who have perished either directly at the hands of the Chinese or indirectly through starvation and hardship. The International Commission of Jurists in the Hague has held the People's Republic of China to be guilty of genocide.

Meanwhile, the profile of the **Tibetan Government in Exile** based in Dharamsala in northern India, representing some 130,000 Tibetan refugees and led by the Dalai Lama, continues to increase. The world community has refused to take a stand for the Tibetans, yet the Dalai Lama, known to the Tibetans as Gyalwa Rinpoche and regarded as the earthly incarnation of the god Chenresi, has never faltered from advocating a peaceful solution for Tibet, a stance which led to his being awarded the 1989 Nobel Peace Prize.

For the Tibetans who remain here the reality of life in Tibet is harsh. China admits that the inhabitants of a quarter of the TAR counties cannot feed or clothe themselves, one third of children do not go to school and Tibet's literacy rate is about thirty percent, the lowest in China. Between 1952 and 1998 it is estimated that China subsidized the TAR to the tune of 40 billion yuan – yet Tibetans are among the poorest people in China and have the lowest life expectancy in the country. As Tibet provides the Chinese with land for their exploding population along with almost untold natural resources, the influx of Han Chinese settlers threatens to swamp the Tibetan population, culture and economy.

Tibet practicalities

The **best time to visit** is April to October, outside the coldest months. June to September are the wettest months when blocked roads and swollen rivers can make travel difficult but the countryside will be at its greenest. However, health considerations should be taken seriously at any time of the year, and even in relatively balmy Lhasa temperatures fall below freezing on a regular basis. In winter, as long as you come fully prepared for the cold (most hotels have no heating) and possible delays due to snow-covered passes, the lack of tourists and the preoccupation of the security forces with staying warm can make for a pleasant trip.

It's worth noting that the Chinese authorities are much pricklier around **festival times** (see box, p.1117) and the week before and after certain historically significant dates, when they'll be much more likely to **clamp down** on unregulated travel and demand permits for inspection. Dates to bear in mind include March 5 and 10 (the anniversaries of uprisings in 1988 and 1989), July 6 (the Dalai Lama's birthday), September 27 and October 1 (the anniversary of protests in 1987), and December 10 (International Human Rights Day and the anniversary of the Dalai Lama's Nobel Peace Prize).

Getting there

Officially you need only a **Chinese visa** to travel to Tibet. However, the authorities control entry into the country by insisting that independent travellers purchase a "**permit**" when they buy travel tickets for the region. You will probably not see this permit and once you are in Tibet nobody is interested in it. **Visa extensions** can be problematic in Tibet; you can apply for extensions at any PSB but, at best, they will ask to see proof that you are on your way out of the country and then only give you one week.

Tour operators outside Tibet – notably those in Chengdu – will exaggerate the difficulty of independent travel in Tibet; don't believe anything they say and talk to other travellers instead. Once in Tibet, you are fairly independent.

By air

Domestic flights operate daily to Lhasa from Chengdu (¥1200), and there are also services from Beijing (via Chengdu), Xining (see p.1056) and Deqin airport in Zhongdian (see p.890). There are also flights from Chongqing, but as the PSB there isn't geared up to handing out the required permits, the only time you just might be using this route is when leaving. At the time of writing, you could not buy a flight in Chengdu or Beijing without being booked onto a tour. Arriving from **Beijing**, you need to be on one of the very pricey tours arranged with the Tibet Tourism Bureau, obscurely located in the basement of the Poly Plaza; you're better off going to **Chengdu** and arranging

Traveller's Tibetan

Although some people involved in the tourist industry are now conversant in several languages including English, most Tibetans speak only their native language with perhaps a smattering of Mandarin. Even a few words of Tibetan are not only greeted enthusiastically but are well nigh essential if you're heading off the beaten track or going trekking.

Tibetan belongs to the small Tibeto-Burmese group of languages and has no similarity at all to Mandarin or Hindi. Tibetan script was developed in the seventh century and has thirty consonants and five vowels which are placed either beside, above or below other letters when written down. There are obvious inaccuracies when trying to render this into the Roman alphabet and the situation is further complicated by the many dialects across the region; the Lhasa dialect is used in the vocabulary below. Word order is back-to-front relative to English, and verbs are placed at the ends of sentences – "this noodle soup is delicious" becomes "tukpa dee shimbo do", literally "noodle soup this delicious is". The only sound you are likely to have trouble with is **ng** at the beginning of words – it is pronounced as in sa**ng**.

Basic phrases

Hello	*tashi delay*
Goodbye, to someone staying	*kalay shu*
Goodbye, to someone going	*kalay pay*
Thank you	*tuk too jay*
Sorry	*gonda*
Please	*coochee*
How are you?	*kusu debo yinbay?* or *kam sangbo dugay?*
I'm . . .	*nga . . .*
Fine	*debo yin*
Cold	*kya*
Hungry	*throko-doe*
Thirsty	*ka gom*
Tired	*galay ka*
I don't understand	*nga ha ko ma-song*
What is your name?	*kayranggi mingla karay ray?*
My name is . . .	*ngeye mingla . . . sa*
Where are you from?	*kayrang kanay ray?*
I'm from . . .	*nga . . . nay yin*
Britain	*injee*
Australia	*otaleeya*
America	*amerika*
How old are you?	*kayrang lo katsay ray?*
I'm . . .	*nga lo . . . yin*
Where are you going?	*kaba drogee yin?*

your trip from there. The tour operators around the *Traffic Hotel* in Chengdu run a cartel, their cheapest tour weighing in at ¥2700, which includes your flight in and three days in a budget hotel. It's simple to arrange, and a ticket for the next day is usually available. Once in Lhasa, you can buy flights back to China at the standard price.

Flights from **Kathmandu** leave twice weekly (Tues & Sat) can be booked only as part of a tour operated by a travel agent there; expect to pay upwards of US$360 for a flight and a three-day tour. If you don't already have a Chinese visa, you'll only get in as part of a group, on a group visa. You can change this to an individual visa in Lhasa but the process is complex, expensive (around ¥300) and depends on how well connected your travel agent is.

By land

Overland routes to Tibet are well established, although they can be physi-

I'm going to . . .	*nga . . . la drogee yin*
Where is the . . .?	*. . . kaba doo?*
hospital	*menkang*
monastery	*gompa*
temple/chapel	*lhakhang*
restaurant	*sakang*
convent	*ani gompa*
caretaker	*konyer*
Is there . . . ?	*. . . doo gay?*
hot water	*chu tsa-bo*
a candle	*yangla*
I don't have . . .	*nga . . . mindoo*
Is this OK/can I do this?	*deegee rebay?*
It's (not) OK	*deegee (ma)ray*
(Not) Good	*yaggo (min)doo*
This is delicious	*dee shimbo doo*
Do you want . . . ?	*kayrang . . . gobay?*
I want tea	*nga cha go*
I don't want this	*dee me-go*
What is this/that?	*dee/day karray ray?*
When?	*kadoo?*
Now	*danta*
Today	*dering*
Yesterday	*kezang*
Tomorrow	*sangnyee*
Sunday	*sa nima*
Monday	*sa dowa*
Tuesday	*sa mingma*
Wednesday	*sa lagba*
Thursday	*sa purbur*
Friday	*sa pasang*
Saturday	*sa pemba*
How much is this?	*gong kadso ray?*

Numbers

1	*chee*
2	*nyee*
3	*soom*
4	*zhee*
5	*nga*
6	*droo*
7	*doon*
8	*gyay*
9	*goo*
10	*chew*
11	*chew chee*
12	*chew nyee*
etc	
20	*nyi shoo*
21	*nyi shoo chee*
etc	
30	*soom chew*
40	*shib chew*
50	*ngab chew*
60	*drook chew*
70	*doon chew*
80	*gyay chew*
90	*goop chew*
100	*gya*
200	*nyee gya*
etc	
1000	*dong*

cally taxing. From within China, **Golmud to Lhasa** (1160km, and thirty to fifty jarring hours) is the only officially permitted land route (see p.1066). CITS are the baddies here, charging an outrageous ¥1700 for a return ticket (they won't sell singles). The return leg is dated three days from the date of the inbound trip; you can change your date of return at the bus station in Lhasa, though most people throw the ticket away and fly out – no one wants to do that trip twice. Some travellers have got around the CITS scam by standing on the road outside Golmud, waiting for the bus, and then making a deal with the driver; others make shady deals with characters who hang around the bus station. It's worth trying, if only to put one over on CITS. It's also possible to go overland from Zhongdian as part of a tour (see p.891 for details).

The overland routes from Sichuan (over 2000km from Chengdu to Lhasa) and Kashgar (1100km to Ali) are officially closed to foreigners, although a few intrepid travellers manage to get through. If you're caught by the authorities you may well be imprisoned, fined and/or deported and drivers caught transporting you face at the least large fines and maybe more serious trouble – some drivers have been given very severe beatings.

Entering Tibet overland **from Kathmandu** via Kodari on the Nepal side and Zhangmu on the Tibetan side is a popular option, but travellers on this route are vulnerable to snap changes in entry regulations, and also to landslides in summer and snow-blocked passes in winter. Under no circumstances apply for a Chinese visa in Kathmandu if you want to travel independently to Tibet – the Chinese embassy will not issue these unless you are booked on an organized tour through a Kathmandu travel agent. Independent travellers must have their Chinese visa before arrival in Kathmandu, and even then Aliens' Travel Permits (see below) for the route to Lhasa (which cost US$30 in Kathmandu) were being issued only if an organized tour through to the capital was booked. Expect to pay around US$380 for an organized seven-day tour overland trip to Lhasa, or around US$240 for a three-day trip. An agency that will group individual travellers together is Nature Trail Trekking at Durbar Marg in Kathmandu (Ⓣ241452, Ⓦwww.allnepal.com), which charges US$300 for a five-day overland "tour" to Lhasa. They will tell you that a ticket out of Tibet is necessary, but some people who don't have one still get in. The best advice is to spend some time in Kathmandu to get a feel for the current situation and check out your options.

At the time of writing, **cyclists** on this route were unable to persuade the authorities to issue a permit without being part of a tour, but this might change. If you're going to attempt cycling in, bear in mind that most of the road between Zhangmu and Shigatse is unpaved and very rough. The altitude gain from Kodari to Zhangmu is 530m in about 9km, then 1450m in the 33km to Nyalam followed by a tough 1300m in the 57-kilometre climb to the Lalung Pass at 5050m. Allow around twenty days to cycle from Kathmandu to Lhasa. You'll need camping equipment, food (plus stove) and adequate warm-weather gear. Dogs are a particular hazard near villages.

Getting around

Aliens' Travel Permits (¥50) are issued by the PSB and give you permission to visit specified places within specified time limits. At the time of writing the only parts of Tibet where you did not need an Aliens' Travel Permit were Lhasa, Shigatse, Zhangmu and Tsetang. For all other areas you need to apply to the PSB in the district capital for a permit; the best place to apply is at the comparatively lenient and friendly PSB office in Shigatse. There are some areas where a permit will not be given under any circumstances, such as the highly militarized Chumbi Valley. However, the status of other areas seems to change from one day to the next. Penalties for being caught somewhere without a permit can be fairly heavy: travellers have faced big fines, been harangued at length, forced to write "confessions" and had passports confiscated. In practice, there are some areas with no checkposts on the way and no PSB officers, for example Namtso Lake, and there's little point in alerting the PSB to the fact you're going.

The **public transport** system in Tibet, such as it is, consists of large public **buses** and the smaller, nippier **minibuses**. For Tibetans these are largely interchangeable, but for foreigners the difference is highly significant. There are, as yet, no problems with foreigners travelling on the public buses, but minibuses come under the label of "private vehicles" and foreigners are banned from

Arranging private transport in Tibet

For specific excursions, most travellers end up **hiring a jeep** with a driver and perhaps a guide as well (this last may be obligatory, depending on your destination). There are many private **tour companies** in **Lhasa** who can arrange this: all the hotels have agencies for the purpose, and they adorn Beijing Dong Lu and Mentsikhang Lu. You'll need to decide your exact itinerary, get together five people to fill up the jeep, write a contract detailing timings and costs and pay the deposit (usually half the agreed fee) before you go. You should check that the quoted price includes the cost of permits (which the tour company should arrange) plus fees, lodging and food for the driver and guide and the cost of fuel – in fact everything except your own food and lodging and the cost of your admission to monasteries. It pays to be precise in your itinerary (so, for example, don't say Rongbuk Monastery if you mean Everest Base Camp), as well as to work out what the extra cost should be if one of your party falls ill and you are delayed (about ¥200 a day is reasonable). The most popular option, a five-day tour to the Nepalese border taking in Gyantse, Shigatse and Everest Base Camp, should cost around ¥4000. Hopefully you'll have no problems, but in the event of a misunderstanding, you may wish to **complain** to the Tour Service Inspection Office of Lhasa's **Tibet Tourism Bureau**, 208 Yuan Lin Lu (☎0891/6333476 or 6334193).

travelling on these (although the minibuses that operate within Lhasa itself seem exempt from this ban). This is regardless of the fact that minibuses are often the best, and sometimes the only, public transport between two points. This ban also means foreigners cannot travel in trucks and private cars, which effectively rules out hitchhiking. Drivers face huge fines and big trouble if they are caught breaking these rules, but the zeal with which the PSB enforces the regulations changes from month to month. The situation with regard to the large **pilgrim buses** which operate daily to Ganden and Tsurphu monasteries is even more confused; while most travellers report few problems using them, drivers may be hesitant about taking you when the local situation is particularly tense. Given that the rules as regards travel in Tibet are in a constant state of flux, it's essential to talk to **other travellers** to try to get an up-to-date picture of things.

Of the **maps** available, recommended is the Mapping Bureau of the TAR's English-language *China Tibet Tour Map* and *Lhasa Tour Map*. Both are available at the Xinhua Bookstore, where they cost ¥7, and at most hotels, where they are a little pricier. The *Yak Hotel* has a dated but detailed hand-drawn city map (¥3). See "Basics", p.24, for advice on maps available outside Tibet. The *On This Spot Lhasa Map* published by the International Campaign for Tibet shows another side to the city, marking prisons, security facilities and army bases – though don't take it there with you.

Health

Tibet poses particular health hazards to travellers. Almost every visitor is affected by **altitude** as most of Tibet is over 3000m with plenty of passes over 5000m. For your first two or three days at altitude rest as much as possible and drink plenty of water. You can buy oxygen canisters in most hotel receptions (¥30) though whether they're much use is debatable. A few painkillers should help to relieve any aches and pains and headaches, but more serious problems can develop; see "Basics", p.30 for more details. Trekkers and anyone travelling long distances in the backs of trucks need also to be particularly aware of the dangers of **hypothermia**.

Travellers to Tibet should have **rabies immunization** before they travel. The dogs here are very aggressive, bites are common and, if you get bitten, Kathmandu is the nearest place stocking rabies serum. A significant number of travellers to Tibet also suffer from **giardiasis**, an unpleasant and debilitating intestinal complaint (see p.28), although there is some controversy over whether it is endemic to the region or brought in from outside. The treatment is Tinadozol or Flagyl, which is not reliably available in Lhasa; bring a course along if you can.

Accommodation

In most Tibetan towns simple **guesthouses** offer accommodation to foreigners, pilgrims and truck drivers. You can expect dormitory accommodation with bedding, of variable cleanliness, provided. The communal toilets are usually pit latrines and there are few washing facilities, although most places have bowls. You can expect hot water in vacuum flasks, for drinks and washing, everywhere. Lighting may be by candle.

There is a greater choice of accommodation in the main tourist centres of Lhasa, Shigatse, Gyantse, Tsetang and Zhangmu, where international-standard hotels provide comfortable rooms with attached bathrooms and at least some hours of hot water. In the administrative centres of Lhasa and Shigatse foreigners are allowed to stay at **mid-range hotels**, with rooms of a similar quality and generally offering very reasonable value for money.

If you are trekking, you can **camp** wherever the fancy takes you, although many trekkers find accommodation in village houses or with nomadic yak-herders. You should not expect them to feed you, and should pay ¥15 or so per night.

Lhasa

Situated in a wide, mountain-fringed valley on the north bank of the Kyichu River, **LHASA** (Ground of the Gods), at 3700m, is a sprawling, rapidly expanding, modern Chinese city with a population of around 200,000. An important settlement for well over a thousand years, it was originally called Rasa, but was renamed by King Songtsen Gampo in the seventh century when he moved his capital here from the Yarlung Valley. Following the collapse of the Yarlung dynasty two centuries later, power dispersed among local chieftains and the city lost its pre-eminence. It was not until the seventeenth century, with the installation of the Fifth Dalai Lama as ruler by the Mongolian emperor, Gushri Khan, that Lhasa once again became the seat of government. It continues now as the capital of the TAR and while glorious sites from earlier times are spread throughout the area, it is this third period of growth, following the Chinese invasion, that has given the city its most obvious features – wide boulevards and concrete-and-glass blocks. The Chinese population of Lhasa is highly active economically, with two Chinese businesses to every Tibetan one, a ratio that reflects the city's population.

There are plenty of sights in and around the city to keep most visitors occupied for at least a week; the **Potala**, **Jokhang** and **Barkhor** district are unmissable, and at least one trip to an outlying monastery is a must. It's also worth taking time to see some of the smaller, less showy temples and simply to absorb the atmosphere of the "Forbidden City"; large numbers of explorers died in their vain efforts to reach Lhasa around a hundred years ago.

Offering tourists better **facilities**, with more choice of accommodation, restaurants and shopping than anywhere else in Tibet, Lhasa is the best place to arrange trips to other parts of the region (see box, p.1125). Whatever the comforts of Lhasa, remember that the city is just one face of Tibet – 88 percent of the population live in the countryside.

Orientation, arrival and city transport

The **central areas** of Lhasa are along and between three main roads that run east–west, parallel to and north of the Kyichu River: Chingdol Lu, Beijing Lu and Lingkor Lu. Lhasa is at its most sprawling to the west, where there is very little countryside between the outskirts of the city and the monastery of Drepung, 8km away from the centre of town, and north where the city virtually merges into the Sera monastery complex, 4km distant. So far the river has prevented a spread south, while to the east the city peters out within a couple of kilometres as the road towards Ganden deteriorates quickly. The Potala

Moving on from Lhasa

Public bus departures are mostly from the bus station. It's advisable to buy tickets a day in advance – there's a foreigners' ticket office and staff are generally helpful, though bring your passport as you might need to show it when buying your ticket. Pilgrim buses and minibuses leave from various points but note the possible restrictions on your use of these (p.1124). Further details are given in the accounts of the destinations and in "Travel details" at the end of the chapter. For information on arranging private transport for a customized itinerary, see p.1125.

Leaving Tibet

You can buy **flight** tickets at CAAC in Lhasa or at the ticket agency in the *Tibet Hotel*. Destinations served are: Kathmandu (Tues & Sat; ¥1800), Chengdu (daily; ¥1200), Xi'an (Wed; ¥1320), Chongqing (Tues & Fri; ¥1300) and Beijing (daily except Mon; ¥2690). You'll also have to pay a departure tax of ¥90 to Kathmandu or ¥50 into China. Airport buses leave from outside the CAAC office in Lhasa, at 6am, 6.30am, 10am, 3pm and 5pm (¥35). An early morning jeep-taxi from Lhasa to the airport costs ¥350 for five people plus luggage, or you can arrange a taxi in advance through the *Pentoc Hotel* for only ¥200.

At the time of writing, **cycling out** of Tibet was a lot easier than cycling in – you just have to be wary of two checkpoints, one outside Lhatse and one outside Shekar. See "Getting there", p.1121, and "Shopping", p.1141. The only destination outside Tibet that you can reach **by bus** is Golmud, for which buses leave the main bus station daily at 8.30am. There's a choice between luxury buses with reclining seats (¥400) or more basic ones with upright seats (¥210). There's no longer any public service to **Nepal**. Most people heading to Nepal make their own arrangements through **tour companies** in Lhasa, hiring jeep and driver plus guide. Expect to be quoted ¥4500 upwards for a six-day, seven-night trip taking in Rongbuk Monastery. Alternatively, you could cadge a lift with one of the minibuses and jeeps which leave Lhasa regularly to collect tour parties at the Nepal border. You have to ask around a bit to arrange transport this way as the companies would rather you took a more expensive tour. They complete the trip in two days, and it will cost around ¥350 per person.

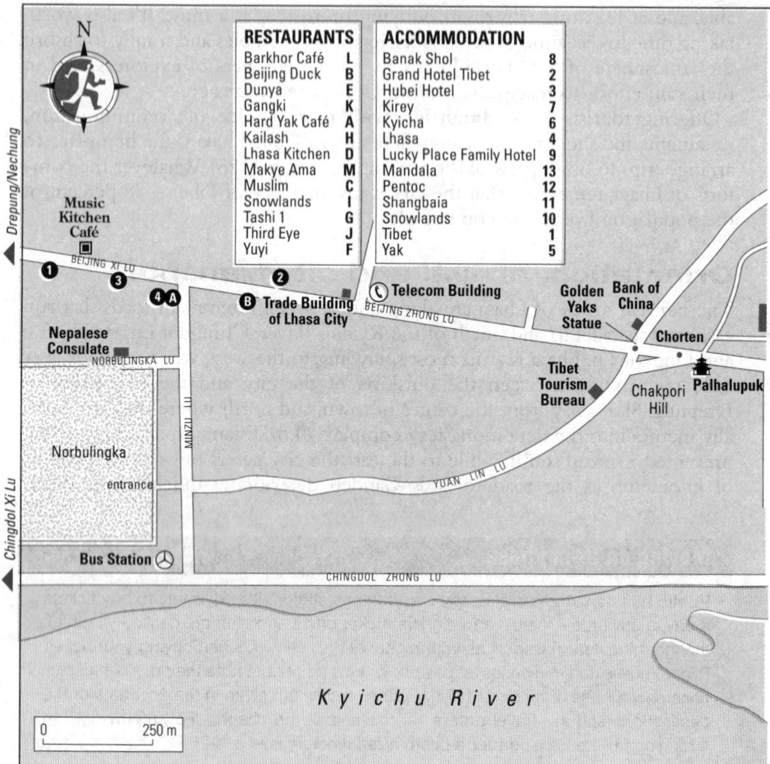

Palace, on Beijing Zhong Lu, is the major landmark visible throughout the city and, together with the Tibetan enclave around the Jokhang temple, known as the Barkhor, forms the centre of interest for most visitors. The Golden Yaks Statue, at the junction of Beijing Zhong Lu and Yuan Lin Lu in the west of the city, erected in 1991 to celebrate the fortieth anniversary of the "liberation" of Tibet, is another useful landmark.

Arriving by air, you'll land at **Lhasa airport** at Gongkhar, a hefty 93km to the southeast of the city. CAAC buses (¥35) bring you to the CAAC office on Nyangrain Lu in around two hours, though foreigners coming on tours will be met by guides with jeeps. Although a few minibuses and pilgrim buses (notably from Shigatse, Ganden and Tsurphu) ply into the middle of town, usually Barkhor Square, if you come by bus, you'll probably be dropped at the main **bus station** west of the centre at the junction of Chingdol Zhong Lu and Minzu Lu. From here either take a tractor into town (¥5), or use the #2 minibus (¥2) which will take you most of the way (see "City transport", below).

City transport

The easiest way to get around the city and its environs is by **minibus** (daily 7am–10pm; ¥2 flat fare) or on a **cycle-rickshaw**, though you'll have to barter

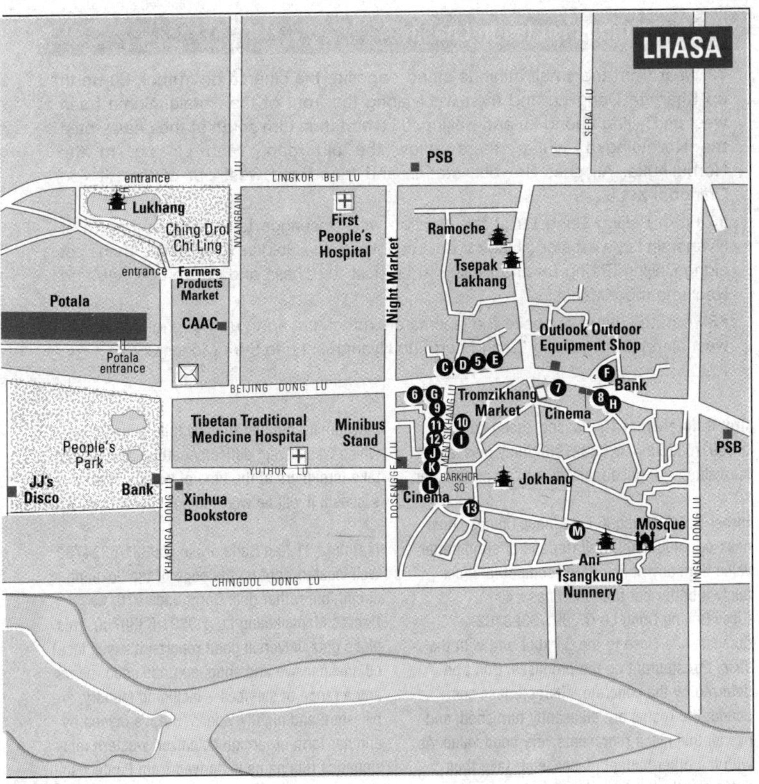

a little for the latter (¥2–4 for most trips). These days there are plenty of **taxis** around too, which have a ¥10 basic rate. **Bike rental** is available at some of the hotels; expect to pay about ¥3 per hour and to leave a deposit of up to ¥300. Apart from the altitude there are few problems with cycling in Lhasa; roads are wide, the traffic isn't overwhelming and there are traffic lights and traffic police at the main junctions to control the flow.

Accommodation

Most foreigners stay near the Barkhor in the long-standing budget stalwarts of the *Snowlands*, *Yak*, *Banak Shol*, *Pentoc* or *Kirey*. The mid- and upper-range hotels in the outskirts are standard Chinese style. Note that, uniquely, these places all advertise rooms by the hour – an indication of Lhasa's new and worrying reputation as a sleazy Chinese resort. If you're considering a tour that puts you up at the *Tibet Hotel*, think twice – not only is it badly located in the west of the city, it's very shabby and unfriendly.

Banak Shol Beijing Dong Lu ☎0891/6323829. Offers clean and homely dorms and a range of rooms with and without bath, and even manages a bit of garden in the courtyard. Beware the rooms at the front which can be noisy. The *Kailash* restaurant is conveniently on the premises. There's a chaotic free laundry service. It's not the best-run budget hotel but it's characterful, with a very Tibetan feel – there are always plenty of locals hanging round. ❷–❹

Useful minibus routes in Lhasa

#2 West from the small minibus stand opposite the cinema on Yuthok Lu north up Kharnga Dong Lu and then west along the front of the Potala. Some head west on Beijing Zhong Lu and Beijing Xi Lu and then turn south at the *Lhasa*, past the Norbulingka, while others follow the old road, Yuan Lin Lu, to the Norbulingka. All pass the bus station and then head west out of the city on Chingdol Xi Lu .

#3 From Beijing Dong Lu at the junction with Dosengge Lu, then loops north at Nyangrain Lu, west along Lingkor Bei Lu, down to the Golden Yaks Statue, then east along Beijing Zhong Lu and Beijing Xi Lu past the *Lhasa* and out to Drepung and Nechung monasteries.

#5 From the stand opposite the cinema on Yuthok Lu, north up Dosengge Lu, then west along Beijing Dong Lu and north up Nyangrain Lu to Sera Monastery.

Grand Hotel Tibet 196 Beijing Zhong Lu ⓣ0891/6826096, ⓕ6832195. Shiny new, and fair value, with good facilities and an oxygen bar. ❺

Hubei Hotel Beijing Xi Lu. A new, Chinese business-oriented hotel, well run and offering better value than any of its nearby competitors; certainly a better bet than the *Lhasa*. ❻

Kirey Beijing Dong Lu ⓣ0891/6323462. Conveniently close to the Barkhor and with the *Tashi 2* restaurant on the premises. Don't be deterred by the concrete, characterless compound; the rooms are pleasantly furnished, and overall this place represents very good value. As with the other budget places, staff take their duties lightly, but there is a free laundry service. Dorm beds ¥15, ❶

Kyichu 19 Beijing Dong Lu ⓣ0891/6338824. Centrally located, good value, with friendly Tibetan staff, this is certainly the best mid-range choice. There's a restaurant on site as well as an antiques shop. ❺

Lhasa Minzu Lu ⓣ0891/6324509, ⓕ6334117. Formerly the *Holiday Inn* (as a sign outside informs you), this is Lhasa's most luxurious hotel, with 460 rooms, a range of restaurants including the *Hard Yak Café,* swimming pool (summer only), business centre and in-house doctor. However, the real *Holiday Inn* would never tolerate present lax standards and this place is certainly not value for money. ❽

Lucky Place Family Hotel Mentsikhang Lu. A new, family-run and friendly little guesthouse, which was having difficulty getting a licence to take foreigners at the time of writing. If they succeed, it will be worth a look. Dorm beds ¥20, ❷

Mandala 31 Nan Barkhor Jie ⓣ0891/6324783. Well located right on the edge of the Jokhang circuit, but rather dull. Dorm beds ¥70, ❻

Pentoc Mentsikhang Lu ⓣ0891/6330700. This place gets universal good reports: it's well located, inexpensive and snug, and has good rooms and a range of services – including laundry, bike-hire and nightly videos. But it's owned by another form of foreign colonizer, western missionaries (the name is derived from Pentecostal). Dorm beds ¥30, ❷

Shangbala Mentsikhang Lu. A new, Chinese three-star place, well run and well located but lacking character. ❻

Snowlands Mentsikhang Lu ⓣ0891/6323687. Well situated near the Jokhang, though the place has a rather faded feel to it. Dorm beds ¥15, ❷

Yak Beijing Dong Lu ⓣ0891/6323496. Another budget favourite offering a range of options from variable-quality dorms to rooms with attached bathroom, all built around two courtyards. There's a communal area inside a Tibetan tent in one courtyard, but it's far from peaceful as the courtyard doubles as a car park. The horns of the stuffed yaks here are useful for drying your clothes on. The double rooms are clean, but the toilets are pungent. Dorm beds ¥20, ❶–❺

The City

With its mix of ascendant Chinese modernity set side by side with ancient Tibetan traditions, Lhasa is a vibrant, fast-changing city that throws up some bizarre juxtapositions – witness the pilgrims on their rounds of prostrations passing the ATM machines of the Bank of China. Construction sites abound,

△ Strolling around Lhasa

but it is still easy to get around to all the major monuments, many of which are within walking distance of the two central landmarks, the **Potala** and **Jokhang**.

The Potala

Perched atop Marpo Ri (Red Mountain), and named after Riwo Potala in India, holy mountain of the god Chenresi, the **Potala Palace** is dazzling both inside and out, an enduring landmark of the city of Lhasa. As you glory in the views from the roof, gaze at the glittering array of gold and jewels and wend your way from chapel to chapel, you'll rub shoulders with excited and awestruck pilgrims from all over ethnic Tibet, making offerings at each of the altars. But be aware that you're in a sad shell of a place: most of the rooms are off limits, part of a UNESCO World Heritage Grant was spent on a CCTV system, and the caretaker monks are not allowed to wear their robes. And don't tackle the Potala on your first day at altitude – the palace is a long climb up, and even the Tibetans huff and puff on the way up; you'll enjoy it more when you're acclimatized.

Rising thirteen dramatic storeys and consisting of over a thousand rooms, the palace complex took a workforce of at least seven thousand builders and fifteen hundred artists and craftsmen over fifty years to complete. The man mass of the Potala is the **White Palace** (Potrange Karpo), while the central building rising from the centre of this is the **Red Palace** (Potrang Marpo). There's a huge amount to take in on one visit and a second look helps to put it in perspective, though the **entrance fee** is a painful ¥70. The **opening hours** (officially daily 9am–6pm) are a source of major confusion as they seem to change frequently, so check with other travellers before you set off; at the time of writing, the palace was open to all in the morning, but in the afternoon you can only visit as part of a (loosely) guided tour that leaves at 3.30pm. Morning is certainly the best time to come, when the place bustles with excited pilgrims; in the afternoon a few foreigners are shown around on a (loosely) guided tour that leaves at 3.30pm. The policy on **photography** also varies: inside, it's either pricey or banned altogether. However, there seems to be little problem with taking pictures on the roof or on the balconies outside the chapels.

Built for several purposes, the Potala served as administrative centre, seat of government, monastery, fortress and the home of all the Dalai Lamas from the Fifth to the Fourteenth, although from the end of the eighteenth century, when the Norbulingka was built as the summer palace, they stayed here only in winter. It was King Songtsen Gampo who built the first palace on this site in the seventh century, though it was later destroyed by invaders. Today's White Palace (1645–1648) was built during the reign of the Fifth Dalai Lama, who took up residence in 1649, while the Red Palace, begun at the same time, was completed in 1693. Both palaces survived the Cultural Revolution relatively unscathed; apparently Zhou Enlai ordered their protection.

Into the palace

The #2 minibus passes the gate in the front wall of the massive compound. You enter here and walk through Shol village, once the red-light district of Lhasa, now lined with souvenir shops and vendors, then turn right through the gates and climb to the inner courtyard of the White Palace, the **Deyang Shar**, where you'll find the ticket office. The courtyard is surrounded by monks' rooms and stores, with the **Quarters of the Dalai Lama** at its eastern end. The opulently carved and painted Official Reception Hall beyond is dominated by the bulk of the high throne and hung with fabulous brocade and *thangkas* (embroidered or painted religious scrolls) with a small doorway leading into the private quarters of the Fourteenth Dalai Lama next door. There's a small audience chamber, a chapel, a hallway and finally the bedroom with an extremely well-painted mural of Tsongkhapa, founder of the Gelugpa school to which the Dalai Lama belongs, over the bed. On the other side of the Official Reception Hall are the private quarters of the previous Dalai Lamas but these are closed to the public.

Stairs lead from the inner courtyard up into the **Red Palace** and continue straight to the roof for fabulous views across Lhasa. You can then descend a floor at a time to tour the palace, moving clockwise all the way. The first room on the **upper floor** is the **Maitreya Chapel**, its huge number of fabulously ornate statues setting the tone for the remainder of the chapels. It's dominated by a seated statue of Maitreya made at the time of the Eighth Dalai Lama and said to contain the brain of Atisha, the eleventh-century Indian scholar responsible for a Buddhist revival in Tibet (see p.1118). On the far left of the Dalai Lama's throne is a statue of the Fifth Dalai Lama commissioned soon after his death and supposedly containing some of his hair.

The Red Palace is the final resting place of the Fifth to Thirteenth Dalai Lamas, except for the Sixth who died on his way to China and is said to be buried near Qinghai Hu in Qinghai Province. However, not all the tombs are open. Although they vary in size, all are jewel-encrusted golden *chortens* (traditional multi-tiered Tibetan Buddhist monuments that usually contain sacred objects) supporting tier upon tier of fantastic engraving; encased deep within are the bodies of the Dalai Lamas preserved in dry salt. You should at least be able to see either the Tomb of the Thirteenth Dalai Lama or Tomb of the Eighth Dalai Lama on the upper floor.

Considered the oldest and holiest shrines in the Potala, the **Lokeshvara Chapel** on the upper floor and the **Practice Chamber of the Dharma King**, directly below on the **upper middle floor**, date back to Songtsen Gampo's original construction, and are the focus of all Potala pilgrims. It's easy to miss the Practice Chamber, entered from a small corridor from the balcony. King Songtsen Gampo supposedly meditated in this dark, dingy room now dominated by statues of the king and his ministers, Tonmi Sambhota and Gawa. At the base of the main pillar is a stove, apparently used by Songtsen Gampo himself.

Although you pass through the lower middle floor, the chapels here are all closed and the remainder of the open rooms are on the **lower floor** leading off the large, many-columned Assembly Hall. The highlight down here is the grand **Chapel of the Dalai Lamas' Tombs**, containing the awesome golden *chorten* of the Fifth Dalai Lama which is three storeys high and consists of 3700kg of gold. To the left and right are smaller *chortens* with the remains of the Tenth and Twelfth Dalai Lamas and the *chortens* on either side of these main ones are believed to contain relics of Buddha himself. Visitors leave the Red Palace by a door behind the altar in the **Chapel of the Holy Born**, from where the path winds down the west side of the hill to the western gate.

Around the Potala

The area around the Potala offers plenty of enjoyable sights. Opposite the front of the palace, on the south side of Beijing Dong Lu, **People's Park** is a market and recreation area complete with fountain, dodgem cars, photographers' stalls and a monument celebrating "liberation". Farther west along Beijing

Dong Lu, the new *chorten* in the middle of the road marks the site of the old West Gate to the city. Due south from here, **Chakpori Hill**, the previous site of the medical college, is now topped by a radio transmitter. For a scenic view of the Potala, climb the hill using the path that goes in front of the public toilets just south of the *chorten*; you'll be able to go only as far as a massive tree laden with prayer flags before the guards at the transmitter start shouting.

From just east of the public toilets at the *chorten* a path leads a couple of hundred metres to the fabulously atmospheric **Palhalupuk Temple**, built around an ancient cave. You'll spot the ochre and maroon, and far less interesting, Neten Temple on the cliff first; Palhalupuk is the smaller, white building below. Entered from an ante-chapel, the cave, about 5m square, was King Songtsen Gampo's retreat in the seventh century and is lined with rock carvings, many of which date from that time. The most important altar is in front of the huge rock pillar that supports the roof, the main image here being of Sakyamuni flanked by his chief disciples. At the far right-hand corner stands a jewel- and *katag*-bedecked statue of Pelden Lhamo, the fierce protective deity of Tibet, on a tiny altar. The back wall has been left untouched, and it's said that the jewels of Songtsen Gampo's Nepalese wife, Princess Bhrikuti, are hidden behind. They don't get many tourists here, and the caretaker and monks are welcoming.

The main area of **rock carvings**, numbering around five thousand, are on the west and southern sides of Chakpori Hill. Back on the road, continue west from the *chorten* along the left fork. Just as you get to the junction with Yuan Lin Lu that leads down from the Golden Yaks Statue, you'll find a rough track leading off to the left. Follow it beside a stream for a couple of hundred metres and you'll arrive at the start of the rock paintings and carvings, which supposedly represent the visions seen by King Songtsen Gampo during his meditation. The carvers at work here copy ancient texts and prayers or sacred *mantras*; they work partly for alms but also produce work for sale.

North of the Potala

Around the other side of the Potala, the park of **Ching Drol Chi Ling** (¥2) has fine views up to the north facade of the Potala and sports a large area of ill-kept trees and a boating lake formed by the removal of earth during the construction of the palace. The park is entered from the north side of the lake or via the entrance at the end of the Farmers Products Market. On an island in the lake is the small, pleasant **Lukhang**, built by the Sixth Dalai Lama in honour of the *naga* king and for use as a retreat. Legend tells of a pact between the builder of the Potala and the king of the *nagas,* subterranean creatures who resemble dragons – the earth could be used as long as a chapel was built in their honour. The temple is famed for the very old and detailed murals on the middle and top floors, but you'll need a flashlight if you want to study them in detail, and the protective wire in front doesn't help. The top-floor pictures showing the stages of human life, the journey of the soul after death and various legends are somewhat esoteric, but the middle-floor murals, depicting the construction of the great monasteries of Sera and Drepung among others, are far more comprehensible.

The Jokhang

From afar the **Jokhang**, sometimes called Tshuglakhang ("cathedral"), the holiest temple in the Tibetan Buddhist world, is somewhat unprepossessing, but draw close and you'll get infected by the anticipation of the pilgrims and the almost palpable air of veneration. Inside you're in for one of the most

THE JOKHANG

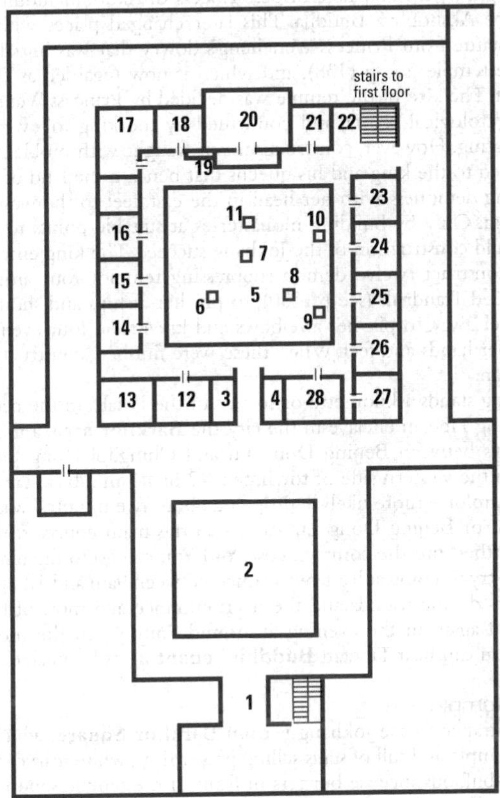

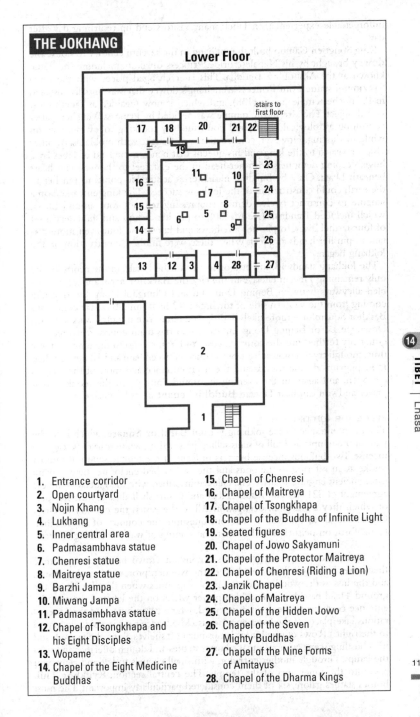

1. Entrance corridor
2. Open courtyard
3. Nojin Khang
4. Lukhang
5. Inner central area
6. Padmasambhava statue
7. Chenresi statue
8. Maitreya statue
9. Barzhi Jampa
10. Miwang Jampa
11. Padmasambhava statue
12. Chapel of Tsongkhapa and his Eight Disciples
13. Wopame
14. Chapel of the Eight Medicine Buddhas
15. Chapel of Chenresi
16. Chapel of Maitreya
17. Chapel of Tsongkhapa
18. Chapel of the Buddha of Infinite Light
19. Seated figures
20. Chapel of Jowo Sakyamuni
21. Chapel of the Protector Maitreya
22. Chapel of Chenresi (Riding a Lion)
23. Janzik Chapel
24. Chapel of Maitreya
25. Chapel of the Hidden Jowo
26. Chapel of the Seven Mighty Buddhas
27. Chapel of the Nine Forms of Amitayus
28. Chapel of the Dharma Kings

unforgettable experiences in Tibet; many visitors end up returning day after day.

King Songtsen Gampo built the Jokhang in the seventh century to house the **dowry** brought by his Nepalese bride, Princess Bhrikuti, including the statue known as the Akshobhya Buddha. This later changed places with the Jowo Sakyamuni statue from Princess Wencheng's dowry that was initially installed in Ramoche temple (see p.1138), and which is now regarded as Tibet's most sacred object. The **site** of the temple was decided by Princess Wencheng after consulting astrological charts, and confirmed by the king following a vision while meditating. However, construction was fraught with problems. Another vision revealed to the king and his queens that beneath the land of Tibet lay a huge, sleeping demoness with her head in the east, feet to the west and heart beneath Lhasa. Only by building monasteries at suitable points to pin her to the earth could construction of the Jokhang succeed. The king embarked on a scheme to construct twelve demon-suppressing temples: four around Lhasa, which included Trandruk (see p.1150), to pin her at hips and shoulders; a set of four farther away, to pin her at elbows and knees; and four even more distant to pin her hands and feet. When these were finished, construction on the Jokhang began.

The Jokhang stands a kilometre or so east of the Potala, in the centre of the only remaining Tibetan enclave in the city, the **Barkhor area**, a maze of cobbled alleyways between Beijing Dong Lu and Chingdol Dong Lu. If you're coming from the western side of town, the #2 or #3 minibus may come into Barkhor Square or – more likely – drop you about five minutes' walk away on Dosengge Lu or Beijing Dong Lu. Access to the main courtyard is free, but going any further into the complex costs ¥40. You can go to the temple at any time, though try to come at least twice: once between 9am and 12.30pm, when most pilgrims do the rounds and the front entrance and most of the chapels are open, and again in the evening at around 7pm, when the monks are at prayer and you can hear Tibetan **Buddhist chant** in its homeland.

Inside the temple

The main entrance to the Jokhang is from **Barkhor Square**, which is to the west of the temple and full of stalls selling prayer flags, white scarves (*katag*) and incense. Two bulbous incense burners in front of the temple send out juniper smoke as an offering to the gods and the two walled enclosures here contain three ancient engraved pillars. The tallest is inscribed with the Tibetan–Chinese agreement of 821 AD and reads: "Tibet and China shall abide by the frontiers of which they are now in occupation. All to the east is the country of Great China; and all to the west is, without question, the country of Great Tibet. Henceforth on neither side shall there be waging of war nor seizing of territory."

In front of the huge temple doors a constant crowd of pilgrims prostrate themselves – you can hear the clack of the wooden protectors on their hands and the hiss as the wood moves along the flagstones when they lie flat on the ground. Head past the giant golden prayer wheel on the left and through the entrance corridor to the open **courtyard**, where ceremonies and their preparations take place. (If the front entrance is closed, access is via a side courtyard to the right.) Rows of tiny butter lamps burn on shelves along the far wall and it's a bustling scene as monks make butter statues and dough offerings and tend the lamps. Through another corridor, with small chapels to left and right, you pass into the inner area of the temple. The central section, **Kyilkhor Thil**, houses statues galore, six of them considered particularly important. The most dramatic are the six-metre-high Padmasambhava on the left, which dates from 1955, and the half-seated figure of Maitreya, the Buddha of the Future, to the right.

Devout pilgrims turn left to move clockwise and enter each chapel in turn to pray and make offerings. They don't hang around, though; stand still to admire the statues and you'll get trampled in the rush. Some of the wooden door frames and columns are original – in particular, the door frame of the Chapel of Chenresi and the columns in front of the Chapel of Jowo Sakyamuni were created by Niwari craftsmen from Nepal during the temple's early years. As with all temples in Tibet, it's often difficult to know exactly what you are looking at. Some of the statues are original, others were damaged during the Cultural Revolution and have been restored either slightly or extensively, and others are replicas. Whatever their age, all are held in deep reverence by the pilgrims.

It's easy to feel overwhelmed, but if you manage only one chapel it should be the **Chapel of Jowo Sakyamuni** in the middle of the back wall of the temple. The 1.5-metre-high Sakyamuni is depicted at 12 years of age, with a sublimely beautiful golden face. Draped in heavy brocade and jewels, this is the most deeply venerated statue in Tibet. Although the Jokhang was originally built to house the statue, the Jowo Sakyamuni first stood in the temple of Ramoche until rumours of a Tang invasion late in the seventh century led to its removal to a hiding place in the Jokhang. During the reign of Trisong Detsen, the Bon opponents of Buddhism removed the statue and buried it, but it was found and sent out of Lhasa for safety. The statue was again buried during King Langdarma's attempt to annihilate Buddhism, but eventually returned to the Jokhang where it rests today. Although there is a rumour that the original was destroyed in the eighteenth century by Mongol invaders, neither it nor the chapel was harmed during the Cultural Revolution and the statue is widely regarded as the original. Monks here keep the butter lamps topped up while the pilgrims move around the altar, bowing their heads to Jowo Sakyamuni's right leg and then his left.

By the time you reach the **upper floor** you'll probably be punch-drunk and there is less to detain you up here than down below, although most of the chapels are now open after restoration. Of most interest here is the **Chapel of Songtsen Gampo**, directly above the main entrance in the west wall and featuring a large statue of the king flanked by his two queens. Continue up the stairs in the southwest corner of the chapel to one fierce and one peaceful image of **Pelden Lhamo**, who is regarded as the protective deity of Tibet and is particularly popular with pilgrims.

From the temple **roof**, the views down over Barkhor Square, into the temple courtyard and as far as the Potala in the distance are wonderful, the golden statues even more impressive close to. You can get up to the roof using any one of a number of staircases, located just to the right of the main entrance, in the far southeast corner of the temple itself, or at the far end of the side courtyard to the right of the main entrance.

The Barkhor

Traditionally pilgrims to Lhasa circled the city on two clockwise routes: an outer circuit called the Lingkhor, now vanished under two-lane highways and rebuilding, and the shorter **Barkhor** circuit through the alleyways a short distance from the Jokhang walls. This has survived, a maze of picturesque streets a world away from the rest of Lhasa. It's now lined with the stalls of an outdoor market selling all manner of goods – saddles and stirrups, Chinese army gear, *thangkas*, jewellery, blankets, cassette tapes, carpets, tin trunks and pictures of lamas, to mention a fraction only. The pilgrims, too, are an amazing sight: statuesque Khampa men with their traditional knives and red-braided hair, decorated with huge chunks of turquoise; Amdo women dripping jewels with their hair in 108 plaits; and old ladies spinning their tiny prayer wheels and intoning *mantras*. The Barkhor circuit is actually at its most interesting in the evening when the stalls clear their tourist junk and vendors start selling what the locals actually want – straw hats, kung-fu T-shirts and abject plastic. The clockwise-strolling masses come here to browse and socialize.

The whole Barkhor area is worth exploring – with huge wooden doors set in long white walls and leading into hidden courtyards – but try not to miss **Tromzikhang market** to the north of the Jokhang; take the main alleyway into the Barkhor that leads off Beijing Dong Lu just east of Ramoche Lu and it's just down on your left. The two-storey modern building is a bit soulless, but nowhere else in the world can you see (or smell) so much yak butter in one place.

One other sight to seek out here is the **Ani Tsangkung Nunnery** (¥6) to the southeast of the Jokhang; you'll probably need to ask the way. With over a hundred nuns in residence, several of whom speak good English, there is a lively but devout atmosphere here, especially around prayer time at 11am. The main chapel is dominated by a fabulous Chenresi in a glass case. From the back of the chapel, facing the main door, you can head right, round the outside, to visit the long, narrow room containing King Songtsen Gampo's meditation chamber in a pit at the end. Supposedly his meditation here altered the course of the Kyichu River when it looked likely to flood the construction of the Jokhang.

Ramoche

The three-storey, robust **Ramoche** (daily 9am–6; ¥20, plus up to ¥50 per chapel for photographs) is small but intriguing, and second only in importance to the Jokhang. A short walk north of the Barkhor, on Ramoche Lu between Beijing Dong Lu and Lingkor Bei Lu, it was built in the seventh century by Songtsen Gampo's Chinese wife, Princess Wencheng, to house the Jowo Sakyamuni statue that she brought to Tibet. The statue later ended up in the Jokhang and was replaced by the Akshobhya Buddha, a representation of Sakyamuni at the age of 8. This much-revered statue was broken in two during the Cultural Revolution, with one part taken to China and narrowly saved from being melted down, while the other was later discovered on a factory scrap heap in Tibet. However, it's fairly unlikely that the statue in position today in the main shrine, the **Tsangkhang** at the back of the temple, is the original.

While you're in the area, call in on the tiny **Tsepak Lakhang** to the south of Ramoche. The little entrance is just beside a huge incense burner and once inside you pass along a small alley lined with a row of prayer wheels. There are two small chapels in this hugely popular temple, and the 55 friendly monks in residence chant their daily prayers around noon. You can walk the small circuit around the walls of Tsepak Lakhang, where the murals have been newly painted.

Norbulingka

Situated in the west of town, on the route of the #2 minibus, the **Norbulingka** (Jewel Park), the Summer Palace of the Dalai Lamas (daily 9.30am–12.30pm & 2.30pm–6pm; ¥35), is not in the top league of Lhasa sights, but worth a look if you've time on your hands. If you're in Lhasa during the festivals of the Worship of the Buddha (July) or during Shotun, the Yoghurt Festival (Aug/Sept), when crowds flock here for picnics and to see masked dances and traditional opera, you should definitely make the trip out. The forty-hectare park has been used as a recreation area by the Dalai Lamas since the time of the Seventh incarnation. The first palace to be built was the **Palace of the Eighth Dalai Lama**, constructed towards the end of the eighteenth century and the closest to the entrance. This palace became the official summer residence to which all Dalai Lamas moved, with due ceremony, on the eighteenth day of the third lunar month. Other buildings open to the public are the **Palace of the Thirteenth Dalai Lama** in the far northwest corner – beyond the appalling zoo – and, the highlight of the visit, the **New Summer Palace**, built in 1956 by the Fourteenth Dalai Lama; it was from here that he fled Lhasa in 1959. Visitors pass through the audience chamber via an anteroom to the meditation chamber, on to his bedroom and then into the reception hall dominated by a fabulously carved golden throne, before passing through to the quarters of the Dalai Lama's mother. The Western plumbing and radio sit beside fabulous *thangkas* and religious murals. It's all very sad and amazingly evocative, the forlorn rooms bringing home the reality of exile.

Eating, drinking and entertainment

The traditional **Tibetan diet** – constrained by what little will grow at over 4000m – consists in large part of **butter tea**, a unique mixture of yak butter, tea and salt, all churned into a blend that most Westerners find largely undrinkable, but which Tibetans consume in huge quantities. Into this is stirred **tsampa**, roasted barley flour, to form a dough with the consistency of raw pastry and a not unpleasant nutty flavour. **Yak meat**, yoghurt and cheese (often dried into bite-sized cubes to preserve it) and sometimes a soup of a few vegetables supplement this. **Thukpa** (pronounced tukpa) is a noodle soup with a few bits and pieces of whatever is available thrown in. If you're lucky, you'll find **momos**, tiny steamed or fried dough parcels containing meat or vegetables (a *thri momo* is a solid dough parcel without a filling). The local brew, **chang**, is a sweet, yellow beer made from a mixture of grains.

Besides the vast number of restaurants in Lhasa, there's an excellent, cheap **night market** along Dosengge Lu, noodle places near Tromzikhang market, and bakeries outside the mosque selling tasty Muslim bread. For **trekking food** like muesli and chocolate, try the counters at the *Kailash* or *Snowland Restaurants*, or the new **supermarket** at the east end of Yuthok Lu. Shops along Beijing Dong Lu sell tasteless but filling army rations in green wrappers.

Restaurants and cafés

Barkhor Café Barkhor Square. A good to place to sit with a chocolate milkshake, though the food is pretty bad – the draw here is the rooftop terrace at the southwest corner of Barkhor Square. Reach the café by the spiral staircase to the right and look down on the evening bustle of the crowds as the setting sun bounces golden rays off the Jokhang roof.

Beijing Duck Restaurant Beijing Xi Lu, opposite and a little west of the *Grand Hotel Tibet*; there's a sign in English (but no English menu inside). No prizes for guessing the house speciality here. You'll pay about ¥50 per person.

Dunya Beijing Dong Lu. Foreign-run, very civilized and not very Tibetan. A diverse range of specials, good Western, Indian and Nepali food and even half-decent Australian wine. Expect to pay around ¥60 a head.

Gangki Restaurant Corner of Mentsikhang Lu and Barkhor Square. This rooftop place is good value and has great views of the Jokhang. Very popular with Tibetans and often extremely busy. Main dishes cost ¥10–30; Tibetan tea and *tsampa* are also available.

Hard Yak Café *Lhasa Hotel*, Minzu Lu. Offering starched linen, muzak, old magazines and a range of Western food, this place is an expensive retreat for the culture-shocked. Expect to pay ¥60–80 for a main meal; the Yak Burger (¥68) is the only thing on the menu that's almost worth the price, though it should only be tackled by the seriously hungry.

Kailash In the *Banak Shol*, Beijing Dong Lu. Their set breakfast includes eggs, toast, hash browns and tomatoes for ¥20. Also on offer are yak burgers, spaghetti and various vegetarian options. The Japanese dishes are well done, and the Japanese room at the back is a good place to relax, as it's usually empty.

Lhasa Kitchen Beijing Dong Lu, beside the *Yak Hotel*. Ignore the tacky lampshades and concentrate on the excellent Tibetan cuisine served in this upmarket but inexpensive place. Try soup with *shaphali* (meat and vegetable patties) followed by *deysee* (rice, raisins and yoghurt).

Makye Ama Behind the Jokhang, southeast corner of the Barkhor. The kind of New Age café you might expect to find in the arty quarter of any Western city. Try the Nepali and Indian dishes. The main draw is the great view over the Jokhang perambulators. The restaurant library has a small collection of English-language books you can borrow.

Muslim Restaurant Beijing Dong Lu, 50m west of the *Banak Shol Hotel*. Run by one of the many Hui families who now live in Lhasa, this little place cooks up some great yak dishes.

Sichuan Restaurants Beijing Dong lu, just west of the *Yak Hotel*. Perhaps it's preferable to patronize Tibetan traders, but it has to be admitted that Chinese restaurants make much better food – the three little places here do inexpensive and delicious Sichuan food and hotpots.

Shangrila In the courtyard of the *Kirey Hotel*. Pleasant Tibetan furnishings, with a large menu, though the food is bland – it's designed not to tax the palate of any of the tour groups who sometimes take over here. There's some rather lacklustre Tibetan singing and dancing every evening at 7pm.

Tashi 1 Corner of Beijing Dong Lu and Mentsikhang Lu. Along with its sister restaurant, *Tashi 2*, in the *Kirey Hotel*, this is the mainstay of budget travellers in Lhasa. Both offer the same small and inexpensive menu, including a range of Tibetan *momos* and delicious, tortilla-like *bobis* with sour cream and vegetables or meat, as well as French fries, spaghetti, mashed potatoes and fried yak meat. The cheesecake and the chocolate cake are excellent.

Third Eye Mentsikhang Lu, opposite the *Snowlands Hotel*. Good Tibetan fare; on some nights a Western action movie is shown.

Yuyi Opposite the *Banak Shol Hotel*, Beijing Dong Lu. Sichuan cuisine served up in an informal atmosphere. No MSG is used but the food isn't as spicy as it should be, unless you make it clear that you want the genuine article.

Entertainment

Not many foreigners realize it, but Lhasa is renowned for sleaze – it reputedly has more brothels than any other Chinese city, catering to Chinese sex tourists and the many soldiers billeted here. A wander in the western half of the city at night reveals rashes of karaoke bars and "hairdressers" doing brisk business. It's now common for Tibetans to say that corruption by Chinese values is as damaging to their culture as oppression.

A less controversial form of entertainment is the discos. **JJs**, opposite the Potala on the southwest side of People's Park, is the biggest, and one of the few places you'll see Chinese and Tibetans mixing freely. There's a ¥30 cover charge, for which you get two live acts and a mix of slushy love songs and techno-lite. There's also a scattering of **bars** aimed at the well-off Chinese; most are on Beijing Zhong Lu, close to the *Lhasa Hotel*, and charges are comparable to those in the West. Best is the *Music Kitchen Café*, where beers are ¥20.

Sadly, there's not much chance to see **Traditional Tibetan** music, dance and opera, unless you happen to be here during a festival. There are occasional shows put on for tourists; ask in your hotel or check for notices in the *Lhasa Hotel* or *Tibet Hotel*, or look in on the *Shangrila Restaurant*. In season, shows of Tibetan opera are sometimes held at the *Potala Hotel*, at the base of the Potala in Shol village. Performances begin at 8pm and 9.30pm and last one hour. Tickets cost ¥100, and should be bought in advance.

The **cinemas** on Yuthok Lu at the junction with Dosengge Lu, and on Beijing Dong Lu between the *Banak Shol* and *Kirey* hotels, have some films from the West, but check whether they've been dubbed in Chinese before you bother; otherwise, it's kung-fu movies which are the staple fare. Western videos are shown nightly at 8pm at the *Pentoc Hotel* and occasionally at the *Third Eye Restaurant* and *Barkhor Café*.

Shopping

A major tourist activity in Lhasa is **shopping**. The main area for browsing is the **Barkhor** (see p.1137), where the better stuff is in the shops behind the stalls, but they're much more expensive than vendors outside. The vendors on the street outside the *Lhasa Hotel* have essentially the same range, but in smaller quantities, and they start off at even higher prices. The shop at the *Pentoc Hotel* has a good range of souvenirs, including **yak-wool jumpers** and socks. Another good gift is the **handmade paper** sold from a shop beside the *Lhasa Kitchen*.

The search for **postcards** can be frustrating and expensive as sets on offer at the main sights are generally pricey; those at the post office and the Xinhua Bookstore are the best value. For **film**, check out the photography shops on Kharnga Dong Lu opposite People's Park. Processing is also available here; expect to pay about ¥1 per print, although the quality is variable – it's best to ask around among travellers to get a current recommendation.

Some travellers buy **bikes** here and ride them to Nepal, where they can be sold, sometimes at a profit. The sturdiest bike for this is the Pegasus, which costs ¥700. You can buy it in the department store just east of the intersection of Dosengge Lu and Beijing Dong Lu.

Finally, if you feel like doing some shopping *for* rather than *from* Tibetans, buy notebooks and pens to donate to an orphanage and give them to Neema at the *Snowlands Restaurant*. Alternatively, turn up at the orphanage itself at 42 Beijing Xi Lu.

Books

The two Xinhua Bookstores on Yuthok Lu and on Beijing Xi Lu, just east of the *Tibet Hotel*, are pretty much useless; if you're very lucky you might find the odd classic English novel here. If you're amused by rabid Chinese propaganda, search out the comic book in Tibetan about the British invasion in 1904. There are a few pricey English coffee-table books, which you can also get in the lobby of the *Lhasa Hotel*. The best on offer is the paperback *Potala Palace* with good pictures of many of the treasures in the Potala that either will be closed off when you're there or you'll fail to notice as you're too overwhelmed. The hardback glossies, *Tibet* and *Snowland Tibet*, are both pricey and heavy to carry around, but have evocative photographs taken throughout the country. If you're into Buddhist art, take a look at the even glossier and heavier *Precious True Word Picture Album of the Buddha, Images of Buddhism*.

For a Tibetan **novel**, get hold of *The Secret Tale of Tesur House*, sold in the *Banak Shol Hotel* and the shop at the *Pentoc*. The first fiction translated from Tibetan into English, it's not a bad read, with a strong plot centring around gory murders and business intrigue, and it's full of fascinating descriptions of Tibetan life and customs – the kind of minutiae that you won't find described anywhere else. Bear in mind, though, that the fact that it's been translated meant it was deemed acceptable by the Chinese authorities. For Western novels, try the library at the *Makye Ama Restaurant*. You can borrow the books for free, but you have to leave a hefty deposit.

Carpets

If it's carpets you're after, visit Khawachen, at 103 Chingdol Xi Lu (Mon–Sat 9am–6.30pm; ⓣ0891/6333255, ⓕ6333250), on the route of the #2 minibus. This government-affiliated and US-financed organization offers the best selection of carpets in Lhasa and the chance to watch them being produced, and can also arrange to ship the merchandise home for you. Available in muted, attractive traditional designs, plus some with a modern slant, the carpets range from 50cm square (US$25) to 2.7m x 3.6m (US$1300). The Lhasa Carpet Factory, Chingdol Dong Lu (Mon–Fri 9am–1pm & 3.30–6pm, Sat 9am–1pm; ⓣ0891/6323447), is a bigger operation where you can watch huge carpets being woven; an extensive range of traditional and modern patterns is available here, costing from ¥140 to ¥32,000. Shipping can also be arranged. Despite its name, the Traditional Tibetan Carpet and Rug Factory, on the left as you approach the ticket office to Norbulingka, is just a small shop, but it has plenty of traditional carpets and also some more unusual contemporary hangings (¥550–1200).

Paintings

Tibetan **thangkas** (religious scrolls) and religious and secular **paintings** would appear to be obvious souvenirs, but many are of poor quality – you'll need to spend some time browsing before you buy. The least expensive *thangkas* – you'll find masses of these in the Barkhor – have a printed religious picture in the middle while the better-quality, higher-priced ones have a hand-painted image. Look carefully, though, at the quality of the painting itself; the best ones have finely drawn and highly detailed backgrounds, but the less skilled artists leave larger areas of the canvas blank with less meticulously painted details. The asking prices are high; bargain hard. An excellent range of good-quality, hand-painted *thangkas* is available at the Tibet Traditional Art Gallery, next door to the Ramoche – expect prices starting at ¥3000. Look also in the shops in Shol village just inside the Potala gate and the *Lhasa Hotel* lobby shop (daily 9am–8pm) which has a range of paintings (¥500–2500) and will give you some idea of the top end of the scale.

Clothes and tents

There are plenty of **tailors** in town, both Chinese and Tibetan, who can make traditional Tibetan or Western dress; look on Beijing Dong Lu west of the *Yak Hotel*. A huge range of materials, from light, summer-weight stuff, to heavier, warmer textiles, is available. Prices depend on the material, but light jackets start at around ¥100, while skirts, trousers or a floor-length Tibetan woman's dress (*chuba*) cost ¥80 and up. Many places have samples made up and you can simply shop around until you find the style and material you want. From first measuring to collecting the finished item usually takes 24 hours.

Rather like marquees, **Tibetan tents** are used on religious and ceremonial occasions and are usually white with auspicious symbols appliquéd in blue. They're available at the Tibetan Tent Factory, just off the unnamed alley that heads north a couple of hundred metres west of the *Yak Hotel*; take the right fork just inside the alley and the factory is on the left. Expect to start negotiating at around ¥2500 for a tent and ¥100 for a door curtain. Cheaper door curtains of differing qualities are available in the Barkhor.

Trekking equipment

For rucksacks, sleeping bags and serious **hiking gear**, check out Outlook Outdoor Equipment on Beijing Dong Lu, opposite the *Kirey Hotel*

Trekking Tibet

For the experienced walker Tibet offers plenty of enticing **trekking routes**. The popular Ganden–Samye trek (see box, p.1152) has the advantages that both the start and finish points are relatively accessible to Lhasa and that it takes only three to four days. Also worth considering are treks to the cave hermitage of **Drak Yerpa** from Lhasa (allow a full day and be prepared to camp), and the five-day trek from Tingri to **Everest Base camp** via Rongbuk. The more challenging options include the sixteen-day mammoth trek to the **Kangshung** face of Everest, exploring the valleys east of the mountain; the 24-day circumnavigation of Namtso Lake, including the arduous exploration of the Shang Valley to the southwest; or the great thirty-day circuit (a Tibetan guide is highly recommended) from Lhatse to **Lake Dangra** up on the Chang Tang plateau.

Spring (April–June) and autumn (September–November) are the best **seasons** in which to trek, though cold-weather threats such as hypothermia and frostbite should be taken seriously even in these months. While trekking is possible at any time in the valleys, high altitudes become virtually impossible in the winter; anyone contemplating trekking at this time should be sure to get local information about the terrain and likely conditions. During the wettest months (June–September), rivers are in flood and crossing them can be difficult, even impossible.

Once you start trekking you get off the beaten track extremely quickly and there is no infrastructure to support trekkers and no rescue service; you therefore need to be fit, acclimatized, totally self-reliant and prepared to do some research before you go. There are two essential books: *Tibet Handbook: a Pilgrimage Guide* by Victor Chan (Moon) and *Trekking in Tibet* by Gary McCue (Cordee), which is especially good for shorter day-treks that anyone can do without all the gear.

(Ⓦ www.ontheway.com.cn). Export-quality Chinese sleeping bags cost ¥600 to buy (¥20–30 a day to rent), and two- or three-person tents, rucksacks, Karrimats and stoves are ¥30–40 per day to rent. The North Col Mountaineering Shop, opposite the Potala in the northwest corner of People's Park, has a similar selection. You can rent sleeping bags from the *Snowlands Restaurant* for ¥8 a night.

Listings

Airlines CAAC, Nyangrain Lu (daily 9am–8.30pm; ⓣ0891/6833446).

Banks and exchange There are several branches of the *Bank of China* around town, but the main one on Lingkor Bei Lu, north of the Golden Yaks Statue (Mon–Fri 9am–1pm & 3.30–6pm) is the only place in Tibet for cash advances on credit cards. The branch on Beijing Dong Lu is conveniently located close to the *Banak Shol* (Mon–Fri 9.30am–6pm, Sat & Sun 11am–3pm).

Bike rental The *Snowlands Hotel* has the usual clunky bikes for ¥3/hr plus deposit, while the *Pentoc Hotel* has mountain bikes for ¥6/hr and ¥15/hr, plus deposit.

Consulates The Nepalese Consulate, 13 Norbulingka Lu (Mon–Fri 10am–12.30pm; ⓣ0891/682281), has a next-day visa service, for which you'll need to submit one passport photograph. Single-entry visas cost ¥135 for fifteen days, ¥225 for thirty days; multiple-entry visas are ¥360 for thirty days, ¥540 for sixty days. You can get single-entry visas at Kodari (see p.1169), but payment there has to be in US dollars.

Hospital First People's Hospital, Lingkor Bei Lu (Mon–Fri 10am–12.30pm & 4–6pm; at weekends emergencies only). It's better to go in the morning when more staff are available and you'll need to take a Chinese translator. There is no dental treatment available in Lhasa, only extraction. Rabies serum is not available (see "Health", p.1125). You could also try the traditional Tibetan Medicine Hospital (Mentsikhang), Yuthok Lu (hours as above). Go upstairs and look for the only sign in English, which says "Outpatients' Office" – this is where the doctor who deals with foreigners works. Otherwise, as some staff are Tibetan and some Chinese, a translator who speaks both is ideal.

Internet access The cybercafé opposite the

Banak Shol Hotel is open 24hr and charges ¥5/hr. There are a couple of smaller places with similar rates on Mentsikhang Lu. Be aware that email from Tibet is monitored, so don't mention any Tibetans by name.

Mail and telephones The main post office is on Beijing Dong Lu, just east of the Potala (daily 9am–8pm). Poste restante and international customs (Mon–Fri 9.30am–1pm & 3.30–6pm) is the counter facing you on the far left as you enter. Mail to be collected here should be addressed Poste Restante, Main Post Office, Lhasa, Tibet, China. Check both the book that lists mail received at the office and ask to see new mail. There's a charge of ¥1.50 per item received. EMS is next door to the post office, and also next door is a 24hr office with direct-dialling facilities and a fax service.

Pharmacies Most are along Yuthok Lu around the junction with Dosengge Lu. There is a pharmacy specializing in Tibetan medicine on the north side of Barkhor Square. Again, you'll need a translator.

PSB Lingkor Bei Lu and also Beijing Dong Lu (Mon–Fri 9.30am–1pm & 3.30–7pm). While PSB offices should be the place to go for factual information about closed and open areas, the information is rarely reliable and frequently inconsistent from one office to the next. The office on Beijing Dong Lu is larger and handles permits and visa extensions.

Around Lhasa

Not only is Lhasa awash with enough sights to keep even the most energetic visitor busy for several days, but the major monasteries of **Sera**, **Drepung** and **Ganden** are easily accessible from the city as half-day or day-trips. Indeed, Sera and Drepung have virtually been gobbled up in the urban sprawl that now characterizes Lhasa, while going on the trip to Ganden is a good chance to get out into the countryside. Morning visits to any of them are likely to be in the company of parties of devout pilgrims who'll scurry around the temples making their offerings before heading on to the next target. Follow on behind them and you'll visit all the main buildings; don't worry too much if you aren't sure what you are looking at – most of the pilgrims haven't a clue either. The monasteries are generally peaceful and atmospheric places where nobody minds you ambling at will, and sooner or later you're bound to come across some monks who want to practise their English.

Sera

To reach **Sera Monastery** (Mon–Sat 9am–noon & 2–4pm; ¥35), 4km north of Lhasa, by public transport, take a #5 **minibus** from the southern end of Nyangrain Lu or from the small minibus stand opposite the cinema on Yuthok Lu. You'll either be dropped on the road, about 500m outside the white-walled monastery compound, or be taken along the track to the entrance. To get transport back, it's better to walk back out to the road. The last minibuses leave just after the end of the debating at about 5pm.

Founded in 1419 by Sakya Yeshe, one of the main disciples of Tsongkhapa, founder of the Gelugpa order, Sera is situated below a hermitage where the great man spent many years in retreat. Spared during the Cultural Revolution, the buildings are in good repair although there is always a fair amount of ongoing building work. Pilgrims proceed on a clockwise circuit, visiting the three main **colleges**, Sera Me, Sera Ngag-Pa and Sera Je, and the main assembly hall, Tsokchen. All are constructed with chapels leading off a central hall and more chapels on an upper floor. They're great places to linger and watch the pilgrims rushing about their devotions. However, if you just want to catch the flavour of the most dramatic buildings, head straight up the hill from the main entrance. After a couple of hundred metres you'll reach the **Tsokchen**, Sera's largest building, built in 1710. The hall is supported by over a hundred columns

Life in the great monasteries

Fifty years ago, there were still six great, functioning **Gelugpa monasteries**: Sera, Drepung and Ganden near Lhasa, plus Tashilunpo in Shigatse (see p.1160), Labrang (see p.1034) and Kumbum (see p.1060). They each operated on a similar system to cope with the huge numbers of monks that were drawn to these major institutions from all over Tibet. In their heyday, Sera and Ganden had five thousand residents each and Drepung (possibly the largest monastery the world has ever known) had between eight and ten thousand.

Each monastery was divided into colleges, **dratsang**, which differed from each other in the type of studies undertaken. Each college was under the management of an abbot (*khenpo*), and a monk responsible for discipline (*ge-kor*). Attached to each college were a number of houses or *khangsten,* where the monks lived during their time at the monastery. Usually these houses catered for students from different geographical regions, and admission to the monastery was controlled by the heads of the houses to whom aspirant monks would apply. Each college had its own assembly hall and chapels, but there was also a main assembly hall where the entire community could gather.

Not every member of the community spent their time in scholarly pursuits. Communities the size of these took huge amounts of organization and the largest monasteries also maintained large estates worked by serfs. About half the monks might be engaged in academic study while the other half worked at administration, the supervision of the estate work and the day-to-day running of what was essentially a small town.

The most obvious feature of these monasteries **today** is their emptiness; hundreds of monks now rattle around in massive compounds built for thousands. Such has been the fate of religious establishments under the Chinese and the flow of lamas into exile that there are now questions about the quality of the Buddhist education available at the monasteries inside Tibet. Monks and nuns nowadays need to be vetted and receive Chinese government approval before they can join a monastery or convent and, although there are persistent rumours of tourists being informed on by monks, it's also apparent that both monks and nuns have been, and continue to be, at the forefront of open political opposition to the Chinese inside Tibet.

and it's here, between statues of the Fifth and Thirteenth Dalai Lamas, that you'll find the main statue of Sakya Yeshe, the founder of the monastery. The Sakya Yeshe statue is a reproduction of the original one in Sera Ngag-Pa college. When there were plans to move the original to the Tsokchen, the story goes that the statue itself said that it wished to stay in the college, so a copy was made.

At the top of the path the walled and shady **debating courtyard** is definitely worth a visit at 3.30pm, when the monks assemble in small animated groups to practise their highly stylized debating skills, involving much posturing, clapping and stamping. They're used to visitors – indeed, it's hard not to suspect the whole circus is put on for visitors – and there seems to be no problem about taking photographs.

To the left of the courtyard, the college of **Sera Je** is the best college to visit if you manage only one. Its spacious assembly hall is hung with fine *thangkas*, but the focus for pilgrims here is the Hayagriva Chapel (Hayagriva or Tamdrin, "the Horse-Headed One", is the protective deity of Sera) reached via an entrance in the left-hand wall.

If you're feeling energetic, take the path up the hillside, from behind the Tsokchen (follow the telegraph wires) to **Tsongkhapa's Hermitage**

(Choding Khang), which is a reconstruction of the original – his meditation cave is a bit farther up. There are splendid views over Lhasa from here.

Drepung and Nechung

Once the largest monastery in the world, **Drepung** (daily 9am–6pm, chapels closed noon–3pm; ¥35) was founded in 1416 by Jamyang Choje, a leading disciple of Tsongkhapa. It was an immediate success and a year after opening there were already two thousand monks in residence and ten thousand by the time of the Fifth Dalai Lama (1617–82). Although it has been sacked three times – in 1618 by the king of Tsang, in 1635 by the Mongols and in the early eighteenth century by the Dzungars – there was relatively little damage during the Cultural Revolution.

To reach Drepung, 8km west of Lhasa, catch the #3 **minibus** on Dossenge Lu at the junction with Beijing Dong Lu. It may drop you on the main road (¥2), leaving you with a thirty-minute walk, or carry on up the hill to the entrance of the massive walled monastery (¥3). Minibuses come back to Lhasa infrequently from the monastery itself, and it's better to walk down the hill to Nechung and then out to the main road to pick up transport there.

Drepung is a huge place, and it's easy to attempt to see everything and get overloaded. One thing to make sure to do is to go up onto the **roofs**; the views across the Kyichu Valley are splendid, and it's definitely worth spending a bit of time just wandering the alleyways, courtyards and ancient doorways.

The easiest way to find your way around is to follow the clockwise pilgrim circuit. This leads left from the entrance up to the grand and imposing **Ganden Palace**, built in 1530 by the Second Dalai Lama and home to the Dalai Lamas until the Fifth incarnation moved to the Potala. The private quarters of the Dalai Lama are behind the balcony at the top right-hand side of the building, but there's little to see inside.

The next stop is the **Tsokchen**, the main assembly hall, its entrance via a small door on the left-hand side facing the building. Its roof supported by over 180 solid wooden columns, the hall is the highlight of Drepung, a space of awesome size and scale. The *thangkas* and brocade hangings add to the incredible ambience, with dust motes highlighted by the rays of the sun slanting down from the high windows. The main chapel at the rear of the hall is the **Buddha of the Three Ages Chapel**, the most impressive in Drepung, with statues crammed together in such profusion the mind reels. The central figures are Sakyamuni with his two main disciples, Shariputra and Maudgalyayana.

There are two upper storeys, both definitely worth a visit. On the next floor up, the **Maitreya Chapel** contains the head and shoulders of a massive statue of Maitreya at a young age, commissioned by Tsongkhapa himself, while the **Tara Chapel** contains a version of the *Kanjur,* sacred Buddhist scriptures, dating from the time of the Fifth Dalai Lama. In the middle of the volumes, which are loose leaves stored between wooden planks and wrapped in brocade, sits a statue of Prajnaparamita, the Mother of Buddhas; the amulet on her lap is said to contain a tooth of Tsongkhapa's. Of the three chapels on the top floor, the highlight is the central **Maitreya Chapel** with a stunning statue of the head of Maitreya, boasting exquisite gold ornamentation.

Behind the Tsokchen there's a tiny **Manjusri Temple**, obligatory for the pilgrims who make offerings to the image of the Bodhisattva of Wisdom carved out of a large rock. The remainder of the circuit is taken up with the **Ngag-Pa College**, to the northwest of the Tsokchen, and **Loseling**, **Gomang and Deyang colleges** to the southeast. They all have items of interest – the stuffed goat at the entrance to the Protector Chapel on the upper storey of Loseling, the cosy Deyang, and the wonderful array of statues in the central chapel of Gomang – but don't feel too bad if you've had enough by now. The main steps of the Tsokchen, looking across the huge courtyard in front of the building, are a good place to sit and admire the view and watch the comings and goings of the other visitors.

Nechung

Easily combined with a trip to Drepung is the eerie **Nechung Monastery** (daily 9am–6pm, chapels closed noon–3pm; Y10), less than a kilometre south-east of Drepung, and reached by a well-trodden path. The monastery was, until 1959, the seat of the **state oracle of Tibet**. By means of complex ritual and chanting, an oracle enters a trance and becomes the mouthpiece of a god, in this case Dorje Drakden, the chief minister of the main spiritual protector of Tibet, Pehar Gyalpo; no important decisions are made by the Dalai Lama or government without reference to Drakden. The original shrine on the site was built in the twelfth century and the Fifth Dalai Lama built the temple later. It was much damaged during the Cultural Revolution, but restoration work is now proceeding quickly. The state oracle fled Tibet in the footsteps of the Dalai Lama in 1959, having questioned Dorje Drakden himself as to what he should do. He died in 1985 in Dharamsala but a successor has been identified there.

Nechung's spookiness begins outside. The beggars are abject, the villagers seem sullen. Inside you are confronted by a panoply of gore – the doors are decorated with images of flayed human skins and the murals in the courtyard depict torture by devils and people drowning in a sea of blood. In the chapels, unusually subdued supplicants are more likely to offer booze than apples. Bloodshot eyes sunk into the sockets of grinning skulls seem to follow you around.

Upstairs, the main room is the audience chamber, where the Dalai Lama would come to consult the oracle. The inner chapel is dedicated to Tsongkhapa, whose statue is between those of his two main disciples, Gyeltsab Je and Khedrup Je. In the only chapel at roof level is the statue of Padmasambhava which, though it dates from the early 1980s, is gloriously bedecked in old Chinese brocade. It's worth the climb up here, if only to escape from the air of sinister corruption below.

Ganden

Situated farther from Lhasa than the other main temples, **Ganden** (daily 9am–noon & 2–4pm; ¥35) is 45km east of Lhasa, the final 6km of the journey being along a winding track off the Lhasa–Sichuan Highway. It is also the most dramatically situated, high up on the Gokpori Ridge, with excellent views over the surrounding countryside. To get here, take the **pilgrim bus** which leaves Lhasa daily at 6.30am from the west side of Barkhor Square (3–4hr; ¥20) and returns at 2pm. You can buy tickets in advance from a tin shack just south of the Jokhang.

Founded by Tsongkhapa himself in 1410 on a site associated with King Songtsen Gampo and his queens, the main hall was not completed until 1417, two years before Tsongkhapa died after announcing his disciple, Gyeltsab Je, as the new **Ganden Tripa**, the leader of the Gelugpa order. The appointment is not based on reincarnation but on particular academic qualifications. Ganden has always been particularly targeted by the Chinese, possibly because it is the main seat of the Dalai Lama's order, and what you see today is all reconstruction.

While it is possible, as always, to follow the pilgrims through the various buildings on their circuit, the highlight is the imposing **Serdung Lhakhang**, on the left side as you follow the main path north from the car park. This temple contains a huge gold and silver *chorten*. The original contained the body of Tsongkhapa, who was said to have changed into a 16-year-old youth when he died. The body was embalmed and placed in the *chorten* and, when the Red Guards broke it open during the Cultural Revolution, they supposedly found the body perfectly preserved, with the hair and fingernails still growing. Only a few pieces of skull survived the destruction and they are in the reconstructed *chorten*. Up the hill and to the right, the **Sertrikhang** houses the golden throne of Tsongkhapa and all later Ganden Tripas; the bag on the throne contains the yellow hat of the present Dalai Lama.

Be sure to allow time to walk the **Ganden kora**, the path around the monastery. The views are startling and it takes about an hour to follow round. There is a basic **guesthouse** at the monastery, used mostly by people heading off on the Ganden–Samye **trek** (see p.1152).

Tsetang and around

The town of **Tsetang**, southeast of Lhasa and just south of the Tsangpo River, and the nearby valleys of **Yarlung** and **Chongye** are steeped in ancient history. Legend claims the first Tibetans originated on the slopes of Gongpo Ri to the east of Tsetang, and that the Yarlung Valley was where the first king of Tibet descended from the heavens to earth upon a sky-cord. This king then fathered the first royal dynasty, many members of which are buried in the nearby **Chongye Valley**. The Yarlung Valley was also where, in the fourth century, the first Buddhist scriptures fell from the sky upon the first king's palace at **Yumbulakhang**. To the west of Tsetang, the walled combined village and monastery of **Samye** is not only the most ancient in Tibet, but also a lively and interesting place to spend a day or two.

Tsetang and Samye are easily accessible via a good road and public transport from Lhasa. However, there is no public transport in the Yarlung and Chongye valleys, although **getting around** by hitching lifts on tractors is feasible for the Yarlung Valley. Transport out to Chongye is more limited. The best way to explore is to hire a vehicle and driver in Tsetang to take you to Chongye and Yumbulakhang on a day-trip. For vehicle rental try the *Tsetang Hotel* first, then the *Gesar Restaurant* opposite – after hard bargaining expect to pay around ¥350 for the day.

Unfortunately, accommodation in Tsetang is not particularly good, terribly expensive (typical costing over ¥500 for a double room) and the **permit** situation is unclear. You should check in Lhasa whether you need a permit for Tsetang. The PSB in Tsetang should issue permits to Yarlung, Chongye, Samye and Lhamo Lhatso but at the time of writing refused to do so unless you were on an organized tour with your own transport and guide – for which purpose, you'll be quoted ¥2000–2500 in Lhasa to rent a jeep for three days and two nights.

Tsetang is also the starting point for a trip to **Lhamo Lhatso**, a sacred lake 115km northeast of Tsetang where visions on the surface of the water are believed to contain prophecies. Regents searching for the next incarnations of high lamas come here for clues and Dalai Lamas have traditionally visited for hints about the future. Buses leave the main Tsetang intersection on

Monday and Friday for **Gyatsa** (returning the next day), where you have to walk across the bridge and pick up another ride up to Chokorgye Monastery and then trek for around five hours up to the lake. You should bring your own food and be prepared to camp unless you're intending a long day's walking.

Tsetang

There is little to recommend an extended stay in the town of **TSETANG**, administrative centre of Lhoka Province, a region stretching from the Tsangpo down to the Bhutan border. While it's lively enough, accommodation is a problem and much of the town is very unattractive, although you could spend an interesting few hours exploring the maze-like alleyways of the small Tibetan quarter. However, Tsetang is largely unavoidable as a base for explorations of the area.

Heading south from the main traffic intersection along Naidong Lu, take a narrow left turn through the small, bustling market into the **Tibetan area** of town, a typical jumble of walled compounds swarming with unwelcoming dogs and children scrapping in the dust. The largest monastery and the first you'll come to is **Ganden Chukorlin** (¥5), now bright and gleaming from restoration, having been used as a storeroom for many years. It was founded in the mid-eighteenth century on the site of an earlier monastery, and there are good views of the Tibetan quarter from the roof. At the nearby fourteenth-century **Narchu Monastery** (¥5), restoration is less complete, but it's worth stopping by for the three unusual brown-painted Sakyamuni statues on the altar. A little farther up the hill, the **Sanarsensky Nunnery** (¥5) was one of the first of its kind in Tibet. It was founded in the fourteenth century in the Sakya tradition but later became a Gelugpa establishment. It's smaller and less ornate than the other two temples, with just one chapel open at present.

Practicalities

Daily **public buses** leave Lhasa between 7am and 8am from Barkhor Square and run as far as the Samye ferry point (4hr; ¥26). You'll then need to pick up another bus or a minibus for the remaining 33km on to Tsetang (¥15) – it's a bit hit-and-miss but you shouldn't have to wait more than an hour or so. Alternatively, direct **minibuses** leave the main bus station in Lhasa for Tsetang from 8am onwards (3hr; ¥35), but they may not be willing to take foreigners, although there are no checkposts between Lhasa and Tsetang.

Tsetang's **bus station** is about 500m west of the main traffic intersection in town. Turn right at the intersection onto Naidong Lu past the post office and numerous restaurants and you'll come to the only comparatively cheap hotel that will take foreigners, the *Postal House* (❹), though with dingy rooms and sullied corridors it's far from a bargain. Continue down the road and you'll come to the grossly over-priced *Tsetang Hotel* (Ⓣ0893/21899, Ⓕ21688; ❽). Naidong Lu itself is lined with bars and **restaurants**.

The Yarlung Valley

Though the **Yarlung Valley** is renowned as the seat of the first Tibetan kings, these days it is the dramatically sited and picturesque **Yumbulakhang**, the first Tibetan palace, that draws visitors to the area. The road due south from Naidong Lu in Tsetang to Yumbulakhang is fairly busy, and it's possible to get a lift without too much trouble (there's no public transport).

Trandruk

The small but extremely significant **Trandruk Monastery** (¥25), 7km south of Tsetang, is undergoing massive reconstruction, although you can still appreciate its grand and imposing structure. One of the earliest Buddhist temples in Tibet, Trandruk was built in the seventh century during the reign of King Songtsen Gampo, and is one of the twelve demon-suppressing temples (see p.1136) – Trandruk anchors the demon's left shoulder to the earth. Legend tells how the site chosen for Trandruk was covered by a large lake containing a five-headed dragon. King Songtsen Gampo emerged from a period of meditation with such power that he was able to summon a supernatural falcon to defeat the dragon and drink the water of the lake, leaving the earth ready for Trandruk (meaning Falcon-Dragon). Damaged during the Bon reaction against Buddhism in the ninth century and again by Dzungar invaders in the eighteenth century, the temple then suffered the loss of many highly prized religious relics and objects following the Chinese invasion. Its remaining glory is the **Pearl Thangka**, an image of King Songtsen Gampo's wife, Princess Wencheng, as the White Tara, created from thousands of tiny pearls meticulously sewn onto a pink background. This is in the central chapel upstairs, which also houses an original statue of Padmasambhava at the age of eight.

Yumbulakhang

From afar, the fortress temple of **Yumbulakhang**, 12km south of Tsetang, appears dwarfed by the scale of the Yarlung Valley. But once you get close, and make the thirty-minute climb up the spur on which it is perched, the drama of the position and the airiness of the site are apparent. Widely regarded as the work of the first king of Tibet, Nyatri Tsenpo, when he arrived in Yarlung, the original Yumbulakhang would have been over 2000 years old and the oldest building in Tibet when it was almost totally destroyed during the Cultural Revolution. The present building is a 1982 reconstruction in two parts with a small two-storey chapel and an eleven-metre-high tower. The lower floor of the **chapel** is dedicated to the early Tibetan kings; Nyatri Tsenpo is to the left and Songtsen Gampo to the right of the central Buddha statue. The delightful and unusual upper-storey chapel, with Chenresi as the central image, is built on a balcony. Some of the modern murals up here show legendary events in Tibetan history; look out on the left for Nyatri Tsenpo and for the Buddhist scriptures descending from heaven. The energetic can ascend by ladders almost to the top of the tower where King Nyatri Tsenpo supposedly meditated. The deep, slit windows at knee level mean the views aren't that wonderful, however; for the best scenery, take a walk up to the ridge behind the temple.

The Chongye Valley

From Tsetang it's a bumpy 27km south along unsurfaced roads through the attractive **Chongye Valley** to the village of **CHONGYE**, a sleepy little place currently expanding with plenty of new buildings. There are a couple of restaurants and a basic guesthouse here, but you'll need to ask to find it. The target for most visitors, the **Tombs of the Kings**, is around a kilometre farther south from the village. The entire valley is an agricultural development area and the patchwork of fields is interspersed with irrigation work. There's no **public transport** out here from Tsetang and very little traffic either.

Tangboche

On the east side of the valley, about 20km from Tsetang, **Tangboche Monastery** is situated at the base of the hill and somewhat difficult to spot among the village houses. It was founded in the eleventh century and the great Tsongkhapa, founder of the Gelugpa tradition, is thought to have stayed here in the fourteenth century. Take a flashlight so you can really appreciate the most interesting features here – genuine old murals, commissioned in 1915 by the Thirteenth Dalai Lama and too numerous to list. Look out in particular for Pelden Lhamo on the left as you enter and, on the right-hand wall, Padmasambhava, Trisong Detsen and Shantarakshita. The artistry and detail of subject and background make an interesting comparison with some of the more modern painting you'll see in Tibet. A couple of hundred metres up the hill is the **hermitage** where the scholar Atisha spent some time in the eleventh century. It's small and recently renovated and, not surprisingly, dominated by rather lurid images of the Indian master. A much-revered statue of Atisha and a set of texts brought by him from India were lost in the Cultural Revolution.

The Tombs of the Kings

One kilometre south of Chongye, the **Tombs of the Kings** are scattered over a vast area on and around the slopes of Mura Ri. Some are huge, up to 200m in length and 30m high. The body of each king was buried along with statues, precious objects and, some sources suggest, live servants. Some of the greatest kings of the Yarlung dynasty were buried here, although there is disagreement over the precise number of tombs – some sources claim it's 21, but far fewer are visible and there is uncertainty about which tomb belongs to which king.

For the best view of the entire area, climb the largest tomb, **Bangso Marpo** (Red Tomb), belonging to **Songtsen Gampo**, just beside the road that heads south along the valley and is easily identifiable by the chapel on the top. Songtsen Gampo, supposedly embalmed and incarcerated in a silver coffin, was entombed with huge numbers of precious gems, gifts from neighbouring countries (India sent a golden suit of armour), his own jewelled robes and objects of religious significance, all of which were looted long ago. The cosy chapel (¥10), originally built in the twelfth century, has central statues of Songtsen Gampo, his wives and principal ministers, Gar and Thonmi Sambhota.

If you look east from this viewpoint, the large tomb straight ahead belongs to Songtsen Gampo's grandson, Mangsong Mangtsen (646–676), who became king at the age of 4. The tomb some distance to the left is that of Tri Ralpachan (805–836), and the nearby enclosure contains an ancient pillar, recording the events of his reign, and constructed on top of a stone turtle symbolizing the foundation of the universe. Originally every tomb had one of these pillars on top but the others have long since disappeared.

The ruins of **Chingwa Tagste Dzong**, perched high on the mountainside to the west, give an idea of the scale of the fortress and capital of the early Yarlung kings before Songtsen Gampo moved to Lhasa. To the left, the monastery of **Riwo Dechen** is visible and a rough road means you can drive to within ten minutes' walk of this now thriving Gelugpa community of around eighty monks. Originally founded in the fifteenth century, it was later expanded by the Seventh Dalai Lama and restored in the mid-1980s. There are three main chapels, the central one dominated by a large Tsongkhapa figure.

Samye

A visit to **SAMYE** on the north bank of the Tsangpo River is a highlight of Tibet. A unique monastery and walled village rolled into one, it's situated in wonderful scenery and, however you arrive, the journey is splendid. You can

The Ganden–Samye trek

Though popular, the Ganden–Samye trek is no less serious and demanding than other treks. The route, which takes three or four days to complete, crosses the mountains that divide the **Kyichu Valley** from that of the Tsangpo and travels through high mountain passes and alpine pasture to the dry, almost desert-like countryside around Samye. The trek goes by **Hebu** village and involves camping out or sleeping in caves or nomad encampments, long climbs to the Jooker La and Sukhe La passes and some deep river wading.

There is also an alternative ancient pilgrim route from Dechen Dzong, 21km east of Lhasa, to Samye, which takes four days and crosses the same mountain range via Changju nomad camp and Gokar La Pass (the name translates as "white eagle" – apparently these birds also struggle to get over it). A third option is the four-day trek from the Gyama Valley, Songtsen Gampo's birthplace, via two five-hundred-metre passes.

climb the sacred Hepo Ri to the east of the complex for excellent views (1hr); it was here that Padmasambhava is said to have subdued the local spirits and won them over to Buddhism.

The monastery

Tibet's first monastery, **Samye** was founded in the eighth century during King Trisong Detsen's reign, with the help of the Indian masters Padmasambhava and Shantarakshita whom he had invited to Tibet to help spread the Buddhist faith. The first Tibetan Buddhist monks were ordained here after examination and are referred to as the "Seven Examined Men". Over the years Samye has been associated with several of the schools of Tibetan Buddhism – Padmasambhava's involvement in the founding of the monastery makes it important in the Nyingma school, and later it was taken over by the Sakya and Gelugpa traditions. Nowadays, followers of all traditions worship here, and Samye is a popular destination for Tibetan pilgrims, some of whom travel for weeks to reach it.

The design of the extensive monastery complex, several hundred metres in diameter, is of a giant **mandala**, a representation of the Buddhist universe, styled after the Indian temple of Odantapuri in Bihar. The main temple, the **utse**, represents Buddha's palace on the summit of Mount Meru, the mythical mountain at the centre of the Buddhist universe. The four continents in the vast ocean around Mount Meru are represented by the *lingshi* temples, a couple of hundred metres away at the cardinal points, each flanked by two smaller temples, *lingtren,* representing islands in the ocean. The utse is surrounded by four giant *chortens,* each several storeys high, at the corners, and there are *nyima* (Sun) and *dawa* (Moon) temples to the north and south respectively. The whole complex is flanked by a newly renovated enclosing wall topped by 1008 tiny *chortens* with gates at the cardinal points. This sounds hugely ordered, but the reality is far more confusing and fun. Samye has suffered much damage and restoration over the years and today you'll find the temples dotted among houses, barns and animal pens, with only a few of the original 108 buildings on the site remaining in their entirety.

The utse

The **utse** (daily 9am–12.30 & 3–5pm; ¥35) is a grand six-storeyed construction and needs a couple of hours to see thoroughly. It is still undergoing renovation and will become even more impressive in the future. Be sure to take a powerful flashlight as there are some good murals tucked away in shadowy corners.

The **first floor** is dominated by the grand main assembly hall with fine old *mandalas* on the high ceiling. On either side of the entrance to the main chapel are statues of historical figures associated with the monastery. Those on the left include Shantarakshita, Padmasambhava (said to be a good likeness of him), Trisong Detsen and Songtsen Gampo. The impressive main chapel, **Jowo Khang**, is reached through three tall doorways and is home to a Sakyamuni statue showing Buddha at the age of 38. To the left of the assembly hall is a small temple, **Chenresi Lhakhang**, housing a gorgeous statue of Chenresi with an eye meticulously painted on the palm of each of his thousand hands – if you look at nothing else in Samye, search this out. To the right of the main assembly hall is the **Gonkhang**, a protector chapel, with all the statues heavily and dramatically draped. Most of the deities here were established as the demons of the Bon religion and were adopted by Buddhism as the fierce protectors – the chapel is a dark and eerie place, laden with the fear of centuries.

Although the first floor is the most impressive, the upper storeys are worth a look. The **second floor** is an open roof area, where monks and local people carry out the craft work needed for the temple. The highlight of the **third floor** is the **Quarters of the Dalai Lama**, consisting of a small anteroom, a throne room and a bedroom. A securely barred, glass-fronted case in the bedroom is stuffed full of fantastic relics, including Padmasambhava's hair and walking stick, a Tara statue that is reputed to speak and the skull of the Indian master Shantarakshita, among many others. The Tibetan pilgrims take this room very seriously and the crush of bodies may mean you can't linger as long as you would like. From the **fourth floor** up, you'll see only recent, obvious and uncompleted reconstruction, but the views from the balconies are extensive.

The other buildings

The surrounding buildings in the complex are in varying stages of renovation. The reconstruction of the four coloured **chortens** is almost complete. Unashamedly modern, they are each slightly different, and visitors seem to love or hate them. There are internal stairs and tiny interior chapels, but generally they are more dramatic from a distance. It's difficult to locate the outer temples accurately and many are still awaiting renovation, some serving as barns and stables, some showing the effects of the Cultural Revolution. The most finely worked murals in Samye are in **Mani Lhakhang**, now a chapel in a house compound in the northwest of the complex, but the occupants are happy for visitors to look around.

Practicalities

Permits are needed for Samye, but the PSB in Tsetang will issue them only if you have arranged a tour. That said, the PSB rarely check up on foreigners except at festival times. The Lhasa–Tsetang road runs along the south bank of the Tsangpo and is served by public transport from both ends. To reach the monastery, you'll need to cross the river via the **Samye ferry**, 33km from Tsetang and 150km from Lhasa. Ferries leave when full and are more frequent in the morning, but run until mid-afternoon. The crossing (¥3, although foreigners are charged ¥10) is highly picturesque and takes an hour or more as the boats wind their way among the sandbanks inhabited by Brahmini ducks, grebes and plovers. On the other side, tractors (¥5; 45min) and trucks (¥3; 30min) ply the bumpy 8km to Samye through rolling, deforested sand dunes newly planted here and there with willows. The small, white-painted *chortens* carved out of the hillside about halfway along mark the place where King Trisong Detsen met Padmasambhava when he came to Samye in the eighth century. **Leaving**, a very useful truck departs from the front of the utse each morning at 8am to connect with the ferry and a Lhasa-bound bus on the other side of the river. In addition, local tractors and trucks run until mid-afternoon, but you may well have to wait at the ferry and on the other side of the river for connections.

The only place to stay at Samye is the **guesthouse** next to the utse, which provides comfortable, cheap dorm accommodation. The monastery **restaurant** is just north of the utse, but a better option is the newer establishment opposite the east reception office near the east gate. There's no menu in either place; you negotiate based on what they have. There are several small shops in the monastery complex which are well stocked with tinned goods, beer, confectionery and even Chinese wine.

Tsurphu and Namtso

One of the most rewarding and popular trips in Tibet is to **Namtso Lake**, around 230km northwest of Lhasa, taking in Tsurphu Monastery and Yangbajing on the way. All these sights can be combined into a two-night/three-day trip in a rented jeep, for which you can expect to pay around ¥1800. There are no checkposts on the roads between Lhasa and Namtso, so you should be all right without a permit but, as always, check the current situation with other travellers in case. If you don't have your own transport, Tsurphu and the town of Damxhung are still reachable, although you may find pilgrim-bus and minibus drivers unwilling to risk carrying you. There is only very infrequent transport (every day or two) from Damxhung across to Namtso Qu on the shores of Namtso.

Tsurphu Monastery

It takes two to three hours by jeep to travel the 70km or so northeast of Lhasa to **Tsurphu Monastery** (daily 9am–1pm; ¥10), at a height of 4480m. A **pilgrim bus** for the monastery leaves Lhasa daily between 7am and 8am (¥25) from the western end of Barkhor Square, returning at 2pm. The monastery is the seat of the **Karmapa Lama**, though it's a seat that's pretty cold these days as the present incumbent, the seventeenth, Urgyen Trinley Dorge, fled to India in 1999. Identified in 1992 at the age of 7, Urgyen is the second holiest Tibetan after the Dalai Lama and seems charismatic and able, and is regarded by many in the government in exile as a natural successor for the role of leader when the Dalai Lama dies.

Founded in the twelfth century by Dusun Khenyapa, the Karmapa order is a branch of the Kagyupa tradition, where members are known as the **Black Hats** after the Second Karmapa was presented with one by Kublai Khan. Most powerful during the fifteenth century, when they were close to the ruling families of the time, they were eventually eclipsed in 1642 when the Fifth Dalai Lama and the Gelugpa order, aided by the Mongol army, gained the ascendancy. The Karmapa were the first order to institute the system of reincarnated lamas, *tulkus*, a tradition later adopted by the Gelugpa school.

Tsurphu is now undergoing reconstruction after being damaged in the years after the Chinese invasion. The solid **Zhiwa Tratsang** has a splendidly ornate gold roof and houses the main assembly hall, dominated by statues of Sakyamuni and a *chorten* containing the relics of the Sixteenth Karmapa Lama, who played a major part in establishing the order overseas and died in Chicago in 1981. The murals here depict the successive Karmapa lamas. The festival of **Saga Dawa**, on the full moon of the fourth lunar month, usually in May or June, is especially fine at Tsurphu, as the massive new *thangka*, completed in recent years, is displayed at this time.

A visit to the monastery can be exhausting as it's at a considerably higher altitude than Lhasa. In addition, the clockwise path, the **kora**, climbs steeply up the hill behind the monastery from the left of the temple complex and circles around high above and behind the monastery before descending on the right. The views are great and the truly fit can even clamber to the top of the ridge, but you need to allow two to three hours for the walk.

There's little reason to stay at Tsurphu unless you're trekking in the area, although there is a basic monastery **guesthouse** (❶) – you'll need to take your own sleeping bag, food and candles.

Yangbajing hot springs, Damxhung and Namtso

Don't get carried away by romantic images of the **Yangbajing hot springs** (daily 8am–8pm; ¥10), which flow unspectacularly into a thirty-metre-long concrete pool (though, at 4270m, this is probably the highest swimming pool you'll ever get to use) at the base of a geothermal power station which provides electricity for Lhasa. **Yangbajing village** itself is 45km northeast of the Tsurphu turn-off along the main Tibet–Qinghai Highway. This is a scenic road with dramatically striated rock formations clearly visible until the valley narrows into impressive gorges. About a kilometre beyond the village, take a left turn and the pool is 3km farther on, on the left, opposite the power station, pretty unmissable and ugly as hell, with chimneys belching steam.

If you're heading up to Namtso, you'll need to continue on the main highway past the Yangbajing turning for another 80km to **DAMXHUNG** (4360m), a bleak truck-stop town. The road is good, and the awesome Nyanchen Tanglha mountain range to the north is dramatically topped by the peak of Nyanchen Tanglha itself (7117m). Minibuses bound here leave Lhasa from just east of the *Yak Hotel* around 7am each morning (3–4hr; ¥30). The turning north to Namtso is about halfway through the town, where a large concrete bridge crosses the river towards the mountains. For **accommodation** in Damxhung there are several unmemorable places, including the noisy and basic *Tang Shung Shey* (❶), opposite the new petrol station at the far end of town. In front stands the cavernous, friendly and atmospheric Muslim restaurant, *Ching Jeng*, and there are plenty of Chinese restaurants around, too.

Namtso

Set at 4700m and frozen over from November to May, **Namtso** (Sky Lake) is 70km long and 30km wide, the second largest saltwater lake in China (only Qinghai Hu is bigger; see p.1063). The scenery comes straight from a dream image of Tibet, with snow-capped mountains towering behind the massive lake and yaks grazing on the plains around nomadic herders' tents.

From Damxhung, it takes around two hours to pass through the Nyanchen Tanglha mountain range at Lhachen La (5150m) and descend to **NAMTSO QU**, the district centre numbering just a couple of houses at the eastern end of the lake. Here you'll be charged the annoying "entrance fee" of ¥40. The target of most visitors is **Tashi Dor Monastery**, considerably farther west (a hefty 42km from Lhachen La), tucked away behind two massive red rocks on a promontory jutting into the lake. At Tashi Dor (¥10), a small Nyingma monastery is built around a cave and there's a dirt-floored **guesthouse** (❶) between the monastery and lake. It's a glorious site, but facilities are limited – bring your own food and flashlights. Although some bedding is provided, you'll be more comfortable in your own sleeping bag, and your own stove and fuel would be an advantage. You can walk around the rock at the end of the promontory and also climb to the top for even more startling views. For true devotees, a circuit of the lake can be attempted, though this takes twenty days and involves camping on the way.

The old southern road and Gyantse

The road west from Lhasa divides at the Chusul Bridge and most vehicles follow the paved Friendship Highway along the course of the Yarlung Tsangpo to Shigatse. However, there is an alternative route, the longer but extremely picturesque **old southern road** that heads southwest to the shores of **Yamdrok Tso**, before turning west to **Gyantse** and then northwest to Shigatse.

There is no public transport between Lhasa and Gyantse, and most people rent jeeps to explore the area or include it on the way to or from the border with Nepal. Allow around six or seven hours' driving time from Lhasa to Gyantse in a good jeep. Day-trips to Yamdrok Tso from Lhasa are feasible; you'll start negotiating at about ¥1000 per jeep for these.

Yamdrok Tso

From Chusul Bridge, on the western outskirts of Lhasa, the southern road climbs steeply up to the Kampa La Pass (4794m) with stunning views of the turquoise waters of the sacred **Yamdrok Tso**, the third largest lake in Tibet. It is said that if it ever dries up then Tibet itself will no longer support life – a tale of heightened importance now that Yamdrok Tso, which has no inflowing rivers to help keep it topped up, is powering a controversial hydroelectric scheme. From the pass, the road descends to Yamtso village before skirting the northern and western shores amid wild scenery dotted with a few tiny hamlets, yaks by the lakeside and small boats on the water.

On the western side of the lake, 57km beyond the Kampa La Pass, the dusty village of **NAKARTSE** (4500m) is the birthplace of the mother of the Great Fifth Dalai Lama. There is basic **accommodation** in the village (ask for directions), but there have been instances of midnight awakenings here as the PSB move foreigners on. There are several Chinese **restaurants**, but the favourite with visitors is the Tibetan restaurant with tables in a tiny courtyard hidden away in the middle of the village, where you can eat rice with potato and meat curry (they fish out the meat for vegetarians) under the eyes of the local dogs. Jeep drivers seem to come here instinctively; otherwise look for the tourist vehicles parked outside.

Yamdrok Tso has many picturesque islands and inlets visible from the road, and there's a seven-day circular **trek** from Nakartse exploring the major promontory into the lake. The climb up from Nakartse to the **Karo La Pass** (5045m) is long and dramatic, with towering peaks on either side as the road heads south and then west towards apparently impenetrable rock faces. From the pass, the road descends gradually, via the mineral mines at Chewang, to the broad, fertile and densely farmed **Nyang Chu Valley** leading to Gyantse.

Gyantse

On the eastern banks of the Nyang Chu at the base of a natural amphitheatre of rocky ridges, **GYANTSE** is an attractive, relaxed town, offering the splendid sights of the **Kumbum** – famous among scholars of Tibetan art throughout the world – and the old **Dzong** and, despite the rapidly expanding Chinese section of town, it has retained a pleasant, laid-back air. It lies 263km from Lhasa on the southern route and 90km southeast of Shigatse.

Little is known about the history of any settlement at Gyantse before the fourteenth century, when it emerged as the capital of a small kingdom ruled by a lineage of princes claiming descent from the legendary Tibetan folk hero, King Gesar of Ling. Hailing originally from northeast Tibet, they allied themselves to the powerful Sakya order. Also at this time, Gyantse operated as a staging post in the **wool trade** between Tibet and India, thanks to its position between Lhasa and Shigatse. By the mid-fifteenth century, the Gyantse Dzong, Pelkor Chode Monastery and the Kumbum had been built, although decline followed as other local families increased their influence.

Gyantse rose to prominence again in 1904 when Younghusband's British expedition, equipped with modern firearms, approached the town via the trade route from Sikkim, routed 1500 Tibetans at Tuna, killing over half of them, and then marched on Gyantse. In July 1904, the British took the Dzong with four casualties while three hundred Tibetans were killed. From here the British marched on to Lhasa. As part of the ensuing agreement between Tibet and Britain, a British Trade Agency was established in Gyantse and as relations between Tibet and the British in India thawed, the trade route from Calcutta up through Sikkim and on to Gyantse became an effective one.

The Town

The best way to get your bearings in Gyantse is to stand at the main traffic intersection at the base of the Dzong. The entrance to the fortress is along the road to the right of the hill, while the road to its left leads to the Kumbum. The road from Shigatse arrives at the intersection to the south, opposite the Dzong, and the old road from Lhasa comes from the southeast.

The original **Gyantse Dzong** (Mon–Sat 7am–7pm; ¥15) dates from the mid-fourteenth century, though, given the extensive damage caused by the British in 1904, today's remains are a lot more recent. Guides will escort you part of the way around the ruins, unlocking the reconstructed buildings on the way, but then you're free to wander at will. Currently visitors are shown the **Meeting Hall**, housing a waxworks tableau; the **Exhibition Hall**, detailing the "Anti-British War" of 1904 in English; and the

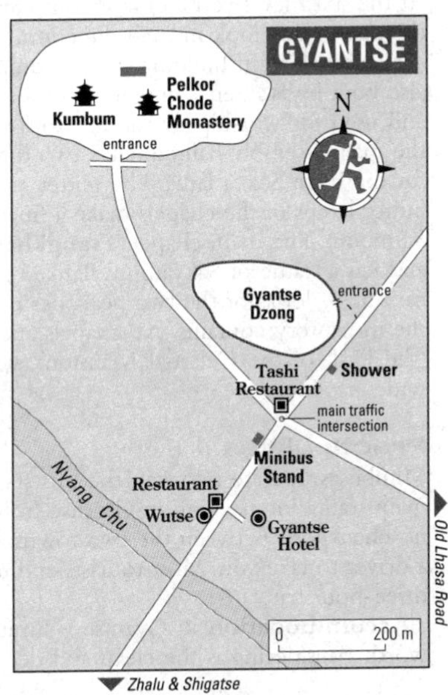

upper and lower chapels of the **Sampal Norbuling Monastery**. A few of the murals in the upper chapel probably date from the early fifteenth century, but most of the other artefacts are modern. The best views are from the top of the tallest tower in the north of the complex. You'll need to clamber up some very rickety ladders, but the scenery is well worth it.

Pelkor Chode and the Gyantse Kumbum

At the northern edge of town, the rather barren monastic compound which now contains Pelkor Chode Monastery and the glorious Kumbum was once home to religious colleges and temples belonging to three schools of Tibetan Buddhism: the Gelugpa, Sakya and Bu (the last of these is a small order whose main centre is at Zhalu; see opposite).

Constructed around 1440 by Rabten Kunsang, the Gyantse prince most responsible for the town's fine buildings, the **Gyantse Kumbum** (Mon–Sat 9am–noon & 3–6pm; ¥35, additional ¥10 for photographs) is a remarkable building, a huge *chorten* crowned with a golden dome and umbrella, with chapels bristling with statuary and smothered with paintings at each level. It's a style unique to Tibetan architecture and, while several such buildings have survived, Gyantse is the best preserved (despite some damage in the 1960s) and most accessible. The word *kumbum* means "a hundred thousand images" – which is probably an overestimate, but not by that much. Many of the statues have needed extensive renovation, and most of the murals are very old – take a flashlight if you want a good look.

The structure has eight levels, decreasing in number and size as you ascend; most of the chapels within, except those on the uppermost floors, are open. With almost seventy chapels on the first four levels alone, there's plenty to see. The highlights, with the densest, most lavish decoration, include the two-storey chapels at the cardinal points on the first and third levels and the four chapels on the fifth level. The views of the town and surrounding area get better the higher you go and some of the outside stucco work is especially fine. At the sixth level you'll emerge onto an open platform, level with the eyes of the *chorten* that look in each direction.

The other main building in the compound is **Pelkor Chode Monastery**, also built by Rabten Kunsang around twenty years earlier than the Kumbum, and used for worship by monks from all the surrounding monasteries. Today the main assembly hall contains two thrones, one for the Dalai Lama and one for the main Sakya lama. The glitter and gold and the sunlight and flickering butter lamps in the chapels make a fine contrast to the gloom of much of the Kumbum. The main chapel, **Tsangkhang**, is at the back of the assembly hall and has a statue of Sakyamuni flanked by deities, amid some impressive wood carvings – look for the two peacocks perched on a beam. The second floor of the monastery contains five chapels and the top level just one, **Shalyekhang** (the Peak of the Celestial Mansion), with some very impressive two-metre-wide *mandalas*.

Practicalities

Minibuses operate between the bus station in Shigatse and just south of the main traffic intersection in Gyantse from around 8am to 4pm daily. There are no checkposts between the two towns, but you may still have trouble getting a driver to take you. Most tourists end up paying close to ¥30 for the two- to three-hour trip.

Accommodation in Gyantse is limited. At the budget end, the only place worth considering is the clean and decent new *Wutse* (❶) south of the main crossroads. The *Gyantse Hotel* opposite is the most comfortable place (☎0892/8172222; ❻), with a spacious lobby and 24-hour hot water. Coming from the old Lhasa road, turn left at the crossroads and it's 50m down the road, its entrance marked by a green stone arch. Note that it's open in the evening only. Dusty arrivals may appreciate the local **shower**, though take flip-flops as the floor is very grungy.

The most obvious **restaurant** in town is the tourist-friendly *Tashi*, at the intersection, which does serviceable *momos*; everything here is ¥10–20. For Chinese food, head west towards the *Gyantse Hotel*. The restaurants around here have English menus. Highly recommended is the place close to the hotel with a red sign that begins "Warmly welcome". The Sichuanese owner is very friendly and a superb cook.

Zhalu Monastery

Accessible enough for a day-trip from Shigatse or an easy side trip between Gyantse and Shigatse, **Zhalu Monastery** is around 22km from Shigatse, 75km from Gyantse and 4km south of the village of Tsungdu between kilometre markers 18 and 19 on the Gyantse–Shigatse road. Originally built in the eleventh century, Zhalu has a finely colonnaded courtyard decorated with luck symbols, but is most remarkable for the green-glazed tiles that line the roof. It rose to prominence as the seat of the Bu tradition of Tibetan Buddhism founded by Buton Rinchendrub in the fourteenth century. Buton's claim to fame is as the scholar who collected, organized and copied the Tengyur commentaries by hand into a coherent whole, comprising 227 thick volumes in all. However, his original work and pen were destroyed during the Cultural Revolution. Although there were once about 3500 monks living here, the tradition never had as many followers as the other schools, but it had a fair degree of influence – Tsongkhapa, among others, was influenced by Buton's teaching. Major renovations are currently underway and chapels have been closed and rearranged, but the monks are friendly and the village is a quiet and pleasant place. For the energetic, it's a one- to two-hour walk up in the hills southwest of Zhalu to the hermitage of **Riphuk** where Atisha (see p.1118) is supposed to have meditated. You'll need directions or a guide from Zhalu as you can't see it from the monastery.

About a kilometre north of Zhalu, **Gyankor Lhakhang** dates from 997. Sakya Pandita, who established the relationship between the Mongol Khans and the Sakya hierarchy in the thirteenth century (see p.1118), was ordained here as a monk and the stone bowl over which he shaved his head prior to ordination is in the courtyard. Just inside the entrance is a conch shell, said to date from the time of Buton Rinchendrub – and to be able to sound without human assistance.

Shigatse

Sadly most people use **SHIGATSE**, Tibet's second city, as an overnight stop on the way to or from Lhasa. While one day is long enough to see the two main sights, **Tashilunpo Monastery** and **Shigatse Dzong**, it's worth spending at least an extra night here simply to do everything at a more leisurely pace, take in the market and spend a bit of time absorbing the atmosphere and wandering the attractive, tree-lined streets. Basing yourself here also gives you the opportunity to explore some of the sights along the old southern road to Lhasa (see p.1156).

The City

Although the city is fairly spread out, about 2km from end to end, most of the sights and the facilities that you'll need are in or near the north–south corridor around Jiefang Tong Lu and Beijing Bei Lu, extending north along Kesang Ke Lu to the market and Dzong. The main exception is Tashilunpo Monastery which is a bit of a hike west. Shigatse offers an adequate range of accommodation, a variety of shops and some pleasant restaurants, and the dramatic Drolma Ridge rising up on the northern side of town helps you get your bearings easily. The pace of life here is unhurried, but there's a buzz provided by the huge numbers of Tibetan pilgrims and foreign visitors. Although most of the city is modern, you'll find the traditional Tibetan houses concentrated in the area west of the market where you can explore the narrow alleyways running between high whitewashed walls.

Tashilunpo Monastery

Something of a showcase for foreign visitors, the large complex of **Tashilunpo Monastery** (Mon–Sat 9.30am–noon & 3.30–5pm; ¥45) is situated on the western side of town just below the Drolma Ridge – the gleaming, golden roofs will lead you in the right direction. The monastery has some of the most fabulous chapels outside Lhasa and it takes several hours to do it justice.

Tashilunpo was founded in 1447 by Gendun Drup, Tsongkhapa's nephew and disciple, who was later recognized as the First Dalai Lama. It rose to prominence in 1642 when the Fifth Dalai Lama declared that Losang Chokyi Gyeltsen, who was his teacher and the abbot of Tashilunpo, was a manifestation

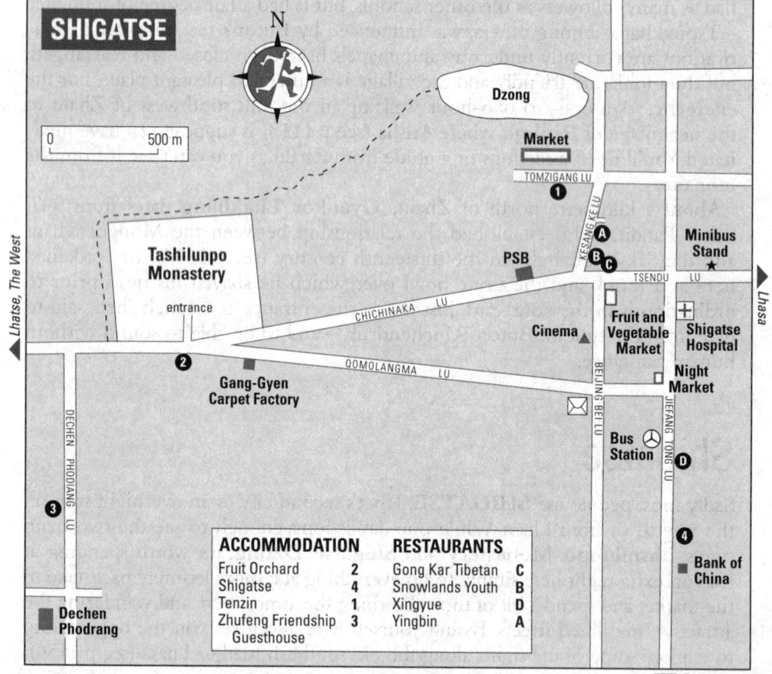

The Panchen Lama controversy

The life of the **Tenth Panchen Lama** (1938–89) was a tragic one. Identified at 11 years of age by the Nationalists in 1949 in Xining, without approval from Lhasa, he fell into Communist hands and was for many years the most high-profile collaborator of the People's Republic of China. His stance changed in 1959 when he openly referred to the Dalai Lama as the true ruler of Tibet. In 1961, in Beijing, the Panchen Lama informed Mao of the appalling conditions in Tibet at that time and pleaded for aid, religious freedom and an end to the huge numbers of arrests. Mao assured the Panchen Lama these would be granted, but nothing changed. Instructed to give a speech condemning the Dalai Lama, he refused and was prevented from speaking in public until the 1964 Monlam Great Prayer Festival in Lhasa. With an audience of ten thousand people he again ignored instructions and spoke in the Dalai Lama's support, ending with the words, "Long live the Dalai Lama". He was immediately placed under house arrest and the Chinese instituted a campaign to "Thoroughly Smash the Panchen Reactionary Clique". The Panchen Lama's **trial** in August 1964 lasted seventeen days, following which he vanished into Qin Cheng Prison No.1, north of Beijing, for fourteen years, where he was tortured and attempted suicide. He was released in February 1978, following the death of Zhou Enlai two years earlier, and the Chinese used him as evidence that there was a thawing of their hardline attitude towards Tibet. He never again criticized the Chinese in public and in private he argued that Tibetan culture must survive at all costs, even if it meant giving up claims for independence. Some Tibetans saw this as a sell-out, others worshipped him as a hero when he returned on visits to Tibet. On the night of January 28, 1989, he died, the Chinese say from a heart attack, others claim from the poison of a vengeful China.

The search for the **Eleventh Panchen Lama** was always likely to be fraught. The central issue is whether the Dalai Lama or the Chinese government have the right to determine the identity of the next incarnation. Stuck in the middle was the abbot of Tashilunpo, Chadrel Rinpoche, who initially led the search according to the normal pattern, with reports of unusual children relayed to the abbot and then checked out by high-ranking monks. On January 25, 1995, the Dalai Lama decided that Gendun Choekyi Nyima, the son of a doctor from Nagchu in Central Tibet, was the reincarnation, but – concerned for the child's safety – he hesitated about a public announcement. The search committee headed by Chadrel Rinpoche supported the same child.

However, the Chinese decreed that the selection should take place by the drawing of lots from the Golden Urn, an eighteenth-century gold vase, one of a pair used by the Qing emperor Qianlong to resolve disputes in his lands. Chadrel Rinpoche argued against its use. In May, the Dalai Lama, concerned about the delay of an announcement from China, publicly recognized Gendun Choekyi Nyima and the following day Chadrel Rinpoche was arrested while trying to return to Tibet from Beijing. Within days, Gendun Choekyi Nyima and his family were taken from their home by the authorities, put on a plane and disappeared. The Chinese will only admit they are holding them "for protection". Fifty Communist Party officials then moved into Tashilunpo to identify monks still loyal to the Dalai Lama and his choice of Panchen Lama. In July there was open revolt by the monks quelled by riot police and across Tibet the Chinese slowly repressed dissent in the other religious institutions. By the end of 1995 they had re-established enough control to hold the Golden Urn ceremony in the Jokhang in Lhasa where an elderly monk drew out the name of a boy called Gyaincain Norbu. In December he was enthroned at Tashilunpo and taken to Beijing for publicity appearances. Meanwhile, the whereabouts of Gendun Choekyi Nyima and his family are unknown and more than fifty people have been imprisoned in Tibet for maintaining that he is the true incarnation of the Panchen Lama.

of the Amitabha Buddha and the Fourth reincarnation of the **Panchen Lama** (Great Precious Teacher) in what has proved to be an ill-fated lineage (see box, p.1161). The Chinese have consistently sought to use the Panchen Lama in opposition to the Dalai Lama, beginning in 1728 when they gave the Fifth Panchen Lama sovereignty over Western Tibet.

The **temples** and shrines of most interest in Tashilunpo stand in a long line at the northern end of the compound. From the main gate head uphill and left to the **Jamkhang Chenmo**. Several storeys high, this was built by the Ninth Panchen Lama in 1914 and is dominated by a 26-metre gold, brass and copper statue of Maitreya, the Buddha of the Future. Hundreds of small images of Maitreya and Tsongkhapa and his disciples are painted on the walls.

To the east, the next main building contains the gold and jewel-encrusted **Tomb of the Tenth Panchen Lama**, which was consecrated in 1994 and is reported to have cost US$8 million. Near the top is a small window cut into a tiny niche, containing his picture. The next building, the **Palace of the Panchen Lamas**, built in the eighteenth century, is closed to the public, but the long building in front houses a series of small, first-floor chapels. The Yulo Drolma Lhakhang, farthest to the right, is worth a look and contains 21 small statues showing each of the 21 manifestations of Tara, the most popular goddess in Tibet.

To the east again, the **Tomb of the Fourth Panchen Lama** contains his eleven-metre-high *chorten* with statues of Amitayus, White Tara and Vijaya, the so-called Longevity Triad, in front. His entire body was supposedly interred in the *chorten* in a standing position, together with an ancient manuscript and *thangkas* sent by the second Manchu emperor. Next comes the **Kelsang Lhakhang**, the largest, most intricate and confusing building in Tashilunpo, in front of the Tomb of the Fifth Panchen Lama. The Lhakhang consists of a courtyard, the fifteenth-century assembly hall and a whole maze of small chapels, often interconnecting, in the surrounding buildings. The flagged **courtyard** is the setting for all the major temple festivals; the surrounding three-level colonnaded cloisters are covered with murals, many recently renovated. Dominating the **assembly hall** are the huge throne of the Panchen Lama and the hanging *thangkas*, depicting all his incarnations. If you've got the energy, it's worth trying to find the **Thongwa Donden Lhakhang**, one of the most sacred chapels in the complex, containing burial *chortens*, including that of the founder of Tashilunpo, the First Dalai Lama, Gendun Drup, as well as early Panchen Lamas and abbots of Tashilunpo.

Spare an hour or so to walk the three-kilometre **kora**, the pilgrim circuit, which follows a clockwise path around the outside walls of the monastery. Turn right on the main road as you exit the monastery and continue around the walls; a stick is useful as some of the dogs are aggressive. The highlight of the walk is the view of the glorious golden roofs from above the top wall. The massive white-painted wall at the top northeast corner is where the forty-metre, giant appliquéd *thangka* is displayed annually at the festival on the fifteenth day of the fifth lunar month (usually in July). At this point, instead of returning downhill to the main road, you can follow the track that continues on around the hillside above the Tibetan part of town and leads eventually to the old Dzong.

Shigatse Dzong and the market

Shigatse Dzong is now a dramatic pile of ruins. It was built in the seventeenth century by Karma Phuntso Namgyel when he was king of the Tsang region and held sway over much of the country, and it's thought that its design was used as the basis for the later construction of the Potala. The structure was initially ruined by the Dzungars in 1717, and further damage took place in the 1950s. Unlike at Gyantse, there has been no attempt at rebuilding and the main reason to climb up is for the fantastic views. To get here from town head west along Tomzigang Lu until the paved surface runs out. A little farther along, a motorable track heads up the hill between some houses to a small pass from where you can climb right up to the Dzong.

The **market**, opposite the *Tenzin Hotel*, is worth a browse if you're looking for souvenirs. There's the usual range of jewellery, "antiques" and religious objects, but the scale of the place is a bit easier to manage than the Barkhor in Lhasa. You'll need to brush up on your bargaining skills and be patient as the stallholders here are used to hit-and-run tourists, so the first asking price is often sky-high.

If you're interested in **carpets**, drop into the Tibet Gang-Gyen Carpet Factory (Mon–Fri 9am–12.30pm & 2.30–7pm) on Qomolangma Lu, a few minutes from the entrance of Tashilunpo. Their carpets are made from ninety percent sheep's wool and ten percent cotton, and you can watch the whole process from the winding of the wool through to the weaving and finishing. They have a good range of traditional and modern designs ranging in price from US$24 up to US$370, and can also arrange shipping.

Practicalities

From Lhasa, public **buses** run to Shigatse from the bus station (¥38), and there are also **minibuses** (¥40) from Beijing Dong Lu, just east of the *Yak Hotel*. Public buses terminate at the **bus station** on Jiefang Tong Lu, returning to Lhasa from here several times a day. Minibuses to and from **Gyantse** use the minibus stand on Tsendu Lu, running until around 4pm. There are plenty of **tractors** operating as taxis (¥3 for a destination in town) or it's about a twenty-minute walk from the bus station to the *Tenzin Hotel*.

Conveniently situated on Chichinaka Lu, Shigatse's **PSB** (Mon–Fri 9.30am–1pm & 3.30–7pm) is one of the more friendly offices; apply here for permits to Gyantse and west as far as Sakya. They may extend your visa, too, if you say you are headed to the border and don't have enough time to make it before your existing visa runs out. The **Bank of China** (Mon–Sat 10am–4pm), just beyond the *Shigatse Hotel*, cashes traveller's cheques. If you're

Moving on to Nepal

If you are heading independently to the **border with Nepal**, you may be able to get a ride all the way to Zhangmu on the minibus which leaves irregularly from in front of the *Shigatse Hotel* between 7 and 8am (¥300). Failing this, you can get as far as Lhatse on a minibus that leaves from the gate of the Tashilunpo at 8.30am; or you can get to the Sakya turn-off on the Friendship Highway, 126km from Shigatse (see p.1165), by taking the 8.30am bus to Sakya, which runs on Monday, Wednesday and Friday from the main bus station. On Tuesday and Thursday a minibus leaves for Sakya (¥27) at the same time from the minibus stand on Tsendu Lu. Be aware that you may well have to hitch the last stretch of the way from Lhatse (see p.1167).

As far as **permits** go, apply for them at the relatively friendly office in Shigatse, or not at all. At the time of writing, it was advisable to skip side-trips to Sakya and Everest (both places have checkposts), but travellers were having no difficulty getting through the two checkposts outside Lhatse and Segar, thanks to the laid-back guards, who usually just check your visa or wave you through.

heading west, stock up here on local currency as there are no more facilities until Zhangmu. At the **post office**, on the corner of Beijing Bei Lu and Qomolangma Lu (daily 9am–7pm), you can send international letters and faxes, but not parcels, and they don't stock postcards – go to the *Shigatse Hotel* for those. There are also international **telephones** here (7am–12pm), but no poste restante service. The Shigatse **hospital** on Jiefang Tong Lu has a first-aid post (daily 10am–12.30pm & 4–6pm) – take a Chinese translator with you.

Accommodation

Accommodation options are not huge as many of the mid-range Chinese hotels will not accept foreigners. The long-standing travellers' haunt is the *Tenzin Hotel* (☎0892/8822018; ❷), opposite the market. The cosy six-bed dorms (¥25) are excellent value, while the "Dalai Lama suite" suffers from lack of use and is not. Make sure the owners understand you expect to have a shower in the evening, otherwise they won't bother to stoke the boiler. There's an excellent roof terrace for basking in the sunshine. The other budget choice is the boxy *Fruit Orchard Hotel*, opposite the monastery (❸, dorm beds ¥15). It's clean but dull and has none of the charisma of the *Tenzin*. There's hot water available from 5 to 8pm. At the other end of the range, the *Shigatse Hotel* is the tour-group hotel, a bit out of the way on Jiefang Tong Lu (☎0892/8822556; ❼), but it's rather cavernous if there aren't plenty of people around. The lobby shop stocks a good range of books and souvenirs and even oxygen canisters. The best mid-range place is the comfortable *Zhufeng Friendship Guesthouse* (☎0892/8821929; ❻) on Dechen Phodrang Lu, which has 24-hour hot water, although it is a bit out of town.

Eating and drinking

There's no shortage of **restaurants** in Shigatse. Of the Chinese ones lining Kesang Ke Lu, head for the *Yingbin*. There's no English sign, but underneath the red Chinese characters it says "Warm welcome to our foreign guests". Inside it's chintzy but spotless, and the chef serves up superb Sichuan food that makes no concessions to wimpy Western palates. On the same street, the Nepali-run *Snowlands Youth Restaurant*, the haunt of some grizzled looking characters, serves excellent yak dishes. Slightly farther away, on Tsendu Lu, the *Gong Kar Tibetan Restaurant* has fabulously painted pillars outside and comfortable sofas within. Adventurous carnivores can try yak's heart salad, pig's trotters and ears here, although there are also more mainstream meat and vegetable dishes (¥12–20). Upmarket Chinese food can be had at the *Xingyue Restaurant*, north of the *Shigatse Hotel,* which caters mainly for groups. There's a small **night market** on the corner of Qomolongma Lu and Jiefang Tong Lu, where you can sit on sofas on the pavement and eat spicy kebabs and nourishing bowls of noodles. If you're getting a **picnic** together, visit the market off Beijing Bei Lu for fresh fruit and the like.

West to Zhangmu

From Shigatse, the Friendship Highway **west to Zhangmu** on the Nepalese border is partly surfaced, but generally rough and quite slow. The only public buses in this direction are the unreliable Shigatse to Sakya, Lhatse and Zhangmu services. From the broad plain around Shigatse, the road gradually climbs to the pass of Tsuo La (4500m) before the steep descent to the Sakya Bridge and the turn-off to Sakya village. If you have time, a detour off the Friendship Highway to Sakya is worthwhile; the valleys are picturesque, the villages retain the rhythm of their rural life and **Sakya Monastery** is a dramatic sight, unlike anything you'll encounter elsewhere in Tibet.

Sakya

The small but rapidly growing village of **SAKYA**, set in the midst of an attractive plain, straddles the small Trum River and is highly significant as the centre of the Sakya school of Tibetan Buddhism. The main reason to visit is to see the remaining monastery, a unique Mongol-style construction dramatically visible from miles away. The village around is now a burgeoning Chinese community, full of ugly concrete, and has been corrupted by tourism; children everywhere will try to sell you quartz or fossils, or sometimes just rocks, and food is very expensive.

Sakya Monastery

Experiences of visiting **Sakya Monastery** (Mon–Sat 9am–noon & 4–6pm; ¥35, photographs inside the chapels ¥80) vary considerably. Some people find the monks rude and offhand, others find them friendly and eager to talk.

Originally there were two monasteries at Sakya: the imposing, Mongol-style structure of the **Southern Monastery** that most visitors come to see today, and the **Northern Monastery** across the river, which was a more typical monastic complex containing 108 chapels. The latter was completely destroyed during the Cultural Revolution and has been largely replaced by housing. Prior to the Chinese occupation, there were around five hundred monks in the two monasteries; there are now about a hundred. The Northern Monastery was founded in 1073 by Kong Chogyal Pho, a member of the Khon family, whose son, Kunga Nyingpo, did much to establish Sakya as an important religious centre. He married and had four sons; three became monks but the fourth remained a layman and continued the family line. The Sakya order has remained something of a family affair and while the monks take vows of celibacy, their lay brothers ensure the leadership remains with their kin. One of the early leaders was a grandson of Kunga Nyingpo, known as Sakya Pandita. He began the most illustrious era of the order in the thirteenth century when he journeyed to the court of the Mongol emperor, Godan Khan, and established the Sakya lamas as religious advisers to subsequent emperors and effective rulers of Tibet. This state of affairs lasted until the overthrow of the Mongols in 1354.

The Southern Monastery

The **entrance** to the Southern Monastery is in its east wall. On the way there, note the unusual decoration of houses in the area – grey, with white and red vertical stripes; this dates back to a time when it denoted their taxable status within the Sakya principality.

A massive fortress, the Southern Monastery was built in the thirteenth century on the orders of Phagpa, nephew of Sakya Pandita. The five main temples in the complex are surrounded by a huge wall with turrets at each corner. On the left of the entrance, the tall, spacious chapel on the second floor of the **Puntsok Palace**, the traditional home of one of the two main Sakya lamas who now lives in the USA, is lined with statues – White Tara is nearest to the door and Sakya Pandita farther along the same wall. The central figure of

Kunga Nyingpo, the founder of the Northern Monastery, shows him as an old man. The *chortens* contain the remains of early Sakya lamas. As you move clockwise around the courtyard, the next chapel is the **Phurkhang**, with statues of Sakyamuni to the left and Manjusri to the right of Sakya Pandita. The whole temple is stuffed with thousands of small statues and editions of sacred texts with murals on the back wall.

Facing the entrance to the courtyard, the **Great Assembly Hall** is an imposing chapel with walls 3.5m thick. Its roof is supported by forty solid wooden columns, one of which was said to be a personal gift from Kublai Khan and carried by hand from China; another was supposedly fetched from India on the back of a tiger, a third brought in the horns of a yak and yet another is said to weep the black blood of the *naga* water spirit that lived in the tree used for the column. The chapel is overwhelmingly full of brocade hangings, fine statues, butter lamps, thrones, murals and holy books. The grandest statues, of Buddha against a golden, carved background, contain the remains of previous Sakya lamas.

Next along, the **Silver Chorten Chapel** houses eleven *chortens* with more in the chapel behind. Completing the circuit, the **Drolma Lhakhang** is on the second floor of the building to the right of the entrance. This is the residence of the other principal Sakya lama, the Sakya Trizin, currently residing in India where he has established his seat in exile in Rajpur. Be sure to take time to walk around the top of the walls for fine views both into the monastery and over the surrounding area.

Practicalities

Situated 150km southwest of Shigatse, Sakya is an easy side-trip off the Friendship Highway if you've got your own transport. Public **buses** run here from Shigatse on weekdays (see box, p.1163), returning from Sakya at 11am the next morning; it's a surprisingly slow trip – allow six hours or more each way. If you want to continue from Sakya to Lhatse, get the bus to drop you at the Friendship Highway turn-off, which it reaches around 1pm. The bus from Shigatse to Lhatse passes here about 1.30pm, so you shouldn't have to wait for long. The **permit** situation is variable: there's a checkpoint just before the village, but some travellers without permits have been waved through by the lazy guards. Don't rely on this, however; if you haven't got a permit and you're trying to get to Nepal, it might be best to give Sakya a miss.

On arrival, avoid the miserable **accommodation** at the bus station; turn right out of the bus station entrance and walk straight ahead for 150m to the *Tibetan Hotel* opposite the north wall of the monastery. Only dorms are on offer, there is bedding but no sheets, electricity is temperamental and pit latrines are the only facilities. The best **restaurant** in Sakya, the *Sichuan Flavour Restaurant*, is just west of the hotel entrance, next to a small shop sporting a *Simone Soda and Cigs* sign. This tiny Chinese restaurant has a surprisingly lengthy menu, written in English, with the usual range of meat, vegetable, rice and noodle dishes (¥10–20); their pancakes make a good breakfast. Alternatively, there is basic accommodation on the Friendship Highway at the turn-off for Sakya (❶) – there's no sign, so ask in the compound there.

Sakya to Everest

Just 24km west of Sakya Bridge (there's no checkpost between the two), the truck-stop town of **Lhatse** (4050m) lines the Friendship Highway and has plenty of restaurants and basic accommodation. There's little to detain you, but most drivers stop here. Another 6km west from Lhatse, there's a checkpoint after which the road divides: the Friendship Highway continues to the left and the route to the far west of the region heads right. If you're hitching in to Western Tibet walk a couple of kilometres along this right fork until you reach the ferry crossing. All the drivers have to stop and wait for the ferry here. If you're hitching to Nepal, walk past the checkpoint and wait there. You are more likely to be picked up by a tour bus heading to the border than by a local.

The continuation of the Friendship Highway is diabolical; allow about four hours in a good jeep, up over the Lhakpa La Pass (5220m) to the checkpost and turn-off to **Shekar** (also known as New Tingri). Avoid the much-advertised but over-priced *Chomolungma Hotel* (❻), a couple of hundred metres towards Shekar off the Friendship Highway, and stay at the new and comfortable, if basic, *Pelbar Family Hotel* (❶), on the highway. There are a few cosy restaurants around here, too. The village itself is 7km farther on, with the Shekar Chode Monastery on the hillside above. There's basic accommodation (❶) in the village, but you'll have to ask, and there's little reason to hang around.

Shekar boasts another checkpost on the highway about 5km from the *Pelbar Family Guesthouse*, and some visitors have reported that the guards here are particularly assiduous in confiscating printed material specifically about Tibet from travellers entering the country (books on China which include Tibet seem to be fine). Just 7km west of this checkpost, the small turning to **Rongbuk Monastery** and on up to **Everest Base Camp** is on the south side of the road. It's a long, bumpy and spellbinding 90km to Rongbuk and worth every tortured minute of the three- or four-hour drive along the rough track. About 3km from the turning, the checkpost at Chay will collect entrance fees (¥400 per jeep, ¥65 per person) for the Everest area.

From Chay the road zigzags steeply up to the Pang La Pass (5150m), from where the glory of the Everest region is laid out before you – the earlier you go in the day the better the views, as it clouds over later. There's a **lookout** spot with a plan to help you identify individual peaks such as Cho Oyu (8153m), Lhotse (8501m) and Makalu (8463m) as well as the mighty Everest (8848m; Chomolungma in Tibetan, Zhumulangma in Chinese). From here the road descends into a network of fertile valleys with small villages in a patchwork of fields. You'll gradually start climbing again and pass through Peruche (19km from Pang La), Passum (10km farther), where there is accommodation just beside the road at the *Passumpembah Teahouse* (❶), and Chodzom (another 12km) before the scenery becomes rockier, starker and you eventually reach Rongbuk Monastery, 22km farther on.

Rongbuk and Everest Base Camp

The highest monastery in the world, **Rongbuk** (4980m) was founded in 1902 by the Nyingma Lama, Ngawang Tenzin Norbu, although a hardy community of nuns had used meditation huts on the site for about two hundred years before this. The chapels themselves are of limited interest; Padmasambhava is in pride of place and the new murals are attractive, but the position of the monastery, perched on the side of the Rongbuk Valley leading straight towards the north face of Everest, is stunning. Just to sit outside and watch the play of light on the face of the mountain is the experience of a lifetime.

Everest Base Camp (5150m) is a farther 8km due south. The road is motorable but it's mostly flat and the walk alongside the river through the boulder-strewn landscape past a small monastery on the cliff is glorious. Base camp is often a bit of a surprise, especially during the climbing seasons (Mar–May, Sept & Oct), when you'll find a colourful tent city festooned with Calor Gas bottles and satellite dishes. It's possible to camp near the monastery where there's also a guesthouse offering dorm **accommodation**. Grubby quilts are provided, but you'll be more comfortable with your own sleeping bag. Each room has a stove and pot to boil water (you collect it from up the valley) and the monks will provide fuel (although if you can manage to buy some in the villages on the way this would be insurance against a shortage – a night here without heat would be grim). There's a small monastery shop selling mostly leftovers from mountaineering expeditions – take your own food. Don't be surprised if you suffer with the **altitude** here. However well you were acclimatized in Lhasa, base camp is around 1500m higher, so be sensible and don't contemplate a trip here soon after arrival up on the Tibetan plateau.

To the border

From the Rongbuk and Everest Base Camp turning on the Friendship Highway, it's a fast 50km south to **TINGRI** (4342m). The road is good and you should allow about an hour in a jeep. Tingri is a convenient stop before the final day's drive to Zhangmu and has good views south towards Everest. To get the best of these, climb up to the old fort that stands sentinel over the main part of the village. The three **accommodation** options are on the northern side of the main road. The first, the *Snow Leopard* (❸), is best avoided as it's twice as expensive as the others and has nothing they don't, except carpets. The *Himalaya Hotel* (❶) and *Everest Veo* (❶) are a little farther east, and both offer dorm accommodation, latrines with a view, and seats in the sunshine. In both, also, the family's living room doubles as a restaurant, and they produce good basic fare. For something fancier, try the Sichuan restaurant opposite – look for the red sign.

The road west of Tingri is good quality and lined with ruins of buildings destroyed in an eighteenth-century Gurkha incursion from Nepal. The road climbs gradually for 85km to the double-topped **Lalung La Pass** (5050m) from where the views of the Himalayas are great, especially looking west to the great slab of Shishapangma (8013m). The descent from the pass is steep and startling as the road drops off the edge of the Tibetan plateau and heads down the gorge of the Po Chu River. Vegetation appears and it becomes noticeably warmer as you near Nyalam, around four hours by jeep from Tingri.

Although difficult to spot if you're coming from the north, **Milarepa's Cave** (10km north of Nyalam) is worth a halt – look out for a white *chorten*, to the left of the road on the edge of the gorge. Milarepa (1040–1123) was a much revered Tibetan mystic who led an ascetic, itinerant life in caves and was loved for his religious songs. The Kagyu order of Tibetan Buddhism was founded by his followers and the impressions in the walls and roof are believed to have been made by Milarepa himself. A temple has been built around the cave, the main statue being of Padmasambhava. Perched on the side of the Matsang Zangpo river gorge, **Nyalam** (3750m) is a small village with several Chinese restaurants and a variety of basic accommodation, although there is little to recommend staying the night here rather than continuing to Zhangmu.

The steep descent through the Himalayas continues on a twisty and dramatic road that winds in and out of the forested mountainsides and feels almost tropical as it descends the 33km to the border town of **ZHANGMU** (2300m). This

Chinese–Tibetan–Nepalese hybrid clings gamely to the sheer mountain, a collection of tin shacks, construction sites, wooden huts, shops, brothels and offices. It's a great place with a Wild-West-comes-to-Asia atmosphere, although good-quality **accommodation** is limited. The choice is between the *Zhangmu Hotel* (☎08074/882272; ❻) at the bottom end of town with no hot water in the private bathrooms, although there's a shower on the top floor of a building opposite, and the *Himalaya Hotel and Lodge* (❶), on the right heading down through town, offering clean dorms and great views down the valley. There are no washing facilities, but there's a shower operation just up the hill and putrid latrines across the street. The **PSB** is tucked away in an alley close to the *Zhangmu Hotel*. Zhangmu boasts two branches of the **Bank of China** (Mon–Fri 10am–1pm & 3.30–6.30pm, Sat 10am–2pm), one near the border post at the bottom of town and one just above the *Himalaya Hotel and Lodge*. Despite production of exchange certificates they refuse to change Chinese money into either Nepalese or other hard currency, so if you've got excess you'll be forced onto the thriving black market. Follow the music and flashing lights for the nightly disco/hostess/**karaoke bar** in the middle of town, where everyone dances the waltz.

Entering Nepal

Border formalities are fairly cursory if you're leaving Tibet for Nepal. The **border posts** (both open daily 9.30am–5pm Chinese time) on the Chinese and Nepalese side, at **Kodari** (1770m), are an extremely steep 9km apart. You can either rent a truck (¥300 for four people), hire a porter (about ¥10 per bag) or carry your own stuff for the ninety-minute walk down (either follow the road or take the short cuts that slice across the zigzags) to the Friendship Bridge, where there is another Chinese checkpost before you cross the bridge into Kodari. The **Nepalese Immigration** post is a couple of hundred metres over the bridge on the left. You can get only single entry visas here, and you have to pay in US dollars and produce one passport photograph (see "Listings", p.1143 for details of Nepali visas available in Lhasa). Don't forget to put your watch back (2hr 15min) when you cross into Nepal.

To head to Kathmandu, either take the express bus there or the cheaper local service to Barabise and then change for Kathmandu. Alternatively, there are taxis in Kodari, or you can negotiate for space in a tourist bus that has just dropped its group at the border – bargain hard and you'll end up paying Rp400–500 per person for the four-hour trip.

Western Tibet

Travellers in Lhasa spend huge amounts of time and energy plotting and planning trips to the highlights of **Western Tibet**: Mount Kailash, Lake Manasarova and, less popular but just as enticing, the hot springs at Tirthapuri and the remains of the tenth-century Guge kingdom, its capital at Tsaparang and main monastery at Tholing. However, this is no guarantee of reaching any of these destinations.

Regulations regarding visits to the west change frequently and you shouldn't underestimate the time it will take to set up a trip. Tour companies in Lhasa arrange journeys for trucks of travellers, generally quoting around ¥12,000 per truck for a two- to three-week return trip. Unless you have huge amounts of time and are willing to persevere, there is little realistic alternative to going on an organized tour; there is no public transport beyond the Sakya turning and plenty more people give up trying to hitchhike than make it. A couple of travellers have died in the attempt.

The **southern route passes** through Saga, Dongpa and Horpa, a stunningly picturesque journey, parallel to the Himalayas, but with rivers that become swollen and passes that get blocked by snow. This route is most reliable from May through to the beginning of July, and again in October and November, although luck plays a big part. The distance is around 1400km from Lhasa to Mount Kailash. The alternative **northern route** via Tsochen, Gertse and Gakyi is longer; Lhasa to Ali (Shiquanhe) is over 1700km and then it's another 300km or so southeast to Kailash. It is also less scenic but more reliable and there's more traffic using it. Many tours plan to go on one route and return on the other – expect at least a week travelling time on either.

Mount Kailash and the other sights

Top of most itineraries is **Mount Kailash** (6714m), Gang Rinpoche to the Tibetans, the sacred mountain at the centre of the universe for Buddhists, Hindus and Jains. Access is via **DARCHEN**, where there's a guesthouse used as a base by visiting pilgrims. The 58-kilometre tour around the mountain takes around three days; you might consider hiring a porter and/or yak (from about ¥45 per day each) as it's a tough walk and you need to carry all your gear including a stove, fuel and food. On the first day you should aim to reach Drirapuk Monastery, on the second day you climb over the Dolma La Pass (5636m) to Zutrulpuk Monastery and the third day you arrive back in Darchen.

After the exertions of Kailash most tours head south 30km to **Lake Manasarova** (Mapham Yutso), the holiest lake in Asia for Hindus and Tibetan Buddhists alike. For the energetic it's a four-day, ninety-kilometre trek to get around the lake, but plenty of travellers just relax by the lakeside for a day or two. At the time of writing, the only agency in Lhasa permitted to sell tours is FIT at the *Snowlands Hotel;* they charge ¥22,000 for one jeep for a seventeen-day trip. Other agencies might be willing to go for a lot less, though allow plenty of time in Lhasa to sort this trip out.

The third major pilgrimage site in Western Tibet is **Tirthapuri** hot springs, which are closely associated with Padmasambhava; they're situated about 80km northwest of Kailash and accessible by road. Pilgrims here immerse themselves in the pools, visit the monastery containing his footprint and the cave that he used, and dig for small pearl-like stones that are believed to have healing properties.

The only remains of the tenth-century kingdom of **Guge**, where Buddhism survived while eclipsed in other parts of Tibet, are the main monastery of **Tholing**, 278km from Ali, and the old capital of **Tsaparang**, 26km west of Tholing. Both places are famous for their extensive ruins, some of which are around a thousand years old, and there are many well-preserved murals, but it's all even less accessible than Kailash and Manasarova.

The major town in the area, **ALI** (also known as Shiquanhe) is the largest town for several hundred kilometres and is a modern Chinese-style settlement at the confluence of the Indus and Gar rivers. The only official foreigners' **accommodation** is the over-priced *Ali Hotel* (❸) west of the main crossroads.

Travel details

Buses

Gyantse to: Shigatse (frequent minibuses; 2–3hr).
Lhasa to: Damxhung (daily minibus; 3–4hr); Ganden (daily pilgrim bus; 3–4hr); Golmud (daily bus; 30–40hr); Samye ferry crossing (daily bus; 4hr); Shigatse (daily bus; 5–6hr; frequent minibuses; 6–7hr); Tsetang (frequent minibuses; 3hr); Tsurphu (daily pilgrim bus; 2–3hr); Xining (daily bus; 40–50hr); Zhangmu (3 buses monthly; 3–4 days) .
Sakya to: Shigatse (daily; 6–7hr).
Shigatse to: Gyantse (frequent minibuses; (2–3hr); Lhasa (daily bus; 5–6hr; frequent minibuses; 6–7hr); Lhatse (one minibus daily; 8hr); Sakya (5 buses weekly; 6–7hr).
Tsetang to: Lhasa (frequent minibuses; 3hr).

Flights

Lhasa to: Beijing (daily except Mon; 4hr 30min); Chengdu (2 daily; 2hr); Chongqing (3 weekly; 2hr); Kathmandu (Nepal; 3 weekly; 1hr); Xi'an (1 weekly; 2hr 40min); Xining (2 weekly; 2hr).

Contexts

Contexts

History

As modern archeology gradually confirms ancient records of the country's earliest times, it seems that, however far back you go, China's history is essentially the saga of its **dynasties**, a succession of warring rulers who ultimately differed only in the degree of their autocracy. Although this generalized view is inevitable in the brief account below, bear in mind that, while the concept of being Chinese has been around for over two thousand years, the closer you look, the less "China" seems to exist as an entity – right from the start, **regionalism** played an important part in the country's history. And while concentrating on the great events, it's also easy to forget that the lot of those ruled was often appalling. The emperors may have lived in splendour while their courts produced talented writers, poets and artisans, but among the peasantry taxes, famine and early death were the norm. While the Cultural Revolution, ingrained corruption, and clampdowns on political dissent in Beijing and Tibet may not be a good track record for the People's Republic, it's also true that only since its birth in 1949 – which seems like yesterday in China's immense timescale – has even the possibility of a decent quality of life been imaginable for the ordinary citizen.

Prehistory and the Three Dynasties

Chinese legends hold that the creator, **Pan Ku**, was born from the egg of chaos and grew to fill the space between Yin, the earth, and Yang, the heavens. For eighteen thousand years Pan Ku chiselled the earth to its present state with the aid of a dragon, a unicorn, a phoenix and a tortoise. When he died his body became the soil, rivers and rain, his eyes the sun and moon, while his parasites transformed into human beings. A pantheon of semi-divine rulers known as the **Five Sovereigns** followed, each reigning for a hundred years or more and inventing fire, the calendar, agriculture, silk-breeding and marriage. Later a famous triumvirate included **Yao the Benevolent** who abdicated in favour of **Shu**. Shu toiled in the sun until his skin turned black and then he abdicated in favour of **Yu the Great**, tamer of floods and said to be the founder of China's first dynasty, the **Xia**. The Xia was reputed to have lasted 439 years until their last degenerate and corrupt king was overthrown by the **Shang** dynasty. The Shang was in turn succeeded by the **Zhou**, who ended this legendary era by virtue of leaving court histories behind them. Together, the Xia, Shang and Zhou are generally known as the **Three Dynasties**.

As far as archeology is concerned, **homo erectus** remains from Liaoning, Anhui, Beijing and Yunnan provinces indicate that China was already broadly occupied by human ancestors well before modern mankind began to emerge 200,000 years ago. Excavations of more recent Stone Age sites show that agricultural communities based around the fertile Yellow River and Yangzi basins, such as **Banpo** in Shaanxi and **Homudu** in Zhejiang, were producing pottery and silk by 5000 BC. It was along the Yellow River, too, that solid evidence of the bronze-working Three Dynasties first came to light, with the discovery of a series of large rammed-earth palaces at **Erlitou** near Luoyang, now believed to have been the Xia capital in 2000 BC.

Little is known about the Xia, though their territory apparently encompassed Shanxi, Henan and Hebei. The events of the subsequent Shang dynasty, however, were first documented just before the time of Christ by the historian **Sima Qian**, and his previously discredited accounts have been supported in recent years by a stream of finds. Based over much the same area as their predecessors and lasting from roughly 1750 BC to 1040 BC, Shang society had a king, a class system and a skilled **bronze technology** which permeated beyond the borders into Sichuan, and produced the splendid vessels found in today's museums. Excavations on the site ofYin, the Shang capital, have found tombs stuffed with weapons, jade ornaments, traces of silk and sacrificial victims – indicating belief in **ancestor worship** and an afterlife. The Shang also practised divination by incising questions onto tortoiseshell or bone and then heating them to study the way in which the material cracked around the words. These **oracle bones** provide China's **earliest written records**, covering topics as diverse as rainfall, dreams and ancestral curses.

Around 1040 BC a northern tribe, the **Zhou**, overthrew the Shang, expanded their kingdom west of the Yellow River into Shaanxi and set up a capital at Xi'an. Adopting many Shang customs, the Zhou also introduced the doctrine of the **Mandate of Heaven**, a belief justifying successful rebellion by declaring that heaven grants ruling authority to leaders who are strong and wise, and takes it from those who aren't – still an integral part of the Chinese political perspective. The Zhou consequently styled themselves "Sons of Heaven" and ruled through a hierarchy of vassal lords, whose growing independence led to the gradual dissolution of the Zhou kingdom from around 600 BC.

The decline of the Zhou dynasty

Driven to a new capital at Luoyang, later Zhou rulers exercised only a symbolic role; real power was fought over by some two hundred city states and kingdoms during the four hundred years known as the **Spring and Autumn** and the **Warring States** periods. This time of violence was also a time of vitality and change. As the feudal system broke down, traditional religion gave way to new ideas based on the writings of Kong Fuzi, or **Confucius**, and also on Taoism and Legalism (see pp.1198–201). As the warring states rubbed up against one another, agriculture and irrigation, trade, transport and diplomacy were all galvanized; iron was first smelted for weapons and tools, and great discoveries made in medicine, astronomy and mathematics. Three hundred years of war and annexation reduced the competitors to seven states, whose territories, collectively known as Zhong Guo, the **Middle Kingdom**, had now expanded west into Sichuan, south to Hunan and north to the Mongolian border.

The Qin dynasty

The fighting of the Warring States period came to an end only in the third century BC with the rise of a new dynasty – the **Qin**. For five hundred years the state of Qin – originally based on modern Shaanxi – had gradually been gobbling up its neighbours. In 221 BC its armies conquered the last pocket of resistance in the Middle Kingdom, east-coast Qi (Shandong), uniting the Chinese as a single centralized state for the first time, and implementing systems of currency and writing that were to last millennia. The rule of China's first emperor, **Qin Shi Huang**, was absolute: ancient literature and historical records were destroyed to wipe out any ideas that conflicted with his own, and peasants were forced off their land to work as labourers on his massive construction projects, which saw thousands of kilometres of roads, canals and an early version of the **Great Wall** laid down across the new empire. Burning with ambition to rule the entire known world, Huang's armies gradually pushed beyond the Middle Kingdom, expanding Chinese rule, if not absolute control, west and southeast. But, though he introduced the basis of China's enduring legacy of bureaucratic government, Huang's 37-year reign was ultimately too self-centred – still apparent in the massive tomb (guarded by the famous **Terracotta Army**) he had built for himself at his capital, Xi'an. When he died in 210 BC the provinces rose in revolt, and his heirs soon proved to lack the personal authority which had held his empire together.

The Han dynasty

In 206 BC the rebel warlord **Liu Bang** took Xi'an, and founded the **Han dynasty**. Lasting some four hundred years and larger at its height than contemporary imperial Rome, the Han was the first great empire, one that experienced a flowering of culture and a major impetus to push out frontiers and open them to trade, people and new ideas. In doing so it defined the national identity to such an extent that the main body of the Chinese people still style themselves "**Han Chinese**" after this dynasty.

Liu Bang maintained the Qin model of local government, but to prevent others from repeating his own military takeover, he strengthened his position by handing out large chunks of land to his relatives. This secured a period of stability, with effective taxation financing a growing civil service and the building of a huge and cosmopolitan capital, **Chang'an**, at today's Xi'an. Growing revenue also refuelled the expansionist policies of later ruler **Wu**. From 135 to 90 BC he extended his lines of defence well into Xinjiang and Yunnan, opening up the Silk Road for trade in tea, spices and silk with India, west Asia and Rome. He used his sons and competent generals to beat off northern tribes, enter Korea, and to subdue and colonize the unruly southern states, including Guangdong and even parts of Vietnam. At home Wu stressed the Confucian model for his growing civil service, beginning a two-thousand-year institution of Confucianism in government offices.

But, eventually, the empire's resources and supply lines were stretched to breaking point, while the burden of taxation led to unrest and retrenchment. Gradually the ruling house became decadent and was weakened by power struggles between rival factions of imperial consorts, eunuchs and statesmen, until **Wang Mang**, regent for a child emperor, usurped the rule to found his own brief dynasty in 9 AD. Fifteen years later the **Eastern Han** was re-established from a new capital at Luoyang, where the classical tradition was reimposed under Emperor **Liu Xiu**, though after his reign the dynasty was again gradually undermined by factional intrigue. Internal strife was later fomented by the **Yellow Turbans**, who drew their following from Taoist cults, while local governments and landowners began to set up as semi-independent rulers, with the country once again splitting into warring states. But by this time two major schools of philosophy and religion had emerged to survive the ensuing chaos. Confucianism's ideology of a centralized universal order had crystallized imperial authority; and **Buddhism**, introduced into the country from India, began to enrich aspects of life and thought, especially in the fine arts and literature, while itself being absorbed and changed by native beliefs.

The Three Kingdoms

Nearly four hundred years separate the collapse of the Han in about 220 AD and the return of unity under the Sui in 589. China was under a single government for only about fifty years of that time, though the idea of a unified empire was never forgotten.

From 200 AD the three states of **Wei**, **Wu** and **Shu** struggled for supremacy in a protracted and massively complicated war (later immortalized in the saga *Romance of the Three Kingdoms*; see p.509) that ruined central China and encouraged mass migrations southwards. The following centuries saw China's regionalism becoming entrenched: the **Southern Empire** suffered weak and short-lived dynasties, but nevertheless there was prosperity and economic growth, with the capital at **Nanjing** becoming a thriving trading and cultural centre. Meanwhile, with the borders unprotected, the north was invaded in 386 by the **Tobas**, who established the northern **Wei dynasty** after their aristocracy adopted Chinese manners and customs – a pattern of assimilation that would recur with other invaders. At their first capital, **Datong**, they created a wonderful series of Buddhist carvings, but in 534 their empire fell apart. After grabbing power from his regent in 581, general **Yang Jian** unified the fragmented northern states and then went on to conquer southern China by land and sea, founding the Sui dynasty.

The Three Kingdoms period was in some ways a dark age of war, violence and genocide, but it was also a richly formative one and, when the dust had settled, a very different society had emerged. For much of this time many areas produced a **food surplus** which could support a rich and leisured ruling class in the cities and the countryside, as well as large armies and burgeoning Buddhist communities. So culture developed, literature flourished, calligraphy and sculpture, especially Buddhist carvings, all enriched by Indian and central Asian elements, reached unsurpassed levels. This was a rich legacy for the ensuing Sui and Tang dynasties to build on.

The Sui

The **Sui** get short shrift in historical surveys. Their brief empire was soon eclipsed by their successors, the Tang, but until the dynasty over-reached itself on the military front in Korea and burnt out, two of its three emperors could claim considerable achievements. Until his death in 604 Yang Jian himself – Emperor **Wen** – was an active ruler who took the best from the past and built on it. He simplified and strengthened the bureaucracy, bought in a new legal code, recentralized civil and military authority and made tax collection more efficient. Near Xi'an his architects designed a new capital, **Da Xing Cheng** (City of Great Prosperity), with a palace city, a residential quarter of 108 walled compounds, several vast markets and an outer wall over 35km round – quite probably the largest city in the world at that time. After Wen's death in 604, **Yang Di** elbowed his elder brother out to become emperor. Yang improved administration, encouraged a revival of Confucian learning and promoted a strong foreign policy. But his engineering works – or rather the forced labour needed to complete them – have left him portrayed as a proverbially "Evil Emperor", principally for ordering the construction of the two-thousand-kilometre **Grand Canal** to transport produce between the rice bowl of the southern Yangzi to his capital at Xi'an. Half the total work force of 5,500,000 died, and Yang was assassinated in 618 after popular hatred had inspired a military revolt led by General **Li Yuan**.

Medieval China: Tang to Song

The seventh century marks the beginning of the medieval period of Chinese history. This was the age in which Chinese culture reached its most cosmopolitan and sophisticated peak, a time of experimentation in literature, art, music and agriculture, and one which unified seemingly incompatible elements.

Having changed his name to **Gao Zu**, Li Yuan consolidated his new **Tang dynasty** by spending the rest of his eight-year reign getting rid of all his rivals. Under his son **Tai Zong**, Tang China expanded: the Turks were crushed, the Tibetans brought to heel and relations established with Byzantium. China kept open house for traders and travellers of all races and creeds, who settled in the mercantile cities of Yangzhou and Guangzhou, bringing with them their religions, especially **Islam**, and influencing the arts, cookery, fashion and entertainment. China's goods flowed out to India, Persia, the Near East and many other countries, and her language and religion gained currency in Japan and Korea. At home, **Buddhism** remained the all-pervading foreign influence, with Chinese pilgrims travelling widely in India. The best known of these, **Xuanzang** (see pp.1072–73), set off in 629 and returned after sixteen years in India with a mass of Buddhist sutras, adding greatly to China's storehouse of knowledge.

Xi'an's population swelled to over a million and it became one of the world's great cultural centres, heart of a centralized and powerful state. A decade after Tai Zong's death in 649, his short-lived son **Gao Zong** and China's only empress, **Wu Zetian**, had expanded the Tang empire's direct influence from Korea to Iran, and south into Vietnam. Wu Zetian was a great patron of Buddhism, commissioning the famous Longmen carvings outside Luoyang, and, though widely unpopular, she created a civil service selected on merit rather than birth. Her successor, **Xuan Zong**, began well in 712, but his later infatuation with the beautiful concubine **Yang Guifei** led to the **An Lushan rebellion** of 755, his flight to Sichuan and Yang's ignominious death at the hands of his mutineering army. Xuan Zong's son, **Su Zong**, enlisted the help of Tibetan and Uigur forces and recaptured Xi'an from the rebels; but though the court was re-established, it had lost its authority, and real power was once again shifting to the provinces.

The following two hundred years saw the country split into regional political and military alliances. From 907 to 960 **Five Dynasties** succeeded each other, all too short-lived to be effective. China's northern defences were permanently weakened, while her economic dependence on the south increased and the dispersal of power brought sweeping social changes. The traditional elite whose fortunes were tied to the dynasty gave way to a military and merchant class who bought land to acquire status, plus a professional ruling class selected by examination. In the south the **Ten Kingdoms** (some existing side by side) managed to retain what was left of the Tang civilization, their greater stability and economic prosperity sustaining a relatively high cultural level.

Finally, in 960, a disaffected army in the north put a successful general, **Song Tai Zu**, on the throne. His new ruling house, known as the **Northern Song**, made its capital at **Kaifeng** in the Yellow River basin, well placed at the head of the Grand Canal for transport to supply its million people with grain from the south. By skilled politicking rather than military might the new dynasty consolidated its authority over surrounding petty kingdoms and re-established civilian primacy. But in 1115, northern China was occupied by the **Jin**, who pushed the imperial court south to **Hangzhou** where, guarded by the Yangzi River, their culture continued to flourish from 1126 as the **Southern Song**. Developments during their 150-year dynasty included gunpowder, the magnetic compass, fine porcelain and moveable type printing. But the Song preoccupation with art and sophistication saw their military might decline and led to them underrating their aggressive "barbarian" neighbours, whose own expansionist policies culminated in the thirteenth-century **Mongol Invasion**.

The Yuan dynasty

In fact, Mongolian influence had first penetrated China in the eleventh century, when the Song emperors paid tribute to separate Mongolian states to keep their armies from invading. But these individual fiefdoms were unified by **Genghis Khan** in 1206 to form an immensely powerful army, which swiftly began the conquest of northern China. Despite Chinese resistance and dilatory Mongol infighting, by 1278 the **Yuan dynasty** was on the Chinese throne, with **Kublai Khan**, Genghis Khan's grandson, at the head of an empire that stretched way beyond China's borders. From their capital at Khanbalik (modern **Beijing**), the Yuan's emperors' central control boosted China's economy and helped repair five centuries of civil war. The country was also thrown wide open to foreign travellers, traders and missionaries; Arabs and Venetians were to be found in many Chinese ports, and a Russian came top of the Imperial Civil Service exam of 1341. The Grand Canal was extended from Beijing to Hangzhou, while in Beijing the **Palace of All Tranquillities** was built inside a new city wall, later known as the **Forbidden City**. Descriptions of much of this were brought back to Europe by **Marco Polo**, who put his impressions of Yuan lifestyle and treasures on paper after living in Beijing for several years and serving in the government of Kublai Khan.

The Yuan retained control over all China only until 1368, their power ultimately sapped by a combination of becoming too Chinese for their northern brethren to tolerate, and too aloof from the Chinese to assimilate properly. After northern tribes had rebelled, and famine and disastrous floods brought a series of uprisings in China, a monk-turned-bandit leader from the south, **Zhu Yuanzhang**, seized the throne from the last boy emperor of the Yuan in 1368.

The Ming dynasty

Zhu Yuanzhang took the name **Hong Wu** and proclaimed himself first emperor of the **Ming dynasty**, with Nanjing as his capital. Zhu's influences on

China's history were far-reaching. Aside from his extreme despotism, which saw two appalling purges in which thousands of civil servants and literati died, he also initiated a course of **isolationism** from the outside world which lasted throughout the Ming and Qing eras. Consequently, Chinese culture became inward-looking, and the benefits of trade and connections with foreign powers were lost. Nowhere is this more apparent than in the Ming construction of the current Great Wall, a grandiose but futile attempt to stem the invasion of northern tribes into China, built once military might and diplomacy began to break down in the fifteenth century.

Yet the period also produced fine artistic accomplishments, particularly **porcelain** from the imperial kilns at Jingdezhen, which became famous worldwide. Nor were the Ming rulers entirely isolationist. During the reign of **Yongle**, Zhu's 26th son, the imperial navy (commanded by the Muslim eunuch, Admiral **Zheng He**) ranged right across the Indian Ocean as far as the east coast of Africa on a fact-finding mission. But stagnation set in after Yongle's death in 1424, and the maritime missions were cancelled as being incompatible with Confucian values, which held a strong contempt for foreigners. Thus initiative for world trade and explorations passed into the hands of the Europeans, with the great period of world voyages by Columbus, Magellan and Vasco da Gama. In 1514, **Portuguese** vessels appeared in the Pearl River at the southern port of Guangzhou (Canton), and though they were swiftly expelled from here, Portugal was allowed to colonize nearby **Macao** in 1557. Though all dealings with foreigners were officially despised by the imperial court, trade flourished as Chinese merchants and officials were eager to milk the profit from it.

In later years, the Ming produced a succession of less able rulers who allowed power to slip into the hands of the seventy thousand inner court officials where it was used, not to run the empire, but for intriguing among the "eunuch bureaucracy". By the early seventeenth century, frontier defences had fallen into decay, and the **Manchu tribes** in the north were already across the Great Wall. A series of peasant and military uprisings against the Ming began in 1627, and when the rebel **Li Zicheng**'s forces managed to break into the capital in 1644, the last Ming emperor fled from his palace and hanged himself – an ignoble end to a 300-year-old dynasty.

The Qing dynasty

The Manchus weren't slow in turning internal dissent to their advantage. Sweeping down on Beijing, they threw out Li Zicheng's army, claimed the capital as their own and founded the **Qing dynasty**. It took a further twenty years for the Manchus to capture the south of the country, but on its capitulation China was once again under foreign rule. Like the Mongol Yuan dynasty before them, the Qing initially did little to assimilate domestic culture, ruling the people as separate overlords. Manchu became the official language, the Chinese were obliged to wear the Manchu **pigtail** and intermarriage between a Manchu and a Chinese was strictly forbidden. Under the Qing dynasty the distant areas of Inner and Outer Mongolia, Tibet and Turkestan were fully incorporated into the Chinese empire, uniting the Chinese world to a greater extent than during the Tang period.

Soon, however, the Manchus proved themselves susceptible to Chinese culture, and ultimately became deeply influenced by it. Three outstanding Qing emperors also brought an infusion of new blood and vigour to government early on in the dynasty. **Kangxi**, who began his 61-year reign in 1654 at the age of 6, was a great patron of the arts, leaving endless scrolls of famous calligraphy and paintings blotted with his seals stating that he had seen them. He assiduously cultivated his image as the Son of Heaven by making royal progresses throughout the country and by his personal style of leadership. He did much to bring the south under control and by 1683 the southern **Rebellion of Three Federations** (led by three military governors) had been savagely put down. His fourth son, the Emperor **Yungzheng** (1678–1735), ruled over what is considered one of the most efficient and least corrupt administrations ever enjoyed by China. This was inherited by **Qianlong** (1711–99), whose reign saw China's frontiers widely extended and the economy stimulated by peace and prosperity. In 1750 the nation was perhaps at its apex, one of the strongest, wealthiest and most powerful countries in the world.

But during the latter half of the eighteenth century, China began to experience growing economic problems. Settled society had produced a **population explosion**, putting pressure on food resources and causing a land shortage. This in turn saw trouble flaring as migrants from central China tried to settle the country's remoter western provinces, disposessing the original inhabitants. Meanwhile, expanding European nations were in Asia, looking for financial opportunities. From about 1660, Portuguese traders in Guangzhou had been joined by British merchants shopping for tea, silk and porcelain, and during the eighteenth century the British **East India Company** moved in, eager for a monopoly. But China's rulers, immensely rich and powerful and convinced of their own superiority, had no wish for direct dealings with foreigners. When **Lord Macartney** arrived in 1793 bearing the usual gifts in order to propose a political and trade treaty between King George III and the emperor, he refused to kowtow in submission and his embassy was unsuccessful. The king's "tribute" was accepted but the emperor rejected totally any idea of alliance with one who, according to Chinese ideas, was a subordinate. Macartney was impressed by the vast wealth and power of the Chinese court, but later wrote perceptively that the empire was "like an old crazy first-rate man of war which its officers have contrived to keep afloat to terrify by its appearance and bulk".

The Opium Wars and the Taiping Uprising

Foiled in their attempts at official negotiations with the Qing court, the East India Company decided to take matters into their own hands and create a clandestine market in China for Western goods. Instead of silver, they began to pay for tea and silk with **opium**, cheaply imported from India. As addicts and demand escalated during the early nineteenth century, China's trade surplus became a deficit, as silver drained out of the country to pay for the drug. The emperor pronounced an edict strictly forbidding the trade, then, when this was ignored, suspended the traffic in 1840 by ordering the confiscation and destruction of over twenty thousand chests of opium – the start of the first **Opium War**. After two years of British gunboats shelling coastal ports, the Chinese were forced to sign the **Treaty of Nanjing**, whose humiliating terms included a huge indemnity, the opening up of new ports to foreign trade, and the **cession of Hong Kong**. This was the first in a long series of concessions extracted by Britain and other nations under various unequal treaties.

It was a crushing blow for the Chinese, who failed to understand how alien techniques and organization had secured European superiority. Furthermore, the country now suffered major internal **rebellions** inspired by anti-Manchu feeling and economic hardship – themselves fuelled by rising taxes to pay off China's war indemnity. While serious uprisings occurred in Guizhou and Yunnan, the most widespread was started by the Chinese Christian evangelist **Hong Xiuquan**, who, backed by his million-strong **Taiping army**, stormed through central China in the 1850s to occupy much of the rich Yangzi Valley. Having captured Nanjing as his "Heavenly Capital", however, Hong's reign was weakened by internal dissent; and as the Taipings began to make military forays towards Beijing, the European powers decided to step in, worried that Hong's anti-foreign government might take control of the country. With their support, Qing troops forced the Taipings back to their capital in 1864 and butchered them. Hong Xiuquan committed suicide and the Taiping Uprising was at an end, leaving twenty million people dead and five provinces in ruins.

It was during the uprising that the **Empress Dowager Wu Cixi** first took over the reins of power in China, ruling from behind various emperors from 1861 until 1908. Ignorant, vain and certain that reform would weaken the Qings' grasp of power, she pursued a deep conservatism at a time when China needed desperately to overhaul its ineffectual political and economic structure. On the home front, profitable industries became owned by foreigners – who channelled their wealth out of the country – and increased Christian missionary activity undermined the traditional concepts on which Chinese society was based. In response, radical advisers persuaded Emperor Guangxu to instigate the **Hundred Days Reform** of 1898, an attempt to modernize agriculture, industry and government institutions. But it was crushed by opposition from the Confucian establishment, backed by Cixi, who imprisoned Guangxu, executed the advisers of reform and repealed their measures.

During this period, China's **colonial empire** was fast disintegrating. France took the former vassal states of Laos, Cambodia and Vietnam in 1883–5; Britain gained Burma; and **Tibet**, which had nominally been under China's control since Tang times, began to assert its independence. But perhaps most importantly, in 1894 China sent two thousand troops to support the king of **Korea** when a rebellion broke out. In reply, **Japan** dispatched ten thousand to keep the rebellion going, and within a few months Chinese and Korean forces were beaten. Under the treaty that followed, China was forced to cede the island of **Taiwan**, the Pescadores and the Liaodong Peninsula to Japan. This didn't go down well on the international scene. France, Germany and Russia, fearful of Japan's snowballing power, forced the country to return the Liaodong Peninsula to China. By way of reward the Chinese allowed Russia to build a rail line through Manchuria to their port at Lushun. With the ability to move troops quickly along this line, Russia effectively controlled Manchuria for the next ten years.

The Boxer rebellion – the end of imperial China

By the 1890s the whole of China was in chaos. For fifty years, the Qing rulers had spent fortunes on ruinous wars, allowed foreigners to take control of business, and stood idle while the countryside was ravaged by civil strife. A popular organization was all that was needed to realize the support of the peasants, and it came with the **Boxers**, more fully known as the "Society of Righteous and Harmonious Fists". Claiming invulnerability to bullets for all who followed their mystical faith, they stated their aims as "Overthrow the Qing, destroy the foreigner" – goals which were understandably close to the peasants' hearts. The Boxers suffered an initial defeat at the hands of Cixi's troops in 1899, but Cixi's government then decided that the Boxer army might in fact make a useful tool, and set them loose to slaughter missionaries, Christian converts and any other foreigner they could lay their hands on. By the summer of 1900 the government had made a wild declaration of war on all foreign powers on its lands, and the Boxers were in Beijing besieging the foreign legation compound. The German and Japanese ministers were killed, but the British and others managed to hold out until an international relief force arrived on August 14. In the massacre, looting and confusion which followed, during which the Boxers were totally routed, Cixi and the emperor disguised themselves as peasants and fled to Xi'an in a cart, leaving her ministers to negotiate a peace.

Though they clung feebly on for another decade, this was the end of the Qing, and internal movements to dismantle the dynastic system and build a new China proliferated. The most influential of these was the **Tong Meng Hui** society, founded in 1905 in Japan by the exile **Sun Yatsen**, a doctor from a wealthy Guangdong family. Cixi died three years later, and, in 1911, opposition to foreigners constructing railways drew events to a head in Wuchang, Hubei Province, igniting a popular uprising which finally toppled the dynasty. Two thousand years of dynastic succession ended almost quietly, and Sun Yatsen returned to China to take the lead in the provisional **Republican Government** at Nanjing.

From republic to communism

Almost immediately the new republic was in trouble. Though a **parliament** was duly elected in 1913, it lacked any real political or military force; in addition, northern China was controlled by the former leader of the Imperial Army, **Yuan Shikai** (who had forced the abdication of the last emperor, **Pu Yi**). Sun Yatsen, faced with a choice between probable civil war and relinquishing his presidency at the head of the newly formed Nationalist People's Party, the **Guomindang**, stepped down. Yuan promptly dismissed the government, forced Sun into renewed exile, and attempted to centralize power – clearly with a view to establishing a new dynasty. But his plans were stalled by his generals, who wanted private fiefdoms of their own, and Yuan's sudden death in 1916 marked the last time in 34 years that China would be united under a single authority. While bickering between Yuan's generals plunged the north into civil war, Sun Yatsen returned yet again, this time to found a southern Guomindang government.

Thus divided, China was unable to stem the increasingly bold territorial incursions made by Japan and other colonial powers as a result of **World War I**. Siding with the Allies, Japan had claimed the German port of Qingdao and all German shipping and industry in the Shangdong Peninsula on the outbreak of war, and in 1915 presented China with **Twenty-One Demands**, many of which Yuan Shikai, under threat of a Japanese invasion, was forced to accept. After the war, hopes that the 1919 **Treaty of Versailles** would end Japanese aggression (as well as the unequal treaties and foreign concessions) were dashed when the Western powers, who had already signed secret pacts with Japan, confirmed Japan's rights in China. This ignited what became known as the **May 4 Movement**, the first in a series of anti-foreign demonstrations and riots.

The rise of the CCP

As a reflection of these events, the **Chinese Communist Party** (CCP) formed in Shanghai in 1921, its leadership drawn from two groups who had been active for several years. The first centred around **Li Dazhao**, former librarian at Beijing university, along with the young **Mao Zedong** and

Zhang Gutao, both students. The second was headed by **Zhou Enlai**, who had organized a Marxist study group in Tianjin. The party was guided by Russian advisers, whose instructions, besides concentrating on the Russian example of an urban proletarian revolution – of dubious value given China's largely rural population – invariably included a measure of Soviet foreign policy. When Moscow asked the CCP to support the Guomindang in its military campaigns against the northern warlords, the reality was that Soviet fear of Japan attacking their eastern lands required a strong China, and they considered the Guomindang the most likely party to achieve this.

While the CCP duly joined the Guomindang, they made unlikely bedfellows, especially after Sun Yatsen died in 1925. He was succeeded by his brother-in-law and military chief **Chiang Kaishek** (better known in China as Jiang Jieshe), an extreme nationalist who had no time for the CCP or its plans to end China's class divisions. Under his leadership, the combined Communist and Guomindang forces, as the National Revolutionary Army (NRA), successfully crushed the rogue warlords on the **Northern Expedition**, but then refused to join Chiang in his new headquarters in Nanchang. Moving on to capture Shanghai on March 21, 1927, Communist elements in the NRA organized a general strike against Chiang, seizing the military arsenal and arming workers. But industry bosses and foreign owners quickly retaliated, financing Chiang to disguise hundreds of thugs as members of the NRA, who then turned on the workers' militia and massacred the Communists, along with anyone else Chiang had decided to eradicate. Around five thousand were murdered; Zhou Enlai escaped only by luck, and Li Dazhao was executed by slow strangulation.

With the army now on his side and much of the original Communist hierarchy summarily executed (including Mao's second wife **Yang Kaihui**), Chiang quickly achieved supremacy and was declared head of a national government in 1928. Under him, the Guomindang became a military dictatorship, ignoring the country's general poverty and Japanese encroachments in favour of subduing all internal opposition by brute force. In this Chiang was aided substantially by Western powers – including the Soviet Union, who never let up on the line that the Communists should maintain their alliance with the GMD. Chiang's domestic power base, however, was small, and, despite attempts at limited social reform, the Party quickly came to represent the interests of a social elite. Those Communists who had escaped Chiang's purges regrouped in remote areas across the country, principally at **Jinggang Shan** in Jiangxi Province, under the leadership of Mao Zedong.

Mao Zedong, the Red Army and the Long March

Son of a well-off Hunanese farmer, **Mao** believed social reform lay in the hands of the peasants, a belief hardened by his time as a teacher at the Peasant Training Institute in Guangzhou during the early 1920s. Despite the overthrow of the emperors, peasants still had few rights and no power base. Chronic poverty was rife, caused by taxation, and dissent was crushed by the landlords' private armies. Drawing from Marx's analyses, Mao recognized the parallels between nineteenth-century Europe and twentieth-century China – and that a mass armed rising was the only way the old order could be replaced.

After events in Shanghai, Mao organized the first peasant-worker army in Changsha, in what was later to be called the **Autumn Harvest Uprising**. Moving southeast to the Hunan–Jiangxi border, his troops settled into Jinggang Shan, where they were met by the forces of **Zhu De**, a Guomindang commander from Nanchang who had joined the Communists. Using guerrilla tactics, their combined **Red Army** of peasants, miners and Guomindang deserters achieved unexpected successes against the Nationalist troops sent against them during the early 1930s, until **Li Lisan**, the Communist leader, ordered Mao out of his mountain base to attack the cities. The ensuing open assaults against the vastly superior Guomindang forces were disastrous, and Chiang Kaishek, following up these defeats, mobilized half a million troops and encircled Jinggang Shan with a ring of concrete block-houses and barbed-wire entanglements.

Forced between choosing to fight or flee, Mao organized eighty thousand troops in an epic retreat which became known as the **Long March**: a 9500-kilometre trek on foot across eighteen mountain ranges (five of them snow-capped), 24 rivers and twelve provinces. Starting in October 1934, the journey took a year, with over sixty thousand perishing either of cold or hunger or in the innumerable battles that were fought with GMD factions. But by the time they reached safety in **Yan'an** in Shaanxi province, the Communists had turned a humiliating defeat into an advance towards victory. Along the way, Mao had become undisputed leader of the CCP at the **Zunyi Conference**, severing the Party from its Russian advisers, while thousands of Chinese who had never heard of communism were made aware of their struggles and beliefs. And, despite the death toll, the Long March won the Communists immense respect – an army determined enough to do this could do anything.

Japanese invasion and the United Front

Meanwhile, Japan had taken over Chinese Manchuria in 1933 and installed Pu Yi (last emperor of the Qing dynasty) as puppet leader. They were obviously preparing to invade eastern China, and Mao wrote to Chiang Kaishek (and to the warlords, bandit leaders and secret societies) advocating an end to civil war and a **United Front** against the threat. Chiang's response was to move his Manchurian armies, under **Zhang Xueliang**, down to finish off the Reds in Shaanxi. Zhang, however, saw an alliance as the only way to evict the Japanese from his homeland, and so secretly entered into an agreement with the Communist forces. On December 12, 1936, Chiang was kidnapped by his own troops in what became known as the **Xi'an Incident** and, with Zhou Enlai as a mediator, reluctantly signed an agreement to the United Front on Christmas Day. Briefly, the parties were united, though both sides knew that the alliance would last only as long as the Japanese threat.

Full-scale war broke out in July 1937 when the Japanese attacked Beijing. The GMD, inadequately armed or trained, were rapidly forced west and south, and at the end of the year the Japanese had taken most of eastern China between Beijing and Guangzhou. With a capital-in-occupation at Nanjing, the Japanese concentrated their efforts on routing the GMD, leaving a vacuum in the north that the Communists quickly filled, establishing what amounted to stable government of a hundred million people across the North China Plain.

The outbreak of war in Europe in September 1939 soon had repercussions in China. Nazi Germany stopped supplying the weaponry the GMD relied on, while with the bombing of Pearl Harbour two years later all military aid from the United States to Japan ceased. With the country's heavy industry in Japanese hands, China's United Front government, having withdrawn to **Chongqing** in Sichuan Province, became dependent on the Americans and British flying in supplies over the Himalayas. Chiang's true allegiances were never far below the surface, however, and after he failed to distribute the arms among the Red Army in 1941, the United Front effectively collapsed.

The end of the war . . . and the Guomindang

By the time the two atom bombs ended the Japanese empire and World War II in 1945, the Red Army was close on a million strong, with a widespread following throughout the country; Communism in China was established. It wasn't, however, that secure. Predictably, the US sided with Chiang Kaishek and the GMD but, surprisingly, so did the Soviet Union – Stalin believed that with American aid, the GMD would easily destroy the CCP. All the same, **peace negotiations** between the Nationalist and Communist sides were brokered by the US in Chongqing, where Chiang refused to admit the CCP into government, knowing that its policies were uncontrollable while the Red Army still existed. For their part, it was evident to the CCP that, without an army, they were nothing. The talks ended in stalemate.

Ironically, it was US military aid that decided matters in the Communists' favour, when US equipment was captured en masse from GMD troops, providing the Communists with firepower. Buoyed by a popular support heightened by Chiang's mishandling of the economy, in 1948 the Communists' newly named **People's Liberation Army** (PLA) began a final assault on the GMD, decisively trouncing them that winter at the massive battle of **Huai Hai** in Anhui Province. Demoralized, the Guomindang troops lost the will to fight, and with Shanghai about to fall before the PLA in early 1949, Chiang Kaishek packed the country's entire gold reserves into a plane and took off for **Taiwan** to form the **Republic of China**. Here he would remain until his death in 1975, forlornly waiting to liberate the mainland with the two million troops and refugees who later joined him. Mopping-up operations against mainland pockets of GMD resistance would continue for several years, but in **October 1949** Mao was able to proclaim the formation of the **People's Republic of China** in Beijing. The world's most populous nation was now Communist.

The People's Republic under Mao

With the country laid waste by over a century of economic mismanagement and war, massive problems faced the new republic. Though Russia quickly offered its support, the US refused to recognize Mao's government, maintaining that Chiang Kaishek and the Guomindang alone represented the Chinese people. China's road and rail network were mostly destroyed, industrial output had slumped, much of the agricultural areas had been ravaged, and there were no monetary reserves. But the Chinese people, still in awe of their hard-won victory, took to the task of repairing the country with an obsessive energy. By the mid-1950s all industry had been nationalized and output was back at prewar levels, while, for the first time in China's history, land was handed over to the peasants as their own. A million former landlords were executed, while others were enrolled in "**criticism and self-criticism**" classes, a re-education designed to ingrain Marxism and prevent ideologies of elitism or bourgeois deviance from contaminating the revolutionary spirit. People were forced to criticize themselves, their past and those around them – a traumatic experience and one that broke centuries-old traditions.

With all the difficulties on the home front, the **Korean War** of 1950 was a distraction the government could well have done without. After Communist North Korea invaded the south, US forces had intervened on behalf of the south and, despite warnings from Zhou Enlai, had continued through to Chinese territory. China declared war in June, and sent a million troops to push the Americans back to the 38th parallel and force peace negotiations. As a boost for the morale of the new nation, the incident could not have been better timed. Meanwhile, China's far western borders were seen to be threatened by an uprising in **Tibet**, and Chinese troops were sent there in 1951, swiftly occupying the entire country and instituting de facto Chinese rule. Eight years later, a failed coup against the occupation by Tibetan monks saw a massive clampdown on religion, and the flight of the **Dalai Lama** and his followers to Nepal.

The Hundred Flowers campaign and the Great Leap Forward

By 1956 China's economy was healthy, if not burgeoning, but there were signs that the initial euphoria driving the country was slowing. Mao – whose principles held that constant struggle was part of existence, and thus that acceptance of the status quo was in itself a bad thing – felt that both government and industry needed to be prodded back into gear. To this end, in 1957 he decided to loosen the restrictions on public expression, in the hope that open criticism would shake up the more complacent bureaucrats and Party officials. Following the slogan "Let a hundred flowers bloom, and a hundred schools of thought contend", intellectuals were encouraged to voice their thoughts and complaints. But the plan backfired: instead of picking on inefficient officials as Mao had hoped, the **Hundred Flowers** campaign resulted in blistering attacks on the very Communist system itself. As Mao was never one to take personal criticsm lightly, those who had spoken out swiftly found themselves victims of an **anti-rightist** campaign, confined to jail or undergoing a heavy bout of self-criticism. From this point on, intellectuals as a group were mistrusted and constantly scrutinized.

Agriculture and industry were next to receive a shake-up. In August 1958 it was announced that all land held privately by peasant farmers was to be pooled into collective farms, linked together as self-governing **communes**. Five hundred million peasants were to be spread over 24,000 communes, with the aim of turning small-scale farming units into hyper-efficient agricultural areas. Industry was to be fired into activity by the co-option of seasonally employed workers, who would construct heavy industrial plants, dig canals and drain marshes. Propaganda campaigns promised eternal well-being in return for initial hard work and austerity; in one **Great Leap Forward** China would match British industrial output in ten years, and overtake American in fifteen to twenty years. But, from the outset, the Great Leap Forward was a disaster. Having been given their land (and in many cases having fought for it), the peasants now found themselves losing it once more, and eagerness to work in huge units was low. This situation, combined with the problem of ill-trained commune management, led to an almost immediate slump in agricultural and industrial production. In the face of a stream of ridiculous **quotas** supplied by Beijing – one campaign required the eradication of all agricultural pests, another that all communes must produce certain quantities of steel, regardless of the availability of raw materials – nobody had time to tend the fields. The 1959 and 1960 harvests both failed, and millions starved. As if this wasn't enough, a thaw in US–USSR relations in 1960 saw the Soviet Union stopping all aid to China.

With the economy in tatters, the commune policy was watered down, each peasant was given a private house and his own land, and by the mid-1960s the country was back on its feet. Politically, though, the incident had ruined Mao's reputation, and set some members of the Communist Party Central Committee against his policies. The two most outspoken members were **Liu Shaoqi** as Chief of State, and the General Secretary of the Communist Party, **Deng Xiaoping**, who had diffused the effects of commune policy by creating a limited free-market economy among the country's traders. Behind them and their doctrine of material incentives for workers was a large bureaucracy over which Mao held little political sway. Liu and Deng also supported the Minister of Defence, **Peng Dehuai**, in what Mao considered a treasonous move to secure technological and military aid from the Soviet Union, and to free troops from non-military work – a move popular with sections of the army.

The Cultural Revolution

With his policies discredited, Mao, feeling that he was losing control of the Party, sought to regain his authority. His most influential supporter was **Lin Biao**, Defence Minister and Vice-Chairman of the Communist Party, who in 1964 formed the **Socialist Education Movement** to destroy the "spontaneous desire to become capitalists" among the peasants. Mao himself widened the movement's aims to include the whole bureaucracy that Liu Shaoqi had founded and, with Lin Biao's help, began orchestrating the youth of China in a campaign against his moderate opponents. Initially this **Great Proletarian Cultural Revolution** seemed a straightforward rerun of the anti-rightist campaign following the Hundred Flowers fiasco. But in 1966 a member of Beijing University's Philosophy Department put up a poster there denouncing the university administration and supporting the Revolution. Under Mao's guidance Beijing's students organized themselves into a political militia – the **Red Guard**. Within weeks Mao had arranged their removal out of the university and on to the streets.

The enemies of the Red Guard were the **Four Olds**: old ideas, old culture, old customs and old habits. Brandishing copies of the *Quotations of Chairman Mao Zedong* (the famous **Little Red Book**), the Red Guard attacked anything redolent of capitalism, the West or the Soviet Union. Academics were humiliated and assaulted, books were burned, temples and ancient monuments desecrated. Shops selling anything remotely Western were destroyed along with the gardens of the "decadent bourgeoisie". As under the commune system, quotas were set, this time for unearthing and turning in the "Rightists", "Revisionists" and "Capitalist Roaders" corrupting Communist society. Officials who failed to fill their quotas were likely to become the next victims, as were those who failed to destroy property or denounce others enthusiastically enough. With the police and army forbidden to intervene, offenders were paraded through the streets wearing placards carrying humiliating slogans; tens of thousands were ostracized, imprisoned, beaten to death or driven to suicide – and, in one horrendous episode, eaten (see p.810). On August 5, 1966, Mao proclaimed that reactionaries had reached the highest levels of the CCP. His targets were obvious: Liu Shaoqi was thrown in prison and died there of ill-treatment in 1969; Deng Xiaoping was dismissed from his post and condemned to wait on tables at a Party canteen and turn a lathe at a provincial tractor plant. Peng Dehuai, having been dismissed from his post at the very start of the Cultural Revolution, disappeared, and many other senior officials and army officers were demoted.

It was also during this time that China's standing in the international community sunk to an all-time low after the Red Guard assaulted members of the British Embassy, causing a general recall of foreign ambassadors. It was clear that the violence was getting completely out of control, with rival Red Guard factions turning on each other. In August 1967 Mao intervened, ordering the arrest of the most fanatical Red Guard leaders and instructing the surrender of all weapons to the army, but the Guard's activities were not easily stopped. After nationwide street fighting broke out the following spring, order was restored only when tanks entered the cities and the army stormed the Guard's university strongholds. To clear them out of the way, millions of former Red Guards were rounded up and shipped off into the countryside, ostensibly to reinforce the Communist message amongst the rural community.

The fall of Lin Biao

One effect of the Cultural Revolution was the rise of a **personality cult** surrounding Mao Zedong, more a fatalistic acknowledgement of his absolute power over China than a popular seal of approval for his inhuman domestic policies. His very image attained quasi-religious status – in one incident, a soldier spotted a school on fire: his first thought was to save the portrait of Mao in the classrooms and only then start to save those trapped inside. More importantly, the late 1960s also saw **Lin Biao**, Mao's closest ally during the Cultural Revolution, rise to prominence as Mao's designated successor. But as the chaos of the revolution subsided, the role of the army and Lin, as its chief, were less crucial, and Lin began to feel his power base eroded.

What happened next is conjecture, but Lin may have attempted some form of a **coup** against Mao and organized an assassination attempt. In 1972 it was announced that he had died the previous year when a plane carrying him and his followers had crashed en route to the Soviet Union. The story is plausible but probably fictional; Lin might well have been executed and the tale concocted to underline his treason. What is certain is that with Lin's removal and the uncovering of a plot, Mao needed to broaden his base of support, which he did by rehabilitating some of those who had fallen from grace during the Cultural Revolution, including **Deng Xiaoping** who, as Mao declined in health (he was 80 in 1973), took control of the the day-to-day running of the Communist Party Central Committee.

Ping-pong diplomacy and the rise of the radicals

The US, its foreign policy determined by business and political interests that stood to gain from the collapse of Communism, had continued to support Chiang Kaishek's Guomindang in the postwar period, while also stirring up paranoia over the chance of a Sino–Soviet pact (despite the split between Khrushchev and Mao in 1960). But in 1964 China exploded its first **atomic bomb**, taking it into the league of nuclear powers not automatically friendly to Washington, and the US began to tread a more pragmatic path. In 1970, envoy Henry Kissinger opened communications between the two countries, cultural and sporting links were formed (a tactic that became known as **ping-pong diplomacy**), and in 1971 the People's Republic became the official representative at the UN of the nation called China, invalidating Chiang Kaishek's claims. The following year US President **Richard Nixon** was walking on the Great Wall and holding talks with Mao, trade restrictions were lifted and China began commerce with the West. The "bamboo curtain" had parted, isolationism was over and the damage caused by the Cultural Revolution was slowly being repaired.

This new attitude of realistic reform derived from the moderate wing of the Communist Party, headed by Premier Zhou Enlai – seen as a voice of reason – and his protege Deng Xiaoping. Zhou's tact had given him a charmed political existence which for fifty years kept him at Mao's side despite policy disagreements

– several holy sites such as the carved grottoes at Dazu in Sichuan were apparently saved from the Red Guards at Zhou's direct order. But with Zhou's death early in 1976, the reform movement immediately succumbed to the **Gang of Four**, who, led by Mao's third wife **Jiang Qing**, had become the radical mouthpiece of an increasingly absent Mao. In early April, at the time of the **Qing Ming** festival commemorating the dead, the Heroes Monument in Beijing's Tian'anmen Square was filled with wreaths in memory of Zhou. On April 5 radicals removed the wreaths and moderate supporters flooded into the square in protest; a riot broke out and hundreds were attacked and arrested. The obvious scapegoat for what became known as the **Tian'anmen Incident** was Deng Xiaoping, and he was publicly discredited and thrown out of office for a second time.

The death of Mao and its aftermath

In July 1976 a catastrophic **earthquake** centred on Hebei province killed half a million people. The Chinese hold that natural disasters always foreshadow great events, and no one was too surprised when Mao himself died on September 9. Deprived of their figurehead, and with memories of the Cultural Revolution clear in everyone's mind, his supporters in the Party quickly lost ground to the Right. Just a month after Mao's death, Jiang Qing and the other members of the Gang of Four were arrested. Deng returned to the political scene for the third time and was granted a string of positions that included Vice-Chairman of the Communist Party, Vice-Premier and Chief of Staff to the PLA; titles aside, he was now running the country. **Hua Guofeng**, Mao's lookalike and chosen successor, was ousted a couple of years later, and Deng's associates, Zhao Ziyang and Hu Yaobang, installed as Premier and Party Chairman respectively in his place.

The move away from Mao's policies was rapid: in 1978 anti-Maoist **dissidents** were allowed to display wall posters in Beijing and elsewhere, some of which actually criticized Mao by name. Though such public airing of political grievances was later forbidden, by 1980 Deng and the moderates were secure enough to sanction officially a cautious condemnation of Mao's actions. His ubiquitous portraits and statues began to come down, and his cult was gradually undermined.

Yet Mao still had many powerful supporters in the Party, and his public reputation was partially salvaged by the worst of the Cultural Revolution being attributed to the corrupting influence of Jiang Qing and her clique. In 1981 the Gang of Four were brought to **trial**: though the verdicts were a formality, the sentences were not, for they would be an indication both of the tenor of the new administration, and also how it saw the Cultural Revolution and Mao's part in it. If the sentence was death and if this was actually carried out, Mao's widow might easily become a martyr; if a suspended death sentence was handed down, the ability to execute counter-revolutionaries again would be compromised. The latter course was chosen, and the Gang of Four were given twenty years to reform their ways. All have since died under arrest.

Modern China: reform and repression

Under Deng, China became unrecognizable from the days when Western thought was automatically suspect and the Red Guards enforced ideological purity. Deng's legacy was the "open door" policy, which brought about new social (rather than political) freedoms as well as a massive rise in the trappings of Westernization, especially in the cities, where Western clothes, fast food and music – plus Japanese motorbikes – have become all the rage.

Economic success and social change

The impetus for such sweeping changes has been economic. Deng's statement "I don't care whether the cat is black or white as long as it catches mice" illustrates the pragmatic approach that he took to the economy, one which has guided policy ever since. In a massive modernization, Deng **decentralized production**, allowing more rational decision-making based on local conditions. The state allowed goods to be produced and allocated according to market forces, and factories contracted with each other instead of with the state. In agriculture, the collective economy was replaced and households, after meeting government targets, were allowed to sell their surpluses on the free market. On the coast, **Special Economic Zones** (SEZ) were set up, where foreign investment was encouraged and Western management practices, such as the firing of unsatisfactory workers, cautiously experimented with.

These economic policies have had a massive impact, and there is no doubt that many Chinese are much better off now than ever before. Annual growth has stood at around seven in the 1990s, while in certain areas, such as Shenzhen (the largest SEZ), it has at times reached 45 percent, and Chinese economic planners are in the awkward position of trying to slow it down. In the 1970s the "three big buys" – consumer goods that families could realistically aspire to – were a bicycle, a watch and a radio; in the 1980s they were a washing machine, a TV and a refrigerator. Today, young urban mainland Chinese can aspire to the same lifestyle as their counterparts in Japan and Hong Kong.

But not everyone has benefited from the new system. In the country, those who farm unproductive land are probably worse off, and now that the collectives have gone, many of the poorest Chinese no longer have access to subsidized education or health care. In the cities, with the closure of inefficient state-run factories (whose employees once constituted the Party's core supporters), millions have been thrown out of work into a society that has no welfare provision, while those who have remained in their jobs are on fixed wages and have thus suffered badly from **inflation**. In 2001 widespread, bitter **demonstrations** were staged in Dongbei by industrial workers who were out of work, or owed back pay, or had been laid off on a tiny stipend; these were quickly dealt with by arresting the ringleaders and then meeting many of the marchers' demands. Such actions by the huge and discontented urban workforce that has missed out on the boom represents possibly the biggest internal threat to the state.

With the creation of a new class of wealthy entrepreneurs, social divisions, between city and country, coast and interior, have widened to a sometimes grotesque degree. One of the more visible results of rising living costs (coupled with increased agricultural mechanization) has been the **mass migration** of the working class from the country to the cities, where most remain unemployed or are hired by the day as labourers. Short-term gain has become the overriding factor in planning, with the result that the future is mortgaged for present wealth. Too little thought is given to the environmental effects of modernization and China now boasts eight of the top ten most **polluted cities** in the world.

As success is largely dependent on *guanxi* (connections), the potential for **corruption** is enormous – indeed, graft is thought to be slicing at least a percentage point off growth figures. As in the past, a desperately poor peasantry is at the mercy of corrupt cadres who enrich themselves by setting and purloining local taxes. The fact that even the government's prestige project, the **Three Gorges Dam**, had to be rebuilt as contractors were enriching themselves and using cheap materials illustrates the scale of the problem. To many ordinary Chinese, the price of modernization has become too high, as crime, prostitition and unemployment, formerly seen as Western malaises, have all risen to levels perceived as epidemic.

Political repression and human rights

Economic reform has not precipitated **political reform**, and is really a way of staving it off, with the Party hoping that allowing the populace the right to get rich will halt demands for political rights. However, dissatisfaction with corruption, rising inflation, low wages and lack of freedom was vividly expressed in the demonstrations held in **Tian'anmen Square** in 1989. The immediate cause of the gatherings was the death of **Hu Yaobang**, former Party General Secretary, who had been too liberal for Deng and was dismissed in 1987. An unofficial mourning service in the square soon swelled into a major demonstration, with 150,000 activists holding an impromptu service. Over the next month the crowds swelled until, by mid-May there were nearly a million people around the square. Most were students, but they had now been joined by workers, even cadets from the Party school for cadres. The demonstrators demanded free speech and an end to corruption. When the Party leadership proved unresponsive, three thousand students went on hunger strike. In May, the demonstrators humiliated the leadership during an official visit by Soviet leader Mikhail Gorbachev to Beijing. Immediately after he left, on May 20, **martial law** was declared, and by the beginning of June, 50,000 troops were massed around Beijing. In the early hours of June 4 they moved in, crushing barriers with tanks and firing into the crowds. There are no reliable figures of the death toll, but the figure is thought to be in the hundreds or possibly thousands. Hospital waiting rooms were piled with corpses and doctors were ordered not to treat casualties.

China's most serious human-rights abuses, however, are being perpetrated in **Tibet**, where dissent is ruthlessly suppressed and Tibetan culture is being swamped by Han migration to the region. In 1995, when the exiled Dalai Lama selected a new Panchen Lama following the death of the previous incumbent, the boy he chose was arrested and became one of the world's youngest political prisoners, while the Chinese government enthroned their own representative (see p.1161). Another cause for concern is the Chinese **gulags** – most of them in Xinjiang and Qinhai – in which up to fourteen million prisoners, an estimated ten percent of them political, are kept in punishing conditions and used as slave labour, a situation that has been highlighted by **Harry Wu**, the high-profile dissident and ex-internee now in the US.

Despite hopes for improvement, the government continues to lock up its critics and shows no sign of changing tactics. Recent sufferers have been Xu Wenli and Qin Yongmin, the most prominent dissidents left in China. They were leaders of the Chinese Democratic Party, the first organized opposition to CCP rule. The most daring display of political activism since Tian'anmen, however, came from a very unusual source; in 1999 ten thousand elderly members of **Falun Gong**, a quasi-spiritual sect, sat cross-legged on the pavement outside Zhongnanhai to protest perceived oppression. Their reward has been ruthless suppression ever since.

China's human-rights record is the biggest obstacle to its desire to achieve international standing, though with China's economy set to become among the largest in the world, the international community is finding it easy to lose any moral scruples it may have. In 1989, when the Dalai Lama won the **Nobel Peace Prize**, Western nations were subdued in their congratulations and, in 1995, President Clinton dropped any link between China's human-rights abuses and the country being granted Most Favoured Nation trade status. Relations with the US took a turn for the worse during the war in Kosovo, however, when NATO bombs struck the Chinese embassy in **Belgrade**, triggering a wave of ugly nationalism and anti-foreign feeling. It was mirrored in the US by the outrage that followed the revelation that a Chinese spy had stolen nuclear secrets.

Prospects

Under Deng Xiaoping and his protege and successor (Deng died in 1997), the rather faceless **Jiang Zemin**, China has continued its course of controlled liberalization, a course which, despite the controversies surrounding the current regime, has given the Chinese people one of their most outward-looking and economically astute governments of any time in the last two thousand years. In particular, **2001** was regarded as an annus mirabilis: Beijing secured the summer **Olympics** for 2008, China joined the **World Trade Organization**, and its **football** team made it to the World Cup finals. Even the **9/11** terrorist attacks brought something of a diplomatic dividend for China, which was in the happy position of being seen to support – or at least not protest against – the subsequent actions of the US government; a war against stateless terrorism suits the Chinese government fine, as it adds justification to its own tough stance on "insurrectionary elements", such as in Xinjiang.

In November 2002, at the sixteenth CCP Congress, Jiang officially stepped down – though he will remain a significant force behind the scenes – and passed on power to a new generation of technocrats, led by his protege **Hu Jintao**. Jiang would like his legacy to be his doctrine of the "three represents" – basically the idea that the party should represent all aspects of society rather than just the workers – but is more likely to be remembered for the shift this hints at: the final abandonment of Marxist doctrine. The party's survival is now entirely contingent on its ability to continue to deliver the economic goods. In its pursuit of a "socialist market economy with Chinese characteristics" – whatever that means – the state has continued to retreat from whole areas of life. Mechanisms of state control – the household registration and work-unit systems – have weakened. The private sector now accounts for perhaps a third of the economy, and foreign-funded ventures account for over half of the country's exports. **Private housing** is catching on and graduates who were once told where to work are now thrown into a competitive market.

Though most observers agree that the pace of **political change** is not fast enough, there have been some improvements. The National People's Congress has begun to take its task of monitoring government and drafting laws seriously. Under Prime Minister Zhu Rongji, central government has shrunk. More room has been made in government for meritocratic types, including former Tian'anmen protestors. One of the largest political changes has come at grass roots, where "village" democracy is now practised by two-thirds of the rural population, who have taken with great gusto to their new right to oust incompetent village leaders. No one, though, has dared to apply this idea to any positions higher up in government.

Hong Kong and Taiwan

In 1997 China regained control of **Hong Kong**. In the handover agreement between China and the UK, Hong Kong was to retain a high degree of **autonomy** – part of China's avowed "one country, two systems" approach. In practice, the Chinese government quickly reneged on its promise by replacing LEGCO, the democratically elected legislative council, with a group of carefully selected Beijingers. It also interfered with the rule of law (regarded as vital for prosperity by the inhabitants) by overturning court judgements and preventing the establishment of a Court of Final Appeal. In 2002 Hong Kong's unpopular Chief Executive, **Tung Chee-Hwa**, widely regarded as Bejing's puppet, secured another five-year tenure.

Events in Hong Kong are keenly watched from **Taiwan**. In 1949 the defeated GMD fled to Taiwan and declared itself the legitimate government of China, in opposition to the Communists. Now Taiwan is one of the most successful, and certainly the most democratic, of the Asian tiger economies. Though both Taiwan and China want to be part of the same country, the affluent Taiwanese have no desire to be ruled by Beijing, certainly not after seeing what has happened in Hong Kong. In 1996, presidential elections were held in Taiwan for the first time. The favourite, Lee Tenghui, displeased China by pushing for Taiwan's entry into the UN and the WTO, and by having the temerity, in China's view, of treating Taiwan as a separate country. In an attempt to influence the elections, China conducted intimidating missile tests over the island. The US government responded by parking two aircraft carriers off Taiwan's coast. Lee won the election, despite China's bullying tactics. Relations between Taiwan and China remain extremely cold, though surprisingly Jiang Zemin's responded with only mild condemnation to the remark by Taiwanese President Chen Shui-bian (the first non-GMD president of the island) that China and Taiwan were now "two states on either side of the Taiwan Straits".

Perhaps China's biggest problem, however, is its massive **population**, which stood at 1.29 billion in 2002. If China's population continues to rise all the recent economic progress will be wiped out as an expanding population puts an unbearable pressure on resources. The one-child policy, which began in 1979, has been most successful in the cities, where it is almost impossible for a couple to get away with having a second child. Who is allowed to give birth, as well as when, is controlled by an individual's work unit, and the pressure for an unsanctioned pregnancy to be aborted is high. Couples who have a second child must accept a cut in wages and restricted access to health care and housing. But limiting the size of families has caused much concern; a generation of "little emperors" – spoilt children – is being raised, who will find themselves heavily outnumbered by the elderly when they get to working age. In rural China, the selling of girls as brides is not unusual in village marketplaces, partly thanks to the heavy prejudice towards male children – **female infanticide** is common.

China's future is far from certain. Woeful progress has been made on the markers of genuine modernity – investment in education, the rule of law, the freedom of the press and executive accountability; the party which was designed to change society may now be shown to be incapable of adapting to it. Whether the nation is doomed to implode under internal pressure, as so many autocratic dynasties have before it, or mature into a truly formidable new superpower, depends on the state's ability to reinvent itself in the coming decades.

Chronology

4800 BC ▶ First evidence of **human settlement**. **Banpo** in the Yellow River basin build Bronze Age town of **Erlitou** in Henan. Excavation at **Yin** in Anyang reveals rich and developed culture.

21C–16C BC ▶ **Xia dynasty**.

16C–11C BC ▶ **Shang dynasty**. First extant writing in China.

11C–771 BC ▶ **Zhou dynasty**. The concept of **Mandate from Heaven** introduced.

770 BC–476 BC ▶ **Spring and Autumn** period. Kong Fuzi or **Confucius** (c. 500 BC) teaches a philosophy of adherence to ritual and propriety.

457 BC–221 BC ▶ **Warring States** period. The **Great Wall** "completed".

221 BC–207 BC ▶ **Qin dynasty**. First centralized empire founded by Emperor **Qin Shi Huang**. **Terracotta Army** guards Qin's tomb.

206 BC–220 AD ▶ **Han dynasty**. Han emperors bring stability and great advances in trade; leave **Han tombs** near Xi'an. **Confucianism** and **Buddhism** ascendant. **Silk Road** opens up first trade with central Asia.

220–280 ▶ **Three Kingdoms** period; influence of Buddhist **India** and **Central Asia** enlivens a Dark Age.

265–420 ▶ **Jin dynasty**. Absorption of northern barbarians into Chinese culture.

420–581 ▶ **Southern dynasties and Northern dynasties**: rapid succession of short-lived dynasties brings disunity. Earliest **Longmen caves** near Luoyang.

581–618 ▶ **Sui dynasty**. Centralization and growth under **Wen Di**. Extension and strengthening of **Great Wall**; digging of **Grand Canal**.

618–907 ▶ **Tang dynasty**. Arts and literature reach their most developed stage. **Great Buddha** at Leshan completed.

907–960 ▶ **Five dynasties**. Decline of culture and the northern defences. **Cliff sculptures** of Dazu.

960–1271 ▶ **Song dynasties**. Consolidation of the lesser kingdoms.

1271–1368 ▶ **Yuan dynasty**. **Genghis Khan** invades. Under **Kublai Khan** trade with Europe develops. **Forbidden City** built. **Marco Polo** visits China 1273–92.

1368–1644 ▶ **Ming dynasty**. Imperial investigative fleet under **Admiral Zheng He** reaches Africa. Later isolationist policies restrict contact with rest of world.

1644 **Qing dynasty** begins. **Manchus** gain control over China and extend its boundaries.

Mid- to late 17C ▶ **Potala Palace** in Lhasa rebuilt by Fifth Dalai Lama.

Late 18C ▶ **East India Company** monopolizes trade with Britain. **Summer Palace** in Beijing completed.

1839–62 ▶ **Opium Wars**. As part of the surrender settlement, Hong Kong is ceded to Britain.

1851–64 ▶ **Taiping Uprising**. Conservative policies of Dowager Empress **Cixi** allow foreign powers to take control of China's industry.

1899 ▶ **Boxer Rebellion**.

1911 ▶ **End of imperial China**. **Sun Yatsen** becomes leader of the **Republic**.

1921 ▶ Chinese Communist Party founded in Beijing.

1927 ▶ **Chiang Kaishek** orders massacre of Communists in Shanghai. **Mao Zedong** organizes first peasant-worker army.

1932 ▸ Japan invades Manchuria.

1936–41 ▸ **United Front**.

1945 ▸ Surrender of Japan. Civil war between Nationalist **Guomindang** and the **People's Liberation Army**.

1949 ▸ Communist takeover. Chiang Kaishek flees to **Taiwan**. **People's Republic** of China supports the North in the **Korean War**.

1956 ▸ The **Hundred Flowers** campaign unsuccessfully attempts liberalizations.

1958 ▸ Agricultural and industrial reform in the shape of the **commune system** and **Great Leap Forward**. Widespread famine results.

1964 ▸ China explodes its first atomic weapon.

1966–8 ▸ Red Guards purge anti-Maoist elements in the **Cultural Revolution**, along with much "ideologically unsound" art and architecture.

1971 ▸ People's Republic replaces Taiwan at **United Nations**.

1972 ▸ **President Nixon** visits Beijing.

1976 ▸ The **Tian'anmen Incident** reveals public support for moderate **Deng Xiaoping**. **Mao Zedong dies**, and the **Gang of Four** are arrested shortly afterwards.

1977 ▸ Deng Xiaoping rises to become **Party Chairman**.

1980 ▸ Beginning of the Open Door policy.

1981 ▸ Trial of the **Gang of Four**.

1986 ▸ Agreement reached on **Hong Kong**'s return to China in 1997.

1989 ▸ Suppression of the democracy movement in **Tian'anmen Square**.

1992 ▸ Major **cabinet reshuffle** puts Deng's men in power.

1993 ▸ Yuan floated on the world currency market.

1995 ▸ Death of Chen Yun, last of the hardline Maoists in the Politburo. Work begins on the **Three Gorges Dam**.

1997 ▸ Return of **Hong Kong** to the mainland. Death of **Deng Xiaoping**.

1999 ▸ Return of **Macau** to the mainland. Persecution of **Falun Gong** begins.

2001 ▸ China admitted to the **World Trade Organization**. Beijing wins bid to host **2008 Olympics**. China's population reaches 1.28 billion.

2002 ▸ Jiang Zemin hands premiership to **Hu Jintao**.

Chinese beliefs

The resilience of ancient beliefs in China, and the ability of the Chinese people to absorb new streams of thought and eventually to dominate them, has been demonstrated again and again over the centuries. While China has been periodically dominated by foreign powers, her belief systems have never been overwhelmed. Instead, conquering invaders, such as the Mongolians in the thirteenth and the Manchus in the seventeenth centuries, have found themselves inexorably **sinicized**. On this strength rests the understandable Chinese confidence in the ultimate superiority of their beliefs, a confidence that has survived through the lowest periods in Chinese history.

Yet the visitor to modern China will find few obvious indications of the traditional beliefs which have underpinned the country's civilization for three thousand years. Certainly, the remains of religious buildings litter the cities and the countryside, yet they appear sadly incongruous amid the furious pace of change all around them. The restored temples – now "cultural relics" with photo booths, concession stands, special foreign tourist shops and cheerful throngs of young Chinese on outings – are garish and evoke few mysteries.

This apparent lack of religion is hardly surprising, however: for decades, the old beliefs have been derided by the authorities as feudal **superstition**, and the oldest and most firmly rooted of them all, Confucianism, has been criticized and repudiated for nearly a century. And in actual fact, the outward manifestations of the ancient beliefs are not essential: the traditions are expressed more clearly in how the Chinese think and act than in the symbols and rituals of overt worship.

The "Three Teachings"

The product of the oldest continuous civilization on earth, Chinese religion actually comprises a number of disparate and sometimes contradictory elements. But at the heart of it all, **three basic philosophies** lie intermingled: Confucianism, Taoism and Buddhism. The way in which a harmonious balance has been created among these three is expressed in the often quoted maxim *San Jiao Fa Yi* – "Three Teachings Flow into One".

Both **Confucianism** and **Taoism** are belief systems rooted in the Chinese soil, and they form as much a part of the Chinese collective unconscious as Platonic and Aristotelian thought does in the West. **Buddhism**, though, was brought to China from India along the Silk Road by itinerant monks and missionaries from about the first century AD onwards. Just as the mutual contradictions of Confucianism and Taoism had been accommodated by the Chinese, however, so Buddhism did not long eclipse other beliefs – as it established itself, its tenets transformed into something very different from what had originally come out of India.

Confucianism

China's oldest and greatest philosopher, Kong Zi, known in the West by his Latinized name **Confucius**, was in his lifetime an obscure and unsuccessful scholar. Born in 551 BC, during the so-called Warring States Period, he lived in an age of petty kingdoms where life was blighted by constant war, feuding and social disharmony. Confucius simply saw that society was something that could be improved if individuals behaved properly. Harking back to an earlier, mythic age of peace and social virtues, he preached adherence to **ritual and propriety** as the supreme answer to the horrifying disorder of the world as he found it. He wandered from court to court attempting to teach rulers a better way to rule, though, like his contemporary Socrates far away in Greece, he was largely ignored by men in power. In the centuries after his death, however, Confucianism, as reflected in the **Analects**, a collection of writings on his life and sayings compiled by disciples, became the most influential and fundamental of Chinese philosophies.

Never a religion in the sense of postulating a higher deity, Confucianism is rather a set of **moral and social values** designed to bring the ways of citizens and governments into harmony with each other, and with their ancestors. Through proper training in the scholarly classics and rigid adherence to the rules of propriety, including ancestor-worship, the superior man could attain a level of moral righteousness which would, in turn, assure a stable and righteous social order. As a political theory Confucianism called for the "**wisest sage**", the one whose moral sense was most refined, to be ruler. With a good ruler, one who practised the virtuous ways of his ancestors and was exemplary in terms of the **five Confucian virtues** (benevolence, righteousness, propriety, wisdom and trustworthiness), the world and society would naturally be in order. Force, the ultimate sanction, would be unnecessary. As Confucius said:

Just as the ruler genuinely desires the good, the people will be good. The virtue of the ruler may be compared to the wind and that of the common people to the grass. The grass under the force of the wind cannot but bend.

Gods play no part in this structure – man is capable of perfection in his own right, given a superior ruler whose virtues are mirrored in the behaviour of his subjects. Instead of God, **five hierarchical relationships** are the prerequisites for a well-ordered society, and given proper performance of the duties entailed in these, society should be "at ease with itself". The five relationships outline a strict structure of duty and obedience to authority: ruler to ruled, son to father, younger brother to older, wife to husband, and – the only relationship between equals – friend to friend. The intention is to create order and stability through rule by a moral elite, though in practice adherence to the unbending hierarchy of these relationships as well as to the precepts of filial piety has been used to justify a form of totalitarian rule throughout Chinese history. The supreme virtue of the well-cultivated man and woman was always **obedience**.

From the time of the Han dynasty (206 BC–220 AD) onwards, Confucianism became institutionalized as a **system of government** which was to prevail in China for two thousand years. With it, and with the notion of the scholar-official as the ideal administrator, came the notorious Chinese **bureaucracy**. Men would study half their lives in order to pass the imperial examinations and attain a government commission. These examinations were rigid tests of the scholar's knowledge of the Confucian classics. Right up until the beginning of the twentieth century, power in China was wielded through a bureaucracy steeped in the classics of rites and rituals written five hundred years before Christ.

The Confucian ideal ruler, of course, never quite emerged (the emperor was not expected to sit the exams) and the scholar-officials often deteriorated into corrupt bureaucrats and exploitative landlords. Furthermore, the Confucian ideals of submission to authority would not seem to have much of a shelf-life at the start of the twenty-first century. On the other hand, with its emphasis on **community and social cohesion**, Confucianism has played an enormous role in keeping China free of the bigotry and religious fanaticism that have been bringing war to Europe for two thousand years. And today it is clear that Confucius does still have a role to play, not least in his new incarnation as the embodiment of the much trumpeted "**Asian values**", namely, the non-confrontational (and undemocratic) system of government. On the grass-roots level, too, old practices such as ancestor-worship within the family are making a comeback. Now that the latest foreign religion of Marxism has been thoroughly discredited, it appears that Confucianism is simply reoccupying its rightful position.

Taoism

The **Tao** translates literally as the "Way" and, in its purest form, Taoism is the study and pursuit of this ineffable Way, as outlined in the fundamental text, the **Daodejing** (often written as *Tao Te Ching*) or "The Way of Power". This obscure and mystical text essentially comprises a compilation of the wise sayings of a semi-mythical hermit by the name of **Lao Zi**, who is said to have been a contemporary of Confucius. The Daodejing was not compiled until at least three centuries after his death.

The Tao is never really defined – indeed by its very nature it is undefinable. To the despair of the rationalist, the first lines of the Daodejing read:

The Tao that can be told
is not the eternal Tao.
The name that can be named
is not the eternal name.

In essence, however, it might be thought of as the Way of Nature, the underlying principle and source of all being, the bond which unites man and nature. Its central principle is **Wu Wei**, which can crudely be translated as "no action", though it is probably better understood as "no action which runs contrary to nature". Taoism was originally the creed of the recluse. Whereas Confucianism is concerned with repairing social order and social relationships, Taoism is interested in the relationship of the individual with the natural universe. It simply looks at human problems from another, higher plane: having good relations with one's neighbours is of no use if one is not in harmony with nature.

Taoism's second major text is a book of parables written by one ideal practitioner of the Way, **Zhuang Zi**, another semi-mythical figure. Acknowledged in his lifetime as a great sage, he rejected all offers of high rank in favour of a life of solitary reflection. His works – allegorical tales which have delighted Chinese readers for centuries – reveal humour as well as perception; in the famous butterfly parable Zhuang Zi examines the many faces of reality:

Once upon a time Zhuang Zi dreamed he was a butterfly. A butterfly flying around and enjoying itself. It did not know it was Zhuang Zi again. We do not know whether it was Zhuang Zi dreaming that he was a butterfly, or a butterfly dreaming he was Zhuang Zi.

As it became part of Chinese culture, Taoism offered a contrast to the stern propriety of Confucianism. In traditional China it was said that the perfect lifestyle was that of a man who was a Confucian during the day – a righteous and firm administrator, upholding the virtues of the gentleman/ruler – and a Taoist after the duties of the day had been fulfilled. The practice of Taoism affirms the virtues of withdrawing from public duties and giving oneself up to a life of **contemplation and meditation**. If Confucianism preaches duty to family and to society, Taoism champions the sublimity of withdrawal, non-committedness and "dropping out". In its affirmation of the irrational and natural sources of life, it has provided Chinese culture with a balance to the rigid social mores of Confucianism. The **art and literature** of China have been greatly enriched by Taoism's notions of contemplation, detachment and freedom from social entanglement, and the Tao has become embedded in the Chinese soul as a doctrine of yielding to the inevitable forces of nature.

Buddhism

The first organized religion to penetrate China, **Buddhism** enjoyed a glorious, if brief, period of ascendancy under the Tang dynasty (618–906 AD). In the eighth century there were over three hundred thousand Buddhist monks in China. This was also a time which saw the creation of much of the country's **great religious art** – above all the cave shrines at **Luoyang** (Henan), **Datong** (Shanxi) and **Dunhuang** (Gansu), where thousands of carvings of the Buddha and paintings of holy figures attest to the powerful influence of Indian art and religion.

Gradually, though, Buddhism too was submerged into the native belief system. Most schools of Indian Buddhism of the time taught that life on earth was essentially one of suffering, an endless cycle in which people were born, grew old and died, only to be born again in other bodies; the goal was to break out of this cycle by attaining nirvana, which could be done by losing all desire for things of the world. This essentially individualistic doctrine was not likely to appeal to the highly regimented Chinese, however, and hence it was that the relatively small **Mahayana School** of Buddhism came to dominate Chinese thinking. The Mahayana taught that perfection for the individual was not possible without perfection for all – and that those who had already attained enlightenment would remain active in the world (as **Bodhisattvas**) to help others along the path. In time Bodhisattvas came to be ascribed miraculous powers, and were prayed to in a manner remarkably similar to that of conventional Confucian ancestor-worship. The mainstream of Chinese Buddhism came to be more about maintaining harmonious relations with Bodhisattvas than about attaining nirvana.

Another entirely new sect of Buddhism also arose in China through contact with Taoism. Known in China as **Chan** (and in Japan as Zen) Buddhism, it offered a less extreme path to enlightenment. For a Chan Buddhist it was not necessary to become a monk or a recluse in order to achieve nirvana – instead this ultimate state of being could be reached through life in accord with, and in contemplation of, the Way.

In short, the Chinese managed to marry Buddhism to their pre-existing belief structures with very little difficulty at all. This was facilitated by the general absence of dogma within Buddhist thought. Like the Chinese, the **Tibetans**, too, found themselves able to adapt the new belief system to their old religion, **Bon** (see p.975), rather than simply replacing it. Over the centuries, they established their own schools of Buddhism often referred to as Lamaist Buddhism or Lamaism, which differ from the Chinese versions in minor respects. The now dominant **Gelugpa** (or Yellow Hat) school, of which the Dalai and Panchen Lamas are members, dates back to the teachings of Tsongkhapa (1357–1419) For more on Buddhism in Tibet, see p.1116.

Minority faiths and popular beliefs

Though Buddhism was the only foreign religion to have left a substantial mark on China, it was not the only religion to enter China via the Silk Road. Both **Islam** and **Christianity** also trickled into the country this way, and to this day a significant minority of Chinese, numbering possibly in the tens of millions, are Muslims. Unlike most of the rest of Asia, however, China did not yield wholesale to the tide of Islam – the rigid, all-embracing doctrines of the Koran never stood much of a chance with the flexible Chinese.

When Jesuit missionaries first arrived in China in the sixteenth and seventeenth centuries they were astounded and dismayed by the Chinese **flexibility of belief**. One frustrated Jesuit put it thus: "In China, the educated believe nothing and the uneducated believe everything." For those versed in the classics of Confucianism, Taoism and Buddhism, the normal belief was a healthy and tolerant scepticism. But for the great majority of illiterate peasants, **popular religion** offered a plethora of ghosts, spirits, gods and ancestors who ruled over a capricious nature and protected humanity. If Christian missionaries handed out rice, perhaps Christ too deserved a place alongside them. In popular Buddhism the hope was to reach the "Pure Land", a kind of heaven for believers ruled over by a female deity known as the Mother Ruler. Popular Taoism shared this feminine deity, but its concerns were rather with the sorcerers, alchemists and martial arts aficionados who sought solutions to the riddle of immortality; you may well see some of these figures depicted in Taoist temples (see p.1219).

Superstitions

Though the Chinese are not generally religious in the conventional sense, they are often very **superstitious**, and you'll see evidence of this everywhere you go. Wordplay is used frequently in this context: the Chinese expression for "let luck come", *fudao*, happens to sound similar to "upside-down luck" – hence the inverted *fu* character pasted up outside homes and businesses at Spring Festival, encouraging good fortune to arrive on the premises. Other **lucky symbols** include peaches and cranes (for longevity), fish (prosperity), mandarin ducks (marital fidelity), dragons (male power), phoenixes (female power) and bats (happiness).

Colours are also important. **Red**, the colour of fire, and **gold**, the colour of money, are auspicious colours, used extensively for decorations, packaging, weddings and festive occasions. **White** traditionally represents death or mourning, though traditional Western wedding dresses are becoming increasingly popular. **Yellow** is the colour of heaven, hence the yellow roof tiles used on temples; yellow clothing was formerly reserved for the emperor alone.

Modern China

During the twentieth century, confronted by the superior military and technical power of the West, the Chinese have striven to break free from the shackles of superstition. The imperial examinations were abolished at the start of the century and since then Chinese intellectuals have been searching for a modern yet essentially Chinese philosophy. The **Cultural Revolution** can be seen as the culmination of these efforts to repudiate the past. Hundreds of thousands of temples, ancestral halls and religious objects were defaced and destroyed. Monasteries which had preserved their seclusion for centuries were burnt to the ground and their monks imprisoned. The classics of literature and philosophy – the "residue of the reactionary feudal past" – were burned in huge celebratory bonfires. In 1974, towards the end of the Cultural Revolution, a campaign was launched to "criticize Lin Biao and Confucius", pairing the general with the sage to imply that both were equally reactionary in their opposition to the government.

Yet the very fact that Confucius could still be held up as an object for derision in 1974 reveals the tenacity of traditional beliefs. With the Cultural Revolution now long gone, they are once again being accepted as an essential part of the cultural tradition which binds the Chinese people together. The older generation, despite a lifetime of commitment to the Marxist revolution, are comforted and strengthened by their knowledge of the national heritage. The young are rediscovering the classics, the forbidden fruit of their school days. The welcome result is that Chinese temples of all descriptions are prosperous, busy places again, teeming with people who have come to ask for grandchildren or simply for money. The atmosphere may not seem devout or religious, but then perhaps it never did.

Traditional Chinese medicine

As an agricultural society, the Chinese have long been aware of the importance of the proper **balance** of natural, elemental forces: too much heat causes drought; too much rain, floods; while the correct measure of both encourages farmers' crops to grow. The ancient Chinese saw heaven, earth and humankind existing as an integral whole, such that if people lived in harmony with heaven and earth, then their collective health would be good. The medical treatise *Huang Di Neijing*, attributed to the semi-mythical Yellow Emperor (2500 BC), mentions the importance of spiritual balance, acupuncture and herbal medicine in treating illnesses, and attests to the venerable age of China's medical beliefs – it may well be a compilation of even earlier texts. Acupuncture was certainly in use by the Han period, as tombs in Hebei dated to 113 BC have yielded acupuncture needles made of gold and silver.

The belief in universal balance is known as **Dao** (or Tao) – literally "the Way", but implying "the Way of Nature". As an extension of Daoist principles, life is seen as consisting of opposites – man and woman, sun and moon, right and left, giving and receiving – whereby all things exist as a result of their interaction with their opposites. This is expressed in the black-and-white Daoist diagram which shows two interacting opposites, the **yin** ("female", passive energy) and the **yang** ("male", active energy). At the core of traditional Chinese medicine is the belief that in order for a body to be healthy, its opposites must also be in a state of dynamic balance; there is a constant fluctuation, for example, between the body's heat, depending on its level of activity and the weather, and the amount of water needed to keep the body at the correct temperature. An excess of water in the system creates oedema, too little creates dehydration; too much heat will cause a temperature, and too little cause chills. Chinese medicine therefore views the body as an integrated whole, so that in sickness, the whole body – rather than just the "ill" part of it – requires treatment.

Qi and acupuncture

An underlying feature of Chinese medical philosophy, **qi** (or chi) is the energy of life: in the same way that electricity powers a lightbulb, *qi* enables us to move, see and speak. *Qi* flows along the body's network of **meridians**, or energy pathways, linking the surface tissues to specific internal **organs** which act as *qi* reservoirs; the twelve major meridians are named after the organ to which they are connected. The meridians are further classed as *yin* or *yang* depending on whether they are exposed or protected. In the limbs, for instance, the outer sides' channels are *yang*, and important for resisting disease, while the inner sides' channels are *yin*, and more involved with nourishing the body.

Mental and physical tensions, poor diet, anger or depression, even adverse weather, however, inhibit *qi* flow, causing illness. Needles inserted (and then rotated as necessary) in the body's **acupuncture points**, most of which lie on meridians and so are connected to internal organs, reinforce or reduce the *qi* flow along a meridian, in turn influencing the organs' activities. When the *qi* is balanced and flowing smoothly once more, good health is regained; acupuncture is specifically used to combat inflammation, to regenerate damaged tissue, and to improve the functional power of internal organs.

Herbal medicine

In the 2200 years since the semi-mythical Xia king **Shennong** compiled his classic work on **medicinal herbs**, a vast amount of experience has been gained to help perfect their clinical use. Approximately seven thousand herbs, derived from roots, leaves, twigs and fruit, are today commonly used in Chinese medicine, with another thousand or so of animal or mineral origin (though also classified as "herbs"). Each is first processed by cleaning, soaking, slicing, drying or roasting, or even stir-frying with wine, ginger or vinegar, to influence their effects; the brew is then boiled down and drunk as a tea (typically very bitter and earthy tasting).

Herbs are effective in preventing or combatting a wide variety of diseases. Some are used to treat the underlying cause of the complaint, others to treat symptoms and help strengthen the body's own immune system, in turn helping it to combat the problem. An everyday example is in the treatment of flu: the herbal formula would include a "cold action" herb to reduce the fever, a herb to induce sweating and so clear the body-ache, a purgative to clear the virus from the system and a tonic herb to replenish the immune system. In all treatments, the patient is re-examined each week, and as the condition improves the herbal formula is changed accordingly.

In the same way that Western aspirin is derived from willow bark, many Chinese drugs have been developed from herbs. One example is the anti-malarial herb *qinghaosu*, or artemisinin, which has proved effective in treating chloroquine-resistant strains of malaria with minimal side-effects.

Chinese versus Western medicine

It's difficult to **compare** Chinese and Western medicine directly, as their approaches are so different. Very broadly, Western medical techniques are superior for treating major physical trauma with surgery; the Chinese approach seems more effective on chronic illness or in maintaining long-term health. In 1974 the World Health Organization recognized the **benefits** of acupuncture, while in 1979 the United Nations accepted that Traditional Chinese Medicine (TCM) worked in the treatment of infections, respiratory, circulatory and neurological conditions, and musculoskeletal traumatic injuries as well as arthritic and inflammatory problems. In addition, the fact that traditional medical schools can be found today in Western cities worldwide, as well as every province of China, indicates a growing global acceptance.

The martial arts of China

Given China's tumultuous ancient history – of warring clans, warring states and eventually warring dynasties – it's unsurprising that so much energy has been invested in the development and fine-tuning of the **martial arts**. In a society unable to rely on the government for protection, being a capable martial artist was often an essential skill, especially at times of large-scale revolution. Fighting techniques evolved in almost all isolated communities, from Buddhist and Daoist temples down to clan villages, often acquiring unique characteristics which were taught solely to members of that group. It's only in very recent times that outsiders – even less so, foreigners – have been able to learn these distinctive styles, though some have now become so popular that even the government has approved formal versions of them.

Styles and techniques

Thousands of martial arts have evolved over the centuries in China, but all can be classed into two basic types. **External** or hard styles (*waijia*) concentrate on developing **li**, or physical strength, to literally overpower opponents; for example, conditioning hands by punching plate iron and slapping concrete blocks thousands of times until one is able, by sheer force, to break planks of wood and stones. **Internal** or soft styles (*neijia*) concentrate on developing the internal energy known as **qi**, which circulates around the body along acupuncture meridians and is also one of the central aspects of Chinese medicine (see p.1204). **Qigong** – which means "breath skills" – is used to build up an awareness of *qi* and an ability to move it at will around the body, eventually replacing excess muscular action and making all movements fluid and powerful.

In practice, however, such distinctions are blurred, at least for the beginner. Initial internal training tends to be overwhelmingly physical, as it requires years before sufficient awareness of *qi* develops to allow it to be used effectively in fighting. Many external styles also utilize *qigong* techniques, just as most internal styles rely on some brute force. And, from the outside, internal and external styles can look very similar, as both use **forms** – prearranged sets of movements – to develop the necessary speed, power and timing; both use punches, kicks and open hand strikes as well as a wide variety of **weapons**; and both often incorporate **animal movements** – for instance, in monkey-style kung fu the practitioner behaves and moves like a monkey while fighting. The following gives brief accounts of some of the better-known martial arts, which you might well see being performed in public parks in China.

Shaolin kung fu

One of the most influential people in the development of Chinese external martial arts was the sixth-century Indian Buddhist monk **Boddhidarma**, who spent many years at the **Shaolin temple** (see p.309). Here he taught the monks movement and breathing exercises, which were later combined with indigenous martial arts to form **Shaolin kung fu**. "Shaolin" is a very nebulous term in China today, indiscriminately used to describe a host of fighting styles which probably have very little historical connection with the temple.

Nonetheless, it's a vigorous art best known for its powerful kicks and animal styles – especially eagle, mantis and monkey. The classic Shaolin weapon is the **staff**, and there's even a **drunken form**, where the practitioner behaves as if inebriated – an athletic and surprisingly effective technique.

Xingyi quan

Xingyi quan translates awkwardly as "shape through intent boxing", reflecting its guiding principle that the body should act directly from the mind. Believed to have been developed from Shaolin kung fu spear forms by the famous Song dynasty general **Yue Fei**, *xingyi* is now an internal art, though using *qi* rather differently from either *bagua* or *tai ji*. *Xingyi* schools emphasize either **twelve animal** or **five elements** methods; irrespective of this, attacks are very **linear**, smashing straight through an opponent's defences and defeating them as directly and effectively as possible. In this uncluttered philosophy, and the use of relatively few techniques, *xingyi* is probably the easiest of the internal arts to learn and use for fighting. The health benefits common to all the internal arts are rarely emphasized in *xingyi*.

Bagua zhang

Bagua zhang's history is murky, but its most famous practitioner and stylist was **Dong Hai Chuan** (1798–1879). The name means "*bagua* palm", referring to the eight-sided Daoist divination symbol in the *I Ching*, of which *bagua zhang* is a martial expression, and to the fact that strikes are almost invariably made with the **palm**. *Bagua* is one of the most distinctive martial arts to watch being performed, employing fast footwork and characteristic **twisting movements** to simultaneously evade attacks and place the defender behind the aggressor, and thus in a position to strike back. An internal art, it nonetheless uses some physical force, and tends towards devastating overkill in its response to attacks. The various schools use **circle-walking forms** to develop *qi* – if you see somebody walking endlessly around a tree in a Chinese park, they're practising this – as well as less abstract linear forms to learn fighting skills. Bagua's continuous twisting pumps *qi* from the spine around the body, and *bagua* practitioners are famous for their health and longevity.

Tai ji quan

Tai ji quan (*yinyang* boxing) is the world's most popular martial art, but it's seldom taught as such. The original form, known as **Chen taiji**, is closely related to Shaolin kung fu though emphasizing *qi* usage; a later form developed by **Yang Luchan** (1799–1872), is entirely internal and the hardest of any style to learn for practical fighting. Despite this, these older forms are effective martial arts, relying on acute sensitivity to anticipate attacks and strike first; counter-strikes are made with the entire body in a state of **minimal tension**, creating *tai ji*'s characteristic "soft" appearance, and increasing *qi* flow and power. Strong *qi* flow means good health, and Yang Luchan's grandson, **Yang Chengfu** (1883–1936), slowed *tai ji* movements and stripped it of obvious martial content in order that the elderly or infirm could learn it and so avoid illness – it's versions of this simplified form which are most widely taught today. A two-person sensitivity training technique common to all *tai ji* styles is *tui shou* (**push hands**), where practitioners alternately attack and yield, learning to absorb and redirect their opponent's force.

Studying martial arts

There's been a considerable watering down of martial arts in China in recent years. Since the 1950s, the Chinese government have produced "official" versions of various fighting styles – including Shaolin kung fu, *bagua* and *tai ji* – which are collectively known as **wushu** (literally, "martial arts"). The main intent with *wushu* styles is to promote health and fitness, not fighting ability, and they're taught mainly as competitive sports. In the process, much of what is openly taught today in China is – in martial terms – second rate. Depending on what you're after, therefore, finding competent **instruction** can be difficult.

Choosing a style is the first thing to consider, and you might want to check a few out before leaving home (see box below for some contacts). For learning quickly how to fight, stick with external arts such as Shaolin and its derivatives, or *xingyi* or *bagua*, all of which have a blunt, direct approach to applying their techniques. In China, it's also fairly rare to find *bagua* and *xingyi* practitioners, however, or genuinely competent teachers of the martial *tai ji* styles.

Famous martial arts centres, such as Shaolin and the Taoist temples at **Wudang Shan** (p.551), might seem like the obvious **places to study**, but in practice, their fame has been counter-productive. Shaolin, for example, is surrounded by martial-arts schools all claiming to be the only one to teach the "real" Shaolin techniques. Still, they're used to foreigners turning up, and courses at the schools are very organized; Wudang Shan has yet to become commercialized, however, and they remain choosy in whom they teach. *Wushu* is widely taught at **sports institutes**, including Beijing University of Physical Education, but serious martial content is lacking. Otherwise, visiting a nearest **park** at dawn to see people practising is a good way of finding an instructor or – if you already know a style – meeting up with others to practise with, though outside Hong Kong you'll need to speak some Chinese. As a bonus, you may encounter one of the lesser-known **regional styles** such as Southern Mantis, White Crane kung fu, Long boxing, or tiger boxing. Unless you

Martial arts contacts overseas

The following teachers and resources should be able to give you a taste of genuine Chinese martial arts before you leave home; many have links to other organizations worldwide. See also "Books", p.1249.

Michael Babin Ⓦwww.angelfire.com/mb/taiji. Canadian-based teacher of *tai ji* and *bagua*; his website offers good background on fighting philosophies.

John Bracy Ⓦwww.chiarts.com. US school teaching *bagua* for fighting and healing; the website contains footage of Chinese masters demonstrating their techniques.

Paul Brecher Ⓦwww.taiji.net. UK teacher of old-style Yang *tai ji* with a martial emphasis.

Kumar Frantzis Ⓦwww.energyarts.com. US-based internal-arts stylist concentrating on *tai ji*, *bagua* and *qigong*.

Adam Hsu Ⓦwww.adamhsu.com. US-based practitioner teaching a variety of internal and external styles, including *xingyi*, Shaolin and mantis boxing.

Erle Montaigue Ⓦwww.taijiworld.com. Australian teacher of Yang *tai ji* and *bagua*.

Park Bok Nam Ⓦwww.pa-kua.com. Traditional *bagua* demystified and taught in a very practical, direct way. Frequent training programmes and seminars in the US.

Ⓦwww.martialarts.com.au. Website with information on many different martial arts, and useful links.

practice one of the standardized *wushu* forms, however, expect some **criticism**: nobody performs any one style in exactly the same way, and teachers, having often invested decades in their own training methods, are understandably dogmatic about what you should be doing. Don't be discouraged, but stick to what you know while examining others' techniques and systems with an open mind.

If you can't speak Chinese, you'll be better of considering the travellers' havens of Dali and Yangshuo, which both have martial-arts teachers used to dealing with foreigners; Yangshuo's Budi Zhen school is particularly good (p.792). As teachers who fled to Hong Kong, Taiwan and overseas after the Communist takeover never adopted the *wushu* styles, it's also possible that you'll find more traditional forms – often taught by English speakers - **outside the mainland**.

Astrology

In the **Chinese zodiac**, each **lunar year** (which starts in late January or early February) is represented by one of twelve **animal signs**. These have existed in Chinese folk tradition since the sixth century BC, though it wasn't until the third century BC that they were incorporated into a formal study of astrology and astronomy. (True Chinese astrologers, however, eschew the use of the animal signs in isolation to analyze a person's life, seeing the zodiac signs as mere entertainment.) Quite why animals emerged as the vehicle for Chinese horoscopy is unclear: one story has it that the animals used are the twelve which appeared before the command of Buddha, who named the years in the order in which the animals arrived. Another says that the Jade Emperor held a race to determine the fastest animals. The first twelve to cross a chosen river would be picked to represent the twelve earthly branches which make up the cyclical order of years in the lunar calendar.

Born under the sign of a particular animal, you will have certain characteristics, ideal partners, lucky and unlucky days. The details below will tell you the basic facts about your character and personality, though to go into your real Chinese astrological self, you need to take your precise date and time of birth along to a Chinese astrologer – in China, you'll find plenty of amateurs plying their trade around city parks. The animals always appear in the same order, so that if you know the animal for the current year you can always work out which one is to influence the following Chinese New Year.

The Rat

Characteristics: Usually generous, intelligent and hard-working, but can be petty and idle; has lots of friends, but few close ones; may be successful, likes challenges and is good at business, but is insecure; generally diplomatic; tends to get into emotional entanglements.

Partners: Best suited to Dragon, Monkey and Ox; doesn't get on with Horse and Goat.

The Ox

Characteristics: Healthy; obstinate; independent; usually calm and cool, but can get stroppy at times; shy and conservative; likes the outdoors and old-fashioned things; always finishes a task.

Partners: Best suited to Snake, Rat or Rooster; doesn't get on with Tiger, Goat or Monkey.

The Tiger

Characteristics: Adventurous; creative and idealistic; confident and enthusiastic; can be diplomatic and practical; fearless and forward, aiming at impossible goals, though a realist with a forceful personality.

Partners: Best suited to Horse for marriage; gets on with Dragon, Pig and Dog; should avoid Snake, Monkey and Ox.

The Rabbit

Characteristics: Peace-loving; sociable but quiet; devoted to family and friends; timid but can be good at business; needs reassurance and affection to avoid being upset; can be vain; long-lived.

Partners: Best suited to Pig, Dog and Goat; not friendly with Tiger and Rooster.

The Dragon

Characteristics: Strong, commanding, a leader; popular, athletic; bright, chivalrous and idealistic, though not always consistent; likely to be a believer in equality.

Calendar chart

Date Of Birth	Animal	Date Of Birth	Animal
20.2.1920–7.2.1921	Monkey	25.1.1963–12.2.1964	Rabbit
8.2.1921–27.1.1922	Rooster	13.2.1964–1.2.1965	Dragon
28.1.1922–15.2.1923	Dog	2.2.1965–20.1.1966	Snake
16.2.1923–4.2.1924	Pig	21.1.1966–8.2.1967	Horse
5.2.1924–23.1.1925	Rat	9.2.1967–29.1.1968	Goat
24.1.1925–12.2.1926	Ox	30.1.1968–16.2.1969	Monkey
13.2.1926–1.2.1927	Tiger	17.2.1969–5.2.1970	Rooster
2.2.1927–22.1.1928	Rabbit	6.2.1970–26.1.1971	Dog
23.1.1928–9.2.1929	Dragon	27.1.1971–14.2.1972	Pig
10.2.1929–29.1.1930	Snake	15.2.1972–2.2.1973	Rat
30.1.1930–16.2.1931	Horse	3.2.1973–22.1.1974	Ox
17.2.1931–5.2.1932	Goat	23.1.1974–10.2.1975	Tiger
6.2.1932–25.1.1933	Monkey	11.2.1975–30.1.1976	Rabbit
26.1.1933–13.2.1934	Rooster	31.1.1976–17.2.1977	Dragon
14.2.1934–3.2.1935	Dog	18.2.1977–6.2.1978	Snake
4.2.1935–23.1.1936	Pig	7.2.1978–27.1.1979	Horse
24.1.1936–10.2.1937	Rat	28.1.1979–15.2.1980	Goat
11.2.1937–30.1.1938	Ox	16.2.1980–4.2.1981	Monkey
31.1.1938–18.2.1939	Tiger	5.2.1981–24.1.1982	Rooster
19.2.1939–7.2.1940	Rabbit	25.1.1982–12.2.1983	Dog
8.2.1940–26.1.1941	Dragon	13.2.1983–1.2.1984	Pig
27.1.1941–14.2.1942	Snake	2.2.1984–19.2.1985	Rat
15.2.1942–4.2.1943	Horse	20.2.1985–8.2.1986	Ox
5.2.1943–24.1.1944	Goat	9.2.1986–28.1.1987	Tiger
25.1.1944–12.2.1945	Monkey	29.1.1987–16.2.1988	Rabbit
13.2.1945–1.2.1946	Rooster	17.2.1988–5.2.1989	Dragon
2.2.1946–21.1.1947	Dog	6.2.1989–26.1.1990	Snake
22.1.1947–9.2.1948	Pig	27.1.1990–14.2.1991	Horse
10.2.1948–28.1.1949	Rat	15.2.1991–3.2.1992	Goat
29.1.1949–16.2.1950	Ox	4.2.1992–22.1.1993	Monkey
17.2.1950–5.2.1951	Tiger	23.1.1993–9.2.1994	Rooster
6.2.1951–26.1.1952	Rabbit	10.2.1994–30.1.1995	Dog
27.1.1952–13.2.1953	Dragon	31.1.1995–18.2.1996	Pig
14.2.1953–2.2.1954	Snake	19.2.1996–6.2.1997	Rat
3.2.1954–23.1.1955	Horse	7.2.1997–27.1.1998	Ox
26.1.1955–11.2.1956	Goat	28.1.1998–15.2.1999	Tiger
12.2.1956–30.1.1957	Monkey	16.2.1999–4.2.2000	Rabbit
31.1.1957–17.2.1958	Rooster	5.2.2000–23.1.2001	Dragon
18.2.1958–7.2.1959	Dog	24.1.2001–11.2.2002	Snake
8.2.1959–27.1.1960	Pig	12.2.2002–30.1.2003	Horse
28.1.1960–14.2.1961	Rat	31.1.2003–17.2.2004	Goat
15.2.1961–4.2.1962	Ox	18.2.2004–6.2.2005	Monkey
5.2.1962–24.1.1963	Tiger	7.2.2005–27.1.2006	Rooster

Partners: Best suited to Snake, Rat, Monkey, Tiger and Rooster; avoid Dog.

The Snake

Characteristics: Charming, but possessive and selfish; private and secretive; strange sense of humour; mysterious and inquisitive; ruthless; likes the nice things in life; thoughtful; superstitious.

Partners: Best suited to Dragon, Rooster and Ox; avoid Snake, Pig and Tiger.

The Horse

Characteristics: Nice appearance and deft; ambitious and quick-witted; favours bold colours; popular, with a sense of humour, gracious and gentle; can be good at business; fickle and emotional.

Partners: Best suited to Tiger, Dog and Goat; doesn't get on with Rabbit and Rat.

The Goat

Characteristics: A charmer and a lucky person who likes money; unpunctual and hesitant; too fond of complaining; interested in the supernatural.

Partners: Best suited to Horse, Pig and Rabbit; avoid Ox and Dog.

The Monkey

Characteristics: Very intelligent and sharp, an opportunist; daring and confident, but unstable and egoistic; entertaining and very attractive to others; inventive; has a sense of humour but little respect for reputations.

Partners: Best suited to Dragon and Rat; doesn't get on with Tiger and Ox.

The Rooster

Characteristics: Frank and reckless, and can be tactless; free with advice; punctual and a hard worker; imaginative to the point of dreaming; likes to be noticed; emotional.

Partners: Best suited to Snake, Dragon and Ox; doesn't get on with Pig, Rabbit and Rooster.

The Dog

Characteristics: Alert, watchful and defensive; can be generous and is patient; very responsible and has good organizational skills; spiritual, home-loving and non-materialistic.

Partners: Best suited to Rabbit, Pig, Tiger and Horse; avoid Dragon and Goat.

The Pig

Characteristics: Honest; vulnerable and not good at business, but still materialistic and ambitious; outgoing and outspoken, but naive; kind and helpful to the point of being taken advantage of; calm and genial.

Partners: Best suited to Dog, Goat, Tiger and Rabbit; avoid Snake and Rooster.

Wildlife and the environment

The scale of China's **environmental problems** is sadly comparable to the breadth of its wildlife, which includes such high-profile creatures as tigers, pandas and elephants. To begin with, China's 1.28 billion souls account for a fifth of the world's **population**, but the nation encompasses less than one tenth of the world's arable land. Furthermore, almost the entire population lives in the well-watered eastern half of the country, where virtually every centimetre of farmland has been developed. Indeed, China has very little land that has not been altered in some way by man. The sheer size of the population means that forests and wetlands, grasslands and agricultural fields are stretched beyond the limits of sustainable use. Dramatic growth in the economy and the continuing need to raise living standards for some of Asia's poorest people means that urban areas face a similar crisis: coal dust, untreated factory emissions, vehicle exhaust and wind-blown desert sand make Chinese cities some of the most **polluted** on Earth; many of the nation's rivers are polluted and virtually all water in urban areas is heavily contaminated.

Habitats

The world's third largest country, China rises from sea level in the east to the peak of Mount Everest on the border with Nepal. The south shares tropical **rainforests** with Laos, Vietnam and Burma, while the Da Hinggan Mountains in Inner Mongolia have **tundra** vegetation on top of permafrost. China is also home to East Asia's most important wetlands and Asia's longest river, and is the source of two rivers of inestimable importance to hundreds of millions of people in South and Southeast Asia – the Ganges and the Mekong. **Deserts** make up one-fifth of China's total territory, largely in the northwest. Arid **steppes** cover additional areas in the Altai, Tian and Kunlun mountains in the far west, a region blocked from the southwestern monsoon by the Tibetan plateau and from the southeastern monsoon by its distance from the sea. This massive diversity of geography and habitats has resulted in an extraordinary range of plant and animal life.

Forests and grasslands

China contains a variety of **forest types**. Both the northeast and northwest reaches contain mountains and cold **coniferous** forests, supporting animal species which include moose and Asiatic black bear, along with some 120 types of of birds. Moist conifer forests can have thickets of **bamboo** as an understorey, replaced by **rhododendrons** in higher montane stands of juniper and yew. **Subtropical** forests, which dominate central and southern China, support an astounding 146,000 species of flora, as well as the famous giant panda, golden monkey and South China tiger. **Tropical rainforest** and seasonal rainforests, though confined to Yunnan and Hainan Island, actually contain a quarter of all the plant and animal species found in China.

Grasslands make up about a third of China's total land area. The immense and productive **grasslands** are largely concentrated in Inner Mongolia, Ningxia Autonomous Region, parts of Qinghai and Tibet. The natural wildlife they support includes three species on the verge of extinction: Przewalski's horse, the Asiatic wild ass and the Bactrian camel (the ancestor of domesticated camels). Others, including the Tibetan gazelle, are threatened by the influx of gold miners and truck drivers carrying goods to and from Tibet, who poach animals for food and as trophies. There is often direct competition between domestic animals and wild fauna, and herdsmen poison or trap carnivores, and sometimes set fires to increase pasture area. The government has recently stepped up efforts to control the conversion of grasslands to pasture, but lacks the manpower to enforce policy.

Freshwater ecosystems

Freshwater habitats are of massive importance to China, and a huge percentage of the population is directly dependent on **wetlands** – marshes, rivers, and lakes – for economic activity, flood control and drinking water. Seven of the most important **rivers** in the world begin in the highlands of western China. The Yellow River, Yangzi River, Lancang Jiang (Mekong) and the Salween rise in the east of the Qinghai–Tibet plateau. The Indus, Ganges and Brahmaputra rise in the south. Downstream these rivers serve as sources of irrigation and drinking water, modes of transport and centres of cultural and religious importance for some two billion people in China, India, Pakistan, Bangladesh and throughout Southeast Asia. These rivers rise and gather strength from many of the thousands of freshwater lakes of the region.

China's northeast is the focus for much of the country's freshwater **marshes**. Two million hectares on the Sanjiang Plain of Heilongjiang Province are essentially a collection of shallow freshwater lakes and reed-beds where the Heilongjiang, Sungari and Wusuli rivers come together. Jilin, Liaoning and Inner Mongolia all share these ecosystems. One of the most well-known wildlife areas in this ecosystem is Zhalong Nature Reserve, a 2,000-square-kilometre area which was created in 1979 to protect breeding areas for the red-crowned crane, and other wintering migrants. These marshes are also of great value for reed production, the bulk of which is turned into pulp for paper. Waterfowl and reed production can usually coexist, at least at present levels, so this is a useful confluence of conservation and economic uses. In Tibet and western Sichuan, marshland provides breeding grounds for the black-necked crane and bar-headed goose.

China's **freshwater lakes** include the country's best-known **wetlands**: Jiangxi's Poyang Hu and Hunan's Dongting Hu. **Dongting Hu**, China's second largest freshwater lake, is vitally important for wildlife, including the highly endangered Yangzi river dolphin and Chinese sturgeon, as well as more wintering wildfowl. **Poyang Hu** is a similar complex of small lakes and marsh areas which fluctuates seasonally; summer floods give way in autumn to fertile agricultural land, attractive both to farmers and visiting birds. The importance of the area is hard to overstate, as the lakes provide a wintering habitat for almost the entire world population of two hundred **Siberian cranes**, and as many as five hundred thousand birds may be on Poyang Hu at any one time during the winter months. In recent years, however, some of Poyang's larger lakes have been drained at the end of autumn, leaving waterfowl with inadequate shallow land on which to feed.

Saltwater lakes and coastal wetlands

About half of China's lakes are **saline** and, once again, are important breeding grounds for **waterfowl**. Most are concentrated in northwest China on the inland drainage systems of the North Tibetan Plain and in the Zaidan basin. The largest is Qinghai Hu, a 4,426-square-kilometre reserve which attracts thousands of birds each summer, including cormorants, great black-headed gulls, bar-headed geese and pied avocets. Similarly, the Tarim River basin in Xinjiang supports one of the largest breeding populations of black stork in China. The Ordos plateau area of Inner Mongolia as well as the Xinjiang's Taolimiao-Alashan Nur (lake) support breeding sites for the endangered relict gull. Most of these lakes and marshes fluctuate seasonally and are threatened by increased diversion of water for human use.

China's **coastline** is approximately 18,000km long, extending from the Bohai Gulf, which freezes in the winter, to the tropical waters of the South China Sea. Coastal wetlands are important as fuel stops for waterfowl on the migratory route between Siberia and Australia. Chongming Island in the Yangzi River Delta near Shanghai – China's largest city and one of its fastest growing regions – is vital for these migrants.

Threats to China's wildlife

Currently, China's **endangered flora and fauna** includes the familiar, endemic and scarce giant panda; South China tiger; Yangzi river dolphin; crested ibis; and a host of other plants and animals. Of these, the giant panda is most populous with approximately a thousand individuals left in the wild, while the entire known population of crested ibis is perhaps 45, and Yangzi dolphins number less than 20. Other endangered animals include the snow leopard, which depends on western China for over half its range; the Asian elephant, a resident of Xishuangbanna near Laos and Vietnam; the golden monkey; the Yangzi alligator; and migratory species such as the red-crowned crane and black-necked crane.

Ultimately, wildlife has declined because conserving it is not considered a productive use of land. **Intensive cultivation** of land for food production has led to diminishing habitat for wildlife, just as reclamation of wetlands for agriculture, and construction of power stations and water conservancy have diminished the area of freshwater ecosystems. Millions of domesticated sheep and cows are **grazed** on the grasslands of Inner Mongolia, leading to an increased threat of **desertification**, a situation heightened by serious droughts and fires in 2002. Demand has outstripped supply for virtually all **natural resources**, including water (shortages are faced throughout the country), timber, animal products and wild plants. The current economic boom (accompanied by a massive spurt in car-buying) has only served to worsen **pollution** and thus damage to habitats.

The extent of **deforestation** for commercial timber, fuel and the creation of new farmland over the last half-century has had massive consequences – most recently it has been blamed for the extent of the appalling flooding through the Yangzi Basin during the late 1990s. An acute illustration of the impact on wildlife is the case of the **giant panda**. Giant pandas require vast quantities of bamboo, which grows as an understorey to the moist subtropical forests of mountainous Sichuan, Gansu and Shaanxi provinces. Without an upper storey of trees, bamboo will wither. The logging which has diminished the forest areas of these provinces has shrunk panda habitat as well. Another animal to suffer from deforestation is the **tiger**, of which there are probably fewer than one hundred remaining in China – it was deliberately hunted out during the 1950s and 60s. Very little suitable habitat remains for the species to recover in numbers and one endemic variety, the **South China tiger**, is critically endangered.

Conservation efforts

As any traveller to China would confirm, **environmental conservation** enjoys a low priority in a country rushing to throw off years of economic stagnation by uncontrolled development. That said, there has been progress in recent years. China's first wildife refuge, at **Dinghu Shan** in Guangdong province, was created in 1956, since when the number has grown to over seven hundred nature reserves covering almost six percent of the country. The government agencies managing these reserves have collaborated with a variety of external organizations since 1980, when the World Wide Fund for Nature (WWF) helped establish a giant panda conservation programme. UNESCO counts ten Chinese reserves among its international network, a status which has encouraged international funding for further conservation projects. Spurred by the growing **international focus** on China through its entry into the WTO, the **government** itself has shown a growing commitment to conservation in recent years, for instance by earmarking a billion US dollars for the creation of some two hundred new wetlands reserves over the next decade.

There are specific success stories to relate. Increasing siltation and land reclamation, which caused Dongting Hu to shrink by almost fifty percent between 1950 and 1998, has been partially reversed by the recent resettling of 300,000 farmers away from the lake – though pollution from nearby Yueyang city remains problematic, even if pesticides and fertilizers are now banned in the area. Although forest clearing continues at a frightening rate, China's overall forest cover has recently risen to almost fourteen percent. This increase has been brought about by the **"Green Great Wall"** campaign – the planting of a huge belt of trees across the Northwest to help stop encroaching erosion – and associated reafforestation efforts, currently focused at the upper reaches of major river systems such as the Yangzi, Yellow and Liao rivers, while anti-desertification projects focus on north-central China in Ningxia and Inner Mongolia. (Sadly though, the biological value of these replanted forests is far lower than that of the natural forests they replace. Replanted forest can provide timber for industrial and household use, but it does not adequately replace the role of natural forests in protecting soil, retaining water or supporting wildlife.)

Much more encouraging are signs that the Chinese **public** are beginning to take the environment very seriously too. The national campaign to save the **snub-nosed monkey**, a creature found only in western Yunnan, is a case in point, and was the first of its kind in China. Some of the monkey's habitat is protected, but Deqin county, which became the focus of the issue, relies on timber for 95 percent of its government revenue – and thus for the salaries of its employees as well as for funding schools and health clinics. A local wildlife videographer took special interest in the monkeys' plight and produced a television programme which was broadcast nationally, leading to something akin to a national outcry. When, as a result, the Ministry of Forestry expressed its concern, this was naturally met with demands for compensation from Deqin county's government. To stop logging would undoubtedly bring economic hardship to the county, already mired in poverty of the most dramatic kind, and with few income options beyond the sale of its one valuable resource. To date, no long-term solution has been identified, though recent increases in regional tourism might provide alternative incomes. Indeed, the biggest problem in instituting new reserves is how to redeploy hundreds of thousands of loggers hitherto working in those areas.

In 2002, Chinese university students were involved in a programme sponsored by the WWF and China's State Forestry Administration to promote environmental awareness among farmers and local officials. Several environmentally minded non-governmental organizations also exist and, though few of these would count as pressure groups in the Western sense, they indicate the growing space for public debate over these issues. Environmental television and radio programmes abound on China's airwaves, further fuelling conservation awareness. Most significantly, younger, technically trained specialists are taking over responsibility for official conservation programmes and, while often subordinate to the anachronistic policies of politically appointed superiors, this new generation is developing influence in key areas around the country.

For up-to-date information on China's environmental problems and how they're being tackled, one useful resource is Ⓦwww.enviroinfo.org.cn, which also has links to relevant NGOs, plus clippings from national newspapers about current issues.

Daniel A. Viederman,
with additional contributions by David Leffman

Architecture

After several weeks in China, it seems that – apart from minor regional variations – one temple looks much like another, even that the differences between a palace, a temple or a substantial private house are negligible, and that there is little sign of historical development. Nor does it take even this long to tire of the cheaply built and disappointingly Westernized appearance of the majority of China's cities. But this overall uniformity in no way reflects China's long architectural heritage; it is rather that several factors have conspired to limit variety. For a start, little has survived from different periods to emphasize their individual characteristics: early wooden structures were vulnerable to natural disasters, war and revolutions, while new dynasties often demolished the work of the old to reinforce their takeover. Another reason for the strong streak of conservatism inherent in all traditional Chinese architecture is *feng shui*, a departure from which would risk upsetting the cosmos. And today, with a huge economic boom sweeping the country, a lust for "modernization" is seeing vast new cityscapes being built on the sites of the old.

Compounding these factors is a passion for precedent, which meant that certain basic rules governing building designs were followed from the earliest times, minimizing the variations which separate the works of different periods. This is not to say that it's impossible to tell a Tang pagoda from a Qing one, but it does mean that a certain **homogeneity** pervades traditional Chinese architecture, making it all the more exciting on the occasions when you do come across distinctive temples, dwellings or even towns.

Feng shui

Whatever the scale of a building project, the Chinese consider divination using **feng shui** an essential part of the initial preparations. Literally meaning "wind and water", *feng shui* is a form of **geomancy**, which assesses how buildings must be positioned so as not to disturb the spiritual attributes of the surrounding landscape. This reflects **Taoist cosmology**, which believes that all components of the universe exist in balance with one another, and therefore the disruption of a single element can cause potentially dangerous alterations to the whole. It's vital, therefore, that sites – whether for peasant homes, the Hong Kong Bank's skyscraper headquarters, entire cities such as Beijing or the underground tomb of the first Qin emperor – are favourably orientated according to points on the compass and protected from local "unlucky directions" by other buildings, walls, hills, mountain ranges, water or even a Terracotta Army. Geomancy further proposes **ideal forms** for particular types of structure, and carefully arranges spaces and components within a building according to time-honoured formulae.

Monumental architecture

Chinese monumental architecture – as represented in temples, palaces and city plans – is notable for constantly repeating **cosmological themes**, the most central of which can be traced right back to the Bronze Age – though the specific details of *feng shui* were only formulated during the Song dynasty. Four

Getting around a Chinese temple

Whether Buddhist or Taoist, Chinese temples share the same broad **features**. Like cities, they generally **face south** and are surrounded by walls. Gates are sealed by heavy doors, usually guarded by paintings or statues of warrior deities to chase away approaching evil. The doors open onto a courtyard, where further protection is ensured by a **spirit wall** which blocks direct entry; although easy enough for the living to walk around, this foils spirits, who are unable to turn corners. Once inside, you'll find a succession of halls arranged in ornamental courtyards. In case evil influences should manage to get in, the area nearest the entrance contains the least important rooms or buildings, with those of greater significance – living quarters or main temple halls – set deeper inside the complex.

One way to tell Buddhist and Taoist temples apart is by the colour of the **supporting pillars** – Buddhists use bright red, while Taoists favour black. **Animal carvings** are more popular with Taoists, who use decorative good luck and longevity symbols such as bats and cranes; some Taoist halls also have distinctive raised octagonal cupolas sporting the black-and-white *yinyang* symbol. Most obviously, however, each religion has its own **deities**. Inside the entrance of a **Buddhist temple** (*sì*) you'll be flanked by the Four Heavenly Kings of the Four Directions, and faced by portly **Maitreya**, the Laughing Buddha; there's also likely to be a statue of **Wei Tuo**, the God of Wisdom. The main hall is dominated by three large statues sitting side by side on lotus flowers, representing Buddhas of the past, present and future, while the walls are decorated by often grossly caricatured images of Buddhist saints (*arhats*) – these are sometimes given a separate hall to themselves. Around the back of the Buddhist trinity is a statue of **Guanyin**, the multi-armed, vase-bearing Goddess of Mercy, who likewise is sometimes given her own room. **Taoist temples** (*miao* or *gong*) are similar, but their halls might be dedicated to any number of mythical and legendary figures. Taoism has its own holy trinity, collectively known as the **Three Purities** or Immortals: **Fuxi**, who taught mankind fishing, hunting and animal husbandry; **Shennong** or **Yan Di**, who created farming, tools and medicine; and **Xuan Yuan** or **Huang Di**, the Yellow Emperor and the first Xia king. Other figures include a further Eight Immortals and historical people who were canonized – the Three Kingdoms characters **Guan Yu** (the red-faced God of War and Healing) and **Zhuge Liang** are popular choices, as are local heroes. Strangely, statues to Guanyin are often also found in Taoist halls as her help in childbirth makes her universally popular.

thousand years ago, **cities** were already laid out in a spiritually favourable **rectangular pattern**, typically facing south on a north–south axis and surrounded by a defensive **wall**. Aside from the business and residential districts, the central focus (though not necessarily centrally located) was a separately walled quarter; this later became the seat of the emperor or his local representative. As the emperor was styled "Son of Heaven", this plan – still apparent in the layout of cities such as Xi'an and Beijing – was a representation of the cosmos, with the ruler at the centre. The same general formula is echoed in the ground plan of palaces, temples and even large family mansions, complexes of buildings whose organization in many ways represented a microcosm of city life. All these are surrounded by a wall, and all have their own central spiritual focus: a main hall in temples where statues of deities are displayed; a similar building in palaces, where the emperor or governor would hold court; or an ancestral shrine in a mansion.

As far as individual buildings are concerned, spiritual considerations also ensured that traditional temples and palaces (the two are virtually identical) followed a basic **building structure**, which can be seen in subjects as diverse as

2000-year-old pottery models and the halls of Beijing's Ming–Qing Forbidden City. The foundations formed a raised platform of earth, brick or stone according to the building's importance. Columns rested on separate bases with the heads of the columns linked by beams running lengthways and across. Above this, beams of diminishing length were raised one above the other on short posts set on the beam below, creating an interlocking structure which rose to the point of the roof where single posts at the centre supported the roof ridge. The arrangement produced a characteristic **curved roof line** with upcurled eaves, felt to confer good luck. **Cantilevered brackets**, introduced in the eighth century, allowed the curving eaves to extend well beyond the main pillars and acquire an increasingly decorative value, supplemented by lines of carved animals and figures on the gable ends of the roof. Though scale and space were ultimately limited by a lack of arches, essential in supporting the massive walls found in European cathedrals, this structural design was solid enough to allow the use of heavy **ceramic roof tiles**.

Development of these features reached a peak of elegance and sophistication during the **Tang and Song** eras, never to be entirely recaptured. Though almost nothing survives intact from this time, later restorations of Tang edifices, such as the temples at Wudang Shan in Hubei Province, or Xi'an's central bell tower, convey something of the period's spirit. Two **regional styles** also developed: **northern** architecture was comparatively restrained and sober, while that from the **south** eventually exaggerated curves and ornamentation to a high degree; Guangdong's Foshan Ancestral Temple is a classic of the latter type. Inside both, however, spaces between the columns were filled by screens providing different combinations of wall, door and latticework, which could be removed or changed to order differently the spaces within. The columns themselves were sometimes carved in stone, or otherwise painted, with different colours denoting specific religions in temples, or the rank of the occupant in palaces. Similarly, **imperial buildings** might be distinguished by four-sided roofs, by higher platforms reached by wide staircases and by special yellow glazed tiles for the roofs. In rare instances, buildings created their own styles without offending *feng shui*; Beijing's circular Temple of Heaven, for example, manages to break with convention by symbolizing the universe in its overall shape.

Pagodas are another important type of monumental structure, originally introduced from India with **Buddhism**. Intended to house saintly relics, they have intrinsically "positive" attributes, are often used to guard cities or buildings from unlucky directions, or are built along rivers to quell (and indicate) dangerous shoals. Their general design in China was probably influenced by the shape of indigenous wooden watchtowers, though the earliest surviving example, at Shendong Si in Shandong Province, is stone and more closely resembles the equivalent Indian stupa. Most, however, are polygonal, with a central stairway rising through an uneven number of storeys – anything from three to seventeen. Buddhism also gave rise to the extraordinary **cave temples** and grottoes, best preserved in the Northwest at Mogao.

Domestic architecture

In general, the other major group of buildings, **domestic architecture**, shares many of the guiding principles of temple and palace design: curved roof lines are desirable, and larger groups of buildings might also be walled off and include spirit walls or **mirrors**, the latter placed over external doorways to repulse demons. Older homes with these basic features can be found all over the country but, in many cases, practical considerations – principally the climate – overrode optimum spiritual designs and created very distinctive **local styles**, which are once again most obvious in a basic north–south divide. **Northern** China's intensely cold winters and hot summers have spawned solidly insulated brick walls, while more stable, subtropical **southern** temperatures encourage the use of open eaves, internal courtyards and wooden lattice screens to allow air to circulate freely.

Rural areas are good places to find some of the more traditional or unusual types of residential architecture; aside from the climate, many of these also reflect local cultures. Striking examples exist in the mountainous border areas between Guizhou and Guangxi provinces, where ethnic **Dong** and **Miao** build large, two- or three-storeyed wooden houses from local cedar. The Dong are further known for their wooden **drum towers** and **wind-and-rain bridges**, which have a spiritual as well as practical function. Another ethnic group building distinctive houses is the **Hakka**, a Han sub-group, whose immense stone circular clan or family mansions – some of which can accommodate hundreds of people – were built for defensive purposes in their Guangdong–Fujian homelands. Extreme adaptation to local conditions can be seen in Shaanxi Province, where **underground homes** have been excavated in prehistoric sedimentary soils deposited by the Yellow River; these are cool in summer and warm in winter.

Traditional **urban architecture** survives, too, though it tends to be less varied. Wood almost invariably formed at least the framework of these buildings, but if fire hasn't claimed them, demolition and replacement by city authorities – who are either safety-conscious or simply eager to modernize – generally has. Scattered examples of old town houses can still be seen even in large cities such as Beijing, Kunming and Chengdu, however, while the ethnic **Naxi** town of Lijiang in Yunnan sports hundreds of traditional wooden homes, the largest such collection anywhere in China. In the east, the area surrounding Tunxi in Anhui Province contains whole villages built in the immensely inflential seventeenth-century "**Huizhou style**", comprising a two-storeyed house plan built around a courtyard, which epitomized the basic forms of contemporary east-coast provincial architecture.

Modern architecture

China's **modern architecture** tends to reflect political and economic, rather than ethnic or climatic, considerations. From the mid-nineteenth century onwards, treaty ports were built up in the **European** colonial manner by the foreign merchants, banks, shipping firms and missionaries who conducted their affairs there. Today, the former offices, warehouses and churches – often divided up for Chinese use – still give certain cities a distinctive look. Hankou, part of Wuhan, has a Customs House and whole streets of colonial buildings, as do the former east-coast concessions of Shanghai, Qingdao, Yantai, Shantou, Xiamen and Guangzhou. European-inspired building continued on into the 1930s.

After the **Communist takeover**, there were various attempts to unite Chinese styles with modern materials. When used, this was successful, and many modern rural dwellings still follow traditional designs, simply replacing adobe walls with concrete. But during the 1950s, while Russia was China's ally, a brutally functional **Soviet style** became the urban norm, requiring that everything from factories to hotels be built as identical drab, characterless grey boxes. Since China opened up to the Western world and capitalism in the late 1970s, however, there's been a move towards a more "international" look, as seen in the concrete-and-glass high-rises going up across the country. While brighter than the Russian model, these are, in general, hardly any more inspirational or attractive, and are afflicted by a mania for facing new buildings in bathroom tiles. Perhaps the most distressing aspect of this trend is that any indigenous characteristics are seen as old-fashioned, and yet, compared with similar buildings in the West, these new buildings are very poor imitations. Yet even here there are occasional attempts to marry the traditional Chinese idiom with current needs, and in a few cases you'll see apartment buildings surrounded by walled compounds and topped with curled roof tiles.

Art

This very brief survey aims to reflect, and to help you to follow, what you are likely to see most of in Chinese provincial and city museums – and to an extent *in situ*. In looking at the art displayed in Chinese museums it should be remembered that while for more than two thousand years an empire with a splendid court produced an incredible wealth of art objects, from the mid-nineteenth century onwards, many of these were acquired – more or less legitimately – or looted, by Westerners. Later, too, some of the great imperial collections were removed by the Nationalists to Taiwan, where they are now in the National Palace Museum.

Pottery, bronzes and sculpture

The earliest Chinese objects date back to the Neolithic farmers of the **Yangshao** culture – well-made **pottery** vessels painted in red, black, brown and white with geometrical designs. You'll notice that the decoration is usually from the shoulders of the pots upwards; this is because what has survived is mostly from graves and was designed to be seen from above when the pots were placed round the dead. From the same period there are decorated clay heads, perhaps for magic or ritual, and pendants and small ornaments of polished stone or jade, with designs that are sometimes semi-abstract – a simplified sitting bird in polished jade is a very early example of the powerful Chinese tradition of animal sculpture. Rather later is the Neolithic **Longshan** pottery – black, very thin and fine, wheel-turned and often highly polished, with elegantly, sharply defined shapes.

The subsequent era, from around 1500 BC, is dominated by **Shang and Zhou bronze** vessels used for preparing and serving food and wine, and for ceremonies and sacrifices. There are many distinct shapes, each with its own name and specific usage. One of the most common is the *ding*, a three- or four-legged vessel which harks back to the Neolithic pots used for cooking over open fires. As you'll see from the museums, these bronzes have survived in great numbers. The **Shang** bronze industry appears already fully developed with advanced techniques and designs and no sign of a primitive stage. Casting methods were highly sophisticated, using moulds, while design was firm and assured and decoration often stylized and linear, with both geometric and animal motifs, as well as grinning masks of humans and fabulous beasts. There are some naturalistic animal forms among the vessels, too – fierce tigers, solid elephants and surly-looking rhinoceroses. Other bronze finds include weapons, decorated horse harnesses and sets of bells used in ritual music. Later, under the **Zhou**, the style of the bronzes becomes more varied and rich: some animal vessels are fantastically shaped and extravagantly decorated; others are simplified natural forms; others again seem to be depicting not so much a fierce tiger, for example, as utter ferocity itself. You'll also see from the Shang and Zhou small objects – ornaments, ritual pieces and jewellery pendants – with highly simplified but vivid forms of tortoises, salamanders and flying birds. From the end of this period there are also painted clay funeral figures and a few carved wooden figures.

The Shang produced a few small sculptured human figures and animals in marble, but **sculptures** and works in stone begin to be found in great quantities in **Han-dynasty** tombs. The decorated bricks and tiles, the bas-reliefs and the terracotta figurines of acrobats, horsemen and ladies-in-waiting placed in the tombs to serve the dead, even the massive stone men and beasts set to guard the Spirit Way leading to the tomb, are all lifelike and reflect concern with everyday activities and material possessions. The scale models of houses with people looking out of the windows and of farmyards with their animals have a spontaneous gaiety and vigour; some of the watchdogs are the most realistic of all. Smaller objects like tiny statuettes and jewellery were also carved, from ivory, jade and wood.

It was the advent of **Buddhism** which encouraged stone carving on a large scale in the round, with mallet and chisel. **Religious sculpture** was introduced from India and in the fourth-century caves at **Datong** (see p.232) and the earlier caves at **Longmen**, near Luoyang (see p.305), the Indian influence is most strongly felt in the stylized Buddhas and attendants. Sometimes of huge size, they have an aloof grace and a rhythmic quality in their flowing robes, but also a smooth, bland and static feel. Not until the **Tang** do you get the full flowering of a native Chinese style, where the figures are rounder, with movement, and the positions, expressions and clothes are more natural and realistic. Some of the best examples are to be seen at **Dunhuang** (see p.1047) and in the later caves at Longmen. The **Song** continued to carve religious figures and at **Dazu** in Sichuan (see p.956) you'll find good examples of a highly decorative style which had broadened its subject matter to include animals, ordinary people and scenes of everyday life; the treatment is down to earth, individual, sometimes even comic. The Dazu carvings are very well preserved and you see them painted, as they were meant to be. In later years less statuary was produced until the **Ming** with their taste for massive and impressive tomb sculptures. You can see the best of these in **Nanjing** and **Beijing**.

Ceramics

In **ceramics** the Chinese tradition is very old. From the Neolithic painted pottery described above onwards, China developed a high level of excellence, based on the availability of high-quality materials. Its pre-eminence was recognized by the fact that for more than four hundred years the English language has used the word "china" to mean fine-quality ceramic ware. In some of the early wares you can see the influence of shapes derived from bronzes, but soon the rise of regional potteries using different materials, and the development of special types for different uses, led to an enormous variety of shapes, textures and colours. This was noticeable by the **Tang dynasty** when an increase in the production of pottery for daily use was partly stimulated by the spread of tea drinking and by the restriction of the use of copper and bronze to coinage. The Tang also saw major technical advances; the production of true **porcelain** was finally achieved and Tang potters became very skilled in the use of polychrome glazing. You can see evidence of this in the *san cai* (three-colour) statuettes of horses and camels, jugglers, traders, polo players, grooms and court ladies, which have come in great numbers from imperial tombs, and which reflect in vivid, often humorous, detail and still brilliant colours so many aspects of the life of the time. It was a cosmopolitan civilization open to foreign influences and this is clearly seen in Tang art.

The **Song** dynasty witnessed a great refinement of ceramic techniques and of regional specialization, many wares being named after the area which produced them. The keynote was simplicity and quiet elegance, both in colour and form. There was a preference for using a **single pure colour** and for incised wares made to look like damask cloth. In the museums you'll see the famous green celadons, the thin white porcelain *ding* ware and the pale grey-green *ju* ware reserved for imperial use. The Mongol **Yuan** dynasty, in the early fourteenth century, enriched Chinese tradition with outside influences – notably the introduction of **cobalt blue underglaze**, early examples of the blue and white porcelain which was to become so famous. The **Ming** saw the flowering of great potteries under imperial patronage, especially **Jingdezhen**. Taste moved away from Song simplicity and returned to the liking for vivid colour which the Tang had displayed – deep **red**, **yellow** and **orange** glazes, with a developing taste for pictorial representation. From the seventeeth century, Chinese export wares flowed in great quantity and variety to the West to satisfy a growing demand for chinoiserie, and the efforts of the Chinese artists to follow what they saw as the tastes and techniques of the West produced a style of its own. The early **Qing** created delicate enamel wares and *famille rose* and *verte*. So precise were the craftsmen that some porcelain includes the instructions for the pattern in the glaze.

You can visit several potteries such as at **Jingdezhen** in Jiangxi province, where both early wares and modern trends are on display. Not so long ago they were turning out thousands of figurines of Mao and Lu Xun sitting in armchairs; now the emphasis is on table lamp bases in the shape of archaic maidens in flowing robes playing the lute, or creased and dimpled Laughing Buddhas.

Painting and calligraphy

While China's famous ceramics were produced by nameless craftsmen, with **painting and calligraphy** we enter the realm of the amateur whose name has survived and who was often scholar, official, poet or all three. It has been said that the four great treasures of Chinese painting are the brush, the ink, the inkstone and the paper or silk. The earliest brush found, from about 400 BC, is made out of animal hairs glued to a hollow bamboo tube. Ink was made from pine soot mixed with glue and hardened into a stick which would be rubbed with water on an inkstone made of non-porous, carved and decorated slate. Silk was used for painting as early as the third century BC and paper was invented by **Cai Lun** in 106 AD. The first known painting on silk was found in a **Han** tomb; records show that there was a great deal of such painting but in 190 AD the vast imperial collection was destroyed in a civil war – the soldiers used the silk to make tents and knapsacks. All we know of Han painting comes from decorated tiles, lacquer, painted pottery and a few painted tombs, enough to show a great sense of movement and energy. The British Museum has a scroll in ink and colour on silk attributed to **Gu Kaizhi** from around 400 AD and entitled *Admonitions of the Instructress to Court Ladies*, and we know that the theory of painting was already being discussed by this date, as the treatise *The Six Principles of Painting* dates from about 500 AD.

The **Sui–Tang** period, with a powerful stable empire and a brilliant court, was exactly the place for painting to develop, and a great tradition of figure painting grew up, especially of court subjects – portraits and pictures of the emperor receiving envoys and of court ladies were produced, several of which are to be seen in Beijing. Although only a few of these survived, the walls of Tang tombs, such as those near Xi'an, are rich in vivid frescoes which provide a realistic portrayal of court life. Wang Wei in the mid-eighth century was an early exponent of monochrome **landscape** painting, but the great flowering of landscape painting came with the **Song dynasty**. An academy was set up under imperial patronage and different schools of painting emerged which analyzed the natural world with great concentration and intensity; their style has set a mark on Chinese landscape painting ever since. There was also lively **figure painting** – a famous horizontal scroll in Beijing showing the Qing Ming River Festival is the epitome of this. The last emperor of the Northern Song, **Hui Zong**, was himself a painter of some note, which indicates the status of painting in China at the time. The Southern Song preferred a more intimate style and such subjects as flowers, birds and still life grew in popularity.

Under the **Mongols** there were many officials who found themselves unwanted or unwilling to serve the alien Yuan dynasty and who preferred to retire and paint. This produced the **"literati" school**, with many painters harking back to the styles of the tenth century. One of the great masters was **Ni Can**. He, among many others, also devoted himself to the ink paintings of bamboo which became important at this time. In this school, of which there are many extant examples, the highest skills of techniques and composition were applied to the simplest of subjects, such as plum flowers. Both ink painting as well as more conventional media continued to be employed by painters of the next three or more centuries. From the **Yuan** onwards a tremendous quantity of paintings has survived. Under the **Ming** dynasty there was a great interest in collecting the works of previous ages and a linked willingness by painters to be influenced by tradition. There are plenty of examples of bamboo and plum blossom, and bird and flower paintings being brought to a high decorative pitch, as well as a number of schools of landscape painting firmly rooted in traditional techniques. The arrival of the Manchu **Qing** dynasty did not disrupt the continuity of Chinese painting, but the art became wide open to many influences. It included the Italian **Castiglione** (Lang Shi-ning in Chinese) who specialized in horses, dogs and flowers under imperial patronage, the Four Wangs who reinterpreted Song and Yuan styles in an orthodox manner, and the individualists such as the Eight Eccentrics of Yangzhou and some Buddhist monks who objected to derivative art and sought a more distinctive approach to subject and style. But, on the whole, the weight of tradition was powerful enough to maintain the old approach.

Calligraphy

The word "**calligraphy**" is derived from the Greek for "beautiful writing", and was crystallized into a high art form in China, where the use of the brush saw the development of handwriting of various styles, valued on a par with painting. There are a number of different scripts: the **seal script** is the archaic form found on oracle bones; the **lishu** is the clerical style and was used in inscriptions on stone; the **kaishu** is the regular style closest to the modern printed form; and **cao shu** (grass script), a cursive style, is the most individual handwritten style. Emperors, poets and scholars over centuries have left examples of their calligraphy cut into stone at beauty spots, on mountains and in grottoes, tombs and temples all over China; you can see some early examples in the caves at Longmen (see p.305). At one stage during the Tang dynasty, calligraphy was so highly thought of that it was the yardstick for the selection of high officials.

Other arts

Jade and lacquerware have also been constantly in use in China since earliest times. In Chinese eyes, **jade**, in white and shades of green or brown, is the most precious of stones. It was used to make the earliest ritual objects, such as the flat disc **Pi**, symbol of Heaven, which was found in Shang and Zhou graves. Jade was also used as a mark of rank and for ornament, in its most striking form in the jade burial suits which you will see in the country's museums.

Lacquer, made from the sap of the lac tree, is also found as early as the Zhou. Many layers of the stuff were painted on a wood or cloth base which was then carved and inlaid with gold, silver or tortoiseshell, or often most delicately painted. There are numerous examples of painted lacquer boxes and baskets from the Han and, as with jade, the use of this material has continued ever since.

Music

The casual visitor to China could be forgiven for thinking that the only traditional style to compete with bland pop is that of the kitsch folk troupes to be heard in hotels and concert halls. But an earthy traditional music still abounds throughout the countryside; it can be heard at weddings, funerals, temple fairs, and New Year celebrations – and even downtown in teahouses. A very different, edgier sound can be heard in certain smokey city bars – the new Chinese rock, energetic expressions of urban angst.

Traditional music

Han music (like Irish music) is heterophonic – the musicians play differently decorated versions of a single melodic line – and its melodies are basically **pentatonic**. Percussion plays a major role, both in instrumental ensembles, and as accompaniment to opera, narrative-singing, ritual music and dance.

Chinese musical roots date back millennia – among archeological finds are a magnificent set of 65 bronze bells from the fifth century BC – and its forms can be directly traced to the Tang dynasty, a golden age of great poets such as Li Bai and Bai Juyi, who were also avid musicians. Several *qin* (zithers) from this period are still played today, and there's a good market in fake ones, too. In fact, the industry in fake antiques extends to the music itself, as tourists may be regaled with Hollywood-style routines marketed as the music and dance of the Tang court. In recent years, the rather soulless Confucian rituals of the bygone imperial courts have been revived in Qufu and some other towns like Nanjing, largely for tourists. The reality, of course, is that there are no "living fossils" in music, and most traditional forms in the countryside are the product of gradual accretion over the centuries, and especially over the past hundred years.

After China's humiliation at the hands of foreign imperial powers, and in the turbulent years after 1911, **Western ideas** gained ground, at least in the towns. Some intriguing urban forms sprang up from the meeting of East and West, such as the wonderfully sleazy Cantonese music of the 1920s and '30s. As the movie industry developed, people in Shanghai, colonial Canton (Guangzhou) and nearby Hong Kong threw themselves into the craze for Western-style jazz and dancehalls, fusing the local traditional music with jazz, and adding saxophone, violin and xylophone to Chinese instruments such as the *gaohu* (high-pitched fiddle) and the *yangqin* (dulcimer). Composers **Lü Wencheng** and **Qiu Hechou** (Yau Hokchau), the violinist **Yin Zizhong** (Yi Tzuchung) and **He Dasha** ("Thicko He"), guitarist and singer of clown roles in Cantonese opera, made many wonderful commercial 78s during this period. While these musicians kept their roots in Cantonese music, the more Westernized (and even more popular) compositions of **Li Jinhui** and his star singer **Zhou Xuan** subsequently earned severe disapproval from Maoist critics as decadent and pornographic. Today, though, you can still hear these 1930s classics, played in modern arrangements, over street loudspeakers.

New "**revolutionary**" music, composed from the 1930s on, was generally march-like and optimistic and, after the Communist victory of 1949, the whole ethos of traditional music was challenged. Anything "feudal" or "superstitious" – which included a lot of traditional folk customs and music – was severely restricted, while Chinese melodies were "cleaned up" with the addition of rudimentary harmonies and bass lines. The communist anthem "**The East is Red**", which began life as a folksong from the northern Shaanxi province (from where Mao's revolution also sprang), is symptomatic. Its local colour was ironed out as it was turned into a conventionally harmonized hymn-like tune. It was later adopted as the unofficial anthem of the Cultural Revolution, during which time musical life was driven underground, with only eight model operas and ballets permitted on stage.

The **conservatoire style** of **guoyue** (national music), which was about the only Chinese music recorded until recently, was an artificial attempt to create a pan-Chinese style for the concert hall, with composed arrangements in a style akin to Western light music. There are still many conservatoire-style chamber groups – typically including *erhu* (fiddle), *dizi* (flute), *pipa* (lute) and *zheng* (zither) – playing evocatively titled pieces, some of which are newly composed. While the plaintive pieces for solo *erhu* by musicians such as **Liu Tianhua** and the blind beggar **Abing** (also a Daoist priest), or atmospheric tweetings on the *dizi*, have been much recorded by *guoyue* virtuosos like **Min Huifen** or **Lu Chunling** respectively, there is much more to Chinese music than this. Folk music has a life of its own and tends to follow the Confucian ideals of moderation and harmony, in which showy virtuosity is out of place.

The qin and solo traditions

Instrumental music is not as popular as vocal music in China, and many of the short virtuosic pieces that you hear played on the *erhu* or *dizi* are in fact the product of modern composers writing in a pseudo-romantic Western style for the concert hall. The genuine solo traditions going back to the scholar-literati of imperial times, and which live on in the conservatoires today, are for the *pipa*, *zheng* and *qin*.

The **qin** (also known as *guqin*) is the most exalted of these instruments. A seven-string plucked zither, it has been a favourite subject of poets and painters for over a thousand years, and is the most delicate and contemplative instrument in the Chinese palette. It is the most accessible, too, producing expressive slides and ethereal harmonics. Though primarily associated with the moderation of the Confucian scholar, the *qin* is also steeped in the mystical Daoism of ancient philosophy – the contemplative union with nature, where silence is as important as sound. The only instruments which may occasionally blend with the *qin* are the voice of the player, singing ancient poems in an utterly introverted style, or the *xiao* end-blown flute.

With its literate background, *qin* music has been written in a unique and complex notation since the Tang dynasty. The *Shenqi mipu* written by the Ming prince, Zhu Quan, in 1425, which included pieces handed down from earlier dynasties, is still commonly used, though most *qin* pieces today have been transmitted from master to pupil since at least the eighteenth century. Since the 1950s there has been a drive to revive other early pieces, comparable to the early-music movement in the West.

The *qin* is best heard in meetings of aficionados rather than in concert. The **Beijing Qin Association**, led by Li Xiangting of the Central Conservatoire, meets on the first Sunday of each month and is open to visitors. In Shanghai, the professor of *guqin* at the Conservatoire, Lin Youren, will introduce you to any get-togethers of qin enthusiasts in the area. Many of the master musicians play instruments dating back to the fifteenth (and in some cases the ninth) century.

Modern traditions of the **pipa** (lute) and **zheng** (zither) also derive from regional styles, transmitted from master to pupil, although "national" repertoires developed during the twentieth century. For the *zheng*, the northern styles of Henan and Shandong and the southern Chaozhou and Hakka schools are best known. The *pipa*, on the other hand, has thrived in the Shanghai region. It makes riveting listening, with its contrast between intimate "civil" pieces and the startlingly modern-sounding martial style of traditional pieces such as "Ambush from All Sides" (*Shimian maifu*), with its frenetic percussive evocation of the sounds of battle.

The poetic titles of many so-called classical solo pieces – like "Autumn Moon in the Han Palace" or "Flowing Streams" – often relate to an identification with nature or to a famous historical scene. Correspondingly, the music is often pictorial, underlining the link with the artistic background of the educated classes of imperial times. The similar titles of the pieces played by folk ensembles, however, are rarely illustrative, serving only as identification for the musicians.

The North: blowers and drummers

Today what we might call classical traditions – derived from the elite of imperial times – live on not just with these solo instruments but still more strongly in **folk ensembles**. Such traditions have survived best in life-cycle and calendar rituals for the gods. The most exciting examples of this music are to be heard at **weddings and funerals**, known as "red and white business" – red being the auspicious colour of the living, white the colour of mourning.

These occasions usually feature raucous **shawm** (a ubiquitous instrument in China, rather like a crude clarinet) and percussion groups called **chuigushou** – "blowers and drummers". While wedding bands naturally tend to use more jolly music, funerals may also feature lively pieces to entertain the guests. The "blowers and drummers" play not only lengthy and solemn suites but also the latest pop hits and theme tunes from TV and films. They milk the audience by sustaining notes, using circular breathing, playing even while dismantling and reassembling their shawms, or by balancing plates on sticks on the end of their instruments while playing. Nobly laying down their lives for their art, shawm players also love to perform while successively inserting cigarettes into both nostrils, both ears, and both corners of the mouth. Some of the more virtuoso shawm bands are found in southwestern Shandong around Heze county.

The **sheng** is one of the oldest Chinese instruments (mentioned as far back as the tenth century BC). It comprises a group of (usually 17) bamboo pipes of different lengths bound in a circle and set in a wooden or metal base into which the player blows. Frequently used for ceremonial music, it adds an incisive rhythmic bite to the music. Long and deafening strings of fire-crackers are another inescapable part of village ceremony. Some processions are led by a Western-style brass band with a shawm-and-percussion group behind, competing in volume, oblivious of key. In northern villages, apart from the blowers and drummers, ritual **shengguan** ensembles are also common, with their exquisite combination of mouth organs and oboes, as well as darting flutes and the shimmering halo of the *yunluo* gong-frame, accompanied by percussion. Apart from this haunting melodic music, they perform some spectacular ritual percussion – the intricate arm movements of the cymbal players almost resemble martial arts.

Around Xi'an, groups performing similar wind and percussion music, misleadingly dubbed **Xi'an Drum Music** (**Xi'an guyue**), are active for temple festivals not only in the villages but also in the towns, especially in the sixth moon, around July. The Xi'an Conservatoire has commercialized these folk traditions, but the real thing is much better. If you remember the tough shawm bands and haunting folksong of Chen Kaige's film *Yellow Earth*, or the harsh falsetto narrative in Zhang Yimou's *The Story of Qiuju*, go for the real thing among the barren hills of northern Shaanxi. This area is home to fantastic folk singers, local opera (such as the Qinqiang and Meihu styles), puppeteers, shawm bands, and folk ritual specialists. Even *yangge* dancing, which in the towns is often a geriatric form of conga dancing, has a wild power here, again accompanied by shawms and percussion.

The South: silk and bamboo

In southeast China, the best-known instrumental music is that of **sizhu** ("silk and bamboo") ensembles, using flutes (of bamboo) and plucked and bowed strings (until recently of silk). More mellifluous than the outdoor wind bands of the north, these provide perhaps the most accessible Chinese folk music.

There are several regional styles, but the most famous is that of **Shanghai**. In the city's teahouses, old-timers – and some youngsters too – get together in the afternoons, sit round a table and take it in turns to play a set with Chinese fiddles, flutes and banjos. You can't help thinking of an Irish session, with Chinese tea replacing Guinness. The most celebrated teahouse is the **Chenghuang miao** (see p.396), a picturesque two-storeyed structure on an island in the old quarter, where there are Monday afternoon gatherings. The contrasting textures of plucked, bowed and blown sounds are part of the attraction of this music with their individual decorations to the gradually unfolding melody. Many pieces consist of successive decorations of a theme, beginning with the most ornate and accelerating as the decorations are gradually stripped down to a fast and bare final statement of the theme itself. Above the chinking of tea bowls and subdued chatter of the teahouse, enjoy the gradual unravelling of a piece like "Sanliu", or feel the exhilarating dash to the finish of "Xingjie", with its breathless syncopations.

There are amateur *sizhu* clubs throughout the lower Yangzi area including the cities of Nanjing and Hangzhou. Although this music is secular and recreational in its urban form, the *sizhu* instrumentation originated in ritual ensembles and is still so used in the villages and temples of southern Jiangsu. In fact, amateur ritual associations are to be found all over southern China, as far afield as Yunnan, punctuating their ceremonies with sedate music reminiscent of the Shanghai teahouses, although often featuring the *yunluo* gong-frame of northern China.

Another fantastic area for folk music is the coastal region of **southern Fujian**, notably the delightful cities of Quanzhou and Xiamen. Here you can find not only opera, ritual music and puppetry, but the haunting **nanguan ballads**. Popular all along the coast of southern Fujian, as in Taiwan across the strait, *nanguan* features a female singer accompanied by end-blown flute and plucked and bowed lutes. The ancient texts depict the sorrows of love, particularly of women, while the music is mostly stately and the delivery restrained, yet anguished.

Still further south, the coastal regions of **Chaozhou** and **Shantou**, and the **Hakka** area (inland around Meixian and Dabu), also have celebrated string ensembles featuring a high-pitched *erxian* (bowed fiddle) and *zheng* (plucked zither), as well as large and imposing ceremonial percussion bands, sometimes accompanied by shrill flutes.

Discography

In China it is easier to find good recordings of opera than instrumental music, but authentic recordings of Chinese instrumental and religious music are finally beginning to match the conservatoire-style recordings of souped-up arrangements that used to dominate the market. All the recordings listed are available on CD.

General traditional

Li Xiangting *Chine: l'Art du Qin* (Ocora, France).
Li is professor of *qin* at the Central Conservatoire in Beijing and also a poet, painter and calligrapher. This album is a fine introduction to the refined meditation of the *qin*, though it actually ends with the celebrated "Guangling san", a graphic depiction of the assassination of an evil tyrant, contrasting with the instrument's tranquil image.

Lin Shicheng *Chine: l'Art du Pipa* (Ocora, France).
Includes not only favourites such as a version of the popular ensemble piece "Spring – River – Flowers – Moon – Night" and the martial piece "The Tyrant Removes his Armour" (also on the Wu Man CD below), but also some rarer intimate pieces.

The Uyghur Musicians from Xinjiang *Music from the Oasis Towns of Central Asia* (Globestyle, UK).
Enjoyable introduction to the Uigur music of the Northwest, recorded on a spare day during a UK concert tour. Features some fine playing of the long-necked, lute-like *tambur* and *satar*, plus the *surnay*, a small twin-reeded shawm.

Wu Man *Traditional and Contemporary Music for Pipa and Ensemble* (Nimbus, UK).
From the southern town of Hangzhou, Wu studied with masters such as Lin Shicheng in Beijing. Since making her home in the USA she has championed new music for the instrument.

Wu Zhaoji *Wumen Qin Music* (Hugo, Hong Kong).
The late Wu Zhaoji's playing typified the contemplative ethos of the *qin*, eschewing mere technical display. Wumen refers here to the Wu style of the canal city of Suzhou.

Compilations

An Anthology of Chinese and Traditional Folk Music: a Collection of Music played on the Guqin (China Record Co., China; Cradle Records, Taiwan).
This is an eight-CD set for serious *qin* enthusiasts, featuring some fantastic reissues of the great masters of the 1950s.

China: Folk Instrumental Traditions (VDE-Gallo/AIMP, Switzerland).
A two-CD set of archive and recent recordings of village ensembles from north and south compiled by Stephen Jones. Includes earthy shawm bands, mystical *shengguan* ritual ensembles, refined silk and bamboo, and some awesome percussion. Features some of the master musicians from before the Cultural Revolution, such as the Daoist priests An Laixu on *yunluo* and Zhu Qinfu on drums.

Chine: Musique Classique (Ocora, France).
A selection of solo and ensemble pieces featuring the *qin*, *pipa*, *sheng*, *guanzi* (oboe), *dizi*, *xiao*, *erhu* and *yangqin*, played by outstanding instrumentalists of the 1950s, including Guan Pinghu, Cao Zheng and Sun Yude.

Songs of the Land in China: Labour Songs and Love Songs (Wind Records, Taiwan).
Two CDs featuring beautiful archive recordings of folk singing, mostly unaccompanied, from different regions of China, including rhythmic songs of boatmen, Hua'er songs from the northwest, and the plaintive songs from northern Shaanxi. A surprisingly varied and captivating selection.

Special Collection of Contemporary Chinese Musicians (Wind Records, Taiwan).
A more comprehensive two-CD set of archive recordings of some of the great 1950s instrumentalists, including masters of the *qin*, *zheng*, *pipa*, *suona* and *guanzi*.

Northern traditions

Compilations

China: Music of the First Moon. Shawms from Northeast China Vol. 1 (Musique du Monde, France).
Ear-cleansing shawm and percussion, featuring a succession of groups from the Dalian playing music for New Year festivities. Earthy stuff with good notes.

Chine: Musique Ancienne de Chang'an (Inédit, France).
The wind pieces on this conservatoire recording are impressive, though lacking the subtlety of tuning, complexity of tempi and sheer guts of the folk ensembles.

Xi'an Drums Music (Hugo, Hong Kong).
Majestic wind and percussion music performed for funerals and calendrical pilgrimages around Xi'an, including some rarely heard vocal hymns (weirdly translated as "rap music").

The Li Family Band *Shawms from Northeast China Vol. 2* (Musique du Monde, France).
Led by the senior Li Shiren, this band typifies northern shawm and percussion groups. The disc features a spectrum of music from doleful funereal music for large shawms to more popular festive pieces.

Southern traditions

Tsai Hsiao-Yueh *Nan-kouan: Chant Courtois de la Chine du Sud Vol. 1* (Ocora, France).
The senior *nanguan* singer Tsai Hsiao-yueh (Cai Xiaoyue), with her group based in Tainan, Taiwan, maintain the proud amateur tradition of this exalted genre originating just across the strait in Fujian. This album features haunting chamber ballads, the female voice accompanied by end-blown flute and plucked and bowed lutes.

Compilations

China: Chuida Wind and Percussive Instrumental Ensembles (UNESCO/Auvidis, France).
Three traditional ensembles from southern China, including some unusual silk and bamboo from Shanghai and ceremonial music for weddings and funerals from Fujian and Zhejiang.

Rain Dropping on the Banana Tree (Rounder, US).
Taking its title from a popular Cantonese melody, this collection of reissued 78s from 1902 to 1930 features early masters of Cantonese music such as Yau Hokchau, as well as excerpts from Beijing and Cantonese opera.

Sizhu/Silk Bamboo: Chamber Music of South China (Pan, Netherlands).
Several styles of chamber ensemble along the southeastern coast, from silk and bamboo from Shanghai to the refined instrumental *nanguan* music from Xiamen, to Chaozhou and Hakka pieces featuring *zheng*, and also examples of the more modern Cantonese style. Excellent notes.

continued overleaf

Discography continued

Temple music

Compilations

China: Buddhist Music of the Ming Dynasty (JVC, Japan).
Exquisite music played by the monks of the Zhihua temple, Beijing, in collaboration with musicians from the Central Conservatoire. Features double-reed pipes, flutes, Chinese mouth organs, a frame of pitched gongs and percussion.

Tianjin Buddhist Music Ensemble (Nimbus, UK).
Buddhist ritual *shengguan* music played by a group of musicians in their 70s, with some wonderful *guanzi*. Good notes too.

Chinese opera

Compilations

China: Ka-lé, Festival of Happiness (VDE-Gallo/AIMP, Switzerland).
Mainly instrumental music from the operas of the Quanzhou Puppet Troupe.

Chinese Classical Opera: Kunqu. The Peony Pavilion (Inédit, France).
A two-CD set featuring excerpts from the great opera by the early-seventeenth-century Tang Xianzu. The vocal sections give a better idea of the tradition than the kitsch harmonized orchestral arrangements.

An Introduction to Chinese Opera (Hong Kong Records, Hong Kong).
A series of four CDs illustrating the different styles, including Beijing, Cantonese, Shanghai, Huangmei, Henan, Pingju and Qinqiang operas.

Opera du Sichuan: la Legende de Serpent Blanc (Musique du Monde, France).
A double CD of traditional opera from Sichuan, featuring the distinctive female chorus and ending with the attractive bonus of a "bamboo ballad" on the same theme sung by a narrative-singer.

Contemporary/new wave

Wu Man and the Kronos Quartet *Ghost Opera* by Tan Dun (Nonesuch, US).
An extraordinary multimedia piece "with water, stones, paper, and metal", and incorporating traditional shamanistic sounds of the composer's childhood in remote Hunan province, alongside Bach and Shakespeare. Totally original.

Yo-Yo Ma *Symphony 1997* by Tan Dun (Sony Classical).
Ma's cello provides the narrative element here, blending his classical technique with gliding tones reminiscent of *erhu* music. The theatrical musical panorama includes the 2400-year-old bells, Cantonese opera recorded on the streets of Hong Kong, a dragon dance plus quotations from Beethoven's "Ode to Joy" and Puccini's *Turandot*. Naïve, yet sophisticated and certainly colourful.

The temples

All over China, particularly on the great religious mountains like **Wutai Shan**, **Tai shan**, **Qingcheng Shan**, **Wudang Shan** and **Putuo Shan**, temples are not just historical monuments but living sites of worship. Morning and evening services are held daily, and larger rituals on special occasions. The priests mainly perform vocal liturgy accompanied by percussion – few now use melodic instruments. They intone sung hymns with long melismas, alternating with chanted sections accompanied by the relentless and hypnotic beat of the woodblock. Drum, bell, gongs and cymbals also punctuate the service.

Melodic instrumental music tends to be added when priests perform rituals outside the temples. These styles are more earthy and accessible even to ears unaccustomed to Chinese music. The Daoist priests from the Xuanmiao Guan in **Suzhou**, for example, perform wonderful mellifluous pieces for silk-and-bamboo instruments, gutsy blasts on the shawm, music for spectacularly long trumpets and a whole battery of percussion.

Opera and other vocal music

Chinese musical drama dates back at least two thousand years and became an overwhelmingly popular form with both the elite and common people from the Yuan dynasty (late thirteenth century). There are several hundred types of regional opera, of which **Beijing Opera**, a rather late hybrid form dating from the eighteenth century, is the most widely known – it's now heard throughout China and is the closest thing to a "national" theatre. The rigorous training the form demands – and the heavy hand of ideology which saw it as the most important of "the peoples' arts" – is graphically displayed in Chen Kaige's film *Farewell My Concubine*. Many librettos now performed date back to the seventeenth century and describe the intrigues of emperors and gods, as well as love stories and comedy. Northern "**clapper operas**" (*bangzi xi*), named after the high-pitched woodblock that insistently runs through them, are earthy in flavour – for example, the "Qinqiang" of Shaanxi province. **Sichuan opera** is remarkable for its female chorus. **Ritual masked opera** may be performed in the countryside of Yunnan, Anhui and Guizhou. Chaozhou and Fujian also have beautiful ancient styles of opera: **Pingju** and **Huangmei Xi** are genteel in style, while **Cantonese opera** is more funky. If you're looking for more music and less acrobatics, try to seek out the classical but now rare **Kunqu**, often accompanied by the sweet-toned *qudi* flute. There are also some beautiful **puppet operas**, often performed for ritual events; Quanzhou in Fujian has a celebrated marionette troupe, and other likely areas include northern Shaanxi and the Tangshan and Laoting areas of eastern Hebei.

While Chinese opera makes a great visual spectacle, musically it is an acquired taste. One must acclimatize to tense, guttural and high-pitched singing styles from both men and women. The music is dominated by the bowed string accompaniment of the *jinghu*, a sort of sawn-off *erhu*. There are also plucked lutes, flutes and – for transitional points – a piercing shawm. The action is driven by percussion, with drum and clappers leading an ensemble of gongs and cymbals in a variety of set patterns. There are professional opera troupes in the major towns, but rural opera performances, which are given for temple fairs and even weddings, tend to be livelier. Even in Beijing you will see groups of old men meeting in parks or, incongruously, at spaghetti junctions where the old gateways used to be, going through their favourite Beijing Opera excerpts.

Narrative-singing, sadly neglected in recordings, also features long classical stories. You may find a teahouse full of old people following these story-songs avidly, particularly in Sichuan, where one popular style is accompanied by the *yangqin* (dulcimer). In Beijing, or more often in Tianjin, amateurs sing through traditional *jingyun dagu* ballads, accompanied by drum and sanxian banjo. In Suzhou, *pingtan*, also accompanied by a plucked lute, is a beautiful genre. In Beijing and elsewhere there is also *xiangsheng*, a comic dialogue with a know-all and a straight man, though its subtle parodies of traditional opera may elude the outsider.

Traditional **folk songs** (as opposed to sentimental bel canto arrangements warbled by ball-gowned divas) are more difficult for the casual visitor to find in Han Chinese areas than among the ethnic minorities, but the beautiful songs of areas like northern Shaanxi and Sichuan are thankfully captured on disc.

New waves

Though the resistance of rural traditions to official ideology during three decades of Maoism has been remarkable, pop music seems to be encroaching more on traditional repertories than revolutionary music ever did. That said, the way that the shawm and percussion bands have been able to produce their own take on film themes and pop songs shows the adaptability that has kept their music alive.

One novel angle on traditional music is in the imaginative use being made of it by new-wave Chinese composers (mostly resident in the US) like **Tan Dun** and **Qu Xiaosong**. Part of the talented generation of novelists and film-makers which grew up during the intellectual vacuum of the Cultural Revolution, they have an experience of folk music that is far from the sentimental patriotism of earlier composers, incorporating an uncompromising Chinese spirituality into a radical avant-garde language. Tan Dun composed the vast "Symphony 1997" to celebrate the return of Hong Kong to mainland China. It incorporates the aforementioned set of 65 *bianzhong* bronze bells (with a range of five octaves) found buried in a royal tomb dating to 433 BC.

Chinese rock

China's indigenous rock, although often connected to the Hong Kong/Taiwanese entertainment industry, is a different beast, one which has its traditions in passionate and fiery protest, and which still possesses a cultural and political self-awareness. The rock scene was nonexistent in China until the mid-1980s, when foreign students on cultural exchange brought tapes of their favourite rock and pop music (and their own electric guitars) to the Chinese mainland, and shared them with their fellow students. Their music quickly caught the imagination of Chinese university youths and the urban vanguard.

Chinese **protest-rock** really began with singer-trumpeter-guitarist, Cui Jian, who cites the Sex Pistols, Sting, Rolling Stones and Beatles as his major influences. Cui also credits the influence of the Taiwanese singer **Teresa Teng** (known to the Chinese by her original name, Deng Lijun; 1953–95). Teng's singing style can be directly traced to Zhou Xuan and 1930s Shanghai. She was probably the most popular Chinese singer of her time, whose recordings were circulated in China on the black market from the late 1970s, when such music was officially banned, as it was held to represent such bourgeois ideas as paid entertainment and social dancing, as well as for lyrics thought to be lowering sexual morals. The ban was lifted by the late 1980s, when the state loosened its grip on the popular music market, knowing that it was a sign of "openness to capitalism".

Cui Jian

A Beijinger born of parents of Korean descent, **Cui Jian** studied the trumpet at an early age, trained as a classical musician and joined the Beijing Symphony Orchestra in 1981. After being introduced to Anglo-American rock in the mid-1980s, however, he forged an independent path and his gritty voice became the primary reference point of Chinese rock.

Cui's song "Nothing To My Name", ostensibly a love song, became a democracy movement anthem since its lyrics could be interpreted as a political monologue of the ruled about his ruler:

I used to endlessly ask
When will you go away with me?
You laugh at me always.
I have nothing to my name.
I want to give you my dreams
And also my freedom.
You laugh at me always.
I have nothing to my name.
I must tell you, I have waited too long.
I'll tell you my last request:
I'll hold your two hands
To take you away with me.

This song evoked a memorable complaint from General Wang Zhen, a veteran of the Long March: "What do you mean, you have nothing to your name? You've got the Communist Party haven't you?"

Even though Cui's lyrics have always been ambiguous, his voice has occasionally been muffled in the 1990s. A nationwide tour was cancelled midway because of his actions on stage (blindfolded in red cloth – the colour of Communism) that mesmerized his fans but enraged officials. He upset the authorities, too, with his recording of "Nanni Wan", a revolutionary song closely associated with the Communist Party and its ideals, glorifying Chinese peasants and their contribution to society. Cui's rock interpretation was understood by many as a challenge to (or mockery of) authority.

Like most of China's rockers, Cui turned more introspective as the Nineties progressed. His 1994 album *Hongqi Xiade Dan* (*Eggs Under the Red Flag*) reflected the shifting concerns of China's youth from politics to the realities of earning a living. But the powerful title track neatly encapsulated both:

Money floats in the air,
We have no ideals.
Although the air is fresh,
We cannot see into the distance.
Although the chance is here,
We are too timid.
We are wholly submissive,
Like eggs under the red flag.

Cui's 1998 album, *Wuneng de Liliang* (*The Power of the Powerless*), his most recent at time of writing, continued to explore global rock and personal lyrical themes, with songs such as "Bird in the Cage" and "Spring Festival" – far from the politics of his early recordings. Over the past few years, Cui has had successful tours in Europe and the US. Nevertheless, he is also keenly aware of the limitations "official China" imposes on his musical freedom. For the latest on Cui Jian's music and concert dates, check out ⓦwww.cuijian.com.

Stephen Jones and Joanna Lee,
with additional contributions from Simon Lewis

Film

Film came early to China. The first moving picture was exhibited in 1896 at a "teahouse variety show" in Shanghai, where the country's first cinema would be built just twelve years later. By the 1930s, cinema as we know it today was already playing an important role in the cultural life of Shanghai, though the huge number of resident foreigners ensured a largely Western diet of films – at least eighty percent of them were from Hollywood. Nevertheless, local Chinese films were also starting to be made, mainly by the so-called **May Fourth intellectuals** (middle-class liberals inspired by the uprising of May 4, 1919), who wanted to turn China into a modern country along Western lines. Naturally, Western stylistic influences on these films were very strong, and early Chinese films have little to do with the highly stylized, formal world of traditional performance arts such as Beijing Opera or shadow-puppet theatre. However, early film showings often employed a traditional style "storyteller" who sat near the screen reading out the titles as they came up, for the benefit of those who could not read.

The Shanghai studios

Of the few important **studios** in Shanghai operating in the 1920s and 1930s, perhaps the most famous was the **Mingxing**, whose films were generally of a left-leaning, anti-imperialist nature quite at odds with the general tenor of Hollywood. The film *Sister Flower* (1933) tells the story of twin sisters separated at birth, one of whom ends up a city girl living in Shanghai, while the other remains a poor villager. During the course of reuniting the sisters, the film contrasts in some detail the lives of ordinary city dwellers and peasants. Another film from the same year, *Spring Silk Worm*, an adaptation of a short story written by the well-known contemporary writer Mao Dun, portrays economic decline and hardship in Zhejiang province outside Shanghai, and implicitly levels the finger of accusation at Japanese imperialism. Finally, *The Goddess* (1934), from the **Lianhua** studio, depicts the struggle of a prostitute to have her son educated, against all the prejudices of the age. The improbably glamorous prostitute was played by the woman often referred to as China's own Garbo, the languorous Ruan Lingyu. Despite the liberal pretensions of these films, it was inevitable – given that audiences comprised just a tiny elite of China's total population – that they would later be derided by the Communists as excessively bourgeois.

After the **Japanese occupation** of Shanghai along with other large tracts of China in 1937, "subversive" studios such as the Mingxing and Lianhua were immediately closed, though some of the film-making talent managed to flee into the interior, where work continued. The experience of war undoubtedly put film-makers in closer touch with their potential future audiences, the Chinese masses. China's great wartime epic, **Spring River Flows East** (1947–8) was the cinematic result of this experience. The story spans the whole duration of the anti-Japanese war – and the ensuing civil war – through the lives of a single family, who are themselves torn apart by the conflict. The heroine, living in simple poverty, contrasts with her husband, who has long since abandoned his wife for a decadent urban existence in Shanghai. Traumatized by a decade of war, the Chinese who saw this film appreciated it as an authentic and representative account of the sufferings through which the entire nation had lived. Over three-quarters of a million people saw the film at the time of its release, which was a remarkable figure given that the country was still at war.

Communism and the cinema

Chinese film-making under the **Communists** is a story which really dates back to 1938, when Mao Zedong and his fellow Long Marchers finally set up their base in **Yan'an**, deep in Shaanxi province, and began to prepare for the seizure of power. There could have been no world farther removed from the glamour of Shanghai than dusty, poverty-stricken Yan'an, full of peasants and simple farmers. This was the ideal location for the film-makers of the future People's Republic to practise their skills. Talent escaping through Japanese lines was soon trickling through in search of employment, among them an obscure actress of high ambitions, one **Jiang Qing**, later to become Mao's wife and self-appointed empress of Chinese culture. One thing that all the leading Communists in Yan'an agreed on was the importance of film as a **centralizing medium**, which could and should be used to unify the culture of the nation after the war had been won.

The immediate consequence of the Communist victory in 1949 was that the showing of foreign films was severely curtailed. The days of the private Shanghai studios, too, were numbered, though they still managed to produce a few films in the years immediately after 1949. In 1950, a **Film Guidance committee** was set up, comprising 32 members whose task would be to set standards and, effectively, decide upon all film output for the entire nation. In addition to Mao's wife, Jiang Qing, the members of the committee included Yan'an film-makers as well as May Fourth intellectuals, and the established pre-war film-makers drew some confidence from the range of voices represented. By 1953 a unified national system for film production was in place and the first major socialist epic, **Bridge**, appeared in 1949, depicting mass mobilization of workers and peasantry rushing enthusiastically to construct a bridge in record time. Although predictably dull in terms of character and plot, the cast still contained a number of prewar Shanghai actors to divert audiences. The end of the film is marked, for the first time in Chinese cinema, by the entire cast gathering to shout "Long live Chairman Mao!", a scene that was to be re-enacted time and again over the coming years.

A year after *Bridge,* one of the very last non-government Shanghai studio films appeared, **The Life of Wu Xun**. This was a huge project that had started well before 1949, and, surprisingly, had been allowed to run through to completion despite the change of regime. The subject of the film is the famous nineteenth-century entrepreneur, Wu Xun, who started out life as a beggar and eventually rose to enormous riches, whereupon he set out on his lifetime's ambition to educate the peasantry. Despite the addition of a narrator's voice at the end of the film, pointing out that it was revolution and not education that peasants really needed, the film turned out a disaster for the Shanghai film industry. Mao himself wrote a damning critique of it for idolizing a "Qing landlord", and a full-scale campaign was launched against the legacy of the entire Shanghai film world, studios, actors, critics and audiences alike.

The remains of the May Fourth Movement struggled on. *New Year's Sacrifice*, a film based on a short story from the great prewar intellectual Lu Xun, was released in 1956, though with most of the intelligence and all of the irony taken out. The consolation for the old guard was that newer generations of Chinese film-makers had not yet solved the problem of how to portray life in the contemporary era either. The 1952 screen adaptation of Lao She's short story "Dragon's Beard Ditch", for example, was supposed to contrast the miserable pre-1949 life of a poor district of Beijing with the happy, prosperous life that was being lived under the Communists. The only problem, as any audience could immediately see, was that the supposedly miserable pre-1949 scenes actually looked a good deal more human and heart-warming than the later ones.

Nevertheless, the Communists did achieve some of their original targets during the **1950s**. The promotion of a universal culture and language was one of them. All characters in all films – from Tibetans to Mongolians to Cantonese – were depicted as speaking in flawless **Mandarin Chinese**. Film production, too, fanned out across China, and was no longer confined to the eastern coastal cities. Above all, there was an explosion in audiences, from around 47 million tickets sold in 1949, to 600 million in 1956, to over 4 billion in 1959. The latter figure should be understood in the context of the madness surrounding the Great Leap Forward, a time of crazed overproduction in all fields, film included. Film studios began sprouting in every town in China, though with a catastrophic loss of quality – a typical studio in Jiangxi Province comprised one man, his bicycle and an antique stills camera. The colossal output of that year included uninspiring titles such as *Loving the Factory as One's Home*.

The conspicuous failure of the Great Leap Forward did, however, bring some short-lived advantages to the film industry. While Mao was forced temporarily into the political sidelines in the late 1950s and early 1960s, the cultural bureaucrats signalled that in addition to "revolutionary realism", a certain degree of "**revolutionary romanticism**" was also to be encouraged. Chinese themes and subjects, as opposed to pure Marxism, were looked upon with more favour. A slight blossoming occurred, with improbable films such as *Lin Zexu* (1959), which covered the life of the great Qing-dynasty official who stood up to the British at the time of the Opium Wars. There was even a tentative branching out into comedy, with the film *What's Eating You?* based on the relatively un-socialist antics of a Suzhou waiter. Unusually, the film featured local dialects, as well as a faintly detectable parody of the "Learn from Lei Feng" campaign, by which the government was seeking to encourage greater sacrifices from individuals by promoting the mythical heroic worker Lei Feng. Generally, films from these years took to depicting so-called "middle" characters, who were neither class heroes nor class villains.

The Cultural Revolution

Unfortunately, this bright period came to a swift end in 1966 with the launching of Mao's Cultural Revolution. Essentially, no interesting work would take place in China for nearly fifteen years, and indeed, no film was produced anywhere in China in the years 1966 to 1970. The few films which did subsequently appear before Mao's death were made under the personal supervision of Jiang Qing, all on the revolutionary model, a kind of ballet with flag waving. Attendance at these dreadful films was virtually **compulsory** for people who did not wish to be denounced for a lack of revolutionary zeal. Ironically, Jiang Qing herself, in the privacy of her home, was a big fan of Hollywood productions.

Recovery from the trauma of the Cultural Revolution was bound to take time, but the years 1979 and 1980 saw a small crop of films attempting for the first time to assess the horror of what the country had just lived through. The best-known of these is **The Legend of Tianyun Mountain**, made in Shanghai in 1980, which featured two men, one of whom had denounced the other for "Rightism" in 1958. The subsequent story is one of guilt, love, emotions and human relationships, all subjects that had been banned during the Cultural Revolution. Understandably, the film was an enormous popular success, though before audiences had time to get too carried away, a subsequent film, *Unrequited Love* (1981), was officially criticized for blurring too many issues.

The 1980s and beyond

In **1984** the Chinese film industry was suddenly brought to international attention for the first time by the arrival of the so-called "**Fifth Generation**" of Chinese film-makers. This was the year that director **Chen Kaige** and his cameraman **Zhang Yimou**, both graduates from the first post-Cultural Revolution class (1982) of the Beijing Film School, made the superb art-house film **Yellow Earth**. The story of *Yellow Earth* is a minor feature; the interest is in the images and the colours. Still shots predominate, recalling traditional Chinese scroll painting, with giant landscapes framed by hills and the distant Yellow River. The film was not particularly well received in China, either by audiences, who expected something more modern, or by the authorities, who expected something more optimistic. Nevertheless, the pattern was now set for a series of increasingly foreign-funded (and foreign-watched) films comprising stunning images of a "traditional" China, irritating the censors at home and delighting audiences abroad.

Chen Kaige's protege Zhang Yimou was soon stealing a march on his former boss with his first film **Red Sorghum** in 1987, set in a remote wine-producing village of northern China at the time of the Japanese invasion. This film was not only beautiful, and reassuringly patriotic, but it also introduced the world to **Gong Li**, the actress who was to become China's first international heart-throb. The fact that Gong Li and Zhang Yimou were soon to be lovers added to the general media interest in their work, both in China and abroad. They worked together on a string of hits, including *Judou*, *The Story of Qiu Ju*, *Raise the Red Lantern*, *Shanghai Triads* and *To Live*. None of these could be described as art-house in the way that *Yellow Earth* had been, and the potent mix of Gong Li's sexuality with exotic, mysterious locations in 1930s China was clearly targeted at Western rather than Chinese audiences. Chinese like to point out that the figure-hugging Chinese dresses regularly worn by Gong Li are entirely unlike the period costume they purport to represent.

One of Zhang's most powerful – and from the point of view of the Chinese authorities, controversial – films is **To Live** (1994), which follows the fortunes of a single family from the final, decadent years of the old regime, right through the Communist era to the present day. The various stages of Mao's Communist experiment, from "liberation" to the Great Leap Forward and the Cultural Revolution, are depicted in terms of the disasters they bring upon the family, including the traumatic deaths of both children in needless accidents for which the regime seems to be responsible. The essence of the story is that life cannot be lived to prescription. Its power lies in the fact that it is a very real reflection of the experience of millions of Chinese people. Similarly, Chen Kaige's superb **Farewell My Concubine** (1994) incorporates the whole span of modern Chinese history, and although the main protagonist – a homosexual Chinese opera singer – is hardly typical of modern China, the tears aroused by the film are wept for the country as a whole. **Not One Less** (1998) re-creates the true story of a country teacher who travels to the city to track down a pupil who has run away. All the characters are portrayed by themselves and give magnificent performances, but ultimately the film is sentimental, suggesting that Zhang is losing his progressive edge.

Inevitably, the fifth generation was followed by a sixth, who castigated their predecessors for being too bland, for selling out to commercial interests and giving the West a false image of China. The sixth generation produced underground movies, generally shot in black and white, depicting what they consider to be the true story of contemporary China – ugly cities, cold flats, broke and depressed people. One of these, **Beijing Bastards**, had a role for the famous rock singer and rebel **Cui Jian**, who is depicted drinking, swearing and playing the guitar. Unsurprisingly, the Sixth Generation fared even worse than the Fifth in terms of getting its work screened in China, and had to rely on foreign funds for production.

In recent years, most Chinese directors, sadly, have concentrated on trying to mimic Hollywood slickness. Appalling propaganda films are still being made and are actually quite entertaining if approached in the spirit of irony. **Opium War** shows the British employing all kinds of underhand tactics to secure Hong Kong. Those naughty Brits are at it again in **Red Valley**, this time invading Tibet. Fortunately, there are also plenty of genuinely good films still being made. Notable is **In the Heat of the Sun, directed by Jiang Wen**, which chronicles the antics of a Beijing street gang in the 1970s. It's written by Wang Shuo, the bad boy of contemporary Chinese literature, and displays his characteristic irreverence and earthy humour. **Lei Feng is Gone** is based on the true story of the man who accidentally killed the iconic hero of Maoist China, the soldier Lei Feng. The potent personal story also works as a metaphor for the state of the nation, and as such was highly controversial when it was released. **Xiao Wu**, the intimate portrayal of a pickpocket, is a fantastic film that has never been shown in China as it takes no moral stance against its criminal main character. Its young director, **Jia Zhangke**, is a rising star to watch for. The hottest commercial director is **Feng Xiaogang**, who makes mainstream but intelligent genre comedies; look out for *Be There or Be Square*, *Sorry Baby* and *Big Shot's Funeral*.

At present, though, the most famous Chinese director is **Ang Lee**, who is Taiwanese. His domestic comedies (*The Wedding Banquet*; *Eat, Drink, Man, Woman*; *Sense and Sensibility* and *The Ice Storm*) are touching and well observed, but his most well-known picture is *Crouching Tiger, Hidden Dragon*, where a Hollywood slickness (and budget) is added to a typical Chinese martial-arts yarn. Perhaps it seemed rather more novel to Western audiences than it actually was (Chinese audiences were unimpressed and it drew poor reviews on the mainland), but its popularity abroad showed that Chinese film has become a significant force in world cinema.

Hong Kong

The movies which have the least difficulty with the Chinese censors are those produced in **Hong Kong**, the world's third largest movie producer, behind

India and the USA. Hong Kong film-makers, despite their profligate output, have avoided awkward political subjects, presumably for commercial reasons. Indeed, there was little indication that, with their home-grown, high-speed, action-comedy format, they were interested in the rest of the world at all, until the arrival of **John Woo** in 1985, with his film *A Better Tomorrow*, starring the manly Chow Yun Fat alongside a natural counterpart, the effeminate Leslie Cheung. Woo's work (and that of the dare-devil stuntman and comic actor, Jackie Chan) has been credited with inspiring the films of Quentin Tarantino; Woo introduced a whole new class of camera dexterity to the genre, and began specializing in mind-boggling special effects of explosions and scenes of reckless violence. **Hard Boiled** and **Bullet in the Head** are his best creations, masterpieces of relentless, beautiful savagery. In 1992, Hong Kong lost Woo to the financial lure of Hollywood but in the meantime Jackie Chan, Chow Yun Fat and Leslie Cheung have become international megastars, particularly in mainland China, where Hong Kong films have taken to outgrossing their Hollywood rivals.

Although the Hong Kong film industry is almost entirely devoted to entertainment rather than "art", there has been interaction with the more earnest mainland directors. Leslie Cheung played the leading role in *Farewell My Concubine*, and actress Gong Li appears regularly in Hong Kong blockbusters. There is, however, only one important Hong Kong director seriously interested in the avant-garde, and his work has led him in a totally different direction from that of his mainland counterparts. **Wong Karwai**, in his extraordinary films *Chungking Express*, *Fallen Angels*, *Happy Together* and *In the Mood for Love*, with their blurred-motion shots, coffee-bar soundtracks and disjointed plots depicting a disjointed society, is right at the cutting edge of modern film-making.

Books

The following is a personal selection of the books that have proved most useful during the preparation of this guide. Don't expect to find much variety of English-language reading available in China, even in Hong Kong. Translations of some of the great classics of Chinese literature are published in Britain and the US, however; there are also a good many cheap editions published by the Foreign Languages Press (FLP) and Panda Books in Beijing, which you'll find in the foreign-language sections of bookshops in China. We've not listed the publishers below except for titles which are produced in mainland China or other parts of the Far East (in the latter case we also give the country of publication). Titles marked ★ are particularly recommended, while those marked o/p are out of print.

History

Patricia Ebrey *Cambridge Illustrated History of China.* An up-to-date, easy-going historical overview, excellently illustrated and clearly written.

Peter Fleming *The Siege at Peking.* An account of the events which led up to June 20, 1900, when the foreign legations in Beijing were attacked by the Boxers and Chinese imperial troops. The siege, which lasted 55 days, led to a watershed in China's relations with the rest of the world.

Peter Hopkirk *Foreign Devils on the Silk Road* and *The Great Game. Foreign Devils* is the story of the machinations of the various international booty-hunters and archeologists who operated in Eastern Turkestan and the Gobi Desert around the turn of the last century – essential for an appreciation of China's northwest regions. *The Great Game* is a hugely entertaining account of the nineteenth-century struggle between Britain and Russia for control of central Asia. In tracing the roots of the Chinese occupations of Tibet and Xinjiang, and also detailing what has invariably happened to foreign powers who have meddled with Afghanistan, it's also disturbingly topical.

Kong Demao *In The Mansion of Confucius' Descendants* (Beijing New World Press). Though rather turgidly written, this account of life in the Confucius mansion in Qufu, by one of Confucius' descendants, provides a rare insider's view of the life of aristocrats in imperial China.

Harrison Salisbury *The Long March* and *The New Emperors.* The former is a comprehensive account by the American China expert, who retraced the route of the actual march in 1983. Access to previously undisclosed archives and interviews with survivors throw new light on the march. The latter is a highly readable account of the lives of China's two twentieth-century "emperors", Mao Zedong and Deng Xiaoping, which tries to demonstrate that Communist rule in China is no more than an extension of the old imperial Mandate of Heaven.

Edgar Snow *Red Star Over China.* Definitive firsthand account of the early days of Mao and the Communist "bandits", written in 1936 after Snow, an American journalist, wriggled through the Guomindang blockade and spent months at the Red base in Shaanxi.

Sima Qian *Historical Records* (aka *Records of the Historian*; FLP). Written in the Han era, *Records* is a masterpiece, using contemporary court documents and oral tradition to illuminate key characters – everyone from emperors to famous con men – from Chinese history up to that point. Long discredited, Sima Qian's accounts have now been partial corroborated by recent archeology.

Jonathan Spence *The Gate of Heavenly Peace*, *The Search for Modern China* and *God's Chinese Son*. The first of these is a narrative tour de force which traces the history of twentieth-century China through the eyes of the men and women caught up in it – writers, revolutionaries, poets and politicians. One of the best books for getting to grips with China's complex modern history. *The Search for Modern China* is quite hard for a straight-through read, but it's compendious and authoritative and probably the best overall history of China available. Also difficult, *God's Chinese Son* tells the sensational story of the most terrible civil war in world history, the nineteenth-century Taiping Uprising, focusing on the extraordinary life of its leader, Hong Xiuquan, who saw himself as a modern-day Jesus Christ.

Justin Wintle *Rough Guide Chronicle: China*. Pocket-sized but surprisingly detailed timeline of China's history, the key events and people put neatly into context in a year-by-year format.

Sally Hovey Wriggins *Xuanzang*. Accessible biography of the famous Tang-dynasty monk, retracing his sixteen-year pilgrimage to India where he studied various Buddhist doctrines at their source, and his subsequent return to Xi'an with a caravan-load of scriptures.

Frances Wood *No Dogs and Not Many Chinese – Treaty Port Life in China*. A history of the foreign enclaves forced on China as a result of the Opium Wars, from their turbulent beginnings in the 1840s through to their demise as the Communists took power after World War II. Greatly enlivened by firsthand accounts and Wood's dry wit.

Tibet

John Avedon *In Exile from the Land of Snows*. A detailed and moving account of modern Tibetan history, covering both those who remained in the country and those who fled into exile. Required reading for anyone contemplating a trip.

Graham Coleman (ed) *A Handbook of Tibetan Culture: a Guide to Tibetan Centres and Resources Throughout the World*. The subtitle says it all; the book exhaustively documents cultural organizations, teaching centres and libraries across the globe which have a Tibetan focus. It also includes biographies of major Tibetan lamas, brief histories of the major schools of Tibetan Buddhism and an illustrated glossary.

Isabel Hilton *The Search for the Panchen Lama*. Details the whole sorry story of the search for the Eleventh Panchen Lama.

★ **Peter Hopkirk** *Trespassers on the Roof of the World: the Race for Lhasa*. Around the turn of the twentieth century, imperial Britain, with the help of a remarkable band of pundits and wallahs from the Indian Survey, was discreetly charting every nook of the most inaccessible part of the earth, the High Tibetan plateau. Peter Hopkirk has researched his subject thoroughly and come up with a highly readable account of this fascinating backwater of history.

David Snellgrove and Hugh Richardson *A Cultural History of Tibet.* An excellent and amazingly gripping introduction to early Tibetan history and religion. Especially good on the effects on ordinary people of the great events of history.

Culture and society

Catriona Bass *Inside the Treasure House.* An account of a year spent working in Tibet in the mid-1980s. The author eloquently explores the everyday lives of the Tibetans and their relationship with the Han Chinese.

David Bonavia *The Chinese: a Portrait.* A highly readable introduction to contemporary China, focusing on the human aspects as a balance to the socio-political trends. Highly recommended.

Jacques Gernet *Daily Life in China on the Eve of the Mongol Invasion 1250–1276.* Based on a variety of Chinese sources, including local gazetteers, letters and anecdotes, this is a fascinating and detailed survey of southern China under the Song, focusing on the capital, Hangzhou, then the largest and richest city in the world. Gernet also deals with the daily lives of a cross-section of society, from peasant to leisured gentry, covering everything from cookery to death.

★ **John Gittings** *Real China.* A series of essays on rural China giving a very different picture from the descriptions of the economic miracle that most Western commentators have focused on, though lacking in depth. The chapter on cannibalism during the Cultural Revolution is morbidly fascinating.

★ **Heinrich Harrer** *Seven Years in Tibet.* A classic account of a remarkable journey to reach Lhasa and of the years there prior to the Chinese invasion, when Harrer was tutor to the Fourteenth Dalai Lama. The book has some excellent observations of Tibetan life of the time, and has been made into a movie starring Brad Pitt.

Joe Studwell *The China Dream.* Mandatory reading for foreign business people in China, this is a cautionary tale, written in layman's terms, debunking the myth that there's easy money to be made from China's vast markets. A great read for anyone interested in business, economics or human greed.

Tiziano Terzani *Behind the Forbidden Door* (o/p). In 1980 Terzani was one of the first Western journalists to be allowed to live in China. He was kicked out after four years for the unacceptable honesty of his writing. There is no better evocation of the bad old days of the pre-reform years than this collection of essays on such varied subjects as the rebirth of kung fu, mass executions and the training of crickets.

Thubten Jigme and Colin Turnbull *Tibet, its History, Religion and People.* Co-authored by the brother of the Fourteenth Dalai Lama, this is the best account around of the traditional everyday lives of the Tibetan people.

★ **Zhang Xinxin and Sang Ye** *Chinese Lives.* This Studs Terkel-like series of first-person narratives from interviews with a broad range of Chinese people is both readable and informative, full of fascinating details of day-to-day existence that you won't read anywhere else.

Travel writing

Charles Blackmore *The Worst Desert on Earth*. Sergeant-majorly account of an arduous and possibly unique trip across the Taklamakan Desert in northwest China.

Mildred Cable with Francesca French *The Gobi Desert*. Cable and French were missionaries with the China Inland Mission in the early part of this century. *The Gobi Desert* is a poetic description of their life and travels in Gansu and Xinjiang, without the sanctimonious and patronizing tone adopted by some of their contemporary missionaries.

Peter Fleming *One's Company: a Journey to China* and *News from Tartary*. The first is an amusing account of a journey through Russia and Manchuria to China in the 1930s. En route, Peter Fleming (brother of Ian) encounters a wild assortment of Chinese and Japanese officials and the puppet emperor Henry Pu Yi himself. *News from Tartary* records a journey of 3500 miles across the roof of the world to Kashmir in 1935.

★ **Peter Hessler** *River Town – Two Years on the Yangtze*. Latest and one of the best of the mini-genre "how I taught English for a couple of years in China and survived". Thoughtful and well written, the book accepts China's positive aspects without becoming romantic, and also avoids cynicsm when dealing with the country's ingrained social problems and inherent contradictions. Especially worth a read if you're planning a lengthy stay in China.

Somerset Maugham *On a Chinese Screen*. Brief, sometimes humorous and often biting sketches of the European missionaries, diplomats and businessmen whom Maugham encountered in China between 1919 and 1921; worth reading for background detail.

★ **Marco Polo** *The Travels*. Said to have inspired Columbus, *The Travels* is a fantastic read, full of amazing details picked up during his 26 years of wandering in Asia between Venice and the court of Kublai Khan. It's not, however, a coherent history, having been ghost-written by a novelist from notes supplied by Marco Polo.

Vikram Seth *From Heaven Lake: Travels through Sinkiang and Tibet*. A student for two years at Nanjing University, Seth set out in 1982 to return home to Delhi via Tibet and Nepal. This account of how he hitched his way through four provinces, Xinjiang, Gansu, Qinghai and Tibet, is in the best tradition of the early travel books.

Colin Thubron *Behind the Wall*. A thoughtful and superbly poetic description of an extensive journey through China just after it opened up in the early 1980s. This is the single best piece of travel writing to have come out of modern China.

Simon Winchester *The River at the Centre of the World: a Journey Up the Yangtze and Back in Chinese Time*. An account of the author's journey from the mouth of the Yangtze to its source in Tibet, recounting Chinese history, – most of it twentieth century, despite the title – along the way.

Guides and reference books

Stephen Bachelor *The Tibet Guide.* Illustrated with glorious photos, the guide gives a scholarly and detailed account of the main temples and monasteries across Tibet.

Victor Chan *Tibet Handbook: a Pilgrimage Guide.* A hugely detailed guide to the pilgrimage sites and treks and how to reach them. Absolutely essential if you're considering a trek.

Kit Chow and Ione Kramer *All the Tea in China.* Everything you need to know about Chinese teas, from variations in growing and processing techniques to a rundown of fifty of the most famous brews. Good fun and nicely illustrated.

Rodolphe De Schauensee *Birds of China.* About the only portable book on Chinese birds that could be used as a field guide, though the illustrations are selective and patchy in quality.

Zhao Ji *The Natural History of China.* A mine of beautiful photographs of rare wildlife, though the text is disappointingly general through obsessively trying to mention as many species as possible.

Gary McCue *Trekking in Tibet: a Traveller's Guide.* Essential reading, together with Chan, above, for anyone planning on trekking during their stay in Tibet. The maps are especially clear and useful, and there are excellent ideas for day treks.

Jessica Rawson *Ancient China: Art and Archaeology.* By an oriental antiquities specialist at the British Museum, this scholarly introduction to Chinese art puts the subject in its historical context. Beginning in Neolithic times, the book explores the technology and social organization which shaped its development up to the Han dynasty.

Mary Tregear *Chinese Art.* Authoritative summary of the main strands in Chinese art from Neolithic times, through the Bronze Age and up to the twentieth century. Clearly written and well illustrated.

Cookery

★ **Hsiang Ju Lin and Tsuifeng Lin** *Chinese Gastronomy* (o/p). A classic work, relatively short on recipes but strong on cooking methods and philosophy – essential reading for anyone serious about learning the finer details of Chinese cooking. Wavers in and out of print, sometimes under different titles; look for Lin as the author name.

★ **Kenneth Lo** *Chinese Food.* Good general-purpose cookbook covering a wide range of methods and styles, from Westernized dishes to regional specialities.

Wang Wenqiao and Gang Wenbin *Chinese Vegetarian Cuisine* (New World Press). Compendium of Chinese vegetarian cooking, from simple dishes like boiled beans with ginger to complex, imitation meat dishes such as sweet-and-sour "spareribs". The recipes are derived from the famous *Gongdelin* restaurant in Beijing.

Wei Chuan Cultural Education Foundation *Vegetarian Cooking* and *Chinese Dim Sum* (Chin Chin, Taiwan). Two in a series of a score or more of excellent, easy-to-follow cookbooks published by the Taiwanese Wei Chuan cooking school; simplified versions of classic dishes produce good results. Not available in China, but easy enough to find in major bookstores in the West.

Martial arts

Paul Brecher *Principles of Tai Chi* and *Secrets of Energy Work*. Two excellent books by a long-time internal martial artist: the first maps out the fundamentals behind *tai ji*, whichever style you practice; the second is a manual on using *qigong* for health.

Kumar Frantzis *The Power of Internal Martial Arts*. Trawl through Frantzis' forty years of experience studying the internal martial arts in Japan, China, Taiwan and the US, with personal accounts of different masters and their styles. Articulate and interesting even if you don't know your *li* from your *jing*, though fellow practitioners will find plenty of gems.

Erle Montaigue *Power Taiji*. For those that think *tai ji* is just a series of pretty movements, this book – based on the Yang long form – lifts the lid on an infinitely subtle art that can be used for both healing or combat.

Wang Xuanjie and J. Moffett *Traditional Chinese Theraputic Exercises – Standing Pole* (FLP). Straightforward introduction to one of the most popular and effective forms of *qigong*, and one which requires no athletic ability.

Religion and philosophy

Asiapac series (Asiapac Books, Singapore). These entertaining titles, available in Hong Kong and Beijing, present ancient Chinese philosophy in comic-book format, making it accessible without losing its complexity. They are all well written and well drawn. Particularly good is the *Book of Zen*, a collection of stories and parables, and the *Sayings of Confucius*.

Kenneth Chen *Buddhism in China*. Very helpful for tracing the origin of Buddhist thought in China, the development of its many different schools and the four-way traffic of influence between India, Tibet, Japan and China.

Confucius *The Analects*. Good modern translation of this classic text, a collection of Confucius's teachings focusing on morality and the state.

Lao Zi *Tao Te Ching*. The collection of mystical thoughts and philosophical speculation that forms the basis of Taoist philosophy.

Arthur Waley (trans) *Three Ways of Thought in Ancient China*. Translated extracts from the writings of three of the early philosophers – Zhuang Zi, Mencius and Han Feizi. A useful introduction.

Biographies and autobiographies

Anchee Min *Red Azalea*. Half-autobiography, half-novel, this beautifully written book is an unusually personal and highly romantic account of surviving the Cultural Revolution.

Ba Jin *Family*. Born in 1904 into a wealthy Chengdu family, Ba Jin attacks the old family feudal system, chronicles his anarchist phase from age 15 until 1949 and traces the strong influence exerted on him by Russian writers such as Turgenev.

Dalai Lama *Freedom in Exile*. The autobiography of the charismatic,

Nobel Prize-winning Fourteenth Dalai Lama.

Richard Evans *Deng Xiaoping*. The basic handbook to understanding the motives and inspirations behind one of the most influential men in modern China.

Jung Chang *Wild Swans*. Enormously popular in the West, this family saga covering three generations was unsurprisingly banned in China for its honest account of the horrors of life in turbulent twentieth-century China. It serves as an excellent introduction to modern Chinese history, as well as being a good read.

★ **Ma Jian** *Red Dust*. Facing arrest for spiritual pollution, writer and artist Ma Jian escaped from Bejing to travel around China's remotest corners for three years in the 1980s, living off his wits, often in extreme poverty. The picaresque tale of this Kerouackian bum meandering across China in the first phase of its opening up is told in lively prose and offers the kind of insights only an alienated insider could garner.

Naisingoro Pu Yi *From Emperor to Citizen* (FLP). The autobiography of the young boy, born into the Qing imperial family and chosen by the Japanese to become the puppet emperor of the state of Manchukuo in 1931.

Philip Short *Mao: A Life*. Despite its length, an extremely readable account of Mao and his times – even if the Great Helmsman's ideologies are becoming ever less relevant in contemporary China.

Jonathan Spence *Emperor of China: Self Portrait of Kang Xi*. A magnificent portrait of the longest reigning and greatest emperor of modern China.

★ **Hugh Trevor-Roper** *Hermit of Peking: the Hidden Life of Sir Edmund Backhouse*. Sparked by Backhouse's thoroughly obscene memoirs, *Hermit of Peking* uses external sources in an attempt to uncover the facts behind the extraordinary and convoluted life of Edmund Backhouse – Chinese scholar, eccentric recluse and phenomenal liar – who lived in Beijing from the late nineteenth century until his death in 1944.

Marina Warner *The Dragon Empress*. Exploration of the life of Cixi, one of only two women rulers of China. Warner lays bare the complex personality of a ruthless woman whose conservatism, passion for power, vanity and greed had such great impact on the events which culminated in the collapse of the imperial ruling house and the founding of the republic.

Literature

Twentieth-century writing

★ **Pearl S. Buck** *The Good Earth*. The best story from a writer who grew up in China during the early twentieth century, *The Good Earth* follows the fortunes of the peasant Wang Lung from his wedding day to his dotage, as he struggles to hold onto his land for his family through a series of political upheavals.

Chen Yuanbin *The Story of Qiuju* (Panda Books). A collection of four tales of which the title story, about a peasant woman pushing for justice after her husband is assaulted by the village chief, was made into a film by award-winning director Zhang Yimou.

Deng Ming-Dao *Chronicles of Tao*. Pitched as a true story, this is a martial-arts novel aimed at Western audiences, based around the life of a Taoist monk growing up in China during the turbulent years before the Communists came to power.

Feng Jicai *The Miraculous Pigtail* (Panda Books). For Western readers, Feng Jicai is one of China's most accessible authors – compassionate, humorous, and uncomplicated – though his longer stories tend to sag with rather obvious morals.

Lao She *Rickshaw Boy* (FLP). One of China's great modern writers, who was driven to suicide during the Cultural Revolution. The story is a haunting account of a young rickshaw puller in pre-1949 Beijing.

★ **Lu Xun** *The True Story of Ah Q* (FLP). Widely read in China today, Lu Xun is regarded as the father of modern Chinese writing. *Ah Q* is one of his best tales, short, allegorical and cynical, about a simpleton who is swept up in the 1911 revolution.

Mo Yan *The Garlic Ballads*. Banned in China, this is a hard-hitting novel of rural life by one of China's greatest modern writers.

Amy Tan *The Joy Luck Club*. Uneven but moving story of four Chinese mothers and their first-generation daughters, chronicling the life of American Chinese with a perceptive touch and some brilliant set-pieces.

Wang Shuo *Playing For Thrills* and *Please Don't Call Me Human*. The enormously popular bad boy of contemporary Chinese literature, Wang Shuo writes in colourful Beijing dialect about the city's wide boys and chancers. *Playing For Thrills* is fairly representative – a mystery story whose boorish narrator spends most of his time drinking, gambling and chasing girls. Banned in mainland China, *Please Don't Call Me Human* is a biting satire portraying modern China as a place where pride is nothing and greed is everything, as the Party turns a dignified martial artist into a vacuous, emasculated dancer in order to win an Olympic gold medal.

Zhang Xianliang *Grass Soup* and *Half Man is Woman*. *Grass Soup* is a hellish account of the 22 years the author spent in Maoist labour camps, expanded from the cryptic diary entries he was able to make at the time. Far more uplifting, *Half Man is Woman* is a semi-autobiographical tale about Zhang's love affair with and subsequent marriage to a fellow prisoner. Often touching and romantic in Western eyes, the book caused a storm in China for its open treatment of sexuality.

Classics

Asiapac series (Asiapac Books, Singapore). Renders Chinese classics and folk tales into cartoon format. Titles include *Journey to the West*, *Tales of Laozhai* and *Chinese Eunuchs*.

Cyril Birch (ed) *Anthology of Chinese Literature from Earliest Times to the Fourteenth Century*. This survey spans three thousand years of literature, embracing poetry, philosophy, drama, biography and prose fiction, with interesting variations of translation.

Cao Xueqing and Gao E. *Dream of Red Mansions/Story of the Stone*. This intricate eighteenth-century tale of manners follows the fortunes of the Jia Clan through the emotionally charged adolescent lives of Jia Baoyu and his two girl cousins, Lin Daiyu and Xue Baochai. The full translation fills five paperbacks, but there's also a much simplified English version available in China.

★ **Luo Guanzhong** *Romance of the Three Kingdoms*. Despite being written 1200 years after the events it portrays, this vibrant tale vividly evokes the battles, political schemings and myths surrounding China's turbulent Three Kingdoms period. One of the world's great historical novels.

Shi Nai'an and Luo Guanzhong *Outlaws of the Marsh/ The Water Margin*. A heavy dose of popular legend as a group of Robin Hood-like outlaws take on the government in feudal times. If the full three-volume set is too much to plough through, try to find Pearl Buck's snappier though still large abridgement, *All Men are Brothers*, in your library.

★ **Wu Cheng'en** *Journey to the West* (FLP). Absurd, lively rendering of the Buddhist monk Xuanzang's pilgramage to India to collect sacred scriptures, aided by Sandy, Pigsy and the irrepressible Sun Wu Kong, the monkey king. Arthur Waley's version, *Monkey*, retains the tale's spirit while shortening the hundred-chapter opus to paperback length.

Language

Language

Chinese

As the **most widely spoken** language on earth, Chinese can hardly be overlooked. Chinese is, strictly speaking, a series of **dialects** spoken by the dominant ethnic group within China, the Han. Indeed, the term most commonly used by the Chinese themselves to refer to the language is **hanyu**, meaning "Han-language", though *zhongyu*, *zhongwen* and *zhongguohua* are frequently used as well. However, non-Han peoples such as Uigurs and Tibetans speak languages which have little or nothing to do with Chinese.

The dialects of *hanyu* are a complicated story in themselves. Some of them are mutually unintelligible and – where the spoken word is concerned – have about as much in common as, say, German and English. The better-known and most distinct dialects include those spoken around China's coastal fringes, such as **Shanghainese** (*shanghai hua*), **Fujianese** (*minnan hua*) and **Cantonese** (*guangdong hua* or *yueyu*), though even within the areas covered by these dialects you'll find huge local divergences. Cantonese and Fujianese are themselves languages of worldwide significance, being the dialects spoken by the people of Hong Kong and among Overseas Chinese communities, particularly those in Southeast Asia.

What enables Chinese from different parts of the country to converse with each other is **Mandarin Chinese**. Historically based on the language of Han officialdom in the Beijing area, Mandarin has been systematically promoted over the past hundred years to be the official, unifying language of the Chinese people, much as modern French, for example, is based on the original Parisian dialect. It is known in mainland China as **putonghua** – "common language" – and in Taiwan (and also remoter corners of China) as *guoyu* – "national language". As the language of education, government and the media, Mandarin is understood to a greater or lesser extent by the vast majority of Han Chinese, and by many non-Han as well, though there are two caveats to this generalization: first, that knowledge of Mandarin is far more common among the young, the educated and the urban-dwelling; and second, that many people who understand Mandarin cannot actually speak it. For example, the chances of the average Tibetan peasant being able to speak Mandarin are extremely small. In Hong Kong and Macau, likewise, there has been until recently very little Mandarin spoken, though this situation is now changing fast.

Another element tying the various dialects together is the Chinese **script**. No matter how different two dialects may sound when spoken, once they are written down in the form of Chinese characters they become mutually comprehensible again, as the different dialects use the same written characters. A sentence of Cantonese, for example, written down beside a sentence of the same meaning in Mandarin, will look broadly similar except for occasional unusual words or structures. Having said this, it should be added that some non-Han peoples use their own scripts, and apart from Cantonese it is unusual to see Chinese dialects written down at all. Most Chinese people, in fact, associate the written word inextricably with Mandarin.

From the point of view of foreigners, the main distinguishing characteristic of Chinese is that it is a **tonal** language: in order to pronounce a word correctly, it is necessary to know not only its sound but also its correct tone.

Despite initial impressions, there is nothing too difficult about learning the basics of communication, however, and being able to speak even a few words of Chinese can mean the difference between a successful trip and a nightmare. Given the way tones affect meaning – and the fact that individual characters are monosyllabic – accuracy in **pronounciation** is particularly important in Chinese, for which an understanding of the **pinyin** phonetic system is vital (see opposite). For advance **teach-yourself** grounding in spoken Mandarin, try *Hugo's Chinese in Three Months*, which includes *pinyin* transliteration and tapes and, while a bit dry, is wider in its approach than purely business- or travel-oriented alternatives. On the road, the Rough Guide *Mandarin Chinese Dictionary Phrasebook* provides useful words and phrases in both *pinyin* and characters, while Langenscheidt's *Pocket Dictionary Chinese* is – for its size – perhaps the best available **dictionary** of colloquial usage. Once you're in China, you'll find that any bookshop will have a huge range of inexpensive Chinese–English dictionaries, and perhaps livelier teach-yourself texts than are available overseas.

Chinese characters

There are tens of thousands of **Chinese characters**, in use since at least the Shang dynasty (1600–1100BC), though the vast majority of these are obsolete – you need about 2500 to read a newspaper, and even educated Chinese are unlikely to know more than ten thousand. The characters themselves are **pictograms**, each representing a **concept** rather than a specific pronunciation. This is similar to the use of numerals: there is nothing in the figure "2" which spells out the pronunciation; having learned what the symbol means, we simply know how to say it – whether "two" in English, "deux" in French, and so on. Similarly, Chinese speakers have to memorize the sounds of individual characters, and the meanings attached to them. While the sounds might vary from region to region, the meanings themselves do not – which is how the written word cuts through regional variations in language.

Although to untrained eyes many Chinese characters seem impossibly complex, there is a logic behind their structure which helps in their memorization. Firstly, each character is written using an exact number of brush (or pen) **strokes**: thus the character for "mouth", which forms a square, is always written using only three strokes: first the left side, then the top and right side together, and finally the base. Secondly, characters can very broadly be broken up into two components, which often also exist as characters in their own right: a **main** part, which frequently gives a clue as to the pronunciation; and a **radical**, which usually appears on the left side of the character and which vaguely categorizes the meaning. As an example, the character for "mother" is made up of the character for "horse" (to which it sounds similar), combined with a radical which means "female". In a few cases, it's easy to see the connection between the pictogram and its meaning – the character *mu*, wood, resembles a tree – though others require some lateral thinking or have become so abstract or complex that the meaning is hidden.

Given the time and difficulty involved in **learning characters**, and the negative impact this has had on the general level of literacy, the government of the People's Republic announced in 1954 that a couple of thousand of the most common characters were to be, quite literally, **simplified**, making them not only easier to learn but also quicker to write, as the new characters often use far fewer penstrokes. This drastic measure was not without controversy. Some argued that by interfering with the original structure of the characters, vital clues as to their meaning and pronunciation would be lost, making them harder than ever to learn. These simplified characters were eventually adopted not just in mainland China but also in Singapore; but Hong Kong and Taiwan, as well as many overseas Chinese communities, continue to use the older, traditional forms.

Today, ironically, the traditional forms are also making a **comeback** on the mainland, where they are now seen as sophisticated. Note that some of these traditional forms differ considerably from the simplified forms provided in this book, though their meaning and pronunciation are identical.

Grammar

Chinese **grammar** is relatively simple. There is no need to conjugate verbs, decline nouns or make adjectives agree – being attached to immutable Chinese characters, Chinese words simply cannot have different "endings". Instead, context and fairly rigid rules about word order are relied on to make those distinctions of time, number and gender that Indo-European languages are so concerned with. Instead of cumbersome tenses, the Chinese make use of words such as "yesterday" or "tomorrow"; instead of plural endings they simply state how many things there are, or use quantifier words equivalent to "some" or "many".

Word formation is affected by the fact that the meanings of many Chinese characters have become diffuse over time. For instance, there is a single character, pronounced *ju* with the third tone in Mandarin, which is a verb meaning "to lift", "to start" or "to choose", an adjective meaning "whole" and a noun meaning "deed". In a very dim way we might perhaps see the underlying meaning of *ju* on its own, but to make things clear in practice, many concepts are referred to not by single characters but by combining two or more characters together like building blocks. In the case of *ju* above, the addition of character for "world" creates a word meaning "throughout the world"; and the addition of "eye" creates a word meaning "look".

For English speakers, **Chinese word order** follows the familiar subject-verb-object pattern, and you'll find that by simply stringing words together you'll be producing fairly grammatical Chinese. Just note that adjectives, as well as all qualifying and describing phrases, precede nouns.

Pronunciation and pinyin

Back in the 1950s it was hoped eventually to replace Chinese characters altogether with a regular alphabet of Roman letters, and to this end the **pinyin** system was devised. Basically, *pinyin* is a way of using the Roman alphabet (except the letter "v") to write out the sounds of Mandarin Chinese, with Mandarin's four tones represented by **accents** above each syllable. Other dialects of Chinese, such as Cantonese – having nine tones – cannot be written in *pinyin*.

The aim of replacing Chinese characters with *pinyin* was abandoned long ago, but in the meantime *pinyin* has one very important function, that of helping foreigners to pronounce Chinese words. However, in *pinyin* the letters do not all have the sounds you would expect, and you'll need to spend an hour or two learning these. You'll often see *pinyin* in China, on street signs and shop displays, but only well-educated locals know the system well. Occasionally, you will come across **other systems** of rendering Mandarin into Roman letters, such as **Wade-Giles**, which writes Mao Zedong as Mao Tse-tung, and Deng Xiaoping as Teng Hsiao-p'ing. These forms are no longer used in mainland China, but you may see them in Western books about China, or in Taiwanese publications.

The Chinese terms in this book have been given both in characters and in *pinyin*; the pronunciation guide below is your first step to making yourself comprehensible. Don't get overly paranoid about your tones: with the help of context, intelligent listeners should be able to work out what you are trying to say. If you're just uttering a single word, however, for example a place name – without a context – you need to hit exactly the right tone, otherwise don't be surprised if nobody understands you.

The tones

There are **four tones** in Mandarin Chinese, and every syllable of every word is characterized by one of them, except for a few syllables which are considered toneless. This emphasis on tones does not make Chinese a particularly musical language – English, for example, uses all of the tones of Chinese and many more. The difference is that English uses tone for effect – exclaiming, questioning, listing, rebuking and so on. In English, to change the tone is to change the mood or the emphasis; in Chinese, to change the tone is to change the word itself.

First or "High" *ā ē ī ō ū*. In English this level tone is used when mimicking robotic or very boring, flat voices.

Second or "Rising" *á é í ó ú*. Used in English when asking a question showing surprise, for example "eh?".

Third or "Falling-rising" *ǎ ě ǐ ǒ ǔ*. Used in English when echoing someone's words with a measure of incredulity. For example, "John's dead." "De-ad?!".

Fourth or "Falling" *à è ì ò ù*. Often used in English when counting in a brusque manner – "One! Two! Three! Four!".

Toneless A few syllables do not have a tone accent. These are pronounced without emphasis, such as in the English **u**pon.

Note that if there are two consecutive characters with the third tone, the first character is pronounced as though it carries the second tone.

Consonants

Most consonants are pronounced in a similar way to their English equivalents, with the following exceptions:

c as in ha**ts**
g is hard as in **g**od (except when preceded by "n" when it sounds like sa**ng**)
q as in **ch**eese
x has no direct equivalent in English, but you can make the sound by sliding from an "s" sound to a "sh" sound and stopping midway between the two
z as in su**ds**
zh as in fu**dge**

Vowels and diphthongs

As in most languages, the vowel sounds are rather harder to quantify than the consonants. The examples here give a rough description of the sound of each vowel followed by related combination sounds.

a usually somewhere between f**a**r and m**a**n
ai as in **eye**
ao as in c**ow**
e usually as in f**ur**
ei as in g**ay**
en is an unstressed sound as at the end of hyph**en**
eng as in s**ung**
er as in f**ur** (ie with a stressed "r")
i usually as in t**ea**, except in *zi*, *ci*, *si*, *ri*, *zhi*, *chi* and *shi*, when it is a short clipped sound like the American military "sir"
ia as in **ya**k
ian as in **yen**
ie as in **yeah**
o as in b**o**re
ou as in sh**ow**
ü as in the German ü (make an "ee" sound and glide slowly into an "oo"; at the mid-point between the two sounds you should hit the ü-sound)
u usually as in f**oo**l except where *u* follows j, q, x or y, when it is always pronounced **ü**
ua as in s**ua**ve
uai as in **why**
ue as though contracting "you" and "air" together, **you'air**
ui as in **way**
uo as in **wo**re

Useful words and phrases

Chinese put their **family names first** followed by their given names, exactly the reverse of Western convention. The vast majority of Chinese family names comprise a single character, while given names are either one or two characters long. So a man known as Zhang Dawei has the family name of Zhang, and the given name of Dawei.

When asked for their name, the Chinese tend to provide either just their family name, or their whole name. In **formal situations**, you might come across the terms "Mr" (*xiansheng*), "Mrs" (*taitai*, though this is being replaced by the more neutral term *airen*) or "Miss" (*xiaojie*), which are attached after the family name: for example, Mr Zhang is *zhang xiansheng*. In more casual encounters, people use familiar terms such as "old" (*lao*) or "young" (*xiao*) attached in front of the family name, though "old" or "young" are more relative terms of status than indications of actual age in this case: Mr Zhang's friend might call him "Lao Zhang", for instance.

Basics

I	我	wǒ
You (singular)	你	nǐ
He	他	tā
She	她	tā
We	我们	wǒmén
You (plural)	你们	nǐmén
They	他们	tāmén
I want...	我要	wǒ yào...
No, I don't want...	我不要	wǒ bú yào...
Is it possible...?	可不可以.....?	kěbùkěyǐ....?
It is (not) possible.	(不)可以	(bù) kěyǐ
Is there any/Have you got any...?	有没有.....?	yǒuméiyoǔ...?
There is/I have.	有	yǒu
There isn't/I haven't.	没有	méiyǒu
Please help me	请帮我忙	qǐng bāng wǒ máng
Mr...	.....先生	xiānshēng
Mrs...	.....太太	tàitài
Miss...	.....小姐	xiǎojiě

Communicating

I don't speak Chinese.	我不会说中文	wǒ bú huì shuō zhōngwén
My Chinese is terrible.	我的中文很差	wǒ de zhōngwén hěn chà
Can you speak English?	你会说英语吗?	nǐ huì shuō yīngyǔ ma?
Can you get someone who speaks English?	请给我找一个会说英语的人	qǐng gěi wǒ zhǎo yí ge huì shuō yīngyǔ de rén?
Please speak slowly.	请说地慢一点	qǐng shuōde màn yīdiǎn
Please say that again.	请再说一遍	qǐng zài shuō yí biàn
I understand.	我听得懂	wǒ tīngdedǒng
I don't understand.	我听不懂	wǒ tīngbudǒng
I can't read Chinese characters	我看不懂汉字	wǒ kànbudóng hànzi
What does this mean?	这是什么意思?	zhè shì shěnme yìsi?
How do you pronounce this character?	这个字怎么念?	zhè ge zì zénme niàn?

Greetings and basic courtesies

Hello/How do you do/ How are you?	你好	nǐ hǎo
I'm fine.	我很好	wǒ hěn hǎo
Thank you.	谢谢	xièxie
Don't mention it/ You're welcome	不客气	búkèqi
Sorry to bother you...	麻烦你	máfan nǐ
Sorry/I apologize.	对不起	duìbùqǐ
It's not important/ No problem.	没关系	méi guānxi
Goodbye.	再见	zài jiàn

Chitchat

What country are you from?	你是哪个国家的?	nǐ shì ná ge guójiā de?
Britain	英国	yīngguó
Ireland	爱尔兰	àiérlán
America	美国	měiguó
Canada	加拿大	jiānădà
Australia	澳大利亚	àodàlìyà
New Zealand	新西兰	xīnxīlán
China	中国	zhōngguó
Outside China	外国	wàiguó
What's your name?	你叫什么名字?	nǐ jiào shěnme míngzi?
My name is...	我叫....	wǒ jiào...
Are you married?	你结婚了吗?	nǐ jiéhūn le ma?
I am (not) married.	我(没有)结婚(了)	wó (méiyoǔ) jiéhūn
Have you got (children)?	你有没有孩子?	nǐ yǒu méiyǒu háizi?
Do you like...?	你喜不喜欢.....?	nǐ xǐ bù xǐhuan....?
I (don't) like...	我不喜欢....	wǒ (bù) xǐhuan...
What's your job?	你干什么工作?	nǐ gàn shěnme gōngzuò?
I'm a foreign student.	我是留学生	wǒ shì liúxuéshēng
I'm a teacher.	我是老师	wǒ shì lǎoshī
I work in a company.	我在一个公司工作	wǒ zài yí ge gōngsī gōngzuò
I don't work.	我不工作	wǒ bù gōngzuò
Clean/dirty	干净/脏	gānjìng/zāng

Hot/cold	热/冷	rè/lěng
Fast/slow	快/慢	kuài/màn
Pretty	漂亮	piàoliang
Interesting	有意思	yǒuyìsi

Numbers

Zero	零	líng
One	一	yī
Two	二/两	èr/liǎng*
Three	三	sān
Four	四	sì
Five	五	wǔ
Six	六	liù
Seven	七	qī
Eight	八	bā
Nine	九	jiǔ
Ten	十	shí
Eleven	十一	shíyī
Twelve	十二	shíèr
Twenty	二十	èrshí
Twenty-one	二十一	èrshíyī
One hundred	一百	yībǎi
Two hundred	二百	èrbǎi
One thousand	一千	yīqiān
Ten thousand	一万	yīwàn
One hundred thousand	十万	shíwàn
One million	一百万	yībǎiwàn
One hundred million	一亿	yīyì
One billion	十亿	shíyì

*liáng is used when enumerating, for example "two people" liǎng ge rén. èr is used when counting.

Time

Now	现在	xiànzài
Today	今天	jīntiān
(In the) morning	早上	zǎoshàng
(In the) afternoon	下午	xiàwǔ
(In the) evening	晚上	wǎnshàng
Tomorrow	明天	míngtiān
The day after tomorrow	后天	hòutiān
Yesterday	昨天	zuótiān
Week/month/year	星期/月/年	xīngqī/yuè/nián
Monday	星期一	xīngqī yī
Tuesday	星期二	xīngqī èr
Wednesday	星期三	xīngqī sān
Thursday	星期四	xīngqī sì
Friday	星期五	xīngqī wǔ
Saturday	星期六	xīngqī liù
Sunday	星期天	xīngqī tiān
What's the time?	几点了?	jǐdiǎn le?
10 o'clock	十点钟	shídiǎn zhōng
10.20	十点二十	shídiǎn èrshí
10.30	十点半	shídiǎn bàn

Travelling and getting about town

North	北	běi
South	南	nán
East	东	dōng
West	西	xī
Airport	机场	jīchǎng
Ferry dock	船码头	chuánmǎtóu
Left luggage office	寄存处	jìcún chù
Ticket office	售票处	shòupiào chù
Ticket	票	piào
Can you buy me a ticket to...?	可不可以给我买到.....的票?	kěbùkěyǐ gěi wǒ mǎi dào... de piào?
I want to go to...	我想到.....去	wǒ xiǎng dào ... qù
I want to leave at (8 o'clock)	我想(八点钟)离开	wǒ xiǎng (bā diǎn zhōng) líkāi
When does it leave?	什么时候出发?	shěnme shíhòu chūfā?
When does it arrive?	什么时候到?	shěnme shíhòu dào?
How long does it take?	路上得多长时间?	lùshàng děi duōcháng shíjiān?
CAAC	中国民航	zhōngguó mínháng
CITS	中国国际旅行社	zhōngguó guójì lǚxíngshè
Train	火车	huǒchē
(Main) Train station	主要火车站	(zhǔyào) huǒchēzhàn
Bus	公共汽车	gōnggòng qìchēzhàn
Bus station	汽车站	qìchēzhàn
Long distance bus station	长途汽车站	chángtú qìchēzhàn
Hard seat	硬座	yìngzuò
Soft seat	软座	ruǎnzuò
Hard sleeper	硬卧	yìngwò
Soft sleeper	软卧	ruǎnwò
Soft seat waiting room	软卧候车室	ruánzuò hòuchēshì
Upgrade ticket	补票	bǔpiào
Platform	站台	zhàntaí
Express train/bus	特快车	tèkuài chē
Fast train/bus	快车	kuài chē
Ordinary train/bus	普通车	pǔtōng chē
Minibus	小车	xiǎo chē

Getting about town

Map	地图	dìtú
Where is...?	......在哪里?	...zài nǎlǐ?
Go straight on	往前走	wàng qián zǒu
Turn right	往右拐	wàng yòu guǎi
Turn left	往左拐	wàng zuǒ guǎi
Taxi	出租车	chūzū chē
Please use the meter	请打开记价器	qǐng dǎkāi jìjiàqì
Underground/Subway station	地铁站	dìtiě zhàn
Rickshaw	三轮车	sānlún chē
Bicycle	自行车	zìxíngchē
I want to rent a bicycle	我想租自行车	wǒ xiǎng zū zìxíngchē
How much is it per hour?	一个小时得多少钱?	yí gè xiǎoshí děi duōshǎo qián?

Can I borrow your bicycle?	能不能借你的自行车	néng bùnéng jiè nǐ de zìxíngchē?
Bus	公共汽车	gōnggòngqìchē
Which bus goes to...?	几路车到......去?	jǐ lù chē dào … qù?
Number (10) bus	(十)路车	(shí) lù chē
Does this bus go to...?	这车到......去吗?	zhè chē dào … qù ma?
When is the next bus?	下一班车几点开?	xià yì bān chē jǐ diǎn kāi?
The first bus	头班车	tóubān chē
The last bus	末班车	mòbān chē
Please tell me where to get off	请告诉我在哪里下车	qǐng gàosu wǒ zài nǎlǐ xià chē
Museum	博物馆	bówùguǎn
Temple	寺院	sìyuàn
Toilet (men's)	南厕所	nán cèsuǒ
Toilet (women's)	女厕所	nǚ cèsuǒ

Accommodation

Hotel (upmarket)	宾馆	bīnguǎn
Hotel (downmarket)	招待所，旅馆	zhāodàisuǒ, lǚguǎn
Hostel	旅社	lǚshè
Foreigner's guesthouse (at universities)	外国专家楼	wàiguó zhuānjiā loú
Is it possible to stay here?	能不能住在这里?	néng bù néng zhù zài zhèlǐ ?
Can I have a look at the room?	能不能看一下房间 ?	néng bù néng kàn yíxià fángjiān?
I want the cheapest bed you've got.	我要你最便宜的床位	wǒ yào nǐ zuì piányi de chuángwèi
Single room	单人间	dānrén jiān
Double room	双人间	shuāngrén jiān
Three-bed room	三人间	sānrén jiān
Dormitory	多人间	duōrén jiān
Suite	套房间	tàofángjiān
Bed	床位	chuángwèi
Passport	护照	hùzhào
Deposit	押金	yājīn
Key	钥匙	yàoshi
When is the hot water on?	什么时候有热水?	shénme shíhòu yǒu rèshuí?
I want to change my room	我想换一个房间	wǒ xiǎng huàn yí ge fángjiān

Shopping, money and banks, and visa extensions

How much is it?	这是多少钱?	zhè shì duōshǎo qián?
That's too expensive	太贵了	tài guì le
I haven't got any cash	我没有现金	wǒ méiyǒu xiànjīn
Have you got anything cheaper?	有没有便宜一点的?	yǒu méiyǒu pían yí yìdiǎn de?
Do you accept credit cards?	可不可以用信用卡?	kě bù kěyí yòng xìnyòngkǎ?
Department store	百货商店	bǎihuò shāngdián
Market	市场	shìchǎng
¥1 (RMB)	一块(人民币)	yí kuài (rénmínbì)
US$1	一块美金	yí kuài měijīn
£1	一个英磅	yí gè yīngbàng

HK$1	一块港币	yí kuài gǎngbì
Change money	换钱	huàn qián
Bank of China	中国银行	zhōngguó yínháng
Traveller's cheques	旅行支票	lǚxíngzhīpiào
PSB	公安局	gōng'ān jú

Mail and telephones

Post Office	邮电局	yóudiànjú
Envelope	信封	xìnfēng
Stamp	邮票	yóupiào
Airmail	航空信	hángkōngxìn
Surface mail	平信	píngxìn
Post restante	邮件侯领处	yóujiàn hòulǐngchù
Telephone	电话	diànhuà
International telephone call	国际电话	guójì diànhuà
Reverse charges/ collect call	对方付钱电话	duìfāngfùqián diànhuà
Fax	传真	chuánzhēn
Telephone card	电话卡	diànhuàkǎ
I want to make a telephone call to (Britain)	我想给(英国)打电话	wǒ xiǎng gěi (yīngguó) dǎ diànhuà
I want to send a fax to (USA)	我想给(美国)发一个传真	wǒ xiǎng gěi (měiguó) fā yí ge chuánzhēn
Can I receive a fax here?	能不能在这里收传真?	néng bù néng zài zhèlǐ shōu chuánzhēn

Health

Hospital	医院	yīyuàn
Pharmacy	药店	yàodiàn
Medicine	药	yào
Chinese medicine	中药	zhōngyào
Diarrhoea	腑泻	fǔxiè
Vomit	呕吐	outù
Fever	发烧	fāshāo
I'm ill	我生病了	wǒ shēngbìng le
I've got flu	我感冒了	wǒgǎnmào le
I'm (not) allergic to...	我对.....(不)过敏	wǒ duì ... (bù) guòmǐn
Antibiotics	抗生素	kàngshēngsù
Quinine	奎宁	kuíníng
Condom	避孕套	bìyùntào
Mosquito coil	蚊香	wénxing
Mosquito netting	蚊帐纱	wénzhàngshā

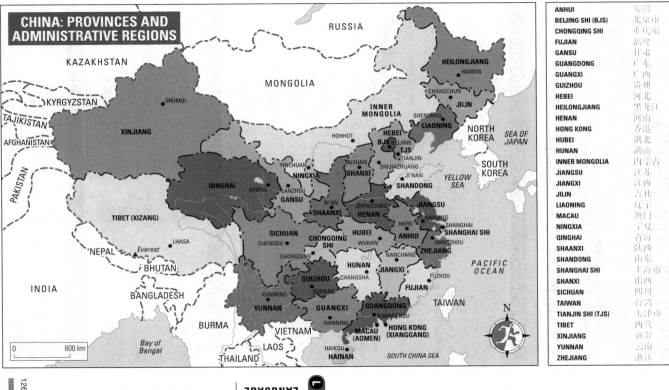

CHINA: PROVINCES AND ADMINISTRATIVE REGIONS

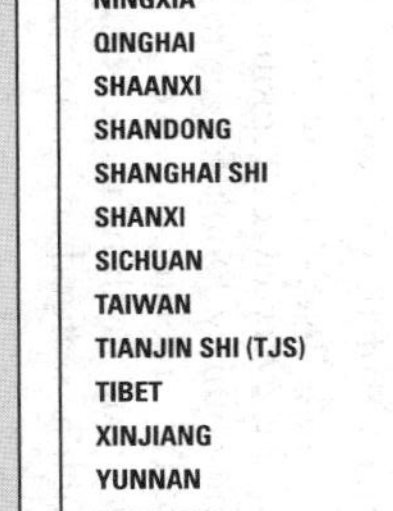

ANHUI	安徽
BEIJING SHI (BJS)	北京市
CHONGQING SHI	重庆市
FUJIAN	福建
GANSU	甘肃
GUANGDONG	广东
GUANGXI	广西
GUIZHOU	贵州
HEBEI	河北
HEILONGJIANG	黑龙江
HENAN	河南
HONG KONG	香港
HUBEI	湖北
HUNAN	湖南
INNER MONGOLIA	内蒙古
JIANGSU	江苏
JIANGXI	江西
JILIN	吉林
LIAONING	辽宁
MACAU	澳门
NINGXIA	宁夏
QINGHAI	青海
SHAANXI	陕西
SHANDONG	山东
SHANGHAI SHI	上海市
SHANXI	山西
SICHUAN	四川
TAIWAN	台湾
TIANJIN SHI (TJS)	天津市
TIBET	西藏
XINJIANG	新疆
YUNNAN	云南
ZHEJIANG	浙江

A food and drink glossary

The following lists should help out in deciphering the characters on a Chinese menu – if they're written clearly. If you know what you're after, try sifting through the staples and cooking methods to create your order, or sample one of the everyday or regional suggestions, many of which are available all over the country. Don't forget to tailor your demands to the capabilities of where you're ordering, however – a street cook with a wok isn't going to be able to whip up anything more complicated than a basic stir-fry. Note that some items, such as seafood and *jiaozi*, are ordered by weight.

General

Restaurant	餐厅	cāntīng
Chopsticks	筷子	kuàizi
House speciality	拿手好菜	náshǒuhǎocài
How much is that?	多少钱?	duōshǎo qián?
I don't eat (meat)	我不吃(肉)	wǒ bù chī (ròu)
I'm Buddhist/I'm vegetarian	我是佛教徒/我只吃素	wǒ shì fójiàotú/wǒ zhǐ chī sù
I would like...	我想要....	wǒ xiǎng yào...
Local dishes	地方菜	dìfāng cài
Menu/set menu/English menu	菜单/套菜/英文菜单	càidān/tàocài/yīngwén càidān
Small portion	少量	shǎoliàng
Spoon	勺	sháo
Waiter/waitress	服务员/小姐	fúwùyuán/xiǎojiě
Bill/cheque	买单	mǎidān
Cook these ingredients together	一快儿	yíkuàir
50 grams	两	liǎng
250 grams	半斤	bànjīn
500 grams	斤	jīn
1 kilo	公斤	gōngjīn

Drinks

Beer	啤酒	píjiǔ
Sweet fizzy drink	汽水	qìshuǐ
Coffee	咖啡	kāfēi
Tea	茶	chá
(Mineral) water	(矿泉)水	(kuàngquán) shuǐ
Wine	葡萄酒	pútáojiǔ
Spirits	白酒	báijiǔ
Soya milk	豆浆	dòujiāng

Staple foods

Aubergine	茄子	qiézi
Bamboo shoots	笋尖	sǔnjiān
Beans	豆	dòu
Bean sprouts	豆芽	dòuyá

Beef	牛肉	niúròu
Bitter gourd	葫芦	húlu
Black bean sauce	黑豆豉	hēidòuchǐ
Buns (plain)	馒头	mántou
Buns (filled)	包子	bāozi
Carrot	胡萝卜	húluóbo
Cashew nuts	坚果	jīanguǒ
Cauliflower	菜花	càihuā
Chicken	鸡	jī
Chilli	辣椒	làjiāo
Coriander (leaves)	香菜	xiāngcài
Crab	蟹	xiè
Cucumber	黄瓜	huángguā
Dog	狗肉	gǒuròu
Duck	鸭	yā
Eel	鳝鱼	shànyú
Fish	鱼	yú
Fried dough stick	油条	yóutiáo
Frog	田鸡	tiánjī
Garlic	大蒜	dàsuàn
Ginger	姜	jiāng
Green pepper (capsicum)	青椒	qīngjiāo
Green vegetables	绿叶素菜	lǜyè sùcài
Jiaozi (ravioli, steamed or boiled)	饺子	jiǎozi
Lamb	羊肉	yángròu
Lotus root	莲心	liánxīn
MSG	味精	wèijīng
Mushrooms	磨菇	mógū
Noodles	面条	miàntiáo
Omelette	炒鸡蛋	chǎojīdàn
Onions	洋葱	yángcōng
Oyster sauce	蚝油	háoyóu
Pancake	摊饼	tānbǐng
Peanut	花生	huāshēng
Pork	猪肉	zhūròu
Potato	土豆	tǔdòu
Prawns	虾	xiā
Preserved egg	皮蛋	pídàn
Rice, boiled	白饭	báifàn
Rice, fried	禾粉	héfěn
Rice noodles	炒饭	chǎofàn
Rice porridge (aka "congee")	粥	zhōu
Salt	盐	yán
Sesame oil	芝麻油	zhīma yóu
Shuijiao (ravioli in soup)	水铰	shuǐjiǎo
Sichuan pepper	四川辣椒	sìchuān làjiāo
Snails	蜗牛	wōniú
Snake	蛇肉	shéròu
Soup	汤	tāng
Star anise	茴香	huíxiāng
Straw mushrooms	草菇	cǎogū
Soy sauce	酱油	jiàngyóu

Sugar	糖	táng
Squid	鱿鱼	yóuyú
Tofu	豆腐	dòufu
Tomato	蕃茄	fānqié
Vinegar	醋	cù
Water chestnuts	马蹄	mǎtí
White radish	白萝卜	báiluóbo
Wood ear fungus	木耳	mùěr
Yam	芋头	yùtóu

Cooking methods

Casseroled	焙	bèi
Boiled	煮	zhǔ
Deep fried	油煎	yóujiān
Fried	炒	chǎo
Poached	白煮	báizhǔ
Red-cooked (stewed in soy sauce)	红烧	hóngshāo
Roast	烤	kǎo
Steamed	蒸	zhēng
Stir-fried	清炒	qīngchǎo

Everyday dishes

Braised duck with vegetables	炖鸭素菜	dùnyā sùcài
Cabbage rolls (stuffed with meat or vegetables)	卷心菜	juǎnxīncài
Chicken and sweetcorn soup	玉米鸡丝汤	yùmǐ jīsī tāng
Chicken with bamboo shoots and babycorn	笋尖嫩玉米炒鸡片	sǔnjiān nènyùmǐ chǎojīpiàn
Chicken with cashew nuts	坚果鸡片	jiānguǒ jīpiàn
Crispy aromatic duck	香酥鸭	xiāngsūyā
Egg flower soup with tomato	蕃茄蛋汤	fānqié dàn tāng
Egg fried rice	蛋炒饭	dànchǎofàn
Fish ball soup with white radish	萝卜鱼蛋汤	luóbo yúdàn tāng
Fish casserole	焙鱼	bèiyú
Fried shredded pork with garlic and chilli	大蒜辣椒炒肉片	dàsuàn làjiāo chǎoròupiàn
Hotpot	火锅	huǒguō
Kebab	串肉	chuànròu
Noodle soup	汤面	tāngmiàn
Pork and mustard greens	芥末肉片	jièmò ròupiàn
Pork and water chestnut	马蹄猪肉	mǎtí zhūròu
Pork and white radish pie	白萝卜肉馅饼	báiluóbo ròuxiànbǐng
Prawn with garlic sauce	大蒜炒虾	dàsuàn chǎoxiā
Roast duck	烤鸭	kǎoyā
Sandpot	沙锅	shāguō
Scrambled egg with pork on rice	滑蛋猪肉饭	huádàn zhūròufàn

Sliced pork with yellow bean sauce	黄豆肉片	huángdòu ròupiàn
Squid with green pepper and black beans	豆豉青椒炒鱿鱼	dòuchǐ qīngjiāo chǎoyóuyú
Steamed eel with black beans	豆豉蒸鳝	dòuchǐ zhēngshàn
Steamed rice packets wrapped in lotus leaves	荷叶蒸饭	héyè zhēngfàn
Stewed pork belly with vegetables	回锅肉	huíguōròu
Stir-fried chicken and bamboo shoots	笋尖炒鸡片	sǔnjiān chǎojīpiàn
Stuffed beancurd soup	豆腐汤	dòufutāng
Stuffed beancurd with aubergine and green pepper	茄子青椒煲	qiézi qīngjiāobāo
Sweet and sour spare ribs	糖醋排骨	tángcù páigǔ
Sweet bean paste pancakes	赤豆摊饼	chìdòu tānbǐng
White radish soup	白萝卜汤	báiluóbo tāng
Wonton soup	馄饨汤	húntun tāng

Vegetables and eggs

Aubergine with chilli and garlic sauce	大蒜辣椒炒茄子	dàsuàn làjiāo chǎoqiézi
Aubergine with sesame sauce	拌茄子片	bànqiézipiàn
Beancurd and spinach soup	菠菜豆腐汤	bōcài dòufu tāng
Beancurd slivers	豆腐花	dòufuhuā
Beancurd with chestnuts	马蹄豆腐	mǎtí dòufu
Braised mountain fungus	炖香菇	dùnxiānggū
Monks' vegetarian dish (stir-fry of mixed vegetables and fungi)	罗汉斋	luóhànzhāi
Pressed beancurd with cabbage	卷心菜豆腐	juǎnxīncài dòufu
Egg fried with tomatoes	蕃茄炒蛋	fānqié chǎodàn
Fried beancurd with vegetables	豆腐素菜	dòufu sùcài
Fried bean sprouts	炒豆芽	chǎodòuyá
Spicy braised aubergine	香茄子条	xiāngqiézitiáo
Stir-fried bamboo shoots	炒冬笋	chǎodōngsǔn
Stir-fried mushrooms	炒鲜菇	chǎoxiāngū
Vegetable soup	素菜汤	sùcài tāng

Regional dishes

Northern

Aromatic fried lamb	炒羊肉	chǎoyángròu
Fish with ham and vegetables	火腿素菜鱼片	huǒtuǐ sùcài yúpiàn
Fried prawn balls	炒虾球	chǎoxiāqiú
Mongolian hotpot	蒙古火锅	ménggǔ huǒguō
Beijing (Peking) duck	北京烤鸭	běijīng kǎoyā
Red-cooked lamb	红烧羊肉	hóngshāo yángròu
Lion's head (pork rissoles casseroled with greens)	狮子头	shīzitóu

Eastern

Beggars' chicken (baked)	叫花鸡	jiàohuājī
Crab soup	蟹肉汤	xièròu tāng
Dongpo pork casserole (steamed in wine)	东坡焙肉	dōngpō bèiròu
Drunken prawns	醉虾	zuìxiā
Five flower pork (steamed in lotus leaves)	五花肉	wǔhuāròu
Fried crab with eggs	蟹肉鸡蛋	xièròu jīdàn
Pearl balls (rice-grain-coated, steamed rissoles)	珍珠球	zhēnzhūqiú
Soup dumplings	汤饱	tāngbāo
Steamed sea bass	清蒸鲈鱼	qīngzhēnglúyú
Stuffed green peppers	馅青椒	xiànqingjiāo
West Lake fish (braised in a sour sauce)	西湖鱼	xīhúyú
"White-cut" beef (spiced and steamed)	白切牛肉	báiqiè niúròu
Yangzhou fried rice	杨州炒饭	yángzhōu chǎofàn

Sichuan and western China

Crackling-rice with pork	爆米肉片	bàomǐ ròupiàn
Crossing-the-bridge noodles	过桥面	guòqiáomiàn
Carry-pole noodles (with a chilli-vinegar-sesame sauce)	棒棒面	bàngbàngmiàn
Deep-fried green beans with garlic	大蒜刀豆	dàsuàn dāodòu
Dong'an chicken (poached in spicy sauce)	东安鸡子	dōng'ān jīzi
Doubled-cooked pork	回锅肉	huíguōròu
Dry-fried pork shreds	油炸肉丝	yóuzhá ròusī
Fish-flavoured aubergine	鱼香茄子	yúxiāng qiézi
Gongbao chicken (with chillies and peanuts)	宫爆鸡丁	gōngbào jīdīng
Green pepper with spring onion and black bean sauce	豆豉青椒	dòuchǐ qīngjiāo
Hot and sour soup (flavoured with vinegar and white pepper)	酸辣汤	suānlà tāng
Hot-spiced beancurd	妈婆豆腐	māpódòufu
Wind-cured ham	火腿	huǒtuǐ
Smoked duck	熏鸭	xūnyā
Strange flavoured chicken (with sesame-garlic-chilli)	怪味鸡	guàiwèijī
Stuffed aubergine slices	馅茄子	xiànqiézi
Tangerine chicken	桔子鸡	júzijī
"Tiger-skin" peppers (pan-fried with salt)	虎皮炒椒	hupí chǎojiāo

Southern Chinese/Cantonese

Baked crab with chilli and black beans	辣椒豆豉焙蟹	làjiāo dòuchǐ bèixiè
Casseroled beancurd stuffed with pork mince	豆腐煲	dòufubāo

Claypot rice with sweet sausage	香肠饭	xiāngchángfàn
Crisp-skinned pork on rice	脆皮肉饭	cuìpíròufàn
Fish-head casserole	焙鱼头	bèiyútóu
Fish steamed with ginger and spring onion	清蒸鱼	qīngzhēngyú
Fried chicken with yam	芋头炒鸡片	yùtóu chǎojīpiàn
Honey-roast pork	叉烧	chāshāo
Kale in oyster sauce	蚝油白菜	háoyóu báicài
Lemon chicken	柠檬鸡	níngméngjī
Litchi (lychee) pork	荔枝肉片	lìzhīròupiàn
Salt-baked chicken	盐鸡	yánjī
Scallops in taro patties	带子	dàizi
White fungus and wolfberry soup (sweet)	枸杞炖银耳	gǒuqǐ dūnyíněr

Dim sum

Dim sum	点心	diǎnxīn
Barbecue pork bun	叉烧包	chāshāo bāo
Chicken feet	凤爪	fèngzhuǎ
Crab and coriander dumpling	蟹肉虾饺	xièròu xiājiǎo
Custard tart	蛋挞	dàntà
Doughnut	炸面饼圈	zhá miànbǐngquān
Pork and prawn dumpling	烧麦	shāomài
Fried taro and mince dumpling	蕃薯糊饺	fānshǔ hújiāo
Lotus paste bun	莲蓉糕	liánrónggāo
Moon cake (sweet bean paste in flaky pastry)	月饼	yuèbǐng
Paper-wrapped prawns	纸包虾	zhǐbāoxiā
Prawn crackers	虾片	xiāpiàn
Prawn dumpling	虾饺	xiājiǎo
Prawn paste on fried toast	芝麻虾	zhīmaxiā
Shanghai fried meat and vegetable dumpling ("potstickers")	锅帖	guōtiē
Spring roll	春卷	chūnjuǎn
Steamed spare ribs and chilli	排骨	páigǔ
Stuffed rice-flour roll	肠粉	chángfěn
Stuffed green peppers with black bean sauce	豆豉馅青椒	dòuchǐ xiànqīngjiāo
Sweet sesame balls	芝麻球	zhīma qiú
Turnip-paste patty	萝卜糕	luóbo gāo

Glossary

General terms

Arhat Buddhist saint.

Bei North.

Binguan Hotel; generally a large one, for tourists.

Bodhisattva A follower of Buddhism who has attained enlightenment, but has chosen to stay on earth to teach rather than enter nirvana; Buddhist god or goddess.

Boxers The name given to an anti-foreign organization which originated in Shandong in 1898. Encouraged by the Qing Empress Dowager Cixi, they roamed China attacking Westernized Chinese and foreigners in what became known as the Boxer rebellion (see p.1183).

CITS China International Travel Service. Tourist organization primarily interested in selling tours, though they can help with obtaining train tickets.

CTS China Travel Service. Tourist organization similar to CITS.

Concession Part of a town or city ceded to a foreign power in the nineteenth century.

Cultural Revolution Ten-year period beginning in 1966 and characterized by destruction, persecution and fanatical devotion to Mao (see p.1189).

Dagoba Another name for a stupa.

Dong East.

Dougong Large, carved wooden brackets, a common feature of temple design.

Fandian Restaurant or hotel.

Fen Smallest denomination of Chinese currency – there are one hundred fen to the yuan.

Feng Peak.

Feng shui A system of geomancy used to determine the positioning of buildings (see p.1218).

Gang of Four Mao's widow and her supporters who were put on trial immediately after Mao's death for their role in the Cultural Revolution, for which they were convenient scapegoats.

Gong Palace; usually indicates a Taoist temple.

Grassland Steppe; areas of land too high or cold to support anything other than grass, and agriculturally useful only as pastureland for sheep or cattle. Found especially in Inner Mongolia, Qinghai and Xinjiang.

Guan Pass.

Guanxi Literally "connections": the reciprocal favours inherent in the process of official appointments and transactions.

Guanyin The ubiquitous Buddhist Goddess of Mercy, the most popular Bodhisattva in China, who postponed her entry into paradise in order to help ease human misery. Derived from the Indian deity Avalokiteshvara, she is often depicted with up to a thousand arms.

Gulou Drum tower; traditionally marking the centre of a town, this was where a drum was beaten at nightfall and in times of need.

Guomindang (GMD) The Nationalist Peoples' Party. Under Chiang Kaishek, the GMD fought Communist forces for 25 years before being defeated and moving to Taiwan in 1949, where it remains a major political party.

Hai Sea.

Han Chinese The main body of the Chinese people, as distinct from other ethnic groups such as Uigur, Miao, Hui or Tibetan.

He River.

Hu Lake.

Hui Muslim minority, mainly based in Gansu and Ningxia. Visually they are often indistinguishable from Han Chinese.

Hutong A narrow alleyway.

I Ching The Book of Changes, an ancient handbook for divination that includes some of the fundamental concepts of Chinese thought, such as the duality *yin* and *yang*.

Inkstones Decoratively carved blocks traditionally used by artists and calligraphers as a palette for mixing ink powder with water. The most famous, smooth-grained varieties come from Anhui and Guangdong provinces.

Jiang River.

Jiao (or mao) Ten fen.

Jiaozi Crescent-shaped, ravioli-like dumpling, usually served fried by the plateful for breakfast.

Jie Street.

Kang A raised wooden platform in a Chinese home, heated by the stove, on which the residents eat and sleep.

Kazakh A minority, mostly nomadic, in Xinjiang.

Lamian "Pulled noodles", a Muslim speciality usually served in a spicy soup.

Ling Tomb.

Little Red Book A selection of "Quotations from Chairman Mao Zedong", produced in 1966 as a philisophical treatise for Red Guards during the Cultural Revolution.

Lohan Buddhist disciple.

Long March The Communists' 9500-kilometre tactical retreat in 1934–35 from Guomindang troops advancing on their base in the Jinggan Shan ranges, Jiangxi, to Yan'an in Shaanxi Province.

Lu Street.

Mandala Mystic diagram which forms an important part of Buddhist iconography, especially in Tibet.

Mantou Steamed bread bun (literally "bald head").

Men Gate/door.

Miao Temple, usually Confucian.

Middle Kingdom A literal translation of the Chinese words for China.

Nan South.

PLA The People's Liberation Army, the official name of the Communist military forces since 1949.

PSB Public Security Bureau, the branch of China's police force which deals directly with foreigners.

Pagoda Tower with distinctively tapering structure, often associated with pseudo-science of *feng shui*.

Pinyin The official system of transliterating Chinese script into Roman characters.

Putonghua Mandarin Chinese; literally "Common Language".

Qianfodong Literally, "Thousand Buddha Cave", the name given to any Buddhist cave site along the Chinese section of the Silk Road.

Qiao Bridge.

RMB Renminbi. Another name for Chinese currency literally meaning "the people's money".

Red Guards The unruly factional forces unleashed by Mao during the Cultural Revolution to find and destroy brutally any "reactionaries" among the populace.

Renmin The people.

SEZ Special Economic Zone. A region in which state controls on production have been loosened and Western techniques of economic management are experimented with.

Sakyamuni Name given to future incarnation of Buddha.

Shan Mountain.

Shi City or municipality.

Shui Water.

Shuijiao Similar to *jiaozi* but boiled or served in a thin soup.

Si Temple, usually Buddhist.

Spirit wall Wall behind the main gateway to a house, designed to thwart evil spirits, which, it was believed, could move only in straight lines.

Spirit Way The straight road leading to a tomb, lined with guardian figures.

Stele Freestanding stone tablet carved with text.

Stupa Multi-tiered tower associated with Buddhist temples that usually contains sacred objects.

Sutra Buddhist texts, often illustrative doctrines arranged in prayer form.

Ta Tower or pagoda.

Taiping Uprising Peasant rebellion against Qing rule during the mid-nineteenth century, which saw over a million troops led by the Christian fanatic Hong Xiuquan establish a capital at Nanjing before their later annihilation at the hands of imperial forces.

Tian Heaven or the sky.

Treaty port A port in which foreigners were permitted to set up residence, for the purpose of trade, under nineteenth-century agreements between China and foreign powers.

Uigur Substantial minority of Turkic people, living mainly in Xinjiang.

Waiguoren Foreigner.

Xi West.

Yuan China's unit of currency. Also a courtyard or garden (and the name of the Mongol dynasty).

Yurt Round, felt tent used by nomads. Also known as *ger*.

Zhan Station.

Zhao Temple; term used mainly in Inner Mongolia.

Zhong Middle; China is referred to as *zhongguo*, the Middle Kingdom.

Zhonglou Bell tower, usually twinned with a Gulou. The bell it contained was rung at dawn and in emergencies.

Zhou Place or region.

Notable people

Chiang Kaishek (1887–1975) Sun Yatsen's brother-in-law and, as leader of the Guomindang from 1925, relentless opponent of the Communist Party.

Cixi (d. 1908) A proud and ruthless autocrat – known as the Empress Dowager – who ruled China for thirty years, presiding over the shabby demise of the Qing dynasty.

Deng Xiaoping China's premier from 1977 until the early 1990s; he died in 1997. A veteran political survivor, he was discredited three times during Mao's rule; he was also a controversial leader, popular for his pragmatic policies which abandoned communist ideology for economic results.

Hu Jintao Jiang Zemin's protege; he took over as head of the CCP in 2002.

Jiang Qing Mao's wife, a former Shanghai movie star who helped orchestrate the Cultural Revolution and was later blamed for its excesses as one of the Gang of Four.

Jiang Zemin Rather characterless CCP Chairman from the time of Deng Xiao Ping's retirement in the early 1990s until 2002.

Kangxi (1661–1722) One of the greatest Qing emperors.

Lao She (1898–1966) One of China's greatest twentieth-century writers, persecuted during the Cultural Revolution but rehabilitated after his death. His most famous novel is *The Rickshaw Boy*, which, like most of his work, tells the story of the daily life of the poor in popular language, with an ear for the comic.

Li Peng Senior hard-line politician, who was premier from 1987 until 1998. A professional engineer, he's credited with being the driving force behind the Three Gorges Dam project.

Lin Biao From 1968 to 1971 the heir apparent to Mao Zedong and a patron of extreme left-wing factions. Died in a mysterious plane crash while attempting to flee China after a power struggle with Mao.

Lu Xun (1881–1936) China's greatest twentieth-century writer and satirist who gave up a promising medical career to write novels with the aim of curing the Chinese of their apathy. *The Story of Ah Q* and *Diary of a Madman* are the most influential of his works.

Mao Zedong (1893–1976) The Great Helmsman; poet, genius and despot who led China on its rocky course from 1949 until his death. The present official Chinese line on Mao is that he was seventy percent right and thirty percent wrong. His legacy is becoming irrelevant to the increasingly materialistic generation who have grown up since his death.

Puyi The last emperor, who ascended to the throne in 1908 at the age of two. The Qing dynasty collapsed soon afterwards and he was later used as a puppet emperor by the Japanese to legitimize their occupation of Manchuria.

Qianlong (1736–96) Qing emperor under whose reign the Chinese empire reached a zenith of size and prosperity.

Qin Shi Huang (221–210 BC) The first

emperor of all China, famous for megalomania and tyranny, and for the Terracotta Army which guards his tomb.

Qu Yuan (340–280 BC) One of China's great poets, whose suicide by drowning is commemorated nationwide by annual dragon-boat races.

Sima Qian (145–85 BC) Having succeeded his father as court astrologer, Sima Qian spent his life compiling the *Historical Records*, the first history of China. After falling from court favour and being castrated as punishment, he consoled himself with the thought that now he could finish his book without distractions.

Su Dongpo (1036–1101) Sichuanese Song-dynasty official and famous poet, also known as Su Shi, whose politics saw him exiled from the court to Hunan and then Hainan Island.

Sun Yatsen (1866–1925) President of the short-lived Chinese Republic and revered by Communists and Guomindang alike for his life-long efforts to unify China and enfranchise the people.

Xuan Zang (602–664) A Tang-dynasty Buddhist monk who made the long trek to India alone in 629, studied under the finest Indian masters for sixteen years, then returned to spend the rest of his life translating the Buddhist classics into Chinese. His travels are the basis for the classic tale *Journey to the West.*

Zhou Enlai China's premier (prime minister) from 1949 to 1976. His memory is much loved in China.

Zhu Rongji Prime Minister from 1998 to 2002.

Zhuge Liang (Kongming) The renowned *Three Kingdoms* strategist and governor of the state of Shu (Sichuan) from about 220 AD.

Index

and small print

Index

Map entries are in **colour**.

The following abbreviations are used throughout this index:		
AH Anhui	**HEB** Hebei	**QH** Qinghai
BJ Beijing	**HEN** Henan	**SAX** Shaanxi
CQ Chongqing	**HN** Hainan	**SC** Sichuan
DB Dongbei	**HUB** Hubei	**SD** Shandong
FJ Fujian	**HUN** Hunan	**SX** Shanxi
GD Guangdong	**IM** Inner Mongolia	**T** Tibet
GS Gansu	**JS** Jiangsu	**XJ** Xinjiang
GX Guangxi	**JX** Jiangxi	**YN** Yunnan
GZ Guizhou	**NX** Ningxia	**ZJ** Zhejiang

A

B

INDEX

C

D

INDEX

INDEX

I

J

N

O

P

Q

R

S

INDEX

T

U

V

W

X

Y

Z

Twenty Years of Rough Guides

In the summer of 1981, Mark Ellingham, Rough Guides' founder, knocked out the first guide on a typewriter, with a group of friends. Mark had been travelling in Greece after university, and couldn't find a guidebook that really answered his needs.There were heavyweight cultural guides on the one hand – good on museums and classical sites but not on beaches and tavernas – and on the other hand student manuals that were so caught up with how to save money that they lost sight of the country's significance beyond its role as a place for a cool vacation. None of the guides began to address Greece as a country, with its natural and human environment, its politics and its contemporary life.

Having no urgent reason to return home, Mark decided to write his own guide. It was a guide to Greece that tried to combine some erudition and insight with a thoroughly practical approach to travellers' needs. Scrupulously researched listings of places to stay, eat and drink were matched by careful attention to detail on everything from Homer to Greek music, from classical sites to national parks and from nude beaches to monasteries. Back in London, Mark and his friends got their Rough Guide accepted by a farsighted commissioning editor at the publisher Routledge and it came out in 1982.

The Rough Guide to Greece was a student scheme that became a publishing phenomenon. The immediate success of the book – shortlisted for the Thomas Cook award – spawned a series that rapidly covered dozens of countries. The Rough Guides found a ready market among backpackers and budget travellers, but soon acquired a much broader readership that included older and less impecunious visitors. Readers relished the guides' wit and inquisitiveness as much as the enthusiastic, critical approach that acknowledges everyone wants value for money – but not at any price.

Rough Guides soon began supplementing the "rougher" information – the hostel and low-budget listings – with the kind of detail that independent-minded travellers on any budget might expect. These days, the guides – distributed worldwide by the Penguin group – include recommendations spanning the range from shoestring to luxury, and cover more than 200 destinations around the globe. Our growing team of authors, many of whom come to Rough Guides initially as outstandingly good letter-writers telling us about their travels, are spread all over the world, particularly in Europe, the USA and Australia. As well as the travel guides, Rough Guides publishes a series of dictionary phrasebooks covering two dozen major languages, an acclaimed series of music guides running the gamut from Classical to World Music, a series of music CDs in association with World Music Network, and a range of reference books on topics as diverse as the Internet, Pregnancy and Unexplained Phenomena. Visit **www.roughguides.com** to see what's cooking.

Rough Guide Credits

Text editor: Richard Lim and Jo Mead
Series editor: Mark Ellingham
Editorial: Martin Dunford, Jonathan Buckley, Kate Berens, Ann-Marie Shaw, Helena Smith, Olivia Swift, Ruth Blackmore, Geoff Howard, Claire Saunders, Gavin Thomas, Alexander Mark Rogers, Polly Thomas, Joe Staines, Duncan Clark, Peter Buckley, Lucy Ratcliffe, Clifton Wilkinson, Alison Murchie, Matthew Teller, Andrew Dickson, Fran Sandham, Sally Schafer (UK); Andrew Rosenberg, Yuki Takagaki, Richard Koss, Hunter Slaton (US)
Production: Susanne Hillen, Andy Hilliard, Link Hall, Helen Prior, Julia Bovis, Michelle Draycott, Katie Pringle, Zoë Nobes, Rachel Holmes, Andy Turner, Dan May
Cartography: Maxine Repath, Melissa Baker, Ed Wright, Katie Lloyd-Jones
Cover art direction: Louise Boulton
Picture research: Sharon Martins, Mark Thomas
Online: Kelly Martinez, Anja Mutic-Blessing, Jennifer Gold, Audra Epstein, Suzanne Welles, Cree Lawson (US)
Finance: John Fisher, Gary Singh, Edward Downey, Mark Hall, Tim Bill
Marketing & Publicity: Richard Trillo, Niki Smith, David Wearn, Chloë Roberts, Demelza Dallow, Claire Southern (UK); Simon Carloss, David Wechsler, Megan Kennedy (US)
Administration: Julie Sanderson, Karoline Densley

Publishing Information

This third edition published April 2003 by
Rough Guides Ltd,
80 Strand, London WC2R 0RL.
345 Hudson St, 4th Floor,
New York, NY 10014, USA.
Distributed by the Penguin Group
Penguin Books Ltd,
80 Strand, London WC2R 0RL
Penguin Putnam, Inc.
375 Hudson Street, NY 10014, USA
Penguin Books Australia Ltd,
487 Maroondah Highway, PO Box 257,
Ringwood, Victoria 3134, Australia
Penguin Books Canada Ltd,
10 Alcorn Avenue, Toronto, Ontario,
Canada M4V 1E4
Penguin Books (NZ) Ltd,
182–190 Wairau Road, Auckland 10,
New Zealand
Typeset in Bembo and Helvetica to an original design by Henry Iles.

Printed in Italy by LegoPrint S.p.A

1296pp includes index
A catalogue record for this book is available from the British Library.
ISBN 1-84353-019-8

Help us update

We've gone to a lot of effort to ensure that the third edition of **The Rough Guide to China** is accurate and up-to-date. However, things change – places get "discovered", opening hours are notoriously fickle, restaurants and rooms raise prices or lower standards. If you feel we've got it wrong or left something out, we'd like to know, and if you can remember the address, the price, the time, the phone number, so much the better.

We'll credit all contributions, and send a copy of the next edition (or any other Rough Guide if you prefer) for the best letters. Everyone who writes to us and isn't already a subscriber will receive a copy of our full-colour thrice-yearly newsletter. Please mark letters: **"Rough Guide China Update"** and send to: Rough Guides, 80 Strand, London WC2R 0RL, or Rough Guides, 4th Floor, 345 Hudson St, New York, NY 10014. Or send an email to **mail@roughguides.com**

Have your questions answered and tell others about your trip at **www.roughguides.atinfopop.com**

Acknowledgements

Thanks from **David** to Narrell. Also many thanks to Linda Zhou, Hou Qiang, Rong Yin Qing, Zhou Hui Huan, the Gaos, Jack, Sam Skinner and Wu Chong Xiao. Plus a big thanks to all the early risers in parks who let me practise *tui shou* and *da lu* with them, and to Craig, Neil, Paul, Rob & Mause, Steve, and Erle Montaigue for much more of the same.

Simon thanks Qian Fan, Howard, Ade, Wilder and Lily, Du and Kathryn.

From **Mike**, thanks to Frances Feng, Michael Goettig, Peter Hessler and Travis Klingberg for lodging, train rides and frisbee on the Mongolian grasslands.

Susie thanks Donna Mongan at the Hong Kong Tourist Board; the Macau Government Tourist Office, especially Lucia in Hong Kong and endlessly informative Joao in Macau. And a huge thank you to Kirstie Bullock for eating for Britain and lugging around bags!

The editors thank Katie Pringle for typesetting; Feng Dan and Link Hall for sorting out the *pinyin* and Chinese characters; Richard and Hazel Watson of the Map Studio and Maxine Repath, Katie Lloyd-Jones and Ed Wright for the maps; Sharon Martins for picture research; Kate Davis for additional Basics research; and Susannah Wight and Sam Skinner for proofreading.

Readers' letters

Thanks to all the readers who took the trouble to write in with their comments and suggestions (and apologies to anyone whose name we've misspelt or omitted):

Tiiu Adamek, Jerry Alder, Mark Alexander, Helen Bicknell, Graeme Brock, Mandi Brooker, Ian Brown, Ruth Brown, Hannah Bullock, Tara Burke, John Burton, Andy Carn, Gez Collins, Robert Cox, Françoise Cremet, E. Davey, Koe Delaere, Nicola and Peter Dickinson, Chris Dieckmann, Alison Dong, Richard Fish, D.T. Fisk, Robert Franquinet, Wyn Grant, Wendy Hampton, Alison Harrison, Fredrik S. Heffermehl, Judy Heiser, Tamara Herrmann, Patrick Hickey, Ashley Hughes, Ingrid and Manuel, Venetia Jackson, Steve Jones, Wendy Kershaw, Kate Lawson, Jim Leffman, Lida, Arjen van Loenen and Edith Beerdsen, Gary Loke, Jane Lucks, Steve McDermott, Alexandre Maier, Joke Meindersma, Rob Minnee, Christian Monks and Michelle Merry, Nick Morley and Teresa Eng, Ann Morrison, Dave Nicel, Jessie Normaschild, Eva Notteboom, Jose Ortega, Piergiorgio Pescali, Anthony Rawlinson, Dawn Regan, Alison Rigby, Nicky Rothon, Daniel Rutter, Richard Salt, Ryno Sauerman, Carol Schrecengost, Ulrik Skibstead, Andrew Sutton, David G. Thomas, Robin Tilston, Paul Tomic, Bryan Wagner, E.O. Wagner and Maureen Moore, Anne Heding Westenholz, Iris Wolong, Karen Wong, Yen Khanh Do, Yung-Sheng Yu.

Photo Credits

Cover credits

Main front picture Leshan © Robert Harding
small top picture Mingga Dunes © Robert Harding
small lower picture Pukuozongcheng © Robert Harding
back top picture Li River © Imagestate
back lower picture Great Wall © Robert Harding

Introduction

Pingyao city walls © Fang Zhongda/Imaginechina
Golden Summit temple, Sichuan © Ran Yujie/Imaginechina
Chillies © Gordon D. R. Clements/AXIOM
Prayer in Jokhang Temple © Zhang Chaoran/Imaginechina
Woman on scooter with facemask © Jiang Ren/Imaginechina
Peking opera © Liu Ligun/Imaginechina
Panda © David Leffman
Dim Sum on table © Zhu Fan/Imaginechina
Letter writing service, Xi'an © Jerry Dennis
Camels in desert © Gao Zhiqiang/Imaginechina
Taiji students, Wudang Shan © David Leffman
Stall selling worship supplies, Wong Tai Sin Temple © Robert Harding
Picking vegetables below Jade Dragon Mountain, Yunnan © Michael Matthews

Things Not To Miss

The Great Wall – Mutianyu in winter © Li Shaobai/Imaginechina
Boating around Cao Hai, Guizhou © David Leffman
Winter ice festival, Harbin © Zhao Gang/Imaginechina
Eating dim sum © Adina Tovey/Robert Harding
Chengde Temple © Li Shaobai/Imaginechina
Dai village, with traditional wooden house on stilts © Wu Xiaohui/Imaginechina
Buddhist grottoes at Mogao Caves, Dunhuang, Gansu © Zhang Chaoyin/Imaginechina
Lijiang street © Liu Quanju/Imaginechina
Beijing duck, chef putting duck into oven © Gao Feng/Imaginechina
Forbidden City, Beijing © Li Shaobai/Imaginechina
Hanging Temple © Amar Grover
Labrang monastery, Xiahe, Gansu © Imaginechina
Li River scenery © K. Cardwell/TRIP
Leshan Buddha (Dafo), Sichuan © Huang Jinguo/Imaginechina
Hong Kong cityscape © Hong Kong Tourism Board
Longmen grottoes, Luoyang © Lu Guangwei/Imaginechina
Jokhang, Lhasa © Wang Jianxin/Imaginechina
Siberian tiger © Zhang Bin/Imaginechina
Mount Everest, Tibet © Zhang Guosheng/Imaginechina
Shanghai Bund (Nanjing Lu), Shanghai © Lv Baohe/Imaginechina
Pilgrims ascending stone staircase up mountain, Tai Shan © Li Ming/Imaginechina
Suzhou garden © Shen Yu/Imaginechina
Sisters' Meal festival, Taijiang, Guizhou © David Leffman
Skiing at Yabuli © Zhao Gang/Imaginechina
Confucius Family Mansion, Qufu, Main hall of residence © Liu Liqun/Imaginechina
The Terracotta Army © B. Turner/TRIP
Ruined Silk Road city, Xinjiang – Flaming Mountains (Huoyanshan) © Ma Kang/Imaginechina
Old Yalu Bridge to Korea, Dandong © Liang Weijie/Imaginechina
A cruise down the Yangzi river © Liu Liqun/Imaginechina
Hukou Falls, Yellow River © Han lu/Imaginechina
Open-air Sichuanese teahouse – T. O'Brien/TRIP
Yonghe Gong, Beijing © Michael Matthews
Colonial architecture, Gulangyu Island, near Xiamen in Fujian province © Amar Grover
The Fort, Jiayuguan, Gansu © Michael Matthews
Sunday Market, Kashgar, Xinjiang © Amar Grover

Black and whites

Great hall of the People, Tian'anmen Square © Li Guiming/Imaginechina (p.72)
Soldiers taking photos, Tian'anmen Square © Olivia Savoure/Imaginechina (p.97)
Chengde Bishushanzhuang © Jiao Xiaojiang/Imaginechina (p.148)
Shanhaiguan Great Wall © Li Shaobai/Imaginechina (p.170)
Man with skis © Du Huaiyu/Imaginechina (p.186)
Changbaishan Nature Reserve in winter © Zhao Gang/Imaginechina (p.213)
Hukou Falls, Yellow River © Han lu/Imaginechina (p.226)
Pingyao wall © Li Shaobai/Imaginechina (p.259)
Pingyao street © Liu Quanju/Imaginechina (p.259)
German style buildings, Qingdao, Shandong © Jan Siefke/Imaginechina (p.359)
Pudong Avenue © Wang Ju/Imaginechina (p.370)
Nanjing Dong, Shanghai © Neil Setchfield (p.389)
Lake Tai © Zhou Kang/Imaginechina (p.414)
Suzhou canal © Yu Liyi/Imaginechina (p.462)
Suzhou garden © Shen Yu/Imaginechina (p.498)
Three Gorges Dam site, Yangtze River © Zhou Lixin/Imaginechina (p.506)
Jingdezhen pottery © Li Wei/Imaginechina (p.544)
Hakka roundhouses in Fujian © Yue Sheng/Imaginechina (p.590)
Monkeys, Wuyishan Nature Reserve © Fan Chongzhi/Imaginechina (p.616)
Peak tram © Hong Kong Tourism Board (p.704)
Old photos for sale © Alain Evrard/Robert Harding (p.758)
Threshers and a Dong minority Wind and Rain bridge © Amar Grover (p.782)
Huangguoshu waterfall © Zhang Guosheng/Imaginechina (p.821)
Kunming street © Michael Matthews (p.850)
Bai seamstress © Amar Grover (p.903)
Open air teahouse in Sichuan © Hou Jianhua/Imaginechina (p.918)
Id Kah mosque, Kashgar © Olivia Savoure/Imaginechina (p.984)
Pulling Lamian noodles © Amar Grover
Samye monastery © Lin Weijian/Imaginechina (p.1085)
Jokhang, Lhasa © Amar Grover (p.1112)

EXPERIENCE CHINA DIFFERENTLY
ADVENTURE TRAVEL
IN CHINA
WILDCHINA
TEL(8610)6403 9737
INFO@WILDCHINA.COM
WWW.WILDCHINA.COM